Fodor's 27th Edition

KU-215-123

USA

The complete guide, thoroughly up-to-date

Packed with details that will make your trip

The must-see sights, off and on the beaten path

What to see, what to skip

Mix-and-match vacation itineraries

City strolls, countryside adventures

Smart lodging and dining options

Essential local dos and taboos

Transportation tips, distances and directions

Key contacts, savvy travel tips

When to go, what to pack

Clear, accurate, easy-to-use maps

Fodor's Travel Publications • New York, Toronto, London, Sydney, Auckland
www.fodors.com

EDITOR: David S. Cashion

Editorial Contributors: Caroline Haberfeld and Helayne Schiff
Editorial Production: Stacey Kulig
Maps: David Lindroth, *cartographer*; Rebecca Baer and Bob Blake, *map editors*
Design: Fabrizio La Rocca, *creative director*; Guido Caroti, *art director*; Jolie Novak, *picture editor*
Cover Design: Pentagram
Production/Manufacturing: Mike Costa
Cover Photograph: Richard Nowitz

Copyright

Twenty-Seventh Edition

ISBN 0–679–00561–7

ISSN 1043–0253

Important Tip

Although all prices, opening times, and other details in this book are based on information supplied to us at press time, changes occur all the time in the travel world, and Fodor's cannot accept responsibility for facts that become outdated or for inadvertent errors or omissions. So **always confirm information when it matters,** especially if you're making a detour to visit a specific place.

Special Sales

Fodor's Travel Publications are available at special discounts for bulk purchases for sales promotions or premiums. Special editions, including personalized covers, excerpts of existing guides, and corporate imprints, can be created in large quantities for special needs. For more information, contact your local bookseller or write to Special Markets, Fodor's Travel Publications, 280 Park Avenue, New York, NY 10017. Inquiries from Canada should be directed to your local Canadian bookseller or sent to Random House of Canada, Ltd., Marketing Department, 2775 Matheson Boulevard East, Mississauga, Ontario L4W 4P7. Inquiries from the United Kingdom should be sent to Fodor's Travel Publications, 20 Vauxhall Bridge Road, London SW1V 2SA, England.

PRINTED IN THE UNITED STATES OF AMERICA

10 9 8 7 6 5 4 3 2 1

CONTENTS

⊕ *Italic entries are maps.*

ON THE ROAD WITH FODOR'S

WHEN I PLAN A VACATION, the first thing I do is cast around among my friends to find someone who's just been where I'm going. Unfortunately, such friends are few and far between. So it's nice to know that there's *Fodor's USA,* a book that's written and updated by people you would hit up for travel tips if you knew them.

Connections

We're pleased that the American Society of Travel Agents continues to endorse Fodor's as its guidebook of choice. ASTA is the world's largest and most influential travel trade association, operating in more than 170 countries, with 27,000 members pledged to adhere to a strict code of ethics reflecting the Society's motto, "Integrity in Travel." ASTA shares Fodor's devotion to providing smart, honest travel information and advice to travelers, and we've long recommended that our readers—even those who have guidebooks and traveling friends—consult ASTA member agents for the experience and professionalism they bring to your vacation planning.

On Fodor's Web site (www.fodors.com), check out the Resource Center, an online companion to the Smart Travel Tips A to Z section of this book, complete with hot links to related sites. In our forums, get advice from other travelers and tips from Fodor's experts worldwide.

Fodor's Choice

We hope you'll have a chance to experience Fodor's choices yourself while traveling in the United States. For detailed information about each entry, refer to the appropriate chapters in this guidebook.

Natural Wonders

The Northeast
Niagara Falls (NY)

The Middle Atlantic States
Delaware Water Gap (PA/NJ)
Natural Bridge (Natural Bridge, VA)
New River Gorge National River (Glen Jean, WV)

The Southeast
Everglades (FL)
Okefenokee (GA)
Jockey's Ridge (NC)

The Mississippi Valley
Buffalo National River (AR)
Mammoth Cave (KY)
Bayou Teche (Acadiana, LA)
The Natchez Trace (Natchez, MS)
Great Smoky Mountains National Park (Gatlinburg, TN)

The Midwest and Great Lakes
Pictured Rocks National Lakeshore (Munising, MI)
Boundary Waters Canoe Area Wilderness (MN)
Apostle Islands National Lakeshore (WI)

The Great Plains
Badlands (ND/SD)

The Southwest
Grand Canyon (AZ)
Carlsbad Caverns (NM)
White Sands National Monument (NM)
Palo Duro Canyon (TX)

The Rockies
Glacier National Park (MT)
Bryce and Zion canyons (UT)
Old Faithful Geyser (Yellowstone, WY)

The West Coast
El Capitan and Half Dome (Yosemite National Park, CA)
Joshua Tree National Park (CA)
La Jolla Cove (La Jolla, CA)
Muir Woods (Mill Valley, CA)
17-Mile Drive (Pebble Beach, CA)
Crater Lake National Park (OR)
Hoh Rain Forest (Olympic Peninsula, WA)

The Pacific
Mt. McKinley (AK)
Kīlauea Volcano (The Big Island, HI)

Historic Buildings and Sites

The Northeast
Victoria Mansion (Portland, ME)
Bunker Hill (Boston, MA)
Historic Deerfield (Deerfield, MA)

Old North Church (Boston, MA)

Plimoth Plantation (Plymouth, MA)

Canterbury Shaker Village (Canterbury, NH)

Ellis Island (New York, NY)

Statue of Liberty (New York, NY)

Hunter House (Newport, RI)

John Brown House (Providence, RI)

The Middle Atlantic States

Antietam National Battlefield (Sharpsburg, MD)

Washington Crossing State Park (Titusville, NJ)

Gettysburg National Military Park (Gettysburg, PA)

Independence National Historical Park (Philadelphia, PA)

Monticello (Charlottesville, VA)

Mount Vernon (Alexandria, VA)

Frederick Douglass National Historic Site (Washington, D.C.)

Vietnam Veterans Memorial (Washington, D.C.)

Washington Monument (Washington, D.C.)

The White House (Washington, D.C.)

Harpers Ferry National Park (Harpers Ferry, WV)

The Southeast

Dexter Avenue King Memorial Baptist Church (Montgomery, AL)

Art Deco District (Miami Beach, FL)

Andersonville National Historic Site (Andersonville, GA)

Johnston Hay House (Macon, GA)

Biltmore House (Asheville, NC)

Old Salem (Winston-Salem, NC)

Wright Brothers National Memorial (Kill Devil Hills, NC)

Drayton Hall (Charleston, SC)

Fort Sumter National Monument (Charleston, SC)

The Mississippi Valley

Old State House (Little Rock, AR)

Old Washington Historic State Park (Washington, AR)

Shaker Village of Pleasant Hill (Harrodsburg, KY)

Old Ursuline Convent (New Orleans, LA)

Rosalie (Natchez, MS)

The Hermitage (Nashville, TN)

The Midwest and Great Lakes

Sears Tower (Chicago, IL)

George Rogers Clark National Historic Park (Vincennes, IN)

Pabst Mansion (Milwaukee, WI)

The Great Plains

George Washington Carver National Monument (MO)

Liberty Memorial (Kansas City, MO)

Crazy Horse Memorial (SD)

Deadwood National Historic Landmark (SD)

Mt. Rushmore National Memorial (SD)

The Southwest

Palace of the Governors (Santa Fe, NM)

The Alamo (San Antonio, TX)

Mission Ysleta (near El Paso, TX)

The Strand (Galveston, TX)

Texas School Book Depository (Dallas, TX)

The Rockies

Mesa Verde National Park (CO)

Little Bighorn Battlefield National Monument (MT)

Salt Lake Mormon Tabernacle and Temple (Salt Lake City, UT)

The West Coast

Olvera Street (Los Angeles, CA)

Hearst Castle (San Simeon, CA)

Sutter's Mill (Coloma, CA)

Fort Clatsop National Memorial (Astoria, OR)

The Pacific States

The Pacific Ketchikan Totem Parks (Ketchikan, AK)

'Iolani Palace (Honolulu, HI)

Museums

The Northeast

Wadsworth Atheneum (Hartford, CT)

Isabella Stewart Gardner Museum (Boston, MA)

Hood Museum of Art (Hanover, NH)

American Museum of Natural History (New York, NY)

Metropolitan Museum of Art (New York, NY)

Museum of Modern Art (New York, NY)

Rhode Island School of Design Museum of Art (Providence, RI)

The Middle Atlantic States

B&O Railroad Museum (Baltimore, MD)

Walters Art Gallery (Baltimore, MD)

Chesapeake Bay Maritime Museum (St. Michaels, MD)

Neighborhoods

Parks and Gardens

Shenandoah National Park
(Shenandoah Valley of VA)

Dumbarton Oaks (Washington, D.C.)

The Southeast

Bellingrath Gardens and Home
(Theodore, AL)

Callaway Gardens (Pine Mountain,
GA)

Town squares (Savannah, GA)

Biltmore Estate Gardens (Asheville,
NC)

Magnolia Plantation (Charleston, SC)

Middleton Place (Charleston, SC)

The Mississippi Valley

Cheekwood–Tennessee Botanical
Gardens and Museum of Art
(Nashville, TN)

Memphis Botanic Garden (Memphis,
TN)

The Midwest and Great Lakes

Lincoln Park (Chicago, IL)

Mitchell Park Domes (Milwaukee, WI)

The Great Plains

International Forest of Friendship
(Atchison, KS)

International Peace Garden (ND)

Theodore Roosevelt National Park
(ND)

Custer State Park (SD)

The Southwest

Arizona–Sonora Desert Museum
(Tucson, AZ)

Desert Botanical Garden (Phoenix, AZ)

Fair Park (Dallas, TX)

Water Gardens Park (Fort Worth, TX)

The West Coast

Balboa Park (San Diego, CA)

Golden Gate Park (San Francisco, CA)

Huntington Library, Art Collections,
and Botanical Gardens (San Marino,
CA)

Washington Park International Rose
Test Garden and Japanese Gardens
(Portland, OR)

Beaches

The Northeast

Cape Cod National Seashore (MA)

Jones Beach (Long Island, NY)

The Middle Atlantic States

Assateague Island (MD/VA)

Island Beach State Park (NJ)

The Southeast

Gulf State Park (AL)

Crandon Park (Miami, FL)

Grayton Beach State Recreation Area
(Seaside, FL)

Cumberland Island National Seashore
(GA)

Cape Hatteras National Seashore (NC)

Hilton Head Island (SC)

The Mississippi Valley

Gulf Islands National Seashore (Ocean
Springs, MS)

The Midwest and Great Lakes

Indiana Dunes National Lakeshore (IN)

The Great Plains

Lake McConaughy State Recreation
Area (NE)

The Southwest

Lake Powell (AZ/UT)

Padre Island National Seashore (TX)

The West Coast

Corona del Mar (CA)

Pismo State Beach (CA)

Oregon Dunes National Recreation
Area (OR)

The Pacific States

Wailea's five crescent beaches (Maui,
HI)

Restaurants

The Northeast

Good News Café (Woodbury, CT; $$–
$$$$)

White Barn Inn (Kennebunk, ME;
$$$$)

Biba (Boston, MA; $$$–$$$$)

Daniel (New York, NY; $$$$)

Al Forno (Providence, RI; $$–$$$)

The Middle Atlantic States

Tio Pepe (Baltimore, MD; $$–$$$)

Le Bec-Fin (Philadelphia, PA; $$$$)

Meskerem (Washington, D.C.; $–$$)

L'Auberge Chez François (Great Falls,
VA; $$$–$$$$)

Red Fox (Snowshoe, WV; $$$)

The Southeast

Highlands Bar & Grill (Birmingham,
AL; $$–$$$$)

Norman's (Coral Gables, FL; $$$$)

Louie's Backyard (Key West, FL; $$$$)

Elizabeth on 37th (Savannah, GA; $$$–
$$$$)

Seeger's (Atlanta, GA; $$$$)

The Dining Room, Ritz Carlton
(Buckhead, GA; $$$$)

Woodlands Inn (Summerville, SC;
$$$$)

L'Auberge Provencale (White Post, VA; $$$–$$$$)

The Mississippi Valley

Lilly's (Louisville, KY; $$$)

Commander's Palace (New Orleans, LA; $$$–$$$$)

Nola (New Orleans, LA; $$–$$$)

Charlie Vergos' Rendezvous (Memphis, TN; $–$$)

The Midwest and Great Lakes

Charlie Trotter's (Chicago, IL; $$$$)

Lelli's Inn (Detroit, MI; $$–$$$$)

Sanford (Milwaukee, WI; $$$–$$$$)

The Great Plains

Stroud's (Kansas City, MO; $$)

Mandan Drug (Mandan, ND; $)

Cattlemen's Steakhouse (Oklahoma City, OK; $–$$)

Jakes (Deadwood, SD; $$)

The Southwest

Café Terra Cotta (Tuscon & Scottsdale, AZ; $$–$$$$)

The Mansion on Turtle Creek (Dallas, TX; $$$$)Cafe Annie (Houston, TX; $$$–$$$$)

Star Canyon (Dallas, TX; $$–$$$$)

The Rockies

Strings (Denver, CO; $$–$$$)

Glitretind (Deer Valley, UT; $$$–$$$$)

The West Coast

Campanile (Los Angeles, CA; $$–$$$$)

Chez Panisse (Berkeley, CA; $$–$$$$)

Geno (Portland, OR; $$$$)

Rover's (Seattle, WA; $$$$)

The Pacific

The Double Musky (Anchorage, AK; $$–$$$$)

A Pacific Café (Kaua'i, HI; $$$$)

Hotels

The Northeast

The Mayflower Inn (Washington, CT; $$$$)

Charlotte Inn (Edgartown, MA; $$$$)

Fairmont Copley Plaza (Boston, MA; $$$$)

Mount Washington Hotel (Bretton Woods, NH; $$$$)

The Carlyle (New York, NY; $$$$)

The Point (Saranac Lake, NY; $$$$

The Middle Atlantic States

Harbor Court (Baltimore, MD; $$$$)

Stone Manor (Middletown, MD; $$$–$$$$)

The Homestead (Hot Springs, VA; $$$$)

Keswick Hall at Monticello (Charlottesville, VA; $$$$)

Hay-Adams Hotel (Washington, D.C.; $$$$)

The Greenbrier (White Sulphur Springs, WV; $$$$)

The Southeast

The Breakers (Palm Beach, FL; $$$$)

Delano Hotel (Miami Beach, FL; $$$$)

The Four Seasons (Atlanta, GA; $$$$)

Grove Park Inn (Asheville, NC; $$$–$$$$)

Charleston Place Hotel (Charleston, SC; $$$$)

John Rutledge House Inn (Charleston, SC; $$$$)

The Mississippi Valley

The Seelbach Hilton (Louisville, KY; $$$–$$$$)

Windsor Court Hotel (New Orleans, LA; $$$$)

Cedar Grove (Vicksburg, MS; $$–$$$)

The Peabody (Memphis, TN; $$$–$$$$)

The Midwest and Great Lakes

Ritz-Carlton (Chicago, IL; $$$$)

Ritz-Carlton (Cleveland, OH; $$$$)

Pfister Hotel (Milwaukee, WI; $$$–$$$$)

The Great Plains

The Raphael (Kansas City, MO; $$$)

Island Guest Ranch (Ames, OK; $$)

The Bullock Hotel (Deadwood, SD; $$)

The Southwest

Arizona Biltmore (Phoenix, AZ; $$$$)

The Boulders (Carefree, AZ; $$$$)

Bellagio (Las Vegas, NV; $$–$$$$)

The Mansion on Turtle Creek (Dallas, TX; $$$$)

Menger Hotel (San Antonio, TX; $$$)

The Rockies

Oxford (Denver, CO; $$$–$$$$)

Cliff Lodge at Snowbird Resort (Snowbird, UT; $$$–$$$$)

Old Faithful Inn (Yellowstone, WY; $–$$$)

The West Coast

Ritz-Carlton Laguna Niguel (Dana Point, CA; $$$–$$$$)

The Heathman (Portland, OR; $$$–$$$$)

Stephanie Inn (Cannon Beach, OR; $$$–$$$$)

The Four Seasons Olympic Hotel (Seattle, WA; $$$$)

The Pacific States

Camp Denali (Denali National Park, AK; $$$$)

Four Seasons Resort Hualālai (Ka'ūpūlehu/Kona, HI; $$$$)

Don't Forget to Write

You can use this book in the confidence that all prices and opening times are based on information supplied to us at press time; Fodor's cannot accept responsibility for any errors. Time inevitably brings changes, so always confirm information when it matters—especially if you're making a detour to visit a specific place.

Were the restaurants we recommended as described? Did you find a museum we recommended a waste of time? Keeping a travel guide up-to-date is a big job, and we welcome your feedback. If you have complaints, we'll look into them and revise our entries when the facts warrant it. If you've discovered a special place that we haven't included, we'll pass the information along to our correspondents and have them check it out. So send us your thoughts via e-mail at editors@fodors.com (specifying the name of the book on the subject line) or on paper in care of the USA editors at Fodor's, 280 Park Avenue, New York, NY 10017. In the meantime, have a wonderful trip!

Karen Cure
Editorial Director

The United States

Amtrak Rail Passenger System

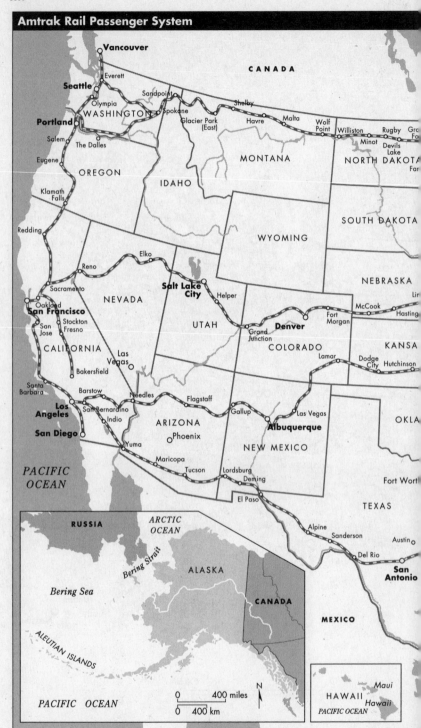

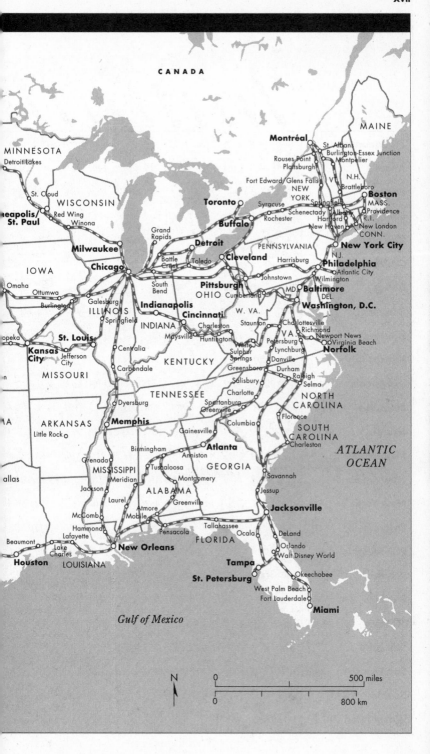

Mileages Between Major U.S. Cities

	Albuquerque	Atlanta	Boston	Chicago	Cincinnati	Cleveland	Dallas	Denver	Houston	Kansas City	Los A...
Albuquerque	—	1409	2225	1343	1402	1608	666	446	876	818	790
Atlanta	1409	—	1105	703	466	715	791	1404	800	801	2199
Boston	2225	1105	—	1018	861	657	1765	2006	1857	1414	3007
Chicago	1343	703	1018	—	296	365	940	1013	1107	511	2014
Cincinnati	1402	466	861	296	—	249	943	1195	1079	592	2192
Cleveland	1608	715	657	365	249	—	1193	1354	1328	797	2355
Dallas	666	791	1765	940	943	1193	—	825	241	523	1440
Denver	446	1404	2006	1013	1195	1354	825	—	1075	606	1004
Houston	876	800	1857	1107	1079	1328	241	1075	—	764	1545
Kansas City	818	801	1414	511	592	797	523	606	764	—	1610
Los Angeles	790	2199	3007	2014	2192	2355	1440	1004	1545	1610	—
Memphis	1004	401	1309	533	487	736	456	1113	592	474	1798
Miami	2009	695	1524	1388	1149	1251	1342	2088	1215	1485	2759
Minneapolis	1255	1121	1435	417	713	782	962	916	1202	437	1889
New Orleans	1178	473	1529	928	818	1067	511	1273	350	842	1894
New York	2002	878	226	814	634	463	1538	1802	1630	1192	2803
Orlando	1770	446	1314	1149	912	1041	1104	1850	976	1247	2521
Philadelphia	1949	779	326	798	581	437	1462	1742	1554	1139	2738
Phoenix	463	1859	2687	1805	1865	2071	1068	832	1173	1280	372
Portland, OR	1411	2599	3046	2126	2370	2466	2009	1241	2205	1796	963
St. Louis	1050	555	1175	293	352	558	647	852	819	249	1840
Salt Lake	646	1876	2396	1403	1647	1743	1290	518	1500	1073	689
San Francisco	1095	2505	3125	2132	2376	2472	1761	1247	1923	1802	381
Seattle	1463	2651	3085	2067	2328	2432	2117	1293	2274	1848	1136
Washington, DC	1875	641	462	733	488	377	1323	1649	1415	1045	2665

Memphis	Miami	Minneapolis	New Orleans	New York	Orlando	Philadelphia	Phoenix	Portland, OR	St. Louis	Salt Lake	San Francisco	Seattle	Washington, DC
008	2009	1255	1178	2002	1770	1949	463	1411	1050	646	1095	1463	1875
01	685	1121	473	878	446	779	1859	2599	555	1876	2505	2651	641
309	1524	1435	1529	226	1314	326	2687	3046	1175	2396	3125	3085	462
33	1388	417	928	814	1149	798	1805	2126	293	1403	2132	2067	733
87	1149	713	818	634	912	581	1865	2370	352	1647	2376	2328	488
36	1251	782	1067	453	1041	437	2071	2466	558	1743	2472	2432	377
56	1342	962	511	1538	1104	1462	1068	2009	647	1290	1761	2177	1323
113	2088	916	1273	1802	1850	1742	832	1241	852	518	1247	1293	1649
92	1215	1202	350	1630	976	1554	1173	2205	819	1500	1923	2274	1415
74	1485	437	842	1192	1247	1139	1280	1796	249	1073	1802	1848	1045
798	2759	1889	1894	2803	2521	2738	372	963	1840	689	381	1136	2665
—	1045	848	398	1082	807	1006	1471	2276	286	1553	2104	2328	867
045	—	1805	887	1298	245	1203	2387	3284	1239	2561	3137	3336	1066
48	1805	—	1243	1231	1567	1215	1718	1737	575	1264	1994	1651	1150
98	887	1243	—	1302	649	1226	1512	2505	681	1802	2272	2574	1087
082	1298	1231	1302	—	1088	95	2465	2915	952	2192	2921	2881	237
07	245	1567	649	1088	—	994	2149	3046	1061	2322	2899	3098	856
006	1203	1215	1226	95	994	—	2412	2899	899	2176	2905	2751	142
471	2387	1718	1512	2465	2149	2412	—	1333	1513	673	750	1489	2337
276	3284	1737	2505	2915	3046	2899	1333	—	2048	765	634	173	2835
86	1239	575	681	952	1061	899	1513	2048	—	1324	2054	2100	806
553	2561	1264	1802	2192	2322	2176	673	765	1324	—	735	817	2111
104	3137	1994	2272	2921	2899	2905	750	634	2054	735	—	807	2841
328	3336	1651	2574	2881	3098	2751	1489	173	2100	817	807	—	2800
67	1066	1150	1087	237	856	142	2337	2835	806	2111	2841	2800	—

SMART TRAVEL TIPS A TO Z

Basic Information on Traveling in the United States, Savvy Tips to Make Your Trip a Breeze, and Companies and Organizations to Contact

AIR TRAVEL

BOOKING

Price is just one factor to consider when booking a flight: frequency of service and even a carrier's safety record are often just as important. Major airlines offer the greatest number of departures. Smaller airlines—including regional and no-frills airlines—usually have a limited number of flights daily. On the other hand, so-called low-cost airlines usually are cheaper, and their fares impose fewer restrictions, such as advance-purchase requirements. Safety-wise, low-cost carriers as a group have a good history—about equal to that of major carriers.

When you book **look for nonstop flights** and **remember that "direct" flights stop at least once.** Try to avoid connecting flights, which require a change of plane. Two airlines may jointly operate a connecting flight, so ask if your airline operates every segment—you may find that your preferred carrier flies you only part of the way.

Ask your airline if it offers electronic ticketing, which eliminates all paperwork. There's no ticket to pick up or misplace. You go directly to the gate and give the agent your confirmation number—a blessing if you've lost your ticket or made last-minute changes in travel plans. There's no worry about waiting on line at the airport while precious minutes tick by.

CARRIERS

➤ MAJOR AIRLINES: **Air Canada** (☎ 888/247–2262). **Alaska Airlines** (☎ 800/426–0333). **America West** (☎ 800/433–7300 or 800/235–9292). **Continental** (☎ 800/525–0280). **Delta** (☎ 800/221–1212). **Northwest** (☎ 800/225–2525). **TWA** (☎ 800/221–2000). **United** (☎ 800/241–

6522). **US Airways** (☎ 800/428–4322).

➤ SMALLER AIRLINES: **Aloha** (☎ 800/367–5250). **Hawaiian** (☎ 800/367–5320). **IslandAir** (☎ 800/323–3345). **Mesa Airlines** (☎ 800/637–2247). **SkyWest** (☎ 800/453–9417). **Southwest Airlines** (☎ 800/435–9792). **Tower Air** (☎ 800/348–6937).

➤ FROM THE U.K.: **American** (☎ 0345/789–789). **British Airways** (☎ 0845/773–3377). **Continental** (☎ 01293/776–464, 0800/776–464 toll-free). **Delta** (☎ 0800/414–767). **Northwest** (☎ 0870/507–4074). **TWA** (☎ 0181/815–0707). **United** (☎ 0845/844–4777). **Virgin Atlantic** (☎ 01293/747–747). Most serve at least the New York area plus their own U.S. hubs. British Airways serves the largest number of U.S. cities—an impressive 20 destinations, including Atlanta, Boston, Charlotte, Chicago, Dallas, Detroit, Houston, Los Angeles, Miami, New York, Orlando, Philadelphia, San Francisco, Seattle, and Washington, DC. A few cities not served by British Airways can be reached by connections with other major carriers.

➤ FROM AUSTRALIA: **Air New Zealand** (☎ 1800/063–385). **Qantas** (☎ 131313).

CHECK-IN & BOARDING

Assuming that not everyone with a ticket will show up, airlines routinely overbook planes. When everyone does, airlines ask for volunteers to give up their seats. In return, these volunteers usually get a certificate for a free flight and are rebooked on the next flight out. If there are not enough volunteers, the airline must choose who will be denied boarding. The first to get bumped are passengers who checked in late and those flying on discounted tickets, so **get to the gate and check in as early as possible,** especially during peak periods.

Although the trend on international flights is to drop reconfirmation requirements, many airlines still ask you to reconfirm each leg of your international itinerary. Failure to do so may result in your reservation being canceled.

Always **bring a government-issued photo ID to the airport.** You may be asked to show it before you are allowed to check in.

CUTTING COSTS

The least expensive airfares to the United States must usually be purchased in advance and are nonrefundable. It's smart to **call a number of airlines, and when you are quoted a good price, book it on the spot**—the same fare may not be available the next day. Always **check different routings** and look into using different airports. Travel agents, especially low-fare specialists (☞ Discounts & Deals, *below*), are helpful.

Consolidators are another good source. They buy tickets for scheduled international flights at reduced rates from the airlines, then sell them at prices that beat the best fare available directly from the airlines, usually without restrictions. Sometimes you can even get your money back if you need to return the ticket. Carefully read the fine print detailing penalties for changes and cancellations, and **confirm your consolidator reservation with the airline.**

When you **fly as a courier,** you trade your checked-luggage space for a ticket deeply subsidized by a courier service. There are restrictions on when you can book and how long you can stay.

On flights within the United States, most airlines offer non-U.S. residents discounted Visit USA fares, with savings of 25%–30%, provided the arrangements are made outside the United States. **Look for air-pass programs that give you a fixed number of domestic flights for a flat fee;** discount passes are available from many airlines, including America West, American, Delta, Hawaiian, Northwest, TWA, and United but must be booked or purchased before

you come to America. Check details with the airline or a travel agent.

➤ CONSOLIDATORS: **Cheap Tickets** (☎ 800/377–1000). **Discount Airline Ticket Service** (☎ 800/576–1600). **Unitravel** (☎ 800/325–2222). **Up & Away Travel** (☎ 212/889–2345). **World Travel Network** (☎ 800/409–6753).

➤ COURIERS: **Now Voyager** (☎ 212/431–1616).

ENJOYING THE FLIGHT

For more legroom, **request an emergency-aisle seat.** Don't sit in the row in front of the emergency aisle or in front of a bulkhead, where seats may not recline. If you have dietary concerns, **ask for special meals when booking.** These can be vegetarian, low-cholesterol, or kosher, for example. On long flights, try to maintain a normal routine, to help fight jet lag. At night, **get some sleep.** By day, **eat light meals, drink water** (not alcohol), and **move around the cabin** to stretch your legs.

FLYING TIMES

Flying time from London is 7 hours to New York; 8 hours, 40 minutes to Chicago; 9 hours, 45 minutes to Miami; and 11 hours to Los Angeles.

Flying time from Sydney is 22–23 hours to New York; and 13 hours, 25 minutes to Los Angeles on a direct flight.

Flying time from Toronto is 1½ hours to New York and 5¼ hours to Los Angeles. Flying time from Vancouver is 23 hours to Los Angeles, 4 hours to Chicago.

HOW TO COMPLAIN

If your baggage goes astray or your flight goes awry, complain right away. Most carriers require that you **file a claim immediately.**

➤ AIRLINE COMPLAINTS: U.S. Department of Transportation **Aviation Consumer Protection Division** (✉ C-75, Room 4107, Washington, DC 20590, ☎ 202/366–2220, airconsumer@ost.dot.gov, www.dot.gov/airconsumer). **Federal Aviation Administration Consumer Hotline** (☎ 800/322–7873).

AIRPORTS

The major gateways to the United States include New York, Miami, Chicago, and Los Angeles.

➤ AIRPORT INFORMATION: *See* Arriving and Departing by Plane *in* New York City, Miami, Chicago, and Los Angeles for specific information about airports in these cities, or the appropriate Arriving and Departing by Plane section under whatever city or region you are planning to fly into.

BIKE TRAVEL

Biking the nation's byways, you'll discover farms and factories, forests and strip malls, antique mansions and trailer parks. Stick to roads and bike paths or go mountain biking on the designated trail systems in city, county, and state parks. **Check the area's policy on mountain bikes before you hop on the trail,** as many parks have banned them to protect the terrain. If you ignore the ban, you could be issued a fine or, worse, have your bicycle impounded. Many ski resorts open their slopes, trails, and chairlifts to mountain bikers during the off-season.

➤ RESOURCES: **Adventure Cycling** (✉ Box 8308, 150 E. Pine St., Missoula, MT 59807, ☎ 406/721–1776 or 800/721–8719, FAX 406/721–8754, www.adv-cycling.org). **Rails to Trails Conservancy** (✉ 1100 17th St. NW, 10th fl., Washington, DC 20036, ☎ 202/331–9696, FAX 202/331–9680, www.railtrails.org) has information on the more than 10,000 mi of abandoned railroad beds that have been turned into bike trails.

BIKES IN FLIGHT

Most airlines accommodate bikes as luggage, provided they are dismantled and boxed. For bike boxes, often free at bike shops, you'll pay about $5 from airlines (at least $100 for bike bags). International travelers can sometimes substitute a bike for a piece of checked luggage at no charge; otherwise, the cost is about $100. Domestic and Canadian airlines charge $25–$50.

BUS TRAVEL

Aside from the two coasts and the major cities, long-distance buses (motor coaches) serve more of the United States than trains do. Various regional bus companies serve their areas of the country; the most extensive long-haul service is provided by Greyhound Lines. Generally no reservations are needed—**buy your tickets before boarding** (allow 15 minutes in advance in small towns, up to 45 minutes in larger cities). Long-distance buses often have reclining seats, individually controlled reading lights, rest rooms, and air-conditioning and heating.

CUTTING COSTS

Visitors from overseas can sometimes receive substantial savings on Greyhound by purchasing an Ameripass through their travel agent prior to arriving in the United States. Student discount cards are available at local bus stations.

Students age 15 and over can buy a Student Advantage Card for $22.50, which gives the user a 15% discount on all Greyhound bus tickets. The cards are valid for one academic year (August to August) and also entitle the holder to discounts at participating hotels, restaurants, car rental agencies, and retail stores.

➤ DISCOUNT PASSES: **Greyhound International** (✉ Port Authority, 625 8th Ave., New York, NY 10018, ☎ 212/971–0492 or 800/246–8572). **Greyhound** (☎ 888/454–7277, www.greyhound.com). **Student Advantage** (☎ 800/333–2920, www.studentadvantage.com).

➤ BUS INFORMATION: **Greyhound** (☎ 800/231–2222, 800/345–3109 TDD).

BUSINESS HOURS

Banks are generally open weekdays from 9 AM until 3 PM, post offices weekdays between 8 AM and 5 PM; many branches operate Saturday morning hours. Business hours tend to be weekdays from 9 to 5, a little later on the East Coast and earlier the farther west you go. Many stores may not open until 10 or 11, but they remain open until 6 or 7; most carry on brisk business on Saturday as well. Large suburban shopping malls, the focus of most Americans' shopping activity, are generally open seven days a week, with evening hours every day except Sunday. Large all-purpose stores like Wal-Mart are often open 24 hours a day, seven days a week, even in small towns. All across the country, so-called convenience stores sell food and sundries until about 11 PM. Along the highways and in major cities you can usually find all-night diners, supermarkets, drugstores, and convenience stores.

CAMERAS & PHOTOGRAPHY

➤ PHOTO HELP: **Kodak Information Center** (☎ 800/242–2424). *Kodak Guide to Shooting Great Travel Pictures,* available in bookstores or from Fodor's Travel Publications (☎ 800/533–6478; $16.50 plus $5.50 shipping).

EQUIPMENT PRECAUTIONS

Always **keep your film and tape out of the sun.** Carry an extra supply of batteries, and **be prepared to turn on your camera or camcorder** to prove to security personnel that the device is real. Always **ask for hand inspection of film,** which becomes clouded after repeated exposure to airport X-ray machines, and **keep videotapes away from metal detectors.**

CAR RENTAL

➤ MAJOR AGENCIES: **Alamo** (☎ 800/327–9633, 0181/759–6200 in the U.K.). **Avis** (☎ 800/331–1212, 800/879–2847 in Canada, 02/9353–9000 in Australia, 09/525–1982 in New Zealand). **Budget** (☎ 800/527–0700, 0144/227–6266 in the U.K.). **Dollar** (☎ 800/800–4000; 0181/897–0811 in the U.K., where it is known as Eurodollar; 02/9223–1444 in Australia). **Hertz** (☎ 800/654–3131, 800/263–0600 in Canada, 0181/897–2072 in the U.K., 02/9669–2444 in Australia, 03/358–6777 in New Zealand). **National InterRent** (☎ 800/227–7368; 0345/222525 in the U.K., where it is known as Europcar InterRent).

CUTTING COSTS

To get the best deal, **book through a travel agent, who will shop around.** Also **price local car-rental companies,** although the service and maintenance may not be as good as those of a major player. Remember to ask about required deposits, cancellation penal-

ties, and drop-off charges if you're planning to pick up the car in one city and leave it in another. If you're traveling during a holiday period, also make sure that a confirmed reservation guarantees you a car.

Do **look into wholesalers,** companies that do not own fleets but rent in bulk from those that do and often offer better rates than traditional car-rental operations.

➤ WHOLESALERS: **Auto Europe** (☎ 207/842–2000 or 800/223–5555, FAX 800/235–6321, www.autoeurope. com). **Kemwel Holiday Autos** (☎ 800/678–0678, FAX 914/825–3160, www.kemwel.com).

INSURANCE

When driving a rented car you are generally responsible for any damage to or loss of the vehicle as well as for any property damage or personal injury that you may cause. Before you rent see what coverage your personal auto-insurance policy and credit cards already provide.

For about $15 to $20 per day, rental companies sell protection, known as a collision- or loss-damage waiver (CDW or LDW), that eliminates your liability for damage to the car. Some states, including [California/Nevada], have capped the price of the CDW and LDW. You pay for only the first $100 of damage to the car in New York State, for only the first $200 in Illinois. No CDW or LDW is available in either state.

In Arizona, Maryland, Massachusetts, and Utah the car-rental company must pay for damage to third parties up to a preset legal limit, beyond which your own liability insurance kicks in. However, **make sure you have enough coverage to pay for the car.** If you do not have auto insurance or an umbrella policy that covers damage to third parties, purchasing liability insurance and a CDW or LDW is highly recommended.

REQUIREMENTS & RESTRICTIONS

In the United States you must be 21 to rent a car, and rates may be higher if you're under 25. In New York you must be 18 to rent a car. You'll pay extra for child seats (about $3 per day), which are compulsory for children under five, and for additional drivers (about $2 per day). Non-U.S. residents will need a reservation voucher, a passport, a driver's license, and a travel policy that covers each driver, when picking up a car.

SURCHARGES

Before you pick up a car in one city and leave it in another, **ask about drop-off charges or one-way service fees,** which can be substantial. Note, too, that some rental agencies charge extra if you return the car before the time specified in your contract. To avoid a hefty refueling fee, **fill the tank just before you turn in the car,** but be aware that gas stations near the rental outlet may overcharge.

CAR TRAVEL

AUTO CLUBS

Consider joining the American Automobile Association (AAA), a federation of state auto clubs that offers maps, route planning, and emergency road service to its members; members of Britain's Automobile Association (AA) are granted reciprocal privileges. Check local phone directories under AAA for the nearest club or contact the national organization.

➤ IN AUSTRALIA: **Australian Automobile Association** (☎ 02/6247–7311).

➤ IN CANADA: **Canadian Automobile Association (CAA,** ☎ 613/247–0117).

➤ IN NEW ZEALAND: **New Zealand Automobile Association** (☎ 09/377–4660).

➤ IN THE U.K.: **Automobile Association (AA,** ☎ 0990/500–600). **Royal Automobile Club (RAC,** ☎ 0990/722–722 for membership, 0345/121–345 for insurance).

➤ IN THE U.S.: **American Automobile Association** (☎ 800/564–6222).

EMERGENCY SERVICES

From any phone, **dial 911** in an emergency to reach the police, fire, or ambulance services. If your car breaks down on an interstate highway, try to pull over onto the shoulder of the road and either wait for the state police to find you or, if you have other passengers who can wait in the car, walk to the nearest emergency roadside phone and call the state police. When calling for help, note your location according to the small green mileage markers posted along the highway. Other highways are also patrolled but may not have emergency phones or mileage markers.

GASOLINE

Gasoline is relatively inexpensive in the United States, though of course the price varies from region to region and fluctuates over time. At press time the price of gas throughout the United States ranged from about $1 to $2.40 a gallon.

In many parts of the United States, long stretches of road present challenges to unwary drivers. Be sure to stock up on gasoline whenever you have the chance. Most gas stations are open late, and many large highways and big cities have 24-hour stations. However, many stations close early on Sunday night.

HIGHWAYS

The fastest routes are usually the interstate highways, each numbered with a prefix "I." Even numbers (I–80, I–40, and so on) are east–west roads; odd numbers (I–91, I–55, and so on) run north–south. These are fully signposted, limited-access highways, with at least two lanes in each direction. In some cases they are toll roads (the Pennsylvania Turnpike is I–76; the Massachusetts Turnpike is I–90). Near large cities, interstates usually intersect with a circumferential loop highway (I–295, and so on) that carries traffic around the city.

Another highway system is the U.S. highway (designated U.S. 1, and so on); they are not necessarily limited access, but well paved and usually multilane. State highways are also well paved and often have more than one lane in each direction. Large cities usually have a number of limited-access expressways, freeways, and parkways, referred to by names rather than numbers (the Merritt Parkway, the Kennedy Expressway, the Santa Monica Freeway).

ROAD CONDITIONS

Road and highway conditions vary from state to state, depending on the climate and budget allocations of a given area. In general, interstates and parkways are well maintained through revenue generated from tolls charged to all motorists. These can be collected at periodic tollbooths along the road or where you exit, depending on the distance traveled. Large highways also have the advantage of well-spaced roadside stops with public rest rooms and stores selling fast food, maps, and other sundries. Major interstates are frequented by state police and tow trucks, whose drivers can lend assistance in the event of an accident or breakdown.

ROAD MAPS

Maps can usually be purchased at gas stations, convenience stores, and rest stops for about $3. If you plan to cover an entire region within the United States, consider a detailed road atlas; these generally cost about $10 and can be purchased in the same locations mentioned above, as well as in bookstores.

RULES OF THE ROAD

Driving in the United States is done on the right side of the road. Speed limits vary and are signposted along roads and highways. **Adhere to speed limits.** Recent federal legislation allows each state to set individual speed limits; they may range from 55 or 65 miles per hour to 75 miles per hour west of the Mississippi. Watch for lower speed limits on back roads. Except for limited-access roads, highways usually post a lower speed limit in towns, so slow down when houses and buildings start to appear. Most states require front-seat occupants to wear seat belts, and in all states **children under age 4 must ride in approved child-safety seats.**

In most communities, it is permissible to make a right turn at a red light once the car has come to a full stop and there is no oncoming traffic. When in doubt about local laws, however, wait for the green light. In New York City, making a right on red is strictly prohibited.

Beware of weekday rush-hour traffic—anywhere from 6 AM to 10 AM and 4 PM to 7 PM—around major cities. To encourage car sharing, some crowded expressways may reserve an express lane for cars carrying more than one passenger. In downtown areas, watch signs carefully—there are lots of one-way streets, "no-left-turn" intersections, and blocks closed to car traffic, all in the name of easing congestion.

CHILDREN & TRAVEL

Be sure to plan ahead and **involve your youngsters** as you outline your trip. When packing, include things to keep them busy en route. On sightseeing days try to schedule activities of special interest to your children. If you are renting a car, don't forget to **arrange for a car seat** when you reserve.

FLYING

If your children are two or older, **ask about children's airfares.** As a general rule, infants under two not occupying a seat fly at greatly reduced fares or even for free. Experts agree that it's a good idea to use safety seats aloft for children weighing less than 40 pounds. Airlines set their own policies: U.S. carriers usually require that the child be ticketed, even if he or she is young enough to ride free, since the seats must be strapped into regular seats. Do **check your airline's policy about using safety seats during take-off and landing.** And since safety seats are not allowed just everywhere in the plane, get your seat assignments early.

When reserving, **request children's meals or a freestanding bassinet** if you need them. But note that bulkhead seats, where you must sit to use the bassinet, may lack an overhead bin or storage space on the floor.

LODGING

Most hotels in the United States allow children under a certain age to stay in their parents' room at no extra charge, but others charge for them as extra adults; be sure to **find out the cutoff age for children's discounts.**

SIGHTS & ATTRACTIONS

Places that are especially appealing to children are indicated by a rubber duckie icon in the margin.

THE GOLD GUIDE / SMART TRAVEL TIPS

COMPUTERS ON THE ROAD

Checking your e-mail or surfing the World Wide Web can sometimes be done in the business centers of major hotels, which usually charge an hourly rate. Web access is also available at many fax and copy centers, many of which are open 24 hours and on weekends. In major cities look for cyber cafés, where tabletop computers allow you to log on while sipping coffee or listening to live jazz.

Do check out the World Wide Web when you're planning. You'll find everything from up-to-date weather forecasts to virtual tours of famous cities. Fodor's Web site (www.fodors.com) is a great place to start your on-line travels.

CONSUMER PROTECTION

Whenever shopping or buying travel services in the United States, **pay with a major credit card** so you can cancel payment or get reimbursed if there's a problem. If you're doing business with a particular company for the first time, **contact your local Better Business Bureau and the attorney general's offices** in your own state and the company's home state, as well. Have any complaints been filed? Finally, if you're buying a package or tour, always **consider travel insurance** that includes default coverage (☞ Insurance, *below*).

➤ BBBs: **Council of Better Business Bureaus** (✉ 4200 Wilson Blvd., Suite 800, Arlington, VA 22203, ☎ 703/276–0100, FAX 703/525–8277, www.bbb.org).

CUSTOMS & DUTIES

When shopping, **keep receipts** for all purchases. Upon reentering the country, **be ready to show customs officials what you've bought.** If you feel a duty is incorrect or object to the way your clearance was handled, note the inspector's badge number and ask to see a supervisor. If the problem isn't resolved, write to the appropriate authorities, beginning with the port director at your point of entry.

IN AUSTRALIA

Australian residents who are 18 or older may bring home $A400 worth of souvenirs and gifts (including jewelry), 250 cigarettes or 250 grams of tobacco, and 1,125 ml of alcohol (including wine, beer, and spirits). Residents under 18 may bring back $A200 worth of goods. Prohibited items include meat products. Seeds, plants, and fruits need to be declared upon arrival.

➤ INFORMATION: **Australian Customs Service** (Regional Director, ✉ Box 8, Sydney, NSW 2001, ☎ 02/9213–2000, FAX 02/9213–4000).

IN CANADA

Canadian residents who have been out of Canada for at least 7 days may bring home C$500 worth of goods duty-free. If you've been away less than 7 days but more than 48 hours, the duty-free allowance drops to C$200; if your trip lasts 24–48 hours, the allowance is C$50. You may not pool allowances with family members. Goods claimed under the C$500 exemption may follow you by mail; those claimed under the lesser exemptions must accompany you. Alcohol and tobacco products may be included in the 7-day and 48-hour exemptions but not in the 24-hour exemption. If you meet the age requirements of the province or territory through which you reenter Canada, you may bring in, duty-free, 1.14 liters (40 imperial ounces) of wine or liquor *or* 24 12-ounce cans or bottles of beer or ale. If you are 16 or older you may bring in, duty-free, 200 cigarettes and 50 cigars. Check ahead of time with Revenue Canada or the Department of Agriculture for policies regarding meat products, seeds, plants, and fruits.

You may send an unlimited number of gifts worth up to C$60 each duty-free to Canada. Label the package UNSOLICITED GIFT—VALUE UNDER $60. Alcohol and tobacco are excluded.

IN NEW ZEALAND

Homeward-bound residents 17 or older may bring back $700 worth of souvenirs and gifts. Your duty-free allowance also includes 4.5 liters of wine or beer; one 1,125-ml bottle of spirits; and either 200 cigarettes, 250 grams of tobacco, 50 cigars, or a combination of the three up to 250 grams. Prohibited items include meat products, seeds, plants, and fruits.

➤ INFORMATION: New Zealand Customs (Custom House, ✉ 50 Anzac Ave., Box 29, Auckland, New Zealand, ☎ 09/359–6655, FAX 09/359–6732).

IN THE U.K.

From countries outside the EU, including the United States, you may bring home, duty-free, 200 cigarettes or 50 cigars; 1 liter of spirits or 2 liters of fortified or sparkling wine or liqueurs; 2 liters of still table wine; 60 ml of perfume; 250 ml of toilet water; plus £136 worth of other goods, including gifts and souvenirs. If returning from outside the EU, prohibited items include meat products, seeds, plants, and fruits.

➤ INFORMATION: **HM Customs and Excise** (✉ Dorset House, Stamford St., Bromley, Kent BR1 1XX, ☎ 0171/202–4227).

IN THE U.S.

➤ INFORMATION: **U.S. Customs Service** (✉ 1300 Pennsylvania Ave. NW, Washington, DC 20229, www.customs.gov; inquiries ☎ 202/354–1000; complaints c/o ✉ Office of Regulations and Rulings; registration of equipment c/o ✉ Resource Management, ☎ 202/927–0540).

DINING

The restaurants we list are the cream of the crop in each price category. Properties indicated by an ✕🏠 are lodging establishments whose restaurant warrants a special trip. Price categories are as follows:

CATEGORY	COST*
$$$$	over $40
$$$	$30–$40
$$	$20–$30
$	under $20

cost of a 3-course meal excluding drinks, tips, and taxes

MEALTIMES

Breakfast is served anywhere from 6 to 11, lunch 11 to 2, dinner from 5 until late. Like business hours in general, mealtimes tend to become earlier when you leave the cities and as you go farther west.

RESERVATIONS & DRESS

Reservations are always a good idea: we mention them only when they're essential or not accepted. Book as far ahead as you can, and reconfirm as soon as you arrive. We mention dress only when men are required to wear a jacket or a jacket and tie.

DISABILITIES & ACCESSIBILITY

LODGING RESERVATIONS

When discussing accessibility with an operator or reservations agent, **ask hard questions.** Are there any stairs, inside *or* out? Are there grab bars next to the toilet *and* in the shower/tub? How wide is the doorway to the room? To the bathroom? For the most extensive facilities meeting the latest legal specifications, **opt for newer accommodations.**

➤ COMPLAINTS: **Disability Rights Section** (✉ U.S. Department of Justice, Civil Rights Division, Box 66738, Washington, DC 20035-6738, ☎ 202/514–0301 or 800/514–0301; TTY 202/514–0301 or 800/514–0301, FAX 202/307–1198) for general complaints. **Aviation Consumer Protection Division** (☞ Air Travel, *above*) for airline-related problems. **Civil Rights Office** (✉ U.S. Department of Transportation, Departmental Office of Civil Rights, S-30, 400 7th St. SW, Room 10215, Washington, DC 20590, ☎ 202/366–4648, FAX 202/366–9371) for problems with surface transportation.

TRAVEL AGENCIES

In the United States, the Americans with Disabilities Act requires that travel firms serve the needs of all travelers. Some agencies specialize in working with people with disabilities.

➤ TRAVELERS WITH MOBILITY PROBLEMS: **Access Adventures** (✉ 206 Chestnut Ridge Rd., Rochester, NY 14624, ☎ 716/889–9096, dltravel@prodigy.net), run by a former physical-rehabilitation counselor. **Accessible Vans of the Rockies** (✉ 2040 W. Hamilton Pl., Sheridan, CO 80110, ☎ 303/806–5047 or 888/837–0065, FAX 303/781–2329, www.access-able.com/avr/avrockies.htm). **CareVacations** (✉ 5-5110 50th Ave., Leduc, Alberta T9E 6V4, ☎ 780/

986–6404 or 877/478–7827, FAX 780/986–8332, www.carevacations.com), for group tours and cruise vacations. **Flying Wheels Travel** (⊠ 143 W. Bridge St., Box 382, Owatonna, MN 55060, ☎ 507/451–5005 or 800/535–6790, FAX 507/451–1685, thq@ll.net, www.flyingwheels.com).

➤ TRAVELERS WITH DEVELOPMENTAL DISABILITIES: **New Directions** (⊠ 5276 Hollister Ave., Suite 207, Santa Barbara, CA 93111, ☎ 805/967–2841 or 888/967–2841, FAX 805/964–7344, newdirec@silcom.com, www.silcom.com/ȧnewdirec). **Sprout** (⊠ 893 Amsterdam Ave., New York, NY 10025, ☎ 212/222–9575 or 888/222–9575, FAX 212/222–9768, sprout@interport.net, www.gosprout.org).

DISCOUNTS & DEALS

Be a smart shopper and **compare all your options** before making decisions. A plane ticket bought with a promotional coupon from travel clubs, coupon books, and direct-mail offers may not be cheaper than the least expensive fare from a discount ticket agency. And always keep in mind that what you get is just as important as what you save.

DISCOUNT RESERVATIONS

To save money, **look into discount reservations services** with toll-free numbers, which use their buying power to get a better price on hotels, airline tickets, even car rentals. When booking a room, always **call the hotel's local toll-free number** (if one is available) rather than the central reservations number—you'll often get a better price. Always ask about special packages or corporate rates.

➤ AIRLINE TICKETS: ☎ 800/FLY–4–LESS. ☎ 800/FLY–ASAP.

➤ HOTEL ROOMS: **Accommodations Express** (☎ 800/444–7666, www.accommodationsexpress.com). **Central Reservation Service (CRS)** (☎ 800/548–3311). **Hotel Reservations Network** (☎ 800/964–6835, www.hoteldiscounts.com). **Players Express Vacations** (☎ 800/458–6161, www.playersexpress.com). **Quickbook** (☎ 800/789–9887, www.quickbook.com). **RMC Travel** (☎ 800/245–5738, www.rmcwebtravel.com). **Steigenberger Reservation Service** (☎ 800/223–5652, www.srs-worldhotels.com). **Turbotrip.com** (☎ 800/473–7829, www.turbotrip.com).

PACKAGE DEALS

Don't confuse packages and guided tours. When you buy a package, you travel on your own, just as though you had planned the trip yourself. Fly/drive packages, which combine airfare and car rental, are often a good deal.

ELECTRICITY

Overseas visitors will need to bring adapters to convert their personal appliances to the U.S. standard: AC, 110 volts/60 cycles, with a plug of two flat pins set parallel to one another.

EMBASSIES

In addition to their principal headquarters, most embassies have offices in Washington, D.C.

➤ AUSTRALIA: **Australian Embassy** (⊠ 1601 Massachussetts Ave. NW, Washington, DC 20036, ☎ 202/797–3000, FAX 202/797–3040, www.austemb.org).

➤ CANADA: **Canadian Embassy** (⊠ 501 Pennsylvania Ave. NW, Washington, DC 20001, ☎ 202/682–1740, FAX 202/682–7726, www.canadianembassy.org).

➤ NEW ZEALAND: **New Zealand Embassy** (⊠ 37 Observatory Circle NW, Washington, DC 20008, ☎ 202/328–4800, FAX 202/667–5227, www.nzemb.org).

➤ UNITED KINGDOM: **British Embassy** (⊠ 19 Observatory Circle NW, Washington, DC 20008, ☎ 202/588–7800, FAX 202/588–7850, www.britainusa.com).

EMERGENCIES

In most communities, **dial 911** in an emergency for police, fire, or ambulance services. In some outlying areas the quickest way to get help in an emergency is to dial 0 for an operator.

GAY & LESBIAN TRAVEL

➤ GAY- AND LESBIAN-FRIENDLY TOUR OPERATORS: **R.S.V.P. Travel Productions** (✉ 2800 University Ave. SE, Minneapolis, MN 55414, ☎ 612/379–4697 or 800/328–7787, FAX 612/379–0484), for cruises and resort vacations for gays. **Hanns Ebensten Travel** (✉ 513 Fleming St., Key West, FL 33040, ☎ 305/294–8174, FAX 305/292–9665), one of the oldest operators in the gay market. **Toto Tours** (✉ 1326 W. Albion Ave., Suite 3W, Chicago, IL 60626, ☎ 773/274–8686 or 800/565–1241, FAX 773/274–8695), for groups.

➤ GAY- & LESBIAN-FRIENDLY TRAVEL AGENCIES: **Different Roads Travel** (✉ 8383 Wilshire Blvd., Suite 902, Beverly Hills, CA 90211, ☎ 323/651–5557 or 800/429–8747, FAX 323/651–3678, leigh@west.tzell.com). **Kennedy Travel** (✉ 314 Jericho Tpk., Floral Park, NY 11001, ☎ 516/352–4888 or 800/237–7433, FAX 516/354–8849, main@kennedytravel.com, www.kennedytravel.com). **Now Voyager** (✉ 4406 18th St., San Francisco, CA 94114, ☎ 415/626–1169 or 800/255–6951, FAX 415/626–8626, www.nowvoyager.com). **Skylink Travel and Tour** (✉ 1006 Mendocino Ave., Santa Rosa, CA 95401, ☎ 707/546–9888 or 800/225–5759, FAX 707/546–9891, skylinktvl@aol.com, www.skylinktravel.com), serving lesbian travelers.

➤ GAY TRAVEL ASSOCIATIONS: The **International Gay and Lesbian Travel Association** (✉ 4331 N. Federal Hwy., Suite 304, Ft. Lauderdale, FL 33308, ☎ 800/448–8550, www.iglta.com) has more than 1,500 travel-industry members. Upon request they will provide a listing of gay-friendly travel agents and tour operators for any specified region. There is no fee for this service.

➤ PUBLICATION: *Fodor's Gay Guide to the USA,* available in bookstores or from Fodor's Travel Publications (☎ 800/533–6478; $20).

HOLIDAYS

Major national holidays include New Year's Day (Jan. 1); Martin Luther King Jr. Day (3rd Mon. in Jan.); President's Day (3rd Mon. in Feb.); Memorial Day (last Mon. in May); Independence Day (July 4); Labor Day (1st Mon. in Sept.); Thanksgiving Day (4th Thurs. in Nov.); Christmas Eve and Christmas Day (Dec. 24 and 25); and New Year's Eve (Dec. 31).

INSURANCE

The most useful travel insurance plan is a comprehensive policy that includes coverage for trip cancellation and interruption, default, trip delay, and medical expenses (with a waiver for preexisting conditions).

Without insurance you will lose all or most of your money if you cancel your trip, regardless of the reason. Default insurance covers you if your tour operator, airline, or cruise line goes out of business. Trip-delay covers expenses that arise because of bad weather or mechanical delays. Study the fine print when comparing policies.

British and Australian citizens need extra medical coverage when traveling overseas. Always **buy travel policies directly from the insurance company;** if you buy them from a cruise line, airline, or tour operator that goes out of business you probably will not be covered for the agency or operator's default, a major risk. Before making any purchase, **review your existing health and homeowner's policies** to find what they cover away from home.

➤ TRAVEL INSURERS: In the U.S.: **Access America** (✉ 6600 W. Broad St., Richmond, VA 23230, ☎ 804/285–3300 or 800/284–8300, FAX 804/673–1583, www.previewtravel.com), **Travel Guard International** (✉ 1145 Clark St., Stevens Point, WI 54481, ☎ 715/345–0505 or 800/826–1300, FAX 800/955–8785, www.noelgroup.com). In Canada: **Voyager Insurance** (✉ 44 Peel Center Dr., Brampton, Ontario L6T 4M8, ☎ 905/791–8700, 800/668–4342 in Canada).

➤ INSURANCE INFORMATION: In the U.K.: **Association of British Insurers** (✉ 51–55 Gresham St., London EC2V 7HQ, ☎ 0171/600–3333, FAX 0171/696–8999, info@abi.org.uk, www.abi.org.uk). In Australia: **Insurance Council of Australia** (☎ 03/9614–1077, FAX 03/9614–7924).

LIQUOR LAWS

Liquor laws vary from state to state, affecting such matters as bar and liquor-store opening times and whether restaurants can sell liquor by the glass or only by the bottle. A few states—mostly in the South or Midwest—allow each county to choose its own policy, resulting in so-called dry counties, where no alcoholic beverages are sold, next to counties where the bars do a roaring business.

The drinking age is 21 in all states, and you should **be prepared to show identification** in order to be served. Restaurants must obtain a license to sell alcoholic beverages on the premises, so some inexpensive establishments, or places that have recently opened, may not sell drinks at all or may sell only beer or wine. In many of these restaurants, however, you can bring your own beer or wine to drink with your meal.

Local laws against driving while intoxicated are growing stricter. Many bars now serve nonalcoholic drinks for the "designated driver," so at least one person in a group is sober enough to drive everyone else safely home.

LODGING

A wide variety of lodging facilities is available in the United States, from gilded suites with marble bathrooms and sweeping views to bare-bones rooms with concrete walls and plastic furniture. An ultralavish hotel or resort room can easily run $500-plus a night, while a spartan roadside motel in a small town could cost $20–$30 per night. Prices vary dramatically depending on location and level of luxury. Whether you're looking for the best, the cheapest, or something in between, there are ample accommodation options to choose from.

Motels are geared to motorists, with locations close to highways and convenient parking. **Airport hotels,** within a few minutes' drive of major airports, are geared to plane travelers in transit, with a strong business-travel clientele; noise may be a problem, although the best ones are soundproofed. **Convention hotels** have hundreds of guest rooms, warrens of meeting rooms (usually on separate floors), and big ballrooms used for exhibits and banquets; when a large convention is staying at one, other guests sometimes feel overwhelmed. Other **downtown hotels** cater more to individual guests and may offer more in the way of health facilities and à la carte restaurants. **Suburban hotels** in many cities attract travelers who want to be close to the circumferential highway and to suburban office parks, shopping malls, or theme parks; they may be larger and more upscale than motels, offering more restaurants, health facilities, and other amenities. **Resorts** tend to be destinations in and of themselves—complete with golf courses, tennis courts, beaches, several restaurants, on-site entertainment, and so on. The setting usually emphasizes a particular outdoor activity, whether skiing, water sports, or golf. One variation on this is the **dude ranch,** where paying guests sample horseback riding, hiking, lake fishing, cookouts, and such western-style activities as rodeos. **Country inns and bed-and-breakfasts** are generally charming older properties that, unlike European B&Bs, tend to be pricey and upscale. They may not have private bathrooms, an in-room phone, or TVs, and as they are frequently meticulously furnished with antiques, they may not be the best place to take young children. There is often an inviting common room where guests can gather for quiet conversation in front of a roaring fireplace or nestle in the folds of a big, soft chair with a good book. Breakfast is usually included in the room rate, but verify this when you make a reservation.

The lodgings we list are the cream of the crop in each price category. We list facilities that are available—but we don't specify whether they cost extra: When pricing accommodations, always ask what's included and what costs extra. Properties indicated by an ✕⚏ are lodging establishments whose restaurant warrants a special trip.

CATEGORY	COST*
$$$$	over $200
$$$	$125–$200
$$	$75–$125
$	under $75

*cost of a standard double room for two during peak season, excluding tax and service charges

Assume that hotels operate on the **European Plan** (EP, with no meals) unless we specify that they use the **Continental Plan** (CP, with a Continental breakfast), **Breakfast Plan** (BP, with a full breakfast), **Modified American Plan** (MAP, with breakfast and dinner), or the **Full American Plan** (FAP, with all meals).

APARTMENT & VILLA RENTALS

If you want a home base that's roomy enough for a family and comes with cooking facilities, **consider a furnished rental.** These can save you money, especially if you're traveling with a group. Home-exchange directories sometimes list rentals as well as exchanges.

➤ INTERNATIONAL AGENTS: **Europa-Let/Tropical Inn-Let** (✉ 92 N. Main St., Ashland, OR 97520, ☎ 541/482–5806 or 800/462–4486, FAX 541/482–0660). **Hideaways International** (✉ 767 Islington St., Portsmouth, NH 03801, ☎ 603/430–4433 or 800/843–4433, FAX 603/430–4444, info@hideaways.com, www.hideaways.com; membership $99).

Hometours International (✉ Box 11503, Knoxville, TN 37939, ☎ 865/690–8484 or 800/367–4668, hometours@aol.com, thor.he.net/áhometour/). **Interhome** (✉ 1990 N.E. 163rd St., Suite 110, N. Miami Beach, FL 33162, ☎ 305/940–2299 or 800/882–6864, FAX 305/940–2911, interhomeu@aol.com, www.inter-home.com). **Vacation Home Rentals Worldwide** (✉ 235 Kensington Ave., Norwood, NJ 07648, ☎ 201/767–9393 or 800/633–3284, FAX 201/767–5510, vhrww@juno.com, www.vhrww.com).

B&BS

A quaint and sometimes inexpensive option for those interested in getting to know the people as well as the local flavor of a town is to check into a bed-and-breakfast inn. These are often run by individuals or families who open up their homes to paying visitors. Accommodations range from modest to museum-like but often entail shared bathrooms and a limited number of bedrooms.

The fastest way to learn about current availability in a specific town or city is to call the local chamber of commerce for a list of the names and phone numbers of B&Bs in the area.

CAMPING

Some of the most reasonably priced campgrounds with the most compelling sites operate under the auspices of the National Park system (☞ National Parks, *below*). If, however, you opt for private commercial operations, your best source for nationwide information on both public and private parks is the National Association of RV Parks and Campgrounds. You can also look for annually updated directories published by the American Automobile Association for camping assessments.

An overnight stay at a commercial campground can cost from $15 to $30, depending on three factors: the amenities, location, and time of year. Tent camping, of course, is the least expensive form of accommodation; if you want water, electric, and sewage hookups, you move into the higher end of the price range.

Many private campgrounds are not open year-round, so it's important to **call ahead.** You can make reservations over the phone, and, customarily, a one-night deposit is required. The peak summer months of June, July, and August are very busy at the more desirable locations; the sooner you book, the more you can count on being awarded an attractive site.

➤ INFORMATION: **National Association of RV Parks and Campgrounds** (113 Park Ave., Fall Church, VA 22046, ☎ 703/241–8801, www.gocampingamerica.com).

➤ PUBLICATIONS: *National Parks of the West* and *National Parks and Seashores of the East*; both are available in bookstores or from Fodor's Travel Publications (☎ 800/533–6478; $17.50 and $17).

HOME EXCHANGES

If you would like to exchange your home for someone else's, **join a home-exchange organization,** which will send you its updated listings of available exchanges for a year and will include your own listing in at least one of them. It's up to you to make specific arrangements.

➤ EXCHANGE CLUBS: **HomeLink International** (✉ Box 650, Key West, FL 33041, ☎ 305/294–7766 or 800/638–3841, FAX 305/294–1448, usa@homelink.org, www.homelink.org; $98 per year). **Intervac U.S.** (✉ Box 590504, San Francisco, CA 94159, ☎ 800/756–4663, FAX 415/435–7440, www.intervac.com; $89 per year includes two catalogs).

HOSTELS

No matter what your age, you can **save on lodging costs by staying at hostels.** In some 5,000 locations in more than 70 countries around the world, Hostelling International (HI), the umbrella group for a number of national youth-hostel associations, offers single-sex, dorm-style beds and, at many hostels, rooms for couples and family accommodations. Membership in any HI national hostel association, open to travelers of all ages, allows you to stay in HI-affiliated hostels at member rates; one-year membership is about $25 for adults (C$26.75 in Canada, £9.30 in the U.K., $30 in Australia, and $30 in New Zealand); hostels run about $10–$25 per night. Members have priority if the hostel is full; they're also eligible for discounts around the world, even on rail and bus travel in some countries.

➤ ORGANIZATIONS: **Hostelling International—American Youth Hostels** (✉ 733 15th St. NW, Suite 840, Washington, DC 20005, ☎ 202/783–6161, FAX 202/783–6171, www.hiayh.org). **Hostelling International—Canada** (✉ 400–205 Catherine St., Ottawa, Ontario K2P 1C3, ☎ 613/237–7884, FAX 613/237–7868, www.hostellingintl.ca). **Youth Hostel Association of England and Wales** (✉ Trevelyan House, 8 St. Stephen's Hill, St. Albans, Hertfordshire AL1 2DY, ☎ 01727/855215 or 01727/845047, FAX 01727/844126, www.yha.uk). **Australian Youth Hostel Association** (✉ 10 Mallett St., Camperdown, NSW 2050, ☎ 02/9565–1699, FAX 02/9565–1325, www.yha.com.au). **Youth Hostels Association of New Zealand** (✉ Box 436, Christchurch, New Zealand, ☎ 03/379–9970, FAX 03/365–4476, www.yha.org.nz).

HOTELS

Hotel chains dominate the lodging landscape in the United States. Some of the large chains, such as Holiday Inn, Hilton, Hyatt, Marriott, and Ramada, are even further subdivided into chains of budget properties, all-suite properties, downtown hotels, or luxury resorts, each with a different name. Though some chain hotels may have a standardized look to them, this "cookie-cutter" approach also means that you can rely on the same level of comfort and efficiency at all properties in a well-managed chain, and at a chain's premier properties—its so-called flagship hotels—decor and services may be outstanding.

Most hotels will hold your reservation until 6 PM; **call ahead if you plan to arrive late.** Hotels will be more willing to hold a late reservation for you if you reserve with a credit-card number.

When you call to make a reservation, **ask all the necessary questions up front.** If you are arriving with a car, ask if the hotel has a parking lot or covered garage and whether there is an extra fee for parking. If you like to eat your meals in, ask if the hotel has a restaurant or whether it has room service (most do, but not necessarily 24 hours a day—and be forewarned that it can be expensive). Most hotels have in-room telephones, but double-check this at inexpensive properties and bed-and-breakfasts. Most hotels and motels have in-room TVs, often with cable movies (usually pay-per-view), but verify this if you like to watch TV. If you want an in-room crib for your child, there will probably be an additional charge. All hotels listed have private bath unless otherwise noted.

➤ TOLL-FREE NUMBERS: **Adam's Mark** (☎ 800/444–2326, www.adamsmark.com). **Baymont Inns** (☎ 800/428–3438, www.baymontinns.com). **Best Western** (☎ 800/528–1234, www.bestwestern.com). **Choice** (☎ 800/221–2222, www.hotelchoice.com). **Clarion** (☎ 800/252–7466, www.choicehotels.com). **Colony** (☎ 800/777–1700, www.colony.com). **Comfort** (☎ 800/228–5150, www.comfortinn.com). **Days Inn** (☎ 800/325–

2525, www.daysinn.com). **Doubletree and Red Lion Hotels** (☎ 800/222–8733, www.doubletreehotels.com). **Embassy Suites** (☎ 800/362–2779, www.embassysuites.com). **Fairfield Inn** (☎ 800/228–2800, www.marriott.com). **Four Seasons** (☎ 800/332–3442, www.fourseasons.com). **Hilton** (☎ 800/445–8667, www.hiltons.com). **Holiday Inn** (☎ 800/465–4329, www.holiday-inn.com). **Howard Johnson** (☎ 800/654–4656, www.hojo.com). **Hyatt Hotels & Resorts** (☎ 800/233–1234, www.hyatt.com). **Inter-Continental** (☎ 800/327–0200, www.interconti.com). **La Quinta** (☎ 800/531–5900, www.laquinta.com). **Le Meridien** (☎ 800/543–4300, www.forte-hotels.com). **Marriott** (☎ 800/228–9290, www.marriott.com). **Nikko Hotels International** (☎ 800/645–5687, www.nikko.com). **Omni** (☎ 800/843–6664, www.omnihotels.com). **Quality Inn** (☎ 800/228–5151, www.qualityinn.com). **Radisson** (☎ 800/333–3333, www.radisson.com). **Ramada** (☎ 800/228–2828. www.ramada.com), **Renaissance Hotels & Resorts** (☎ 800/468–3571, www.hotels.com). **Ritz-Carlton** (☎ 800/241–3333, www.ritzcarlton.com). **Sheraton** (☎ 800/325–3535, www.sheraton.com). **Sleep Inn** (☎ 800/753–3746, www.sleepinn.com). **Westin Hotels & Resorts** (☎ 800/228–3000, www.starwood.com). **Wyndham Hotels & Resorts** (☎ 800/822–4200, www.wyndham.com).

MOTELS

➤ TOLL-FREE NUMBERS: **Budget Hosts Inns** (☎ 800/283–4678). **Econo Lodge** (☎ 800/553–2666). **Friendship Inns** (☎ 800/453–4511). **Motel 6** (☎ 800/466–8356). **Rodeway** (☎ 800/228–2000). **Super 8** (☎ 800/848–8888).

MAIL & SHIPPING

Every address in the United States belongs to a specific zip-code district, and each zip code has five digits. Some addresses include a second sequence of four numbers following the first five numbers, but although this speeds mail delivery for large organizations, it is not necessary to use it. Each zip-code district has at least one post office, where you can buy stamps and aerograms, send parcels, or conduct other postal business. Occasionally you may find small stamp-dispensing machines in airports, train stations, bus terminals, large office buildings, hotel lobbies, drugstores, or grocery stores, but don't count on it. Most Americans go to the post office to buy their stamps, and the lines can be long.

Official mailboxes are either the stout, royal blue steel bins on city sidewalks or mail chutes on the walls of post offices or in large office buildings. A schedule posted on mailboxes and mail slots should indicate when the mail is picked up.

POSTAL RATES

First-class letters weighing up to 1 ounce can be sent anywhere within the United States with a 33¢ stamp; each additional ounce costs 22¢. Postcards need a 20¢ stamp. A half-ounce airmail letter overseas takes 60¢, an airmail postcard 55¢. For Canada, you'll need a 55¢ stamp for a 1-ounce letter, 45¢ for a postcard. For Mexico, you'll need 46¢ for a half-ounce letter, 40¢ for a postcard. For 60¢, you can buy an aerogram—a single sheet of lightweight blue paper that folds into its own envelope, already stamped for overseas airmail delivery.

RECEIVING MAIL

If you wish to receive mail while traveling in the USA, **have it sent c/o General Delivery** at the city's main post office (be sure to use the right zip code). It should be held there for up to 30 days. You must pick it up in person, and bring identification with you. American Express offices in the United States do not hold mail.

Prices throughout this guide are given for adults. Substantially reduced fees are almost always available for children, students, and senior citizens. For information on taxes, *see* Taxes, *below*.

ATMS

A debit card, also known as a check card, deducts funds directly from your checking account and helps you stay within your budget. When you want to rent a car, though, you may still need an old-fashioned credit card. Although you can always *pay* for your car with a debit card, some agencies will not allow you to *reserve* a car with a debit card.

Otherwise, the two types of plastic are virtually the same. Both will get you cash advances at ATMs worldwide if your card is properly programmed with your personal identification number (PIN). Both offer excellent, wholesale exchange rates. And both protect you against unauthorized use if the card is lost or stolen. Your liability is limited to $50, as long as you report the card missing.

CREDIT CARDS

Should you use a credit card or a debit card when traveling? Both have benefits. A credit card allows you to delay payment and gives you certain rights as a consumer (☞ Consumer Protection, *above*). Throughout this guide, the following abbreviations are used: **AE**, American Express; **D**, Discover; **DC**, Diners Club; **MC**, MasterCard; and **V**, Visa.

➤ REPORTING LOST CARDS: To report lost or stolen credit cards, use the following toll-free numbers: **American Express** (☎ 800/327–2177), **Discover Card** (☎ 800/347–2683), **Diners Club** (☎ 800/234–6377), **Master-Card** (☎ 800/307–7309), or **Visa** (☎ 800/847–2911).

BANKS

In general, U.S. banks will not cash a personal check for you unless you have an account at that bank (it doesn't have to be at that branch). Only in major cities are large bank branches equipped to exchange foreign currencies. Therefore, it's best to rely on credit cards, cash machines, and traveler's checks to handle expenses while you're traveling.

CURRENCY

The basic unit of U.S. currency is the dollar, which is subdivided into 100 cents. Coins are the copper penny (1¢) and four silver coins: the nickel (5¢), the dime (10¢), the quarter (25¢), and the half-dollar (50¢). Silver $1 coins are rarely seen in circulation. Paper money comes in denominations of $1, $5, $10, $20, $50, and $100. All these bills are the same size and green in color; they are distinguishable only by the dollar amount indicated on them and by pictures of various famous American people and monuments.

At press time (May 2000), the exchange rate was $1.53 to the pound sterling, 67¢ to the Canadian dollar, and 58¢ to the Australian dollar.

EXCHANGING MONEY

In the United States, it is not as easy to find places to exchange currency as it is in European cities. In major international cities, such as New York and Los Angeles, currency may be exchanged at some bank branches, as well as at currency-exchange booths in airports and at foreign-currency offices such as American Express Travel Service and Thomas Cook (check local directories for addresses and phone numbers). The best strategy is to **buy traveler's checks in U.S. dollars** before you come to the United States; although the rates may not be as good abroad, the time saved by not having to search constantly for exchange facilities far outweighs any financial loss.

For the most favorable rates, **change money through banks.** Although fees charged for ATM transactions may be higher abroad than at home, Cirrus and Plus exchange rates are excellent, because they are based on wholesale rates offered only by major banks. You won't do as well at exchange booths in airports or rail and bus stations, in hotels, in restaurants, or in stores, although you may find their hours more convenient. To avoid lines at airport exchange booths, **get a bit of local currency before you leave home.**

➤ EXCHANGE SERVICES: **Chase *Currency To Go*** (☎ 888/242–7384). **International Currency Express** (☎ 888/842–0880 on the East Coast, 888/278–6628 on the West Coast). **Thomas Cook Currency Services** (☎ 800/287–7362 for telephone orders and retail locations).

MONEY ORDERS, FUNDS TRANSFERS

Any U.S. bank is equipped to accept transfers of funds from foreign banks.

It helps if you can plan dates to pick up money at specific bank branches. Your home bank can supply you with a list of its correspondent banks in the United States.

If you have more time, and you have a U.S. address where you can receive mail, you can have someone send you a certified check, which you can cash at any bank, or a postal money order (for as much as $700, obtained for a fee of up to 85¢ at any U.S. post office and redeemable at any other post office). From overseas, you can have someone go to a bank to send you an international money order (also called a bank draft), which will cost a $15–$20 commission plus airmail postage. Always bring two valid pieces of identification, preferably with photos, to claim your money.

TRAVELER'S CHECKS

Do you need traveler's checks? It depends on where you're headed. If you're going to rural areas and small towns, go with cash; traveler's checks are best used in cities. Lost or stolen checks can usually be replaced within 24 hours. To ensure a speedy refund, buy your own traveler's checks—don't let someone else pay for them, as this can cause delays. The person who bought the checks should make the call to request a refund.

NATIONAL PARKS

Look into discount passes to save money on park entrance fees. The Golden Eagle Pass ($50) gets you and your companions free admission to all parks for one year. (Camping and parking are extra.) Both the Golden Age Passport ($10), for those 62 and older, and the Golden Access Passport (free), for travelers with disabilities, entitle holders to free entry to all national parks, plus 50% off fees for the use of many park facilities and services. You must show proof of age and of U.S. citizenship or permanent residency (such as a U.S. passport, driver's license, or birth certificate) and, if requesting Golden Access, proof of disability. All three passes are available at all national parks wherever entrance fees are charged. Golden Eagle and Golden Access passes are also available by mail.

➤ PASSES BY MAIL: **National Park Service** (✉ National Park Service National Office, 1849 C St. NW, Washington, DC 20240-0001, ☎ 202/208–4747).

PACKING

The American lifestyle is generally casual: Women may wear slacks and men may go without a jacket and tie virtually anywhere, except expensive restaurants in larger cities. If you prefer to dress up for dinner or the theater, though, go right ahead. As a rule, people in the Northeast dress more formally, while people in such places as Florida, Texas, and southern California are relatively informal. In beach towns, many hotels and restaurants post signs announcing that they will not serve customers who are shoeless, shirtless, or dressed in bathing suits or other skimpy attire, so tote along some shoes and cover-ups.

The United States has a wide range of climates. When deciding what weather to dress for, **read the "When to Go" sections in chapter introductions** for each region you'll be visiting. One caveat: Even in warm destinations, you may want an extra layer of clothing to compensate for overactive air-conditioning or to protect against brisk ocean breezes. Although you can count on all modern buildings being well heated in winter, historic inns and hunting lodges in rugged climates—New England, the Great Lakes states, the Rockies, or the Pacific Northwest—may be poorly insulated, drafty, or heated only by wood-burning fireplaces. Pack accordingly.

If you'll be sightseeing in historic cities, you'll spend a lot of time walking, so **bring sturdy, well-fitting, flat-heeled shoes.** Don't forget deck shoes if you want to go sailing and sandals for walking across the burning-hot sand of sunny beaches. If you plan to hike in the country, pack shoes or boots with strong flexible soles and wear long pants to protect your legs from brambles and insect bites.

Bring sunscreen lotion if you expect to be out in the sun, because prices may be high at beachside stores. These days most upscale hotels provide a basket of toiletries—soaps, shampoo, conditioner, bath gel—but if you prefer using a certain brand, bring your own. Hand-held hair dryers are sometimes provided, but don't rely on this. You can generally request an iron and ironing board from the front desk.

In your carry-on luggage, **pack an extra pair of eyeglasses or contact lenses** and **enough of any medication you take** to last the entire trip. You may also ask your doctor to write a spare prescription using the drug's generic name, since brand names may vary from country to country. In luggage to be checked, **never pack prescription drugs or valuables.** To avoid customs delays, carry medications in their original packaging. And don't forget to carry with you the addresses of offices that handle refunds of lost traveler's checks.

CHECKING LUGGAGE

How many carry-on bags you can bring with you is up to the airline. Most allow two, but not always, so make sure that everything you carry aboard will fit under your seat or in the overhead bin, and get to the gate early. Note that if you have a seat at the back of the plane, you'll probably board first, while the overhead bins are still empty.

If you are flying internationally, note that baggage allowances may be determined not by piece but by weight—generally 88 pounds (40 kilograms) in first class, 66 pounds (30 kilograms) in business class, and 44 pounds (20 kilograms) in economy.

Airline liability for baggage is limited to $1,250 per person on flights within the United States. On international flights it amounts to $9.07 per pound or $20 per kilogram for checked baggage (roughly $640 per 70-pound bag) and $400 per passenger for unchecked baggage. You can buy additional coverage at check-in for about $10 per $1,000 of coverage, but it excludes a rather extensive list of items, shown on your airline ticket.

Before departure, **itemize your bags' contents** and their worth, and label the bags with your name, address, and phone number. (If you use your home address, cover it so potential thieves can't see it readily.) Inside

each bag, **pack a copy of your itinerary.** At check-in, **make sure that each bag is correctly tagged** with the destination airport's three-letter code. If your bags arrive damaged or fail to arrive at all, file a written report with the airline before leaving the airport.

PASSPORTS & VISAS

➤ CONTACTS: **U.S. Embassy Visa Information Line** (☎ 01891/200–290; calls cost 49p per minute, 39p per minute cheap rate) for U.S. visa information. **U.S. Embassy Visa Branch** (✉ 5 Upper Grosvenor Sq., London W1A 1AE) for U.S. visa information; send a self-addressed, stamped envelope. **U.S. Consulate General** (✉ Queen's House, Queen St., Belfast BTI 6EO) if you live in Northern Ireland. **Office of Australia Affairs** (✉ 59th floor, MLC Centre, 19–29 Martin Pl., Sydney, NSW 2000) if you live in Australia. **Office of New Zealand Affairs** (✉ 29 Fitzherbert Terr., Thorndon, Wellington) if you live in New Zealand.

PASSPORT OFFICES

The best time to apply for a passport or to renew is in fall and winter. Before any trip, check your passport's expiration date, and, if necessary, renew it as soon as possible.

➤ AUSTRALIAN CITIZENS: **Australian Passport Office** (☎ 131–232, www.dfat.gov.au/passports).

➤ CANADIAN CITIZENS: **Passport Office** (☎ 819/994–3500 or 800/567–6868, www.dfait-maeci.gc.ca/passport).

➤ NEW ZEALAND CITIZENS: **New Zealand Passport Office** (☎ 04/494–0700, www.passports.govt.nz).

➤ U.K. CITIZENS: **London Passport Office** (☎ 0990/210–410) for fees and documentation requirements and to request an emergency passport.

SENIOR-CITIZEN TRAVEL

To qualify for age-related discounts, **mention your senior-citizen status up front** when booking hotel reservations (not when checking out) and before you're seated in restaurants (not when paying the bill). When renting a car, ask about promotional car-rental discounts, which can be cheaper than senior-citizen rates.

➤ EDUCATIONAL PROGRAMS: **Elderhostel** (✉ 75 Federal St., 3rd floor, Boston, MA 02110, ☎ 877/426–8056, FAX 877/426–2166, www.elderhostel.org). **Interhostel** (✉ University of New Hampshire, 6 Garrison Ave., Durham, NH 03824, ☎ 603/862–1147 or 800/733–9753, FAX 603/862–1113, www.learn.unh.edu).

STUDENTS IN THE UNITED STATES

➤ IDs & SERVICES: **Council Travel** (CIEE; ✉ 205 E. 42nd St., 14th floor, New York, NY 10017, ☎ 212/822–2700 or 888/268–6245, FAX 212/822–2699, info@councilexchanges.org, www.councilexchanges.org) for mail orders only, in the United States. **Travel Cuts** (✉ 187 College St., Toronto, Ontario M5T 1P7, ☎ 416/979–2406 or 800/667–2887, www.travelcuts.com) in Canada.

TAXES

HOTEL

Many states and cities levy hotel taxes, usually as a percentage of the room rate. For example, in New York City, there is a 13.25% progressive hotel tax and an additional 2% per-room, per-night occupancy tax. When you make room reservations **ask how much tax will be added to the basic rate.**

SALES TAX

There is no U.S. value-added tax, but sales taxes are set by most individual states, and they can range anywhere from 3% to 8¼%. In some states, localities are permitted to add their own sales taxes as well. Exactly what is taxable, however, varies from place to place. In some areas, food and other essentials are not taxable, although you might pay tax for restaurant food. Luxury items such as cigarettes and alcohol are sometimes subject to an extra tax (known colloquially as a "sin tax"), as is gasoline, on the theory that car users should provide funds used to improve local roads.

TELEPHONES

All U.S. telephone numbers consist of 10 digits—the three-digit area code, followed by a seven-digit local number. If you're calling a number from another area-code region, dial "1" then all 10 digits. If you're calling

from a distance but within the same area code, dial "1" then the last seven digits. For calls within the same local calling area, just dial the seven-digit number. A map of U.S. area codes is printed in the front of most local telephone directories; throughout this book, we have listed each phone number in full, including its area code.

Four special prefixes, "800," "888," "877," and "900," are not area codes but indicators of particular kinds of service. "800," "888," and "877" numbers can be dialed free from anywhere in the country—usually they are prepaid commercial lines that make it easier for consumers to obtain information, products, or services. The "900" numbers charge you for making the call and generally offer some kind of entertainment, such as horoscope readings, sports scores, or sexually suggestive conversations. These services can be very expensive, so **know what you're getting into before you dial a "900" number.**

COUNTRY CODES

The country code for the United States is 1.

CREDIT-CARD CALLS

U.S. telephone credit cards are not like the magnetic cards used in some European countries, which pay for calls in advance; they simply represent an account that lets you charge a call to your home or business phone. On any phone, you can make a credit-card call by punching in your individual account number or by telling the operator that number. Certain specially marked pay phones (usually found in airports, hotel lobbies, and so on) can be used only for credit-card calls. To get a credit card, contact your long-distance telephone carrier, such as AT&T, MCI, or Sprint.

DIRECTORY & OPERATOR INFORMATION

For assistance from an operator, dial "0". To find out a telephone number, call directory assistance, 555–1212 in every locality. These calls are free from a pay phone or 45¢ from a private phone. If you want to charge a long-distance call to the person you're calling, you can call collect by

THE GOLD GUIDE / SMART TRAVEL TIPS

dialing "0" instead of "1" before the 10-digit number, and an operator will come on the line to assist you (the party you're calling, however, has the right to refuse the call).

INTERNATIONAL CALLS

International calls can be direct-dialed from most phones; dial "011," followed by the country code and then the local number (the front pages of many local telephone directories include a list of overseas country codes). To have an operator assist you, dial "0" and ask for the overseas operator. The country code for Australia is 61; New Zealand, 64; and the United Kingdom, 44. To reach Canada, dial "1" + area code + number.

LONG-DISTANCE CALLS

Competitive long-distance carriers make calling within the United States relatively convenient and let you avoid hotel surcharges. By dialing an 800 number, you can get connected to the long-distance company of your choice.

➤ LONG-DISTANCE CARRIERS: **AT&T** (☎ 800/225–5288). **MCI** (☎ 800/888–8000). **Sprint** (☎ 800/366–2255).

PUBLIC PHONES

Instructions for pay telephones should be posted on the phone, but generally you insert your coins—anywhere from 10¢ to 35¢ for a local call—in a slot and wait for the steady hum of a dial tone before dialing the number you wish to reach. If you dial a long-distance number, the operator will come on the line and tell you how much more money you must insert for your call to go through.

TIPPING

Tipping is a way of life in the United States, and some individuals may even be rude if you don't give them the amount of tip they expect. At restaurants, a 15% to 20% tip is standard for waiters. The same goes for taxi drivers, bartenders, and hairdressers. Coat-check facilities usually expect $1; bellhops and porters should get about 50¢ per bag; hotel maids in upscale hotels should get about $1 per day of your stay. On package tours, conductors and drivers usually get about $2–$3 per day from each

group member; check whether this has already been figured into your cost. For local sightseeing tours, you may individually tip the driver-guide $1 if he or she has been helpful or informative. Ushers in theaters do not expect tips.

TOURS & PACKAGES

Because everything is prearranged on a prepackaged tour or independent vacation, you'll spend less time planning—and often get it all at a good price.

BOOKING WITH AN AGENT

Travel agents are excellent resources. But it's a good idea to collect brochures from several agencies as some agents' suggestions may be influenced by relationships with tour and package firms that reward them for volume sales. If you have a special interest, **find an agent with expertise in that area**; ASTA (☞ Travel Agencies, *below*) has a database of specialists worldwide.

Make sure your travel agent knows the accommodations and other services of the place being recommended. Ask about the hotel's location, room size, beds, and whether it has a pool, room service, or programs for children, if you care about these. Has your agent been there in person or sent others whom you can contact?

Do some homework on your own, too: local tourism boards can provide information about lesser-known and small-niche operators, some of which may sell only direct.

BUYER BEWARE

Each year consumers are stranded or lose their money when tour operators—even large ones with excellent reputations—go out of business. So **check out the operator.** Ask several travel agents about its reputation, and try to **book with a company that has a consumer-protection program.** (Look for information in the company's brochure.) In the United States, members of the National Tour Association and the United States Tour Operators Association are required to set aside funds to cover your payments and travel arrangements in the event that the company defaults. It's also a good idea to choose a company that participates in the American Society of Travel Agents' Tour Operator Program (TOP); ASTA will act as mediator in any disputes between you and your tour operator.

Remember that the more your package or tour includes the better you can predict the ultimate cost of your vacation. Make sure you know exactly what is covered, and **beware of hidden costs.** Are taxes, tips, and transfers included? Entertainment and excursions? These can add up.

➤ TOUR-OPERATOR RECOMMENDATIONS: **American Society of Travel Agents** (☞ Travel Agencies, *below*). **National Tour Association** (NTA; ✉ 546 E. Main St., Lexington, KY 40508, ☎ 606/226–4444 or 800/682–8886, www.ntaonline.com). **United States Tour Operators Association** (USTOA; ✉ 342 Madison Ave., Suite 1522, New York, NY 10173, ☎ 212/599–6599 or 800/468–7862, FAX 212/599–6744, ustoa@aol.com, www.ustoa.com).

THEME TRIPS

➤ OUTDOORS TRIPS: **Appalachian Mountain Club** (✉ 5 Joy St., Boston, MA 02108, ☎ 617/523–0636, FAX 617/523–0722); **Gorp Travel** (✉ Box 1486, Boulder, CO 80306, ☎ 800/444–0099, FAX 303/444–3999, www.gorptravel.com); **Mountain Travel Sobek** (✉ 6420 Fairmount Ave., El Cerrito, CA 94530-3606, ☎ 800/227–2384, FAX 510/525–7710, www.mtsobek.com); the **Nantahala Outdoor Center/NOC** (✉ 13077 U.S. 19W, Bryson City, NC 28713, ☎ 828/488–2175 or 800/232–7238). **National Audubon Society** (✉ Nature Odysseys, 700 Broadway, New York, NY 10003, ☎ 212/979–3066, FAX 212/979–8947); the **Sierra Club** (✉ 85 2nd St., 2nd floor, San Francisco, CA 94105, ☎ 415/977–5522, FAX 415/977–5795, www.sierraclub.org/outings).

➤ BICYCLING: **Adventure Cycling** (☞ Bike Travel, *above*); **Backcountry Tours** (✉ Box 4029, Bozeman, MT 59772, ☎ 406/586–3556 or 800/575–1540, FAX 406/586–4288, www.backcountrytours.com); Back-roads (✉ 801 Cedar St., Berkeley, CA 94710, ☎ 510/527–1555 or 800/462–2848, FAX 510/527–1444, www.backroads.com); **Brooks Country Cycling Tours** (✉ Box 20792, New York, NY 10025, ☎ 212/874–5151 or 800/284–8954, FAX 212/932–2529); **Cycle America** (✉ Box 485, Cannon Falls, MN 55009, ☎ 507/263–2665 or 800/245–3263, FAX 507/263–0873, www.CycleAmerica.com); **Timberline Bicycle Tours** (✉ 7975 E. Harvard St., Unit J, Denver, CO 80231, ☎ 303/759–3804 or 800/417–2453, FAX 303/368–1651, www.timbertours.com); and **Vermont Bicycle Touring** (✉ Box 711, Bristol, VT 05443, ☎ 800/245–3868).

➤ CLIMBING AND MOUNTAINEERING: **Colorado Mountain School** (✉ Box 1846, Estes Park, CO 80517, ☎ 970/586–5758 or 888/267–7783, FAX 970/586–5798, www.cmschool.com); **Exum Mountain Guides** (✉ Box 56, Moose, WY 83012, ☎ 307/733–2297, FAX 307/733–9613, www.Exumguides.com), in the Tetons; and **Yosemite Mountaineering School** (✉ Yosemite National Park, Yosemite, CA 95389, ☎ 209/372–8344, www.yosemitepark.com).

Offering a good mix of guided climbs and lessons at beginner-to-advanced levels are the **Alpine Adventures** (✉ Box 179, Keene, NY 12942, ☎ 518/576–9881, FAX 518/576–9574, www.alpineadven.com); **American Alpine Institute** (✉ 1515 12th St., Bellingham, WA 98225, ☎ 360/671–1505, FAX 360/734–8890, www.aai.cc); **Eastern Mountain Sports Climbing School** (✉ Main St., Box 514, North Conway NH 03860, ☎ 603/356–5433 or 800/310–4504, FAX 603/356–9469, www.emsclimb.com); **Fantasy Ridge Mountain Guides** (✉ Box 1679, Telluride, CO 81435, ☎ 970/728–3546, www.fantasyridge.com); **Mountain Skills Climbing School** (✉ 595 Peak Rd., Stone Ridge, NY 12484, ☎ 914/687–9643). **Nantahala Outdoor Center/NOC** (✉ 13077 U.S. 19W, Bryson City, NC 28713, ☎ 828/488–2175 or 800/232–7238); and **Sierra Wilderness Seminars** (✉ Box 988, Mt. Shasta, CA 96067, ☎ 530/926–6003, FAX 877/797–6867, www.swsmtns.com).

➤ FISHING SCHOOLS: **Bud Lilly's Trout Shop** (✉ Box 530, 39 Madison Ave., West Yellowstone, MT 59758, ☎ 406/646–7801 or 800/854–9559, www.budlillys.com). **Orvis Fly Fishing Schools** (✉ Rte. 7A, Manchester, VT 05254, ☎ 802/362–3622 or 800/235–9763, www.orvis.com). **Wulff School of Fly Fishing** (✉ Box 948, Livingston Manor, NY 12758, ☎ 914/439–5020, FAX 914/439–8055, www.royalwulff.com).

➤ GOLF CLINICS: **Craft-Zavichas Golf School** (✉ 600 Dittmer Ave., Pueblo, CO 81005, ☎ 719/564–4449 or 800/858–9633, FAX 719/564–2616 www.czgolfschool.com). **Golf Digest Schools** (✉ 5520 Park Ave., Box 395, Trumbull, CT 06611-0395, ☎ 203/373–7130 or 800/243–6121, FAX 203/373–7088, www.golfdigest.com).

➤ HIKING AND BACKPACKING TRAILS: **Appalachian Trail** (✉ Appalachian Trail Conference, Box 807, Harpers Ferry, WV 25425, ☎ 304/535–6331, www.appalachiantrail.org). The **Continental Divide Trail** (✉ Box 30002, Bethesda, MD 20824, ☎ no phone). The **Long Trail** (✉ Green Mountain Club, R.R. 1, Rte. 100, Box 650, Waterbury Center, VT 05677, ☎ 802/244–7037, FAX 802/244–5867). **Pacific Crest Trail Association** (✉ 5325 Elk Horn Blvd., P.M.B 256, Sacramento, CA 95842, ☎ 916/349–2109, FAX 916/349–1268, www.pcta.org).

➤ OFFBEAT GUIDED BACKPACKING TRIPS: **Country Inns Along the Trail** (✉ 834 Van Cortland Rd., Brandon, VT 05733, ☎ 802/247–3300). **Knapsack Tours** (✉ 2586 Chinook Dr., Walnut Creek, CA 94598, ☎ 925/944–9435, FAX 925/472–0536, www.knapsacktours.com).

➤ INN-TO-INN HORSEBACK RIDES: **Kedron Valley Stables** (✉ Box 368, South Woodstock, VT 05071, ☎ 802/457–1480 or 800/225–6301, FAX 802/457–3029, www.kedron.com). **Vermont Icelandic Horse Farm** (✉ Box 577, Waitsfield, VT 05673, ☎ 802/496–7141, FAX 802/496–5390, www.icelandichorses.com).

➤ DUDE RANCHES: **G Bar M** (✉ Box 29, Clyde Park, MT 59018, ☎ 406/686–4687). **Lone Mountain** (✉ Box 160069, Big Sky, MT 59716, ☎ 406/995–4644 or 800/514–4644, FAX 406/995–4670, www.lmranch.com). **Rancho de los Caballeros** (✉ 1551 S. Vulture Mine Rd., Wickenburg, AZ 85390, ☎ 520/684–5484 or 800/684–5030, FAX 520/684–2267, www.sunc.com).

➤ NATURE CAMPS: **Audubon Ecology Workshops** (✉ 613 Riversville Rd., Greenwich, CT 06831, ☎ 203/869–5272, FAX 203/869–4437, www.audubon.org). **Chewonki Foundation** (✉ 485 Chewonki Neck Rd., Wiscasset, ME 04578, ☎ 207/882–7323, FAX 207/882–4074, www.chenowiki.org). **National Wildlife Federation Summits** (✉ 8925 Leesburg Pike, Vienna, VA 22184, ☎ 703/790–4363 or 800/245–5484, FAX 703/790–4468). **Sierra Club Outings** (✉ 85 2nd St., 2nd floor, San Francisco, CA 94105, ☎ 415/977–5522, FAX 415/977–5795, www.sierraclub.org/outings).

➤ NATURE CAMPS IN THE NATIONAL PARKS: **Canyonlands Field Institute** (✉ Box 68, Moab, UT 84532, ☎ 435/259–7750, FAX 435/259–2335, www.canyonlandsfieldinst.org). **Glacier Institute** (✉ Box 7457, Kalispell, MT 59904, ☎ 406/755–1211, FAX 406/755–7154, www.glacierinstitute.org). **Olympic Park Institute** (✉ 111 Barnes Point Rd., Port Angeles, WA 98363, ☎ 360/928–3720 or 800/775–3720, FAX 360/928–3046, www.yni.org/opi). **Point Reyes Field Seminars** (✉ Point Reyes National Seashore, Point Reyes Station, CA 94956, ☎ 415/663–1200, FAX 415/663–8174, www.ptreyes.org). **Yellowstone Association Institute** (✉ Box 117, Yellowstone National Park, WY 82190, ☎ 307/344–2294, FAX 307/344–2485, www.yellowstoneassociation.org).

➤ NATURALIST-LED TOURS AND CRUISES: **Nature Expeditions International** (✉ 7860 Peters Rd., Suite F103, Plantation, FL 33324, ☎ 954/693–8852 or 800/869–0639, FAX 954/693–8854, www.naturexp.com).

➤ WILDERNESS SKILLS PROGRAMS: The **National Outdoor Leadership School** (✉ 288 Main St., Lander, WY 82520, ☎ 307/335–5300, FAX 307/335–1220, www.nols.edu). **Outward Bound** (✉ 100 Mystery Point Rd., Garrison, NY

10524-9729, ☎ 914/424–4000 or 800/243–8520, FAX 914/424–4280, www.outwardbound.com).

➤ RIVER RAFTING: **American River Touring Association** (⊠ 24000 Casa Loma Rd., Groveland, CA 95321, ☎ 209/962–7873 or 800/323–2782, FAX 209/962–4819, www.arta.org). **Dvoák Kayak & Rafting Expeditions** (⊠ 17921 U.S. 285, Nathrop, CO 81236, ☎ 719/539–6851 or 800/ 824–3795, FAX 719/539–3378, www. dvorakexpeditions.com). **OARS** (Outdoor Adventure River Specialists; ⊠ Box 67, Angels Camp, CA 95222, ☎ 209/736–4677 or 800/346–6277, FAX 209/736–2902, www.oars.com).

➤ SAILING SCHOOLS: **Annapolis Sailing School** (⊠ 601 6th St., Annapolis, MD 21403, ☎ 410/267–7205 or 800/638–9192, FAX 410/268–3114, www.annapolissailing.com) has a branch in the U.S. Virgin Islands. **Offshore Sailing School** (⊠ 16731 McGregor Blvd., Fort Myers, FL 33908, ☎ 941/454–1700 or 800/ 221–4326, FAX 941/454–1191, www. offshore-sailing.com.com).

➤ GROUP SKI TRIPS: **Country Inns Along the Trail** (⊠ 834 Van Cortland Rd., Brandon, VT 05733, ☎ 802/ 247–3300). **Paragon Guides** (⊠ Box 130, Vail, CO 81658, ☎ 970/926– 5299 or 877/926–5299, FAX 970/926– 5298, www.paragonguides.com).

➤ TENNIS CAMPS AND CLINICS: **Bollettieri Tennis Academy** (⊠ 5500 34th St. W, Bradenton, FL 34210, ☎ 941/755–1000 or 800/872–6425, FAX 941/752–2531, www.zonetennis. com). **Harry Hopman/Saddlebrook International Tennis** (⊠ 5700 Saddlebrook Way, Wesley Chapel, FL 33543, ☎ 813/973–1111 or 800/ 729–8383, FAX 813/973–2936, www. saddlebrookresort.com). **John Gardiner's Tennis Camp** (⊠ Box 228, Carmel Valley, CA 93924, ☎ 831/ 659–2207 or 800/453–6225, FAX 831/ 659–2492, www.jgtr.com). **John Newcombe's Tennis Ranch** (⊠ Box 310–469, New Braunfels, TX 78131, ☎ 830/625–9105 or 800/444–6204, FAX 830/625–2004, www.newktennis.com). **Tennis Camps, Ltd.** (⊠ 444 E. 82nd St., Suite 31-D, New York, NY 10028, ☎ 212/879–0225 or 800/223–2442, FAX 212/452–

0816). **Van Der Meer Tennis University** (⊠ Box 5902, Hilton Head Island, SC 29938, ☎ 843/785–8388 or 800/845–6138, FAX 843/785–7032, www.vandermeertennis.com). **Vic Braden Tennis College** (⊠ 1871 W. Canyon View Dr., St. George, UT 84770, ☎ 435/628–8060 or 800/ 237–1068, FAX 435/673–4084, www. vicbradentennis.com).

➤ HISTORY TOURS: **Studies Tours Program/National Trust for Historic Preservation** (⊠ 1785 Massachusetts Ave. NW, Washington 20036, ☎ 202/ 588–6300 or 800/944–6847, FAX 202/ 588–6246, www.nationaltrust.org). **Smithsonian Study Tours and Seminars** (⊠ 1100 Jefferson Dr. SW, Room 3077, Washington, DC 20560, ☎ 202/357–4700, FAX 202/633–9250, www.si.edu/tsa/sst.com).

➤ INTENSIVE COURSES AT COOKING SCHOOLS: **California Culinary Academy** (⊠ 625 Polk St., San Francisco, CA 94102, ☎ 415/771–3536 or 800/229–2433, FAX 415/292–8290, www.baychef.com). **Culinary Institute of America** (⊠ 433 Albany Post Rd., Hyde Park, NY 12538, ☎ 914/452– 2230 or 800/888–7850, FAX 914/451– 1066, www.ciachef.edu).

➤ CRAFTS WORKSHOPS: **Anderson Ranch Arts Center** (⊠ Box 5598, Snowmass Village, CO 81615, ☎ 970/923–3181, FAX 970/923–3871, www.andersonranch.org). **Arrowmont School of Arts and Crafts** (⊠ Box 567, Gatlinburg, TN 37738, ☎ 865/436–5860, FAX 865/430–4101, www.arrowmount.org). **Haystack Mountain School of Crafts** (⊠ Box 518, Deer Isle, ME 04627-0518, ☎ 207/348–2306, FAX 207/348–2307, www.haystack-mtn.org). **John C. Campbell Folk School** (⊠ 1 Folk School Rd., Brasstown, NC 28902, ☎ 828/837–2775 or 800/365–5724, FAX 828/837–8637). **Penland School of Crafts** (⊠ Box 37, Penland Rd., Penland, NC 28765, ☎ 828/765– 2359, FAX 828/765–7389, www. penland.org).

➤ PRINTMAKING AND FINE ARTS PROGRAMS: **Art Institute of Boston** (⊠ Continuing Education, 700 Beacon St., Boston, MA 02215, ☎ 617/262– 1223). **Dillman's Bay Resort** (⊠ Box 98, Lac du Flambeau, WI 54538,

☎ 715/588–3143). **Maine Coast Art Workshops** (✉ 2 Park St., Suite 501, Rockland, ME 04841, ☎ 207/594–2300).

➤ GUIDED PHOTOGRAPHY TOURS: **Close-Up Expeditions** (✉ 858 56th St., Oakland, CA 94608, ☎ 510/654–1548 or 800/457–9553, FAX 510/654–3043, www.cuephoto.com). **Photo Adventure Tours** (✉ 2035 Park St., Atlantic Beach, NY 11509, ☎ 516/371–0067 or 800/821–1221, FAX 516/371–1352, www.photoadventuretours.homestead.com).

➤ FIELD RESEARCH: **Earthwatch Institute** (✉ 3 Clock Tower Pl., Suite 100, Box 75, Maynard, MA 01754, ☎ 978/461–0081, FAX 978/461–2332, www.earthwatch.org). **University Research Expeditions Program** (✉ University of California, One Shields Ave., Davis, CA 95616, ☎ 530/752–0692, FAX 530/752–0681, urep.ucdavis.edu).

➤ ARCHAEOLOGICAL RESEARCH: **Four Corners School** (✉ Box 1029, Monticello, UT 84535, ☎ 435/587–2156, FAX 435/587–2193, www.sw-adventures.org).

➤ SOCIAL SERVICE: **Council on International Educational Exchange** (✉ 205 E. 42nd St., New York, NY 10017, ☎ 212/822–2600 or 888/268–6245, www.ciee.org). **Points of Light Foundation** (✉ 1737 H St. NW, Washington, DC 20005, ☎ 202/729–8000, www.pointsoflight.org).**Volunteers for Peace International Workshops** (✉ 1034 Tiffany Rd., Belmont, VT 05730, ☎ 802/259–2759, FAX 802/259–2922, www.vfp.org.)

TRAIN TRAVEL

Amtrak is the national passenger rail service. It runs a limited number of routes; the northeast coast from Boston down to Washington, D.C., is generally well served. Chicago is a major rail terminus as well.

Some trains travel overnight, and you can sleep in your seat or book a couchette at additional cost. Most trains have diner cars with acceptable food, but you may prefer to bring your own. Excursion fares, when available, may save you nearly half the round-trip fare.

FARES & SCHEDULES

Train schedules can be obtained at ticket counters or special displays in train terminals. Automated schedule and fare information is often available 24 hours a day on local or toll-free numbers.

➤ TRAIN INFORMATION: **Amtrak** (☎ 800/872–7245, 800/523–6590 TDD, ☎ 800/872–7245; 800/523–6590 TDD).

CHILDREN

Children under 2 ride free (one child per adult) if they don't occupy a seat; children 2–15 accompanied by a fare-paying adult pay half-price (two children per adult); children 16 and over pay the full adult fare.

CUTTING COSTS

The USA Railpass allows overseas visitors 15 or 30 days of unlimited nationwide travel for $440 or $550 (peak season, June 1–September 5) and $295–$385 (off peak, September 8–May 31), respectively. Fifteen- and 30-day regional rail passes can be purchased by non-U.S. citizens for the Far West ($245/$320, peak season; $190/$250, off-peak), Western ($325/$405, peak; $200/$270, off-peak), Eastern ($260/$320, peak; $210/$265, off-peak), and Northeast ($205/$240, peak; $185/$225, off-peak) areas of the United States; 30-day passes are also offered for rail travel along the East Coast and West Coast (each is $285, peak; $235, off-peak) regions of the country. You can purchase these rail passes in the United States at any Amtrak station, but to qualify you must show a valid non-U.S. passport. If you're a student, ask about student discounts that may apply to certain passes.

SENIOR CITIZENS

Senior citizens (over 62) are entitled to a 15% discount on the lowest available fares.

TRAVELERS WITH DISABILITIES

Amtrak requests 48 hours' advance notice to provide redcap service, special seats, or wheelchair assistance at stations equipped to provide these services.

Passengers with disabilities receive 15% off an adult one-way fare.

TRAVEL AGENCIES

A good travel agent puts your needs first. Look for an agency that has been in business at least five years, emphasizes customer service, and has someone on staff who specializes in your destination. In addition, **make sure the agency belongs to a professional trade organization.** The American Society of Travel Agents (ASTA), with 27,000 agents in some 170 countries, is the largest and most influential in the field. Operating under the motto "Integrity in Travel," it maintains and enforces a strict code of ethics and will step in to help mediate any agent-client disputes if necessary. ASTA also maintains a Web site that includes a directory of agents. (If a travel agency is also acting as your tour operator, *see* Buyer Beware *in* Tours & Packages, *above*.)

➤ LOCAL AGENT REFERRALS: **American Society of Travel Agents** (ASTA; ☎ 800/965–2782 24-hr hot line, FAX 703/ 684–8319, www.astanet.com). **Association of British Travel Agents** (✉ 68– 71 Newman St., London W1P 4AH, ☎ 0171/637–2444, FAX 0171/637– 0713, www.abtanet.com). **Association of Canadian Travel Agents** (✉ 1729 Bank St., Suite 201, Ottawa, Ontario K1V 7Z5, ☎ 613/521–0474, FAX 613/ 521–0805, acta.ntl@sympatico.ca). **Australian Federation of Travel Agents** (✉ Level 3, 309 Pitt St., Sydney 2000, ☎ 02/9264–3299, FAX 02/9264–1085, www.afta.com.au). **Travel Agents' Association of New Zealand** (✉ Box 1888, Wellington 10033, ☎ 04/499–0104, FAX 04/499– 0827, taanz@tiasnet.co.nz).

VISITOR INFORMATION

State tourism offices, city tourist bureaus, and local chambers of commerce, which are usually the best sources of information about their communities, are listed throughout this book at the beginning of each state, city, or regional section. Government agencies can be an excellent source of inexpensive travel information. When planning your trip, **find out what government materials are available.**

➤ IN CANADA: **Travel USA** (☎ 905/ 890–5662).

➤ IN THE U.K.: There is no single tourist organization for the United States; U.S. states have their own agencies. Call **Visit USA** (☎ 0891/ 600–530) for contact addresses and telephone numbers; calls cost 50p per minute peak times, 45p per minute all other times.

➤ U.S. GOVERNMENT RESOURCES: Contact the **Consumer Information Center** (✉ Consumer Information Catalogue, Pueblo, CO 81009, ☎ 888/878–3256, FAX 719/948–9724, www.pueblo.gsa.gov) for a free catalog that includes travel titles.

WEB SITES

Do check out the World Wide Web when you're planning. You'll find everything from current weather forecasts to virtual tours of famous cities. Fodor's Web site (www.fodors.com) is a great place to start your online travels. When you see a 🕸 in this book, go to www.fodors.com/urls for an up-to-date link to that destination's site.

For contact information on state tourism offices go to www.information-USA.com.

WHEN TO GO

Although there is no country-wide tourist season, various regions may have high and low seasons that are reflected in airfares and hotel rates. Unless the weather is a real drawback (as in Alaska in the winter or Miami in August), **visit areas during their off-season to save money and avoid crowds.**

CLIMATE

For climate information in specific regions of the country, **read the "When to Go" sections in United States Region-by-Region chapter.**

➤ FORECASTS: **Weather Channel Connection** (☎ 900/932–8437), 95¢ per minute from a Touch-Tone phone.

THE UNITED STATES
REGION-BY-REGION

The United States of America occupies a vast expanse of land and is a treasure of climates and cultures. From mountains and oceans to deserts and meadows, from sprawling cities of towering skyscrapers to villages with roots still firmly planted in the past, the U.S.A. cannot be summed up easily. This chapter attempts to make sense of it all by dividing the country into 10 regions.

THE NORTHEAST

Connecticut, Maine, Massachusetts, New Hampshire, New York, Rhode Island, Vermont

T HE TWO MAJOR METROPOLITAN areas of the Northeast—New York and Boston—offer the best of modern city life, the hurly-burly and intensity that come with so many ambitious citizens pursuing their dreams. New York City—one of the world's leading financial and cultural capitals—belongs to the world as much as to the country. Boston, the nation's oldest (and still leading) college town, has redefined itself as a hub of service and high-tech industries. As distinguished as each metropolis is, neither entirely defines the region: Captured in a single wide-angle lens, the six states of New England and massive New York State are decidedly un-urban, with a wider variety of landscapes and outdoor diversions per square mile than any other part of the country.

Beyond the glitz and grime of New York City, the Northeast fans out in waves of increasingly soothing vistas, from the placid charms of the Connecticut River valley and Rhode Island's Narragansett Bay, through the forests of Vermont and New Hampshire's Green and White mountains, to the pristine hinterland of Maine's remote Allagash Wilderness Waterway. Similarly, the "wilderness" of upstate New York begins within an hour's drive of the Bronx: The Hudson River valley lures frazzled urban dwellers northward past the Catskill resorts to the 6.2-million-acre Adirondack Park. At the western end of the state, the wonders of Niagara Falls attract visitors from around the world.

The region was historically defined by the coastline, where the Pilgrims first established a toehold in the New World. Until it veers inland north of Yarmouth, Maine, I–95 skirts the inlets and harbors that sheltered the whaling and trading vessels of 17th- to 19th-century settlers—Mystic, Connecticut; Providence, Rhode Island; Cape Cod, Nantucket, and Plymouth, Massachusetts; and Portland, Maine. Beyond the interstate's exits, in-between the museums and tourist centers, lies a region with a wealth of diversions—cerebral, spiritual, athletic. Every season brings its own recreations—fishing in New York and in Vermont's Lake Champlain, skiing in the White and Green mountains, camping on the Appalachian Trail, biking along Maine's rocky coast, sailing on Long Island Sound, applauding world-class musicians in the Berkshires, watching whales cavort off Cape Cod.

When to Go

Spring blooms start in April along the southern coastal regions and begin later the farther north you go. This tends to be the quietest period throughout the region because of rains and melting snows. **Summer,** which ranges from an average monthly high of 85°F in the southern region to an average monthly low of 59°F in the north, attracts beach lovers to the islands and coastal regions; those preferring cooler climes head to the lakes in New York State, the mists of Maine, or the mountains of Massachusetts, Vermont, and New Hampshire. **Autumn** is a kaleidoscope of colors as leaves change from green to burning gold. Temperatures remain around 55°F into October in many places. **Winter** brings snow and skiers to the mountain slopes of most states in the region (Vermont is the most popular).

Prices during an area's peak season—summer along coastal regions, winter in ski areas, and autumn inland and in the mountains—climb accordingly. Newport hotel rooms in summer, for example, typically go for double the winter prices. Room rates also rise during festivals, such as the outdoor music festival at Tanglewood, in Massachusetts's Berkshire hills. During peak seasons, reserve hotel rooms well ahead.

Festivals and Seasonal Events

Winter

➤ EARLY DEC.: The **Nantucket Stroll** (☎ 508/228–1700), the best known of the many Christmas-season celebrations held throughout **Cape Cod**, takes place on the first Saturday of the month.

➤ DEC.: The little town of **Bethlehem (CT)** is the site of a large annual Christmas festival (☎ 203/266–5557).

➤ NEW YEAR'S EVE: The final day of the year is observed with festivals and entertainment in many locations during **First Night** celebrations. Among the cities hosting such events are **Providence, Rhode Island** (☎ 401/227–2601); **Portland, Maine** (☎ 207/772–9012); **Boston, Massachusetts** (☎ 617/542–1399); and **Danbury, Hartford,** and **Stamford, Connecticut.** In New York City, the **Ball Drop in Times Square** (☎ 212/768–1560) is the New Year's Eve party the whole world watches.

➤ MID-JAN.: Vermont's **Stowe Winter Carnival** (☎ 802/253–7321) is among the country's oldest such celebrations.

➤ FEB.: Well-bred canines take over Madison Square Garden in New York City for the **Westminster Kennel Club Dog Show** (☎ 212/465–6000 or 212/465–6741). In the invitational **Annual Empire State Building Run-Up** (☎ 212/736–3100, 212/860–4455 for The New York Roadrunners Club), 125 runners scramble up the 1,576 stairs from the lobby of the Empire State Building to the 86th-floor observation deck.

In New York, Saranac Lake's weeklong **Winter Carnival** (☎ 518/891–1990), with its trademark ice palace, is the oldest winter carnival in the eastern United States.

Spring

➤ MAR.: At **maple-sugaring festivals,** held throughout the month and into April, the sugarhouses of Maine, New Hampshire, Vermont, Massachusetts, and Connecticut demonstrate procedures like maple-tree tapping and sap boiling.

➤ MAR. 17: All of Boston turns out for the **St. Patrick's Day Parade** (☎ 888/733–2678).

➤ MID-APR.: On Patriot's Day in Boston, celebrants reenact **Paul Revere's ride** (☎ 888/733–2678 or 800/888–5155) while the **Boston Marathon** (☎ 617/236–1652) fills the streets from Hopkinton to Back Bay.

➤ LATE APR.: In Massachusetts, Nantucket's four-day **Daffodil Festival** (☎ 508/228–1700) celebrates spring with a flower show, shop-window displays, and a procession of antique cars that ends with tailgate picnics at Siasconset.

➤ EARLY MAY: New York's **Cherry Blossom Festival** (☎ 718/623–7200) is held at the Brooklyn Botanic Garden.

Summer

➤ JUNE: New York City's Lincoln Center hosts the **Annual American Crafts Festival** (☎ 973/746–0091) a couple of weekends during the month.

➤ EARLY JUNE: The **Belmont Stakes** (☎ 718/641–4700, ext. 732), Thoroughbred racing's final Triple Crown event, takes place at Belmont Park, in Elmont, New York.

➤ MID-JUNE: The **Festival of Historic Houses** (☎ 401/831–7440) celebrates the Colonial, Greek Revival, and Victorian homes of **Providence, Rhode Island.**

➤ LATE JUNE: **Lesbian and Gay Pride Week** (☎ 212/807–7433) in New York City includes the world's largest lesbian and gay pride parade. The **Texaco New York Jazz Festival** (☎ 212/219–3006) showcases more than 200 groups spread in venues all over town. Besides classic acts, you'll find acid, Latin, and avant-garde jazz.

➤ LATE JUNE–EARLY JULY: Boston's weeklong Fourth of July celebration, **Harborfest** (☎ 617/227–1528), includes a concert synchronized to fireworks over the harbor.

➤ LATE JUNE–AUG.: The **Jacob's Pillow Dance Festival** (☎ 413/243–0745), at Becket, Massachusetts, in the Berkshires, hosts performers from various dance traditions.

➤ EARLY JULY: **Schooner Days** and the **North Atlantic Blues Festival** showcase top blues singers in a **Rockland, Maine,** harbor-front park (☎ 207/596–0376).

➤ JULY–AUG.: The **Mid-Summer Night Swing** (☎ 212/875–5400) fills the Fountain Plaza of New York City's Lincoln Center with swinging couples and live music; swing lessons are given before the dance. The **Tanglewood Music Festival** (☎ 413/637–1600 or 617/638–9235), in Lenox, Massachusetts, the summer home of the Boston Symphony Orchestra, schedules top performers.

➤ JULY 4: The **Fourth of July Parade** (☎ 401/245–0750) in Bristol, Rhode Island, is the oldest Independence Day parade in the country, attracting thousands of visitors and an array of bands and military units.

➤ MID-JULY: Held in the picturesque village of Wickford, Rhode Island, the **Wickford Art Festival** (☎ 401/295–5566) is

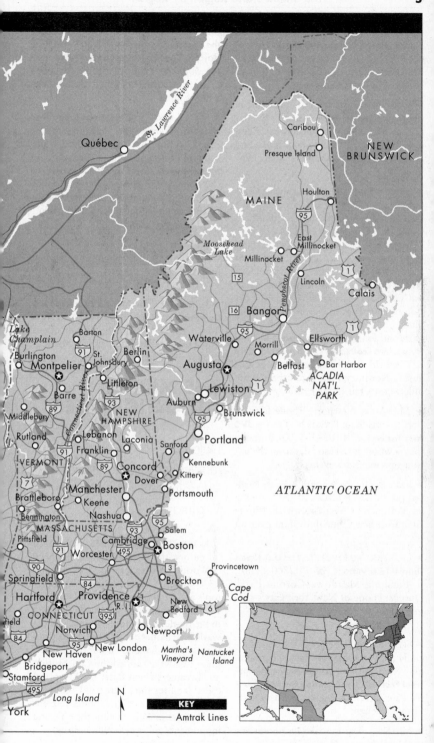

Québec

St. Lawrence River

NEW BRUNSWICK

MAINE

Caribou

Presque Island

Houlton

95

Moosehead Lake

East Millinocket

Millinocket

Penobscot River

15

Lincoln

Calais

Bangor

16

95

1

Waterville

Ellsworth

Morrill

1

Lake Champlain

Barton

Berlin

Augusta

Belfast

Bar Harbor

Burlington

91

St. Johnsbury

ACADIA NAT'L. PARK

Montpelier

Lewiston

Littleton

Barre

Auburn

1

89

93

Brunswick

Middlebury

NEW HAMPSHIRE

95

Connecticut River

Rutland

Lebanon

Laconia

Portland

91

Franklin

Sanford

VERMONT

89

Kennebunk

ATLANTIC OCEAN

7

Concord

Manchester

Dover

Kittery

Brattleboro

Keene

Portsmouth

Bennington

Nashua

MASSACHUSETTS

95

Pittsfield

93

Salem

Cambridge

Worcester

91

Boston

90

495

Springfield

3

Provincetown

84

Brockton

Cape Cod

Hartford

Providence

New Bedford

6

CONNECTICUT

R.I.

395

84

Norwich

Newport

95

New London

Martha's Vineyard

Nantucket Island

New Haven

Bridgeport

Stamford

495

York

Long Island

N

one of the oldest, largest, and most diversified art festivals on the East Coast. Rhode Island's **Newport Music Festival** (☎ 401/846–1133) brings together celebrated musicians for two weeks of concerts in **Newport** mansions.

➤ LATE JULY: Forty wineries take part in the **Finger Lakes Wine Festival** (☎ 607/535–2481), which also brings hay rides, arts and crafts, food, and jazz, blues, and bluegrass music to **Watkins Glen, New York**.

➤ EARLY AUG.: The **Maine Lobster Festival** (☎ 207/596–0376) is a public feast held on the first weekend of the month in **Rockland**. The **Maine Festival** (☎ 207/772–9012) in **Portland** is the state's largest and most diverse art and cultural event showcasing music, dance, theater, and literary readings. **Ben & Jerry's Folk Festival** (☎ 401/847–3700), held in Fort Adams State Park in **Newport, Rhode Island**, books top names like the Indigo Girls and Joan Baez. The **League of New Hampshire Craftsmen's Festival** (603/224–3375), held during the first week of August in **Newbury, New Hampshire**, is the oldest crafts fair in the nation.

➤ MID-AUG.: Newport, Rhode Island's Fort Adams State Park is host to the **JVC Jazz Festival** (☎ 401/847–3700), formerly the Newport Jazz Festival, one of the nation's premier jazz events.

➤ LATE AUG.: The **Rhythm & Roots Festival** (☎ 401/351–6312), at the Stepping Stone Ranch in **West Greenwich, Rhode Island**, attracts Cajun music fans from all over.

➤ LATE AUG.–EARLY SEPT.: The **U.S. Open Tennis Tournament** (☎ 718/760–6200), in Flushing Meadows–Corona Park, Queens, is one of **New York City**'s premier sport events.

Autumn

➤ SEPT.: Labor Day fairs in the region include the **Vermont State Fair,** in Rutland, and Rhode Island's **Providence Waterfront Festival.** The **Common Ground Country Fair,** in Unity, Maine, is an organic farmer's delight.

➤ MID SEPT.: The annual **New Hampshire Highland Games** (☎ 800/358–7268) is a four-day event held in **Lincoln** featuring Scottish music, dancing, food, and athletic events.

➤ OCT.: College Crew teams and spectators come from all over for the **Head of the Charles Regatta** (☎ 617/864–8415) in Boston. The **Nantucket Cranberry Harvest** (☎ 508/228–1700) is a three-day celebration that includes bog and inn tours and a crafts fair.

➤ EARLY OCT.: The **Columbus Day Parade** (☎ 800/888–5515) in **Boston** moves from East Boston to the North End, while south of Boston on the same weekend, the **Massachusetts Cranberry Harvest Festival** (☎ 508/295–5799 May–October) takes place in both **Plymouth** and neighboring South Carver's Edaville Cranberry Bog.

➤ EARLY NOV.: The **New York City Marathon** (☎ 212/860–4455) is the world's largest; it winds through all five boroughs of the city and finishes at the Tavern on the Green in Central Park.

➤ LATE NOV.: The **Macy's Thanksgiving Day Parade** (☎ 212/494–5432) is a New York City tradition; huge balloons float down Central Park West at 77th Street to Broadway and Herald Square.

THE MIDDLE ATLANTIC STATES

Delaware, Maryland, New Jersey, Pennsylvania, Virginia, Washington, D.C., West Virginia

IN THE CLOSING DECADES of the 18th century, the major action in the New World was here, in five of the original 13 colonies. General George Washington's audacious crossing of the Delaware River made possible the colonists' victory in the Battle of Trenton; Virginia saw the war's final battles and surrender; the Constitution was hammered out in Philadelphia; Delaware ratified the Constitution and became the first state; and Maryland ceded land for the District of Columbia. Today the people of these states remember the past, proudly tending their historic monuments and welcoming visitors.

The Middle Atlantic countryside of rolling farmland and woods, ancient, soft-edged mountains, broad rivers, and green valleys is a livable land in a manageable climate—

a land much walked through and fought over. Besides the Revolution, the region suffered many of the battles of the Civil War and today commemorates their sites. On its eastern edge (part of the densely populated urban corridor that runs from Boston to Richmond), you'll find the cities and most of the history. The international, multiracial population produces every possible cuisine, and you can buy anything on earth in the upscale boutiques, department stores, and antiques shops.

Beyond the New Jersey Turnpike are long beaches, casino-filled Atlantic City, and Victorian Cape May to the east; horse country, ski resorts, and Philadelphia to the west. The Eastern Shore's Delaware and Maryland beaches are sedate or swinging; Virginia Beach is both. And the seafood anywhere near the Chesapeake Bay is superb. Baltimore combines historic buildings with new restaurants and shops; Annapolis and Oxford are ports for boaters tooling around the Chesapeake. Washington, D.C., the nation's seat of government, is a wonderful showplace for visitors, with myriad treasures set off by cherry trees. Alexandria's historic district, in Virginia, and Georgetown's splendid town houses recall the capital's early years. In Williamsburg you'll hear echoes of the Revolution and sample 18th-century life.

West of the Tidewater, or the coastal region, the towns are smaller and farther apart. Continuing on a circuit past Richmond, with its glorious capitol, you'll come to Charlottesville, Thomas Jefferson's hometown; farther west rise the Blue Ridge Mountains and West Virginia's Appalachians, sprinkled with palatial 19th-century resorts. At the stunning confluence of the Shenandoah and Potomac rivers sits Harpers Ferry, where John Brown met his fate; and back in Pennsylvania are Gettysburg and Amish country. These are the habitats of the country auction, the wonderful local restaurant, and the farmhouse bed-and-breakfast—the secret places off the beaten track that you'll love to discover for yourself.

When to Go

In the cool early **spring** Washington's pink cherry blossoms are at their peak for a few spectacular days. The many equestrian events in Maryland and Virginia also her-ald the season. **Summer** is swampy in Washington, Baltimore, and Philadelphia, with temperatures in the 80s, yet thousands flock to all three for monuments or baseball. Ocean bathers head to the Jersey shore, Rehoboth, Ocean City, and Virginia Beach. The dazzling **autumn** foliage in Virginia's Shenandoah Valley and West Virginia's Potomac Highlands draws hordes and also signals the opening of the orchestra, theater, and ballet seasons in the cities, most notably Philadelphia. In **winter,** when temperatures average in the 40s, workaday Washington grinds to a halt after just a sprinkling of snow, but Maryland, Pennsylvania, Virginia, and West Virginia offer downhill and cross-country skiing, weather permitting.

Festivals and Seasonal Events

Winter

➤ EARLY DEC.–JAN. 1: The **National Christmas Tree Lighting/Pageant of Peace** (☎ 202/619–7222), in **Washington, D.C.,** begins on the second Thursday in December, when the president lights the tree, and is followed by nightly choral performances at the Ellipse, a grassy area on the White House complex.

➤ JAN. 1: The **Mummers Parade** (☎ 215/636–1666, 215/336–3050 for Mummer's Museum), in **Philadelphia,** ushers in the year with some 20,000 sequined and feathered marchers between Broad Street and city hall.

➤ JAN. 22: The **Presidential Inaugural Parade** (☎ 202/789–7000) promenades down **Washington D.C.'s** Pennsylvania Avenue from the Capitol to the White House.

➤ MID-FEB.: **George Washington's Birthday** (☎ 703/838–4200) is celebrated in **Alexandria, Virginia,** with a parade and reenactment of a Revolutionary War skirmish at nearby Fort Ward.

Spring

➤ EARLY MAR.: The **Philadelphia Flower Show** (☎ 215/988–8800), the nation's largest indoor flower show, has acres of exhibits and themed displays.

➤ LATE MAR.: **Maryland Days** (☎ 301/862–0990) of **St. Mary's City, Maryland,** commemorates the founding of the colony at its original birthplace. The **Virginia Festival of the Book** (☎ 804/924–3296) in **Charlottesville** celebrates the book with

The Middle Atlantic States

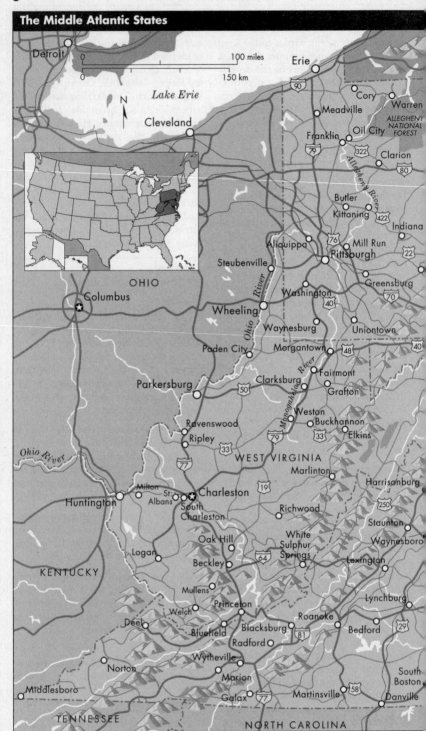

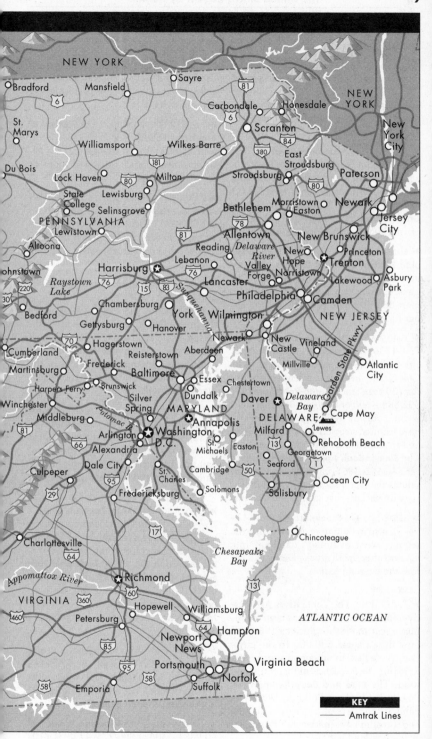

programs for all ages, panel discussions, readings, and the participation of more than 100 writers.

➤ LATE MAR.–EARLY APR.: The two-week-long **National Cherry Blossom Festival** (☎ 202/728–1137, 202/547–1500, or 202/619–7275) takes place in Washington, D.C., with a parade, a marathon, and a Japanese lantern-lighting ceremony.

➤ MID-APR.: The **Azalea Festival** (☎ 757/622–2312) in Norfolk, Virginia, features a parade, an air show, concerts, a ball, and the coronation of a queen from a NATO nation. Throughout Virginia during **Historic Garden Week** (☎ 804/644–7776), grand private homes open their doors to visitors.

➤ LATE APR.–EARLY MAY: The **Philadelphia Festival of World Cinema** (☎ 800/969–7392) presents more than 100 features, documentaries, and short films from more than 30 countries at venues throughout the city.

➤ EARLY MAY: **Old Dover Days** (☎ 302/734–1736) celebrates Delaware's capital city with a parade, dancing, and tours of Colonial homes and gardens. For more than 20 years, the **Point-to-Point Races** (☎ 302/888–4600 or 800/448–3883) at Winterthur outside Wilmington, Delaware, have featured steeplechase and pony races and an annual tailgate picnic competition. The **Shenandoah Apple Blossom Festival** (☎ 540/662–3863) in Wichester, Virginia, salutes the regions apple-growing industry with parades, live music, and a circus.

➤ MID MAY: The **Preakness** (☎ 410/542–9400), held in Baltimore, Maryland, is the second event of horse racing's Triple Crown, after the Kentucky Derby and before the Belmont Stakes.

Summer

➤ EARLY JUNE: The **Three River Arts Festival** (☎ 412/281–8723) has been an annual event in Pittsburgh since 1960 and now draws some 600,000 to the city's Point State Park for its commissioned and juried art, theater, dance, music, crafts, and food. The **Blue and Grey Reunion** (☎ 304/457–4265), in Philippi, West Virginia, is four days of music, food, crafts, and a costumed reenactment of the Civil War's first land battle.

➤ JUNE: Philadelphia's **First Union U.S. Pro Cycling Championship** (☎ 215/636–1666), the country's premier bicycle race,

attracts the world's top cyclists to its 156-mi course; a two-week celebration leads up to the event.

➤ LATE JUNE: The **Hampton Jazz Festival** (☎ 757/838–4203), in Hampton, Virginia, brings together top performers in various styles of jazz.

➤ LATE JUNE–EARLY JULY: The **Festival of American Folklife** (☎ 202/357–2700), held on the Mall in Washington, D.C., celebrates music, arts, crafts, and foods of regional cultures.

➤ EARLY JULY: Philadelphia's **Sunoco Welcome America Festival** (☎ 215/636–1666 or 800/537–7676) includes parades, hot-air balloon races, ceremonies at Independence Hall, a restaurant festival, and July 4 fireworks.

➤ JULY 4: **Independence Day** celebrations in Baltimore (☎ 410/837–4636) culminate in a major show of fireworks over the Inner Harbor. Celebrations in Washington, D.C. (☎ 202/619–7222), include a grand parade, a National Symphony Orchestra performance on the steps of the Capitol, and fireworks over the Washington Monument.

➤ EARLY AUG.: The **Virginia Highlands Festival** (☎ 540/623–5266 or 540/676–2282), in Abingdon, has crafts and farm animals on exhibit, antiques for sale, painting and writing workshops, hot-air balloon rides, and a variety of musicians in concert.

➤ LATE AUG.: The **Wine Festival** (☎ 410/267–6711) in The Plains, Virginia, features tastings of vintages from about 45 Virginia wineries, plus grape stomping and musical entertainment. The **Philadelphia Folk Festival** (☎ 215/242–0150) is America's oldest (1962) continuous folk festival; performers at the three-day event range from young crooners to folk superstars.

Autumn

➤ LABOR DAY WEEKEND: At the **Crafts Festival** (☎ 302/888–4600 or 800/448–3883), at Winterthur, Delaware, 200 craftspeople sell high-quality contemporary and traditional work.

➤ EARLY–MID-OCT.: **Victorian Week** (☎ 609/884–5404 or 800/275–4278) is a 10-day celebration of Cape May, New Jersey's Victorian heritage; historic house tours and craft and antiques shows are a highlight. **United States Sailboat and Power-**

boat Shows (☎ 410/268–8828), the world's largest events of their kind, take place in **Annapolis, Maryland.**

➤ MID-OCT.: The **Taste of DC Festival** (☎ 202/724–5430) presents dishes from a variety of **Washington, D.C.,** eateries. In **Harpers Ferry, West Virginia,** the park service stages **Election Day 1860** (☎ 304/535–6298), when people portraying the presidential candidates of the region's 1860 ballot come to debate the hot topics of that day: states' rights versus a strong federal union.

➤ LATE OCT.: **Fiddler's and Sea Witch Weekend Festival** (☎ 302/227–2233), in **Rehoboth Beach, Delaware,** is a madcap Halloween spectacular that welcomes visitors with fiddler's contests, music, parades, hayrides, and the antics of masked marauders. The **Marine Corps Marathon** (☎ 703/784–2225) is nicknamed the "Marathon of the Monuments," starting at the Marine Corps War Memorial in **Arlington, Virginia,** and winding through **Washington, D.C.**

➤ LATE OCT.–EARLY NOV.: New Hollywood and independent movies are screened at the **Virginia Film Festival** (☎ 804/982–5277) in **Charlottesville, Virginia;** it's fast becoming a major event in the film biz.

➤ EARLY NOV.: Backyard inventors test their pumpkin-throwing contraptions at the **Punkin Chunkin** (☎ 800/515–9095), in **Lewes, Delaware;** the current record, set by a gourd-hurling, homemade pneumatic cannon, is a whopping 3,718 ft.

➤ NOV.–DEC.: **Yuletide at Winterthur** (☎ 302/888–4600 or 800/448–3883) is a Christmas-theme tour of the treasure-filled rooms at this vast museum near **Wilmington, Delaware.**

THE SOUTHEAST

Alabama, Florida, Georgia, North Carolina, South Carolina

F ROM PINE TO PALM, lapped by the Atlantic Ocean and the Gulf of Mexico, stretch North and South Carolina, Georgia, Florida, and Alabama. Celluloid stereotypes portray Southerners as dreaming life away on the veranda, julep in hand, among the magnolias and Spanish moss. Certainly, there are verandas. Magnolias still bloom. Spanish moss drapes trees growing along coastal lowlands. And certainly, too, the Southeast retains its taste for history, especially its own, but nowadays the Southeast is clearly dealing in the present and planning for tomorrow as it vigorously competes with the rest of the country and, indeed, the world for business and economic development.

With the exception of Florida, all these states have both mountains (with resorts and sports) and seashore (with beaches and boating); in Florida the coast is never more than 70 mi away. It's a good thing, too, because the region's temperatures and humidity are fierce, although air-conditioning has transformed the summers. Southerners, chiefly wealthy ones, often sought refuge from the region's legendary heat in the highlands and piney woods of the Carolinas and northern Georgia. Today these areas are highly regarded resort destinations.

It's commonly held that following the Civil War the South entered a period of economic decay from which it has only recently emerged. In fact, huge fortunes—consider Coca-Cola—were made in the South after the war. It was the Great Depression that brought much economic disruption to the region. Post-depression poverty prevented much of the tearing down and rebuilding common in the rest of the East and forced people to make do with that outmoded old Empire and Victorian furniture they had hoped to replace with the new machine-made marvels. It also caused many of the classic homes to suffer decay and, sometimes, to be demolished. But much has been retained and restored. Today dozens of Greek Revival and Victorian mansions containing their original furnishings are open during special festival times to visitors, while others have become house museums open to the public on a regular basis. White-columned houses, some in advanced states of disrepair, have been rescued and restored, often converted into bed-and-breakfast inns, so that travelers may today sleep in those tall mahogany and walnut beds in which wealthy 19th-century plantation owners once slumbered.

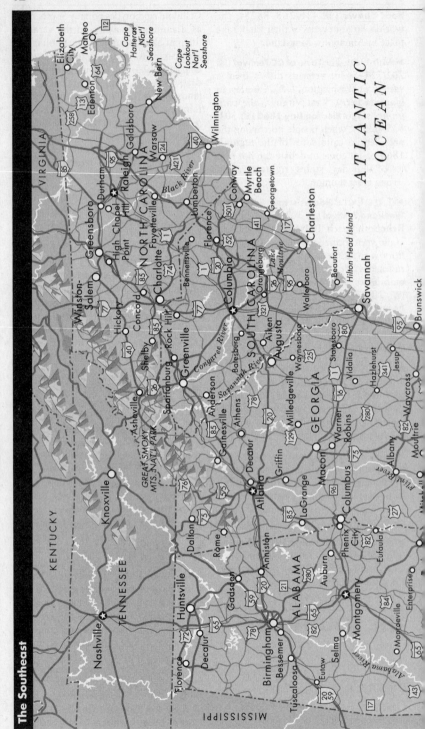

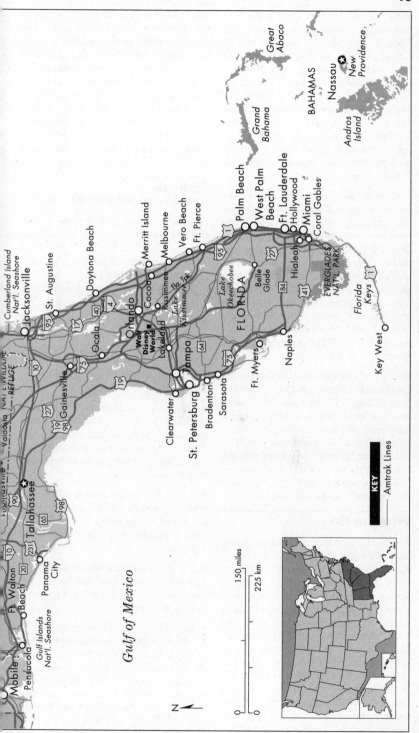

Some of the cities are charmingly old-fashioned; in Savannah and Charleston, Edenton, and Mobile, you can wander through houses on shady squares with brick courtyards and gardens of astonishing fecundity. There are modern cities, too: the dynamic, high-tech Research Triangle region of Raleigh–Durham–Chapel Hill; the booming transportation hub that is Atlanta; Birmingham, the city that grew up on steel-making and is today a major medical center; and Miami, infused with Cuban culture.

Food in the Southeast today is as adventurous as regional fare can be: You may savor anything from fancy nouvelle cuisine to down-home country food and dishes drawn from the plantation tradition. To come South and fail to taste barbecue, with all its subregional variations, is to miss the treat of a lifetime. Spicy Cajun and Caribbean restaurants, authentic Asian and Mexican restaurants reflecting the tastes of new immigrants, and classic Italian and French fare all make dining in the Southeast a rich experience.

And there's always that well-regarded southern hospitality, perhaps inherited from the region's Celtic roots. "Y'all come, hear?" is an oft-heard, and oft-parodied, invitation, but it is usually extended in earnest. If you take it seriously and show up, you can bet you'll be greeted warmly. Southerners are an easygoing bunch—talkative, courteous, and witty, with a talent for laughing and enjoying life.

When to Go

The best times to visit the South are **spring** and **fall,** when temperatures are in the 70s and 80s. That's when golf and tennis buffs converge on the region en masse. Spring also brings the magnificent azaleas, magnolias, and other flora of the region to life, and visitors come to "ooh" and "aah" their way through the gardens and historic homes that traditionally open to the public at this time of year. Fall, when colors reach their peak in the mountains of Alabama, Georgia, and the Carolinas, draws thousands of leaf worshipers. Autumn is also a popular season for senior citizens to visit the region, taking advantage of smaller crowds and lower rates in beach and resort areas. **Winter** can be quite pleasant in the Southeast, especially in the more temperate, lower coastal regions of Georgia and Florida. In the higher elevations of western North Carolina and Georgia, temperatures often drop to freezing between mid-November and mid-March, producing ideal conditions for area ski resorts. **Summer** tends to be hot and muggy, with temperatures often soaring into the 90s, especially in Florida and at the lower elevations of Alabama, Georgia, and the Carolinas. That's when flatlanders (mountain slang for nonresidents) flock to the mountains to cool off.

Festivals and Seasonal Events

Festivals are a way of life in the Southeast. Even the smallest communities have planned celebrations around offbeat and often obscure themes, such as chitterlings (pronounced chitlins), hog-calling and hollering contests, and the woolly worm.

Winter

➤ EARLY NOV.–LATE DEC.: **Salem Christmas** (☎ 336/721–7300 or 888/653–7253) is celebrated in Old Salem, the restored 18th-century village once home to the Moravians, a Protestant sect, in **Winston-Salem, North Carolina.**

➤ LATE NOV.–DEC.: **Christmas at Biltmore** (☎ 800/543–2961) brings six weeks of festive decorations, musical concerts, and candlelit tours to this estate, the largest private home in America, near **Asheville, North Carolina.**

➤ EARLY DEC.: The **Atlanta Festival of Trees** (☎ 404/264–9348) celebrates the Christmas season with a parade and exhibit of elaborately decorated trees and wreaths.

➤ MID-JAN.: **Art Deco Weekend** (☎ 305/539–3000) spotlights **Miami Beach's** historic district with a street fair, a gala, and live entertainment.

➤ LATE JAN.–EARLY FEB.: For more than 15 years, the **Cloister Food and Wine Classic** (☎ 912/638–3611 or 800/732–4752), on **Sea Island, Georgia,** has enjoyed an international reputation for quality classes, seminars, tastings, and dinners matching food and wine. **Gasparilla Pirate Fest** (☎ 888/224–1733), in **Tampa, Florida,** celebrates Tampa's historic heritage with a parade and other street festivities.

➤ LATE JAN.–EARLY MAR.: The **Winter Equestrian Festival** (☎ 561/793–5867 or

813/623–5801), at the Palm Beach Polo Equestrian Grounds in Wellington in **West Palm Beach, Florida,** includes more than 3,000 horses and three grand prix equestrian events.

➤ FEB.: **Black History Month** is observed throughout the South, with special events at many bookstores, universities, and other cultural venues, including **Tuskegee University** (☎ 334/727–8837), in Tuskegee, Alabama; **Southern University** (☎ 225/771–4500), in Baton Rouge, Louisiana; and in **Atlanta, Georgia,** at the **Martin Luther King Jr. Center for Nonviolent Social Change** (☎ 404/526–8900).

➤ MID-FEB.: **Mardi Gras** in Mobile, Alabama (☎ 334/208–2000 or 800/252–3862), is an uproarious, pre-Lenten celebration similar to its more famous cousin in New Orleans. The **Miami Film Festival** (☎ 305/377–3456) screens 10 days of international, U.S., and local films. The **Florida Manatee Festival** (☎ 352/795–3149), in **Rock Crusher Canyon,** near Crystal River, focuses on fine art from around the country as well as manatee education.

Spring

➤ EARLY MAR.: The long-running **Annual Sanibel Shell Fair** (☎ 941/472–2155), which begins the first Thursday of the month and lasts four days, is the largest event of the year on **Sanibel Island, Florida.**

➤ MID-MAR.: In **South Carolina,** the **Aiken Triple Crown** (☎ 803/641–1111), with its Thoroughbred trials, harness races, and steeplechases, draws thousands of equestrian enthusiasts. **Macon, Georgia**'s annual **Cherry Blossom Festival** (☎ 912/751–7429) celebrates the city's more than 200,000 cherry trees with tours of classic antebellum and Victorian homes, concerts, art exhibitions, and assorted special events. The charming streets of downtown **Fairhope, Alabama,** are filled with fine art as well as an assortment of crafts at the **Fairhope Arts and Crafts Festival** (☎ 334/928–6387).

➤ MID-MAR.–EARLY MAY: **Springtime Tallahassee** (☎ 904/224–5012) is a major cultural, sporting, and culinary event in Florida's capital.

➤ MAR. 17: The **St. Patrick's Day Celebration** (☎ 800/444–2427), in **Savannah, Georgia,** is one of the country's largest, honoring Ireland's patron saint.

➤ EARLY APR.: The **Masters Golf Tournament** (☎ 800/726–0243), in **Augusta, Georgia,** attracts top golf pros and spectators to this tournament of tournaments. Atlanta's springtime launches with the **Atlanta Steeplechase** (☎ 404/237–7436), a benefit for the Atlanta Speech School. It's held at Kingston Downs, near Cartersville, Georgia, just north of Atlanta (advance tickets only). **The Atlanta Dogwood Festival** (☎ 404/329–0501) has craft shows, hot-air balloons, concerts, and other cultural events in Piedmont Park. The **North Carolina Azalea Festival** (☎ 910/763–0905) in **Wilmington** celebrates the brilliantly colored blooms with entertainers, a parade, street fairs, home and garden tours, plant sales, and visits to nearby ships.

➤ LATE APR.–EARLY MAY: Florida's **Daytona Beach Music Festival** (☎ 800/654–3018), held over two consecutive weekends, includes concerts by marching, jazz, and stage bands, choirs, and orchestras.

➤ LATE MAY: In Beaufort, South Carolina, the annual **Gullah Festival** (☎ 843/525–0628) highlights the fine arts, customs, language, and dress of Lowcountry African-Americans. Over Memorial Day weekend Anderson, South Carolina, celebrates **Freedom Weekend Aloft** (☎ 864/232–3700), one of the largest balloon rallies in the country. There are also amusement rides, arts and crafts, and special events.

➤ LATE MAY–EARLY JUNE: **Spoleto Festival USA** (☎ 843/722–2764), which draws world-renowned performers and artists to **Charleston, South Carolina,** gets global attention (advance tickets necessary for most events). Running concurrently, the Piccolo Spoleto Festival offers cultural events that are either free or very inexpensive.

Summer

➤ EARLY JUNE: The **Sun Fun Festival** (☎ 843/916–7239), in Myrtle Beach, South Carolina, features beauty-queen contests, sand sculpting, and other activities.

➤ MID-JULY: The **Annual Highland Games and Gathering of the Scottish Clans** (☎ 828/733–1333 or 800/468–7325), held in the high meadows of **Grandfather Mountain** in North Carolina, is one of the largest Scottish celebrations in the world.

➤ MID-LATE JULY: The **Hemingway Days Festival** (☎ 305/294–1136) holds look-alike contests as well as first-novel and short-story competitions in Key West, Florida. The **Folkmoot USA: North Carolina International Folk Festival** (☎ 828/452–2997), held in locales throughout western North Carolina over a two-week period, spotlights dancers and singers from around the globe.

➤ EARLY–MID-AUG.: The **Georgia Mountain Fair** (☎ 706/896–4191), a mountain craft and music extravaganza, is held near Hiawasee, Georgia.

Autumn

➤ EARLY OCT.: The annual **Indian Key Festival** (☎ 305/664–4815), in Florida, celebrates the Key's history the first weekend of the month.

➤ MID-OCT.: The second full week in October, the **Alabama's National Shrimp Festival** (☎ 334/968–6904), held in Gulf Shores, celebrates with seafood, arts and crafts, fine art, and music. **Big Pig Jig** (☎ 912/268–8275), in Vienna, Georgia, attracts more than 100 entrants to compete for championships in several barbecue categories (ribs, shoulders, whole hog), plus hollering competitions, a beauty pageant, a parade, and music.

➤ MID-NOV.: The annual **Miami Book Fair International** (☎ 305/237–3258), one of the largest book fairs in the United States, is held on the Miami-Dade Community College Wolfson Campus.

THE MISSISSIPPI VALLEY

Arkansas, Kentucky, Louisiana, Mississippi, Tennessee

S TAND ON A SHORE of the Mississippi River, and you're swept with emotions: Here are the waters that have sweetened the delta and fed the imagination of the South. The five states that constitute the Mississippi Valley all sweat history; each has Civil War battlefields and citizens with long, long memories. You can find the New South here, of course, but the Old South—of Cotton Is King, of Christ Is Coming, of aristocracy and its flip side, poverty—is never far away.

The soil is rich: No sight in the world affects a Southerner like the fields of cotton ready for harvest. The region isn't only farmland, though; Tennessee, Kentucky, and Arkansas are blessed with some of the most beautiful mountain scenery in America. The metropolises, from Louisville to Shreveport to Jackson, have their big-city grandeur and decay. Outside them you'll see the regal old plantation houses, but you'll also pass along godforsaken stretches of state road with tumbledown shanties that can look more desolate than any city slum.

Yet the folk culture that sprouted among the poor people of these states took root and spread its branches far out into the world. Nashville calls itself the capital of country music; Memphis will always mean rhythm and blues; New Orleans is the cradle of jazz. And all three cities—all three musics—had a hand in delivering rock and roll. Graceland, the Memphis mansion where Elvis lived and died in tacky majesty, stands now as an unofficial monument to the best American art and the worst American taste.

The region gave the world not only music beloved the world over but also its own revered cuisine. A visitor can find ambrosial ribs in the barbecue palaces of Memphis or at hole-in-the-wall luncheonettes on Arkansas roadsides. Those lucky enough to have tasted fried chicken or fried catfish down here have been known to lose their taste for chicken and catfish anywhere else. The scent of collard greens stewing in pork fat, of sweet potatoes glistening with sugar and butter, emanates from some deep place as central to the culture as the one that produced the Mississippi blues of Muddy Waters and the long, hypnotic phrases of Faulkner.

Farther downriver the spirit changes. The sauces become more complex; the music turns airier, and so does the mood. The fundamentalism of the Bible Belt loosens into a kind of good-time Catholicism whose motto is *Laissez les bons temps rouler*—Let the good times roll. Cajun festivals, for everything from gumbo to petroleum, are just about always happening—any excuse for a party. The biggest excuse, of course, is Mardi Gras (Fat Tuesday), the day before Lent begins, which is celebrated throughout southern Louisiana and all along the Gulf Coast.

By the time the Mississippi gets this close to the Gulf, its width is monumental, but the water is warm, unhurried. And so is New Orleans. It's as though the river chose this city as the place to deposit all the richness it has picked up on its long journey. You come here to slow down, relax, enjoy the good life, and dedicate your days to pleasure.

When to Go

The best times to visit the Mississippi Valley states are **April** and **October,** when temperatures and humidity are comfortable: in Louisiana and Mississippi, the mid-70s; in the mountains of Arkansas, Kentucky, and Tennessee, the 60s, cooling off to the mid-40s at night. In **spring** everything is in glorious bloom; in the **fall** the trees, especially in the mountains, are bright with turning leaves. You can tour magnificent historic mansions in spring and fall.

If you dislike crowds, avoid New Orleans during Mardi Gras (February or March, depending on when Easter falls) and Louisville during the Kentucky Derby (the first Saturday in May). Visits during these times require flight and hotel reservations long in advance; also, expect hotel prices to jump.

Festivals and Seasonal Events

Winter

➤ JAN.–FEB.: The **Dixie National Rodeo/Western Festival/Livestock Show** (☎ 601/961–4000 or 800/354–7695) in Jackson, Mississippi, features rodeos and other events.

➤ FEB. 27: **Mardi Gras** (☎ 504/566–5031) in New Orleans, Louisiana, caps several weeks of madness: street festivals, parades with fantastic floats, marching bands, and eye-popping costumes.

Spring

➤ LATE MARCH: The **Tennessee Williams New Orleans Literary Festival** (☎ 504/581–1144) presents lectures and workshops on Williams, as well as modern authors and literary issues.

➤ MAR.–APR.: In **Mississippi, spring pilgrimages** to elegant antebellum mansions are held throughout the state, with Natchez (☎ 800/647–6724 or 800/647–6742) claiming grande-dame status, followed by **Columbus** (☎ 800/327–2686) and **Vicksburg** (☎ 800/221–3536). On the coast, the annual tour stretches from state line to state line and is free (☎ 888/467–4853).

➤ LATE APR.: The **Annual Arkansas Folk Festival** (☎ 501/269–8068), in Mountain View, salutes the folk culture of the Ozarks with music, dance, crafts, a parade, and a rodeo. The **Festival International de Louisiane** (☎ 318/232–3737), in Lafayette, brings together more than 600 local and far-flung performers in music, visual arts, theater, dance, cinema, and cuisine for a dizzying globe-grazing extravaganza.

➤ LATE APR.–EARLY MAY: The **New Orleans Jazz & Heritage Festival** (☎ 504/522–4786) draws hundreds of thousands of musicians, fans, and artisans for a 10-day all-out jam session.

➤ MAY: The **Memphis in May International Festival** (☎ 901/525–4611), a monthlong salute to the city, includes music on Beale Street and the **World Championship Barbecue Cooking Contest.**

➤ MAY 6: In Louisville the **Kentucky Derby,** one of horse racing's premier events, is preceded by a two-week festival (☎ 502/584–6383 or 502/636–4402) with parades, riverboat races, and many a mint julep. For racing information, call Churchill Downs (☎ 502/584–6383 or 502/636–4402).

Summer

➤ EARLY JUNE: The **Great French Market Tomato Festival** (☎ 504/522–2621), in New Orleans, is one of many food festivals held throughout the state this month.

➤ MID-JUNE: The **International Country Music Fan Fair** (☎ 615/889–7503), in Nashville, Tennessee, lets country music fans mix with their favorite stars in a weeklong celebration featuring live shows, exhibits, autograph sessions, and special concerts.

➤ AUG.: Memphis, Tennessee, pulls out all the stops for the **Elvis International Tribute Week** (☎ 901/543–5333 or 901/332–3322).

➤ LATE AUG.: **Louisville's Kentucky State Fair** (☎ 502/367–5000) draws some half-million people, with rooster-crowing contests, top-name concerts, a horse show, and an amusement park.

The Mississippi Valley

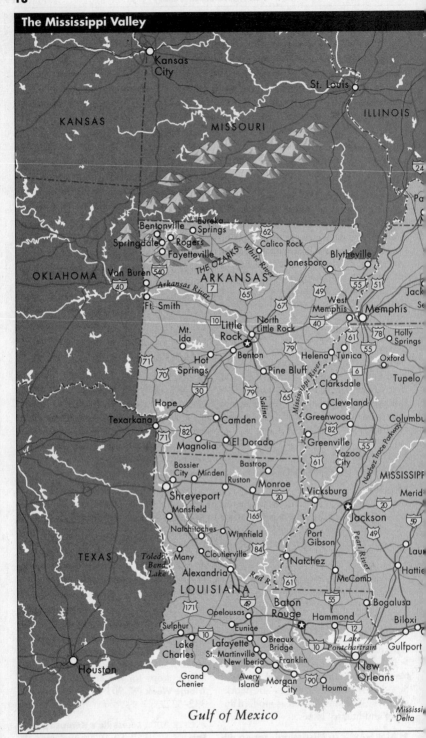

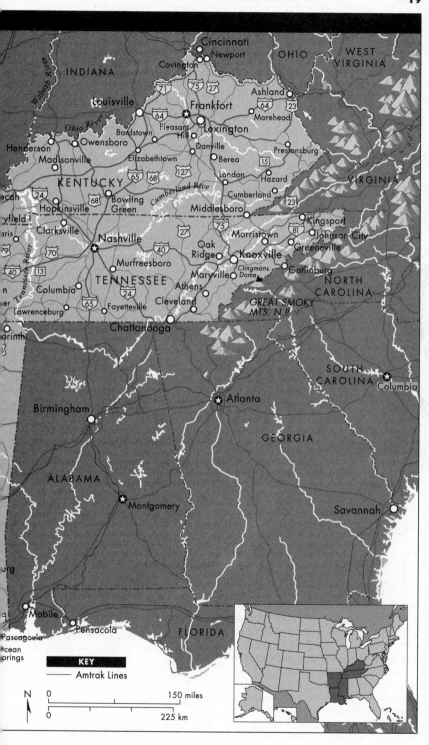

KEY
— Amtrak Lines

N

0   150 miles
0   225 km

Autumn

➤ EARLY SEPT.: The **Zydeco Music Festival** (☎ 318/942–2392), in Plaisance, Louisiana, is the original festival devoted to the state's indigenous musical genre.

➤ LATE SEPT.: The **Festivals Acadiens** (☎ 318/232–3737) attract more than 100,000 annually to see, hear, taste, and experience Cajun life in Lafayette, the capital of French Louisiana.

➤ EARLY OCT.: The first full weekend of the month, Allardt, Tennessee, hosts the two-day **Great Pumpkin Festival** (☎ 931/879–9948), with contests, crafts, and gospel singing.

➤ EARLY OCT.: Held on the weekend preceding Columbus Day, the **King Biscuit Blues Festival** (☎ 888/274–0907), named after the King Biscuit Flour Co. and a revered local blues radio-program broadcast since the 1940s, draws national and regional blues and gospel acts to Helena, Arkansas.

➤ LATE OCT.: The **Canton Flea Market Arts and Crafts Festival** (☎ 601/859–1307 or 800/844–3369), the largest one-day crafts show in the Southeast, takes place on Courthouse Square in Canton, Mississippi.

THE MIDWEST AND GREAT LAKES

Illinois, Indiana, Michigan, Minnesota, Ohio, Wisconsin

T**HE MIDWEST IS AMERICA,** that prototypical vision of neat farmland, affluent suburbs, and compact, skyscrapered downtowns strung together along purposefully straight silver highways. Sauk Centre, Minnesota, was the setting for Sinclair Lewis's *Main Street*; Muncie, Indiana, was the subject of the sociological study called *Middletown, USA*. It is no accident that stand-up comedians use midwestern town names—Peoria, Sheboygan, Kokomo, Kalamazoo—to mean "the heart of the country." Transplanted Midwesterners spend the rest of their lives longing for broad, clear horizons; thick, shady stands of beech and maple trees; and hazy summer afternoons when kids sell lemonade from sidewalk stands. People

seem genuinely friendlier and more down-to-earth here.

Six states—Ohio, Indiana, Michigan, Illinois, Wisconsin, and Minnesota—occupy what was originally the Northwest Territory, a vast tract of forest and meadow awarded to the United States in the 1783 Treaty of Paris. Unlike the stark Great Plains to the west, this is gently rolling landscape, punctuated by rivers, woods, and trees. It is defined by great geological features: to the east, the Appalachian Mountains; to the north, the Great Lakes; to the south, the Ohio River; to the west, the majestic Mississippi River.

Smarting from years of being labeled "the sticks," midwestern cities are always trying to prove themselves, cheerfully rehabilitating their downtowns, rooting for their major-league ball teams, and building gleaming convention centers and festival malls. Ohio has no fewer than five important cities (Cleveland, Cincinnati, Columbus, Dayton, and Toledo). Minnesota's major population center comprises two cities, Minneapolis and St. Paul, which means that there are twice as many parks and museums as you'd expect. Indiana's capital, Indianapolis, is a beautifully laid-out city that's also the amateur-sports capital of the country. In Michigan, Detroit is the home of America's auto industry. Surprisingly, it also has the greatest number of theater seats outside of New York City. Milwaukee, Wisconsin, poised on the western shore of Lake Michigan, is a rich melting pot of immigrant cultures, as is vibrant and powerful Chicago, Illinois, the region's one great metropolis.

But it's never more than an hour's drive from these cities to northern lake resorts, historic villages along sleepy back roads, utopian colonies, and pleasant university towns. Big swatches of forest and lakeshore are protected as parkland, and gorgeous scenic drives edge the Great Lakes and the dramatic bluffs of the Mississippi and Ohio river valleys.

When to Go

Summer is the most popular time to visit the Midwest and the Great Lakes. Generally, the farther north you go, the fewer people you'll find. Prices in most places peak in July and August. Daily temperatures average in the 80s in Illinois, Indiana, and Ohio, though July and August heat waves can push them high into the 90s. In Michigan, Wisconsin, and Minnesota, temperatures run 10° cooler. These three states have the best **fall** foliage, though you can see good color in all six. Depending on the weather, the leaves usually begin to turn in mid-September and reach their most colorful by mid-October. In **winter** Michigan has the only significant downhill skiing in the region, but cross-country is all the rage in Wisconsin and Minnesota. The Midwest usually gets at least one subzero cold snap every year. For the rest of winter expect temperatures in the 20s and 30s and about 10°F colder in northern Michigan, Wisconsin, and Minnesota. Sudden snowstorms can make winter driving unpredictable and treacherous. **Spring** is damp and clammy, with erratic weather and temperatures ranging from the 30s to the 60s.

Festivals and Seasonal Events

Winter

➤ JAN.: International Falls, Minnesota, hosts **Ice Box Days** (☎ 218/283–9400), a long-weekend festival of snow sculpture, skating, cross-country skiing, and the Freeze Your Gizzard Blizzard Run. The six-day **Plymouth International Ice Sculpture Spectacular** (☎ 734/459–6969), in Plymouth, Michigan, features 150 carvers from around the world, in addition to nightly light shows and a life-size ice carousel. The best snowmobile racers in the country gather in Eagle River, Wisconsin, to compete on a half-mile banked ice track at the **World's Championship Snowmobile Derby** (☎ 715/479–4424).

➤ LATE JAN.–EARLY FEB.: Minnesota's 10-day **St. Paul Winter Carnival** (☎ 612/223–4700 or 800/488–4023) celebrates winter with a sleigh and cutter parade, an ice palace, car races on the ice, and ice sculptures by artists from around the world.

➤ LATE FEB.: The three-day **DYNO American Birkebeiner** (☎ 715/634–5025), which starts in Cable, Wisconsin and ends in Hayward, Wisconsin, is the largest cross-country ski marathon in North America.

Spring

➤ MARCH: During **Eagle Watch Weekend** (☎ 800/657–4972) the spring migration of bald eagles can be viewed along the Mississippi River in the vicinity of **Winona, Minnesota.**

➤ MAY: The monthlong **Indianapolis 500 Festival** (☎ 317/237–3400) culminates in the most famous car race in the United States. The **Holland Tulip Time Festival** (☎ 800/822–2770), in Holland, Michigan, showcases flowers and Dutch traditions.

Summer

➤ EARLY JUNE: The **Detroit Grand Prix** (☎ 313/393–7749), held on scenic **Belle Isle**, in Detroit, is the cornerstone of a three-day downtown event that includes parties and several support races.

➤ LATE JUNE–EARLY JULY: **Milwaukee** holds **Summerfest** (☎ 414/273–2680 or 800/837–3378), a lakefront festival with rock, jazz, and popular music.

➤ JULY: The **Minneapolis Aquatennial** (☎ 612/331–8371) celebrates the lakes of Minnesota with sailing regattas, water-skiing competitions, and other events on and around the city lakes. The 330-mi **Chicago-to-Mackinac Boat Race** (☎ 312/861–7777) is one of the most challenging sailboat races in the country. Some 350,000 people flock to Traverse City, Michigan, during the **National Cherry Festival** (☎ 616/947–4230) to sample the best of the local orchards. During the **Great Circus Parade** (☎ 414/273–7877) antique circus wagons from Baraboo's famous Circus World Museum ride through the streets of Milwaukee, Wisconsin.

➤ LATE JULY: The **Pro Football Hall of Fame Game** (☎ 330/456–8207) and induction ceremonies, in Canton, Ohio, kick off the football season. The **Cincinnati Riverfront Stadium Festival** (☎ 513/871–3900) is the largest festival in the country devoted to rhythm and blues.

➤ LATE JULY–EARLY AUG.: The **Experimental Aircraft Association Fly-In** (☎ 920/426–4800), in Oshkosh, Wisconsin, gathers close to a million people and 30,000 aircraft from around the world.

➤ AUG.: The **Wisconsin State Fair** (☎ 414/266–7000) attracts crowds to Milwaukee for livestock and crop shows, midway attractions, and stage shows. The **Illinois State Fair** (☎ 217/782–6661), in Springfield, has livestock shows, car and horse races, food, and entertainment. The citizens of **Young America, Minnesota,** recall

The Midwest and Great Lakes

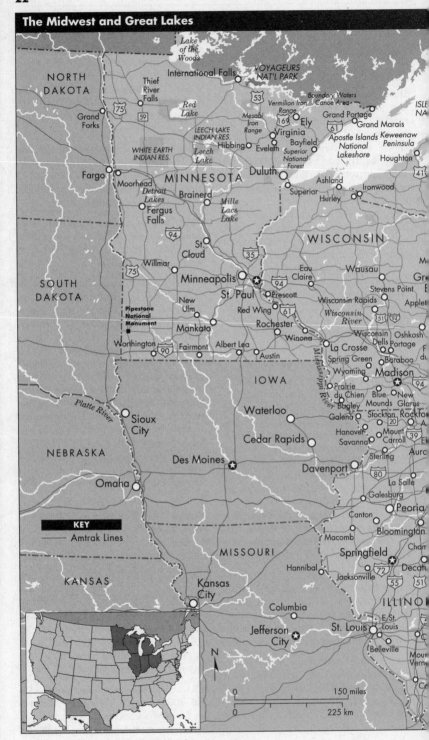

NORTH DAKOTA

Thief River Falls

International Falls

Lake of the Woods

VOYAGEURS NAT'L PARK

53

Grand Forks

75

59

Red Lake

Vermilion Iron Range

Mesabi Iron Range

169 Ely

Virginia

Boundary Waters Canoe Area

Grand Portage

61

Grand Marais

ISLE NA

Hibbing Eveleth

Bayfield

Apostle Islands National Lakeshore

Keweenaw Peninsula

LEECH LAKE INDIAN RES.

Leech Lake

Superior National Forest

Houghton

WHITE EARTH INDIAN RES.

Duluth

41

Fargo

Moorhead

Detroit Lakes

MINNESOTA

Ashland

Ironwood

Brainerd

Superior

Hurley

Fergus Falls

Mille Lacs Lake

WISCONSIN

94

SOUTH DAKOTA

Willmar

75

St. Cloud

35

Minneapolis

St. Paul

94

Eau Claire

Wausau

Stevens Point

Appl

Gr

E

M

New Ulm

Prescott

Red Wing

61

Wisconsin Rapids

51

94

Pipestone National Monument

Mankato

Rochester

Wisconsin River

Oshkosh

Worthington

90

Fairmont

Albert Lea

Winona

Wisconsin Dells

Portage

F

du

Austin

La Crosse

Spring Green

Baraboo

IOWA

Mississippi River

Wyoming

Madison

94

Prairie du Chien

Blue Mounds

New Glarus

Sioux City

Platte River

Waterloo

Bagley

Galena

Stockton

Rockfo

A

NEBRASKA

Cedar Rapids

Hanover

Savanna

Mount Carroll

39

El

20

Des Moines

Davenport

Sterling

Aurc

80

Omaha

La Salle

Galesburg

Peoria

KEY

Amtrak Lines

Canton

Bloomington

Macomb

Chan

MISSOURI

Springfield

Decat

KANSAS

Hannibal

Jacksonville

72

55

51

Kansas City

ILLINO

Columbia

E. St. Louis

Jefferson City

St. Louis

Belleville

Mou Vern

N

0   150 miles

0   225 km

their German roots with **Stiftungsfest** (☎ 612/467–3365), which features a parade, an arts fair, and ethnic food and music.

➤ LATE AUG.–EARLY SEPT.: The **Michigan State Fair** (☎ 313/369–8250), in Detroit, is the nation's oldest state fair, with an animal birthing center and top musical acts performing inside the band shell.

Autumn

➤ EARLY SEPT.: On Labor Day weekend, the **Montreux Detroit Jazz Festival** (☎ 313/963–7622) attracts more than 700,000 jazz fans.

➤ OCT.: On the third weekend of the month, the **LaSalle Bank Chicago Marathon** (☎ 312/904–9800) draws runners from all over the world. The **Circleville Pumpkin Show** (☎ 614/474–7000) is Ohio's oldest, with a huge harvest party afterwards.

THE GREAT PLAINS

Iowa, Kansas, Missouri, Nebraska, North Dakota, Oklahoma, South Dakota

THE NAME GREAT PLAINS EVOKES an image of flat farmland stretching to the horizon, unbroken save for the occasional cluster of buildings marking a town or farmstead. Those who go there, however, know this limitless terrain destroys as many preconceived images as it confirms. The seemingly uniform landscape actually encompasses geography as diverse as the towering buttes that loom over the horizons of northwestern South Dakota and the fertile river valleys that crisscross the eastern boundaries of Missouri and Kansas.

The cultural legacy of the Great Plains owes as much to such artists as Louis Sullivan and Grant Wood as to the cowboy and Native American artifacts that stud the region. And although extensive European settlement came later here, St. Louis existed more than a decade before the signing of the Declaration of Independence; and Coronado had already explored Kansas two centuries before that.

Much is owed to the 1804–06 expedition led by explorers Lewis and Clark who followed the Missouri River from St. Louis through the Dakotas, and then crossed the mountains to the Pacific coast. After fur traders came the railroad companies and thousands of immigrant farmers drawn by the vast and inexpensive land; towns sprang up along rail lines and pioneer trails; and Native Americans were inexorably forced into smaller and smaller territories. The sod-breaking plow and hardy winter wheat helped transform the long- and short-grass prairies of the high plains into America's breadbasket. In the remaining grasslands cattle fed where bison once reigned.

Life on the Great Plains in the 19th century was harsh and sometimes violent, yet it's a life that today's residents love to recreate. Countless historical theme parks and Old West towns dot the region, along with abundant archaeological and Civil War battle sites, U.S. Army forts, pioneer trail markers, and museums of Native American and pioneer lore. Great Plains folk think nothing of journeying 100 mi to see a building covered with thousands of bushels of corn (the Corn Palace in Mitchell, South Dakota), wrecked cars arranged to resemble the monoliths of Stonehenge (Carhenge in Alliance, Nebraska), or Mt. Rushmore, where the 60-ft faces of four U.S. presidents have been carved into a wall of South Dakota granite.

But alongside these landmarks and oddities lies another Great Plains. To know it, you must drive its hundreds of miles of roads bisecting fields of grain or leave the highway for one of its small towns, just to walk the Main Street and see the serene, mellow old houses. Here, somewhere between myth and reality, the true spirit of this region is revealed.

When to Go

The traditional tourist season for most of the Great Plains is **summer,** despite the soaring temperatures and high humidity. Many tourist attractions are open only during June, July, and August. Northern states, such as the Dakotas and Nebraska, are generally cooler, but you should be prepared for anything in this variable region. **Winter** weather can be equally extreme, especially in Nebraska and the Dakotas, where subzero temperatures and snowy conditions are common. North and South Dakota offer cross-country and downhill skiing and snowmobiling, but again, make sure hotels and restaurants are open. In Oklahoma, winter is generally mild and may be more pleasant than during the summer heat. **Spring** and **fall** can be excellent times to visit, with moderate temperatures and crowds at a minimum. Fall in the Ozarks or in such places as the eastern border of Iowa has the added attraction of colorful foliage.

Festivals and Seasonal Events

Winter

➤ EARLY DEC.: **Christmas on the River** (☎ 816/505–2227), in Parkville, Missouri, rings in the holiday season with a 1,000-voice children's choir, Santa's arrival by riverboat, and performances of Dickens's *A Christmas Carol*.

Spring

➤ APR.: Nearly 1 million people enjoy fine art, food, and performances during **Oklahoma City's Festival of the Arts** (☎ 405/297–3995), a 34-year-old springtime tradition, held in Festival Plaza and Myriad Gardens.

Summer

➤ JUNE: See a reenactment of the **Pawnee Bill Wild West Show** (☎ 918/762–2108) in Pawnee, Oklahoma. Crafts, food, and fast-draw competitions are available for visitors wanting to experience the Wild West. **Nebraskaland Days** (☎ 308/532–7939) is a Western hootenanny in North Platte that's highlighted by the Buffalo Bill Rodeo. The **Red Earth Native American Cultural Festival** (☎ 405/427–5228), in Oklahoma City, attracts hundreds of Native American dancers from the United States and Canada for competitions and performances. Native American artists and artisans, storytellers, films, and children's activities make this three-day event fun for all ages.

➤ LATE JUNE–EARLY JULY: DeSmet, South Dakota, hosts the annual **Laura Ingalls Wilder Pageant** (☎ 605/854–3383 or 605/692–2108).

➤ JULY: **Kansas City Blues & Jazz Festival** (☎ 816/753–3378 or 800/530–5266) features performances by nationally known blues and jazz artists on three stages. On Independence Day weekend, **National Tom Sawyer Days** (☎ 573/221–2477) has Americana-oriented activities such as fence

painting in Mark Twain's hometown of Hannibal, Missouri. The **North Dakota State Fair** (☎ 701/852–3247)in Minot attracts 250,000 annually to its traditional grand exhibit of rodeos, livestock and horse shows, concerts, and carnival entertainment. **Black Hills Heritage Festival** (☎ 605/394–4115) combines music, dance, and crafts.

➤ LATE JULY: The annual **Bix Beiderbecke Jazz Festival** (☎ 319/324–7170) is held in LeClaire Park in Davenport, Iowa, and three other indoor venues.

➤ JULY–AUG.: In Kansas, the **Dodge City Roundup Rodeo** (☎ 316/225–2244) takes place over five days during the Dodge City Days festival.

➤ AUG.: The **Iowa State Fair** (☎ 515/262–3111), in Des Moines, is a short course in farm machinery, animals, crops, and crafts; less bucolically minded visitors can enjoy carnival rides and musical entertainment. **Days of '76** (☎ 605/578–1876), in Deadwood, South Dakota, celebrates the town's wild and woolly gold rush days with a parade, a rodeo, and other activities. **Pioneer Days at Bonanzaville USA** (☎ 701/282–2822) transforms the pioneer village near West Fargo, North Dakota, into a living museum for two days, with costumed shopkeepers, tradespeople, and townspeople.

➤ MID-AUG.: Sturgis, South Dakota's **Sturgis Motorcycle Rally** (☎ 605/347–9190) draws more than 200,000 bike buffs from around the world each year. During the weeklong event many businesses turn their buildings over to sellers of leather goods, rally T-shirts, and other biker-related paraphernalia.

Autumn

➤ SEPT.: **Santa-Cali-Gon Days** (☎ 816/252–4745), in Independence, Missouri, celebrates the opening of the West through the Santa Fe, California, and Oregon trails, all of which originated in this gateway town. The **United Tribes International Powwow** (☎ 701/255–3285) brings Native Americans from around the country to Bismarck, North Dakota, to hold dance competitions and celebrate cultural ties.

➤ OCT.: **Octoberfest** (☎ 573/486–2744) in Hermann, Missouri, draws thousands of people each weekend to celebrate this Missouri River town's German and wine-making heritage. **Norsk Hostfest** (☎ 701/

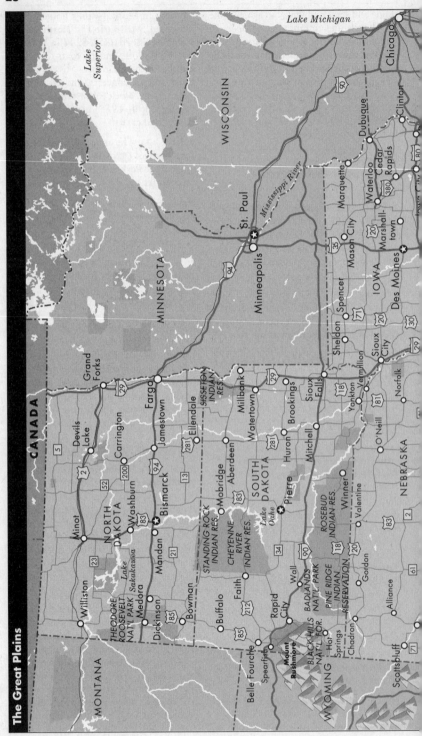

852–2368) in **Minot, North Dakota**, brings international crowds to sample Scandinavian culture through food, dancing, and costumes. **Buffalo Roundup** (☎ 605/255–4515) in **Custer State Park, South Dakota**, allows visitors to witness one of the great remaining roundups in the West. The **Covered Bridge Festival** (☎ 515/462–1185) in **Winterset, Iowa**, includes tours of Madison County's six restored covered bridges as well as visits to sights made famous by the eponymous book and movie.

➤ Nov.: The **American Royal** (☎ 816/221–5242 or 800/767–7700), an annual celebration of **Kansas City**'s heritage, has rodeos, horse shows, livestock shows, and a no-holds-barred barbecue.

THE SOUTHWEST

Arizona, Nevada,
New Mexico, Texas

A REGION THAT DEMANDS superlatives, the Southwest is the ruggedly beautiful, wide-open land out of which America's myths continue to emerge. Cowboys and Indians, Old World conquistadors and new religions, rising and falling fortunes in gold, copper, and oil—all feed into the vision of an untamed territory with limitless horizons.

Of course, Phoenix and Dallas are sophisticated metropolises, and Santa Fe is becoming a rival Los Angeles in wealth and number of art galleries per square foot. Las Vegas is sui generis, an unbridled, peculiarly American phenomenon. Foodies all over the country sing the praises of the delicately spiced southwestern cuisine, an outgrowth of Asian immigration into the area, now duplicated in cosmopolitan restaurants nationwide. Nor is there a region that has better Mexican food, whether you like it Tex-Mex, Sonoran, or New Mexican style. Southwestern furnishings—an eclectic blend that might include mission chests, Navajo blankets, Mexican tinwork mirrors, *yristras* (strings of red chili peppers), and even bleached cow skulls à la Georgia O'Keeffe—have become so popular in upscale homes that they're a bit of a cliché.

But other, more ancient cultures vie here with contemporary ones. The country's largest Native American reservation, that of the Navajo Nation, occupies millions of acres and traverses state boundaries, and dozens of other tribes—among them Hopi, Zuni, and Apache—live in the region as well. It is their vanishing civilization and, above all, the area's natural phenomena—spectacular canyons, eerily towering rock formations, and clear, lambent light—that continue to capture the imagination of all who visit or live in the area. The southwestern landscape is a glorious lesson in geologic upheaval to be learned at such sites as Carlsbad Caverns in New Mexico, the Grand Canyon in Arizona, and the Rio Grande in Texas.

Clearly anything is possible in such an unrestrained place. The heyday of the western movie may be over, but when today's screen heroines Thelma and Louise light out for freedom, they find it in the Southwest, still the most natural setting for outlandish deeds and grand gestures.

When to Go

In the semiarid climate of most of the Southwest, **spring** is the season of choice, with cool, fresh, clear weather. In March and April, when temperatures average in the 70s, short-lived wildflowers produce carpets of extravagant color in many parts of the region, including some deserts as well as in temperate areas like East Texas. **Summer** is dry and often very hot, sometimes unpleasantly so, across the Southwest; but water sports abound, and dramatic mountain chains provide cool respite. Summer thunderstorms are typical in most areas. After spring, **fall**—from September to November, in general—is the preferred time to visit, with temperatures falling back into the 70s and 80s, and gorgeous foliage to be seen in many areas. Skiers flock to slopes across the Southwest in **winter.** In general, temperatures vary greatly even within the same state and season because of the great variety of microclimates in the Southwest's mountains, deserts, plains, and forests.

Festivals
and Seasonal Events

Winter

➤ EARLY DEC.: The ghost town of **Madrid, New Mexico**, is reawakened with streetlights and an arts-and-crafts festival during its **Christmas Open-House Celebration** (☎ 505/471–1054).

➤ LATE JAN.: The **Cowboy Poetry Gathering** (☎ 702/738–7508), in Elko, Nevada, has become famous both for the authentic characters it draws from around the Southwest and for the gentle quality of the verse these rough-hewn men and women produce. **KidFilm Festival** (☎ 214/821–3456), the country's largest media event for children, takes place in Dallas.

➤ MID.-FEB.: **Washington's Birthday Celebration** (☎ 956/722–0589), in Laredo, Texas, is a binational celebration of parades and fiestas honoring the first successful New World revolutionary.

➤ FEB.–MAR.: Twenty thousand animals are shown at Houston's **Livestock Show & Rodeo** (☎ 713/791–9000), a truly Texas-size event held under the curved roof of the Astrodome. Rodeos and country music abound. Galveston Island, Texas, decks out in green, gold, and purple as **Mardi Gras** (☎ 888/425–4753) celebrations take over the town. Parades, beads, and bands are part of the tropical carnival.

➤ MAR.: The **North Texas Irish Festival** (☎ 214/821–4174) brings more than 47 bands to Dallas's Fair Park. High-quality artwork is the norm at the **Heard Museum Guild Indian Fair and Market** (☎ 602/252–8840), a juried invitational for Native American artists held in Phoenix, Arizona. Hundreds of rock bands, along with filmmakers and Internet artists, descend on Austin, Texas, during the 10-day **South by Southwest** (☎ 512/467–7979) music and multimedia conference. The **Dallas Video Festival** (☎ 214/999–8999) is a four-day event featuring independently produced and experimental videos, from animated clips to documentaries. Call for the schedule, since it's subject to change.

Spring

➤ EARLY APR.: **The Houston International Festival** (☎ 713/654–8808) in Texas features a different country each year for a 10-day celebration in the heart of Downtown. Music, dance, bazaars, food tastings, and kids zones are capsuled with the hilarious Art Car parade.

➤ APR.: In Dallas, film buffs rub elbows with professional filmmakers from around the world at the **USA Film Festival** (☎ 214/821–3456).

➤ LATE APR.: Native Americans celebrate **American Indian Week** (☎ 505/843–7270) in Albuquerque, New Mexico, with dance, arts and crafts, a trade show at the Indian Pueblo Cultural Center, and The Gathering of Nations Pow Wow. Texas's 10-day **Fiesta San Antonio** (☎ 210/227–5191), more than a century old, commemorates the Battle of San Jacinto with a festival of music, food, sports, art shows, and the River Parade.

➤ APR.–JUNE: Waxahachie, Texas, just outside Dallas, is the setting of **Scarborough Faire** (☎ 972/938–1888), an English Renaissance festival with games, period foods, and performances.

➤ MAY 5: **Cinco de Mayo,** a fiesta celebrating Mexican history and heritage, is held in many cities and towns across the Southwest.

Summer

➤ LATE JUNE: New Mexico's craftspeople are world famous, and some of the best display and sell their work at the **New Mexico Arts & Crafts Fair** (☎ 505/884–9043) in Albuquerque, New Mexico.

➤ EARLY JULY: The **National Basque Festival** (☎ 702/738–3418), in Elko, Nevada, celebrates the heritage of the Basque people (recruited to the area from northern Spain because of their remarkable shepherding abilities) in the American West.

➤ LATE JULY: The **Fiesta de Santiago y Santa Ana** (☎ 505/758–3873 or 800/732–8267), a colorful street party and fair, began as a trade fair nearly 300 years ago; today it's a major annual event in Taos, New Mexico.

➤ LATE AUG.: The weeklong **Nevada State Fair** (☎ 702/688–5767), in Reno, Nevada, features rides, farm animal competitions, livestock shows, fast food, and all the other accoutrements of a real state fair.

Autumn

➤ MID-SEPT.: On the first weekend after Labor Day, Zozobra, or "Old Man Gloom," is burned to open the annual **Fiestas de Santa Fe** (☎ 505/984–6760 or 800/777–2489), in Santa Fe, New Mexico. During the celebration, Santa Fe Plaza is filled with music, dancing, and food vendors.

The Southwest

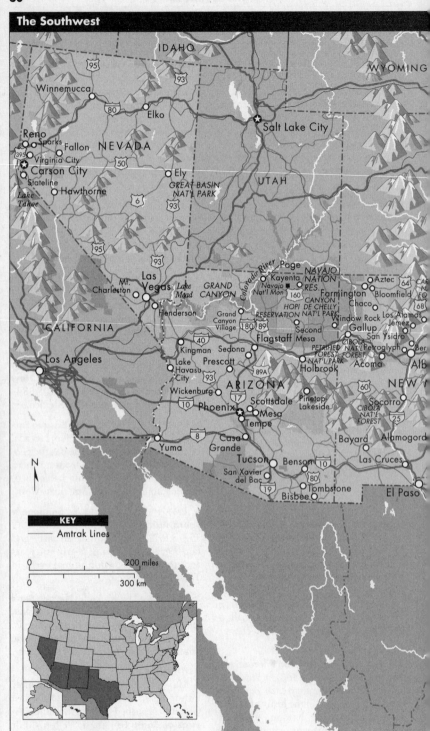

KEY

— Amtrak Lines

0 _____ 200 miles
0 _____ 300 km

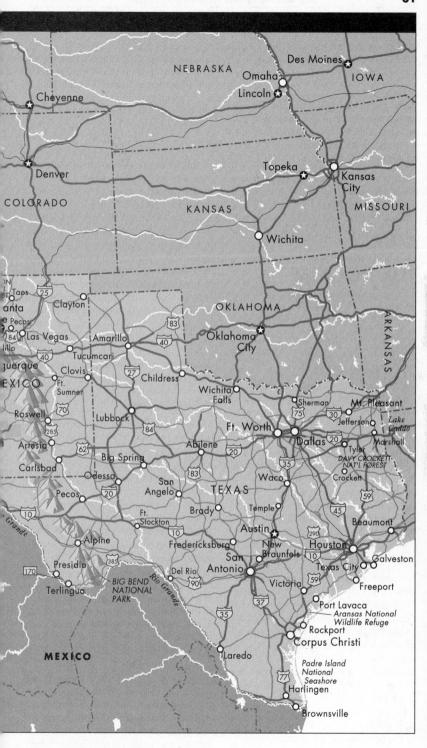

➤ SEPT.: Professional open-wheel circuit racing (CART) pulses through the streets of downtown **Houston, Texas,** for the **TEXACO-Havoline Grand Prix** (☎ 713/739–7223).

➤ LATE SEPT.–MID-OCT.: The **State Fair of Texas** (☎ 214/565–9931), the nation's largest state fair, holds its three-week annual run at **Dallas's** Fair Park, declared a National Historic Landmark in 1986 for its Art Deco architecture.

➤ MID-OCT.: The **Albuquerque International Balloon Fiesta** (☎ 505/821–1000), in which more than 850 colorful hot-air balloons rise in spectacular unison with the dawn, is probably **New Mexico's** best-known event.

THE ROCKIES

Colorado, Idaho, Montana, Wyoming, Utah

To MANY MINDS, the term Rocky Mountains conjures up images of wolves and outlaws, the click of cowboy spurs and the rustling of leather chaps. Indeed, it's hard to forget the broken treaties and betrayals to Native Americans, the energy and innocence of wide-open spaces, boomtowns, and the search for precious metals that have figured so heavily in the making of Idaho, Colorado, Montana, Wyoming, and Utah. The unpredictable charms and crimes of nature and human action that thrived in the Old West have marked the Rocky Mountains with a crude but poetic beauty.

But most enduring of all are the mountains—a 4,000-mi-long chain that stretches from Alaska to northern New Mexico. Begun about 70 million years ago, when sandstone, shale, granite, marble, and volcanic rock surged and split and gave under the plow of glacial ice, the Rockies emerged to run intermittently along what is now the Idaho–Montana boundary down to a central section sloping through western Wyoming's Yellowstone and Grand Teton national parks and into northern Colorado and Utah.

This mountain backdrop still inspires the kind of fear and wonder it once did from mountain folk and Native Americans.

What you'll see from atop these summits is a landscape of breathtaking beauty and variety. The westernmost state, Idaho, has terrain encompassing everything from fruit orchards to the tallest sand dunes in the United States. Utah has 84,990 square mi of mind-bogglingly varied topography—a vast salt lake, mountain peaks and lush evergreen forests, and improbable red-rock canyons in the southern reaches. Montana claims 25 million acres of public land, most of it aloft in the northern Rockies. Its Glacier National Park is home to the grizzly bear, wolf, mountain goat, and moose. Wyoming, the ninth-largest and least populated state in the Union, is dotted with thermal pools, bubbling hot springs, and, within a square-mile area in Yellowstone National Park, a quarter of the earth's geysers. In Colorado, the ski capital of the United States, high-country lakes, meadows frosted with blue columbine, and treeless alpine tundra assemble in one sweeping vista, while Denver—the Mile-High City—and the university town of Boulder attract visitors and settlers from all corners of the globe.

When to Go

Many visitors think the Rockies have only two seasons: skiing and hiking. But for those willing to risk sometimes capricious weather, fall and spring are the Rockies' best-kept secrets. **Spring** is a good time for fishing, rafting the runoff, or birding and viewing wildlife. **Fall** may be the prettiest season of all, with golden splashes of aspen on the mountainsides, more wildlife at lower elevations, and excellent fishing during spawning. You will also pay less during these shoulder seasons, and you may have a corner of Yellowstone all to yourself. Driving in the **winter** can be chancy, and although the interstates are usually kept open even in fearsome weather, highway passes like the Going-to-the-Sun Highway in Glacier National Park and the Mirror Lake Highway between Park City and the Utah/Wyoming border can be blocked from late October to June. High altitude (over 7,000 ft above sea level) and high latitude (the nearer you get to Canada) result in longer winters. Winter visitors should prepare for the possibility of temperatures below zero. Wilderness snowbanks can linger through June, so backcountry hikers generally crowd in from July through Labor Day. **Summer** temperatures rarely rise into the 90s (except in southern Utah, where the mercury may top 100°F), but the thinner atmosphere at high altitudes makes it necessary for visitors to shield themselves from ultraviolet rays.

Festivals and Seasonal Events

Winter

➤ JAN.: **National Western Stock Show and Rodeo** (☎ 303/295–1660), in Denver, is the biggest indoor rodeo in the world, attracting all the stars of the rodeo circuit for two weeks. The **Western Montana Wine Festival** (☎ 406/728–3100) in **Missoula** features tastings of regional wines, accompanied by superb food. Utah's **Sundance Film Festival** (☎ 801/328–3456), founded by Robert Redford, brings independent filmmakers to **Park City** and **Salt Lake City** for one of the country's premier film screening events. During **Ullr Fest** (☎ 970/453–6018), the town of **Breckenridge, Colorado,** declares itself an independent kingdom and pays homage to the Norse God of snow in a weeklong wild revel.

➤ FEB.: **Race to the Sky** (☎ 406/442–4008), near **Helena, Montana,** is a 500-mi dogsled race that crisscrosses the Continental Divide at elevations up to 7,000 ft. Spectators can watch a shorter (300-mi) race at check-in sites. A wide range of huge ice sculptures line the streets of **McCall, Idaho,** during the **Winter Carnival** (☎ 208/634–7631).

Spring

➤ MAR.: The Irish and other wearers of the green flock to **Butte, Montana,** for one of the West's largest and most rollicking **St. Patrick's Day** parades. Collectors from around the world gather in **Great Falls, Montana,** for the **C. M. Russell Auction of Original Western Art** (☎ 800/803–3351).

➤ LATE MAY: Memorial Day brings the annual **Bolder Boulder** run (☎ 303/444–7223) to **Boulder, Colorado,** where a top international field and 40,000 ordinary citizens race through the closed streets of town. In Missoula, Montana, the annual **International Wildlife Film Festival** (☎ 406/728–9380) is the longest running such festival in the world (since 1978).

Summer

➤ LATE JUNE: In Colorado, the **Telluride Bluegrass & Country Music Festival** (☎ 800/624–2422) has become so popular the organizers have had to limit the number of spectators to 10,000. The nation's best bluegrass players gather in **Weiser, Idaho,** for the **National Oldtime Fiddlers Contest and Festival** (☎ 208/549–0452 or 800/437–1280). The **Boise River Festival** (☎ 800/437–1280) is a three-day outdoor extravaganza of concerts, specialty acts, a hot air balloon rally, and a parade of illuminated floats.

➤ JULY: The popular **Mormon Miracle Pageant** (☎ 435/835–3000) is a musical drama of American and Mormon history set against the backdrop of the temple in **Manti, Utah.** Wyoming's **Cheyenne Frontier Days** (☎ 307/778–7222 or 800/227–6336), the rodeo daddy of 'em all since 1897, includes evening shows featuring the biggest names in country music, as well as parades, Native American dancing, and very popular pancake breakfasts. The Grant-Kohrs Ranch in **Deer Lodge, Montana,** celebrates cowboy lore and skills during **Western Heritage Days** (☎ 406/846–2070) with roping, branding, chuck-wagon cooking, and traditional cowboy music.

➤ JUNE–AUG.: **Colorado Shakespeare Festival** (☎ 303/492–0554), in **Boulder,** presents three outdoor and one indoor Shakespearean productions Tuesday–Sunday nights. The actors are recruited from around the country. At the **Aspen Music Festival and School** (☎ 970/925–3254) students from around the world perform with faculty, and world-class soloists and conductors are also featured. **Grand Teton Music Festival** (☎ 307/733–1128), the most important classical music concert series in the northern Rockies, attracts musicians from the nation's finest orchestras. The **Idaho Shakespeare Festival** (☎ 208/336–9221) in **Boise** presents top-rate productions with hilarious pre-show entertainment in a lovely outdoor theater along the Boise River.

➤ LATE JULY–EARLY AUG.: The **Festival of the American West** (☎ 800/225–3378), near **Logan, Utah,** includes a Great West Fair and a multimedia pageant, "The West: America's Odyssey." In Colorado, the **Vail International Dance Festival** (☎ 970/949–1999) is set amid wildflowers in the outdoor Ford Amphitheater.

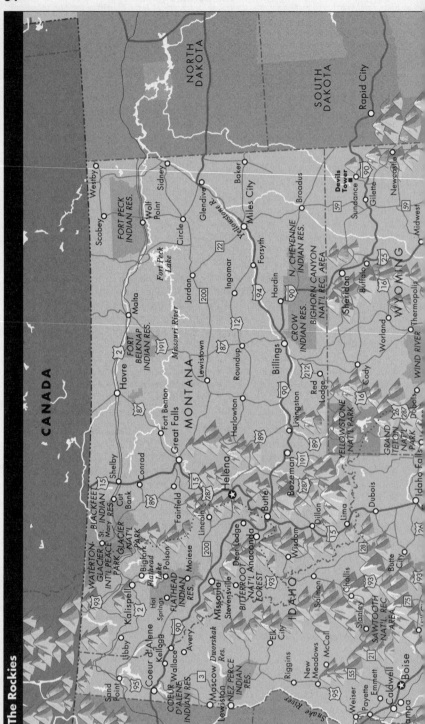

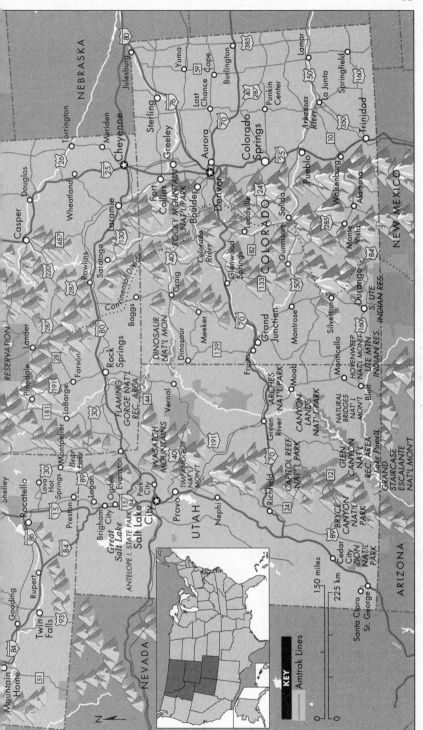

➤ AUG.: At the **Cowboy Poetry Gathering** (☎ 406/538–5436) in **Lewiston, Montana,** U.S. and Canadian performers share verses about a man and a horse following a cow. The **Crow Fair** and Rodeo (☎ 406/638–2601) celebrates native culture and customs in **Crow Agency, Montana,** tepee capital of the world. Cowboy songs and Range Ballads are revived at the annual **Frontier Festival** sponsored by the Buffalo Bill Historical Center in **Cody, Wyoming** (☎ 307/587–4771).

➤ LATE JULY–AUG.: In **Sandpoint, Idaho,** the **Festival at Sandpoint** (☎ 208/263–0887) presents classical, jazz, and pop concerts under the stars.

➤ LATE JUN.–EARLY SEPT.: **Cedar City** is the setting of the **Utah Shakespearean Festival** (☎ 435/586–7878 or 800/752–9849), with feasts, bawdy Elizabethan skits, and performances in an open-air replica of the Globe Theatre.

Autumn

➤ SEPT.: **Libby, Montana**'s four-day **Nordicfest** (☎ 800/785–6541) celebrates Scandinavian food, costumes, music, dance, and crafts.

➤ EARLY OCT.: In **Denver,** the **Great American Beer Festival** (☎ 303/447–0126) is the country's largest and longest running beer fest, with samples of about 2,000 brews.

➤ OCT.–LATE DEC.: Join the **Eagle Watch** (☎ 406/475–3128) to see hundreds of bald eagles gather annually in Canyon Ferry State Park, near **Helena, Montana,** during freshwater salmon spawning.

THE WEST COAST

California, Oregon, Washington

SOME VISITORS FROM THE EAST picture the West Coast as America's frontier, but the shoreline of California, Oregon, and Washington presents no barrier to the region's businesspeople, who carry the pioneering spirit to the Pacific Rim. West Coast entrepreneurs generate high-tech products and services the world will take for granted in the new millennium, while "fusion" chefs reinvent classic cooking techniques with Asian influences.

Throughout its history the West Coast has been a destination for trendsetters and fortune seekers. The gold-hungry Spanish built missions and huge ranchos in what is now California, long before modern empire builders headed for Silicon Valley in a race to lead the nation's communications, information, and technology revolution.

Others have migrated to the West Coast because of its magnificent natural beauty and (for the most part) temperate weather. Washington and Oregon are similar in topography and climate, cooler than California, and are bisected by the Cascade Mountains. The Seattle and Tacoma are of Washington is home to one of the world's busiest container ports as well as the legendary Bill Gates, chairman of Microsoft. Portland, a busy inland port at the head of Oregon's lush Willamette River valley, is known for its curtain of fog, rain, and evergreens.

Despite development, nature continues to provide a critical perspective on human pursuits. The ragged edges of Washington's Olympic Peninsula and the Oregon coast illustrate the power of the ocean; the mountains surrounding Seattle evoke a sobering sense of scale, as does the view from Yosemite's valley floor; and tremors along the San Andreas Fault remind California residents that the earth is an unstable place. Every town along the West Coast sits amid some grand gesture of nature.

The great West Coast cities—Seattle, Portland, San Francisco, Los Angeles, and San Diego—continue to attract a hopeful, worldly mix of immigrants in search of personal freedom and economic opportunity. In contrast to the urban areas, the extraordinary rural landscapes of these states feature wild climatic changes and altitudes—deserts, forests, a 1,500-mi seashore, mountains, and rich agricultural valleys. In addition to the athletic attractions of rock climbing, deep-sea fishing, wilderness camping, surfing, skiing, and snowboarding, tourists and residents enjoy five-star resorts, historic western towns, Disneyland, Hollywood studios, world-class museums, and topnotch art and entertainment from grunge to opera.

When to Go

You can take a West Coast vacation any time of the year. Weather in coastal areas is generally mild year-round, with the rainy season running from **late fall through early spring**—though rain may occur any time of year, especially in Washington. Ski season in the High Sierra and Cascades runs from November through March, occasionally into April and May. These same months are also ideal for those who want to enjoy the sun-drenched delights of the desert; wildflowers are at their peak in April. **Summer** is the busiest tourist season, when you can expect the most congestion and the highest prices. It's also a time of heavy fog in the coastal areas (Mark Twain once remarked that the coldest winter he ever spent was a summer in San Francisco). Inland areas such as Napa Valley, the Columbia Gorge, and the High Sierra can be hot in summer, with temperatures reaching up to 90°F in the plains and mountains; in California's Central Valley and desert regions, summer temperatures can soar to 110°F. Whenever you visit the West Coast, expect temperatures to vary widely from night to day, sometimes by as much as 40°F. Most West Coast attractions are open daily year-round.

Festivals and Seasonal Events

Winter

➤ JAN. 1: The **Tournament of Roses** (☎ 626/449–4100), in Pasadena, California, features a parade of more than 50 floral floats, equestrian units, and marching bands and is followed by the Rose Bowl football game.

➤ LATE JAN.–EARLY FEB.: California's **AT&T Pebble Beach National Pro-Am** (☎ 831/649–1533 or 800/541–9091) pairs 180 top professional golfers with amateurs from the business, sports, and entertainment worlds.

➤ FEB.: **Chinese New Year** celebrations are held in San Francisco (☎ 415/982–3000) and Los Angeles (☎ 213/617–0396), complete with dragon parades, fireworks, and feasts.

Spring

➤ EARLY MAR.: The **Mendocino Whale Festival** (☎ 707/961–6300), in Mendo-

cino, **California,** combines whale-watching with art viewing, wine tasting, lighthouse tours, music, and merriment.

➤ LATE MAR.–EARLY APR.: **Washington's Skagit Valley Tulip Festival** (☎ 360/428–5959) showcases millions of colorful tulips and daffodils in bloom.

➤ MEMORIAL DAY WEEKEND: The **Sacramento Jazz Jubilee** (☎ 916/372–5277) brings more than 100 jazz bands to **Sacramento, California,** for four days of jamming.

➤ LATE MAY: The **Northwest Folklife Festival** (☎ 206/684–7300) lures musicians and artists to **Seattle** for one of the largest folk festivals in the United States.

Summer

➤ MID-FEB.–LATE OCT.: The **Oregon Shakespeare Festival** (☎ 541/482–4331), held in **Ashland,** presents four plays by Shakespeare—plus seven other plays by both classical and contemporary playwrights—plus tours, concerts, and lectures.

➤ JUNE: The **Portland Rose Festival** (☎ 503/227–2681) includes a rose show, carnivals, celebrity entertainment, a hot-air balloon race, two parades, an air show, bands, and a world-class auto show. The sand becomes an art form at **Oregon's Cannon Beach Sandcastle Contest** (☎ 503/436–2623), attended by thousands each year.

➤ MID-JUNE–EARLY JULY: The **Oregon Bach Festival** (☎ 541/346–5666 or 800/457–1486) brings stellar musicians to **Eugene** for concerts, recitals, lectures, chamber music, and opera.

➤ MID-JUNE–EARLY SEPT.: Contemporary and classical performances of music, dance, and theater are held in an outdoor amphitheater during **Jacksonville,** Oregon's annual **Britt Festivals** (☎ 541/773–6077 or 800/882–7488).

➤ LATE JULY: The **Pacific Northwest Arts Fair** (☎ 425/454–3322) brings the work of Northwest artists to **Bellevue,** Washington.

➤ EARLY AUG.: In California, **Old Spanish Days Fiesta** (☎ 805/962–8101) is Santa Barbara's biggest event, with parades, a carnival, a rodeo, and dancers in the Spanish marketplace. At Linfield College in McMannville, Oregon, the **Inter-**

West Coast (Northern)

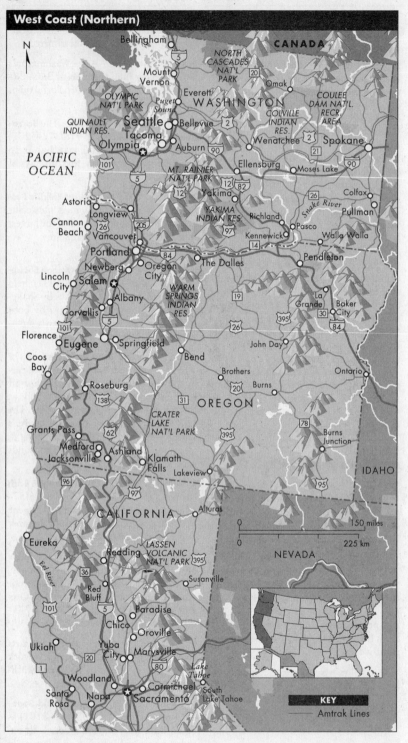

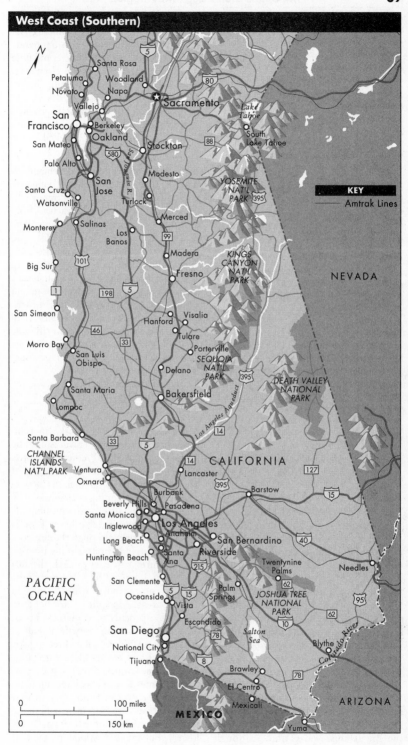

West Coast (Southern)

Santa Rosa
Petaluma
Novato
Woodland
Napa
Vallejo
Sacramento
Lake Tahoe
South Lake Tahoe
San Francisco
Berkeley
Oakland
San Mateo
Stockton
Palo Alto
Modesto
San Jose
Santa Cruz
Watsonville
Turlock
YOSEMITE NAT'L PARK
Monterey
Salinas
Los Banos
Merced
Big Sur
Madera
KINGS CANYON NAT'L PARK
NEVADA
San Simeon
Fresno
Hanford
Visalia
Morro Bay
Tulare
San Luis Obispo
Porterville
SEQUOIA NAT'L PARK
Delano
Santa Maria
Bakersfield
DEATH VALLEY NATIONAL PARK
Lompoc
Los Angeles Aqueduct
Santa Barbara
CHANNEL ISLANDS NAT'L.PARK
Ventura
Oxnard
Lancaster
CALIFORNIA
Barstow
Burbank
Beverly Hills
Pasadena
Santa Monica
Inglewood
Los Angeles
Anaheim
Long Beach
San Bernardino
Huntington Beach
Santa Ana
Riverside
Twentynine Palms
Needles
San Clemente
Palm Springs
JOSHUA TREE NATIONAL PARK
Oceanside
Vista
San Diego
Escondido
Salton Sea
National City
Blythe
Tijuana
Colorado River
Brawley
El Centro
ARIZONA
Mexicali
MEXICO
Yuma
PACIFIC OCEAN

KEY
Amtrak Lines

0   100 miles
0   150 km

national **Pinot Noir Celebration** (☎ 800/ 775–4762) features Oregon wines and foods.

➤ EARLY AUG.: The **Mt. Hood Festival of Jazz** (☎ 503/231–0161) brings acclaimed jazz musicians to **Gresham, Oregon,** for a tuneful weekend.

➤ EARLY AUG.: Seattle's **Seafair** (☎ 206/ 728–0123) transforms the waterfront into a showplace of hydroplane racers, Blue Angels flyers, Navy ships, and fireboats.

➤ LATE AUG.–EARLY SEPT.: **Bumbershoot** (☎ 206/281–8111), a **Seattle** festival of the arts, presents more than 450 performers in music, dance, theater, comedy, and the visual and literary arts.

Autumn

➤ LATE AUG.–OCT.: The **Renaissance Pleasure Faire** (☎ 800/523–2473) draws revelers in Elizabethan-style costumes to the **San Francisco Bay Area** for many weekends of music, merriment, and theater.

➤ LATE NOV.–EARLY DEC.: The **Hollywood Christmas Parade** (☎ 323/469–2337) features celebrities riding festively decorated floats.

THE PACIFIC STATES

Alaska, Hawai'i

THE TWO YOUNGEST STATES in the union, Alaska and Hawai'i, have more in common than their images might suggest. Both are thousands of miles from the U.S. mainland, both have dramatic landscapes, and both have significant populations of indigenous people. The two states also share a reliance on water—rivers, lakes, and the Pacific Ocean—which supplies a means of transportation, a source of food, and countless recreational possibilities. Humpback whales also forge a link, summering in Alaska's Inside Passage and Prince William Sound, then swimming 4,000 mi to Hawai'i to mate, calve, and nurse their young in the warm waters off Maui, the Big Island, and O'ahu. Although Alaskan and Hawaiian stores are stocked with the same goods found on the mainland, each state retains its unique exotic flavor.

Alaska, with its vast, austere wilderness and extreme weather, is demanding, but it rewards exploration with temperate summers, a frontier atmosphere, and flora and fauna rarely accessible elsewhere. From the nation's highest mountain, Mt. McKinley, to the islands, glaciers, and fjords of the southeast, the state provides superb hiking, boating, and fishing—and scenery as majestic and unspoiled as any in North America.

Hawai'i's gentle climate and tremendous diversity make it welcoming and endlessly fascinating. Each of the eight major volcanic islands has its own character—from lush tropical scenery and stunning white beaches to towering dramatic cliffs and rugged volcanic terrain. If you enjoy rampant commercialism in a spotlessly clean environment, O'ahu's Waikīkī is the place for you, but for pineapple plantations and active volcanoes, cheerful small towns, and remote natural refuges, head for Maui and the Big Island. Kaua'i is worthwhile for its Nā Pali Coast and gorgeous Waimea Canyon; Moloka'i and Lāna'i are more tranquil getaways.

When to Go

Alaska

Most visitors come to Alaska in **summer,** when milder temperatures and the midnight sun prevail. Predictably, hotels and campgrounds are crowded, and prices are often higher than in the off-season: Advance planning is essential. The farther north you go in summer, the longer the days; Fairbanks in June is never really dark, although the sun does set for a couple of hours. In the interior temperatures can easily reach the 80s and 90s in June and July. The rest of the state is cooler, and rain is common in coastal areas. Mosquitoes are fierce in summer, especially in wilderness areas; never travel without repellent. **Fall** in Alaska is an abbreviated three weeks, when trees and bushes blaze with color and daytime temperatures are still pleasant. It comes as early as late August in the interior and in September farther south. **Winters** are extremely cold in the interior (daytime temperatures of 0°F or lower), but many Alaskans prefer that season, because it opens up most of the state for travel by snowmobile and dogsled. In the southeast's temperate maritime climate, though, temperatures rarely dip below freezing. **Spring** is often a monthlong soggy period of thawing and freezing, starting at the beginning of April.

Hawai'i

Hawai'i's long days of sunshine and fairly mild year-round temperatures allow for 12 months of pleasurable island travel. In resort areas near sea level the average afternoon temperature during the coldest months of December and January is 80°F; during the hottest months of August through October, temperatures can reach the low 90s. The northern shores of each island usually receive more rain than those in the south. Mid-December through mid-April and July through August are peak travel times, which means accommodation rates can be 10%–15% higher than those in other seasons.

Festivals and Seasonal Events

Alaska

➤ MID-FEB.: The **Anchorage Fur Rendezvous** (☎ 907/277–8615) brings a three-day world-championship sled-dog race through city streets, plus hundreds of other winter activities.

➤ EARLY MAR.: The **Iditarod Trail Sled Dog Race** (☎ 907/376–5155) officially covers 1,049 mi from Anchorage to Nome and can take up to two weeks to complete, though the record is less than 10 days.

➤ EARLY MAY: **Kachemak Bay Shorebird Festival** (☎ 907/235–7740) celebrates the return of migrating shorebirds to **south central Alaska**.

➤ JUNE: Enjoy chamber music by world-renowned musicians in a beautiful setting at the **Sitka Summer Music Festival** (☎ 907/277–4852).

➤ EARLY JULY: The **July 4th Mount Marathon Race and Celebration** in Seward (☎ 907/224–8051) is a grueling race up a 3,022-ft mountain, followed by a parade and festival of crafts, games, and food booths.

➤ LATE AUG.–EARLY SEPT.: **Alaska State Fair** (☎ 907/745–4827) in **Palmer**, north of Anchorage, is a traditional celebration complete with cooking, handicrafts, livestock, and brewing competitions.

➤ EARLY NOV.: Dancing, guitar playing, and fiddling are all part of the **Athabascan Fiddling Festival** (☎ 907/456–5774) in **Fairbanks**.

Hawai'i

➤ LATE MAR.–EARLY APR.: Reserve tickets months in advance for the **Merrie Monarch Festival** (☎ 808/935–9168) in **Hilo** on the Big Island—a full week of hula competitions beginning Easter Sunday.

➤ MAY 1: The statewide **Lei Day** (☎ 808/547–7393) is an annual flower-filled celebration with lei-making competitions and exquisite leis for sale.

➤ JUNE: On **King Kamehameha Day** (☎ 808/586–0333), twin statues of the king who united Hawai'i's various islands are draped in giant leis in **Honolulu, O'ahu**, and **Hāwī** on the Big Island.

➤ AUG.: A world-class marlin-fishing competition, the **Hawaiian International Billfish Tournament** (☎ 808/329–6155) in **Kailua-Kona** on the Big Island, includes a parade with amusing entries.

➤ SEPT.–OCT.: **Aloha Festivals** (☎ 808/545–1771) celebrate Hawaiian culture with street parties, canoe races, craft exhibits, music, and dance events statewide.

➤ OCT.: Watch some of the world's fittest athletes swim, cycle, and run in the **Ironman Triathlon World Championships** (☎ 808/329–0063). The race begins with a 2.4-mi open-water swim from Kailua Pier in Kailua-Kona, then proceeds with a 112-mi bike race and 26.2-mi run along the Ka'ahumanu Highway.

➤ NOV.: The **Hawai'i International Film Festival** (☎ 808/528–3456), on O'ahu and Neighbor Islands, showcases films from the United States, Asia, and the Pacific and includes seminars with filmmakers and critics.

Barrow

Chukchi Sea

BROOKS

Noatak
National
Preserve

RUSSIA

Cape Krusenstern
National
Monument

ARCTIC CIRCLE

Kotzebue

*Gates of the Arctic
National Park
and Preserve*

Kobuk Valley
National
Park

A R C

Strait

Bering
Land Bridge
National
Preserve

Selawik
National
Wildlife
Refuge

Bettles

Bering

Teller

Koyukuk
National
Wildlife
Refuge

Kanuti Flats
National
Wildlife
Refuge

Council

*Saint
Lawrence
Island*

Nome

Yukon River

Norton Sound

Nowitna National
Wildlife Refuge

I N T E R

*Bering
Sea*

Innoko
National
Wildlife
Refuge

Denali
National Park
and Preserve

KUSKOKWIM

MOUNTAINS

ALASKA RR

Mt. McKinley

Cantwell

R A

GEORGE PARKS
HWY

Yukon Delta
National
Wildlife
Refuge

ALASKA

SOUTH

Willow

Bethel

Palm

*Nunivak
Island*

Anchorage

Lake Clark
National Park
and Preserve

Tyonek

Whittier

Kenai

Kuskokwim Bay

Togiak
National
Wildlife
Refuge

Soldotna

Seward

Dillingham

Iliamna Lake

Homer

Kenai
Fjords
National
Park

Cook

Inlet

U

N

D

Kenai National
Wildlife Refuge

O

S

Katmai
National Park
and Preserve

Bristol Bay

PRIBILOF
ISLANDS

Port Lions

Chugach
National
Forest

Kodiak
National
Wildlife
Refuge

Kodiak

Izembek
Wildlife
Refuge

ALASKA PENINSULA

Aniakchak
National Monument
and Preserve

ALEUTIAN
ISLANDS

Becharof National
Wildlife Refuge

Alaska Peninsula
National Wildlife
Refuge

P A C

ALASKA MARITIME
NATIONAL WILDLIFE REFUGE

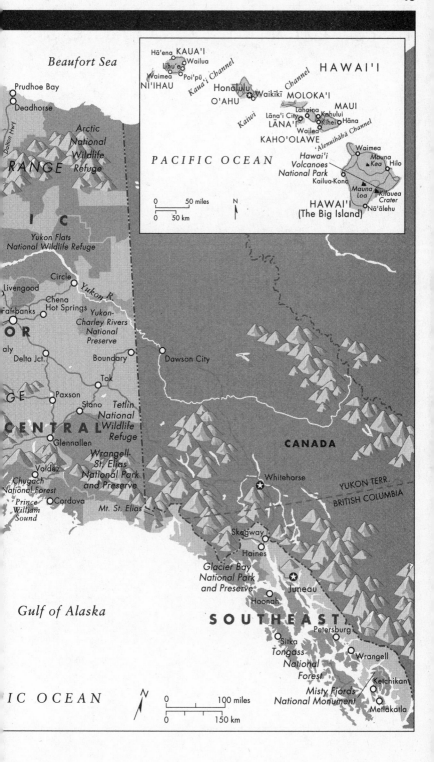

Beaufort Sea

Prudhoe Bay
Deadhorse

Arctic
National
Wildlife
Refuge

RANGE

I   C

Yukon Flats
National Wildlife Refuge

Circle
Livengood
Chena
Hot Springs
Fairbanks
Yukon R.
Yukon-
Charley Rivers
National
Preserve

aly
Delta Jct.
Boundary
Dawson City

Tok

G E
Paxson
Slano
Tetlin
National
CENTRAL
Wildlife
Refuge
Glennallen
Wrangell-
St. Elias
National Park
and Preserve
Valdez
Chugach
National Forest
Prince
Cordova
William
Sound
Mt. St. Elias

CANADA

Whitehorse
YUKON TERR.
BRITISH COLUMBIA

Skagway
Haines

Glacier Bay
National Park
and Preserve
Juneau
Gulf of Alaska
Hoonah

SOUTHEAST
Petersburg
Sitka
Tongass
National
Forest
Wrangell
Ketchikan
Misty Fjords
National Monument
Metlakatla

IC OCEAN

0   100 miles
0   150 km

Hawaii inset

Hā'ena   KAUA'I
Līhu'e   Wailua
Waimea   Poi'pū
NI'IHAU
Kaua'i Channel
HAWAI'I

Honolulu
Waikīkī   Channel
O'AHU   MOLOKA'I
MAUI
Lāna'i City   Lahaina   Kahului
Kā'iwi   LĀNA'I   Kīhei   Hāna
Wailea
KAHO'OLAWE
Alenuihāhā Channel

PACIFIC OCEAN
Waimea
Mauna
Kea
Hilo
Hawai'i
Volcanoes
National Park
Kailua-Kona
Mauna   Kīlauea
Loa   Crater
HAWAI'I
(The Big Island)
Nā'ālehu

0   50 miles
0   50 km
N

THE UNITED STATES

Each state is a unique entity with its own
character. (In the case of some of the larger
states, you'll find multiple personalities.)
Each chapter contains sections on major
cities, the most popular sights, and
worthwhile but lesser-known destinations,
along with good suggestions on where to
stay, eat, and explore.

ALABAMA

Updated by
Michelle
Roberts

Capital	Montgomery
Population	4,319,000
Motto	We Dare Defend Our Rights
State Bird	Yellowhammer
State Flower	Camellia
Postal Abbreviation	AL

State Visitor Information

Alabama Bureau of Tourism and Travel (✉ 401 Adams Ave., Box 4927, Montgomery 36103, ☎ 334/242–4169 or 800/252–2262). **Welcome centers:** I–59 near Valley Head, I–20/59 at Cuba, I–65 at Elkmont, I–10 north of Seminole, I–10 at Grand Bay, I–20 east of Heflin, I–85 at Lanett, U.S. 231 south of Dothan.

Scenic Drives

Talladega Scenic Drive begins at U.S. 78 near Heflin and winds through Talladega National Forest to Adams Gap, southwest of Cheaha State Park. The 25-mi drive has scenic views, especially in March and April and mid-October through mid-November. In and around Mobile, the **Azalea Trail** twines for 27 mi; flowering time is February and March.

State Parks

Alabama's 24 state parks include a wide variety of recreational activities and lodging accommodations. Visitors have the choice of resort lodges, hotels, campgrounds, chalets, and cabins, both modern and rustic. Several parks have marinas, golf courses, and tennis facilities. **De-Soto State Park,** in northern Alabama, has the spectacular Little River Canyon and falls. **Lake Guntersville State Park,** also in the northern part of the state, is home of the annual Eagle Awareness programs. **Gulf State Park,** near Gulf Shores, has one of the most popular beach areas along the Alabama coast. Contact **Alabama State Parks** (✉ 64 N. Union St., Folsom Administrative Bldg., Suite 547, Montgomery 36130, ☎ 800/252–7275) for reservations or information on state parks.

CENTRAL ALABAMA

This region encompasses the hilly Highlands around Birmingham, the state's largest city, and the state capital, Montgomery, with its antebellum history, 90 mi south of Birmingham.

Visitor Information

Birmingham: Convention and Visitors Bureau (✉ 2200 9th Ave. N, 35203-1100, ☎ 205/458–8000 or 800/458–8085). **Montgomery:** Convention & Visitors Center (✉ 401 Madison Ave., 36104, ☎ 334/261–1100 or 800/240–9452).

Arriving and Departing

By Bus

Greyhound (✉ 618 N. 19th St., Birmingham; 950 W. South Blvd., Montgomery; ☎ 800/231–2222) serves major towns.

By Car

I–59 runs northeast from Birmingham into Georgia and Tennessee and southwest into Mississippi. I–20 runs east–west through Birmingham. I–65 is the north–south route connecting Birmingham with Montgomery. I–85 leads southwest from Atlanta to Montgomery.

By Plane

Major airlines serve **Birmingham International Airport** (⊠ 5900 Airport Hwy., ☎ 205/599–0500). Montgomery's **Dannelly Field** (⊠ 4445 Selma Hwy., ☎ 334/281–5040) is served by many carriers.

By Train

Amtrak (☎ 800/872–7245) serves Birmingham and Mobile.

Exploring Central Alabama

Birmingham blossomed with the development of the iron industry and coal mines in the 19th century. Today its primary employer is the University of Alabama at Birmingham, home to one of the country's largest medical centers. The city has restored many of its 19th-century buildings and is an attractive, welcoming metropolis.

The **Birmingham Museum of Art,** the Southeast's largest municipal museum, has some 18,000 works, from Italian Early Renaissance to contemporary American. The museum houses the region's largest collection of Asian art and has the finest collection of Wedgwood outside England. ⊠ *2000 8th Ave. N,* ☎ *205/254–2565.* ⊡ *Free. Closed Mon.*

The **Alabama Sports Hall of Fame and Museum** (⊠ 2150 Civic Center Blvd., ☎ 205/323–6665; ⊡ $5), adjacent to the Civic Center, displays memorabilia of such Alabama athletic heroes as coach Bear Bryant, Jesse Owens, Willie Mays, and Hank Aaron.

In the Kelly Ingram Park area, southwest of the Civic Center, is the **16th Street Baptist Church,** a civil rights landmark where numerous protests were staged in the 1960s. A bomb planted by white supremacists exploded here in 1963, killing four black children. There is a plaque in their memory. ⊠ *1530 16th St.,* ☎ *205/251–9402.* ⊡ *$2. No tours Sun.–Mon.; Sat. tours by appointment only.*

★ The **Birmingham Civil Rights Institute** documents the civil rights movement from the 1920s to the present using exhibits, multimedia presentations, music, and oral histories. ⊠ *520 16th St. N,* ☎ *205/328–9696.* ⊡ *$5. Closed Mon.* ✎

The **Alabama Jazz Hall of Fame,** two blocks from the Civil Rights Institute, has photos and memorabilia of the state's jazz legends, including Nat "King" Cole, Duke Ellington, and Lionel Hampton. ⊠ *1631 4th Ave. N,* ☎ *205/254–2720.* ⊡ *Free. Closed Mon.*

The **Sloss Furnaces,** a massive ironworks, used ore from the hills around Birmingham when it was in operation between 1882 and 1971. Guided tours of this National Historic Landmark are given weekends. During October, the site is transformed into a scary Halloween phenomenon known as Sloss Fright Furnace (☎ 205/324–6881). ⊠ *20 32nd St.,* ☎ *205/324–1911.* ⊡ *Free. Closed Mon.*

☾ With 800 animals, the **Birmingham Zoo** (⊠ 2630 Cahaba Rd., ☎ 205/879–0408; ⊡ $5) is one of the Southeast's largest zoos. Birmingham's
☾ **McWane Center** (⊠ 200 19th St. N, ☎ 205/714–8300; ⊡ $7.50 museum, $7.50 IMAX, $11 for both) is a hands-on science museum with an IMAX theater.

VisionLand Theme Park (⊠ VisionLand Pkwy., Bessemer, ☎ 205/481–4750; ⊡ $23) is 16 mi southwest of Birmingham on I–20/59 near I-

459. It has more than 20 rides including Rampage, a giant wooden roller coaster; River Rapids, a water park with a white-water raft ride; and Dino Domain by Dinomation, a walk-through section with 36 robot dinosaurs, including one that's 26 ft tall and 40 ft long.

★ ☾ **DeSoto Caverns Park** (☎ 256/378–7252 or 800/933–2283, 🎫 $9.99 for 1 hr. guided tour), 40 mi from Birmingham (head southeast on U.S. 280 to Childersburg, then east on Route 76), is a network of caves that were used as a Native American burial ground 2,000 years ago. Rediscovered by Spanish explorer Hernando De Soto in 1540, the caverns later served as a Confederate gunpowder mining center and a Prohibition speakeasy. Tours begin with a sound, water, and laser-light show in the 12-story Great Onyx Cathedral.

More than 300 Confederate veterans and their wives are buried in **Confederate Memorial Park** (✉ 437 C.R. 63, Marbury, ☎ 205/755–1990; 🎫 free), southwest of Childersburg, off U.S. 31 near Mountain Creek.

Montgomery, 90 mi south of Birmingham via I–65, is a city steeped in antebellum history. Today many of its old houses have been restored, and the city is known as a cultural capital of the South. The **visitor center** (☞ Visitor Information, *above*) shows a brief video. Park your car at the center and you can walk to many attractions.

The handsome **state capitol** (✉ Bainbridge St. at Dexter Ave., ☎ 334/242–3935), built in 1851, served as the first capitol for the Confederate States of America. Dr. Martin Luther King Jr. began his career as a minister in 1954 at the **Dexter Avenue King Memorial Baptist Church** (✉ 454 Dexter Ave., ☎ 334/263–3970). A basement mural depicts people and events associated with the civil rights movement. The first **White House of the Confederacy** (☎ 334/242–1861; 🎫 free) stands at the corner of Washington Avenue and Union Street. Built in 1835, it has Civil War artifacts and many items that belonged to Jefferson Davis, the Confederate president.

★ At the **Civil Rights Memorial** (✉ 400 Washington Ave., ☎ 334/264–0286), a circular black granite table records names of 40 people who lost their lives in the civil rights movement and chronicles its history in lines radiating like the hands of a clock. Water emerges from the table's center and flows evenly across the top. On a curved black granite wall behind the table are engraved the words from the Bible that Dr. Martin Luther King Jr. often quoted, "Until justice rolls down like waters and righteousness like a mighty stream."

Dining and Lodging

Throughout Alabama, Old South dishes—fried chicken, barbecue, roast beef, country-fried steak—prevail. In recent years, though, a number of upscale restaurants with more varied fare have opened in Birmingham and Montgomery. Hotels and motels offer weekend specials, but football games in Auburn can book up Montgomery hotels; legislative sessions also make rooms scarce, so it's best to call ahead.

Birmingham

$$–$$$$ ✕ **Highlands Bar and Grill.** Known for his French-inspired southern
★ cuisine, owner-chef Frank Stitt offers freshly prepared, creative comfort food in a sophisticated setting. Although the menu changes daily, baked grits is Stitt's signature dish. ✉ 2011 11th Ave. S, ☎ 205/939–1400. *Reservations essential. AE, MC, V. Closed Sun.–Mon.*

$–$$ ✕ **Nabeel's Cafe.** Greek-born John Krontiras, his Italian-born wife, Ottavia, and their son, Anthony, serve food prepared with artistry, whether it's an eggplant casserole, spinach-and-feta croissant, or spinach pie.

The adjacent gourmet market has Mediterranean products at modest prices. ⊠ *1706 Oxmoor Rd., Homewood,* ☎ *205/879–9292. AE, MC, V. Closed Sun.*

$–$$ ✕ **Silvertron Cafe.** Since 1986 owner Alan Potts has done wonders with chicken, Black Angus beef, orange roughy, and fresh pasta sauces. Linger under tin ceilings, fresh flowers, and photos of early Birmingham while you make room for a Bailey's Brownie. ⊠ *3813 Clairmont Ave.,* ☎ *205/591–3707. AE, DC, MC, V.*

$$$ 🏨 **The Tutwiler.** This National Historic Landmark with a European am-
★ bience was built in 1913 as a luxury apartment building and was con-
verted in 1986 into a hotel. The elegant lobby has marble floors, chandeliers, and lots of flowers. ⊠ *2021 Park Pl., at 21st St. N, 35203,* ☎ *205/322–2100 or 800/996–3426,* FAX *205/325–1183. 147 rooms. Restaurant. AE, D, DC, MC, V.* ♻

$$–$$$ 🏨 **Wynfrey Hotel.** Rising 15 stories above the Riverchase Galleria mall (☞ Shopping, *below*), this deluxe hotel has a gracious lobby with an Italian marble floor, Chippendale-style furniture, and a brass esca-
lator. Rooms are done in English and French traditional styles. ⊠ *1000 Riverchase Galleria (U.S. 31S), 35244,* ☎ *205/987–1600 or 800/996–3739,* FAX *205/987–9552. 329 rooms. Restaurant, pool, health club. AE, D, DC, MC, V.* ♻

$–$$ 🏨 **Mountain Brook Inn.** This hotel at the foot of Red Mountain has an eight-story glass-exterior, a marble-floor lobby, and bilevel suites with spiral staircases. ⊠ *2800 U.S. 280, 35223,* ☎ *205/870–3100 or 800/523–7771,* FAX *205/414–2128. 170 rooms. Restaurant, pool. AE, D, DC, MC, V.* ♻

Montgomery

$–$$$ ✕ **Jubilee Seafood Company.** In this small café setting you'll find some of the finest and freshest seafood in town. ⊠ *1057 Woodley Rd., Cloverdale Plaza,* ☎ *334/262–6224. Reservations not accepted. AE, MC, V. Closed Sun. and Mon.*

$–$$$ ✕ **Sahara Restaurant.** Proprietors Joe and Mike Deep carry on a fam-
★ ily tradition of friendly service at one of the city's finest restaurants. Their broiled snapper, shrimp scampi, and certified Angus beef are per-
fectly prepared. ⊠ *511 E. Edgemont Ave.,* ☎ *334/262–1215. AE, D, DC, MC, V. Closed Sun.*

$ ✕ **Chris' Hot Dog Stand.** A Montgomery tradition for more than 80 years, this small eatery is always busy at lunchtime. Chris's famous sauce contains chili peppers, onions, and a variety of herbs that give his hot dogs a one-of-a-kind flavor. ⊠ *138 Dexter Ave.,* ☎ *334/265–6850. Reservations not accepted. No credit cards. Closed Sun.*

$$ 🏨 **Red Bluff Cottage.** In this delightful cottage in the heart of down-
town, guests can relax on a veranda overlooking the Alabama River plain. Rooms have ceiling fans and antiques. The sitting room with a fireplace and the music room–library are good places to relax. ⊠ *551 Clay St., 36104,* ☎ *334/264–0056 or 888/551–2529. 4 rooms. AE, D, MC, V. BP.* ♻

Motels

🏨 **Hampton Inn** (⊠ 1401 East Blvd., Montgomery 36117, ☎ 334/277–2400), 105 rooms; pool, breakfast; *$.*

🏨 **Motel Birmingham** (⊠ 7905 Crestwood Blvd., Birmingham 35210, ☎ 205/956–4440 or 800/338–9275, FAX 205/956–3011), 108 rooms; pool; *$.*

The Arts

In Montgomery at the world-class **Alabama Shakespeare Festival** (⊠ 1 Festival Dr.; Eastern Bypass Exit off I–85, ☎ 334/271–5353 or 800/

841–4273), Shakespearean plays, contemporary dramas and comedies, and musicals are performed on two stages.

Shopping

Birmingham's **Riverchase Galleria** (☎ 205/985–3039), at the intersection of I–459 and U.S. 31S, is one of the Southeast's largest malls, with more than 200 stores. The **Summit** (☎ 205/967–0111), one of Birmingham's newest and most upscale malls, is a pedestrian-friendly, one-level shopping center located at the intersection of I–459 and U.S. 280. **Boaz**, about 60 mi north of Birmingham, has more than 100 outlet and specialty stores (☎ 800/746–7262).

MOBILE AND THE GULF COAST

In Mobile, a busy port and one of Alabama's oldest cities (celebrating her 300th birthday in 2002), antebellum buildings survive as a bridge to the past, and a springtime explosion of azaleas shows why Mobile is known as "the Azalea City." The country's first Mardi Gras was held here (not in New Orleans), and today the city still exults in two weeks of pre-Lenten parades, balls, and merrymaking. South of Mobile, across Mobile Bay, the area around Gulf Shores has 32 mi of white-sand beaches. On the eastern shore of Mobile Bay in Fairhope and Point Clear, live oaks are laced with Spanish moss, and sprawling clapboard houses with wide porches overlook the bay and its spectacular sunsets.

Visitor Information

Alabama Gulf Coast area–Gulf Shores/Orange Beach: Convention and Visitors Bureau (✉ Drawer 457, Gulf Shores 36542; 3150 Gulf Shores Pkwy., Gulf Shores 36547; 23685 Perdido Beach Blvd., Orange Beach 36561; ☎ 800/745–7263). **Eastern Shore:** Eastern Shore Chamber of Commerce (✉ 327 Fairhope Ave., Fairhope 36532, ☎ 334/928–6387; ✉ 29750 Larry Dee Cawyer Dr., Daphne 36527, ☎ 334/621–8222). **Mobile:** Mobile Convention and Visitors Corporation (✉ 1 Water St., 36602, ☎ 800/566–2453).

Arriving and Departing

By Bus
Greyhound (☎ 800/231–2222) has stations in **Mobile** (✉ 2545 Government Blvd.) and **Pensacola, Florida** (✉ 505 W. Burgess Rd.).

By Car
I–10 leads west from Florida to Mobile and continues into Mississippi. I–65 leads south from Birmingham and Montgomery and ends at Mobile. Twenty miles east of Mobile, along Baldwin County's eastern shore of Mobile Bay, the communities of Fairhope and Point Clear are accessible via U.S. 98 and Alternate U.S. 98A. Gulf Shores is connected with Mobile via I–10 and Route 59; Routes 180 and 182 are the main beach routes.

By Plane
Mobile Regional Airport (✉ 8400 Airport Blvd., ☎ 334/633–0313) is served by a number of major domestic carriers. Florida's **Pensacola Regional Airport** (✉ 2430 Airport Blvd., ☎ 850/435–1746), about 40 mi east of Gulf Shores/Orange Beach, has service from many carriers.

By Train
Amtrak (☎ 800/872–7245) connects Mobile with the east and west coasts.

Exploring Mobile and the Gulf Coast

In 1711 **Fort Condé** (⊠ 150 S. Royal St., ☎ 334/208–7304; ☞ free) was the name the French gave to the Colonial outpost that would one day expand and become Mobile. Today, the city's French origins endure in its Creole cuisine. One hundred fifty years after the fort was destroyed, its remains were discovered during construction of the I–10 interchange. A reconstructed portion houses the city's **visitor center**, as well as a museum. Costumed guides conduct tours.

The visitor center has information on major annual events hosted by Mobile, the biggest of which is **Mardi Gras,** with balls, parties, and parades. The **Azalea Trail Festival** is held in March. The two-day **Historic Mobile Homes Tour,** also in March, opens private homes for viewing.

Oakleigh (⊠ 350 Oakleigh Pl., ☎ 334/432–1281; ☞ $5), 1½ mi from Fort Condé, is an antebellum, Greek Revival–style mansion, built between 1833 and 1838. Costumed guides give tours of the home, which features fine period furniture, portraits, silver, jewelry, kitchen implements, toys, and more. Tickets include a tour of neighboring **Cox-Deasy House,** an 1850s cottage furnished with simple 19th-century pieces.

★ Mobile Bay, just east of downtown, is the site of the 155-acre **Battleship Park** (⊠ 2703 Battleship Pkwy., ☎ 334/433–2703 or 800/426–4929, ☞ $8), where the battleship USS *Alabama* is anchored. A tour gives a fascinating glimpse into the operation of the World War II vessel, which had a crew of 2,500. Anchored next to it is the USS *Drum,* a World War II submarine. Other exhibits include the B-52 bomber *Calamity Jane.*

★ **Bellingrath Gardens and Home,** 20 mi south of Mobile, is the site of one of the world's most magnificent azalea gardens. Here, amid a 905-acre semitropical landscape, 65 acres of gardens bloom in all seasons: 200 species of azaleas in spring, 3,000 rosebushes in summer, 60,000 chrysanthemum plants in autumn, and fields of poinsettias in winter. Built by Coca-Cola bottling pioneer Walter D. Bellingrath, who started the gardens with his wife in 1917, the house has a fine collection of antiques, including porcelain. Sightseeing cruises along Fowl River are available aboard the *Southern Belle.* ⊠ *12401 Bellingrath Gardens Rd., Theodore,* ☎ *334/973–2217.* ☞ *Gardens $8, gardens and home $14.*

Fairhope, on the eastern shore of Mobile Bay, is noted for its public pier and beaches, quaint downtown shops (selling everything from toys to nautical gear), art shows, and crafts festivals. A growing art colony with antiques shops and several potteries, the village provides ample opportunities for fishing and boating. Stay in one of its charming B&Bs. **Point Clear,** a bend in the road, is a leading resort destination because of Marriott's Grand Hotel (☞ Dining and Lodging, *below*).

The **Eastern Shore Art Center** hosts monthly exhibits of oils, watercolors, graphics, mixed-media, photography, sculpture, and ceramics. ⊠ *401 Oak St., Fairhope,* ☎ *334/928–2228.* ☞ *Free. Closed Sun. and Mon.*

The family-operated **Punta Clara Kitchen** (⊠ 17111 Scenic Hwy. 98, Point Clear, ☎ 334/928–8477) sells exquisite confections, preserves, and other treats from an 1897 Victorian home.

From Mobile take I–10 and Route 59 south to **Gulf Shores,** a family-oriented beach area with hotels, restaurants, and attractions. There's ample free parking along the white-as-snow beach, though the traffic can be bumper to bumper at peak times. Star-shape **Fort Morgan** (⊠ Mobile Point, ☎ 334/540–7125) sits at the western tip of Pleasure Island, 20 mi west of Gulf Shores at the end of Route 180. The fort was

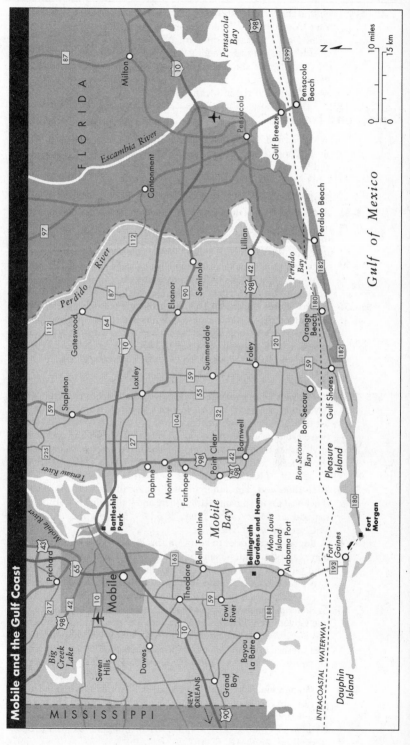

Mobile and the Gulf Coast

built in the early 1800s to guard the entrance to Mobile Bay. In 1864, after Confederate torpedoes sank the ironclad *Tecumseh,* Union admiral David Farragut shouted, "Damn the torpedoes! Full speed ahead!" The rest of Farragut's fleet pushed its way to the bay, forcing the Confederates' surrender. The museum at the site tells the story. From Wednesday through Sunday, actors in period dress present plays of the events that occurred inside the fort.

Dining and Lodging

In Mobile and throughout the Gulf Coast area, fresh seafood abounds. Shrimp, crab claws, and oysters (fried, stewed, or nude) as well as gumbo and West Indies salad are staples on the menu at most seafood restaurants.

Gulf Shores

$–$$ ✕ **Original Oyster House.** Dining at this nautically themed restaurant
★ overlooking the bayou has become a local tradition. Oysters, plucked fresh from nearby Perdido Bay, are the specialty of the house. The Cajun-style gumbo—with crab claws, shrimp, amberjack, grouper, redfish, okra and other vegetables, and Cajun spices—has won 20 culinary awards. ⊠ *Bayou Village Shopping Center, Rte. 59,* ☎ *334/948–2445. Reservations not accepted. AE, D, DC, MC, V.*

$$–$$$ ▦ **Gulf Shores Plantation.** This 320-acre family resort, 8 mi east of Fort Morgan on the Gulf, has condominiums with fully equipped kitchens in high-rises overlooking the beach. Many recreational activities are available. ⊠ *Rte. 180 W (Box 1299), 36547,* ☎ *334/540–5000 or 800/ 554–0344,* FAX *334/540–6055. 524 units. Pools, tennis. AE, MC, V.* ⊛

Mobile

$$$–$$$$ ✕ **Justine's Courtyard and Carriageway.** Just blocks from the Mobile
★ River in the heart of the city, Justine's features two beautiful settings for outdoor dining—in the courtyard or the carriageway—as well as two elegant inside dining rooms. Owner-chef Matt Shipp concocts creative dishes from southern staples, like his butterbean cakes with feta cheese, leeks, and red peppers. ⊠ *80 St. Michael St.,* ☎ *334/438–4535. AE, D, DC, MC, V. Closed Tues. No lunch Mon. or Sat.*

$–$$ ✕ **La Louisiana.** This family-owned restaurant, in a renovated house, is beloved for its romantic atmosphere and Italian dishes featuring fresh seafood. ⊠ *2400 Airport Blvd.,* ☎ *334/476–8130. AE, D, DC, MC, V. Closed Sun. No lunch.*

$ ✕ **Roussos.** Next door to Fort Condé is Roussos, one of the most popular seafood restaurants in the Mobile area. The outstanding service, family-friendly atmosphere, and excellent seafood—fried, broiled, or Greek style—make Roussos a fun place. ⊠ *166 S. Royal St.,* ☎ *334/ 433–3322. AE, D, DC, MC, V. Closed Sun.*

$$ ▦ **Radisson Admiral Semmes Hotel.** This downtown hotel, next to Mobile Government Plaza, is popular with local politicians. Revelers appreciate its excellent location on the Mardi Gras parade route. Rooms are furnished in Queen Anne and Chippendale styles. ⊠ *251 Government St., 36602,* ☎ *334/432–8000,* FAX *334/405–5942. 170 rooms. Restaurant, pool. AE, D, DC, MC, V.*

$–$$ ▦ **Malaga Inn.** Rooms at this delightful, historic inn surround a lush, gaslit courtyard with a fountain. The large, airy rooms are furnished with period antiques, and many have original hardwood floors. ⊠ *359 Church St., 36602,* ☎ *334/438–4701 or 800/235–1586. 40 rooms. Restaurant, pool. AE, D, MC, V.*

Orange Beach

$$–$$$ ✕ **The Outrigger.** Perched at the tip of Alabama Point on Perdido Pass, this clean, contemporary restaurant has panoramic views of the water.

The fried seafood (served with hush puppies) is hard to pass up, but fish also comes broiled or blackened. Shrimp Perdido and veal are specialties. ⊠ *27500 Perdido Beach Blvd.,* ☎ *334/981–6700. Reservations not accepted. AE, D, DC, MC, V.*

$–$$$ ✕ **Bayside Grill.** The nautical decor here blends smartly with the marina view. Fresh seafood is the specialty, along with pastas, steaks, salads, and chicken. A New Orleans–born chef creates such down-home fare as coconut shrimp, black bean soup, Cajun-style gumbo, and bananas Foster strudel. Sunday brunch is bountiful. The early-dinner menu, served from 4 until 6 in the fall and winter months, is a bargain. ⊠ *27842 Canal Rd.,* ☎ *334/981–4899. AE, D, DC, MC, V.*

$–$$ ✕ **Franco's.** If you're craving Italian food, come to this popular restaurant for such specialties as stuffed mushrooms, seafood fettuccine, veal, and steak—all prepared with the freshest ingredients. Ask about nightly specials. ⊠ *26651 Perdido Beach Blvd.,* ☎ *334/981–9800. Reservations not accepted. AE, D, DC, MC, V.*

$–$$ ✕ **Hazel's Family Restaurant.** This plain family-style restaurant serves a full menu: there's a hearty breakfast (with great biscuits and a popular omelet bar), soup-and-salad lunches, and buffet dinners with seafood. There's also a self-service ice cream bar. ⊠ *Gulf View Square Shopping Center, Rte. 182,* ☎ *334/981–4628. Reservations not accepted. AE, D, DC, MC, V.*

$$–$$$ ☷ **Original Romar House.** This unassuming beach cottage is full of surprises—from the Caribbean-style upstairs sitting area to the Purple Parrot Bar to the luxurious art deco–style guest rooms. In the evening, wine and cheese are served. ⊠ *23500 Perdido Beach Blvd., 36561,* ☎ *334/974–1625 or 800/487–6627,* ⅢⅩ *334/974–1163. 6 rooms, 1 cottage. AE, MC, V. BP.*

$$–$$$ ☷ **Perdido Beach Resort.** The exteriors of these Mediterranean-style
★ eight- and nine-story hotel towers are stucco and red tile, and the lobby is tiled in terra-cotta and has mosaics by Venetian artists. Luxurious rooms have beach views and balconies. ⊠ *27200 Perdido Beach Blvd., 36561,* ☎ *334/981–9811 or 800/634–8001,* ⅢⅩ *334/981–5670. 345 rooms. 3 restaurants, pools, tennis court, exercise room. AE, D, DC, MC, V.* ✆

Point Clear

$$–$$$$ ✕☷ **Marriott's Grand Hotel.** The Grand, set within 550 acres of beau-
★ tifully landscaped grounds on Mobile Bay, has been cherished since 1847. A small beach, Jubilee Point pavilion, and a fishing pier provide access to the bay, and an oversize pool is the favorite gathering spot for families. The award-winning weekend brunch, featuring made-to-order crabmeat omelets, is worth the drive from Mobile. ⊠ *1 Grand Blvd., Point Clear 36564,* ☎ *334/928–9201 or 800/544–9933,* ⅢⅩ *334/ 928–1149. 306 rooms, 9 cottages. 3 restaurants, pool, golf, tennis court. AE, D, DC, MC, V.* ✆

Outdoor Activities and Sports

Canoeing

Sunshine Canoe Rentals (☎ 334/344–8664) runs canoe trips at Escatawpa River, 15 mi west of Mobile. The river has no rapids, so you travel at a leisurely pace past lots of white sandbars.

Fishing

Fishing here is excellent. You can obtain a fishing license from most bait shops. For information contact the **Department of Conservation and Natural Resources** (☎ 334/242–3829). In Gulf Shores, **Gulf State Park** (☞ State Parks, *above*) has fishing from an 825-ft pier; you can also rent flat-bottom boats for lake fishing. Deep-sea fishing from charter boats is very popular. Orange Beach has more than 100 charter boats including the **Moreno Queen** (☎ 334/981–8499), which offers four- and six-hour fishing trips.

Golf

In recent years, coastal Alabama has developed into one of the most popular golfing destinations in the Southeast. With winter temperatures averaging in the 60°F range and pleasant breezes, the area has become a true year-round spot. Prices range from about $32 to $70 for greens fees and cart rental. The **Robert Trent Jones Golf Trail** (☎ 800/949–4444 for reservations and information) includes challenging, scenic courses in eight locations around the state, including Mobile.

The spectacular **Kiva Dunes** course, adjacent to Gulf Shores Plantation Resort (⊠ 12 mi west of Gulf Shores on Rte. 180, ☎ 334/540–7000), designed by Jerry Pate, combines oceanfront dunes golf with Scottish-style links golf. The **Craft Farms** complex (⊠ Rte. 59 just north of Gulf Shores, ☎ 334/968–7500) has 36 holes on two Arnold Palmer–designed courses at **Cotton Creek** and another 18 on the **Woodlands course** designed by Larry Nelson. About 12 mi north of Gulf Shores in Foley, the **Glenlakes Golf Club** (⊠ 9530 Clubhouse Dr., ☎ 334/955–1220 or 800/435–5253), a course designed by Bruce Devlin, has 18 challenging holes that play over 7,000 yards and another 9 holes stretching 3,100 yards. The course at **Gulf State Park** (⊠ 20115 Rte. 135, ☎ 334/948–7275) in Gulf Shores sits on 3,600 resort acres. The **Earl Stone–designed course** (☎ 334/948–4653), built in 1972, is challenging and well bunkered. Senior citizens get a 15% discount.

Water Sports

In Orange Beach **Fun Marina** (☎ 334/980–5122) rents Jet Skis, pontoon boats, and 16-ft bay-fishing boats. In Gulf Shores **Island Recreation Services** (☎ 334/948–7334) rents Jet Skis, bikes, body boards, surfboards, and sailboats.

ELSEWHERE IN ALABAMA

Huntsville

Arriving and Departing

Huntsville is 100 mi north of Birmingham via I–65 and U.S. 72E.

Visitor Information

Huntsville Convention and Visitors Bureau (⊠ 700 Monroe St., Huntsville 35801, ☎ 256/533–5723 or 800/772–2348).

What to See and Do

Huntsville has a cluster of attractions including golf courses, historic homes, and a variety of museums. The **U.S. Space and Rocket Center** (⊠ 1 Tranquility Base, ☎ 256/837–3400 or 800/637–7223; ☞ $14.95) is home to the **U.S. Space Camp, Space Academy,** and **Aviation Challenge.** The center runs a bus tour of the NASA labs and shuttle test sites, hands-on exhibits in the museum, and an outdoor park filled with spacecraft; the **Spacedome Theater** shows IMAX movies.

EarlyWorks is a hands-on history center comprising four properties. **Alabama Constitution Village** is the site of Alabama's Constitutional Convention of 1819. Craftspeople in period dress demonstrate skills such as woodworking, printing, cooking, and weaving. At the **EarlyWorks Museum,** visitors can hear stories from a talking tree, build a house at an interactive architectural exhibit, and examine a 46-ft keelboat. The **Decorative Arts Center** features special exhibits in a restored 1848 home. A few blocks from the village, the **Historic Huntsville Depot** gives a glimpse of railroad life in the early 19th century. ⊠ *404 Madison St.,* ☎ *256/564–8100 or 800/678–1819.* ⌐ *$10. Closed Sun.*

Dining and Lodging

$–$$ ✕ **Cafe Berlin.** Paintings and photographs of European café scenes adorn the walls, and taped music ensures that the German theme is not forgotten. Schnitzel and wurst are prepared a number of ways; other choices are fish, chicken, steak, and enormous salads. ⊠ *505 Airport Rd.,* ☎ *256/880–9920. AE, D, MC, V.*

$–$$ 🏨 **Huntsville Hilton.** The location is prime, as the Hilton is within walking distance of the historic district and museums, and many rooms overlook either Big Spring Park and Lake or the Von Braun Civic Center. The spacious rooms have irons, hair dryers, and coffeemakers. ⊠ *401 Williams Ave., 35801,* ☎ *256/533–1400,* 𝐅𝐀𝐗 *256/534–7787. 277 rooms. Restaurant, pool, exercise room. AE, D, DC, MC, V.* 🐾

Tuscumbia

Arriving and Departing

Tuscumbia is 120 mi northwest of Birmingham via I–65 and U.S. Alternate 72. Take Exit 310 off I–65 at Cullman.

Visitor Information

Colbert County Tourism and Convention Bureau (⊠ U.S. 72, Tuscumbia 35674, ☎ 256/383–0783 or 800/344–0783).

What to See and Do

Tuscumbia and the adjoining towns of Florence, Sheffield, and Muscle Shoals form a quad-city area known throughout Alabama simply as the Shoals. Spreading out on both sides of the Tennessee River basin, this area is rich in culture and history.

Ivy Green (⊠ 300 W. North Commons, ☎ 256/383–4066; ⌐ $5) is the birthplace of author and lecturer Helen Keller, who was left unable to hear or see at the age of 19 months. With the help of her teacher, Annie Sullivan, she graduated from Radcliffe with honors in 1904 and became a champion for all those with similar disabilities. Tours are year-round. *The Miracle Worker,* the play about Keller's childhood, is performed outdoors from mid-June through late July.

The **Alabama Music Hall of Fame and Museum** celebrates the history of Alabama's musical heritage and holds the original contracts of Elvis Presley's deal with Sun Records, the actual touring bus of the band Alabama, and exhibits on the likes of Hank Williams, Lionel Richie, and Nat "King" Cole. August's annual **Concert Series** (⊠ U.S. 72, ☎ 256/381–4417 or 800/239–2643; ⌐ $6) draws performers and fans from across the country.

Lodging

$–$$ 🏨 **Sharlotte's House Bed and Breakfast.** Two blocks from Helen Keller's birthplace in Tuscumbia's historic district, this stately Victorian home has been renovated and redecorated by proprietors Coy and Sharlotte Roper. ⊠ *105 E. North Commons, Tuscumbia 35674,* ☎ *256/386–7269. 3 rooms. AE, D, MC, V.*

$ 🏨 **Key West Inn.** This is a clean, comfortable, and affordable motel. Rooms have microwaves and small refrigerators. ⊠ *1800 U.S. 72, Tuscumbia 35674,* ☎ *256/383–0700. 41 rooms. AE, D, DC, MC, V.*

ALASKA

Updated by	**Capital**	Juneau
Bill Sherwonit	**Population**	620,000
	Motto	North to the Future
	State Bird	Willow ptarmigan
	State Flower	Forget-me-not
	Postal Abbreviation	AK

Statewide Visitor Information

The **Alaska Division of Tourism** (✉ Box 110801, Juneau 99811, ☎ 907/465–2010, FAX 907/465–2287) provides general visitor information. The **Alaska Public Lands Information Center** (✉ 605 W. 4th Ave., Suite 105, Anchorage 99501, ☎ 907/271–2737) is a clearinghouse of information on state and federal lands, including hiking trails, cabins, and campgrounds. The **Department of Fish and Game** (✉ Box 25526, Juneau 99802, ☎ 907/465–4180 for seasons and regulations; 907/465–2376 for licenses) can answer questions about sportfishing. The **Alaska Native Tourism Council** (✉ 1577 C St., Suite 304, Anchorage 99501, ☎ 907/274–5400, FAX 907/263–9971) represents the state's Native-run attractions. For bed-and-breakfast reservations throughout Alaska, call **Alaska Private Lodging: Stay with a Friend** (✉ Box 200047, Anchorage 99520, ☎ 907/258–1717, FAX 907/258–6613).

Cruising

More than a third of Alaska's visitors arrive by cruise ship. Most cruises leave from Vancouver, British Columbia, on a weeklong itinerary up the Inside Passage of Alaska's Southeast Panhandle. All cruise lines stop at Ketchikan, Juneau, and Skagway, while some also visit Sitka, Haines, and Petersburg. Many include a day in Glacier Bay National Park, but call ahead to be sure. Some cruises also continue across the Gulf of Alaska, to the south-central towns of Seward and Valdez. The major cruise tour operators serving Alaska are **Princess Cruises and Tours** (✉ 2815 2nd Ave., Suite 400, Seattle, WA 98121, ☎ 206/366–6000 or 800/426–0442) and **Holland America Line/Westours** (✉ 300 Elliott Ave. W, Seattle, WA 98119, ☎ 206/281–3535 or 800/426–0327). For a small-ship cruise tour, contact **Cruise West** (✉ 2401 4th Ave., Suite 700, Seattle, WA 98121, ☎ 206/441–8687 or 800/888–9378). State ferries provide year-round budget service for passengers and vehicles (☞ Arriving and Departing *in* Southeast, *below*) on similar routes.

National and State Parks

Alaska has more land in national parks, wilderness areas, and national wildlife refuges than all the other states combined.

National Parks

Denali National Park and Preserve (☞ The Interior, *below*) is home to North America's tallest peak, Mt. McKinley; admission to the park is $5 per person, or $10 per family. **Glacier Bay National Park and Preserve** (☞ Southeast, *below*) is a marine preserve where 17 spectacular glaciers meet tidewater and seals float on icebergs. **Katmai National Park and Preserve** (☞ Southwest, *below*), a mixture of volcanic moonscape, rugged coast, large lake systems, mountains, and forested lowlands on the Alaska Peninsula, is home to huge coastal brown bears that fish for salmon in the Brooks River. On the Kenai Peninsula south of Anchorage is **Kenai Fjords National Park** (☞ South Central, *below*), known for its tidewater glaciers, rugged fjords, and abundant marine wildlife. The country's largest national park, **Wrangell–St. Elias** (☞ South Central, *below*), east of Anchorage along the Canadian border, is six times the size of Yellowstone.

The nation's largest national forest, the **Tongass** (☞ Southeast, *below*), stretches the length of the Panhandle. **Chugach National Forest** (☞ South Central, *below*) encompasses much of the Kenai Peninsula and Prince William Sound.

State Parks

Chugach State Park (⊠ HC 52, Box 8999, Indian 99540, ☎ 907/345–5014), near Anchorage, has more than 100 mi of hiking trails, wildlife viewing, and easily accessible wilderness. **Denali State Park** (⊠ HC 32, Box 6706, Wasilla 99654, ☎ 907/745–3975) has a ridge-top trail with views of the Alaska Range, and public-use cabins.

SOUTHEAST

Southeast Alaska is a maritime region of thousands of islands blanketed by old-growth spruce forest. The waters abound in Pacific salmon (five species) and sea mammals, and the shore is home to deer, bears, and coastal communities that cling to the mountainsides. The wet climate inspires locals to call galoshes "Juneau tennis shoes," although summer does bring some breathtakingly beautiful sunny days. The villages of Tlingit, Haida, and Tsimshian Indians, as well as museums and cultural centers in the region's larger communities, give insights into Native American cultures.

Visitor Information

Southeast: Tourism Council (⊠ Box 20710, Juneau 99802, ☎ 907/586–4777, FAX 907/463–4961). **Juneau:** Log Cabin Information Center (⊠ 134 3rd St., 99801, ☎ 907/586–2201 or 888/581–2201, FAX 907/586–6304). **Ketchikan:** Visitors Bureau (⊠ 131 Front St., 99901, ☎ 907/225–6166 or 800/770–3300; 800/770–2200 for brochures; FAX 907/225–4250). **Sitka:** Convention and Visitors Bureau (⊠ 303 Lincoln Street, Suite 4, Box 1226, 99835, ☎ 907/747–5940, FAX 907/747–3739) provides brochures and advice.

Arriving and Departing

Southeast Alaska is accessible mainly by air or water. The mainland road system (from Anchorage, through the Canadian Yukon) connects only with tiny northern communities after hundreds of miles of wilderness road. Cruise ships (☞ Cruising, *above*) and state ferries are the most common means of visitor transportation.

By Car

Ferries that will transport vehicles to southeast Alaska leave from Bellingham, Washington, and from Prince Rupert, British Columbia. From the north, the Alaska and Haines or Klondike Highway lead to Skagway and Haines, and ferries continue south through the region.

By Ferry

The **Alaska Marine Highway System** (⊠ 1591 Glacier Ave., Juneau 99801, ☎ 907/465–3941 or 800/642–0066, FAX 907/465–2476) is an extensive network of large and small vessels that link most southeast communities. All ferries take cars (reservations necessary in summer) and have cafeterias or restaurants; most also have staterooms, but many Alaskans camp on deck in tents—or on the lounges' floors. The system makes connections with BC Ferries in Prince Rupert, British Columbia.

By Plane

Regular jet service is available from Pacific Coast and southwestern U.S. cities to Ketchikan, Wrangell, Petersburg, Sitka, and **Juneau International Airport** (☎ 907/789–7821). The southeast is served year-round by **Alaska Airlines** (☎ 800/426–0333). Flight service to the villages is available from the region's larger communities.

Exploring the Southeast

Ketchikan

Ketchikan is a fishing and logging town at the southern end of the Panhandle. Its centerpiece is **Creek Street,** the historic red-light district, now home to quaint shops built on stilts over Ketchikan Creek. Ten miles

★ north of town, **Totem Bight State Historic Park** (⊠ 9883 N. Tongass Hwy., ☎ 907/247–8574) displays beautiful, historic totem poles. The village of **Saxman** (☎ 907/225–5163), 2½ mi south of Ketchikan, also has many totem poles. Original totem poles, some 200 years old, can be seen at the **Totem Heritage Center** (⊠ 601 Deermont St., ☎ 907/ 225–5900; ☎ $4) from May through September. The city, in fact, contains the world's largest collection of totem poles.

Sitka

This historic town was the capital of Russian America before Alaska was sold to the United States in 1867. Russian cannons still crown **Castle Hill,** and the flagpole where the Stars and Stripes replaced the czarist Russian standard still stands. **St. Michael's Cathedral** (⊠ 240 Lincoln St., ☎ 907/747–8120; ☎ $2) is a 1976 replica of the 1848 church. During the 1966 fire that destroyed the original, townspeople entered the burning building to rescue precious icons and other religious objects, which are now on display.

Open daily in summer and by appointment in winter, the **Russian Bishop's House** (⊠ Monastery and Lincoln Sts., ☎ 907/747–6281; ☎ $3) is a log structure built in 1842 that's been restored by the National Park Service; call ahead October through April, when it's open by appointment only. The **Sheldon Jackson Museum** (⊠ 104 College Dr., ☎ 907/747–8981; ☎ $4) has a fine collection of priceless Tlingit, Haida, Tsimshian, Athabascan, Aleut, and Eskimo artwork and crafts. In **Sitka National Historical Park** (⊠ 106 Metlakatla St., 99835, ☎ 907/ 747–6281), Tlingit carvers still work at the venerable craft of carving totems; a forest trail winds among 15 totems, both old and new.

Juneau

The state capital clings to the mountainside along a narrow saltwater channel. It was born as a gold rush town in 1880 and remained an active gold-mining center until World War II. Today its number one employer is the state government, with transportation and tourism important runners-up.

Although Juneau's hills are steep, you can still explore the charming town on foot. Houses downtown date from the gold rush. On South Franklin Street, the **Red Dog Saloon** (☎ 907/463–3777) preserves the rough-and-tumble spirit of 1898. The Victorian **Alaskan Hotel** (☞ Dining and Lodging, *below*) is a more genteel relic of the gold rush era. The tiny, onion-domed **St. Nicholas Russian Orthodox Church** (⊠ 5th and Gold Sts., ☎ 907/586–1023), constructed in 1894, is the oldest original Russian church in Alaska. The **Alaska State Museum** (⊠ 395 Whittier St., ☎ 907/465–2901; ☎ $5 mid-May–mid-Sept., $3 mid-Sept.–mid-May), near the waterfront, highlights the state's rich Russian-American cultural heritage, along with Native American artifacts, gold rush memorabilia, and natural history displays.

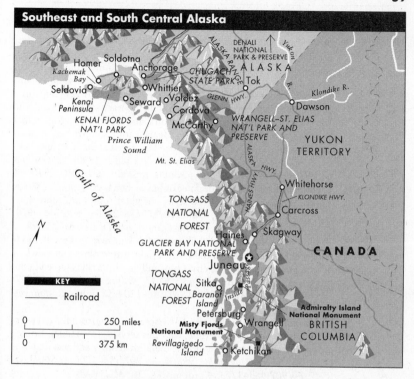

Southeast and South Central Alaska

Glacier Bay National Park and Preserve

★ Whales, porpoises, sea otters, sea lions, seals, and seabirds inhabit the 62-mi-long **Glacier Bay** (⌂ Box 140, Gustavus 99826, ☎ 907/697–2230), a remote and wild marine park wilderness accessible only by boat. In addition to wildlife, the bay has 17 tidewater glaciers and about a dozen inlets or arms to explore, making it a favorite destination for sea kayaking as well as wildlife viewing from charter boats and cruise ships; contact **Glacier Bay Tours and Cruises** (☎ 800/622–2042) for details. Visitor services are available in the nearby community of Gustavus, 30 minutes by plane from Juneau.

Tongass National Forest

The largest of the nation's forests, the **Tongass** (⌂ Centennial Hall, 101 Egan Dr., Juneau 99801, ☎ 907/586–8751) encompasses 16.8 million acres, or nearly three-fourths of Southeast Alaska. Mostly covered by old-growth temperate rain forest, the Tongass is a breeding ground for black and brown bears, bald eagles, Sitka black-tailed deer, mountain goats, and wolves. **Misty Fjords** (☎ 907/225–2148) and **Admiralty Island** (☎ 907/586–8800), two national monuments, have rugged shorelines and breathtaking vistas.

Dining and Lodging

Juneau

$–$$$$ ✕ **The Waterfront Summit.** Housed in a converted turn-of-the-20th-century brothel, this restaurant serves its meals in a small, candlelit room. You have a choice of nearly 15 local fish and shellfish dishes. ⌂ 455 S. Franklin St., ☎ 907/586–2050. AE, D, DC, MC, V.

$–$$$ ✕ **The Fiddlehead.** Downstairs, you'll find healthy, eclectic dishes such as black beans with rice served in a cozy room with stained glass, historic photos, and a view of Mt. Juneau. Upstairs, you can dine in a more elegant setting with Tuscan-Italian decor; pastas and fresh fish are featured dishes. The homemade bread is delectable and the restaurant features one of Alaska's finest wine lists. ⊠ *429 Willoughby Ave.,* ☎ *907/586–3150. AE, D, MC, V.*

$–$$ ✗🍴 **Silverbow Inn.** Remodeled from a bakery dating from the 1890s, this is a B&B built in European style and adorned with antiques and personal memorabilia. Each guest room is individually decorated in a specific style that blends history with contemporary art and design. The Backroom restaurant has settings, chairs, and tables (no two are alike) from the turn of the 20th century. Meals feature sandwiches, with an international flavor. Next door you can buy bagels at the Silverbow bakery, the oldest operating bakery in the state (circa 1890). ⊠ *120 2nd St., 99801,* ☎ *907/586–4146. 6 rooms. Restaurant. D, MC, V. BP.* 🐾

$$$ 🍴 **Baranof Hotel.** This grande dame of Juneau hotels still reflects its 1930s origins. The lobby is Art Deco style, but guest rooms are contemporary. ⊠ *127 N. Franklin St., 99801,* ☎ *907/586–2660 or 800/544–0970,* FAX *907/586–8315. 196 rooms. Restaurant. AE, D, DC, MC, V.* 🐾

$$$ 🍴 **The Prospector.** A short walk west of downtown, this small, modern hotel has very large rooms with bright watercolors and views of the channel, mountains, or city. Outstanding prime rib is served in the McGuires' dining room and lounge. ⊠ *375 Whittier St., 99801,* ☎ *907/ 586–3737 or 800/331–2711,* FAX *907/586–1204. 58 rooms. Restaurant. AE, D, DC, MC, V.* 🐾

$$ 🍴 **Alaskan Hotel.** This historic 1913 hotel is 15 mi from the ferry ter-
★ minal and 9 mi from the airport (city bus service is available). Rooms are on three floors and have turn-of-the-20th-century antiques and iron beds. ⊠ *167 S. Franklin St., 99801,* ☎ *907/586–1000 or 800/327– 9347,* FAX *907/463–3775. 42 rooms. D, DC, MC, V.* 🐾

Ketchikan

$$–$$$$ ✗ **Salmon Falls Resort.** It's a half-hour drive from town, but the fresh seafood and steaks served in the huge, octagonal dining room make the trip more than worthwhile. The pine-log restaurant overlooks the waters of Clover Passage, where sunsets can be vivid red and remarkable. This is a convenient stop after a visit to Totem Bight Park. ⊠ *Mile 17, N. Tongass Hwy.,* ☎ *907/225–2752. AE, MC, V.*

Sitka

$–$$$$ ✗ **Channel Club.** Fine steaks and seafood are served in nautical surroundings, including glass and fishnet floats and whalebone carvings. ⊠ *2906 Halibut Point Rd.,* ☎ *907/747–9916. AE, DC, MC, V.*

$$$ 🍴 **Westmark Shee Atika.** Southeast Alaskan Native artwork illustrates the history, legends, and exploits of the Tlingit people at this rustic Westmark chain outpost. Many rooms overlook Crescent Harbor and the islands beyond; others have mountain and forest views. Fried halibut nuggets in the Raven Room restaurant are not to be missed. ⊠ *330 Seward St., 99835,* ☎ *907/747–6241 or 800/544–0970,* FAX *907/ 747–5486. 101 rooms. Restaurant. AE, D, DC, MC, V. EP.* 🐾

Campgrounds

State and national forest campgrounds are available near all southeast communities (☞ Alaska Public Lands Information Center *in* Statewide Visitor Information, *above*). *The Milepost,* available in most Alaska and Washington bookstores, lists campgrounds throughout the state.

Outdoor Activities and Sports

Fishing

Southeast Alaskans are blessed with great salmon fishing off city docks and on beaches where creeks meet saltwater. You can also take an air taxi to a remote spot for a day's fishing or an extended stay. Fishing licenses are available in most grocery and sporting-goods stores.

Kayaking and Rafting

You can bring your own kayak aboard state ferries or hire a local outfitter—such as **Alaska Discovery Wilderness Adventures** (✉ 5310 Glacier Hwy., Juneau 99801, ☎ 907/780–6226 or 800/586–1911)—for a guided Inside Passage or Glacier Bay excursion. The company also guides kayak trips on Admiralty Island and at Icy Bay, near Yakutat, and float trips on the Tatshenshini and Alsek rivers. For rafting on the Mendenhall River as well as glacial travel, canoe and kayak trips, and hiking, contact **Alaska Travel Adventures** (✉ 9085 Glacier Hwy., Suite 301, Juneau 99801, ☎ 907/789–0052; 800/478–0052 in AK). Guided sea-kayaking tours of nearby Misty Fjords National Monument in Tongass National Forest are available from **Southeast Exposure** (✉ 515 Water St., Box 9143, Ketchikan 99901, ☎ 907/225–8829); the company also does day trips in the Ketchikan area and rents both kayaks and bikes.

Wildlife Viewing

Southeast Alaska is renowned for its whales, eagles, and brown bears (the coastal cousins of grizzlies). **Glacier Bay National Park** is a prime viewing area for several species of whales, including humpbacks and orcas. **Alaska Discovery Wilderness Adventures** (☞ Kayaking and Rafting, *above*) leads whale-watching tours at Icy Strait, near Chichagof Island. Popular bear-viewing areas are **Pack Creek,** within Admiralty Island National Monument (☞ Tongass National Forest, *above*), and **Anan Creek** in the Tongass Forest near Wrangell (contact U.S. Forest Service in Wrangell, ☎ 907/874–2323). The **Alaska Chilkat Bald Eagle Preserve** (☎ 907/766–2292), near Haines, hosts the world's largest gathering of bald eagles: Between 1,000 and 4,000 eagles gather here each November and December.

Ski Areas

The **Eaglecrest** ski area, across the channel from Juneau on Douglas Island, has 31 trails, three lifts, a ski school, cafeteria, and equipment rental. ✉ *155 S. Seward St., Juneau 99801, ☎ 907/586–5284; 907/586–5330 for recorded ski conditions. Closed May–Nov.*

Check with local visitor centers for **cross-country ski trails** groomed for either diagonal or skate skiing.

Shopping

Silver Lining Seafoods (✉ 1705 Tongass Ave., ☎ 907/225–9865), north of Ketchikan's city dock, has locally smoked seafood and fish-motif postcards and T-shirts by local artist Ray Troll.

In Juneau the **Alaska Steam Laundry Building,** on South Franklin Street, has shops and a good coffeehouse downstairs. The **Senate Building Mall,** also on South Franklin, houses a Christmas store and other import shops. In the Senate Building Mall, **Taku Smokeries** has two retail outlets selling locally smoked seafood.

SOUTH CENTRAL

South-central Alaska is home to most of the state's population and many of its most sought-out attractions. Many visitors start their trips in Anchorage, then continue south to the fishing and artists' communities of the Kenai Peninsula.

Visitor Information

Anchorage: Convention and Visitors Bureau (⊠ 524 W. 4th Ave., 99501, ☎ 907/276–4118; 907/276–3200 for events hot line; FAX 907/278–5559), Log Cabin and Downtown Visitor Information Center (⊠ W. 4th Ave. and F St., ☎ 907/274–3531). **Homer:** Visitor Center (⊠ 135 Sterling Hwy., Box 541, 99603, ☎ 907/235–7740, FAX 907/235–8766). **Kenai Peninsula:** Tourism Marketing Council (⊠ 150 N. Willow, Suite 29, Kenai 99611, ☎ 907/283–3850; 800/535–3624 to order a vacation planner, FAX 907/283–2838). **Seward:** Visitor Information Center (⊠ Mile 2, Seward Hwy., Box 749, 99664, ☎ 907/224–8051, FAX 907/224–5353). **Soldotna:** Visitor Information Center (⊠ 44790 Sterling Hwy., 99669, ☎ 907/262–1337, FAX 907/262–3566).

Arriving and Departing

By Bus

Gray Line of Alaska (☎ 907/277–5581 in Anchorage; 907/456–7741 in Fairbanks) serves Anchorage, Denali, and Fairbanks and also makes runs to Seward, Valdez, Skagway, and Whitehorse.

By Car

To get to Anchorage from Tok, on the Alaska Highway near the Canadian border, head southwest on the Glenn Highway. From Fairbanks travel south on the George Parks Highway. South of Anchorage, the Seward and Sterling highways connect with communities on the Kenai Peninsula.

By Ferry

The south-central section of the **Alaska Marine Highway** ferry system (☞ Southeast, *above*) links communities on Prince William Sound, the Gulf of Alaska, and Cook Inlet. Road connections to and from Anchorage can be made in Whittier and Seward. There is no regular ferry service between the south-central and southeast regions.

By Plane

Anchorage International Airport (☎ 907/266–2437), about 6 mi from downtown, is served by Alaska Airlines, American West, Continental, Northwest, Delta Airlines, and United. Commuter plane service is available to Denali National Park, Homer, Kenai, and other destinations within the region. A cab from the Anchorage airport to downtown costs about $15 plus tip. Some hotels have shuttles.

By Train

The **Alaska Railroad** (☎ 800/544–0552; 907/265–2494 in Anchorage; 907/458–6025 or 800/895–7245 in Fairbanks, FAX 907/265–2323) has mainline service between Seward, Anchorage, Denali National Park, and Fairbanks and secondary service between Portage and Whittier.

Exploring South Central

Anchorage

Anchorage is a young, spirited city in a spectacular setting between mountains and sea. Nearly half the state's population resides here, which may explain why you can find everything from oil industry high-rises to backwoods cabins with resident sled-dog teams.

The **Anchorage Museum of History and Art** (⊠ W. 7th Ave. and A St., ☎ 907/343–6173; ☏ $6.50) has an outstanding exhibit on Native Alaskan life and a permanent display of artwork depicting Alaska as seen by explorers, resident painters, and latter-day visitors. The **Imaginarium** (⊠ 737 W. 5th Ave., Suite G, ☎ 907/276–3179; ☏ $5) is an interactive science museum with a shop selling educational toys. At **Ship**

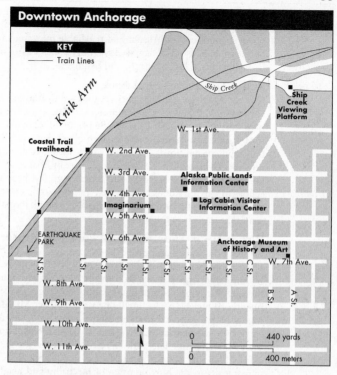

Downtown Anchorage

KEY
— Train Lines

Knik Arm

Ship Creek

Ship Creek Viewing Platform

W. 1st Ave.

Coastal Trail trailheads

W. 2nd Ave.

W. 3rd Ave.

Alaska Public Lands Information Center

W. 4th Ave.

Log Cabin Visitor Information Center

Imaginarium

W. 5th Ave.

EARTHQUAKE PARK

W. 6th Ave.

Anchorage Museum of History and Art

W. 7th Ave.

N St.   L St.   K St.   I St.   H St.   G St.   F St.   E St.   D St.   C St.   B St.   A St.

W. 8th Ave.

W. 9th Ave.

W. 10th Ave.

W. 11th Ave.

N

0   440 yards
0   400 meters

Creek, just north of downtown, you can see salmon jump in summer as they head upstream to spawn; there's a platform for easy viewing.

A display at **Earthquake Park,** at the west end of Northern Lights Boulevard, shows the damage wrought by the 1964 quake, when houses tumbled into the ocean. Trees have claimed the earth mounds and ponds created by the quake's force. The **floatplane base at Lake Hood,** near the Anchorage International Airport, is the world's largest and busiest. Plan a sunset stroll by the scenic **Coastal Trail,** which runs along Cook Inlet, with several trailhead access points in mid- and downtown.

The Kenai Peninsula

Thrusting into the Gulf of Alaska south of Anchorage, the Kenai Peninsula is a glacier-hewn landscape with magnificent wildlife viewing and fishing from its spectacular coastline. In summer the Alaska Railroad runs a passenger train daily to **Seward,** a small fishing and tourist town on Resurrection Bay, but most people drive the three hours from Anchorage. Tour boats leave Seward's busy downtown harbor for excursions that include visits to sea lion and bird rookeries and close-up views of tidewater glaciers.

Seward is the jumping-off point for **Kenai Fjords National Park** (☞ *below*). **Mariah Tours** (☎ 800/270–1238), run out of Seward, has wildlife and glacier tours of the park.

At the southern terminus of the Seward Highway, 225 mi from Anchorage, lies **Homer,** in a breathtaking setting that includes a sand spit jutting into Kachemak Bay. The town's buildings are picturesque, and you can comb the beach, fish off the docks, or charter a boat for halibut fishing (☞ Outdoor Activities and Sports, *below*). Wildlife abounds in the bay, and fishing charters may give you a close-up view of seals, porpoises, birds, and, more rarely, whales. If you walk along the docks at the end of the day, you can see fishermen unloading their catch. Across from the end of the Homer spit is **Halibut Cove,** one of the prettiest spots in south-central Alaska and reachable by water taxi. **Seldovia,** on the other side of Kachemak Bay from Homer, has an onion-domed Russian church, lots of shops, and fishing.

Kenai Fjords National Park

★ One of only three national parks connected to Alaska's highway system, the 670,000-acre **Kenai Fjords** (✉ 1212 4th Ave., at the small-boat harbor, Box 1727, Seward 99664, ☎ 907/224–3175) is known for its abundant marine wildlife, deep-blue tidewater glaciers, waterfalls, and coastal fjords (long and steep-sided glacially carved valleys now filled with seawater). People come here by boat to see whales, porpoises, seals, and seabirds; fish for salmon; and hear the booming echoes of calving tidewater glaciers. Yet the park's most popular visitor attraction is on land: **Exit Glacier** is a short walk from the one gravel road that leads into the park.

Wrangell–St. Elias National Park and Preserve

Bridging the Canadian border, 13-million-acre **Wrangell–St. Elias** (✉ Box 29, Glennallen 99588, ☎ 907/822–5234) could fit six Yellowstones within its borders. Known to some as Alaska's Mountain Kingdom, the park encompasses four major mountain ranges and six of the continent's 10 highest peaks, including the 18,008-ft **Mt. St. Elias.** Here, too, is North America's largest subpolar ice field, the Bagley, which calved several gigantic glaciers; one of them, the **Malaspina,** is larger than Rhode Island. The park has two main entryways: On the north side is Nabesna Road; on the east is 60-mi-long McCarthy Road, which leads to the historic town of **McCarthy** and neighboring **Kennecott Mine** (now closed), two of the park's key attractions if you don't want to venture far from the road system.

Chugach National Forest

Second only to the Tongass in size, **Chugach National Forest** (✉ 3301 C St., Suite 300, Anchorage 99503, ☎ 907/271–2500) encompasses much of Prince William Sound, the Kenai Peninsula, and the Copper River delta region. Its 5.8 million acres include forested hills and valleys, rugged coastal mountains, one of the world's largest tidewater glaciers, and wetlands that support migrating waterfowl and shorebirds. About an hour's drive south of Anchorage, **Portage Glacier** and the **Begich-Boggs Visitor Center** are two of Alaska's premier visitor attractions.

Dining and Lodging

For bed-and-breakfast reservations, call **Alaska Private Lodging: Stay with a Friend** (✉ Box 200047, Anchorage 99520, ☎ 907/258–1717, FAX 907/258–6613, ✑).

Anchorage

$$$–$$$$ ✕ **Seven Glaciers Restaurant.** A high-speed tram transports you to this alpine restaurant, perched on the side of Mt. Alyeska at 2,300 ft. You are assured a culinary adventure that emphasizes fresh local ingredients, including Alaska fish and wild game. ✉ *The Westin Alyeska Prince Hotel, 1000 Arlberg, Girdwood,* ☎ *907/754–2237. Reservations essential. AE, D, MC, V. Closed Sun.–Thurs. from Nov.–Apr. No lunch.*

$$–$$$$ ✕ **Marx Brothers Cafe.** The second-oldest house in Anchorage was orig-
★ inally constructed for the engineers who built the Alaska Railroad; now it's a restaurant serving sophisticated fare such as macadamia-crusted halibut and, for dessert, wild-berry crisp with Alaskan birch syrup. There are more than 500 selections on the award-winning wine list. ✉ *627 W. 3rd Ave.,* ☎ *907/278–2133. AE, DC, MC, V. Closed Sun. Oct.–Apr. No lunch.*

$$–$$$$ ★ ✕ **Double Musky.** It's worth the 40-mi trip south of town and the wait once you arrive. The little building set among spruce trees is casually decorated with Mardi Gras memorabilia, the better to prepare you for the fine Cajun dishes and huge, tender steaks to come. ✉ *Crow Creek Rd., Girdwood,* ☎ *907/783–2822. Reservations not accepted. AE, D, DC, MC, V. Closed Mon. No lunch.*

$$–$$$$ ✕ **Sacks Cafe.** A favorite before- or after-show dining option for those attending concerts and plays at Anchorage's Performing Arts Center, this downtown restaurant serves fresh seafood, pasta, and dinner salads. It also has takeout service for sandwiches, salads, and espresso. Sunday brunch is served until 2:30. ✉ *328 G St.,* ☎ *907/276–3546. AE, MC, V.*

$$–$$$$ ✕ **Simon and Seafort's Saloon and Grill.** A bustling place, especially in summer, this longtime local favorite is known for its fresh local seafood, salt-rock-roasted prime rib, and the large windows that look out across Cook Inlet and afford views of the Alaska Range. ✉ *420 L St.,* ☎ *907/ 274–3502. AE, DC, MC, V. No lunch Sun.*

$–$$ ✕ **Downtown Deli.** Alaska's governor owns this classic delicatessen, where you can get anything from deli classics like chopped-liver sandwiches to local specialties such as reindeer stew. Nestle into a wooden booth inside, or watch the street action from a sidewalk table outside. ✉ *525 W. 4th Ave.,* ☎ *907/276–7116. AE, D, DC, MC, V.*

$$$$ 🏨 **Anchorage Hotel.** Built in 1916, this charming hotel has its original sinks and tubs, and the hallways upstairs are lined with old photos of the city. There's a fireplace in the lobby. ✉ *330 E St., 99501,* ☎ *907/272–4553 or 800/544–0988,* FAX *907/277–4483. 26 rooms. AE, D, DC, MC, V. CP.*

$$$$ 🏨 **Hotel Captain Cook.** This three-tower hotel takes up a full city block. Teak paneling lines most public walls, recalling Captain Cook's voyages in the South Pacific. ✉ *939 W. 5th Ave., 99501,* ☎ *907/276– 6000 or 800/843–1950,* FAX *907/343–2298. 547 rooms. 3 restaurants, pool, health club. AE, D, DC, MC, V.* ✧

$$$–$$$$ 🏨 **The Westin Alyeska Prince Hotel.** Seven glaciers and lush forests surround this château-style luxury hotel at the base of Mt. Alyeska. Rooms have refrigerators, safes, heated towel racks, ski-boot storage, bathrobes, and slippers, and all have views of the Chugach Mountains. A tram taking you to Seven Glaciers Restaurant (☞ *above*) leaves from the hotel. ✉ *1000 Arlberg, Box 429, Girdwood 99587,* ☎ *907/754– 1111 or 800/880–3880,* FAX *907/754–2200. 307 rooms. 4 restaurants, pool, exercise room. AE, D, DC, MC, V.* ✧

$$$ 🏨 **Voyager Hotel.** All the rooms in this small four-story hotel are nosmoking; they have full kitchens and bathrooms with pedestal sinks and wainscoting. Upstairs, west-side rooms look out on the Cook Inlet. ✉ *501 K St., 99501,* ☎ *907/277–9501 or 800/247–9070,* FAX *907/ 274–0333. 38 rooms. Restaurant. AE, D, DC, MC, V.*

$$ 🏨 **Alaskan Samovar Inn.** This well-worn but clean motel is east of downtown on one of the city's main thoroughfares. Victorian-style rooms are small and dark, but each has a whirlpool tub, cable TV, and refrigerator. ✉ *720 Gambell St., 99501,* ☎ *907/277–1511 or 800/478– 1511,* FAX *907/272–5192. 68 rooms. Restaurant. AE, D, MC, V.*

$ 🏨 **Hosteling International Anchorage.** At this cinder-block building downtown, most guests share dorm-style rooms, though there's a limited number of private rooms (all with shared bathrooms). There's a 1 AM curfew and a five-night minimum stay in summer. ✉ *700 H St., 99501,* ☎ *907/276–3635,* FAX *907/276–7772, 6 rooms, 95 beds. MC, V.*

The Kenai Peninsula

$–$$$ ✕ **Harbor Dinner Club.** Run by the same family since 1958, this eatery serves local halibut and salmon in a dining room with a view of Resurrection Bay and the mountains. There's dancing in the lounge. ✉ *220 5th Ave., Seward,* ☏ *907/224–3012. AE, D, DC, MC, V.*

$–$$ ✕ **The Saltry.** A 45-minute ride from Homer Harbor on the Kachemak
★ Bay Ferry takes you to this restaurant with a deck over the water. Once there, sample some of south-central Alaska's best seafood dishes, including fine sushi. Arrange for boat and dining reservations through the Central Charter Booking Agency. ✉ *Halibut Cove,* ☏ *907/235– 7847; 800/478–7847 in AK. MC, V. Closed Oct.–May.*

$$$–$$$$ ☷ **Best Western Hotel Seward.** Gold rush–style rooms in this downtown hotel have VCRs and refrigerators, and some have views of Resurrection Bay. The hotel runs a shuttle to the harbor in summer and is close to the ferry. ✉ *221 5th Ave., Seward 99664,* ☏ *907/224–2378 or 800/ 528–1234,* 𝖥𝖠𝖷 *907/224–3112. 38 rooms. AE, D, DC, MC, V.* ✑

$$–$$$ ☷ **Land's End.** The three wings of this beachfront hotel at the far end of the Homer Spit have a contemporary nautical theme. All rooms facing Kachemak Bay have small balconies for watching the sunset. ✉ *4786 Homer Spit Rd., Homer 99603,* ☏ *907/235–2500; 800/478–0400 in AK (reservations only);* 𝖥𝖠𝖷 *907/235–0420. 61 rooms. Restaurant. AE, D, DC, MC, V.* ✑

Campgrounds

In Anchorage, the city-operated ⚠ **Centennial and Lions Campground** (✉ Box 196650, 99519, ☏ 907/333–9711) has 88 spaces for tent camping, showers, and a dump station; it's closed from mid-October through April. Near Anchorage, ⚠ **Chugach State Park** (✉ HC52 Box 8999, Indian 99540, ☏ 907/345–5014) has three public campgrounds. For **Kenai Peninsula** and other area campgrounds, contact the Alaska Public Lands Information Center (☞ Statewide Visitor Information, *above*).

Nightlife and the Arts

The **Alaska Center for the Performing Arts** (✉ 621 W. 6th Ave., ☏ 907/ 263–2900) is home to a local symphony orchestra and theater companies and also presents operas, symphonies, concerts, and plays by national and international touring companies. The **Fly-by-Night Club** (✉ 3300 Spenard Rd., ☏ 907/279–7726) features everything from pop rock and blues to poetry readings and stage revues with tacky jokes. The *Anchorage Daily News* publishes a weekend activity guide every Friday, and the *Anchorage Press* includes a calender of events in its weekly editions.

Outdoor Activities and Sports

Biking

Most south-central highways are suitable for biking on the shoulder. Anchorage has more than 125 mi of bike trails. The **Matanuska Valley** is an increasingly popular place for farm-road rides. Bikes are available for rent at many hotels and at **Downtown Bicycle Rental** (✉ 5th Ave. and C St., Anchorage, ☏ 907/279–5293) and **Anchorage Coastal Bicycle Rentals** at the **Adventure Café** (✉ 414 K St., Anchorage, ☏ 907/276–8282).

Fishing

All south-central coastal communities have fishing charters, outfitters, and guides. Although Anchorage does not have good saltwater fishing—glacial runoff makes the water too murky—the freshwater lakes are stocked, and hatchery-enhanced runs of salmon return to Ship and Campbell creeks each summer. In Homer, **Central Charter Booking Agency** (✉ 4241 Homer Spit, 99603, ☏ 907/235–7847; 800/478–7847 in AK) arranges salmon and halibut charters. **Alaska Wildland Adventures** (✉ Box 389, Girdwood 99587, ☏ 800/334–8730; 800/478–

4100 in AK) sells float and fish packages on the Kenai River, world famous for its huge salmon runs. Licenses are sold in most grocery and other retail stores.

Hiking and Backpacking

There are public cabins for rent along many hiking trails in south-central Alaska (☞ Alaska Public Lands Information Center *in* Statewide Visitor Information, *above*). **Chugach State Park** (☎ 907/345–5014), just east of Anchorage, has approximately 30 trails totaling more than 150 mi. Trails are also maintained within **Chugach National Forest** (☞ *above*), on the Kenai Peninsula.

Kayaking and Rafting

Floating is available on hundreds of rivers within a small area. **Nova River Runners** (☒ Box 1129, Chickaloon 99674, ☎ 907/745–5753 or 800/746–5753) leads guided day trips on the Chickaloon, Matanuska, and Six-Mile rivers and overnighters on the Matanuska, Talkeetna, and Copper rivers. **Ketchum Air Service** (☒ Box 190588, Anchorage 99519, ☎ 907/243–5525 or 800/433–9114) provides drop-off and pickup service and gear for wilderness float trips.

Sled-Dog Racing

On winter weekends the **Alaska Sled Dog and Racing Association** (☎ 907/562–2235) hosts races at the Tudor Track in mid-Anchorage. The three-day **Fur Rendezvous World-Championship Sled Dog Race** is staged in downtown Anchorage in mid-February. March brings the famous, 1,049-mi **Iditarod,** which begins in Anchorage and ends in Nome.

Wildlife Viewing

Some of Alaska's best wildlife viewing is possible right outside Anchorage in **Chugach State Park:** Look for moose, Dall sheep, bears, and many smaller mammals and bird life in this accessible wilderness. Along the coastline of the **Kenai Peninsula,** you'll often see whales, sea lions, sea otters, seals, and seabirds.

Ski Areas

The **Alyeska Resort** (☒ Box 249, Girdwood 99587, ☎ 907/754–1111 or 800/880–3880; 907/754–7669 for recorded ski conditions), about 40 mi south of Anchorage, is the largest in the state, with 786 acres of skiable terrain, a 2,600-ft vertical drop, 68 trails, six chair lifts, two cable tows, a 60-passenger tram, and a half-pipe course for snowboarders. It also has a 307-room hotel, a ski school, and two mountaintop restaurants (☞ Seven Glaciers *in* Dining, *above*). **Hilltop Ski Area** (☒ 7015 Abbott Rd., Anchorage 99516, ☎ 907/346–1446; 907/346–2167 for recorded ski conditions), 10 mi from downtown Anchorage, has one lift, one surface lift, one rope tow, nine trails, a vertical drop of 300 ft, ski instruction, cross-country trails, and a national-grade half-pipe for snowboarders.

Anchorage also has a vast and diverse Nordic ski-trail system, with more than 100 mi of groomed trails for both diagonal skiers and skate-skiers. The **Nordic Skiing Association of Anchorage** (☎ 907/276–7609) has a ski hot line (☎ 907/248–6667) that gives grooming and trail condition updates.

Shopping

The shops along 4th and 5th avenues sell T-shirts, trinkets, and Alaskan arts and crafts. The **Cook Inlet Book Company** (☒ 415 W. 5th Ave., ☎ 907/258–4544) has the largest collection of books on Alaska. In summer, Anchorage's **Saturday Market** at 3rd Avenue and E Street is filled with vendors selling fresh produce from Matanuska-Susitna farms, Alaska-made crafts, plus snacks and fast-food meals.

THE INTERIOR

The Alaska and George Parks highways give access to this diverse area, a vast wilderness of birch and spruce forest, high mountains, tundra valleys, and abundant wildlife. Its crown jewel is Denali National Park, 240 highway miles north of Anchorage. En route here from Anchorage, you'll travel through green Matanuska Valley farm country. North of Fairbanks, two hot springs retreats are open year-round.

Visitor Information

Denali National Park and Preserve (⊠ Superintendent, Box 9, Denali National Park 99755, ☎ 907/683–2294 year-round; 907/683–1266 in summer; FAX 907/683–9612 year-round). **Fairbanks:** Convention and Visitors Bureau Information Cabin (⊠ 550 1st Ave., 99701, ☎ 907/456–5774 or 800/327–5774; 907/456–4636 for events hot line; FAX 907/452–2867).

Arriving and Departing

By Car

Much of the Interior is inaccessible by road, but some major roadways do pass through the region. Fairbanks is connected to Anchorage in south-central Alaska by the George Parks Highway. The Steese, Elliot, and Dalton highways provide access north of Fairbanks. Hardy RVers and campers drive the Alaska Highway through British Columbia and the Yukon to Fairbanks; the drive takes at least a week.

By Plane

Year-round, Alaska Airlines and Delta have daily nonstop jet service between Anchorage and the **Fairbanks International Airport** (☎ 907/474–2500); Alaska Airlines also flies nonstop between Seattle and Fairbanks. Also in summer Northwest flies to Fairbanks from Minneapolis. A number of bush carriers originate in Fairbanks and will take you to otherwise inaccessible destinations in the region.

By Train

The **Alaska Railroad** (☎ 800/544–0552; 907/265–2494 in Anchorage; 907/458–6025 or 800/895–7245 in Fairbanks; FAX 907/265–2323) runs between Anchorage and Fairbanks via Denali.

Exploring the Interior

Denali National Park

★ Denali encompasses 6 million acres of wilderness, including the majestic **Mt. McKinley**—at 20,320 ft the highest peak in North America. Along with panoramic vistas of unspoiled taiga and tundra, the park is the natural habitat of bears, wolves, moose, Dall sheep, and caribou. The only road through the park is closed to private vehicles beyond Mile 15. You can, however, take a **shuttle bus** (☎ 800/622–7275), which costs $12–$30 depending on turnaround point, on an 11-hour round-trip excursion to **Wonder Lake,** famous for its views of wading moose and Mt. McKinley. If you tire of the ride, you can get out and walk, then catch another bus (they leave from the park entrance every half hour starting at 5 AM) in either direction. Check with the **visitor center,** near the park entrance, for the day's schedule of naturalist walks and sled-dog demonstrations. Denali is open year-round, but services and accommodations are minimal from September to May. For information on camping *see* Campgrounds *in* Dining and Lodging, *below.*

Fairbanks

Built on the banks of the Chena River, Fairbanks was founded by gold miners early in the 20th century and later became a transportation hub for all the Interior. Today it's the state's second-largest city, although its atmosphere is more that of a frontier town. Its residents cope with incredible winter temperatures (lows reach −50°F) and only three to four hours of daylight in the dead of winter.

One of Fairbanks's main attractions is the **University of Alaska** (⊠ 501 Yukon Dr., ☎ 907/474–7211). On its grounds are the **Large Animal Research Station** (☎ 907/474–7207; ⊡ $5), where live musk ox and caribou can be seen on one-hour tours in summer, and the **University of Alaska Museum** (☎ 907/474–7505; ⊡ $5), whose collection includes a 36,000-year-old mummified steppe bison, a whale skull, dinosaur fossils, and ivory carvings. In summer, daily programs focus on Alaska's northern Native peoples and the aurora borealis (a.k.a. the northern lights); you are welcome to explore and touch such items as Native masks and tools, wolf pelts, and historic artifacts. The **Geophysical Institute** (☎ 907/474–7558) shows a free video on the aurora borealis on Thursday afternoon from June through August. The west ridge of the campus has a view of the Alaska Range to the south.

Another big draw in Fairbanks is **Alaskaland Park** (⊠ Airport Way and Peger Rd., ☎ 907/459–1087), on the Chena River near downtown. Among its numerous free attractions are museums, a theater, an art gallery, a native village, and a reconstructed gold rush town. The park's visitor attractions are closed between Labor Day and Memorial Day.

Hot Springs Retreats

The discovery of natural hot springs in the frozen wilderness just north of Fairbanks sent early miners scrambling to build communities around this heaven-sent phenomenon. Today, Fairbanks residents come to soak in pools filled with hot spring water and to enjoy excellent fishing, hiking, and cross-country skiing. The springs are also a favorite viewing point for the famed northern lights.

Dining and Lodging

Denali

$–$$ ✕ **Lynx Creek Pizza & Pub.** Young park workers as well as park visitors enjoy beer, pizza, and Mexican dishes while dining at picnic tables in this funky frame building just outside Denali. Try the reindeer-sausage pizza topping. ⊠ *Parks Hwy., 1½ mi north of park entrance,* ☎ *907/683–2548. Reservations not accepted. AE, D, MC, V. Closed Sept.–May.*

$$$ ⊞ **Denali National Park Hotel.** The park's only official hotel is 1½ mi inside the park entrance. The original 1939, 200-room structure burned down and in 1972 was replaced by the present modular structure designed for function rather than luxury. Naturalists present nightly programs in summer in the hotel's auditorium. ⊠ *241 W. Ship Creek Ave., Anchorage 99501,* ☎ *907/276–7234 or 800/276–7234,* ☎ *907/258–3668. 103 rooms. Restaurant. AE, D, MC, V. Closed early Sept.–Memorial Day weekend.* ✨

$$$ ⊞ **Denali Princess Lodge.** This large log complex above the Nenana River has suites with whirlpools, landscaped walkways, and a lounge with fireplace. ⊠ *Parks Hwy., 1 mi north of park entrance. Reservations:* ⊠ *2815 2nd Ave., Suite 400, Seattle, WA 98121,* ☎ *907/683–2282 in summer, 800/426–0500 for reservations;* ☎ *907/683–2545 in summer, 206/443–1979 for reservations. 280 rooms. 3 restaurants. AE, DC, MC, V. Closed mid-Sept.–mid-May.* ✨

$ 🏠 **Denali Hostel.** A log building with two dormitory-style bunkhouses, this independent hostel offers bus service to and from the park. There's also a family-style apartment if you want privacy. The hostel is 10 mi north of the park entrance, near Healy. ⊠ *Box 801, Denali National Park 99755,* ☎ *907/683–1295,* FAX *907/683–2106. No credit cards. Bunkhouses closed mid-Sept.–mid-May.*

WILDERNESS CAMPS AND LODGES

$$$$ 🏠 **Camp Denali.** This rustic compound in the heart of the park has cab-
★   ins lighted by gaslight. Its authentic charm, delicious home cooking, and views of Mt. McKinley make it a favorite place to stay in Denali. A knowledgeable staff and naturalist programs will acquaint you with the surrounding wilderness. Visits are arranged according to a fixed schedule, with a three-night minimum stay. ⊠ *Wonder Lake, Box 67, Denali National Park 99755,* ☎ *907/683–2290,* FAX *907/683–1568. 17 cabins. No credit cards. Closed early Sept.–early June. FAP.* 🐾

$$$$ 🏠 **Denali Wilderness Lodge.** Built as a hunting camp to supply gold rush–era miners, this complex of more than two dozen log buildings is reachable only by bush plane. Activities include horseback riding, hiking, bird-watching, and nature walking. ⊠ *30 mi east of Denali Park entrance; mailing address: Box 120, Trout Lake, WA 98650 Sept. 13– May 30; Box 50, Denali Park, AK 99755 May 31–Sept. 12;* ☎ *907/ 683–1287 in summer, 800/541–9779 year-round;* FAX *907/683–1286 in summer, 509/395–2710 in winter. 23 rooms. Closed mid-Sept.–late May. FAP.* 🐾

CAMPGROUNDS

There are seven campgrounds in Denali. Three are open to private ve-hicles for tent and RV camping, three others are reached by shuttle bus and are restricted to tent camping, and one is for backpackers only. For reservations call 🚌 **Denali Park Resorts** (☎ 907/272–7275 or 800/ 622–7275). For more information contact the park superintendent (☞ Visitor Information, *above*). Several private campgrounds are outside the park along the highway; try 🚌 **McKinley RV Park and Campground** (⊠ Mile 248.5, Parks Hwy., Denali Park 99755, ☎ 907/683–2379 or 800/478–2562). For general campsite information and availability, contact the **Alaska Public Lands Information Center** (☞ Statewide Vis-itor Information, *above*).

Fairbanks

$$–$$$$ ✕ **Two Rivers Lodge.** Once a wilderness homestead, this rustic log building is now a full-service restaurant with acclaimed cuisine. In sum-mer you can sit on a deck that overlooks a pond and sample tapas, ap-petizer-size portions of Mediterranean dishes cooked in a wood-fired oven. The wine list is one of Alaska's largest. ⊠ *Mile 16, Chena Hot Springs Rd., Fairbanks,* ☎ *907/488–6815. AE, D, DC, MC, V. No lunch.*

$$$$ 🏠 **Westmark Fairbanks.** This full-service member of Alaska's biggest chain is built around a courtyard on a quiet street in downtown Fair-banks. Some rooms have exercise equipment. ⊠ *813 Noble St., Fair-banks 99701,* ☎ *907/456–7722; 800/544–0970 for central reservations;* FAX *907/451–7478. 244 rooms. Restaurant. AE, D, DC, MC, V.* 🐾

$$$ 🏠 **Sophie Station.** Every room has a full-size kitchen and refrigerator at this all-suite hotel near Fairbanks International Airport. ⊠ *1717 Uni-versity Ave., Fairbanks 99709,* ☎ *907/479–3650 or 800/528–4916,* FAX *907/479–7951. 147 rooms. Restaurant. AE, D, DC, MC, V.* 🐾

Hot Springs

$$$ ✕🏠 **Chena Hot Springs Resort.** This resort, just 60 mi from Fairbanks on Chena Hot Springs Road, is the local favorite. There's a campground, as well as antiques-filled hotel rooms and rustic cabins with electric-ity but no water. Nonguests can pay to use the heated pool and eat in the restaurant. ⊠ *Box 73440, Fairbanks 99707,* ☎ *907/452–7867; 800/ 478–4681 in AK;* FAX *907/456–3122. 80 rooms, 6 cabins. Restaurant, pool, health club. AE, D, DC, MC, V.* ☜

$–$$$ ✕▣ **Arctic Circle Hot Springs Resort.** A three-hour drive from Fairbanks on the Steese Highway, this four-story spa-hotel dates from 1930 and includes everything from hostel-style rooms (for your sleeping bags and pads) to luxury suites. There are also one- and two-bedroom cabins with whirlpool baths and kitchenettes. The entire complex is naturally heated by hot springs. ⊠ *Box 30069, Central 99730,* ☎ *907/520–5113,* FAX *907/520–5116. 24 rooms, 14 cabins. Restaurant, pool. MC, V.* ☜

Outdoor Activities and Sports

Canoeing
The Chena River attracts canoeists, both in Fairbanks and out in the wilderness. Entry points are marked along Chena Hot Springs Road. Avoid the Tanana River, with its hidden sandbars and swift current.

Fishing
Char, grayling, and pike are abundant in the lakes and rivers of the Interior. The Chena River between Fairbanks and Chena Hot Springs is known for its grayling fishing.

Hiking and Backpacking
Skilled outdoorspeople can hike virtually anywhere in Denali National Park's northern foothills and tundra, though they should be prepared for the park's trailless wilderness. There are well-marked beginner trails near the park entrance.

Ice Hockey
The **University of Alaska Nanooks** (☎ 907/474–7205) draw big crowds of ice hockey fans.

Rafting
Several companies run white-water trips on the thrilling Nenana River, which parallels the George Parks Highway near the Denali entrance. Try **Denali Raft Adventures** (⊠ Drawer 190, Denali National Park 99755, ☎ 907/683–2234) or **McKinley Raft Tours** (⊠ Box 138, Denali National Park 99755, ☎ 907/683–2773).

Sled-Dog Racing
The **North American Open Sled Dog Championship** is held in downtown Fairbanks in March. Check with the visitor center (☞ Visitor Information, *above*) for details.

Wildlife Viewing
Few places in North America can equal the wildlife-viewing opportunities at Denali National Park, where you can most likely see grizzly bears, caribou, moose, and Dall sheep. Wolves and golden eagles can also sometimes be spied.

Shopping

In Fairbanks, **Beads and Things** (⊠ 537 2nd Ave., ☎ 907/456–2323) sells native handicrafts from around the state. On College Road, near the University of Alaska Fairbanks campus, **Apocalypse Design** (⊠ 101 College Rd., ☎ 907/451–7555) makes its own specialized cold-weather clothing for mushers and cyclists, as well as miscellaneous outdoor gear accessories. In Ester, just outside Fairbanks, **Judie Gumm Designs** (⊠ 3600 Main St., Ester, ☎ 907/479–4568) sells silver and gold jewelry patterned after Alaska's best-known wildlife and plants.

In North Pole, about 15 mi southeast of Fairbanks, the **Santa Claus House Gift Shop** (⊠ Mile 349, Richardson Hwy., 101 St. Nicholas Dr., ☎ 907/488–2200) has a variety of toys and Alaskan handicrafts.

SOUTHWEST

Visitor Information

Southwest Alaska Municipal Conference (⊠ 3300 Arctic Blvd., Suite 203, Anchorage 99503, ☎ 907/562–7380, FAX 907/562–0438).

Arriving and Departing

Alaska Airlines (☎ 800/426–0333) runs daily nonstop jet service to Kodiak Island from Anchorage. For packages to Kodiak contact **Alaska Airlines Vacations** (⊠ SEARV, Box 68900, Seattle, WA 98168, ☎ 800/468–2248).

Commuter planes serve the town of King Salmon, which is just a short floatplane ride from Katmai National Park and Preserve, 290 mi southwest of Anchorage. Airlines serving King Salmon include Alaska Airlines (☞ *above*), **PenAir** (☎ 907/243–2323 or 800/448–4226), and Reeve Aleutian Airways (☞ *below*).

Contact **Reeve Aleutian Airways** (⊠ 4700 W. International Airport Rd., Anchorage 99502, ☎ 907/243–4700 or 800/544–2248) for flight and package-tour information on the Aleutian and Pribilof islands, in the remote Bering Sea region.

Getting Around

The **Alaska Marine Highway System** (☞ Southeast, *above*) serves some Alaska Peninsula and Aleutian Islands communities in summer.

Exploring the Southwest

Kodiak

The largest island in the United States, Kodiak is home to the brown bear, one of North America's largest land mammals. Before the seat of colonial government was moved to Sitka, Kodiak was the original capital of Russian Alaska. Today the town is a commercial fishing center: You can go halibut fishing, sea kayaking, or flightseeing for bears. Much of the rain-forest-covered island lies within 1.6-million-acre **Kodiak Island National Refuge** (☎ 907/487–2600).

Katmai National Park and Preserve

Katmai National Park and Preserve (⊠ Box 7, King Salmon 99613, ☎ 907/246–3305) is a more remote and less developed park than Denali, but therein lies its charm. A lush valley within what is now the park became a land of steaming fumaroles after the 1912 eruption of Mt. Novarupta and the collapse of nearby Mt. Katmai's peak. The eruption forced residents to flee surrounding areas and produced the Valley of Ten Thousand Smokes. These days the area is known for its trophy rainbow trout and salmon, as well as brown bears, which congregate near **Brooks River**. Hiking, boat touring, and coastal kayaking are other Katmai attractions. **Katmailand Inc.** (⊠ 4125 Aircraft Dr., Suite 2, Anchorage 99502, ☎ 907/243–5448 or 800/544–0551) offers tours and backcountry lodging.

The Aleutian and Pribilof Islands

For most people package tours are the only practical way to see these areas. Schedules are changeable, depending on the weather.

The **Aleutian Islands,** a volcanic, treeless archipelago of 20 large and several hundred smaller islands, stretch 1,000 mi from the Alaska Peninsula toward Japan. The Aleuts who live in the tiny settlements here work in canneries or as commercial fishermen and guides; many continue to lead subsistence lifestyles. Out here, where the wind blows constantly and fog is common, bird-watching opportunities are limitless: Look for terns, guillemots, murres, and puffins. The Japanese invaded the Aleutian Islands during World War II, and at Dutch Harbor on Unalaska Island you can still see concrete bunkers, gun batteries, and a partially sunken ship. The **Grand Aleutian Hotel** (⊠ Box 921169, Dutch Harbor 99692, ☎ 800/891–1194, FAX 907/581–7150), in Dutch Harbor, offers guided activities and tours as well as lodging.

Every spring the largest herd of northern fur seals in the world—nearly 1 million seals—comes to the tiny, volcanic **Pribilof Islands,** in the Bering Sea about 200 mi northwest of Cold Bay. Tours fly to **St. Paul Island,** largest of the Pribilofs and home to the world's largest Aleut community (about 600 of the island's 750 year-round residents are Aleuts). The island is also the summer home of legions of birds. Contact **Reeve Aleutian Airways** (☞ Arriving and Departing, *above*) for tour information. Next to St. Paul Island, **St. George Island** is the only other island in the Pribilof chain to be inhabited by humans. It is also a birder's paradise; more than 1½ million seabirds nest here each summer.

THE ARCTIC

Visitor Information

Barrow and **Kotzebue:** Alaska Native Tourism Council (☞ Statewide Visitor Information, *above*). **Nome:** Convention and Visitors Bureau (⊠ Box 240, Nome 99762, ☎ 907/443–5535, FAX 907/443–5832).

Arriving and Departing

Nearly all destinations in the Arctic are accessible only by plane. The only public highway that leads to the Arctic—the Dalton Highway—is open to traffic all the way to Deadhorse, on the North Slope, but is impassable in winter due to snow conditions. **Alaska Airlines Vacations** (⊠ SEARV, Box 68900, Seattle, WA 98168, ☎ 800/468–2248) runs air tours of the Arctic from Anchorage and Fairbanks.

Exploring the Arctic

Gold was discovered in 1898 in **Nome,** just below the Arctic Circle. Colorful saloons and low-slung, ramshackle buildings help perpetuate its vintage gold-camp aura. **Kotzebue** is a proud Eskimo community north of Nome where salmon dries on wooden racks and Eskimo boats rest in yards. The **Living Museum of the Arctic** (☎ 907/442–3301; ⌨ free) preserves Nome's Eskimo heritage, as does a cultural camp where elders pass on traditions to the next generation. The museum is open for tour groups or upon request; in summer, daily cultural shows are performed for visitors. The cost to attend the shows is $20. At the top of the state, tours of the **Prudhoe Bay** area explore the oil industry life here, as well as the wildlife and tundra surrounding it. Fees range from $25 for a 1-hour tour to $50 for a 2½-hour tour; call **Tour Arctic** (☎ 907/659–2368) for information. In **Barrow,** the northernmost community in the United States, the sun rises on May 10 and doesn't set for nearly three months.

In the northernmost portion of the Brooks Range, the 18-million-acre

★ **Arctic National Wildlife Refuge** (☎ 907/456–0250) contains the United States' only protected Arctic coastal lands as well as millions of acres of mountains and alpine tundra. The refuge is home to one of the world's largest groups of caribou, the 130,000-member Porcupine Caribou Herd. Other residents are grizzly and polar bears, Dall sheep, wolves, musk ox, and myriad bird species. Accessible only by boat, plane, or foot, the refuge can be explored by backpacking or river running.

ARIZONA

By Laura
Randolph

Updated by
D. Elliott,
C. LaBrie,
A. Moore,
D. Randolph,
K. Westerman,
and G. Young

Capital	Phoenix
Population	4,555,000
Motto	God Enriches
State Bird	Cactus wren
State Flower	Saguaro cactus
Postal Abbreviation	AZ

Statewide Visitor Information

Arizona Office of Tourism (⊠ 2702 N. 3rd St., Suite 4015, Phoenix 85004, ☎ 602/230–7733 or 800/842–8257, ⨳ 602/240–5475).

Scenic Drives

The drive from the South Rim to the North Rim of the Grand Canyon follows U.S. 89 through the **Arizona Strip,** a starkly beautiful, largely uninhabited part of the state. Almost all the Grand Canyon drives are breathtaking, especially West Rim Drive on the South Rim and the dirt road to Point Sublime on the North Rim. Fall foliage is spectacular on U.S. 89A from Flagstaff to Sedona via **Oak Creek Canyon.** From Tucson, I–10 east of Benson passes through the startling rock formations of **Texas Canyon.**

National and State Parks

National Parks

Among the state's national parks are **Grand Canyon National Park** (☞ Grand Canyon National Park, *below*), **Petrified Forest National Park** (☞ Northeast Arizona, *below*), and **Saguaro National Park** (☞ Tucson, *below*); **Canyon de Chelly** (☞ Northeast Arizona, *below*) is a national monument. For Native American ruins in scenic settings, visit **Walnut Canyon National Monument** and **Wupatki National Monument** (☞ Flagstaff, *below*), in the Flagstaff area; **Tuzigoot National Monument** (⊠ Broadway Rd., Clarkdale 86324, ☎ 520/634–5564; ⨳ $2 per person), south of Sedona; and **Navajo National Monument** (☞ Northeast Arizona, *below*). Little-visited spots of unusual beauty include **Sunset Crater Volcano National Monument** (☞ Flagstaff, *below*), west of Flagstaff, and **Chiricahua National Monument** (⊠ Hwy. 191 to Hwy. 181, 58 mi northeast of Douglas 85643, ☎ 520/824–3560; ⨳ $4 per car), in the southeastern part of the state.

State Parks

Arizona's 24 state parks run a wide spectrum, from the relatively tiny 54-acre **Slide Rock,** near Sedona (⊠ 6871 N. Hwy. 89A, Box 10358, Sedona 86339, ☎ 520/282–3034; ⨳ $5 per vehicle, $1 per pedestrian or bicycle) to 13,000-acre **Lake Havasu** (⊠ 1801 Hwy. 95, Lake Havasu 86406, ☎ 520/855–9394; ⨳ $4–$7 per vehicle), notable for **London Bridge,** a transplanted 18th-century bridge. Boating and watersports enthusiasts congregate at **Alamo Lake State Park** (⊠ U.S. 60, 37 mi north of Wenden, Box 38, Wenden 85357, ☎ 520/669–2088; ⨳ $4 per vehicle, $1 per pedestrian or bicycle) and **Roper Lake State Historic Park** (⊠ 101 E. Roper Lake Rd., Rte. 2, Box 712, Safford 85546, ☎ 520/428–6760; ⨳ $4 per vehicle, $1 per pedestrian or bicycle). Desert rats will like **Catalina State Park** (⊠ 11570 N. Oracle Rd., Box 36986,

Tucson 85740, ☎ 520/628–5798; ⊒ $4 per vehicle, $1 per pedestrian or bicycle) and the **Boyce Thompson Southwestern Arboretum** (⊠ 37615 E. Hwy. 60, Superior 85273, ☎ 520/689–2723; ⊒ $5 per person), an hour east of Phoenix. Head to **Red Rock State Park** (⊠ 4050 Red Rock Loop Rd., Sedona 86336, ☎ 520/282–6907; ⊒ $5 per vehicle, $1 per pedestrian or bicycle) and **Tonto Natural Bridge State Historic Park** (⊠ Hwy. 87, 10 mi north of Payson, Box 1245, Payson 85547, ☎ 520/476–4202; ⊒ $5 per vehicle, $1 per pedestrian or bicycle), for dramatic scenery. For a taste of the state's lively frontier history, visit **Riordan Mansion State Park** (⊠ 1300 Riordan Ranch St., Riordan 86001, ☎ 520/779–4395; ⊒ $4); **Jerome State Historic Park** (⊠ Douglas Rd., Box D, Jerome 86331, ☎ 520/634–5381), in north-central Arizona; **Tombstone Courthouse State Historic Park** (⊠ 219 Toughnut St., Tombstone 85638, ☎ 520/457–3311) and **Tubac Presidio Historic Park** (⊠ 1 Burruel St., Box 1296, Tubac 85646, ☎ 520/398–2252; ⊒ $5 per vehicle, $1 per pedestrian or bicycle), in the southeast; and **Yuma Territorial Prison State Historic Park** (⊠ 100 N. Prison Hill Rd., Yuma 85364, ☎ 520/343–2500), in the southwest. The **Arizona State Parks Department** (⊠ 1300 W. Washington St., Phoenix 85007, ☎ 602/542–4174) provides information on all the parks.

GRAND CANYON NATIONAL PARK

Not even the finest photographs convey a fraction of the impact of a personal encounter with the Grand Canyon. This awesome, vastly silent, ancient erosion of the surface of our planet is 277 mi long, 17 mi across at its widest spot, and more than 1 mi deep at its lowest point. Its twisted and contorted layers of rock reveal a fascinating geological profile of the earth. All around you, otherworldly stone monuments change colors with the hours.

Visitor Information

Before you go, write to **Grand Canyon National Park** (⊠ Box 129, Grand Canyon 86023, ☎ 520/638–7888) for a complimentary *Trip Planner*. Accommodations: **Amfac Parks and Resorts** (⊠ 14001 E. Iliff, Suite 600, Aurora, CO 80014, ☎ 303/297–2757; 520/638–2631 for same-day reservations). North and South Rim camping: **National Park Reservation Service** (⊠ Box 85705, San Diego, CA 92186-5705, ☎ 800/365–2267, 301/722–1257 outside the U.S.). A free newspaper, the *Guide*, which contains a detailed area map, is available at both rims.

Arriving and Departing

By Bus

Greyhound (☎ 800/231–2222) stops at Flagstaff and Williams. **Nava-Hopi Tours** (☎ 800/892–8687, 520/774–5003 in Flagstaff) provides bus service to and from the canyon's South Rim. Schedules change frequently; call or check the Web site for information.

By Car

From the east, west, or south, the fastest route to the Grand Canyon is via Flagstaff, either northwest on U.S. 180 (81 mi) to Grand Canyon Village on the South Rim or, for a more scenic route, north on U.S. 89 to Route 64W; from Utah, take U.S. 89S. To visit the North Rim, some 210 mi from Flagstaff, follow U.S. 89 north to Bitter Springs, and then take U.S. 89A to the junction of Route 67. Travel south on AZ 67 for approximately 40 mi to the North Rim. From the west on I–40, the most direct route to the South Rim is via Route 64 to U.S. 180. Summer traffic approaching the South Rim is very congested around Grand

Canyon Village. Facilities at the more remote North Rim open May 15. From October 15 through December 1 or until heavy snows close the road, the North Rim remains open for day use only.

The quickest route from Los Angeles is U.S. 93, which intersects with I-40 in Kingman, Arizona.

By Plane

McCarran International Airport (☎ 702/261–5743), in Las Vegas, Nevada, is the primary hub for flights to **Grand Canyon National Park Airport** (☎ 520/638–2446). Carriers include **Eagle Scenic Airlines** (☎ 800/446–4584), **Air Vegas** (☎ 702/736–3599), and **Scenic Airlines** (☎ 800/535–4448). You can make connections from **Sky Harbor International Airport** (☎ 602/273–3300), in Phoenix, with the commuter line, **West Wind** (☎ 602/991–5557). The **Canyon Airport Shuttle Services, Inc.** (☎ 520/638–0821) operates between Grand Canyon airport and the nearby towns of Tusayan and Grand Canyon Village. The **Fred Harvey Transportation Company** (☎ 520/638–2822 or 520/638–2631) provides taxi service.

By Train

Flagstaff is the town closest to the Grand Canyon that is served by **Amtrak** (☎ 520/774–8679 or 800/872–7245). From Williams you can take the historic **Grand Canyon Railway** (☎ 800/843–8724) to the South Rim.

Exploring Grand Canyon National Park

Access to both the South Rim and North Rim areas of the Grand Canyon is carefully managed by the National Park Service. Large crowds converge on the South Rim every summer, and a light-rail Visitor Transportation System is currently under construction to ease the congestion. The most trafficked spots are popular for good reason, but a walk into the canyon itself opens up extraordinary perspectives.

South Rim

From **Mather Point**, at the outskirts of Grand Canyon Village, you'll get your first glimpse of the canyon from one of the most impressive and accessible overlooks on the rim.

Scenic overlooks on the 25-mi-long East Rim Drive include **Yaki Point**, where the much-traveled Kaibab Trail starts the canyon descent to the inner gorge; **Grandview Point**, which supports large stands of ponderosa and piñon pine, oak, and juniper; and **Moran Point**, a favorite of photographers. At the **Tusayan Ruins and Museum** (☎ 520/638–2305), 3 mi east of Moran Point, partially intact rock dwellings are evidence of early habitation in the gorge. **Lipan Point** is the widest part of the canyon. The highest points along the tour are **Watchtower** (☎ 520/638–2736), site of a lookout tower with a panoramic view of the Grand Canyon and a trading post with Native American art.

Back in Grand Canyon Village, the paved Village Rim Trail (about 1 mi round-trip) starts at **Hopi House**, one of the canyon's first curio stores (☞ Shopping, *below*). Stops along the way include the historic **El Tovar Hotel** (☞ Dining and Lodging, *below*), the jewel in the crown of the country's national park system; **Lookout Studio**, a combination lookout point, museum, and gift shop; **Bright Angel Trailhead**, the starting point for the best-known trail to the bottom of the canyon; and **Bright Angel Lodge** (☞ Dining and Lodging, *below*), with a fireplace made of regional rocks arranged in layers that match those of the canyon.

On West Rim Drive you can get an unobstructed view from **Trailview Overlook** of the distant San Francisco Peaks, Arizona's highest mountains. At **Maricopa Point** you'll see the remnants of an early Grand

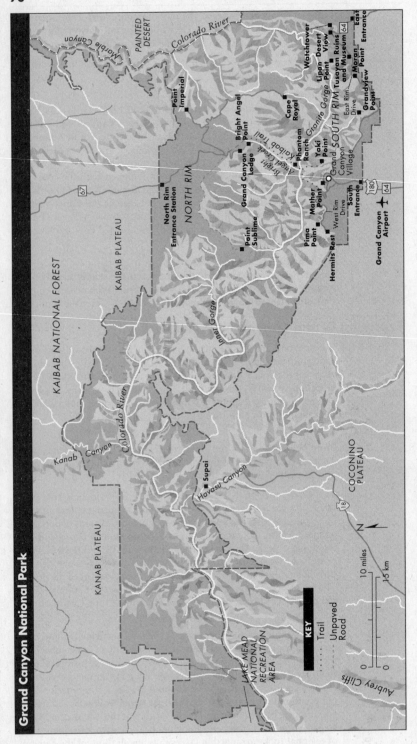

Grand Canyon National Park

PAINTED DESERT

Marble Canyon

Colorado River

Colorado River

KAIBAB NATIONAL FOREST

KAIBAB PLATEAU

67

North Rim Entrance Station

NORTH RIM

Point Imperial

Bright Angel Point

Grand Canyon Lodge

Point Sublime

Bright Angel Creek Trail

Kaibab Trail

Cape Royal

Phantom Ranch

Yaki Point

Mather Point

Pima Point

Hermit's Rest

West Rim Drive

Watchtower

Lipon Point

Desert View

Tusayan Ruins and Museum

SOUTH RIM

Grand Canyon Village

East Rim Drive

Grandview Point

Moran Point

East Entrance

64

South Entrance

180

64

Grand Canyon Airport

Granite Gorge Scenic Drive

Inner Gorge

Kanab Canyon

Colorado River

KANAB PLATEAU

Supai

Havasu Canyon

LAKE MEAD NATIONAL RECREATION AREA

COCONINO PLATEAU

18

Aubrey Cliffs

N

KEY

······· Trail

– – – Unpaved Road

10 miles

15 km

0

Canyon mining operation. The **Abyss** reveals a sheer canyon drop of 3,000 ft. **Pima Point** provides a bird's-eye view of the Tonto Plateau and the Tonto Trail, which winds for more than 90 mi through the canyon. **Hermits Rest,** the westernmost viewpoint, and **Hermit Trail** (☞ Outdoor Activities and Sports, *below*), which descends from it, were named for Louis Boucher, a 19th-century prospector and recluse who had a roughly built home in the canyon. The West Rim Drive is closed to auto traffic in summer; from early May through September free shuttle buses leave daily from Grand Canyon Village for Hermits Rest.

North Rim

The relative solitude of the North Rim, set in deep forest near the 9,000-ft crest of Kaibab Plateau in the isolated Arizona Strip, is well worth the extra miles. From central Arizona, the only route into this area is more than 200 mi of lonely road to the northwest of Flagstaff. From late fall through early spring the North Rim and its facilities are closed because heavy snows cut off highway access to the area.

The trail to **Bright Angel Point,** one of the most awe-inspiring overlooks on either rim, starts on the grounds of the Grand Canyon Lodge (☞ Dining and Lodging, *below*), a massive stone structure built in 1928 by the Union Pacific Railroad. At 8,803 ft, **Point Imperial** is the canyon's highest viewpoint. **Cape Royal** is the southernmost viewpoint on the North Rim.

Dining and Lodging

The North Rim is less crowded than the South Rim, but it has limited lodging facilities. It's difficult to find rooms in the South Rim area in summer, so make reservations as much as six months in advance. Year-round, the Fred Harvey Company operates the Grand Canyon National Park Lodges on the South Rim—Bright Angel Lodge, El Tovar, Maswik Lodge, Yavapai Lodge, Moqui Lodge, Kachina Lodge, and Thunderbird Lodge. All are comfortable, if not luxurious (Bright Angel and El Tovar are the nicest); come for the setting, not for the amenities. Moqui is on U.S. 180, just outside the park; the others are in Grand Canyon Village. If you can't find accommodations in the immediate South Rim area, try the nearby communities of Williams, an hour away by car, or Flagstaff. Camping inside the park is permitted only in designated areas. For information on park camping and reservations, contact the National Park Reservation Service (☞ Visitor Information, *above*). The Arizona Office of Tourism (☞ Statewide Visitor Information, *above*) can provide a campground directory.

South Rim

$$-$$$$ ✕▥ **El Tovar Hotel.** Built in 1905 of native stone and heavy pine logs
★ and renovated in 1998, El Tovar has maintained its reputation for excellence throughout its history. Some rooms are small, but all are well appointed, and many have canyon views. For decades the hotel's restaurant has served fine seasonal southwestern cuisine in a hunting lodge–style dining room. Try the seasonal game. ✉ *Amfac Parks and Resorts, 14001 E. Iliff Ave., Suite 600, Aurora, CO 80014,* ☎ *303/ 297–2757,* 𝔽𝔸𝕏 *520/638–2631, 303/297–3175 for reservations. 80 rooms. Restaurant. AE, D, DC, MC, V.* ✪

$-$$$$ ✕▥ **Bright Angel Lodge.** Built in 1935, this log-and-stone structure a few yards from the canyon rim has rooms in the main lodge and somewhat run-down cabins (some with fireplaces) scattered among the pines. The informal steak house overlooks the abyss. You'll find moderately priced, good-quality beef on the menu. ✉ *Amfac Parks and Resorts, 14001 E. Iliff Ave., Suite 600, Aurora, CO 80014,* ☎ *303/297–*

2757, FAX 520/638–2631, 303/297–3175 *for reservations. 30 rooms, 11 with bath; 47 cabins. Restaurant. AE, D, DC, MC, V.* ✿

$$–$$$$ 🏠 **Sheridan House Inn.** This bed-and-breakfast in Williams provides a good alternative to crowded park lodgings. Nicely appointed large rooms in the pines, just a few blocks from Route 66, are quiet, and hearty breakfasts will ready you for the hour's drive to the Grand Canyon. ✉ *460 E. Sheridan Ave., Williams 86046,* ☎ *520/635–9441 or 888/635–9345. 8 rooms. AE, D, MC, V. BP.* ✿

CAMPGROUNDS

In Grand Canyon Village, 🏕 **Mather Campground** (☞ National Park Reservation Service *in* Visitor Information, *above*) has RV and tent sites. 🏕 **Trailer Village** (✉ Amfac Parks and Resorts, 14001 E. Iliff Ave., Suite 600, Aurora, CO 80014, ☎ 303/297–2757) has RV sites. Commercial and Forest Service campgrounds outside the park include 🏕 **Flintstone Bedrock City** (✉ Grand Canyon Hwy., HCR 34, Box A, Williams 86046, ☎ 520/635–2600), with tent and RV sites; 🏕 **Grand Canyon Camper Village** (✉ Hwy. 64, 1 mi south of park entrance, Box 490, Tusayan 86023, ☎ 520/638–2887), with RV and tent sites; and 🏕 **Ten X Campground** (✉ Kaibab National Forest, Tusayan Ranger District, Box 3088, Grand Canyon 86023, ☎ 520/638–2443), with large sites (closed winter).

Bottom of the Canyon

$ ✕🏠 **Phantom Ranch.** Dormitories (with shared bath) and cabins (with outside shower) nestle in a grove of cottonwood trees at the bottom of the canyon. The restaurant has a limited menu of basic American food, with meals served family style. Arrangements—and payment— for both food and lodging should be made 9–11 months in advance. ✉ *Amfac Parks and Resorts, 14001 E. Iliff Ave., Suite 600, Aurora, CO 80014,* ☎ *303/297–2757,* FAX *520/638–2631, 303/297–3175 for reservations. 4 dorms, 11 cabins. AE, D, DC, MC, V.* ✿

CAMPGROUNDS

For information about the campgrounds at **Indian Gardens,** about halfway down the canyon, and **Bright Angel,** near the bottom, contact the Backcountry Reservations Office (☞ Hiking *in* Outdoor Activities and Sports, *below*).

North Rim

$–$$ 🏠 **Grand Canyon Lodge.** This historic stone structure, built in 1928, has comfortable though not luxurious rooms. The lounge area, with hardwood floors and high beamed ceilings, has a spectacular view of the canyon through massive plate-glass windows. ✉ *Amfac Parks and Resorts, 14001 E. Iliff, Suite 600, Aurora, CO 80014,* ☎ *303/297– 2757,* FAX *520/638–2611, 303/297–3175 for reservations. 44 rooms, 157 cabins. Restaurant. AE, D, DC, MC, V.* ✿

CAMPGROUNDS

🏕 **North Rim Campground** (☞ the National Park Reservation Service *in* Visitor Information, *above*), inside the park, has RV and tent sites. Outside the park, 🏕 **Demotte Campground** (✉ Kaibab National Forest, North Kaibab Ranger District, Box 248, Fredonia 86022, ☎ 520/ 643–7395) is run by the Forest Service.

Outdoor Activities and Sports

Hiking

Detailed area maps of the many canyon trails are available at ranger stations and visitor centers. Overnight hikes in the Grand Canyon require a permit that can be obtained only by written or faxed request to the **Backcountry Reservations Office** (⊠ Box 129, Grand Canyon 86023, ☎ 520/638–7875, FAX 520/638–2125). Get one in advance if possible; otherwise, pick one up at the Backcountry Reservations Office, either near the entrance to Maswik Lodge, on the South Rim, or at the North Rim's ranger station. Allow five days to hike the gorge from rim to rim.

Bright Angel Trail, a steep (4,460-ft), demanding ascent, connects the bottom of the canyon to the South Rim (8 mi). The 9-mi **Hermit Trail** provides inspiring views of Hermit Gorge and the Redwall and Supai formations. The steep, 7-mi **South Kaibab Trail** begins near Yaki Point, on East Rim Drive near Grand Canyon Village. The 14-mi **North Kaibab Trail,** the only maintained trail into the canyon from the North Rim, connects at the bottom of the canyon with the South Kaibab Trail.

Mule Trips

Mule trips down the precipitous trails to the inner gorge are nearly as well known as the canyon itself. Inquire via **Amfac** (⊠ 14001 E. Iliff, Suite 600, Aurora, CO 80014, ☎ 303/297–2757) about prices and restrictions for riders. Book as far in advance as possible.

Rafting

Reservations for white-water rafting trips, which last from 3 to 18 days, must often be made more than six months ahead of time. For a complete list of park-service-approved concessionaires, contact the **River Permits Office** (⊠ Grand Canyon National Park, Box 129, Grand Canyon 86023, ☎ 520/638–7888). **Fred Harvey Transportation Company** (☎ 520/638–2822) specializes in smooth-water rafting day trips. **Wilderness River Adventures** (☎ 520/645–3279 or 800/992–8022) is another option.

Shopping

Native American items sold at most of the lodges and at major gift shops are authentic. The **Desert View Trading Post** (⊠ East Rim Dr., ☎ 520/638–2360) sells Southwest souvenirs and Native American crafts. The **El Tovar Hotel Gift Shop** (⊠ near the rim in Grand Canyon Village, ☎ 520/638–2631) features silver jewelry. **Hopi House** (⊠ east of El Tovar Hotel, ☎ 520/638–2631) has some museum-quality Native American artifacts.

NORTHEAST ARIZONA

A vast and magnificent landscape of lofty buttes and towering cliffs, northeast Arizona is the home of the Navajo and Hopi peoples, who call the area "the rez." The mysterious ruins of ancient tribes can be found within the stunning landscapes of Navajo National Monument, Monument Valley, and Canyon de Chelly. All of these monuments lie within the northeastern portion of the Navajo reservation. Homolovi Ruins State Historical Park, an ancient Hopi settlement and active archaeological dig, lies 5 mi northeast of Winslow on I–40. Just below the southeastern boundary of the Navajo reservation, straddling I–40, the Petrified Forest National Park is an intriguing geologic open book of Earth's distant past. Above the far northwest corner of the Navajo reservation on U.S. 80 lies Glen Canyon Dam. Behind it more than 120 mi of Lake Powell's emerald waters are held in precipitous canyons of erosion-carved stone.

Throughout both reservations, excellent traditional Native American arts and crafts may be found for sale in shops, galleries, and trading posts. Visitors are sometimes invited to watch ancient cultural traditions such as Hopi ceremonial dances; however, the privacy, customs, and laws of the tribes should be respected.

Visitor Information

Glen Canyon National Recreation Area (✉ Box 1507, Page 86040-1507, ☎ 520/608–6200 or 520/608–6404). **Hopi Tribe Office of Public Relations** (✉ Box 123, Kykotsmovi 86039, ☎ 520/734–2441). **Navajo Nation Tourism Office** (✉ Box 663, Window Rock 86515, ☎ 520/871–7371, ✇). **Page/Lake Powell:** Chamber of Commerce & Visitor Bureau (✉ 644 N. Navajo, Box 727, Page 86040, ☎ 520/645–2741).

Arriving and Departing

By Bus

Greyhound (☎ 800/231–2222) goes to Phoenix and Flagstaff. Inexpensive but slow and erratic, **Navajo Transit System** (☎ 520/729–4002) provides the only bus service on the reservation.

By Car

From the east or west I–40 passes through Flagstaff, a good entry point to the region. From the north or northwest U.S. 89 brings you to Page. From the northeast U.S. 64 leads west from Farmington, New Mexico. From the northwest out of Page, U.S. 89 and U.S. 98 head respectively south and southeast into the Navajo and Hopi nations. Touring Navajo and Hopi country involves driving long distances among widely scattered communities, so a detailed road map is essential. In this sparsely populated area, service stations are rare, so fuel up wherever you can. Never drive into dips or low-lying road areas during a heavy rainstorm; dangerous flash floods are common. Tune to the following radio stations for news and weather on the Navajo and Hopi reservations: 660 AM, 770 AM, 97.9 FM, and 107.3 FM.

By Plane

No major airlines fly directly to this area. You'll need to make flight connections in Phoenix (☞ Arriving and Departing *in* Metropolitan Phoenix, *below*) to travel on to either **Flagstaff Pullium Airport** (☎ 520/556–1234) or to **Page Municipal Airport** (☎ 800/245–8668), near Lake Powell. **Scenic Airlines** (☎ 800/634–6801) flies from Phoenix and Las Vegas to Page and Monument Valley. **Sunrise Air** (☎ 800/245–8668 or 602/225–9135) also makes daily flights from Phoenix to Page.

By Train

Amtrak (☎ 520/774–8679 or 800/872–7245) stops in Flagstaff, a good jumping-off point for a car trip into the area.

Exploring Northeast Arizona

Some 115 mi east of Flagstaff off I–40, **Petrified Forest National Park** (✉ Box 2217, Petrified Forest 86028, ☎ 520/524–6228, ✎ $10 per vehicle) is strewn with ancient ruins and fossilized tree trunks whose wood cells were replaced over the centuries by brightly hued mineral deposits. The park's 94,000 acres include portions of the **Painted Desert**, a colorful but essentially barren and waterless series of windswept plains, hills, and mesas. Also look for Native American petroglyphs.

Window Rock, northeast of Petrified Forest, is the capital of the Navajo Nation and the business and social center for families from the surrounding rural areas. The **Navajo Nation Museum** (✉ off Rte. 264 just north of the Navajo Nation Inn on Rte. 264, Window Rock, ☎ 520/871–6673; ✎ $1) has exhibits on Navajo art, culture, and history. It is closed weekends in winter. The **Navajo Arts and Crafts Enterprise** (☞ Shopping, *below*), next to the Navajo Nation Inn on Route 264, displays and sells local authentic Navajo arts and crafts.

Northwest of Window Rock, occupying nearly 84,000 acres, **Canyon de Chelly** (✉ Chinle 86503–0588, ☎ 520/674–5500, ☜ free) is one of the Southwest's most extraordinary national monuments. Gigantic sandstone cliffs rise hundreds of feet above small streams, hogans, tilled fields, peach orchards, and grazing lands; thousand-year-old cliff dwellings, petroglyphs, and pictographs made by precursors of the Pueblo people are carved into some of its sheer cliff walls. Paved rim drives afford marvelous views. There are also horseback and Jeep tours of the canyon.

At the approximate center of the Navajo reservation lies the 4,000-square-mi **Hopi reservation,** a series of stone-and-adobe villages built on high mesas. On First Mesa is the town of **Walpi,** built on solid rock and surrounded by steep cliffs. Its 30 residents defy modernity and live without electricity and running water. In Second Mesa's oldest and largest village, **Shungopavi,** the famous Hopi snake dances take place in August of even-numbered years. Currently, the village closes to the public during the dances, but that policy may change in the next few years. **Homolovi Ruins State Historic Park,** south of Second Mesa on State Route 67, offers visitors a close look at an active archaeological dig of an ancient Hopi settlement. Extensive information is available about the Hopi people and their lands. Also on Second Mesa is the **Hopi Cultural Center** (☎ 520/734–2401), with a pueblo-style museum, shops, and a good restaurant and motel (☞ Dining and Lodging, *below*). **Kykotsmovi,** at the eastern base of Third Mesa, is known for its greenery and peach orchards. It is the site of the Hopi Tribal headquarters. Atop Third Mesa, **Oraibi,** established around AD 1150, is widely believed to be the oldest continuously inhabited community in the United States. The Hopi people are much more strict about privacy rules than the Navajo; avoid taking pictures or notes, making sketches, or scanning through binoculars.

Monument Valley (✉ visitor center, 3½ mi off U.S. 163, 24 mi north of Kayenta, ☎ 435/727–3353), near the Utah border north of Kayenta, may look familiar to those who have seen it in westerns and commercials. This sprawling expanse of soaring red buttes, eroded mesas, deep canyons, and naturally sculpted rock formations was populated by the ancestors of the Pueblo people and has been home to generations of Navajo. Within this vast area lies the 30,000-acre **Monument Valley Navajo Tribal Park** and its 17-mi self-guided tour.

At **Navajo National Monument** (✉ HC 71, Box 3, Tonalea 86044, ☎ 520/672–2366; ☜ free), southwest of Monument Valley off U.S. 160, two unoccupied 13th-century cliff pueblos, **Keet Seel** and **Betatakin,** stand under the overhang of soaring orange and ocher cliffs. The largest Native American ruins in Arizona, these pueblos, too, were built by the ancestors of the Pueblo people, whose reasons for suddenly abandoning them prior to AD 1300 are still disputed by scholars. The visitor center is open year-round.

For information on the construction of **Glen Canyon Dam and Lake Powell,** 136 mi north of Flagstaff on U.S. 89, stop at the **Carl Hayden Visitor Center** (✉ Glen Canyon Dam, ☎ 520/608–6404). The best way to see eerie, man-made Lake Powell as it twists through rugged canyon country is by boat (☞ Outdoor Activities and Sports, *below*). Take a half-day excursion to **Rainbow Bridge National Monument,** a 290-ft red-sandstone arch that straddles one of the lake's coves.

Dining and Lodging

Northeast Arizona is a vast and spacious land. Most larger communities offer dining and lodging to the visitor. Good dining is available at Page, Window Rock, Fort Defiance, Ganado, Chinle, Holbrook, Hopi

Second Mesa, Keams Canyon, Tuba City, Kayenta, Goulding's Trading Post/Monument Valley, and Cameron. No alcoholic beverages are sold on the Navajo and Hopi reservations, and possession or consumption of alcohol is against the law in these areas. In summer, lodging reservations are highly advised.

Cameron

$–$$ ✕▥ **Cameron Trading Post and Motel.** This is a good place to fuel up along the drive from the Hopi mesas to the Grand Canyon. Motel rooms and RV sites are available; there's also a wood-beamed dining room serving hearty Navajo fare such as their popular Navajo tacos, green chili, and mutton stew. ✉ *54 mi north of Flagstaff on U.S. 89, Box 339, Cameron 86020,* ☎ *520/679–2231,* 𝖥𝖠𝖷 *520/679–2350. 66 units. Restaurant. AE, DC, MC, V.*

Chinle/Canyon de Chelly

$–$$ ✕▥ **Best Western Canyon de Chelly.** This rustic motel about 2 mi south of Canyon de Chelly has cheerful, modern rooms. There's also an indoor pool. The on-site Junction Restaurant offers a wide variety of standard American and Navajo fare. Lunch features the Navajo taco, fry bread heaped with homemade chili beans, lettuce, tomatoes, olives, and onions. Dinner specials include beef stew and thick broiled T-bone steaks. ✉ *Rte. 7 (¼ mi east of U.S. 191), Box 295, Chinle 86503,* ☎ *520/674–5875, 520/674–5288, or 800/327–0354. 102 rooms. Restaurant, pool. AE, D, DC, MC, V.* ✍

$–$$ ✕▥ **Holiday Inn Canyon de Chelly.** This Navajo-staffed complex stands on the site of a former trading post and incorporates part of the historic structure. Rooms are predictable, but the lobby restaurant serves Navajo specialties like fresh mountain trout dusted in blue cornmeal. A gift shop on the premises features authentic local Indian crafts and arts. ✉ *Indian Rte. 7, Box 1889, Chinle 86503,* ☎ *520/674–5000,* 𝖥𝖠𝖷 *520/674–8264. 108 rooms. Restaurant. AE, D, DC, MC, V.* ✍

$–$$ ✕▥ **Thunderbird Lodge.** At the mouth of Canyon de Chelly is this lodge, with stone-and-adobe units spread over manicured lawns among cottonwood trees. Some rooms have hewn beam ceilings and rustic furniture. An all-Navajo staff prepares inexpensive meals in the cafeteria. Navajo tacos and mutton stew are tasty highlights on the menu. The lodge also offers drives into the Canyon in open Jeeps. ✉ *½ mi south of canyon visitor center on Rte. 7, Box 548, Chinle 86503,* ☎ *520/674–5841 or 800/679–2473. 72 rooms. Restaurant. AE, D, DC, V.*

CAMPGROUNDS

⚠ **Cottonwood Campground** (✉ near the visitor center, Canyon de Chelly National Monument, Chinle 86503, ☎ 520/674–5500) has 52 RV sites and 95 campsites, which are free and available on a first-come, first-served basis. There are flush toilets but no showers. The campground is open year-round.

Hopi Reservation–Second Mesa

$–$$ ✕▥ **Hopi Cultural Center Motel.** High atop Second Mesa is this pueblo-
★ style lodging with immaculate rooms. A comfortable, inexpensive restaurant serves traditional dishes such as Hopi blue-corn pancakes and *nok qui vi* (lamb stew). ✉ *Rte. 264, Box 67, 86043,* ☎ *520/734–2401,* 𝖥𝖠𝖷 *520/734–6651. 33 units. Restaurant. AE, D, DC, MC, V.* ✍

Kayenta

$$ ▥ **Best Western Wetherill Inn.** This clean, cheerful, two-story motel was named for frontier explorer and trader John Wetherill. A gift shop on site offers excellent local Indian arts and crafts. ✉ *U.S. 163, Box 175, 86033,* ☎ *520/697–3231. 54 rooms. Pool. AE, D, DC, MC, V.* ✍

$$ 🏨 **Holiday Inn Monument Valley.** This typical Holiday Inn near Monument Valley has one of the best swimming pools in the area. The gift shop offers authentic native arts and crafts and the on-site restaurant offers standard American and Southwest fare. ☒ *At the junction of U.S. 160 and U.S. 163, Box 307, 86033,* ☎ *520/697–3221 or 800/465–4329,* ℻ *520/697–3349. 164 rooms. Restaurant, pool. AE, D, DC, MC, V.* 🐾

Keams Canyon

$ ✕ **Keams Canyon Restaurant.** At this typical rural roadside café you'll find a few American dishes and Native American standards such as Hopi tacos, which are much like Navajo tacos with slightly spicier seasoning. Closing time on weekends is 3 PM. ☒ *Keams Canyon Shopping Center (off Rte. 264),* ☎ *520/738–2296. D, MC, V.*

Lake Powell/Page

$–$$$ ✕🏨 **Lake Powell Resorts and Marinas—Wahweap Lodge.** On a promon-
★ tory above Lake Powell, the rustic Wahweap Lodge serves as a base for boating, fishing, and other outdoor pursuits. All rooms have balconies or patios, and many have lake views. The circular Rainbow Room, with a panoramic lake view, has a seasonal menu of southwestern and Continental fare. ☒ *U.S. 89, 7 mi north of Page, Box 1597, Page 86040,* ☎ *520/645–2433 or 800/528–6154. 350 rooms. Restaurant, bar, exercise room. AE, D, DC, MC, V.* 🐾

$$ 🏨 **Best Western at Lake Powell.** On the main street of Page, overlooking Glen Canyon Dam, this friendly motel has a fitness room, pool and hot tub, and complimentary breakfast. Many good restaurants are nearby. ☒ *208 N. Lake Powell Blvd., Box 4899, 86040,* ☎ *520/645–5988,* ℻ *520/645–2578. 132 rooms. Pool, exercise room. AE, D, DC, MC, V. BP.* 🐾

$$ 🏨 **Canyon Colors Bed & Breakfast.** The oldest B&B in Page, this cozy and friendly lodging offers visitors a personal touch. Each of its four large rooms accommodates up to five people, and each room is air-conditioned. A full breakfast is included. It's best to make reservations far in advance as this popular B&B books up fast. ☒ *225 S. Navajo Dr., Box 3657, 86040,* ☎ ℻ *520/645–5979, 520/645–5979, or 800/536–2530. 3 rooms. AE, D, MC, V. BP.* 🐾

Monument Valley, Utah

$–$$ ✕🏨 **Goulding's Lodge.** Built near the base of an immense red sandstone butte, the lodge has private balconied rooms with spectacular views of Monument Valley. The on-premises Stagecoach Restaurant serves tasty fare such as its New York–cut Fiesta steak with fry bread, chili, and southwestern salsa or the always-popular Navajo taco. A landing strip for Scenic Airlines out of Phoenix is just across the street. ☒ *2 mi west of U.S. 163, just north of UT border, Box 360001, Monument Valley, UT 84536,* ☎ *435/727–3231 or 435/727–3231,* ℻ *435/727–3344. 62 rooms. Restaurant, pool. AE, D, DC, MC, V.* 🐾

Tuba City, Arizona

$ ✕ **Kate's Cafe.** A local favorite, this all-American café serves a great breakfast, lunch, and dinner at reasonable prices. The dinner house specialty is fettuccine Alfredo. ☒ *264 Main St., 86045,* ☎ *435/283–6773. No credit cards.*

$–$$ ✕🏨 **Quality Inn Tuba City.** This Quality Inn offers 56 fully appointed and spacious rooms, each with queen beds and cable TV. The facility also has a trading post for gifts, art, and crafts that dates back to 1870. On-site Hogan Restaurant offers standard southwestern fare at reasonable prices. ☒ *Box 247, at S.R. 264 and U.S. 160, 86045,* ☎ *520/283–4545 or 800/644–8383,* ℻ *520/283–4144. Restaurant. AE, D, DC, MC, V.*

CAMPGROUNDS

⚠ **Mitten View Campground** (⊠ Monument Valley Navajo Tribal Park, near visitor center, off U.S. 163, 86003, ☎ 435/727–3287) offers decks, grills, tables, and water. RV and tent sites are $10 in summer, $5 in winter; the price includes a 17-mi loop tour of Monument Valley. There's limited service in winter. ⚠ **Good Sam Campground** (⊠ off U.S. 163 near Goulding's Lodge, 86003, ☎ 435/727–3231) offers full-service hookups March 15 through October 31 but is open year-round. Registration for Good Sam Campground is at Goulding's Lodge (☞ *above*).

Navajo National Monument

CAMPGROUNDS

⚠ **Navajo National Monument** (☞ Exploring Northeast Arizona, *above*) has single and group sites. RVs longer than 25 ft are discouraged.

Outdoor Activities and Sports

Boating

Rental boats, water-sports equipment, and excursion boats are available at **Wahweap Marina** (⊠ U.S. 89, 5 mi north of Page, ☎ 520/645–2433 or 800/528–6154). Rentals are also available at **Hall's Crossing Marina** (⊠ ☎ 435/684–7000), **Hite Marina** (⊠ ☎ 435/684–2278), and **Bullfrog Marina & Resort** (⊠ ☎ 435/684–3000).

Hiking

There's excellent hiking in **Canyon de Chelly** (☎ 520/674–5500 for visitor center). Guides are required for all but the White House Ruin Trail; contact the visitor center. Hike on your own along the rim areas at **Navajo National Monument** (☎ 520/672–2366), or sign up for guided hikes to Betatakin from early May to mid-October. A permit is needed for the unsupervised longer hike to Keet Seel (open only from Memorial Day to Labor Day). **Monument Valley** also has superb hiking trails. Permits are available at the visitor center (☎ 435/727–3287).

Horseback Riding

Sacred Mountain Horseback Tours (☎ 435/727–3227) gives long and short trail rides of Monument Valley. Year-round guided trail rides in and around Monument Valley are also offered by **Ed Black** (☎ 435/739–4285), who also specializes in San Juan River rafting tours. In the Canyon de Chelly area, contact **Justin's Horse Rental** (☎ 520/674–5678) for horseback tours of the canyon and surrounding areas.

Shopping

You may find exactly what you want at a good price from one of the many roadside vendors in the area, but the following have dependable selections of Native American wares. **Cameron Trading Post** (⊠ 54 mi north of Flagstaff on U.S. 89, ☎ 520/679–2231 or 800/338–7385) sells Navajo, Hopi, Zuni, and New Mexico Pueblo jewelry, rugs, baskets, and pottery. **Navajo Arts and Crafts Enterprise** (⊠ off Rte. 264, next to Navajo Nation Inn, ☎ 520/871–4108 or 800/662–6189), in Window Rock, stocks fine authentic Navajo products. **Hubbell Trading Post** (⊠ Rte. 264, ½ mi west of Ganado, ☎ 520/755–3254) is famous for its "Ganado red" Navajo rugs; it also has a good collection of Native American pottery.

FLAGSTAFF

Few visitors slow down long enough to explore Flagstaff, a town of 58,000. Still, set against a backdrop of pine forests and the snowcapped San Francisco Peaks, "Flag" (as it's known locally) makes a good base for exploring the Grand Canyon and Navajo-Hopi country. Downtown retains a frontier flavor, and motels and restaurants abound.

Visitor Information

The **Flagstaff Visitors Center** (⊠ 1 E. Rte. 66, 86001, ☎ 520/774–9541 or 800/842–7293) has information on the area.

Arriving and Departing

Flagstaff is 138 mi north of Phoenix and 80 mi south of the Grand Canyon, at the junction of I–40 and I–17.

Exploring Flagstaff

The **Historic Downtown District,** where many interesting shops and buildings are concentrated, is near the Santa Fe railroad station. To view an architectural masterpiece built by two lumber-baron brothers, visit the **Riordan State Historic Park** (⊠ 1300 Riordan Ranch St., ☎ 520/779–4395; ☞ $4). The **Lowell Observatory** (⊠ 1400 W. Mars Hill, ☎ 520/774–2096; ☞ $3) has educational displays on astronomy and allows visitors to peer through its 24-inch telescope on some evenings (schedules vary seasonally). Set in a striking native-stone building, the **Museum of Northern Arizona** (⊠ 3101 N. Fort Valley Rd., ☎ 520/774–5213; ☞ $5) traces the natural and cultural history of the Colorado Plateau.

Head to the **Arizona Snowbowl & Flagstaff Nordic Center** (☎ 520/779–1951) for fine downhill and cross-country skiing in winter and excellent views and good hiking trails in summer; you'll see the exit 5 mi north of town on U.S. 180. In a pine forest about 10 mi southeast of Flagstaff, off I–40, is **Walnut Canyon National Monument** (⊠ Walnut Canyon Rd., ☎ 520/526–3367; ☞ $3), the site of 14th-century cliff dwellings. The 2,000-square-mi San Francisco Volcanic Field, about 20 mi north of Flagstaff on U.S. 89, is home to **Sunset Crater Volcano National Monument** (☎ 520/556–7042; ☞ $3, including admission to Wupatki National Monument). You can take a 20-mi loop road from Sunset Crater to **Wupatki National Monument** (☎ 520/556–7040), rich in Indian history.

Dining and Lodging

$$–$$$ ✕ **Cottage Place.** Unexpectedly elegant in a town known for hearty food and drive-through service, this restaurant in a 50-year-old cottage serves Continental cuisine in a series of intimate dining rooms. Try the artichoke chicken breast or chateaubriand for two, carved table-side. ⊠ *126 W. Cottage Ave.,* ☎ *520/774–8431. AE, MC, V. Closed Mon. No lunch.*

$$–$$$ ✕ **The Down Under.** This charming restaurant owned by New Zealanders serves wonderful lamb chops and other regional specialties, including kangaroo. The small wine list features impressive bottlings from both Australia and New Zealand. ⊠ *413 N. San Francisco St.,* ☎ *520/774–6677. AE, MC, V. Closed Sun. No lunch weekends.*

$ ✕ **Café Express.** The menu is largely vegetarian at this wholesome, all-day (Sunday–Thursday 7 AM–9 PM, Friday–Saturday 7 AM–10 PM) natural-food restaurant, whose walls are covered with works by local artists. The baked goods are heavenly. ⊠ *16 N. San Francisco St.,* ☎ *520/774–0541. MC, V.*

$$–$$$ ▦ **Inn at Four Ten.** This quiet and convenient downtown bed-and-breakfast, in a beautifully restored 1907 building, has spacious two-room suites. Fresh-baked cookies are served in the afternoon. ⊠ *410 N. Leroux St., 86001,* ☎ *520/774–0088 or 800/774–2008. 9 suites. MC, V. BP.*

$$ ▦ **Little America of Flagstaff.** The biggest motel in town is deservedly popular: It's surrounded by evergreen forest, and it's one of the few places in Flagstaff with room service. Plush rooms have brass chandeliers and French provincial–style furniture. A courtesy van gives complimentary rides to the airport and bus and train stations. ⊠ *2515 E. Butler Ave. (Box 3900), 86004,* ☎ *520/779–2741 or 800/352–4386,* 𝖥𝖠𝖷 *520/779– 7983. 248 rooms. Restaurant, pool, exercise room. AE, D, DC, MC, V.*

Nightlife and the Arts

Nightlife

There's usually a country-and-western band at the **Museum Club** (⊠ 3404 E. Rte. 66, ☎ 520/526–9434), a lively cowboy honky-tonk. **Main Street Bar and Grill** (⊠ 14 S. San Francisco St., ☎ 520/774–1519) features bluegrass, jazz, and rock. **Charly's** (⊠ 23 N. Leroux St., ☎ 520/779–1919), inside the Weatherford Hotel, attracts a loyal local following to its late-night jazz and blues bands. **Monsoon's** (⊠ 22 E. Rte. 66, ☎ 520/774–7929) books an eclectic array of live music, from alternative to world beat.

The Arts

Between the **Flagstaff Symphony Orchestra** (⊠ Ardrey Auditorium, on campus of Northern Arizona University, corner of Riordan Rd. and Knowles Dr., ☎ 520/774–5107), **Theatrikos Community Theater** (⊠ 11 W. Cherry Ave., ☎ 520/774–1662), and Northern Arizona University's **College of Performing Arts** (☎ 520/523–5661), you're bound to find entertainment. In August the **Flagstaff Festival of the Arts** (☎ 520/774–7750 or 800/266–7740) fills the town with music.

From May through September the **Museum of Northern Arizona** (☞ Exploring, *above*) celebrates Native American art.

SEDONA AND ENVIRONS

Sedona is perhaps the most attractive stopover en route north from Phoenix to the Grand Canyon. Startling formations of deep-red rocks reach up into an almost always clear blue sky, both colors intensified by dark-green pine forests. Filmmakers in the 1940s and '50s saw this as a quintessential Wild West landscape and shot more than 80 films in the area. Now an upscale art colony, Sedona is also a center of interest to New Age enthusiasts, who believe the area contains important vortices (energy centers).

Visitor Information

For information on the area contact **Sedona–Oak Creek Canyon Chamber of Commerce** (⊠ U.S. 89A and Forest Rd., Box 478, Sedona 86339, ☎ 520/282–7722 or 800/288–7336).

Arriving and Departing

By Car

Sedona is 125 mi north of downtown Phoenix and 27 mi south of Flagstaff, at the south end of Oak Creek Canyon on U.S. 89A.

By Plane

There are no commercial flights into Sedona.

Exploring Sedona and Environs

Tlaquepaque Mall (⊠ Rte. 179, ☎ 520/282–4838) has the largest concentration of shops. The **Chapel of the Holy Cross** (⊠ Chapel Rd., ☎ 520/282–4069) is worth a visit for its striking architecture and stunning vistas.

Scenic hiking areas close to town include Long Canyon, Devil's Kitchen, and Boynton Canyon, and there are almost limitless other opportunities for hikes and walks; stop at the **Sedona Ranger District** office (✉ 250 Brewer Rd., ☎ 520/282–4119) between Monday and Saturday for more information. Five miles southwest of Sedona, **Red Rock State Park** (☎ 520/282–6907; 🎟 $5 per car, $1 per pedestrian) has incredible rock formations. Visit **Slide Rock State Park** (☎ 520/282–3034; 🎟 $5 for up to 4 people, $1 for each additional person), 8 mi north of Sedona in Oak Creek Canyon, for a picnic and a plunge into a natural swimming hole.

On Cleopatra Hill, **Jerome** is about 37 mi southwest of Sedona on U.S. 89A. This town was once known as the Billion Dollar Copper Camp, but after the last mines closed in 1953, the booming population of 15,000 dwindled to 50 determined souls, earning Jerome the "ghost town" designation it still holds, even though the population has risen to almost 450. Today, with many artsy boutiques, Jerome is a shopper's haven. The town's mining history is chronicled at the **Mine Museum** (✉ 200 Main St., ☎ 520/634–5477; 🎟 $1) and **Jerome State Historic Park** (✉ State Park Rd., ☎ 520/634–5381; 🎟 $2.50).

Dining and Lodging

$$–$$$ ✕ **Heartline Café.** This plant-filled café west of Sedona serves tasty southwestern-style food, such as grilled salmon marinated in tequila and lime. On nice days you can eat on the rose-planted terrace. ✉ 1610 W. U.S. 89A, ☎ 520/282–0785. AE, D, MC, V. No lunch Sun.

$$–$$$ ✕ **Pietro's.** Good northern Italian cuisine is served by a friendly, attentive staff in a lively (often noisy) room. Creative pastas might include fettuccine with duck, cabbage, and figs; the veal piccata is excellent. ✉ 2445 W. Hwy. 89A, ☎ 520/282–2525. AE, D, DC, MC, V. No lunch.

$$$$ 🏨 **Enchantment Resort.** Designed as a tennis resort, Enchantment has ★ excellent sports facilities (including a putting green), but it's the setting of Boynton Canyon that makes it unique. Rooms are in pueblostyle casitas, many with beehive fireplaces and kitchenettes, and all have dazzling views. ✉ 525 Boynton Canyon Rd., 86336, ☎ 520/282–2900 or 800/826–4180, 📠 520/282–9249. 162 rooms. Restaurant, pools, tennis, health club. AE, D, MC, V.

$$–$$$ 🏨 **Sky Ranch Lodge.** An excellent value in an expensive town, the lodge has simply furnished rooms with southwestern touches, such as Mexican tiles surrounding the dressers. Some rooms have fireplaces and kitchenettes; others have balconies with views of Sedona's red rock formations. ✉ Airport Rd. (Box 2579), 86339, ☎ 520/282–6400, 📠 520/282–7682. 92 rooms, 2 cottages. Pool. MC, V.

PRESCOTT

In a forested bowl among the Mingus Mountains, Prescott was Arizona's first territorial capital and remains the Southwest's richest repository of late-19th-century New England–style architecture. Because of its temperate climate, in summer the town draws escapees from the Phoenix heat—as well as retirees year-round. The town's two institutions of higher learning, Yavapai and Prescott colleges, ensure a younger scene, too. Many visitors come to buy reasonably priced antiques and collectibles on the stretch of Cortez Street east of Courthouse Plaza.

Visitor Information

Prescott Chamber of Commerce (✉ 117 W. Goodwin St., 86303, ☎ 520/445–2000 or 800/266–7534).

Arriving and Departing

By Bus
Greyhound (⊠ 820 E. Sheldon St., ☎ 520/445–5470 or 800/231–2222).

By Car
Prescott is 34 mi southwest of Jerome via U.S. 89A. From Phoenix take I–17 north for 60 mi to Cordes Junction, and then drive northwest on Highway 69 for 36 mi into town.

By Plane
There are daily flights from Phoenix into **Prescott Municipal Airport** (☎ 520/445–7860), 10 mi north of town.

Exploring Prescott

Courthouse Plaza, bounded by Gurley and Goodwin streets to the north and south and Cortez and Montezuma streets to the west and east, is the heart of the city. **Whiskey Row,** named for a string of brawling pioneer taverns, runs along Montezuma Street, flanking the plaza's west side; it was once lined with 20 saloons and houses of pleasure.

Two blocks west of Courthouse Plaza, the **Sharlot Hall Museum** (⊠ 415 W. Gurley St., ☎ 520/445–3122; ☜ $5 donation requested per family), devoted to the area's history, includes the log cabin that housed the territorial governor and three restored late-19th-century houses. The **Phippen Museum of Western Art** (⊠ 4701 Hwy. 89 N, ☎ 520/778–1385; ☜ $3), about 5 mi north of downtown, displays work by many prominent artists of the West, along with the painting and bronze sculptures of George Phippen. The **Prescott Resort Conference Center and Casino** (⊠ 1500 Hwy. 69, Prescott 86201, ☎ 520/776–1666 or 800/967–4637) is nearby.

Dining and Lodging

$ ✕ **Prescott Brewing Company.** In addition to the pub fare you'd expect, including fish-and-chips, you'll also find a surprising range of vegetarian selections. Four good beers are brewed on the premises. ⊠ 130 W. Gurley St., ☎ 520/771–2795. AE, D, DC, MC, V.

$$–$$$ ✕🖭 **Hassayampa Inn.** Built in 1927 for early automobile travelers, the
★   Hassayampa Inn oozes character. Rooms are individually decorated, some with original furnishings such as oak headboards inset with tiles. A cocktail in the elegant lounge and a full breakfast are included in the reasonable rates. The Peacock Room, the hotel's art-nouveau-style dining room, serves impressive Continental cuisine. ⊠ 122 Gurley St., Prescott 86301, ☎ 520/778–9434, 800/322–1927 in AZ. 68 rooms. Restaurant. AE, D, DC, MC, V. BP.

METROPOLITAN PHOENIX

One of America's newest, fastest-growing major urban centers, metropolitan Phoenix lies at the northern tip of the Sonoran Desert, in the Valley of the Sun, named for its 330-plus days of sunshine each year. Now-chic Scottsdale began in 1901 as fewer than a dozen adobe houses and 30-odd tents put up by seekers of healthful desert air. Glendale and Peoria on the west side and Tempe, Mesa, Gilbert, and Chandler on the east constitute the nation's third-largest Silicon Valley. Excellent hiking, golf, shopping, and dining and some of the best luxury resorts in the country make the valley one of the country's leading business and vacation destinations.

Visitor Information

Arizona Office of Tourism (✉ 2702 N. 3rd St., Phoenix 85004, ☎ 602/230–7733 or 888/520–3444). **Greater Phoenix Chamber of Commerce** (✉ Bank One Plaza, 201 N. Central Ave., Suite 2700, Phoenix 85073, ☎ 602/254–5521). **Phoenix and Valley of the Sun Convention and Visitors Bureau** (✉ Arizona Center, 400 E. Van Buren St., Suite 600, Phoenix 85004, ☎ 602/254–6500).

Arriving and Departing

By Bus
Greyhound (✉ 2115 E. Buckeye Rd., ☎ 602/389–4200 or 800/231–2222).

By Car
From the west you'll probably come to Phoenix on I–10. Interstate 40 enters Arizona in the northwest; U.S. 93 continues to Phoenix. From the east I–10 brings you from El Paso into Tucson, then north to Phoenix. The northeastern route, I–40 from Albuquerque, leads to Flagstaff, where I–17 goes south to Phoenix.

By Plane
Sky Harbor International Airport (☎ 602/273–3300), 3 mi east of downtown Phoenix, is home base for America West and a hub for the Southwest. It is also served by other major airlines. By car, downtown Phoenix is 10 minutes from the airport; Scottsdale, about 30 minutes; Tempe, 10 minutes; Glendale and Mesa, 25 minutes; and Sun City, 30–45 minutes. **Valley Metro** (☎ 602/253–5000) buses connect with downtown Phoenix or Tempe for $1.25. A **taxi** trip into downtown Phoenix costs $6.50–$12 plus tip and $1 airport surcharge. **SuperShuttle** (☎ 602/244–9000 or 800/258–3826) can run 25% less than a taxi for longer trips.

By Train
Amtrak (✉ 401 W. Harrison St., ☎ 602/253–0121 or 800/872–7245).

Getting Around Metropolitan Phoenix

If you plan to see anything beyond the pedestrian-friendly downtowns of Phoenix, Scottsdale, or Tempe, you will need a car. Right turns on red are permitted unless otherwise specified.

Exploring Metropolitan Phoenix

★ The **Heard Museum** (✉ 2301 N. Central Ave., ☎ 602/252–8848 or 602/252–8840, ☎ $7), with a stunning expansion, reaffirms its position as the world's foremost showcase of Native American art and culture. The exceptional collection of fine art, basketry, and pottery, including first-class contemporary work, is supplemented by interactive exhibits, a multimedia show, and live demonstrations by artisans and performers. Western painting is a primary focus of the galleries at the **Phoenix Art Museum** (✉ 1625 N. Central Ave., ☎ 602/257–1880; ☎ $6).

A piece of the city as it was at the turn of the 20th century still stands in parklike **Heritage Square** (✉ 6th and Monroe Sts., ☎ 602/262–5071), at the east end of downtown. Within Heritage Square is the **Arizona Science Center** (✉ 600 E. Washington St., ☎ 602/716–2000; ☎ $8, $11 combined admission to science center, planetarium, and theater), where lively hands-on exhibits let kids discover the science of making gigantic soap bubbles, the technology of satellite weather systems, and more. Within the science center are the **Dorrance Planetarium** and the **Irene P. Flinn Theater**, with a 50-ft screen.

Chock-full of amusing oddities, the **Mystery Castle** (⊠ 800 E. Mineral Rd., at the foot of South Mountain Park, ☎ 602/268–1581; ⊒ $4) was constructed out of native stone, railroad refuse, kitchen appliances, and anything else its builder could get his hands on. **Scottsdale,** no suburb anymore but a booming city in its own right, has a downtown rich in historic sites, nationally known art galleries, and smart boutiques. Historic **Old Town,** with its rustic storefronts and wooden sidewalks, has the look of the Old West and souvenirs galore; **Main Street** and **Marshall Way** are the places to go for the area's leading fine art galleries. The **Scottsdale Museum of Contemporary Art** (⊠ 7380 E. 2nd St., ☎ 602/994–2787; ⊒ $5), with a stunning design by architect Will Bruder and constantly changing exhibits of dynamic work, solidifies Scottsdale's reputation as a top-notch arts destination. An hour's drive south of Phoenix, **Casa Grande Ruins National Monument** (⊠ north of Coolidge on Rte. 87, ☎ 520/723–3172; ⊒ $2 per person or $4 per car) is the site of the 35-ft-tall Casa Grande (Big House), built in the early 13th century by the Hohokam Indians. These early inhabitants farmed the area from more than 1,500 years ago until they vanished around 1450. A small museum displays artifacts and archaeological exhibits.

Parks, Gardens, and Zoos

★ The **Desert Botanical Garden** (⊠ 1201 N. Galvin Pkwy., ☎ 602/941–1217; ⊒ $7.50) is an urban oasis with the world's largest collection of desert plants in a natural setting.

Five trails wind through the 125-acre **Phoenix Zoo** (⊠ 455 N. Galvin Pkwy., ☎ 602/273–1341; ⊒ $8.50), where the habitats of an African savanna and a tropical rain forest are expertly replicated. Children can help groom goats and sheep at the zoo's big red barn.

Dining

One of Phoenix's great pleasures is the amount of fine dining to be found in hotels (☞ Lodging, *below*); don't miss **Marquesa** (Scottsdale Princess), **Wright's** (Arizona Biltmore), **T. Cook's** (Royal Palms), and **Lon's** (Hermosa Inn).

$$–$$$$ ✕ **Eddie Matney's Bistro.** This stylish bistro on the ground floor of an office building features winning appetizers like horseradish mashed potato-stuffed shrimp and main courses such as fish cooked in grape leaves or turkey tenderloin on cranberry-sage gnocchi. There's live music on Sundays and Mondays. ⊠ 2398 E. Camelback Rd., Phoenix, ☎ 602/957–3214. Reservations essential. AE, D, DC, MC, V. No lunch weekends.

$$–$$$$ ✕ **RoxSand.** Chef RoxSand Scocos doesn't follow trends; she sets them. ★ Who else would think to stuff tamales with curried lamb moistened in a Thai-style peanut sauce? The air-dried duck entrée, served with a trio of sauces (Szechuan Black Bean, Evil Jungle Prince, Elephant Plum), is a house specialty. ⊠ 2594 E. Camelback Rd. (Biltmore Fashion Park), Phoenix, ☎ 602/381–0444. Reservations essential. AE, DC, MC, V.

$$–$$$$ ✕ **Roy's.** Roy is Roy Yamaguchi, a James Beard award-winning chef and one of the pioneers of Pacific Rim cooking, with branches of his restaurant scattered all over the globe. Look for inventive dishes like steamed pork and crab buns with a spicy Maui onion black-bean sauce or nori-crusted ono fish with a hot-and-sour red-pepper sauce. ⊠ 7001 N. Scottsdale Rd. (Scottsdale Seville), Scottsdale, ☎ 602/905–1155. AE, MC, V. No lunch.

$$–$$$ ✕ **Café Terra Cotta.** The most exciting cooking in the valley can be found ★ at the Scottsdale branch of Donna Nordin's famed Tucson eatery. With appetizers like buffalo carpaccio drizzled with chili-infused oil, followed by entrées like lamb chops in an ancho-chili mole sauce or salmon crusted with sunflower seeds and yellow chili sauce, Terra Cotta raises southwestern cuisine to new levels of sophistication and creativity. ⊠ *The Borgata of Scottsdale, 6166 N. Scottsdale Rd., Scottsdale,* ☎ *602/948–8100. AE, D, DC, MC, V.*

$$–$$$ ✕ **Franco's Trattoria.** Florence-born Franco puts together meals that sing with the flavors of Tuscany. Veal is a specialty: One standout dish is *orecchie d'elefante* (elephant ears—pounded, breaded, fried veal that's splayed across the plate and coated with tomatoes, shallots, and basil). ⊠ *8120 N. Hayden Rd., Scottsdale,* ☎ *602/948–6655. AE, MC, V. Closed Sun. and July. No lunch.*

$$–$$$ ✕ **Rancho Pinot Grill.** The attention to quality paid by the husband-and-
★ wife proprietors—he manages, she cooks—has made this tiny, south-western-style Scottsdale spot one of the town's top restaurants. The inventive menu changes weekly, but you'll usually find favorites like Nonni's Sunday Chicken (braised with white wine and mushrooms) or bay-marinated pork tenderloin with balsamic-bacon potatoes. ⊠ *6208 N. Scottsdale Rd., Scottsdale,* ☎ *602/468–9463. Reservations essential. AE, D, MC, V. Closed Sun.–Mon. and 2 wks in Aug. No lunch.*

$$–$$$ ✕ **Restaurant Hapa.** "Hapa" is Hawaiian slang for "half," which de-scribes the half-Japanese, half-American background of the chef here. But there's nothing halfway about Hapa's flavorful, Asian-inspired cui-sine. Appetizers include skillet-roasted mussels coated in a Thai-inspired broth, and the signature entrée is beef tenderloin, lined with hot Chinese mustard and caramelized brown sugar. ⊠ *6204 N. Scottsdale Rd., Scottsdale,* ☎ *602/998–8220. MC, V. Closed Sun. No lunch.*

$$–$$$ ✕ **Tarbell's.** Sleek modern ambience meets down-home friendliness at Mark Tarbell's popular restaurant. Menus rotate often, but count on such new American specialties as vibrant smoked rock shrimp starter, or aromatic mussels steamed in a heady broth of white wine and shal-lots. ⊠ *3213 E. Camelback Rd., Phoenix,* ☎ *602/955–8100. Reservations essential. AE, D, DC, MC, V. No lunch.*

$ ✕ **Los Dos Molinos.** A hanging Arizona license plate with the word "HH-HHOT" should clue you in that the food's a touch spicy at this beloved Mexican restaurant. Adobada ribs, a specialty, feature fall-off-the-bone meat marinated in red chilies, and the green chili enchilada and beef taco are potentially lethal. This restaurant is a riot of color, sound, and (best of all) taste. ⊠ *8646 S. Central Ave., Phoenix,* ☎ *602/243–9113. AE, D, MC, V. Closed Sun. and Mon.*

$ ✕ **Pizzeria Bianco.** Bronx native Chris Bianco is a craftsman of pizza. His wood-fired crust is a work of art, not too bready, not too light. Toppings include imported cheeses, homemade fennel sausage, wood-roasted mush-rooms or onions, and the freshest herbs and spices. ⊠ *623 E. Adams St., Phoenix,* ☎ *602/258–8300. MC, V. Closed Mon. No lunch weekends.*

Lodging

Phoenix is famous for its world-class resorts. From grand multistoried palaces full of artificially lush greenery to sprawling properties with cac-tus gardens and adobe lodgings, Phoenix's resorts are a major drawing card for visitors. Want to play golf? Hike in the nearby mountains? Maybe you just want to lounge poolside, basking in the warm Arizona sun (and the indulgent service). With a selection of spots in all price ranges, Phoenix and Scottsdale are certainly well equipped to handle the flood of visitors that arrives annually. Off-season rates can be a great savings—sometimes as much as 50% off winter prices, even at the top resorts.

$$$$ ☷ **Arizona Biltmore.** The world's only resort with a direct design link
★ to Frank Lloyd Wright, the Biltmore has set the standard in central Phoenix since it opened in 1929. Every president since Herbert Hoover has stayed here: The landscaped grounds and low-key, southwestern-

style elegance might explain why. Rooms have marble bathrooms and are decorated in earth tones and accented with southwestern-patterned accessories. ✉ *24th St. and Missouri Ave., Phoenix 85016,* ☎ *602/ 955–6600 or 800/950–0086,* ℻ *602/381–7600. 750 rooms, 62 villas. 3 restaurants, pools, golf, tennis, health club. AE, D, DC, MC, V.* ✆

$$$$ ✕🏨 **The Boulders.** The desert setting of the valley's most serene lux-
★ ury resort is its most spectacular feature; buildings nestle among hill-size granite boulders in Carefree (just over the border from Scottsdale). Accommodations have wood-beam ceilings, kiva fireplaces, and huge bath-dressing areas. The golf course is one of the valley's most famous. ✉ *34631 N. Tom Darlington Dr., Carefree 85377,* ☎ *602/488–9009 or 800/553–1717,* ℻ *602/488–4118. 160 casitas, 33 pueblo villas. 5 restaurants, pools, golf, tennis, health club. AE, D, DC, MC, V.*

$$$$ 🏨 **Hermosa Inn.** Once the home and studio of cowboy artist Lon
★ Megargee, the Hermosa lives up to its name (Spanish for "beautiful"), providing a restful alternative to the megaresorts. Individually deco-rated casitas and villas as big as private homes are hung with an en-viable collection of museum-quality art. ✉ *5532 N. Palo Cristi Rd., Paradise Valley 85253,* ☎ *602/955–8614 or 800/241–1210,* ℻ *602/ 955–8299. 4 villas, 3 haciendas, 22 casitas, 17 ranchos. Restaurant, pool, tennis. AE, D, DC, MC, V.* ✆

$$$$ 🏨 **Marriott's Camelback Inn.** Desert landscaping, large rooms (some
★ with private swimming pools), and a world-class spa make this a perennial favorite for those wanting to be pampered in a dramatic set-ting between the Camelback and Mummy mountains. ✉ *5402 E. Lin-coln Dr., Scottsdale 85253,* ☎ *602/948–1700 or 800/242–2635,* ℻ *602/951–8469. 480 rooms. 7 restaurants, pools, golf, tennis, health club. AE, D, DC, MC, V.* ✆

$$$$ 🏨 **The Phoenician.** With its crystal chandeliers, marble floors, cas-cading series of swimming pools (one tiled in mother-of-pearl), and top-notch spa, this swanky resort makes you forget you're in the desert. Rooms are spacious; ask for one facing south to enjoy views of the re-sort's pools and the city. ✉ *6000 E. Camelback Rd., Scottsdale 85251,* ☎ *602/941–8200 or 800/888–8234,* ℻ *602/947–4311. 654 rooms. 7 restaurants, pools, golf, tennis, health club. AE, D, DC, MC, V.* ✆

$$$$ 🏨 **Royal Palms.** A luxurious Mediterranean look prevails, from the tit-ular palms at the entrance to the manicured gardens dotted with an-tique fountains. Casitas are given individually themed treatment by well-known designers. ✉ *5200 E. Camelback Rd., Phoenix 85018,* ☎ *602/840–3610 or 800/672–6011,* ℻ *602/840–6927. 73 rooms, 43 ca-sitas. Restaurant, pool, tennis, health club. AE, D, DC, MC, V.* ✆

$$$$ 🏨 **Scottsdale Princess.** Built around a series of outdoor plazas, the Princess has a Mexican-colonial feel, with spacious rooms in soothing desert tones, beautifully landscaped grounds, and dining that makes you never want to leave the property. ✉ *7575 E. Princess Dr., Scotts-dale 85255,* ☎ *602/585–4848 or 800/344–4758,* ℻ *602/585–0091. 450 rooms, 125 casitas, 75 villas. 4 restaurants, pools, tennis, golf, health club. AE, D, DC, MC, V.* ✆

$$$ 🏨 **Hotel San Carlos.** Built in 1927, this downtown landmark retains historic touches such as pedestal sinks in the rooms and crystal chan-deliers in the lobby. The 3-inch concrete walls in the rooms ensure quiet, and though the rooms aren't huge, the staff is among the valley's friendliest. ✉ *202 N. Central Ave., 85004,* ☎ *602/253–4121 or 800/ 678–8946,* ℻ *602/253–6668. 133 rooms. 3 restaurants, café, pool, exercise room, meeting rooms, parking (fee). AE, D, DC, MC, V.* ✆

$$ 🏨 **Quality Hotel & Resort.** With a 1½-acre Getaway Lagoon complete with rock waterfalls pouring into a free-form pool, and plenty of facilities (a putting green, playground, and business center), the Quality is central Phoenix's best bargain oasis. Cabana suites on the VIP floor have private rooftop pools with great views of the Phoenix skyline. ✉ *3600 N. 2nd Ave., 85013,* ☎ *602/248–0222 or 800/256–1237,* ⅎⰊ *602/265–6331. 280 rooms. Restaurant, pools, exercise room. AE, D, DC, MC, V.* ✍

Nightlife and the Arts

Cultural and entertainment events are listed in the free weekly *New Times* newspaper, distributed Wednesday. The *Rep Entertainment Guide* and Sunday "Arts" section of the *Arizona Republic* also detail the current goings-on.

Nightlife

There are plenty of nightclubs, restaurants, and bars in downtown's **Arizona Center,** but there's no lack of nightlife elsewhere, particularly in Scottsdale and Tempe. On Camelback Road, restaurants abound in the **Biltmore Fashion Park.** Scottsdale's Main Street comes alive for **Art Walk,** held Thursday evenings from 7 to 9. **Mill Avenue,** near the ASU campus, is the center of action in Tempe.

The Arts

Downtown Phoenix's **Symphony Hall** (✉ 225 E. Adams St., ☎ 602/ 262–7272) and **Herberger Theater Center** (✉ 200 W. Washington St., ☎ 602/534–5600) are home to many performing arts groups.

Outdoor Activities and Sports

Golf

The Valley of the Sun has more than 100 courses, from par-3 to PGA-championship links. For a detailed listing contact the **Arizona Golf Association** (✉ 7226 N. 16th St., Suite 200, Phoenix 85020, ☎ 602/944–3035, 800/458–8484 in AZ).

Hiking

Phoenix has some of the best-trod hiking trails in the world, and the area favorite is in **Squaw Peak Park** (✉ 2701 Squaw Peak Dr., north of Lincoln Dr., east of South Peak Pkwy., ☎ 602/262–7901). The 1¼-mi trail to the top is steep; plan for an hour each direction. **Camelback Mountain** (✉ E. McDonald Dr. and Tatum Blvd., ☎ 602/256–3220), the city's most prominent landmark, presents a challenging climb that will take one to three hours. **South Mountain Park** (✉ 10919 S. Central Ave., south of Baseline Rd., ☎ 602/261–8457), the world's largest city park, contains more than 40 mi of multiuse trails. Rangers can help you plan hikes to see some of the 200 Native American petroglyph sites in the park.

Spectator Sports

Baseball: Arizona Diamondbacks (✉ Box 2095, Phoenix 85001, ☎ 602/514–8400) play at the Bank One Ballpark, next to the America West Arena. Several major-league baseball teams train in the Phoenix area during March. Contact the **Cactus League Baseball Association** at the Mesa Convention and Visitor's Bureau (✉ 120 N. Center St., Mesa 85201, ☎ 602/827–4700 or 800/283–6372) for information. **Basketball: Phoenix Suns** (✉ 201 E. Jefferson St., ☎ 602/379–7867). **Football:** The **Arizona Cardinals** (✉ Box 888, Phoenix 85001, ☎ 602/379–0102 or 800/999–1402) play at ASU's Sun Devil Stadium in Tempe. **Golf:** The **Phoenix Open** (✉ 17020 N. Hayden Rd., Scottsdale, ☎ 602/585–3600) is held each January at the Tournament Players Club of Scottsdale. **Hockey: Phoenix Coyotes** (✉ 201 E. Jefferson St., ☎ 602/563–7825). **Rodeo: Parada del Sol** (☎ 602/502–5600) festivities begin in January; the rodeo is held the first week in February.

Shopping

The valley is a shopper's delight, with everything from glitzy malls in Phoenix and Mesa to charming boutiques and galleries in downtown Scottsdale.

Arizona Center (⊠ 400 E. Van Buren St., Phoenix, ☎ 602/271–4000) is a modern, open-air center with two tiers of shops and restaurants. Anchored by Saks Fifth Avenue and Macy's, **Biltmore Fashion Park** (⊠ 24th St. and Camelback Rd., Phoenix, ☎ 602/955–8400) has posh shops as well as some of the city's most popular restaurants.

Souvenir shops and stores selling Native American jewelry and crafts are found along Scottsdale's **5th Avenue,** between Goldwater Boulevard and Scottsdale Road, and in **Old Town,** bordered by Brown Avenue, Scottsdale Road, Indian School Road, and 2nd Street. Head to **Main Street** and **Marshall Way,** just west of Scottsdale Road, for the fine art for which Scottsdale is known. **Scottsdale Fashion Square** (⊠ Scottsdale and Camelback Rds., ☎ 602/990–7800) sprawls across Camelback Road, with a Nordstrom and several other stores including Neiman-Marcus, Robinson's-May, and Dillard's. The ritzy **Borgata of Scottsdale** (⊠ 6166 N. Scottsdale Rd., ☎ 602/998–1822) has more than 50 boutiques in an Italian village–style complex.

Discount outlets also abound: Just east of downtown Phoenix, in Tempe, lies **Arizona Mills** (⊠ 5000 Arizona Mills Circle, Tempe, ☎ 602/491–9700), a mammoth center with almost 200 outlet stores, a food court, cinemas, and a faux rain forest. Thirty miles east of Phoenix, **Superstition Springs Center** (⊠ Superstition Freeway and Power Rd., Mesa), ☎ 480/832–0212) has the usual assortment of shops and eateries, a botanical garden, and a 15-ft Gila monster slide for the kids. The town of Casa Grande, some 45 minutes to the south via I–10, is home to two huge outlet malls, **Factory Stores of America** (⊠ Exit 194 off I–10, ☎ 602/421–0112) and **Tanger Outlet Center** (⊠ Exit 198 off I–10, ☎ 602/836–0897).

TUCSON

Tucson, Arizona's second-largest city, has a small-town atmosphere enriched by its deep Hispanic and Old West roots. Because of its large university, myriad resorts, and desirable climate—the sun shines more than 340 days a year, on the average—Tucson hosts all kinds of recreational and cultural activities, including historical tours, year-round.

Visitor Information

The **Metropolitan Tucson Convention and Visitors Bureau** (⊠ 130 S. Scott Ave., 85701, ☎ 520/624–1817 or 800/638–8350) is open weekdays 8–5 and weekends 9–4.

Arriving and Departing

By Bus
Greyhound (⊠ 2 S. 4th Ave., ☎ 520/792–3475 or 800/231–2222). **Arizona Shuttle Service** (☎ 520/795–6771) runs express buses from Phoenix's Sky Harbor Airport to Tucson.

By Car
From Phoenix, 111 mi to the northwest, or from the east, take I–10 to Tucson. From the south take I–19.

By Plane
Tucson International Airport (☎ 520/573–8000), 8½ mi south of down-town, is served by 10 carriers, some of which serve Mexico as well as domestic destinations.

By Train
Amtrak (⊠ 400 E. Toole Ave., ☎ 520/623–4442 or 800/872–7245).

Exploring Tucson

Tucson covers more than 500 square mi in a valley ringed by moun-tains, so a car is necessary. The downtown area, just east of I–10 off the Broadway-Congress exit, is easy to navigate on foot.

In the El Presidio neighborhood, the **Tucson Museum of Art** (⊠ 140 N. Main Ave., ☎ 520/624–2333; ☜ $2, free Sun.) houses a permanent col-lection of pre-Columbian art and hosts traveling shows, mostly of con-temporary art. The museum lies within Tucson's **Historic Block**—a neighborhood that takes visitors back to a time when the city was a fortress and Arizona was still part of New Spain. The historic buildings on this block are listed in the National Register of Historic Buildings. You can enter **La Casa Cordova** (⊠ 175 N. Meyer Ave.), the **Stevens House** (⊠ 150 N. Main Ave.), and the **J. Knox Corbett House** (⊠ 180 N. Main Ave.). The **Edward Nye Fish House** houses the art museum's western collection.

The city divides **Saguaro National Park** (☎ 520/733–5158 for west, 520/733–5153 for east; ☜ $4 per vehicle or $2 per pedestrian for Saguaro East, free Saguaro West) into two sections; the one west of town is the most heavily visited, in part because of its **Red Hills Visi-tor Center**. Both parks are forested by the huge saguaro cactus, a na-tive of the Sonoran Desert that is known for its towering height (often 50 ft) and for arms that reach out in strange configurations.

★ ⓒ Near Saguaro National Park West is the **Arizona–Sonora Desert Mu-seum** (⊠ 2021 N. Kinney Rd., ☎ 520/883–2702; ☜ $8.95), where birds and animals busy themselves in a desert microcosm. **Old Tucson Studios** (⊠ 201 S. Kinney Rd., in Tucson Mountain Park, ☎ 520/883–0100; ☜ $14.95) is a western theme park that's been used as a loca-tion for 350 movie and television productions over the past 50 years.

Among the museums on the **University of Arizona** campus (⊠ corner of Park Ave. and Speedway Blvd.) are the **Center for Creative Pho-tography** (☎ 520/621–7968), the **Arizona Historical Society's Museum** (☎ 520/628–5774), the **Arizona State Museum** (☎ 520/621–6302), and the **Flandrau Science Center and Planetarium** (☎ 520/621–4515). Entrance to all of these museums is free.

Just southwest of Tucson, the 1692 **Mission San Xavier del Bac** (⊠ I–19, Exit 92, San Xavier Rd., ☎ 520/294–2624; ☜ donations ac-cepted) is the oldest Catholic church in the United States still serving the community for which it was built: the Tohonó O'odham Indian tribe. Painted statues, carvings, and frescoes make this beautiful Span-ish-Moorish-style structure a sight to behold.

Dining

$$$$ ✕ **Janos.** Chef Janos Wilder brings his Southwest hacienda-style cui-
★ sine to the grounds of the Westin La Paloma hotel (☞ Lodging, *below*). Roasted quail stuffed with chihuacle spoonbread on prickly pear com-pote tastes magical as you survey stunning views of the city and desert. ⊠ *3770 E. Sunrise Dr.,* ☎ *520/615–6100. AE, DC, MC, V. Closed Sun. No lunch.*

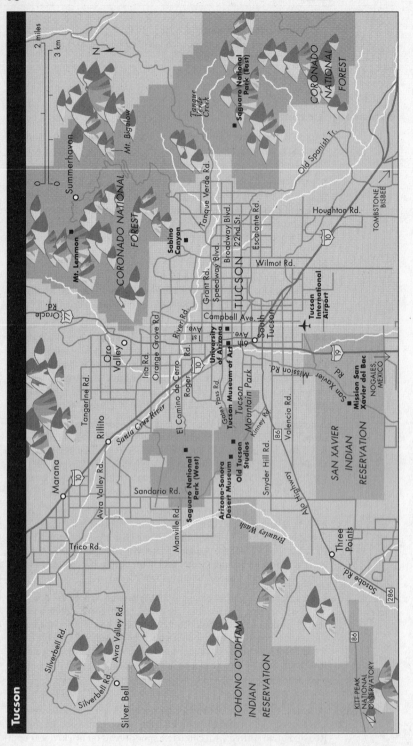

$$–$$$$ ╳ **Café Terra Cotta.** Specialties at this very southwestern restaurant include duck two ways (grilled breast and duck carnitas springroll with sweet ancho-ginger sauce), chiles relleno, and pork tenderloin with black beans. At press time a move to 3500 Sunrise Drive in the nearby foothills was planned, so call to confirm the address. ⊠ *4310 N. Campbell Ave.,* ☎ *520/577–8100. AE, D, DC, MC, V.*

$$–$$$ ╳ **Kingfisher Bar and Grill.** Brick walls and black banquettes create a chic setting for Kingfisher's innovative cuisine. You might find stuffed grilled trout with a pecan-cilantro pesto sauce or braised shank of Colorado lamb on the seasonally changing menu. Added bonuses include an extensive bourbon selection and late hours (food is served until midnight). ⊠ *2564 E. Grant Rd.,* ☎ *520/323–7739. AE, D, DC, MC, V. No lunch weekends.*

$$–$$$ ╳ **Vivace.** Daniel Scordato's involvement with some of the best Italian restaurants in town clearly benefits his latest venture. The industrial-chic dining room has gray columns, black iron chairs, and an open kitchen. Appetizers are a bit pricey, but the wild mushrooms in a phyllo cup with tomato, basil, and garlic sauce are hard to resist. ⊠ *4811 E. Grant Rd., Suite 155,* ☎ *520/795–7221. AE, D, MC, V. No lunch Sun.*

$$ ╳ **Café Poca Cosa.** Chef-owner Susan Davila pays homage to differ-
★ ent regions of her native Mexico in what is arguably Tucson's best restaurant. The chalkboard menu changes daily; ingredients are always fresh. The tiny original restaurant across the street (⊠ 20 S. Scott Ave.) is open for breakfast and lunch during the week. ⊠ *Park Inn, 88 E. Broadway,* ☎ *520/622–6400. MC, V. Closed Sun.*

$–$$ ╳ **Pinnacle Peak Steakhouse.** No nouvelle-cuisine fans welcome here: It's a cowboy steak house all the way. Excellent mesquite-broiled steak comes with salad and pinto beans; for dessert, there's a heavenly hot apple cobbler. The restaurant is part of Trail Dust Town, a re-created turn-of-the-20th-century town where gunfights take place Tuesday through Saturday at 7 and 8 PM. ⊠ *6541 E. Tanque Verde Rd.,* ☎ *520/ 296–0911. Reservations not accepted. AE, D, DC, MC, V. No lunch.*

Dining and Lodging

$$$$ ╳⊞ **Loews Ventana Canyon Resort.** Expect to see desert cottontails around the 93-acre grounds of this luxury resort, along with hummingbirds, quail, and other birds. Rooms are modern and chic; each bath has a miniature TV. At the center of the property, an 80-ft waterfall cascades down the Santa Catalina Mountains into a little lake. The elegant Ventana Room serves seasonal specialties such as grilled loin of venison with pecans. ⊠ *7000 N. Resort Dr. 85750,* ☎ *520/ 299–2020 or 800/234–5117,* ℻ *520/299–6832. 412 rooms. 4 restaurants, pools, golf, tennis, health club. AE, D, DC, MC, V.* ❧

Lodging

Resorts in the area are known for their outdoor-recreation facilities, which often include trails for hiking and horseback riding. Prices for most health-spa resorts include all meals; call individual properties for details.

$$$$ ⊞ **Canyon Ranch.** Since 1979, this health spa has drawn an interna-
★ tional crowd of glitterati. Set on 70 acres in the desert foothills northeast of Tucson, the resort has a full-time staff of dieticians, exercise physiologists, and medical professionals who attend to body and soul. There's a four-night minimum stay. ⊠ *8600 E. Rockcliff Rd., 85715,* ☎ *520/749–9000 or 800/742–9000,* ℻ *520/749–1646. 153 rooms. Restaurant, pools, tennis, health club. AE, D, MC, V.* ❧

$$$$ ☷ **Miraval.** Some 20 mi north of Tucson, Miraval is known for its secluded desert setting, beautiful southwestern rooms, and progressive mind-body programs, many based on Eastern philosophy. Meals and tips are included. ✉ *5000 E. Via Estancia Miraval, Catalina 85739,* ☎ *520/825–4000 or 800/825–4000,* FAX *520/825–5163. 106 rooms. 2 restaurants, pools, tennis, exercise room. AE, D, DC, MC, V. FAP.* ✤

$$$$ ☷ **Sheraton Tucson El Conquistador.** In the rugged Santa Catalina
★   Mountains, this golf and tennis resort has a truly southwestern feel. A mural in the cathedral-ceiling lobby illustrates cowboys and cacti; rooms, either in private casitas or the main hotel building, have balconies or patios, and some suites have kiva-shape fireplaces. ✉ *10000 N. Oracle Rd., 85737,* ☎ *520/544–5000 or 800/325–7832,* FAX *520/544–1224. 428 rooms. 4 restaurants, pools, golf, tennis, exercise rooms. AE, D, DC, MC, V.*

$$$$ ☷ **Tanque Verde Ranch.** One of the oldest guest ranches in the coun-
★   try, Tanque Verde sits on more than 600 acres in the Rincon Mountains between Coronado National Forest and Saguaro National Park. Rooms are in the main ranch house or in private casitas; many have patios and fireplaces. ✉ *14301 E. Speedway Blvd., 85748,* ☎ *520/296–6275 or 800/234–3833,* FAX *520/721–9426. 72 rooms, 2 houses. Restaurant, pools, tennis, exercise room. AE, D, MC, V. FAP.* ✤

$$$$ ☷ **Westin La Paloma.** Vying with the Sheraton for convention business, this sprawling pink resort has top-notch golf, fitness, and beauty centers; there's also a huge pool with Tucson's only swim-up bar and Arizona's longest resort water slide. Child-care programs help parents relax. ✉ *3800 E. Sunrise Dr., 85718,* ☎ *520/742–6000,* FAX *520/577–5878. 487 rooms. 5 restaurants, pools, golf, tennis, exercise room. AE, D, DC, MC, V.* ✤

$$$$ ☷ **White Stallion Ranch.** Many scenes from the television show *High Chaparral* were shot on this family-run ranch, set on 3,000 desert mountain acres. Activities include horseback rides, a weekend rodeo, cookouts, and hikes along mountain trails. Longhorn cattle roam the grounds; there's also a children's petting zoo. Rooms are spare (no phones or TVs) but comfortable. ✉ *9251 W. Twin Peaks Rd., 85743,* ☎ *520/297–0252 or 888/977–2624,* FAX *520/744–2786. 39 rooms. Pool, tennis. No credit cards. Closed June–Aug. FAP.* ✤

$$$–$$$$ ☷ **Arizona Inn.** Though it's close to the university and downtown, this
★   landmark 1930s-era inn is secluded on 14 acres of lushly landscaped grounds. The spacious rooms are spread out in pink stucco houses; all have patios and some have fireplaces. Large groups may rent a guest house. ✉ *2200 E. Elm St., 85719,* ☎ *520/325–1541 or 800/933–1093,* FAX *520/881–5830. 86 rooms, two 5-bedroom guest houses, one 2-bedroom guest house. 2 restaurants, pool, tennis. AE, DC, MC, V.* ✤

$$$ ☷ **Windmill Inn.** In a shopping plaza, this modern inn has 122 suites with microwave, wet bar, two TVs, and three phones. Complimentary coffee, muffins, and a newspaper are delivered to your door. ✉ *4250 N. Campbell Ave., 85718,* ☎ *520/577–0007 or 800/547–4747,* FAX *520/577–0045. 122 suites. Pool. AE, D, DC, MC, V. CP.* ✤

$$ ☷ **Best Western Ghost Ranch Lodge.** The logo of this hotel was designed by Georgia O'Keeffe, a friend of the original owner. The units have Spanish-tile roofs and are spread over 8 acres amid an orange grove and garden with 400 types of cacti. The cottages are a bargain, with separate kitchens and carports. ✉ *801 W. Miracle Mile, 85705,* ☎ *520/791–7565 or 800/456–7565,* FAX *520/791–3898. 72 rooms, 11 cottages. Restaurant, pool. AE, D, DC, MC, V. CP.* ✤

$–$$ ☷ **Hotel Congress.** This downtown hotel, built in 1919 in Art Deco style, has a convenient location, low rates, and a hip young crowd that frequents the popular Club Congress. Rooms have original iron beds. ✉ *311 E. Congress St., 85701,* ☎ *520/622–8848 or 800/722–8848,* FAX *520/792–6366. 40 rooms. Restaurant. AE, D, MC, V.* ✤

Campgrounds

The public campground closest to Tucson is at ⚠ **Catalina State Park** (✉ 11570 N. Oracle Rd., ☎ 520/628–5798). Recreational vehicles can park in any number of facilities around town; the Convention and Visitors Bureau (☞ Visitor Information, *above*) can provide information about specific locations.

Nightlife and the Arts

Nightlife

Cactus Moon (✉ 5470 E. Broadway, ☎ 520/748–0049) and **Maverick** (✉ 4702 E. 22nd St., ☎ 520/748–0456) are lively country-and-western nightclubs.

The Arts

The **Tucson Symphony Orchestra** (☎ 520/882–8585) and the **Arizona Opera Company** (☎ 520/293–4336) perform in the **Tucson Convention Center's Music Hall** (✉ 260 S. Church St., ☎ 520/791–4226). The **Arizona Theatre Company** (☎ 520/884–8210) comes to Tucson's Temple of Music and Art (✉ 330 S. Scott Ave., ☎ 520/622–2823) from September through May.

Outdoor Activities and Sports

Golf

Tucson has five **municipal golf courses** (✉ Tucson Parks and Recreation Dept., ☎ 520/791–4336), as well as many excellent resort courses, such as those at the **Lodge at Ventana Canyon** (✉ 6200 N. Club House La., off Kold Rd., ☎ 520/577–4061), **OmniTucson National Golf Resort and Spa** (✉ 2727 W. Club Dr., ☎ 520/297–2271), **Westin La Paloma** and **Sheraton Tucson El Conquistador** (for the last two, *see* Lodging, *above*). For information about other courses in the area, send $5 for the **Tucson and Southern Arizona Golf Guide** (✉ Madden Publishing, Box 42915, Tucson 85733, ☎ 520/322–0895).

Hiking

For great hiking opportunities around Tucson, head for **Tucson Mountain Park, Mt. Lemmon, Sabino Canyon,** or **Kitt Peak.** A little-visited treasure, **Chiricahua National Monument,** about two hours east of Tucson off I–10, south of Bowie, has spectacular rugged rock vistas. Directly south of Tucson, the Huachuca Mountains, home of **Ramsey Canyon,** are a bird-watcher's paradise. The Santa Ritas, just south of Tucson, host another bird lover's haven, **Madera Canyon.** The local chapter of the **Sierra Club** (☎ 520/620–6401) welcomes out-of-town visitors on its weekend hikes.

Horseback Riding

Tucson stables include **Pusch Ridge Stables** (✉ 13700 N. Oracle Rd., ☎ 520/825–1664). Many resorts also have horseback riding.

Shopping

In Tucson, **Old Town Artisans** (✉ 186 N. Meyer Ave., ☎ 520/623–6024), **Plaza Palomino** (✉ 2970 N. Swan, ☎ 520/795–1177), and **St. Philip's Plaza** (✉ 4380 N. Campbell Ave., ☎ 520/886–7485) all carry a broad selection of fine southwestern jewelry, crafts, and clothing. Hard-core bargain hunters head for **Nogales,** the Mexican border town 63 mi south of Tucson on I–19. For work by regional artists, try the **Tubac** artists' community, 45 mi south of Tucson, just off I–19 at Exit 34.

SOUTHERN ARIZONA

Southeastern Arizona is a relatively undiscovered treasure of mountains, deserts, canyons, and dusty little cowboy towns. Of particular interest are Bisbee and Tombstone, which recall Arizona during its Wild West heyday.

Visitor Information

Bisbee Chamber of Commerce (⊠ 7 Main St., Box BA, 85603, ☎ 520/432–5421). **Tombstone Chamber of Commerce and Visitor Center** (⊠ corner of 4th and Allen Sts., ☎ 520/457–3929).

Arriving and Departing

By Car

East of Tucson, U.S. 80 cuts south from I–10 to Tombstone and Bisbee.

Exploring Southern Arizona

Tombstone

Born on the site of a wildly successful silver mine, this town 67 mi southeast of Tucson on U.S. 80 was headquarters of many of the West's rowdies in the late 1800s. The famous shoot-out at the OK Corral and other gunfights are replayed on Sunday on the town's main drag, **Allen Street.** As you enter Tombstone from the northwest, you'll pass **Boot Hill Graveyard** (⊠ Hwy. 80), where the victims of the OK Corral shoot-out are buried. The **Tombstone Courthouse State Historic Park** (⊠ Toughnut and 3rd Sts., ☎ 520/457–3311; ☑ $2.50) has a reconstruction of the town's original 1882 courthouse, plus area artifacts and old photographs.

Bisbee

Once a mining boomtown, Bisbee, set on a mountainside 24 mi south of Tombstone, is now an artists' colony. Arizona's largest pit mine yielded some 94 million tons of copper ore before mining activity halted in the early 1970s; at the **Lavender Pit Mine** you can still see the huge crater left by the process. The **Mining and Historical Museum** (⊠ 5 Copper Queen Plaza, ☎ 520/432–7071; ☑ $4) is filled with old photos and artifacts from the town's heyday. Behind the museum is the venerable **Copper Queen Hotel** (☞ Dining and Lodging, *below*), home away from home to such guests as "Black Jack" Pershing, John Wayne, and Teddy Roosevelt. The **Copper Queen mine tour** (⊠ 478 N. Dart Rd., ☎ 520/432–2071; ☑ $10.75), led by retired miners, is an entertaining way to learn about the town's history.

Dining and Lodging

Bisbee

$ ✕ **Café Roka.** One of the best bargains in southern Arizona, this chic ★ northern Italian restaurant is in a historic building with exposed brick walls and an original 1906 tinwork ceiling. Generous portions of pasta are served with soup, salad, and sorbet. ⊠ *35 Main St., ☎ 520/432–5153. MC, V. Closed Sun.–Tues. No lunch.*

$$ ▥ **Copper Queen Hotel.** This turn-of-the-20th-century hotel in the ★ heart of downtown has thin walls but a lot of Victorian charm. The boom-days memorabilia throughout is fascinating. ⊠ *11 Howell Ave., Drawer CQ, 85603, ☎ 520/432–2216 or 800/247–5829, FAX 520/432–4298. 47 rooms. Restaurant, pool. AE, D, DC, MC, V.* ✍

Tombstone

$-$$ ✕ **Nellie Cashman's.** Named for the Tombstone pioneer who opened it in 1882, Nellie Cashman's is known for its juicy pork chops, chicken-fried steaks, and country breakfasts complete with biscuits and gravy. ✉ *5th and Toughnut Sts.,* ☎ *520/457–2212. AE, D, MC, V.*

$-$$ ✕🏠 **Tombstone Boarding House Bed & Breakfast.** Two meticulously re-stored 1880s adobes sit side by side in a quiet residential neighborhood. In one of the buildings, a dining room serves a limited but daily-changing menu. Typical selections are chicken breast in a sherry-mushroom sauce and beef Wellington. Next door, spotless rooms with hardwood floors contain period furnishings from surrounding Cochise County. ✉ *108 N. 4th St., Box 906, 85638,* ☎ *520/457–3716 or 877/225–1313,* ℻ *520/457–3038. 8 rooms. Restaurant. AE, D, MC, V. BP.*

$-$$ 🏠 **Best Western Look-Out Lodge.** Western-print bedspreads and wood-hewn clocks give this motel off U.S. 80 a lot of character. Rooms have views of the Dragoon Mountains and desert valley and come with Continental breakfast. ✉ *U.S. 80 W, Box 787, 85638,* ☎ *520/457–2223 or 877/652-6772,* ℻ *520/457–3870. 40 rooms. Pool. AE, D, DC, MC, V. CP.* 🐾

ARKANSAS

By Marcia
Schnedler

Capital	Little Rock
Population	2,538,300
Motto	The People Rule
State Bird	Mockingbird
State Flower	Apple blossom
Postal Abbreviation	AR

Statewide Visitor Information

Arkansas Department of Parks and Tourism (⊠ 1 Capitol Mall, Little Rock 72201, ☎ 501/682–7777 or 800/628–8725). There are 12 state tourist information centers on major highways near the state borders, and one in Little Rock.

Scenic Drives

Arkansas's billing as the Natural State is appropriate: The state has more than 17 million acres of public and private forests, 600,000 acres of lakes, and 9,700 mi of rivers and streams. Its **Ozark** and **Ouachita mountains** rival New England's for scenic vistas and fall colors, which you can see along meandering roadways, including eight state and national scenic byways. **Route 7** between Arkadelphia and Harrison winds over both ranges and through two national forests. The **Talimena Scenic Byway** stretches across mountain crests from Mena to Talihina, Oklahoma, passing through **Queen Wilhelmina State Park.** The **St. Francis Scenic Byway**—part of the **Great River Road** that follows the Mississippi River—leads through wild terrain between Marianna and Helena/West Helena.

National and State Parks

Arkansas boasts 340 public and private campgrounds with some 9,800 campsites and has more than 300 trails stretching over 1,622 mi. The *Camper's and Hiker's Guide* and *Arkansas State Parks* booklet, both available from the state tourism department (☞ Statewide Visitor Information, *above*), provide locations, fees, and other useful information. Arkansas is also prime territory for fly-fishing and warm-water angling, as well as for hunting duck, deer, wild turkey, and small game. Contact the **Arkansas Game and Fish Commission** (☎ 501/223–6346 or 800/364–4263).

National Parks

★ The **Buffalo National River** (⊠ 402 N. Walnut St., Suite 136, Harrison 72601, ☎ 870/741–5443), backed by limestone bluffs, became the first federally protected river in 1972. Its 132 mi are noted for canoeing, white-water rafting, hiking, and fishing spots; wilderness areas; and historic sites. The **Ouachita National Forest** (⊠ USFS, Box 1270, Hot Springs 71902, ☎ 501/321–5202), dotted by crystal lakes, is the oldest and largest in the South. The **Ozark National Forest** (⊠ 605 W. Main St., Russellville 72801, ☎ 501/968–2354) encompasses wild hills, hollows, rivers, and streams, as well as Arkansas's highest peak—the 2,753-ft Mt. Magazine. **Hot Springs National Park** (⊠ Box 1860, Hot Springs 71902, ☎ 501/624–3383 ext. 640) features Bathhouse Row—eight turn-of-the-20th-century spa buildings—plus a campground and hiking trails in mountains and gorges surrounding the town. **Felsenthal National Wildlife Refuge** (⊠ Box 1157, Crossett 71635, ☎ 870/

364–3167) is a mosaic of wetlands, lakes, and rivers that draws anglers, boaters, and wildlife watchers.

State Parks

Arkansas has 50 state parks, museums, and monuments; 27 have campgrounds, and 12 have lodges and cabins. **Devil's Den** (⊠ 11333 W. Ark. 74, West Fork 72774, ☎ 501/761–3325) is set in an Ozark valley full of caves, crevices, bluffs, and Civilian Conservation Corps structures from the 1930s. **Village Creek** (⊠ 201 CR 754, Wynne 72396, ☎ 870/238–9406) lies atop Crowley's Ridge, an unusual forested highland that slices through the Mississippi Delta. Volunteers participate in seasonal excavations in **Parkin Archaeological State Park** (⊠ Box 1110, Parkin 72373-1110, ☎ 870/755–2500) to uncover the remains of a Native American village chronicled by Hernando de Soto's Spanish expedition of 1541. **Petit Jean** (⊠ 1285 Petit Jean Mountain Rd., Morrilton 72110, ☎ 501/727–5441), perched on a mountaintop, comprises canyons, waterfalls, a lake, a lodge, and cabins, plus the Museum of Automobiles. **Lake Chicot** (⊠ 2542 Ark. 257, Lake Village 71653, ☎ 870/265–5480) sits on a 20-mi-long oxbow lake edged by cypress and noted for fishing and bird-watching.

LITTLE ROCK

Little Rock, on the south bank of the Arkansas River, is Arkansas's geographical, governmental, and financial center, as well as a major convention hub. Spanish and French explorers passed the site in the 16th and 17th centuries, naming it La Petite Roche because of a small outcrop that marked the transition from the flat Mississippi Delta region to the Ouachita Mountain foothills. A simple translation turned the town into Little Rock when it became the territorial capital in 1821—the capital had been at Arkansas Post, the first European settlement in the lower Mississippi River valley. Within an hour of Little Rock's downtown are world-renowned duck hunting in rice-growing regions to the southeast and wild scenic vistas, streams, and trails in forested mountains to the north and west.

Visitor Information

Little Rock Convention & Visitors Bureau (⊠ Box 3232, Little Rock 72203, ☎ 501/376–4781 or 800/844–4781).

Arriving and Departing

By Car

I–40 and I–30 lead to Little Rock, as do U.S. 65 and U.S. 67.

By Plane

Most major airlines fly into **Little Rock National Airport** (⊠ 1 Airport Dr., ☎ 501/372–3439), 5 mi east of downtown off I–440. Major Little Rock hotels provide airport shuttles. Cab fare to downtown is about $12; for a taxi, call **Black & White/Yellow Cabs** (☎ 501/374–0333) or **Capitol Cab** (☎ 501/568–0462).

Getting Around Little Rock

By Bus

Central Arkansas Transit (☎ 501/375–1163) serves Little Rock and North Little Rock.

By Car

Little Rock is easily negotiated by interstate highways and major streets. There are plenty of parking facilities and taxis.

Exploring Little Rock

A series of free walking-driving tours lead through several historic areas in and near downtown. The **MacArthur Park Historic District** takes in some antebellum buildings, including the 1843 **Trapnall Hall** (⊠ 423 E. Capitol Ave.), as well as fine Victorian architecture. The birthplace of General Douglas MacArthur, in the eponymous park, is part of an 1838 arsenal. MacArthur Park also includes the modern **Arkansas Arts Center** (⊠ 9th and Commerce Sts., ☎ 501/372–4000; ⌨ free), with nine galleries, an outstanding children's theater, a museum school, a gift shop, and a restaurant. Changing exhibits are mounted at the **Decorative Arts Museum** (⊠ 7th and Rock Sts., ☎ 501/372–4000; ⌨ free), set in an 1840 mansion.

The area surrounding the **governor's mansion** (⊠ 1800 Center St., ☎ 501/324–9805; ⌨ free) encompasses elegant post–Civil War and turn-of-the-20th-century churches and homes; tours of the mansion are by appointment. The 1881 Italianate **Villa Marre** (⊠ 1321 S. Scott St., ☎ 501/371–0075; ⌨ $3; closed Sat.), whose facade was featured in the TV series *Designing Women,* is now open by appointment to the public, complete with period furnishings.

The **Empress of Little Rock Bed & Breakfast and Tour Home** (⊠ 2120 S. Louisiana, ☎ 501/374–7966; ⌨ $5), open Tuesday and Thursday, offers public tours of the beautifully restored 1888 Gothic Queen Anne house that is described in the National Register of Historic Places as the best example of ornate Victorian architecture in Arkansas.

★   Historic public buildings in the riverfront district include the **Old State House** (⊠ 300 W. Markham St., ☎ 501/324–9685, ⌨ free), built between 1833 and 1842 and recently restored as a museum devoted to Arkansas history. Bill Clinton used this building as his backdrop for victory speeches on gubernatorial election nights. The **Arkansas Territorial Restoration** (⊠ 200 E. 3rd St., ☎ 501/324–9351; ⌨ $2) shows off restored and furnished frontier buildings on living-history tours and galleries displaying Arkansas-made fine and decorative arts. The shop features the work of local craftspeople.

The neoclassical **state capitol** (⊠ Capitol Ave. and Woodlane, ☎ 501/682–5080; ⌨ call for free guided tour), built between 1899 and 1915 on a hilltop west of downtown, has an imposing rotunda, grand marble staircases and columns, stained-glass skylights, murals, and six intricately crafted 4-inch-thick brass doors from Tiffany & Co.

The **Central High School Museum Visitor Center** (⊠ 2125 W. 14th St., ☎ 501/374–1957; ⌨ free), a National Historic Site, features exhibits and audiovisual programs commemorating the school's integration in 1957, when nine black students were enrolled under the protection of

☺   federal troops. In historic Union Train Station, the interactive **Children's Museum of Arkansas** (⊠ 1400 W. Markham St., ☎ 501/374–6655; ⌨ $4) lets kids make stationery in the post office, shop at the farmers' market, or contribute to the Kids Gallery of collectibles.

☺   The **Aerospace Education Center** (⊠ 3301 E. Roosevelt Rd., ☎ 501/376–4629) has an **IMAX theater** (⌨ $6.50), a small free museum, and

☺   a library. The **Museum of Discovery** (⊠ 500 E. Markham St., ☎ 501/396–7050 or 800/880–6475; ⌨ $5) explores science and culture with hands-on exhibits.

Outside Little Rock

Just 15 mi west of downtown is **Pinnacle Mountain State Park** (⊠ 11901 Pinnacle Valley Rd., Roland 72135, ☎ 501/868–5806; ⌨ free), whose habitats range from high peaks to river bottomlands lined with hardwoods and ancient cypress.

Less than 30 minutes east of downtown on U.S. 165 is the state park–operated **Plantation Agriculture Museum,** whose displays interpret the history of cotton agriculture. ⊠ *4815 Hwy. 161, Scott,* ☎ *501/961–1409.* ⊠ *$2.25. Closed Mon. except holidays.*

Several miles beyond Scott off U.S. 165 sits **Toltec Mounds Archaeological State Park,** the remains of a large Native American ceremonial and governmental complex inhabited from AD 600 to AD 950. ⊠ *490 Toltec Mounds Rd., Scott,* ☎ *501/961–9442.* ⊠ *$2.25. Closed Mon.*

Parks, Gardens, and Zoos

War Memorial Park (⊠ north off I–630 at Fair Park Ave. and W. Markham St., ☎ 501/371–4770), one of Little Rock's oldest and most popular parks, contains a public golf course, tennis courts, a football stadium, and the baseball park of the minor-league Arkansas Travelers. It also has a fitness center (open to the public) and a zoo.

Riverfront Park edges both sides of the Arkansas River. On the Little Rock side it lies behind the Old State House and Convention Center, with playgrounds, a history pavilion, and an amphitheater. The site of the future **Bill Clinton Presidential Library** is east of I–30 adjacent to the park. In North Little Rock, across the river from Riverfront Park, the **Alltel Arena** (⊠ 312 Main St., ☎ 501/340–5660) is the home of the Glacier-Cats minor-league hockey team and the site of other sports and entertainment events. East of the Main Street bridge in North Little Rock is the dock for the *Spirit* (☎ 501/376–4150), a paddle-wheel riverboat that makes both excursion and dining cruises. The **Little Rock Zoo** (⊠ 1 Jonesboro Dr., ☎ 501/663–4733; ⊠ $5) has gorillas, giant anteaters, and 175 other species.

Dining and Lodging

Note: Some of the counties outside the city are dry.

$–$$$ ✕ **Alouette's.** This prestigious French Continental restaurant offers ca-
★ sual-elegant dining and an innovative menu that changes seasonally. An extensive wine list includes older vintages. ⊠ *11401 N. Rodney Parham Rd.,* ☎ *501/225–4152. AE, D, DC, MC, V. Closed Sun. and Mon.*

$–$$ ✕ **Spaule.** This relaxed but stylish spot has won numerous national and regional awards for its new American cuisine. The menu and wine list change monthly but often feature such dishes as cornmeal-crusted fried oysters and roasted veal. ⊠ *5713 Kavanaugh Blvd.,* ☎ *501/664–3663. Reservations not accepted. AE, MC, V. Closed Sun.*

$–$$ ✕ **Trio's.** Intriguing international-eclectic lunch and dinner menus show southwestern, Caribbean, Pan-Asian, Italian, Creole, and contemporary influences. Desserts are delectable, and there's a full bar. ⊠ *8201 Cantrell Rd.,* ☎ *501/221–3330. AE, D, DC, MC, V. Closed Sun.*

$ ✕ **Franke's Cafeteria.** This family-owned local institution serves good, simple food for lunch at all locations or early dinner at its restaurants on Rodney Parham Road and in University Mall. ⊠ *11121 N. Rodney Parham Rd.,* ☎ *501/225–4487;* ⊠ *300 S. University Ave.,* ☎ *501/663–4461; 400 W. Capitol St.,* ☎ *501/372–1919. D, MC, V. Capitol location closed weekends.*

$$$ ▥ **Arkansas Excelsior Hotel.** Atop the Statehouse Convention Center on the banks of the Arkansas River, the Excelsior offers both concierge and standard floors. Among its three stylish restaurants is the award-winning Josephine's Library. Business facilities and an airport shuttle are pluses. ⊠ *3 Statehouse Plaza, 72201,* ☎ *501/375–5000 or 800/527–1745,* ℻ *501/375–4721. 417 rooms. 3 restaurants, exercise room. AE, D, DC, MC, V.* 🐾

$$$ 🏨 **Capital Hotel.** A careful restoration of this 1872 National Historic Landmark has called attention to the classic cast-iron facade; the high-ceiling dining rooms; and the atrium lobby's mosaic floors, lead-glass skylight, and handsome columns. The restaurant, Ashley's, offers fine dining, with casual lunches and dinners served in the lounge. ✉ *111 W. Markham St., 72201,* ☎ *501/374–7474 or 800/766–7666,* FAX *501/370–7091. 125 rooms. Restaurant. AE, D, DC, MC, V.*

$$–$$$ 🏨 **Embassy Suites.** This all-suite hotel lies in West Little Rock, 10–15 minutes from downtown. The two-room suites have sofa beds and kitchenettes. ✉ *11301 Financial Centre Pkwy., 72211,* ☎ *501/312–9000,* FAX *501/312–9455. 251 suites. Restaurant, pool, exercise room. AE, D, DC, MC, V. BP.* 🐾

$$ 🏨 **Holiday Inn–Select.** This West Little Rock hotel is convenient to downtown as well as nearby restaurants and businesses. Business facilities and an airport shuttle are provided. ✉ *201 S. Shackleford Rd., 72211,* ☎ *501/223–3000,* FAX *501/223–2833. 261 rooms. 2 restaurants, bar, pool, exercise room. AE, D, DC, MC, V.* 🐾

Motels

🏨 **La Quinta–North** (✉ 4100 McCain Blvd., North Little Rock 27117, ☎ 501/945–0808, FAX 501/945–0393), 122 rooms; pool; CP; $–$$.

🏨 **Hampton Inn I–30** (✉ 6100 Mitchell Dr., 72209, ☎ 501/562–6667, FAX 501/568–6832), 122 rooms; pool, exercise room; CP; $.

🏨 **Motel 6** (✉ 10524 W. Markham St. [at I–430], 72205, ☎ 501/225–7366, FAX 501/227–7426), 146 rooms; pool; $.

Nightlife and the Arts

The "Weekend" section of Friday's *Arkansas Democrat-Gazette* and the weekly *Arkansas Times* list nightlife and arts events, and you can call a recorded "What's Happening" line (☎ 501/372–3399).

Nightlife

The **After Thought** (✉ 2721 Kavanaugh Blvd., ☎ 501/663–1196) provides a variety of music nightly, with Jazz & Heritage Foundation performances on Monday nights. The DJ'd **Bobbisox Lounge,** at the Holiday Inn Airport (✉ I–440 Airport Exit, ☎ 501/490–1000), is a popular spot for dancing. **Juanita's Cantina** (✉ 1300 S. Main St., ☎ 501/372–1228) serves up Mexican fare daily along with an eclectic mix of evening entertainment—rock, blues, reggae, and other touring groups. **Vino's** (✉ 923 W. 7th St., ☎ 501/375–8466) presents avant-garde Red Octopus theater productions and is home to the Little Rock Folk Club and other concert organizations; it also has a microbrewery and delicious pizzas.

The Arts

The **Robinson Center** (✉ Markham St. and Broadway, ☎ 501/376–3291) is the city's major venue for the performing arts. The **Arkansas Repertory Theater** (✉ 601 Main St., ☎ 501/378–0405) stages popular and avant-garde works. The **Arkansas Symphony Orchestra** (☎ 501/666–1761), at various locations, performs both classical and pops music. **Celebrity Attractions** (✉ 1501 N. University Ave., Suite 813, 72207, ☎ 501/661–1500) brings in national touring companies of Broadway shows. At **Murry's Dinner Playhouse** (✉ 6323 Asher Ave., ☎ 501/562–3131) a buffet accompanies Broadway comedies and musicals or solo performances. The **UALR Fine Arts Galleries & Theatre** (✉ 2801 S. University Ave., ☎ 501/569–3291 for theater; 501/569–3183 for galleries) sponsors concerts and theater as well as art exhibits. **Wildwood Park for the Performing Arts** (✉ 20919 Denny Rd., ☎ 501/821–7275) offers opera, jazz, cabaret, chamber music, and festivals.

Shopping

Major department stores are at **Park Plaza** and **University Mall,** on either side of Markham Street at University Avenue in Little Rock, and at **McCain Mall** at Arkansas 67/U.S. 167 and McCain Boulevard in North Little Rock. In a restored warehouse alongside Riverfront Park, the **River Market** (✉ 400 E. Markham St., ☎ 501/375–2552) has blossomed into a lively center of gourmet shops, boutiques, cafés, and ethnic-food stalls, with an outdoor farmers' market spring through late fall. It has become the anchor for a revitalized neighborhood that now has the Museum of Discovery (☞ Exploring Little Rock, *above*), galleries, restaurants, and year-round special events. Galleries, specialty shops, and boutiques lie along winding **Kavanaugh Boulevard** and **Rodney Parham Road.**

THE ARKANSAS OZARKS

The forested mountains and hollows, sparkling waters, and calcite caverns of the Arkansas highlands provide a breathtaking backdrop for gatherings of self-taught folk musicians in town squares, for the display of handicrafts from pioneer days, and for tiny towns barely changed in the last century. Yet, the Ozarks also encompass upscale shopping malls, fine-arts centers, and sophisticated restaurants. The area's rivers offer superb fishing and canoeing; its lakes, boating and water sports. Networks of trails lace the mountains, from easygoing, accessible paths to the rugged, 178-mi-long Ozark Highlands trail. Dozens of scenic byways lead past exquisite vistas. Civil War battlefields at Pea Ridge and Prairie Grove, ecotours exploring natural and human history, railway excursions, antiques, outdoor theater, great golfing, and lively festivals and fairs round out the appeal of this scenic playground.

Visitor Information

Northwest Arkansas Tourism Association (✉ Box 5176, Bella Vista 72714, ☎ 888/398–3444). **Ozark Gateway Tourist Council** (✉ Box 4049, Batesville 72503, ☎ 870/793–9316 or 800/264–0316) handles the eastern Ozarks. **Ozark Mountain Region** (✉ Box 137, Yellville 72687, ☎ 800/544–6867) covers the central Ozarks.

Arriving and Departing

By Car

To reach northwest Arkansas from Little Rock, take I–40 west, and then turn north on I–540. The fastest route to other parts of the Ozarks from Little Rock is U.S. 65 north from I–40 at Conway and then the appropriate highway to your destination. At Harrison, U.S. 62 leads from U.S. 65 to Eureka Springs, Pea Ridge National Military Park, and U.S. 71 at Rogers.

By Plane

American Eagle, Trans World Express, Atlantic Southeast Airline, Northwest Airlink, and US Airways all have scheduled flights into **Northwest Arkansas Airport** (✉ 1 Airport Blvd., Bentonville, ☎ 501/205–1000), west of U.S. 71 Bypass and Bentonville.

Exploring the Arkansas Ozarks

Fayetteville, Springdale, Rogers, and Bentonville—together Arkansas's fastest-growing metropolitan area—feature walking-driving tours of each of their fascinating historic districts. The **Shiloh Museum of Ozark History,** in Springdale (✉ 118 W. Johnson Ave., ☎ 501/750–8165, 🎫 free; closed Sun.), and the **Rogers Historical Museum** (✉ 322 S. 2nd St., Rogers,

☎ 501/621–1154; ✉ free; closed Sun.) lead you through the history and culture of the region. **Headquarters House,** in Fayetteville (✉ 118 E. Dickson St., ☎ 501/521–2970; ✉ $3 for living-history tours of house and historic district; closed Sun., Tues., and Fri.), served as both Union and Confederate headquarters during the Civil War. Bentonville's **Peel Mansion Museum & Gardens** belonged to a pioneer businessman and U.S. Congressman. Its shop is in a restored log cabin. ✉ *400 S. Walton Blvd.,* ☎ *501/273–9664.* ✉ *$3. Closed Sun. and Mon.*

Pea Ridge National Military Park (☎ 501/451–8122; ✉ $2), 10 mi northeast of Rogers on U.S. 62, and **Prairie Grove Battlefield Park** (☎ 501/846–2990; ✉ $2.25, $4 for museum and interpreter-led tour), 10 mi southwest of Fayetteville on U.S. 62, are the sites of decisive Civil War battles. The **University of Arkansas** (☎ 501/575–2000) in Fayetteville, home of the hallowed Razorback teams, has museums and a lively arts calendar. President Bill Clinton and Hillary Rodham Clinton taught law here. Vintage cars on the **Arkansas and Missouri Railroad** in Springdale make daylong round-trips through the Ozarks to Van Buren, and two-hour excursions from Van Buren. ✉ *306 E. Emma St.,* ☎ *501/751–8600 or 800/687–8600.* ✉ *Round-trips $29–$44; Van Buren excursions $17–$25, depending on day of wk and season. Closed Nov.–Mar.*

Eureka Springs, with more than 50 B&Bs and 60 motels and hotels plus cabins and campsites, has greeted visitors since its early days as a Victorian-era spa. Now it's as much a scene for family holidays as for romantic weddings and honeymoons, serving as a base for scenic mountain drives, visits to colorful caverns, and general outdoor activities. The town and its attractions host a packed schedule of music, crafts and other shows, and festivals.

Victorian homes and shops, including fine-arts and crafts galleries that sponsor monthly evening events, line Main and Spring streets as they wind uphill from a narrow valley. The tall, airy **Thorncrown Chapel** (✉ U.S. 62W, ☎ 501/253–7401; ✉ free) takes advantage of its woodland setting. The 33-acre **Eureka Springs Gardens** sprawls up the hillsides from a spring (✉ U.S. 62W, ☎ 501/253–9256; ✉ $6.45; closed Dec.–Feb.). The **Belle of the Ozarks** (✉ Starkey Marina off U.S. 62W, ☎ 501/253–6200 or 800/552–3803; ✉ $12) floats along 60 mi of Beaver Lake shoreline; and vintage steam locomotives of the **Eureka Springs & North Arkansas Railway** (✉ 299 N. Main St., ☎ 501/253–9623; ✉ $8) chug into the Ozarks from a historic depot. Both are closed November–February.

★   The **Ozark Folk Center** (✉ Box 500, Mountain View 72560, ☎ 870/269–3851, ✉ $7.50 each for crafts area and evening show or $13.25 for combination ticket) is a unique state park devoted to the perpetuation and lively demonstration of traditional Ozark Mountain crafts, acoustic music, and dance. The park has a lodge, a gift shop, and the **Iron Skillet Restaurant.** In **Mountain View,** the music continues in informal sessions on the **courthouse square,** surrounded by crafts, antiques, and other shops in old stone buildings.

★   The U.S. Forest Service leads year-round tours of **Blanchard Springs Caverns** (✉ Box 1279, Mountain View 72560, ☎ 870/757–2211; ✉ $9), 15 mi northwest of Mountain View off Arkansas 14, providing the state's premier underground experience.

At **Ozark Ecotours** (✉ Box 513, Jasper 72641, ☎ 870/446–5898; ✉ $50 and up) local guides take small groups on one-day and overnight trips into the rugged Buffalo River landscape to learn about Native American, pioneer, Civil War, and outlaw history and lore in the areas where events actually happened, as well as to explore its bountiful natural history. Some trips involve easygoing hikes; others include canoeing, caving, and horseback riding.

Dining and Lodging

Eureka Springs

$$$-$$$$ ✕ **Chez Charles.** This fine-dining spot in the Grand Hotel presents Amer-
★ ican staples with high style, using imaginative spices and sauces. The luncheon menu is à la carte. Dinner is a five-course menu that changes monthly. Dinner seatings are at 6 and 9 PM, 6 PM only December–March. ⊠ *37 N. Main St.,* ☎ *501/253–9509 or 888/253–1003. Reservations essential at dinner. AE, D, MC, V. Closed Tues. and Wed. Apr.–Dec.; Mon.–Wed. Jan.–Mar.*

$-$$ ✕ **Cottage Inn.** The fresh Mediterranean cuisine at this highly regarded establishment includes salmon and roasted rack of lamb. The wine list is extensive. ⊠ *U.S. 62W,* ☎ *501/253–5282. MC, V. Closed Mon.*

$-$$ ✕ **Ermilio's.** This cozy spot serves creative meals derived from northern and southern Italian family recipes. ⊠ *26 White St.,* ☎ *501/253–8806. Reservations not accepted. MC, V. Closed Thurs. No lunch Sun.–Wed.*

$ ✕ **Center Street South Restaurant & Bar.** Enjoy authentic and innovative Latin American and Caribbean cuisine—from Mexico to Brazil. Try the mango and habanero shrimp or fillet of red snapper *mojo de ajo.* There's live entertainment Friday and Saturday. ⊠ *10 Center St.,* ☎ *501/253–8102. MC, V. Closed Tues. and Wed. Apr.–Oct.; Tues.–Thurs. Nov.–Mar.*

$$-$$$ ▥ **Heartstone Inn and Cottages.** Eureka Springs's largest B&B offers accommodations graced with antiques in both a Victorian home and in two cottages with refrigerators and kitchenettes. Sit back on their shaded decks or gazebo, or try their on-site massage therapy studio. All rooms and cottages are no-smoking. Children are welcome. ⊠ *35 Kingshighway, 72632,* ☎ *501/253–8916 or 800/494–4921. 10 rooms, 2 cottages. Golf privileges. AE, D, MC, V. BP.*

$-$$ ▥ **Basin Park Hotel.** This 1905 hotel is in the center of the town's bustling shopping, dining, and entertainment district. Remodeled and refurbished in 2000, the Basin Park has a billiards room, which features a piano, a bar, and antique game tables. Children are welcome, pets accepted. New Moon Spa privileges are available. ⊠ *12 Spring St., 72632,* ☎ *501/253–7837 or 800/643–4972,* ☒ *501/253–6985. 59 rooms. Restaurant, golf and tennis privileges. AE, D, MC, V. CP.* ✍

Fayetteville

$-$$ ✕ **AQ Chicken House.** Since 1947 AQ has been serving chicken as fresh as it gets. The menu, served at two sites, also has a full range of other entrées. ⊠ *1925 N. College Ave., Fayetteville,* ☎ *501/443–7555; U.S. 71B, Springdale,* ☎ *501/751–4633. AE, D, DC, MC, V.*

$-$$ ▥ **Fayetteville Clarion.** This hotel is near the University of Arkansas and historic districts. ⊠ *1255 S. Shiloh Dr., Fayetteville 72701,* ☎ *501/521–1166 or 800/223–7275,* ☒ *501/521–1204. 197 rooms. Restaurant, indoor pool, exercise room. AE, D, DC, MC, V.*

Johnson

$$-$$$$ ✕ **James at the Mill.** One of Arkansas's finest dining spots, this restau-
★ rant serves seasonal variations of Ozark Plateau cuisine—traditional southern dishes updated with a twist, including game, dry-aged rib-eye steaks, and fresh local produce. ⊠ *3906 Greathouse Springs Rd., Johnson,* ☎ *501/443–1400,* ☒ *501/443–3879. AE, D, DC, MC, V. Closed Sun. No lunch Sat.*

$$ ▥ **Inn at the Mill.** Next to James at the Mill (☞ *above*), this inn in a rural setting is built around a restored 1835 mill and pond. ⊠ *3906 Greathouse Springs Rd., Johnson 72741,* ☎ *501/443–1800 . 48 rooms. Exercise room. AE, D, DC, MC, V. CP.*

Lakeview

$–$$$
★
✕ ⚏ **Gaston's White River Resort.** This lodge draws serious anglers and families with first-class cottages, a marina, fishing guides, an outstanding restaurant serving steak and seafood, and lovely scenery. ✉ *1777 River Rd., Lakeview 72642,* ☎ *870/431–5202,* ⏛ *870/431–5216. 36 rooms, 38 cottages. Restaurant, pool, tennis. MC, V.*

Rogers

$$
✕ **Tale of the Trout.** This country spot, east of Exit 64 on U.S. 71, has raised its own trout for 50 years and also serves steak, quail, and seafood. ✉ *Hwy. 94 (New Hope Rd.), Rogers,* ☎ *501/636–0508. AE, D, DC, MC, V. Closed Sun.*

Silver Hill

$$–$$$
⚏ **Buffalo River Outfitters.** Seven log cabins above the Buffalo National River have furnished kitchens, fireplaces, and barbecue grills. An additional lodge sleeps 10. The extensive array of outdoor activities includes hiking trails; canoe and raft floats; kayaking, fishing, and hunting guide service; mountain biking, horseback riding, and hot-air ballooning. ✉ *Rte. 1, Box 56, U.S. 65 at Silver Hill, St. Joe 72675,* ☎ *501/ 439–2244 or 800/582–2244,* ⏛ *870/439–2211. 10 units. D, MC, V.*

Springdale

$$–$$$
⚏ **Holiday Inn Northwest Arkansas.** Convenient to interstates, this hotel has an eight-story atrium and five-story waterfall along with a sports bar and grill. ✉ *1500 S. 48th St., Springdale 72762,* ☎ *501/751–8300,* ⏛ *501/751–4640. 206 rooms. Restaurant, pool, golf privileges, exercise room. AE, D, DC, MC, V.* ✑

Nightlife and the Arts

Friday's "Northwest Arkansas Weekend" section in the *Arkansas Democrat-Gazette* lists nightlife and arts events.

The **Arts Center of the Ozarks** (✉ 214 S. Main St., ☎ 501/751–5441; ✉ free), in Springdale, has an active schedule of visual and performing arts. Northwest Arkansas's major club and café scene is along Fayetteville's **Dickson Street,** between the University of Arkansas campus and Walton Arts Center. The **Walton Arts Center** in Fayetteville (✉ 495 Dickson St., ☎ 501/443–5600) presents a wide range of fine- and performing-arts events.

WESTERN ARKANSAS

Western Arkansas reaches south from Fort Smith and Van Buren—which preserve the region's wild and woolly frontier heritage as well as its Victorian era—through the ancient forests and rivers of the Ouachita (pronounced *Wash*-i-taw) Mountains. The quartz-rich mountains cradle Hot Springs (nicknamed Spa City), the boyhood home of President Bill Clinton. The five crystal-clear Diamond Lakes also lure vacationers who love water and beautiful scenery. The region's rivers offer whitewater rafting trips and scenic canoeing and fishing, and the Ouachitas are laced with top-notch trail systems and campsites.

Visitor Information

Fort Smith Convention and Visitors Bureau (✉ 2 N. B St., 72901, ☎ 501/783–8888 or 800/637–1477). The **Hot Springs Convention & Visitors Bureau** (✉ mailing: Box K, Hot Springs 71902; walk-in center: 629 Central Ave., ☎ 800/772–2489) provides information for the city and surrounding five-county region.

Arriving and Departing

By Car

The easiest way to arrive and get around is by car. From Little Rock, I–30 and U.S. 70 lead to Hot Springs. I–40 reaches Fort Smith and Van Buren.

By Plane

Lone Star/Aspen Mountain Air flies from Dallas–Fort Worth to the Hot Springs municipal airport, and there is shuttle service (☎ 800/643–1505) between Hot Springs and Little Rock National Airport. **American Eagle, Atlantic Southeast Airlines, Trans World Express,** and **Northwest Airlink** fly into Fort Smith Regional Airport.

Exploring Western Arkansas

Native Americans called today's Hot Springs the Valley of the Vapors. This cluster of 47 thermal springs was first encountered by Spanish explorer Hernando de Soto in 1541. In 1832 the U.S. Congress created the first federal reservation around the springs, and in 1921 they became a national park. From the 1920s to the early 1960s, Hot Springs was a gambling town famed for its therapeutic bathhouses. Get a feel

★ for this opulent era on Bathhouse Row at the **Fordyce Bathhouse,** now the **Hot Springs National Park Visitor Center** (⊠ 369 Central Ave., Box 1860, 71902, ☎ 501/624–3383; ⌨ free). Only a handful of spas providing mineral baths remain, including the old-fashioned **Buckstaff** (⊠ 509 Central Ave., ☎ 501/623–2308; ⌨ $14–$32; closed Sun.), a 1912 National Historic Landmark, and five hotels and health spas.

Hot Springs offers a host of activities and events, including a wax museum; country-music, magic, and comedy shows; a Christian musical drama; and land-and-lake tours on amphibious World War II "ducks." The 400-passenger **Belle of Hot Springs** sails Lake Hamilton daily on sightseeing, lunch, and dinner-dance cruises (⊠ 5200 Central Ave./Ark. 7S, ☎ 501/525–4438; ⌨ $9.99 for excursion only, $18.99–$25.99 for dinner cruise). At the restored headquarters of **Mountain Valley Spring Company** (⊠ 150 Central Ave., ☎ 501/623–6671; ⌨ free; closed

☾ Sun.) you can try samples of natural spring water. The **Mid-America Science Museum** explores science and nature in interactive exhibits. ⊠ *500 Mid-America Blvd., off U.S. 270W, ☎ 501/767–3461 or 800/632–0583. ⌨ $6. Closed Mon.*

☾ There's a great view from the top of the 216-ft **Hot Springs Mountain Tower** (⊠ Hot Springs Mountain Dr. off Fountain St., ☎ 501/623–6035; ⌨ $4). **President Bill Clinton's boyhood homes,** at 1011 Park Avenue and 213 Scully Street—along with his schools, church, and favorite teenage hangouts—are detailed in a brochure and map available at the Hot Springs Convention & Visitors Bureau (☞ Visitor Information, *above*).

Dig for crystals or browse among those already cleaned and polished at **Coleman's Crystal Mine & Rock Shop** (☎ 501/984–5328; ⌨ $10 to dig), in Jessieville, 14 mi north of Hot Springs on Arkansas 7.

Fort Smith was established in 1817 on the Indian frontier. The Fort Smith visitor center is in **Miss Laura's** (⊠ 2 N. B St., ☎ 501/783–8888 or 800/637–1477), a stylishly decorated former brothel on the National Register of Historic Places. From there a trolley (⌨ $1) carries visitors

☾ to museums, historic homes, and other sights. The **Fort Smith National Historic Site** (⊠ 3rd St. and Rogers Ave., ☎ 501/783–3961; ⌨ $2) includes the remains of two successive frontier forts and a reproduction of Hanging Judge Isaac Parker's 1870s gallows—big enough to hang 12

☾ outlaws at once. The **Fort Smith Museum of History** traces regional history (⊠ 320 Rogers Ave., ☎ 501/783–7841; ⌨ $3; closed Mon.). The

Hot Springs and the Ozarks

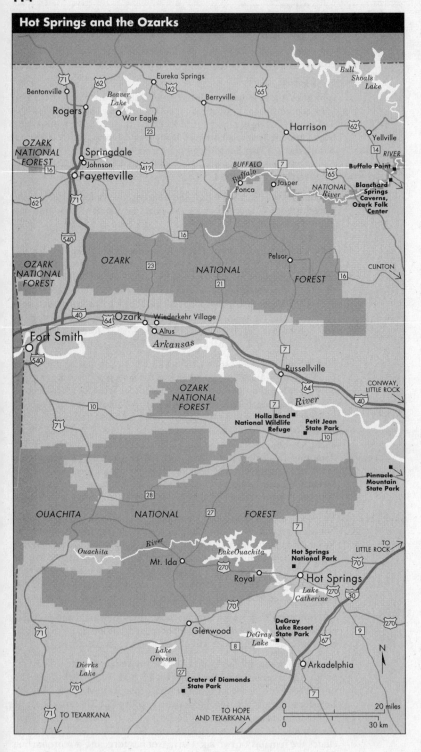

⏱ **Fort Smith Trolley Museum** (⊠ 100 S. 4th St., ☎ 501/783–0205; 🎫 free; closed Mon.) contains a 1926 streetcar and other transportation memorabilia. The **Patent Model Museum** (⊠ 400 N. 8th St., ☎ 501/782–9014; 🎫 free; closed weekends) demonstrates American inventiveness. The **Darby House** (⊠ 311 N. 8th St., ☎ 501/782–3388; 🎫 free; closed Mon. and Tues.) was the boyhood home of General William O. Darby, who organized and commanded Darby's Rangers in World War II.

The **Clayton House,** built in the 1850s and extensively amended after 1870, features hand-carved woodwork. Many of its period furnishings belonged to the Clayton family. ⊠ *514 N. 6th St.,* ☎ *501/783–3000.* 🎫 *$2. Closed Mon. and Tues.*

Van Buren, just north of Fort Smith over the Arkansas River, was also settled in the early 1800s as a riverboat stop and prospered as a trade and supply center. Van Buren's century-old **Main Street,** which runs six blocks from the Old Frisco Depot to the county courthouse, is an architectural and historic delight, with shops filled with antiques and country crafts, as well as cafés, restaurants, and a theater. From the foot of Main the ***Frontier Belle*** (⊠ Box 1241, 72956, ☎ 501/471–5441; 🎫 excursion $7, luncheon cruise $12) cruises the Arkansas River April–October.

Dining and Lodging

Fort Smith

$–$$$ ✕ **Folie à Deux.** This fine restaurant has won awards for its Continental dishes and for its extensive wine list. ⊠ *2909 Old Greenwood Rd.,* ☎ *501/648–0041. AE, D, DC, MC, V. Closed Sun.*

$–$$ ✕ **Emmy's.** Hearty German cuisine is served in this old-line restaurant. ⊠ *602 N. 16th St.,* ☎ *501/783–0012. AE, D, DC, MC, V. Closed Sun. and Mon.*

$$ 🏨 **Holiday Inn Fort Smith Civic Center.** Many historic sites are within walking distance, as is the convention center. ⊠ *700 Rogers Ave., 72901,* ☎ *501/783–1000,* 🆀 *501/783–0312. 255 rooms. Restaurant, pool, exercise room. AE, D, DC, MC, V.* ⏱

$–$$ 🏨 **Hampton Inn.** This motel is convenient to I–540, restaurants, and shopping. ⊠ *6201-D Rogers Ave., 72901,* ☎ *501/452–2000,* 🆀 *501/ 452–6668. 143 rooms. Pool, tennis, exercise room. AE, D, DC, MC, V. CP.* ⏱

Hot Springs

$–$$$$ ✕ **Hamilton House.** Housed in an historic Mediterranean-style villa, this award-winning restaurant overlooks Lake Hamilton and has a patio and fountain. It serves steak, prime rib, quail, and fresh seafood and has an extensive wine list. ⊠ *130 Van Lyell Terr.,* ☎ *501/525–2727. AE, D, DC, MC, V. Closed most Sun.*

$ ✕ **McClard's.** Bill Clinton loved this old-fashioned barbecue spot as a teenager—and for good cause. ⊠ *505 Albert Pike,* ☎ *501/624–9586. No credit cards. Closed Sun. and Mon.; mid-Dec.–mid-Jan.; 1 wk in July.*

$$ 🏨 **Arlington.** This historic spa hotel is a slightly faded grande dame featuring an old-fashioned bathhouse-spa and a beautiful setting in Hot Springs's historic district. ⊠ *239 Central Ave., 71901,* ☎ *501/623– 7771 or 800/643–1502,* 🆀 *501/623–2243. 481 rooms. 2 restaurants, 2 pools, hot springs, outdoor hot tub, massage, mineral baths, sauna, spa, steam room, 2 18-hole golf courses, 1 9-hole course, tennis courts, exercise room. AE, D, DC, MC, V.*

$$ 🏨 **Lake Hamilton Resort.** Rooms in this luxurious all-suite resort have balconies and lake views. ⊠ *2803 Albert Pike, 71913,* ☎ *501/767– 5511 or 800/426–3184,* 🆀 *501/767–8576. 104 suites. Restaurant, 2 pools, tennis. AE, D, DC, MC, V. Closed Christmas week.* ⏱

Outdoor Activities and Sports

For information on trails, scenic drives, and campsites, contact **Ouachita National Forest** (⊠ USFS, Box 1270, Hot Springs 71902, ☎ 501/321–5202). Nearby is the **DeGray Lake Resort State Park** (⊠ Rte. 3, Box 490, Bismarck 71929–8194, ☎ 501/865–2801 or 800/737–8355), with a lodge, golf course, marina, campsites, horseback riding, tennis, biking, and interpretive activities such as eagle watches.

Spectator Sports

Thoroughbred racing: Hot Springs's **Oaklawn Jockey Club** (⊠ 2705 Central Ave., ☎ 800/625–5296; ⊡ live racing $2, simulcasts $1) has racing from late January through mid-April and simulcasts the rest of year.

Shopping

Dozens of artists and gallery owners have transformed Hot Springs's Victorian downtown into a vibrant, cosmopolitan arts district. There's a self-guided **gallery walk** the first Friday of each month. Several **malls** lie south of downtown on Arkansas 7/Central Avenue.

ELSEWHERE IN ARKANSAS

Texarkana

Visitor Information

Texarkana Chamber of Commerce (⊠ Box 1468, Texarkana, TX 75504, ☎ 903/792–7191).

Arriving and Departing

From Little Rock take I–30 to Texarkana, which straddles the Arkansas-Texas border.

What to See and Do

The **Post Office** and Photographer's Island (⊠ 500 State Line Ave.) are half in Arkansas, half in Texas. Winnings from a poker game built the 1885 **Ace of Clubs House** (⊠ 5th and Pine Sts., ☎ 903/793–4831; ⊡ $5; closed Sun. and Mon.), designed, fittingly, in the shape of a playing card. The **Texarkana Historical Museum** (⊠ 219 State Line Ave., ☎ 903/793–4831; ⊡ $2; closed Sun. and Mon.) is in the city's oldest brick building. Opened in 1924, the elaborate **Perot Theater** (⊠ 219 Main St., ☎ 903/792–4992) was restored thanks to a major donation by native son and presidential hopeful H. Ross Perot. Across the street, a mural pays tribute to another native son, ragtime composer Scott Joplin.

Dining and Lodging

$–$$$ ✕ **Cattleman's Steak House.** Its specialty of prime rib, plus T-bones, rib eyes, and other choice cuts, will make you think you're deep in the heart of Texas. The menu also includes shrimp, fish, and sandwiches. ⊠ *4018 N. State Line Ave.*, ☎ *870/774–4481. AE, D, MC, V. Closed Sun.*

$–$$$ ✕ **Lake Country.** Market-fresh Continental specialties with Mediterranean touches are served in a historic building. The wine list is extensive. ⊠ *217 Walnut*, ☎ *870/773–1550. AE, D, MC, V. Closed Sun. and Mon.*

$–$$ 🏨 **Four Points Hotel.** This conveniently located and service-oriented hotel has a concierge floor with business services. Airport-shuttle service is available. ⊠ *5301 N. State Line Ave., 75503*, ☎ *903/792–3222*, FAX *903/793–3930. 147 rooms. Restaurant, pool, exercise room. AE, D, DC, MC, V. CP.*

$ 🏨 **Hampton Inn.** Convenient to the interstate as well as the downtown historic district, this hotel offers guests free access to a nearby health club. ⊠ *300 N. State Line Ave., at I–30, 71854*, ☎ *870/774–4444*, FAX *870/779–1303. 60 rooms. Pool. AE, D, DC, MC, V. CP.* ✍

Hope

Visitor Information

The **Hope Visitor Center** (✉ S. Main and Division Sts., ☎ 870/722–2580) is in the restored 1912 railroad depot; it provides a map showing Clinton sites.

Arriving and Departing

I–30 leads from Little Rock to Hope.

What to See and Do

Hope is Arkansas's watermelon capital, growing some of the world's largest and tastiest melons. It's also the birthplace of President Bill Clinton, who lived here until he was six. The **Clinton Center,** where the President was born and lived with his grandparents until age four, is now a restored home and gardens open to the public. ✉ *117 S. Hervey St., at 2nd St.,* ☎ *870/777–4455.* ✈ *$5 (purchase tickets at Clinton Center on 2nd St.). Closed Mon.; also Sun. in winter.*

★ Near Hope is **Old Washington Historic State Park** (✉ Box 98, Washington, ☎ 870/983–2684). Established in 1824 on the Southwest Trail, this was the Confederate state capital after Little Rock's capture. Some 40 buildings remain from the 1820s–70s. Tours and museum admissions range from $2.75 to $12. **Crater of Diamonds State Park** (✉ Rte. 1, Box 364, Murfreesboro, ☎ 870/285–3113; ✈ $4.50), near Murfreesboro, is North America's only public diamond mine where you can keep what you find.

Dining and Lodging

$–$$ ✕ **Little B's.** This casual steak house serves all the usual cuts as well as Mexican dishes. ✉ *2406 N. Hervey St. (Hwy. 4),* ☎ *870/777–3377. AE, D, MC, V.*

$ ✕ **Williams Tavern.** This tavern was built in 1832 on a plantation northeast of town. Before it was moved to its present location in Old Washington Historic State Park, it served as a residence, post office, and stagecoach stop. It serves a simple, southern-style lunch, and dinner for special events. ✉ *Morrison and Carroll Sts., Washington,* ☎ *870/ 983–2890. AE, D, MC, V.*

$ 🏨 **Best Western of Hope.** This chain property is convenient to interstates and Clinton sites. ✉ *I–30 and Hwy. 4 (Box 6611), 71801,* ☎ *870/777–9222,* ✉AX *870/777–9077. 74 rooms. Restaurant, pool. AE, D, DC, MC, V.* ✎

$ 🏨 **Holiday Inn Express.** This hotel is convenient to highways and Clinton sites. Guests have privileges at a nearby health club. ✉ *2600 N. Hervey St., 71801,* ☎ *870/722–6262,* ✉AX *870/722–1922. 61 rooms. Pool. AE, D, DC, MC, V. CP.* ✎

Helena

Visitor Information

Helena Tourism Commission (✉ 226 Perry St., 72342, ☎ 870/338–9831).

Arriving and Departing

From Little Rock take I–40, turning south on U.S. 49.

What to See and Do

One of the oldest Mississippi River settlements and a Civil War battle site, Helena is home to the **Delta Cultural Center** (✉ 95 Missouri St. and 141 Cherry St., ☎ 870/338–4350; ✈ free), which documents the roots of the Delta blues, pioneer days, and the river life described by Mark Twain. Helena shows off numerous antebellum and postwar mansions, several of which are now B&Bs. The 1896 **Pillow-Thompson House** is one of the South's finest examples of Queen Anne architecture (✉ 718 Perry St., ☎ 870/338–8535; ✈ Free; closed Mon.).

Each October Helena hosts the **King Biscuit Blues Festival** (✉ Box 247, 72342, ☎ 870/338–9144), which has gained international acclaim.

Dining and Lodging

$ ✕ **Pasquale's Tamales.** This casual eatery, in a historic building, serves up dynamite tamales, chili with trimmings, New Orleans muffulettas, roast beef poboys, and meatball sandwiches among other dishes. It's open 9 AM–5 PM Monday–Thursday and serves until 9 PM Friday. ✉ *201 Missouri St.,* ☎ *870/338–6722 or 800/390–3992. MC, V. Closed weekends.*

$–$$ 🏨 **Edwardian Inn.** Elegantly restored and decorated in 1912 Colonial Revival style, this bed-and-breakfast has many rooms with 14-ft ceilings and fireplaces; all have VCRs. You'll also find a common room, a garden room, decks, and a wide front porch. Children are welcome and guests may use the laundry facilities. ✉ *317 Biscoe St., 72342,* ☎ *870/338–9155. 12 rooms. AE, D, DC, MC, V. BP.*

$ 🏨 **Delta Inn.** Conveniently located on the main highway into West Helena/Helena, this simple motel serves both business travelers and families. ✉ *1207 Hwy. 49N, 72390,* ☎ *870/572–7915 or 877/748–8802,* FAX *870/572–3757. 96 rooms. Pool. AE, D, DC, MC, V. CP.*

CALIFORNIA

Capital	Sacramento
Population	34,036,000
Motto	Eureka
State Bird	Valley quail
State Flower	Golden poppy
Postal Abbreviation	CA

Statewide Visitor Information

California Division of Tourism (⊠ 801 K St., Suite 1600, Sacramento 95814, ☎ 916/322–2881 or 800/862–2543, FAX 916/322–3402 or 916/322–0501).

Scenic Drives

The land- and seascapes along the nearly 400 mi of coastline between San Francisco Bay and the Oregon border are beautiful and rugged; switchbacked **Highway 1** is punctuated by groves of giant redwood trees, tiny coastal towns, and secluded coves and beaches. **U.S. 395** north from San Bernardino rises in elevation gradually from the Mojave Desert to the Sierra foothills and on past the east entrance to Yosemite National Park. **Highway 49** winds 325 mi through northern California's historic Gold Country.

National and State Parks

National Parks

California has eight national parks: Death Valley, Joshua Tree, Lassen Volcanic, Redwood, Sequoia, Kings Canyon, Yosemite, and the Channel Islands (☞ *below*). National monuments include Cabrillo, in San Diego, and Muir Woods, north of San Francisco. For information contact the western regional office of the **National Park Service** (⊠ Fort Mason Center, Bldg. 201, San Francisco 94123, ☎ 415/556–0560).

State Parks

The **California State Park System** (⊠ Dept. of Parks and Recreation, Box 942896, Sacramento 94296, ☎ 916/653–6995) includes more than 200 sites; many are recreational and scenic, others historic or scientific. In an effort to make the park system more accessible for everyone, the state recently reduced the fees to state parks by about 50%. Camping fees that were $12 or more will be $12, and those less than $12 will stay the same. All weekend, premium, and seasonal rates as well as boating fees were eliminated. In addition, state museums and historical site admissions were also reduced by half.

SAN FRANCISCO

San Francisco's approximately 800,000 residents nest on a 46½-square-mi tip of land between San Francisco Bay and the Pacific Ocean. Experiencing San Francisco means visiting its neighborhoods: the eclectic Mission District, gay-friendly Castro, countercultural Haight Street, serene Pacific Heights, bustling Chinatown, and still-bohemian North Beach.

Visitor Information

San Francisco Convention and Visitors Bureau (⊠ Box 429097, San Francisco 94142, ☎ 415/974–6900); contact the bureau by phone or

visit its Web site for an information kit or pick one up at the lower
level of Hallidie Plaza, at the corner of Market and Powell streets.

Arriving and Departing

By Bus
Greyhound (☎ 800/231–2222) serves San Francisco's **Transbay Terminal** (✉ 1st and Mission Sts.).

By Car
I–80 comes into San Francisco from the east, crossing the Bay Bridge
from Oakland. U.S. 101 runs north–south through the city and across
the Golden Gate Bridge.

By Plane
San Francisco International Airport (SFO; ☎ 800/736–2008), 30 minutes south of the city off U.S. 101, is served by most major airlines.
Several domestic airlines serve **Oakland Airport** (☎ 510/577–4000),
across the bay. **SuperShuttle** (☎ 415/558–8500) will take you from SFO
to anywhere within the city limits ($12–$15). **Taxis** between downtown
and either airport take 20–30 minutes and cost about $35.

By Train
Amtrak (☎ 800/872–7245) trains stop in **Oakland** (✉ Jack London
Sq., 245 2nd St.) and **Emeryville** (✉ 5885 Landregan St.); shuttle
buses connect the Emeryville station and San Francisco's Ferry Building, on the Embarcadero. **CalTrain** (✉ 4th and Townsend Sts., ☎ 800/
660–4287) connects the city with the region to the south.

Getting Around San Francisco

By Car
Watch out for one-way streets, curb your wheels when parking on hills,
and check street signs for parking restrictions. Public parking garages
(look for the city seal) tend to be less expensive than private lots.
Hotel garages charge as much as $32 per day. Except at a few marked
intersections, a right turn at a red light is legal, as is a left turn on red
at two intersecting one-way streets.

By Public Transportation
Most of the light-rail and bus lines of the Municipal Railway System,
called **Muni** (☎ 415/673–6864), operate continuously; standard fare
is $1, and exact change (coins or a dollar bill) is required. If you'll be
changing buses, get a transfer (good for 90 minutes) when you board.
Three **cable car** lines crisscross downtown; information and tickets ($2)
are available on board. Multiday tourist passes can be obtained at the
lower level of Hallidie Plaza, at Powell and Market streets. **BART** (Bay
Area Rapid Transit; ☎ 650/992–2278) trains service the East Bay and
beyond to Daly City, Concord, Dublin, and Richmond; wall maps list
destinations and fares.

By Taxi
Rates are high—$2.50 to get in and about a $1.80 a mile after that.
It's difficult to hail a cab in most neighborhoods. Call **Yellow Cab Co.**
(☎ 415/626–2345), but expect long waits during peak periods. When
possible, book in advance.

Orientation Tours

Gray Line (✉ 350 8th St., ☎ 415/558–9400 or 800/826–0202) offers
tours on buses and double-deckers ranging in price from $15 to $48.
The **Great Pacific Tour** (✉ 518 Octavia St., ☎ 415/626–4499) lasts 3½

hours at a cost of $32; multilingual guides are available, and the company will pick you up at most downtown hotels.

Walking Tours

The **Chinese Culture Center** (☎ 415/986–1822) offers a Heritage Walk and a Culinary Walk through Chinatown. Elaine Sosa's **Javawalk** (☎ 415/673–9255) visits some of the city's cafés.

Exploring San Francisco

Touring San Francisco is best done on foot—although the hills are a challenge. Dependable walking shoes are essential. You'll need a jacket for the dramatic temperature swings, especially in summer, when fog rolls in during the afternoon.

Union Square

The landmark of Union Square is the **Westin St. Francis Hotel** (✉ 335 Powell St., ☎ 415/397–7000). The hotel's Art Deco **Compass Rose** lounge is a stylish place to sip afternoon tea.

Boutiques and sidewalk cafés line two-block **Maiden Lane,** across Union Square from the St. Francis. The building that holds **Folk Art International/Boretti Amber/Xanadu** (✉ 140 Maiden La., ☎ 415/392–9999) galleries is the only Frank Lloyd Wright building in the city. It's said to have been the architect's model for the Guggenheim Museum in New York City.

Chinatown

The dragon-crowned **Chinatown Gate** (✉ Bush St. and Grant Ave.) is the main entrance to colorful, fragrant Chinatown. Among the many interesting architectural examples here is the **Chinese Six Companies** building (✉ 843 Stockton St.). The **Old Chinese Telephone Exchange** (✉ 743 Washington St.), a three-tier pagoda that's now the Bank of Canton, was built just after the 1906 earthquake. To learn about the area's history, visit the **Chinese Culture Center** (✉ Holiday Inn, 750 Kearny St., 3rd floor, ☎ 415/986–1822; ⌨ free), which is closed on Monday.

Nob Hill

Nob Hill, north of Union Square, is home to some of the city's finest hotels. The 1906 earthquake destroyed the mansions of railroad barons and gold- and silver-rush millionaires, with the exception of the shell of James Flood's brownstone, now the **Pacific Union Club** (✉ 1000 California St.). The Episcopal **Grace Cathedral** (✉ 1100 California St.) has bronze doors cast from Ghiberti's *Gates of Paradise* in Florence. The **Mark Hopkins Inter-Continental Hotel** (✉ 1 Nob Hill, ☎ 415/392–3434) is known for the view from its **Top of the Mark** lounge.

Civic Center

City Hall (✉ Polk St. between Grove and McAllister Sts.), a granite-and-marble masterpiece, faces **Civic Center Plaza**, which has a lawn, walkways, and flower beds. Many transients frequent the plaza, and caution is advised after dark. City Hall, which positively gleams now, reopened in 1999 to general acclaim after a long renovation. The **Performing Arts Center** complex, on Van Ness Avenue between McAllister and Hayes streets, includes the **War Memorial Opera House** and the **Louise M. Davies Symphony Hall.**

In the Western Addition, a neighborhood due west of the Civic Center area, is the much-photographed row of six identical Victorian houses along **Steiner Street,** at the east end of Alamo Square. If you're walking, the safest route is up Fulton Street to Steiner Street. Avoid the area at night.

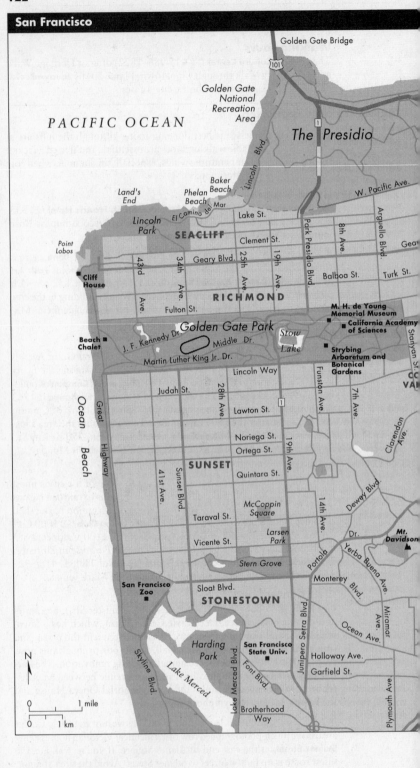

Golden Gate Bridge

101

Golden Gate
National
Recreation
Area

The Presidio

PACIFIC OCEAN

1

W. Pacific Ave.

Baker
Beach

Phelan
Beach

Land's
End

El Camino del Mar

Lake St.

Lincoln
Park

SEACLIFF

Clement St.

Park Presidio Blvd.

8th Ave.

Arguello Blvd.

Gea

Point
Lobos

Geary Blvd.

25th Ave.

19th Ave.

Balboa St.

Turk St.

43rd Ave.

34th Ave.

Cliff
House

RICHMOND

Fulton St.

M. H. de Young
Memorial Museum

California Academy
of Sciences

Beach
Chalet

J. F. Kennedy Dr.

Golden Gate Park

Middle Dr.

Stow
Lake

Strybing
Arboretum and
Botanical
Gardens

Stanyan St.

Martin Luther King Jr. Dr.

Lincoln Way

Funston Ave.

7th Ave.

CO
VAL

Judah St.

28th Ave.

1

Lawton St.

Noriega St.

Ortega St.

19th Ave.

Clarendon Ave.

SUNSET

Quintara St.

14th Ave.

Dewey Blvd.

41st Ave.

Sunset Blvd.

McCoppin
Square

Taraval St.

Larsen
Park

Vicente St.

Dr.

Mt.
Davidson

Stern Grove

Portola

Yerba Buena Ave.

San Francisco
Zoo

Sloat Blvd.

Monterey

Blvd.

Miramar Ave.

STONESTOWN

Ocean Ave.

Junipero Serra Blvd.

Ocean Beach

Great Highway

N

Harding
Park

San Francisco
State Univ.

Holloway Ave.

Garfield St.

Skyline Blvd.

Lake Merced

Lake Merced Blvd.

Font Blvd.

Plymouth Ave.

0   1 mile

0   1 km

Brotherhood
Way

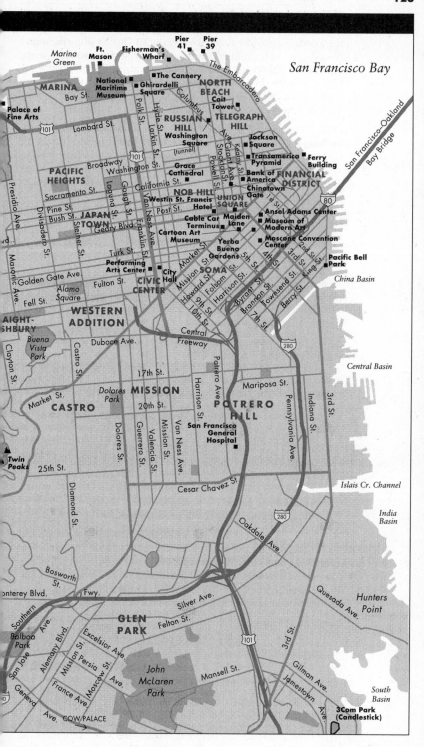

San Francisco Bay

Marina
Green

Ft.
Mason

Fisherman's
Wharf

Pier
41

Pier
39

The Embarcadero

MARINA

National
Maritime
Museum

Ghirardelli
Square

The Cannery

**NORTH
BEACH**

Coit
Tower

San Francisco–Oakland
Bay Bridge

Bay St.

Columbus

**Palace of
Fine Arts**

Lombard St.

Polk St.

Hyde St.

Larkin St.

**RUSSIAN
HILL**

Washington
Square

**TELEGRAPH
HILL**

Grant Ave.

Kearny St.

Jackson
Square

Transamerica
Pyramid

Ferry
Building

**PACIFIC
HEIGHTS**

Broadway

Washington St.

Stockton St.

Powell St.

(tunnel)

Grace
Cathedral

NOB HILL

Bank of
America

Chinatown
Gate

**FINANCIAL
DISTRICT**

Sacramento St.

California St.

Pine St.

Laguna St.

Gough St.

Van Ness Ave.

Franklin St.

Bush St.

**JAPAN
TOWN**

Geary Blvd.

Post St.

Westin St. Francis
Hotel

**UNION
SQUARE**

Ansel Adams Center

Museum of
Modern Art

Cable Car
Terminus

Maiden
Lane

Presidio Ave.

Divisadero St.

Steiner St.

Cartoon Art
Museum

Moscone Convention
Center

Pacific Bell
Park

Turk St.

Yerba
Buena
Gardens

5th St.

4th St.

3rd St.

King St.

China Basin

Masonic Ave.

Golden Gate Ave.

Performing
Arts Center

City
Hall

SOMA

Mission St.

Howard St.

Folsom St.

Harrison St.

Bryant St.

Brannan St.

Townsend St.

Berry St.

Pacific Bell
Park

Fulton St.

**CIVIC
CENTER**

9th St.

10th St.

7th St.

Fell St.

Alamo
Square

**HAIGHT–
ASHBURY**

**WESTERN
ADDITION**

Duboce Ave.

Central
Freeway

Buena
Vista
Park

Clayton St.

Castro St.

17th St.

MISSION

Potrero Ave.

Harrison St.

Mariposa St.

**POTRERO
HILL**

Pennsylvania Ave.

Indiana St.

3rd St.

Central Basin

Market St.

CASTRO

Dolores
Park

20th St.

Van Ness Ave.

Mission St.

Valencia St.

Guerrero St.

Dolores St.

San Francisco
General
Hospital

India
Basin

**Twin
Peaks**

25th St.

Diamond St.

Cesar Chavez St.

Islais Cr. Channel

280

Oakdale Ave.

Bosworth
St.

Monterey Blvd.

Fwy.

Silver Ave.

Felton St.

Quesada Ave.

**Hunters
Point**

Southern

Balboa
Park

San Jose Ave.

Alemany Blvd.

Mission St.

Persia St.

Moscow St.

Excelsior Ave.

France Ave.

**GLEN
PARK**

John
McLaren
Park

Mansell St.

Gilman Ave.

Jamestown Ave.

South
Basin

Geneva Ave.

Ave.

COW PALACE

101

3rd St.

**3Com Park
(Candlestick)**

The Financial District and the Barbary Coast

Bounded by the Union Square area, Telegraph Hill, Market Street, and the Embarcadero, San Francisco's Financial District is distinguished from the rest of town by its steel-and-glass high-rises and older, more decorative architectural monuments to commerce. The city's signature high-rise is the 853-ft **Transamerica Pyramid** (⊠ Clay and Montgomery Sts.). Dominating the Financial District skyline is the 52-story **Bank of America** (⊠ California and Kearny Sts.).

Other notable structures in the Financial District include the **Pacific Stock Exchange** (⊠ 301 Pine St.). The ceiling and entry are black marble in the **Stock Exchange Tower** (⊠ 155 Sansome St.), an Art Deco gem. **Jackson Square** is at the heart of what used to be called the Barbary Coast, a late-19th-century haven for brawling and boozing. The brick buildings and narrow alleys in the area bordered by Pacific Avenue and Washington, Sansome, and Montgomery streets recall the romance and rowdiness of early San Francisco.

The Embarcadero and South of Market (SoMa)

The beacon of the port area is the **Ferry Building,** at the foot of Market Street on the Embarcadero. The clock tower is 230 ft high and was modeled after the campanile of Seville's cathedral. A **waterfront promenade** that extends from the piers north of the Ferry Building to the San Francisco–Oakland Bay Bridge is great for watching sailboats on the bay or enjoying a picnic.

Across the Embarcadero from the Ferry Building, the **Hyatt Regency Hotel** (⊠ 5 Embarcadero, ☎ 415/788–1234) is noted for its lobby and 17-story hanging garden. On the waterfront side of the Hyatt Regency is **Justin Herman Plaza,** often the site of arts-and-crafts shows and political rallies.

★ The **Center for the Arts at Yerba Buena Gardens** (⊠ 701 Mission St., ☎ 415/978–2787; ☜ $5), in the SoMa (South of Market Street) area, which presents dance, music, performance, theater, visual arts, film, and video, is closed on Monday. The **San Francisco Museum of Modern Art** (⊠ 151 3rd St., ☎ 415/357–4000; ☜ $9), which is closed on Wednesday, has a fine permanent collection.

The **Ansel Adams Center** (⊠ 655 Mission St., ☎ 415/495–7000; ☜ $5) exhibits photography. The **Cartoon Art Museum** (⊠ 814 Mission St., Suite 200, ☎ 415/227–8666; ☜ $5), which is closed on Monday, is a worthwhile stop.

North Beach and Telegraph Hill

★ The streets of **North Beach** are packed with Italian delicatessens and bakeries, coffeehouses, and, increasingly, Chinese markets. Grant and Columbus avenues contain intriguing vintage clothing and other shops.

Telegraph Hill rises to the east of North Beach. From Filbert Street above Grant Avenue, the Greenwich Stairs climb to **Coit Tower,** a monument to the city's volunteer firemen. Inside are the works of 25 muralists. From the top there's a panoramic view of the bay, bridges, and islands.

The Northern Waterfront and Fisherman's Wharf

Fisherman's Wharf and the waterfront are at the end of the Powell-Hyde cable car line from Union Square. The **National Maritime Museum** (⊠ Polk St. at Beach St., ☎ 415/556–3002; ☜ donation suggested) and Ghirardelli Square are west of the Hyde Street cable car turnaround; Fisherman's Wharf and Pier 39 are east of it. The historic vessels at the **Hyde Street Pier** (⊠ Hyde St. at Jefferson St., ☎ 415/556–3002; ☜ $5) are a delight to explore. **Bay cruises** leave from Piers 39, 41, and 43½ (☎ 415/705–5555 for Blue and Gold ferries, 415/447–0591 or 800/229–2784 for Red and White line).

The renovated factory buildings of **Ghirardelli Square** (⊠ 900 N. Point St., between Polk and Larkin Sts.) are filled with shops, restaurants, and galleries. East of the Hyde Street Pier is the **Cannery** (⊠ 2801 Leavenworth St. at Beach St.), a former fruit and vegetable cannery that houses shops, restaurants, and the **Museum of the City of San Francisco** (☎ 415/928–0289; ☒ free).

★ **Lombard Street,** better known as "the crookedest street in the world," is south of the waterfront area between Hyde and Leavenworth streets.

The shopping and entertainment options at the popular **Pier 39** include **Underwater World at Pier 39,** which surveys Bay Area marine life. Above ground are a carousel, food stalls, and some noisy sea lions that bask on the pier's north side.

To the west of the waterfront area, at the edge of the Marina District, is the **Palace of Fine Arts** (⊠ Baker and Beach Sts.), with massive columns, an imposing rotunda, and a swan-filled lagoon. Built for the 1915 Panama-Pacific International Exposition, the palace is a cherished
★ ℭ San Francisco landmark. The **Exploratorium** (⊠ Palace of Fine Arts, ☎ 415/561–0360, ☒ $9) contains imaginative interactive exhibits.

To reach the **Golden Gate Bridge,** walk along the bay from the Marina District or take Muni Bus 28 to the toll plaza. Conditions are sometimes gusty and misty, but a walk across the nearly 2-mi-long bridge offers unparalleled views of the skyline, the bay, the Marin Headlands, and the Pacific Ocean.

Golden Gate Park and the Western Shore

★ **Golden Gate Park,** in the northwestern part of town, is ideal for strolling. On Sunday many of its streets are closed to car traffic. Several museums are in the park's eastern section. The strengths of the **M. H. de Young Memorial Museum** (☎ 415/863–3330; ☒ $7, good also for Asian Art Museum) include its collection of American art. Adjoining the de Young is the **Asian Art Museum** (☎ 415/668–8921; ☒ $7, good also for de Young Museum). The Asian and de Young are closed on Monday. Inside the **California Academy of Sciences** (☎ 415/750–7145; ☒ $8.50), a fine natural history museum, are the Steinhart Aquarium and the Morrison Planetarium. The **Strybing Arboretum and Botanical Gardens** (⊠ 9th Ave. at Lincoln Way, ☎ 415/661–1316; ☒ free) shelters Californian, Australian, Mediterranean, and South African plants.

The **Beach Chalet,** at the park's west end, contains a visitor center and a brewpub restaurant with views of Ocean Beach. At the north end of Ocean Beach is the **Cliff House** (⊠ 1090 Point Lobos Ave., ☎ 415/386–3330),
ℭ a restaurant where you can dine to the sound of crashing surf. The **San Francisco Zoo** (⊠ Sloat Blvd. at 45th Ave., ☎ 415/753–7080; ☒ $9), at the south end of Ocean Beach, has a petting corral for children.

Dining

$$$–$$$$ ✕ **Hawthorne Lane.** On a quiet alley a block or so from the Museum
★ of Modern Art, patrons in the somewhat formal, light-flooded dining room find contemporary fare all turned out with Mediterranean and Asian touches. ⊠ *22 Hawthorne St. (SoMa),* ☎ *415/777–9779. Reservations essential. D, DC, MC, V. No lunch weekends.*

$$$–$$$$ ✕ **Jardinière.** This is *the* place to dine before a performance at the nearby
★ Opera House and Symphony Hall. The sophisticated interior, with its eye-catching oval atrium, plays host to a contemporary menu with mem-

orable first courses of sweetbreads, duck confit, and foie gras. A three-course "staccato menu" puts music-loving diners in their orchestra seats before the curtain goes up. ⊠ *300 Grove St. (Civic Center),* ☎ *415/861–5555. Reservations essential. AE, DC, MC, V. No lunch.*

$$–$$$ ✕ **B44.** With its spare, modern decor and open kitchen, B44 draws lo-
★ cals who love the menu of authentic Catalan tapas and paellas. ⊠ *44 Belden Pl. (downtown),* ☎ *415/986–6287. AE, MC, V. Closed Sun. No lunch Sat.*

$$–$$$ ✕ **Delfina.** This clean, modern, and very popular spot attracts a loyal
★ crowd with chef-owner Craig Stoll's simple yet exquisite Italian fare. ⊠ *3621 18th St. (Mission),* ☎ *415/552–4055. MC, V. No lunch.*

$$–$$$ ✕ **Rose Pistola.** Chef-owner Reed Hearon celebrates North Beach's Lig-
★ uran roots with a wide assortment of small antipasti plates, such as roasted peppers and house-cured fish, in addition to pizzas from a wood-burning oven and cioppino, the classic San Francisco Italian seafood stew. ⊠ *532 Columbus Ave. (North Beach),* ☎ *415/399–0499. Reservations essential. AE, MC, V.*

$$–$$$ ✕ **Scala's Bistro.** Smart leather-and-wood booths, an extravagant mural along one wall, and an appealing menu of Italian plates make this one of downtown's most attractive destinations. ⊠ *432 Powell St. (Union Sq.),* ☎ *415/395–8555. AE, D, DC, MC, V.*

$–$$ ✕ **Helmand.** Authentic Afghani cooking, elegant surroundings, and amazingly low prices are Helmand hallmarks. Look for *aushak* (leek-filled ravioli served with yogurt and ground beef) and exceptional lamb dishes. There's free validated parking at night at 468 Broadway. ⊠ *430 Broadway (North Beach),* ☎ *415/362–0641. AE, MC, V. No lunch.*

$–$$ ✕ **Thep Phanom.** The fine Thai food and the lovely interior at this Lower
★ Haight institution keep local food critics and restaurant goers singing its praises. ⊠ *400 Waller St. (The Haight),* ☎ *415/431–2526. AE, D, DC, MC, V. No lunch.*

$–$$ ✕ **Ton Kiang.** The lightly seasoned Hakka cuisine of southern China,
★ rarely found in this country, was introduced to San Francisco at this restaurant. The dim sum is arguably the finest in the city. ⊠ *5821 Geary Blvd. (Richmond District),* ☎ *415/387–8273. MC, V.*

$ ✕ **Café Claude.** Order a *salade niçoise* or simple daube from the French-speaking staff at this café in a Financial District alley, and you might forget what country you're in. On weekends the boisterous crowds regularly spill out into the alleyway. ⊠ *7 Claude La. (downtown),* ☎ *415/392–3505. AE, DC, MC, V. Closed Sun.*

$ ✕ **La Taqueria.** This attractive taqueria in the Mission is one of the finest among many. The tacos—with a spoonful of perfectly fresh salsa—are superb. ⊠ *2889 Mission St. (Mission),* ☎ *415/285–7117. No credit cards.*

$ ✕ **Mifune.** Bowls of thin brown *soba* (buckwheat) and thick white *udon* (wheat) are the traditional Japanese specialties served at this outpost of an Osaka-based noodle empire. ⊠ *Japan Center, Kintetsu Bldg., 1737 Post St. (Japantown),* ☎ *415/922–0337. Reservations not accepted. AE, D, DC, MC, V.*

Lodging

For assistance with hotel reservations try **San Francisco Reservations** (☎ 800/677–1500).

$$$$ ⊞ **Hotel Monaco.** This very hip hotel with a yellow Beaux-Arts facade
★ has small but comfortable and inviting guest rooms. In the evening, there's a complimentary wine and appetizer hour featuring a tarot reader and massage therapist. ⊠ *501 Geary St. (Union Sq.), 94102,* ☎ *415/292–0100 or 800/214–4220,* FAX *415/292–0111. 201 rooms. Restaurant. AE, D, DC, MC, V.* ⌨

$$$$ ⚂ **Mandarin Oriental.** Since the Mandarin comprises the top 11 floors
★ (38 to 48) of the California Center, all rooms provide sweeping
panoramic vistas of the city and beyond; those facing west fill up
quickly because of their views of the Golden Gate Bridge and the Pacific Ocean. Touches like loofah sponges, plush robes, binoculars, and
fresh fruit make guests feel very pampered. ⊠ *222 Sansome St. (Financial District), 94104,* ☎ *415/276–9888 or 800/622–0404,* FAX *415/
433–0289. 158 rooms. Exercise room. AE, D, DC, MC, V.* ⚐

$$$$ ⚂ **Sir Francis Drake Hotel.** Beefeater-costumed doormen welcome you
into the regal lobby of this 1928 landmark property. The guest rooms
look neoclassical, with boldly striped fabrics and mahogany and cherry-
wood furniture. On the top floor, Harry Denton's Starlight Room is
one of the city's plushest skyline bars. ⊠ *450 Powell St. (Union Sq.),
94102,* ☎ *415/392–7755 or 800/227–5480,* FAX *415/391–8719. 417
rooms. 2 restaurants, exercise room. AE, D, DC, MC, V.* ⚐

$$$–$$$$ ⚂ **Hotel Milano.** Adjacent to the San Francisco Shopping Centre and
near all the museums and attractions south of Market Street, the eight-
story hotel features spacious and handsomely decorated guest rooms.
Enjoy a soak, steam, or sauna in the split-level fitness center. ⊠ *55 5th
St. (SoMa), 94103,* ☎ *415/543–8555 or 800/398–7555,* FAX *415/543–
5885. 108 rooms. Restaurant, exercise room. AE, D, DC, MC, V.* ⚐

$$$–$$$$ ⚂ **The Maxwell.** This handsome, stylish hotel is just a block from Union
Square. Rooms have a clubby, retro feel, with classic Edward Hopper
prints on the walls. ⊠ *386 Geary St. (Union Sq.), 94102,* ☎ *415/986–
2000 or 888/734–6299,* FAX *415/397–2447. 153 rooms. Restaurant. AE,
D, DC, MC, V.* ⚐

$$$ ⚂ **Clarion Bedford Hotel.** Guests pass under Art Nouveau arches to
enter the bright lobby of this handsome 1929 building. Most of the
light and airy rooms with white furniture and canopied beds have gorgeous bay and city views. ⊠ *761 Post St. (Union Sq.), 94109,* ☎ *415/
673–6040 or 800/227–5642,* FAX *415/563–6739. 144 rooms. Restaurant. AE, D, DC, MC, V.* ⚐

$$–$$$ ⚂ **Hotel Del Sol.** Once a typical '50s-style motor court, the Hotel Del
★ Sol has a sunny courtyard and yellow-and-blue three-story building that
are candy for the eyes. Rooms evoke a beach-house feeling with plantation shutters and rattan chairs. Some have brick fireplaces. ⊠ *3100
Webster St. (Marina), 94123,* ☎ *415/921–5520 or 877/433–5765,* FAX
415/931–4137. 57 rooms. Pool, sauna. AE, D, DC, MC, V. ⚐

$$ ⚂ **Golden Gate Hotel.** This homey, family-run B&B is set in a four-
story Edwardian with bay windows. The original "birdcage" elevator
takes guests to their rooms, which are individually decorated with an-
tiques, wicker pieces, and floral bedding and curtains. ⊠ *775 Bush St.
(Union Sq.), 94108,* ☎ *415/392–3702 or 800/835–1118,* FAX *415/392–
6202. 25 rooms, 14 with bath. AE, DC, MC, V. CP.* ⚐

$ ⚂ **Adelaide Inn.** The bedspreads don't match the curtains, but the rooms
are clean and cheap at this friendly small hotel popular with Europeans.
There are sinks in every room, but the baths down the hall are shared.
⊠ *5 Isadora Duncan Ct., at Taylor St. between Geary and Post Sts.,
94102,* ☎ *415/441–2474,* FAX *415/441–0161. 18 rooms. AE, MC, V.*

Nightlife and the Arts

For club and events listings, see the pink "Datebook" section of the
Sunday *Examiner-Chronicle* or pick up the weekly *Bay Guardian* or
S.F. Weekly, available throughout the city. You can charge tickets from
BASS (☎ 415/776–1999 or 510/762–2277) by phone. Half-price same-
day tickets to many stage shows go on sale at 11 AM Tuesday–Satur-
day at the **TIX Bay Area** (☎ 415/433–7827) ticket booth, on the
Stockton Street side of Union Square. Cash only is accepted.

Nightlife

DANCE CLUBS

El Rio (⊠ 3158 Mission St., ☎ 415/282–3325) features a mix of salsa, Arab, and world dance events. **Hi-Ball Lounge** (⊠ 473 Broadway, ☎ 415/397–9464), a small North Beach club, is where the swing set gathers to jump and twist to live bands. Enthusiastic beginners are welcome.

MUSIC CLUBS

Bimbo's 365 Club (⊠ 1025 Columbus Ave., ☎ 415/474–0365) is a plush place for a variety of rock acts, often with a retro feel. **Bottom of the Hill** (⊠ 1233 17th St., ☎ 415/621–4455) showcases alternative rock and blues. **Cafe Du Nord** (⊠ 2170 Market St., ☎ 415/861–5016) presents jazz, blues, and alternative music. The **Great American Music Hall** (⊠ 859 O'Farrell St., ☎ 415/885–0750) hosts top blues, folk, jazz, and rock entertainers. Count on **Slim's** (⊠ 333 11th St., ☎ 415/522–0333) for high-quality rock, jazz, and blues.

SAN FRANCISCO'S FAVORITE BARS

The eccentric **Cypress Club** (⊠ 500 Jackson St., ☎ 415/296–8555) restaurant hosts live jazz nightly. Combos at the famously kitschy **Tonga Room** (⊠ Fairmont Hotel, 950 Mason St., ☎ 415/772–5278) play Top 40 pop on a floating barge. **Vesuvio Cafe** (⊠ 255 Columbus Ave., ☎ 415/362–3370) recalls the heyday of the beat poets, with memorabilia from the era covering nearly every surface.

GAY AND LESBIAN NIGHTLIFE

The **CoCo Club** (⊠ 139 8th St.; enter on Minna St., ☎ 415/626–2337) hosts theme nights, including a drag cabaret, a coed erotic cabaret, and a women's speakeasy. The **Stud** (⊠ 399 9th St., ☎ 415/252–7883) hosts a gender-bending mix of straight, lesbian, gay, and bisexual urbanites and suburbanites.

The Arts

The **American Conservatory Theater** (⊠ Geary Theater, 415 Geary St., ☎ 415/749–2228), a repertory company, specializes in classics and contemporary dramas. The **San Francisco Ballet** (⊠ War Memorial Opera House, 301 Van Ness Ave., ☎ 415/865–2000) performs from February to May. The **San Francisco Opera** (⊠ War Memorial Opera House, 301 Van Ness Ave., ☎ 415/864–3330) performs September to January and June to July. The **San Francisco Symphony** (⊠ Louise M. Davies Symphony Hall, 201 Van Ness Ave., ☎ 415/864–6000) plays from September to May.

Spectator Sports

Baseball: San Francisco Giants (⊠ Pacific Bell Park, at the intersection of 3rd and King Sts. in the China Basin District, ☎ 415/972–2000). **Oakland A's** (⊠ Oakland Coliseum, off I–880 at 66th Ave., ☎ 510/638–0500).

Basketball: Golden State Warriors (⊠ Oakland–Alameda County Arena, ☎ 510/762–2277).

Football: San Francisco 49ers (⊠ 3Com Park, ☎ 415/468–2249). **Oakland Raiders** (⊠ Network Associates Coliseum [former Oakland Coliseum], ☎ 510/762–2277).

Shopping

Shopping Districts

Union Square is surrounded by Macy's, Saks Fifth Avenue, and Neiman Marcus. On or near the square are Tiffany & Co., Disney, Border's Books and Music, Niketown, and Virgin Megastore. **Fisherman's**

Wharf, the **Embarcadero Center,** and **Chinatown** are three shopping areas near tourist attractions. The **SoMa** area, between 2nd, 10th, Townsend, and Howard streets, contains many clothing, houseware, and other discount outlets. The **Haight-Ashbury District** has some interesting shops, particularly on the 1500 block of Haight Street.

Antiques
Telegraph Hill Antiques (✉ 580 Union St., ☎ 415/982–7055) stocks fine china and porcelain, crystal, cut glass, Victoriana, and bronzes.

Books
City Lights (✉ 261 Columbus Ave., ☎ 415/362–8193), stomping ground of the 1950s beat poets, is well stocked with poetry, contemporary literature and music, and translations of Third World literature.

Clothing
Solo Mia (✉ 1599 Haight St., ☎ 415/621–0342) sells women's clothes made of luxurious fabrics, many designed in-house.

Gifts
Gordon Bennett (✉ Ghirardelli Sq., ☎ 415/351–1172) carries housewares, dried-flower arrangements, ceramics, and other creations, many by local artists.

Side Trip to Berkeley and Oakland

Arriving and Departing
By car, follow I–80 across the Bay Bridge; exit at University Avenue for Berkeley or pick up I–580 and exit at Grand Avenue for Oakland. By BART, Berkeley is 30 to 45 minutes from the city; exit at the downtown Berkeley stop, and then take the shuttle to campus. Oakland is a 45-minute BART ride from San Francisco; exit at the Lake Merritt station for the museum.

What to See and Do
Berkeley is the home of the **University of California at Berkeley.** Along Telegraph Avenue south of the campus is a student-oriented business district with a dog-eared counterculture ambience.

Oakland has the second-largest port in California. **Jack London Square** (✉ Embarcadero at Broadway, ☎ 510/814–6000), along the waterfront, holds shops, restaurants, small museums, and historic sites. The **Oakland Museum** (✉ 1000 Oak St., ☎ 510/238–2200 or 888/625–6873; ☞ $6) displays California art, history, and natural sciences through engaging exhibits and films.

Dining
$$–$$$$ ✕ **Chez Panisse.** This culinary institution was one of the birthplaces
★   of California cuisine. Meals at the formal downstairs restaurant are pricey; things are less expensive upstairs in the informal café. ✉ *1517 Shattuck Ave., north of University Ave.,* ☎ *510/548–5525 for restaurant, 510/548–5049 for café. Reservations essential for restaurant. AE, D, DC, MC, V. Closed Sun.*

Side Trip to Sausalito and Muir Woods

Arriving and Departing
To reach Sausalito by car, cross the Golden Gate Bridge and drive north a few miles to the Sausalito exit. **Golden Gate Ferry** (☎ 415/923–2000) crosses the bay to Sausalito from the south wing of the Ferry Building at Market Street and the Embarcadero; the trip takes 30 minutes. **Blue and Gold Fleet** (☎ 415/705–5555) ferries depart daily for Sausalito from Fisherman's Wharf. To drive to Muir Woods, continue north on U.S. 101 to the Highway 1–Stinson Beach exit and follow the signs.

What to See and Do

Sausalito, a hillside town on Richardson Bay, an inlet of San Francisco Bay in Marin County, has usually sunny weather and superb views. The main street, Bridgeway, has waterfront restaurants, shops, and hotels.

★ The 550-acre **Muir Woods National Monument** contains majestic redwoods, some nearly 250 ft tall and 1,000 years old. To avoid traffic congestion visit between 8 and 10 AM or after 4 PM. ✉ *Panoramic Hwy. off Hwy. 1,* ☎ *415/388–2595.* 🎫 *$2 parking.*

SAN JOSE

Visitor Information

San Jose Convention and Visitors Bureau (✉ 150 W. San Carlos St., 95110, ☎ 408/977–0900 or 408/295–2265).

Arriving and Departing

By Car

San Jose is 44 mi south of San Francisco; the easiest route to downtown is I–280 south to the Guadalupe Parkway (also known as Highway 87) north to the Santa Clara Street exit east.

By Plane

San Jose International Airport (✉ 1661 Airport Blvd. off Hwy. 87, ☎ 408/277–4759) is served by major airlines. **South & East Bay Airport Shuttle** (☎ 408/559–9477) transports visitors to and from the airport.

By Train

CalTrain (☎ 800/660–4287) runs from 4th and Townsend streets in San Francisco to San Jose's Rod Diridon station ($5.25 one-way). A **shuttle bus** (☎ 408/321–2300) links downtown San Jose to the CalTrain station during morning and evening commute hours.

Getting Around

By Bus or Train

Light-rail trains pass near most major attractions and historic sites downtown. Tickets cost $1.25 one-way or $3 for a day pass. The **Downtown Customer Service Center** (✉ 2 N. 1st St., ☎ 408/321–2300) has information about local bus routes.

Exploring San Jose

In 1777, El Pueblo de San Jose de Guadalupe became California's first civil settlement under Spanish rule. Today, strikingly modern architecture contrasts with restored 19th-century and mission-style buildings.

Much of downtown San Jose can be toured on foot. The **Children's Discovery Museum** (✉ 180 Woz Way, at Auzerais St., ☎ 408/298–5437; 🎫 $6) contains interactive installations on science, the humanities, and the arts. At the northeast corner of the Plaza de Cesar Chavez is the **San Jose Museum of Art** (✉ 110 S. Market St., ☎ 408/294–2787; 🎫 $7). The adjacent multidome **Cathedral Basilica of St. Joseph** (✉ 90 S. Market St., ☎ 408/283–8100), built in 1877, has extraordinary stained-glass windows and murals. On the square's western edge at Park ★ Avenue is the dazzling **Tech Museum of Innovation** (✉ 201 S. Market St., ☎ 408/294–8324, 🎫 $8.95), which has many hands-on exhibits about technology and an IMAX dome theater.

Follow Market Street north from the plaza and turn left on Santa Clara Street. Turn right on San Pedro Street, and continue two blocks—past the sidewalk cafés and restaurants—to St. John Street and turn left. The **Fallon House** (⊠ 175 W. St. John St., ☎ 408/993–8182; ⌨ $6 for Fallon House and Peralta Adobe) was built in 1855 by San Jose's seventh mayor. Across the street is the circa-1797 **Peralta Adobe** (⊠ 184 W. St. John St., ☎ 408/993–8182; ⌨ $6 for Peralta Adobe and Fallon House), the last remaining structure from the pueblo that was once San Jose. The **Rosicrucian Egyptian Museum** (⊠ 1342 Nagle Ave., ☎ 408/947–3636, ⌨ $7 museum) exhibits Egyptian and Babylonian antiquities, including mummies.

Dining and Lodging

$$$–$$$$ ✗ **Emile's.** The cuisine of Swiss chef and owner Emile Mooser has classical and contemporary Californian influences. Specialties include house-cured gravlax, rack of lamb, fresh game, and a Grand Marnier soufflé. ⊠ 545 S. 2nd St., ☎ 408/289–1960. AE, D, DC, MC, V. Closed Sun. and Mon. No lunch.

$–$$$ ✗ **Gordon Biersch Brewery Restaurant.** San Jose's younger set feasts on the kitchen's legendary garlic fries, ahi tuna, specialty pastas, and burgers. ⊠ 33 E. San Fernando St., ☎ 408/294–6785. AE, D, DC, MC, V.

$$$$ 🏨 **Hotel De Anza.** This lushly appointed 1931 Art Deco hotel has hand-painted ceilings, a warm color scheme, and an enclosed terrace with towering palms and dramatic fountains. ⊠ 233 W. Santa Clara St., 95113, ☎ 408/286–1000 or 800/843–3700, FAX 408/286–0500. 99 rooms. Restaurant, exercise room. AE, D, DC, MC, V. ☜

Nightlife and the Arts

Agenda (⊠ 399 N. 1st St., ☎ 408/287–3991) consists of a restaurant, lounge, and nightclub. The **Center for Performing Arts** (⊠ 255 Almaden Blvd., ☎ 408/277–3900, 408/998–2277 for BASS tickets) is a venue for drama, musical-theater, symphony, opera, and ballet performances. **San Jose Repertory Theatre** (⊠ 101 Paseo de San Antonio, ☎ 408/291–2255) is a well-regarded company.

Outdoor Activities and Sports

The 17,483-seat **San Jose Arena** (⊠ Santa Clara St. at Autumn St., ☎ 408/287–9200 or 408/998–2277) hosts many events and is home to the San Jose Sharks of the National Hockey League.

THE WINE COUNTRY

Napa and Sonoma counties produce some of the world's finest wines. Napa Valley becomes crowded on weekends, when visitors jam the gift shops and restaurants. The pace is less frenetic in Sonoma County. Along the coast in the city of **Mendocino,** things slow down even more. Admission is free to the wineries listed below, but most have nominal tasting fees, either by the glass or for a set number of wines.

Visitor Information

Fort Bragg–Mendocino Coast Chamber of Commerce (⊠ Box 1141, Fort Bragg 95437, ☎ 800/726–2780). **Napa Valley Conference and Visitors Bureau** (⊠ 1310 Napa Town Center, 94559, ☎ 707/226–7459). **Sonoma Valley Visitors Bureau** (⊠ 453 1st St. E, Sonoma 95476, ☎ 707/996–1090).

Arriving and Departing

By Bus

Greyhound (☎ 800/231–2222) runs buses from San Francisco to the cities of Sonoma and Santa Rosa in Sonoma County; the line's buses stop along U.S. 101 in inland Mendocino County. **Sonoma County Area Transit** (☎ 707/585–7516) and **Napa Valley Transit** (☎ 707/255–7631) provide local transportation.

By Car

The best way to get around the Wine Country is by car. From San Francisco cross the Golden Gate Bridge and follow U.S. 101 north to Highway 37 east to Highway 121 north and east. Take Highway 12 north from Highway 121 for Sonoma wineries; continue east on Highway 121 to Highway 29 north for Napa wineries. From the East Bay take I–80 north to Highway 37 east to Highway 29 north for Napa; Highway 12 heads west from Highway 29 toward Sonoma. To get to Mendocino from San Francisco, take U.S. 101 north to Highway 128 west to Highway 1 north.

By Train

The **Napa Valley Wine Train** (☎ 707/253–2111 or 800/427–4124) serves lunch ($69), dinner ($75), and a weekend brunch ($60) on restored Pullman cars that run between Napa and St. Helena.

Exploring the Wine Country

The Napa Valley

Along Highway 29 north of the town of **Napa** and parallel to the highway on the Silverado Trail are some of California's most important wineries. **Domaine Chandon** (✉ California Dr., Yountville, ☎ 707/944–2280) is owned by Moët-Hennessey and Louis Vuitton. **Stag's Leap** (✉ 5766 Silverado Trail, Yountville, ☎ 707/944–2020) produces a superb chardonnay.

The **Napa Valley Museum** (✉ 55 Presidents Circle, Yountville, ☎ 707/944–0500; ⊠ $3.50) has an innovative, permanent exhibit devoted to regional wine making as well as changing art shows. Some of the largest wine caves in America are below **Rutherford Hill** (✉ 200 Rutherford Hill Rd., Rutherford, ☎ 707/963–7194). **Beaulieu Vineyard** (✉ 1960 St. Helena Hwy., Rutherford, ☎ 707/963–2411) utilizes the same wine-making process it did in the last century. At **Robert Mondavi** (✉ 7801 St. Helena Hwy., Oakville, ☎ 707/259–9463), the 60-minute tour is encouraged before imbibing. Visitors ride up the side of a hill in a gondola to reach **Sterling Vineyards** (✉ 1111 Dunaweal La., Calistoga, ☎ 707/942–3300).

Calistoga, at the Napa Valley's north end, was founded as a spa and remains notable for its mineral water, hot mineral springs, mud baths, steam baths, and massages. **Indian Springs Resort and Spa** (✉ 1712 Lincoln Ave., ☎ 707/942–4913) has full spa amenities.

The Sonoma Valley

East of U.S. 101 and west of the Napa Valley, Highway 12 runs through the hills of Sonoma County. The historic central plaza in the town of Sonoma is the site of **Mission San Francisco Solano** (✉ 114 Spain St. E, ☎ 707/938–1519; ⊠ $3), which is a re-creation of the original early 19th-century structure.

California's wine-making industry got its start at the **Buena Vista Carneros Winery** (✉ 18000 Old Winery Rd., Sonoma, ☎ 707/938–1266) in 1857. The **Benziger Family Winery** (✉ 1883 London Ranch Rd., Glen Ellen, ☎ 707/935–3000) specializes in premium estate and Sonoma County wines. The rustic grounds at **Kenwood Vineyards** (✉ 9592 Sonoma Hwy., Kenwood, ☎ 707/833–5891) complement the attractive tasting room. The charred but evocative ruins of the author's dream home, Wolf House, and the House of Happy Walls museum are among the highlights at **Jack London State Historic Park** (✉ 2400 London Ranch Rd., Glen Ellen, ☎ 707/938–5216; ⊠ $6 per vehicle).

Mendocino

This coastal city on windswept headlands 153 mi north of San Francisco was a logging center in the late 1800s, but its chief industry these days is tourism.

The **Mendocino Art Center** (✉ 45200 Little Lake St., ☎ 707/937–5818) contains a gallery and a theater. The restored 1854 **Ford House** (✉ 735 Main St., west of Lansing St., ☎ 707/937–5397; ☐ free) holds the

★ visitor center for Mendocino Headlands State Park. The **Mendocino Coast Botanical Gardens** (✉ 18220 N. Hwy. 1, ☎ 707/964–4352; ☐ $6) contains a splendid array of flowers and other plant life within three distinct microclimates.

Husch (✉ 4400 Hwy. 128, Philo, ☎ 707/895–3216) sells award-winning chardonnays and a superb gewürztraminer. At **Roederer Estate** (✉ 4501 Hwy. 128, Philo, ☎ 707/895–2288), you can taste sparkling wines produced by the American affiliate of the famous French champagne maker.

Dining and Lodging

Calistoga

$$–$$$ ✗ **Catahoula Restaurant and Saloon.** Chef Jan Birnbaum employs a large wood-burning oven to churn out such California-Cajun dishes as spicy gumbo with andouille sausage and oven-braised lamb shank with red beans. ✉ *Mount View Hotel, 1457 Lincoln Ave.,* ☎ *707/942–2275. Reservations essential. MC, V. Closed Tues. and Jan.*

$$$–$$$$ ▥ **Mount View Hotel.** This historic hotel has a small but full-service European spa offering state-of-the-art pampering. Three cottages here are equipped with private redwood decks, Jacuzzis, and wet bars. ✉ *1457 Lincoln Ave., 94515,* ☎ *707/942–6877,* ℻ *707/942–6904. 32 rooms. Restaurant, pool. AE, MC, V.*

Mendocino

$$–$$$ ✗ **Cafe Beaujolais.** All the rustic charm of peaceful, backwoods Men-
★ docino is here, with great country cooking to boot. The ever-evolving, cross-cultural dinner menu includes delicacies like Yucatecan Thai crab cakes. ✉ *961 Ukiah St.,* ☎ *707/937–5614. No credit cards.*

$$–$$$$ ▥ **Whitegate Inn.** With a white picket fence, a latticework gazebo, and
★ a romantic garden, the Whitegate is a picture-book Victorian. Guest rooms and public spaces have high ceilings and floral fabrics. ✉ *499 Howard St., 95460,* ☎ *707/937–4892 or 800/531–7282,* ℻ *707/937–1131. 7 rooms. AE, D, DC, MC, V.* ☜

Rutherford

$$$$ ✗▥ **Auberge du Soleil.** The dining terrace of this hilltop inn, looking
★ down across groves of olive trees to the Napa Valley vineyards, is the closest you can get to the atmosphere, charm, and cuisine of southern France without a passport. The inn itself is a luxurious retreat with full spa facilities. ✉ *180 Rutherford Hill Rd., off Silverado Trail north of Rte. 128, 94573,* ☎ *707/963–1211 or 800/348–5406,* ℻ *707/963–8764. 50 rooms. Restaurant, pool, exercise room. AE, D, DC, MC, V. CP.* ☜

St. Helena

$$$$ ▥ **Meadowood Resort.** Croquet lawns, a nine-hole golf course, tennis courts, and gorgeous hiking trails add to the glamour of this sprawling 256-acre resort with a rambling country lodge and bungalow suites. ✉ *900 Meadowood La., 94574,* ☎ *707/963–3646 or 800/458–8080,* ℻ *707/963–3532. 85 rooms. 2 restaurants, pools. AE, D, DC, MC, V.*

Santa Rosa

$$$–$$$$ ✕ **John Ash & Co.** The chef emphasizes presentation, innovation, and
★   freshness and uses mainly seasonal foods grown in Sonoma County.
This is a favorite spot for Sunday brunch. ✉ *4430 Barnes Rd.,* ☎ *707/
527–7687. Reservations essential weekends. AE, MC, V. No lunch Mon.*

Sonoma

$$$–$$$$ ⊞ **Thistle Dew Inn.** Half a block from Sonoma Plaza is this Victorian
inn with Arts and Crafts furnishings and antique quilts. Welcome
bonuses include a hot tub and free use of the inn's bicycles. ✉ *171 W.
Spain St., 95476,* ☎ *707/938–2909, 800/382–7895 in CA. 6 rooms.
AE, MC, V. BP.* ✿

Yountville

$$$$ ✕ **French Laundry.** This intimate, cottage-style restaurant, surrounded
★   by gardens, offers exquisite prix-fixe French menus of four or five courses.
✉ *6640 Washington St.,* ☎ *707/944–2380. Reservations essential. AE,
MC, V. Closed 1st 2 wks in Jan.; lunch hrs and days vary.*

Outdoor Activities and Sports

Hot-Air Ballooning

Many hotels arrange excursions, or contact **Napa Valley Balloons** (☎
707/944–0228, 800/253–2224 in CA). For Sonoma trips try **Above the
Wine Country Balloons and Tours** (☎ 707/538–7359 or 800/759–5638).

YOSEMITE NATIONAL PARK

Yosemite's U-shape valleys were formed by the action of glaciers dur-
ing recent ice ages. A pass to the park, good for a week, costs $20 per
car or $10 per person if you don't arrive in a car.

Visitor Information

Yosemite National Park (✉ Box 577, Yosemite National Park 95389,
☎ 209/372–0264, 209/372–0200 for 24-hr information).

Arriving and Departing

By Bus

Yosemite VIA (☎ 209/384–1315 or 800/369–7275) runs three daily
buses from Merced to Yosemite Valley. **Greyhound** (☎ 800/231–2222)
serves Merced from the California coast.

By Car

Yosemite is a four- to five-hour drive from San Francisco (take I–80
to I–580 to I–205 to Highway 120) and a six-hour drive from Los An-
geles (take I–5 north to Highway 99 to Fresno, and Highway 41 north
to Yosemite). Highways 41, 120, and 140 all intersect with Highway
99, which runs north–south through California's Central Valley.

By Plane

Fresno Air Terminal (✉ 5175 E. Clinton Ave., ☎ 559/498–4095), the
nearest major airport, is served by national and regional carriers.

Exploring Yosemite National Park

★   The highlights of **Yosemite Valley** include **Yosemite Fall,** the highest
waterfall in North America; the famous **El Capitan** and **Half Dome**
granite peaks; misty **Bridalveil Fall;** and **Glacier Point,** which affords
a phenomenal bird's-eye view of the entire valley. Near **Wawona** at
the park's south entrance are the historic **Wawona Hotel** and the Mari-

posa Grove of Big Trees. A free **shuttle bus** runs around the east end of Yosemite Valley year-round. A summer shuttle runs from Wawona to the Mariposa Grove of Big Trees.

Dining and Lodging

Besides the Ahwahnee Hotel's classy restaurant, dining options in Yosemite Valley include fast food and picnic fixings from a grocery store. **Yosemite Concession Services Corporation** (☎ 559/252–4848) handles reservations for the park's fancy hotels, modest lodge rooms, and Yosemite Valley tent cabins and tent sites.

ELSEWHERE IN NORTHERN CALIFORNIA

The Gold Country

Arriving and Departing

Sacramento International Airport (⊠ 6900 Airport Blvd., off I–5, ☎ 916/874–0700) is served by major domestic airlines.

Greyhound (☎ 800/231–2222) serves Sacramento, Auburn, Grass Valley, and Placerville from San Francisco.

The most convenient way to see the area is by car. I–80 intersects with Highway 49, the main route through the region, at Auburn; U.S. 50 intersects with Highway 49 at Placerville.

What to See and Do

When gold was discovered at **Coloma** in 1848, people came from all over the world to search for the treasure. Today, clustered along Highway 49 are restored villages and ghost towns, antiques shops, crafts stores, and vineyards. The heart of the Gold Country lies on Highway 49 between Nevada City and Mariposa.

★ **Empire Mine State Historic Park** (⊠ 10791 E. Empire St., Grass Val-
★ ley, ☎ 530/273–8522, ⊡ $1) has exhibits on gold mining. The **Marshall Gold Discovery State Historical Park** (⊠ Hwy. 49, Coloma, ☎ 530/622–3470, ⊡ $2) has a replica of Sutter's Mill, where the gold
★ rush started. In **Columbia State Historic Park** (⊠ Hwy. 49, ☎ 209/532–4301, ⊡ free) you can ride a stagecoach, pan for gold, or watch a blacksmith working at his anvil. At the **California State Mining and Mineral Museum** (⊠ Mariposa County Fairgrounds, Hwy. 49, Mariposa, ☎ 209/742–7625; ⊡ $2) a glittering 13-pound crystallized gold nugget vividly illustrates what the gold rush was all about. The museum is closed on Tuesday year-round and on Monday between October and April.

Sacramento, the California state capital, is also the largest Gold Country city. The **Visitor Information Center** (⊠ 1101 2nd St., ☎ 916/442–7644) has the latest on key attractions, plus lodging, reservations, and ↻ other services. The **Discovery Museum** (⊠ 101 I St., ☎ 916/264–7057; ⊡ $5) presents a streamlined introduction to Sacramento's history. The
★ **California State Railroad Museum** (⊠ 125 I St., ☎ 916/445–6645, ⊡ $3) displays restored locomotives and railroad cars.

Dining and Lodging
SACRAMENTO

$$–$$$$ ✕ **Biba.** The capitol crowd flocks here for delicate pasta dishes, veal
★ specials, and homemade ravioli, as well as specialties from the Emilia-Romagna region of Italy. ⊠ 2801 Capitol Ave., ☎ 916/455–2422. AE, DC, MC, V. Closed Sun. No lunch Sat.

$$–$$$ ✕⌂ **Best Western Sutter House.** This downtown property has rooms that open onto a courtyard surrounding a pool. The restaurant, Grape's,

serves contemporary cuisine. The no-smoking rule lets you know you're in California. ⊠ *1100 H St., 95814,* ☎ *916/441–1314, 800/ 830–1314 in CA;* 🖷 *916/441–5961. 98 rooms. Restaurant, pool. AE, D, DC, MC, V. CP.* ✿

Lake Tahoe

Arriving and Departing
Reno–Tahoe International Airport (⊠ U.S. 395, Exit 65B, Reno, NV, ☎ 702/328–6400), about 40 mi from Lake Tahoe, is served by several domestic airlines. **Tahoe Casino Express** (☎ 702/785–2424 or 800/446–6128) provides shuttle service from the airport to Stateline casinos.

Amtrak (☎ 800/872–7245) and **Greyhound** (☎ 800/231–2222) also serve the Tahoe area. **South Tahoe Area Ground Express** (☎ 530/573–2080) and **Tahoe Area Regional Transit** (☎ 530/581–6365) are the local bus companies. Lake Tahoe is 198 mi northeast of San Francisco. The drive takes about four hours. The major route is I–80 through the Sierra Nevadas; U.S. 50 from Sacramento is the direct route to the south shore. Tire chains are regularly necessary in winter.

What to See and Do
Visitors to Lake Tahoe's California side—where gambling isn't legal—come to ski, hike, fish, camp, and boat in the spectacular Sierra Nevada range, 6,000 ft to 10,000 ft above sea level. Ski resorts, such as Alpine Meadows and Squaw Valley, open at the end of November and operate as late as May. Tourist information is provided by the **Lake Tahoe Visitors Authority** (☎ 530/544–5050 or 800/288–2463). Ride the
★ **Heavenly Tram** (⊠ north on Ski Run Blvd. off U.S. 50 and follow signs, ☎ 775/586–7000; ⊡ $12) for a view of the lake from 8,200 ft.

The 72-mi Lake Tahoe shoreline is best seen along a route through wooded flatlands and past beaches, climbing to vistas on the rugged west side of the lake. The drive should take about three hours but can be slow going in summer and on holiday weekends.

West of South Lake Tahoe on Highway 89 is the **Pope-Baldwin Recreation Area** (☎ 530/541–5227; ⊡ free), where three grand century-old mansions (fees to enter vary) are open to the public. The **Lake Tahoe Visitors Center** (☎ 530/573–2674), on Taylor Creek, is near the site of a onetime Washoe Indian settlement; there are trails through meadow,
★ marsh, and forest. Tahoe's **Emerald Bay** is famed for its shape and color.

The **Hornblower's Tahoe Queen** (⊠ Ski Run Marina, off U.S. 50, South Lake Tahoe, ☎ 530/541–3364; ⊡ $18–$45), a glass-bottom sternwheeler, cruises on the lake and swings by Emerald Bay year-round. Beyond Emerald Bay is **D. L. Bliss State Park** (☎ 530/525–7277; ⊡ $5), with 6 mi of shorefront and 168 family campsites. At Tahoe City Highway 89 turns north to **Squaw Valley,** site of the 1960 Winter Olympics.

Dining and Lodging
$$–$$$$ ✕🏨 **Harvey's Resort Hotel/Casino.** Any description of Harvey's runs
★ to superlatives. Rooms have custom furnishings, oversize marble baths, and minibars. The health club, spa, and pool are free to guests, a rarity for this area. Among the resort's restaurants, Llewellyn's is outstanding. ⊠ *U.S. 50, Box 128, Stateline, NV 89449,* ☎ *702/588–2411 or 800/648–3361,* 🖷 *775/782–4889. 741 rooms. 8 restaurants, pool, health club. AE, D, DC, MC, V.*

$$–$$$$ 🏨 **Inn by the Lake.** Across the road from a beach, this luxury motel has spacious rooms, all with balconies. You can summon a casino shuttle from a direct-dial phone in the lobby. ⊠ *3300 Lake Tahoe Blvd.,*

South Lake Tahoe 96150, ☎ 530/542–0330 or 800/877–1466, ᴀ̇ᴄ 530/ 541–6596. 99 rooms. Pool. AE, D, DC, MC, V. CP.

THE CENTRAL COAST

Raging surf, rugged rocks, hidden tidal pools, and wind-warped trees mark the coastline south from San Francisco. Several towns provide entertainment, but the Pacific Ocean dominates. Coast-hugging Highway 1, sometimes precariously narrow, is the route of choice. It's slow and winding, but the views are worth the extra time.

Visitor Information

Monterey Peninsula Visitors and Convention Bureau (⊠ 380 Alvarado St., Monterey 93942, ☎ 831/649–1770). **Santa Barbara Conference and Visitors Bureau** (⊠ 12 E. Carrillo St., 93101, ☎ 805/966–9222 or 800/549–5133).

Arriving and Departing

By Car

Highway 1 heads south from San Francisco through the region. The quickest (if less scenic) route to Monterey from San Francisco or San Jose is I–280 south to Highway 17 west to Highway 1 south. U.S. 101 is the quickest route to Santa Barbara from Los Angeles or San Francisco. To get to Monterey from Los Angeles, take U.S. 101 to Salinas and head west on Highway 68.

By Plane

Airlines serving **Monterey Peninsula Airport** (⊠ 200 Fred Kane Dr., ☎ 831/648–7000) and **Santa Barbara Municipal Airport** (⊠ 500 Fowler Rd., ☎ 805/683–4011) include America West, American Eagle, United, United Express, and Skywest/Delta.

By Train

Amtrak's *Coast Starlight* makes stops in Santa Barbara, San Luis Obispo, and Salinas on its run from Los Angeles to Seattle.

Exploring the Central Coast

About 125 mi south of San Francisco, the city of **Monterey** is rich in California history. The Path of History is a 2-mi self-guided tour
★ through **Monterey State Historic Park** (☎ 831/649–7118). Two highlights are the **Custom House** (⊠ 1 Custom House Plaza, ☎ 831/649–2909; ▣ free), built by the Mexican government in 1827, and the **Pacific House** (⊠ 10 Custom House Plaza, ☎ 831/649–7118; ▣ $2), a former hotel and saloon that is now a museum of early California life.

Monterey's barking sea lions are best seen along **Fisherman's Wharf,** a touristy pier. A footpath leads from Fisherman's Wharf to **Cannery Row,** where the old tin-roof canneries made famous by John Steinbeck's eponymous book have been converted into restaurants, art galleries,
★ and minimalls. The outstanding **Monterey Bay Aquarium** (⊠ 886 Cannery Row, ☎ 831/648–4888, 800/756–3737 in CA for tickets, ▣ $15.95) is a window on the sea waters beyond.

Pacific Grove recalls its Victorian heritage in tiny board-and-batten cottages and in stately mansions. For years migrating monarch butterflies from Canada and the Pacific Northwest have made Pacific Grove their winter home. **Monarch Grove Sanctuary** (⊠ 1073 Lighthouse Ave.) is a good viewing spot.

★ Celebrated **17-Mile Drive** offers a chance to explore an 8,400-acre microcosm of the Monterey Peninsula's coastal landscape. You'll find the weather-sculpted **Lone Cypress** tree here. At **Seal Rock** and **Bird Rock,** just offshore, you can watch the creatures sunning themselves en masse. Also along the drive is the famous **Pebble Beach Golf Links.**

Carmel was an important religious center for Spanish California. The stone buildings and tower dome of the 1770 **Carmel Mission** (✉ Rio Rd. and Lasuen Dr., ☎ 831/624–3600; 🎫 $2) have been beautifully restored. Another example of Carmel's architectural heritage is the late poet Robinson Jeffers's **Tor House** (✉ 26304 Ocean View Ave., ☎ 831/624–1813 or 831/624–1840; 🎫 $7). The house is open only on Friday and Saturday; reservations are recommended to view it.

Carmel's greatest beauty is in the rugged coastline and surrounding cypress forests, best seen at **Carmel River State Park,** off Scenic Road and south of Carmel Beach, and the larger **Point Lobos State Reserve** (☎ 831/624–4909 for both), a 350-acre headland south of Carmel. At the latter, the Sea Lion Point Trail is a good spot to observe sea lions, otters, harbor seals, and seasonally migrating whales.

You can catch the quintessential view of California's coast from the elegant concrete arc of **Bixby Creek Bridge,** 13 mi south of Carmel. **Big Sur** begins at the Point Sur Light Station, atop a sandstone cliff south of Bixby Creek. At **Pfeiffer Big Sur State Park** (☎ 831/667–2315) a trail leads up a small valley to a waterfall. One of the few places where you can actually reach the water is **Pfeiffer Beach** (follow the road just past the Big Sur Ranger Station for 2 mi).

★ **Hearst Castle** reigns in solitary splendor a few miles north of Cambria. William Randolph Hearst's grandiose mansion contains extravagant marble halls, ornate swimming pools, and an extensive European art and antiquities collection. A film ($6) at the giant-screen theater details Hearst's life and the castle's construction. Tour reservations are necessary. ☎ 805/927–2020 or 800/444–4445. 🎫 *$10 day tours.* ✍

The coastal ribbon of Highway 1 ends at **Morro Bay.** Morro Rock, with the sheltered harbor on one side and the Pacific surf on the other, is a preserve for peregrine falcons. At **San Luis Obispo,** south of Morro Bay, halfway between San Francisco and Los Angeles, are such historic sites as the 1772 **Mission San Luis Obispo de Tolosa** (☎ 805/543–6850) downtown. Drop by the garish, goofy **Madonna Inn** (✉ 100 Madonna Rd., off U.S. 101, ☎ 805/543–3000 or 800/543–9666) if only for a drink and a look at the kitschy accoutrements.

Temperate **Santa Barbara** seems like the most relaxed place in the world. It retains its Spanish character with wide tree-shaded streets, red-tile-roof arcades downtown, and courtyards filled with upscale boutiques and restaurants. Scenic murals adorn the interior walls of the Span-
★ ish-Moorish-style **Santa Barbara County Courthouse** (✉ 1100 Anacapa St., ☎ 805/962–6464), well worth a visit. The Spanish built what is now **El Presidio State Historic Park** (✉ 123 E. Cañon Perdido St., ☎ 805/965–0093) as a military stronghold in 1782. Along the Santa Barbara waterfront, not far from downtown, is **Stearns Wharf** (✉ Cabrillo Blvd. at State St.), a pier holding shops, eateries, and the Museum of

★ Natural History's Sea Center (☎ 805/962–0885). The landmark **Mission Santa Barbara** (✉ 2201 Laguna St., ☎ 805/682–4713; 🎫 $4) lies a bit north of Stearns Wharf. In the Santa Ynez foothills, the **Santa Barbara Botanic Garden** (✉ 1212 Mission Canyon Rd., ☎ 805/682–4726; 🎫 $3) contains 65 acres of native plants.

Dining and Lodging

Big Sur

$$$–$$$$ ✕ **Nepenthe.** On an 800-ft cliff overlooking lush meadows and the ocean, the house now occupied by this restaurant was once owned by Orson Welles. The food—from roast chicken to sandwiches and hamburgers—is only adequate; it's the location that warrants a stop. ⊠ *Hwy. 1 at south end of town,* ☎ *831/667–2345. AE, MC, V.*

$$$$ ✕⌂ **Post Ranch Inn.** Each unit at this cliff-top resort has its own spa
★ tub, stereo, private deck, fireplace, and massage table. The inn's restaurant, serving a prix-fixe menu of cutting-edge American fare, is the best in the area. ⊠ *Hwy. 1 (Box 219), 93920,* ☎ *831/667–2200 or 800/ 527–2200,* FAX *831/667–2512 or 831/687–2824. 30 rooms. Restaurant, pool, exercise room. AE, MC, V. CP.* ⊗

$$$$ ✕⌂ **Ventana.** The activities at this quintessential California getaway with
★ lodge-style rooms are purposely limited to sunning at poolside—there is a clothing-optional deck—and walks in the hills nearby. The hotel's stone-and-wood restaurant serves California cuisine with Continental influences (weekend brunch on the terrace is a real event). ⊠ *Hwy. 1, 93920,* ☎ *831/667–2331 or 800/628–6500,* FAX *831/667–2419. 59 rooms, 3 houses. Restaurant, pools, exercise room. AE, D, DC, MC, V. CP.* ⊗

$$–$$$ ⌂ **Big Sur Lodge.** Motel-style cottages at this lodge within Pfeiffer Big Sur State Park—some with fireplaces or kitchens—are set around a meadow surrounded by redwood and oak trees. ⊠ *Hwy. 1 (Box 190), 93920,* ☎ *831/667–3100 or 800/424–4787,* FAX *831/667–3110. 61 rooms. Restaurant, pool. AE, MC, V.* ⊗

Cambria

$$–$$$ ✕ **Sea Chest.** Perched on the sea's edge, the best seafood joint in Cam-
★ bria has a very popular oyster bar. ⊠ *6216 Moonstone Beach,* ☎ *805/ 927–4514. Reservations not accepted. No lunch. No credit cards.*

$–$$$ ✕ **Hamlet at Moonstone Gardens.** In the middle of 3 acres of luxuriant
★ gardens, this restaurant, open for lunch and dinner, has a lovely patio that's perfect for lunch. An upstairs dining room overlooks the Pacific. Salmon comes poached in white wine; meat entrées range from hamburgers to rack of lamb. ⊠ *Hwy. 1 on east side,* ☎ *805/927–3535. MC, V.*

$$–$$$ ⌂ **Cypress Cove Inn.** This romantic getaway was designed in the Welsh style, with outside walls made of old stone. Ask for a room facing the Pacific. ⊠ *6348 Moonstone Beach Dr., 93428,* ☎ *805/927–2600 or 800/568–8517. 22 rooms. AE, MC, V.* ⊗

$$ ⌂ **San Simeon Pines Resort.** The accommodations at this motel-style resort include cottages with landscaped backyards. Rooms in parts of the complex are for adults only; others are reserved for families. ⊠ *7200 Moonstone Beach Dr. (Box 117), San Simeon 93452,* ☎ *805/927–4648. 58 rooms. Pool. AE, MC, V.* ⊗

Carmel

$$–$$$ ✕ **Casanova.** Southern French and northern Italian cuisine come together
★ at Casanova, one of the most romantic restaurants in Carmel. A heated outdoor garden and the more than 1,000 domestic and imported wines enhance the dining experience. The menu changes monthly. All entrées come with an antipasto plate and choice of appetizers. ⊠ *5th Ave. between San Carlos and Mission Sts.,* ☎ *831/625–0501. MC, V.*

$–$$ ✕ **Caffé Napoli.** Redolent of garlic and olive oil, this small Italian restaurant is a favorite of locals, who come for the crisp-crusted pizzas, house-made pastas, and fresh seafood. ⊠ *Ocean Ave. at Lincoln,* ☎ *831/625–4033. Reservations essential on weekends. MC, V.*

$$$–$$$$ ⌂ **Carmel River Inn.** This motel-cabins complex is away from the crowds of downtown. Some cabins have kitchenettes. ⊠ *Hwy. 1, at* the Carmel River Bridge (Box 221609), 93922, ☎ 831/624–1575 or 800/882–8142, ℻ 831/624–0290. 43 rooms. Pool. MC, V. ✺

$$$–$$$$ ⊞ **Cypress Inn.** When Doris Day became part owner of this inn, she ★ added her own touches, such as posters from her many movies and photo albums of her favorite canines. (Pets are welcome in most rooms here.) In nice weather, enjoy your Continental breakfast in a garden courtyard surrounded by bougainvillea. ⊠ *Lincoln St. and 7th Ave., Box Y, 93921*, ☎ *831/624–3871 or 800/443–7443*, ℻ *831/624–8216. 34 rooms. AE, D, MC, V. CP.*

Monterey

$$$–$$$$ ✕ **Fresh Cream.** The cuisine at this harbor-view restaurant is French, with imaginative Californian accents. Typical dishes on the menu (which changes weekly) are rack of lamb Dijonnaise and roast boned duck in black-currant sauce. ⊠ *99 Pacific St., Suite 100C*, ☎ *831/375–9798. AE, D, DC, MC, V. No lunch.*

$–$$$ ✕ **Paradiso Trattoria and Oyster Bar.** Mediterranean specialties and pizzas from a wood-burning oven are the luncheon fare at this Cannery Row eatery. Seafood is a good choice for dinner, served in a dining room overlooking a lighted beachfront or at the gleaming oyster bar. ⊠ *654 Cannery Row*, ☎ *831/375–4155. AE, D, DC, MC, V.*

$–$$$ ✕ **Tarpy's Roadhouse.** Fun, dressed-down roadhouse lunch and dinner are served in a renovated farmhouse built in the early 1900s. The kitchen cooks everything Mom used to make, only better. ⊠ *2999 Monterey–Salinas Hwy. (Hwy. 68), at Canyon Del Rey Rd.*, ☎ *831/647–1444. AE, D, MC, V.*

$$$$ ⊞ **Spindrift Inn.** This Cannery Row hotel has beach access and a ★ rooftop garden. Rooms are spacious, with hardwood floors, fireplaces, canopied beds, sitting areas, down comforters, and other luxuries. ⊠ *652 Cannery Row, 93940*, ☎ *831/646–8900 or 800/841–1879*, ℻ *831/646–5342. 42 rooms. AE, D, DC, MC, V. CP.* ✺

$$–$$$$ ⊞ **Quality Inn Monterey.** Some rooms at this friendly property have fireplaces; all have refrigerators, microwaves, and VCRs. ⊠ *1058 Munras Ave., 93940*, ☎ *831/372–3381*, ℻ *831/372–4687. 55 rooms. Pool. AE, D, DC, MC, V. CP.* ✺

Morro Bay

$$–$$$ ⊞ **Embarcadero Inn.** A drab metallic exterior hides a more welcoming interior of sparkling clean rooms, all of them with balconies that face the sea. The two hot tubs are a plus. ⊠ *456 Embarcadero, 93442*, ☎ *805/772–2700 or 800/292–7625*, ℻ *805/772–1060. 32 rooms. AE, D, DC, MC, V.* ✺

Pacific Grove

$$$–$$$$ ✕ **Old Bath House.** This romantic converted bathhouse overlooks the ★ water at Lovers Point. The menu makes the most of local seafood and produce. ⊠ *620 Ocean View Blvd.*, ☎ *831/375–5195. AE, D, DC, MC, V. No lunch.*

Santa Barbara

$$$–$$$$ ✕ **Citronelle.** The accent at this offspring of Citron in Los Angeles is on ★ French Riviera–style dishes: light and delicate but loaded with intriguing good tastes. Sweeping harbor views can be had from the dining room. ⊠ *901 E. Cabrillo Blvd.*, ☎ *805/963–0111. AE, D, DC, MC, V.*

$$–$$$ ✕ **Brophy Bros.** The seafood salads at this boisterous harbor-front restaurant are excellent, as are the daytime ocean views. Arrive hungry—the straightforward fish and seafood entrées are huge. ⊠ *119 Harbor Way*, ☎ *805/966–4418. AE, MC, V.*

$ ✕ **La Super-Rica.** Fans of this food stand with a patio drive for miles ★ to fill up on soft tacos and incredible beans. ⊠ *622 N. Milpas St., at Alphonse St.*, ☎ *805/963–4940. No credit cards.*

$ ✕ **Roy.** This downtown storefront is a real bargain. Owner-chef Leroy Gandy serves a $15 prix-fixe dinner that includes a small salad, fresh soup, and a selection from a rotating roster of Cal-Mediterranean main courses. Expect a wait on weekends. ⊠ *7 W. Carrillo St.,* ☎ *805/ 966–5636. AE, D, DC, MC, V.*

$$$$ ⊞ **Four Seasons Biltmore.** This grande dame of Santa Barbara hostel-
★ ries is more formal than other city accommodations, with lush gardens and palm trees galore. ⊠ *1260 Channel Dr., Montecito 93108,* ☎ *805/ 969–2261 or 800/332–3442,* ℻ *805/565–8329. 230 rooms. 2 restau-rants, pool, health club. AE, DC, MC, V.* ✍

$$–$$$$ ⊞ **Glenborough Inn.** One of the best B&Bs in Santa Barbara County,
★ this inn is composed of four buildings constructed around the dawn of the 20th century. ⊠ *1327 Bath St., 93101,* ☎ *805/966–0589 or 800/ 962–0589,* ℻ *805/564–8610. 14 rooms. AE, D, DC, MC, V. BP.* ✍

$$–$$$$ ⊞ **Hotel Santa Barbara.** The location is central and the rooms are ser-viceable; from the top floors, guests can see the ocean. Rooms in the back are quieter. ⊠ *533 State St., 93101,* ☎ *888/259–7700. 75 rooms. AE, D, DC, MC, V.* ✍

$ ⊞ **Motel 6.** Low price and great location near the beach are the pluses for this no-frills motel. ⊠ *443 Corona Del Mar Dr., 93103,* ☎ *805/ 564–1392,* ℻ *805/963–4687. 51 rooms. Pool. AE, D, DC, MC, V.* ✍

Nightlife and the Arts

The Carmel-Monterey area's top performing arts venue is the **Sunset Community Cultural Center** (⊠ San Carlos St. between 8th and 10th Aves., Carmel, ☎ 831/624–3996), which presents concerts, lectures, and headline performers. The **Arlington Theater** (☎ 805/963–4408) is home to the Santa Barbara Symphony.

Outdoor Activities and Sports

Biking

The Monterey Peninsula is prime biking territory, with paths follow-ing parts of the shoreline. **Bay Bikes** (⊠ 640 Wave St., Monterey, ☎ 831/646–9090) rents bikes. Rent bikes, quadricycles, and skates from **Beach Rentals** (⊠ 22 State St., Santa Barbara, ☎ 805/966–6733). In Santa Barbara the **Cabrillo Bike Lane** passes the city zoo, a bird refuge, beaches, and the harbor.

Fishing

Charter boats leave from Monterey, Morro Bay, and Santa Barbara. Most trips—from such outfits as **Monterey Sport Fishing and Whale Watch-ing** (⊠ 96 Fisherman's Wharf, Monterey, ☎ 831/372–2203) or **Sea Land-ing Aquatic Center** (⊠ Cabrillo Blvd. at Bath, Santa Barbara, ☎ 805/ 963–3564)—include equipment rental, bait, fish cleaning, and a license.

Golf

Pebble Beach Golf Links (⊠ 17-Mile Dr., ☎ 831/624–3811), with its sweeping ocean views, is one of the world's most famous courses; reser-vations are essential. At **Spyglass Hill** (⊠ Spyglass Hill Rd., ☎ 831/ 622–1300), the holes are unforgiving, but the views offer consolation. The **Santa Barbara Golf Club** (⊠ Las Positas Rd. and McCaw Ave., ☎ 805/687–7087) and **Sandpiper Golf Course** (⊠ 7925 Hollister Ave., Goleta, ☎ 805/968–1541) are two options farther south.

Whale-Watching

On their annual migration between the Bering Sea and Baja Califor-nia, 45-ft gray whales can be spotted at many points not far off the coast. The migration south takes place from December through February; the journey north, from March to mid-May. Other species of whales can be seen in the summer and autumn.

Beaches

In general, the shoreline north of San Luis Obispo is rocky and backed by cliffs, the water rough and often cold, and sunbathing limited to only the warmest hours of the early afternoon. Still, **Point Carmel, Big** ★ **Sur,** and **Morro Bay** provide unparalleled beach experiences. **Pismo Beach** marks the first of the classic southern California beaches, with long, low stretches of sand. From Point Concepción down through Santa Barbara and into Ventura County are some fine beaches. Santa Barbara's **East Beach** has lifeguards, volleyball courts, a jogging-and-biking trail, a jungle-gym play area, and a bathhouse with a gym, showers, and changing rooms. **Arroyo Burro County Beach,** near Santa Barbara, is a state preserve, with a small grassy area that has picnic tables and with sandy beaches below the cliffs. **El Capitan, Refugio,** and **Gaviota state beaches** near Santa Barbara have campsites, picnic tables, and fire pits.

LOS ANGELES

Los Angeles is a wholly modern city, created, defined, dependent on, and thrust into prominence by the advances of the modern age: automobiles, airplanes, and the movies. It is among the nation's most ethnically diverse cities, with thriving Hispanic, Korean, Chinese, Japanese, and Middle Eastern communities.

Visitor Information

Convention and Visitors Bureau (✉ 633 W. 5th St., Suite 6000, 90071, ☎ 213/624–7300).

Arriving and Departing

By Bus
Greyhound (✉ 1716 E. 7th St., at Alameda St., ☎ 800/231–2222).

By Car
The main north–south route into Los Angeles is I–5 (called the Golden State or Santa Ana Freeway here). U.S. 101 (called the Hollywood Freeway) travels south through Los Angeles. I–10 (called the Santa Monica Freeway) runs east–west across the United States; its western terminus is Santa Monica. I–15 travels north from San Diego to Los Angeles, then heads northeast toward California's border with Nevada.

By Plane
Los Angeles International Airport (LAX; ☎ 310/646–5252), about 25 mi west of downtown and 10 mi from Beverly Hills, is served by more than 85 major airlines. Four smaller regional airports—in Burbank, Long Beach, Orange County, and Ontario—also serve the greater L.A. area. Taxis to downtown cost $24–$30 (request a flat fee—metered fares are more) and take 20–60 minutes, depending on traffic. **SuperShuttle** (☎ 310/782–6600) services downtown hotels for about $12 ($13 to Disneyland hotels); fares to private residences vary. **Airport Bus** (☎ 714/938–8900 or 800/772–5299) provides service from LAX to the Pasadena ($12 one-way, $20 round-trip) and Anaheim ($14 and $22) areas.

By Train
Amtrak (☎ 800/872–7245) serves Los Angeles's Union Station (✉ 800 N. Alameda St.).

Getting Around Los Angeles

Freeways, whose names can change along the route, are the most efficient way to get from one end of the city to another.

By Public Transportation

The **Southern California Metropolitan Transit Authority** (MTA; ☎ 213/626–4455) provides bus and light-rail service. Bus fare is $1.35 plus 25¢ for a transfer. **DASH** (Downtown Area Short Hop; ☎ 213/626–4455) is a system of minibuses serving the downtown area. DASH runs weekdays 6 AM–7 PM, Saturday 10–5. Stops are every two blocks or so, and you pay 25¢ every time you get on, no matter how far you go.

By Taxi

All cabs must be ordered by phone; companies include **Independent Cab. Co.** (☎ 213/385–8294) and **United Independent Taxi** (☎ 323/653–5050). The metered rate is $1.90 at the flag drop and $1.60 per mile thereafter. A flat fee is available in the downtown area.

Orientation Tours

Starline Tours of Hollywood (☎ 323/463–3333 or 800/959–3131) offers tours of movie stars' homes, Disneyland, Universal Studios, Sea World of California, the J. Paul Getty Museum, and other attractions.

Exploring Los Angeles

Downtown

★ Pyramidal skylights mark the **Museum of Contemporary Art at California Plaza** (⊠ 250 S. Grand Ave., ☎ 213/626–6222, ⊠ $6; free Thurs. 5–8), which was designed by renowned Japanese architect Arata Isozaki. The 5,000-piece permanent collection is split between the Geffen Contemporary (⊠ 152 Central Ave., ☎ 213/621–1727) and the galleries at this site. The collection includes works from the 1940s to the present; artists represented include Mark Rothko, Franz Kline, Susan Rothenberg, Diane Arbus, and Robert Frank.

On weekends especially, **Chinatown**'s colorful shops, exotic markets, and restaurants attract crowds of shoppers. Fiestas are held nearly every weekend on **Olvera Street,** a Mexican-style marketplace with shops, stalls, restaurants, and the oldest downtown building (1818). Olvera Street is part of the 44-acre **El Pueblo de Los Angeles Historical Monument** (⊠ Sepulveda House visitor center, 622 N. Main St., ☎ 213/628–1274), which celebrates the birthplace of Los Angeles (no one knows exactly where the original 1781 settlement was). First Street and Central Avenue are in the heart of **Little Tokyo.** The **Japanese American**
★ **National Museum** (⊠ 369 E. 1st St., ☎ 213/625–0414, ⊠ $6) chronicles the Japanese-American experience.

Amid shops and sidewalk vendors along Broadway catering to the Hispanic community, **Grand Central Market** (⊠ 317 S. Broadway, ☎ 213/624–2378) has exotic produce, herbs, and meats. Across the street, the Victorian-era **Bradbury Building** (⊠ 304 S. Broadway, ☎ 213/626–1893) has a filigreed, glassed-in courtyard and open balconies.

A few miles south of Broadway is **Exposition Park** (⊠ Figueroa St. at Exposition Blvd.), site of 1932 and 1984 Olympics events and home to the impressive **California Science Center** (☎ 323/724–3623; ⊠ free, IMAX prices vary, parking $5) and **Natural History Museum of Los Angeles County** (☎ 213/763–3466; ⊠ $8, free 1st Tues. of month).

Los Angeles

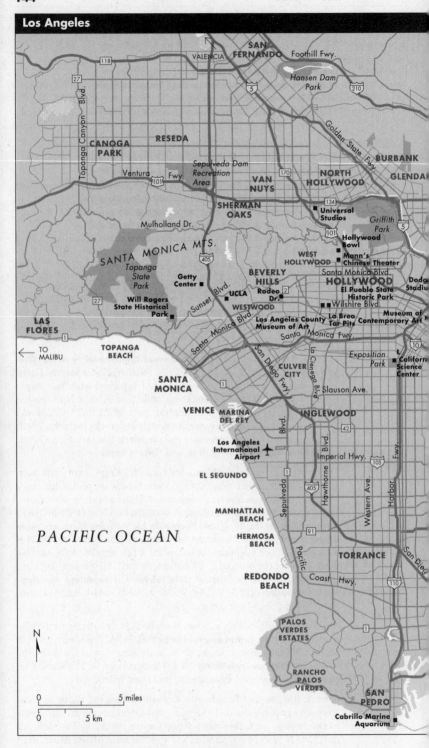

SAN FERNANDO

VALENCIA

Foothill Fwy.

Hansen Dam Park

BURBANK

GLENDA

CANOGA PARK

RESEDA

Topanga Canyon Blvd.

Sepulveda Dam Recreation Area

VAN NUYS

NORTH HOLLYWOOD

Ventura Fwy

Golden State Fwy.

SHERMAN OAKS

Universal Studios

Mulholland Dr.

Griffith Park

SANTA MONICA MTS.

Hollywood Bowl

WEST HOLLYWOOD

Mann's Chinese Theater

Topanga State Park

Getty Center

BEVERLY HILLS

Santa Monica Blvd.

HOLLYWOOD

Will Rogers State Historical Park

UCLA

Rodeo Dr.

El Pueblo State Historic Park

Dodg Stadiu

Sunset Blvd.

WESTWOOD

Wilshire Blvd.

LAS FLORES

Santa Monica Blvd.

Los Angeles County Museum of Art

La Brea Tar Pits

Museum of Contemporary Art

TO MALIBU

TOPANGA BEACH

Santa Monica Fwy.

Santa Monica Blvd.

Exposition Park

Californ Science Center

SANTA MONICA

CULVER CITY

San Diego Fwy.

La Cienega Blvd.

Slauson Ave.

VENICE

MARINA DEL REY

INGLEWOOD

Los Angeles International Airport

Sepulveda Blvd.

Imperial Hwy.

Hawthorne Blvd.

Western Ave.

Harbor Fwy.

EL SEGUNDO

MANHATTAN BEACH

PACIFIC OCEAN

HERMOSA BEACH

TORRANCE

San Die

REDONDO BEACH

Pacific Coast Hwy.

N

PALOS VERDES ESTATES

RANCHO PALOS VERDES

SAN PEDRO

0   5 miles

0   5 km

Cabrillo Marine Aquarium

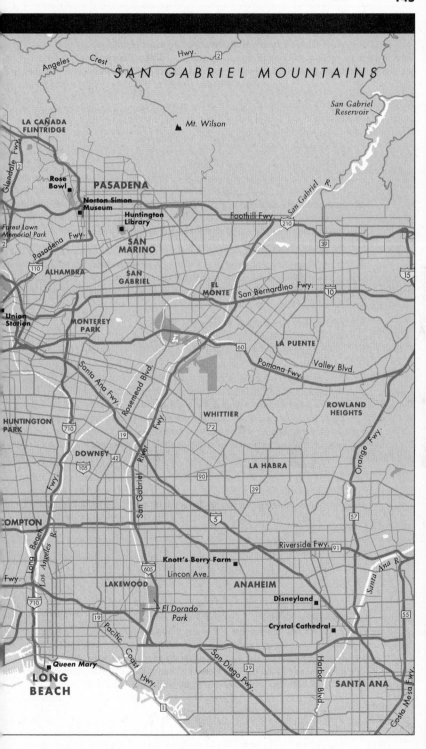

Hollywood

The cradle of the movie industry is rife with landmarks of its glamorous past. The 50-ft-tall **HOLLYWOOD** sign in the hills above the movie colony can be seen miles away. The **Griffith Observatory** (✉ Griffith Park, ☎ 323/664–1191) is recognizable from films like *Rebel Without a Cause*. At **Paramount Pictures** (✉ 5555 Melrose Ave., ☎ 323/956–5575, ✆ $15), walking tours are offered of the only major motion picture studio still in Hollywood. The **Capitol Records Tower** (✉ 1750 N. Vine St.) was built in 1956 to resemble a stack of records. Along Hollywood Boulevard, **Frederick's of Hollywood** (✉ 6608 Hollywood Blvd., ☎ 323/466–8506), the famous name in risqué lingerie, has a bra museum. **Mann's Chinese Theatre** (✉ 6925 Hollywood Blvd., ☎ 323/464–8111), originally Grauman's Chinese, invented the gala movie premiere; its famous courtyard holds the footprints and other bodily impressions of more than 160 celebrities. The **Hollywood Entertainment Museum** (✉ 7021 Hollywood Blvd., ☎ 323/485–7900; ✆ $7.50) tracks the evolution of Hollywood through multimedia exhibits.

The **Hollywood Walk of Fame** immortalizes the names of movie and other entertainment greats on brass plaques embedded in pink stars along the city's sidewalks. Marlon Brando is at 1765 Vine Street, Clark Gable at 1608 Vine, John Wayne at 1541 Vine, and Marilyn Monroe at 6774 Hollywood Boulevard.

Museum Row and Farmers Market

Wilshire Boulevard begins its grand, 16-mi sweep to the sea in downtown Los Angeles. Along the way, it passes through formerly grand but now run-down neighborhoods near MacArthur Park, the elegant old-money enclave of Hancock Park, the showy city of Beverly Hills, and the high-priced, high-rise condo corridor in Westwood before ending its march at the cliffs above the Pacific Ocean. For most visitors, the three-block stretch of Wilshire Boulevard east of Fairfax Avenue, with its six museums of widely varying themes and a prehistoric tar pit to boot, turns out to be the most entertaining portion to explore.

At **La Brea Tar Pits** more than 100 tons of fossils have been removed. Many fossils are on view next door at the **Page Museum** (✉ 5801 Wilshire Blvd., ☎ 323/934–7243; ✆ $6, free 1st Tues. of month). Next door is the **Los Angeles County Museum of Art** (✉ 5905 Wilshire Blvd., ☎ 323/857–6000, ✆ $7, free 2nd Tues. of month), containing fine collections of American and Asian art, and a small sculpture garden. The **Petersen Automotive Museum** (✉ 6060 Wilshire Blvd., ☎ 323/930–2277; ✆ $7) traces the history of the automobile. North of Museum Row is **Farmers Market** (✉ 6333 W. 3rd St., ☎ 323/933–9211), a partly covered marketplace with food stalls, produce vendors, and a few boutiques located near CBS Television Studios.

Beverly Hills

Beverly Hills lures armies of visitors on the lookout for a famous face and a glimpse of opulence—especially along the ritzy **Rodeo Drive** shopping district. For years the Pink Palace, the **Beverly Hills Hotel** (✉ 9641 Sunset Blvd., ☎ 310/276–2251), has been a landmark of the Hollywood high life. The **Museum of Television and Radio** (✉ 465 N. Beverly Dr., ☎ 310/786–1000, ✆ $6) has a collection of 90,000 radio and TV shows spanning eight decades.

The Westside

The Westside districts of Westwood, Brentwood, and Bel Air are among L.A.'s most exclusive, with palatial homes, chic shops, and fine restaurants. The **Museum of Tolerance** (✉ 9786 W. Pico Blvd., ☎ 310/553–8403, ✆ $8.50) uses state-of-the-art technology to confront bigotry and racism. **Westwood,** which straddles the hillsides between Wilshire and Sunset boulevards, is home to the **University of California at Los Angeles.** UCLA has sculpture and botanical gardens, the **Fowler Museum of Cultural History** (☎ 310/825–4361), and offers walking tours of the campus (☎ 310/825–8764). The university operates the nearby **Armand Hammer Museum of Art and Cultural Center** (✉ 10899 Wilshire Blvd., ☎ 310/443–7000; ✍ $4.50, free Thurs. 11–9, parking $2.75). Northwest of Beverly Hills in the Santa Monica Mountains is the Richard Meier–designed **Getty Center** (✉ 1200 Getty Center Dr., ☎ 310/440–7300, ✍ free, $5 parking), the home of most of oil billionaire J. Paul Getty's art collection.

Santa Monica and the Beach Cities

Wilshire Boulevard ends at Ocean Avenue in **Santa Monica.** The **Santa Monica Pier** (☎ 310/458–8900) has a 46-horse antique carousel, an amusement park, gift shops, arcade, cafés, and a psychic adviser. A sandy beach stretches north and south of the pier. Palm-shaded **Palisades Park** overlooks the beach from the cliffs above. North from Santa Monica along the Pacific Coast Highway is **Malibu,** site of the beachfront homes of many stars.

Venice, immediately south of Santa Monica, is known for its active scenes—street vendors, musicians, in-line skaters, guys and gals pumping iron, and folks simply tanning—on **Ocean Front Walk** and the **Venice Boardwalk.**

San Fernando Valley

Universal Studios Hollywood, 5 mi north of Hollywood in the San Fernando Valley via the Hollywood Freeway, is a tremendously popular theme park, with five- to seven-hour tram tours of its attractions, which feature plenty of special effects and stage shows. ✉ *100 Universal City Pl.,* ☎ *818/508–9600.* ✍ *$41 adults, $31 children. AE, MC, V.* ❧

NBC studios (✉ 3000 W. Alameda, Burbank, ☎ 818/840–3537; ✍ $7) offers a walking tour of its facility.

Warner Bros. Studios provides a behind-the-scenes walking tour of its television and film operations. Reserve tickets at least one week in advance. ✉ *4000 Warner Blvd., Burbank,* ☎ *818/954–1744.* ✍ *$30. AE, MC, V. No children under 8.*

Pasadena

The communities northeast of downtown L.A. were the first suburbs of the city, established by wealthy Angelenos in the 1880s. In Highland Park the **Southwest Museum** (✉ 234 Museum Dr., ☎ 323/221–2163; ✍ $5), which is closed on Monday, houses a collection of Native American art and artifacts. In San Marino the **Huntington Library, Art Collections, and Botanical Gardens** (✉ 1151 Oxford Rd., ☎ 626/405–2100, ✍ $8.50, free 1st Thurs. of month) are spread over 207 hilly acres. The complex's collections number more than 4 million items, including a Gutenberg Bible, the Ellesmere manuscript of Chaucer's *Canterbury Tales,* and first editions by Shakespeare.

In Pasadena the **Norton Simon Museum** (✉ 411 W. Colorado Blvd., ☎ 626/449–6840; ✍ $6) houses Impressionist paintings, as well as masterpieces by Rembrandt, Goya, and Picasso. **Gamble House** (✉ 4 Westmoreland Pl., ☎ 626/793–3334, built by Charles and Henry Greene in 1908, is the ultimate in California Craftsman–style architecture. The restored historic buildings of **Old Town Pasadena** now house many popular cafés and shops.

Long Beach

To the south, in Long Beach, is the **Queen Mary** (⊠ Pier J, ☎ 562/435–3511), the famous ocean liner that now houses a hotel, shops, and restaurants. Also in or near Long Beach are two aquariums: the **Long Beach Aquarium of the Pacific** (⊠ 100 Aquarium Way, ☎ 562/590–3100; ☎ $14.95) and the smaller **Cabrillo Marine Aquarium** (⊠ 3720 Stephen White Dr., San Pedro, ☎ 310/548–7562; ☎ $2 donation requested, parking $6.50), designed by Frank Gehry.

Outside Los Angeles

Santa Catalina Island, 26 mi offshore, is a good day trip or weekend getaway from Los Angeles. No private cars are permitted on the island (golf carts can be rented), but the main town of Avalon can be easily explored on foot. From San Pedro and Long Beach, **Catalina Express** (310/519–1212 or 800/995–4386) provides boat service. **Santa Catalina Island Co.** (☎ 310/510–8687) and **Catalina Adventure Tours** (☎ 310/510–2888) operate escorted bus tours of the interior, coastal cruises, and glass-bottom-boat rides.

Parks, Gardens, and Zoos

★ **Griffith Park** (⊠ Ventura and Golden State Fwys., ☎ 213/665–5188) has acres of picnic areas, hiking and bridle trails, a carousel, and pony rides. Also in the park are the **Los Angeles Zoo** (☎ 323/644–6400; ☎ $8.25); **Travel Town** (⊠ 5200 Zoo Dr., ☎ 323/662–5874; ☎ free), with railcars, planes, and classic cars; and the **Planetarium and Observatory** (⊠ enter at Los Feliz Blvd. and Vermont Ave., ☎ 323/664–1191; ☎ $4; ☞ Exploring Los Angeles, *above*).

Dining

Parking can be difficult; most restaurants listed here offer valet parking.

$$$$ ✕ **Citrus.** One of L.A.'s most prominent chefs, Michel Richard, cre-
★ ates superb dishes by blending French and American cuisines. You can't miss with the artichoke terrine or crab cakes with tomato-mustard sauce. ⊠ *6703 Melrose Ave., Hollywood,* ☎ *323/857–0034. Reservations essential. AE, MC, V. No lunch weekdays.*

$$$$ ✕ **L'Orangerie.** French specialties at this elegant restaurant (jacket
★ and tie advised) include duck with foie gras, John Dory with roasted figs, rack of lamb for two, and a sublime apple tart. ⊠ *903 N. La Cienega Blvd., West Hollywood,* ☎ *310/652–9770. Reservations essential. AE, D, DC, MC, V. Closed Mon. No lunch.*

$$$–$$$$ ✕ **Granita.** The menu at this Wolfgang Puck eatery favors seafood items.
★ ⊠ *23725 W. Malibu Rd., Malibu,* ☎ *310/456–0488. Reservations essential. D, DC, MC, V. Brunch weekends. No lunch.*

$$$–$$$$ ✕ **Spago Hollywood.** At this restaurant that propelled Wolfgang Puck into the culinary spotlight, the proof is in the tasting: tempura Maryland soft-shell crabs and grilled Alaskan salmon with lemongrass. ⊠ *1114 Horn Ave., West Hollywood,* ☎ *310/652–4025. Reservations essential. D, DC, MC, V. Closed Mon. No lunch.*

$$–$$$$ ✕ **Campanile.** The restaurant in Charlie Chaplin's former office com-
★ plex serves dishes that include celery-root soup with pesto, lobster risotto, and loin of venison with quince puree. ⊠ *624 S. La Brea Ave., Hollywood,* ☎ *323/938–1447. Reservations essential. AE, D, DC, MC, V. Brunch weekends. No dinner Sun.*

$$–$$$$ ✕ **Dining Room at the Regent Beverly Wilshire.** The classy California
★ cuisine served here includes Chilean sea bass with bok choy and lemongrass essence. Adjoining the Dining Room is a cocktail lounge, with romantic lighting and a pianist playing show tunes. ⊠ *Regent Beverly*

Wilshire Hotel, 9500 Wilshire Blvd., Beverly Hills, ☎ *310/275–5200. Jacket required. AE, D, DC, MC, V.*

$$–$$$$ ✕ **La Cachette.** Owner-chef Jean-François Meteigner's modern French
★ cuisine manages to be both light and appealing. ⊠ *10506 Little Santa Monica Blvd., West Los Angeles,* ☎ *310/470–4992. Reservations essential. AE, MC, V. No lunch weekends.*

$$–$$$$ ✕ **Valentino.** The light, modern Italian dishes at this top-notch restau-
★ rant include carpaccio with arugula and shaved Parmesan and lamb shank with saffron risotto. Order from the lengthy list of daily specials. ⊠ *3115 Pico Blvd., Santa Monica,* ☎ *310/829–4313. Reservations essential. AE, DC, MC, V. Closed Sun. No lunch Sat. and Mon.–Thurs.*

$$–$$$$ ✕ **Yujean Kang's Gourmet Chinese Cuisine.** Start with the tender slices
★ of veal on a bed of enoki mushrooms and topped with a tangle of quick-fried shoestring yams or the sea bass with kumquats and a passion-fruit sauce; then finish with poached plums or with watermelon ice under a mantle of white chocolate. ⊠ *67 N. Raymond Ave., Pasadena,* ☎ *626/585–0855. AE, D, DC, MC, V.*

$$–$$$ ✕ **Ca'Brea.** The modern Italian fare includes roast leg of lamb with
★ black-truffle-and-mustard sauce and whole boneless chicken marinated and grilled with herbs. ⊠ *346 S. La Brea Ave., Hollywood,* ☎ *323/938–2863. AE, D, DC, MC, V. Closed Sun. No lunch weekends.*

$–$$$ ✕ **Chan Dara.** Try any of the Thai noodle dishes here, especially those
★ with crab and shrimp. Also tops on the extensive menu are *satay* (skewered meat appetizers with peanut sauce) and barbecued chicken and catfish. ⊠ *310 N. Larchmont Blvd., Hollywood,* ☎ *323/467–1052. AE, D, DC, MC, V. No lunch weekends.*

$$ ✕ **Border Grill.** The eclectic menu here ranges from grilled tandoori
★ skirt steak marinated in garlic and cilantro to grilled fish tacos to vinegar-and-pepper-grilled turkey. ⊠ *1445 4th St., Santa Monica,* ☎ *310/451–1655. AE, D, DC, MC, V. No lunch Mon.*

$$ ✕ **Broadway Deli.** Whatever you feel like eating at this brasserie-cum-
★ upscale-diner, you will probably find it on the menu, from a platter of assorted smoked fish or Caesar salad to shepherd's pie, carpaccio, steak, and grilled swordfish. ⊠ *1457 3rd St. Promenade, Santa Monica,* ☎ *310/451–0616. Reservations not accepted. AE, MC, V.*

$$ ✕ **El Cholo.** This restaurant serves zesty margaritas and tacos (includ-
★ ing some you make yourself), along with L.A.-Mex versions of chicken enchiladas and other standards. ⊠ *1121 S. Western Ave., Mid-Wilshire,* ☎ *323/734–2773. AE, DC, MC, V.*

Lodging

Because L.A. is so sprawling, you'll want to select a hotel close to where you'll be touring.

$$$$ 🏨 **Mondrian.** Mod apartment-size accommodations at this ultrahip Ian
★ Schrager–run property have floor-to-ceiling windows, slipcovered sofas, and marble coffee tables; many have kitchens. ⊠ *8440 Sunset Blvd., West Hollywood 90069,* ☎ *323/650–8999 or 800/525–8029,* 𝔽𝔸𝕏 *323/650–5215. 238 rooms. Restaurant, pool, health club. AE, D, DC, MC, V.* 🐾

$$$$ 🏨 **Regal Biltmore Hotel.** Many historic details at this elegant landmark building remain. Guest rooms have overstuffed beds, flowing draperies, and period furnishings. ⊠ *506 S. Grand Ave., downtown, 90071,* ☎ *213/624–1011 or 800/245–8673,* 𝔽𝔸𝕏 *213/612–1545. 769 rooms. 3 restaurants, pool, health club. AE, D, DC, MC, V.* 🐾

$$$$ 🏨 **Regent Beverly Wilshire.** Known as the *Pretty Woman* hotel (a pres-
★ idential suite was showcased in the film), the Regent is a longtime classic. Accommodations have appropriate period furnishings and glorious

marble bathrooms with deep tubs. ⊠ *9500 Wilshire Blvd., Beverly Hills 90212,* ☏ *310/275–5200 or 800/427–4354 in CA, 800/421–4354 outside CA;* FAX *310/274–2851. 511 rooms. 2 restaurants, pool, health club. AE, DC, MC, V.* ✍

$$$$ 🖬 **Shutters on the Beach.** Locals looking to get away from it all often
★   come to Los Angeles's only hotel sitting directly on the sand. Amenities include fluffy beds with Frette linens, lavish tubs, and complimentary classic movies for the VCR. ⊠ *1 Pico Blvd., Santa Monica 90405,* ☏ *310/458–0030 or 800/334–9000,* FAX *310/458–4589. 198 rooms. 2 restaurants, pool, health club. AE, D, DC, MC, V.* ✍

$$–$$$$ 🖬 **Carlyle Inn.** The contemporary four-story hotel gives guests extras such as a buffet breakfast in the morning and wine and cheese in the afternoon. Modern rooms have amenities including bathrobes and hair dryers. ⊠ *1119 S. Robertson Blvd., near Beverly Hills 90035,* ☏ *310/275–4445 or 800/322–7595,* FAX *310/859–0496. 32 rooms. Exercise room. AE, D, DC, MC, V. BP.* ✍

$$$ 🖬 **Beverly Hills Inn.** This European-style inn is a nice alternative to the
★   town's more mammoth (and more expensive) luxury hotels. The address is trendy, the service is excellent, and a complimentary breakfast is delivered to your door each morning. ⊠ *125 S. Spalding Dr., Beverly Hills 90212,* ☏ *310/278–0303 or 800/463–4466,* FAX *310/278–1728. 50 rooms. Pool, exercise room. AE, DC, MC, V. CP.*

$$$ 🖬 **Clarion Hotel Hollywood Roosevelt.** A landmark hotel with a hip Art Deco lobby, the Hollywood Roosevelt hosted Tinseltown's golden-age elite. The room decor isn't as grand as in the old days, but the hotel is convenient to some attractions (Mann's Chinese Theater is across the street). ⊠ *7000 Hollywood Blvd., Hollywood 90028,* ☏ *323/466–7000 or 800/950–7667,* FAX *323/462–8056. 359 rooms. Restaurant, pool, exercise room. AE, D, DC, MC, V.* ✍

$$$ 🖬 **Sportsmen's Lodge.** An English country–style structure, this hotel has attractive grounds and rooms done in soft colors. Studio suites with private patios are available. ⊠ *12825 Ventura Blvd., Studio City 91604,* ☏ *818/769–4700 or 800/821–8511,* FAX *213/877–3898. 191 rooms. 3 restaurants, pool, exercise room. AE, D, DC, MC, V.* ✍

$$$ 🖬 **Westin Los Angeles Airport.** Here's a great place to stay if you want
★   to be pampered but also need to be close to the airport. Many suites have private outdoor hot tubs. ⊠ *5400 W. Century Blvd., 90045,* ☏ *310/216–5858 or 800/937–8461,* FAX *310/670–1948. 765 rooms. Restaurant, pool, exercise room. AE, D, DC, MC, V.* ✍

$$–$$$ 🖬 **Crescent Hotel.** A rare value in its swank zip code, this small-European-style hotel is lean on services but provides little extras such as complimentary snacks and fresh fruits. Standard rooms are on the spartan side, but the price is right. ⊠ *403 N. Crescent Dr., Beverly Hills 90210,* ☏ *310/247–0505 or 800/451–1566,* FAX *310/247–9053. 41 rooms. AE, D, DC, MC, V. CP.* ✍

$$–$$$ 🖬 **Hotel Carmel.** Price and location (near the beach and shopping) make this hotel a popular choice. Basic rooms are spacious, some with ocean views. ⊠ *201 Broadway, Santa Monica 90401,* ☏ *310/451–2469 or 800/445–8695,* FAX *310/393–4180. 102 rooms. AE, D, DC, MC, V. CP.* ✍

$$ 🖬 **Figueroa Hotel and Convention Center.** The Spanish feel of this 12-story hotel built in 1926 is accented by terra-cotta-color rooms, hand-painted furniture, wrought-iron beds, and, in many rooms, ceiling fans. ⊠ *939 S. Figueroa St. (downtown), 90015,* ☏ *213/627–8971 or 800/421–9092,* FAX *213/689–0305. 287 rooms. 2 restaurants, pool. AE, DC, MC, V.* ✍

$$ 🖬 **Kawada Hotel.** Akin to a small European hotel, this property near the Music Center and local government buildings has good service, immaculate (if smallish) rooms, and an excellent restaurant. ⊠ *200 S.*

Hill St. (downtown), 90012, ☎ 213/621–4455 or 800/752–9232, FAX 213/687–4455. 116 rooms. 2 restaurants. AE, DC, MC, V.

$ 🖬 **Banana Bungalow Hotel and International Hostel.** You'll get good value for your money at this friendly, no-smoking inn, which is open only to those heading in or out of the country—show proof in the form of a passport and ticket. ⊠ *2775 Cahuenga Blvd. W, Hollywood 90068, ☎ 323/851–1129 or 800/446–7835, FAX 323/851–1569. 22 dorm rooms, 13 private rooms. Restaurant, pool, exercise room. MC, V.*

$ 🖬 **The InnTowne.** This modern three-story hotel 1½ blocks from the convention center has large rooms with beige-and-white or gray-and-white color schemes. A bar and coffee shop are on site. ⊠ *913 S. Figueroa St. (downtown), 90015, ☎ 213/628–2222 or 800/457–8520, FAX 213/687–0566. 171 rooms. Pool. AE, D, DC, MC, V.*

Nightlife and the Arts

For the most complete listing of weekly events, consult the current issue of *Los Angeles* magazine. The "Calendar" section of the *Los Angeles Times* also lists a wide survey of Los Angeles arts events, as do the more alternative publications, the *L.A. Weekly* and the *New Times Los Angeles* (both free). Most tickets can be purchased by phone from **Ticketmaster** (☎ 213/480–3232). For an additional charge, tickets can also be purchased from **Good Time Tickets** (☎ 323/464–7383).

Nightlife

COMEDY

The **Comedy Store** (⊠ 8433 Sunset Blvd., West Hollywood, ☎ 323/656–6225) showcases comedians, including top names. The **Improvisation** (⊠ 8162 Melrose Ave., West Hollywood, ☎ 323/651–2583) features comedy and some music. The **Laugh Factory** (⊠ 8001 Sunset Blvd., West Hollywood, ☎ 323/656–8860) offers stand-up comedy and improvisation.

DANCE CLUBS

A dressed-to-impress, upscale crowd frequents the **Century Club** (⊠ 10131 Constellation Blvd., Century City, ☎ 310/553–6000), where dance grooves range from Latin to hip hop to electronic. If you're nostalgic for the 1960s, stop by the tourist-friendly **Crush Bar** (⊠ 1743 Cahuenga Ave., Hollywood, ☎ 323/461–9017), open Friday through Sunday. **Sugar** (⊠ 814 Broadway, Santa Monica, ☎ 310/899–1989) is one of the most popular West Side dance clubs, with DJs spinning (house, drum and bass, techno) Friday and Saturday.

LIVE MUSIC

At the **Atlas Bar and Grill** (⊠ 3760 Wilshire Blvd., Los Angeles, ☎ 213/380–8400) you'll hear jazz and torch in a classy, historic Art Deco supper club. Crowds squeeze in to hear powerhouse jazz and blues at the tiny **Baked Potato** (⊠ 3787 Cahuenga Blvd. W, North Hollywood, ☎ 818/980–1615). You can hear exceptional jazz performers at **Club Brasserie** (⊠ Bel Age Hotel, 1020 N. San Vicente Blvd., West Hollywood, ☎ 310/358–7776) from Thursday through Saturday.

The **Roxy** (⊠ 9009 Sunset Blvd., West Hollywood, ☎ 310/276–2222), classy and comfortable, is L.A.'s premier rock club, though it presents stage productions as well. The **Viper Room** (⊠ 8852 Sunset Blvd., West Hollywood, ☎ 310/358–1880) is a notorious hangout for musicians and movie stars. The live music is loud and purely contemporary, with an alternative bent. The **Whiskey A Go Go** (⊠ 8901 Sunset Blvd., West Hollywood,, ☎ 310/652–4202) is the most famous rock-and-roll club on the Sunset Strip, with up-and-coming alternative, very hard rock, and punk bands. For the most current alternative sounds, head to **Spaceland** (⊠ 1717 Silver Lake Blvd., Silver Lake, ☎ 213/833–2843).

The Arts

MUSIC

The **Dorothy Chandler Pavilion** (✉ 135 N. Grand Ave., ☎ 213/972–7211) is home to the Los Angeles Philharmonic Orchestra and presents other large-scale productions. The **Hollywood Bowl** (✉ 2301 Highland Ave., Hollywood, ☎ 323/850–2000) offers an outdoor summer season of classical jazz, international, and popular music. The outdoor **Greek Theater** (✉ 2700 N. Vermont Ave., ☎ 323/665–1927) presents big-name performers in its mainly pop-rock-jazz schedule from June through October.

THEATER

Plays are presented at two of the three theaters at the **Performing Arts Center of Los Angeles County** (✉ 135 N. Grand Ave.): the Ahmanson Theatre (☎ 213/628–2772) and the **Mark Taper Forum** (☎ 213/628–2772). The **James A. Doolittle Theatre** (✉ 1615 N. Vine St., Hollywood, ☎ 323/462–6666) presents dramas, comedies, and musicals. The **Geffen Playhouse** (✉ 10886 Le Conte Ave., Westwood, ☎ 310/208–6500 or 310/208–5454) presents musicals and comedies year-round. Many of the productions here are on their way to or from Broadway.

Spectator Sports

Baseball: Los Angeles Dodgers (✉ Dodger Stadium, 1000 Elysian Park Ave. [downtown], ☎ 323/224–1448). **Basketball: Los Angeles Lakers** (✉ The Staples Center, 1111 S. Figueroa St. [downtown], ☎ 310/426–6000). **Los Angeles Clippers** (✉ The Staples Center, 1111 S. Figueroa St. [downtown], ☎ 213/742–7500). **Hockey: Los Angeles Kings** (✉ The Staples Center, 1111 S. Figueroa St. [downtown], ☎ 213/742–7100). **Horse Racing: Santa Anita Race Track** (✉ Huntington Dr. and Colorado Pl., Arcadia, ☎ 626/574–7223), late December–April, October–mid-November; **Hollywood Park** (✉ Century Blvd. and Prairie Ave., Inglewood, ☎ 310/419–1500), April–mid-July, mid-November–December 24. **Soccer: Galaxy** (✉ Rose Bowl, Arroyo Blvd., Pasadena, ☎ 888/657–5425).

Beaches

Los Angeles County beaches (and state beaches operated by the county) have lifeguards. Public parking (for a fee) is widely available, most state beaches have picnic and rest-room facilities, and most city beaches (some local favorites are listed below from north to south) are lined with a boardwalk that has plenty of services.

Leo Carrillo State Beach (✉ 35000 Pacific Coast Hwy. [PCH], Malibu, ☎ 818/880–0350) is fun at low tide, when tide pools emerge. There are hiking trails, sea caves, and tunnels, and you can often see whales, dolphins, and sea lions.

Zuma Beach Park (✉ 30050 PCH, Malibu, ☎ 310/457–9891), Malibu's largest and sandiest beach, is a favorite surfing spot and teen hangout.

Westward Beach–Point Dume (✉ south end of Westward Beach Rd., Malibu, ☎ 310/457–9891) has tide pools and sandstone cliffs. It's a favorite surfing spot among older surfers because of its slow, long-breaking waves.

Surfrider Beach/Malibu Lagoon State Beach (✉ 23200 PCH, Malibu, ☎ 818/880–0350), north of Malibu Pier, has steady 3- to 5-ft waves that make it great for long-board surfing. The International Surfing Contest is held here each September. The lagoon is a sanctuary for many birds.

Topanga County Beach (✉ 18700 block of PCH, Malibu, ☎ 310/394–3266), rocky but a favorite with surfers, stretches from the mouth of Topanga Canyon down to Coastline Drive.

Will Rogers County Beach (⊠ 15100 PCH, Pacific Palisades, ☎ 310/394–3266) is a wide, sandy beach with a steady, even surf. There's plenty of beach, volleyball, and bodysurfing action parallel to the pedestrian bridge. Parking is limited.

Santa Monica State Beach (⊠ Santa Monica Blvd. and Ocean Ave., Santa Monica, ☎ 310/394–3266), the widest stretch of beach on the Pacific coast, is also one of the most popular, with bike paths, facilities for people with disabilities, playgrounds, and volleyball.

Manhattan Beach (⊠ west of Strand, Manhattan Beach, ☎ 310/372–2166) is a sandy beach with swimming, diving, surfing, fishing, and picnicking.

Redondo Beach (⊠ foot of Torrance Blvd., Redondo Beach, ☎ 310/372–2166) is usually packed in summer, and parking is limited.

Shopping

Shopping Districts
Rodeo Drive in Beverly Hills is the world-famous street where pricey shops sell designer fashions. In downtown L.A., the **Citadel Factory Stores** (⊠ 5675 E. Telegraph Rd., ☎ 323/888–1220) has Benetton, Joan & David, Betsey Johnson, and other outlets. For vintage styles or the just plain weird, go to **Melrose Avenue** between La Brea and Crescent Heights. The **Beverly Center** (⊠ Beverly Blvd. at La Cienega Blvd.) holds more than 200 upscale stores and boutiques. The **Santa Monica Promenade** and **Montana Avenue** feature boutique after boutique of quality goods.

Department Stores
Los Angeles has branches of many national and regional chains, including Bloomingdales, Barneys, Neiman Marcus, Saks Fifth Avenue, Sears, Macy's, Nordstrom, and Robinsons-May.

Gifts and More
Tesoro (⊠ 401 N. Cañon Dr., ☎ 310/273–9890) features highly unusual dishware and art objects. **Star Wares on Main** (⊠ 2817 Main St., ☎ 310/399–0224) sells authentic and duplicate costumes from films, and memorabilia of stars such as Loretta Swit to Liz Taylor.

Vintage Clothing
Golyester (⊠ 136 S. La Brea Ave., ☎ 323/931–1339) sells funky used clothing and home furnishings.

ORANGE COUNTY

Orange County sits between Los Angeles to the north and San Diego to the south. Though primarily suburban, it is one of the top tourist destinations in California, with attractions such as Disneyland, pro sports, and miles of beaches.

Visitor Information

Anaheim Area: Convention and Visitors Bureau (⊠ Anaheim Convention Center, 800 W. Katella Ave., 92802, ☎ 714/765–8888).

Arriving and Departing

By Bus
Greyhound (☎ 714/999–1256) serves Santa Ana and Anaheim.

By Car
I–405 (San Diego Freeway) and I–5 (Santa Ana Freeway) run north–south through Orange County. I–405 merges into I–5 at Irvine.

By Plane

John Wayne Airport Orange County (✉ MacArthur Blvd. at I–405, Santa Ana, ☎ 949/252–5252) is served by a number of major carriers.

By Train

Amtrak (☎ 800/872–7245) trains stop in Fullerton, Anaheim, Santa Ana, Irvine, San Juan Capistrano, and San Clemente.

Exploring Orange County

Inland Orange County

★ ☾ Anaheim is the home of **Disneyland.** Visitors enter the Magic Kingdom by way of Walt Disney's idealized circa-1900 Main Street. Along with the various thrill rides and high-tech wizardry are the strolling Disney characters, a daily parade on Main Street, a dazzling nighttime "Fantasmic" show, and fireworks nightly in summer. The rides in **Fantasyland** are based on children's stories. **Frontierland** depicts the Wild West. The highlight of **Adventureland** is the Indiana Jones thrill ride. New Orleans Square is the setting for **Pirates of the Caribbean**—a boat ride through a scene lavish with animated characters—and the Blue Bayou restaurant. The nearby **Haunted Mansion** is full of holographic ghosts. In Critter Country is **Splash Mountain,** a flume ride that drops 52 ft at 40 mph. **Mickey's Toontown** is a child-size interactive community that gives kids the feeling of being inside a cartoon with Mickey and other characters. **Tomorrowland** has a Buck Rogers–ish feel. The lures here are Space Mountain, Honey I Shrunk the Audience, and Innoventions. ✉ *1313 Harbor Blvd.,* ☎ *714/781–4565.* ⌑ *$38.* ✍

★ ☾ **Knott's Berry Farm,** a 150-acre complex of food, shops, rides, and other attractions, is near Disneyland, in Buena Park. **Ghost Town** re-creates an 1880s mining town; the **Gold Mine** ride descends into a replica of a working gold mine. **Camp Snoopy** is a kid-size High Sierra wonderland where Snoopy and the *Peanuts* gang hang out. At **Wild Water Wilderness** riders can brave white water in an inner tube in the **Big Foot Rapids** or commune with Native peoples of the northwest coast in the spooky **Mystery Lodge.** Thrill rides are placed throughout the park, including the **Wind Jammer, Boomerang, Jaguar!,** and **Montezooma's Revenge** roller coasters. The **Boardwalk** includes dolphin and sea lion shows at the Pacific Pavilion, along with the Good Time and 3-D Nu Wave theaters. And don't forget what made Knott's famous: the fried chicken dinners and boysenberry pies at **Mrs. Knott's Chicken Dinner Restaurant,** outside the park gates in Knott's California MarketPlace. ✉ *8039 Beach Blvd., Buena Park,* ☎ *714/220–5200.* ⌑ *$38.* ✍

The **Movieland Wax Museum** (✉ 7711 Beach Blvd., Buena Park, ☎ 714/522–1155; ⌑ $12.95) re-creates the famous in wax.

Garden Grove is the site of the **Crystal Cathedral** (✉ 12141 Lewis St., Garden Grove, ☎ 714/971–4013), the domain of televangelist Robert Schuller.

The Coast

Pacific Coast Highway (PCH; Highway 1) is the main thoroughfare for all the beach towns along the Orange County coast. **Huntington Beach** is a popular surfer hangout; you can watch the action from the Huntington Pier. South of Huntington Beach is **Newport Beach,** a Beverly-Hills-by-the-sea. Nearly 10,000 boats bob in the U-shape Newport Harbor, which arcs around eight small islands. **Balboa Peninsula,** with its Victorian Balboa Pavilion and active Fun Zone, is a popular visitor area. The **Orange County Museum of Art** (✉ 850 San Clemente Dr., ☎ 949/759–1122; ⌑ $5) emphasizes works by California artists.

★ Farther south is **Corona del Mar,** a small jewel of a town with exceptional beaches. You can walk clear out over the bay on a rough-and-tumble rock jetty, or you can wander about tide pools and hidden caves. Protected by small cliffs, the beaches here resemble those of northern California's coastline. In **Laguna Beach** art galleries in town coexist with volleyball games and sun worship on nearby Main Beach; in July and August the **Pageant of the Masters** (☎ 949/494–1145) features living models re-creating famous paintings. Below Laguna the small harbor town of **Dana Point** is reminiscent of northern California's beaches. In March migrating swallows and spectacle-loving tourists flock to **Mission San Juan Capistrano** (✉ Camino Capistrano and Ortega Hwy., ☎ 949/248–2049).

Dining and Lodging

Anaheim

$$–$$$$ ✕ **JW's Steak House.** This subdued steak house specializes in aged beef but also serves seafood. It's a great place for business or romance. ✉ *Anaheim Marriott, 700 W. Convention Way,* ☎ *714/750–8000. AE, D, DC, MC, V. No lunch.*

$$–$$$$ ✕ **Mr. Stox.** Prime rib, mesquite-grilled rack of lamb, and fresh fish specials are popular at this cozy restaurant. The pastas, breads, and pastries are made on the premises, and the wine list has won awards. ✉ *1105 E. Katella Ave.,* ☎ *714/634–2994. AE, D, DC, MC, V. No lunch weekends.*

$–$$$$ ✕ **Luigi's D'Italia.** Though the surroundings are simple, the Italian cuisine, from spaghetti marinara to cioppino, is excellent. ✉ *801 S. State College Blvd.,* ☎ *714/490–0990. AE, MC, V.*

$$$–$$$$ 🏨 **Disneyland Hotel.** There's a 1950s charm to the buildings at this
★ Disney-owned resort. A stay here can be on the expensive side but is worth it for the true Disney vacation experience. You can save a few dollars with combined room-ticket packages. ✉ *1150 W. Cerritos Ave., 92802,* ☎ *714/778–6600,* ℻ *714/956–6582. 990 rooms. 5 restaurants, pools, health club. AE, D, DC, MC, V.* ✪

$$ 🏨 **Candy Cane Inn.** The name of this motel speaks volumes about the
★ fanciful, family-friendly feel inside. Rooms are spacious. Free Disneyland shuttles run every 30 minutes. ✉ *1747 S. Harbor Blvd., 92802,* ☎ *714/774–5284 or 800/345–7057,* ℻ *714/772–5462 or 714/772–1305. 172 rooms. Pool. AE, D, DC, MC, V.*

$$ 🏨 **Radisson Maingate.** Some of the handsomely decorated rooms in the two eight-story buildings here have pull-out sofas as well as beds. Regular shuttles can zip you over to Disneyland or Knotts Berry Farm, and parking is free. ✉ *1850 S. Harbor Blvd., 92802,* ☎ *714/750–2801 or 800/624–6855,* ℻ *714/971–4754. 314 rooms. Restaurant, pool. AE, D, DC, MC, V.* ✪

$–$$ 🏨 **Best Western Stovall's Inn.** Nice touches at this well-kept motel include a topiary garden, a free shuttle to Disneyland, and Nintendo and movie rentals. ✉ *1110 W. Katella Ave., 92802,* ☎ *714/778–1880 or 800/854–8175,* ℻ *714/778–3805. 290 rooms. Pools. AE, D, DC, MC, V.* ✪

Brea

$$$–$$$$ ✕ **La Vie en Rose.** In this reproduction Norman farmhouse complete
★ with a large turret, traditional French cuisine is served. The menu includes seafood, lamb, and veal. For dessert try the silky crème brûlée or a Grand Marnier soufflé. ✉ *240 S. State College Blvd., across from the Brea Mall,* ☎ *714/529–8333. AE, DC, MC, V. Closed Sun.*

Costa Mesa

$–$$ ✕ **Memphis Soul Café and Bar.** The gumbo here is the best in the county,
★ bar none. The turkey sandwich with pesto is addicting, and the pork chops
are superb. ⊠ *2920 Bristol St.,* ☎ *714/432–7685. AE, DC, MC, V.*

Dana Point

$–$$$ ✕ **Luciana's.** This intimate Italian restaurant is a real find. The well-
prepared food—linguine with clams, prawns, calamari, and green-lip
mussels in a light tomato sauce; veal medallions with haricot verts and
oven-dried tomatoes—is served with care. ⊠ *24312 Del Prado Ave.,*
☎ *949/661–6500. AE, DC, MC, V. No lunch.*

$$$–$$$$ ✕☎ **Ritz-Carlton–Laguna Niguel.** One of California's most highly re-
★ spected hotels, the Ritz has beach access, a spectacular ocean view, the
award-winning Dining Room restaurant, a lavishly decorated lobby,
and spacious rooms. ⊠ *1 Ritz-Carlton Dr., 92629,* ☎ *949/240–2000
or 800/241–3333,* 𝖥𝖠𝖷 *949/240–1061. 332 rooms. 3 restaurants, pools,
tennis, health club. AE, D, DC, MC, V.* ☙

Irvine

$$–$$$ ✕ **Prego.** Reminiscent of a Tuscan villa, this restaurant with an out-
★ door patio glows with soft lighting and golden walls. Try the spit-roasted
meats and chicken, charcoal-grilled fresh fish, or pizzas from the oak-
burning oven. ⊠ *18420 Von Karman Ave.,* ☎ *949/553–1333. AE, DC,
MC, V. No lunch weekends.*

$–$$ ✕ **Kitima Thai Cuisine.** Orange County's best Thai restaurant is tucked
away in an office building. The names may be gimmicky—"Rock and
Roll Shrimp Salad," "Rambo Chicken"—but fresh ingredients are
used in every dish. ⊠ *2010 Main St., Suite 170,* ☎ *949/261–2929. AE,
MC, V. Closed Sun.*

$$$–$$$$ ☎ **Irvine Marriott.** Towering over Koll Business Center, the Marriott is
convenient for business travelers. Despite its size, the hotel has an inti-
mate feel. Weekend discounts and packages are usually available. ⊠ *1800
Von Karman Ave., 92612,* ☎ *949/553–0100,* 𝖥𝖠𝖷 *949/261–7059. 492
rooms. 2 restaurants, pool, tennis, health club. AE, D, DC, MC, V.* ☙

Laguna Beach

$$–$$$$ ✕ **Five Feet.** Delicate pot stickers and Five Feet Catfish are two of the
★ scrumptious dishes here. The setting is pure Laguna: exposed ceiling, open
kitchen, high noise level, and brick walls hung with works by local artists.
⊠ *328 Gleneyre St.,* ☎ *949/497–4955. AE, D, DC, MC, V. No lunch.*

$$–$$$ ✕ **Ti Amo.** A romantic setting and creative Mediterranean cuisine have
earned this place acclaim. Try the seared ahi with a sesame crust or
farfalle with smoked chicken and tomato brandy cream sauce. To
maximize romance, request a table in the enclosed garden in back. ⊠
31727 S. Coast Hwy., ☎ *949/499–5350. AE, D, DC, MC, V. No lunch.*

$$$$ ☎ **Inn at Laguna Beach.** This oceanfront Mediterranean-style inn on
★ a bluff has luxurious amenities and many rooms with views. ⊠ *211
N. Coast Hwy., 92651,* ☎ *949/497–9722 or 800/544–4479,* 𝖥𝖠𝖷 *949/
497–9972. 70 rooms. Pool. AE, D, DC, MC, V.* ☙

Newport Beach

$$–$$$$ ✕ **Aubergine.** A husband-and-wife team runs this restaurant. He heads
★ up the kitchen and she handles the dining room. Classic French dishes
are prepared with modern flair, using only the freshest ingredients. ⊠
508 29th St., ☎ *949/723–4150. Reservations essential. AE, MC, V.
Closed Sun. and Mon. No lunch.*

$–$$ ✕ **El Torito Grill.** The tortilla soup is to die for, as is the carne asada. Just-
★ baked tortillas with fresh salsa replace the usual chip basket. The bar
serves hand-shaken margaritas and 80 brands of tequila. ⊠ *Fashion Island, 951 Newport Center Dr.,* ☎ *949/640–2875. AE, D, DC, MC, V.*

$$$$ 🏨 **Four Seasons Hotel.** A suitably stylish hotel in an ultrachic neigh-
★   borhood (it's across the street from the tony Fashion Island mall), the
20-story Four Seasons caters to luxury seekers by offering weekend golf
packages and extensive fitness facilities. Guest rooms have spectacular views and private bars. ⊠ *690 Newport Center Dr., 92660,* ☎ *949/
759–0808 or 800/332–3442,* ℻ *949/759–0568. 378 rooms. 3 restaurants, pool, tennis, health club. AE, D, DC, MC, V.* ☜

$$$–$$$$ 🏨 **Sutton Place Hotel.** This ultramodern hotel has an eye-catching zig-
gurat design. The luxuriously appointed rooms all have minibars. ⊠ *4500
MacArthur Blvd., 92660,* ☎ *949/476–2001,* ℻ *949/476–0153. 463
rooms. 2 restaurants, pool, tennis, health club. AE, D, DC, MC, V.*

Nightlife and the Arts

The **Orange County Performing Arts Center** (⊠ 600 Town Center Dr.,
Costa Mesa, ☎ 714/556–2787) presents symphony orchestras, opera
companies, and musicals. Next door to the center is the **South Coast
Repertory Theater** (⊠ 655 Town Center Dr., Costa Mesa, ☎ 714/708–
5555), which presents traditional and contemporary works. The **Irvine
Meadows Amphitheater** (⊠ 8800 Irvine Center Dr., ☎ 949/855–8095)
presents summer concerts.

Outdoor Activities and Sports

Biking

A **bike path** runs from Marina del Rey down to San Diego with only
minor breaks. For rentals try **Rainbow Bicycles** (⊠ Laguna, ☎ 949/
494–5806) or **Team Bicycle Rentals** (⊠ Huntington Beach, ☎ 714/969–
5480).

Water Sports

Water-sports equipment rentals are near most piers, including **Hobie Sports**
(⊠ Dana Point, ☎ 949/496–2366; Laguna, ☎ 949/497–3304). **Balboa
Boat Rentals** (☎ 949/673–7200), in Newport Harbor, and **Embarcadero
Marina** (☎ 949/496–6177), at Dana Point, rent sail and powerboats.

Spectator Sports

Baseball: Anaheim Angels (⊠ Edison Field, 2000 Gene Autry Way, ☎
714/634–2000). **Hockey: Mighty Ducks of Anaheim** (⊠ The Arrow-
head Pond of Anaheim, 2695 E. Katella, ☎ 714/740–2000).

Beaches

The beaches along Highway 1 in Orange County are among the finest
and most varied in southern California, with fine swimming, great surf-
ing, and many services. Take posted warnings about undertow seriously.

Huntington State Beach is a long stretch of flat, sandy beach with
changing rooms, concessions, fire pits, and lifeguards. **Lower Newport
Bay** is a sheltered 740-acre preserve for ducks and geese. **Newport Dunes
Resort** offers picnic facilities, changing rooms, and a boat launch.
Corona del Mar State Beach has sandy beaches backed by rocky bluffs
and tide pools and caves. **Laguna** has the county's best spot for scuba
diving—the **Marine Life Refuge**, which runs from Seal Rock to Diver's
Cove. **Main Beach,** a sandy arc steps from downtown Laguna, is a pop-
ular picnic and sand volleyball venue. In South Laguna **Aliso County
Park** has recreational facilities and a playground. **Doheny State Park,**
near Dana Point Harbor, has food stands, camping, and a fishing pier.
San Clemente State Beach has camping facilities and food stands and
is renowned for its surf.

SAN DIEGO

San Diego is the birthplace of Spanish California. Its pleasant climate and beaches encourage plenty of outdoor activities. Downtown is lively with shops and restaurants, and a cluster of museums and the zoo lie within Balboa Park.

Visitor Information

International Visitor Information Center (⊠ 11 Horton Plaza, 92101, ☎ 619/236–1212). **San Diego Visitor Information Center** (⊠ 2688 E. Mission Bay Dr., off I–5, 92109, ☎ 619/276–8200).

Arriving and Departing

By Bus
Greyhound (⊠ 120 W. Broadway, ☎ 800/231–2222).

By Car
I–5 runs north–south. I–8 comes into San Diego from the east, I–15 from the northeast.

By Plane
San Diego International Airport (⊠ N. Harbor Dr., ☎ 619/231–2100) is 3 mi northwest of downtown and is served by most domestic and many international air carriers. The **Cloud 9 Shuttle** (☎ 858/278–8877) has door-to-door service to anywhere in San Diego County, often for less than the cost of a taxi. **San Diego Transit** (☎ 619/233–3004) buses leave the airport every 10–15 minutes and cost $2. Taxi fare is $7–$9 (plus tip) to most center-city hotels.

By Train
Amtrak (☎ 800/872–7245) trains arrive at the **Santa Fe Depot** (⊠ Kettner Blvd. and Broadway, ☎ 619/239–9021).

Getting Around San Diego

It's best to have a car, but avoid the freeways during rush hours. The **San Diego Trolley** (☎ 619/233–3004) travels the 20 mi from downtown to within 100 ft of the Mexican border; other trolleys on the line serve Seaport Village, the Convention Center, Qualcomm Stadium, and inland areas. The **San Diego–Coronado Ferry** (☎ 619/234–4111) provides service from the Broadway Pier to Coronado.

Exploring San Diego

Central San Diego
★ **Balboa Park** encompasses 1,200 acres of cultural, recreational, and environmental delights, including a theater complex and gardens. Among the park's several museums are the **Mingei International Museum of Folk Art** (☎ 619/239–0003; 🎟 $5), devoted to folk art; the **Museum of Photographic Arts** (☎ 619/239–5262; 🎟 $6), with works by Ansel Adams and Henri Carier-Bresson; the **San Diego Museum of Art** (☎ 619/232–7931; 🎟 $8), which hosts major traveling shows; and the **San Diego Aerospace Museum and International Aerospace Hall of Fame** (☎ 619/234–8291; 🎟 $8). Wide-format films are shown on the Omnimax screen of the **Reuben H. Fleet Space Theater and Science Center** (☎ 619/238–1233; 🎟 $6.50).

★ Balboa Park's most famous attraction is the **San Diego Zoo** (⊠ 2920 Zoo Dr., ☎ 619/234–3153, 🎟 $18), where more than 4,000 animals of 800 species roam in habitats like the Gorilla Tropics, Tiger River,

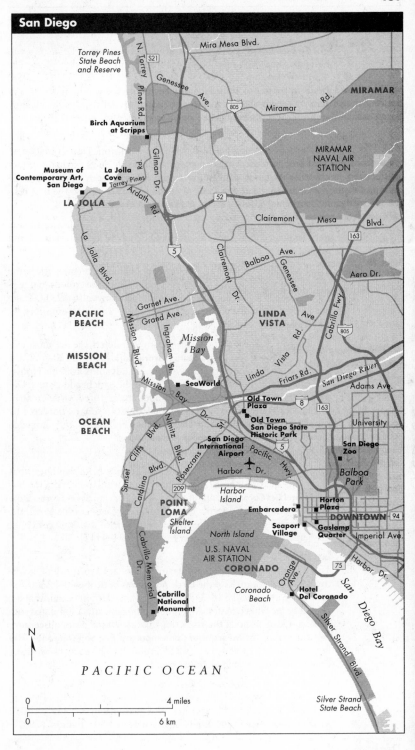

San Diego

Torrey Pines State Beach and Reserve

Mira Mesa Blvd.

S21
N. Torrey Pines Rd.
Genessee Ave.
805
Miramar
Miramar Rd.

MIRAMAR

Birch Aquarium at Scripps

Gilman Dr.

MIRAMAR NAVAL AIR STATION

Museum of Contemporary Art, San Diego

La Jolla Cove
Torrey Pines

Ardath Rd.
52

LA JOLLA

Clairemont Mesa Blvd.
163

5

Clairemont Dr.
Balboa Ave.
Genessee Ave.
Aero Dr.
Cabrillo Fwy
805

La Jolla Blvd.

Garnet Ave.
Grand Ave.

PACIFIC BEACH

Mission Blvd.
Ingraham St.

Mission Bay

LINDA VISTA

Linda Vista Rd.

MISSION BEACH

Mission Bay

Friars Rd.
San Diego River
Adams Ave.

8
163

Sports Arena
SeaWorld

Old Town Plaza
Old Town San Diego State Historic Park

University

OCEAN BEACH

Sunset Cliffs Blvd.
Catalina Blvd.
Nimitz Blvd.
Rosecrans St.

San Diego International Airport

Pacific Hwy
5

San Diego Zoo

Balboa Park

Harbor Dr.

Harbor Island

209

Cabrillo Memorial Dr.

POINT LOMA

Shelter Island

North Island

Embarcadero

Horton Plaza

DOWNTOWN
94

Seaport Village
Gaslamp Quarter
Imperial Ave.

U.S. NAVAL AIR STATION

CORONADO

Orange Ave.
75
Harbor Dr.

Cabrillo National Monument

Coronado Beach

Hotel Del Coronado

San Diego Bay

N

Silver Strand Blvd.

PACIFIC OCEAN

0 ___ 4 miles
0 ___ 6 km

Silver Strand State Beach

and Polar Bear Plunge. The young giant panda, Hua Mei, is the zoo's darling. Call 888/697–2632 to learn about viewing times.

The **Embarcadero,** at the foot of Ash Street on Harbor Drive, is a waterfront walkway lined with restaurants and cruise-ship piers. The **Maritime Museum** (✉ 1306 N. Harbor Dr., ☎ 619/234–9153, ✇ $5) has a collection of restored ships, including the windjammer *Star of India.* **Seaport Village,** a bustling array of specialty shops, snack bars, and restaurants, spreads out across 14 acres and connects the harbor with the San Diego Convention Center.

The **Gaslamp Quarter** is a 16-block National Historic District containing most of San Diego's Victorian-era commercial buildings and many restaurants. At the fringe of the quarter, the **William Heath Davis House** (✉ 410 Island Ave., at 4th Ave., ☎ 619/233–4692), one of the first residences in town, serves as the information center.

Mission Bay, with ocean and bay-shore beaches, is a 4,600-acre aquatic park dedicated to action and leisure. On land are joggers, skaters, and bikers.

The traditional favorite at **SeaWorld of California** theme park is the Shamu show, with giant killer whales entertaining the crowds, but performing dolphins, sea lions, and otters at other shows also delight. There are wet amusement rides too. ✉ *1720 S. Shores Rd., Mission Bay,* ☎ *619/226–3815.* ✇ *$39.*

San Diego's Spanish and Mexican history and heritage are most evident in **Old Town San Diego State Historic Park** (☎ 619/220–5422), a six-block district north of downtown. The **Robinson-Rose House,** once the commercial center of San Diego, is the park headquarters. **Old Town Plaza** contains 20 historic buildings, restored or re-created. **Bazaar del Mundo** resembles a colonial Mexican square, bordered by shops with Latin American crafts. Ballet Folklorico and flamenco dancers perform here on weekend afternoons.

Coronado
The villagelike city of Coronado across the bay from San Diego has numerous Victorian houses. The most prominent landmark is the historic **Hotel Del Coronado,** all turrets and gingerbread. **Silver Strand State Beach** is one of San Diego's nicest. You can reach Coronado via the 2¼-mi San Diego–Coronado Bridge, which yields a stunning view of the San Diego skyline, or by **ferry** (☎ 619/234–4111).

La Jolla
The attractions in the upscale village of La Jolla, 13 mi north of downtown San Diego, include the **Birch Aquarium at Scripps** (✉ 2300 Expedition Way, ☎ 858/534–3474; ✇ $8.50), the largest oceanographic exhibit in the United States. A 70,000-gallon tank and a simulated submarine ride are among the attractions. Works of the past half-century are featured at the **Museum of Contemporary Art, San Diego** (✉ 700 Prospect St., ☎ 858/454–3541; ✇ $4). Palms line the sidewalk on Coast Boulevard along scenic **La Jolla Cove.**

Torrey Pines State Beach and Reserve (☎ 858/755–2063), north of La Jolla, has hiking trails with ocean views. About 30 mi north, Highway 76 east of I–5 leads to the well-preserved **Mission San Luis Rey** (✉ 4050 Mission Ave., Oceanside, ☎ 442/757–3651; ✇ $4), built in 1798.

Dining

$$$–$$$$ ✕ **George's at the Cove.** Enjoy a a view of La Jolla Cove and an imaginative menu heavy on seafood but that also includes pasta, beef, and

lamb. Casual dining and a sweeping view are available on the rooftop terrace. ✉ *1250 Prospect St., La Jolla,* ☎ *619/454–4244. Reservations essential for main dining room on weekends. AE, D, DC, MC, V.*

$$$–$$$$ ✕ **Star of the Sea.** The flagship of this local fleet of seafood restau-
★ rants has a changing menu but expect contemporary preparations, such as roasted salmon with spinach, champagne, and sorrel sauce; and sauté of Gulf prawns. There's a formal dining room and an outdoor patio on the waterfront. ✉ *1360 N. Harbor Dr.,* ☎ *619/232–7408. AE, D, DC, MC, V. No lunch.*

$$–$$$$ ✕ **Dobson's.** A superb mussel bisque is Dobson's signature dish among
★ its contemporary entrées. A business crowd lunches here and theater-goers come for dinner. ✉ *956 Broadway Circle (downtown),* ☎ *619/ 231–6771. AE, DC, MC, V. Closed Sun. No lunch Sat.*

$$–$$$$ ✕ **Laurel.** Polished service and a smart decor set the stage for an imag-inative, expertly prepared menu that takes its inspiration from Mediter-ranean cuisine. ✉ *505 Laurel St. (uptown),* ☎ *619/239–2222. AE, D, DC, MC, V. No lunch.*

$–$$$$ ✕ **Fish Market.** Downstairs, families enjoy fresh fish in a bustling, in-formal dining room whose enormous windows look directly onto the harbor. Upstairs, the more formal Top of the Market serves a distinc-tive menu of exquisitely prepared seafood. ✉ *750 N. Harbor Dr. (downtown),* ☎ *619/232–3474 for the Fish Market, 619/234–4867 for Top of the Market. AE, D, DC, MC, V.*

$$–$$$ ✕ **California Cuisine.** The menu in this minimalist-chic dining room is con-
★ sistently innovative. You can count on careful preparation and elegant presentation. The staff is knowledgeable and attentive, the wine list is good, and the baked desserts and sorbets beckon. ✉ *1027 University Ave.,* ☎ *619/543–0790. AE, D, DC, MC, V. Closed Mon. No lunch weekends.*

$$–$$$ ✕ **Fio's.** Contemporary variations on traditional northern Italian cui-sine are served in a high-ceiling, brick-and-wood dining room over-looking the Gaslamp Quarter scene. The menu includes a range of imaginative pizzas baked in the wood-burning oven and classic Ital-ian dishes. ✉ *801 5th Ave. (downtown),* ☎ *619/234–3467. AE, D, DC, MC, V. No lunch.*

$–$$$ ✕ **Panda Inn.** This dining room at the top of Horton Plaza serves sub-
★ tly seasoned Mandarin and Szechuan dishes in an elegant setting that feels far removed from the rush of commerce below. Try the honey wal-nut shrimp, the Peking duck, the spicy bean curd, and the Panda beef. ✉ *506 Horton Plaza,* ☎ *619/233–7800. AE, D, DC, MC, V.*

$–$$ ✕ **Bayou Bar and Grill.** Seafood gumbo and fresh Louisiana Gulf seafood dishes are among the Cajun and creole specialties served here. Sunday brunches are hearty. ✉ *329 Market St. (downtown),* ☎ *619/ 696–8747. AE, D, DC, MC, V.*

$–$$ ✕ **Berta's Latin American Restaurant.** Berta's serves wonderful Latin American dishes that manage to be tasty and health-conscious at the same time. The simple dining room is small, but there's also a little patio. ✉ *3928 Twiggs St., Old Town,* ☎ *619/295–2343. AE, MC, V.*

$–$$ ✕ **Palenque.** This Pacific Beach restaurant serves a wonderful selec-
★ tion of regional Mexican dishes, including chicken with mole and *ca-marones en chipotle,* large shrimp cooked in a chili-tequila cream sauce (an old family recipe of the proprietor). ✉ *1653 Garnet Ave., Pacific Beach,* ☎ *619/272–7816. AE, D, DC, MC, V. No lunch Mon.*

$ ✕ **Hob Nob Hill.** The French toast, corned beef, and fried chicken taste truly homemade at this restaurant whose dark-wood booths lend a vin-tage feel. ✉ *2271 1st Ave. (uptown),* ☎ *619/239–8176. AE, D, MC, V.*

Lodging

$$$$ 🏨 **La Valencia.** This centrally located pink-stucco Spanish-Mediterranean
★   confection is a La Jolla landmark. It has a courtyard for patio dining
and an elegant lobby where guests congregate to enjoy the ocean view.
Rooms have a romantic European style. ⊠ *1132 Prospect St., La Jolla
92037,* ☎ *858/454–0771 or 800/451–0772,* ⅊⅄ *858/456–3921. 100
rooms. 3 restaurants, pool, exercise room. AE, D, DC, MC, V.* ☟

$$$$ 🏨 **Westgate Hotel.** Antiques, Italian marble counters, and bath fixtures
★   with 24-karat-gold overlays typify the opulent furnishings here. High
tea, breathtaking views from the ninth floor up, and nearby Horton Plaza
are other highlights. ⊠ *1055 2nd Ave. (downtown), 92101,* ☎ *619/
238–1818 or 800/221–3802, 800/522–1564 in CA;* ⅊⅄ *619/557–3737.
223 rooms. 2 restaurants, exercise room. AE, D, DC, MC, V.* ☟

$$$–$$$$ 🏨 **Hotel Del Coronado.** Rooms and suites in the 1888 whimsical Vic-
torian building were redone in 1999–2000 with a Victorian theme. The
Ocean Towers rooms have modern decor. The hotel has a great beach-
front and new terraces for dining. ⊠ *1500 Orange Ave., Coronado
92118,* ☎ *619/435–6611 or 800/468–3533,* ⅊⅄ *619/522–8262. 676
rooms. 2 restaurants, pool. AE, D, DC, MC, V.* ☟

$$–$$$$ 🏨 **Heritage Park Bed & Breakfast Inn.** This romantic 1889 Queen Anne
mansion is full of 19th-century antiques. Rooms run from small to ample.
⊠ *2470 Heritage Park Row, Old Town 92110,* ☎ *619/299–6832 or
800/995–2470,* ⅊⅄ *619/299–9465. 12 rooms. AE, MC, V.*

$$ 🏨 **Gaslamp Plaza Suites.** Listed on the National Registry of Historic
Places, this 11-story structure built in 1913 was San Diego's first
"skyscraper." Although most rooms are rather small, they are well dec-
orated with dark wood furnishings that give the hotel an elegant flair.
Guests can enjoy the view and a complimentary Continental break-
fast on the rooftop terrace. ⊠ *520 E St. (downtown), 92101,* ☎ *619/
232–9500 or 800/874–8770,* ⅊⅄ *619/238–9945. 52 suites. Restau-
rant. AE, D, DC, MC, V.*

$$ 🏨 **Ramada Limited–Old Town.** An excellent value for Old Town, this
★   cheerful property completed a major renovation in 1999 to give the
rooms a European look. You'll find modern conveniences such as coffeemakers, microwave ovens, and refrigerators. ⊠ *3900 Old Town Ave.,
Old Town 92110,* ☎ *619/299–7400 or 800/451–9846,* ⅊⅄ *619/299–
1619. 125 rooms. Pool. AE, D, DC, MC, V. CP.* ☟

$ 🏨 **Point Loma Travelodge.** You'll get the same view here as at the higher-
priced hotels—for far less money. Of course, there are fewer amenities and the neighborhood isn't as serene, but the rooms are adequate
and clean. ⊠ *5102 N. Harbor Dr., 92106,* ☎ *619/223–8171, 800/578–
7878 for central reservations,* ⅊⅄ *619/222–7330. 45 rooms. Pool. AE,
D, DC, MC, V.* ☟

Nightlife and the Arts

The daily *San Diego Union-Tribune* and weekly *Reader* have nightlife
and cultural-event listings. Half-price tickets to most theater, music,
and dance events can be bought on the day of performance at **Times
Arts Tix** (⊠ Horton Plaza, ☎ 619/497–5000). Only cash is accepted.
Advance full-price tickets are also sold. **Ticketmaster** (☎ 619/220–8497)
sells tickets to many cultural and entertainment events. Service charges
vary, and most tickets are nonrefundable.

Nightlife

San Diego's nightlife ranges from quiet piano bars to cutting-edge
rock. The **Casbah** (⊠ 2501 Kettner Blvd., ☎ 619/232–4355) is a small
club with a national reputation for showcasing promising rock bands.

The **Comedy Store La Jolla** (✉ 916 Pearl St., La Jolla, ☎ 619/454–9176) books local and national talent. **Humphrey's by the Bay** (✉ 2241 Shelter Island Dr., ☎ 619/523–1010) presents outdoor concerts in the summer. For cowgirls, cowboys, and city slickers alike, **In Cahoots** (✉ 5373 Mission Center Rd., Mission Valley, ☎ 619/291–8635) gives free dance lessons every day except Wednesday, when seasoned two-steppers strut their stuff on the large dance floor. Happy Hour seven days a week is one of this bar's many lures. The best local Latin, jazz, and blues bands alternate appearances during the week at the classy bar at the **U. S. Grant Hotel** (✉ 326 Broadway [downtown], ☎ 619/232–3121).

The Arts

The **Old Globe Theatre** (✉ Simon Edison Centre, Balboa Park, ☎ 619/239–2255) presents classics, experimental works, and a summer Shakespeare festival. **Spreckels Organ Pavilion** (✉ Balboa Park, ☎ 619/702–8138) holds a giant outdoor pipe organ. Civic organist Robert Plimpton gives concerts on most Sunday afternoons and on most Monday evenings in summer. **Lamb's Players Theatre** (✉ 1142 Orange Ave., Coronado, ☎ 619/437–0600) has a season of five productions from February through November and stages a period musical, "Festival of Christmas."

Outdoor Activities and Sports

Baseball: San Diego Padres (✉ Qualcomm Stadium, 9449 Friars Rd., ☎ 619/280–4636). **Football: San Diego Chargers** (✉ Qualcomm Stadium, ☎ 619/280–2121). **Horse Racing: Del Mar Thoroughbred Club** (✉ 2260 Jimmy Durante Blvd.; take I–5 to the Via de la Valle exit, ☎ 619/755–1141); July–September.

Beaches

The following beaches are listed geographically from north to south.

La Jolla Cove is one of the prettiest spots in the world. A palm-lined park sits on top of the cliffs. Rough-water swimmers like the cove and divers and snorkelers can explore the underwater delights of the San Diego–La Jolla Underwater Ecological Reserve. Children's Pool, a shallow lagoon at the south end, is a good place to watch marine mammals—so many seals and sea lions frequent the cove that it is now closed to swimmers due to contamination. Follow Coast Boulevard north to the signs; or take the La Jolla Village Drive exit from I–5, head west to Torrey Pines Road, turn left, and drive down the hill to Girard Avenue, then turn right.

Mission Beach has a boardwalk that's popular with strollers, roller skaters, and cyclists. To the north, Pacific Beach is crowded in summer, and parking is a challenge. Exit I–5 at Garnet Avenue and head west to Mission Boulevard. Turn south for parking.

Ocean Beach is a haven for volleyball players, sunbathers, and swimmers (beware of unusually vicious rip currents). You can fish off the pier, which has a restaurant at the middle. The beach is south of the channel entrance to Mission Bay. You'll find food vendors and fire rings; limited parking is available. Take I–8 west to Sunset Cliffs Boulevard and head west; turn right on Santa Monica Avenue.

Coronado Beach is perfect for sunbathing or Frisbee throwing. There are rest rooms and fire rings; parking can be difficult on busy days. From the bridge turn left on Orange Avenue; then follow signs.

Silver Strand State Beach, Coronado, has relatively calm water, an RV campground ($12–$16 per night), and places to rollerblade or ride bikes. Parking is $4 per car, but collection is lax from Labor Day through

February. From the Coronado Bridge turn left onto Orange Avenue, which becomes Highway 75, and follow signs.

Shopping

Horton Plaza (⊠ Broadway and G St. from 1st to 4th Ave., ☎ 619/238–1596), occupying several square blocks downtown, is a uniquely festive, postmodern mall. Major department stores anchor the huge **Fashion Valley Center** (⊠ 452 Fashion Valley Dr., Mission Valley, ☎ 619/297–3386).

The **Gaslamp Quarter** (☞ Exploring San Diego, *above*) is home to art galleries, antiques shops, and other specialty stores. Trendy boutiques and galleries line Girard Avenue and Prospect Street in **La Jolla. Old Town** has the **Bazaar del Mundo, La Esplanade,** and the **Old Town Mercado,** with international goods, toys, souvenirs, and arts and crafts. Gay and funky **Hillcrest** is home to many gift, book, and music stores, and coffeehouses. **Coronado's** shops are at the ferry landing and along upscale Orange Avenue.

ELSEWHERE IN SOUTHERN CALIFORNIA

Palm Springs

A desert playground for Hollywood celebrities since the 1930s, Palm Springs has plenty of attractions: luxurious resorts, nearly year-round golf and tennis, and fine upscale and outlet shopping.

Visitor Information

Palm Springs Desert Resorts Bureau (⊠ 69–930 Hwy. 111, Suite 201, Rancho Mirage 92270, ☎ 760/770–9000 or 800/967–3767). **Palm Springs Visitor Information Center** (⊠ 2781 N. Palm Canyon, Palm Springs 92262, ☎ 800/347–7746). Both can make reservations for accommodations in the area and have lists of golf courses that are open to the public.

Arriving and Departing

Palm Springs is about a two-hour drive east of Los Angeles and a three-hour drive northeast of San Diego. From L.A. take I–10 east to Highway 111. From San Diego take I–15 north to Highway 60, then I–10 east to Highway 111. **Palm Springs International Airport** (⊠ 3400 E. Tahquitz Canyon Way) is served by national and regional airlines.

What to See and Do

★ For an overview of the area, ride up the **Palm Springs Aerial Tramway** (⊠ 1 Tramway Rd., ☎ 760/325–1391 or 888/515–8726, ☞ $17.65).

★ The region's natural attractions include **Joshua Tree National Park** (⊠ Hwy. 62 northeast from Hwy. 111, ☎ 760/367–7511). Its oddly shaped trees, with their branches raised like arms, and its weather-sculpted rocks are entrancing. Come eyeball to eyeball with coyotes, ℭ mountain lions, cheetahs, and golden eagles at the **Living Desert Wildlife and Botanical Park** (⊠ 47-900 Portola Ave., Palm Desert, ☎ 760/346–5694; ☞ $7.50). Easy to challenging trails traverse desert gardens populated with plants of the Mojave, Colorado, and Sonoran deserts.

The **Palm Springs Desert Museum** (⊠ 101 Museum Dr., ☎ 760/325–7186; ☞ $7.50) has a fine collection that emphasizes natural science and 20th-century art. The museum's Annenberg Theater presents plays, concerts, lectures, operas, and other cultural events. The hottest ★ ticket in the desert is the **Fabulous Palm Springs Follies** (⊠ Plaza Theater, 128 S. Palm Canyon Dr., ☎ 760/327–0225, ☞ $30–$65), a vaudeville-style revue that stars extravagantly costumed retired (but very much in shape) showgirls, singers, and dancers.

Dining and Lodging

$$$–$$$$
★ ✕ **Cuistot.** Signature dishes at chef-owner Bernard Dervieux's French restaurant include grilled shrimp with spinach linguine, Chinese-style duck in a mango-Madeira-ginger sauce, and rack of lamb with rosemary. ✉ *73-111 El Paseo, Palm Desert,* ☎ *760/340–1000. Reservations essential. AE, DC, MC, V. Closed Mon. No lunch Sun.*

$$–$$$$ ✕ **Shame on the Moon.** The kitchen here turns out consistently delicious Continental fare like roasted salmon with horseradish crust and calves' liver and onions with a bourbon glaze. The desserts are alluringly decadent. ✉ *69-950 Frank Sinatra Dr., Rancho Mirage,* ☎ *760/324–5515. Reservations essential. AE, MC, V. Closed Aug. No lunch.*

$$–$$$ ✕ **Palomino Euro Bistro.** The cuisine at this ultrapopular restaurant ranges from pizza and snacking items to grilled and roasted entrées with Mediterranean influences. ✉ *73–101 Hwy. 111, Palm Desert,* ☎ *760/773–9091. AE, D, DC, MC, V. No lunch.*

$$$$ ▥ **Merv Griffin's Resort Hotel and Givenchy Spa.** Indulgence is the word for this French-style resort with opulent rooms, perfectly manicured gardens, and fine restaurants. Personalized spa services include everything from facials to marine mud wraps to aromatherapy. ✉ *4200 E. Palm Canyon Dr., Palm Springs 92264,* ☎ *760/770–5000 or 800/276–5000,* ℻ *760/324–6104. 93 rooms. 2 restaurants, pool, health club. AE, D, DC, MC, V.* ▨

$$–$$$$ ▥ **Ingleside Inn.** Many rooms at this 1920s hacienda-style inn have antiques, fireplaces, and private patios; many have two-person whirlpool tubs and steam showers. ✉ *200 W. Ramon Rd., Palm Springs 92264,* ☎ *760/325–0046 or 800/772–6655,* ℻ *760/325–0710. 30 rooms. Restaurant, pool. AE, D, DC, MC, V. CP.* ▨

$$ ▥ **Hampton Inn.** Appointments here are basic but clean. There are barbecues available for guest use. ✉ *200 N. Palm Canyon Dr., Palm Springs 92262,* ☎ *760/320–0555 or 800/732–7755,* ℻ *760/320–2261. 93 rooms. Pool. AE, D, DC, MC, V. CP.* ▨

Death Valley

Arriving and Departing

To reach Death Valley from the west (about 300 mi from Los Angeles), exit U.S. 395 at either Highway 190 or 178. From the southeast (about 140 mi from Las Vegas), take Highway 127 north from I–15 and Highway 178 past Badwater and Artists Palette to Highway 190 at Furnace Creek. Zabriskie Point and Dante's View are off Highway 190 heading back southeast to Highway 127. Reliable maps are a must.

What to See and Do

★ **Death Valley National Park** (visitor center: ✉ Furnace Creek, Hwy. 190, ☎ 760/786–2331) is a desert wonderland of sand dunes, crusty salt flats, 11,000-ft mountains, and hills and canyons of many hues. In the northwestern section is **Scotty's Castle** (✉ Hwy. 190, north from Furnace Creek, ☎ 760/786–2392; ▦ $8), a Moorish-style mansion built by a onetime performer in Buffalo Bill's Wild West Show. **Harmony Borax Works** (✉ Hwy. 190, near Furnace Creek) illustrates the mining history of the valley, from which the 20-mule teams hauled borax to the railroad at Mojave. **Dante's View** (✉ Hwy. 190, south of Furnace Creek), 5,000 ft up in the Black Mountains, has views of the lowest (Badwater) and highest (Mt. Whitney) points in the contiguous United States.

COLORADO

By Sandra
Widener

Updated by
Eric Peterson

Capital	Denver
Population	4,167,000
Motto	Nothing Without Providence
State Bird	Lark bunting
State Flower	Columbine
Postal Abbreviation	CO

Statewide Visitor Information

Colorado Travel and Tourism Authority (⊠ 1127 Pennsylvania St., Denver 80203, ☎ 800/265–6736).

Scenic Drives

Colorado has 17 designated scenic routes, which are marked by signs that have blue columbines. The 232-mi **San Juan Skyway** traverses historic ranching and mining towns such as Durango, Silverton, Ouray, Telluride, and Cortez. The **Peak-to-Peak Highway** follows Routes 119, 72, and 7 through gold-mining towns to Rocky Mountain National Park.

National and State Parks

National Parks

Black Canyon of the Gunnison National Park (⊠ 15 mi northeast of Montrose on U.S. 50 and CO Hwy. 347, Gunnison 81230, ☎ 970/641–2337) is a small but striking park centered on a uniquely narrow and deep canyon. **Great Sand Dunes National Monument** (⊠ 35 mi northeast of Alamosa off Rte. 150, Mosca 81146, ☎ 719/378–2312), with sand dunes almost 750 ft high, has a year-round campground and a nature trail. **Mesa Verde National Park** (⊠ U.S. 160, 9 mi east of Cortez, Mesa Verde National Park 81330, ☎ 970/529–4465) has well-preserved cliff dwellings of the ancient Anasazi Indians. **Rocky Mountain National Park** (⊠ 5 mi west of Estes Park on U.S. 36, Estes Park 80517, ☎ 970/586–1206) presents a 265,000-acre picture-book vision of craggy mountains, abundant wildlife, and deep-blue mountain lakes, with camping, hiking, and scenic drives.

State Parks

In the state's 40 parks you can hike, fish, sail, and take in idyllic views. Contact the **Colorado Division of Parks** (⊠ 1313 Sherman St., Room 618, Denver 80203, ☎ 303/866–3437) for information.

DENVER

In Denver winter weather reports frequently begin with skiing conditions. After the lifts shut down for the summer, weekends are often occupied with trips to the mountains to hike, camp, and fish. The sharp-edged skyscrapers, clean streets, and dozens of well-used parks evoke the image of a young, progressive city, but much of the essence of Denver lies in its western past. Areas like LoDo, a historic part of lower downtown, buzz with jazz clubs, restaurants, and art galleries housed in century-old buildings.

Visitor Information

Denver Metro Convention and Visitors Bureau (✉ 1555 California St., Suite 300, 80202, ☎ 303/892–1112).

Arriving and Departing

By Bus
Greyhound (✉ 1055 19th St., ☎ 800/231–2222).

By Car
I–70 (east–west) and I–25 (north–south) intersect just north of downtown.

By Plane
Denver International Airport (✉ 8500 Peña Blvd., ☎ 303/342–2000), 23 mi from downtown Denver, is served by most major carriers. Cab fare downtown should average about $50; **RTD,** the local bus service (☞ Getting Around Denver, *below*), can also get you there. The **Denver-Boulder Super Shuttle** (☎ 800/525–3177) provides express bus service from the airport to locations in Denver and surrounding areas; a trip to downtown Denver costs about $20 depending on your destination. Reservations are essential.

By Train
Amtrak (☎ 800/872–7245) serves **Union Station** (✉ 17th St. at Wynkoop St.).

Getting Around Denver

By Car
Despite many one-way streets, driving in Denver is not difficult, and finding a spot in a parking lot is usually easy. Traffic on I–25 and I–70 can be congested during rush hours.

By Public Transportation
A free shuttle bus operates frequently down the length of the 16th Street Mall. The region's public bus service, **RTD** (☎ 303/299–6000 or 303/299–6700), has routes throughout Denver and to outlying towns such as Boulder, Longmont, and Nederland. RTD's **light-rail system** serves the downtown and southwestern regions. Buy bus tokens (🖙 75¢ or $1.25, depending on time of day) at grocery stores or pay on board; rail tickets are available from machines in the train stations.

By Taxi
Yellow Cab (☎ 303/777–7777) and **Metro Taxi** (☎ 303/333–3333) are two 24-hour taxi services.

Orientation Tours

Gray Line (☎ 303/289–2841) conducts a 3½-hour city tour and a mountain-parks tour.

Exploring Denver

At the **Civic Center,** a three-block park, lawns, gardens, and a Greek amphitheater present Denver's official face to the world. The backdrop for the Civic Center is the **state capitol** (✉ 200 E. Colfax Ave., ☎ 303/866–2604). As a reminder of the state's mining heritage, the dome of the 1886 building is periodically recovered with hammered gold leaf. The balcony affords a panoramic view of the Rockies. The capitol is closed weekends. Just off the Civic Center park is the **Colorado History Museum** (✉ 1300 Broadway, ☎ 303/866–3682; 🖙 $4.50), with

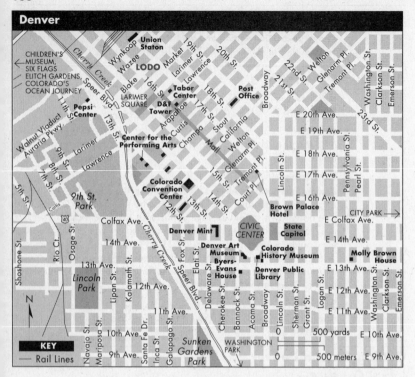

Denver

CHILDREN'S MUSEUM, SIX FLAGS ELITCH GARDENS, COLORADO'S OCEAN JOURNEY

KEY
— Rail Lines

Colorado and western memorabilia and dioramas, plus special exhibits.

★ The **Denver Art Museum** (⌂ 100 W. 14th Ave. Pkwy., ☎ 303/640–2793, ⌸ $4.50) has an excellent collection of Native American art, as well as superlative holdings in pre-Columbian and Spanish colonial art. The museum is closed Monday. Connected to the art museum by an underground walkway is the **Denver Public Library** (⌂ 10 W. 14th Ave. Pkwy., ☎ 303/640–6200). This Michael Graves–designed building houses a world-renowned collection of books, photographs, and newspapers that chronicle the American West.

Adjacent to the Denver Art Museum, the elaborate redbrick Victorian **Byers-Evans House,** built in 1883, is an elegantly restored house-museum (⌂ 1310 Bannock St., ☎ 303/620–4933; ⌸ $3).

Near the Civic Center is the **Denver Mint** (⌂ W. Colfax Ave. and Cherokee St., ☎ 303/405–4761; ⌸ free)—officially known as the United States Mint—where an average of 10 billion coins are stamped yearly. Free tours take place on weekdays; the mint is closed on weekends.

Free shuttle buses are the only vehicles allowed on the **16th Street Mall,** which has shade trees, outdoor cafés, historic buildings, and shops. Be

★ sure to peek inside the **Brown Palace Hotel** (⌂ 321 17th St., ☎ 303/297–3111), the grande dame of Denver hotels, built in 1892 and still proud of her antique charms.

The 330-ft **D&F Tower** (⌂ 16th St. at Arapahoe St.) emulates the campanile of St. Mark's Cathedral in Venice. **Denver Center for the Performing Arts** (⌂ 14th and Curtis Sts.) is a huge space-age complex of theaters and a symphony hall.

Denver's most charming shopping area is historic **Larimer Square** (⌂ Larimer and 15th Sts.), which showcases some of the city's oldest retail buildings and finest specialty shops. **LoDo,** north of Larimer Street between Speer Boulevard and 22nd Street, is a quirky historic area filled with art galleries, nightclubs, brewpubs, and restaurants.

West of LoDo is **Denver Children's Museum** (⊠ 2121 Crescent Dr., ☎ 303/433–7444; ☜ $5), where interactive exhibits include a working TV station, a child-size grocery store, and an outdoor ski hill.

In the newly redeveloped Platte River valley between LoDo and I–25, **Colorado's Ocean Journey** (⊠ 700 Water St., ☎ 303/561–4450; ☜ $14.95) features river ecosystems replicated via state-of-the-art technology at the largest aquarium between Chicago and Monterrey. Across the Platte River from the aquarium sits **Six Flags Elitch Gardens** (⊠ Speer Blvd. and I–25, ☎ 303/595–4386; ☜ $29; closed Nov.–late Apr.), the nation's only downtown amusement park and a popular destination for roller coaster fanatics during the summer months.

East of downtown, the **Molly Brown House Museum** (⊠ 1340 Pennsylvania St., ☎ 303/832–4092; ☜ $6), a Victorian confection, celebrates the life and times of the scandalous Ms. Brown, whose story was made into the film *The Unsinkable Molly Brown*.

★ ⵌ Northeast of downtown in City Park is the **Denver Museum of Natural History** (⊠ 2001 Colorado Blvd., ☎ 303/322–7009, ☜ $7), with traditional collections and hands-on exhibits, plus an IMAX movie theater with a four-story screen. The museum's planetarium is being renovated and will be closed until midyear 2001. The Prehistoric Journey exhibit invites you to walk through the seven stages of the earth's development, beginning 3½ billion years ago.

Parks, Gardens, and Zoos

Denver has one of the largest city park systems (☎ 303/698–4900 for park headquarters office) in the country, with more than 360 parks and 14,000 acres of outlying mountain lands. Flower gardens and lakes abound in **Washington Park,** east of Downing Street between Virginia and Louisiana avenues. **City Park** has lakes, tennis, golf, and museums (☞ Exploring Denver, *above*). Also in City Park is the **Denver Zoo** (⊠ E. 23rd St. between York St. and Colorado Blvd., ☎ 303/376–4800; ☜ $8), with a nursery for baby animals and the Primate Panorama, where visitors can view 29 primate species in simulated natural habitats.

★ Southeast of downtown are the **Denver Botanic Gardens** (⊠ 1005 York St., ☎ 303/331–4000, ☜ $4.50). The conservatory houses a rain forest; outside are a Japanese garden, an alpine rock garden that blooms with brilliant wildflowers in spring, and other horticulture displays. **Platte River Greenway** includes more than 20 mi of biking and jogging paths that follow Cherry Creek and the Platte River, much of it through downtown Denver.

Dining

Beef, buffalo, and burritos are prominent in Denver's culinary history, but more sophisticated fare can also be found. Cruise LoDo or 17th Avenue East for inventive kitchens, and check out Federal Street for cheap ethnic eats.

$$–$$$$ ✕ **Buckhorn Exchange.** The neighborhood has deteriorated, but this Denver landmark with handsome men's-club decor is still a great place to eat elk, buffalo, and beef and to gawk at the deer and other trophies mounted on the walls. ⊠ *1000 Osage St., ☎ 303/534–9505. AE, D, DC, MC, V. No lunch weekends.*

$$–$$$$ ✕ **Denver Chophouse & Brewery.** The best of the many LoDo brewpubs and restaurants surrounding the ballpark, the Chophouse, all dark wood and exposed brick, is housed in the old Union Pacific Railroad warehouse. The food is basic American and plenty of it: steak, seafood, and chicken served with hot corn bread and honey-butter and "bottomless" salad tossed at the table. ⊠ *1735 19th St., Suite 100,* ☎ *303/296–0800. AE, DC, MC, V.*

$$–$$$$ ✕ **European Café.** In a space gleaming with polished brass and crystal, this mainstay of fine dining serves beautifully presented dishes that pay homage to French master chefs. Try the mesquite charbroiled duck breast in apricot sauce. ⊠ *1040 15th St.,* ☎ *303/825–6555. Reservations essential. AE, D, DC, MC, V. No lunch weekends.*

$$–$$$$ ✕ **The Fort.** This adobe structure, complete with a piñon bonfire in the ★ courtyard, is a perfect replica of Bent's Fort, a Colorado fur trade center. Buffalo meat and game are the specialties; elk with huckleberry sauce and mesquite-grilled ostrich are especially good. Costumed characters from the fur trade wander the restaurant, playing mandolins and telling tall tales. ⊠ *U.S. 285 and Hwy. 8,* ☎ *303/697–4771. AE, D, DC, MC, V. No lunch.*

$$–$$$$ ✕ **Today's Gourmet Highlands Garden Café.** The menu changes daily at chef-owner Patricia Perry's intimate northwest Denver establishment, which occupies a pair of joined Victorian houses with seating inside and on gardened patios. The varied menu usually features a wide variety of creatively presented seafood, as well as pasta, beef, and poultry, all prepared with great attention to detail. ⊠ *3927 W. 32nd Ave.,* ☎ *303/458–5920. Reservations essential. AE, MC, V. Closed Sun. and Mon. No lunch.*

$$–$$$$ ✕ **Zenith.** Chef Kevin Taylor has created a simple, sublime menu full of inventive variations on southwestern and Mediterranean dishes. The soaring, column-laden space, in the former Guarantee National Bank building, has become a favorite hangout of Denver's movers and shakers. ⊠ *815 17th St.,* ☎ *303/293–2322. AE, DC, MC, V. Closed Sun. No lunch weekends.*

$$–$$$ ✕ **Barolo Grill.** This restaurant looks like a chichi farmhouse—dried flowers in brass urns, straw baskets, and hand-painted porcelain. Choose from duckling stewed with red wine, house-made gnocchi, or a number of other rotating Italian specialties. ⊠ *3030 E. 6th Ave.,* ☎ *303/393–1040. Reservations essential. AE, D, DC, MC, V. Closed Sun. and Mon. No lunch.*

$$–$$$ ✕ **Strings.** This light, airy spot with its wide-open kitchen is a preferred ★ hangout for visiting celebs, whose autographs are mounted. The food is casual-contemporary. One specialty is the cashew-encrusted sea bass with vanilla butter sauce. ⊠ *1700 Humboldt St.,* ☎ *303/831–7310. Reservations essential. AE, D, DC, MC, V. No lunch Sun.*

$–$$ ✕ **Bayou Bob's.** Housed in the Paramount Theatre Building downtown, Bayou Bob's features Cajun classics—gumbo, jambalaya, étouffée—in a casual atmosphere. Don't miss the panfried alligator tail. ⊠ *1635 Glenarm St.,* ☎ *303/573–6828. Reservations not accepted. AE, D, DC, MC, V.*

$–$$ ✕ **T-WA Inn.** This South Asian hole-in-the-wall serves a broad range of great food, including delicate Vietnamese spring rolls and daily specials. ⊠ *555 S. Federal Blvd.,* ☎ *303/922–4584. AE, D, DC, MC, V.*

$–$$ ✕ **Wynkoop Brewing Company.** The beer is brewed on the premises, ★ and the pub fare is hearty. Try the shepherd's pie or charbroiled elk medallions with brandy peppercorn sauce; then check out the pool hall and cabaret for a full night's entertainment. ⊠ *1634 18th St.,* ☎ *303/297–2700. AE, D, DC, MC, V.*

$ ✕ **Blue Bonnet Café.** Its location in a fairly seedy neighborhood southeast of downtown doesn't stop the crowds from lining up early. The western decor, Naugahyde, and jukebox set an upbeat mood for killer margaritas and great burritos. ⊠ *457 S. Broadway,* ☎ *303/778–0147. Reservations not accepted. MC, V.*

Lodging

Denver's lodging choices range from the stately Brown Palace to budget chain motels, with bed-and-breakfasts and other options in between. **Bed & Breakfast Innkeepers of Colorado** (⊠ Box 38416, Dept. S-95, Colorado Springs 80937-8416, ☎ 800/265–7696) handles B&Bs throughout the state. **Hostelling International–Rocky Mountain Council** (⊠ Box 2370, Boulder 80306, ☎ 303/442–1166) provides information about hostels in nine Colorado locations.

$$$$ ★ 🏨 **Brown Palace Hotel.** This downtown grande-dame hotel has hosted President Eisenhower, the Beatles, and other illustrious guests. The eight-story lobby is topped by a glorious stained-glass ceiling. Rooms are Victorian in style. ⊠ *321 17th St.,* 80202, ☎ 303/297–3111 or 800/321–2599, FAX *303/312–5900. 230 rooms. 4 restaurants, exercise room. AE, D, DC, MC, V.* 🐾

$$$–$$$$ ★ 🏨 **Loews Giorgio.** A 12-story steel-and-black glass facade conceals the delightful Italian Baroque motif within. Rooms are spacious and elegant, with Continental touches. The hotel is halfway between downtown and the Denver Tech Center, a local business hub. ⊠ *4150 E. Mississippi Ave.,* 80222, ☎ 303/782–9300 or 800/235–6397, FAX *303/758–6542. 183 rooms. Restaurant. AE, D, DC, MC, V.* 🐾

$$$–$$$$ ★ 🏨 **Oxford.** The city's most charming small hotel was a Denver fixture in the Victorian era. Guest rooms have antiques and reproductions. ⊠ *1600 17th St.,* 80202, ☎ 303/628–5400 or 800/228–5838, FAX *303/628–5413. 80 rooms. 2 restaurants, health club. AE, D, DC, MC, V.* 🐾

$$–$$$$ 🏨 **Westin Tabor Center.** Oversize rooms at this high-rise overlooking the 16th Street Mall are done in gray and taupe and have paisley duvets. A view of the Denver skyline from the indoor-pool room makes swimming laps a pleasure. One of the hotel restaurants is a branch of the Palm, the Manhattan-based steak house. ⊠ *1672 Lawrence St.,* 80202, ☎ 303/572–9100, FAX *303/572–7288. 430 rooms. 2 restaurants, pool, health club. AE, D, DC, MC, V.* 🐾

$$$ 🏨 **Adam's Mark.** In the mid-1990s the I. M. Pei–designed Radisson and the old May D&F department store across the street from it were converted into a convention-oriented property—one of the 25 largest hotels in the country. The location, at the south end of the 16th Street Mall, is ideal. ⊠ *1550 Court Pl.,* 80202, ☎ 303/893–3333 or 800/444–2326, FAX *303/626–2543. 1,225 rooms. 2 restaurants, pool, exercise room. AE, D, DC, MC, V.* 🐾

$$–$$$ 🏨 **Castle Marne.** This B&B with balconies, a four-story turret, and intricate stone- and woodwork is east of downtown and near several fine restaurants. Rooms are full of antiques and art. Three of the rooms have hot tubs. ⊠ *1572 Race St.,* 80206, ☎ 303/331–0621 or 800/926–2763, FAX *303/331–0623. 9 rooms. AE, D, DC, MC, V. BP.* 🐾

$$–$$$ 🏨 **Comfort Inn/Downtown.** The advantages to this hotel are its reasonable rates and its location, right across from—and connected to—the Brown Palace (☞ *above*). Rooms higher up have panoramic views. ⊠ *401 17th St.,* 80202, ☎ 303/296–0400 or 800/221–2222, FAX *303/297–0774. 229 rooms. Restaurant. AE, D, DC, MC, V.*

$$–$$$ 🏨 **Holiday Chalet.** This B&B is in the heart of Capitol Hill, immediately east of downtown. It's full of charm, with stained-glass windows and family heirlooms; each room has a full kitchen. ⊠ *1820 E. Colfax Ave.,* 80218, ☎ 303/321–9975 or 800/626–4497, FAX *303/377–6556. 10 rooms. AE, D, DC, MC, V. CP.* 🐾

$$–$$$ ★ 🏨 **Queen Anne Inn.** North of downtown in a reclaimed historic area, this B&B (composed of two adjacent Victorian houses) makes a romantic

getaway, with fresh flowers and antiques. An afternoon Colorado-wine tasting is free. ⊠ *2147 Tremont Pl., 80205,* ☎ *303/296–6666 or 800/ 432–4667,* FAX *303/296–2151. 14 rooms. AE, D, DC, MC, V. BP.* ✎

Nightlife and the Arts

Friday's *Denver Post* and *Rocky Mountain News* list entertainment events, as does the weekly *Westword*. **TicketMan** (☎ 303/430–1111) sells tickets to major events. The **Ticket Bus** (⊠ 16th St. Mall at Curtis St.) is open weekdays from 10 to 6 and sells same-day half-price tickets.

Nightlife

Downtown and **LoDo** host most of Denver's nightlife. Downtown is where you'll find mainstream entertainment. LoDo is home to rock clubs and small theaters. Remember that Denver's high altitude makes you react more quickly to alcohol.

COMEDY

Comedy Works (⊠ 1226 15th St., ☎ 303/595–3637) features local and nationally known stand-up comics.

COUNTRY AND WESTERN

The **Grizzly Rose** (⊠ I–25 Exit 215, ☎ 303/295–1330), with its miles of dance floor, hosts national bands.

JAZZ

El Chapultepec (⊠ 20th St. at Market St., ☎ 303/295–9126) is a smoky dive where visiting jazz musicians often jam after hours.

ROCK

Herman's Hideaway (⊠ 1578 S. Broadway, ☎ 303/777–5840) is a favorite for both hot local bands and national acts; there's some blues and reggae, too. **Bluebird Theatre** (⊠ 3317 E Colfax Ave., ☎ 303/322–2308), one of Denver's oldest theaters (1912), features edgy entertainment—live rock music and cult movies—every night. The **Mercury Café** (⊠ 2199 California St., ☎ 303/294–9281) triples as a health-food restaurant, fringe theater, and music venue featuring a wide variety of rock and world music artists.

The Arts

The modern **Denver Center for the Performing Arts** (⊠ 14th and Curtis Sts., ☎ 303/893–3272) houses most of the city's large concert halls and theaters.

DANCE

The **Colorado Ballet** (☎ 303/837–8888) presents classics in the performing arts center.

MUSIC

The **Colorado Symphony Orchestra** (⊠ 13th and Curtis Sts., ☎ 303/ 986–8742) performs at Boettcher Concert Hall.

THEATER

The **Denver Center Theater Company** (☎ 303/893–4100) presents fine repertory theater. **Robert Garner Attractions** (☎ 303/893–4100) brings Broadway-caliber plays to the city.

Spectator Sports

Baseball: Colorado Rockies (⊠ Coors Field, 2001 Blake St., downtown, ☎ 303/762–5437). **Basketball: Denver Nuggets** (⊠ Pepsi Center, 1000 Chopper Cir., west of downtown at Auraria Pkwy. and Speer Blvd., ☎ 303/405–1100). **Football: Denver Broncos** (⊠ Mile High Stadium, 1900 Eliot St., ☎ 303/433–7466). **Hockey: Colorado Avalanche** (⊠

Pepsi Center, 1000 Chopper Cir., west of downtown at Auraria Pkwy. and Speer Blvd., ☎ 303/405–1100).

Shopping

Denver is one of the top places to buy recreational equipment and clothing. Pick up a pair of cowboy boots and other western apparel at any western store.

Shopping Districts

The Cherry Creek shopping district, 2 mi from downtown, is Denver's best. On one side of 1st Avenue at Milwaukee Street is the **Cherry Creek Shopping Mall,** a granite-and-glass behemoth containing some of the nation's finest retailers. On the other side is **Cherry Creek North,** with art galleries and specialty shops. On the **16th Street Mall** are Tabor Center and other large downtown retailers. **South Broadway** between 1st Avenue and Evans Street has blocks of antiques stores; prices are sometimes lower than those elsewhere. **LoDo** has the trendiest galleries, many in restored warehouses.

Books

Tattered Cover (⊠ 2995 E. 1st Ave., ☎ 303/322–7727; ⊠ 1628 16th St., ☎ 303/436–1070) has overstuffed armchairs, four floors of books (more than 250,000 titles), afternoon lectures and musical presentations, and a knowledgeable staff. The original location, at 1st Avenue and Milwaukee Street, is more active and bigger.

Sporting Goods

Gart Brothers Sports Castle (⊠ 1000 Broadway, ☎ 303/861–1122) is a huge, multistory shrine to the Colorado sporting lifestyle.

Western Wear

Denver Buffalo Company Trading Post (⊠ 1109 Lincoln St., ☎ 303/832–0884) has top-of-the-line western clothing and souvenirs.

Side Trip to Boulder

Arriving and Departing

From Denver take I–25 north to the Boulder Turnpike (Highway 36). Denver's RTD buses make the 27-mi commute regularly. The turnpike is notorious for traffic, especially during rush hours.

What to See and Do

Home of the University of Colorado, Boulder is a quintessential college town, but it's also the headquarters of a hard-core group of professional athletes who live to bike and run. The atmosphere is peaceful, new age, and cultural, with a gorgeous backdrop of mountains. One of the city's main attractions is the **Pearl Street Mall,** a see-and-be-seen pedestrian street with benches, grassy spots, great shopping, and outdoor cafés. Weekdays from 10 to 3, the **Celestial Seasonings Plant** (⊠ 4600 Sleepytime Dr., ☎ 303/581–1202) conducts free tours; you'll see raw tea ingredients (the Mint Room is off-limits because of its potent scent), then watch them being blended. Rich in lectures, theater, and music year-round, Boulder celebrates classical music each summer at its **Colorado Music Festival** (⊠ Chautauqua Park, ☎ 303/449–1397).

Side Trip to Central City and Blackhawk

Arriving and Departing

From I–70 take Highway 58 to Golden, then Highway 6 up Clear Creek Canyon, and finally Highway 119 northwest 1 mi past Blackhawk to Central City. The town is 35 mi from Denver. Many of the towns' casinos offer inexpensive shuttles from metro Denver locations.

What to See and Do

Abandoned mines along the scenic road that leads to these historic towns testify to the silver- and gold-mining heritage of the area. Now that low-stakes gambling has arrived, the jingle of slot machines is a constant. The narrow, winding streets are edged with brick storefronts from the last century. The **Central City Opera House** (☎ 303/292–6700), a small Victorian jewel in the center of town, stages opera in summer.

Side Trip to Georgetown

Arriving and Departing

Take I–70 west to the Georgetown exit, 46 mi from Denver.

What to See and Do

With gingerbread Victorian houses on quiet streets, Georgetown provides a tantalizing glimpse of Colorado's heady mining past. This National Historic District has restaurants, small shops, and the **Georgetown Loop Railroad** (☎ 303/569–2403), a 3-mi narrow-gauge line that travels into the mountains and back during the summer.

Side Trip to Golden

Arriving and Departing

From I–70 take Highway 58 to Golden, 12 mi west of Denver.

What to See and Do

Coors (✉ 13th and Ford Sts., ☎ 303/277–2337) operates the world's largest brewery. Daily tours (except on Sundays) cover the basics of brewing beer and end with a trip to the tasting rooms. The drive up Lookout Mountain to the **Buffalo Bill Grave and Museum** (✉ Rte. 5 off I–70 Exit 256, or 19th Ave. out of Golden, ☎ 303/526–0747; ✉ $3) affords a sensational panoramic view of Denver. Contrary to popular belief, Bill Cody never expressed a burning desire to be buried here: The *Denver Post* bought the corpse from Bill's sister and bribed her to concoct a teary story about his dying wish. Apparently, rival towns were so outraged that the National Guard had to be called in to protect the grave from robbers.

COLORADO SPRINGS AND ENVIRONS

At the center of the state, 65 mi south of Denver, is Colorado Springs, Colorado's second-largest city. In addition to its natural wonders such as Pike's Peak, the region has such man-made attractions as the Air Force Academy and the Broadmoor resort.

Visitor Information

Colorado Springs: Convention and Visitors Bureau (✉ 104 S. Cascade Ave., Suite 104, 80903, ☎ 719/635–7506 or 800/368–4748).

Arriving and Departing

By Bus

Greyhound (✉ 120 S. Weber St., ☎ 800/231–2222) serves national routes, and **Springs Transit Scheduling** (✉ 127 E. Kiowa St., ☎ 719/385–7433) serves local ones.

By Car

From Denver take I–25 south.

By Plane

Colorado Springs Airport (✉ 7770 Drennan Rd., ☎ 719/550–1900), 14 mi southeast of the city, is served by domestic airlines.

Exploring Colorado Springs and Environs

A mix of attractions surrounding **Colorado Springs** complements the city's Victorian houses and wide tree-lined streets. **U.S. Olympic Training Center** (⊠ 1 Olympic Plaza, ☎ 719/578–4500; ☒ free) conducts tours of the sprawling complex where hundreds of athletes train. The **Broadmoor** (⊠ 1 Lake Ave.) is a rambling ensemble of pink-stucco Italian Renaissance–style hotel buildings combined with gardens and a picture-perfect lake skimmed by black swans. The **Carriage House Museum** (⊠ Lake Circle, ☎ 719/634–7711; ☒ free), on the Broadmoor's grounds, displays an old stagecoach, vintage cars, and carriages used at presidential inaugurals.

The **Cheyenne Mountain Zoo** (⊠ 4250 Cheyenne Mountain Zoo Rd., ☎ 719/633–9925; ☒ $8.50), set on a mountainside, is a haven for more than 50 endangered species and hundreds of other animals. You can hike 224 steep steps or take an elevator to the top of **Seven Falls** (⊠ Cheyenne Blvd., ☎ 719/632–0765; ☒ $6.50), a series of falls plunging into a tiny pool, set in a breathtaking red-rock canyon.

Two routes—a **cog railway** (⊠ 515 Ruxton Ave., Manitou Springs, ☎ 719/685–5401) and a **toll road** (⊠ 10 mi west on Hwy. 24, left at marked exit at Cascade)—lead to breathtaking views atop **Pike's Peak,** the summit Zebulon Pike claimed could never be scaled. The railway is $24.50 round-trip; the toll road, $10. The **Air Force Academy** (⊠ 10 mi north on I-25, Exits 156B and 150B, ☎ 719/333–2025) has a futuristic **Cadet Chapel,** with 17 spires, each rising 150 ft. The academy sometimes gives guided tours in summer; self-guided tours are always available. The **Garden of the Gods** (⊠ off Ridge Rd., north of U.S. 24, ☎ 719/634–6666) has picnic spots and hikes among 1,350 acres of weird, windswept red-rock formations and unusual plant life.

Cripple Creek—24 mi west from Colorado Springs to Divide, then 20 mi south on Highway 67—was once known for vast deposits of gold and has gone upscale with the legalization of low-stakes gambling. The **Cripple Creek and Victor Narrow Gauge Railroad** (☎ 719/689–2640; ☒ $8 round-trip), on the north end of town, runs a 4-mi route (May–October) past old mines and older mountains.

Southwest of Colorado Springs on U.S. 50 is **Cañon City,** gateway to one of the Rockies' most powerful sights. The 1,053-ft-deep **Royal Gorge** (☎ 719/275–7507; ☒ $12.95 toll, including aerial tram), often called the Grand Canyon of Colorado, was carved by the Arkansas River more than 3 million years ago. It's spanned by the world's highest **suspension bridge.** Other activities include riding the 2,200-ft long aerial tram and traveling aboard the **Scenic Railway,** the world's steepest incline rail. For kids, there's a miniature train trolley and a carousel. A theater presents a 25-minute multimedia show, and there's outdoor musical entertainment in summer.

Famous films such as *True Grit* and *Cat Ballou* were shot in **Buckskin Joe Frontier Town and Railway** (⊠ Off Hwy. 50, Cañon City, ☎ 719/275–5149; ☒ $12), which vividly evokes the Old West. Children love the horse-drawn trolley rides, horseback rides, and gold-panning. Adults enjoy the live entertainment in the Crystal Palace and Saloon.

Dining and Lodging

Steak and other basic western foods, along with Mexican dishes, are the mainstays hereabouts. The Colorado Springs Convention and Visitors Bureau (☞ Visitor Information, *above*) provides lodging assistance.

Central Colorado

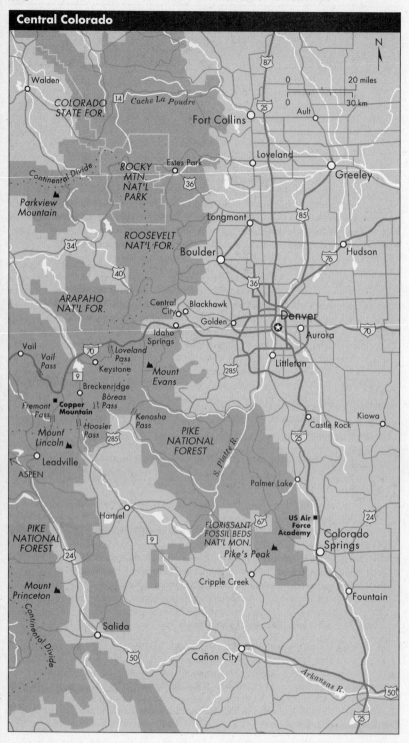

N

0   20 miles
0   30 km

Walden

COLORADO
STATE FOR.

14   Cache La Poudre

Fort Collins

Ault

87

25

Loveland

Greeley

Continental Divide

ROCKY
MTN.
NAT'L
PARK

Estes Park

36

85

Parkview
Mountain

Longmont

34

ROOSEVELT
NAT'L FOR.

Boulder

Hudson

76

40

36

ARAPAHO
NAT'L FOR.

Central
City

Blackhawk

Denver

70

Golden

Aurora

Idaho
Springs

Vail

70

Loveland
Pass

Keystone

Mount
Evans

285

Littleton

Vail
Pass

9

Breckenridge

Bóreas
Pass

Fremont
Pass

Copper
Mountain

Kenosha
Pass

PIKE
NATIONAL
FOREST

Castle Rock

Kiowa

25

Mount
Lincoln

Hoosier
Pass

285

S. Platte R.

Leadville

ASPEN

Palmer Lake

Hartsel

9

FLORISSANT
FOSSIL BEDS
NAT'L MON.

67

US Air
Force
Academy

24

PIKE
NATIONAL
FOREST

24

Pike's Peak

Colorado
Springs

Mount
Princeton

Cripple Creek

Fountain

Continental Divide

Salida

50

Cañon City

Arkansas R.

50

25

Colorado Springs

$$–$$$ ✕ **The Ritz Grill.** This hip and lively downtown restaurant is centered
★ on a horseshoe-shape marble bar and features an art deco style. It is
known for its Cajun food and chicken and shrimp pasta, and it transforms into a nightclub after 9:30 PM. ⊠ *15 S. Tejon St.,* ☎ *719/635–
8484. AE, MC, V.*

$–$$ ✕ **El Tesoro.** This historic building doubles as a restaurant and art gallery;
★ exposed brick walls, colorful rugs, and *ristras* (strings) of chilies complement the northern New Mexican food, a savory blend of Native American, Spanish, and Anglo influences. The *posole* (hominy with pork and
red chili), green chili, and originals like mango quesadillas are heavenly. ⊠ *10 N. Sierra Madre St.,* ☎ *719/471–0106. AE, D, MC, V. Closed
Sun. No lunch Sat., no dinner Mon.*

$$$$ ✕▥ **The Broadmoor.** This resort is a Colorado legend. The 1918 build-
★ ings house plush, traditional rooms; the restaurants serve everything
from formal French food to Sunday brunch. The parklike grounds have
golf, tennis, horseback riding, and paddle-boating facilities. The spa
provides such treatments as the Broadmoor Falls water massage, which
uses 17 jets of water. Substantially lower rates are available in fall and
spring. ⊠ *1 Lake Ave., 80906,* ☎ *719/634–7711 or 800/634–7711,*
℻ *719/577–5700. 700 rooms. 9 restaurants, 2 pools, spa, health club,
tennis, golf, horseback riding, boating. AE, D, DC, MC, V.* ☙

$$–$$$ ▥ **The Crescent Lily.** This elegant 1898 Victorian home just north of down-
★ town serves gourmet breakfasts. Rooms may have whirlpools, fireplaces, or balconies. ⊠ *6 Boulder Crescent, 80902,* ☎ *719/442–2331
or 800/869–2721,* ℻ *719/442–6947. 5 rooms. AE, MC, V. BP.* ☙

Manitou Springs

$$–$$$$ ✕ **Briarhurst Manor.** An 1878 stone mansion provides the setting for
chef Sigi Krauss's fine cuisine. Dishes such as chateaubriand are pre-
pared with Colorado ingredients and a European touch. ⊠ *404 Man-
itou Ave.,* ☎ *719/685–1864. AE, DC, MC, V. Closed Sun. No lunch.*

Motels

▥ **Best Western Le Baron Hotel** (⊠ 314 W. Bijou, Colorado Springs
80905, ☎ 719/471–8680 or 800/477–8610, ℻ 719/471–0894), 202
rooms; restaurant, pool, exercise room; $$.

▥ **Palmer House Best Western** (⊠ I–25 near Exit 145, 3010 North Chestnut St., Colorado Springs 80907, ☎ 719/636–5201 or 800/223–9127,
℻ 719/636–3108), 150 rooms; restaurant, pool; $$.

Outdoor Activities and Sports

Biking
Mountain-bike trails thread through **Pike National Forest** (⊠ U.S.
Ranger District Office, 601 S. Weber St., Colorado Springs 80903, ☎
719/636–1602).

Fishing
There's excellent trout fishing in the streams of the **South Platte** (⊠ Rte.
67, 28 mi north of Woodland Park). **Elevenmile Reservoir** (⊠ Hwy. 24W
to town of Lake George) has rainbow trout, kokanee salmon, and pike.

Golf
The **Broadmoor** (⊠ 1 Lake Ave., ☎ 719/634–7711) has three 18-hole
courses.

Hiking and Backpacking
Ask the **El Paso County Parks Department** (☎ 719/520–6375) for sug-
gestions. Some of the best trails are in **Pike National Forest** (☞ Bik-
ing, *above*).

Horseback Riding

Academy Riding Stables (⊠ 4 El Paso Blvd., ☎ 719/633–5667) rents horses for one- to two-hour guided tours through Garden of the Gods park (☞ Exploring Colorado Springs and Environs, *above*). Reservations are essential.

NORTHWESTERN COLORADO

As you climb west from Denver, the mountains rear up, pine forests line the road, and the legendary Colorado of powder skiing, alpine scenery, and the great outdoors begins. As once-primitive mining towns have attracted skiers and scenery buffs, sophisticated dining and lodging have followed.

Visitor Information

Aspen Chamber Resort Association (⊠ 425 Rio Grande Pl., 81611, ☎ 970/925–1940). **Glenwood Springs Chamber Resort Association** (⊠ 1102 Grand Ave., 81601, ☎ 970/945–6589). **Steamboat Springs Chamber Resort Association** (⊠ 1255 S. Lincoln Ave., 80477, ☎ 970/879–0880). **Summit County Chamber of Commerce** (⊠ Summit Ave. at Main St., Frisco 80443, ☎ 800/530–3099). **Vail Valley Tourism and Convention Bureau** (⊠ 100 E. Meadow Dr., Suite 34, 81657, ☎ 970/476–1000 or 800/525–3875).

Arriving and Departing

By Bus
Greyhound (☎ 800/231–2222).

By Car
I–70 is the main route to the Summit County resorts, Vail, and Glenwood Springs. From Glenwood Springs, Highway 82 heads to Aspen. From Denver, Highway 36 leads to Rocky Mountain National Park and Estes Park; from Empire, Highway 40 heads to Steamboat Springs.

By Plane
Aspen Airport (⊠ 0233 E. Airport Rd., ☎ 970/920–5385) is 7 mi east of town; most flights connect from Denver. **Steamboat Springs Airport** (⊠ 3495 Airport Circle, ☎ 970/879–1204) is 3 mi northwest of town. **Eagle County Airport** (⊠ 0219 Eldon Wilson Rd., Gypsum 81637, ☎ 970/524–9490), 35 mi west of Vail, serves Vail Valley. Regional and national airlines fly to all three airports.

By Train
Amtrak (☎ 800/872–7245) stops in Glenwood Springs, Granby, and Winter Park.

Exploring Northwestern Colorado

Estes Park is the northern gateway to **Rocky Mountain National Park** (☞ National and State Parks, *above*), where **Trail Ridge Road** (closed in winter) provides a spectacular ride on one of the highest auto routes in the world. On the west side of Estes Park is **Grand Lake,** the largest natural lake in Colorado, with the world's highest yacht club. The turn-of-the-20th-century town of the same name is also a snowmobiling mecca in winter.

The resort skiing closest to Denver is off I–70 at **Winter Park,** a family-oriented resort with more challenging terrain on the Mary Jane side of the mountain. Denverites often come here via the Ski Train (☎ 303/296–4754; ⊠ $40 round-trip) on weekends. The mountains of **Sum-**

mit County, 70 mi from Denver off I–70, attract climbers, hikers, and skiers. **Copper Mountain,** the first Club Med in North America, has terrain for most abilities, with an emphasis on intermediate and advanced skiers. **Keystone Resort** encompasses the peaks of **Keystone,** for beginning and intermediate skiers, and the **Outback** and **North Peak** for serious skiers. **Breckenridge** is an old mining town transformed into a resort. For a change from resort atmosphere and prices, head to **Lake Dillon,** a large reservoir popular with boaters. Up U.S. 40 from I–70, **Steamboat Springs** has great, uncrowded skiing for all abilities and a decidedly western feel.

West of Summit County is **Vail,** celebrated home of the largest ski mountain in North America. Constructed from the ground up to look like a European ski village, the town is huge, varied in its attractions, and pricey. It tends to be more conservative and family oriented than Aspen. **Beaver Creek** was created for those seeking an even more exclusive atmosphere than that of Vail; everything here lives up to its billing, from the billeting to the bill of fare. The ski area is geared to intermediate and advanced skiers.

At the turnoff for Aspen on I–70 is **Glenwood Springs,** where the main attraction besides scenery is **Yampah Hot Springs** (✉ 709 E. 6th St., ☎ 970/945–0667; 🎫 $8.75), which is heated by the world's largest outdoor mineral hot springs.

You know all about **Aspen,** the glitzy resort where actors and moguls vacation in ski season. It's expensive—and worth it if your passions are people-watching and great skiing. Many prefer the other seasons, though, for the beauty of the setting or for the summer **Aspen Music Festival** (☎ 970/925–3254), a renowned classical series.

Within Aspen's orbit are several **ski areas,** each geared to a different level of ability. Skiers can get a multiday ticket to all four mountains: **Buttermilk,** serving primarily beginners and low-intermediate skiers; **Aspen Highlands,** for intermediate skiers, with some of the highest vertical drops and best views; **Snowmass,** a perfect intermediate hill; and, for experts, **Aspen Mountain,** which hosts international competitions.

Dining and Lodging

The celebrity atmosphere of towns like Aspen and Vail attracts celebrity chefs, and hot restaurants come and go here as quickly as in New York. If you don't want to spend the money to eat with stars, consider heading to nearby towns, where the atmosphere and prices are more down-home western. The ski resorts make getting accommodations easy. Calling the following numbers can hook you up with many different kinds of lodgings: **Aspen** (☎ 800/262–7736), **Beaver Creek** (☎ 800/622–3131), **Breckenridge** (☎ 800/221–1091), **Copper Mountain** (☎ 800/458–8386), **Keystone** (☎ 800/222–0188), **Steamboat Springs** (☎ 800/922–2722), **Vail** (☎ 800/525–3875), and **Winter Park** (☎ 800/729–5813). Condos are the most common and, because they have kitchens, can help cut down on food expenses.

Aspen

$$$$ ✕ **Renaissance.** In this mountain-elegant space finished with shades of French country, owner-chef Charles Dale artfully transforms ordinary ingredients into culinary gold. Opt for his menu degustation—six courses matched with the appropriate glass of wine. Upstairs, the R Bistro is more casual and less expensive. ✉ *304 E. Hopkins St., Aspen,* ☎ *970/925–2402. Reservations essential. AE, D, DC, MC, V. Closed May and Oct.–Thanksgiving. No lunch.*

$$$–$$$$ ✕ **Ajax Tavern.** This is a bright, bustling restaurant with mahogany paneling, leather banquettes, and an open kitchen. The menu emphasizes Mediterranean flavors prepared with classic French techniques, using regional ingredients whenever possible. ⊠ *685 E. Durant Ave.,* ☏ *970/920–9333. Reservations essential. AE, D, DC, MC, V.*

$$$–$$$$ ✕ **Syzygy.** Upstairs and unmarked, this restaurant is for those who like
★   sleek modern design and sophisticated food that blends international flavors. Live jazz artists perform here every night during the ski season. ⊠ *520 E. Hyman,* ☏ *970/925–3700. Reservations essential. AE, D, DC, MC, V. Closed May and Oct.–Thanksgiving. No lunch.*

$$$$ ☷ **Hotel Jerome.** Rooms and suites in this brick building have retained
★   their Victorian charm with period furnishings such as carved cherry armoires; many bathrooms have Jacuzzis and separate showers. The J-Bar is a lively local's hangout; the Library Bar has more of a gentlemen's club atmosphere. ⊠ *330 E. Main St., 81611,* ☏ *970/920–1000 or 800/331–7213,* 🆆 *970/925–2784. 93 rooms. 2 restaurants, pool. AE, D, DC, MC, V.* ☙

$$$$ ☷ **St. Regis at Aspen.** The imposing châteaulike facade surrounds a central courtyard; the lobby showcases a $5 million art collection. ⊠ *315 E. Dean St., 81611,* ☏ *970/920–3300 or 888/454–9005,* 🆆 *970/925–8998. 257 rooms. Restaurant, pool, health club. AE, D, DC, MC, V.* ☙

$$$–$$$$ ☷ **Snowflake Inn.** The wide-ranging accommodations here are all quite comfortable. Most are decorated in tartans or bright colors. During ski season, hot spiced cider and cheese and crackers are served in the wood-beamed lobby around a stone fireplace. ⊠ *221 E. Hyman Ave., 81611,* ☏ *970/925–3221 or 800/247–2069,* 🆆 *970/925–8740. 38 rooms. Pool. AE, D, DC, MC, V. CP.* ☙

Beaver Creek

$$$$ ☷ **Hyatt Regency Beaver Creek.** An antler chandelier, huge stone fire-
★   places, and upholstered comfort characterize the public rooms here. Guests exiting the hotel step into their warmed and waiting ski boots and skis. Nonskiers can take advantage of the full spa and health club, as well as a top-notch children's program. Watch for much lower rates off-season. ⊠ *136 E. Thomas Pl. (Box 1595), Avon, 81620,* ☏ *970/949–1234 or 800/554–9288,* 🆆 *970/949–4164. 275 rooms. 3 restaurants, pool, health club. AE, D, DC, MC, V.* ☙

Breckenridge

$$–$$$ ☷ **B&Bs on North Main St.** Two picture-perfect five-room inns date from
★   the 1880s; a rustic timber-frame barn is a more modern addition. ⊠ *303 N. Main St., 80424,* ☏ *970/453–2975 or 800/795–2975,* 🆆 *970/453–5258. 10 rooms, 1 3-bedroom cottage. AE, D, MC, V. BP.* ☙

Glenwood Springs

$$ ☷ **Hotel Colorado.** Teddy Roosevelt stayed at this hotel, now listed in the National Historic Register, to take advantage of the adjacent hot springs. The imposing sandstone structure has a grand marble lobby. Bedrooms are huge and sparsely furnished. ⊠ *526 Pine St., 81601,* ☏ *970/945–6511 or 800/544–3998,* 🆆 *970/945–7030. 128 rooms. Restaurant, exercise room. AE, D, DC, MC, V.* ☙

Grand Lake

$–$$$ ☷ **Grand Lake Lodge.** Set majestically above Grand Lake and bordering Rocky Mountain National Park, the lodge is actually a collection of rustic cabins. Some have wood-burning stoves for heat, and all are comfortable and well worn. ⊠ *15500 U.S. Hwy. 34 (Box 569), 80447,* ☏ *970/627–3967 or 303/759–5848. 56 cabins. Restaurant, pool. AE, D, MC, V. Closed mid-Sept.–May.* ☙

Keystone

$$–$$$ ✕🏨 **Ski Tip Lodge.** This premium B&B reflects its 1880s origins with
★   four-poster beds, handmade quilts, and log-cabin decor. In the main
room, huge picture windows overlook a forest. The dining room's American regional cuisine is exceptional. The lodge is ½ mi from the slopes.
✉ Box 38, Keystone 80435, ☎ 970/496–4950 or 800/222–0188. 11
rooms. Restaurant, bar. AE, D, DC, MC, V. 🐾

Steamboat Springs

$$–$$$$ ✕ **Antares.** In a splendid Victorian building, you'll find fieldstone
★   walls, pressed-tin ceilings, stained glass, and exciting cuisine inspired
by America's rich ethnic stew. Creative dishes like trout with mango
and jícama chutney might be on the menu. ✉ 57½ 8th St., ☎ 970/879–
9939. Reservations essential. AE, MC, V. No lunch.

$–$$$$ ✕ **La Montaña.** Among the standouts at this southwestern establish-
★   ment are red-chili pasta in a shrimp, garlic, and cilantro sauce; inter-
woven strands of mesquite-grilled chorizo, lamb, and elk sausages; and
pecan-crusted elk loin with bourbon cream sauce. ✉ 2500 Village Dr.,
☎ 970/879–5800. AE, D, MC, V. No lunch.

$$–$$$ 🏨 **Sky Valley Lodge.** Glorious scenery surrounds this homey property
a few miles from downtown. Rooms are English country style. ✉
31490 E. U.S. Hwy. 40, 80477, ☎ 970/879–7749 or 800/499–4759,
FAX 970/879–7752. 24 rooms. AE, D, DC, MC, V. CP. 🐾

Vail

$$$–$$$$ ✕ **Sweet Basil.** A meal here will wake up your taste buds. The creative
★   menu includes such preparations as linguine with seafood and double-
cut pork chops with sweet apple stuffing. ✉ 193 E. Gore Creek Dr.,
☎ 970/476–0125. Reservations essential. AE, MC, V.

$$–$$$$ ✕ **Terra Bistro.** In the Vail Athletic Club, where a warm fireplace con-
★   trasts with black-iron chairs and black-and-white photographs, this soar-
ing space has an innovative, seasonally changing menu that caters to
both meat-and-potatoes diners and vegans. Everything is crisply tex-
tured and pungently seasoned. Organic produce and free-range meat
and poultry are used whenever possible. ✉ 352 E. Meadow Dr., ☎
970/476–6836. Reservations essential. AE, D, DC, MC, V. No lunch.

$$$$ 🏨 **Sonnenalp Resort of Vail.** A German family runs this centrally lo-
★   cated Bavarian-style hotel, where small but luxurious rooms have an
authentically German alpine feeling. It features a full-service spa and
an 18-hole golf course. ✉ 20 Vail Rd., 81657, ☎ 970/476–5656 or
800/654–8312, FAX 970/476–1639. 90 suites. 2 restaurants, pool, spa,
health club. AE, DC, MC, V. 🐾

Winter Park

$$–$$$$ ✕🏨 **Gasthaus Eichler.** This is Winter Park's most romantic dining
★   room, with quaint Bavarian decor, antler chandeliers, and stained-glass
windows. Veal and grilled items round out the menu of German clas-
sics such as sauerbraten. The Eichler also has 15 cozy Old World
rooms, with down comforters, lace curtains, armoires, cable TVs, and
whirlpool tubs. ✉ Hwy. 40, 80482, ☎ 970/726–5133 or 800/543–
3899, FAX 970/726–5175. 15 rooms. Restaurant. AE, MC, V.

Ranches

$$$$ 🏨 **C Lazy U Ranch.** Near Rocky Mountain National Park, this ram-
★   bling southwestern-style wooden lodge has fireplaces and Navajo rugs
in its rooms and cabins. Activities include horseback riding, ice skat-
ing, and dogsledding. The fare ranges from old-fashioned ranch food
(steak and barbecue) to contemporary cuisine. ✉ 3640 Colorado Hwy.
125 (Box 379), Granby 80446, ☎ 970/887–3344, FAX 970/887–3917.
19 rooms, 20 cabins. Restaurant, pool, exercise room. No credit cards.
Closed Apr.–May and Oct.–Dec. 21. FAP. 🐾

$$$$ ★   🏠 **Home Ranch.** This rustic yet luxurious western lodge in the Steamboat Springs area is a member of the prestigious Relais & Châteaux group. Each log cabin has a wood-burning stove and hot tub. Hiking, fishing, and horseback riding are the main summer activities; in winter, lift tickets to Steamboat Springs are included in the price. ⌧ *54880 County Rd. 129 (Box 822), Clark 80428,* ☏ *970/879–1780,* FAX *970/879–1795. 8 cabins, 6 lodge rooms. Restaurant, pool. AE, MC, V. Closed Apr.–May and Oct.–Nov.* 🐎

Campgrounds

You can reserve **camping spaces** at many of the national forest campgrounds by calling 800/280–2267. △ **Tiger Run Resort** (⌧ 3 mi north of Breckenridge on Hwy. 9, 80424, ☏ 970/453–9690) is a retreat for RVs, with tennis courts, a pool, and a recreation room. △ **Winding River Resort Village** (⌧ 1447 County Rd. 491, Box 629, Grand Lake 80447, ☏ 970/627–3215) is a combination campground and low-cost dude ranch in a beautiful forest.

Outdoor Activities and Sports

Boating

Sailing regattas are common at Grand Lake during the summer. Rent fishing boats and motorboats at **Beacon Landing Marina** (⌧ Grand County Rd. 64, 6 mi south of Grand Lake off Hwy. 34, ☏ 970/627–3671). **Lake Dillon Marina** (⌧ Dillon, ☏ 970/468–5100) rents sailboats and motorboats.

Fishing

Grand Lake and the connected reservoirs Shadow Mountain Lake and Lake Granby are known for their trout fishing. Dillon Reservoir is stocked with salmon and trout. The Lower Blue River, below Dillon Reservoir, is a Gold Medal catch-and-release area, as is the Fryingpan River near Aspen.

Golf

Sheraton Steamboat Golf Club (⌧ 2200 Village Inn Ct., ☏ 970/879–2220) was designed by Robert Trent Jones Jr. Reservations are essential at the Jack Nicklaus–designed **Breckenridge Golf Club** (⌧ 200 Clubhouse Dr., ☏ 970/453–9104). The difficult **Eagle/Vail Golf Course** (⌧ 0431 Eagle Dr., Avon, ☏ 970/949–5267) has reduced fees in fall and spring.

Hiking and Backpacking

To find out about parks and wilderness areas with hiking and backpacking trails, contact the **Holy Cross Ranger District Office** (⌧ 24747 Hwy. 24, Minturn, near Vail, ☏ 970/827–5715), the **Aspen Ranger District Office** (⌧ 806 W. Hallam St., ☏ 970/925–3445), or the **Dillon Ranger District Office** (⌧ 680 Blue River Pkwy., Silverthorne, ☏ 970/468–5400).

Rafting

The Colorado River lures both white-water enthusiasts and beginners, as does the Arkansas River near Buena Vista. Contact rafting firms through the **Colorado River Outfitters Association** (⌧ Box 440021, Aurora 80044, ☏ 303/280–2554).

Ski Areas

For **snow conditions** at Colorado resorts, call 303/825–7669.

Cross-Country

Aspen Cross-Country Center (☏ 970/925–2145) contains 35 mi of trails through the Roaring Fork Valley. **Breckenridge Nordic Ski Center** (☏

970/453–6855) maintains 14 mi of trails. **Copper Mountain/Trak Cross-Country Center** (☎ 970/968–2318, ext. 6342) has 16 mi of groomed track and skate lanes. **Devil's Thumb Ranch** (✉ Devil's Thumb, 7 mi north of Winter Park, ☎ 970/726–5632) is a full-service resort with 63 mi of groomed trails. **Frisco Nordic Center** (✉ 18454 Colorado Hwy. 9, ☎ 970/668–0866) has nearly 25 mi of one-way loops. **Snowmass Cross-Country Training Center** (☎ 970/923–3148) offers solitude in 40 mi of trails in the backcountry. **Steamboat Ski Touring Center** (☎ 970/879–8180) has trails emanating from the golf course. **Vail Cross-Country Ski Centers** (☎ 970/479–4390) has information on Vail Valley trails.

Downhill

Aspen Highlands (✉ 1498 Maroon Creek Rd., Aspen 81611, ☎ 970/925–1220) has 675 acres of runs, 4 lifts, and a 3,635-ft vertical drop. **Aspen Mountain** (✉ Box 1248, Aspen 81612, ☎ 970/925–1220) has 675 acres of runs, a gondola, 7 lifts, and a 3,267-ft drop. **Beaver Creek** (✉ Box 7, Vail 81658, ☎ 970/476–5601) has 1,625 acres of runs, 14 lifts, and a 4,040-ft drop. **Breckenridge** (✉ Box 1058, Breckenridge 80424, ☎ 970/453–5000) has 2,043 acres of runs, 23 lifts, and a 3,398-ft drop. **Buttermilk** (✉ Box 1248, Aspen 81612, ☎ 970/925–1220) has 420 acres of runs, 7 lifts, and a 2,030-ft drop. **Copper Mountain** (✉ Box 3001, Copper Mountain 80443, ☎ 970/968–2882) has 2,433 acres of runs, 21 lifts, and a 2,601-ft drop. **Keystone** (✉ Box 38, Keystone 80435, ☎ 970/468–2316) has 1,861 acres of runs, 22 lifts, and a 2,900-ft drop. **Snowmass** (✉ Box 5566, Snowmass Village 80446, ☎ 970/925–1220) has 3,010 acres of runs, 20 lifts, and a 4,406-ft drop. **Steamboat** (✉ 2305 Mt. Werner Circle, Steamboat Springs 80487, ☎ 970/879–6111) has 2,939 acres of runs, a gondola, 19 lifts, and a 3,668-ft drop. **Vail** (✉ Box 7, Vail 81658, ☎ 970/845–2500 or 800/525–2257) has 5,164 acres of runs, a gondola, 32 lifts, and a 3,360-ft drop. **Winter Park** (✉ Box 36, Winter Park 80482, ☎ 970/726–5514) has 2,886 acres of runs, 22 lifts, and a 3,060-ft drop.

Shopping

The town of **Silverthorne** has an outlet shopping complex (✉ I–70 at Silverthorne, ☎ 970/468–9440) with nearly 80 stores.

SOUTHWESTERN COLORADO

Ski areas and red-rock deserts, cowboy hangouts and haunts of ancient cultures mark this region. The feeling is down-home—you may see a cowboy in the distance riding off after a stray or walk into a bar where ranchers discussing stock prices sit next to climbers enthusing over an ascent route.

Visitor Information

Southwest Colorado Travel Region (✉ Box 2102, Montrose 81402, ☎ 800/933–4340). **Durango:** Chamber of Commerce (✉ 111 S. Camino del Rio, Box 2587, 81302, ☎ 970/247–0312 or 800/525–8855). **Telluride:** Chamber of Commerce (✉ 700 W. Colorado Ave., Box 653, 81435, ☎ 970/728–3041 or 800/525–3455).

Arriving and Departing

By Bus

Greyhound (☎ 800/231–2222) serves Durango and major mountain towns such as Purgatory, Silverton, Ouray, Ridgeway, and Montrose.

By Car

Highway 141 from Grand Junction to Highway 145 leads to Telluride; Highway 550 is the route from Durango to Silverton and Ouray.

By Plane

Durango–La Plata Airport (⊠ 1000 Airport Rd., ☎ 970/247–8143) is 14 mi east of Durango, and **Montrose Regional Airport** (⊠ 2100 Airport Rd., ☎ 970/249–3203) is 1 mi north of Montrose. **Gunnison County Airport** (⊠ 711 Rio Grande Rd., ☎ 970/641–2304) is 23 mi south of Crested Butte. **Telluride Regional Airport** (⊠ 1500 Last Dollar Rd. ☎ 970/728–5313) is 3 mi west of Telluride.

Exploring Southwestern Colorado

Telluride is another old mining town turned ski resort but with a difference: Its relative isolation in a box canyon makes it more laid-back than many other Colorado resorts, and its beauty is legendary. Skiers of all abilities will find suitable terrain. The summer brings nationally known **festivals** of film (☎ 603/433–9202), bluegrass (☎ 800/624–2422), and jazz (☎ 970/728–7009). South of Telluride is a complete change of scene: **Mesa Verde** (☞ National and State Parks, *above*), where the forests give way to dramatic red-rock cliff dwellings. The structures were fashioned more than 700 years ago by the Anasazi, believed to be the ancestors of the Pueblos.

East of Mesa Verde is **Durango,** a surprisingly large town with dramatic views of the San Juan Mountains, and strong frontier traditions. A trip on the **Durango and Silverton Narrow Gauge Railroad** (⊠ 479 Main Ave., ☎ 970/247–2733; ☞ $53 round-trip) is worth the trouble of reserving well in advance. The nine-hour round-trip takes you over tracks laid between the two towns in 1881, past unspoiled scenery, dramatic gorge crossings, and rails dug into the mountainside. **Silverton** is a smaller, more untouched frontier mining town.

Ouray, about 25 mi up the twisty, breathtaking Million-Dollar Highway, is a sleepy western town surrounded by the magnificent red San Juan Mountains. Dive into the **Ouray Hot Springs Pool** (☎ 970/325–4638; ☞ $7) or, for a more rustic dip, **Orvis Hot Springs** (☎ 970/626–5324; ☞ $8). Northeast of Ouray is **Crested Butte,** an old Victorian mining town tucked away in another gorgeous setting; the town serves as base for the excellent Crested Butte Mountain Resort ski area, 2 mi away and best suited for high-intermediate and expert skiers.

Dining and Lodging

Crested Butte

$$$–$$$$ ✗ **Soupçon.** Peter McCurrach, chef of Soupçon ("soup's on," get it?) ★   prepares innovative variations on classic bistro cuisine. The duck and fish are sublime, as is the intimate dining room inside a log cabin. ⊠ *Just off 2nd St. behind the Forest Queen,* ☎ 970/349–5448. *Reservations essential. AE, MC, V. Closed late Apr.–mid-June and Oct.–Thanksgiving. No lunch.*

$ ✗ **Slogar.** A soul-satisfying prix-fixe meal of plump fried chicken, ★   flaky buttermilk biscuits, coleslaw, mashed potatoes, and homemade ice cream costs just $12.95 inside this Victorian tavern with a lace and stained-glass motif. ⊠ *2nd and Whiterock Sts.,* ☎ 970/349–5765. *AE, MC, V. Closed late Apr.–mid-June and Oct.–mid-Nov. No lunch.*

$$$–$$$$ ☷ **Crested Butte Club.** This quaint, stylish inn has cherry-wood antiques ★   and claw-foot brass tubs. The bar is a convivial gathering spot, and the full-scale health club is a great place to relax after skiing or bik-

ing. ✉ *512 2nd St., 81224,* ☎ *970/349–6655 or 800/815–2582,* 𝖥𝖠𝖷 *970/349–7580. 8 rooms. Pool, health club. D, MC, V. CP.*

Durango

$$–$$$ ✕ **Ariano's.** Pasta made fresh daily and a sure touch with meats make this northern Italian restaurant one of Durango's most popular. The veal scallopini sautéed with fresh sage and garlic is excellent. ✉ *150 E. College Dr.,* ☎ *970/247–8146. Reservations not accepted. AE, MC, V. No lunch.*

$–$$ ✕ **Cypress Café.** The Greek-influenced menu, with flavorful vegetarian, lamb, and chicken dishes, is a welcome respite from the region's standard meat-and-potatoes fare. The outdoor patio, shaded by fruit trees, is one of the nicest places to dine in Durango on a summer day. ✉ *725 E. 2nd Ave.,* ☎ *970/385–6884. AE, DC, MC, V. Closed Sun. and Mon. during winter.*

$$–$$$ 🏨 **New Rochester Hotel.** This former flophouse was built in 1892. Its spacious rooms are full of western artifacts and are named for the many movies shot in the area, such as *Butch Cassidy and the Sundance Kid.* ✉ *726 E. 2nd Ave., 81301,* ☎ *970/385–1920 or 800/664–1920,* 𝖥𝖠𝖷 *970/385–1967. 15 rooms. AE, D, DC, MC, V. BP.* 🐾

Ouray

$$–$$$ 🏨 **China Clipper Inn.** A welcome relief from the area's typical western- and Victorian-style inns, the China Clipper is tastefully decorated with Oriental and nautical antiques. Innkeeper Earl Yarbrough is warm and interesting. ✉ *525 2nd St., 81427,* ☎ *970/325–0565 or 800/ 315–0565,* 𝖥𝖠𝖷 *970/325–4190. 11 rooms. AE, D, MC, V. BP.* 🐾

Telluride

$$$–$$$$ ✕ **Campagna.** Oak and terra-cotta floors and vintage photos of the Italian countryside give this place the feel of a Tuscan farmhouse; its assured, classically simple cuisine comes as no surprise. Wild mushrooms (porcini or Portobello) and wild boar chops are among the enticing possibilities. Finish off your meal with a perfect tiramisu and a shot of fiery grappa. ✉ *435 W. Pacific Ave.,* ☎ *970/728–6190. Reservations essential. MC, V. Closed mid-Apr.–mid-June and mid-Oct.– Thanksgiving. No lunch.*

$$$–$$$$ ✕ **La Marmotte.** At this rustic restaurant decorated like a French country cottage, the Gallic owners and chefs change the menu seasonally, ★ serving such dishes as duck breast with raspberry vinegar sauce or rack of lamb with tomato marmalade sauce. ✉ *150 W. San Juan Ave.,* ☎ *970/728–6232. Reservations essential. AE, MC, V. Closed mid-Apr.– mid-June and mid-Oct.–Thanksgiving. No lunch.*

$$$$ 🏨 **The Wyndham Peaks Resort and Golden Door Spa.** The prisonlike ★ exterior can be excused at this ski-in/ski-out luxury resort, thanks to its invigorating spa treatments, some of which purport to have their roots in indigenous Native American rites. But the biggest kick is the two-story water slide, which deposits you into the glorious pool, with Mt. Wilson looming in the background. ✉ *136 Country Club Dr., 81435,* ☎ *970/728–6800,* 𝖥𝖠𝖷 *970/728–6567. 174 rooms. 2 restaurants, 3 pools, exercise room. AE, D, DC, MC, V.* 🐾

$$$–$$$$ 🏨 **San Sophia Inn.** If you eschew Victorian frills, this is the inn for you: ★ There's no trace of Laura Ashley here, except for the brass beds and handmade quilts. Rooms, although smallish, are luxurious. ✉ *330 W. Pacific St., 81435,* ☎ *970/728–3001 or 800/537–4781. 16 rooms. AE, MC, V. BP.* 🐾

$$–$$$$ 🏨 **New Sheridan Hotel.** William Jennings Bryan delivered his rousing "Cross of Gold" speech here in 1896, garnering a presidential nomination in the process. Victoriana abounds, with exposed brick walls, brass beds, red-velour love seats, and wicker rocking chairs. Complimentary breakfast and afternoon wine service complete the experience of fin-de-siècle gracious living. The bar is a local institution. ✉ *231 W. Colorado Ave., 81435,* ☎ *970/728–4351 or 800/200–1891. 32 rooms. Restaurant, exercise room. AE, D, MC, V. BP.* ◈

Ranch

$$$–$$$$
★

🏠 **Skyline Ranch.** Burlap walls, pine furniture, and down comforters deck the rooms in the slab-wood buildings of this rustic western ranch, which has prime horseback riding and fly-fishing. In winter, guests cross-country ski or head to Telluride for downhill skiing. The cuisine is Continental in winter and casual American in summer. ✉ *7214 Hwy. 145, 8 mi south of Telluride, 81435,* ☎ *970/728–3757 or 888/754–1126,* FAX *970/728–6728. 10 lodge rooms, 6 cabins. Restaurant. AE, MC, V. Closed mid-Apr.–mid-June and mid-Oct.–mid-Dec. FAP summer, BP winter.* ◈

Campgrounds

Ranger district offices (☞ Hiking and Backpacking *in* Outdoor Activities and Sports, *below*) have information on campgrounds in the state and national forests. Near Durango is a ⚠ **KOA** campground (✉ east on Hwy. 160, ☎ 970/247–0783), which is closed mid-October–April.

Outdoor Activities and Sports

Biking

Crested Butte is a mountain-biking destination; Durango is home to many world-class road cyclists because of its great riding terrain. Bike rental locations abound in both towns.

Fishing

The Dolores River, in the San Juan National Forest (☞ Hiking and Backpacking, *below*), and the Animas River, near Durango, are good for trout. The Vallecito Reservoir, also near Durango, has pike, trout, and salmon. At **Ridgway State Park** (☎ 970/626–5822), 15 mi north of Ouray, you can catch rainbow trout.

Golf

Some of the best 18-hole courses in the area are **Crested Butte Country Club** (✉ 385 Country Club Dr., outside Crested Butte, ☎ 970/349–6127), **Hillcrest Golf Course** (✉ 2300 Rim Dr., Durango, ☎ 970/247–1499), **Tamarron** (✉ 40292 U.S. Hwy. 550N, north of Durango, ☎ 970/259–2000), and **Telluride Golf Club** (✉ Telluride Mountain Village, ☎ 970/728–3856).

Hiking and Backpacking

The 460-mi **Colorado Trail,** from Durango to Denver, is a major route. The **San Juan National Forest Supervisor's Office** (✉ 15 Burnett Ct., Durango, ☎ 970/247–4874) has information on trails in the area.

Rafting

Rafting is popular on the San Miguel, Dolores, Gunnison, and Animas rivers. Arrange trips through the **Colorado River Outfitters Association** (✉ Box 440021, Aurora 80044, ☎ 303/280–2554).

Ski Areas

For **snow conditions** at Colorado resorts, call ☎ 303/825–7669.

Cross-Country

Trails abound; check with local tourist offices for details. **Purgatory Ski Touring Center** (✉ Purgatory Ski Area, 1 Skier Pl., Durango 81301, ☎ 970/247–9000) manages 26 mi of trails; **Telluride Nordic Center** (✉ Box 1784, Telluride 81435, ☎ 970/728–1144) has 15 mi of trails and a free shuttle from the alpine ski area.

Downhill

Crested Butte (⊠ off Rte. 135, Box A, 81225, ☎ 970/349–2333) has 1,434 acres of runs, 14 lifts, and a 3,062-ft vertical drop. **Purgatory** (⊠ Hwy. 550, 81301, ☎ 970/247–9000) has 1,200 acres of runs, 11 lifts, and a 2,029-ft drop. **Telluride** (⊠ 565 Mountain Village Blvd., Box 11155, 81435, ☎ 970/728–3856) has 1,050 acres of runs, 12 lifts, and a 3,522-ft drop.

Shopping

Western Goods

Toh-Atin Gallery (⊠ 145 W. 9th St., Durango, ☎ 970/247–8277) and the related **Toh-Atin's Art on Main** (⊠ 865 Main Ave., ☎ 970/247–4540), around the corner, are perhaps the foremost western, Native American, and southwestern fine art and crafts galleries in Colorado. **North Moon** (⊠ 801 Main St., Ouray, ☎ 970/325–4885) carries southwestern hand-painted furniture, fine photography, and contemporary Native American jewelry.

ELSEWHERE IN COLORADO

South Central Colorado

Arriving and Departing

Buena Vista is 90 mi west of Colorado Springs on U.S. 24; the only way to get there is by car. Pueblo is a half hour south of Colorado Springs on I–25 south; Trinidad is just over an hour farther. **Pueblo Memorial Airport** (⊠ 31201 Bryan Circle,, ☎ 719/948–3355) is served by United Express.

What to See and Do

Hiking, biking, and climbing are king in **Buena Vista,** where the Collegiate Peaks Wilderness Area has 14,000-ft peaks. During the summer on the Arkansas River, Buena Vista also bills itself as "the white-water-rafting capital of the world." Contact **Dvorak Kayak & Rafting Expeditions** (⊠ Nathrop, ☎ 800/824–3795) or **Rio Expeditions** (⊠ Arvada, ☎ 800/291–2080) for trip information. After a full day of activities, head to the **Mt. Princeton Hot Springs** (⊠ 5 mi west of Nathrop, CR 162, ☎ 719/395–2447; ⊡ $6) for a restorative soak. The **Buena Vista Heritage Museum** (⊠ E. Main St., ☎ 719/395–8458; ⊡ $2) contains artifacts from the life and times of the regional pioneers. It is open during the summer only.

Pueblo, a multiethnic working-class steel town in the shadow of Colorado Springs, has some glorious historical neighborhoods, such as the **Union Avenue Historic District.** Walking-tour brochures are available at the **Chamber of Commerce** (⊠ 302 N. Santa Fe Ave., 81003, ☎ 719/542–1704). The **Rosemount Victorian Museum** (⊠ 419 W. 14th St., ☎ 719/545–5290; ⊡ $5) is an opulent mansion whose rooms are virtually intact. The **Sangre de Cristo Arts Center** (⊠ 210 N. Santa Fe Ave., ☎ 719/543–0130; ⊡ free) celebrates regional arts and crafts.

U.S. 50 roughly follows the faded tracks of the **Santa Fe Trail** from the Kansas border through La Junta, where U.S. 350 picks up the scent, traveling southwest to Trinidad. If you detour onto the quiet county roads, you can still discern the faint outline of the trail. Here, amid the magpies and prairie dogs, it takes little imagination to conjure visions of the pioneers struggling to travel just 10 mi a day by oxcart over vast stretches of territory. Just east of La Junta, **Bent's Fort** (⊠ 35110 Hwy. 194 E, ☎ 719/383–5010; ⊡ $2), now a living museum, was the most important stop along the route.

The **Trinidad History Museum** (⊠ 300 E. Main St., ☎ 719/846–7217; ☜ $5), occupying a historic city block, has exhibits chronicling the area's history and the effect of the Santa Fe Trail on the community. It is open weekdays during the summer and by reservation the rest of the year.

Dining and Lodging

$–$$ ✕ **Irish Brew Pub & Grille.** Pub grub is elevated to an art form here.
★ The grilled smoked-duck sausage with goat cheese is a standout, as are beaver (yes, beaver) sandwiches. Seven varieties of beer are brewed on the premises. ⊠ 108 W. 3rd St., Pueblo, ☎ 719/542–9974. AE, D, DC, MC, V. Closed Sun.

$–$$ 🏨 **Abriendo Inn.** With original parquet floors, stained glass, and Min-
★ nequa oak wainscoting, this exquisite 1906 home is on the National Register of Historic Places. Cookies and snacks are available around the clock. ⊠ 300 W. Abriendo Ave., Pueblo 81004, ☎ 719/544–2703, FAX 719/542–6544. 10 rooms. AE, DC, MC, V. BP. 🐾

$–$$ 🏨 **River Run Inn.** On the Arkansas River, this historic Victorian home has breathtaking mountain prospects. There's a large room available that sleeps from 5 to 13 people. ⊠ 8495 CR 160, east off Hwy. 285, Salida 81201, ☎ 719/539–3818 or 800/385–6925. 8 rooms. AE, MC, V. BP. 🐾

The San Luis Valley

Arriving and Departing

Alamosa is 150 mi east of Durango on U.S. 160 or 115 mi from Pueblo on U.S. 160E to I–25N. Great Sand Dunes National Monument is on Route 150 north of U.S. 160; San Luis is on Route 159 south of U.S. 160. The **Durango–La Plata Airport** (⊠ 1000 Airport Rd., ☎ 970/247–8143) receives daily flights from American, America West, Reno Air, and United Express.

What to See and Do

Nestled between the San Juan Mountains and the Sangre de Cristo range and watered by the mighty Rio Grande and its tributaries, the 8,000-square-mi **San Luis Valley** is the world's largest alpine valley. The **Alamosa National Wildlife Refuge** (⊠ 9383 El Rancho La., ☎ 719/589–4021) is an important sanctuary for the nearly extinct whooping crane and its cousin, the sandhill. The terrain of the San Luis Valley ranges from the stark moonscape of the Wheeler Geologic Area to the tawny, un-
🌤 dulating **Great Sand Dunes National Monument** (⊠ 35 mi from Alamosa, east on U.S. 160 and north on Rte. 150, ☎ 719/378–2312). Created by windswept grains from the Rio Grande floor, the sand dunes—which rise up to 750 ft and stretch for 55 square mi—are an improbable, unforgettable sight, as curvaceous as Rubens's nudes.

San Luis, founded in 1851, is the oldest incorporated town in Colorado. Its Hispanic heritage is celebrated in the **San Luis Museum and Cultural Center** (⊠ 401 Church Pl., ☎ 719/672–3611; ☜ $2). Murals depicting famous stories and legends of the area adorn the town's tree-lined streets.

Dining and Lodging

$–$$ ✕ **True Grit Steakhouse.** This popular steak house serves outstanding chicken-fried steaks, hand-cut steaks, and prime rib accompanied by huge salads and baked potatoes. If you're a John Wayne fan, you'll think you've gone to heaven. Everything here is named for the Duke. ⊠ 100 Santa Fe Ave., Alamosa, ☎ 719/589–9954. D, MC, V.

$ ✕ **Taqueria Calvillo.** This informal eatery serves seven kinds of fresh salsas and will wow you with authentic, homemade tortillas, fajitas, chile rellenos, and slow-cooked carnitas. ⊠ *119 Broadway, Alamosa,* ☎ *719/587–5500. No credit cards.*

$$ ⊞ **Cottonwood Inn B&B.** This pretty cranberry-and-azure house, built
★ in 1908, features Stickley furniture and regional photographs and watercolors. It's also a gathering place for cooking and writing workshops. Rooms are sunny, with country-French washed walls; some have clawfoot tubs. ⊠ *123 San Juan Ave., Alamosa 81101,* ☎ *719/589–3882 or 800/955–2623. 9 rooms. AE, D, MC, V. BP.* 🐾

CONNECTICUT

Updated by
Michelle
Bodak Acri

Capital	Hartford
Population	3,274,069
Motto	He Who Transplanted Still Sustains
State Bird	American robin
State Flower	Mountain laurel
Postal Abbreviation	CT

Statewide Visitor Information

Office of Tourism (⊠ 505 Hudson St., Hartford 06106, ☎ 800/282–6863 for brochure).

Scenic Drives

The narrow roads that wind through the **Litchfield Hills** in northwestern Connecticut offer scenic delights, especially in the spring and autumn. Each road bridge crossing the beautiful and historic **Merritt Parkway** (Route 15) between Greenwich and Stratford has its own architecturally significant design. **Routes 57 to 53 to 107 to 302,** which connect Exit 42 of the Merritt Parkway in Westport to Exit 10 of I–84 in Newtown, take you by Colonial homesteads, over steep ridges, and alongside the **Saugatuck Reservoir.** In northeastern Connecticut, **Route 169** from Norwich to North Woodstock has been designated a National Scenic Byway.

National and State Parks

National Park
Dapper, wooded Wilton is home to **Weir Farm National Historic Site,** former home of celebrated impressionist painter J. Alden Weir. The 60 acres here include hiking paths, picnic areas, and restored rose and perennial gardens. Tours of Weir's studio and sculptor Mahonri Young's studio are conducted, and you can take a self-guided tour of Weir's painting sites. ⊠ *735 Nod Hill Rd.,* ☎ *203/834–1896.* ✉ *Free.* ☺ *Visitor center closed Mon. and Tues.*

State Parks
Connecticut has nearly 100 state parks. For information on state parks contact the **State Parks Division, Bureau of Outdoor Recreation** (⊠ 79 Elm St., Hartford 06106, ☎ 860/424–3200).

COASTAL CONNECTICUT

The state's 253-mi coastline contains a series of bedroom communities serving New York City with smaller towns linked to Connecticut's major cities of Stamford, Bridgeport, New Haven, and New London. Along with its Colonial heritage and 21st-century urban sprawl, the region has nature centers and wilderness preserves for hiking and birdwatching, as well as restored 18th- and 19th-century townships and museums dedicated to bringing Connecticut's past alive.

Visitor Information

Southeastern Connecticut: Connecticut's Mystic and More (⊠ Box 89, New London 06320, ☎ 860/444–2206 or 800/863–6569). **Southwestern Connecticut:** Coastal Fairfield County Convention and Visitors Bureau (⊠ 297 West Ave., The Gate Lodge–Mathews Park, Norwalk 06850, ☎ 203/899–2799 or 800/866–7925). **New Haven:**

Greater New Haven Convention and Visitors Bureau (⊠ 59 Elm St., New Haven 06510, ☎ 203/777–8550 or 800/332–7829).

Arriving and Departing

By Bus

Greyhound (☎ 800/231–2222) provides bus service from throughout the United States. **Bonanza** (☎ 800/556–3815) offers service from various points in New England. **Connecticut Transit** (☎ 203/327–7433) provides bus service in the Stamford, Hartford, and New Haven areas. **Southeast Area Transit** (☎ 860/886–2631) serves Norwich, New London, Mystic, and Niantic.

By Car

The Merritt Parkway and I–95, both known for severe traffic jams during rush hour, are the principal coastal highways between New York and New Haven. I–95 continues beyond New Haven into Rhode Island. From Hartford, I–91 goes south to New Haven.

By Ferry

The **Bridgeport and Port Jefferson Steamboat Company** (☎ 888/443–3779 or 516/473–0286) has ferries connecting Bridgeport with the north shore of New York's Long Island. **Cross Sound Ferry** (☎ 860/443–5281) connects New London with northeastern Long Island's Orient Point.

By Plane

The state's chief airport is **Bradley International Airport** (⊠ Rte. 20, Exit 40 off I–91, ☎ 860/292–2000), 12 mi north of Hartford, with daily flights by most major U.S. airlines. US Airways Express flies into **Tweed/New Haven Airport** (⊠ Burr St. off I–95, ☎ 203/466–8833), 5 mi southeast of New Haven.

By Train

Amtrak (☎ 800/872–7245) stops at Stamford, Bridgeport, New Haven, Hartford, New London, and Mystic. **Metro North** (☎ 212/532–4900 or 800/638–7646) runs between New York City and New Haven, with stops at a few inland stations and many towns along the coast.

Exploring Coastal Connecticut

Greenwich, which borders New York State, epitomizes affluent Fairfield County, with gourmet restaurants and chic boutiques. The **Bruce Museum** (⊠ 1 Museum Dr., ☎ 203/869–0376; ☑ $3.50), closed Monday, has a mineral collection, a small but worthwhile collection of American Impressionist paintings, and a 16th-century-era woodland diorama. The 280-acre **Audubon Center** (⊠ 613 Riversville Rd., ☎ 203/869–5272; ☑ $3) has exhibits on the local environment and 8 mi of secluded hiking trails. The small barn-red **Putnam Cottage** was built about 1690 and was operated as Knapp's Tavern during the Revolutionary War. Inside are Colonial-era furnishings; outside is a lush herb garden. ⊠ 243 E. Putnam Ave., Rte. 1, ☎ 203/869–9697. ☑ $4. ☉ Open Apr.–Dec.; Wed., Fri., and Sun. 1–4.

Cos Cob is a village within the township of Greenwich. The **Bush-Holley Historic Site,** built circa 1732, has paintings by Childe Hassam and John Twachtman, sculptures by John Rogers, and pottery by Leon Volkmar. ⊠ 39 Strickland Rd., ☎ 203/869–6899. ☑ $6. Closed Jan.–Mar., weekdays; Apr.–Dec., Mon. and Tues.

Stamford's shoreline is given over primarily to industry and commerce, but to the north some beautiful nature areas remain. The 118-acre **Stamford Museum and Nature Center** (⊠ 39 Scofieldtown Rd., ☎ 203/322–1646; ☑ $5) has five galleries with changing exhibits on natural his-

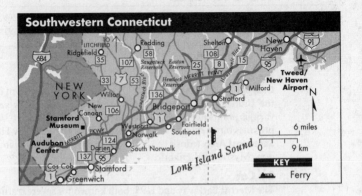

Southwestern Connecticut

tory, art, and Americana; a working New England farm; and a permanent exhibit on local Native American history. Shows are offered at the center's observatory and planetarium. Downtown, in the Champion International Corporation building, the **Whitney Museum of American Art at Champion** presents exhibits of primarily 20th-century American painting and photography that often include works from the Whitney's collection in New York City. ⊠ *Atlantic St. and Tresser Blvd.,* ☎ *203/358–7630.* 🖼 *Free. Closed Sun. and Mon.*

★ Affectionately dubbed SoNo, **South Norwalk,** off I–95's Exit 15, has
🖼 restored art galleries, restaurants, and boutiques. The **Maritime Aquarium at Norwalk** (⊠ 10 N. Water St., ☎ 203/852–0700; 🖼 Aquarium $7.75, IMAX $6.50) includes a huge aquarium, marine vessels, and an IMAX theater.

Wilton, a brief detour from the coast, up Routes 7 and 33 from Norwalk, is a well-preserved community with a wooded countryside and good antiques shopping. Wilton has Connecticut's first national park, **Weir Farm National Historical Site** (☞ National and State Parks, *above*). **Ridgefield,** with its sweeping lawns and stately mansions, is where you'll find northwestern Connecticut atmosphere within an hour of Manhattan. Ridgefield is home to the **Aldrich Museum of Contemporary Art,** which has changing exhibits of cutting-edge works and one of the finest sculpture gardens in the Northeast. ⊠ *258 Main St.,* ☎ *203/438–4519.* 🖼 *$5. Closed Mon.*

★ **Westport** has long been an artistic and literary community and now is also a trendy hub of shops and eateries. In summer visitors flock to **Sherwood Island State Park** (⊠ I–95 Exit 18, ☎ 203/226–6983; 🖼 $5–$12) for its 1½-mi sweep of sandy beach.

The exclusive Colonial village of **Southport** is on the Pequot River. To get there from Sherwood Island, head east along Greens Farms Road. **Fairfield** was almost destroyed in a raid by the British in 1779—four houses survived the attack and still stand on Beach Road. In the northern part of town, the **Connecticut Audubon Center of Fairfield** (⊠ 2325 Burr St., ☎ 203/259–6305; 🖼 $2), America's oldest nature center, maintains a 160-acre wildlife sanctuary.

Despite a poor reputation because of economic difficulties, **Bridgeport** is improving thanks to the hard work of city leaders. This fact, and a
🖼 handful of unique attractions, makes it a worthwhile stop. **Beardsley Park and Zoological Gardens** (⊠ 1875 Noble Ave., ☎ 203/394–6565; 🖼 $5) is Connecticut's only zoo. Here you'll find more than 350 animals as well as a South American rain forest and a carousel. The **Barnum Museum,** associated with onetime mayor P. T. Barnum, has exhibits

depicting the great showman's career and a scaled-down model of his famous creation, the five-ring circus. ⊠ *820 Main St.,* ☎ *203/331–1104.* ☑ *$5. Closed Mon.*

★ **New Haven** is a city of extremes: Although it's prosperous in the area around the green—encompassing the Yale University campus and the numerous shops, museums, and restaurants of Chapel Street—20% of the city's residents live below the poverty level. Stay near the campus and city common, especially at night, and get a good street map. Knowledgeable guides give one-hour walking tours of the **Yale University campus** (⊠ 149 Elm St., ☎ 203/432–2300; ☑ free). Part of Yale University, the **Beinecke Rare Book Library** (⊠ 121 Wall St., ☎ 203/432–2977; ☑ free), closed Sunday, houses a world-class collection of rare books and manuscripts—including a Gutenberg Bible and original Audubon bird prints—in a stunning building made from panels of translucent marble. The **Yale University Art Gallery** (⊠ 1111 Chapel St., ☎ 203/432–0600; ☑ free), closed Monday, has a collection that spans the centuries and the continents. The **Yale Center for British Art** (⊠ 1080 Chapel St., ☎ 203/432–2800; ☑ free), closed Mondays, has the most extensive collection of British artwork and rare books out-
Ⓒ side the United Kingdom. The **Peabody Museum of Natural History** (⊠ 170 Whitney Ave., ☎ 203/432–5050; ☑ $5), part of Yale University, is the largest of its kind in New England.

The urban buildup that characterizes the Connecticut coast west of New Haven dissipates as you drive east on I–95 toward New London. **Old Saybrook** was once a lively shipbuilding and fishing town; today the bustle comes mostly from its many summer vacationers. **Old Lyme,** on the other side of the Connecticut River from Old Saybrook, has a rich artistic history. The **Florence Griswold Museum** (⊠ 96 Lyme St., ☎ 860/434–5542; ☑ $4) once housed an art colony that included Childe Hassam. The museum displays the artists' works, along with 19th-century furnishings and decorative items. The **Lyme Academy of Fine Arts** (⊠ 84 Lyme St., ☎ 860/434–5232; ☑ donation suggested) shows works by students and other contemporary artists.

The seagoing community of **New London** is the home of the **U.S. Coast Guard Academy** (⊠ 15 Mohegan Ave., ☎ 860/444–8270; ☑ free), whose 100-acre cluster of traditional redbrick buildings includes a museum. The three-masted training bark *Eagle* may be boarded when in port.

In **Groton,** across the Thames River from New London, is a U.S. submarine base. The world's first nuclear-powered submarine, the *Historic Ship Nautilus,* was launched here in 1954 and is now permanently berthed here and is open to visitors. The **Submarine Force Museum,** next to the base, contains memorabilia, artifacts, and displays, including working periscopes and controls. ⊠ *Crystal Lake Rd.,* ☎ *860/694–3558 or 800/343–0079.* ☑ *Free. Closed Tues. late Oct.–early May.*

★ Ⓒ **Mystic** is a celebrated whaling seaport. **Mystic Seaport** (⊠ 75 Greenmanville Ave., ☎ 860/572–0711, ☑ $16)—the nation's largest maritime museum, on 17 riverfront acres—has 19th-century sailing vessels you can board, including the *Charles W. Morgan,* the last wooden whaling ship afloat. There is also a maritime village with historic homes, a spectacular collection of sailing-related artifacts, and craftspeople who give demon-
Ⓒ strations. At the **Mystic Marinelife Aquarium and Institute for Exploration** (⊠ Off I–95 on Coogan Blvd., ☎ 860/572–5955; ☑ $15) you can see more than 6,000 specimens and 50 live exhibits of sea life.

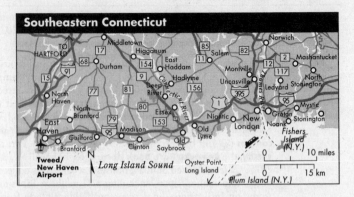

Southeastern Connecticut

Stonington is a quiet fishing community clustered around white-spired churches. Past the historic buildings that surround the town green is the **Old Lighthouse Museum,** where you'll find displays about shipping, whaling, and other subjects. You can climb to the top of the granite tower for a view of Long Island Sound and three states. ⊠ *7 Water St.,* ☎ *860/ 535–1440.* ⊡ *$4. Closed Nov.–Apr. and Mon. May, June, Sept., and Oct.*

Ledyard was a quiet town that has been transformed by the local Native American tribe, the Pequots, into a major tourist center. The **Mashantucket Pequot Museum and Research Center** (⊠ 110 Pequot Trail, ☎ 800/411–9671; ⊡ $12), a vast, innovative museum, uses state-of-the-art technology to explore more than 18,000 years of Northeastern Woodland tribes' history. The gambling and entertainment complex **Foxwoods** (⊠ 39 Norwich Westerly Rd., ☎ 860/312–3000) is the world's largest casino, with more than 5,500 slot machines, a high-stakes bingo parlor, poker rooms, a smoke-free gaming area, and more.

The **Mohegan Sun** casino (⊠ Mohegan Sun Blvd., ☎ 888/226–7711), in Uncasville, offers similar facilities as Foxwoods on a smaller scale.

Dining and Lodging

The **Covered Bridge B&B Reservation Service** (☎ 860/542–5944) and **Nutmeg B&B Agency** (☎ 860/236–6698) are reliable statewide services for B&Bs and small inns. **B&B, Ltd.** (☎ 203/469–3260) is a service for small B&Bs, inns, and rooms rented in private homes. Rooms are costliest in summer and autumn. A 12% lodging tax is added to each bill.

Greenwich

$$$$ ✕ **Restaurant Jean-Louis.** Roses, Limoges china, and crisp, white table-
★ cloths with lace underskirts complement extraordinary food, carefully served. The fixed-price menu might include diced vegetables cooked in saffron broth with mussels, or endive salad accompanied by American caviar and followed by a sliced breast of duck on a bed of spinach. ⊠ *61 Lewis St.,* ☎ *203/622–8450. Jacket required. AE, D, DC, MC, V. No lunch Mon.–Thurs.*

$$$ ✕🔲 **Homestead Inn.** Each bedroom in this Italianate mansion is decorated with antiques and reproductions. The restaurant ($$$$; jacket required) serves up-to-the-minute French cuisine. ⊠ *420 Field Point Rd., 06830,* ☎ *203/869–7500,* 𝖥𝖠𝖷 *203/869–7502. 23 rooms. Restaurant. AE, MC, V.*

Mystic

$$–$$$$ ✕🔲 **Inn at Mystic.** The highlight of this inn, which sprawls over 15 hilltop acres and overlooks Pequotsepos Cove, is the five-bedroom Georgian Colonial mansion in which Lauren Bacall and Humphrey Bogart honeymooned. Almost as impressive are the four-bedroom gatehouse and the unusually attractive motor lodge. The sun-filled Floodtide Restaurant serves traditional New England fare. ⊠ *Rtes. 1 and 27, 06355,* ☎ *860/536–9604 or 800/237–2415,* ℻ *860/572–1635. 67 rooms. Restaurant, pool. AE, D, DC, MC, V.* ⊛

$$–$$$ 🏠 **Whaler's Inn and Motor Court.** A perfect compromise between a chain motel and a country inn, this complex is one block from the Mystic River and downtown. The rooms are decorated in a Victorian style with quilts and reproduction four-poster beds. ⊠ *20 E. Main St., 06355,* ☎ *860/536–1506; 800/243–2588 outside CT;* ℻ *860/572–1250. 41 rooms. 3 restaurants. AE, MC, V.*

New Haven

$ ✕ **Frank Pepe's.** The big ovens on the back wall of this New Haven
★   institution bake pizzas that are revered throughout the country. On weekend evenings the wait for a table can be more than an hour, but the pizza—the sole item on the menu—is worth it. ⊠ *157 Wooster St.,* ☎ *203/865–5762. Reservations not accepted. No credit cards. Closed Tues. No lunch Mon., Wed., or Thurs.*

$$$ 🏠 **Three Chimneys Inn.** This 1870 Victorian mansion is one of the most
★   polished small inns in the state. Rooms have posh Georgian furnishings: mahogany four-poster beds, oversize armoires, and Chippendale desks. The sitting room and library have working fireplaces. ⊠ *1201 Chapel St., 06511,* ☎ *203/789–1201,* ℻ *203/776–7363. 10 rooms. AE, D, MC, V. BP.*

North Stonington

$$–$$$ ✕🏠 **Randall's Ordinary.** Famed for its open-hearth cooking of authentic Colonial dishes, the Ordinary creates tasty lunches and three-course fixed-price dinners (reservations essential), served by staff in period costume. Accommodations are available in the 17th-century John Randall House, where rooms are simply furnished with antiques, or in the converted barn. ⊠ *Rte. 2, Box 243, 06359,* ☎ *860/599–4540,* ℻ *860/ 599–3308. 15 rooms. Restaurant. AE, MC, V.* ⊛

Norwalk

$$$ ✕ **Meson Galicia.** The inventive tapas served in this restored trolley barn
★   stimulate the taste buds. Ingredients might include sweetbreads, capers, asparagus, or chorizo. Come with an empty stomach and an open mind, and let the enthusiastic staff spoil you. ⊠ *10 Wall St.,* ☎ *203/866– 8800. AE, D, DC, MC, V. Closed Mon. No lunch weekends.*

Norwich

$$$–$$$$ ✕🏠 **The Spa at Norwich Inn.** This luxurious Georgian-style inn is set on 42 acres high on a bluff a few hundred yards from the Thames River. Topnotch treatments and fitness classes are offered in the newly renovated and expanded spa facility. Kensington's restaurant ($$–$$$$) serves Continental delicacies as well as lighter spa cuisine. ⊠ *607 W. Thames St. (Rte. 32), 06360,* ☎ *860/886–2401 or 800/275–4772,* ℻ *860/886–4492. 145 rooms. Restaurant, indoor pool, health club. AE, DC, MC, V.* ⊛

Old Lyme

$$–$$$ ✕🏠 **Bee & Thistle Inn.** This three-story 1756 Colonial contains period
★   antiques, sunlit porches, and a formal garden. Most rooms have canopy or four-poster beds. Fireplaces and candlelight create a romantic atmosphere in the restaurant (closed on Tuesday and the first three weeks in January), where classic American cuisine is served with style. ⊠ *100 Lyme St., 06371,* ☎ *860/434–1667; 800/622–4946 outside CT;* ℻ *860/ 434–3402. 12 rooms. Restaurant. AE, DC, MC, V.* ⊛

Old Saybrook

$$–$$$ ✕ **Aleia's.** Light, bright, and bountiful as the Italian countryside, this restaurant has raffia, silk flowers, and hand-painted plates from Capri

on the walls. Trompe l'oeil fruits, vegetables, and herbs adorn the table-tops. Chef-owner Kimberly Snow takes a contemporary approach to Italian cuisine by applying nouvelle touches to her mother's tried-and-true recipes. ⊠ *1687 Boston Post Rd.,* ☎ *860/399–5050. AE, MC, V. Closed Mon. No lunch.*

Stamford

$$$–$$$$ ✕ **Amadeus.** One of a dozen great restaurants along its stretch of Summer Street, Amadeus leads the pack. The fare, like the decor, is Continental with a Viennese flair. Try the Mediterranean fish and shellfish soup, followed by the trademark Vienna schnitzel, served with golden panfried potatoes. ⊠ *201 Summer St.,* ☎ *203/348–7775. AE, D, DC, MC, V. No lunch weekends.*

Westbrook

$$$–$$$$ 🏨 **Water's Edge Inn & Resort.** With a spectacular setting on Long Island Sound and its own beach, this weathered gray-shingle compound is one of the Connecticut shore's premier resorts. Rooms in the main building, though not as large as the suites in surrounding outbuildings, have better views and nicer furnishings. ⊠ *1525 Boston Post Rd., 06498,* ☎ *860/ 399–5901 or 800/222–5901,* ℻ *860/399–6172. 167 rooms. Restaurant, indoor and outdoor pools, spa, health club. AE, D, DC, MC, V.* ☜

Westport

$$$–$$$$ ✕ **Splash.** Cutting-edge Pacific Rim cuisine is served in a white-clap-board country club. The funky made-for-sharing dishes include *Baang* chicken salad—shredded white meat tossed with Asian vegetables and sesame oil. Don't miss the soups or a chance to sit on the stunning white wraparound porch where locals go to see and be seen. ⊠ *260 Compo Rd. S.,* ☎ *203/454–7798. AE, D, MC, V. Closed Mon.*

$$$–$$$$ ✕🏨 **Inn at National Hall.** The inn's redbrick building on the down-
★ town banks of the Saugatuck River belies its whimsical, exotic interior. Each room is a study in innovative restoration. New chef Todd English, a Boston superstar, prepares such dishes as grilled sirloin over Tuscan bruschetta and tortelli of butternut squash with brown butter and sage. ⊠ *2 Post Rd. W, 06880,* ☎ *203/221–1351 or 800/628–4255,* ℻ *203/221–0276. 15 rooms. Restaurant. AE, DC, MC, V. CP.* ☜

Campgrounds

🏕 **Riverdale Farm Campsite** (⊠ 111 River Rd., Clinton, ☎ 860/669–5388). 🏕 **Hammonasset Beach State Park** (⊠ I–95, Exit 62, Madison, ☎ 203/245–1817).

Nightlife and the Arts

Nightlife

Bars and clubs are sprinkled throughout southern Connecticut. The best of them are concentrated in Westport, South Norwalk, New Haven's Chapel West area, and along New London's Bank Street.

With two dance floors, the **Art Bar** (⊠ 84 W. Park Pl., Stamford, ☎ 203/973–0300) is the best dance spot in the area. Music ranges from 1980s pop to New Wave to Gothic and Industrial. The crowd is sometimes on the young side. **The Brook Café** (⊠ 919 Post Rd. E, Westport, ☎ 203/222–2233), one of the oldest gay clubs in the world, is in a ramshackle shack that looks great inside, with a hot-pink bathroom and other eclectic designs. Alternative and traditional rock bands play at **Toad's Place** (⊠ 300 York St., New Haven, ☎ 203/624–8623).

The Arts

The Connecticut coast's wealth of successful repertory and Broadway-style theaters includes the **Long Wharf Theatre** (⊠ 222 Sargent Dr., New

Haven, ☎ 203/787–4282), known for its revivals of neglected classics and imaginative productions of new work. The **Shubert Performing Arts Center** (⊠ 247 College St., New Haven, ☎ 203/562–5666) presents an array of full-scale productions. **Stamford Center for the Arts** (⊠ 307 Atlantic St., ☎ 203/325–4466) offers everything from one-act plays to musicals to film festivals. In summer the **Westport Country Playhouse** (⊠ 25 Powers Ct., ☎ 203/227–4177) presents first-rate plays. The **Yale Repertory Theatre** (⊠ 222 York St., New Haven, ☎ 203/432–1234) is known for its fresh interpretations of classics.

Most coastal towns have outdoor summer concerts and music festivals, and some have smaller regional theaters. Call tourist offices for details (☞ Visitor Information, *above*).

Outdoor Activities and Sports

Fishing

Saltwater fishing is best from June through October; bass, bluefish, and flounder are popular catches. Boats are available from **Hel-Cat Dock** (⊠ Groton, ☎ 860/445–5991) and **Sea Sprite Charters** (⊠ Old Saybrook, ☎ 860/669–9613).

Golf

Danbury's 18-hole **Richter Park Golf Course** (⊠ 100 Aunt Hack Rd., ☎ 203/792–2550) is one of the top public courses in the nation. Three 18-hole courses in the area are the **H. Smith Richardson Golf Course** (⊠ 2425 Morehouse Hwy., Fairfield, ☎ 203/255–7300) and the courses designed by Robert Trent Jones and Gary Player at the **Lyman Orchards Golf Club** (⊠ Rte. 147, Middlefield, ☎ 860/349–8055).

Shopping

Southwestern Connecticut

Route 7, which runs through Wilton and Ridgefield, has dozens of antiques sheds and boutiques. **Cannondale Village** (⊠ Off Rte. 7, Wilton, ☎ 203/762–2233) is a pre–Civil War farm village turned shopping complex. Washington Street in **South Norwalk** (SoNo) has galleries and crafts dealers. The **Stamford Town Center** (⊠ 100 Greyrock Pl., ☎ 203/356–9700) houses 130 mostly upscale shops. Main Street in **Westport** is like an outdoor mall, with J. Crew, Ann Taylor, Coach, and dozens of other fashionable shops. **New Canaan, Darien,** and **Greenwich** are renowned for their swank stores and boutiques.

Southeastern Connecticut

The New Haven and New London areas have typical shopping centers. **Clinton Crossing Premium Outlets** (⊠ I–95, Exit 63, Clinton, ☎ 860/664–0700) has 70 upscale shops. **Westbrook Factory Stores** (⊠ I–95, Exit 65, Westbrook, ☎ 860/399–8656) has 65 outlets. Downtown **Mystic** has an interesting collection of boutiques and galleries. **Olde Mistick Village** (⊠ I–95, Exit 90, Mystic, ☎ 860/536–1641), a re-created Colonial village, has crafts and souvenir shops. The **Tradewinds Gallery** (⊠ 20 W. Main St., Mystic, ☎ 860/536–0119) specializes in antique prints and maps. The **Essex–Saybrook Antiques Village** (⊠ 345 Middlesex Tpke., Old Saybrook, ☎ 860/388–0689) has more than 120 dealers. **Old Lyme, Guilford,** and **Stonington** are good sources for antiques.

THE LITCHFIELD HILLS

Here, in the foothills of the Berkshires, is some of the most unspoiled scenery in the state. Grand old inns are plentiful, as are surprisingly sophisticated eateries. Rolling farmlands abut thick forests, and engaging trails traverse state parks. Two rivers, the Housatonic and Farmington, attract anglers and canoeing enthusiasts, and there are three sizable lakes—Waramaug, Bantam, and Twin lakes. Most towns are anchored by sweeping greens and stately homes and offer a glimpse of New England life as it existed two centuries ago.

Visitor Information

Litchfield Hills Visitors Council (⊠ Box 968, Litchfield 06759, ☎ 860/567–4506).

Exploring the Litchfield Hills

The mountainous northern towns of **Sharon, Lakeville, Salisbury,** and **Norfolk** are crisscrossed by scenic winding roads. From late April to mid-October auto-racing fans come to **Lime Rock Park** (⊠ Rte. 112, Lakeville, ☎ 860/435–5000), home to the Northeast's best road racing.

The crossroads village of **New Preston** is packed with antiques shops. North of downtown is Lake Waramaug. Route 478, a scenic drive around the lake (8 mi), will take you past stately homes and beautiful old inns, many of which serve outstanding Continental cuisine. **Kent,** to the northwest of New Preston, is home to the area's greatest concentration of art galleries, some of them nationally recognized. **Bull's Bridge** (⊠ off Rte. 7), in Kent, is one of the state's three remaining covered bridges. Within **Kent Falls State Park** (⊠ Rte. 7, ☎ 860/927–3238) is one of the state's most impressive waterfalls.

Everything seems on a larger scale in **Litchfield** than in neighboring towns: Great white Colonials line broad streets shaded by majestic elms, and serene Litchfield Green is surrounded by lovely shops and restaurants. Near the green is the **Tapping Reeve House and Law School** (⊠ 82 South St., ☎ 860/567–4501; ☑ $5), America's first law school, which was founded in 1773. It's closed on Monday and late-November–mid-April. The **Litchfield History Museum** (⊠ Rtes. 63 and 118, ☎ 860/567–4501; ☑ $5), closed on Monday and late-November–mid-April, has galleries, a reference library, and information on the town's historic buildings. **White Flower Farm** (⊠ Rte. 63, ☎ 860/567–8789), where much of America shops in person or by mail for perennials and bulbs, is a restful stop.

The villages of **Washington, Roxbury,** and **Bridgewater** offer a gentle landscape, with pastoral rolling hills, in which numerous actors and writers seek refuge from the din of Manhattan and Hollywood. You can buy the ingredients for a gourmet picnic lunch—try the **Pantry** (⊠ Titus Rd., Washington, ☎ 860/868–0258)—and laze on the shores of sparkling Lake Waramaug or enjoy a leisurely drive along precipitous ridges, passing gracious farmsteads and meadows alive with wildflowers.

☾ In Bristol are two amusements for the child in everyone. The **Carousel Museum of New England** (⊠ 95 Riverside Ave., ☎ 860/585–5411; ☑
☾ $4) displays carousel art. **Lake Compounce** (⊠ Rte. 229 N, I–84, Exit 31, ☎ 860/583–3631; ☑ $6.95 general admission, $23.95 with rides) is the country's oldest continually operating amusement park. Highlights of the 325-acre park include an antique carousel, a classic wooden roller coaster, a new water playground, and a lake with a beach.

Dining and Lodging

Litchfield

$$–$$$$ ✕ **West Street Grill.** This stylish dining room on Litchfield's historic green is the favorite of local glitterati, but all are warmly welcomed. Imaginative grilled fish, steak, poultry, and lamb dishes are served with

fresh vegetables and pasta or risotto. The desserts are superb. ⊠ *43 West St. (Rte. 202),* ☎ *860/567–3885. AE, MC, V.*

New Preston

$$$$ ✕▥ **Boulders Inn.** This is the most idyllic and prestigious of the inns
★ along Lake Waramaug's uneven shoreline. The Boulders opened in 1940 but still looks like the private home it was at the turn of the 20th century. Apart from the main house, a carriage house and several guest houses command panoramic views of the countryside and the lake. Rooms contain Victorian antiques and wood-burning fireplaces; four have double whirlpool baths. The exquisite menu at the Boulders' window-lined, stone-wall dining room ($$$) changes seasonally. ⊠ *E. Shore Rd. (Rte. 45), 06777,* ☎ *860/868–0541 or 800/552–6853,* ℻ *860/868–1925. 17 rooms. Restaurant. AE, MC, V. MAP.* ✎

Norfolk

$$$–$$$$ ▥ **Greenwoods Gate.** The cheerful George Shumaker, a former Hilton executive with a penchant for playing cupid, runs Connecticut's foremost romantic hideaway. Every room holds countless amenities, from chocolates and cognac to soaps, fresh flowers, and powders to board games with titles like "Romantic Liaisons"; champagne or deep massages are available with notice, and for a fee. George prepares a huge breakfast—a spread of muffins and fresh fruit followed by a hearty hot meal—and lays out snacks and afternoon wine and cheese. ⊠ *105 Greenwoods Rd. E (Rte. 44), 06058,* ☎ *860/542–5439,* ℻ *860/542–5897. 4 suites. No credit cards. BP.* ✎

Washington

$$$$ ✕▥ **Mayflower Inn.** Though some suites at this inn will set you back
★ $1,000 a night, the place is always booked well ahead—with good reason. The Mayflower is impeccably decorated: Guest rooms have fine 18th- and 19th-century antiques and four-poster canopy beds; oversize baths have mahogany wainscotting and marble throughout. Streams and trails crisscross the 28-acre grounds. The mouthwatering cuisine might include roast Muscovy duck breast. ⊠ *118 Woodbury Rd. (Rte. 47), 06793,* ☎ *860/868–9466,* ℻ *860/868–1497. 25 rooms. Restaurant, pool, health club. AE, MC, V.* ✎

Woodbury

$$–$$$$ ✕ **Good News Café.** The emphasis is on healthful, innovative fare: venison filet mignon with a horseradish crust on grilled onions and snow
★ peas with a cherry-cabernet sauce is a tasty example. Or you can bounce in for cappuccino and munchies—there's a separate room just for this purpose, decorated with a fascinating collection of vintage radios. ⊠ *694 Main St. S,* ☎ *203/266–4663. AE, MC, V. Closed Tues.*

Nightlife and the Arts

World-renowned artists and ensembles perform Friday and Saturday evening June–August at the **Norfolk Chamber Music Festival** (☎ 860/542–3000), at the Music Shed on the Ellen Battell Stoeckel Estate at the northwest corner of the Norfolk green. Yale School of Music students perform at the festival Thursday evening and Saturday morning.

Outdoor Activities and Sports

Canoeing

Clarke Outdoors (⊠ 163 Rte. 7, West Cornwall, ☎ 860/672–6365) offers canoe and kayak rentals as well as 10-mi trips from Falls Village to Housatonic Meadows State Park.

Hiking

The Litchfield Hills area has terrific hiking terrain, with **Haystack Mountain and Dennis Hill** (⊠ Rte. 272, Norfolk, ☎ 860/482–1817) and the 758-acre **Sharon Audubon Center** (⊠ 325 Cornwall Bridge Rd., ☎ 860/364–0520) offering the region's best opportunities.

Ski Areas

Mohawk Mountain (⊠ 46 Great Hollow Rd., Cornwall, ☎ 860/672–6100). **Ski Sundown** (⊠ 126 Ratlum Rd., New Hartford, ☎ 860/379–9851). **Woodbury Ski Area** (⊠ 785 Washington Rd., Woodbury, ☎ 203/263–2203).

Shopping

The best antiques and crafts shopping is along Route 6 in **Woodbury** and **Southbury,** Route 45 in **New Preston,** U.S. 7 in **Kent,** Route 128 in **West Cornwall,** and U.S. 202 in **Bantam.**

ELSEWHERE IN CONNECTICUT

The Connecticut River Valley and Hartford

Visitor Information

Connecticut River Valley and Shoreline Visitors Council (⊠ 393 Main St., Middletown 06457, ☎ 860/347–0028 or 800/486–3346). **Greater Hartford Tourism District** (⊠ 234 Murphy Rd., Hartford 06114, ☎ 860/244–8181 or 800/793–4480).

Arriving and Departing

Amtrak, Greyhound, and **Bonanza** provide service to the Hartford area (☞ Arriving and Departing *in* Coastal Connecticut, *above*). By car take I–91 north from New Haven or I–84, which cuts diagonally southwest–northeast through the state. Head north along Route 9 from Old Saybrook for a scenic drive through this historic area.

What to See and Do

The Connecticut River valley meanders through rolling hills, offering a taste of Colonial history as well as sophisticated inns. **Essex,** on the west bank of the Connecticut River, is where the first submarine, the *American Turtle,* was built. A full-size reproduction of the *Turtle* is at the **Connecticut River Museum** (⊠ Steamboat Dock, ☎ 860/767–8269; ☒ $4). In **East Haddam** is the region's leading oddity: a 24-room oak-and-fieldstone hilltop castle that is part of **Gillette Castle State Park** (⊠ 67 River Rd., off Rte. 82, ☎ 860/526–2336; ☒ grounds free, castle $4). East Haddam is also the home of the **Goodspeed Opera House** (⊠ Rte. 82, ☎ 860/873–8668). The upper floors of this elaborate structure have served as a venue for theatrical performances for more than a century.

Hartford, known as the insurance capital of America, is also the state capital. The Federal **Old State House** (⊠ 800 Main St., ☎ 860/522–6766; ☒ free) was designed by Charles Bulfinch, architect of the U.S. Capitol. **The Mark Twain House** (⊠ 351 Farmington Ave., ☎ 860/493–6411; ☒ $9) is named after the author who made his home here in this extravagant Victorian mansion. The 50,000 artworks and artifacts ★ at the **Wadsworth Atheneum** (⊠ 600 Main St., ☎ 860/278–2670, ☒ $7), the nation's first public art museum, span 5,000 years and include paintings from the Hudson River School, the Impressionists, and 20th-century painters.

Dining and Lodging

$$$–$$$$ ✕ **Restaurant du Village.** A black wrought-iron gate beckons you away from the tony antiques shops of Chester's quaint Main Street to this Colonial storefront, painted in Newport blue and adorned with flower boxes. Sample classic French cuisine—escargots in puff pastry, filet mignon—while recapping the day's shopping coups. ✉ *59 Main St., Chester,* ☎ *860/526–5301. AE, MC, V. Closed Mon. and Tues. No lunch.*

$$–$$$$ ✕ **Max Downtown.** Upscale Max Downtown serves cuisine from around the world—miso-saki glazed Chilean sea bass, Portobello mushroom napoleons, aged New York strip steaks, and grilled veal loin chops. A separate cigar bar serves classic port and single-malt liquor. ✉ *185 Asylum St., CityPlace, Hartford,* ☎ *860/522–2530. Reservations essential. AE, DC, MC, V. No lunch weekends.*

$$–$$$ ✕🏠 **Copper Beech Inn.** A magnificent copper beech tree shades the imposing main building of this Victorian inn, which is furnished in period pieces. Each of the main house's four guest rooms has an old-fashioned tub; the nine rooms in the carriage house are more modern and have decks. Seven acres of wooded grounds and terraced gardens create an atmosphere of privileged seclusion. The country French menu in the romantic dining rooms ($$$–$$$$; reservations essential; jacket and tie) changes seasonally. ✉ *46 Main St., Ivoryton 06442,* ☎ *860/767–0330 or 888/809–2056. 13 rooms. Restaurant. AE, DC, MC, V. CP.* ☙

$$–$$$ ✕🏠 **Griswold Inn.** The decor at what's billed as America's oldest inn is kaleidoscopic—some Colonial, a touch of Federal, a little Victorian, and just as much modern (air-conditioning, phones, but no in-room TVs) as is necessary to meet present-day expectations. The chefs at the restaurant prepare country-style and gourmet dishes—try the famous 1776 sausages, which come with sauerkraut and German potato salad, or the risotto croquettes. ✉ *36 Main St., Essex 06426,* ☎ *860/767–1776,* 🖷 *860/767–0481. 30 rooms. Restaurant. AE, MC, V. CP.*

$$–$$$$ 🏠 **Goodwin Hotel.** Considering this grand city hotel's stately exterior,
★ rooms are not as opulent as you might expect, though they're large and have Italian marble baths. The clubby, mahogany-paneled Pierpont's Restaurant serves commendable new American fare. ✉ *1 Haynes St., Hartford 06103,* ☎ *860/246–7500 or 800/922–5006,* 🖷 *860/247–4576. 124 rooms. Restaurant, exercise room. AE, D, DC, MC, V.* ☙

DELAWARE

Anne
Dubuisson
Anderson

Capital	Dover
Population	743,000
Motto	Liberty and Independence
State Bird	Blue hen
State Flower	Peach blossom
Postal Abbreviation	DE

Statewide Visitor Information

Delaware State Visitors Center (⊠ 406 Federal St., Dover 19901, ☎ 302/739–4266). **Delaware Tourism Office** (⊠ 99 Kings Hwy., Box 1401, Dover 19903, ☎ 800/441–8846). **Visitor centers:** I–95, between Routes 896 and 273 (☎ 302/737–4059); at **Delaware Memorial Bridge** (☎ 302/571–6340); and **north of Smyrna**, on U.S. 13 north (☎ 302/653–8910).

Scenic Drives

From Wilmington's western edge, a **30-mi loop** follows winding Route 100 past well-screened estates, a state park, and the meandering Brandywine Creek; and then into Pennsylvania on a section of U.S. 1 west, which takes you past several historical attractions; and finally back into Delaware, where you'll travel on Route 52 (locally called Château Country) to villages lined with antiques shops, to horse farms, and to Winterthur, a major du Pont estate turned museum. A drive south along **Route 9** from New Castle to Dover slides past tidal marshes and across creeks on one-lane bridges; side roads veer into bird sanctuaries or out to points of land with a view of Delaware Bay.

National and State Parks

National Parks
Bombay Hook National Wildlife Refuge (⊠ 2591 Whitehall Neck Rd., Smyrna 19977, ☎ 302/653–6872) is more than 15,000 acres of ponds and fields filled between April and November with both resident and migrating waterfowl. **Prime Hook National Wildlife Refuge** (⊠ Rte. 236, just off Rte. 16; R.D. 3, Box 195, Milton 19968, ☎ 302/684–8419) is a smaller, well-developed preserve with boat ramps, canoe trails, and a boardwalk trail through marshes.

State Parks
Fourteen parks run by the **Delaware Division of Parks and Recreation** (⊠ 89 Kings Hwy., Richardson and Robbins Bldg., Dover 19901, ☎ 302/739–4702) are set up for hiking, fishing, and picnicking. The chief inland parks, with freshwater ponds, add seasonal boat rentals to basic amenities. All parks are free from November through April and charge $2.50 per Delaware car or $5 per out-of-state car on weekends between April and November and daily from Memorial Day through Labor Day.

Brandywine Creek State Park (⊠ Rtes. 92 and 100, Box 3782, Greenville 19807, ☎ 302/577–3534), about 5 mi from Wilmington, is the state's best picnic park with more than 1,000 acres of open fields and wooded grounds, a nature center, 12 mi of hiking trails, and perfect sledding slopes in winter. **Cape Henlopen** (⊠ 42 Henlopen Dr., Lewes 19958, ☎ 302/645–8983; Seaside Nature Center, ☎ 302/645–6852), east of Lewes, has more than 150 campsites in pinelands. **Bellevue State Park** (⊠ 800 Carr Rd., Wilmington 19809, ☎ 302/577–3390), once a du Pont family estate, offers summer concerts, horseback riding, and tennis. **Delaware Seashore State Park** (⌧ 850 Inlet, Rehoboth Beach 19971, ☎ 302/227–2800; Marina, ☎ 302/227–3071) has both ocean surf and calm bay waters, large bathhouses with showers, and nearly 300 campsites with hookups. **Lums Pond State Park** (⌧ U.S. 301 and Rte. 71 south of Newark; 1068 Howell School Rd., Bear 19701, ☎ 302/368–6989) has more than 70 campsites. **Trap Pond** (⌧ off Rte. 24 east of Laurel; R.D. 2, Box 331, Laurel 19956, ☎ 302/875–5153) includes part of the Great Cypress Swamp and has more than 140 rustic sites under a canopy of loblolly pines. **Kellens Pond State Park** (⌧ 5025 Kellens Pond Rd., Felton 19943, ☎ 302/284–4526) has a 66-acre millpond for boating and fishing, plus a water park, campground, and set of rustic cabins.

WILMINGTON

Wilmington, the state's commercial hub and largest city, was founded in 1638 as a Swedish settlement and successively taken over by the Dutch and the English. More recently it has been populated by employees of DuPont's company headquarters, credit-card banks, and nearby poultry ranches. The city boasts handsome architecture with good examples of styles such as Federal, Greek Revival, Queen Anne and Art Deco, as well as abundant cultural attractions. Outside the compact city center are several outstanding museums, including some that are legacies of the duPonts.

Two nearby towns—Newark, home of the University of Delaware, and New Castle, the state's beautifully restored Colonial capital—are linked to Wilmington by a few miles of neighborhoods and strip malls. The wide ribbon of I–95, which crosses the state, connects Wilmington at the eastern edge to Newark at the western border. This nondescript, 20-minute drive is all many travelers ever see of the First State.

Visitor Information

Greater Wilmington: Convention and Visitors Bureau (⌧ 100 W. 10th St., 19801-1661, ☎ 302/652–4088 or 800/422–1181).

Arriving and Departing

By Bus
Greyhound (⌧ 101 N. French St., ☎ 302/652–7391 or 800/231–2222).

By Car
Situated between Baltimore and Philadelphia, Wilmington is bisected by I–95 north–south and linked to small-town Pennsylvania by U.S. 202 and routes 52 and 41.

By Plane
Philadelphia International Airport (⌧ 8000 Essington Ave., ☎ 217/937–6937), about 30 mi north of downtown Wilmington, is served by all major U.S. and international airlines. **Taxi** fare is about $25 to Wilmington.

By Train
Wilmington Train Station (⌧ Martin Luther King Blvd. and French St., ☎ 302/429–6523) has **Amtrak** (☎ 800/872–7245) service, as well as **SEPTA** (☎ 215/580–7800) commuter service to Philadelphia.

Getting Around Wilmington

Downtown is compact enough to stroll, but visits to New Castle, Newark, or the museums and parks ringing Wilmington require a car.

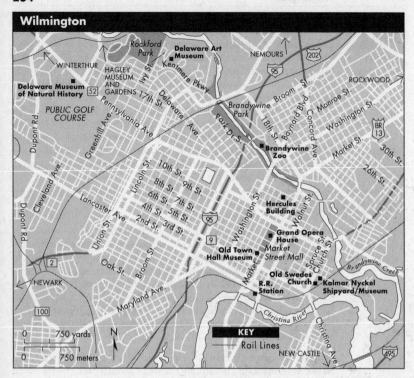

Wilmington

Downtown parking is moderately priced in garages and impossible to find on the streets in the jam-packed office district. Buses are geared to commuters, not explorers.

Exploring Wilmington

The four-block **Market Street Mall** marks the city center. The **Grand Opera House** (⊠ 818 Market St. Mall, ☎ 302/658–7897) is a working theater. Built by the Masonic Order in 1871 and restored in 1971, the four-story Grand's facade is cast iron painted white in French Second Empire style to mimic the old Paris Opéra. The recently constructed adjoining Giacco Building houses a smaller theater and art galleries.

The **Delaware History Museum** (⊠ 504 Market St., ☎ 302/656–0637; ☞ $4) in a restored 1940s Woolworth's building, has three galleries and a changing exhibit of Delaware history. The **Old Town Hall Museum** (⊠ 512 Market St., ☎ 302/655–7161; ☞ free with Delaware History Museum admission) is a two-story Georgian-style structure with changing exhibits and restored jail cells to tour. The hall and museum shop were restored as headquarters for the **Historical Society of Delaware**.

The **Hercules Building** (⊠ 1313 N. Market St., ☎ 302/594–5000), north of the mall, was built in the 1980s with ziggurat walls and a 20-ft-diameter clock. The core of the building is a 14-story atrium, with ground-level shops and a jungle of plants.

East of the mall and surrounded by some of the city's poorest neighborhoods, a monument to the 1638 landing of a Swedish expedition marks the first permanent settlement in the Delaware Valley.

Two 17th-century structures are worth a visit: **Old Swedes Church,** built in 1698, retains its original hipped roof and high wooden pulpit and is still used regularly for religious services. The **Hendrickson House Mu-**

seum, a farmhouse built in 1690 by Swedish settlers, is furnished with period pieces. *Both:* ⊠ *606 Church St.,* ☎ *302/652–5629.* ☞ *Free.*

★ Children who visit the **Delaware Museum of Natural History** (⊠ 4840 Kennett Pike, ☎ 302/658–9111, ☞ $5), 5 mi northwest of Wilmington, can explore the mysteries of Australia's Great Barrier Reef and examine an African water hole, dinosaur replicas, and a 500-pound clam. The museum's hands-on, interactive discovery room encourages children to use all their senses.

☾ The **Delaware Art Museum,** a few miles west of the city center and I–95, houses a major collection of post-1840 American paintings and illustrations, including works by major figures such as Homer, Eakins, Hopper, Wyeth, Sloan, and illustrator Howard Pyle, as well as the foremost assemblage of English Pre-Raphaelite paintings and decorative arts in the United States. Children create their own masterpieces on the peg board in the **Pegasaurus Room.** ⊠ *2301 Kentmere Pkwy.,* ☎ *302/571–9590.* ☞ *$7. Closed Mon.*

Nemours Mansion and Gardens shows the Alfred du Pont family's preference for fine automobiles, European antiques, Louis XVI–style architecture, and formal French gardens. The estate, a 102-room mansion on 300 acres, is open only to those 12 and over. ⊠ *1600 Rockland Rd.,* ☎ *302/651–6912.* ☞ *$10. Reservations essential. Closed Mon. and Dec.–Apr.*

The **Hagley Museum and Library,** one of three former du Pont family properties on the northwest edges of Wilmington, recalls the DuPont company's beginnings in 1802 as an explosives manufacturer. You can tour gunpowder mills, a 19th-century machine shop, and the family home and gardens, all set on 240 acres. ⊠ *Rte. 141,* ☎ *302/658–2400.* ☞ *$9.75. Hrs vary seasonally.*

Outside Wilmington

New Castle, 5 mi south of Wilmington on Route 9, is a barely commercialized gem of a town with restored Colonial houses, cobblestone streets, and historic sites along the Delaware River. William Penn's first landing in North America is noted in **Battery Park.** Two blocks west of the waterfront, the **New Castle Courthouse,** Delaware's Colonial capital until 1777, is a pristine museum of state history, with three brick wings and a white cupola and spire. ⊠ *211 Delaware St.,* ☎ *302/323–4453.* ☞ *Free. Closed Mon.*

New Castle's **George Read II House** and formal gardens was built in 1801 in Federal style by a signer of both the Declaration of Independence and the Constitution. Twelve rooms of the big brick house are open, including three furnished in period style. ⊠ *42 The Strand,* ☎ *302/322–8411.* ☞ *$4. Closed Mon., weekdays Jan. and Feb.*

★ **Winterthur Museum, Garden, and Library** (⊠ Rte. 52, Winterthur, ☎ 302/888–4600 or 800/448–3883, ☞ price varies depending on tour and season) focuses on Henry Francis du Pont's passion for collecting furniture and decorative arts made or used in America from 1640 to 1860. The nine-story, 175-room hillside stucco mansion and museum wing shelter a world-class collection of furniture, silver, paintings, and textiles in period settings. There are three exhibition galleries and an elegant pavilion that houses the museum shop and glass-enclosed restaurant. The 966 acres of naturalistic gardens showcase native and exotic plants.

Odessa is a tiny, mostly residential village set on the banks of the Appoquinimink River, about 23 mi south of Wilmington off U.S. 13. Originally a grain-shipping port, it stopped growing in the mid-19th century when disease attacked its peach crops and the railroad passed it by.

Today this tiny community is a living-history lesson—until a few years ago, muskrat still topped the menu at the town's one-and-only restaurant. A branch of the Winterthur Museum includes two 18th- and 19th-century Quaker mansions, the **Corbitt Sharp House** and the **Wilson Warner House.** Also open to visitors is the **Brick Hotel Gallery,** which houses rotating exhibits of American furniture and decorative arts. ☎ *302/378–4069.* ⌑ *$8 for all 3 buildings. Closed Mon. and Jan.–Feb.*

Parks, Gardens, and Zoos

In **Brandywine Park** (⊠ *1021 W. 18th St.*), shady paths pass Colonial stone walls and a tiny brick church that was built in 1740 and used for British wounded during the Revolutionary War. Lush Brandywine Creek and a millrace attract fishermen and splash-happy children. Wilmington's **Brandywine Zoo** tucks outdoor exhibits into cliffs along Brandywine Creek. ⊠ *1001 N. Park Dr.,* ☎ *302/571–7747.* ⌑ *$3 Apr.–Oct., free Nov.–Mar. Exotic-animal house closed Nov.–Mar.*

Rockwood Museum, a 19th-century country estate with a Gothic manor house displays 19th-century decorative arts and furnishings and features 6 acres of landscaped grounds and 62 acres of woodlands. ⊠ *610 Shipley Rd.,* ☎ *302/761–4340.* ⌑ *$5. Closed Mon.*

Dining

$$$–$$$$ × **Green Room.** French cuisine is served in 19th-century opulence at
★ the Hotel duPont (☞ Lodging, *below*). Seafood entrées such as sautéed sea scallops over tomato fettuccine and crab cakes with chive oil and deep-fried leeks are especially well handled. Lunch is served Monday through Saturday, dinner only on Saturday. The hotel's clubby **Brandywine Room,** with its original Wyeth paintings and Continental cuisine, is open for dinner Sunday through Thursday from 6 to 11. ⊠ *Hotel duPont, 11th and Market Sts.,* ☎ *302/594–3154. Reservations essential. Jacket and tie for dinner. AE, D, DC, MC, V.*

$$–$$$$ × **Deep Blue.** When chef Dan Butler closed Tavola Toscona his loyal following swore they'd never find a replacement; when Butler opened this contemporary fish house, they swore they had. The eclectic menu, with smooth tuna carpaccio and grilled octopus in olive oil and garlic, deserves all the kudos it's received. ⊠ *111 W. 11 St.,* ☎ *302/777–2040. AE, D, DC, MC, V. Closed Sun.*

$$–$$$ × **Black Trumpet Bistro.** With candlelight and room for just 45 diners, the atmosphere here is elegant and intimate. Meals are a cut above ordinary bistro cuisine; the menu includes lamb, chicken, beef, veal, and a fish of the day. You're in luck if they have the white-pepper ice cream for dessert. ⊠ *1828 West 11th St.,* ☎ *302/777–0454. Reservations essential in the main dining room. AE, D, DC, MC, V. Closed Sun.*

$$–$$$ × **Eclipse.** This intimate bistro is a Wilmington favorite. The innovative seasonal menu has included grilled ostrich loin with fennel and vidalia onion, as well as lamb chops in a lingonberry and green peppercorn demi-glace. ⊠ *1020B N. Union St.,* ☎ *302/658–1588. AE, MC, V.*

$$–$$$ × **Harry's Savoy Grill.** Residents come for the friendly service, great
★ food, and warm atmosphere. The slow-roasted prime rib is a top seller; and in season nobody does soft-shell crab better. ⊠ *2020 Naamans Rd.,* ☎ *302/475–3000. AE, DC, MC, V.*

$–$$$ × **Jessop's Tavern & Colonial Restaurant.** In a tiny space just steps from New Castle's waterfront park, chef Tim Bell presents a menu inspired by the English, Dutch, and Swedish founders of the region. The rich oyster chowder, double-crusted chicken potpie, and crusty flat bread can be topped off with an English bread pudding. ⊠ *114 Delaware St., New Castle,* ☎ *302/322–6111. AE, MC, V. Closed Mon.*

$-$$ ✕ **Saigon Vietnam.** This authentic, well-run Vietnamese eatery is in a
★ spacious, beautifully decorated space in a revived shopping center at
the end of Newark's Main Street. Don't miss the crispy spring rolls,
sweet-yet-spicy lemongrass chicken, or clay-cooked specialties. ⌧ *207
Main St., Newark,* ☎ *302/737–1590. AE, D, DC, MC, V. Closed Mon.*

$ ✕ **Iron Hill Brewery & Restaurant.** Beer brewed in-house, good burg-
ers, and a satisfying selection of regional American entrées make this
place perfect for a casual meal. Don't miss the Louisiana barbecue shrimp
and Jamaican jerk pork chop. ⌧ *147 E. Main St., Newark,* ☎ *302/
266–9000. AE, D, MC, V.*

Lodging

Most Wilmington-area hotels are business-oriented. For variety there
are restored Colonial inns (not modern adaptations) and a few bed-
and-breakfasts. A reservation service—**Bed & Breakfast of Delaware,
Inc.** (⌧ 701 Landon Dr., Suite 200, Wilmington 19810, ☎ 302/479–
9500) helps locate moderately priced lodgings.

$$$–$$$$ ▦ **Inn at Montchanin Village.** These painstakingly restored 19th-century
★ buildings once housed DuPont powder mill workers. Each elegant guest
unit is unique, with antique reproduction furniture and luxurious linens.
The village is only five minutes from the Winterthur Museum and Gar-
dens, in the heart of Château Country. At the excellent four star restau-
rant, Krazy Kat's, guests are treated to breakfast. ⌧ *Rte. 100 and Kirk
Rd., Montchanin 19710,* ☎ *302/888–2133 or 800/269–2473,* ℻ *302/
888–0389. 37 rooms. Restaurant. AE, D, DC, MC, V. BP.* ✆

$$–$$$$ ▦ **Hotel duPont.** This posh and popular 12-story downtown hotel with
an old-world feel has large rooms with living areas set off by mahogany
dividers. The furnishings are 18th-century reproductions. ⌧ *11th and
Market Sts., 19801,* ☎ *302/594–3100 or 800/441–9019,* ℻ *302/594–
3108. 217 rooms. 3 restaurants, health club. AE, D, DC, MC, V.* ✆

$$$ ▦ **Brandywine Suites.** This former store, tucked into a nondescript
★ downtown block, has dramatic contemporary architecture, suites
with rich traditional furnishings, and a popular lounge. ⌧ *707 King
St., 19801,* ☎ *302/656–9300,* ℻ *302/656–2459. 49 suites. Restau-
rant. AE, DC, MC, V.*

$$ ▦ **Darley Manor Inn.** Once the home of Felix Darley, the mid-Victorian
illustrator of titles including *The Scarlet Letter* and *Rip Van Winkle,* today
this inn caters to business travelers and weekend visitors of the nearby
Longwood Gardens and Brandywine Valley. Rooms have modern amenities including data ports. ⌧ *3701 Philadelphia Pike (U.S. 13), Claymont
19703,* ☎ *302/792–2127. 6 rooms. AE, DC, MC, V. BP.* ✆

$–$$ ▦ **Marriott Courtyard.** Centrally located in downtown Wilmington, this
affordable hotel has a Brandywine Valley ambience—lots of hunter green
and cranberry red along with Wyeth reproductions. Many businesspeople stay here (there are two meeting rooms), but the Courtyard also
specializes in wedding parties and family reunions. ⌧ *1102 West St.,
19801,* ☎ *302/429–7600 or 800/321–2211,* ℻ *302/429–9167. 125
rooms. Restaurant, exercise room. AE, D, DC, MC, V.*

$ ▦ **Boulevard Bed & Breakfast.** This stately 1913 home adorned with
fluted columns is in one of Wilmington's fine older neighborhoods near
downtown. The rooms are simple and comfortable with reading chairs,
desks, and floral wallpaper. A full breakfast is served on an enclosed
side porch. ⌧ *1909 Baynard Blvd., Wilmington 19802,* ☎ *302/656–
9700,* ℻ *302/454–0233. 6 rooms. AE, MC, V. BP*

$ ▦ **Fairfield Inn.** Close to the University of Delaware and about 9 mi
west of Wilmington, this Marriott-owned inn is spartan but convenient.
⌧ *65 Geoffrey Dr., Newark 19713,* ☎ *302/292–1500. 135 rooms. Pool.
AE, D, DC, MC, V.*

$ ▣ **Rodeway Inn.** No-smoking rooms and proximity to historic New Castle are two advantages of this simple motor inn. ⊠ *111 S. DuPont Hwy., New Castle 19702,* ☎ *302/328–6246 or 800/321–6246,* ℻ *302/328–9493. 40 rooms. AE, D, DC, MC, V.*

Shopping

The **Greenville Shopping Center** (⊠ Rte. 52 near the Rte. 141 interchange) has tony dress, shoe, and jewelry stores where merchants cater to the Château Country crowd. Newark's **Christiana Mall** (⊠ Rte. 7 at I–95 Exit 4S, ☎ 302/731–9815) has 130 stores, including Macy's and Strawbridge & Clothier. **Concord Mall** (⊠ 4737 Concord Pike, ☎ 302/478–9271) has 95 stores and two department store biggies: Strawbridge & Clothier and Boscov's.

THE ATLANTIC COAST

Whether you have a day, a weekend, or the whole summer, a visit to Delaware's beaches will likely be a highlight of a trip to the First State. From Cape Henlopen State Park at the northern end to Fenwick Island at the southern border are 23 mi of Atlantic shoreline. The main route south gets you to shore points the fastest, but if you have time, drive scenic Route 9 (it runs from New Castle to Dover) between farm fields and stands of 10-ft-high grasses. The most scenic stretch of shoreline is south of Dewey Beach, where sand dunes and wide, white Atlantic beaches are just an arm's reach from Route 1.

Visitor Information

Bethany-Fenwick: Chamber of Commerce and Information Center (⊠ Rte. 1N, Fenwick Island; Box 1450, Bethany Beach 19930, ☎ 302/539–2100 or 800/962–7873). **Lewes:** Chamber of Commerce and Visitors Bureau (⊠ Savannah Rd. and Kings Hwy., Box 1, 19958, ☎ 302/645–8073). **Milton:** Chamber of Commerce (⊠ 104 Federal St., 19968, ☎ 302/684–1101). **Rehoboth Beach–Dewey Beach:** Chamber of Commerce (⊠ 501 Rehoboth Ave., Box 216, Rehoboth Beach 19971, ☎ 302/227–2233 or 800/441–1329).

Delaware Today magazine (☎ 302/656–1809 or 800/285–0400), published monthly, covers events and region-wide restaurants.

Arriving and Departing

By Bus
Greyhound (☎ 800/231–2222) links Rehoboth Beach with Wilmington, New Castle, and Dover.

By Car
From the north take I–95 south to U.S. 13 south (in Wilmington). Then pick up U.S. 113 at Dover and take it to Route 1 (in Milford). From the south the scenic route to Delaware's northern shores crosses Chesapeake Bay at Annapolis and continues east via U.S. 301/50; follows U.S. 50 to Route 404 at Wye Mills, Maryland; then crosses Delaware on Routes 404, 18, and 9 to Route 1 at Lewes.

By Ferry
Cape May–Lewes Ferry (☎ 302/645–6346 or 302/645–6313) is a 70-minute ride from Cape May, New Jersey, to Lewes, Delaware.

Exploring the Atlantic Coast

There is ample public access to the Atlantic surf and to the 23 mi of sand, though crowds pour in from Washington, D.C., and points west on holidays and summer weekends. The Broadkill River, Rehoboth Bay, Indian River Bay, and Little Assawoman Bay have sheltered coves.

Just west of the beaches are some of the state's historic villages and scenic bay-side parks (☞ National and State Parks, *above*). In **Milton,** once a major shipbuilding center at the head of the Broadkill River, the whole downtown area is a historic district of 18th- and 19th-century architecture, including old cypress-shingle houses. **Lewes,** a 1631 Dutch settlement at the mouth of Delaware Bay, cherishes its seafaring past with a marine museum and draws visitors with good restaurants, shops, and lodging away from the hectic beach resorts.

Coastal towns include **Rehoboth Beach,** the largest, with a busy boardwalk for strolling and shopping. Rehoboth is the main gay getaway destination for the Middle Atlantic region. Next door is **Dewey Beach,** popular with young singles. Adjacent **Bethany Beach, South Bethany,** and **Fenwick Island** (founded as a church camp and known for its fishing), south of the Indian River inlet, are quieter resorts.

Dining and Lodging

Once upon a time this sleepy resort area was full of basic motels and guest houses with kitchens that served generic fried seafood and burgers. Today, the coast is lined with swank hotels and restaurants run by talented young chefs. Rehoboth Beach is the center of the culinary boom, which has spread as far north as Milford and southward to the state line at Fenwick Island.

Bethany Beach

$$$ ✕ **Sedona.** Among the restaurant's creative dishes are grilled ahi tuna, spicy almond-encrusted salmon, and West Texas crab cakes with Santa Fe salsa. The casual aesthetic is more reminiscent of Santa Fe or Albuquerque than Bethany or Dewey Beach. ⊠ *26 Pennsylvania Ave.,* ☎ *302/539–1200. AE, D, DC, MC, V. Closed Nov.–Jan.*

Dewey Beach

$–$$$ ✕ **Rusty Rudder.** In this barnlike, nautical-themed space overlooking Rehoboth Bay, the specialties are down-home service and local seafood, such as crab imperial. A land-and-sea buffet of seafood and chicken specialties is served every Friday year-round and several times weekly during summer months. There's also a Sunday brunch. ⊠ *113 Dickinson St., on the bay,* ☎ *302/227–3888. AE, D, DC, MC, V.*

Lewes

$$ ✕ **Lazy Susan's.** For the fattest, sweetest, steamed blue-shell crabs, this simple roadside eatery is the place. Eating inside can be stifling, and the outside deck overlooks the highway, so takeout may be your best bet. Call ahead to make sure the crabs are fresh. ⊠ *Rte. 1 at Tenley Ct., Lewes,* ☎ *302/645–5115. MC, V.*

$$–$$$ ▥ **Inn at Canal Square.** Valued for its waterfront location, this modern inn built to fit in with its older neighbors has rooms with balconies overlooking the harbor. ⊠ *122 Market St., 19958,* ☎ *302/644–3377 or 888/644–1911,* ℻ *302/645–7083. 19 rooms. AE, D, DC, MC, V. CP.* ⊛

$–$$$ ▥ **New Devon Inn.** The inn was built in 1926 and is listed in the Na★ tional Register of Historic Places. The lobby and parlor are treasuries of Early Americana. Ask about the self-guided biking inn-to-inn package. ⊠ *2nd and Market Sts., Box 516, 19958,* ☎ *302/645–6466 or 800/824–8754,* FAX *302/645–7196. 23 rooms. AE, MC, V.*☜

Milford

$$ 🏨 **The Marshall House and Towers Bed and Breakfast.** This restored
★ Victorian bank building has traditionally decorated guest rooms, some with fireplaces. ⊠ *112 N.W. Front St., 19963,* ☎ *302/422–5708 or 302/422–3814. 3 rooms. Restaurant. DC, MC, V. BP.*☜

$ 🏨 **Traveler's Inn Motel.** Rooms in this two-story, balconied motel are plain, with two double beds and minimal furnishings (a hanging rack, no closet). ⊠ *1036 N. Walnut St., 19963,* ☎ *302/422–8089. 38 rooms. AE, MC, V.*

Rehoboth Beach

$$$–$$$$ ✕ **Blue Moon.** Since 1980, the Blue Moon has been Rehoboth's best and hippest restaurant. The Pan Asian–influenced menu sometimes includes seafood lasagna and baked salmon stuffed with scallops and leeks. The charming old house has a sunny front porch, and the restaurant is adjacent to the town's main gay bar. ⊠ *35 Baltimore Ave.,* ☎ *302/ 227–6515. AE, DC, MC, V.*

$$–$$$ ✕ **La La Land.** In a tiny beach house, this magical restaurant serves eclec-
★ tic French–cum–Southwest–meets–Pacific Rim cuisine. Try lobster claw risotto or the wild mushroom barley with three pestos and truffle oil. ⊠ *22 Wilmington Ave.,* ☎ *302/227–3887. AE, DC, MC, V. Closed Mon.–Wed.*

$$–$$$ ✕ **Sydney's Blues and Jazz.** New Orleans–influenced American cooking issues from the kitchen with such specialties as oysters Rockefeller and authentic gumbo and jambalaya. Wine-flight tastings—samples of three wines served in small portions—are also offered. The innovative grazing menu is great for light eaters and the bar menu features po'boys. There's live blues and jazz music. ⊠ *25 Christian St.,* ☎ *302/227–1339 or 800/808–1924. AE, D, DC, MC, V.*

$–$$ ✕ **Dogfish Head Brewery.** Delaware's first brewpub, Dogfish Head is
★ owned by two young entrepreneurs who keep their clientele happy with a changing menu of in-house brews, pizzas, and musical performers. ⊠ *320 Rehoboth Ave.,* ☎ *302/226–2739. AE, MC, V.*

$ ✕ **Nicola's Pizza.** Home of the original Nic-O-Boli, this family-run pizzeria ships its trademarked neo-stromboli all over the world to demanding fans. The bustling shop is packed until the wee hours of the morning. ⊠ *8 N. 1st St.,* ☎ *302/226–2654. MC, V.*

$$$$ 🏨 **Boardwalk Plaza Hotel.** The most deluxe hotel on the boardwalk has grand Victorian trappings. Rooms for guests with disabilities are available; you can have breakfast on a terrace right on the boardwalk. ⊠ *2 Olive Ave., 19971,* ☎ *302/227–7169 or 800/332–3224. 84 rooms. Restaurant, pool, exercise room. AE, D, MC, V.*☜

$$–$$$ 🏨 **Brighton Suites.** Each suite has a bedroom with king-size bed and a living room with refrigerator and wet bar. ⊠ *34 Wilmington Ave., 19971,* ☎ *302/227–5780 or 800/227–5788. 66 suites. Pool. AE, D, DC, MC, V.*☜

$–$$$ 🏨 **Best Western Gold Leaf.** A half block from the beach and across the street from the bay, this Best Western has traditionally styled guest rooms, some with water views. ⊠ *1400 Rte. 1, 19971,* ☎ *302/ 226–1100 or 800/422–8566,* FAX *302/226–9785. 75 rooms. Pool. AE, D, DC, MC, V.*☜

$ 🏨 **Atlantic Budget Inn.** Rooms in this two-story brick inn are crowded, with double or king-size beds and hanging clothes racks (no closets). ⊠ *4353 Rte. 1, 19971,* ☎ *302/227–0401 or 800/245–2112. 74 rooms. AE, DC, MC, V.*

Outdoor Activities and Sports

Fishing

Charter boats for either deep-sea or bay (trout, bluefish) fishing can be booked for either day or half-day trips, including all the gear. Book through your hotel or try **Fisherman's Wharf** (☎ 302/645–8862) in Lewes, or **Delaware Seashore State Park Marina** (☎ 302/422–8940) at the Indian River inlet.

Water Sports

Marinas on Rehoboth Bay and Delaware Bay (at Lewes) rent sailboards, sailboats, and motorboats. Catamarans are for rent at **Fenwick Island State Park** (⊠ ½ mi north of Fenwick Island on Rte. 1, ☎ 302/539–9060), among others.

Shopping

On the Atlantic coast bargain hunters scour the shops at **Rehoboth Outlets** (⊠ Rte. 1, Rehoboth Beach, ☎ 302/226–9223), a manufacturers' outlet center touting 140 stores that sprawl along both sides of the busy, four-lane highway. Farther north, on the southbound side of the highway, the same owner operates a 35-unit outlet mall that is anchored by an L. L. Bean factory store. Just north of Lewes is the **Lighthouse Outlet** (⊠ 753 Rte. 1, Lewes, ☎ 302/645–1207), which sells discounted fixtures and ceiling fans.

ELSEWHERE IN DELAWARE

Dover

Arriving and Departing

The north and south approaches to Dover are on U.S. 13; Route 10 links it with Goldsboro, Maryland; Route 1 bypasses Dover and heads toward Dover from the coastal towns. **DART** (☎ 800/652–3278), a statewide public bus system, serves Wilmington, Newark, Middletown, Dover, and the Atlantic beaches, with various intermediate points.

What to See and Do

An oasis of Colonial preservation in a busy government center, the **capitol complex** historic area is on a square laid out in 1722 according to William Penn's 1683 plan. Information about Delaware's historic sites and attractions is available at the **Delaware State Visitors Center** (⊠ 406 Federal St., 19901, ☎ 302/739–4266); the Sewell C. Biggs Museum of American Decorative Arts (⊠ free) occupies the building's upper floors. The **Dover Air Force Base,** southeast of town, and its C-5 Galaxies are visible from U.S. 113. The **Air Mobility Command Museum** (☎ 302/677–5938; ⊠ free) is housed in a 20,000-square-ft hangar that's filled with planes and airlift memorabilia, including a Medal of Honor hall of fame. The hangar itself served as a rocket test center during World War II.

The **John Dickinson Plantation** (⊠ 340 Kitts Hummock Rd., ☎ 302/739–3277) gives visitors a glimpse of 18th-century plantation life in Kent County, Delaware. A horse-drawn wagon, a crop duster, threshers, a corn house, and a privy are only part of the fascinating collection of tools and structures exhibited at the **Delaware Agricultural Museum and Village** (⊠ 866 N. DuPont Hwy., ☎ 302/734–1618). A re-created 1890s village and farmstead, the operation is devoted to Delaware's rich agrarian past and present (agriculture is still the state's number one industry).

Had enough culture? Then head straight for **Dover Downs International Speedway** (⊠ North of Dover on U.S. 13, ☎ 302/674–4600 or 800/

441–7223), where the grandstands can handle up to 5,000 spectators for stock car and harness racing; there's also a casino.

Dining and Lodging

$–$$ ✕ **Where Pigs Fly.** With family-style food that's a notch above most, this is a kid-friendly place that's easy on the wallet. Try the "pulled pig" (hickory smoked pork pulled from the bone) or the baby back ribs. ⊠ *E. 617 Loockerman St., at U.S. 13,* ☎ *302/678–0586. AE, D, DC, MC, V.*

$$$ 🏨 **Sheraton Dover Hotel.** Convenient, comfortable, and well appointed, the Sheraton features spacious meeting rooms and a conference center. ⊠ *1570 N. DuPont Hwy., 19901,* ☎ *302/678–8500 or 800/325–3535,* FAX *302/678–9073. 153 rooms. Restaurant, pool. AE, D, DC, MC, V.* 🐾

FLORIDA

Updated by
Pamela
Acheson, Diane
Marshall, Gary
McKechnie,
and Gretchen
Schmidt

Capital	Tallahassee
Population	14,654,000
Motto	In God We Trust
State Bird	Mockingbird
State Flower	Orange blossom
Postal Abbreviation	FL

Statewide Visitor Information

Florida Division of Tourism (✉ 661 E. Jefferson St., Suite 300, Tallahassee 32301, ☎ 850/488–5607 or 888/7FLA–USA). **Information centers:** on U.S. 231 in Campbellton Graceville, I–75 near Jennings, I–10 at Pensacola, I–95 near Yulee, and in the lobby of the capitol in Tallahassee.

Scenic Drives

In **Everglades National Park** the 38-mi drive from the Main Visitor Center to Flamingo reveals a patchwork of ecosystems, including mangrove and cypress forests and saw-grass marshes. Although traffic jams abound during the winter tourist season, the **Overseas Highway** (U.S. 1) from Key Largo to Key West affords spectacular vistas of the Atlantic, Florida Bay, the Gulf of Mexico, and the myriad islands of the Keys. **Route 789,** along the Gulf Coast south from Holmes Beach in Bradenton to Lido Beach in Sarasota and from Casey Key south of Osprey to Nokomis Beach, passes over several picturesque barrier islands. Along the Atlantic coast, north of Jacksonville, the **Buccaneer Trail** (Route A1A) from Mayport to the old seaport town of Fernandina Beach passes through marshlands and along pristine beaches. **U.S. 98** winds east from historic Pensacola through the lush coastal landscape of the Panhandle.

National and State Parks

National Parks

Everglades and Biscayne national parks (☞ Elsewhere in Florida, *below*) are in Homestead, just south of Miami. In southwestern Florida **Big Cypress National Preserve** (✉ 20 mi east of Ochopee on U.S. 41; HCR 61, Box 110, Ochopee 33943, ☎ 941/695–2000 or 941/262–1066), noted for the bald and dwarf cypress trees that line its marshlands, is a sanctuary for alligators, bald eagles, and the endangered Florida panther.

Florida has three national forests. The 556,500-acre **Apalachicola National Forest** (✉ Rte. 65; Edward Ball Wakulla Spring State Park, Wakulla Spring Rd., Wakulla 32305, ☎ 904/653–9419) is great for canoeing and hiking and has a recreational facility designed for people with disabilities. **Ocala National Forest** (✉ Forest Visitor Center, 10863 E. Rte. 40, Silver Springs 34488, ☎ 904/625–7470) has lakes, springs, hiking trails, campgrounds, and historic sites. **Osceola National Forest** (✉ Osceola Ranger District, Box 70, 10090 Rte. 90, Olustee 32072, ☎ 904/752–2577) is dotted with cypress swamps and offers good fishing and hunting. In addition, the state has five national monuments, two national seashores, and eight national wildlife refuges.

State Parks

The state administers hundreds of parks, nature preserves, and historic sites. Among these are **Blackwater River State Park** (✉ Rte. 1, Box 57C, Holt 32564, ☎ 850/623–2363), 40 mi northeast of Pensacola on I–10, popular with canoeists; **Delnor-Wiggins Pass State Recreation Area**

(✉ 1100 Gulfshore Dr. N, Naples 33963, ☎ 941/597–6196), with miles of beaches, picnic areas, and fishing spots; **Florida Caverns State Park** (✉ 3345 Caverns Rd., Mariana 32446, ☎ 850/482–9598), two hours north of Panama City on Route 167, comprising 1,783 acres of caves and nature trails; **Ft. Clinch State Park** (☞ Elsewhere in Florida, *below*); **St. Andrews State Recreation Area** (✉ 4415 Thomas Dr., Panama City Beach 32408, ☎ 850/233–5140), in the Panhandle, encompassing 1,038 acres of beaches, pinewoods, and marshes for swimming, pier fishing, and dune hiking; and the **John Pennekamp Coral Reef State Park** (✉ Box 487, U.S. Hwy. 1, MM 102.5, Key Largo 33037, ☎ 305/451–1202), with the only coral reef in the continental United States. For more information contact the **Florida Department of Natural Resources** (✉ Marjory Stoneman Douglas Bldg., MS 525, 3900 Commonwealth Blvd., Tallahassee 32399, ☎ 904/488–9872).

MIAMI

Running with the energy and passion of Rio, Monte Carlo, and Hemingway's Paris, Miami is arguably the most exotic city that Americans can visit without a passport. More than half of its population is Hispanic in origin, and Miami is sometimes called the capital of Latin America. Indeed, Miami is a city of superlatives. This ever-growing metropolis has one of the busiest airports and cruise-ship ports in the world; more than 150 companies base their international operations here; four professional sports teams attract the faithful; and fashion models are photographed for a worldwide audience. Add Miami's architectural treasures, exotic foods, and outdoor recreation, and you have America's favorite sun-drenched tropical playground.

Visitor Information

Greater Miami: Convention & Visitors Bureau (✉ 701 Brickell Ave., Suite 2700, 33131, ☎ 305/539–3084 or 800/283–2707). **Miami Beach:** Chamber of Commerce (✉ 1920 Meridian Ave., 33139, ☎ 305/672–1270, FAX 305/538–4336). **Coconut Grove:** Chamber of Commerce (✉ 2820 McFarlane Rd., 33133, ☎ 305/444–7270, FAX 305/444–2498). **Coral Gables:** Chamber of Commerce (✉ 50 Aragon Ave., 33134, ☎ 305/446–1657, FAX 305/446–9900). **South Miami–Dade County:** Tropical Everglades Visitors Center (✉ 160 U.S. 1, Florida City 33034, ☎ 305/245–9180 or 800/388–9669, FAX 305/247–4335).

Arriving and Departing

By Bus
Greyhound (☎ 800/231–2222) stops at five terminals in Greater Miami, including a terminal at the airport.

By Car
I–95, which runs north–south along Florida's east coast, flows into the heart of Miami. From the northwest I–75 leads to the city. Route 836 (also called East–West Expressway or Dolphin Expressway), connecting the airport to downtown (toll eastbound only, 50¢), continues across I–395 and the MacArthur Causeway to lower Miami Beach and the Art Deco District. Route 112 (Airport Expressway) connects the airport with midtown (toll eastbound only, 50¢) and continues across I–195 and the Julia Tuttle Causeway to mid–Miami Beach.

By Plane
Miami International Airport (MIA; ✉ N.W. 21 St. and 45 Ave., ☎ 305/876–7000), 6 mi west of downtown via Route 836, is served by most major carriers and many minor ones. The flat rate is about $24 (per

trip, with tolls and $1 airport surcharge) to any point in Miami Beach from South Beach to 63rd Street. **SuperShuttle** (☎ 305/871–2000 or 800/874–8885) vans transport passengers 24 hours a day between MIA and local hotels, the Port of Miami, and individual residences. The cost to downtown hotels runs $9–$10. At MIA, the vans pick up at the ground level of each concourse (look for clerks with yellow shirts who'll flag one down for you). **Bus service** is available from Miami–Dade County's updated **Metrobus** (☎ 305/770–3131) and still costs $1.25 (transfer 25¢; exact change required). Look for them in the lower-level lanes in the center of the airport.

By Train
Amtrak (✉ 8303 N.W. 37th Ave., ☎ 305/835–1223 or 800/872–7245).

Getting Around Miami

Greater Miami resembles Los Angeles in its urban sprawl and traffic congestion. You'll need a car to get from one area of the city to another. **Metromover** (☞ *below*), a light-rail mass-transit system, travels above the heart of the city. It's a cheap (25¢) way to tour downtown Miami. South Beach and Coconut Grove are best explored on foot.

By Car
Miami is laid out in quadrants: northwest, northeast, southwest, southeast. These meet at Miami Avenue, which separates east from west, and Flagler Street, which separates north from south. Avenues and courts run north–south; streets, terraces, and ways run east–west. Roads run diagonally, northwest–southeast. In Miami Beach avenues run north–south; streets, east–west. Streets in Coral Gables have names, not numbers. In other words, be prepared to ask directions early and often.

By Public Transportation
The **Metro–Dade Transit Agency** (☎ 305/770–3131) runs the Metrorail, Metromover, and Metrobus and provides free maps and schedules. **Metrorail** (fare $1.25) runs from downtown Miami north to Hialeah and south along U.S. 1 to Dadeland. **Metromover** (fare 25¢), a separate system, has two loops that circle downtown Miami, linking major hotels, office buildings, and shopping areas. **Metrobus** (fare $1.25) stops are marked by blue-and-green signs with a bus logo and route information. Frequency of service varies widely, but a quick call to the agency will end confusion.

By Taxi
Be on your guard when traveling by cab in Miami. Some drivers are rude and unhelpful and may take advantage of visitors unfamiliar with their destinations. To avoid this, connect with a consortium of drivers who have banded together to provide good service: This nameless group can be reached through its **dispatch service** (☎ 305/888–4444). If you have to use another company, try to be familiar with your route and destination. Major cab companies include **Diamond Cab Company** (☎ 305/545–5555) and **Yellow Cab Company** (☎ 305/444–4444). Miami is divided into five zones, each with a flat rate. The driver can tell you the fare in advance, based on where you are traveling. Outside of the five zones, fares are $3.50 for the first mile, and $2 per mile thereafter, plus possible tolls.

Orientation Tours

Boat Tours
Island Queen, Island Lady, and *Pink Lady* (☎ 305/379–5119; ✏ $12) take passengers on 90-minute narrated water tours of the Port of

Miami and Millionaires' Row. The three boats depart from the center of Bayside Marketplace between the bandstand and the giant shark.

Walking Tours

The **Miami Design Preservation League** (☎ 305/672–2014) runs several tours. The most popular walking tour covers the Art Deco District and departs at 10:30 AM Saturday and 6:30 PM Thursday, leaving from the Art Deco Welcome Center on Ocean Drive (⊠ 1001 Ocean Dr.). Self-guided, tape-narrated tours are also available. The **Miami Beach Bicycle Center** (⊠ 601 5th St., ☎ 305/674–0150; ⬧ tour $6, tour and bike rental $10) offers bicycle tours of the Art Deco District twice a month. Miami–Dade Community College history professor **Paul George** (☎ 305/375–1492) leads fact-filled walking tours through downtown and other historic districts.

Exploring Miami

Downtown

★ Begin your tour of downtown Miami at the **Miami-Dade Cultural Center** (⊠ 101 W. Flagler St.), a 3.3-acre postmodern Mediterranean-style complex. You may recognize it from the movie *There's Something About Mary*. The elevated plaza provides a serene haven from the city's commotion, and within the complex are several arts venues, including the **Miami Art Museum** (MAM; ☎ 305/375–3000; ⬧ $5), which has both a permanent collection and major touring exhibitions focusing on work completed since 1945. The **Historical Museum of Southern Florida** (☎ 305/375–1492; ⬧ $5), also in the cultural center, has artifacts including Tequesta and Seminole ceramics, a 1920s streetcar, cigar and citrus labels, and a railroad exhibit—pure Floridiana. Another cultural center tenant, the **Main Public Library** (☎ 305/375–2665; ⬧ free) has nearly 4 million holdings and art exhibits in its auditorium and second-floor lobby.

Bayside Marketplace (☎ 305/577–3344; ⬧ free), between Bayfront Park and the entrance to the Port of Miami, is a massive waterside entertainment and shopping center that includes shops, outdoor cafés, and a food court. Street performers entertain throughout the day and evening, and free concerts take place every day of the year. Scenic boat tours and disco cruises depart from here (☞ Orientation Tours, *above*).

Bordering the Bayside Marketplace, between Biscayne Boulevard and Biscayne Bay, is the **Mildred and Claude Pepper Bayfront Park.** An urban landfill in the 1920s, it now includes a memorial to the *Challenger* astronauts, two amphitheaters, and a fountain honoring the late Florida congressman, Claude Pepper, and his wife.

★ The beauty of the **Gusman Center for the Performing Arts** (⊠ 174 E. Flagler St., ☎ 305/374–2444 for information; 305/372–0925 for box office), a former movie palace, is startling. The inside, with its cool, vivid colors, resembles a Moorish courtyard with twinkling stars. The Florida Philharmonic performs here year-round, except when the Miami Film Festival takes over in late January–early February. If the hall is closed, call the office and ask to take a look around.

Miami Beach

Made up of 17 islands in Biscayne Bay, Miami Beach is a separate city from Miami. In recent years this so-called "American Riviera" has re-
★ vived the carefree spirit of the early 1920s by renewing its **South Beach** area. Today South Beach revels in world glory as a lure for models and millionaires. The hub of South Beach is the 1-square-mi **Art Deco District,** which stretches along Ocean Drive and is the most talked-about beachfront in America. About 800 significant buildings in the district

are listed on the National Register of Historic Places—it's the nation's first 20th-century district to be honored as such.

Begin your tour of the Art Deco District at the **Art Deco District Welcome Center** (⊠ 1001 Ocean Dr., ☎ 305/531–3484). Proceed north past pastel-hued Art Deco hotels (outlined in brilliant neon at night) on your left, and the palm-fringed beach on your right. You'll also pass the magnificently restored **Casa Casuarina** (⊠ 1114 Ocean Dr.), home of the late fashion designer Gianni Versace, who was murdered outside the front gate in July 1997. The neighborhood's two main commercial streets are **Collins Avenue**, one block west of Ocean Drive, and, one block farther west, **Washington Avenue**. The latter is a colorful mix of Jewish, Cuban, Haitian, and more familiar American cultures, containing delicatessens, avant-garde stores, produce markets, shops selling religious artifacts, and many of the city's best restaurants and nightclubs. Just off Washington, **Espanola Way** is a quaint avenue with a youth hostel, clubs, restaurants, and ethnic shops—a late-afternoon flea market is held here each Sunday. Three blocks north is the **Lincoln Road Mall,** a lively pedestrian shopping street with upscale restaurants, eclectic shops, and great people-watching.

The **Holocaust Memorial** (⊠ 1933–1945 Meridian Ave., ☎ 305/538–1663; ✉ free), across from the Miami Beach Convention Center, is a chilling sculpture and a graphic record in memory of 6 million Jewish victims. The **Bass Museum of Art** (⊠ 2121 Park Ave., ☎ 305/673–7530; ✉ $5), four blocks north of South Beach proper, has a diverse collection of European works including pieces by Albrecht Dürer and Henri de Toulouse-Lautrec. A new expansion has doubled the museum's size to nearly 40,000 square ft. A 70,000-plus-item collection of modern design and "propaganda arts" lies within the **Wolfsonian—Florida International University** (⊠ 1001 Washington Ave., ☎ 305/531–1001; ✉ $5, free Thurs. 6–9), an elegantly renovated 1927 storage facility. The gallery is closed Wednesday.

The striking triumphal archway that looms on Collins Avenue is a mural of illusionary art by Richard Haas that depicts the **Fontainebleau Hilton Resort and Towers** (⊠ 4441 Collins Ave., ☎ 305/538–2000), which actually sits behind it.

Little Havana
More than 40 years ago the tidal wave of Cubans fleeing the Castro regime flooded an older neighborhood just west of downtown with refugees. The area became known as **Little Havana,** although today more than half a million Cubans live throughout the greater Miami area. **Calle Ocho** (⊠ S.W. 8th St.) is Little Havana's main commercial thoroughfare.

At the **Plaza de la Cubanidad** (⊠ S.W. 17th Ave.; ✉ free), on the southwest corner of Flagler Street and Teddy Roosevelt Avenue, redbrick sidewalks surround a monument inscribed with words from José Martí, a leader in Cuba's struggle for independence from Spain: LAS PALMAS SON NOVIAS QUE ESPÉRAN (The palm trees are girlfriends who will wait).

Visit **Versailles** (⊠ 3555 S.W. 8th St., ☎ 305/445–7614), a Cuban restaurant that will immerse you in Cuban-American popular culture with its menu and decor. The **Brigade 2506 Memorial** (⊠ S.W. 8th St. and S.W. 13th Ave.), which stands at Calle Ocho and Memorial Boulevard, commemorates the victims of the unsuccessful 1961 Bay of Pigs invasion of Cuba by an exile force. **El Credito** (⊠ 1106 S.W. 8th St., ☎ 305/858–4162 or 800/726–9481) is a cigar shop seemingly transported from the Cuban capital lock, stock, and stogie.

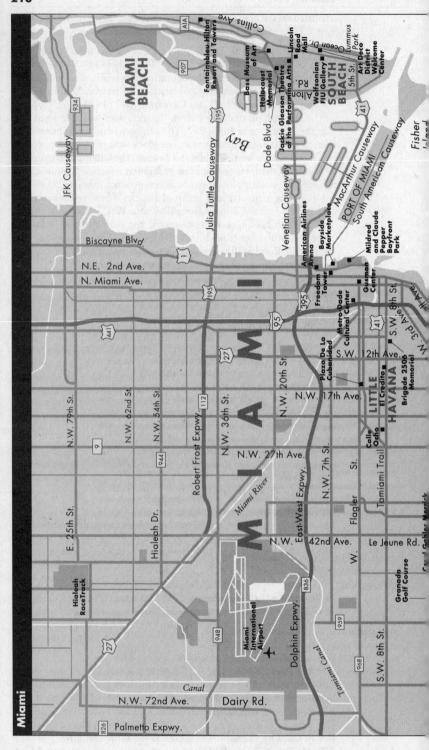

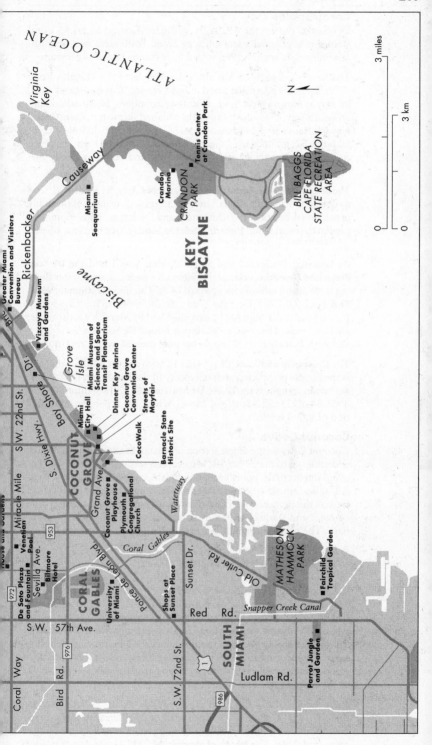

Coral Gables

Developed during the 1920s by visionary George Merrick, Coral Gables is a planned community of broad boulevards and Spanish-Mediterranean architecture, with a busy commercial downtown.

The heart of downtown Coral Gables stretches from Douglas Road (37th Avenue) to LeJeune Road (42nd Avenue). This four-block area, known as **Miracle Mile,** has a mixture of boutiques, bridal salons, and an assortment of restaurants along the Mile and side streets. **Coral Gables Merrick House and Gardens,** (⊠ 907 Coral Way, ☎ 305/460–5361; 🖃 house $2, grounds free), George Merrick's boyhood home, has been restored to its original 1920s appearance and contains family furnishings and artifacts.

The dazzling **Biltmore Hotel** (⊠ 1200 Anastasia Ave., ☎ 305/445–1926), a replica of Seville's Giralda Tower, features a charming lobby, richly ornamented Beaux Arts architecture, and the largest hotel swimming pool in the continental United States. On Sunday, free tours are offered at 1:30, 2:30, and 3:30 PM.

At Granada Boulevard and Sevilla Avenue you'll find the **De Soto Plaza and Fountain,** a classical column on a pedestal, with water flowing from the mouths of four sculpted faces. This and the stunning **Venetian Pool** (⊠ 2701 De Soto Blvd., ☎ 305/460–5356; 🖃 $8, free parking across De Soto Blvd.) were designed by Merrick's artist-uncle, Denman Fink. The pool, on northeast-bound De Soto Boulevard, is a fantastic, fantasy-themed municipal pool created from a rock quarry.

The **University of Miami** (⊠ off U.S. 1), with almost 14,000 students, is the largest private research university in the Southeast. On its 260-acre main campus is the **Lowe Art Museum** (⊠ 1301 Stanford Dr., ☎ 305/284–3535; 🖃 $5; closed Mon.), which has a permanent collection of 8,000 works.

Coconut Grove

Coconut Grove is the oldest section of Miami, begun during the 1870s and annexed to the city in 1925. Its earliest settlers included New England intellectuals, bohemians, Bahamians, and—later—artists, writers, and scientists who established winter homes here. The Grove still reflects the pioneers' eclectic origins, with posh estates next to rustic cottages and starkly modern dwellings, all amid lush subtropical foliage. The tone of Coconut Grove today is upscale and urban.

Before exploring the restaurants and shops of the Grove, you may want to visit the **Plymouth Congregational Church** (⊠ 3400 Devon Rd., ☎ 305/444–6521; 🖃 free), a handsome coral-rock Mexican mission–style structure dating from 1917. Also on the 11-acre grounds are natural sunken gardens; the first schoolhouse in Dade County (one room), which was moved to this property; and the site of the original Coconut Grove water and electric works. Main Highway returns you to the historic

★ **Village of Coconut Grove,** a trendy commercial district with redbrick sidewalks and more than 300 restaurants, stores, and art galleries. Parking is often a problem at night, so be prepared to walk several blocks to the heart of the district.

In Coconut Grove's village center is **CocoWalk** (⊠ 3015 Grand Ave., ☎ 305/444–0777), a multilevel open mall of Mediterranean-style brick courtyards and terraces overflowing with restaurants, bars, movie theaters, and shops. The **Streets of Mayfair** (⊠ 2911 Grand Ave., Coconut Grove, ☎ 305/448–1700), next to CocoWalk, is another entertainment and retail center. The Spanish rococo–style **Coconut Grove Playhouse** (⊠ 3500 Main Hwy., ☎ 305/442–4000) opened in 1926 as a movie theater and now presents Broadway-bound plays, musical revues, and experimental productions. The **Barnacle State Historic Site** (⊠ 3485 Main Hwy., ☎ 305/448–9445; ⊡ $1), a 19th-century pioneer residence, was built by Commodore Ralph Munroe in 1891. The house, which is open Fridays and weekends, is the oldest in Miami still on its original site.

North on Bayshore Drive is **Dinner Key Marina** (⊠ 3400 Pan American Dr., ☎ 305/579–6980), Greater Miami's largest marina. Antiques, boat, and home furnishings shows are held annually at the 105,000-square-ft **Coconut Grove Convention Center** (⊠ 2700 S. Bayshore Dr., ☎ 305/579–3310). **Miami City Hall** (⊠ 3500 Pan American Dr., ☎ 305/250–5400; ⊡ free) is known for its nautical-motif Art Deco trim. It was built in 1934 as the terminal for the Pan American Airways seaplane base at Dinner Key. Sadly, the interior is now generic government decor.

You can manipulate and marvel at the many hands-on sound, gravity, and electricity exhibits at the **Miami Museum of Science and Space Transit Planetarium** (⊠ 3280 S. Miami Ave., ☎ 305/854–4247 or 305/854–2222; ⊡ $9, laser concerts $6), which also features traveling exhibits and virtual reality, life science demonstrations, and Internet technology.

★ Overlooking Biscayne Bay on South Miami Avenue is **Vizcaya Museum and Gardens** (⊠ 3251 S. Miami Ave., ☎ 305/250–9133, ⊡ $10), an estate with an Italian Renaissance–style villa that was built in the early 20th century as the winter residence of Chicago industrialist James Deering.

South Miami

South Miami is a former pioneer farming community that has managed to retain its small-town charm, while growing into a major suburb. Contrary to what its name implies, South Miami is a city, not just a geographical moniker.

Fine old homes and mature trees line **Sunset Drive,** the city-designated "historic and scenic road" to and through downtown South Miami. At the **Parrot Jungle and Garden** (⊠ 11000 S.W. 57th Ave., ☎ 305/666–7834; ⊡ $14.95), you can marvel at postcard-perfect flamingos, watch a trained-bird show, or stroll among orchids.

Not far from Parrot Jungle is the 83-acre **Fairchild Tropical Garden** (⊠ 10901 Old Cutler Rd., ☎ 305/667–1651; ⊡ $8), the largest tropical botanical garden in the continental United States. Old Cutler Road traverses Miami–Dade County's oldest and most scenic park, **Matheson Hammock Park** (⊠ 9610 Old Cutler Rd., ☎ 305/665–5475; ⊡ free, $3.50 parking), which dates from the days of the Civilian Conservation Corps in the 1930s. The park has a bathing beach, sailing school, marina, restaurant, and changing facilities.

A few miles south on Old Cutler Road, the **Deering Estate at Cutler** (⊠ 16701 S.W. 72nd Ave., ☎ 305/235–1668; ⊡ $9) contains the 1913 Mediterranean Revival stone house of Charles Deering on a site rich in archaeological, historical, and natural treasures. A huge Environmental Education and Visitor's Center presents programs for children and adults. Nature tours and canoe trips are available.

Virginia Key and Key Biscayne

The waters of Government Cut and the Port of Miami separate densely populated Miami Beach from two of Greater Miami's playground islands, Virginia Key and Key Biscayne—the latter no longer the laid-back village where Richard Nixon set up his presidential vacation compound. Parks and stretches of dense mangrove swamp occupy much of both keys. To reach the keys, take the **Rickenbacker Causeway** across Biscayne Bay at Brickell Avenue and Southwest 26th Road, about 2 mi south of downtown Miami. The causeway links several islands in the bay.

★ On Virginia Key, the **Miami Seaquarium** (✉ 4400 Rickenbacker Causeway, ☎ 305/361–5705, 🎟 $21.95, parking $4) features sea lion, dolphin, and killer whale performances and a 235,000-gallon tropical-reef aquarium. Many educated beach enthusiasts rate **Crandon Park** (✉ 4000 Crandon Blvd., ☎ 305/361–5421; 🎟 $3.50 per vehicle) among the top 10 beaches in North America.

The commercial center of Key Biscayne is a mix of shops and stores catering to neighborhood needs. At the key's south end is the **Bill Baggs Cape Florida State Recreation Area** (✉ 1200 S. Crandon Blvd., ☎ 305/361–5811; 🎟 $4 per vehicle; $1 per person on foot, bicycle, or bus), with a 1¼-mi expanse of palm-topped white-sand beach, several boardwalks, fishing piers, picnic shelters, a café, and the **Cape Florida Lighthouse**, South Florida's oldest structure.

Dining

Dining in Miami is an essential part of nightlife, whether in the Cuban restaurants on Calle Ocho or in the exclusive eateries of South Beach. Here you can taste New World cuisine—fresh, inventive dishes that make ample use of indigenous ingredients such as mango, local seafood, and peppers, while drawing on influences from the Caribbean, Mexico, and South America. The sizzle in Miami's food scene means fierce competition among restaurateurs, such that hopefuls open and failures close almost every week. Restaurants listed here have passed the test of time, but you might double-check by phone before you set out for the evening.

$$$$ ✕ **Blue Door at Delano.** The flavors of classic French cuisine are com-
★ bined with South American influences to create dishes like the Big Raviole, filled with taro-root mousseline and white-truffle oil. Equally pleasing is dining with the crème de la crème of Miami (and New York and Paris) society. ✉ *1685 Collins Ave.,* ☎ *305/674–6400. Reservations essential. AE, D, DC, MC, V.*

$$$$ ✕ **China Grill.** This crowded, noisy place has no view, but that doesn't
★ detract from its popularity or that of the original China Grill in New York. Come for "world cuisine," in portions large and meant for sharing, and celeb sightings. Crispy duck with caramelized black vinegar sauce and scallion pancakes is a nice surprise. ✉ *404 Washington Ave.,* ☎ *305/534–2211. AE, DC, MC, V. No lunch Sat. and Sun.*

$$$$ ✕ **Norman's.** At this elegantly casual restaurant, the art of New World
★ cuisine has been perfected—a combination rooted in Latin, North American, Caribbean, and Asian influences. Highlights of the inventive and bold menu include pan-cooked crab cakes with Indian guacamole, island chips and salsa, and rum-and-pepper-painted grouper on a mango-*habanero mojo* sauce. ✉ *21 Almeria Ave.,* ☎ *305/446–6767. AE, DC, MC, V. Closed Sun. No lunch.*

$$$–$$$$ ✕ **Astor Place.** Expect such exquisite treats as lobster knuckle chow-
★ der flavored with orange and coconut milk, cilantro-seared sea bass with rock shrimp mashed potatoes, and beef two ways—a flavorful filet mignon with olive butter and braised short ribs in a Rioja reduction. ✉ *956 Washington Ave.,* ☎ *305/672–7217. AE, DC, MC, V.*

$$$–$$$$ ✕ **Chef Allen's.** You'll find innovative new world cuisine like no other,
★ with such signature creations as pistachio-crusted grouper with a fricasee of rock shrimp, mango, leeks, and peppers as well as Bahamian lobster–crab cakes with tropical fruit chutney and vanilla beurre blanc. Try the chocolate banana almond soufflé for dessert. ✉ *19088 N.E. 29th Ave., Aventura,* ☎ *305/935–2900. AE, DC, MC, V.*

$$$–$$$$ ✕ **Joe's Stone Crab Restaurant.** "Before SoBe, Joe Be," touts this fourth-generation family restaurant. The centerpiece of the menu is, of course, stone crab, served with drawn butter, lemon wedges, and

piquant mustard sauce. Hash brown potatoes and garlic creamed spinach are musts. Save room for dessert—key lime pie or apple pie—and come prepared to wait. ✉ *227 Biscayne St.,* ☎ *305/673–0365; 305/673–4611 for takeout; 800/780–2722 for overnight shipping. Reservations not accepted. AE, D, DC, MC, V. Closed mid-May–mid-Oct. No lunch Mon.*

$$$–$$$$ ✗ **Nemo.** The open-air atmosphere, bright colors, copper fixtures, ★ and tree-shaded courtyard lend casual comfort. The menu, which blends Caribbean, Japanese, and Southeast Asian influences, includes garlic-cured salmon rolls with *tobiko* caviar and a grilled Indian-spiced pork loin. There's a terrific Sunday brunch. ✉ *100 Collins Ave.,* ☎ *305/532–4550. AE, MC, V.*

$$$–$$$$ ✗ **Ortanique on the Mile.** New World Caribbean cuisine is delivered with vibrant style in a setting of tropical elegance, next to the restored Actors' Playhouse. Start with a selection of ceviches and follow with a Caribbean bouillabaisse of sea bass, shrimp, littleneck clams, and mussels in a curry broth. Save room for sweets, such as the chocolate mango tower or the drunken banana fritters served with cinnamon ice cream. ✉ *278 Miracle Mile, Coral Gables,* ☎ *305/446–7710. AE, DC, MC, V.*

$$$–$$$$ ✗ **Pacific Time.** This superb eatery has a high blue ceiling and banquettes, ★ accents of mahogany and brass, and an open-window kitchen. The American-Asian cuisine includes such entrées as grilled wild river salmon, rosemary-roasted chicken, and dry-aged Colorado beef grilled with shiitake mushrooms. Desserts include Baked Alaska Key West and a warm Chocolate Bomb. There's an extensive international wine list. ✉ *915 Lincoln Rd.,* ☎ *305/534–5979. AE, DC, MC, V.*

$$$–$$$$ ✗ **Yuca.** The Cuban food here rises to high standards: traditional corn ★ tamales filled with smoked turkey, freshly cut corn, kalamata olives and sliced tomatoes, yucca stuffed with *mamacita's picadillo* and dressed in wild mushrooms, and plantain-coated dolphinfish served with tamarind sauce. Call ahead to see if popular Cuban chanteuse Albita is performing on Saturday nights, and if so, make a reservation. ✉ *501 Lincoln Rd.,* ☎ *305/532–9822. AE, DC, MC, V.*

$$–$$$ ✗ **Osteria del Teatro.** Orchids grace the tables in the intimate gray-on-★ gray room with a low laced-canvas ceiling and Deco lamps. Try an appetizer such as grilled Portobello mushrooms topped with fontina cheese. One standout entrée is the linguine sautéed with chunks of jumbo shrimp, roasted peppers, capers, black olives, diced tomato, and herbs. ✉ *1443 Washington Ave.,* ☎ *305/538–7850. AE, DC, MC, V. Closed Sun. No lunch.*

$–$$$ ✗ **News Café.** An Ocean Drive landmark, this 24-hour café attracts ★ a big crowd around the clock with snacks, light meals, drinks, and the sidewalk people parade. There's a bar in back, but most diners prefer sitting outside. The popular eatery expanded to a second location in Coconut Grove in 1997. ✉ *800 Ocean Dr.,* ☎ *305/538–6397; 2901 Florida Ave., Coconut Grove,* ☎ *305/774–6397. AE, DC, MC, V.*

$–$$ ✗ **Café Prima Pasta.** Consistently intense flavors, high-quality ingre-★ dients, and just plain good cooking are the hallmarks of this cozy spot in the emerging North Beach neighborhood. After fresh-made bread with a dipping oil with garlic, parsley, and crushed red pepper arrives at the table, diners can choose from such favorites as penne *alla vodka* and black linguine with seafood and creamy lobster sauce. ✉ *414 71st St.,* ☎ *305/867–0106. No credit cards.*

$ ✗ **Pollo Tropical.** This fast-food chain serves up some of Miami's tastiest (and healthiest) Latin-Caribbean food with a tropical touch. Try succulent grilled chicken, marinated in fruit juices; fried yucca and sweet plantains; and savory black beans and rice with spicy fresh salsa on the side. Top it off with the ultrasweet Nicaraguan *tres leches* dessert. Most locations have drive-throughs. ✉ *2710 S. Dixie Hwy., Coconut*

Grove, and many other locations throughout the county, ☎ *305/448–9892. No credit cards.*

$ ✕ **Shorty's Bar-B-Q.** Family friendly and affordable, this local chain features meaty hickory-smoked ribs and chicken, baked beans, corn on the cob, and coleslaw. Finish off with tart key lime pie, flan, or rice pudding. ⊠ *9200 S. Dixie Hwy., 11575 S.W. 40th St., and University Dr. at Sterling Rd.,* ☎ *305/670–7732. D, MC, V.*

Lodging

Lodgings are concentrated in Miami Beach and downtown Miami, around the airport, and in Coral Gables, Coconut Grove, and Key Biscayne. For historic bed-and-breakfast accommodations contact **Miami Area Bed-and-Breakfast Inns and Boutique Hotels** (⊠ Box 331891, Miami 33233–1891, ☎ 305/665–2274 or 800/339–9430, FAX 305/666–1186). Winter is peak season; summer is also busy but rates are much lower.

$$$$ 🏨 **Alexander Hotel.** Every room is a large suite with two baths and a
★ kitchen, ocean or bay view, and antique or reproduction furnishings. The hotel is renowned for its service. ⊠ *5225 Collins Ave., Miami Beach 33140,* ☎ *305/865–6500 or 800/327–6121,* FAX *305/341–6553. 150 suites. 2 restaurants, 2 pools, health club. AE, DC, MC, V.* ☙

$$$$ 🏨 **Biltmore Hotel.** The 1926 Biltmore rises like a sienna-color wedding
★ cake in the heart of a residential district. The vaulted lobby has hand-painted rafters on a twinkling sky-blue background. The huge swimming pool is breathtaking. Large guest rooms are done in a restrained Moorish style. For a slightly higher nightly rate ($2,650) you can book the Everglades (a.k.a. Al Capone) Suite. ⊠ *1200 Anastasia Ave., Coral Gables 33134,* ☎ *305/445–1926 or 800/727–1926,* FAX *305/913–3159. 280 rooms. Restaurant, pool, golf, tennis, health club. AE, DC, MC, V.* ☙

$$$$ 🏨 **Delano Hotel.** If Calvin Klein had teamed with Salvador Dalí to build a hotel, this weird and wonderful property would be it. Miami's hotel du jour, owned by New Yorker Ian Schrager, appeals to female fashion models and men of independent means. Tourists enjoy the surreal atmosphere and fantasy pool. ⊠ *1685 Collins Ave., Miami Beach 33139,* ☎ *305/672–2000 or 800/555–5001,* FAX *305/532–0099. 208 rooms. Restaurant, pool, health club. AE, D, DC, MC, V.*

$$$$ 🏨 **Grand Bay Hotel.** Artwork and fresh flowers enhance the elegant
★ lobby of this modern high-rise with easterly views of Biscayne Bay. Whoopi Goldberg and Bruce Willis have stayed here, perhaps enjoying the hotel's pyramid-like stepped profile that gives each room facing the bay a private terrace. ⊠ *2669 S. Bayshore Dr., Coconut Grove 33133,* ☎ *305/858–9600 or 800/327–2788,* FAX *305/859–2026. 177 rooms. Restaurant, pool, health club. AE, DC, MC, V.*

$$$$ 🏨 **Sonesta Beach Resort Key Biscayne.** With its 750-ft beach, this
★ hotel has always been one of Miami's best. Some rooms are in villas with full kitchens and screened-in pools. Facilities include parasailing, catamaran rental, and children's programs. The grand size of the property, Olympic pool, and range of activities make this a good family getaway. ⊠ *350 Ocean Dr., Key Biscayne 33149,* ☎ *305/361–2021 or 800/766–3782,* FAX *305/361–3096. 299 rooms, 4 villas. 3 restaurants, pool, tennis, health club. AE, D, DC, MC, V.* ☙

$$$$ 🏨 **Turnberry Isle Resort & Club.** Guests can choose from the Mediter-
★ ranean-style annex, the intimate Marina Hotel, the Yacht Club on the Intracoastal Waterway, or the Ocean Club Hotel beside the golf course at this 300-acre resort and condominium complex in North Miami–Dade County. The marina has moorings for 117 boats up to 150 ft, and there's a free shuttle to the beach club and the Aventura Mall. ⊠ *19999 W. Country Club Dr., Aventura 33180,* ☎ *305/932–6200 or*

800/327–7028, ⓕ︎ᴀ︎ˣ︎ 305/933–6560. 340 rooms. 3 restaurants, pools, golf, tennis, health club. AE, D, DC, MC, V.

$$$–$$$$ 🏨 **Indian Creek Hotel.** This 1936 pueblo-inspired Deco jewel may be
★ Miami's most charming accommodation. Owner Marc Levin rescued the inn and was fortunate enough to find original Deco furniture in the basement (which no doubt helped him win the Miami Design Preservation League's award for outstanding restoration). The hotel restaurant, Mezzo Mezzo, now flows outside to a secluded poolside dining area. ✉️ 2727 Indian Creek Dr., Miami Beach 33140, ☎️ 305/531–2727 or 800/491–2772, ⓕ︎ᴀ︎ˣ︎ 305/531–5651. 61 rooms. Restaurant, pool. AE, D, DC, MC, V. ✎

$$$–$$$$ 🏨 **Omni Colonnade Hotel.** The twin 13-story towers of this swank hotel,
★ office, and shopping complex dominate downtown Coral Gables. Oversize rooms have sitting areas and built-in armoires. Rooms have data ports, and business facilities, such as meeting rooms, attract an abundance of conferences. ✉️ 180 Aragon Ave., Coral Gables 33134, ☎️ 305/441–2600, ⓕ︎ᴀ︎ˣ︎ 305/445–3929. 157 rooms. Restaurant, pool, exercise room. AE, D, DC, MC, V. ✎

$$$–$$$$ 🏨 **Park Central.** Across the street from a glorious stretch of beach, this seven-story Art Deco hotel is a favorite of visiting fashion models and other trendsetters. Rooms are decorated with restored 1940s-era Philippine mahogany furnishings. ✉️ 640 Ocean Dr., Miami Beach 33139, ☎️ 305/538–1611 or 800/727–5236, ⓕ︎ᴀ︎ˣ︎ 305/534–7520. 128 rooms. Restaurant, pool, exercise room. AE, D, DC, MC, V. ✎

$$–$$$ 🏨 **Hotel Place St. Michel.** The finest boutique hotel in metropolitan Miami
★ is in the heart of downtown Coral Gables. Art nouveau chandeliers are suspended from vaulted lobby ceilings, and the scent of fresh flowers is circulated through the public spaces by paddle fans. Each room is unique, and count on English, French, and Scottish antiques. ✉️ 162 Alcazar Ave., Coral Gables 33134, ☎️ 305/444–1666 or 800/848–4683, ⓕ︎ᴀ︎ˣ︎ 305/529–0074. 27 rooms. Restaurant. AE, DC, MC, V, CP. ✎

$$–$$$ 🏨 **Miami River Inn.** Ten minutes by foot from the heart of downtown,
★ this turn-of-the-20th-century inn consists of five clapboard buildings on a grassy, palm-studded compound. Don't be put off by the neighborhood—the setting is lovely, and rooms are filled with antiques. ✉️ 118 S.W. South River Dr., Miami 33130, ☎️ 305/325–0045, ⓕ︎ᴀ︎ˣ︎ 305/325–9227. 40 rooms. Pool. AE, D, DC, MC, V. CP.

$$–$$$ 🏨 **Nassau Suite Hotel.** This renovated 1937 hotel consists of 22 spacious and smart-looking suites. King beds, fully equipped kitchens, hardwood floors, white-wood blinds, free local calls, and privileges at the Beachcomber's bistro make one wonder how the rates remain so reasonable. ✉️ 1414 Collins Ave., Miami Beach 33139, ☎️ 305/534–2354, ⓕ︎ᴀ︎ˣ︎ 305/534–3133. 22 suites. AE, D, DC, MC, V. ✎

$–$$ 🏨 **Bayliss.** Rooms are abnormally large, surprisingly inexpensive, and clean. An easy three blocks west of the ocean, this place is in a residential neighborhood that's comfortably close to—but far enough away from—the din of the Deco District. You can't do much better than this for the price. ✉️ 500 14th Ave., Miami Beach 33139, ☎️ 305/531–3755 or 888/305–4683, ⓕ︎ᴀ︎ˣ︎ 305/673–8609. 19 rooms. AE, DC, MC, V.

Nightlife and the Arts

The best sources for events are the widely distributed free weeklies *New Times, Miami Today,* and *Street.* The *Miami Herald* publishes a "Weekend" section on Friday and a "Lively Arts" section on Sunday. If you read Spanish, rely on *El Nuevo Herald* (the Spanish-language version of the *Miami Herald*).

Nightlife

The liveliest scenes are in South Beach (Miami Beach's Art Deco District—especially on Washington Avenue) and Coconut Grove, but clubs can be found in the suburbs, downtown, Little Havana, and Little Haiti.

BARS WITH MUSIC

Mac's Club Deuce (✉ 222 14th St., Miami Beach, ☎ 305/673–9537) is a funky, working-class South Beach spot, where top international models come to shoot pool. **Tobacco Road** (✉ 626 S. Miami Ave., Miami, ☎ 305/374–1198) holds Miami's oldest liquor license (Number 0001!) and is one of the city's oldest bars, with excellent blues nightly. **Zeke's Road House** (✉ 625 Lincoln Rd., ☎ 305/532–0087), a sandwich shop and beer bar hidden amid new South Beach businesses, is a neighborhood bar that transcends trends.

DANCE CLUBS

Nightclubs are the lifeblood of Miami. Although many clubs fall out of favor quickly, these seem to have withstood the test of time: **Bash** (✉ 655 Washington Ave., Miami Beach, ☎ 305/538–2274) is a grottolike bar that mostly plays loud disco. **Chaos** (✉ 743 Washington Ave., at 7th St., ☎ 305/674–7350) draws a dressy, upscale crowd. Unique concepts turn the club into a different place—Thailand, Rio, London—each Sunday night. The still hot, still happenin' **Groove Jet** (✉ 323 23rd St., ☎ 305/532–2002) plays hypnotic dance music. **Living Room at the Strand** (✉ 671 Washington Ave., ☎ 305/532–2340) draws A-list celebs and sheiks who drop $1,000 tips. **Penrod's** (✉ 1 Ocean Dr., ☎ 305/538–1231) has seven bars at its beautiful beachfront location, including the Nikki Beach Club, fast becoming a celeb hangout.

The Arts

To order tickets for performing arts events by telephone, call **Ticketmaster** (☎ 305/358–5885).

BALLET

Miami City Ballet (✉ 2200 Liberty Ave., Miami Beach, ☎ 305/929–7000) is an acclaimed troupe under the direction of Edward Villella, now housed in a new three-story, custom-built facility, one that allows visitors to watch dancers practicing. Catch a performance between September and March at the **Jackie Gleason Theater of the Performing Arts** (☞ *below*).

MUSIC

New World Symphony (✉ 541 Lincoln Rd., Miami Beach, ☎ 305/673–3331), conducted by Michael Tilson Thomas, is also a national orchestral academy for young music-school graduates. **Concert Association of Florida** (✉ 555 Hank Meyer Blvd., at 17th St., Miami Beach, ☎ 305/532–3491) is the Southeast's largest presenter of classical artists, dance, and music—concerts are held at a variety of venues. Past performers have included Itzhak Perlman, Mikhail Baryshnikov, and Luciano Pavarotti.

OPERA

Florida Grand Opera (✉ 1200 Coral Way, Miami, ☎ 305/854–1643) presents five operas a year at the Dade County Auditorium. Operas are sung in the original language, with English subtitles projected above the stage.

THEATER

The **Coconut Grove Playhouse** (✉ 3500 Main Hwy., ☎ 305/442–4000) stages Broadway-bound plays and musical revues as well as experimental productions. **Colony Theater** (✉ 1040 Lincoln Rd., Miami Beach, ☎ 305/674–1026), once a movie theater, is now a city-owned 465-seat performing arts center featuring dance, drama, music, and experimental cinema. **Jackie Gleason Theater of the Performing Arts** (✉ 1700 Washington Ave., Miami Beach, ☎ 305/673–7300) is home of the Broadway Series and other stage events. The **Miami–Dade County Auditorium** (✉ 2901 W. Flagler St., Miami, ☎ 305/545–3395) hosts opera, concerts, and touring musicals. **Teatro de Bellas Artes** (✉ 2173 S.W. 8th St., Miami, ☎ 305/325–0515), a 255-seat theater on Little Havana's Calle Ocho, presents Spanish plays and musicals year-round.

Outdoor Activities and Sports

Diving

Summer diving conditions in Greater Miami have been compared with those in the Caribbean. Winter can bring rough, cold waters. Fowey, Triumph, Long, and Emerald reefs are good for snorkelers and beginning divers. For charters, rentals, and instruction, try **Divers Paradise of Key Biscayne** (✉ 4000 Crandon Blvd., Key Biscayne, ☎ 305/361–3483) or the **Diving Locker** (✉ 223 Sunny Isles Blvd., N. Miami Beach, ☎ 305/947–6025). **Bubbles Dive Center** (✉ 2671 S.W. 27th Ave., Miami, ☎ 305/856–0565) is an all-purpose dive shop. Most dive shops host night and wreck dives.

Fishing

Smaller charter boats can cost $350–$400 for a half day and provide everything but food and drinks. If you're on a budget, book a passage on a larger fishing boat for around $25. Charter boats depart from **Crandon Marina** (✉ 4000 Crandon Blvd., Key Biscayne, ☎ 305/361– 1281 for marina office), **Haulover Park** (✉ 10800 Collins Ave., Miami Beach, ☎ 305/947–3525), and the **Miami Beach Marina** (✉ 300 Alton Rd., MacArthur Causeway, Miami Beach, ☎ 305/673–6000).

Golf

Miami–Dade County has more than 30 private and public golf courses (☎ 305/857–3350 for Miami–Dade County; 305/673–7730 for Miami Beach). Call ahead for discount afternoon-twilight rates. A few of Miami's more notable courses include the **Biltmore Golf Course** (✉ 1210 Anastasia Ave., Coral Gables, ☎ 305/460–5364); the "Blue Monster" at the **Doral Golf Resort and Spa** (✉ 4400 N.W. 87th Ave., Doral, ☎ 305/592–2000 or 800/713–6725); and **Turnberry Isle Resort & Club** (✉ 19999 W. Country Club Dr., Aventura, ☎ 305/933–6929), with 36 holes designed by Robert Trent Jones—this course is only open to hotel guests. The **Granada Golf Course** (✉ 2001 Granada Blvd., ☎ 305/460– 5367) is one of Coral Gables's two public courses.

Sailing

The center of sailing in Greater Miami remains at the **Dinner Key** and the **Coconut Grove** waterfronts, although moorings and rentals are found elsewhere up the bay and up the Miami River.

Tennis

Greater Miami has more than 60 private and public tennis centers. All public courts charge nonresidents an hourly fee. If you're on a schedule, call in advance; some courts take reservations on weekdays. **Biltmore Tennis Center** (✉ 1150 Anastasia Ave., Coral Gables, ☎ 305/460–5360) has 10 hard courts. **Flamingo Tennis Center** (✉ 11th St. and Alton Rd., Miami Beach, ☎ 305/673–7761) has 19 clay courts. **Tennis Center at Crandon Park** (✉ 7300 Crandon Blvd., Key Biscayne, ☎ 305/365–2300), which hosts the annual Ericsson Championships in March, has 2 grass, 8 clay, and 17 hard courts.

Windsurfing

You can rent windsurfing equipment and take lessons at **Sailboards Miami** (✉ Key Biscayne, ☎ 305/361–7245), on Hobie Island just past the tollbooth for the Rickenbacker Causeway to Key Biscayne.

Spectator Sports

In addition to the usual spectator sports, in Miami you can watch jai alai, known as the fastest game on earth. Pelotas (hard balls) are thrown from handheld baskets called cestas, traveling at speeds of more than 170 mph. Locals place bets on the winning team or on the order in which teams will finish.

Baseball: The 1997 World Series champion **Florida Marlins** play at Pro Player Stadium (⊠ 2269 N.W. 199th St., Miami, ☎ 305/626–7400). **Basketball: Miami Heat,** American Airlines Arena (⊠ Biscayne Blvd. between N.E. 8th and 9th Sts., Miami, ☎ 305/577–4328). **Football:** Miami's favorite team, the **Miami Dolphins,** play at Pro Player Stadium (⊠ 2269 N.W. 199th St., Miami, ☎ 305/620–2578). **Hockey: Florida Panthers** (⊠ 13611 Green Toad Rd., Sunrise, ☎ 954/845–9292). **Jai Alai: Miami Jai Alai** (⊠ 3500 N.W. 37th Ave., Miami, ☎ 305/633–6400).

Beaches

Millions visit the beaches in Miami–Dade County each year. **Miami Beach** extends continuously for 10 mi. A boardwalk runs from 23rd to 44th Street, and along this stretch various groups congregate in specific areas. **Lummus Park,** the stretch of beach opposite the Art Deco District, between 5th and 15th streets, attracts all ages, with volleyball courts, inline skating along a paved upland path, and children's playgrounds. Gays frequent the beach between 11th and 13th streets. Sidewalk cafés parallel the entire beach area. **North Beach,** along Ocean Terrace between 72nd and 75th streets, is more serene.

Two of metropolitan Miami's best beaches are on Key Biscayne. Nearest the causeway is the 3½-mi county beach in **Crandon Park** (⊠ 4000 Crandon Blvd., ☎ 305/361–5421). **Bill Baggs Cape Florida State Recreation Area** (⊠ 1200 S. Crandon Blvd., ☎ 305/361–5811) has beaches, boardwalks, bicycle paths, and nature trails.

Shopping

Malls, an international free zone, and specialty shopping districts are the attractions in Miami. Many shopping areas have an ethnic flavor.

Shopping Districts

Just north of downtown Miami (⊠ N.E. 2nd Ave, at 39–42 Sts.), the **Miami International Arts & Design District** consists of 1 square mi of furniture, eclectic accessories, antiques, art studios, and interior design firms that are open to the public. Most stores in the district are open Monday–Saturday 9–5, some by appointment. More than 500 garment manufacturers sell their clothing in more than 30 factory outlets and discount fashion stores in the **Fashion District,** east of I–95 along 5th Avenue from 25th to 29th Street. Most stores in the district are open Monday–Saturday 9–5. The **Miami Free Zone** (⊠ 2305 N.W. 107th Ave., ☎ 305/591–4300) is a vast international wholesale trade center where you can buy goods duty-free for export, or pay duty on goods released for domestic use. More than 140 companies sell products from more than 100 countries, including clothing, computers, cosmetics, electronics, liquor, and perfumes. At **Historic Cauley Square** (⊠ 22400 Old Dixie Hwy., Goulds, ☎ 305/258–3543), a complex of clapboard, coral-rock, and stucco buildings that housed railroad workers at the turn of the 20th century, shops primarily sell antiques and crafts. To get there, exit U.S. 1 at Southwest 224th Street; it's usually closed on Monday.

WALT DISNEY WORLD™ AND THE ORLANDO AREA

Once upon a time about the only things to see in Orlando were at the Walt Disney World Resort. Today, however, cosmopolitan Orlando is an international business center and tourist mecca. Universal Orlando and the Busch Entertainment Corporation have their own smaller but burgeoning theme park empires, and many other attractions, shopping areas, and nightspots make the area an exciting, if sometimes frenetic and crowded, vacation destination. Away from the tourist areas, hundreds of spring-fed lakes surrounded by oak trees recall Orlando's bucolic past. About an hour's drive on the Atlantic coast are the Cocoa Beach area and the Kennedy Space Center.

Visitor Information

Kissimmee/St. Cloud: Convention and Visitors Bureau (⊠ 1925 E. Irlo Bronson Memorial Hwy., Kissimmee 34744, ☎ 407/847–5000 or 800/327–9159). **Orlando/Orange County:** Convention & Visitors Bureau (⊠ 6700 Forum Dr., Suite 100, Orlando 32821-8087, ☎ 407/363–5800).

Arriving and Departing

By Bus
Greyhound (☎ 800/231–2222) provides service from major Florida cities and from outside the state.

By Car
From Jacksonville take I–95 south, then I–4 from Port Orange. From Tampa/St. Petersburg take I–4 east. From Miami take I–95 north and connect with Florida's Turnpike going northbound at White City. From Atlanta take I–75 south and connect with Florida's Turnpike.

By Plane
Orlando International Airport (⊠ 6086 McCoy Rd., off the Bee Line Expressway, ☎ 407/825–2001) is served by major airlines.

By Train
Amtrak (☎ 800/872–7245) operates the *Silver Star* and the *Silver Meteor,* which stop at Winter Park, Orlando, and Kissimmee. Amtrak's Auto Train runs between Sanford and Lorton, Virginia.

Exploring Walt Disney World and the Orlando Area

Walt Disney World Resort
★ ℭ The focal point of an Orlando vacation is **Walt Disney World Resort** (⊠ Box 10040, Lake Buena Vista 32830, ☎ 407/824–4321), a collection of theme parks and attractions connected by an extensive bus, monorail, motor-launch, and tram network (access is included in the price of a multiday pass or available for a small fee). Admission is not cheap: A one-day adult ticket (including tax) costs $48.76; a child's ticket is $39.22 (as of spring 2000) and admits you to only one of the parks: Magic Kingdom, Epcot, Disney–MGM Studios, or Disney's Animal Kingdom. Depending on how many parks you want to visit in what amount of time, it may pay to purchase a Park Hopper (four days $186.56 adults, $150.52 children; five days $218.36 adults, $177.02 children) or an all-in-one Park Hopper Plus (five days $250.18 adults, $203.53 children; six days $281.99 adults, $230.03 children; seven days $313.79 adults, $256.54 children). All admit you to the four major parks, but not all include the minor Disney parks or allow you to visit more than one park in a day.

The Magic Kingdom is divided into seven lands. To do the Kingdom justice, try to visit all (or at least most) of them. For an overview, or a rest on a hot afternoon, hop aboard the **Walt Disney World Railroad** and take a 1½-mi ride around the perimeter of the park. You can board at the Victorian-style station by the park entrance, in Frontierland, or at Mickey's Toontown Fair.

Sprawling before you when you enter the Magic Kingdom is **Main Street, U.S.A.**—a shop-filled boulevard with Victorian-style stores and restaurants. Stop at **City Hall** (on your left as you enter) to get information or to snap a picture with the Disney characters who make their rounds. A cinema that runs vintage Disney cartoons is another attraction here. If you walk two blocks along Main Street, you'll enter Central Plaza, with Cinderella Castle rising directly in front of you. The plaza is the hub of the Kingdom; all the lands radiate from it.

Adventureland is a mishmash of tropical and swashbuckling attractions that are among the most crowded in the Magic Kingdom. Visit first thing in the morning, late in the afternoon, or in the evening. The **Swiss Family Treehouse** is a good way to get both exercise and a view of the park. You walk single file up the many-staired tree and past the imaginatively furnished "rooms," a trip that can take up to a half hour. The **Jungle Cruise** takes you along the Nile, the Mekong, the Congo, and the Amazon rivers. The tour guide's narration is corny but worth a few chuckles. **Pirates of the Caribbean** is a journey through a world of pirate strongholds and treasure-filled dungeons.

Frontierland's major draw is **Splash Mountain,** an elaborate flume ride based on Disney's 1946 film *Song of the South*, with characters and some songs from the movie. An eight-person hollowed-out log takes a meandering journey through Brer Rabbit's habitat before plummeting down a long, sharp flume drop. **Big Thunder Mountain Railroad,** the "runaway train," takes twists and turns through a mountain but has none of the huge drops serious roller coaster fans adore. The gold rush scenery is great, and it's scarier after dark when you can't anticipate the curves. The lines here are often shorter than they are for Splash Mountain or Space Mountain.

Liberty Square is a journey back to Colonial America. The **Hall of Presidents** is a 30-minute multimedia tribute to the Constitution and the nation's 42 presidents. The star attraction here is the **Haunted Mansion.** Scary but not terrifying, this "doom buggie" ride takes you past a plethora of dust, cobwebs, tombstones, and creepy characters.

Fantasyland is, as the map says, "where storybook dreams come true." Gingerbread houses, gleaming gold turrets, and streams sparkling with shiny pennies dot the landscape, and its rides are based on Disney's animated movies. Unlike many other Magic Kingdom stage shows, **Legend of the Lion King** does not draw on human talent. Simba, Mufasa, Scar, and the rest are played by "humanimals," larger-than-life figures that are manipulated by hidden human "animateers." Other attractions include the rides **Dumbo the Flying Elephant, Peter Pan's Flight, Snow White's Scary Adventures,** and the **Mad Tea Party.** Kids of all ages love the antique **Cinderella's Golden Carrousel.** Small children adore **It's a Small World,** a boat ride accompanied by the now-famous theme song of international brotherhood. The newest Fantasyland attraction is the **Many Adventures of Winnie the Pooh.**

Mickey's Toontown Fair is filled with all manner of things child size. Kids can visit **Mickey and Minnie's country houses; Barnstormer at Goofy's Wiseacres Farm,** a kid-size roller coaster; and **Toon Park,** a spongy green meadow filled with foam topiary in the shapes of goats, cows, pigs, and horses. This is a good opportunity for weary parents to rest their feet while their children run around.

Tomorrowland had a face-lift in the mid-'90s. **Space Mountain** is still here, however, and the needlelike spires of this space-age roller coaster are a Magic Kingdom landmark. Although the ride's speed never exceeds 28 mph, the experience in the dark, with everyone screaming, is thrilling. Prepare to scream at **ExtraTERRORestrial Alien Encounter,** where you'll have a very close encounter with an "extraTERRORestrial" creature. Those less into raising their heart rate can opt for **Timekeeper,** a time-traveling movie adventure for older kids and adults (small children won't be able to see unless held up), or **Buzz Lightyear's Space Ranger Spin,** for children ages five to seven.

EPCOT

Epcot is that rare paradox—an educational theme park—and a very successful one at that. Although rides have been added, the thrills are mostly for the mind. As such, Epcot is best for older children and adults.

Epcot comprises two distinct parts separated by the 40-acre World Showcase Lagoon. The northern half, **Future World,** itself consists of two concentric circles of pavilions. In the inner core are the **Spaceship Earth** geosphere—the giant, golf-ball-shape Epcot icon whose ride explores the development of human communication—and just beyond it, the **Innoventions** buildings, whose exhibits highlight new technology that affects daily living. Making up the circle's outer ring are seven corporate-sponsored pavilions with rides and interactive displays on such topics as energy, the human body, the earth, and imagination.

The southern half, **World Showcase,** stretches 1⅓ mi around the lagoon; in this space you can circumnavigate the globe—or at least explore it. Eleven pavilions present a Disney version of life in various countries with food, entertainment, and wares. Models of some of the world's best-known monuments, such as the Eiffel Tower, a Maya temple, and a majestic Japanese pagoda, are painstakingly re-created.

Except for the boat rides in **Mexico** and **Norway,** World Showcase has no amusement-park-type rides. Instead, it has breathtaking films, ethnic art, cultural entertainment, Audio-Animatronics presentations, and dozens of fine shops and restaurants featuring national specialties. Throughout the day there are live street shows featuring comedy, song, or dance and demonstrations of folk arts and crafts.

DISNEY–MGM STUDIOS

At this combination theme park and fully functioning movie and television production center, exhilarating rides are blended with instructional tours, nostalgia with high-tech wonders.

Sunset Boulevard is a destination for thrill seekers. At the **Rock 'n' Roller Coaster,** rock music booms as a high-speed launch sets you off for a ride with multiple complete inversions. Board the giant elevator in the **Twilight Zone Tower of Terror** and head upward 13 stories past seemingly deserted hallways. Suddenly, the creaking vehicle will plunge in a terrifying 130-ft free-fall drop—and then go back up to do it again! The ride is for older children and adults.

At **Animation Courtyard,** several attractions reveal the secrets of moviemaking. One of the funniest is the **Magic of Disney Animation,** a 30-minute self-guided tour through the Disney animation process, complete with views of actual artists at work. The **Walt Disney Theater** usually runs *The Making of . . . ,* a behind-the-scenes look at Disney's latest smash hit (produced for the Disney Channel). The **Studios**

Backlot Tour, a combination tram ride and walking tour, takes you on a 60-minute behind-the-scenes tour exploring the set design, costumes, props, lighting, and special effects of movies. At Catastrophe Canyon, for example, the tram starts bouncing up and down in a simulated earthquake, and a water tower crashes to the ground, touching off a flash flood.

The **Echo Lake** area packs several popular attractions. The 30-minute **Indiana Jones Epic Stunt Spectacular!,** presented in a 2,200-seat amphitheater, features the stunt choreography of veteran coordinator Glenn Randall (*Raiders of the Lost Ark, E.T.,* and *Jewel of the Nile* are among his credits). **Star Tours** is a flight-simulator thrill ride. Created under the direction of George Lucas, the five 40-seat theaters become spaceships, and you're off to the moon of Endor.

DISNEY'S ANIMAL KINGDOM

At Walt Disney World's fourth major theme park, lifelike experiences with fictional animals and dinosaurs combine with high-adventure encounters including real exotic animals. Sprawling over 500 acres, the park resembles the animal reserves of Africa and Asia and is a habitat for more than 1,000 animals, including endangered species.

Enter at the **Oasis,** a cool green grotto filled with waterfalls and gardens alive with exotic birds, reptiles, and animals. **Safari Village,** the centerpoint of the park, is home to the **Tree of Life,** which serves as the park's great icon. Its trunk features intricate carvings of animal forms symbolizing the richness of life on earth. Beneath the tree roots is a theater for **"It's Tough to be a Bug!,"** a humorous 3-D film and special effects show modeled after the animated film *A Bug's Life.* From the Oasis, bridges connect to the other lands.

The largest of Disney's Animal Kingdom is **Africa.** It starts in the village of **Harambe,** featuring the architecture of an East African port city on the northern banks of the Discovery River. Board a safari vehicle for the exciting **Kilmanjaro Safaris,** where herds of wild animals roam among the trees, lakes, and grasslands of Africa. The safari also includes a race to save elephants from ivory poachers. At the end of the trip, you can follow the **Pangani Forest Exploration Trail** to see lowland gorillas, hippos, meerkats, and warthogs. By **Wildlife Express** steam train, you can journey to **Conservation Station** to investigate the worldwide efforts to save endangered animals and preserve wild habitats. Here you can experience interactive displays and take a backstage look at how the park's animals are kept happy and healthy. At the **Affection Station,** you can observe and touch small animals; Disney educators are on hand to help you find information on ways to connect with conservation efforts in your own community.

Another major land, **Asia** opened in 1999. The main attractions are **Kali River Rapids,** a thrilling white-water rafting journey, and **Maharajah Jungle Trek,** a hike with an up-close view of jungle animals. Pause at the outdoor **Caravan Stage** to catch Flights of Wonders, spectacular demonstrations by falcons, hawks, and other fascinating birds.

In **DinoLand U.S.A.,** youngsters can climb, crawl, and slide in a simulated paleontological dig at the **Boneyard,** which is complete with scaffolding, excavations, dinosaur skeletons, and fascinating "fossils." Nearby is a primeval forest, **Cretaceous Trail,** which gives walkers a visit with some of the survivors of the dinosaur age. Dinosaurs are brought back to life in the most thrilling of all the new adventures, **Countdown to Extinction.** Passengers are whisked back 65 million years on a journey to save the last dinosaur from extinction when the crash of a fiery asteroid threatens everything in sight. At the 1,500-seat outdoor

Theater in the Wild, a live musical performance of *Journey into the Jungle Book* features stars from the film classic.

Camp Minnie-Mickey is a character meet-and-greet location. Stars from many Disney favorites sign autographs and pose for pictures. Theaters host the *Festival of the Lion King* and *Colors of the Wind,* in which Pocahontas introduces live animal performers.

OTHER ATTRACTIONS

Blizzard Beach (⌨ $29.63 adults, $23.85 children) promises the seemingly impossible—a seaside playground with an alpine theme. **River Country** (⌨ $16.91 adults, $13.25 children), the first of Walt Disney World Resort's water parks, is a rustic and rugged swimming hole. **Typhoon Lagoon** (⌨ $29.63 adults, $23.85 children), four times the size of River Country, contains everything from an artificial coral reef with tropical fish (closed in winter) to a lazy river that circles the entire park.

The Orlando Area

Universal Studios is saucy, sassy, and hip. A theme park *and* working film studio, it features the special-effects magic of creative consultant Steven Spielberg as well as the animation wizardry of Hanna-Barbera. Here you can view live shows, participate in movie-themed attractions, and tour back-lot sets. **Universal Orlando Islands of Adventure** is fun for the young and young-at-heart. It's the permanent home of some of the world's most beloved characters, including the Cat in the Hat, Spider-Man, Popeye, the Incredible Hulk, Sinbad, and the dinosaurs of *Jurassic Park.* ⌂ *1000 Universal Studios Plaza, Orlando,* ☎ *407/363–8000 or 888/331–9108; 407/363–8265 TTY.* ⌨ *$48.76 adults, $39.22 children 3–9; 2-day combination with Islands of Adventure $84.74 adults, $68.84 children.*

Performing dolphins, killer whales, and a walk-through Plexiglas tunnel that lets you view sharks and barracudas capture your attention at **SeaWorld Orlando.** The park also has penguins, tropical fish, manatees, seals and sea lions, and other educational diversions. **Discovery Cove** (☎ 877/347–2683), across the street from SeaWorld, is a new, reservations only, daylong experience where you can swim with dolphins and interact with tropical sea creatures and birds in an exotic setting. Take Exit 27A or 28 off I–4. ⌂ *7007 Sea Harbor Dr., Orlando,* ☎ *407/351–3600 or 800/327–2424.* ⌨ *$48.76 adults, $39.22 children.*

The **Orlando Science Center** has 10 themed display halls housing exciting hands-on exhibits as well as an eight-story theater for Iwerks films, planetarium programs, and laser light shows. ⌂ *777 E. Princeton St.,* ☎ *407/514–2000.* ⌨ *$9.50–$14.25 adults, $6.75–$11 children.*

Cypress Gardens is a land of exotic gardens, with bird shows and a famous waterskiing revue. Take I–4 to the U.S. 27S exit and follow signs. ⌂ *Off Rte. 540 east of Winter Haven,* ☎ *941/324–2111 or 800/237–4826; 800/282–2123 in FL.* ⌨ *$33.87 adults, $15.85 children.*

A big hit with children, **Gatorland** is a campy attraction with thousands of alligators, crocodiles, and other Florida wildlife. ⌂ *14501 S. Orange Blossom Trail, between Orlando and Kissimmee,* ☎ *407/855–5496 or 800/393–5297.* ⌨ *$16.93 adults, $7.48–$9.95 children, one child free with each full-paying adult.*

Splendid China—12 mi southwest of Orlando—has more than 60 scaled-down replicas of China's greatest landmarks, including the Great Wall, the Imperial Palace of Beijing's Forbidden City, and the Dalai Lama's Potala Palace. ⌂ *3000 Splendid China Blvd., Kissimmee,* ☎ *407/396–7111 or 800/244–6226; 407/397–8800 recording.* ⌨ *$26.99 adults, $16.99 children.*

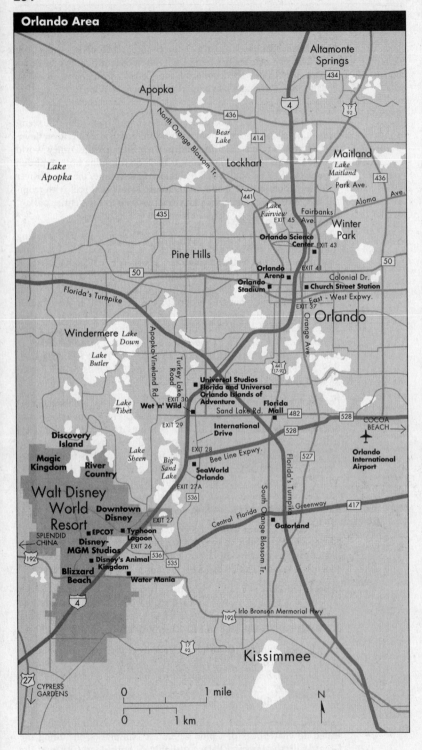

Orlando Area

★ ☾ In the Cocoa Beach area, 47 mi east of Orlando via Route 50 or the Bee Line Expressway, is the **Kennedy Space Center Visitor Complex.** You can see it on two narrated bus tours: One passes by some of NASA's office and assembly buildings, including current launch facilities and the space shuttle launching and landing sites. The other goes to Cape Canaveral Air Force Station, where early launch pads and unmanned rockets that were later adapted for manned use illuminate the history of the early space program. Even more dramatic is the IMAX film *The Dream Is Alive,* shown hourly in the Galaxy Theater. ⊠ *Rte. 405, Kennedy Space Center,* ☎ *407/452–2121 or 800/572–4636.* 🎫 *Free, bus tours $8, IMAX film $6.* ☙

Dining and Lodging

Even dining is an adventure in the Orlando area, where international cuisines, fresh fish and seafood, and such exotic local dishes as grilled alligator tail are all on hand. Besides hotels in Walt Disney World Resort, you'll find accommodations in Orlando; Kissimmee, just east of Walt Disney World; and other outlying towns.

Cocoa Beach

$$$–$$$$ ✗ **Mango Tree Restaurant.** Dine in elegance amid orchid gardens, with piano music playing in the background. Broiled grouper topped with scallops, shrimp, and hollandaise sauce is a favorite. ⊠ *118 N. Atlantic Ave.,* ☎ *407/799–0513. AE, MC, V. Closed Mon. No lunch.*

$$–$$$ 🏨 **Inn at Cocoa Beach.** The spacious rooms in this charming oceanfront inn are each decorated differently, but all have some combination of reproduction 18th- and 19th-century armoires and four-poster beds, plus balconies or patios with ocean views. ⊠ *4300 Ocean Beach Blvd., 32931,* ☎ *407/799–3460; 800/343–5307 outside FL;* FAX *407/784–8632. 50 rooms. Pool. AE, D, MC, V. CP.* ☙

Kissimmee

$ 🏨 **Sevilla Inn.** One of the best buys in the area, this motel has stucco and wood outside and up-to-date rooms inside. The tropical pool looks like something you'd find at a fancier resort. ⊠ *4640 W. Irlo Bronson Memorial Hwy., 34746,* ☎ *407/396–4135 or 800/367–1363,* FAX *407/396–4942. 50 rooms. Pool. AE, D, MC, V.* ☙

Orlando

$$–$$$ ✗ **Le Coq au Vin.** The traditional French fare served at this modest,
★ charming little house in south Orlando is as expertly prepared as any you'll find in town. Fresh rainbow trout with champagne sauce and Long Island duck with green peppercorns are topped off with crème brûlée for dessert. Take I–4 to Exit 34 or 35. ⊠ *4800 S. Orange Ave.,* ☎ *407/851–6980. AE, DC, MC, V. Closed Mon.*

$$$$ 🏨 **Peabody Orlando.** The bland facade gives no hint of this 27-story hotel's
★ beautifully decorated interior, with marble floors, fountains, and modern art. Many rooms have views of Walt Disney World Resort, but the real show is watching the Peabody's ducks waddle their way to the marble fountain, where they pass the day. ⊠ *9801 International Dr., 32819,* ☎ *407/352–4000 or 800/732–2639,* FAX *407/351–9177. 891 rooms. 3 restaurants, pools, golf, tennis, health club. AE, D, DC, MC, V.* ☙

$$$ 🏨 **Buena Vista Palace Resort and Spa at WDW Resort.** Don't be fooled by the corporate-looking sand-color tower; this resort—the largest at Lake Buena Vista—is a very elegant establishment featuring the largest health and beauty spa in the area. The best rooms look out toward Epcot's Spaceship Earth. ⊠ *1900 Buena Vista Dr., 32830,* ☎ *407/827–2727 or 800/327–2990,* FAX *407/827–6034. 1,014 rooms. 4 restaurants, 3 pools, tennis, health club. AE, D, DC, MC, V.*

Walt Disney World

Thanks to the park's **central reservations line** (☎ 407/939–3463) reservations for restaurants within Walt Disney World are especially easy to make. For the very popular Epcot restaurants, you can make reservations at any of the WorldKey Information System terminals in the park. Reserve early in the day before beginning your sightseeing.

World Showcase, in Epcot, offers some of the best dining in the Orlando area, with specialties from various nations that will appeal to every taste.

L'Originale Alfredo di Roma Ristorante ($$$–$$$$), in Italy of course, is known for its namesake dish, fettuccine Alfredo, served by singing waiters.

Marrakesh ($$–$$$$) delights the palate with such Moroccan fare as couscous with vegetables, exotic to some Americans.

The **Rose and Crown** pub ($$–$$$), in the United Kingdom, serves hearty portions of fish-and-chips with a Guinness stout.

Although hotels and resorts on Disney property cost more than comparable facilities elsewhere, their convenience is a significant advantage, and you don't have to drive or pay for parking when visiting Disney parks. Book all Disney hotels—including the following—through **Walt Disney World Central Reservations** (☎ 407/934–7639).

$$$$ ★ 🏨 **Grand Floridian.** With its brick chimneys, gabled roof, sweeping verandas, and stained-glass domes, this resort exudes Victorian charm but has all the conveniences of a modern hotel. Water sports are a focal point at the marina. ☎ 407/824–3000, FAX 407/824–3186. 990 rooms. 6 restaurants, pool, tennis, health club. AE, MC, V.

$$–$$$ 🏨 **Caribbean Beach Resort.** On a 42-acre lake, this resort has several villages named after Caribbean islands, each with a pool, but all share a beach. There's a promenade around the lake, and Parrot Cay, an island in the lagoon with bike paths, trails, and a play area. ☎ 407/934–3400, FAX 407/934–3288. 2,112 rooms. Restaurant, 7 pools. AE, MC, V.

Motels

U.S. 192 is crammed with motels convenient to Walt Disney World Resort. Rates range from inexpensive to moderate, and most have a pool but few other extras. Among these are **Best Western, Quality Suites,** and **Residence Inn** (☞ Toll-Free Numbers *in* Smart Travel Tips A to Z).

Campgrounds

⚠ **Fort Wilderness Resort and Campground** (⊠ Walt Disney World Central Reservations; 🛏 $49–$234; ☞ Walt Disney World, *above*) encompasses 700 acres of scrubby pine and tiny streams within Walt Disney World Resort. You can rent a trailer or bring your own tent or RV to campsites equipped with electrical outlets, outdoor grills, running water, and waste disposal. Tent sites with water and electricity are also available.

Nightlife and the Arts

Nightlife

Inside Walt Disney World Resort every hotel has bars and lounges. Nightly shows include Epcot's **IllumiNations,** with fireworks, lasers, and special effects, and the **Polynesian Luau** (☎ 407/939–3463 in advance; 407/824–1593 day of show), at the Polynesian Resort. **Pleasure Island** (⊠ off Buena Vista Dr., I–4, Exit 27, ☎ 407/934–7781 or 407/824–2222) has eight clubs and a few restaurants. In Orlando **Church Street Station** (⊠ 129 W. Church St., ☎ 407/422–2434) is an entertainment complex in an authentic 19th-century setting. **Cirque du Soleil** in Downtown Disney West Side (⊠ off Buena Vista Dr., ☎ 407/939–7600) combines extraordinary acrobatics, avant-garde stagings, costumes, and choreography. **CityWalk** (☎ 888/331–9108) is the latest addition to Orlando's nightlife, containing stores, dining and drinking establishments, and a 20-screen multiplex with stadium seating. **Medieval Times** (⊠ 4510 W. Irlo Bronson Memorial Hwy., Kissimmee, ☎ 407/239–0214 or 800/229–8300) has a dinner show with knights, nobles, and maidens.

The Arts

Carr Performing Arts Centre (⊠ 401 W. Livingston St., Orlando, ☎ 407/849–2577) routinely features dance, music, and theater performances. The **Civic Theater of Central Florida** (⊠ 1001 E. Princeton St., Orlando, ☎ 407/896–7365) presents a variety of shows. **Orange County Convention and Civic Center** (⊠ south end of International Dr., Orlando, ☎ 407/345–9800) presents big-name performers.

Outdoor Activities and Sports

Biking

The most scenic biking in Orlando is on Walt Disney World Resort property. Two good bike trails were created from former railroad lines: the **West Orange Trail,** running through western Orlando and Apopka, and the **Cady Way Trail,** connecting east Orlando with the suburb of Winter Park. Serious cyclists head to the rolling hills of nearby Lake County.

Golf

The **Celebration Golf Club** (⊠ 700 Golf Park Dr., Celebration, ☎ 407/566–4653) was designed by Robert Trent Jones Jr. and Sr. and is just 1 mi off the U.S. 192 strip. The course at **Falcon's Fire Golf Club** (⊠ 3200 Seralago Blvd., Kissimmee, ☎ 407/239–5445) was designed by Rees Jones. **Grand Cypress Resort** (⊠ 1 N. Jacaranda Dr., Orlando, ☎ 407/239–1909 or 800/297–7377) has 45 holes. **Timacuan Golf and Country Club** (⊠ 550 Timacuan Blvd., Lake Mary, ☎ 407/321–0010) has a front nine that's open, with lots of sand, and a back nine that's heavily wooded. There are five championship courses within **Walt Disney World** (☎ 407/824–4321).

Horseback Riding

⚠ **Fort Wilderness Campground** (⊠ Walt Disney World Resort, ☎ 407/824–2832) offers tame trail rides through backwoods.

Spectator Sports

Basketball: Orlando Magic (☎ 407/839–3900) play in **Orlando Arena** (⊠ 600 W. Amelia St., 2 blocks west of I–4 Amelia St. exit, Orlando). The new WNBA team, the **Orlando Miracle** (☎ 407/916–2255), started playing at the Orlando Arena in 1999.

Beaches and Water Sports

A plethora of water sports is available in the Orlando area. Marinas at resorts in **Walt Disney World** rent all types of boats, from pontoon boats and pedal boats to catamarans and outrigger canoes. Just north of the Kennedy Space Center, the **Canaveral National Seashore** (⊠ 7611 S. Atlantic Ave., between New Smyrna Beach and Titusville, ☎ 904/428–3384) has 24 mi of unspoiled, uncrowded beaches.

Shopping

Much of the Walt Disney World Resort shopping that isn't in the theme parks is concentrated in the area known as **Downtown Disney,** comprising the Marketplace, Pleasure Island, and West Side. Universal has answered the shopping-entertainment challenge with its own complex, **Uni-**

versal Studios CityWalk. **Florida Mall** (⊠ 8001 S. Orange Blossom Trail, Orlando) is the largest mall in central Florida, with department stores, 200 specialty shops, seven theaters, and one of the area's better food courts. The festive **Mercado Mediterranean Village** (⊠ 8445 International Dr., Orlando) has specialty shops and a large food court with cuisines from around the world. **Renninger's Twin Markets,** near the charming village of Mount Dora (30 mi northwest of Orlando on U.S. 441), hosts hundreds of flea market and antiques dealers every weekend. The really big shows take place the third weekends of November, January, and February, when some 1,400 antiques dealers converge. **Belz Factory Outlet World** (⊠ 5401 W. Oak Ridge Rd., northern tip of International Dr., Orlando) is the area's largest collection of outlet stores—more than 180, in two malls and four nearby annexes. **Pointe*Orlando** (⊠ 9101 International Dr., Orlando) is home to 70 specialty shops.

THE FLORIDA KEYS

The string of 31 islands—or keys—placed like a comma between the Atlantic Ocean and the Gulf of Mexico, at the southern tip of Florida, presents a paradox to the visitor. On the one hand, the Keys are natural wonders of lush vegetation, tropical birds, and wildlife, washed by waters teeming with more than 600 kinds of fish; a place where swimming, fishing, and boating are a way of life. On the other hand, the Keys are a highly commercialized tourist attraction that has brought a clutter of unsightly billboards, motels, and shopping malls to U.S. 1 (also known as the Overseas Highway), which links the islands to the mainland. Although the 110-mi drive from Key Largo to Key West is often clogged with traffic on weekends and holidays, it is still a mesmerizing journey into expanses of blue water and blue sky, especially where the road is the only thing separating the ocean from the Gulf. A note about addresses, which are listed by island or mile marker (MM) number: Residents use the abbreviation BS for the Bay Side of the Overseas Highway (U.S. 1) and OS for the Atlantic Ocean side of the highway.

Visitor Information

Florida Keys & Key West: Visitors Bureau (⊠ 402 Wall St., 33040, ☎ 800/352–5397). **Greater Key West:** Chamber of Commerce (⊠ 402 Wall St., 33040, ☎ 305/294–2587 or 800/527–8539, FAX 305/294–7806). **Islamorada:** Chamber of Commerce (⊠ MM 82.5, BS, Box 915, 33036, ☎ 305/664–4503 or 800/322–5397). **Key Largo:** Chamber of Commerce (⊠ MM 106, BS, 106000 Overseas Hwy., 33037, ☎ 305/451–1414 or 800/822–1088). **Key West:** Business Guild (oriented toward gays and lesbians) (⊠ Box 1208, 33041, ☎ 305/294–4603 or 800/535–7797). **Lower Keys:** Chamber of Commerce (⊠ MM 31, OS, Box 430511, Big Pine Key 33043, ☎ 305/872–2411 or 800/872–3722, FAX 305/872–0752). **Marathon:** Chamber of Commerce & Visitor Center (⊠ MM 53.5, BS, 12222 Overseas Hwy., 33050, ☎ 305/743–5417 or 800/842–9580).

Arriving and Departing

By Boat

You can travel to Key West via the Intracoastal Waterway through Florida Bay or in Hawk Channel along the Atlantic coast. Marinas abound in the Keys, but be sure to make docking reservations in advance. For more information contact the **Florida Marine Patrol** (⊠ MM 48, BS, 2796 Overseas Hwy., Suite 100, State Regional Service Center, Marathon 33050, ☎ 305/289–2320; 800/342–5367 after 5 PM).

By Bus

Greyhound (☎ 800/231–2222) runs a Keys shuttle three times a day between Miami International Airport's Concourse E, lower level) and the Keys. Fares run from $12–$13 one-way weekday/weekend and $24/$26 round-trip for Key Largo (MM 102) to $30/$32 one-way and $60/$63 round-trip for Key West (MM1).

By Car

From Miami take Florida's Turnpike (toll road) or State Highway 826/874 to the Homestead Extension of Florida's Turnpike south until it links with U.S. 1 in Florida City. Just south of here U.S. 1 becomes the Overseas Highway.

By Plane

Continuous improvements in service now link airports in Miami, Fort Lauderdale/Hollywood, Naples, Orlando, and Tampa directly with **Key West International Airport** (✉ 3491 S. Roosevelt Blvd., ☎ 305/296–5439). Service is provided by **American Eagle** (☎ 800/433–7300), **Cape Air** (☎ 800/352–0714), **Comair/Delta Connection** (☎ 800/354–9822), **Gulfstream/Continental Connection** (☎ 800/525–0280), and **US Airways/US Airways Express** (☎ 800/428–4322). Direct service between Miami and **Marathon** (✉ MM 52, BS, 9000 Aviation Blvd., ☎ 305/743–2155) is provided by American Eagle.

Exploring the Florida Keys

The Keys are divided into the Upper Keys (from Key Largo to Long Key Channel), the Middle Keys (from Long Key Channel to Seven Mile Bridge), and the Lower Keys (from Seven Mile Bridge to Key West). Pause to explore the flora and fauna of the backcountry and the fragile reefs and aquatic life of the surrounding waters as you weave your way south to historically rich Key West.

Upper Keys

The Upper Keys are dominated by **Key Largo,** with its wildlife refuges and nature parks. Bikers, walkers, and rollerbladers can cruise along the 1¼-mi paved road (one way) through the 2,400-acre **Key Largo Hammocks State Botanical Site** (✉ 1 mi north of U.S. 1 on Rte. 905, OS, ☎ 305/451–1202; ☞ free), the largest remaining stand of West Indian tropical hardwood hammock and mangrove wetland in the Keys. It recently added rest rooms, information kiosks, picnic tables, and interpretive signs. **John Pennekamp Coral Reef State Park** (✉ MM 102.5, OS, Box 487, 102601 Overseas Hwy., ☎ 305/451–1202, ☞ $4 per vehicle, $2 for walk-ins and cyclists) encompasses 78 square mi of coral reefs, which contain 40 species of coral and more than 650 varieties of fish. Diving and snorkeling here are exceptional. A concessionaire rents watercraft and offers boat trips to the reef. The visitor center–aquarium has a new floor-to-ceiling aquarium surrounded by numerous smaller tanks, a video room, and exhibits.

The small **Maritime Museum of the Florida Keys** has exhibits depicting the history of shipwrecks and salvage efforts along the Keys, including retrieved treasures, reconstructed wreck sites, and artifacts in various stages of preservation. ✉ *MM 102.5, BS, Key Largo,* ☎ *305/451–6444.* ☞ *$2. Closed weekends.*

Get a close-up look at bird life at the **Florida Keys Wild Bird Rehabilitation Center** (✉ MM 93.6, BS, 93600 Overseas Hwy., Tavernier, ☎ 305/852–4486; ☞ donations welcome), where at any time the resident population can include ospreys, hawks, pelicans, cormorants, terns, and herons. When the Florida East Coast Railway drilled, dynamited, and carved Windley Key's limestone bed, it exposed the once-living fossilized coral reef that was laid down about 125,000 years ago. Explore the five trails and Alison Fahrer Environmental Education Center on a tour or on your own at the **Windley Key Fossil Reef State Geologic Site** (✉ MM 85.5, BS, ☎ 305/664–2540; ✉ free, trail access $1.50; closed Tues. and Wed.).

Theater of the Sea (✉ MM 84.5, OS, Islamorada, ☎ 305/664–2431; ✉ $17.25) has dolphin and sea lion shows, a touch tank, a pool where sharks are fed by a trainer, and several small aquariums. For $110, you can swim with the dolphins (reservations recommended). At **Robbie's Marina** (✉ MM 77.5, BS, Islamorada, ☎ 305/664–9814; ✉ dock access $1), 50 or so tarpon—some as long as 5 ft—gather below the docks, waiting to be fed. The following two sites are accessible only by boat; you can take a ferry ($15 for one site, $25 for both) or rent a boat or kayak from the official state concessionaire, **Robbie's Marina** (☞ *above*). **Indian Key State Historic Site** (✉ MM 78.5, OS, Islamorada, ☎ 305/664–4815; ✉ tour $1, free if you arrive by ferry), inhabited by Indians for several thousand years before Europeans arrived, was also a base for early 19th-century shipwreck salvagers until an Indian attack wiped out the settlement in 1840. A virgin hardwood forest still cloaks **Lignumvitae Key State Botanical Site** (✉ MM 78.5, BS, Islamorada; ✉ tour $1, free if you arrive by ferry), punctuated only by the house and gardens built by chemical magnate William Matheson in 1919. For information and reservations contact **Long Key State Recreation Area** (✉ MM 67.5, OS, Box 776, Long Key, ☎ 305/664–4815; ✉ $3.25, plus 50¢ per each additional person; canoe rental $4 per hr).

The Middle Keys

Once you cross **Long Key Viaduct** (MM 65), one of 42 bridges in the island chain, the Keys become more rustic. The second-longest bridge on the former rail line (known informally as the Overseas Railroad), this 2-mi-long structure has 222 reinforced-concrete arches. The nonprofit **Dolphin Research Center** (✉ MM 59, BS, ☎ 305/289–1121; ✉ $12.50 tour, Dolphin Encounter $110) runs educational tours and dolphin interaction programs.

The Florida Keys Land Trust owns the **Museums of Tropical Crane Point Hammock** (✉ MM 50, BS, 5550 Overseas Hwy., Marathon, ☎ 305/743–9100; ✉ $7.50), which houses the **Museum of Natural History of the Florida Keys** and the **Florida Keys Children's Museum** and features a 1-mi loop trail, the remnants of a Bahamian village, and the

George Adderly House, the oldest surviving example of Conch-style architecture outside Key West. From November to Easter, weekly docent-led hammock tours may be available; call for times. Bring good walking shoes and bug repellent. At the end of Marathon are the Old Seven Mile Bridge and the new Seven Mile Bridge. Visitors can walk 2.2 mi or take a shuttle (from Knight's Key MM 47, OS) across the old bridge to tour **Pigeon Key** (✉ MM 45, OS, Box 500130, Pigeon Key 33050, ☎ 305/289–0025 general information, 305/743–7655 eco-tour information, ✉ $7.50), a former work camp for the Overseas Railroad, and visit a museum that recalls the history of the railroad, the Keys, and railroad baron Henry M. Flagler.

The Lower Keys

Just south of Marathon, the **Seven Mile Bridge,** believed to be the world's longest segmented bridge, is the gateway to the Lower Keys. The delicate Key deer can be viewed at **National Key Deer Refuge** (✉ Headquarters, MM 30.5, BS, Big Pine Shopping Center, ☎ 305/872–2239; ✉ free; headquarters closed weekends), on Big Pine Key.

The final key is **Key West**, famous for its climate, laid-back lifestyle, sizable gay population, colorful heritage, and 19th-century architecture.

Key West's rich ethnic past comes alive in the **Bahama Village** area (⊠ Thomas and Petronia Sts.), with the peach, yellow, and pink homes of early Bahamian settlers. The **San Carlos Institute** (⊠ 516 Duval St., ☎ 305/294–3887; ☞ $3; closed Mon.) is a Cuban-American heritage center, with a museum and research library focusing on the history of Key West and 19th- and 20th-century Cuban exiles. **Fort Zachary Taylor State Historic Site** (⊠ Southard St., ☎ 305/292–6713; ☞ $2.50 per vehicle, $1.50 per pedestrian or bicyclist) was an important fort during the Civil and Spanish-American wars. It's 88 steps to the top of the 92-ft lighthouse at the **Lighthouse Museum** (⊠ 938 Whitehead St., ☎ 305/294–0012; ☞ $6). The adjacent keeper's cottage displays ship models and lighthouse artifacts. The **Audubon House and Gardens** (⊠ 205 Whitehead St., ☎ 305/294–2116; ☞ $8.50) has beautiful tropical gardens and a large

★ collection of Audubon engravings. The **Hemingway House** (⊠ 907 Whitehead St., ☎ 305/294–1575, ☞ $8) is dedicated to the life and work of the author who wrote 70% of his works in Key West, including *For Whom the Bell Tolls*. **Harry S. Truman Little White House Museum** (⊠ 111 Front St., ☎ 305/294–9911; ☞ $8), a winter White House for Presidents Truman, Eisenhower, and Kennedy, features a photographic review of visiting dignitaries and exhibits. It's on the grounds of **Truman Annex,** a 103-acre former military parade grounds and barracks. The island's newest attraction is the **Key West Museum of Art & History** (⊠ 281 Front St., ☎ 305/295–6616; ☞ $6), a former U.S. Customs House. The impressive redbrick and terra-cotta Richardsonian Romanesque–style building houses permanent and rotating exhibits about the history of Key West.

Nancy Forrester's Secret Garden (⊠ 1 Free School La., ☎ 305/294–0015; ☞ $6) is one of the prettiest spots in Key West. It features rare palms and cycads, trails lined with ferns, bromeliads, bright gingers, heliconias, and towering native gumbo-limbos strewn with hanging orchids and twining vines. Many brides and grooms have exchanged vows here.

☺ At the **Key West Aquarium** (⊠ 1 Whitehead St., ☎ 305/296–2051; ☞ $8) kids learn about the marine life found around the Keys in an up-close-and-personal experience with turtles, rays, sharks, parrot fish, eels, and tarpon swimming in glass tanks, coral pools, a pond, and touch tanks.

Sharon Wells, who conducts **Island City Strolls** (☎ 305/294–8380) walking tours, was the state historian in Key West for nearly 20 years and has authored numerous books about Key West, including the *Walking and Biking Guide to Historic Key West,* available free at Key West bookstores. In addition to publishing guides to the Keys, the **Historic Florida Keys Foundation** (☎ 305/292–6718) conducts tours of Key West's City Cemetery Tuesday and Thursday at 9:30.

Dining and Lodging

Local specialties include conch chowder, Florida lobster, and key lime pie. Accommodations, from historic hotels and guest houses to large resorts and run-of-the-mill motels, are more expensive here than elsewhere in southern Florida.

Islamorada

$$–$$$$ ✕ **Morada Bay.** This bayfront restaurant has a spectacular water view,
★ traditional wooden Conch architecture, and a contemporary menu featuring tapas and innovative dishes, mostly from the sea. There's frequently live entertainment, especially on weekends. ⊠ MM 81, BS, 81590 Overseas Hwy., ☎ 305/664–0604. AE, MC, V.

$–$$$ ✕ **Squid Row.** Along with local fish grilled, divinely flaky, or in bread crumbs and sautéed, this affable seafood eatery offers a nightly special of bouillabaisse ($26.95) thick with fish and shellfish—even stone crab claws–that is simply wonderful. Finish it by yourself and they'll serve you a free slice of key lime pie. ✉ *MM 81.9, OS, Overseas Hwy.*, ☎ *305/664–9865. AE, D, DC, MC, V.*

$–$$ ✕ **Manny & Isa's.** This Keys institution has no frills, fancy decor, or pretense, but it does have delicious Cuban and Spanish dishes, local seafood, and daily fish, chicken, and pork chop specials. Manny's key lime pies are heavenly. To avoid the wait for dinner on weekends and in high season, call for takeout. ✉ *MM 81.6, OS, 81610 Old Hwy.*, ☎ *305/664–5019. AE, D, MC, V. Closed Tues. and mid-Oct.–mid-Nov.*

$$$$ ☷ **Cheeca Lodge.** This classy, 27-acre, low-rise resort combines a sense of luxury with a sense of familiarity. Suites have kitchens and screened balconies; fourth-floor rooms in the main lodge have ocean or bay views. The resort is the local leader in green activism with everything from recycling to ecotours. ✉ *MM 82, OS, Box 527, 33036, ☎ 305/664–4651 or 800/327–2888, ℻ 305/664–2893. 203 rooms. 2 restaurants, 4 pools, golf, tennis. AE, D, DC, MC, V.* ✍

Key Largo

$–$$$$ ✕ **Fish House.** Expect nautical, Keys-y casual decor and friendly, dili-
★ gent servers at this perennial favorite. Nightly specials like shrimp and lobster Creole in a spicy tomato sauce served over rice are another reason why locals and visitors come back. Their new next-door annex, the Gift House, features coffees, fabulous desserts, and souvenirs. ✉ *MM 102.4, OS, Overseas Hwy.*, ☎ *305/451–4665. AE, D, MC, V. Closed early Sept.–early Oct.*

$–$$ ✕ **Cafe Largo.** This bistro-style eatery prepares seafood and traditional Italian dishes quite well. The penne with shrimp and broccoli has tender shrimp, al dente broccoli, and garlic. There's lobster and shrimp scampi, too. The dessert list is short but sweet. ✉ *MM 99.5, BS, Overseas Hwy.*, ☎ *305/451–4885. AE, MC, V. No lunch.*

$–$$ ✕ **Mrs. Mac's Kitchen.** The architecture, atmosphere, and decor of this rustic screened, open-air restaurant hark back to the 1950s, when the Keys had more fishermen than well-heeled visitors. They still prepare traditional American foods like sandwiches, burgers, barbecue, and seafood. ✉ *MM 99.4, BS, 99336 Overseas Hwy.*, ☎ *305/451–3722. No credit cards. Closed Sun.*

$ ✕ **Chad's Deli & Bakery.** Each morning the namesake owner bakes eight kinds of fresh breads, which he uses to make American sandwiches ($5–$6) large enough to feed two hungry adults. The menu also features salads, sides, soft drinks, and cookies. Residents have voted it number one for best sandwiches in the Upper Keys. ✉ *MM 92.3, BS, Overseas Hwy.*, ☎ *305/853–5566. No credit cards. Closed Sun.*

$$$–$$$$ ☷ **Westin Beach Resort, Key Largo.** This large resort with lush landscaping is tucked away among the trees of a hardwood hammock. The spacious, comfortable rooms have tropical decor. Lighted nature trails and boardwalks wind through the woods to a small beach. Both restaurants overlook the water. ✉ *MM 96.9, BS, 97000 Overseas Hwy., 33037, ☎ 305/852–5553 or 800/826–1006, ℻ 305/852–8669. 200 rooms. 2 restaurants, 2 pools. AE, D, DC, MC, V.* ✍

$$$ ☷ **Kona Kai Resort.** A sidewalk links landscaped cottages to a sandy
★ beach at this stylish, laid-back resort. There are no room phones, and maid service is every third morning. Studios and one- and two-bedroom suites—with full kitchens—are spacious and light-filled. Beachfront hammocks and a toasty pool make it easy to while away the day. Smoking is not permitted; neither are guests under 16 years old. ✉ *MM 97.8, BS, 97802 Overseas Hwy., 33037, ☎ 305/852–7200 or 800/365–7829. 11 units. Pool, tennis. AE, D, MC, V.* ✍

$$ ☷ **Largo Lodge.** A palpable calm hangs over the 1950s-vintage adults-
★ only cottages hidden in a garden of palms, sea grapes, and orchids. Cozy

accommodations are fully equipped with kitchens and screened porches but no phones. There's 200 ft of bay frontage. ⊠ *MM 101.5, BS, 101740 Overseas Hwy., 33037,* ☎ *305/451–0424 or 800/468–4378. 7 units. MC, V.* ☙

Key West

$$$$
★ ✕ **Louie's Backyard.** This oceanfront contemporary restaurant with a steal-your-breath view consistently offers an enticing menu that changes seasonally. Dine outside under a mahoe tree. Come for lunch if you're on a budget; the menu is less expensive and there's that view. For night owls, the Afterdeck Bar serves cocktails on the water until the wee hours. ⊠ *700 Waddell Ave.,* ☎ *305/294–1061. AE, DC, MC, V.*

$$–$$$$
★ ✕ **Alice's at La Te Da.** Chef-owner Alice Weingarten moved her contemporary restaurant across the street to a tropical poolside location, added breakfast and brunch, and was named one of the area's top 10 chefs by South Florida Gourmet. What hasn't changed is the exemplary selection of wines that complement the creative mix of seafood, game, beef, pork, and poultry dishes. A sizzling Key West yellowtail features an aromatic blend of Thai red curry and Asian vegetables served over coconut basmati rice. ⊠ *1125 Duval St.,* ☎ *305/296–6706. AE, D, MC, V. Closed Mon.*

$–$$
✕ **Mangia Mangia.** Diners select a fresh pasta from the daily selection and match it with one of Mangia Mangia's freshly made Italian sauces: alfredo, marinara, meaty, or with pesto. Tables are arranged in a brick garden and in a nicely dressed-up old-house dining room. It's one of the best restaurants in Key West, and one of its best values. The wine list of more than 350 selections contains many under $20. ⊠ *900 Southard St.,* ☎ *305/294–2469. AE, MC, V. No lunch.*

$$$$
★ ⊞ **Marquesa Hotel.** This coolly elegant restored 1884 home is Key West's finest lodging. Guests relax among richly landscaped pools and gardens against a backdrop of brick steps rising to the villalike suites on the property's perimeter. Elegant rooms contain eclectic antique and reproduction furnishings and botanical print fabrics. Although the clientele is mostly straight, the hotel is very gay-friendly. ⊠ *600 Fleming St., 33040,* ☎ *305/292–1919 or 800/869–4631,* 🖷 *305/294–2121. 27 rooms. Restaurant, 2 pools. AE, DC, MC, V.* ☙

$$$$
★ ⊞ **Paradise Inn.** Gloriously chic best describes this romantic palm-shaded inn composed of renovated cigar makers' cottages and authentically reproduced Bahamian-style houses with sundecks and balconies. The lush tropical garden with a heated pool and lily pond are light-years away from the bustle of Key West. Complimentary breakfast pastries are from Louie's Pantry. ⊠ *819 Simonton St., 33040,* ☎ *305/293–8007 or 800/888–9648,* 🖷 *305/293–0807. 18 units. Pool. AE, D, DC, MC, V. CP.* ☙

$$$–$$$$
⊞ **Cuban Club Suites.** Originally built as a social club for cigar makers, the "club" was rebuilt as a luxury hotel. Eight fully equipped townhouse units have either two bedrooms and two baths or one bedroom and 1½ baths. Grouped in two buildings that feel like an exclusive apartment complex, they have wide balconies that overlook the excitement of Duval Street. Guests have pool and beach privileges at the Wyndham Reach, a resort nearby, and pets are allowed. ⊠ *1108 Duval St., 33040,* ☎ *305/296–0465 or 800/432–4849,* 🖷 *305/293–7669. 8 suites. AE, MC, V.* ☙

$$–$$$$
★ ⊞ **Popular House/Key West Bed & Breakfast.** Local art—large, splashy canvases; a mural in the style of Gauguin—hangs on the walls, and tropical gardens and music set the mood. You'll find both inexpensive rooms with shared bath (whose rates haven't been raised in more than 10 years) and luxury rooms. ⊠ *415 William St., 33040,* ☎ *305/296–7274 or 800/438–6155,* 🖷 *305/293–0306. 9 rooms. AE, D, DC, MC, V. CP.* ☙

Marathon

$–$$$$ ✕ **Barracuda Grill.** For those who think Keys food is limited to grilled dolphinfish and coconut shrimp, Barracuda Grill will be a revelation. This contemporary eatery presents an eclectic menu that capitalizes on the local bounty—fresh fish—but is equally represented by tender, aged Angus beef; rack of lamb; and even a meat loaf that defies the stereotype. ✉ *MM 49.5, BS,* ☎ *305/743–3314. AE, MC, V. Closed Sun. No lunch.*

$ ✕ **7 Mile Grill.** This nearly 50-year-old weatherworn, open-air seafood
★   restaurant could serve as a movie set for a 1950s movie. Situated at the Marathon end of the Seven Mile Bridge, it serves up friendly service and casual food. Favorites on the mostly seafood menu include fresh-squeezed orange juice, creamy shrimp bisque, and fresh grouper and dolphinfish grilled, broiled, or fried. ✉ *MM 47, BS, 1240 Overseas Hwy.,* ☎ *305/743–4481. MC, V. Closed Wed.; also Thurs. mid-Apr.–mid-Nov.; and at owner's discretion Aug.–Sept.*

$$–$$$ 🏨 **Seascape Ocean Resort.** The charming lobby filled with soothing
★   sea colors and original artwork gives way to nine pastel-color guest rooms decorated with more artwork, hand-painted headboards, and fresh flowers and fruit. The 5-acre oceanfront property with a large, two-story house is an exclusive yet unsnobbish retreat. Guests can swim in the pool or ocean, paddle a kayak, or relax under a shade tree. Continental breakfast and afternoon cocktails and hors d'oeuvres are served. Rooms are nonsmoking and have no phones. ✉ *MM 50.5, OS, 1075 75th St., 33050,* ☎ *305/743–6455 or 800/332–7327,* 🖷 *305/743–8469. 9 rooms. Pool. AE, MC, V. CP.* ✍

$–$$ 🏨 **Coral Lagoon.** This little resort has cheerfully painted duplex cottages with kitchens, private sundecks with lazy hammocks, views of a deep-water canal, and pretty landscaping. Extras not usually found at this price include videocassette players, safes, hair dryers, morning coffee, tennis rackets, fishing equipment, dockage, and barbecues. ✉ *MM 53.5, OS, 12399, Marathon 33050,* ☎ *305/289–0121,* 🖷 *305/289–0195. 18 cottages. Pool, tennis. AE, D, MC, V.*

Nightlife and the Arts

Key West is the Keys' hub for artistic performances and nightlife. This city alone claims among its current residents 55 full-time writers and 500 painters and craftspeople. The most popular entertainment is the nightly gathering of street vendors, performers, and visitors on **Mallory Square Dock** to celebrate the sunset. The **Tennessee Williams Fine Arts Center** (✉ Florida Keys Community College, 5901 College Rd., ☎ 305/296–9081) offers dance, music, plays, and star performers from November to April. **Capt. Tony's Saloon** (✉ 428 Greene St., ☎ 305/294–1838), a landmark bar noted for its connection with Ernest Hemingway, features nightly entertainment. Hemingway liked to gamble in the club room at **Sloppy Joe's** (✉ 201 Duval St., ☎ 305/294–5717), a popular, noisy bar.

Outdoor Activities and Sports

Biking

Cyclists are now able to ride all but a tiny portion of the bike path that runs along the Overseas Highway from Mile Marker 106 south to Mile Marker 73, then picks up again at Mile Marker 70 to Mile Marker 66, then again from Mile Marker 53 to the Seven Mile Bridge. Trails crisscross the Marathon area; most popular is the 2-mi section of the old **Seven Mile Bridge** leading to Pigeon Key. For rentals in Key Largo and Marathon, contact **Equipment Locker Sport & Cycle** (✉ Tradewinds Plaza, MM 101, OS, 101487 Overseas Hwy., Key Largo, ☎ 305/453–0140; ✉ MM 53, BS, 11518 Overseas Hwy., Marathon, ☎ 305/289–1670). For moped rentals, contact **Keys Moped & Scooter** (✉ 523 Tru-

When it Comes to Getting Cash at an ATM,

Same Thing.

Whether you're in Yosemite or Yemen, using your Visa® card or ATM card with the PLUS symbol is the easiest and most convenient way to get cash. Even if your bank is in Minneapolis and you're in Miami, Visa/PLUS ATMs make getting cash so easy, you'll feel right at home. After all, Visa/PLUS ATMs are open 24 hours a day, 7 days a week, rain or shine. And if you need help finding one of Visa's 627,000 ATMs in 127 countries worldwide, visit **visa.com/pd/atm**. We'll make finding an ATM as easy as finding the Eiffel Tower, the Pyramids or even the Grand Canyon.

It's Everywhere You Want To Be.®

ONE LAST TRAVEL TIP:

Pack an easy way to reach the world.

123 456 7891 2345
J.D. SMITH

Wherever you travel, the MCI WorldCom Card℠ is the easiest way to stay in touch. You can use it to call to and from more than 125 countries worldwide. And you can earn bonus miles every time you use your card. So go ahead, travel the world. MCI WorldCom℠ makes it even more rewarding. For additional access codes, visit **www.wcom.com/worldphone**.

EASY TO CALL WORLDWIDE

1. Just dial the WorldPhone® access number of the country you're calling from.

2. Dial or give the operator your MCI WorldCom Card number.

3. Dial or give the number you're calling.

Aruba (A) ⊹	800-888-8
Australia ◆	1-800-881-100
Bahamas ⊹	1-800-888-8000

Barbados (A) ⊹	1-800-888-8000
Bermuda ⊹	1-800-888-8000
British Virgin Islands (A) ⊹	1-800-888-8000
Canada	1-800-888-8000
Costa Rica (A) ◆	0800-012-2222
New Zealand	000-912
Puerto Rico	1-800-888-8000
United States	1-800-888-8000
U.S. Virgin Islands	1-800-888-8000

(A) Calls back to U.S. only. ⊹ Limited availability. ◆ Public phones may require deposit of coin or phone card for dial tone.

EARN FREQUENT FLIER MILES

man Ave., Key West, ☎ 305/294–0399) or **Moped Hospital** (✉ 601 Truman Ave., Key West, ☎ 305/296–3344).

Diving and Snorkeling

Miles of living coral reefs are populated with 650 species of tropical fish, as well as four centuries of explorable shipwrecks. Outstanding diving areas include **John Pennekamp Coral Reef State Park** (✉ MM 102.5, OS, Key Largo, ☎ 305/451–1202) and **Looe Key Reef,** 5 mi off Ramrod Key (✉ MM 27.5). **American Diving Headquarters** (✉ MM 105.5, BS, 10550 Overseas Hwy., Key Largo, ☎ 305/451–0037) and **Looe Key Dive Center** (✉ MM 27.5, OS, Ramrod Key, ☎ 305/872– 2215 or 800/942–5397) lead dives in the area.

Fishing and Boating

Anglers can enjoy deep-sea fishing on the ocean or Gulf and flat-water fishing in the backcountry shallows. Numerous marinas rent all types of boats and water-sports equipment. Particularly popular are the glass-bottom-boat tours to the coral reefs. Check with chambers of commerce for information on charter- and party-boat operators. Sandy Moret is one of the most recognizable names in Keys fly-fishing. He operates **Florida Keys Outfitters** (✉ MM 82, BS, ☎ 305/664–5423), home to a store and the Florida Keys Fly Fishing School, which attracts anglers from around the world. There are classes, fishing trips, and fishing and accommodations packages (at Cheeca Lodge). Try **Hubba Hubba** for backcountry fishing (✉ MM 79.8, OS, Islamorada, ☎ 305/664–9281). Third-generation Key Wester Bill Wickers and his wife run sportfishing outings on the **Linda D III** and **Linda D IV** (☎ 305/296–9798 or 800/299–9798), which operate out of Key West City Marina, at the corner of U.S. 1 and Palm Avenue.

Golf

Key Colony Beach Par 3 (✉ MM 53.5, OS, 8th St., Key Colony Beach near Marathon, ☎ 305/289–1533) is a 9-hole public course. **Key West Resort Golf Club** (✉ 6450 E. College Rd., Stock Island, ☎ 305/294– 5232) is an 18-hole public course.

Beaches

Keys beaches, particularly in Key West, have been closed periodically to swimming because of sewage contamination. Observe signs about the water's health conditions. Since the natural shorelines of the Keys are a combination of marshes, rocky outcroppings, and grassy wetlands, most beaches for sunbathing and swimming are man-made from imported sand. The exception is **Bahia Honda State Park** (✉ MM 37, OS, Bahia Honda Key, ☎ 305/872–2353), which has a naturally sandy beach, plus a nature trail, campground and waterfront cabins (reserve up to 11 months in advance), marina, and dive shop. **Anne's Beach** (✉ MM 73.5, OS, Islamorada, ☎ 305/852–2381) has a ½-mi elevated wooden boardwalk that crosses a wetlands hammock at the edge of the shore. Information on **Curry Hammock State Park** (✉ MM 57, OS) is provided by Long Key State Recreation Area (☞ Long Key *in* Exploring, *above*). It comprises upland hammock, wetlands, mangroves, and a long sandy beach with a bathhouse and picnic tables. **Sombrero Beach** (✉ MM 50, OS, Sombrero Rd., Marathon, ☎ 305/289–6077 or 888/227–8136) has areas for swimmers, jet boats, and windsurfers. Behind the narrow, sandy beach is a large, grassy park with grills, picnic kiosks, showers, and a playground. **Ft. Zachary Taylor State Historic Site** (✉ end of Southard St., through Truman Annex, ☎ 305/292– 6713) is the best of the several Key West beaches. It's uncrowded and has picnic areas, grills, and an historic fort.

Shopping

The Keys are a thriving artists' community, so art is in good supply here. Original works by major international artists—including American Everglades photographer Clyde Butcher, French painter Jalinepol W, and French sculptor Polles—are shown at the **Gallery at Kona Kai** (⊠ MM 97.8, BS, 97802 Overseas Hwy, ☎ 305/852–7200. **Rain Barrel** (⊠ MM 86.7, BS, 86700 Overseas Hwy., Islamorada, ☎ 305/852–3084) is a 3-acre crafts village with eight resident artists and works by scores of others, plus a delightful restaurant serving primarily vegetarian dishes. Across the street, an enormous fabricated lobster by artist Richard Blaes stands in front of **Treasure Village** (⊠ MM 86.7, OS, 86729 Old Hwy., Islamorada, ☎ 305/852–0511), which has a dozen crafts and specialty shops. **Redbone Gallery** (⊠ MM 81, OS, 200 Industrial Dr., Islamorada, ☎ 305/664–2002) specializes in art with a fishing and marine theme. The **Gallery at Morada Bay** (⊠ MM 81.6, BS, Overseas Hwy., Islamorada, ☎ 305/664–3650) carries fine arts and crafts, including blown glass, jewelry, and paintings by top South Florida artists. **World Wide Sportsman** (⊠ MM 82.5, BS, Overseas Hwy., Islamorada, ☎ 305/664–4615) is a two-level attraction–retail center–lounge, selling upscale fishing equipment. Key West has numerous fine art galleries and unique specialty shops, such as **Fast Buck Freddie's** (⊠ 500 Duval St., ☎ 305/294–2007), which sells housewares, clothing, and furnishings with a tropical theme. In a town with a gazillion T-shirt shops, **Last Flight Out** (⊠ 706A Duval St., ☎ 305/294–8008) stands out for its selection of classic namesake T's, collectibles, and specialty clothing and gifts that appeal to aviation types and those reaching for the stars.

SOUTHWEST FLORIDA

Swimming, sunbathing, sailing, and shelling draw increasing numbers of visitors to the 200-mi coastal stretch between the Tampa Bay area and the Everglades. Venturing inland from the miles of sun-splashed beaches along the Gulf of Mexico, many visitors discover the culturally rich and ethnically diverse towns, interesting historical sites, and stellar attractions, such as Busch Gardens. This area tends to be more affordable than other parts of Florida. The region is divided into three areas: Tampa Bay (including Tampa, St. Petersburg, Clearwater, and Tarpon Springs), Sarasota (including Bradenton and Venice), and Fort Myers/Naples.

Visitor Information

Greater Tampa: Chamber of Commerce (⊠ Box 420, 33601, ☎ 813/228–7777). **Lee County:** Visitor and Convention Bureau (⊠ 2180 W. 1st St., Fort Myers 33950, ☎ 941/338–3500 or 800/533–4753). **Greater Naples Area:** Chamber of Commerce (⊠ 3620 Tamiami Tr. N, 33940, ☎ 941/262–6141). **St. Petersburg:** Chamber of Commerce (⊠ 100 2nd Ave. N, 33701, ☎ 727/821–4069). **Sanibel-Captiva:** Chamber of Commerce (⊠ Causeway Rd., Sanibel 33957, ☎ 941/472–1080). **Sarasota:** Convention and Visitors Bureau (⊠ 655 N. Tamiami Trail, 34236, ☎ 941/957–1877 or 800/522–9799). **Tampa/Hillsborough:** Convention and Visitors Association (⊠ 111 Madison St., Suite 1010, Tampa 33601, ☎ 800/826–8358).

Arriving and Departing

By Bus

Greyhound (☎ 800/231–2222) provides statewide service, including stops at Tampa, St. Petersburg, Sarasota, Fort Myers, and Naples. For local bus service contact **Hillsborough Area Regional Transit** (☎ 813/

254–4278) for the Tampa area, **Sarasota County Area Transit** (☎ 941/951–5850) for Sarasota, and **Lee County Transit System** (☎ 941/275–8726) for the Fort Myers area.

By Car

From the Georgia-Florida border, it's a three-hour drive via I–75 south to Tampa, four hours to Sarasota, five to Fort Myers, and six to Naples. U.S. 41 (the Tamiami Trail) also traverses the region, but because it pierces many towns' business districts, traffic can be extremely heavy, particularly from Tampa south. Naples is linked to Fort Lauderdale, on the eastern side of the state, via Alligator Alley (I–75).

By Plane

Most major U.S. airlines serve at least one of the region's airports. **Tampa International** (☒ 5507 Spruce St., ☎ 813/870–8700), 6 mi from downtown, is also served by international airlines. **Sarasota-Bradenton Airport** (☒ 6000 Airport Circle, ☎ 941/359–5200) is 5 mi north of downtown Sarasota off U.S. 41. **Southwest Florida International Airport** (☒ 16000 Chamberlin Pkwy., ☎ 941/768–1000), served by regional and some international carriers, is about 12 mi south of Fort Myers and 25 mi north of Naples.

By Train

Amtrak (☎ 800/872–7245) connects most of the country with Tampa's station.

Exploring Southwest Florida

The Tampa Bay Area

Tampa is the commercial center of southwestern Florida, with a bustling international port and the largest shrimp fleet in the state. Known as the City by the Bay, Tampa pays homage to its waterfront setting with ★ the **Florida Aquarium** (☒ 701 Channelside Dr., ☎ 813/273–4000, ☒ $11.95), whose 83-ft-high glass dome is already a landmark. More than 4,300 specimens of fish, other animals, and plants represent 550 species native to Florida. The 35,000-square-ft **Tampa Museum of Art** (☒ 600 N. Ashley Dr., ☎ 813/274–8130; ☒ $5) has a permanent collection of more than 7,000 works, including the most comprehensive collection of Greek, Roman, and Etruscan antiquities in the southeastern United States and an excellent collection of 20th-century American art.

☾ Reserve a day in Tampa for a journey through **Busch Gardens** (☒ 3000 E. Busch Blvd., ☎ 813/987–5082; ☒ $41.15), a 335-acre African-inspired theme park with rides, live shows, and a monorail "safari."

☾ Busch Gardens' water-park cousin, 25-acre **Adventure Island** (☒ 10001 Malcolm McKinley Dr., ☎ 813/987–5660; ☒ $24.45) has water slides and man-made waves. It's closed late October–mid-March.

★ With cobblestone streets and wrought-iron balconies, Tampa's **Ybor City** (pronounced *Ee*-bor) is one of only three National Historic Landmark districts in Florida. Cubans expanded their cigar-making industry to this city in 1866. The ornately tiled **Columbia Restaurant** and the stores lining 7th Avenue are representative of this enclave's ethnic history and vitality. Today once-empty cigar factories, like the one at **Ybor Square** (☒ 1901 13th St.), house boutiques, shops, restaurants, and nightclubs. To get here, take I–4 west to Exit 1 (22nd Street) and go south five blocks to 7th Avenue.

On the Gulf about 25 mi north of Tampa is colorful **Tarpon Springs.** Famous for its sponge divers, the town reflects the heritage of its predominantly Greek population. At **Weeki Wachee Spring** (☒ 45 mi north of Tampa on U.S. 19 and Rte. 50, Weeki Wachee, ☎ 352/596–2062;

$16.95), 27 mi north of Tarpon Springs, "mermaids" have been presenting shows in an underwater theater for more than 50 years.

You can watch manatees up close at **Homosassa Springs State Wildlife Park** (⊠ 1 mi west of U.S. 19 on Fish Bowl Dr., Homosassa Springs, ☎ 352/628–2311; ⊡ $7.95). Here you can also see reptile and alligator shows, cruise the Homosassa River, and view sea life in a floating observatory.

Head south from Tampa and cross Old Tampa Bay on I–275 to get to the heart of **St. Petersburg.** Set on a peninsula whose three sides border bays and the Gulf of Mexico, this city has beautiful beaches. With more than 1,500 pieces, the **Salvador Dalí Museum** (⊠ 1000 3rd St. S, ☎ 727/823–3767; ⊡ $8) has the world's largest collection of originals by the Spanish surrealist. **Great Explorations!** (⊠ 800 2nd Ave. NE, ☎ 727/821–8885; ⊡ $6) is a hands-on museum with mind-stretching puzzles and games and a 90-ft-long pitch-black maze you crawl through.

The Sarasota Area

Known for its plentiful, clean beaches and profusion of golf courses, the Sarasota area, south of Tampa Bay via U.S. 41 or U.S. 301, is also a growing cultural center and winter home of the Ringling Brothers Barnum & Bailey Circus. Midway between Tampa and Sarasota, the low-key beach city of Bradenton is the site of **De Soto National Memorial** (⊠ 75th St. NW, ☎ 941/792–0458; ⊡ free), where costumed guides recount Spanish conquistador Hernando de Soto's 16th-century landing and expedition. Near Bradenton is **Gamble Plantation and Confederate Memorial State Historical Site** (⊠ 3708 Patten Ave., Ellenton, ☎ 941/723–4536; ⊡ $3), the only surviving pre–Civil War plantation house in South Florida.

★ In the smart resort city of Sarasota you'll find the **Ringling Museums** (⊠ ½ mi south of Sarasota-Bradenton Airport on U.S. 41, ☎ 941/359–5700, ⊡ $8.50), which include the Venetian-style mansion of circus magnate John Ringling, his art museum with its collection of Rubens paintings, and a circus museum. The **Marie Selby Botanical Gardens** (⊠ 811 S. Palm Ave., ☎ 941/366–5730; ⊡ $7) has world-class orchid displays as well as a small museum of botany and art, all contained in a restored mansion on the grounds. Kids enjoy the bird and reptile shows at **Sarasota Jungle Gardens** (⊠ 3701 Bayshore Rd., ☎ 941/355–5305; ⊡ $9). A petting zoo and a museum displaying seashells and butterflies are also here. For a good beach escape head for the barrier island of **Siesta Key,** across the water from Sarasota. To reach Siesta Key, take U.S. 41 south from southern Sarasota to either Siesta Drive or Stickney Point Road, both of which lead west to the island.

The Fort Myers/Naples Area

The bustle of commercially oriented Fort Myers gives way to the relaxed atmosphere of the Gulf communities elsewhere in growing Lee County. Beach lovers head for the resort islands of Estero (popular with young singles); Captiva and Sanibel; and the Lover's Key State Recreation Area—all of which are known for superb shelling and fishing. Most of the beautiful residences here are hidden by Australian pines, but the beaches and tranquil Gulf waters are readily accessible.

Fort Myers is a small inland city; although it's a half hour from the nearest beach, its downtown business district overlooks the broad, flat Caloosahatchee River. One of the most scenic stretches of highway in southeastern Florida, **McGregor Boulevard** is framed by hundreds of towering palms. Fort Myers's premier attraction, **Thomas A. Edison's Winter Home** (⊠ 2350 McGregor Blvd., ☎ 941/334–3614; ⊡ $12, including access to Mangoes), on a 14-acre estate, houses Edison's laboratory and a museum devoted to his inventions. Next door is **Mangoes,** the winter house of the inventor's longtime friend, automaker Henry Ford.

The refined city of **Naples** is fast becoming Florida's west-coast version of Palm Beach, with excellent beaches and golf courses, luxury high-rise condos, and several upscale shopping and dining districts. About 30 mi northeast of Naples you can return to Florida's unspoiled past at the **Corkscrew Swamp Sanctuary** (⊠ 16 mi east of I–75 on Rte. 846, ☎ 941/ 348–9151; ⊡ $8), an 11,000-acre tract that the National Audubon Society set aside to protect 500-year-old trees and endangered birds.

Dining and Lodging

Around **Tampa** the ethnic diversity of the region makes for some adventurous dining, from honey-soaked Greek baklava to Cuban saffron rice casserole. A generous mix of roadside motels, historic hotels, and sprawling resorts can be found here.

Raw bars and seafood restaurants are everywhere in and around **Sarasota.** Tamiami Trail (U.S. 41), which traverses the region, is lined with inexpensive motels, while the islands have more expensive resort complexes and high-rise hotels.

In **Fort Myers** and **Naples,** seafood reigns supreme. A particular treat is a succulent claw of the native stone crab, usually served with drawn butter or a tangy mustard sauce; stone crabs are in season mid-October–mid-May. It's hard to find restaurants on Sanibel and Captiva islands that aren't expensive. For budget options (both dining and lodging) you'll have better luck in Fort Myers and Naples along the Tamiami Trail.

Bradenton

$$–$$$ 🏨 **Holiday Inn Riverfront.** Suites overlook a courtyard at this Spanish-style motor inn near the Manatee River. Rooms, with burgundy carpeting and mahogany furnishings, are a bit dark, but a third have river views. ⊠ *100 Riverfront Dr. W, 34205,* ☎ *941/747–3727,* ℻ *941/746–4289. 153 rooms. Restaurant, pool, exercise room. AE, DC, MC, V.* ♻

Captiva

$$$$ 🏨 **South Seas Plantation Resort and Yacht Harbor.** More neighborhood
★   than resort, this busy 330-acre property has many styles of accommodations, among them harborside villas, Gulf cottages, and private homes. Activities include sailing, shelling, and strolling on the 2½ mi of beach and landscaped grounds. There are 18 swimming pools on the grounds. ⊠ *South Seas Plantation Rd., 33924,* ☎ *941/472–5111 or 800/227–8482,* ℻ *941/472–7541. 620 units. 4 restaurants, 18 pools, golf, tennis, exercise room. AE, DC, MC, V.*

Fort Myers and Fort Myers Beach

$$$–$$$$ ✕ **Peter's La Cuisine.** Smack in the middle of downtown Fort Myers,
★   two blocks off the river, is this charming restaurant in a restored brick building. The dining room's extra-high ceiling gives a spacious feel, and exposed brick walls, dim lighting, and a refined atmosphere provide a pleasant background for Continental cuisine with a twist. After dinner wander upstairs for a cordial and some great blues. ⊠ *2224 Bay St.,* ☎ *941/332–2228. AE, MC, V. No lunch weekends.*

$$–$$$$ ✕ **Prawnbroker Restaurant and Fish Market.** This popular restaurant has an abundance of seafood and shellfish seemingly just plucked from Gulf waters, plus some selections for culinary landlubbers. It's almost always crowded—and for good reason. ⊠ *13451 McGregor Blvd.,* ☎ *941/489–2226. AE, MC, V. No lunch.*

$$–$$$ ✕ **Snug Harbor.** This harbor-front restaurant serves absolutely fresh seafood—courtesy of the restaurant's private fishing fleet—in a casual,

rustic atmosphere. ⊠ *645 San Carlos Blvd., Fort Myers Beach,* ☎ *941/463–4343. Reservations not accepted. AE, MC, V.*

$$–$$$ 🏨 **Amtel Marina Hotel & Suites.** This modern, 25-story high-rise has a commanding position in the downtown skyline, rising above the river and yacht basin. Rooms have panoramic views of the water and the city. ⊠ *2500 Edwards Dr., Fort Myers 33901,* ☎ *941/337–0300 or 800/833–1620,* FAX *941/479–4180. 427 rooms. Restaurant, pool, tennis, exercise room. AE, DC, MC, V.*

$$–$$$ 🏨 **Outrigger Beach Resort.** This informal, family-oriented resort is set on a wide beach overlooking the Gulf of Mexico. There's a broad deck for sunning, plus tiki huts to sit under when you want to escape from the heat, and a beachfront pool. ⊠ *6200 Estero Blvd., Fort Myers Beach 33931,* ☎ *941/463–3131 or 800/749–3131,* FAX *941/463–6577. 144 units. Pool. MC, V.* ✦

Naples

$$–$$$ ✕ **Bistro 821.** The decor for this trendy restaurant is spare and sophisticated. Entrées include marinated leg of lamb with basil mashed potatoes, snapper baked in parchment, wild mushroom pasta, vodka penne, risotto, and a seasonal vegetable plate. ⊠ *821 5th Ave. S,* ☎ *941/261–5821. Reservations essential. AE, DC, MC, V. No lunch.*

St. Petersburg Beach

$$$$ 🏨 **Don CeSar Beach Resort.** Still echoing with the ghosts of Scott and
★ Zelda Fitzgerald, this sprawling beachfront "Pink Palace" has long been a Gulf Coast landmark. Turn-of-the-20th-century elegance abounds, and service is first-rate. You can indulge in various treatments and sea scrubs at the beach spa. ⊠ *3400 Gulf Blvd., 33706,* ☎ *727/360–1881,* FAX *813/367–3609. 295 rooms. 3 restaurants, 2 pools, tennis, exercise room. AE, DC, MC, V.* ✦

Sarasota

$$$–$$$$ ✕ **Cafe L'Europe.** This art-filled café is on fashionable St. Armand's Cir-
★ cle, on Lido Key. The menu may include such dishes as Wiener schnitzel sautéed in butter and topped with anchovies, olives, and capers, or Dover sole served with fruit. ⊠ *431 St. Armand's Circle,* ☎ *941/388–4415. AE, DC, MC, V.*

$$$ 🏨 **Hyatt Sarasota.** This contemporary hotel is ideally located, near the city center and the major art and entertainment venues. The spacious rooms overlook Sarasota Bay or the marina. ⊠ *1000 Blvd. of the Arts, 34236,* ☎ *941/953–1234,* FAX *941/952–1987. 297 rooms. 2 restaurants, pool, health club. AE, DC, MC, V.* ✦

Siesta Key

$$–$$$ ✕ **Ophelia's on the Bay.** Sample mussel soup, eggplant crepes, chicken potpie, seafood linguine, or cioppino, among other eclectic dishes, at this waterfront restaurant. ⊠ *9105 Midnight Pass Rd.,* ☎ *941/349–2212. AE, D, DC, MC, V. No lunch.*

Tampa

$$$–$$$$ ✕ **Bern's Steak House.** This nationally known steak house has more
★ than just steak. Organically grown vegetables from the owner's farm are the specialty here, and scrumptious desserts are served upstairs in intimate glass-enclosed rooms. ⊠ *1208 S. Howard Ave.,* ☎ *813/251–2421. AE, DC, MC, V. No lunch.*

$$–$$$ ✕ **Columbia.** An institution in Ybor City since 1905, this light and spacious Spanish restaurant serves excellent paella, with some flamenco dancing on the side. ⊠ *2117 E. 7th Ave.,* ☎ *813/248–4961. AE, DC, MC, V.*

$$ 🏨 **Holiday Inn Busch Gardens.** This well-maintained motor lodge is just 1 mi west of Busch Gardens. Rooms are bright and spacious;

some look out on a central courtyard. ⊠ *2701 E. Fowler Ave., 33612,* ☎ *813/971–4710 or 800/206–2747,* FAX *813/977–0155. 402 rooms. Restaurant, pool, exercise room. AE, DC, MC, V.* 🍃

Tarpon Springs

$–$$$ ✕ **Louis Pappas' Riverside Restaurant.** This waterfront landmark is always crowded with diners savoring the fine Greek fare, including moussaka, Greek meatballs, and *spanakopita* (white cheese and spinach baked into phyllo pastry). ⊠ *10 W. Dodecanese Blvd.,* ☎ *727/937–5101. AE, DC, MC, V. No lunch Sun.*

Nightlife and the Arts

The region between Tampa and Sarasota hums with cultural activities. Professional theater, dance, and music events are presented at **Tampa Bay Performing Arts Center** (⊠ 1010 W. C. MacInnes Pl., Tampa, ☎ 813/229–7827 or 800/955–1045) and **Ruth Eckerd Hall** (⊠ 1111 McMullen Booth Rd., Clearwater, ☎ 727/791–7400). Broadway touring companies of plays, concerts, dance, ice-skating, and other shows are held at Sarasota's **Van Wezel Performing Arts Hall** (⊠ 777 N. Tamiami Trail, Sarasota, ☎ 941/953–3366). Other major venues in the city are the **Florida West Coast Symphony Center** (⊠ 709 N. Tamiami Trail, ☎ 941/953–4252), the **Sarasota Opera** (⊠ Opera House, 61 N. Pineapple Ave., ☎ 941/953–7030), and the **Asolo Center for the Performing Arts** (⊠ 5555 N. Tamiami Trail, ☎ 941/351–8000).

The **Naples Philharmonic Center for the Arts** (⊠ 5833 Pelican Bay Blvd., ☎ 941/597–1111) presents plays, concerts, and art exhibits.

Outdoor Activities and Sports

Biking

Sanibel Island has the best biking in the region, with extensive paths along the waterways and through wildlife refuges. On Sanibel you can rent bicycles by the hour at **Bike Route** (⊠ 2330 Palm Ridge Rd., ☎ 941/472–1955).

Boating and Sailing

Sailing is popular on the calm bays and Gulf waters. Sailing schools include **Seacoast Yacht Charters** (⊠ Port Sanibel Yacht Club, South Fort Myers, ☎ 941/540–8050). For powerboat rentals contact **Boat House of Sanibel** (⊠ Sanibel Marina, 634 N. Yachtman Dr., ☎ 941/472–2531). **Jensen's Marina** (⊠ Captiva, ☎ 941/472–5800) rents little powerboats perfect for fishing and shelling.

Canoeing

Canoeists can explore many waterways here, including those at **Myakka River State Park** (⊠ Rte. 72, 15 mi south of Sarasota, ☎ 941/365–0100). **Tarpon Bay Marina** (⊠ 900 Tarpon Bay Rd., Sanibel, ☎ 941/472–8900) has canoes and equipment for exploring the waters of the J. N. "Ding" Darling National Wildlife Refuge. With several locations throughout Florida, **Canoe Outpost** offers canoe and camping trips on the Little Manatee River (⊠ 18001 U.S. 301S, Wimauma, 20 mi southeast of Tampa, ☎ 813/634–2228) and the Peace River (⊠ Rte. 7, Arcadia, ☎ 941/494–1215).

Fishing

The Tampa Bay area and Fort Myers are major fishing centers. Speckled trout and kingfish are often caught in the Tampa Bay inlets. Deep-sea fishing enthusiasts can charter boats or join a party boat to catch tarpon, marlin, grouper, redfish, and shark. Charter outfitters include **Florida Deep Sea Fishing** (⊠ 60 Corey Ave., St. Petersburg Beach, ☎

727/360–2082). Fishing is popular in Sanibel. Call **Captain Pat Lovetro** (✉ Sanibel Marina, 634 N. Yachtman Dr., ☎ 941/472–2723) for half-day, six-hour, and full-day trips.

Golf

Championship and other courses abound here. All of these have 18 holes: **Babe Zaharias Golf Course** (✉ 11412 Forest Hills Dr., Tampa, ☎ 813/932–8932); **Lely Flamingo Island Club** (✉ 8004 Lely Resort Blvd., Naples, ☎ 941/793–2223); the **Fort Myers Country Club** (✉ 3591 McGregor Blvd., Fort Myers, ☎ 941/936–2457); **Resort at Longboat Key Club** (✉ 301 Gulf of Mexico Dr., Longboat Key, ☎ 941/383–8821); **Pelican's Nest Golf Course** (✉ 4450 Pelican's Nest Dr. SW, Bonita Springs, ☎ 941/947–4600); and the **Dunes** (✉ 949 Sandcastle Rd., Sanibel, ☎ 941/472–2535).

Spectator Sports

Baseball: Tampa Bay Devil Rays (✉ Tropicana Field, 1 Tropicana Dr., ☎ 727/825–3120). **Football: Tampa Bay Buccaneers** (✉ Tampa Stadium, 4201 N. Dale Mabry Hwy., ☎ 813/870–2700 or 800/282–0683), August–December. **Hockey: Tampa Bay Lightning** (✉ 401 Channelside Dr., ☎ 813/229–2658). **Horse Racing: Tampa Bay Downs** (✉ Race Track Rd., off Rte. 580, Oldsmar, ☎ 813/855–4401), Thoroughbred races from mid-December to early May.

Beaches

The waters of the Gulf of Mexico tend to be cloudy, so snorkeling and diving are best on the Atlantic side of the state. The southwestern beaches are good for shelling and sunbathing on quiet stretches of sand. Sunsets are spectacular here.

In the Bradenton area the **Manatee County Beach,** on Anna Maria Island, has picnic facilities, a snack bar, showers, lifeguards, and rest rooms. **Estero Island (Fort Myers Beach),** 18 mi from downtown Fort Myers, attracts families and young singles; hotels, restaurants, and condominiums run its length. The island's shores slope gradually into the usually tranquil and warm Gulf waters. Along Gulf Shore Boulevard in Naples, **Lowdermilk Park** has 1,000 ft of beach, picnic tables, showers, rest rooms, and a pavilion with vending machines.

In the St. Petersburg area the 900-acre **Fort De Soto Park** encompasses six islands. Its 7 mi of beaches include two fishing piers, picnic sites, and a waterskiing and boating area. **Old Lighthouse Beach,** at the southern end of Sanibel Island, attracts a mix of singles, families, and shellers. Beautiful **Siesta Beach,** on Siesta Key near Sarasota, features a concession stand, picnic areas, nature trails, and facilities for soccer, softball, volleyball, and tennis. **Caspersen Beach,** on Beach Drive in South Venice, is one of the county's largest parks. Beachcombers find lots of shells and sharks' teeth here.

Shopping

Seven blocks of fine shops and restaurants line Tampa's Swan Avenue in **Old Hyde Park Village** (☎ 813/251–3500). If you're looking for Cuban cigars, try **Ybor City** on Tampa's east side. In Pinellas Park **Wagonwheel** (✉ 7801 Park Blvd., ☎ 727/544–5319) is a weekend flea market with about 2,000 vendors. For unique gifts, shop for natural sponges on **Dodecanese Boulevard** in Tarpon Springs.

Art lovers can browse through the art galleries on **Main Street** and **Palm Avenue** in downtown Sarasota. A British telephone booth or an Australian boomerang is available for a price at the unique shops of Harding Circle on fashionable **St. Armand's Circle,** west of downtown Sarasota across the Ringling Causeway.

For a great display of shells, coral, and jewelry, visit the **Shell Factory** (⊠ 2787 N. Tamiami Trail, North Fort Myers, ☎ 888/995–2141). For boutiques selling resort wear, designer fashions, and jewelry, try the **Royal Palm Square** area (⊠ Colonial Blvd., between McGregor Blvd. and U.S. 41) in Fort Myers. The largest shopping area in Naples is **Old Naples,** an eight-block area bordered by Broad Avenue on the north and 4th Street South on the east. The classy **Village on Venetian Bay** (⊠ 4200 Gulf Shore Blvd.) has more than 60 shops and restaurants built over the bay. The **Waterside Shops** (⊠ Seagate Dr. and U.S. 41), known by locals as Bell Tower because of its landmark bell tower, are anchored by a Saks Fifth Avenue and a Jacobson's department store and house 50 shops and several noteworthy eating spots.

THE GOLD AND TREASURE COASTS

The Gold Coast exudes wealth and opulence, but it's also steeped in natural beauty. Once famous as a spring-break haven for the college crowd, Fort Lauderdale now attracts families by offering a variety of recreational, sports, cultural, and historical activities. Farther north is the international high-society resort of Palm Beach, with its elegant mansions and world-class shopping. Following downtown Fort Lauderdale's lead, West Palm Beach is trying to renew itself through a combination of governmental efforts and the arts to become the hub of Palm Beach County and the Treasure Coast. Inland about 50 mi is 448,000-acre Lake Okeechobee, noted for catfish, bass, and perch fishing. Heading north from West Palm Beach to Sebastian Inlet, the Treasure Coast offers barrier islands, beaches, and sea-turtle havens to the east and citrus groves and cattle ranches to the west.

Visitor Information

Greater Fort Lauderdale: Convention & Visitors Bureau (⊠ 1850 Eller Dr., Suite 303, 33301, ☎ 954/765–4466). **Palm Beach County:** Convention & Visitors Bureau (⊠ 1555 Palm Beach Lakes Blvd., Suite 204, West Palm Beach 33401, ☎ 561/471–3995 or 800/833–5733); Chamber of Commerce of the Palm Beaches (⊠ 401 N. Flagler Dr., West Palm Beach 33401, ☎ 561/833–3711).

Arriving and Departing

By Bus

Greyhound (☎ 800/231–2222) stops in Fort Lauderdale and West Palm Beach, and **Broward Transit** (☎ 954/357–8400) serves the surrounding county. **CoTran** buses (☎ 561/233–1111) ply the Greater Palm Beach area.

By Car

Two major north–south routes, I–95 and U.S. 1, connect the region with Miami to the south and Jacksonville to the north. Alligator Alley (I–75) runs east–west from Fort Lauderdale to Naples. Florida's Turnpike is a less congested and less direct route from Orlando to the Gold and Treasure Coasts.

The four-lane route Okeechobee Boulevard (Route 704) carries traffic from west of downtown West Palm Beach, near the Amtrak station in the airport district, directly into Palm Beach. Plans are under way to turn Flagler Drive pedestrian-only in the next several years.

By Plane

Major foreign and domestic carriers serve the **Fort Lauderdale–Hollywood International Airport** (⊠ 4 mi south of downtown Fort Lauderdale off U.S. 1, ☎ 954/359–6100) and **Palm Beach International Airport** (⊠ Congress Ave. and Belvedere Rd., West Palm Beach, ☎ 561/471–7400).

By Train

Amtrak (☎ 800/872–7245) provides daily service to Fort Lauderdale, Hollywood, and Deerfield Beach in Broward County and to West Palm Beach.

Exploring the Gold and Treasure Coasts

Fort Lauderdale and Palm Beach dazzle with their fabulous homes and pricey shops, shimmering beaches, plentiful sports activities, first-class museums, and cultural events. North of Palm Beach are the Treasure Coast's 70 mi of soothing sand, sea, and nature refuges.

Don't miss a visit to the splendidly redesigned **Fort Lauderdale beachfront,** along Route A1A. The beach side remains open and uncluttered, and trendy shops and restaurants (plus a mix of new and dated hotels) line the opposite side of the street. From the beach, picturesque **Las Olas Boulevard** takes you inland through the Isles, where expensive homes line canals dotted with yachts. After this the boulevard becomes an upscale shopping street, with Spanish colonial buildings housing boutiques and galleries. The **Museum of Art** (⊠ 1 E. Las Olas Blvd., ☎ 954/763–6464; ☞ $10; closed Mon.) has an extensive early 20th-century European and American art collection.

Palm-lined **Riverwalk,** which begins around U.S. 1 south of Broward Boulevard, is a lovely paved promenade with fine shops, restaurants, popular nightspots, and views of New River. Riverwalk leads into the city's newly burgeoning **Arts and Science District,** which has spawned a slew of new shops, restaurants, and entertainment venues in the heart of downtown. The top attraction in the Arts and Science District is the **Museum of Discovery and Science** (⊠ 401 S.W. 2nd St., ☎ 954/467–6637 for museum; 954/463–4629 for IMAX, ☞ museum $6, IMAX $9, both $12.50), with an IMAX theater and interactive exhibits on ecology, health, and outer space. For an interesting side trip, head south a few miles to the **Seminole Native Village** (⊠ 3551 N. Rte. 7, Hollywood, ☎ 954/961–4519; ☞ self-guided tour $5, guided tour including alligator wrestling and snake demonstrations $10; closed Mon.), a reservation where you can pet a cougar, hold a baby alligator, and watch other wildlife demonstrations. The Seminole Indians also sell their arts and crafts.

★

As you travel north from Fort Lauderdale along U.S. 1, pause to admire the 1920s Spanish-style architecture in affluent **Boca Raton.** In the posh island community of **Palm Beach,** you can rub shoulders with the rich and famous as you stroll along the 12-mi-long island's **Worth Avenue,** one of the world's premier shopping streets. To recapture the glitter and flamboyance of Florida's boom years, when railroad magnate Henry M. Flagler first established Palm Beach as a playground for the wealthy, visit his ornate hotel, the **Breakers,** a legendary bastion of wealth and privilege (☞ Dining and Lodging, *below*). Henry Flagler's palatial 73-room Whitehall Mansion, known as the **Henry Morrison Flagler Museum** (⊠ 1 Whitehall Way, ☎ 561/655–2833; ☞ $7, closed Mon.), contains original furnishings and an art collection.

After visiting Palm Beach, take a drive past the secluded mansions along **County Road** and around the northern tip of the island. Directly across the Fort Worth inlet from Palm Beach is the rapidly gentrifying mainland city of **West Palm Beach.** Long considered Palm Beach's impov-

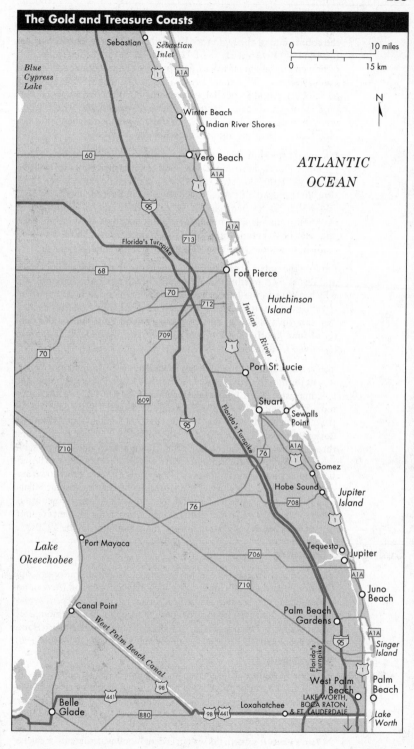

The Gold and Treasure Coasts

erished cousin, West Palm is now economically vibrant in its own right—it's become the cultural, entertainment, and business center of the county and of the region to the north. The **Norton Museum of Art** (⊠ 1451 S. Olive St., ☎ 561/832–5194; ⊠ $6) has a fine collection of French Impressionist works. Southwest of West Palm Beach, at **Lion Country Safari** (⊠ Southern Blvd. W [U.S. 98], ☎ 561/793–1084; ⊠ $15.50, van rental $6 per hr), you can drive (with car windows closed) on 8 mi of paved roads through a 500-acre cageless zoo where 1,000 wild animals roam free. Lions, giraffes, zebras, ostriches, and elephants are among the animals in residence.

It's an abrupt shift from the man-made world of Palm Beach into primitive Florida at **Arthur R. Marshall Loxahatchee National Wildlife Refuge** (⊠ 10119 Lee Rd., off U.S. 441 between Boynton Beach Blvd. [Rte. 804] and Atlantic Ave. [Rte. 806], west of Boynton Beach, ☎ 561/734–8303; ⊠ $5 per vehicle, $1 per pedestrian), a wilderness of marshes, wetlands, and bountiful wildlife south of West Palm Beach and west of Boynton Beach. Stroll the nature trails, fish for bass and panfish, or paddle your own canoe through the waterways.

Explore the upper Treasure Coast at a leisurely pace by taking U.S. 1 and Route A1A north from West Palm Beach along the Indian River, which separates the barrier islands from the mainland. Of major interest from April to August are the sea turtles that nest on the beaches. You can learn about the turtles at **Loggerhead Park Marine Life Center of Juno Beach.** ⊠ *1200 U.S. 1,* ☎ *561/627–8280.* ⊠ *Donations welcome. Closed Mon.*

You can drive through sand dunes at **Jupiter,** on the Intracoastal Waterway at the mouth of the scenic Loxahatchee River. Pause to photograph the impressive 105-ft **Jupiter Inlet Lighthouse** (⊠ Rte. 707 to Captain Armour's Way, ☎ 561/747–8380; ⊠ tour $5; closed Thurs.–Sat.), one of the oldest lighthouses on the Atlantic coast. At Jupiter Island's **Blowing Rocks Preserve** (⊠ Rte. 707, ☎ 561/575–2297), water sprays burst through holes in the shore's limestone facade at high tide. The preserve is home to large bird communities and a wealth of plants native to beachfront dune, marsh, and hammock. The revival of historic downtown **Stuart** (⊠ at the St. Lucie Inlet) is transforming this onetime fishing village into a magnet for people who want to live and work in a small-town atmosphere. About 30 mi farther north along the coast, the affluent community of **Vero Beach** has elegant houses, many dating from the 1920s.

Dining and Lodging

The Gold and Treasure coasts have a mix of American, European, and Caribbean cuisines, all emphasizing local fish and seafood. Accommodations are expensive in the Palm Beach area, but many inexpensive motels line U.S. 1 and the major exits of I–95 throughout the region. B&B accommodations are popular in Palm Beach County; contact **Open House Bed & Breakfast** (⊠ Box 3025, Palm Beach 33480, ☎ 561/842–5190).

Boca Raton

$$$–$$$$ ✗ **La Vieille Maison.** Closets transformed into private dining nooks are
★ part of the charm of this 1920s home turned elegant French restaurant serving such dishes as venison chop with red currant–pepper sauce and roasted chestnuts. ⊠ *770 E. Palmetto Park Rd.,* ☎ *561/391–6701. AE, D, DC, MC, V. Closed early July–Aug.*

$ ✗ **Tom's Place.** It's worth the wait in line for mouthwatering ribs or chicken in homemade barbecue sauce and the sweet-potato pie in this casual, family-run eatery. ⊠ *7251 N. Federal Hwy.,* ☎ *561/997–0920. Reservations not accepted. MC, V. Closed Sun., also Mon. May–mid-Nov.*

Fort Lauderdale

$$$–$$$$ ✕ **Burt & Jack's.** This local favorite—operated by veteran restaurateur Jack Jackson and actor Burt Reynolds since 1984—offers seafood, steaks, and chops, and scenic views of Port Everglades. ✉ *Berth 23, Port Everglades,* ☎ *954/522–2878 or 954/525–5225. AE, D, DC, MC, V. No lunch.*

$$ ✕ **Shirttail Charlie's.** After dining on crab balls or coconut shrimp with piña colada sauce on the outdoor deck or in the upstairs dining room of this 1920s-style restaurant, enjoy a free cruise on the New River. ✉ *400 S.W. 3rd Ave.,* ☎ *954/463–3474. AE, D, MC, V.*

$$$ 🏨 **Riverside Hotel.** This 1936 hotel amid the upscale shops on Las Olas Boulevard has an attentive staff, murals by well-known artist Bob Jenny (one of which stretches across 725 square ft of the building's facade), and antique oak furnishings in the guest rooms. ✉ *620 E. Las Olas Blvd., 33301,* ☎ *954/467–0671 or 800/325–3280,* ℻ *954/462–2148. 110 rooms. 2 restaurants, pool. AE, DC, MC, V.*

Hutchinson Island

$$$$ ✕🏨 **Indian River Plantation Marriott Beach Resort.** This luxury resort on 200 island acres evokes a Victorian seaside ambience with its latticework trim, tin roofs, and cool verandas. Feast on steak Diane or fresh snapper at the intimate Inlet Restaurant ($$–$$$$), or try the Sunday champagne brunch at Scalawags. ✉ *555 N.E. Ocean Blvd., Stuart 34996,* ☎ *561/225–3700 or 800/775–5936,* ℻ *561/225–0003. 476 units. 5 restaurants, pool, tennis. AE, DC, MC, V.* ♨

Palm Beach

$$–$$$$ ✕ **Ta-boo.** Dressed in gorgeous pinks, greens, and florals, the spaces of
★ this Worth Avenue landmark are divided into discreet salons: One resembles a courtyard, another an elegant living room with a fireplace, and a third a skylighted gazebo. Expect eclectic fare including chicken and arugula from the grill, prime rib, steaks, frogs' legs, main-course salads, and pizzas. ✉ *221 Worth Ave.,* ☎ *561/835–3500. AE, DC, MC, V.*

$$$$ ✕🏨 **The Breakers.** Dating from 1926 and enlarged in 1969, this op-
★ ulent Italian Renaissance–style resort sprawls over 140 splendidly manicured acres. Cupids frolic in the Florentine fountain at the main entrance, while majestic ceiling vaults and frescoes grace the lobby. A recent $100 million renovation included the construction of the fabulous Spa and Beach Club. You can dine on Continental specialties such as herb-crusted rack of lamb in the hotel's tapestry-filled Florentine Dining Room. ✉ *1 S. County Rd., 33480,* ☎ *561/655–6611 or 800/833–3141,* ℻ *561/659–8403. 620 rooms. 5 restaurants, pool, tennis, health club. AE, D, DC, MC, V.* ♨

$$–$$$ 🏨 **Palm Beach Hawaiian Ocean Inn.** Families gravitate to this casual, two-story resort, which is reasonably priced and right on the beach. Large rooms and spacious suites face tropical gardens or look out to the ocean and are simply but adequately furnished and have bedspreads and draperies in colorful striped pastels. ✉ *3550 S. Ocean Blvd., 33480,* ☎ ℻ *561/582–5631. 58 rooms. Restaurant, pool. D, MC, V.* ♨

Spas

Fort Lauderdale

$$$–$$$$ 🏨 **Wyndham Resort & Spa Fort Lauderdale.** The resort's spacious rooms have tropical decor and balconies overlooking a lake or a golf course. Menus follow the nutritional guidelines of the American Heart Association and the American Cancer Society. Fitness programs are available, and the resort offers combination spa-tennis and spa-golf packages. ✉ *250 Racquet Club Rd., 33326,* ☎ *954/389–3300 or 800/327–8090,* ℻ *954/384–0563. 496 units. 4 restaurants, 5 pools, golf, tennis, health club. AE, D, MC, V.* ♨

$$–$$$$ 🏨 **Palm-Aire Spa Resort.** This 750-acre resort has both a luxurious resort hotel and a spa complex that promotes physical fitness and stress reduction. Large guest rooms have separate dressing rooms and private terraces. Guests can play 94 holes of golf. ✉ *2601 Palm-Aire Dr. N, Pompano Beach 33069,* ☎ *954/972–3300 or 888/266–3287. 204 units. Restaurant, pool, tennis, exercise room. AE, D, MC, V.*

Palm Beach

$$$$ 🏨 **PGA National Resort & Spa.** At this sybaritic getaway where golf and tennis pros exercise during tournaments, the spa facilities include the signature mineral pools with salts from around the world. Choose from large guest rooms with tropical decor or cottage units with two bedrooms and a kitchen. ✉ *400 Ave. of the Champions, Palm Beach Gardens 33418,* ☎ *561/627–2000 or 800/633–9150,* ℻ *561/622–0261. 419 units. 4 restaurants, 9 pools, tennis, exercise room. AE, D, DC, MC, V.* ✍

Nightlife and the Arts

Fort Lauderdale and the Palm Beach area offer a full roster of performing arts events. Major venues include **Broward Center for the Performing Arts** (✉ 201 S.W. 5th Ave., Fort Lauderdale, ☎ 954/462–0222) and **Raymond F. Kravis Center for the Performing Arts** (✉ 701 Okeechobee Blvd., ☎ 561/832–7469), the cultural center of Palm Beach. Many of the cultural events in Vero Beach take place at the **Center for the Arts** (✉ 3001 Riverside Park Dr., ☎ 561/231–6990). Fort Lauderdale has the liveliest nightlife, with comedy clubs, discos, and clubs featuring music for all ages and tastes; popular ones include **Baja Beach Club** (✉ 3339 N. Federal Hwy., ☎ 954/563–7889), with karaoke and performing bartenders, and **O'Hara's Pub & Sidewalk Cafe** (✉ 722 E. Las Olas Blvd., ☎ 954/524–1764), which has nightly live jazz and blues.

Outdoor Activities and Sports

Biking

The beautiful **Palm Beach Bicycle Trail** runs for 10 mi along the shoreline of Lake Worth. For bike rentals try **Palm Beach Bicycle Trail Shop** (✉ 223 Sunrise Ave., ☎ 561/659–4583). In Fort Lauderdale, some of the most popular routes are along A1A—the beach road. For bike rentals, contact the **International Bicycle and Skate Shop** (✉ 1900 E. Sunrise Blvd., ☎ 954/792–2298).

Diving

A popular place to dive is the 23-mi-long, 2-mi-wide **Fort Lauderdale Reef,** one of 80 dive sites in Broward County. Palm Beach County offers excellent drift diving and anchor diving off the Atlantic coast. Try **Pro Dive** (✉ Radisson Bahia Mar Beach Resort, 801 Seabreeze Blvd., Fort Lauderdale, ☎ 954/761–3413 or 800/772–3483) for diving equipment and packages.

Fishing

Anglers can deep-sea or freshwater fish year-round. Pompano, amberjack, and snapper are caught off the numerous piers and bridges, while Lake Okeechobee yields bass and perch. Sailfish are a popular catch on deep-sea charters, offered at **Hillsboro Inlet Marina** (✉ 2629 N. Riverside Dr., Pompano Beach, ☎ 954/943–8222) and **B-Love Fleet** (✉ 314 E. Ocean Ave., Lantana, ☎ 561/588–7612).

Golf

Among the 50-plus golf courses in Greater Fort Lauderdale is **Colony West Country Club** (✉ 6800 N.W. 88th Ave., Tamarac, ☎ 954/726–8430). The **Breakers Hotel Golf Club** (✉ 1 S. County Rd., ☎ 561/655–6611 or 800/833–3141) has 36 holes. **Palm Beach Par 3** (✉ 2345 S.

Ocean Blvd., ☎ 561/547–0598) has 18 holes, including 4 on the Atlantic and three on the inland waterway.

Spectator Sports

Horse Racing: Gulfstream Park Race Track (✉ 901 S. Federal Hwy., Hallandale, ☎ 954/454–7000), January–mid-March. **Pompano Harness Track** (✉ 1800 Race Track Rd., Pompano Beach, ☎ 954/972–2000), Monday and Wednesday–Saturday, October–August.

Polo: Palm Beach Polo and Country Club (✉ 13198 Forest Hill Blvd., West Palm Beach, ☎ 561/793–1440) has games on Sunday, January–April.

Beaches

Crystal-clear warm waters are the main draw of the miles of beaches along the Atlantic coast. Each coastal town has a public beach area; many, like **Pompano Beach** and **Deerfield Beach,** have fishing piers. The area is popular with snorkelers and divers.

The **beachfront,** along Route A1A between Las Olas Boulevard and Sunrise Boulevard in Fort Lauderdale, is a very popular beach; shops, restaurants, and hotels line the road. In Dania the **John U. Lloyd Beach State Recreation Area** (✉ 6503 N. Ocean Dr., ☎ 954/923–2833), the locals' favorite, is a fine beach with picnicking, fishing, and canoeing facilities and 251 acres of mangroves to explore. **Bathtub Beach,** on Hutchinson Island north of Jupiter, has placid waters and a gentle sea slope, making it ideal for children.

Shopping

Both Palm Beach and Fort Lauderdale have shopping districts that cater to an upscale clientele. In Fort Lauderdale expensive boutiques are clustered along tree-lined **Las Olas Boulevard.** In Palm Beach more than 250 specialty shops and pricey boutiques, with such famous names as Gucci and Cartier, beckon to well-heeled shoppers along **Worth Avenue.** A few miles west of Fort Lauderdale, bargain shoppers flock to **Sawgrass Mills Mall** (✉ 12801 W. Sunrise Blvd., at Flamingo Rd., Sunrise), which has 270 stores.

ELSEWHERE IN FLORIDA

Everglades and Biscayne National Parks

Arriving and Departing

Miami International Airport (☞ Miami, *above*) is about 35 mi from Homestead and Florida City, gateways to the national parks. Traveling south by car, use Florida's Turnpike or Routes 826 and 874 and the Florida's Turnpike Extension to reach the gateway towns.

What to See and Do

★ **Everglades National Park** (✉ Main Visitor Center, 40001 Rte. 9336, Homestead 33034, ☎ 305/242–7700), the country's largest remaining subtropical wilderness, contains more than 1.4 million acres—half land, half water—that can be explored by boat, by bike, on foot, and partly by car. This slow-moving "river of grass" is a maze of saw-grass marshes, mangrove swamps, salt prairies, and pinelands that shelter a variety of plants and animals, even though increased pollution by pesticide runoff from local farms has reduced the number of birds and brought the Florida panther to near extinction. The visitor center is superb; the three park entrances are in Homestead, along U.S. 41 (Tamiami Trail), and, on the west coast of Florida, in Everglades City.

Biscayne National Park (⊠ 9700 S.W. 328th St., Box 1369, Homestead 33090, ☎ 305/230–7275) is the nation's largest marine park and the largest national park with a living coral reef in the continental United States. It covers about 274 square mi, mostly underwater, and has several ecosystems. Shallow Biscayne Bay is home to the manatee, the upper Florida Keys harbor moray eels, and brilliantly colored parrot fish in a 150-mi coral reef, and bald eagles and other large birds inhabit the mainland mangrove forests. A visitor center with interactive exhibits, a glass-bottom-boat tour, canoeing, snorkeling, and scuba diving are popular ways to experience the park.

The Panhandle: Northwestern Florida

Visitor Information

Destin: Chamber of Commerce (⊠ 1021 U.S. 98E, Destin 32541, ☎ 850/837–6241 or 850/837–0087). **Emerald Coast:** Convention & Visitors Bureau (⊠ 1540 Miracle Strip Pkwy. SE, Fort Walton Beach 32549, ☎ 850/651–7122 or 800/322–3319). **Panama City Beach:** Convention & Visitors Bureau (⊠ 12015 W. Front Beach Rd., Panama City Beach 32407, ☎ 850/233–6503 or 800/722–3224). **Pensacola:** Visitor Information Center (⊠ 1401 E. Gregory St., Pensacola 32501, ☎ 850/434–1234 or 800/874–1234).

Arriving and Departing

Pensacola Regional Airport (☎ 850/435–1746) serves the region. I–10 and U.S. 90 are the main east–west highways across the top of the state, U.S. 98 runs along the coast, and U.S. 231, 331, and 29 and Route 85 traverse the Panhandle north–south.

What to See and Do

The Panhandle, in Florida's northwest corner, stretches between the Gulf of Mexico and the Alabama and Georgia state lines. This area is lush with thick pine forests, magnolias, live oaks draped in Spanish moss, and pristine rivers and lakes more common to the Deep South than Florida. Dubbed the Emerald Coast due to the color of the Gulf's blue-green emerald water and the snow-white beaches, the region draws visitors with its historical and archaeological sites, golf, hiking, water sports, and outstanding fishing.

Stroll through the historic districts of **Pensacola** and absorb some of the city's colorful Spanish, French, British, and Civil War past. **Fort Walton Beach** is a family vacation playground famous for its beaches and spectacular sand dunes. **Eglin Air Force Base** (⊠ Rte. 85, ☎ 850/882–3931), in Fort Walton Beach, includes 10 auxiliary fields and a total of 21 runways. Visitors can tour the base and the **Airforce Armament Museum,** which contains vintage aircraft, guns, and other weapons. Kids especially enjoy the **Indian Temple Mound Museum** (⊠ 139 Miracle Strip Pkwy. [U.S. 98], Fort Walton Beach, ☎ 850/833–9595), where they can learn all about the prehistoric peoples who lived in the region during the past 10,000 years.

Destin, Fort Walton Beach's neighbor, a once-quiet fishing village, has developed into a bustling seaside vacation spot popular with anglers, sun worshipers, and gourmets and offers some of the area's finest restaurants. Just east of Destin are the quiet, family-friendly **Beaches of South Walton** including **Grayton Beach State Recreation Area** (⊠ Rte. 30A), near the quaint, Victorian-style community of Seaside, which has one of the most scenic beaches along the Gulf Coast, if not the country.

For sun-up until sun-down action, head for the snow-white beaches, miles of waterways, and amusement parks of **Panama City Beach,** a prime vacation area and *the* spot for students on spring break.

Northeastern Florida

Visitor Information

Amelia Island–Fernandina Beach: Chamber of Commerce (✉ 102 Centre St., Fernandina Beach 32034, ☎ 904/261–3248). **Daytona:** Destination Daytona! (✉ 126 E. Orange Ave., 32120, ☎ 904/255–0415 or 800/854–1234). **Jacksonville and its beaches:** Convention and Visitors Bureau (✉ 6 E. Bay St., Suite 200, 32202, ☎ 904/798–9111). **St. Augustine:** Visitor Information Center (✉ 10 Castillo Dr., 32084, ☎ 800/653–2489).

Arriving and Departing

Jacksonville International Airport (☎ 904/741–4902) and **Daytona Beach International Airport** (☎ 904/248–8069) serve the region. I–10 is the major east–west artery through the north, and I–4 from Tampa and Orlando enters the region to the south, near Daytona Beach. The primary north–south routes are I–95 along the east coast and I–75 through the center of the state.

What to See and Do

Variety is the key word for northeastern Florida: You can see live-oak-framed roads and plantations that recall the Old South all along St. Johns River; Thoroughbred horse farms in Ocala; impressive savannas in Gainesville; and the cosmopolitan city of Jacksonville. The beaches range from rocky shorelines to the glistening sand beaches of Jacksonville and the famous hard-packed, drivable beach at Daytona. The **Daytona 500** auto race is held annually in February at Daytona International Speedway (✉ U.S. 92, ☎ 904/254–2700). Jacksonville is the host of collegiate football's New Year's Day **Gator Bowl** (☎ 904/396–1800).

St. Augustine, the oldest permanent settlement in the United States, dates to 1565. Explore the 300-year-old Spanish fortress of **Castillo de San Marcos National Monument** (✉ 1 Castillo Dr., ☎ 904/829–6506; ⊠ $4), which guards Matanzas Bay. Stroll down St. George Street through St. Augustine's restored **Spanish Quarter** for a glimpse of life in the 1700s. Drink from the spring reputed to be the fountain of youth discovered by Ponce de León in 1513 at the **Fountain of Youth Archaeological Park** (✉ 155 Magnolia Ave., ☎ 904/829–3168; ⊠ $5.50).

Silver Springs (✉ Rte. 40, 1 mi east of Ocala, ☎ 352/236–2121; ⊠ $26.95), the state's oldest attraction and the world's largest formation of clear artesian springs, offers glass-bottom-boat tours and a jungle cruise.

Amelia Island, just north of Jacksonville, contains the historic town of Fernandina Beach, with its 19th-century mansions and many posh resorts. North of Fernandina Beach lies 1,086-acre **Fort Clinch State Park** (✉ N. 14th St., ☎ 904/277–7274; ⊠ $3.25 per vehicle), with a brick fort, nature trails, swimming, and living history reenactments.

GEORGIA

Updated by
Michael P.
Hagearty

Capital	Atlanta
Population	7,788,240
Motto	Wisdom, Justice, and Moderation
State Bird	Brown thrasher
State Flower	Cherokee rose
Postal Abbreviation	GA

Statewide Visitor Information

Georgia Department of Industry, Trade and Tourism (✉ Box 1776, Atlanta 30301, ☎ 404/656–3590 or 800/847–4842). There are 11 **visitor centers** at various border points and 45 locally operated **welcome centers** in Atlanta, Savannah, and throughout the state.

Scenic Drives

Along the coast Jekyll Island's **North Riverview Drive** passes scenery ranging from historic homes in the Jekyll Island Historic District to glimpses of marshland. **Route 157** north from Cloudland Canyon State Park to the Tennessee border at Lookout Mountain has views of northwestern Georgia's mountains. **U.S. 76** east from Dalton to the Chattooga River traverses the North Georgia mountains.

National and State Parks

National Parks

The **Andersonville National Historic Site** (✉ Georgia Hwy. 49N [Rte. 1, Box 800], Andersonville 31711, ☎ 912/924–0343; ▦ free), formerly a Confederate prison camp, is now the site of the National Prisoner of War Museum. **Chattahoochee River National Recreation Area** (✉ 1978 Island Ford Pkwy., Dunwoody 30350, ☎ 770/399–8070; ▦ $2 parking fee) has picnic areas, hiking trails, and rivers with swimming areas. **Kennesaw Mountain National Battlefield** (✉ 900 Kennesaw Mountain Dr., Kennesaw 30152, ☎ 770/427–4686; ▦ free), a 2,884-acre park outside Atlanta, commemorates one of the Civil War's most decisive battles and has 16 mi of hiking trails.

State Parks

Georgia's state parks charge $2 per day per vehicle for all-day parking passes. **Cloudland Canyon State Park** (✉ 122 Cloudland Canyon Park Rd., Rising Fawn 30738, ☎ 706/657–4050), on the west side of Lookout Mountain in the state's northwest corner, has cabin facilities, camping, and dramatic scenery. **Vogel State Park** (✉ 7485 Vogel State Park Rd., Blairsville 30512, ☎ 706/745–2628), a 280-acre park surrounded by the Chattahoochee National Forest, includes a 22-acre lake. The park has cottages and campsites. **Providence Canyon** (✉ Rte. 1, Box 158, Lumpkin 31815, ☎ 912/838–6202), known as Georgia's Grand Canyon, is a day park for picnicking, exploring, and hiking.

ATLANTA

Atlanta is one of the fastest-growing cities in the United States, with a skyline that is constantly changing. Initially founded as a railroad center, the city has blossomed into a major metropolis with more than 3 million people. It is an aviation hub and a regional leader in commerce and industry. You can still feel the buzz that came to Atlanta when it hosted the 1996 Summer Olympic Games. But for all its modernity, the city's winning character is defined by its southern hospitality and its near-picture-perfect residential neighborhoods.

Visitor Information

Atlanta Chamber of Commerce (⊠ 235 International Blvd., 30303, ☎ 404/880–9000). **Convention and Visitors Bureau visitor centers** (⊠ Peachtree Center Mall, 233 Peachtree St., 30303, ☎ 404/222–6688 or 800/285–2682; Underground Atlanta, 65 Upper Alabama St., ☎ 404/577–2148; Georgia World Congress Center, 285 International Blvd., 30313, ☎ 404/233–4017; Hartsfield International Airport, North Terminal at West Crossover, 30320, ☎ 404/305–8426; Lenox Square, 3393 Peachtree Rd., 30324, ☎ 404/266–1398).

Arriving and Departing

By Bus

Greyhound (⊠ 232 Forsyth St., ☎ 404/584–1731 or 800/231–2222) provides transportation to downtown Atlanta, Decatur, Hapeville, Marietta, Conyers, Douglasville, and Norcross.

By Car

Atlanta is called the Crossroads of the South for good reason. Between South Carolina and Alabama, I–85 runs northeast–southwest through Atlanta and I–20 runs east–west; I–75 runs north–south through the state. I–285 makes a 65-mi loop around the metro area. If driving from I–75 north to Decatur, use I–675 to connect to I–285 on the east side of the metro Atlanta area.

By Plane

Hartsfield Atlanta International Airport (⊠ 6000 N. Terminal Pkwy., 30320, ☎ 404/530–6600) has scheduled flights by most major domestic and foreign carriers. Cab fare to downtown Atlanta, 13 mi north of the airport via I–75 and I–85, is about $18 for one person, $20 for two people, and $8 each additional for three or more. From the airport, the **MARTA** (☎ 404/848–4711) rapid-rail subway system is one of the quickest and easiest ways to reach many areas including downtown.

By Train

Amtrak (☎ 404/881–3060 or 800/872–7245) serves Brookwood Station (⊠ 1688 Peachtree St.).

Getting Around Atlanta

By Car

Major public parking lots downtown are at the **CNN Center** (⊠ entrance off Techwood Dr.), the **Georgia World Congress Center** (⊠ off International Blvd.), **Peachtree Center** (☞ Exploring Atlanta, *below*), **Macy's** (⊠ Carnegie Way, 1 block off Peachtree St.), and **Underground Atlanta** (⊠ 65 Upper Alabama St.). Buckhead and Midtown have on-street parking and more lots.

By Public Transportation

MARTA (☎ 404/848–4711) operates buses and a modern rapid-rail subway system. Fare for either is $1.50; exact change or a token is required. The rapid-rail trains operate weekdays every 8–10 minutes from 5 AM to 1 AM and weekends from 6 AM to 12:30 AM. Bus schedules depend on the route. Information is available in five languages.

By Taxi

You can hail a cab fairly easily at hotels in the downtown or Buckhead district. **Buckhead Safety Cab** (☎ 404/233–1152 or 404/233–1153) and **Checker Cab** (☎ 404/351–1111) have 24-hour service. With advance reservations, **Carey Executive Limousine** (☎ 404/223–2000 or 800/241–3943) also provides 24-hour service.

Orientation Tours

Bus and Van Tours

Atlanta Discovery Tours (☎ 770/667–1414) and **American Sightseeing Atlanta** (☎ 404/233–9140 or 800/572–3050) pick you up at area hotels for customized sightseeing tours. **Gray Line of Atlanta** (⊠ 705 Lively Ave., Norcross 30071, ☎ 770/449–1806 or 800/593–1818, ℻ 770/246–9397) offers tours of downtown, Midtown, Buckhead, and the King Center.

Walking Tours

Atlanta Preservation Center (⊠ Suite 3, 156 7th St., ☎ 404/876–2041; 404/876–2040 for tour hot line; ☜ $5) has guided tours of 10 historic neighborhoods, from March through November, and a tour of the Fox Theatre that's available year-round.

Exploring Atlanta

Because Atlanta is a sprawling city, a car is a necessity, though there are a number of walkable neighborhoods and districts with interesting architecture and attractions. Beginning downtown, you can move north past an eclectic mix of Renaissance Revival towers and contemporary skyscrapers; through Midtown's genteel, garden-filled neighborhoods punctuated by parks and museums; and into upscale Buckhead, lined with mansions and glitzy shopping centers.

Downtown

Atlanta had its inauspicious beginning as a 19th-century settlement and later became a railway hub; a few sites from the earliest days are preserved downtown. A three-level, six-block entertainment and shopping center called **Underground Atlanta** (⊠ 50 Upper Alabama St., ☎ 404/523–2311) encompasses some of the original city center's 19th-century storefronts and streets. The **World of Coca-Cola** (⊠ 55 Martin Luther King Jr. Dr., ☎ 404/676–5151; ☜ $6) gives free samples and has three floors of memorabilia from the two-centuries-old soft drink company.

At the corner of Marietta Street and Techwood Drive is the **CNN Center** (⊠ 1 CNN Center, ☎ 404/827–2300; ☜ $8), headquarters of Cable News Network. There are daily guided behind-the-scenes tours, including newscasters in action. Children under six are not admitted to the tours.

Thrusting into the sky a block north of Woodruff Park are the striking angles of the red-marble **Georgia-Pacific Building** (⊠ 133 Peachtree St., at John Wesley Dobbs Ave.). Built between 1979 and 1982 on the site of Loew's Grand Theatre, where *Gone With the Wind* premiered in 1939, the 50-story corporate flagship building houses the **High Museum of Folk Art and Photography Galleries** (⊠ 30 John Wesley Dobbs Ave., ☎ 404/577–6940; ☜ free), a branch of the High Museum of Art (☞ Midtown, *below*).

★ Walking tours of the **Martin Luther King, Jr., National Historic District** start from the **King Center** (⊠ 449 Auburn Ave., ☎ 404/526–890, ☜ free), established by King's widow, Coretta Scott King. Inside the center there's a museum, a library, and a gift shop; King's tomb is marked by an eternal flame.

The Queen Anne–style clapboard house that was **Dr. King's Birth Home** (⊠ 501 Auburn Ave., ☎ 404/331–3920; ☜ free) is open for tours. Three generations of the King family have preached at **Ebenezer Baptist Church** (⊠ 407 Auburn Ave., ☎ 404/688–7263; ☜ free).

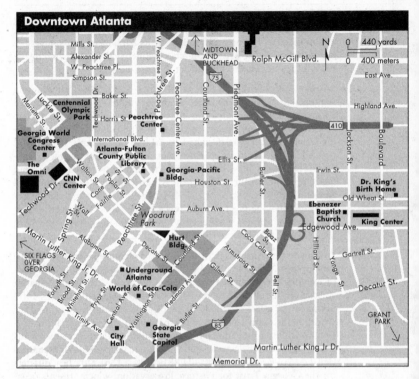

Downtown Atlanta

The **Georgia State Capitol** (⊠ Washington St. at Martin Luther King Jr. Dr., ☎ 404/656–2844; ☞ free) houses government offices and a museum. Built in 1889, it has a dome gilded with gold leaf from ore mined in nearby Dahlonega. The capitol building is now under extensive renovation. After years of restoration, the **Georgia Capitol Museum** is scheduled to welcome exhibits on the history of the Capitol Building back to its galleries in early 2001.

Atlantan John Portman designed the **Peachtree Center** (☎ 404/524–3787), built between 1960 and 1992. The climate-controlled complex, filled with shops, restaurants, hotels, and offices, is on the city's main thoroughfare, **Peachtree Street.** In the lobby of the center's Marriott Marquis Two Tower is the **Atlanta International Museum of Art, Design and Culture** (⊠ 285 Peachtree Center Ave., ☎ 404/688–2467; ☞ free), which specializes in international art and design.

★ ☾ In Grant Park, 2 mi southeast of downtown, is the unique **Atlanta Cyclorama** (⊠ Grant Park, 800 Cherokee Ave., ☎ 404/624–1071 for tickets; 404/658–7625 for information; ☞ $5), designed in 1921 by John Francis Downing. Within its walls hangs a huge circular painting that depicts the Battle of Atlanta (1864), when the city was burned by General William T. Sherman.

☾ **Six Flags over Georgia** (⊠ I–20 at 7561 Six Flags Rd., Austell, ☎ 770/739–3400; ☞ $37, $18.50 if under 48″ tall), a large theme park 10 mi west of downtown, has dozens of rides (including roller coasters and water rides), musical revues, and concerts. It is closed from November through February.

Midtown

Midtown, just north of downtown, was the heart of Atlanta's hippie scene during the 1960s and early '70s and now is the city's primary art and theater district and the home of a large segment of Atlanta's gay population, as well as young families, young professionals, artists, and musicians. The area is popular for its bars, restaurants, and specialty shops. Like downtown, it has a distinctive skyline created by the many office towers erected during the past decade.

☺ **SciTrek** (✉ 395 Piedmont Ave., ☎ 404/522–5500; 🎟 $7.50) is among the top science museums in the country, with hands-on exhibits and Kidspace, a special area for two- to seven-year-olds. The Egyptian-style **Fox Theatre** (✉ 660 Peachtree St., ☎ 404/881–2100), the city's oldest movie palace, was designed by Marye, Alger, and Vinour and opened in 1929. It hosts splashy events ranging from touring companies of Broadway plays to rock concerts; tours are offered year-round (☞ Orientation Tours, *above*). In Midtown, the **Margaret Mitchell House** (✉ 990 Peachtree St., ☎ 404/249–7012; 🎟 $10), the thrice-renovated (having been torched twice by arsonists) apartment building in which Margaret Mitchell wrote her famous novel *Gone With the Wind,* pays tribute to the famous Georgia author.

Designed by architect Richard Meier, the **High Museum of Art** (✉ 1280 Peachtree St., ☎ 404/733–4444; 🎟 $6) showcases a major collection of American contemporary and decorative art as well as sub-Saharan African art. It's closed Monday. The **Center for Puppetry Arts** (✉ 1404 Spring St., ☎ 404/873–3391; 🎟 $8) displays puppets from around the world, holds puppet-making workshops, and stages original productions for children and adults. It's closed Sunday. Atlanta architect Willis Denny's impressive Romanesque Victorian mansion, **Rhodes Memorial Hall** (✉ 1516 Peachtree St., ☎ 404/881–9980; 🎟 $5), is the headquarters for the **Georgia Trust for Historic Preservation,** which presents occasional traveling exhibits on Georgia architecture. The **Fernbank Science Center** (✉ 156 Heaton Park Dr., ☎ 404/378–4311; 🎟 free, planetarium shows $2), with an *Apollo* spacecraft and a planetarium, is in Druid Hills, a tree-lined neighborhood just north of Ponce de Leon Avenue.

Buckhead

Buckhead, 5 mi north of Midtown on Peachtree Street, is to Atlanta what Beverly Hills is to Los Angeles. This residential and shopping area is home to fine dining, designer boutiques, and expensive homes. To see the manicured lawns and mansions of Atlanta's elite, take a scenic drive along Tuxedo, Valley, and Habersham roads.

The white-columned, neoclassical **Georgia Governor's Mansion** (✉ 391 W. Paces Ferry Rd., ☎ 404/261–1858; 🎟 free) has many Federal-period antiques; it's open for tours Tuesday through Thursday. The **Atlanta History Center** (✉ 130 W. Paces Ferry Rd., ☎ 404/814–4000; 🎟 $10)—comprising the **Atlanta History Museum,** the **Tullie Smith Farm** (🎟 $1), the neoclassic **Swan House** mansion (🎟 $2), and **McElreath Hall**—is a 33-acre forested and garden-filled site.

Parks, Gardens, and Zoos

☺ **Zoo Atlanta** (✉ 800 Cherokee Ave., ☎ 404/624–5600; 🎟 $12) is in Grant Park, just southeast of downtown. Nearly 1,000 animals live here in naturalistic habitats, including the newest main attraction—two giant pandas.

Near the CNN Center, **Centennial Olympic Park** (✉ Marietta St. and Techwood Dr.), a legacy of the 1996 Centennial Olympic Games, enhances the streetscape with green space and sculpture. The fountains are especially popular for cooling off during the late summer heat. **Piedmont Park,** in Midtown between 10th Street and the Prado, is the city's premier urban green space, with paved paths for biking, running, and roller skating. You can rent bikes and in-line skates from **Skate Escape** (⊠ 1086 Piedmont Ave., ☎ 404/892–1292), across the street.

🕭 Adjoining Piedmont Park is the 30-acre **Atlanta Botanical Garden** (⊠ 1345 Piedmont Ave., ½ mi north of 14th St., ☎ 404/876–5859; 🎫 $7, free Thurs. after 3 PM), with landscaped gardens and the climate-controlled Fuqua Conservatory. Exhibits are closed Monday.

🕭 **Stone Mountain Park** (⊠ U.S. 78, ☎ 770/498–5690; 🎫 $6 parking, additional fees for individual attractions and special events), 7 mi northeast of the city, features the world's largest sculpture, a memorial to Confederate heroes Jefferson Davis, Robert E. Lee, and Stonewall Jackson (a cable car takes you 825 ft up the mountain face for a closer look). The 3,200-acre park contains an antebellum plantation and museums, plus a railroad, a riverboat, and nightly laser shows in summer.

Dining

Atlanta prides itself on a wide selection of international restaurants but has plenty of places to sample the traditional and new-style fare of the Deep South.

$$$$ ✕ **Bacchanalia.** The best ingredients from America's farms are used
★ to craft a unique cuisine. Savor such dishes as foie gras with nectarines, dates with cheese, and salmon with green lentils. The imaginative vegetable tasting menu is outstanding. ⊠ *1198 Howell Mill Rd.,* ☎ *404/365–0410. Reservations essential. AE, DC, MC, V. Closed Sun. and Mon. No lunch.*

$$$$ ✕ **The Dining Room, the Ritz-Carlton, Buckhead.** French basics are
★ deftly blended with Asian techniques and ingredients. Thai soup with crab roll and fresh coriander appears on the table next to a plate of fromage blanc with cucumber gelée. The fare changes daily, but the best deal is the tasting menu ($82). ⊠ *3434 Peachtree Rd.,* ☎ *404/ 237–2700. Reservations essential. Jacket and tie. AE, D, DC, MC, V. Closed Sun. No lunch.*

$$$$ ✕ **Seeger's.** The roulade of foie gras with onion marmalade and puree
★ of red wine, apple, and quince is characteristic of the restaurant. Local ingredients also appear, as in grilled lamb chops with Vidalia onions. Fixed-price menus (including a vegetable menu) may be paired with selected wines for an additional charge. ⊠ *111 W. Paces Ferry Rd.,* ☎ *404/846–9779. Reservations essential. Jacket and tie. AE, D, DC, MC, V. Closed Sun. No lunch*

$$$–$$$$ ✕ **The Atlanta Fish Market.** It's busy and it's noisy, but there is no better seafood in the local area. An intimidating menu is made simple by the quick and knowledgeable wait staff, but many still choose the simpler favorites like the clam and cod chowder or the shrimp and scallops en brochette. ⊠ *265 Pharr Rd.,* ☎ *404/262–3165. AE, D, DC, MC, V. No lunch Sun.*

$$$–$$$$ ✕ **Le Saint Amour.** The flavors and colors of Provence make a gastronomic and cultural statement in this freestanding house in Midtown. What could be more transporting than a terrine of foie gras with redwine–onion compote or a fish soup with garlic and grated cheese? ⊠ *1620 Piedmont Ave.,* ☎ *404/881–0300. Reservations essential. AE, D, DC, MC, V. No lunch Sat.*

$$–$$$$ ✕ **City Grill.** The grand setting of this restaurant in the historic Hurt Building includes high ceilings and romantic table lamps. The menu is American with a southern flair as seen in such dishes as Creole barbecued shrimp and hickory-grilled pork fillet with Tennessee whiskey sauce. Save room for the chocolate pecan soufflé. ⊠ *50 Hurt Plaza,* ☎ *404/524–2489. AE, D, DC, MC, V. Closed Sun. No lunch Sat.*

$$–$$$$ ✕ **South City Kitchen.** The cuisine at this bright, popular restaurant is the traditional Low Country style of coastal South Carolina and Georgia. The she-crab soup, crab hash with poached eggs, buttermilk fried chicken, and chocolate pecan pie are all superb. ⊠ *1144 Crescent Ave.,* ☎ *404/873–7358. AE, DC, MC, V.*

$$–$$$ ✕ **Luna Si.** Funky meets uptown chic at this delightfully relaxed loft restaurant. The menu, which changes weekly, is dominated by seafood. Signature dishes include salmon with a ginger crust and roasted chicken with mashed potatoes. ⊠ *1931 Peachtree Rd.,* ☎ *404/355–5993. AE, DC, MC, V. Reservations essential.*

$–$$$ ✕ **Colonnade Restaurant.** For traditional southern cuisine, such as
★ oyster stew, Parker House rolls, crab cakes, and ham steak, insiders head for the Colonnade, an Atlanta institution since 1927. ⊠ *1879 Cheshire Bridge Rd.,* ☎ *404/874–5642. Reservations not accepted. No credit cards.*

$ ✕ **Thelma's Kitchen.** Thelma Grundy's down-home self-service restaurant on the street level of a somewhat renovated Roxy Hotel has some of the best southern food in town. Unique okra pancakes are not to be missed. Fried catfish, "cold" slaw, macaroni and cheese, and pecan pie are all special. ⊠ *768 Marietta St. NW,* ☎ *404/688–5855. Reservations not accepted. No credit cards. Closed weekends. No dinner.*

Lodging

The city's booming convention business means hotel and motel options in all price ranges. The downtown, Buckhead, and north I–285 areas have the greatest concentration of accommodations.

$$$$ 🏨 **Four Seasons Hotel.** A sweeping staircase at the entrance leads up to a welcoming, refined bar with cozy seating and Park 75, the hotel's fine restaurant. Rooms have marble bathrooms, brass chandeliers, and data ports. ⊠ *75 14th St., 30309,* ☎ *404/881–9898,* FAX *404/873–4692. 246 rooms. Restaurant, pool, health club. AE, D, DC, MC, V.* ⊛

$$$$ 🏨 **Ritz-Carlton, Buckhead.** The elegant lobby with fine art, a fireplace,
★ and comfortable, authentic antique furniture is perfect for lingering over afternoon tea before returning to rooms containing luxury linens, marble baths, and reproduction period furnishings. ⊠ *3434 Peachtree Rd., 30326,* ☎ *404/237–2700,* FAX *404/239–0078. 553 rooms. 2 restaurants, pool, health club. AE, D, DC, MC, V.* ⊛

$$$–$$$$ 🏨 **Atlanta Marriott Marquis.** The lobby of this convention hotel stretches to the skylighted roof 50 stories above. Traditionally furnished guest rooms open onto this central atrium. A skywalk connects the hotel to the Peachtree Center and its shops. ⊠ *265 Peachtree Center Ave., 30303,* ☎ *404/521–0000,* FAX *404/586–6299. 1,675 rooms. 5 restaurants, 2 pools, health club. AE, D, DC, MC, V.* ⊛

$$$–$$$$ 🏨 **JW Marriott.** Handsome Chippendale-style furniture graces both the lobby and the guest rooms of this elegant 25-story hotel, which connects with Lenox Square mall. Some rooms also have spacious marble baths with separate shower stalls. ⊠ *3300 Lenox Rd., 30326,* ☎ *404/262–3344,* FAX *404/262–8689. 371 rooms. Restaurant, pool, health club. AE, D, DC, MC, V.* ⊛

$$$–$$$$ 🏨 **Swissôtel.** An international clientele frequents this European-style luxury hotel, with its chic, modern glass exterior; sophisticated Biedermeier-style interiors; and fabulous art on view in the public spaces. Palm, an outpost of the popular Manhattan restaurant of the same name, is famous for its steaks. ⊠ *3391 Peachtree Rd., 30326,* ☎ *404/365–0065 or 800/253–1397,* FAX *404/365–8787. 365 rooms. Restaurant, pool, health club. AE, D, DC, MC, V.* ⊛

$$$ 🏨 **Embassy Suites.** This Buckhead high-rise is just blocks from two of the city's top shopping centers, Phipps Plaza and Lenox Square (☞

Shopping, *below*). Suites range from basic bedroom and sitting-room combinations to luxurious rooms with wet bars. All units have microwaves and refrigerators. ⊠ *3285 Peachtree Rd., 30305,* ☎ *404/261–7733,* 🖷 *404/261–6857. 317 suites. Restaurant, pool. AE, D, DC, MC, V. BP.* ☻

$$$ 🏨 **Sierra Suites Atlanta Brookhaven.** Studio-style suites with kitchens are decorated in earth tones and forest green. Light wood modern-style furniture with an oak finish is standard. This place, just north of Buckhead, is a good value. ⊠ *3967 Peachtree Rd., 30319,* ☎ *404/237–9100,* 🖷 *404/237–0055. 92 suites. Pool. AE, D, DC, MC, V. CP.* ☻

$$ 🏨 **Quality Hotel Downtown.** Rooms in this quiet hotel have views of downtown; some have balconies. The marble lobby is lit by crystal chandeliers, and modest-size rooms are done in teal and navy. ⊠ *89 Luckie St., 30303,* ☎ *404/524–7991,* 🖷 *404/524–0672. 89 rooms. Pool. AE, DC, MC, V. BP.*

Nightlife and the Arts

Arts and nightlife events are listed in the *Atlanta Journal and Constitution* and *Creative Loafing* newspapers, as well as *Symbol,* the *Season, WHERE ATLANTA,* and *KNOW ATLANTA* magazines, available at visitor information centers and in hotels. Ticket brokers include **Ticketmaster** (☎ 404/249–6400 or 800/326–4000) and **Ticket-X-Press** (☎ 404/231–5888).

Nightlife

Buckhead, Virginia-Highland, East Atlanta, and **Little Five Points** neighborhoods are Atlanta's nightlife centers. Virginia-Highland's **Atkins Park Bar & Grill** (⊠ 794 N. Highland Ave., ☎ 404/876–7249), one of the city's oldest neighborhood bars, attracts a 30-something crowd. The venerable **Blind Willie's** (⊠ 828 N. Highland Ave., ☎ 404/873–2583) offers New Orleans– and Chicago-style blues. **Eddie's Attic** (⊠ 515B N. McDonough St., ☎ 404/377–4976), next to the MARTA station in nearby Decatur, is the best venue for local acoustic acts. For contemporary rock try **Echo Lounge** (⊠ 551 Flat Shoals Ave., ☎ 404/681–3600) or the **EARL** (⊠ 488 Flat Shoals Ave., ☎ 404/522–3950). **Backstreet** (⊠ 845 Peachtree St., ☎ 404/873–1986), drawing both men and women, has been Midtown's mainstay gay club for nearly two decades. But nongay couples often enjoy the all-hours club as well.

In Buckhead, Latin music invites dancing Thursday to Saturday night at **Sanctuary** (⊠ 128 E. Andrews Dr., ☎ 404/262–1377) and **Havana Club** (⊠ East Village Square, 247 Buckhead Ave., ☎ 404/869–8484). At **Churchill Arms** (⊠ 3223 Cain Hill Pl., ☎ 404/233–5633) folks of all ages gather to shoot pool, sing old-time songs, and listen to live piano music. **Tongue & Groove** (⊠ 3055 Peachtree Rd., ☎ 404/261–2325) is Buckhead's see-and-be-seen nightspot. **Sambuca Jazz Cafe** (⊠ 3102 Piedmont Rd., ☎ 404/237–5299) attracts a chic young set to its decent table dining, lively bar, and good live jazz.

The Arts

Most touring **Broadway productions** make their way to Atlanta's **Fox Theatre** (☞ Midtown *in* Exploring Atlanta, *above*) or the **Civic Center** (⊠ 395 Piedmont Ave., ☎ 404/523–6275). The **Alliance Theater Company** (⊠ 1280 Peachtree St., ☎ 404/733–5000) is one of the city's leading theatrical groups. Woodruff Arts Center's **Symphony Hall** (⊠ 1280 Peachtree St., ☎ 404/733–5000) is the home of the **Atlanta Symphony Orchestra.** The **Atlanta Ballet Company** (☎ 404/892–3303) performs at the Fox Theatre. In summer the **Atlanta Opera** (☎ 404/881–8801) usually presents four operas at the Fox Theatre.

Outdoor Activities and Sports

Golf

The only public course near downtown, **Bobby Jones Golf Course** (⊠ 384 Woodward Way, ☎ 404/355–1009) has some of the city's worst fairways and greens; still, the 18-hole, par-71 course is always crowded. The **Alfred Tup Holmes Club** (⊠ 2300 Wilson Dr., ☎ 404/753–6158), with 18 par-72 holes, is known for doglegs and blind shots. With 18 holes, the par-71 **North Fulton Golf Course** (⊠ 216 W. Wieuca Rd., ☎ 404/255–0723) in Chastain Park has one of the best layouts in the city. Outside I–285, in the suburbs, **Stone Mountain Park** (⊠ U.S. 78, ☎ 770/498–5715) offers two courses: Stonemont, an 18-hole, par-71 course; and par-70 Lakemont, with 18 holes.

Tennis

Bitsy Grant Tennis Center (⊠ 2125 Northside Dr., ☎ 404/609–7193) has 13 clay courts, 6 of which are lighted, and 10 lighted hard courts; it's the area's best public facility. **Piedmont Park** (⊠ Piedmont Ave. between 10th St. and the Prado, ☎ 404/853–3461) has 12 hard courts with lights. Access the tennis center from Park Drive off Monroe Drive; even though the sign reads DO NOT ENTER, the security guard will show you the parking lot.

Spectator Sports

Tickets for the teams listed below are available through **Ticketmaster** (☎ 800/326–4000).

Baseball: Atlanta Braves (⊠ Turner Field, 755 Hank Aaron Dr., ☎ 404/522–7630). **Basketball: Atlanta Hawks** (⊠ Philips Arena, 1 Philips Dr., ☎ 404/827–3865). **Football: Atlanta Falcons** (⊠ Georgia Dome, 1 Georgia Dome Dr., ☎ 404/223–8000). **Hockey: Atlanta Thrashers** (⊠ Philips Arena, 1 Philips Dr., ☎ 404/584–7825).

Shopping

Antiques Stores

Shops selling antique pine pieces, collectibles, and crafts line **Bennett Street** in Buckhead. European furnishings and fine art are offered in more than 25 shops in Buckhead's **2300 Peachtree Road** complex. **Miami Circle,** a street on the northern edge of Buckhead off Piedmont Road, is a hot spot for lovers of antiques, with such stores as **Gables Antiques** (⊠ 711 Miami Circle, ☎ 404/231–0734) and **Williams Antiques** (⊠ 699 Miami Circle, ☎ 404/231–9818). **Chamblee Antique Row** (⊠ turn east at the intersection of Broad St. and Peachtree Industrial Blvd., Chamblee, ☎ 770/458–1614) has more than 200 dealers in its numerous antiques stores and malls.

Shopping Districts

Atlanta's shopping centers are generally open Monday through Saturday 10 to 6 and Sunday noon to 5; many stay open until 9 or 9:30 several weeknights and most weekends. The primary downtown shopping areas are **Underground Atlanta,** where specialty boutiques, chain stores, and pushcarts mix with restaurants and nightclubs; and the stretch of Peachtree between **Macy's** and **Peachtree Center Mall.** North of downtown in Buckhead, **Lenox Square** (⊠ 3393 Peachtree St.) and **Phipps Plaza** (⊠ 3500 Peachtree Rd.) attract shoppers from throughout the Southeast. Lenox's second level has more than 250 stores, while Phipps's now has more than 100 stores. **Perimeter Mall** (⊠ 4400 Ashford-Dunwoody Rd., Dunwoody) serves the Dunwoody area, and **Cumberland Mall** (⊠ I–285 at Cobb Pkwy.) and **Galleria** (⊠ 1 Galleria Pkwy.) are the most convenient to I–75/I–285.

SAVANNAH

Four hours southeast of Atlanta, but a world away from the bustling, modern metropolis, lies Savannah, wrapped in a mantle of Old World grace. Established in 1733, the city preserves its heritage in a 2½-square-mi historic district, the nation's largest urban landmark. Here 1,000 structures have been restored, and families still live in the 19th-century mansions and town houses. Known as the City of Festivals, Savannah rarely lets a weekend pass without some sort of celebration, from the St. Patrick's Day bash in March and the Riverfront Seafood Festival in April to the spring azalea and dogwood festivals to the house tours and concerts at Christmas.

Visitor Information

Convention and Visitors Bureau (⊠ 101 E. Bay St., 31402, ☎ 877/728-2662). **Visitors Center** (⊠ 301 Martin Luther King Jr. Blvd., 31401, ☎ 912/944-0455).

Arriving and Departing

By Bus
Greyhound (⊠ 610 W. Oglethorpe Ave., ☎ 912/232-2135 or 800/231-2222).

By Car
I-95, running north-south along the coast, and I-16, leading east from Macon, intersect west of Savannah; I-16 dead-ends in downtown. The Coastal Highway (U.S. 17) runs north-south through town, and U.S. 80 runs east-west.

By Plane
Savannah International Airport (⊠ 400 Airways Ave., 31408, ☎ 912/964-0514) served by major airlines, is 18 mi west of town on I-16. There is no bus service into town, but **McCall's Shuttle** (☎ 912/966-5364) runs a van between the airport and the city for $16 per person one-way.

By Train
The **Amtrak** station (⊠ 2611 Seaboard Coastline Dr., ☎ 912/234-2611 or 800/872-7245) is 4 mi southwest of downtown.

Getting Around Savannah

Savannah's historic district is best seen on foot as you can better observe the intricate architectural details. It's laid out in a grid pattern, and strategically placed benches allow for frequent rests. If you bring a car, park it in one of the metered and off-street pay lots.

Exploring Savannah

A good way to start a tour is by picking up information at the **Visitors Center** (☞ Visitor Information, *above*) in the old Central Georgia railway station. For entertainment of every sort, visit the restored **City Market** (⊠ W. St. Julian St. between Ellis and Franklin Sqs.), a four-block area of shops, art galleries, restaurants, and music venues. Near the riverfront, narrow cobblestone streets wind from Bay Street down to Factors Walk and, below, to River Street and the **River Front** district, a nine-block area with shops, restaurants, taverns, and some wonderfully restored old buildings. The **Ships of the Sea Museum** (⊠ 41 Martin Luther King Jr. Blvd., ☎ 912/232-1511; ☜ $5) displays memorabilia ranging from models of the earliest ships and nuclear submarines to nautical folk art. This William Jay–designed building dates to 1819.

Savannah

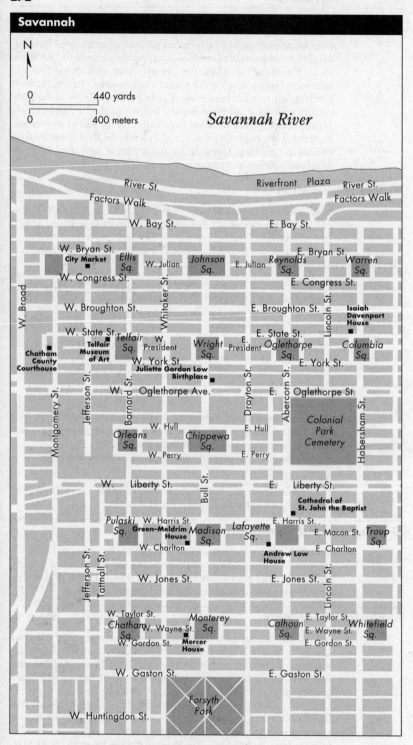

N

0 ———— 440 yards
0 ———— 400 meters

Savannah River

River St.
Factors Walk
Riverfront Plaza
River St.
Factors Walk

W. Bay St.
E. Bay St.

W. Bryan St.
City Market
Ellis Sq.
W. Julian
Johnson Sq.
E. Julian
Reynolds Sq.
E. Bryan St.
Warren Sq.

W. Congress St.
E. Congress St.

W. Broughton St.
E. Broughton St.
Isaiah Davenport House

W. Broad

Whitaker St.

Lincoln St.

W. State St.
Telfair Sq.
W. President
Wright Sq.
E. President
E. State St.
Oglethorpe Sq.
Columbia Sq.

Telfair Museum of Art

Chatham County Courthouse

W. York St.
E. York St.

Juliette Gordon Low Birthplace

Montgomery St.

Jefferson St.

Barnard St.

Drayton St.

Abercorn St.

Habersham St.

W. Oglethorpe Ave.
E. Oglethorpe St.

W. Hull
E. Hull
Colonial Park Cemetery

Orleans Sq.
Chippewa Sq.

W. Perry
E. Perry

W. Liberty St.
Bull St.
E. Liberty St.

Cathedral of St. John the Baptist

Pulaski Sq.
W. Harris St.
Green-Meldrim House
Madison Sq.
Lafayette Sq.
E. Harris St.
E. Macon St.
Troup Sq.

Jefferson St.

Tattnall St.

W. Charlton
Andrew Low House
E. Charlton

W. Jones St.
E. Jones St.

Lincoln St.

W. Taylor St.
Monterey Sq.
E. Taylor St.

Chatham Sq.
W. Wayne St.
Calhoun Sq.
E. Wayne St.
Whitefield Sq.

W. Gordon St.
Mercer House
E. Gordon St.

W. Gaston St.
E. Gaston St.

Forsyth Park

W. Huntingdon St.

★ The **Isaiah Davenport House** (⊠ 324 E. State St., ☎ 912/236–8097; ⊠
$6), which master builder Davenport built for himself in 1820, is one
of the city's finest examples of Federal architecture. It has Chippendale,
Hepplewhite, and Sheraton antiques. Within the graceful **Telfair Museum
of Art** (⊠ 121 Barnard St., ☎ 912/232–1177; ⊠ $6, free on Sun.), de-
signed by William Jay and built in 1818, is the South's oldest public art
museum, displaying American, French, and German paintings from the
18th and 19th centuries. The now-famous "Bird Girl" that graced the
cover of *Midnight in the Garden of Good and Evil* is now on exhibit
here. The **Juliette Gordon Low Birthplace/Girl Scout National Center** (⊠
142 Bull St., ☎ 912/233–4501; ⊠ $6), in a Regency town house that
was the city's first National Historic Landmark, displays memorabilia
of the founder of the Girl Scouts of America.

At the corner of Oglethorpe Avenue and McDonough Street, **Colonial
Park Cemetery** is the burial ground for some of the city's earliest and
most notable residents, such as Button Gwinnett, a signatory of the
Declaration of Independence. **Cathedral of St. John the Baptist** (⊠ 222
E. Harris St., ☎ 912/233–4709; ⊠ free), a late-19th-century structure,
contains Austrian stained-glass windows, an Italian marble altar, and
German-made stations of the cross. Tours are by appointment only and
are offered when services are not in progress.

The **Andrew Low House** (⊠ 329 Abercorn St., ☎ 912/233–6854; ⊠
$7; closed Thurs.) was built in 1848 for Andrew Low by New York
architect John Norris, who also designed the Green-Meldrim (☞
below). The home later belonged to his son, William, who married Juliette Gordon, founder of the Girl Scouts. Some of the city's most impressive ironwork decorates the exterior; inside is a fine collection of
★ 19th-century antiques. The **Green-Meldrim House** (⊠ 1 W. Macon St.,
☎ 912/233–3845; ⊠ $5; closed Mon. and Wed.) is a splendid Gothic
Revival mansion built in 1852 for cotton merchant Charles Green. Now
a parish house for St. John's Episcopal Church, it is furnished with 16th-
through 19th-century antiques.

Midnight in the Garden of Good and Evil

In his 1994 best-seller, *Midnight in the Garden of Good and Evil,* John
Berendt focuses on the action surrounding the mysterious death of one
Savannahian and the ensuing trials of Jim Williams (who was acquit-
ted). Read the book before you visit the city. *Note: Unless otherwise
indicated, the sites mentioned in the book are not open to the public.*

Songwriter Johnny Mercer's great-grandfather began building **Mercer
House** (⊠ 429 Bull St., on Monterey Sq.) in 1860. The redbrick Italianate mansion became the home of Jim Williams, the book's main character. Here his sometime house partner Danny Hansford was shot and
killed, and Williams himself died in the house in 1990. Today, Williams's
sister lives here quietly. Jim Williams lived and worked in **Armstrong
House** (⊠ 447 Bull St.) before purchasing the Mercer House. **Lee
Adler's home** (⊠ 425 Bull St.), residence of one of Williams's biggest
adversaries, is half of the double town house facing West Wayne Street.

At **the first of Joe Odom's homes** (⊠ 16 E. Jones St.), Odom, a combination tax lawyer, real estate broker, and piano player, hosted a
steady stream of visitors. Author Berendt loaded up on greasy-spoon
breakfasts at **Clary's Cafe** (⊠ 404 Abercorn St., ☎ 912/233–0402).
Hamilton-Turner Inn (⊠ 330 Abercorn St., ☎ 912/233–1833 or 888/
448–8849), a Second Empire mansion built in 1873, was acquired by
Mandy Nichols, Joe Odom's fiancée. The sturdily elegant towering hulk
now is a bed-and-breakfast inn (☞ Lodging, *below*).

The three Williams murder trials took place at **Chatham County Court-house** (⊠ 133 Montgomery St.) over the course of about eight years.

Club One Jefferson (⊠ 1 Jefferson St., ☎ 912/232–0200), the gay club where Lady Chablis still occasionally bumps and grinds down the cat-walk, is a must stop. Call to find out when Chablis sings. Emma Kelly sings at **Hard Hearted Hannah's East** (☞ Nightlife, *below*). She moved here after her club went bankrupt under Joe Odom's direction.

Bonaventure Cemetery (⊠ 330 Bonaventure Rd., ☎ 912/651–6843), east of downtown, is the final resting place for Danny Hansford. The haunting female tombstone figure from the book's cover has been re-moved to protect surrounding graves from overenthusiastic fans.

Outside Savannah

From Savannah a 30-minute drive east on Victory Drive (U.S. 80/ Tybee Rd.) leads across a bridge to **Tybee Island.** About 5 mi long and 2 mi wide, Tybee has white-sand beaches for shelling, crabbing, and swimming, as well as covered picnic facilities, a marina, and a wide variety of seafood restaurants, motels, and shops. The **Tybee Museum** (⊠ 30 Meddin Dr., ☎ 912/786–4077; ☒ both lighthouse and museum $3), which faces the **Tybee Lighthouse,** the state's oldest and tallest, traces the island's history from early Native American days.

Parks and Gardens

★ Integral to Savannah's design is its park system: 22 **town squares**— large and small and each with a historic monument or a graceful foun-tain—dot the historic district. The earliest square is Johnson Square, near City Market; food carts are typically parked along its edges. On West Macon Street is **Forsyth Park,** site of frequent outdoor concerts; at the center of its shady 20 acres, which include a jogging path and the Fragrant Garden for the Blind, is a graceful white fountain.

Dining

$$$–$$$$ ✕ **Elizabeth on 37th.** This restaurant in a turn-of-the-20th-century
★ mansion has earned a national reputation for its fine seafood and del-icate sauces. Regional foods such as stone-ground grits, black-eyed peas, country ham, and succulent white Georgia shrimp grace the seasonal menu. Finish with Savannah Cream Cake. ⊠ *105 E. 37th St.,* ☎ *912/ 236–5547. Reservations essential. AE, D, DC, MC, V. No lunch.*

$$–$$$$ ✕ **Sapphire Grill.** Squab, grits, Georgia white shrimp, and fried green
★ tomatoes are expertly used in contemporary Low Country and eclec-tic dishes. The chocolate flan is sinful. ⊠ *110 W. Congress St.,* ☎ *912/ 443–9962. Reservations essential. AE, D, DC, MC, V. No lunch.*

$$–$$$ ✕ **Bistro Savannah.** This establishment, housed in a circa 1878 build-
★ ing, specializes in fresh regional fare that uses both farmed and wild ingredients. Crab cakes with lemon-caper aioli and chowchow, and shrimp and tasso ham with stone ground grits are among the highlights. ⊠ *309 W. Congress St.,* ☎ *912/233–6266. AE, MC, V. No lunch.*

$–$$ ✕ **Johnny Harris.** What started as a small roadside stand in 1924 is now one of the city's culinary mainstays. The menu includes steaks, fried chicken, seafood, and barbecued meats smothered in the restau-rant's famous sauce. There's live piano or guitar music on Friday night and dancing on Saturday night. ⊠ *1651 E. Victory Dr.,* ☎ *912/354– 7810. AE, DC, MC, V. Closed Sun.*

$–$$ ✕ **The Lady & Sons.** Yes, it is run by a mother and her sons. Visitors and locals stand in line patiently waiting to attack the buffet ($12.95 at dinner). They come for moist and crispy fried chicken, great baked spaghetti, crab stew, and fresh lemonade. An à la carte menu and a decent wine list are also available. ⊠ *311 W. Congress St.,* ☎ *912/233–2600. AE, D, MC, V.*

$ ✕ **Mrs. Wilkes Dining Room.** Come to this unassuming basement
★ restaurant for comfort food served family style. Folks line up at breakfast and lunch for such quintessentially southern dishes as biscuits, grits, collard greens, mashed potatoes, and fried chicken. ⊠ *107 W. Jones St.,* ☎ *912/232–5997. Reservations not accepted. No credit cards. Closed weekends. No dinner.*

$ ✕ **Nita's Place.** Just a half block from the Colonial Cemetery, this lit-
★ tle steam-table operation offers nothing in decor. But Juanita Dixon has established a reputation for down-home southern cooking with her salmon patties, baked chicken, perfectly cooked okra, outstanding squash casserole, and homemade desserts. ⊠ *140 Abercorn St.,* ☎ *912/238–8233. Reservations not accepted. D, MC, V. No dinner.*

Lodging

$$$–$$$$ 🏨 **Ballastone Inn.** This sumptuous inn occupies a mansion dating from
★ 1838 that once served as a bordello. Each room is decorated differently. On the garden level, rooms are small and cozy, with exposed brick walls and beamed ceilings. Afternoon tea, hors d'oeuvres, robes, movies, and bicycles are among the amenities. ⊠ *14 E. Oglethorpe Ave., 31401,* ☎ *912/236–1484 or 800/822–4553,* 🏧 *912/236–4626. 16 rooms. AE, MC, V. BP.* 🐾

$$$–$$$$ 🏨 **Gaston Gallery.** The city's most deluxe accommodations are found
★ at this 1868 inn two blocks from Forsyth Park. All rooms have working fireplaces and antiques from the Georgian and Regency periods. Breakfast might include ginger pancakes, and pralines await you at turndown. ⊠ *220 E. Gaston St., 31401,* ☎ *912/232–2869 or 800/671–0716,* 🏧 *912/232–0710. 17 rooms. AE, D, MC, V. BP.* 🐾

$$$–$$$$ 🏨 **Hamilton-Turner Inn.** Experience *Midnight in the Garden of Good and Evil* with a stay in this 1873 Second Empire mansion built by wealthy Savannah jeweler Samuel Hamilton. Until recently, the house belonged to Mandy Nichols, one of the principal figures in the John Berendt book. It is furnished with fine antiques. Complimentary afternoon tea, robes, and a film library are among the amenities. All rooms have desks and data ports. ⊠ *330 Abercorn St., 31401,* ☎ *912/233–1833 or 888/448–8849,* 🏧 *912/233–0291. 15 rooms. AE, D, DC, MC, V. BP.* 🐾

$$$–$$$$ 🏨 **Kehoe House.** A fabulously appointed bed-and-breakfast inn, the
★ Victorian Kehoe House has brass-and-marble chandeliers, a courtyard garden, and a music room. On the main floor, a double parlor with a 14-ft ceiling holds two fireplaces. Here, guests enjoy sumptuous breakfasts, wine with hors d'oeuvres, and lavish afternoon tea. Guests have access to the Downtown Athletic Club. ⊠ *123 Habersham St., 31401,* ☎ *912/232–1020 or 800/820–1020,* 🏧 *912/231–0208. 18 rooms. AE, D, DC, MC, V. BP.*

$$$–$$$$ 🏨 **The President's Quarters.** At this inn composed of two 19th-century
★ town houses, guests are greeted with wine and fruit, and afternoon tea comes with sumptuous cakes. A renovated house across the street features two suites and a guest room, each with fireplaces and whirlpool tubs. ⊠ *225 E. President St., 31401,* ☎ *912/233–1600 or 800/592–1812,* 🏧 *912/238–0849. 19 rooms. AE, D, DC, MC, V. CP.* 🐾

Nightlife

Savannah's nightlife is a reflection of the city's laid-back, easygoing personality. Some clubs have live reggae, hard rock, and other contemporary music, but most stay with traditional blues, jazz, and piano-bar vocalists. At **Hard Hearted Hannah's East** (⊠ Pirate's House, 20 E. Broad St., ☎ 912/233–2225) Emma Kelly, the famed Lady of 6,000

Songs, performs Tuesday through Saturday. Irish music fills the air Wednesday through Saturday at **Kevin Barry's Irish Pub** (⊠ 117 W. River St., ☎ 912/233–9626). If you're in the mood for a low-key evening, drop in for coffee at **Savannah Coffee House and Café** (⊠ 102 W. Congress St., ☎ 912/233–5311).

Shopping

Savannah's many specialty shops sell such merchandise as English antiques, antiquarian books, and Low Country handmade quilts. Stores in the historic district are housed in ground floors of mansions and town houses or in renovated warehouses along the waterfront. The **River Front** and **City Market** areas have a variety of shops, and Downtown is becoming a draw for antiques and collectibles hunters.

THE GOLDEN ISLES

An hour south of Savannah lie the Golden Isles, a chain of barrier islands stretching along Georgia's coast to the Florida state line. The three most developed—Jekyll Island, Sea Island, and St. Simons Island—are the only ones accessible by car; they are connected to the mainland near Brunswick by a network of causeways. A ferry from St. Marys connects Cumberland Island National Seashore with the mainland, and a launch transports visitors from St. Simons to Little St. Simons, a private vacation retreat. Spring, when temperatures are mild, is the ideal time for a visit; the superb beaches attract large crowds in summer.

Visitor Information

Cumberland Island National Seashore (⊠ National Park Service, Box 806, St. Marys 31558, ☎ 912/882–4335). **Jekyll Island:** Welcome Center (⊠ 45 S. Beachview Dr., 31527, ☎ 912/635–3636 or 800/841–6586). **St. Simons Island:** Visitors Bureau (⊠ 4 Glynn Ave., 31520, ☎ 912/265–0620 or 800/933–2627).

Arriving and Departing

By Bus
Greyhound (☎ 800/231–2222) connects Brunswick with surrounding towns and cities, including Savannah and Jacksonville, Florida.

By Boat
To reach Cumberland Island, you must reserve passage on the *Cumberland Queen* ferry, which leaves from St. Marys for the 45-minute journey. For a schedule, reservations, and fare information, contact Cumberland Island National Seashore (☞ Visitor Information, *above*).

By Car
From Brunswick take the **Jekyll Island Causeway** ($2 per car) to Jekyll Island or the **F. J. Torras Causeway** (35¢) to St. Simons. From St. Simons you can reach Sea Island via the **Sea Island Causeway.** Only residents and park service personnel are allowed to drive cars on Cumberland Island.

By Plane
Glynco Jetport (⊠ 500 Connole St., 31525, ☎ 912/265–2070), on the mainland 6 mi outside Brunswick, is served by Delta affiliate Atlantic Southeast Airlines (☎ 800/282–3424). International airports are in Savannah, an hour's drive north, and in Jacksonville, Florida, an hour's drive south, but there are no scheduled international flights operating at either airport. Jekyll and St. Simons islands maintain small airstrips for private planes.

Exploring the Golden Isles

Little St. Simons Island

Accessible by private boat, Little St. Simons is a Robinson Crusoe–style getaway just 6 mi long and less than 3 mi wide. The island's only development is a rustic but comfortable guest compound (☞ Dining and Lodging, *below*). The island's forests and marshes are inhabited by wildlife and more than 200 species of birds. There's a 7-mi stretch of beach for swimming and water sports.

Sea Island

Five-mile-long Sea Island's main attraction is the Cloister (☞ Dining and Lodging, *below*), a Spanish Mediterranean–style resort. This luxurious, low-key property has a beach club with a health spa, formal and casual restaurants, and many outdoor activities. Outside the resort, beautiful mansions line Sea Island Drive.

St. Simons Island

The contrasting beauties of white-sand beaches and salt marshes characterize St. Simons, north of Jekyll and Cumberland islands. As large as Manhattan and with more than 14,000 residents, it's the Golden Isles' most complete and commercial resort destination.

At the island's south end, the **Village** is dotted with T-shirt and souvenir shops, boutiques, restaurants, and a public pier for fishing and crabbing. Overlooking the ocean is **Neptune Park,** with a playground, a miniature golf course, and picnic tables shaded by live oaks. Also in the park are the **St. Simons Lighthouse** and the **Museum of Coastal History** (☒ 101 12th St., ☎ 912/638–4666; ☒ both lighthouse and museum $3) in the former lightkeeper's cottage.

Fort Frederica National Monument, on the island's north end, contains the foundation ruins of a fort and buildings inhabited by English soldiers and civilians in the mid-18th century. Tours begin at the **National Park Service visitor center** (☒ off Frederica Rd., ☎ 912/638–3639; ☒ $4 per vehicle). Visit the Gothic-style, cruciform **Christ Church** (☒ 6329 Frederica Rd., ☎ 912/638–8683), where the stained-glass windows illustrate local history and religious themes. One of the windows is by Louis Tiffany. The church was rebuilt in 1886.

Jekyll Island

The golf courses and system of bike paths here can be enjoyed year-round. Jekyll Island was once the favored retreat of the Vanderbilts, Rockefellers, Morgans, and other American aristocrats. Many of these millionaires' mansions are part of the **Jekyll Island Historic District.** Stop for maps and information at the **visitor center** (☒ 45 S. Beachview Dr., ☎ 877/453–5955; 912/635–3636 locally). An 11-acre water park, **Summer Waves** (☒ 210 S. Riverview Dr., ☎ 912/635–2074; ☒ $14.95; closed Oct.–Apr.), ranks as a top summer attraction.

Cumberland Island National Seashore

The largest and most remote of the Golden Isles, **Cumberland Island** (☒ $4 day use fee), is a 200-square-mi sanctuary of marshes, dunes, beaches, forests, ponds, estuaries, and inlets. You can tour the unspoiled terrain and the ruins of Thomas Carnegie's **Dungeness** estate on your own or join history and nature walks led by park rangers (☞ Visitor Information, *above*). You must bring along whatever food, beverages, sunscreen, and insect repellent you may need; the island has no shops.

Dining and Lodging

Cumberland Island

$$$$ ✕⊡ **Greyfield Inn.** This turn-of-the-20th-century house, built by the Carnegie family, is the island's only lodging; its wide, colonnaded porches beckon invitingly. The inn is furnished with Asian and English antiques; burnished hardwood floors are warmed by Persian rugs. ⊠ *Box 900, Fernandina Beach, FL 32035,* ☎ *904/261–6408. 17 rooms. Restaurant. AE, D, MC, V. FAP.* 🍽

Jekyll Island

$$–$$$ ✕⊡ **Jekyll Island Club Hotel.** Built in 1886, the four-story clubhouse
★ with wraparound verandas and Queen Anne–style towers and turrets once served as the winter hunting retreat for wealthy financiers. Rooms are custom-decorated with mahogany beds, armoires, and plush sofas and chairs. The nearby Sans Souci Apartments, built in 1896 by a group of club members, have been converted into spacious guest rooms. The Grand Dining Room serves southern cuisine, such as famed Georgia white shrimp and fried green tomatoes with black-eyed-pea relish; meal plans are available. ⊠ *371 Riverview Dr., 31527,* ☎ *912/635–2600; 800/535–9547; 912/635–2400 for dining room;* FAX *912/635–2818. 134 rooms. 2 restaurants, pool, tennis. AE, D, DC, MC, V.* 🍽

Little St. Simons Island

$$$$ ⊡ **Lodge on Little St. Simons Island.** Guests stay in spacious rooms in
★ one of four buildings: a two-bedroom cottage; the 1917 Hunting Lodge, with two antiques-filled guest rooms; or one of two houses with four guest rooms each. All buildings have screened porches or decks. Meals are served family-style in the main dining room; platters are heaped with fresh fish, home-baked breads, and pies. All rooms are air-conditioned. ⊠ *Box 21078, 31522,* ☎ *912/638–7472 or 888/733–5774,* FAX *912/634–1811. 15 rooms. Pool. AE, D, MC, V. FAP.*

St. Simons Island

$–$$ ✕ **Blanche's Courtyard.** Seafood, such as blue crab soup, and simple but delicious steak and chicken dinners are among the local favorites. The apple fritters, renamed "sweet puppies" on the menu, are unforgettable. Reservations are recommended. ⊠ *440 King's Way,* ☎ *912/638–3030. AE, DC, MC, V. Closed Mon. No lunch.*

$$–$$$ ⊡ **King and Prince Beach and Golf Resort.** This beachfront hotel-and-condominium complex has spacious guest rooms and two- and three-bedroom villas. Villas are privately owned, so the total number available for rent varies from time to time. ⊠ *201 Arnold Rd. (Box 20798), 31522,* ☎ *912/638–3631 or 800/342–0212,* FAX *912/634–1720. 140 rooms, 43 villas. 2 restaurants, 5 pools, golf, tennis. AE, D, DC, MC, V.* 🍽

$$–$$$ ⊡ **Sea Palms Golf and Tennis Resort.** A contemporary resort complex with fully furnished villas, most with kitchens, nestles on an 800-acre site. ⊠ *5445 Frederica Rd., St. Simons Island 31522,* ☎ *912/638–3351 or 800/841–6268,* FAX *912/634–8029. 156 rooms. 2 restaurants, 3 pools, golf, tennis, health club. AE, DC, MC, V.* 🍽

Sea Island

$$$$ ✕⊡ **The Cloister.** At this classic resort, modern ocean-side villas, condos, and rental homes have grown up around a 1920s Spanish Mediterranean–style hotel. Formal dining, casual grill lunches, and seafood and breakfast buffets are included in the rate. A spa offers a fitness room and beauty treatments. ⊠ *The Cloister, Sea Island 31561,* ☎ *912/638–3611 or 800/732–4752,* FAX *912/638–5159. 286 rooms. 4 restaurants, 2 pools, golf, tennis. AE, MC, V. FAP.* 🍽

Campgrounds

⚕ **Cumberland Island National Seashore** (☞ Visitor Information, *above*) maintains a tent campground with rest rooms, showers, and freshwater sources (bring your own container). Known as Seacamp, this area costs $4 per person, per night. Hikers may want to explore the backcountry, where there are no amenities. The fee for camping in the backcountry is $2 per person per night. Reserve well in advance.

Outdoor Activities and Sports

Biking

Sea Island, Jekyll Island, and St. Simons have paved bike paths. You can rent bikes from **Barry's Beach Service** (⊠ 1300 Ocean Blvd., ☎ 912/638–8053), which also has other recreational equipment, and **Benjy's Bike Shop** (⊠ 130 Retreat Pl., ☎ 912/638–6766), both on St. Simons.

Fishing

The Intracoastal Waterway and the Atlantic Ocean are teeming with trout, barracuda, snapper, amberjack, and other fish. On St. Simons, **Ducky II Charter Boat Service** (⊠ 402 Kelsall Ave., ☎ 912/634–0312) organizes deep-sea and inshore fishing. **Capt. Martin Noble Charter Fishing** (☎ 912/634–1219) handles both offshore and inshore fishing for St. Simons. **St. Simons Transit Company** (⊠ 105 Marina Dr., ☎ 912/638–5678) organizes river and deep-sea fishing expeditions, dolphin tours, and land tours and operates a water taxi service between the coastal islands. **Taylor Fish Camp** (⊠ Lawrence Rd., ☎ 912/638–7690) offers guided fishing trips.

Golf

St. Simons Island has four courses: **Hampton Club** (⊠ 100 Tabbystone, ☎ 912/634–0255), with 18 holes at par 72; **St. Simons Island Club** (⊠ 100 King's Way, ☎ 912/638–5130), with 18 holes at par 72; and **Sea Palms Golf and Tennis Resort** (⊠ 5445 Frederica Rd., ☎ 912/638–3351), with 27 holes, par 72 on any two nines. Though it has several courses, Jekyll Island is known for two in particular: **Oceanside** (⊠ N. Beachview Dr., ☎ 912/635–2170), with 9 holes, par 36; and **Jekyll Island Golf Club** (⊠ 322 Captain Wylly Rd., ☎ 912/635–2368 or 912/635–3464), with three 18-hole courses—Indian Mound, Oleander, and Pine Lake—all par 72.

Tennis

Jekyll Island Tennis CourtsCenter (⊠ 400 Captain Wylly Rd., ☎ 912/635–3154) offers 13 clay courts, 7 of which are lighted. The center hosts USTA-sanctioned tournaments and offers tennis camps. **Sea Palms Golf and Tennis Resort** (⊠ 5445 Frederica Rd., ☎ 912/638–3351) offers 12 Rubico courts, 3 of which are lighted.

Beaches

Wide expanses of clean, sandy beaches skirt all the islands. St. Simons's **East Beach** attracts large groups and families and has sailboat rentals. The beaches rimming **Jekyll Island** are usually not too busy during the week but become crowded on weekends. On **Sea Island** you can rent sailboats, sea kayaks, and boogie boards. The dunes and beaches of **Cumberland Island National Seashore** offer peaceful isolation.

ELSEWHERE IN GEORGIA

Historic Sites Along I–75

Arriving and Departing

Take I–75 north to the Tennessee state line and look for the brown state historic markers that indicate historic sites.

What to See and Do

New Echota State Historic Site (⊠ Rte. 225, 1 mi east of I–75 [Exit 317], near Calhoun, ☎ 706/624–1321; ⊒ $3) is the location of the 1825–38 capital of the Cherokee Nation, whose constitution was patterned after that of the United States. Some buildings have been reconstructed. Native Americans frequently hold special events at the site.

The **Chief Vann House** (⊠ 82 Rte. 225, 17 mi east of New Echota, Chatsworth, ☎ 706/695–2598; ⊒ $3), a three-story brick edifice, was built in 1804 by Moravian artisans hired by Chief James Vann, a leader of the Cherokee Nation. To get here, take Exit 317 from I–75 to Route 52A going west. It's closed Monday.

The **Chickamauga and Chattanooga National Military Park** (⊠ U.S. 27 off I–75, Exit 350, south of Chattanooga, TN, ☎ 706/866–9241; ⊒ free), established in 1890, was the nation's first military park. In 1863, this was the site of one of the Civil War's bloodiest battles (30,000 casualties), which ended in the Union Capture of Chattanooga. Monuments, battlements, and weapons adorn the road that traverses the 8,000-acre park, with markers explaining the action. An excellent visitor center offers reproduction memorabilia, superb books, and a film on the battle.

Dining and Lodging

$ ✕ **J. J.'s.** Locals enjoy the "day-old" ribs for their crispy tenderness, but the standout is the smoked catfish. Collard greens and fruit cobblers are good, too. The posted menu only notes the specials, so ask for details. Rome is about 30 mi southwest of New Echota from Calhoun via Georgia Highway 53. ⊠ *1517 Dean St., Rome,* ☎ *706/234–7895. Reservations not accepted. No credit cards. Closed Sun.*

$$ ▨ **Claremont House.** This beautifully restored 1890s Victorian inn has huge rooms furnished with period antiques. Breakfast is sumptuous, with stuffed French toast and the like. ⊠ *906 E. 2nd Ave., Rome 30161,* ☎ *706/291–0900 or 800/254–4797,* ℻ *706/802–0551. 6 rooms. AE, D, MC, V. BP.*

Callaway Gardens

Arriving and Departing

Callaway Gardens is on U.S. 27 in Pine Mountain, 70 mi southwest of Atlanta. From Atlanta drive south on I–85, I–185, and U.S. 27.

What to See and Do

★ **Callaway Gardens** is a 14,000-acre, year-round horticultural fantasyland and family-style golf and tennis resort, best known for its impressive gardens developed in the 1930s by a couple determined to breathe new life into the area's dormant cotton fields. On the grounds are 10 tennis courts, bicycling trails, a lakefront beach, and four nationally recognized golf courses. The **Cecil B. Day Butterfly Center,** the largest glass-enclosed tropical conservatory of living butterflies in North America, and the **John A. Sibley Horticultural Center** (⊠ Both: U.S. 27, Pine Mountain, ☎ 706/663–2281 or 800/282–8181, ℻ 706/663–5049, ⊒ $10), one of the most advanced garden greenhouse complexes in the world, are part of the gardens. Trails and paved paths traverse the world's largest collection of hollies and more than 700 varieties of azaleas and wildflowers.

Just 15 mi east of Callaway Gardens on Route 85 is the **Little White House Historic Site** (⊠ 401 Little White House Rd., Warm Springs, ☎ 706/655–5870; ⊒ $5), where in 1932 President Franklin Delano Roosevelt built the "Little White House," the simple, three-bedroom cottage in which he died in 1945.

Macon

Arriving and Departing

Take I–75 south from Atlanta 90 mi. There are several exits into Macon from I–75; get off at Exit 2, Martin Luther King Jr. Blvd., to get to downtown and the attractions listed below.

What to See and Do

Founded in 1823, Macon lies at the state's geographic center. Its rich architecture includes both antebellum and Victorian residences and commercial buildings. Visitors marvel at the stained-glass windows and marble mantels of the Italianate **Hay House** (⊠ 934 Georgia Ave., ☎ 912/742–8155; ⊑ $6). Famous artists who have called Macon home include flutist and pre–Civil War poet laureate of the United States Sidney Lanier, Little Richard, the Allman Brothers, and Otis Redding. Experience the state's contribution to American music at the **Georgia Music Hall of Fame** (⊠ 200 Martin Luther King Jr. Blvd., ☎ 912/750–8555; ⊑ $8). It's closed Sunday. Directly across the street, the **Georgia Sports Hall of Fame** (⊠ 301 Cherry St., ☎ 912/752–1585; ⊑ $6) has the look of an old ballpark. The **Tubman African American Museum** (⊠ 340 Walnut St., ☎ 912/743–8544; ⊑ $3) salutes the former slave who led more than 300 people to freedom and displays African artifacts and African-American art.

Dining and Lodging

$ ✕ **The Cherry Corner.** This taste of Italy is the perfect spot for lunch, a quick snack of pizza or soup, or coffee and a pastry. Dine at one of the sidewalk tables when it's warm. ⊠ 502 Cherry St., ☎ 912/741–9525. MC, V. Closed Sun.

$$$ 🏨 **1842 Inn.** With its grand, white-pillared front porch and period antiques, this place offers a taste of antebellum Macon. From here, it's an easy walk to downtown. ⊠ 353 College St., 31201, ☎ 800/336–1842. 21 rooms. AE, MC, V.

Andersonville

Arriving and Departing

Take I–75 south from Macon to Route 49 and follow the signs that read THE ANDERSONVILLE TRAIL to Andersonville.

What to See and Do

The tiny town of Andersonville grew up around a railway stop. The depot is the **Andersonville Welcome Center** (⊠ 114 Church St., 31711, ☎ 912/924–2558). Antiques and memorabilia fill the restored storefront shops that form the town center. Two Civil War festivals, both with crafts and collectibles, take place here: the Andersonville Historic Fair (first weekend in October) and the smaller Memorial Day weekend fair.

★ The **Andersonville National Historic Site** (☞ National and State Parks, *above*) marks the Civil War's most notorious prisoner-of-war camp, which opened in 1864: 13,000 Union prisoners died here. Today it is the site of the National Prisoner of War Museum and serves as a final resting place for U.S. veterans and their spouses. The site's living history event takes place in spring.

Dining and Lodging

$$ ✕🏨 **Windsor Hotel.** Americus, only 10 mi southwest of Andersonville via Route 49, has one of America's most intriguing historic hotels. This Romanesque structure dominates downtown, and its lobby, rich in Moorish detail, is breathtaking. In the elegant dining room, the fine menu focuses on southern fare, with such dishes as barbecued shrimp on linguine, crab cakes, and pecan-crusted salmon. ⊠ 125 W. Lamar St., Amer-

*icus 31709, ☎ 912/924–1555 or 888/297–9567, ℻ 912/928–0533.
53 rooms. Restaurant. AE, D, MC, V. No dinner Sun.*

Okefenokee National Wildlife Refuge

Arriving and Departing

The refuge is near the Georgia-Florida border, 40 minutes northwest of Jacksonville, Florida, and 40 minutes southwest of the Golden Isles. From Atlanta take I–75 south to U.S. 82 into Waycross. From the Golden Isles take U.S. 84 to U.S. 301.

What to See and Do

★ **Okefenokee National Wildlife Refuge** (✉ Folkston, ☎ 912/496–3331 for canoe rental and reservations; 912/496–7836 for information; 🖙 $5 per vehicle), covering about 730 square mi, is a vast peat bog once part of the ocean floor and now 100 ft above sea level. Its thick vegetation is inhabited by at least 54 reptile species (including alligators), 49 mammal species, and 234 types of birds.

The **Okefenokee Swamp Park** (✉ 8 mi south of Waycross, ☎ 912/283–0583; 🖙 $10) offers guided tours ($14 per person) of the refuge. Boardwalks lead to an observation tower; guided boat tours are available, or you can rent a canoe ($16 per person). A 1½-mi train tour passes by a Seminole village and stops at Pioneer Island for a 30-minute walking tour. There's an eastern entrance at the **Suwanee Canal Recreation Area** (✉ near Folkston, ☎ 912/496–7156 or 800/792–6796); the 11-mi waterway was built more than two centuries ago. Wilderness canoeing and camping in the Okefenokee's interior are by reserved fee permit only. Permits are tough to get, especially in cool weather. Call **refuge headquarters** (☎ 912/496–3331) *exactly 60 days* in advance of the desired starting date. There's also a western entrance at **Stephen C. Foster State Park** (✉ Rte. 177, off U.S. 441, Fargo, ☎ 912/637–5274), an 80-acre park with boat rides through a swamp, a ½-mi nature trail, restored homesteads, and cypress and black gum trees.

Lodging

$$ 🖾 **Inn at Folkston.** This restored 1920s bungalow is right in the center of town. Two of the guest rooms feature a front veranda and gas-log fireplaces, and all of them are individually decorated. ✉ *509 W. Main St., Folkston 31537, ☎ 912/496–6256 or 888/509–6246. 4 rooms. AE, MC, V. BP.* ❧

HAWAI'I

Capital	Honolulu
Population	1,186,600
Motto	The Life of the Land Is Perpetuated in Righteousness
State Bird	Nēnē (Hawaiian goose)
State Flower	Hibiscus
Postal Abbreviation	HI

Statewide Visitor Information

Hawai'i Visitors and Convention Bureau (⊠ Waikīkī Business Plaza, 2270 Kalākaua Ave., Suite 801, Honolulu 96815, ☎ 808/923–1811, 800/464–2924 for brochures). **Surf Report** (☎ 808/596–7873).

Scenic Drives

On the eastern tip of O'ahu the 10-mi stretch of **Kalaniana'ole Highway** from Hanauma Bay to Waimānalo is a cliff-side road resembling Highway 1 up the California coast. On the Big Island **Highway 19** north out of Hilo runs along the lush and rugged Hāmākua Coast to Waipi'o Valley, past sugarcane fields and spectacular ocean views. From Pā'ia to Hāna, Maui's **Hāna Highway** (Highway 36) is a winding 55-mi coastal route that spans rivers and passes tropical waterfalls. From the town of Waimea, Kaua'i's **Waimea Canyon Drive** meanders upward past panoramas of Waimea Canyon, culminating at the 4,120-ft Kalalau Lookout.

National and State Parks

National Parks

Some of Hawai'i's best National Park Service attractions are **Hawai'i Volcanoes National Park** (⊠ National Park Service, Box 52, Hawai'i Volcanoes National Park, 96817; ⊠ $10 per car, $5 on foot or by bike), 30 mi southeast of Hilo on Highway 11; **Pu'uhonua o Hōnaunau National Historic Park** (⊠ Pu'uhonua o Hōnaunau, Box 129, Hōnaunau 96726, ☎ 808/985–6000; ⊠ $2), 20 mi south of Kailua-Kona, on Highway 160; **Pu'ukoholā National Historic Site** (⊠ Hwy. 270, Kawaihae, ☎ 808/882–7218; ⊠ free); **Haleakalā National Park** (☞ Maui, *below*); **Kalaupapa** (☞ Elsewhere in Hawai'i, *below*); and the **USS Arizona Memorial** (⊠ 1 Arizona Memorial Pl., Honolulu 96818-3145, ☎ 808/422–0561; ⊠ free). A 20-minute drive west from downtown Honolulu, the memorial bridges the hulk of the USS *Arizona,* which sank with 1,102 men aboard during the attack on Pearl Harbor on December 7, 1941.

State Parks

Popular state parks include **Hāpuna State Recreation Area** (☞ The Big Island of Hawai'i, *below*), **Kōke'e State Park** (☞ Kaua'i, *below*), and **Wailua River State Park** (⊠ Wailua Marina, Kapa'a, Kaua'i 96746, ☎ 808/822–5065), where you can see the sites of ancient villages and an enormous fern-laced lava tube. For information write to the **District Office of the Hawai'i Department of Land and Natural Resources,** Division of State Parks (⊠ Box 621, Honolulu 96809, ☎ 808/587–0300).

HONOLULU AND WAIKĪKĪ

Honolulu, on the island of O'ahu, is the urban metropolis of the Aloha State. Here, differing cultures blend harmoniously, yet each retains its distinct character. Downtown, royal history contrasts with the modern-day action of a major government and business capital. Just 3½ mi from downtown is the tourist mecca of Waikīkī. Set on the sunny, dry side of O'ahu, Waikīkī provides a stunning physical setting along with the buzz of international hotel and shopping destinations.

Arriving and Departing

By Plane

Honolulu International Airport (⊠ 300 Rodgers Blvd., ☎ 808/836–6413) is only 20 minutes from Waikīkī. U.S. carriers serving Honolulu include American, Continental, Delta, Hawaiian, Northwest, TWA, and United. A cab from the airport to downtown or to Waikīkī costs about $20 plus tip. **TransHawaiian Services** (☎ 808/566–7333) runs a shuttle service to Waikīkī (⊠ $7 one-way, $13 round-trip). Some hotels also provide pickup and shuttle service; ask when you make reservations.

Getting Around Honolulu and Waikīkī

By Car

Don't bother renting a car unless you're planning to travel outside Waikīkī. When making hotel or plane reservations, ask if there's a car tie-in. Driving in rush hour (6:30 AM–8:30 AM and 3:30 PM–5:30 PM) is frustrating because of traffic, parking limitations, and numerous one-way streets. At peak times—summer, Christmas vacation, and February—reservations are a must. **Avis** (☎ 800/333–1212), **Hertz** (☎ 800/654–8200), and **Budget** (☎ 800/527–0700) are among the many national agencies with locations in Honolulu.

By Public Transportation

You can go anywhere on the island for $1 on Honolulu's municipal transportation system, affectionately known as the **Bus** (☎ 808/848–5555); *and* you'll receive a free transfer if you ask for it when boarding. Exact change is required, and dollar bills are accepted. A four-day pass for visitors costs $10 and is sold at the more than 30 ABC Stores in Waikīkī. Monthly passes are available for $25.

By Taxi

You can usually get a cab outside your hotel. Meter rates are $1.50–$2 at the drop of the flag, plus $1.50 for each additional mile. The two biggest cab companies are **Charley's** (☎ 808/531–1333) and **SIDA of Hawai'i** (☎ 808/836–0011).

Orientation Tours

The **Pearl Harbor and Punchbowl Tour** offered by Polynesian Adventure Tours (☎ 808/833–3000) includes a Navy launch out to the *Arizona* Memorial. In downtown Honolulu the **Chinatown Walking Tour** (☎ 808/533–3181) provides a look at O'ahu's oldest neighborhood.

Exploring Honolulu and Waikīkī

In Hawai'i directions are often given as *mauka* (toward the mountains) and *makai* (toward the ocean), or they may refer to Diamond Head (east, toward the famous volcanic landmark) and *'ewa* (west).

Downtown Honolulu

Aloha Tower Marketplace (⊠ 101 Ala Moana Blvd., at Piers 8, 9, and 10, ☎ 808/528–5700) has two stories of shops, kiosks, and indoor and outdoor restaurants—some with live entertainment—right next to Honolulu Harbor. The landmark 10-story Aloha Tower is its anchor; to view the harbor take the free ride up to the observation deck. A trolley runs regularly between the marketplace and Waikīkī.

Honolulu and Waikīkī

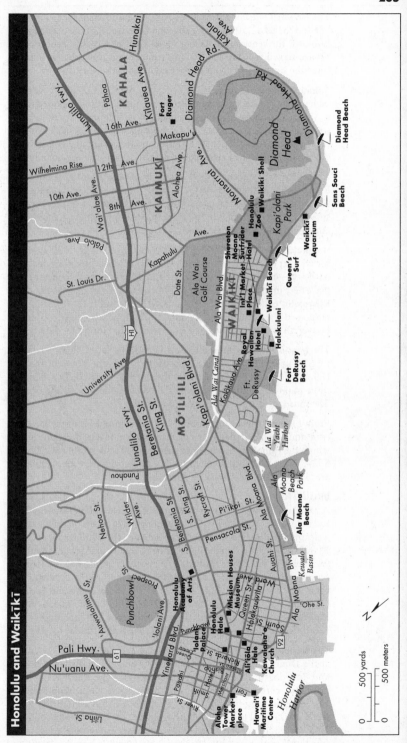

The **Hawai`i Maritime Center** (⊠ Ala Moana Blvd. at Pier 7, ☎ 808/536–6373; 🎫 $7.50) is on the Diamond Head side of the marketplace. Look for the century-old sailing vessel *Falls of Clyde,* a four-masted, square-rigged tall ship moored out front. Lively, informative exhibits trace the history of Hawai`i's love affair with the sea.

`Iolani Palace** (⊠ King St. at Richards St., ☎ 808/522–0832; 🎫 $15), built in 1882 on the site of an earlier palace and beautifully restored today, is America's only royal palace built with the assistance of American Masons. It contains the thrones of King Kalākaua and his successor (and sister) Queen Lili`uokalani. The palace is closed on Sunday and Monday. Reservations are essential, and children under five are not allowed.

Across the street from `Iolani Palace is **Ali`iōla Hale** (⊠ King St. at Richards St., ☎ 808/539–4919; 🎫 free), the old judiciary building that served as parliament hall under the monarchy and now houses the state supreme court. In front is the gilded statue of Kamehameha I, the Hawaiian chief who unified the islands.

Honolulu Hale (⊠ 530 S. King St., at Punchbowl St., ☎ 808/527–5666 for concert information; 🎫 free), the city hall, is a Mediterranean Renaissance–style building constructed in 1929. Free live concerts take place here in the evenings. Built in 1842 of massive blocks of solid coral, **Kawaiaha`o Church** (⊠ 957 Punchbowl St., ☎ 808/522–1333; 🎫 free) witnessed the coronations, weddings, and funerals of generations of Hawaiian royalty; it's across King Street from Honolulu Hale.

The **Mission Houses Museum** (⊠ 553 S. King St., ☎ 808/531–0481; 🎫 $8), next door to Kawaiaha`o Church, was the home of the first U.S. missionaries to Hawai`i after their arrival in 1820. The mission's three main structures are among the oldest buildings on the islands. The museum is closed Sunday and Monday.

From here it's three long blocks toward Diamond Head to Ward Avenue and one block mauka (toward the mountains) to Beretania Street, where the **Honolulu Academy of Arts** (⊠ 900 S. Beretania St., ☎ 808/532–8700; 🎫 $7) houses a world-class collection of western and Asian art. The academy is closed on Monday.

Waikīkī

A paved ocean walk leads up to the pink **Royal Hawaiian Hotel** (⊠ 2259 Kalākaua Ave., ☎ 808/923–7311), built in 1921 when Waikīkī was still a sleepy paradise. **International Market Place** (⊠ 2330 Kalākaua Ave., ☎ 808/923–9871) is on the mauka side of Kalākaua Avenue, about 100 yards east of the Royal Hawaiian. With its spreading banyan tree, the outdoor bazaar retains a little authentic flavor among the dozens of souvenir stands. The oldest hotel in Waikīkī, the **Sheraton Moana Surfrider** (⊠ 2365 Kalākaua Ave., ☎ 808/922–3111) is on the makai side of Kalākaua Avenue. The beautifully restored Beaux Arts building is worth visiting to get a sense of what Hawai`i was like before the days of jet travel.

The **Honolulu Zoo** (⊠ 151 Kapahulu Ave., ☎ 808/971–7171; 🎫 $6), at the Diamond Head end of Waikīkī, is home to thousands of furry and finned creatures. It's not the biggest zoo in the country, but its 40 lush acres certainly make it one of the prettiest. **Kapi`olani Park** is a vast green playing field adjoining the Honolulu Zoo. Here you'll find the **Waikīkī Shell** (⊠ 2805 Monsarrat Ave., ☎ 808/924–8934), Honolulu's outdoor concert arena, where locals spread out on "grass seats" (the lawn) with picnics to hear some of Hawai`i's best musicians and visiting pop stars. Most concerts are held between May 1 and Labor Day. Check the newspapers to see what's playing. Next door to the Waikīkī Shell, the **Kodak Hula Show** (☎ 808/627–3379; 🎫 free) has been wowing crowds for more than 50 years. It takes place on Tuesday, Wednesday, and Thursday mornings at 10.

The **Waikīkī Aquarium** (⊠ 2777 Kalākaua Ave., ☎ 808/923–9741; 🎟 $7) harbors more than 300 species of marine life.

The steep hike to the summit of **Diamond Head** (⊠ Monsarrat Ave. near 18th Ave., ☎ 808/971–2525) gives you a marvelous view of O'ahu's southern coastline. The entrance is about 1 mi above Kapi'olani Park. Drive through the tunnel to the inside of the crater, and then park and start walking.

Dining

The Aloha State is known for fine ethnic food—especially Chinese, Japanese, and Thai—and the culinarily spectacular Hawai'i Regional cuisine, based on fresh local produce and seafood.

$$$$ ✗ **Bali by the Sea.** The glorious ocean-side views of Waikīkī Beach might
★ be upstaged here by the menu with its blend of French and Asian influences. Enjoy entrées such as casserole of Hawaiian lobster and 'ōpakapaka (blue snapper) with Kaffir lime sauce. Another favorite is the rack of lamb crusted with macadamia nuts and herbs. ⊠ *Hilton Hawaiian Village, 2005 Kālia Rd., Waīkīki, ☎ 808/941–2254. Reservations essential. AE, D, DC, MC, V. No dinner Sun.*

$$$$ ✗ **La Mer.** This exotic, oceanfront Mandalay mansion serves some of
★ Hawai'i's best contemporary cuisine. A standout entrée is *onaga* (red snapper) fillet accompanied by a confit of tomato, truffle juice, and fried basil. ⊠ *Halekūlani, 2199 Kālia Rd., Waīkīki, ☎ 808/923–2311. Reservations essential. Jacket required. AE, MC, V. No lunch.*

$$$–$$$$ ✗ **Sam Choy's.** His motto is "Never trust a skinny chef," and indeed,
★ Choy's broad girth and even broader smile let you know you'll be well taken care of. The theme is upscale local, as the Hawai'i-born chef modernizes the foods he grew up with. The result? Brie-stuffed wontons with pineapple marmalade, seared ahi seasoned with ginger, and roasted duck with orange sauce. Portions are huge. ⊠ *449 Kapahulu Ave., 2nd level, Honolulu, ☎ 808/732–8645. AE, MC, V. No lunch.*

$$–$$$$ ✗ **Alan Wong's.** In his fabulous, low-key restaurant, Wong relies on
★ Hawaiian-grown products to keep the flavors super-fresh, and he's utterly creative, turning local "grinds" into gourmet treats. Garlic-mashed potatoes come with a black-bean salsa, grilled pork chops with a coconut-ginger sweet potato puree. Finding the restaurant can be difficult: Look for a white apartment building and a small sign after a parking garage, where your car can be valet parked. ⊠ *McCully Court, 1857 S. King St., 3rd floor, ☎ 808/949–2526. AE, MC, V. No lunch.*

$$–$$$$ ✗ **Golden Dragon.** Chef Steve Chiang is known for his unconven-
★ tional Cantonese and nouvelle-Chinese cuisine; signature dishes include stir-fried lobster with curry sauce and Szechuan beef. ⊠ *Hilton Hawaiian Village, 2005 Kālia Rd., Waīkīki, ☎ 808/946–5336. Reservations essential. AE, D, DC, MC, V. No lunch.*

$$–$$$$ ✗ **Hau Tree Lāna'i.** Right beside the sand at Kaimana Beach you can dine
★ under graceful hau trees, listening to the waves. For breakfast try the Belgian waffle or salmon omelet. Two standout dinner entrées are the jumbo shrimp fettuccine and a blue-cheese-and-herb-crusted New York steak. ⊠ *New Otani Kaimana Beach Hotel, 2863 Kalākaua Ave., Waīkīki, ☎ 808/921–7066. Reservations essential. AE, D, DC, MC, V.*

$$–$$$$ ✗ **3660 On The Rise.** Ten minutes from Waikīkī, in the up-and-com-
★ ing culinary center of Kaimukī, this stellar restaurant is known for home-grown ingredients combined with European flavors: Dungeness crab cakes served atop angel-hair pasta with a ginger-cilantro aioli. Light hardwoods, frosted glass, green marble, and black granite create a ca-

sual yet high-style ambience. ⊠ *3660 Wai`alae Ave., Honolulu,* ☎ *808/ 737–1177. AE, DC, MC, V.*

$$–$$$ ✕ **Keo's Thai Cuisine.** Hollywood celebrities have discovered this or-
★ chid-filled nook, where the Evil Jungle Prince (chicken, shrimp, or vegetables in a sauce of fresh basil, coconut milk, and red chili) is tops.
⊠ *Ambassador Hotel, 2040 Kūhiō Ave., Waikīkī,* ☎ *808/951–9355. Reservations essential. AE, D, DC, MC, V. No lunch.*

$$–$$$ ✕ **Roy's.** Two walls of windows allow you to gaze out at Maunalua
Bay and Diamond Head in the distance. The noisy two-story restaurant has a devoted following, thanks to its Euro-Asian-Hawaiian cuisine. It's hard to find a better blackened ahi in a hot, soy-mustard sauce.
⊠ *Hawai`i Kai Corporate Plaza, 6600 Kalaniana`ole Hwy., Honolulu,*
☎ *808/396–7697. AE, D, DC, MC, V.*

$–$$ ✕ **California Pizza Kitchen.** A glass atrium with tiled and mirrored walls
and one side open to the shopping mall creates a sidewalk-café effect.
Pizzas have unusual toppings: Thai chicken, Peking duck, Caribbean
shrimp. Pasta is made fresh daily on the premises. ⊠ *Kāhala Mall, 4211
Wai`alae Ave., Honolulu,* ☎ *808/737–9446. Reservations not accepted.
AE, D, DC, MC, V.*

$ ✕ **`Ono Hawaiian Foods.** There's usually a line outside after about 5
PM at this no-frills storefront restaurant. Locals come for Island innovations such as poi, *lomilomi* salmon (salmon massaged until tender
and served with minced onions and tomatoes), and *laulau* (steamed
bundle of ti leaves containing pork, butterfish, and taro tops). ⊠ *726
Kapahulu Ave., Honolulu,* ☎ *808/737–2275. Reservations not accepted. No credit cards. Closed Sun.*

Lodging

O`ahu's best accommodations are in or near Waikīkī, with a few places
of note in Honolulu. Except for Christmas week and the peak months
of January, February, and August, you'll have no trouble getting a room
if you call first. For bed-and-breakfasts contact **Bed and Breakfast
Hawai`i** (⊠ Box 449, Kapa`a 96746, ☎ 808/822–7771 or 800/733–
1632, FAX 808/822–2723).

$$$$ 🏨 **Halekūlani.** This serene and elegantly modern hotel has beautifully
★ detailed marble-and-wood rooms, some with breathtaking ocean views,
plus three of the finest restaurants in Honolulu. It's right on Waikīkī
beach, with lovely views of Diamond Head. ⊠ *2199 Kālia Rd., Waikīkī
96815,* ☎ *808/923–2311 or 800/367–2343,* FAX *808/926–8004. 456
rooms. 3 restaurants, pool, exercise room AE, DC, MC, V.* 🐢

$$$$ 🏨 **Hilton Hawaiian Village.** Waikīkī's largest resort includes four towers, a botanical garden, and a pond with penguins. Rooms are done
in raspberry or aqua, with rattan and bamboo furnishings. ⊠ *2005
Kālia Rd., Waikīkī 96815,* ☎ *808/949–4321 or 800/445–8667,* FAX *808/
947–7898. 2,545 rooms. 6 restaurants, pools, exercise room. AE, D,
DC, MC, V.* 🐢

$$$$ 🏨 **`Ihilani Resort & Spa.** At press time, `Ihilani was in the process of
★ conversion to a JW Marriott Resort, making it only the 10th Marriott
hotel to carry this designation. Guest rooms have marble bathrooms
with deep soaking tubs, and private lanai, many with ocean views. The
35,000-square-ft `Ihilani Spa presents everything from seaweed baths
to stair-climbers. ⊠ *92–1001 `Ōlani St., Kapolei 96707,* ☎ *808/679–
0079 or 800/626–4446,* FAX *808/679–0295. 387 rooms. 4 restaurants,
pools, golf, tennis, health club. AE, DC, MC, V.*

$$$$ 🏨 **Kāhala Mandarin Oriental Hawai`i.** Minutes away from Waikīkī,
on the quiet side of Diamond Head, this elegant oceanfront hotel is an
oasis of peace and comfort. Guest rooms are in off-white hues, with

touches of Asia and old Hawai'i in the art and furnishings. ⊠ *5000 Kāhala Ave., Honolulu 96816,* ☎ *808/739–8888 or 800/367–2525,* FAX *808/739–8800. 370 rooms. 3 restaurants, pool, exercise room. AE, D, DC, MC, V.*

$$$$ 🏨 **Outrigger Waikīkī on the Beach.** At this beachfront property in the heart of the best shopping and dining action, rooms have a Polynesian motif, and each has a lanai. ⊠ *2335 Kalākaua Ave., Waikīkī 96815,* ☎ *808/923–0711 or 800/688–7444,* FAX *800/622–4852. 530 rooms. 6 restaurants, pool. AE, D, DC, MC, V.*

$$$–$$$$ 🏨 **Aston at the Waikīkī Banyan.** Families enjoy this high-rise condominium resort near Diamond Head, one block from Waikīkī Beach and two blocks from the Honolulu Zoo. One-bedroom suites have daily maid service and private lanai. Look for the fishpond in the lobby area. ⊠ *201 'Ōhua Ave., Honolulu 96815,* ☎ *808/922–0555 or 800/922–7866,* FAX *808/922–0906. 307 suites. Pool, tennis. AE, D, DC, MC, V.*

$$$–$$$$ 🏨 **Waikīkī Parc.** Though its main entrance is down a narrow side street, this hotel is just one block from Waikīkī's beach. Guest rooms are done in cool blues and whites, with lots of rattan and plush carpeting. Added draws are the fine Japanese restaurant, Kacho; and the lovely Parc Café, known for its reasonably priced all-you-can-eat buffets. ⊠ *2233 Helumoa Rd., Waikīkī 96815,* ☎ *808/921–7272 or 800/422–0450,* FAX *808/ 931–6638. 298 rooms. 2 restaurants, pool. AE, D, DC, MC, V.*

$$–$$$$ 🏨 **New Otani Kaimana Beach Hotel.** Polished to a shine, this hotel is ★ open to the trade winds—right on the beach at the quiet end of Waikīkī, practically at the foot of Diamond Head. Get a room with an ocean view, if possible, and dine at least once at the Hau Tree Lānai. ⊠ *2863 Kalākaua Ave., Honolulu 96815,* ☎ *808/923–1555 or 800/356–8264,* FAX *808/922–9404. 125 rooms. 2 restaurants. AE, D, DC, MC, V.*

$$–$$$ 🏨 **Mānoa Valley Inn.** Tucked away in Mānoa Valley, just 2 mi from Waikīkī, this stately hotel built in 1919 features a complimentary Continental breakfast buffet on a shady lanai, and fresh tropical fruit and cheese in the afternoon. The country-style rooms have antique four-poster beds. ⊠ *2001 Vancouver Dr., Honolulu 96822,* ☎ *808/947– 6019 or 800/535–0085,* FAX *808/922–2421. 8 rooms, 4 with bath; 1 cottage. AE, DC, MC, V. CP.*

$$–$$$ 🏨 **Outrigger Royal Islander.** This inexpensive link in the Outrigger hotel chain is just a two-minute walk from a very nice section of Waikīkī Beach. Some rooms have ocean or park views and a few suites have kitchenettes; all accommodations have private lanai. Guests have access to pools at other Outrigger hotels. ⊠ *2164 Kālia Rd., Honolulu 96815,* ☎ *808/922–1961 or 800/688–7444,* FAX *808/923–4632. 101 rooms. AE, D, DC, MC, V.*

$–$$ 🏨 **Waikīkī Ha'na.** One block from the beach in Waikīkī, this eight-story hotel is convenient and clean; many rooms have private lanai. For a little extra you can rent a refrigerator for your room. ⊠ *2424 Koa Ave., Honolulu 96815,* ☎ *808/926–8841 or 800/367–5004,* FAX *808/586–0158. 72 rooms. Restaurant. AE, DC, MC, V.*

$ 🏨 **Royal Grove Hotel.** This small flamingo-pink hotel has rooms with kitchenettes. ⊠ *15 Uluniu Ave., Waikīkī 96815,* ☎ *808/923–7691,* FAX *808/922–7508. 85 rooms. Pool. AE, D, DC, MC, V.*

Nightlife and the Arts

Cocktail and Dinner Shows

Waikīkī's old pro, **Don Ho** (⊠ Waikīkī Beachcomber Hotel, 2300 Kalākaua Ave., ☎ 808/923–3981), still packs them in to his Polynesian revue with its cast of attractive Hawaiian performers. There's a cocktail and dinner show Sunday–Thursday at 7. Magician John Hirokawa displays mystifying sleight-of-hand in **Magic of Polynesia** (⊠

Waikīkī Beachcomber Hotel, 2300 Kalākaua Ave., ☎ 808/539–9460), with hula dancers and island music. Shows are nightly at 6:30 and 8:45.

Dinner Cruises

Patterned after an ancient Polynesian vessel, *Ali'i Kai* **Catamaran** (✉ Pier 5, Honolulu, ☎ 808/539–9400) takes passengers on a deluxe dinner cruise, complete with two open bars and a Polynesian show. **Royal Hawaiian Cruises** (✉ Honolulu Harbor, ☎ 808/848–6360) ferries you along O'ahu's south shores on the sleek *Navatek,* with gourmet food by Honolulu chef George Mavrothalassitis.

Lū'au

Royal Hawaiian Lū'au (✉ 2259 Kalākaua Ave., Waikīkī, ☎ 808/923–7311) takes place at the venerable Royal Hawaiian and is a notch above many other commercial lū'au presentations on the island.

Nightclubs

At **Lewers Lounge** (✉ Halekūlani, 2199 Kālia Rd., ☎ 808/923–2311), Bruce Hamada and friends perform contemporary jazz and standards Tuesday–Saturday from 10:30 to midnight. A vocalist-pianist sits in Sunday and Monday. The **Paradise Lounge,** at Hilton Hawaiian Village (✉ 2005 Kālia Rd., ☎ 808/949–4321), has all kinds of acts, such as island band Olomana (Friday–Saturday 8–midnight). **Nick's Fishmarket** (✉ Waikīkī Gateway Hotel, 2070 Kalākaua Ave., ☎ 808/955–6333) is probably the most comfortable of Waikīkī's upscale dance lounges, with an elegant crowd, smooth music, and an intimate, dark atmosphere. At **Rumours** (✉ Ala Moana Hotel, 410 Atkinson St., ☎ 808/955–4811), there's disco dancing with high-tech lights on Saturdays from 9 PM to 4 AM.

Theater

The **Diamond Head Theater** (✉ 520 Makapu'u Ave., ☎ 808/734–0274) is five minutes away from Waikīkī, right next to Diamond Head. Its repertoire includes a little of everything: musical comedies as well as experimental, contemporary, and classical dramas. The **John F. Kennedy Theater** (✉ 1770 East–West Rd., ☎ 808/956–7655) at the University of Hawai'i's Manoa campus is the setting for eclectic dramatic offerings—everything from Kabuki, Noh, and Chinese opera to contemporary musical comedy.

Outdoor Activities and Sports

Golf

Ala Wai Golf Course (✉ 404 Kapahulu Ave., ☎ 808/733–7387), on Waikīkī's mauka end, is quite popular; call ahead. Advance reservations are also recommended at the 6,222-yard **Hawai'i Kai Championship Course** and the neighboring 2,386-yard **Hawai'i Kai Executive Course** (✉ 8902 Kalaniana'ole Hwy., Honolulu, ☎ 808/395–2358 for either).

Tennis

In the Waikīkī area there are 4 free public courts at **Kapi'olani Tennis Courts** (✉ 2748 Kalākaua Ave., ☎ 808/971–2525); 9 at the **Diamond Head Tennis Center** (✉ 3908 Pākī Ave., ☎ 808/971–7150); and 10 at **Ala Moana Park** (✉ Makai side of Ala Moana Blvd., ☎ 808/522–7031).

Water Sports

Seemingly endless ocean options—from sailing to surfing—can be arranged through any hotel travel desk or beach concession. Try the **Waikīkī Beach Center,** next to the Sheraton Moana Surfrider, or the **C & K Beach Service,** by the Hilton Hawaiian Village (no phone).

Sailing lessons may be arranged through **Tradewind Charters** (☎ 808/973–0311). For scuba diving, **South Seas Aquatics** (☎ 808/922–0852) offers two-tank boat dives for $75. **Captain Bruce's Scuba Charters** (☎ 808/373–3590) leads intimate dive trips off O'ahu's west coast.

Hanauma Bay is famous for snorkeling. **Hanauma Bay Snorkeling Excursions** (☎ 808/373–5060) runs to and from Waikīkī. You can also get masks, fins, and snorkels at the park's **rental stand** (☎ 808/395–4725).

Beaches

Honolulu

Ala Moana Beach Park, across from Ala Moana Shopping Center, has a protective reef that keeps waters calm. Facilities include bathhouses, indoor and outdoor showers, lifeguards, concession stands, and tennis courts. **Hanauma Bay,** a 30-minute drive (or a $1 bus ride) east of Waikīkī, is a designated marine preserve with coral reefs and turquoise waters. Food and snorkel-equipment rental concessions, changing rooms, and showers are among the facilities.

Waikīkī

Fort DeRussy Beach, the widest part of Waikīkī Beach, has volleyball courts, picnic tables, showers, dressing rooms, and food stands. **Queen's Surf,** across from the Honolulu Zoo, is named for Queen Liliʻuokalani's beach house, which once stood here. The sand is soft, and there are plenty of shade trees and picnic tables; there's also a changing house with showers. The beach attracts a mixture of families and gays and lesbians.

Shopping

Just outside Waikīkī is the **Ala Moana Shopping Center** (✉ 1450 Ala Moana Blvd., ☎ 808/946–2811), a 50-acre open-air mall with a host of major department stores, including Liberty House, Hawaiʻi's home-grown department store chain. **Ward Centre** (✉ 1200 Ala Moana Blvd., ☎ 808/591–8451) has upscale boutiques and eateries. **Ward Warehouse** (✉ 1050 Ala Moana Blvd.) is a two-story mall with 65 shops and restaurants. **Aloha Tower Marketplace** (☞ Exploring Honolulu and Waikīkī, *above*) bills itself as a festival marketplace. Along with food and entertainment, it has shops and kiosks selling mostly visitor-oriented merchandise, from expensive sunglasses to refrigerator magnets.

In Waikīkī shopping options include the **International Market Place** (☞ Exploring Honolulu and Waikīkī, *above*). The **Royal Hawaiian Shopping Center** (✉ 2201 Kalākaua Ave., ☎ 808/922–0588) is three stories high and three blocks long, with 120 stores.

Side Trip to the North Shore

Arriving and Departing

From the Diamond Head end of Waikīkī go toward the mountains on Kapahulu Avenue and follow the signs to the Lunalilo Freeway (H–1). Take H–1 northwest to H–2 through Wahiawa. Then follow the signs to Haleʻiwa, which marks the official beginning of the North Shore.

What to See and Do

The **North Shore** of Oʻahu is the flip side of Honolulu. Instead of high-rises there are old homes and stores, some converted into businesses catering to tourists, surfers, and beach bums. The area's wide and uncrowded beaches, rural countryside, and slower pace are reminiscent of Hawaiʻi's other islands.

Haleʻiwa is a sleepy plantation town that has come of age with contemporary boutiques and galleries. Northeast of Haleʻiwa the road continues past such beaches as **Waimea Bay,** where winter waves can crest at 30 ft. **Waimea Valley** (✉ 59–864 Kamehameha Hwy., Haleʻiwa, ☎ 808/638–8511), once an ancient Hawaiian community, is a lush garden setting with wildlife, walks, and cliff-diving shows. You can have a free hula lesson here.

East of Hale'iwa is the **Polynesian Cultural Center** (⊠ 55–370 Kamehameha Hwy., Laie, ☎ 808/293–3333 or 808/923–1861; ⊡ $49, $65 with dinner), 40 acres containing lagoons and seven re-created South Pacific villages, with a spectacular evening lū'au and revue. The center is closed on Sunday.

THE BIG ISLAND OF HAWAI'I

Nearly twice as large as all the other Hawaiian Islands combined, this youngest of the chain is still growing: Since 1983 lava flowing from Kīlauea, the world's most active volcano, has added more than 70 acres to the island. In a land of South Seas superlatives, the Big Island is also the Aloha State's most diverse region. You can hike into volcanic craters, catch marlin, visit *paniolo* (cowboy) country, tour orchid farms and waterfalls, or simply sunbathe along 266 mi of coastline.

Visitor Information

Information and brochures are dispensed at the **Big Island Visitors Center** (HVCB) booths at Big Island airports and at HVCB offices in Hilo and Kailua-Kona. ⊠ *250 Keawe St., Hilo,* ☎ *808/961–5797,* ℻ *808/961–2126; 75-5719 Ali'i Dr., Kailua-Kona,* ☎ *808/329–7787,* ℻ *808/326–7563.* ✎

Arriving and Departing

Visitors to the west side of the island fly into **Kona International Airport** (☎ 808/329–2484). Those staying on the east side fly into **Hilo International Airport** (☎ 808/934–5801). Both airports are served by Aloha and Hawaiian airlines; United has direct flights from the mainland to Keāhole Kona International.

Exploring the Big Island

The Big Island is so large and varied that it's best to split up your exploring itinerary. You might spend a night in the county seat of Hilo, visit the paniolo town of Waimea, head to Volcanoes National Park for some hiking, then wind up on the west coast, home of the best beaches, weather, and nightlife.

Hilo and the Hāmākua Coast

Hilo is nicknamed the City of Rainbows because of its frequent showers, but rain or shine, this east coast town is truly beautiful. You can take a self-guided walking tour of downtown Hilo and its historic buildings with the help of a map from the **Lyman House Memorial Museum** (⊠ 276 Haili St., Hilo, ☎ 808/935–5021; ⊡ $7 includes guided tour of Museum and Mission House, map $1.50).

Banyan Drive, in Hilo, is lined with huge, leafy banyan trees with dangling aerial roots. They were planted along here in the 1930s by visiting luminaries such as Amelia Earhart and Franklin Delano Roosevelt; look for their names on plaques on the trees.

'Akaka Falls State Park (☎ 808/974–6200), where two waterfalls provide dramatic photo opportunities, is about 10 mi north of Hilo and 5 mi inland off Highway 19. **Honoka'a,** one of the sleepy little towns along Highway 19 north of Hilo, is where the first macadamia trees were planted in Hawai'i in 1881. **Waipi'o** lies 8 mi west of Honoka'a on Highway 240. Arrange here for a four-wheel-drive tour of

Waipi'o Valley (☎ 808/775–7121)—the least strenuous way to visit the valley's dramatic 2,000-ft cliffs and 1,200-ft waterfalls. The view from an overlook at the end of the highway is spectacular.

If you drive cross-island over to the west coast from here, stop at **Waimea** (also known by its older name, Kamuela), home to the **Parker Ranch Visitor Center and Museum** (✉ Off Hwy. 19, ☎ 808/885–7655). Several residences are open on the property and a prestigious art collection is on display. It's a 90-minute drive from Hilo.

Hawai'i Volcanoes National Park

Hawai'i Volcanoes National Park, a 359-square-mi park established in 1916, features an abundance of attractions inspired by Kīlauea. Just beyond the park entrance, 30 mi southwest of Hilo on Highway 11, is **Kīlauea Visitor Center** (☎ 808/985–6011), open daily 6:45–5, where displays and a movie focus on past eruptions. **Volcano House** (☎ 808/967–7321), dating from 1941, is a charming lodge with a huge stone fireplace. Windows in the restaurant and bar provide picture-perfect views of Kīlauea Caldera and its steaming fire pit, Halema'uma'u Crater. Drive around the caldera to see the **Thomas A. Jaggar Museum** (☎ 808/985–6049), with seismographs and filmstrips of current and previous eruptions. *Park Headquarters: ✉ Highway Belt Rd. (Hwy. 11), Box 52, Hawai'i Volcanoes National Park 96718, ☎ 808/985–6000. ⚐ $10 per car, $5 on foot or bike, $20 annual pass.*

Kailua-Kona

Kailua Pier is the center of much of the action in this seaside village on the west coast. During the sportfishing tournaments each summer, daily catches are weighed in here. In October it's the jumping-off point for the **Ironman Triathlon** (☞ Festivals and Seasonal Events *in* the United States Region by Region chapter). A short walk from the pier, **Hulihe'e Palace** (✉ 75-5718 Ali'i Dr., ☎ 808/329–1877; ⚐ $5) is one of only three royal palaces in America. Tour guides can fill you in on the royal lifestyle here, but the oversize doors and koa-wood furniture will more graphically illustrate how huge some of the early Hawaiian people were. During weekday afternoons hula *hālau* (schools) rehearse on the grounds.

A boat shuttles passengers from Kailua Pier to the 65-ft *Atlantis IV* submarine (✉ 75–5669 Ali'i Dr., ☎ 808/329–6626; ⚐ $79), which feels more like an amusement park ride than the real thing. A large glass dome in the bow and 13 viewing ports on the sides give up to 48 passengers clear views of the watery world outside.

Kohala Coast

Tour the Kohala Coast by driving north from Kailua-Kona on Highway 19 along the base of Mt. Hualālai, past sweeping stretches of old lava flows. When you get to the split in the road 33 mi from Kailua-Kona, turn left on Highway 270 toward Kawaihae and stop at the **Pu'ukoholā National Historic Site.** The visitor center tells the story of the three stone *heiau* (temples), one of them submerged just offshore, built here by King Kamehameha's men in 1791.

Dining and Lodging

With so many good restaurants on the scene, choosing a place to eat in the western part of the Big Island is difficult. The Kohala Coast is somewhat pricey, although Hilo dining has remained fairly inexpensive and family oriented. You can find good deals on charming accommodations by contacting **Hawai'i's Best Bed and Breakfasts** (✉ Box 563, Kamuela 96743, ☎ 808/885–4550 or 800/262–9912).

Hilo

$$–$$$$ ✕ **Café Pesto.** This is not your ordinary pizza place: Sample pizza *al pesto*, with sun-dried tomatoes, eggplant, and fresh basil pesto. Not in the mood for a pie? Order seafood risotto made with sweet Thai chili, Hawaiian spiny lobster, jumbo scallops, and tiger prawns. ⊠ *308 Kamehameha Ave.,* ☎ *808/969–6640. AE, D, DC, MC, V.*

$$–$$$ ✕ **Harrington's.** A popular and reliable steak-and-seafood restaurant, Harrington's has a dining lanai that extends out over the water. The mahimahi meunière and the Slavic steak (thinly sliced and slathered with garlic butter) are outstanding. ⊠ *135 Kalaniana'ole Ave.,* ☎ *808/ 961–4966. MC, V.*

$$–$$$$ ⊞ **Hawai'i Naniloa Hotel.** Ask for a room with an ocean or bay view when you book at this attractively modern hotel. The glass-walled exercise room has wraparound oceanfront views. ⊠ *93 Banyan Dr., 96720,* ☎ *808/969–3333 or 800/367–5360,* FAX *808/969–6622. 325 rooms. 2 restaurants, pools, golf, health club. AE, DC, MC, V.*

$–$$ ⊞ **Dolphin Bay Hotel.** All units have kitchens in this clean, homey hotel in a lovely, green Hawaiian garden setting four blocks from Hilo Bay. ⊠ *333 'Iliahi St., Hilo 96720,* ☎ *808/935–1466,* FAX *808/935–1523. 18 rooms. MC, V.*�@

Kailua-Kona

$$$–$$$$ ✕ **Jameson's by the Sea.** Sit outside next to the ocean or inside by the picture windows for glorious sunset views over Magic Sands Beach. Choose from three or four daily Island fish specials, or try stir-fried ocean scallops or Jameson's creamy clam chowder. ⊠ *77-6452 Ali'i Dr.,* ☎ *808/329–3195. AE, D, DC, MC, V. No lunch weekends.*

$$–$$$ ⊞ **King Kamehameha's Kona Beach Hotel.** Although its rooms are not particularly special, this is the only centrally located Kailua-Kona hotel— right next to the pier—with a white-sand beach. ⊠ *75-5660 Palani Rd., Kailua-Kona 96740,* ☎ *808/329–2911 or 800/367–6060,* FAX *808/329– 4602. 455 rooms. 2 restaurants, pool, tennis. AE, D, DC, MC, V.*@

$$ ⊞ **Kona Bay Hotel, Uncle Billy's.** These two- and four-story motel-type units are right in the center of town, across the street from the ocean. The atmosphere is friendly and fun-loving. Open-air dining around the pool is casual. Some rooms have kitchenettes. ⊠ *75-5739 Ali'i Dr., Kailua-Kona 96740,* ☎ *808/329–1393 or 800/367–5102,* FAX *808/ 329–9210. 146 rooms. Restaurant, pool. AE, D, DC, MC, V.*@

Kohala Coast and Waimea

$$$–$$$$ ✕ **CanoeHouse.** In this open-air beachfront restaurant surrounded by
★ fishponds, you can enjoy Pacific Rim cuisine with imaginative entrées such as grilled New York steak with a sauce of merlot and *panini* (local wild cactus fruit). ⊠ *Mauna Lani Bay Hotel, 68–1400 Mauna Lani Dr., Kohala Coast,* ☎ *808/885–6622. AE, D, DC, MC, V.*

$$–$$$$ ✕ **Merriman's.** Peter Merriman earns rave reviews for his imaginative
★ use of fresh, local ingredients, including vegetarian selections. Wok-charred *ahi* fish—a favorite entrée—originated here. ⊠ *Opelo Plaza, corner of Hwy. 19 and Opelo Rd., Kamuela,* ☎ *808/885–6822. Reservations essential. AE, MC, V.*

$$$$ ⊞ **Four Seasons Resort Hualālai.** At historic Ka'ūpūlehu, four clusters of bungalows house six or eight rooms each in this romantic oceanfront hotel. Sisal carpeting, natural slate floors, and Hawaiian artwork create a peaceful haven. Six suites have outdoor garden showers. The resort's golf course annually hosts the Senior PGA Tournament of Champions. ⊠ *Box 1269, Kailua-Kona),* ☎ *808/325–8000 or 800/ 332–3442,* FAX *808/325–8100. 274 rooms. 4 restaurants, pools, tennis. AE, DC, MC, V.*@

$$$$ ⊞ **Hāpuna Beach Prince Hotel.** This luxury hotel fronts the white sand
★ of Hāpuna, considered one of the best beaches in the country. The hotel

is a glitzy beauty with floors of rare slate tile, and 350 ocean-view rooms decorated in cool sand- and soft-green tones with marble bathrooms. ⊠ *62–100 Kauna'oa Dr., Kohala Coast 96743,* ☎ *808/880–1111 or 800/882–6060,* FAX *808/880–3142. 386 rooms. 5 restaurants, pool, golf, tennis, health club. AE, D, DC, MC, V.*

$$$$ 🏨 **Kona Village Resort.** Accommodations at this resort 15 mi north
★ of Kailua-Kona are in thatched-roof bungalows by the sea or around fishponds. The extra-large rooms, in soft earth-tone colors, are quiet and spacious and don't have telephones, TVs, or radios. ⊠ *Hwy. 19, 15 mi north of Kailua-Kona (Box 1299), 96745,* ☎ *808/325–5555 or 800/367–5290,* FAX *808/325–5124. 125 units. 2 restaurants, pools, tennis, health club. AE, DC, MC, V. Closed 1 wk in Dec. FAP.*

$$ 🏨 **Waimea Country Lodge.** Rooms, all with kitchenettes, look out on the green pastures of the island's cool Upcountry. ⊠ *65–1210 Lindsey Rd., Kamuela 96743,* ☎ *808/885–4100,* FAX *808/885–6711. 21 rooms. AE, D, DC, MC, V.*

Nightlife

Lulu's (⊠ 75–5819 Ali'i Dr., Kailua-Kona, ☎ 808/331–2633). A crowd dances every evening here to hot dance music selected by a professional DJ. From Tuesday through Saturday you might be able to find some easy-listening jazz at the **Honu Bar,** in the Mauna Lani Bay Hotel and Bungalows (⊠ 68–1400 Mauna Lani Dr., Kohala Coast, ☎ 808/885–6622).

In Hilo **Fiascos** (⊠ 200 Kanoelehua Ave., Hilo, ☎ 808/935–7666) sometimes has live music.

Outdoor Activities and Sports

Camping and Hiking

Popular areas are the 13,796-ft **Mauna Kea,** in the northeast, and **Hawai'i Volcanoes National Park.** For more information contact the **Department of Parks and Recreation** (⊠ 25 Aupuni St., Hilo 96720, ☎ 808/961–8311).

Fishing

More than 50 charter boats are available for hire, most of them out of Honokōhau Harbor, just north of Kailua. For bookings call the **Kona Activities Center** (☎ 808/329–3171 or 800/367–5288).

Golf

On the Kohala Coast the **Mauna Kea Beach Resort** (⊠ 1 Mauna Kea Beach Dr., ☎ 808/882–5400) has a well-regarded 18-hole course. The North and South courses of the **Francis I'i Brown Golf Course** (⊠ Mauna Lani Resort, ☎ 808/885–6655) have 36 holes.

Sailing/Snorkeling

Captain Zodiac Raft Expedition (☎ 808/329–3199) offers a four-hour snorkel cruise off the Kona Coast. From January through April you may see humpback whales.

Scuba Diving

The Kona Coast has calm waters for diving. Outfitters include **Big Island Divers** (☎ 808/329–6068). Many Kohala Coast resorts, such as Waikoloa Resort, hold scuba diving classes for guests.

Beaches

Onekahakaha Beach Park, a protected white-sand beach 3 mi south of Hilo, is a favorite of local families. Close to Kailua-Kona the most popular beach is **Kahalu'u Beach Park,** where the swimming, snorkeling, and fine facilities attract weekend crowds. Currents can pull swimmers away from the beach when the surf is high. On the Kohala Coast **Anaeho'omalu Beach** (⊠ Royal Waikoloan Resort) is an expanse perfect for water sports. Instruction and equipment rentals are available at the north end. The long, white-sand **Kauna'oa Beach** (⊠ Mauna Kea Beach Resort) is one of the most beautiful on the island, but beware of the high surf that pounds the shore in winter. Amenities here are hotel owned. Between the Mauna Kea Beach and Mauna Lani resorts, **Hāpuna State Recreation Area** is a ½-mi crescent of sand flanked by rocky points. The surf can be hazardous in winter, but calmer summer water makes it ideal for swimming, snorkeling, and scuba diving.

Shopping

Many talented artists seek out the solitude and beauty of the Big Island. Consequently, galleries abound in Kailua-Kona, Waimea, North Kohala, Volcano, Hilo, and even in such out-of-the-way bergs as Holualoa and Kukuihaele, where you can purchase original artwork, fine woodwork, or other handmade crafts. Kailua-Kona has souvenirs from far-flung corners of the globe. In general, major stores and shopping centers on the Big Island open at 9 or 9:30 AM and close by 5:30 PM. Hilo's **Prince Kūhiō Shopping Plaza** (⊠ 111 E. Puainako St., Hilo, ☎ 808/959–8451) has specialty boutiques and larger stores; it stays open until 9 Monday through Friday. In Kona, most of the stores at the **Kona Coast Shopping Center** (⊠ Palani Rd.) are open daily 9–9, though the **KTA Super Stores** (☎ 808/329–1677) outlet (a supermarket) is open from 6 AM to midnight. **Ali'i Drive** is lined with small shopping malls. On the makai side, extending an entire block, is **Kona Inn Shopping Village** (☎ 808/329–6573). Much of this shopping arcade was once Kona Inn, a hotel built in 1929 that was a longtime landmark. Broad lawns on the ocean side are lovely for afternoon picnics.

MAUI

Maui is known for its perfect beaches, lively nightlife, and sophisticated resorts. Presiding over everything—from the sunny, active western Maui Gold Coast to laid-back Hāna, on the east side—is Haleakalā, the 10,023-ft dormant volcano whose peak is among the finest sunrise-viewing vantage points in the world.

Visitor Information

Maui Visitors Bureau (⊠ 1727 Wili Pa Loop, Wailuku 96793, ☎ 808/244–3530).

Arriving and Departing

Maui's major airport, **Kahului Airport** (☎ 808/872–3894), at the center of the island, is served by United, American, Delta, Hawaiian, and Aloha airlines. If you're staying in West Maui, you might be better off flying into **Kapalua–West Maui Airport** (☎ 808/669–0623), served by Aloha Airlines. The landing strip at **Hāna Airport** (☎ 808/248–8208) is served by Aloha Airlines.

Exploring Maui

West Maui

The road that follows the island's northwest coast passes through the beach towns of **Nāpili, Kahana,** and **Honokōwai,** which are all packed with condos and have a few restaurants. To the south is **Lahaina,** former capital of the islands and a 19th-century whaling town, where many old buildings have been renovated. On the ocean side of Lahaina's **Front**

Street is a banyan tree planted in 1873 and the largest of its kind in
Hawai'i. Docked at Lahaina Harbor is the brig **Carthaginian II** (☎ 808/
661–3262; ⌨ $3), a replica of a whaler now open as a museum. Also
worth a visit is the **Baldwin Home** (✉ 696 Front St., ☎ 808/661–3262;
⌨ $3), where missionary doctor Dwight Baldwin lived in the 1830s.
The **Wo Hing Temple** (✉ 858 Front St., ☎ 808/661–3262) was built
in 1912 as a mutual aid society headquarters for Chinese immigrants.

Central Maui

Kahului is an industrial town that most tourists pass through on their way
to the airport. The **Alexander & Baldwin Sugar Museum** (✉ 3957 Hansen
Rd., Pu'unēnē, ☎ 808/871–8058; ⌨ $4), which details the rise of sug-
arcane in the Islands, is about 2 mi from Ka'ahumanu Avenue (Highway
32), Kahului's main street. A right onto Pu'unēnē Avenue (Highway 350)
from Highway 32 will take you there. The museum is closed on Sunday.

Wailuku's Historical District centers on Main Street—drive out of Kahului on Kahumanu Avenue. **ʻĪao Valley State Park** is the home of **ʻĪao
Needle,** a 1,200-ft rock spire rising from the valley floor. Drive toward
the mountains on Wailuku's Main Street to reach the park.

Haleakalā and Upcountry

Haleakalā, a 10,023-ft dormant volcano, is the font from which all of
East Maui flowed and the centerpiece of a 27,284-acre national park—
the terrain and views are unmatched anywhere else in the world. Bring a
sweater or jacket since it's chilly at the top. From Kahului, drive on
Haleakalā Highway (Highway 37) toward the volcano's slopes. Turn left
on Highway 377. After about 6 mi make a left onto Haleakalā Crater
Road, where the switchback ascent begins. You can stop and learn something of the volcano's origins and eruption history at the **Park Head-
quarters/Visitor Center,** at 7,000-ft elevation on Haleakalā Highway. Maps,
posters, and other memorabilia are available at the gift shop here.
Haleakalā Visitor Center, at 9,740-ft elevation, has exhibits inside and a
trail that leads to a small crater nearby. The road ends at **Pu'u 'Ula'ula
Overlook,** the highest point on Maui, where you'll find a glass-enclosed
lookout. On a clear day you can see the islands of Moloka'i, Lāna'i,
Kaho'olawe, and Hawai'i. Before you head up Haleakalā, call (☎ 808/
871–5054) for the latest park weather conditions. ✉ *Haleakalā Crater
Rd. (Hwy. 378), Makawao,* ☎ *808/572–4400.* ⌨ *$10 per car. Park
headquarters and visitor center close at 4; Haleakalā visitor center closes
at 3.*

Upcountry, as the western slopes of Haleakalā are known, encompasses the fertile land responsible for much of Hawai'i's produce and
flowers. Heading down from the volcano's summit on Highway 377,
stop at **Kula Botanical Gardens** (✉ Upper Kula Rd., Kula, ☎ 808/878–
1715; ⌨ $4) to admire the tropical flora.

East Maui

The **Road to Hāna** is 55 mi of hairpin turns and spectacular scenery.
It begins in Pā'ia on the north coast and passes **Ho'okipa Beach.** At
Mile Marker 11 stop at the bridge over **Puohokamoa Stream,** where
there are pools, waterfalls, and picnic tables. Another mile takes you
to **Kaumahina State Wayside Park,** which has a picnic area and a
lovely overlook to the Keanae Peninsula. Past **Honomanū Valley,** with
its 3,000-ft cliffs and a 1,000-ft waterfall, is the **Ke'anae Arboretum**
(✉ Hāna Hwy., Mile Marker 17, Ke'anae; ⌨ free), devoted to native
plants and trees. Nearby is the **Ke'anae Overlook,** with views of taro
farms and the ocean; it's an excellent spot for photos. As you continue
on toward Hāna, you'll pass **Wai'ānapanapa State Park** (✉ Hāna

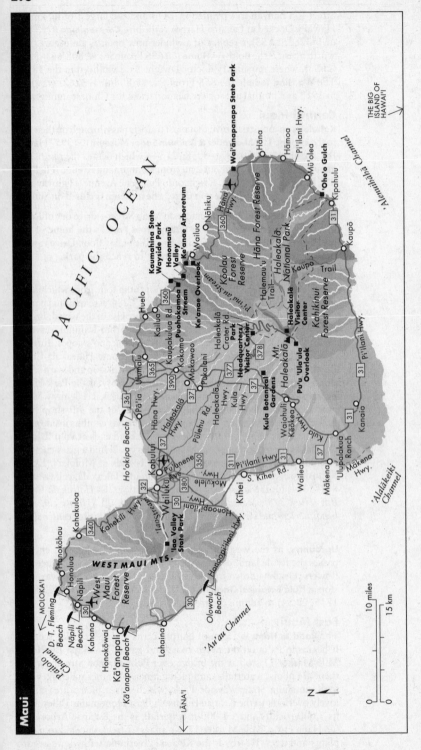

Maui

PACIFIC OCEAN

MOLOKA'I

Pailolo Channel

D. T. Fleming Beach
Honokōhau
Honolua
Kahakuloa
Nāpili Beach
Nāpili
Kahana
West Maui Forest Reserve
Honokōwai
Kā'anapali Beach
Kā'anapali
Lahaina

LĀNA'I

'Au'au Channel

340
Kahekili Hwy.

Waihe'e
Waiehu
Wailuku
Kahului
32
30
380
Honoapi'ilani Hwy.
30
'Īao Valley State Park
WEST MAUI MTS.

Olowalu Beach
Honoapi'ilani Hwy.

Ho'okipa Beach
Pā'ia
36
37
Hāna Hwy.
Pu'unēnē
Mokulele Hwy.
S. Kīhei Rd.
Kīhei
Pi'ilani Hwy.
31
311
350
Wailea
Mākena
Mākena Hwy.

'Alalākeiki Channel

Huelo
365
Kailua
360
Kaupakulua Rd.
Kokomo
390
Makawao
37
Pā'ia
Pukalani
377
Haleakalā Hwy.
Kula Hwy.
Pūlehu Rd.
37
Haleakalā Hwy.
Waiakoa
Keōkea
Kula Hwy.
31
'Ulupalakua Ranch
Kanaio

Pu'ohokamoa Stream
Ke'anae Overlook
Ke'anae
Pi'ina'au Stream
Ko'olau Forest Reserve
Haleakalā Crater Rd.
Park Headquarters/ Visitor Center
378
Mt. Haleakalā
Haleakalā Visitor Center
Pu'u 'Ula'ula Overlook
Kula Botanical Gardens

Kaumahina State Wayside Park
Honomanū Valley
Ke'anae Arboretum
Wailua
Nāhiku
360
Hāna Hwy.
Halemau'u Trail
Haleakalā National Park
Kahikinui Forest Reserve
Pi'ilani Hwy.
31
Kaupō
Trail
Kaupō

Wai'ānapanapa State Park
Hāna
Hāmoa
Pi'ilani Hwy.
Mu'olea
'Ohe'o Gulch
Kīpahulu
31

Hāna Forest Reserve
Halemau'u Trail

'Alenuihāhā Channel

THE BIG ISLAND OF HAWAI'I →

N

0   10 miles
0   15 km

Hwy. near Mile Marker 32, Hāna, ☎ 808/248–8061; ⚏ free), which has state-run cabins and picnic areas.

Hāna is just down the road from Wai'ānapanapa State Park. **'Ohe'o Gulch** and its famous pools are about 10 mi past Hāna on a bumpy stretch of road called Pi'ilani Highway; swimming is hazardous here, but it's a great place to sit in the sun or take pictures.

Dining and Lodging

Some of Maui's best restaurants are at resort hotels, which are mainly in West Maui and South Maui.

For B&B accommodations contact **Affordable Accommodations Maui** (⊠ 2825 Kauhale St., Kīhei 96753, ☎ 808/879–7865).

East Maui

$$$$ ★ ✕ **A Pacific Cafe.** The two Maui-based restaurants of Kaua'i's superstar chef, Jean-Marie Josselin, serve food from lands bordering the Pacific including dishes such as pan-seared mahimahi with a garlic sesame crust and ginger-lime sauce. ⊠ *Azeka Place II, Kīhei,* ☎ *808/879–0069; 3350 Lower Honoapi'ilani Rd., Lahaina,* ☎ *808/669–2724. AE, DC, MC, V. No lunch.*

$$–$$$$ ★ ✕ **Hali'imaile General Store.** It was a camp store in the 1920s, and now its painted tin exterior looks a little out of place in an Upcountry pineapple field, but the classic cuisine here has become a Maui institution. Sample fine smoked duck with pineapple chutney or dynamite barbecued ribs. ⊠ *900 Hali'imaile Rd., 2 mi north of Pukalani,* ☎ *808/ 572–2666. MC, V.*

$$–$$$$ ✕ **Makawao Steak House.** This Upcountry steak joint is one of the best on the island—a tender New York strip goes for less than $25. The fresh fish and fresh-baked bread are just as good. ⊠ *3612 Baldwin Ave.,* ☎ *808/572–8711. D, DC, MC, V. No lunch.*

$$$$ ★ 🏨 **Four Seasons Resort.** Low-key elegance defines this stunning property with open-air public areas and access to one of Maui's best beaches. Most rooms have ocean views and elegant marble bathrooms with high ceilings. ⊠ *3900 Wailea Alanui, Wailea 96753,* ☎ *808/874– 8000 or 800/334–6284,* ℻ *808/874–6449. 380 rooms. 3 restaurants, pool, health club. AE, D, DC, MC, V.* ✍

$$$$ ★ 🏨 **Hotel Hāna-Maui.** One of the best places to stay in Hawai'i is this small, secluded Hāna hotel surrounded by a 7,000-acre ranch. Rooms have bleached-wood floors, overstuffed furniture in natural fabrics, and local art. ⊠ *Box 9, Hāna Hwy., Hāna 96713,* ☎ *808/248–8211 or 800/321–4262,* ℻ *808/248–7264. 96 rooms. Restaurant, pools, exercise room, tennis. AE, D, DC, MC, V.*

$$ 🏨 **Heavenly Hāna Inn.** An impressive Japanese gate marks the entrance to this small upscale inn. The three suites, one a two-bedroom unit, all have TVs. Decor is spare, with Japanese overtones. ⊠ *Box 790, Hāna 96713,* ☎ *808/248–8442. 3 suites. AE, D, MC, V.*

West Maui

$$$$ ★ ✕ **Gerard's.** One of Hawai'i's most talented chefs, owner Gerard Reversade changes the French menu daily: You might find confit of duck or shiitake and oyster mushrooms in puff pastry. Prepare to do some stargazing, as this is a celebrity favorite. ⊠ *Plantation Inn, 174 Lahainaluna Rd., Lahaina,* ☎ *808/661–8939. AE, D, DC, MC, V. No lunch.*

$$–$$$$ ✕ **Roy's Kahana Bar & Grill.** Anyone who's ever eaten at one of Roy Yamaguchi's restaurants knows how good the cuisine is, and this Roy's is no exception. Such Asian-Pacific specialties as shrimp with sweet, spicy chili sauce keep regulars returning for more. ⊠ *Kahana Gate-*

way Shopping Center, 4405 Honoapi`ilani Hwy., Kahana, ☎ 808/669–6999. *AE, D, DC, MC, V.*

$–$$$ ✕ **Lahaina Coolers.** This breezy little café with a surfboard hanging from
★ its ceiling serves up such tantalizing fare as shrimp-pesto linguine with
prawns, basil, garlic, and cream, as well as pizzas, steaks, and burgers.
For dessert, try a chocolate taco filled with tropical fruit and berry "salsa."
⊠ *180 Dickenson St., Lahaina,* ☎ 808/661–7082. *AE, MC, V.*

$$–$$$ 🏨 **Lahaina Inn.** The 12 rooms here have antique beds and wardrobes,
and country-print curtains and spreads. You can sit in a wicker chair
on your balcony right in the heart of town. ⊠ *127 Lahainaluna Rd.,
Lahaina 96761,* ☎ *808/661–0577 or 800/669–3444,* ℻ *808/667–9480.
12 rooms. AE, D, MC, V. CP.* ✆

$$$$ 🏨 **Kapalua Bay Hotel.** Flowering orchids fill the lobby of this resort
★ hotel; there's a fine view of the ocean beyond. Rooms are spacious and
appealing. ⊠ *1 Bay Dr., Kapalua 96761,* ☎ *808/669–5656 or 800/
367–8000,* ℻ *808/669–4694. 194 rooms, 135 condo units. 3 restau-
rants, pools, tennis. AE, D, DC, MC, V.* ✆

$$$$ 🏨 **Ritz-Carlton.** This quietly luxurious Kapalua resort has spacious, com-
★ fortable rooms with oversize marble bathrooms and individual lanai,
most with panoramic ocean views. Service and business facilities are
first rate. ⊠ *1 Ritz-Carlton Dr., Kapalua 96761,* ☎ *808/669–6200 or
800/262–8440,* ℻ *808/669–3908. 550 rooms. 4 restaurants, pool, golf,
tennis, health club. AE, D, DC, MC, V.* ✆

Nightlife

The best options are in resort areas and Lahaina. **Moose McGilly-
cuddy's** (⊠ 844 Front St., Lahaina, ☎ 808/667–7758) has live music
Tuesday and Thursday evenings. **Molokini Lounge** (⊠ Maui Prince Hotel,
Mākena Resort, ☎ 808/874–1111) is a pleasant bar with live Hawai-
ian music, a dance floor, and an ocean view. The best lū`au on Maui
is the **Old Lahaina Lū`au** (⊠ 1287 Front St., Lahaina, ☎ 808/667–1998),
performed daily from 5:30 to 8:30.

Outdoor Activities and Sports

Golf

Maui's major resorts all have golf courses, and all are open to the pub-
lic. Most lower their greens fees after 2:30 on weekday afternoons. **Ka-
palua Golf Club** (⊠ 300 Kapalua Dr., Kapalua, ☎ 808/669–8044) has
three 18-holers. **Kā`anapali Golf Courses** (⊠ Kā`anapali Beach Resort,
Kā`anapali, ☎ 808/661–3691) contains two of Maui's most famous.
The **Wailea Golf Club** (⊠ 100 Wailea Golf Club Dr., Wailea, ☎ 808/
875–5111) has three courses.

Fees are lower at Maui's municipal courses such as **Waiehu Municipal
Golf Course** (⊠ off Hwy. 340 in West Maui, ☎ 808/244–5934), on
the northeast coast, a few miles past Wailuku.

Tennis

The finest facilities are at the **Wailea Tennis Club** (⊠ 131 Wailea Ike
Pl., Kīhei, ☎ 808/879–1958), often called Wimbledon West because
of its grass courts.

Water Sports

Fishing. You can fish year-round in Maui for such catch as Pacific blue
marlin and wahoo. Plenty of fishing boats run out of Lahaina and
Mā`alaea harbors, including those from **Lucky Strike Charters** (⊠ Box
1502, Lahaina 96767, ☎ 808/661–4606).

Sailing, Snorkeling, and Scuba Diving. Many outfitters provide com-
bination sailing and snorkeling cruises or scuba expeditions; some

also have whale-watching expeditions and sunset cruises. Call **Ocean Activities Center** (⊠ 1847 S. Kīhei Rd., Suite 203, Kīhei, ☎ 808/879–4485 or 800/798–0652); **Trilogy Excursions** (⊠ 180 Lahainaluna Rd., Lahaina, ☎ 808/661–4743 or 800/874–2666); or **Maui–Moloka'i Sea Cruises** (⊠ 831 Eha St., Wailuku, ☎ 808/242–8777).

Surfing. Although on land it may not look as if there are seasons on Maui, the tides tell another story. In winter the surf is up on the northern shores of the Hawaiian Islands, while summer brings big swells to the southern side. You can rent surfboards and boogie boards at many surf shops, such as **Second Wind** (⊠ 111 Hāna Hwy., Kahului, ☎ 808/877–7467), **Lightning Bolt Maui** (⊠ 55 Ka'ahumanu Ave., Kahului, ☎ 808/877–3484), and **Ole Surfboards** (⊠ 277 Wili Ko Pl., Lahaina, ☎ 808/661–3459).

Whale-Watching. Quite a few operations run whale-watching excursions off the coast of Maui, with many boats departing from the wharves at Lahaina and Ma'alaea each day. **Pacific Whale Foundation** (⊠ Kealia Beach Plaza, 101 N. Kīhei Rd., Kīhei 96753, ☎ 808/879–8811) pioneered whale-watching back in 1979 and now runs four boats, plus sea kayak excursions and special trips to encounter turtles and dolphins.

Windsurfing. Ho'okipa Bay, 10 mi east of Kahului, is the windsurfing capital of the world. Rent a board or take lessons from **Maui Ocean Activities** (⊠ 104 Wahikuli Rd., Lahaina, ☎ 808/667–1964).

Beaches

If you start at the northern end of West Maui and work your way down the coast, you'll find many beaches. **D. T. Fleming Beach,** 1 mi north of Kapalua, is a sandy cove better for sunbathing than swimming. **Nāpili Beach,** a secluded crescent, is right outside the Nāpili Kai Beach Club. **Kā'anapali Beach** is best for people-watching; cruises, windsurfers, and parasails launch from here. Farther south of Kā'anapali are **Wailea**'s five crescent-shape beaches, which stretch for nearly 2 mi with little interruption. South of Wailea are **Big Beach,** a 3,000-ft-long, 100-ft-wide strand, and **Little Beach,** popular for nude sunbathing (officially illegal here).

Shopping

You can browse through the stores of Front Street in Lahaina or the boutiques in the major hotels. Maui also has several major shopping malls. **Ka'ahumanu Center** (⊠ 275 Ka'ahumanu Ave., Kahului, ☎ 808/877–3369) has nearly 100 shops and restaurants. Also in Kahului is the **Maui Mall Shopping Center** (⊠ Corner of Ka'ahumanu and Pu'unēnē Aves., ☎ 808/877–7559), with 33 stores and a 12-screen megaplex. **Whalers Village** (⊠ 2435 Kā'anapali Pkwy., Kā'anapali, ☎ 808/661–4567) in the Kā'anapali resort area has good restaurants and upscale boutiques such as Tiffany & Co. and Louis Vuitton.

KAUA'I

Kaua'i's natural beauty is amazingly diverse. The cooler, damper north shore has lush landscaping, mist-shrouded peaks, and world-class golf courses; the southern shore has the sunshine; and the west coast is home to two geologic wonders: Waimea Canyon—the Grand Canyon of the Pacific—and the Nā Pali Coast.

Visitor Information

Hawai'i Visitors and Convention Bureau (⊠ 4334 Rice St., Suite 101, Līhu'e 96766, ☎ 808/245–3971 or 800/262–1400, ℻ 808/246–9235). **Po'ipū Resort Association** (⊠ Box 730, Kōloa 96756, ☎ 808/742–7444 or 888/744–0888, FAX 808/742–7887) is the central source of information about the south shore.

Arriving and Departing

Līhu'e Airport (☎ 808/246–1400), 3 mi east of the county seat of Līhu'e, handles most of Kaua'i's air traffic; it is served by Aloha and Hawaiian airlines.

Exploring Kaua'i

A coastal road runs around the rim of Kaua'i and dead-ends on either side of the rugged Nā Pali Coast. If you're looking for sunshine, head to the southern resort of Po'ipū; for greener scenery and a wetter climate, try Hanalei and Princeville to the north. For a bird's-eye view of the whole island, consider a helicopter excursion.

The Road North

Kīlauea Lighthouse (☎ 808/828–1413; ☎ $2), built in 1913, is now part of a wildlife refuge near the former plantation town of Kīlauea, north of Wailua on Highway 56. The **Hanalei Valley Overlook** encompasses a view of more than ½ mi of taro, the staple plant of the Hawaiian diet, plus a 900-acre endangered-waterfowl refuge. **Hanalei** is the site of the **Waioli Mission** (☒ Kūhiō Hwy., ☎ 808/245–3202; ☎ suggested donation $5), founded by Christian missionaries in 1837. It's closed Monday, Wednesday, Friday, and Sunday.

Smith's Tropical Paradise (☒ 174 Wailua Rd., Kapa'a, ☎ 808/821–6895; ☎ $5) is a 30-acre expanse of jungle, exotic foliage, tropical birds, and lagoons. From Wailua Marina, on the east coast, boats cruise up Wailua River to **Fern Grotto** (☒ Smith's Motor Boat Service, 174 Wailua Rd., Kapa'a, ☎ 808/821–6892; ☎ $15), a yawning lava tube with enormous fishtail ferns.

To the South and West

Kaua'i Museum (☒ 4428 Rice St., Līhu'e, ☎ 808/245–6931; ☎ $5) is chock-full of exhibits about the island's history. **Kilohana** (☒ 3–2087 Kaumuali'i Hwy., ☎ 808/245–5608; ☎ free), a historic sugar plantation, is now a 35-acre visitor attraction with upscale shops. **Po'ipū** is the premier resort town of Kaua'i's south shore and a mecca for body surfers. **Spouting Horn,** a waterspout that shoots up through an ancient lava tube, lies just west of Po'ipū along Highway 52.

Waimea, a sleepy little town, marks the first landfall of British captain James Cook to the Sandwich Islands in 1778. **Waimea Canyon,** created by an ancient fault in the earth's crust, stretches inland from Waimea. Spectacular views of the ever-changing reds, greens, and golden browns of the canyon—3,600 ft deep, 2 mi wide, and 10 mi long—can be seen from Pu'uka-pele and Pu'uhinahina lookouts. Waimea Canyon Drive passes through **Kōke'e State Park** (☎ 808/335–5871; ☎ free), a 4,345-acre wilderness. The drive ends 4 mi above the park at the 4,120-ft **Kalalau Lookout,** the best viewpoint in Kaua'i.

For a flightseeing adventure you won't easily forget—the rugged splendor of the Nā Pali Coast or the hidden waterfalls of Waimea Canyon—call the **South Sea Tour Company** (☒ Main Terminal, Līhu'e Airport, ☎ 808/245–2222 or 800/367–9214). The spectacular Nā Pali Coast is not accessible by land, so this may be your best way to have a good look.

Dining and Lodging

For an insider's look at Kaua'i, book with **Bed and Breakfast Hawai'i** (☒ Box 449, Kapa'a 96746, ☎ 808/822–7771 or 800/733–1632).

East and North Kaua'i

$$$-$$$$ ✕ **A Pacific Cafe.** With its cutting-edge cuisine, chef Jean-Marie Josselin's
★ restaurant has won many awards. The daily-changing menu might in-
clude grilled moonfish with black-olive polenta, sun-dried tomatoes,
pancetta, and shiitake mushrooms. The macadamia-nut torte sprinkled
with toasted coconut is tops. ⊠ *Kaua'i Village Shopping Center, Hwy.
56, Kapa'a,* ☎ *808/822–0013. AE, D, DC, MC, V. No lunch.*

$$$-$$$$ ✕ **La Cascata.** Terra-cotta floors and trompe l'oeil paintings give the restau-
rant the feel of an Italian villa, an influence that shows up in the cuisine
as well: Savor sautéed shrimp, lobster, clams, and scallops on pasta with
a spicy tomato-fennel sauce. ⊠ *Princeville Hotel, Princeville,* ☎ *808/
826–9644. Reservations essential. AE, D, DC, MC, V. No lunch.*

$-$$ ✕ **Bull Shed.** This A-frame restaurant is rustic, with exposed wood,
ocean views, and family-style tables. Alaskan king crab and prime rib
are on the menu. ⊠ *796 Kūhiō Ave., Kapa'a,* ☎ *808/822–3791. AE,
D, DC, MC, V. No lunch.*

$$$$ ⛨ **Princeville Hotel.** This splendid cliff-side property has breathtaking
★ views of Hanalei Bay. Bathrooms have gold-plated fixtures and picture windows that cloud up for privacy at the flick of a switch. The
setting and service are unmatched. ⊠ *5520 Ka Haku Rd., Princeville
96722,* ☎ *808/826–9644 or 800/826–4400,* ☏ *808/826–1166. 252
rooms. 3 restaurants, pool, golf, tennis. AE, D, DC, MC, V.* ✆

$$ ⛨ **Kapa'a Sands.** Furnishings in this intimate condominium are bun-
galow style, with rustic wood and ceiling fans. Ask for an oceanfront
room with open-air lanai and Pacific views. ⊠ *380 Papaloa Rd., Kapa'a
96746,* ☎ *808/822–4901 or 800/222–4901. 20 units. Pool. MC, V.*

South and West

$$$-$$$$ ✕ **Beach House.** This may be the best ocean view from any restaurant
★ on the south shore. The cuisine is equally superlative: The menu
changes often, but you might find grilled salmon with spinach won-
ton and shrimp-tomato broth. ⊠ *5022 Lawai Rd., Kōloa,* ☎ *808/742–
1424. AE, D, DC, MC, V. No lunch.*

$$-$$$$ ✕ **Piatti.** Gardens with torch-lit paths surround this historic home, once
the residence of a plantation manager, that serves Italian food in a Poly-
nesian atmosphere. Sit inside or on a wide veranda. Herbs come from
the manager's garden, and the fish might have been caught only hours
before it arrives at your table. ⊠ *2253 Po'ipū Rd., Kiahuna Plantation, Kōloa,* ☎ *808/742–2216. AE, DC, MC, V. No lunch.*

$$-$$$$ ✕ **Roy's Po'ipū Bar & Grill.** Hawai'i's culinary superstar Roy Yamaguchi
★ serves first-rate Euro-Asian-Pacific cuisine. Who but Roy could team
fresh seared 'aōpakapaka with orange shrimp butter and Chinese
black-bean sauce? ⊠ *Po'ipū Shopping Village, 2360 Kiahuna Planta-
tion Dr., Po'ipū Beach,* ☎ *808/742–5000. AE, D, DC, MC, V. No lunch.*

$-$$$$ ✕ **Brennecke's Beach Broiler.** At this veteran restaurant with picture
windows overlooking the ocean, the chef specializes in wood-broiled
foods and homemade desserts. ⊠ *Ho'one Rd., Po'ipū,* ☎ *808/742–7588.
AE, D, DC, MC, V.*

$-$$$ ✕ **Green Garden.** In business since 1948, this family-run no-frills
restaurant is brightened by an assortment of hanging and standing plants.
Local fare includes breaded mahimahi fillet and passion-fruit chiffon
pie. ⊠ *Hwy. 50, Hanapēpē,* ☎ *808/335–5422. AE, MC, V. Closed Tues.*

$$$$ ⛨ **Hyatt Regency Kaua'i Resort and Spa.** Low-rise, plantation-style
★ architecture with dramatic open-air courtyards, lush tropical landscaping, and spectacular rock-enclosed swimming lagoons make this
the most Hawaiian of Hyatts—and one of the most striking hotel resorts anywhere. Two-thirds of the rooms have ocean views. The 25,000-
square-ft spa is first-rate. ⊠ *1571 Po'ipū Rd., Koloa 96756,* ☎ *808/*

742–1234 or 800/233–1234, ℻ 808/742–6265. *607 rooms. 5 restaurants, pools, golf, tennis, health club. AE, D, DC, MC, V.* ✋

$$$ 🏨 **Garden Isle Cottages.** Tropical flower gardens surround these spacious ocean-side cottages five minutes from the restaurants of Po'ipū. One of the cottages, Hale Waipahu, sits on the highest point in Po'ipū, with a 360-degree ocean vista that takes in Brennecke's Beach. Six units have kitchens with microwaves, ceiling fans, and a washer and dryer; there are no telephones. ✉ *2666 Pu'uholo Rd., Kōloa 96756,* ☎ *808/742–6717 or 800/742–6711. 7 cottages. No credit cards.* ✋

$ 🏨 **Kōke'e Lodge.** Twelve mountaintop cabins are surrounded by pine trees and hiking trails. Furnishings are rustic (prices vary according to quality), but each is cozy, with a fireplace and fully equipped kitchen. ✉ *Box 819, Waimea 96796),* ☎ *808/335–6061. 12 cabins. Restaurant. AE, MC, V.*

Nightlife

Weekends, people gather at **Duke's Barefoot Bar** (✉ Kalapaki Beach, Lihu'e, ☎ 808/246–9599) to hear contemporary Hawaiian tunes. Of Kaua'i's lū'au options, **Kaua'i Coconut Beach Resort Lū'au** (✉ Coconut Plantation, Kapa'a, ☎ 808/822–3455 or 800/760–8555) is regarded by many as the best on the island.

Outdoor Activities and Sports

Fishing

For deep-sea fishing, **Sportfishing Kaua'i** (☎ 808/639–0013) has a 28-ft and a 38-ft six-passenger custom sportfisher.

Golf

Best known are the Makai and Prince courses at **Princeville Resort** (✉ Princeville, ☎ 808/826–3580).

Hiking

Kōke'e State Park (✉ Kōke'e Rd., Kōke'e, ☎ 808/335–5871) has 45 mi of hiking trails. The **Department of Land and Natural Resources** (✉ Līhu'e, ☎ 808/241–3446) provides hiking information.

Snorkeling and Scuba Diving

Explore spectacular underwater reefs with **Dive Kaua'i** (✉ 4–976 Kūhiō Hwy., Suite 4, Kapa'a, ☎ 808/822–0452). **Hanalei Sea Tours** (☎ 808/826–7254) has a four-hour snorkeling cruise off the Nā Pali coast.

Tennis

Princeville Tennis Center (☎ 808/826–9823) has six courts.

Beaches

The waters that hug Kaua'i are clean, clear, and inviting, but be careful where you go in: The south shore sees higher surf in the summer, and north-shore waters are treacherous in winter.

North Shore

On the winding section of Highway 56 west of Hanalei is **Lumahai Beach,** flanked by high mountains and lava rocks. There are no lifeguards here, so swim only in summer. **Hanalei Beach Park** has views of the Nā Pali coast and shaded picnic tables, but swimming here can be treacherous. Near the end of Highway 56, **Ha'ēna State Park** is good for swimming when the surf is down in summer. Highway 56 dead-ends at **Kē'ē Beach,** a fine swimming beach in summer.

South and West Shores

Kalapak i Beach, a sheltered bay ideal for water sports, fronts the Marriott in Līhu'e. Small- to medium-size waves make **Brennecke's Beach**

in Po'ipū a bodysurfer's heaven, and there are showers, rest rooms, and lifeguards. At the end of Highway 50 is **Polihale Beach Park,** a long, wide strand flanked by huge cliffs. Swim here only when the surf is small; there are no lifeguards.

Shopping

In Līhu'e is **Kukui Grove Center** (⊠ 3–2600 Kaumuali'i Hwy., ☎ 808/245–7742), Kaua'i's largest mall. **Coconut Marketplace** (⊠ 4–484 Kūhiō Hwy., Kapa'a, ☎ 808/822–0744) is a standout among east-coast malls. **Kaua'i Village Shopping Center** (⊠ 4–831 Kūhiō Hwy., Kapa'a, ☎ 808/822–4904) has 19th-century plantation-style architecture and 25 shops. **Princeville Shopping Center** (⊠ 5–4280 Kūhiō Hwy., Kapa'a, ☎ 808/826–3040), in the north end of the island, has interesting shops.

ELSEWHERE IN HAWAI'I

Moloka'i

With its slow pace and emphasis on Hawaiiana, Moloka'i drowses in another era. There are no high-rises, no traffic jams, and no stoplights on the 10- by 38-mi island. The fanciest hotels are bungalow style, and there's plenty of undeveloped countryside.

Visitor Information

Moloka'i Visitors Association (⊠ Box 960, Kaunakakai 96748, ☎ 808/553–3876 or 800/800–6367). **Maui Visitors Bureau** (⊠ 1727 Wili Pa Loop, Wailuku, Maui 96793, ☎ 808/244–3530).

Arriving and Departing

Ho'olehua Airport (☎ 808/567–6140), a tiny strip just west of central Moloka'i, is served by Hawaiian, Island, and Pacific Wings airlines.

What to See and Do

The **R. W. Meyer Sugar Mill and Moloka'i Museum** (⊠ Hwy. 470, 2 mi southwest of Pālā'au State Park, Kala'e, ☎ 808/567–6436; ⊠ $2.50) was built in 1877 and reconstructed to teach visitors about sugar's importance to the local economy. It's closed on Sunday.

Kalaupapa National Historic Park (⊠ Box 2222, Moloka'i 96742, ☎ 808/567–6802) was a leper colony until 1888. The pretty little town is now a National Historic Landmark. It's most accessible via **Damien Tours** (☎ 808/567–6171) or **Moloka'i Mule Rides** (⊠ 100 Kala'e Hwy., Kualapu'u 96757, ☎ 808/567–6088).

Lāna'i

Visitor Information

For visitor information contact **Destination Lāna'i** (⊠ 730 Lāna'i Ave., Suite 102, Lāna'i City 96763, ☎ 808/565–7600).

Arriving and Departing

Hawaiian Airlines and **Island Air** serve this tiny island, whose **airport** (☎ 808/565–6757) is a 10-minute drive from Lāna'i City.

What to See and Do

For decades Lāna'i was known as the Pineapple Island, with hundreds of acres devoted to growing the golden fruit. Today this 140-square-mi island has been called Hawai'i's most secluded island, and the pineapple industry has given way to tourism. There are two upscale hotels and two championship golf courses, but despite these additions, Lāna'i—the third smallest of the islands—remains remote and intimate.

Lāna'i is for those who love the outdoors, because the island has no commercial attractions other than those offered at the two resorts. You can visit such sights as the **Garden of the Gods,** where rocks and boulders are scattered across a crimson landscape; spend a leisurely day at **Hulopo'e Beach,** where the waters are brilliantly blue and clear; or hike to the top of **Lāna'ihale,** a 3,370-ft perch with a view of every inhabited Hawaiian island except Kaua'i and Ni'ihau.

IDAHO

Updated by
Kristin Rodine

Capital	Boise
Population	1,210,200
Motto	Esto Perpetua (It Is Perpetual)
State Bird	Mountain bluebird
State Flower	Syringa
Postal Abbreviation	ID

Statewide Visitor Information

Idaho Travel Council (⊠ Dept. of Commerce, 700 W. State St., Box 83720, Boise 83720-0093, ☎ 208/334–2470 or 800/635–7820).

Scenic Drives

Eighteen historic or scenic byways and segments of 10 historic trails are shown on the Official Idaho Highway Map, available from the Idaho Travel Council (☞ Statewide Visitor Information, *above*). The 35-mi **Lewis and Clark Back Country Byway,** 11 mi southeast of Salmon off Route 28 at Tendoy, traces the passage of explorers Meriwether Lewis and William Clark through the Continental Divide, along the crest of the Bitterroot and Beaverhead mountains near the Montana state line. The **Lake Coeur d'Alene Scenic Byway** cuts southwest on Route 3 through thick pine forests for 25 mi and then heads north on Route 97, shadowing the lake's crooked eastern shore for 35 mi.

National and State Parks

National Parks

With 40% of its acreage in trees, Idaho is the most heavily forested of the Rocky Mountain states. For information on all of Idaho's forests, contact **Boise National Forest** (⊠ 1750 Front St., Boise 83702, ☎ 208/373–4007). The Snake River Canyon plunges more than 1 mi at **Hells Canyon National Recreation Area** (⊠ 2535 Riverside Dr., Clarkston, WA 99403, ☎ 509/758–0616 or 800/523–1235), making it the deepest river gorge in the nation. Idaho has 3,000 mi of white-water river action, the most in the nation. Legend has it that the main Salmon River was nicknamed the River of No Return by Lewis and Clark boatmen after they witnessed the waters churning "with great violence from one rock to another . . . foaming and roaring . . . so as to render the passage of anything impossible." Reconsidering, the expedition party backtracked to Montana and pursued an alternate route via Lolo Pass over the Continental Divide. Today the main Salmon and its Middle Fork, an acclaimed stretch of white water, are surrounded by the 2-million-acre **Frank Church–River of No Return Wilderness Area** (⊠ Rte. 2, Grangeville 83530, ☎ 208/983–1950). Once used as a training site for U.S. astronauts because of its strikingly lunar appearance, the **Craters of the Moon National Monument** (⊠ Box 29, Arco 83213, ☎ 208/527–3257; ☑ $4 per vehicle) covers 83 square mi, with spatter cones, lava caves, and other eerie volcanic-formed features. In the **Sawtooth National Recreation Area** (⊠ Star Rte., Ketchum 83340, ☎ 208/727–5013 or 800/260–5970; ☑ $5 per vehicle), the jagged Sawtooth Mountains (often called America's Alps, with 42 peaks reaching at least 10,000 ft), join the Boulder and White Cloud ranges to stretch across 1,180 square mi, beginning just north of Ketchum on Route 75. Additional National Park Service properties include **Nez Percé National Historical Park** (⊠ Hwy. 95, Box 93, Spalding 83551, ☎ 208/843–2261);

Hagerman Fossil Beds National Monument (⊠ Box 570, Hagerman 83332, ☎ 208/837–4793); and **City of Rocks National Reserve** (⊠ Box 169, Almo 83312, ☎ 208/824–5519). Other federal land in Idaho is under the jurisdiction of the **Bureau of Land Management Idaho State Office** (⊠ 3380 Americana Terr., Boise 83706, ☎ 208/384–3000).

State Parks

The **Idaho Department of Parks & Recreation** (⊠ Box 83720, Boise 83720, ☎ 208/334–4199 or 800/635–7820) maintains 24 state parks. **Heyburn State Park** (⊠ Rte. 1, Box 139, Plummer 83851, ☎ 208/686–1308; ☜ $2), at the southern tip of Lake Coeur d'Alene on Route 5, encompasses nearly 8,000 acres of land and water and is known for its migratory herons, eagles, and osprey as well as an annual fall harvest of wild rice. Rising 470 ft, North America's tallest single-structured sand dunes are the centerpiece of **Bruneau Dunes State Park** (⊠ HC 85, Box 41, Mountain Home 83647, ☎ 208/366–7919; ☜ $3), just a stone's throw from the Snake River and roughly 60 mi southeast of Boise on Route 78. Fly fishers and a third of the Rocky Mountain trumpeter swan population flock to Henry's Fork of the Snake River, which winds through **Harriman State Park** (⊠ HC 66, Box 500, Island Park 83429, ☎ 208/558–7368; ☜ $3), on U.S. 20, 33 mi southwest of West Yellowstone, Montana.

Outdoor Activities and Sports

The **Idaho Travel Council** (☞ Statewide Visitor Information, *above*) has information about private campgrounds. For camping on federal and state lands, phone the national and state parks listed above. For information about hiking, backpacking, and rafting, contact the regional travel associations and local chambers of commerce (☞ Visitor Information, *below*) or **Idaho Outfitters and Guides Association** (⊠ Box 95, Boise 83701, ☎ 208/342–1919 or 800/847–4843).

The fishing season generally runs from the Saturday before Memorial Day through November. The **Idaho Department of Fish & Game** (⊠ 600 S. Walnut St., Box 25, Boise 83707, ☎ 208/334–3700 or 800/554–8685) provides licenses and information, including the excellent "Official Guide to Fishing in Idaho." A visitor's fishing permit costs $7.50 for the first day and $3 for each additional consecutive day. The department also publishes a wildlife viewing guide that lists the best and most easily accessible viewing sites in the state.

SOUTHERN IDAHO

Idaho's longest river, the Snake, carves a steely blue course of nearly 1,000 mi through southern Idaho, linking a diverse mix of terrain. Vast stretches of fertile farmland give way to desert plateaus blanketed in jet-black lava. Sweeps of sand dunes anchor the southwestern and eastern portions of the state. In between, waterfalls and springs spill into deep, rugged canyons. Pine-and-sage-clad mountains along the upper fringe of the Snake River plain hint of the taller Northern Rockies that rise within the state's borders.

Visitor Information

Southwest Idaho Travel Association (⊠ 168 N. 9th St., Suite 200, Box 2106, Boise 83702, ☎ 208/344–7777 or 800/635–5240). **South Central Idaho Travel Association** (⊠ 858 Blue Lakes Blvd., Twin Falls 83301, ☎ 208/733–3974 or 800/255–8946). **Southeastern Idaho Travel Association** (⊠ Box 498, Lava Hot Springs 83246, ☎ 208/776–5273 or 800/

423–8597). **Yellowstone/Teton Territory Travel Association** (✉ 505 Lindsay Blvd., Idaho Falls 83402, ☎ 208/523–1010 or 800/634–3246).

Arriving and Departing

By Bus

Greyhound (✉ 1212 W. Bannock St., Boise, ☎ 800/231–2222) serves Boise, Twin Falls, Pocatello, and Idaho Falls. **Sun Valley Express** (✉ Boise Municipal Airport, ☎ 800/634–6539) runs several daily round-trip van shuttles between Boise and Sun Valley. **Sun Valley Stages** (✉ Boise Municipal Airport, ☎ 800/821–9064) runs daily round-trip motor coaches between the airport, Sun Valley, and Twin Falls.

By Car

Boise is reached by I–84 from the east and the west. Route 55 heads south.

By Plane

Boise Airport (✉ 3201 Airport Way, ☎ 208/383–3110), 3 mi from downtown, is served by America West, Delta, Horizon, Northwest, Sky West, Southwest, United, and regional airlines.

Orientation Tours

The **Boise Tour Train** (✉ Capitol Blvd., ☎ 208/342–4796 or 800/999–5993; ☞ $6.50) provides a one-hour introduction to the city from May through October; tours depart from the depot across from the rose garden in Julia Davis Park.

Exploring Southern Idaho

Boise

The name Boise, French for "wooded," is traced to French-Canadian trappers who found a tree-laced greenway on the Boise River, a sight for sore eyes after trekking across the area's semiarid plain. Boise and surrounding Ada County now form a modern center of government and business. A mean temperature of 51°F and annual rainfall averaging about 18 inches create a hospitable setting for the headquarters of seven major corporations and a countywide population of more than 250,000.

Next to the Boise River, the grassy expanse of **Julia Davis Park** is home to two museums and **Zoo Boise** (✉ 355 N. Julia Davis Dr., ☎ 208/384–4260; ☞ $4), where zebras and Bengal tigers roam. An Old West saloon and relics from Idaho's early days as an Oregon Trail outpost fill the **Idaho State Historical Museum** (✉ 610 N. Julia Davis Dr., ☎ 208/334–2120; ☞ free). The adjacent **Boise Art Museum** (✉ 670 S. Julia Davis Dr., ☎ 208/345–8330; ☞ $4) focuses on American realism, but visiting exhibits showcase a wide range of artists and media.

Lady Bluebeard and Diamondfield Jack were among the more notorious felons who did time at the **Old Idaho Penitentiary** (✉ 2445 Penitentiary Rd., ☎ 208/368–6080; ☞ $4). The jail was in operation from 1870 until 1973; today it welcomes visitors for shorter stays. You can also tour a garden of Idaho native plants, a garden for children, a garden for butterflies and hummingbirds, and other theme gardens within the penitentiary confines at the **Idaho Botanical Garden** (✉ 2355 Penitentiary Rd., ☎ 208/343–8649; ☞ $3), open Tuesday–Sunday from April through October.

★ The **Discovery Center of Idaho** (✉ 131 W. Myrtle St., ☎ 208/343–9895, ☞ $4), a hands-on science learning center open from Tuesday to Sunday, has more than 120 displays on the northern edge of Julia Davis Park. The **Morrison-Knudsen Nature Center** (✉ 600 S. Walnut Ave., ☎

Idaho

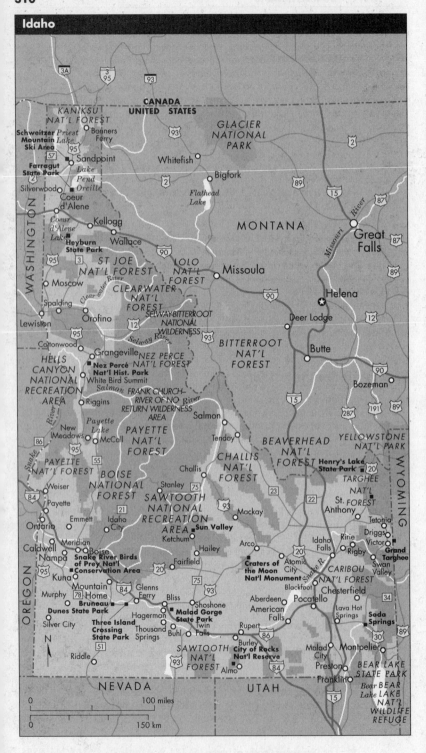

208/334–2225; ✉ donations accepted) features walk-through ecosystem exhibits of wetlands, plains, high-desert terrain, and mountain streams where fish can be viewed from above and below the surface. Outdoor exhibits are open daily; the visitor center is closed Monday.

★ Eight miles south of downtown Boise (take South Cole Road from I–84's Exit 50 and follow signs), the **World Center for Birds of Prey** (✉ 5666 Flying Hawk La., ☎ 208/362–8687, ✉ $4), open year-round, has live falcons, eagles, and other birds of prey. Guided 1½-hour tours throughout the day leave from the visitor center; special float tours through the nearby Snake River Birds of Prey Conservation Area are offered in summer. The largest concentration of Basque people in the United States has called Idaho's Snake River plain home since the late 1800s. You can visit a restored 1864 former boardinghouse, then go next door to the **Basque Museum and Cultural Center** (✉ 611 Grove St., ☎ 208/343–2671; ✉ donations accepted) to see colorful costumes, relics, and exhibits on Basque culture. The center is closed Sunday and Monday.

The Owyhee Uplands and the South-Central Region

South of Boise, from the Owyhee Mountains and arid Uplands east along the verdant Snake River canyon to Twin Falls, you'll find Oregon Trail wagon ruts, rocky gorges, hushed waterfalls, and springs trickling from canyon walls behind a veil of moss and ferns.

Just south of Murphy a 25-mi dirt road off Route 78 leads to the one-time queen of Idaho's mining region, **Silver City** (☎ 208/495–2319), now a ghost town with 70 rustic buildings. **Three Island Crossing State Park** (✉ Rte. 78 off I–84 near Glenns Ferry, ☎ 208/366–2394; ✉ $3) marks an important Oregon Trail wagon-train fording site on the Snake River. At **Malad Gorge State Park** (✉ off U.S. 30 north of Hagerman, ☎ 208/837–4505; ✉ $2) a suspension footbridge spans a 250-ft chasm as a 60-ft waterfall gushes into the Devil's Washbowl below. Warmed by geothermal springs, the **Hagerman Valley**—a patchwork of melon fields, orchards, and trout farms off U.S. 30—is the gateway to the **Thousand Springs Scenic Byway,** where springs gush from the north canyon wall. Five miles north of the town of Twin Falls (take Falls Avenue east from U.S. 30 and head north on 3300 East Road), **Shoshone Falls** (☎ 208/736–2240 or 800/255–8946; ✉ $3 per vehicle) cascade 21 ft–52 ft farther than Niagara Falls. They are most dramatic in spring.

Blackfoot, Bear Lake, and Lava Hot Springs

Billionaire J. R. Simplot made Idaho famous for its potatoes beginning in the 1940s. Today much of southeastern Idaho's fertile Snake River crescent, stretching from Burley to Idaho Falls, is devoted to agriculture.

★ A must-see is the **World Potato Exposition** (✉ 130 N. Main St., Blackfoot, ☎ 208/785–2517, ✉ $3), open from Tuesday through Saturday between May and October. Exhibits explain potato production and display spud oddities. The gift shop sells potato cookbooks and fudge and hands out "free 'taters for out-of-staters." **Bear Lake State Park** (☎ 208/945–2790; ✉ $3), south of Montpelier off U.S. 89 at St. Charles, is known for its dip-net fishing. Light reflecting off limestone particles suspended in the 80,000-acre lake (roughly half of which is in Utah) give it a stunning turquoise color that has earned it the moniker Caribbean of the Rockies. **Bear Lake National Wildlife Refuge** (☎ 208/847–1757; ✉ free), on the north shore of the lake, has one of the largest Canada geese populations in the western United States. The **National Oregon/California Trail Center** (☎ 208/847–0375) at the junction of U.S. 89 and 30 in Montpelier depicts life on a wagon train and in frontier settlements. A continuous flow of warm spring water at the base of lava cliffs has spawned the charming resort community of **Lava Hot Springs** (☎ 208/776–5221), 21 mi west of Soda Springs on U.S. 30.

Yellowstone/Teton Territory

Sixty miles of interconnecting scenic byways yield breathtaking views of the back sides of the Grand Tetons and Yellowstone Park. The **Mesa Falls Scenic Byway** (Route 47) travels through a 23-mi-wide caldera (volcanic crater) before traversing the Idaho portions of the **Targhee National Forest** (☎ 208/624–3151), which shelters pristine Upper and Lower Mesa Falls. The **Teton Scenic Byway** (Routes 32, 33, and 31 as the byway heads south from Ashton) passes through the small farming communities of Tetonia, Driggs, and Victor, all dwarfed by the Tetons just to the east. In winter hundreds of inches of dry, powdery snow draw skiers to the resort of **Grand Targhee** (⊠ Box SKI, Alta, WY 83422, ☎ 800/827–4433) just over the state line near Driggs.

Dining and Lodging

Boise

$–$$ ✕ **Doughty's Bistro.** The marble floor and high ceiling of this charm-
★   ing eatery reveal its history as a bank. Now chef Joyce Doughty provides a wealth of delicious, artfully presented dishes like chicken parmigiana with roasted vegetables ragout, goat cheese, and sage. There's an impressive wine list, and brunch is offered on Saturdays. ⊠ 199 N. 8th St., ☎ 208/336–7897. AE, D, MC, V. Closed Sun.–Mon.

$–$$ ✕ **Onati–The Basque Restaurant.** Photographs and memorabilia of Basque culture and history in Idaho line the walls of this roomy eatery set in the back of a casual bar. Savory lamb stew, chorizo sausage and rice, and squid in tomato sauce are standouts on the authentic Basque menu. ⊠ 3544 Chinden Blvd., ☎ 208/343–6464. AE, DC, MC, V.

$–$$ ✕ **Sandpiper.** High ceilings, oak tables, a nautical motif and live music on weekends create a fun atmosphere for dining on steak, seafood, and prime rib. ⊠ 1100 W. Jefferson St., ☎ 208/344–8911. AE, D, DC, MC, V. No lunch Sun.

$ ✕ **Harrison Hollow Brewhouse.** The massive timbers in this cozy brewpub nestled against the Boise foothills are echoed by huge portions of tasty fare such as overstuffed sandwiches and red beans and rice. Hot sauces and other condiments are packed in wooden toolboxes. An open fire adds to the ski-lodge atmosphere. Six to nine home-crafted ales are available at all times. ⊠ 24555 Harrison Hollow Rd., ☎ 208/343–6820. AE, MC, V.

$ ✕ **Noodles.** Locals flock to this casual downtown spot perched atop a wine bar for its trademark "pizza, pasta, and pizzazz." ⊠ 800 W. Idaho St., ☎ 208/342–9300. AE, MC, V. Closed Sun.

$$–$$$ ✕▥ **Owyhee Plaza.** Giant light fixtures and rich oak paneling remain from 1910, when this three-story downtown hotel was built. The elegant Gamekeeper restaurant specializes in flaming presentations. ⊠ 1109 Main St., 83702, ☎ 208/343–4611 or 800/233–4611, FAX 208/381–0695. 100 rooms. 2 restaurants, pool. AE, D, DC, MC, V.

$$ ▥ **Doubletree Hotel Riverside.** Nestled along the river, this modern hotel features airy public areas; spacious, well-equipped rooms; and complimentary chocolate chip cookies. ⊠ 2900 Chinden Blvd., 83714, ☎ 208/343–1871, FAX 208/344–1079. 304 rooms. 2 restaurants, pool, spa, sauna. AE, D, DC, MC, V. ⊜

$–$$ ▥ **Idaho Heritage Inn.** Each room has its own personality and politically
★   themed name at this lovingly restored B&B in a former governor's residence, about a mile east of downtown. Antiques, wallpaper, and old-style bed frames capture an early 1900s mood. Each room boasts a private bath. Breakfasts feature such fare as apple skillet cakes or French toast

stuffed with apricot cream cheese. ⊠ *109 W. Idaho St., 83702,* ☎ *208/ 342–8066,* ⅢX *208/343–2325. 6 rooms. AE, D, DC, MC, V. BP.*✎

Idaho Falls

$ ✕ **Mama Inez.** Five homemade salsas head the menu at this friendly Mexican restaurant two blocks from the scenic Snake River Falls. Try the braised-pork burritos heaped with green-chili sauce. ⊠ *344 Park Ave.,* ☎ *208/525–8968. MC, V. Closed Sun.*

$–$$ ⊡ **Best Western Driftwood.** Rooms in this two-story motel have refrigerators or kitchenettes. Picture windows gaze across the lawn to the falls of the Snake River, a short walk away. On the grounds are a rose garden and lush landscaped niches with benches and chairs. ⊠ *575 River Pkwy., 83402,* ☎ *208/523–2242 or 800/528–1234. 74 rooms. Pool. AE, D, DC, MC, V.*✎

Lava Hot Springs

$–$$ ✕⊡ **Riverside Inn and Hot Springs.** This restored 1914 inn by the Portneuf River has indoor and outdoor mineral hot tubs and an immaculate interior. Originally called the Honeymoon Hotel because it was so romantic, the inn has cozy rooms with colorful quilts and ceiling fans. President Truman once stayed here. TV and phones are limited to the lobby. ⊠ *255 E. Portneuf Ave., Box 127, 83246,* ☎ *208/776– 5504 or 800/773–5504,* ⅢX *208/776–5504. 16 rooms, 12 with bath. Restaurant. D, MC, V. CP.*✎

Twin Falls

$–$$ ✕ **Rock Creek.** There's a massive salad bar to accompany your steak, prime rib, or seafood—plus a wide range of wine, vintage ports, and single-malt whiskeys. ⊠ *200 Addison Ave. W,* ☎ *208/734–4154. AE, MC, V. No lunch.*

$ ✕ **Buffalo Café.** Ask anybody in town where to go for breakfast, and
★ you'll get the same answer: this tiny café. The house specialty is the Buffalo Chip, a concoction of eggs, fried potatoes, cheese, bacon, peppers, and onion. ⊠ *218 4th Ave. W,* ☎ *208/734–0271. No credit cards. No dinner.*

$$ ⊡ **Ameritel Inn–Twin Falls.** Built in 1993, this motel offers large rooms with dark wood furnishings. Fresh-baked cookies are served in the evening, and a generous Continental breakfast helps start your day. ⊠ *1377 Blue Lakes Blvd. N, 83301,* ☎ *208/736–8000 or 800/822–8946,* ⅢX *208/734–7777. 118 rooms. Indoor pool, spa. AE, D, DC, MC, V.*

Nightlife and the Arts

The **Idaho Shakespeare Festival** puts on first-rate performances in its beautiful open-air theater on Boise's eastern edge (⊠ 5657 Warm Springs Ave., ☎ 208/336–9221) from June through September. The **Boise River Festival** (☎ 208/344–7777 or 800/635–5240), held the last Thursday through Sunday in June, boasts more than 300 events, a huge nighttime parade, and entertainment on six stages.

Outdoor Activities and Sports

Fishing

The **Silver Creek Preserve** (⊠ Box 165, Sun Valley, ☎ 208/788–2203; ☒ free), northeast of Shoshone in south-central Idaho, offers catch-and-release fishing for rainbow, brown, and brook trout. In eastern Idaho, Henry's Fork of the Snake River and Henry's Lake in **Henry's Lake State Park** (☎ 208/558–7532) are renowned fly-fishing waters, with enormous rainbow and cutthroat trout. The **Targhee National Forest** (⊠ 420 N. Bridge St., St. Anthony 83445, ☎ 208/624–3151) watershed is home to Big Springs, spawning grounds for rainbow trout, which can be viewed from a bridge. **Bear Lake** (☞ Blackfoot, Bear Lake, and Lava Hot Springs, *above*), in the southeast corner of the state, is the only place where fishing for sardinelike ciscoes with dip nets is allowed. Fishing licenses are required.

Ski Areas

DOWNHILL

Bogus Basin (⊠ 2405 Bogus Basin Rd., Boise, ☎ 208/332–5151), 48 runs, 7 lifts, 1,800-ft drop. **Grand Targhee** (⊠ Driggs, ☎ 800/827–4433), 68 runs, 5 lifts, 2,200-ft drop. **Kelly Canyon** (⊠ Box 367, Ririe, ☎ 208/538–6261), 23 runs, 4 lifts, 1,000-ft drop.

Shopping

The **8th Street Marketplace** (⊠ Capitol Blvd. and Front St., Boise), a brick warehouse converted into more than 30 stores, sits on the east side of 8th Street across from the convention center. Near the marketplace, **Capitol Terrace** (⊠ Idaho and Main Sts., Boise) looks like a New Orleans French Quarter building, with a balcony level of shops. **Boise Factory Outlets** (⊠ Gowen Rd. off I–84, Exit 57, Boise) stretches along the freeway in southeast Boise with offerings from London Fog to Corning Revere. Power shoppers find bliss at **Boise Towne Square Mall** (⊠ Franklin Rd. exit off I–84, ☎ 208/378–4400), a giant indoor mall with 185 stores and a wide array of surrounding shopping plazas and restaurants.

CENTRAL IDAHO

Idaho's midsection is a dense mosaic of rugged wilderness terrain so impenetrable that even cartographers are hard-pressed to sketch roadways across the northern part of this region. A teeming waterway system fed by the **Snake** and **Salmon rivers** spins a lacy web across the bumpy landscape and has been the favored mode of transportation since the days of Lewis and Clark. The 420-mi Salmon is the longest undammed river in the lower 48 states.

Visitor Information

Hells Canyon and Lewiston–Clarkston: North Central Idaho Travel Association (⊠ 2207 E. Main St., Suite G, Lewiston 83501, ☎ 208/743–3531 or 800/473–3543). **McCall:** Visitors Information (⊠ Box D, McCall 83638, ☎ 208/634–7631). **Ketchum–Sun Valley:** Chamber of Commerce (⊠ Box 2420, Sun Valley 83353, ☎ 208/726–3423 or 800/634–3347). **Sawtooth Mountains:** Stanley/Sawtooth Chamber of Commerce (⊠ Hwy. 75, Box 8, Stanley 83278, ☎ 208/774–3411).

Arriving and Departing

From Montana, take U.S. 93. From Oregon, take U.S. 12 to U.S. 95. From Boise, take I–84 to U.S. 20/26.

Exploring Central Idaho

Sun Valley–Ketchum

At the precise point where alpine and desert climes converge, the legendary **Sun Valley** resort opened in 1935. Its signature pedestrian mall is patterned after an Austrian village.

Ketchum, a mile away, is an old mining town with an impressive array of shops and restaurants. Just outside Ketchum, beside Trail Creek, the **Ernest Hemingway Memorial** commemorates the writer's last years there. He is buried in the town cemetery.

McCall

The 108-mi drive north from Boise on Route 55 to the resort town of McCall runs along the shore of the Payette River as it rushes down mountains, over boulders, and through forests. The arid plains of the Snake River give way to higher and higher mountains covered by tremendous stands of pines. McCall lies at the southern end of lovely **Payette Lake.**

Hells Canyon and Lewiston-Clarkston

The ragged Seven Devils Range stands at 9,000 ft, rimming the southeastern lip of the Snake River Canyon, a deep, dark basalt abyss within the **Hells Canyon National Recreation Area** (☞ National Parks, *above*). Route 71 traces a portion of the gorge, but the best way to take in the scenery is by jet boat or raft (☞ Rafting *in* Outdoor Activities and Sports, *below*). North of Hells Canyon, Lewiston and its sister city, Clarkston, Oregon, owe their lifeblood to the confluence of the Clearwater and Snake rivers. Ships ply the waters 470 mi from the ocean via the Columbia River to Lewiston's inland seaport. Route 12, among the few east–west motor routes in this part of the state, travels from Lewiston to **Lolo Pass** on the Montana border, following the route that Sacagawea, Lewis and Clark's Native American guide, traced through the rugged wilderness. The **Nez Percé National Historical Park** (☞ National Parks, *above*) displays Nez Percé artifacts and outlines the history and culture of the Native American nation and its famous leader, Chief Joseph.

Dining and Lodging

McCall

$ ✕ **Romano's Ristorante.** This attractive and casual restaurant on the ground floor of the Yacht Club offers reliable pasta dishes and lovely views of Payette Lake. ⊠ *203 E. Lake St., 83638,* ☎ *208/634–4396. AE, MC, V.*

$–$$$ ▦ **Hotel McCall.** This hybrid between a hotel and a B&B is in the center of town. Rooms (and prices) vary widely; six are small and share a bath, while others are almost grand and have lots of light and antique furnishings. Some have views of Payette Lake. ⊠ *3rd and Lake Sts., Box 1778, 83638,* ☎ *208/634–8105,* 𝔽𝔸𝕏 *208/634–8755. 22 rooms, 16 with bath. AE, MC, V. CP.*

Sun Valley–Ketchum

$$–$$$ ✕ **Michel's Christiania.** Among the highlights at this Sun Valley classic are roast lamb in a parsley crust, sautéed ruby Idaho trout with hazelnuts and cream, and similarly elegant treatments of elk, duckling, and fresh seafood. The atmosphere blends white-linen elegance with rustic timbers and gigantic wrought-iron chandeliers. ⊠ *Sun Valley Rd. and Walnut St., Ketchum,* ☎ *208/726–3388. AE, D, MC, V.*

$ ✕ **Desperado's.** Huge burritos, black beans, and four kinds of salsa headline the menu at this popular Mexican restaurant in the heart of Ketchum. ⊠ *4th St. and Washington Ave.,* ☎ *208/726–3068. AE, D, MC, V.*

$$$–$$$$ ✕▦ **Knob Hill Inn.** Rooms at this modern luxury hotel with an alpine motif have large tubs, wet bars, and balconies with mountain views. Intermediate rooms, suites, and penthouses have fireplaces. ⊠ *960 N. Main St., Box 800, Ketchum 83340,* ☎ *208/726–8010 or 800/526–8010,* 𝔽𝔸𝕏 *208/726–2712. 24 rooms. 2 restaurants, pool, exercise room. AE, MC, V. BP.* ♨

$$–$$$$ ✕▦ **Sun Valley Resort.** The area's biggest resort includes a family-oriented inn, lodge-style accommodations, and condominiums. On the grounds are three pools, 18 tennis courts, and an ice-skating rink. Within the lodge complex, the Lodge Dining Room is the area's signature restaurant, known for its Sunday brunch. The resort is surrounded by towering pines; some rooms on the back side overlook the ice rink and the

ski-run carved face of ski mecca Baldy Mountain, 1 mi away. ⊠ *Sun Valley Resort, Sun Valley 83353,* ☎ *208/622–4111 or 800/786–8259, 208/622–2150 for dining room,* FAX *208/622–3700. 260 rooms, 280 condos. 5 restaurants, 3 pools. AE, D, DC, MC, V.* 🐾

$–$$ 🏨 **Lift Tower Lodge.** Look for the lift tower and chair (Western-style lawn art) in front of this basic motel. Half of the rooms face the ski mountain; the rest front Route 75, Ketchum's heavily traveled main drag. Ski lifts and restaurants are about three blocks away. ⊠ *703 S. Main St., Box 185, Ketchum 83340,* ☎ *208/726–5163 or 800/462–8646,* FAX *208/726–2614. 14 rooms. AE, D, DC, MC, V.*

Wilderness Camps and Lodges

$$$$ ✕🏨 **The Lodge at Riggins Hot Springs.** About 10 mi north of Riggins next to the Salmon River, this massive wood A-frame is nestled among pine trees overlooking the banks of the Salmon River, which is visible from all 10 rooms. Rafting, jet boating, and fishing trips can be arranged, and the huge outdoor pool is fed by hot springs. Meals are outstanding. ⊠ *Box 1247, Riggins 83549,* ☎ FAX *208/628–3725. 10 rooms. Restaurant, sauna. MC, V. FAP.* 🐾

$$$$ 🏨 **Twin Peaks Ranch.** Nestled in a mile-high valley between the Salmon River and the Frank Church–River of No Return Wilderness Area, Twin Peaks was one of America's first dude ranches. The 2,300-acre property, 2 mi off U.S. 93, contains cabins, the original 1923 ranch house, and an apple orchard set on several acres of lawn. Experienced wranglers teach horsemanship in the full-size rodeo arena; guided day rides and overnight pack trips are also available. Stocked trout ponds attract anglers, and guided fishing and white-water rafting trips can be arranged. ⊠ *Box 774, Salmon 83467,* ☎ *208/894–2290 or 800/659–4899,* FAX *208/894–2429. 13 cabins. Dining room, pool, hot tub. MC, V. Closed Jan.–Apr.* 🐾

$$$–$$$$ 🏨 **Idaho Rocky Mountain Ranch.** The ranch's 8,000-square-ft lodgepole-pine lodge remains much the same as when it was constructed in the 1930s. Period photographs hang on the walls, and animal trophies, rustic artifacts, and a massive rock fireplace immediately catch the eye. Lodge rooms and most of the duplex cabins have Oakley stone showers and handcrafted log furniture. Activities on the ranch's 1,000 acres range from hot-springs swimming to volleyball to horseback riding. ⊠ *HC 64, off Rte. 75; Box 9934, Stanley 83278,* ☎ *208/774–3544,* FAX *208/774–3477. 2 lodge rooms, 8 duplex cabins. Dining room, pool. D, MC, V. Closed May, Oct. MAP.* 🐾

Outdoor Activities and Sports

Fishing

Steelhead fishing is a major attraction in the **Frank Church–River of No Return Wilderness Area** (☞ National Parks, *above*). The 20-pound fish swim 1,800 mi to the ocean and back again to spawn in the Salmon River.

Hiking and Backpacking

The **Sawtooth National Recreation Area** (☞ National Parks, *above*) draws hikers and backpackers from afar. In winter, yurts (tents made of skins) in the Boulder, Smoky, and Sawtooth mountains are accessible for day ski trips or backcountry multiday trips. Extensive trail systems run through the **Selway Bitterroot** and **Frank Church–River of No Return** wilderness areas.

Rafting

Salmon and Stanley are launching points for trips on the **Salmon River,** including the famous **Middle Fork,** which runs 100 mi with 100 rapids. Reserve well ahead for summer. Riggins and White Bird are the takeoff points for trips down the northern portion of the Salmon and **Snake** rivers. The **Selway** and **Clearwater** rivers are other prime rafting waterways.

Ski Areas

Cross-Country

The central Idaho mountain valleys and backcountry are ideal for Nordic skiing. The **Wood River Trails** (⊠ Blaine County Recreation District, 308 N. Main, Hailey, ☎ 208/788–2117) system in the Ketchum–Sun Valley area grooms more than 100 mi of trails. The **Sun Valley Nordic Center** (⊠ Box 10, Sun Valley, ☎ 208/622–2250 or 800/786–8259) includes almost 25 mi of groomed trails spread across the Sun Valley Golf Course, just north of the Sun Valley Resort (☞ Dining and Lodging, *above*).

Downhill

Brundage (⊠ Box 1062, McCall, ☎ 208/634–4151 or 800/888–7544), 36 runs, 5 lifts, 1,800-ft drop. **Sun Valley** (⊠ Sun Valley 83353, ☎ 800/635–8261 or 800/786–8259), 78 runs, 20 lifts, 3,400-ft drop. **Soldier Mountain** (⊠ Box 465, Fairfield, ☎ 208/764–2526), 35 runs, 2 lifts, 1,400-ft drop.

NORTHERN IDAHO

Water reigns supreme in wooded northern Idaho, which claims more than 140 lakes (the highest concentration in the western United States) and 2,000 mi of streams and rivers. Six major lakes, including **Coeur d'Alene** and the state's largest, **Pend Oreille,** dominate the Panhandle.

Visitor Information

Coeur d'Alene: Convention & Visitors Bureau (⊠ Box 1088, 83816, ☎ 208/664–0587). **North Idaho Travel Committee:** (⊠ Box 877, Coeur d'Alene 83814, ☎ 208/769–1537). **Silver Valley:** Wallace Chamber of Commerce (⊠ 10 River St., Wallace 83873, ☎ 208/753–7151).

Arriving and Departing

By Bus
Greyhound (⊠ 1527 Northwest Blvd., Coeur d'Alene, ☎ 800/231–2222).

By Car
The major highways serving northern Idaho are I–90 (east–west) and U.S. 95 (north–south).

By Plane
The nearest airport is **Spokane International** (☎ 509/455–6455), 20 mi from Coeur d'Alene in eastern Washington. Delta, Horizon, Northwest, Southwest, and United fly into Spokane.

By Train
Amtrak (☎ 800/872–7245) serves Sandpoint, about 40 mi north of Coeur d'Alene.

Exploring Northern Idaho

Coeur d'Alene and the Silver Valley

Nestled in a pine-green mantle beside a gem of a lake, **Coeur d'Alene** has perhaps the most idyllic setting of any Idaho town. Restaurants with waterfront dining, a 3,300-ft floating boardwalk, and resort hotels cluster along the water's edge. American bald eagles and the largest population of osprey in the western United States make their homes here; the watery playground attracts sailors and water-skiers as well. With more than 29 golf courses within an hour's drive of Coeur d'Alene, it's a golfer's paradise; sightseeing cruises pass by the floating 14th hole of the golf course at the Coeur d'Alene Resort (☞ Dining and Lodging, *below*).

About 14 mi north of Coeur d'Alene on U.S. 95, **Silverwood Amusement Park** (☎ 208/683–3400; 🎫 $22) features a perfectly reconstructed turn-of-the-20th-century mining town. Rides range from a vintage biplane to an eight-story roller coaster called Tremors.

Silver Valley, the world's largest silver-mining district, is centered in the towns of Kellogg and Wallace along I–90. The entire town of **Wallace** is listed on the National Register of Historic Places. Throughout July and August, the **Sixth Street Melodrama** (☎ 208/752–8871; 🎫 $8) recalls Wallace's colorful past. The **Wallace District Mining Museum** (☎ 208/753–7151; 🎫 $1.50) contains a mother lode of mining history. From May to mid-October, the Sierra Silver Mine Tour (☎ 208/752–5151; 🎫 $7.50) provides a peek into an old mine.

The Northern Lakes

The resort town of **Sandpoint,** on the northwestern shores of Lake Pend Oreille, is completely surrounded by mountains; it has been a railroad depot and a mining town but now survives on tourism and lumber. At the southern end of Lake Pend Oreille, 4,000-acre **Farragut State Park** (☎ 208/683–2425; 🎫 $3) supports a diverse wildlife population.

Route 57 provides access to remote **Priest Lake,** with 70 mi of densely wooded shoreline, and the **Upper Priest Lake Scenic Area,** just a jump from the Canadian border. The **Grove of Ancient Cedars,** on the west side of Priest Lake, is a virgin forest with trees up to 12 ft across and 150 ft high.

Dining and Lodging

Coeur d'Alene

$–$$ ✕ **Cedars Floating Restaurant.** This restaurant is actually *on* the lake, giving it wonderful views. Beer-marinated charbroiled steak is a specialty. ⊠ *U.S. 95, ¼ mi south of I–90,* ☎ *208/664–2922. AE, DC, MC, V. No lunch.*

$ ✕ **Hudson's Hamburgers.** These folks have been in business since 1907 with a six-item menu. Even rivals admit that Hudson's serves the town's favorite burgers. ⊠ *207 Sherman Ave.,* ☎ *208/664–5444. No credit cards. Closed Sun. No dinner.*

$$–$$$$ ✕🏨 **Coeur d'Alene Resort.** The plush rooms at this lakeside resort have either fireplaces or balconies with terrific views of the water. The lower-priced rooms are high-standard motel fare. Its top-of-the-line restaurant, Beverly's, is known for its fine Northwest cuisine, superb wine cellar, and incomparable views of the lake and mountains. ⊠ *2nd and Front Sts., 83814,* ☎ *208/765–4000 or 800/688–5253,* 🖷 *208/667–2707. 336 rooms. 4 restaurants, pool, golf, exercise room. AE, D, DC, MC, V.* 🕭

$–$$ 🏨 **Blackwell House.** This B&B in a Victorian jewel of a house is close to the lake and shopping. The quaintly elegant rooms have wing chairs, antique beds, and rich wood paneling, and the bathtubs are big and old-fashioned. ⊠ *820 Sherman Ave., 83814,* ☎ *208/664–0656 or 800/899–0656. 8 rooms, 6 with bath. AE, D, MC, V. BP.*

Priest Lake

$$–$$$$ ✕🏨 **Hill's Resort.** Cabins or condos all have kitchenettes, and some have fireplaces. The acclaimed restaurant features cream of morel soup, barbecued baby back ribs, and huckleberry pie. There's dancing in the summer. Nearby are hiking trails, a golf course, tennis courts and a boat launch. ⊠ *HCR 5, Box 162A, 83856,* ☎ *208/443–2551,* 🖷 *208/443–2363. 52 units. Restaurant. D, MC, V.* 🕭

Outdoor Activities and Sports

Fishing

Lake Pend Oreille is famous for kamloops (large rainbow trout), Priest Lake for mackinaw, and Lake Coeur d'Alene for cutthroat trout and chinook salmon. The St. Joe and Coeur d'Alene rivers are good for stream angling.

Ski Areas

DOWNHILL

Schweitzer Mountain (✉ Box 815, Sandpoint, ☎ 208/263–9555 or 800/831–8810), 55 runs, 6 lifts, 2,400-ft vertical drop. **Silver Mountain** (✉ 610 Bunker Ave., Kellogg, ☎ 208/783–1111), 50 runs, gondola, 5 lifts, 2,200-ft drop.

Shopping

Plaza Shops at the Coeur d'Alene (✉ 210 Sherman Ave., at 2nd St., Coeur d'Alene) is an enclosed mini-mall with 22 small shops offering a wide array of crafts and other goodies.

ILLINOIS

Updated by	**Capital**	Springfield
Joanne Cleaver	**Population**	11,895,849
	Motto	State Sovereignty—National Union
	State Bird	Cardinal
	State Flower	Purple violet
	Postal Abbreviation	IL

Statewide Visitor Information

Illinois Bureau of Tourism (✉ James R. Thompson Center, 100 W. Randolph St., Suite 3-400, Chicago 60601, ☎ 800/226–6632).

Scenic Drives

The Illinois part of the **Lake Michigan Circle Tour** follows the shoreline along Lake Shore Drive through Chicago and passes through the elegant suburbs of the North Shore: Evanston, Winnetka, Glencoe, Highland Park, and Lake Forest. **Great River Road** follows the Mississippi River, stretching the length of Illinois (more than 500 mi) from East Dubuque to Cairo (pronounced *kay*-ro).

National and State Parks

National Park
Shawnee National Forest (✉ 50 Rte. 145S, Harrisburg 62946, ☎ 618/253–7114 or 800/699–6637) blankets the southern tip of Illinois with 275,000 acres; it is here that glaciers stopped flattening the state during the last Ice Age.

State Parks
Illinois has more than 260 state parks, conservation areas, fish and wildlife areas, and recreation areas. For a magazine on state parks, including descriptions of state-owned resorts and lodges, contact the **Illinois Department of Natural Resources** (✉ 524 S. 2nd St., Springfield 62701-1787, ☎ 217/782–7454). **Illinois Beach State Park** (✉ Lake Front, Zion 60099, ☎ 847/662–4828), on Lake Michigan near the Wisconsin border, has sandy beaches along 6½ mi of shoreline. **Rend Lake/Wayne Fitzgerrell State Park** (✉ 11094 Ranger Rd., Whittington 62897, ☎ 618/629–2320) has the state's second-largest inland lake, where you can fish, sail, and swim. **Starved Rock State Park** (✉ Box 509, Utica 61373, ☎ 815/667–4726), on the Illinois River between LaSalle and Ottawa, has 18 canyons formed during the melting of the glaciers. The park is about a two-hour drive from downtown Chicago.

CHICAGO

From the elegance of Michigan Avenue's shops to the stunning sweep of the lakefront skyline, Chicago has much to offer. The Loop, the city's central business district, is a living museum of skyscraper architecture, while many outlying neighborhoods retain the grace and homey quality of pre–World War II America. Chicago's arts community is world class, and strong ethnic communities embrace immigrants from countries as disparate as Croatia and Cambodia, all of whom leave their cultural stamp on the city.

Visitor Information

Chicago Office of Tourism: Visitor Information Center (⊠ Chicago Cultural Center, 77 E. Randolph St., 60602, ☎ 312/744–2400 or 800/226–6632) and **walk-in centers** (⊠ historic Water Tower, 806 N. Michigan Ave.). **Mayor's Office of Special Events:** General Information and Activities (⊠ 121 N. La Salle St., Room 703, 60602, ☎ 312/744–3315; 312/744–3370 for recordings on events and festivals).

Arriving and Departing

By Bus
Greyhound (⊠ 630 W. Harrison St., ☎ 312/408–5980 or 800/231–2222).

By Car
From the east the Indiana Toll Road (I–80/90) leads to the Chicago Skyway (also a toll road), which runs into the Dan Ryan Expressway (I–90/94); take the Dan Ryan west to any downtown exit. From the south, take I–57 to the Dan Ryan. From the west follow I–80 to I–55, which is the major artery from the southwest and leads into Lake Shore Drive. From the north I–94 and I–90 eastbound merge about 10 mi north of downtown to form the John F. Kennedy Expressway (I–90/94).

By Plane
Every national airline, most international airlines, and a number of regional carriers fly into **O'Hare International Airport** (⊠ I–90W, ☎ 773/686–2200), some 20 mi northwest of downtown Chicago. One of the world's busiest airports, it is a hub for United and American airlines. The **Chicago Transit Authority** (☎ 312/836–7000) subway station is in the underground concourse between terminals; for $1.50, trains will take you into the Loop. **Airport Express** (☎ 312/454–7799 or 800/654–7871) provides express coach service from O'Hare to major downtown and Near North hotels for a fare of $16 one-way. Metered taxicab service is available at O'Hare; expect to pay $27–$32 (plus tip) to Near North and downtown locations.

Many major carriers also use **Midway Airport** (⊠ 5700 S. Cicero, ☎ 773/838–0600) on the city's southwest side, close to downtown. The **Chicago Transit Authority**'s Orange Line train runs from Midway to the Loop, where you can transfer to other lines. Or for $11 you can take an **Airport Express** bus from Midway to hotels in the Loop and Near North. Cabs from Midway cost $17–$22, plus tip.

By Train
Amtrak serves Chicago's Union Station (⊠ 225 S. Canal St., at Jackson St., ☎ 800/872–7245).

Getting Around Chicago

The best way to see Chicago is on foot, supplemented by public transportation or taxi. Streets are laid out in a grid, the center of which is the intersection of Madison Street, which runs east–west, and State Street, which runs north–south.

By Car
Leave your car behind if you're visiting the Loop, the Near North Side, or Lincoln Park. You'll need a car to go to the suburbs or outlying city neighborhoods. Downtown parking lots charge $8–$20 a day.

By Public Transportation
The **Chicago Transit Authority** and the **Regional Transportation Authority** (☎ 312/836–7000 for both) provide information on how to get around

on city rapid-transit and bus lines, suburban bus lines, and commuter trains; the base fare is $1.50. On the subway and the El, you must use a fare card, which can be purchased at the station. Buses accept either cash (exact change only) or fare cards.

By Taxi

Taxis are metered. The base fare is $1.60, plus $1.40 for each additional mile or minute of waiting time. Taxi drivers expect a 15% tip. Major companies are **American United Cab** (☎ 773/248–7600), **Checker Taxi Association** (☎ 312/243–2537), and **Yellow Cab** (☎ 312/829–4222).

Orientation Tours

The **Chicago Architecture Foundation** (✉ 224 S. Michigan Ave., ☎ 312/922–3432) operates downtown walking tours of historic and contemporary architecture; bus tours; a river cruise; neighborhood tours; and, during summer, tours of two historical Prairie Avenue house museums—the Glessner House and the Henry B. Clarke House. **Wendella Sightseeing Boats** (✉ Lower Michigan Ave. at the Wrigley Bldg., ☎ 312/337–1446) and **Mercury Chicago Skyline Cruiseline** (✉ Michigan Ave. at Wacker Dr., ☎ 312/332–1353) run guided tours of the Chicago River and Lake Michigan throughout the spring, summer, and early fall.

Exploring Chicago

The Loop and Magnificent Mile epitomize the city's practical, savvy style. The patchwork of ethnic neighborhoods composing the rest of the city reflects the waves of immigrants who contribute to Chicago's cultural wealth.

The Loop

Walking through Chicago's central business district (defined by and named for the loop of the elevated train that circles it) is like taking a course in the history of American commercial architecture. From the Monadnock Building, the tallest load-bearing masonry structure in the world, to the Sears Tower, technically the tallest building of any kind in North America, Chicago's skyscrapers have unique personalities. Adorning the plazas of many buildings are sculptures by Picasso, Calder, Miró, and other artists.

The **Chicago Cultural Center** (✉ 78 E. Washington St., at Michigan Ave., ☎ 312/346–3278; 🎫 free) used to be the city's main library; now it's used primarily for free art and history exhibits, lectures, and performances. Two splendid, backlit interior Tiffany-glass domes are among its treasures.

The terra-cotta **Reliance Building** (✉ 32 N. State St., at Washington St.), designed by John Root and Charles Atwood in 1894, has the distinctive Chicago window, an innovation in early skyscrapers: two small panes of glass, which open to catch the Lake Michigan breezes, flanking a large center panel. The **Richard J. Daley Center** (✉ Dearborn and Washington Sts.), named for the late mayor, father of the current mayor Richard Daley, is headquarters for the Cook County court system; in the plaza is a 52-ft Cor-Ten steel sculpture by Picasso.

Spacious halls, high ceilings, and plenty of marble define the handsome neoclassical **Chicago City Hall** (✉ 121 N. La Salle St.) and the **Cook County Building** (✉ 118 N. Clark St.), designed by Holabird & Roche in 1911. If you're lucky, you may catch the city council in session—usually a good show, with plenty of hot air. Helmut Jahn's 1985 **James R. Thompson Center** (✉ Clark and Randolph Sts.), which houses state offices, has a jarring futuristic design in striking contrast to the city's classically styled civic structures.

A softly curving building emphasizing the bend in the Chicago River, **333 West Wacker Drive** was constructed in an irregular shape dictated by the triangular parcel on which it sits. The building, designed by Kohn Pedersen Fox in 1983 and set in a spacious plaza, has forest-green marble columns and a shimmering green-glass skin resembling the color of the river.

The graceful 1969 **First National Bank** (⊠ Dearborn and Madison Sts.) was one of the first skyscrapers to slope upward from its base like the capital letter *A*. The adjoining plaza is a summer lunchtime hangout. A Chagall mosaic, *The Four Seasons,* is at the northeast corner.

Chicago has some handsome examples of very early skyscrapers. The 1894 **Marquette Building** (⊠ 140 S. Dearborn St.), by Holabird & Roche, features an exterior terra-cotta bas-relief and interior reliefs and mosaics depicting scenes from early Chicago history. The darkly handsome **Monadnock Building** (⊠ 53 W. Jackson Blvd., at Dearborn St.) has walls 6 ft thick at the base. Groundbreaking architects Burnham & Root and Holabird & Roche worked out their structural engineering concepts on the building, erecting the north half of the building by 1891 and the south half in 1893.

The Gothic-style **Fisher Building** (⊠ 343 S. Dearborn St.), designed by D. H. Burnham & Co. in 1895, is exquisitely ornamented with carved terra-cotta cherubs and fish. The **Chicago Board of Trade** (⊠ 141 W. Jackson Blvd., at La Salle St.), a 1930 design by Holabird & Root, is one of the few important Art Deco buildings in Chicago. At the top is a gilded statue of Ceres, the Roman goddess of agriculture—an apt overseer of the frenetic commodities trading within.

★ The **Sears Tower** (⊠ 233 S. Wacker Dr., at Jackson Blvd., ☎ 312/875–9696, 🎟 $8.50) has 110 stories and reaches to 1,454 ft. A Skidmore, Owings & Merrill design of 1974, the tower affords unbeatable views from the sky deck, but there are long lines on weekends. The Wacker Drive lobby has a jolly mobile by Alexander Calder. In 1999, the Tower turned 25, and the sky deck was revamped. It now boasts a 4-ft-tall Chicago cityscape for children to explore. The imposing red-stone **Rookery Building** (⊠ 209 S. La Salle St., ☎ 312/553–6150), east of the Sears Tower, was designed in 1888 by Burnham & Root; Frank Lloyd Wright remodeled the magnificent lobby in 1905.

The Chicago Symphony Orchestra performs in Orchestra Hall, part of **Symphony Center** (⊠ 220 S. Michigan Ave.), known for its excellent acoustics and elegant 1904 design.

★ ☻ The **Museum of the Art Institute of Chicago** (⊠ 111 S. Michigan Ave., ☎ 312/443–3600, 🎟 $8), across the street from the Symphony Center, is one of the finest art museums in the world. In addition to its renowned collections of Impressionist and Postimpressionist paintings and medieval and Renaissance works, the museum contains the Thorne Miniature Rooms, illustrating interior decoration in every historical style; a renowned collection of Chinese, Japanese, and Korean art spanning five millennia; and a meticulous reconstruction of the trading room of the old Chicago Stock Exchange. The **Kraft Education Center** educates kids on artistic traditions and features an ever-changing gallery of original illustrations from well-known children's books. Reserve tickets for special museum exhibits as early as you can; only a few same-day tickets are available, and the line is usually long.

Largely unchanged since 1898, the **Fine Arts Building** (⊠ 410 S. Michigan Ave.) contains movie theaters showing foreign and art films. The handsome detailing on the exterior previews the marble and woodwork in the lobby. Around the corner from the Fine Arts Building, the 4,000-

Chicago

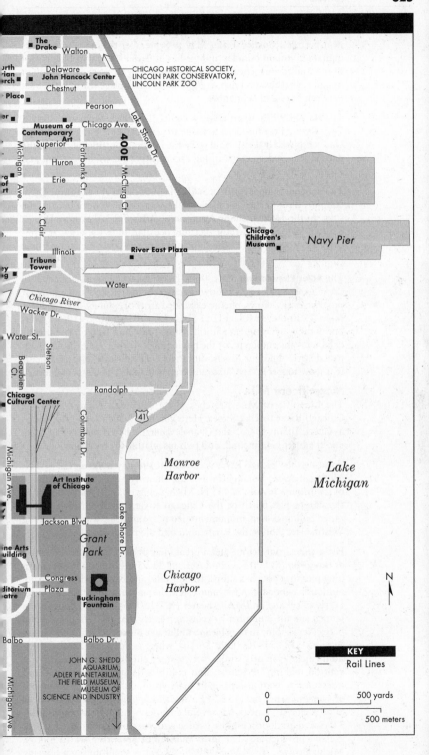

The Drake
Walton
Delaware
John Hancock Center
Chestnut
orth rian rch
Place
Pearson
Chicago Ave.
Museum of Contemporary Art
Superior
Huron
Erie

Michigan Ave.
St. Clair
Fairbanks Ct.
McClung Ct.
400 E
Lake Shore Dr.

CHICAGO HISTORICAL SOCIETY, LINCOLN PARK CONSERVATORY, LINCOLN PARK ZOO

Illinois
Tribune Tower
Water
River East Plaza
Chicago Children's Museum
Navy Pier

Chicago River
Wacker Dr.
Water St.
Stetson
Beaubien Ct.

Chicago Cultural Center
Columbus Dr.
Randolph
41
Monroe Harbor
Lake Michigan

Michigan Ave.
Art Institute of Chicago
Lake Shore Dr.
Jackson Blvd.
Grant Park
Chicago Harbor

ne Arts uilding
Congress Plaza
Buckingham Fountain
N

ditorium atre

Balbo
Balbo Dr.

KEY
Rail Lines

Michigan Ave.
JOHN G. SHEDD AQUARIUM, ADLER PLANETARIUM, THE FIELD MUSEUM, MUSEUM OF SCIENCE AND INDUSTRY

0   500 yards
0   500 meters

seat **Auditorium Theatre** (⊠ 50 E. Congress Pkwy., ☎ 312/922–2110), built in 1889 by Adler and Sullivan, has unobstructed sight lines and near-perfect acoustics. From May to September the mammoth **Buckingham Fountain** bubbles and gushes in **Grant Park,** two blocks east of the Auditorium Theatre. It's worth a detour to see the profusion of nymphs, cherubs, and fish. A light show takes place from 9 to 11 PM between May and September.

The **Harold Washington Library Center** (⊠ 400 S. State St., ☎ 312/747–4999), a postmodern homage to classical-style public buildings, was completed in 1991. Said to be the largest municipal library in the nation, it includes a performing arts auditorium, winter garden, and nearly 71 mi of shelves.

The museum campus north of Soldier Field and east of Lake Shore Drive contains three venues, with free trolleys running between each of the sites. At the **John G. Shedd Aquarium** (⊠ 1200 S. Lake Shore Dr., ☎ 312/939–2438; ☜ $13) the dazzling oceanarium is the draw. It replicates a portion of the Pacific Northwest ocean coastline and is home to beluga whales, Pacific dolphins, and a lively family of sea otters.

The **Adler Planetarium** (⊠ 1300 S. Lake Shore Dr., ☎ 312/322–0300; ☜ $5 general, $3 for sky show) has astronomy exhibits and a popular program of sky shows, plus an expanded array of exhibits. The **Field Museum** (⊠ Roosevelt Rd. at Lake Shore Dr., ☎ 312/922–9410, ☜ $8) is one of the country's great natural history museums. Don't miss the eerie exhibit on ancient Egypt, or the fascinating Life over Time display, with its extensive dinosaur fossils, dioramas, and full-scale models. Its current showstopper is "Sue," the most complete adult T-rex fossil ever found.

Magnificent Mile

The Magnificent Mile stretches along Michigan Avenue from the Chicago River to Oak Street. Here you'll find such high-price shops as Gucci, Tiffany & Co., and Chanel; venerable hotels such as the Drake and the Inter-Continental; and two fascinating art museums.

Fronting the Chicago River is the ornate **Wrigley Building** (⊠ 410 N. Michigan Ave.), headquarters of the chewing-gum empire. The base of the **Tribune Tower** (⊠ 435 N. Michigan Ave.), a 1930s Gothic-style skyscraper just north of the Chicago River, incorporates pieces of other buildings and monuments from around the world, including Westminster Abbey, the Parthenon, and the pyramids.

For a waterfront detour and a great view of the skyline, make a stop at **Navy Pier** (⊠ 600 E. Grand Ave., ☎ 312/595–7437), a former shipping pier that now has shops, restaurants, and bars. **Skyline Stage,** an outdoor pavilion for music, dance, and drama performances, has a huge Ferris wheel and an **IMAX theater** (☎ 312/595–0090). Skyline is the launch site for a number of cruising vessels that ply Lake Michigan.

Navy Pier is home to the **Chicago Children's Museum** (⊠ 700 E. Grand Ave., ☎ 312/527–1000; ☜ $6.50), where educational hands-on exhibits include an arts studio, a two-story climbing structure, an "invention making" machine, and exhibits on intergenerational and intercultural relationships. In its massive, modular home, the **Museum of Contemporary Art** (⊠ 220 E. Chicago Ave., ☎ 312/280–2660; ☜ $7.50), closed Monday, has several galleries of modern art; there's also a terraced outdoor sculpture garden and a performance space for progressive productions. The **Terra Museum of American Art** (⊠ 664 N. Michigan Ave., ☎ 312/664–3939; ☜ $7), a small museum housing industrialist Daniel Terra's superb private collection, includes works by almost every major American painter, including Whistler, Sargent, the Wyeths, and Cassatt; it is closed Monday.

One of the few buildings to survive the Chicago Fire of 1871, the **Water Tower** (⊠ Michigan Ave. at Pearson St.) sits like a giant sand castle at the heart of the Magnificent Mile. Inside is a visitor center.

The gray-marble high-rise called **Water Tower Place** (⊠ 835 N. Michigan Ave., ☎ 312/440–3165) has restaurants, a cinema, two department stores, and boutiques. You can view the city—and, on a clear day, Indiana and Wisconsin—from a height of 1,000 ft at the **observatory and outdoors skydeck** on the 94th floor of the 100-story **John Hancock Center** (⊠ 875 N. Michigan Ave., ☎ 312/751–3681; ⊒ $8.75); or enjoy the same view while you have a drink in the bar on the 96th floor. A change of pace from the North Michigan Avenue shops, the **Fourth Presbyterian Church** (⊠ 126 E. Chestnut St., ☎ 312/787–4570) is a Gothic-style jewel with a quiet courtyard. On Fridays, the sanctuary often holds organ recitals and concerts.

Lincoln Park

Lincoln Park is the area that stretches from North Avenue to Diversey Parkway and from the lakefront on the east to about Racine Avenue on the west. The adjoining lakefront park is also called Lincoln Park (causing visitors occasional confusion), though it stretches several miles farther north than the neighborhood.

The **Chicago Historical Society** (⊠ 1601 N. Clark St., ☎ 312/642–4600; ⊒ $5) contains a costumes alcove, as well as history galleries where you can view Lincoln's deathbed and artifacts and first-hand testimonials from the great Chicago Fire of 1871. Children love to climb aboard the *Pioneer* locomotive, Chicago's first train.

You'll find elegant town houses and small apartment buildings from the late 1800s and early 1900s in the **Lincoln Park neighborhood,** the heart of which is the intersection of Fullerton Avenue, Lincoln Avenue, and Halsted Street. The area declined after World War II as residents moved to the suburbs, but it was rediscovered in the 1970s; now it's full of million-dollar homes, coffeehouses, and funky boutiques. The **Biograph Cinema** (⊠ 2433 N. Lincoln Ave., ☎ 773/348–4123), where the gangster John Dillinger met his end at the hands of the FBI, is on the National Register of Historic Places and shows first-run movies.

Other Attractions

River North—a former warehouse neighborhood west of Michigan Avenue, bounded roughly by Clark Street, Chicago Avenue, Orleans Street, and the Chicago River—bloomed during the mid-1980s gentrification craze and now is home to a number of art galleries and trendy restaurants. **The Visitor Welcome Center** in the historic Water Tower (⊠ Michigan Ave. at Pearson St.) carries the *Chicago Gallery News*, which lists addresses, hours, and current exhibits.

The **Museum of Science and Industry** (⊠ E. 57th St. and S. Lake Shore Dr., ☎ 773/684–1414; ⊒ $7), on the lake in Hyde Park about 7 mi south of the Loop, is a treasure trove of historic and high-tech engineering marvels, applied science, and hands-on exhibits. There's a genuine German U-boat, a reproduction coal mine, Colleen Moore's Fairy Castle (a dollhouse to end all dollhouses), actual spacecraft from early NASA missions, and a giant-screen Omnimax theater.

Parks, Gardens, and Zoos

Most of Chicago's more than 20 mi of shoreline is parkland or beach reserved for public use. A 19-mi path stretches along the lakefront, snaking through **Lincoln Park, Grant Park** (just east of the Loop), and **Jackson Park** (just south of the Museum of Science and Industry, with a wooded island and the Osaka Japanese garden) and winding past half a dozen harbors, two golf courses, Navy Pier, Buckingham Fountain, the lakefront museum campus, McCormick Place, and all the city's popular beaches. Bikes are the best way to cover maximum territory; they can be rented in summer at the concession near the Lincoln Park entrance at Fullerton Avenue and Cannon Drive. Beware of bicycle thieves along the comparatively deserted stretch south of McCormick Place, especially on weekdays and at night.

★ ℃ The 35-acre **Lincoln Park Zoo** (✉ 2200 N. Cannon Dr., ☎ 312/742–2000, 🎫 free), the nation's oldest, is home to all the requisite zoo denizens, including koalas, reptiles, great apes, and lowland gorillas. Bring the kids to the **Children's Zoo** and the **Farm-in-the-Zoo,** which features farm animals plus a learning center with films and demonstrations. In Lincoln Park's **South Pond,** just south of the Lincoln Park Zoo, you can rent paddleboats May–October. The **Lincoln Park Conservatory** (✉ 2400 N. Stockton Dr., ☎ 312/742–7736; 🎫 free), which borders the Lincoln Park Zoo, has a palm house, a fernery, special exhibits, and large outdoor gardens.

There are hundreds of parks in neighborhoods throughout the city and suburbs. The **Garfield Park Conservatory** (✉ 300 N. Central Park Blvd., ☎ 312/746–5100; 🎫 free) maintains 5 acres of plants and flowers under glass and holds four shows a year. The **Chicago Botanic Garden** (✉ 1000 Lake Cook Rd., Glencoe, ☎ 847/835–5440; 🎫 $7 per car), north of the city in Glencoe, covers 385 acres and has 15 separate gardens and three biodomes. The **Morton Arboretum** (✉ Rte. 53 north of I–88, Lisle, ☎ 630/719–2465; 🎫 $7 per car), in the western suburbs, has 1,700 acres of woody plants, woodlands, and outdoor gardens, plus 13 mi of walking trails.

Dining

Most places listed below are in the Near North, River North, and Loop areas, within walking distance of the major hotel districts. For clusters of ethnic restaurants too numerous to mention here, try Greektown, at Halsted and Madison streets; Chinatown, at Wentworth Avenue and 23rd Street; Little Italy, on Taylor Street between Racine and Ashland avenues; Argyle Street between Broadway and Sheridan Road (for Chinese and Vietnamese); Devon Avenue between, Leavitt Street and Sacramento Avenue (Indian); and Clark Street, from Belmont Avenue to Addison Street (Thai, Japanese, Chinese, Korean, Ethiopian, Italian, and Mexican).

$$$$ ✕ **Ambria.** In an art nouveau building in Lincoln Park, Ambria has a seasonal, contemporary French menu that complements entrées with natural juices and vegetable reductions. Finish with the sensational dessert soufflé. ✉ *2300 N. Lincoln Park W,* ☎ *773/472–5959. Reservations essential. Jacket required. AE, D, DC, MC, V. Closed Sun. No lunch.*

$$$$ ✕ **Charlie Trotter's.** This top-of-the-line Lincoln Park town house ac-
★ commodates 28 tables. Chef-owner Charlie Trotter prepares stellar, innovative American cuisine with French and Asian overtones. Dishes are presented in a multicourse degustation format; there's even a nightly vegetable-based (but not vegetarian) tasting menu. ✉ *816 W. Armitage Ave.,* ☎ *773/248–6228. Reservations essential. AE, D, DC, MC, V. Closed Sun. and Mon. No lunch.*

$$$$ ✕ **Everest.** On the 40th floor of a postmodern skyscraper in the heart
★ of the financial district, Everest continues to scale heights by reinventing classic French cuisine with a contemporary twist. ✉ *440 S. La Salle St.,* ☎ *312/663–8920. Reservations essential. AE, D, DC, MC, V. Closed Sun. and Mon. No lunch.*

$$$$ ✕ **Le Français.** In a country-French setting, this restaurant in the northwestern suburbs turns out contemporary French creations that are vi-

sual masterpieces. Portions are substantial for cuisine this fine, and the desserts are delectable. ✉ *269 S. Milwaukee Ave., Wheeling,* ☎ *847/541–7470. Reservations essential. Jacket required. AE, D, DC, MC, V. Closed Sun. No lunch Mon. and Sat.*

\$\$\$\$ ✕ **Spiaggia.** In elegant pink-and-teal quarters overlooking the lake, Spi-
★ aggia is the most opulent Italian restaurant in town, with elaborate stuffed pastas, veal chops in a vodka-cream sauce, and other inventive dishes. Sample the kitchen's talents next door at Café Spiaggia, with lower prices but equally excellent meals. ✉ *980 N. Michigan Ave.,* ☎ *312/280–2750. Reservations essential. Jacket required. AE, D, DC, MC, V. No lunch Sun.*

\$\$\$\$ ✕ **Trio.** Creative touches distinguish Trio's elaborate contemporary cui-
★ sine; dishes may be served on such unique objects as painters' palettes. An eight-course degustation menu, priced at \$85, includes the chef's choice of specialties. ✉ *1625 Hinman Ave., Evanston,* ☎ *847/733–8746. AE, D, DC, MC, V. Closed Mon. No lunch.*

\$\$\$–\$\$\$\$ ✕ **Morton's of Chicago.** Chicago's best steak house serves beautiful, hefty steaks cooked to perfection. Excellent service, a classy ambience, and a very good wine list add to the appeal. Vegetarians should look elsewhere. ✉ *1050 N. State St.,* ☎ *312/266–4820. AE, D, DC, MC, V. No lunch.*

\$\$\$–\$\$\$\$ ✕ **Signature Room at the 95th.** The main draw here is the view—it's at the top of the John Hancock Center—though the elegant restaurant also has good food. At \$8.95, the weekday lunch buffet is a good bargain. Dinner is a very formal affair; the expensive Sunday brunch is splendid. ✉ *John Hancock Center, 875 N. Michigan Ave.,* ☎ *312/787–9596. AE, D, DC, MC, V.*

\$\$–\$\$\$\$ ✕ **Arun's.** Long considered the city's best—and most expensive—Thai restaurant, Arun's is also known for its congenial staff, its elegant dining room with Thai art, and, most importantly, superb dishes made with fresh ingredients. Try the 12-course tasting menu. ✉ *4156 N. Kedzie Ave.,* ☎ *773/539–1909. AE, D, DC, MC, V. Closed Mon. No lunch.*

\$\$–\$\$\$\$ ✕ **Marché.** This hip restaurant west of the Loop draws a see-and-be-seen crowd that includes many celebs. Standouts on the bistro menu are spit-roasted chicken and tempting desserts such as crème brûlée and chocolate truffle cake. ✉ *833 W. Randolph St.,* ☎ *312/226–8399. AE, D, DC, MC, V. No lunch weekends.*

\$\$–\$\$\$\$ ✕ **Philander's.** One of Oak Park's few fine restaurants, Philander's is also a prime place to hear live jazz every night. The hotel dining room feels like a classy tavern and serves reliable seafood, pastas, and vegetarian dishes, in addition to Peterson's ice cream—a local institution. ✉ *Carleton Hotel, 1120 Pleasant St., Oak Park,* ☎ *708/848–4250. AE, D, DC, MC, V. Closed Sun. No lunch.*

\$\$–\$\$\$\$ ✕ **Rosebud Cafe.** Specializing in good, old-fashioned southern Italian cuisine, Rosebud serves a superior red sauce, and the roasted peppers, homemade sausage, chicken Vesuvio, and exquisitely prepared pastas are not to be missed. ✉ *1500 W. Taylor St.,* ☎ *312/942–1117. AE, D, DC, MC, V. No lunch weekends.*

\$\$–\$\$\$\$ ✕ **Spago.** At this Wolfgang Puck spin-off, guests go for the stir-fry lamb and house-smoked salmon in the beautiful, modern dining room. The service is excellent. ✉ *520 N. Dearborn St.,* ☎ *312/527–3700. Reservations essential. AE, D, DC, MC, V. No lunch weekends.*

\$–\$\$\$\$ ✕ **Maggiano's Little Italy.** This convivial restaurant serves up enormous portions of red-sauce Italian food in a wide-open dining room. Lunchtime sandwiches are especially good. Additional locations are spreading throughout the suburbs. ✉ *516 N. Clark St.,* ☎ *312/644–7700. AE, D, DC, MC, V.*

\$\$–\$\$\$ ✕ **Printer's Row.** Named after its chic loft neighborhood in the South Loop, this warm and attractive restaurant specializes in game meats and seafood, with notable venison preparations. ✉ *550 S. Dearborn St.,* ☎ *312/461–0780. AE, D, DC, MC, V. Closed Sun. No lunch Sat.*

$–$$$ ✕ **Brasserie Jo.** Discerning diners come here to sample Everest chef Jean
★   Joho's food at relatively moderate prices. Don't miss the shrimp in a phyllo-dough bag or classic coq au vin. ✉ *59 W. Hubbard St.,* ☎ *312/ 595–0800. AE, D, DC, MC, V. No lunch weekends.*

$–$$$ ✕ **Frontera Grill/Topolobampo.** In Frontera Grill's cozy, colorful store-
★   front, genuine regional Mexican cooking goes way beyond burritos and chips. At Topolobampo, next door, slightly higher prices give the chef an opportunity to experiment with more expensive ingredients. ✉ *445 N. Clark St.,* ☎ *312/661–1434. Reservations essential at Topolobampo. AE, D, DC, MC, V. Closed Sun. and Mon. No lunch Sat. at Topolobampo.*

$–$$$ ✕ **Heaven on Seven.** Enter at Rush and Ontario streets to sample au-
thentic Cajun and Creole specialties—shrimp étouffée, jambalaya, gumbo, and the like—served in lively surroundings. ✉ *600 N. Michigan Ave.,* ☎ *312/280–7774. AE, D, DC, MC, V.*

$–$$$ ✕ **Yoshi's Cafe.** Chef Yoshi Katsumura's restaurant specializes in Asian-
influenced French bistro cuisine. Dishes are gorgeously presented; try the fresh seafood, such as tuna tartare with homemade guacamole. ✉ *3257 N. Halsted St.,* ☎ *773/248–6160. AE, DC, MC, V. Closed Mon. No lunch.*

$–$$ ✕ **The Berghoff.** This Loop institution has two huge, oak-paneled din-
ing rooms and a splendid bar with Berghoff beer on tap. Expect a wait of 15 minutes or so at midday. American favorites augment the menu of German classics (Wiener schnitzel, sauerbraten). ✉ *17 W. Adams St.,* ☎ *312/427–3170. AE, MC, V. Closed Sun.*

$–$$ ✕ **Le Bouchon.** Chef-owner Jean-Claude Poilevey serves reasonably
priced bistro fare at this intimate 45-seat French restaurant in Bucktown. The onion tart is a signature appetizer. Typical entrées include duck for two and sautéed rabbit with shallots and mustard. ✉ *1958 N. Damen Ave.,* ☎ *773/862–6600. AE, D, DC, MC, V. Closed Sun. No lunch.*

$–$$ ✕ **Mia Francesca.** Why is this tiny restaurant so insanely popular? Prin-
cipally because of its very good, authentic Italian cooking; its moder-ate prices don't hurt. Try the classic bruschetta or full-flavored pasta and chicken dishes. ✉ *3311 N. Clark St.,* ☎ *773/281–3310. Reservations not accepted. AE, MC, V. No lunch.*

$ ✕ **Ann Sather.** The line often stretches down the street for home-style
breakfasts at this large Swedish restaurant in the far north Anderson-ville neighborhood of Chicago. Specialties include omelets, Swedish pan-cakes, homemade cinnamon rolls, potato sausage, chicken croquettes, and sandwiches. ✉ *929 W. Belmont Ave. and 2 additional Lincoln Park locations (3416 N. Southport; 3411 N. Broadway),* ☎ *773/348–2378. AE, DC, MC, V.*

$ ✕ **Pizzeria Uno/Pizzeria Due.** This is where Chicago deep-dish pizza got
★   its start. There's usually a shorter wait for a table at Pizzeria Due (same ownership and menu, different decor and longer hours), a block away. ✉ *Uno: 29 E. Ohio St.,* ☎ *312/321–1000; Due: 619 N. Wabash Ave.,* ☎ *312/943–2400. Reservations not accepted. AE, D, DC, MC, V.*

Lodging

Chicago is the country's biggest convention town, and accommoda-tions can be tight when major events are scheduled. Most hotels run weekend specials when no big shows are on. Accommodations are con-centrated in the Loop and the Near North Side. **Bed and Breakfast Chicago** (✉ Box 14088, 60614, ☎ 773/248–0005, FAX 773/248–7090) handles more than 50 B&Bs in the downtown area.

$$$$ ▥ **The Drake.** The grandest of Chicago's traditional hotels was built
★   in 1920 in the style of an Italian Renaissance palace. The Palm Court,

with its fountain and harpist, is a lovely setting for afternoon tea. Asian art and lamps bring a touch of class to the rooms, many of which have splendid lake views. ⊠ *140 E. Walton Pl., 60611,* ☎ *312/787–2200 or 800/553–7253,* FAX *312/787–1431. 535 rooms. 3 restaurants, exercise room. AE, D, DC, MC, V.* ✎

$$$$ 🏨 **The Fairmont.** This 37-story neoclassical structure of Spanish pink granite is next to the Illinois Center complex (where guests have access to a huge athletic facility). Many of the sizable rooms have views of the lake and Grant Park. ⊠ *200 N. Columbus Dr., 60601,* ☎ *312/565–8000,* FAX *312/856–1032. 692 rooms. 2 restaurants. AE, D, DC, MC, V.* ✎

$$$$ 🏨 **Four Seasons.** Though it feels more like a grand English manor house
★ than an urban skyscraper, the Four Seasons has spectacular lake and city views. Rooms have handcrafted armoires and beds piled with throw pillows. The sumptuous afternoon tea is the perfect pick-me-up for weary shoppers. ⊠ *120 E. Delaware Pl., 60611,* ☎ *312/280–8800,* FAX *312/280–9184. 343 rooms. 2 restaurants, pool, health club. AE, D, DC, MC, V.* ✎

$$$$ 🏨 **Renaissance Chicago Hotel.** The modern stone-and-glass exterior
★ houses a tidy '90s interpretation of turn-of-the-20th-century splendor. Lavish floral carpets, crystal-beaded chandeliers, and French provincial furniture create rich-looking public areas. Rooms have separate sitting areas. ⊠ *1 W. Wacker Dr., 60601,* ☎ *312/372–7200 or 800/ 468–3571,* FAX *312/372–0093. 553 rooms. 2 restaurants, pool, exercise room. AE, D, DC, MC, V.* ✎

$$$$ 🏨 **Ritz-Carlton.** The Ritz-Carlton, run by Four Seasons Hotels and Re-
★ sorts, sits atop the Water Tower Place shopping mall. Magnificent flower arrangements adorn the public areas, and the two-story greenhouse lobby serves afternoon tea. The luxurious, spacious rooms are a tasteful blend of European styles. ⊠ *160 E. Pearson St., 60611,* ☎ *312/266–1000 or 800/621–6906,* FAX *312/266–1194. 430 rooms. 3 restaurants, pool, health club. AE, D, DC, MC, V.* ✎

$$$$ 🏨 **Sutton Place Hotel.** This ultramodern hotel has a sleek, Art Deco lobby and similarly stylish guest rooms, with black leather headboards and photographs by Robert Mapplethorpe (not to worry, the subjects are floral). ⊠ *21 E. Bellevue Pl., 60611,* ☎ *312/266–2100 or 800/606– 8188,* FAX *312/266–2103. 246 rooms. Restaurant, exercise room. AE, D, DC, MC, V.* ✎

$$$–$$$$ 🏨 **Chicago Hilton and Towers.** Built in 1927, this huge grand hotel in the South Loop has a lavishly restored lobby filled with gilt and crystal. The large ballroom is worthy of Marie Antoinette. ⊠ *720 S. Michigan Ave., 60605,* ☎ *312/922–4400,* FAX *312/922–5240. 1,543 rooms. 3 restaurants, pool, health club. AE, D, DC, MC, V.* ✎

$$$–$$$$ 🏨 **Lenox Suites.** Conveniently located near North Michigan Avenue, the hotel has one-room "suites" with a Murphy bed, sofa bed, and kitchenette, in addition to one-bedroom suites with a separate living room and kitchen. ⊠ *616 N. Rush St., 60611,* ☎ *312/337–1000 or 800/445– 3669,* FAX *312/337–7217. 324 suites. 2 restaurants, exercise room. AE, D, DC, MC, V.*

$$$–$$$$ 🏨 **Palmer House Hilton.** Built in 1871 by the Chicago merchant Potter Palmer, this hotel has public areas that reflect the opulence of that era, including a frescoed rococo lobby. Its modern guest rooms are more ordinary. The high-tech golf simulator will tell you where your ball would land on a real course. ⊠ *17 E. Monroe St., 60603,* ☎ *312/726–7500,* FAX *312/917–1707. 1,639 rooms. 3 restaurants, pool, exercise room. AE, D, DC, MC, V.* ✎

$$$–$$$$ 🏨 **Sheraton Chicago Hotel and Towers.** This enormous hotel attracts business travelers with its modern appointments and lighthouselike location on the Chicago River, which guarantees unobstructed views. Standard rooms are uninspiring, with gray carpet and bedspreads, though

the marble bathrooms are full of amenities. ✉ *301 E. North Water St., 60611,* ☎ *312/464–1000 or 800/233–4100,* FAX *312/464–9140. 1,204 rooms. 5 restaurants, pool, exercise room. AE, D, DC, MC, V.* ✎

$$–$$$$ 🏨 **Hotel Inter-Continental Chicago.** A grand architectural gem, the Inter-Continental has a dramatic lobby, ornately painted ceilings, marble steps, and a second-floor terra-cotta fountain. The Italianate junior-Olympic-size pool helped earn the hotel a spot on the National Register of Historic Places. Its North Tower is less inspiring. ✉ *505 N. Michigan Ave., 60611,* ☎ *312/944–4100 or 800/628–2112,* FAX *312/944–1320. 844 rooms. Restaurant, pool, health club. AE, D, DC, MC, V.* ✎

$$–$$$$ 🏨 **The Raphael.** On a quiet street off the Magnificent Mile, this hotel has old-world charm. Some guest rooms have quirky touches such as chaise lounges and arched entries. ✉ *201 E. Delaware Pl., 60611,* ☎ *312/943–5000,* FAX *312/943–9483. 172 rooms. Restaurant. AE, D, DC, MC, V.*

$$$ 🏨 **Best Western River North.** This former warehouse in the thriving River North entertainment district has an undistinguished exterior, but inside are large, reasonably priced guest rooms with pinstriped duvets, buffalo-plaid blankets, and black-and-white tiled bathrooms. Sofa sleepers in the suites and an indoor pool make it a family favorite. ✉ *125 W. Ohio St., 60610,* ☎ *312/467–0800 or 800/727–0800,* FAX *312/467–1665. 150 rooms. Indoor pool, exercise room. AE, D, DC, MC, V.* ✎

$$$ 🏨 **Claridge Hotel.** Nestled among Victorian houses on a tree-lined Near North street, this simply outfitted 1930s building is intimate and homey. ✉ *1244 N. Dearborn Pkwy., 60610,* ☎ *312/787–4980 or 800/245–1258,* FAX *312/266–0978. 163 rooms. Restaurant. AE, D, DC, MC, V.*

$$ 🏨 **City Suites Hotel.** Ten minutes north of the Loop in the Lakeview neighborhood is this small, European-style hotel with a fireplace in the lobby and cozy guest rooms with chic black-and-white tile baths. The location is unbeatable. ✉ *933 W. Belmont Ave., 60657,* ☎ *773/404–3400 or 800/248–9108,* FAX *773/404–3405. 45 rooms. AE, D, DC, MC, V.* ✎

Motels

🏨 **Comfort Inn of Lincoln Park** (✉ 601 W. Diversey Pkwy., 60614, ☎ 773/348–2810, FAX 773/348–1912), 74 rooms; *$$.*

🏨 **Hojo Inn** (✉ 720 N. La Salle St., 60610, ☎ 312/664–8100, FAX 312/664–2365), 71 rooms; restaurant; *$$.*

🏨 **Ohio House** (✉ 600 N. La Salle St., 60610, ☎ 312/943–6000, FAX 312/943–6063), 50 rooms; restaurant; *$$.*

Nightlife and the Arts

For listings of arts and entertainment events, check the monthly *Chicago* magazine (on newsstands) or the Friday edition of the *Chicago Tribune* or the *Chicago Sun-Times.* Two free weeklies, the *Reader* (available Friday) and *New City* (available Thursday), which can be found at bookstores, restaurants, and bars, are the best sources for what's happening in clubs and small theaters and for showings of noncommercial films.

Nightlife

Chicago comes alive at night. Shows usually begin at 9; cover charges range from $3 to $10, depending on the day. Most bars are open until 2 AM, and some larger dance clubs until 4 AM.

BLUES CLUBS

In the years following World War II, Chicago-style blues grew into its own musical form. After fading in the 1960s, Chicago blues is coming back, although more strongly on the trendy North Side than on the South Side, where it all began. **Kingston Mines** (✉ 2548 N. Halsted St., ☎ 773/477–4646) has been king of Chicago blues clubs for more than 30 years, with bands on two stages weekends. The intimate **B.L.U.E.S.** (⊠ 2519 N. Halsted St., ☏ 773/528–1012) pulses with music in a rather small space. The elaborate **House of Blues** (⊠ 330 N. State St., ☏ 312/527–2583) features top-notch groups playing in an ornate, theater-like setting with unconventional art adorning the walls. **Buddy Guy's Legends** (⊠ 754 S. Wabash Ave., ☏ 312/427–0333), owned by the famous blues man, sits in a spacious former storefront. The **Checkerboard Lounge** (⊠ 423 E. 43rd St., ☏ 773/624–3240) is in a rough neighborhood but has a long pedigree.

COMEDY CLUBS

Many comedy clubs have a drink minimum instead of or in addition to a cover charge. The granddaddy of all comedy clubs is **Second City** (⊠ 1616 N. Wells St., ☏ 312/337–3992), which usually has two different revues playing at once. The best stand-up comedy in town is found at **Zanies** (⊠ 1548 N. Wells St., ☏ 312/337–4027). **Improv Olympic** (⊠ 3541 N. Clark St., ☏ 773/880–0199) presents improv troupes as well as staged shows.

DANCE CLUBS

Drink, eat, and dance at **Drink** (⊠ 702 W. Fulton St., ☏ 312/733–7800), a trendy spot west of the Loop with five crowded rooms. **Polly Esther's** (⊠ 213 W. Institute Pl., ☏ 312/664–0777) plays 1970s and '80s dance music. **Liquid** (⊠ 1997 N. Clybourn Ave., ☏ 773/528–3400) hosts popular swing nights on Sunday, Tuesday, and Thursday; other nights range from rock to salsa. **Mad Bar** (⊠ 1640 N. Damen Ave., ☏ 773/227–2277), a see-and-be-seen Bucktown bar, has bands, DJs, and dancing.

FOLK CLUBS

No Exit Cafe/Gallery (⊠ 6970 N. Glenwood Ave., ☏ 773/743–3355), a coffeehouse right out of the 1960s, has folk, jazz, and poetry readings. **Old Town School of Folk Music** (⊠ 4544 N. Lincoln Ave., ☏ 773/525–7793) mixes local talent and outstanding nationally known performers.

JAZZ CLUBS

Jazz Showcase (⊠ 59 W. Grand Ave., ☏ 312/670–2473) books nationally known groups in its classy River North home. **Pops for Champagne** (⊠ 2934 N. Sheffield Ave., ☏ 773/472–1000) has jazz combos and a champagne bar. The **Green Mill** (⊠ 4802 N. Broadway, ☏ 773/878–5552), a Chicago institution off the beaten track, books solid, sizzling local acts in an ornate 1940s space. **Green Dolphin Street** (⊠ 2200 N. Ashland Ave., ☏ 773/395–0066) plays bossa, bebop, Latin, and world jazz in a large, open club.

ROCK CLUBS

Metro (⊠ 3730 N. Clark St., ☏ 773/549–0203) presents progressive nationally known and local artists. Downstairs from Metro, **Smart Bar** (☏ 773/549–4140) throbs with punk and funk dance tunes. The **Cubby Bear** (⊠ 1059 W. Addison St., ☏ 773/327–1662), across from Wrigley Field, plays rock, fusion, and country-tinged acts. In the hip Wicker Park neighborhood, the **Double Door** (⊠ 1572 N. Milwaukee Ave., ☏ 773/489–3160) books top and up-and-coming local artists. **Wild Hare** (⊠ 3530 N. Clark St., ☏ 773/327–4273) is the city's premier reggae club.

FOR SINGLES

Chicago's legendary Rush Street singles scene is actually on **Division Street** between Clark and State; here you'll find such bars as **Original Mother's** (⊠ 26 W. Division St., ☏ 312/642–7251), featured in the movie . . . *About Last Night*. **Butch McGuire's** (⊠ 20 W. Division St., ☏ 312/337–9080) is jammed with out-of-towners on the make. River East Plaza (⊠ 435 E. Illinois St. and McClurg Crescent) has several popular singles spots, including **Dick's Last Resort** (☏ 312/836–7870). There's a cluster of bar life in the neighborhood around **Halsted and Armitage streets** in Lincoln Park.

GAY BARS

The area around Halsted Street—approximately between Belmont and Waveland avenues—has the city's highest concentration of gay bars, including the yuppified **Roscoe's Tavern & Cafe** (✉ 3356 N. Halsted St., ☏ 773/281–3355). **Berlin** (✉ 954 W. Belmont Ave., ☏ 773/348–4975) attracts a mixed crowd to its dance floor, video bar, and theme nights. **Gentry** (✉ 440 N. State St., ☏ 312/836–0933), a prime meeting spot downtown, has a piano bar and video bar.

The Arts

Chicago is a splendid city for the arts, with more than 50 theater groups, world-class orchestra and opera companies, and dozens of smaller musical ensembles.

DANCE

Ballet Chicago (☏ 312/251–8838) is the city's oldest resident classical ballet company. You can also enjoy the **Joffrey Ballet of Chicago** (☏ 312/739–0120), which relocated from New York a few years ago. **Hubbard Street Dance Chicago** (☏ 312/850–9744) is known for its contemporary, jazzy vitality.

FILM

In addition to the usual commercial theaters, Chicago has several venues for the avant-garde, vintage, or merely offbeat. The **Film Center of the Art Institute** (✉ Columbus Dr. at Jackson Blvd., ☏ 312/443–3737) sometimes presents lectures in conjunction with its films. The **Fine Arts Theatre** (✉ 418 S. Michigan Ave., ☏ 312/939–3700) shows first-run avant-garde and foreign flicks. The ornate **Music Box Theatre** (✉ 3733 N. Southport Ave., ☏ 773/871–6604), a 1920s movie palace, shows many independent films.

MUSIC

The **Chicago Symphony Orchestra** performs from September to May at the Orchestra Hall (✉ 220 S. Michigan Ave., ☏ 312/294–3000 or 800/223–7114) under the direction of Daniel Barenboim. In summer the Chicago Symphony moves outdoors to take part in the **Ravinia Festival** (☏ 847/266–5100), in suburban Highland Park.

OPERA

From September to March the **Lyric Opera of Chicago** (✉ 20 N. Wacker Dr., ☏ 312/332–2244) performs grand opera with international stars; tickets are difficult to come by. The **Chicago Opera Theater** (☏ 312-704-8414) presents innovative versions of traditional favorites and contemporary American pieces, all sung in English.

THEATER

Half-price theater tickets are available for many productions on the day of performance, and on Friday afternoon for many weekend performances at **Hot Tix** booths (✉ 163 E. Pearson St.; 108 N. State St.; ☏ 312/977–1755 for both). With excellent acoustics, the **Auditorium Theatre** (✉ 50 E. Congress Pkwy., ☏ 312/922–2110) shows popular Broadway musicals. The grand **Shubert Theatre** (✉ 22 W. Monroe St., ☏ 312/977–1700), built in 1906, is home to touring Broadway plays, musicals, and dance companies. The **Chicago Theatre** (✉ 175 N. State St., ☏ 312/443–1130), a restored 1920s-era movie palace, presents musicals, concerts, and special events. The **Athenaeum Theatre** (✉ 2936 N. Southport Ave., ☏ 773/935–6860) hosts provoking music, opera, dance, and drama performances.

Several local ensembles have made the big jump into national prominence, most notably the successful **Steppenwolf** (⊠ 1650 N. Halsted St., ☎ 312/335–1650). **Victory Gardens** (⊠ 2257 N. Lincoln Ave., ☎ 773/871–3000) presents plays by local playwrights on its four stages. The city's oldest repertory theater, the **Goodman Theatre** (⊠ 200 S. Columbus Dr., ☎ 312/443–3800), features contemporary works and classics.

Spectator Sports

Baseball: Chicago Cubs (⊠ Wrigley Field, 1060 W. Addison St., ☎ 773/404–2827); **Chicago White Sox** (⊠ Comiskey Park, 333 W. 35th St., ☎ 312/831–1769). **Basketball: Chicago Bulls** (⊠ United Center, 1901 W. Madison St., ☎ 312/455–4000). **Football: Chicago Bears** (⊠ Soldier Field, 425 E. McFetridge Dr., ☎ 847/295–6600). **Hockey: Chicago Blackhawks** (⊠ United Center, 1901 W. Madison St., ☎ 312/455–7000). **Horse racing: Hawthorne Race Course** (⊠ 3501 S. Laramie Ave., Stickney, ☎ 708/780–3700) has Thoroughbred racing July–November. **Sportsman's Park** (⊠ 3301 S. Laramie Ave., Cicero, ☎ 708/652–2812) has Thoroughbred racing May–June. **Maywood Park** (⊠ North and 5th Aves., Maywood, ☎ 708/343–4800) has harness racing year-round.

Shopping

Shopping Districts

The **Loop** and the **Magnificent Mile** (☞ Exploring Chicago, *above*, for both) are filled with major department and upscale specialty stores. **Oak Street,** between Michigan Avenue and State Street, has such top-of-the-line stores as **Barneys New York** (⊠ 25 E. Oak St., ☎ 312/587–1700), **Ultimo** (⊠ 114 E. Oak St., ☎ 312/787–1171), and **Giorgio Armani** (⊠ 113 E. Oak St., ☎ 312/427–6264). Three vertical (multiple-story) malls combine department stores and specialty shops: **Water Tower Place** (☞ Exploring Chicago, *above*); the **900 North Michigan Shops** (☎ 312/915–3916); and **Chicago Place** (⊠ 700 N. Michigan Ave., ☎ 312/642–4811). The **Lincoln Park neighborhood** has several worthwhile shopping strips. Clark Street between Armitage and Diversey avenues is home to clothing boutiques and specialty stores. From Diversey north to Addison Street are several large antiques stores, more boutiques, and some bookstores.

Department Stores

In the Loop, **Marshall Field's** (⊠ 111 N. State St., at Randolph St., ☎ 312/781–1000), the city's biggest department store, takes up an entire city block. With 500 departments, it's the second-largest retail store in the country and is revered for its extravagant window displays and signature Frango mints. **Carson Pirie Scott** (⊠ 1 S. State St., ☎ 312/641–7000) doesn't have the style or selection of its North Michigan Avenue competitors, but it does have spectacular ornamental ironwork around the main entrance. To keep up with the latest fashion trends, visit **Bloomingdale's** (⊠ 900 N. Michigan Ave., ☎ 312/440–4460). For couture clothing don't miss **Neiman Marcus** (⊠ 737 N. Michigan Ave., ☎ 312/642–5900). **Saks Fifth Avenue** (⊠ Chicago Place, 700 N. Michigan Ave., ☎ 312/944–6500) is a must for those in search of classy high style.

Specialty Stores

Crate & Barrel (⊠ 646 N. Michigan Ave., ☎ 312/787–5900) sells its own stylish brand of home accessories, cookware, and furniture. **Nike-Town** (⊠ 669 N. Michigan Ave., ☎ 312/642–6363) draws tourists with its displays of sports memorabilia and merchandise. Girls flock to **American Girl Place** (⊠ 111 E. Chicago Ave., ☎ 877/247–5223), the only retail outlet in the country for the Pleasant Company's popular brand of dolls, accessories, and clothing. Reservations are required for its live **revue show** (☎ $25), and for lunch or tea at the **AG Restau-**

rant. In the Loop, **Illinois Artisans Shop** (⌧ James R. Thompson Center, 100 W. Randolph St., ☎ 312/814–5321) culls the best work from artists and craftspeople from around the state. For clever souvenirs, browse in the shops at major museums and at the quirky stalls of **Navy Pier** (☞ Magnificent Mile *in* Exploring Chicago, *above*).

Side Trip to Oak Park

Arriving and Departing

Take I–290 west to Harlem Avenue and exit from the left lane. Turn right at the top of the ramp, head north on Harlem Avenue to Lake Street, turn right, and proceed to Oak Park Avenue.

What to See and Do

Founded in the 1850s, just west of the Chicago border, is Oak Park, one of Chicago's oldest suburbs and a living museum of Prairie School residential architecture. The **Frank Lloyd Wright Home and Studio** (⌧ 951 Chicago Ave., corner of Forest Ave., ☎ 708/848–1976; ⌧ $8) looks just as it did in 1889, when it was built for Wright, who lived and worked here until 1909. The poured-concrete **Unity Temple** (⌧ 875 Lake St., ☎ 708/383–8873; ⌧ $5), which Frank Lloyd Wright designed in 1905, was the architect's first public building. Learn about Ernest Hemingway's first 20 years at the **Ernest Hemingway Museum** (⌧ 200 N. Oak Park Ave., ☎ 708/848–2222), closed Monday through Wednesday. The **Ernest Hemingway Birthplace** (⌧ 339 N. Oak Park Ave., ☎ 708/848–2222), closed Monday–Wednesday, is the Victorian home where the Nobel Prize–winning author was born in 1899. Combined admission to the Hemingway museum and birthplace costs $6. The **Oak Park Visitors Center** (⌧ 158 N. Forest Ave., ☎ 708/848–1500 or 888/625–7275) sells tour tickets and provides information.

Side Trip to Baha'i House of Worship

Arriving and Departing

Take Lake Shore Drive north until it ends at Hollywood; then turn right onto Sheridan Road and follow it about 10 mi.

What to See and Do

Baha'i House of Worship (⌧ 100 Linden Ave., Wilmette, ☎ 847/853–2300; ⌧ free) is a lovely nine-sided building whose architectural styles and icons from the world's religions symbolize unity. The symmetry and harmony of the building are paralleled in the surrounding formal gardens.

Side Trip to Woodstock

Arriving and Departing

Take I–90 west and exit on Route 47 going north. Make a left on Calhoun Street and then a right on Dean Street.

What to See and Do

Woodstock, 65 mi north of Chicago, is a Victorian oasis set in rolling countryside. The city square, lined with antiques stores and restaurants, is home to summer band concerts and ice cream socials. Most of *Groundhog Day,* starring Bill Murray, was filmed here. Orson Welles and Paul Newman cut their teeth at the **Woodstock Opera House** (⌧ 121 Van Buren St., ☎ 815/338–5300), which was built in 1890 and still houses musical and theatrical productions. The **Old Court House Arts Center** (⌧ 101 N. Johnson St., ☎ 815/338–4525; ⌧ free), built in 1857, showcases local artists' works. In the basement is the former jail, now the **Tavern on the Square** restaurant (☎ 815/334–9540), where meals are served from Tuesday through Sunday in the old cell blocks.

The center is closed from Monday through Wednesday. The **Chester Gould–Dick Tracy Museum** (☎ 815/338–8281; ⊠ $1), in the Old Court House Arts Center (☞ *above*), displays the artwork of Chester Gould, the creator of the *Dick Tracy* comic strip, who lived and worked in Woodstock. It, too, is closed from Monday through Wednesday. Contact the **Woodstock Chamber of Commerce** (⊠ 136 Cass St., 60098, ☎ 815/338–2436) for more information.

Side Trip to Naperville

Arriving and Departing

Naperville is about 35 mi west of the Loop. Take I–290 west to I–88 west, and exit south on Naperville Road. Proceed south to Diehl Street, take Diehl west to Washington Street, and Washington south to downtown Naperville.

What to See and Do

A living history museum, the 19th-century **Naper Settlement** (⊠ 523 S. Webster St., Naperville, ☎ 630/420–6010; ⊠ $6.50) has many buildings with hands-on activities and demonstrations. Start at the visitor center, and then visit the 1864 American Gothic Revival chapel, the Victorian Martin-Mitchell Mansion, and the Greek Revival Murray Mansion House. Children enjoy the re-created log-picket Fort Payne and the rough-hewn, one-room Paw Paw post office.

Just a block north of Naper Settlement, **downtown Naperville** is a charming area bordered to the west by the DuPage River. Stroll along the river walk, stopping to enjoy its shrubbery-shaded nooks, playgrounds, and even a covered bridge. Specialty clothing stores, home accessory shops, and antiques stores abound here. For more information on the area, call the **Naperville Chamber of Commerce** (⊠ 131 N. Jefferson St., 60540, ☎ 630/355–4141).

GALENA AND NORTHWESTERN ILLINOIS

The tiny town of Galena (population: 3,600) has beautifully preserved pre–Civil War architecture, with houses in Federal, Italianate, and Gothic Revival styles; a large concentration of specialty shops; and (rare in the Midwest) hilly terrain. There's good biking, cross-country skiing, fishing, hunting, and camping in the region.

Lead mining took off here in the 1820s, and Galena had a near-monopoly on the shipping of ore down the Mississippi until the railroad came through in 1854. A depression later that decade and then the Civil War disrupted the lead trade and sent the city into an economic decline from which it never recovered. As a result, Galena today looks much as it did in the 1850s; 85% of the town is on the National Register of Historic Places. This was once the home of Ulysses S. Grant, commander of the Union Army in the Civil War and later the 18th president of the United States.

The region surrounding Galena is dotted with tiny towns that have been similarly bypassed by modern life. Among their offbeat charms are an antique-tractor museum (in Stockton) and the world's largest mallard hatchery (in Hanover). Stockton is also a time capsule of turn-of-the-20th-century architecture, and much of Mount Carroll is registered as a National Historic District.

Visitor Information

Galena/Jo Daviess County: Call the **Galena/Jo Daviess County Convention and Visitors Bureau** (☎ 815/777–3557 or 800/747–9377), or visit the Galena Area Chamber of Commerce's **Visitor Information Center** (✉ 101 Bouthillier St., Galena 61036).

Arriving and Departing

By Car

From Chicago take I–90 86 mi to Rockford, then Route 20 west 81 mi to Galena. From Iowa pick up Route 20 at Dubuque and continue 16 mi east across the Mississippi.

Exploring Galena and Northwestern Illinois

In Galena the **Ulysses S. Grant Home** (✉ 500 Bouthillier St., ☎ 815/ 777–0248; ☑ $2), built in 1860 in the Italianate bracketed style, was presented to Grant in 1865 by Galena residents in honor of his service to the Union. The Grant family lived there until Grant's victory in the 1868 presidential election. In 1904 Grant's children gave the house to the city of Galena. Now a state historic site, the house has been meticulously restored to its 1868 appearance.

The heart of the **Belvedere Mansion and Gardens** (✉ 1008 Park Ave., ☎ 815/777–0747; ☑ $5) is the 1857 Italianate mansion built for a steamboat magnate. Some might consider its lavishness gaudy; accoutrements include the famous green drapes from the movie *Gone With the Wind* and furnishings from Liberace's estate. The mansion is closed from November through May.

The **Galena/Jo Daviess County History Museum** (✉ 211 S. Bench St., ☎ 815/777–9129; ☑ $3.50) provides interesting background on the area. A large Civil War exhibit shows the effect of the war on Galena's development. Display cases house period dolls, toys, clothing, and household artifacts.

Galena's oldest house is the 1826 **Dowling House** (✉ 220 Diagonal St., ☎ 815/777–1250; ☑ $3.50), which is open daily in summer and only on weekends in winter. **Galena Trolley Tours** (✉ 314 S. Main St., ☎ 815/777–1248; ☑ $8) offers tours of the town.

A huge swath of rolling countryside east of town, the **Galena Territory** started as a vacation-home development in the early 1980s but has taken on a life of its own as a recreation area with hunting, fishing, and golf. Watch out for deer and turkey on the back roads; they're everywhere.

Mallards outnumber people 200 to 1 in **Hanover,** southeast of Galena, off Route 20 on Route 84. The **Whistling Wings Hatchery** (✉ 113 Washington St., ☎ 815/591–3512) hatches 200,000 mallards a year; a viewing window lets you see the baby ducks in incubators. **Savanna,** on Route 84 along the Mississippi, has many large, well-preserved 19th-century houses. In **Mount Carroll,** east of Savanna on Route 52, rolling hills and gracious 19th-century frame and masonry buildings recall a small New England town, complete with a town square.

Stockton, about 30 mi east of Galena on Route 20, is the highest town in Illinois, at 1,000 ft; the business district preserves many lacy, cupola-topped Victorian structures. **Arlo's Tractor Collection and Museum** (✉ 7871 S. Ridge Rd., ☎ 815/947–2593; ☑ free) contains 60 restored antique tractors, all in working order. The museum is closed from November through April; tours are by appointment only.

Dining and Lodging

Restaurant fare here tends toward hearty steaks, burgers, and ribs. Several bakeries along Galena's Main Street sell tempting cookies and pastries. A stay in one of the area's 40-plus B&Bs is almost de rigueur; some are right in town, and others are in the Galena Territory or other rustic outlying areas. The Convention and Visitors Bureau (☞ Visitor Information, *above*) has a complete list of B&Bs and other types of lodging.

East Dubuque

$–$$$ ✕ **Timmerman's Supper Club.** This swanky restaurant across the parking lot from Timmerman's Motor Lodge (but under separate ownership) has spectacular views, rib-eye steaks, and DJs on weekends. ⊠ *7777 Timmerman Dr.,* ☎ *815/747–3316. AE, D, MC, V.*

$ ▥ **Timmerman's Motor Lodge.** Perched on a bluff near the Mississippi River, this modern complex is frequented by riverboat gamblers in neighboring Dubuque, Iowa. Most of the rooms are 1980s Holiday Inn style. ⊠ *7777 Timmerman Dr., 61025,* ☎ *815/747–3181 or 800/336–3181,* FAX *815/747–6556. 74 rooms. Restaurant, pool. AE, D, MC, V.*

Galena

$$–$$$$ ✕ **El Dorado.** Wild game specials include a mixed grill of locally raised
★   venison, Texas antelope, and wild boar sausage. A Southwest motif prevails in the lofted space with exposed brick walls. ⊠ *219 N. Main St.,* ☎ *815/777–1224. AE, D, MC, V. Closed Tues. and Wed. No lunch.*

$–$$$ ✕ **Café Italia and Twisted Taco Café.** Featured in the movie *Field of Dreams,* this cozy wood-and tile restaurant serves minestrone, lasagna, veal parmigiana, and other Italian standards, in addition to a full Mexican menu. ⊠ *301 N. Main St.,* ☎ *815/777–0033. AE, D, DC, MC, V. Closed Mon. and Tues.*

$$–$$$ ✕▥ **DeSoto House Hotel.** Opened in 1855, the DeSoto House served as presidential campaign headquarters for Ulysses S. Grant, and Lincoln really did sleep here. The spacious rooms recall the 1860s. The stately Generals' Restaurant serves straightforward steaks, chops, and seafood; the Courtyard Restaurant is open for breakfast and lunch. ⊠ *230 S. Main St., 61036,* ☎ *815/777–0090 or 800/343–6562,* FAX *815/ 777–9529. 55 rooms. 2 restaurants. AE, D, DC, MC, V.* ☜

$–$$$ ▥ **Chestnut Mountain Resort.** Looking like a Swiss chalet, the resort sits atop a bluff above the Mississippi, 8 mi southeast of downtown Galena; bedrooms overlook the ski slopes. There are mountain bikes for rent and ski packages that include lodging and meals. ⊠ *8700 W. Chestnut Rd., 61036,* ☎ *815/777–1320 or 800/397–1320,* FAX *815/777– 1068. 119 rooms. Restaurant, pool, tennis. AE, D, DC, MC, V.* ☜

Galena Territory

$$$–$$$$ ✕▥ **Eagle Ridge Inn and Resort.** This rustic yet elegant "inn resort for golf" is set on 6,800 acres; horseback riding, boating, and cross-country skiing opportunities abound. Guest rooms have views of lake or woodland. The formal Woodlands restaurant serves excellent American cuisine. ⊠ *444 Eagle Ridge Dr., Galena 61036,* ☎ *815/777–2444 or 800/892– 2269,* FAX *815/777–4502. 80 rooms; 320 condominiums, town houses, and homes. 2 restaurants, pool, exercise room. AE, D, DC, MC, V.* ☜

Motels

▥ **Best Western Quiet House Suites** (⊠ 9923 Rte. 20W, Galena 61036, ☎ 815/777–2577, FAX 815/777–0584), 42 suites; pool, exercise room.

▥ **Grant Hills Motel** (⊠ Rte. 20E, Galena 61036, ☎ 815/777–2116), 35 rooms; pool.

▥ **Karen's Neat Lodging** (⊠ 11383 Rte. 20W, Galena 61036, ☎ 815/ 777–2043, FAX 815/777–2625), 64 rooms.

Nightlife

The **Depot Theater** (⊠ 314 S. Main St., ☎ 815/777–1248), at the Galena Trolley Depot, presents cabaret-style theater in a candlelit space. Shows tend to be historical, such as Jim Post's *Mark Twain and the Laughing River.*

Outdoor Activities and Sports

Biking

Bicyclists will find plenty of hilly back roads around Galena. The **Old Stagecoach Trail** runs parallel to Route 20, winding from Lena through Apple River and Warren to Galena. **Chestnut Mountain Resort** (☞ Dining and Lodging, *above*) rents mountain bikes. The Visitor Information Center (☞ Visitor Information, *above*) has maps.

Fishing

Licenses can be purchased at marinas, bait shops, hardware stores, and other outlets, or contact the **Illinois Bureau of Tourism** (☞ Statewide Visitor Information, *above*) or the **Illinois Department of Natural Resources** (⊠ 2612 Locust St., Sterling 61081, ☎ 815/625–2968).

Golf

Eagle Ridge Inn and Resort (☞ Dining and Lodging, *above*), in Galena Territory, has three championship 18-hole courses and one 9-hole course. **Galena Golf Club** (⊠ Rte. 20W, Galena, ☎ 815/777–3599) has one 18-hole course and a driving range. **Lacoma Golf Course** (⊠ 8080 Timmerman Dr., East Dubuque, ☎ 815/747–3874) has one 18-hole course, two regulation 9-hole courses, and one 9-hole par-three course.

Hiking and Backpacking

Mississippi Palisades State Park (⊠ 16327A Rte. 84N, Savanna, ☎ 815/273–2731), about 30 mi south of Galena, has hiking trails with river views and nature preserves with accessible lookouts. More cliffs and canyons, in addition to camping, fishing, and five 1-mi-long hiking trails, can be found at **Apple River Canyon State Park** (⊠ 8763 E. Canyon Rd., north of Rte. 20 between Stockton and Warren, ☎ 815/745–3302).

Horseback Riding

Shenandoah Riding Center (⊠ Galena Territory, 200 N. Brodrecht Rd., off Rte. 20E, Galena, ☎ 815/777–2373) offers riding lessons and hay and sleigh rides.

Ski Areas

Cross-Country

Eagle Ridge Inn and Resort (☞ Dining and Lodging, *above*) maintains more than 35 mi of groomed trails. **Lacoma Golf Course** (☞ Golf *in* Outdoor Activities and Sports, *above*) opens its 260-acre course to skiers, but you have to break your own trails. **Mississippi Palisades State Park** (☞ Hiking and Backpacking *in* Outdoor Activities and Sports, *above*) also has marked trails.

Downhill

It's not the Alps, or even the Catskills, but if you want downhill skiing in Illinois, try **Chestnut Mountain Resort** (☞ Dining and Lodging, *above*), with 19 runs that overlook the Mississippi, plus a 7-acre snowboard park and a children's learn-to-ski program.

Shopping

Galena's Main Street is lined with more than 30 shops selling antiques, folk art, contemporary collectibles, and locally produced wine and foodstuffs. **Stockton, Warren,** and **Elizabeth** have antiques stores and artists' studios.

ELSEWHERE IN ILLINOIS

Springfield

Visitor Information
Springfield Convention and Visitors Bureau (⊠ 109 N. 7th St., 62701, ☎ 217/789–2360 or 800/545–7300).

Arriving and Departing
Loop I–55 runs north–south through the city. Interstate–72 comes from Champaign and Decatur to the east. The Amtrak route from Chicago to St. Louis stops in Springfield.

What to See and Do
A surprisingly generous slice of Abraham Lincoln's life is preserved and re-created in Springfield, Illinois's capital. The importance of preserving artifacts from the president's life was recognized even as his funeral plans were being made, and so the historic sites here offer an amazing array of personal and family artifacts, from a desk where he wrote his legal briefs to family furniture and decorations on the mantelpiece in the only home he owned. In the summer, you might want to visit New Salem, which is about a 45-minute drive northwest of Springfield. The Illinois State Fair held there in mid-August is a two-week extravaganza of midwestern farming and domestic triumphs. If you want to go, though, make your hotel reservations long in advance—rooms are impossible to find then.

In Springfield, start early in the day and pick up a free admission ticket at the visitor center of the **Lincoln Home National Historic Site** (⊠ 426 S. 7th St., ☎ 217/492–4150) across the street from the Lincoln Home. An interpretive film provides a concise and moving biography of this quintessential American figure. The two blocks surrounding the Lincoln House are being restored to their mid-19th-century state, and biographies of the neighbors who befriended Mary Lincoln and baby-sat the Lincoln boys are being pieced together in exhibits in those neighbors' restored homes. Exhibits about the neighborhood, the gradual expansion of the Lincolns' house and economic rise, and Illinois life of the period are steadily being expanded as more neighborhood homes are restored. Springfield's Oak Ridge Cemetery is home to the **Lincoln Tomb State Historic Site** (⊠ 1500 N. Monument Ave., ☎ 217/782–2717; ☎ free), the final resting place for Lincoln, Mary Todd, and three of their four sons. On Tuesday nights in summer, catch the Civil War Retreat Ceremony held at the tomb. The **Lincoln-Herndon Law Offices** (⊠ 6th and Adams Sts., ☎ 217/785–7960; ☎ $2) provide glimpses into Lincoln's life and career before he became president. The **Old State Capitol** (⊠ 5th and Adams Sts., ☎ 217/785–7961; ☎ $2), where Lincoln delivered his "House Divided" speech and where he lay in state before burial, has been restored to the way it looked during Lincoln's legislative years. **Lincoln's New Salem State Historic Site** (⊠ Rte. 97 near Petersburg, ☎ 217/632–4000; ☎ free), which lies about 20 mi northwest of Springfield, is a reconstructed village where Lincoln spent his early adulthood; in summer volunteers in period dress re-create village life. The visitor center at New Salem explores the hardscrabble life in this tiny hamlet where Lincoln toiled as a shopkeeper and erstwhile law student. In summer, the site hosts a corny but touching musical of Lincoln's young adulthood in its outdoor amphitheater.

Aside from Lincolniana, Springfield is also home to the **Dana-Thomas House** (⊠ 301 E. Lawrence Ave., ☎ 217/782–6776; ☎ $3), built by

Frank Lloyd Wright from 1902 to 1904 for a local socialite and now a state historic site. Elaborately restored in the late 1980s, it's among the most perfectly preserved examples of early Wright architecture, art glass, and furniture. It's closed Monday and Tuesday.

Dining and Lodging

$$ ✕ **Café Brio.** Colorful and lively, Brio serves aromatic Mexican, Caribbean, and Mediterranean cuisine. Margaritas are made with fresh lime juice. ⊠ *524 E. Monroe St.,* ☎ *217/544–0574. AE, MC, V. No dinner Sun.*

$–$$ ✕ **Maldener's.** Hangout for local politicians, Maldener's still has its original turn-of-the-20th-century decor, right up to the pressed-tin ceiling. Lunches are classic midwestern fare—especially the hot sandwiches smothered in gravy. Maldener's is just down the block from the Lincoln-Herndon law offices. ⊠ *222 S. 6th St.,* ☎ *217/522–4313. AE, D, MC, V. Closed Sun.*

$$–$$$ ▥ **Springfield Hilton.** The 30-story hotel has good city views and spacious rooms. In the heart of downtown, it's within walking distance of Lincoln historical sites. ⊠ *700 E. Adams St., 62701,* ☎ *217/789–1530,* ℻ *217/789–0709. 367 rooms. 3 restaurants, pool, health club. AE, D, DC, MC, V.* ☜

$$ ▥ **The Inn at 835 Bed & Breakfast.** Just around the corner from the Dana-Thomas House, this stately late-19th-century inn has a Classical Revival exterior and is filled with oak detailing and large fireplaces. Rooms are spacious and decorated in authentic midwestern Victorian—fancy, but not fussy. ⊠ *835 S. 2nd St., 62701,* ☎ *217/523–4466,* ℻ *217/523–4468. 10 rooms. MC, V.* ☜

INDIANA

Updated by
Peggy Sailors

Capital	Indianapolis
Population	5,544,159
Motto	The Crossroads of America
State Bird	Cardinal
State Flower	Peony
Postal Abbreviation	IN

Statewide Visitor Information

Indiana Department of Commerce, Division of Tourism (✉ 1 N. Capitol Ave., Suite 700, Indianapolis 46204, ☎ 317/232–8860 or 800/291–8844).

Scenic Drives

Charming 19th-century river towns front the **Ohio River Scenic Route** from Madison to Aurora on Routes 56 and 156. Trace Indiana's early frontier history along the **Chief White Eyes Trail** from Madison to Dillsboro on Route 62. The 50-mi **Lincoln Heritage Trail–George Rogers Clark Trail,** on Routes 462, 62, and 162 from Corydon to Gentryville, takes a gentle ride across southern hill country. From Newburgh to Sulphur the **Hoosier Heritage Trail Scenic Route** follows the Ohio River's squiggly course, then cuts north through state forests on Route 66. Indiana's 40-mi portion of the 1,100-mi **Lake Michigan Circle Tour** around the second largest of the Great Lakes follows U.S. 12 from Illinois to Michigan.

National and State Parks

National Parks

The murals and statue of George Rogers Clark in the columned, circular-stone memorial at **George Rogers Clark National Historic Park** (✉ 401 S. 2nd St., Vincennes 47591, ☎ 812/882–1776) commemorate Clark's capture of Britain's Fort Sackville in 1779 and the subsequent acquisition of the Northwest Territory, the largest land conquest of the Revolutionary War. The 13,400-acre **Indiana Dunes National Lakeshore** (✉ 1100 N. Mineral Springs Rd., Porter 46304, ☎ 219/926–7561) encompasses dune grasses, arctic bearberries, and prickly pear cacti. A living historical farm and a replica of Abraham Lincoln's boyhood home are the lures at the **Lincoln Boyhood National Memorial** (✉ Box 1816, Lincoln City 47552, ☎ 812/937–4541). Ridge-topped trails at the 194,000-acre **Hoosier National Forest** (✉ 811 Constitution Ave., Bedford 47421, or 248 15th St., Tell City 47586, ☎ 812/547–7933) border quiet lakes and pass through dense woodlands in the state's south-central corridor, which stretches to the banks of the Ohio River.

State Parks

Indiana's 23 state parks are operated by the **Department of Natural Resources** (✉ 402 W. Washington St., Room W298, Indianapolis 46204, ☎ 317/232–4124; 800/622–4931 in IN) and are open daily year-round. **Falls of the Ohio** (✉ Box 1327, Jeffersonville 47131, ☎ 812/280–9970) has 220 acres of 386-million-year-old exposed Devonian fossil beds in the Ohio River. At **Spring Mill** (✉ Rte. 60, Box 376, Mitchell 47446, ☎ 812/849–4129) you can tour a reconstructed 1800s pioneer village and gristmill on its original site, hike an 80-acre tract of virgin hardwood forest, then explore two caves on foot or by boat. Just 15 mi apart, **Turkey Run** (✉ Rte. 1, Box 164, Marshall 47859, ☎ 765/597–

2635) and **Shades** (⊠ Rte. 1, Box 72, Waveland 47989, ☎ 765/435–2810) are linked by Sugar Creek and steep sandstone ravines covered with moss and ferns. With central's Indiana's largest unbroken forest canopy, **Fort Harrison State Park** (⊠ 5753 Glenn Rd., Indianapolis 46216, ☎ 317/591–0904) is a 1,700-acre patch of rugged woodlands just minutes from downtown Indianapolis. There are also hiking trails and paved biking paths, and a hilly, challenging golf course. Climb to the top of 123-ft Mt. Baldy at the **Indiana Dunes State Park** (⊠ 1600 N. 25E, Chesterton 46304, ☎ 219/926–1952) for a view of Lake Michigan's 26-mi shoreline and, on a clear day, the Chicago skyline.

INDIANAPOLIS

For a city of its size, Indianapolis has a surprising assortment of museums and performance halls, plus plenty of green space. One of the most recent additions to the parks system is a network of Greenways trails. The popular Monon Rail-Trail, currently a 7.6-mi paved trail, will eventually stretch 12 mi from the northern suburbs and Broad Ripple Village to downtown. Finally, there's Circle Centre, a swanky, villagelike enclosed complex of shops and entertainment attractions that has helped transform a formerly sleepy downtown into a revitalized urban center.

Visitor Information

Indianapolis City Center (⊠ 201 S. Capitol Ave., Pan American Plaza, 46225, ☎ 317/237–5200 or 800/824–4639). **Convention & Visitors Association** (⊠ 1 RCA Dome, Suite 110, 46225, ☎ 317/639–4282).

Arriving and Departing

By Bus
Greyhound Bus Terminal (⊠ 350 S. Illinois St., ☎ 317/267–3071 or 800/231–2222).

By Car
With more segments of interstate highway (I–65, I–69, I–70, I–74, and I–465) intersecting here than anywhere else in the country, Indianapolis is indisputably a driving city. Car rentals are available at major hotels and at the airport.

By Plane
The **Indianapolis International Airport** (⊠ 1500 S. High School Rd., ☎ 317/487–9594) is served by major and commuter airlines. The trip from the airport to downtown or to the west side of town is about 20–25 minutes. To the other parts of town it's a 30- to 45-minute drive. By taxi or limo, the cost is $13–$23 to downtown, $23–$30 to most other destinations. **Carey Indiana** (☎ 317/241–7100 or 317/241–2522) charges $8 per passenger for shared rides from the airport to downtown.

By Train
Amtrak (⊠ Union Station, 350 S. Illinois St., ☎ 317/267–0700 or 800/872–7245) offers limited service.

Getting Around Indianapolis

It's easy to get around, and the center is perfectly walkable. Street numbers are based on a rectangular coordinate system, with each block roughly equal to 100. The intersection of Washington and Meridian streets, just south of Monument Circle, is the zero point for numbering in all directions. **Indy Go** buses (☎ 317/635–3344) run from 4:45 AM to 11:45 PM on heavily traveled routes, with shorter schedules in the suburbs. Fares ($1) are payable upon boarding. **Yellow Cab** (☎ 317/

487–7777) taxis are radio dispatched; call ahead to be sure of getting a cab, unless you're at the airport or downtown. The fare is $1.25 for the first ⅕ mi and 36¢ each additional ⅕ mi. **Carey Indiana** provides shared-ride limousine service from the airport to outlying parts of the city for up to $28 per passenger (☎ 317/241–7100 or 317/241–2522).

Exploring Indianapolis

Attractions extend into a wider metropolitan area than the square-mile downtown area. Many of the museums, arts and entertainment venues, and shopping areas, all generally within a 45-minute drive, are scattered around, both downtown and beyond in the contiguous counties.

Downtown
Monument Circle is Indianapolis's centerpiece. Avenues radiate from it across the grid of streets, as in Washington, D.C. (Indianapolis architect Alexander Ralston was a protégé of Pierre L'Enfant). At the center is the **Soldiers' and Sailors' Monument,** a 284-ft spire crowned by the 30-ft bronze statue *Victory,* better known as *Miss Indiana.* There's also a Civil War museum and an **observation area** (☎ 317/232–7615; ⊠ free) with a panoramic view. Also on Monument Circle is the city's oldest church, **Christ Church Cathedral** (⊠ 55 Monument Cir., ☎ 317/636–4577; ⊠ free), an 1857 Gothic country–style masterpiece, with a spire, steep gables, bell tower, and arched Tiffany windows. Tours are Sunday at noon or by appointment.

The **Indiana State Museum** (⊠ 202 N. Alabama St., ☎ 317/232–1637; ⊠ free), in the Old City Hall, chronicles the state's history and culture. The massive limestone-and-marble **Indiana World War Memorial** (⊠ 431 N. Meridian, ☎ 317/232–7615; ⊠ free) pays tribute to fallen Hoosier veterans of World War I, World War II, the Korean War, and the Vietnam War. The circa-1929 Gothic Tudor–style Masonic **Scottish Rite Cathedral** (⊠ 650 N. Meridian St., ☎ 317/262–3100; ⊠ free) contains a 54-bell carillon and a 7,000-pipe organ.

There's lunchtime entertainment most Fridays at the historic 1886 **Indianapolis City Market** (⊠ 222 E. Market St., ☎ 317/634–9266; ⊠ free), where shops sell ethnic and deli fare.

Housed in a contemporary adobe building, the **Eiteljorg Museum of American Indians and Western Art** (⊠ 500 W. Washington St., ☎ 317/636–9378; ⊠ $5) displays works by Frederic Remington and Georgia O'-Keeffe, among others. Next door is an **IMAX 3D Theater** (☎ 317/233–4629; ⊠ $8).

At the **NCAA Hall of Champions** (⊠ 700 W. Washington St., ☎ 317/916–4255 or 800/735–6222), just opened in White River State Park (☞ Parks, Gardens, and Zoos, *below*), visitors can see college games on a 144-ft video monitor, watch championship games in one of four theaters, and tour the multimedia exhibits to learn about past NCAA champs at the 40,000-square-ft museum. Across from White River State Park, the Indiana Historical Society has erected a stunning neoclassical-style building, the **Indiana Historical Society Headquarters** (⊠ 450 W. Ohio St., ☎ 317/232–1882; ⊠ free). The complex includes a museum of Indiana history, a 30,000-square-ft library, and the Cole Porter Room, where you can listen to music by such Hoosiers as Porter, Hoagy Carmichael, and John Mellencamp.

The **Indiana Convention Center & RCA Dome** (⊠ 100 S. Capitol Ave., ☎ 317/639–3452; 317/237–2663 tours; ⊠ free, tours $5), reaching 19 stories and one of just six major air-supported domed stadiums in the world, is the home of the NFL's Indianapolis Colts.

Indianapolis

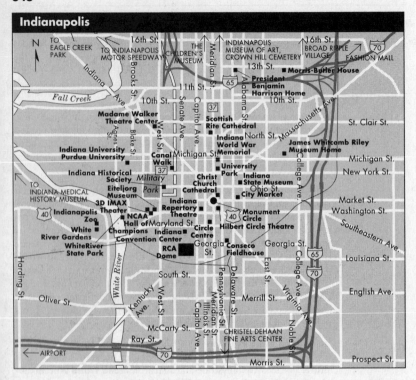

Ornate Victorian furnishings, political mementos, and period ball gowns of the nation's 23rd president and first lady fill the 1875 **President Benjamin Harrison Home** (⊠ 1230 N. Delaware St., ☎ 317/631–1898; ⊡ $5). The **Morris-Butler House** (⊠ 1204 N. Park Ave., ☎ 317/636–5409; ⊡ $5), a restored 1865 Second Empire–style gem, is filled with fancy furnishings, dazzling chandeliers, and rich woodwork.

In the historic **Lockerbie Square** neighborhood, the **James Whitcomb Riley Museum Home** (⊠ 528 Lockerbie St., ☎ 317/631–5885; ⊡ $3), acclaimed as one of the nation's finest examples of Victoriana, remains almost as the noted poet left it.

Midtown/Crosstown

Named for the country's first black female self-made millionaire and once frequented by jazz legends Ella Fitzgerald and Wes Montgomery, today the 1927 **Madame Walker Theatre Center** (⊠ 617 Indiana Ave., ☎ 317/236–2099; ⊡ free, tours by appointment) presents "Jazz on the Avenue" on Friday nights.

The world's largest water clock, a planetarium, the nation's first Cine-Dome Theater, a science center, Playscape, and nine other major galleries make up the **Children's Museum of Indianapolis** (⊠ 3000 N. Meridian St., ☎ 317/334–3322; ⊡ $8). With 11,000 artifacts on five floors, the museum ranks as one of the nation's 20 most-visited museums. Be sure to take a spin on the turn-of-the-20th-century carousel and explore the replica limestone cave.

The **Indianapolis Museum of Art** (⊠ 1200 W. 38th St., ☎ 317/923–1331; ⊡ free), a five-pavilion complex and botanical gardens on 152 acres of manicured lawns, houses works by J. M. W. Turner, the old masters, and the neoimpressionists, along with major Asian, African, and decorative arts collections. At the **Crown Hill Cemetery** (⊠ 700

W. 38th St., ☎ 317/920–2726; ⊠ free), the nation's third largest, notorious criminal John Dillinger cozies up to President Benjamin Harrison and a host of American authors.

South Side

The stunning **Christel DeHaan Fine Arts Center** (⊠ 1400 E. Hanna Ave., ☎ 317/788–3211; ⊠ free) at the University of Indianapolis has exhibition space and a 500-seat concert hall renowned for its acoustics.

West Side

The **Indianapolis Motor Speedway Hall of Fame Museum** (⊠ 4790 W. 16th St., ☎ 317/484–6747; ⊠ $3) displays winning cars of the Indianapolis 500, as well as classic and antique autos. The new road course, added for the Formula One Race, is the first change in the track's configuration since 1909. **Indiana Medical History Museum** (⊠ 3045 W. Vermont St., ☎ 317/635–7329; ⊠ $5), a turn-of-the-20th-century pathology laboratory, exhibits 15,000 medical treatment and health-care artifacts.

Parks, Gardens, and Zoos

There are jogging, biking, hiking, golfing, and swimming facilities at the rustic 4,200-acre **Eagle Creek Park** (⊠ 7840 W. 56th St., ☎ 317/327–7110; ⊠ $2 per car). An exceptionally well planned network of woodland trails and riverfront boardwalks traverses hilly terrain at **Holliday Park** (⊠ 6349 Spring Mill Rd., ☎ 317/327–7180; ⊠ free).

White River State Park (⊠ 801 W. Washington St., ☎ 317/634–4567; ⊠ free) is a 250-acre greenbelt straddling White River with sculptures dotting grassy areas, a waterfall, paved walkways, and a ½-mi walled gardenlike riverside trail, the River Promenade. Within the park is the **Indianapolis Zoo** (⊠ 1200 W. Washington St., ☎ 317/630–2001; ⊠ $9). Next door is the **White River Gardens** (⊠ 1200 W. Washington St., ☎ 317/630–2001; ⊠ $6), a 3.3-acre complex with a 5,000-square-ft glass conservatory, a gift shop, more than 1,000 species of plants, and 1½ mi of pathways.

The downtown **Canal Walk,** a 10½-block vestige of the historic 400-mi canal system linking the Great Lakes and the Ohio River, is an urban haven, with benches, fountains, and wide walkways lining both sides of the canal. The Indy Parks Greenways pedestrian trail, the 7.6-mi paved **Monon Rail-Trail** (☎ 317/327–7431), connects northern suburbs and Broad Ripple Village (☞ Shopping, *below*) to the Indiana State Fairgrounds on East 38th Street.

Dining

$$$–$$$$ ✕ **Peter's Restaurant & Bar.** The seasonal menu here may include pomegranate-glazed Indiana duckling with sweet-potato custard and mustard greens. Chilean sea bass is seared and basted with a spicy orange-chili marinade. ⊠ 8505 Keystone Crossing Blvd., ☎ 317/465–1155. AE, D, MC, V. Closed Sun. No lunch.

$$–$$$$ ✕ **The Restaurant at the Canterbury.** Inside the Canterbury Hotel (☞ Lodging, *below*), this is one of the city's best restaurants. The clubby dining room has wood paneling and crisp white linens. The traditional dishes—Dover sole, pepper-crusted rack of lamb—are expertly prepared. ⊠ 123 S. Illinois St., ☎ 317/634–3000, ext. 7230. AE, D, DC, MC, V.

$$$–$$$$ ✕ **St. Elmo.** Since 1909 this has been the place for big steaks, large martinis, and eye-watering shrimp cocktail sauce. Visiting celebrities often book a table here or stop by the cigar room. ⊠ 127 S. Illinois St., ☎ 317/635–0636. AE, MC, V. No lunch.

$$–$$$$ ✕ **Something Different/Snax.** Tapas at Snax are just enough to whet your appetite for dinner next door. Sister restaurant Something Different

serves dinners that consistently push the envelope with inspired, well-prepared fare. The setting is chic, the menu innovative American. ⊠ *4939 E. 82nd St.,* ☎ *317/570–7700. AE, D, MC, V. Closed Sun. No lunch.*

$$$ ✕ **Palomino.** This upscale European bistro is a hot restaurant for fine contemporary food. The oven-roasted mussels in rosemary-lemon butter and authentic paella casserole are not to be missed. ⊠ *49 W. Maryland St.,* ☎ *317/974–0400. AE, D, DC, MC, V.*

$ ✕ **Shapiro's Delicatessen & Cafeteria.** The strawberry cheesecake and huge corned-beef sandwiches on rye are signature items at this nationally known deli, an Indianapolis institution since 1904. ⊠ *808 S. Meridian St.,* ☎ *317/631–4041; 2370 W. 86th St.,* ☎ *317/872–7255. Reservations not accepted. No credit cards.*

Lodging

$$$ 🏨 **Canterbury Hotel.** The luxurious guest rooms at this 60-year-old
★ hostelry have armoires, queen-size four-poster beds, and elegant baths. A covered skywalk leads to Circle Centre. ⊠ *123 S. Illinois St., 46225,* ☎ *317/634–3000 or 800/538–8186,* ℻ *317/685–2519. 99 rooms. Restaurant, health club. AE, D, DC, MC, V. CP.*

$$$ 🏨 **Omni Severin Hotel.** This hotel, with crystal chandeliers, a marble staircase, and cast-iron balustrades recalling its 1913 origins, stands across from historic Union Station. Guest rooms are a blend of traditional and Mediterranean styles. ⊠ *40 W. Jackson Pl., 46225,* ☎ *317/634–6664 or 800/843–6664,* ℻ *317/687–3619. 424 rooms. 2 restaurants, pool, health club. AE, D, DC, MC, V. CP.*

$$–$$$ 🏨 **University Place Conference Center & Hotel–A Doubletree Hotel.** Rooms in this hotel on the shared campus of Indiana and Purdue universities are handsomely appointed, with desks, easy chairs, and 18th-century reproduction furnishings. ⊠ *850 W. Michigan St., 46202,* ☎ *317/269–9000 or 800/627–2700,* ℻ *317/231–5168. 278 rooms. 2 restaurants, pool, health club. AE, D, DC, MC, V. BP.* 🐾

$$–$$$ 🏨 **The Westin Suites Indianapolis North.** This upscale high-rise hotel is smack in the middle of the north side of Indianapolis at the Fashion Mall Keystone at the Crossing shopping and entertainment complex (☞ Shopping, *below*), a 40-minute drive from downtown or the airport. A covered skywalk connects to 100 shops and restaurants. ⊠ *8787 Keystone Crossing, 46240,* ☎ *317/574–6770,* ℻ *317/574–6755. 159 rooms. Restaurant, pool, health club. AE, D, DC, MC, V. CP.*

Nightlife and the Arts

Nightlife

Pub crawling is best in out-of-the-way neighborhoods such as **Broad Ripple Village** (☞ Shopping, *below*). Cruise the offbeat **Massachusetts Avenue Arts District** scene for interesting art galleries, unusual shops, and neighborhood eateries and taverns. There are Christmas lights and checkered flags year-round at the **Chatterbox** (⊠ 435 Massachusetts Ave., ☎ 317/636–0584), where a varied clientele stops by for late-night jazz. On Level 4 of **Circle Centre** (☞ Shopping, *below*), there are nightclubs, nine cinemas, and virtual reality and arcade games.

The Arts

NUVO Newsweekly, Indianapolis Monthly magazine, and the Friday and Sunday editions of the *Indianapolis Star* list arts and events. Tickets for plays and concerts are available through **Court Side Tickets, Inc.** (⊠ 6100 N. Keystone Ave., Suite 103, ☎ 317/254–9500 or 800/627–1334), **Ticketmaster** (⊠ 2 W. Washington St., ☎ 317/239–5151), **Tickets + Travel** (⊠ 1099 N. Meridian St., Suite 100, ☎ 317/633–6400), or **Premium Tickets & Tours** (⊠ 2113 Broad Ripple Ave., ☎ 317/251–

0163 or 800/768–0898). Ticket scalping is permitted. Check newspaper ads and the Yellow Pages for listings.

MUSIC

Indianapolis Symphony Orchestra (⊠ 45 Monument Circle, ☎ 317/262–1100 for tickets) performs at the Hilbert Circle Theatre from September through May and outdoors at Conner Prairie in summer (☞ Hamilton County *in* Side Trips from Indianapolis, *below*). The **Indianapolis Opera** (⊠ 250 E. 38th St., ☎ 317/283–3531 or or 317/239–1000) stages productions from its grand opera repertoire and new works each season.

About 20 mi northeast of downtown Indianapolis, **Deer Creek Music Center** (⊠ 12880 E. 146th St., Noblesville, ☎ 317/776–3337 or 317/841–8900) brings top-name performers to its outdoor facility.

THEATER

Indiana's only resident professional theater, the **Indiana Repertory Theatre** (⊠ 140 W. Washington St., ☎ 317/635–5227 or 317/635–5252) presents major works in a restored 1927 movie palace downtown. The resident troop at **Beef & Boards Dinner Theatre** (⊠ 9301 N. Michigan Rd., ☎ 317/872–9664), on the northwest side, stages Broadway shows with a dinner buffet. Original musical revues play at **American Cabaret Theatre** (⊠ 401 E. Michigan St., ☎ 317/631–0334), and avant-garde plays take the stage at **Phoenix Theatre** (⊠ 749 N. Park Ave., ☎ 317/635–7529).

Spectator Sports

Baseball: Indianapolis Indians (⊠ Victory Field, 501 W. Maryland St., ☎ 317/269–3545). **Basketball: Indiana Pacers** (⊠ Conseco Fieldhouse, 125 S. Pennsylvania St., ☎ 317/917–2500 or 317/239–5151 for tickets). **Football: Indianapolis Colts** (⊠ 7001 W. 56th St., ☎ 317/297–7000). **Ice hockey: Indianapolis Ice** (⊠ 1202 E. 38th St., ☎ 317/925–4423 or 317/239–5151). **Soccer: Indiana Blast/Indiana Blaze** (⊠ Kuntz Memorial Soccer Stadium, 1502 W. 16th St., ☎ 317/595–9203 or 317/327–7194).

Shopping

Downtown, **Nordstrom** (☎ 317/636–2121) and **Parisian** (☎ 317/971–6200) department stores headline the roster of more than 120 shops at **Circle Centre** (⊠ 1 W. Washington St., ☎ 317/971–6200). On the north side of town, the **Fashion Mall Keystone at the Crossing** (⊠ 9000 Keystone Crossing, ☎ 317/574–4000) is anchored by the upscale Jacobson's (☎ 317/574–0088) and **Parisian** (☎ 317/581–8200) department stores. About 6 mi north of downtown, **Broad Ripple Village** (⊠ 62nd St. at Broad Ripple and College Aves., ☎ 317/251–2782) has art galleries, gift shops, and boutiques.

Side Trips from Indianapolis

Bloomington, Brown County, and Columbus

About an hour's drive south of the capital city on Route 46, the flat expanse of farmland dominating the upper two-thirds of the state gives way to hilly terrain. In **Bloomington,** home of Indiana University, ethnic restaurants, boutiques, galleries, and shops surround the courthouse square and fill the block-long mall, **Fountain Square** (⊠ 308 Fountain Square, Kirkwood and College Aves., ☎ 812/336–3681), distinguished by its historic storefront facades. For information contact the **Monroe County Convention and Visitors Bureau** (⊠ 2855 N. Walnut St., Bloomington 47404, ☎ 812/334–8900 or 800/800–0037).

Columbus is a forward-thinking city with more than 50 contemporary-style structures by world-renowned architects. Contact the **Columbus Area Visitors Center** (✉ Box 1589, 5th and Franklin Sts., 47202, ☎ 812/378–2622 or 800/468–6564) for information.

In picturesque Brown County, the quaint village of **Nashville** was a gathering place for artists in the early 1900s. Today, country-cooking eateries and shops nestle in alongside artists' studios and galleries throughout town. Contact the **Nashville/Brown County Convention and Visitors Bureau** (✉ Box 840, Main and Van Buren Sts., Nashville 47448, ☎ 812/988–7303 or 800/753–3255) for information.

Centerville and Richmond

Beginning in the 1820s, historic **Centerville** and **Richmond,** on the Ohio state line, saw as many as 200 wagons pass daily on the National Road, a western immigration trail (now U.S. Highway 40). Today this stretch of road is known as Antiques Alley, with more than 800 dealers. The **Richmond–Wayne County Convention and Visitors Bureau** (✉ 5701 National Rd. E, Richmond 47374, ☎ 765/935–8687 or 800/828–8414) has information on the area.

Hamilton County

Towns in this county northeast of downtown were once simply bedroom communities for Indianapolis. But restoration of the stately county courthouse in Noblesville coincided with a renaissance of museums, shops, and restaurants. It's always 1836 at **Conner Prairie** (✉ 13400 Allisonville Rd., Fishers 46038, ☎ 317/776–6000 or 800/966–1836), a re-created pioneer village complex in Fishers. For information contact the **Hamilton County Convention & Visitors Bureau** (✉ 11601 Municipal Dr., Fishers 46038, ☎ 317/598–4444 or 800/776–8687).

Parke County

Dubbed the Covered-Bridge Capital of the World, Parke County has 32 covered bridges scattered within an hour's drive west of Indianapolis (take Route 136). Every October Rockville and seven nearby towns welcome 1 million visitors to the 10-day **Covered Bridge Festival,** with crafts fairs, quilts and antiques shows, and barbecue beef and bean soup dinners. During the **Maple Syrup Festival** in early spring, sugar shacks open their doors to let visitors peek inside and taste the sweet treats. The **Covered Bridge Capital** visitors information office (✉ Box 165, 401 E. Ohio St., Rockville 47872, ☎ 765/569–5226) provides details about the area.

Zionsville

Brick streets and Stick-style, early 19th-century wood cottages create a fairy-tale setting for the town's quaint shops and intimate restaurants. Though just a 30-minute drive from downtown's domed stadiums and shiny new high-rises, Zionsville seems to be perfectly preserved. Contact the **Greater Zionsville Chamber of Commerce** (✉ Box 148, 135 S. Elm St., 46077, ☎ 317/873–3836).

SOUTHERN INDIANA

Dense stands of oak, hickory, and maple crown the rolling terrain that dominates southern Indiana. Tucked among the hills and valleys are 19th-century riverfront towns, caves that beg to be explored, and vast stretches of clear blue water.

Visitor Information

Southern Indiana: Clark/Floyd Counties Convention and Tourism Bureau (✉ 305 S. Indiana Ave., Jeffersonville 47130, ☎ 812/280–5566 or 800/552–3842). **Lincoln Hills Area:** Lincoln Hills/Patoka Lake Recreation Region (⊠ 125 S. 8th St., Courthouse Annex, Cannelton 47520, ☎ 812/547–7028). **Madison Area:** Madison Area Convention and Visitors Bureau (⊠ 301 E. Main St., Madison 47250, ☎ 812/265–2956 or 800/559–2956). **Vincennes Area:** Vincennes/Knox County Convention and Visitors Bureau (⊠ 27 N. 3rd St., Box 602, Vincennes 47591, ☎ 812/886–0400 or 800/886–6443). **Evansville and New Harmony:** Evansville Convention and Visitors Bureau (⊠ 401 S.E. Riverside Dr., Evansville 47713, ☎ 812/421–2200 or 800/433–3025).

Arriving and Departing

By Bus
Service between Indianapolis, Evansville, and Vincennes is available on **Greyhound** (☎ 812/425–8274 or 800/231–2222).

By Car
The major road through this region is I–64. From Indianapolis take I–70 and U.S. 41 to Vincennes and Evansville, I–65 and Route 7 to Madison, and I–65 to Clarksville and Jeffersonville. From Louisville, Kentucky, take I–65; from Cincinnati, Ohio, take I–74.

By Plane
Evansville Regional Airport (⊠ 7801 Bussing Dr., ☎ 812/421–4401) is served by commuter and regional airlines.

Exploring Southern Indiana

Three-hundred-year-old **Vincennes** brims with history. **Grouseland** (⊠ 3 W. Scott St., ☎ 812/882–2096; ☑ $3) was the home of the ninth U.S. president, William Henry Harrison. The log-and-mud **Old French House and Indian Museum** (⊠ 509 N. 1st St., ☎ 812/882–7886 or 800/886–6443; ☑ $1) is a French-Creole cottage constructed by a French fur trader in 1806. In the southwesternmost corner of Indiana, quaint **New Harmony** was the site of two 19th-century utopian communities; contact Historic New Harmony, Inc. (⊠ Box 579, New Harmony 47631, ☎ 812/682–4488 or 800/231–2168; ☑ $8) for information. Special tours are held at Christmas.

In the historic Riverside District of **Evansville**, columned mansions such as the **Historic Reitz Home** (⊠ 224 S.E. 1st St., ☎ 812/426–1871; ☑ $2) overlook the Ohio River. The **Evansville Museum of Arts and Science** (⊠ 411 S.E. Riverside Dr., ☎ 812/425–2406; ☑ free) has American and European art from the 1700s to the present, a planetarium, and a reconstructed turn-of-the-20th-century village.

In **Corydon,** Indiana's first capital, you can browse through 10,000 square ft of antiques in two downtown malls. Corydon's Federal-style **Corydon Capitol State Historic Site** (⊠ 202 E. Walnut St., ☎ 812/738–4890; ☑ free) is where the state's first constitution was drafted. The **Corydon 1883 Scenic Railroad** (⊠ 210 Walnut St., ☎ 812/738–8000; ☑ $9) makes a 16-mi (90-minute) trip through the countryside in the summer and fall.

Dubbed the Williamsburg of the Midwest, **Madison** is an antebellum-era town whose entire main street and 100 additional blocks are listed on the National Register of Historic Places. See the gleaming white Greek Revival **Lanier Mansion State Historic Site** (⊠ 511 W. 1st St., ☎ 812/265–3526; ☑ free), whose portico overlooks the Ohio River. Exhibits trace the heydays of steamboating and trains in southeastern Indiana at the **Jefferson County Historical Society Museum and 1895 Madison Railroad Station** (⊠ 615 W. 1st St., ☎ 812/265–2335; ☑ $2).

Dining and Lodging

Contact the **Indiana Bed & Breakfast Association** (☏ no phone) for information on the area's coziest accommodations.

Corydon

$–$$ 🏠 **Kintner House Inn.** Once the headquarters of Confederate general John Hunt Morgan, the inn dates from the mid-1800s. The large rooms have Victorian furnishings and antique light fixtures. ⊠ *101 S. Capitol St., at Chestnut St., 47112,* ☏ *812/738–2020. 15 rooms. AE, D, DC, MC, V. BP.*

New Harmony

$$ ✕🏠 **New Harmony Inn.** On spacious grounds overlooking a small lake, this contemporary-style inn has two fine restaurants, the Red Geranium and the Bayou Grill. Rooms are furnished sparsely, with Shaker-style furniture, original artwork, and antiques. ⊠ *506 North St. (Box 581), 47631,* ☏ *800/782–8605. 90 rooms. 2 restaurants, pool, tennis, health club. AE, D, MC, V. CP.* 🐾

Outdoor Activities and Sports

Biking

Six routes on the **Bikeways** system managed by the Outdoor Recreation Division of the Indiana Department of Natural Resources (⊠ 402 W. Washington St., Room W271, Indianapolis, 46204, ☏ 317/232–4070) run through this area.

Fishing

Each season at **Patoka Lake** (⊠ R.R. 1, Box 290, Birdseye, ☏ 812/685–2464) and **Markland Dam,** on the Ohio River off Route 156 near Vevay in Florence, record catches of bass, carp, and catfish are recorded. The dam has free picnic facilities and vantage points to watch river traffic go through the locks. Contact the **Indiana Department of Natural Resources, Division of Fish and Wildlife** (⊠ 402 W. Washington St., Room W273, Indianapolis 46204, ☏ 317/232–4080) for permits and information.

NORTHERN INDIANA

Stretches of dunes and inviting beaches along Lake Michigan give way to a neat grid of lush farmland dotted with Amish communities in northeastern Indiana. The state's second-largest city, Fort Wayne, has lake country to the west and charming Amish towns like Grabill to the northwest and east.

Visitor Information

Amish Country: Elkhart County Convention and Visitors Bureau (⊠ 219 Caravan Dr., Elkhart 46514, ☏ 219/262–8161 or 800/262–8161). **Fort Wayne:** Convention and Visitors Bureau (⊠ 1021 S. Calhoun St., 46802, ☏ 219/424–3700 or 800/767–7752). **Lake Country:** Kosciusko County Convention and Visitors Bureau (⊠ 111 Capital Dr., Warsaw 46580, ☏ 219/269–6090 or 800/800–6090). **North Coast:** Lake County Convention and Visitors Bureau (⊠ 7770 Corinne Dr., Hammond 46323, ☏ 219/989–7770 or 800/255–5253); Porter County Convention and Visitors Bureau (⊠ 800 Indian Boundary Rd., Chesterton 46304, ☏ 219/926–2255 or 800/283–8687); LaPorte County Convention and Visitors Bureau (⊠ 1503 S. Meer Rd., LaPorte 46360, ☏ 219/872–5055 or 800/685–7174). **South Bend/Mishawaka:** Convention and Visitors Bureau (⊠ 401 E. Colfax Ave., South Bend 46617, ☏ 219/234–0051 or 800/282–2230).

Arriving and Departing

By Bus

United Limo (☎ 219/674–6993) in Osceola provides daily service to and from Chicago. Other service is available on **Greyhound** (✉ 4671 Terminal Dr., South Bend, ☎ 800/231–2222).

By Car

Major east–west roads are I–80/90 and U.S. 12 and 20. Traversing the region north–south are I–65, I–69, and U.S. 31 and 41.

By Plane

The **South Bend Regional Airport** (✉ 4477 Terminal Dr., South Bend, ☎ 219/233–2185) is served by national and regional carriers.

By Train

Connecting South Bend, northwestern Indiana, and Chicago is the **South Shore Line** (✉ 2702 W. Washington St., South Bend, ☎ 219/233–3111 or 800/356–2079). **Amtrak** (✉ 2702 Washington Ave., South Bend, ☎ 800/872–7245) offers limited service.

Exploring Northern Indiana

In one of the nation's earliest conservation efforts, the poet Carl Sandburg fought to save the land that is now the 2,200-acre **Indiana Dunes State Park** (☞ National and State Parks, *above*) in the northeastern corner of the state. Visitors can reach 40 mph on twin ¼-mi refrigerated toboggan tracks at **Pokagan State Park** (✉ 450 Lane 100, Lake James, Angola, ☎ 219/833–2012; 🎟 park $2 per car residents, $5 nonresidents; toboggan $4 per hr).

In **Michigan City**, the 1905 **Barker Mansion and Civic Center** (✉ 631 Washington St., ☎ 219/873–1520; 🎟 $3) illustrates the opulent lifestyle of freight car magnate John H. Barker with its lavish interior and marble fireplaces. **Old Lighthouse Museum** (✉ Heisman Harbor Rd., ☎ 219/872–6133; 🎟 $2) is the only Indiana lighthouse along Lake Michigan. The 1858 lighthouse—which hasn't shone a light since 1904—has lighthouse furnishings and city-history exhibits.

Fans flock to **South Bend** each year to see the **University of Notre Dame**'s Fighting Irish. Be sure to stop by the landmark **Golden Dome** (✉ U.S. 33 N, ☎ 219/239–7367) and the **College Football Hall of Fame** (✉ 111 S. St. Joseph St., ☎ 219/235–9999; 🎟 $9), with a plaza modeled after a football field, talking statues, and a 360-degree video projection inside a "stadium" theater. Downtown South Bend's **East Race Waterway** (✉ U.S. 31 N, ☎ 219/235–9401) attracts tubers, rafters, and Olympic kayakers. The **Studebaker National Museum** (✉ 525 S. Main St., ☎ 219/235–9479; 🎟 $4.50) celebrates the company's 114-year history with exhibits of 75 Studebaker-related vehicles, from Conestoga wagons to automobiles, including the last Studebaker built in South Bend, a red 1964 hardtop.

The 75-mi corridor from South Bend southeast to Fort Wayne goes through Indiana's **Amish Country. Amish Acres** (✉ Rte. 19, 1600 W. Market St., Nappanee, ☎ 219/773–4188; 🎟 $6.95) is an 80-acre restored Amish farm with a dinner theater in the round and a restaurant and inn with Amish furnishings. The **Borkhholder Dutch Village** (✉ County Rd. 101, Nappanee, ☎ 219/773–2828 🎟 free) has more than 500 arts, crafts, and antiques booths. More than 1,000 vendors crowd the 40-acre open-air **Shipshewana Auction & Flea Market** (✉ Rte. 5S, Shipshewana, ☎ 219/768–4129) every Tuesday and Wednesday from May to October, drawing 35,000 visitors daily. The **Old Bag Factory** (✉ 1100 Chicago Ave., Goshen, ☎ 219/534–2502; 🎟 free), a massive redbrick structure dating from 1895, houses 18 shops, including a custom hardwood-furniture maker. Just outside Fort Wayne, **Grabill** (⌧ Chamber of Commerce, Box 7, Grabill 46741, ☎ 219/627–522 or 800/939–3216) seems caught in a time warp, with Amish buggies hitched up all around town. West of Fort Wayne, hundreds of kettle lakes, as well as **Lake Wawasee and Lake Maxinkuckee,** attract summer vacationers in the **Lake County** of Kosciusko County.

Dining and Lodging

For inn bookings contact the **Indiana Bed & Breakfast Association** (⌧ Box 1127, Goshen 46526, ☎ no phone).

Amish Country

$$$ 🏨 **Checkerberry Inn.** On 100 acres, this elegant hostelry has the state's only professional croquet course, a walking lane, and woodlands. The guest rooms' decor reminds visitors this is Amish country. A cup of tea in the solarium is a must. ⌧ *62644 County Rd. 37, Goshen 46526,* ☎ FAX *219/642–4445. 14 rooms. Restaurant, tennis court. AE, MC, V. CP.*☻

$$–$$$ 🏨 **Essenhaus Country Inn.** The three-story, softly lit atrium with a potbellied stove is the centerpiece of this inn. Locally handcrafted Amish quilts and furniture make guest rooms simple but inviting. ⌧ *240 U.S. 20, Middlebury 46540,* ☎ FAX *219/825–9447 or* ☎ *800/ 455–9471. 33 rooms. Restaurant. AE, D, MC, V.*

Indiana's North Coast

$–$$$ ✕ **Miller Bakery Cafe.** This cozy bakery turned eatery has received rave reviews for its inventive fare. Start dinner with savory bread pudding with cilantro pesto or wild mushroom ragout. Then, move on to New Zealand rack of lamb with coarse whole-grain mustard sauce, or sautéed veal medallions with carmelized mushrooms. ⌧ *555 S. Lake St., Gary,* ☎ *219/938–2229. MC, V. Closed Sun.*

$$–$$$ 🏨 **Hutchinson Mansion Inn.** This 1876 mansion spanning almost a city block is filled with stained-glass windows and marble fireplaces. Antiques and fresh flowers fill the guest rooms and public spaces. ⌧ *220 W. 10th St., Michigan City 46360,* ☎ *219/879–1700. 10 rooms. AE, MC, V. BP.*

South Bend/Mishawaka

$$–$$$ 🏨 **Book Inn.** High ceilings, original woodwork, and a homemade breakfast served with silver and Waterford crystal make this downtown South Bend inn a favorite. The decor in the Charlotte Brontë, Louisa May Alcott, and Jane Austen guest rooms reflects the era of its respective namesakes; amenities, such as data ports, reflect this one. ⌧ *508 W. Washington St., South Bend 46601,* ☎ *219/288–1990. 5 rooms. AE, MC, V. BP.*☻

IOWA

Updated by
Diana Lambdin
Meyer

Capital	Des Moines
Population	2,829,000
Motto	Our Liberties We Prize and Our Rights We Will Maintain
State Bird	Eastern goldfinch
State Flower	Wild rose
Postal Abbreviation	IA

Statewide Visitor Information

The **Division of Tourism** (✉ Iowa Department of Economic Development, 200 E. Grand Ave., Des Moines 50309, ☎ 515/242–4705 or 800/345–4692) has 23 welcome centers along I–35 and I–80 and in towns throughout the state. For regional visitor information call or write **Eastern Iowa Tourism Association** (✉ 216 W. 4th St., Vinton 52349, ☎ 319/472–5135 or 800/891–3482), **Central Iowa Tourism Region** (✉ Box 454, Webster City 50595–0454, ☎ 515/832–4808 or 800/285–5842), and **Western Iowa Tourism Region** (✉ 502 Coolbaugh St., Red Oak 51566, ☎ 712/623–4232 or 888/623–4232).

Scenic Drives

Iowa's most beautiful scenic drive may be the series of roads that take you south along the high bluffs and verdant banks of the Mississippi River on the state's eastern border (☞ Dubuque and the Great River Road, *below*). In western Iowa, the **Loess Hills Scenic Byway** crisscrosses the Missouri River valley, featuring ancient soil gathered by ice-age winds. Follow Route 12 north from Sioux City. In southeast Iowa **Route 5** from Des Moines to Lake Rathbun, near Centerville, makes a nice detour from I–35; to return to the interstate, take **Route 2W** from Centerville for about 50 mi.

National and State Parks

National Parks

Effigy Mounds National Monument (☞ Exploring Dubuque and the Great River Road, *below*) has scenic hiking trails along prehistoric burial mounds. Iowa has four federal reservoir areas around large man-made lakes: **Coralville Lake** (✉ 2850 Prairie du Chien Rd. NE, Iowa City 52240, ☎ 319/338–3543), **Rathbun Lake** (✉ Rte. 3, Centerville 52544, ☎ 515/647–2464), **Lake Red Rock** (✉ 1105 Hwy. T15, Knoxville 50138-9522, ☎ 515/828–7522), and **Saylorville Lake** (✉ 5600 N.W. 78th Ave., Johnston 50131, ☎ 515/276–4656).

The **Neal Smith National Wildlife Refuge** (✉ 9981 Pacific St., Prairie City 50228, ☎ 515/994–3400), 20 mi east of Des Moines on I–80, has 8,600 acres of reconstructed tallgrass prairie, 5 mi of hiking trails accessible to travelers with disabilities, a prairie education center, and an elk and bison viewing area.

State Parks

Iowa's 70 state parks include 5,383 campsites, many with shower facilities and electrical hookups. Some well-developed parks with modern campsites, cabins, lodge rentals, and boat rentals are **Clear Lake** (☎ 515/357–4212), near Mason City; **George Wyth Memorial** (☎ 319/232–5505), near Waterloo; **Lacey-Keosauqua** (☎ 319/293–3502), near Keosauqua; and **Lake of Three Fires** (☎ 712/523–2700), near Bedford. Virgin prairie areas, state parks without facilities, include **Cayler Prairie**, near the Great Lakes area in northwestern Iowa; **Hayden Prairie,** near the Minnesota border in the northeastern corner of the state; **Kalsow Prairie,** about 90 mi northwest of Des Moines; and **Sheeder Prairie,** about 50 mi west of Des Moines. Contact the **Iowa Department of Natural Resources** (☎ 515/281–5145) for more information.

DES MOINES

If you were to peer down from an airplane or the top of a hill, the capital of Iowa would look like a cluster of office towers popping out of a green corduroy landscape. Downtown straddles the confluence of two rivers—the Raccoon and the Des Moines. The skyline of historic buildings and modern structures faces granite government buildings and a classic gold-domed capitol across four bridges. Although hardly a glittering metropolis, Des Moines is a relatively hassle-free city with a number of museums, historic districts, and parks, as well as Drake University.

Visitor Information

The Des Moines Convention and Visitors Bureau (⊠ 2 Ruan Center, 601 Locust St., No. 222, 50309, ☎ 800/451–2625) operates visitor centers in three locations, including the **airport** lobby (☎ 515/287–4396), the **Living History Farms** (☎ 515/278–2400), and in the **skywalk** above the corner of 6th and Locust streets downtown (☎ 515/286–4960).

Arriving and Departing

By Bus
Greyhound (☎ 800/231–2222) and **Jefferson** (☎ 515/283–0074) share a terminal at Keosauqua Way and 12th Street.

By Car
I–80, the major east–west thoroughfare through the state, and I–35, Iowa's main north–south route, intersect northwest of Des Moines and link with I–235, which runs across the northern part of the city.

By Plane
Des Moines International Airport (⊠ 5800 Fleur Dr., ☎ 515/256–5100), about 3 mi south of downtown, has scheduled service by major domestic airlines. The drive into town takes about 10 minutes in normal traffic. Cab fare, including tip, is less than $10. Hotel shuttles serve the route, and major car-rental companies are in the airport.

Getting Around Des Moines

Streets both in the city and in suburban Urbandale and West Des Moines are laid out in a grid, which makes getting around fairly easy. A car, however, is essential, as attractions are scattered about the city and suburbs. Downtown is compact enough to explore in comfortable shoes.

Exploring Des Moines

Downtown
Start a walking tour of downtown Des Moines at the **capitol complex** (⊠ E. 9th St. and Grand Ave., ☎ 515/281–5591; ☞ free), on the east bank of the Des Moines River. There you can see the elaborate murals in the rotunda of the capitol and climb into the dome, covered in 22-karat gold leaf. Near the capitol, the **Botanical Center** (⊠ 909 E. River Dr., ☎ 515/323–8900; ☞ $1.50) has flower displays and a three-story, dome-topped jungle. The **Iowa Historical Building** (⊠ 600 E. Locust St., ☎ 515/281–5111; ☞ free), one block west of the capitol, shakes off any dusty-old-stuff image with its postmodern design, abstract

sculpture of neon and glass, and striking fountain display. The building houses the state archives, library, and museum.

Just west of downtown in Greenwood Park, the **Des Moines Art Center** (✉ 4700 Grand Ave., ☎ 515/277–4405; ⌨ free) houses a permanent collection of contemporary art. The **Science Center of Iowa** (✉ 4500 Grand Ave., ☎ 515/274–4138; ⌨ $5.50), in Greenwood-Ashworth Park, has interactive programs that include laser shows, a planetarium, and a space shuttle simulator appropriate for all ages.

Terrace Hill, an 1866 Victorian mansion known as the "palace of the prairie," is the Iowa governor's mansion. ✉ 2300 Grand Ave., ☎ 515/ 281–3604. ⌨ $5. Closed Sat.–Mon. and Jan. and Feb.

Some of the city's most interesting historic buildings can be found on the west side of the Des Moines River (follow Locust Street from the east side). Self-guided walking tours are detailed in brochures from **Downtown Partnership, Inc.** (✉ Suite 255, 400 Locust St., ☎ 515/243–6625). The **Sherman Hill Historic District** has impressive Victorian houses. The **Court Avenue District** contains a number of restored 19th-century warehouses and other commercial buildings, many of which now house shops, restaurants, and entertainment venues.

Outside the City

Spend a half day exploring **Living History Farms,** a 600-acre open-air museum a few miles northwest of Des Moines. The farms are a trip back in time via the sights, sounds, and smells of an 18th-century Native American village, two working farms from 1850 and 1900, and an 1875 town. ✉ 2600 N.W. 111th St., Urbandale 50322, ☎ 515/278–2400. ⌨ $10. Closed Nov.–Apr. Call for special events in winter.

Dining

$$ ✕ **Cafe Su.** Dim sum appetizers are the specialty at this chic restaurant in the Valley Junction shopping area in West Des Moines. Contemporary decor complements the traditional Chinese cuisine. ✉ 225 5th St., ☎ 515/274–5102. AE, D, DC, MC, V. Closed Sun. and Mon.

$–$$ ✕ **Chezwicks.** Located in the historic Savery Hotel, Chezwicks attracts a downtown business crowd for breakfast, lunch, and dinner who enjoy Iowa pork and roast beef served with pastas, soup, and salad. The restaurant features intimate booth seating and is decorated with original art. ✉ 401 Locust St., ☎ 515/244–2151. AE, D, MC, V.

$–$$ ✕ **Jesse's Embers.** Just west of downtown, Jesse's is prized for grilled prime steaks cooked over an open pit in the main dining room. The room is small, plain, and crowded with neighborhood people waiting in the bar, but service is swift. ✉ 3301 Ingersoll Ave., ☎ 515/255– 6011. AE, MC, V. Closed Sun.

$–$$ ✕ **Trostel's Greenbriar.** The large menu at this restaurant in the northern suburb of Johnston mixes elegant and basic fare; choices include Iowa pork chops, rack of lamb, and seafood. Frosted glass and dark wood accent the three dining rooms and bar. ✉ 5810 Merle Hay Rd., Johnston, ☎ 515/253–0124. AE, D, MC, V. Closed Sun. No lunch.

$–$$ ✕ **Tursi's Latin King.** This family-owned restaurant has served traditional Italian-American food since 1947. ✉ 2200 Hubble Ave., ☎ 515/ 266–4466. AE, D, MC, V. Closed Sun. and Mon.

$–$$ ✕ **Waterfront Seafood Market.** Saltwater and freshwater fish are flown in daily from around the world to this supercasual seafood market and restaurant. ✉ 2900 University Ave., West Des Moines, ☎ 515/223– 5106. AE, D, MC, V. Closed Sun.

$ ✕ **Drake Diner.** Students from nearby Drake University mix with older
★ patrons at this chrome-and-neon spot, with a traditional soup, salad, and sandwich menu. ✉ *1111 25th St.,* ☎ *515/277–1111. AE, D, DC, MC, V.*

$ ✕ **El Patio.** Southwestern artifacts fill this converted bungalow just west of downtown, where diners sit in colorful rooms and on a covered patio. More Tex than Mex, the food is still a cut above the fare found at chains. ✉ *611 37th St.,* ☎ *515/274–2303. AE, MC, V. No lunch.*

$ ✕ **India Cafe.** Classic aromatic dishes range from zingy lamb vindaloo
★ to mild tandoori chicken. The restaurant's peach-color walls have Indian paintings, and seating is at booths and tables with armchairs. ✉ *Parkwood Plaza, 86th and Douglas Sts., Urbandale,* ☎ *515/278–2929. AE, D, MC, V.*

Lodging

Contact the **Iowa Bed and Breakfast Innkeepers' Association** (✉ 250 W. Maple, Hartley 51346, ☎ 800/888–4667) for information on B&Bs.

$$$ ☷ **Des Moines Marriott.** The location, downtown on the skywalk, which connects several buildings, is a plus. Rooms on higher floors have unobstructed views of the city. The restaurant, Quenelle's, serves rich Continental fare. ✉ *700 Grand Ave., 50309,* ☎ *515/245–5500 or 800/228–9290,* ℻ *515/245–5567. 415 rooms. 2 restaurants, pool, health club. AE, D, MC, V.* ✺

$$–$$$ ☷ **Embassy Suites Hotel on the River.** This hotel across the bridge from
★ the Court Avenue District has seven balconies around an atrium with a waterfall. Beyond this, the Embassy Suites lacks flash but dazzles with attentive service. ✉ *101 E. Locust St., 50309,* ☎ *515/244–1700,* ℻ *515/244–2537. 234 suites. Restaurant, pool, health club. AE, D, DC, MC, V. BP.* ✺

$$–$$$ ☷ **Hotel Fort Des Moines.** Some of the greatest names in world history
★ have stayed in this grand hotel since its opening in 1919. Marble floors and walnut woodwork original to the structure are just a couple of the reasons why it's been placed on the National Register of Historic Places. ✉ *1000 Walnut St., 50309,* ☎ *515/243–1161 or 800/532–1146,* ℻ *515/243–4317. 295 rooms. AE, D, MC, V. CP.* ✺

$$ ☷ **Holiday Inn Downtown.** Expect fresh but ordinary rooms and a few suites with whirlpool baths at this chain motel north of downtown. ✉ *1050 6th Ave., 50314,* ☎ *515/283–0151,* ℻ *515/283–0151. 253 rooms. Restaurant, pool. AE, D, MC, V.* ✺

$–$$ ☷ **Valley West Inn.** The three-story inn next to West Des Moines's big mall has simply furnished rooms decorated in rosy fabrics and blond woods. ✉ *3535 Westown Pkwy., West Des Moines 50266,* ☎ *515/225–2524 or 800/833–6755,* ℻ *515/225–9058. 136 rooms. Restaurant, pool. AE, D, DC, MC, V.* ✺

$ ☷ **Airport Comfort Inn.** This three-story hotel is two blocks from the airport. Meeting rooms are available. ✉ *5231 Fleur Dr., 50321,* ☎ *515/287–3434. 55 rooms. Pool. AE, D, DC, MC, V. CP.*

$ ☷ **Heartland Inn.** The inn, a rustic three-story building on the north-
★ eastern edge of Des Moines, is next to an amusement complex. ✉ *5000 N.E. 56th St., Altoona 50009,* ☎ *515/967–2400 or 800/334–3277,* ℻ *515/967–0150. 86 rooms. Pool. AE, D, DC, MC, V. CP.*

The Arts

The **Des Moines Art Center** (✉ 4700 Grand Ave., ☎ 515/277–4405), just west of downtown in Greenwood-Ashworth Park, hosts poetry readings, lectures, and film presentations. It also has a permanent collection of contemporary art (☞ Exploring, *above*). The **Des Moines**

Symphony (✉ 221 Walnut St., ☎ 515/243–1160) presents impressive local musicians and guest performers throughout the year.

Spectator Sports

Track and Field: The Drake Relays (✉ Drake University, Forest and 27th Sts., ☎ 515/271–3791), held in late April, draw track and field athletes from 744 colleges, universities, and high schools, as well as some big-name Olympians and professional athletes. Call for ticket packages.

Arena Football: Iowa Barnstormers (✉ 319 7th St., No. 222, ☎ 515/282–3596) is growing in popularity in the Midwest, thanks in part to this team's three consecutive division titles.

Shopping

Valley Junction (☎ 515/222–3642), six square blocks located 5 mi west of downtown on 5th Street in West Des Moines, has a mix of antiques stores and contemporary shops selling country furnishings, collectibles, and Iowa souvenirs.

EAST-CENTRAL IOWA

This region east of Des Moines is a mix of historic towns, trim farm-steads, and forested river valleys. Cedar Rapids is the largest town in the area. Iowa City, about 25 mi south, is the home of the University of Iowa. The Amana Colonies, a cluster of seven villages west of Iowa City that were founded in the 19th century as a utopian religious community, are the major attraction.

Visitor Information

Amana Colonies: Welcome Center (✉ 39 38th Ave., Suite 100, near U.S. 151 and Rte. 220, Amana 52203, ☎ 319/622–7622 or 800/579–2294), with information and a lodging reservation service. **Cedar Rapids area:** Convention and Visitors Bureau (✉ 119 1st Ave. SE, 52401, ☎ 319/398–5009 or 800/735–5557). **Iowa City/Coralville:** Visitors Bureau (✉ 408 1st Ave., Coralville 52241, ☎ 319/337–6592 or 800/283–6592).

Arriving and Departing

By Car
I–80, the state's major east–west thoroughfare, runs from Des Moines east to Iowa City. From Iowa City I–380 passes Lake MacBride on the way north to Cedar Rapids. From Cedar Rapids U.S. 151 meanders southwest for about 25 mi through a rural farmscape to Middle Amana, the start of the cluster of Amana colonies.

By Plane
The **Eastern Iowa Regional Airport** (✉ 2515 Wright Brothers Blvd. West, ☎ 319/362–3131), 7 mi south of Cedar Rapids and just off I–380, is served by American Eagle, Delta Connection, Northwest/Northwest Airlink, United, US Airways, and TWA.

Exploring East-Central Iowa

★ Begin at the **Amana Colonies,** as the seven villages of Amana are known (☞ Visitor Information, *above*). Although descendants of the German-Swiss immigrants who founded the community voted to end its communal way of life in 1932, little has visibly changed since then. The 30-square-mi area of the Amana Colonies region encompasses nearly 500 restored buildings, including barns and kitchens now housing

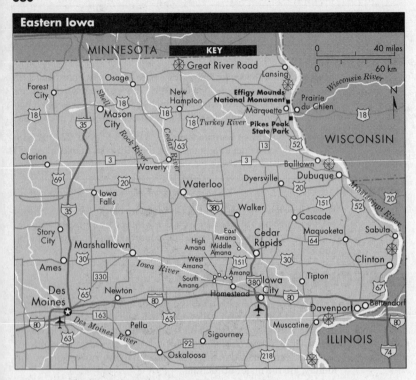

Eastern Iowa

museums, and a schoolhouse, which together have been designated a National Historic Landmark. Members of the Amana community still manufacture prized woolen goods, furniture, wine, cheese, and baskets. The original **Amana Appliance Store** (⊠ 836 48th Ave., ☎ 319/622–7655), founded after residents voted to abandon their communal life, is still in business, although the appliances are no longer manufactured by the Amanites. The **Museum of Amana History** is filled with historical artifacts and documents relating to the settlement of the area. ⊠ 4310 220th Trail, ☎ 319/622–3567. ☞ $5. Closed Jan. and Feb., limited hrs until late spring.

Cedar Rapids is on U.S. 151 in east-central Iowa, just north of the Amana Colonies. In the 19th and early 20th centuries, waves of Czechoslovakian immigrants settled in this manufacturing town. A sampling of Czech heritage is on view at the **National Czech & Slovak Museum & Library.** ⊠ 30 16th Ave. SW, ☎ 319/362–8500. ☞ $5. Closed Mon.

Cedar Rapids has the world's largest permanent collection of paintings by renowned native son Grant Wood, at its **Museum of Art.** ⊠ 410 3rd Ave. SE, ☎ 319/366–7503. ☞ $4. Closed Mon.

Iowa City, in east-central Iowa, served as the seat of state government until the capital moved to Des Moines in the mid-19th century. The golden dome of the **Old Capitol** (⊠ 24 Old Capitol Dr., ☎ 319/335–0548) is now the center of the beautiful, hilly campus of the **University of Iowa** on the banks of the Iowa River.

West Branch, a community of 2,000 with more than two dozen buildings listed on the National Register of Historic Places, is just west of Iowa City on I–80. The **Herbert Hoover Presidential Library and Birthplace** (⊠ Parkside Dr. and Main St., ☎ 319/643–5301; ☞ $2), the cottage where the future president was born to Quaker parents in 1874, contains period furnishings, many of them original.

Dining and Lodging

Amana kitchens bustle with rich German meals, often served family style. Try the locally made rhubarb wine. Hotels in Cedar Rapids tend to cater to business travelers, but the Amanas, like many other Iowa towns, are home to a growing number of B&Bs (**Iowa Bed and Breakfast Innkeepers' Association**; ⊠ 250 W. Maple Dr., Hartley 51346, ☎ 800/888–4667). Decent chain hotels and motels dominate in Iowa City.

Amana Colonies

$ ✕ **Brick Haus Restaurant.** Large portions of Wiener schnitzel *mit* spaetzle are a specialty at this place in the middle of prime Amana shopping. Food is served at long tables covered in checkered cloths. ⊠ *728 47th Ave., Amana,* ☎ *319/622–3278. AE, MC, V.*

$ ✕ **Ox Yoke Inn.** Come for traditional German-American food in an
★ Old Country–inspired setting. ⊠ *Main St., Amana,* ☎ *319/622–3441. AE, D, MC, V. Closed Mon. in Jan. and Feb.*

$ ✕ **Zuber's Restaurant.** The comfortable surroundings haven't changed much since the 1950s, nor has the menu, a primer on German cuisine: hearty portions of oven-baked steak, country-style chicken, salad, vegetables, and dessert, served family style. ⊠ *Main St., Homestead,* ☎ *319/622–3911. AE, D, MC, V.*

$$ 🏨 **Amana Holiday Inn.** The rustic setting of the pool and sauna enlivens this good-size hotel located just off the interstate. ⊠ *Exit 225 off I–80 (Box 187, Little Amana 52203),* ☎ *319/668–1175 or 800/633–9244,* FAX *319/668–2853. 155 rooms. Restaurant, pool. AE, D, MC, V.* 🐾

$ 🏨 **Die Heimat Country Inn.** This two-story B&B is the oldest in the colonies. It has small rooms with locally made, traditional furnishings and deluxe units with canopy beds. ⊠ *4430 V St. (Box 160, Homestead 52236),* ☎ *319/622–3937. 19 rooms. D, MC, V. BP.*

$ 🏨 **Rawson's Bed & Breakfast.** When Homestead still practiced com-
★ munal living, this unique B&B was a kitchen workers' dormitory. There are two large, distinctive rooms, with exposed beams and brick walls, and one suite; all have period furnishings and fabrics, and lavish baths. ⊠ *4424 V St. (Box 118, Homestead 52236),* ☎ *319/622–6035 or 800/637–6035. 4 rooms. D, MC, V. BP.* 🐾

Cedar Rapids

$–$$ 🏨 **Collins Plaza.** In this hotel north of downtown, rooms are large, with traditional furnishings and pastel colors. There's an airport shuttle. ⊠ *1200 Collins Rd. NE, 52402,* ☎ *319/393–6600 or 800/541–1067,* FAX *319/393–2308. 221 rooms. Restaurant, pool, exercise room. AE, D, DC, MC, V.* 🐾

Iowa City

$ ✕ **Givanni's.** Neon lights enhance the exposed-brick walls at this Italian-American-vegetarian restaurant in the downtown pedestrian mall. ⊠ *109 E. College St.,* ☎ *319/338–5967. AE, D, DC, MC, V.*

$ ✕ **Iowa River Power Company.** The former power station for much of eastern Iowa, set on the banks of the Iowa River, was turned into a restaurant serving classic American cuisine. ⊠ *501 1st Ave., Coralville,* ☎ *319/351–1904. AE, DC, MC, V.*

Walcott

$ ✕ **Iowa 80 Kitchen.** The native stone fireplace, beamed ceiling, and spacious dining room make this one of the most elegantly furnished truck stops in the country. With a 48-ft salad bar, an in-house bakery, laundry facilities, and a warehouse store, it's also a traveler's dream. Walcott is about 55 mi east of Iowa City. ⊠ *395 W. Iowa 80 Rd.,* ☎ *319/284–6965. D, MC, V.*

Motel

🏨 **Heartland Inn** (⊠ 3315 Southgate Ct. SW, Cedar Rapids 52404, ☎ 319/362–9012 or 800/334–3277, ⅎᴬˣ 319/362–9694), 114 rooms; pool; $.

Shopping

The commercial hub of Amana shopping is the eight-block center of Amana, just east of the visitor center. The **Woolen Mill Salesroom** (⊠ 800 48th Ave., ☎ 319/622–3432) sells all manner of woolens, from clothing to blankets; take a self-guided tour of the mill. On weekdays at the **Furniture and Clock Shop** (⊠ 724 48th Ave., ☎ 319/622–3291) you can watch craftspeople making the products sold here. The fragrant, creaky **Old Fashioned High Amana Store** (⊠ 1308 G St., ☎ 319/622–3797), 2 mi west of the visitor center, stocks old-time-type gifts. The **Amana Arts Guild Center** (⊠ 1210 G St., ☎ 319/622–3678) sells high-quality quilts and crafts. **Little Amana**, at I–80 and U.S. 151, is more of a quick-stop outlet for woolens, gifts, and souvenirs than a typical Amana village. The **Tanger Factory Outlet Center** (⊠ Exit 220 off I–80, Williamsburg, ☎ 800/406–2887) has 70 stores selling designer clothing and accessories, housewares, and brand-name shoes.

DUBUQUE AND THE GREAT RIVER ROAD

The mighty Mississippi River forms the eastern border of Iowa; the top third of the border, from the Minnesota line to Dubuque, has the oldest settlements, highest bluffs, and closest river access of the entire stretch. The **Great River Road** is a network of federal, state, and county roads that wind along this magnificent stretch of riverbank, highlighting wildlife refuges and the river's complicated locks and dams system. Routes 26, 52, and 99 make up this road in Iowa.

Visitor Information

Tourist Information Center (⊠ Port of Dubuque Welcome Center, 400 3rd St., Dubuque 52001, ☎ 319/556–4372 or 800/798–8844).

Arriving and Departing

By Bus

Greyhound (☎ 800/231–2222) links Dubuque to most major cities; its local bus station is in the lower level of the Julien Inn (⊠ 200 Main St.).

By Car

You can join Iowa's **Great River Road** from the north on U.S. 18 at Prairie du Chien, Wisconsin, or pick up the scenic route anywhere on Iowa's eastern border. The entire length of the Great River Road is marked by signs with a 12-spoke pilot's wheel symbol.

Exploring Dubuque and the Great River Road

Just 11 mi south of the Minnesota border, the **Municipal Park,** in Lansing, Iowa, provides spectacular views of the Mississippi River. The **Effigy Mounds National Monument** (⊠ Rte. 76, ☎ 319/873–3491; ⊡ $2 per person, up to $4 per car; free Nov.–Mar.), 3 mi north of McGregor along the Great River Road, has hiking trails that run alongside eerie, animal-shape prehistoric Native American burial mounds.

One-, four-, and six-hour walks lead to cliff-top views of the upper Mississippi River valley.

Pikes Peak State Park (☎ 319/873–2341), 3 mi south of McGregor, has a view of the Wisconsin River as it links up with the Mississippi. The stretch of road approaching **Balltown,** 7 mi north of Dubuque, reveals green hills rolling down to the river.

Dubuque is full of river merchants' homes, some of them lavish Victorian houses turned B&Bs, snuggled against the limestone cliffs that back this small harbor town. Get out of the car here and explore **Cable Car Square** (☎ 319/583–5000), at 4th and Bluff streets, site of two dozen shops and restaurants. From April through November you can ride the **Fenelon Place Elevator** (☎ 319/582–6496; ☜ $1.50) to the top of a 200-ft bluff for a sweeping view of the city.

☾ **Dyersville,** 25 mi west of Dubuque on U.S. 20, found fame as a setting for the 1989 movie *Field of Dreams.* The **Field of Dreams Movie Site** (⊠ 28963 Lansing Rd., ☎ 319/875–8404 or 888/875–8404; ☜ free), about 3 mi north of town, has been preserved as a tourist attraction. Bring your own equipment to play in the continual pickup game; the field is closed November–March. There are several museums, including the **National Farm Toy Museum,** which has more than 30,000 old farm toys. ⊠ *1110 16th Ave. SE,* ☎ *319/875–2727.* ☜ *$4.*

Dining and Lodging

Ethnic and family-style restaurants line Dubuque's 4th Street at Cable Car Square. As in the rest of the state, B&Bs are abundant (**Iowa Bed and Breakfast Innkeepers' Association,** ⊠ 250 W. Maple, Hartley 51346, ☎ 800/888–4667).

Balltown

$ ✕ **Breitbach's Country Dining.** This funky, rambling piece of folk ar-
★ chitecture has a good home-style kitchen. ⊠ *563 Balltown Rd.,* ☎ *319/552–2220. MC, V.*

Dubuque

$–$$ ✕ **Yen Ching.** The café serves predictable Chinese food, with a few spicy Hunan dishes for variety. ⊠ *926 Main St.,* ☎ *319/556–2574. AE, MC, V. Closed Sun.*

$$–$$$ ⊞ **Hancock House.** This meticulously restored Victorian perched halfway
★ up a bluff has four-poster beds, lace-covered windows, ornate fireplaces, and a rare Tiffany lamp collection. ⊠ *1105 Grove Terr., 52001,* ☎ *319/557–8989,* ℻ *319/583–0813. 9 rooms. D, MC, V. BP.* ☙

$$ ⊞ **Redstone Inn.** Bedrooms are grand and baths lavish at this British manor–like establishment on the prairie. ⊠ *504 Bluff St., 52001,* ☎ *319/582–1894,* ℻ *319/582–1893. 15 rooms. AE, D, MC, V. BP.*

ELSEWHERE IN IOWA

Iowa's Great Lakes

Visitor Information
Iowa Great Lakes Chamber of Commerce (⊠ 56 N. Okoboji Grove Rd., Box 9, Arnolds Park 51331, ☎ 800/270–2574).

Arriving and Departing
Take I–80 west from Des Moines and U.S. 71 north to Spirit Lake or take I–35 north from Des Moines to U.S. 18, which leads west to the Great Lakes area.

What to See and Do

The Iowa Great Lakes lie in the northwest corner of the state. The region has six lakes (including West Okoboji—one of only three true bluewater lakes in the world) and dozens of vacation resorts. The **Queen II** excursion boat (✉ Arnolds Park, ☎ 712/332–5159) gives tours of West Okoboji.

Dining and Lodging

Lodging rates may drop substantially in this area between late fall and spring.

$ ✕ **Lighthouse Bar & Grill.** Guests come by boat, bike, or car to dine inside or out in the nautical atmosphere here. Steak and seafood get top billing on the menu, which has everything from sandwiches to full dinners. ✉ U.S. 71 at East Oak Mall, Okoboji, ☎ 712/332–5995. AE, MC, V.

$ ✕ **Maxwell's on the Lake.** A lovely view, elegant dining, fine service, and an extensive menu (with lots of seafood and steak) make dining here a memorable experience. ✉ 144 Lakeshore Dr., Arnold's Park, ☎ 712/332–7578. AE, MC, V.

$$$ 🏨 **Village East Resort.** This resort overlooking Brooks Golf Course and East Lake Okoboji has indoor and outdoor pools. Additional draws are a pro shop and weight room. ✉ Box 499, Okoboji 51355-0499, ☎ 712/332–2161 or 800/727–4561. 101 rooms. Restaurant, 2 pools, tennis, health club. AE, D, DC, MC, V.

$$ 🏨 **Beaches Resort.** On the quiet north end of West Lake Okoboji, these clapboard cottages offer simple but comfortable furnishings at a family-oriented resort. At day's end, you can gather around the fire pit on the sandy beach for complimentary s'mores. ✉ 15109 215th Ave., Spirit Lake 51360, ☎ 712/336–2230. 6 cottages, 5 apartments, 1 house. Restaurant. D, MC, V.

The Quad Cities

Visitor Information

Quad Cities Visitors Bureau (✉ 102 S. Harrison St., Davenport 52801, ☎ 309/788–7800 or 800/747–7800).

Arriving and Departing

From Des Moines take I–80 east to Davenport.

What to See and Do

Davenport and **Bettendorf** make up Iowa's side of the Quad Cities (the others are Rock Island and Moline in Illinois), which straddle the Mississippi River. The **President Riverboat Casino** (✉ 130 W. River Dr., ☎ 800/262–8711), a National Historic Landmark, is as big as a football field and has five decks decorated in Victorian splendor. Hotels, restaurants, and antiques shops are within walking distance. The **Bix Beiderbecke Jazz Festival** (☎ 319/324–7170) is held each July in Davenport's riverfront park.

The **Village of East Davenport** (☎ 319/322–0546) is Iowa's second-largest historic district and home to about 50 specialty shops and restaurants.

Dining and Lodging

$ ✕ **Iowa Machine Shed.** Enjoy Iowa pork chops and beef, homemade desserts, and fresh vegetables served in a farmhouse atmosphere. Drinks are served in Mason jars. ✉ 7250 Northwest Blvd., Davenport, ☎ 319/391–2427. MC, V.

$$ 🏨 **Jumer's Castle Lodge.** Impressive both inside and out, this lodge is furnished with heavy walnut carvings, rich carpets, and elegant ac-

cessories. ⊠ *900 Spruce Hill Dr., Bettendorf 52722,* ☎ FAX *800/285–8637. 210 rooms. Restaurant, pool, exercise room. AE, D, MC, V.*

The Covered Bridges Region

Arriving and Departing

Take I–35 south from Des Moines to U.S. 92, which leads west into Madison County.

What to See and Do

Made famous by Robert James Waller's novel *The Bridges of Madison County* and the eponymous 1995 movie, **Madison County,** 50 mi southwest of Des Moines, is home to six covered bridges that date from the 1880s. **Bus tours** (☎ 515/462–1185) of the bridges take place all day, or you can take a self-guided one. Maps are available at the Chamber office (⊠ 73 Jefferson St.). Tours are also available at Francesca's Farmhouse and other buildings used as sites for the movie. The Covered Bridge Festival is held here each October. In Winterset, the **birthplace of John Wayne** (⊠ 224 S. 2nd St., ☎ 515/462–1044; ☎ $2.50) is furnished with family memorabilia and authentic turn-of-the-20th-century pieces; you can watch Wayne's films in the gift shop.

Dining and Lodging

$–$$ ✕ **Summerset House.** An Italianate Victorian mansion just two blocks from the courthouse square now serves as a tearoom. Lunch fare includes elegant sandwiches and quiche; choices for the five-course dinner are salmon steaks, apricot-glazed game hens, and prime rib. ⊠ *204 W. Washington St., Winterset,* ☎ *515/462–9099. Reservations essential. MC, V.*

$ ✕ **Northside Cafe.** You'll find typical café fare—meat loaf, fried chicken, mashed potatoes, and homemade pie—at this spot, where Clint Eastwood ate in the movie *The Bridges of Madison County.* ⊠ *61 W. Jefferson St., Winterset,* ☎ *515/462–1523. No credit cards.*

$ ▨ **Hutchings-Wintrode Bed and Breakfast.** This 1886 brick home, just four blocks from the courthouse, has been refurbished with antiques and period decor. ⊠ *503 E. Jefferson St., Winterset 50273,* ☎ *515/462–3095. 3 rooms. MC, V. BP.*

KANSAS

By Janet
Majure

Updated by
Diana Lambdin
Meyer

Capital	Topeka
Population	2,595,000
Motto	To the Stars Through Difficulties
State Bird	Western meadowlark
State Flower	Wild native sunflower
Postal Abbreviation	KS

Statewide Visitor Information

Kansas Department of Commerce, Travel & Tourism Division (✉ 700 S.W. Harrison St., Suite 1300, Topeka 66603-3712, ☎ 785/296–2009 or 800/252–6727). There are **visitor information centers** on I–70W in **Kansas City** (☎ 913/299–2253), on I–70E in **Goodland** (☎ 785/899–6695), on I–35 at **Belle Plaine** (☎ 316/326–5123), on I–35 at **Olathe** (☎ 913/768–6155), and in **Topeka** (☎ 785/296–3966).

Scenic Drives

Route 177 south from I–70 to historic Council Grove provides lovely views of the undulating Flint Hills, especially in late afternoon or early morning.

National and State Parks

National Parks

Federal sites include the **Fort Larned National Historic Site** (☞ The Santa Fe Trail Region, *below*); the **Fort Scott National Historic Site** (✉ Box 918, Old Fort Blvd., Fort Scott 66701, ☎ 316/223–0310 or 800/245–3678; ⛁ $2), which centers on a fort built in 1842 to keep the peace in Native American territory and includes exhibits on pivotal confrontations of the Civil War; the **Tallgrass Prairie National Preserve** (✉ Rte. 1, Box 14, Strong City 66869, ☎ 316/273–8494; ⛁ donations accepted), which offers self-guided and ranger-escorted tours of tallgrass prairie that once covered much of the Great Plains; and the **Cimarron National Grassland** (✉ Box J, 242 E. Hwy. 56, Elkhart 67950, ☎ 316/697–4621; ⛁ free), less than a mile from central Elkhart, which offers a self-guided auto tour of key Santa Fe Trail sites.

State Parks

Kansas has 22 state parks, most associated with recreational lakes, run by the **Department of Wildlife and Parks** (✉ 512 S.E. 25th Ave., Pratt 67124, ☎ 316/672–5911). Two of the best are **Scott County State Park** (✉ 520 W. Scott Lake Dr., Scott City 67871, ☎ 316/872–2061), containing archaeological evidence of the northernmost Native American pueblo and one of the first white settlements in Kansas, and **Milford State Park** (✉ 8811 State Park Rd., Milford 66514, ☎ 785/238–3014), with a 37,000-acre reservoir, a nature center, and a fish hatchery.

EAST-CENTRAL KANSAS

Heading west from Kansas City across east-central Kansas, you'll follow in the footsteps of pioneers who blazed the Oregon, Santa Fe, Smoky Hill, and Chisholm trails. Native American history, Civil War sites, and the Old West loom large along this 150-mi stretch of prairie.

Visitor Information

Abilene: Convention & Visitors Bureau (⊠ 201 N.W. 2nd St., 67410, ☎ 785/263–2231 or 800/569–5915). **Atchison:** Visitor Center (⊠ 200 S. 10th St., 66002, ☎ 913/367–2427 or 800/234–1854). **Kansas City, Kansas:** Convention & Visitors Bureau (⊠ 727 Minnesota Ave., 66117, ☎ 913/321–5800 or 800/264–1563). **Lawrence:** Convention & Visitors Bureau (⊠ 734 Vermont St., 66044, ☎ 785/865–4411). **Overland Park:** Convention & Visitors Bureau (⊠ 10975 Benson Dr., Suite 360, 66210, ☎ 913/491–0123 or 800/262–7275). **Topeka:** Convention & Visitors Bureau (⊠ 1275 S.W. Topeka Blvd., 66612, ☎ 785/234–1030 or 800/235–1030).

Arriving and Departing

By Bus

Greyhound (☎ 800/231–2222) connects Kansas City, Lawrence, Topeka, and Abilene en route to Denver, Colorado. **Jefferson Lines** (☎ 800/735–7433) serves Kansas City, Overland Park, and Lawrence.

By Car

I–70W enters Kansas from Kansas City, Missouri; I–70E, from Colorado. Most attractions are just off the interstate. Note: Kansas weather is extremely variable. Listen to the radio for forecasts, as ice storms, heavy snowfalls, flash floods, and high winds can make driving treacherous. Road conditions are also posted at toll booths along I–70.

By Plane

The biggest airport serving east-central Kansas is **Kansas City International Airport** (☞ Missouri). US Airways Express serves Topeka's **Forbes Field** (⊠ Box 19053, J St. and First N St., ☎ 785/862–2362).

By Train

Amtrak (☎ 800/872–7245) serves Lawrence, Topeka, and Kansas City.

Exploring East-Central Kansas

Along I–70 you'll encounter an array of historic sites. Kansas City, which straddles the border between Kansas and Missouri, was a major provisioning point for frontier travelers in the 19th century.

The **Mahaffie Farmstead & Stagecoach Stop** (⊠ 1100 Kansas City Rd., Olathe 66061, ☎ 913/782–6972; ⊡ $3) once served the Santa Fe Trail, one of the routes established in the 19th century for trade and later for westward expansion. There are guided tours of the stone house, one of three farmstead buildings here listed on the National Register of Historic Places. The farmstead is closed in January and on weekends from February through April.

In Fairway, a Kansas City suburb, the **Shawnee Indian Mission** (⊠ 3403 W. 53rd St., ☎ 913/262–0867; ⊡ free) was created in 1839 as a school to teach English and trade skills to Native Americans. You can tour two of its three buildings every day except Monday.

About 40 mi west of Kansas City on I–70 is **Lawrence.** The town was rebuilt after being raided and burned by William Quantrill and a band of Confederate sympathizers for the antislavery stance of its citizens during the Civil War; many structures from this time remain. Stroll along Massachusetts Street through the lovely downtown area, where turn-of-the-20th-century buildings and retail shops retain a small-town flavor.

A few blocks away from Massachusetts Street is the scenic main campus of the 29,000-student **University of Kansas.** Lining Jayhawk Boulevard is an assortment of university buildings, including the Romanesque native-limestone building that houses the **University of Kansas Natural History Museum** (✉ Dyche Hall, ☎ 785/864–4540; ⌑ donations accepted), one of the school's four museums. The Natural History Museum has fossils, mounted animals, and rotating exhibits; kids will enjoy the dinosaur bones and live snakes. Also in Lawrence is **Haskell Indian Nations University** (✉ 155 Indian Ave., ☎ 785/749–8450), which has provided higher education for Native Americans since 1884 and includes several **Stan Herd Earth Works** sculptures for viewing on the southwest corner of the campus.

Fifty miles northwest of Kansas City on Route 7, overlooking the Missouri River, is **Atchison,** the birthplace of famed aviator Amelia Earhart. The **Amelia Earhart Birthplace Museum** (✉ 223 N. Terrace St., 66002, ☎ 913/367–4217; ⌑ $2), owned by the International Ninety-Nines, Inc., a group of women pilots, displays flying memorabilia and childhood treasures of the famed pilot.

Trees from 50 states and 38 countries grow in harmony at the **International Forest of Friendship** (✉ 1½ mi southwest of Atchison at Warnock Lake, ☎ 913/367–1419; ⌑ free), a gift to the United States for its bicentennial from the city and International Ninety-Nines, Inc. The forest is accessed through Memory Lane, which is paved with plaques that list the names of more than 600 pilots, astronauts, and manufacturers who have contributed to aviation. About 70 mi west of Kansas City on I–70 is **Topeka,** with its outstanding classical state **capitol** (✉ 300 W. 10th St., ☎ 785/296–3966), begun in 1866 and completed nearly 40 years later. Lobby murals include a striking depiction of abolitionist John Brown by John Steuart Curry. Be sure to visit the ornate senate chambers, which have magnificent bronze columns and variegated-marble accents. Topeka holds a place in history as the site of the *Brown* v. *Board of Education* lawsuit, the 1954 case that outlawed segregation in public schools. The **Monroe School** (✉ 424 S. Kansas Ave., ☎ 785/354–4273), the focal point of the case, is now part of the National Park system. West of downtown Topeka, the **Kansas Museum of History** (✉ 6425 S.W. 6th St., ☎ 785/272–8681; ⌑ free), perversely situated in a modernist box of a building, traces Kansas's history from the Native American era to the present. Kids like **Discovery Place,** a hands-on exhibit involving 19th-century tools, clothes, and household items. Just outside Topeka, the **Combat Air Museum** (✉ Hangars 602 and 604, Forbes Field, ☎ 785/862–3303; ⌑ $5) has two hangars full of military aircraft dating from World War I. **Historic Ward-Meade Park** (✉ 124 N. Fillmore St., ☎ 785/295–3888) is as lovely as it is historic, with a restored mansion, a cabin, a train depot, a one-room schoolhouse, and botanical gardens. **Gage Park** (✉ 635 Gage Blvd., ☎ 785/368–3838) has a carousel and is home to the **Topeka Zoo** (☎ 785/272–5821; ⌑ $4.50).

Tallgrass Prairie National Preserve (✉ Rte. 1, Box 14, Strong City 66869, ☎ 316/273–8494; ⌑ donations accepted), contains the last large vestiges of the bluestem, or tallgrass, prairie that once covered much of the Great Plains. Tours include a stone mansion and barn built in 1881. The historic **Grand Central Hotel** (✉ 215 Broadway St., ☎ 316/273–6763 or 800/951–6763) in Cottonwood Falls has been welcoming guests since 1884.

The small town of **Abilene,** about 85 mi west of Topeka, is famous for cattle drives and for Dwight D. Eisenhower.

The **Eisenhower Center complex** (⊠ 200 S.E. 4th St., ☎ 785/263–4751 or 877/746–4453; ⊡ $3) includes the late president's **boyhood home** as well as the Eisenhower Museum, the Eisenhower Presidential Library, and the **Place of Meditation**, a chapel where the president, his wife, Mamie, and their son, Doud Dwight, are interred. The museum displays memorabilia from Eisenhower's youth in Abilene to his success as a World War II general through his popular presidency.

Also in Abilene is the **Dickinson County Historical Museum** (⊠ 412 S. Campbell St., ☎ 785/263–2681; ⊡ $2.50), with exhibits on the life of the Plains Indians and cowboys on the Chisholm Trail and a fully restored 1901 C.W. Parker carousel available for rides. The **Greyhound Hall of Fame** (⊠ 407 S. Buckeye St., ☎ 785/263–3000; ⊡ donations accepted) documents the history of the illustrious canine breed.

Dining and Lodging

Typical Kansas roadhouse fare is chicken-fried steak and fried chicken. Restaurants in east-central cities and towns also serve good barbecue and Mexican food. Accommodations range from business-class hotels in the Kansas City suburb of Overland Park to basic roadside motels in the western part of the region to bed-and-breakfasts (contact **Kansas Bed & Breakfast Association,** ⊠ Rte. 1, Box 93, WaKeeney 67672).

Abilene

$$ ✕ **Kirby House.** The traditional midwestern fare is nothing special, but the modestly elegant setting, in a restored Victorian mansion, makes this place worthwhile. ⊠ *205 N.E. 3rd St.,* ☎ *785/263–7336. MC, V.*

$ ✕ **Mr. K's Farmhouse.** Once a favorite of Dwight and Mamie Eisenhower, the "house on the hill" serves fried chicken and homemade desserts. ⊠ *407 S. Van Buren,* ☎ *785/263–7995. D, MC, V. Closed Mon.*

Kansas City

$$ ✕ **Kansas Machine Shed.** Kansas farm cooking—including corn-fed hams, homemade cottage cheese, and apple dumplings the size of a dinner plate—along with antique farm machinery and a gift shop make this stop just off the interstate an attraction in its own right. ⊠ *12080 Strang Line Rd., Olathe,* ☎ *913/780–2697. AE, D, DC, MC, V.*

$ ✕ **Dick Clark's American Bandstand Grill.** Rock-and-roll history comes alive in this diner, owned by America's perpetual teenager. Vintage posters, gold albums, and artists' contracts on the walls complement a varied menu. Clark and other music celebrities often stop in. ⊠ *10975 Metcalf Ave., Overland Park,* ☎ *913/451–1600. AE, D, MC, V.*

$ ✕ **Hayward's Pit Bar-B-Que.** Locals flock to this hillside restaurant for
★ piles of succulent smoked beef, ribs, chicken, pork, and sausage. ⊠ *11051 Antioch Rd., Overland Park,* ☎ *913/451–8080. AE, MC, V.*

$$$ ⊞ **Double Tree Hotel.** Adjacent to two major highways, a business park, and a scenic public jogging trail, this 18-story hotel is convenient to shopping, restaurants, and a bowling alley. ⊠ *10100 College Blvd., Overland Park 66210,* ☎ *913/451–6100,* ⒻⒶⓍ *913/451–0386. 357 rooms. Restaurant, pool, health club. AE, D, DC, MC, V.* ✺

$$$ ⊞ **Overland Park Marriott Hotel.** This upscale hotel in a suburban business area has a marble-floor lobby and traditionally styled rooms. ⊠ *10800 Metcalf Ave., Overland Park 66210,* ☎ *913/451–8000,* ⒻⒶⓍ *913/451–5914. 390 rooms. 2 restaurants, pool, health club. AE, D, DC, MC, V.* ✺

Lawrence

$ ✕ **Free State Brewing Co.** Kansas's first legal brewpub, opened in
★ 1989, serves dishes like fish-and-chips and a Burgundy beef sandwich (shredded beef brisket on a baguette, smothered with gravy) to com-

plement the selection of beers. ⊠ *636 Massachusetts St.,* ☎ *785/843–4555. AE, D, DC, MC, V.*

$$ 🏨 **Eldridge Hotel.** Listed on the National Register of Historic Places,
★ this downtown hotel has attractive suites with parlors and wet bars.
Rooms on the top (fifth) floor have great views. The downtown loca-
tion means some traffic noise but great convenience. ⊠ *701 Massa-
chusetts St., 66044,* ☎ *785/749–5011 or 800/527–0909,* ℻ *785/749–
4512. 48 suites. Restaurant. AE, D, DC, MC, V.* ✲

Topeka

$$ ✕🏨 **Heritage House.** Rooms range from dramatic to cozy at this turn-
of-the-20th-century clapboard home. The intimate restaurant serves a
frequently changing Continental menu for lunch and dinner. ⊠ *3535
S.W. 6th St., 66606,* ☎ *785/233–3800,* ℻ *785/233–9793. 11 rooms.
Restaurant. Jacket and tie. AE, D, DC, MC, V.*

$$ 🏨 **Club House Inn.** In western Topeka near the Kansas Museum of His-
tory, this modern white-stucco hotel has spacious rooms, many over-
looking a landscaped courtyard, and suites with kitchenettes. ⊠ *924
S.W. Henderson St., 66615,* ☎ *785/273–8888,* ℻ *785/273–5809. 121
rooms. Pool. AE, D, DC, MC, V.* ✲

Motels

I–70 is lined with chain hotels (☞ Lodging *in* Chapter 1).

🏨 **Best Western Inn** (⊠ 2210 N. Buckeye St., Abilene 67410, ☎ 785/
263–2050, ℻ 785/263–7230), 62 rooms, restaurant, pool; *$.*

Campgrounds

🏕 **Four Seasons RV Acres** (⊠ 6 mi east of Abilene off I–70; 2502 Mink
Rd., Abilene 67410, ☎ 785/598–2221 or 800/658–4667). 🏕 **KOA Camp-
grounds of Lawrence** (⊠ 1473 Hwy. 40, Lawrence 66044, ☎ 785/842–
3877). 🏕 **KOA Campground** (⊠ Rte. 1, Grantville 66429, ☎ 785/246–
3419). Camping is also available in state parks at reservoirs.

Nightlife

The **New Theatre Restaurant** (⊠ 9229 Foster St., Overland Park
66212, ☎ 913/649–7469), an Equity theater and restaurant, stages first-
run and recent musicals and comedies.

Outdoor Activities and Sports

Fishing

Most of east-central Kansas follows the Kansas River (called the Kaw
River locally), where a series of large-scale flood-control reservoirs yield
good fishing for walleye, bass, and crappie. Good sites include **Clinton
State Park** (⊠ 798 N. 1415 Rd., Lawrence 66049); **Perry State Park**
(⊠ 5441 West Lake Rd., Ozawkie 66070), near Topeka; **Tuttle Creek
State Park** (⊠ 5020-B Tuttle Creek Blvd., Manhattan 66502); and **Mil-
ford State Park** (☞ National and State Parks, *above*). Licenses, which
are required, can be purchased at county clerks' offices, state parks of-
fices, and some retail outlets. The **Kansas Department of Fish and Game**
(☎ 316/672–5911) has further information.

Hiking

Kansas's reservoirs are bordered by state parks with marked nature
trails. The **Konza Prairie** (⊠ 5 mi off I–70 at Exit 307, McDowell Creek
Rd., ☎ 785/587–0441), an 8,600-acre section of tallgrass prairie set
aside for research and preservation, has a self-guided nature trail.

Spectator Sports

Basketball: Jayhawks (⊠ Memorial Stadium, 11th and Mississippi Sts.,
☎ 785/864–3141 or 800/344–2957).

Shopping

Lawrence Riverfront Factory Outlets (⊠ 1 Riverfront Plaza, ☎ 785/842–5511), at the north end of downtown, has nearly 50 stores. The mall's north-side picture windows have excellent views of the nearly 20 bald eagles that live in the cottonwood trees on the banks of the Kansas River, which rushes past the front of the mall. The **Tanger Center** (⊠ 1035 N. 3rd St., Lawrence, ☎ 800/406–4215), about a mile north of downtown, has 25 factory-outlet stores from major manufacturers of clothing, shoes, and other goods. **Johnson County,** which incorporates the Kansas City suburbs of Overland Park, Lenexa, and Olathe, has abundant shopping in several fashionable centers and strip malls. There are also a number of unique shops along Metcalf Avenue at I–435, at 95th and I–35, and at the 150 stores of the **Great Mall of the Great Plains** (☎ 913/829–6277) at I–35 and 151st St.

THE SANTA FE TRAIL REGION

Although the Santa Fe Trail spans the entire state, the towns in western Kansas are most closely associated with its lore and history. This is the Kansas we know from film and myth: remote, flat, treeless, littered with tumbleweeds, and windy, but imbued with a romance identified with such names as Wyatt Earp and Dodge City. Towns sprang up here first along the trail, then near the railroad lines that followed. Today the mainstay is agriculture and natural gas. Tourism is growing, but don't expect resorts.

Visitor Information

Dodge City: Convention & Visitors Bureau (⊠ Box 1474, 400 W. Wyatt Earp Blvd., 67801, ☎ 316/225–8186). **Hutchinson:** Convention & Visitors Bureau (⊠ 117 N. Walnut St., 67501, ☎ 316/662–3391). **Larned:** Chamber of Commerce (⊠ 502 Broadway, 67550, ☎ 316/285–6916 or 800/747–6919).

Arriving and Departing

By Bus
Greyhound (☎ 800/231–2222) connects with **TNM&O Coaches** (☎ 316/276–3731) to provide service to Dodge City and Garden City from Wichita. **Salt City Shuttle** (☎ 316/664–6117) connects several small towns throughout the state.

By Car
From Kansas City or Topeka take I–70 west and I–135 south, then Route 61 to Hutchinson. Eastbound travelers enter Dodge City via U.S. 50 or U.S. 56.

By Plane
Dodge City Regional Airport (⊠ 100 Airport Rd.), about 2 mi east of downtown, is served by US Airways Express from Denver (☎ 316/227–8679) and United Airlines Express from Kansas City (☎ 316/225–5065).

By Train
Amtrak (☎ 800/872–7245) serves Hutchinson, Newton, Garden City, and Dodge City.

Exploring the Santa Fe Trail Region

★ Hutchinson is home to the state fairgrounds and some of the world's largest grain elevators, but what really makes this small town worth a visit is the **Kansas Cosmosphere & Space Center** (⊠ 1100 N. Plum St., ☎ 316/662–2305 or 800/397–0330, ☞ $5). Housing more than $100 million worth of space exhibits, the center's museum has the largest such collection outside the Smithsonian Institution. Various displays, including interactive exhibits, trace the history of space exploration and solutions to the many challenges of human flight. Exhibits include the *Apollo 13 Odyssey* command module and the world's largest display of Soviet space artifacts; the center also has a planetarium and an Omnimax theater. Tickets are an additional fee and advance purchase is recommended.

Travel west out of Hutchison on 4th Street (which becomes County Road 636) for about 30 mi, and you'll see signs to the **Quivira National Wildlife Refuge** (⌧ Rte. 3, Box 48A, Stafford 67578, ☎ 316/486–2393; ⌨ free). More than 250 bird species have been spotted on these 21,000 acres, including bald eagles, pelicans, and whooping cranes.

Drive north through the Quivira refuge, and then turn west on County Road 484, which becomes Route 19, to **Larned,** a well-preserved Old West town. Two miles west of Larned on Route 156, the **Santa Fe Trail Center** (⌧ Rte. 3, ☎ 316/285–2054; ⌨ $3) details the history of the trail and displays artifacts from early 20th-century prairie life. About 4 mi west of Larned on Route 156 is **Fort Larned National Historic Site** (⌧ R.R. 3, ☎ 316/285–6911; ⌨ $2), a meticulous restoration of an 1868 prairie fort that protected travelers and railroad workers on the Santa Fe Trail. Buffalo Soldiers (post–Civil War regiments of black soldiers) were stationed here. The nine-building site includes a museum, restored barracks, and a nature trail; a slide show depicts the fort's history.

Turn south on the first road west of Fort Larned, which intersects with U.S. 56. Follow this southwest to **Dodge City,** which capitalizes on its 19th-century reputation as the "wickedest little city in America." Founded 5 mi west of Fort Dodge in anticipation of the arrival of the Santa Fe Railroad, the town thrived on the drinking and gambling of buffalo hunters and cowboys until it burned down in 1885. It was here that lawmen Bat Masterson and Wyatt Earp earned their fame.

Dodge City's **Boot Hill Museum** (⌧ Front St., ☎ 316/227–8188; ⌨ $6) includes exhibits on Native American history, the Santa Fe Trail, and the town's early life; Front Street, a reconstruction of the town's original houses, saloons, and other businesses; and a re-creation of the Boot Hill cemetery (the remains of those buried here were moved years ago). In summer, gunfights, medicine shows, and stagecoach rides are staged daily.

From Dodge City, follow U.S. 50 west for 9 mi to the **Santa Fe Trail tracks,** a 140-acre preserve where ruts from wagons on the trail are still visible in the sandy prairie earth more than 130 years later.

Dining and Lodging

Motels hold sway in this part of the state, and you'll find few fancy restaurants. If you're traveling in summer, make reservations early for lodging, and try to make reservations for dinner on weekends. Note: The term *red beer* on menus means beer mixed with tomato juice (it's better than it sounds). Kansas liquor laws vary from county to county; in dry counties alcohol is served only in private clubs, to which many hotels offer courtesy memberships (ask when you call to reserve).

Dodge City

$$$ ✕ **Casey's Cowtown Steakhouse.** A little more elegant than the name implies, Casey's is known for steak dinners served in a fine dining atmosphere and features an extensive wine list. ⌧ *503 East Trail,* ☎ *316/ 227–5225. MC, V. Closed Sun.*

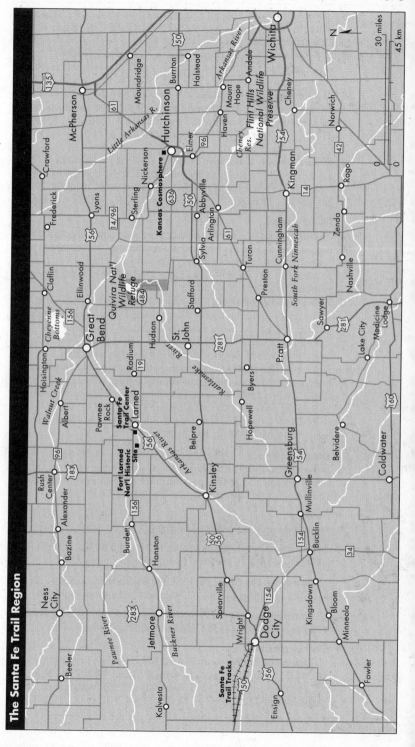

The Santa Fe Trail Region

$ ✕ **Big Art's.** Those in search of basic American sandwiches, steaks, and shakes will be satisfied here. ✉ *1005 W. Wyatt Earp Blvd.,* ☎ *316/227-2424. AE, D, MC, V.*

$ ✕ **El Charro.** Mexican dishes such as "enchilada delights," topped with cheese, lettuce, tomato, and sour cream, make this a favorite. ✉ *1209 W. Wyatt Earp Blvd.,* ☎ *316/225-0371. MC, V. Closed Sun.*

$$ ▣ **Boot Hill Bed & Breakfast.** In a Colonial Dutch home, the owners incorporate a Wild West theme into the elegance of fine linens, home-made pastries, and beautiful gardens. ✉ *603 W. Spruce St., 67801,* ☎ *316/225-7600 or 888/255-7655,* 🄵🄰🄷 *316/225-6585. 6 rooms. AE, D, MC, V.* ✆

$ ▣ **Best Western Silver Spur Lodge.** You'll find pleasant but undistinguished rooms at this sprawling complex, just five minutes from Front Street. ✉ *1510 W. Wyatt Earp Blvd., 67801,* ☎ *316/227-2125,* 🄵🄰🄷 *316/227-2030. 121 rooms. 2 restaurants, pool. AE, D, DC, MC, V.* ✆

Hutchinson

$
★ ✕ **Anchor Inn.** Two large brick-walled rooms in older downtown buildings are the setting for Mexican dishes that use the restaurant's distinctive homemade flour tortillas. Portions are bounteous. ✉ *126–128 S. Main St.,* ☎ *316/669-0311. Reservations not accepted weekend evenings. MC, V.*

$ ✕ **Roy's Hickory Pit BBQ.** This tiny restaurant seating 36 serves barbecued pork spareribs, beef brisket, sausage, ham, and turkey. There's nothing else on the menu except beans, salad, and bread—but what more do you want? ✉ *1018 W. 5th St.,* ☎ *316/663-7421. Reservations not accepted. No credit cards. Closed Sun. and Mon.*

$$
★ ▣ **Ramada Inn Hutchinson.** Rooms in the "minidome" section of this busy convention hotel look onto a quiet, landscaped courtyard. "Maindome" rooms open onto a recreation area with a putting green and swimming pool. ✉ *1400 N. Lorraine St., 67501,* ☎ *316/669-9311 or 800/362-5018,* 🄵🄰🄷 *316/669-9830. 220 rooms. Restaurant, pool, exercise room. AE, D, DC, MC, V.* ✆

Larned

$ ✕ **Harvest Inn.** Chicken, steaks, and seafood are on the menu at this family restaurant; pub grub is served in the accompanying bar, the Grain Club. ✉ *718 Ft. Larned Ave.,* ☎ *316/285-3870. D, MC, V.*

Motels

EconoLodge and **Super 8** (☞ Lodging *in* Chapter 1) are in Dodge City.

▣ **Best Western Townsman Inn** (✉ 123 E. 14th St., Larned 67550, ☎ 316/285-3114, 🄵🄰🄷 316/285-7139), 44 rooms, pool; **$**.

▣ **Quality Inn City Center** (✉ 15 W. 4th St., Hutchinson 67501, ☎ 316/663-1211, 🄵🄰🄷 316/663-1211), 98 rooms, restaurant, pool; **$$**.

▣ **Scotsman Inn** (✉ 322 E. 4th St., Hutchinson 67501, ☎ 316/669-8281 or 800/950-7268, 🄵🄰🄷 316/669-8282), 48 rooms; **$**.

Campgrounds

⛺ **Gunsmoke Campground** (✉ R.R. 2, W. Hwy. 50, Dodge City 67801, ☎ 316/227-8247). ⛺ **Melody Acres RV Park** (✉ 1009 E. Blanchard St., Hutchinson 67501, ☎ 316/665-5048). ⛺ **Watersports Campground** (✉ 500 E. Cherry St., Dodge City 67801, ☎ 316/225-9003).

Nightlife

In Dodge City, the **Boot Hill Museum** (☞ Boot Hill Museum *in* Exploring the Santa Fe Trail Region, *above*) puts on the 19th-century-style Long Branch Variety Show. Also in Dodge City, the **Longhorn Saloon** (✉ 706

N. 2nd St., ☎ 316/225–3546) has a restaurant and a 1,350-square-ft wooden dance floor for western stomping.

Outdoor Activities and Sports

Hiking

☾ At **Dillon Nature Center,** in Hutchinson (✉ 3002 E. 30th St., ☎ 316/663–7411), a 2-mi National Recreation Trail takes in woods, prairie, wetlands, and a prairie-dog town. Inside the Discovery Center, both kids and adults can use hands-on exhibits to learn about the Kansas outdoors.

Spectator Sports

Rodeo: The biggest Professional Rodeo Cowboys Association–affiliated rodeo in Kansas is the **Dodge City Roundup Rodeo** (☎ 316/225–2244), held for five days each summer during the Dodge City Days festival.

SOUTHEAST KANSAS

Wichita

Visitor Information

Convention and Visitors Bureau (✉ 100 S. Main St., Suite 100, 67202, ☎ 316/265–2800 or 800/288–9424).

Arriving and Departing

Wichita lies about 190 mi southwest of Kansas City on the Kansas Turnpike (I–35). Most visitors arrive by car or fly into **Wichita Mid-Continent Airport** (✉ 2299 Airport Rd., ☎ 316/946–4700), served by most major domestic carriers. **Greyhound Lines** ☎ (800/231–2222) stops in Wichita en route between Kansas City and Dallas.

What to See and Do

Originally a frontier town, **Wichita** is known today as one of the world's capitals of airplane production—Beech, Cessna, and Learjet are based here, and Boeing has a major installation. The city is also home to such corporate giants as Coleman, makers of camping equipment, and Pizza Hut.

The **Indian Center Museum** (✉ 650 N. Seneca St., ☎ 316/262–5221; ☎ $2) displays artifacts from numerous tribes, including the Crow and the Sioux. The **Old Cowtown Museum** (✉ 1871 Sim Park Dr., ☎ 316/264–0671; ☎ $7; Closed Nov.–Mar.) is a re-created 19th-century town. At **Botanica, the Wichita Gardens** (✉ 701 N. Amidon, ☎ 316/264–0448; ☎ $4.50 Apr.–Dec., free Jan.–Mar.), more than 9 acres of perennials and woody plants are displayed among dozens of fountains and pools. The **Wichita Greyhound Park** (✉ 10 mi north of downtown Wichita on I–135, ☎ 316/755–4000 or 800/872–2894) offers live horse and greyhound racing, as well as simulcast races from around the country, year-round.

Just 15 minutes north of Wichita on I–35 is El Dorado, home of the **Coutts Museum of Art** (✉ 110 N. Main St., ☎ 316/321–1212, ☎ free), with an impressive collection of Renoirs, Remingtons, and works by local artists.

Dining and Lodging

$$ ✕ **Scotch & Sirloin.** Hearty comfort food is served amid red carpets and brass candelabras. Prime rib is the specialty, but you can opt for seafood or poultry. ✉ 5325 Kellogg, 67218, ☎ 316/685–8701. AE, D, MC, V.

$ ✕ **River City Brewery.** This rustic pub lives up to its slogan: "Fresh ales, flavorful food, and fair prices." Venison is a regular favorite. ✉ 150 N. Mosely, ☎ 316/263–2739. AE, D, MC, V.

$$-$$$ ☒ **Hyatt Regency.** Located on the east bank of the Arkansas River, the Hyatt is connected to the Century II Convention Center. ☒ *400 W. Waterman St., 67202,* ☎ *316/293–1923 or 800/233–1234,* FAX *316/293–1200. 303 rooms. Restaurant, pool, health club. AE, D, DC, MC, V. CP.* ☜

$–$$ ☒ **Hotel at Old Town.** In the center of the city's renovated historic district, the hotel has an atmosphere of the early 20th century with modern amenities. ☒ *830 E. 1st St., 67202,* ☎ *316/267–4800 or 877/256–3869,* FAX *316/267–4840. 115 rooms. Bar. AE, D, DC, MC, V.* ☜

Nightlife
Old Town Wichita (☎ 316/262–3555), located between 1st and 3rd in downtown Wichita, is an entertainment district of 60 restored buildings with raised boardwalks and antique lighting, and a wide array of dance clubs, restaurants, and cigar bars.

Fort Scott

Visitor Information
The **Fort Scott Visitor Center** (☒ 231 E. Wall St., ☎ 800/245–3678) runs an hourly trolley tour (from April through December only) of town highlights.

Arriving and Departing
Fort Scott is an easy 100-mi drive south of Kansas City on Route 69. Designated a National Military Highway, the route is sparsely populated but dotted with several historical markers describing the Indian and Civil War battles that took place around here.

What to See and Do
Some historians argue that the violence and bloodshed that plagued this part of the Kansas-Missouri border in the years leading up to the Civil War had a greater impact on the start of the war than the shots
★ fired at Fort Sumter. Today, nine of the original buildings at the **Fort Scott National Historic Site** (☒ Box 918, Old Fort Blvd., ☎ 316/223–0310, ☒ $2, free Dec.–Feb.) are fully restored, and frequent reenactments demonstrate life in this frontier post. Summer and fall bring numerous festivals and activities.

Dining and Lodging
$ ✕ **Papa Don's.** Feast on excellent pizza and pasta, and then finish up with ice cream and cookies at this charming stop on historic Main Street. ☒ *22 N. Main,* ☎ *316/223–4171. D, MC, V.*

$$ ☒ **The Lyons Victorian Mansion.** One of two identical homes built side-by-side in the 1860s for daughters of a wealthy banker, this three-story Victorian home is completely restored in rich velvets, tapestries, and detailed walnut carvings. ☒ *742 S. National, 66701,* ☎ *316/223–3644 or 800/784–8378. 5 rooms. AE, MC, V.* ☜

KENTUCKY

Updated by
Susan Reigler

Capital	Frankfort
Population	3,908,000
Motto	United We Stand, Divided We Fall
State Bird	Cardinal
State Flower	Goldenrod
Postal Abbreviation	KY

Statewide Visitor Information

Kentucky Department of Travel Development (⊠ 2200 Capital Plaza Tower, Frankfort 40601, ☎ 502/564–4930 or 800/225–8747). **Welcome centers:** I–75S at Florence, I–65N at Franklin, I–64W at Grayson, I–24E at Paducah, I–75N at Williamsburg, and U.S. 68 at Maysville.

Scenic Drives

The loop around rugged **Red River Gorge** in the eastern Kentucky mountains starts near Natural Bridge State Park, on **Route 77** near Slade. **Forest Development Road 918** is a 9-mi National Scenic Byway in the Daniel Boone National Forest, near Morehead. In the fall, the oak hickory maples along the 35-mi stretch of **Little Shepherd Trail** (U.S. 119), between Harlan and Whitesburg, have brilliant foliage. **Old Frankfort Pike** between Lexington and Frankfort passes through classic bluegrass countryside.

National and State Parks

National Parks

Daniel Boone National Forest (⊠ U.S. 27, Whitley City; mailing address: ⊠ 100 Vaught Rd., Winchester 40391, ☎ 606/745–3100) has spectacular mountain scenery, especially in the Red River Gorge Geological Area, known for its natural arches, native plants, and 300-ft cliffs. **Land Between the Lakes** (⊠ 100 Van Morgan Dr., Golden Pond 42211, ☎ 502/924–2000), a demonstration project in environmental education and resource management, occupies an uninhabited 40-mi-long peninsula between Kentucky and Barkley lakes. **Mammoth Cave National Park** (⊠ entrances on Rte. 70, 10 mi west of Cave City, and on Rte. 255, 8 mi northwest of Park City, Mammoth Cave 42259, ☎ 502/758–2328) is a 350-mi-long system of twisting underground passages full of colorful mineral formations.

State Parks

Kentucky's 50 state parks are ideal for hiking or simply enjoying the countryside; most also have facilities for picnicking, camping, water sports, and horseback riding. Sixteen resort parks have rustic but comfortable lodges and/or cottages; 16 have tent and trailer sites, available April–October; 14 have year-round campgrounds. For information contact **Kentucky Department of Parks** (⊠ Capital Plaza Tower, Frankfort 40601, ☎ 502/564–2172 or 800/255–7275).

LOUISVILLE

Louisville (locally pronounced *loo*-uh-vul) was founded in 1778 by Revolutionary War hero General George Rogers Clark and named for King Louis XVI as gratitude for France's help during the war. The city's charter was signed in 1780 by Thomas Jefferson, then the governor of Virginia, of which Kentucky was the westernmost district. Louisville's location—on a bend of the mighty Ohio River and smack in the center of the eastern half of the nation—has molded its culture and history. During the first half of the 19th century the city was a bustling river port. Then, with the invention of the train, it became a railroad hub. Waves of European immigrants settled into colorful neighborhoods that still retain their character. Today, the city is an international air hub for United Parcel Service. Every May crowds of visitors come to Louisville for the nation's premier horse race: the Kentucky Derby.

Visitor Information

Greater Louisville, Inc. (⊠ 600 W. Main St., 40202, ☎ 502/625–0060). **Convention & Visitors Bureau** (⊠ 400 S. 1st St., 40202, ☎ 502/584–2121 or 800/792–5595).

Arriving and Departing

By Bus
Greyhound (⊠ 720 W. Muhammad Ali Blvd., ☎ 800/231–2222).

By Car
Interstates run all over Louisville: I–64 runs east–west, I–71 northeast, and I–65 north–south. I–264, also known as the Henry Watterson Expressway, rings the city, as does the outermost ring road, the Gene Snyder Freeway (I–265). These interstates converge downtown in a ramp-ridden tangle known as Spaghetti Junction, where confusion can result in a quick trip to Indiana.

By Plane
Louisville International Airport (⊠ 600 Terminal Dr., ☎ 502/367–4636) is 15 minutes south of downtown on I–65. It has a comfortable, modern terminal and is served by most major carriers. Cab fare from the airport to downtown Louisville runs about $20.

Getting Around Louisville

The downtown area is defined north–south by Broadway and the Ohio River, east–west by Preston and 18th streets. The **Transit Authority of River City** (⊠ 1000 W. Broadway, ☎ 502/585–1234) operates local buses ($1 at peak times, 75¢ other times), as well as a free trolley along 4th Avenue between Broadway and the river. For explorations beyond downtown, a car is a must.

Exploring Louisville

Downtown
Historic sites abound in the heart of Louisville. **West Main Street** has more examples of 19th-century cast-iron architecture than anyplace else in the country except New York City's SoHo. The facade of the **Hart Block** (⊠ 728 W. Main St.), a five-story building designed in 1884 at the height of Louisville's Victorian era, is a jigsaw puzzle of cast-iron pieces bolted together. The tiny **St. Charles Hotel** (⊠ 634 W. Main St.) was constructed before 1832. The Roman Catholic **Cathedral of the Assumption** (⊠ 443 S. 5th St.), a Gothic Revival structure built between 1849 and 1852, was restored between 1985 and 1994. The **Jefferson County Courthouse** (⊠ 531 W. Jefferson St.), a Greek Revival landmark designed by Gideon Shyrock, was built in 1835 with the intent of luring the state government to Louisville.

The 35-story **Aegon Center** (⊠ 400 W. Market St.) dominates Louisville's skyline and holds court as the tallest building in Kentucky. A dramatic geodesic dome tops the 1992 art deco–style structure, designed by New York architect John Burgee. Another contemporary work, the grand

Central Kentucky

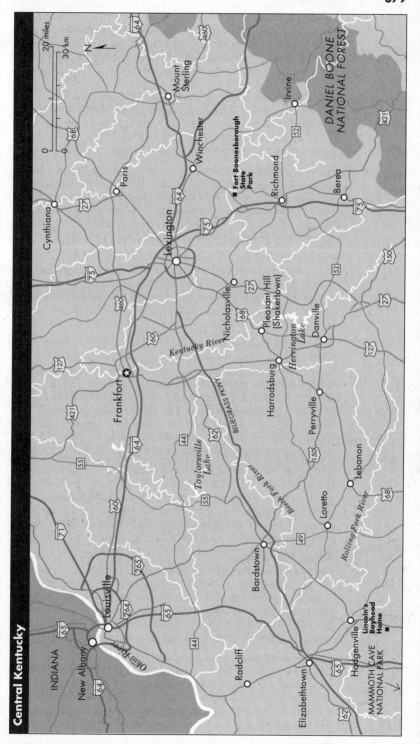

20 miles
30 km

N

DANIEL BOONE NATIONAL FOREST

64
460
Mount Sterling
Irvine
121
66
Winchester
52
Fort Boonesborough State Park
Paris
27
Richmond
Berea
Cynthiana
75
75
150
Lexington
64
75
460
52
Nicholasville
27
Pleasant Hill (Shakertown)
Danville
27
60
68
Herrington Lake
122
Kentucky River
Harrodsburg
127
Frankfort
BLUEGRASS PKWY
62
Perryville
150
421
44
Taylorsville Lake
55
64
55
Beech Fork River
Loretto
Lebanon
68
60
Rolling Fork River
49
71
265
Bardstown
264
Louisville
65
INDIANA
New Albany
64
Ohio River
65
44
Radcliff
Hodgenville
Lincoln's Boyhood Home
62
Elizabethtown
65
MAMMOTH CAVE NATIONAL PARK
62

Humana Building (⊠ 500 W. Main St.) of 1985, is the eclectic creation of architect Michael Graves. The **American Life and Accident Building** (⊠ 3 Riverfront Plaza), designed by Mies van der Rohe and completed in 1973, is called the Rusty Building, after its oxidized Cor-Ten steel covering. The **Kentucky Center for the Arts** (☞ Nightlife and the Arts, *below*), on Riverfront Plaza, has a distinguished collection of 20th-century sculpture by artists such as Louise Nevelson, Alexander Calder, and Jean Dubuffet. The **Louisville Science Center/IMAX Theatre** (⊠ 727 W. Main St., ☎ 502/561–6103; ⊡ $7.50), a 19th-century warehouse full of science arcades and demonstrations, has an Egyptian mummy's tomb, a Foucault pendulum, and lots of hands-on exhibits.

★ ☟ Look for the giant baseball bat in front of the **Louisville Slugger Museum** (⊠ 800 W. Main St., ☎ 502/588–7228, ⊡ $5), and the giant baseball seemingly lodged in a pane of the plate glass factory next door. Try interactive exhibits such as a "virtual pitch," in which a computerized baseball comes hurtling at you at 90 mph. A tour of the adjoining Hillerich & Bradsby factory, where the famous baseball bats are made, is included.

Ten blocks east of the bat museum is Louisville's newest sports venue, a place where the home runs are real, not virtual. **Louisville Slugger Field** is a 12,000-seat jewel box of a baseball stadium that incorporates architectural elements from a 19th-century redbrick warehouse. Opened in spring of 2000, it's home to the Louisville RiverBats, the AAA affiliate team to the Cincinnati Reds. ⊠ *401 E. Main St.,* ☎ *502/367–9121.* ⊡ *$7.*

Scenic 6.9-mi **RiverWalk** stretches from downtown's 4th Street Wharf westward to Chickasaw Park. The path parallels the Ohio shore and has a variety of views, from the locks and dam on the shipping channel to quiet, wooded portions where the occasional deer roams. Parking is available at 4th Street, 8th Street, 10th Street, 31st Street, and at Lannan, Shawnee, and Chickasaw Parks. One-quarter mile east of RiverWalk,
☟ **Linear Park** has a playground with attractions for all age groups. Between the playground and the wharf is the **Great Lawn,** an outdoor concert and recreation area where visitors can stroll to the river's edge.

At the river, check out the *Belle of Louisville* (☎ 502/574–2355; ⊡ $9). It's usually moored at City Wharf at 4th and River streets. The gingerbread-trim steamboat, built in 1914, is the oldest Mississippi-style stern-wheeler still afloat. If you grow tired, you can hire a horse-drawn carriage from **River City Horse Carriage** (☎ 502/895–7268) or **Louisville Horse Trams** (☎ 502/581–0100).

Other Attractions

Butchertown was settled in the 1830s, mostly by Germans who worked in meatpacking plants and lived in "shotgun" and "camelback" houses under the shadow of the abandoned **Bourbon Stock Yards.** In 1814 French immigrants settled in **Portland,** where goods came ashore to be portaged past the falls of the Ohio River. Today barges carry 5 million tons of cargo per month through the **McAlpine Locks and Dam** (⊠ 27th St.).

The **Cherokee Triangle,** a classic Victorian village of grand homes on broad tree-lined streets, was built between 1870 and 1910. A few miles out Bardstown Road from the triangle is **Farmington** (⊠ 3033 Bardstown Rd., ☎ 502/452–9920; ⊡ $4), a Federal-style mansion built in 1810 from a design by Thomas Jefferson. The president's special touches include two octagonal rooms and an adventurously steep hidden staircase.

★ **Old Louisville** is the most elegant of Louisville's neighborhoods. Its architectural styles include Victorian Gothic, Richardsonian Romanesque, Queen Anne, Italianate, Châteauesque, and Beaux Arts. Look for lead- and stained-glass windows, turrets, and gargoyles as you explore. The

Conrad-Caldwell House (⊠ 1402 St. James Ct., ☎ 502/636–5023; ▦ $4), a Victorian Romanesque Revival building, has an intricately carved stone exterior and elaborate interior woodwork. It's open for tours Saturday 10–4 and Sunday and Wednesday noon–4. On the southern edge of Old Louisville is the **University of Louisville** campus.

★ Its **J. B. Speed Art Museum** innovatively displays masterworks by artists such as Rembrandt, Rubens, Picasso, and Caravaggio and has frequent contemporary exhibits. ⊠ 2035 S. 3rd St., ☎ 502/636–2893. ▦ *Free. Closed Mon.*

South of the university is **Churchill Downs,** the world-famous home of the Kentucky Derby. Since the track's opening in 1875, scores of heroic three-year-old Thoroughbreds have thundered past its famous twin spires into legend. During the regular racing season don't miss **"Dawn at the Downs"** (☎ 502/636–3351; ▦ $10.95), when the track opens shortly after daybreak on Saturday, allowing visitors to watch the horses exercise and see the infield grass and flower beds peaceful and still covered in dew. The **Kentucky Derby Museum** (☎ 502/637–1111; ▦ $6) documents the careers of champions. During the annual Kentucky Derby Festival—the two weeks leading up to and including Derby Day (the first Saturday in May)—be prepared to pay more for everything in Louisville, from lodging to transportation. ⊠ 700 Central Ave., ☎ 502/636–4400. Closed Dec.–Mar. and July–Sept.

East of downtown is peaceful **Locust Grove** (⊠ 561 Blankenbaker La., ☎ 502/897–9845; ▦ $4), the former home of Louisville's founder. Three presidents—James Monroe, Andrew Jackson, and Zachary Taylor—have slept here.

☾ **Six Flags Kentucky Kingdom,** near Louisville International Airport, has rides and games, including three roller coasters, a water park, and a playground for young children. ⊠ 937 Phillips La., ☎ 502/366–2231. ▦ $25; $14.80 children under 54"; free children 3 or younger. Closed Nov.–Mar.

Outside Louisville

Bernheim Forest (⊠ Rte. 245 just off I–65, Clermont, ☎ 502/543–2451) is about 25 mi south of the city, in bourbon country. The 14,000-acre preserve has 1,800 species of plants, a nature center, a museum, picnic areas, hiking trails, and lakes; in spring it gives the state's best show of rhododendrons and azaleas. The forest is free on weekdays; weekends and holidays it's $5 per vehicle. In Clermont, a half mile southeast of Bernheim Forest on scenic Route 245, is the **Jim Beam American Outpost Museum** (☎ 502/543–9877; ▦ free), which has a collection of the famous Jim Beam bourbon decanters and a film about making bourbon.

Farther southeast on Route 245 is **Bardstown,** a historic city in a rural setting, best known as the site of **My Old Kentucky Home State Park** (⊠ 501 E. Stephen Foster Ave., ☎ 502/348–3502). It's closed January–February. Stephen Foster visited **Federal Hill** (▦ $4), the Georgian Colonial mansion that is the park's centerpiece, in 1852 shortly before he wrote the state song, "My Old Kentucky Home," sung at every Kentucky Derby.

Southeast of Bardstown, in Loretto, is **Maker's Mark Distillery** (⊠ 3350 Burks Spring Rd., ☎ 502/865–2881; ▦ free), a National Historic Landmark and a working distillery. Southwest of Bardstown is the **Abraham Lincoln Birthplace National Historic Site** (⊠ 3 mi south of Hodgenville on U.S. 31E/Rte. 61, ☎ 502/358–3137; ▦ free), where Lincoln was born February 12, 1809. The 116-acre park includes about 110 acres of the original Thomas Lincoln farm.

Parks, Gardens, and Zoos

In 1891 Louisville's Board of Parks hired Frederick Law Olmsted, designer of New York's Central Park, to design a system of public lands that would be "free to all forever." Among his creations were **Shawnee Park** in the west, a plain of river bottomland; **Cherokee Park** in the east, where Beargrass Creek wanders among woods and meadows; and **Iroquois Park** in the south, a tall, rugged escarpment offering views of the city. Another Olmsted jewel, little **Tyler Park,** on Baxter Avenue, is a spot of solitude in the city bustle. The **Louisville Zoo** (⊠ 1100 Trevilian Way, ☎ 502/459–2181; ☞ $7.95) has more than 1,600 animals in naturalistic environments.

Dining

The two major Restaurant Rows are east of downtown on Bardstown Road and on Frankfort Avenue. Many of Louisville's finer restaurants put a new twist on regional products such as country ham, grits, and bourbon.

$$$$ ✕ **English Grill.** An oak-paneled dining room evokes a 19th-century Lon-
★ don gentlemen's club. The menu, a blend of Continental and Kentucky specialties, changes with the seasons; typical choices are pork tenderloin marinated with apple butter, grenadine of beef tenderloin with oxtail vol-au-vent, and a bourbon dessert soufflé. ⊠ *335 W. Broadway, in the Camberly Brown Hotel,* ☎ *502/583–1234. AE, D, DC, MC, V.*

$$$$ ✕ **The Oakroom.** Specialties include bluegrass free-range chicken with coun-
★ try ham-pesto stuffing, Kentucky beef Wellington, and a bananas Foster with bourbon instead of rum. The formal dining room radiates southern hospitality, and the wine list is one of the best in the Ohio Valley. ⊠ *500 S. 4th St., in the Seelbach Hotel,* ☎ *502/585–3200. AE, D, DC, MC, V.*

$$$ ✕ **Cafe Metro.** Come for the Art Deco and the creative Continental cuisine. All entrées have a set price; they include quail stuffed with veal, currants, and pine nuts, and seafood in puff pastry. Decadent desserts are de rigueur. ⊠ *1700 Bardstown Rd.,* ☎ *502/458–4830. AE, DC, MC, V. Closed Sun.*

$$$ ✕ **Lilly's.** Innovative "haute Kentucky" fare centers on farm-fresh pro-
★ duce and meats. Dishes such as sweetbreads and morels cooked with country ham, and slow-roasted rabbit with lamb sausage fill her seasonal menu. The stylish dining room is green, black, and purple. ⊠ *1147 Bardstown Rd.,* ☎ *502/451–0447. AE, MC, V. Closed Sun.*

$$$ ✕ **Pat's Steak House.** Traditional southern cooking and scents of bourbon and tobacco fill this cozy, old-fashioned restaurant and bar. Waiters wear white coats and call most customers by name as they serve plates of marvelous fried chicken livers, country ham, fried chicken, and tender aged steaks. ⊠ *2437 Brownsboro Rd.,* ☎ *502/893–2062. No credit cards. Closed Sun.*

$$$ ✕ **Vincenzo's.** Deep leather chairs, 17th-century paintings, and crisp tablecloths are the setting for impeccable service and Italian meals such as *vitello alla Sinatra* (spinach-stuffed veal scallopini with wine sauce). The award-winning wine list has many Italian and California vintages. ⊠ *Humana Bldg., 150 S. 5th St.,* ☎ *502/580–1350. AE, D, DC, MC, V. Closed Sun.*

$$ ✕ **Asiatique.** Euro-Asian preparations and modern art prevail in this casual suburban eatery. Try the smoked salmon quesadilla with Asianstyle salsa, roasted quail on a noodle pancake, or lemongrass beef medallions. Dessert specialties include ginger ice cream. ⊠ *106 Sears Ave.,* ☎ *502/899–3578. AE, DC, MC, V.*

$$ ✕ **Bobby J's Club Cafe.** Cigar smokers crowd the balcony of this Art Deco bistro hoping for a good view of the Flying Martinis, the in-house jazz band. Mussels steamed in white wine, roasted chicken, and spicy

pasta dishes are favorites from the predominately Italian menu. ⊠ *1314 Bardstown Rd.,* ☎ *502/452–2665. AE, D, DC, MC, V. Closed Mon.*

$$ ✕ **Lynn's Paradise Cafe.** There's a giant red coffeepot and cup-and-saucer
★ fountain out front; inside, portions are enormous. Best bets are the breakfast burrito and Dagwood-size sandwiches. Dinner (Tuesday through Saturday only) features a famous meat loaf and a bourbon-teriyaki salmon. ⊠ *984 Barret Ave.,* ☎ *502/583–3447. MC, V. Closed Mon.*

$$ ✕ **Uptown Café.** A remarkable Caesar salad, shrimp bisque, and such
★ entrées as duck ravioli and salmon croquettes make this a local favorite for fine food at moderate prices. Like its sister bistro, the upscale Cafe Metro, the Uptown specializes in imaginative combinations. Ask for a booth in the cozy back room. ⊠ *1624 Bardstown Rd.,* ☎ *502/458–4212. AE, DC, MC, V. Closed Sun.*

$$ ✕ **Zephyr Cove.** From vegetarian entrées to game, there's something for everyone at this California-style bistro. Dishes include rabbit loin, Portobello duck breast, and vegetable moussaka. The outstanding wine list was chosen to match the fare. ⊠ *2330 Frankfort Ave.,* ☎ *502/893–0106. AE, MC, V.*

$ ✕ **Baxter Station Bar and Grill.** Just east of downtown, this former neighborhood bar serves pub grub like crab cakes, calamari, burgers, and fried-fish sandwiches with flair. Grilled entrées include Asian, Cajun, French, and Latin American dishes. The bar has an excellent selection of imported and microbrewed beers on tap. In good weather, sit outside. ⊠ *1201 Payne St.,* ☎ *502/584–1635. AE, MC, V. Closed Sun.*

$ ✕ **Check's Cafe.** The food at this Germantown eatery—like the atmosphere and service—is down-home. Bratwurst sandwiches, chili, and fish are some favorites. ⊠ *1101 E. Burnett Ave.,* ☎ *502/637–9515. No credit cards.*

$ ✕ **Come Back Inn.** This neighborhood hangout serves South Side Chicago Italian cuisine. Beef sandwiches, pastas with homemade marinara, and traditional pizzas are highlights. ⊠ *909 Swan St.,* ☎ *502/627–1777. AE, MC, V. No dinner Mon.*

$ ✕ **El Mundo.** This hole-in-the-wall Mexican cantina serves up some of the city's most authentic south-of-the-border fare. The self-serve hot sauces compliment the great food like chile rellenos (stuffed green peppers) and enchiladas. ⊠ *2345 Frankfort Ave.,* ☎ *502/899–9930. No credit cards. Closed Sun.*

$ ✕ **Mazzoni's Oyster Cafe.** Here's the place to try rich oyster stew, real panfried oysters, and a Louisville invention—deep-fried oysters rolled in cornmeal batter. ⊠ *2804 Taylorsville Rd.,* ☎ *502/451–4436. No credit cards. Closed Sun.*

Lodging

Like any other port city, Louisville has a long tradition of hospitality. Choose either a lovingly restored, pricey downtown hotel or a budget room in a place that feels like home. Bed-and-breakfast accommodations can be found through **Kentucky Homes B&B** (⊠ 1219 S. 4th Ave., Louisville 40203, ☎ 502/635–7341).

$$$–$$$$ ⬚ **Hyatt Regency Louisville.** Hyatt's familiar plant-filled atrium and glass-and-brass lobby are the focus of this 18-story hotel. The rooms have a back-to-nature theme, with redwood and pastels. ⊠ *320 W. Jefferson St., 40202,* ☎ *502/587–3434,* 𝖥𝖠𝖷 *502/581–0133. 388 rooms. 2 restaurants, pool, tennis, exercise room. AE, D, DC, MC, V.* ✺

$$$–$$$$ ⬚ **The Seelbach Hilton.** The refurbished guest rooms in this 11-story
★ landmark have four-poster beds, armoires, and marble baths with gold fixtures. ⊠ *500 4th Ave., 40202,* ☎ *502/585–3200 or 800/333–3399,* 𝖥𝖠𝖷 *502/585–9239. 322 rooms. Restaurant. AE, D, DC, MC, V.* ✺

$$–$$$$ ⬚ **Camberly Brown Hotel.** This 16-story historic hotel, built in 1923, has been fully restored with Old English–style furnishings. The artwork, atmosphere, and service are impeccable. The English Grill (☞ *Dining, above*) is one of the city's finest restaurants. ⊠ *335 W. Broadway, 40202,* ☎ *502/583–1234 or 800/866–7666,* FAX *502/587–7006. 294 rooms. Restaurant, exercise room. AE, D, DC, MC, V.* ✍

$$–$$$ 🏨 **Galt House East.** Overlooking the river, this downtown hotel has an elaborately landscaped, modern 18-story atrium, but the room furnishings emphasize old-fashioned comfort. ⊠ *141 N. 4th Ave., 40202,* ☎ *502/589–3300 or 800/843–4258,* FAX *502/585–4266. 600 rooms. Restaurant, pool. AE, D, DC, MC, V.* ✍

$$–$$$ 🏨 **Old Louisville Inn Bed & Breakfast.** The guest rooms in this 1901 brick house have elaborately carved mahogany woodwork and antiques. The atmosphere and service make it feel just like old times. ⊠ *1359 S. 3rd St., 40208,* ☎ *502/635–1574,* FAX *502/637–5892. 10 rooms. AE, D, MC, V. BP.* ✍

$–$$$ 🏨 **Breckinridge Inn.** This is a clean, plain, and comfortable two-story motor hotel where most rooms have art deco designs. ⊠ *2800 Breckinridge La., at I–264, 40220,* ☎ *502/456–5050,* FAX *502/451–1577. 123 rooms. Restaurant, pool, tennis. AE, D, DC, MC, V.*

$$ 🏨 **Executive Inn.** An English Tudor style characterizes every part of this six-story hotel near the airport. Some rooms have private patios or balconies. ⊠ *978 Phillips La., off I–64, 40209,* ☎ *800/626–2706; 800/222–8284 in KY;* FAX *502/363–1880. 465 rooms. Restaurant, 2 pools, exercise room. AE, D, DC, MC, V.* ✍

$ 🏨 **Red Roof Inn East.** Basic, inexpensive accommodations are available in this motor inn about 20 minutes east of downtown via I–64 at Hurstbourne Parkway. Rooms are clean and spare. Pets are allowed. ⊠ *9330 Blairwood Rd., 40222,* ☎ *502/426–7621,* FAX *502/426–7933. 108 rooms. AE, D, DC, MC, V.* ✍

$ 🏨 **Travelodge.** A cinder-block exterior disguises this centrally located, inexpensive motel. Rooms are spacious and clean. ⊠ *401 S. 2nd St., 40202,* ☎ *502/583–2841 or 800/255–3050,* FAX *502/583–2629. 98 rooms. Restaurant. AE, D, DC, MC, V.* ✍

Nightlife and the Arts

For arts and entertainment events, look for *Louisville* magazine on newsstands, and the Friday and Saturday editions of the *Courier-Journal* newspaper. Daily arts updates can be found on the *Courier-Journal*'s entertainment Web page (www.louisvillescene.com).

Nightlife

The **Comedy Caravan Nightclub** (⊠ 1250 Bardstown Rd., in the Mid-City Mall, ☎ 502/459–0022) and the **Legends Comedy Club** (⊠ 9700 Bluegrass Pkwy., in the Hurstbourne Hotel & Conference Center, ☎ 502/459–0022) have stand-up circuit comics. The **Connection** (⊠ 130 S. Floyd St., ☎ 502/585–5752), a giant entertainment complex, has a restaurant and the biggest dance floor in town. There are talent shows in the bar on Thursday nights, and a female impersonator does revues on the weekends in the theater. **Country Palace Jamboree** (⊠ 421 N. Main St., Mount Washington, about 20 minutes south of Louisville, ☎ 502/955–8452) is a good place for families to go for country music and dancing. **Coyote's** (⊠ 116 W. Jefferson St., ☎ 502/589–3866) has live country music, a raucous but friendly clientele, and free two-step and line dancing instruction. **Rick's Square Piano** (⊠ 20 Theatre Sq., at 4th St. and Broadway, ☎ 502/583–6090) has a bustling cocktail scene with live piano jazz by owner Rick Bartlett.

The Arts

Actors Theatre of Louisville (⊠ 316 W. Main St., ☎ 502/585–1210) is a Tony Award–winning repertory theater in a bank building (circa 1837) designated a National Historic Landmark. Each February, the Actors Theatre sponsors the **Humana Festival of New American Plays,** which has premiered several plays that have gone on to New York and London. The **Broadway Series** (⊠ 611 W. Main St., ☎ 502/584–7469) hosts touring productions of Broadway's best. **Shakespeare in the Park** (⊠ Central Park at S. 4th St., ☎ 502/634–8237) transforms Louisville into the Bard's town on summer weekends. **Stage One: The Louisville Children's Theatre** (⊠ 425 W. Market St., ☎ 502/584–7777 or 800/283–7777) offers professional productions on weekends from October to May.

The three stages at the **Kentucky Center for the Arts** (⊠ 5 Riverfront Plaza, ☎ 502/562–0100 or 800/283–7777) are alive with entertainment, from Broadway to Bach and bagpipes to bluegrass. The **Louisville Orchestra** (⊠ 609 W. Main St., ☎ 502/584–7777 or 800/283–7777) has received international attention for its recordings of contemporary works. The **Louisville Ballet** and **Kentucky Opera** (☎ 502/584–7777 or 800/283–7777) also perform at the arts center.

Spectator Sports

Baseball: The Louisville RiverBats, a farm team of the Cincinnati Reds, play in the new **Louisville Slugger Stadium** near the riverfront (⊠ 402 E. Main St., ☎ 502/361–3100 for ticket information), which opened in spring 2000.

Horse racing: The Kentucky Derby at **Churchill Downs** (☞ Exploring Louisville, *above*) is a *very* tough ticket—unless you're willing to join tens of thousands of seatless young revelers in the infield, where you're unlikely to get even a glimpse of a horse. Races occur from late April to mid-July and October to November.

Shopping

Shopping Districts

The **Galleria** (⊠ 4th Ave. between Liberty St. and Muhammad Ali Blvd., ☎ 502/584–7170), a glass-enclosed mall with 80 stores and 11 fast-food restaurants, is a city melting pot and the best place to shop downtown. **Bardstown Road,** southeast of downtown, is a 2-mi strip of antiques shops, bookstores, and boutiques. The **Jefferson Mall** (☎ 502/968–4101), 10 mi south of downtown on Outer Loop, is a huge enclosed mall with more than 100 stores. The **Mall St. Matthews** (☎ 502/893–0311) and **Oxmoor Center** (☎ 502/426–3000) are both located at the intersection of the Watterson Expressway with Shelbyville Road. Together they house more than 300 stores, including outlets of such retailers as Brooks Brothers, the Nature Company, and Eddie Bauer.

Department Stores

Louisville has several department stores; most are in the suburban shopping malls: **Jacobson's** (⊠ Oxmoor Center, ☎ 502/327–0200); **Lazarus** (⊠ Jefferson Mall, ☎ 502/966–1800; ⊠ Oxmoor Center, ☎ 502/423–3000); and **Lord & Taylor** (⊠ The Mall St. Matthews, ☎ 502/895–8887; Jefferson Mall, ☎ 502/968–6080). **Bigg's** "hypermarket" (⊠ 12975 Shelbyville Rd., Middletown, ☎ 502/244–4760) has everything from pastries to chain saws at bargain prices.

Specialty Stores

The **Kentucky Art & Craft Gallery** (⊠ 609 W. Main St., ☎ 502/589–0102) sells top-quality crafts. **Baer Fabrics** (⊠ 515 E. Market St., ☎ 502/583–5521) has been building its world-renowned collection of buttons since 1905. **Joe Ley Antiques** (⊠ 615 E. Market St., ☎ 502/583–4014) has an outstanding 2-acre litter of hardware, fixtures, and doodads.

LEXINGTON AND THE BLUEGRASS

Lexington, the world capital of racehorse breeding and burley tobacco (a thin-bodied, air-cured variety), was named by patriotic hunters who camped here in 1775 shortly after hearing news of the first battle of the Revolutionary War at Lexington, Massachusetts. A log structure built by a member of that historic hunting party is preserved on the campus of Transylvania University. The Bluegrass is a lush region of rolling hills, meandering streams, and manicured horse farms.

Visitor Information

Frankfort/Franklin County: Tourist and Convention Commission (⊠ 100 Capital Ave., Frankfort 40601, ☎ 502/875–8687 or 800/960–7200). **Lexington:** Greater Lexington Convention & Visitors Bureau (⊠ Suite 363, 430 W. Vine St., 40507, ☎ 606/233–1221 or 800/845–3959). **Richmond:** Tourism Commission (⊠ Box 250, City Hall, 40476, ☎ 606/623–1000).

Arriving and Departing

By Car

The Lexington area and the Bluegrass are well served by I–64 east–west, I–75 north–south, and the state parkway system, a toll network that bisects the state east–west.

By Plane

Lexington Bluegrass Airport (⊠ 4000 Versailles Rd., ☎ 606/254–9336), 4 mi west of downtown Lexington, is served by Delta, US Airways, and regional lines.

Exploring Lexington and the Bluegrass

Lexington

Lexington Livery Company (☎ 606/259–0000) gives horse-drawn carriage rides ($25 for a 30-minute tour). In the **Gratz Park Historic District,** near 2nd Street and Broadway, are two fine houses from 1814: the lavish, privately owned **Gratz House** (⊠ 231 N. Mill St., ☎ no phone), built by a rich hemp manufacturer, and the **John Hunt Morgan House** (⊠ 201 N. Mill St., ☎ 606/233–3290; ☜ $4), which passed from the swashbuckling Confederate general to his great-grandson, Thomas Hunt Morgan, who won a Nobel Prize in 1933 for proving the existence of the gene. The Morgan house is closed December 15–February and Mondays the rest of year. A statue of General Morgan stands on the lawn of the **Fayette County Courthouse** (⊠ 215 W. Main St.). When it was unveiled in 1911, its portrayal of the Rebel raider astride a stallion caused quite a stir as his best-known mount was a mare, Black Bess.

The Greek Revival campus of **Transylvania University** (⊠ 300 N. Broadway, ☎ 606/233–8120), the first college west of the Alleghenies (established in 1780), has left its mark on two U.S. vice presidents, 50 senators, 34 ambassadors, and 36 Kentucky governors. The 1832 **Mary Todd Lincoln House** (⊠ 578 W. Main St., ☎ 606/233–9999; ☜ $4) belonged to the parents of Abraham Lincoln's wife and displays Lincoln and Todd family memorabilia. The museum is closed Sunday and Monday and December through mid-March. U.S. senator Henry Clay, the Great Compromiser, was a green 20-year-old lawyer when he came to Lexington in 1797 and opened his **law office** (⊠ 176–178 N. Mill St., ☎ no phone).

Two attractions at the **University of Kentucky** (⊠ Euclid Ave. and S. Limestone St., ☎ 606/257–3595) are an **anthropology museum** (⊠ 201 Lafferty Hall, ☎ 606/257–7112; ☜ free), with exhibits on evolution and Kentucky culture, and an **art museum** (⊠ 121 Singletary Center for the Arts, ☎ 606/257–5716; 🖼 free), which has a fine permanent collection and frequent special exhibits; both are closed on Monday.

☺ The interactive exhibits at the **Lexington Children's Museum** (⊠ 401 W. Main St., ☎ 606/258–3256; 🖼 $3) include an archaeology dig. A Lexington curiosity is the huge **castle** (⊠ just west of the city on Versailles Rd.), with eight turrets and 70-ft-tall corner towers. A Fayette County developer began, but never finished, construction in 1969 on what was to be his private residence. The **Headley-Whitney Museum** houses an eclectic, personal three-building collection of Asian porcelains, masks, paintings, shells, and jeweled bibelots. ⊠ *Old Frankfort Pike,* ☎ 606/255–6653. 🖼 *Free. Closed Mon.*

The Bluegrass

Kentucky's **Bluegrass** area has more than 400 horse farms, some with Thoroughbred barns as elegant as French villas. Among the famous breeding farms is **Calumet** (⊠ just west of the city on Versailles Rd./U.S. 60, ☎ no phone), which has produced a record eight Kentucky Derby winners. The antebellum mansion at **Manchester Farm** (⊠ Van Meter Rd., ☎ no phone) is said to have been the inspiration for Tara in *Gone with the Wind.* **Spendthrift** (⊠ Ironworks Pike, ☎ 606/299–5271) is one of the few farms that routinely welcome visitors. Famous horses from the **C. V. Whitney Farm,** on Paris Pike, have included Regret, the first filly to win the Kentucky Derby, and the appropriately named Upset, the only horse ever to finish ahead of the legendary Man o' War. **Normandy** (⊠ Paris Pike, ☎ no phone) has a famous L-shape barn, built in 1927, with a clock tower and animal-shape roof ornaments.

A number of Lexington-based companies conduct tours that take in several farms and the Keeneland Racecourse (☞ Spectator Sports, *below*). They include **Bluegrass Tours** (⊠ Box 1176, 40589, ☎ 606/ 252–5744; 🖼 $20) and **Historic and Horse Farm Tours** (⊠ Box 22593, 40522, ☎ 606/268–2906, 𝙁𝘼𝙓 606/266–8603; 🖼 $23). A showcase for
☺ Thoroughbreds and other horses, **Kentucky Horse Park** has a museum, an art gallery, and campgrounds. It also offers films, a breeds show, and farm tours. ⊠ *4089 Iron Works Pike, off I–75, Lexington,* ☎ *606/233–4303.* 🖼 *$6.50. Closed Mon. and Tues.*

The most historic bourbon distillery in Kentucky is **Labrot & Graham,** surrounded on all sides by horse farms. The whiskey is made in copper-pot stills housed in a limestone building dating from the early 1800s. ⊠ *7855 McCracken Pike off U.S. 60,* ☎ *606/879–1812.* 🖼 *Free. Closed Sun. and Mon.*

Southward on scenic U.S. 25 is **Fort Boonesborough State Park** (☎ 606/ 527–3131 or 800/255–7275; 🖼 $4.50), a reconstruction of one of Daniel Boone's early forts, with a museum and demonstrations of pioneer crafts. In Richmond is the **White Hall State Historic Site** (⊠ 500 White Hall Shrine Rd., ☎ 606/623–9178; 🖼 $4), home of the abolitionist Cassius Marcellus Clay, a cousin of Henry Clay and an ambassador to Russia. The elegant mansion combines two houses and two styles, Georgian and Italianate.

In Berea, where the Bluegrass meets the mountains, charming, tuition-free **Berea College** (☎ 606/986–9341), founded in 1855, has 1,500 students—most from Appalachia—who work for their education. On the campus is the **Appalachian Museum** (⊠ Jackson St., ☎ 606/986– 9341 or 606/986–6078; 🖼 free), which charts regional history through arts and crafts.

★ The **Shaker Village of Pleasant Hill** (⊠ Hwy. 68, ☎ 606/734–5411, 🖼 $9.50), 25 mi southwest of Lexington, has 27 restored buildings of frame, brick, or stone erected between 1805 and 1859 by members of a religious sect noted for industry, architecture, and furniture making. In Harrodsburg, the first permanent settlement in Kentucky, **Old Fort Harrod State Park** (☎ 606/734–3314; ☒ $3.50) has a full-scale reproduction of the old fort, built on its original 1774 site.

About 15 mi south of Lexington the beautiful, deep blue-green **Kentucky River** flows gently but relentlessly through the Bluegrass. The combination of rolling river and rugged rock faces creates dramatic landscapes. Take Jacks Creek Pike from Lexington through one of the most enchanting parts of Kentucky to **Raven Run Nature Sanctuary** (☎ 606/272–6105), a place of rugged, forested hills and untouched wildlife along the Kentucky River.

In lovely Danville, 30 mi southwest of Lexington, the **McDowell House and Apothecary Shop** (☒ 125 S. 2nd St., ☎ 606/236–2804; ☒ free), the residence and shop of Dr. Ephraim McDowell (a noted surgeon of the early 19th century), is refurnished with period pieces. The house is closed November–March. West of Danville on U.S. 150 and north on U.S. 68 is **Perryville Battlefield** (☎ 606/332–8631), the site of Kentucky's most important (and bloodiest) Civil War battle, where 4,241 Union soldiers and 1,822 Confederates were killed or wounded.

Frankfort, between Louisville and Lexington on I–64, was chosen as the state capital in 1792 as a compromise between the cities' rival claims and has been caught in the middle ever since. The **state capitol** (☎ 502/564–3449), overlooking the Kentucky River at the south end of Capitol Avenue, is noted for its Ionic columns, high central dome, and lantern cupola; guided tours are given. Outside the capitol is the famous **Floral Clock**, a working outdoor timepiece whose face—made of thousands of plants—is swept by a 530-pound minute hand and a 420-pound hour hand.

In Frankfort Cemetery, on East Main Street, you can visit **Daniel Boone's grave** (he died in Missouri, but his remains were returned to Kentucky in 1845). The restored Georgian-style **Old Governor's Mansion** (☒ 420 High St., ☎ 502/564–5500; ☒ free), built in 1798, served as the residence of 33 governors until a new mansion was built in 1914. The later **governor's mansion** (☎ 502/564–3449; ☒ free) is styled after the Petit Trianon, Marie Antoinette's villa at Versailles. Both mansions are open for tours Tuesday and Thursday.

Dining and Lodging

Although Lexington offers varied dining options, most restaurants outside the city are down-home. Menus tend toward country-fried steak, country ham, and fried chicken. Many of the best places to dine are out of the way and unimpressive looking—so don't be bashful about asking the locals for guidance.

Restored historic properties, often modestly priced, are short on amenities but long on charm. State park lodges and cottages are bargains, rustic but comfortable. In many rural areas you'll have to settle for barebones accommodations. In Lexington **Dial Accommodations** (☒ 430 W. Vine St., ☎ 606/233–7299) can help with reservations.

Berea

$–$$ ✕🏨 **Boone Tavern.** This grand old Colonial-style hotel (1909) is operated by Berea College and outfitted with furniture handmade by students. The restaurant ($; jacket and tie required for dinner) is famous for its spoon bread, chicken flakes in bird's nest, and Jefferson Davis pie. ☒ *Main and Prospect Sts. (Box 2345), 40403,* ☎ *606/986–9358 or 606/986–9359. 57 rooms. Restaurant. AE, D, DC, MC, V.*

Frankfort

$ ✕ **Smile of Siam.** A few travel posters of Thailand are the only decoration, but the food is elegant and delicious. Coconut milk, lemongrass, lime leaves, peanuts, and cilantro flavor dishes including Thai beef stick, chicken red curry, and *pad Thai* (stir-fried rice noodles). ⊠ *19 Century Plaza,* ☎ *502/227–9934. MC, V. Closed Sun.*

Harrodsburg

$$ ✕▥ **Inn at Pleasant Hill.** Rooms in 27 restored buildings (circa 1800)—some with four stories and no elevators—are furnished with Shaker reproductions and handwoven rugs and curtains. The restaurant, Trustees' House at Pleasant Hill, serves hearty family-style meals and specializes in a tangy Shaker lemon pie for which people have been known to drive a hundred miles; reservations are essential. ⊠ *3500 Lexington Rd., 40330,* ☎ ⅎⱯⱵ *606/734–5411. 80 rooms. Restaurant. MC, V.* ✍

$ ✕▥ **Beaumont Inn.** Guest rooms at this exemplar of southern hospitality are scattered among four timeworn (but polished) buildings furnished with antiques. The restaurant specializes in corn pudding and cured Kentucky country ham. ⊠ *638 Beaumont Dr., 40330,* ☎ *606/734–3381,* ⅎⱯⱵ *606/734–6897. 33 rooms. Restaurant, pool, tennis. AE, D, DC, MC, V. Closed mid-Dec.–mid-Mar. CP.*

Lexington

$$$ ✕ **A la Lucie.** The tin roof, terrazzo floors, hot colors, green plants, and eclectic art give this chef-owned eatery a Parisian Left Bank ambience. French, German, and American dishes appear on the menu, but the specialty is seasonal seafood. ⊠ *150 N. Limestone St.,* ☎ *606/252–5277. AE, DC, MC, V. Closed Sun.*

$$$ ✕ **Roy & Nadine's.** An overstuffed sofa, fringed lamp shades, and Erté prints set the tone in this suburban restaurant famous for its list of 25 "shaken, not stirred" martinis. The food is eclectic and international: pepper-seared carpaccio, a black bean ancho-Caesar salad, cumin-spiced chicken, and grilled rack of lamb. ⊠ *3775 Harrodsburg Rd., in the Palomar Shopping Center,* ☎ *606/223–0797. AE, MC, V.*

$$ ✕ **Alfalfa Restaurant.** The food in this small, woody, old-fashioned
★ restaurant is organically grown vegetarian and ethnic. The menu, written on a chalkboard, may include ham-and-apple quiche; the house salad is lavish. Each Wednesday a different cuisine—Greek, Italian, Indian—is served. ⊠ *557 S. Limestone St.,* ☎ *606/253–0014. MC, V. No dinner Mon.*

$$ ✕ **Atomic Cafe.** The Bluegrass region may not seem like the place for Caribbean cuisine, but the conch fritters taste fresh off the boat. Jerk chicken and pork dishes are fiery. Shrimp lovers should check out the coconut-battered variety served here. Decor is tropical, with evocative murals. ⊠ *265 N. Limestone St.,* ☎ *606/254–1969. MC, V. Closed Sun. and Mon.*

$$ ✕ **Dudley's Restaurant.** Huge tulip trees shade the courtyard of this chic, unpretentious restaurant in a 100-year-old schoolhouse. A favorite on the Continental menu is pasta with chicken, sun-dried tomatoes, and vegetables. ⊠ *380 S. Mill St.,* ☎ *606/252–1010. AE, MC, V.*

$$ ✕ **Merrick Inn.** The spacious, comfortable, not-too-formal restaurant is housed in a sprawling, white-columned building that was once a horse farm (circa 1890). On the extensive menu are steak, lamb, and a variety of pastas, but the specialty is fresh seasonal seafood. ⊠ *3380 Tates Creek Rd.,* ☎ *606/269–5417. AE, DC, MC, V. Closed Sun.*

$$ ✕ **Phil Dunn's Restaurant.** The quilt made from jockey silks hanging on one wall identifies the bluegrass roots of this sophisticated bistro. Remodeled in spring 2000, the white-tablecloth establishment is decorated with mahogany and brushed metal accents. Continental entrées include oven-roasted lamb chops, grilled Long Island duck, and spinach fettuccine with grilled vegetables. ⊠ *431 Old E. Vine St.,* ☎ *606/231–0099. AE, MC, V. No dinner Sun.*

$ ✕ **Joe Bologna's.** This old college hangout occupies a church built in
★ 1890; the original stained-glass windows are still in place. Feast on pasta and pizza. ⊠ *120 W. Maxwell St.,* ☎ *606/252–4933. MC, V.*

$ ✕ **Lexington City Brewery.** This microbrewery and brewpub in a shopping center on the edge of the tobacco warehouse district serves excellent wood-oven pizzas and German sausage platters to go with the topflight beer. Winner's Gold Ale and Smiley Pete's stout are must-sips. ⊠ *1050 S. Broadway,* ☎ *606/259–2739. AE, MC, V.*

$$$–$$$$ ▥ **Camberly Club Hotel at Gratz Park.** The guest rooms in this elegantly refurbished three-story medical building from 1887 are furnished with antiques. Continental breakfast, afternoon tea, and evening cordials are available. ⊠ *120 2nd St., 40507,* ☎ *606/231–1777 or 800/227–4362,* FAX *606/233–7593. 52 rooms. Restaurant. AE, D, DC, MC, V. CP.*

$$–$$$$ ▥ **Marriott's Griffin Gate Resort.** This gleaming, contemporary seven-
★ story resort caters to a youngish crowd that likes physical activities and physical comforts. The rooms have private patios or balconies. ⊠ *1800 Newtown Pike, 40511,* ☎ *606/231–5100,* FAX *606/255–9944. 409 rooms. Restaurant, pool, tennis, health club. AE, D, DC, MC, V.* ☙

$–$$$ ▥ **Campbell House Inn.** The friendly, attentive staff gives guests a warm welcome at this three-story motel. Rooms are modern but homey. ⊠ *1375 Harrodsburg Rd., 40504,* ☎ *606/255–4281 or 800/354–9235; 800/432–9254 in KY;* FAX *606/254–4368. 370 rooms. Restaurant, pool, tennis. AE, D, DC, MC, V.* ☙

$$ ▥ **Courtyard by Marriott.** The trademark of this motel is a sunny, gardenlike central courtyard. The green, brown, and mauve rooms are modern, with light woodwork and oversize desks. ⊠ *775 Newtown Ct., 40511,* ☎ *606/253–4646,* FAX *606/253–9118. 146 rooms. Restaurant, pool, exercise room. AE, D, DC, MC, V.* ☙

Nightlife and the Arts

Nightlife

After-dark events in Lexington are sparse and tame. From Thursday through Sunday check out the **Brewery** (⊠ 509 W. Main St., ☎ 606/255–2822), a friendly Texas-roadhouse-style bar with classic rock and country tunes. Or visit **Comedy Off Broadway** (⊠ 3199 Nicholasville Rd., ☎ 606/271–5653), where stand-up comics make wisecracks.

The Arts

Lexington's performing arts scene is vivacious. For information on performances contact the **Actors' Guild** (☎ 606/233–0663), **Lexington Ballet** (☎ 606/233–3925), **Lexington Philharmonic** (☎ 606/233–4226), and **Opera of Central Kentucky** (☎ 606/231–6994). Concerts, plays, and lectures are also presented at **Transylvania University** and the **University of Kentucky** (☞ Exploring Lexington and the Bluegrass, *above*).

☾ The **Lexington Children's Theatre** (☎ 606/254–4546) offers performances for young audiences.

Outdoor Activities and Sports

Kentucky's lakes and streams provide great fishing for more than 200 species. You're rarely more than a 30-minute drive from a public golf course. The state parks and national forests are full of hiking trails. Eastern Kentucky has several rivers with mild to moderate whitewater rafting opportunities. For information contact the **Department of Parks** (☞ National and State Parks, *above*), tourism offices (☞ Visitor Information, *above*), or the state **Department of Fish and Wildlife Resources** (⊠ 1 Game Farm Rd., Frankfort 40601, ☎ 502/564–4336).

Spectator Sports

College Basketball: Rupp Arena (⊠ 430 W. Vine, ☎ 606/233–4567) is the home of the University of Kentucky Wildcats basketball team. A warning: Home games are often sold out, as hoards of regular fans buy season tickets to cheer the 1996 and 1998 NCAA champions.

Horse racing: Keeneland Race Course (⊠ 4201 Versailles Rd., Lexington, ☎ 606/254–3412 or 800/456–3412) holds races in April and in October.

Shopping

In Lexington **Fayette Mall** (⊠ 3473 Nicholasville Rd., ☎ 606/272–3493) has more than 100 stores and a dozen places to eat. For something out of the ordinary, try **Dudley Square** (⊠ 380 S. Mill St., ☎ no phone), in a restored 1881 school building; its shops sell antiques, prints, quilts, and the like. **Victorian Square** (⊠ 401 W. Main St., ☎ 606/252–7575) is an entire downtown block of renovated Victorian buildings that now have elegant retail and dining establishments. Lexington also has many **antiques shops**; the Convention & Visitors Bureau (☞ Visitor Information, *above*) maintains a list.

LOUISIANA

By Honey
Naylor

Updated by
Baty Landis

Capital	Baton Rouge
Population	4,342,000
Motto	Union, Justice, and Confidence
State Bird	Pelican
State Flower	Magnolia
Postal Abbreviation	LA

Statewide Visitor Information

Louisiana Office of Tourism (⊠ Box 94291, Baton Rouge 70804-9291, ☎ 800/334–8626).

Scenic Drives

Gators laze along the exotic **Creole Nature Trail,** a circular drive out of Lake Charles designated a National Scenic Byway. **Routes 56 and 57** also form a circular drive south of Houma, where shrimp boats dock along the bayous from May to December. **Route 82** runs through the coastal marshes and wildlife refuges along the Gulf of Mexico. The **Longleaf Trail Scenic Byway,** south of Natchitoches, is a 17-mi highway through the Kisatchie National Forest linking Routes 117 and 119. **Route 182** runs alongside Bayou Teche in southern Louisiana. **Route 93,** between Grand Coteau and Lafayette, passes through farmland and small Cajun towns.

National and State Parks

National Parks

The **Jean Lafitte National Historical Park and Preserve** (⊠ 365 Canal St., New Orleans 70130, ☎ 504/589–3882) maintains seven separate parks throughout the state and offers nature trails and canoeing through exotic swampland. The 100,000-acre Kisatchie Ranger District of the **Kisatchie National Forest** (⊠ Rte. 6 W, Box 2128, Natchitoches 71457, ☎ 318/352–2568) has hiking and equestrian trails through hardwood and pine forests.

State Parks

A prehistoric Native American site dating from between 1800 BC and 500 BC, the 400-acre **Poverty Point State Commemorative Area** (⊠ Rte. 577, Box 276, Epps 71237, ☎ 318/926–5492 or 888/926–5492) is one of the country's most important excavations, with hiking trails and an interpretive center in addition to the ancient Native American mounds. The 600-acre **Louisiana State Arboretum** (⊠ Rte. 3042, Ville Platte 70586, ☎ 337/363–6289), lush with trees and plants native to the state, has 2½ mi of nature trails. Fishing, boating, and camping (cabins are available) are all possibilities in the 6,500-acre **Chicot State Park** (⊠ Rte. 3042, Box 494, Ville Platte 70586, ☎ 337/363–2403 or 888/677–2442); **Bayou Segnette,** near New Orleans (⊠ 7777 Westbank Expressway, Westwego 70094, ☎ 504/736–7140 or 888/677–2296); **Lake Bistineau State Park** (⊠ Box 589, Doyline 71023, ☎ 318/745–3503 or 888/677–2478); **Lake Fausse Point State Park** (⊠ 5400 Levee Rd., along Rte. 3083, Box 5648, St. Martinville 70582, ☎ 337/229–4764); and **North Toledo Bend State Park** (⊠ Box 56, Zwolle 71486, ☎ 318/645–4715 or 888/677–6400).

NEW ORLEANS

Tucked beyond miles of marsh and isolated from the surrounding area, New Orleans sometimes seems closer in spirit to the Caribbean than to

Our Town, USA. New Orleanians are often oblivious to national trends and styles, while the European, African, and Caribbean cultures that settled here are intact and even thriving—often, as during Mardi Gras, in exuberant contiguity. Creole cuisine, the continuing legacy of New Orleans jazz, and the unabashed prioritizing of pleasure that define life here are all part of a culture that is by geographical dictate self-contained. Visitors are treated to that oh-so-rare mixture of modernity and true individuality, found in the frank indifference of leisure-seeking locals no less than in the raucous revelry of the touristed French Quarter.

Visitor Information

New Orleans Metropolitan Convention & Visitors Bureau (⊠ 1520 Sugar Bowl Dr., 70112, ☎ 504/566–5011 or 800/672–6124, FAX 504/566–5021). **New Orleans Welcome Center** (⊠ 529 St. Ann St., in the French Quarter, 70116, ☎ 504/568–5661).

Arriving and Departing

By Boat

You can arrive from northern ports in grand 19th-century style aboard one of the authentic overnight steamboats that home-port in New Orleans—the *Delta Queen*, the *Mississippi Queen*, or the *American Queen*—all run by the **Delta Queen Steamboat Company** (⊠ 30 Robin St. Wharf, 70130, ☎ 504/586–0631 or 800/543–1949, FAX 504/585–0630).

By Bus

Greyhound (☎ 800/231–2222) operates out of **Union Passenger Terminal** (⊠ 1001 Loyola Ave., ☎ 504/528–1610).

By Car

I–10 is the major east–west artery through the city; I–55, which runs north–south, connects with I–10 west of town. I–59 heads for the northeast. U.S. 61 and U.S. 90 also run through the city.

By Plane

New Orleans International Airport (also known as Moisant Field; ⊠ 900 Airline Dr., ☎ 504/464–0831), 15 mi west of New Orleans in Kenner, is served by many carriers. Cab fare for the 20- to 30-minute trip to downtown runs $21–$32, depending on the number of passengers. The 24-hour **Airport Shuttle** (☎ 504/522–3500; ⊇ $10 one-way) drops passengers off downtown and at French Quarter hotels, St. Charles Avenue, and major universities. Buses operated by **Louisiana Transit** (☎ 504/737–9611) run between the airport and the Central Business District; the fare is $1.50 (exact change in coins).

By Train

Amtrak (☎ 800/872–7245) serves New Orleans's Union Passenger Terminal (☞ By Bus, *above*).

Getting Around New Orleans

The French Quarter is best savored on leisurely strolls; the Central Business District (CBD) and Warehouse District are also highly walkable.

By Car

French Quarter streets are often clogged with traffic, and street parking is strictly monitored by meter maids and tow trucks. Elsewhere, traffic is light, though a lack of urgency on the part of local drivers can slow things up.

By Ferry

A ferry, the *Crescent City Connection* (☎ 504/364–8100), crosses the Mississippi from the Canal Street Wharf to Algiers. It's free outgoing and $1 returning per car or person.

By Public Transportation

The **Regional Transit Authority** (RTA; ☎ 504/248–3900) operates the bus and streetcar system and staffs a 24-hour information line.

Bus and **St. Charles Streetcar** fare is $1.25 (exact change); the **Riverfront Streetcar** ($1.50 exact change) links attractions along the Mississippi. The **Vieux Carré Shuttle** ($1.25 exact change) runs from Elysian Fields Avenue and Royal Street through the French Quarter, CBD, and Warehouse District to the Convention Center. VisiTour passes, good on all RTA buses and streetcars and the Vieux Carré shuttle, cost $5 (one day) and $12 (three days).

By Taxi

Cabs cruise the French Quarter, the CBD, and St. Charles Avenue but not beyond. Reliable companies with 24-hour service are **United Cabs** (☎ 504/522–9771) and **Yellow-Checker Cabs** (☎ 504/943–2411). The fare is $2.10 at the flag drop, 20¢ for each additional ¼ mi, and 75¢ for each additional passenger.

Orientation Tours

Bus and Van Tours

Gray Line (☎ 504/587–0861) offers city, plantation, trolley, and combination bus–paddle wheeler tours. **Le'Ob's Tours** (☎ 504/288–3478) runs a three-hour daily bus tour and a plantation tour, focusing on the contributions of African-Americans. **New Orleans Tours** (☎ 504/592–0560, 504/592–1991, or 800/543–6332) has city, swamp, and plantation tours and combination city–paddle wheeler outings. **Tours by Isabelle** (☎ 504/391–3544 or 888/223–2093) does city, swamp, plantation, and combination swamp-and-plantation tours.

Cruises

Riverboat sightseeing and dinner-jazz cruises are offered by the **New Orleans Steamboat Company** (☎ 504/586–8777) and **New Orleans Paddle Wheels** (☎ 504/524–0814). Bayou tours are given by **Honey Island Swamp Tours** (☎ 504/641–1769) and **Cypress Swamp Tours** (☎ 504/581–4501).

Walking Tours

Gray Line (☞ Bus and Van Tours, *above*) conducts walking tours through the French Quarter and Garden District. **Heritage Tours** (☎ 504/949–9805) offers literary walking tours of the French Quarter. **Le'Ob's Tours** (☞ Bus and Van Tours, *above*) has a two-hour French Quarter walking tour focusing on African-American heritage. **Pat Bernard's Classic Tours** (☎ 504/899–1862) is operated by a native New Orleanian who is in love with the city; her chatty tours cover art, antiques, architecture, and history. **Save Our Cemeteries** (☎ 504/525–3377) conducts lively guided tours of St. Louis Cemetery No. 1 and Lafayette Cemetery No. 1. Voodoo haunts and such are covered by both **Magic Walking Tours** (☎ 504/588–9693) and the **New Orleans Historic Voodoo Museum** (☎ 504/523–7685).

Exploring New Orleans

The French Quarter, the CBD, and the Warehouse District

★ The **French Quarter** is the original colony founded in 1718 by French Creoles. A carefully preserved historic district that's also a residential district, the Quarter is home to famous Creole restaurants and many a jazz club. An eclectic crowd ambles in and out of small two- and three-story frame, old-brick, and pastel stucco buildings, most of which date from the mid-19th century. Baskets of splashy subtropical plants dangle from the eaves of buildings with filigreed galleries, dollops of gingerbread, and dormer windows. Secluded courtyards are awash in greenery and brilliant blossoms.

The heart of the Quarter is **Jackson Square,** a formally landscaped park surrounded by a flagstone pedestrian mall and centered by an equestrian statue of Andrew Jackson. The mall is alive with sidewalk artists, food vendors, Dixieland bands, and clowns. The promenade of **Washington Artillery Park,** across Decatur Street from Jackson Square, affords a splendid perspective on the square and Ol' Man River.

St. Louis Cathedral (⊠ 615 Père Antoine Alley, ☎ 504/525–9585) is a quiet reminder of the city's spiritual life. The present church dates from 1794 and was restored in 1849. Free tours are conducted daily. **Pirate's Alley** and **Père Antoine's Alley,** two flagstone passageways redolent of bygone days, run alongside St. Louis Cathedral.

The **Louisiana State Museum** (⊠ 751 Chartres St., ☎ 504/568–6968) operates three properties on or near Jackson Square, all closed Monday. If you visit two or more state museum properties within a three-day period, you can receive a 20% discount on admission. Transfer papers for the Louisiana Purchase of 1803 were signed on the second floor of the **Cabildo** (🖾 $5). New Orleans's rich multicultural history is explored through historic documents and artifacts, among them a death mask of Napoléon—one of only three in the world. The **Presbytère** (🖾 $5), originally built as a home for priests, today houses a Mardi Gras museum. You can see what life was like for wealthy 19th-century Creole apartment dwellers in the **1850s House** (⊠ 523 St. Ann St.; 🖾 $3), which contains period furnishings, antique dolls, and a quaint kitchen.

The **Pontalba Buildings,** which line Jackson Square on St. Ann and St. Peter streets, are among the oldest apartment houses in the country. Built between 1849 and 1851, they have some of the city's loveliest ironwork galleries.

The **French Market** (⊠ along Decatur St. between Jackson Sq. and Esplanade Ave.) is a complex of shops, offices, and eating places in a row of renovated buildings that once housed markets during Spanish and
★ French rule. Here in the French Market, **Café du Monde** (⊠ 800 Decatur St., ☎ 504/525–4544) provides a 24-hour haven for café au lait and beignets (a unique New Orleans concoction: squares of fried dough dusted with powdered sugar).

The **Old U.S. Mint** houses exhibits on jazz and Mardi Gras. This was the first branch of the U.S. Mint, in operation from 1838 until 1861. It's now part of the Louisiana State Museum (☞ *above*). ⊠ *400 Esplanade Ave.,* ☎ *504/568–6968.* 🖾 *$5. Closed Mon.*

★ The **Old Ursuline Convent,** erected in 1749 by order of Louis XV, is the only building remaining from the original colony. The Sisters of Ursula, who arrived here in 1727, occupied the building from 1749 to 1824.

New Orleans

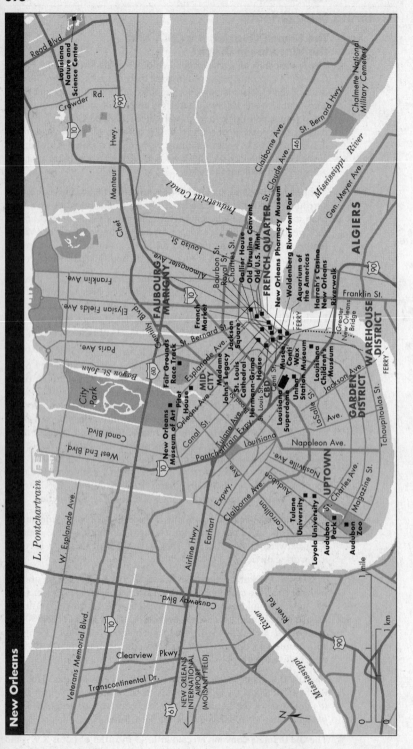

Guided tours of the complex take in the splendid **St. Mary's Church.** ⊠ *1112 Chartres St.,* ☎ *504/529–3040.* ☜ *Tours $5. Closed Mon.*

The **Gallier House** was built about 1857 by famed architect James Gallier Jr. as his family home. This is one of the best-researched house-museums in the city and a fine example of how well-heeled Creoles lived. ⊠ *1118–32 Royal St.,* ☎ *504/525–5661.* ☜ *$6, combination ticket to Hermann-Grima House $10. Closed Sun.*

The newest branch of the Louisiana State Museum (☞ *above*) is **Madame John's Legacy** (⊠ 632 Dumaine St., ☎ 504/568–8788; ☜ $3), a former residence and one of the few structures to survive the great fire of 1794. A recent archaeological excavation yielded a fascinating series of structural foundations, as well as artifacts including pottery and documents. There are also changing exhibits by Louisiana artists.

The **LaBranche House** (⊠ 740 Royal St.), a private residence dating from about 1840, wraps around the corner of Royal and St. Peter streets. Its filigreed double galleries are the most photographed in the city.

The **New Orleans Pharmacy Museum** is a musty old place where the nation's first licensed pharmacist lived and worked in the 1820s. It's full of ancient and mysterious medicinal things. ⊠ *514 Chartres St.,* ☎ *504/565–8027.* ☜ *$2. Closed Mon.*

★ At the **Hermann-Grima House** guides take you through the Georgian-style town house, built in 1831, and its picturesque outbuildings. On Thursdays, October through May, you can watch Creole cooking demonstrations—sorry, no tastings! ⊠ *820 St. Louis St.,* ☎ *504/525–5661.* ☜ *$6, combination ticket to Gallier House $10. Closed Sun.*

☾ Not to be missed are the tableaux in the **Musée Conti Wax Museum** (⊠ 917 Conti St., ☎ 504/525–2605; ☜ $6.25), which immortalizes such Louisiana legends as Andrew Jackson, Jean Lafitte, and Marie Laveau, the 19th-century voodoo queen.

Canal Street forms the upriver border of the French Quarter. Across Canal Street from the French Quarter and the nerve center of the nation's second-largest port, the **Central Business District (CBD)** has the city's newest high-tech convention hotels, along with ritzy shopping malls, fast-food chains, stores, foreign agencies, and the mammoth Superdome.

Harrah's Casino New Orleans (⊠ 4 Canal St., ☎ 504/533–6000 or 877/277–4263), the city's first land-based casino, opened in 1999, with 100,000 square ft of space, a slew of slots and table games, and New Orleans–style decor.

★ ☾ The **Aquarium of the Americas** (⊠ 1 Canal St., ☎ 504/565–3033, ☜ aquarium $13; IMAX $7.75; aquarium and IMAX $17.25) offers an IMAX theater and close encounters with aquatic creatures in 60 displays. The 16-acre **Woldenberg Riverfront Park,** which fronts the Aquarium of the Americas, affords excellent river views.

The **Riverwalk** (☞ Shopping, *below*), a busy area near the ferry landing, comprises Spanish Plaza, a broad, open expanse of mosaic tile with a magnificent fountain; the Riverwalk shopping mall; and riverboat docks.

The **Warehouse District** is home to converted warehouse apartment buildings, art galleries, and a growing number of trendy bars and restaurants. **Julia Street** is the main arts drag; the first Saturday evening of every month is alive with openings and music. The **Contemporary Arts Center** (⊠ 900 Camp St., ☎ 504/523–1216; ☜ $3) presides over the gallery scene with changing exhibits, many by local and regional artists.

A café in the center offers free web access, and two theaters have plays and live music in the evenings (☞ Theater, *below*).

The **Louisiana Children's Museum** emphasizes hands-on activities that are both educational and fun. ⊠ *420 Julia St.,* ☎ *504/523–1357.* ☞ *$5. Closed Mon.*

The Garden District and Uptown

Nestled between St. Charles, Louisiana, and Jackson avenues and Magazine Street, the **Garden District** is aptly named. Shunned by the French Creoles when they arrived in the early 19th century, American settlers built palatial estates upriver and surrounded them with lavish lawns. Many of the elegant Garden District houses were built during New Orleans's golden age, from 1830 until the Civil War. Some of these private homes are open to the public during **Spring Fiesta tours** (☎ 504/581–1367), which generally occur in late March.

Uptown is the area just upriver of the Garden District. Here, **Tulane** and **Loyola** universities stand side by side on St. Charles Avenue, across from Audubon Park (☞ Parks, Gardens, and Zoos, *below*).

St. Charles Avenue is the beautiful, oak-lined street that strings together the French Quarter, the Garden District, and Uptown. The **St. Charles Streetcar** (☞ Getting Around, *above*), the oldest operating streetcar line anywhere, is a wonderful way to trace the development of the city as it spread upriver.

Mid-City

Mid-City is between the French Quarter and Lake Pontchartrain. One of Mid-City's major draws is the **Fair Grounds Race Track** (☞ Spectator Sports, *below*), the third-oldest racetrack in the nation. The **New Orleans Museum of Art** (⊠ 1 Collins-Diboll Circle, ☎ 504/488–2631; ☞ $6) displays Italian paintings from the 13th to the 18th century, 20th-century European and American paintings and sculptures, Chinese jade, and the *Imperial Treasures,* a large collection of Fabergé eggs. It's closed on Monday.

The **Pitot House** is a West Indies–style house built in the late 18th century. Inside are many antiques from 19th-century Louisiana. ⊠ *1440 Moss St.,* ☎ *504/482–0312.* ☞ *$5. Closed Sun.–Thurs.*

North of town, **Lake Pontchartrain** is a boating and fishing destination with marinas, picnic grounds, and seafood restaurants. The **Treasure Chest** (☎ 504/443–8000 or 800/298–0711) and Bally's **Belle of Orleans** (☎ 504/568–9376) are riverboat casinos afloat on Lake Pontchartrain.

Parks, Gardens, and Zoos

City Park (⊠ City Park Ave., ☎ 504/482–4888), in Mid-City, is a 1,500-acre urban oasis shaded by majestic live oak trees. Its offerings include golf courses, tennis courts, and an ice-skating rink; lagoons for boating, canoeing, and fishing; botanical gardens; and a children's amusement park with a carousel and pony rides.

The lush 400-acre **Audubon Park** (⊠ 6500–6800 blocks of St. Charles Ave.) has a 2-mi jogging trail with exercise stations, a riding stable, a swimming pool, tennis courts, a golf course, and a zoo.

The **Audubon Zoo** (⊠ 6500 Magazine St., ☎ 504/861–2537; ☞ $9) covers 58 acres of Audubon Park. Wooden walkways afford an up-close look at more than 1,800 animals in natural-habitat settings, including a Louisiana swamp and an African savanna. There's also a petting zoo; sea lion and elephant feedings are festive events.

Dining

Updated by
Gene Bourg

New Orleans is renowned for Creole and Cajun cuisine. The essence of Creole is in its classic French-style sauces and distinctive seasonings; Cajun cooking, with its hearty ingredients, tends to be more rustic in style.

$$$$ ✕ **Grill Room.** New American cuisine with strong Continental overtones
★ is served here in an opulent setting highlighted by original artwork. As the name suggests, there's a grill, over which much good fish is prepared. ✉ *Windsor Court Hotel, 2nd level, 300 Gravier St., CBD,* ☎ *504/522–1992. Reservations essential. Jacket required. AE, D, DC, MC, V.*

$$$–$$$$ ✕ **Arnaud's.** Beveled glass, ceiling fans, and tile floors create an aura of traditional southern dining. The big, ambitious menu includes classic dishes such as rich shrimp bisque and beef Wellington. Cigar aficionados will feel at home in Arnaud's Bar, and the Richelieu Room is open for late-night live music, supping, and dancing. ✉ *813 Bienville St., French Quarter,* ☎ *504/523–5433. Reservations essential. Jacket required in main dining room. AE, D, DC, MC, V.*

$$$–$$$$ ✕ **Commander's Palace.** Housed in a renovated Victorian mansion,
★ this elegant restaurant offers the best sampling in New Orleans of old Creole cooking, prepared with a combination of American and French touches. Chef Jamie Shannon's classics include trout with roasted pecans and poached oysters in a seasoned cream sauce with Oregon caviar. ✉ *1403 Washington Ave., Garden District,* ☎ *504/899–8221. Reservations essential. Jacket required. AE, D, DC, MC, V.*

$$–$$$$ ✕ **K-Paul's Louisiana Kitchen.** National celebrity chef Paul Prud-
★ homme's restaurant is a shrine to New Orleans Cajun cooking. Inventive gumbos, fried crawfish tails, blackened tuna, and sweet-potato–pecan pie are just a few of the jewels on the menu. Prices are steep at dinner but moderate at lunch; servings are generous. ✉ *416 Chartres St., French Quarter,* ☎ *504/524–7394. AE, DC, MC, V. Closed Sun.*

$$–$$$ ✕ **Bayona.** In an early 19th-century Creole cottage on a quiet street,
★ chef Susan Spicer skillfully prepares such dishes as turnovers filled with spicy crawfish tails; a bisque of corn, leeks, and chicken; and fresh salmon fillet in white-wine sauce with sauerkraut. In good weather drinks and meals are served on a patio overflowing with tropical greenery. ✉ *430 Dauphine St., French Quarter,* ☎ *504/525–4455. Reservations essential. AE, DC, MC, V. Closed Sun.*

$$–$$$ ✕ **Galatoire's.** Operated by the fourth generation of the family owners, Galatoire's is a tradition in New Orleans. Every imaginable Creole dish is served in a large, narrow dining room lit with brass chandeliers. ✉ *209 Bourbon St., French Quarter,* ☎ *504/525–2021. Jacket required. AE, DC, MC, V. Closed Mon.*

$$–$$$ ✕ **Nola.** This Emeril Lagasse spin-off serves down-to-earth southern
★ Louisiana dishes in energetic and colorful surroundings. The trout swathed in a horseradish-citrus crust and plank-roasted in a wood oven is unforgettable, as is the coconut cream pie with cinnamon ice cream. ✉ *534 St. Louis St., French Quarter,* ☎ *504/522–6652. Reservations essential. AE, D, DC, MC, V. No lunch Sun.*

$$–$$$ ✕ **Palace Cafe.** Just a few blocks from the Mississippi riverfront, the Palace, with its drugstore-tile floors and stained-cherry booths, is a convivial spot to try some of the more imaginative contemporary Creole dishes like crab chops, rabbit ravioli in piquant sauce, and seafood Napoléon. Wait till you see the menu of chocolate desserts. ✉ *605 Canal St., CBD,* ☎ *504/523–1661. Reservations essential. AE, DC, MC, V.*

$–$$ ✕ **Praline Connection.** Down-home cooking in the southern Creole style is the forte of these laid-back restaurants. The fried or stewed chicken, smothered pork chops, barbecued ribs, and collard greens are definitively done. ✉ *542 Frenchmen St., Faubourg Marigny,* ☎ *504/943–*

3934; 901 S. Peters St., Warehouse District, ☎ 504/523–3973. Reservations not accepted. AE, D, DC, MC, V.

$–$$ ✕ **Ralph & Kacoo's.** Getting past the door to the vast dining spaces usually means first taking a ticket and waiting your turn in a crowded bar decorated in a bayou theme. Freshness and consistency are trademarks here. You'll find them in the boiled shrimp, raw oysters, shrimp rémoulade, trout meunière, and fried seafood platter. This restaurant is popular with families. ✉ 519 Toulouse St., French Quarter, ☎ 504/522–5226. Reservations not accepted. AE, D, MC, V.

$ ✕ **Camellia Grill.** This classy lunch counter with linen napkins and a maître d' serves the best omelets in town all day long, as well as great hamburgers, pecan pie, cheesecake, and banana cream pie. Expect long lines on weekends for breakfast. ✉ 626 S. Carrollton Ave., Uptown, ☎ 504/866–9573. No credit cards.

Lodging

Reserve well in advance of your New Orleans stay, especially during Mardi Gras, the bacchanalian celebration the day before Lent, or other seasonal events. Hotels frequently offer special packages at reduced rates, but never during Mardi Gras, when rates are much higher.

$$$$ ★ 🏨 **Fairmont Hotel.** The Fairmont is one of the oldest grand hotels in America. Its lobby is decked out in blue-and-gold Victorian splendor. Special touches in every room include down pillows and terry-cloth robes. ✉ 123 Baronne St., CBD, 70140, ☎ 504/529–7111 or 800/527–4727, FAX 504/529–4764. 785 rooms. 3 restaurants, pool, tennis, exercise room. AE, D, DC, MC, V.

$$$$ ★ 🏨 **Windsor Court Hotel.** Exquisite, gracious, elegant, eminently civilized—these words try to but cannot capture the wonderful quality of this hotel. Four blocks from the French Quarter, the Windsor Court has plush carpeting, canopy and four-poster beds, stocked wet bars, marble vanities, oversize mirrors, and dressing areas. ✉ 300 Gravier St., CBD, 70130, ☎ 504/523–6000 or 800/262–2662, FAX 504/596–4513. 326 rooms. 2 restaurants, pool, health club. AE, D, DC, MC, V. ✦

$$$–$$$$ ★ 🏨 **Royal Orleans Hotel (Omni).** An elegant white-marble hotel, the Royal O is reminiscent of a bygone era. Rooms, though not exceptionally large, are well appointed, with marble baths (telephone in each) and marble-top dressers and tables. ✉ 621 St. Louis St., French Quarter, 70140, ☎ 504/529–5333, FAX 504/529–7089. 362 rooms. Restaurant, pool, exercise room. AE, D, DC, MC, V. ✦

$$–$$$$ 🏨 **Chateau Le Moyne Holiday Inn.** Old-world atmosphere and decor can be found just one block off Bourbon Street. Eight suites are in Creole cottages off a tropical courtyard; all rooms are furnished with antiques and reproductions and have coffeemakers, hair dryers, and irons and ironing boards. ✉ 301 Dauphine St., French Quarter, 70112, ☎ 504/581–1303, FAX 504/523–5709. 171 rooms. Restaurant, pool. AE, D, DC, MC, V. ✦

$$–$$$ 🏨 **Josephine Guest House.** European antiques fill the rooms of this restored Italianate mansion built in 1870. The bathrooms are impressive in both size and decor. A complimentary Continental breakfast, served on Wedgwood china from a silver tray, can be brought to your room. ✉ 1450 Josephine St., Garden District, 70130, ☎ 504/524–6361 or 800/779–6361, FAX 504/523–6484. 6 rooms. AE, D, DC, MC, V. CP.

$$–$$$ ★ 🏨 **Le Richelieu.** This small, friendly hotel offers many amenities usually found in luxury high-rises. Some rooms have mirrored walls, walk-in closets, and refrigerators; all have hair dryers. Luxury suites are available. ✉ 1234 Chartres St., French Quarter, 70116, ☎ 504/529–2492 or 800/535–9653, FAX 504/524–8179. 86 rooms. Pool. AE, D, DC, MC, V.

$$–$$$ 🏨 **Pontchartrain Hotel.** Maintaining the grand tradition is the hallmark of this quiet, elegant European-style hotel, which has reigned on St.

Charles Avenue since it was built in 1927. Accommodations range from lavish sun-filled suites to small pension-style rooms with shower-baths. ⊠ *2031 St. Charles Ave., Garden District, 70140,* ☎ *504/524–0581 or 800/777–6193,* FAX *504/524–7828. 122 rooms. 2 restaurants. AE, D, DC, MC, V.* 🐾

$$–$$$ 🏨 **Rue Royal Inn.** This circa-1850 home has balcony rooms overlooking a courtyard and Royal Street; two suites have Jacuzzis. Each room has a coffeemaker and a small refrigerator. ⊠ *1006 Royal St., French Quarter, 70116,* ☎ *504/524–3900 or 800/776–3901,* FAX *504/ 558–0566. 17 rooms. AE, D, DC, MC, V. CP.* 🐾

$–$$ 🏨 **St. Charles Guest House.** Simple and affordable, this European-style pension is in four buildings one block from St. Charles Avenue. Rooms in the A and B buildings are larger. The small "backpacker" rooms share a bath and do not have air-conditioning. ⊠ *1748 Prytania St., Garden District, 70130,* ☎ *504/523–6556,* FAX *504/522–6340. 36 rooms, 8 with shared bath. Pool. AE, MC, V. CP.* 🐾

Nightlife and the Arts

The Friday edition of the *Times-Picayune* and the weekly *Gambit* (free) carry comprehensive calendars of arts and entertainment events. *New Orleans* magazine (on newsstands) and *This Week in New Orleans* and *Where: New Orleans* (both available free in hotels) also publish calendars of events. The best dirt on the local music scene comes courtesy of *Offbeat,* a free monthly. Credit-card purchases of tickets for events at the Saenger Performing Arts Center and Kiefer UNO Lakefront Arena can be made through **Ticketmaster** (☎ 504/522–5555 or 800/488–5252).

Nightlife

New Orleans is a 24-hour town, meaning there are no legal closing times. Bourbon Street in the French Quarter is lined with clubs; many local hangouts are Uptown.

BARS

The heavily touristed **Pat O'Brien's** (⊠ 718 St. Peter St., French Quarter, ☎ 504/525–4823) has three lively bars. At **Lafitte's Blacksmith Shop** (⊠ 941 Bourbon St., French Quarter, ☎ 504/523–0066) drinks are served in a rustic 18th-century cottage. According to legend the cottage was once a front for pirate Jean Lafitte's smuggling and slave trade. **Napoleon House** (⊠ 500 Chartres St., French Quarter, ☎ 504/524–9752) is a longtime favorite hangout. In the French Quarter, **Oz** (⊠ 800 Bourbon St., ☎ 504/593–9491) is a popular dance bar for young gays and lesbians, and **Bourbon Pub** (⊠ 801 Bourbon St., ☎ 504/529–2107) is a popular gay bar for young men. In the Warehouse District, **Ernst Café** (⊠ 600 S. Peters St., ☎ 504/525–8544) is a friendly, atmospheric old bar.

JAZZ

You can catch live traditional jazz at the two-stage **Storyville District** (⊠ 125 Bourbon St., French Quarter, ☎ 504/410–1000), the Funky Butt (⊠ 714 N. Rampart St., French Quarter, ☎ 504/558–0872), **Pete Fountain's** (⊠ 2 Poydras St., in the Hilton hotel, CBD, ☎ 504/523–4374), **Snug Harbor** (⊠ 626 Frenchmen St., Faubourg Marigny, across Esplanade Ave. from the French Quarter, ☎ 504/949–0696), or the lovably ramshackle **Preservation Hall** (⊠ 726 St. Peter St., French Quarter, ☎ 504/522–2841).

R&B, CAJUN, ROCK, NEW WAVE

An institution, **Tipitina's** (⊠ 501 Napoleon Ave., Uptown; 233 N. Peters St., French Quarter, ☎ 504/897–3943) is a laid-back place with a mixed bag of music. **Jimmy's Music Club** (⊠ 8200 Willow St., Uptown, ☎ 504/861–8200) is popular with the college crowd. You can enjoy a good R&B or blues act at the **Maple Leaf Bar** (⊠ 8316 Oak

St., Uptown, ☎ 504/866–9359). Cajun two-stepping can be found at **Mulate's** (✉ 201 Julia St., Warehouse District, ☎ 504/522–1492) or **Michaul's** (✉ 840 St. Charles Ave., CBD, ☎ 504/522–5517). **House of Blues** (✉ 225 Decatur St., French Quarter, ☎ 504/529–2583) has a contrived atmosphere but nonetheless books top-notch acts.

The Arts

CONCERTS

The up-and-coming **Louisiana Philharmonic Orchestra** (☎ 504/523–6530) performs classical music in the **Orpheum Theater** (✉ 129 University Pl., ☎ 504/524–3285). Nationally known artists perform at **Kiefer UNO Lakefront Arena** (✉ 6801 Franklin Ave., ☎ 504/280–7222).

THEATER

The avant-garde and the satirical are among the offerings at **Contemporary Arts Center** (✉ 900 Camp St., ☎ 504/523–1216). **Le Petit Théâtre du Vieux Carré** (✉ 616 St. Peter St., ☎ 504/522–2081) presents more traditional fare as well as children's theater. **Southern Repertory Theater** (✉ Canal Pl. at Canal St., ☎ 504/861–8163) puts on local productions. Touring Broadway shows and top-name talent appear at the **Saenger Performing Arts Center** (✉ 143 N. Rampart St., ☎ 504/524–2490).

Outdoor Activities and Sports

Biking

New Orleans is entirely flat, and many distances can be easily covered on two wheels. Bikes can be rented at **Bicycle Michael's** (✉ 622 Frenchmen St., ☎ 504/945–9505) and **French Quarter Bicycles** (✉ 522 Dumaine St., ☎ 504/529–3136). **French Louisiana Bike Tours** (✉ 3216 W. Esplanade Ave., PMB 302, ☎ 504/488–9844 or 800/346–7989) conducts guided bike tours of the River Road and of Cajun Country.

Boating

Canoes, rowboats, and pedal boats can be rented for lazing along **City Park's lagoons** (✉ 1 Dreyfous Ave., ☎ 504/483–9371).

Golf

There are four 18-hole courses at **City Park**, as well as a 100-tee double-decker driving range (✉ 1040 Fillmore Ave., ☎ 504/483–9396). There is an 18-hole course at **Audubon Park** (✉ 473 Walnut St., ☎ 504/865–8260).

Ice Skating

The city's only ice-skating rink opened in late 1999 in City Park, adjacent to the Wisner Tennis Center. **Holiday Ice Rink** (✉ Dreyfous Ave. at Victory Ave., ☎ 504/522–7465) has daily skating sessions, as well as lessons, figure skating exhibitions, and hockey demonstrations.

Tennis

There are 39 courts at **City Park's Wisner Tennis Center** (✉ Victory Ave., ☎ 504/483–9383) and 10 courts in **Audubon Park** (✉ rear of park, 6320 Tchoupitoulas St., ☎ 504/895–1042).

Spectator Sports

Baseball (Minor League): New Orleans Zephyrs (✉ Zephyr Stadium, 6000 Airline Hwy., Metairie, ☎ 504/734–5155). **Football: New Orleans Saints** (✉ Superdome, 1 Sugar Bowl Dr., ☎ 504/731–1700). The **Sugar Bowl Classic** (☎ 504/525–8573) is played annually in the Superdome on New Year's Day. **Horse Racing:** There is Thoroughbred racing from Thanksgiving Day to April at the **Fair Grounds** (✉ 1751 Gentilly Blvd., ☎ 504/944–5515). **Hockey: New Orleans Brass** of the East Coast Ice Hockey League (✉ New Orleans Arena, 1501 Girod St., ☎ 504/522–7825).

Shopping

You will find all types of shopping in New Orleans, but the city is exceptional for antiques and local arts and crafts. Louisiana's **tax-free shopping** program grants shoppers from other countries a sales-tax rebate. Retailers who display the tax-free sign issue vouchers for the 9% sales tax, which can be redeemed on departure. Present the vouchers with your passport and international plane ticket at the tax-rebate office at New Orleans International Airport and receive up to $500 in cash back. If the amount redeemable exceeds $500, a check for the difference will be mailed to you.

Shopping Districts

Most of the **French Quarter**'s ritzy antiques stores, musty bazaars, art galleries, and boutiques are housed in quaint 19th-century structures. The sleek indoor malls of the **CBD** include **Riverwalk** (⊠ 1 Poydras St., ☎ 504/522–1555), with more than 200 specialty shops and restaurants; **Canal Place** (⊠ 365 Canal St., ☎ 504/522–9200), with more than 40 tony shops, a food court, and cinemas; and **New Orleans Centre** (⊠ 1400 Poydras St., ☎ 504/568–0000), connected by a walkway to the Superdome and a hotel. The **Warehouse District,** especially Julia Street off St. Charles Avenue, is a major center for art galleries. **Magazine Street** has 6 mi of antiques stores and boutiques, many in once-grand Victorian houses, as well as trendy shopping and artisan shops. **Riverbend** has specialty shops and restaurants, many cradled in small Creole cottages.

Specialty Stores

ANTIQUES

Royal Street in the Quarter is lined with elegant antiques stores. The three-story **French Antique Shop** (⊠ 225 Royal St., ☎ 504/524–9861) has excellent chandeliers and 18th-century furniture. **Keil's Antiques** (⊠ 325 Royal St., ☎ 504/522–4552) specializes in jewelry. **Let's Go Antiquing** (⊠ 1424 Fourth St., 70130, ☎ 504/899–3027) arranges individual shopping sprees. **Mirror, Mirror** (⊠ 301 Chartres St., ☎ 504/566–1990) sells reflective glass in all shapes and sizes. The Royal Street Guild and the Magazine Street Merchants' Association publish pamphlets that are available free at the **New Orleans Welcome Center** (☞ Visitor Information, *above*).

FLEA MARKET

Locals as well as tourists turn out for the **Community Flea Market** held daily from 7 to 7 in the French Market (☞ Exploring New Orleans, *above*).

FOOD

Louisiana Products (⊠ 507 St. Ann St., on Jackson Sq., ☎ 504/524–7331) and the **Louisiana General Store** (⊠ 524 St. Louis St., ☎ 504/525–2665) have packaged Louisiana food products. **Old Town Praline Shop** (⊠ 627 Royal St., ☎ 504/525–1413) sells the best pralines in town.

JAZZ RECORDS

The **Louisiana Music Factory** (⊠ 210 Decatur St., ☎ 504/586–1094) stocks the best supply of local music.

MASKS

Handmade Mardi Gras masks are available at **Little Shop of Fantasy** (⊠ 523 Dumaine St., ☎ 504/529–4243) and **Rumors** (⊠ 513 Royal St., ☎ 504/525–0292).

Side Trip to Baton Rouge and Plantation Country

Although the Baton Rouge and Plantation Country area is worth an extended visit, several of these locations can be visited on day trips from New Orleans.

Visitor Information

Baton Rouge Area Convention and Visitors Bureau (⊠ 730 North Blvd., 70802, ☎ 504/383–1825 or 800/527–6843).

Arriving and Departing

The quickest way to reach plantations along River Road between New Orleans and Baton Rouge by car is to follow I–10 or U.S. 61 to the appropriate exit. From Baton Rouge, U.S. 61 continues on to St. Francisville.

What to See and Do

You can see what went with the wind and hear tales of Yankee invaders and ghosts in some of the fine restored antebellum plantations sprinkled around Baton Rouge, including **Oak Alley** (⊠ 3645 Rte. 18, Vacherie, ☎ 225/261–2151 or 800/442–5539; ☞ $8), named for the stunning 300-year-old live oaks that stretch out in front of the house; **Houmas House** (⊠ Rte. 942, ½ mi off Rte. 44, near Burnside, ☎ 888/323–8314; ☞ $8), a Greek Revival mansion famed for its three-story spiral staircase; and **Nottoway Plantation** (⊠ 2 mi north of White Castle, ☎ 225/346–8263; ☞ $10), an extravagant Italianate mansion with elegant, antiques-filled rooms.

As state capitol, **Baton Rouge** harbors much of Louisiana's history, especially its colorful (some might say scandalous) political history. In the Art Deco **Louisiana State Capitol** (⊠ State Capitol Dr., ☎ 225/342–7317; ☞ free), you can see impressive documents and legislative chambers, as well as the site of Governor Huey P. Long's assassination in 1935. The Gothic Revival **Old State Capitol** (⊠ 100 North Blvd. at River Rd., ☎ 225/342–0500 or 800/488–2968; ☞ $4) was the capitol from 1850 to 1932; it now houses the **Center for Political and Governmental History**, a museum with some interactive exhibits. The **Enchanted Mansion** (⊠ 190 Lee Dr., ☎ 225/769–0005; ☞ $4.50) has an enchanting collection of more than 2,000 dolls. The restored **Old Governor's Mansion** (⊠ 502 N. Blvd., ☎ 225/343–3989; ☞ $4), built in 1930 during Huey Long's administration, is a museum with rooms dedicated to governors who have served since the house was built. Architecturally, the house features some lovely wood paneling and frieze work. Slightly out of the ordinary, the **Rural Life Museum and Windrush Gardens** (⊠ Essen La. at I–10, ☎ 225/765–2437; ☞ $5) is a fascinating combination of buildings and artifacts outlining Louisiana's rural history. There are beautiful landscaped gardens, with European statuary, beyond the buildings. The **Magnolia Mound Plantation** (⊠ 2161 Nicholson Dr., ☎ 225/343–4955; ☞ $5) and grounds are a lovely example of West Indies influence in southern Louisiana.

North of Baton Rouge, **St. Francisville** is the heart of English Louisiana. A walk down **Ferdinand Street** takes you by a number of gift and antiques shops. **Grace Episcopal Church** (⊠ 11621 Ferdinand St., ☎ 225/635–4065) is splendidly set in a park of old, moss-draped live oaks.

The **West Feliciana Parish Tourist Commission** (⊠ 11757 Ferdinand St., ☎ 225/635–6330 or 800/789–4221) has historical exhibits and brochures.

St. Francisville is surrounded by eight plantation homes open for tours. Perhaps the grandest of them is **Rosedown** (⊠ 12501 Rte. 10, ☎ 225/635–3110; ☞ $10), with expansive formal gardens in addition to the stately Greek Revival house itself. James J. Audubon stayed a spell at the West Indies–style **Oakley House** (⊠ 11788 Rte. 965, in the Audubon State Commemorative Area, ☎ 225/635–3739; ☞ $2), where he tutored the owner's daughter for several months. The graceful **Greenwood Plantation** (⊠ 6838 Highland Rd., ☎ 225/655–4475; ☞ $6) still produces pecans, hay, and cattle. Inside, some original antiques and portraits remain.

Near St. Francisville, the **Angola Prison Museum** (⊠ Angola, end of
Rte. 66, ☎ 225/655–2592; ⌨ free) houses a fascinating, eerie, and often
moving collection of photographs documenting the people and events
that have been a part of Angola; items such as prisoner weapons and
the electric chair used for executions until 1991 are also on display.

CAJUN COUNTRY

Cajun Country, or Acadiana, comprises 22 parishes (counties) of southern Louisiana to the west of New Orleans. Cajuns are descendants of
17th-century French settlers who established a colony they called l'A-
cadie (*Cajun* is a corruption of *Acadian*) in the present-day Canadian
provinces of Nova Scotia and New Brunswick. After the British ex-
pelled the Acadians in the mid-18th century (their exile is described in
Longfellow's epic poem *Evangeline*), many eventually found a home
in southern Louisiana. They have been here since 1762, imbuing the
region with a distinctive flavor summed up in the Cajun phrase "Laissez les bons temps rouler!" ("Let the good times roll!")

Visitor Information

Southwest Louisiana Convention & Visitors Bureau (⊠ 1205 Lakeshore
Dr., Lake Charles 70601, ☎ 337/436–9588 or 800/456–7952). **Lafayette
Convention & Visitors Bureau** (⊠ 1400 N.W. Evangeline Thruway, Box
52066, Lafayette 70505, ☎ 337/232–3737 or 800/346–1958; 800/543–
5340 in Canada).

Arriving and Departing

By Bus
Greyhound (☎ 800/231–2222) has frequent daily service to Lafayette
and environs. **Gray Line** (☎ 504/587–0861 or 800/535–7788) offers
orientation tours of Cajun country.

By Car
The fastest route from New Orleans through Cajun Country is west
on I–10. U.S. 90 is a slower but more scenic drive. If you have time,
take the back roads for exploring this area. A ferry across the Mississippi costs $1 per car; most bridges are free.

By Plane
Lafayette Regional Airport (⊠ 200 Terminal Dr., ☎ 318/266–4400)
is served by American Eagle, Atlantic Southeast (Delta), Continental,
and Northwest Airlink.

By Train
Amtrak (☎ 800/872–7245) serves Lafayette and New Iberia.

Exploring Cajun Country

U.S. 90 dips down south of New Orleans into Terrebonne Parish, a
major center for shrimp and oyster fisheries (the blessing of the shrimp
fleets in Chauvin and Dulac is a colorful April event). A slew of swamp
tours are based here, including **Annie Miller's Terrebonne Swamp &
Marsh Tours** (☎ 504/879–3934). **Hammond's Cajun Air Tours** (☎ 504/
876–0584) takes passengers up for a gull's-eye view of the alligators
and other critters that inhabit the coastal wetlands.

Route 182 west of Morgan City branches off U.S. 90 and ambles
northwest toward Lafayette, traveling for much of the way along
★ **Bayou Teche,** the largest of the state's many bayous. (*Teche* is a Native America word meaning "snake." According to an ancient legend,

the death throes of a giant snake carved the bayou.) The road runs by rice paddies and canebrakes, and on the bayous you can see Cajun pirogues (canoelike boats) and cypress cabins built on stilts. In the picturesque town of **Franklin,** near the Bayou Teche, old-fashioned street lamps line Main Street, which rolls out beneath an arcade of live oaks. Six antebellum homes are open for tours.

New Iberia, founded in 1779 by Spanish settlers who named it for their homeland, is also known as the "Queen City of the Teche." **Shadows-on-the-Teche** (✉ 317 E. Main St., ☎ 337/369–6446; 💲 $8), one of the South's best-known plantation homes, was built in 1834 for sugar planter David Weeks. The recent discovery of 40 trunks of documents tracing the various residents' activities provides for a tour filled with lively detail. At the **Konrico Company Store** (✉ 309 Ann St., ☎ 337/367–6163 or 800/551–3245; 💲 $2.75), you can tour the nation's oldest rice mill.

★ Red-hot Tabasco sauce is a 19th-century Louisiana creation; on **Avery Island** at McIlhenny's Tabasco Company (✉ Rte. 329, ☎ 337/373–6129 or 800/634–9599; 💲 free), you can tour the factory where it's still being manufactured by descendants of its creator. Here also are the 200-acre **Jungle Gardens,** lush with tropical plants, and **Bird City,** a sanctuary with flurries of snow-white egrets (☎ 337/369–6243; 💲 $5.75).

★ Like Avery Island, **Rip Van Winkle Gardens** (✉ 5505 Rip Van Winkle Rd., off Rte. 675, ☎ 337/365–3332, 💲 house and gardens $9), on Jefferson Island, is actually a salt dome, capped by lush vegetation. The 19th-century American actor Joseph Jefferson, who toured the country portraying Rip Van Winkle, built a winter home here. His three-story house is surrounded by lovely formal and informal gardens.

Along **Route 31,** a pretty country road that hugs the banks of the Teche between New Iberia and Opelousas to the north, you'll find **St. Martinville,** a little town awash with legends. Now a sleepy village, it was known in the 18th century as Petit Paris, a refuge for aristocrats fleeing the French Revolution. It was also a major debarkation point for exiled Acadians. Longfellow's poem *Evangeline* was based on the true story of two young lovers who were separated for years during the Acadian exile. The **Evangeline Oak** (✉ Evangeline Blvd. at Bayou Teche) is said to be the place where the ill-starred lovers met again—albeit briefly. On the town square are **St. Martin de Tours,** mother church of the Acadians, and the **Petit Paris Museum** (✉ 103 S. Main St., ☎ 337/394–7334; 💲 $1), which showcases the local Mardi Gras traditions. Be sure to visit the small cemetery behind the church, where a bronze statue depicts the real-life Evangeline. The **Longfellow-Evangeline State Commemorative Area** (✉ 1200 N. Main St., ☎ 337/394–3754 or 888/677–2900; 💲 $2) includes a small museum tracing the history of the Acadians, a Creole plantation cottage, and a Cajun cabin. Tours are self-guided, and at the back of the park, picnic tables line the bayou.

Tiny **Breaux Bridge,** just north of St. Martinville, calls itself the "crawfish capital of the world." Some decades ago, when crawfish were still viewed as a low-class meat, this town brazenly threw a **Crawfish Festival.** These days the festival, held each May, draws more than 100,000 people. **Café des Amis** (☞ Dining and Lodging, *below*) is at the forefront of a bubbling artistic and commercial revival in town; the restaurant's walls are lined with the work of regional artists.

Lafayette proudly proclaims itself the capital of French Louisiana. In this part of the state some 40% of the residents speak Cajun French, a 17th-century dialect. As most Cajuns also speak standard French as well as English, this is a superb place to test your language skills. **Cajun Mardi Gras** rivals its sister celebration in New Orleans. Lafayette, though it's short on the charm that typifies this region, has a few note-worthy attractions and is a good base for exploring the region.

★ The **Acadian Cultural Center** (⊠ 501 Fisher Rd., ☎ 337/232–0789 or 318/232–0961, 🖳 free), a unit of the **Jean Lafitte National Historical Park and Preserve**, traces the history of the Acadians through numer-ous audiovisual exhibits. The **Children's Museum of Acadiana** has ed-ucational hands-on exhibits (⊠ 201 E. Congress St., ☎ 337/232–8500; 🖳 $5). The **Alexandre Mouton House** (⊠ 1122 Lafayette St., ☎ 337/234–2208; 🖳 $3), formerly the home of wealthy Creoles, is filled with early to mid-19th-century period furniture and documen-tation of the Mouton family. The main attraction at **St. John the Evan-gelist Cathedral** (⊠ 914 St. John St., at Cathedral St.) is the gargantuan, 400-plus-year-old **Cathedral Oak** beside it.

The **Acadian Village** (⊠ 200 Greenleaf Dr., ☎ 337/981–2364; 🖳 $6) is a re-creation of an old-style Acadian village, featuring authentic houses, shops, and a church. **Vermilionville** (⊠ , ☎ 337/233–4077 or 800/992–2968; 🖳 $8) is a re-created village with more replicas than authentic struc-tures, but it also showcases local artists, cooks, and craftspeople at work.

★ Among the small towns that dot the flatlands west of Lafayette and whose residents are called Prairie Cajuns is tiny **Eunice.** In the **Prairie Acadian Cultural Center** (⊠ corner of S. 3rd St. and Park Ave., ☎ 337/457–8499, 🖳 free) displays, films, and the occasional cooking demonstration paint the historical picture of the Prairie Cajuns. In a former railroad depot, the home-style **Eunice Museum** (⊠ 220 C. C. Duson Dr., ☎ 337/457–6540; 🖳 free) contains displays on Cajun culture, including its music and Mardi Gras. The **Cajun Music Hall of Fame** (⊠ 240 C. C. Duson St., ☎ 337/457–6534; 🖳 free) proudly honors Acadian musical heritage.

Grand Coteau is a religious and educational center, and the entire peaceful little village is on the National Register of Historic Places. Of particular note in Grand Coteau is the **Church of St. Charles Borromeo,** a simple wooden structure with an ornate high-Baroque-style interior. A splendid antebellum mansion, **Chretien Point** (⊠ 665 Chretien Point Rd., 12 mi north of Lafayette, ☎ 337/662–5876 or 800/880–7050; 🖳 $6.50) is now a bed-and-breakfast (☞ Dining and Lodging, *below*). The staircase in Tara, Scarlett O'Hara's home in *Gone With the Wind,* was modeled on the one in this house.

Opelousas is the third-oldest town in the state. Founded by the French in 1720, the town was named for the Appalousa Indians, who lived here centuries before the French and Spanish arrived. For a brief pe-riod during the Civil War, Opelousas served as the state capital. At the intersection of I–49 and U.S. 190, the **Opelousas Tourist Information Center** (☎ 337/948–6263 or 800/424–5442) houses memorabilia of Jim Bowie, the Alamo hero who spent his boyhood here. The **Opelousas Museum and Interpretive Center** (⊠ 329 N. Main St., ☎ 337/948–2589; 🖳 free) traces the history of this region. A tour through **Tony Chachere's,** a Creole seasoning factory (⊠ 533 N. Lombard St., ☎ 800/551–9066; 🖳 free), includes nose masks to filter the pepper in the air. During the last full week in October, Opelousas stages the **Yambilee Festival,** a cel-ebration of the superior local sweet potatoes.

The small town of **Washington** is home to O'Connor's Antique School Mall (☞ Shopping, *below*). The old plantation home at **Magnolia Ridge** (⊠ Prescott St.) is closed to the public, but the surrounding grounds are beautiful for rambling. There are nice picnic spots by the bayou and a rich bit of swamp right in the middle of the property.

South of Lafayette, Route 82 (Hug-the-Coast Highway) whips along the windswept coastal marshes to the **Rockefeller Wildlife Refuge** (☎ 337/538–2165), in **Grand Chenier**. At this 84,000-acre preserve, thousands of ducks, geese, gators, wading birds, and otters while away the winter months.

Dining and Lodging

With the state's wealth of waterways, it is no surprise that Louisiana tables are laden with seafood in every variety. In southern Louisiana sea creatures are prepared with a Cajun flair, meaning rich, heavily seasoned sauces; local ingredients; and a frugal approach to seafood. Warning: Tolerance for hot, spicy foods is very high around here. Sleeping accommodations run from homey B&Bs to chain motels to luxury hotels to elegant antebellum mansions open for overnighters.

Breaux Bridge

$$–$$$ ★ ✕ **Café des Amis.** Enjoy rich Cajun fare in this open, art-lined restaurant. Owner and chef Dickie Breaux (descended from Breaux Bridge's founders) prides himself on an authentic approach to Cajun cuisine. The saucy house specialty, barbecue shrimp, comes with a bib. A zydeco band entertains for Saturday breakfasts. ⊠ *140 E. Bridge St.,* ☎ *337/332–5273. Reservations essential. AE, D, MC, V. Closed Mon. No dinner Tues., Wed., or Sun.*

$–$$ ★ ✕ **Mulate's.** This renowned roadhouse with tables covered in checkered plastic has Cajun seafood and dancing to live Cajun music every night. ⊠ *325 W. Mills Ave.,* ☎ *337/332–4648 or 800/422–2586. AE, MC, V.*

Grand Coteau

$$–$$$ ✕ **Catahoula's.** "New Louisiana cooking" is the self-proclaimed approach at this restaurant. Cajun Country does not normally embrace the trendy, but Catahoula's, with its warehouse-inspired interior and photographs on the walls, is an exception. You'll find familiar ingredients in new guises, such as a savory crabmeat cheesecake or a roulade of snapper with scallop-crab stuffing. They also do a nice Sunday brunch. ⊠ *234 King Dr.,* ☎ *337/662–2275 or 888/547–2275. AE, D, MC, V. Closed Mon.*

Lafayette

$$$–$$$$ ✕ **Café Vermilionville.** Lafayette rivals New Orleans when it comes to fine dining, and Café Vermilionville is one of the best bets in town. The restaurant occupies an antebellum house, formerly an inn. The seasonal menu is essentially Cajun, so expect rich and spicy preparations. Constant favorites include the crawfish beignets and fire-roasted smoked salmon. ⊠ *1304 W. Pinhook Rd.,* ☎ *337/237–0100. Jacket required. AE, D, DC, MC, V. Closed Sun.*

$$–$$$ ★ ✕ **Prejean's.** Housed in a cypress cottage, this local favorite has a cozy oyster bar, red-checked cloths, and live music nightly. Platters of traditional and new Cajun seafood are the specialties. ⊠ *3480 U.S. 167N, next to Evangeline Downs,* ☎ *337/896–3247. AE, DC, MC, V.*

$$ 🏨 **Holiday Inn Central–Holidome.** Built around an atrium that's banked with greenery, this modern motel has rooms done in contemporary decor and 17 acres within which you can find almost every diversion you'd ever need for a long life. ⊠ *2032 N.E. Evangeline Thruway, Box 91807, 70501,* ☎ *337/233–6815 or 800/942–4868,* ℻ *337/235–1954. 243 rooms. Restaurant, pool, tennis. AE, D, DC, MC, V.* ♨

$$ ★ 🏨 **T'Frere's House.** Warm hospitality pervades this reputedly haunted old house. The casual rooms are warmly outfitted with thick beds and sitting areas, and breakfast—an excellent, multicourse affair—is always jovial. Hosts Pat and Maugie Pastor serve cocktails when you arrive; cordials are available throughout the day. ⊠ *1905 Verot School Rd., 70508,* ☎ *800/984–9347,* ☎ ℻ *337/984–9347. 6 rooms. D, MC, V. BP.* ♨

New Iberia

$$ ✕▦ **leRosier.** Across the street from Shadows-on-the-Teche, leRosier is a six-room B&B whose shining star is the restaurant ($$$–$$$$, reservations essential for dinner), presided over by chef Hallman Woods III. Among other accomplishments, Woods has prepared a five-course crawfish degustation for the James Beard Foundation. Expect fresh ingredients and succulent seafood in his small white-cloth dining room. Rooms are sparsely decorated but modern and clean. ✉ *314 E. Main St., 70560,* ☎ *888/804–7673,* ☎ FAX *337/367–5306. 6 rooms. Restaurant. AE, MC, V. BP.* ☜

Opelousas

$–$$ ✕ **Palace Café.** This down-home coffee shop on the town square, operated by the same family since 1927, serves steak, fried chicken, sandwiches, burgers, and seafood. Locals flock here for the homemade baklava. ✉ *167 W. Landry St.,* ☎ *337/942–2142. MC, V.*

$$ ▦ **The Estorge House.** Many of the original furnishings—as well as details such as antique nightgowns in the closets—fill the eminently comfortable old rooms of this antebellum house near the center of Opelousas. Guests are treated lavishly and encouraged to make themselves at home. ✉ *427 N. Market St., 70570,* ☎ *337/942–8151. 2 rooms. MC, V. BP.*

St. Martinville

$–$$ ✕▦ **La Place d'Evangeline.** Rooms are spacious at this B&B on the banks of the Bayou Teche. The restaurant (closed Sunday–Monday) serves hearty portions of seafood and Cajun dishes; the homemade bread is superb. ✉ *220 Evangeline Blvd., 70582,* ☎ *337/394–4010,* FAX *337/394–7983. 7 rooms. Restaurant. AE, D, MC, V. BP.*

Sunset

$$–$$$$ ▦ **Chretien Point.** This stately home sits in luxurious isolation near a bayou. The rather formal rooms are furnished with period antiques. The French Greek Revival layout of the house provides for large, comfortable sitting areas. There was a Civil War battle here, and Jean Lafitte was smuggling in cahoots with the original owner, so stories of hauntings abound. ✉ *665 Chretien Point Rd., across the highway from Grand Coteau, 70584,* ☎ *800/880–7050,* ☎ FAX *337/662–5876. 5 rooms. Pool, tennis. AE, D, MC, V. BP.*

Nightlife and the Arts

Cajun and Zydeco Music

Mulate's in Breaux Bridge, **Prejean's** in Lafayette (☞ Dining and Lodging, *above*), and **Randol's** (✉ 2320 Kaliste Saloom Rd., Lafayette, ☎ 337/981–7080) regularly feature Cajun music and dancing. **Slim's Y-Ki-Ki** (✉ U.S. 167, Washington Rd., Opelousas, ☎ 337/942–9980), a rural club, is one of the best zydeco dance venues in the state. **Fred's Lounge** (✉ 420 6th St., Mamou, ☎ 337/468–5411), open Saturday morning only (8–1), is a legendary bar with live radio broadcasts and plenty of dancing. **Rendez-Vous des Cajuns** (✉ Liberty Theatre, Park Ave. at 2nd St., Eunice, ☎ 337/457–7389; ☎ $5) is a live Saturday-night radio show, mostly in French, that's been described as a combination of the *Grand Ole Opry,* the *Louisiana Hayride,* and the *Prairie Home Companion.*

Outdoor Activities and Sports

Pack & Paddle (✉ 601 E. Pinhook Rd., Lafayette, ☎ 337/232–5854 or 800/458–4560) is an excellent resource for outdoor gear for almost any sport, and for information about outdoor sports in the area.

Biking

French Louisiana Bike Tours (⊠ 3216 W. Esplanade Ave., PMB 302, Metairie, LA 70002, ☎ 504/488–9844 or 800/346–7989) offers four- and seven-day tours of Cajun Country that include the rental of a Cannondale hybrid bike (equipped with smooth tires, Avocet computer, backrack and handlebar pack), van support, lodging, and meals.

Fishing

Sportsman's Paradise (⊠ Rte. 56, Cocodrie, ☎ 504/594–2414) and **Salt, Inc. Charter Fishing Service** (⊠ Rte. 56, Cocodrie, ☎ 504/594–6626 or 800/648–2626), both about 20 mi south of Houma, offer fishing trips in the bays and barrier islands of lower Terrebonne Parish as well as into the Gulf of Mexico.

Golf

City Park Golf Course (⊠ Mudd Ave. and Louisiana Ave., Lafayette, ☎ 337/291–5557) and **Vieux Chêne Golf Course** (⊠ Rte. 89, Broussard, ☎ 337/837–1159) have 18-hole courses.

Hiking and Nature Trails

The **Louisiana State Arboretum** (☞ National and State Parks, *above*) in Ville Platte is a 300-acre facility with several miles of nature trails. There are 6 mi of hiking trails in the **Port Hudson State Commemorative Area,** north of Baton Rouge (⊠ 756 W. Plains–Port Hudson Rd. [U.S. 61], Zachary, ☎ 225/654–3775).

Spectator Sports

Home games of the **Ice Gators**, of the East Coast Hockey League, as well as NBA exhibition and collegiate basketball, professional soccer exhibition games, wrestling, and other sports events take place at the **Cajundome** (⊠ 444 Cajundome Blvd., Lafayette, ☎ 337/265–2100). There's Thoroughbred racing April–Labor Day at **Evangeline Downs** (⊠ 3620 N.W. Evangeline Thruway, I–10 at I–49, Carencro, ☎ 337/896–7223).

Shopping

For Cajun spices and ingredients, try the **Cajun Country Store** (⊠ 401 E. Cypress St., Lafayette, ☎ 337/233–7977) and **B. F. Trappey's & Sons** (⊠ 900 E. Main St., New Iberia, ☎ 337/365–8281).

Antiques hunting is a favorite pastime here. In Lafayette, the **Jefferson Street Market** (⊠ 528 Jefferson St., ☎ 337/233–2589) houses many local antiques dealers and craftspeople. You can root fruitfully around **Ruins & Relics** (⊠ 900 Evangeline Dr., off University Ave., ☎ 337/233–9163).

In Washington, **O'Connor's Antique School Mall** (⊠ 210 Church St., ☎ 337/826–3580), closed Sunday, houses more than 100 dealers in a former school and gym.

Cajun artist Rodrigue has gained international attention with his Blue Dog paintings. The house where Tiffany, Rodrigue's canine inspiration, once lived with the artist's family now houses the artist's works and is known as the **Rodrigue** gallery (⊠ 1206 Jefferson St., ☎ 337/232–6398).

What Bayou Trading Company (⊠ 153 W. Landry St., ☎ 337/942–2575) is a wonderful small store in Opelousas packed with neat local crafts and artistry, as well as Cajun CDs, cookbooks, and other souvenirs.

ELSEWHERE IN LOUISIANA

Natchitoches and North-Central Louisiana

Visitor Information

Natchitoches Parish Tourist Commission (⊠ 781 Front St., Box 411, 71457, ☎ 318/352–8072 or 800/259–1714).

Arriving and Departing

I–49 cuts diagonally from southeast to northwest, connecting Lafayette with Natchitoches. Route 1 runs diagonally from the northwest corner all the way to Grand Isle on the Gulf of Mexico.

What to See and Do

Nestled in the piney hills of north-central Louisiana, **Natchitoches** (pronounced *nak*-a-tish) is the oldest permanent European settlement of the Louisiana Purchase, four years older than New Orleans. The town has a quaint 33-block Historic Landmark District, with brick-paved streets and buildings garbed in lacy ironwork. In the center of the downtown area is pretty Cane River Lake, edged with live oak trees and rolling green lawns. Natchitoches appeared in the film version of *Steel Magnolias*. Tours of the town are conducted in miniature trolleys. Popular events include the **Christmas Festival of Lights,** which draws about 150,000 people annually, and the **October Pilgrimage,** when several historic houses are open for tours. Near Natchitoches, backpackers and hikers explore the 8,700-acre **Kisatchie Hills Wilderness** with its Backbone Trail, part of the Kisatchie National Forest (☞ National and State Parks, *above*).

Route 494 follows the Cane River Lake southward from Natchitoches, bordered by arching trees and dotted with handsome plantation houses. Famed primitive artist Clementine Hunter lived and worked at **Melrose Plantation** (⊠ 3533 Rte. 119, Melrose, ☎ 318/379–0055; ☑ $6), where nine quaint buildings can be toured. Twenty miles south of ★ Natchitoches, the **Kate Chopin House** (⊠ 243 Rte. 495, Cloutierville, ☎ 318/379–2233, ☑ $6) was home in the 19th century to Kate Chopin, author of *The Awakening*. It now houses the **Bayou Folk Museum** in addition to some memorabilia and documents of the writer.

Hodges Gardens (⊠ U.S. 171, ☎ 318/586–3523; ☑ $5), west of Natchitoches, has 4,700 acres of rolling pine forests with streams, waterfalls, and multilevel formal botanical gardens, where flowers and shrubs bloom year-round. The huge **Toledo Bend Lake** (☎ 800/259–5253), a camping, boating, and bass-fishing delight, lies along the Texas border.

Dining and Lodging

NATCHITOCHES

$–$$$ ✕ **The Landing.** This popular white-cloth bistro offers pasta, chicken, veal, and seafood dishes; the spicy country-fried steak is a specialty. ⊠ *530 Front St.,* ☎ *318/352–1579. AE, MC, V. Closed Mon.*

$ ✕ **Lasyone's Meat Pie Kitchen.** Natchitoches meat pies are known throughout the state, and this casual little spot does them better than anywhere else. ⊠ *622 2nd St.,* ☎ *318/352–3353. No credit cards. Closed Sun.*

$–$$ ▥ **Fleur-de-lis.** The town's oldest B&B, expanded in 1999, now includes two houses: a 1903 rose-color Victorian and, next door, a 1920s Craftsman-style guest house. Proprietors make guests feel right at home, and a full breakfast is served family style. ⊠ *336 2nd St., 71457,* ☎ *318/352–6621 or 800/489–6621. 8 rooms. AE, MC, V. BP.*

$ ▥ **Ryders Inn.** Comfortable and predictable rooms can be found in this former Holiday Inn. ⊠ *Hwy. 1 South Bypass, 71457,* ☎ *318/357–8281 or 888/252–8281,* FAX *318/352–9907. 145 rooms. Restaurant, lobby lounge, pool. AE, D, DC, MC, V.*

MAINE

By Ed and
Roon Frost

Updated by
Hilary M.
Nangle

Capital	Augusta
Population	1,242,000
Motto	I Lead
State Bird	Chickadee
State Flower	White pinecone and tassel
Postal Abbreviation	ME

Statewide Visitor Information

Maine Office of Tourism (⊠ DECD, 33 Stone St., 59 State House Station, Augusta 04333, ☎ 207/287–5711, FAX 207/287–8070). **Maine Tourism Association** (⊠ 325B Water St., Box 2300, Hallowell 04347, ☎ 207/623–0363; 800/533–9595 outside ME; FAX 207/623–0388). **Maine Innkeepers Association** (⊠ 305 Commercial St., Portland 04101, ☎ 207/773–7670).

Scenic Drives

See Exploring sections, *below,* for recommended coastal routes. For a leisurely inland excursion, try **Routes 37** and **35** from Bridgton north through the Waterfords to Bethel, continuing north on **Route 26** past the Sunday River ski resort to Grafton Notch State Park and into northern New Hampshire.

National and State Parks

National Park

★ **Acadia National Park** (⊠ Box 177, Bar Harbor 04609, ☎ 207/288–3338; 🎫 $10 per car or free, depending on where and when you enter), with fine stretches of shoreline and the highest mountains along the East Coast, offers camping, hiking, biking, and boating.

State Parks

More than two dozen state parks offer outdoor recreation along the coast and in less-traveled interior sections. For information contact the **Bureau of Parks and Lands** (⊠ State House Station 22, Augusta 04333, ☎ 207/287–3821).

THE SOUTHERN COAST

Maine's southern coast has sandy beaches, historic towns, fine restaurants, and factory-outlet malls within an easy day's trip of many points in New England. Maine's largest city, Portland, is small enough to be seen in a day or two. Near Portland are Freeport, a mecca for shoppers, and Boothbay Harbor, the state's boating capital.

Visitor Information

Bath-Brunswick Region: Chamber of Commerce of the Bath-Brunswick Region (⊠ 45 Front St., Bath 04530, ☎ 207/443–9751; ⊠ 59 Pleasant St., Brunswick 04011, ☎ 207/725–8797). **Boothbay Harbor Region:** Chamber of Commerce (⊠ 192 Townsend Ave., Boothbay Harbor 04538, ☎ 207/633–2353 or 800/266–2628). **Freeport:** Merchants Association (⊠ Box 452, 04032, ☎ 207/865–1212 or 800/865–1994). **Kennebunk-Kennebunkport:** Chamber of Commerce (⊠ 17 Western Ave., Kennebunk 04043, ☎ 207/967–0857). **Ogunquit:** Chamber of Commerce (⊠ Box 2289, 03907, ☎ 207/646–2939). **Portland:** Greater

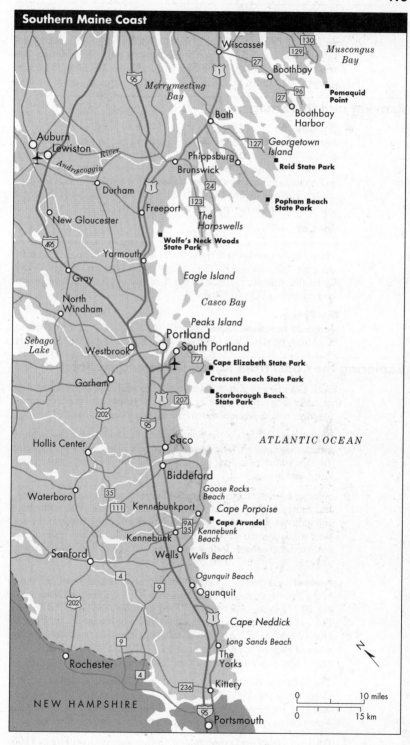

Southern Maine Coast

Wiscasset

Muscongus
Bay

130
129

27

Boothbay

96

27

Pemaquid
Point

Merrymeeting
Bay

Bath

95

Boothbay
Harbor

Auburn
Lewiston

River
Androscoggin

127

Georgetown
Island

Phippsburg

Reid State Park

Brunswick

Durham

1

24

Popham Beach
State Park

123

Freeport

New Gloucester

The
Harpswells

Wolfe's Neck Woods
State Park

495

Yarmouth

Eagle Island

Gray

Casco Bay

North
Windham

Peaks Island

Sebago
Lake

Portland

Westbrook

South Portland

77

Cape Elizabeth State Park

Gorham

Crescent Beach State Park

1

207

Scarborough Beach
State Park

202

95

ATLANTIC OCEAN

Hollis Center

Saco

Biddeford

Waterboro

35

Goose Rocks
Beach

111

Kennebunkport

Cape Porpoise

9A
35

Cape Arundel

Kennebunk
Beach

Kennebunk

Sanford

Wells

Wells Beach

4

9

Ogunquit Beach

202

Ogunquit

1

Cape Neddick

9

Long Sands Beach

Rochester

The
Yorks

4

Kittery

236

N

NEW HAMPSHIRE

0   10 miles

95

0   15 km

Portsmouth

Portland Chamber of Commerce (⊠ 145 Middle St., Portland, ☎ 207/772–2811) and Greater Portland Convention and Visitors Center (⊠ 305 Commercial St., Portland, ☎ 207/772–5800). Additional information is available from the **Maine State Visitor Information Centers** (⊠ Rte. 1 [Exit 17 off I–95], Yarmouth, ☎ 207/846–0833; Rte. 1 and I–95, Kittery, ☎ 207/439–1319).

Arriving and Departing

By Bus
Vermont Transit (☎ 207/772–6587) provides service to Portland and Brunswick on the coast as well as inland to Lewiston, Augusta, Waterville, and Bangor. **Greyhound** (☎ 207/772–6587) provides service to Portland and Bangor. **Concord Trailways** (☎ 800/639–3317) has daily service between Boston and Bangor (via Portland); a coastal route connects towns between Brunswick and Searsport.

By Car
From Boston take U.S. 1 north to I–95, passing through the short New Hampshire seacoast to Kittery, the first town in Maine. I–95 continues past Portland (I–295 gives access to the city) and Freeport (Exit 20 for the outlet stores). Pick up U.S. 1 in Brunswick to reach the coastal communities of Down East.

By Plane
Portland International Airport (⊠ 1001 Westbrook St., ☎ 207/772–0690), 3 mi from Portland, has scheduled daily flights by major U.S. carriers.

Exploring the Coast from Kittery to Pemaquid Point

York County, and Kittery in particular, is probably better known for its outlet shopping than for its beaches. But those who crave the scenic coastline will appreciate the maritime scenery of Routes 103 and 1A.

Route 1A passes through fashionable York Harbor and the chockablock summer cottages of **York Beach. Ogunquit,** a few miles north of the Yorks, is famed for its long white-sand beach and galleries, shops, restaurants, and homes.

★ Summer tourists flock to **Kennebunkport** to soak up salt air, seafood, and sunshine. Dock Square is the busy town center, lined with shops and galleries. **Ocean Avenue** follows the Kennebunk River to the sea, then winds around Cape Arundel. Trolley rides are the order of the ☙ day at the **Seashore Trolley Museum** (⊠ Log Cabin Rd., Kennebunkport, ☎ 207/967–2800; ☞ $7).

Portland is a thriving seaport whose restaurants, coffeehouses, and shops evoke a romantic mood. On Congress Square, the **Portland Museum of Art** (⊠ 7 Congress Sq., ☎ 207/775–6148 or 207/773–2787; ☞ $6; free Fri. evenings 5–9), which is closed on Monday, has works by Winslow ☙ Homer, John Marin, Andrew Wyeth, and others. At the **Children's Museum of Maine** (⊠ 142 Free St., ☎ 207/828–1234; ☞ $5), little ones can pretend they are lobster catchers, shopkeepers, or computer experts.

The Italianate-style Morse-Libby Mansion **Victoria Mansion** (⊠ 109 Danforth St., ☎ 207/772–4841; ☞ $6; closed Mon. and Nov.–Apr.) was built between 1858 and 1860 and is widely regarded as the most sumptuously ornate dwelling of its period remaining in the country.

★ Portland's **Old Port Exchange,** built following the Great Fire of 1866, was revitalized in the 1960s by artists and craftspeople. Now it is the city's shopping and dining hub. Allow a couple of hours to stroll on

Market, Exchange, Middle, and Fore streets. On a sunny day, while away the hours aboard a ferry on **Casco Bay.**

Freeport, 17 mi north of Portland, is the home of L. L. Bean, which attracts 3½ million shoppers a year. Nearby, more than 100 other outlets have sprouted (☞ Shopping, *below*).

Bath is farther up the coast. The **Maine Maritime Museum and Shipyard** (⊠ 243 Washington St., ☎ 207/443–1316; ☞ $8.50) has a collection to stir many a nautical dream. You can watch boatbuilders wield their tools on classic Maine vessels at the restored shipyard.

Wiscasset bills itself as "Maine's prettiest village" and lives up to it with historic homes, antiques shops, and museums overlooking the Sheepscot River.

Boothbay Harbor swells in summer with visitors and seasonal residents.
★ Wander the shops and waterfront or ride an excursion boat to **Monhegan Island.** At **Pemaquid Point** be sure your camera stand is at the ready for a shot of a much-photographed lighthouse. At **Colonial Pemaquid Restoration,** view the excavations that have turned up thousands of artifacts of a 17th-century English settlement and of earlier Native American life. ⊠ *Rte. 130,* ☎ *207/677–2423.* ☞ *$2. Closed Labor Day–Memorial Day.*

Dining and Lodging

For most visitors Maine means lobster, and this delectable crustacean is served at most Maine restaurants. Aficionados prefer to eat them "in the rough" at classic lobster pounds, where you choose your lobster from a pool and enjoy it at a picnic table. B&Bs and Victorian inns have joined the family-oriented motels in the coastal towns.

Bath

$$–$$$$ ✕ **Robinhood Free Meetinghouse.** Multiethnic cuisine is served in an
★ 1855 Greek Revival meetinghouse. Begin with the artichoke strudel, move on to a classic veal saltimbocca or a confit of duck, and finish up with Obsession in Three Chocolates. ⊠ *Robinhood Rd., Georgetown,* ☎ *207/371–2188. D, MC, V. Call ahead in winter.*

$–$$ ✕ **Kristina's Restaurant & Bakery.** This frame house turned restaurant bakes some of the finest pies, pastries, and cakes on the coast. Satisfying dinners are mainly new American cuisine. ⊠ *160 Centre St.,* ☎ *207/ 442–8577. D, MC, V. Closed Jan. No dinner Sun. Call ahead in winter.*

$$–$$$ 🏨 **The Inn at Bath.** In Bath's Historic District, this handsome 1810 Greek Revival inn is a convenient and comfortable base for exploring Bath on foot. It is filled with antiques, and five guest rooms have wood-burning fireplaces; two also have two-person whirlpool tubs. ⊠ *969 Washington St., 04530,* ☎ *207/443–4294,* 🆔 *207/443–4295. 9 rooms. AE, D, MC, V. BP.* 🐾

Boothbay Harbor

$–$$$ ✕ **Christopher's Boathouse.** You can't beat the view over the harbor or the food at this renovated boathouse, where you can watch the chefs prepare your dinner. Begin with the award-winning lobster and mango bisque with hot and spicy lobster wontons, then move on to the lobster succotash or Asian-spiced tuna steak with Caribbean salsa, and finish off with the raspberry almond flan. ⊠ *25 Union St.,* ☎ *207/633– 6565,* 🆔 *207/633–6178. MC, V. Call ahead mid-Oct.–mid-May.*

$ ✕ **Lobstermen's Co-op.** Lobster lovers and landlubbers alike will find something at this dockside lobster pound. Eat indoors or outside while watching the lobstermen at work. ⊠ *Atlantic Ave.,* ☎ *207/633–4900. Closed mid-Oct.–mid-May.*

$–$$ 🏨 **Admiral's Quarters Inn.** This renovated 1830 sea captain's house is ideally situated for exploring Boothbay Harbor by foot, a good thing since in-town parking is limited and expensive. ⊠ *71 Commercial St., 04538,* ☎ *207/633–2474,* 🖷 *207/633–5904. 6 rooms. D, MC, V. Closed mid-Dec.–mid-Feb. BP.*

Brunswick

$–$$ ✕ **Great Impasta.** At this storefront restaurant, try the seafood lasagna or match your favorite pasta and sauce. ⊠ *42 Maine St.,* ☎ *207/729–5858. Reservations not accepted. D, DC, MC, V.*

$$–$$$$ 🏨 **Harpswell Inn.** Spacious lawns and neatly pruned shrubs surround this stately white-clapboard, dormered inn. Half the rooms have water views. ⊠ *108 Lookout Point Rd., Harpswell 04079,* ☎ *207/833–5509 or 800/843–5509. 12 rooms. No smoking. MC, V. BP.* 🐾

Freeport

$ ✕ **Harraseeket Lunch & Lobster Co.** At this bare-bones lobster pound beside the town landing, fried-seafood baskets and lobster dinners, eaten in the dining room or at picnic tables, are what it's all about. ⊠ *Main St., South Freeport,* ☎ *207/865–4888. Reservations not accepted. No credit cards. Closed mid-Oct.–Apr.*

$$$–$$$$ ✕🏨 **Harraseeket Inn.** Despite modern appointments such as elevators and whirlpool baths, this 1850 Greek Revival home retains an old-fashioned country-inn feel. The formal Maine Dining Room ($$$–$$$$) specializes in contemporary American regional cuisine. The casual Broad Arrow Tavern ($$–$$$), with an open kitchen and a wood-fired oven and grill, serves heartier fare. ⊠ *162 Main St., 04032,* ☎ *207/ 865–9377 or 800/342–6423,* 🖷 *207/865–1684. 84 rooms. 2 restaurants, indoor pool. AE, D, DC, MC, V. BP.* 🐾

Kennebunkport

$$$$ ✕🏨 **Cape Arundel Inn.** This shingle-style inn commands a magnificent ocean view that takes in the Bush estate at Walker Point. The spacious rooms are furnished with country-style furniture and antiques, and most have sitting areas with ocean views. In the candlelighted dining room ($$$–$$$$), every table has a view of the surf. ⊠ *108 Ocean Ave., 04046,* ☎ *207/967–2125,* 🖷 *207/967–1199. 14 rooms. Restaurant. AE, D, MC, V. Closed Jan.–early May. BP.* 🐾

$$$$ ✕🏨 **White Barn Inn.** Known for its attentive service, this 19th-century
★   inn has meticulously appointed rooms decorated with hand-painted pieces and period furniture; some have fireplaces and whirlpool baths. The rustic but elegant dining room ($$$$; jacket required for dinner) serves updated New England cuisine. ⊠ *Box 560C, 37 Beach St., 04046,* ☎ *207/967–2321,* 🖷 *207/967–1100. 25 rooms. Restaurant, pool. AE, MC, V. CP.* 🐾

$$$–$$$$ 🏨 **Captain Lord Mansion.** This sumptuously appointed 1812 Federal-style mansion—with a suspended elliptical staircase, a widow's walk, gas fireplaces in 15 rooms, and near–museum quality decor—has a formal but not stuffy atmosphere. ⊠ *Box 800, Pleasant and Green Sts., 04046,* ☎ *207/967–3141. 16 rooms. D, MC, V. BP.*

Newcastle

$$–$$$$ ✕🏨 **Newcastle Inn.** This classic country inn overlooks the Damariscotta River. Guests spread out in the cozy pub, comfortable living room, and spacious sunporch overlooking the river; some rooms have fireplaces and whirlpools. In the dining room, the four-course, fixed-price menu ($39.50, reservations essential) emphasizes Maine seafood. ⊠ *60 River Rd., 04553,* ☎ *207/563–5685 or 800/832–8669,* 🖷 *207/563–6877. 16 rooms. 2 dining rooms. AE, MC, V. Dining room closed Mon. in summer, Mon.–Wed. in winter. BP.* 🐾

Ogunquit

$$–$$$$ ✕ **Hurricane.** Don't let the weather-beaten exterior deter you—this com-
★ fortable bar-and-grill offers first-rate cooking and spectacular views
of the crashing surf. ✉ *Perkins Cove,* ☎ *207/646–6348. AE, D, DC,
MC, V. Closed late Dec.–mid-Jan.*

Portland

$$$–$$$$ ✕ **Gabriel's.** Hand-painted murals on the walls let diners view the sea
as they savor appetizers like Great Hill Blue Cheese Tart with caramelized
walnuts and onion confit and entrées like whole French turbot with
roasted vegetables. The adventurous can choose the five-course Chef's
Dinner ($65). ✉ *47 Middle St.,* ☎ *207/775–1510. AE, D, DC, MC,
V. Closed Mon. No lunch.*

$$–$$$ ✕ **Fore Street.** Two of Maine's best chefs opened this restaurant in an
★ old warehouse. Every table in the main dining room has a view of the
huge brick oven and hearth and the open kitchen, where entrées such
as apple-wood-grilled Atlantic swordfish and roasted lobster are pre-
pared. Reservations are recommended. ✉ *288 Fore St.,* ☎ *207/775–
2717. AE, MC, V. No lunch.*

$$–$$$ ✕ **Street and Co.** At what may be the best seafood restaurant in Maine,
★ you enter through the kitchen, with all its wonderful aromas, and dine
at a copper-topped table amid dried herbs and shelves of grocery sta-
ples. ✉ *33 Wharf St.,* ☎ *207/775–0887. AE, MC, V. No lunch.*

$$$$ ✕🏠 **Inn by the Sea.** On Greater Portland's most prime real estate, this
all-suites inn is set back from the shoreline and has views of the ocean.
The architecture is typical New England; the dining room ($$–$$$$),
open to nonguests, serves seafood and other regional cuisine. ✉ *40 Bow-
ery Beach Rd., Cape Elizabeth (7 mi south of Portland) 04107,* ☎ *207/
799–3134 or 800/888–4287,* ℻ *207/799–4779. 43 suites. Restaurant, pool, tennis. AE, D, MC, V.* ✍

$$$–$$$$ 🏠 **Portland Regency Hotel.** The only major hotel in the center of the
Old Port Exchange, the Regency building was Portland's armory in the
late 19th century. Rooms have tall standing mirrors, floral curtains,
and love seats; many have four-poster beds. ✉ *20 Milk St., 04101,* ☎
207/774–4200 or 800/727–3436, ℻ *207/775–2150. 95 rooms. Restau-
rant, nightclub, meeting rooms, health club. AE, D, DC, MC, V.* ✍

$$$ 🏠 **Inn on Carleton.** This elegant brick town house on the city's West-
ern Promenade is a quiet retreat furnished with antiques and decorated
with artwork by contemporary Maine artists. The entryway features
a restored faux painting by Charles Schumacher. ✉ *46 Carleton St.,
04102,* ☎ *207/775–1910, or 207/761–0956, or 800/639–1779,* ℻ *207/
761–1779. 6 rooms. D, MC, V. BP.* ✍

$$$ 🏠 **Pomegranate Inn.** The classic architecture of this handsome inn gives
no hint to the surprises that await within. Hand-painted walls, floors,
and woodwork combine with contemporary artwork to create a vivid
ambience that is somehow both challenging and comforting. Rooms
are individually decorated, but all have telephones and TVs, and five
have fireplaces. ✉ *49 Neal St., 04102,* ☎ *207/772–1006 or 800/356–
0408,* ℻ *207/773–4426. 8 rooms. MC, V. BP.* ✍

Scarborough

$$$$ 🏠 **Black Point Inn.** At the tip of a peninsula 12 mi south of Portland
stands a tastefully updated old-time resort with views up and down
the coast. On the grounds are beaches, a bird sanctuary, hiking trails,
and sports facilities, including boats and bicycles. The dining room menu
is strong in seafood. Rates include breakfast, afternoon tea, and din-
ner (jacket required). ✉ *510 Black Point Rd., 04074,* ☎ *207/883–4126
or 800/258–2500,* ℻ *207/883–9976. 80 rooms. Restaurant, 2 pools,
golf, tennis court. AE, D, MC, V. MAP.* ✍

The Yorks

$$–$$$$
★

✕⊡ **York Harbor Inn.** A mid-17th-century fishing cabin with dark timbers and a fieldstone fireplace forms the heart of this inn, to which various wings and outbuildings have been added. Rooms are furnished with antiques and country pieces; many have decks overlooking the water, and a few have whirlpool tubs or fireplaces. The dining room has country charm and great ocean views. Try the lobster-stuffed chicken breast. ⊠ *Box 573, Rte. 1A, York Harbor 03911,* ☎ *207/363–5119 or 800/343–3869,* ᶠᴬˣ *207/363–7151. 40 rooms. AE, DC, MC, V. No lunch off-season (usually between Columbus Day and Memorial Day). CP.* ❧

Nightlife and the Arts

Nightlife

Asylum (⊠ 121 Center St., Portland, ☎ 207/772–8274) has live entertainment and dancing. For blues, head to the **Big Easy** (⊠ 55 Market St., ☎ 207/871–8817). **Stone Coast Brewery** (⊠ 14 York St., Portland, ☎ 207/773–2337) is a brewpub with entertainment. **Wine Bar** (⊠ 38 Wharf St., Portland, ☎ 207/772–6976) is a wine and espresso bar with a light menu and desserts.

The Arts

Bowdoin Summer Music Festival (⊠ Bowdoin College, Brunswick, ☎ 207/725–3322 for information; 207/725–3895 for tickets) is a six-week concert series featuring performances by students, faculty, and prestigious guest artists. **Cumberland County Civic Center** (⊠ 1 Civic Center Sq., Portland, ☎ 207/775–3458) is a 9,000-seat auditorium that hosts concerts, family shows, and sporting events. **Maine State Music Theater** (⊠ Pickard Theater, Bowdoin College, Brunswick, ☎ 207/725–8769) stages musicals from mid-June through August. **Ogunquit Playhouse** (⊠ Rte. 1, Ogunquit, ☎ 207/646–5511) mounts plays and musicals from late June to Labor Day. **Portland Performing Arts Center** (⊠ 25A Forest Ave., Portland, ☎ 207/744–0465) hosts music, dance, and theater. **Portland City Hall's Merrill Auditorium** (⊠ 20 Myrtle St., Portland, ☎ 207/874–8200) is home to the Portland Symphony Orchestra and Portland Concert Association and the site of numerous theatrical and musical events.

Outdoor Activities and Sports

Boat Trips

From Perkins Cove in Ogunquit, **Finestkind** (☎ 207/646–5227) runs boats to Nubble Light and schedules lobstering trips. In Portland, for tours of the harbor, Casco Bay, and the islands, try **Bay View Cruises** (☎ 207/761–0496), **Casco Bay Lines** (☎ 207/774–7871), or **Old Port Mariner Fleet** (☎ 207/775–0727). In Boothbay Harbor, *Balmy Days II* (☎ 207/633–2284 or 800/298–2284) makes day trips to Monhegan Island, and **Cap'n Fish's Boat Trips** (☎ 207/633–3244 or 800/636–3244) offers sightseeing cruises throughout the region. From New Harbor, **Hardy Boat Cruises** (☎ 207/677–2026 or 800/278–3346) offers lighthouse and seal cruises and sails daily to Monhegan Island.

Canoeing

The **Maine Audubon Society** (☎ 207/781–2330; 207/883–4100 mid-June–Labor Day) leads daily guided canoe trips in Scarborough Marsh (on Route 9 in Scarborough), the largest salt marsh in Maine.

Deep-Sea Fishing

Venture Inn Charters (⊠ Performance Marine, near the Rte. 9 bridge, ☎ 207/967–0005 or 800/853–5002) operates full- and half-day deep-sea fishing trips.

Beaches

Goose Rocks, north of Kennebunkport, is the largest area beach and a favorite of families with small children; the Kennebunkport Town Office (✉ Elm St., ☎ 207/967–4244) sells parking permits. **Kennebunk Beach** is actually three beaches, with cottages and Victorian boardinghouses nearby; for parking permits go to the Kennebunk Town Office (✉ 1 Summer St., ☎ 207/985–2102). **Ogunquit Beach,** a fine stretch at the mouth of the river, is protected from the surf. Families gravitate to the ends, while gay visitors camp at the beach's middle. **Old Orchard Beach,** with an amusement park reminiscent of Coney Island, is only a few miles north of Biddeford on Route 9. At the end of Route 209 south of Bath, **Popham Beach State Park** (Phippsburg, ☎ 207/389–1335) has a good sand beach and picnic tables. **Reid State Park** (☎ 207/371–2303), on Georgetown Island off Route 127, has three beaches, bathhouses, picnic tables, and a snack bar.

Shopping

More than 100 **factory outlets** along U.S. 1 around Kittery sell clothing, shoes, glassware, and other products from top manufacturers and specialty companies. The big names of designer outlets are in **Freeport,** from Coach and Polo Ralph Lauren to Hartmann and Dansk. Across from **L. L. Bean**'s main store (✉ Rte. 1, ☎ 800/341–4341), an L. L. Bean factory outlet has seconds and discontinued merchandise at discount prices. The *Freeport Visitors Guide* (☎ 207/865–1212; 800/865–1994 for a copy) lists the more than 100 shops and factory outlet stores that can be found on Main Street, Bow Street, and elsewhere. **Portland** also has shopping. In the **Old Port Exchange** the better shops are concentrated along Fore and Exchange streets. **L. L. Bean** has a store on Congress Street. The **Portland Public Market** (✉ 25 Preble St., ☎ 207/228–2000) has more than 20 locally owned businesses specializing in fresh foods, organic produce, and imported specialty foods.

Antiques shops line the main and side streets of **Wiscasset** and overflow across the bridge into Edgecomb. Just south of town on Route 1 in Woolwich is the **Montsweag Flea Market,** a trash-and-treasure trove open Wednesday and Friday–Sunday.

PENOBSCOT BAY AND ACADIA

Purists hold that the Maine coast begins at Penobscot Bay, where water vistas are wider and bluer, with the shore a jumble of broken granite boulders, cobblestones, and gravel. East of Penobscot Bay, Acadia is the informal name for Mount Desert (pronounced *dessert*) Island and environs. Mount Desert, Maine's largest island, encompasses most of Acadia National Park, the state's principal tourist attraction. Camden, on Penobscot Bay, and Bar Harbor, on Mount Desert, offer accommodations and restaurants.

Visitor Information

Acadia National Park (✉ Box 177, Bar Harbor 04609, ☎ 207/288–3338). **Bar Harbor:** Chamber of Commerce (✉ 93 Cottage St., Box 158, 04609, ☎ 207/288–3393, 207/288–5103, or 800/288–5103). **Rockland–Thomaston Area:** Chamber of Commerce (✉ Harbor Park, Box 508, Rockland 04841, ☎ 207/596–0376 or 800/562–2529). **Rockport, Camden, and Lincolnville:** Chamber of Commerce (✉ Public Landing, Box 919, Camden 04843, ☎ 207/236–4404 or 800/223–5459). **Southwest Harbor/Tremont:** Chamber of Commerce (✉ Box 1143, Main St., Southwest Harbor 04679, ☎ 207/244–9264 or 800/423–9264).

Arriving and Departing

By Car

U.S. 1 follows the west coast of Penobscot Bay, linking Rockland, Camden, and Ellsworth. From Ellsworth, Route 3 will take you onto Mount Desert Island.

By Plane

Bangor International Airport (⊠ 287 Godfrey Blvd., ☎ 207/947–0384), 30 mi north of Penobscot Bay, is served by Business Express, Delta Airlines/Comair, Finnair, and US Airways. **Knox County Regional Airport** (⊠ Ash Point Dr., Owls Head, ☎ 207/594–4131), 3 mi south of Rockland, is served by Colgan Air/Continental Connection. **Hancock County Airport** (⊠ Rte. 3., Trenton, ☎ 207/667–7329), 8 mi northwest of Bar Harbor, is served by Colgan Air/Continental Connection.

Exploring Penobscot Bay and Acadia

Tenants Harbor is a quintessential Maine fishing town. Port Clyde, south of Tenants Harbor, is the point of departure for the mail boat that serves tiny, remote **Monhegan Island.** Known to Basque, Portuguese, and Breton fishermen well before Columbus "discovered" America, it was discovered again by some of America's finest painters, including Rockwell Kent, Robert Henri, and Edward Hopper, who sailed out to paint its meadows, cliffs, wild ocean views, and fishermen's shacks. Tourists followed, and Monhegan is now overrun with visitors in summer. Nevertheless, the island's 17 mi of hiking trails offer places to escape as well as mesmerizing views of pounding surf and cathedral pines.

Rockland, home of the Seafood Festival (a.k.a. the Lobster Festival), ranks as the coast's commercial hub, with fishing boats moored alongside a growing flotilla of windjammers. Day trips to Vinalhaven and North Haven islands depart from the harbor, the outer portion of which is bisected by a nearly mile-long granite breakwater. Art galleries line the main

★ and side streets around the **Farnsworth Art Museum,** which specializes in American art, with a focus on Maine-related works. The **Wyeth Center** is devoted to Maine-related works of Andrew Wyeth and other members of the Wyeth family. The new **Jamien Morehouse Wing** displays new works by living Maine artists as well as pieces from the museum's permanent collection. The museum also operates the **Olson House** in Cushing, which was depicted in Andrew Wyeth's famous painting *Christina's World.* ⊠ *356 Main St.,* ☎ *207/596–6457.* ☞ *$9. Closed Mon. Oct.–May.*

☾ The **Shore Village Museum** displays many lighthouse and Coast Guard artifacts and has exhibits of maritime and Civil War memorabilia. ⊠ *104 Limerock St.,* ☎ *207/594–0311.* ☞ *Donation suggested. Mid-Oct.– May by appointment only.*

☾ **Owls Head Transportation Museum** has antique aircraft, cars, and engines and stages air shows every other weekend May–October. ⊠ *Rte. 73, Owls Head (2 mi south of Rockland),* ☎ *207/594–4418.* ☞ *$6.*

★ In **Camden,** mountains tower over the harbor, and the fashionable waterfront is home to a large windjammer fleet; such cruises are a superb way to explore the ports and islands of Penobscot Bay. The 5,500-acre **Camden Hills State Park** (☎ *207/236–3109*), 2 mi north of Camden on U.S. 1, contains 20 mi of trails. Hike or take the toll road up Mt. Battie for a magnificent view over the bay.

☾ **Kelmscott Farm** is a rare-breed animal farm with a nature trail, children's activities, heirloom gardens, and frequent special events. ⊠ *Rte. 52, Lincolnville,* ☎ *207/763–4088.* ☞ *$5. Closed Mon.*

Searsport claims to be the antiques capital of Maine, with shops and a seasonal weekend flea market. Historic **Castine,** over which French, British, Dutch, and Americans fought, has two museums and the ruins of a British fort. But the finest thing about Castine is the town itself: the lively, welcoming town landing; the serene Federal and Greek Revival houses; and the town common.

Ellsworth has an array of outlets including an L. L. Bean store. It's also the gateway to Bar Harbor and Acadia; it's where you pick up Route 3 to Mount Desert Island. Although most of **Bar Harbor**'s grand mansions were destroyed in a 1947 fire, this busy resort town on Frenchman Bay has retained its beauty. Shops, restaurants, and hotels are clustered along Main, Mount Desert, and Cottage streets. To escape the crowds, head to quiet **Southwest Harbor** or elite **Northeast Harbor.**

★ The Hulls Cove approach to **Acadia National Park** (☞ National and State Parks, *above,* and Hiking, *below*) is northwest of Bar Harbor on Route 3. Though often clogged with traffic, the 27-mi Park Loop Road provides the best introduction to the park. The visitor center shows a free 15-minute film and has trail maps. The Ocean Trail is an easily accessible walk with some of Maine's most spectacular scenery. For a mountaintop experience without the hike, drive to the summit of **Cadillac Mountain,** the highest point on the eastern coast. The view from the bald summit is spectacular, especially at sunset. The **Abbe Museum** (✉ Sieur de Mont Spring exit from Rte. 3 or Acadia National Park Loop Rd., ☎ 207/288–3519; ✆ $2; closed mid-Oct.–mid-May) is in a National Historic Register building that survived the 1947 fire. Within its octagonal walls is a treasure trove of Maine Native American artifacts, including arrowheads, moccasins, tools, jewelry, and a well-documented collection of baskets.

Dining and Lodging

Bar Harbor

$$$ ✗ **George's.** Candles, flowers, and linens grace the tables and art fills
★ the walls of the four small dining rooms in this old house. The menu's Mediterranean influences can be tasted in the phyllo-wrapped lobster; the lamb and wild-game entrées are superb. Jazz musicians perform nightly in peak season. ✉ 7 Stephen's La., ☎ 207/288–4505. AE, D, DC, MC, V. Closed Nov.–mid-June. No lunch.

$$–$$$ ✗ **Café This Way.** Jazz music, unmatched tables and chairs, and a few couches provide a relaxing background for the creative, internationally inspired menu at this restaurant tucked down a back street in Bar Harbor. Reservations are recommended. ✉ 14½ Desert St., ☎ 207/ 288–4483. MC, V.

$$$–$$$$ ✗▥ **Bar Harbor Inn.** The roots of this genteel inn date from the 1880s. Rooms are spread out over three buildings on nicely landscaped waterfront property, just a short walk to town. Most rooms have balconies, hot tubs, fireplaces, and great views. The formal waterfront Reading Room serves mostly Continental fare but has some Maine specialties. ✉ Newport Dr., 04609, ☎ 207/288–3351 or 800/248–3351, ℻ 207/ 288–5296. 153 rooms. 2 restaurants, pool, exercise room, business services. AE, D, DC, MC, V. CP. ✿

$$$–$$$$ ▥ **Ullikana.** Inside the stucco and timber walls of this traditional
★ Tudor cottage is a riotous decor that juxtaposes traditional antiques with contemporary country pieces, vibrant color with French country wallpapers, and abstract art with folk art. Rooms are large, most have at least a glimpse of the water, many have fireplaces, and some have decks. Across the drive, the owners have refurbished and opened the Yellow House, with an additional six rooms decorated in Old Bar Har-

bor style. ⊠ *16 The Field, 04609,* ☎ *207/288–9552,* FAX *207/288–3682. 16 rooms. MC, V. Closed Nov.–May. BP.* ⊛

$$$ ⚍ **Inn at Canoe Point.** Seclusion and privacy are the main attributes
★ of this snug, 100-year-old Tudor-style house on the water at Hulls Cove, 2 mi from Bar Harbor and ¼ mi from Acadia National Park's Hulls Cove Visitor Center. The large living room has huge windows that look out on the water, a granite fireplace, and a waterfront deck where breakfast is served in summer. ⊠ *Box 216, Rte. 3, 04609,* ☎ *207/288–9511,* FAX *207/288–2870. 5 rooms. D, MC, V. BP.*

Camden

$$–$$$ ✕ **Waterfront Restaurant.** Come for a ringside seat on Camden Harbor; the best view is from the outdoor deck, open in warm weather. The fare is primarily seafood. ⊠ *Bay View St.,* ☎ *207/236–3747. Reservations not accepted. MC, V.*

$$$ ✕⚍ **Whitehall Inn.** Camden's best-known inn, a white-clapboard ship captain's home with a wide porch, was built in 1843. Rooms are small and sparsely furnished, with dark-wood bedsteads and claw-foot bathtubs; some have ocean views. The dining room, open to nonguests for dinner and breakfast, serves traditional and creative American cuisine. ⊠ *52 High St., Box 558, 04843,* ☎ *207/236–3391 or 800/789–6565,* FAX *207/236–4427. 44 rooms. Restaurant, tennis. AE, MC, V. Closed mid-Oct.–mid-May. MAP, BP.* ⊛

$$–$$$ ✕⚍ **Youngtown Inn.** Inside this white Federal farmhouse are a French-inspired country retreat and a well-respected French restaurant ($$$). The country location guarantees quiet, and the inn is a short walk to the Fernald Neck Preserve on Lake Megunticook. ⊠ *Rte. 52 at Youngtown Rd., Lincolnville 04849,* ☎ *207/763–4290 or 800/291–8438,* FAX *207/763–4078. 6 rooms, 1 suite. AE, MC, V. BP.* ⊛

$$$$ ⚍ **Inn at Oceans Edge.** This shingle-style inn perched on the ocean's
★ edge looks as if it has been here for decades. In actuality, it's a new structure in which each room has an ocean view as well as a king-size bed, fireplace, and whirlpool for two. TV, VCR, and individually controlled heat and air-conditioning are standard. The Lincolnville setting is private, yet minutes from Camden. ⊠ *U.S. 1, Lincolnville (Box 704, Camden 04843),* ☎ *207/236–0945,* FAX *207/236–0609. 15 rooms. Exercise room. AE, MC, V. BP.* ⊛

Castine

$$–$$$ ✕⚍ **Castine Inn.** Upholstered easy chairs and fine prints and paintings are typical appointments in this inn's light, airy guest rooms. The third floor has the best views: overlooking the gardens and the harbor on one side, the village on the other. The creative menu in the dining room ($$–$$$$) makes use of local ingredients. The inn also has a pub. ⊠ *Main St. (Box 41), 04421,* ☎ *207/326–4365,* FAX *207/326–4570. 19 rooms. Restaurant. MC, V. Restaurant hrs limited mid-Oct.–mid-Dec. Inn closed mid-Dec.–Apr. BP.* ⊛

Hancock

$$$ ✕⚍ **Le Domaine.** Owner-chef Nicole L. Purslow whips up classic haute cuisine. Le Domaine is known primarily for its food ($$$), but its French-country-style guest rooms are also inviting. Ask for a room in the rear, overlooking the lawns and gardens and away from the noise of Route 1. ⊠ *HC77, Box 496, Rte. 1, 04640,* ☎ *207/422–3395 or 800/554–8495,* FAX *207/422–2316. 7 rooms. Restaurant. AE, D, MC, V. Closed late Oct.–mid-May. MAP; BP available.* ⊛

Monhegan

$$–$$$$ ⚍ **Island Inn.** This three-story inn, which dates from 1807, has a commanding presence on Monhegan's harbor. The waterside rooms, though mostly small, are the nicest, with sunset views over the harbor and stark

Manana Island. ✉ *Box 128, Monhegan Island 04852,* ☎ *207/596–0371,* FAX *207/594–5517. 34 rooms. Restaurant. MC, V. Closed Columbus Day–Memorial Day. BP.* ✧

Rockland

$–$$$ ✕ **Amalfi.** Delicious Mediterranean cuisine, a well-chosen and af-
★ fordable wine list, and excellent service made this Mediterranean bistro in a Main Street storefront an immediate hit. The Amalfi fish stew and the lobster risotto are especially good. ✉ *421 Main St.,* ☎ *207/596–0012. D, MC, V. Closed Sun.*

$$ ✕ **Café Miranda.** Expect to wait for a table at this cozy bistro, where the daily-changing menu reflects fresh, seasonal ingredients and the chef's creative renditions of both new American and traditional home-style foods. ✉ *15 Oak St.,* ☎ *207/594–2034. MC, V. Closed Sun. and Mon. No lunch.*

$$$–$$$$ ⌂ **Samoset Resort.** On the Rockland-Rockport town line next to the breakwater, this sprawling oceanside resort has excellent facilities, including indoor and outdoor pools, racquetball, and children's programs. Ask about special packages. ✉ *220 Warrenton St., Rockport 04856,* ☎ *207/594–2511; 800/341–1650 outside ME;* FAX *207/594–0722. 178 rooms. Restaurant, 2 pools, golf, tennis, exercise room. AE, D, DC, MC, V.* ✧

$$–$$$ ⌂ **Limerock Inn.** You can walk to the Farnsworth museum from this
★ magnificent Queen Anne–style Victorian on a quiet residential street. The rooms are meticulously decorated; some have fireplaces and whirlpool tubs. ✉ *96 Limerock St., 04841,* ☎ *207/594–2257 or 800/546–3762,* FAX *207/594–1846. 8 rooms. MC, V. BP.* ✧

Southwest Harbor

$–$$$$ ✕ **Beal's Lobster Pier.** You can watch lobstermen bringing in their catch at this working lobster pound. Order lobster at one take-out window, fried foods, burgers, and dessert at another. ✉ *End of Clark Point Rd.,* ☎ *207/244–3202, 207/244–7178, or 800/245–7178. Closed mid-Oct.–mid-May.*

$$ ⌂ **Island House.** This sweet B&B on the island's quiet side has simply decorated bedrooms in the main house and a carriage house suite, complete with sleeping loft and kitchenette. ✉ *Box 1006, 04679,* ☎ *207/244–5180. 5 rooms. MC, V. BP.* ✧

Tenants Harbor

$$–$$$ ✕⌂ **East Wind Inn & Meeting House.** On a knob of land overlooking the harbor and the islands, the East Wind offers unadorned but comfortable guest rooms (nine with bath), suites, and efficiencies in three buildings. The restaurant, which welcomes nonguests, serves breakfast, dinner, and Sunday brunch. ✉ *Mechanic St. (Rte. 131), 10 mi off Rte. 1 (Box 149, 04860),* ☎ *207/372–6366 or 800/241–8439,* FAX *207/372–6320. 26 rooms, 4 apartments. 2 restaurants. AE, D, MC, V. Closed Dec.–Apr. No lunch.* ✧

Campgrounds

The two campgrounds in Acadia National Park—⌂ **Blackwoods** (☎ 800/365–2267) and ⌂ **Seawall** (☎ 207/244–3600)—fill up quickly in summer. Nearby ⌂ **Lamoine State Park** (☎ 207/667–4778) has a great location on Frenchman Bay.

The Arts

Bay Chamber Concerts (✉ Rockport Opera House, 6 Central St., Rockport, ☎ 207/236–2823) presents chamber music on Thursday and Friday nights during July and August; concerts are given once a month from September through June. **Arcady Music Festival** (☎ 207/288–3151) schedules concerts (primarily classical) at locations around Mount

Desert Island and at some off-island sites, year-round. **Bar Harbor Music Festival** (⊠ 59 Cottage St., ☎ 207/288–5744) has concerts from early July to early August.

Outdoor Activities and Sports

Biking

The carriage paths that wind through **Acadia National Park** are ideal for biking; pick up a map from the Hulls Cove visitor center. Bikes can be rented in Bar Harbor from **Acadia Bike & Canoe** (⊠ 48 Cottage St., ☎ 207/288–9605 or 800/526–8615) and **Bar Harbor Bicycle Shop** (⊠ 141 Cottage St., ☎ 207/288–3886 or 800/824–2453).

Boat Trips

Port Clyde is the point of departure for the *Laura B.* (☎ 207/372–8848 for schedules), the mail boat that serves Monhegan Island. From Bar Harbor, the *Acadian Whale Watcher* (☎ 207/288–9794 or 800/421–3307) runs whale-watching cruises. **Whale Watcher Inc.** (⊠ 1 West St., ☎ 207/288–3322 or 800/508–1499) operates the windjammer *Bay Lady,* the nature-sightseeing cruise vessel *Acadian,* and the 300-passenger *Atlantis* in summer.

The four-masted schooner *Margaret Todd* (⊠ Bar Harbor Inn Pier, ☎ 207/288–4585) offers 1½- to 2-hour tours daily between mid-May and October. Camden and Rockland are the East Coast **windjammer** headquarters. For information contact **Maine Windjammer Association** (⊠ Box 1144, Blue Hill 04614, ☎ 800/807–9463). In Southwest Harbor, **Manset Yacht Service** (⊠ Shore Rd., Manset, ☎ 207/244–4040) rents powerboats and sailboats.

For guided kayak tours, try **National Park Sea Kayak Tours** (⊠ 39 Cottage St., Bar Harbor, ☎ 207/288–0342 or 800/347–0940) or **Coastal Kayaking Tours** (⊠ 48 Cottage St., Bar Harbor, ☎ 207/288–9605 or 800/526–8615).

Hiking

Acadia National Park maintains nearly 200 mi of paths. Among the more rewarding hikes are the Precipice Trail to Champlain Mountain, the Great Head Loop, the Gorham Mountain Trail, and the path around Eagle Lake.

Shopping

In Camden, the best shopping streets are Main and Bayview. Antiques shops (abundant in **Searsport**) are scattered around the outskirts of villages; yard sales abound in summer. Galleries and boutiques can be found in **Rockland, Blue Hill, Deer Isle,** and **Stonington. Bar Harbor** is a good place to browse for gifts. For bargains head for the outlets along Route 3 in **Ellsworth.**

WESTERN LAKES AND MOUNTAINS

Less than 20 mi northwest of Portland, the lakes and mountains of western Maine stretch along the New Hampshire border to Quebec. The Sebago–Long Lake region has antiques stores and lake cruises on a 42-mi waterway. Kezar Lake, in a fold of the White Mountains, is a hideaway of the wealthy. Bethel is a classic New England town, while the less-developed Rangeley Lakes area is a fishing paradise; both become ski country in winter.

Visitor Information

Bethel Area: Chamber of Commerce (☒ Box 439, Bethel 04217, ☎ 207/824–2282 or 800/442–5526); Maine Tourism Association Welcome Center (☒ Box 1084, Rte. 2, Bethel 04217, ☎ 207/824–4582). **Bridgton–Lakes Region:** Chamber of Commerce (☒ Box 236, Bridgton 04009, ☎ 207/647–3472). **Rangeley Lakes Region:** Chamber of Commerce (☒ Box 317, Rangeley 04970, ☎ 207/864–5571 or 800/685–2537). **Sugarloaf Area Chamber of Commerce** (☒ R.R. 1, Box 2151, Kingfield 04947, ☎ 207/235–2100).

Arriving and Departing

By Car

U.S. 302 provides access to the region from I–95. U.S. 2, which runs east–west, links Bangor to Bethel.

Exploring the Western Lakes and Mountains

Sebago Lake State Park (☎ 207/693–6613 mid-June–Sept.; 207/693–6231 Oct.–mid-June) offers opportunities for swimming, picnicking, camping, boating, and fishing. To the north is **Naples,** with cruises and boat rentals on Long Lake. **Songo Lock** connects the northern tip of Sebago Lake with Long Lake. The **Songo River Queen II,** a 92-ft sternwheeler, takes passengers on hour-long cruises on Long Lake and longer voyages down the Songo River and through Songo Lock. ☒ *Rte. 302, Naples Causeway,* ☎ *207/693–6861.* ☺ *Songo River ride $11, Long Lake cruise $8. Closed Oct.–May; limited schedule in June and Sept.*

Bridgton, near Highland Lake, has antiques shops in and around town. U.S. 302/Route 5 through Lovell and Route 37 through the Waterfords are scenic routes to **Bethel,** a town with white-clapboard houses, antiques stores, and a mountain vista at the end of every street. Keep this route in mind for the first and second week of October—Maine's forests are usually at their most spectacular then.

The area from Bethel to **Rangeley Lake** is beautiful, too, particularly in autumn. In **Grafton Notch State Park** (☎ 207/824–2912) you can hike to stunning gorges and waterfalls and into the Baldpate Mountains. For a century, **Rangeley** has lured people who fish and hunt to its more than 40 lakes and ponds. **Rangeley Lake State Park** (☎ 207/864–3858) has superb scenery, swimming, picnicking, and boating. Campsites are set well apart. In the shadow of Sugarloaf Mountain, **Kingfield** is prime ski country—a classic New England town with a general store, historic inns, and a white-clapboard church. **Sandy River & Rangeley Lakes Railroad** has a century-old train that traverses the woods. ☒ *Bridge Hill Rd., Phillips (20 mi southeast of Rangeley),* ☎ *207/639–3352.* ☺ *$3. Closed Nov.–May.*

Dining and Lodging

Bethel has the largest concentration of inns and B&Bs, and its chamber of commerce has a **lodging reservations service** (☎ 207/824–3585).

Bethel

$$ ✕🏠 **Victoria Inn.** It's hard to miss this turreted inn, with its beige-,
★ mauve-, and teal-painted exterior. Inside, Victorian details include ceiling rosettes, stained-glass windows, elaborate fireplace mantels, and gleaming oak trim. The restaurant, open to the public for dinner ($$–$$$), offers entrées such as beef tenderloin au poivre and rack of lamb. ☒ *Box 249, 32 Main St., 04217,* ☎ *207/824–8060 or 888/774–1235,* FAX *207/824–3926. 15 rooms. Restaurant. MC, V. Restaurant closed Mon. and Tues. BP.* ✿

$$$$ ⊡ **Bethel Inn and Country Club.** Choice rooms in this old-fashioned resort hotel are either new or recently renovated. Many have fireplaces and whirlpool tubs. Condos on the fairway are a bit sterile. ⊠ *Box 49, Village Common, 04217,* ☎ *207/824–2175 or 800/654–0125,* 𝔽𝔸𝕏 *207/824–2233. 54 rooms, 40 condo units. Restaurant, pool, golf, tennis, health club. AE, D, DC, MC, V. MAP.* ✎

Kingfield

$$–$$$ ⊡ **Grand Summit Hotel.** This six-story brick structure at the base of the Sugarloaf lifts combines a New England ambience with European-style service. Ski tuning, lockers, and mountain guides are available through the concierge. There's a pub in the hotel, as well as a hot tub and sauna. ⊠ *R.R. 1, Box 2299, Carrabassett Valley 04947,* ☎ *207/237–2222 or 800/527–9879,* 𝔽𝔸𝕏 *207/237–2874. 119 rooms. Restaurant, exercise room. AE, D, DC, MC, V.*

Lovell

$–$$$ ✕⊡ **Center Lovell Inn.** The current owners won this rambling, old-fashioned country inn in an essay contest in 1993. The eclectic decor mixes pieces from the mid-19th to mid-20th century in a pleasing, homey style. The best tables for dining are on the wraparound porch, which has sunset views over Kezar Lake and the White Mountains. Entrées may include veal scallopini, chateaubriand, or chicken breast Toscano. ⊠ *Box 261, Rte. 5 04016,* ☎ *207/925–1575 or 800/777–2698. 9 rooms. Restaurant. MC, V. Closed Nov.–Apr. MAP available.* ✎

Rangeley

$$ ✕⊡ **Rangeley Inn and Motor Lodge.** From Main Street you see only the three-story, blue inn building (circa 1907), but behind it is a newer motel wing with views of Haley Pond, a lawn, and a garden. Some of the inn's sizable rooms have iron-and-brass beds, some have claw-foot tubs, and others have whirlpool tubs. The dining room, open for dinner, serves entrées such as bouillabaisse, fresh fish, and New Zealand rack of lamb. Casual fare is served in the tavern. ⊠ *Box 160, 51 Main St., 04970,* ☎ *207/864–3341 or 800/666–3687,* 𝔽𝔸𝕏 *207/864–3634. 51 rooms, 2 cabins. 2 restaurants. AE, D, MC, V. EP; MAP available.* ✎

Waterford

$$
★ ⊡ **Bear Mountain Inn.** After a swim at the private beach on Bear Lake or a hike up Bear Mountain across the street, it's nice to return to this rambling farmhouse inn, meticulously decorated with a woodsy theme. Four of the rooms share two baths. Among the activities are badminton, croquet, volleyball, boating, fishing, ice-skating, cross-country skiing, and snowmobiling. ⊠ *Rte. 35, South Waterford 04081,* ☎ *207/583–4404. 9 rooms, 2 cottages. MC, V. BP.* ✎

Outdoor Activities and Sports

Boating

Sebago, Long, Rangeley, and Mooselookmeguntic are the most popular lakes for boating. Contact tourist offices for rentals.

Canoeing

The **Saco River** and **Rangeley** and **Mooselookmeguntic lakes** are favorites for canoeing. For rentals try **Canal Bridge Canoes** (⊠ Rte. 302, Fryeburg Village, ☎ 207/935–2605), **Oquossoc Cove Marina** (⊠ Oquossoc, ☎ 207/864–3463), **Dockside Sports Center** (⊠ Town Cove, Rangeley, ☎ 207/864–2424), or **River's Edge Sports** (⊠ Rte. 4, Oquossoc, ☎ 207/864–5582).

Fishing

Fishing licenses (required) can be obtained at many sporting goods and hardware stores and at town halls. The **Department of Inland Fisheries and Wildlife** (⊠ 284 State St., Augusta 04333, ☎ 207/287–2871) has further information.

Skiing

Sugarloaf/USA (⊠ Kingfield 04947, ☎ 207/237–2000) has both downhill and cross-country trails. **Sunday River** (⊠ Box 450, Bethel 04217, ☎ 207/824–3000) has downhill trails.

ELSEWHERE IN MAINE

The North Woods

Visitor Information

Baxter State Park Authority (⊠ 64 Balsam Dr., Millinocket 04462, ☎ 207/723–5140). **Katahdin Area Chamber of Commerce** (⊠ 1029 Central St., Millinocket 04462, ☎ 207/723–4443). **Maine Sporting Camp Association** (⊠ Box 89, Jay 04239) publishes a list of its members, with details on the facilities available at each camp. **Moosehead Lake Region Chamber of Commerce** (⊠ Rtes. 6 and 15, Box 581, Greenville 04441, ☎ 207/695–2702). **North Maine Woods** (⊠ Box 425, Ashland 04732, ☎ 207/435–6213) maintains 500 primitive campsites on commercial forest land.

Arriving and Departing

Charter planes can be arranged from Bangor. Route 6 wends its way from I–95 to Greenville; Route 11 provides access from I–95 to Millinocket.

What to See and Do

Moosehead Lake, Maine's largest, offers rustic camps, restaurants, guides, and outfitters. Its 420 mi of shorefront are virtually uninhabited and in most places accessible only by floatplane or boat. **Greenville** is the locus for canoe rentals, outfitters, and basic lodging. **Moosehead Marine Museum** (⊠ Box 1151, Main St., ☎ 207/695–2716; ☜ $3; closed early Oct.–late May) has exhibits on the local logging industry and the steamship era on Moosehead Lake.

★ The Moosehead Marine Museum also offers three-hour and six-hour trips on Moosehead Lake aboard the *Katahdin* (⊠ Main St., ☎ 207/695–2716; ☜ $18–$24; closed Columbus Day–July 1), a 1914 steamship (now diesel). The 115-ft *Katahdin,* fondly called *The Kate,* carried passengers to Kineo until 1942 and then was used in the logging industry until 1975. Dam-controlled flows ensure good white-water rafting from May through September on the Kennebec, Dead, and Penobscot rivers. For information contact **Raft Maine** (☎ 800/723–8633).

Baxter State Park (⊠ 64 Balsam Dr., Millinocket 04462, ☎ 207/723–5140) is a 200,000-acre wooded wilderness. There are 46 mountains in the park, including **Katahdin,** Maine's highest. They're all accessible from a 150-mi trail network.

Even more remote is the **Allagash Wilderness Waterway,** a 92-mi corridor of lakes and rivers. **Ripogenus Dam,** 30 mi northwest of Millinocket on lumbering roads, is the most popular jumping-off point for Allagash trips. The **Maine Department of Conservation, Bureau of Parks and Lands** (⊠ State House Station 22, Augusta 04333, ☎ 207/287–3821) has information on camping and canoeing.

Dining and Lodging

$–$$ ✕ **Kelly's Landing.** This family-oriented restaurant on the Moosehead shorefront has indoor and outdoor seating, excellent views, and a dock for boaters. The fare includes sandwiches, burgers, lasagna, seafood dinners, and prime rib. ✉ *Rtes. 6 and 15, Greenville Junction,* ☎ *207/695–4438. MC, V.*

$$$ ✕🏠 **Greenville Inn.** This rambling lumber baron's mansion, built more than a century ago, is a block from town on a rise over Moosehead Lake. The decor includes ornate cherry and mahogany paneling, Oriental rugs, and leaded glass. Cottages have mountain and lake views, and some have decks. The restaurant ($$–$$$, reservations essential, no lunch) has water views. The menu, revised daily, reflects the owners' Austrian background. ✉ *Box 1194, Norris St., Greenville 04441,* ☎ *207/695–2206 or 888/695–6000,* 𝔽𝔸𝕏 *207/695–0335. 6 rooms, 6 cottages. Restaurant. D, MC, V. BP.* ✍

$$$–$$$$ 🏠 **Lodge at Moosehead Lake.** All rooms in this luxurious mansion have
★   a whirlpool, fireplace, and hand-carved four-poster bed; most have lake views. The dining room, where breakfast is served, has a spectacular view of the lake. ✉ *Lily Bay Rd., Greenville 04441,* ☎ *207/695–4400,* 𝔽𝔸𝕏 *207/695–2281. 8 rooms. D, MC, V. Closed late Oct.–mid-Jan. and mid-Mar.–mid-May. BP.* ✍

$–$$ 🏠 **Birches Resort.** The living room in the main lodge of this family-oriented resort is dominated by a fieldstone fireplace. Log-cabin cottages have wood-burning stoves or fireplaces and sleep from 2 to 15 guests. There's a hot tub and sauna on the premises. ✉ *Off Rtes. 6 and 15, on Moosehead Lake (Box 41, Rockwood 04478),* ☎ *207/534–7305 or 800/825–9453,* 𝔽𝔸𝕏 *207/534–8835. 4 rooms, 15 cottages. Dining room. AE, D, MC, V. Dining room closed Apr. and Dec. BP; MAP available June–Aug.* ✍

MARYLAND

By Francis X.
Rocca

Updated by
Greg Tasker

Capital	Annapolis
Population	5,171,634
Motto	Manly Deeds, Womanly Words
State Bird	Baltimore oriole
State Flower	Black-eyed Susan
Postal Abbreviation	MD

Statewide Visitor Information

The **Maryland Office of Tourism Development** (⊠ 217 E. Redwood St., Baltimore 21202, ☎ 410/767–3400 or 800/543–1036) provides free publications and operates 13 information centers.

Scenic Drives

Alternate U.S. Route 40, between Frederick and Hagerstown, rolls gently through the rural land and picturesque towns of a region steeped in Civil War history. Early autumn foliage blankets much of Western Maryland in shades of crimson, yellow, and orange. **I–68,** between Hancock and Cumberland in western Maryland, passes through a narrow, 340-ft-deep cut in the rocky crest of a mountain, then opens to sweeping views of the Appalachians. **U.S. 50/301,** at the eastern end of Kent Island on Maryland's Eastern Shore, traverses the elevated **Chesapeake Bay Bridge,** which looks over the fishing boats, pleasure craft, and sailboats on the inlet below.

National and State Parks

National Parks

★ National Park Service attractions include **Antietam National Battlefield** (☎ 301/432–5124; ⌑ $2 per person, $4 per family), **Assateague Island National Seashore** (☎ 410/641–1441; ⌑ $5 per vehicle, $2 pedestrian), **Blackwater National Wildlife Refuge** (☎ 410/228–2677; ⌑ $3 per vehicle, $1 per pedestrian), **Catoctin Mountain Park** (☎ 301/663–9330; ⌑ free), **Chesapeake & Ohio Canal National Historic Park** (☎ 301/739–4200; ⌑ free), **Fort McHenry National Monument and Shrine** (☎ 410/962–4290; ⌑ $5), and **Fort Washington Park** (☎ 301/763–4600; ⌑ $4 per vehicle, free weekdays Nov.–Apr.).

State Parks

Maryland has 47 parks and forests on more than 280,000 acres of land. The Office of Tourism Development (☞ Statewide Visitor Information, *above*) has information about each of the parks. At **Swallow Falls State Park** (☎ 301/334–9180), in far western Maryland, paths wind along the Youghiogheny River past rocky gorges, rapids, towering hemlocks, and the 63-ft Muddy Creek Falls. North of Baltimore, more than 100 mi of hiking and biking trails run through the 13,200-acre **Gunpowder Falls State Park** (☎ 410/592–2897), in the picturesque Gunpowder River valley. **Sandy Point State Park** (☎ 410/974–2149) on the western shore of the Chesapeake Bay, has bay beaches and park land perfect for picnicking, fishing, and bird-watching. The **Department of Natural Resources** (☎ 410/260–8367) organizes guided canoe trips, hiking, backpacking, wildflower walks, forest walks, and guided mountain-bike trips.

BALTIMORE

Baltimore transformed its moribund Inner Harbor into a bustling destination two decades ago, and today the old port city is in the midst of another renaissance. The city's old hulking Power Plant now thrives as a harborside entertainment and retail complex. The retro Oriole Park at Camden Yards got a new (and much bigger) neighbor with the 1998 opening of the Baltimore Ravens' football stadium, PSINET Stadium. Northeast of the Inner Harbor, Port Discovery, a children's museum with exhibits designed by the Walt Disney Co., opened in a former fish market. In 2001, a luxury Wyndham Hotel is expected to tower along the eastern banks of the harbor. Despite the recent development blitz, history, tradition, and a small-town feeling still prevail in Baltimore. Beyond the Inner Harbor, historic neighborhoods such as Federal Hill, Mount Vernon, and Fells Point beckon with an eclectic mix of restaurants, shops, pubs, and splendid architecture—from Colonial row houses to massive brownstones. Though the cityscape is modernizing, no bulldozer could remove the history from a city synonymous with the "Star-Spangled Banner" and local legends Babe Ruth, Edgar Allan Poe, and H. L. Mencken.

Visitor Information

Baltimore Area Convention & Visitors Association (⌧ 301 E. Pratt St., 21202, ☎ 410/837–4636 or 800/282–6632). **Office of Promotion** (⌧ 200 W. Lombard St., 21201, ☎ 410/752–8632).

Arriving and Departing

By Bus
Greyhound (⌧ 210 W. Fayette St., ☎ 800/231–2222).

By Car
Baltimore is on I–95, the major East Coast artery.

By Plane
Baltimore–Washington International Airport (⌧ 7062 Friendship Rd., ☎ 410/859–7111), 10 mi south of town, is a destination for most major domestic and foreign carriers. Taxi fare to downtown runs about $20. **Washington Dulles International Airport** and **Ronald Reagan Washington National Airport** (☞ Arriving and Departing *in* Washington, D.C.) are a bit farther from Baltimore but sometimes have cheaper and more frequent direct flights. **Amtrak** (☞ By Train, *below*) and **MARC** (☎ 800/325–7245) trains run between the airport station (10 minutes from the terminal via free shuttle bus) and Penn Station, about 20 minutes away. **BWI SuperShuttle** (☎ 410/859–0800) has van service to downtown hotels for $20 round-trip and to most suburban hotels.

By Train
Amtrak serves Baltimore's Penn Station (⌧ Charles St. at Mt. Royal Ave., ☎ 800/872–7245). **Central Light Rail Line** (☎ 410/539–5000) has service from Hunt Valley, north of the city, through downtown and south to Glen Burnie and BWI Airport. **MARC** (☎ 800/325–7245) trains travel between Baltimore and Washington, D.C.

Getting Around Baltimore

Most attractions are a walk or a short tour bus ride (☞ Orientation Tours, *below*) from the Inner Harbor. **Water taxis** (☎ 410/563–3901) stop at Fells Point and at Inner Harbor locations. Beyond that, a car is useful as the metro line is limited, and riding the bus often means transferring. Call **Mass Transit Administration** (☎ 410/539–5000) for information.

Orientation Tours

From spring through fall, **Harbor City Tours** (☎ 410/254–8687; 🎫 $10) offers 90-minute, narrated minibus tours four times daily. You can board at Light and Conway streets or at major hotels and can get on and off at attractions. **Ed Kane's Water Taxi** rides (☎ 410/563–3901 or 800/658–8947; 🎫 $4.50 for day pass) stop at 16 sights, including the Inner Harbor, Fells Point, Canton, Fort McHenry, and the Baltimore Museum of Industry.

Exploring Baltimore

The city fans out northward from the Inner Harbor, with newer attractions such as the National Aquarium and Oriole Park concentrated at the city center, and more historic neighborhoods and sites toward the edges. Baltimore's major northbound artery is Charles Street; cross streets are labeled "East" or "West" relative to it.

Inner Harbor and Environs

★ The **American Visionary Art Museum** (⌖ 800 Key Hwy., at Covington St., ☎ 410/244–1900, 🎫 $6), in a complex with a former whiskey warehouse near Federal Hill, shows thought-provoking works by self-trained and self-taught artists. Its exhibits include paintings, sculpture, and drawings.

The **Maryland Science Center** (⌖ 601 Light St., ☎ 410/685–5225; 🎫 $9.75) has hundreds of hands-on exhibits, a planetarium, and a five-story IMAX theater, recently upgraded to feature 3-D films. For a panoramic view of the harbor and downtown, head for the **Top of the World,** the observation deck on the 27th floor of the World Trade Center (⌖ 401 E. Pratt St., ☎ 410/837–8439; 🎫 $3).The **Baltimore Maritime Museum** (⌖ Piers 3 and 4, Pratt St., ☎ 410/396–3453; 🎫 $5.50) glimpses maritime history aboard the World War II submarine USS *Torsk,* the lightship *Chesapeake,* and the Coast Guard cutter *Taney.*

★ The **National Aquarium in Baltimore** (⌖ 501 E. Pratt St., ☎ 410/576–3800, 🎫 $14) has more than 10,000 creatures representing 600 species of fish, birds, amphibians, and marine mammals. Simulated habitats include the new Amazon River Forest, as well as the South American Rain Forest, the Atlantic Coral Reef, and the Marine Mammal Pavilion.

At the **Power Plant** (⌖ Inner Harbor at Pratt St.), a hulking, turn-of-the-20th-century building houses chains such as the Hard Rock Cafe, Barnes & Noble, and ESPN Zone, a sports-theme restaurant with actual and virtual sports games.

President Street Station, the oldest surviving big-city depot in the country, has been restored and reopened as the **Baltimore Civil War Museum** (⌖ 601 President St., ☎ 410/385–5188; 🎫 $2). Exhibits focus on Baltimore's role in the Civil War.

🕒 **Port Discovery** (⌖ 35 Market Pl., ☎ 410/727–8120; 🎫 $10) designed by the Walt Disney Co., occupies an old fish market a few blocks northeast of the Inner Harbor. The children's museum has exhibits that make learning fun, including a re-created Egypt, complete with the Nile River, pyramids, and mazes.

East of Inner Harbor is the the **Star-Spangled Banner Flag House and 1812 Museum** (⌖ 844 E. Pratt St., ☎ 410/837–1793; 🎫 $5), where Mary Pickersgill wove the flag that inspired the national anthem.

★ A 15-minute stroll on the waterfront promenade, or a short taxi ride (water or land) from the Inner Harbor, takes you to **Fells Point,** where antiques shops, galleries, restaurants, and bars line the cobblestone streets

Baltimore

Broadway

Madison Square

Eden St.

Chase St.

Eager St.

Madison St.

Monument St.

Old Town Mall

McElderry St.

Aisquith St.

Ensor St.

Orleans St.

Main Post Office

Fayette St.

Fairmount Ave.

Low St.

Gay St.

KEY

Rail lines

Johnson Square

Harford Ave.

Biddle St.

Greenmount Ave.

The Fallsway

Gay St.

Holliday St.

Front St.

Hillen St.

0   1 500 yards
0   1 500 meters

N

Guilford Ave.

Davis St.

Pleasant St.

Chase St.

Calvert St.

Read St.

Peabody Library

Saint Paul St.

BALTIMORE MUSEUM OF ART
JOHNS HOPKINS UNIVERSITY
BALTIMORE ZOO

Saint Paul St.

Washington Monument

Eager St.

Washington Pl.

Charles St.

Cathedral St.

Mt. Vernon Place

Walters Art Gallery

Centre St.

Basilica of the Assumption

Liberty St.

Read St.

Enoch Pratt Main Library

Park Ave.

Saratoga St.

Howard St.

Monument St.

Maryland Historical Society

Madison St.

Franklin St.

Mulberry St.

Howard St.

Biddle St.

Eutaw St.

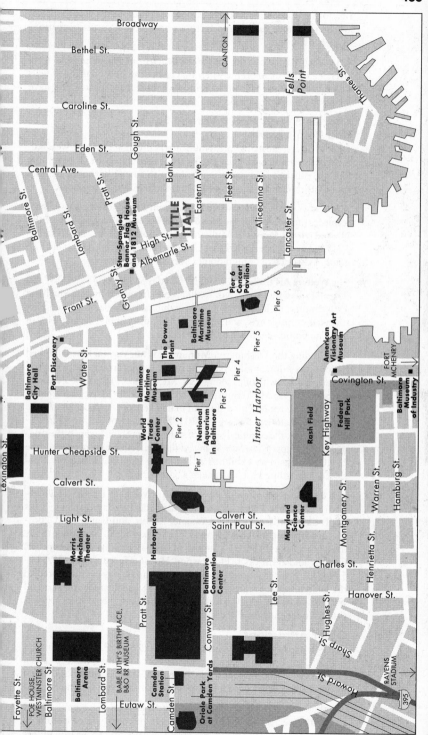

Broadway

Bethel St.

Caroline St.

Eden St.

Central Ave.

Pratt St.

Lombard St.

Baltimore St.

CANTON

Fells Point

Thames St.

Gough St.

Bank St.

Star-Spangled Banner Flag House and 1812 Museum

Granby St.

High St.

Albemarle St.

LITTLE ITALY

Eastern Ave.

Fleet St.

Aliceanna St.

Lancaster St.

Front St.

Pier 6 Concert Pavilion

Pier 6

Port Discovery

Water St.

The Power Plant

Baltimore Maritime Museum

Pier 5

Baltimore City Hall

Baltimore Maritime Museum

Pier 4

American Visionary Art Museum

FORT McHENRY

Hunter Cheapside St.

World Trade Center

Pier 3

National Aquarium in Baltimore

Inner Harbor

Covington St.

Baltimore Museum of Industry

Calvert St.

Pier 2

Key Highway

Lexington St.

Light St.

Harborplace

Pier 1

Rash Field

Federal Hill Park

Morris Mechanic Theater

Calvert St.
Saint Paul St.

Maryland Science Center

Montgomery St.

Warren St.

Hamburg St.

Charles St.

Henrietta St.

Baltimore Convention Center

Lee St.

Hanover St.

Pratt St.

Conway St.

Hughes St.

Sharp St.

Fayette St.

POE HOUSE, WESTMINSTER CHURCH

Baltimore St.

Baltimore Arena

Lombard St.

Eutaw St.

BABE RUTH'S BIRTHPLACE, B&O RR MUSEUM

Camden Station

Camden St.

Oriole Park at Camden Yards

Howard St.

RAVENS STADIUM

395

of a former shipbuilding center. Farther east is **Canton,** a neighborhood whose renovated homes and factories have become artistic creations in their own right.

On a nice day, walk the **Baltimore Waterfront Promenade,** a 6-mi stretch a block or so off the water that goes from Canton through Fells Point and the Inner Harbor to South Baltimore. Restaurants here have views of the downtown skyline.

Charles Street, Mount Vernon Square, and Points North

Charles Street, the main northbound artery dividing East and West Baltimore, has some of the city's most striking architecture. Restaurants and art galleries lend an urbane tone to this neighborhood, with its mix of 19th-century brownstones and modern office buildings.

A block west of Charles Street is Benjamin Latrobe's neoclassic masterpiece, the **Basilica of the National Shrine of the Assumption of the Blessed Virgin Mary** (⊠ Mulberry St. at Cathedral St., ☎ 410/539–5741; ☙ free). America's oldest Catholic cathedral, it was built in 1812 and has distinctive "onion domes" on the belfry towers.

★ The **Walters Art Gallery** (⊠ 600 N. Charles St., ☎ 410/547–2787, ☙ $5), an Italianate palace, has 30,000 pieces from antiquity through the 19th century, including Egyptology exhibits, medieval armor and artifacts, decorative arts, and paintings. The adjacent Hackerman House has a magnificent gallery of Asian art.

Surrounding the Washington Monument is **Mt. Vernon Place,** flanked by four block-long parks. Note the bronze sculptures in the parks and the elegant brownstones along East Mt. Vernon Place. The **Peabody Library** (⊠ 17 E. Mt. Vernon Pl., ☎ 410/659–8179; ☙ free) has a handsome reading room with a skylight in its five-story-high ceiling. At the **Maryland Historical Society** (⊠ 201 W. Monument St., ☎ 410/685–3750; ☙ $4), the eclectic display of state memorabilia includes the original manuscript of *The Star-Spangled Banner.* The society now has some 250,000 items once exhibited at Baltimore City Life Museums (now closed), including H. L. Mencken's baby grand.

The **Baltimore Museum of Art** (⊠ 10 Art Museum Dr., ☎ 410/396–7101; ☙ $6, free Thurs.), closed Monday and Tuesday, displays works by Rodin, Matisse, Picasso, Cézanne, Renoir, and Gauguin. A 20th-century art wing includes 19 Andy Warhol paintings. Next door to the museum is the 140-acre campus of **Johns Hopkins University** (⊠ Charles and 34th Sts.). **Homewood House Museum** (☎ 410/516–5589; ☙ $6), set on a grassy knoll on campus, has been restored to the Federal-style country house it was in 1800 when Charles Carroll Jr., the son of Charles Carroll of Carrollton, a signer of the Declaration of Independence, lived here.

Other Attractions

The **Poe House** (⊠ 203 N. Amity St., ☎ 410/396–7932; ☙ $3) is where Edgar Allan Poe wrote his first horror story. You may want to take a cab or drive if you visit, as it's in a rough neighborhood. Poe is buried at the **Westminster Church Grave** (⊠ W. Fayette and Greene Sts.).

North of Inner Harbor is the **Great Blacks in Wax Museum** (⊠ 1601 E. North Ave., ☎ 410/563–6415; ☙ $6), the only one of its kind in the United States. Rosa Parks, Frederick Douglass, and Dr. Martin Luther King Jr. are among the figures you'll see.

Though it opened in the early 1990s, **Oriole Park at Camden Yards** (⊠ Camden and Howard Sts., ☎ 410/685–9800) looks like the ballparks of the early 1900s but has skyboxes, lounges, and restaurants. Behind-the-scenes **guided ballpark tours** (☎ 410/685–9800; ⊠ $5) are scheduled year-round. Just south of the baseball park is the home of the NFL's Baltimore Ravens, **PSINET Stadium** (⊠ 1101 Russell St., ☎ 410/547–8100). MARC trains from Washington, the Central Light Rail trains from the suburbs, and numerous bus park-and-ride routes serve both stadiums. Two blocks west of Oriole Park, the **Babe Ruth Birthplace & Orioles Museum** (⊠ 216 Emory St., ☎ 410/727–1539; ⊠ $6) has exhibits, photos, and films on the Babe, the Orioles, and Maryland baseball history.

★ The **B&O Railroad Museum** (⊠ 901 W. Pratt St., ☎ 410/752–2490, ⊠ $6.50), one of the world's largest train museums, is on the site of the country's first railroad station and displays locomotives and railroad cars.

Inside a former oyster cannery, the **Baltimore Museum of Industry** (⊠ 1415 Key Hwy., ☎ 410/727–4808; ⊠ $5) celebrates the city's industrial heritage. Hands-on exhibits include the Kids' Cannery, where children shuck, pack, and can oyster shells. The flag that flew over **Fort McHenry National Monument and Shrine** (⊠ Fort Ave. off Key Hwy., ☎ 410/962–4290; ⊠ $5) the morning of September 14, 1814, inspired Francis Scott Key to pen the lyrics to *The Star-Spangled Banner*. Tours, exhibits, films, and restored barracks trace the star-shape fort's successful defense against the British attack in the War of 1812.

Parks, Gardens, and Zoos

Sherwood Gardens (⊠ Stratford Rd. and Greenway, 3 mi from Inner Harbor east of St. Paul St., ☎ 410/323–7982; ⊠ free) explodes with color when 80,000 tulips peak in April or early May. South of Inner Harbor, **Federal Hill Park** (⊠ Battery St. and Key Hwy.) has an excellent view of the downtown skyline and the remnants of the city's industrial heritage. It's safer during the day.

More than 1,200 animals, including polar bears and penguins, inhabit the 150 acres of the **Baltimore Zoo** (⊠ Druid Park Lake Dr., I-83 to Exit 7, ☎ 410/366–5466; ⊠ $9.50).

Dining

Baltimore, known for its fabulous Chesapeake Bay seafood and great steaks, has broadened its dining options in recent years. You'll find old favorites like Tio Pepe for Spanish, while swanky newcomers serve Afghan, Greek, and Indian food.

$$$–$$$$ ✕ **Boccaccio.** A formal, dimly lit dining room and consistently excellent Italian food make this Little Italy restaurant a Baltimore favorite. Some say the veal is the best in town. ⊠ *925 Eastern Ave.,* ☎ *410/234–1322. AE, DC, MC, V.*

$$$–$$$$ ✕ **Charleston Restaurant.** Diners come back for specialties such as grilled
★ venison medallions and cornmeal-crusted oysters in a lemon-cayenne sauce. Peek into the open kitchen and watch the chef create. ⊠ *1000 Lancaster St.,* ☎ *410/332–7373. AE, MC, V.*

$$$–$$$$ ✕ **The Prime Rib.** Black walls, leopard-print carpeting, and a baby grand
★ add to the elegance and romance of this Baltimore fixture. Along with top cuts, including prime rib and New York Strip, the traditional menu features superb crab cakes. ⊠ *1101 N. Calvert St.,* ☎ *410/539–1804. Reservations essential. Jacket required. AE, DC, MC, V.*

$$–$$$$ ✕ **The Black Olive.** At this Greek tavern in Fells Point diners can pick their own whole fish from the fridge. The seafood kabobs, rack of lamb, and veal chops are also good bets. ⊠ *814 S. Bond St.,* ☎ *410/276–7141. AE, D, DC, MC, V.*

$$–$$$ ✕ **Tio Pepe.** The candlelit cellar with its whitewashed walls is like a little piece of Spain. Try the saffron rice with chicken, veal, lobster, chorizo, shrimp, and mussels. ⊠ *10 E. Franklin St.,* ☎ *410/539–4675. Reservations essential. Jacket required. AE, D, DC, MC, V.*

$$–$$$ ✕ **Windows.** Located on the fifth floor of the Renaissance Harborplace Hotel (☞ Lodging, *below*), Windows is well known for its contemporary American menu and great views of the Inner Harbor. Radiatore pasta with sea scallops, tossed with shrimp, garlic, and Reggiano cheese, is a favorite. ⊠ *202 E. Pratt St.,* ☎ *410/547–1200. AE, D, DC, MC, V.*

$–$$ ✕ **The Helmand.** Afghani textiles decorate the walls, and candles light the noisy dining room. Try specialties such as flaky sea bass with raisins and ginger tomatoes. ⊠ *806 N. Charles St.,* ☎ *410/752–0311. AE, DC, MC, V.*

$–$$ ✕ **Mughal Garden.** Mughal Garden has made a name for itself with fine Indian food, lavish decor, dancing, and moderate prices. ⊠ *920 N. Charles St.,* ☎ *410/547–0001. AE, D, DC, MC, V.*

Lodging

Staying around the Inner Harbor means ready access to major attractions. Away from the water, as far north as Mt. Vernon, are reminders of an older Baltimore and some relative bargains in accommodations.

$$$$ 🏨 **Harbor Court.** This redbrick tower with marble floors, crystal chan-
★ deliers, and fine reproduction furniture is Baltimore's most prestigious and luxurious hotel. Its Hampton's Restaurant, with a formal Continental menu, ranks among the country's best. ⊠ *550 Light St., 21202,* ☎ *410/234–0550 or 800/824–0076,* FAX *410/659–5925. 203 rooms. 2 restaurants, pool, exercise room. AE, D, DC, MC, V.* ✇

$$$$ 🏨 **Hyatt Regency Baltimore.** A walkway across Light Street links the Hyatt to one of the pavilions of Harborplace and to the Baltimore Convention Center. Rooms facing the water have incomparable harbor views. ⊠ *300 Light St., 21202,* ☎ *410/528–1234 or 800/233–1234,* FAX *410/ 685–3362. 486 rooms. 2 restaurants, pool, tennis, exercise room. AE, D, DC, MC, V.* ✇

$$$$ 🏨 **Renaissance Harborplace Hotel.** Across from the Inner Harbor shopping pavilions, waterfront tourist sights, this is one of the most conveniently located hotels in the city. Don't miss the view from the Window's restaurant. ⊠ *202 E. Pratt St., 21202,* ☎ *410/547–1200,* FAX *410/539–5780. 622 rooms. Restaurant, pool, exercise room. AE, D, DC, MC, V.* ✇

$$$–$$$$ 🏨 **The Admiral Fell Inn.** Eight adjoining buildings have been transformed
★ into an elegant, European-style inn a block from the water in the heart of Fells Point. Many rooms have canopied beds; some have Jacuzzis and fireplaces. ⊠ *888 S. Broadway, 21231,* ☎ *410/522–7377 or 800/292–4667,* FAX *410/522–0707. 80 rooms. 2 restaurants. AE, DC, MC, V. CP.* ✇

$$$–$$$$ 🏨 **Sheraton Inner Harbor.** Just two blocks from Harborplace and Oriole Park, the official hotel of the Baltimore Orioles is within walking distance of most downtown attractions. ⊠ *300 S. Charles St., 21201,* ☎ *410/962–8300,* FAX *410/962–8211. 357 rooms. 2 restaurants, pool, exercise room. AE, D, DC, MC, V.* ✇

$$$ 🏨 **Tremont Plaza Hotel.** This plain, gray, 37-story tower has suites with
★ kitchens. Those numbered "06" have the best views. ⊠ *222 St. Paul Pl., 21202,* ☎ *410/727–2222 or 800/873–6668,* FAX *410/685–4215. 231 suites. Restaurant, pool, exercise room. AE, D, DC, MC, V.*

$$–$$$ 🏨 **Celie's Waterfront Bed & Breakfast.** This romantic waterfront B&B in Fells Point has two front rooms that overlook the harbor and have fireplaces and whirlpool tubs. Guests have access to a garden and a rooftop deck. ⊠ *1714 Thames St., 21231,* ☎ *410/522–2323 or 800/ 432–0184,* FAX *410/522–2324. 7 rooms. AE, D, DC, MC, V.* ✇

Motels
☎ **Hampton Inn Hunt Valley** (✉ 11200 York Rd., Hunt Valley 21031, ☎ 410/527–1500, 🖷 410/771–0819), 126 rooms; AE, D, DC, MC, V; CP; $$.

Nightlife and the Arts

Check the *City Paper,* a free weekly, for the most complete events listings. The Thursday *Baltimore Sun* and the monthly *Baltimore* magazine also have listings.

Nightlife
For blues and rock, head to the hip South Baltimore club the **Eight by Ten** (✉ 8 E. Cross St., ☎ 410/625–2000). Along the streets of the **Fells Point** waterfront you'll find bars and clubs with live performances of everything from Irish folk music to blues. The **Full Moon Saloon** (✉ 1710 Aliceanna St., ☎ 410/276–6388) features live blues seven nights a week in an intimate, neighborhood-style bar. Just east of the Inner Harbor, **Bohager's** (✉ 701 S. Eden St., ☎ 410/563–7220) attracts top local, regional, and, occasionally, national acts to its indoor and outdoor stages. Just north of the Inner Harbor, the **Havana Club** (✉ 600 Water St., ☎ 410/783–0033) is a busy, upscale cigar lounge; the music varies from swing to disco.

The Arts
Center Stage (✉ 700 N. Calvert St., ☎ 410/332–0033) is the state theater of Maryland. Other major venues include **Friedberg Hall** (✉ Peabody Conservatory, E. Mt. Vernon Pl. and Charles St., ☎ 410/659–8124), **Lyric Opera House** (✉ Mt. Royal Ave. and Cathedral St., ☎ 410/685–5086), **Joseph Meyerhoff Symphony Hall** (✉ 1212 Cathedral St., ☎ 410/783–8000), **Morris A. Mechanic Theater** (✉ Baltimore and Charles Sts., ☎ 410/625–4230), and **Pier Six Concert Pavilion** (✉ Pier 6 at Pratt St., ☎ 410/752–8632).

Spectator Sports

Baseball: Orioles (✉ Oriole Park at Camden Yards, Camden and Howard Sts., ☎ 410/685–9800). **Football: Ravens** (✉ PSINET Stadium, 1101 Russell St., ☎ 410/261–7283).

Shopping

Baltimore offers an impressive mix of shops in and around the downtown district. **Antique Row** (✉ 700 and 800 blocks, N. Howard St.; 200 block, W. Read St.) has more than three dozen first-rate antiques shops. Old homes at **Fells Point** now house antiques shops, art galleries, and boutiques. The two waterfront pavilions of **Harborplace** (✉ 200 E. Pratt St., ☎ 410/332–4191) have chains such as California Pizza Kitchen as well as independent restaurants and boutiques. Across Pratt Street, the multilevel **Gallery** has upscale shops and a food court. Small and quirky shops, restaurants, and cafés line **Charles Street,** just north of the harbor. For a taste of old Baltimore, stop by one of the indoor markets with fresh food stands and shops: **Broadway Market** (✉ Broadway and Fleet Sts.), **Cross Street Market** (✉ Light and Cross Sts.), and **Lexington Market** (✉ Lexington and Eutaw Sts.).

MARYLAND'S CHESAPEAKE

The beauty of Maryland's Chesapeake Bay region has enchanted visitors for more than three centuries. Attractions here are, naturally, water oriented. Annapolis is a world yachting capital with a small-town feel. From there, cross one of the soaring dual spans of the Bay Bridge to the Eastern Shore of the Delmarva Peninsula, and you'll find water-side towns perfect for a getaway, opulent country inns on former plantations, and some of the world's best seafood. On the other side of the peninsula is Ocean City, a busy Atlantic resort.

Visitor Information

Annapolis & Anne Arundel County: Visitors Center (✉ 26 West St., Annapolis 21401, ☎ 410/280–0445). **Calvert County:** Department of Economic Development (✉ 175 Main St., Prince Frederick 20678, ☎ 410/535–4583 or 800/331–9771). **Charles County:** Tourism Office (✉ Box B, LaPlata 20646, ☎ 800/766–3386). **Dorchester County:** Dorchester County Tourism (✉ 2 Rose Hill Pl., Cambridge 21613, ☎ 410/228–1000 or 800/522–8687). **Kent County:** Kent County Tourism (✉ 100 N. Cross St., Chestertown 21620, ☎ 410/778–0416). **Ocean City:** Convention and Visitors Bureau at the Visitor Information Center (✉ 4001 Coastal Hwy., Ocean City 21842, ☎ 410/289–8181 or 800/626–2326). **Queen Anne's County:** Office of Tourism (✉ 425 Piney Narrows Rd., Chester 21619, ☎ 410/604–2100). **St. Mary's County:** Division of Travel and Tourism (✉ 23115 Leonard Hall Dr., Leonardtown 20650, ☎ 301/475–4411 or 800/327–9023). **St. Michaels:** Talbot County Conference and Visitors Bureau (✉ 210 Marlboro Ave., Suite 3, Easton 21601, ☎ 410/822–4606). **Wicomico:** Convention and Visitors Bureau (✉ 8480 Ocean Hwy., Delmar 21875, ☎ 410/548–4914). **Worcester County:** Tourism Office (✉ 113 Franklin St., Snow Hill 21863, ☎ 410/632–3617 or 800/852–0335).

Arriving and Departing

By Bus

Maryland's **Mass Transit Administration** (☎ 410/539–5000) has express service on weekdays, local service on weekends, between Annapolis and Baltimore. **Greyhound** (☎ 410/727–5014) has service between Baltimore, Annapolis, and some Eastern Shore towns, including Ocean City.

By Car

To Annapolis: From Baltimore follow Route 97 to U.S. 50 (Rowe Blvd. exit). **To southern Maryland:** From Annapolis take Route 2 south, which becomes Route 4 in Calvert County. **To the Eastern Shore:** From Baltimore or Annapolis cross the Bay Bridge ($2.50 toll eastbound only) northeast of Annapolis and stay on U.S. 50/301.

Exploring Maryland's Chesapeake

Annapolis

Start on the waterfront. Sailboats dock right at the edge of **Market Square,** where there is a visitor information booth. Stop by the square's **Market House** for seafood and fresh fruits and vegetables. At **City Dock** look for the sidewalk plaque commemorating the arrival of Kunta Kinte, the African slave immortalized in Alex Haley's *Roots*.

At the **Museum Store and Historic Annapolis Foundation** (✉ 77 Main St., ☎ 410/268–5576; ▣ free, $5 for tape) you can rent an audiocassette and let narrator Walter Cronkite be your guide on a walking tour of the Historic District.

Start your visit to the **United States Naval Academy** at the **Armel-Leftwich Visitors Center** (✉ 52 King George St., Gate 1, ☎ 410/263–6933; ▣ free, tours $6) on the Academy's riverside campus. Towering over the pretty waterfront grounds is the bronze-domed **U.S. Naval Chapel**, burial place of Revolutionary War hero John Paul ("I have not yet begun to fight!") Jones. Outdoors, full-dress parades of midshipmen are a stirring sight.

Annapolis, once briefly the capital of the United States, has one of the finest collections of 18th- and 19th-century buildings in the country. Many of its stately brick buildings have been restored as homes, inns, shops, and restaurants. The three-story redbrick **Hammond-Harwood House** (⊠ 19 Maryland Ave., ☎ 410/269–1714; 🎫 $5) is the only verified full-scale example of the work of William Buckland, Colonial America's most prominent architect. Across the street, the grand Georgian **Chase-Lloyd House** (⊠ 22 Maryland Ave., ☎ 410/263–2723; 🎫 $2) was built by Samuel Chase, lawyer and signer of the Declaration of Independence. In 1765, another signer of the Declaration of Independence and governor of Maryland built the 37-room redbrick **William Paca House and Garden** (⊠ 186 Prince George St., ☎ 410/263–5553; 🎫 $5 house only; $4 gardens only; $7 house and gardens combined). **St. John's College** (⊠ 60 College Ave., ☎ 410/263–2371) is the third-oldest college in the country and alma mater of Francis Scott Key, writer of the *The Star-Spangled Banner*.

★ The **Maryland State House** (⊠ State Circle, ☎ 410/974–3400, 🎫 free) is the oldest state capitol in continuous legislative use and the only one that has housed the U.S. Congress. Charles Willson Peale's painting *Washington at the Battle of Yorktown* hangs inside. Free 30-minute tours take place daily at 11 and 3.

Southern Maryland

The less-traveled routes through southern Maryland have bayside scenery, historic sites, romantic B&Bs, and great restaurants. **Calvert Cliffs** rise 100 ft over bay beaches where visitors can collect Miocene-era fossils. To see the cliffs and beaches, stop at **Calvert Cliffs State Park** (⊠ Rte. 2/4, Lusby, ☎ 301/872–5688; 🎫 $2). The fossil sites are about a 2-mi walk from the park entrance. For a glimpse of the Eastern Shore on a clear day, try the observation deck at the **Calvert Cliffs Nuclear Power Plant** (☎ 410/495–4600; 🎫 free) next door. The **Battle Creek Cypress Swamp Sanctuary** (⊠ Rte. 2/4 to Rte. 506, ☎ 410/535–5327; 🎫 free) is home to the northernmost naturally occurring strand of the ancient bald cypress tree in the United States.

At the tip of the peninsula, **Solomons** has become popular among boaters and nonboaters for its quiet, small-town feel. The **Calvert Marine Museum** (⊠ Rte. 2/4 at Solomons Island Rd., ☎ 410/326–2042; 🎫 $5) exhibits fossils, boats from various eras, and a 19th-century lighthouse.

You'll find vintage aircraft and all sorts of failed flying contraptions like the improbable Goodyear "Inflatoplane" at the **Patuxent River Naval Air Museum** (⊠ Rte. 235 and Shangri-la Dr., ☎ 301/863–7418; 🎫 free) in Lexington Park, south of Solomons.

Maryland's history began at **Historic St. Mary's City** (⊠ Rte. 5, ☎ 301/862–0990 or 800/762–1634; 🎫 $7.50). The first colonists, dispatched by Lord Baltimore, settled here in 1634. Until 1695, St. Mary's served as Maryland's capital. Reconstructions of the first State House and the supply ship that accompanied the settlers, along with a typical tobacco plantation, compose the "living history" museum. The complex includes the **Godiah Spray Plantation** (⊠ Rosecroft Rd., St. Mary's City, ☎ 301/862–0990) with demonstrations of planting, cooking, and building from 17th-century plantation life. When John Wilkes Booth ended up at the **Dr. Samuel A. Mudd House** (⊠ Dr. Samuel A. Mudd Rd., ☎ 301/934–8464; 🎫 $3; closed Dec.–Mar.), Dr. Mudd had no idea his patient was a wanted man. The **Thomas Stone National Historic Site** (⊠ Rosehill Rd., between Rtes. 6 and 225, ☎ 301/934–6027; 🎫 $2), the Charles County home of Thomas Stone, one of four Marylanders to sign the Declaration of Independence, has been painstakingly rebuilt.

The Eastern Shore

The William Preston Lane Jr. Memorial Bridge links Annapolis to the Eastern Shore, crossing the Chesapeake at **Kent Island,** the bay's largest island. Agents of Virginia's governor set up a trading post here in 1631, making Kent Maryland's first English settlement. Route 50 continues south past historic towns near the bay and then leads east to the Atlantic.

In **Chestertown,** boutiques, cafés, and ornate 18th-century homes line the wide brick sidewalks. In the affluent town of **Easton,** well-preserved buildings from Colonial and Victorian times fill the charming downtown; visit the 17th-century Quaker meetinghouse, 18th-century courthouse, and restored Art Deco Avalon Theater.

★ **St. Michaels,** once a shipbuilding center, is now a quaint, fashionable destination on the Miles River. The **Chesapeake Bay Maritime Museum** (✉ Navy Point, ☎ 410/745–2916, ☞ $7.50) chronicles the history of the bay and its traditions in boatbuilding, commercial fishing, and navigation.

The **Oxford-Bellevue Ferry** (☎ 410/745–9023; ☞ $5 one-way, $8 round-trip) has been running since 1683. Today it takes cars and pedestrians across the Tred Avon River from a spot 7 mi south of St. Michaels to the 17th-century town of Oxford. Few of the surviving buildings in **Oxford** date before the mid-1800s, but the bigger (and less charming) town of Cambridge, 15 mi to the southeast, has several from the 1700s. Many roads in the area have special bike lanes.

Southwest of Cambridge is the **Blackwater National Wildlife Refuge** (✉ 2145 Key Wallace Dr., ☎ 410/228–2677; ☞ car $3, pedestrian or cyclist $1), with more than 22,000 acres of marsh, woods, waters, and open fields inhabited by Canada geese, ospreys, and bald eagles.

The marshland replicas at the **Ward Museum of Wildfowl Art** (✉ 3416 Schumaker Pond at Beaglin Park Dr., Salisbury, ☎ 410/742–4988; ☞ $4) give visitors a sense of the wild. From May to October **Smith Island Cruises** (☎ 410/425–2771; ☞ $20) leave from Crisfield's Somers Cove Marina for the 70-minute trip to Smith Island, which has been sustained by commercial fishing for more than three centuries.

On the Atlantic side of the peninsula is **Ocean City,** with 10 mi of white-sand beach and a flashy 27-block boardwalk. The Coastal Highway, with blocks of high-rise condos, runs down the center of town. More than 8 million vacationers flock here every summer. **Trimper's Amusement Park** (✉ Boardwalk and S. 1st St., ☎ 410/289–8617), with a vintage carousel and huge roller coaster, recently celebrated its 110th birthday.

Dining and Lodging

The bay area's traditional seafood kitchens and crab houses are now joined by chic bistros and ethnic restaurants. Lodging reservations should be made up to a year in advance of the Annapolis sailboat and power boat shows in October, the Naval Academy commencement in May, and Easton's Waterfowl Festival in November.

Annapolis

$$$–$$$$ ✕ **The Corinthian.** With cushioned armchairs, oil-lamp lighting, and a courtyard view, this formal hotel restaurant has the elegant feel of an old Maryland home. The crab cakes have an angel hair–pasta binder, and the New York strip has been aged three weeks. ✉ *Loews Annapolis Hotel, 126 West St.,* ☎ 410/263–7777. AE, D, DC, MC, V.

$–$$$ ✕ **Cantler's Riverside Inn.** Tucked off back roads just outside Annapolis, this former watermen's bar is now a seafood house. Feast on crabs, clams, shrimp, and oysters in season on the screened waterfront deck or inside the casual dining room. ✉ *158 Forest Beach Rd.,* ☎ *410/757–1467. AE, D, DC, MC, V.*

$–$$$ ✕ **McGarvey's Saloon and Oyster Bar.** This casual saloon and restau-
★ rant is a popular hangout with locals, tourists, and sailors. The kitchen serves standard American fare—burgers, steaks, seafood, and finger foods. ✉ *8 Market Space, at northeast corner of Market House,* ☎ *410/263–5700. AE, MC, V.*

$–$$ ✕ **Middleton Tavern.** Since 1750 this cozy inn by City Dock has been a popular place to eat and drink; former guests include George Washington, Thomas Jefferson, and Ben Franklin. The seafood is excellent, as are the pasta and southwestern dishes. Fireplaces blaze in all four dining rooms in winter; when it's warm, diners can watch the harbor bustle from the tables out front. ✉ *2 Market Space,* ☎ *410/263–3323. AE, D, MC, V.*

$$$–$$$$ 🏠 **Annapolis Marriott Waterfront.** Amenities such as bathroom phones typify the rooms, which face the water, the historic district, or—from private balconies—City Dock. Pusser's Landing is a casual restaurant with a Caribbean flair, Jamaican and English fare, and a waterside setting. ✉ *80 Compromise St., 21401,* ☎ *410/268–7555,* 🅵🅰🆇 *410/269–5864. 150 rooms. Restaurant. AE, D, DC, MC, V.* ✎

$$$–$$$$ 🏠 **Historic Inns of Annapolis.** Three charming inns take guests back in time. Guest rooms are tastefully furnished in original and reproduction antiques and have private baths. Guest can use a local health club. ✉ *58 State Circle, 21401,* ☎ *410/263–2641. 128 rooms. Restaurant, bar. AE, D, DC, MC, V.* ✎

$–$$ 🏠 **Gibson's Lodgings.** Three detached houses—two of them historic— stand together across the street from the United States Naval Academy. The inn has the character of a bed-and-breakfast; a Continental breakfast is served in the formal dining room. ✉ *110–114 Prince George St., 21401,* ☎ *410/268–5555,* 🅵🅰🆇 *410/268–2775. 21 rooms. AE, MC, V. CP.* ✎

Calvert County

$–$$$ ✕ **CD Café.** Overlooking the Patuxent River and the main road into Solomons, this cozy café describes itself as a coffeehouse with bistro flair. The limited menu has inventive dishes such as pan-seared chicken breast with pecans, apples, onions, and schnapps. The homemade desserts are spectacular. ✉ *14350 Solomons Island Rd., Solomons,* ☎ *410/326–3877. MC, V.*

$$–$$$ 🏠 **Back Creek Inn.** Rooms in this 19th-century wood-frame house have brass beds with colorful quilts and views of the water, a garden, or a quiet street. Guests have use of an outdoor hot tub. ✉ *Calvert and Alexander Sts., Solomons 20688,* ☎ *410/326–2022. 6 rooms, 1 cottage. AE, MC, V.*

Chestertown

$$–$$$ 🏠 **The White Swan Tavern** This inn, in the heart of Chestertown, has formal guest rooms with canopy beds. The most requested room, the tavern's original kitchen, has a brick floor and a huge fireplace. Afternoon tea conjures the 18th century. ✉ *231 High St., Chestertown 21620,* ☎ *410/778–2300. 6 rooms. MC, V. CP.* ✎

Ocean City

$$–$$$ ✕ **The Hobbit.** Murals and carved lamps portray J. R. R. Tolkien characters in this dining room with a two-angled view of Assawoman Bay. Try the veal with pistachios or the sautéed catch of the day. ✉ *101 81st St.,* ☎ *410/524–8100. AE, D, MC, V.*

$$$–$$$$ 🏠 **Inn on the Ocean.** A wraparound veranda affords sweeping views of the Atlantic, not to mention the crowds along the boardwalk—literally outside the front door. The small Victorian inn has a cozy liv-

ing room with a working fireplace, to ease the chill in the winter. ⊠ *1001 Atlantic Ave., 21842,* ☎ *410/289–8894 or 888/226–6223. 6 rooms. AE, D, MC, V. BP.*

$$$–$$$$ ☷ **Sheraton Fountainbleau Hotel.** One of Ocean City's larger hotels, this place has great service and spacious ocean-view rooms. ⊠ *10100 Coastal Hwy. (Oceanfront at 101st St.), 21842,* ☎ *410/524–3535 or 800/638–2100. 250 rooms. 2 restaurants, pool, exercise room AE, D, DC, MC, V.* ✎

Oxford

$$–$$$ ✕☷ **Robert Morris Inn.** Conveniently located near the Oxford-Bellevue Ferry terminal, this friendly inn has efficiencies, river cottages, and simple bedrooms—some with bay windows, others with porches. The inn is known for its excellent food, especially the crab cakes. ⊠ *314 N. Morris St., Box 70, Oxford 21654,* ☎ *410/226–5111,* F̅A̅X̅ *410/226–5744. 35 rooms. AE, MC, V. Restaurant and inn closed Jan.–Mar.* ✎

St. Mary's County

$–$$$ ✕ **Evans Seafood.** Ask for a water view, and then order lobster stuffed with crab imperial, or the spicy hard-shell crab made from a secret recipe. ⊠ *Rte. 249, Piney Point,* ☎ *301/994–2299. MC, V. Closed Mon. No lunch weekdays in Apr.–Aug. and Fri. and Sat. in Sept.–Mar.*

$–$$ ☷ **Potomac View Farm.** This former nun's retreat, built in the late 19th century, has been converted into a bed-and-breakfast inn. Rooms are spacious, with views of the Potomac River. The 27-acre retreat includes a pond. ⊠ *15914 Camp Merryelande Rd., St. George Island 20674,* ☎ *301/994–2311. 6 rooms, 9 cottages. AE, D, MC, V. BP.* ✎

St. Michaels

$$$–$$$$ ✕ **208 Talbot.** An antiques-filled late-19th-century house is the setting
★ for regional cuisine: soft-shell crab in season, Maryland rockfish with wild mushrooms in an oyster-cream sauce, and fresh bay oysters with a champagne-cream sauce, prosciutto, and pistachio nuts. ⊠ *208 N. Talbot St.,* ☎ *410/745–3838. D, MC, V.*

$$–$$$ ✕ **Crab Claw.** Bang-them-yourself steamed blue crabs are first rate at this harborside eatery. Spicy deep-fried hard crab is worth a try, too, as is the vegetable crab soup. ⊠ *Navy Point,* ☎ *410/745–2900. No credit cards. Closed Dec.–mid-Mar.*

$$$–$$$$ ✕☷ **The Inn at Perry Cabin.** The guest rooms at this inn set on 25 acres
★ have Laura Ashley fabrics and antique furnishings. Come for the luxuries: afternoon tea, fresh flowers, and heated towel racks. The formal dining room serves excellent fresh seafood and international fare. ⊠ *308 Watkins La., St. Michaels 21663,* ☎ *410/745–2200 or 800/722–2949. 41 rooms. Restaurant, pool, exercise room. AE, DC, MC, V.* ✎

$$$–$$$$ ☷ **Chesapeake Wood Duck Inn.** Stay at this intimate Victorian on Tilghman Island, a short drive from St. Michaels, and you're likely to avoid the summer crowds. Freshly baked muffins and great omelets make breakfast a treat. ⊠ *Gibsontown Rd., Tilghman Island 21671,* ☎ *410/886–2070 or 800/956–2070. 6 rooms. MC, V.* ✎

Nightlife and the Arts

Nightlife

Come sunset, Ocean City is lit with neon and hopping with nightlife, from big band to rock and roll. Try the **Purple Moose** (⊠ 108 S. Boardwalk, ☎ 410/289–6953) or, on the waterfront, the crowded **Seacrets** (⊠ 49th St. on the bay, ☎ 410/524–4900). Annapolis bars are packed on the weekends; grab a beer at the **Ram's Head Tavern** (⊠ 33 West St., ☎ 410/268–4545), or catch some live jazz at **King of France Tavern** (⊠ 16 Church Circle, ☎ 410/269–0990). In St. Michaels, nightlife is a bit more subdued; the **Town Dock** (✉ 125 Mulberry St., ☎ 410/745–5577) has a piano lounge. In Solomons, the thatched **Tiki Bar** (✉ 1 Main St., ☎ 410/326–4075) overflows with revelers on warm nights.

The Arts

In summer the **U.S. Naval Academy Band** performs at Annapolis's City Dock on Tuesday evenings. **Ocean City** sponsors free boardwalk concerts; call the **Convention and Visitors Bureau** (☎ 410/289–2800 or 800/626–2326) for schedules. When the **Colonial Players** (✉ 108 East St., Annapolis, ☎ 410/268–7373) go on vacation the **Annapolis Summer Garden Theater** (✉ Compromise and Main Sts., ☎ 410/268–0809) takes over.

Outdoor Activities and Sports

Biking

Viewtrail 100 is a 100-mi circuit in Worcester County, between Berlin and Pocomoke City. In **Ocean City** the right-hand lanes of Coastal Highway are for buses and bikes. Several boardwalk shops rent bikes.

Fishing

The principal catches are rock fish, black drum, channel bass, flounder, bluefish, white perch, weakfish, croaker, trout, and largemouth bass. One-week **licenses** are sold at many sporting-goods stores; one-year licenses are available from the **Department of Natural Resources** (✉ Box 1869, Annapolis 21404, ☎ 410/260–8367). Bay charters are available through **Bunky's Charter Boats** (✉ Solomons Island Rd., Solomons, ☎ 410/326–3241), the **Fishing Center** (✉ Shantytown Rd., West Ocean City, ☎ 410/213–1121), and **Bahia Marina** (✉ 22nd St. on the bay, Ocean City, ☎ 410/289–7438).

Golf

Eisenhower Golf Course (✉ Generals Hwy., Crownsville, northwest of Annapolis, ☎ 410/571–0973) has 18 holes, and the **Bay Club** (✉ 9122 Libertytown Rd., Berlin, west of Ocean City, ☎ 410/641–4081) has 36 holes. **Ocean City Golf and Yacht Club** (✉ 11401 Country Club Dr., Berlin, ☎ 410/641–1779) has 36 holes.

Sailing

Annapolis Sailing School (✉ 601 6th St., ☎ 410/267–7205 or 800/638–9192) offers outfitting and instruction. **Sailing, Etc.** (✉ 46th St., Bayside, Ocean City, ☎ 410/723–1144) has a wide range of sailboats for rent. **Schooner Woodwind** (✉ 80 Compromise St., Annapolis, ☎ 410/263–7837 or 410/263–8994) runs public and chartered cruises on a 74-ft yacht and rents sailboats and powerboats.

Beaches

Southern Maryland beaches are mainly for strolling, looking, and fossil-collecting. **Sandy Point State Park** (✉ Rte. 50, 12 mi east of Annapolis) is a good area for fishing, swimming, or launching boats. South of Ocean City, the northern portion of **Assateague Island National Seashore** (☞ National and State Parks, *above*) is pristine; wild horses roam the beaches.

Shopping

Prime Outlets at Queenstown (✉ Rte. 50, 10 mi east of the Bay Bridge) has more than 60 factory outlet stores. Galleries, crafts shops, and stores line the streets of Annapolis, Chestertown, and St. Michaels. **Ocean City Factory Outlets** (✉ Rte. 50 and Golf Course Rd.) has about 40 national retail stores, including Ann Taylor, Bass, and Jones New York.

WESTERN MARYLAND

Western Maryland

The region has beautiful mountains, lakes, and rivers, as well as skiing, boating, swimming, fishing, and more than 100 mi of biking trails.

Visitor Information

Allegany County: Convention & Visitors Bureau (⊠ Western Maryland Station Center, 13 Canal St., Cumberland 21502, ☎ 301/777–5132 or 800/508–4748). **Frederick County:** Tourism Council (⊠ 19 E. Church St., 21701, ☎ 301/663–8687 or 800/999–3613). **Hagerstown/Washington counties:** Convention and Visitors Bureau (⊠ 16 Public Sq., 21740, ☎ 301/791–3246 or 800/228–7829).

Arriving and Departing

From Baltimore I–70 runs westward through Frederick and up to the state's narrowest point, pinched between West Virginia and Pennsylvania. U.S. 40 passes through the Narrows into the Panhandle. From Hancock, I–68—the National Highway—is the quickest route to Cumberland, Deep Creek Lake, and several state parks and forests.

What to See and Do

According to legend and poetry, an old woman defied Stonewall Jackson by waving the Stars and Stripes from the **Barbara Fritchie House and Museum** (⊠ 154 W. Patrick St., Frederick, ☎ 301/698–0630; ☜ $2), which is closed January through March.

Mount Olivet Cemetery (⊠ 515 S. Market St., Frederick, ☎ 301/662–1164; ☜ free) is the final resting place of some of Maryland's most famous citizens, including Barbara Fritchie and Francis Scott Key, author of *The Star-Spangled Banner.*

The **National Museum of Civil War Medicine** (⊠ 48 E. Patrick St., Frederick, ☎ 301/695–1864; ☜ $2.50), with more than 3,000 medical artifacts, gives a chilling look at battlefield medical care.

★ At **Antietam National Battlefield** (⊠ Rte. 65, Sharpsburg, ☎ 301/432–5124, ☜ $2) Union troops repelled Lee's invasion in 1862. At the annual **Memorial Illumination,** held the first Saturday in December, the glow of 23,100 candles—one for each of the battle's casualties—illuminates the battlefield.

The **Western Maryland Scenic Railroad** (⊠ 13 Canal St., Cumberland, ☎ 301/759–4400 or 800/872–4650; ☜ $17.50 May–Sept., $19.50 Oct.–Dec.) takes passengers on a vintage 1916 locomotive through mountains and a mile-long gorge. Visitors who arrive in Frostburg via the Scenic Railroad get in free to the **Thrasher Carriage Museum** (⊠ 19 Depot St., Frostburg, ☎ 301/689–3380; closed Jan.–Apr.), which displays early 19th- and 20th-century horse-drawn carriages, such as Theodore Roosevelt's inaugural carriage.

Dining and Lodging

Allegany County

$$–$$$ ✕🖼 **The Inn at Walnut Bottom.** Guest rooms at this cozy, 19th-century inn have comfortable country charm. The Oxford House Restaurant, on the inn's lower level, serves traditional yet inventive dishes. ⊠ *118 Greene St., Cumberland 21502, ☎ 301/777–0003. 12 rooms, 8 with bath. AE, D, MC, V. BP.* ✎

$$–$$$$ 🖼 **Rocky Gap Lodge & Golf Resort.** In the heart of Rocky Gap State Park, this contemporary lodge is in the center of an 18-hole tournament-grade golf course designed by Jack Nicklaus. ⊠ *16701 Lakeview*

Rd. NE, Flintstone 21502, ☎ *301/784–8400 or 800/724–0828,* FAX *301/784–8408. 220 rooms. Restaurant, pool, golf. AE, D, DC, MC, V.*

Frederick County

$–$$$ ✕ **Tauraso's.** In a renovated downtown warehouse, this popular Frederick restaurant serves brick-oven pizza and Italian specialties. ⊠ *6 East St.,* ☎ *301/663–6600. AE, D, DC, MC, V.*

$$$–$$$$ ⊞ **Stone Manor.** Secluded among the rolling hills west of Frederick, this 19th-century stone manor remains a working 114-acre farm. The house has 10 working fireplaces, and antique reproductions fill individually decorated suites. ⊠ *5820 Carroll Boyer Rd., Middletown 21769,* ☎ *301/473–5454. 6 suites. AE, MC, V. BP.*

Washington County

$$–$$$ ⊞ **Antietam Overlook Farm.** This elegant, 19th-century farmhouse overlooks Antietam National Battlefield. Each suite has a fireplace and screened porch with a tub. The inn serves evening cordials and a big breakfast. ⊠ *Porterstown Rd., Keedysville 21756,* ☎ *301/432–4200 or 800/878–4241. 6 rooms. AE, D, MC, V. BP.*

Outdoor Activities and Sports

Deep Creek Lake has year-round recreation: boating, fishing, bicycling, mountain-climbing, hiking, and water and downhill skiing.

Biking

To ride along the C&O Canal, rent bikes at **Potomac Pushbikes** (⊠ 11 E. Potomac St., Williamsport, ☎ 301/582–4747).

Shopping

Prime Outlets at Hagerstown (⊠ 495 Prime Outlets Blvd., at I–70 and Rte. 65) is Maryland's newest factory outlet center, with 76 brand-name outlet stores. Head to the small shops of **New Market** and **Frederick** for antiques.

MASSACHUSETTS

Updated by
A. Copps,
C. Heller,
R. Hertzog,
L. Gibbons
Paul, K. & W.
Scheller,
A. Stuart, and
M. Zanger

Capital	Boston
Population	6,118,000
Motto	By the Sword We Seek Peace, But Peace Only Under Liberty
State Bird	Chickadee
State Flower	Mayflower
Postal Abbreviation	MA

Statewide Visitor Information

Massachusetts Office of Travel and Tourism (⊠ 10 Park Plaza, Suite 4510, Boston 02116, ☎ 617/973–8500 or 800/227–6277; 800/447–6277 for brochures).

Scenic Drives

Much of Cape Cod's **Route 6A,** from Sandwich to Orleans, is a National Historic District preserving traditional New England seacoast towns. **Routes 133 and 1A** on the North Shore, from Gloucester to Newburyport, cover some of the earliest settlements in the United States, dating to the 1630s. In the Berkshires, the **Mohawk Trail,** running 63 mi along Route 2 between Greenfield and North Adams, is famous for its fall foliage, which peaks in late September and early October. In the southwest, **Route 23** from Great Barrington to Westfield travels through wooded hills and rural towns.

National and State Parks

National Park

★ **Cape Cod National Seashore** (☞ Cape Cod and the Islands, *below*), a 30-mi stretch of dune-backed beach between Eastham and Provincetown, has excellent swimming, bird-watching, and nature-trail walking.

State Parks

The **Executive Office of Environmental Affairs** (⊠ Division of Forests and Parks, 100 Cambridge St., Boston 02202, ☎ 617/727–3159) has information on all state parks, including the Heritage state parks, which have exhibits on the state's industrial history.

Mt. Greylock State Reservation (⊠ Rockwell Rd. off Rte. 7, Lanesborough, ☎ 413/499–4262 or 413/499–4263) has the state's highest peak. **Nickerson State Park** (⊠ 3488 Main St. [Rte. 6A], ☎ 508/896–3491; 877/422–6762 for camping reservations), on Cape Cod, has nearly 2,000 acres of forest with walking trails, trout-stocked ponds, and campsites. **Tolland State Forest** (⊠ Rte. 8, Otis, ☎ 413/269–6002), in the Berkshires, has camping facilities and hiking trails.

BOSTON

New England's largest and most important city, and the cradle of American independence, Boston is more than 360 years old. Its most famous buildings are not merely civic landmarks but national icons; its greatest citizens—John Hancock, Paul Revere, and the Adamses—live at the crossroads of history and myth.

Boston is also New England's center of high finance and higher technology, a place of granite-and-glass towers rising along what were once rutted village lanes. Its enormous population of students, academics, artists, and young professionals makes the town a haven for the arts, bookstores, alternative music, and unconventional local politics.

Visitor Information

For general information and brochures, contact the **Greater Boston Convention and Visitors Bureau** (⊠ 2 Copley Pl., Suite 105, 02116, ☎ 617/536–4100 or 800/888–5515), which runs a visitor center near the Park Street station on the T. The **Boston Welcome Center** (⊠ 140 Tremont St., 02111, ☎ 617/451–2227) has general information.

Boston magazine (on newsstands) and *Where: Boston* (free in hotels and visitor centers) list arts and entertainment events. The *Boston Travel Planner,* available from the Greater Boston Convention and Visitors Bureau (☞ *above*), contains a calendar of events, sports and regional activities, and information on hotel weekend packages.

Arriving and Departing

By Bus
Bonanza Bus Lines (☎ 800/556–3815), **Greyhound** (☎ 800/231–2222), **Peter Pan Bus Lines** (☎ 617/426–7838 or 800/237–8747), and **Plymouth & Brockton Street Railway Buses** (☎ 508/746–0378) serve Massachusetts. The depot in Boston for these bus companies is **South Station** (⊠ Atlantic Ave. and Summer St., ☎ 617/345–7451).

By Car
Boston is the traffic hub of New England: I–95 (which is the same as Route 128 in parts) skirts the city along the coast, while I–90 (the Massachusetts Turnpike toll road) heads west. I–93 connects Boston to the north and New Hampshire; the highway runs through the city as the Fitzgerald Expressway. This section of I–93 is scheduled to be turned into an underground highway as part of the massive Central Artery Project; expect construction and delays here into 2004.

By Plane
Logan International Airport (⊠ I–93N, Exit 24, ☎ 617/561–1800 or 800/235–6426) has scheduled flights by most major domestic and foreign carriers. Cab fare to downtown is about $20 including tip. For 24-hour information on parking, bicycle access, and bus, subway, and water-shuttle transportation, call Logan's **Ground Transportation Desk** (☎ 800/235–6426). The **Massachusetts Bay Transportation Authority** (MBTA; ☎ 617/722–3200; 800/392–6100; 617/722–5146 TTY) Blue Line subway from the Airport station (85¢) goes downtown; free shuttle buses connect the station with airline terminals and run every 8–12 minutes from 5:30 AM to 1 AM.

By Train
Amtrak (☎ 800/872–7245) serves Boston. All trains stop at South Station; some stop at Back Bay station and the easy-access Route 128 station in Canton, south of the city. At press time (summer 2000) Amtrak had plans to begin high-speed Acela service along its Northeast Corridor line; this was to replace Metroliner service.

Getting Around Boston

Boston is meant for walking; a majority of its historic and architectural attractions are found in compact areas.

By Car
Due to a profusion of one-way streets and streets with the same name, Boston is not an easy city to drive in. It's a good idea to look at a map

Boston

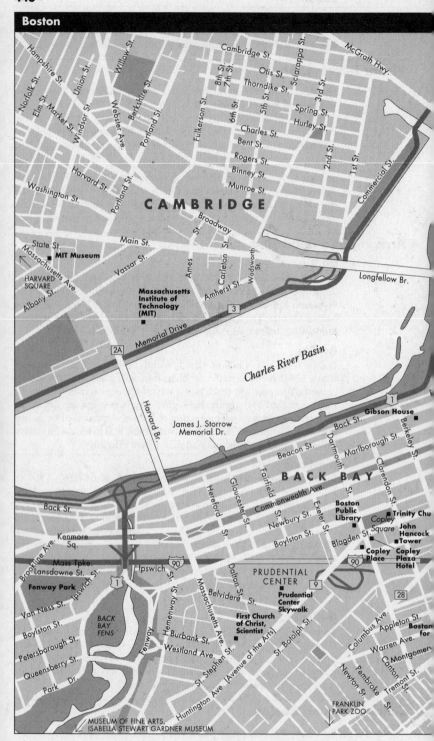

Hampshire St.

Norfolk St.

Elm St.

Market St.

Union St.

Willow St.

Windsor St.

Webster Ave.

Berkshire St.

Portland St.

Cambridge St.

8th St.

7th St.

6th St.

5th St.

Otis St.

Thorndike St.

Fulkerson St.

Sciarappa St.

3rd St.

Spring St.

Hurley St.

2nd St.

1st St.

McGrath Hwy.

Charles St.

Bent St.

Rogers St.

Binney St.

Munroe St.

Harvard St.

Washington St.

Portland St.

Commercial St.

CAMBRIDGE

Broadway

Main St.

State St.

■ MIT Museum

Massachusetts Ave.

HARVARD SQUARE

Albany St.

Vassar St.

Ames St.

Carleton St.

Wadsworth St.

Massachusetts Institute of Technology (MIT) ■

Memorial Drive

Amherst St.

Longfellow Br.

[2A]

[3]

Harvard Br.

Charles River Basin

James J. Storrow Memorial Dr.

Back St.

Gibson House

Berkeley St.

Beacon St.

Dartmouth St.

Marlborough St.

Clarendon St.

BACK BAY

Fairfield St.

Hereford St.

Gloucester St.

Commonwealth Ave.

Newbury St.

Exeter St.

Boylston St.

Boston Public Library ■

Copley Square

■ **Trinity Chu**

John Hancock Tower ■

Blagden St.

Copley Place ■

■ **Copley Plaza Hotel**

Back St.

Kenmore Sq.

Brookline Ave.

Mass Tpke.

Lansdowne St.

Ipswich St.

Ipswich

Fenway Park ■

[1]

[90]

[9]

[28]

PRUDENTIAL CENTER

Prudential Center Skywalk ■

Dalton St.

Belvidere St.

Massachusetts Ave.

Van Ness St.

Boylston St.

Petersborough St.

Queensberry St.

Park Dr.

BACK BAY FENS

Fenway

Hemenway St.

Burbank St.

Westland Ave.

St. Stephen St.

First Church of Christ, Scientist ■

Huntington Ave. (Avenue of the Arts)

St. Botolph St.

Columbus Ave.

Warren Ave.

Pembroke St.

Newton St.

Canton St.

Tremont St.

Appleton St.

Montgomery

Bosto for

FRANKLIN PARK ZOO ↓

MUSEUM OF FINE ARTS, ISABELLA STEWART GARDNER MUSEUM ↓

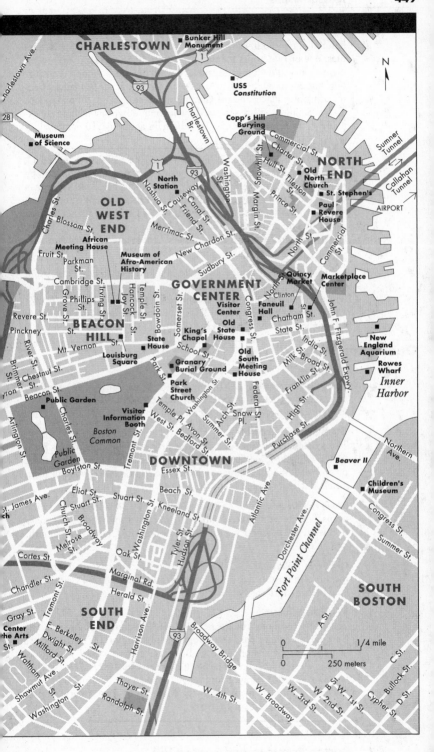

first and keep one with you at all times. Furthermore, parking is a tricky business. Some neighborhoods have residents-only rules, with just a handful of two-hour visitor spaces; others have meters (25¢ for 15 minutes, one or two hours maximum). Major public lots are at Government Center and Quincy Market, beneath Boston Common (entrance on Charles Street), beneath Post Office Square, at the Prudential Center, at Copley Place, and off Clarendon Street near the John Hancock Tower. Smaller lots are scattered throughout downtown. Most are expensive; the few city garages are a bargain at about $10 per day.

By Public Transportation

The **MBTA** (☎ 617/722–3200; 800/392–6100; 617/722–5146 TTY), known as the T, operates subways, elevated trains, and trolleys along four connecting lines—Red, Blue, Green, and Orange. Trains run from 5:30 AM to about 12:30 AM daily; adult base fare is 85¢. Visitor passes, available for $5 for one day, $9 for three days, and $18 for seven days, can be bought at the following MBTA stations: Airport, South Station, North Station, Back Bay, Government Center, and Harvard Square.

By Taxi

Cabs are not easily hailed; if you're in a hurry, try a hotel taxi stand or telephone for a cab. Fares run about $2 per mile. Companies offering 24-hour service include **Cambridge Checker Cab** (☎ 617/497–1500), **Checker** (☎ 617/536–7000), and **Independent Taxi Operators Association** (ITOA; ☎ 617/426–8700).

Orientation Tours

By Boat

Boston Harbor Cruises (✉ 1 Long Wharf, ☎ 617/227–4321) operates several cruises departing from Long Wharf, including a whale-watching cruise from mid-April to October.

By Bus and Trolley

The red **Beantown Trolleys** (✉ Transportation Bldg., 14 Charles St. S, ☎ 617/236–2148 or 800/343–1328) makes more than 20 stops; get on and off as many times as you like. The $20 tickets are available from hotel concierges and at many attractions.

Brush Hill/Gray Line (☎ 617/236–2148 or 800/343–1328) buses pick up passengers from several suburban and downtown hotels for tours of Boston and neighboring towns like Lexington, Concord, Plymouth, and Salem.

Old Town Trolley (☎ 617/269–7010) runs tours from several different locations in Boston every 30 minutes from 9 AM to 3 or 4 PM for $21. Cambridge tours are also available.

Walking Tours

The 2½-mi **Freedom Trail** (☎ 617/242–5642), marked on the sidewalk by a red line, winds past 16 of Boston's most important historic sites, beginning at the visitor center at Boston Common, where you'll find maps and other brochures. The **Black Heritage Trail**® (☎ 617/742–5415) begins at Boston Common and moves through the Beacon Hill neighborhood. Maps are available at the Museum of Afro American History on Smith Court, off Joy Street.

Exploring Boston

Boston Common and Beacon Hill

★ **Boston Common**, the oldest public park in the United States and the site of festivals, political rallies, and family outings, is the heart of Boston. At the Congregationalist **Park Street Church** (✉ 1 Park St., ☎ 617/523–

3383), finished in 1810, Samuel Smith's hymn "America" was first sung in 1831. The **Granary Burying Ground** (⊠ Tremont St.), next to Park Street Church, is where Revolutionary heroes Samuel Adams, John Hancock, and Paul Revere lie.

★ At the summit of Beacon Hill is Charles Bulfinch's magnificent neoclassical **State House** (⊠ Beacon St. between Hancock and Bowdoin Sts., ☎ 617/727–3676; ⊠ free), its dome both sheathed in copper from Paul Revere's foundry and gilded after the Civil War. Tours are given on weekdays and Saturday; you can also visit on your own.

★ With its brick row houses, most built between 1800 and 1850, the classic face of **Beacon Hill** is in a style never far from the early Federal norm. **Chestnut and Mt. Vernon streets** are distinguished not only for their individual houses but also for their general atmosphere and character. Henry James lived on Mt. Vernon, which opens out on **Louisburg Square**, the heart of Beacon Hill. Once the home address of William Dean Howells and Louisa May Alcott, the square was an 1840s model for town house development.

On the north slope of Beacon Hill is the 1806 **African Meeting House** (⊠ 8 Smith Ct., ☎ 617/739–1200), the oldest African-American church building in the United States. The New England Anti-Slavery Society was formed here in 1832. The site marks the end of the Black Heritage Trail®. At press time, the African Meeting House was expected to be closed for extensive renovations, due for completion sometime in 2001. Call ahead for the latest information. Adjacent to the meeting house is the newly renovated **Abiel Smith School**, the first public school for black children in the United States, and **Museum of Afro American History**.

The North End and Charlestown

In the 17th century the **North End** *was* Boston, as much of the rest of the peninsula was still under water. Since the 20th century the North End has been Italian Boston, full of restaurants, bakeries, churches, social clubs, cafés, and festivals honoring saints and food.

Off Hanover Street, the North End's main thoroughfare is North Square. The **Paul Revere House,** the oldest home still standing in Boston, was built nearly a century before its illustrious tenant's midnight ride. Colonial-era furniture decorates the rooms. ⊠ *19 North Sq., ☎ 617/523–2338. ⊠ $2.50. Closed Mon., Jan.–Mar.*

Past North Square on Hanover Street is **St. Stephen's** (⊠ 401 Hanover St., ☎ 617/523–1230), the only Charles Bulfinch–designed church still standing in Boston. The steeple of Christ Church, more commonly ★ known as the **Old North Church** (⊠ 193 Salem St., ☎ 617/523–6676)—where Paul Revere hung the two lanterns to signal Cambridge residents on the night of April 18, 1775—can be seen on Tileston Street. It's the oldest church building in Boston.

Cross the Charlestown Bridge to reach the **USS Constitution,** nicknamed "Old Ironsides" for the strength of its oaken hull, which seemed to repel cannon fire. Launched in 1797, it is the oldest commissioned ship in the U.S. Navy and is moored at the Charlestown Navy Yard. During its service against the Barbary pirates and in the War of 1812, the ship never lost an engagement. Nearby is the **Constitution Museum,** which tells the story of the ship with artifacts, maps, photos, and videos. ⊠ *Charleston Navy Yard, off Water St., ☎ 617/242–5670; 617/ 426–1812 for the museum. ⊠ Constitution free, museum free.*

★ The Battle of Bunker Hill was actually fought on Breed's Hill, and this is where Solomon Willard's **Bunker Hill Monument** (⊠ Main St. to Monument St., then straight uphill, ☎ 617/242–5641, ⊠ free)—a 221-ft shaft of Quincy granite—stands. It rises from the spot where on June 17, 1775, a citizens' militia—reputedly commanded not to fire "until you see the whites of their eyes"—inflicted more than 1,100 casualties on British regulars (who eventually did seize the hill). The views from the top are worth the 294-step ascent.

Downtown Boston

Downtown is east of Boston Common. There is little logic to the streets here because they were once village lanes; they are now lined with 40-story office towers. The granite **King's Chapel** (⊠ 58 Tremont St., at School St., ☎ 617/227–2155), built in 1754, houses Paul Revere's largest and—in his own judgment—sweetest-sounding bell.

The **Old South Meeting House** (⊠ 310 Washington St., ☎ 617/482–6439; ☞ $3), built in 1729, is Boston's second-oldest church. Many of the fiery town meetings that led to the Revolution were held here, including the one called by Samuel Adams concerning some dutiable tea that activists wanted returned to England.

A brightly gilded lion and unicorn, symbols of British imperial power, adorn the facade of the **Old State House** (⊠ 206 Washington St., ☎ 617/720–3290; ☞ $3). This was the seat of the Colonial government from 1713 until the Revolution. The museum within the structure surveys Boston's revolutionary history. The site of the Boston Massacre is marked by a circle of stones in the traffic island in front of the building.

☾ The **Children's Museum** (⊠ 300 Congress St., ☎ 617/426–6500; ☞ $7) contains hands-on exhibits, many designed to help children understand science, cultural diversity, their bodies, and the nature of disabilities.

★ **Faneuil Hall** (⊠ Faneuil Hall Sq., ☎ 617/338–2323; ☞ free), erected in 1742 to serve as both a town meeting hall and a public market, is where in 1772 Samuel Adams first suggested that Massachusetts and the other colonies organize a Committee of Correspondence to maintain semi-clandestine lines of communication in the face of hardening British repression. In national election years the hall usually hosts debates among contenders in the Massachusetts presidential primary. On the top floors are the headquarters and museum of the Ancient and Honorable Artillery Company of Massachusetts, the oldest militia in the nation (1638).

Quincy Market (⊠ off State St., ☎ 617/338–2323), near Faneuil Hall, has served as a retail and wholesale distribution center for meat and produce for 150 years. It houses retail shops, restaurants, and offices. Some people consider it all hopelessly trendy, but the 50,000 visitors who come here in the peak summer season seem to enjoy it. **Marketplace Center,** at the waterfront end of Quincy Market, is another complex that houses more shops, eateries, and boutiques.

The most glittering addition to Boston's waterfront can be found on **Rowes Wharf**—a 15-story redbrick Skidmore, Owings & Merrill extravaganza, gaily adorned with white trim and home to chic restaurants, shops, and the Boston Harbor Hotel (☞ Lodging, *below*).

Seals, penguins, a variety of sharks, and other sea creatures reside at the **New England Aquarium** (⊠ Central Wharf, ☎ 617/973–5200; ☞ $12.50), which has a four-story, 187,000-gallon coral reef tank. The glass-and-steel exterior of the West Wing mimics fish scales.

When you cross Fort Point Channel on the Congress Street Bridge, you encounter the *Beaver II,* a faithful replica of a Boston Tea Party ship, like the ones forcibly boarded and unloaded on the night Boston Harbor itself became a teapot. ⊠ *Congress St. Bridge,* ☎ *617/338–1773.* ☞ *$8. Closed Dec.–Feb.*

Back Bay and the South End

Southwest of Boston Common is **Back Bay,** once a tidal flat that formed the south bank of a distended Charles River until it was filled as far as the Fens in the 19th century. Back Bay is a living museum of urban Victorian residential architecture. One of the first Back Bay residences (1859), the **Gibson House** (⊠ 137 Beacon St., ☎ 617/267–6338; ☞ $5) has been preserved with all its Victorian fixtures and furniture intact.

Newbury Street, Boston's poshest shopping district, is lined with sidewalk cafés and dozens of upscale specialty shops offering clothing, china, antiques, and art.

From the 60th-floor observatory of the tallest building in New England, the 62-story **John Hancock Tower** (⊠ Observatory ticket office, Trinity Pl. and St. James Ave., ☎ 617/247–1977; ☞ $6), you'll have one of the best vantage points in the city.

Copley Square, where the Boston Marathon runners end their 26-mi race, is dominated by monumental architecture. The 1912 **Copley Plaza Hotel** (⊠ 138 St. James Ave.) is a stately, bowfront structure. **Trinity Church** (⊠ 206 Clarendon St., ☎ 617/536–0944) is Henry Hobson Richardson's Romanesque Revival masterwork of 1877. The **Boston Public Library** (⊠ Dartmouth St. at Copley Sq., ☎ 617/536–5400) confirmed the status of McKim, Mead & White as apostles of Renaissance Revival in 1895. The modern complex **Copley Place** comprises two major hotels (the Westin and the Marriott; ☞ Lodging, *below*), dozens of shops and restaurants, and a cinema.

The headquarters of the **First Church of Christ, Scientist** (⊠ 175 Huntington Ave., at Massachusetts Ave., ☎ 617/450–3790) is a striking mixture of old and new architecture. Mary Baker Eddy's original church structure (1894) and the domed Renaissance basilica added to the site in 1906 are now surrounded by the offices of the *Christian Science Monitor* and by I. M. Pei's 1973 complex of church administration buildings with its distinctive reflecting pool. Tours of the church are available every day except Saturday. Overlooking the Christian Science Church, the **Prudential Center Skywalk** (⊠ 800 Boylston St., ☎ 617/859–0648; ☞ $4) is a 50th-floor observatory with great views of the city and suburbs.

The **South End,** eclipsed by the Back Bay more than a century ago, has now been gentrified, with galleries and restaurants catering to young professionals, including a large concentration of Boston's gay population. The houses here continue the pattern established on Beacon Hill (in a uniformly bowfront style) but have more florid decoration.

The South End has a strong African-American presence, particularly along Columbus Avenue and Massachusetts Avenue, which marks the beginning of the Roxbury neighborhood. The early integration of the South End set the stage for its transformation into a remarkably polyglot population. At the northeastern extreme of the South End, Harrison Avenue and Washington Street connect the area with Chinatown.

On Tremont Street you'll find blocks of trendy restaurants and the **Boston Center for the Arts** (⊠ 539 Tremont St., ☎ 617/426–5000; ☞ free), which has a gallery, several small theaters, and the "Cyclorama," a large space now devoted to antiques shows, exhibits, and other events.

The Fens

The **Fens,** a park designed by Frederick Law Olmsted, consists of still, irregular, and reed-bound pools surrounded by broad meadows, trees, and flower gardens.

★ The **Museum of Fine Arts** (✉ 465 Huntington Ave., ☎ 617/267–9300,
💲 $12) has holdings of American art surpassing those of all but two or
three other U.S. museums; an extensive collection of Asian art; and European artwork from the 11th century through the present. Count on
staying a while to have *any* hope of seeing even a smidgen of what is here.
The museum has two restaurants, a cafeteria, and a popular gift shop.

★ The **Isabella Stewart Gardner Museum** is a monument to one woman's
taste. The emphasis among the 2,000 spectacular paintings, sculptures, furniture, and textiles is on Italian Renaissance and 17th-cen-
tury Dutch masters. Friend to John Singer Sargent, Edith Wharton, and
Henry James, Gardner shocked proper Bostonians with the flamboyance of her Venetian-style palazzo. The highlight of the collection—
and according to some scholars, the greatest painting in an American
museum—is Titian's *Rape of Europa*. At the center of the building is
a soaring courtyard planted with flowers. ✉ *280 The Fenway,* ☎ *617/*
566–1401. 💲 *$12. Closed Mon. except for some holidays.*

The Boston shrine known as **Fenway Park** (✉ 4 Yawkey Way, ☎ 617/
267–8661; 617/267–1700 for tickets) is one of the smallest and oldest baseball parks in the major leagues. It was built in 1912 and still
has real grass on the field. **Kenmore Square** (✉ Commonwealth Ave.,
Brookline Ave., and Beacon St. intersection) is home to fast-food parlors, alternative rock clubs, an abundance of students from nearby Boston
University, and the enormous neon CITGO sign, an area landmark.

Cambridge

In 1636 the country's first college was established in Cambridge, across
the Charles River from Boston. Three years later it was named in
honor of John Harvard, a young Charlestown clergyman who had died,
leaving the college his entire library and half his estate. **Harvard** was
the only college in the American colonies until 1693. The **Harvard University Events and Information Center** (✉ 1350 Massachusetts Ave.,
☎ 617/495–1573), in Holyoke Center, offers area maps and a free one-
hour tour of Harvard Yard most days. Near the Cambridge Common
is **Radcliffe College,** founded in 1897; since 1975 Radcliffe students have
shared classes and degrees with Harvard students.

Harvard University has three celebrated art museums, each a treasure
in itself. A $5 admission price covers all three museums. The **Fogg Art
Museum** (✉ 32 Quincy St., ☎ 617/495–9400) is the most famous of
the Harvard museums. Founded in 1895, it now owns 80,000 works
of art from every major period and from every corner of the world. Its
focus is primarily on European and American art from the 14th century to the present. The museum's most significant works are a Van Gogh
self-portrait and Edgar Degas's ballet-theme painting, *The Rehearsal*.
In Werner Otto Hall the **Busch-Reisinger Museum,** which is entered
through the Fogg Art Museum, has a collection that specializes in Ger-
manic and Central and Northern European art from the 16th century
to the present. Across the street from the Fogg, the **Arthur M. Sackler
Museum** (✉ 485 Broadway, ☎ 617/495–9400) concentrates on ancient
Greek and Roman, Egyptian, Islamic, Chinese, and other Eastern art.

The **Massachusetts Institute of Technology (MIT),** which borders the
Charles River southeast of Harvard Square, boasts distinctive architecture by I. M. Pei and Eero Saarinen. The **Information Center** (✉ 77 Massachusetts Ave., Bldg. 7, ☎ 617/253–4795) offers free tours of the MIT campus
weekdays at 10 and 2. Art and science meet in the **MIT Museum** (✉ 265
Massachusetts Ave., ☎ 617/253–4444; 💲 $5), which showcases scien-
tific instruments and memorabilia. Of special interest are the museum's
alluring collection of holograms and stop-motion photography.

Parks, Gardens, and Zoos

★ The **Boston Public Garden,** next to Boston Common, is the oldest botanical garden in the United States. Its pond has been famous since 1877 for its foot pedal–powered Swan Boats, which offer leisurely cruises during the warm months of the year. The **Franklin Park Zoo** (⊠ 1 Franklin Park Rd., ☎ 617/442–2002 or 617/442–4896; ☞ $7) includes lions and cheetahs in its roster of exotic animals.

Dining

$$$$ ✕ **L'Espalier.** An elegantly modernized Victorian Back Bay town house is the setting for an intoxicating blend of new French and contemporary New England cuisine. You can simplify the opulent menu by choosing a prix-fixe tasting menu, such as the innovative vegetarian degustation. ⊠ 30 Gloucester St., Back Bay, ☎ 617/262–3023. Reservations essential. Jacket and tie. AE, D, DC, MC, V. Closed Sun. No lunch.

$$$–$$$$ ✕ **Biba.** The menu at Boston's best restaurant encourages inventive com-
★ binations, unusual cuts of meat and produce, haute comfort food, and big postmodern desserts. Take your time, and don't settle for the "classic lobster pizza" if something like "vanilla chicken with chestnut puree" is available. The wine list is an adventure. ⊠ 272 Boylston St., Back Bay, ☎ 617/426–7878. Reservations essential. AE, D, DC, MC, V.

$$$–$$$$ ✕ **Mamma Maria.** One of the most elegant and romantic restaurants
★ in the North End, Boston's remarkable Little Italy, Mamma Maria sneaks in a lot of serious cuisine, like the smoked-seafood ravioli appetizer, among the homemade pasta entrées you might expect. ⊠ 3 North Sq., North End, ☎ 617/523–0077. AE, D, DC, MC, V.

$$$–$$$$ ✕ **Olives.** This bistro sets the local standard for grilled pizza and sig-
★ nature offerings like the smoked beef short ribs. The crowded seating, noise, long lines, and abrupt service only add to the legend. Come early or late—or be prepared for an extended wait: Reservations are taken only for groups of six or more at 5:30 or 8:30 PM, and there are few nearby alternatives. ⊠ 10 City Sq., ☎ 617/242–1999. AE, DC, MC, V. Closed Sun. No lunch.

$$$–$$$$ ✕ **Union Oyster House.** At Boston's oldest continuing restaurant (it was established in 1826), it's best to have what Daniel Webster had—oysters on the half shell at the ground-floor raw bar, which is the oldest part of the restaurant and still the best. The rooms at the top of the narrow staircase are very Ye Olde New England. Uncomfortably small tables and chairs tend to undermine the simple, decent, but expensive food. ⊠ 41 Union St., Faneuil Hall, ☎ 617/227–2750. AE, D, DC, MC, V.

$$–$$$$ ✕ **Grill 23 & Bar.** Dark paneling, comically oversized flatware, and waiters in white jackets lend this steak house a men's-club ambience. The rotisserie tenderloin with Roquefort mashed potatoes is a winner, as is the meat loaf with mashed potatoes and truffle oil. Seafood actually outsells beef by a narrow margin; grilled Maine salmon is one reason why. Break out your jacket and tie. ⊠ 161 Berkeley St., ☎ 617/542–2255. Reservations essential. AE, D, DC, MC, V. No lunch.

$$–$$$$ ✕ **Hamersley's Bistro.** Gordon Hamersley has earned renown for such
★ signature dishes as a grilled mushroom–and–garlic sandwich, duck confit, and souffléed lemon custard. His place has a full bar, a café area with 10 tables for walk-ins, and a larger dining room that's a little more formal and decorative. ⊠ 553 Tremont St., South End, ☎ 617/423–2700. AE, D, DC, MC, V.

$$–$$$$ ✕ **Legal Sea Foods.** The hallmark here is top-quality seafood; dishes come to the table in whatever order they leave the kitchen, since freshness is key. The smoked bluefish pâté is one of the finest appetizers anywhere, and don't miss the chowders. ⊠ 26 Park Sq., ☎ 617/426–4444; 255 State St., ☎ 617/227–3115; ⊠ Cambridge: 5 Cambridge Center,

Kendall Sq., ☎ *617/864–3400;* ☒ *Logan Airport: Terminal C,* ☎ *617/569–4622. Reservations not accepted. AE, D, DC, MC, V.*

$$–$$$ ✕ **Les Zygomates.** This restaurant serves up classic French bistro fare
★ that dares to be simple and simply delicious. Prix-fixe menus are offered for both lunch and dinner. Pan-seared catfish with house vinaigrette and roasted rabbit leg stuffed with vegetables typify the taste. ☒ *129 South St., Downtown,* ☎ *617/542–5108. Reservations essential. AE, D, DC, MC, V. No lunch weekends.*

$–$$$ ✕ **Sonsie.** This restaurant, which opens at 7 AM, is famous for breakfasts that extend well into the afternoon. In warm weather, the entire front of Sonsie becomes an open-air café looking out on upper Newbury Street. The dishes on the menu are basic bistro with an American twist, such as a pan-seared fish sandwich with spicy tartar sauce. ☒ *327 Newbury St., Back Bay,* ☎ *617/351–2500. AE, DC, MC, V.*

$–$$ ✕ **Chau Chow.** Seafood is the speciality at this Chinese restaurant: Try the clams in black bean sauce, steamed sea bass, or any dish with their famous ginger sauce. Chau Chow has expanded to a larger storefront called **Grand Chau Chow** (☎ *617/426–6266*) across the street and to an enormous two-block-wide palace, **Chau Chow City** (☎ *617/338–8158*), at 83 Essex Street. Seating at old Chau Chow is very tight. ☒ *50–52 Beach St., Chinatown,* ☎ *617/292–5166. No credit cards.*

$ ✕ **Mr. and Mrs. Bartley's Burger Cottage.** It may be perfect cuisine for the student metabolism: a huge variety of variously garnished thick burgers, french fries, and onion rings. (There's also a competent veggie burger.) The nonalcoholic "raspberry lime rickey," made with fresh limes, raspberry juice, sweetener, and soda water, is the must-try drink. Tiny tables in a crowded space make it a convenient place for Phi Beta eavesdropping. ☒ *1246 Massachusetts Ave., Cambridge,* ☎ *617/354–6559. Reservations not accepted. No credit cards. Closed Sun.*

Lodging

Many of the city's most costly lodgings offer attractively priced weekend packages. Consult the *Boston Travel Planner* (☞ Visitor Information, *above*) for current rates. Bed-and-breakfasts can be a less-expensive alternative.

$$$$ 🏨 **Boston Harbor Hotel at Rowes Wharf.** Everything here is done on a
★ grand scale, starting with the dramatic entrance through an 80-ft archway. Guest rooms—all being renovated to include marble bathrooms, fresh flowers, and a custom-made desk—have city or water views. ☒ *70 Rowes Wharf, 02110,* ☎ *617/439–7000 or 800/752–7077,* FAX *617/330–9450. 230 rooms. 2 restaurants, pool, health club. AE, D, DC, MC, V.*☜

$$$$ 🏨 **Fairmont Copley Plaza.** The public spaces of this 1912 landmark are
★ grand, with high gilded and painted ceilings, mosaic floors, marble pillars, and crystal chandeliers; guest rooms have antique and repro-antique furniture, elegant marble bathrooms, and fax machines. ☒ *138 St. James Ave., 02116,* ☎ *617/267–5300 or 800/527–4727,* FAX *617/375–9648. 379 rooms. 2 restaurants, exercise room. AE, D, DC, MC, V.*☜

$$$$ 🏨 **Four Seasons.** The Four Seasons is famed for luxurious personal service of the sort demanded by celebrities and heads of state. It has huge
★ rooms with king-size beds and new carpeting, spreads, and artwork. The Bristol Lounge serves afternoon tea daily. ☒ *200 Boylston St., 02116,* ☎ *617/338–4400 or 800/332–3442,* FAX *617/423–0154. 288 rooms. 2 restaurants, pool, health club. AE, D, DC, MC, V.*☜

$$$$ 🏨 **Lenox Hotel.** The guest rooms here have custom-made traditional furnishings and marble baths; some of the corner rooms have working wood-burning fireplaces. The Samuel Adams Brew House and the popular bistro Anago are both worthy stops. ☒ *710 Boylston St., 02116,* ☎ *617/536–5300 or 800/225–7676,* FAX *617/267–1237. 212 rooms. 3 restaurants, exercise room. AE, D, DC, MC, V.*☜

$$$$ ★ **🏨 Ritz-Carlton.** Suites in the older section have parlors with working fireplaces and views of the public garden. Standard rooms are small but stately. Public rooms include the dining room, with its stunning chandelier; the Roof Restaurant; and the lounge. ⊠ *15 Arlington St., 02117,* ☎ *617/536–5700 or 800/241–3333,* 🇫🇦🇽 *617/536–1335. 275 rooms. 3 restaurants, exercise room. AE, D, DC, MC, V.* 🐾

$$$–$$$$ ★ **🏨 Eliot Hotel.** The luxurious suites at the Eliot have Italian marble bathrooms, two cable-equipped televisions, and tasteful pastel-hue decor. The airy restaurant, Clio, has been garnering rave reviews for its serene ambience and contemporary French-American cuisine. The Eliot is steps from Newbury Street and a short walk to Kenmore Square. ⊠ *370 Commonwealth Ave., 02215,* ☎ *617/267–1607 or 800/443–5468,* 🇫🇦🇽 *617/ 247–1997. 95 suites. Restaurant. AE, D, DC, MC, V.* 🐾

$$–$$$$ **🏨 A Cambridge House Bed and Breakfast.** This Greek Revival B&B is a haven of peace and otherworldliness, with richly carved cherry paneling, a grand cherry fireplace, elegant Victorian antiques, and polished wood floors overlaid with Oriental rugs. Harvard Square is a distant walk, but public transportation is nearby. ⊠ *2218 Massachusetts Ave., Cambridge 02140,* ☎ *617/491–6300 or 800/232–9989,* 🇫🇦🇽 *617/868– 2848. 15 rooms. AE, D, DC, MC, V. No smoking. BP.* 🐾

$$–$$$ **🏨 The Gryphon House.** Each suite in this four-story brownstone is thematically decorated—one evokes a Victorian parlor, another a medieval castle—and each is rich with amenities like fireplaces, wet bars, refrigerators, TV/VCRs, and CD players. ⊠ *9 Bay State Rd., 02215,* ☎ *617/ 375–9003,* 🇫🇦🇽 *617/425–0716. 8 suites. AE, D, DC, MC, V. CP.* 🐾

$–$$ **🏨 Chandler Inn.** This cozy little hotel with its friendly staff is one of the best bargains in the city. Located at the end of one of the South End's prettiest streets, it's an easy walk to the T, the Amtrak station, Newbury Street's boutiques, or any of Tremont Street's trendy restaurants. Rooms are small but comfortable. ⊠ *26 Chandler St., 02115,* ☎ *617/ 482–3450,* 🇫🇦🇽 *617/542–3428. 56 rooms. AE, D, DC, MC, V. CP.*

$–$$ **🏨 John Jeffries House.** This turn-of-the-20th-century house has rooms with French country decor. Triple-glazed windows block virtually all noise from busy Charles Circle. Most rooms have kitchenettes and many have views of the Charles River. At the foot of Beacon Hill, the inn is an easy walk from public transportation and most of downtown. ⊠ *14 David G. Mugar Way, 02114,* ☎ *617/367–1866,* 🇫🇦🇽 *617/742– 0313. 46 rooms. AE, D, DC, MC, V. CP.*

Motels

🏨 Holiday Inn Boston Airport (⊠ 225 McClellan Hwy., East Boston, 02128, ☎ 617/569–5250 or 800/798–5849, 🇫🇦🇽 617/569–5159), 354 rooms; restaurant, pool, exercise room; $$–$$$.

🏨 Susse Chalet Inn (⊠ 211 Concord Tpke., 02140, ☎ 617/661–7800 or 800/524–2538, 🇫🇦🇽 617/868–8153), 78 rooms; CP; $.

Nightlife and the Arts

The *Boston Globe* calendar and the weekly *Boston Phoenix,* both published on Thursday, provide listings of events for the coming week. Also see the *Globe*'s Sunday "Arts" section and *Boston* magazine's arts listings.

Nightlife

Faneuil Hall Marketplace and **Kenmore Square** in Boston and **Harvard and Central squares** in Cambridge are centers of nightlife.

BARS AND LOUNGES

Bay Tower Room (⊠ 60 State St., ☎ 617/723–1666) offers piano music and dancing every night but Sunday; dress up. The **Black Rose**

(✉ 160 State St., Faneuil Hall, ☎ 617/742–2286) is the city's best-known Irish pub, complete with live Celtic music. **Boston Beer Works** (✉ 61 Brookline Ave., near Fenway Park, ☎ 617/536–2337) brews up regular and seasonal brews for a youngish crowd. **Bull & Finch Pub** (✉ 84 Beacon St., at Hampshire House, ☎ 617/227–9605) was the inspiration for the TV series *Cheers*. **John Harvard's Brew House** (✉ 33 Dunster St., Harvard Sq., ☎ 617/868–3585) serves up ales, lagers, pilsners, and stouts brewed on the premises; take a close look at the stained-glass windows depicting celebrity beer drinkers. **Top of the Hub** (✉ Prudential Center, Back Bay, ☎ 617/536–1775) has expensive drinks—a worthwhile trade-off for a 52nd-floor view and live jazz.

CAFÉS AND COFFEEHOUSES

Caffé Vittoria (✉ 296 Hanover St., ☎ 617/227–7606) is a great after-dinner stop for coffee and desserts such as tiramisu and cannoli; check out the historic jukebox. **Lulu's Tealuxe** (✉ Zero Brattle St., Harvard Sq., Cambridge, ☎ 617/441–0077) is a tiny "tea bar" with more than 100 different blends. **Roasters** (✉ 85 Newbury St., Back Bay, ☎ 617/867–9967) has both indoor and outdoor seating for sipping coffee and people-watching.

COMEDY

Comedy Connection (✉ Faneuil Hall Marketplace, ☎ 617/248–9700) books local and nationally known acts. **Dick Doherty's Comedy Vault** (✉ 124 Boylston St., Theater District, ☎ 781/938–8088) and other area locations have stand-up, improv, and open-mike comedy. **Nick's Comedy Stop** (✉ 100 Warrenton St., Theater District, ☎ 617/482–0930) presents local comics every night except Monday.

DANCE CLUBS

Axis (✉ 13 Lansdowne St., ☎ 617/262–2424), near Kenmore Square, has high-energy dancing for more than 1,000 people; themes include the techno-music X Nights (Friday) and Gay Night (Sunday). **M-80,** part of the **Paradise Rock Club** (✉ 967 Commonwealth Ave., ☎ 617/562–8800), offers dancing for a young, largely international, designer-clothes-clad crowd. **Man Ray** (✉ 21 Brookline St., Inman Sq., Cambridge, ☎ 617/864–0400) is the home of Boston's goth and alternative scenes, with Friday Fetish Nights. **Roxy** (✉ 279 Tremont St., Theater District, ☎ 617/338–7699), Boston's biggest nightclub, has theme nights ranging from reggae to Latin to swing. **Venu** (✉ 100 Warrenton St., Theater District, ☎ 617/338–8061) brings a Miami feel to Boston; local DJs provide dance music.

MUSIC

Avalon (✉ 15 Lansdowne St., near Kenmore Sq., ☎ 617/262–2424), famous for state-of-the-art light-and-sound systems, has alternative, rock, and dance concerts. **Club Passim** (✉ 47 Palmer St., Harvard Sq., Cambridge, ☎ 617/492–7679) hosts folk music. **House of Blues** (✉ 96 Winthrop St., Harvard Sq., Cambridge, ☎ 617/491–2583) offers blues nightly and a gospel brunch on Sunday. **Marketplace Café** (✉ 300 Faneuil Hall, ☎ 617/227–9660) has a nightly blues or jazz show and no cover charge. The **Paradise Rock Club** (✉ 967 Commonwealth Ave., near Boston University, ☎ 617/227–9660) and **Middle East Café** (✉ 472 Massachusetts Ave., Central Sq., Cambridge, ☎ 617/497–0576) host live rock and other acts. **Regattabar** (✉ Charles Hotel, Harvard Sq., Cambridge, ☎ 617/864–1200; 617/876–7777 for tickets) and **Scullers Jazz Club** (✉ DoubleTree Guest Suites Hotel, 400 Soldiers Field Rd., ☎ 617/783–0811) headline top names in jazz.

The Arts

BosTix (⌧ Faneuil Hall Marketplace, Copley Sq. and Harvard Sq., ☎ 617/723–5181) sells half-price tickets for same-day performances and full-price advance tickets. With major credit cards, you can charge tickets for many events by phone through **Ticketmaster** (☎ 617/931–2000) and **NEXT Ticketing** (☎ 617/423–6398).

DANCE

Boston Ballet (⌧ 19 Clarendon St., ☎ 617/695–6950), the city's premier dance company, performs at the Wang Center. **Ballet Theatre of Boston** (⌧ 186 Massachusetts Ave., ☎ 617/262–0961), an exciting young troupe, performs in downtown theaters. **Dance Umbrella** (☎ 617/482–7570) presents contemporary dance at the Emerson Majestic Theatre (☞ Theater, *below*) and other locations.

MUSIC

Berklee Performance Center (⌧ 136 Massachusetts Ave., ☎ 617/266–1400; 617/266–7455 for recorded information) is best known for jazz programs. **Jordan Hall at the New England Conservatory** (⌧ 30 Gainsborough St., ☎ 617/536–2412) is home to the Boston Philharmonic. **Symphony Hall** (⌧ 301 Massachusetts Ave.,☎ 617/266–1492 or 800/274–8499), renowned for its acoustics, is home to the Boston Symphony Orchestra and the Boston Pops.

OPERA

The **Boston Lyric Opera Company** (⌧ 114 State St., ☎ 617/542–6772) presents three productions each season.

THEATER

The **Boston Center for the Arts** (⌧ 539 Tremont St., ☎ 617/426–7700) houses several quirky low-budget troupes. **Charles Playhouse** (⌧ 74 Warrenton St., Theater District, ☎ 617/426–6912; 617/426–5225 for *Shear Madness*) presents two long-running shows: the avant-garde *Blue Man Group* and *Shear Madness,* an audience-participation whodunit. The **Colonial Theatre** (⌧ 106 Boylston St., Theatre District, ☎ 617/426–9366) hosts major visiting dance and theater productions. **Emerson Majestic Theatre** (⌧ 219 Tremont St., Theater District, ☎ 617/824–8000) hosts everything from dance to drama to classical concerts. The **Huntington Theatre Company** (⌧ 264 Huntington Ave., ☎ 617/266–0800), affiliated with Boston University, performs five plays annually. **Loeb Drama Center** (⌧ 64 Brattle St., Harvard Sq., Cambridge, ☎ 617/495–2668) is home to the American Repertory Theater, which showcases a variety of classic and experimental works on two stages.

Outdoor Activities and Sports

The **Dr. Paul Dudley White Bikeway,** approximately 18 mi long, follows both banks of the Charles River as it winds from Watertown Square to the Museum of Science.

Baseball: Boston Red Sox (⌧ Fenway Park, 4 Yawkey Way, ☎ 617/267–1700). **Basketball: Boston Celtics** (⌧ FleetCenter, Causeway St. at Haverhill St., ☎ 617/624–1000; 617/931–2000 for tickets). **Football: New England Patriots** (⌧ Foxboro Stadium, 45 mins south of Boston, Foxborough, ☎ 800/543–1776). **Hockey: Boston Bruins** (⌧ FleetCenter, Causeway St. at Haverhill St., ☎ 617/624–1000; 617/931–2000 for tickets).

Shopping

Most Boston stores are in the area bounded by Quincy Market, the Back Bay, downtown, and Copley Square. Though locals complain that there are too many chain stores, Boston's strength remains its idiosyncratic boutiques, handicrafts shops, and art and crafts galleries. Because such places like to keep inventory fresh, it's usually easy to find a bargain even though there are few outlet stores in the city. Boston's two daily newspapers, the *Globe* and the *Herald,* are the best places to learn about sales.

Shopping Districts

Charles Street on Beacon Hill is a mecca for antiques lovers. **Copley Place** (✉ 100 Huntington Ave., ☎ 617/369–5000), an indoor shopping mall connecting two hotels in Back Bay, has 87 stores, restaurants, and cinemas that blend the elegant, the glitzy, and the overpriced. **Downtown Crossing,** between Summer and Washington streets, is a pedestrian mall with outdoor food and merchandise kiosks, street performers, and benches. **Faneuil Hall Marketplace** (☎ 617/338–2323) has crowds, small shops, and kiosks of every description, and one of the area's great food experiences, Quincy Market. **Harvard Square,** in Cambridge, has more than 150 stores; it is a book lover's paradise. On **Newbury Street** in the Back Bay, the funky and the trendy give way to the chic and the expensive.

Department Stores

Filene's (✉ 426 Washington St., ☎ 617/357–2100; ✉ CambridgeSide Galleria, Cambridge, ☎ 617/621–3800) carries name-brand men's and women's clothing. **Filene's Basement** (✉ 426 Washington St., ☎ 617/542–2011) pioneered the idea of discounting; it reduces prices according to the number of days items have been on the rack.

Specialty Stores

Flat of the Hill (✉ 60 Charles St., ☎ 617/619–9977) will have something for everyone on your list—with seasonal items, gourmet foods, hard-to-find toiletries, dolls, toys, pillows, and pet products. **Louis, Boston** (✉ 234 Berkeley St., ☎ 617/262–6100) carries elegantly tailored designs and subtly updated classics. South American culture is represented by the boldly colored textiles and hand-painted tchotchkes at **Mayan Weavers** (✉ 268 Newbury St., ☎ 617/262–4342). **Shreve, Crump & Low** (✉ 330 Boylston St., ☎ 617/267–9100) is an old, well-respected store that carries the finest in jewelry, china, crystal, and silver.

Side Trip to Lexington and Concord

The events of April 19, 1775—the first military encounters of the American Revolution—are very much a part of present-day Lexington and Concord, two quintessential New England towns. Concord is also rich in literary history: This is the site of Walden Pond, immortalized by Thoreau. Several historic houses can be visited.

Visitor Information

Lexington Visitor Center (✉ 1875 Massachusetts Ave., 02173, ☎ 781/862–1450). **Minute Man National Historical Park Visitor Center** (✉ Rte. 2A, ½ mi west of Rte. 128, ☎ 978/369–6993 or 781/862–7753).

Arriving and Departing

To reach Lexington and Concord by car from Boston, take Memorial Drive in Cambridge to the Fresh Pond Parkway, and then follow Route 2 west. Alternatively, follow I–90 (Massachusetts Turnpike) west to I–95/Route 128 north. Exit at Route 2 east for Lexington, Route 2 west for Concord. From Lexington to Concord, follow Route 2A west. Both towns are about a 30- to 40-minute drive from the metropolitan Boston area. The MBTA (☞ Getting Around Boston, *above*) operates buses to Lexington and commuter trains to Concord.

What to See and Do

Lexington comes alive each Patriot's Day (the Monday nearest April 19), when costume-clad "Minutemen" re-create battle maneuvers and "Paul

Revere" reenacts his midnight ride. On April 19, 1775, Minuteman captain John Parker assembled his men on the **Battle Green,** a 2-acre triangular piece of land, to await the arrival of the British, who were marching to Concord to "teach rebels a lesson." Parker's role is commemorated in Henry Hudson Kitson's renowned sculpture, the **Minuteman Statue.**

Buckman Tavern, built in 1690, is where the Minutemen gathered the morning of April 19, 1775. A tour takes in the tavern's seven rooms. ⊠ *1 Bedford St.,* ☎ *781/862–5598.* ▣ *$4. Closed Nov.–mid-Apr.*

Though small, the **Museum of Our National Heritage** (⊠ 33 Marrett Rd., Rte. 2A at Massachusetts Ave., ☎ 781/861–6559; ▣ free) does a superb job of displaying items and artifacts from all facets of American life, as well as putting them in a social and political context.

The **Minute Man National Historical Park Visitor Center** (⊠ Rte. 2A, ½ mi west of Rte. 128, ☎ 978/369–6993 or 781/862–7753) is part of the 800-acre Minuteman National Historical Park, which extends into Lexington, Concord, and Lincoln. The center's exhibits and its captivating multimedia presentation focus on the Revolutionary War.

Concord includes sites of historic and literary interest. If you're heading from Lexington to Concord on Route 2A, you may want to stop off at the point where Revere's midnight ride ended with his capture by the British; it's marked with a boulder and plaque. At the **Old North Bridge** off Monument St., ½ mi north of the Concord town center, the tables were turned on the British on April 19, 1775, by the Concord Minutemen. Daniel Chester French's famous statue *The Minuteman* (1875) honors the country's first freedom fighters.

Author Nathaniel Hawthorne and essayist-poet Ralph Waldo Emerson both lived at the **Old Manse** at different times. ⊠ *269 Monument St.,* ☎ *978/369–3909.* ▣ *$6. Closed late Oct.–mid-Apr.*

From 1835 until his death in 1882, Ralph Waldo Emerson lived in the **Ralph Waldo Emerson House,** where he wrote his *Essays.* The Emerson House furnishings have been preserved as the writer left them, down to his hat resting on the newel post. ⊠ *28 Cambridge Tpke., at Lexington Rd.,* ☎ *978/369–2236.* ▣ *$4.50. Closed mid-Oct.–mid-Apr.*

The "Why Concord?" exhibit at the **Concord Museum** (⊠ 200 Lexington Rd. [entrance on Cambridge Tpke.], ☎ 978/369–9763; ▣ $7) provides a good overview of the town's history. The museum also has Emerson and Thoreau artifacts and one of the two lanterns hung at the Old North Church the night of April 18, 1775.

Louisa May Alcott's family home, **Orchard House,** is where the author wrote *Little Women.* Many of the original furnishings and the artwork of May Alcott (the model for Amy in *Little Women*) remain. ⊠ *399 Lexington Rd.,* ☎ *978/369–4118.* ▣ *$6. Closed Jan. 1–15.*

The **Wayside,** at different times home to Nathaniel Hawthorne, Louisa May Alcott, and Margaret Sydney, has exhibits on the former literary residents and a tour of Hawthorne's preserved tower-study. ⊠ *455 Lexington Rd.,* ☎ *978/369–6975.* ▣ *$4. Closed Nov.–early May.*

Walden Pond (⊠ Rte. 126, ☎ 978/369–3254; ▣ free; parking Memorial Day–Labor Day, $2 per vehicle; free parking rest of year) is Henry David Thoreau's most famous residence. Thoreau published *Walden* (1854), a collection of essays on observations he made while living at his cabin here in the woods. You can see an authentically furnished full-size replica of the cabin, and you can swim and hike here.

Side Trip to Plymouth

On December 21, 1620, 102 weary pilgrims disembarked from the *Mayflower* to found the first permanent European settlement north of Virginia. Today, Plymouth is characterized by narrow streets, clapboard mansions, quaint shops, and antiques stores.

Visitor Information

Destination Plymouth (✉ 170 Water St., Suite 10C, Plymouth 02360, ☎ 800/872–1620).

Arriving and Departing

To get to Plymouth from Boston, take I–93 south to Route 3 (toward Cape Cod); Exits 6 and 4 lead to downtown Plymouth and Plimoth Plantation, respectively; it's about an hour's drive. **Plymouth & Brockton Street Railway Buses** (☎ 508/746–0378) call at Plymouth en route to Cape Cod. **MBTA** commuter rail service (☞ Getting Around Boston, *above*) is available to Plymouth and nearby Kingston.

What to See and Do

★ The **Plimoth Plantation** living history museum painstakingly re-creates a 1627 Pilgrim village, complete with thatched roofs, longhorn livestock, and "residents" with quaint accents and mannerisms. ✉ *Warren Ave. (Rte. 3A),* ☎ *508/746–1622.* ✆ *Plantation only $16, Plantation and Mayflower II $19. Closed Dec.–Mar.*

At the waterfront is the ***Mayflower II*** (☎ 508/746–1622; ✆ $6.50 or as part of combined Plimoth Plantation fee), a replica of the ship that brought the Pilgrims from England. **Plymouth Rock** is believed to be the very spot on which the Pilgrims first set foot in 1620 after unsuccessfully scouting the Provincetown area as a potential settlement.

Side Trip to the North Shore

The beautiful North Shore extends from the northern suburbs to the Cape Ann region and beyond to the New Hampshire border.

Visitor Information

North of Boston Visitors and Convention Bureau (✉ 17 Peabody Sq., Peabody 01960, ☎ 978/977–7760 or 800/742–5306, ℻ 978/977–7758).

Arriving and Departing

It's about 40 mi from Boston to Gloucester. The primary link between Boston and the North Shore is I–93 north to Route 128, which then follows the line of the coast as far north as Gloucester. A more scenic route is along coastal Route 1A (which leaves Boston via the Callahan Tunnel) to Route 127.

What to See and Do

The narrow, winding streets of **Marblehead** hold ancient clapboard houses and sea captains' mansions whose occupants impress neighbors and visitors with an annual window-box competition. **Salem,** now infamous for the witchcraft hysteria of 1692, includes compelling museums, trendy waterfont stores and restaurants, and a traffic-free shopping area. **Rockport** brims with crafts shops, galleries, and artists' studios. **Gloucester** is the oldest seaport in America. **Newburyport** has a gorgeous redbrick center and rows of clapboard Federal mansions.

Crane Beach (✉ 290 Argilla Rd., Ipswich, ☎ 978/356–4354) and **Parker River Wildlife Refuge** (✉ Plum Island, Newburyport, ☎ 978/465–5753) are two undeveloped beach sanctuaries. **Newburyport Whale Watch** (✉ 54 Merrimac St., Newburyport, ☎ 978/465–9885 or 800/848–1111) and **Cape Ann Whale Watch** (✉ 415 Main St., Gloucester, ☎ 978/283–5110 or 800/877–5110) take you to the high seas. The **Thomas E. Lannon** (✉ 63R Rogers St., Seven Seas Wharf, ☎ 978/281–6634) schooner takes guests for ocean sails. The **Essex River Cruises** (✉ 35 Dodge St., Essex Marina, Essex, ☎ 978/768–6981 or 800/748–3706) head for the area's salt marshes and rivers.

CAPE COD AND THE ISLANDS

Separated from the mainland by the 17½-mi-long Cape Cod Canal, the Cape curves 70 mi from end to end. Every summer crowds are attracted to its charming villages of weathered-shingle houses and white-steepled churches and to its natural beauty of pinewoods, grassy marshes, and beaches backed by rolling dunes. To the south, Martha's Vineyard and Nantucket are resort islands ringed with beautiful sandy beaches; Nantucket preserves a near-pristine whaling-era town.

Visitor Information

Cape Cod: Chamber of Commerce (✉ Rtes. 6 and 132, Hyannis 02601, ☎ 508/862–0700 or 888/332–2732). **Martha's Vineyard:** Chamber of Commerce (✉ Box 1698, Beach Rd., Vineyard Haven 02568, ☎ 508/ 693–0085). **Nantucket:** Chamber of Commerce (✉ 48 Main St., Nantucket 02554, ☎ 508/228–1700).

Arriving and Departing

By Bus

Bonanza Bus Lines (☞ Arriving and Departing *in* Boston, *above*) operates direct service to Bourne, Falmouth, and Woods Hole from Boston and Providence. **Plymouth & Brockton Street Railway** (☞ Arriving and Departing *in* Boston, *above*) provides bus service to Provincetown from Boston and Logan Airport, with stops in several Cape towns en route.

By Car

From Boston take I–93 South to Route 3 South to the Sagamore Bridge. From New York take I–95 North to Providence, where you'll pick up I–195 East to Route 25 East to the Bourne Bridge.

By Ferry

Ferries connect Martha's Vineyard and Nantucket to the mainland from Woods Hole, Hyannis, Falmouth, and New Bedford. The **Steamship Authority** (☎ 508/477–8600), **Hy-Line Cruises** (☎ 508/778–2600), and the **Island Queen** (☎ 508/548–4800) serve Martha's Vineyard from the Cape. The **Schamonchi** (☎ 508/997–1688) travels between New Bedford and the Vineyard. The **Steamship Authority** and **Hy-Line** serve Nantucket.

By Plane

Barnstable Municipal Airport (✉ 480 Barnstable Rd., Rte. 28 rotary, Hyannis, ☎ 508/775–2020) is Cape Cod's air gateway, with flights from Cape Air/Nantucket Airlines (☎ 508/771–6944 or 800/352–0714), Colgan Air/Continental Connection (☎ 800/272–5488), and US Airways Express (☎ 800/428–4322). Cape Air/Nantucket Airlines also flies to **Martha's Vineyard Airport, Provincetown Municipal Airport,** and **Nantucket Memorial Airport**; US Airways Express serves the Vineyard as well.

Exploring Cape Cod and the Islands

U.S. 6 traverses the relatively unpopulated center of the Cape. Paralleling U.S. 6 but following the north coast is Route 6A, which passes through some of the Cape's old but well-preserved New England towns. The south shore, encompassing Falmouth, Hyannis, and Chatham and traced by Route 28, is heavily populated and is the most commercially developed region of the Cape. The sparse outer portion

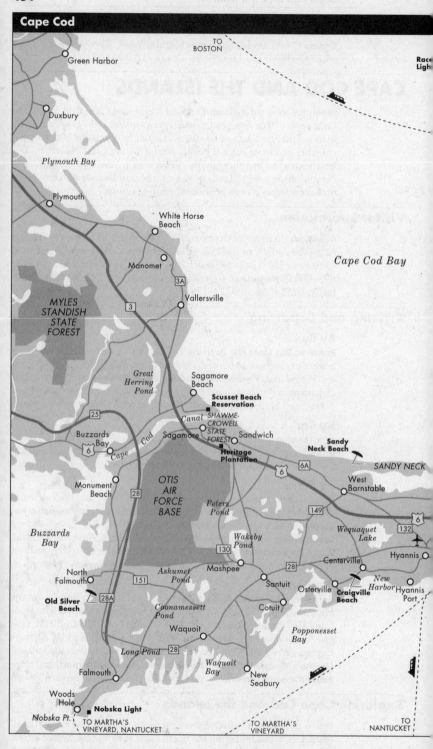

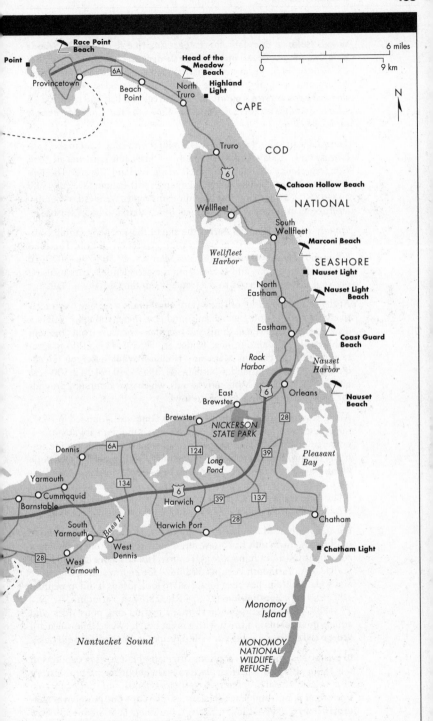

of the Cape, from Orleans to Provincetown, is edged with white-sand beaches and nature preserves. At the Cape's southwestern corner is **Woods Hole,** an international center for marine research. The **Woods Hole Oceanographic Institute Exhibit Center** (⊠ 15 School St., ☎ 508/289–2663; 🎫 $2 suggested donation) is a good place to learn about oceans and oceanography. The 16 tanks at the modest **National Marine Fisheries Service Aquarium** contain regional fish and shellfish. ⊠ *Albatross and Water Sts.,* ☎ *508/495–2267.* 🎫 *Free. Closed weekends mid-Sept.–late June.*

The village green in **Falmouth** was a military training field in the 18th century and is today flanked by Colonial homes, fine inns, and an 1856 Congregational church with a bell made by Paul Revere. The **Falmouth Historical Society** (⊠ Village Green, off Palmer Ave., ☎ 508/548–4857; 🎫 $3) maintains two museums (open Wednesday–Sunday afternoons in summer) and conducts free walking tours in season.

Quietly wealthy **Hyannis Port** is the site of the Kennedy family compound. **Hyannis** is the Cape's year-round commercial hub. The **John F. Kennedy Hyannis Museum** (⊠ 397 Main St., ☎ 508/790–3077; 🎫 $3) has photographs and videos from the presidential years focusing on John F. Kennedy's ties to the Cape. It's in the Old Town Hall.

At the southeastern tip of Cape Cod, **Chatham** is a seaside town relatively free of the commercialism found elsewhere, though it offers a downtown of traditional shops and fine inns. The view from **Chatham Lighthouse** (⊠ Main St., near Bridge St., ☎ 508/945–5199) is spectacular. Off the coast is **Monomoy National Wildlife Refuge** (Headquarters: ⊠ Morris Island, Chatham, ☎ 508/945–0594), a 2,500-acre preserve including the Monomoy Islands, which provide nesting grounds for 285 species of birds and waterfowl.

Along Route 6A on the Cape's bay side is **Sandwich,** founded in 1637, the oldest town on the Cape. Centered by a pond with a waterwheel-powered gristmill, this picturesque town remains famous for the colored glass produced here in the 19th century. Off Route 130 is **Heritage Plantation,** a complex of museum buildings displaying classic and historic cars, antique military-related items, Currier & Ives prints, and other Americana—all set amid extensive gardens. ⊠ *Grove and Pine Sts., Sandwich,* ☎ *508/888–3300.* 🎫 *$9. Closed Nov.–mid-May.*

Barnstable, east of Sandwich on Route 6A, is a lovely town of large old houses. **Yarmouth** has a few attractions for children, including a zoo-aquarium and a miniature golf course. **Hallet's Store** (⊠ 139 Main St./Rte. 6A, Yarmouth Port, ☎ 508/362–3362), a working drugstore and soda fountain, has been preserved to look just as it did more than 100 years ago. **ZooQuarium** (⊠ 674 Rte. 28, West Yarmouth, ☎ 508/775–8883; 🎫 $8) has sea-lion shows, a petting zoo, pony rides, and aquariums. **Dennis** is a town with a great beach (West Dennis Beach). **Scargo Hill** offers a spectacular view of Cape Cod Bay and Scargo Lake.

Brewster has numerous mansions originally built for sea captains in the 1800s. It's also a perfect place to learn about the natural history of the Cape: The area contains conservation lands, state parks, forests, freshwater ponds, and brackish marshes. The **Cape Cod Museum of Natural History** (⊠ 869 Main St./Rte. 6A, Brewster, ☎ 508/896–3867; 🎫 $5) has environmental and marine exhibits, and trails through 80 acres rich in wildlife.

In **Orleans,** Nauset Beach is a 10-mi-long sweep of sandy beach with low dunes and large waves good for body surfing or board surfing. ★ The **Cape Cod National Seashore** preserves 30 mi of landscape along the Lower Cape, including superb beaches and lighthouses. With several fine beaches, hiking trails, and bike paths, **Eastham** is a good place to enjoy the outdoors. Off Route 6 in Eastham, the National Seashore's **Salt Pond Visitor Center** has a museum with displays, tours, lectures, and films (⊠ Doane Rd., off U.S. 6, ☎ 508/255–3421; closed weekdays Jan. and Feb.).

★ **Wellfleet** was a Colonial whaling and cod-fishing port and is now home to fishermen, artists, and artisans. The **Massachusetts Audubon Wellfleet Bay Sanctuary** (⊠ Off Rte. 6, S. Wellfleet, ☎ 508/349–2615, ☏ $3), a 1,000-acre haven for more than 250 species of birds, is a superb place for bird-watching, walking, and watching the sun set over the salt marsh and bay. **Truro** is popular with writers and artists for its high dunes and virtual lack of development. At the National Seashore's **Pilgrim Heights Area,** trails meander through terrain explored by the *Mayflower* crew before they moved on to Plymouth.

In **Provincetown,** which is filled with first-rate shops and galleries, Portuguese and American fishermen mix with painters, poets, whale-watchers, and a large gay and lesbian community. The National Seashore's **Province Lands** (Visitor center: ⊠ Race Point Rd., ☎ 508/487–1256) allow access to Provincetown's spectacular beaches and dunes, as well as walking, biking, and horse trails; they are closed December–mid-April. The **Pilgrim Monument** (⊠ High Pole Hill Rd., ☎ 508/487–1310; ☏ $5), on a hill above the town center, commemorates the landing of the Pilgrims in 1620. From atop the 252-ft tower the view of the entire Cape is lovely.

Martha's Vineyard, a hot spot with celebrities, is less developed than Cape Cod yet more cosmopolitan than Nantucket. On the island the lively town of **Oak Bluffs** has a warren of some 300 candy-color Victorian cottages. The historic **Flying Horses Carousel** (⊠ Oak Bluffs Ave., ☎ 508/693–9481; ☏ $1) delights youngsters. The main port of **Vineyard Haven** has a street of shops and a backstreet preserved to reflect the way it appeared in whaling days. Tidy **Edgartown** has upscale boutiques, elegant sea captains' houses, and beautiful flower gardens. **Chappaquiddick Island,** laced with nature preserves, is accessible by ferry from Edgartown. The dramatically striated red-clay **Aquinnah Cliffs** (formerly Gay Head Cliffs), a major tourist sight, stand in a Wampanoag Indian township on the island's western tip.

The island of **Nantucket** is covered with moors that are scented with bayberry, wild roses, and cranberries; ringing it are miles of clean, white-sand beaches. **Nantucket Town,** an exquisitely preserved National Historic District, encapsulates the island's whaling past in more than a dozen historical museums along its cobblestone streets. The beach community of **Siasconset** offers an unhurried lifestyle in beautiful surroundings; tiny rose-covered cottages and white-clamshell drives abound.

Dining and Lodging

On Martha's Vineyard only Edgartown and Oak Bluffs allow the sale of liquor. For summer, lodgings should be booked as far in advance as possible. **DestINNations** (☎ 800/333–4667) and **Martha's Vineyard and Nantucket Reservations** (☎ 508/693–7200; 800/649–5671 in Massachusetts) are reservations services.

Brewster

$$$$ × **Chillingsworth.** This crown jewel of Cape restaurants is extremely ★ formal, terribly pricey, and completely upscale. The classic French menu and wine cellar win award after award. Recent favorites have been roast lobster and grilled venison. At dinner, a more modest bistro

menu is served in the Garden Room. ✉ *2449 Main St., Rte. 6A,* ☎ *508/896–3640. Reservations essential. AE, DC, MC, V. Closed Thanksgiving–Memorial Day and some weekdays rest of year.*

$$$–$$$$
★
🏨 **Captain Freeman Inn.** The opulent details at this 1866 Victorian include a marble fireplace, herringbone-inlay flooring, ornate Italian ceiling medallions, and 12-ft ceilings. Guest rooms have hardwood floors, antiques, and eyelet spreads. ✉ *15 Breakwater Rd., 02631,* ☎ *508/ 896–7481 or 800/843–4664,* ℻ *508/896–5618. 12 rooms. Pool. AE, MC, V. No smoking. BP.* 🐾

Chatham

$–$$
★
✕ **Vining's Bistro.** The wood grill, where the chef employs zesty spices from all over the globe, is the center of attention here. Spit-roasted Jamaican chicken and the Portobello mushroom sandwich are the restaurant's signature dishes. ✉ *595 Main St.,* ☎ *508/945–5033. Reservations not accepted. AE, D, MC, V. Closed mid-Jan.–Apr.*

$$$–$$$$
★
🏨 **Captain's House Inn.** Fine architectural details and a feeling of quiet comfort make this inn one of the Cape's finest. Some rooms in the four buildings are lacy and feminine, others refined and elegant. ✉ *371 Old Harbor Rd., 02633,* ☎ *508/945–0127,* ℻ *508/945–0866. 19 rooms. AE, D, MC, V. No smoking. BP.* 🐾

Falmouth

$$$
★
🏨 **Mostly Hall.** Set in a landscaped yard, this imposing 1849 house has a wraparound porch and a cupola. Accommodations are in corner rooms with leafy views, reading areas, antique pieces, and canopy beds. ✉ *27 Main St., 02540,* ☎ *508/548–3786 or 800/682–0565,* ℻ *508/ 457–1572. 6 rooms. AE, D, MC, V. Closed Jan.–mid-Feb. BP.* 🐾

Hyannis

$$–$$$
✕ **The Paddock.** For more than 30 years, the Paddock has been synonymous with excellent formal dining. Steak au poivre and Pacific Rim chicken (a grilled breast topped with oranges and mangoes) are among the traditional yet innovative preparations. Manhattans are popular in the lounge, where musicians perform in the evening. ✉ *W. Main St. rotary, next to Melody Tent,* ☎ *508/775–7677. AE, DC, MC, V. Closed mid-Nov.–Mar.*

$$
🏨 **Sea Breeze Inn.** The rooms at this cedar-shingle seaside B&B have antique or canopy beds. The nicest of the three detached cottages is the three-bedroom Rose Garden, which has two baths, a TV room, a fireplace, and a washer and dryer. ✉ *397 Sea St., 02601,* ☎ *508/771– 7213,* ℻ *508/862–0663. 14 rooms, 3 cottages. AE, D, MC, V. CP.* 🐾

Martha's Vineyard

$$–$$$
✕ **Black Dog Tavern.** This island landmark serves basic chowders, pastas, and fish. Waiting for a table is something of a tradition, although locals have generally adopted Yogi Berra's line: "It's so crowded, no one goes there anymore." ✉ *Beach St. Ext., Vineyard Haven,* ☎ *508/ 693–9223. Reservations not accepted. AE, D, MC, V. BYOB.*

$$$$
★
✕🏨 **Charlotte Inn.** Come to this tasteful inn for an Edwardian fantasy, an escape in one of the luxurious suites, a tranquil winter holiday with the island nearly to yourself, or a sumptuous meal at L'étoile (reservations essential), one of the Vineyard's finest traditional restaurants. ✉ *27 S. Summer St., Edgartown 02539,* ☎ *508/627–4751,* ℻ *508/ 627–4652. 25 rooms. Restaurant. AE, MC, V. CP.*

$$$–$$$$
✕🏨 **Inn at Blueberry Hill.** The restaurant at this secluded property on 56 acres is relaxed and elegant, and the chefs prepare innovative, healthful dishes. Shaker-inspired island-made furniture and fresh flowers decorate the rooms, which have a sparse but tasteful ambience. Some of the less expensive ones are on the small side. ✉ *R.R. 1, Box 309, 74 North Rd., Chilmark 02535,* ☎ *508/645–3322 or 800/356–3322,*

FAX *508/645–3799. 25 rooms. Pool, tennis, exercise room. AE, MC, V. Closed Nov.–Apr. BP.* ❧

$$$ ✕🏠 **Lambert's Cove Country Inn.** Rooms in the 1790 farmhouse of this secluded inn have light floral wallpapers and a sweet country feel. Rooms in outbuildings have screened porches or decks. Enjoy excellent Continental cooking by soft candlelight in the restaurant (reservations essential; BYOB). Especially good are the crisp-baked soft-shell crab appetizer and the grilled Muscovy duck breast on caramelized onions. ✉ *Off Lambert's Cove Rd., W. Tisbury (R.R. 1, Box 422, Vineyard Haven 02568),* ☎ *508/693–2298,* FAX *508/693–7890. 15 rooms. Restaurant, tennis. AE, MC, V. BP.* ❧

Nantucket

$$$$ ✕ **Chanticleer.** Anne and Jean-Charles Berruet serve superb French food in a formal country setting, complete with gorgeous clematis cascading down the weathered shingles. The food is unimpeachable and the desserts are profoundly rich. ✉ *9 New St., Siasconset,* ☎ *508/257–6231. Jacket required. AE, MC, V. Closed Mon. and mid-Oct.–early May.*

$$$$ ✕🏠 **Harbor House.** This family-oriented complex prides itself on its service. Standard rooms are done in English-country style but feature phones and TVs. The hotel's restaurant serves simple New England fare; it has five separate stations—an extensive salad bar, a pasta section, a meat-carving table, a children's section, and a dessert table. ✉ *Box 1139, S. Beach St., Nantucket Town 02554,* ☎ *508/228–1500; 800/475–2637 for reservations;* FAX *508/228–7639. 109 rooms. Restaurant. AE, D, DC, MC, V.* ❧

$$$$ ✕🏠 **Wauwinet.** Eight miles from Nantucket Town, this deluxe establishment has country-style rooms with pine antiques; some rooms have spectacular views of the ocean. The chic restaurant specializes in fresh seafood. ✉ *Box 2580, 120 Wauwinet Rd., 02584,* ☎ *508/228–0145 or 800/426–8718,* FAX *508/228–7135. 25 rooms, 5 cottages. Restaurant, tennis. AE, DC, MC, V. Closed Nov.–Apr. BP.* ❧

Provincetown

$$–$$$ ✕ **Café Edwige.** Delicious contemporary cuisine is served in a homey set-
★   ting at Café Edwige. Appetizers include Maine crab cake and warm goat cheese on crostini. Among the choices for entrées are lobster and Wellfleet scallops over pasta with a wild mushroom and tomato broth. ✉ *333 Commercial St.,* ☎ *508/487–2008. AE, DC, MC, V. Closed Nov.–May.*

$$ ✕ **Bubala's by the Bay.** Personality abounds at this restaurant inside
★   a bright yellow building adorned with campy carved birds. The kitchen serves three meals, with lots of local seafood. The wine list is priced practically at retail. The bar scene picks up in the evening. ✉ *183 Commercial St.,* ☎ *508/487–0773. AE, D, MC, V. Closed Oct. 31–Apr.*

$$$–$$$$ 🏠 **Bayshore.** This apartment complex on the water, ½ mi from the town
★   center, is great for long stays. Many of the units have decks and large water-view windows; all have full kitchens, modern baths, and phones. Rentals are mostly by the week in season. ✉ *493 Commercial St., 02657– 2413,* ☎ FAX *508/487–9133. 25 apartments. AE, MC, V.*

$$–$$$ 🏠 **The Masthead.** The Masthead is a charming cluster of shingled houses that overlook a lush lawn, a 450-ft-long boardwalk, and a private beach. Spacious rooms, efficiencies, apartments, and cottages are among the lodging options. ✉ *Box 577, 31–41 Commercial St., 02657,* ☎ *508/487–0523 or 800/395–5095,* FAX *508/487–9251. 7 apartments, 3 cottages, 2 efficiencies, 9 rooms. AE, D, DC, MC, V.* ❧

Campgrounds

🏕 **Nickerson State Park** (☞ National and State Parks, *above*). 🏕 **Shawme–Crowell State Forest** (✉ Rte. 130, Sandwich 02563, ☎ 508/ 888–0351; 877/422–6762 for reservations) has 285 sites and a beach.

Nightlife and the Arts

Nightlife

Hyannis has many nightclubs and bars featuring live rock and jazz (☎ 508/394–5277 Jazz Hot Line). Circuit Avenue in **Oak Bluffs** has rowdy bars and a year-round dance club. There are rock clubs, as well as restaurants with sedate piano bars, in **Nantucket Town.**

The Arts

Actors Theatre of Nantucket (⊠ Methodist Church, 2 Centre St., at Main St., Nantucket Town, ☎ 508/228–6325) presents several Broadway-style plays each summer. The **Cape Playhouse** (⊠ 820 Main St./Rte. 6A, Dennis, ☎ 508/385–3911) and the **Wellfleet Harbor Actors Theater** (⊠ 1 Kendrick St., ☎ 508/349–6835) present summer stock. The **Vineyard Playhouse** (⊠ 24 Church St., Vineyard Haven, ☎ 508/693–6450) hosts Equity productions and community theater year-round.

Outdoor Activities and Sports

Biking

Cape Cod Rail Trail, a 25-mi paved railroad right-of-way from Dennis to Wellfleet, is the Cape's premier bike path. On either side of the **Cape Cod Canal** is an easy 7-mi straight trail. The **Cape Cod National Seashore** and **Nickerson State Park** also maintain bicycle trails. On **Martha's Vineyard,** scenic well-paved paths follow the coast from Oak Bluffs to Edgartown and inland from Vineyard Haven to South Beach; some connect with rougher trails that weave through the state forest. **Nantucket** has several-miles-long bike paths that meander through the moorland.

Fishing

Tuna, mako and blue sharks, bluefish, and bass are the main ocean catches. The necessary license to fish the Cape's freshwater ponds is available at tackle shops, such as **Eastman's Sport & Tackle** (⊠ 150 Main St., Falmouth, ☎ 508/548–6900) and **Goose Hummock Shop** (⊠ 15 Rte. 6A off the Rte. 6 rotary, Orleans, ☎ 508/255–0455). **Dick's Bait & Tackle** (⊠ New York Ave., Oak Bluffs, ☎ 508/693–7669) on Martha's Vineyard and **Barry Thurston's Fishing Tackle** (⊠ Harbor Sq., ☎ 508/228–9595) on Nantucket rent equipment and can point out good fishing spots. Rental boats are available from **Cape Water Sports** (⊠ 337 Main St., Harwich Port, ☎ 508/432–7079), **Vineyard Boat Rentals** (⊠ Dockside Marketplace, Oak Bluffs Harbor, ☎ 508/693–8476), and **Nantucket Boat Rentals** (⊠ Slip 1, ☎ 508/325–1001).

Cap'n Bill & Cee Jay (⊠ Macmillan Wharf, Provincetown, ☎ 508/487–4330 or 800/675–6723), **Hy-Line** (⊠ Ocean St. Dock, Hyannis, ☎ 508/790–0696), and **Patriot Party Boats** (⊠ Falmouth Harbor, ☎ 508/548–2626; 800/734–0088 in MA) operate deep-sea fishing trips. On **Martha's Vineyard** the party boat *Skipper* (☎ 508/693–1238) leaves from Oak Bluffs Harbor. On **Nantucket** charters sail out of Straight Wharf.

Horseback Riding

To ride horseback try **Moby Dick Farm** (⊠ 179 Great Fields Rd., Brewster, ☎ 508/896–3544), **Haland Stables** (⊠ 878 Rte. 28A, West Falmouth, ☎ 508/540–2552), **Nelson's Riding Stable** (⊠ 43 Race Pt. Rd., Provincetown, ☎ 508/487–1112), **Misty Meadows Horse Farm** (⊠ Old County Rd., West Tisbury, Martha's Vineyard, ☎ 508/693–1870), or **Scrubby Neck Farm** (⊠ Edgartown–West Tisbury Rd., across from airport entrance, West Tisbury, Martha's Vineyard, ☎ 508/693–3770).

Water Sports

Arey's Pond Boat Yard (⊠ Off Rte. 28, South Orleans, ☎ 508/255–0994) has a sailing school. **Cape Water Sports** (☎ 508/432–7079), in

Harwich Port, offers sailboat, canoe, and other rentals and lessons. Lessons and rentals are also available at **Wind's Up!** (⌧ 199 Beach Rd., Vineyard Haven, ☎ 508/693–4252) on Martha's Vineyard and at **Nantucket Island Community Sailing** (⌧ Jetties Beach, ☎ 508/228–5358).

Whale-Watching

The proximity of the Cape to the whales' feeding grounds at Stellwagen Bank (about 6 mi off the tip of Provincetown) affords the rare opportunity of spotting several species of whales. **Hyannis Whale Watcher Cruises** (⌧ Millway Marina, off Phinney's La., Barnstable, ☎ 508/362–6088 or 800/287–0374), **Dolphin Fleet** (⌧ Macmillan Wharf, Provincetown, ☎ 508/349–1900 or 800/826–9300), and **Ranger V** (ticket office: ⌧ Bradford and Standish Sts., Provincetown, ☎ 508/487–3322 or 800/992–9333) operate whale-watching excursions.

Beaches

★ Beaches fronting on **Cape Cod Bay** generally have cold water and gentle waves. The Cape's south-side beaches, on **Nantucket Sound,** have rolling surf and are warmer. Open-ocean beaches on the **Cape Cod National Seashore** are cold, with serious surf. These beaches, backed by high dunes, have lifeguards and rest rooms. In summer, parking lots can fill up by 10 AM. On **Martha's Vineyard and Nantucket,** the beaches facing the sound are warmer than the Atlantic beaches.

Shopping

Provincetown has many fine galleries. **Wellfleet** has emerged as a vibrant center for arts and crafts. There's a giant **flea market** (⌧ 51 U.S. 6, Eastham–Wellfleet town line, ☎ 508/349–2520) on weekends and Monday holidays from April to October, plus Wednesday and Thursday in July and August. **Cape Cod Mall** (⌧ between Rtes. 132 and 28, Hyannis, ☎ 508/771–0200) holds 120 shops.

The chief shopping town on **Martha's Vineyard** is **Edgartown,** with the best selection of antiques and crafts shops. The **West Tisbury Farmers' Market** (⌧ South Rd., West Tisbury, ☎ 508/693–9549), open on Wednesday and Saturday in summer, is the largest of its kind in Massachusetts. **Nantucket**'s specialty is lightship baskets—expensive woven baskets, often decorated with scrimshaw or rosewood.

THE PIONEER VALLEY

The Pioneer Valley, a string of historic settlements along the Connecticut River from Springfield in the south up to the Vermont border, formed the western frontier of New England from the early 1600s until the late 18th century. The northern regions of the Pioneer Valley remain rural and tranquil; farms and small towns have typical New England architecture. Farther south, the cities of Holyoke and Springfield are more industrial. Educational pioneers came to this region as well—to form major colleges and some well-known prep schools.

Visitor Information

Greater Springfield Convention and Visitors Bureau (⌧ 1441 Main St., Southfield 01103, ☎ 413/787–1548 or 800/723–1548).

Arriving and Departing

By Bus

Peter Pan Bus Lines (☞ Arriving and Departing *in* Boston, *above*) links Boston, Springfield, Northampton, Amherst, and South Hadley.

By Car

I–91 runs north–south the entire length of the Pioneer Valley, from Greenfield to Springfield; I–90 (the Mass Pike) links Springfield to Boston; and Route 2 connects Boston with Greenfield in the north.

By Plane

The most convenient airport for flying into the Pioneer Valley is **Bradley International Airport** (☞ Arriving and Departing *in* Coastal Connecticut).

By Train

Amtrak (☞ Arriving and Departing *in* Boston, *above*) stops in Springfield on routes from Boston and New York.

What to See and Do

Four museums have set up shop near downtown Springfield at the **museum quadrangle** (⊠ State and Chestnut Sts.). The **Connecticut Valley Historical Museum** surveys the history of the Pioneer Valley. There's also a permanent Dr. Seuss exhibit in honor of Theodore Geisel, the children's books writer who grew up in the area. The **George Walter Vincent Smith Art Museum** contains Japanese armor, ceramics, and textiles and a gallery of American paintings. The **Museum of Fine Arts** has paintings by Gauguin, Renoir, Degas, and Monet, as well as 18th-century American paintings and contemporary works. The **Springfield Science Museum** has an "Exploration Center" of touchable displays, a planetarium, and dinosaur exhibits. ☎ 413/263–2800. ⊠ *$4 pass valid for all museums. Closed. Mon. and Tues.*

The large **Riverside Park,** outside Springfield, has more than 160 rides including the Mind Eraser, a giant roller coaster. The admission price includes entry to a water theme park. ⊠ *1623 Main St., Agawam,* ☎ *413/786–9300 or 800/370–7488.* ⊠ *$27.99 for adults, $17.99 for kids under 4 ft. Closed Nov.–Apr. and weekdays Apr.–Memorial Day and Labor Day–Oct.*

Deerfield, in the north, has many historic buildings and is the site of the prestigious Deerfield Academy. The **Street** (⊠ Rte. 5, ☎ 413/774–5581; ⊠ $12 pass for all houses, $6 for single house) is a tree-lined avenue of 18th- and 19th-century Deerfield homes maintained as a museum site; 14 of the preserved buildings are open to the public year-round. In **Amherst** are three of the valley's five major colleges—the University of Massachusetts, Amherst College, and Hampshire College. The **Emily Dickinson Homestead,** which can be viewed by tour only, is the house in which the poet spent her entire life. Reservations are recommended. ⊠ *280 Main St.,* ☎ *413/542–8161.* ⊠ *$4. Closed Sun.–Tues.*

Northampton, once home to the 30th U.S. president, Calvin Coolidge, is now the site of Smith College, a lively arts scene, and good bookstores. The village of **South Hadley** is best known for Mount Holyoke, founded in 1837 as the country's first women's college.

East of the southern end of the valley is **Old Sturbridge Village** (⊠ 1 Old Sturbridge Village Rd., Sturbridge, ☎ 800/733–1830; ⊠ $16, good for 2 consecutive days), a living, working model of an early 1800s New England town, with more than 40 buildings on a 200-acre site.

Dining and Lodging

Amherst

$$–$$$ ✕☰ **Lord Jeffery Inn.** Many bedrooms at this gabled brick inn have a floral decor; others have stencils and pastel woodwork. The formal dining room, where traditional dishes are served, has old wood panels,

heavy drapery, and a large fireplace. Burgers, salads, and the like are served at Boltwood's Tavern, which has a small bar and a wraparound porch. ⊠ *30 Boltwood Ave., 01002,* ☎ *413/253–2576 or 800/742–0358,* FAX *413/256–6152. 48 rooms. 2 restaurants. AE, DC, MC, V.* 🐾

$–$$$
★ 🏨 **Allen House.** Busy, colorful wall coverings reach to the high ceilings of this restored inn. Antiques include wicker "steamship" chairs, screens, and carved golden-oak beds. Lace curtains grace the windows in the rooms, whose comfortable beds have goose-down comforters. Allen House is a short walk from the center of Amherst. ⊠ *599 Main St., 01002,* ☎ *413/253–5000. 7 rooms. MC, V. BP.* 🐾

Deerfield

$$$
★ ✕ **Sienna.** The atmosphere at Sienna is soothing, but the food is what really shines. Choices from the ever-changing menu might include an appetizer of smoked-salmon samosas on a champagne beurre blanc and entrées like tuna loin on a light stir-fry of zucchini, fennel, and gnocchi with a mustard sauce. ⊠ *6 Elm St., S. Deerfield,* ☎ *413/665–0215. Reservations essential. MC, V. Closed Mon. and Tues. No lunch.*

$$$–$$$$
★ ✕🏨 **Deerfield Inn.** Period wallpapers decorate the rooms in the main inn, which was built in 1884; the rooms in an outbuilding have identical papers but are newer (1981) and closer to the parking lot. All rooms have antiques and replicas, sofas, and bureaus. The menu in the sunny dining room changes monthly, but you'll always find duck and Indian pudding. ⊠ *81 Old Main St., 01342,* ☎ *413/774–5587; 800/926–3865 outside MA;* FAX *413/773–8712. 23 rooms. Restaurant, coffee shop. AE, DC, MC, V. No smoking. BP.*

$$
✕🏨 **Whately Inn.** Antiques and four-poster beds slope gently on old-wood floors at the Whately. Prime Angus steaks, baked lobster with shrimp stuffing, and other entrées come with salad, appetizer, and dessert. ⊠ *Chestnut Plain Rd., Whately Center 01093,* ☎ *413/665–3044 or 800/942–8359. 4 rooms. Restaurant. AE, D, DC, MC, V.*

Northampton

$–$$
✕ **Paul and Elizabeth's.** Plants fill this high-ceiling natural-foods restaurant. Among the seasonal specials are butternut-squash soup, corn muffins and Indian pudding, Japanese tempura, and innovative fish entrées. ⊠ *150 Main St.,* ☎ *413/584–4832. AE, MC, V.*

Northfield

$–$$
★ 🏨 **Northfield Country House.** Truly remote, this large English manor house, built in the late 1800s, sits on 16 acres amid thick woodlands. Rooms are decorated with antiques; several have brass beds and three have working fireplaces. The living room has massive oak beams and a 12-ft fieldstone fireplace. ⊠ *181 School St., 01360,* ☎ *413/498–2692 or 800/498–2692. 7 rooms. Pool. MC, V. BP.*

THE BERKSHIRES

Though only about a 2½-hour drive west from Boston or north from New York City, the Berkshires live up to storybook images of rural New England, with wooded hills; narrow, winding roads; and compact, charming villages. Summer offers a variety of cultural events, not the least of which is the Tanglewood festival of classical music, in Lenox. Fall brings a blaze of brilliant foliage. In winter the Berkshires are a popular ski area. Springtime visitors can enjoy maple-sugaring. The region can be crowded any weekend.

Visitor Information

Mohawk Trail Association (⊠ Box 2031, Charlemont 01339, ☎ 413/664–6256). **Berkshire Visitors Bureau** (⊠ Berkshire Common Plaza, Pittsfield

01201, ☎ 413/443–9186 or 800/237–5747). **Lenox Chamber of Commerce** (✉ Lenox Academy Bldg., 75 Main St., 01240, ☎ 413/637–3646).

Arriving and Departing

By Bus
Peter Pan Bus Lines (☎ 413/426–7838 or 800/237–8747) serves Lee and Pittsfield from Boston and Albany. **Bonanza Bus Lines** (☞ Arriving and Departing *in* Boston, *above*) connects the Berkshires with Albany, New York City, and Providence.

By Car
The Massachusetts Turnpike (I–90) connects Boston with Lee and Stockbridge. The scenic Mohawk Trail (Route 2) parallels the northern border of Massachusetts. To reach the Berkshires from New York City, take the New York Thruway (I–87) or the Taconic State Parkway. Within the Berkshires the main north–south road is Route 7.

By Plane
The closest airports are in Boston (☞ Arriving and Departing *in* Boston, *above*), Albany and New York City (☞ New York), and Hartford (☞ Connecticut).

Exploring the Berkshires

Williamstown is the northernmost Berkshires town, at the junction of Route 2 and U.S. 7. **Williams College** opened in 1793, and the town still revolves around it. Gracious campus buildings lining the wide main street are open to visitors. The **Sterling and Francine Clark Art Institute** is an outstanding small museum, with paintings by Renoir, Monet, and Degas. ✉ *225 South St., Williamstown,* ☎ *413/458–9545.* ✆ *$5 July–Oct., free Nov.–June. Closed Mon. Sept.–June.*

The **Mohawk Trail,** a scenic 7-mi stretch of Route 2, follows a former Native American path east from Williamstown. **Mt. Greylock,** south of Williamstown off Route 7, is, at 3,491 ft, the highest point in the state. **Pittsfield,** county seat and geographic center of the Berkshires, has a lively small-town atmosphere. **Hancock Shaker Village** (☎ 413/443–0188 or 800/817–1137; ✆ $10 for 2 consecutive days; $13.50 for self-guided tour, good for 10 consecutive days), 5 mi west of Pittsfield on Route 20, was founded in the 1790s as the third Shaker community in America. The religious community closed in 1960, and the site, complete with living quarters, round stone barn, and working crafts shops, is now a museum.

The village of **Lenox,** 5 mi south of Pittsfield on Route 7, epitomizes the Berkshires for many visitors. In the thick of the summer-cottage region, it's rich with old inns and majestic mansions. Novelist Edith Wharton designed the house and grounds for her summer home the **Mount,** a turn-of-the-20th-century classical American mansion. ✉ *Plunkett St.,* ☎ *413/637–1899.* ✆ *$6. Closed Nov.–late May.*

★ **Tanglewood** (☞ The Arts *in* Nightlife and the Arts, *below*) is summer headquarters of the Boston Symphony. Thousands flock to the 200-acre estate every summer weekend to picnic on the lawns as musicians perform on the open-air stage.

The touristy, archetypal New England small town of **Stockbridge** has a history of literary and artistic inhabitants, including painter Norman Rockwell and writers Norman Mailer and Robert Sherwood. The **Norman Rockwell Museum** (✉ Rte. 183, ☎ 413/298–4100; ✆ $9) holds the world's largest collection of the artist's original paintings.

Chesterwood was for 33 years the summer home of the sculptor Daniel Chester French, who created *The Minuteman* in Concord and the Lincoln Memorial in Washington, D.C. Tours are given of the house and of the studio, where one can see the casts and models French used to create the Lincoln Memorial. ⊠ *Williamsville Rd. off Rte. 183,* ☎ *413/ 298–3579.* ⚲ *$6.50. Closed Nov.–May.*

Great Barrington is the largest town in the southern Berkshires and a mecca for antiques hunters. **Bartholomew's Cobble** (⊠ Rte. 7A, ☎ 413/ 229–8600; ⚲ $3.50), south of Great Barrington, is a natural rock garden beside the Housatonic River (the Native American name means "river beyond the mountains"). The 277-acre site is filled with trees, ferns, wildflowers, and hiking trails. The visitor center has a museum.

Mt. Washington State Forest (⊠ Rte. 23, ☎ 413/528–0330) is 16 mi southwest of Great Barrington on the New York State border. The free primitive camping area is open year-round, but there's a catch—you have to hike 1½ mi from the parking lot. The forest's Bash Bish Brook (say that 10 times, fast) flows through a gorge and over a 50-ft waterfall into a clear natural pool.

Dining and Lodging

Lenox

$$–$$$ ✕ **Church St. Café.** Original art covers the walls, the tables are surrounded by ficus trees, and classical music wafts through the air at this café. The seasonal menu might include roast duck with thyme and Madeira sauce, rack of pork with wild mushrooms, or crab cakes. ⊠ *69 Church St.,* ☎ *413/637–2745. MC, V. Closed Sun. and Mon., Nov.–Apr.*

$$$$ 🏨 **Blantyre.** Modeled after a castle in Scotland, Blantyre is awe-inspiring, ★ with massive public rooms and 88 acres of beautiful grounds. Huge and lavishly decorated, the rooms in the main house have hand-carved four-poster beds, overstuffed chaise longues, and Victorian bathrooms. The rooms in the carriage house are well appointed but can't compete with the grandeur of the main house. ⊠ *16 Blantyre Rd., off Rte. 20, 01240,* ☎ *413/637–3556,* ℻ *413/637–4282. 23 rooms. Restaurant, pool, tennis. AE, DC, MC, V. Closed Dec.–Apr. CP.*

South Egremont

$$–$$$ ✕🏨 **Egremont Inn.** The public rooms in this 1780 inn are enormous, and each has a fireplace. The bedrooms are on the small side but have four-poster beds, claw-foot baths, and unpretentious furnishings. Windows sweep around two sides of the stylish restaurant (reservations essential summer and fall weekends). The menu changes frequently but always includes fresh fish, a homemade pasta, and a hearty meat dish. ⊠ *Box 418, Old Sheffield Rd., 01258,* ☎ *413/528–2111 or 800/859–1780,* ℻ *413/ 528–3284. 20 rooms. Restaurant, pool, tennis. AE, D, MC, V. CP.* ✆

Stockbridge Area

$$–$$$$ ✕🏨 **Red Lion Inn.** An inn since 1773, the Red Lion has a large main building and seven annexes. The rooms in the annex houses tend to be nicer. All the rooms are furnished with antiques and reproductions. The same menu is served in both dining rooms and (in season) in the garden. New England specialties include clam chowder; broiled scallops prepared with sherry, lemon, and paprika; and steamed or stuffed lobster. ⊠ *Main St., 02162,* ☎ *413/298–5545,* ℻ *413/298–5130. 122 rooms, 14 with shared bath. 2 restaurants, pool, exercise room. AE, D, DC, MC, V.* ✆

$$–$$$ 🏨 **Historic Merrell Inn.** Built in the 1790s and meticulously main- ★ tained, the inn has an unfussy yet authentic style, with polished wide- board floors, several working fireplaces, and Federal and Victorian antiques and reproductions. ⊠ *1565 Pleasant St. (Rte. 102), South Lee*

01260, ☎ 413/243–1794 or 800/243–1794, ☒ 413/243–2669. 10 rooms. MC, V. BP. ✎

Williamstown

$$ ✕ **Mezze Bistro.** Veal sweetbreads with artichoke hearts and radicchio, sautéed pork with roasted shallots, prosciutto over soft polenta, and oven-roasted fennel gazpacho are among the zesty offerings at this hip and happening place featuring live cabaret entertainment. ☒ *84 Water St., ☎ 413/458–0123. AE, MC, V. Closed Mon. Sept.–May, Sun. and Mon. Dec. except for Sun. brunch. No lunch.*

$$–$$$ 🔲 **Field Farm Guest House.** Built in 1948 on 296 acres, this house, which
★ resembles a modern museum, is now run as a B&B by a nonprofit organization. Three rooms have private decks; two have working fireplaces with tiles depicting animals, birds, and butterflies. ☒ *554 Sloan Rd. (off Rte. 43), 01267, ☎ 413/458–3135. 5 rooms. Dining room, pool, tennis, fishing. D, MC, V. BP.*

Nightlife and the Arts

Listings appear daily in the *Berkshire Eagle* from June to Columbus Day. *Berkshires Week* is the summer bible for events listings. Weekly listings appear in the *Williamstown Advocate*. Major concerts are listed in the Thursday *Boston Globe*.

Nightlife

The most popular local nightspot is the **Lion's Den** (☎ 413/298–5545), at the Red Lion Inn in Stockbridge (☞ Dining and Lodging, *above*), which has nightly folk music and some contemporary local bands.

The Arts

DANCE

Jacob's Pillow Dance Festival (☒ George Carter Rd. at Rte. 20, Becket, ☎ 413/637–1322; 413/243–0745 for box office in summer) happens over 10 weeks each summer. The participants range from well-known classical ballet companies to Native American dance groups.

MUSIC

The **Berkshire Performing Arts Theater** (☒ 70 Kemble St., Lenox, ☎ 413/637–1800) attracts top-name artists in jazz, folk, rock, and blues each summer. The season at **Tanglewood** (☎ 413/637–5165 or 617/266–1492 for information; 617/266–1200 for tickets only; ☞ Exploring the Berkshires, *above*), where the Boston Symphony Orchestra performs, runs from June to August.

THEATER

The **Berkshire Theatre Festival** (☒ Rte. 102, Box 797, Stockbridge 01262, ☎ 413/298–5576) stages nightly performances in summer at a century-old theater. The **Williamstown Theatre Festival** (☒ Adams Memorial Theatre, 1000 Main St., Box 517, Williamstown 01267, ☎ 413/597–3400) presents classics and contemporary works each summer.

Outdoor Activities and Sports

Biking

The back roads of Berkshire County can be hilly, but the views and the countryside are incomparable. **Mountain Goat Bicycle Shop** (☒ 130 Water St., Williamstown, ☎ 413/458–8445) rents mountain bikes and can provide information on routes in the Mt. Greylock area.

Boating

The **Housatonic River** flows south from Pittsfield between the Berkshire Hills and the Taconic Range toward Connecticut. **Onota Boat Livery** (☒ 463 Pecks Rd., Pittsfield, ☎ 413/442–1724) rents canoes, rowboats, and other small craft; provides dock space on Onota lake; and sells fishing tackle and bait.

Fishing

The area's rivers, lakes, and streams abound with bass, pike, perch, and trout. **Points North Fishing and Hunting Outfitters** (✉ Rte. 8, Adams, ☎ 413/743–4030) organizes summer fly-fishing schools.

Golf

Waubeeka Golf Links (✉ Rte. 7, Williamstown, ☎ 413/458–5869) and the **Cranwell Resort and Hotel** (✉ 55 Lee Rd., Lenox 02140, ☎ 413/637–1364 or 800/272–6935) have 18-hole courses open to the public.

Hiking

The **Appalachian Trail** goes through Berkshire County. Hiking is particularly rewarding in the higher elevations of **Mt. Greylock State Reservation** (☞ National and State Parks, *above*). **Tolland State Forest** (☞ National and State Parks, *above*) has camping facilities and hiking trails.

Ski Areas

Cross-Country

Brodie (✉ Rte. 7, New Ashford 01237, ☎ 413/443–4752). **Butternut Basin** (✉ Rte. 23, Great Barrington 01230, ☎ 413/528–2000).

Downhill

Berkshire East (✉ Box 727, S. River Rd., Charlemont 01339, ☎ 413/339–6617). **Bousquet Ski Area** (✉ Dan Fox Dr., Pittsfield 01201, ☎ 413/442–8316 or 413/442–2436). **Brodie** (☞ Cross-Country, *above*). **Butternut Basin** (☞ Cross-Country, *above*). **Jiminy Peak** (✉ Corey Rd., 01237, ☎ 413/738–5500; 413/738–7325 for snow conditions). **Otis Ridge Ski Area** (✉ Rte. 23, Otis 01253, ☎ 413/269–4444).

Shopping

Antiques

The greatest concentration of antiques stores is around Great Barrington, South Egremont, and Sheffield. For a list of storekeepers who belong to the **Berkshire County Antiques Dealers Association** and guarantee the authenticity of their merchandise, send a self-addressed, stamped envelope to R.D. 1, Box 1, Sheffield 01257.

Outlet Stores

Along Route 7 north of Lenox are two factory-outlet malls, **Lenox House Country Shops** and **Brushwood Farms**.

MICHIGAN

Updated by
Khristi Zimmeth

Capital	Lansing
Population	9,774,000
Motto	If You Seek a Pleasant Peninsula, Look About You
State Bird	Robin
State Flower	Apple blossom
Postal Abbreviation	MI

Statewide Visitor Information

Travel Michigan (⌧ Box 30226, Lansing 48909, ☎ 800/543–2937). **Information centers:** I–94 at New Buffalo and Port Huron; I–69 at Coldwater; U.S. 23 at Dundee; U.S. 2 at Ironwood and Iron Mountain; U.S. 41 at Marquette and Menominee; I–75 at St. Ignace, Sault Sainte Marie, and Monroe; U.S. 27 in a rest area 1 mi north of Clare; and Route 108 in Mackinaw City.

Scenic Drives

Route BR–15 between Pentwater and Montague follows the Lake Michigan shoreline for about 25 mi. **Route M–23** between Tawas City and Mackinaw City follows the Lake Huron shoreline for more than 160 mi. In the Upper Peninsula **Route M–28** follows the Lake Superior shoreline between Marquette and Munising.

National and State Parks

National Parks

Isle Royale National Park (⌧ 800 E. Lakeshore Dr., Houghton 49940, ☎ 906/482–0984), 48 mi off the Michigan coast in Lake Superior, is a wilderness park, accessible by ferry from Houghton or Copper Harbor or by seaplane from Houghton. **Pictured Rocks National Lakeshore** (⌧ Box 40, Munising 49862, ☎ 906/387–2607), in the Upper Peninsula, extends 40 mi along Lake Superior between Munising and Grand Marais. **Sleeping Bear Dunes National Lakeshore** (⌧ 9922 Front St., Empire 49630, ☎ 231/326–5134) encompasses 35 mi of lower Michigan's Lake Michigan shore and includes the Manitou Islands; the 71,000-acre preserve has the highest sand dunes outside the Sahara.

★

State Parks

Michigan has 96 state parks, including 21 in the Upper Peninsula, many with spectacular waterfalls. Admission to all state parks is $4 per car, per day or $20 for an unlimited, annual pass. Most parks allow camping. A motor-vehicle permit, available at each park entrance, is required for admission. The *Michigan Travel Ideas and State Park Guide,* available from Travel Michigan (☞ Statewide Visitor Information, *above*), details park facilities.

Brimley State Park (⌧ 9200 W. 6 Mile Rd., Brimley 49715, ☎ 906/248–3422), overlooking Lake Superior's Whitefish Bay, is one of 14 parks where you can rent a tent that's already set up and equipped with two cots and two sleeping pads. **Porcupine Mountains Wilderness State Park** (⌧ 412 S. Boundary Rd., Ontanagon 49953, ☎ 906/885–5275), on the rugged western edge of the Upper Peninsula, is one of 13 parks with cabins for rent. At **J. W. Wells State Park** (⌧ N7670 Hwy. M–35, Cedar River 49813, ☎ 906/863–9747), some cabins are a mere few yards from the softly lapping Lake Michigan shoreline.

DETROIT

Founded seven decades before the American Revolution, the oldest city in the Midwest is a busy industrial center, producing roughly a quarter of the nation's autos, trucks, and tractors. The riverfront harbor is one of the busiest ports on the Great Lakes. Downtown, a constant flow of traffic moves in and out of the Detroit–Windsor Tunnel and across the Ambassador Bridge, both of which connect Detroit with Windsor, Ontario, directly across the Detroit River.

Though the city nicknamed itself the "Renaissance City" in the 1970s, it did little to deserve the title until recently. The 1990s have brought major changes, including a new mayor, plans for new sports stadiums, and a number of revitalized downtown areas, including the glitzy theater district—now second only to New York's Great White Way in number of seats.

Visitor Information

Detroit Metropolitan Convention and Visitors Bureau (⊠ 211 W. Fort St., Ste. 1000, 48226, ☎ 313/202–1800).

Arriving and Departing

By Bus
Greyhound (⊠ 1001 Howard St., ☎ 800/231–2222).

By Car
I–75 enters Detroit from the north and south, U.S. 10 from the north. Approaching from the west and northeast is I–94; from the west, I–96 and I–696. From the east, Canadian Route 401 becomes Route 3 upon entering Detroit from Windsor via the Ambassador Bridge and Route 3B upon entering via the Detroit–Windsor Tunnel.

By Plane
Detroit Metropolitan Wayne County Airport (1 Rogell Dr., ☎ 734/247–7265) is in Romulus, about 26 mi west of downtown Detroit. It's served by most major airlines, with nearly 1,000 arrivals and departures daily.

Commuter Express (☎ 800/488–7433) runs buses from the metropolitan airport to major downtown hotels from 6:45 AM to midnight; the fare is $15 one-way, $28 round-trip. Taxis to and from the airport take about 45 minutes; the fare is about $33 one-way.

By Train
Amtrak (⊠ 16121 Michigan Ave., Dearborn, ☎ 800/872–7245).

Getting Around Detroit

By Car
Detroit is the Motor City, and everyone does drive. Many downtown streets are one-way; a detailed map is a necessity. The main streets into downtown are Woodward Avenue (north–south) and Jefferson Avenue (east–west). Rush hours should be avoided.

By Public Transportation
The **Department of Transportation** (☎ 313/933–1300) operates bus service throughout Detroit; the fare is $1.25. **Suburban Mobility Authority Regional Transportation (SMART)** (☎ 313/962–5515) provides suburban bus service. The **People Mover** (☎ 313/224–2160) is an elevated, automated monorail that makes a 14-minute, 3-mi circuit of 13 downtown stations. Trains run about every three minutes; the fare is 50¢ (tokens are sold at each station).

By Taxi

The taxi fare is $1.40 for the first half mile, $1.40 for each additional mile. Taxis can be ordered by phone or hired at stands at most major hotels. The two largest companies are **Checker Cab** (☎ 313/963–7000) and **City Cab** (☎ 313/833–7060).

Exploring Detroit

Starting from the riverside Renaissance Center, downtown, you can move outward to east Detroit and then on to the northwest side, the cultural heart of the city.

Downtown

Detroit's most prominent landmark, the big, brassy **Renaissance Center,** known as the Ren Cen, dominates the city's skyline with six office towers and the spectacular 73-story Marriott Hotel, one of the tallest hotels in the world. A city within a city, the waterfront complex has retail stores, services, and popular restaurants. It was purchased in 1997 by General Motors, which then moved in and established its new world headquarters here. There's a People Mover stop right out front.

Old Mariners' Church (⊠ 170 E. Jefferson Ave., ☎ 313/259–2206) was made famous in Gordon Lightfoot's song "The Wreck of the *Edmund Fitzgerald*." The 75-acre **Civic Center,** next to Old Mariners' Church, is a riverfront center for entertainment, festivals, and sports. At the heart of the Civic Center is **Philip A. Hart Plaza,** designed by Isamu Noguchi. In warm weather lunchtime crowds come here to enjoy the open spaces, sculptures, and computer-controlled **Dodge Fountain.**

Randolph Rogers, who created the bronze doors of the U.S. Capitol, also designed **Cadillac Square,** site of many presidential speeches and the 1872 **Civil War Soldiers' and Sailors' Monument.** The blinking red light atop the 47-story **Penobscot Building** (⊠ 645 Griswold, ☎ 313/961–8800), the state's tallest office tower, has been part of the skyline since 1928. A statue of Steven T. Mason, Michigan's first governor, stands over his grave in **Capitol Park,** site of the state's first capitol.

Grand Circus Park was envisioned as a full circus (as open circular spaces were then known) when Detroit was rebuilt after a disastrous fire in 1805; only half the park was completed. A fountain in the west park honors Thomas A. Edison. Nearby is the opulent **Fox Theatre** (⊠ 2211 Woodward Ave., ☎ 313/596–3200), which opened in 1928 as America's largest movie palace. Today it's an Art Deco showcase for top musical acts and large-screen movies.

Greektown, one of Detroit's most popular entertainment districts, is centered on Monroe Street. It percolates day and night with markets, bars, coffeehouses, shops, and restaurants serving authentic Greek fare with an American flair.

Second Baptist Church (⊠ 441 Monroe, ☎ 313/961–0920), organized in 1836, is Detroit's oldest black congregation and an important stop on the Underground Railroad. African-Americans gathered here to celebrate the Emancipation Proclamation. **Old St. Mary's Catholic Church** (⊠ 646 Monroe Ave., ☎ 313/961–8711), built in 1885, began as a parish of German and Irish immigrants in 1833.

Bricktown, characterized by its brick facades, is a refurbished industrial corner of downtown filled with restaurants and bars; it's a good place for a leisurely lunch, a shopping spree, or cocktails.

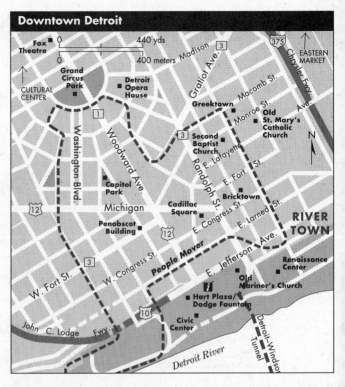

Downtown Detroit

Detroit East

In the 1880s the section east of the Renaissance Center, between the river and Jefferson Avenue, exploded with lumberyards, shipyards, and railroads. Known as **Rivertown,** the area is seeing new life today, with parks, shops, restaurants, and nightspots set in rejuvenated warehouses and carriage houses. **Stroh River Place,** opened in 1988, has attracted businesses, restaurants, and shops to a 21-acre site that stood empty for years.

Rivertown is the home of **Pewabic Pottery** (⊠ 10125 E. Jefferson Ave., ☎ 313/822–0954; ⊇ free), founded in 1907, which produced the brilliantly glazed ceramic Pewabic tiles found in buildings throughout the nation, including the Detroit Public Library and Washington National Cathedral. The pottery now houses a ceramics museum, a workshop, and a learning center.

Farmers and city slickers alike have gathered in the historic open-air **Eastern Market** (⊠ 2934 Russell St., ☎ 313/833–1560) since 1892 to bargain and barter over fresh produce, meats, fish, and plants. Public shopping hours start Saturday at 5 AM. Stores stay open until 5 PM; open-air markets shut down around 2 PM, when the stock runs out.

Near Northwest Detroit

Two and a half miles from downtown via Woodward Avenue is the **University Cultural Center,** a collection of art, history, and science museums and institutions clustered throughout some 40 city blocks near Wayne State University.

The main exhibit at the **Detroit Historical Museum** (⊠ 5401 Woodward Ave., ☎ 313/833–1805; ⊇ $4.50, free Wed.) explores the city's ties to the automobile. Other worthwhile exhibits are the Lawrence Scripps Wilkinson toy collection and the Streets of Old Detroit—a walk through the city's long history.

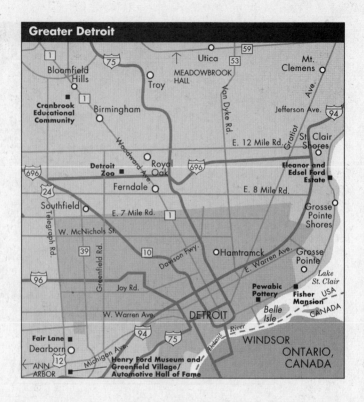

With more than 100 galleries, the **Detroit Institute of Arts** (⊠ 5200 Woodward Ave., ☎ 313/833–7900; 🎫 $4) displays 5,000 years of art treasures, including works by van Gogh, Rembrandt, and Renoir. Diego Rivera's *Detroit Industry,* four immense frescoes, is a must-see. The institute is open from Wednesday through Sunday.

With 1.3 million books, the Cultural Center branch of the **Detroit Public Library** (⊠ 5201 Woodward Ave., ☎ 313/833–1000, 313/833–1722 for recorded information) is the system's largest. Its Burton Historical Collection is the state's most comprehensive on city, state, Great Lakes lore, and genealogy. The library is open from Tuesday through Saturday.

The **International Institute of Metropolitan Detroit** (⊠ 111 E. Kirby St., ☎ 313/871–8600; 🎫 free) is a museum, a working resource center for foreigners, and a lunchtime café. Its Gallery of Nations displays the arts and crafts of 43 countries. The **Charles H. Wright Museum of African-American History** (⊠ 315 E. Warren Ave., ☎ 313/494–5800; 🎫 $5), the largest museum of its kind in the world, tells the story of the black experience in America through exhibits and audiovisual presentations.

Other Attractions

Scattered around Detroit are the lavish homes of four of the city's famed auto barons. Henry Ford's **Fair Lane** (⊠ 4901 Evergreen Rd., Dearborn, ☎ 313/593–5590; 🎫 $8) blends a Scottish Baronial style with a simple Arts and Crafts design. Here, you'll get a look at the bowling alley where Ford used to shoot pins with his friends Thomas Edison and naturalist John Burroughs. Ford's son Edsel built the **Eleanor and Edsel Ford Estate** (⊠ 1100 Lakeshore Rd., Grosse Pointe Shores, ☎ 313/884–4222; 🎫 $8), a 1929 Cotswold–style residence with beautiful artwork and gardens. The largest of the auto baron's homes, the opulent **Meadow Brook Hall** (⊠ Oakland University, Rochester, ☎ 248/

370–3140; $8) was built in the late 1920s for Matilda Dodge, widow of auto pioneer John Dodge. Among its more than 100 rooms is a two-story ballroom; there are also formal gardens. The most lavish residence in its day, **Fisher Mansion** (⊠ 383 Lenox Ave., ☎ 313/331–6740; ✉ $6) is the only auto baron's mansion within city limits. With 24-karat gold-leaf ceilings, it was modeled after William Randolph Hearst's San Simeon and is now a vegetarian restaurant and cultural center.

☾ Dearborn's **Henry Ford Museum and Greenfield Village** (⊠ 20900 Oakwood Blvd., ☎ 313/271–1620; ✉ $12.50 each for museum or village; $22 for both) is America's largest indoor-outdoor museum. It charts the country's evolution from a rural to an industrial society through exhibits covering communications, transportation, domestic life, agriculture, and industry. Greenfield Village preserves 80 famous historic structures, including the bicycle shop where the Wright brothers built their first airplane; Thomas Edison's laboratory; an Illinois courthouse where Abraham Lincoln practiced law; and the Dearborn farm where Ford himself was born. The Automobile in American Life is a lavish collection of chrome and neon that traces the country's love affair with cars. The adjacent **Automotive Hall of Fame** (⊠ 21400 Oakwood Blvd., ☎ 888/298–4748; ✉ $6) has profiles of the men behind the machines, a mural of automotive history, and a full-size replica of the world's first gas-powered car.

Cranbrook, in Bloomfield Hills, is a cultural and educational center with a graduate art academy and college-preparatory schools. **Historic Cranbrook House and Gardens** (⊠ 380 Lone Pine Rd., ☎ 248/645–3149 or 800/GO–CRANB; ✉ $6), a mansion built for newspaper publisher George Booth, has lead-glass windows, art objects, and formal gardens with fountains and sculpture. The **Cranbrook Art Museum** (⊠ 1221 N. Woodward Ave., ☎ 248/645–3312 or 800/GO–CRANB; ✉ $5) has major exhibitions of contemporary art and a permanent collection
☾ that includes works by Eliel and Eero Saarinen and Charles Eames. **Cranbrook Institute of Science** (⊠ 1221 N. Woodward Ave., ☎ 248/645–3200 or 800/GO–CRANB; ✉ $7) has intriguing hands-on physics experiments, geology displays, and dinosaur-excavation findings.

Parks, Gardens, and Zoos

More than 1,200 animals from 300 species live uncaged in natural habitats at the **Detroit Zoo** (⊠ 8450 W. Ten Mile Rd., Royal Oak, ☎ 248/398–0900; ✉ $7.50). Highlights include the world's largest "penguinarium," a walk-through aviary with tropical birds and plants, and a wildlife interpretive gallery with a butterfly house.

Belle Isle (☎ 313/852–4075), 3 mi southeast of the city center on a 1,000-acre island in the Detroit River, is reached by way of East Jefferson Avenue and East Grand Boulevard. Here are woods, walking trails, sports facilities, a 9-hole golf course, and a ½-mi-long beach.

Among Belle Isle's other attractions is the **Anna Scripps Whitcomb Conservatory** (☎ 313/852–4065; ✉ $2), with one of the largest orchid collections in the country. **Belle Isle Aquarium** (☎ 313/852–4141; ✉ $2), the nation's oldest freshwater aquarium, exhibits more than 200 species of fish, reptiles, and amphibians, including a popular electric eel. The **Belle Isle Nature Center** (☎ 313/852–4075; ✉ donations accepted) has changing exhibits and presentations on local natural history. The **Belle Isle Zoo** (☎ 313/852–4083; ✉ $3), closed from November through April, has an elevated walkway that gives you a bird's-eye view of animals roaming in natural settings.

Also on Belle Isle, the **Dossin Great Lakes Museum** (⊠ 100 Strand Dr., ☎ 313/852–4051; ✉ $2) has displays on Great Lakes shipping and the Prohibition era in Detroit. The ongoing exhibit, "The Storm of 1913," recounts the Great Lakes' worst storm ever. You can also listen to ship-to-shore radio messages and view the river and city through a periscope. The museum is open from Wednesday through Sunday.

Dining

Each wave of immigrants to Detroit has made a culinary mark: You'll find soul food in the inner city, a vibrant Mexican community on the west side, and Greek restaurants in Greektown. Detroiters often dine across the river in Windsor, Ontario, where a favorable rate of exchange makes for excellent values.

$$$–$$$$ ✕ **The Summit.** This revolving restaurant on the 71st floor of the Westin Hotel has a superb view of Detroit; unfortunately the food is not always as memorable. Charbroiled steaks and swordfish à la Louisiana are staples. ⊠ *Renaissance Center,* ☏ *313/568–8600. Jacket and tie. AE, D, DC, MC, V.*

$$$–$$$$ ✕ **The Whitney.** Once the mansion of lumber baron David Whitney,
★   this posh restaurant turns out creative American dishes, snappy pastas, and very fresh seafood. Brunch is served on Sunday. ⊠ *4421 Woodward Ave.,* ☏ *313/832–5700. Reservations essential. Jacket and tie. AE, D, MC, V.*

$$–$$$$ ✕ **Caucus Club.** This venerable Detroit institution recalls a time when elegant restaurants had boardroom decor, lots of oil paintings, and wood. The menu is of similar vintage: corned-beef hash, steaks, chops, Dover sole, and the club's famous baby-back ribs. ⊠ *150 W. Congress St.,* ☏ *313/965–4970. AE, D, DC, MC, V. Closed weekends.*

$$–$$$$ ✕ **Fishbone's Rhythm Kitchen Cafe.** This authentic New Orleans–style
★   restaurant in the heart of Greektown is loud, brash, funky, and fun. The spicy Creole fare on the seasonal menu includes gator, gumbo, crawfish, and gulf oysters on the half shell. The whiskey ribs are tops year-round. If you're staying in the suburbs, check out the branches in St. Clair Shores and West Bloomfield. ⊠ *400 Monroe Ave.,* ☏ *313/965–4600. AE, D, DC, MC, V.*

$$–$$$$ ✕ **Lelli's Inn.** When Detroiters think Italian, Lelli's comes to mind. Ex-
★   ceptional veal, minestrone, red sauce, and homemade ice creams are served in a cavernous, 650-seat dining room. ⊠ *7618 Woodward Ave.,* ☏ *313/871–1590. Jacket and tie. AE, DC, MC, V. Closed Mon.*

$$–$$$$ ✕ **Rattlesnake Club.** There are innovative pickerel, salmon, and veal dishes, but the signature dish is rack of lamb. The dining room is all marble and rosewood, with terrific views of the Detroit River and Windsor skyline. ⊠ *300 River Pl.,* ☏ *313/567–4400. AE, D, DC, MC, V.*

$–$$$$ ✕ **Pegasus Taverna.** Specialties such as *pastitsio* (Greek-style lasagna) and *avgolemono* (chicken-lemon soup) are prepared in a huge open kitchen at this Greek tavern. You'll also find American classics like Caesar salad and sandwiches. ⊠ *558 Monroe Ave.,* ☏ *313/964–6800. AE, D, DC, MC, V.*

$–$$$ **Beans & Cornbread.** This upscale eatery in suburban Southfield pays homage to its southern roots with period music from earlier this century, vintage *Life* magazine posters featuring famous African-Americans, and mounds of solidly prepared soul food. ⊠ *29508 Northwestern Hwy.,* ☏ *248/208–1680. AE, DC, MC, V.*

$–$$$ ✕ **Blue Nile.** Detroit's only Ethiopian restaurant is, oddly enough, in
★   the heart of Greektown. Richly seasoned meats and vegetables are served on communal platters with *injera,* a crepe-like flat bread used to scoop up the foods. ⊠ *Trappers Alley, 508 Monroe Ave.,* ☏ *313/964–6699. AE, D, DC, MC, V.*

$–$$$ ✕ **Traffic Jam & Snug.** The menu changes often, but you can count on wheatberry and other interesting breads, inventive salads, and daily specials like spinach lasagna and Caesar salad. Dessert is key: opt for a sweet "death by chocolate" sundae. ⊠ *511 W. Canfield St.,* ☎ *313/ 831–9470. Reservations not accepted. D, DC, MC, V. No dinner Mon.; no lunch weekends.*

$ ✕ **Lafayette Coney Island.** Detroit's contribution to the world of gastronomy is the so-called Coney Island: loose beef in a hot-dog bun, smothered with cheese, onions, and chili. At 3 AM, suburbanites and visiting celebrities in stretch limos share counter stools with workers getting off the night shift at this area institution. ⊠ *115 Lafayette St.,* ☎ *313/964–8198. Reservations not accepted. No credit cards.*

$ **The Mini.** Worth the drive across the border to Windsor, the tiny Mini is one of those places locals rave about, with spicy Vietnamese fare and wonderful fresh-fruit slushes. The Canadian exchange makes the meal that much tastier. ⊠ *475 University W, Windsor,* ☎ *519/254–2221. AE, D, MC, V.*

$ ✕ **Under the Eagle.** As with most of Hamtramck's modestly priced Polish cafés, the Eagle's food is first-rate, with generous portions of stick-to-your-ribs roast duckling and kielbasa. For the adventuresome there's *czarnina* (duck-blood soup). ⊠ *9000 Joseph Campau St., Hamtramck,* ☎ *313/875–5905. No credit cards. Closed Wed.*

Lodging

In addition to those in downtown Detroit, accommodations are available in suburban Troy, with its high concentration of corporate headquarters, and in Dearborn, where the Ford Motor Company is based. Most hotels, motels, and inns offer reduced-price weekend packages.

$$$$ 🏨 **Ritz-Carlton, Dearborn.** Like Ritz-Carlton hotels around the world,
★ Dearborn's is known for impeccable taste and service. Its mahogany-paneled walls, overstuffed settees, and antique art suggest a clubby, British elegance. Reinforcing that image is a traditional afternoon tea and hors d'oeuvres served in the lobby lounge. ⊠ *300 Town Center Dr., Dearborn 48126,* ☎ *313/441–2000 or 800/241–3333,* 🖷 *313/441–2051. 308 rooms. Restaurant, pool, exercise room. AE, D, DC, MC, V.* 🐾

$$$–$$$$ 🏨 **Atheneum Suite Hotel.** Business travelers and visiting celebrities favor this downtown newcomer. The spacious, individually decorated suites have Greek overtones, and the lobby bar bustles with activity. ⊠ *1000 Brush St., 48226,* ☎ *313/962–2323 or 800/772–2323,* 🖷 *313/ 962–2424. 174 suites. Restaurant, pool, health club. AE, DC, MC, V.*

$$$ 🏨 **Embassy Suites.** This all-suites hotel is a feast for the eyes, with an eight-story atrium full of trees, flowers, and ivy. It's centrally located for Troy business and the nearby Somerset Mall. ⊠ *850 Tower Dr., Troy 48098,* ☎ *248/879–7500 or 800/424–2900,* 🖷 *248/879–9139. 251 suites. Restaurant, pool, health club. AE, D, DC, MC, V. BP.* 🐾

$$$ 🏨 **Hotel Pontchartrain.** The Pontch, as it is familiarly known, has light, airy rooms done in neutral shades accented by green-and-rose fabrics. Most rooms have wonderful views of the city and the river; do not, however, accept a room at the back of the hotel—which is across the street from a fire station—unless you are a heavy sleeper. ⊠ *2 Washington Blvd., 48226,* ☎ *313/965–0200,* 🖷 *313/965–9464. 413 rooms. Restaurant, pool, health club. AE, DC, MC, V.*

$$$ 🏨 **Marriott.** At 73 stories and 1,342 rooms, this hotel is known for its
★ size more than anything else. Guest rooms are neither large nor special, but each commands a waterfront view of the city and of neighboring Windsor, Ontario. Formerly a Westin property, the hotel was taken over by the Marriott chain in 1998. ⊠ *Renaissance Center, Jefferson Ave. at Randolph St., 48243,* ☎ *313/568–8000 or 800/228–9290,* 🖷 *313/568–8146. 1,342 rooms. Restaurant, pool, health club. AE, D, DC, MC, V.* 🐾

$$–$$$ 🖼 **Dearborn Inn–A Marriott Hotel.** Henry Ford built this hotel in 1931 to house foreign dignitaries and inventors such as Thomas Edison and Charles Lindbergh. The Colonial-inspired property is across from the Henry Ford Museum and Greenfield Village; adjacent to the main building are five historic homes associated with such famous Americans as Patrick Henry, Edgar Allan Poe, and Walt Whitman. ✉ *20301 Oakwood Blvd., Dearborn 48124,* ☎ *313/271–2700 or 800/228–9290,* FAX *313/271–7464. 220 rooms, 5 cottages. 2 restaurants, pool, tennis, exercise room. AE, D, DC, MC, V.* 📧

$$–$$$ 🖼 **Hyatt Regency Dearborn.** Opposite Ford's world headquarters, this large, modern and recently renovated hotel with a trademark Hyatt atrium is five minutes from the Henry Ford Museum and Greenfield Village. ✉ *Fairlane Town Center, Dearborn 48126,* ☎ *313/593–1234 or 800/233–1234,* FAX *313/593–3366. 771 rooms. 2 restaurants, pool. AE, D, DC, MC, V.* 📧

$$–$$$ 🖼 **Somerset Inn.** In the heart of Troy's corporate district, 25 mi north of Detroit, the Somerset is a favorite of the business set. Guest rooms are small and standard, but the entry level is lovely, with several small sitting rooms tucked around the perimeter. ✉ *2601 W. Big Beaver Rd., Troy 48084,* ☎ *248/643–7800 or 800/228–8769,* FAX *248/643–2296. 250 rooms. Restaurant, pools, health club. AE, D, DC, MC, V.*

$$ 🖼 **Courtyard by Marriott Downtown.** One of Detroit's most modern
★   hotels, the Courtyard (formerly a Doubletree and an Omni) is connected by skywalk to the Renaissance Center, and by People Mover to the rest of downtown. Rooms are bright and large. ✉ *333 E. Jefferson Ave., 48226,* ☎ *313/222–7700 or 800/222–8733,* FAX *313/222–8517. 254 rooms. Restaurant, pool, tennis, health club. AE, D, DC, MC, V.* 📧

$–$$ 🖼 **Shorecrest Motor Inn.** This pleasant, no-frills two-story hotel is two blocks east of the Renaissance Center and within walking distance of downtown attractions. ✉ *1316 E. Jefferson Ave., 48207,* ☎ *313/ 568–3000 or 800/992–9616,* FAX *313/568–3002. 54 rooms. Restaurant. AE, D, DC, MC, V.*

Nightlife and the Arts

Nightlife

Much of Detroit's nightlife is centered downtown and in suburban Royal Oak, home to cutting-edge restaurants and smoky coffeehouses. In Greektown, tourists crowd the **Bouzouki Lounge** (✉ 432 E. Lafayette St., ☎ 313/964–5744) for traditional Greek music, folk singers, and belly dancers. On the west side of the city is **Baker's Keyboard Lounge** (✉ 20510 Livernois Ave., ☎ 313/345–6300), a dimly lighted, smoke-filled club with nightly jazz and great soul food.

Poetry readings, art exhibitions, and no-nonsense live acts give **Alvin's** (✉ 5756 Cass St., ☎ 313/832–2355) a bohemian appeal, especially among students at nearby Wayne State University. More alternative music can be had at **St. Andrews Hall** (✉ 431 E. Congress St., ☎ 313/961–8137) or at the techno tough hangout **Venues** (3515 Caniff, Hamtramck, ☎ 313/369–0080).

The Arts

Metro Times, a free weekly available throughout the metropolitan area, has a comprehensive calendar of events. Also check the arts sections of the *Detroit News* and *Detroit Free Press,* and the calendar section of *Hour Detroit.*

The **Detroit Repertory Theater** (✉ 13103 Woodrow Wilson Ave., ☎ 313/868–1347) is one of the city's oldest resident theater companies. Touring Broadway shows and nationally known entertainers appear at the **Fisher Theater** (✉ 3011 W. Grand Blvd., ☎ 313/872–1000) and the **Masonic Temple** (⊠ 500 Temple St., ☎ 313/832–7100). **Detroit Symphony Orchestra Hall** (⊠ 3663 Woodward Ave., ☎ 313/576–5100) is home to the **Chamber Music Society of Detroit** and the **Detroit Symphony.** The **Detroit Opera House** (⊠ 1526 Broadway, ☎ 313/327–3279) is the newly restored home of the acclaimed Michigan Opera Theatre; it also hosts visiting ballet and musical troupes from around the country. Across the street is the relocated **Gem Theater** (⊠ 333 Madison Ave., ☎ 313/963–9800), which used to stand across from the Fox but was moved to make way for the new Detroit Tigers ballpark.

Spectator Sports

Baseball: The 2000 season was the first at the new Comerica Park in the heart of downtown. The glitzy stadium has all the bells and whistles, but purists still reminisce about classic Tiger Stadium, closed in 1999. **Detroit Tigers** (⊠ 2121 Trumbull at Michigan Ave., ☎ 313/962–4000). **Basketball: Detroit Pistons** (⊠ The Palace of Auburn Hills, 2 Championship Dr., 30 mi north of Detroit, Auburn Hills, ☎ 248/377–0100). **Football: Detroit Lions** (⊠ Pontiac Silverdome, 30 mi north of Detroit, Pontiac, ☎ 248/335–4131). **Hockey: Detroit Red Wings** (⊠ Joe Louis Arena, downtown on the riverfront, ☎ 313/983–6606).

Shopping

Shopping is scarce downtown, where once-fashionable Woodward Avenue is now a forlorn and mostly abandoned strip; these days, most shopping is concentrated in the suburbs. Near the University Cultural Center, **New Center One** attracts office workers during lunchtime. In suburban Troy, the **Somerset Collection and Somerset North** has tony boutiques and prominent upscale chains such as Neiman Marcus, Saks Fifth Avenue, and Nordstrom. **Suburban Birmingham** is home to some of the Midwest's finest art galleries as well as exclusive boutiques. In funky **Royal Oak,** you'll find small stores stocking everything from leather clothing and paraphernalia to fine antiques.

The area leader in fashion and home furnishings is **J. L. Hudson's.** Its onetime beloved downtown flagship was imploded in 1998 but has been replaced by a suburban headquarters at Northland Mall in Southfield. Other stores and malls are scattered throughout the suburbs, including a luxurious outlet in the Somerset Collection in Troy.

ELSEWHERE IN MICHIGAN

Ann Arbor

Visitor Information

Ann Arbor: Convention and Visitors Bureau (⊠ 120 W. Huron St., 48104, ☎ 800/888–9487).

Arriving and Departing

Ann Arbor, 50 mi west of downtown Detroit, is intersected by U.S. 23 and I–94.

What to See and Do

Leafy, liberal, and young (thanks to the student population of the University of Michigan), Ann Arbor is consistently rated among the country's most desirable communities. The downtown shopping district, which extends along **Main Street,** is known for its funky specialty stores, run by knowledgeable, independent owners. The State Street area, closer to campus, has one of the finest concentrations of book and music stores in the country. Among them is the original **Borders Books and Music**

(⊠ 612 E. Liberty, ☎ 734/668–7100), started in 1971 by two University of Michigan graduates. On campus are three exceptional free museums. The **University of Michigan Museum of Art** (⊠ 525 S. State St., ☎ 734/764–0395) has a permanent collection of 13,000 pieces, including works by Rodin, Picasso, and Monet. Exhibits at the **University of Michigan Exhibit Museum of Natural History** (⊠ 1109 Geddes Ave., ☎ 734/763–6085) range from miniature dioramas to towering dinosaur skeletons. The **Kelsey Museum of Archaeology** (⊠ 434 S. State St., ☎ 734/764–9304) houses ancient Greek, Egyptian, Roman, and Near Eastern artifacts. Try your hands at the 250 working-science exhibits at the **Ann Arbor Hands-On Museum** (⊠ 219 E. Huron St., ☎ 734/995–5439; ⊡ $5), housed in an 1882 firehouse downtown.

Dining and Lodging

$$$$ ✕ **Zanzibar.** Amid tropical decor and a lively atmosphere, this hip, centrally located eatery serves entrées from tropical countries around the equator. ⊠ 216 S. State St., ☎ 734/994–7777. AE, DC, MC, V.

$–$$$$ ✕ **Gandy Dancer.** Housed in a 19th-century railroad depot on the edge of town, this flagship of Joe Muer's popular seafood chain specializes in fresh seafood and tasty pastas. The Sunday brunch is a lavish, diet-busting spread. ⊠ 401 Depot St., ☎ 734/769–0592. AE, DC, MC, V.

$$$–$$$$ ✕▥ **Bell Tower.** The only hotel in the heart of campus has a traditional, intimate, European style. The elegant restaurant, Escoffier, serves old-style French cuisine such as baked rainbow trout stuffed with scallop mousse, and sautéed sweetbreads with grapes and Madeira. ⊠ 300 S. Thayer St., 48104, ☎ 734/769–3010 or 800/562–3559, ℻ 734/769–4339. 66 rooms. Restaurant. D, DC, MC, V.

Mackinac Island

Visitor Information

Mackinac Island Chamber of Commerce (⊠ Box 451, Mackinac Island 49757, ☎ 906/847–3783).

Arriving and Departing

By car, take I–75 north from Detroit to Mackinaw City. Island ferries depart from Mackinaw City and St. Ignace, at the northern end of the Mackinac Bridge.

What to See and Do

No autos are allowed on **Mackinac Island** (island, town, and straits are all pronounced *mack*-i-naw), but the quaint Victorian village begs to be explored on foot. A small park at the eastern end of the village, along the boardwalk, affords terrific views of the Mackinac Bridge and ships passing through the straits. Farther afield, 8 mi of paved roads circle the island; bicycles rent by the hour or day at concessions near the ferry docks on Huron Street. **Mackinac Island Carriage Tours** (⊠ Main St., ☎ 906/847–3573) conducts horse-drawn tours covering historic points of interest, including Fort Mackinac, Arch Rock, Skull Cave, Surrey Hill, and the Grand Hotel.

On a bluff above the harbor, **Fort Mackinac** (☎ 906/847–3328) was a British stronghold during the American Revolution and the War of 1812. Fourteen original buildings are preserved as a museum; costumed guides conduct tours and reenactments. **Marquette Park,** directly below the fort along Main Street, commemorates the work of French missionary Jacques Marquette with a bark chapel patterned after those built on the island in the 1600s. The venerable **Grand Hotel** (☎ 906/847–3331), now more than a century old, charges visitors $10 just to look, but the Victorian opulence of the public rooms and the view from the world's longest porch are worth it.

Dining and Lodging

$$$–$$$$ ✕⌂ **Island House.** The island's oldest hotel and a registered historic site is also the home of Governor's Dining Room, one of the area's most acclaimed restaurants. Fish and steak are served in a formal dining room with views of the lake and nearby islands. ✉ *1 Lakeshore Dr., 49757,* ☎ *906/847–3347,* FAX *906/847–3819. 97 rooms. Restaurant, pool. MC, V.* ⊛

Keweenaw Peninsula

Visitor Information

Keweenaw Tourism Council (✉ 326 Shelden Ave., Houghton 49931, ☎ 906/482–2388 or 800/338–7982).

Arriving and Departing

The Keweenaw, in the northwestern section of the Upper Peninsula, is reached by U.S. 41.

What to See and Do

Curving into Lake Superior like a crooked finger, the Keweenaw (*key-wa-naw*) was the site of extensive copper mining from the 1840s to the 1960s. In Hancock, you can take a guided tour of now-defunct mine workings, **Quincy Mine Hoist** (☎ 906/482–5569; ⊡ $10). **Houghton** is home to Michigan Technical University, whose **Seaman Mineral Museum** (☎ 906/487–2572; ⊡ $4) has displays of minerals native to the Upper Peninsula.

North on U.S. 41, the Victorian stone architecture in **Calumet** gives just a hint of the wealth in the copper towns during the boom days. Stars such as Sarah Bernhardt and Douglas Fairbanks Sr. once performed at the circa-1900 **Calumet Theater** (☎ 906/337–2610). At **Coppertown, U.S.A.** (☎ 906/337–4579; ⊡ $3), a visitor center and museum tells the story of the mines, towns, and hearty people of the Keweenaw. Michigan's northernmost community, **Copper Harbor,** at the tip of the Keweenaw peninsula, is a crowd-free biking and camping destination. **Fort Wilkins State Historic Park** (☎ 906/289–4215) contains the restored buildings of an Army post established in 1844 and abandoned in 1870; the complex also has copper-mine shafts, hiking trails, and campgrounds. **Brockway Mountain Drive** climbs 900 ft above Copper Harbor for magnificent views of the peninsula and Lake Superior.

Lake Michigan Shore

Visitor Information

The **West Michigan Tourist Association** (✉ 1253 Front St., Grand Rapids 49504, ☎ 616/456–8557) provides information on the Lake Michigan Shore area.

Arriving and Departing

U.S. 31 edges Lake Michigan from St. Joseph to Mackinaw City.

What to See and Do

The Lake Michigan shoreline, which extends from the southwestern corner of the state up to the Mackinac Bridge, is one of Michigan's greatest natural resources. Its placid waters, cool breezes, and sugary beaches (including some of the largest sand dunes in the world) have attracted generations of tourists, including such regulars as Al Capone, Ernest Hemingway, and L. Frank Baum (who wrote many of his books about Oz over the course of several summer vacations here).

Resort towns, some of which triple in population between Memorial Day and Labor Day, dot the shoreline. **St. Joseph** is a picturesque community whose turn-of-the-20th-century downtown and two 1,000-ft-long piers make it ideal for walkers. The artists' colony of **Saugatuck** has many fine restaurants and shops, an active gay and lesbian community, and enough B&Bs to make it the bed-and-breakfast capital of the state. **Saugatuck Dune Rides** (☎ 616/857–2253) offers freewheeling dune-buggy rides along Lake Michigan. In **Douglas,** the **S. S. Keewatin** (☎ 616/857–2701), one of the Great Lakes' last passenger steamboats, is permanently docked as a maritime museum.

Near Douglas is **Holland,** home of the **Tulip Time Festival** in May (☞ Festivals and Seasonal Events *in* the United States Region by Region chapter). The **De Klomp Wooden Shoe and Delftware Factory** (⊠ 12755 Quincy St., ☎ 616/399–1900; ☑ free) is the only place outside the Netherlands where earthenware is hand-painted and fired using Delft blue glaze.

North of Holland is the eastern shore's largest city, **Muskegon,** an industrial town known mainly as the home of the **Muskegon Winter Sports Complex** (☎ 231/744–9629), with the only luge run in the Midwest. The Art Deco **Frauenthal Center for the Performing Arts** (⊠ 425 W. Western St., ☎ 231/722–4538) hosts traveling Broadway-quality plays, silent films, and the West Shore Symphony Orchestra. Eight miles north of Muskegon is **Michigan's Adventure Amusement Park** (⊠ 4750 Whitehall Rd., ☎ 231/766–3377; ☑ $20), with more than 20 rides, 10 water slides, a wave pool, shows, games, food, and the only two roller coasters in Michigan.

A two-hour drive north of Muskegon is **Traverse City,** Michigan's premier sports-vacation destination. Much to the chagrin of longtime residents, the area south of Grand Traverse Bay was "discovered" by sportsmen—and developers—about 25 years ago. Unfortunately, the roads have not kept pace with the boom in sailors, golfers, and skiers: The two-lane highways can resemble parking lots, particularly during the popular **National Cherry Festival** (☞ Festivals and Seasonal Events *in* the United States Region by Region chapter). For a pleasant diversion follow Route 37 around the **Old Mission Peninsula,** filled with the cherry orchards and vineyards that are the area's main industry next to tourism. A good time to visit is in the spring, when crowds are small.

Savor some of the finest views of Lake Michigan from the **Leelanau Peninsula,** the finger that juts into Little Traverse Bay. Follow Route 119 to **Harbor Springs,** a resort village overlooking Little Traverse Bay.

MINNESOTA

By Don
Davenport and
Karin Winegar

Updated by
Jim Umhoefer

Capital	St. Paul
Population	4,725,420
Motto	Star of the North
State Bird	Common loon
State Flower	Pink lady's slipper
Postal Abbreviation	MN

Statewide Visitor Information

Minnesota Office of Tourism (✉ 500 Metro Sq., 121 7th Pl. E, St. Paul 55101, ☎ 651/296–5029 or 800/657–3700). There are 12 visitor centers around the state.

Scenic Drives

U.S. 61, along the Mississippi River between Red Wing and Winona, is often compared with the Rhine Valley in beauty; between Duluth and the Canadian border (☞ Duluth and the North Shore, *below*), it hugs the edge of Lake Superior for 160 mi, providing spectacular views of the lake and its rocky shoreline. **Route 59,** between Fergus Falls and Detroit Lakes, traverses some of central Minnesota's prime lake country.

National and State Parks

National Parks

Voyageurs National Park (☞ The Iron Range and Boundary Waters, *below*), in far northern Minnesota, has 30 major lakes and is part of the watery highway that makes up the state's northern border with Canada.

Pipestone National Monument, in southwestern Minnesota, protects the red stone quarry mined for centuries by Native Americans for material to carve their ceremonial pipes. The quarry is still in use, and traditional stone craft is practiced at the **cultural center** in the Monument Headquarters (✉ Hwy. 75, Pipestone 56164, ☎ 507/825–5464).

State Parks

Minnesota has 68 state parks, 62 with camping facilities. For information contact the **Department of Natural Resources** (✉ DNR Information Center, 500 Lafayette Rd., Box 40, St. Paul 55155–4040, ☎ 651/296–6157).

Fort Snelling State Park, just south of downtown St. Paul (✉ Rte. 5 and Post Rd., St. Paul 55111, ☎ 612/725–2389), preserves the historic fort built at the junction of the Mississippi and Minnesota rivers in 1819. **Itasca State Park** (✉ HC05, Box 4, Lake Itasca 56460, ☎ 218/266–2100) is Minnesota's oldest state park, established in 1891 to protect the headwaters of the Mississippi River, which rises from Lake Itasca. **Soudan Underground Mine State Park** (✉ 1379 Stuntz Bay Rd., Soudan 55782, ☎ 218/753–2245) has hiking trails and tours of the Soudan Mine, Minnesota's oldest and largest iron mine, which operated until 1962. **Gooseberry Falls State Park** (✉ 1300 Hwy. 61E, Two Harbors 55616, ☎ 218/834–3855) and **Temperance River State Park** (✉ Hwy. 61, Box 33, Schroeder 55613, ☎ 218/663–7476), with their roaring waterfalls and scenic views, are typical of the parks along Lake Superior's shore.

MINNEAPOLIS AND ST. PAUL

Though both Minneapolis and St. Paul straddle the Mississippi River, the two cities have completely different personalities. St. Paul feels slightly reserved and antique, as it has preserved much of its architectural heritage; downtown Minneapolis is newer, hipper, noisier, and busier. Both cities have tall, gleaming glass skylines; St. Paul's blends with its Art Deco and Victorian architecture, and Minneapolis's skyline is eclectic. Riverboat traffic calls at the Twin Cities from as far away as New Orleans.

There are 2.5 million people in the Greater Minneapolis/St. Paul metropolitan area, and 375,090 of them live in Minneapolis, the region's most populated city. To bear the harsh winter climate, the cities have constructed several-mile-long skyway systems. Using the skyway, you can drive downtown, park, walk to work, go to lunch, shop, see a show, and return to your car without once setting foot outdoors—a blessing in the blustery Minnesota winters.

Visitor Information

Minneapolis: Convention and Visitors Association (⊠ 4000 Multifoods Tower, 33 S. 6th St., 55402, ☎ 612/661–4700 or 888/676–6757). **St. Paul:** Convention and Visitors Bureau (⊠ 175 W. Kellogg Blvd., Suite 502, 55102, ☎ 612/297–6985 or 800/627–6101).

Arriving and Departing

By Bus
Greyhound has stations in St. Paul (⊠ 166 W. University Ave., ☎ 651/222–0509) and in Minneapolis (⊠ 1100 Hawthorne Ave., ☎ 612/371–3325).

By Car
The major north–south route through the area is I–35, which divides into I–35W bisecting Minneapolis and I–35E through St. Paul. I–94 goes east–west through both cities. A beltway circles the Twin Cities, with I–494 looping through the southern suburbs and I–694 cutting through the north.

By Plane
Minneapolis/St. Paul International Airport (⊠ 4300 Glumack Dr., St. Paul 55111, ☎ 612/726–5555) lies between the cities on I–494, 8 mi south of downtown St. Paul and 10 mi south of downtown Minneapolis. It is served by most major domestic airlines and several foreign carriers. From the airport to either city, **Metropolitan Transit Commission** (☎ 612/349–7000) buses cost $1 ($2 during rush hour); taxis take about 30 minutes and charge $17–$25 to both downtown Minneapolis and St. Paul.

By Train
St. Paul's **Amtrak** station (⊠ 730 Transfer Rd., ☎ 651/644–1127) serves both cities.

Getting Around Minneapolis and St. Paul

Both cities are laid out on a grid, with streets running north–south and east–west. However, many downtown streets parallel the Mississippi River and run on a diagonal, and not all streets cross the river. Both downtowns have extensive skyway systems. Many St. Paul attractions can be reached on foot, but most of those in Minneapolis require wheels. Express fare on **Metropolitan Transit Commission** (☎ 612/349–7000) buses between Minneapolis and St. Paul during rush hour is $2. Within each city's central business district the fare is 50¢. Outside the downtown area the fare is $1, $1.50 during peak hours (6–9 AM and 3:30–6:30 PM).

Taxi fare is $3.40 for the first mile and $1.60 for each additional mile. Minimum fares apply. The largest taxi firms in St. Paul are **Yellow** (☎ 651/222–4433) and **City Wide** (☎ 651/489–1111); in Minneapolis, **Blue** and White (☎ 612/333–3333) and **Yellow** (☎ 612/824–4444). **Town Taxi** (☎ 612/331–8294) serves all suburbs.

Exploring Minneapolis and St. Paul

Minneapolis

Downtown Minneapolis is easily walkable in any season. The climate-controlled skyway system connects hundreds of shops and restaurants. In general, skyways remain open during the business hours of the buildings they connect.

The Mississippi River's **Falls of St. Anthony,** discovered by Father Louis Hennepin, drop 16 ft at the eastern edge of downtown. Harnessed by dams and diminished in grandeur, the historic falls are today bypassed by the **Upper St. Anthony Lock** (⊠ foot of Portland Ave.), which allows river traffic to reach industrial sections of Minneapolis. An observation deck provides views of lock operations.

The **Stone Arch Bridge,** a railroad bridge over the Mississippi River near the Upper St. Anthony Lock, was built in the late 19th century by railroad baron James J. Hill and later restored and opened to foot and bicycle traffic. Guided walking tours of the **St. Anthony Falls Historic District** (☎ 612/627–5433) are available from April through October.

With an enrollment of close to 60,000, the **University of Minnesota** is one of the largest campuses in the country. **Dinkytown,** on the east bank, and **Seven Corners,** on the west bank, are good places to find campus bars, nightspots, university shops, record emporiums, and bookstores.

The University of Minnesota's **James Ford Bell Museum of Natural History** (⊠ University Ave. SE at 17th Ave., ☎ 612/624–7083; ⊡ $3) has dioramas of Minnesota wildlife, an art gallery of wildlife paintings, and a touch-and-see room for kids. The most talked-about building on campus is the **Weisman Art Museum** (⊠ 333 E. River Rd., ☎ 612/625–9494; ⊡ free), a wild-looking metallic structure designed by famed avantgarde architect Frank Gehry. The permanent collection includes works and installations by American pop artists and modernists like Andy Warhol, Roy Lichtenstein, and Georgia O'Keeffe.

Much of Minneapolis's towering downtown was built in the past 25 years, several blocks west of the university. Two of the downtown's most recent additions are the 57-story **Norwest Center** (⊠ 77 S. 7th St.), designed by Cesar Pelli, and its smaller companion, **Gaviidae Common** (⊠ 651 Nicollet Mall), the latest downtown shopping hub. The mirrored, 51-story **IDS Building** (⊠ 80 S. 8th St.) contains **Crystal Court,** a focal point of the skyway system, with shops, restaurants, and offices. The 42-story **Piper Jaffray Tower** (⊠ 222 S. 9th St.), sheathed in aqua-color glass, and the 17-story **Lutheran Brotherhood Building** (⊠ 625 4th Ave. SE), in copper-color glass, are sparkling members of the skyline. At the **Foshay Tower** (⊠ 821 Marquette Ave., ☎ 612/341–2522)—Minneapolis's first skyscraper, constructed in 1929—the 31st-floor observation deck has spectacular views of the city.

Nicollet Mall, a mile-long pedestrian mall, runs from Washington Avenue South to Grant Street East, with an extensive system of skyways connecting its many shops and the public library. Inside the library, the **Minneapolis Planetarium** (⊠ 300 Nicollet Mall, ☎ 612/630–6150; ⊡ $2.50–$4.50) gives shows that tour the night sky and investigate the latest discoveries in space science.

Another downtown landmark, the inflated **Hubert H. Humphrey Metrodome** (⊠ 900 S. 5th St., ☎ 612/332–0386), is home to the Minnesota Twins baseball team and the Minnesota Vikings and Univer-

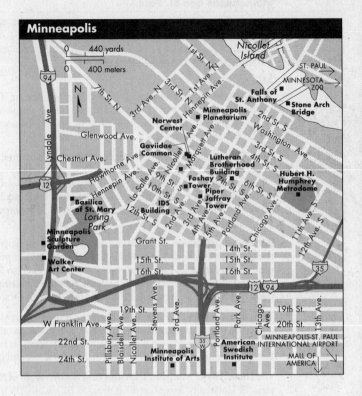

Minneapolis

sity of Minnesota football teams. Behind-the-scenes tours of the locker rooms, playing field, and press box are available.

The **Minneapolis Institute of Arts** (⊠ 2400 3rd Ave. S, ☎ 612/870–3131; ☞ free, except during special exhibits), 1 mi south of downtown and west of I–35W, displays more than 80,000 works of art from every age and culture, including works by the French Impressionists, rare Chinese jade, and a photography collection from 1863 to the present. The building also houses the **Children's Theatre Company,** which puts on adventurous plays for all ages. The institute and theater company are both closed on Monday.

The **American Swedish Institute** (⊠ 2600 Park Ave., ☎ 612/871–4907; ☞ $4) is set in a 33-room Romanesque château filled with decorative woodwork. The museum, five blocks east of the Minneapolis Institute of Arts, displays art, pioneer items, Swedish glass, ceramics, and furniture relating to the area's Swedish heritage.

★ The **Walker Art Center** (⊠ Vineland Pl., adjoining Guthrie Theater, ☎ 612/375–7600; ☞ $4, free Thurs. and 1st Sat. of the month; closed Mon.) houses an outstanding collection of 20th-century American and European sculpture, prints, and photography, as well as traveling exhibits. The center also brings national and international acts to Minneapolis. Adjacent to the museum is the **Minneapolis Sculpture Garden,** the nation's largest outdoor urban sculpture garden. The **Irene Hixon Whitney Footbridge,** designed by sculptor Siah Armajani, connects the arts complex to Loring Park, across I–94. The footbridge provides a clear view of the 250-ft dome of the **Basilica of St. Mary** (⊠ 88 N. 17th St.). The exterior was completed in 1914, when the basilica celebrated its first mass. It became the United States' first designated basilica in 1926.

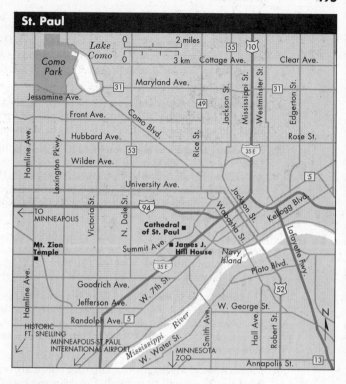

St. Paul

Like its twin, downtown St. Paul is easily explored on foot thanks to its all-weather, climate-controlled skyway system. The Mississippi River runs east–west through the city.

City Hall and the **Ramsey County Courthouse** (⌧ 15 W. Kellogg Blvd., ☎ 651/266–8000) look out across the Mississippi River from a 20-story building of a design known as American Perpendicular. Here, Memorial Hall (4th Street entrance) features Swedish sculptor Carl Milles's towering *Vision of Peace* statue, which at 36 ft and 60 tons is the largest carved-onyx figure in the world.

Rice Park, at the corner of West 5th and Washington streets, is St. Paul's oldest urban park, dating from 1849. It's a favorite with downtowners. Facing Rice Park on the north is the **Landmark Center** (⌧ 75 W. 5th St., ☎ 651/292–3225), which is the restored Federal Courthouse, constructed in 1902. This towering Romanesque Revival structure has a six-story indoor courtyard, stained-glass skylights, and a marble-tile foyer. Of particular interest inside the Landmark Center are a branch of the **Minnesota Museum of American Art** (☎ 651/292–4355; ✉ donation requested), which has strong holdings in Asian and 19th- and 20th-century American art, as well as changing exhibits of contemporary sculpture, paintings, and photography; and the **Schubert Club Musical Instrument Museum** (☎ 651/292–3268), with an outstanding collection of keyboard instruments dating from the 1700s.

On the south side of Rice Park is the block-long Italian Renaissance Revival **St. Paul Public Library.** On the west side of Rice Park is the **Ordway Music Theater** (☞ Nightlife and the Arts, *below*), a state-of-the-art auditorium with faceted-glass walls set in a facade of brick and copper.

West of Rice Park is the **Alexander Ramsey House** (✉ 265 S. Exchange St., ☎ 651/296–8760; 🎟 $5), home to the first governor of the Minnesota Territory. Built in 1872, the restored French Second Empire mansion has 15 rooms, elegantly appointed with period furnishings. The house contains ornate marble fireplaces and fine collections of silver and china. It's open from May through December.

The **Minnesota Children's Museum** (✉ 10 W. 7th St., ☎ 651/225–6000; 🎟 $5.95), has educational, hands-on exhibits, plus story times and singalongs. It's closed Monday from Labor Day to Memorial Day.

The **Science Museum of Minnesota** (✉ 120 W. Kellogg Blvd., ☎ 651/221–9488; 🎟 $7, films extra) has exhibits on archaeology, technology, and biology and many hands-on exhibits for kids. In the **McKnight Omnitheater** 70mm films are projected overhead on a massive tilted screen. Between Labor Day and late December the theater and museum are closed Monday.

Constructed of more than 25 varieties of marble, sandstone, and granite, the **Minnesota State Capitol** (✉ Aurora and Cedar Sts., ☎ 651/296–2881) is just northwest of downtown St. Paul. Its 223-ft-high marble dome is the world's largest.

The **Cathedral of St. Paul** (✉ 239 Selby Ave., ☎ 651/228–1766), a classic Renaissance-style domed church like St. Peter's in Rome, lies ½ mi southwest of the capitol. Inside are beautiful stained-glass windows, statues, paintings, and other works of art, as well as a small historical museum on the lower level.

★ **Summit Avenue,** which runs 4½ mi from the cathedral to the Mississippi River, has the nation's longest stretch of intact residential Victorian architecture. F. Scott Fitzgerald was living at 599 Summit in 1918 when he wrote *This Side of Paradise.* The **James J. Hill House** (✉ 240 Summit Ave., ☎ 651/297–2555; 🎟 $5), once the home of the builder of the Great Northern Railroad, is a Richardsonian Romanesque mansion, with carved woodwork, tiled fireplaces, and a skylighted art gallery with changing exhibits. **Mt. Zion Temple** (✉ 1300 Summit Ave., ☎ 651/698–3881) is the home of the oldest (1856) Jewish congregation in Minnesota.

At the confluence of the Mississippi and Minnesota rivers is **Historic Fort Snelling** (✉ Rtes. 5 and 55, near the International Airport south of St. Paul, ☎ 612/726–1171; 🎟 $5 per vehicle). As the northernmost outpost in the old Northwest Territories, it remained an active military post until after World War II. Seventeen buildings have been restored, and costumed guides portray 1820s fort life with demonstrations of blacksmithing, carpentry, and military ceremonies. Exhibits and short films on the fort are shown in the **History Center,** which is closed weekends from November through April. (The fort is closed every day from November through April.)

Parks, Gardens, and Zoos

Minneapolis

Minnehaha Park, on the Mississippi near the airport, is the site of Minnehaha Falls, which was made famous by Longfellow's *Song of Hiawatha.* Above the waterfall is a statue of Hiawatha and Minnehaha. Minnehaha Parkway follows Minnehaha Creek, providing miles of jogging, biking, and in-line-skating trails that run west to Lake Harriet, one of the many lakes in Minneapolis.

Wirth Park (✉ Plymouth Ave. and Theodore Wirth Pkwy., just west of downtown) has bicycling and walking paths through wooded areas and the **Eloise Butler Wildflower Garden**—a little Eden of local forest and prairie flora. Wirth also has a moderately challenging 18-hole public golf course, which doubles as a cross-country ski area in winter.

In Minneapolis's Apple Valley suburb, the **Minnesota Zoo** (⊠ 13000 Zoo Blvd., Apple Valley, ☎ 612/431–9500; ⌨ $8) houses some 1,700 animals in natural settings along six year-round trails. There's also a monorail, the Zoo Lab, a seasonal children's zoo, bird and animal shows, and daily films and slide shows.

St. Paul

Como Park (⊠ N. Lexington Ave. at Como Ave.) has picnic areas, walking trails, playgrounds, and tennis and swimming facilities. **Como Park Zoo** (☎ 651/487–8201) is home to large cats, land and water birds, primates, and aquatic animals. The adjacent **Como Park Conservatory**, in a domed greenhouse, has sunken gardens, a fern room, biblical plantings, and seasonal flower shows.

Dining

Although Minnesotans are known for the culinary traditions of their Scandinavian and German ancestors, the growing immigrant population is introducing ethnic food to the Twin Cities' cuisine.

Minneapolis

$$–$$$$ ✕ **Murray's.** This local institution has been serving steak since 1946. Silver Butter Knife steaks, hickory-smoked shrimp, and Murray's signature garlic toast are served in a plush atmosphere with piano and violin accompaniment. ⊠ *26 S. 6th St.,* ☎ *612/339–0909. AE, D, DC, MC, V.*

$$–$$$ ✕ **Aquavit.** In an unornamented but sleek atmosphere on the ground floor of the IDS Tower downtown, try herring tacos or miso-grilled bass. The restaurant even serves its own aquavits—clear liquors flavored with cloudberries and other delicacies. ⊠ *80 S. 8th St.,* ☎ *612/ 343–3333. AE, D, DC, MC, V.*

$$–$$$ ✕ **D'Amico Cucina.** From the gleaming white linens to the marble floors and leather chairs, this is a haute place. The seasonal menu has a modern Italian accent and includes artistically presented pastas. ⊠ *Butler Sq., 100 N. 6th St.,* ☎ *612/338–2401. AE, D, DC, MC, V.*

$$–$$$ ✕ **Goodfellow's.** The changing menu at this plush restaurant includes regional game such as venison, pheasant, and trout in season, as well as excellent presentations of lamb, veal, and pork. ⊠ *City Center, 40 S. 7th St.,* ☎ *612/332–4800. AE, D, MC, V. Closed Sun.*

$$–$$$ ✕ **Loring Cafe.** There's a terrific view of Loring Park from this bohemian-chic café. The menu changes nightly and includes pasta, vegetarian, and meat dishes. The artichoke ramekin appetizer stands out. ⊠ *1624 Harmon Pl.,* ☎ *612/332–1617. AE, MC, V.*

$–$$$ ✕ **Kincaid's Steak, Chop and Fish House.** Kincaid's imposing interior of marble, brass, glass, and wood sets the mood for all-American standards such as filet mignon, mesquite-grilled salmon, grilled-rosemary lamb, and roasted chicken Dijon. ⊠ *8400 Normandale Lake Blvd., Bloomington,* ☎ *612/921–2255. AE, D, DC, MC, V.*

$–$$$ ✕ **New French Cafe & Bar.** This café in Minneapolis's Warehouse District has actually been a favorite for the past 20 years. The open kitchen turns out French and Mediterranean specialties, including beef tenderloin and tuna. French bread and pastries are baked in the bakery next door. ⊠ *128 N. 4th St.,* ☎ *612/338–3790. AE, D, MC, V.*

$–$$$ ✕ **Whitney Grille.** In the lavish Whitney Hotel (☞ Lodging, *below*), the Grille has a flower-filled garden plaza and a hushed main room with rich woods and muted floral fabrics. The regional American specialties change seasonally and have included beef tenderloin with goose-liver pâté and port wine demi-glacé, and crisp whole red snapper. ⊠ *150 Portland Ave.,* ☎ *612/372–6405. AE, D, DC, MC, V.*

$ ✕ **Bryant-Lake Bowl.** This 1930s-era eight-lane bowling alley has one of the Twin Cities' hippest restaurants. Impressive wine and beer lists complement such specials as soft-shell tacos and fresh ravioli with four cheeses. After your meal, bowl a few frames or catch a live performance in the attached 99-seat theater. Breakfast is a bargain. ⊠ *810 W. Lake St.,* ☎ *612/825–3737. AE, D, DC, MC, V.*

St. Paul

$$–$$$ ✕ **Pazza Luna.** A floor-to-ceiling mural of the face of Botticelli's Venus overlooks this artfully designed trattoria, which manages to be busy and tranquil at once. Pazza Luna stakes its growing reputation on innovative dishes such as the fritto misto calamari but brings panache to standards like handmade fettuccine in a Bolognese meat sauce. ⊠ *360 St. Peter St.,* ☎ *651/223–7000. AE, D, DC, MC, V.*

$–$$$ ✕ **Ristorante Luci.** This intimate, family-run neighborhood trattoria serves carefully crafted regional Italian dishes such as *vitello saltimbucca,* pounded veal medallions with prosciutto and fontina cheese. Reservations are recommended. ⊠ *470 Cleveland Ave. S,* ☎ *651/699–8258. MC, V.*

$–$$$ ✕ **St. Paul Grill.** The Saint Paul Hotel's (☞ Lodging, *below*) stylish, contemporary bistro has a view of Rice Park. The menu is American with dry-aged steaks, fresh fish, pastas, chicken potpie, homemade roast beef hash, and weekly specials. ⊠ *350 Market St.,* ☎ *651/224–7455. AE, D, DC, MC, V.*

$–$$ ✕ **Dakota Bar and Grill.** The Twin Cities' best jazz club also serves creative midwestern fare, including grilled rainbow trout and salmon-walleye croquettes. Like the music, the atmosphere is contemporary and cool. There's also a Sunday brunch. ⊠ *Bandana Sq., 1021 E. Bandana Blvd.,* ☎ *651/642–1442. AE, D, DC, MC, V. No lunch.*

$ ✕ **Khyber Pass Cafe.** An unassuming storefront across from a coin laundry encloses a small slice of Afghani culture and cuisine. Tangy spice combinations enliven dishes such as *baba ghanoush* (eggplant dip) and *shola* (mung beans) with chunks of tender stewed lamb. ⊠ *1399 St. Clair Ave.,* ☎ *651/698–5403. No credit cards.*

$ ✕ **Mickey's Diner.** This quintessential 1930s diner, with lots of chrome and vinyl, a lunch counter, and a few tiny booths, is listed on the National Register of Historic Places. The stick-to-the-ribs fare and great breakfasts make it a local institution. ⊠ *36 W. 7th St., at St. Peter St.,* ☎ *651/222–5633. D, MC, V.*

Lodging

Accommodations are plentiful in each city's downtown, along I–494 in the suburbs, in the industrial parks of Bloomington and Richfield (known as the Strip), and near the Minneapolis/St. Paul International Airport and the Mall of America. Some hotels in downtown Minneapolis and St. Paul are connected to the Skyway system, making it possible to avoid—at least part of the time—Minnesota's fierce winter cold.

Minneapolis

$$$–$$$$ 🏨 **Hyatt Regency Hotel.** This hotel is in the heart of downtown Minneapolis, connected by skyways to restaurants and shopping areas. The building's design centers on a sweeping lobby with a fountain and trees. Many rooms have a view of the city skyline. ⊠ *1300 Nicollet Mall, 55403,* ☎ *612/370–1234,* ℻ *612/370–1463. 554 rooms. Restaurant. AE, D, DC, MC, V.* ✍

$$$–$$$$ 🏨 **Hyatt Whitney Hotel.** The 1880s flour mill converted into a small
★   European-style hotel has suites only; half of them overlook the Mississippi. The lobby is warm with rich woods, brass, and marble. ⊠ *150 Portland Ave., 55401,* ☎ *612/375–1234 or 800/233–1234,* ℻ *612/ 339–1333. 96 suites. Restaurant. AE, D, DC, MC, V.* ✍

$$$ ⊞ **Marriott City Center Hotel.** This sleek, 31-story hotel is located within the City Center shopping mall. In the restaurant, members of the waitstaff, most of whom are professional singers, may entertain you. ⊠ *30 S. 7th St., 55402,* ☎ *612/349–4000,* FAX *612/332–7165. 626 rooms. 2 restaurants, health club. AE, D, DC, MC, V. CP.* ⊛

$$–$$$ ⊞ **Holiday Inn Metrodome.** A 10-minute bus ride from downtown, this hotel is in the heart of the theater and entertainment district and is close to both the Metrodome and the University of Minnesota. ⊠ *1500 Washington Ave. S, 55454,* ☎ *612/333–4646 or 800/448–3663,* FAX *612/333–7910. 265 rooms. Restaurant, pool. AE, D, DC, MC, V. BP.* ⊛

$$–$$$ ⊞ **Nicollet Island Inn.** This charming 1893 limestone inn is on Nicollet Island in the middle of the Mississippi River, with downtown Minneapolis on one shore and the Riverplace and St. Anthony Main on the other. There's early American reproduction furniture in the rooms, some of which have river views. ⊠ *95 Merriam St., 55401,* ☎ *612/331–1800,* FAX *612/331–6528. 24 rooms. Restaurant. AE, D, DC, MC, V. BP.* ⊛

$$–$$$ ⊞ **Regal Minneapolis Hotel.** This recently remodeled 14-story hotel is in the middle of Minneapolis's downtown. Rooms are contemporary, with sweeping views of the city. ⊠ *1313 Nicollet Mall, 55403,* ☎ *612/332–6000 or 800/522–8856,* FAX *612/359–2160. 325 rooms. Restaurant, pool, exercise room. AE, DC, MC, V. EP.* ⊛

St. Paul

$$$–$$$$ ⊞ **The Covington Inn.** Relax on the spacious decks of the historic towboat *Covington,* moored on the Mississippi River across from downtown St. Paul. Rooms feature private baths and fireplaces. ⊠ *Pier One, Harriet Island, 55107,* ☎ *651/292–1411. 4 rooms. Restaurant (closed winter). MC, V. BP.* ⊛

$$–$$$$ ⊞ **Saint Paul Hotel.** This stately stone hotel, built in 1910, overlooks Rice Park and is within walking distance of St. Paul's shopping and entertainment district. Rooms are traditional in style. ⊠ *350 Market St., 55102,* ☎ *651/292–9292 or 800/292–9292,* FAX *651/228–9506. 255 rooms. 2 restaurants. AE, D, DC, MC, V.* ⊛

$$–$$$ ⊞ **Embassy Suites–St. Paul.** With terra-cotta, brickwork, tropical plants, and a courtyard fountain, this hotel has a neo–New Orleans Garden District style. It is close to I–35E and within walking distance of major downtown businesses. ⊠ *175 E. 10th St., 55101,* ☎ *651/224–5400,* FAX *651/224–0957. 210 suites. Restaurant, pool. AE, D, DC, MC, V. BP.* ⊛

$$–$$$ ⊞ **Holiday Inn Express.** In what was once a paint shop for the Pacific Northern Railroad, this hotel is connected by skyway to the Bandana Square shopping center. Rooms are contemporary. ⊠ *1010 W. Bandana Blvd., 55108,* ☎ *651/647–1637,* FAX *651/647–0244. 109 rooms. Pool. AE, D, DC, MC, V. CP.* ⊛

$$–$$$ ⊞ **Radisson Hotel Saint Paul.** This 22-story riverside tower has a lobby with Asian touches and traditional American–style rooms, many with river views. ⊠ *11 E. Kellogg Blvd., 55101,* ☎ *651/292–1900,* FAX *651/224–8999. 494 rooms. Restaurant, pool, exercise room. AE, D, DC, MC, V.* ⊛

$$ ⊞ **Best Western Kelly Inn.** Visiting legislators have frequented this clean, efficient hotel for the past 30 years, as it's within walking distance of the state capitol. ⊠ *161 St. Anthony St., 55103,* ☎ *651/227–8711,* FAX *651/227–1698. 126 rooms. Restaurant, pool. AE, DC, MC, V.*

Nightlife and the Arts

Nightlife

With closing time at 1 AM, "the wee small hours" does not apply to the Twin Cities. Most bars and clubs attract a youngish crowd. Plenty of nightspots serve the the Twin Cities' sizable gay and lesbian community.

Clubs and bars are generally clustered in three areas—downtown Minneapolis, Uptown, and Seven Corners. Downtown, the intimate **Fine Line Music Café** (⊠ 318 1st Ave. N, ☎ 612/338–8100) presents locally and nationally known jazz and rock musicians. In a former bus station, **First Avenue** (⊠ 29 N. 7th St., ☎ 612/332–1775) attracts top rock groups and is a great place for dancing; the club was featured in the movie *Purple Rain*. Blues, rock, and alternative bands take the stage six nights a week at the **Cabooze** (⊠ 917 Cedar Ave. S, ☎ 612/338–6425). The best gay bar in downtown Minneapolis is the **Gay Nineties** (⊠ 408 S. Hennepin Ave., ☎ 612/333–7755).

St. Paul is said to close down with the end of the business day, but there are several good nightspots downtown and on Grand Avenue. The **Dakota Bar and Grill** (⊠ Bandana Sq., 1021 E. Bandana Blvd., ☎ 651/642–1442) is one of the best jazz bars in the Midwest, featuring some of the Twin Cities' finest performers. The **Artist's Quarter** (⊠ 366 Jackson St., ☎ 651/292–1359) hosts local and national jazz performers in a dark, jazz-minimalist space. For blues check out **Lucy's** (⊠ 601 Western Ave. N, ☎ 651/228–9959).

The Arts

The "About Town" section of the monthly *Minneapolis St. Paul* magazine has extensive listings of events. Check out the *St. Paul Pioneer Press,* the Minneapolis-based *Star Tribune,* and the free newsweekly *City Pages* for events. **Ticketmaster** (☎ 651/989–5151) sells tickets for sporting events, concerts, theater, attractions, and special events.

The Hennepin Avenue Theatre District, between 8th and 10th streets in downtown Minneapolis, is home to the city's hottest entertainment. The Twin Cities Broadway Theatre season brings national touring productions to the historic **State Theater** (⊠ 805 Hennepin Ave., ☎ 612/339–7007) and **Orpheum Theater** (⊠ 910 Hennepin Ave., ☎ 612/339–7007). The **Hey City Theater** has almost nightly performances of the smash hit *Tony n' Tina's Wedding* (⊠ 824 Hennepin Ave., ☎ 612/333–9202).

The **Guthrie Theater** (⊠ 725 Vineland Pl., ☎ 877/447–8243) has a repertory company praised for its balance of classic and avant-garde productions. High-caliber national acts come to the **Walker Art Center** (⊠ Vineland Pl., ☎ 612/375–7622). The **Brave New Workshop** (⊠ 3001 Hennepin Ave. S, ☎ 612/377–8445) will keep you laughing with original sketch comedy. The acclaimed Minnesota Orchestra performs in **Orchestra Hall** (⊠ 1111 Nicollet Mall, ☎ 612/371–5656).

The **Great American History Theater** (⊠ 30 E. 10th St., ☎ 651/292–4323) presents plays about Minnesota and midwestern history. The **Penumbra Theater Company** (⊠ 270 N. Kent St., ☎ 651/224–3180) is Minnesota's only black professional theater company. The **Ordway Music Theater** (⊠ 345 Washington St., ☎ 651/224–4222) is home to the St. Paul Chamber Orchestra, the Minnesota Opera, and other performing-arts groups.

Outdoor Activities and Sports

Beaches

Quite a few of Minnesota's 10,000 lakes are in or near the Twin Cities' metro area. For the best of the urban beaches, try sunbathing on the shores of Cedar Lake, Lake Harriet, or Lake Calhoun. More information about the city's famous chain of lakes is available from the Minneapolis Parks and Recreation Board (☎ 612/661–4800).

Spectator Sports

Baseball: Minnesota Twins (✉ Hubert H. Humphrey Metrodome, 501 Chicago Ave. S, Minneapolis, ☎ 612/335–3370). **Basketball: Minnesota Timberwolves** (✉ Target Center, 600 1st Ave. N, Minneapolis, ☎ 612/337–3865). **Football: Minnesota Vikings** (✉ Hubert H. Humphrey Metrodome, 501 Chicago Ave. S, Minneapolis, ☎ 612/333–8828).

Shopping

The skyway systems in each of the Twin Cities connect hundreds of stores, shops, and enclosed shopping malls.

Minneapolis

Among the many shops along **Nicollet Mall** (☞ Exploring Minneapolis and St. Paul, *above*) are **Dayton's** (✉ 700 Nicollet Mall), the city's largest department store, and **Gaviidae Common** (✉ 651 Nicollet Mall), with three levels of upscale shops, including branches of Saks Fifth Avenue and Neiman Marcus. **City Center** (✉ 7th and Nicollet) has three floors of shopping and the largest food court downtown. There are more than 40 mostly one-of-a-kind, hip urban shops and several restaurants at **Uptown** (✉ Lake and Hennepin Aves.), a smaller shopping center on Calhoun Square.

St. Paul

The **World Trade Center** (✉ 30 E. 7th St.), downtown, has more than 100 specialty shops and restaurants, including Dayton's. **Victoria Crossing** (✉ 850 Grand Ave.) is a collection of small shops and specialty stores anchoring the 100-plus other stores along Grand Avenue's 26 blocks. **Bibelot** (✉ 1082 Grand Ave. and 2276 Como Ave.) combines an extensive array of truly unusual and tasteful gift items with locally designed and made women's fashions.

Bloomington

Bloomington, south of Minneapolis, is Minnesota's third-largest city and home to the **Mall of America** (✉ 24th Ave. S and Killebrew Dr., ☎ 612/883–8800), the nation's largest enclosed mall. Appropriately nicknamed the Megamall, it has more than 500 stores and shops, including Macy's, Bloomingdale's, Sears, and Nordstrom. Beneath its central dome is Camp Snoopy, a large amusement park.

ELSEWHERE IN MINNESOTA

Southeastern Minnesota

Visitor Information

Red Wing Chamber of Commerce (✉ 420 Levee St., Box 133, 55066, ☎ 651/385–5934 or 800/498–3444).

Winona Chamber and Convention Bureau (✉ 67 Main St., Box 870, 55987, ☎ 507/452–2272 or 800/657–4972).

Arriving and Departing

From the Twin Cities follow U.S. 61 southeast along the Mississippi River.

What to See and Do

This picturesque corner of the state has high, wooded bluffs that provide vast panoramas of the Mississippi River. The river towns and villages are noted for their charming 19th-century architecture. **Red Wing** is famous for boots and pottery bearing its name. Levee Park, Bay Point Park, and Covill Park have stunning views of the Mississippi, which widens into Lake Pepin here. The Victorian **St. James Hotel** (☞ Dining and Lodging, *below*), built in 1875, has boutiques, shops, and an art gallery as well as grand public spaces recalling the heyday of riverboats.

Frontenac State Park (☎ 651/345–3401), 10 mi south of Red Wing on U.S. 61, has a picnic area with a 400-ft-high bluff and great views of Lake Pepin, as well as a bird sanctuary. Just outside the park is **Old Frontenac**, a Civil War–era village with a charming 1865 Craftsman-style bed-and-breakfast inn.

Winona is an early lumbering town settled by New Englanders and Germans. Here **Garvin Heights Scenic Lookout** (✉ Huff St. past U.S. 14 and U.S. 61) has picnic facilities, hiking trails, and scenic views from atop a 575-ft bluff. The **Julius C. Wilkie Steamboat Center** (✉ foot of Main St. in Levee Park, ☎ 507/454–1254; ☎ $2), open from Memorial Day through Labor Day, is a steamboat replica with exhibits on steamboating and river life. Exhibits of the local Polish heritage found at the **Polish Cultural Institute** (✉ 102 N. Liberty St., ☎ 507/454–3431; ☎ free) include family heirlooms and many religious artifacts. The museum is open from May through November.

Dining and Lodging

$–$$ × **Staghead Restaurant.** At this casual eatery with pressed-tin ceilings, oak tables, and brick walls, the menu usually includes pork, chicken, and pasta, as well as scones and muffins for breakfast. ✉ *219 Bush St., Red Wing,* ☎ *651/388–6581. MC, V. Closed Sun. No dinner Mon.*

$$–$$$ ×🏨 **St. James Hotel.** This 1875 hotel is the area's most stately lodging. The elegant, lower-level Port of Red Wing restaurant serves sophisticated meals such as smoked, roasted duckling and lobster-stuffed chicken. ✉ *406 Main St., Red Wing 55066,* ☎ *651/388–2846,* FAX *651/388–5226. 61 rooms. 3 restaurants. AE, D, DC, MC, V.* 🐾

Duluth and the North Shore

Visitor Information

Duluth Convention and Visitors Bureau (✉ 100 Lake Place Dr., 55802, ☎ 218/722–4011 or 800/438–5884).

Arriving and Departing

From the Twin Cities head north on I–35.

What to See and Do

Set at the edge of the north-woods wilderness and the western end of Lake Superior is **Duluth,** a city of gracious old homes with one of the largest ports on the Great Lakes. **Skyline Parkway,** a 16-mi scenic boulevard above the city, has views of Lake Superior and the Duluth-Superior Harbor, with its 50 mi of dock line. **Vista Fleet Excursions** (✉ 5th Ave. W and the waterfront, ☎ 218/722–6218) operates narrated boat tours of the harbor. The **Aerial Lift Bridge** (✉ Canal Dr.), an unusual 386-ft elevator bridge, spans the canal entrance to the harbor. Not far from the harbor, the **Depot** (✉ 506 W. Michigan St., ☎ 218/727–8025), an 1892 landmark train station, houses the **Lake Superior Museum of Transportation** (☎ $8), with an extensive collection of locomotives and rolling stock. **Lake Superior Zoological Gardens** (✉ 7210 Fremont St., ☎ 218/723–3748) has a children's zoo and animals from all over the world.

Lake Superior's rugged **North Shore** is best viewed from U.S. 61 north of Duluth. **Gooseberry Falls State Park** (✉ 1300 Hwy. 61, Two Harbors, ☎ 218/834–3855) and **Temperance River State Park** (✉ Hwy. 61, Box 33, Schroeder, ☎ 218/663–7476) are typical of parks found along Lake Superior's shore, with roaring waterfalls and scenic vistas.

North of Grand Marais, the **Gunflint Trail** attracts cross-country skiers with about 100 mi of groomed trails leading deep into Superior National Forest. **Gunflint Lake** was once a busy route traveled by voyagers and modern pioneers such as Justine Kerfoot, author of *Woman of the Boundary Waters*. Kerfoot's son and his wife now run the famous **Gunflint Lodge** (⊠ 143 S. Gunflint Lake, Grand Marais 55604, ☎ 218/388–2294 or 800/328–3325) and its restaurant.

Dining and Lodging

$–$$ ✕ **Grandma's Saloon & Grill.** Duluth's famous Grandma's Marathon is sponsored by this lively restaurant on the waterfront. The hands-down favorite dish is chicken tetrazzini, fettuccine and sautéed chicken in a mozzarella-Mornay sauce. ⊠ *522 S. Lake Ave.,* ☎ *218/727–4192. AE, D, DC, MC, V.*

$–$$$$ 🏨 **Fitger's Inn.** All the rooms in this cozy inn have lake views; some also have fireplaces and skylights. Newer suites have double whirlpools. The building—the old Fitger's Brewery—dates to the 1850s and is part of the Fitger's Brewery Complex, a cluster of nightclubs and retail shops four blocks from downtown. ⊠ *600 E. Superior St., 55802,* ☎ *218/722–8826 or 888/348–4377,* FAX *218/722–8826. 60 rooms. Restaurant. AE, D, DC, MC, V. CP.* 🍽

The Iron Range and Boundary Waters

Visitor Information

The **Ely Chamber of Commerce** (⊠ 1600 Sheridan St., 55731, ☎ 218/365–6123 or 800/777–7281) provides information on canoe outfitters and trips. The **Rainy Lake Visitor Center** (⊠ 11 mi east of International Falls on Rte. 11, ☎ 218/286–5258) is at Voyageurs National Park.

Arriving and Departing

From Duluth take U.S. 53 north.

What to See and Do

The discovery of iron ore in the north woods brought an influx of immigrants who wove a rich and varied cultural heritage. Known as the Range because it encompasses the huge Mesabi and Vermilion iron ranges, the region is ringed by deep forests and many lakes.

Eveleth, which produces taconite, a form of processed iron ore, is home to the **United States Hockey Hall of Fame** (⊠ 801 Hat Trick Ave., ☎ 218/744–5167; 🎫 $3.50), where pictures, films, and artifacts tell the story of hockey in America. In Virginia, 2 mi north of Eveleth, rimmed with open-pit mines and reserves of iron ore, the **Mine View in the Sky observation platform,** at the southern edge of town, overlooks part of the vast Rochleau Mine works. Chisholm is home to the **Ironworld Discovery Center** (⊠ W. Hwy. 169, Box 392, ☎ 800/372–6437; 🎫 $8), depicting the saga of the region's settlers through entertainment and interpretation.

West of Virginia on U.S. 169 is **Hibbing,** the largest town in the Mesabi Range and the place where the Greyhound bus system began in 1914. The **Greyhound Origin Center** (⊠ 1201 Greyhound Blvd., ☎ 218/263–6485; 🎫 $3) features displays and artifacts on the history of the company. Tours of the **Hull-Rust Mahoning Mine** (⊠ 211 E. Howard St., Box 727, 55746, ☎ 218/262–3895; 🎫 free), the world's largest open-pit iron ore mine, may be arranged during the summer at the Hibbing Area Chamber of Commerce. The **Paulucci Space Theater** (⊠ U.S. 169 and 23rd St., ☎ 218/262–6720; 🎫 $4.50) has programs on astronomy and space exploration.

Ely, east of Virginia on U.S. 169, lies in the heart of the Superior National Forest. It is the gateway to the western portion of the **Boundary Waters Canoe Area Wilderness,** a federally protected area of more than 1,000 pristine lakes surrounded by dense forests. Area outfitters rent canoes and camping equipment and provide assistance in planning canoe trips. The **Vermilion Interpretive Center** (⊠ 1900 E. Camp St., ☎ 218/365–3226), closed in winter, has exhibits on the Vermilion iron range, the fur trade, and Native Americans. The **International Wolf Center** (⊠ 1396 Hwy. 169, ☎ 218/365–4695 or 800/359–9653), celebrates and studies the wolf, which still thrives in northern Minnesota; more than 2,000 live in the state's wilderness. The center has exhibits, programs, and a few live examples of *canis lupus.*

International Falls, at the northern terminus of U.S. 53 on the Canadian border, is known as the "icebox of the nation" because of its severe winters. The town lies at the western edge of **Voyageurs National Park** (☞ National and State Parks, *above*), where the **Rainy Lake Visitor Center** (☞ Visitor Information, *above*) has a slide show, exhibits, maps, and information, as well as guided boat tours of the lake and other points in the park. In town is the **Koochiching County Historical Museum** (⊠ 214 6th Ave., Box 1147, ☎ 218/283–4316), with exhibits on early settlement, gold mining, and Native Americans. The **International Falls Chamber of Commerce** (⊠ 301 2nd Ave., 56649, ☎ 218/283–9400 or 800/325–5766) has brochures and information on area outfitters, camping, and attractions.

Dining and Lodging

$ ✕🏨 **Hibbing Park Hotel.** The best hotel in the Range has a lovely lobby with a marble fireplace, and an excellent restaurant, Reflections. ⊠ *1402 Howard St., Hibbing 55746, ☎ 218/262–3481 or 800/262–3481,* FAX *218/262–1906. 121 rooms. Restaurant, pool. AE, D, DC, MC, V.*

MISSISSIPPI

Updated by
Karen S.
Bryant

Capital	Jackson
Population	2,731,000
Motto	By Virtue and Arms
State Bird	Mockingbird
State Flower	Magnolia
Postal Abbreviation	MS

Statewide Visitor Information

Mississippi Division of Tourism Development (⊠ 550 High St., 11th floor, Jackson 39205, ☎ 601/359–3297 or 800/927–6378).

Scenic Drives

The **Natchez Trace Parkway** cuts a 313-mi swath across Mississippi from northeast of Tupelo to Natchez in the southwest, passing through Jackson at the center of the state. **U.S. 90** runs along the Mississippi Sound from Alabama to Louisiana, offering views of Gulf Coast beaches, ancient live oaks, and historic homes. Along the Mississippi River, **U.S. 61**—also known as Blues Alley and the birthplace of that musical form—runs through flat Delta cotton land to the hills of Vicksburg, then through Natchez to Louisiana.

National and State Parks

National Parks

Gulf Islands National Seashore (☞ The Gulf Coast *in* Elsewhere in Mississippi, *below*) includes Ship, Horn, and Petit Bois islands; there are nature trails and expeditions into the marsh. Vicksburg's **National Military Park** (☞ Vicksburg *in* Elsewhere in Mississippi, *below*) rivals Gettysburg in historic appeal and scenic beauty.

State Parks

Just north of Port Gibson is **Grand Gulf Military Monument Park** (☞ Exploring the Natchez Trace, *below*). **J. P. Coleman State Park** (⊠ Rte. 5, 13 mi north of Iuka off Rte. 25, 613 County Rd. 321, Iuka 38852, ☎ 601/423–6515) includes scenic Pickwick Lake, which has a lodge, cabins, camping, and swimming. **Tishomingo State Park** (⊠ Rte. 1, 15 mi south of Iuka and 3 mi north of Dennis off Rte. 25, Box 880, Tishomingo 38873, ☎ 601/438–6914), which vies with J. P. Coleman for the title of most spectacular Mississippi park, lies in the Appalachian foothills, making its terrain unique in Mississippi. Bring your own provisions to enjoy hiking and water sports. Canoe and float trips can be arranged at the park, and there's fishing in Haynes Lake.

THE NATCHEZ TRACE

The Natchez Trace Parkway, a long, thin park running for almost 450 mi from Nashville to Natchez, crosses early paths worn by the Choctaw and Chickasaw, flatboatmen, outlaws, itinerant preachers, post riders, soldiers, and settlers. The parkway extends for more than 300 mi in Mississippi, with other sections in Alabama and Tennessee. Meticulously manicured by the National Park Service, it is unmarred by billboards, and commercial traffic is prohibited.

Visitor Information

Natchez–Adams County: Convention & Visitors Bureau (✉ 640 S. Canal St., Box C, Natchez 39120, ☎ 601/446–6345 or 800/647–6724). **Natchez Trace Parkway:** Visitor Center (✉ 2680 Natchez Trace Pkwy., Tupelo 38801, ☎ 601/680–4025 or 800/305–7417). **Jackson:** Metro Jackson Convention and Visitors Bureau (✉ Box 1450, 39215, ☎ 601/960–1891 or 800/354–7695).

Arriving and Departing

By Car

The Natchez Trace is interrupted at Jackson; I–55, I–220, and I–20, which run through the city, connect the two segments. Natchez, at the southwestern end of the Natchez Trace Parkway, is also bisected by U.S. 61.

By Plane

Jackson's **International Airport** (✉ 100 International Dr., ☎ 601/939–5631), east of the city off I–20, 10 minutes from downtown, is served by American, Continental Express, Delta, Northwest Airlink, Southwest Airlines, and US Airways.

By Train

Amtrak (☎ 800/872–7245) stops in Jackson on its way south from Memphis to New Orleans.

Exploring the Natchez Trace

The Mississippi segment of the Natchez Trace begins near Tupelo, in the northeast corner of the state, in a hilly area of dense forests and sparkling streams. Enjoy this natural beauty at **J. P. Coleman State Park** or at **Tishomingo State Park** (☞ National and State Parks, *above*).

Tupelo

Tupelo (named after the gum tree), the largest city in northern Mississippi, sits in scenic hill country. It's the site of the 1864 Civil War battle of the same name.

At Milepost 266 in Tupelo is the **Natchez Trace Parkway Visitor Center** (☞ Visitor Information, *above*), which has exhibits pertaining to the history of the Trace and the area's agricultural business. On display are early surveying equipment, old maps of the area, examples of the indigenous wildlife, a few pioneering tools, and more. Pick up a copy of the *Official Map and Guide,* with detailed mile-by-mile information on places along the parkway from Nashville to Natchez.

Tupelo is probably best known for **Elvis Presley's Park & Museum** (✉ 306 Elvis Presley Dr., ☎ 601/841–1245; ⊟ birthplace $2, museum $4). Here you will find the tiny two-room shotgun house where the singer was born on January 8, 1935. The surrounding park includes a museum, a gift shop, and the **Elvis Presley Memorial Chapel.**

From Tupelo to Jackson

The three-hour trip from Tupelo to Jackson can easily take an entire day if you stop to read the brown wooden markers describing historic sites, explore nature trails, and admire the neat fields, trees, and wildflower meadows along the way. At Ridgeland, housed in a dogtrot cabin, the **Mississippi Crafts Center** (✉ Trace Milepost 102.4, ☎ 601/856–7546) sells high-quality crafts created by members of the Craftsman's Guild of Mississippi. Rest rooms and picnic tables are present.

Jackson

Jackson, the state capital, has an interesting downtown, with many small museums and most of the city's notable architecture. The **Jim Buck Ross**

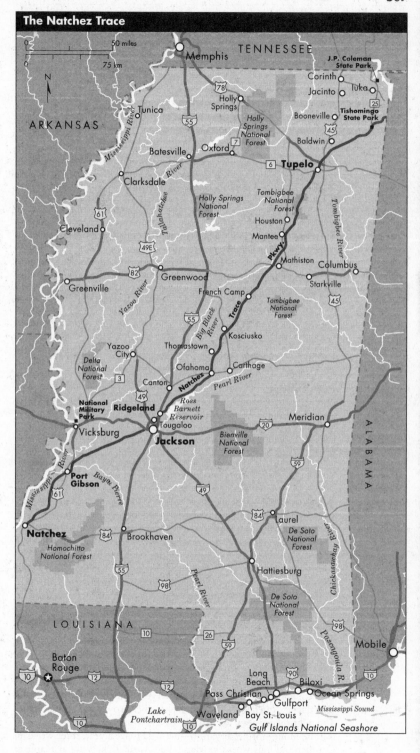

The Natchez Trace

Mississippi Agriculture and Forestry Museum (⊠ 1150 Lakeland Dr., ☎ 601/354–6113; ☎ $4) includes 10 old Mississippi farm buildings, as well as a farm (operational during harvest time) and a 1920s cross-roads town. The general store sells snacks and souvenirs. Just outside the gates a shop sells Mississippi crafts, and a down-home restaurant serves blue-plate lunches (veggies, crisp fried catfish).

The **Mississippi Museum of Art** has changing exhibits and a permanent collection of more than 3,600 works, including 19th- and 20th-century American, southern, and Mississippi art. ⊠ *201 E. Pascagoula St.,* ☎ *601/960–1515.* ☎ *$3. Closed Sun.–Mon.*

The **Governor's Mansion** has been the official home of the state's first family since its completion in 1842. Reservations are required to view the antiques-filled interior on free tours that leave on the half-hour between 9:30 and 11 AM. ⊠ *300 E. Capitol St.,* ☎ *601/359–6421.* ☎ *Free. Closed Sat.–Mon.*

The **New Capitol** (⊠ 400 High St., ☎ 601/359–3114; ☎ free), dating from 1903, sits in Beaux Arts splendor, its dome topped by a gold-plated copper eagle with a 15-ft wingspan. Elaborate interior architectural details include two stained-glass skylights and a painted ceiling.

The **Manship House,** built in 1857, is a restored Gothic Revival home built by the mayor who surrendered the city to General Sherman during the Civil War. ⊠ *420 E. Fortification St. (enter parking area from Congress St.),* ☎ *601/961–4724.* ☎ *Free. Closed Sun.–Mon.*

☾ Jackson's **Zoological Park** (⊠ 2918 W. Capitol St., ☎ 601/352–2585; ☎ $4) has animals, including endangered species, in natural settings.

Port Gibson

Port Gibson, about 60 mi southwest of Jackson, is one of the oldest surviving towns along the Trace. Along **Church Street** many houses and churches have been restored; here, too, is the much-photographed **First Presbyterian Church** (1859), its spire topped by a 10-ft hand pointing heavenward. Information on the town's historic sites is available from the **Port Gibson Chamber of Commerce** (⊠ south end of Church St., ☎ 601/437–4351).

☾ **Grand Gulf Military Monument Park** (⊠ Rte. 2 off U.S. 61, ☎ 601/437–5911; ☎ $1.50), just north of Port Gibson, was built on the site of the town of Grand Gulf, once the most thriving river port between New Orleans and St. Louis. Grand Gulf was partially destroyed in the 1850s when capricious currents caused the Mississippi to change its course and flood much of the town. Already in decline, Grand Gulf was completely destroyed by Union gunners during the Civil War. Children especially love the steep trail, the observation tower, the waterwheel, and the bloodstained Civil War uniforms on display.

Natchez

Because Natchez had little military significance, it survived the Civil War almost untouched. Today it is famous for the opulent plantation homes and stylish town houses built between 1819 and 1860, when cotton plantations and the bustling river port poured riches into the city. A number of these houses are open year-round, but others are open only during Natchez Pilgrimage weeks, when crowds flock to see them. The pilgrimages—started in 1932 by the women of Natchez as a way to raise money for preservation—are held twice a year: three weeks in October and four weeks in March and April. Tickets are available at **Pilgrimage Tour Headquarters** (⊠ 220 State St., 39121, ☎ 601/446–6631 or 800/647–6742; ☎ 4-house pass $24, pageants $12), where all tours originate. **Carriage tours** (✉ $9) of downtown Natchez also begin at Pilgrimage Tour Headquarters.

★ **Rosalie** (⊠ 100 Orleans St., ☎ 601/445–4555; ✉ $6), built in 1823, established the ideal form of the southern mansion, with its white columns, hipped roof, and red bricks. Furnishings purchased for the house in 1858 include a rare parlor set. A trip down south is not complete without a visit to the grand and gracious **Stanton Hall** (⊠ 401 High St., ☎ 601/442–6282; ✉ $6), one of the most photographed houses in the country. Built around 1857 for cotton broker Frederick Stanton, the palatial former residence is now run as a house-museum by the Pilgrimage Garden Club.

☾ **Longwood** (⊠ 140 Lower Woodville Rd., ☎ 601/442–5193; ✉ $6) is the largest octagonal house in North America. Construction began in 1860, but the outbreak of the Civil War prevented its completion; unfinished and mysterious, it will interest both adults and children.

Dining and Lodging

Jackson

$$–$$$ ★ ✗ **BRAVO!** This cheery, bustling restaurant in a shopping mall serves traditional regional Italian cuisine: pastas, wood-fired pizzas, antipasti, and grilled meats with inventive sauces, chutneys, and herb rubs. ⊠ *244 Highland Village, South Plaza,* ☎ *601/982–8111. AE, D, DC, MC, V. Closed Mon.*

$$–$$$ ✗ **Nick's.** Large and elegant, this restaurant serves nouvelle versions of regional dishes. Lunch specialties are pasta salad and fish; for dinner another choice is beef tenderloin. ⊠ *1501 Lakeland Dr.,* ☎ *601/ 981–8017. Jacket and tie. AE, MC, V.*

$–$$$ ★ ✗ **Schimmel's.** The hot new place to eat, Schimmel's specializes in prime meat and fresh Gulf seafood. Signature dishes include the veal chop, breadless crab cake, fried lobster tails, and the Asiago-crusted flounder, which nestles tender flounder under a layer of Italian cheese. ⊠ *2615 N. State St.,* ☎ *601/957–0702. AE, MC, V.*

$ ✗ **Broad Street Baking Co. & Café.** You can enjoy breakfast, lunch, or dinner here, where some dozen different breads are baked fresh daily using European and old family recipes. Specialties include pizzas, sandwiches, pastries, and croissants. ⊠ *101 Banner Hall, I–55 at Northside Dr.,* ☎ *601/362–2900. MC, V. Closes Sun. at 3.*

$$–$$$ ★ ▥ **Millsaps-Buie House.** This 1888 Queen Anne Victorian, restored as a bed-and-breakfast in 1987, is listed on the National Register of Historic Places. Guest rooms are decorated with antiques, and the staff is attentive. ⊠ *628 N. State St., 39202,* ☎ *800/784–0221. 11 rooms. AE, DC, MC, V. BP.* ☙

$$ ▥ **Edison Walthall Hotel.** The cornerstone and huge brass mailbox are about all that remain of the original 1920s Walthall Hotel, but the marble floors and paneled library–cum–writing room almost fool you into thinking this is a restoration. The rooms have upscale hotel decor. ⊠ *225 E. Capitol St., 39201,* ☎ *601/948–6161 or 800/932–6161,* ﬁ *601/ 948–0088. 208 rooms. Restaurant, pool. AE, DC, MC, V.* ☙

$$ ▥ **Jackson Hilton and Convention Center.** This high-rise convention hotel in the north end of town is sleekly contemporary. ⊠ *1001 County Line Rd., 39211,* ☎ *601/957–2800,* ﬁ *601/957–3191. 300 rooms. 2 restaurants, pool. AE, DC, MC, V.* ☙

Natchez

$–$$ ✗ **Cock of the Walk.** The famous original of a regional franchise, this restaurant, in an old train depot overlooking the Mississippi River, specializes in fried catfish fillets, fried dill pickles, hush puppies, mustard greens, and coleslaw. ⊠ *200 N. Broadway, on the Bluff,* ☎ *601/446–8920. AE, D, DC, MC, V.*

$–$$ ✕ **John Martin's.** This fine-dining restaurant features signature dishes of seared breast of Muscovy duck topped with a three-pepper Mayhaw jelly as well as redfish, lamb loin, and a 22-ounce bone-in rib eye. ⊠ *21 Silver St., Under-the-Hill,* ☎ *601/445–0605. AE, MC, V.*

$–$$ ✕ **Pearl Street Pasta.** The fresh pasta dishes at this intimate restaurant, including pasta primavera and breast of chicken with *tasso* (spiced ham), onions, and mushrooms over angel-hair pasta, suggest a taste of Italy in the Mississippi heartland. ⊠ *105 S. Pearl St.,* ☎ *601/442–9284. AE, D, DC, MC, V.*

$$–$$$ ⊞ **Dunleith.** At stately, colonnaded Dunleith a wing for overnight guests has rooms with antiques, fireplaces, and wonderful views of the landscaped grounds. ⊠ *84 Homochitto St., 39120,* ☎ *601/446–8500 or 800/433–2445. 19 rooms. AE, MC, V. BP.* ☜

$$–$$$ ⊞ **Monmouth.** This plantation mansion (circa 1818) was owned by Mississippi governor John A. Quitman from 1826 until his death in 1858. Guest rooms are in the main house, as well as, a courtyard building, garden cottages, and other outbuildings. ⊠ *36 Melrose Ave., 39120,* ☎ *601/442–5852 or 800/828–4531,* ℻ *601/446–7762. 31 rooms. AE, D, MC, V. BP.* ☜

$ ⊞ **Ramada Hilltop Motel.** This motel sits on a bluff overlooking the Mississippi River to the north and Louisiana to the west. ⊠ *130 John R. Junkin Dr., 39120,* ☎ *601/446–6311,* ℻ *601/446–6321. 162 rooms. Restaurant, pool. AE, DC, MC, V.* ☜

Tupelo

$–$$ ✕ **Harvey's.** A local favorite, Harvey's serves consistently good chow. Specialties are prime rib, steaks, seafood, and pasta. ⊠ *424 S. Gloster St.,* ☎ *601/842–6763. AE, D, MC, V. Closed Sun.*

$–$$ ✕ **Jefferson Place.** This rambling late-Victorian house is lively inside, with red-checked tablecloths and bric-a-brac. It's popular with the college crowd and specializes in short orders and steaks. ⊠ *823 Jefferson St.,* ☎ *601/844–8696. AE, D, MC, V. Closed Sun.*

$–$$ ✕ **Vanelli's.** Family pictures and scenes of Greece decorate this comfortably nondescript restaurant. Specialties include pizza with a choice of 10 toppings, lasagna, and Greek salad. ⊠ *1302 N. Gloster St.,* ☎ *601/844–4410. AE, D, DC, MC, V.*

$ ⊞ **Ramada Inn.** This modern hotel caters to business travelers and conventioneers, as well as families. Breakfast and lunch buffets are served. ⊠ *854 N. Gloster St., 38804,* ☎ *662/844–4111,* ℻ *662/840–7960. 230 rooms, 8 minisuites, 8 executive suites. Restaurant, 2 pools, convention center. AE, DC, MC, V.* ☜

$ ⊞ **Trace Inn.** This old, rustic inn on 15 acres near the Natchez Trace offers neat rooms and friendly service. ⊠ *3400 W. Main St., 38801,* ☎ *662/842–5555,* ℻ *662/844–3105. 95 rooms. Restaurant, pool. AE, D, MC, V.*

Nightlife

Jackson

For live entertainment, from bluegrass to Celtic, try **Hal and Mal's** (⊠ 200 S. Commerce St., ☎ 601/948–0888) on weekends. At the **Dock** (⊠ Main Harbor Marina at Ross Barnett Reservoir, ☎ 601/856–7765), the mood is set by people who step off their boats to dine, drink, and listen to rock or rhythm and blues. **Rodeo's** (⊠ 6107 Ridgewood Rd., ☎ 601/957–9300) is a spot where patrons line up outside to line-dance inside.

Natchez

Under-the-Hill is a busy strip of restaurants, gift shops, and bars on the river. Gambling is offered at the permanently docked riverboat casino the **Lady Luck** (☎ 601/445–0605), and there's live music on weekends at **Under-the-Hill Saloon** (✉ 25 Silver St., ☎ 601/446–8023).

Shopping

In Jackson, **Everyday Gourmet** (✉ 2905 Old Canton Rd., ☎ 601/362–0723; ✉ 1625 E. County Line Rd., ☎ 601/977–9258) stocks state products including pecan pie, muscadine jelly, jams, cookbooks, fine ceramic tableware, and bread and biscuit mixes.

OXFORD AND HOLLY SPRINGS

Holly Springs and Oxford, in northern Mississippi, are sophisticated versions of the Mississippi small town. In these courthouse towns incorporated in 1837, you'll find historic architecture, arts and crafts, literary associations, and those unhurried pleasures of southern life that remain constant from generation to generation: entertaining conversation, good food, and nostalgic walks at twilight. Oxford and Lafayette counties were immortalized as "Jefferson County" and "Yoknapatawpha County" in the novels of Oxford native William Faulkner.

Visitor Information

Holly Springs: Chamber of Commerce (✉ 154 S. Memphis St., 38365, ☎ 662/252–2943). **Oxford:** Chamber of Commerce (✉ Jackson Ave., across from the fire station, Box 147, 38655, ☎ 662/234–4651).

Arriving and Departing

By Bus
Greyhound has a station in Holly Springs (✉ 490 Craft St., ☎ 800/231–2222).

By Car
Oxford is accessible from I–55; it is 23 mi east of Batesville on Route 6. **Holly Springs,** 29 mi north of Oxford on Rte. 7, near the Tennessee state line, is reached via U.S. 78 and Routes 4, 7, and 311.

By Train
Amtrak (☎ 800/872–7245) stops in Batesville, 23 mi west of Oxford.

Exploring Oxford and Holly Springs

Oxford
Even if you're not a Faulkner fan, this is a great place to experience small-town living. You won't be bored; the kinds of characters who fascinated Faulkner still live here, and the University of Mississippi keeps things lively. Oxford's **Courthouse Square** is a National Historic Landmark. At its center is the white-sandstone **Lafayette** (pronounced luh-*fay*-it) **County Courthouse**, rebuilt in 1873 after Union troops burned it; the courtroom on the second floor is original. There's an information center at the nearby city hall.

University Avenue, from South Lamar Boulevard to the university, is one of the state's most beautiful sights when the trees flame orange and gold in the fall or when the dogwoods blossom in spring. The **University of Mississippi,** the state's beloved Ole Miss, opened in 1848. Its tree-shaded campus centers on the **Grove,** surrounded by historic buildings. Facing it is the beautifully restored antebellum **Barnard Observatory**

(☎ 662/232–5993; ⌨ free), which houses the **Center for the Study of Southern Culture,** with exhibits on southern music, folklore, and literature and the world's largest blues archive (40,000 records). The **Mississippi Room** (☎ 662/915–7408), in the John Davis Williams Library, contains a permanent exhibit on Faulkner, including the Nobel Prize for literature he won in 1949, as well as first editions of works by other Mississippi authors. The room is closed on weekends.

★ **Rowan Oak,** built in 1848, was William Faulkner's home from 1930 until his death in 1962. The two-story white-frame house is now a National Historic Landmark owned by the university. The writer's typewriter, desk, and other personal items still evoke his presence. ⊠ *Old Taylor Rd.,* ☎ *662/234–3284.* ⌨ *Free. Closed Mon.–Wed.*

Faulkner's funeral was held at Rowan Oak, and he was buried in the family plot in **St. Peter's Cemetery** (⊠ Jefferson and N. 16th Sts.; ⌨ free). Another Faulkner pilgrimage site is **College Hill Presbyterian Church** (⊠ 8 mi northwest of Oxford on College Hill Rd., ☎ 662/234–5020; ⌨ free), where he and Estelle Oldham Franklin were married June 20, 1929.

Holly Springs

Holly Springs, 29 mi north of Oxford on Route 7, contains more than 200 structures (61 of which are antebellum homes) listed on the National Register of Historic Places. These include the 1858 **Montrose** (⊠ 307 E. Salem Ave., ☎ 662/252–2943; ⌨ $5), open by appointment only, and the privately owned Salem Avenue mansions **Cedarhurst** and **Airliewood.**

Dining and Lodging

Holly Springs

$ ✕ **City Cafe.** Breakfast and lunch specials pack them in at this "meat-and-three" (meat with three side orders) eatery, serving homemade soups, roast beef, and fried chicken livers. ⊠ *135-E Van Dorn Ave.,* ☎ *662/ 252–9895. No credit cards.*

$ ✕ **Phillips Grocery.** The building was constructed in 1882 as a saloon for railroad workers. Decorated with antiques and crafts, the grocery serves big, old-fashioned hamburgers. ⊠ *541-A Van Dorn Ave.,* ☎ *662/ 252–4671. No credit cards. Closed Sun. No dinner.*

$ 🏨 **Heritage Inn.** Rooms are comfortable if nondescript, with either a king-size bed or two doubles, and the restaurant's lunch buffet has home-style southern cooking. The motel is on U.S. 78, where it meets Routes 7 and 4. ⊠ *U.S. 78, Box 476, 38635,* ☎ FAX *662/252–1120. 48 rooms. Restaurant, pool, lounge. AE, DC, MC, V.*

Oxford

$$–$$$ ✕ **City Grocery.** The menu at this trendy bistro in a former grocery store
★ on Oxford's historic Courthouse Square is more suggestive of New Orleans than north Mississippi. A signature dish is the shrimp and grits, and the bananas Foster bread pudding is divine. ⊠ *152 Courthouse Sq.,* ☎ *662/232–8080. AE, MC, V. Closed Sun.*

$$–$$$ ✕ **Downtown Grill.** The Grill could be a club in Oxford, England, but the balcony overlooking the square is pure Oxford, Mississippi. Specialties include shrimp étouffée and Cajun-style spicy catfish Lafitte. ⊠ *110 Courthouse Sq.,* ☎ *662/234–2659. AE, D, DC, MC, V. Closed Sun.*

$ ✕ **Smitty's.** Look for home-style cooking here: red-eye gravy and grits, biscuits with blackberry preserves, fried catfish, chicken and dumplings, corn bread, and black-eyed peas. The atmosphere is down-home. ⊠ *208 S. Lamar Blvd.,* ☎ *662/234–9111. No credit cards.*

$ 🏨 **Downtown Inn.** The guest rooms are functional and comfortable, but don't expect high style. The restaurant prepares breakfast and a noon buffet. ⊠ *400 N. Lamar Blvd., 38655,* ☎ *662/234–3031,* FAX *662/ 234–2834. 123 rooms. Restaurant, pool. AE, D, DC, MC, V.*

$ ⛤ **Oliver-Britt House.** In a restored circa-1900 house, this conveniently located B&B has pleasant rooms. ⊠ *512 Van Buren Ave., 38655,* ☎ *662/234–8043. 5 rooms. AE, D, MC, V. Full breakfast weekends.*

Nightlife

In Oxford, **Proud Larry's** (⊠ 211 S. Lamar Blvd., ☎ 662/232–5993) schedules regional bands playing blues, folk, funk, jazz, and rock.

Shopping

At Oxford's well-stocked **Square Books** (⊠ 160 Courthouse Sq., ☎ 662/236–2262), you can chat with the knowledgeable staff about local writers and savor cappuccino or dessert.

ELSEWHERE IN MISSISSIPPI

The Delta

Visitor Information

Mississippi Welcome Center (⊠ 4210 Washington St., Vicksburg 39180, ☎ 601/638–4269). **Greenville/Washington County Convention and Visitors Bureau** (⊠ 410 Washington Ave., Greenville 38701, ☎ 662/ 334–2711 or 800/467–3582).

Arriving and Departing

U.S. 61 runs from Memphis through the Delta to Vicksburg, Natchez, and Baton Rouge, Louisiana.

What to See and Do

Between Memphis and Vicksburg (☞ Vicksburg, *below*) is the **Delta,** a vast agricultural plain created by the Mississippi River. Drive through the Delta on U.S. 61, which will take you past **Tunica**'s gambling halls and their towering new hotels, or down Route 1 (the Great River Road) or Route 8 for good views of the Mississippi.

Stop for lunch in **Clarksdale,** where a renovated train depot houses the **Delta Blues Museum.** The exhibits and programs at the museum trace the history of the blues and its influence on other music. ⊠ *1 Blues Alley,* ☎ *662/627–6820.* ⊡ *Free. Closed Sun.*

The historic port city of **Greenville** has produced an extraordinary number of writers, including William Alexander Percy, Ellen Douglas, Hodding Carter, and Shelby Foote. The area was also home to the late Jim Henson, creator of Kermit the Frog. It's also noted as the home of Doe's (☞ Dining and Lodging, *below*).

Dining

CLARKSDALE

$-$$ ✕ **Rest Haven.** The Delta's large Lebanese community influences the food, making Middle Eastern cuisine a regional specialty. Among the favorites are *kibbe* (seasoned lean ground steak with cracked wheat), spinach and meat pies, and cabbage rolls. Daily plate-lunch specials include chicken and dumplings, salmon croquettes, and catfish. Patrons choose from three meats and seven vegetables. Breakfast is also served. ⊠ *419 State St. (U.S. 61),* ☎ *662/624–8601. No credit cards. Closed Sun.*

CLEVELAND

$$-$$$$ ✕ **KC's Restaurant.** The eclectic, sophisticated menu at this funky but fabulous restaurant changes seasonally, but it always has French, Italian, Asian, and southwestern influences. Count on sampling wild

game, fresh fish, free-range meats, and organic vegetables. ⊠ *U.S. 61N at 1st St.,* ☎ *662/843–5301. AE, MC, V. No lunch Sat., no dinner Sun.*

GREENVILLE

$$–$$$$ ✕ **Doe's.** This tumbledown building is visually uninspiring, but when
★   you see that huge steak hanging off your plate, you'll know why this place is famous. Hot tamales (a popular takeout item) are a specialty. ⊠ *502 Nelson St.,* ☎ *662/334–3315. AE, D, DC, MC, V. No lunch.*

The Gulf Coast

Visitor Information

Mississippi Beach Convention and Visitors Bureau (⊠ Box 6128, Gulfport 38506, ☎ 228/896–6699 or 800/237–9493). **Ocean Springs Chamber of Commerce** (⊠ Box 187, 39566, ☎ 228/875–4424).

Arriving and Departing

U.S. 90 runs through the heart of Ocean Springs, Biloxi, and Gulfport.

What to See and Do

Oak-shaded **Ocean Springs** originated in 1699 as a French fort. It is now known as the former home of artist Walter Anderson. The **Walter Anderson Museum of Art** (⊠ 510 Washington Ave., ☎ 228/872–3164; ☞ $4) displays Anderson's work, including his cottage studio with intricately painted walls. The artist (1903–65) revealed his ecstatic communion with nature in thousands of drawings and watercolors, most kept secret until his death.

★ Ocean Springs is the headquarters of the **Gulf Islands National Seashore** (⊠ 3500 Park Rd., Ocean Springs 39564, ☎ 228/875–9057). On the mainland there are nature trails and ranger programs. Out in the Gulf, pristine Ship, Horn, and Petit Bois islands have beaches as white and soft as sugar. Excursion boats to Ship, rimmed by about 7 mi of this remarkable sand, leave from Biloxi in summer and from Gulfport from May through October. Charter operators regularly take wilderness lovers to Horn and Petit Bois, both nationally designated wilderness areas, where camping is permitted.

A string of casino openings has turned **Biloxi** and its quiet beach into a mini–Las Vegas. Along with the neon lights and traffic jams have come big-name entertainment and more dining choices. In **Gulfport,** two casinos share the waterfront with the shrimp boats and banana warehouses vital to the area's economy.

Dining and Lodging

BILOXI

$$–$$$ ✕ **La Cucina.** Located inside the Beau Rivage casino, La Cucina takes
★   advantage of fresh seafood to put a Gulf Coast twist on Italian cuisine. The food is tasty, the service attentive. ⊠ *875 Beach Blvd.,* ☎ *228/386–7111. AE, D, DC, MC, V.*

$$–$$$ ✕ **Mary Mahoney's Old French House.** This longtime favorite of locals prepares fresh seafood dishes, steaks, lamb, and veal. Among its most tantalizing fare is the lobster Georgio, the snapper stuffed with shrimp and crab au gratin, and the veal Antonio, topped with three cheeses and sautéed crabmeat. ⊠ *116 Rue Magnolia,* ☎ *228/374–0163. AE, D, DC, MC, V. Closed Sun.*

$–$$$$ 🏨 **Beau Rivage.** This hotel has all the elegance that its owner, Steve Wynn of Mirage Resorts, is famous for—plus a casino. In keeping with its southern theme, the hotel has graced its lobby with huge live magnolias, the state's flower, and other fragrant flowers that are changed regularly. ⊠ *875 Beach Blvd., 39530,* ☎ *228/386–7111 or 888/567–*

6667. *1,800 rooms. 6 restaurants, coffee shop, deli, pools, spa, meeting rooms. AE, D, DC, MC, V.* 🐾

GULFPORT

$$–$$$ ✕ **Vrazel's.** Dining nooks with windows facing the beach add charm here. Special attractions include the red snapper, Gulf trout, flounder, and shrimp prepared every which way. ✉ *3206 W. Beach Blvd. (U.S. 90),* 🕾 *228/863–2229. AE, D, DC, MC, V. Closed Sun. No lunch Sat.*

$–$$$ ▦ **Grand Casino Gulfport Oasis Resort & Spa.** The Oasis features an Olympic-size swimming pool, surrounded by a grotto with waterfall and a "lazy river" that takes guests on a 15-minute inner tube float ride. There are also outside Jacuzzis and a cabana bar. ✉ *3215 W. Beach Blvd., 39501,* 🕾 *228/769–7777 or 800/946–7777. 600 rooms. Restaurant, pools, golf, tennis, exercise room. AE, D, DC, MC, V.*

Vicksburg

Visitor Information

Vicksburg: Convention and Visitors Bureau (✉ Box 110, Vicksburg 39181, 🕾 601/636–9421 or 800/221–3536).

Arriving and Departing

I–20 runs east–west and U.S. 61 north–south through Vicksburg.

What to See and Do

During the Civil War the Confederacy and the Union vied for control of this strategic location on the Mississippi Delta across the river from Louisiana. After a 47-day siege the city surrendered to Ulysses S. Grant on July 4, 1863, giving the Union control of the river and sounding the death knell for the Confederacy. Vicksburg's **National Military Park** (✉ Visitor Center, 3201 Clay St., I–20, Exit 4B onto U.S. 80, Vicksburg 39180, 🕾 601/636–0583) details the events of these turbulent times. Battle positions are marked, and monuments line the 16-mi drive through the park. Tours of grand antebellum homes and 24-hour riverfront gambling are other draws.

Dining and Lodging

$ ✕ **Walnut Hills.** If you're yearning for authentic regional cooking, this restaurant is a must. Diners eat round-table style, sampling two or three meats, seven vegetables, and desserts such as blackberry cobbler. Don't pass up the outstanding fried chicken, fresh snap beans, or purple-hull peas. ✉ *1214 Adams St.,* 🕾 *601/638–4910. AE, DC, MC, V. Closed Sat. No dinner Sun.*

$$–$$$ ▦ **Cedar Grove.** This 1840s mansion and its grounds cover a full city
★ block. The entire house is furnished with period antiques. You can hear nearby river traffic from the quiet, gaslit grounds or survey the scene from the rooftop veranda. A house tour and hearty breakfast are included. Croquet and bicycles are available. ✉ *2200 Oak St., 39180,* 🕾 *601/636–1000 or 800/862–1300,* ℻ *601/634–6126. 29 rooms. Restaurant, pool, tennis. AE, D, MC, V. BP.*

$$–$$$ ▦ **Duff Green Mansion.** This 1856 mansion was used as a hospital dur-
★ ing the Civil War. Each guest room is decorated with antiques, including half-tester beds. A large southern breakfast and a tour of the home are included. ✉ *1114 1st East St., 39180,* 🕾 *601/636–6968 or 800/992–0037. 4 rooms. Pool. AE, MC, V. BP.* 🐾

MISSOURI

Updated by	**Capital**	Jefferson City
Diana Lambdin	**Population**	5,117,000
Meyer	**Motto**	Let the Welfare of the People Be the Supreme Law
	State Bird	Eastern bluebird
	State Flower	Hawthorn
	Postal Abbreviation	MO

Statewide Visitor Information

The **Missouri Division of Tourism** (⊠ Truman State Office Bldg., Box 1055, Jefferson City 65102, ☎ 573/751–4133; 800/877–1234 in MO) operates six visitor centers.

Scenic Drives

Route 21 from St. Louis to Doniphan, in extreme southern Missouri, passes through national forests and rugged hill country. Scenic routes in southwestern Missouri's Ozark Mountains include **Route 76, Route 248,** and **U.S. 65** south of Springfield.

National and State Parks

National Parks

The **Ozark National Scenic Riverways** (⊠ National Park Service, Box 490, Van Buren 63965, ☎ 573/323–4236) includes the Current and Jacks Fork rivers, two south-central Missouri rivers that were the first to be federally protected. Both offer good canoeing. The **Mark Twain National Forest** (⊠ 401 Fairgrounds Rd., Rolla 65401, ☎ 573/364–4621) is in southern Missouri.

State Parks

Lake of the Ozarks State Park (⊠ U.S. 54, ☎ 573/348–2694) is the largest state park in Missouri. The popular **Missouri River State Trail,** known to locals as the Katy Trail, is a walking-and-cycling path, much of it along the Missouri River between Sedalia and St. Charles. Other significant parks include **Elephant Rocks** (⊠ Box 509, Pilot Knob 63663, ☎ 573/546–3454), **Johnson's Shut-Ins** (⊠ Middle Brook 63656, ☎ 573/546–2450), **Mastodon State Park** (⊠ Imperial 63052, ☎ 314/464–3079), and **Onondaga Cave State Park** (⊠ Leasburg 65535, ☎ 573/245–6576). For more information contact the **Missouri Department of Natural Resources** (Division of State Parks, ⊠ Box 176, Jefferson City 65101, ☎ 573/751–2479 or 800/334–6946).

ST. LOUIS

Founded by the French in 1764 as a fur-trading settlement on the west bank of the Mississippi River, St. Louis is best known for the soaring silver arch that so impresses travelers entering the city from the east. In its early days the city thrived as a river port, then as a rail hub, and today it's the world headquarters for such mega-corporations as Anheuser-Busch and McDonnell Douglas. The construction of the Gateway Arch in 1965 did more than commemorate the city's role in westward expansion—it helped spark the rebirth of a downtown that had been abandoned in the rush for the suburbs.

Visitor Information

Convention and Visitors Commission (⊠ One Metropolitan Square, Suite 1100, 63102, ☎ 314/421–1023 or 800/888–3861) is open weekdays from 8:30 to 5. There are **visitor centers** at the airport and downtown (⊠ 308 Washington Ave., ☎ 314/241–1764). The **Missouri Tourist Information Center** (⊠ I–270 at the Riverview exit, ☎ 314/869–7100) is just west of the Missouri-Illinois border.

Arriving and Departing

By Bus
Greyhound (⊠ 1450 N. 13th St., ☎ 800/231–2222).

By Car
From I–70, I–55, and I–44 follow the exits for downtown St. Louis. From U.S. 40 (I–64), exit at Broadway.

By Plane
Lambert–St. Louis International Airport (⊠ 10701 Lambert International Blvd., ☎ 314/426–8000), 10 mi northwest of downtown on I–70, has scheduled flights on most major domestic and foreign carriers. It's about a 20-minute drive from the airport to downtown St. Louis; taxis cost about $22. Transportation is also provided to downtown stops by the **Bi-State** bus and **MetroLink** (both ☎ 314/231–2345) and to downtown hotels by **Airport Express** shuttle vans (☎ 314/429–4950).

By Train
Amtrak (⊠ 550 S. 16th St., ☎ 314/331–3300 or 800/872–7245).

Getting Around St. Louis

Explore the downtown sights on foot; elsewhere you'll need a car. **MetroLink** (☎ 314/231–2345), the city's light-rail system, stops near major attractions downtown. A one-way ticket costs $1.25. Rides are free between Laclede's Landing and Union Station weekdays from 10 to 3.

Exploring St. Louis

Downtown
A ride to the top of the 630-ft **Gateway Arch** is a must. The centerpiece of the 91-acre **Jefferson National Expansion Memorial Park**, the arch was built in 1965 to commemorate the city where thousands of 19th-century pioneers stopped for provisions before traveling west. For $6, a tram takes you up through one of the arch's legs to an observation room with a terrific view of the city and the Mississippi. Beneath the arch is the underground visitor center and the **Museum of Westward Expansion**. ⊠ *On the riverfront at Market St.,* ☎ *314/655–1700.*

Just down the steps from the Gateway Arch is the Mississippi riverfront and its cobblestone levee, where permanently moored **riverboats** house a handful of mostly fast-food restaurants. The *Tom Sawyer* and *Becky Thatcher* (☎ 314/621–4040 or 800/878–7411), replicas of 19th-century steamboats, offer one-hour sightseeing trips and two-hour dinner cruises. Nearby is the *President Casino on the Admiral* (☎ 314/622–1111 or 800/772–3647; ▨ $2), a noncruising riverboat that offers casino gambling in a Las Vegas–style environment. Other riverboat casinos in the St. Louis area include the **Casino St. Charles** (⊠ S. 5th St., ☎ 636/949–7777 or 800/325–7777) and, upriver, the **Alton Belle Riverboat Casino** (⊠ 219 Piasa St., Alton, IL, ☎ 618/223–7568 or 800/336–7568). Northwest of the Gateway Arch is **Laclede's Landing,** nine square blocks

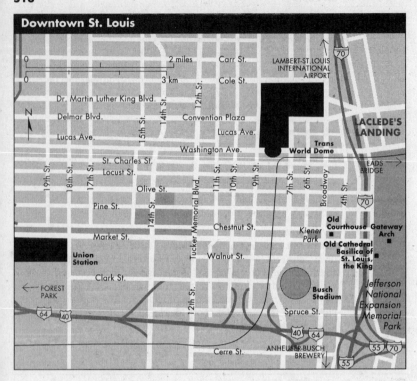

Downtown St. Louis

of cobblestone streets and restored 19th-century warehouses now filled with shops, galleries, restaurants, and nightspots.

West of the Gateway Arch is St. Louis's oldest church, the **Old Cathedral Basilica of St. Louis, the King** (⌂ 209 Walnut St., ☎ 314/231–3250), a simple Greek Revival structure built in 1834 that still holds daily masses. On Market Street, the **Old Courthouse** (⌂ 11 N. 4th St., ☎ 314/655–1700) has displays and photographs of early St. Louis.

South of the Old Courthouse is **Busch Stadium,** home of the St. Louis Cardinals (☞ Spectator Sports, *below*). Just across the street is the **International Bowling Hall of Fame** (111 Stadium Plaza, ☎ 314/231–6340; ⌂ $6), where you can bowl in a 1930s alley and learn more about the history of the sport. On the northeast side of the stadium is the **St. Louis Cardinals Hall of Fame,** with sports memorabilia and audio and video highlights of the history of St. Louis baseball. ⌂ *Off I–40 (exit at 9th St.),* ☎ *314/421–3060.* ⌂ *$6. Closed weekends Jan.–Mar.*

Other Attractions

St. Louis is home to the world's largest brewer, **Anheuser-Busch,** maker of Budweiser beer. Tours of the company's world headquarters, in south St. Louis, include the stables where the famous Clydesdale horses are kept. ⌂ *12th and Lynch Sts.,* ☎ *314/577–2626.* ⌂ *Free. Closed Sun.*

On the western edge of town is **Forest Park** (⌂ north of U.S. 40 between Kingshighway and Skinker Blvds.), whose grounds include a variety of attractions. Within the park, the **St. Louis Zoo** (⌂ 1 Government Dr., ☎ 314/781–0900; ⌂ free) has a high-tech education center. The **St. Louis Art Museum** (⌂ 1 Fine Arts Dr., ☎ 314/721–0072; ⌂ free), next to the St. Louis Zoo, has outstanding pre-Columbian and German expressionist collections. The **St. Louis Science Center** (⌂ 5050

Oakland Ave., ☎ 314/289–4444; 🎫 free), in the southeast part of Forest Park, contains more than 600 hands-on exhibits on ecology, space, and humanity. **The Magic House** (✉ 516 S. Kirkwood Rd., ☎ 314/822–8900; 🎫 $5.50) is a restored Victorian house with interactive learning experiences.

A mind-boggling collection of mosaics covers the walls, ceilings, and three domes of the **Cathedral of St. Louis** (✉ Lindell Blvd. and Newstead Ave., ☎ 314/533–2824 or 314/533–0544), also known as the New Cathedral.

The **Missouri Botanical Garden** (✉ 4344 Shaw Ave., ☎ 314/577–5100; 🎫 $5), known locally as Shaw's Garden for founder Henry Shaw, is a 15-minute drive southwest of downtown. Highlights include an impressive Japanese garden and a tropical rain forest.

The **St. Louis City Museum** (✉ 701 N. 15th St., ☎ 314/231–2489, 🎫 $6) is not like any museum you've been to before, unless you've crawled through fish-head trees, participated in a real circus, and escaped from an enchanted castle via a slide and tunnel system.

Six Flags over Mid-America–St. Louis (✉ I–44 and Allenton Rd., Eureka, ☎ 314/938–4800; 🎫 $34.99 adults, $17.49 children under 48″), about 30 mi southwest of St. Louis, has rides, shows, and a water park. **Grant's Farm** (✉ 10501 Gravois, ☎ 314/843–1700), open April through October, is a favorite with St. Louis children for its 160-acre petting zoo, animal preserve, and train ride to visit the Clydesdales.

Dining

St. Louis's Hill neighborhood has an Italian restaurant on nearly every corner; even the abundant steak houses carry an Italian dish or two. Other ethnic restaurants are scattered throughout the city. The Central West End and Laclede's Landing have a number of restaurants, as does Clayton, the St. Louis County seat, about 7 mi west of downtown.

$$$$ ✕ **Cardwell's.** At this sophisticated Clayton establishment, you can eat in either the airy café, with marble-top tables and French doors, or in the more formal, elegant dining room. The changing menu may include duck breast or roasted rack of lamb, among other specialties. ✉ *8100 Maryland St., ☎ 314/726–5055. AE, DC, MC, V. Closed Sun.*

$$$$ ✕ **Tony's.** This four-star, family-owned restaurant has been a St. Louis favorite since the 1950s. Superb Italian dishes, prime steaks, and superior service make it well worth the price. ✉ *410 Market St., ☎ 314/231–7007. Reservations essential. Jacket and tie. AE, D, DC, MC, V. Closed Sun. No lunch.*

$$ ✕ **Blue Water Grill.** Grilled seafood with a southwestern flair is the specialty at this small, festive Kirkwood restaurant. On Monday night diners can mix and match "Flying Saucers," miniature entrées. ✉ *343 S. Kirkwood, ☎ 314/821–5757. AE, MC, V. Closed Sun.*

$$ ✕ **Mike Shannon's Steaks & Seafoods.** The name Mike Shannon is synonymous with the glory days of Cardinal baseball thanks to his extensive career as an announcer on KMOX Radio. People flock to this downtown steak house as much for Shannon's impressive sports-memorabilia collection as for the fine steaks and gourmet desserts. ✉ *100 N. 7th St., ☎ 314/421–1540. AE, MC, V.*

$–$$ ✕ **Cunetto's House of Pasta.** There's usually a wait at this popular Hill
★ restaurant, but relaxing in the cocktail lounge is part of the experience. Once seated, you'll find plenty of veal and beef dishes as well as more than 30 different pastas. ✉ *5453 Magnolia Ave., ☎ 314/781–1135. Reservations not accepted. AE, DC, MC, V. Closed Sun.*

$ ✕ **Big Sky Café.** Owned and operated by the same family as the Blue Water Grill (☞ *above*), this casual café is popular with the business-lunch crowd in Webster Groves. Try the pungent garlic mashed potatoes or the corn-bread-stuffed chicken breast. ✉ *47 S. Old Orchard,* ☎ *314/962–5757. AE, DC, MC, V.*

$ ✕ **Blueberry Hill.** Dart competitions and live local bands draw crowds to this gathering spot in trendy University City. A burger, a locally brewed Rock 'n Roll beer, and a quarter in the famous 2,000-tune jukebox gets the good times going. ✉ *6504 Delmar Blvd.,* ☎ *314/727–0880. Reservations not accepted on weekends. AE, D, DC, MC, V.*

$ ✕ **Rigazzi's.** Generous, inexpensive servings of homemade pasta keep locals coming back to this no-frills, family-style restaurant on the Hill. ✉ *4945 Daggett St.,* ☎ *314/772–4900. AE, DC, MC, V. Closed Sun.*

Lodging

Most of St. Louis's big hotels are downtown or in Clayton, about 7 mi west. For bed-and-breakfasts in town, call or write **Bed and Breakfasts of St. Louis, River Country of Missouri and Illinois** (✉ 1900 Wyoming St., St. Louis 63118, ☎ 314/771–1993).

$$$$ 🏨 **Hyatt Regency St. Louis at Union Station.** Most of these rooms are in a contemporary garden setting beneath the arched trusses of Union Station's original train station. Deluxe rooms and suites are available in the Regency Club. ✉ *1 St. Louis Union Station, 63103,* ☎ *314/231–1234 or 800/233–1234,* 🖷 *314/436–6827. 536 rooms. 2 restaurants, pool, exercise room. AE, D, DC, MC, V.* ✍

$$$$ 🏨 **Ritz-Carlton, St. Louis.** Chandeliers and museum-quality oil paintings fill this luxury hotel in Clayton. Some rooms on the top floors have views of the downtown St. Louis skyline. ✉ *100 Carondelet Plaza, Clayton 63105,* ☎ *314/863–6300 or 800/241–3333,* 🖷 *314/863–3525. 301 rooms. 2 restaurants, pool, exercise room. AE, D, DC, MC, V.* ✍

$$$ 🏨 **Omni Majestic.** This small, European-style hotel downtown is a frequent choice of visiting celebrities. It was built in 1913 and is filled with reproduction antiques. ✉ *1019 Pine St., 63101,* ☎ *314/436–2355 or 800/843–6664,* 🖷 *314/436–0223. 91 rooms. Restaurant, exercise room. AE, D, DC, MC, V.* ✍

$$ 🏨 **Drury Inn–Union Station.** Lead-glass windows and marble columns
★ give historic charm to this former YMCA. Among its assets are free parking and an excellent location, next to Union Station. ✉ *201 S. 20th St., 63103,* ☎ *314/231–3900,* 🖷 *314/231–3900. 176 rooms. Restaurant, pool, exercise room. AE, D, DC, MC, V. CP.* ✍

Motels

🏨 **Red Roof Inn** (✉ 5823 Wilson Ave., 63110, ☎ 314/645–0101, 🖷 314/645–0119, 110 rooms; *$$.* 🏨 **Baymont Inn & Suites, West Port** (✉ 12330 Dorsett Rd., 63043, ☎ 314/878–1212, 🖷 314/878–3409), 145 rooms; *$.*

🏨 **Fairfield Inn by Marriott** (✉ 9079 Dunn Rd., 63042, ☎ 314/731–7700, 🖷 314/731–1891), 135 rooms; pool; *$.*

Nightlife and the Arts

Nightlife

Much of St. Louis's nightlife can be found in the jazz and blues clubs in the redeveloped areas of **Laclede's Landing,** on the riverfront, and in **Soulard,** on the southern edge of downtown. To find out who's playing where, consult the Thursday calendar section in the *St. Louis Post-Dispatch* or the free, weekly *Riverfront Times.* Dinner theater is popular throughout the city; the **Royal Dumpe** (✉ 711 1st St., ☎ 314/621–5800) and **Bissell Mansion Dinner Theatre** (✉ 4426 Randall Pl., ☎ 314/533–9830) are solid choices. St. Louis is home to the country's oldest and largest outdoor theater, the **Muny**(☎ 314/361–1900), in Forest Park, with Broadway shows from June to August. Those who like to dance will enjoy the 5,000-square-ft **Casa Loma Ballroom** (✉ 3354 Iowa Ave., ☎ 314/664–8000).

The Arts

The **Fabulous Fox Theatre** (✉ 527 N. Grand Blvd., ☎ 314/534–1678) hosts major shows and concerts. The **Riverport Amphitheatre** (✉ 14141 Riverport Dr., ☎ 314/298–9944) stages big-name concerts. The St. Louis Symphony Orchestra performs at **Powell Symphony Hall** (✉ 718 N. Grand Blvd., ☎ 314/534–1700). For tickets to major events call **Ticketmaster** (☎ 314/241–1888) or for arts events call **MetroTix** (☎ 314/534–1111).

Spectator Sports

Baseball: St. Louis Cardinals (✉ Busch Stadium, 250 Stadium Plaza, ☎ 314/421–3060). **Football: St. Louis Rams** (✉ Trans World Dome, 801 Convention Plaza, ☎ 314/425–8830). **Ice hockey: St. Louis Blues** (✉ Kiel Center, 1401 Clark Ave., ☎ 314/969–1800). **Incline roller hockey: St. Louis Vipers** (✉ 1819 Clarkson Blvd., ☎ 636/530–1967). **Soccer: St. Louis Ambush** (✉ 7547 Ravensridge, ☎ 314/962–4625).

Shopping

For browsing in boutiques and specialty shops, try **Union Station** (✉ 1820 Market St.), an impressive former train station with more than 100 shops and restaurants, and **Laclede's Landing** (☞ Exploring St. Louis, *above*). The **Central West End,** along Euclid Avenue east of Forest Park, is an area of hip boutiques and restaurants. The city's most sophisticated shoppers head for **Plaza Frontenac** (✉ Clayton Rd. and Lindbergh Blvd., ☎ 314/432–0604), home to nearly 50 upscale stores, including Neiman Marcus and Saks Fifth Avenue. Antiques and crafts lovers should visit historic downtown **St. Charles** (✉ I–70 and First Capital Dr.), seven cobblestone blocks of shops and restaurants on the banks of the Missouri River. For more contemporary crafts, try the **Apropos Gallery** (✉ 7750 Forsyth Blvd., ☎ 314/212–5500) or **Coyote's Paw** (✉ 6388 Delmar, ☎ 314/721–7576).

KANSAS CITY

With upwards of 200 fountains—more than any city except Rome—and more boulevard miles (155) than Paris, Kansas City is attractive and cosmopolitan. This sprawling metropolitan area straddling the Missouri-Kansas line has a rich history as a frontier river port and trade center, where wagon trains were outfitted before heading west on the Santa Fe and Oregon trails. Through the years it has been home to the nation's second-largest stockyards, to saxophone player Charlie "Bird" Parker and his Kansas City–style bebop, and to some of the best barbecue in the world. Today, it is also home to the world's leading pharmaceutical companies, telecommunications giants, and Hallmark Cards, the preeminent name in greeting cards.

Visitor Information

Greater Kansas City: Convention and Visitors Bureau (✉ 1100 Main St., Suite 2550, 64105, ☎ 816/221–5242 or 800/767–7700) is in City Center Square in downtown Kansas City. Its recorded visitor information (☎ 816/691–3800) provides a weekly list of activities. The **Missouri Information Center** (✉ I–70 and Blue Ridge Cutoff; 4010 Blue Ridge Cutoff, 64133, ☎ 816/889–3330) overlooks the Truman Sports Complex.

Arriving and Departing

By Bus
Greyhound (✉ 11th St. and Troost Ave., ☎ 800/231–2222).

By Car
From I–70 or I–35 exit at Broadway for downtown. From the airport, I–29 from the north merges with I–35 north of the city.

By Plane
Kansas City International Airport (✉ 601 Brasilia, ☎ 816/243–5237), 20 minutes northwest of downtown on I–29, is served by major domestic airlines. Taxi service is zoned; the maximum fare from the airport to downtown Kansas City is $26. **KCI Shuttle** buses (☎ 816/243–5950) will take you to major downtown hotels for $12.

By Train
Amtrak (✉ 2200 Main St., ☎ 816/421–3622 or 800/872–7245).

Getting Around Kansas City

Attractions are scattered throughout the metropolitan region, making a car important for travelers. However, **Kansas City Trolley Co.** (☎ 816/221–3399; ⊞ $9, exact change required) runs replica trolleys between the sites downtown and the River Market area, as well as Crown Center, Westport, and the Country Club Plaza. The drivers are usually entertaining and well versed in local history.

Exploring Kansas City

Plaza, Midtown, Downtown
Kansas City's **Country Club Plaza** (✉ 47th and Main Sts., ☎ 816/753–0100) is known for its more than 180 fine shops and restaurants, its Spanish-style architecture, and its annual display of holiday lights from Thanksgiving to January, when hundreds of thousands of gaily colored bulbs outline its buildings. Here you'll also find many of Kansas City's fountains and statues. Several blocks east of the plaza ★ is the **Nelson-Atkins Museum of Art** (✉ 4525 Oak St., ☎ 816/561–4000, ⊞ $5, free on Sat.), known for its outstanding Asian-art collection and the Henry Moore Sculpture Garden on the south grounds.

The **Kemper Museum of Contemporary Art and Design** (✉ 4420 Warwick Blvd., ☎ 816/753–5784; ⊞ free) has a permanent collection of 400 works in a broad range of media. Next to the Kemper Museum is the **Kansas City Art Institute** (✉ 4415 Warwick Blvd., ☎ 816/472–4852; ⊞ free), a four-year college of art and design spread across 4 acres dotted with sculptures. A campus tour includes a visit to the institute's student-run gallery, which displays two- and three-dimensional contemporary artwork.

Before there was a Kansas City, there was a **Westport** (✉ north of the Plaza at Broadway and Westport Rd., ☎ 816/756–2789), built along the Santa Fe Trail as an outfitting center for wagon trains heading west. Today the area is filled with renovated and new buildings housing trendy shops, restaurants, and nightspots.

On the crest of a hill at the northern edge of Penn Valley Park, north of Westport, is the **Liberty Memorial** (✉ 100 W. 26th St., ☎ 816/221–1918), dedicated to those who served in World War I. Extensive structural renovation has temporarily closed the tower's 217-ft observation deck and the museum, which is scheduled to reopen on November 11, 2001.

Across Pershing Road from the memorial is the newest jewel in Kansas ★ ☾ City's attractions, the **Union Station/Science City** (✉ 30 W. Pershing

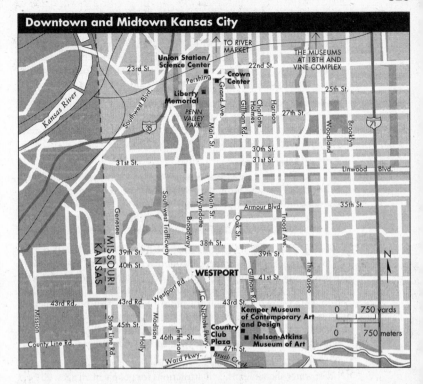

Rd., ☎ 816/460–2222, ⌧ $12.50), a 55,000-square-ft science museum in the recently restored train station, which was once the second largest in the country. The old station now houses 50 hands-on learning environments, including a space center and media lab, as well as restaurants, shops, and theaters.

Just across Main Street from the Liberty Memorial and Union Station is **Crown Center** (⊠ 2450 Grand Ave., ☎ 816/274–8444), an 85-acre shopping mall and entertainment, office, and hotel complex. In summer, free concerts are held on the terrace on Friday nights; in winter, there's a covered outdoor ice-skating rink. Hallmark Cards, the largest maker of greeting cards in the world, built Crown Center and has its headquarters here. Monday through Saturday you can stop by the **Hallmark Visitors Center** (⊠ 2501 McGee St., ☎ 816/274–3613), which features a display on the history of the greeting-card industry and a machine that makes those big round bows (you can keep the bow). **Kaleidoscope** (⊠ 2501 McGee St., ☎ 816/274–8300; ⌧ free, reservations required) is a hands-on creative-arts center for children staffed as a public service by Hallmark employees.

North of downtown, the River Market area has some of the city's most distinctive ethnic restaurants and markets. In the summer months, a Saturday-morning farmers' market draws thousands, as does a Sunday-morning artists' market. Year-round, tourists and locals enjoy the ★ ***Arabia*** Steamboat Museum (⊠ 400 Grand Ave., ☎ 816/471–4030, ⌧ $7.50), which houses goods—from French perfume to buttons to coffeepots—salvaged from the *Arabia*'s muddy grave 132 years after it sank in the Missouri River in 1856.

In the Museums at 18th and Vine complex, the cornerstone of the historic 18th and Vine district, the **Negro Leagues Baseball Museum** (⊠ 1616 E. 18th St., ☎ 816/221–1920; ⌧ $6, $8 joint ticket with American Jazz Museum) documents the history of African-Americans in baseball through films and a multimedia gallery. The **American Jazz Museum** (⊠ 1616 E. 18th St., ☎ 816/474–8463; 🎟 $6, $8 joint ticket with Negro Leagues Baseball Museum), in the same building, honors Louis Armstrong, Duke Ellington, Ella Fitzgerald, and Charlie Parker. You can listen to hundreds of jazz CDs in the interactive studio and sound library.

Riverboat gambling is popular along the banks of this Missouri River town. Two noncruising boats in the Kansas City area are the **Argosy** (⊠ Hwy. 9 and I–635, Riverside, ☎ 816/741–7568) and **Harrah's Casino** (⊠ Armour Rd., North Kansas City, ☎ 816/471–3364).

Other Attractions

Just east of Kansas City is **Independence,** once the home of President Harry S. Truman. Truman's life and career are the focus at the **Harry S. Truman Library and Museum** (⊠ U.S. 24 and Delaware St., ☎ 816/833–1225; 🎟 $5). The **Truman Home** (⊠ 219 N. Delaware St.; ticket center: 223 Main St., ☎ 816/254–9929; 🎟 $2) was the Trumans' summer White House.

Ⓒ **Fleming Park** (⊠ 22807 Woods Chapel Rd., ☎ 816/795–8200), in Blue Springs, south of Independence, contains the 970-acre Lake Jacomo, which hosts sailing regattas each weekend from April through October. Also in Fleming Park is **Missouri Town 1855** (🎟 $3), a reproduction 1800s town created from more than 30 transplanted period houses, barns, stores, and outbuildings. The staff and volunteers wear period clothing. It's closed from Monday through Friday in fall and winter, and Monday and Tuesday in spring and summer.

★ Ⓒ **Worlds of Fun/Oceans of Fun** are two adjoining theme parks with shows, rides, water shenanigans, and attractions for people of all ages. ⊠ *East loop of I–435 at Exit 54,* ☎ *816/454–4545.* 🎟 *Worlds of Fun $31.95, Oceans of Fun $21.95, combination ticket $41.95, children ages 4 and up or under 48″ tall $7.95 for both parks, children 3 and under free. Closed mid-Oct.–mid-Apr.*

Ⓒ The **Kansas City Zoo** (⊠ I–435 and 63rd St., ☎ 816/871–5701; 🎟 $5) includes a 5,000-acre African-plains exhibit as well as an **IMAX** theater (☎ 816/871–5858; 🎟 $6).

Just north of downtown Kansas City is the historic riverboat community of **Weston** (☎ 816/640–2909). Every building in the five-block downtown shopping area is on the National Register of Historic Places.

Dining

Kansas City is best known for its steaks and barbecue. Both Country Club Plaza and Westport have a variety of good restaurants.

$$$ ✕ **Plaza III—The Steakhouse.** This handsome, nationally known restaurant at Country Club Plaza serves excellent steaks, prime rib, and
★ seafood. The steak soup is legendary. ⊠ *4749 Pennsylvania Ave.,* ☎ *816/753–0000. AE, D, DC, MC, V. No lunch Sun.*

$$ ✕ **Golden Ox.** Down the street from Kemper Arena, this popular steak house serves prime rib in a comfortable western atmosphere. ⊠ *1600 Gennessee St.,* ☎ *816/842–2866. AE, D, DC, MC, V. No lunch Sun.*

$$ ✕ **Savoy Grill.** Locals often choose this historic, turn-of-the-20th-century beauty when celebrating a special occasion. Maine lobster and a T-bone steak from the restaurant's own herd are good choices. ⊠ *219 W. 9th St.,* ☎ *816/842–3890. AE, D, DC, MC, V. No lunch Sun.*

$$ ✕ **Stroud's.** This sprawling building on Kansas City's north side was
★ once the first stagecoach stop for travelers on their way to St. Joseph. After feasting on fried chicken and homemade pies, take a stroll around

the grounds, complete with ponds, geese, and swans. ⊠ *5410 N.E. Oak Ridge Dr.,* ☏ *816/454–9600. AE, DC, MC, V.*

$–$$ ✕ **Lidia's.** Northern Italian cuisine, such as veal with spinach tagliatelle, is the house specialty in this simple but classic restaurant in Kansas City's midtown, an area growing with galleries and ethnic food. ⊠ *101 W. 22nd St.,* ☏ *816/221–3722. AE, D, DC, MC, V. Closed Mon.*

$ ✕ **Arthur Bryant's.** Although there are reportedly more than 70 bar-
★ becue joints in Kansas City, Bryant's—low on decor but high on taste—tops the list for locals, who don't mind standing in long lines to order at the counter. ⊠ *1727 Brooklyn Ave.,* ☏ *816/231–1123. AE, MC, V.*

Lodging

Kansas City offers a core of major hotels within walking distance of Country Club Plaza and Westport or in the Crown Center complex. For a listing of B&Bs contact **Bed & Breakfast Kansas City** (⊠ Box 14781, Lenexa 66285, ☏ 913/888–3636).

$$$–$$$$ 🏨 **Ritz-Carlton.** Crystal chandeliers, imported marble, and fine art fill
★ this luxury hotel. Some rooms have balconies and views of the plaza. ⊠ *401 Ward Pkwy., 64112,* ☏ *816/756–1500,* ℻ *816/756–1635. 366 rooms. Restaurant, pool, health club. AE, D, DC, MC, V.* ✎

$$$–$$$$ 🏨 **Westin Crown Center.** Part of the Crown Center complex, the Westin has a bustling lobby complete with a five-story waterfall and a natural limestone cliff. All rooms have views; the best ones face Crown Center Square to the east. ⊠ *1 Pershing Rd., 64108,* ☏ *816/474–4400 or 800/228–3000,* ℻ *816/391–4490. 774 rooms. 3 restaurants, pool, health club. AE, D, DC, MC, V.* ✎

$$$ 🏨 **The Raphael.** Built in 1927 as an apartment house, the Raphael today
★ is the only intimate, European-style hotel in Kansas City. Yet, many of the rooms are large, with excellent views of the plaza. ⊠ *325 Ward Pkwy., 64112,* ☏ *816/756–3800 or 800/821–5343,* ℻ *816/756–3800. 123 rooms. Restaurant. AE, D, DC, MC, V.*

$$$ 🏨 **Southmoreland on the Plaza.** Within walking distance of the Country Club Plaza and the Nelson-Atkins Museum, the rooms of this urban inn are named and decorated according to some of the big names of local history, such as William Rockhill Nelson and Satchel Paige. ⊠ *116 E. 46th St., 64112,* ☏ *816/531–7979,* ℻ *816/531–2407. 13 rooms. AE, D, DC, MC, V. BP.* ✎

$$ 🏨 **Quarterage Hotel.** This intimate brick hotel in the Westport area is central to many activities in the metropolitan area. ⊠ *560 Westport Rd., 64111,* ☏ *816/931–0001 or 800/942–4233,* ℻ *816/931–8891. 123 rooms. Health club. AE, D, DC, MC, V. BP.* ✎

$–$$ 🏨 **Drury Inn–Stadium.** Across from the sports complex, this chain hotel offers clean, comfortable rooms. Make reservations well ahead of time during sporting events. ⊠ *3830 Blue Ridge Cutoff, 64133,* ☏ ℻ *816/923–3000. 133 rooms. Pool. AE, D, DC, MC, V. CP.* ✎

Nightlife and the Arts

Nightlife

Much of Kansas City's nightlife happens in the Westport and Plaza areas. The **Grand Emporium** (⊠ 3832 Main St., ☏ 816/531–1504) has twice been honored as the best blues club in the nation by the Blues Foundation of America. The city is justly proud of its jazz heritage. Several venues host live performances; for information call the **Jazz Hotline** (☏ 816/763–1052). The **Blue Room** (☏ 816/474–8463, ext. 215/216), in the American Jazz Museum (☞ Exploring Kansas City, *above*), reels jazz fans in on Monday and from Thursday through Saturday nights with live bands.

Standford's Comedy House (✉ 504 Westport Rd., ☎ 816/756–1450; ⌨ $8 weeknights, $12 weekends) features local and national comedians. Several dinner theaters draw crowds, including the **American Heartland Theatre** in Crown Center (☞ Exploring Kansas City, *above*; ☎ 816/842–9999) and the **New Theatre Restaurant** (✉ 9229 Foster, ☎ 816/649–7469).

The Arts

The **Folly Theater** (✉ 12th and Central Sts., ☎ 816/842–5500) stages comedy acts, ballet, operas, and theater. The **Midland Center for the Performing Arts** (✉ 1228 Main St., ☎ 816/471–8600) has shows and concerts. The Lyric Opera of Kansas City and the Kansas City Symphony perform at the **Lyric Theatre** (✉ 11th and Central Sts., ☎ 816/471–7344). For information on upcoming events check the Friday and Sunday editions of the *Kansas City Star*. Call **Ticketmaster** (☎ 816/931–3330) for tickets to main events.

Spectator Sports

Baseball: Kansas City Royals (✉ Kauffman Stadium, Truman Sports Complex, I–70 and Blue Ridge Cutoff, ☎ 816/921–8000). **Football: Kansas City Chiefs** (✉ Arrowhead Stadium, Truman Sports Complex, ☎ 816/924–9400). **Ice Hockey: Kansas City Blades** (✉ Kemper Arena, 1800 Gennessee, ☎ 816/842–5233). **Indoor soccer: Kansas City Attack** (✉ Kemper Arena, 1800 Gennessee, ☎ 816/474–2255). **Outdoor soccer: Kansas City Wizards** (✉ Arrowhead Stadium, Truman Sports Complex, ☎ 816/920–9300).

Shopping

Kansas City's finest shopping is at **Country Club Plaza,** and a number of specialty shops and boutiques are clustered in **Westport, Crown Center,** and the **River Market** (for all, ☞ Exploring Kansas City, *above*). **Parkville,** an historic river town just 10 minutes north of downtown Kansas City, offers antiques, crafts, and one of the finest quilt shops in the country.

THE OZARKS

The Ozark hill region of southern Missouri is famed for its wooded mountaintops; clear, spring-fed streams; and water playgrounds, the Lake of the Ozarks and Table Rock Lake. Branson, the nation's second country-music capital after Nashville, attracts 7 million visitors a year to its star-studded theaters.

Visitor Information

Branson: Branson Lakes Area Chamber of Commerce (✉ Box 1897, 65616, ☎ 417/334–4136 or 800/214–3661). **Greater Lake of the Ozarks:** Convention and Visitors Bureau (✉ Box 1498, Osage Beach 65065, ☎ 573/348–1599 or 800/386–5253). **Springfield:** Convention and Visitors Bureau and Tourist Information Center (✉ 3315 E. Battlefield Rd., 65804-4048, ☎ 417/881–5300 or 800/678–8766). **Table Rock Lake/Kimberling City Area:** Chamber of Commerce (✉ Box 495, Kimberling City 65686, ☎ 417/739–2564).

Arriving and Departing

By Car

Many of the towns and attractions in this vast region can be reached from I–44, which cuts diagonally across the state from St. Louis to Springfield, or south out of Kansas City on U.S. 71. Branson lies about 40 mi south of Springfield on U.S. 65. The Lake of the Ozarks is centrally located between St. Louis and Kansas City.

Exploring the Ozarks

Central Missouri's **Lake of the Ozarks,** formed by the damming of the Osage River in 1931, is the state's largest lake, with 1,300 mi of shoreline sprawling over 58,000 acres. In summer crowds of vacationing families descend on the numerous resorts, motels, and tourist attractions; better times to visit may be spring, when the dogwoods are in bloom, and fall, when the wooded hills come alive with color.

Lake of the Ozarks State Park (☞ National and State Parks, *above*), just south of Osage Beach, encompasses 90 mi of shoreline and offers hiking trails, boating, fishing, and other diversions, plus tours of **Ozark Caverns** (☎ 573/346–2500; ☞ $4); it's open April through October.

You're deep in the country's Bible Belt when you reach **Springfield** (off I–44), home to two Bible colleges and a theological seminary and near several sights and cultural events with religious themes. For many people, however, the first stop in Springfield has little to do with religion. The enormous **Bass Pro Shops Outdoor World** (⊠ 1935 S. Campbell Ave., ☎ 417/887–7334), dubbed the "Sportsman's Disney World," has cascading waterfalls, a wildlife-trophy collection, a boat showroom, and sporting-goods shops.

The visitor center at **Wilson's Creek National Battlefield** (⊠ 6424 W. Farm Rd. 182, Republic 65738, ☎ 417/732–2662; ☞ $2), southwest of Springfield, documents the first major Civil War battle fought west of the Mississippi. In Mansfield, roughly 40 mi east of Springfield on U.S. 60, is the **Laura Ingalls Wilder Home** (⊠ Rte. A, ☎ 417/924–3626; ☞ $6), a National Historic Landmark, where the much-loved children's author wrote her *Little House* books; it's open March through October. About 70 mi

★ west of Springfield near the town of Diamond is the **George Washington Carver National Monument** (⊠ 5646 Carver Rd., ☎ 417/325–4151, ☞ free), honoring the birthplace of the famous black botanist and agronomist. North of the Carver Monument, in Carthage, you can tour the **Precious Moments Chapel** (⊠ 4321 Chapel Rd., ☎ 800/543–7975; ☞ donations accepted), which features 30 stained-glass windows and 52 colorful murals designed by Sam Butcher, creator of the Precious Moments dolls and figurines. A gift shop on the premises sells these popular items.

About 40 mi south of Springfield on U.S. 65 is **Lake Taneycomo,** the first of Missouri's man-made lakes. Its larger, more developed neighbor, **Table Rock State Park** (⊠ Branson, ☎ 417/334–4704), offers boating, picnicking, and plenty of motels, resorts, and commercial campgrounds. **Kimberling City** is the main resort town serving Lake Taneycomo and Table Rock.

With more than a dozen glittering music halls (☞ Nightlife and the Arts, *below*), **Branson** rivals Nashville as a country-music mecca. Most growth has occurred along Route 76, already crowded with miniature-golf courses, bumper-car concessions, souvenir and hillbilly-crafts shops, motels, and resorts.

♻ **White Water** (⊠ Rte. 76, Branson, ☎ 417/334–7488; ☞ $24.45) is the place for water-soaked rides and activities.

★ ♻ At **Silver Dollar City** (⊠ Rte. 76, ☎ 800/952–6626, ☞ $32.85, $22.25 children under 18), just west of Branson, Ozark artisans demonstrate traditional crafts, and rides and music shows keep all amused. Also west of Branson is the **Shepherd of the Hills Homestead and Outdoor Theatre,** a working pioneer homestead, with a gristmill, a sawmill, and smith and wheelwright shops. The inspirational drama *Shepherd of the Hills* is performed here. ⊠ *Rte. 76,* ☎ *417/334–4191.* 🖭 *$19. Closed Jan.–Apr.*

Dining and Lodging

For information on B&Bs in this area, contact the **Ozark Mountain Country Bed and Breakfast** reservation service (⊠ Box 295, Branson 65615, ☎ 417/334–4720 or 800/695–1546).

Branson Area

$$$ ★ ✕ **Candlestick Inn.** Fresh seafood and prime rib rubbed in garlic and seared on the grill are the specialties at this elegant restaurant overlooking Lake Taneycomo. ⊠ *Rte. 76E, Branson,* ☎ *417/334–3633. AE, D, MC, V.*

$–$$$ 🏨 **Kimberling Inn Resort and Conference Center.** This small resort motel on Table Rock Lake is walking distance from Kimberling City Shopping Village's crafts shops and restaurants. ⊠ *Box 159B, Kimberling City 65686,* ☎ *417/739–4311 or 800/833–5551. 120 rooms, 120 condos. 4 restaurants, 4 pools, tennis. AE, D, DC, MC, V.* 🐾

$ 🏨 **Dogwood Inn.** This modern hotel is not right on Lake Taneycomo, but you can see the lake from some rooms. Service is friendly, and the location is convenient to area attractions. ⊠ *1420 Rte. 76W (Box 6288), Branson 65616,* ☎ *417/334–5101,* FAX *417/334–0789. 220 rooms. Restaurant, pool. AE, D, DC, MC, V.*

Lake of the Ozarks

$$$ ✕ **Blue Heron.** Enjoy cocktails poolside before moving to the lake-view dining room at this seasonal restaurant. Steak and seafood are the mainstays. ⊠ *Business Rte. 54 and Rte. HH, Osage Beach,* ☎ *573/365–4646. Reservations not accepted. AE, D, MC, V. Closed Dec.–Mar. and Sun. and Mon. No lunch.*

$$$$ ★ ✕🏨 **Lodge of the Four Seasons.** Golf is the draw here (45 holes). There's also fine dining in the Toledo Room. Rates drop dramatically in winter, but you'll still get the pampering of a first-class resort. ⊠ *Box 215, Lake Ozark 65049,* ☎ *573/365–3000 or 800/843–5253,* FAX *573/365–8525. 311 rooms. 3 restaurants, 2 pools, tennis. AE, D, DC, MC, V.* 🐾

$$$ ★ ✕🏨 **Marriott's Tan-Tar-A Resort and Golf Club.** One of the top choices in the region for both vacations and business meetings, the Tan-Tar-A offers two golf courses and fine dining in the Windrose Restaurant. ⊠ *Rte. KK, Osage Beach 65065,* ☎ *573/348–3131 or 800/826–8272,* FAX *573/348–3206. 938 rooms. 5 restaurants, 2 pools, golf, tennis, exercise room. AE, D, DC, MC, V.* 🐾

$$$ 🏨 **Holiday Inn Resort and Conference Center.** You don't have lake access, but for a slightly higher rate you can have a lake view. ⊠ *Business Rte. 54 (Box 1930), Lake Ozark 65049,* ☎ *573/365–2334 or 800/532–3575,* FAX *573/365–6887. 217 rooms. Restaurant, 2 pools, exercise room. AE, D, DC, MC, V. BP.* 🐾

Springfield

$$–$$$ ✕ **Hemingway's Blue Water Cafe.** This restaurant, part of the Bass Pro Shops Outdoor World (☞ Exploring the Ozarks, *above*), serves seafood, steak, pasta, and poultry. ⊠ *1935 S. Campbell Ave.,* ☎ *417/887–3388. AE, D, MC, V.*

$$ 🏨 **Clarion Inn.** Rooms at this hotel in the southern end of town are clean and comfortable. ⊠ *3333 S. Glenstone Ave., 65804,* ☎ *417/883–6550,* FAX *417/883–5720. 200 rooms. Restaurant, pool. AE, D, DC, MC, V.* 🐾

$$ 🏨 **University Plaza Holiday Inn.** Boasting the largest conference center in Missouri, this hotel has guest rooms arranged around a nine-story atrium. ⊠ *333 John Q. Hammons Pkwy., 65806,* ☎ *417/864–7333,* FAX *417/831–5893. 271 rooms. 2 restaurants, 2 pools, tennis, exercise room. AE, D, DC, MC, V.* 🐾

Motels

🏨 **EconoLodge** (⊠ 2808 N. Kansas Expressway, Springfield 65803, ☎ 417/869–5600), 83 rooms; *$.*

🏨 **Red Roof Inn** (⊠ 2655 N. Glenstone Ave., Springfield 65803, ☎ 417/831–2100), 112 rooms; *$.*

Campgrounds

Missouri Association of RV Parks and Campgrounds (⊠ 3020 S. National Ave., No. D149, Springfield 65804). In the Lake of the Ozarks area: ⚠️ **Deer Valley Park and Campground** (⊠ Sunrise Beach, ☎ 573/374–5277; closed mid-Oct.–mid-Apr.); ⚠️ **Lake of the Ozarks State Park** (☞ Exploring the Ozarks, *above*). **In the Branson area:** ⚠️ **Blue Mountain Campground** (⊠ Branson, ☎ 800/779–2114); ⚠️ **Port of Kimberling Marina and Campground** (⊠ Kimberling City, ☎ 417/739–5377); ⚠️ **Silver Dollar City Campground** (⊠ Branson, ☎ 417/338–8189 or 800/477–5164; closed Oct.–Apr.).

Nightlife and the Arts

Music theaters in Branson include the **Andy Williams Moon River Theater** (⊠ 2500 W. Hwy. 76, ☎ 417/334–4500 or 800/666–6094), **Baldknobbers Hillbilly Jamboree Show** (⊠ 2635 W. Hwy. 76, ☎ 417/334–4528), **Grand Palace** (⊠ 2700 W. Hwy. 76, ☎ 417/336–1220), **Jim Stafford Theater** (⊠ 1340 W. Hwy. 76, ☎ 417/335–8080), **Mel Tillis Theater** (⊠ 2527 State Hwy. 248, ☎ 417/335–6635), **Mickey Gilley's Family Theater** (⊠ 3455 W. Hwy. 76, ☎ 417/334–3210), **Presley's Country Music Jubilee** (⊠ 2920 76 Country Blvd., ☎ 417/334–4874), **Hughes' Brothers Celebrity Theater** (⊠ 3425 W. Hwy. 76, ☎ 417/334–0076), **Shoji Tabuchi Show** (⊠ 3260 Shepherd of the Hills Expressway, ☎ 417/334–7469), and **Lawrence Welk Champagne Theatre** (⊠ 1984 U.S. 165, ☎ 800/505–9355). Contact the Branson Lakes Area Chamber of Commerce (☞ Visitor Information, *above*) for a complete list.

Outdoor Activities and Sports

Canoeing

The Ozarks have some of the finest streams in the country, including the **Current** and **Jacks Fork rivers,** two waterways protected as the **Ozark National Scenic Riverways** (☞ National and State Parks, *above*). For a list of canoeing outfitters contact the Missouri Division of Tourism (☞ Statewide Visitor Information, *above*).

Fishing

Bull Shoals Lake, Lake Taneycomo, and **Table Rock Lake** all offer excellent fishing for bass, catfish, trout, and other fish. Other good spots include **Lake of the Ozarks** and **Truman Lake.** Contact the **Missouri Department of Conservation** (⊠ Box 180, Jefferson City 65102, ☎ 573/751–4115) for information on permits, costs, and seasons.

Hiking and Backpacking

The partially completed **Ozark Trail** passes through national and state forest and parkland as well as private property. For information and maps contact the **Missouri Department of Natural Resources** (⊠ Division of State Parks, 101 Adams St., Jefferson City 65101, ☎ 573/751–2479 or 800/334–6946) or individual state parks (☞ National and State Parks, *above*).

Shopping

Osage Village (⊠ U.S. 54, Osage Beach, ☎ 573/348–2065) is a major factory-outlet mall with about 115 stores, restaurants, and theaters. For crafts and antiques in Osage Beach, try the **Poverty Flats Shopping**

Mall (⊠ U.S. 54, ☎ 573/348–5101). Crafts and souvenir shops dominate Highway 76 in Branson, but for more consolidated shopping, try the 90 stores at the **Factory Merchants Outlet Mall** (☎ 417/335–6686).

ELSEWHERE IN MISSOURI

Hannibal

Visitor Information
Hannibal Visitors and Convention Bureau (⊠ 505 3rd St., 63401, ☎ 573/221–2477).

Arriving and Departing
Hannibal is about two hours north of St. Louis on U.S. 61.

What to See and Do
Hannibal is Mark Twain country. The author's boyhood home is preserved at the **Mark Twain Home and Museum** (⊠ 208 Hill St., ☎ 573/221–9010; ⊡ $6). The **Mark Twain Cave** (⊠ Rte. 79, ☎ 573/221–1656; ⊡ $10) is where Tom Sawyer and Becky Thatcher got lost in Twain's classic *Adventures of Tom Sawyer.*

Dining
$$ ✕ **Lula Belle's Cafe and Bed & Breakfast.** Listed on the National Register of Historic Places, this former bordello attracts a more family-minded clientele today for a wide selection of soups and salads for lunch, shrimp and prime rib for dinner. ⊠ *111 Bird St., ☎ 573/221–6662 or 800/882–4890. AE, D, MC, V. Closed Sun.*

Ste. Genevieve

Arriving and Departing
Ste. Genevieve is about one hour south of St. Louis on I–55.

What to See and Do
Numerous historic homes in this small river town—the oldest permanent settlement in Missouri—include examples of 18th-century French-Creole architecture, characterized by vertical log construction. The **Great River Road Interpretive Center** (⊠ 66 S. Main St., 63670, ☎ 573/883–7097 or 800/373–7007) houses the visitor center and sells tickets for the ferryboat ride across the Mississippi River to Illinois.

Lodging
$$–$$$ ▣ **The Southern Hotel.** Housed in a 1790 Federal-style brick building, this inn invites you to relax in historic gardens or shoot a game of pool on the 1870 pool table. Some guest rooms have fireplaces. ⊠ *146 S. 3rd St., 63670, ☎ 573/883–3493 or 800/275–1412. 8 rooms. D, MC, V.*✺

$–$$ ▣ **Main Street Inn.** One of the many inns and restaurants in the National Historic District, this 1883 home is fully furnished with period antiques and offers a pleasant view of the Mississippi River. Complimentary wine is served in the evening. ⊠ *221 N. Main St., 63670, ☎ 573/883–9199 or 800/918–9199. 8 rooms. AE, D, MC, V. BP.*✺

St. Joseph

Visitor Information
St. Joseph Convention and Visitors Bureau (⊠ Box 445, 109 S. 4th St., 64502, ☎ 816/233–6688 or 800/785–0360).

Arriving and Departing
St. Joseph is about one hour north of Kansas City on I–29.

What to See and Do

During the short experiment called the Pony Express, riders set out on the 2,000-mi trip to Sacramento, California, from what is now St.

★ Joseph's **Pony Express National Memorial** (✉ 914 Penn St., ☎ 816/ 279–5059; ⌨ $3). The **Jesse James Home** (✉ 12th and Penn Sts., ☎ 816/232–8206; ⌨ $3.50) is where a member of James's own gang shot and killed the notorious outlaw in pursuit of reward money. You can still see a bullet hole in the wall.

Dining

$ ✕ **Hoof and Horn.** In business since 1898, this is the oldest restaurant in St. Joseph and serves some of the best prime rib and steak in the Midwest. The decor in the rustic building recalls the days when cattle drivers would walk in fresh from the trail. ✉ *429 Illinois Ave.,* ☎ *816/ 238–0742. AE, DC, MC, V. Closed Sun.*

$ ✕ **Jerre Anne's Cafeteria and Bakery.** Although this restaurant is small and often crowded, locals return for the heaping portions of meat loaf, mashed potatoes, and homemade pie. ✉ *2640 Mitchell St.,* ☎ *816/ 232–6585. No credit cards. Closed Sun. and Mon.*

MONTANA

Updated by
Kristin Rodine

Capital	Helena
Population	879,400
Motto	Oro y Plata (Gold and Silver)
State Bird	Western meadowlark
State Flower	Bitterroot
Postal Abbreviation	MT

Statewide Visitor Information

Travel Montana (✉ Dept. of Commerce, 1424 9th Ave., Helena 59620, ☎ 406/444–2654 or 800/847–4868).

Scenic Drives

Beartooth Highway, the stretch of U.S. 212 from Red Lodge to Yellowstone National Park, is a slow but spectacular 68-mi route over a 10,947-ft mountain pass; it's generally open from mid-June to mid-October. For 187 mi between Helena and East Glacier, **I–15, U.S. 287,** and **U.S. 89** parallel the Rocky Mountain Front as it rises from the eastern plains. The 50-mi-long **Going-to-the-Sun Road** runs through Glacier National Park (☞ Exploring the Flathead and Western Montana, *below*).

National and State Parks

Millions of acres of Big Sky Country—Montana's nickname for its vast wide-open spaces—are public reserves, including national parks, monuments, and recreation areas. There are eight national wildlife refuges, 10 national forests, and 15 wilderness areas. Yellowstone National Park is also a logical part of a Montana itinerary.

National Parks

Glacier National Park (☞ Exploring the Flathead and Western Montana, *below*) crowns the Continental Divide on the Montana-Canada border. **Little Bighorn Battlefield National Monument** (☞ Bighorn Country, *below*) preserves the battle site in southeastern Montana.

State Parks

The **Montana Department of Fish, Wildlife and Parks** (✉ 1420 E. 6th Ave., Helena 59620, ☎ 406/444–2535) manages 41 state parks, including **Bannack State Park,** west of Dillon, a ghost town of homes, saloons, and a gallows; **Missouri Headwaters State Park,** near Three Forks, where Lewis and Clark came upon the confluence of the three rivers that form the Missouri; and **Makoshika State Park,** northeast of Billings near Glendive, which features dramatic badlands formations and dinosaur fossils.

THE FLATHEAD AND WESTERN MONTANA

The northwestern, or Flathead, region is a destination resort area, with such attractions as Flathead Lake and Glacier National Park. In western Montana south of the Flathead, forests, lakes, and meadows mix with ranch country and small valley towns.

Visitor Information

Glacier Country: Regional Tourism Commission (✉ Box 1035, Bigfork 59911, ☎ 406/837–6211 or 800/338–5072).

Arriving and Departing

By Bus
Intermountain Bus Co. (☎ 406/755–4011) stops in Kalispell. **Greyhound** (☎ 800/231–2222) serves Missoula.

By Car
I–90 and U.S. 93 pass through Missoula. U.S. 93 and Route 35 lead off I–90 to Kalispell, in the Flathead; from there U.S. 2 leads to Glacier National Park. From Great Falls take I–15 and then U.S. 89 to St. Mary, at the east entrance to Glacier's Going-to-the-Sun Road, which is open from mid-June through September, depending on snowfall. In winter, skirt along the southern edge of the park by taking U.S. 2 west from U.S. 89 at Browning.

By Plane
Glacier Park International Airport (☎ 406/257–5994), northeast of Kalispell, and **Missoula International Airport** (☎ 406/728–4381) are served by major domestic airlines, including Delta and Northwest.

By Train
Amtrak (☎ 800/872–7245) stops in Essex, Whitefish, West Glacier, and East Glacier.

Exploring the Flathead and Western Montana

The Flathead
The relatively close proximity of Flathead's towns is atypical of Montana. Bigfork, Kalispell, and Whitefish make good touring bases.

★ **Glacier National Park** (✉ West Glacier 59936, ☎ 406/888–7800, ☞ $10 per vehicle for 7 days) preserves more than a million spectacular acres of peaks, waterfalls, lakes, and wildlife best seen from a hiking trail (☞ Outdoor Activities and Sports, *below*) or on horseback. Mountain goats and bighorn sheep often can be seen ambling along the 52-mi **Going-to-the-Sun Road**, the park's only through road. The narrow, winding roadway is a cliff-hanger and unsuitable for oversize vehicles. A **shuttle service** and guided **bus tours** (☎ 602/207–6000) leave from either end. **Sun Tours** (☎ 800/786–9220) runs trips highlighting Blackfeet Indian culture from East Glacier. Most of the park, including this road, is closed to vehicles in winter.

South of Kalispell is **Flathead Lake,** the largest freshwater lake west of the Mississippi. An 85-mi loop drive around it takes in cherry orchards, parks, sweeping views of the Mission and Swan ranges, and the arts community of **Bigfork,** which has a summer repertory theater company and rows of galleries and shops along Electric Avenue.

Western Montana
Scenic, outdoorsy **Missoula**, 60 mi south of Kalispell via U.S. 93, is home to the **University of Montana** (☎ 406/243–5874 to arrange a free guided tour) and to a thriving community of writers and artists. The Clark Fork, Bitterroot, and Blackfoot rivers converge here—it's not unusual to see anglers casting just downstream of the movie theater. The **Missoula Museum of the Arts** (✉ 335 N. Pattee St., ☎ 406/728–0447; ☞ $2; free on Tues.) exhibits contemporary works. Hand-carved steeds circle 'round **A Carousel for Missoula** (☎ 406/549–8382; ☞ $1) in downtown Caras Park, along the Clark Fork River.

The **Rocky Mountain Elk Foundation Wildlife Visitor Center** (✉ 2291 W. Broadway, ☎ 406/523–4545 or 800/225–5355; ☞ donations accepted) offers engaging natural history, art, and wildlife displays. At **Smokejumper Visitor Center** (✉ W. Broadway/Old Hwy. 10, ☎ 406/

Glacier National Park

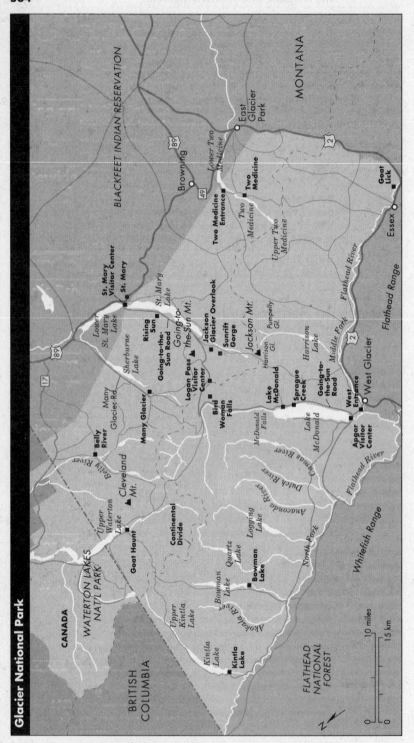

CANADA

BRITISH COLUMBIA

WATERTON LAKES NATL PARK

BLACKFEET INDIAN RESERVATION

MONTANA

Browning

East Glacier Park

Lower Two Medicine

Two Medicine

Two Medicine Entrance

Two Medicine

Upper Two Medicine

Goat Lick

Essex

St. Mary Visitor Center

St. Mary

St. Mary Lake

Lower St. Mary Lake

Rising Sun

Sherburne Lake

Going-to-the-Sun Road

Going-to-the-Sun Mt.

Jackson Glacier Overlook

Sunrift Gorge

Jackson Mt.

Pumpelly Gl.

Flathead River

Flathead Range

Many Glacier Rd.

Many Glacier

Logan Pass Visitor Center

Bird Woman Falls

Harrison Gl.

Harrison Lake

Lake McDonald

Sprague Creek

Going-to-the-Sun Road

West Entrance

West Glacier

Middle Fork

Belly River

Belly River

Cleveland Mt.

Upper Waterton Lake

Goat Haunt

Continental Divide

McDonald Falls

Lake McDonald

Camas River

Dutch River

Anaconda River

Logging Lake

North Fork

Apgar Visitor Center

Flathead River

Whitefish Range

Quartz Lake

Bowman Lake

Bowman Lake

Akokala River

Upper Kintla Lake

Kintla Lake

Kintla Lake

FLATHEAD NATIONAL FOREST

10 miles

15 km

0

N

329–4934; ✉ donations accepted), firefighter-guides conduct summer tours peppered with firsthand accounts of forest fires and smoke jumping. View bison, elk, deer, antelope, and bighorn sheep through your
★ car window at the **National Bison Range** (☎ 406/644–2211, ✉ $4 per vehicle) at Moiese, north of Missoula en route to the Flathead. A visitor center explains the history, habits, and habitat of bison.

East of Missoula, Route 200 leads to **Seeley-Swan Valley,** densely forested and dotted with easily accessed lakes. View loons and other waterfowl from turnouts along the scenic 18-mi **Clearwater Chain-of-Lakes** (⊠ Rte. 83, from Salmon Lake to Rainy Lake).

South of Missoula on U.S. 93, **Bitterroot Valley** stretches between the Sapphire Mountains and the Bitterroots, one of the northern Rockies' most rugged ranges. Jesuit missionaries founded **St. Mary's Mission** (☎ 406/777–5734; ✉ $3) in 1841 at Stevensville. Guided tours are offered April through October.

Dining and Lodging

Reserve well in advance for Glacier and for Flathead's summer and ski seasons.

Bigfork

$-$$ ✕ **Swan River Cafe and Dinner House.** This relaxed yet elegant eatery serves prime rib and seafood inside or on the terrace overlooking Bigfork Bay. The Sunday brunch and dinner buffets attract throngs of hungry locals. ⊠ 360 Grand Ave., Bigfork, ☎ 406/837–2220. AE, D, MC, V.

$$ ▥ **O'Duach'ain Country Inn Bed & Breakfast.** In a quiet lodgepole-pine
★ forest near Flathead Lake and the Swan River, this log house and neighboring cabin are filled with Old West antiques and Navajo rugs; two stone fireplaces warm the main house. Hiking opportunities abound, and the breakfasts are both gourmet and comforting. ⊠ 675 Ferndale Dr., 59911, ☎ 406/837–6851, ℻ 406/837–0778. 5 rooms, 4 with bath. AE, MC, V. BP. ☙

Glacier National Park

Glacier Park, Inc. runs Glacier's **grand lodges,** which were built by the Great Northern Railroad at the turn of the 20th century. All three offer outdoor activities such as horseback riding, hiking, and fishing. Rooms are rustic—no TVs—but comfortable. The hotels are open in summer only; make reservations far in advance by calling the Glacier Park corporate office in Arizona. ⊠ Greyhound Tower, Station 1210, Phoenix, AZ 85077, ☎ 602/207–6000. ☙

$$$-$$$$ ✕▥ **Glacier Park Lodge.** On the east side of the park across from the Amtrak station, this beautiful 1913 hotel is constructed of giant timbers. 154 rooms. Restaurant, pool, golf. D, MC, V. Closed mid-Sept.–mid-May.

$$-$$$ ✕▥ **Many Glacier Hotel.** On the east side of the park, 12 mi west of Babb, the park's largest lodge has commanding views of Swiftcurrent Lake and the mountains. The nearby Swiftcurrent Motor Inn offers 62 standard motel rooms and 26 cottages for about half the price of lodge rooms. 211 rooms in lodge. Restaurant. D, MC, V. Closed mid-Sept.–mid-May.

$$ ✕▥ **Lake McDonald Lodge.** This former hunting refuge near West Glacier has four-person cabins, plus motel units and a lodge on the lake. Boating, fishing, and horseback riding are prime activities. 100 rooms. Restaurant. D, MC, V. Closed mid-Sept.–mid-May.

Hot Springs

$$ ✕▥ **Fairmont Hot Springs.** This family-friendly resort offers naturally heated indoor and outdoor pools, a water slide, a petting zoo, and 18

holes of golf in a beautiful setting. ⊠ *1500 Fairmont Rd., Gregson 59711,* ☎ *406/797–3241 or 800/332–3272,* 𝖥𝖠𝖷 *406/797–3337. 140 rooms. Restaurant, 4 pools, massage, golf, tennis, ski area. AE, D, MC, V.* ✑

$–$$ ✕🖈 **Lost Trail Hot Springs Resort.** Hot springs feed the swimming pool and a hot tub at this resort 90 mi south of Missoula in the Bitterroot National Forest. RV spaces are available. ⊠ *8321 Hwy. 93 S, Box 8321, Sula 59871,* ☎ *406/821–3574,* 𝖥𝖠𝖷 *406/821–4012 or 800/825–3574. 8 rooms, 9 cabins. Restaurant, pool, hot tub. AE, D, MC, V.* ✑

Missoula

$–$$ ✕ **Guy's Lolo Creek Steak House.** This quintessentially Montana restau-
★   rant in a massive log structure 8 mi south of Missoula feels like a hunting lodge, complete with stuffed wildlife on the walls. Guy's signature
sirloins are cooked over an open-pit barbecue and come in three sizes.
Chicken, pork, and seafood offerings round out the menu. Portions
are hearty and the fare is fresh, straightforward, and well prepared.
⊠ *6600 U.S. 12W, Lolo,* ☎ *406/273–2622. AE, D, MC, V.*

$ ✕ **The Shack.** Innovative omelets and hash browns with herb-scented
★   gravy draw a crowd of locals to this attractive eatery at breakfast time;
creative lunch and dinner specials are served throughout the rest of the
day. ⊠ *222 W. Main St.,* ☎ *406/549–9903. MC, V.*

$$–$$$ 🖈 **Goldsmith's Inn.** Built in 1911 as the residence of the University of
Montana's first president, this prairie-style redbrick B&B has big white
eaves and a huge porch. It's on the shore of the Clark Fork River, near
the university campus. Beautiful rooms have hardwood floors, period
furniture, and hand-painted tiles in the private bath; four rooms have
balconies with lovely views. ⊠ *809 E. Front St., 59801,* ☎ *406/721–
6732. 7 rooms. AE, D, MC, V. BP.* ✑

Ranches

Montana's guest ranches range from working ranches to deluxe spreads
with nary a cow in sight; check Travel Montana's directory (☞
Statewide Visitor Information, *above*). Those listed throughout this chap-
ter are categorized as either $$ (less than $1,000 per person per week),
$$$ ($1,000–$1,900 per person per week), or $$$$ (more than $1,900
per person based on double occupancy). Meals and recreation are in-
cluded unless otherwise noted.

$$$$ ✕🖈 **Averill's Flathead Lake Lodge.** Reserve a year in advance (one-week
minimum) for this deluxe 2,000-acre dude ranch on the shores of Flat-
head Lake. Each of the rustic western lodges has a big stone fireplace.
Horseback riding, boating, tennis, basketball, volleyball, waterskiing,
and fishing are among the activities. ⊠ *Box 248, Bigfork 59911,* ☎
406/837–4391, 𝖥𝖠𝖷 *406/837–6977. 18 rooms, 20 cottages. Dining
room, pool. MC, V. Closed Oct.–May. FAP.* ✑

Motels

🖈 **Doubletree Hotel Edgewater** (⊠ 100 Madison St., Missoula 59801,
☎ 406/728–3100 or 800/237–7445, 𝖥𝖠𝖷 406/728–2530), 172 rooms;
2 restaurants, pool; *$$.*

🖈 **Aero Inn** (⊠ 1830 Hwy. 93S, Kalispell 59901, ☎ 406/755–3798,
𝖥𝖠𝖷 406/752–1304), 62 rooms; CP; *$.*

Campgrounds

Glacier National Park's 13 campgrounds are available on a first-come,
first-served basis; they often fill up before noon. Other public campgrounds are in national forests and state parks. Look for private campgrounds with RV services near towns or check Travel Montana's
directory (☞ Statewide Visitor Information, *above*).

Outdoor Activities and Sports

Biking

Glacier's Going-to-the-Sun Road is a challenging ride. **Backcountry Bicycle Tours** (⊠ Box 4029, Bozeman 59772, ☎ 406/586–3556) organizes five- to seven-day trips in Glacier National Park as well as the rest of the state.

Fishing

In the Flathead Valley, fish for cutthroat and bull trout in the Flathead River or perch, whitefish, and lake trout in Flathead Lake. **Pointer Scenic Cruises** (⊠ Bigfork, ☎ 406/837–5617) operates custom charter tours on Flathead Lake. For western Montana waterways, fish the Clark Fork, Bitterroot, and Blackfoot rivers; Rock Creek, a blue-ribbon trout stream; or Seeley Lake. Local stores sell two-day fishing licenses for $10, or $45 for the season.

Golf

Eagle Bend Golf Club (⊠ Box 960, Bigfork 59911, ☎ 406/837–7300 or 800/255–5641) is a 27-hole championship course with splendid views.

Hiking and Backpacking

Glacier National Park has 730 mi of trails. **Glacier Wilderness Guides** (⊠ Box 535, West Glacier 59936, ☎ 406/888–5466 or 800/521–7238) leads backcountry trips. The **Great Bear, Bob Marshall,** and **Scapegoat wilderness areas** (⊠ Flathead National Forest, 1935 3rd Ave. E, Kalispell 59901, ☎ 406/755–5401) constitute a million-acre refuge along the Continental Divide. The **Jewel Basin Hiking Area,** 13 mi east of Bigfork off Route 83, is a short, minimal-ascent trail to high-country lakes and superb views. For information on backcountry hiking, contact the **U.S. Forest Service Northern Region Office** (⊠ 2000 E. Broadway Ave., Missoula 59807, ☎ 406/329–3511).

Rafting and Canoeing

Rafting outfitters include **Glacier Raft Co.** (⊠ Box 218M, West Glacier 59936, ☎ 406/888–5454 or 800/332–9995). Canoes take the calmer waters of Glacier Park's Lake McDonald. For canoe rentals try **Glacier Park Boat Company** (⊠ Box 5262, Kalispell 59903, ☎ 406/888–5727 May–Sept.; 406/752–5488 Oct.–Apr.).

Most stretches of the Clark Fork and Bitterroot can be run by raft or canoe; the Blackfoot is more difficult. A good outfitter is **Western Waters** (⊠ 5455 Keil Loop, Missoula, ☎ 406/543–3203). Northeast of Missoula near Seeley Lake, the **Clearwater River Canoe Trail** follows an easy 4-mi stretch.

Water Sports

Flathead Lake supports a large sailing community, countless water-skiers and windsurfers, and cruises on the **Port Polson Princess** (⊠ Polson, ☎ 406/883–2448 or 800/882–6363).

Ski Areas

For **ski reports** call ☎ 406/444–2654 or 800/847–4868.

Cross-Country

Trails are found at Glacier National Park, in the Flathead National Forest, and in Lolo National Forest near Missoula. On Glacier's southern border, the **Izaak Walton Inn** (⊠ U.S. 2, Essex 59916, ☎ 406/888–5700, FAX 406/888–5200) has 18 mi of groomed trails along with food and lodging.

Downhill

Big Mountain (⊠ Box 1400, Whitefish 59937, ☎ 406/862–1900 or 800/858–5439) has 63 runs, 9 lifts, and a 2,300-ft vertical drop.

SOUTHWESTERN MONTANA

Montana's pioneer history began here, and evidence of the early mining frontier—from rough-and-tumble camps to the mansions of the magnates—is inescapable. In the high country north and west of Yellowstone National Park you'll find world-class fishing and some of the state's best ski terrain.

Visitor Information

Gold West Country: Regional Tourism Commission (⊠ 1155 Main St., Deer Lodge 59722, ☎ 406/846–1943 or 800/879–1159). **Yellowstone Country:** Regional Tourism Commission (⊠ Box 1490, West Yellowstone 59758, ☎ 406/646–4383 or 800/736–5276).

Arriving and Departing

By Bus

Intermountain Bus Co. (☎ 406/442–5860, 406/723–3287, 406/442–5860, or 406/723–3287) stops in Helena and Butte. **Greyhound** serves Bozeman (☎ 800/231–2222). In summer **Karst Stages** (☎ 800/332–0504) runs between Bozeman, Livingston, and Yellowstone.

By Car

I–15 passes through Helena. Use I–90 for Butte and Bozeman. U.S. 191, 89, 287, and 212 link the region with Yellowstone.

By Plane

Helena Regional Airport (☎ 406/442–2821), Bozeman's **Gallatin Field Airport** (☎ 406/388–6632), and Butte's **Bert Mooney Airport** (☎ 406/494–3771) are served by major domestic airlines.

Exploring Southwestern Montana

The humble mining origins of **Helena,** Montana's capital, are visible in its earliest commercial district, **Reeder's Alley.** By 1888, the "Queen City of the Rockies" had 50 resident millionaires and a legacy of major gold rushes. The mansions on the **West Side** and commercial buildings on the main street, **Last Chance Gulch,** preserve the era's opulence.

Helena's vibrant arts scene includes dramatic performances and movies in the two auditoriums within the **Myrna Loy Theater** (⊠ 15 N. Ewing St., ☎ 406/443–0287). Free tours are conducted at the **Archie Bray Foundation** (⊠ 2915 Country Club Ave., ☎ 406/443–3502), a nationally known center for ceramic arts. The **Montana Historical Society Museum** (⊠ 225 N. Roberts St., ☎ 406/444–2694; ⌑ donations accepted) showcases valuable collections of western paintings and historic memorabilia across from the state capitol. In front of the museum, the **Last Chancer** automotive tour train (☎ 406/442–1023; ⌑ $5) departs on the hour in summer.

The millionaires may have resided in Helena, but the miners lived in **Butte,** a tough, wily town with a rich ethnic mix. The **Berkeley Pit,** a mile-wide open-pit copper mine, sits at the edge of the **Butte National Historic District,** a downtown area of ornate buildings with an Old West feel. Self-guided tour brochures are available at the Chamber of Commerce (⊠ 1000 George St., ☎ 406/723–3177 or 800/735–6814.) On the northern edge of Deer Lodge, 24 mi north of Butte, the **Grant-Kohrs**

Ranch National Historic Site (✉ 316 Main St., ☎ 406/846–2070; 🎫 $2) preserves the home and outbuildings of a 19th-century ranch, still worked by cowboys and draft horses.

★ Montana's oldest state park, **Lewis and Clark Caverns** (✉ Rte. 2, off I–90, ☎ 406/287–3032; 🎫 $3 entry, $7 tour) lies near Whitehall, 40 mi east of Butte. Two-hour tours lead through narrow passages and vaulted chambers past colorful, intriguingly varied limestone formations. The park is closed from mid-October through April.

Bozeman, 50 mi east of Butte on I–90, is a cowboy town, a regional trade center, and a place crazy for food, art, and the outdoors. At Montana
★ ⬤ State University, the **Museum of the Rockies** (✉ 600 W. Kagy Blvd., ☎ 406/994–3466, 🎫 $6) presents paleontology exhibits, a hands-on dinosaur playroom, planetarium shows, and western art and history exhibits.

South of town, U.S. 191 follows the Gallatin River to West Yellowstone, the gateway to **Yellowstone National Park** (☞ Wyoming). On the U.S. 89 approach to Yellowstone, **Livingston**—former home of Calamity Jane and now a haven for hiking, fishing, and other outdoor activities—sits at the head of Paradise Valley, which is bisected by the Yellowstone River. U.S. 212, the most spectacular route to Yellowstone, passes through **Red Lodge.** The coal mines here drew immigrants from Great Britain, Italy, Finland, Yugoslavia, and other nations at the turn of the last century. The town celebrates its diverse heritage each August with a weeklong celebration.

Dining and Lodging

Big Sky

$$$–$$$$ ✕🏨 **Big Sky Ski and Summer Resort.** After enjoying a stint of golfing, fishing, horseback riding, or skiing, come back to large, bright rooms in the ski lodge or condominiums of this resort in gorgeous Gallatin Canyon, 43 mi south of Bozeman and 18 mi from Yellowstone National Park. ✉ *Box 160001, 59716,* ☎ *406/995–5000 or 800/548–4486,* 🆃🆇 *406/995–5001. 298 rooms. 24 restaurants, pool, health club. AE, D, DC, MC, V. Closed mid-Apr.–late May, early Oct.–late Nov.* ✎

Bozeman

$ ✕ **Mackenzie River Pizza Co.** Zesty gourmet pizzas are baked in a brick oven. Tasty salads, sandwiches, and bread sticks round out the offerings. ✉ *232 E. Main St.,* ☎ *406/587–0055. Reservations not accepted. AE, MC, V.*

$$ 🏨 **Voss Inn.** Afternoon tea is served in the parlor of this antiques-filled,
★ 1883 Victorian B&B in Bozeman's historic district. The lovely English garden is perfect for an afternoon stroll. ✉ *319 S. Willson Ave., 59715,* ☎ *406/587–0982,* 🆃🆇 *406/585–2964. 6 rooms. MC, V. BP.* ✎

Butte

$–$$ ✕ **Uptown Café.** Fresh seafood, steaks, and pasta are served in this informal café. ✉ *47 E. Broadway,* ☎ *406/723–4735. AE, MC, V.*

Helena

$ ✕ **The Windbag Saloon and Grill.** This historic, cherrywood-paneled saloon, once a sporting house called Big Dorothy's, was named in honor of the hot political debates you're likely to overhear while dining on burgers, quiche, salads, and sandwiches. ✉ *19 S. Last Chance Gulch,* ☎ *406/443–9669. AE, D, MC, V.*

$$ 🏨 **The Sanders.** Wilbur Fisk Sanders, frontier politician and vigilante,
★ once lived in this 1875 Queen Anne mansion, now a centrally located B&B on the National Register of Historic Places. Most furnishings are original. Breakfasts boast innovative entrées; free sherry, fruit, and cook-

ies are offered each afternoon. ⊠ *328 N. Ewing St., 59601,* ☎ *406/442–3309,* ℻ *406/443–2361. 7 rooms, 6 with bath. AE, D, MC, V. BP.*

Motels

🏨 **Jorgenson's Holiday Motel** (⊠ 1714 11th Ave., Helena 59601, ☎ 406/442–1770, 800/272–1770 in MT, ℻ 406/449–0155), 117 rooms; restaurant, pool; *$–$$.*

🏨 **War Bonnett Inn** (⊠ 2100 Cornell Ave., Butte 59701, ☎ 406/494–7800), 131 rooms; restaurant, pool, exercise room; *$–$$.*

🏨 **Bozeman Inn** (⊠ 1235 N. 7th Ave., Bozeman 59715, ☎ 406/587–3176 or 800/648–7515, ℻ 406/585–3591), 49 rooms; restaurant, pool; *$.*

Ranch

$$$ ✕🏨 **Rainbow Ranch Lodge.** Nestled in the breathtaking Gallatin River Canyon 15 minutes from Yellowstone National Park, this ranch blends blue-ribbon fishing and trail rides with gourmet meals and a hot tub that boasts its own fireplace. The 21 guest rooms feature river views and lodgepole beds with thick down comforters. Meals are not included in the lodging price. ⊠ *Box 160336, Big Sky 59716,* ☎ *406/995–4132 or 800/937–4132,* ℻ *406/995–2861. 21 rooms. Restaurant, spa. AE, D, MC, V.*✎

Campgrounds

Public campgrounds are in national forests and state parks; private ones with RV services are near towns. Check Travel Montana's directory (☞ Statewide Visitor Information, *above*). In peak season campgrounds near Yellowstone fill early in the day.

The Arts

The String Orchestra of the Rockies performs at the **Big Sky Arts Festival** at the Big Sky Ski and Summer Resort (☞ Dining and Lodging, *above*) in July. Big Timber hosts August's **Montana Cowboy Poetry Gathering** (⊠ Sweet Grass Chamber of Commerce, ☎ 406/932–5131).

Outdoor Activities and Sports

Fishing

Few trout streams rival the Missouri, Beaverhead, and Big Hole rivers; the **Complete Fly Fisher** (⊠ Wise River, ☎ 406/832–3175) provides lodging.

Livingston, Ennis, and West Yellowstone are base towns for the superb fly-fishing on the Yellowstone, Madison, and other local rivers; **Dan Bailey's Fly Shop** (⊠ 209 W. Park St., Livingston, ☎ 406/222–1673 or 800/356–4052) is a Montana legend. Licenses are sold at local stores (residents: full-season $17; nonresidents: full-season $50, or $15 for the first two days and $10 for every other two days).

Golf

Big Sky Golf Course (⊠ Rte. 64, Big Sky, ☎ 406/995–4706), 18 holes.

Hiking and Backpacking

Wilderness areas include the **Gates of the Mountains** (☎ 406/449–5201), near Helena; the **Anaconda-Pintler Wilderness** (☎ 406/496–3400), near Anaconda; the **Lee Metcalf Wilderness** (☎ 406/587–6701), near Bozeman; and **Absarokee-Beartooth Wilderness** (☎ 406/587–6701), near Livingston.

Rafting and Canoeing

The Missouri River north of Helena is easy for rafts and canoes. Bear Trap Canyon, on the Madison River near Ennis, and Yankee Jim, on the Yellowstone near Gardiner, require white-water experience or an outfitter, such as the **Yellowstone Raft Co.** (☎ 406/848–7777 or 800/858–7781).

Ski Areas

For **ski reports** call ☎ 406/444–2654 or 800/847–4868.

Cross-Country

In winter many national forest roads and trails become backcountry ski trails. **Lone Mountain** (✉ Box 160069, Big Sky 59716, ☎ 406/995–4644 or 800/514–4644, FAX 406/995–4670) has 45 mi of groomed and tracked trails, food, lodging, and even guided cross-country ski tours of nearby Yellowstone National Park.

Downhill

Big Sky Ski and Summer Resort (☞ Dining and Lodging, *above*) has 75 runs, 16 lifts, and a 4,180-ft vertical drop.

BIGHORN COUNTRY

Despite the heavy influence of cowboy culture, southeastern Montana is Native American land. The Northern Cheyenne and the Crow still inhabit this stunning country of rimrock, badlands, wide-open grass-lands, and rugged mountains. Billings is a convenient base for touring.

Visitor Information

Custer Country: Regional Tourism Commission (✉ Rte. 1, Box 1206A, Hardin 59034, ☎ 406/665–1671 or 800/346–1876).

Arriving and Departing

By Bus

Greyhound (☎ 800/231–2222) and **Rimrock Stages** (☎ 406/549–2339 or 800/255–7655) serve Billings.

By Car

The main routes between Yellowstone and Broadus, in the southeast-ern corner of the state, are I–94, I–90, U.S. 212, and Route 59.

By Plane

Major domestic airlines including Delta, Northwest, and United fly to **Logan International Airport** (☎ 406/657–8495), in Billings.

Exploring Bighorn Country

Booms in coal, oil, and gas made **Billings** Montana's largest town. Sprawled between steep-face rimrocks and the Yellowstone River, it has big-city services and a stockman's heart. Rodeos are held on weekend nights throughout the summer. The **Moss Mansion** (✉ 914 Division St., ☎ 406/256–5100; ☞ $6) is an elegantly restored 1903 red sandstone dwelling, with hourly tours. A broader view of the social history of the Yellowstone Valley can be found in the varied exhibits of the **Western Heritage Center** (✉ 2822 Montana Ave., ☎ 406/256–6809; ☞ dona-tions accepted). The **Yellowstone Art Center** (✉ 401 N. 27th Ave., ☎ 406/256–6804; ☞ $3) showcases regional art in the original county jail.

Southeast of Billings on I–94 lie the Crow and Northern Cheyenne In-dian reservations. **Crow Fair** (☎ 406/638–2601), held in Crow Agency for five days in August, draws visitors from all over the West for pa-rades, rodeos, traditional dancing, and horse races.

★ Sixty miles southeast of Billings on I–90, **Little Bighorn Battlefield Na-tional Monument** (✉ National Park Service, Crow Agency 59022, ☎ 406/638–2621, ☞ $6 per vehicle) preserves the site where in 1876 the Cheyenne and Sioux defended their homeland in a bloody battle with Lt. Col. George Armstrong Custer. You can explore the windswept prairie on your own or with a guided tour. A new interpretive display includes items from recent archaeological digs that help explain what might have happened in the battle.

Dining and Lodging

Billings

$–$$ ✕ **CJ's Restaurant.** Mesquite-grilled ribs, steaks, chicken, and seafood dominate the fare, with barbecue sauces ranging from mild to three-alarm. ⊠ 2456 Central Ave., ☎ 406/656–1400. AE, D, DC, MC, V.

$$ ✕🏨 **Radisson Northern Hotel.** Though a fire destroyed the original 1905 building in 1940, this hotel retains its American West theme, with woven rugs, bedspreads, and a gaming table. A massive fireplace dominates the lobby. The Golden Belle restaurant serves fine Continental cuisine. ⊠ Broadway at 1st Ave. N, Box 1296, 59101, ☎ 406/245–5121 or 800/333–3333, FAX 406/259–9862. 160 rooms. Restaurant. AE, D, DC, MC, V. 🐾

Motel

🏨 **Ponderosa Inn Best Western** (⊠ 2511 1st Ave. N, Billings 59101, ☎ 406/259–5511 or 800/628–9081, FAX 406/245–8004), 130 rooms; restaurant, pool, exercise room; $.

Campgrounds

Public campgrounds are in **Custer National Forest** and **Bighorn Canyon National Recreation Area**; for private campgrounds check Travel Montana's listing (☞ Statewide Visitor Information, *above*).

Outdoor Activities and Sports

Fishing

Trout anglers fish the Yellowstone River above Columbus. Walleye, bass, and warmer-water fish are found downriver. The Bighorn River below Yellowtail Dam near Pryor is trout heaven; lake species inhabit the reservoir above the dam.

Hiking and Backpacking

The northern region of the arid Pryor Mountains, south of Billings, is on the Crow Reservation; permits for backcountry travel are issued by the **Crow Tribal Council** (⊠ Crow Agency 59022, ☎ 406/638–2601). The southern Pryors are in **Custer National Forest** (⊠ 2602 1st Ave. N, Billings 59103, ☎ 406/657–6361).

Rafting and Canoeing

Canoes, rafts, and drift boats ply the Yellowstone River and the Bighorn River below Yellowtail Dam. **Elk River Outfitters** (☎ 406/252–5959) has float trips, fishing excursions, and trail rides.

Ski Area

Red Lodge Mountain (⊠ Box 750, Red Lodge 59068, ☎ 406/446–2610 or 800/444–8977), an hour southwest of Billings, has 45 runs, 8 lifts, and a 2,350-ft vertical drop.

ELSEWHERE IN MONTANA

Central and Eastern Montana

Visitor Information

Russell Country Regional Tourism Commission (⊠ Box 3166, Great Falls 59403, ☎ 406/761–5036 or 800/527–5348).

Arriving and Departing

I–15 and U.S. 89 traverse the region north–south; U.S. 2 and I–94 run east–west.

What to See and Do

Montana's heartland is open grasslands and, rising abruptly from the plains, the sheer escarpment of the Rocky Mountain Front. In **Great** ★ **Falls**, the **C. M. Russell Museum** (✉ 400 13th St. N, ☎ 406/727–8787, 🎞 $4) has a formidable collection of works by the cowboy artist, along with his original log-cabin studio. Cowboy life thrives 146 mi northeast of Billings in Miles City, which in May hosts the **Miles City Bucking Horse Sale** (☎ 406/232–0635), three days of horse trading, rodeo, and street dances.

Dining

$–$$ ✗ **Jaker's.** Arrive hungry for heaping plates of ribs, steaks, and seafood. ✉ *1500 10th Ave. S, Great Falls,* ☎ *406/727–1033. AE, D, MC, V.*

NEBRASKA

Updated by
Diana Lambdin
Meyer

Capital	Lincoln
Population	1,657,000
Motto	Equality Before the Law
State Bird	Western meadowlark
State Flower	Goldenrod
Postal Abbreviation	NE

Statewide Visitor Information

The **Nebraska Department of Economic Development, Division of Travel and Tourism** (⊠ Box 98907, Lincoln 68509-8907, ☎ 402/471–3796 or 800/228–4307) staffs 24 rest and information areas along I–80.

Scenic Drives

Route 2, from Grand Island west to Crawford, is a long, lonesome road through the Sandhills, traversing 332 mi of delicate wildflowers, tranquil rivers, and grazing cattle. The 130-mi drive north on **U.S. 83** from North Platte to Valentine affords views of the Sandhills' native short-grass prairie. **U.S. 26** from Ogallala to Scottsbluff is a 128-mi historic segment of the Oregon Trail, passing such natural landmarks as Ash Hollow; Courthouse, Jail, and Chimney Rocks; and Scotts Bluff National Monument.

National and State Parks

National Parks

Homestead National Monument (⊠ 8523 W. State Hwy. 4, 68310, ☎ 402/223–3514; ⊠ free), near Beatrice, includes walking trails and a museum that commemorate the Homestead Act of 1862 and the pioneers who settled the prairies between 1863 and 1936. **Nebraska National Forest** (⊠ Box 38, 69142, ☎ 308/533–2257; ⊠ free), at Halsey, is the largest planted forest in the country, with more than 20,000 acres of conifers.

State Parks

The **Nebraska Game and Parks Commission** (⊠ Box 30370, Lincoln 68503, ☎ 402/471–0641 or 800/826–7275) manages and provides information on all eight state parks. Among these are **Fort Robinson State Park** (☞ Exploring Northwest Nebraska, *below*); **Eugene T. Mahoney State Park** and **Platte River State Park** (☞ Exploring Southeast Nebraska, *below*); and **Indian Cave State Park** (⊠ 2 mi north and 5 mi east of Shubert; Box 30, 68437, ☎ 402/883–2575) in the state's southeast corner. You can buy a day pass ($2.50) or an annual pass ($14) at any state park; they're good for admission to all eight.

SOUTHEAST NEBRASKA

This is a land of both city sophistication and country charm. Here you can tour museums and historic buildings, shop in restored warehouses, and ride riverboats.

Visitor Information

Beatrice: Chamber of Commerce (⊠ 226 S. 6th St., 68310, ☎ 402/223–2338 or 800/755–7745). **Lincoln:** Convention and Visitors Bureau (⊠ 1135 M St., Suite 200, 68508, ☎ 402/434–5335 or 800/423–8212). **Nebraska City:** Convention and Visitors Bureau (⊠ 806 1st Ave., 68410, ☎ 402/873–6654 or 800/514–9113). **Omaha:** Greater Omaha

Convention and Visitors Bureau (⊠ 6800 Mercy Rd., Suite 202, 68106, ☎ 402/444–4660 or 800/332–1819).

Arriving and Departing

By Bus

Omaha and Lincoln are served by **Greyhound** (☎ 800/231–2222). Local bus service is provided in Lincoln by **StarTran** (☎ 402/476–1234) and in Omaha by **Metro Area Transit** (☎ 402/341–0800).

By Car

I–80 links Des Moines with Omaha (I–480 serves downtown Omaha) and Lincoln. U.S. 75S from Omaha leads to Nebraska City. From Lincoln, Route 2 goes to Nebraska City. To get to Beatrice, take U.S. 77 south from Lincoln.

By Plane

Eppley Airfield (⊠ 4501 Abbott Dr., ☎ 402/422–6800), about 3 mi from downtown Omaha, is served by most domestic carriers including **United Express** (☎ 800/554–5111). Cab fare from the airport to downtown is about $9.50. **Lincoln Municipal Airport** (⊠ 2400 W. Adams, ☎ 402/474–2770), about 3 mi from downtown Lincoln, is served by several major airlines; taxis to downtown cost about $10. **Eppley Express** (☎ 308/234–6066 or 800/888–9793) runs an airport van from Lincoln Municipal Airport to Eppley Airfield ($19 fare).

By Train

Amtrak's (☎ 800/872–7245) *Desert Wind, Pioneer,* and *California Zephyr* stop in Lincoln and Omaha.

Exploring Southeast Nebraska

Nebraska's state capitol dominates the Lincoln skyline; the river city of Omaha is the region's center of commerce and industry. Minutes away from both downtowns are expansive prairies, state parks, and attractions that chronicle the opening of the West to settlement.

Omaha is a quintessentially friendly midwestern city with a refurbished 12-block market area by the river, known as **Old Market,** where shoppers may choose from more than 100 shops and boutiques.

The **Henry Doorly Zoo** (⊠ 3701 S. 10th St., ☎ 402/733–8401, ⊞ $7.75) has the world's largest indoor rain forest—the Lied Jungle—and a saltwater aquarium with one of the country's largest penguin exhibits. "Ride the rails" at the **Western Heritage Museum** (⊠ 801 S. 10th St., ☎ 402/444–5071; ⊞ $5), where you're invited to climb aboard at Nebraska's largest restored Art Deco railroad station. Formerly Omaha's Union Station, the museum highlights the history of the Omaha and Union Pacific railroads through interactive exhibits. Lifelike sculptures of soldiers, salesmen, and other rail travelers of the 1930s and '40s sit in restored train cars and "talk" about the politics, music, and the society of the time.

Father Flanagan's **Boys Town** (⊠ 13628 Flannigan Blvd., 68010, ☎ 402/498–1140; ⊞ free), just outside Omaha about 2 mi west of I–680, remains the only official village in the nation created just for children. Founded in 1917 and made famous by the 1938 movie starring Spencer Tracy and Mickey Rooney, the town includes schools, churches, and farmland.

In Fremont, about 50 mi northwest of Bellevue, you can board the historic **Fremont and Elkhorn Valley Railroad** (⊠ 1835 N. Somers Ave., ☎ 402/727–0615; ⊞ $11) for a tour through the lush Elkhorn River valley. Hop the **Fremont Dinner Train** (⊠ 650 N. H St., ☎ 800/942–7245; ⊞ $44.95) for a dining experience that recalls rail travel in the

1940s. The scenic, 30-mi round-trip takes about three hours and includes a five-course meal.

About 60 mi south of Fremont on I–80W, halfway between Lincoln and Omaha, are the **Eugene T. Mahoney State Park** (✉ 28500 W. Park Hwy., Ashland 68003, ☎ 402/944–2523; 🖪 $2.50) and the **Platte River State Park** (✉ Hwy. 50, then 2 mi west on Hwy. 66 near Louisville, ☎ 402/234–2217; 🖪 $2.50). You'll find campsites at Mahoney and cabins and teepees at Platte River. In both areas you can hike, swim, canoe, and ride horseback. Platte River has buffalo-stew cookouts on Friday and Saturday nights in summer.

At the **Strategic Air Command Museum** (✉ I–80, Exit 426, Ashland, ☎ 402/944–3100 or 800/358–5029; 🖪 $6), displays include real aircraft that have changed the course of history, missiles, rare film footage, and an extensive collection of military artifacts.

Lincoln, home of the University of Nebraska and the state government, rises to meet you as you drive along I–80W. You can scan the city's skyline from atop the **Nebraska State Capitol Building** (✉ 1445 K St., ☎ 402/471–0448), with its 400-ft spire that towers over the surrounding plains. Free tours are given daily between 9 and 4.

A five-minute drive north from the capitol will take you to the **University of Nebraska,** at 14th and U streets. There you'll find the State Museum of Natural History (☎ 402/472–2642; 🖪 $2), nicknamed Elephant Hall for its exhibit of elephant fossils, collected from animals that once roamed the Great Plains. Within the State Museum is the Ralph Mueller Planetarium (☎ 402/472–2641), with regularly scheduled laser and astronomy shows. Call for ticket information. At **Nine-Mile Prairie** (✉ 1 mi west of N.W. 48th St. and Fletcher Ave.; 🖪 free) you can park your car and hop out to hike the natural prairies.

From Lincoln you can take Route 2 southeast to U.S. 75, then U.S. 136 southeast to Brownville. At the **Brownville State Recreation Area,** the *Spirit of Brownville* riverboat (☎ 402/825–6441) makes various sightseeing, dining, and dancing cruises on the mighty Missouri River.

U.S. 75N brings you to **Nebraska City,** a tidy town rimmed with historic sites and apple orchards, including the **Arbor Day Farm** (✉ 100 Arbor Ave., ☎ 402/873–8710), where you can buy apples in season and apple cider year-round. Lip-smacking desserts are served in the Pie Garden from May through October.

★ While at the Arbor Day Farm, peek into the past with a visit to the **Arbor Lodge State Historical Park and Arboretum** (✉ 2nd and Centennial Aves., ☎ 402/873–7222, 🖪 $3). On these grounds are the 52-room mansion and carriage house of J. Sterling Morton, the 19th-century politician and lover of trees who inaugurated the first Arbor Day. The mansion was later inhabited by his son, Morton Salt baron Joy Morton.

Hop the **Nebraska City Trolley** (☎ 402/873–4293; 🖪 $4) at stops throughout town. It links historic sites to 11 downtown factory outlets clustered around 8th and 1st Corso streets and to the **Factory Stores of America Mall** (✉ 1001 Rte. 2, ☎ 402/873–7727). The trolley also stops at **John Brown's Cave and Historical Village** (✉ 1908 4th Corso St., ☎ 402/873–3115; 🖪 $5), where you can visit a cave and a passageway that were once part of the Underground Railroad. It's open from May through November.

Dining and Lodging

For information on B&Bs contact the **Nebraska Association of Bed and Breakfasts** (⊠ 7 Valleyview Heights, Kearney 68845-4031, ☎ 308/234–1670).

Lincoln

$$ ✕ **Misty's Restaurant.** Adorned with Cornhusker football paraphernalia, this is, by locals' accounts, the prime-rib palace of the Plains. ⊠ *6235 Havelock Ave.,* ☎ *402/466–8424. AE, D, MC, V.*

$–$$ ✕ **Billy's.** A fascinating collection of political memorabilia and antiques
★ decorates this upscale restaurant. The menu covers all the classics—steak, lamb, veal, duck—and has nightly fresh-fish specials. ⊠ *1301 H St.,* ☎ *402/474–0084. AE, D, DC, MC, V.*

$–$$ ✕ **Valentino's Restaurant.** Besides pizza with original or home-style crust,
★ this restaurant also serves Italian specials and "dessert pizzas" with such toppings as cherries and cream cheese. ⊠ *3457 Holdrege St.,* ☎ *402/467–3611. AE, D, MC, V.*

$ ✕ **Arturo's Restaurant & Cantina.** Lincoln's first Mexican restaurant serves a wide variety of traditional Mexican dishes, all made with fresh ingredients, plus "tasha," a family recipe made with refried beans and cheese in a corn tortilla. ⊠ *803 Q St.,* ☎ *402/475–8226. D, MC, V.*

$ ✕ **Rock 'n' Roll Runza.** Waitresses on roller skates serve Runzas—hamburger-cabbage sandwiches—at this 1950s-style restaurant, a chain only found in Nebraska. ⊠ *210 N. 14th St.,* ☎ *402/474–2030. AE, D, MC, V.*

$$$ ▦ **The Cornhusker.** The lobby of this elegant hotel has a grand curving staircase, hand-painted murals, and an Italian-marble floor. Rooms in the east and south wings have good views of downtown Lincoln. ⊠ *333 S. 13th St., 68508,* ☎ *402/474–7474 or 800/793–7474, ︻FAX︼ 402/474–1847. 290 rooms. 2 restaurants, pool, exercise room. AE, D, DC, MC, V.* ✆

$$ ▦ **Rogers House Bed and Breakfast.** Built in 1914, this ivy-covered brick
★ mansion was converted into a B&B by the current owners in 1984. The antiques-filled public areas, with oak floors, include a living room with a fireplace and a sunroom where guests eat breakfast. ⊠ *2145 B St., 68502,* ☎ *402/476–6961, ︻FAX︼ 402/476–6473. 12 rooms. AE, D, MC, V. BP.* ✆

Nebraska City

$ ✕ **Teresa's Family Restaurant.** Booths line the walls of this casual
★ country kitchen, where old-fashioned fare such as meat loaf and homemade lemon pie is served at yesterday's prices. ⊠ *812 Central Ave.,* ☎ *402/873–9100. MC, V.*

$ ✕ **Ulbrick's.** This converted gas station and café is nothing fancy, but
★ the made-from-scratch family-style dinners of fried chicken, creamed corn and cabbage, and homemade egg noodles are exceptional. ⊠ *1513 S. 11th St.,* ☎ *402/873–5458. No credit cards.*

$–$$ ▦ **Arbor Day Farm Lied Conference Center.** In a 260-acre educational complex devoted to environmental programs, Arbor Day Farm is surrounded by arboretums and interpretive nature trails. ⊠ *2700 Sylvan Rd., 68410,* ☎ *402/873–8733 or 800/546–5433, ︻FAX︼ 402/873–4999. 144 rooms. Pool. AE, D, MC, V.* ✆

$ ▦ **Whispering Pines.** Nestled among pines on 6½ quiet acres, this 1886 two-story brick house has been completely refurbished as a B&B and filled with antiques. Take a dip in the six-person hot tub before you turn in for the night. ⊠ *21st St. and 6th Ave., 68410,* ☎ *402/873–5850. 5 rooms. D, MC, V. BP.* ✆

Omaha

$$ ✕ **Johnny's Café.** Johnny's has been *the* place in Omaha for mouth-watering steaks, seafood, and midwestern dishes since 1922. ⊠ *4702 S. 27th St.,* ☎ *402/731–4774. AE, D, DC, MC, V.*

$ ✕ **Austins.** Feel free to throw your peanut shells on the floor at this casual eatery, where the atmosphere is western and the food pure country. Chicken-fried steak, prime rib, and barbecued ribs are house specialties. ⊠ *12020 Anne St.,* ☎ *402/896–5373. AE, MC, V.*

$ ✕ **Bohemian Cafe.** Gaily painted Czech plates hang on the walls of this family-style restaurant, where you can try Eastern European favorites such as goulash. ⊠ *1406 S. 13th St.,* ☎ *402/342–9838. D, MC, V.*

$ ✕ **Garden Café.** Home-style cooking with everything made from scratch is what this café in the historic Old Market is known for. Highlights are the potato casseroles, soups, salads, and desserts. ⊠ *12th and Harvey Sts.,* ☎ *402/422–1574. AE, DC, MC, V.*

$ ✕ **Mr. C's.** Christmas lights surround you at this Italian steak house, ★ where the sirloin is as good as the lasagna and manicotti. ⊠ *5319 N. 30th St.,* ☎ *402/451–1998. AE, MC, V.*

$$$ 🏨 **Marriott Hotel.** This six-story hotel in suburban Omaha is near the upscale Regency Fashion Court shopping area. ⊠ *10220 Regency Circle, 68114,* ☎ *402/399–9000,* FAX *402/399–0223. 301 rooms. 2 restaurants, pool, exercise room. AE, D, DC, MC, V.* 🐾

$$–$$$ 🏨 **Double Tree Hotel.** In the heart of the downtown business and enter-★ tainment district, the Double Tree is close to the Old Market and Henry Doorly Zoo and only 10 minutes from Eppley Air Field. Rooms on all of its 19 stories are spacious. ⊠ *1616 Dodge St., 68102,* ☎ *402/346–7600,* FAX *402/346–5722. 413 rooms. Restaurant, pool. AE, D, DC, MC, V.* 🐾

Motels
🏨 **Oak Creek Inn** (⊠ 2808 S. 72nd St., Omaha 68124, ☎ 402/397–7137, FAX 402/397–3492), 102 rooms; pool, exercise room; *$.*

Campgrounds
⚠ **Indian Cave State Park** (☞ National and State Parks, *above*) and ⚠ **Eugene T. Mahoney State Park** (☞ Exploring Southeast Nebraska, *above*) have excellent tent and RV camping.

Outdoor Activities and Sports

Fishing
The 13 Salt Valley lakes surrounding Lincoln, especially **Branched Oak** (⊠ N.W. 140th St. and W. Raymond Rd.) and **Pawnee** (⊠ N.W. 98th and W. Adams Sts.), contain a variety of fish, including largemouth bass, northern pike, walleye, and channel catfish. For more information about fishing in Nebraska, contact the **Game and Parks Commission** (☎ 402/471–0641).

Spectator Sports
Football: University of Nebraska Cornhuskers (⊠ 117 S. Stadium St., ☎ 402/472–3111).

Shopping

The **Nebraska Furniture Mart** (⊠ 700 S. 72nd St., Omaha, ☎ 402/397–6100 or 800/359–1200) is said to be the largest furniture store west of the Mississippi. Omaha's **Old Market** (⊠ Between 10th and 13th Sts., ☎ 402/346–4445) is a collection of boutiques, galleries, and restaurants in the oldest part of town. Lincoln's charming, restored warehouse shopping district, **Historic Haymarket** (⊠ Between 7th and 9th Sts. and between O and S Sts., ☎ 402/435–7496), has quaint antiques stores, novelty gift shops, and some fine restaurants.

NORTHWEST NEBRASKA

Rugged and beautiful, this is true Old West territory, with dramatic buttes and bluffs, ponderosa pines, craggy ridges, and canyons.

Visitor Information

Alliance: Box Butte Visitors Committee (⊠ Alliance Chamber of Commerce, Box 571, 69301, ☏ 308/762–1520). **Chadron:** Chamber of Commerce (⊠ Box 646, 69337, ☏ 308/432–4401). **Scottsbluff:** Scotts Bluff County Tourism (⊠ 1517 Broadway, 69361, ☏ 308/632–2133 or 800/ 788–9475).

Arriving and Departing

By Car

From Omaha and Lincoln take I–80 west about 275 mi to U.S. 26, which closely follows the Oregon and Mormon trails as it takes you to Scottsbluff. To bypass Kearney and North Platte, take I–80 to Grand Island, then scenic Route 2 to the north, which runs parallel to I–80 through Nebraska's Sandhills.

Exploring Northwest Nebraska

You can retrace the route of the wagon trains by exiting I–80 near Ogallala and heading west on U.S. 26. Four miles south of Bridgeport on Route 88, you can see **Courthouse** and **Jail rocks,** sandstone outcroppings that pioneers used as landmarks on the trail west. One mile south of the junction of U.S. 26 and Route 92 and 4 mi south of Bayard, the **Chimney Rock National Historic Site** (☏ 308/586–2581; ☞ $2) is an impressive outcrop that pioneers described as "towering to the heavens." The visitor center, open year-round, commemorates those who traveled the Oregon Trail. Oregon Trail wagon traces are still visible at the **Scotts Bluff National Monument** (⊠ 3 mi west of Gering on Rte. 92, ☏ 308/436–4340; ☞ $5), an enormous bluff that rises out of the rocky plains. Once described as the "Lighthouse of the Plains," it now has a museum at its base.

About 35 mi north of Mitchell on Route 29, the **Agate Fossil Beds National Monument** has fossil deposits dating back 20 million years. A museum (☏ 308/668–2211; ☞ $2) preserves and displays fossils and Native American artifacts.

North on Route 29 to Harrison, then east on U.S. 20 is **Fort Robinson State Park** (☏ 308/665–2900; ☞ $2.50), where activities include trail rides, historic tours, cookouts, swimming, trout fishing, hiking, and stagecoach rides. From late May to late August there's also a summer-theater program. Tent sites, electrical hookups, and lodge rooms are available, as well as horse corrals.

Dining and Lodging

Travelers to northwest Nebraska chow down at casual, out-of-the-way restaurants, wagon train–style cookouts, and ranches. Inexpensive cattle ranches and B&Bs (contact the **Nebraska Association of Bed and Breakfasts,** ⊠ 7 Valleyview Heights, Kearney 68845-4031, ☏ 308/234-1670) provide charming alternatives to chain motels.

Bayard

$–$$ ✕▣ **Oregon Trail Wagon Train.** Sleep under the stars and dine on
★ cookouts of fire-grilled rib eyes, stew, spoon bread, and vinegar pudding on covered-wagon tours through some of Nebraska's remaining short-grass prairies. One- to four-day treks are available. ⊠ *Rte. 2, Box*

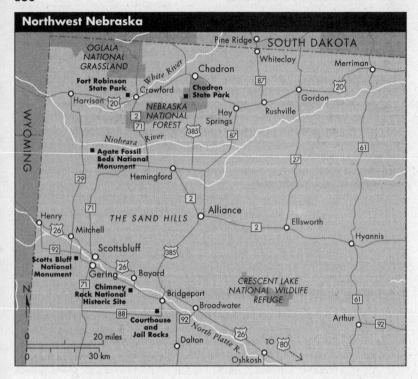

Northwest Nebraska

502, 69334, ☎ 308/586–1850, FAX 308/586–1848. 3 cabins (each sleeps 6). Reservations essential. MC, V.

Crawford

$ 🏠 **Fort Robinson State Park Lodge.** Dating from the 1800s, this historic fort in Fort Robinson State Park includes a two-story lodge with large verandas and tall columns. Built in 1909 as an enlisted men's barracks, the lodge now has 22 modern rooms with private baths (but no telephones or TVs). Cabins, which sleep up to 12 people, are also available, and then there are the officers' quarters, a group facility that can sleep up to 60. ⊠ *3 mi west of Crawford, Box 392, Crawford 69339, ☎ 308/665–2900, FAX 308/665–2906. 22 rooms, 31 cabins. Restaurant. MC, V.*

Scottsbluff

$ ✕ **Grampy's Pancake House.** This large family-style restaurant is divided into three dining rooms. Besides strawberry and other varieties of pancakes, there are omelets, blintzes, and other breakfast treats, as well as simple lunch and dinner fare. ⊠ *1802 E. 20th Pl., ☎ 308/632–6906. AE, D, MC, V.*

Motels

🏠 **Landmark Inn** (⊠ 246 Main St., Bayard 69334, ☎ 308/586–1375 or 800/658–4424), 10 rooms; *$*. 🏠 **Scottsbluff Inn** (⊠ 1901 21st Ave., Scottsbluff 69361, ☎ 308/635–3111; 800/597–3111 for reservations only, FAX 308/635–7646), 138 rooms; restaurant, pool, exercise room; *$*. 🏠 **Town Line Motel** (⊠ Box 423, 3591 Hwy. 20, Crawford 69339, ☎ 308/665–1450 or 800/903–1450), 24 rooms; *$*.

Ranches

$$ 🏠 **Meadow View Ranch Bed and Breakfast Bunkhouse.** Guests stay in the converted bunkhouse of this 5,000-acre working ranch 18 mi from the South Dakota border. Accommodations include a kitchenette,

a living room, and two bedrooms. Complimentary breakfast is served in the ranch kitchen, and picnic lunches are packed on request. Activities include horseback riding, fishing, hiking in the nearby Sandhills, and going on wagon rides and cattle drives. ⊠ *HC 91, Box 29, Gordon 69343,* ☎ *308/282–0679,* 𝔽𝔸𝕏 *308/282–1078. Bunkhouse sleeps 8. No credit cards. Closed Nov.–Apr.* ✎

Campgrounds

🏕 **Chadron State Park** (☞ Hiking and Backpacking *in* Outdoor Activities and Sports, *below*) is a favorite. 🏕 **Fort Robinson State Park** (☞ Exploring Northwest Nebraska, *above*) has tent and RV camping.

Outdoor Activities and Sports

Hiking and Backpacking

Fort Robinson State Park (☞ Exploring Northwest Nebraska, *above*) and **Chadron State Park** (⊠ 8 mi south of Chadron on U.S. 385, ☎ 308/432–6167) have hiking trails, four-wheel-drive rides, paddleboats, fishing, a swimming pool, and tennis courts.

ELSEWHERE IN NEBRASKA

Lake McConaughy and Ogallala

Arriving and Departing

From Lincoln and Omaha take I–80 west to Ogallala.

What to See and Do

★ The white-sand beaches of **Lake McConaughy State Recreation Area and the Kingsley Dam** (⊠ 9 mi north of Ogallala on Rte. 61, ☎ 308/284–3542; ⊚ $2.50) attract thousands every year. In Ogallala, **Front Street** (☎ 308/284–6000) depicts an 1880s Main Street, complete with a wooden boardwalk, jail, barbershop, and cowboy museum. The restaurant proudly serves Nebraska steaks and puts on nightly western shows from Memorial Day through Labor Day. The **Mansion on the Hill** (⊠ W. 10th and Spruce, ☎ 308/284–4066; ⊚ $2) is a museum with exhibits on 19th-century cattle drives. Ogallala is also home to the infamous **Boot Hill Cemetery** (⊠ W. 10th and Parkhill Dr.), so named because the outlaws first buried there were left in graves so shallow that their boots stuck out.

Red Cloud

Arriving and Departing

From Lincoln and Omaha take I–80 west to Grand Island, then U.S. 34 south to U.S. 281, and continue south.

What to See and Do

Red Cloud was the home of Pulitzer Prize–winning author Willa Cather. The **Willa Cather Historical Center** (⊠ 326 N. Webster St., ☎ 402/746–2653; ⊚ $1) is dedicated to the writer, who loved the Plains ; 610 acres are preserved as the **Cather Memorial Prairie** (⊠ 5 mi south of Red Cloud).

On the National Register of Historic Places is the **Starke Round Barn,** 4 mi east of Red Cloud on Highway 136. Built in 1902 by four brothers from Milwaukee named Starke, this three-story barn is held together by balanced tension and stress rather than nails or pegs.

The Great Platte River Road

Arriving and Departing

From Omaha and Lincoln take I–80 west.

What to See and Do

Westward-bound pioneers on the Mormon and Oregon trails once hugged the shores of the Platte River, a verdant natural pathway. Today I–80 follows the same route, cutting through the state's heartland and affording glimpses of the pioneer past. **Sculpture gardens** dot the landscape along the highway for 500 mi across the Nebraska plains. At nine rest areas, large stone-and-metal artworks constitute what some have called a "museum without walls."

The **Stuhr Museum of the Prairie Pioneer** (⊠ junction of U.S. 34 and U.S. 281, ☎ 308/385–5316; ☞ $7.25), in Grand Island, houses Native American and Old West artifacts and features the 60-building Railroad Town, which includes the birthplace of actor Henry Fonda, antique farm machinery, a restored 19th-century farmhouse, and folks in period costumes. It's open from May through mid-October.

From early March to mid-April, people flock to an area near Grand Island and Kearney to witness the migration of thousands of Sandhill cranes as they pause here before resuming their flight north. The **Crane Meadows Nature Center** (⊠ ½ mi south of I–80 at the Alda exit, ☎ 308/382–1820; ☞ tours $15) and the **Lillian Rowe Audubon Sanctuary** (☎ 308/468–5282; ☞ tours $15) offer tours. The Crane Meadows Nature Center also has a **visitor center** (☞ $2) with wildlife displays.

Fort Kearny State Historical Park (⊠ 2 mi south of I–80 on Rte. 44 and then 4 mi east on L–50A, ☎ 308/865–5305; ☞ $2.50) has a re-created stockade and interpretive exhibits detailing the role of the outpost on the frontier.

★ **Harold Warp's Pioneer Village** (⊠ Junction of U.S. 6, U.S. 34, and Hwy. 10 in Minden, ☎ 308/832–1181, ☞ $7) has an extensive collection of pioneer memorabilia; horse-drawn covered-wagon rides; and craftwork demonstrations. The Old West comes alive in **North Platte,** where Buffalo Bill Cody and his famous Wild West show began. You can tour his ranch house, enjoy trail rides, or chow down on buffalo stew in the **Buffalo Bill Ranch State Historical Park** (☎ 308/535–8035; ☞ $2.50), 6 mi northwest of I–80. In Hastings, which lies near the junction of U.S. 34 and Highway 281, you'll find the **Hastings Museum** (⊠ 1330 N. Burlington Ave., ☎ 402/461–4629 or 800/508–4629; ☞ $5), which has exhibits on natural history and frontier days; related films are shown in its IMAX theater.

Two-hour tours of the **Dancing Leaf Earth Lodge Cultural Learning Center** (⊠ 6100 E. Opal Springs Rd., Wellfleet, ☎ 308/963–4233; ☞ $8) give modern travelers the opportunity to experience Native American life as it was about 1,000 years ago. Earth lodges, a natural trail, and archaeological sites are among the attractions.

Lodging

$ 🏠 **Home Comfort B&B.** On 15 acres of Nebraska farmland, this comfortable bed-and-breakfast is within walking distance of Harold Warp's Pioneer Village (☞ *above*) and provides complimentary transportation to the Sandhill-crane migration. ⊠ *1523 N. Brown, Minden 68959,* ☎ *308/832–0533. 4 rooms. No credit cards.*

Sandhills/Valentine Region

Visitor Information

Valentine: Visitor Center (⊠ Box 201, 69201, ☎ 402/376–2969 or 800/658–4024).

Arriving and Departing

From Lincoln and Omaha take I–80 west to Grand Island. Go north on U.S. 281 to Route 22; then follow it west 9 mi and go north on Route 11. At Burwell follow Route 91 west, U.S. 183 north, and U.S. 20 west to Valentine.

What to See and Do

Fort Hartsuff State Historical Park (✉ 3 mi north of Elyria off Hwy. 11, ☎ 308/346–4715; 💲 $2.50), open May through October, is a restored 1870s infantry post with guides in period uniforms and costumes.

For a view of the Great Plains as it once was, you can take a drive through hundreds of miles of mixed-grass prairie, where numerous outdoor attractions beckon. The **Niobrara River** draws canoeists from throughout the state; outfitters include **Dryland Aquatics** (✉ Box 33C, Sparks 69220, ☎ 800/337–3119), **A&C Canoe Rentals** (✉ 518 N. Ray St., Valentine 69201, ☎ 402/376–2839), **Brewers Canoers** (✉ 433 E. U.S. 20, Valentine 69201, ☎ 402/376–2046), **Graham Canoe Outfitters** (✉ HC 13, Box 16A, Valentine 69201, ☎ 402/376–3708), and **Little Outlaw Canoe & Tube Rentals** (✉ Box 15, Valentine 69201, ☎ 402/376–1822). Native wildlife is abundant at the **Valentine National Wildlife Refuge** (✉ HC 14, Box 67, Valentine 69201, ☎ 402/376–1889), south of Valentine on U.S. 83. Its 70,000 acres of prairie and wetlands shelter ducks, geese, hawks, eagles, deer, coyotes, beavers, and other species. Trails encourage both driving and hiking through this open country; there are information kiosks at entrances to the refuge.

The **Fort Niobrara National Wildlife Refuge** (✉ HC 14, Box 67, Valentine 69201, ☎ 402/376–3789), 5 mi east of Valentine on Route 12, has forested terrain and sizable species, such as bison, elk, and longhorn cattle. A visitor center and picnic facilities are available.

Two sites on Main Street in Valentine are worth a visit. **Backporch Friends Factory** (✉ 227 N. Main St., ☎ 402/376–3369) makes soft-filled hand-sewn dolls sold around the world. Also, the front of the **First National Bank** (✉ 253 N. Main St., ☎ 402/376–2470) includes the largest brick mural in the country created by sculptor Jack Curran, which celebrates the spirit of discovery of early pioneers to the region.

Dining and Lodging

$ ✕ **The Peppermill.** As nice as it comes in this part of the country, this local favorite known for steaks and seafood has mirrored walls, linen tablecloths, and mixed drinks, in addition to an outdoor beer garden open in appropriate weather. ✉ *112 N. Main St.,* ☎ *402/376–1440. AE, D, MC, V.*

$–$$ ☷ **The Niobrara Inn.** Within walking distance of downtown shops, this 1912 American four-square home is highlighted by warm woodwork and an large grand piano in the parlor. ✉ *525 N. Main St., Valentine 69201,* ☎ *402/376–1779. 6 rooms. No credit cards.* ✍

NEVADA

Updated by
Deke
Castleman

Capital	Carson City
Population	1,880,000
Motto	Battle Born
State Bird	Mountain bluebird
State Flower	Sagebrush
Postal Abbreviation	NV

Statewide Visitor Information

Nevada Commission on Tourism (⊠ Capitol Complex, Carson City 89710, ☎ 702/687–4322 or 800/638–2328).

Scenic Drives

The **"Loneliest Road in America"** is U.S. 50 in Nevada, which winds across the central part of the state from Carson City to Ely. **U.S. 93** runs from north of Las Vegas through more than 500 mi of long desert valleys and passes 13,061-ft **Wheeler Peak,** the second-highest point in the state. For a good look at some southwestern desert, particularly in the spring, take **U.S. 93/95** southeast from Las Vegas, turning east onto Route 147 in Henderson, which takes you through Lake Mead National Recreation Area to Valley of Fire State Park (☞ Las Vegas, *below*).

National and State Parks

National Park
Great Basin National Park (⊠ off U.S. 50 at the Nevada-Utah border, Baker 89311, ☎ 702/234–7331; ☜ free) is 77,092 acres of dramatic mountains, lush meadows, alpine lakes, limestone caves, and a stand of bristlecone pines (the oldest living trees in the world), with many camping, hiking, and picnicking areas.

State Parks
For information on Nevada's 23 state parks, contact the state tourism office (☞ Statewide Visitor Information, *above*). **Washoe Lake State Recreation Area** (⊠ off U.S. 395; 4855 E. Lake Blvd., Carson City 89704, ☎ 702/687–4319), with views of the majestic Sierra Nevada, is popular for fishing and horseback riding.

LAS VEGAS

Las Vegas is known worldwide as a fantasyland for adults. It was given its name, which means "The Meadows," by a Spanish scouting party who found a spring in the area in the 1820s. Mormons settled the valley briefly in 1855, but until the turn of the 20th century it was little more than a handful of ranches and homesteads. The San Pedro, Los Angeles, and Salt Lake Railroad founded the town of Las Vegas in 1905 as a watering stop for its steam trains. The construction of the Hoover Dam in the 1930s brought a large wave of settlers seeking jobs.

Las Vegas as we know it was born shortly after World War II, when mobster Benjamin "Bugsy" Siegel decided to build a gambling resort in the desert (Nevada had legalized gambling in 1931). Bugsy built his Flamingo with money borrowed from fellow mobsters, who rubbed him out when the casino flopped. The resort eventually recovered, and casino-hotels on the Las Vegas Strip caught on. The city is now home to 18 of the 21 largest hotels in the world.

Visitor Information

Las Vegas Chamber of Commerce (✉ 711 E. Desert Inn Rd., 89109, ☎ 702/735–1616). **Las Vegas Convention and Visitors Authority** (✉ 3150 Paradise Rd., 89109, ☎ 702/892–0711).

Arriving and Departing

By Bus
Greyhound (✉ 200 S. Main St., ☎ 800/231–2222).

By Car
Major highways leading into Las Vegas are I–15 from Los Angeles and Salt Lake City, U.S. 95 from Reno, and U.S. 93 from Arizona.

By Plane
McCarran International Airport (✉ 1 Wayne Newton Dr., ☎ 702/261–5743), about 2 mi from the southern end of the Strip, is served by major airlines. Taxi fare from the airport to Strip hotels is about $9–$12; to the downtown hotels, about $15–$18; but the least expensive way to reach your hotel ($4.40–$6.60 per person) is by **Gray Line Airport Transportation** (☎ 702/739–5770), which you'll find near the taxis.

By Train
Amtrak passenger service to Las Vegas has been discontinued.

Getting Around Las Vegas

Taxis, in ready supply at every hotel, are the most convenient way to get around. The **Strip bus** (Citizens Area Transit, or CAT, ☎ 702/228–7433) costs $1.50 and links the Strip and the downtown with stops near major hotels. You can rent a car to drive out of town or explore the desert, but be sure to fuel up before you go; you won't find many stations out there.

Exploring Las Vegas

Las Vegas is a relatively small city; downtown and small sections of the Strip are easy to explore on foot. Just beware the extremely hot months of June, July, and August, when walking outdoors for an extended length of time is not recommended. The massive casino-hotels along the Strip make distances deceptive; a stroll "next door" may take 10 minutes, because properties are so large. Take taxis or buses for longer distances along the Strip or between the Strip and downtown.

The downtown casino center occupies the most brightly lit four blocks in the world, thanks to **Fremont Street Experience,** a four-block pedestrian mall covered by an arched, 100-ft-high awning illuminated by 2 *million* lightbulbs. After dark, a kaleidoscopic light-and-sound show is presented here on the hour until midnight. A focal point of downtown is **Jackie Gaughan's Plaza** (✉ 1 N. Main St., ☎ 702/386–2110), built on the site of the old Union Pacific train station. Freight trains still rumble past the back door at all hours.

Among the downtown casino-hotels, the **Golden Nugget** (✉ 129 E. Fremont St., ☎ 702/385–7111) has a particularly attractive lobby, where you can gawk at a 61-pound gold nugget. **Binion's Horseshoe** (✉ 128 E. Fremont St., ☎ 702/382–1600) is an old-fashioned gambling joint with a huge crap pit and a display of custom guns nearby.

Lied Discovery Children's Museum (✉ 833 Las Vegas Blvd. N, ☎ 702/382–5473; ✄ $5) has hands-on science exhibits. **Southern Nevada Zoological Park** (✉ 1775 N. Rancho Dr., ☎ 702/648–5955; ✄ $6) is a small but enjoyable zoo.

Las Vegas

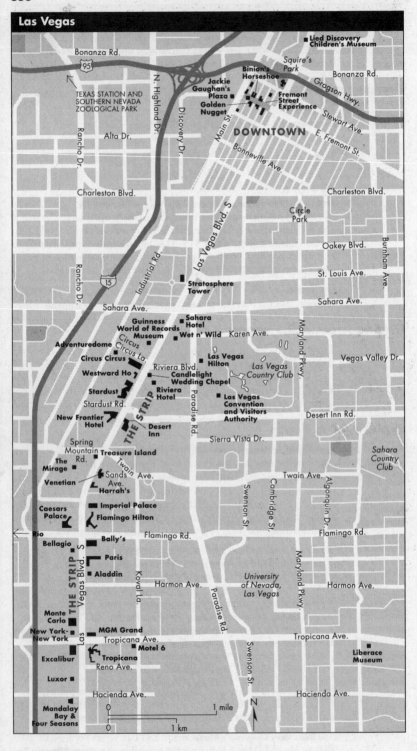

Bonanza Rd.

95

TEXAS STATION AND
SOUTHERN NEVADA
ZOOLOGICAL PARK

Lied Discovery
Children's Museum

Squire's
Park

Bonanza Rd.

Binion's
Horseshoe

Jackie
Gaughan's
Plaza

Golden
Nugget

Fremont
Street
Experience

Gragson Hwy.

Stewart Ave.

DOWNTOWN

E. Fremont St.

Bonneville Ave.

Charleston Blvd.

Charleston Blvd.

Circle
Park

Oakey Blvd.

Burnham Ave.

St. Louis Ave.

Las Vegas Blvd. S.

Industrial Rd.

Rancho Dr.

Alta Dr.

N. Highland Dr.

Discovery Dr.

Main St.

Sahara Ave.

Sahara Ave.

15

Stratosphere
Tower

Guinness
World of Records
Museum

Sahara
Hotel

Wet n' Wild

Karen Ave.

Maryland Pkwy.

Vegas Valley Dr.

Adventuredome

Circus
Circus La.

Circus Circus

Westward Ho

Stardust

Stardust Rd.

New Frontier
Hotel

Las Vegas
Hilton

Riviera Blvd.

Candlelight
Wedding Chapel

Riviera Hotel

THE STRIP

Paradise Rd.

Las Vegas
Country
Club

Las Vegas
Convention
and Visitors
Authority

Desert Inn Rd.

Desert Inn

Sierra Vista Dr.

Spring
Mountain
Rd.

Treasure Island

The
Mirage

Venetian

Twain
Ave.

Sands
Ave.

Harrah's

Twain Ave.

Swenson St.

Cambridge St.

Algonquin Dr.

Sahara
Country
Club

Caesars
Palace

Imperial Palace

Flamingo Hilton

Rio

Bellagio

Bally's

Flamingo Rd.

Flamingo Rd.

Maryland Pkwy.

THE STRIP

Vegas Blvd. S.

Paris

Aladdin

Koval La.

Harmon Ave.

University
of Nevada,
Las Vegas

Paradise Rd.

Harmon Ave.

Monte
Carlo

New York-
New York

Excalibur

Luxor

Las

MGM Grand

Tropicana Ave.

Motel 6

Tropicana

Reno Ave.

Swenson St.

Tropicana Ave.

Liberace
Museum

Hacienda Ave.

Hacienda Ave.

Mandalay
Bay &
Four Seasons

0   1 mile

0   1 km

N

At 1,149 ft, the **Stratosphere Tower** (✉ 2000 Las Vegas Blvd. S, ☎ 702/380–7777; 🎫 $5) is the tallest building west of the Mississippi. High-speed elevators whisk you to a 12-story pod with a revolving restaurant, bar, and meeting rooms. The tower's most unusual features, however, are its roller coaster (which runs 900 ft above ground!) and the Big Shot thrill ride, which thrusts up and free-falls down the needle. Only in Las Vegas.

The famous **Strip** is a 3½-mi stretch of Las Vegas Boulevard South. It begins at the **Sahara** (✉ 2535 Las Vegas Blvd. S, ☎ 702/737–2111), whose newest addition is Speed, the fastest of five roller coasters on the Strip. **Wet n' Wild** (✉ 2600 Las Vegas Blvd. S, ☎ 702/737–3819; 🎫 $24.95) is a 26-acre amusement park with every water ride imaginable.

The **Guinness World of Records Museum** (✉ 2780 Las Vegas Blvd. S, ☎ 702/792–3766; 🎫 $4.95) honors such record holders as the tallest man in the world and has videos of some records being set. Next door to Guinness is **Circus Circus** (✉ 2880 Las Vegas Blvd. S, ☎ 702/734–0410), the first Las Vegas hotel to cater to families with children. It has a midway with carnival games, free circus acts, and a 5-acre indoor amusement park called **Adventuredome** (☎ 702/794–3939; 🎫 free), with the world's largest indoor roller coaster. The **Candlelight Wedding Chapel** (✉ 2855 Las Vegas Blvd. S, ☎ 702/735–4179) is the busiest chapel in town.

The **Riviera** (✉ 2901 Las Vegas Blvd. S, ☎ 702/734–5110) is noted for its four showrooms. The reclusive billionaire Howard Hughes lived in the penthouse of the **Desert Inn** (✉ 3145 Las Vegas Blvd. S, ☎ 702/733–4444), one of the smallest and most upscale casino-hotels on the Strip. Hughes once owned the **New Frontier Hotel** (✉ 3120 Las Vegas Blvd. S, ☎ 702/794–8200); today it caters to a young crowd, with good, cheap food and low table minimums. The Mirage-owned **Treasure Island** resort (✉ 3300 Las Vegas Blvd. S, ☎ 702/894–7111) is loosely based on Robert Louis Stevenson's novel—pirates and sailors engage in ship-to-ship cannon battles in Buccaneer Bay out front. At the $670 million palace known as the **Mirage** (✉ 3400 Las Vegas Blvd. S, ☎ 702/791–7111), a volcano erupts in a front yard landscaped with a towering waterfall, lagoons, and tropical plants; inside is a glassed-in tigers' den.

Across from the Mirage, the **Venetian** (✉ 3335 Las Vegas Blvd. S, ☎ 702/733–5000) opened in April 1999. It features replicas of historic Venice landmarks, including a 1,200-ft Grand Canal—running through a 90-store shopping mall.

Imperial Palace (✉ 3535 Las Vegas Blvd. S, ☎ 702/731–3311; 🎫 $6.50) is the home of the Imperial Palace Auto Collection, a display of more than 300 antique and classic cars, many once owned by such famous and notorious figures as Adolf Hitler and Al Capone. The **Flamingo Hilton** (✉ 3555 Las Vegas Blvd. S, ☎ 702/733–3111) grew from the first luxury resort on the Strip, opened by Bugsy Siegel in 1946, and still has the city's most lush and luxurious pool area.

The high stakes at the opulent **Caesars Palace** (✉ 3570 Las Vegas Blvd. S, ☎ 702/731–7110) attract serious gamblers; the indoor Forum Shops mall resembles an ancient Roman streetscape. **Bally's** (✉ 3645 Las Vegas Blvd. S, ☎ 702/739–4111) is a giant among giants.

Next door to Bally's is the 2,900-room megaresort, **Paris** (✉ 3645 Las Vegas Blvd. S, ☎ 702/739–4612), which debuted in September 1999. The centerpiece is a half-scale replica of the Eiffel Tower, with a restaurant on the 17th floor and a glass elevator to an observation deck on the 44th.

Across from Paris, the Mirage company has opened **Bellagio** (✉ 3600 Las Vegas Blvd. S, ☎ 702/693–7111), the most expensive hotel ever built. Bellagio features a $30 million dancing-waters show on an 11-

acre lake; an indoor botanical garden; and a Cirque du Soleil extravaganza with tickets at $100 a pop.

Next door to Paris, the new **Aladdin** (⊠ 3667 Las Vegas Blvd. S, ☎ 877/333–WISH) is rising from the ashes of the old; at press time the 2,600-room megaresort was scheduled to open in August 2000.

The Victorian-theme **Monte Carlo** (⊠ 3770 Las Vegas Blvd. S, ☎ 702/730–7777) has 3,000 rooms and the largest microbrewery in town. Megaresort **New York–New York** (⊠ 3790 Las Vegas Blvd. S, ☎ 702/740–6969) has 2,035 rooms, a replica of the New York City skyline, a food court modeled after Greenwich Village, a Central Park–theme casino, and a roller coaster. The emerald-green **MGM Grand** (⊠ 3799 Las Vegas Blvd. S, ☎ 702/891–1111) houses the second-largest casino in the world, so large that it's divided into four parts, distinguished mainly by their carpet patterns. The sprawling grounds of the **Tropicana** (⊠ 3801 Las Vegas Blvd. S, ☎ 702/739–2222) are attractively landscaped; some of the plantings are more than 40 years old. The blue-and-pink quasi-castle **Excalibur** (⊠ 3850 Las Vegas Blvd. S, ☎ 702/597–7777) has a medieval theme. **Luxor** (⊠ 3900 Las Vegas Blvd. S, ☎ 702/262–4000) is a 30-story Egyptian-style pyramid with an ultra-high-tech arcade, a 3-D IMAX theater, and motion simulators. In March 1999, **Mandalay Bay** (⊠ 3950 Las Vegas Blvd. S, ☎ 702/632–7777) welcomed the first guests to the 3,200-room megaresort. Floors 35 through 39 of the same building are occupied by the 400-room Four Seasons hotel. The **Liberace Museum** (⊠ 1775 E. Tropicana Ave., ☎ 702/798–5595; ☞ $6.95), 2 mi east of the Strip, has three buildings: one for the entertainer's pianos and cars, one for his costumes, and the third for general memorabilia.

Outside Vegas

The awe-inspiring **Hoover Dam** (⊠ Rte. 93, east of Boulder City, ☎ 702/293–8321; ☞ tour $8), about 35 mi east of Las Vegas, was built in the 1930s to tame the destructive waters of the Colorado River and produce electricity. Tours into the 727-ft-high, 660-ft-thick dam are conducted daily.

The construction of Hoover Dam created **Lake Mead** (⊠ Alan Bible Visitor Center, U.S. 93 and Lakeshore Dr., ☎ 702/293–8906), the largest man-made lake in the western hemisphere, with more than 500 mi of shoreline. It's popular for boating, fishing, and swimming. For water tours of the lake and Hoover Dam, contact **Lake Mead Cruises** (☎ 702/293–6180).

Dramatic **Valley of Fire State Park** (⊠ Rte. 169, Overton, ☎ 702/397–2088), 55 mi northeast of Lake Mead, contains distinctive polychrome sandstone formations and mysterious Anasazi petroglyphs.

Red Rock Canyon (⊠ Rte. 159, ☎ 702/363–1921; ☞ $5) is closer to Las Vegas (only 20 mi west) than Valley of Fire, but slightly less spectacular. Still, its sheer sandstone cliffs and twisting canyons are an internationally known rock-climbing destination. A 13-mi loop drive begins at the Red Rock visitor center.

For a respite from the bustle of Las Vegas and the heat of the desert, travel 35 mi northwest of the city on U.S. 95 and Route 157 to **Mt. Charleston,** with a forest, canyons, and a 12,000-ft peak. There's excellent skiing, both cross-country and downhill, in winter (at Lee Canyon) and hiking, camping, and picnicking the rest of the year.

Though it isn't exactly in the vicinity (five hours by car; one hour by small plane; 40 minutes by jet), Las Vegas does consider itself a gateway to the awesome, vastly silent **Grand Canyon National Park** (⊠ Box 129, Grand Canyon, AZ 86023, ☎ 520/638–7888; ☞ Arizona). One of the seven wonders of the natural world, the canyon is stunning in depth and size, and its layers of rock reveal a fascinating geological profile of the planet Earth. **South Rim Travel** (☎ 520/638–2748 or 800/682–4393), a full-service travel agency, can arrange rooms, cars, and Colorado River trips. **Eagle Canyon Airlines** (☎ 702/736–3333), based in Las Vegas, is one of several Grand Canyon flightseeing companies.

Casino Gambling

Most major hotels in Las Vegas (as well as in Reno and Lake Tahoe) are centered on large casinos. The largest casinos in town are at the MGM Grand, Bellagio, and Riviera. The games are slot machines, blackjack, baccarat, craps, roulette, keno, video poker, Let It Ride, Caribbean Stud, wheel of fortune, and race and sports betting. Admission to the casinos is free—until you start playing, of course. Most larger casinos give free gaming lessons, usually during the slower, weekday-morning hours. Slot machines are by far the favorite game; thanks to progressive computer-linked slot jackpots, such as Megabucks and Quartermania, wins have gone into the millions.

With more than 60 major casino-hotels competing for visitors and their dollars in Vegas, most try to separate themselves from the pack with some distinguishing characteristic. We list those with the most imaginative themes or attractive particulars.

Bellagio (✉ 3600 Las Vegas Blvd. S, ☎ 702/693–7111) is the second-largest casino in Las Vegas: sprawling, luxurious, and a bit overdecorated. The race and sports book features arena seating and massive electronic reader boards; each station is equipped with its own TV monitor. Club Bellagio is one of Las Vegas's most user-friendly slot clubs.

Binion's Horseshoe (✉ 128 E. Fremont St., ☎ 702/382–1600) hosts the world's highest-paying gambling tournament, the World Series of Poker, and sees some of the largest wagers in the world thanks to its no-limit policy.

Caesars Palace (✉ 3570 Las Vegas Blvd. S, ☎ 702/731–7110), a sprawling ersatz temple for serious gamblers with money to burn, lays on the antiquity, complete with toga-clad cocktail waitresses and a lounge called (and styled after) Cleopatra's Barge.

Circus Circus (✉ 2880 Las Vegas Blvd. S, ☎ 702/734–0410), arranged under a pink-and-white big top, takes on the hurly-burly atmosphere of a three-ring circus. For such a huge hotel, it has surprisingly low minimums.

Desert Inn (✉ 3145 Las Vegas Blvd. S, ☎ 702/733–4444) is small, relaxed, elegant, and—best of all—quiet, appealing to one of the most exclusive clienteles in town.

Excalibur (✉ 3850 Las Vegas Blvd. S, ☎ 702/597–7777) recalls the days of King Arthur. The casino is cavernous and cacophonous—with 2,630 slot machines, it couldn't be otherwise.

Flamingo Hilton (✉ 3555 Las Vegas Blvd. S, ☎ 702/733–3111) bears no resemblance to the "classy little joint" built by Bugsy Siegel in 1946. The splendiferous pink-flamingo theme is rampant in the huge casino, which is typical of a center-Strip megaresort: sprawling and raucous, with all the $5-minimum tables jammed with players.

Golden Nugget (✉ 129 E. Fremont St., ☎ 702/385–7111) is more Hollywood than Vegas, with white marble, gold leaf, and brass-plated elevators. The casino combines high Strip class with low downtown minimums.

Jackie Gaughan's Plaza (⊠ 1 N. Main St., ☎ 702/386–2110) is low-roller heaven, with penny slots, full-pay nickel video poker, 25¢ craps, and $3 blackjack galore.

Las Vegas Hilton (⊠ 3000 W. Paradise Rd., ☎ 702/732–5111) has a NASA-esque sports book, with 46 video screens, and the imaginative Space Quest casino, which fronts the Star Trek attraction.

Luxor (⊠ 3900 Las Vegas Blvd. S, ☎ 702/262–4000) recalls ancient Egypt with its 29-million-cubic-ft pyramid. The casino is roomy, regal, and round, with surprisingly fresh air throughout.

MGM Grand (⊠ 3805 Las Vegas Blvd. S, ☎ 702/891–1111) is the world's second-largest casino (Foxwoods in Ledyard, Connecticut, is the largest), with 3,500 slot machines, more than 100 gaming tables, and a Hollywood-entertainment theme.

The **Mirage** (⊠ 3400 Las Vegas Blvd. S, ☎ 702/791–7111) transports you to the South Seas, with thatch-roof gaming areas and tropical plants and flowers flanking an indoor stream and pond. Some of the machines in the high-roller slot area take $500 tokens.

Tropicana (⊠ 3801 Las Vegas Blvd. S, ☎ 702/739–2222) is lush and tropical, with a stunning pool area complete with swim-up blackjack in summer.

Getting Married in Las Vegas

Nevada is one of the easiest—and least-expensive—states in which to get married. There is no blood test or waiting period; all you need is a license ($35) from the **Marriage License Bureau** (⊠ 200 S. 3rd St., ☎ 702/455–4415), and you're ready to go. In Las Vegas there are about 25 chapels along the Strip, not including the numerous chapels in the casino-hotels (☞ Exploring Las Vegas, *above*). Services start at around $50.

Dining

Las Vegas has become the hottest restaurant market in the United States. On average, a new dining establishment opens here every week. Most hotels have multiple restaurants, including a buffet for which the city is justly famous: breakfast, on average, is $4–$5, lunch $6–$8, and dinner $8–$12. One of the cheapest buffets is at Circus Circus; two of the best are at Bellagio and Paris. Bally's has the best Sunday champagne brunch (the Sterling) in town.

$$$$ ✕ **Picasso.** By almost all accounts, the best restaurant in town is this
  ★   Mediterranean-French eatery, operated by celebrity-chef Julian Serrano. Choose between the tasting and prix-fixe menus—and marvel over the original Picasso artwork surrounding you. ⊠ *Bellagio Hotel, 3600 Las Vegas Blvd. S, ☎ 702/693–7111. AE, D, DC, MC, V.*

$$$–$$$$ ✕ **Pamplemousse.** The loving creation of Georges LaForges, a former Las Vegas maître d', this restaurant looks like a little French country inn. Classic French food is served *sans* menu; the waiter recites the daily specials. ⊠ *400 E. Sahara Ave., ☎ 702/733–2066. Jacket required. AE, D, DC, MC, V. No lunch.*

$$–$$$$ ✕ **Top of the World.** Floor-to-ceiling windows provide 360-degree views of the valley as this airy eatery rotates near the top of the 1,149-ft-tall Stratosphere Tower. Continental fare is spiced with a few twists: tequila-and-lime shrimp, spinach-and-wild-mushroom salad, and the like. ⊠ *Stratosphere Tower, 2000 Las Vegas Blvd. S, ☎ 702/380–7731. AE, D, DC, MC, V. No lunch.*

$$–$$$ ✕ **Bertolini's.** This sidewalk café inside the Forum Shops at Caesars can be noisy, but the northern Italian fare is first-rate. Order individual pizzas, soups, salads, and luscious gelato and sorbet. ⊠ *3570 Las Vegas Blvd. S,* ☎ *702/735–4663. AE, DC, MC, V.*

$$–$$$ ✕ **Mayflower Cuisinier.** Head to this off-Strip restaurant for creative
★ Chinese dishes with eclectic accents such as pan-seared ostrich with brandy sauce and an Asian Portobello mushroom burrito. ⊠ *4750 W. Sahara Ave.,* ☎ *702/870–8432. AE, D, DC, MC, V.*

$$–$$$ ✕ **Second Street Grill.** Although you'll find steaks, lamb chops, and veal on the menu, seafood—flown in fresh daily from around the Pacific Rim—is the specialty. This place has been around for years, but it's fairly unknown in the Las Vegas fine-dining firmament, so you can almost always get a reservation. ⊠ *Fremont Hotel, 200 E. Fremont St.,* ☎ *702/385–3232. AE, D, DC, MC, V. No lunch.*

$–$$$ ✕ **The Broiler.** A good, popular, and fairly inexpensive steak house, the Broiler has an excellent salad bar (including soups and desserts) as well as mesquite-grilled steaks, veal, and chicken. ⊠ *Boulder Station, 4111 Boulder Hwy.,* ☎ *702/432–7777. AE, D, DC, MC, V. No lunch.*

$–$$ ✕ **Battista's Hole in the Wall.** Battista Locatelli, a former opera singer, roams his domain here, a short walk from the Strip. Decorated with wine bottles, garlic, and celebrity photos, this Italian restaurant offers lots of specials and all the free wine you can drink. ⊠ *4041 Audrie St.,* ☎ *702/732–1424. AE, D, DC, MC, V. No lunch.*

$–$$ ✕ **Roberta's.** Las Vegas's most venerable "bargain gourmet" room is at the historic El Cortez downtown. You won't believe the prices, especially for a 16-ounce prime rib or a pound of king-crab legs. ⊠ *El Cortez, 600 E. Fremont St.,* ☎ *702/386–0692. AE, MC, V. No lunch.*

$–$$ ✕ **Viva Mercado's.** Don't let the shopping-center location fool you: This is one of the most popular Mexican restaurants in town. The room is cozy, and the food is low-fat and creative. ⊠ *6182 W. Flamingo Rd.,* ☎ *702/871–8826. Reservations not accepted. AE, MC, V.*

$ ✕ **Roxy's Pipe Organ Pizza.** The late 1999 expansion at the Fiesta, a locals casino in North Las Vegas, included a two-story pizzeria, featuring Regina's pizza (famous in Boston since the 1920s) and the 16-ton organ, complete with 3,000 pipes, flutes, and horns, from the Roxy Theater in New York City. ⊠ *Fiesta Hotel, 2400 N. Rancho Dr.,* ☎ *702/631–7000. Reservations not accepted. AE, D, MC, V.*

Lodging

Las Vegas lodging ranges from virtual palaces to simple motels. The hotels are better for cleanliness and location; the motels, while a little frayed around the edges, can be great bargains. In general, lodging in Vegas is far less expensive than lodging in other major U.S. resorts, though rates fluctuate widely according to supply and demand. The largest and most lavish hotels are on the Strip; downtown hotels are often less expensive. The range we're quoting is generally from a standard room (on a regular weekday) to a deluxe suite (on a busy weekend).

$$$–$$$$ 🏨 **Venetian.** All 3,036 standard guest rooms at the Venetian, the world's
★ largest convention center–hotel, are 700-square-ft suites, nearly twice the size of the average Las Vegas hotel room. There's a sunken living room, two 27-inch TVs, a 130-square-ft-bathroom with separate tub and shower and telephone, a minibar, a fax machine–copier–printer, three dual-line telephones, and a queen-size hide-a-bed. ⊠ *3355 Las Vegas Blvd. S, 89109,* ☎ *702/693–7111 or 888/283–6423,* 𝔽𝔸𝕏 *702/733–5000. 3,036 rooms. 14 restaurants, pools. AE, D, DC, MC, V.* ☜

$$–$$$$ 🏨 **Bellagio.** Las Vegas's greatest mousetrap is also one of its most expensive and exquisite. It caters only to adults (families are actively discouraged from staying here), and preferably high rollers, though the standard rooms are fairly ordinary. ⊠ *3600 Las Vegas Blvd. S, 89109,*

☎ 702/693–7111 or 888/987–6667, ℻ 702/697–7111. *3,025 rooms. 10 restaurants, pools. AE, D, DC, MC, V.* ✍

$$–$$$$ 🏨 **Caesars Palace.** Caesars caters to an upscale clientele, with world-
★   class service, lavish restaurants, and headliners such as David Copper-
field. The casino is full of handsome people making sizable wagers, but
there are plenty of nickel slots, too. Most guest rooms are opulent, even
by Las Vegas standards, and many have Roman-style bathtubs. ⊠ *3570
Las Vegas Blvd. S, 89109,* ☎ *702/731–7110 or 800/634–6661,* ℻ *702/
731–6636. 2,512 rooms. 19 restaurants, pools. AE, D, DC, MC, V.* ✍

$$–$$$$ 🏨 **Desert Inn.** Surrounded by the Strip's last golf course and offering
suites, town houses, and even villas, this hotel is one of the city's classi-
est. The elegant rooms have a southwestern theme. ⊠ *3145 Las Vegas
Blvd. S, 89109,* ☎ *702/733–4444 or 800/634–6906,* ℻ *702/733–
4774. 715 rooms. 4 restaurants, health club. AE, D, DC, MC, V.*

$$–$$$$ 🏨 **Las Vegas Hilton.** With 29 floors and three wings, this megasize hotel
seems even larger next to the low-rise Convention Center; it's one of
the most recognizable hotels in town. The rooms are spacious, and those
on the higher floors have great views. The high-tech Star Trek virtual-
reality show draws crowds. ⊠ *3000 Paradise Rd., 89109,* ☎ *702/732–
5111 or 800/732–7117,* ℻ *702/794–3611. 3,174 rooms. 9 restaurants,
pool. AE, D, DC, MC, V.* ✍

$$–$$$$ 🏨 **MGM Grand.** This movie-theme megaresort is the largest in the
world. Four emerald-green hotel towers bring to mind the *Wizard of
Oz;* a 33-acre theme park re-creates Hollywood back lots with rides
and performances. ⊠ *3799 Las Vegas Blvd. S, 89119,* ☎ *702/891–
1111 or 800/929–1111,* ℻ *702/891–1030. 5,005 rooms. 10 restaurants, pool, health club. AE, D, DC, MC, V.* ✍

$$–$$$$ 🏨 **The Mirage.** When this extravagant hotel opened in 1989, it launched
the current Las Vegas building boom. It's still the centerpiece of the Strip,
with its lush tropical landscaping, minimal neon, efficient use of recy-
cled water, rain-forest dome, and exemplary service. ⊠ *3400 Las Vegas
Blvd. S, 89109,* ☎ *702/791–7111 or 800/627–6667,* ℻ *702/791–7446.
3,049 rooms. 8 restaurants, pool, exercise room. AE, D, DC, MC, V.* ✍

$–$$$$ 🏨 **Flamingo Hilton.** The first luxury hotel in Las Vegas—it was sur-
rounded only by desert in 1946, when it was built—the Flamingo has
been completely reconstructed over the years and is now the fifth-largest
hotel in Las Vegas. With a time-share tower; a lush, 15-acre pool area
and wildlife park (yes, it has flamingos); and very reasonable rates, it
would still make founder Bugsy Siegel proud. ⊠ *3555 Las Vegas Blvd.
S, 89109,* ☎ *702/733–3111 or 800/732–2111,* ℻ *702/733–3528.
3,530 rooms. 8 restaurants, pools. AE, D, DC, MC, V.* ✍

$–$$$$ 🏨 **Golden Nugget.** The largest and classiest joint in Glitter Gulch, the
Nugget runs the gamut from traditional downtown bargain (dollar draft
beer) to Strip-style exclusivity (a segregated baccarat pit for high
rollers). The lobby is all marble and etched glass; guest rooms reflect
the same elegance. ⊠ *129 E. Fremont St., 89101,* ☎ *702/385–7111
or 800/634–3454,* ℻ *702/386–8362. 1,909 rooms. 5 restaurants,
pool, health club. AE, D, DC, MC, V.* ✍

$–$$$$ 🏨 **Rio Suite.** These four red-and-blue towers contain only suites. Ask
★   for a unit on the east side of one of the top floors, facing the Strip. The
41-story tower has the most festive casino in town: singers, dancers,
and jugglers in Mardi Gras costumes perform in a Masquerade Show
wherein parade floats inch along a 950-ft track suspended from the
high ceiling. ⊠ *3700 W. Flamingo Rd. (at Valley View), 89109,* ☎ *702/
252–7777 or 800/888–1808,* ℻ *702/253–6090. 2,569 suites. 15
restaurants, pool, health club. AE, D, DC, MC, V.* ✍

$–$$$ 🏨 **Excalibur.** This pastel-hue turreted castle is the third-largest resort
hotel in Las Vegas. Families come for the medieval theme, complete
with a King Arthur jousting tournament, old-world midway, and

strolling minstrels, mimes, and musicians. ⊠ *3850 Las Vegas Blvd. S, 89109,* ☎ *702/597–7777 or 800/937–7777,* ℻ *702/597–7009. 4,032 rooms. 7 restaurants, pool. AE, D, DC, MC, V.* ✇

$–$$$ 🏨 **Harrah's Las Vegas.** In 1997 Harrah's replaced its signature riverboat facade with a more tasteful design, but it's still the flagship of Harrah's extensive national gambling fleet. The rooms are modest by Strip standards. ⊠ *3475 Las Vegas Blvd. S, 89109,* ☎ *702/369–5000 or 800/ 634–6765,* ℻ *702/369–5008. 2,700 rooms. 6 restaurants, pool, exercise room. AE, D, DC, MC, V.* ✇

$–$$$ 🏨 **Luxor.** This bronze-color pyramid recalls its ancient Egyptian namesake with a sphinx out front and a replica of King Tut's tomb inside. "Inclinators" rise to the top floor at a 39-degree angle; the Egyptian theme continues in the large guest rooms. ⊠ *3900 Las Vegas Blvd. S, 89119,* ☎ *702/262–4000 or 800/288–1000,* ℻ *702/262–4454. 4,476 rooms. 7 restaurants, pool. AE, D, DC, MC, V.* ✇

$–$$$ 🏨 **Riviera.** One of the most famous hotels in Las Vegas, the Riviera also has one of the largest casinos in the world. It is convenient to both the upper Strip and the Convention Center. ⊠ *2901 Las Vegas Blvd. S, 89109,* ☎ *702/734–5110 or 800/634–6753,* ℻ *702/794–9663. 2,220 rooms. 5 restaurants, pool, health club. AE, D, DC, MC, V.* ✇

$–$$$ 🏨 **Stardust.** From its first incarnation as a motor hotel to its more recent 32-story tower, the Stardust has been one of the best-known hotels on the Strip. The rooms are large, attractive, and usually available when the rest of the Strip is sold out. ⊠ *3000 Las Vegas Blvd. S, 89109,* ☎ *702/732–6111 or 800/634–6757,* ℻ *702/732–6296. 2,500 rooms. 6 restaurants, pool, health club. AE, D, DC, MC, V.* ✇

$–$$$ 🏨 **Treasure Island.** This hotel's theme is loosely based on Robert Louis Stevenson's novel, and the landscaping and decor are ersatz South Seas. There's a monorail to the Mirage. Rooms are smallish, but they were remodeled in 1999. ⊠ *3300 Las Vegas Blvd. S, 89109,* ☎ *702/894– 7111 or 800/944–7444,* ℻ *702/894–7446. 2,912 rooms. 6 restaurants, pool, health club. AE, D, DC, MC, V.* ✇

$–$$$ 🏨 **Tropicana.** Two high-rise towers loom above beautiful grounds, complete with waterfalls and swans. Rooms have a tropical theme, with bamboo and pastels. ⊠ *3801 Las Vegas Blvd. S, 89109,* ☎ *702/739– 2222 or 800/634–4000,* ℻ *702/739–2469. 1,912 rooms. 6 restaurants, pools, health club. AE, D, DC, MC, V.*

$–$$ 🏨 **Sahara.** Like many of its neighbors, the Sahara began as a small motor hotel and built itself up by adding towers. It has a casino and serves as a business hotel for the Convention Center down the street. Tower rooms are large, and those that face south overlook the Strip. ⊠ *2535 Las Vegas Blvd. S, 89109,* ☎ *702/737–2111 or 800/634–6666,* ℻ *702/791– 2027. 1,710 rooms. 5 restaurants, health club. AE, D, DC, MC, V.*

$–$$ 🏨 **Sam's Town.** This hotel caters mostly to local residents and their families. Some rooms have views of the desert and mountains; those facing inside overlook an 18-story courtyard with trees, creeks, and a waterfall. ⊠ *5111 Boulder Hwy., 89122,* ☎ *702/456–7777 or 800/ 634–6371,* ℻ *702/454–8014. 650 rooms. 7 restaurants, pool. AE, D, DC, MC, V.* ✇

$ 🏨 **Circus Circus.** Catering primarily to families with children, the hotel has painted circus tents in the hallways and a generally chaotic atmosphere. The brightly colored rooms (red carpets and chairs; red-, pink- , and blue-striped wallpaper) are small but clean. ⊠ *2880 Las Vegas Blvd. S, 89109,* ☎ *702/734–0410 or 800/634–3450,* ℻ *702/734– 2268. 3,774 rooms. 7 restaurants, pools. AE, D, DC, MC, V.* ✇

$ 🏨 **Jackie Gaughan's Plaza.** This casino-hotel was built on the original site of the Union Pacific train station; the rooms facing front look down at Glitter Gulch, and those in back face the railroad yards. Rooms are done in light mauve tones. ⊠ *1 Main St., 89101,* ☎ *702/*

386–2110 or 800/634–6575, FAX 702/382–8281. 1,037 rooms. 3 restaurants, pool. AE, D, DC, MC, V.

Motels

🏨 **Days Inn–Town Hall** (⊠ 4155 Koval La., 89109, ☎ 702/731–2111 or 800/634–6541, FAX 702/731–1113), 360 rooms; restaurant, pool; *$*.

🏨 **Motel 6** (⊠ 195 E. Tropicana Ave., 89109, ☎ 702/798–0728, FAX 702/798–5657), 877 rooms; pools; *$*.

🏨 **Westward Ho** (⊠ 2900 Las Vegas Blvd. S, 89109, ☎ 702/731–2900 or 800/634–6651, FAX 702/731–6154), 1,000 rooms; restaurant, pools; *$*.

Nightlife and the Arts

Nightlife

Las Vegas may have more nocturnal activities than any other city in America—if not the world.

SHOWS

Hotel showrooms seat from several hundred to 2,000. Most are luxurious and intimate, with few, if any, bad seats. The old-style seating system involves arriving early and tipping the maître d' or captain. The new trend is reserved seating, which eliminates the waiting and "survival of the tippest." When a show is expected to sell out, hotel guests are given preference.

Showrooms present five main types of entertainment: headliner shows, such as David Copperfield, Tom Jones, and Liza Minnelli; big production shows, such as Bally's *Jubilee!* or the Tropicana's *Folies Bergères,* which include elaborate song-and-dance numbers, smaller specialty acts, and topless showgirls; small production shows, with song and dance on a smaller scale, such as *Forever Plaid* at the Flamingo Hilton; the ubiquitous lounge shows, where pop bands play dance music and the only admission charge is the purchase of a drink or two; and two productions of Cirque du Soleil, a new-age circus with an international cast.

The major hotels' entertainment venues are as follows: **Bally's,** large production show; **Bellagio,** Cirque du Soleil; **Desert Inn,** headliners; **Excalibur,** large production show; **Flamingo Hilton,** large and small production shows; **Harrah's Las Vegas,** small production show; **Imperial Palace,** small production show; **Luxor,** small production show; **MGM Grand,** headliners and large production shows; **Mirage,** large production show; **Paris,** small production show; **Rio Suite,** small production show; **Riviera,** large and small production shows; **Stardust,** large production show; **Treasure Island,** Cirque du Soleil; **Tropicana,** large production show, **Venetian,** small production show. *See* Exploring Las Vegas *and* Lodging (both *above*) for addresses and phone numbers.

COMEDY CLUBS

MGM Grand: **Catch a Rising Star.** Harrah's: **The Improv.** Tropicana: **The Comedy Stop.** Riviera: **The Comedy Club.**

The Arts

Most arts events in Las Vegas are associated with the **University of Nevada, Las Vegas** (☎ 702/895–3011). For additional information call the **Allied Arts Council** (☎ 702/731–5419).

Outdoor Activities and Sports

Spectator Sports

Boxing: Caesars Palace and **MGM Grand** present championship bouts.
Golf: PGA Las Vegas Invitational (⊠ Desert Inn, ☎ 702/382–6616),

October. **Rodeo: National Finals Rodeo** (✉ Thomas & Mack Center, University of Nevada, ☎ 702/731–2115), early December.

Shopping

The chichi retail area at the hotel **Bellagio** (✉ 3600 Las Vegas Blvd. S, ☎ 702/693–7111) is now the most upscale shopping in Las Vegas with Gucci, Prada, Tiffany's, and restaurants such as Le Cirque. Some of Las Vegas's best shopping is on the Strip at the **Fashion Show Mall** (✉ 3200 Las Vegas Blvd. S, ☎ 702/369–8382), a collection of 150 shops and department stores, including Saks Fifth Avenue and Neiman Marcus. The **Forum Shops at Caesars** (✉ 3570 Las Vegas Blvd. S, ☎ 702/893–4800), a complex of 135 specialty stores adjoining Caesars Palace, dazzles shoppers with two replicated Roman markets, complete with fountains, a simulated sky above, and two shows with animatronic-statues, enormous figures that talk and move. You'll find the likes of Gucci, Ann Taylor, the Museum Company, and F.A.O. Schwarz, along with half a dozen popular restaurants. **Boulevard Mall** (✉ 3528 S. Maryland Pkwy., ☎ 702/735–8268), about 3 mi from the Strip, is the largest shopping mall in Nevada. **Meadows Mall** (✉ 4300 Meadows La., ☎ 702/878–4849) is on the northwest side of town and has a big merry-go-round for kids. **Gamblers General Store** (✉ 800 S. Main St., ☎ 702/382–9903) carries all manner of gambling paraphernalia.

RENO

Reno, once the gambling and divorce capital of the country, is smaller, less crowded, friendlier, and prettier than Las Vegas. Established in 1859 as a trading station at a bridge over the Truckee River, Reno grew along with the silver mines of nearby Virginia City (starting in 1860), the railroad (railroad officials named the town in 1868), and gambling (legalized in 1931). Today Reno is getting a boost from the National Bowling Stadium—the only one of its kind in the country—as well as the 1,700-room Silver Legacy downtown.

Visitor Information

Reno-Sparks Convention and Visitors Authority (✉ 4590 S. Virginia St., Reno 89502, ☎ 775/827–7600 or 800/367–7366).

Arriving and Departing

By Bus
Greyhound (✉ 155 Stevenson St., ☎ 775/322–2970 or 800/231–2222).

By Car
The major highways leading to Reno are I–80 (east–west) and U.S. 395 (north–south).

By Plane
Reno–Tahoe International Airport (✉ 2001 E. Plumb La., ☎ 775/328–6400), served by national and regional airlines, is on the east side of the city, just minutes from downtown.

By Train
Amtrak (✉ 135 E. Commercial Row, ☎ 775/329–8638 or 800/872–7245).

Getting Around Reno

Reno is such a small city that it's easy to get around on foot or by cab. Taxis are easily hired at the airport and in front of the major hotels; the main taxi firms are **Reno-Sparks Cab Co.** (☎ 775/333–3333), **Whittlesea Taxi** (☎ 775/322–2222), and **Star Taxi** (☎ 775/355–5555).

There are rental-car agencies at the airport. **Reno Citifare** (☎ 702/348–7433) provides local bus service. Many large hotels run courtesy buses around town and to and from the airport.

Exploring Reno

One advantage Reno has over Las Vegas is weather: Its summer temperatures are much more temperate, making strolling a pleasure. The city's focal point is the famous Reno Arch, a sign over the upper end of Virginia Street proclaiming it "The Biggest Little City in the World."

As in Las Vegas, gambling is a favorite pastime. Although not as garish as their Vegas counterparts, Reno's casinos still offer plenty of glitz. With the exception of the Reno Hilton, Peppermill, Atlantis, and John Ascuaga's Nugget, they are crowded into five square blocks downtown.

Circus Circus (✉ 500 N. Sierra St., ☎ 775/329–0711 or 800/648–5010), marked by a neon clown sucking a lollipop, is the best stop for families with children. Complete with clowns, games, fun-house mirrors, and circus acts, the midway on the mezzanine above the casino floor is open from 10 AM to midnight.

Club Cal-Neva (✉ 38 E. 2nd St., ☎ 775/323–1046 or 877/777–7303) is the best place in town to gamble, with low limits and optimal rules.

Eldorado (✉ 345 N. Virginia St., ☎ 775/786–5700 or 800/648–5966) is action-packed, with tons of slots, good bar-top video poker, and one of the largest roulette tables around.

Flamingo Hilton (✉ 255 N. Sierra St., ☎ 775/322–1111 or 800/648–4882) is a scaled-down version of its Vegas counterpart, complete with a pink-feathered neon flamingo and a bar-restaurant on the top floor.

Harrah's (✉ 219 N. Center St., ☎ 775/786–3232 or 800/648–3773) debuted in 1937 as the Tango Club and now occupies two city blocks, with a sprawling casino, a race and sports book, and an outdoor promenade; it also has a 29-story Hampton Inn annex. Minimums are low, and service is friendly.

Silver Legacy (✉ 407 N. Virginia St., ☎ 775/329–4777 or 800/687–7833) is a classy, Victorian-themed casino with a 120-ft-tall mining rig that mints silver-dollar tokens.

Four casinos lie outside the downtown area. The **Reno Hilton** (✉ 2500 E. 2nd St., ☎ 775/789–2000 or 800/648–5080) is the largest casino in Reno, with 100,000 square ft. The **Peppermill** (✉ 2707 S. Virginia St., ☎ 775/826–2121 or 800/648–6992) is the gaudiest, glitziest, and noisiest. The **Atlantis** (✉ 3800 S. Virginia St., ☎ 775/825–4700 or 800/723–6500) has a lush Polynesian decor. Orozko, the newest restaurant at **John Ascuaga's Nugget** (✉ 1100 Nugget Ave., Sparks, ☎ 775/356–3300 or 800/648–1177), gives the small casino a new flair with its Pyrenees village square design.

Besides the casino-hotels, Reno has a number of cultural and family-friendly attractions. On the University of Nevada campus, the sleekly designed **Fleischmann Planetarium** (✉ 1600 N. Virginia St., ☎ 775/784–4811; ✉ free) has films and astronomy shows. The **Nevada Museum of Art** (✉ 160 W. Liberty St., ☎ 775/329–3333; ✉ $3), the state's largest art museum, has changing exhibits. More than 220 antique and classic automobiles, including an Elvis Presley Cadillac, are on display at the **National Automobile Museum** (✉ Mill and Lake Sts., ☎ 775/333–9300; ✉ $7.50).

C Wilbur D. May Great Basin Adventure (✉ 1502 Washington St., ☎ 775/785–4153; ⌨ $3) in Rancho San Rafael Park has a petting zoo, a flume ride, and a mining exhibit that traces the evolution of the Great Basin.

C In the town of Sparks, the family amusement park **Wild Island** (✉ 250 Wild Island Ct., ☎ 775/331–9453; ⌨ call for prices) includes a water park; a 36-hole minigolf course; Indy, sprint, and bumper cars; and a state-of-the-art video arcade.

The always-festive **Downtown River Walk** (✉ S. Virginia St. and the river, ☎ 775/334–2077) often hosts special events featuring street performers, musicians, dancers, food, art exhibits, and games. **Victorian Square** (✉ Victorian Ave. between Rock and Pyramid) is fringed by restored turn-of-the-20th-century houses and Victorian-dressed casinos and storefronts; its bandstand is the focal point for the many festivals held here.

Outside Reno

Virginia City, only 25 mi from Reno (U.S. 395 south to Rte. 341), was once the largest population center in Nevada, with more than 20,000 residents, 110 saloons, and—ahem—one church. The Comstock Lode, one of the largest gold and silver deposits ever discovered, was responsible for the city's boom (1860–80), and it's still one of the liveliest historic mining towns in the West.

Visitor Information

Contact the **Virginia City Chamber of Commerce** (✉ C St. across from the post office, Box 464, 89440, ☎ 775/847–0311).

You can still belly up to the grand mahogany bar and hear honky-tonk piano music at the **Bucket of Blood** (☎ 775/847–0322) saloon on C Street. The lavish interiors of **Mackay Mansion** (✉ 129 D St., ☎ 775/847–0173; ⌨ $3) and the **Castle** (✉ B St. just south of Taylor, ☎ 775/847–0275; ⌨ $3) offer a glimpse of the past with such adornments as Oriental rugs, Italian marble, and Brussels lace, as well as table settings made from the silver mined beneath their floors. The **Virginia & Truckee Railroad** (✉ Washington and F Sts., ☎ 775/847–0380; ⌨ $5.50) can take you through the Comstock mining region on a historic, steam-powered locomotive. Virginia City's most famous resident was Mark Twain, who lived here from 1861 to 1864 while working as a reporter for the *Territorial Enterprise*; the **Mark Twain Museum** (✉ 47 S. C St., ☎ 775/847–0525; ⌨ $1) occupies the newspaper's pressroom and displays 19th-century printing equipment.

South of Virginia City is **Carson City,** the state capital. The **Carson City Chamber of Commerce** (✉ 1900 S. Carson St., ☎ 775/882–1565) has information on the town's attractions.

The **Nevada State Museum** (✉ 600 N. Carson St., ☎ 775/687–4811; ⌨ $3), once a U.S. mint, is packed with exhibits on Nevada's natural history, the early mining days, CC-minted silver and gold coins, and willow baskets woven by Washoe artists. The **Nevada State Railroad Museum** (✉ 2180 S. Carson St., ☎ 775/687–6953; ⌨ $2) has an extensive collection of historical passenger and freight cars and two restored Virginia & Truckee trains; be sure to take the tour of the restoration shop.

Genoa (pronounced juh-*no*-uh), the oldest settlement in Nevada, is a quaint Victorian town about 20 mi south of Carson City, just west of U.S. 395. **Mormon Station State Historic Park** (✉ Foothill Rd. and Genoa La., ☎ 775/687–4379; ⌨ free) contains an early log cabin and Mormon artifacts. **Walley's Hot Springs Resort** (✉ 2001 Foothill Rd., ☎ 775/782–8155) has hot mineral pools dating from 1862.

Dining

As in Las Vegas, your most economical meals are the casino-hotel breakfast, lunch, and dinner buffets. Favorites are those at the **Atlantis, John Ascuaga's Nugget** (☞ Exploring Reno, *above*), and the **Peppermill** (☞ Lodging, *below*).

$$$–$$$$ ✕ **19th Hole.** This posh restaurant on the Lakeridge Golf Course has a great view of the city and nearby mountains and serves well-prepared American and Continental food. ⊠ *1200 Razorback Rd.,* ☎ *775/ 825–1250. D, MC, V.*

$$–$$$$ ✕ **Pimparel's La Table Française.** In a converted house off the beaten track, Pimparel's specializes in award-winning French provincial cuisine. It's popular with locals for special occasions. ⊠ *3065 W. 4th St.,* ☎ *775/323–3200. AE, D, DC, MC, V. No lunch.*

$$–$$$ ✕ **Harrah's Steak House.** This casino-hotel's dark and romantic restaurant has been serving prime beef and fresh seafood since 1967. ⊠ *219 N. Center St.,* ☎ *775/786–3232. AE, D, DC, MC, V.*

$$–$$$ ✕ **La Strada.** The excellent northern Italian cuisine is served upstairs from the Eldorado Casino. The pastas and sauces are homemade, and the gourmet pizzas bake in a wood-fired oven. ⊠ *345 N. Virginia St.,* ☎ *775/786–5700. AE, D, DC, MC, V. No lunch.*

$–$$ ✕ **Café de Thai.** The soups, salads, stir-fries, and curries are expertly prepared by a Thai national trained at the Culinary Institute. ⊠ *3314 S. McCarran,* ☎ *775/829–8424. MC, V.*

$–$$ ✕ **John A's Oyster Bar.** Entirely nautical in theme, John A's restaurant and bar serves the best steamers, pan roasts, cioppino, chowder, shrimp Louie, and cocktails this side of Fisherman's Wharf. ⊠ *1100 Nugget Ave., Sparks,* ☎ *775/356–3300. AE, D, DC, MC, V.*

$ ✕ **Bertha Miranda's Mexican Restaurant.** Begun as a hole-in-the-wall, this has grown into a highly successful establishment. The food is made fresh by Bertha's family, and the salsa is the best in town. ⊠ *336 Mill St.,* ☎ *775/786–9697. MC, V.*

$ ✕ **Blue Heron.** Here's one of the few natural-food restaurants in this meat-and-potatoes state. Choose from grains, veggies, and tofu and tempeh dishes, even macrobiotic meals; many of the offerings are grown fresh on the owner's farm. ⊠ *1091 S. Virginia St.,* ☎ *775/786– 4110. DC, MC, V.*

$ ✕ **Louis' Basque Corner.** Basque shepherds once populated northern Nevada; sample their heritage at this family-style restaurant, which specializes in oxtail, lamb, and tongue. ⊠ *301 E. 4th St.,* ☎ *775/323– 7203. AE, DC, MC, V.*

$ ✕ **Nugget Diner.** Think classic Americana diner: Seating is on stools at front and back counters. The Awful Awful Burger is renowned, as is the prime rib. ⊠ *Nugget Casino, 233 N. Virginia St.,* ☎ *775/323– 0716. MC, V.*

Lodging

Most of Reno's hotels are downtown.

$–$$$$ 🏨 **Eldorado.** Owned by fourth-generation locals, the Eldorado is known for its fine food and attention to detail. Rooms, including an all-suite tower, overlook the mountains. ⊠ *345 N. Virginia St., 89501,* ☎ *775/786–5700 or 800/648–5966,* 🖷 *702/322–7124. 836 rooms. 8 restaurants, pool. AE, D, DC, MC, V.* ✍

$–$$$$ 🏨 **Silver Legacy.** This two-tower megaresort centers on a 120-ft-tall mining machine that coins dollar tokens. Skywalks connect it to Circus Circus (☞ *below*) and the Eldorado (☞ *above*). ⊠ *407 N. Virginia St., 89501,* ☎ *775/329–4777 or 800/687–8733. 1,700 rooms. 5 restaurants. AE, D, DC, MC, V.* ✍

$–$$$ ⊞ **Flamingo Hilton.** This sister hotel of the Las Vegas and Laughlin Flamingos has a $1 million sign and a 21-story tower. The guest rooms facing west have nice views of the mountains. ⊠ *255 N. Sierra St., 89501,* ☎ *775/322–1111 or 800/648–4822,* FAX *702/322–1111. 604 rooms. 4 restaurants. AE, D, DC, MC, V.* ✆

$–$$$ ⊞ **Harrah's.** This is one of the most luxurious hotels in downtown Reno. Large guest rooms decorated in blues and mauves overlook downtown and the entire mountain-ringed valley. ⊠ *219 N. Center St., 89501,* ☎ *775/786–3232 or 800/648–3773. 565 rooms. 6 restaurants, pool, health club. AE, D, MC, V.* ✆

$–$$$ ⊞ **John Ascuaga's Nugget.** This casino-hotel in neighboring Sparks offers some of the largest and most luxurious rooms around—as well as the only indoor pool in town. ⊠ *1100 Nugget Ave., Sparks 89431,* ☎ *775/356–3300 or 800/648–1177,* FAX *775/356–3434. 1,983 rooms. 7 restaurants, pool. AE, D, DC, MC, V.* ✆

$–$$$ ⊞ **Peppermill.** Three miles from downtown, the Peppermill has Reno's most colorful casino. It has eight room sizes (and styles) to choose from; their photos are on display in the lobby. ⊠ *2707 S. Virginia St., 89502,* ☎ *775/826–2121 or 800/648–6992,* FAX *775/826–5205. 1,070 rooms. 5 restaurants, pool, health club. AE, D, DC, MC, V.* ✆

$–$$$ ⊞ **Reno Hilton.** This 27-story hotel near the airport is Nevada's largest hotel north of Las Vegas. In fact, almost everything here is the area's largest: the buffet, race and sports books, showroom, convention facilities, bowling alley, arcade, wedding chapel, driving range, and RV park. ⊠ *2500 E. 2nd St., 89595,* ☎ *775/789–2000 or 800/648–5080,* FAX *775/789–2418. 2,001 rooms. 6 restaurants, pool, health club. AE, D, DC, MC, V.* ✆

$–$$ ⊞ **Comstock.** The lobby and casino have an Old West theme, and spectacular neon lights simulate exploding fireworks on the exterior tower walls. The Victorian-style rooms are small, with city or mountain views. ⊠ *200 W. 2nd St., 89501,* ☎ *775/329–1880 or 800/648–4866,* FAX *775/348–0539. 310 rooms. 3 restaurants, pool, health club. MC, V.*

$ ⊞ **Circus Circus.** This smaller version of the giant Las Vegas hotel has the same family-oriented atmosphere. The rooms, though small and garish, are good values—when you can get one. ⊠ *500 N. Sierra St., 89503,* ☎ *775/329–0711 or 800/648–5010,* FAX *775/329–0599. 1,625 rooms. 3 restaurants. AE, DC, MC, V.* ✆

Nightlife and the Arts

Nightlife

As in Las Vegas, Reno area nightlife breaks down into several categories: headliners, big production shows, small production shows, and lounge acts. Here are the options at the major Reno hotels (for addresses and phone numbers, *see* Lodging, *above*). **Circus Circus** has continual circus acts. **Eldorado** has a small production show. **Harrah's Reno** has headliners and small production shows. Mostly country-and-western headliners play **John Ascuaga's Nugget**. **Reno Hilton** has headliners, a large production show, and a comedy club.

The Arts

Most of the arts in Reno—such as the **Nevada Festival Ballet** (☎ 775/785–7915), the **Nevada Opera Association** (☎ 775/786–4046), the **Reno Philharmonic** (☎ 775/323–6393), and the **Performing Arts Series** (☎ 775/348–9413)—center on the **University of Nevada, Reno** (☎ 775/784–1110).

Shopping

Arlington Gardens (⊠ 600 W. Plumb La., ☎ 775/828–1911) is a trendy mall with a cookbook store, a bath-and-body shop, clothiers, and a café.

The **Meadowood Mall** (⊠ Virginia St. at McCarran Blvd., ☎ 775/827–8450) is the Reno area's big mall, with 90 stores and a food court. **AAA Slots of Fun** (⊠ 2800 Dickerson Rd., ☎ 775/324–7711) sells a large selection of new and used slot and video-poker machines.

LAKE TAHOE

Southwest of Reno, Lake Tahoe's vast expanse of crystal-blue water surrounded by rugged peaks is a playground for both locals and visitors. Half in Nevada and half in California, it's the largest alpine lake in North America, 22 mi long and 12 mi wide. The region is known for outstanding skiing in winter; boating, fishing, and mountain sports in summer; and casino entertainment year-round.

Visitor Information

Tahoe-Douglas Chamber of Commerce (⊠ U.S. 50 at the Round Hill Shopping Center, Box 7139, Stateline 89449, ☎ 775/588–4591). **Incline Village/Crystal Bay Visitors and Convention Bureau** (⊠ 969 Tahoe Blvd., Incline Village 89451-9508, ☎ 775/832–1606 or 800/468–2463).

Arriving and Departing

By Car
From Reno take U.S. 395 south through Carson City to U.S. 50, which leads to South Lake Tahoe; U.S. 395 south to Route 431 leads to North Lake Tahoe.

By Plane
The closest major airport to Lake Tahoe is **Reno–Tahoe International Airport** (☞ Reno, *above*). No scheduled commercial flights serve the **Lake Tahoe Airport** (⊠ 1901 Airport Rd., ☎ 530/542–6180), near Stateline.

Exploring Lake Tahoe

The scenic drive encircling Lake Tahoe (Routes 28 and 89) affords stunning lake, forest, and mountain vistas. You can also explore the lake from on board the **MS *Dixie II*** (⊠ Zephyr Cove, ☎ 775/588–3508; ☎ $18–$42). **Crystal Bay,** the northernmost community on the Nevada side, has a small-town, outdoorsy feel and several casinos. Affluent **Incline Village,** 2 mi east of Crystal Bay, has lakeshore residences, weekend condos, and inviting shopping areas. South of Incline Village, the **Ponderosa Ranch** (⊠ Rte. 28, ☎ 775/831–0691; ☎ $8.50–$10.50) is a Hollywood-style western "town" based on the TV series *Bonanza*, open from early May through October.

At the south end of the lake are the neon lights of **Stateline,** where four towering and two low-rise casinos cluster in two long blocks. Across the border in California is **South Lake Tahoe,** the most populous town on the lake. Ski Run Boulevard takes you southeast to the **Heavenly Ski Area** (☎ 775/586–7000; ☎ $12), where the tram lifts you to fantastic skiing in winter and unbeatable views over the water year-round.

Dining and Lodging

Incline Village

$$–$$$ ✕ **Lone Eagle Grille.** This restaurant in the Hyatt Regency Hotel has a fantastic view of the lake. Specialties include duck, fish, and steak. ⊠ *Country Club Dr. at Lakeshore,* ☎ *775/831–1111. AE, D, DC, MC, V.*

$–$$ ✕ **Azzara's.** This typical trattoria serves excellent food—a dozen different pasta dishes, along with pizza, chicken, lamb, veal, and shrimp—

with understated elegance. ✉ *930 Tahoe Blvd.,* ☎ *775/831–0346. AE, MC, V. No lunch.*

$$–$$$$ 🏨 **Hyatt Regency Lake Tahoe.** Rooms are large and attractive, with warm color schemes and lake views. Amenities include a private beach, water sports, Camp Hyatt for kids, and a casino with a forest theme. ✉ *Country Club Dr. at Lakeshore, Incline Village 89450,* ☎ *775/832–1234 or 800/233–1234,* FAX *775/831–7508. 460 rooms. 3 restaurants, pool, health club. AE, DC, MC, V.* ✧

Stateline

$$$$ ✕ **The Summit.** The view from this 16th-floor restaurant is spectacular. The creative menu includes artfully presented salads, seafood entrées, and decadent desserts. ✉ *Harrah's Casino/Hotel Lake Tahoe, U.S. 50,* ☎ *775/588–6611. AE, D, DC, MC, V.*

$$$–$$$$ ✕ **Sage Room Steak House.** This romantic restaurant is descended from the Wagon Wheel Saloon and Gambling Hall—the origins of Harvey's Resort. The sautéed prawns are excellent. ✉ *Harvey's Resort Hotel/Casino, U.S. 50,* ☎ *775/588–2411. AE, D, DC, MC, V.*

$–$$$ ✕ **Empress Court.** Plush velvet booths and etched-glass partitions are the backdrop for traditional Chinese cuisine. The grilled-squab salad is a standout. ✉ *Caesars Tahoe, U.S. 50,* ☎ *775/588–3515. AE, DC, MC, V. No lunch.*

$–$$ ✕ **El Vaquero.** Wrought iron, a fountain, and tiles give this restaurant a touch of Old Mexico. The fare is traditional Mexican. ✉ *Harvey's Resort Hotel/Casino, U.S. 50,* ☎ *775/588–2411. AE, D, DC, MC, V.*

$ ✕ **The Forest Buffet.** On the 18th floor of Harrah's, the Forest has the best view of any buffet in Nevada and simulates its namesake inside. ✉ *Harrah's Casino/Hotel Lake Tahoe, U.S. 50,* ☎ *775/588–6611. Reservations not accepted. AE, DC, MC, V.*

$$$–$$$$ 🏨 **Harrah's Casino/Hotel Lake Tahoe.** Rooms are large and comfort-
★ able, and each has two full bathrooms, complete with telephone and TV. Most rooms also have excellent views. ✉ *U.S. 50 (Box 8), 89449,* ☎ *775/588–6606 or 800/648–3773,* FAX *775/586–6607. 533 rooms. 7 restaurants, pool, health club. AE, DC, MC, V.*

$$$–$$$$ 🏨 **Harvey's Resort Hotel/Casino.** Harvey's is Lake Tahoe's oldest and largest resort. Rooms have a conventional style; most look out on the lake and the mountains. ✉ *U.S. 50 (Box 128), 89449,* ☎ *775/588–2411 or 800/648–3361,* FAX *775/588–6643. 740 rooms. 8 restaurants. AE, D, DC, MC, V.*

$$–$$$ 🏨 **Caesars Tahoe.** Once you negotiate the lobby staircase and casino areas, you'll find hallways with faux Corinthian columns and plush rooms in fantastical color schemes, such as hot pink with mint green. The indoor pool has a waterfall and a swim tunnel. ✉ *U.S. 50 (Box 5800), 89449,* ☎ *775/588–3515 or 800/648–3353,* FAX *775/586–2050. 440 rooms. 5 restaurants, pool, health club. AE, D, DC, MC, V.*

Nightlife

Lake Tahoe nightlife centers on the top-name entertainment and production shows at the casino-hotels. **Caesars Tahoe** and **Harrah's** (☞ Dining and Lodging, *above*) both present headliners.

Outdoor Activities and Sports

Fishing

The lake is renowned for mighty Macinkaw and rainbow trout. Non-resident fishing permits are available at most sporting goods stores. For more information call the **Department of Wildlife** (☎ 775/688–1500).

Golf

Edgewood at Tahoe (✉ Stateline, ☎ 775/588–3566) has 18 holes. **Glenbrook Golf Course** (✉ Glenbrook, ☎ 775/749–5201) has 9 holes. **Incline Village Championship Golf Course** (✉ 955 Fairway Blvd., ☎ 775/832–1144) has 18 holes. **Incline Village Executive Course** (✉ 690 Wilson Way, ☎ 775/832–1150) has 18 holes.

Hiking

More than 250 mi of hiking trails traverse this area, many through high mountain passes or along streams and meadows with sweeping views. Contact the **U.S. Forest Service** (☎ 530/573–2600) for information.

Ski Areas

Lake Tahoe has more than 15 world-class downhill resorts and nearly a dozen cross-country ski centers, all within an hour of one another. Elevations range from 6,000 to 10,000 ft, with vertical drops up to nearly 4,000 ft. More than 150 lifts operate during the season, which usually lasts from November through May.

Cross-Country

Diamond Peak (✉ 1210 Ski Way, Incline Village 89450, ☎ 775/832–1177) has 22 mi of groomed high-elevation track, including skating lanes.

Downhill

Diamond Peak (☞ *above*) has 7 lifts, 30 runs, and a 1,840-ft vertical drop. **Heavenly Ski Area** (✉ Box 2180, Stateline 89449, ☎ 775/586–7000 or 800/243–2836), straddling the Nevada-California border, has 26 lifts, 72 trails (including the longest run in Tahoe), and a 3,600-ft drop. **Mt. Rose** (✉ 22222 Mt. Rose Hwy., Reno 89511, ☎ 775/849–0704) has one of the highest base elevations in the area, with unequaled powder skiing, 5 lifts, 41 runs, and a 1,440-ft drop.

NEW HAMPSHIRE

By Ed and
Roon Frost

Updated by
Paula J.
Flanders

Capital	Concord
Population	1,173,000
Motto	Live Free or Die
State Bird	Purple finch
State Flower	Purple lilac
Postal Abbreviation	NH

Statewide Visitor Information

New Hampshire Office of Travel and Tourism Development (⊠ Box 1856, Concord 03302, ☎ 603/271–2343 or 800/386–4664). **Alpine ski and foliage hot line** (☎ 800/258–3608). **Cross-country ski conditions** (☎ 800/262–6660).

Scenic Drives

The **Kancamagus Highway** (Route 112) rolls through 35 mi of the White Mountains between Lincoln and Conway. The 32-mi stretch of **Route 113** between Holderness and South Tamworth is full of hills and curves, and winds between mountains and lakes. **Routes 12A and 12** parallel the Connecticut River along the Vermont border between Lebanon and Keene, with views of the river and the picturesque towns.

National and State Parks

National Forest

The **White Mountains National Forest** (⊠ U.S. Forest Service, 719 N. Main St., Laconia 03246, ☎ 603/528–8721; ☞ $5 day-use fee, good for 7 consecutive days) occupies 790,000 acres of northern New Hampshire (☞ The White Mountains, *below*). There are good hiking trails throughout the area and 20 campgrounds with more than 900 sites.

State Parks

The **Division of Parks and Recreation** (⊠ Box 1856, Concord 03302, ☎ 603/271–3556) maintains about 70 state parks, beaches, and historic sites.

THE SEACOAST

The southern end of New Hampshire's 18-mi coastline is dominated by Hampton Beach—5 mi of sand, sunbathers, motels, arcades, and a boardwalk. At the northern end is Portsmouth, with its beautifully restored historic area, one-of-a-kind restaurants, and the state's only working port. In between are dunes, beaches, salt marshes, and state parks where you can picnic, hike, swim, boat, and fish.

Visitor Information

Greater Portsmouth Chamber of Commerce (⊠ 500 Market St., Portsmouth 03801, ☎ 603/436–1118). **Hampton Beach Area Chamber of Commerce** (⊠ 836 Lafayette Rd., Hampton 03842, ☎ 603/926–8718).

Arriving and Departing

By Bus

C&J (☎ 603/431–2424). **Concord Trailways** (☎ 800/639–3317). **Vermont Transit** (☎ 603/436–0163 or 800/451–3292).

By Car

I–95 provides access to the Hamptons (Exit 2), central Portsmouth (Exits 3–6), and Portsmouth harbor and historic district (Exit 7).

Exploring the Seacoast

The Atlantic is rarely out of sight from Route 1A, and there are plenty of spots for pulling over. In summer, stop to see the 2,000 rosebushes at **Fuller Gardens** (⊠ 10 Willow Ave., ☏ 603/964–5414; ⚐ $5).

Rye has great beaches, and **Wallis Sands State Beach** (⊠ Rte. 1A, ☏ 603/436–9404; ⚐ parking $8 weekends, $5 weekdays) is one of the nicest. Although there's no beach, **Odiorne Point State Park** (⊠ Rte. 1A, ☏ 603/436–1552; ⚐ $2.50) has more than 350 acres of tidal pools and footpaths. The **Seacoast Science Center** (☏ 603/436–8043; ⚐ $1), in the park, has exhibits and an aquarium. From Rye Harbor inlet, **New Hampshire Seacoast Cruises** (☏ 603/964–5545 or 800/964–5545) makes whale-watching trips and trips to the Isles of Shoals, a Colonial fishing settlement.

★ Walkable **Portsmouth**, a city with a working port, is an easy day trip from Boston. The **Portsmouth Historical Society** (⊠ 43 Middle St., ☏ 603/436–8420; ⚐ $5), housed in the **John Paul Jones House**, is one stop on a self-guided walking tour that includes six historic houses open to the public in summer.

Showcasing Portsmouth's architectural diversity is **Strawbery Banke Museum,** a 10-acre village-museum whose 46 buildings date from 1695 to 1950. The gardens are splendid. ⊠ *Marcy St.,* ☏ *603/433–1100 or 603/433–1106.* ⚐ *$12. Closed Nov.–mid-Apr., except 1st 2 weekends in Dec.*

Historic **Prescott Park** has a formal garden and lively fountains. Kids will want to start with Portsmouth's lively hands-on **Children's Museum** (⊠ 280 Marcy St., ☏ 603/436–3853; ⚐ $4). The **Port of Portsmouth Maritime Museum**, home to the **USS Albacore** (⊠ 600 Market St., ☏ 603/436–3680; ⚐ $4), a vintage submarine, is another attraction that appeals to youngsters.

Dining and Lodging

Hampton

$$–$$$ 🏠 **Victoria Inn.** Built as a carriage house in 1875, this romantic B&B is done in the style Victorians loved best: wicker, chandeliers, and lace. The honeymoon suite has a private sunroom. ⊠ *430 High St. (½ mi from Hampton Beach), 03842,* ☏ *603/929–1437,* ⨳ *603/929–0747. 5 rooms, 1 cottage. MC, V. BP.* ✉

Hampton Beach

$$–$$$$ ✕ **Ron's Landing at Rocky Bend.** This casually elegant restaurant serving fresh seafood and pasta has a second-floor porch that affords a sweeping ocean view. ⊠ *379 Ocean Blvd.,* ☏ *603/929–2122. AE, D, DC, MC, V.*

$$–$$$$ ✕🏠 **Ashworth by the Sea.** At this centrally located favorite of generations of beachgoers, most rooms have decks. Some rooms have queen-size four-poster beds and glowing cherry-wood furnishings. ⊠ *295 Ocean Blvd., 03842,* ☏ *603/926–6762 or 800/345–6736,* ⨳ *603/926–2002. 105 rooms. 3 restaurants, pool. AE, D, DC, MC, V.* ✉

$$$ 🏠 **Oceanside Inn.** Rooms with carefully selected antiques and such
★ thoughtful touches as reading lights and comfortable chairs and love seats give the Oceanside the feel of a turn-of-the-20th-century home. ⊠ *365 Ocean Blvd., 03842,* ☏ *603/926–3542,* ⨳ *603/926–3549. 10 rooms. AE, D, MC, V. Closed mid-Oct.–mid-May. BP.* ✉

Portsmouth

$$$ ✕ **Dunfey's Aboard the John Wanamaker.** Portsmouth's only floating restaurant, aboard an elegantly restored tugboat, offers such delicacies as shiitake-encrusted halibut with wild mushroom ravioli. The upper-level deck is a favorite on starry summer nights. ⊠ *1 Harbour Pl.,* ☎ *603/433–3111. AE, MC, V.*

$–$$$ ✕ **Blue Mermaid World Grill.** The stately exterior of this 1810 house belies the hot Jamaican-style dishes that come from the wood-burning grill. The grilled Maine lobster with mango butter is a favorite. ⊠ *409 Hanover St., The Hill,* ☎ *603/427–2583. AE, D, DC, MC, V.*

$$$ ✕▥ **Sheraton Harborside Portsmouth Hotel.** Portsmouth's only luxury hotel has a harbor view and a central location. The main restaurant ($$–$$$$) serves fresh seafood and American cuisine, such as lamb T-bones marinated in stout and molasses. The Krewe Orleans restaurant prepares Cajun specialties. ⊠ *250 Market St., 03801,* ☎ *603/431–2300 or 800/325–3535,* ℻ *603/433–5649. 205 rooms. 2 restaurants, pool, exercise room. AE, D, DC, MC, V.* ☙

$$$–$$$$ ▥ **Sise Inn.** This Queen Anne town house, full of chintz and gleaming armoires, is convenient for waterfront strolls. No two rooms are alike; some have whirlpool baths. ⊠ *40 Court St., 03801,* ☎ *800/267–0525,* ☎ ℻ *603/433–1200. 34 rooms. Meeeting rooms. AE, DC, MC, V. CP.*

Nightlife and the Arts

Summer concerts draw crowds at the **Hampton Beach Casino Ballroom** (⊠ 169 Ocean Beach Blvd., ☎ 603/926–4541). The 1878 **Music Hall** (⊠ 28 Chestnut St., Portsmouth, ☎ 603/436–2400) hosts touring events and an ongoing film series. Catch jazz, folk, or blues at the **Press Room** (⊠ 77 Daniel St., Portsmouth, ☎ 603/431–5186). The **Prescott Park Arts Festival** (⊠ 105 Marcy St., ☎ 603/436–2848) presents theater, dance, and musical events outdoors during the months of June, July, and August.

Outdoor Activities and Sports

Boating and Fishing

Rentals and charters are available from **Atlantic Fishing Fleet** in Rye Harbor (☎ 603/964–5220 or 800/942–5364). **Al Gauron Deep Sea Fishing** (☎ 603/926–2469) and **Smith & Gilmore** (☎ 603/926–3503) are in Hampton Beach.

Shopping

The streets radiating out from Market Square in **Portsmouth** are filled with crafts shops, galleries, and clothing boutiques. For regional crafts, try **Kumminz Gallery** (⊠ 65 Daniels St., ☎ 603/433–6488). **W. Barrett** (⊠ 53 Market St., ☎ 603/431–4262) also carries a wide selection. Antiques stores, including **Antiques at Hampton Falls** (☎ 603/926–1971), line Route 1 in the towns of Hampton and Hampton Falls.

THE LAKES REGION

The eastern half of central New Hampshire is scattered with beautifully preserved 18th- and 19th-century villages nestled among sparkling lakes—Winnipesaukee (Smile of the Great Spirit) is the largest—that echo with squeals and splashes all summer long.

Visitor Information

Greater Laconia Chamber of Commerce (⊠ 11 Veterans Sq., Laconia 03246, ☎ 603/524–5531 or 800/531–2347). **Lakes Region Association**

(✉ Box 589, Center Harbor 03226, ☎ 603/253–8555 or 800/925–2537). **Squam Lakes Area Chamber of Commerce** (✉ Box 65, Ashland 03217, ☎ 603/968–4494). **Wolfeboro Chamber of Commerce** (✉ Railroad Ave., Box 547-WT7, Wolfeboro 03894, ☎ 603/569–2200 or 800/516–5324).

Arriving and Departing

By Bus

Concord Trailways (☎ 603/228–3300; 800/639–3317 in New England) serves Laconia, Meredith, Center Harbor, and Moultonborough.

By Car

I–93 is the principal north–south artery. From the coast, Route 11 goes to southern Lake Winnipesaukee; en route to the White Mountains, north–south Route 16 accesses spurs to the lakes.

Exploring the Lakes Region

Alton Bay, at Winnipesaukee's southernmost tip, has the lake's cruise-boat docks and a Victorian bandstand. In affluent Colonial **Gilford** you'll find **Ellacoya State Beach** (✉ Rte. 11, ☎ 603/293–7821). The **Gunstock Recreation Area** (✉ Rte. 11A, ☎ 603/293–4341 or 800/486–7862) has swimming, hiking, mountain biking, horseback riding, and camping. At **Canterbury Shaker Village** (✉ Canterbury, ☎ 603/783–9511 or 800/982–9511; ✆ $10 for 2 consecutive days), southwest of Winnipesaukee, crafts demonstrations and guided tours illuminate 19th-century Shaker life.

In honky-tonk **Weirs Beach,** fireworks light up summer nights. Here you can board the **M/S Mount Washington** for lake cruises (☎ 603/366–5531 or 888/843–6686). The **Winnipesaukee Scenic Railroad** (☎ 603/279–5253; ✆ $7.50 and up) carries passengers alongside the lake. **Amusement centers** like Funspot (☎ 603/366–4377), **Surf Coaster** (☎ 603/366–4991), and **Water Slide** (☎ 603/366–5161) line Route 3.

Commercial **Meredith,** on the north shore, has restaurants and shops. **Moultonborough** has a country store and several miles of lakeside shoreline. The 5,000-acre **Castle in the Clouds** estate (✉ Rte. 171, ☎ 603/476–2352 or 800/729–2468; ✆ $11) is anchored by an odd and elaborate stone mansion built by an eccentric millionaire. Tours include the mansion and the Castle Springs Microbrewery located on the property. At the **Loon Center** (✉ Lees Mills Rd., ☎ 603/476–5666; ✆ free), run by the Audubon Society, you'll learn about the popular black-and-white birds whose calls haunt New Hampshire's lakes. **Holderness** is the gateway to Squam Lake, one of New Hampshire's most pristine. The **Squam Lakes Natural Science Center** (✉ intersection of Route 3 and Route 113, ☎ 603/968–7194; ✆ $9) has hands-on activities, nature trails, and indigenous animals.

President Grover Cleveland summered in tiny **Tamworth.** His son, Francis, returned to stay and founded the Barnstormers Theater. The **Remick Country Doctor Museum and Farm** (✉ 58 Cleveland Hill Rd., ☎ 603/323–7591; ✆ free) illustrates the life of a country doctor and the activities of a working farm.

Scenic, lake-hugging Route 109 leads from Moultonborough to **Wolfeboro,** an old-line resort. Uniforms, vehicles, and other artifacts at the **Wright Museum** (✉ 77 Center St., ☎ 603/569–1212; ✆ $5) illustrate the contributions of those on the home front to America's World War II effort.

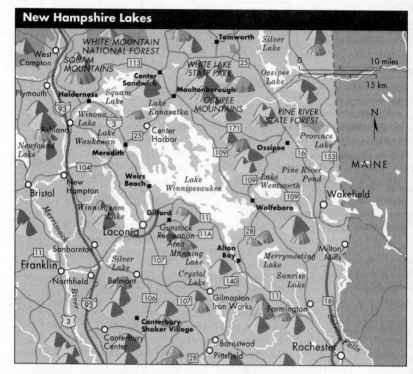

New Hampshire Lakes

Dining and Lodging

Since summer and fall are peak seasons—and in winter many businesses close down, making your options more scarce—you'll always want to make hotel and restaurant reservations in advance.

Center Harbor

$$–$$$ ✕▥ **Red Hill Inn.** Victorian pieces and country furniture decorate this B&B; 20 of the rooms have fireplaces, one has a mural of nursery-rhyme characters. For dinner, try the goat cheese bruschetta followed by rack of lamb encrusted in fresh rosemary and garlic. ⊠ *Rte. 25B (R.D. 1, Box 99M), 03226,* ☎ *603/279–7001 or 800/573–3445,* ℻ *603/279–7003. 26 rooms. Restaurant, bar, outdoor hot tub, pool. AE, D, DC, MC, V. BP.* 🐾

Holderness

$$$$ ✕▥ **Manor on Golden Pond.** This dignified inn has a dock on Squam
★ Lake, the setting for the movie *On Golden Pond,* so boating and swimming are part of the fun. Guests can stay in the main inn, carriage-house suites, or cottages. The five-course prix-fixe dinner may include such specialties as rack of lamb, filet mignon, and nonpareil apple pie. ⊠ *Rte. 3, 03245,* ☎ *603/968–3348 or 800/545–2141,* ℻ *603/968–2116. 21 rooms, 4 cottages. Restaurant, pool, tennis. AE, MC, V. BP.*

Moultonborough

$$–$$$ ✕ **The Woodshed.** Farm tools and antiques decorate this former barn, built in 1860. Make your way through the raw bar or try the New England section of the menu, which includes clam chowder, tender sea scallops, and Indian pudding for dessert. ⊠ *Lee's Mill Rd., 03254,* ☎ *603/476–2311. AE, D, DC, MC, V. Closed Mon.*

Sanbornton

$$ 🏠 **Ferry Point House.** Built in the 1800s as a summer retreat for the Pillsbury family, this red Victorian farmhouse B&B has superb views of Lake Winnisquam and a gazebo by the water's edge. There's a beach, boating, and fishing. The pretty rooms have Oriental-style rugs and antique Victorian furniture. ⊠ *100 Lower Bay Rd., 03269,* ☎ *603/524–0087,* FAX *603/524–0959. 6 rooms. No credit cards. Closed Nov.–Apr. BP.* 🍃

Tamworth

$$–$$$ ✕🏠 **Tamworth Inn.** Recently renovated inside and out, this Victorian inn features a cozy beamed ceiling pub and a formal dining room with seasonal specialties like lobster-stuffed black ravioli. Guest rooms have brass or antique beds. Beautifully landscaped grounds border the Swift River. ⊠ *Main St., 03886,* ☎ *603/323–7721 or 800/642–7352,* FAX *603/323–2026. 16 rooms. Restaurant, pool. MC, V. Closed Nov.–Apr. BP.* 🍃

Wolfeboro

$$$–$$$$ ✕🏠 **Wolfeboro Inn.** This landmark waterfront resort, partly dating from the 19th century, has polished cherry and pine pieces, stenciled borders, and country quilts. There's a bar, beach, and boating. ⊠ *90 N. Main St. (Box 1270), 03894,* ☎ *603/569–3016 or 800/451–2389,* FAX *603/569–5375. 45 rooms. 2 restaurants. AE, D, MC, V. CP.*

Campgrounds

⚠ **Gunstock Campground** (⊠ Gilford, ☎ 603/293–4341 or 800/486–7862). ⚠ **Meredith Woods** (⊠ Meredith, ☎ 603/279–5449 or 800/848–0328). ⚠ **White Lake State Park** (⊠ Tamworth, ☎ 603/323–7350; 603/271–3627 for reservations). ⚠ **Yogi Bear's Jellystone Park** (⊠ Ashland, ☎ 603/968–9000, FAX 603/968–7349).

Nightlife and the Arts

The **Belknap Mill Society** (⊠ Mill Plaza, Laconia, ☎ 603/524–8813) has year-round concerts in an early 19th-century brick mill building. **Barnstormers** (⊠ Main St., Tamworth, ☎ 603/323–8500), New Hampshire's oldest professional theater company, performs in July and August. The **M/S Mount Washington** (⊠ Weirs Beach, ☎ 603/366–5531) has moonlight cruises with dinner and dancing; it docks in Weirs Beach, Alton Bay, and Wolfeboro.

Outdoor Activities and Sports

Biking

Not too hilly, the Lakes Region is fun for even inexperienced bikers—though summer's heavy traffic can be a bit much. Lakeside roads make for pleasant pedaling. **Gunstock Recreation Area** (⊠ Rte. 11A, Gilford, ☎ 603/293–4341) has trails for mountain biking and rentals available.

Boating

Rent at **Thurston's** (☎ 603/366–4811 or 800/834–4812) in Weirs Beach, or the **Meredith Marina and Boating Center** (☎ 603/279–7921) or **Wild Meadow Canoes and Kayaks** (☎ 603/253–7536 or 800/427–7536), both in Meredith. In Wolfeboro, go to **Winnipesaukee Kayak Company** (☎ 603/569–9926) or **Wetwolfe Boat Rentals** (☎ 603/569–1503).

Fishing

Local waters yield trout; Winnipesaukee also has salmon. The **New Hampshire Department of Fish and Game**'s local office (⊠ New Hampton, ☎ 603/744–5470) can tell you where the action is.

Beaches

Most beaches are private, so it's good to know about **Ellacoya State Beach,** in Gilford, a 600-ft beach that's the area's major public strand. **Wentworth State Beach** is at Wolfeboro.

Shopping

Summer folk prowl area galleries and boutiques, such as the **Burlwood Antique Center** (⊠ Rte. 3, Meredith, ☎ 603/279–6387), a 170-dealer shop, and **Mill Falls Marketplace** (⊠ Rte. 3, Meredith, ☎ 603/279–7006). The **League of New Hampshire Craftsmen** (⊠ Rte. 3, ☎ 603/279–7920) runs a shop stocked with one-of-a-kind items in Meredith. The **Lakes Region Factory Stores** (⊠ 120 Laconia Rd., Tilton, ☎ 603/286–7880) is the place to go for bargains of all kinds.

THE WHITE MOUNTAINS

Northern New Hampshire is the home of New England's highest mountains and the 790,000-acre White Mountain National Forest. Rivers start here, gorges slash the forests, and summer brings hikers, climbers, and Sunday drivers to marvel at it all. In winter, skiers, both alpine and Nordic, and snowboarders flock to the region's peaks. Year round, shoppers hunt bargains in North Conway's outlets. But it's the short foliage season that draws the biggest crowds.

Visitor Information

Mt. Washington Valley Chamber of Commerce (⊠ North Conway 03860, ☎ 603/356–3171 or 800/367–3364). **Jackson Chamber of Commerce** (⊠ Box 304, Jackson 03846, ☎ 603/383–9356 or 800/866–3334).

Arriving and Departing

By Bus
Concord Trailways (☎ 603/228–3300; 800/639–3317 in New England) serves Littleton, Jackson, Berlin, Conway, Plymouth, and other towns.

By Car
North–south routes include I–93 and Route 3 in the west, and Route 16 in the east. The Kancamagus Highway (Route 112) and Route 302 are the main east–west thoroughfares.

Exploring the White Mountains

One-street **North Conway** overflows with outlet stores, restaurants, and inns. Trails from **Echo Lake State Park** (⊠ off Rte. 302, ☎ 603/356–2672 in summer; ⊆ $2.50), in North Conway, lead up to White Horse and Cathedral ledges, both 1,000-ft cliffs overlooking the town. Youngsters love the antique steam- and diesel-powered **Conway Scenic Railroad** (⊠ Rtes. 16/302, North Conway, ☎ 603/356–5251 or 800/232–5251; ⊆ $8.50–$52).

Intervale, just north of North Conway, has another attraction for railroad buffs. **Hartmann's Model Railway Museum** (⊠ Rte. 16 and Town Hall Rd., Intervale, ☎ 603/356–9922 or 603/356–9933; ⊆ $5) houses 14 operating layouts.

Glen is home to two family-oriented attractions. **Story Land** (⊠ Rte. 16, ☎ 603/383–4186; ⊆ $19) has life-size nursery-rhyme characters and themed rides. At **Heritage New Hampshire** (⊠ Rte. 16, ☎ 603/383–4186; ⊆ $10) theatrical sets, sound effects, and animation are used to immerse you in New England history.

Mountain-rimmed **Jackson** has retained its storybook New England character and is nationally known as a destination for cross-country skiers. Dramatic **Pinkham Notch,** in the **White Mountain National Forest,** is the departure point for hikes to the top of the Northeast's highest mountain, 6,288-ft **Mt. Washington** (be sure to carry warm clothing year-round in case of sudden, nasty storms). In summer and fall, weather permitting, you can corkscrew up via the **Mt. Washington Auto Road** (⊠ Glen House, Rte. 16, Pinkham Notch, ☎ 603/466–3988; ▭ $16 per car and driver and $6 per passenger or $22 van fare), either in your own car or by guided van tour. In winter, the tour goes to just above tree line, and you can cross-country ski or snowshoe down.

In summer, **Attitash Bear Peak** (⊠ Rte. 302, Bartlett, ☎ 603/374–2368) has two dry alpine slides, water slides, a children's play pool, horseback riding, mountain biking, and a driving range. The steam-powered ★ ered **Mt. Washington Cog Railway** (⊠ Off Rte. 302, Bretton Woods, ☎ 603/846–5404 or 800/922–8825, ▭ $44) has been carrying passengers to and from the top of Mt. Washington since 1869; reserve ahead.

Many famous writers have stopped by **Franconia.** You can visit poet **Robert Frost's home** (⊠ Ridge Rd., ☎ 603/823–5510; ▭ $3). **Franconia Notch State Park** (☎ 603/745–8391; ▭ $7 for Flume) is known for the Old Man of the Mountains, a rock formation that looks like a human profile, and the 800-ft-long natural chasm known as the Flume.

Lincoln, on the western end of the Kancamagus Highway, is home to ⟳ the **Whale's Tale** (⊠ Rte. 3, ☎ 603/745–8810; ▭ $20), site of watersliding fun for the whole family. In summer and fall at **Loon Mountain** (⊠ Kancamagus Hwy., ☎ 603/745–8111; ▭ gondola $9.50), you can ride New Hampshire's longest gondola to the summit, where daily activities include lumberjack shows, storytelling by a mountain man, and nature tours. At the base, there's lift-serviced mountain biking, horseback riding, and skating.

The **Kancamagus Highway,** 32 mi of mountain scenery in the **White Mountain National Forest** (with bumper-to-bumper traffic during foliage season), starts in the resort town of Lincoln and passes campgrounds, scenic overlooks, and trailheads en route to Conway.

Dining and Lodging

Reservations are essential in fall and during winter vacations.

Bretton Woods

$$$$ ✕▥ **Mount Washington Hotel.** The 1902 construction of this leviathan
★   was one of the most ambitious projects of its day. Noted for its 900-ft-long veranda, which affords a full view of the mountains, this jewel retains a turn-of-the-20th-century formality; jacket and tie are required in the dining room. Although the menu changes daily, you'll find such entrées as lemon lobster ravioli with shrimp and scallops. In winter, guests can cross-country ski. ⊠ *Rte. 302, 03575,* ☎ *603/278–1000 or 800/258–0330,* ℻ *603/278–8838. 200 rooms. 2 restaurants, pools, golf, tennis. AE, MC, V. MAP.* ✦

Dixville Notch

$$$$ ✕▥ **Balsams Grand Resort Hotel.** This resort on 15,000 acres is a real
★   Victorian, built in 1866. Accommodations are bright and homey, and the array of activities, including downhill and cross-country skiing, gives you no reason to leave the grounds. In the restaurant ($–$$$, reservations essential, jacket and tie), the summer buffet lunch is heaped upon a 100-ft-long table. ⊠ *Rte. 26, 03576,* ☎ *603/255–3400 or 800/ 255–0600,* ℻ *603/255–4221. 202 rooms. Restaurant, pool, golf, ten-*

nis. AE, D, MC, V. Closed Apr.–mid-May and mid-Oct.–mid-Dec. MAP winter; FAP summer. 🐾

Franconia

$$-$$$ ✕🏨 **Franconia Inn.** Play tennis, ride horseback, cross-country ski, swim, hike, or soak in the hot tub at this family resort. Rooms have canopy beds and country furnishings; some have whirlpool baths or fireplaces. At the restaurant, savor medallions of veal with apple-mustard sauce or filet mignon with green-chili butter and Madeira sauce. ⊠ *1300 Easton Rd., 03580,* ☎ *603/823–5542 or 800/473–5299,* 🗚 *603/823–8078. 34 rooms. Restaurant, pool, tennis. AE, MC, V. Closed Apr.–mid-May. BP; MAP.* 🐾

Glen

$$-$$$ ✕🏨 **Bernerhof.** This Old World–style hotel is right at home in its alpine setting. Rooms have hardwood floors with hooked rugs, antiques, and reproductions. The menu at the Prince Palace restaurant features such Swiss specialties as fondue and Wiener schnitzel. The Black Bear pub pours many microbrewery beers. ⊠ *Box 240, Rte. 302, 03838,* ☎ *603/383–9132 or 800/548–8007,* 🗚 *603/383–0809. 9 rooms. Restaurant. AE, D, MC, V. BP.*

Jackson

$$$-$$$$ ✕🏨 **Inn at Thorn Hill.** Dark wood furniture and rose-motif wallpaper
★ patterns recall the inn's origins as a home designed by Stanford White. Yet the comforts are strictly up-to-date—many of the rooms have spa tubs and gas fireplaces. The restaurant is one of the area's best, serving such contemporary dishes as panfried Maine scallops with a ravioli of root vegetables, apples, and prosciutto. ⊠ *Thorn Hill Rd. (Box A), 03846,* ☎ *603/383–4242 or 800/289–8990,* 🗚 *603/383–8062. 19 rooms. Restaurant, pool. AE, D, DC, MC, V. MAP; BP.* 🐾

Lincoln

$$-$$$$ 🏨 **Mountain Club on Loon.** This first-rate slopeside resort hotel has an assortment of accommodations: suites that sleep as many as eight, studios with Murphy beds, and 117 units with kitchens. Entertainers perform in the lounge on most winter weekends. ⊠ *Rte. 112, Kancamagus Hwy., 03251,* ☎ *603/745–2244 or 800/229–7829,* 🗚 *603/745–2317. 234 rooms. Restaurant, pool, health club. AE, D, DC, MC, V.*

North Conway

$$$-$$$$ ✕🏨 **Snowvillage Inn.** To complement this inn's tome-jammed bookshelves, guest rooms are named for famous authors. The nicest, with 12 windows overlooking the Presidential Range, honors native son Robert Frost. The candlelit dining room ($$-$$$, reservations required) serves such specialties as roasted rack of lamb with Provençal herbs. On-site cross-country skiing and snowshoeing are popular winter activities. ⊠ *Box 68, Stuart Rd., Snowville 03849,* ☎ *603/447–2818 or 800/447–4345,* 🗚 *603/447–5268. 18 rooms. Restaurant. AE, D, DC, MC, V. BP; MAP.* 🐾

Nightlife and the Arts

Look into the **Mt. Washington Valley Theater Company** (⊠ Eastern Slope Playhouse, Main St., North Conway, ☎ 603/356–5776). Catch some music or theater at the **North Country Center for the Performing Arts** (⊠ Mill at Loon Mountain, Lincoln, ☎ 603/745–6032). Or sample the bars. The **Red Parka Pub** (⊠ Rte. 302, Glen, ☎ 603/383–4344) is favored by under-30s.

Outdoor Activities and Sports

Biking
Great Glen Trails Outdoor Center (⊠ Rte. 16, Pinkham Notch, ☎ 603/466–2333) rents mountain bikes by the day and half day for use on their extensive network of trails at the base of Mt. Washington.

Fishing
Clear White Mountain streams and lakes yield trout, salmon, and bass. The **New Hampshire Fish and Game Department**'s regional office (☎ 603/788–3164) has the latest information. You can take lessons in fly-fishing at **Great Glen Trails** (☞ Biking *in* Outdoor Activities and Sports, *above*).

Hiking
The White Mountains are crisscrossed with footpaths. The Maine-to-Georgia **Appalachian Trail** crosses the state. The **Appalachian Mountain Club** (⊠ Box 298, Gorham 03851, ☎ 603/466–2727 for reservations or a free guide to huts; 603/466–2725 for trail information) suggests routes, operates hikers' huts and the Joe Dodge Lodge in Pinkham Notch, and runs year-round outdoor skills workshops. The **White Mountains National Forest** Office (☎ 603/528–8721) is a good source of hiking information and the place to obtain the recreation permit needed to park in national forest areas. **New England Hiking Holidays–White Mountains** (⊠ Box 1648, North Conway 03860, ☎ 603/356–9696 or 800/869–0949) conducts scheduled guided hikes with lodging at country inns.

Ski Areas

New Hampshire's best skiing is in the White Mountains. For the latest conditions statewide, contact **SKI New Hampshire** (☎ 800/887–5464, FAX 603/745–3002).

Cross-Country
In Jackson nearly 100 mi of trails maintained by the **Jackson Ski Touring Foundation** (⊠ Main St., ☎ 800/927–6697) string together inns, restaurants, and woodlands and connect to another 40 mi of trails maintained by the Appalachian Mountain Club (☞ Hiking *in* Outdoor Activities and Sports, *above*). Other well-maintained areas with reasonable selections of terrain, both groomed and backcountry trails, and rental equipment include the **Balsams Grand Resort Hotel** (☞ Dining and Lodging, *above*). **Bear Notch Ski Touring Center** (⊠ Rte. 302, Bartlett, ☎ 603/374–2277). **Bretton Woods** (⊠ Rte. 302, ☎ 603/278–3300 or 800/232–2972). **Franconia Village Cross-Country Center** (⊠ Easton Rd., Franconia, ☎ 603/823–5542 or 800/473–5299). **Great Glen Trails** (☞ Biking *in* Outdoor Activities and Sports, *above*). **Waterville Valley** (⊠ Rte. 49, Waterville Valley, ☎ 603/236–8311; 603/236–4144 for conditions).

Downhill
For New Hampshire's largest ski areas, the 1990s were a decade of growth. But plenty of smaller, low-key areas still offer a pleasant counterpoint. **Waterville Valley** (⊠ Rte. 49, Waterville Valley, ☎ 603/236–8311; 603/236–4144 for conditions). **Loon Mountain** (⊠ Kancamagus Hwy., Lincoln, ☎ 603/745–8111; 603/745–8100 for conditions). **Black Mountain** (⊠ Rte. 16B, Jackson, ☎ 603/383–4490 or 800/698–4490). **Attitash Bear Peak** (⊠ Rte. 302, Bartlett, ☎ 603/374–2368; 800/223–7669 for conditions). **Mt. Cranmore** (⊠ Snowmobile Rd., North Conway, ☎ 603/356–5543; 603/356–8516 for conditions). **Wildcat** (⊠ Rte. 16, Pinkham Notch, ☎ 603/466–3326; 800/643–4521 for conditions). **Cannon Mountain** (⊠ Franconia, ☎ 603/823–8800; 603/823–7771 for conditions). **Bretton Woods** (☞ Cross-Country, *above*) has undergone a major expansion so that it now compares well with

better known ski areas. The **Balsams Wilderness** (☞ Dining and Lodging, *above*) is a small area at one of the grand old resort hotels.

Shopping

Route 16 through **Conway** and **North Conway** is the major shopping area of the region. More than 150 outlets and shops line this busy route, including craft stores, boutiques, and antiques shops. You can pick up a guide to the shopping opportunities at visitor centers in either town and at most stores.

WESTERN AND CENTRAL NEW HAMPSHIRE

The countryside bordered by the Connecticut River on the west, Interstate 93 on the east, and Massachusetts and the southern slope of the White Mountains is a land of covered bridges, calendar-page villages, hardwood forests, jewel-like lakes, and lonely mountains. New Hampshire's largest cities, such as Manchester and Nashua, are clustered along the central I–93 corridor, as is the capital, Concord.

Visitor Information

Concord Chamber of Commerce (⊠ 244 N. Main St., 03301, ☎ 603/224–2508). **Hanover Chamber of Commerce** (⊠ Box A-105, 03755, ☎ 603/643–3115). **Lake Sunapee Business Association** (⊠ Box 400, Sunapee 03782, ☎ 603/763–2495; 800/258–3530 in New England). **Manchester Chamber of Commerce** (⊠ 889 Elm St., 03101, ☎ 603/666–6600). **Monadnock Travel Council** (⊠ 8 Central Sq., Keene 03431, ☎ 603/355–8155). **Peterborough Chamber of Commerce** (⊠ Box 401, 03458, ☎ 603/924–7234).

Arriving and Departing

By Bus
Concord Trailways (☎ 800/639–3317) operates within the state and **Advance Transit** (☎ 802/295–1824) within the area.

By Car
I–89 cuts southeast–northwest into Vermont. North–south, I–93 provides scenic travel while I–91 follows the Connecticut River on its Vermont shore; in New Hampshire, Routes 12 and 12A are slow but beautiful. Route 4 winds between Lebanon and the coast.

By Plane
Manchester Airport (⊠ 1 Airport Rd., Manchester 03103, ☎ 603/624–6539), the state's largest airport has scheduled flights by Continental, Delta, United, Southwest, and US Airways.

Exploring Western & Central New Hampshire

Concord, New Hampshire's capital, is undergoing an awakening. The "Concord on Foot" walking trail covers the historic district and includes the **Pierce Manse,** once home to Franklin Pierce, the nation's 14th president. ⊠ *14 Penacook St.,* ☎ *603/225–2068 or 603/224–5954.* ☒ *$3. Closed Sept.–mid-June.*

Reserve seats for shows at Concord's high-tech **Christa McAuliffe Planetarium** (⊠ 3 Institute Dr., ☎ 603/271–7827; ☒ $6).

Visit the **Museum of New Hampshire History** to see exhibits spanning the days of the Abenaki Indians to the present. ✉ *6 Eagle Sq.,* ☎ *603/ 226–3189.* 🖾 *$5. Closed Mon. Nov.–June.*

Three governors were born in **Warner.** Now the quiet town is home to the **Kearsarge Indian Museum** (✉ Kearsarge Mountain Rd., ☎ 603/ 456–2600; 🖾 $6), where you'll find exhibits on Native American crafts. Mountains and parks set off bright, clear **Lake Sunapee.** You can cruise the water on the **M/V *Mt. Sunapee II*** (✉ Main St., Sunapee, ☎ 603/763–4030), or you can picnic by the side at quiet, woodsy **Sunapee State Beach** (✉ Rte. 103, Newbury, ☎ 603/763–5561; 🖾 $2.50). At **Mt. Sunapee** (✉ Rte. 103, Newbury, ☎ 603/763–2356), the region's largest ski area, you can take the Express Quad to the summit and hike to Lake Solitude, try lift-serviced mountain biking, or enjoy the in-line skate park at the base. Also in **Newbury,** you'll find the **Fells** (✉ Rte. 103A, ☎ 603/763–4789; 🖾 $3), a National Historic Site and former summer estate of John M. Hay, who served as private secretary to Abraham Lincoln and as Secretary of State for Presidents Mckinley and T. Roosevelt.

Tiny Enfield is home to the **Enfield Shaker Museum,** which displays and explains Shaker artifacts and crafts. ✉ *2 Lower Shaker Village Rd.,* ☎ *603/632–4346.* 🖾 *$7. Closed weekdays mid-Oct.–May.*

★ **Dartmouth College,** in Hanover, is an Ivy League archetype of redbrick and white clapboard around a village green. Its **Hood Museum of Art** (✉ Wheelock St., ☎ 603/646–2808; 🖾 free) houses works from Africa, Asia, Europe, and America. In modest **Cornish,** to the south of Hanover via Route 12A, you can cross four covered bridges. The **Saint-Gaudens National Historic Site** (✉ off Rte. 12A, ☎ 603/675–2175; 🖾 $4) displays some of the sculptor's heroic, sensitive work.

☾ In Charlestown is the **Fort at No. 4,** a frontier outpost in Colonial times. Today costumed interpreters demonstrate crafts and reenact the lives of the settlers. ✉ *Rte. 11,* ☎ *603/826–5700.* 🖾 *$6. Closed late Oct.– late May.*

In **Monadnock State Park** (✉ Off Rte. 124, Jaffrey, ☎ 603/532–8862; 🖾 $2.50) 20 trails ascend to the bald summit of 3,165-ft Mt. Monadnock, one of the world's most climbed mountains. Near **Dublin,** where proper Bostonians summer and locals publish the *Old Farmer's Almanac,* you can exit Monadnock State Park onto Route 101.

Beautifully preserved **Fitzwilliam,** spreading from the edges of an oval common, warrants a detour. Acres of wild rhododendrons burst into bloom in mid-July at **Rhododendron State Park** (✉ off Rte. 12, 2½ mi northwest of the common, ☎ 603/532–8862).

The four villages that make up **Hillsborough** include Hillsborough Center, where 18th-century houses surround a picture-perfect town green. The Hillsborough Historical Society operates the **Pierce Homestead** (✉ Rte. 31, 03244, ☎ 603/478–3165; 🖾 $3; closed mid-Oct.–May) where 14th President Franklin Pierce was reared.

Manchester is the state's largest city and home to some of its prime cultural attractions. The **Currier Gallery of Art** (✉ 201 Myrtle Way, ☎ 603/ 669–6144; 🖾 $5, $7 for Zimmerman House), in a 1929 Beaux Arts Italianate building, has European and American paintings, sculpture, and decorative arts from the 13th to the 20th century. The museum also owns and arranges tours of the Frank Lloyd Wright–designed **Zimmerman House.**

Dining and Lodging

Charlestown

$$ 🏨 **MapleHedge.** Guest rooms in the 1820 Federal-style section are decorated with considerable flair. The Cobalt Room, for example, features a light-catching collection of cobalt glass and mahogany furnishings. Freshly ironed linens and a three-course breakfast are among the amenities. ⊠ *355 Main St. (Box 638), 03603,* ☎ *603/826–5237 or 800/962–7539,* ᴀ̶x̶ *603/826–5237. 5 rooms. MC, V. BP.* 🐾

Chesterfield

$$$–$$$$ ✕🏨 **Chesterfield Inn.** Rooms in this B&B, which is surrounded by gardens, are spacious and tastefully decorated with antiques and period-★ style fabrics. Favorites from the dining room ($$–$$$) include crab cakes with rémoulade and lime coconut chicken. ⊠ *Rte. 9 (Box 155), 03443,* ☎ *603/256–3211 or 800/365–5515,* ᴀ̶x̶ *603/256–6131. 15 rooms. Restaurant. AE, D, DC, MC, V. BP.* 🐾

Concord

$–$$ ✕ **Hermanos Cocina Mexicana.** The food at this popular two-level restaurant is standard Mexican, but with fresher ingredients and more subtle sauces than one might expect. ⊠ *11 Hills Ave.,* ☎ *603/224–5669. Reservations not accepted. D, MC, V.*

$$–$$$ ✕🏨 **Centennial Inn.** Each room in this charming brick and stone structure, built for widows of Civil War veterans in 1896, is individually decorated with antiques and reproductions. In the Franklin Pierce dining room ($$–$$$$), the menu changes seasonally. ⊠ *96 Pleasant St., 03301,* ☎ *603/225–7102 or 800/360–4839,* ᴀ̶x̶ *603/225–5031. 32 rooms. Restaurant. AE, D, DC, MC, V.*

Cornish

$$ 🏨 **Chase House Bed & Breakfast Inn.** The birthplace of Salmon P. Chase—who was Abraham Lincoln's secretary of the treasury and a founder of the Republican Party—this B&B has been gracefully restored with Colonial furnishings and Waverly wall coverings. Ask for a room with a view of the Connecticut River valley and Mt. Ascutney. ⊠ *Rte. 12A (1½ mi south of the Cornish-Windsor covered bridge), R.R. 2, Box 909, 03745,* ☎ *603/675–5391 or 800/401–9455,* ᴀ̶x̶ *603/675–5010. 8 rooms. Exercise room. MC, V. No smoking. Closed Nov. BP.*

Enfield

$$–$$$ ✕🏨 **The Shaker Inn.** Built between 1837 and 1841, the Great Stone Dwelling here is the largest main dwelling ever built by a Shaker community. Now an inn, it is adjacent to the Enfield Shaker Museum. The guest rooms in the original sleeping chambers have reproduction Shaker furniture and are decorated with simplicity and style. The dining room serves Shaker-inspired cuisine that relies heavily on regional ingredients. ⊠ *447 Rte. 4A, 03748,* ☎ *603/632–7810 or 888/707–4257. 24 rooms. Restaurant. AE, D, MC, V.* 🐾

Fitzwilliam

$–$$ 🏨 **Hannah Davis House.** The original beehive oven still sits in the kitchen of this 1820 Federal-style B&B, and one suite has two Count ★ Rumford fireplaces. The inn is just off the village green. Your host has the scoop on area antiquing. ⊠ *186 NH Rte. 119 W, 03447,* ☎ *603/ 585–3344. 6 rooms. D, MC, V. BP.*

Hanover

$$$$ ✕🏨 **Hanover Inn.** Three stories of white-trimmed brick, this embodiment of American traditional architecture, owned by Dartmouth College, is handsomely furnished with 19th-century antiques and reproductions. You can get regional cuisine, such as roast rack of veni-

son and sautéed striped bass, in the Daniel Webster Room ($$–$$$$), and lighter bites in Zins, the inn's wine bistro. ⊠ *Box 151, The Green 03755,* ☎ *603/643–4300 or 800/443–7024,* FAX *603/646–3744. 92 rooms. 2 restaurants. AE, D, DC, MC, V.*

Nightlife and the Arts

The arts flourish at the **Capitol Center for the Arts** (⊠ 46 S. Main St., Concord, ☎ 603/225–1111). The **Colonial Theater** (⊠ 95 Main St., Keene, ☎ 603/352–2033) has folk, rock, jazz, and movies. **Monadnock Music** (⊠ Box 255, Peterborough 03458, ☎ 603/924–7610 or 800/ 868–9613) has concerts in July and August. Nashua is home to the state's largest professional theater, the **American Stage Festival** (⊠ 14 Court St., ☎ 603/886–7000).

Outdoor Activities and Sports

Biking

Try **Route 10** along the Ashuelot River south of Keene; spurs lead to covered bridges. You can rent bikes or get yours serviced at **Spokes and Slopes** (☎ 603/924–9961) in Peterborough.

Boating

The Connecticut River, while usually safe after June 15, is not for beginners. Rent gear at **Northstar Canoe Livery** (⊠ Rte. 12A, Balloch's Crossing, ☎ 603/542–5802).

Fishing

To find out where the action is on the area's 200 lakes and ponds, call the **Department of Fish and Game**'s regional office in Keene (☎ 603/ 352–9669).

Hiking

Networks of trails can be found in many state parks and forests, among them the rugged **Pillsbury State Park** (⊠ Washington, ☎ 603/ 863–2860) and **Fox State Forest** (⊠ Center Rd., Hillsborough, ☎ 603/464–3453).

Shopping

This part of the state is perfect for shopping for crafts directly from the maker. Look for artisans' studios marked by blue-and-white New Hampshire state signs. Antiques dealers sell "by chance or by appointment"; keep an eye peeled along Route 119 west of Fitzwilliam and along Route 101 east of Marlborough.

Keene has malls and **Colony Mill Marketplace** (⊠ 222 West St., ☎ 603/ 357–1240). **Antiques at Colony Mill** (⊠ Colony Mill Marketplace, ☎ 603/358–6343) is a group shop with more than 240 dealers. In Peterborough, you can buy outdoor gear at **Eastern Mountain Sports** (⊠ Vose Farm Rd., ☎ 603/924–7231) and local crafts and artwork at **Sharon Arts Downtown** (⊠ Depot Sq., ☎ 603/924–7256). In Concord, visit the **League of New Hampshire Craftsmen** (⊠ 36 N. Main St., ☎ 603/ 228–8171) for a wide variety of juried crafts.

NEW JERSEY

Updated by
Robert
DiGiacomo

Capital	Trenton
Population	8,053,000
Motto	Liberty and Prosperity
State Bird	Eastern goldfinch
State Flower	Common meadow violet
Postal Abbreviation	NJ

Statewide Visitor Information

New Jersey Department of Commerce and Economic Development (⊠ Division of Travel and Tourism, Box 820, Trenton 08625-0820, ☎ 609/292–2470 or 800/537–7397, FAX 609/633–7418). There are nine visitor information centers at major destinations around the state. For information on state parks contact the **Department of Environmental Protection, Division of Parks and Forestry** (⊠ Box 404, Trenton 08625, ☎ 609/984–0370 or 800/843–6420).

Scenic Drives

For Hudson River views take the **Palisades Interstate Parkway** north from the George Washington Bridge to the state line or take **River Road** from Weehawken north to Fort Lee. Both **Route 23,** northwest from Newfoundland through High Point State Park, and **Route 15,** northwest from I–80, give you glimpses of lakes, rural estates, and higher-elevation vistas. The backroads off **Routes 202** and **206** in central New Jersey pass by horse farms, antiques shops, and historic sites. Along the southern shore, **Ocean Drive** is a causeway that links barrier islands.

National and State Parks

National Parks

Sandy Hook Unit of Gateway National Recreation Area (⊠ Box 530, Fort Hancock 07732, ☎ 732/872–0115) preserves sandbar ecology and fortifications built to protect New York Harbor. On the Delaware River boundary between New Jersey and Pennsylvania is the **Delaware Water Gap National Recreation Area** (⊠ Visitor Center, Kittatinny Point, off I–80, Bushkill, PA 18324, ☎ 908/496–4458 or 570/588–2451), the largest national recreation area in the Northeast. The 40,000-acre **Edwin B. Forsythe National Wildlife Refuge's Brigantine Division** (⊠ Great Creek Rd., Box 72, Oceanville 08231, ☎ 609/652–1665) has an 8-mi wildlife drive, mainly through diverse coastal habitat, and two short, circular nature trails that are especially worthwhile during spring and fall bird migrations.

State Parks

New Jersey has the third-largest state park system in the nation, with 36 parks, 11 forests, 4 recreation areas, 42 natural areas, 23 historic sites, 4 marinas, and 1 golf course. **Wharton State Forest** (⊠ Rte. 542, Hammonton 08037, ☎ 609/561–3262), New Jersey's largest, contains the **Batsto State Historic Site** (⊠ Rte. 542, ☎ 609/561–7310), a restored late-18th- and 19th-century Pinelands ironworking village. **High Point State Park** is named after the state's tallest peak. Many of New Jersey's 19 **lighthouses** are preserved in state parks, including Barnegat Lighthouse, Cape May Point Lighthouse, and Sandy Hook Lighthouse (☞ Exploring the Jersey Shore, *below*).

THE JERSEY SHORE

The Jersey Shore is 127 mi of public beachfront stretching like a pointing finger along the Atlantic Ocean from the Sandy Hook Peninsula in the north to Cape May at the southern tip. There is no one description of what it's like "down the shore." Things change town by town and sometimes season by season—winter storms have a habit of rearranging beaches and boardwalks. Activities along the shore include saltwater fishing from pier, bridge, dock, or boat (licenses not required); all kinds of water sports; bird-, whale-, and dolphin-watching; and bicycling or strolling on the ubiquitous wood-plank or concrete boardwalks. In Atlantic City are the famed gambling casinos; in Cape May, Victorian bed-and-breakfasts; and in between—in Seaside Heights, Point Pleasant, and Wildwood—quintessential seaside amusements.

Visitor Information

Atlantic City: Convention & Visitors Authority (⌧ 2314 Pacific Ave., 08401, ☎ 609/348–7100 or 888/248–4748, ☏ 609/348–3426). **Cape May:** Chamber of Commerce of Greater Cape May (⌧ 609 Lafayette St., Box 556, 08204, ☎ 609/884–5508); Mid-Atlantic Center for the Arts (⌧ Box 340, 08204, ☎ 609/884–5404). **Cape May County:** Chamber of Commerce (⌧ Box 74, Cape May Court House 08210, ☎ 609/465–7181, ☏ 609/465–5017); Department of Tourism and Economic Development (⌧ Box 365, Cape May Court House 08210, ☎ 609/463–6415 or 800/227–2297). **Monmouth County:** Department of Promotion and Tourism (⌧ 31 E. Main St., Freehold 07728, ☎ 732/431–7476 or 800/523–2587, ☏ 732/294–5930). **Ocean County:** Tourism Advisory Council (⌧ Box 2191, Toms River 08754, ☎ 732/929–2138 or 800/365–6933, ☏ 732/506–5000). **Wildwoods:** Information Center (⌧ Box 609, Wildwood 08260, ☎ 609/522–1407 or 800/992–9732).

Arriving and Departing

By Bus

New Jersey Transit (☞ By Train, *below*) provides bus service to most Jersey Shore towns. **Academy Lines** (☎ 732/291–1300) also runs buses between New York City and shore points. **Greyhound** (☎ 609/345–6617 or 800/231–2222) serves Atlantic City. Ask Atlantic City casino-hotels about direct service to their properties.

By Car

The main road serving the Jersey Shore is the Garden State Parkway, a north–south toll road that ends in Cape May. From New York City, I–80 and the New Jersey Turnpike (toll) connect with the Garden State. From Philadelphia and southern New Jersey suburbs, take the Atlantic City Expressway (toll). From the south take the Delaware Memorial Bridge and continue north on the New Jersey Turnpike. Toms River, Barnegat, and Tuckerton are linked by U.S. 9.

By Ferry

The **Cape May–Lewes Ferry** (☎ 609/886–1725, 800/643–3779 for reservations) is a year-round 70-minute car ferry (800 passengers, 100 cars per ferry) across the Delaware Bay (☞ Delaware).

By Plane

Philadelphia International (☞ Pennsylvania), **Newark International Airport** (⌧ Tower Rd., ☎ 973/961–6000), and the **New York City airports** (☞ New York) are closest to Atlantic City and shore points. **Atlantic City International Airport** (☎ 609/645–7895 or 888/235–9229) serves the southern shore.

By Train

Amtrak (⊠ 1 Atlantic City Expressway, near Kirkman Blvd., ☎ 800/872–7245 or 973/762–5100) serves Atlantic City. **New Jersey Transit** (☎ 800/772–2222 from northern NJ; 800/582–5946 from southern NJ) operates local commuter service to Atlantic City from Philadelphia and to the shore towns in Monmouth and Ocean counties from New York City.

Exploring the Jersey Shore

The **New Jersey Coastal Heritage Trail** (☎ 856/447–0103), under joint development by the National Park Service, the state of New Jersey, and other organizations, connects significant natural and cultural resources along the Atlantic coast and Delaware Bay. A network of routes (primarily vehicular) stretches more than 275 mi, from Perth Amboy south along the Atlantic coast to Cape May, then north along the Delaware Bay coast to the Delaware Memorial Bridge in Deepwater. The project area has been divided into five regions: Sandy Hook, Barnegat Bay, Absecon, Cape May, and the Delsea region on the western shore. Each area will have its own regional welcome centers to provide interpretive information; two centers have opened, one at Fort Mott State Park in Salem County and another at Milepost 18.3 of the Garden State Parkway near Cape May Oceanview Service Area. Five theme routes—wildlife migration, maritime history, historic settlements, relaxation and inspiration, and coastal habitats—highlight the heritage of this region of the state.

At the shore's north end the **Sandy Hook Lighthouse**, the oldest continuously operating lighthouse in the country (built in 1764), stands in the **Sandy Hook Unit of Gateway National Recreation Area** (☞ National Parks, *above*), 4 mi east of Atlantic Highlands on Route 36. On this peninsula of barrier beach you can splash in the usually gentle, shallow surf; explore sleepy **Fort Hancock**, established in 1895; and glimpse the New York City skyline, 19 mi across the harbor from North Beach.

Just south on Route 36, **Long Branch** was founded in the 18th century as one of America's first resorts; over the years it has hosted seven presidents, from Grant to Wilson.

A century ago **Asbury Park** was the shore's toniest resort, but efforts to revive that glory have so far been disappointing. It is still known for its place in rock history, as the young Bruce Springsteen performed here in the 1960s; but the club where he played, the Stone Pony, was torn down in 1998. By contrast, neighboring **Ocean Grove** was established in 1859 by Methodists as a camp-meeting area and still serves that purpose. The town's dignified tone echoes in its Victorian hotels and inns; relatively quiet beaches; a short, gameless boardwalk; and shops and cafés. Ocean Grove is also one of two shore towns that do not sell alcohol—the other is **Ocean City**, a Methodist town patterned after it. The imposing **Great Auditorium** (⊠ Pilgrim Pathway, ☎ 732/775–0035 or 800/773–0097) presents a summer schedule of concerts—everything from big bands to country and jazz.

In Belmar the **Municipal Marina** (⊠ Rte. 35, ☎ 732/681–2266), on the Shark River, has party and charter boats that head for the ocean daily in search of blackfish, blues, fluke, tuna, and shark. Neighboring **Spring Lake** has an uncommercialized boardwalk, three spring-fed lakes with swans, a small town center, and numerous romantic B&Bs. At the family-oriented **Point Pleasant Beach**, Jenkinson's Aquarium (⊠ Ocean Ave., ☎ 732/899–1659; ☜ $7), on the boardwalk at the Broadway Beach area, is a nice rainy-day diversion.

★ ☙ **Six Flags Great Adventure**, inland from Spring Lake, comprises both an amusement park with a multitude of the newest rides and a drive-

The Jersey Shore

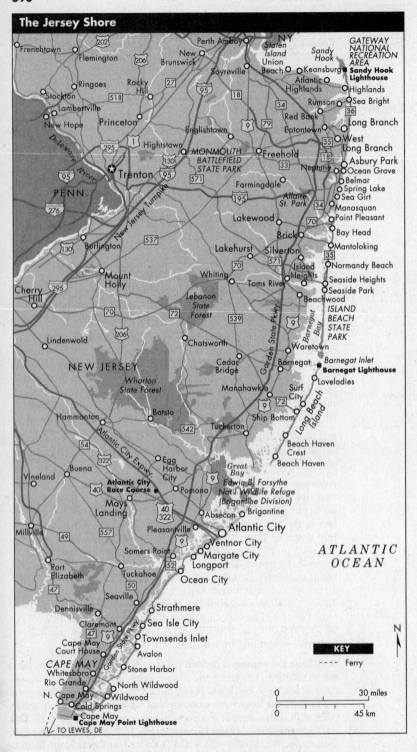

Frenchtown
Flemington
202
Ringoes
206
Rocky Hill
27
New Brunswick
Perth Amboy
NY
Staten Island
Union Beach
Keansburg
GATEWAY NATIONAL RECREATION AREA
Sandy Hook
Sandy Hook Lighthouse
Stockton
518
Atlantic Highlands
Highlands
Lambertville
95
18
Rumson
Sea Bright
New Hope
Princeton
Englishtown
9
79
34
Red Bank
Eatontown
36
Long Branch
295
Hightstown
1
MONMOUTH BATTLEFIELD STATE PARK
Freehold
35
18
West Long Branch
Delaware River
95
Trenton
130
95
571
33
Neptune
Asbury Park
Ocean Grove
PENN.
Farmingdale
195
Allaire St. Park
34
Belmar
Spring Lake
Sea Girt
276
Lakewood
Manasquan
Point Pleasant
Burlington
537
70
Brick
Bay Head
Mantoloking
130
Lakehurst
Silverton
571
Island Heights
Normandy Beach
Mount Holly
Whiting
70
Toms River
Seaside Heights
Seaside Park
Beachwood
Cherry Hill
295
70
Lebanon State Forest
72
539
Garden State Pkwy
Barnegat Bay
ISLAND BEACH STATE PARK
Lindenwold
206
Chatsworth
Waretown
NEW JERSEY
Cedar Bridge
Barnegat
Barnegat Inlet
Barnegat Lighthouse
Wharton State Forest
Manahawkin
Loveladies
Surf City
Hammonton
Batsto
542
Ship Bottom
Long Beach Island
54
Atlantic City Expwy
Tuckerton
9
72
322
Egg Harbor City
Great Bay
Beach Haven Crest
Buena
Edwin B. Forsythe Nat'l Wildlife Refuge (Brigantine Division)
Beach Haven
Vineland
40
Atlantic City Race Course
Pomona
9
Mays Landing
40
322
Absecon
Brigantine
Millville
49
557
Pleasantville
Atlantic City
Port Elizabeth
52
Somers Point
9
Ventnor City
Margate City
Longport
ATLANTIC OCEAN
47
Tuckahoe
Ocean City
Dennisville
50
Seaville
Strathmere
Claremont
Sea Isle City
47
9
Cape May Court House
Townsends Inlet
Garden State Pkwy
Avalon
CAPE MAY
Stone Harbor
Whitesboro
Rio Grande
North Wildwood
N. Cape May
Wildwood
Cold Springs
Cape May
Cape May Point Lighthouse
TO LEWES, DE

KEY
---- Ferry

0   30 miles
0   45 km

N

through safari park. ⊠ *Rte. 537, I–195, Exit 16, Jackson,* ☎ *732/928–2000, 732/928–1821 for recording.* 🎫 *$39.99, safari only $15, safari–theme park combination $42.99. Closed late Oct.–mid-Apr.* 🐾

On Barnegat Peninsula, the side-by-side resorts of **Seaside Heights** and **Seaside Park** have two major amusement piers plus water rides. Don't miss a turn on the antique Dentzel-Looff carousel. Just south, but seemingly a world away, is narrow **Island Beach State Park** (☎ 732/793–0506, 🎫 Labor Day–Memorial Day $4; Memorial Day–Labor Day $6 weekdays, $7 weekends), 10 mi of ocean and bay beaches with almost no evidence of human habitation.

Return inland over Barnegat Bay to Toms River, once a pirate and privateering port, and today the center of a booming region of retirement communities. The **Ocean County Historical Museum** (⊠ 26 Hadley Ave., ☎ 732/341–1880; 🎫 donations accepted) has Victorian artifacts, a research library for tracing genealogy, and exhibits on the dirigibles that flew from the Lakehurst Naval Air Station, site of the 1937 *Hindenburg* tragedy.

Head south on U.S. 9 and east on Route 72 over Barnegat Bay to **Long Beach Island. Barnegat Lighthouse** (☎ 609/494–2016), known locally as Old Barney, completed in 1858, is at the northern tip of the island. To the south is **Beach Haven,** the island's commercial center, with Victorian houses set around a town square. In one of these houses you'll find the **Long Beach Island Museum** (⊠ Engleside and Beach Aves., ☎ 609/492–0700), which conducts walking tours of the historic district from late June to early September.

Back on the mainland, the Garden State Parkway and U.S. 9 lead to **Atlantic City,** the gambling capital of the East Coast (bettors drop about $8 million daily). A visitor welcome center, situated just off the Atlantic City Expressway at the city limits, offers information on the resort and other local attractions. Between the games and the nationally famous nightclub acts, nightlife is fierce at the **Atlantic City casino-hotels.** Read the street signs and you'll find the roads that made the board game Monopoly famous, including the **Boardwalk,** the nation's first elevated wood walkway (1870), where saltwater taffy is still sold. The resort's earlier 19th-century stone hotels have been replaced by 12 **casino-hotels**—outrageous in design and entertainment, from the Mardi Gras festivity of the Showboat to the onion domes of the Taj Mahal. While there are still pockets of down-at-the-heels buildings and pawnshops in Atlantic City, renovations, increased security, and infusions of capital have decreased the incidence of crime and given the entire city a more optimistic tone. Hey, Atlantic City even has its own **Planet Hollywood, Hard Rock Cafe, and Ripley's Believe It Or Not** museum.

You can still see some of Atlantic City's famous ocean **amusement piers,** but only the **Central Pier** (⊠ St. James Pl. and Tennessee Ave.), on the boardwalk, retains its original 1884 appearance. The **Garden Pier** (⊠ New Jersey Ave. and the Boardwalk) has been converted to an art center; don't miss the terrific little **Atlantic City Historical Museum and Cultural Center** (☎ 609/347–5839; 🎫 free), with an evocative collection of memorabilia and a thorough video on the history of the seaside resort. The **Steel Pier** is now an amusement pier and arcade. The annual **Miss America Pageant** (☎ 609/345–7571) has moved its headquarters to the **Sheraton Convention Center,** but the pageant itself remains at the old boardwalk **convention hall** (⊠ 2301 Boardwalk, ☎ 609/348–7100), which is slated to reopen in fall 2001 after a major renovation. The new convention center has pageant memorabilia. The **Ocean Life Center** (☎ 609/348–2880; 🎫 $6) on the bay at Historic Gardner's Basin offers 10 themed exhibits and eight aquariums filled with area fish and sea animals, all designed to create an awareness of the wonders of the ocean.

🕐 In Margate **Lucy the Elephant** (✉ Atlantic and Decatur Aves., ☎ 609/823–6473; 🎟 $3), an elephant-shape building six stories high and a National Historic Landmark, has been drawing the curious of all ages since 1881. It is open from April through October.

🕐 Farther south is **Ocean City,** across Great Egg Harbor, whose **boardwalk** and boardwalk parades are family-oriented. Summer-evening concerts at the **Music Pier** (✉ Moorlyn Terr., ☎ 609/525–9248) are a tradition.

🕐 **Strathmere Beach** is a great place for a quiet walk. Take time out to explore the **Wetlands Institute** (☎ 609/368–1211; 🎟 $5), in Stone Harbor, a research and education center on coastal ecology; the institute is open Tuesday through Saturday between October 15 and May 15. The **Wings 'n Water Festival** is held here and in neighboring towns the third weekend of September.

🕐 Ocean Drive leads to the little boroughs known as the **Wildwoods.** The best known, loudest, kitschiest, and wildest is **Wildwood** itself. Its 2-mi **boardwalk** has the greatest concentration of outdoor amusement rides on the shore, including seven amusement piers. In the last few years, the town's funky, original 1950s architecture, echoing the postwar optimism of the space program and new technologies, has become a launching pad for a renewed interest in this seashore resort.

★ At the southern tip of the shore, the meticulously restored Victorian town of **Cape May** offers a dramatic change of pace and scenery. The state's oldest ocean resort, it was named for the Dutch captain, Cornelius Mey, who sighted it in 1620. Cape May today has plenty of bed-and-breakfasts, many in elaborate gingerbread-style Victorian houses. **Victorian Week** (☞ Festivals and Seasonal Events in the United States Region by Region chapter) combines madcap frivolity with house tours, dinners, and lectures (make reservations well in advance). The July 4 celebration is vintage Americana, while Christmastime has Dickensian flair, with trolley, candlelight, and walking tours of houses decorated in traditional Victorian finery.

Cape May, at the southern tip of New Jersey, is one of the strategic stops along the Atlantic Flyway, so it attracts flocks of birds and bird-watchers, especially during the spring and fall migrations. A favorite birding locale is **Cape May Point State Park** (✉ Lighthouse Ave., ☎ 609/884–2159), site of the **Cape May Point Lighthouse** (☎ 609/884–5404 or 800/275–4278), built in 1859, which marks the end of the Jersey Shore. Another popular activity is whale-watching; several boats ply the Atlantic spring through fall, often coming upon pods of dolphins as well as whales. Not far from the lighthouse, **Sunset Beach** (✉ Sunset Blvd., Cape May Point) is the place to collect "Cape May diamonds," pebbles of pure quartz that wash up on the beach, and to watch the sun set over Delaware Bay.

Dining and Lodging

Seafood is the Jersey Shore's strongest suit, with local catches featured on most menus. Ocean City and Ocean Grove do not allow the sale of liquor.

Lodgings should be booked far in advance in summer. Beachfront rooms are more expensive. Rooms in Atlantic City casino-hotels are the most popular, the most costly, and the most difficult to reserve, especially on weekends from mid-June to Labor Day. Chambers of commerce (☞ Visitor Information, *above*) can provide assistance.

The **Bed & Breakfast Innkeepers Association of New Jersey** (☎ 732/449–3535) offers a free guidebook featuring 85 inns statewide.

Atlantic City

$$$$ ✕ **Peregrines'.** Named for the peregrine falcons that nest on the pent-
★ house ledge, this small, elegant, yet friendly gourmet restaurant has both à la carte and prix-fixe menus. Among the specialties are Belon oysters from France, truffles from Belgium, and quinoa from the Indies. ✉ *Atlantic City Hilton Casino Resort, Boston Ave. and Boardwalk,* ☎ *609/347–7111. AE, D, DC, MC, V. Closed Mon.–Wed. No lunch.*

$$$–$$$$ ✕ **Le Palais.** Favorites such as rack of lamb with rosemary and hazel-
★ nuts and sautéed Dover sole with panfried banana, and individual dessert soufflés are elegantly served in this lavish mirrored dining room. ✉ *Resorts Atlantic City, N. Carolina Ave. and Boardwalk,* ☎ *609/344–6000 or 888/771–1SUN. AE, D, DC, MC, V. Closed Mon.–Tues.*

$–$$$ ✕ **Angelo's Fairmount Tavern.** Locals flock here for lots of good Ital-
★ ian fare, dished out by the Mancuso family, owners since 1935. ✉ *2300 Fairmount Ave.,* ☎ *609/344–2439. AE, MC, V.*

$–$$$ ✕ **Dock's Oyster House.** Owned and operated by the Dougherty family since 1897, the city's oldest restaurant serves seafood in a setting of wood and stained glass engraved with nautical scenes. ✉ *2405 Atlantic Ave.,* ☎ *609/345–0092. AE, DC, MC, V. Closed Dec.–Feb.*

$–$$ ✕ **Los Amigos.** South-of-the-border specialties such as Mexican pizza, burritos, and margaritas, served in the dimly lighted back room, are good bets at this small bar and restaurant two blocks from the boardwalk casinos. ✉ *1926 Atlantic Ave.,* ☎ *609/344–2293. AE, DC, MC, V.*

$ ✕ **White House Sub Shop.** The White House claims to have sold more than 17 million overstuffed sandwiches since 1946. Celebrities seem to love it; check out the photos on the walls. ✉ *Mississippi and Arctic Aves.,* ☎ *609/345–1564 or 609/345–8599. Reservations not accepted. No credit cards.*

$$$–$$$$ 🏨 **Bally's Park Place Casino Hotel & Tower.** Guests can stay in the Art
★ Deco rooms of the historic Dennis Hotel, built in 1860, or in the newer 37-story tower, whose spacious, angular rooms have picture windows even in the marble-tile bathrooms. The spa facilities are exceptional. ✉ *Park Pl. at Boardwalk, 08401,* ☎ *609/340–2000 or 800/225–5977,* 🖷 *609/340–4713. 1,268 rooms. 8 restaurants, pool, exercise room. AE, D, DC, MC, V.* ✇

$$$ 🏨 **Sheraton Atlantic City Convention Center Hotel.** The 16-story Art Deco hotel, connected to the convention center by an enclosed walkway, showcases Miss America Pageant memorabilia in display windows. Inside, a grand circular staircase leads to the Miss America–theme Shoe Bar, restaurant, and meeting rooms. Every room has a coffeemaker and a stash of Ellis coffee. ✉ *2 Ocean Way, 08401,* ☎ *609/344–3535 or 800/325–3535,* 🖷 *609/348–4336. 502 rooms. 2 restaurants, tennis, health club. AE, D, MC, V.* ✇

$$–$$$ 🏨 **Quality Inn Atlantic City.** Half a block from the boardwalk, one of
★ Atlantic City's best values has a 17-story modern guest wing above a Federal-style base. Rooms are outfitted with handsome Colonial reproductions. Resorts Atlantic City is next door. ✉ *S. Carolina and Pacific Aves., 08401,* ☎ *609/345–7070 or 800/356–6044,* 🖷 *609/345–0633. 203 rooms. Restaurant. AE, D, DC, MC, V.* ✇

$$–$$$ 🏨 **Trump Marina Hotel Casino.** Blandly modern on the outside, this bayside marina is removed from some of the boardwalk glitz. Service is first-rate. ✉ *Huron Ave. and Brigantine Blvd., 08401,* ☎ *609/441–2000 or 800/777–8477,* 🖷 *609/345–7604. 728 rooms. 8 restaurants, pool, tennis, health club. AE, D, DC, MC, V.*

$–$$$ 🏨 **Flagship Resort.** This pleasant, modern, salmon-color condo hotel is across from the boardwalk (facing Brigantine and the Absecon Inlet), away from the casino action. Every suite has a private terrace with a view, as well as a microwave, refrigerator, and wet bar. ⊠ *60 N. Main Ave., 08401,* ☎ *609/343–7447 or 800/647–7890,* FAX *609/343–1608. 300 suites. Restaurant, pool, health club. AE, D, MC, V.*

Cape May

$$–$$$$ ✕ **Mad Batter.** Eclectic contemporary cuisine is served in the sky-lighted Victorian dining room or outside on the porch or the garden terrace. Breakfasts are imaginative, albeit pricey; Belgian waffles and eggs Benedict are favorites. For lunch try the crab-cake sandwich; for dinner, crab *mappatello* (crabmeat, spinach, ricotta, and onions in a puff pastry). Upstairs is Carroll Villa, a 21-room B&B. ⊠ *19 Jackson St.,* ☎ *609/884–5970. AE, MC, V. Closed Jan.*

$$$–$$$$ 🏨 **Angel of the Sea.** A stunning, sprawling Victorian presence in Cape May, this 1850s inn consistently winds up on "best-of" lists nation-wide; it also won the Restoration of the Year Award from the National Trust for Historic Preservation. Complimentary afternoon tea and wine and cheese are served daily. ⊠ *5–7 Trenton Ave., 08204,* ☎ *609/ 884–3369 or 800/848–3369. 27 rooms. AE, MC, V. BP.*

$$$–$$$$ 🏨 **Queen Victoria B&B and the Queen's Hotel.** In the center of the historic district, three restored Victorian houses (two devoted to the B&B, the other to the hotel) pay homage to the queen and the period named for her. Rooms, though full of antiques, also have modern touches, including refrigerators, whirlpool baths in some rooms, and TVs in the suites. ⊠ *102 Ocean St. (B&B), 601 Columbia Ave. (hotel), 08204,* ☎ *609/884– 8702 B&B, 609/884–1613 hotel. 21 rooms. AE, MC, V. CP (B&B only).*

$$$–$$$$ 🏨 **The Virginia Hotel.** With turndown and room service, a morning news-paper, and privileges at local golf clubs, the Virginia is a full-service hotel on an intimate scale. Rooms, which vary in size, have cherry and poplar furnishings with Victorian lines. Grilled seafood and meats and rich desserts are served at the Ebbitt Room Restaurant. ⊠ *25 Jackson St., 08204,* ☎ *609/884–5700 or 800/732–4236,* FAX *609/884– 1236. 24 rooms. Restaurant. AE, D, DC, MC, V. CP.*

$$–$$$$ 🏨 **Captain Mey's Inn.** A wraparound veranda and a small, walled court-yard and tulip garden bring charm to this 1890 house close to the Wash-ington Mall and the beach. The Victorian antiques include a collection of Delft china. Two guest rooms have whirlpool tubs. ⊠ *202 Ocean St., 08204,* ☎ *609/884–7793 or 800/981–3702. 8 rooms. AE, MC, V. BP.*

$$$ 🏨 **The Mainstay Inn.** This 1872 men's gambling club reincarnated as
★ a B&B captures the feel of another era with 14-ft ceilings, stenciling, historic wallpapers, and harmoniously arranged antiques. Across the street is a suites-only sister property in another restored building. ⊠ *635 Columbia Ave., 08204,* ☎ *609/884–8690. 16 rooms. No credit cards. CP or BP, depending on season and building.* ✎

$$–$$$ 🏨 **Manor House.** On a quiet, tree-lined street two blocks from the beach, this 1905 guest house mixes antiques, stained glass, art, and eclectic touches, such as an old-fashioned player piano. Innkeepers Tom and Nancy Mc-Donald prepare the four-course breakfasts from scratch. ⊠ *612 Hughes St., 08204,* ☎ *609/884–4710. 10 rooms. D, MC, V. Closed Jan. BP.*

$–$$ 🏨 **Chalfonte.** With its simple original furnishings, this authentic Vic-torian summer hotel attracts a mix of longtime guests, families, and new clientele. Special programs include evening entertainment; volunteer work weekends during which students and other volunteers pay a small reg-istration fee but basically stay free at the hotel in return for help with its upkeep; and a supervised children's dining room, where youngsters eat from a special menu while parents dine on the inn's famous, mostly southern home-style cooking. ⊠ *301 Howard St., 08204,* ☎ *609/884– 8409,* FAX *609/884–4588. 78 rooms, 2 cottages. Restaurant. AE, D, MC, V. Closed Columbus Day–Memorial Day weekend. MAP.*

Ocean City

$–$$ ⊞ **Serendipity Bed & Breakfast.** At this beautifully restored inn a half block from the beach, owners Clara and Bill Plowfield place an emphasis on natural-foods cooking, serving breakfast throughout the year and dinners from October to May. ⊠ *712 9th St., 08226,* ☎ *609/ 399–1554 or 800/842–8544. 6 rooms. AE, D, MC, V. BP.*

Spring Lake

$$$–$$$$ ⊞ **Sea Crest by the Sea.** This 1885 Queen Anne Victorian is one of many in town. Eight rooms have gas-log fireplaces, and seven have ocean views; all have feather beds and luxurious fabrics. Buttermilk scones are a breakfast standard; there's also daily afternoon tea. ⊠ *19 Tuttle Ave., 07762,* ☎ *732/449–9031 or 800/803–9031,* FAX *732/974–0403. 11 rooms. AE, MC, V. BP.*

$$–$$$ ⊞ **Hollycroft.** Overlooking Lake Como at the northern edge of town, Hollycroft is a mountain-style lodge without the mountains. A 16-ft ironstone fireplace and walls of knotty pine in the living room make it a charming getaway. ⊠ *North Blvd. (Box 448), 07762,* ☎ *732/681– 2254 or 800/679–2254. 7 rooms. AE, D, MC, V. BP.*

$$–$$$ ⊞ **Normandy Inn.** This huge 1888 Italianate mansion has been a guest house since 1909. Owners Michael and Susan Ingino have filled it with museum-quality American Victorian antiques. The Tower Room, with windows on four sides, has views of the ocean, which is a two-minute walk away. ⊠ *21 Tuttle Ave., 07762,* ☎ *732/449–7172 or 800/449– 1888,* FAX *732/449–1070. 18 rooms. AE, D, DC, MC, V. BP.*

Toms River

$–$$$ ✕ **Old Time Tavern.** Italian dishes, steaks, seafood, and sandwiches are the lures at this restaurant and taproom. Early birds can get soup-to-dessert meals at bargain prices. ⊠ *N. Main St., Rte. 166 off Rte. 37,* ☎ *732/349–8778. AE, DC, MC, V.*

Motels

⊞ **Ascot Motel** (⊠ Iowa and Pacific Aves., Box 1824, Atlantic City 08404, ☎ 609/344–5163 or 800/225–1476), 80 rooms; pool; $$.

⊞ **Clarion Bayside Resort at Golf & Tennis World** (⊠ 8029 Black Horse Pike, W. Atlantic City 08232, ☎ 609/641–3546 or 800/999–9466, FAX 609/641–4329), 110 rooms; restaurant, pools, tennis, health club; $$.

⊞ **Sandpiper** (⊠ Long Beach Blvd. at 10th St., Ship Bottom 08008, ☎ 609/494–6909), 20 rooms; pool; closed Nov.–Apr.; $–$$.

Nightlife and the Arts

PNC Bank Arts Center (⊠ Garden State Pkwy., Exit 116, Holmdel, ☎ 732/335–0400) has a summer roster of performing-arts groups, big-name pop acts, and ethnic festivals.

Outdoor Activities and Sports

Biking

Boardwalks are grand for biking if you don't mind dodging weekend walkers and joggers. Many towns restrict riding to the early-morning hours, before the crowds gather. The road around **Cape May Point** takes you past Cape May Point State Park and its lighthouse.

Canoeing

Try the many freshwater creeks, streams, and tributaries in the 1.1-million-acre **Pinelands National Reserve** (☎ 609/894–7300), the country's first national reserve.

Fishing

Monmouth County has more charter and party boats than any other area along the shore; most popular is the **Belmar Marina** (☞ Exploring the Jersey Shore, *above*). In Ocean County numerous party and charter boats sail from Point Pleasant and Long Beach Island. Fishing boats sail from state marinas in **Leonardo** (☎ 732/291–1333) and **Atlantic City** (☎ 609/441–8482).

Gardens

New Jersey is, after all, nicknamed the Garden State, and in Swainton is one of its most charming. **Leaming's Run Gardens** (⊠ 1845 Rte. 9N, ☎ 609/465–5871), with 25 designed and planted gardens, is the largest annual garden in the country.

Spectator Sports

Horse Racing: Before Atlantic City began staging big-name boxing events, horse racing was the shore's most popular spectator sport. **Monmouth Park Racetrack** (⊠ Rte. 36 and Oceanport Ave., Oceanport, ☎ 732/222–5100) is the area's best-known track, with Thoroughbred races from Memorial Day through Labor Day. The **Atlantic City Racetrack** (⊠ 4501 Black Horse Pike, Mays Landing, ☎ 609/641–2190) has Thoroughbred racing for five days in May only and simulcasting year-round. There's harness racing at **Freehold Raceway** (⊠ U.S. 9 and Rte. 33, Freehold, ☎ 732/462–3800) from mid-August through May.

Baseball: The national pastime, begun in Hoboken more than a century ago, has come to New Jersey in a big way: In 1998 Atlantic City opened a new, 5,900-seat minor-league stadium for its own pro team, the Atlantic City Surf. Catch a game at the stadium, the **Sandcastle** (⊠ 545 N. Albany Ave., Atlantic City, ☎ 609/344–8873), from mid-May to mid-September.

Beaches

From Memorial Day to Labor Day the **Water Information Hotline** (☎ 800/648–7263) supplies reports on the shore's water quality and beach
★ conditions. **Island Beach State Park** (☞ Exploring the Jersey Shore, *above*) is the most scenic natural beach on the Jersey Shore. Beaches usually charge a fee from Memorial Day or mid-June to Labor Day. Windsurfing is especially good in the calm waters of the open bays. Sailing, rowing, and powerboating are superb on sheltered Barnegat Bay in Ocean County.

Shopping

The **Shore Antique Center** (⊠ 300 Richmond Ave. [Rte. 35], Point Pleasant Beach, ☎ 732/295–5771) is a warren of high-quality merchandise, including folk art, lawn ornaments, and fine art, from more than 40 dealers. Nearby are several other treasure chests, including the **Antique Emporium** (⊠ Bay and Trenton Aves., ☎ 732/892–2222). Another nexus of happy hunting is Red Bank, where you'll find more than a dozen antiques markets; the largest of these is the three-building **Red Bank Antique Center** (⊠ 195, 195B, and 226 W. Front St., ☎ 732/842–3393) with pieces from more than 150 dealers.

ELSEWHERE IN NEW JERSEY

The Northwest Corner

Arriving and Departing

There's easy access from northwestern New Jersey to Manhattan via I–80 and Routes 23 and 15.

What to See and Do

This sparsely developed region of small lakes and low mountains attracts skiers in winter; the rest of the year brings outdoorsy types who come to enjoy water sports on the Delaware River and Lake Hopatcong, scenic roads, hikes on the Appalachian Trail, and historical sites from the 18th and 19th centuries.

The state's highest elevation (1,803 ft) is in **High Point State Park** (☞ State Parks, *above*), 7 mi northwest of Sussex. Hugging the river from
★ I–80 to the northern tip of the state is the **Delaware Water Gap National Recreation Area** (☞ National Parks, *above*). **Waterloo Village** (⊠ Waterloo Rd., Stanhope, ☎ 973/347–0900) is a restored early 19th-century canal town. Children's activities, such as face painting and storytelling, are ongoing. The summer concert series attracts renowned jazz, classical, rock, and country performers. **Skylands Park** (⊠ Rte. 565 E, Augusta, ☎ 973/579–7500 or 888/652–2737), home to the minor-league New Jersey Cardinals, is a great place to see a ball game for under $10 or catch the park's occasional fireworks show. There is also a baseball museum and batting cages.

The most popular ski areas—clustered around the nondescript town of **McAfee**—have snowmaking equipment, offer both day and evening skiing on terrain for various abilities, and are generally family-oriented.

Mountain Creek (⊠ Rte. 94, Vernon, ☎ 973/827–2000), formerly Vernon Valley/Great Gorge, was taken over in 1998 by Intrawest, which owns resorts throughout North America. Mountain Creek is the biggest resort in New Jersey—in the first year alone, Intrawest invested $20 million in renovations and upgrades. Among the changes was the replacement of the aging lift system with state-of-the-art equipment (a gondola, nine chairlifts, and two "magic carpet" lifts for beginners). There are 52 trails on three mountains. **Hidden Valley** (⊠ Rte. 515, Vernon, ☎ 973/764–4200) is a lively alternative, with three chairlifts and 12 trails. **Craigmeur Ski Area** (⊠ Rte. 513, Rockaway, ☎ 973/697–4500)—small (one chairlift, one rope tow, one T-bar, four trails) and friendly—is best for beginners or families with younger children. **Campgaw Mountain Ski Area** (⊠ 200 Campgaw Rd., Mahwah, ☎ 201/327–7800)—is also very compact (two chairlifts, two handle-tows, one T-bar, eight trails), and a good place to learn how to ski or snowboard.

Dining and Lodging

MILFORD

$–$$ ✕ **Ship Inn.** New Jersey's first brewpub serves half a dozen home brews and more than a dozen British draught ales. The fare includes burgers and British specialties such as shepherd's pie. ⊠ *61 Bridge St.*, ☎ *908/995–7007 or 800/651–2537. AE, MC, V.*

$$ 🏠 **Chestnut Hill on the Delaware.** The rocker-lined veranda of this 1860-vintage B&B has some beautiful views. There's also a country cottage with carousel horses, modern conveniences, and absolute privacy. ⊠ *63 Church St. (Box N), 08848,* ☎ *908/995–9761,* FAX *908/995–0608. 6 rooms, 1 cottage. No credit cards. No smoking. BP.*

STANHOPE

$$–$$$ 🏠 **Whistling Swan Inn.** Tiger-oak woodwork and an octagonal tower room with a conical ceiling are among the features of this 1904 house, now a lovely Victorian B&B. In a tiny village in New Jersey's highlands, the inn is close to winter skiing and ice-skating, summer water sports on the lakes, and cultural activities in Waterloo Village; the Delaware River is a 25-minute drive away. ⊠ *110 Main St., 07874,* 🕾 *973/347–6369,* FAX *973/347–3391. 10 rooms. AE, D, MC, V. BP.*

WALPACK CENTER

$–$$$ ✕ **Walpack Inn.** The only restaurant within the boundaries of the Delaware Water Gap National Recreation Area has been here since 1949. Lobster comes solo (two tails) or with steak. The Swedish brown bread is so popular it's sold by the loaf. Deer usually prance by in the field beyond the skylit greenhouse dining room. The rustic piano bar, with a fieldstone fireplace and mounted moose, bear, and deer heads, is worth the trip in itself. ⊠ *Rte. 615, 4 mi due south of Walpack Center Historic District,* 🕾 *973/948–9849 or 973/948–6505. MC, V. Closed Mon.–Thurs. No lunch.*

Along the Delaware

Arriving and Departing

From Manhattan the New Jersey Turnpike skirts the area, and U.S. 1 and I–195 are key access roads. From Philadelphia I–95 runs up the Pennsylvania side of the river, crossing north of Trenton, while I–295 and the New Jersey Turnpike parallel it on the Jersey side.

What to See and Do

Forming New Jersey's "other shore" (its border with Pennsylvania), the Delaware slowly changes from a relatively small, often rock-studded river in the north to a mighty, navigable river as it flows past Philadelphia and empties into Delaware Bay. The towns that line it change as well. Part of the way down the state, quaint towns like **Milford, Frenchtown, Stockton,** and, the largest of these, **Lambertville** hug the river below ridges and rolling hills beyond. Gracing the pastoral scenery are 18th-century buildings, galleries, antiques and crafts stores, excellent restaurants, and B&Bs and inns. Across the bridge from Lambertville is the artsy town of **New Hope,** in Bucks County (☞ Pennsylvania). Inland a bit, **Flemington** also has some antiques stores but is best known for its outlets. Flemington's **Liberty Village** (⊠ 1 Church St., 🕾 908/782–8550) has more than 60 factory and designer outlets.

Follow the river south of Lambertville to find an area where George Washington really did sleep for 10 critical days in 1776–77 (in fact, Washington and the Continental Army spent about one-third of the war in New Jersey). **Washington Crossing State Park** (⊠ Rte. 546, Titusville, 🕾 609/737–0623) is the site of Washington's Christmas-night 1776 crossing (reenacted each Christmas Day). Follow Washington's trail south to the state capital, **Trenton,** previously a Colonial pottery and manufacturing center, today a small city struggling with a quiet rebirth. One of Trenton's gems is **Chambersburg,** also known as the Burg, a residential neighborhood with dozens of superb Italian restaurants. Washington surprised the sleeping Hessians in the **Old Barracks** (⊠ Barrack St., 🕾 609/396–1776; 🖙 $6), now a museum. Also in Trenton is the two-centuries-old **New Jersey State Museum** (⊠ 205 W. State St., 🕾 609/292–6464; 🖙 free), with holdings in archaeology and ethnology, cultural history, fine arts, and natural history. The museum has a planetarium, which offers nighttime laser rock shows on the weekend. Washington followed his victory in Trenton with one in **Princeton,** just to the north. The two battles were the first major victories for the Continental Army. Princeton is now a pretty university town, with upscale shops and the governor's mansion, **Drumthwacket** (⊠ 354 Stockton St., ☎ 609/683–0057; ☞ free), which is open March through July and September through December, Wednesday from noon to 2 PM.

South of Trenton, the aging industrial town of **Camden** is enjoying some degree of revitalization along its waterfront. Central to the project is the **Thomas H. Kean New Jersey State Aquarium** (⊠ 1 Riverside Dr., ☎ 856/365–3300; ☞ $11.95), built in 1992 and updated in 1995 with the award-winning **Ocean Base Atlantic exhibit,** which features interactive displays and an artful underwater effect that makes you feel like you're entering the marine home of more than 4,000 fish. Adjacent to the aquarium is the **Camden Children's Garden,** a 4-acre interactive horticultural playground with such exhibits as a giant tree house, dinosaur fossil area, and a carousel ride (⊠ 3 Riverside Dr., ☎ 856/365–8733; ☞ $5; $11.95 combination ticket that includes admission to aquarium and Children's Garden).

Within walking distance along the waterfront is the $56 million **Blockbuster–Sony Music Entertainment Centre** (⊠ 1 Harbour Blvd., ☎ 856/365–1300). The state-of-the-art amphitheater accommodates 25,000 people, including 18,000 on the lawn; it is the first such venue to be converted to a year-round indoor theater. Camden also boasts **Walt Whitman's house** (⊠ 328–330 Mickle Blvd., ☎ 856/964–5383; ☞ free) and his **tomb** in the Harleigh Cemetery (⊠ Vesper and Haddon Aves.); the house is open Wednesday through Sunday.

Dining and Lodging

FRENCHTOWN

$$$–$$$$ ✕ **Frenchtown Inn.** This 1805 former tavern and boardinghouse is one of the state's most romantic restaurants. Top-notch, modern, French-influenced cuisine is served in three beautiful dining rooms, including the less-formal Grill Room, which serves wonderful salads, meat, pasta dishes, and fish entrées, such as seared salmon with Hollandaise sauces and red wine au jus. ⊠ *5 Bridge St.,* ☎ *908/996–3300. AE, MC, V.*

$$–$$$ ☷ **Hunterdon House.** This 1864 Italianate Victorian mansion, in a landscaped garden overlooking this charming river town, has high ceilings, tall shuttered windows, and period antiques. Guest rooms are dominated by huge, carved Victorian bedroom sets. ⊠ *12 Bridge St., 08825,* ☎ *908/996–3632 or 800/382–0375,* FAX *908/996–2921 (call first). 7 rooms. AE, MC, V. CP.*

$–$$ ☷ **National Hotel.** Established in 1851, the National is a major presence in town. Lunch and dinner are served in two lovely old-fashioned dining rooms, and an aviation theme enlivens the atmospheric lounge. Service is friendly, and the ambience relaxed. Each guest room has its own period style. ⊠ *31 Race St., 08825,* ☎ *908/996–4871,* FAX *908/ 996–3642. 5 rooms. Restaurant. AE, D, DC, MC, V.*

LAMBERTVILLE

$$–$$$$ ☷ **Chimney Hill Bed & Breakfast.** This circa-1820 stone manor house sits on 8 acres above the town of Lambertville. Rooms have canopy beds and fireplaces; there are four with kitchens and studies. The candlelight breakfast includes homemade pastries, Belgian waffles, and French toast. Afternoon port, sherry, and tea are served. ⊠ *207 Goat Hill Rd., 08530,* ☎ *609/397–1516 or 800/211–4667. 8 rooms. AE, MC, V. CP.*

$$–$$$ ☷ **Inn at Lambertville Station.** This well-run small hotel overlooks the Delaware River. ⊠ *11 Bridge St., 08530,* ☎ *609/397–8300 or 800/ 524–1091,* FAX *609/397–9744. 45 rooms. AE, MC, V.*

STOCKTON

$$–$$$ 🏨 **The Woolverton Inn.** This pretty inn in a 1792 stone manor house is situated on a 10-acre, tree-lined property. ✉ *6 Woolverton Rd., 08559,* ☎ *609/397–0802 or 888/264–6648. 8 rooms, 1 cottage. AE, MC, V. CP.*

$–$$$ 🏨 **The Stockton Inn.** In 1934 Richard Rodgers and Lorenz Hart escaped from Manhattan to this inn, which inspired their musical *On Your Toes* and its song "There's a Small Hotel with a Wishing Well." The wishing well still stands in the terraced garden. Built as a private home in 1710, the inn became a stagecoach stop in 1796 and a hotel in 1832 (it now comprises five houses). Historic touches remain—eight bedrooms and the five dining rooms have working fireplaces. The restaurant serves contemporary American and Continental fare. ✉ *1 Main St., Box C, 08559,* ☎ *609/397–1250. 11 rooms. Restaurant. AE, DC, MC, V. CP.*

North Jersey

Arriving and Departing

From Manhattan take either the Lincoln Tunnel or the George Washington Bridge, and you're in North Jersey. I–80, to the north, and I–78, through Jersey City and Newark, connect with the New Jersey Turnpike, the Garden State Parkway, and I–287, which all run northeast–southwest through the region.

What to See and Do

Although Newark International Airport is all some travelers experience of this part of the state, a wealth of activities is available to those who care to linger. Among the suburban bedroom communities of Manhattan-bound commuters are parks, performing-arts venues, museums, great shopping, and some of the state's finest restaurants and lodgings.

Jersey City, at first glance merely gritty and urban, is nonetheless worth a visit—most obviously for its superb views of the broad Hudson River and the Manhattan skyline. It is also the site of **Liberty State Park** (✉ New Jersey Turnpike, Exit 14B, ☎ 201/915–3400), where ferries leave for the Statue of Liberty and the Ellis Island Immigration Museum on the site of the restored two-centuries-old former immigration facility, less than 2,000 ft offshore. Within Liberty State Park is the **Liberty Science Center** (✉ 251 Phillip St., ☎ 201/200–1000; 🎫 $9.50), with three floors of hands-on and interactive exhibits and a Kodak Omni Theater (a domed screen 88 ft across and 125 ft high); and the restored, open-sided 1889 **Central Railroad of New Jersey Terminal,** now used for special events and exhibits. The science center is closed Mondays. You can also stroll along **Liberty Walkway,** a waterfront promenade.

The "mile-square" city of **Hoboken** has several claims to fame. It was the setting for the movie *On the Waterfront;* the birthplace of baseball, first played on Elysian Fields (at the site of the now-defunct Maxwell House plant) in 1846; and the hometown of Frank Sinatra. Though its relationship with Old Blue Eyes was a love-hate one—Sinatra spurned his hometown after being pelted with fruits at a concert there in 1952—hard feelings seem to have been put aside since his death in 1998. A plaque marks **Sinatra's birthplace** (✉ 415 Monroe St.), destroyed by fire in 1967. **Frank Sinatra Way,** hugging the bank of the Hudson River, commands some of the best views in town. A new waterfront park was named in Sinatra's honor shortly after his death, and many of the town's long-standing businesses display faded photos of the singer. Music is also part of the draw for a new generation; yuppified **Washington Street** is the main drag for the trendy and boisterous, who drop into its many music clubs. **Maxwell's** (✉ 1039 Washington St., ☎ 201/798–0406) is the granddaddy, with live, mostly alternative music most nights. Hoboken has always been a big artist community, and many artists open their studios for an annual tour in October. Washington Street is a suitably arty mix of boutiques, antiques shops, hole-in-the-wall restaurants and liquor stores, and fast-food chain restaurants. Parking is Manhattan-style impossible, especially on weekends.

Newark, the state's largest city, is making a remarkable comeback from many years of economic stagnation and urban decay. The **New Jersey Performing Arts Center** (⊠ 1 Newark Ctr., between Military Park and waterfront, ☎ 888/466–5722) is one of the major factors in this renewal. Since its debut in the fall of 1997, it has attracted internationally recognized performers, such as Itzhak Perlman and the Alvin Ailey dance troupe, and sellout crowds to its intimate 514-seat Victoria Theater and 2,750-seat Prudential Hall. The $180 million facility has two restaurants, parking facilities, and a landscaped plaza and is the home of the New Jersey Symphony Orchestra. The **Newark Museum** (⊠ 49 Washington St., ☎ 973/596–6550; ☎ free) has outstanding fine-arts, science, and industry collections; its restored Ballantine House, a National Historic Landmark, has two floors of Victorian period rooms and decorative arts. It's open Wednesday through Sunday. Newark's **Ironbound District** is a Portuguese neighborhood popular for its ethnic restaurants.

★ The **Edison National Historic Site** (⊠ Main and Lakeside Ave., West Orange, ☎ 973/736–0550, ☎ $2), on the site of Thomas Alva Edison's former home, includes the inventor's main laboratory, machine shop, and library, and replicas of many of his creations. The site is scheduled to reopen in spring 2001, after undergoing an $80 million renovation.

In Millburn, the **Paper Mill Playhouse** (⊠ Brookside Dr., ☎ 973/376–4343) has long been regarded as one of the finest off-Broadway theaters, with a constantly changing slate of plays and musicals. In winter the New Jersey Ballet Company performs the *Nutcracker*.

To the west, outside suburban Morristown, is the **Morristown National Historical Park/Jockey Hollow** (⊠ Washington Pl., ☎ 973/539–2085; ☎ $4), where George Washington and his Continental Army camped during the winter of 1779–80. The park includes the elegant Ford Mansion, once Washington's quarters, and replicas of the soldiers' log huts. From Morristown U.S. 202 leads south past antiques shops and farm stands. This is horse country, with estates and meadows edged with wood fencing, especially around **Bedminster.** Many horse farms are off U.S. 202 on Route 523. At the headquarters of the **U.S. Equestrian Team** (⊠ Rtes. 512 and 206, Gladstone, ☎ 908/234–1251; ☎ free), you can visit the stables and the trophy room, which displays the team's Olympic medals, photos, and other mementos. Competitions, including a major festival in June, are held throughout the year. The complex is open on weekdays. **Far Hills** is the home of the U.S. Golf Association and its museum, **Golf House** (⊠ Rte. 512, ☎ 908/234–2300; ☎ free).

The **Great Swamp National Wildlife Refuge** (⊠ Basking Ridge, ☎ 973/425–1222; ☎ free) encompasses 7,300 acres of wildlife sanctuary, crossed with 8½ mi of trails, blinds, and boardwalks.

For wildlife of a different sort, the **Meadowlands Racetrack,** at the Meadowlands Sports Complex (⊠ Rte. 3 and NJ Turnpike, East Rutherford, ☎ 201/935–8500), has Thoroughbred racing in the fall, with harness racing and simulcasts from other tracks the rest of the year. Check local newspapers for gate times. **Pegasus** (⊠ 600 Meadowlands Pkwy., Secaucus, ☎ 201/843–2446) is the most upscale of the four restaurants on site. South of the track, in **Secaucus,** are acres and acres of the **outlet shops** that put this city on the map.

Dining and Lodging

BERGENFIELD

$$$$ ✕ **Chez Dominique.** Tables at this romantic French restaurant are small and candlelit, and the mood is elegantly cozy. The menu changes often but has included seafood risotto, coq au vin, and duck with foie gras immersion. Bring your own wine. ✉ *Bedford Ave.,* ☎ *201/384–7637. Reservations essential. DC, MC, V. Closed Sun.–Mon.*

EAST RUTHERFORD

$$–$$$ ✕ **Park & Orchard.** Vegetarians appreciate the many meatless dishes, including meat- and dairy-free lasagna and vegetarian meat loaf, at this cavernous, noisy, and always busy spot. Non–red meat entrées such as boneless chicken breast and blackened tuna steak are also available. The 1,900-bottle wine list has won many awards; the house wines are usually terrific choices. Save room for the peanut-butter pie. ✉ *240 Hackensack St.,* ☎ *201/939–9292. AE, D, DC, MC, V.*

SHORT HILLS

$$$–$$$$ ✕🖬 **Hilton Short Hills Hotel and Spa.** This is one of New Jersey's finest
★   hotels. Its gourmet restaurant, the Dining Room, receives raves for its Continental cuisine, and the hotel's beautiful spa is reason enough for a visit. The Mall at Short Hills, across the road, is great for tony shopping, including a Neiman Marcus—and, unlike in the town of Paramus, it's open on Sunday. ✉ *41 JFK Pkwy., 07078,* ☎ *973/379–0100 or 800/445–8667,* ℻ *973/379–6870. 304 rooms. 2 restaurants, pool, health club. AE, D, MC, V.* ✸

TENAFLY

$$$ 🖬 **Clinton Inn Hotel.** Tucked into a pretty suburban neighborhood, the Clinton Inn is especially popular for weddings and other special occasions. Good food and personalized service are the hallmarks. ✉ *145 Dean Dr., 07670,* ☎ *201/871–3200 or 800/275–4411,* ℻ *201/871–3435. 112 rooms. Restaurant, exercise room. AE, DC, MC, V.*

WEST ORANGE

$$–$$$$ ✕ **The Manor.** Countless romantic evenings have been lived out at this local institution, which serves American and Continental cuisine. The menu changes seasonally but may include oyster-cappuccino soup; fillet of salmon with potato crust; and, for dessert, a Sacher torte or frozen Grand Marnier soufflé. There's live piano music in the Terrace Lounge and dancing weekends in Le Dome nightclub—which now has a cigar bar, too. ✉ *111 Prospect Ave.,* ☎ *973/731–2360. Jacket required. AE, D, DC, MC, V. Closed Mon.*

NEW MEXICO

Updated by
Kathleen
McCloud,
Sharon
Niederman,
and Jeanie
Fleming
Pulseston

Capital	Santa Fe
Population	1,655,172
Motto	It Grows as It Goes
State Bird	Roadrunner
State Flower	Yucca
Postal Abbreviation	NM

Statewide Visitor Information

New Mexico Department of Tourism (⊠ Lamy Bldg., 491 Old Santa Fe Trail, Santa Fe 87503, ☎ 505/827–7400 or 800/733–6396, ℻ 505/827–8594). For outdoor activity information, contact the **USDA Forest Service, Southwestern Region** (⊠ Public Affairs Office, 517 Gold Ave. SW, Albuquerque 87102, ☎ 505/842–3292). For information about New Mexico's Native American reservations, contact the **Indian Pueblo Cultural Center** (⊠ 2401 12th St. NW, Albuquerque 87102, ☎ 505/843–7270).

Scenic Drives

The old **High Road** is not the most direct route from Santa Fe to Taos, but it takes you through rolling hillsides studded with orchards and tiny picturesque villages set against a rugged mountain backdrop. No visit to northern New Mexico is complete without the 100-mi trip along the **Enchanted Circle,** a breathtaking panorama of deep canyons, passes, alpine valleys, and towering mountains of the verdant Carson National Forest. **Route 66,** America's most nostalgic highway, includes a colorful stretch that now constitutes Albuquerque's Central Avenue. A scenic route between Albuquerque and Santa Fe, the **Turquoise Trail** (Route 14) snakes up through a portion of Cibola National Forest and several mining semi–ghost towns.

National and State Parks

National Parks
Carlsbad Caverns National Park is a spectacular system of caves and rock formations while **White Sands National Monument** is a white wonderland of gypsum sand dunes (☞ Elsewhere in New Mexico, *below*).

State Parks
New Mexico's 33 state parks range from the high mountain lakes and pine forests of the north to the Chihuahuan Desert lowlands in the south. Pristine and unspoiled, they have every conceivable outdoor recreational facility. For maps and brochures contact the **State Parks and Recreation Division** (⊠ Energy, Minerals, and Natural Resources Dept., 2040 S. Pacheco St., Box 1147, Santa Fe 87504-1147, ☎ 505/827–7173 or 888/667–2757, ℻ 505/827–1376).

Native American Reservations

Pueblo Indians established an agricultural civilization here many centuries ago. Nomadic tribes—the Navajo, Mescalero Apache, and Jicarilla Apache—came into the area much later. The settlements of various **Pueblo** tribes are described in the Albuquerque and Santa Fe sections. Note: When visiting Indian lands, it's important to respect all rules and requests regarding photography, videotaping, recording, and sketching. Some pueblos charge a fee for these activities; others ban them outright. The pueblos welcome visitors, but expect their sovereignty to be respected.

The **Jicarilla Apache Tribe** (✉ Box 507, Dulce 87528, ☎ 505/759–3242, FAX 505/759–3005) live on a 750,000-acre reservation in north-central New Mexico. The tribe has a tourist program promoting big-game hunting, fishing, and camping on a 15,000-acre game preserve.

A reservation of a half-million acres of timbered mountains and green valleys in southeastern New Mexico is home to the **Mescalero Apache Tribe** (✉ Tribal Office, 101 Central, Box 227, Mescalero 88340, ☎ 505/671–4494). The tribe owns and operates one of the most elegant luxury resorts in the state, Inn of the Mountain Gods, as well as Ski Apache, 16 mi from Ruidoso.

The Navajo Reservation, home to the largest Native American group in the United States, covers 17.6 million acres in New Mexico, Arizona, and Utah. There are a few towns on the reservation, but for the most part it is a vast area of stark pinnacles, colorful rock formations, high desert, and mountains. The tribe encourages tourism; write or call the **Navajo Nation Tourism Office** (✉ Box 663, Window Rock, AZ 86515, ☎ 520/871–6436 or 520/871–7371, FAX 520/871–7381).

ALBUQUERQUE

A large city—its population is nearing the half-million mark—Albuquerque spreads out in all directions. The hot-air balloons that take part in the annual October Kodak Albuquerque International Balloon Fiesta are an apt simile for the city's free spirit. As in the rest of New Mexico, Albuquerque's Native American, Spanish, and Anglo cultures are well blended. The city began as an important trade and transportation station on the Camino Real–Chihuahua Trail, which wound down into Mexico and remains a travel crossroads today. The original four-block core, known as Old Town, is the city's tourist hub, with unique shops, galleries, museums, and restaurants.

Visitor Information

Convention and Visitors Bureau (✉ 20 First Plaza NW, Box 26866, 87125, ☎ 505/842–9918 or 800/284–2282).

Arriving and Departing

By Bus
Albuquerque is served by **Greyhound** (✉ 300 2nd St. SW, ☎ 800/231–2222) and **TNMO Coaches Transportation Center** (✉ 300 2nd St. SW, ☎ 505/243–4435 or 800/231–2222).

By Car
I–25 enters Albuquerque from points north and south; I–40, from points east and west.

By Plane
Albuquerque International Airport (☎ 505/842–4366) is 5 mi south of downtown; the trip takes 10–15 minutes. Taxis charge $15–$20 plus tip. In Albuquerque, **Sun Tran** buses (☎ 505/843–9200) pick up on the baggage claim level about every 20 minutes; the fee is 75¢.

By Train
Amtrak (☎ 800/872–7245) serves the Albuquerque station (✉ 214 1st St. SW, ☎ 505/842–9650).

Exploring Albuquerque

Albuquerque sprawls in all directions, so it's best to see the city by car. Historic and colorful Route 66 is Albuquerque's Central Avenue, unifying as nothing else can the diverse areas of the city: Old Town, to the west, cradled at the bend of the Rio Grande; the downtown business and government centers; the University of New Mexico, to the east; and, farther east, Nob Hill, a lively strip of restaurants, boutiques, galleries, and shops. The railroad tracks, running north and south, and east–west Central Avenue divide the city into quadrants: southwest (SW), northwest (NW), southeast (SE), and northeast (NE).

The city began in 1706 in what is now Old Town, and tree-shaded **Old Town Plaza** remains the heart of Albuquerque's heritage. The massive adobe walls of **San Felipe de Neri Church** (⊠ 2005 Plaza NW, ☎ 505/243–4628) date from 1793 and still serve an active congregation. Most of the old adobe houses surrounding the plaza have been converted into charming shops, galleries, and restaurants.

The **Albuquerque Museum of Art and History** (⊠ 2000 Mountain Rd. NW, ☎ 505/243–7255; ⊠ free) showcases traditional and contemporary art of New Mexico and has an outstanding collection of Spanish colonial art that illustrates 400 years of Rio Grande valley history.

The striking glass-and-sandstone **New Mexico Museum of Natural History and Science** (⊠ 1801 Mountain Rd. NW, ☎ 505/841–2800; ⊠ $5.25) presents a simulated volcano and frigid Ice Age cave, dinosaurs, and an Evolator (short for Evolution Elevator)—a six-minute high-tech ride through 35 million years of New Mexico's geologic history.

The spectacular two-story **Indian Pueblo Cultural Center** (⊠ 2401 12th St. NW, ☎ 505/843–7270; ⊠ free, museum $4) has a museum that holds one of the largest collections of Native American arts and crafts in the Southwest. At the center, the 19 Pueblo tribes of New Mexico each operate separate alcoves devoted to their own arts and crafts. Fine examples of these are for sale. Free performances of ceremonial dances are given on most weekends and on special holidays.

Sandia Peak Aerial Tramway (⊠ 10 Tramway Loop NE, ☎ 505/856–7325; ⊠ $14), among the world's longest aerial tramways, makes an awesome 2¾-mi climb from the edge of the city to a point near 10,678-ft Sandia Crest for an overview of Albuquerque—and half of New Mexico. At sunset the sky is a kaleidoscope of colors over the desert. The tram closes for servicing during two weeks of fall and spring; call ahead.

On the city's western fringe lies **Petroglyph National Monument** (⊠ 4735 Unser Blvd. NW, ☎ 505/899–0205; ⊠ weekdays $1 per car, weekends $2 per car), which contains more than 15,000 ancient rock drawings inscribed as early as AD 1300 in the volcanic rocks and cliffs.

☾ Spend an afternoon at the **Albuquerque Biological Park** (⊠ 903 10th St. SW, ☎ 505/764–6200; ⊠ $4.50), an environmental museum that includes the **Albuquerque Aquarium, Rio Grande Zoo,** and **Rio Grande Botanic Garden.** The eel cave and shark tank are real kid pleasers, and the zoo is home to more than 1,000 animals, including elephants, bison, koalas, and endangered Mexican wolves, known as *lobos.* Wander through the beautiful gardens, which showcase plants from the Southwest and other climates.

☾ At the **Albuquerque Children's Museum** (⊠ Winrock Shopping Center, I–25 and Louisiana NE, ☎ 505/842–1537; ⊠ $4), arts and cultural exhibits, a computer lab, and the Make-It-Take-It Art Room keep youngsters entertained for hours. Don't miss the Bubble Room, where kids can enclose themselves in a giant bubble. Within the Children's Museum is **Explora!,** a hands-on science center where changing exhibits allow kids to conduct their own experiments such as using wind to make sand dunes and mini-tornadoes.

Outside Albuquerque

Coronado State Monument and Park (✉ off I–25 on Rte. 44, Box 95, Bernalillo 87004, ☎ 505/867–5351), a prehistoric Native American pueblo once known as Kuaua, sits on a bluff overlooking the Rio Grande near Bernalillo, 20 mi north of Albuquerque; it is believed to have been the headquarters of Coronado's army of 1,200, who came seeking the legendary Seven Cities of Gold in 1540.

Pueblos near Albuquerque

Made up of a series of terraced adobe structures and dominated by the massive mission church of San Estevan del Rey, **Acoma Pueblo** (☎ 505/470–4966 or 800/747–0181; ✇ $9, including guided tour) sits atop a 367-ft mesa that rises abruptly from the valley floor 64 mi west of Albuquerque. Most of its residents now live on the valley floor but retain traditional residences without electricity or running water on the mesa. Also known as Sky City, the pueblo may be visited only on paid, guided tours. Pueblo artists sell their prized thin-walled pottery.

Santo Domingo Pueblo (☎ 505/465–2214; ✇ free), off I–25 at the Santo Domingo exit between Albuquerque and Santa Fe, operates a Tribal Cultural Center, where its outstanding *heishi* (shell) jewelry is sold. The August 4 Corn Dance is one of the most colorful and dramatic of all the Pueblo ceremonial dances.

The sun symbol appearing on New Mexico's flag was adopted from the **Zia Pueblo** (✉ 135 Capital Square Dr., ☎ 505/867–3304; ✇ free), which has been at its present site (40 mi northwest of Albuquerque) since the early 1300s. Skillful Zia potters make polychrome wares, and painters produce highly prized watercolors.

Jemez Pueblo (☎ 505/834–7359; ✇ free), 51 mi northwest of Albuquerque, is the state's sole Towa-speaking pueblo. It is noted for its polychrome pottery and fine yucca-frond baskets. The beautiful **San Jose de los Jemez Mission** (☎ 505/829–3530; ✇ $2), a stone structure built in 1622, is at the Jemez State Monument, 13 mi north of Jemez Pueblo in Jemez Springs.

Dining

$$$$ ✗ **High Finance Restaurant and Tavern.** To get to this restaurant in the center of Cibola National Park, you must either take the Sandia Peak Tram, hike 3 mi into the park, or ski through the Sandia Ski Area. On the edge of Sandia Peak, more than 10,000 ft above sea level, it's a sublime place to watch a New Mexico sunset; every seat in the house has a view that spans 11,000 square mi. Entrées run along the steak, seafood, and pasta lines. ✉ *40 Tramway Rd. NE,* ☎ *505/243–9742. Reservations essential. AE, D, DC, MC, V. Closed Apr. and Nov.*

$$$ ✗ **Maria Teresa.** This nationally preserved landmark in Old Town, next to the Sheraton, is a restored 1840s adobe with 32-inch-thick brick adobe walls, fireplaces, early Spanish-American furnishings, and gardens. Aged beef, seafood, chicken, and New Mexican specialties, such as *carne adovada* (cubed pork marinated and baked in red chili), are served. ✉ *618 Rio Grande Blvd. NW,* ☎ *505/242–3900. AE, DC, MC, V.*

$$–$$$ ✗ **Artichoke Café.** Grilled duck, pumpkin ravioli with fresh spinach ★ and butternut squash, and rack of lamb with rosemary-merlot sauce are a few specialties served in this turn-of-the-20th-century brick building just east of downtown. The large, modern, bi-level dining room spills onto a small courtyard. ⊠ *424 Central Ave. SE,* ☎ *505/243–0200. AE, D, DC, MC, V. Closed Sun. No lunch Sat.*

\$\$ ✕ **Monte Vista Fire Station.** Now a national historic landmark, this spacious, airy restaurant was once a working firehouse. The American menu includes a wide variety of seafood, beef, and pasta dishes; highlights are crab ravioli and duck with raspberry coulis. ⊠ *3201 Central Ave. NE,* ☎ *505/255–2424. AE, D, DC, MC, V. No lunch weekends.*

\$\$ ✕ **Scalo Northern Italian Grill.** Bankers and bikers gather at this lively,
★ informal restaurant with an open kitchen and full-service bar. In addition to excellent pizza, Scalo serves such dishes as spinach-and-ricotta-stuffed pasta in a light cream sauce and grilled salmon with a balsamic-citrus glaze. ⊠ *3500 Central Ave. SE, in the Nob Hill Business Center,* ☎ *505/255–8781. AE, D, MC, V. No lunch Sun.*

Lodging

\$\$\$–\$\$\$\$ 🏨 **Brittania & W. E. Mauger Estate B&B.** Popular with professionals because of its downtown location and updated business services, this fine B&B is situated in an 1897 Queen Anne Victorian with an Old West front veranda and hardwood floors. ⊠ *701 Roma Ave. NW, 87102,* ☎ *505/242–8755 or 800/719–9189,* 𝖥𝖠𝖷 *505/842–8835. 8 rooms. AE, D, DC, MC, V. BP.* ✎

\$\$\$ 🏨 **Albuquerque Marriott.** Kachina dolls and Native American pottery and art are combined elegantly at this 17-story uptown property decorated in the colors of the region's natural environment. Shoppers will enjoy being near the city's largest malls. ⊠ *2101 Louisiana Blvd. NE, 87110,* ☎ *505/881–6800 or 800/228–9290,* 𝖥𝖠𝖷 *505/888–2982. 411 rooms. Restaurant, pool, health club. AE, D, DC, MC, V.* ✎

\$\$\$ 🏨 **La Posada de Albuquerque.** A tiled lobby fountain, an encircling balcony, massive vigas, and Native American war-dance murals are a few of the atmospheric touches that set this historic hotel apart—thanks to New Mexico native Conrad Hilton, who opened the hotel in 1939. Hopi pottery and R. C. Gorman prints lend character to the rooms. ⊠ *125 2nd St. NW, 87102,* ☎ *505/242–9090 or 800/777–5732,* 𝖥𝖠𝖷 *505/242–8664. 114 rooms. Restaurant. AE, D, DC, MC, V.*

\$\$ 🏨 **Barcelona Suites.** This colorful hotel just off I–40 has the feel of Old Mexico, with tiles and wrought iron—though rooms have more of a Southwest ambience. Complimentary breakfast and evening cocktails are served around the atrium fountain. Each two-room suite has a galley kitchen with a wet bar and microwave oven. ⊠ *900 Louisiana Blvd. NE, 87110,* ☎ *505/255–5566 or 877/227–7848,* 𝖥𝖠𝖷 *505/266–6644. 64 suites. Pools. AE, D, MC, V.* ✎

\$\$ 🏨 **Best Western Rio Grande Inn.** Rooms in this Best Western have handcrafted wood furniture, tin sconces, and artwork from local artisans. The hotel is conveniently just off I–40, and within an easy walk of Old Town. ⊠ *1015 Rio Grande Blvd. NW, 87104,* ☎ *505/843–9500 or 800/959–4726,* 𝖥𝖠𝖷 *505/843–9238. 174 rooms. Restaurant, pool.* ✎

\$\$ 🏨 **Radisson Albuquerque Airport.** Arched balconies, desert colors, and indoor and outdoor dining add to the Spanish-southwestern flavor of this two-story motor hotel near the airport. ⊠ *1901 University Blvd. SE, 87106,* ☎ *505/247–0512,* 𝖥𝖠𝖷 *505/843–7148. 148 rooms. Restaurant, pool. AE, D, DC, MC, V.* ✎

Campgrounds

Fifteen minutes south of Albuquerque on I–25, the 🛆 **Isleta Lakes and Recreation Area** (⊠ Box 383, Isleta 87022, ☎ 505/877–0370) has complete campground facilities with tent sites and RV hookups. Within Albuquerque, there are tent sites and RV facilities at the 🛆 **Albuquerque KOA Central** (⊠ 12400 Skyline Rd. NE, 87123, ☎ 505/296–2729).

Just north of town is the ⚐ **Albuquerque North Bernalillo KOA** (✉ 555 S. Hill Rd., Box 758, Bernalillo 87004, ☎ 505/867–5227).

Nightlife and the Arts

To find out what's on in town, check the *Albuquerque Journal* on Friday and Sunday or the *Albuquerque Tribune* on Thursday.

The Arts
The **New Mexico Symphony Orchestra** (✉ 3301 Menaul Blvd. NE, Suite 4, ☎ 505/881–8999) is among the state's largest performing arts organizations.

Outdoor Activities and Sports

Contact the **Albuquerque Parks and Recreation Department** (✉ 7701 San Pedro NE, Bldg. A, Box 1293, 87103, ☎ 505/857–8640) for information on its network of parks and recreational programs, including golf courses, paved tracks for biking and jogging, pools, tennis courts, playing fields, playgrounds, and even a shooting range.

Hot-Air Ballooning
The **Kodak Albuquerque International Balloon Fiesta** (☞ Festivals and Seasonal Events *in* the United States Region by Region chapter) is the world's largest gathering of balloonists. You can also hire a pilot and balloon for your own ride. **Rainbow Ryders** (✉ 11520 San Bernadino NE, ☎ 505/823–1111 is a reliable firm. **World Balloon Corporation** (✉ 4800 Eubank NE, ☎ 505/293–6800) can safely take you up and away.

Shopping

To find dozens of one-of-a-kind shops, meander down the tiny lanes and small plazas of **Old Town. Winrock Center** (✉ Louisiana Blvd. exit off I-40, ☎ 505/888–3038) and **Coronado Center** (✉ Louisiana and Menaul Blvds., ☎ 505/881–4600) are two of the area's main malls. **Cottonwood Mall** (✉ Coors Blvd. at Coors Bypass, ☎ 505/899–7467) has 147 shops. **Nob Hill**, a seven-block strip of shops stretching along Central Avenue from Girard to Washington Street, is the city's newest and trendiest shopping district. Neon-lighted boutiques, restaurants, galleries, and performing-arts spaces encourage strolling and people-watching.

SANTA FE

Updated by
Kathleen
McCloud

With its crisp, clear air and bright, sunny weather, New Mexico's capital couldn't be more welcoming. Perched on a 7,000-ft plateau at the base of the Sangre de Cristo Mountains, Santa Fe is surrounded by the remnants of a 2,000-year-old Pueblo civilization and filled with evidence of the Spanish, who founded the city as early as 1607. Rows of chic art galleries (Santa Fe claims to be the country's third most important arts center, after New York and Los Angeles), smart restaurants, and shops selling southwestern furnishings and apparel combine to give the city an unusual cosmopolitan flair. Its population, an estimated 70,000, swells to nearly double that during the peak summer season and to a lesser degree in the winter, with the arrival of skiers lured by the challenging slopes of the Santa Fe Ski Area and nearby Taos Ski Valley.

Visitor Information

Chamber of Commerce (✉ 510 N. Guadalupe St., Suite N, De Vargas Center N, 87504, ☎ 505/983–7317). **Convention and Visitors Bureau** (✉ 201 W. Marcy St., Box 909, 87504, ☎ 505/984–6760 or 800/777–2489, ℻ 505/984–6679).

Arriving and Departing

By Bus
Santa Fe can be reached via **Greyhound** (⊠ 858 St. Michael's Dr., ☎ 505/471–0008 or 800/231–2222).

By Car
Santa Fe is accessible from points north and south on I–25 or U.S. 84/285. It is 60 mi north of Alburquerque on I–25.

By Plane
Albuquerque International Airport (☎ 505/842–4366) serves Santa Fe, too. **Shuttle bus** service is available from **Sandia Shuttle** (☎ 505/474–5696); the trip takes 70 minutes and runs 10 times per day. The cost is $20 one-way. For charter flights between Albuquerque and Santa Fe, contact the Albuquerque airport or the **Santa Fe Municipal Airport** (☎ 505/473–7243), which is 20 minutes southwest of downtown.

By Train
The **Amtrak** station (☎ 800/872–7245) nearest to Santa Fe is in **Lamy** (☎ 505/466–4511); Amtrak runs a **shuttle-bus service** (☎ 505/982–8829 in Santa Fe) the 17 mi to Santa Fe.

Getting Around Santa Fe

Santa Fe's downtown core is easily maneuvered on foot. The city's public bus system is limited in scale, so you'll need a car to visit attractions in the outer reaches. Otherwise, call **Capital City Cab Company** (☎ 505/438–0000).

Exploring Santa Fe

★ The heart of Santa Fe is its historic **Plaza.** Established as early as 1607 as the city's social and political hub, it was later the terminus of the Santa Fe Trail, where freight wagons unloaded after completing their arduous journeys. Today the Plaza is lined with shops, art galleries, and restaurants. (Museum goers should consider purchasing the $10 four-day museum pass, which can be used at the four state museums as well as the Georgia O'Keeffe Museum.)

Fronting the Plaza is the oldest public building in the United States:
★ the Pueblo-style **Palace of the Governors,** which houses the **State History Museum.** Under the palace's portal, Native American artisans display and sell their wares. ⊠ N. Plaza, ☎ 505/476–5100. ☞ $5, free with museum pass, free 5–8 on Fri. Closed Mon. ✆

The building that began Santa Fe's Pueblo Revival style is the **Museum of Fine Arts.** On display are the works of regional artists, as well as those of early Modernist painters who migrated to Santa Fe and Taos in the early 20th century, putting Taos and Santa Fe on the national map as vibrant arts communities. ⊠ 107 W. Palace Ave., ☎ 505/476–5072. ☞ $5, free with museum pass. Closed Mon. Jan.–June.

The **Georgia O'Keeffe Museum** (⊠ 217 Johnson St., ☎ 505/995–0785; ☞ $5, free with museum pass) opened in July 1997. Its founders plan eventually to house the world's largest collection of art by O'-Keeffe, one of the many artists who have drawn their inspiration from the unique beauty of the New Mexico landscape but one of the few whose work has achieved worldwide fame.

A block east of the Plaza, the magnificent French Romanesque–style **St. Francis Cathedral** (⊠ 231 Cathedral Pl., ☎ 505/982–5619) houses the crypt of Jean Baptiste Lamy, Santa Fe's first archbishop, and the statue La Conquistadora (Our Lady of the Conquest), carried to Santa

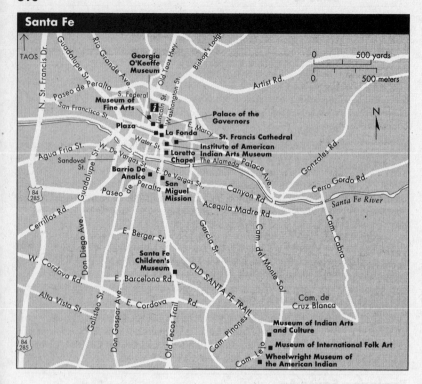

Santa Fe

Fe in 1692 by Don Diego de Vargas. If you walk to the southern edge of the cathedral grounds, you will come to the **Archives of the Archdiocese** (✉ free), a small museum with historic church artifacts that is open weekdays 9–4.

Facing St. Francis Cathedral, in a renovated former post office, is the **Institute of American Indian Arts Museum** (✉ 108 Cathedral Pl., ☎ 505/988–6281; ✉ $4), which houses the more than 8,000-object **National Collection of Contemporary Indian Art**. Its paintings, photography, and traditional crafts showcase the work of students and teachers, past and present, of the prestigious **Institute of American Indian Arts**, which was founded as a one-room studio classroom in the early 1930s.

A number of the city's sights trace the path of the **Old Santa Fe Trail**. The **Loretto Chapel** (✉ 211 Old Santa Fe Trail, ☎ 505/982–0092) is known for its Miraculous Staircase—an engineering marvel leading to the choir loft; many of the faithful believe the staircase was built by St. Joseph. The adobe **San Miguel Mission** (✉ 401 Old Santa Fe Trail, ☎ 505/983–3974; ✉ $1), built in about 1625 by the Tlaxcala Indians and the oldest church still in use in the continental United States, houses a number of priceless statues and paintings and the San Jose Bell, said to have been cast in Spain in 1356. This site has been known to close early in winter, so schedule accordingly. **Barrio De Analco** (now called East De Vargas Street), lined with historic houses, is believed to be one of the oldest continuously inhabited streets in the United States.

★ ☪ The fascinating **Museum of International Folk Art** contains textiles, dolls, jewelry, ornaments, and other folk art objects from many countries. It is among the premier museums of its kind in the world. ✉ 706 *Camino Lejo*, ☎ 505/476–1200. ✉ *$5, free with museum pass. Closed Mon.* ☪

Rearing up from a piñon-and-juniper forest behind the Museum of International Folk Art is the privately owned **Wheelwright Museum of the American Indian** (⊠ 704 Camino Lejo, ☎ 505/982–4636; ⊡ free), housed in a building shaped like a traditional Navajo hogan; works of many Native American cultures are on display.

The **Museum of Indian Arts and Culture** (⊠ 710 Camino Lejo, ☎ 505/476–1250; ⊡ $5, free with museum pass) interweaves the history and contemporary culture of New Mexico's Pueblo, Navajo, and Apache tribes.

The **Santa Fe Children's Museum** has hands-on exhibits on the arts and sciences. Older kids enjoy the climbing wall. ⊠ *1050 Old Pecos Trail,* ☎ *505/989–8359.* ⊡ *$3. Closed Mon.–Wed. in Sept.–May; closed Mon. and Tues. in June–Aug.*

Outside Santa Fe

Forty-five minutes (about 40 mi) northwest of Santa Fe, **Los Alamos,** birthplace of the atomic bomb, spreads over fingerlike mesas at an altitude of 7,300 ft. This is a dull, modern town that by itself is not very scenic but for nearby Bandelier. Though research continues at the Los Alamos National Laboratory on off-limits nuclear weaponry, visitors can drop in on the interesting **Bradbury Science Museum** (⊠ 15th St. at Central Ave., ☎ 505/667–4444; ⊡ free). The area abounds with archaeological sites, including **Bandelier National Monument** (⊠ HCR1, off Rte. 4 about 12 mi from Los Alamos, ☎ 505/672–3861; ⊡ $10 per car for 7 days), which contains the remains of one of the largest Anasazi centers.

A kind of Williamsburg of the Southwest, **El Rancho de las Golondrinas,** 15 mi south of Santa Fe off I–25, is a reconstruction of a small, traditional 19th-century New Mexico farming village, complete with grinding mills, a blacksmith shop, animals, working fields, homes, and a *morada* (meeting place) of the Penitente order. ⊠ *334 Los Pinos Rd., in the village of La Cienega,* ☎ *505/471–2261.* ⊡ *$5, $7 during festivals. Closed Nov.–Mar.* ⊛

About 25 mi southeast of Santa Fe via I–25 north, **Pecos National Historical Park** (⊠ Rte. 63, Box 418, Pecos 87552, ☎ 505/757–6032; ⊡ $4 per car) is the site of a once-flourishing Native American pueblo. An early trading center, Pecos was the largest and easternmost pueblo reached by the Spanish conquistadors in 1541. Franciscan priests built a mission church here in the 1620s, but the pueblo was abandoned in 1838 because of disease and raiding nomadic tribes.

Pueblos near Santa Fe

The Native American pueblos near Santa Fe vary in their craft specialties and in the recreational facilities they offer tourists. On feast days, most have ceremonial dances that are open to the public, but call ahead for regulations. To find out when events are held, call the **Eight Northern Pueblos** office (☎ 505/852–4265).

About 20 mi north of Santa Fe on U.S. 84/U.S. 285, **Pojoaque Pueblo** (⊠ Rte. 11, Santa Fe, ☎ 505/455–2278) features the **Poeh Museum** (☎ 505/455–2489; ⊡ free), a cultural center focusing on the Tewa-speaking Native Americans. The pueblo also operates an official **state tourist center** on U.S. 285/U.S. 84, with an extensive selection of northern New Mexican arts and crafts.

San Ildefonso Pueblo (⊠ Rte. 5, Santa Fe, ☎ 505/455–3549; ⊡ $3 per car), just north of Route 502, about 15 mi east of Los Alamos, was the home of the most famous of all pueblo potters, Maria Martinez, whose exquisite polished black-on-black pottery is revered among collectors. The pueblo still boasts a number of highly acclaimed potters, as well as other artists and craftspeople.

San Juan Pueblo (⊠ U.S. 74 [take Rte. 68 1 mi north of Espanola, turn left onto U.S. 74 at sign, entrance is 1 mi farther], ☎ 505/852–4400) is headquarters of the Eight Northern Indian Pueblos Council. In its beautiful arts center, the **Oke Oweenge Crafts Cooperative**, the pueblo's distinctive redware and micaceous clay pottery can be purchased. Two handsome kivas and a New England–style church are other attractions.

Santa Clara Pueblo (⊠ Rte. 30, 4 mi south from Espanola, crossing the Rio Grande, Espanola, ☎ 505/753–7326) is home of the beautiful 740-room **Puyé Cliff Dwellings** (☒ $5), a national landmark believed to have been built between the 13th and 14th centuries. It is also famous for its shiny red-and-black engraved pottery and for its many well-known painters and sculptors. Tours are conducted on weekdays.

Dining

$$$$ ✕ **Coyote Cafe.** Try the "Cowboy"—a 22-ounce rib-eye steak served
★ with barbecued black beans and red-chili-dusted onion rings. Other favorites are the squash-blossom and corn-cake appetizers. The three-course prix-fixe menu is $42.50. From April through October, the restaurant opens its less-expensive Rooftop Cantina, which serves Mexican fare. ⊠ 132 W. Water St., ☎ 505/983–1615. AE, D, DC, MC, V. Closed Tues. and Wed. Jan. and Feb.

$$$$ ✕ **The Compound.** This restaurant prides itself on old world elegance. The American-Continental menu includes chicken in champagne, roast loin of lamb, Russian caviar, and New Zealand raspberries. ⊠ 653 Canyon Rd., ☎ 505/982–4353. Reservations essential. AE. Closed Jan.–Feb. and Sun.–Mon. No lunch.

$$$ ✕ **Café Pasqual's.** Only a block southwest of the Plaza, this cheerful, in-
★ formal café decked out with piñatas is known for fabulous brunches of huevos rancheros and quesadillas with apple-smoked bacon (the Wall Street Journal named it the best breakfast in the nation), as well as chicken mole and grilled Chimayo chili–rubbed New York steak with serrano mayonnaise. Expect a line. Pasqual's also serves dinner with Asian-French specialties like bouillabaisse, Thai shrimp and lemongrass sauce, along with Latin favorites. ⊠ 121 Don Gaspar Ave., ☎ 505/983–9340. AE, MC, V.

$$$ ✕ **El Nido.** Since 1920 this former dance hall and trading post has been known for its cozy, firelit rooms and menu of choice aged beef and seafood. ⊠ U.S. 285, 6 mi north of Santa Fe to Tesuque exit, then 1½ mi to restaurant, ☎ 505/988–4340. AE, D, DC, MC, V. Closed Mon. No lunch.

$$$ ✕ **Pink Adobe.** The old adobe walls add a magical touch to the dining experience in this cozy restaurant that has been operating for more than 50 years. Perennial specials on the menu are steak Dunnigan, smothered in green chili and mushrooms; and savory shrimp Louisianne—fat and crispy deep-fried shrimp. ⊠ 406 Old Santa Fe Trail, ☎ 505/983–7712. AE, D, DC, MC, V. No lunch weekends.

$$–$$$ ✕ **Ore House on the Plaza.** Margaritas and great people-watching rather than great cooking are the mainstay of this restaurant. Margaritas come in more than 80 flavors and may be sipped on the balcony, which overlooks the active Plaza. ⊠ 50 Lincoln Ave., ☎ 505/983–8687. AE, MC, V.

$–$$ ✕ **Guadalupe Café.** A local favorite, this informal café features New Mexican dishes, including sizable sopapillas (fluffy fried bread). The seasonal raspberry pancakes are one of many breakfast favorites that keep the place crowded every morning. Generous salads, homemade bread, and guacamole enchiladas are all popular. ⊠ 422 Old Santa Fe Trail, ☎ 505/982–9762. Reservations not accepted. D, DC, MC, V.

$–$$ ✕ **The Shed.** It's in the rambling adobe hacienda that once belonged to the Sena family, dating from 1692. Try the red-chili enchiladas or posole (hominy stew). Expect a line at lunchtime. ⊠ 113½ E. Palace

Ave., ☎ 505/982–9030. *Reservations not accepted for lunch. AE, DC, MC, V. No dinner Sun.–Tues.*

$ ✕ **Plaza Café.** The red-leather banquettes, black Formica tables, tile floors, and coffered tin ceiling haven't changed much since 1918. Standard American fare is served along with southwestern and Greek specialties. There is continuous service from early morning until 10 PM, so it's a good place to go for a late lunch when other restaurants are closed. ⊠ *54 Lincoln Ave.*, ☎ *505/982–1664. Reservations not accepted. AE, D, MC, V.*

Lodging

Hotel rates fluctuate considerably from place to place, but most are dramatically lower from November through April (excluding the Thanksgiving and Christmas holidays)—after which they soar. Bed-and-breakfasts are a less expensive alternative; contact **Bed & Breakfast of New Mexico** (⊠ Box 2805, Santa Fe 87504, ☎ 505/982–3332). Also, note that all the major chains—often with less expensive rooms—are represented along Cerrillos Road, south of downtown.

$$$$ 🏨 **Bishop's Lodge.** Three miles north of downtown Santa Fe, in the foothills of the Sangre de Cristo Mountains, this 1,000-acre resort has rooms in 11 one- and three-story lodges. The restaurant, which serves steaks and Continental fare, is one of the area's best. Organized outdoor activities abound, and there's a children's program. ⊠ *Bishop's Lodge Rd., Santa Fe 87504*, ☎ *505/983–6377 or 800/732–2240*, FAX *505/989–8739. 88 rooms. Restaurant, pool, tennis, exercise room, hot tub, horseback riding. AE, D, MC, V.* ❧

$$$$ 🏨 **Eldorado Hotel.** One of the city's most luxurious hotels, in the heart of downtown, it has southwestern-style rooms in desert colors; many have balconies with mountain views. The Old House restaurant is outstanding. Evenings, there's live music in the lounge. ⊠ *309 W. San Francisco St., 87501*, ☎ *505/988–4455 or 800/955–4455*, FAX *505/995–4455. 219 rooms, 55 casitas. 2 restaurants, pool, health club, sauna, hot tub, shops. AE, D, DC, MC, V.* ❧

$$$$ 🏨 **Inn of the Anasazi.** One of Santa Fe's finer hotels, the inn has rooms
★ with beamed ceilings, kiva fireplaces, and handcrafted furnishings. The excellent restaurant serves a mix of American and cowboy cuisines. ⊠ *113 Washington Ave., 87501*, ☎ *505/988–3030 or 800/688–8100*, FAX *505/988–3277. 59 rooms. Restaurant. AE, D, DC, MC, V.* ❧

$$$$ 🏨 **La Fonda.** The oldest hotel in Santa Fe may be the only one that can boast having had both Kit Carson and John F. Kennedy as guests. Each room is unique, with hand-carved and -painted Spanish colonial–style furniture and motifs painted by local artists. ⊠ *100 E. San Francisco St., 87501*, ☎ *505/982–5511 or 800/523–5002*, FAX *505/988–2952. 164 rooms. Restaurant, pool, 2 hot tubs. AE, D, DC, MC, V.* ❧

$$$$ 🏨 **La Posada de Santa Fe Resort & Spa.** In 1999 La Posada underwent a change of ownership and a major renovation. The result is a top-drawer establishment with valet parking and a bellman at every turn. The spa has a full-time staff for body treatments at additional charge. Most rooms have fireplaces, beamed ceilings, Native American rugs, and Spanish flair; the five rooms in the main building are drenched in Victoriana. ⊠ *330 E. Palace Ave., 87501*, ☎ *505/986–0000 or 800/727–5276*, FAX *505/982–6850. 159 rooms. Restaurant, pool, exercise room. AE, DC, MC, V.* ❧

$$$–$$$$ 🏨 **Hotel Santa Fe.** This posh Native American–owned hotel has rooms with locally handmade furniture and Pueblo paintings. Its gift shop sells works by Picurís and other Pueblo Indian artists at prices lower than those of most nearby retail stores; guests get an additional 25% discount. Native American–performed dances are during peak season (May–October). The Corn Dance Cafe serves Native American cuisine with nouvelle twist. ⊠ *1501 Paseo de Peralta, 87505*, ☎ *505/982–*

1200 or 800/825–9876, FAX 505/984–2211. 128 rooms. Restaurant. AE, D, DC, MC, V. ✍

$$–$$$$ 🏠 **Inn of the Turquoise Bear.** This rambling inn on the edge of downtown was fashioned out of the 30-room estate of the late poet Witter Bynner, who hosted Willa Cather, W. H. Auden, Thornton Wilder, and Errol Flynn, among other notables. Rooms, in many shapes and sizes, are tastefully furnished; though not lavish, they exude character. Most have fireplaces, and some open onto private courtyards. ⊠ 342 E. Buena Vista St., 87501, ☎ 505/983–0798 or 800/396–4104, FAX 505/988–4225. 11 rooms. AE, D, MC, V. CP. ✍

$$$ 🏠 **Inn of the Governors.** This unpretentious inn, one of the nicest in town, is two blocks from the Plaza. Rooms have a Mexican theme, with bright colors, hand-painted folk art, southwestern fabrics, and handmade furnishings. ⊠ 234 Don Gaspar Ave., at Alameda St., 87501, ☎ 505/982–4333 or 800/234–4534, FAX 505/989–9149. 100 rooms. Restaurant, pool. AE, DC, MC, V. ✍

$$–$$$ 🏠 **Territorial Inn.** This elegant, 100-year-old Victorian home is just two blocks from the Plaza. Some rooms have their own fireplaces, and there's a hot tub on the back patio. ⊠ 215 Washington Ave., 87501, ☎ 505/989–7737, FAX 505/984–8482. 10 rooms. AE, D, MC, V. CP. ✍

Campgrounds

La Bajada Welcome Center (⊠ La Bajada Hill, 13 mi southwest of Santa Fe on I–25, ☎ 505/471–5242) provides information on private campgrounds near Santa Fe. ⚠ **Babbitt's Los Campos RV Park** (⊠ 3574 Cerrillos Rd., 87505, ☎ 505/473–1949) is the only full-service RV park within city limits. The ⚠ **Santa Fe National Forest** (⊠ 1220 S. St. Francis Dr., Box 1689, 87504, ☎ 505/438–7840), right in Santa Fe's backyard, has public sites open from May through October. For a one-stop information about recreational sites in the area, call **New Mexico Public Lands Information Center** (☎ 505/438–7542).

Nightlife and the Arts

Check the entertainment listings in Santa Fe's daily newspaper, the *New Mexican*, for performances and events. On Friday, the paper includes the arts and entertainment supplement, the *Pasatiempo*, which covers the gamut of gallery openings, movies, and community happenings, among other events. Or, check the free weekly *Santa Fe Reporter*, published on Wednesday, for its listing of current events.

Nightlife

The lounges, hotels, and nightspots of Santa Fe present many entertainment options. **Club Alegria** (⊠ Aqua Fria, just west of Siler Rd., ☎ 505/471–2324) offers salsa dancing to live music on weekends. Downtown, **Evangelo's** (⊠ 200 W. San Francisco St., ☎ 505/982–9014) has Hawai'i à la New Mexico decor, 200 imported beers, and pool tables in a funky basement; bands play upstairs on weekends. **Paramount** (⊠ 331 Sandoval St., ☎ 505/982–8999) features dancing to live music and DJs. They host theme evenings, which include swing, salsa, and disco. **El Farol** (⊠ 808 Canyon Rd., ☎ 505/983–9912) features live blues, jazz, folk, and flamenco music in a rustic centuries-old adobe that's the oldest restaurant and cantina in Santa Fe. **Rodeo Nites** (⊠ 2911 Cerrillos Rd., ☎ 505/473–4138) attracts a country-and-western crowd.

The Arts

Artistically and visually the city's crown jewel, the famed **Santa Fe Opera** (⊠ U.S. 285, ☎ 505/986–5900) is housed every summer in a modern open-air amphitheater carved into a hillside 7 mi north of the city. The **Santa Fe Symphony** (☎ 505/983–1414) performs from September through May at Sweeney Center (⊠ 201 W. Marcy St.). The **Santa Fe**

Pro Musica plays at the Lensic Theater (⊠ 211 W. San Francisco St., ☎ 505/988–4640) from September through May. The **Santa Fe Chamber Music Festival** (☎ 505/983–2075) brings internationally known musicians to the St. Francis Auditorium at the Museum of Fine Arts from July to August. Hopefully, by spring 2001, festival performances will be held in the new **Lensic Performing Arts Center,** which is situated in the totally renovated old Lensic theater (⊠ 107 W. Palace Ave., ☎ 505/988–7050).

Outdoor Activities and Sports

Horseback Riding

Bishop's Lodge (⊠ Bishop's Lodge Rd., ☎ 505/983–6377) conducts trail rides from April through November. **Broken Saddle Riding Co.** (⊠ High Desert Ranch in Cerrillos, ☎ 505/470–0074) leads excursions into the historic and scenic canyons of the Cerrillos hills, 23 southeast of Santa Fe. **Santa Fe Detours** (⊠ 54½ E. San Francisco St., ☎ 505/983–6565 or 800/338–6877) leads excursions for private groups.

Shopping

Santa Fe's downtown shops display goods that are as enigmatic as the town itself. Sure, the T-shirt shops are there, but don't miss the dramatic array of clothing at **Origins** (⊠ 135 W. San Francisco St. ☎ 505/988–2323). **Mirá** (⊠ 101 W. Marcy St. ☎ 505/988–3585) is a Latin American–style mercado that sells ethnographic and urban-chic women's clothing along with folk art. **Jane Smith** (⊠ 550 Canyon Rd., ☎ 505/988–4775) is the place to go for extraordinary handmade western wear for men and women, from cowboy boots to beaded tunics.

Peruse a fine collection of antique and Native American artifacts (Navajo weavings, Pueblo pottery, Plains Indian beadwork) at **Morning Star Gallery** (⊠ 513 Canyon Rd., ☎ 505/982–8187). A Santa Fe landmark for unusual and kitschy gifts is **Doodlet's** (⊠ 120 Don Gaspar Ave., ☎ 505/983–3771).

For an all-inclusive Santa Fe shopping experience with a global twist, drive north of town near the village of Tesuque for the weekend **Tesuque Pueblo Flea Market** (⊠ U.S. 84/285, 7 mi north of Santa Fe). It's open Friday as well, May–October, and closed January–mid-February. Art galleries make up the majority of shops on Canyon Road. **Gerald Peters Gallery** (⊠ 1011 Paseo de Peralta, ☎ 505/954–5700) has approximately 30,000 square ft of outstanding 19th- and 20th-century American and European art and a large western art collection. For contemporary art on the Plaza, visit **LewAllen Contemporary** (⊠ 129 W. Palace Ave., ☎ 505/988–8997).

TAOS

At the base of the rugged Sangre de Cristo Mountains about 60 mi northeast of Santa Fe, Taos is a small, old frontier town steeped in the history of New Mexico. Stately elms and cottonwood trees, narrow streets, and a profusion of adobe all cast a lingering spell on the memory; the charming old Plaza, surrounded by art galleries and boutiques, adds to the allure. Georgia O'Keeffe, Ansel Adams, and D. H. Lawrence are among Taos's former residents; so are such Wild West figures as Kit Carson and New Mexico's first governor, Charles Bent. Taos Ski Valley is a famed ski resort in winter and a hiking and mountain-biking venue in the summer.

Visitor Information

Taos County Chamber of Commerce (✉ 1139 Paseo del Pueblo Sur, Drawer 1, Taos 87571, ☎ 505/758–3873 or 800/732–8267).

Arriving and Departing

By Bus

Texas, New Mexico & Oklahoma Coaches, a subsidiary of Greyhound/Trailways, runs buses once a day from Albuquerque to the Taos Bus Station (✉ 1006 Paseo del Pueblo Sur, ☎ 505/758–1144). The trip is about three hours. **Pride of Taos** (☎ 505/758–8340) runs daily shuttle service between Taos and Santa Fe ($20 one-way, $40 round-trip); reserve in advance.

By Car

The main route from Santa Fe to Taos is via U.S. 84/U.S. 285 to Route 68—a 70-mi drive with stunning river and canyon views. For spectacular mountain scenery, the High Road to Taos (☞ Scenic Drives, *above*) is tops and well worth the slightly longer drive (about two hours). From points north, take Route 522; from points east or west, take U.S. 64.

By Plane

The **Taos Municipal Airport** (✉ U.S. 64, ☎ 505/758–4995), 12 mi west of the city, services only private planes and air charters. For air-charter information, call 888/884–4350. **Pride of Taos** (☎ 505/758–8340) runs daily shuttle service from downtown Taos to the Albuquerque airport ($35 one-way, $65 round-trip); reserve in advance. **Faust's Transportation** (☎ 505/758–3410 or 505/758–7359), in nearby El Prado, provides radio-dispatched taxis between the Taos airport and town (about $20) and between the Albuquerque airport and Taos ($35 one-way, $65 round-trip).

By Train

Amtrak (☎ 800/872–7245) provides service into Lamy Station (✉ Rte. 41, Lamy 87500), a half hour outside Santa Fe, in the opposite direction of Taos, but still the closest train station to Taos. **Faust's Transportation** (☎ 505/758–3410 or 505/758–7359) dispatches taxis to the train station.

Getting Around

Taos radiates around a central plaza. The main street through town is Paseo del Pueblo Norte, coming down from Colorado; the route then becomes Paseo del Pueblo Sur and heads out toward Santa Fe. A car is a big help for exploring Taos, unless you choose an accommodation right downtown and don't plan on venturing out to Taos Pueblo or Ranchos de Taos. **Faust's Transportation** (☎ 505/758–3410 or 505/758–7359), in nearby El Prado, has a fleet of radio-dispatched cabs.

Orientation Tours

Pride of Taos Tours (☎ 505/758–8340) provides 70-minute narrated trolley tours of Taos highlights. The departure point for tours, shuttles, and pickups is next to the Taos County Chamber of Commerce (☞ Visitor Information, *above*) and the Plaza.

Exploring Taos

The **Taos Pueblo** (☎ 505/758–9593; ⊠ $4), 2 mi north of the Plaza, at the base of the 12,282-ft Taos Mountain, is the home of the Taos Tiwa-speaking Indians, whose apartment house–style pueblo dwelling is one of the oldest continuously inhabited communities in the United

States. Life here predates Marco Polo's 13th-century travels in China and the arrival of the Spanish in America in 1540. Unlike many nomadic Native American tribes forced to relocate to government-designated reservations, these people have resided at the base of the Taos Mountain for centuries; this continuity has made possible the link between pre-Columbian inhabitants who originally lived in the Taos Valley and their descendants who reside there now. Special feast days are the Corn Dance held May 3 and San Geronimo Day, September 30.

Four miles south of town is the farming and ranching community **Ranchos de Taos** (✉ Ranchos de Taos, ☎ 505/758–2754), site of the beautiful **San Francisco de Asís Church.** Its massive, buttressed adobe walls and graceful towers are a prime example of early Mission architecture. Generations of painters and photographers, including Georgia O'Keeffe and Ansel Adams, have been inspired by the earthy, clean lines of the exterior walls and supporting bulwarks, which cast eerie shapes and shadows.

Dining and Lodging

$$–$$$$ ✕ **Trading Post Cafe.** Perfectly marinated salmon gravlax; first-rate paella; excellent pasta, fowl, and fresh fish; a great wine list; and homemade raspberry sorbet are some of the reasons this chic yet comfortable restaurant attracts a crowd. ✉ 4179 Rte. 68, at Rte. 518, Rancho de Taos, ☎ 505/758–5089. MC, V. Closed Sun.

$$$ ✕ **Doc Martin's.** This pleasant, casual restaurant in the Historic Taos Inn (☞ below) might feature piñon-crusted salmon with anchovy pesto sauce and Southwest lacquered duck. Don't skip the superb desserts: Aztec chocolate mousse with roasted-banana sauce or coconut-milk crème brûlée. ✉ 125 Paseo del Pueblo Norte, ☎ 505/758–1977. AE, D, MC, V.

$–$$$ ✕ **Apple Tree.** Named for the large tree in the umbrella-shaded courtyard, this is a great lunch and early dinner spot in an historic adobe one block from the Plaza. The food is fresh—among the well-crafted dishes are grilled lamb and chicken fajitas. The restaurant has received regular awards for its wine selection. Sunday brunch is served. ✉ 123 Bent St., ☎ 505/758–1900. AE, D, DC, MC, V.

$ ✕ **Fred's Place.** A friendly young waitstaff delivers Fred's northern New Mexican specialties, including *carne adovada* (a spicy marinated meat dish) and blue-corn enchiladas, to a devoted group of regulars. Expect to wait for a table—you'll be glad you did. ✉ 332 Paseo del Pueblo Sur, ☎ 505/758–0514. Reservations not accepted. MC, V. Closed Sun. No lunch.

$ ✕ **Taos Cow.** Taos Cow has expanded its world headquarters for tasty
★ ice cream (made from growth-hormone-free milk featured in area health food stores) into the former Casa Fresen Bakery building. The remodeled covered porch is a fine spot to enjoy coffee, tea, chai, pastries, cookies, and fresh-baked bread from the kitchen inside. Favorites among the three-dozen ice-cream flavors are Cherry Ristra, Piñon Caramel, and—the true test—Vanilla. ✉ 591 Hondo Seco Rd., ☎ 505/776–5640.

$$–$$$$ 🏨 **Touchstone Inn.** Nestled against the Taos Pueblo land, this elegant B&B enjoys magnificent views of the mountains. Each luxury suite has a kiva fireplace, a whirlpool bath, and antiques. The owner, Bren Price, is an artist, and her work is displayed throughout the inn. ✉ 110 Mabel Dodge La., 87571, ☎ 800/758–0192, FAX 505/758–3498. 8 suites. MC, V. ❧

$$$ 🏨 **Historic Taos Inn.** Only steps from Taos Plaza, this local landmark is listed on the National Register of Historic Places. The lobby, with its popular Adobe Bar, is built around an old town well, from which a fountain now bubbles forth. Rooms have Native American–style wood-burning fireplaces and furniture built by local artists. ✉ 125 Paseo del

Pueblo Norte, 87571, ☎ 505/758–2233 or 800/826–7466, ℻ 505/758–5776. 36 rooms. Restaurant. AE, D, MC, V. ✍

$$–$$$ 🏨 **Mabel Dodge Luhan House.** D. H. and Frieda Lawrence, Georgia
★ O'Keeffe, and Willa Cather have all been guests at this National Historic Landmark hotel, once the home of heiress and Taos socialite Mabel Dodge Luhan. The guest rooms in the main house are simple but tasteful; there's also a two-bedroom gatehouse cottage. Five of the rooms do not have private baths. ✉ 240 Morada La., 87571, ☎ 505/751–9686 or 800/846–2235, ℻ 505/751–0431. 17 rooms, 12 with bath; 1 cottage. AE, MC, V. BP. ✍

$$ 🏨 **Austing Haus.** The Taos Ski Valley forms a stunning backdrop to this
★ soaring timber-frame B&B—especially when viewed through the glass-paneled front of the establishment. Many of the spotless rooms have four-poster beds; there are also three hot tubs. The dining room calls to mind an alpine resort, with huge etched-glass windows and a breakfast table covered with apple strudel or other freshly baked goods. ✉ 1282 Rte. 150, Box 8, Taos Ski Valley 87525, ☎ 505/776–2649 or 800/748–2932, ℻ 505/776–8751. 22 rooms, 3 chalets. AE, DC, MC, V. ✍

$$ 🏨 **Casa Europa.** Pastures and mountains surround this spacious 17th-century pueblo-style adobe B&B outside town. The delightful rooms have kiva fireplaces and marble bathrooms; there's also a five-room suite with a hot tub. Gourmet breakfasts are served every morning and European-style homemade pastries every afternoon—except during ski season, when there are fireside hors d'oeuvres in the evenings instead. A hot tub and sauna soothe ski-weary muscles. ✉ 840 Upper Ranchitos Rd., HC 68, Box 3F, 87571, ☎ ℻ 505/758–9798, ☎ 888/758–9798. 7 rooms. MC, V. BP.

$$ 🏨 **San Geronimo Lodge.** Set on 2½ acres just outside of Carson National Forest, this lodge was originally constructed in 1925 by an Oklahoma socialite wanting to accommodate her friends. Rooms have handcrafted furniture, and most have kiva fireplaces. A hot tub and massage services are added bonuses. ✉ 1101 Witt Rd., 87571, ☎ 505/751–3776 or 800/894–4119, ℻ 505/751–1493. 18 rooms. Pool. MC, V. BP.

Campgrounds

⛺ **Carson National Forest Service** (✉ 208 Cruz Alta Rd., Taos 87571, ☎ 505/758–6200) provides information about the many camping sites in the forest. ⛺ **Taos RV Park** (✉ Rte. 68, Box 729TCVG, Ranchos de Taos 87557, ☎ 505/758–1667 or 800/323–6009), with 29 spaces, is open year-round.

Ski Areas

Within a 90-mi radius of Taos are plenty of winter ski resorts with beginning, intermediate, and advanced slopes, as well as snowmobile and cross-country skiing trails. All provide excellent lodging accommodations and child-care programs at reasonable prices.

Cross-Country

Carson National Forest (✉ 208 Cruz Alta Rd., Taos 87571, ☎ 505/758–6200) has 440 mi of trails. **Enchanted Forest/Miller's Crossing Cross-Country Ski Area** (✉ Box 219, Red River 87558, ☎ 505/754–2374), about 40 mi NE of Taos, has 24 mi of trails.

Downhill

Angel Fire Resort (✉ Drawer B, Angel Fire 87710, ☎ 505/377–6401 or 800/633–7463) has a 2,180-ft drop, 59 trails, and 6 lifts. **Red River Ski Area** (✉ Box 900, Red River 87558, ☎ 505/754–2223, ℻ 505/754–6184) has a 600-ft drop, 44 trails, and 7 lifts. **Sipapu Lodge and Ski Area** (✉ Box 29, Vadito 87579, ☎ 505/587–2240) has a 865-ft drop, 19 trails, and 3 lifts. **Taos Ski Valley** (✉ Box 90, Taos Ski Valley 87525, ☎ 505/776–2291, FAX 505/776–8596) has a whopping 2,612-ft drop, 72 trails, and 11 lifts.

ELSEWHERE IN NEW MEXICO

Carlsbad Caverns National Park

Arriving and Departing

The park is in the southeastern part of the state, 320 mi from Albuquerque via I–25, U.S. 380, and U.S. 285, and 167 mi west of El Paso, Texas, via U.S. 180. **Mesa Airlines** (☎ 800/637–2247, 505/885–0245 in Carlsbad) provides air-shuttle service between the Albuquerque airport and **Cavern City Air Terminal** in Carlsbad.

What to See and Do

★ **Carlsbad Caverns National Park** (⊠ 3225 National Parks Hwy., Carlsbad 88220, ☎ 505/785–2232, 800/967–CAVE for ranger tours; ⌑ $6) contains one of the world's largest and most spectacular cave systems: 83 caves, with huge subterranean chambers, fantastic rock formations, and delicate mineral sculptures. Only two caves, Carlsbad and Slaughter Canyon, are open to the public for regular tours, but some off-trail viewing options are available during special trips. At **Carlsbad Cavern** the descent to the 750-ft level is made by foot or elevator; either way, you will see the Big Room, large enough to hold 14 football fields. Reservations are essential a day in advance for the much less accessible **Slaughter Canyon Cave,** 25 mi from the main cavern. The last few miles of the road are gravel, and there's a ½-mi trek up a 500-ft rise to reach the cave's entrance.

The park is the area's main lure, but the town of **Carlsbad** is an interesting place to see as well. For information contact the **Chamber of Commerce** (⊠ 302 S. Canal St., 88220, ☎ 505/887–6516). The **Living Desert State Park** (⊠ 1504 Miehls Dr., Carlsbad 88220, ☎ 505/887–5516; ⌑ $4) is also worth a visit while you're in the area.

Dining and Lodging

$ ✕ **Lucy's Mexicali Restaurant & Entertainment Club.** All the standards are prepared at this family-owned oasis of great Mexican food, along with some not-so-standard items such as chicken fajita burritos, and Tucson-style chimichangas. Low-fat and fat-free Mexican dishes and 12 microbrewery beers are served. Live entertainment is offered on weekends. ⊠ 701 S. Canal St., ☎ 505/887–7714. AE, D, DC, MC, V.

$ ✕ **Red Chimney.** If you hanker for sweet and tangy barbecue, try this restaurant, which has log-cabin decor and an Early American atmosphere. Sauce from an old family recipe is slathered on chicken, pork, beef, turkey, and ham. ⊠ 817 N. Canal St., ☎ 505/885–8744. MC, V. Closed weekends.

$$ ⌑ **Holiday Inn Carlsbad Downtown.** The rugs, paintings, and room decor ★ of this two-story lodge harmonize with the building's Territorial theme. Ventanas, the gourmet restaurant, serves fine Continental cuisine. ⊠ 601 S. Canal St., 88220, ☎ 505/885–8500 or 800/742–9586, FAX 505/887–5999. 100 rooms. 2 restaurants, pool, exercise room. AE, D, DC, MC, V. BP. ⊛

$ ⌑ **Best Western Stevens Inn.** Classy accommodations and reliable service make this reasonably priced inn a steal. Some of the spacious rooms ★ have kitchenettes. Prime rib and steaks are served in the evening at the motel's Flume Room, and Mexican food and sandwiches are served throughout the day at the Green Tree Room. ⊠ 1829 S. Canal St. (Box 580), 88220, ☎ 505/887–2851 or 800/730–2851, FAX 505/887–6338. 202 rooms. 2 restaurants, bar. AE, D, DC, MC, V. ⊛

White Sands National Monument

Arriving and Departing

The park is in the south-central part of the state. The visitor center is located off U.S. 70/82, 15 mi southwest of Alamogordo or 52 mi east of Las Cruces.

What to See and Do

White Sands National Monument. With shifting sand dunes 60 ft high, the park encompasses 145,344 acres and the largest deposit of gypsum sand in the world. The monument, one of the few landforms recognizable from space, has displays in its visitor center that describe how the dunes were formed. A 17-minute introductory video that's very helpful if you intend to hike among the dunes is screened at the visitor center, where there's a gift shop, a snack bar, and a bookstore. A walk on the 1-mi **Big Dune Trail** will give you a good overview of the site. Backpackers' campsites are available by permit, obtainable at the visitor center, but there aren't any facilities. ⊠ *Off U.S. 70/82, 15 mi southwest of Alamogordo or 52 mi east of Las Cruces,* ☎ *505/679–2599.* ☞ *$3 (day use or camping).*

Dining And Lodging

$–$$ ✕ **Margo's.** *Chalupas* (beans, meat, and cheese served on crisp tortillas) is the specialty Mexican dish at family-owned Margo's. In winter, *menudo,* made of hominy and tripe, is served hot and steaming. The southwestern decor includes colorful blankets. ⊠ *504 1st St.,* ☎ *505/ 434–0689. AE, D, MC, V.*

$ ▥ **Days Inn.** Contemporary rooms with standard chain-motel quality have extra nice touches such as hair dryers and microwaves in every room. ⊠ *907 S. White Sands Blvd., 88310,* ☎ *505/437–5090,* ℻ *505/ 434–5667. 40 rooms. Pool, exercise room. AE, D, DC, MC, V. CP.*

NEW YORK

Updated by
K. Clifford,
M. Davis,
K. Deaver,
J. Donohue,
D. Downing,
M. Feldstein,
R. King

Capital	Albany
Population	18,138,000
Motto	Excelsior
State Bird	Bluebird
State Flower	Rose
Postal Abbreviation	NY

Statewide Visitor Information

New York State Division of Tourism (✉ 1 Commerce Plaza, Albany 12245, ☎ 518/474–4116 or 800/225–5697).

Scenic Drives

The **Taconic Parkway,** particularly the stretch from Hopewell Junction to East Chatham, passes through rolling hills, orchards, woods, and pastures reminiscent of England's Yorkshire countryside. To make a dramatic loop around the Adirondacks' **High Peaks** region, pick up Route 73 off the Northway (I–87) at Exit 30, drive northwest through Lake Placid, proceed on Route 86 through Saranac Lake, then head southwest on Route 3 to Tupper Lake, due south on Route 30 to Long Lake, and east on Route 28N to North Creek. For information on the dozen officially designated scenic drives, call **New York State Travel Information Center** (☎ 800/225–5697).

National and State Parks

National Parks

The **Gateway National Recreation Area** (✉ Floyd Bennett Field, Bldg. 69, Brooklyn 11234, ☎ 718/338–3338) extends through Brooklyn, Queens, Staten Island, and into New Jersey. It includes the **Jamaica Bay Wildlife Refuge,** a good spot to see migrating birds; **Jacob Riis Park,** where a boardwalk stretches along the surfy Atlantic; plus various beaches, parklands, and facilities for outdoor and indoor festivals. **Fire Island National Seashore** (✉ 120 Laurel St., Patchogue 11772, ☎ 516/289–4810) offers Atlantic surf and beaches on a barrier island.

State Parks

New York has 150 state parks. The **Empire State Passport,** permitting unlimited entrance to the parks for a year (April–March), is available for $49 at most parks; you can also contact the **State Office of Parks and Recreation** (☎ 518/474–0456) or write for an application (✉ Passport, State Parks, Albany 12238).

NEW YORK CITY

Whatever you're looking for in a big-city vacation, you'll find it in New York. The city has a rich history, from the arrival of early Dutch settlers and the swearing in of George Washington as the first U.S. president to the influx of millions of immigrants in the late 19th and early 20th centuries. Today's New York City is known around the world for its distinctive skyline, its first-rate museums and performing arts companies, and its status as the capital of finance, fashion, art, publishing, broadcasting, theater, and advertising. And, of course, New Yorkers themselves are world famous—if not always for their charm, at least for their panache, ethnic diversity, and street smarts.

Beyond the allure of must-see sights, from the Statue of Liberty to Times Square, from Central Park to the Metropolitan Museum of Art, New York has an indefinable aura all its own. It's a special intensity that comes from being in the big leagues, where everybody's chasing a dream and still keeping score. To paraphrase a slogan originally coined for the Plaza Hotel, you get the feeling that "nothing unimportant ever happens in New York."

Visitor Information

Convention and Visitors Bureau (⊠ 810 7th Ave., at 53rd St., 10019, ☎ 212/484–1222, FAX 212/246–6310).

Arriving and Departing

By Bus

The **Port Authority Terminal** (⊠ 40th to 42nd Sts., between 8th and 9th Aves., ☎ 212/564–8484) handles all long-haul and commuter bus lines. Among the bus lines serving New York are **Greyhound** (☎ 800/231–2222), **Bonanza** (☎ 800/556–3815 for travel from New England), **Peter Pan Trailways** (☎ 800/237–8747) in the northeast, **Martz Trailways** (☎ 800/233–8604) from northeastern Pennsylvania, and **New Jersey Transit** (☎ 973/762–5100) from New Jersey.

By Car

A complex network of **bridges and tunnels** provides access to Manhattan. I–95 enters via the George Washington Bridge. I–495 enters from Long Island via the Midtown Tunnel. From upstate the city is accessible via the New York (Dewey) Thruway (I–87), which is known as the Major Deegan Expressway within New York City.

By Plane

Virtually every major U.S. and foreign airline serves one or more of New York's three airports. **La Guardia** (☎ 718/533–3400) and **John F. Kennedy International** (☎ 718/244–4444) airports are in Queens. **Newark International Airport** (☎ 973/961–6000) is in New Jersey. Cab fare to midtown Manhattan runs $17–$29 plus tolls and tip from La Guardia, $30 plus tolls and tip from JFK, and $34–$38, plus tolls and tip, from Newark. Both the **Gray Line Airport Shuttle** (☎ 212/315–3006 or 800/451–0455) and **Olympia Trails Airport Express** (☎ 908/354–3330) connect all three airports to various locations in Manhattan. By public transportation, the **A train (subway)** to Howard Beach connects with a free airport shuttle bus to JFK.

By Train

All train lines servicing Manhattan arrive or depart from either Pennsylvania Station or Grand Central Terminal, including **Amtrak** ☎ (800/872–7245), **MTA Metro-North Railroad** (☎ 212/532–4900 or 800/638–7646), and **New Jersey Transit** (☎ 973/762–5100).

Getting Around New York City

New York is a city of neighborhoods best explored at a leisurely pace, up close, and on foot. Extensive public transportation easily bridges gaps between areas of interest.

By Car

If you're traveling by car, don't plan to use it much in Manhattan. Driving in the city can be a nightmare of gridlocked streets and aggressive fellow motorists. Free parking is almost nonexistent in midtown, and parking lots everywhere are exorbitant ($10 for half an hour is not unusual in midtown).

By Public Transportation

The 714-mi **subway** system, the fastest and cheapest way to get around the city, serves Manhattan, Brooklyn, Queens, and the Bronx and operates 24 hours a day. Tokens cost $1.50 each, with reduced fares during nonrush hours for people with disabilities (note: the subways are not wheelchair-accessible) and for senior citizens, and are sold in subway stations. Pay-Per-Ride MetroCards, purchased for any amount between $3 and $80, are also available at all subway stations; to use one, swipe it through a reader at the turnstile; the fare is automatically deducted from the card's value. When you purchase a MetroCard for $15 or more you get an additional 10% credit. For $17 you can purchase an unlimited-ride MetroCard offering as many rides as you desire within a seven-day period—a good deal if you plan to take more than 12 rides. Transfers among subway lines are free at designated interchanges. Most **buses** follow easy-to-understand routes along the Manhattan grid, and some run 24 hours. Routes go up or down the north–south avenues, east and west on the major two-way crosstown streets: 96th, 86th, 79th, 72nd, 57th, 42nd, 34th, 23rd, and 14th. To find a bus stop, look for a light blue sign (or green for an express bus) on a green pole. Bus fare is $1.50 in exact coins (no pennies or bills) or a subway token; a MetroCard can also be used on all city buses. If you need to transfer to a connecting bus line and you are not using a MetroCard, request a free transfer coupon when paying the fare. Transfers between the bus and the subway are also free if you use a MetroCard. For **24-hour bus and subway information** call 718/330–1234. For subway or bus **maps** ask at token booths or write to the **New York City Transit Authority** (✉ Customer Assistance, 370 Jay St., Room 702, Brooklyn 11201).

By Taxi

Taxis (official, licensed ones are yellow) are usually easy to hail on the street, in front of major hotels, and by bus and train stations. The fare is $2 for the first ⅕ mi, 30¢ for each ⅕ mi thereafter, and 20¢ for each 60 seconds not in motion. A 50¢ surcharge is added to rides begun between 8 PM and 6 AM. Bridge and tunnel tolls are extra, and drivers expect a 15% tip. Barring performance above and beyond the call of duty, don't feel obliged to give more.

Orientation Tours

Boat Tour

From March to mid-December **Circle Line Cruises** (✉ Pier 83, at 42nd St. and 12th Ave., ☎ 212/563–3200) offers a three-hour circumnavigation of Manhattan. Semi-Circle tours run from mid-December through March.

Bus Tours

Gray Line New York Tours (✉ 900 Eighth Ave., at 42nd St., ☎ 212/397–2600) offers a number of standard city and double-decker bus tours in several languages, plus trolley tours and day trips to Atlantic City. **New York Doubledecker Tours** (☎ 718/361–5788) covers the major attractions. Both tour lines allow you to hop on and off.

Walking Tours

Heritage Trails New York (☎ 212/269–1500) is a self-guided walking tour through the downtown area. **New York City Cultural Walking Tours** (☎ 212/979–2388) focuses on the city's landmarks, memorials, and outdoor art. The **Municipal Art Society** (☎ 212/935–3960) offers walking tours featuring history and architecture.

Exploring Manhattan

Midtown is the heart of New York City, so it makes sense to start your exploration here. Then move on to the museum-rich Upper West and Upper East sides, downtown to Chelsea, Greenwich Village, SoHo, Little Italy, and Chinatown, and finally to Lower Manhattan, the city's financial center.

Midtown

★ At the center of midtown is **Rockefeller Center,** a complex of 19 buildings occupying nearly 22 acres of prime real estate between 5th and 7th avenues and 47th and 52nd streets. The outdoor ice rink, on the Lower Plaza between 49th and 50th streets, is the center's trademark. The ice rink becomes an open-air café in warm weather. In December the plaza is decorated with a huge Christmas tree. The center's 6,000-seat Art Deco **Radio City Music Hall** (✉ 6th Ave. at 50th St., ☎ 212/247–4777; ☛ tour $15), is America's largest indoor theater. It produces major concerts, Christmas and Easter extravaganzas, awards presentations, and other special events and is home of the fabled Rockettes chorus line.

The stretch of **5th Avenue** between Rockefeller Center and 59th Street glitters with world-famous shops, including Saks Fifth Avenue, F.A.O. Schwarz, Prada, and Tiffany & Co. Gothic-style **St. Patrick's** (✉ 5th Ave. at 50th St., ☎ 212/753–2261), the Roman Catholic cathedral of New York, is dedicated to the patron saint of the Irish. The stone structure was begun in 1859, consecrated in 1879, and completed in 1906.

The **Museum of Television and Radio** (✉ 25 W. 52nd St., ☎ 212/621–6600 or 212/621–6800 for recorded general information and daily events; ☛ donations suggested; closed Mon.) has three galleries of photographs and artifacts documenting the history of broadcasting. The collection contains more than 60,000 television shows and radio programs, as well as several thousand commercials; you can watch your selections at individual consoles.

★ The **Museum of Modern Art** (MoMA; ✉ 11 W. 53rd St., ☎ 212/708–9480, ☛ $10; donations suggested Fri. 4:30–8:30; closed Wed.) is the city's foremost showcase for 20th-century art, housed in an airy structure built around a sculpture garden. All the great modern artists, from van Gogh to Picasso, Matisse to Warhol, are represented. Photography, prints, architecture, and design all have their own galleries. Afternoon and evening film showings are free with the price of admission. A major renovation is scheduled to be completed in 2001; in the meantime call for gallery changes while work progresses.

Times Square, one of New York's principal energy centers, is southwest of the Museum of Modern Art. Known as the Crossroads of the World, it is perhaps best known as the core of the Broadway Theater District. Most Broadway theaters are actually on streets west of Broadway. Redevelopment on and around 42nd Street has dramatically transformed the area, especially 42nd Street between 7th and 8th avenues. Construction will continue well into the year 2001.

At the historic **New Amsterdam Theater** (✉ 214 W. 42nd St., ☎ 212/282–2900), the acclaimed stage version of *The Lion King* draws crowds nightly. Across from the New Amsterdam another renovated theatrical jewel, the **New Victory Theater** (✉ 209 W. 42nd St., ☎ 212/239–6255), stages productions mostly by and for children. Next door the **Ford Center for the Performing Arts** (✉ 43rd St. between 7th and 8th Aves., ☎ 212/307–4100) opened in 1998 with a production of E. L. Doctorow's novel *Ragtime*.

Two crouching marble lions guard the entrance to the **New York Public Library (NYPL) Center for the Humanities** (☎ 212/930–0800; ☒ free), between 40th and 42nd streets on 5th Avenue. This 1911 Beaux Arts masterpiece has frequent exhibits and a majestic renovated **main reading room.**

United Nations (☎ 212/963–7713; ☒ tour $7.50) headquarters is on a lushly landscaped riverside tract along 1st Avenue between 42nd and 48th streets. A line of flagpoles flies the flags of member nations when the General Assembly is in session inside the striking 505-ft-high slab of the Secretariat Building. Tours depart from the General Assembly lobby.

The **Morgan Library** (☒ 29 E. 36th St., at Madison Ave., ☎ 212/685–0008; ☒ donations suggested; closed Mon.), at the southern end of midtown, is a small, patrician museum centered on the famous banker's red-damask-lined study and his majestic personal library, with tiers of handsomely bound rare books, letters, and illuminated manuscripts; both rooms were completed in 1906. Rotating exhibitions from the permanent collection showcase drawings, prints, manuscripts, and books.

★ The 1931 Art Deco **Empire State Building** (☒ 5th Ave. and 34th St., ☎ 212/736–3100, ☒ $7 for observatory), two blocks southwest of the Morgan Library, is no longer the world's tallest building, but it is one of the world's best-loved skyscrapers. Go to the concourse level to buy a ticket for the 86th- and 102nd-floor observation decks.

Upper East Side

The **Upper East Side,** east of Central Park between 59th and 96th streets, is the focus of the wealthy, high-society New York glamorized in literature and film. The neighborhood includes singles bars and high-rise apartment buildings on 1st Avenue, sedate town houses in the East 60s, and an outstanding concentration of art museums and galleries. Along **Madison Avenue** between 59th and 79th streets are patrician art galleries, unique specialty stores, and the boutiques of many of the world's major fashion designers. **Museum Mile** is a strip of cultural institutions devoted to a broad spectrum of subjects and artistic styles, on or near 5th Avenue between 70th and 104th streets.

★ The **Frick Collection** (☒ 1 E. 70th St., at 5th Ave., ☎ 212/288–0700, ☒ $7; closed Mon.), housed in a Beaux Arts–style palace built by Pittsburgh Coke-and-steel baron Henry Clay Frick, is the city's finest small art museum. Specializing in European works from the late 13th to the late 19th century, it has masterpieces by Rembrandt, Fragonard, Bellini, Turner, and Vermeer, among others.

The **Whitney Museum of American Art** (☒ 945 Madison Ave., at 75th St., ☎ 212/570–3676; ☒ $12.50; free 1st Thurs. of every month 6–8; closed Mon.), a gray granite vault with cantilevered construction and startling trapezoidal windows that project outward, is devoted exclusively to 20th-century American works, from naturalism and impressionism to pop art, abstract expressionism, postmodernism, and whatever comes next.

★ The **Metropolitan Museum of Art** (☒ 5th Ave. at 82nd St., ☎ 212/535–7710, ☒ donations suggested; closed Mon.), on the edge of Central Park, is the largest art museum in the western hemisphere. Galleries display prehistoric to postindustrial works from around the world, including impressive Greek and Egyptian collections and an entire wing devoted to tribal arts. The museum has the world's most comprehensive collection of American art, and its holdings of European art are unequaled outside Europe. Also here are the Temple of Dendur, an entire Egyptian temple (circa 15 BC), and galleries devoted to musical in-

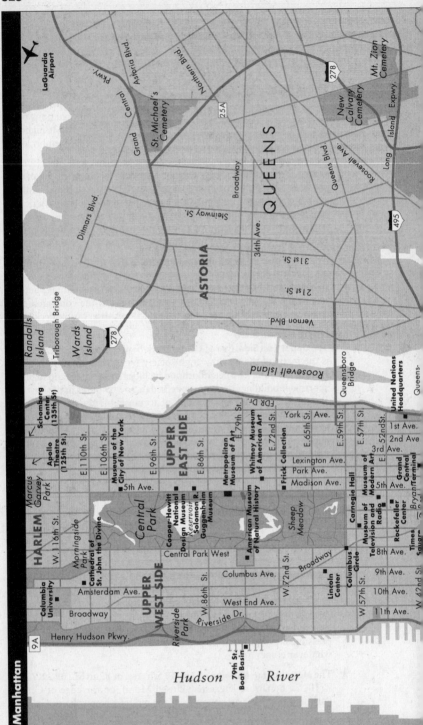

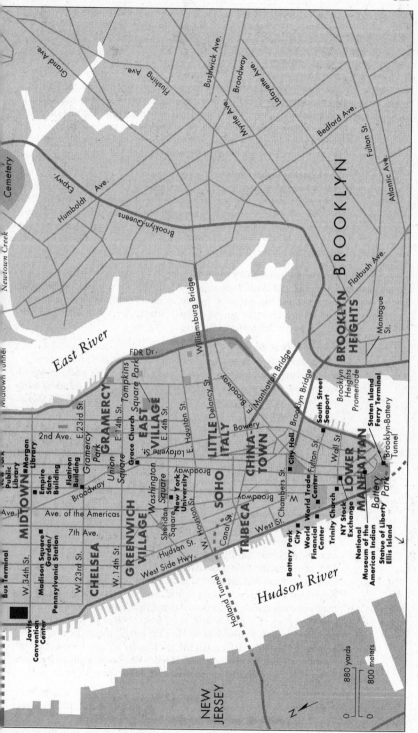

Neutown Creek

Cemetery

Grand Ave.

Flushing Ave.

Bushwick Ave.

Broadway

Lafayette Ave.

Bedford Ave.

Fulton St.

BROOKLYN

Humboldt Ave.

Expwy.

Brooklyn-Queens

Atlantic Ave.

BROOKLYN HEIGHTS

Flatbush Ave.

Montague St.

East River

FDR Dr.

Midtown Tunnel

Williamsburg Bridge

Manhattan Bridge

Brooklyn Heights Promenade

E. 23rd St.

GRAMERCY

Tompkins Square Park

EAST VILLAGE

E. 14th St.

E. 4th St.

Delancy St.

LITTLE ITALY

E. Broadway

Brooklyn Bridge

South Street Seaport

Staten Island Ferry Terminal

2nd Ave.

New York Public Library

Morgan Library

Grace Church

Gramercy Park

Union Square

Washington Square

Lafayette St.

E. Houston St.

Bowery

CHINA TOWN

City Hall

Fulton St.

Wall St.

Brooklyn-Battery Tunnel

Empire State Building

Flatiron Building

Broadway

SOHO

New York University

Broadway

Chambers St.

LOWER MANHATTAN

Battery Park

Ave. of the Americas

Sheridan Square

GREENWICH VILLAGE

Hudson St.

W. Houston St.

Canal St.

Broadway

W. Broadway

West St.

W.

World Trade Center

Trinity Church

NY Stock Exchange

Ave. J

MIDTOWN

7th Ave.

W. 14th St.

CHELSEA

W. 23rd St.

TRIBECA

West Side Hwy.

West St.

Battery Park City

World Financial Center

National Museum of the American Indian

Statue of Liberty Ellis Island

Bus Terminal

W. 34th St.

Madison Square Garden/ Pennsylvania Station

Holland Tunnel

Hudson River

Javits Convention Center

NEW JERSEY

880 yards

0

0

800 meters

N

struments and arms and armor. Walking tours and lectures are free with admission. The museum's separate **Cloisters** (☎ 212/923–3700), an amalgam of monastery buildings transported stone by stone from Europe, overlooks the Hudson River in Fort Tryon Park at the top of Manhattan; it houses the museum's medieval collection.

★ The **Solomon R. Guggenheim Museum** (⊠ 1071 5th Ave., at 89th St., ☎ 212/423–3500, ☜ $12; donations suggested Fri. 6–8; closed Thurs.), designed by Frank Lloyd Wright and expanded and restored in 1992, is a six-story spiral filled with fine examples of modern art. Exhibits alternate between new artists and modern masters; the permanent collection includes more than 20 Picassos.

The **Cooper-Hewitt National Design Museum** (⊠ 2 E. 91st St., ☎ 212/849–8400; ☜ $8; free Tues. 5–9; closed Mon.), a branch of the Smithsonian Institution, was once the residence of industrialist and philanthropist Andrew Carnegie. Changing exhibitions focus on various aspects of contemporary or historical design. Major holdings include drawings and prints, textiles, wall coverings, applied arts and industrial design, and graphic design.

The **Museum of the City of New York** (⊠ 5th Ave. at 103rd St., ☎ 212/534–1672; ☜ donations suggested; closed Mon.–Tues.) brings the history of the Big Apple to life, from its seafaring beginnings to yesterday's headlines, in period rooms, videos, clever displays of memorabilia, and a dollhouse collection.

Upper West Side

The **Upper West Side** is one of New York's most desirable neighborhoods, with boutiques and cafés lining the avenues and renovated brownstones on the side streets. **Lincoln Center** (⊠ W. 62nd to 66th Sts. between Broadway and Amsterdam Ave., ☎ 212/546–2656 for general information; 212/875–5350 for tour schedule and reservations; ☜ tour $9.50) is the area's cultural anchor. Flanking the central fountain are three major concert halls: **Avery Fisher Hall,** where the New York Philharmonic Orchestra performs; the glass-fronted **Metropolitan Opera House,** home of the Metropolitan Opera and the American Ballet Theatre; and the **New York State Theater,** home of the New York City Ballet and the New York City Opera.

The **American Museum of Natural History** (⊠ Central Park West at W. 79th St., ☎ 212/769–5200 for museum tickets and programs; 212/769–5100 for museum general information; 212/769–5034 for IMAX Theater show times; ☜ museum: donations suggested; IMAX theater: $14; combination tickets available; closed Mon.), with more than 36 million artifacts and specimens, is the largest and most important museum of natural history in the world. Forty-two exhibition halls display an awe-inspiring collection of items, including dinosaur skeletons, a 94-ft replica of a blue whale, the 563-carat Star of India sapphire, and the 4-billion-year-old *Ahnighito,* the largest meteorite ever recovered on the earth's surface. An **IMAX Theater** screens films about nature; the adjacent newly renovated **Hayden Planetarium,** inside the Rose Center for Earth and Space, features high-tech space shows.

Founded in 1754, **Columbia University** (☎ 212/854–4900) is New York City's only Ivy League school. Bounded by 114th and 120th streets, Broadway, and Amsterdam Avenue, the campus is so effectively walled off from the city by buildings that it's easy to believe you're in the country. Enter at 116th Street and Broadway for a look around. Close to Columbia University is the **Cathedral of St. John the Divine** (⊠ 1047 Amsterdam Ave., at 112th St., ☎ 212/316–7540; 212/932–7347 to arrange tours; ✉ tours: donations suggested), an immense limestone-and-granite church that, when finished, will be the largest Gothic structure in the world. Until then, you can have a rare, fascinating glimpse of a cathedral in progress.

Harlem

Harlem has been a center of African-American culture for nearly a century. In the 1920s, during the Harlem Renaissance, black novelists, playwrights, musicians, and artists gathered here. By the 1960s crowded housing, poverty, and crime had turned the neighborhood into a simmering ghetto. Today Harlem is restoring itself. Mixed in with some seedy remains of the past are old jewels like the refurbished **Apollo Theatre** (✉ 253 W. 125th St., ☎ 212/749–5838; 212/531–5337 to arrange tours), where such music greats as Ella Fitzgerald and Duke Ellington brought black musicians into the limelight. **Schomburg Center for Research in Black Culture** (✉ 515 Lenox Ave., at 135th St., ☎ 212/491–2200; ✉ free) contains more than 5 million items in its collection, including rare manuscripts, art and artifacts, motion pictures, records, and videotapes. It hosts regular exhibits, performing arts programs, and lectures.

Chelsea and the Flatiron District

Chelsea has quiet side streets graced by lovingly renovated town houses. The neighborhood stretches from 5th Avenue west to the Hudson River and from 14th to 29th Street. The city's diversity shows up here in the 19th-century **Third Cemetery of the Spanish & Portuguese Synagogue**, the literary landmark **Chelsea Hotel**, and the ultramodern **Chelsea Piers Sports and Entertainment Complex**. An active gay community frequents the lively stores and restaurants on 8th and 7th avenues. A hot **gallery scene** flourishes west of 10th Avenue from 20th to 29th Street. Several blocks north along 9th Avenue, **Hell's Kitchen** is home to great ethnic eateries.

Eastern Chelsea merges with the **Flatiron District**, which lies between 14th and 34th streets and spreads east to Park Avenue South. The neighborhood, centered around the awe-inspiring **Flatiron Building**, owes its identity and flavor to the scores of photographic studios and design firms that have set up shop in former manufacturing and warehouse lofts. Along **5th Avenue in the 20s**, shops offer the latest fashions, and on the side streets you can find the latest in home furnishings. Models and producers graze at the area's noteworthy restaurants, many of which cluster near **Union Square** and **Madison Square** parks.

Greenwich Village and the East Village

With its narrow tree-lined streets, brick town houses, and hidden
★ courtyards, **Greenwich Village** is like a small town in Manhattan. The Village is ideal for strolling, window-shopping, and café hopping; it extends from 14th Street south to Houston Street and from the Hudson River to 5th Avenue. For generations the haunt of writers, artists, and musicians, the Village is synonymous with many of the avant-garde artists of this century, including abstract expressionist painters like Franz Kline and Mark Rothko, Beat writers and poets such as Jack Kerouac and Allen Ginsberg, and folk musicians and poets, notably Bob Dylan and Peter, Paul, and Mary.

Washington Square, at the foot of 5th Avenue, is a good place to begin a walking tour of the Village. At the top of the square is the Washington Arch, designed by Stanford White and built in 1889 to commemorate the 100th anniversary of George Washington's inauguration. The surrounding area attracts New York University students to its shops, bars, jazz clubs, Off-Broadway theaters, cabarets, coffeehouses, and cafés.

To the northwest, **Sheridan Square** anchors Christopher Street, a hub of New York's gay community and a busy shopping strip. West of 7th Avenue South, the Village turns into a picture-book warren of twisting streets filled with **historical buildings,** quaint houses, and tiny restaurants. At different times Edna St. Vincent Millay and John Barrymore each lived at 75½ Bedford Street—at 9½ ft wide, New York's narrowest house. Theodore Dreiser wrote *An American Tragedy* at 16 St. Luke's Place. The stretch of West 4th Street is particularly pleasant.

As far west as the Hudson, on 14th Street and just below, is the **Meatpacking District,** which was once just that but now shares its sidewalks with shoppers and gallery hunters, gourmands and club kids.

The **East Village,** east of 4th Avenue (Lafayette Street), has housed Jewish, Ukrainian, and Puerto Rican immigrants; beatniks; hippies; punks; students, artists; and, most recently, affluent young professionals. Soak up the eclectic atmosphere along St. Marks Place and 9th Street east of 3rd Avenue, and along avenues A and B between East Houston (pronounced *How*-stun) and 12th streets. You'll find restaurants and bars both chic and cheap, vintage and cutting-edge clothing boutiques, cafés, and offbeat shops. To the south, bounded by the Bowery and East Houston, Pitt and Delancey streets, the **Lower East Side,** once a neighborhood of Jewish immigrants, offers more of the same, with an even more mod twist, side by side with vestiges of the past.

SoHo, NoLita, and TriBeCa

SoHo (so named because it is the district *So*uth of *Ho*uston Street, bounded by Broadway, Canal Street, and 6th Avenue) defines urban elegance—a mix of artists, young Wall Streeters, pricey boutiques, art spaces, and restaurants with a modernist approach to both food and design. **West Broadway,** paralleling Broadway four blocks to the west, is SoHo's main strip. On Saturday, the big day for shopping and gallery hopping, it can be crowded but still great for people-watching. At 28–30 and 72–76 Greene Street you'll find two fine examples of the abundant **cast-iron architecture** for which SoHo is world-famous.

South of SoHo is its offspring **TriBeCa** (from *Tri*angle *be*low *Ca*nal Street). Its glamorous loft apartments, converted from prewar industrial spaces, are among the city's most coveted and expensive. Correspondingly excellent and expensive restaurants occupy the stunning storefronts. SoHo's stylish character has also spread east into **NoLita,** as in *No*rth of *Li*ttle *Ita*ly. Mulberry, Mott, and Elizabeth streets between Houston and Spring streets have sprouted trendy clothing, design, and secondhand boutiques as well as restaurants and cafés worth exploring.

Chinatown and Little Italy

In booming **Chinatown,** Canal and Grand streets abound with food shops and outdoor markets bursting with fresh seafood, Chinese vegetables, almond cookies, and roasted ducks. The main drag is narrow and twisting **Mott Street,** crammed with souvenir shops in pagoda-style buildings, and crowded with pedestrians at all hours. Within a few dense blocks, hundreds of restaurants serve every type of Chinese cuisine, from simple noodles and dumplings to sumptuous Hunan, Szechuan, Cantonese, Mandarin, and Shanghai feasts.

Squeezed between Chinatown and East Houston Street, **Little Italy** is a shrinking enclave of Italian life. **Mulberry Street,** lined with tenement buildings, long the heart of Little Italy, is now virtually the entire body. Between Broome and Canal streets, Mulberry consists of restaurants, cafés, bakeries, food shops, and souvenir stores. Each September the Feast of San Gennaro turns the streets into a bright and bustling Italian kitchen.

Lower Manhattan

Lower Manhattan is compact and packed with attractions: narrow streets and immense skyscrapers, Wall Street and Colonial-era houses, South Street Seaport and Battery Park City. The city did not expand beyond these precincts until the middle of the 19th century. Today Wall Street dominates Lower Manhattan; the thoroughfare is both an actual street and a shorthand name for the vast, powerful financial community that clusters around the New York and American stock exchanges.

Outside the **Staten Island Ferry Terminal,** at the southernmost tip of Manhattan, is a good place to start your exploration. For great harbor views of the Statue of Liberty, Ellis Island, and the Lower Manhattan skyline, consider the free ferry ride to Staten Island. **Battery Park,** a verdant landfill loaded with monuments and sculpture, and the point of embarkation for visits to the Statue of Liberty and Ellis Island, is a short walk up the Battery Park waterfront from the ferry terminal. Buy your ticket for the boat to the Statue of Liberty or Ellis Island at **Castle Clinton National Monument** (☎ 212/269–5755; ⊠ ferry $7 roundtrip), inside the park; arrive early and be prepared to wait.

★ The **Statue of Liberty** (☎ 212/363–3200, ⊠ free) is one of America's greatest symbols of freedom. Once on Liberty Island you may have to wait as many as four hours to take the elevator 10 stories to the top of the pedestal. The strong of heart and limb can climb another 12 stories to the crown.

★ **Ellis Island** (☎ 212/363–3200, ⊠ free), which reopened in 1990 after restoration rescued it from decades of neglect, was once the main East Coast federal immigration facility. Between 1892 and 1954, 12 million men, women, and children—the ancestors of more than 40% of the Americans living today—were processed here.

The **National Museum of the American Indian** (⊠ 1 Bowling Green, ☎ 212/668–6624; ⊠ free), in a stunning Beaux Arts–style building, is the first national museum dedicated solely to Native American culture, and its exhibits of fascinating objects from around the Americas are accompanied with good documentation.

Fraunces Tavern (⊠ Broad and Pearl Sts., ☎ 212/425–1778; ⊠ museum $2.50) occupies a Colonial house built in 1719 and restored in 1907. It is best remembered as the site of George Washington's 1783 farewell address to his officers celebrating the British evacuation of New York and contains two fully furnished period rooms and other displays on 18th- and 19th-century American history.

A **statue of George Washington** on Wall Street stands at the spot where, in 1789, he was sworn in as the first U.S. president. After the nation's capital moved to Philadelphia in 1790, the original Federal Hall became New York's city hall but was demolished in 1812. The current **Federal Hall National Memorial** (⊠ 26 Wall St., ☎ 212/825–6888; ⊠ free), built in 1842, contains exhibits on New York and Wall Street; it is closed weekends. **Trinity Church** (⊠ Broadway and Wall St., ☎ 212/602–0800) was New York's first Anglican parish (1697). The graves of Alexander Hamilton and Robert Fulton are in the churchyard. The present structure (1846) ranked as the city's tallest building for most of the last half of the 19th century.

The **New York Stock Exchange** (⊠ 20 Broad St., ☎ 212/656–5165; ⊠ free; closed weekends) has its august Corinthian main entrance around the corner from Wall Street, on Broad Street. A self-guided tour, a multimedia presentation, and staff members help you interpret the chaos that seems to reign on the trading floor. Free tour tickets are distributed beginning at 8:45 AM; come before 1 PM to assure entrance.

The **World Trade Center** (Ticket booth: ⊠ 2 World Trade Center, mezzanine level, ☎ 212/323–2340; ⊡ $12.50), a 16-acre complex, boasts New York's two tallest buildings (each 1,350 ft). Elevators to the observation deck on the 107th floor of 2 World Trade Center glide a quarter of a mile into the sky in only 58 seconds.

South Street Seaport is an 11-block historic district on the East River that encompasses a museum, shopping, historic ships, cruise boats, a multimedia presentation, and innumerable places to eat and drink. You can view the historic ships from Pier 16, which is the departure point for the one-hour Seaport Liberty Cruise (☎ 212/630–8888).

★ The **Brooklyn Bridge,** New York's oldest and best-known, is north of the South Street Seaport. The bridge was designed by John Augustus Roebling. When completed in 1883, it was the world's longest suspension bridge and the tallest structure in the city. Walking across the Brooklyn Bridge is a peak New York experience.

Parks, Gardens, and Zoos

★ **Central Park** was designed by landscape architects Frederick Law Olmsted and Calvert Vaux on 843 acres of land acquired by the city in 1856. Bounded by 59th and 110th streets, 5th Avenue, and Central Park West, the park contains grassy meadows, wooded groves, and formal gardens; numerous fountains, sculptures, and bodies of water; paths for jogging, strolling, horseback riding, and biking; playing fields; a small zoo; two ice-skating rinks; a carousel; and an outdoor theater.

★ The **Bronx Zoo** (⊠ Bronx River Pkwy. and Fordham Rd., Bronx, ☎ 718/367–1010, ⊡ Apr.–Oct., Thurs.–Tues. $7.75; Nov.–Dec., Thurs.–Tues. $6; Jan.–Mar., Thurs.–Tues. $4; Children's Zoo $2) is the nation's largest urban zoo, with nearly 6,500 animals on 265 acres of woods, ponds, streams, and parkland.

New York's **Aquarium for Wildlife Conservation** (⊠ W. 8th St. and Surf Ave., Coney Island, Brooklyn, ☎ 718/265–3474; ⊡ $8.75), just off the Coney Island Boardwalk, has more than 20,000 creatures on display, plus performing dolphins and sea lions.

The **New York Botanical Garden** (⊠ 200th St. and Kazimiroff Blvd., Bronx, ☎ 718/817–8700; ⊡ Nov.–Mar. $1.50, Apr.–Oct. $3; free Sat. 10–noon and Wed.; Enid A. Haupt Conservatory $3.50; parking $5), a 250-acre botanical treasury around the dramatic gorge of the Bronx River, is within Bronx Park. Its 40-acre forest, conservatory, museum, and outdoor gardens draw nature enthusiasts from around the world.

Dining

By Mitchell Davis and Jane Miller

New York is the restaurant capital of the country, maybe even the world. Dining options run the gamut, from small, out-of-the-way ethnic eateries to formal French temples of gastronomy. You can spend $5 on dinner or $500, and some of the better restaurants offer real deals at lunch. When they are accepted, reservations are essential (make them well in advance); when they aren't you may have to wait. Don't fret. In general—though not always—a long line augurs a good experience.

$$$$
★ ✕ **Daniel.** Traditional French dishes like stuffed pig's feet and whole-roasted halibut mingle with contemporary innovations like sea bass in a potato crust or scallops in black tie (dressed with truffles). The neo-Renaissance dining room provides an extremely formal setting, but the

attentive service alleviates any intimidation. Dinner in the lounge is a more relaxed experience. ⊠ *60 E. 65th St., between Park and Madison Aves.,* ☎ *212/288–0033. Reservations essential. Jacket required. AE, D, DC, MC, V. Closed Sun.*

$$$$ ✕ **Gramercy Tavern.** This urbanely rustic restaurant is divided into two
★   rooms—the first-come, first-served tavern in the front offers a light menu that features foods prepared in the wood-burning oven while you watch; the more formal but still unintimidating dining room in the back features a carefully conceived American table d'hôte menu. Friendly service and a terrific cheese selection complete the experience. ⊠ *42 E. 20th St., between Broadway and Park Ave. S,* ☎ *212/477–0777. Reservations essential. AE, DC, MC, V.*

$$$$ ✕ **Jean Georges.** The main dining room here, with dramatic picture windows overlooking Central Park, features luxurious but understated furnishings. Chef Jean-Georges Vongerichten presents unusual combinations that intrigue the palate without overwhelming it: sea scallops in caper-raisin emulsion with caramelized cauliflower, and spring garlic soup perfumed with thyme and dotted with nuggets of boned, sautéed frogs' legs are stellar examples. ⊠ *1 Central Park W, at 59th St.,* ☎ *212/299–3900. Reservations essential. Jacket and tie. AE, DC, MC, V. Closed Sun.*

$$$$ ✕ **Kuruma Zushi.** Only a sign in Japanese indicates the location of this extraordinary restaurant that, in the tradition of the best restaurants in Japan, serves nothing but sushi. The best way to enjoy the exotic delicacies available here is to bypass the tables in the spartan dining room, sit at the sushi bar, and put yourself in the hands of the talented sushi chef who imports hard-to-find fish from Japan, as well as other traditional choices. ⊠ *7 E. 47th St., 2nd Floor, between 5th and Madison Aves.,* ☎ *212/317–2802. AE, MC, V. Closed Sun.*

$$$$ ✕ **Le Cirque 2000.** The plush Blue Room with modern velvet banquettes is preferred by celebrities, and the sprightlier Red Room with a view of the open kitchen by European dignitaries. Favorites include artichokes barigoule, fresh-made ravioli, lobster salad "Le Cirque," broiled salmon with cranberry beans, duck magret (boned breast grilled with the skin on), and chicken fricassee. ⊠ *455 Madison Ave., between 50th and 51st Sts.,* ☎ *212/794–9292. Reservations essential. Jacket and tie. AE, DC, MC, V. Closed Sun.*

$$$$ ✕ **March.** With its travertine floor, working fireplace, and burled teak and elm wainscoting, this romantic restaurant tucked into a small town house is warmly understated. The polished service and expert wine list complement the inspired cuisine on the all–table d'hôte menu, which changes frequently. Dishes often include a Japanese-influenced sashimi of Japanese yellowfin tuna with olive oil and soy sauce, as well as such luxury offerings as the whimsical "Beggar's Purses" filled with caviar and crème fraîche or lobster and truffles. ⊠ *405 E. 58th St., between 1st Ave. and Sutton Pl.,* ☎ *212/754–6272. Reservations essential. AE, DC, MC, V. No lunch.*

$$$$ ✕ **Nobu.** A curved wall of river-worn black pebbles, bare wood tables,
★   birch trees, and a hand-painted beech floor serve as the dramatic setting for the Japanese-inspired food. You can sample classic Japanese sushi and sashimi, among the best in town, or contemporary dishes such as the defyingly delicious seared black cod with sweet miso or Peruvian-style sashimi. If you can't get a reservation, try the new Next Door Nobu, where you can get highlights of the Nobu menu on a first-come, first-served basis. ⊠ *105 Hudson St., off Franklin St.,* ☎ *212/219–0500; 212/219–8095 for same-day reservations. Reservations essential. AE, DC, MC, V. Closed Sun. No lunch.*

$$$$ ✕ **Peter Luger Steak House.** You cannot find a better porterhouse
★ steak anywhere. Period. Sure, you can find better lighting, a more sophisticated atmosphere, a more comfortable chair. But if prime aged
beef is what you want (and maybe a shrimp cocktail, some home fries
and some creamed spinach), and if you don't want to dress up, then
Peter Luger's is where you should be. Take a taxi there and a private
car service will carry you back to Manhattan. ✉ *178 Broadway, at
Driggs Ave., Brooklyn,* ☎ *718/387–7400. Reservation essential. No
credit cards.*

$$$$ ✕ **Picholine.** Named for a small green Mediterranean olive, this mellow restaurant is designed to look like a Provençal farmhouse. The French
food with Mediterranean accents is among the finest in Manhattan. Top
dishes include the signature grilled octopus with fennel, potato, and lemon-
pepper dressing; Moroccan-spiced loin of lamb with vegetable couscous
and mint-yogurt sauce, and tournedos of salmon with horseradish
crust, cucumbers, and salmon caviar. The wine list and cheese selection
are superlative. ✉ *35 W. 64th St., off Broadway,* ☎ *212/724–8585. Reservations essential. AE, DC, MC, V. Closed Sun. No lunch Mon.*

$$$$ ✕ **Sparks Steak House.** Magnums and jeroboams of fine wine decorate the large dining rooms of this classic New York steak house. Although seafood is given fair play on the menu, Sparks is about steak.
The menu includes dry-aged cuts of every description—sirloin, fillet,
and rib among them. For something besides beef, order the double-
cut lamb chops, so tender and flavorful they will spoil you. ✉ *210 E.
46th St., between 2nd and 3rd Aves.,* ☎ *212/687–4855. Reservations
essential. AE, DC, MC, V. No lunch weekends.*

$$$$ ✕ **Tabla.** From the time the waiter sets down the bread—freshly baked
roti and nan served with an apple and onion purée—you know you're
about to embark on a delicious culinary journey. Dishes like lamb and
turmeric ravioli with tomato *kasundi* (sauce) and mint oil and tandoori
rabbit with *Goan bacalao* (salt-cod) set the tone. A downstairs "bread
bar" affords a more casual, less expensive experience. ✉ *11 Madison
Ave., at 25th St.,* ☎ *212/889–0667. Reservations essential. AE, DC,
MC, V.*

$$$$ ✕ **'21' Club.** This four-story brownstone landmark, a former speakeasy,
first opened on December 31, 1929. Here is one of the world's great
wine cellars, with some 50,000 bottles. The Grill Room is *the* place to
be, with its banquettes, red-checked tablecloths, and a ceiling hung with
toys; it serves such standbys as the signature '21' burger and a host of
more exciting dishes, such as Asian-style seared tuna. ✉ *21 W. 52nd
St., between 5th and 6th Aves.,* ☎ *212/582–7200. Reservations essential.
Jacket and tie. AE, DC, MC, V. Closed Sun. No lunch Sat.*

$$$–$$$$ ✕ **Babbo.** After your first bite of the kitchen's ethereal homemade pasta
★ or the tender suckling pig, you'll know that this is Italian food as it
was meant to be, combining the finest ingredients with impeccable tech-
nique and a passion for adventure. A five-course pasta tasting menu
is the best way to get your fill of fresh noodles. Babbo's owners opened
Lupa (✉ 170 Thompson St., between Bleecker and Houston Sts., ☎
212/982–5089), a casual trattoria, with excellent food and friendly ser-
vice. ✉ *110 Waverly Pl., between MacDougal St. and 6th Ave.,* ☎ *212/
777–0303. Reservations essential. AE, MC, V. No lunch.*

$$$–$$$$ ✕ **Balthazar.** One of the city's most difficult reservations to score, Balt-
hazar has vintage French ambience straight out of movie-set Paris. The
food matches the atmosphere and the breads are superb. For a first-
come, first-served alternative, try Balthazar's baby cousin **Pastis** (✉ 9
9th Ave., at Little W. 12th St., ☎ 212/929–4844) in the meatpacking
district. ✉ *80 Spring St., between Broadway and Lafayette St.,* ☎ *212/
965–1414. Reservations essential. AE, DC, MC, V. No lunch Mon.*

\$\$\$–\$\$\$\$ ✕ **Café Boulud.** At this "casual bistro," only the atmosphere is relaxed;
★ the food and service are as serious and as disciplined as can be. The
changing four-part menu features dishes from the classic French repertoire, others based on seasonal ingredients, still others adapted from
cuisines of the world, and a number of vegetarian options. ⊠ *Surrey
Hotel, 20 E. 76th St., at Madison Ave.,* ☎ *212/772–2600. Reservations essential. AE, DC, MC, V. No lunch Sun. and Mon.*

\$\$\$–\$\$\$\$ ✕ **Firebird.** Housed in two brownstones renovated to resemble a pre-
revolutionary St. Petersburg mansion, Firebird has captured the former
Russian Tearoom celebrity crowd. Staples of the Russian regional cuisine range from caviar and *zakuska* (assorted Russian hors d'oeuvres)
to tea with cherry preserves, and signature desserts. Don't fail to sample the extraordinary vodka selection. The elegant caviar presentation—steaming hot blini drenched in butter, slathered with sour cream,
and filled with beluga, sevruga, or osetra by waiters in white gloves, is
a giddy indulgence. ⊠ *365 W. 46th St., between 8th and 9th Aves.,* ☎
212/586–0244. Reservations essential. AE, DC, MC, V. No lunch Sun.

\$\$\$–\$\$\$\$ ✕ **I Trulli.** Rough-hewn gold walls, a fireplace, a garden for summer
dining, and a whitewashed open grill distinguish this Italian winner.
Start with a glass of wine from a little-known producer and one of the
enticing appetizers. Almost all of the pasta is made by hand, and the
special preparations of the day shouldn't be overlooked. A lovely casual wine bar next door (**Enoteca**) offers a simple menu of the same
exquisite food and an impressive selection of wines. ⊠ *122 E. 27th
St., between Lexington and Park Ave. S,* ☎ *212/481–7372. Reservations essential. AE, DC, MC, V. Closed Sun. No lunch Sat.*

\$\$\$–\$\$\$\$ ✕ **The Mercer Kitchen.** The sleek, modern, industrial space is surpris-
ingly comfortable, and the room sizzles with the palpable energy of
the New York downtown elite. Dinner might include black sea bass
carpaccio with lime juice, coriander, and mint; figs with Italian prosciutto, aged balsamic vinegar, and rosemary flat bread; or Alsatian tarte
flambée with fromage blanc, onions, and bacon. ⊠ *The Mercer Hotel,
99 Prince St., at Mercer St.,* ☎ *212/966–5454. Reservations essential.
AE, DC, MC, V. No dinner Sun.*

\$\$\$–\$\$\$\$ ✕ **Rosa Mexicano.** When the staff slips open the parchment package
that contains a lamb shank braised in a three-chili sauce, the room fills
with the fragrance of Oaxaca. A better guacamole, prepared table-side
and served with warm corn tortillas, cannot be found—not even in Mexico. The lively, jam-packed barroom in the front makes you feel as though
you've happened upon a Mexican fiesta. ⊠ *1063 1st Ave., at 58th St.,*
☎ *212/753–7407. Reservations essential. AE, DC, MC, V. No lunch.*

\$\$\$ ✕ **Blue Ribbon.** Open for dinner from 4 PM until 4 AM, this small
★ American bistro is a popular hangout for off-duty chefs and other night
crawlers. There is a raw bar in the front where a shucker turns out ter-
rifically fresh oysters and other seasonal delicacies from the sea. The
something-for-everyone menu offers a mix of dishes from around the
world—excellent sautéed sweetbreads, a towering pupu platter, a duck
club sandwich, and matzoh ball soup. ⊠ *97 Sullivan St., between
Prince and Spring Sts.,* ☎ *212/274–0404. Reservations essential. AE,
DC, MC, V. Closed Mon. No lunch.*

\$\$–\$\$\$ ✕ **Churrascaria Plataforma.** This sprawling, boisterous shrine to meat,
best experienced with a group, is a popular Brazilian spot. Order a full
pitcher of *caipirinhas* and head for the center of the room, where a vast
salad bar beckons with vegetables, meats, and cheeses. But exercise re-
straint—the real show begins with the parade of lamb, beef, chicken,
ham, sausage, and innards, brought to the table on skewers. Side
dishes include plantains, french fries, rice, mashed potatoes, manioc,
and a tangy vinegar sauce. ⊠ *316 W. 49th St., between 8th and 9th
Aves.,* ☎ *212/245–0505. AE, DC, MC, V.*

$$–$$$ ✕ **Clementine.** This innovative restaurant offers affordable prices and contemporary American cuisine. Whimsical menu items include fried green tomatoes with spareribs salad, squid stuffed with merguez sausage, and steamed salmon with risotto. The lemon caramel icebox cake attracts sweet tooths from all over the city. A well-chosen wine list helps make the main dining room most agreeable. A mobbed bar scene up front attracts a young crowd. ⊠ *1 5th Ave., at 8th St.,* ☎ *212/539–0877. Reservations essential. AE. No lunch.*

$$ ✕ **Pongal.** Service may be a bit slow, but the gentle prices and marvelous dishes more than compensate at this pretty vegetarian Indian restaurant, which happens to be kosher. Magnificent dosas made with lentils and rice flour are wrapped around potatoes and a fiery chutney. The Gujarati thali offers a taste of many dishes. ⊠ *110 Lexington Ave., between 27th and 28th Sts.,* ☎ *212/696–9458. AE, DC, MC, V.*

$$ ✕ **Second Avenue Deli.** A recent face-lift has removed the wrinkles of
★ time, but the strictly kosher, dairy-free Jewish food here is as good as ever. The deli's bevy of classics includes chicken in the pot, matzo ball soup, chopped liver, Romanian tenderloin, and *cholent* (a Sabbath dish of meat, beans, and grain). A better pastrami sandwich you can't find (don't ask for it lean). A welcome bowl of pickles, sour green tomatoes, and coleslaw satisfies from the start, but at the finish, don't order dessert. ⊠ *156 2nd Ave., at 10th St.,* ☎ *212/677–0606. AE.*

$–$$ ✕ **Barney Greengrass.** This place hasn't changed much since it opened in 1908. Order anything with smoked salmon or sturgeon in it: scrambled eggs with onions; bagels or bialys with cream cheese, tomato, and red onion; or the austere platters of fish. A full range of Jewish food includes glasses of chilled beet borscht with sour cream, potato knishes that are split in half and toasted, and chopped liver. End with an individual chocolate babka "muffin" and you will have forgotten the long wait to get in. ⊠ *541 Amsterdam Ave., between 86th and 87th Sts.,* ☎ *212/724–4707. Reservations not accepted. MC, V. No credit cards on weekends. Closed Mon.*

$–$$ ✕ **Holy Basil.** Holy Basil serves distinctive Thai food in a second-floor dining room decorated like the living quarters of a nobleman. Dishes are beautifully presented: spicy *som tum* (green papaya salad), better-than-average *pad thai* (rice noodles with shrimp and tamarind), and rich *tom kah gai* (chicken and coconut milk soup), not to mention anything in *kaw praw* (a traditional curried preparation). Vegetarian selections abound, and a large and informative wine list is an added bonus. ⊠ *149 2nd Ave., between 9th and 10th Sts.,* ☎ *212/460–5557. AE, DC, MC, V. No lunch.*

$–$$ ✕ **Moustache.** No New York spot serves Middle-Eastern food as fresh,
★ flavorful, or appealingly presented as Moustache. The focal point is the pita, steam-filled pillows of dough baked in a searingly hot oven. Use it to scoop up the tasty salads—lemony chickpea and spinach, creamy hummus, and hearty lentil and bulghur among them. For entrées, try the leg of lamb or merguez sausage sandwiches or the ouzi, a large phyllo package stuffed with chicken and fragrant rice. For quickest seating, arrange to eat at off-peak times; otherwise expect a line. ⊠ *90 Bedford St., between Barrow and Grove Sts.,* ☎ *212/229–2220; 265 E. 10th St., between Ave. A and 1st Ave.,* ☎ *212/228–2022. Reservations not accepted. No credit cards.*

$–$$ ✕ **Virgil's.** This massive roadhouse in the Theater District looks just the way a barbecue place should. Start with stuffed jalapeños or buttermilk onion rings with blue-cheese dip. Then go for the Pig Out: a rack of pork ribs, Texas hot links, pulled pork, rack of lamb, chicken, and more. Wash it all down with beer from a good list. ⊠ *152 W. 44th St., between 6th Ave. and Broadway,* ☎ *212/921–9494. Reservations essential. AE, MC, V.*

$ ✕ **Cafe Habana.** When they opened this small Latin-themed restaurant in 1998, the owners wanted to sustain the neighborhood-hangout quality cultivated by the previous occupants. The simple Cuban-Mexican menu reflects the friendly, casual atmosphere: Cubano sandwiches, rice and beans, and *camarones al ajillo* (shrimp in garlic sauce), all at budget prices. A second location in Greenwich Village is bigger, but the food is every bit as good. ✉ *17 Prince St., at Elizabeth St.,* ☎ *212/625–2001; 11 Abingdon Sq., between W. 12th and Bleecker Sts.,* ☎ *212/989–6883. AE, MC, V.*

$ ✕ **Pepe Giallo.** The crown of a growing chain of tiny Italian eateries, this Chelsea outpost is the most spacious and charming of the lot. (Other locations include Pepe Rosso in SoHo and Pepe Verde in the East Village.) A long list of specials changes daily, but the menu always includes a variety of pastas—prepared fresh in the open kitchen and served in generous portions—antipasti, salads, entrées, and sandwiches.✉ *253 10th Ave., at 25th St.,* ☎ *212/242–6055;* ✉ *Pepe Rosso: 110 St. Mark's Place, between Ave. A and 1st Ave.; or 149 Sullivan St., between Houston and Prince Sts.,* ☎ *212/677–6563 or 212/677–4555;* ✉ *Pepe Verde: 559 Hudson St., between Perry and W. 11th Sts.,* ☎ *212/255–2221. No credit cards.*

$ ✕ **Sweet 'n' Tart Restaurant.** There are several menus at this clean, mul-
★ tilevel restaurant: one is organized according to principles of Chinese medicine, another features more familiar Chinese dishes, and a third lists drinks and curative "teas," which are actually more like soups: little white bowls composed of such exotica as almond milk, black sesame paste, and chestnuts. Don't miss the yam noodle soup with assorted dumplings, the fried rice served in a bamboo container, or the Chinese broccoli in oyster sauce. Colorful fresh-fruit shakes enriched with pearls of tapioca or black balls of sago are also exciting to try. ✉ *20 Mott St., between Chatham Sq. and Pell St.,* ☎ *212/964–0380. No credit cards.*

$ ✕ **Viet Nam.** At this rathskeller Vietnamese hole-in-the-wall, the food is fresh, flavorful, and very cheap. Among the highlights are the green papaya salad with beef jerky, sweet and sour shrimp soup, and anything in black bean sauce. ✉ *11–13 Doyers St., between Bowery and Pell St.,* ☎ *212/693–0725. AE, MC, V.*

Lodging

A sustained boom in tourism has resulted in a constant demand for hotel rooms in New York City, allowing hoteliers to jack up their rates to all-time highs, averaging in the neighborhood of $300. We have scoured the city for good-value hotels and budget properties, and there are more of them than you might think.

$$$$ 🏨 **The Carlyle.** European tradition and Manhattan swank shake hands
★ at this elegant baby grand on Madison Avenue, just steps from Central Park. Everything here suggests refinement, from the Mark Hampton–designed rooms, with their fine antique furniture and artfully framed Audubons and botanicals, to the first-rate service. ✉ *35 E. 76th St., 10021,* ☎ *212/744–1600 or 800/227–5737,* ℻ *212/717–4682. 190 rooms. Restaurant, health club. AE, DC, MC, V.*

$$$$ 🏨 **Essex House.** The lobby of this stately Central Park South property is an Art Deco masterpiece fit for Fred and Ginger. Guest rooms, all with large, marble bathrooms, are outfitted with British Chippendale or French Louis XIV antiques. Views from parkside rooms—which range from tiny queens to suites you could get lost in—are stunning year-round. ✉ *160 Central Park S, 10019,* ☎ *212/247–0300 or 800/645–5687,* ℻ *212/315–1839. 597 rooms. 2 restaurants, health club. AE, D, DC, MC, V.* 🍽

$$$$ ☷ **The Lucerne.** In a handsome brownstone building on a quiet, Upper West Side side street, this newcomer enjoys a constant buzz of activity, thanks to the publike Wilson's Bar & Grill next door. The multi-hued-marble lobby, with its earth-tone walls and comfy olive-green couches, has more pizzazz than the predictable guest rooms. ✉ *201 W. 79th St., 10024,* ☎ *212/875–1000 or 800/492–8122,* FAX *212/721–1179. 250 rooms. Restaurant, exercise room. AE, D, DC, MC, V.* ✤

$$$$ ☷ **Mercer Hotel.** Guest rooms at this minimalist masterpiece are enormous, with long entryways, high ceilings, and walk-in closets; dark African woods and high-tech light fixtures make a subtle statement. Bathrooms steal the show with their decadent two-person tubs, some of them surrounded by mirrors. ✉ *147 Mercer St., 10012,* ☎ *212/966–6060 or 888/918–6060,* FAX *212/965–3838. 75 rooms. Restaurant. AE, DC, MC, V.*

$$$$ ☷ **New York Hilton.** You could easily spend a week in New York without setting foot outside this vast midtown hotel, whose myriad business facilities, eating establishments, and shops are designed for convenience. Considering the size of this property, guest rooms are surprisingly well maintained, and all have coffeemakers, hair dryers, and ironing boards. ✉ *1335 6th Ave., 10019,* ☎ *212/586–7000 or 800/445–8667,* FAX *212/315–1374. 2,061 rooms. 2 restaurants, health club. AE, D, DC, MC, V.* ✤

$$$$ ☷ **New York Marriot Brooklyn.** Manhattan is 10 minutes via subway from this impressive spot with its Olympic-length pool, 1,100-car garage, and 18,000 square-ft Grand Ball Room. Trompe l'oeil ceilings enhance the multilevel foyer; guest rooms have 11-ft ceilings, massaging showerheads, and rolling desks. ✉ *333 Adams St., Brooklyn 11201,* ☎ *718/246–7000 or 800/843–4898,* FAX *718/246–0563. 376 rooms. Restaurant, health club. AE, D, DC, MC, V.* ✤

$$$$ ☷ **Waldorf-Astoria.** This Art Deco masterpiece built in 1931 is a hub of city life; the lobby, with its original murals and mosaics, is a meeting place for the rich and powerful. Guest rooms, each individually decorated, are all traditional and elegant. ✉ *301 Park Ave., 10022,* ☎ *212/355–3000 or 800/925–3673,* FAX *212/872–7272. 1,452 rooms. 4 restaurants, health club. AE, D, DC, MC, V.* ✤

$$$$ ★   ☷ **The Warwick.** Built by William Randolph Hearst in 1927, the Warwick remains a midtown favorite, catercorner from the New York Hilton and well placed for theater and points west. Its handsome, Regency-style rooms have soft pastel color schemes, mahogany armoires, and nice marble bathrooms. ✉ *65 W. 54th St., 10019,* ☎ *212/247–2700 or 800/223–4099,* FAX *212/489–3926. 427 rooms. Restaurant. AE, DC, MC, V.* ✤

$$$–$$$$ ★   ☷ **Gramercy Park Hotel.** Guests at this 1920s curio enjoy clean yet simply appointed rooms, as well as access to the only private park in the city. The combination of comparatively low cost, large accommodations, and quiet surroundings makes the whole of this comfortable spot worth more than the sum of her parts. ✉ *2 Lexington Ave., 10010,* ☎ *212/475–4320 or 800/221–4083,* FAX *212/205–0535. 509 rooms. Restaurant. AE, D, DC, MC, V.*

$$$–$$$$ ★   ☷ **Hotel Beacon.** The Upper West Side's best affordable buy is a short walk from both Central Park and Lincoln Center. All rooms and suites have kitchenettes with coffeemakers, full-size refrigerators, and stoves; some even have microwaves. What's more, the closets are huge, and the bathrooms come complete with Hollywood dressing room–style mirrors. ✉ *2130 Broadway, at 75th St., 10023,* ☎ *212/787–1100 or 800/572–4969,* FAX *212/724–0839. 210 rooms. AE, D, DC, MC, V.* ✤

$$$ ☷ **Washington Square Hotel.** This cozy Greenwich Village hotel has a true European feel and style, from the wrought iron and gleaming brass in the small, elegant lobby to the personal service. Rooms are simple but pleasant and well maintained; some do not have windows, so request one with a window. There's also a good, reasonably priced restaurant, C3. ⌧ *103 Waverly Pl., 10011,* ☎ *212/777–9515 or 800/ 222–0418,* ⒻⒶⓍ *212/979–8373. 165 rooms. Restaurant, exercise room. AE, MC, V. CP.* ⌘

$$–$$$ ⌹ **The Gershwin.** Young travelers flock to this hip budget hotel-cum-hostel, housed in a 13-story Greek Revival. Enter, and be visually assaulted by a giant primary-color cartoony sculpture, one of many works by house artist Brad Howe. Dormitories have four or eight beds and a remarkable $22 rate. ⌧ *7 E. 27th St., 10016,* ☎ *212/545–8000,* ⒻⒶⓍ *212/684–5546. 120 rooms, 15 dorm rooms. Restaurant. MC, V.* ⌘

$$–$$$ ⌹ **Herald Square Hotel.** Vintage magazine covers adorning the hallways inside lend character to this historic hotel, housed in the former *Life* magazine building. Rooms are basic and clean, with deep-green carpets and floral-print bedspreads; all have TVs, phones with voice mail, and in-room safes. ⌧ *19 W. 31st St., 10001,* ☎ *212/279–4017 or 800/727–1888,* ⒻⒶⓍ *212/643–9208. 120 rooms. AE, D, MC, V.* ⌘

$$–$$$ ⌹ **Pickwick Arms Hotel.** This convenient East Side establishment charges $125 a night for standard doubles and has older singles with shared baths for as little as $70; it's routinely booked solid by bargain hunters. Privations you endure to save a buck start and end with the Lilliputian size of some rooms, which have cheap-looking furnishings. ⌧ *230 E. 51st St., 10022,* ☎ *212/355–0300 or 800/742–5945,* ⒻⒶⓍ *212/ 755–5029. 370 rooms, 175 with bath. Café. AE, DC, MC, V.* ⌘

$$ ⌹ **Larchmont Hotel.** You might miss the entrance to this Beaux Arts
★ brownstone, whose geranium boxes and lanterns blend right in with the old New York feel of West 11th Street. If you don't mind shared bathrooms and no room service or concierge, the residential-style accommodations are all anyone could ask for at this price (doubles are just under $100). ⌧ *27 W. 11th St., 10011,* ☎ *212/989–9333,* ⒻⒶⓍ *212/ 989–9496. 55 rooms without bath. AE, D, DC, MC, V. CP.*

$–$$ ⌹ **Broadway Inn Bed & Breakfast.** This comfortable, inexpensive the-
★ ater district gem is one of the best deals in town. The spartan but cheerful rooms, with black-lacquer beds and folding chairs, are impeccably kept. Single travelers can get their own room for as little as $125, and the kitchenette suites are perfect for small families on a New York getaway. ⌧ *264 W. 46th St., 10036,* ☎ *212/997–9200 or 800/826–6300,* ⒻⒶⓍ *212/768–2807. 33 rooms. AE, D, DC, MC, V. CP.* ⌘

$–$$ ⌹ **Malibu Studios Hotel.** This hip, young, budget crash pad could very well pass for a college dorm, especially given its proximity to the Columbia University campus. Though it's farther north than some would care to venture, the neighborhood is lively and safe. Clean, modern double-occupancy rooms with private bath start at $99, and those with shared bath start at $55. Every room has a TV, a desk with a writing lamp, and black-and-white prints of New York. ⌧ *2688 Broadway, at 103rd St., 10025,* ☎ *212/222–2954 or 800/647–2227,* ⒻⒶⓍ *212/678– 6842. 150 rooms, 110 with bath. No credit cards. CP.*

Nightlife and the Arts

Full listings of entertainment and cultural events appear in the weekly magazines *New York* and *Time Out New York*; they include capsule summaries of plays, concerts, and exhibitions, as well as performance times and ticket prices. The *New York Times* has excellent event listings on Fridays, and the "Arts & Leisure" section on Sundays also lists and describes events. The Theater Directory in the daily *New York Times* advertises ticket information for Broadway and Off-Broadway shows. Listings of events also appear weekly in *The New Yorker* and the *Village Voice,* a free weekly newspaper that probably has more nightclub ads than any other rag in the world. For the tattooed and pierced, *Paper* magazine's "P.M. 'Til Dawn" and bar sections have as good a listing as exists of the roving clubs and the best of the fashionable crowd's hangouts.

Nightlife

BAR-LOUNGES

Divine Bar (⊠ 244 E. 51st St., ☎ 212/319–9463) is an uptown spot with zebra-striped bar chairs, cigar area, and cozy, velvet couches upstairs. **Pravda** (⊠ 281 Lafayette St., ☎ 212/226–4696), a Russian-theme bar, has more than 70 brands of vodka and nearly as many types of martinis. The **Screening Room** (⊠ 54 Varick St., ☎ 212/334–2100) offers good food, drinks, and movies all in one congenial TriBeCa space. **Spy** (⊠ 101 Greene St., ☎ 212/343–9000) provides a baroque parlor setting with plush couches and pretty people. **Veruka** (⊠ 525 Broome St., ☎ 212/625–1717) is a SoHo favorite of New York Yankee players and other celebrities.

CABARET

The **Oak Room** at the Algonquin Hotel (⊠ 59 W. 44th St., ☎ 212/840–6800) still offers yesteryear's charms. Just head straight for the long, narrow club–cum–watering hole; you might find the hopelessly romantic singer Andrea Marcovicci.

COMEDY CLUBS

Caroline's Comedy Club (⊠ 1626 Broadway, ☎ 212/757–4100), a high-gloss venue, features established names as well as comedians on the edge of stardom. **Gotham Comedy Club** (⊠ 34 W. 22nd St., between 5th and 6th Aves., ☎ 212/367–9000) is housed in a landmark building in the Flatiron district and showcases popular headliners such as Chris Rock and David Brenner.

DANCE CLUBS

Nell's (⊠ 246 W. 14th St., ☎ 212/675–1567) has an upstairs live-music jazz salon; downstairs is for dancing to music spun by a DJ. **Irving Plaza** (⊠ 17 Irving Pl., ☎ 212/777–6800) has ballroom dancing Sunday nights to live orchestras, organized by the Swing Dance Society. For information on the society, call 212/696–9737. **Webster Hall** (⊠ 125 E. 11th St., ☎ 212/353–1600), a fave among NYU students and similar species, boasts four floors and five eras of music.

JAZZ CLUBS

Many consider the **Blue Note** (⊠ 131 W. 3rd St., ☎ 212/475–8592) the jazz capital of the world. **Iridium** (⊠ 48 W. 63rd St., ☎ 212/582–2121) presents some of the music's top names, in a Gaudí-esque setting. The **Village Vanguard** (⊠ 178 7th Ave. S, ☎ 212/255–4037) is a basement joint that has ridden the crest of every new wave in jazz.

POP, ROCK, BLUES, AND COUNTRY

The **Bitter End** (⊠ 147 Bleecker St., ☎ 212/673–7030) has been giving a break to folk, rock, jazz, and country acts for more than 25 years. The **Bottom Line** (⊠ 15 W. 4th St., ☎ 212/228–6300), an intimate sit-down space, features folk and rock headliners. **Chicago Blues** (⊠ 73 8th Ave., ☎ 212/924–9755) is a just-plain-folksy West Village dive that's often home to Big Time Sarah, Jimmy Dawkins, the Holmes Brothers, and other performers. **Rodeo Bar** (⊠ 375 3rd Ave., ☎ 212/683–6500), a full-scale Texas roadhouse, never charges a cover for its country, rock, rockabilly, and blues bands.

FOR SINGLES (UNDER 30)

At **Coffee Shop** (⊠ 29 Union Sq. W, ☎ 212/243–7969), moonlighting models bring your food and drinks, plus there's usually a flashy, gorgeous crowd. **Hi-Life** (✉ 477 Amsterdam Ave., ☎ 212/787–7199) is big with the Upper West Side's bon vivants. At **Max Fish** (✉ 178 Ludlow St., ☎ 212/529–3959), a kitschy palace with a pool table and a twisted image of a grimacing Julio Iglesias over the bar, a young, grungy crowd gathers around midnight. Put on something black and make your way to **Merc Bar** (✉ 151 Mercer St., ☎ 212/966–2727), in the heart of trendy SoHo.

FOR SINGLES (OVER 30)

At **B Bar** (✉ 358 Bowery, ☎ 212/475–2220), long lines peer through venetian blinds at the fabulous crowd within. If the bouncer says there's a private party going on, ignore him and insist you are on the list. **Monkey Bar** (✉ 60 E. 54th St., ☎ 212/838–2600) is a posh '90s creation that draws mannered banker-types who shoot back Scotch.

GAY AND LESBIAN BARS AND CLUBS

For advice on the bar scene and other assorted topics, call the **Gay and Lesbian National Hotline** (☎ 212/989–0999) or stop by the **Lesbian and Gay Community Services Center** (✉ 1 Little W. 12th St., near 9th Ave., ☎ 212/620–7310). **g** (✉ 223 W. 19th St., ☎ 212/929–1085), an up-to-the-minute Chelsea favorite, draws an upscale, mostly male crowd to its huge circular bar and two airy rooms lined with leather settees. At the **Works** (✉ 428 Columbus Ave., ☎ 212/799–7365), J. Crew-clad Upper West Side men cruise and mingle. The lesbian favorite **Henrietta Hudson** (✉ 438 Hudson St., ☎ 212/924–3347) has two large rooms, a DJ, and a pool table. **Julie's** (✉ 204 E. 58th St., ☎ 212/688–1294) is popular with a slightly older midtown set.

The Arts

CLASSICAL MUSIC

Lincoln Center (☞ Upper West Side *in* Exploring Manhattan, *above*) has magnificent concert halls and theaters showcasing much of New York's serious music scene. Its **Avery Fisher Hall** (☎ 212/875–5030) is home to the New York Philharmonic Orchestra, the Mostly Mozart Festival, and visiting orchestras and soloists. **Carnegie Hall** (✉ 154 W. 57th St., at 7th Ave., ☎ 212/247–7800), the city's most famous classical-music palace, is more than 100 years old. This is where Leonard Bernstein made his conducting debut in 1943; where Jack Benny and Isaac Stern fiddled together; and where the Beatles played one of their first U.S. concerts.

DANCE

The **American Ballet Theatre** (☎ 212/477–3030) in Lincoln Center is the resident dance company of the Metropolitan Opera House. The **New York City Ballet** (☎ 212/870–5570) performs at Lincoln Center's New York State Theater. It reached world-class prominence under the direction of the late George Balanchine; Peter Martins is now ballet master-in-chief. **City Center** (✉ 131 W. 55th St., ☎ 212/581–1212) hosts innovative performance groups and dance companies, such as the Alvin Ailey and the Paul Taylor dance companies. The **Joyce Theater** (✉ 175 8th Ave. at 19th St., ☎ 212/242–0800) schedules a potpourri of international dance troupes.

FILM

On any day of the year film buffs find all the major new releases, plus renowned classics, unusual foreign offerings, and experimental works. For information on schedules and theaters dial 212/777–FILM, the MovieFone, or check the local newspapers. *New York, The New Yorker,* and *Time Out New York* magazines publish programs and reviews. The vast majority of Manhattan theaters are first-run houses. Among the art film and revival houses are the **Walter Reade Theater**

(⊠ 165 W. 65th St., plaza level, between Broadway and Amsterdam Aves., ☎ 212/875–5600), the **Angelika Film Center** (⊠ W. Houston and Mercer Sts., ☎ 212/995–2000), and **Film Forum** (⊠ 209 W. Houston St., between 6th Ave. and Varick St., ☎ 212/727–8110); the **Museum of Modern Art** (☞ Midtown *in* Exploring Manhattan, *above*) also offers several film series every year.

OPERA

The **Metropolitan Opera House** (☎ 212/362–6000), at Lincoln Center, is a sublime setting for mostly classic operas performed by world-class stars. The **New York City Opera** (☎ 212/870–5570), at Lincoln Center's State Theater, offers a diverse repertoire consisting of adventurous and rarely seen works as well as classic opera favorites.

THEATER

Nearly 40 Broadway theaters, three dozen Off-Broadway theaters, and 200 Off-Off-Broadway houses make New York a theater lover's paradise. Most Broadway theaters are in the Theater District, between Broadway and 8th Avenue, from 40th to 53rd streets. Off- and Off-Off-Broadway theaters are scattered all over town, including Greenwich Village, the East Village, SoHo, the Upper West Side, and Theater Row, on 42nd Street between 9th and 10th avenues.

The **TKTS booths** in Duffy Square (⊠ 47th St. and Broadway, ☎ 212/221–0013) and in the **Wall Street area** (⊠ 2 World Trade Center mezzanine, ☎ 212/221–0013) are New York's best-known source of discount tickets. TKTS sells day-of-performance tickets for Broadway and some Off-Broadway plays at discounts of 25% or 50% (plus $2.50 per ticket), depending on a show's popularity. For evening performances Monday–Sunday, the Duffy Square booth is open from 3 to 8; for Wednesday and Sunday matinee shows, from 10 to 2; for Sunday matinee and evening performances, 11–8. The World Trade Center booth is open weekdays 11 to 5:30 and Saturday 11 to 3:30. TKTS accepts only cash or traveler's checks—no credit cards.

Spectator Sports

Baseball: New York Mets (⊠ Shea Stadium, Roosevelt Ave. off Grand Central Pkwy., Flushing, Queens, ☎ 718/507–8499). **New York Yankees** (⊠ Yankee Stadium, 161st St. and River Ave., The Bronx, ☎ 718/293–6000). **Basketball: New York Knicks** (⊠ Madison Square Garden, 7th Ave. between 31st and 33rd Sts., ☎ 212/465–6741; 212/465–5867 for Knicks hot line). **New Jersey Nets** (⊠ Continental Airlines Arena, Rte. 3, East Rutherford, NJ, ☎ 201/935–3900). **New York Liberty** (⊠ Madison Square Garden, 7th Ave. between 31st and 33rd Sts., ☎ 212/465–6741 or 212/564–9622 for Liberty hot line). **Football: New York Giants** (⊠ Giants Stadium, Rte. 3, East Rutherford, NJ, ☎ 201/935–8111 or 201/935–3900). **New York Jets** (⊠ Giants Stadium, Rte. 3, East Rutherford, NJ, ☎ 516/560–8100 or 201/935–3900). **Hockey: New York Rangers** (⊠ Madison Square Garden, 7th Ave. between 31st and 33rd Sts., ☎ 212/465–6741; 212/308–6977 for Rangers hot line). **Running: New York Marathon** (⊠ New York Road Runners Club, 9 E. 89 St., ☎ 212/860–4455). **Tennis: U.S. Open,** late August and early September at the USTA National Tennis Center in Flushing Meadows–Corona Park, Queens (☎ 888/673–6849).

Shopping

You can buy almost anything you might want or need at almost any time of day or night somewhere in New York City, but in general, major department stores and other shops are open every day and keep late hours on Thursday. Many of the high-end shops along upper 5th and Madison avenues close on Sunday. The bargain shops along Orchard Street on the Lower East Side are closed on Saturday, mobbed on Sunday. For specialty stores with several branches in the city we have listed the locations in the busier shopping neighborhoods.

Shopping Neighborhoods

Fifth Avenue from 50th to 58th Street contains many of the world's most famous—and expensive—stores, including several excellent jewelers and department stores. **57th Street** between Park and 5th Avenues is an audacious mix of couture flagships and more accessible retail blockbusters. **Madison Avenue** between 59th and 79th streets has scads of ultraexclusive stores from the best-known American and international designers. **SoHo** is packed with trendy clothing boutiques and housewares shops, plus a recent boom of makeup stores. Lower Broadway, from Prince to Canal Street, is lined with one of the city's best selections of sneakers and streetwear. A few blocks east, the streets of **NoLita** (North of Little Italy), are lined with carefully arranged pocket-size boutiques offering precious housewares and fashions. NoLita's parallel spines are Elizabeth, Mott, and Mulberry streets, between Houston and Broome. **Chinatown,** which abuts NoLita and is ever encroaching on the touristy Little Italy, is a maze of teeming streets where everything from dried shrimp to silk cheongsams to porcelain tea sets is for sale. Check Canal Street for fake Rolexes and Prada (and be sure to bargain). The **Lower East Side** offers bargains of all kinds, from luggage to lingerie, plus the city's most avant-garde shops, which often double as performance spaces or galleries. Directly north, the **East Village** offers eclectic boutiques and inexpensive vintage clothing shops. **West 14th Street** is classic New York City: from Union Square to 7th Avenue, the wide avenue is lined with shops offering bargain goods like $3 kids T-shirts and $15 musical wall clocks. **Chelsea** is scattered with a healthy mix of funky shops, many catering to the neighborhood's gay community. With SoHo's increasing commercialization, many galleries have moved to the western edges of Chelsea. On the Upper West Side, **Columbus Avenue** between 66th and 86th streets is a sturdy stretch of familiar chain stores dotted with a few interesting adults' and kids' clothing boutiques.

Department Stores

Barneys (⊠ 660 Madison Ave. at 60th St., ☎ 212/826–8900) is monied, modern New York to the hilt: floor after floor of cutting-edge designer clothes, cosmetics, and accessories for women and men, plus a tiny boutique for tots. **Bergdorf Goodman** (⊠ 754 5th Ave., ☎ 212/753–7300) is where devastating elegance reigns in a *vieux riches* setting; the men's store, with its vaulted marble lobby, is across the street. **Bloomingdale's** (⊠ 59th St. and Lexington Ave., ☎ 212/355–5900) is a New York institution, with a stupefying maze of cosmetics counters on the main floor and a good, dependable selection of merchandise for women, men, kids, and the home. **Century 21** (⊠ 22 Cortlandt St., between Broadway and Church St., ☎ 212/227–9092) is the mother lode of discount shopping; four large floors are crammed with everything from designer suits to high-quality bedding. **Macy's** (⊠ 34th St. and Broadway, ☎ 212/695–4400) has huge housewares and gourmet-foods departments, as well as not-too-fancy designer clothes for all ages. Not your average department store, Chinatown's **Pearl River Mart** (⊠ 277 Canal St., at Broadway, ☎ 212/431–4770; 200 Grand St., at Mott St., ☎ 212/966–1010) offers imported wares, bamboo steamers, silk pajamas, muscat-flavor candies, and of course perennially popular Chinese slippers at very low prices. **Saks Fifth Avenue** (⊠ 611 5th Ave., at 49th St., ☎ 212/753–4000) is a fashion-only department store, with rack after rack of voguish designer goods for women, men, and children.

Specialty Stores

ANTIQUES

At **Florian Papp** (⊠ 962 Madison Ave., at 75th St., ☎ 212/288–6770) the shine of gilt lures knowledgeable collectors. **Israel Sack, Inc.** (⊠ 730 5th Ave., at 57th St., ☎ 212/399–6562) is widely considered one of the very best places in the country for 18th-century American furniture. **Lost City Arts** (⊠ 275 Lafayette St., at Prince St., ☎ 212/941–8025) is full of 1950s furniture and objects, like neon clocks and vintage radios. At **Manhattan Art & Antiques Center** (⊠ 1050 2nd Ave., at 55th St., ☎ 212/355–4400) more than 100 dealers stock three floors with antiques from around the world.

BOOKS

All the big national **chain bookstores** are here, with branches all over town—Barnes & Noble, Borders, and Waldenbooks—but New York is the perfect place to rediscover the intimate touch of the independent bookseller. **Crawford Doyle Booksellers** (⊠ 1082 Madison Ave., at 81st St., ☎ 212/288–6300) has a thoughtful selection of fiction, nonfiction, biographies, and so on, plus some rare books on the narrow upstairs balcony. **Gotham Book Mart** (⊠ 41 W. 47th St., at 5th Ave., ☎ 212/719–4448) emphasizes literature and the performing arts in books and magazines. **Rizzoli Bookstore** (⊠ 31 W. 57th St., ☎ 212/759–2424; World Financial Center, ☎ 212/385–1400) is a hushed environment with a rich book selection. The **downtown branch** (⊠ 454 W. Broadway, at Prince St., ☎ 212/674–1616) specializes in art and architecture and also offers a quirky boutique section and an espresso bar. Student-filled **Shakespeare & Co. Booksellers** (⊠ 939 Lexington Ave., between 68th and 69th Sts., ☎ 212/570–0201; ⊠ 716 Broadway, at Washington Pl., ☎ 212/529–1330) stocks the latest in just about every field. The scruffy **Strand** (⊠ 828 Broadway, at 12th St., ☎ 212/473–1452; ⊠ 95 Fulton St., at William St., ☎ 212/732–6070), North America's largest used-book store, offers more than 2 million volumes; rare books are located next door at 826 Broadway. The Fulton Street branch is less overwhelming than the Broadway behemoth. **Three Lives & Co.** (⊠ 154 W. 10th St., at Waverly Pl., ☎ 212/741–2069), perched on a picture-perfect West Village corner, has one of the city's most impeccable selection of books.

JEWELRY

Bulgari (⊠ 730 5th Ave., at 57th St., ☎ 212/315–9000; 783 Madison Ave., ☎ 212/717–2300; ⊠ 2 E. 61st St., in the Hotel Pierre, ☎ 212/486–0326) has beautiful, weighty pieces. **Cartier** (⊠ 653 5th Ave., at 52nd, ☎ 212/753–0111) still dazzles with extravagant gems; favorite items include the three-band trinity ring and the gold "love bracelet." Virtually every store is a jewelry shop in the **Diamond District** (⊠ 47th St. between 5th and 6th Aves.); be ready to haggle. **Harry Winston** (⊠ 718 5th Ave., at 56th St., ☎ 212/245–2000) is a long-standing source for outsize stones. **Me & Ro Jewelry** (⊠ 239 Elizabeth St., at Prince St., ☎ 917/237–9215) creates ethnic-inspired designs that are both earthy and delicate. At legendary **Tiffany & Co.** (⊠ 727 5th Ave., at 57th St., ☎ 212/755–8000) prices can be extravagant, but there's always a selection of lower-price gift items, not to mention some of the most creative display windows on 5th Avenue.

MEN'S AND WOMEN'S WEAR

Brooks Brothers (⊠ 666 5th Ave., at 53rd St., ☎ 212/276–9440) defines traditional American style. It's still the place that suits up most of Wall Street, not to mention the Ivy League. Casual wear hasn't changed much since the 1950s, meaning it's back in style. **Calvin Klein** (⊠ 654

Madison Ave., at 59th St., ☎ 212/292–9000) has a stark store right next to Barneys that showcases the luxe end of the designer's clothing line, plus housewares, accessories, and yes, underwear. **Canal Jean** (⊠ 504 Broadway, ☎ 212/226–1130) is a sort of clothing jumble shop—stacks of Levi's, vintage Hawaiian shirts, discounted name brands, and Army-Navy surplus. In **Dolce & Gabbana** (⊠ 825 Madison Ave., ☎ 212/249–4100) it's easy to feel like an Italian movie star amid the extravagant (in every sense) clothes. **Giorgio Armani** (⊠ 760 Madison Ave., ☎ 212/988–9191) displays stunning clothes in a museumlike space, or check **A/X: Armani Exchange** (⊠ 568 Broadway, at Prince St., ☎ 212/431–6000; ⊠ 645 5th Ave., at 51st St., ☎ 212/980–3037) for Armani style at lower prices. Sophisticated from its sunglasses to its shoes, **Gucci** (⊠ 685 5th Ave., ☎ 212/826–2600) epitomizes desirability. **Helmut Lang** (⊠ 80 Greene St., at Spring St., ☎ 212/925–7214) is a shrine to minimalism. Lang's austere designs are perennial favorites with the ultrachic crowd. For a perfectly edited selection of women's clothing that looks like it jumped right out of a fashion magazine, check out **Intermix** (⊠ 125 5th Ave., at 19th St., ☎ 212/533–9720; 1033 Madison Ave., at 77th St., ☎ 212/249–7858). **J. Crew** (⊠ 99 Prince St., ☎ 212/966–2739; ⊠ 203 Front St., ☎ 212/385–3500; 91 5th Ave., ☎ 212/255–4848; ⊠ 30 Rockefeller Plaza, ☎ 212/767–4227) lines up fresh-scrubbed essentials: wool sweaters, button-downs, easy-cut suits, jeans, and some of the best-fitting swimsuits around. The first retail powerhouse to set up shop in the newly chic meatpacking district, **Jeffrey** (⊠ 449 W. 14th St., at 10th Ave., ☎ 212/206–3928) resembles the closet of your wildest dreams: piles of fancy shoes and racks of ultraluxe garments from top designers. There's even a small boutique devoted to luxury beauty goods. SoHo's superboutique **Kirna Zabête** (⊠ 96 Greene St., at Prince St., ☎ 212/941–9656) carries a truly eclectic mix of high-price designers, plus giant gumballs and fresh flowers. The gossamer silks, slick black technofabric, and ultraluxe shoes and leather goods at **Prada** (⊠ 841 Madison Ave., ☎ 212/327–4200; 724 5th Ave., ☎ 212/664–0010; ⊠ Prince St., at Mercer [opened fall 2000], ☎ phone not available at press time) embody one of the great fashion coups of the last millennium. A **smaller branch** (⊠ 45 E. 57th St., ☎ 212/308–2332) carries just the shoes, while the downtown **Prada Sport** (⊠ 116 Wooster St., at Spring St., ☎ 212/925–2221) can sell you mink-lined ski gear or a microfiber golf bag. **Miu Miu** (⊠ 100 Prince St., at Mercer St., ☎ 212/334–5156) is Prada's little sister: more playful (and colorful) versions of Miuccia's grown-up line. Prices are a bit lower too, though that's not saying much. It's hard to top the **Polo/Ralph Lauren** (⊠ 867 Madison Ave., ☎ 212/606–2100) location in its turn-of-the-20th-century mansion; the velvet evening gowns and pinstripe suits look right at home. **Polo Sport** is right across the street.

MUSIC STORES

Bleecker Bob's Golden Oldies Record Shop (⊠ 118 W. 3rd St., ☎ 212/475–9677) is a Greenwich Village spot with good rock on vinyl. Eclectic **Kim's Video & Music** (⊠ 6 St. Mark's Pl., at 2nd Ave., ☎ 212/598–9985; ⊠ 144 Bleecker St., between Thompson St. and La Guardia Pl., ☎ 212/260–1010; 350 Bleecker St., at W. 10th St., ☎ 212/675–8996) crystallizes the downtown music scene. For gigantic spaces where you can browse for books, laser discs, DVDs, and videos—besides thousands of CDs—check out the monoliths: **Tower Records** (⊠ 1961 Broadway, ☎ 212/799–2500; ⊠ 725 5th Ave., ☎ 212/838–8110; ⊠ 692 Broadway, ☎ 212/505–1500), **Virgin Megastore** (⊠ 1540 Broadway, ☎ 212/921–1020; 52 E. 14th St., ☎ 212/598–4666); **HMV** (⊠ 57 W. 34th St., ☎ 212/629–0900; ⊠ 565 5th Ave., ☎ 212/681–6700; ⊠ 1280 Lexington Ave., ☎ 212/348–0800).

Side Trips to Other Boroughs

The Bronx

The 250-acre **New York Botanical Garden,** built around the dramatic gorge of the Bronx River, is considered one of the leading botany centers of the world. Less than a mile from the botanical garden is the world-class **Bronx Zoo** (for both, ☞ Parks, Gardens, and Zoos, *above*).

ARRIVING AND DEPARTING

For the botanical garden, take Metro-North to the New York Botanical Garden stop, or take Subway D or 4 to Bedford Park Boulevard. For the zoo, take Subway 2 to Pelham Parkway and walk three blocks west, or take the **Liberty Line** BxM-11 express bus from Manhattan to the Bronx Zoo (☎ 718/652–8400 for bus schedules, locations of stops, and fares).

Brooklyn

★ **Brooklyn Heights** was New York's first suburb, linked to the city first by ferry and later by the Brooklyn Bridge. In the 1940s and 1950s the Heights was an alternative to the bohemian haven of Greenwich Village—home to writers including Carson McCullers, W. H. Auden, Alfred Kazin, and Norman Mailer. In the late 1960s the neighborhood was designated New York's first historic district. Some 600 buildings more than 100 years old, representing a wide range of American building styles, are lovingly preserved today. The **Plymouth Church of the Pilgrims** (✉ Orange St., between Henry and Hicks Sts., ☎ 718/624–4743) was a center of abolitionist sentiment in the years before the Civil War, thanks to the oratory of the eminent theologian Henry Ward Beecher. **Willow Street,** between Clark and Pierrepont streets, is one of Brooklyn Heights' prettiest and most architecturally varied blocks. Pierrepont Street ends at the **Brooklyn Heights Promenade,** a quiet sliver of park lined with benches offering a dramatic vista of the Manhattan skyline. Just off the promenade's south end, **Montague Street,** the commercial spine of the Heights, offers a flurry of shops, cafés, and restaurants of every ethnicity.

ARRIVING AND DEPARTING

Walk across the Brooklyn Bridge from lower Manhattan near city hall and return on Subway 2 or 3 from the Clark Street station, a few blocks southwest of the walkway terminus.

Queens

Astoria, in Queens, is one of New York's most vital ethnic neighborhoods; once German, then Italian, it is now heavily Greek and is filled with shops and restaurants reflecting the community. Astoria is the site of the **American Museum of the Moving Image,** where a theater features clips from the works of leading Hollywood cinematographers; galleries offer interactive exhibits on filmmaking techniques; and the collection of movie memorabilia contains costumes worn by everyone from Marlene Dietrich to Robin Williams. ✉ *35th Ave. at 36th St.,* ☎ *718/784–0077.* ☜ *$8.50. Closed Mon.*

ARRIVING AND DEPARTING

Take the N train from Manhattan to the Broadway stop. For the Museum of the Moving Image, walk five blocks along Broadway to 36th Street; turn right and walk two blocks to 35th Avenue.

LONG ISLAND

Long Island is not only the largest island on America's East Coast—1,682 square mi—but the most varied. From west to east, Long Island encompasses two New York City boroughs (Brooklyn and Queens), congested commuter towns, the farmland of the North Fork, and the world-famous villages of the Hamptons. It has arguably the nation's finest stretch of white-sand beach, as well as the notoriously clogged Long Island Expressway (LIE).

Visitor Information

Long Island Convention and Visitors Bureau (⊠ 350 Vanderbilt Motor Pkwy., Suite 103, Hauppauge 11788, ☎ 516/951–3440 or 800/441–4601). **Visitor centers,** open late spring–early fall (⊠ Southern State Pkwy., between Exits 13 and 14, Valley Stream; LIE between Exits 52 and 53, Dix Hills–Deer Park; Rte. 24, Flanders). **Fire Island Tourism Bureau** (⊠ 49 N. Main St., Sayville 11782, ☎ 516/563–8448), open Memorial Day through Labor Day.

Arriving and Departing

Although mass transit makes Long Island very accessible, a car is necessary to explore the island's nooks and crannies.

By Bus
Hampton Jitney (☎ 516/283–4600; 800/936–0440 in New York City) links Manhattan and area airports with towns on the southeastern end of Long Island.

By Car
The **Midtown Tunnel** (I–495), **Queensborough Bridge** (Northern Boulevard, Route 25A), and the **Triborough Bridge** (I–278) connect Long Island with Manhattan. The **Throgs Neck Bridge** (I–295) and the **Whitestone Bridge** (I–678) provide access from the Bronx and New England.

By Ferry
There are a few ferries that service Fire Island: The **Sayville Ferry Service** (☎ 516/589–8980) shuttles from Sayville to Cherry Grove, Fire Island Pines, and Sailor's Haven. **Fire Island Ferries, Inc.** (☎ 516/665–2115) runs from Bayshore to several Fire Island communities.

By Plane
In addition to **John F. Kennedy** and **La Guardia** airports, in Queens (☞ Arriving and Departing *in* New York City), Long Island is served by **Long Island MacArthur Airport,** in Islip (☎ 516/467–3210).

By Train
The **Long Island Railroad** (☎ 516/822–5477) has frequent service from Penn Station in Manhattan to major towns on Long Island.

Exploring Long Island

The best way to get a feel for Long Island and explore its museums, stately mansions, nature preserves, and coastal villages is to avoid the traffic-choked LIE and take the more leisurely roads that parallel the coasts. On the North Shore your best bet is Route 25A and, on the North Fork, Route 25; on the South Shore, Route 27 (Sunrise Highway).

The stretch of wealthy suburbs just outside New York City on the **North Shore** is known as the Gold Coast. Families like the Vanderbilts, Whitneys, and Roosevelts built mansions here in the late 19th and early 20th centuries, making this area on Long Island Sound a fashionable playground for the rich. It wasn't until after World War II that vast numbers of the middle class moved out to Long Island. However, some communities such as Oyster Bay still maintain their elite status.

The **Nassau County Museum of Art** is housed in the former country residence of Henry Clay Frick and displays changing exhibits from Botticelli to Frida Kahlo. Outdoor sculptures dot the 145 acres of formal

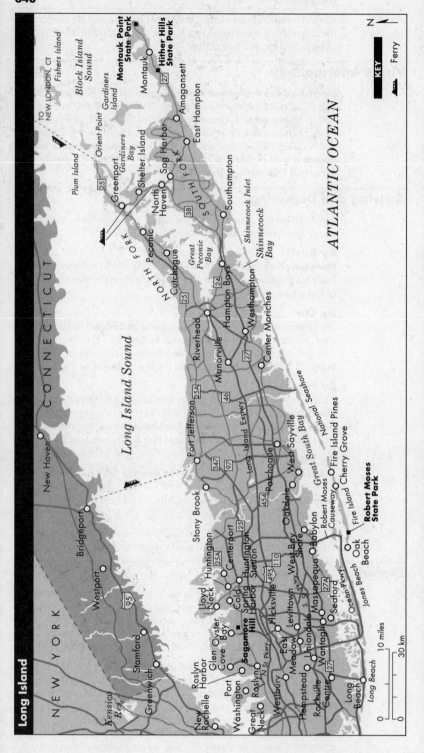

gardens and rolling fields. ⊠ *1 Museum Dr., at Northern Blvd. (Rte. 25A), Roslyn Harbor,* ☎ *516/484–9337.* ☜ *$4. Closed Mon.*

The quaint town of **Oyster Bay** sits on an inlet of the Long Island Sound. The **Planting Fields Arboretum State Historic Park** is yet another stunning Gold Coast property with an impressive estate. The British-born marine-insurance magnate William Robertson Coe bought the place in 1913 and worked with landscape artist James Dawson, of the famed Olmsted Brothers' firm, to plan grand allées of trees, azalea walks, and a rhododendron park on the 490 acres surrounding his mansion, Coe Hall. The grounds are open year-round, the house in the summer, by appointment. ⊠ *Planting Fields Rd., off Oyster Bay–Glen Cove Rd.,* ☎ *516/922–0479.* ☜ *$5 per vehicle. Coe Hall closed Oct.–May.*

You can tour President Theodore Roosevelt's Queen Anne summer White House at **Sagamore Hill National Historic Site** (⊠ Cove Neck Rd., 1.7 mi north of Rte. 25A, ☎ 516/922–4447; ☜ $5).

Cold Spring Harbor, one of the Gold Coast's most enchanting towns, is just east of Oyster Bay. During its heyday in the mid-1800s, this town was home port to a fleet of whaling vessels. Take some time to browse along Main Street, which is lined with shops and restaurants.

The **North Fork,** the upper part of Long Island's eastern tail, is bucolic farm country, with a thriving wine-growing business concentrated in Cutchogue and Peconic. Make a stop at **Hargrave Vineyard,** the pioneer winery in the region, for a tour or tasting. ⊠ *South side of Rte. 48, Cutchogue,* ☎ *516/734–5158.* ☜ *Free. No tours in winter.*

Beautiful and historic **Shelter Island,** in Gardiners Bay nestled between the North and South forks, was among the first parts of Long Island to be settled by the British and is now primarily a summer resort and boating center. You can use the island as a scenic stepping-stone between one fork and the other, taking the ferries that leave from Greenport on the North Fork (⊠ North Ferry, ☎ 516/749–0139) and North Haven on the South Fork (⊠ South Ferry, ☎ 516/749–1200).

Sag Harbor, on the north shore of the South Fork, was an important whaling center from 1775 to 1871. The town looks much as it did in the 1870s, with stately homes of whaling merchants lining Main Street. The **Whaling Museum** displays logbooks, scrimshaw, and harpoons. It's open by appointment. ⊠ *Garden and Main Sts.,* ☎ *516/725–0770.* ☜ *$3. Closed Oct.–mid-May.*

★ The **Hamptons,** on the South Fork, are seaside villages that the East Coast upper crust "discovered" in the late 1800s and transformed into elegant summer resorts. At the pinnacle of fashion and fame is **East Hampton**; despite hordes of tourists and celebrities, from Steven Spielberg to Martha Stewart, who descend each summer, it retains its Colonial heritage. Main Street has a classic white-frame Presbyterian church and stately old homes and inns, which mingle with trendy shops and galleries.

At Long Island's eastern tip, **Montauk** has the double allure of extremity and the sea. Though the village is rather touristy, the beaches are unsurpassed. **Hither Hills State Park** (⊠ Rte. 27, 12 mi west of Montauk village, ☎ 516/668–2461) preserves miles of rolling moors and forests of pitch pine and scrub oak. Campgrounds are here but book up quickly. You can climb the 137 steps that lead to the top of the **Montauk Lighthouse** (⊠ Rte. 27, 6 mi east of village, ☎ 516/668–2544), a famous Long Island landmark. On a clear day, you can see Rhode Island.

Fire Island, a slender 32-mi-long barrier island on Long Island's south shore, encompasses an unspoiled stretch of national seashore. Its half dozen tiny communities include two longtime lesbian and gay enclaves, Cherry Grove and the Pines. To reach the west end of the island, take the Robert Moses Causeway to Robert Moses State Park—you can leave your car here for a small fee. You can reach the central and eastern communities on Fire Island by ferry (☞ Arriving and Departing, *above*).

Dining and Lodging

Long Island restaurants run the gamut from fast-food chains, pizzerias, and family-style eateries to ethnic restaurants and elegant country inns. Not surprisingly, the island draws on the bounty of the surrounding waters, especially on the east end, where commercial fishing remains a vital industry. Recent years have brought all the major motel chains to Long Island. Resort hotels and small inns are concentrated in the Hamptons. In summer prices tend to double, if not triple, and there is often a minimum stay on weekends.

Bridgehampton

$$$–$$$$ ✕ **Bobby Van's.** Although the menu includes something for everyone, this restaurant is best known for its fabulous steaks. There's a definite see-and-be-seen attitude in the air here. ⊠ *2636 Montauk Hwy.,* ☎ *631/537–0590. Reservations essential. AE, D, DC, MC, V.*

East Hampton

$ ✕ **Babette's.** Towering banana trees give a tropical feel to this funky café. Although it's crowded in summer (especially for breakfast), the innovative fare here is worth the wait. There's a large selection of vegetarian dishes; try the smoked tempeh fajitas. ⊠ *66 Newtown La.,* ☎ *631/329–5377. AE, MC, V. Closed Mon.–Thurs. Jan.–Mar.*

$$$–$$$$ ✕🏠 **Maidstone Arms.** Dating to 1740, this inn is the coziest and most
★ comfortable in town. It also has one of the best locations—right across from a pond and a pristine park, surrounded by East Hampton's oldest streets and most beautiful houses. Beach parking permits are available for guests. An East Hampton mainstay, the inn's always-busy restaurant serves new American cuisine, including potato-wrapped striped bass on smothered red beans and crab butter and Long Island duck with coffee glaze and scallion pancake. A breakfast of delicious baked goods is included with the room. ⊠ *207 Main St., 11937,* ☎ *631/324–5006,* 🖷 *631/324–5037. 16 rooms, 3 cottages. Restaurant. AE, DC, MC, V. CP.* ✑

$$$$ 🏠 **J. Harper Poor Cottage.** Gary and Rita Reiswig have created the *definitive* East Hampton retreat, where you will be coddled as you should be in the Hamptons. More mansion than cottage, the inn dates back to the 1600s and has been expanded and renovated several times. Today, exquisite William Morris papers cover the walls, and plush overstuffed furniture graces the sitting rooms, which are filled with fresh flowers and a good collection of books. ⊠ *181 Main St., 11937,* ☎ *516/324–4081,* 🖷 *631/329–5931. 5 rooms. AE, DC, MC, V. BP.* ✑

Greenport

$$–$$$$ ✕ **Claudio's.** This family-run classic seafood restaurant has been around for more than 125 years. Forget fancy culinary creations: Go for the baked clams, fresh mussels, or fried calamari for starters, and the shrimp scampi or grilled swordfish as a main dish. From May to October, you can also dine alfresco at one of the restaurant's more casual locales, both on the piers, within 300 ft of the restaurant. For raw-bar fare, head to the Clam Bar, with live entertainment and tables overlooking Peconic Bay. **Crabby Jerry's,** a self-service seafood shack, is great for families. ⊠ *111 Main St.,* ☎ *631/477–0627. MC, V. Closed Jan.–mid-Apr.*

Montauk

$–$$$ ✕ **Gosman's Dock.** This huge, touristy fish restaurant is jam-packed in the summer. It offers a spectacular location—at the entrance to Montauk Harbor—and the freshest possible fish, served indoors or out. You may have a long wait in peak season. ⊠ *500 W. Lake Dr.,* ☎ *631/668–5330. Reservations not accepted. AE, MC, V. Closed mid-Oct.–Apr.*

$$$$ ▦ **Gurney's Inn Resort and Spa.** Long popular for its fabulous location, on a bluff overlooking 1,000 ft of private ocean beach, Gurney's has become even more famous in recent years for its European-style health-and-beauty spa. The large, luxurious rooms and suites all have ocean views. ⊠ *290 Old Montauk Hwy., 11954,* ☎ *631/668–2345,* FAX *516/668–3576. 129 rooms, 5 cottages. 2 restaurants, pool, health club. AE, D, DC, MC, V. MAP.* ✎

Sag Harbor

$$$$ ✕▦ **The American Hotel.** Try to have lunch or dinner at this small hotel's
★ well-known restaurant, where the kitchen puts out such tasty dishes as crab cakes in chanterelles and truffles and a Porterhouse steak Florentine. The bar is the sort where you'd want to sip brandy and light up a cigar. The rooms upstairs are big with nice modern bathrooms, but the dining room is the real reason to come here. ⊠ *25 Main St., 11963,* ☎ *631/725–3535,* FAX *631/725–3573. 8 rooms. Restaurant. AE, D, DC, MC, V. No lunch weekdays. CP.* ✎

Shelter Island

$$–$$$$ ✕▦ **Ram's Head Inn.** This 1929 center-hall Colonial-style island re-
★ treat makes for the perfect romantic getaway—far from the Hamptons crowds. The inn overlooks 800 ft of beachfront, and sailboats and kayaks are available for guests' use, as is a tennis court. The dining room ($$$–$$$$), regarded as one of the best on eastern Long Island, serves such dishes as warm duck sausage with spinach-grain mustard, pistachios, and strawberries; and peppercorn-crusted tuna over crispy curried noodles with a piquant mango chutney. ⊠ *108 Ram Island Dr., Shelter Island 11965,* ☎ *516/749–0811,* FAX *516/749–0059. 17 rooms. Restaurant. AE, MC, V. Closed Mar. CP.* ✎

Motels

▦ **Drake Motor Inn** (⊠ 16 Penny La., Hampton Bays 11946, ☎ 516/728–1592, FAX 516/728–8770), 15 rooms; pool; *$$–$$$$.*

▦ **Ramada Inn East End** (⊠ 1830 Rte. 25, Riverhead 11901, ☎ 516/369–2200, FAX 516/369–1202), 100 rooms; restaurant, pool; *$$$.*

Campground

⚠ **Hither Hills State Park** (☞ Exploring Long Island, *above*) has both tent and RV sites, although they are hard to come by. You must reserve nearly 11 months before the date you will arrive. Call 800/456-CAMP for reservations.

Nightlife and the Arts

Check the Friday edition of *Newsday,* the Long Island newspaper, which has a weekend supplement containing information about Long Island arts and entertainment, as well as the magazine *Long Island Monthly.*

Nightlife

The Long Island scene is lively, especially in the Hamptons. You can hear live music every night in the summer at the **Stephen Talkhouse** (⊠ Main St., Amagansett, ☎ 516/267–3117), a relaxed place to hang out. In Southampton, nightclubbers head to **Jet East** (⊠ North Sea Rd., ☎ 516/283–0808), but beware: lots of hype has made this place a scene.

The Arts

Jones Beach Marine Theatre (⊠ Jones Beach, Wantagh, ☎ 516/221–1000) hosts major outdoor concerts by contemporary pop artists May–September. **Nassau Veteran's Memorial Coliseum** (⊠ 1255 Hempstead Tpke., Uniondale, ☎ 516/794–9300) has major rock and pop concerts year-round. **Westbury Music Fair** (⊠ 590 Brush Hollow Rd., Westbury, ☎ 516/334–0800) presents live concerts, shows, and theater. Rainy days are a good time to catch a flick at the **East Hampton Cinema** (⊠ 30 Main St., ☎ 516/324–0448); however, everyone else usually thinks of this, too, so buy your tickets in advance.

Outdoor Activities and Sports

Participant Sports

BOATING

Oyster Bay Sailing School (☎ 516/624–7900) offers classes and three- to five-day vacation packages from May through October; charter sailboats are also available.

Spectator Sports

Hockey: New York Islanders (⊠ Nassau Coliseum, Hempstead Tpke., Uniondale, ☎ 516/832–4200). **Horse Racing: Belmont Park Race Track** (⊠ Hempstead Tpke., Elmont, ☎ 718/641–4700) is home to the third jewel in horse racing's triple crown, the Belmont Stakes, held in early June.

Beaches

★　**Jones Beach State Park** (⊠ Wantagh Pkwy., Wantagh, ☎ 516/785–1600), a wide, sandy stretch of ocean beach, is the most crowded but also the biggest and most fully equipped of Long Island's beaches, with a restaurant, concession stands, changing rooms, a boardwalk, a theater, and sports facilities. The **Robert Moses State Park** (⊠ Robert Moses Causeway, Babylon, ☎ 516/631–0449), on Fire Island, is an uncrowded, beautiful, sandy ocean beach. Parking at many of the Hamptons' beaches is difficult; a town permit is usually required.

Shopping

Long Island is known for its shopping malls. The **Roosevelt Field** mall (⊠ Meadowbrook Pkwy., ☎ 516/742–8000), in Garden City, is the largest, with more than 200 stores. **Manhasset's Miracle Mile,** along Route 25A, has department stores and designer boutiques.

THE HUDSON VALLEY

The landscape along the Hudson River for the 140 mi from Westchester County to Albany, the state capital, is among the loveliest in America. Indeed, this natural beauty—dramatic palisades, pine forests, cool mountain lakes and streams—inspired an entire art movement: the Hudson River School, which originated in the 19th century. Still a rich agricultural region, the valley has scores of orchards, vineyards, and farm markets along country roads. Proximity to Manhattan makes this a viable destination for day trips, but the numerous country inns, B&Bs, and resorts make more leisurely journeys especially enjoyable.

Visitor Information

Albany County: Convention and Visitors Bureau (⊠ 25 Quackenbush Sq., Albany 12207, ☎ 518/434–1217 or 800/258–3582). **Columbia County:** Chamber of Commerce (⊠ 507 Warren St., Hudson 12534,

☎ 518/828–4417). **Dutchess County:** Tourism Promotion Agency (✉ 3 Neptune Rd., Suite M, No. 17, Poughkeepsie 12601, ☎ 914/463–4000 or 800/445–3131). **Hudson River Valley:** Hudson Valley Tourism (✉ Box 284, Salt Point 12578, ☎ 800/232–4782).

Arriving and Departing

By Boat

New York Waterways (☎ 800/533–3779) offers boat tours up the Hudson from Manhattan; one includes a stop at Kykuit (☞ Exploring the Hudson Valley, *below*).

By Bus

Adirondack Trailways (☎ 800/225–6815) has daily service between New York's Port Authority Bus Terminal and New Paltz, Kingston, Albany, and other Hudson Valley towns.

By Car

From New York City pick up the New York State Thruway (I–87), which parallels the west bank of the Hudson River, or the more scenic Taconic Parkway, which parallels the east bank. I–84 provides access to the region from southern New England and northeastern Pennsylvania.

By Plane

La Guardia, John F. Kennedy, and **Newark** airports (☞ Arriving and Departing *in* New York City, *above*) are manageable distances from the Hudson Valley. In the Hudson Valley area itself, **Stewart International Airport** (☎ 914/564–2100), in Newburgh, is served by some major airlines. Most major airlines or their shuttles fly into the **Albany County Airport** (☎ 518/869–3021), in Colonie.

By Train

Amtrak (☎ 800/872–7245) provides service to Hudson, Rhinecliff, Rensselaer (Albany), and points west and north of Poughkeepsie. In summer, **Metro North** (☎ 212/532–4900 or 800/638–7646) offers sightseeing packages that include admission to the Hudson Valley's historic sites.

Exploring the Hudson Valley

U.S. 9 hugs the east bank of the Hudson, passing through many picturesque towns, including Tarrytown, Hyde Park, Rhinebeck, and Hudson. U.S. 9W hugs the west bank from Newburgh to Catskill.

Sunnyside, just minutes off the Tappan Zee Bridge, was the romantic estate of Washington Irving, author of *The Legend of Sleepy Hollow.* Guides in Victorian dress give tours regularly; the 10 rooms include Irving's library and many of his original furnishings. ✉ *W. Sunnyside La., off U.S. 9, Tarrytown,* ☎ *914/591–8763.* ⊡ *$8. Closed Jan.–Feb., weekdays Mar., Tues. Apr.–Dec.*

Just north of Sunnyside is **Lyndhurst,** one of America's finest examples of Gothic Revival architecture. The mansion, designed in 1838, has been occupied by three noteworthy New Yorkers and their families: former New York City mayor William Paulding, merchant George Merritt, and tycoon Jay Gould. ✉ *635 S. Broadway, off U.S. 9, Tarrytown,* ☎ *914/631–4481.* ⊡ *$10. Closed Mon. mid-Apr.–Oct., weekdays Nov.–mid-Apr.*

★ You can get a glimpse into the private life of one of America's most famous families at **Kykuit,** the country house of the great American philanthropist John D. Rockefeller and his son John D. Rockefeller, Jr. Two-hour tours of the house, art gallery, and gardens begin at the nearby **Philipsburg Manor,** an 18th-century farm and gristmill. ✉ *U.S. 9,*

Hudson Valley and the Catskills

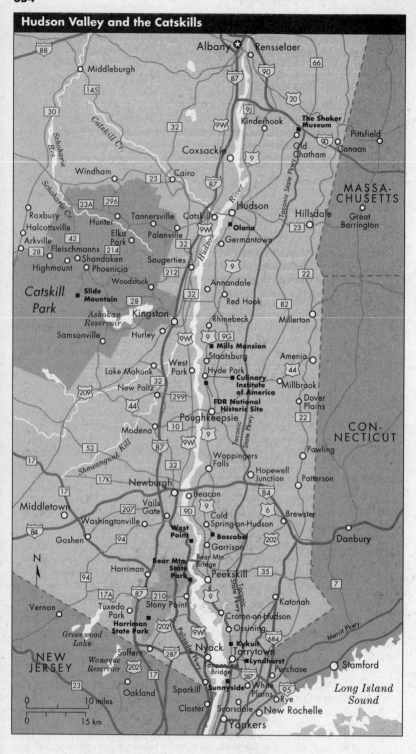

North Tarrytown, ☎ *914/631–9491.* ✉ *$18. Closed Nov.–late Apr., Tues. May–Oct.*

Harriman and Bear Mountain state parks (✉ off Palisades Pkwy., ☎ 914/786–2701; ✉ free; parking $5 at Bear Mountain weekends Labor Day–Memorial Day and daily in summer) are the most famous parks of the vast Palisades interstate system. Outdoor activities include boating, swimming, hiking, fishing, and cross-country skiing on the parks' more than 50,000 acres.

West Point (✉ U.S. 9W, 5 mi north of Bear Mountain State Park, West Point, ☎ 914/938–2638; ✉ free), America's oldest and most distinguished military academy, is on bluffs overlooking the Hudson River. Stop in the visitor center near the Thayer Gate entrance for a map of the grounds. Just next door in Olmstead Hall is the **West Point Museum,** which houses one of the world's foremost military collections.

Across the river from West Point, the small village of **Cold Spring-on-Hudson,** once one of the largest iron foundries in the United States, was founded in the 19th century. Take time to stroll its quiet streets lined with antiques and crafts shops.

Boscobel, in Garrison, is a restored Federal-style mansion surrounded by beautiful gardens with a breathtaking view of the Hudson River. ✉ *Rte. 9D,* ☎ *914/265–3638.* ✉ *$8. Closed Jan.–Feb., Tues. Apr.–Dec.*

The country's most respected cooking school, the **Culinary Institute of America** (✉ U.S. 9, Hyde Park, ☎ 914/471–6608), is housed in a former Jesuit seminary on grounds overlooking the Hudson. Founded in 1946, the institute has 2,100 students enrolled in either culinary arts or baking and pastry arts programs. Facilities include 38 kitchens and bakeshops, plus five student-staffed restaurants open to the public (☞ Dining, *below*).

Up the Hudson River north of Poughkeepsie at Hyde Park is the **Franklin Delano Roosevelt National Historic Site** (✉ U.S. 9, Hyde Park, ☎ 914/229–2501; ✉ $10). The large Roosevelt family home contains original furnishings and a museum displaying personal items.

Nearby the Roosevelt home is **Val-kill,** the cottage where Eleanor Roosevelt lived from 1945 to 1962. It is set on 188 wooded acres. A tour here includes the film biography *First Lady of the World.* ✉ *Rte. 9G, Hyde Park,* ☎ *914/229–9115.* ✉ *$5. Closed weekdays Nov.–Apr.*

North of Hyde Park in Staatsburg is **Mills Mansion,** the opulent country estate of Ogden and Ruth Livingston Mills. You can see the interior by guided tour only. Hiking, picnicking, and cross-country skiing are encouraged. Although the mansion is closed in winter, it opens in December for magical Christmas tours. ✉ *Old Post Rd., Staatsburg,* ☎ *914/889–8851.* ✉ *$3. Closed Oct.–Mar., Mon.–Tues. late Apr.–Sept.*

Quaint **Rhinebeck** is a great spot to spend an afternoon—charming storefronts line the streets, beckoning you to come in and browse; there are several galleries and restaurants worth a stop as well. The village makes a great base for day trips to mansions along the Hudson.

Frederic Church, the leading artist of the Hudson River School, built **Olana,** a 37-room Moorish-style castle, on a hilltop with panoramic vistas of the valley. Persian carpets, decorative arts, and paintings, even some of his own works, are on display. The house is open only for guided tours (reservations recommended); the grounds surrounding Olana are open year-round. ✉ *Rte. 9G, Hudson,* ☎ *518/828–0135.* ✉ *Tours $3; grounds free. House closed Nov.–Mar., Mon.–Tues. Apr.–Oct.*

As you drive north from Hudson toward the villages of Chatham and Old Chatham, the landscape becomes more open and rolling, with sweeping vistas of verdant sheep meadows dotted with large patches of woods; the area is remarkably reminiscent of the English countryside. The **Shaker Museum** in Old Chatham houses the largest collection of Shaker artifacts in the United States. ⊠ *88 Shaker Museum Rd., off Rte. 13,* ☎ *518/794–9100.* 🎟 *$8. Closed Tues.–Wed. and Dec.–Apr.*

A trip to Albany should start in the **Albany Heritage Area** (⊠ 25 Quackenbush Sq., corner of Broadway and Clinton Ave., 12207, ☎ 518/434–0405), which has exhibits depicting Albany's past and present. The **Henry Hudson Planetarium** here presents star shows and a free orientation film about Albany. The center has a great brochure about its walking tour, which will guide you knowledgeably through Albany's historic streets.

Albany's **Empire State Plaza** (☎ 518/474–2418) is a ¼-mi-long concourse with modern art and sculpture and a mix of government, business, and cultural buildings. The plaza includes the **Corning Tower**, with a free observation deck on the 42nd floor. The **New York State Museum** (⊠ Empire State Plaza, ☎ 518/474–5877; 🎟 free), one of the oldest state museums in the country, has life-size exhibits depicting the state's natural and cultural history, including a reproduction of an Iroquois village with a full-size longhouse. It took more than 30 years (1867–99) to complete the **New York State Capitol** (⊠ Empire State Plaza, ☎ 518/474–2418), which incorporates many interesting architectural elements including H.H. Richardson's magnificent Senate chamber. Free tours are conducted; call for times.

Dining and Lodging

Albany

$$–$$$
★
✕ **Ogden's.** On the ground floor of a 1903 brick-and-limestone building, this dining room has two-story arched windows built into 30-ft-high ceilings. The menu focuses on Continental and new American cuisine and includes such dishes as pan-roasted sea bass with a mustard-coriander rub and filet mignon with a zinfandel wine sauce. ⊠ *42 Howard St.,* ☎ *518/463–6605. AE, MC, V. Closed Sun. No lunch Sat.*

$$–$$$
✕🖼 **Albany Mansion Hill Inn and Restaurant.** Standard-issue rooms are eclipsed by the real draw here—the intimate dozen-table restaurant (which doesn't serve lunch). The dinner menu has an imaginative new American flair. If you stay at the inn, breakfast might include items such as blueberry pancakes or frittatas. ⊠ *115 Philip St., 12202,* ☎ *518/465–2038,* FAX *518/434–2313. 8 rooms. Restaurant. AE, D, DC, MC, V. BP.* 🐾

$$$–$$$$
★
🖼 **The Morgan State House.** During the day sunlight pours through the windows of this late-19th-century town house on Washington Park. Mahogany architectural accents complement the interior's hand-glazed walls, high ceilings, fireplaces, and such touches as down comforters. Charming innkeeper Charles Kuhtic oversees things. ⊠ *393 State St., 12210,* ☎ *518/427–6063,* FAX *518/463–1316. 12 rooms. AE, D, DC, MC, V. BP.* 🐾

Bear Mountain

$$
🖼 **Bear Mountain Inn.** For more than 50 years this chalet-style resort has been known for both its bucolic location (in Bear Mountain State Park on the shores of Hessian Lake) and its warm hospitality. Rooms are divided among a main inn and five lodges across the lake. In winter the lobby fireplaces make the lodges cozy; in summer there are great spots nearby for picnicking. Activities abound here, from ice-skating to boating and hiking. ⊠ *U.S. 9W, 10911,* ☎ *914/786–2731,* FAX *914/786–2543. 60 rooms. Restaurant, pool. AE, D, MC, V.*

Cold Spring

$$$ ✗🏠 **Hudson House.** Clean and simple, this historic clapboard inn has a homey feel with country French furnishings and wide-plank floorboards. Tasty American fare is served in the dining room ($$–$$$). The inn is within walking distance of many antiques shops and nearly sits on the Hudson River. ✉ *2 Main St., 10516,* ☎ *914/265–9355. 12 rooms. Restaurant. AE, DC, MC, V.* ✍

Dover Plains

$$$–$$$$ ✗🏠 **Old Drover's Inn.** The oldest continuously operating inn in the country has only four rooms, but guests here are pampered as if it were a luxury hotel. The employees also run the award-winning restaurant, where you might sample such signature dishes as cheddar cheese soup or steak and kidney pie. This early 18th-century inn is one of the state's most romantic hideaways. ✉ *Off Rte. 22, 12522,* ☎ *914/832–9311,* FAX *914/832–6356. 4 rooms. Restaurant. MC, V. Closed Tues.–Wed. MAP weekends, CP weekdays.* ✍

Earlton

$$$–$$$$ ✗ **The Basement Bistro.** Founder and owner Damon Baehrel takes a hands-on approach to his restaurant; he actually built the house in which it's ensconced, and as chef, he's responsible for preparing every dish on its constantly changing menu. À la carte is an option, but you're better off with the tasting menu, 12–18 delectable little courses that add up to a spectacular feast. In the summer, feel free to bring vegetables from your overabundant garden, and see what the chef can do with them. ✉ *776 Rte. 45,* ☎ *518/634–2338. AE, MC, V. Closed Jan.*

Hyde Park

$–$$$$ ✗ **Culinary Institute of America.** The institute (☞ Exploring the Hudson Valley, *above*) has five public restaurants. **Escoffier** features classic French cuisine. **American Bounty** offers American regional fare. **Caterina de Medici** focuses on nouvelle Italian cooking; a four-course prix-fixe menu is offered. **St. Andrew's Cafe** serves low-fat contemporary American cuisine. **Apple Pie Bakery and Cafe** is an informal spot serving lunch and pastries. Reservations are necessary for all but Apple Pie Bakery. ✉ *433 Albany Post Rd., U.S. 9,* ☎ *914/471–6608. AE, DC, MC, V. Closed Sun. and 3 wks in summer.*

New Paltz

$$$$ 🏠 **Mohonk Mountain House.** On a 20,000-acre preserve, this awe-inspiring Victorian-era hotel, with its stone-and-shingled terraces, quiet parlors, and red-tiled turrets, perches on the edge of a quiet lake; extensive hiking trails surround the hotel. You'll find plenty to do here, from golf and tennis to croquet and boccie ball. Rates include three hearty meals, as well as afternoon tea. ✉ *1000 Mountain Rest Rd. (Exit 18 off I–87), Lake Mohonk 12561,* ☎ *914/255–1000 or 800/772–6646,* FAX *914/256–2180. 261 rooms. 3 dining rooms, exercise room. AE, DC, MC, V. FAP.* ✍

Rhinebeck

$$–$$$ ✗🏠 **Beekman Arms.** In all, 10 buildings make up this inn in the village center: the original 1766 building, with its smallish though cheery and comfortable Colonial-style rooms (with modern baths); a motel-like building behind the main inn; and, a block away, the mid-19th-century Delamater House, with primarily Victorian-style rooms. The inn's restaurant, Larry Forgione's **Beekman 1766 Tavern** ($$$–$$$$), which incorporates the old taproom, serves American regional fare, including cedar-plank salmon served with creamy corn pudding and the popular Pennsylvania-Dutch free-range turkey potpie with a cheddar-biscuit topping. ✉ *6387 Mill St. (U.S. 9), 12572,* ☎ FAX *914/876–*

7077, ☎ 914/871–1766 *for restaurant. 63 rooms. Restaurant. AE, D, DC, MC, V.* ✎

Motels
🏨 **Sheraton Civic Center Hotel** (⊠ 40 Civic Center Plaza, Poughkeepsie 12601, ☎ 914/485–5300 or 800/325–3535, FAX 914/485–4720), 175 rooms; café, health club; *$$.*

Nightlife and the Arts

The **Egg** (⊠ Empire State Plaza, Albany, ☎ 518/473–1845) has music, dance, and theater performances. The **Palace Theater** (⊠ 19 Clinton Ave., Albany, ☎ 518/465–4663) is home to the Albany Symphony Orchestra.

Outdoor Activities and Sports

Fishing
The Hudson River estuary contains a remarkable variety of fish, most notably American shad, black bass, smallmouth and largemouth bass, and sturgeon. For information on licenses (required in fresh waters) and restrictions, as well as fishing hot spots and charts, contact the **New York State Department of Environmental Conservation** (⊠ 21 S. Putt Corners Rd., New Paltz 12561, ☎ 914/256–3000; 50 Wolf Rd., Albany 12233, ☎ 518/457–3521).

Golf
Beekman Country Club (⊠ 11 Country Club Rd., Hopewell Junction, ☎ 914/226–7700) has 27 holes. **Dinsmore Golf Course** (⊠ U.S. 9, Staatsburg, ☎ 914/889–4082) has 18 holes.

Ski Areas

Cross-Country
Bear Mountain State Park (⊠ Bear Mountain, 10911, ☎ 914/786–2701) has 5 mi of trails. **Mills-Norrie State Park** (⊠ Old Post Rd., Staatsburg 12580, ☎ 914/889–4100) has 6 mi of trails with views of the Hudson River. **Olana State Historic Site** (⊠ Rte. 9G, Hudson 12534, ☎ 518/828–0135) has 5 mi of trails. **Rockefeller State Park** (⊠ Rte. 117, North Tarrytown 10591, ☎ 914/631–1470) has about 20 mi of trails.

THE CATSKILLS

The Catskill Mountains have a beauty and variety disproportionate to their modest size. Fringing the western side of the upper Hudson Valley and just a few hours by car from New York City, the area offers streams for fly-fishing, paths for hiking, cliffs for rock climbing, slopes for skiing, and back roads for leisurely driving. Once known as the Borscht Belt for the resort complexes that catered to Jewish families, the region now also attracts wilderness lovers and craftspeople.

Visitor Information

Catskill: Association for Tourism Services (⊠ Box 449, Catskill 12414, ☎ 518/943–3223). **Delaware County:** Chamber of Commerce (⊠ 97 Main St., Delhi 13753, ☎ 800/642–4443). **Greene County:** Promotion Department (⊠ Box 527, Catskill 12414, ☎ 518/943–3223 or 800/355–2287). **Sullivan County:** Office of Public Information (⊠ 100 North St., Box 5012, Monticello 12701, ☎ 914/794–3000, ext. 5010 or 800/882–2287).

Arriving and Departing

By Bus

Adirondack Trailways (☎ 800/225–6815) offers regular service from New York City and Albany to several Catskill communities, including Kingston, New Paltz, Hunter, and Fleischmanns. **Shortline** (☎ 800/631–8405) connects New York City with a half dozen Sullivan County communities, including Bloomingburg and Wurtsboro.

By Car

The northern Catskills can be reached from I–87 from Catskill (Routes 23 and 23A) and Kingston (Route 28). The western edge of the resort region is also accessible via Route 17 north, reached from either I–87 at Harriman or from I–84 at Middletown.

By Plane

Albany County Airport (☞ Arriving and Departing by Plane *in* the Hudson Valley, *above*) is an hour's drive from the heart of the Catskills.

Exploring the Catskills

In the northeastern section of the Catskills is the actual village of **Catskill,** which has its share of museums and quaint buildings. The ♻ **Catskill Game Farm,** in Catskill, is home to 2,000 birds and animals, including a large collection of rare hooved species, and has a petting zoo and a playground. ⊠ *400 Game Farm Rd. (off Rte. 32).* ☎ *518/ 678–9595.* 🖆 *13.95. Closed Nov.–Apr.*

To reach the heart of the Catskills, head west on Route 28 beginning by the Hudson River in **Kingston,** a former industrial port city now known for its three historic districts brimming with fine shops and restaurants. At Route 375, consider a brief detour to **Woodstock,** which became a rock music legend after the 1969 concert (actually held 50 mi away, in Bethel). Today, the town is somewhat touristy, but its bohemian element is still evident. Spend the afternoon here—it's a great spot to shop for crafts or New Age crystals, or simply to people-watch.

★ Back on Route 28, if you're the least bit hungry, stop by the **Bread Alone Bakery** (⊠ Rte. 28, Boiceville, ☎ 914/657–3328), where you can sample and purchase some organic hearth-baked breads, from currant buns to *pain levain* (European-style sourdough bread). There are Rhinebeck and Woodstock outposts, too. From the New York State Thruway take Exit 19; it's 16 mi down the road on the right-hand side.

In the area known as the **High Peaks,** from Phoenicia north to the ski resort town of Hunter, Route 214 winds through **Stoney Clove,** a spectacular mountain cleft that has inspired countless tales of the supernatural. Another scenic route out of Phoenicia is across the Esopus River and south up through lovely Woodland Valley to the well-marked trail to **Slide Mountain,** the highest peak in the Catskills.

Delaware County, newly discovered by big-city vacationers and second-home buyers, has gentler terrain than the High Peaks region, which is to its east. Fishermen prize the east and west branches of the Delaware River, and the county's more than 500 farms offer honey, eggs, cider, and maple syrup at numerous roadside stands. **Roxbury,** on Route 30, has the kind of picture-perfect Main Street Norman Rockwell would have loved.

♻ South of Roxbury, in Arkville, is the **Delaware & Ulster Rail Ride,** a scenic trip on a diesel train between Arkville and Highmount or Halcottsville. ⊠ *Rte. 28,* ☎ *607/652–2821.* 🖆 *$7. Closed Nov.–May*

Dining and Lodging

The Catskills are best known for mammoth resort hotels, but there are
plenty of B&Bs and country inns providing a personal touch, as well
as ski-center condos.

Catskill

$$–$$$ ✕ **La Conca D'Oro.** In addition to the usual Italian offerings, the menu
here includes elk, boar, and pheasant prepared with a northern Italian
accent. ⊠ *440 Main St.,* ☎ *518/943–3549. MC, V. Closed Tues. No
lunch weekends.*

Elka Park

$–$$ ✕🏠 **Redcoat's Return.** Driving up a twisting mountain road, you'll en-
counter a bit of the spirit of England in the eastern Catskills. Tom (the
Redcoat) and Peg Wright have owned Redcoat's since 1973; memen-
tos from their trips abroad decorate the inn. The dining room ($–$$$;
closed Mon.–Thurs.), with views of surrounding mountains, serves up
hearty Continental dishes, such as duckling with apples and wild rice
and beef Stroganoff. ⊠ *Dale La., 12427,* ☎ 🖾 *518/589–6379. 14
rooms. Restaurant. AE, D, MC, V. BP.* 🐾

Kingston

$–$$ ✕ **Schneller's.** Schnitzels and wursts are served at this authentic Ger-
★   man tavern in Kingston's Uptown Stockade historic district. After
your meal you may want to stop in the meat market next door for some
imported cheeses or hickory-smoked bacon to take home. The outdoor
beer garden is splendid in summer. ⊠ *61 John St.,* ☎ *914/331–9800.
AE, DC, MC, V. No dinner Mon.–Thurs.*

Lewbeach

$$$$ 🏠 **Beaverkill Valley Inn.** Developed by Laurance Rockefeller, this inn
caters to those who cherish privacy. Its surrounding forests and nearby
fields, preserved as "forever wild," are protected from development.
Fly-fishing is definitely the draw here. But those not hooked on angling can head for the croquet court, indoor basketball court, game
room, help-yourself ice-cream parlor, or the wide front porch lined with
rockers. In winter, there's ice-skating and cross-country skiing on the
property. "Kill," by the way, is the Dutch word for "river." ⊠ *Barn-
hart Rd., off Beaverkill Rd., off Rte. 151/Rte. 152, Box 136, 12753,*
☎ *914/439–4844,* 🖾 *914/439–3884. 28 rooms. Restaurant, pool.
AE, MC, V. FAP.* 🐾

Tannersville

$$–$$$ ✕🏠 **Deer Mountain Inn.** This circa-1900 mansion on a 15-acre wooded
enclave is lushly packed with items that create a mountain ambience:
moose heads, boar heads, bearskin rugs, paintings of European moun-
tain villages, and heavy overstuffed furniture. The dining room ($$;
closed Tuesday, no lunch), bracketed by two huge stone fireplaces, serves
American fare—trout, veal, and seafood—with a European accent. ⊠
Rte. 25, Box 443, 12485, ☎ 🖾 *518/589–6268. 7 rooms. Restaurant.
AE, MC, V. BP.* 🐾

Windham

$$–$$$ ✕ **La Griglia.** Elegant country dining here features northern Italian cui-
sine. A house specialty is the penne *pepperata* (with sautéed sun-dried
tomatoes, sweet red peppers, basil, and a touch of cream). ⊠ *Rte. 296,*
☎ *518/734–4499. AE, DC, MC, V. No lunch weekdays.*

$$–$$$ 🏠 **Albergo Allegria.** This gingerbread Victorian mansion in the north-
ern Catskills is 1 mi from Ski Windham. This B&B is extremely cozy
and has spacious rooms with interesting details, from stained-glass win-
dows and fireplaces to cathedral ceilings and chestnut moldings. There's

also a carriage-house annex with five private-entrance suites. Each room has its own TV and VCR, and there's a video library with more than 200 movies. ⊠ *Rte. 296, 12496,* ☎ *518/734–5560. 21 rooms. MC, V. BP.* ☕

Woodstock

$$ ✕ **Gypsy Wolf Cantina.** Multicolored geckos walk across the ceiling, wolf masks eye a coop of ceramic chickens, and bright red chili-pepper lights enhance the playful vibe of this restaurant. However, from the hearty taco-enchilada combo plates to the chile rellenos, the Mexican food here is seriously delicious. ⊠ *Rte. 212,* ☎ *914/679–9563. MC, V. No lunch.*

$$–$$$ ⌂ **Woodstock Country Inn.** Hidden several hundred yards from the quiet main road, this bed-and-breakfast sits in a beautiful meadow, with mountains rising in the background. Decorated in solid colors from a light palette, the rooms have no fussy prints or ruffles; simple luxuries like 300-thread count cotton sateen sheets are delightful. Whatever your early morning plans, don't pass up the lavish, home-cooked breakfast. ⊠ *Cooper Lake Rd., 2 mi west of Woodstock via Rte. 212, Bearsville 12409,* ☎ *914/679–9380. 4 rooms. D, MC, V. BP.* ☕

Motel

⌂ **Hunter Inn** (⊠ Rte. 23A, Hunter 12442, ☎ 518/263–3777, FAX 518/263–3981), 40 rooms; restaurant, pool, exercise room; $$$–$$$$.

Nightlife and the Arts

Contact the regional visitor centers for schedules of the area's performing arts events. Hunter has some lively nightspots during ski season and summer.

Outdoor Activities and Sports

Canoeing

The 79-mi Upper Delaware Scenic and Recreational River is one of the finest streams for paddling in the region. For a list of trip planners and rental firms, contact the **Sullivan County Office of Public Information** (☞ Visitor Information, *above*).

Fishing

Trout are abundant in Catskill streams; smallmouth bass, walleye, and pickerel can be found in many lakes and in six reservoirs. For the "Catskill Fishing" brochure and map, write to **Catskill Association for Tourism Services** (☞ Visitor Information, *above*).

Golf

The region has nearly 50 golf courses, many of which are at the big resorts. For the "Golf Catskills" brochure, write to **Catskill Association for Tourism Services** (☞ Visitor Information, *above*).

Hiking

The **New York State Department of Environmental Conservation** (⊠ 50 Wolf Rd., Albany 12233, ☎ 518/457–7433) puts out several brochures on Catskill Forest Preserve hiking trails.

Tubing

Town Tinker (⊠ Bridge St., Phoenicia, ☎ 914/688–5553) rents tubes for beginner and advanced routes along Esopus Creek between Shandaken and Mount Pleasant.

Spectator Sports

Horse Racing: You can see harness racing year-round at **Monticello Raceway** (⊠ Rtes. 17 and 17B, Monticello, ☎ 914/794–4100).

Ski Areas

For information on area slopes and trails, contact **Ski the Catskills** (⊠ Box 135, Arkville 12406, ☎ 914/586–1944).

Cross-Country

Belleayre Mountain (☞ Downhill, *below*) has 5 mi of trails. **Mountain Trails Cross-Country Ski Center at Hyer Meadows** (⊠ Box 198, Rte. 23A, 12485, ☎ 518/589–5361) in Tannersville has 20 mi of groomed trails; rentals and lessons are available.

Downhill

Downhill ski areas in the Catskills have snowmaking capabilities. **Belleayre Mountain** (⊠ Box 313, off Rte. 28, Highmount 12441, ☎ 914/254–5600), with 33 runs, 9 lifts, and a 1,404-ft vertical drop, is the only state-run ski facility in the Catskills. **Hunter Mountain** (⊠ Box 295, Rte. 23A, Hunter 12442, ☎ 518/263–4223) has 48 runs, 13 lifts, and a 1,600-ft drop. **Ski Windham** (⊠ C. D. Lane Rd., Windham 12496, ☎ 518/734–4300) has 33 runs, 7 lifts, and a 1,600-ft drop.

Shopping

Shopping is a major diversion in the Catskills, with a scattering of factory outlets, shopping villages, auctions, flea markets, crafts fairs, antiques shops, and galleries. **Woodbury Common Premium Outlets** (⊠ Rte. 32, Exit 16 off I–87, Harriman, ☎ 914/928–6840) has more than 200 discount stores, including Gucci and Barneys.

SARATOGA SPRINGS AND THE NORTH COUNTRY

Saratoga Springs, about 30 mi north of Albany, is one of American high society's oldest summer playgrounds. The six-week Thoroughbred-racing season, starting in mid-July, is the high point of the year. Northwest of Saratoga, and in stark contrast, are the rugged mountains, immense forests, and abundant lakes and streams of Adirondack Park, the largest park expanse in the continental United States. The North Country—anchored by the resort towns of Lake Placid and Lake George—hums year-round. Hikers descend in the summer, autumn brings leaf peepers, and with the snow come many winter-sports enthusiasts.

Visitor Information

Greater Saratoga: Chamber of Commerce (⊠ 28 Clinton St., Saratoga Springs 12866, ☎ 518/584–3255). **Lake George:** Regional Chamber of Commerce (⊠ 2176 Rte. 9, Lake George 12845, ☎ 518/668–5755). **Lake Placid:** Visitors Bureau (⊠ 216 Main St., Olympic Center 12946, ☎ 518/523–2445 or 800/447–5224). **Saranac Lake:** Chamber of Commerce (⊠ 30 Main St., 12983, ☎ 518/891–1990 or 800/347–1992).

Arriving and Departing

By Bus

Adirondack Trailways (☎ 914/339–4230 or 800/225–6815) provides bus service to Saratoga Springs, Lake Placid, Lake George, Chestertown, Bolton Landing (summer only), and many other area towns.

By Car

The primary route through the region is the Northway (I–87), which links Albany and Montréal.

By Plane

The principal airports are in New York City (207 mi south of Lake George) and Montréal (177 mi north of Lake George). Other airports serving the region are in Albany, Syracuse, and Burlington, Vermont.

By Train

Amtrak (☎ 800/872–7245) operates the *Adirondack,* a daily train between New York and Montréal, with many North Country stops.

Exploring Saratoga Springs and the North Country

People have been frequenting **Saratoga Springs** for its medicinal properties since the late 18th century. In the late 19th century it emerged as one of North America's principal resorts, both for its spa waters and its gambling casino. It also became a horse-racing center in the 1890s, and August still brings crowds for the race meet and yearling sale.

You can still see mineral-water springs bubbling from the ground—22 are currently visible—at **Saratoga Spa State Park.** Listed on the National Register of Historic Places, this 2,000-acre park has walking paths to the springs. Mineral baths and massages are available at the Roosevelt and Lincoln Park bathhouses. Tennis courts, swimming pools, and golf courses are available as well. ✉ *19 Roosevelt Dr., between U.S. 9 and Rte. 50, Saratoga Springs 12866,* ☎ *518/584–2000.* ✑ *$5 for parking May–Sept.*

Across from the Saratoga Race Course (☞ Spectator Sports, *below*), site of the renowned horse races, is the **National Museum of Racing.** Its centerpiece is the Hall of Fame, which has video clips of races featuring the horses and jockeys enshrined here. ✉ *191 Union Ave.,* ☎ *518/584–0400.* ✑ *$5.*

Yaddo (✉ Union Ave., ☎ 518/587–4886), once a private home, is now a highly regarded retreat for artists and writers. The rose garden is open to the public.

The **National Museum of Dance** features rotating exhibits on the history and development of the art form, as well as the Hall of Fame, which honors dance luminaries. The studios allow visitors to watch or participate in a dance class. ✉ *99 S. Broadway,* ☎ *518/584–2225.* ✑ *$3.50. Closed Mon. June–Dec.; Jan.–May except by appointment.*

The **Historical Society of Saratoga Springs** is housed in Canfield Casino—an 1870s Italianate building that was a gambling casino. A museum devoted to the town's colorful gambling history occupies three floors of the building. ✉ *Congress Park, Broadway and Circular St.,* ☎ *518/584–6920.* ✑ *$3. Closed Mon.–Tues. Oct.–Apr.*

In the Adirondack Mountain range, the 6-million-acre **Adirondack Park** encompasses 1,000 mi of rivers and more than 2,500 lakes and ponds. The southern sections are more developed, while the High Peaks region, in the north-central sector, offers the greatest variety of wilderness activities. Adirondack Park differs in several important ways from most public lands. Only about 47% of the park is public property; the rest is owned by individuals, corporations, clubs, and municipalities. You can't set foot in these sections without the owner's approval. There are no user fees and no "entrances," other than occasional road signs marking boundaries. Park services are relatively limited. In the middle of the park there are two **Visitor Interpretive Centers** (✉ Rte. 30, 1 mi north of Paul Smith's College, Paul Smiths, ☎ 518/ 327–3000; Rte. 28N, Newcomb, ☎ 518/582–2000).

Lake George, 40 mi north of Saratoga, is a kitschy tourist town catering to families, with amusement parks, souvenir shops, and miniature golf. Cruises from the town dock are extremely popular from May through October; contact **Lake George Shoreline Cruises** (☎ 518/668–4644) and the **Lake George Steamboat Company** (☎ 518/668–5777).

Just south of town is **Great Escape and Splashwater Kingdom,** the North Country's largest theme park. Since it includes a water park, it's a good place to head on a hot day. ⊠ *U.S. 9,* ☎ *518/792–3500.* ☞ *$28.99. Closed Mon.–Thurs. Nov.–mid.-May.*

Kids will love the caves and gorge at **Natural Stone Bridge and Caves.** ⊠ *Exit 26 off I–87, near Pottersville,* ☎ *518/494–2283.* ☞ *$7.50. Closed Sept.–May.*

Those not big on hiking can sample the beauty of the Adirondack region at **Ausable Chasm,** where there are massive stone formations. Visitors amble along paths, up and down quite a few stairs, and over an awesome footbridge. For an extra fee you can raft down the river, too. ⊠ *U.S. 9, just north of Keeseville,* ☎ *518/834–7454.* ☞ *Walking tour $12.95; walking and rafting $19. Closed mid.-Oct.–May.*

Another natural attraction, **High Falls Gorge** (⊠ off Rte. 86, near Wilmington, ☎ 518/946–2278; ☞ $6, up to $20 in winter, includes snowshoes), has three dramatic waterfalls and a self-guided tour on steel bridges and paths along the Ausable River. In winter, you can clamp ice-cleats to your shoes and trek through the frozen gorge, reminiscent of an ice castle. To warm up afterward, roast marshmallows around a campfire.

Lake Placid is the hub of the northern Adirondacks. This mountain town is probably best known for its **1932 and 1980 winter Olympics facilities.** The Ice Arena and speed-skating oval are in the center of town; the ski jump is 2 mi out; **Whiteface Mountain** (scene of the downhill competitions) is a 10-minute drive away, on Route 86; and the bobsled run at Mt. Van Hoevenberg, on Route 73, is 15 minutes away. Call 518/523–1655 or 800/462–6236 for more information.

John Brown Farm was the home and burial place of the famed abolitionist. ⊠ *Off Rte. 73 by the Olympic ski jumps,* ☎ *518/523–3900.* ☞ *Free. House closed Mon.–Tues. and Nov.–Apr.*

The serenity and mountain air of **Saranac Lake** (elevation: 1,600 ft) made it a health resort for the tubercular in the late 19th century. Ten miles west of Lake Placid, it is today the jumping-off point for canoe trips (☞ Outdoor Activities and Sports, *below*). Much of the lake is part of the **St. Regis Canoe Area,** which is off-limits to powerboats.

★ Overlooking Blue Mountain Lake, the open-air **Adirondack Museum** has a day's worth of exhibits on the history, culture, and crafts of the region. The *New York Times* calls it "the best museum of its kind in the world." ⊠ *Rte. 30,* ☎ *518/352–7311.* ☞ *$10. Closed mid-Oct.– mid-June.*

Dining and Lodging

Saratoga is indisputably the North Country's culinary champion in quality and variety, with Lake Placid a distant second. Elsewhere expect large portions, home cooking, and a rustic atmosphere. Lodging runs the gamut from roadside motels to resorts.

Bolton Landing

$$$$ ✕☷ **Sagamore Resort.** The large public rooms and gracious style of this grand resort on an island in Lake George will take you back to another era. The rooms are spread among the main hotel and lakeside lodges. Each of the six dining rooms ($$–$$$$) has its own atmosphere and cuisine, ranging from the formal, slightly nouvelle touches of Trillium (reservations essential, jacket required, no lunch) to the hearty burgers and steaks of Mr. Brown's Pub. You'll find plenty of opportunity for activity here, including boating, tennis, and golf. ⊠ *110 Sagamore Rd., 12814,* ☎ *518/644–9400,* ℻ *518/644–2626. 350 rooms. 6 restaurants, pool, golf, tennis, health club. AE, D, DC, MC, V.* 🕸

Chestertown

$$$–$$$$ ✕🏨 **Friends Lake Inn.** Most of this inn's cozy guest rooms have moun-
★ tain or lake views. There's plenty to do in the area—cross-country skiing, hiking, swimming, or just relaxing in a big Adirondack-style chair on the inn's spacious lawn. The regionally acclaimed restaurant here serves new American cuisine. ⊠ *Friends Lake Rd., 12817,* ☎ *518/494–4751,* ℻ *518/494–4616. 17 rooms. Restaurant. MC, V. MAP.* 🕸

Keene Valley

$ ✕ **Noon Mark Diner.** This classic small-town diner is the perfect spot for lunch, and if you've already eaten, at least stop in for some homemade pie. The food here is better than your average greasy spoon, and you'll get a good sense of the local scene. ⊠ *Rte. 73,* ☎ *518/576–4499. D, MC, V.*

Lake Placid

$ ✕ **Cottage Cafe.** You can sink your teeth into a Stuffed Shirt sandwich at this always-crowded café overlooking Mirror Lake. When the weather's good, the open-air deck is the perfect place for cocktails. Lunch and dinner fare include salads and sandwiches. ⊠ *1 Main St., across from the Mirror Lake Inn,* ☎ *518/523–9845. AE, D, MC, V.*

$ ✕ **Tail o' the Pup.** Conveniently located halfway between Lake Placid
★ and Saranac Lake, this classic roadside restaurant specializes in savory barbecued items, including chicken and ribs. You can dine inside, at the outdoor picnic tables, or in your car—honk twice for service. ⊠ *Rte. 86, Ray Brook,* ☎ *518/891–5092. MC, V. Closed Oct.–May.*

$$$$ ✕🏨 **Lake Placid Lodge.** Originally a rustic lodge built before the turn
★ of the 20th century, this small hotel embodies the spirit of Lake Placid's past *and* cossets guests with the comforts of luxurious amenities. Rooms are furnished with twig and birch-bark furniture and Adirondack antiques; amenities include featherbeds, terry-cloth robes, and soaking tubs. All have granite fireplaces. If seeking privacy, ask about the cabins that sit right on the shores of the lake. The dining room's new American menu ($$$–$$$$) changes seasonally but might include grilled Seattle salmon with lime and ginger, sun-dried-tomato couscous and baby vegetables, roast spring lamb with rosemary-olive polenta, grilled asparagus, and eggplant. ⊠ *Whiteface Inn Rd., Box 550, 12946,* ☎ *518/523–2700,* ℻ *518/523–1124. 17 rooms, 17 cabins. Restaurant. AE, MC, V. BP.* 🕸

$$$–$$$$ 🏨 **Mirror Lake Inn.** On the shores of Mirror Lake, this stately Adirondack inn is within walking distance of downtown Lake Placid. The atmosphere here is truly genteel. The elegant interior includes an antiques-filled library and a living room with stone fireplaces and walnut floors. The rooms are spread among several buildings; those on the lake have private balconies. Guests take advantage of the outdoor sports, spa, and meeting rooms. ⊠ *5 Mirror Lake Dr., 12946,* ☎ *518/523–2544,* ℻ *518/523–2871. 128 rooms. 2 restaurants, pools, tennis. AE, D, DC, MC, V.* 🕸

$$–$$$$ 🏨 **Lake Placid Resort Holiday Inn.** This friendly resort high on a hill above Lake Placid's Main Street is by no means your typical Holiday Inn: The service is personal, original art decorates public spaces, and

amenities range from coffeemakers and microwaves in every room to a Scottish-style links golf course. The lobby's floor-to-ceiling windows overlook Mirror Lake and the mountains beyond. ⊠ *1 Olympic Dr., Lake Placid 12946,* ☎ *518/523–2556,* FAX *518/523–9410. 210 rooms. 4 restaurants, pool, golf, tennis, health club. AE, D, DC, MC, V.* 🍽

Saranac Lake

$$$$ 🛏 **The Point.** Onetime home of William Avery Rockefeller, this all-in-
★ clusive elegantly rustic inn is the Adirondacks' and one of the coun-
try's most exclusive and expensive retreats, with daily rates about $1,000 to $2,000. You pay in advance—that way, you feel more like a guest for the weekend: You can fix yourself a drink from one of several bars, take out one the speedboats for waterskiing, borrow snow-
shoes and trek around the property, and even have a seven-course dinner served in your room, all without having to take out your wallet. There are no signs pointing here; you have to book a room in order to get the address. ⊠ *HCR 1, Box 65, 12983,* ☎ *518/891–5678 or 800/255–
3530,* FAX *518/891–1152. 11 rooms. Restaurant. AE, FAP.* 🍽

Saratoga Springs

$$$–$$$$ ✕ **43 Phila Bistro.** The innovative offerings at this Saratoga hot spot may include duck, ahi tuna, rack of lamb, or steak. ⊠ *43 Phila St.,* ☎ *518/584–2720. MC, V. Closed Sun. Sept.–May.*

$$–$$$ ✕ **Eartha's Kitchen.** This small bistro is a local favorite, especially for
★ the mesquite-grilled seafood and meat dishes that come from Eartha, the wood-fired grill. The ever-changing, eclectic menu incorporates the freshest ingredients available. ⊠ *60 Court St.,* ☎ *518/583–0602. Reser-
vations essential. DC, MC, V. Closed Mon.–Tues. Sept.–May. No lunch.*

$$–$$$$ 🛏 **Adelphi Hotel.** This downtown Saratoga showplace is extravagant and fun. The opulent lobby with slowly rotating fans is done in a style so reminiscent of La Belle Epoque that one could picture the Divine Sarah Bernhardt holding court amid its splendor. No two rooms are the same: furnishings are eclectic—and recherché. ⊠ *365 Broadway, 12866,* ☎ *518/587–4688. 38 rooms. AE, MC, V. Closed Nov.–Apr.*

Motels

🛏 **Days Inn of Lake George** (⊠ 1454 Rte. 9, Suite 1, Lake George 12845, ☎ 518/793–3196 or 800/329–7466), 104 rooms; restaurant, pool; *$$–$$$.*

🛏 **Wildwood on the Lake** (⊠ 88 Saranac Ave., Lake Placid, 12946, ☎ 518/523–2624, FAX 518/523–3248), 35 rooms; pools; *$–$$.*

Campgrounds

⚠ **Adirondack Loj Wilderness Campground** (⊠ Off Rte. 73, Box 867, Lake Placid 12946, ☎ 518/523–3441), on Heart Lake, has 34 tent sites and 15 lean-tos, water, picnic tables, seasonal showers, and toilets, but no gas or electric. It is run by the Adirondack Mountain Club, and staffers will provide information about camping throughout the High Peaks region.

The Arts

Adirondack Lakes Center for the Arts (⊠ Rte. 28, Blue Mountain Lake, ☎ 518/352–7715) is a multipurpose arts center that presents art exhibits and concerts and has coffeehouses and workshops. The **Saratoga Performing Arts Center** (☎ 518/587–3330) hosts the New York City Opera, the New York City Ballet, the Philadelphia Orchestra, and the Newport Jazz Festival–Saratoga, as well as big-name pop stars, from May to September.

Outdoor Activities and Sports

Middle Earth Expeditions (⊠ HCR 1, Box 37, Rte. 73, Lake Placid 12946, ☎ 518/523–9572) leads tours and provides guides for individuals or groups in canoeing, white-water rafting, fishing, and backpacking. The friendly folks at **McDonald's Adirondack Challenge** (⊠ Rte. 30, Lake Clear, ☎ 518/891–1176) sell and rent gear for canoeing, cross-country skiing, snowshoeing, and hiking.

Biking

Roadside signs mark several bike routes, most quite hilly, that wind through the North Country. For a map of routes in the area, contact the **Saranac Lake Chamber of Commerce** (☞ Visitor Information, *above*).

Canoeing

The 170-mi **Raquette River** and the **St. Regis Canoe Area,** east of Saranac Lake, are among the best and most popular canoe routes in the North Country. **Jones Outfitters Ltd.** (⊠ 37 Main St., Lake Placid, ☎ 518/523–3468), on Mirror Lake, rents canoes and kayaks. **Middle Earth Expeditions** (☞ *above*) leads canoeing and white-water trips, and **McDonald's Adirondack Challenge** (☞ *above*) sells and rents gear for canoeing.

Fishing

Brook and lake trout are taken year-round on the lakes and streams of the North Country. Licenses can be obtained at town or county clerk offices, sporting goods stores, and outfitters.

Golf

Among the more challenging courses are those at the **Whiteface Club** (⊠ Whiteface Inn Rd., Lake Placid, ☎ 518/523–2551), 18 holes; the **Sagamore Resort** (⊠ 110 Sagamore Rd., Bolton Landing, ☎ 518/644–9400), 18 holes; and the **Lake Placid Resort** (⊠ Mirror Lake Dr., Lake Placid, ☎ 518/523–4460), 44 holes.

Hiking

The most popular area for hiking is the High Peaks region, accessible from the Lake Placid area in the north, Keene and Keene Valley in the east, and Newcomb in the south. For more information contact the **Adirondack Mountain Club** (⊠ ADK, Box 867, Lake Placid 12946, ☎ 518/523–3441).

Rafting

Hudson River Rafting Company (⊠ 1 Main St., North Creek, ☎ 800/888–7238) offers day trips on the Hudson, the Sacandaga, and the Black River from April to October.

Spectator Sports

Lake Placid summer and winter athletic competitions: Contact the **Olympic Authority** (☎ 518/523–1655 or 800/462–6236). Events include concerts, ski jumping, and figure-skating shows. **Horse Racing:** The six-week Thoroughbred-racing season starts in mid-July at **Saratoga Race Course** (⊠ Union Ave., Saratoga Springs, ☎ 518/584–6200).

Ski Areas

Cross-Country

Mt. Van Hoevenberg, on Route 73, has 30 mi of groomed tracks, which connect with the **Jackrabbit Trail,** a 33-mi network of ski trails through the High Peaks region connecting Lake Placid, Saranac Lake, and Paul Smiths. For information and conditions contact **Adirondack Ski Touring Council** (⊠ Box 843, Lake Placid 12946, ☎ 518/523–1365).

Downhill

Whiteface Mountain Ski Center (✉ 8 mi northeast of Lake Placid, Wilmington 12997, ☎ 518/946–2223) has 65 runs, 10 lifts, a 3,351-ft vertical drop, and snowmaking capabilities.

Shopping

The region's maple syrup and sharp cheddar cheese make great gifts. **Blue Mountain Lake** and **Lake Placid** are good bets for crafts hunting. Look for birch-bark baskets, pottery, and an array of jewelry, leather work, and quilting. Adirondack-style furniture also makes a superb souvenir. The **Adirondack Crafts Center** (✉ Lake Placid Center for the Arts, 93 Saranac Ave., Lake Placid, ☎ 518/523–2062) is a year-round facility where more than 300 local artisans show their wares.

LEATHERSTOCKING COUNTRY AND THE FINGER LAKES

Visitor Information

Cooperstown: Chamber of Commerce (✉ 31 Chestnut St., 13326, ☎ 607/547–9983). **Leatherstocking Country:** (✉ 327 N. Main St., Herkimer 13350, ☎ 315/866–1500 or 800/233–8778). **Finger Lakes Association:** (✉ 309 Lake St., Penn Yan 14527, ☎ 315/536–7488 or 800/548–4386). **Clearly Cayuga:** (✉ 904 E. Shore Dr., Ithaca 14850, ☎ 877/422–9842). **Seneca County:** Chamber of Commerce (✉ Box 294, 2022 Rte. 5/20, Seneca Falls 13148, ☎ 315/568–2906 or 800/732–1848).

Arriving and Departing

The Leatherstocking region is 200 mi to 300 mi from New York City via the New York State Thruway (I–87) and, from Kingston, Route 28. I–90, at this point also called the New York State Thruway, runs east–west through both Leatherstocking Country and the Finger Lakes, connecting Albany with Buffalo. I–88 runs northeast–southwest, leading from Binghamton to just northwest of Albany.

Exploring Leatherstocking Country and the Finger Lakes

The early Yankees in their leather leggings gave the region its nickname; it is quintessential rural America, with gently rolling countryside, community chicken barbecues, and tree-shaded small towns. Cooperstown ★ � is home to the **National Baseball Hall of Fame** (✉ Main St., ☎ 607/547–7200, 🔊 $9.50), where displays and paintings honor the heroes, recall great moments, and trace the history of the game.

Binghamton has the **Roberson Museum and Science Center** (✉ 30 Front St., ☎ 607/772–0660; 🔊 $5), comprising a restored 1910 historic house, a complex of museums, and a planetarium.

� Kids are especially fond of Binghamton's wooded **Ross Park Zoo** (✉ 185 Park Ave., ☎ 607/724–5454; 🔊 $3.50), where animals (including tigers and a timber wolf pack) live in natural environments.

The 11 parallel **Finger Lakes,** from **Conesus Lake,** south of Rochester, to **Otisco Lake,** southwest of Syracuse, stretch north to south like long, narrow fingers through the rolling countryside of western New York. The region's diverse terrain—waterfalls, gorges, rocky hillsides, lush forests—is the perfect backdrop for the area's many vineyards and wineries. The two largest lakes, **Seneca** and **Cayuga,** have wine trails; the visitor center (Visitor Information, *above*) has brochures that map them out.

About 5 mi west of the north end of Cayuga Lake is **Seneca Falls,** where on July 18, 1848, 300 people attended America's first women's rights convention, held at the Wesleyan Methodist Chapel on 126 Falls Street. The **Women's Rights National Historical Park Visitor Center** (⊠ 136 Falls St., ☎ 315/568–2991), next door, has informative exhibits.

The design studios and factory of the **MacKenzie-Childs, Ltd.** empire are housed in an old country house and barn on the eastern shore of Cayuga Lake. You can see artisans creating the company's signature majolica pottery, glassware, and trimmings on weekdays at 9:30 AM. Reservations are recommended. ⊠ *Rte. 90, Aurora,* ☎ *315/364–7123.* ☜ *Tours $9.50. Closed Sun.*

Ithaca, at the tip of Cayuga Lake, is the home of both **Cornell University** and **Ithaca College.** The town is more spectacular than most others in the Finger Lakes because of the deep gorges and more than 100 waterfalls that lace it.

Geneva, at the northern tip of Seneca Lake, seems like a town preserved in time. Its South Main Street, overlooking the lake, is lined with 19th-century houses and century-old trees. The picturesque campuses of Hobart and William Smith colleges are here, too.

The village of Watkins Glen is at the southern end of Seneca Lake adjoining the 1,000-acre **Watkins Glen State Park** (⊠ *Rte. 14,* ☎ *607/535–4511).* The 1½-mi gorge here is highlighted by rock formations and 18 waterfalls. It's a great spot for hiking.

Rochester is the headquarters of the Eastman Kodak Company. The George Eastman House, onetime home of the company founder and photographic innovator, now houses the **International Museum of Photography,** the world's largest museum devoted to photographic art and technology. ⊠ *900 East Ave.,* ☎ *716/271–3361.* ☜ *$6.50. Closed Mon.*

It was in Rochester at **Susan B. Anthony's house** that the 19th-century women's rights advocate wrote *The History of Woman Suffrage.* The house is furnished in the style of the mid-1800s. ⊠ *17 Madison St.,* ☎ *716/235–6124.* ☜ *$5. Closed Mon.–Tues.*

In Corning the vastly expanded **Corning Museum of Glass** (⊠ 1 Museum Way, off Rte. 17, ☎ 607/937–5371; ☜ $6) contains a world-class collection of glass, a library covering everything ever written about the subject, and a self-guided tour of the Steuben glass factory.

Dining and Lodging

Cooperstown

$$$$ 🏨 **Otesaga Hotel.** This grand hotel, built circa 1909 on a smaller scale than most, is still quite formidable in Cooperstown. It wears the frown of age and is a bit set in its ways, but the Otesaga is still known as the fanciest place in town. ⊠ *Rte. 80 (Lake Rd.), 13326,* ☎ *607/547–9931,* FAX *607/547–9675. 135 rooms. 2 restaurants, pool, tennis. AE, D, MC, V. Closed Nov.–mid-Apr. MAP.*

$$–$$$ 🏨 **Fieldstone Farm.** A great place for families, this friendly, informal former farm has 178 acres of fields, big ponds, and woods. There's plenty to keep kids busy, too—from tennis and volleyball to fishing, Ping-Pong, and an 80-ft rec room. The accommodations, with two levels and kitchenettes, are more like town houses than rooms; cabins are available as well. ⊠ *Roses Hill Road off Rte. 26, Box 528, 13326,* ☎ *315/858–0295. 7 apartments, 13 cottages. Pool. D, DC, MC, V.* 🐾

Geneva

$$$$ 🏨 **Geneva on the Lake.** Built in 1910, this impressive Renaissance-style palazzo was modeled after the Villa Lancelotti in Frascati, Rome. Originally a private residence, it has served as a monastery and an apartment complex. Now part of a resort, the rooms here are spacious, some have fireplaces, and almost all have a view of the lake and formal gardens. ⊠ *1001 Lochland Rd., Rte. 14S, 14456,* ☎ *315/789–7190,* FAX *315/789–0322. 30 suites. Restaurant, pool. AE, D, MC, V. CP.* ⊛

Ithaca

$ ✗ **Moosewood Restaurant.** A vegetarian mecca famous for its cookbooks, Moosewood has been creating appealing eclectic fare for more than 25 years. Tall windows, warm yellow walls, and golden-hued wood furnishings provide a relaxing backdrop in which to savor dishes such as creamy sweet potato soup with ginger, *tortino di verdure* (layered roasted eggplant, potatoes, and zucchini with tomatoes, basil, and mozzarella), and Creole beans and rice. ⊠ *215 N. Cayuga St.,* ☎ *607/273–9610. Reservations not accepted. MC, V. No lunch Sun.*

BUFFALO AND NIAGARA FALLS

Visitor Information

Greater Buffalo: Convention and Visitors Bureau (⊠ 617 Main St., Suite 400, 14203, ☎ 716/852–0511 or 800/283–3256). **Niagara Falls:** Convention and Visitors Bureau (⊠ 4th and Niagara Sts., 14303, ☎ 716/284–2000).

Arriving and Departing

By Bus

Greyhound (☎ 800/231–2222) and **New York Trailways** (☎ 800/295–5555) serve Buffalo's bus station (⊠ 181 Ellicott St., at N. Division St.).

By Car

Access to both Buffalo and Chautauqua County is primarily via I–90, the New York State Thruway. From Buffalo, I–190 leads to Niagara Falls.

By Plane

The Buffalo-Niagara area is served by **Buffalo International Airport** (⊠ Genessee St., Cheektowaga, ☎ 716/630–6011). Flying time from New York City to Buffalo is one hour.

Exploring Buffalo, and Niagara Falls

Buffalo is a city of Victorian elegance, with many churches and strongly ethnic neighborhoods. Walk along downtown Buffalo's **Elmwood Avenue** for a taste of the city's eclectic mix of shops and restaurants. **Chippewa Street** (or the Chippewa District), known for its nightclubs and jazz bars, is another lively area in the heart of the city. Just north of downtown Buffalo is the **Albright-Knox Art Gallery** (⊠ 1285 Elmwood Ave., ☎ 716/882–8700). The modern art collection here, including works by Mondrian, Miró, and van Gogh, is superb. The Albright-Knox Gallery is on the western side of **Delaware Park** (⊠ Parkside and Elmwood Ave., ☎ 716/851–5806), a 350-acre park designed by Frederick Law Olmsted (the creator of New York City's Central Park). More than 23 acres of the park are dedicated to one of the oldest zoos in the country, the **Buffalo Zoo** (⊠ 300 Parkside Ave., ☎ 716/837–3900; ⊠ $7).

Niagara Falls, the most accessible and famous waterfall in the world, is actually three cataracts: the **American** and **Bridal Veil** falls, in New York, and **Horseshoe Falls,** in Ontario, Canada. More than 750,000 gallons of water flow each second in the summer.

For a good orientation to the falls, stop at the Niagara Visitor Center in the **Niagara Reservation State Park** (⊠ Prospect Park, Niagara Falls 14303, ☎ 716/278–1701), the oldest state park in the nation. **Goat Island** provides the closest view of the American Falls; cross to the Canadian side for the best view of Horseshoe Falls. The famous *Maid of the Mist* boat ride lets you view the falls from the water.

Dining and Lodging

Buffalo

$$–$$$ ✕ **The Hourglass.** This spot has been open for business for more than
★ 50 years and continues to maintain its reputation as one of greater Buffalo's best restaurants. All the Continental classics are available here— lamb chops, duck breast, sweetbreads—but the kitchen is especially proud of the seafood it turns out; try the Cape scallops or soft-shell crabs when they're available. ⊠ *981 Kenmore Ave., Kenmore,* ☎ *716/ 877–8788. AE, MC, V. Closed Sun.–Mon. No lunch.*

$–$$ ✕ **Just Pasta.** This popular Buffalo eatery is the perfect spot for a casual dinner. You'll find good simple pastas here: spinach-and-egg spaghetti with prosciutto, peas, and cream, and Gorgonzola ravioli with ricotta and tomato sauce. ⊠ *307 Bryant St.,* ☎ *716/881–1888. AE, DC, MC, V. Closed Sun.*

$$ 🏨 **Hyatt Regency Buffalo.** This 16-floor hotel is housed in a historic office building, erected in 1923; the building was converted to a hotel in 1983. ⊠ *2 Fountain Plaza, 14202,* ☎ *716/856–1234,* FAX *716/852– 6157. 395 rooms. 3 restaurants. AE, D, MC, V.* ✒

Niagara Falls

$$–$$$ ✕🏨 **Red Coach Inn.** This 1923 inn has an Old England atmosphere. One- and two-bedroom suites are luxurious, with gas-burning fireplaces and kitchenettes; all but two of the rooms have a spectacular view of the upper rapids. The restaurant's specialties ($$–$$$$) include prime rib—the patio is splendid for summer dining. ⊠ *2 Buffalo Ave., Niagara Falls 14303,* ☎ *716/282–1459. 14 suites. Restaurant. AE, D, DC, MC, V.*

$$–$$$ 🏨 **Holiday Inn Select.** You can't beat the location of this hotel, only 1,600 ft from the falls. This is Niagara's largest hotel, with plenty of amenities, including a whirlpool, saunas, and convention and business services. ⊠ *3rd and Old Falls Sts., Niagara Falls 14303,* ☎ *716/285– 3361,* FAX *716/285–3900. 400 rooms. Restaurant, pool, health club. AE, D, DC, MC, V.* ✒

Nightlife and the Arts

With two State University of New York campuses as well as several other schools, Buffalo has a changing assortment of clubs and bars. Stroll along Elmwood Avenue, near Buffalo State College, or on Main Street, near the University of Buffalo, to sample the college scene.

Shea's Performing Arts Center (⊠ 646 Main St., Buffalo, ☎ 716/847– 1410) presents concerts, opera, dance, and touring theater performances, which have included shows like *Stomp* and *Rent.* Contact the Buffalo Philharmonic Orchestra for performance schedules (⊠ Kleinhans Music Hall, 370 Pennsylvania Ave., Buffalo, ☎ 716/885–5000).

Outdoor Activities and Sports

Spectator Sports

There's always a sports event to see in Buffalo. Check out one of the city's local teams: The **Buffalo Bills Football Team** (⊠ Ralph Wilson Stadium, 1 Bills Dr., Orchard Park, ☎ 716/649–0015); **Buffalo Sabres Hockey** (⊠ Marine Midland Arena, Seymour H. Knox III Plaza, Buffalo, ☎ 716/855–4100); or the minor league **Buffalo Bisons Baseball Team** (⊠ Dunn Tire Park, 275 Washington St., Buffalo, ☎ 716/846–2000).

NORTH CAROLINA

Updated by
Lisa H. Towle

Capital	Raleigh
Population	7,846,220
Motto	To Be Rather Than to Seem
State Bird	Cardinal
State Flower	Dogwood
Postal Abbreviation	NC

Statewide Visitor Information

North Carolina Division of Tourism, Film and Sports Development (⊠ 301 N. Wilmington St., Raleigh 27601, ☎ 919/733–8372 or 800/847–4862). **Welcome centers:** I–77S near Charlotte, I–77N near Dobson, I–85S near Kings Mountain, I–85N near Norlina, I–95S near Rowland, I–95N near Roanoke Rapids, I–26W near Columbus, and I–40W near Waynesville.

Scenic Drives

The **Blue Ridge Parkway** runs from the Virginia state line to the Great Smoky Mountains National Park entrance near Cherokee. In North Carolina the recreation-oriented byway extends more than 250 mi and offers stunning mountain views, nature exhibits, historic sites, parks, picnic areas, and hiking trails. **U.S. 441** from Cherokee to Gatlinburg, Tennessee, cuts through the middle of the national park for about 35 mi, climbing to a crest of 6,643 ft at Clingmans Dome, a short distance from Newfound Gap. Portions of **U.S. 64** travel through the Hickory Nut Gorge between Lake Lure and Chimney Rock and the Cullasaja Gorge between Lake Toxaway and Franklin, affording spectacular views of mountain peaks and cascading waterfalls. **Route 12,** which connects the Outer Banks, offers great views of the ocean and landscapes dotted with lighthouses and weathered beach cottages.

National and State Parks

The state tourism division's travel guide (☞ Statewide Visitor Information, *above*) includes a complete listing of state and national parks and recreation areas as well as state forests.

National Parks

Cape Hatteras National Seashore (⊠ Rte. 1, Box 675, Manteo 27954, ☎ 252/473–2111; ⌨ free), a natural habitat for hundreds of species of birds, wild animals, and aquatic life, stretches 75 mi from Nags Head to Ocracoke and encompasses 30,318 acres of marshland and sandy beaches. **Cape Lookout National Seashore** (⊠ 131 Charles St., Harkers Island 28531, ☎ 252/728–2250; ⌨ free) extends 56 mi from Portsmouth Island to Beaufort Inlet and includes 28,400 acres of uninhabited land and marsh, accessible only by boat or ferry. Portsmouth, a deserted village that was inhabited from 1753 until 1971, has been restored and is open to the public from April through November. **Great Smoky Mountains National Park** (⊠ 107 Park Headquarters Rd., Gatlinburg, TN 37738, ☎ 423/436–1200; ⌨ free), with 9 million visitors a year, is the most visited national park in the country. Its 521,000 acres straddle the North Carolina–Tennessee border and have camping, hiking, fishing, historic sites, and nature lore (☞ Tennessee). To enter the park from North Carolina, take U.S. 441 north from Cherokee.

State Parks

Many of North Carolina's 43 state parks and recreation areas preserve unique geological and biological resources. Home to extremely rare plants and animals is **Lake Waccamaw State Park** (✉ 1866 State Park Dr., Lake Waccamaw 28450, ☎ 910/646–4748), which has boating, camping, fishing, and picnicking. **Jockey's Ridge State Park** (✉ Box 592, Nags Head 27959, ☎ 252/441–7132) offers hang-gliding instruction and flights from the tallest sand dune in the East. **Eno River State Park** (✉ 6101 Cole Mill Rd., Durham 27705, ☎ 919/383–1686) is a green, wild, and watery buffer in an urban area. It includes a swinging bridge, white-water rapids, hiking, fishing, and primitive camping. **Mt. Mitchell State Park** (✉ Rte. 5, Box 700, Burnsville 28714, ☎ 828/675–4611) has tent camping and a picnic area and organizes guided nature walks on the highest mountain in the East (6,684 ft).

THE PIEDMONT

The Piedmont is the heartland of North Carolina, a vast area of rolling hills that extends from the coastal plain, which is east of the Triangle area (Raleigh, Durham, and Chapel Hill), to the foothills of the Blue Ridge Mountains, which are west of Charlotte and the Triad area (Greensboro, Winston-Salem, and High Point). Scattered along I–40, I–77, and I–85, the major arteries of the region, are the state's biggest towns, cities, and industries. Here also are large rivers and woodlands; historic villages dating from the mid-1700s; crafts, antiques, and outlet shops; world-renowned colleges and universities; and one of the largest concentrations of golf courses in the world.

Visitor Information

Charlotte: INFO! Charlotte (✉ 330 S. Tryon St., 28202, ☎ 704/331–2700 or 800/231–4636). **Durham:** Convention & Visitors Bureau (✉ 101 E. Morgan St., 27701, ☎ 919/687–0288 or 800/446–8604). **Greensboro:** Convention & Visitors Bureau (✉ 317 S. Greene St., 27401, ☎ 336/274–2282 or 800/344–2282). **Raleigh:** Capital Area Visitor Center (✉ 301 N. Blount St., 27611, ☎ 919/733–3456); Convention and Visitors Bureau (✉ 421 Fayetteville St. Mall, Suite 1505, 27601, ☎ 919/834–5900 or 800/849–8499). **Winston-Salem:** Convention & Visitors Bureau (✉ 601 N. Cherry St., Suite 100, 27102, ☎ 336/777–3796 or 800/331–7018).

Arriving and Departing

By Bus

Greyhound/Carolina Trailways (☎ 800/231–2222) provides service to Charlotte, Raleigh, Durham, Chapel Hill, Greensboro, and Winston-Salem.

By Car

I–40, U.S. 64, and U.S. 74 run east–west through the Piedmont; I–77 runs north from Charlotte; I–85 runs from Charlotte northeast through Greensboro and the Triangle area.

By Plane

Major carriers serve **Charlotte-Douglas International Airport** (✉ 5501 Josh Birmingham Blvd., Charlotte, ☎ 704/359–4013), **Raleigh-Durham International Airport** (✉ 1600 Terminal Blvd., Morrisville, ☎ 919/840–2123), and **Piedmont Triad International Airport** (✉ 6451 Bryan Blvd., Greensboro, ☎ 336/665–5666). Taxi and limousine services are available at all airports.

By Train

Amtrak's (☎ 800/872–7245) *Carolinian* provides daily service to stations in 12 Piedmont cities, while the *Piedmont* connects nine cities daily. The *Crescent* services five cities and the *Silver Service* trains make local stops.

Exploring the Piedmont

Charlotte, the region's largest city, is known as a financial center and prides itself on its cosmopolitan flair. At **Discovery Place** (⊠ 301 N. Tryon St., ☎ 704/372–6261 or 800/935–0553; ☞ $6.50), an award-winning hands-on science museum, there's a touch tank, aquariums, an indoor rain forest, an Omnimax theater, a planetarium, and special exhibits.

The **Hezekiah Alexander Homesite and Charlotte Museum of History,** built in 1774, is the city's oldest dwelling. The site, which was named for the settler who built it, includes a log kitchen; costumed docents give guided tours. ⊠ *3500 Shamrock Dr.,* ☎ *704/568–1774.* ☞ *Museum $3; museum and homesite $4; grounds free. Closed Mon.*

Though it has displayed art since 1936, the **Mint Museum of Art** was built in 1837 as a U.S. mint. Its permanent collection includes American and European decorative and fine art, as well as pre-Columbian and Spanish colonial objects. It has hosted internationally acclaimed exhibits. ⊠ *2730 Randolph Rd.,* ☎ *704/337–2000.* ☞ *$6. Closed Mon.*

The **Mint Museum of Craft & Design** in Charlotte's center city features collections of ceramics, glass, fiber, metal, and wood. ⊠ *220 N. Tryon Rd.,* ☎ *704/337–2000.* ☞ *$6. Closed Mon.*

Straddling the North Carolina–South Carolina border near Charlotte is **Paramount's Carowinds** (⊠ 14523 Carowinds Blvd., off I–77, ☎ 704/588–2600 or 800/888–4386; ☞ $35), a 100-acre amusement park with water rides and movie-theme rides and shows.

Greensboro, an hour and a half north of Charlotte on I–85, is the largest city in the Triad. **Guilford Courthouse National Military Park** (⊠ 2332 New Garden Rd., ☎ 336/288–1776; ☞ free) has more than 200 acres of wooded hiking trails, monuments, and military memorabilia dating back to the Revolutionary War.

There's a dinosaur gallery, dozens of gems and minerals, and lemurs, snakes, and amphibians at the **Natural Science Center of Greensboro** (⊠ 4301 Lawndale Dr., ☎ 336/288–3769; ☞ $3.50). Young children will enjoy the petting zoo.

Forty minutes south of Greensboro on U.S. 220, the **North Carolina Zoological Park** (⊠ 4401 Zoo Pkwy., ☎ 336/879–7000 or 800/488–0444; ☞ $8), in Asheboro, is home to more than 1,100 animals and 60,000 exotic and tropical plants. The African Plains exhibit alone is larger than most zoos.

A half hour west of Greensboro on I–40 is **Winston-Salem,** whose residents are known for their support of the arts and the city's museums. **Old Salem,** a restored 18th-century village, re-creates the life of the Moravians, a Protestant sect that settled in the area in 1766. The **Museum of Early Southern Decorative Arts,** also in the village, displays period furnishings. ⊠ *600 S. Main St.,* ☎ *336/721–7350.* ☞ *Entry to Old Salem $15, to Old Salem and Museum of Early Southern Decorative Arts $20.*

An hour's drive east from Greensboro on I–85 will bring you to **Durham,** a city once known for its tobacco production but known today as the home of Duke University and an eclectic arts scene.

Duke University Chapel (⊠ Chapel Dr., West Campus, ☎ 919/681–1704; ☜ free), an ornate neo-Gothic cathedral, is open for tours and free organ demonstrations.

The 55-acre **Sarah P. Duke Gardens** (⊠ main entrance at Anderson St., Duke University's West Campus, ☎ 919/684–3698; ☜ free) has landscaped and woodland gardens, a wisteria-draped gazebo, and a Japanese garden with a lily pond filled with goldfish.

☾ The **North Carolina Museum of Life and Science** (⊠ 433 Murray Ave., ☎ 919/220–5429; ☜ $8) has exhibits ranging from life-size dinosaur models and NASA artifacts to Carolina wildlife. The Magic Wings House has tropical plants and 1,000 exotic butterflies in open flight.

In Chapel Hill, 15 minutes south of Durham on U.S. 15/501, you can stargaze, take classes, and attend narrated presentations, including ☾ laser and children's shows, at the University of North Carolina's **Morehead Planetarium** (⊠ 250 E. Franklin St., ☎ 919/962–1236; ☜ $4), one of the largest planetariums in the country.

Raleigh, the state's capital, is a 30-minute drive from Chapel Hill on I–40. Its downtown is easily explored on foot. The Greek Revival–style **state capitol** (⊠ Capitol Square, ☎ 919/733–4994; ☜ free), completed in 1840, commands the highest point in Capitol Square. The **North Carolina Museum of History** (⊠ 5 E. Edenton St., ☎ 919/715–0200; ☜ free) combines artifacts, audiovisual programs, and interactive exhibits to bring the state's history to life. The **Executive Mansion** (⊠ 200 N. Blount St., ☎ 919/733–3456; ☜ free), a turn-of-the-20th-century Queen Anne–style structure in brick with gingerbread trim, is the governor's home.

☾ The **North Carolina Museum of Natural Sciences** (⊠ 11 W. Jones St., ☎ 919/733–7450; ☜ free) is an elegant and airy institution. The skeleton of Acrocanthosaurus, a giant carnivore that lived in the South 110 million years ago and preyed on dinosaurs larger than itself, is featured in a multistory glass-enclosed tower.

☾ In addition to being an architectural showplace, **Exploris** (⊠ 201 E. Hargett St., ☎ 919/834–4040; ☜ $6) is a children's museum and science center focusing on language, culture, geography, global trade, and communications.

The **North Carolina Museum of Art,** on a 140-acre tract near Raleigh's western edge, has exhibits representing 5,000 years of artistic heritage. The Museum Cafe is a favorite for lunch or Friday-night entertainment. ⊠ *2110 Blue Ridge Rd.,* ☎ *919/839–6262.* ☜ *Free. Closed Mon.*

Dining and Lodging

The Piedmont has a growing number of upscale restaurants and ethnic eateries, as well as restaurants that specialize in the more traditional—barbecue, fresh seafood, fried chicken, and country ham. Many city hotels have weekend packages with discounted rates.

Chapel Hill

$$$–$$$$ ✕▥ **Fearrington House.** On a 200-year-old farm, this elegant French-
★ style country inn anchors a bustling village center and is a member of Relais & Châteaux. Rooms are decorated with chintz, antiques, and original art. The restaurant's prix-fixe menu is a blend of regional and French cuisines. ⊠ *Fearrington Village Center, Pittsboro 27312,* ☎ *919/542–2121,* ⅎAX *919/542–4202. 31 rooms. 2 restaurants. AE, MC, V.*

Charlotte

$$–$$$ ✕ **Atlantic Beer & Ice Co.** This uptown eatery has a cigar and Scotch bar with billiards on the top floor, a restaurant and bar on the main floor, and a jazz club on the lower level. The seasonal menu is broad: knockwurst and pastrami sandwiches to tenderloin tips. Beef is always a good bet. ✉ *330 N. Tryon St.,* ☎ *704/339–0566. AE, DC, MC, V.*

$$–$$$ ✕ **Campania.** The walls are golden and textured, the room is full of rich wood and candlelight, and the music is genuinely Italian, from opera to contemporary. The *gamberoni Mergellina,* shrimp sautéed in garlic butter and herbs, and linguini Posillipo, clams paired with red or white sauce, are characteristic of the menu. ✉ *6414 Rea Rd.,* ☎ *704/541–8505. AE, D, MC, V.*

$$–$$$ ✕🏨 **Hyatt Charlotte at Southpark.** Rooms surround a four-story atrium lobby at this modern hotel, popular with business travelers. The restaurant serves northern Italian cuisine. ✉ *5501 Carnegie Blvd., 28209-3462,* ☎ *704/554–1234 or 800/233–1234,* 🅵🅰🆇 *704/554–8319. 262 rooms. Restaurant, pool, health club. AE, D, DC, MC, V.* 🕾

$$ 🏨 **Comfort Inn–Lake Norman.** North of Charlotte on I–77 near Lake Norman and Davidson College, this motel offers rooms with refrigerators and coffeemakers. Some rooms have VCRs, microwaves, and whirlpool baths. Jogging trails are nearby. ✉ *20740 Torrence Chapel Rd., Cornelius 28031,* ☎ *704/892–3500 or 800/848–9751,* 🅵🅰🆇 *704/892–6473. 90 rooms. Pool. AE, D, DC, MC, V. CP.* 🕾

$$ 🏨 **Homeplace.** This spotless turn-of-the-20th-century Victorian gem in a residential neighborhood is now a B&B filled with antiques and memorabilia. Rooms, with four-poster beds and antique reproductions, are country Victorian in style. The no-smoking inn is best for adults and older children. ✉ *5901 Sardis Rd., 28270,* ☎ *704/365–1936,* 🅵🅰🆇 *704/366–2729. 3 rooms. AE, MC, V. BP.*

Durham

$$–$$$ ✕ **Magnolia Grill.** This award-winning bistro is one of the finest, most
★ innovative places to dine in the state. It is especially known for its desserts—co-owner Karen Barker won best pastry chef in America in *Bon Appetit*'s 1999 American Food and Entertaining Awards. ✉ *1002 9th St.,* ☎ *919/286–3609. MC, V. Closed Sun. No lunch.*

$$$–$$$$ ✕🏨 **Washington Duke Inn & Golf Club.** Part of the Duke University
★ campus, this luxurious inn overlooks a Robert Trent Jones golf course. Among the entrées at the elegant Fairview restaurant are Muscovy duck with mashed white beans, roasted garlic, and cranberry sauce; and homemade fettuccine tossed with mussels, clams, shrimp, and scallops. There is also a bar called the Bull Durham. ✉ *3001 Cameron Blvd., 27706,* ☎ *919/490–0999 or 800/443–3853,* 🅵🅰🆇 *919/688–0105. 171 rooms. Restaurant, pool. AE, DC, MC, V.* 🕾

Greensboro

$$–$$$ ✕ **Paisley Pineapple.** The dining is formal in this romantic Old Greensborough restaurant in a restored 1920s building. The menu, heavy on hearty fare such as rack of lamb, grilled veal tenderloin, and sautéed beef tenderloin, is tempered by light soups. Upstairs there's a sofa bar with live jazz. ✉ *345 S. Elm St.,* ☎ *336/279–8488. AE, MC, V. Closed Sun. and Mon.*

$$$ 🏨 **Holiday Inn Four Seasons/Joseph S. Koury Convention Center.** For the most part, the accommodations here are standard. But if it's convenience you want, they've got it at this hotel near major thoroughfares and shopping areas. ✉ *3121 High Point Rd., 27407,* ☎ *336/292–9161 or 800/242–6556,* 🅵🅰🆇 *336/294–3516. 1,092 rooms. 4 restaurants, 2 pools, exercise room. AE, D, DC, MC, V.* 🕾

Raleigh

$$–$$$$ ✕ **Angus Barn, Ltd.** Housed in a huge rustic barn, this Raleigh fixture
★ is known for its steaks, seafood, prime rib, homemade desserts, and extensive wine list. Its Wild Turkey lounge is a favorite gathering spot

among locals. ⊠ *U.S. 70 W at Aviation Pkwy.,* ☎ *919/781–2444. Reservations not accepted Sat. AE, D, DC, MC, V.*

$–$$ ✕ TÍR NA NÓG. The interior is styled in the manner of a traditional Irish pub with lots of stone and even a thatched roof. The name means "land of eternal youth." The fare ranges from pub grub to gourmet, and the popular Sunday brunch has southern specialties (sausage and biscuits) as well as a Bloody Mary bar. There's also live entertainment many evenings. ⊠ *218 S. Blount St.,* ☎ *919/833–7795. AE, DC, MC, V.*

$$–$$$ ⊞ Raleigh Marriott Crabtree Valley. Standard guest rooms have Asian floral prints and dark cherrywood furnishings. You can dine at Crabtree Grill or Quinn's, which serves light fare and drinks daily. An airport shuttle is available. ⊠ *4500 Marriott Dr., 27612,* ☎ *919/781–7000 or 800/228–9290,* ᴘᴀx *919/571–7445. 379 rooms. Restaurant, pool, exercise room. AE, D, DC, MC, V.* ⊜

$$–$$$ ⊞ William Thomas House. A stately but not stuffy Victorian home is now a B&B on the edge of downtown Raleigh a few blocks from the governor's mansion. Rooms are traditionally and elegantly decorated and feature oversize windows, 12-ft ceilings, modem lines, and inconspicuous refrigerators. ⊠ *530 N. Blount St., 27604,* ☎ *919/755–9400 or 800/653–3466,* ᴘᴀx *919/755–3966. 4 rooms. AE, D, DC, MC, V. BP www.williamthomashouse.com.*

Winston-Salem

$$ ✕ Old Salem Tavern Dining Room. Dine on Moravian dishes, such as chicken potpie and beef ragout, in a Moravian setting with costumed servers. In warm months drinks are served under the arbor on the patio. ⊠ *736 S. Main St.,* ☎ *336/748–8585. AE, D, MC, V.*

$$–$$$ ⊞ Henry F. Shaffner House. This majestic Queen Anne, built around
★   1907 with tiger oak paneling and the finest materials, offers luxurious accommodations and lots of personal attention in a wonderfully convenient setting near Old Salem and many downtown attractions. ⊠ *150 S. Marshall St., 27101,* ☎ *336/777–0052 or 800/952–2256,* ᴘᴀx *336/777–1188. 9 rooms. AE, MC, V. BP.*

Nightlife and the Arts

In Winston-Salem, the **Stevens Center at the North Carolina School of the Arts** (⊠ 405 W. 4th St., ☎ 336/721–1945) stages events and performances. The **Eastern Music Festival** (☎ 877/833–6753) presents six weeks of classical music concerts each summer in Greensboro. High Point's **North Carolina Shakespeare Festival** (☎ 800/627–3849) puts on several productions in late summer and early autumn and *A Christmas Carol* in December. **North Carolina Blumenthal Performing Arts Center** (⊠ 130 N. Tryon St., ☎ 704/333–4686), in Charlotte, hosts operas, concerts, plays, and other cultural events. The **North Carolina Symphony Orchestra** (☎ 919/733–2750) performs in Raleigh's BTI Center for the Performing Arts (⊠ 2 E. South St.), which is also home to the **North Carolina Theatre** (☎ 919/831–6941) and the **Carolina Ballet** (☎ 919/856–0083).

Outdoor Activities and Sports

Golf

The Sandhills area, in the southern part of the Piedmont, has more than three dozen courses, including Pinehurst's famous Number 2. For details contact the **Pinehurst Area Convention and Visitors Bureau** (⊠ Box 2270, Southern Pines 28388, ☎ 910/692–3330 or 800/346–5362).

Spectator Sports

Basketball: Charlotte Hornets (⊠ Charlotte Coliseum, 100 Hive Dr., Tyvola Rd. off Billy Graham Pkwy., ☎ 704/357–0252) is the state's NBA team. From November through March, the Piedmont is a college basketball fan's dream, with Atlantic Coast Conference rivals **Duke University** (☎ 919/681–2583 or 800/672–2583) in Durham, **North Carolina State** (☎ 919/515–2106 or 800/310–7225) in Raleigh, the **University of North Carolina** (☎ 919/962–2296 or 800/722–4335) in Chapel Hill, and **Wake Forest University** (☎ 336/758–3322 or 888/758–3322) in Winston-Salem. **Football: Carolina Panthers** (✉ Ericsson Stadium, 800–1 S. Mint St., Charlotte, ☎ 704/358–7800), one of the National Football League's youngest franchises, plays in a 72,000-seat stadium in uptown Charlotte. **Ice Hockey:** The National Hockey League's **Carolina Hurricanes** (☎ 919/467–7825 or 888/645–8491) play in Raleigh at the high-tech, 21,000-seat Entertainment & Sports Arena. **NASCAR Racing:** The Coca-Cola 600 and UAW-GM 500 races draw huge crowds to the **Lowe's Motor Speedway** (☎ 704/455–3200), off I–85 near Concord.

Shopping

The Piedmont is ideal for lovers of **antiques and crafts**; towns such as Waxhaw, Cameron, Pineville, and Matthews are devoted almost entirely to antiques. For more information, call Charlotte's visitor center (☞ Visitor Information, *above*). One of the country's largest antiques centers is **Metrolina Expo** (✉ 7100 N. Statesville Rd., ☎ 704/596–4643 or 800/824–3770), near Charlotte. **Concord Mills** (✉ 15 mi north of Charlotte, intersection of I–85 and Concord Mills Blvd., Concord, ☎ 704/979–3000 or 877/626–4557) offers the latest in "shoppertainment" with more than 200 stores and theme restaurants, a 24-screen movie theater, arcades, even a waterfall and trout pond, arranged around a 1-mi oval walking lane. **High Point,** 20 minutes southwest of Greensboro, is known as the furniture capital of the world.

Replacements, Ltd. (✉ 1089 Knox Rd., at Exit 132 off I–85/40, between Burlington and Greensboro, ☎ 800/737–5223) is the world's largest retailer of discontinued and active china, crystal, flatware, and collectibles. There are more than 6 million pieces of inventory and 125,000 patterns represented. Daily tours are offered between 8:30 AM and 8:30 PM.

The **N.C. Pottery Center** (✉ 250 East Ave., ☎ 336/873–8430) in Seagrove, between Greensboro and Pinehurst, has information about and samples of work by potters from around the state every Tuesday through Saturday. Burlington, between Greensboro and Durham, is a hub for **outlet stores.** Charlotte and Raleigh are retail centers; the latter is home to one of the largest **farmers' markets** in the Southeast.

THE COAST

English settlers came to the shores of the North Carolina coast more than 400 years ago to establish a colony on Roanoke Island and mysteriously disappeared. They were not alone: the Outer Banks came to be called the Graveyard of the Atlantic as its seas swallowed hundreds of ships and provided refuge to marauding pirates in the 1700s. For years the region remained isolated, home only to a few fishermen and their families. But now, linked by bridges and ferries, the islands are a popular vacation spot. The chain of barrier islands that flanks the coast has three main regions. The Outer Banks stretch some 130 mi from the Virginia state line south to Cape Lookout; the Crystal Coast includes the stretch from Cape Lookout to the Bogue Banks; the southern coast, to the South Carolina line, includes the Cape Fear River region and Wilmington, the state's primary port. Nearby, the Albemarle region comprises charming towns full of early architecture. Hundreds of films and television programs have been shot in Wilmington, which has a restored historic district and waterfront.

On the surrounding coast visitors can tour old plantation houses and azalea gardens, study sea life, and bask in the sun at nearby beaches.

Visitor Information

Cape Fear Coast: Convention and Visitors Bureau (⊠ 24 N. 3rd St., Wilmington 28401, ☎ 910/341–4030 or 800/222–4757). **Carteret County:** Crystal Coast Visitors Center (⊠ 3409 Arendell St., Morehead City 28557, ☎ 252/726–8148 or 800/786–6962). **Craven County:** Convention and Visitors Bureau (⊠ 314 S. Front St., New Bern 28563, ☎ 252/637–9400 or 800/437–5767). **Dare County:** Tourist Bureau (⊠ U.S. 64/264, Manteo 27954, ☎ 252/473–2138 or 800/466–6262). **Historic Albemarle Tour, Inc.** (⊠ 1 Harding Sq., Washington 27858, ☎ 252/974–2950). **Ocracoke:** Visitor Center (⊠ Cape Hatteras National Seashore, NC 12 Hwy., Ocracoke 27960-0340, ☎ 252/928–4531).

Arriving and Departing

By Boat

There are nearly 150 marinas along the Intracoastal Waterway, including **Manteo Waterfront Docks** (☎ 252/473–3320) and the National Park Service's **Silver Lake Marina** (☎ 252/928–5111) in Ocracoke. Beaufort is a popular stopover. The Wilmington area has public marinas at **Carolina Beach State Park** (☎ 910/458–7770) and **Wrightsville Beach** (☎ 910/256–6666). The *North Carolina Coastal Boating Guide,* compiled by the North Carolina Department of Transportation (☎ 919/733–7600), lists marinas and other facilities for boaters.

By Bus

Greyhound/Carolina Trailways (☎ 800/231–2222) serves Elizabeth City, on the Albemarle Sound; Wilmington; and Norfolk, Virginia.

By Car

Roads link the mainland to the Outer Banks at their northern end: U.S. 158 enters from the north, near Kill Devil Hills, and U.S. 64/264 enters Manteo on Roanoke Island, from the west. These connect with Route 12, the main route in the region, running south from Corolla to Ocracoke Island. Toll **ferries** (☎ 800/293–3779) connect Ocracoke with Cedar Island, to the south, and with Swan Quarter on the mainland; a free ferry travels between Hatteras Island and Ocracoke Island. From I–95 near Raleigh, U.S. 70 leads to Cedar Island via New Bern and Morehead City, and I–40 serves Wilmington.

By Plane

The closest airports are **Raleigh-Durham International** (☞ Arriving and Departing *in* the Piedmont, *above*); **Wilmington International** (⊠ 1740 Airport Blvd., Wilmington, ☎ 910/341–4333); and Virginia's **Norfolk International Airport** (⊠ 2200 Norview Ave., Norfolk, ☎ 757/857–3351). SouthEast Air (☎ 252/473–3222 or 800/289–8202) and Outer Banks Airways (☎ 252/473–2227) provide charter service from **Dare County Regional Airport** (⊠ 410 Airport Rd., Manteo, ☎ 252/473–2600).

Exploring the Coast

Start your tour of the Outer Banks at Nags Head and Kill Devil Hills, where the Cape Hatteras National Seashore begins (☞ National and State Parks, *above*). You can drive from Nags Head to Ocracoke in a day, but allow plenty of time in summer, when ferries are crowded. During major storms and hurricanes, follow the evacuation signs to safety.

Kill Devil Hills is the site of the first manned flight in history. The **Wright Brothers National Memorial** (⊠ U.S. 158 Bypass, ☎ 252/441–

North Carolina's Outer Banks

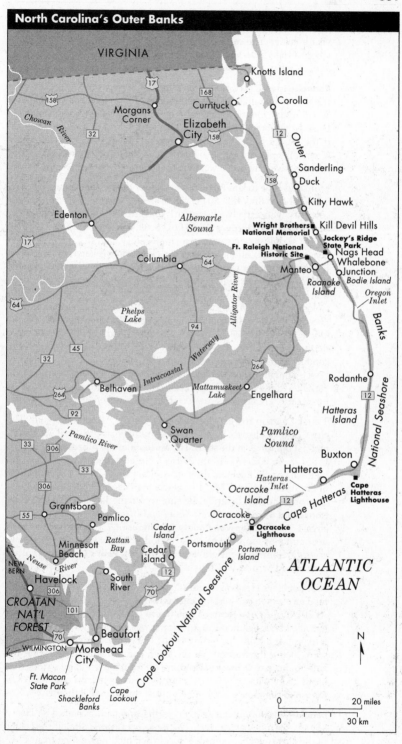

7430; ✆ $2 per adult, $4 per car) is a tribute to Wilbur and Orville's feat of December 17, 1903. A replica of the *Flyer* is displayed in the visitor center. You can fly a kite from the tallest sand dune in the East (about 110 ft) in **Jockey's Ridge State Park** (☞ National and State Parks, *above*), a few miles south of the Wright Brothers National Memorial.

Roanoke Island, accessible from U.S. 158 Bypass via U.S. 64/264, was the site of several ill-fated attempts at English colonization of the New World. Today, four sites alone focus on Sir Walter Raleigh's Lost Colonists. During the summer months the place is a beehive of tourist-related activity. Yet, the island hasn't succumbed to full-scale commercialization; it remains a place of quiet neighborhoods and forests as wild as the days when Native Americans were the only ones to occupy the land.

From mid-June to late August, the outdoor drama *Lost Colony* (✆ 252/473–3414 or 800/488–5012; ✆ $18) reenacts the story of the first colonists, who settled on Roanoke Island in 1587 and then disappeared. The **Elizabethan Gardens** (✉ 1411 U.S. 64, Manteo, ✆ 252/473–3234; ✆ $5) are a lush re-creation of a 16th-century English garden. The gardens, with their antique statuary, are closed on weekends in December, January, and sometimes February. **Fort Raleigh National Historic Site** (✉ off U.S. 64/264 north of Manteo, ✆ 252/473–5772; ✆ free) is a restoration of the original 1585 earthworks that mark the beginning of English Colonial history in America. The history, education, and cultural arts complex opposite the waterfront in Manteo, **Roanoke Island Festival Park** (✉ One Festival Park, ✆ 252/475–1506; ✆ $8) explores the evolution of the Outer Banks from the 16th century to the 20th. Costumed interpreters conduct tours of the *Elizabeth II,* a 69-ft re-creation of a 16th-century vessel. The **North Carolina Aquarium at Roanoke Island** (✉ Airport Rd., ✆ 252/473–3493; ✆ $3) has been extensively renovated to double its former size. The centerpiece tank is the *Graveyard of the Atlantic* exhibit.

Take a day trip to visit **Elizabeth City,** on the Albemarle Sound. The city's historic district has the largest number of pre–Civil War commercial buildings in the state. The **Museum of the Albemarle** (✉ 1116 U.S. 17S, ✆ 252/335–1453; ✆ free), closed Monday, has displays on regional history. **Edenton,** the state capital from 1722 to 1743, lies west of Elizabeth City. In 1774, 51 local women staged the Edenton Tea Party to protest English taxation. Be sure to see the Jacobean-style **Cupola House and Gardens** (✉ West Water and Broad Sts.), which were built circa 1758. The **Chowan County Courthouse** (✉ E. King St.) has been in continuous use since its construction in 1767. Three Colonial governors are buried in the graveyard behind **St. Paul's Church** (✉ corner of S. Broad St. and W. Church St.).

South of Nags Head on Route 12, the Herbert C. Bonner Bridge arches for 3 mi over Oregon Inlet to **Hatteras Island,** where the blue marlin reigns. At 208 ft, the **Cape Hatteras Lighthouse** (✆ 252/995–4474; ✆ free) is the tallest brick lighthouse in America. It was recently moved nearly 3,000 ft to protect it from the shifting sands. The visitor center has a small museum. Board the free ferry at the south end of Hatteras Island for the half-hour trip to **Ocracoke Island,** cut off from the world for so long that locals speak with a distinctive, but now endangered, brogue. The 1823 **Ocracoke Lighthouse** is the state's oldest operating lighthouse.

Beaufort, the third-oldest town in North Carolina, was named for Henry Somerset, Duke of Beaufort. The **Beaufort Historic Site,** in the center of this tiny town, is composed of restored buildings dating from 1767 to 1859, including the **Carteret County Courthouse** and the **Apothecary Shop and Doctor's Office.** Don't miss the **Old Burying Grounds** (1731). Here Otway Burns, a privateer in the War of 1812, is buried under his ship's cannon; a nine-year-old girl who died at sea is buried in a rum keg; and an English soldier saluting the king is buried upright in his grave. Tours on an English-style double-decker bus depart from here. ⊠ *130 Turner St.,* ☎ *252/728–5225 or 800/575–7483.* ☜ *Bus tour only $6, bus and walking tour $10. Closed Sun.*

Beaufort's **North Carolina Maritime Museum** (⊠ 315 Front St., ☎ 252/728–7317; ☜ free) documents the state's seafaring and coastal history. The museum includes the **Watercrafts Center,** which offers boat-building classes. Its education staff also provides year-round programs, including trips to the marsh and barrier islands.

Morehead City is a fishing and boating center across Bogue Sound from Bogue Banks. **Atlantic Beach** and **Emerald Isle** are popular family beaches. The **North Carolina Aquarium at Pine Knoll Shores** (⊠ Salter Path Rd., Milepost 7, Atlantic Beach, ☎ 252/247–4004; ☜ $3), in a maritime forest on Bogue Banks, features a 2,000-gallon salt marsh tank with live alligators and a loggerhead turtle nursery.

New Bern, northwest of Morehead City, was the state capital during English rule until immediately after the Revolution. The reconstructed **Tryon Palace** (⊠ 610 Pollock St., ☎ 252/514–4900 or 800/767–1560; ☜ $12), an elegant Georgian building, was the Colonial capitol and the home of Royal Governor William Tryon in the 1770s. An audio-visual orientation is given, costumed interpreters conduct tours of the house and gardens, and (in summer) actors deliver monologues describing a day in the life of local citizens. Tours of the garden are self-guided. The stately **John Wright Stanly House** (circa 1783), the **Dixon-Stevenson House** (circa 1826), and **New Bern Academy** (circa 1809) are within or very near the 13-acre Tryon Palace complex.

U.S. 17S leads to **Wilmington,** a bustling harbor town and filmmaking center. The **USS *North Carolina* Battleship Memorial** (☎ 910/251–5797; ☜ $8) is permanently docked off U.S. 421. You can park next to the site or take the river taxi from Riverfront Park (in summer only) for a self-guided tour that can last up to 2½ hours.

Wilmington's restored waterfront and historic district, with its 18th-century churches, can be explored with the aid of a self-guided walking-tour map from the Cape Fear Coast Convention and Visitors Bureau (☞ Visitor Information, *above*). The 1770 **Burgwin-Wright House,** on Market Street, is built on the foundation of a jail. Downtown's Italianate **Zebulon Latimer House** was built in 1852 and can be seen from 3rd Street.

The **St. John's Museum of Art** (⊠ 114 Orange St., ☎ 910/763–0281; ☜ $2) is composed of three architecturally distinctive buildings. One houses a permanent collection of etchings by Mary Cassatt; it's closed on Monday. Open from Tuesday through Sunday, the **Cape Fear Museum** (⊠ 814 Market St., ☎ 910/341–7413; ☜ $4), the state's oldest history museum, traces the natural and cultural history of Cape Fear River country.

U.S. 421 leads south from Wilmington to the **Fort Fisher State Historic Site** (⊠ Kure Beach, ☎ 910/458–5538; ☜ free), the largest Confederate earthwork fortification of the Civil War. War relics and artifacts from sunken Confederate blockade runners are on display. The site is closed Monday from November through March. Not far from Kure Beach is the **North Carolina Aquarium at Fort Fisher** (⊠ 2201 Fort Fisher Blvd., ☎ 910/458–8257; ☜ $3). Now closed for expansion, it will reopen in 2002.

On the west side of the Cape Fear River, south of Wilmington on Route 133, a passenger ferry links Southport and **Bald Head Island** (☎ 910/457–5003). On a day trip to the car-free island you can take a historic tour (reservations required) to see the 109-ft Old Baldy Lighthouse, dating from 1817; have a picnic or lunch at one of the restaurants; play golf; swim; or fish.

Dining and Lodging

Fresh seafood is plentiful, prepared almost every way. Hearty southern cooking, with chicken, ham, and fresh vegetables, is also widespread. Cottages, condominiums, motels, resorts, B&Bs, and country inns abound all along the coast. Most places offer lower rates from September through May. Condos and beach cottages can be rented through local realtors by the week or month.

Beaufort

$–$$ ✕ **Clawson's 1905 Restaurant and Pub.** Housed in what was a general store in the early 1900s, Clawson's serves hearty food such as ribs, steaks, pasta, and local seafood. It gets crowded in summer, so arrive early for both lunch and dinner. The coffee bar opens at 7 AM. ⊠ *425 Front St.,* ☎ *252/728–2133. D, MC, V.*

$$ 🏨 **Langdon House.** You'll sleep surrounded by antiques at this three-★ story B&B built in 1733. The host provides everything from sightseeing suggestions to sumptuous southern breakfasts and full beach baskets for picnics. ⊠ *135 Craven St., 28516,* ☎ *252/728–5499. 4 rooms. No credit cards. BP.* 🍽

Duck

$$$$ ✕🏨 **Sanderling Inn Resort & Conference Center.** This remote beach-★ side resort actually encompasses three inns. Ceiling fans, wicker, and neutral tones give rooms a cool and casual feel. The restaurant, in a restored lifesaving station, has such delicacies as crab cakes, roast Carolina duckling with black-cherry sauce, and fricassee of shrimp. ⊠ *1461 Duck Rd., 27949,* ☎ *252/261–4111 or 800/701–4111,* FAX *252/ 261–1638. 88 rooms, 29 efficiencies. Restaurant, pool, tennis, health club. AE, D, MC, V.* 🍽

$$$ 🏨 **Advice 5¢.** This modern B&B in Duck's North Beach is just a short walk from downtown and offers the use of Sea Pines tennis courts and swimming pool. All rooms have crisp, colorful linens; ceiling fans; and decks. ⊠ *111 Scarborough La., 27949,* ☎ *252/255–1050 or 800/238– 4235. 5 rooms. MC, V. CP.* 🍽

Kill Devil Hills

$–$$ ✕ **Flying Fish Cafe.** Brightly colored and casual are the bywords for this downtown café, but the food and wine are taken very seriously; this restaurant is the recipient of a *Wine Spectator* Award of Excellence. A perennial favorite entrée is the shrimp on spinach fettuccine with feta cheese. ⊠ *2003 Croatan Hwy.,* ☎ *252/441–6894. AE, D, MC, V. No lunch weekends.*

$$$ 🏨 **Ramada Inn.** Guest rooms in this convention-style hotel have private balconies, some with ocean views. All rooms are equipped with refrigerators, microwave ovens, and coffeemakers. The hotel restaurant, Peppercorns, which overlooks the ocean, serves breakfast and dinner; lunch is available on the sundeck next to the pool. ⊠ *1701 S. Virginia Dare Trail, off U.S. 158, Milepost 9.5 (Box 2716), 27948,* ☎ *252/441– 2151 or 800/635–1824,* FAX *252/441–1830. 172 rooms. Restaurant, pool. AE, D, DC, MC, V.* 🍽

Manteo

$–$$ ✕ **Weeping Radish Brewery and Restaurant.** This Bavarian-style restaurant and microbrewery is known for its German cuisine and annual post–Labor Day Octoberfest weekend featuring German and blues bands. Free tours of the brewery are given on request. ⊠ *U.S. 64,* ☎ *252/473–1157. D, MC, V.*

$$–$$$ ✕⊞ **Tranquil House Inn.** This waterfront B&B is only a few steps from shops and restaurants; bikes are provided for adventures beyond. The restaurant, named 1587, serves inventive entrées such as sesame-crusted tuna with wasabi vinaigrette and encourages vegetarian requests. It's closed from December through February. ⊠ *405 Queen Elizabeth Ave., 27954,* ☎ *252/473–1404 or 800/458–7069,* ℻ *252/473–1526. 25 rooms. Restaurant. AE, D, MC, V. CP.* ✎

Morehead City

$–$$ ✕ **Sanitary Fish Market & Restaurant.** Sixty-one years ago, when the Sanitary was founded, many fish houses were ill-kept. The owners wanted to signal their difference. Hush puppies are a specialty at this clean, simple waterfront eatery. It can get noisy (the restaurant seats 600), but guests from around the world have gushed about the food. ⊠ *501 Evans St.,* ☎ *252/247–3111. D, MC, V.*

Nags Head

$$ ✕ **Windmill Point.** The menu changes often but you can always count on the signature seafood trio. Dinner, served seven nights a week April through September, promises stunning views of the sound at sunset. Take a look at the memorabilia from the SS *United States.* ⊠ *U.S. 158 Bypass, Milepost 16.5,* ☎ *252/441–1535. AE, D, DC, MC, V.*

$$$–$$$$ ⊞ **First Colony Inn.** Verandas encircle this 1932 B&B. Some rooms have
★ Jacuzzis or ocean views, others have four-poster or canopy beds and armoires. The entire property is smoke-free. ⊠ *6720 S. Virginia Dare Trail, 27959,* ☎ *252/441–2343 or 800/368–9390,* ℻ *252/441–9234. 27 rooms. Pool. AE, D, MC, V. BP.* ✎

New Bern

$$–$$$ ✕⊞ **Harvey Mansion Historic Inn.** Beat and Carolyn Zuttel have opened
★ an inn to go with their award-winning restaurant. It's all under one roof in a striking 1797 house near the confluence of the Trent and Neuse rivers. The mansion serves as an art gallery, and the cellar, with its exposed beams, is a low-key pub. ⊠ *221 S. Front St., 28560,* ☎ *252/638–3205 or 800/ 638–3205. 3 rooms. Restaurant. AE, D, DC, MC, V. CP.* ✎

$$ ⊞ **Harmony House Inn.** At this historic B&B convenient to all the at-
★ tractions, guests sleep in spacious rooms where Yankee soldiers stayed during the Civil War. Today they are furnished with a mixture of antiques and reproductions. The inn serves a hot breakfast buffet and complimentary white and dessert wines in the evening. ⊠ *215 Pollock St., 28560,* ☎ *800/ 636–3113,* ℻ *252/636–3810. 10 rooms. AE, D, DC, MC, V. BP.* ✎

Ocracoke

$–$$ ✕⊞ **Island Inn.** This well-worn turn-of-the-20th-century inn has third-floor rooms with cathedral ceilings and lovely views. Families will be more comfortable in the newer, roomier addition across the street. The dining room is known for its oyster omelets, crab cakes, and hush puppies. ⊠ *Rte. 12 (Box 9), 27960,* ☎ *252/928–4351,* ℻ *252/928–4352. 35 rooms. Restaurant, pool. D, MC, V.* ✎

Southport

$$ ✕⊞ **Bald Head Island Resort.** Reached by ferry from Southport, this self-contained, carless community has its own grocery and general stores, restaurants, and golf course. The bleached-wood villas and shingled cottages have won architectural design awards. Guests travel the island on foot, bicycles, or in golf carts. Historic day tours are $36; this includes parking and ferry fees, lunch, and a guided tour. There are five restaurants on the resort with everything from steaks and steamed seafood to hot dogs and pizza on the menu. ⊠ *Box 3069, Bald Head Island 28461,* ☎ *910/457–5000 or 800/234–1666,* ℻ *910/457–9232. 195 homes/con-dos/villas, 2 B&Bs. 3 restaurants, pool, golf, tennis. AE, DC, MC, V.* ✎

Wilmington

$-$$ ✕ **Pilot House.** This Chandler's Wharf restaurant is known for its Sun-
★ day brunch, Carolina bisque, and shrimp and grits—a lunch favorite.
You can dine indoors or on a riverside deck. ⊠ *2 Ann St.,* ☎ *910/343–
0200. AE, D, MC, V.*

$$$ ⌅ **Hilton-Riverside.** Overlooking the Cape Fear River on one side and
the historic section of the city on the other, the spacious Hilton is one
of the most convenient places to stay in town. The lobby is plush; guest
rooms are traditional, with dark woods and autumnal colors. ⊠ *301
N. Water St., 28401,* ☎ *910/763–5900 or 800/445–8667,* ℻ *910/763–
0038. 178 rooms. Restaurant, pool. AE, D, DC, MC, V.*☜

$$ ⌅ **Inn at St. Thomas Court.** In the heart of the historic district, five for-
★ mer commercial buildings and a convent have been transformed into
luxurious suites, each decorated in a different theme. ⊠ *101 S. 2nd
St., 28401,* ☎ *910/343–1800 or 800/525–0909,* ℻ *910/251–1149. 40
suites. AE, D, DC, MC, V. CP.*☜

Campgrounds

Camping is permitted in designated areas of the ⚠ **Cape Hatteras** and
⚠ **Cape Lookout national seashores** from mid-April through mid-Oc-
tober and at most state parks (☞ National and State Parks, *above*).
Private campgrounds are scattered all along the coast. For more in-
formation contact the state's division of tourism (☞ Statewide Visitor
Information, *above*).

Nightlife and the Arts

A favorite haunt on the Wilmington waterfront is the **Ice House** (⊠
115 S. Water St., ☎ 910/763–2084), an indoor-outdoor bar with live
rhythm and blues. In Wrightsville Beach at the **Blockade Runner Resort Hotel** (⊠ 275 Waynick Blvd., ☎ 910/256–2251), there's a lounge
and entertainment for both adults and children during the summer. In
Wilmington, the **Thalian Hall Center for the Performing Arts** (⊠ 310
Chestnut St., ☎ 910/343–3664 or 800/523–2820), built between 1855
and 1858 and restored to its former grandeur, hosts more than 250
theater, dance, and musical performances each year.

Outdoor Activities and Sports

Boating

You can travel hundreds of miles over the sounds and inlets of this vast
region along the Intracoastal Waterway. For marina and docking information, pick up a copy of the *North Carolina Coastal Boating Guide*
(☞ Arriving and Departing, *above*) or contact the appropriate county
chamber of commerce (☞ Visitor Information, *above*).

Fishing

The region teems with bass, billfish, flounder, mullet, spot, trout, and
other fish. Fishing is permitted from piers all along the coast and from
certain bridges and causeways. Charter boats for deep-sea fishing are
available at the **Oregon Inlet Fishing Center** (☎ 252/441–6301 or 800/
272–5199) on the Outer Banks; **Flapjack & Gung Ho Charters** (☎ 910/
458–4362 or 800/288–3474) at Carolina Beach Municipal Marina; and
the *Carolina Princess* (☎ 252/726–5479 or 800/682–3456) in Morehead City. Fishing licenses are available from the **North Carolina Wildlife
Resources Commission** (☎ 919/773–2881).

Golf

Among the public and semiprivate courses in the Greater Wilmington
area is the breathtaking **Bald Head Island Golf Course** (☎ 910/457–
7310), designed by George Cobb. Ocean Isle, near the South Carolina

state line, also has a number of outstanding courses. Contact the **Cape Fear Coast Convention and Visitors Bureau** (☞ Visitor Information, *above*) or the **South Brunswick Islands Chamber of Commerce** (✉ Box 1380, Shallotte 28459, ☎ 910/754–6644 or 800/426–6644).

Scuba Diving

With more than 1,500 known shipwrecks off the coast of the Outer Banks, diving opportunities are legion. Dive shops include **Outer Banks Dive Center** (✉ 3917 S. Croatan Hwy., Nags Head, ☎ 252/449–8349), **Aquatic Safaris** (✉ 5751-4 Oleander Dr., Wilmington, ☎ 910/392–4386), and **Olympus Dive Center** (✉ 713 Shepard St., Morehead City, ☎ 252/726–9432 or 800/992–1258).

Surfing and Windsurfing

Kitty Hawk Kites (☞ Shopping, *below*), the oldest hang-gliding school on the East Coast, provides gear and instruction. Rentals are also available at shops in Wilmington, Wrightsville Beach, and Carolina Beach.

Beaches

Cape Hatteras and **Cape Lookout national seashores** offer more than 100 mi of beaches. **Atlantic Beach** and **Emerald Isle**, on Bogue Banks near Morehead City; **Wrightsville, Carolina,** and **Kure beaches**, near Wilmington; and **Ocean Isle**, farther south, are other top spots.

Shopping

You can find **nautical items** at antiques shops and **hand-carved wooden ducks and birds** at local crafts shops in Duck, a few miles north of Nags Head, and in Wanchese, at the south end of Roanoke Island. Nags Head is the main retail outlet for **Kitty Hawk Kites** (☎ 252/441–4124 or 800/334–4777). As the largest kite store on the East Coast, it offers every type of kite and wind sock known to man as well as toys and outdoor clothing. New Bern and Wilmington are centers for **antiques**; in Wilmington many shops are at Chandler's Wharf, the Cotton Exchange, and the Water Street Market on the waterfront.

THE MOUNTAINS

The majestic peaks, meadows, and valleys of the Appalachian, Blue Ridge, and Smoky mountains characterize the west end of the state. There are three distinct mountain regions: the southern mountains (home to the Eastern Band of the Cherokee Nation); the northern mountains, known as the High Country (Boone, Blowing Rock, Banner Elk); and the central mountains, anchored by Asheville, for decades a retreat for the wealthy and famous. National parks, national forests, centers for handmade crafts, and the Blue Ridge Parkway are the area's main attractions, providing prime opportunities for shopping, skiing, hiking, bicycling, camping, fishing, canoeing, or just taking in the breathtaking views.

Visitor Information

Appalachian Trail Conference (✉ 160–A Zillicoa St., Box 2750, Asheville 28802, ☎ 828/254–3708). **Asheville:** Convention and Visitors Center (✉ 151 Haywood St., Box 1010, 28802, ☎ 828/258–6111 or 800/257–1300). **Blowing Rock:** Chamber of Commerce (✉ Box 406, 28605, ☎ 828/295–7851). **Blue Ridge Parkway:** Superintendent (✉ 400 BB&T Bldg., 1 Pack Sq., Asheville 28801, ☎ 828/298–0398). **Boone:** Chamber of Commerce (✉ 208 W. Howard St., 28607, ☎ 828/262–3516 or 800/852–9506). **Cherokee:** Cherokee Visitor Center (✉ U.S. 441 Business, ☎ 828/497–9195 or 800/438–1601). **Fall Foliage**

Forecast (☎ 800/847–4862). **NC High Country Host** (✉ 1700 Blowing Rock Rd., Boone 28607, ☎ 828/264–1299 or 800/438–7500). **Smoky Mountain Host of NC** (✉ 4437 Georgia Rd., Franklin 28734, ☎ 828/369–9606 or 800/432–4678).

Arriving and Departing

By Bus
Greyhound/Carolina Trailways (☎ 800/231–2222) serves Asheville.

By Car
You can reach Asheville from the east or the west via I–40. I–26 begins in Asheville and heads south, connecting with I–240, which circles the city. U.S. 23/19A also runs through Asheville.

The High Country is reached off I–40 via U.S. 321 at Hickory, Route 181 at Morganton, and U.S. 221 at Marion. U.S. 421 is a major east–west artery. The Blue Ridge Parkway bisects the region, traveling over mountain crests in the High Country.

By Plane
Asheville Regional Airport (✉ Rte. 280, Fletcher, ☎ 828/684–2226) is 15 mi south of Asheville.

Exploring the Mountains

The town of **Cherokee** is the capital of Qualla Boundary, a 56,000-acre Cherokee Indian Reservation. The **Museum of the Cherokee Indian** (✉ U.S. 441 at Drama Rd., ☎ 828/497–3481; 🖭 $6) covers 10,000 years of Cherokee history with high-tech exhibits and an extensive artifact collection. There's also an art gallery and an outdoor living exhibit of Cherokee life as it was in the 15th century. The **Qualla Arts and Crafts Mutual** (✉ U.S. 441 at Drama Rd., ☎ 828/497–3103; 🖭 free), across the street from the Museum of the Cherokee Indian, is a cooperative that displays and sells baskets, masks, pottery, and wood carvings handcrafted by 300 Cherokee artisans. At **Oconaluftee Indian Village** (✉ U.S. 441 at Drama Rd., ☎ 828/497–2315; 🖭 $10), guides in Native American costumes will lead you through the re-created village of the 1750s, while others demonstrate skills such as weaving, pottery, canoe construction, and hunting techniques. With 2,300 gaming machines, video poker, video blackjack, and video craps **Harrah's Cherokee Casino** (✉ Hwy. 19 off U.S. 441 N, ☎ 828/497–7777) is the largest casino in a 500-mi radius. The complex also has a 1,500-seat concert hall, three restaurants, and a child-care area. You're guaranteed a find at **Smoky Mountain Gold and Ruby Mine** (✉ U.S. 441 N, ☎ 828/497–6574; 🖭 free), on the Qualla Boundary, where gems such as aquamarines, rubies, and sapphires are plentiful. You can purchase the treasures you dig up and pan for. Gold ore costs $5 per bag.

The largest and most cosmopolitan city in the mountains, **Asheville** has been rated America's favorite place to live of cities its size. The city's downtown is a pedestrian-friendly place, with upscale shopping, art galleries, museums, restaurants, and nightlife.

The 92,000-square-ft **Pack Place Education, Arts & Science Center,** in downtown Asheville, houses the Asheville Art Museum, Colburn Gem & Mineral Museum, Health Adventure, and Diana Wortham Theatre. The YMI Cultural Center, also maintained by Pack Place, is directly across the street. ✉ *2 Pack Sq.,* ☎ *828/257–4500.* 🖭 *$6.50. Closed Mon. June–Oct. and Sun. and Mon. Nov.–May.*

East of Asheville is America's largest private residence, the astonish-
★ ing **Biltmore Estate** (✉ Exit 50 off I–40E, ☎ 828/255–1700 or 800/
624–1575, 🎫 $29.95), built in the 1890s as the home of George Van-
derbilt. The 250-room French Renaissance–style château is filled with
priceless antiques and art treasures. The grounds, landscaped by Frederick Law Olmsted, include 75 acres of elaborate gardens, 72 acres of
vineyards, and a state-of-the-art winery.

The **North Carolina Arboretum** (✉ 10 mi southwest of downtown
Asheville, adjacent to the Blue Ridge Pkwy., ☎ 828/665–2492; 🎫 free),
426 acres that were part of the original Biltmore Estate, completes Frederick Law Olmsted's dream of creating a world-class arboretum in the
western part of the state. It features southern Appalachian flora in a
stunning number of settings.

A 45-minute drive from Asheville is Madison County, home to the picturesque village of Hot Springs, a way station for hikers on the Appalachian Trail, and the **Hot Springs Spa** (✉ 1 Bridge St., ☎ 828/622–
7676 or 800/462–0933; 🎫 $7.50–$30 per hr, depending on time of
day and number of guests). These mineral springs maintain a natural
100°F temperature year-round, and since the turn of the 20th century,
they have provided relief for visitors suffering a variety of ailments.

The **Great Smoky Mountains Railway,** just 45 minutes west of Asheville,
is one of the most popular attractions in western North Carolina.
Choose from five excursions on diesel-electric and steam locomotives
(fares vary). Open-sided cars or cabooses are ideal for picture taking
as the spectacular scenery glides by. ✉ *119 Front St., Dillsboro 28725,*
☎ *828/586–8811 or 800/872–4681.* 🎫 *$20–$50; some rides include
a meal. Closed Jan.–Mar.*

The most scenic route from Asheville to the Boone–Blowing Rock
area is via the **Blue Ridge Parkway** (☎ 828/271–4779), a stunningly
beautiful 469-mi road that gently winds through mountains and meadows and crosses mountain streams on its way from Waynesboro, Virginia, to Cherokee, North Carolina. The parkway is generally open
year-round but often closes during heavy snows and icy conditions. Maps
and information are available at visitor centers along the highway.

At Milepost 316.3 on the Blue Ridge Parkway is the **Linville Falls Visitor
Center** (✉ Rte. 1, Box 789, Spruce Pine 28777, ☎ 828/765–1045; 🎫
free), a part of the Linville Falls Recreation Area. From here it's an easy
½-mi hike to one of North Carolina's most photographed waterfalls.

Just off the parkway, on U.S. 221 at Milepost 305, is **Grandfather Mountain,** which soars 6,000 ft and is famous for its mile-high swinging bridge.
Sweaty-palmed visitors cross the 228-ft bridge, which sways over a 1,600
ft drop into Linville Valley. The United Nations has designated Grandfather Mountain a Biosphere Reserve. The **Nature Museum** has exhibits
on native minerals, flora and fauna, and pioneer life. ☎ *828/733–2013
or 800/468–7325.* 🎫 *$10. Closed in inclement weather.*

Blowing Rock refers to both a quiet mountain village and the nearby
4,000-ft rock for which it was named. The **observation tower** (☎ 828/
295–7111; 🎫 $4) offers a 180-degree view of mountaintops, valleys,
and gorges. The tower is closed weekdays in January and February.

☾ The **Tweetsie Railroad** is a popular Wild West theme park where you
can pan for gold, ride a train beset by robbers, and catch a musical
with cancan girls. ✉ *U.S. 321/221, Blowing Rock 28605, ☎ 828/264–
9061 or 800/526–5740.* 🎫 *$20. Closed Nov.–mid-May.*

🖐 **Blue Ridge Gemstone Mine,** midway between Asheville and Boone on the Blue Ridge Parkway, is in a region with one of the richest mineral deposits in the country. Though you can't enter the mine, you can purchase a gem bucket for anywhere from $5 to $100, take it to the flume line, and sort through it for rubies, emeralds, and more. ✉ *Box 327, Little Switzerland 28749,* ☎ *828/765–5264.* 🖙 *Free. Closed Jan.–Mar.*

Boone, named for frontiersman Daniel Boone, is at the convergence of three major highways—U.S. 321, U.S. 421, and Rte. 105. **Horn in the West** (✉ Amphitheater off U.S. 321, ☎ 828/264–2120; 🖙 $12), a project of the Southern Appalachian Historical Association, is an outdoor drama that traces the story of Daniel Boone. The show runs Tuesday through Sunday from mid-June to mid-August. Boone's **Appalachian Cultural Museum** (✉ University Hall near Greene's Motel, U.S. 321, ☎ 828/262–3117; 🖙 $4) is dedicated to the history and culture of the region, including the geographic origins of the mountains, the beginnings of stock car racing, as well as antiques and quilt traditions. The museum is closed Monday.

Dining and Lodging

The spirit of the pioneers who settled the mountains has always been present in the area's food and shelter—basic, hardy, and family-oriented. Be sure to make reservations early for visits in the fall, when every nook and cranny is crammed with leaf peepers.

Asheville

$–$$ ✕ **Cafe on the Square.** The menu for this street-side bistro, which faces historic Pack Square downtown, is heavy on fresh seafood and pastas cooked with various salsas, chutneys, and marinades. The local business crowd frequents the restaurant during lunch, but theatergoers come for dinner. ✉ *1 Biltmore Ave.,* ☎ *828/251–5565. AE, D, MC, V.*

$–$$ ✕ **Mountain Smoke House.** Local musicians entertain here, making dinner much more than just a meal. Yet, the mountain barbecue and pigpickin' buffets may make you want to be a regular at this family-style restaurant. Vegetarians can be accommodated, too. ✉ *802 Fairview Rd.,* ☎ *828/298–8121. AE, D, DC, MC, V. No lunch.*

$$$–$$$$ ✕🖾 **Grove Park Inn.** With its supervised children's activities, racquet-
★ ball and tennis courts, views of the Blue Ridge Mountains, and new spa complex, this is Asheville's premier resort. Since its opening in 1913, the guest list has included Thomas Edison, F. Scott Fitzgerald, and Michael Jordan. The inn, whose two newer wings are in line with the original design, is furnished with oak antiques in the Arts and Crafts style. The restaurants offer plenty of choices. Horizons, which gets creative with game dishes from ostrich to boar, has been recognized with DiRoNA's Fine Dining Award and a Wine Spectator Award. ✉ *290 Macon Ave., 28804,* ☎ *828/252–2711 or 800/438–5800,* ℻ *828/253–7053 for guests; 828/252–6102 for reservations. 510 rooms. 4 restaurants, 2 pools, golf, tennis, health club. AE, D, DC, MC, V.* 🐾

$$$–$$$$ ✕🖾 **Richmond Hill Inn.** This elegant Victorian mansion, once a private
★ residence, is on the National Register of Historic Places. Many of the 12 rooms in the mansion are furnished with canopy beds, Victorian sofas, and other antiques, while the more modern guest rooms have contemporary pine poster beds. The restaurant, Gabrielle's, known for its innovative cuisine, is only open to the public for dinner and Sunday brunch; jacket and tie are required. ✉ *87 Richmond Hill Dr., 28806,* ☎ *828/252–7313 or 888/742–4565,* ℻ *828/252–8726. 27 rooms, 9 cottages. 2 restaurants. AE, MC, V. BP.* 🐾

$$ 🖾 **Comfort Inn.** This hotel, off I–240 near the River Ridge Outlet Mall, has a walking trail and standard but comfortable guest rooms and suites with garden-tub Jacuzzis, private balconies, and dinette areas. ⊠ *800 Fairview Rd., 28803,* ☏ *828/298–9141,* FAX *828/298–6629. 177 rooms. Pool. AE, D, DC, MC, V. CP.* ☜

$ 🖫 **Mountaineer Inn.** A fixture along Tunnel Road for nearly 40 years, this motel is popular with families and others who care less about fancy than they do about affordable, comfortable surroundings. Refrigerators and coffeemakers are in each uniquely styled room. ⊠ *155 Tunnel Rd., 28805,* ☏ *800/255–4080. 79 rooms. AE, D, MC, V. CP.*

Blowing Rock

$ 🖫 **Alpine Village Inn.** In the heart of Blowing Rock, this motel harks back to a simpler time. Its rooms are neat as a pin and are decorated with antiques, quilts, and even flowers on holidays. ⊠ *297 Sunset Dr., 28605,* ☏ *828/295–7206. 15 rooms. AE, D, MC, V.* ☜

Boone

$–$$ ✕🖫 **High Country Inn.** A popular honeymoon choice that also draws skiers, golfers, and other groups interested in the discount packages, the inn, made of native stone and surrounded by ponds, has rooms that range from luxurious to comfortable. The dining choices include Geno's sports lounge and Geno's Restaurant. ⊠ *1785 Hwy. 105, 28607,* ☏ *828/264–1000 or 800/334–5605,* FAX *828/262–0073. 120 rooms, 2 log cabins. Restaurant, pool, exercise room. AE, D, MC, V.* ☜

Cherokee

$ ✕ **Nantahala Village Restaurant.** Located about 10 mi southwest of Cherokee, this restaurant is a favorite of folks in Swain County. The dining area features a locally crafted fireplace. The menu is eclectic, listing everything from trout, chicken, and country ham to Wild Forest Pasta. ⊠ *9400 U.S. 19W, Bryson City,* ☏ *828/488–9616 or 800/438–1507. D, MC, V. Closed late Nov.–early Mar.*

$–$$ 🖫 **Holiday Inn Cherokee.** Guest rooms are standard at this friendly, well-equipped motel. The in-house Chestnut Tree restaurant has dinner buffets that are veritable groaning boards, and the on-site native crafts shop, the Hunting Ground, with works by local artists, is a nice touch. ⊠ *U.S. 19S, 28719,* ☏ *828/497–9181 or 800/465–4329,* FAX *828/497–5973. 154 rooms. Restaurant, 2 pools, exercise room. AE, D, DC, MC, V.* ☜

Hot Springs

$–$$ ✕🖫 **Bridge Street Cafe & Inn.** This renovated storefront, circa 1922, is right on the Appalachian Trail and overlooks Spring Creek. Upstairs are brightly decorated rooms filled with antiques. Two rooms share baths. The café downstairs has a hand-built wood-fired oven and grill for gourmet pizzas. ⊠ *Bridge St. (Box 502), 28743,* ☏ *828/622–0002,* FAX *828/622–7282. 4 rooms. Restaurant. AE, D, MC, V. Closed Nov.–Mar.* ☜

Nightlife

An intimate, smoke-free listening room, **Be Here Now** (⊠ 5 Biltmore Ave., Asheville, ☏ 828/258–2071) offers dancing and concerts. The **Manor House Restaurant** (⊠ N. Main St. off NC 321 Bypass, Blowing Rock, ☏ 828/295–5500) at Chetola Resort is just the number for those in a mellow mood. Entertainment—usually jazz—is live and seasonal.

Outdoor Activities and Sports

Canoeing and White-Water Rafting

Near Boone and Blowing Rock, the New River, a federally designated Wild and Scenic River (Classes I and II), provides hours of excitement for canoeists, as do the Watauga River, Wilson Creek, and the Toe River. The Toe becomes the Nolichucky River as it goes into Tennessee. As the Nolichucky traverses the deepest, most spectacular canyon east of the Grand Canyon, its rapids offer heart-pounding excitement for the adrenaline deprived. **Nantahala Outdoor Center** (☎ 888/662–1662), **Edge of the World Outfitters** (☎ 828/898–9550 or 800/789–EDGE), and **High Mountain Expeditions** (☎ 828/295–4200 or 800/262–9036) run trips down the Nolichucky via raft.

Ski Areas

North Carolina's first ski resort opened 37 years ago, but it wasn't until snowmaking technology was perfected that the sport really took off here. Today there are eight ski areas and, generally, the season runs from mid-November through March. All offer ski schools, programs for children, night skiing, and snowboarding. Downhill skiing is available at **Appalachian Ski Mountain** (☎ 828/295–7828 or 800/322–2373), at Blowing Rock; **Hawksnest Golf & Ski Resort** (☎ 828/963–6561 or 888/429–5763), at Banner Elk; **Ski Beech** (☎ 828/387–2011 or 800/438–2093), at Beech Mountain, the highest resort in eastern North America; and **Sugar Mountain** (☎ 828/898–4521 or 800/784–2768), at Banner Elk.

Shopping

The **Folk Art Center** (☎ 828/298–7928), at Milepost 382 on the Blue Ridge Parkway, sells mountain arts and crafts made by the 700 artisans of the Southern Highland Handicraft Guild. **Biltmore Village,** on the Biltmore Estate, has specialty shops, restaurants, and galleries along its cobbled sidewalks. There's a turn-of-the-20th-century English hamlet feel and a shop for everything from children's books to music, antiques, and wearable art. **Malaprops** (⌧ 55 Haywood St., ☎ 828/254–6734 or 800/441–9829) bookstore and café is a mainstay in Asheville. Its two stories are filled with books about the region. The original **Mast General Store** is in Valle Crucis. There are now five of these nostalgic country stores, including ones in Asheville (⌧ 15 Biltmore Ave., ☎ 828/232–1883) and Boone (⌧ 630 W. King St., ☎ 828/262–0000). They sell everything from jellies to shoes, cradles to caskets.

NORTH DAKOTA

Updated by		
Sue Berg	**Capital**	Bismarck
	Population	641,000
	Motto	Liberty and Union, Now and Forever, One and Inseparable
	State Bird	Western meadowlark
	State Flower	Wild prairie rose
	Postal Abbreviation	ND

Statewide Visitor Information

North Dakota Tourism Department (⊠ Liberty Memorial Bldg., 604 E. Blvd., Bismarck 58505, ☎ 701/328–2525 or 800/435–5663). **Welcome centers:** along I–94E, 1 mi west of Beach; off I–94 at the Oriska Rest Area, 12 mi east of Valley City; off I–29N at the Lake Agassiz Rest Area, 8 mi south of Hankinson interchange; along I–29S, 1 mi north of the Pembina interchange; 1 block west of the junction of U.S. 2 and U.S. 85 in Williston; at the junction of U.S. 12 and U.S. 85 in Bowman; at the 45th Street interchange off I–94W in Fargo; and on U.S. 2, 10 mi east of Grand Forks at Fisher's Landing.

Scenic Drives

The **Pembina Gorge,** in northeastern North Dakota, is a beautiful forested valley created by glaciers and the winding Pembina River; from I–29 at the Joliette exit near the northern border, drive west on Route 5, then north on Route 32 to Walhalla. The South Unit loop road in **Theodore Roosevelt National Park** begins near park headquarters in Medora and winds 36 mi through an eerie world of lonesome pinnacles and spires, steep gorges, and ravaged buttes. The 14-mi **North Unit Road** begins at the park entrance along U.S. 85, 15 mi south of Watford City; the high ground above the Little Missouri River has dramatic overlooks, and a lower area near the visitor center features a series of slump rocks, huge sections of bluff that gradually slid intact to the valley floor.

National and State Parks

National Park

Theodore Roosevelt National Park (☞ Exploring the Badlands, *below*).

State Parks

North Dakota's 16 state parks are open year-round. Among the most scenic are **Cross Ranch State Park** (⊠ 1403 River Rd., Center 58530, ☎ 701/794–3731), 40 mi north of Mandan off Highway 25; two parks on U.S. 2 and Highway 19 that are part of **Devils Lake State Parks** (⊠ 152 S. Duncan Rd., Devils Lake 58301, ☎ 701/766–4015); **Fort Abraham Lincoln State Park** (☞ Exploring the Missouri River Corridor, *below*); and **Icelandic State Park** (⊠ 13571 Hwy. 5, Cavalier 58220, ☎ 701/265–4561), on Route 5, 5 mi west of Cavalier. **Lake Sakakawea State Park** (⊠ Box 732, Riverdale 58565, ☎ 701/487–3315), 1 mi north of Pick City, off Garrison Lake. All of these parks offer camping facilities; for camping reservations during the summer season, contact the **North Dakota Parks and Recreation Department** (⊠ 1835 E. Bismarck Expressway, Bismarck 58554, ☎ 701/328–5357 or 800/807–4723).

MISSOURI RIVER CORRIDOR

The Missouri River is both a geographic and a symbolic barrier between the two North Dakotas, the east and the west. The state capital, Bismarck, on the east bank of the Missouri, is a busy political hub, while at sprawling Lake Sakakawea, a short drive to the northwest, urban life seems a world away. Meriwether Lewis and William Clark followed the Missouri River through North Dakota during their famous exploration of the Louisiana Purchase; on their way west, Lewis and Clark spent the winter of 1804–05 near present-day Washburn, where they were joined by the guide Sakakawea, her husband, and her infant son. Lewis and Clark returned through North Dakota in 1806. Today's Routes 1804 and 1806 mark parts of the Lewis and Clark Trail in North Dakota.

Visitor Information

Bismarck-Mandan: Convention and Visitors Bureau (⊠ Box 2274, Bismarck 58501, ☎ 701/222–4308 or 800/767–3555). **Minot:** Convention and Visitors Bureau (⊠ Box 2066, 58702, ☎ 701/857–8206 or 800/264–2626).

Arriving and Departing

By Bus
Greyhound (☎ 800/231–2222) and **Minot-Bismarck Bus Service** (☎ 701/223–6576 or 701/852–2477) serve Bismarck and Minot.

By Car
I–94, the state's major east–west thoroughfare, runs through the Bismarck–Mandan area. U.S. 83 runs north–south from Bismarck to Minot, the state's second- and fourth-largest cities, respectively. U.S. 2 runs east–west along the top half of the state, including Minot.

By Plane
Bismarck Municipal Airport (⊠ 2301 University Dr., 58504, ☎ 701/222–6502) and **Minot International Airport** (⊠ 25 Airport Rd., Suite 10, 58703, ☎ 701/857–4724) are served by Northwest. Bismarck also is served by United Express. Both are about 5 mi from downtown; cab fare is about $6.

By Train
Amtrak (☎ 800/872–7245) stops in Minot and Williston.

Exploring the Missouri River Corridor

As in the rest of North Dakota, most of these attractions are open in the summer only (often Memorial Day–Labor Day); be sure to call ahead before you visit. The 19-story **state capitol** (⊠ 600 E. Boulevard Ave., 58505, ☎ 701/328–2480), in north Bismarck, is visible for miles across the Dakota prairie; free tours of this limestone-and-marble Art Deco structure, built in the 1930s, are offered on weekdays year-round and also on weekends Memorial Day–Labor Day. The **North Dakota Heritage Center** (⊠ 612 E. Boulevard Ave., ☎ 701/328–2666; ☑ free) is the state's largest museum and archive; exhibits include Native American and pioneer artifacts and natural-history displays. The facility is across the street from the capitol. The **Former Governors' Mansion State Historic Site** (⊠ 4th St. and Ave. B, ☎ 701/328–2666; ☑ free) is an elegant Victorian building containing political memorabilia and period furnishings. The **Lewis and Clark Riverboat**, departing from the Port of Bismarck (⊠ 1700 N. River Rd., ☎ 701/255–4233; ☑ $10.95), offers summer cruises on the Missouri River, plying the route taken by the traders, trappers, and settlers of the late 19th century.

General George Armstrong Custer buffs often visit **Fort Abraham Lincoln State Park** (⊠ Hwy. 1806, Mandan, ☎ 701/663–9571; ☜ $4 per person for park and sites). You can also reach the park from Bismarck by crossing the river on I–94 to Mandan, then either traveling 4 mi south on Route 1806 or taking the 9-mi **Fort Lincoln Trolley** (☎ 701/663–9018; ☜ $4) from south Mandan. Among the reconstructed buildings at the fort are the barracks (where groups can stay overnight for $15 per person) and the **Custer House,** a replica of the 1870s house where Custer lived with his wife, Libby, before his fateful expedition to the Little Big Horn. Nearby is the reconstructed **On-A-Slant Indian Village,** once home to the Mandan tribe.

Travel 44 mi south of Mandan on Route 1806 to the **Prairie Knights Casino** (⊠ HC 1, Box 26A, Fort Yates 58538, ☎ 701/854–7777 or 800/425–8277, FAX 701/854–3795) on Standing Rock Sioux Reservation. The fanciest of North Dakota's five reservation casinos, Prairie Knights features murals by Native American artists and first-class dining. The games, two bars, and two restaurants are open 24 hours a day. Next door is the 69-room Lodge at Prairie Knights ($).

From Bismarck take U.S. 83 north to Washburn, where the **Lewis & Clark Interpretive Center** (⊠ ¼ mi west off U.S. 83, Box 607, 58577, ☎ 701/462–8535; ☜ $3) will be the hub of bicentennial celebrations in 2004. The center is one of only four in the world with a complete set of reproduction prints by Karl Bodmer, the artist-explorer who followed Lewis & Clark's trail some 25 years later.

From Washburn, take Route 200A west to **Fort Clark State Historical Site** (☜ free), a fur trade post along the Missouri River where a steamboat full of passengers with smallpox docked, infecting and wiping out most of the nearby Mandan Indian population.

Knife River Indian Villages National Historic Site (⊠ ¼ mi north of Stanton, Box 9, 58571, ☎ 701/745–3309; ☜ free) preserves depressions formed by the Hidatsa and Mandan tribes' circular, earth-and-timber lodges. The museum and interpretive center displays pottery shards, other artifacts, and a full-scale furnished replica of an earth lodge.

Twenty miles north of Stanton is the 600-square-mi **Lake Sakakawea,** whose countless recreational opportunities include swimming and boating. State parks and small resort communities are sprinkled along its shores. Free tours of the **Garrison Dam power plant** are conducted by the U.S. Army Corps of Engineers (☎ 701/654–7441). A good portion of Lake Sakakawea is surrounded by **Fort Berthold Indian Reservation,** home of the Mandan, Hidatsa, and Arikara. They're organized as the Three Affiliated Tribes with headquarters in New Town. For more information on the lake, contact the tourism department (☞ Statewide Visitor Information, *above*).

About 40 mi north of the big lake on U.S. 83 is Minot, with its popular **Roosevelt Park and Zoo** (⊠ 1219 Burdick Expressway E, 58701, ☎ 701/857–4166; ☜ $3; closed Oct.–Apr.). A miniature train gives passengers park tours, and the zoo shows off more than 200 species of animals, ranging from bison to giraffes.

Dining and Lodging

For a listing of area bed-and-breakfasts, contact the tourism department (☞ Statewide Visitor Information, *above*).

Bismarck

$$–$$$ ✕ **Peacock Alley Bar and Grill.** In what was once the historic Patterson Hotel, this restaurant enjoys local fame as the scene of countless
★

political deals, captured in period photographs. The menu features regional dishes such as pan-blackened prime rib. ✉ *422 E. Main St.,* ☎ *701/255–7917. AE, D, DC, MC, V.*

$–$$ ✕ **Fiesta Villa.** This family-run Mexican restaurant is suitably housed in a mission-style building. Beef or chicken fajitas are a good choice here, and they go well with the excellent margaritas. ✉ *4th and Main Sts.,* ☎ *701/222–8075. AE, D, MC, V.*

$$–$$$ 🏨 **Radisson Inn.** Rooms are spacious and comfortable. The hotel is across from Kirkwood Mall (☞ Shopping, *below*), Bismarck's largest shopping center. ✉ *800 S. 3rd St., 58504,* ☎ *701/258–7700 or 800/333–3333,* 𝔽𝔸𝕏 *701/224–8212. 306 rooms. Restaurant, pool, health club. AE, D, DC, MC, V.*🛴

Mandan

$ ✕ **Mandan Drug.** For a fun lunch, order a sandwich or homemade soup
★ with an old-fashioned cherry soda or a brown cow—that is, a root-beer float with chocolate syrup. The homemade candy is hard to resist. ✉ *316 W. Main St.,* ☎ *701/663–5900. MC, V. Closed Sun.*

$–$$ 🏨 **Best Western Seven Seas Inn and Conference Center.** Nautical decor is the unlikely theme in the public areas, from 200-year-old anchors to carpeting in the pattern of ship's planking. Rooms are also adorned with maritime art. ✉ *I–94, Exit 152; 2611 Old Red Trail, 58554,* ☎ *701/663–7401 or 800/597–7327,* 𝔽𝔸𝕏 *701/663–0025. 103 rooms. Restaurant, pool. AE, D, DC, MC, V.*🛴

Minot

$–$$ 🏨 **Best Western International Inn.** Larger-than-average rooms have con-
★ temporary furnishings at this five-story hotel on a hill above downtown. ✉ *1505 N. Broadway, 58703,* ☎ *701/852–3161 or 800/735–4493,* 𝔽𝔸𝕏 *701/838–5538. 270 rooms. Restaurant, pool. AE, D, DC, MC, V.*🛴

Motel

🏨 **Expressway Inn** (✉ 200 E. Bismarck Expressway, Bismarck 58504, ☎ 𝔽𝔸𝕏 701/222–2900, ☎ 800/456–6388), 163 rooms; pool; CP; $.

Campgrounds

There are campgrounds at 🏕 **Fort Abraham Lincoln State Park** (☞ Exploring the Missouri River Corridor, *above*) and 🏕 **Lake Sakakawea State Park** (☞ National and State Parks, *above*).

Outdoor Activities and Sports

Biking

The 403-mi **CANDISC (Cycling Around North Dakota in Sakakawea Country)** is a bike tour—not a race—along Lake Sakakawea, Fort Berthold Indian Reservation, the badlands, and coal country, following some of the route traveled by Lewis and Clark two centuries earlier. Contact the tourism department (☞ Statewide Visitor Information, *above*) for details. **Dakota Cyclery** (✉ 1606 E. Main Ave., Bismarck, ☎ 701/222–1218) rents bicycles and can provide information about area biking.

Fishing

Walleye, salmon, and northern pike are the big catches on Lake Sakakawea. The **North Dakota Game and Fish Department** (✉ 100 N. Bismarck Expressway, Bismarck 58501, ☎ 701/328–6300) has a list of local fishing guides. The *North Dakota Hunting and Fishing Guide,* available through the tourism department (☞ Statewide Visitor Information, *above*), outlines seasons and regulations.

Hiking

Bismarck/Mandan maintains 30-plus mi of paved paths, including a 12-mi trail that follows the Missouri River from north Bismarck to Fort

Abraham Lincoln State Park south of Mandan. Contact **Bismarck Parks and Recreation Department** (✉ 420 E Front Ave., 58504, ☎ 701/222–6455) for details.

Shopping

Kirkwood Mall, between South 3rd and South 7th streets in Bismarck, has four major department stores and 100 specialty shops, including the locally owned **Maxwell's** (☎ 701/222–4332), a cozy bookstore with a special section on regional interests, including guidebooks, local history, and books by local authors.

Across the river in Mandan, the **Five Nations Arts** (✉ 401 W. Main St., ☎ 701/663–4663) sells handmade Native American star quilts, beadwork, sculptures, and more.

THE BADLANDS

Theodore Roosevelt, who ranched in western North Dakota in the late 1800s, once said, "I would never have been president if it had not been for my experiences in North Dakota." He was referring to the **Badlands,** where a national park that bears his name is now the heart of this wide-open country, largely unchanged since the president's time.

Visitor Information

Medora: Theodore Roosevelt Medora Foundation (✉ c/o Rough Riders, 301 5th St., Box 198, 58645, ☎ 701/623–4444 or 800/633–6721). **Williston:** Convention and Visitors Bureau (✉ 10 Main St., 58801, ☎ 701/774–9041 or 800/615–9041). **Dickinson:** Convention and Visitors Bureau (✉ 72 Museum Dr., 58601, ☎ 701/483–4988 or 800/279–7391).

Arriving and Departing

By Bus
Greyhound (☎ 800/231–2222) stops in Dickinson and Medora.

By Car
I–94 crosses the Badlands, with an exit at Medora for the South Unit of Theodore Roosevelt National Park. U.S. 85 links the park's North and South units.

By Plane
Bismarck Municipal Airport (☞ Missouri River Corridor, *above*) is the nearest large airport. The commuter airline United Express serves **Williston Airport** (✉ Airport Rd., ☎ 701/774–8594) and **Dickinson Airport** (✉ 11168 42R St. SW, ☎ 701/225–1062 or 701/225–3822).

Exploring the Badlands

★ **Theodore Roosevelt National Park** (✉ Box 7, Medora 58645, ☎ 701/623–4466, 🖙 $5 per person, $10 per vehicle) is divided into three units, separated by about 50 mi of Badlands and the **Little Missouri National Grasslands.** Scenic loops through the **South Unit** (☞ Scenic Drives, *above*) are marked with low speed limits to protect the bison, wild horses, mule deer, pronghorn antelope, and bighorn sheep that roam here. You can get a panoramic view of the Badlands from the park's **Painted Canyon Overlook and Visitors Center** (☎ 701/623–4466; 🖙 free), on I–94, 7 mi east of Medora, a good place to start a tour. The center has picnic tables.

The park has 80 mi of marked horse trails; if you're up for a 90-minute horseback ride in the South Unit, contact **Peaceful Valley Ranch** (☎

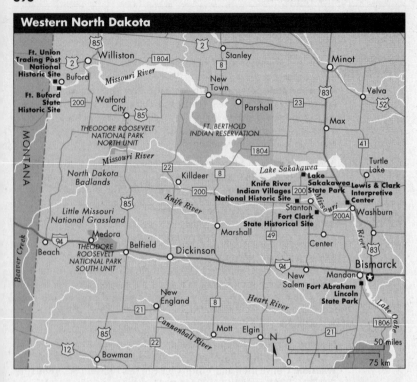

Western North Dakota

701/623–4568), 7 mi north of the park entrance. The visitor center can provide you with maps if you prefer to hike.

The **North Unit,** off U.S. 85 south of Watford City, offers the same scenic driving and hiking opportunities but in a less crowded setting. It's a good place to spot the wildlife you may have missed in the South Unit.

Outside the park, historic **Medora** is a walkable small town with a number of tiny shops, museums, and other attractions. The **Château de Mores State Historic Site** (⊠ ½ mi southwest of Medora on Hwy. 10, ☎ 701/ 623–4355; ☜ $5), an elegant 26-room mansion on a bluff overlooking the town, was built in the mid-1880s by a French nobleman who ran a short-lived cattle and meatpacking enterprise from here.

You can see a collection of antique dolls in the **Medora Doll House** (☜ $3). The **Museum of the Badlands** (☜ $3) has Native American artifacts, wildlife exhibits, and wax figures depicting frontier days. The **Harold Schafer Heritage Center** (☜ free) is an art gallery with an exhibit on Harold Schafer, the inventor of Mr. Bubble, the bubble soap for kids, who has been using his fortune to rebuild Medora since the early 1960s. The Theodore Roosevelt Medora Foundation (☞ Visitor Information, *above*) oversees these three sights, which are open from June through August only; call ahead for more information.

Dickinson, an oil-boom-and-bust community on I–94, is now renowned for its dinosaur deposits. You can see 12 full-scale dinosaurs and other fossil, mineral, and animal collections at the **Dakota Dinosaur Museum.** ⊠ *200 Museum Dr., off I–94, Exit 61,* ☎ *701/225–3466.* ☜ *$5. Closed Nov.–Feb.*

Fort Buford State Historic Site (☎ 701/572–9034; ☜ $4), 22 mi southwest of Williston via Route 1804, is built around the 1866 fort that once imprisoned famous Native American leaders, including Sioux leader Sitting Bull and Nez Percé chief Joseph. It's open from mid-May through mid-September. Two miles west of Fort Buford on Route 1804 is a national historic site, the **Fort Union Trading Post National Historic Site** (☎ 701/572–9083; 🎫 free). A reconstructed fur-trading post used by John Jacob Astor's American Fur Company, Fort Union dominated the fur trade along the upper Missouri River from 1828 to 1867.

Dining and Lodging

Dickinson

$$–$$$$ ✕ **Rattlesnake Creek Brewery and Grill.** If the remarkable beer doesn't bite you, the Killdeer Mountain potatoes will: these escalloped potatoes in cream have secret spices for fiery flavor. The chili is a close second on the inventive meat-and-potatoes menu. ⊠ 2 W. Villard, ☎ 701/225–9518. AE, D, DC, MC, V. Closed Sun.

Medora

$–$$ ✕ **Rough Rider Hotel Dining Room.** Housed in a two-story wood-
★ frame building, this rustic restaurant serves barbecued buffalo ribs, prime rib, and other beef specialties. ⊠ Main St., ☎ 701/623–4444. AE, D, MC, V. Operates as a B&B Oct.–Apr.

$ ✕ **Trapper's Kettle Restaurant.** Be prepared for reminders of the fur trade at this restaurant's two locations—traps, furs, stuffed and mounted animals, and a canoe, which holds the salad bar. Go for chili topped with melted cheese. ⊠ I–94 and U.S. 85, Belfield, ☎ 701/575–8585; ⊠ 3901 2nd Ave. W, Williston, ☎ 701/774–2831. AE, MC, V.

Williston

$–$$ ✕ **El Rancho Restaurant.** This cattle-country restaurant, furnished in earth tones and adorned with southwestern art, is well known for its specialty, prime rib. Seafood and chicken are also on the menu. ⊠ 1623 2nd Ave. W, ☎ 701/572–6321. AE, D, DC, MC, V.

Motels

🏨 **AmericInn Motel & Suites** (⊠ 75 E. River Rd. S, Medora 58645, ☎ 701/623–4800 or 800/634–3444, FAX 701/623–4890), 56 rooms; pool; CP; $–$$.

🏨 **Badlands Motel** (⊠ Box 198, Medora 58645, ☎ 701/623–4444 or 800/633–6721, FAX 701/623–4494), 116 rooms; pool; closed Oct.–Apr.; $–$$.

🏨 **El Rancho Motor Hotel** (⊠ 1623 2nd Ave. W, Williston 58801, ☎ 701/572–6321 or 888/452–3706, FAX 701/572–6321), 91 rooms; restaurant; $.

🏨 **Hospitality Inn** (⊠ I–94 and Rte. 22, Dickinson 58601, ☎ 701/227–1853 or 800/422–0949, FAX 701/225–0090), 149 rooms; restaurant, pool; $.

Campgrounds

⚠ **Cottonwood Campground** (⊠ 5 mi inside Theodore Roosevelt National Park, ☎ 701/623–4466). ⚠ **Medora Campground** (⊠ Medora, ☎ 701/623–4444 or 800/633–6721). ⚠ **Red Trail Campground** (⊠ Box 367, Medora, ☎ 701/623–4317 or 800/621–4317).

Nightlife

The **Medora Musical** (⊠ 1 mi west of Medora, ☎ 701/623–4444; 🎫 $17–$19), in the outdoor Burning Hills Amphitheater, is a theater tribute to western Americana, featuring everything from singing to history to fireworks. Before the show, you can dine at the **Pitchfork Fondue** (🎫 $10–$18), a cowboy name for a steak-dinner picnic held right outside the theater on the prairie bluff.

Outdoor Activities and Sports

Biking

The roads in the north and south units of Theodore Roosevelt National Park are challenging and scenic.

Hiking and Backpacking

All units of Theodore Roosevelt National Park offer spectacular hiking and backpacking. The challenging **Maah Daah Hey Trail** crosses 100 mi of rugged western North Dakota, mostly in badlands territory. Open for hiking, horseback riding, and some biking, the nonmotorized trail is jointly managed by the U.S. Forest Service (☎ 701/225–5151), the National Park Service (☎ 701/623–4466), and the state Parks and Recreation Department (☎ 701/328–5357). The Little Missouri National Grasslands (☞ Exploring the Badlands, *above*), which stretches between the main park units, is also a popular spot.

Shopping

Specialty shops lining Medora's Main Street include **Chateau Nuts** (☎ 701/623–4825), which stocks every nut imaginable in quantities large enough to make a squirrel's heart race.

ELSEWHERE IN NORTH DAKOTA

The Lakes Region

Visitor Information

Devils Lake Tourism & Promotion (✉ Box 879, Devils Lake 58301, ☎ 701/662–4903 or 800/233–8048). **Jamestown Promotion & Tourism Center** (✉ Box 389, Jamestown 58402, ☎ 800/222–4766).

Arriving and Departing

U.S. 2 is the principal east–west route through the region, connecting with I–29 at Grand Forks. U.S. 281 runs north–south, with secondary roads leading to lakes and area attractions. Devils Lake is served by **United Express. Amtrak** (800/872–7245) stops in Devils Lake and Rugby.

What to See and Do

Jamestown, at U.S. 281 and I–94, marks the southern end of this region. The world's largest buffalo sculpture and a live bison herd are both clearly visible from I–94.

Devils Lake, the heart of the lakes region, is surrounded by hundreds of smaller lakes and prairie potholes filled with marsh water. A major breeding ground for North America's migratory waterfowl, Devils Lake offers fine birding. The lake itself has excellent jumbo-perch and walleye fishing. Check ahead, though, before you make fishing or camping plans; rising lake levels have eroded rural roadways. Call the North Dakota Department of Transportation (☎ 701/662–1304) for road reports. For more information on fishing in the area, contact the **Game and Fish Department** (✉ 100 N. Bismarck Expressway, Bismarck 58501, ☎ 701/328–6300).

Within the Spirit Lake Sioux Indian Reservation is the **Fort Totten State Historic Site** (✉ Rte. 57, ☎ 701/766–4441; ☞ $4), the best-preserved military fort west of the Mississippi River. Built in 1867, it later served as one of the nation's largest government-run schools for Native Americans. It's open mid-May through mid-September.

Rugby, west of Devils Lake on U.S. 2, is the geographical center of North America. Marked by a stone monument, the landmark includes a spacious **Geographical Center Pioneer Village and Museum** (☎ 701/776–6414; 💷 $4) containing thousands of objects, such as 19th-century farming equipment and antique cars. It's open mid-May through mid-September. The **International Peace Garden** (⊠ 13 mi north of Dunseith on U.S. 281, ☎ 701/263–4390 or 888/432–6733, 💷 $5 per person, $10 per vehicle, free in winter) is a 2,300-acre garden straddling the border between Canada and the United States and is planted as a symbol of peace between the two nations. Just south of the International Peace Garden is the reservation of the **Turtle Mountain Band of Chippewa,** with headquarters in Belcourt (☎ 701/477–6451).

Dining and Lodging

$–$$ ✕ **Birchwood Steakhouse and Northern Lights Lounge.** Delicious prime rib is a staple at this beautiful lakeside restaurant bordering Canada. ⊠ *North of Rte. 43, Lake Metígoshe,* ☎ *701/263–4283. MC, V.*

$–$$ ✕ **Mr. & Mrs. J's.** The "Pig-out Omelette" is the specialty; a huge salad bar complements traditional fare. ⊠ *U.S. 2E, Devils Lake,* ☎ *701/662–8815. AE, D, MC, V.*

MOTELS

🏨 **Comfort Inn** (⊠ 811 20th St. SW, Jamestown 58401, ☎ 701/252–7125 or 800/228–5150, FAX 701/252–7125), 117 rooms; restaurant, pool; $–$$.

🏨 **Dakota Motor Inn** (⊠ Box 887, Devils Lake 58301, ☎ 701/662–4001 or 888/662–7748, FAX 701/662–4003), 80 rooms; restaurant, pool; CP; $.

CAMPGROUND

⚠ **Grahams Island State Park** (⊠ 152 S. Duncan Rd., Devils Lake 58301, ☎ 701/766–4015) is 15 mi southwest of Devils Lake off Route 19. Check before visiting for updates on lake flooding.

The Red River Valley

Visitor Information

Fargo/Moorhead Convention and Visitors Bureau (⊠ 2001 44th St. SW, Fargo 58103, ☎ 701/282–3653 or 800/235–7654). **Grand Forks Convention and Visitors Bureau** (⊠ 4251 Gateway Dr., 58203, ☎ 701/746–0444 or 800/866–4566). **Wahpeton Visitors Center** (⊠ 118 N. 6th St., 58075, ☎ 701/642–8744 or 800/892–6673).

Arriving and Departing

I–94 links Fargo with Minneapolis–St. Paul to the east and with Billings, Montana, to the west. I–29 connects Fargo with Grand Forks, 75 mi north, and with Sioux Falls, South Dakota, to the south. **Hector International Airport** (⊠ Box 2845, 58108, ☎ 701/241–1501), in Fargo, and **Grand Forks International Airport** (⊠ 2787 Airport Dr., 58203, ☎ 701/795–6981) are served by Northwest and Mesaba; Fargo is also served by United Express. **Amtrak** (☎ 800/872–7245) serves both cities. **Greyhound** (☎ 800/231–2222) provides service to Fargo and Grand Forks.

What to See and Do

The **Red River of the North** forms the eastern boundary of North Dakota with Minnesota. The fertile valley formed by the river attracted northern European immigrants in the late 19th century and still contains more than a third of the state's population. The region is an enormous shopping hub, drawing bargain hunters from Minnesota, Canada, and the rest of North Dakota.

In the southeast corner of the state, off I–29, is **Wahpeton.** You can ride on the restored 1926 **Prairie Rose Carousel** for $1 (⊠ 10 mi east of I–29). Nearby is the **Roger Ehnstrom Learning Center and Chahinkapa**

Park Zoo (☎ 701/642–8709; ▨ $4), with such native species as eagles, bison, and elk. It's open May through mid-September. Ten miles west of I–29 is Mooreton's **Bagg Bonanza Farm** (☎ 701/274–8989; ▨ $3.50), a national historic site that re-creates the *Bonanza*-like farm life of the late 1800s and early 1900s. Nine of the 21 buildings have been restored. The farm is open Friday and weekends June through September. Head north 50 mi on I–29 to **Fargo,** the state's largest city and the setting for the Coen brothers' acclaimed 1996 film of the same name. **Bonanzaville USA** (✉ Exit 65, I–29, West Fargo, ☎ 701/282–2822 or 800/700–5317; ▨ $6; closed Nov.–May) is a pioneer village and museum with 40 original and re-created buildings illustrating life in 1880s Dakota Territory. The **Roger Maris Baseball Museum** (✉ West Acres Shopping Center, I–29 and 13th Ave. S, ☎ 701/282–2222; ▨ free) honors the baseball hero who for 37 years held the single-season home-run record at 61 runs, until Mark McGuire hit 70 in 1998. Hands-on learning is the theme at the **Children's Museum at Yunker Farm** (✉ 1201 28th Ave. N, 58102, ☎ 701/232–6102; ▨ $3).

The **Plains Art Museum** (✉ 704 1st Ave. N, downtown Fargo, ☎ 701/232–3821 or 800/333–0903; ▨ $3; closed Mon.) has one of the largest fine arts collections between Minneapolis and Seattle with traditional Native American and African examples, regional art, and contemporary pieces.

Seventy-five miles north of Fargo on I–29 is **Grand Forks,** the state's cultural and technological center. Grand Forks is home to the **North Dakota Museum of Art** (✉ Centennial Dr., ☎ 701/777–4195; ▨ free) and the **Center for Aerospace Sciences** (✉ 4125 University Ave., ☎ 701/777–2791; ▨ free, by appointment only), both at the **University of North Dakota.** Seventy miles north of Grand Forks via I–29, the **Pembina State Museum** (✉ Box 456, Pembina 58271, ☎ 701/825–6840; ▨ free, $2 for elevator to top of tower) has exhibits on North Dakota's 100-million-year history and an observation tower. Just west, in **Icelandic State Park** (☞ National and State Parks, *above*), the **Pioneer Heritage Interpretive Center** (☎ 701/265–4561; ▨ $3 per vehicle; closed Sat. Sept.–mid-May) uses artifacts and exhibits to showcase the region's ethnic diversity.

Dining and Lodging

$$–$$$$ ✕ **Luigis.** Mismatched antique wooden chairs and tables, quaint fabric screens, and a fabulous 40-ft ceiling evoke nostalgia in the city's famous old music conservatory, built in 1910. Try the filet mignon sautéed in a marsala sauce and balsamic vinaigrette, topped with prosciutto and provolone. ✉ *613 1st Ave. N, Fargo,* ☎ *701/241–4200,* FAX *701/241–4129. AE, D, DC, MC, V.*

MOTELS

▨ **Best Western Doublewood Inn and Conference Center** (✉ 3333 13th Ave. S, Fargo 58103, ☎ 701/235–3333 or 800/528–1234, FAX 701/280–9482), 170 rooms; restaurant, pool; *$$.*

▨ **Road King Inn** (✉ 3300 30th Ave. S, Grand Forks 58201, ☎ 701/746–1391 or 800/707–1391, FAX 701/746–8586), 85 rooms; pool; CP; *$–$$.*

OHIO

Updated by
Nicki Chodnoff

Capital	Columbus
Population	11,256,000
Motto	With God, All Things Are Possible
State Bird	Cardinal
State Flower	Scarlet carnation
Postal Abbreviation	OH

Statewide Visitor Information

Ohio Division of Travel and Tourism (✉ Box 1001, Columbus 43216, ☎ 800/282–5393). **Ohio Historical Society** (✉ 1982 Velma Ave., Columbus 43211, ☎ 614/297–2300).

Scenic Drives

The **Lake Erie Circle Tour** (☎ 888/327–LAKE for information) consists of nearly 200 mi of state routes and U.S. highways along the Lake Erie shoreline from Toledo to Conneaut (☞ Northwest Ohio and the Lake Erie Islands, *below*). **Route 7** (☎ 513/553–1500 for information), which runs parallel to the Ohio River along the state's southeastern border, cuts through the French-settled village of Gallipolis; the site of Ohio's only significant Civil War battle, near Pomeroy; and Marietta, the historic first city of the Northwest Territory.

National and State Parks

National Parks

National monuments include the **Hopewell Culture National Historic Park** (☞ Columbus, *below*) and **Perry's Victory and International Peace Memorial,** in Put-in-Bay (☞ Northwest Ohio and the Lake Erie Islands, *below*). **William Howard Taft National Historic Site** (✉ 2038 Auburn Ave., Cincinnati, ☎ 513/684–3262) is a national historic site. The **Cuyahoga Valley National Recreation Area** (✉ 15610 Vaughn Rd., Brecksville 44141, ☎ 440/526–5256) occupies 22 mi of forested valley between Cleveland and Akron along the Cuyahoga River, and follows the path of the historic Ohio and Erie Canal.

State Parks

Of the 73 state parks, eight are classified as **Ohio State Park Resorts** (☎ 800/282–7275), which have cabins for rent and facilities for swimming, boating, golf, tennis, and dining. For more information contact the **Ohio Department of Natural Resources** (✉ Ohio State Parks Information Center, Fountain Sq., Bldg. C–1, Columbus 43224, ☎ 614/265–7000 or 800/BUCKEYE).

COLUMBUS

Columbus, Ohio's state capital and largest city, is known for its entrepreneurial spirit and economic vitality. The city recently welcomed the country's first stadium built specifically for soccer, introduced a new Arena district, and doubled the size of its favorite science attraction, COSI (Center of Science and Industry). The state's largest university, Ohio State, is here, as are the headquarters of a number of Fortune 500 companies, many of whose executives claim they would not leave the city—even if they were promoted.

Visitor Information

Greater Columbus Convention and Visitors Bureau (⊠ 90 N. High St., Columbus, OH 43215, ☎ 614/221–6623 or 800/345–4386).

Arriving and Departing

By Bus
Greyhound (⊠ E. Town St. at 3rd St., ☎ 800/231–2222) serves Columbus.

By Car
Columbus is in the center of the state, at the intersection of I–70 and I–71.

By Plane
Port Columbus Airport, 10 mi east of downtown Columbus, is served by 21 airlines, including **Air Ontario** (☎ 800/776–3000) and **Midwest Express** (☎ 800/452–2022). A cab from the airport to downtown costs about $18; **Urban Express** (☎ 877/840–0411) airport shuttle from downtown costs $12.

Getting Around Columbus

Downtown is fairly compact and easily walkable. Some government buildings are connected to each other and to nearby buildings through underground walkways. The **Central Ohio Transit Authority** (☎ 614/228–1776), or COTA, operates buses within Columbus.

Exploring Columbus

Crew Stadium, home of the MLS's Columbus Crew, opened in May 1999 at the Ohio Expo Center and is the first stadium in the country built specifically for a professional soccer team. The stadium holds 22,500 soccer fans. The **Nationwide Arena,** on the northern edge of downtown, scheduled to open in the fall of 2000 as the home of the NHL's Columbus Blue Jackets.

At the heart of downtown is the domeless Greek Revival **state capitol** (⊠ Corner of High and Broad Sts., ☎ 614/752–9777), with its distinguished skylights, stained glass, and period details. The Veterans Memorial on the east side of the building is an addition to this historic structure. The lively **Riffe Gallery** (⊠ 77 S. High St., ☎ 614/644–9624), in the Vern Riffe Center for Government and the Arts, has works by Ohio artists. COSI (pronounced co-*sigh*), the **Center of Science and Industry** (⊠ 333 Broad St., ☎ 614/228–2674; ⌨ $12), moved to a building twice the size of the original. Bring the kids for the interactive science exhibits that encourage you to touch, feel, and create.

The **Short North** (☎ 614/421–1030), a strip of trendy shops, clubs, vintage clothing and antiques stores, restaurants, and art galleries north of downtown, holds a Gallery Hop the first Saturday of every month.

★ The **Wexner Center for the Arts** (⊠ N. High St. at 15th Ave., ☎ 614/292–0330 or 614/292–3535), on the Ohio State University campus, shows contemporary art in a dramatic building designed by Peter Eisenmann.

★ **German Village** (☎ 614/221–8888), a neighborhood of tightly packed brick homes built by immigrants in the 19th century, lies just south of downtown. In the **Brewery District,** next to German Village, old breweries are now restaurants and bars.

It looks like the plains of Africa at **The Wilds** (⊠ 14000 International Rd., ☎ 740/638–5030; ⌨ $10), in Cumberland, about 80 mi southeast of Columbus. Camels, giraffes, and bison roam 10,000 square acres of surface-mined land which has been reclaimed as an endangered species center. Guide buses take you within feet of the exotic animals at this facility, the largest of its kind in the United States. The park is closed November–April.

Three generations of gorillas, monkeys, and other animals call the new African Forest exhibit home. The facility is one of four manatee preserves outside of Florida and boasts a new pachyderm area. **Columbus Zoo and Aquarium** (⊠ 9990 Riverside Dr., ☎ 614/645–3550; ☜ $7), about 18 mi northwest of downtown off I–270.

Dining

Though dubbed the "Fast Food Capital of the World," by the *New York Times* and *Wall Street Journal,* Columbus features a lively restaurant scene. Eateries tucked into the Short North, German Village, and surrounding suburbs offers everything from down-home barbecue to haute cuisine.

$$$–$$$$ ✕ **Mitchell's Steakhouse.** Mitchell's, in the heart of downtown near the State House, is called by some the city's most beautiful restaurant. The renovated former bank building retains its ornate 20-ft-high ceilings. This nirvana for carnivores specializes in aged steaks and chops. ⊠ *45 N. 3rd St. at Gay St.,* ☎ *614/621–2333. AE, D, DC, MC, V.*

$$ ✕ **G. Michael's Italian American Bistro and Bar.** In a historic town house in quaint German Village, the atmosphere inside is fancy without feeling stuffy. Don't expect all red sauces and spaghetti and meatballs in their renditions of contemporary Italian American cuisine. Check out the intimate outdoor patio that seats 24 in the summer. ⊠ *595 S. 3rd St.,* ☎ *614/464–0575. AE, D, DC, MC, V.*

$ ✕ **City Barbecue.** Go for the food, not the atmosphere at this no-frills restaurant about 15 minutes northwest of downtown. The tables are crammed together, there's no table service, and the smoker sits in the parking lot. You'll be rewarded with big portions of North Carolina–style barbecue dressed with corn, baked beans, and other traditional fixings. ⊠ *2111 W Henderson Rd.,* ☎ *614/538–8890. AE, D, MC, V.*

$ ✕ **Haiku.** The sushi bar is the center of activity at this stylish Pan-Asian restaurant in the trendy Short North. Hot entrées include healthful, creative Asian dishes like the house specialty, noodles served in sauce or broth. There's a full sake menu to wash down the food. ⊠ *800 N. High St.,* ☎ *614/294–8168. AE, D, DC, MC, V.*

Lodging

Lodging is mostly in downtown Columbus and nearby German Village.

$$$–$$$$ 🏨 **Lofts Hotel, Columbus.** Italian furniture and exposed brick walls make ★ the 44 rooms feel like New York lofts; the Lofts' midwestern charms and courteous service remind you where you are. ⊠ *55 Nationwide Blvd., 43215,* ☎ *614/461–2663 or 800/73–LOFTS,* 🖷 *614/461–5828. 44 rooms. Restaurant, pool. AE, D, DC, MC, V.* ✧

$$$ 🏨 **Adam's Mark Hotel.** A new player in the downtown hotel scene, this modern and elegant hotel caters to a business clientele. ⊠ *50 N. Third St., 43215,* ☎ *614/228–5050 or 800/444–ADAM,* 🖷 *614/228–2525. 415 rooms. Pool, health club. AE, D, DC, MC, V.*

$$$ 🏨 **Westin Hotel, Columbus.** High ceilings, marble floors, and stone ★ columns give this turn-of-the-20th-century hotel a grand air. Rooms are done in a Queen Anne style, with marble baths. ⊠ *310 S. High St., 43215,* ☎ *614/228–3800,* 🖷 *614/228–7666. 196 rooms. Restaurant. AE, D, DC, MC, V.*

$$-$$$ 🏨 **Hyatt Regency, Columbus.** Adjacent to the convention center, this ultramodern high-rise hotel caters mainly to business travelers. (The Hyatt on Capitol Square has a more political crowd.) ⊠ *350 N. High St., 43215,* ☎ *614/463–1234,* 🖷 *614/280–3034. 632 rooms. Restaurant, pool, exercise room. AE, D, DC, MC, V.*

$$ 🏨 **Courtyard by Marriott.** Formerly a warehouse, this unusual hotel has a bi-level, contemporary lobby, and luxurious suites with kitchens. The location is convenient to everything. ⊠ *35 W. Spring St., 43215,* ☎ *614/228–3200,* 🖷 *614/228–6752. 149 rooms. Restaurant. AE, D, DC, MC, V.*

$ 🏨 **German Village Inn.** Friendly service and low rates are the advantages of this no-frills German Village hotel near downtown. ⊠ *920 S. High St., 43206,* ☎ *614/443–6506,* 🖷 *614/443–5663. 43 rooms. AE, D, DC, MC, V.*

Nightlife and the Arts

Two free weekly newspapers—the *Other Paper,* and *Columbus Alive!*—have complete listings of goings-on in the city.

Nightlife

Most of Columbus's hot spots are scattered near the Ohio StateUniversity campus (expect crowds when the OSU Buckeye football andbasketball teams play) and the downtown neighborhoods around GermanVillage, the Short North, and the Brewery District. Live bands play on the weekends at the **Short North Tavern** (⊠ 674 N. High St., ☎ 614/221–2432), which reverts to a neighborhood bar during the week. Live out your fantasy at **Howl at the Moon** (⊠ 450 S. Front St., ☎ 614/224–4695), where you can sing along with the dueling pianos at this 21-and-older club in the Brewery District. Endless rows of televisions line every wall and play the latest music videos at Union Station Video Café (⊠ 630 N. High St. at Goodale, ☎ 614/228–3546). From alternative and country to blues and rock, **Little Brother's** (⊠ 1100 N. High St., ☎ 614/421–2025) showcases the music of local singer-songwriters and bands.

The Arts

After more than 20 years, the **Southern Theater** (⊠ 21 E. Main St., ☎ 614/340–9698), originally built in 1896, was saved from the wrecking ball and fully restored and now opens its doors for such performance groups as the Columbus Jazz Orchestra and the Columbus Light Opera. The **Columbus Association for the Performing Arts** (☎ 614/469–0939) operates the **Capitol Theatre,** in the Riffe Center (⊠ 77 S. High St., ☎ 614/460–7214), and the **Ohio Theater** (⊠ 55 E. State St., ☎ 614/469–1045; 614/469–0939 for tickets), home to the **Columbus Symphony Orchestra** (☎ 614/228–8600) and the **BalletMet** (☎ 614/229–4860, 614/229–4848 for tickets). **Opera/Columbus** and touring Broadway shows take the stage at the **Palace Theatre** (⊠ 34 W. Broad St., ☎ 614/469–9850, 614/431–3600 for tickets).

Shopping

Columbus is the world headquarters of Leslie Wexner's empire of clothing stores, which include the Limited, Express, Structure, Victoria's Secret, and Abercrombie & Fitch, all of which are downtown in **Columbus City Center** (⊠ 111 S. 3rd St., ☎ 614/221–4900). You can't miss **Lazarus** (⊠ 141 S. High St., ☎ 614/463–2121), the granddaddy of Columbus department stores; its old-fashioned water tower sticks up out of the skyline like a Tootsie Roll Pop. **Prime Outlets at Jeffersonville I and II** (⊠ at I–71 exit 65 and 69, Jeffersonville, ☎ 800/746–7644), 35 minutes south of Columbus, has more than 150 outlets. Browse through more than 130 stores at the **Mall at Tuttle Crossing** (⊠ 5043

Tuttle Crossing Blvd., ☎ 614/717–9300) a charming, upscale shopping center just at the edge of Columbus. The **Easton Town Center** (⊠ I–270 and Easton Way, ☎ 614/337–2200), 16 minutes from downtown in the northeast part of the city, is the area's newest shopping and entertainment complex.

CINCINNATI

Cincinnati is a well-regulated city with a proud history, an active riverfront, and a busy downtown. A river's width from the South, in many respects it resembles a southern city: Its summers are hot and humid, a result of being in a basin along the Ohio River, and its politics lean toward the conservative.

Visitor Information

Greater Cincinnati Convention and Visitors Bureau (⊠ 300 W. 6th St., at Plum St., 45202, ☎ 513/621–6994 or 800/344–3445).

Arriving and Departing

By Bus
Greyhound (⊠ 1005 Gilbert Ave., ☎ 800/231–2222).

By Car
I–71, I–75, and I–74 all converge on downtown Cincinnati.

By Plane
Cincinnati/Northern Kentucky International Airport is 12 mi south of downtown, off I–275, in Kentucky. It is served by major airlines and by **ComAir** (☎ 800/354–9822). **Jetport Express** (☎ 606/767–3702) makes regular trips from the airport to downtown hotels ($12 one-way, $16 round-trip). Taxis downtown cost about $25 plus tip.

By Train
Amtrak (⊠ Union Terminal, 1301 Western Ave., ☎ 800/872–7245).

Getting Around Cincinnati

Downtown Cincinnati is entirely walkable. Skywalks connect hotels, convention centers, stores, and garages. **Metro** (☎ 513/621–4455) runs buses out of Government Square (⊠ 5th St. between Walnut and Main Sts.). There is also a downtown loop bus (Bus 79).

Exploring Cincinnati

Fountain Square (⊠ 5th and Vine Sts.) is the center of downtown Cincinnati. The city is laid out along the river, with numbered streets running east–west (2nd Street is Pete Rose Way); north–south streets have names. Vine Street divides the city into east and west.

If you have only an hour in Cincinnati, spend it at **Carew Tower** (⊠ 5th and Race Sts.) looking at the gorgeous Rookwood pottery in the arcade. Also don't miss the **Omni Netherland Plaza Hotel,** whose marble-and-rosewood interior is filled with mirrors and murals.

You can cross the Ohio River from Cincinnati into Covington, Kentucky, on the **Roebling Suspension Bridge,** built by John A. Roebling, who later designed the Brooklyn Bridge. **Covington Landing,** a floating entertainment complex and a wharf, is west of Roebling Bridge. Beyond the Covington wharf is **BB Riverboats** (☎ 606/261–8500), running river tours year-round. **Covington** itself, east of Roebling Bridge, is a neighborhood of fine antebellum mansions, with wonderful views from Riverside Drive.

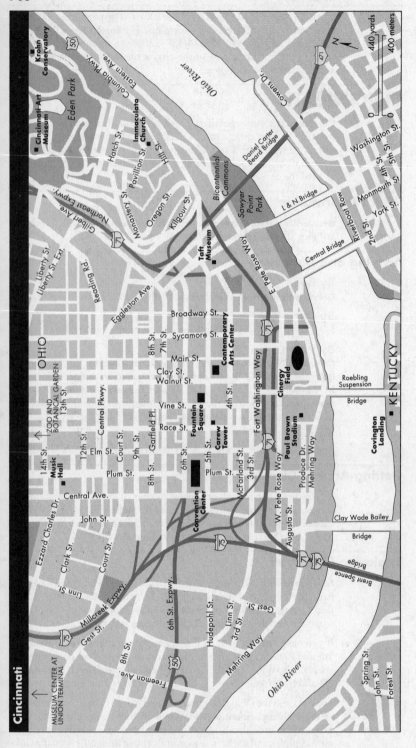

Cincinnati

On the Ohio side of the river, the narrow streets and funky houses of **Mount Adams,** the first hill east of downtown, are reminiscent of San Francisco. The yard of the **Immaculata Church** (⌧ Pavillion and Guido Sts., ☎ 513/721–6544) provides a sterling view of the city.

Eden Park, on Mt. Adams, is the site of the **Krohn Conservatory** (☞ Parks, Gardens, and Zoos, *below*) and the **Cincinnati Art Museum** (☎ 513/721–5204; ☷ $5, free on Sat.; closed Mon.), which has an outstanding collection of Near Eastern and ancient art. Downtown, the **Contemporary Arts Center** (⌧ 115 E. 5th St., ☎ 513/345–8400 or 513/721–0390; ☷ $3.50) presents some of today's most cutting-edge artists. The **Taft Museum of Art** (⌧ 316 Pike St., ☎ 513/241–0343; ☷ $4, free Wed. and Sat.) is famous for its Chinese porcelains.

🔄 You could spend a full day in the magnificently restored **Museum Center at Union Terminal** (⌧ 1301 Western Ave., off I–75 at Ezzard Charles Dr., ☎ 513/287–7000 or 800/733–2077), which looks like a huge Art Deco cabinet radio. This historic former train station houses the **Cinergy Children's Museum,** a delightfully inventive, hands-on museum for children of all ages; the **Museum of Natural History and Science,** which has a cave with real bats; the **Cincinnati History Museum;** and the **Robert D. Lindner Family OmniMax Theater.**

Paramount's **Kings Island Theme Park,** 24 mi north of Cincinnati in Kings Mills, has eight theme areas, including a water park and the world's longest wooden roller coaster. ⌧ *I–71 Exit 24,* ☎ *800/288–0808.* ☷ *$38.99; $20.99 seniors, children 3–6, or under 48". Closed Labor Day–mid-Apr. and weekdays mid-Apr.–Memorial Day.*

Parks, Gardens, and Zoos

Krohn Conservatory (☎ 513/421–4086; ☷ free), in Eden Park, has a greenhouse and gardens with more than 5,000 species of plants.

The **Cincinnati Zoo and Botanical Garden** (⌧ 3400 Vine St., ☎ 513/281–4700; ☷ $11), famous for its white Bengal tigers, is the second-oldest zoo in the country. Follow the paw-print signs off I–75 Exit 6 or I–71 Exit 7.

Bicentennial Commons, an outdoor recreation center at Sawyer Point on the Ohio River, uses monuments to tell the story of Cincinnati's origins as a river town. Look for the famous flying pigs, a playful reminder of the city's prominence as a meatpacking center.

Dining and Lodging

Famous for its chili, Cincinnati has more good restaurants than the most ravenous traveler could sample in one visit, including riverboat restaurants and rathskellers. Downtown Cincinnati has several choice hotels. Many offer weekend packages including tickets to Reds or Bengals games. Staying in the suburbs is less expensive.

$$$$ ✕ **The Maisonette.** Since 1964 the Maisonette has been ranked among the foremost restaurants in the United States. The food is fresh and French, the atmosphere formal. ⌧ *114 E. 6th St.,* ☎ *513/721–2260. Reservations essential. Jacket required. AE, D, DC, MC, V. Closed Sun.*

$$$–$$$$ ✕ **The Celestial.** The views from the top of Mt. Adams are as much of
★ a draw as the French and American cuisine. ⌧ *1071 Celestial St.,* ☎ *513/241–4455. Jacket required. AE, DC, MC, V. Closed Sun.*

$–$$ ✕ **Montgomery Inn at the Boathouse.** The barbecued ribs are famous, and you can't get any closer to the river without jumping in for a swim. Lunchtime and happy hour both draw crowds. ⌧ *925 Eastern Ave.,* ☎ *513/721–7427. AE, D, DC, MC, V. No lunch weekends.*

$ ✕ **Lenhardt's.** Schnitzel, Viennese and Hungarian goulash, sauerbraten, and potato pancakes are served at this casual place. The outdoor beer garden is a great summer escape. ⊠ *151 W. McMillan St.,* ☎ *513/281–3600. AE, D, MC, V. Closed Sun.–Mon., 1st 2 wks in Aug., 2 wks at Christmas.*

$ ✕ **Rookwood Pottery.** The wood-and-brick dining rooms contain what were once the kilns of the famous Mt. Adams pottery. Families come here for giant burgers and other simple fare. ⊠ *1077 Celestial St.,* ☎ *513/721–5456. AE, DC, MC, V.*

$$$–$$$$ ✕⌑ **Cincinnatian Hotel.** This sedate French Second Empire–style hotel has
★ a newly renovated lobby and unusual contemporary interior. This show-place features a wedding suite and a luxury whirlpool room. Reservations are essential at the Palace (☎ 513/381–6006), where the chef delights diners with his regional American cuisine—and his crème brûlée. ⊠ *601 Vine St., 45202,* ☎ *513/381–3000; 800/942–9000 in OH,* ℻ *513/651–0256. 146 rooms. 2 restaurants, health club. AE, D, DC, MC, V.* ☜

$$$–$$$$ ✕⌑ **Omni Netherland Plaza.** Downtown's grand Art Deco hotel is in
★ the Carew Tower (☞ *Exploring Cincinnati, above*). The two-story lobby has bas-relief sculptures and dramatic fountains and light fixtures; guest rooms have 10-ft ceilings and soft pastel colors. The restaurant, Orchids, serves American cuisine in the exquisite Palm Court Café. ⊠ *35 W. 5th St., 45202,* ☎ *513/421–9100,* ℻ *513/421–4291. 621 rooms. 2 restaurants, health club. AE, D, DC, MC, V.* ☜

$$–$$$ ⌑ **Amos Shinkle Townhouse B&B.** The master bedroom in this antebellum mansion, once home to the man who hired John A. Roebling to build a suspension bridge across the Ohio River, has a whirlpool and a crystal chandelier in the bathroom. Covington is a short ride from Cincinnati, on the other side of the Roebling Suspension Bridge. ⊠ *215 Garrard St., Covington, KY 41011,* ☎ *606/431–2118 or 800/972–7012,* ℻ *606/491–4551. 7 rooms. AE, D, DC, MC, V.*

$ ⌑ **Best Western Mariemont Inn.** Even the cash machine is in the Tudor style at this charming inn on the National Register of Historic Places. Amenities include a pub and free parking. ⊠ *6880 Wooster Pike (U.S. 50), Mariemont 45227,* ☎ *513/271–2100 or 800/528–1234,* ℻ *513/ 271–1057. 60 rooms. Restaurant. AE, D, DC, MC, V.* ☜

Nightlife and the Arts

Nightlife

On Riverboat Row, **Howl at the Moon Saloon** (⊠ 101 Riverboat Row, Newport, KY, ☎ 859/581–2800) features dueling piano players and sing-alongs. In Mt. Adams, **Longworth's** (⊠ 1108 St. Gregory St., ☎ 513/579–0900) has a DJ, a garden, and live music on weekends. The **Incline** (⊠ 1071 Celestial St., ☎ 513/241–4455), a sophisticated bar at the Celestial Restaurant, spotlights vocalists.

The Arts

The **Music Hall** (⊠ 1241 Elm St., ☎ 513/621–1919), built in the 18th century in a style since dubbed "sauerbraten Gothic," is home to the Cincinnati Symphony Orchestra as well as the **Cincinnati Pops Orchestra**

(☎ 513/381–3300), which performs from September through May at the Music Hall and June and July at Riverbend; and the **Cincinnati Opera** (☎ 513/241–2742), with performances in June and July. The **Cincinnati Ballet** performs from October through May at the Aronoff Center for the Arts (✉ 650 Walnut St., ☎ 513/621–2787), and holds special shows at the Music Hall.

Spectator Sports

Baseball: Cincinnati Reds (✉ 100 Cinergy Field, ☎ 513/421–4510). **Football: Cincinnati Bengals** (✉ Paul Brown Stadium, 1 Paul Brown Stadium Dr., ☎ 513/621–3550).

Shopping

There are upscale stores in the **Fountain Place Lazarus** (✉ 5th and Race Sts.), with Tiffany & Co. and Brook's Brothers setting the tone for this shopping area. **Tower Place** (✉ at 4th and Race Sts.) is an atrium shopping mall. Skywalks connect Tower Place with **Saks Fifth Avenue** (via Carew Tower). Over the Roebling Bridge in Covington, Kentucky, **Mainstrasse Village** has gift and antiques shops and vintage clothing boutiques.

NORTHWEST OHIO AND THE LAKE ERIE ISLANDS

Between Toledo and Cleveland lie a stretch of the Lake Erie shore and a group of islands that constitute the Riviera and Madeira of Ohio. Families rent cottages at Catawba Point or Put-in-Bay (the port village on South Bass Island) and swim, fish, and boat, topping the week off with a trip to Cedar Point Amusement Park in Sandusky.

Visitor Information

Erie County: Visitors Bureau (✉ 231 W. Washington Row, Sandusky 44870, ☎ 419/625–2984 or 800/255–3743) covers Cedar Point, Kelleys Island, and Sandusky. **Ottawa County:** Visitors Bureau (✉ 109 Madison St., Port Clinton 43452, ☎ 419/734–4386 or 800/441–1271) covers Catawba, Lakeside, Marblehead, Port Clinton, Oak Harbor, and Put-in-Bay. **Greater Toledo:** Convention and Visitors Bureau (✉ SeaGate Convention Center, 401 Jefferson Ave., 2nd floor, 43604, ☎ 419/321–6404 or 800/243–4667). **Kelleys Island:** Chamber of Commerce (✉ Box 783F, 43438, ☎ 419/746–2360). **Put-in-Bay:** Chamber of Commerce (✉ Box 250-BN, 43456, ☎ 419/285–2832).

Arriving and Departing

By Boat

Ferries serve the Lake Erie islands from May through October. **Put-in-Bay Jet Express** (☎ 800/245–1538), from Port Clinton to Put-in-Bay, takes passengers and bicycles only and has late-night service. Starting in March, **Miller Boat Line** (☎ 419/285–2421) takes passengers and cars (reservations required) from Catawba to Lime Kiln Dock (on the opposite side of South Bass Island from Put-in-Bay) and to Middle Bass Island. **Neumann Boat Line** (☎ 419/798–5800 or 800/876–1907) takes passengers from Marblehead to Kelleys Island.

By Bus

Greyhound has national service from Toledo (✉ 811 Jefferson Ave., ☎ 800/231–2222). **Toledo Area Regional Transit Authority** (TARTA; ☎ 419/243–7433) covers Toledo and its suburbs.

By Car

The Ohio Turnpike (I–80/90) runs between 5 and 10 mi south of the Lake Erie shoreline. For Toledo take Exit 4 (I–75) or Exit 5 (U.S. 280); for Port Clinton, Exit 6 (Route 53); for Sandusky, Exit 7 (U.S. 250). Toledo is on I–75. Route 2 hugs the lake between Toledo and Sandusky; Route 269 loops out to Marblehead.

By Plane

Toledo Express Airport is served by six airlines. **Cleveland Hopkins Airport** (☞ Arriving and Departing *in* Cleveland, *below*) is served by major airlines and several commuter lines. **Griffing Island Airlines** (☎ 419/734–3149), out of **Port Clinton Airport** (✉ 3255 E. State Rd.), and **Griffing Flying Service** (☎ 419/626–5161) fly to the Lake Erie Islands out of **Griffing–Sandusky Airport** (✉ 3115 Cleveland Rd., east of Sandusky).

By Train

Amtrak (☎ 800/872–7245) stops in Toledo and Sandusky.

Exploring Northwest Ohio and the Lake Erie Islands

A true lakefront town, **Toledo** combines natural beauty with local artistry such as glassblowing. Its multicultural mix supports great ethnic eats, interesting architecture, and a host of unusual storefront shops. Just down the coastline the shores of Lake Erie teem with wildlife. The Toledo Mud Hens, a Detroit Tigers farm team, play in **Ned Skeldon Stadium,** at Lucas County Recreation Center (✉ 2901 Key St., off U.S. 24, Maumee, ☎ 419/893–9843). The **Toledo Museum of Art** (✉ 2445 Monroe St., at Scottwood Ave., off I–75, ☎ 419/255–8000) has a fine collection of European and American paintings, ancient Greek and Egyptian statues, and regionally produced and internationally recognized blown glass.

Vacationland begins at **Port Clinton,** a center for fishing excursions, at the northern base of the Marblehead Peninsula, some 30 mi east of Toledo on Route 2 (☞ Outdoor Activities and Sports, *below*). Port Clinton is also the base for a ferry to South Bass Island's **Put-in-Bay** (☞ Arriving and Departing, *above*), a port village consisting of a marina, a grassy lakefront park dotted with small cannons, and a strip of shops, bars, and restaurants, with a vintage wooden merry-go-round. Now a town of wild parties, Put-in-Bay was the site of Commodore Oliver Hazard Perry's naval victory over the British in the War of 1812. From the top of **Perry's Victory and International Peace Memorial,** a single massive Doric column east of downtown, you can see all the way to Canada. From May through September you can hop on a ferry to **Middle Bass Island** and sample the wares of the **Lonz Winery** (☎ 419/285–5411), which looks like a European monastery.

Back on the mainland, at the eastern tip of the peninsula, is **Marblehead,** site of the oldest continuously working lighthouse on Lake Erie. From Marblehead it's a short ferry ride to **Kelleys Island,** which has two remarkable geologic features: Glacial grooves (waves in the rock) carved during the Ice Age are visible on the north shore, and the south shore has prehistoric Native American pictographs.

Sandusky, a small port city with lush gardens enlivening its town square, makes a good touring base. It's near the highways and ferries and has thousands of motel rooms as well as a few romantic Victorian hideaways.

Cedar Point Amusement Park (✉ Off U.S. 250N, ☎ 419/627–2350; ✐ $38) is in the *Guinness Book of Records* because it has the most roller coasters in the world (14, and counting), including the new Millennium Force, the tallest and fastest roller coaster in the world. It also has Snake River Falls, the tallest, deepest, and quickest water ride in the world; a water park; and a mile-long sandy beach. The park is open daily in summer and on weekends in September.

Dining and Lodging

The chambers of commerce in Put-in-Bay and on Kelleys Island (☞ Visitor Information, *above*) give advice on lodging, which should be arranged well in advance.

Catawba Point

$-$$ ✕ **Mon Ami.** This well-established winery and restaurant has a chalet-★ style dining room with 4-ft-thick stone walls and a patio surrounded by wooden casks. Pasta and fresh fish are the specialties. Enjoy live jazz during the summer. ⊠ *3845 E. Wine Cellar Rd., off N.E. Catawba Rd. (Rte. 53),* ☏ *419/797–4445 or 800/777–4266. AE, MC, V.*

Grand Rapids

$$ 🏠 **Mill House.** This country-Victorian house on the Maumee River 40 minutes from downtown Toledo was built in 1900 as a working grist-mill. One of the four French Country–style guest rooms has its own private entrance and whirlpool tub. ⊠ *24070 Front St., 43522,* ☏ *419/ 832–6455. 4 rooms. AE, D, MC, V. CP.*

Marblehead

$$ 🏠 **Old Stone House Bed & Breakfast.** Victorian antiques fill this Fed-eral-style mansion. ⊠ *133 Clemons St., 43440,* ☏ *419/798–5922 or 877/798–5922. 13 rooms. D, MC, V. CP.*

Port Clinton

$-$$ ✕ **Garden at the Lighthouse.** American cuisine is served with casual elegance in the terraced garden of this Victorian house originally built for the lighthouse keeper. ⊠ *226 E. Perry St.,* ☏ *419/732–2151. AE, D, DC, MC, V. Closed Sun. and Mon. Sept.–May.*

$$-$$$ ✕🏠 **Island House Inn.** The casual dining room of the 110-year-old red-brick hotel has tall windows and serves fresh fish. ⊠ *102 Madison St., 43452,* ☏ *419/734–2166 or 800/233–7307. 39 rooms. Restaurant. AE, D, DC, MC, V.*

$ 🏠 **Beach Cliff Lodge.** An unpretentious place near the ferry and the state park with freezers and fish-cleaning services. ⊠ *4189 N.W. Catawba Rd., 43452,* ☏ *419/797–4553. 8 rooms, 19 cottages. No credit cards.*

Put-in-Bay

$$ ✕ **Crescent Tavern.** If you're only going to eat one meal in Put-in-Bay, come to this gracious Victorian house for seafood, steak, and pasta. ⊠ *Delaware Ave.,* ☏ *419/285–4211. D, MC, V. Closed Oct.–Mar.*

$ ✕ **Frosty's.** With a bar and a pool table on one side, and Formica ta-bles on the other, this noisy hangout caters to rowdies and families. ⊠ *Delaware Ave.,* ☏ *419/285–4741. D, MC, V. Closed Oct.–Mar.*

$-$$ 🏠 **Park Hotel.** This white-frame hotel, dating from the 1870s, has etched glass and a gracious Victorian lobby. It's also smack in the middle of the island revelry, so bring earplugs. ⊠ *234 Delaware Ave., Box 60, 43456,* ☏ *419/285–3581. 26 rooms. MC, V. Closed Oct.–Mar. CP.*

Sandusky

$$$ 🏠 **Hotel Breakers.** Built in 1905 to resemble a French château, with a ★ five-story rotunda, stained glass, and vintage wicker furniture, this is *the* place to stay on the beach at Cedar Point, especially if you can get a turret room. ⊠ *Cedar Point Amusement Park, Box 5006, 44871,* ☏ *419/627–2106. 400 rooms. 4 restaurants, pool. D, MC, V.*

$$$ 🏠 **Radisson Harbor Inn.** This big hotel is successfully disguised as a rambling, weathered beach house. It's on the property of Cedar Point

Amusement Park, connected via a walkway to many restaurants and shops. ⊠ *2001 Cleveland Rd., at Cedar Point Causeway, 44870,* ☎ *419/627–2500,* FAX *419/627–0745. 237 rooms. Restaurant, pool, exercise room. AE, D, DC, MC, V.*

$$ 🏨 **Wagner's 1844 Inn.** Each of the three guest rooms at this inn a block from downtown has a private bath, canopy beds, and globe lamps. Guests can use the pool table, TV, and travel library. ⊠ *230 E. Washington St., 44870,* ☎ *419/626–1726. 3 rooms. D, MC, V. CP.*

Toledo

$ ✕ **Tony Packo's Cafe.** Before Max Klinger ever mentioned it on *M*A*S*H,* Tony Packo's was famous for its Tiffany lamps and Hungarian hot dogs. (The buns are imprinted with the restaurant's logo, lest you forget where you are.) ⊠ *1902 Front St.,* ☎ *419/691–6054. AE, D, MC, V.*

$–$$$ 🏨 **Wyndham Hotel.** This is the only downtown hotel right on the Maumee River. It's also conveniently connected by walkways to office buildings and the convention center. ⊠ *2 SeaGate/Summit St., 43604,* ☎ *419/241–1411,* FAX *419/241–1855. 241 rooms. Restaurant, pool, exercise room. AE, D, DC, MC, V.*

Motels

The majority of area motels are in and around Sandusky, on the roads to Cedar Point.

🏨 **Best Western Resort Inn** (⊠ 1530 Cleveland Rd., Sandusky 44870, ☎ 419/625–9234), 106 rooms; restaurant, pool; *$$–$$$.*

🏨 **Comfort Inn** (⊠ 11020 U.S. 250, Milan Rd., Milan 44846, ☎ 419/499–4681), 103 rooms; pool; *$$–$$$.*

Campground

⚠ **St. Hazard's Village on the Beach** has tent and RV sites, hot showers, a beach, bike rentals, boat rentals, and charter-fishing packages. ⊠ *1233 Fox Rd. (Box 69), Middle Bass Island 43446,* ☎ *419/285–6121 or 800/837–5211. Closed Oct.–Mar.*

Outdoor Activities and Sports

Beaches and Water Sports

The best Lake Erie beach is at **East Harbor State Park,** off Route 163 on Marblehead Peninsula. **Cedar Point Amusement Park** also has good swimming. You can rent sailboats and take sailing lessons from **Adventure Plus Yacht Charters and Sailing** at the Sandusky Harbor Marina (☎ 419/625–5000).

Fishing

The western Lake Erie Basin is known as the "walleye capital of the world"; Toledo even has a **Walleye Hot Line** (☎ 419/893–9740), which operates from March through May. Smallmouth bass and Lake Erie perch are also plentiful. Nonresident fishing licenses are sold at bait shops, or contact the **Division of Wildlife** (☎ 419/625–8062). There's ice fishing when the lake freezes.

The breakwater in Port Clinton and the pier at Catawba Point are both good fishing areas. Per-head fishing boats leave from **Fisherman's Wharf** in Port Clinton (☎ 419/734–6388) and from **Battery Park Marina** in Sandusky (☎ 419/625–6142), among other places.

CLEVELAND

In recent years Cleveland has emerged with a new cultural identity. Major attractions such as the Rock and Roll Hall of Fame and Museum, the Great Lakes Science Center, and the Gateway sports venues, have been the main catalysts, along with the world-class orchestra, stunning art museum, fully restored downtown theater district, and blooming gardens on the east side of town. The renaissance continues with the completion of Municipal Stadium, the long-anticipated new home of the Cleveland Browns. Neighborhoods such as the Flats, the Warehouse District, the Gateway district, and Northcoast Harbor buzz with restaurants, shops, and nightclubs.

Visitor Information

Cleveland Convention and Visitors Bureau, Visitor Information Center (⊠ 50 Public Sq., Suite 3100, ☎ 216/621–4110 or 800/321–1004).

Arriving and Departing

By Bus

Greyhound (⊠ E. 15th St. and Chester Ave., ☎ 800/231–2222).

By Car

I–90 runs east–west through downtown Cleveland. Interstate–71 and I–77 come up from the south. Driving from the east on the Ohio Turnpike (I–80), take Exit 10 to I–71N.

By Plane

Cleveland Hopkins International Airport (☎ 216/265–6030), 10 mi southwest of downtown, is served by major airlines and several commuter lines. From here the **Rapid Transit Authority** rail system (☎ 216/566–5100) takes 20 minutes to Public Square and costs $1.50. A taxi takes twice as long and costs about $20.

By Train

Amtrak (⊠ 200 Memorial Shoreway NE, ☎ 800/872–7245).

Getting Around Cleveland

The RTA rapid-transit system (☎ 216/566–5100), though not extensive, efficiently bridges east and west, with Tower City as its hub. RTA buses travel from Public Square on five downtown loop routes. A light-rail system, the **Waterfront Line,** links Tower City with the Flats entertainment district, Municipal Stadium, the Rock and Roll Hall of Fame and Museum, the Great Lakes Science Center, downtown shopping, and municipal parking lots.

Exploring Cleveland

Begin your tour of Cleveland at **Terminal Tower,** the city's central landmark. **Tower City Center,** an office and shopping complex, includes the shops of the Avenue (☞ Shopping, *below*). Pick up a copy of "Walks," a brochure outlining some popular Cleveland walking tours, at the **visitor information center** just inside the entrance to Tower City Center. The **Old Arcade** is filled with specialty shops and runs between Superior and Euclid avenues, a short block east of Public Square. Built in 1890, this is still downtown's most architecturally significant building. Like a nave without a cathedral, it rises five stories, with brass railings, ironwork, walkways, and a skylight.

South of Public Square on Ontario Street you'll find **Gund Arena** (⊠ 1 Center Court, ☎ 216/420–2000), a sports venue that hosts basketball, hockey, indoor football, concerts, and other events. Next to the arena is **Jacobs Field** (⊠ 2401 Ontario St., ☎ 216/420–4200), a trapezoid-shape baseball park that looks at once old-fashioned and brand new.

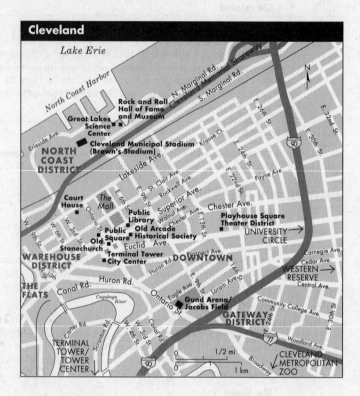

Cleveland

Lake Erie

North Coast Harbor

N. Marginal Rd.
Cleveland Memorial Shoreway
S. Marginal Rd.

Rock and Roll Hall of Fame and Museum

Great Lakes Science Center

Erieside Ave.

Cleveland Municipal Stadium (Brown's Stadium)

NORTH COAST DISTRICT

Lakeside Ave.

E. 6th St. Clair Ave.
Rockwell Ave.

Krause Ct.
Payne Ave.

Court House

The Mall

Public Library

Superior Ave.
Walnut Ave.
Chester Ave.

Chester Ave.

Playhouse Square Theater District

UNIVERSITY CIRCLE →

Public Square
Old Arcade
Historical Society
Old Stonechurch
Euclid Ave.
Terminal Tower
City Center

Prospect Ave.

Carnegie Ave.

WAREHOUSE DISTRICT

DOWNTOWN

Huron Rd.

WESTERN RESERVE →
Central Ave.

THE FLATS

Huron Rd.
Canal Rd.

Cuyahoga River

Eagle Ave.
Lorain Ave.

Ontario St.

Gund Arena/
Jacobs Field

Community College Ave.

GATEWAY DISTRICT

Center Rd.
Scranton Rd.
W. 3rd St.
W. 4th St.
Canal Rd.

Woodland Ave.

TERMINAL TOWER/ TOWER CENTER ↓

Broadway

CLEVELAND METROPOLITAN ZOO ↓

1/2 mi

1 km

For a fabulous view of the lake, take East 9th Street to North Coast
★ Harbor, formerly the East 9th Street Pier. The **Rock and Roll Hall of
Fame and Museum** (⊠ 1 Key Plaza, ☎ 216/781–7625, 800/282–5393
for a brochure, ☎ $14.95) has more than 55 high- and low-tech ex-
hibits including interactive kiosks that provide a video and sound exploration of performers' contributions to the rock genre, and the Sun
recording studio, where Elvis Presley, Carl Perkins, and Roy Orbison
made their first records. Stage costumes that once belonged to Chuck
Berry and Iggy Pop, handwritten lyrics by Jimi Hendrix, Janis Joplin's
Porsche, and a number of thought-provoking films are among the museum's holdings. **The Great Lakes Science Center** (⊠ 601 Erieside, ☎
216/694–2000; ☎ $6.75) focuses on the environment and technology,
particularly in relation to the Great Lakes. The 165,000-square-ft museum has dozens of hands-on exhibits and a 324-seat Omnimax Theater. From June through September, the *Goodtime III* (☎ 216/861–5110)
gives sightseeing tours on the Cuyahoga River and short lake cruises.

University Circle, reached by rapid transit or a 15-minute drive from
downtown, contains more than 50 cultural institutions. The center-
piece of University Circle is the **Cleveland Museum of Art** (⊠ 11150
E. Blvd., ☎ 216/421–7340; ☎ free), a white-marble temple set among
spring-flowering trees and reflected in a lagoon. The museum (closed
Monday) is world renowned for its medieval European collection,
Egyptian art, and European and American paintings. The **Museum of
Natural History** (⊠ 1 Wade Oval Dr., ☎ 216/231–4600, ☎ $6.50) has
an observatory and planetarium. The **Children's Museum** (⊠ 10730
Euclid Ave., ☎ 216/791–5437; ☎ $5) has interactive exhibits on top-
ics such as geography, bridge-building, climate, and weather. Juno, the
see-through woman, and a remodeled 18-ft-high tooth are among the
favorite permanent exhibits at the **Health Museum** (⊠ 8911 Euclid Ave.,
☎ 216/231–5010; ☎ $5); traveling exhibits focus on current health

issues and are designed to be fun and educational for kids. The **Western Reserve Historical Society** (✉ 10825 East Blvd., ☎ 216/721–5722; 🎟 $7.50), closed Monday, has an extensive Napoleonic collection, and just about every old car you'd want to see is in the **Crawford Auto-Aviation Museum**. Also in University Circle is **Severance Hall**, home of the Cleveland Orchestra (☞ Nightlife and the Arts, *below*), with the city's most beautiful Art Deco interior.

Parks, Gardens, and Zoos

Cleveland Metroparks Zoo and Rainforest (✉ Brookside Park Dr. off W. 25th St., ☎ 216/661–6500; 🎟 $7) has tropical plants and animals in a simulated rain-forest environment, as well as an excellent outdoor zoo. At **Edgewater Park,** just west of downtown, you can swim while enjoying a startlingly close-up view of downtown. The park also has a fishing pier, bait shop, fitness course, playgrounds, and picnic facilities. The stiff wind off the lake attracts kite flyers, boomerang enthusiasts, windsurfers, and the occasional hang glider. Drive through the **Cleveland Cultural Gardens** (✉ Martin Luther King Blvd. in University Circle, north of Chester Ave. and south of I–90, ☎ 216/664–2517) to see gardens representing more than 20 nationalities. The **Rockefeller Park Greenhouse** (✉ 750 E. 88th St., ☎ 216/664–3103), the oldest civic horticultural center in the country, houses seasonal flower and plant exhibits indoors; outside you'll find a Japanese garden, a formal English garden, and a talking garden for people with vision impairments. In Aurora, 30 mi southeast of Cleveland, **Sea World** (✉ Rtes. 43 and 82, ☎ 330/995–2121 or 330/562–8101, 800/637–4268 for recording) is a kid-friendly summertime destination. It's closed from September through May.

Dining

Ethnic food reigns in Cleveland, whether it's a spicy burrito or Polish kielbasa smothered with Cleveland's famous Stadium Mustard. There are restaurant rows in the Flats, the Warehouse District, the area around Gund Arena and Jacobs Field, Little Italy, and on Coventry Road in Cleveland Heights.

$$$ ✕ **Watermark.** Located in a converted warehouse on the banks of the busy Cuyahoga River in Cleveland's Flats district, the Watermark serves a mix of fresh seafood specialties and local products like Ohio Italian chicken sausage. ✉ *1250 Old River Rd.,* ☎ *216/241–1600. AE, D, DC, MC, V.*

$$–$$$ ✕ **Moxie.** In the upscale town of Beachwood, 20 minutes southeast of
★ downtown Cleveland by car, this trendy newcomer is a must. It's unassuming from the outside, but once you step into the large, bright room and taste the creatively prepared American fare with a nouvelle twist, you'll understand why they named it Moxie. ✉ *3355 Richmond Rd., off I–271, Beachwood,* ☎ *216/831–5599. AE, D, MC, V.*

$$–$$$ ✕ **Sans Souci.** Sophisticated seafood dishes and contemporary Mediterranean cuisine are served in a comfortably elegant dining room overlooking Public Square. ✉ *24 Public Sq.,* ☎ *216/696–5600. Reservations essential. AE, D, DC, MC, V.*

$$ ✕ **Luchita's.** With great authentic Mexican food, generous portions, good margaritas, and friendly service, it's no wonder this restaurant with two locations is jammed on the weekends. The menu changes every three months. ✉ *3456 W. 117th St.,* ☎ *216/252–1169;* ✉ *13112 Shaker Sq.,* ☎ *216/561–8537. AE, MC, V. Closed Mon.*

$–$$ ✕ **La Dolce Vita.** In addition to trendy Italian food, this neighborhood restaurant has an eclectic schedule of musicians that includes strolling mariachis and live opera performers. On Monday nights there's an eight-course meal; on other days, specials include veal, seafood, and risotto dishes. ⊠ *12112 Mayfield Rd.,* ☎ *216/721–8155. Reservations essential Mon. MC, V.*

$–$$ ✕ **Lola Bistro & Wine Bar.** Chef-owner Michael Simon has received national attention from food and wine critics for the creations he describes as "urban comfort food." Read: homey American classics with a novel twist. Best-sellers on the winter menu are seafood pierogi, and macaroni-and-cheese with fresh rosemary, goat cheese, and roasted chicken. Fish and game are first-rate; desserts are out of this world. ⊠ *900 Literary Rd., Tremont,* ☎ *216/771–5652. Reservations essential. AE, D, DC, MC, V.*

$–$$ ✕ **The Palazzo.** The third generation of the original owners prepare northern Italian cuisine in this romantic hideaway. Whether turning out updated versions of her recipes or new dishes inspired by annual trips back to Italy, they do their grandma proud. ⊠ *10031 Detroit Ave.,* ☎ *216/651–3900. AE, D, MC, V. Closed Sun. and Mon.*

$ ✕ **Nate's Deli and Restaurant.** This breakfast and lunch spot on the near West Side serves traditional deli fare as well as Middle Eastern and vegetarian specialties. The creamy hummus may be the best in town. ⊠ *1923 W. 25th St.,* ☎ *216/696–7529. No credit cards. Closed Sun. No dinner.*

$ ✕ **Tommy's.** A vegetarian institution on hippie-tinged Coventry Road, Tommy's serves hefty salads and sandwiches, and embarrassingly large but delicious milk shakes made with Cleveland's own Pierre's ice cream. ⊠ *1824 Coventry Rd., Cleveland Heights,* ☎ *216/321–7757. MC, V.*

Lodging

Many downtown hotels have weekend packages; those in the suburbs have lower weekday rates.

$$$$ 🏨 **Ritz-Carlton.** The city's only four-star hotel is filled with antiques
★ and original 18th-century art. The Riverview Room restaurant has excellent views of the Flats. ⊠ *1515 W. 3rd St., 44113,* ☎ *216/623–1300,* FAX *216/623–0515. 208 rooms. Restaurant, pool, exercise room. AE, D, DC, MC, V.*❧

$$$–$$$$ 🏨 **Embassy Suites Hotel.** The lobby of this all-suite hotel feels like an old-style ocean liner or a private club. Some rooms have in-suite kitchens. ⊠ *1701 E. 12th St., 44114,* ☎ *216/523–8000,* FAX *216/523–1698. 268 suites. Restaurant, pool, health club. AE, D, DC, MC, V.*

$$$–$$$$ 🏨 **Renaissance Cleveland Hotel.** The city's original grand hotel has a lobby with an ornate Carrara marble fountain. Guest rooms have period furniture and spacious marble bathrooms. ⊠ *24 Public Sq., 44113,* ☎ *216/696–5600,* FAX *216/696–0432. 491 rooms. 2 restaurants, pool, health club. AE, D, DC, MC, V.*

$$$–$$$$ 🏨 **Sheraton Cleveland City Center Hotel.** This hotel is geared to business travelers, with upgraded communications systems and plenty of phones and work space in all rooms. ⊠ *777 St. Clair Ave., 44114,* ☎ *216/771–7600, 800/321–1090 in OH,* FAX *216/566–0736. 470 rooms. Restaurant, health club. AE, D, DC, MC, V.*

$$$–$$$$ 🏨 **The Wyndham Hotel.** The 14 stories of the Wyndham—the newest addition to Cleveland's Playhouse Square—overlook the bright lights of the vibrant theater district. The hotel's airy, modern lobby is flanked by Winsor's, an exceptional restaurant and bar. ⊠ *1260 Euclid Ave., Cleveland, 44106,* ☎ *216/615–7500,* FAX *216/231–3329. 205 rooms. 3 restaurants, pool, exercise room. AE, D, DC, MC, V.*

$$$ 🏨 **Baricelli Inn.** Every room is different in this simple European-style brownstone mansion–turned–bed-and-breakfast. It's convenient to University Circle. The dining room (closed Sunday) serves contemporary European and American dinners. ⊠ *2203 Cornell Rd., 44106,* ☎ *216/791–6500,* FAX *216/791–9131. 7 rooms. Restaurant. AE, DC, MC, V. CP.*

$$$ 🏨 **Cleveland Marriott Key Center.** Attached to Key Tower, the tallest building in Cleveland, this hotel faces the historic Mall "C" and abuts Public Square. Plush accommodations have fantastic views of Lake Erie and the downtown skyline. ⊠ *127 Public Sq., 44114,* ☎ *216/696–9200,* FAX *216/696–0966. 400 rooms. Restaurant, exercise room. AE, D, DC, MC, V.*

$$$ 🏨 **Mario's International Spa and Hotel.** This is a charming country getaway with a spa is full of antiques and Victorian decor. The restaurant, which is open to the public, has a private area for robe-clad spa diners. Meals are wholesome but tasty, ranging from Roman pizza to six-course northern Italian dinners. ⊠ *35 E. Garfield Rd. (Rtes. 82 and 306), Aurora 44202,* ☎ *330/562–9171,* FAX *330/562–2386. 14 rooms. Restaurant, health club. AE, D, DC, MC, V.*

$$–$$$ 🏨 **Holiday Inn–Lakeshore.** Across from Burke Lakefront Airport and convenient to the train station, the Rock and Roll Hall of Fame and Museum, and the Great Lakes Science Center, this hotel has lake views and an unbeatable location. ⊠ *1111 Lakeside, 44114,* ☎ *216/241–5100,* FAX *216/241–5437. 380 rooms. Restaurant, pool, exercise room. AE, D, DC, MC, V.*

$$–$$$ 🏨 **Ramada Inn–Southeast.** This seven-story suburban hotel, with a restful, blue-and-gray lobby, provides easy access to Sea World and nearby Geauga Lake. ⊠ *24801 Rockside Rd. (at I–271), Bedford Heights 44146,* ☎ FAX *330/439–2500. 130 rooms. Restaurant, pool. AE, D, DC, MC, V.*

$ 🏨 **Brooklyn YMCA.** Bare-bones single rooms for men are available on a first-come, first-served basis. ⊠ *3881 Pearl Rd., 44109,* ☎ *216/749–2355. 69 rooms. Pool, exercise room. D, MC, V.*

Motels

Motels are concentrated around the Berea–Middleburg Heights exit off I–71 (near the airport), the Rockside Road/Brecksville exit off I–77, and the Chagrin Boulevard/Beachwood exit off I–271. Closer to Aurora, rates are higher in summer.

🏨 **Six Flag Woodlands Hotel** (⊠ 800 N. Aurora Rd., Aurora 44202, ☎ 330/562–9151 or 800/877–7849), 145 rooms; restaurant, pool, exercise room; $$$.

🏨 **Radisson Inn Beachwood** (⊠ 26300 Chagrin Blvd., Beachwood 44122, ☎ 330/831–5150 or 800/221–2222), 196 rooms; restaurant, pool, exercise room; $$.

🏨 **La Siesta Motel** (⊠ 8300 Pearl Rd., Strongsville 44136, ☎ 440/234–4488), 38 rooms; $$.

🏨 **Quality Inn Airport** (⊠ 16161 Brook Park Rd., Cleveland 44142, ☎ 440/267–5100 or 800/228–5151, FAX 440/267–2428), 158 rooms; restaurant, pools; $.

Nightlife and the Arts

Nightlife

Nightlife is concentrated on both banks of the Flats—where the crowd is young and into everything from bar-hopping to live music—as well as in the more mature Warehouse District.

At the south end of the Flats, the **Powerhouse** is a beautifully restored building that was originally a power station for Cleveland's trolley cars; today it houses the Improv Comedy Club (☎ 216/696–4677) and other shops and restaurants. For a look at the Flats the way it used to be—a blue-collar haven—stop in at the **Harbor Inn** bar (⊠ 1219 Main

Ave., ☎ 216/241–3232). At **Liquid Café & Bar** (✉ 1212 W. 6th St., ☎ 216/479–7717), in the Warehouse District, patrons sit in comfy chairs playing Scrabble and other board games. The rest of the district is lined with dance clubs and fine-dining establishments. Across the river in Ohio City, Market Avenue bustles with sidewalk cafés in the summertime. In the center of the action here is the **Great Lakes Brewing Company** (✉ 2516 Market Ave., ☎ 216/771–4404). **Market Avenue Wine Bar** (✉ 2524 Main Ave., ☎ 216/696–9463) has a brilliant wine list, and simple appetizers.

The Arts

Playhouse Square Center (✉ 1501 Euclid Ave., at E. 17th St., ☎ 216/771–4444) is home to the Cleveland Ballet, Cleveland Opera, and the Great Lakes Theater Festival. The **Cleveland Play House** (✉ 8500 Euclid Ave., ☎ 216/795–7000) and **Karamu House** (✉ 2355 E. 89th St., at Quincy Ave., ☎ 216/795–7070) are near University Circle. **Severance Hall** (✉ 11001 Euclid Ave., ☎ 216/231–1111) is home to the Cleveland Orchestra, except in summer, when the orchestra performs in a pastoral outdoor shed, **Blossom Music Center** (☎ 330/920–8040 or 888/225–6776), between Cleveland and Akron. Tickets to many events are sold through **TicketMaster** (☎ 216/241–5555) and **Advantix** (☎ 216/241–6000).

Spectator Sports

Baseball: Cleveland Indians (✉ Jacobs Field, 2401 Ontario St., at Carnegie Ave., ☎ 216/420–4200). **Basketball: Cavaliers** (✉ Gund Arena, Ontario St. at Huron Rd., ☎ 216/420–2000).

Football: Cleveland Browns (✉ Municipal Stadium, W. 3rd and Lakeside, ☎ 216/891–5000).

Shopping

Cleveland has two glitzy downtown malls, the **Galleria** (✉ 1301 E. 9th St., ☎ 216/861–4343) and the **Avenue** (✉ Tower City Center, ☎ 216/241–8550), with views of the river. The **West Side Market** (✉ Corner of W. 25th St. and Lorain Rd.), the world's largest indoor/outdoor farmers' market, sells freshly baked breads, fruit picked that morning, and perhaps the sharpest cheddar cheese you've ever eaten.

ELSEWHERE IN OHIO

Neil Armstrong Air and Space Museum

Arriving and Departing

The museum is off I–75, halfway between Cincinnati and Toledo (about an hour from either), in Wapakoneta, Neil Armstrong's hometown.

What to See and Do

Ohio is a leading producer of astronauts. At the **Neil Armstrong Air and Space Museum** (✉ I–75 Exit 111, ☎ 419/738–8811 or 800/860–0142; ⌨ $5), you can begin to identify with these explorers. The museum is closed from December through February.

Dayton

Arriving and Departing

Dayton is 54 mi north of Cincinnati on I–75, just below the interchange with I–70. **Dayton International Airport** is served by several major carriers and commuter lines.

What to See and Do

Aviation is central to the history of Dayton. The **Dayton/Montgomery County Convention and Visitors Bureau** (⌧ 1 Chamber Plaza, Suite A, 5th and Main Sts., 45409, ☎ 937/226–8212 or 800/221–8235) publishes a helpful visitors' guide and operates an information center at the United States Air Force Museum (☞ *below*).

The **Dayton Aviation Heritage National Historical Park** (☎ 937/225–7705) includes the field where Dayton natives Orville and Wilbur Wright first practiced flying, as well as the **Wright Cycle Company** (⌧ 22 S. Williams St.), the **Wright Memorial,** and the home of a Wright Brothers associate, noted African-American poet Paul Laurence Dunbar.

The **United States Air Force Museum** (⌧ Wright-Patterson Air Force Base, Springfield Pike, ☎ 937/255–3286; ⌧ free), an internationally known attraction, explains the story of flight, from Icarus to the Space Age and features more than 300 aircraft including *Air Force One* and *Apollo 15.* The **IMAX Theater** shows flight-related films several times daily (☎ 937/253–4629; ⌧ $5). Also here are museum shops, a café, and picnic tables. Take I–75 to the Route 4/Harshman Road Exit.

Southeast of Dayton, the **National Afro-American Museum and Cultural Center** (⌧ 1350 Brush Row Rd., Wilberforce 45384, ☎ 937/376– 4944 or 800/BLK–HIST; ⌧ $4; closed Mon.) is one of the largest African-American museums in the United States—and the only such museum chartered by Congress. Among its many exhibits exploring history and art is the permanent From Victory to Freedom, which examines black politics from the 1940s through the '60s. To get here, take U.S. 35 to Route 42. The museum is closed Monday.

Dining and Lodging

$–$$ ✕ **Pine Club.** Fresh, panfried trout, extra-thick lamb chops, and stewed tomatoes are the house specialties in this aptly named restaurant with pine-paneled walls and a large bar in the center. ⌧ *1926 Brown St.,* ☎ *937/228–7463. Credit cards not accepted. Closed Sun. No lunch.*

$ ✕ **Clifton Mill.** Among America's oldest gristmills, this historic site lies along the scenic Little Miami River. Southern-style breakfasts and lunches are served; just follow the scent of freshly baked breads. ⌧ *75 Water St., Clifton,* ☎ *937/767–5501. AE, MC, V. No dinner.*

$$$ ✕⌷ **Crowne Plaza.** The big plush chairs in the rooms will make you feel right at home. From the rooftop restaurant you can often see military jets cruising to the nearby Air Force base. ⌧ *5th and Jefferson Sts., 45402,* ☎ *937/224–0800,* ⌷ *937/224–3913. 283 rooms. Restaurant, pool. AE, D, DC, MC, V.*

$ ⌷ **Signature Inn.** Guests receive discounts at local eateries, shops, and fitness centers. Some rooms are equipped with Jacuzzis for rest and relaxation. ⌧ *250 Byers Rd., Miamisburg 45342,* ☎ *937/865–0077,* ⌷ *937/865–0077. 125 rooms. Pool. AE, D, DC, MC, V. CP.*

Akron

Arriving and Departing

Akron is about 25 mi south of Cleveland, off I–77.

What to See and Do

The **Akron/Summit Convention and Visitors Bureau** (⌧ 77 Mill St., ☎ 330/374–7560 or 800/245–4254) has information on attractions and events around the Rubber City, where you just might catch the Goodyear blimp landing across from Goodyear Park. **Inventure Place and National Inventors Hall of Fame** (⌧ 221 S. Broadway, at University Ave., ☎ 330/ 762–4463 or 800/968–4332; ⌧ $7.50) honors famous inventors and inventions in a striking museum in downtown Akron. In the spirit of encouraging future inventors, the museum has one room full of computers, which you're invited to play with and even disassemble.

Dining and Lodging

$$–$$$ ✕ **Inn at Turner's Mill.** Just outside of Akron, this country cove is cozy and inviting, with a fireplace and a straightforward menu of midwestern game and fresh vegetables. There's live jazz on weekends. ⊠ *36 E. Streetsborough Rd., Hudson,* ☎ *330/656–2949. AE, D, MC, V.*

$ ✕ **Luigi's.** Come here for crisp-crust pizza, piping-hot pasta, and red wine served in carafes. A miniature big band plays above the entranceway when you put a nickel in the jukebox. ⊠ *105 N. Main St.,* ☎ *330/253–2999. No credit cards.*

$$ ⊞ **Hilton Akron Inn at Quaker Square.** Connected to the Convention Center and Quaker Square retail complex, this hotel on the National Register of Historic Places is actually built from mills and 19th-century grain silos. Each round room takes the shape of the silo and retains the coarse texture of the original walls. ⊠ *135 S. Broadway, Akron 44308,* ☎ *330/253–5970,* FAX *330/253–5970. 150 rooms. Restaurants, pool. AE, D, DC, MC, V.*

$–$$ ⊞ **Comfort Inn–Akron West.** Some rooms in this standard hotel have whirlpool tubs. ⊠ *130 Montrose West Ave. 44321,* ☎ *330/666–5050,* FAX *330/668–2550. 132 rooms. Pool. AE, D, DC, MC, V.*

Canton

Arriving and Departing

Canton is about 50 mi south of Cleveland, off I–77.

What to See and Do

The **Canton/Stark County Convention & Visitors Bureau** (⊠ 229 Wells Ave. NW, Canton 44703, ☎ 330/454–1439 or 800/552–6083) maintains an information center along the approach road to the Pro Football Hall of Fame. The **Pro Football Hall of Fame** (⊠ 2121 George Halas Dr. NW, Fulton Rd. Exit off I–77 and U.S. 62, ☎ 330/456–8207; 🖃 $10) has a dome shaped like a football in kickoff position. Two enshrinement halls are the serious attraction, but displays include a chronology of the game, mementos of the great players, and video replays showing great moments in football.

Dining and Lodging

$$ ✕ **Bender's Tavern.** Jerry Jacob has fresh ingredients flown in for his top-quality American cuisine preparations. The turn-of-the-20th-century barn and livery has been in the Jacob family for more than 60 years and is still going strong. ⊠ *132 Court Ave., SW, Canton,* ☎ *330/453–8424. MC, V.*

$–$$ ✕ **Cité Grille.** The friendly, trendy waitstaff sets a clipping pace for an evening of brisk fun and smart contemporary cuisine. ⊠ *6041 Whipple Ave. NW, North Canton,* ☎ *330/494–6758. AE, MC, V.*

$$–$$$ ⊞ **Sheraton at Belden Village.** You can try your hand at a golf simulator at this hotel in Canton's shopping district. A free shuttle takes guests to the Hall of Fame. ⊠ *6041 Whipple Ave., North Canton 44720,* ☎ *330/494–6494,* FAX *330/494–7129. 152 rooms. Restaurant, pool. AE, D, DC, MC, V.*

$$ ⊞ **Canton Hilton.** Rooms are bright and sunny at this hotel near the Pro Football Hall of Fame and shopping centers. ⊠ *320 Market Ave. S, 44702,* ☎ *330/454–5000,* FAX *330/454–5494. 170 rooms. Restaurant, pool. AE, D, DC, MC, V.*

OKLAHOMA

Updated by Karen Gibson	**Capital**	Oklahoma City
	Population	3,358,000
	Motto	Labor Conquers All Things
	State Bird	Scissor-tailed flycatcher
	State Flower	Mistletoe
	Postal Abbreviation	OK

Statewide Visitor Information

Oklahoma Tourism and Recreation Department (⊠ 15 N. Robinson Ave., Box 52002, Oklahoma City 73152, ☎ 405/521–2409 or 800/652–6552). **State Historical Society** (⊠ 2100 N. Lincoln Blvd., Oklahoma City 73105, ☎ 405/521–2491).

Scenic Drives

Route 49 traverses the prairies and granite peaks of the Wichita Mountains Wildlife Refuge (☞ Exploring Southwestern Oklahoma, *below*). **Route 66,** the road of nostalgia, cruises through Oklahoma, treating travelers to unique historical roadside attractions such as Arcadia's Round Barn and the Giant Blue Whale in Catoosa while surrounded by a backdrop of unblemished scenery. **Route 1,** known as the Talimena Skyline Drive, was built for the breathtaking view winding through the Ouachita National Forest (☞ National and State Parks, *below*). It is known as a prime location for colorful fall foliage.

National and State Parks

National Park

Natural hot springs are the main attraction at the **Chickasaw National Recreation Area** (⊠ Box 201, off I–35, Sulphur 73086, ☎ 580/622–3165), in southern Oklahoma. In southeastern Oklahoma, **Ouachita National Forest** (⊠ HC 64, Box 3467, Heavener 74937, ☎ 918/653–2991), 2 mi south of Heavener on Route 59, is a scenic region of small mountain ranges.

State Parks

Oklahoma has 51 state parks, and all but two have camping facilities. Some of the best are **Alabaster Caverns State Park** (⊠ Rte. 1, Box 32, Freedom 73842, ☎ 580/621–3381), 6 mi south of Freedom on Route 50; **Robbers Cave State Park** (☞ Exploring Southeastern Oklahoma, *below*); **Lake Murray Resort Park** (⊠ 3310 S. Lake Murray Dr., No. 12A, Ardmore 73401, ☎ 405/223–4044); **Quartz Mountain State Park** (☞ Exploring Southwestern Oklahoma, *below*); and **Red Rock Canyon State Park** (⊠ Box 502, Hinton 73047, ☎ 405/542–6344), 1 mi south of Hinton on U.S. 281.

CENTRAL OKLAHOMA

Oklahoma's image as a western state was largely forged in central Oklahoma, where pickup trucks, cowboy boots, and oil wells are still the ultimate status symbols. The Chisholm Trail, the most famous of the cattle trails that moved Texas cattle north through Indian Territory after the end of the Civil War, came through here 130 years ago, and the country's largest live cattle auction still gets under way in Oklahoma City's Stockyards City every Monday and Tuesday morning. Many towns in central Oklahoma, including Guthrie, Oklahoma City, and Norman, share a common heritage: They were born in one day, following the April 22, 1889, land run, which opened a parcel of land in central Oklahoma to non-Indian settlement. Would-be homesteaders lined up on the borders and literally raced for claims.

Visitor Information

Three welcome centers are located in Oklahoma City: State Capital rotunda (⊠ N.E. 23rd and Lincoln; I–35 and N.E. 122nd; and I–40 at the Air Depot exit). **Guthrie:** Chamber of Commerce (⊠ 212 W. Oklahoma St., Box 995, 73044, ☎ 405/282–1947 or 800/299–1889). **Oklahoma City:** Convention and Visitors Bureau (⊠ 189 W. Sheridan St., 73102, ☎ 405/297–8912 or 800/225–5652). **Norman:** Convention and Visitors Bureau (⊠ 224 W. Gray St., Suite 104, 73069, ☎ 405/366–8095 or 800/767–7260).

Arriving and Departing

By Bus
Greyhound (⊠ 427 W. Sheridan St., Oklahoma City, ☎ 405/235–6425 or 800/231–2222).

By Car
Interstate 35 takes travelers north and south through central Oklahoma; I–40 crosses east and west. Interstate 44, which runs diagonally from the northeast to the southwest, intersects both I–35 and I–40 in Oklahoma City.

By Plane
The **Will Rogers World Airport** (⊠ Airport Rd., ☎ 405/680–3200), in southwestern Oklahoma City, is served by major domestic airlines.

By Train
Amtrak's *Heartland Flyer* (☎ 800/872–7245) offers daily service from Oklahoma City south to Ft. Worth with stops also in Norman, Pauls Valley, and Ardmore.

Getting Around Central Oklahoma

A car is a necessity here since public transportation is limited.

Exploring Central Oklahoma

Visiting **Guthrie,** Oklahoma's first capitol, is like taking a trip back in time with a twist. A delightful mix of Victorian architecture and Old West atmosphere, Guthrie is home to more than 100 historical buildings. As the largest urban area on the National Register of Historic Places, Guthrie is home to turn-of-the-20th-century buildings adorned with stained-glass windows and stamped-tin ceilings. The Guthrie Chamber of Commerce (☞ Visitor Information, *above*) conducts guided walking tours. **First Capitol Trolley** (☎ 405/282–6000; 🎫 $2) makes regular tours of downtown Guthrie from the corner of 2nd Street and Harrison Avenue. Stroll over to the **International Scottish Rite Temple** (⊠ 900 E. Oklahoma Ave., ☎ 405/282–1281; 🎫 $2; closed Sun.) for a look at one of the world's largest Masonic lodges. Talented artisans built this impressive structure with 396 stained-glass windows during Oklahoma's oil boom. Experience Guthrie's western heritage at the **Lazy E Arena** (⊠ I–35 south, 4 mi east of Seward Rd.; Rte. 5, Box 393, 73044, ☎ 405/282–3004 or 800/595–7433), 5 mi east of Guthrie. This completely modern arena hosts a variety of western entertainment including world-class rodeo events and championships.

Oklahoma City, 20 mi south of Guthrie, continues to benefit from an extensive downtown renewal project, particularly in the east area known as Bricktown. An industrial area largely abandoned by the 1950s, Bricktown has emerged as Oklahoma City's new entertainment district with the presence of trendy restaurants and clubs, one-of-a-kind shops, and the Bricktown Ballpark. A mile-long canal winding through historic Bricktown features water taxis. To traverse downtown and the outer areas including the Stockyards, State Fairgrounds, and Meridian hotel district, you can take advantage of an inexpensive trolley.

The **Oklahoma City National Memorial** (⊠ N.W. 5th St. between Robinson and Harvey Sts.) opened in the spring of 2000 on the fifth anniversary of the tragic bombing at the former site of the Murrah Federal Building. The 168 glass-and-granite chairs are designed to remember the men, women, and children who will never be able to sit there. A reflecting pool and a tribute to the rescue workers are also part of this outdoor memorial that never closes.

Many Oklahoma City attractions are found east and north of downtown, including the limestone-and-granite **Oklahoma State Capitol** (⊠ N.E. 23rd and Lincoln, ☎ 405/521–3356). Oil derricks mark the sites of seven wells that once surrounded the Capitol. The Oklahoma Capitol is also the only capitol in the world with an oil well underneath the building—Petunia #1. Tours are available weekdays.

An extensive collection of western artifacts and fine art is on display at the **National Cowboy Hall of Fame and Western Heritage Center** (⊠ 1700 N.E. 63rd, ☎ 405/478–2250; ☎ $8.50) north of the capitol off I–44. Three new historical exhibits were added in 1999—the American Cowboy Gallery, the American Gallery, and the re-created western town of Prosperity Junction.

Twenty miles south of Oklahoma City is **Norman,** home to the **University of Oklahoma** and an interesting blend of cultural opportunities. Free walking tours are available of the lovely landscaped university grounds and historical buildings from the OU Visitor Center (⊠ Jacobson Hall, 550 Parrington Oval, ☎ 405/325–1188 or 800/234–6868; ★ closed Sun.). The **Sam Noble Oklahoma Museum of Natural History** (⊠ 2401 Chautauqua,, ☎ 405/325–4712, ☎ $4) opened May 1, 2000. The largest natural history museum in the world connected to a university includes a paleontology exhibit with the world's largest apatosaurus specimen, extensive Native American artifacts, the Hall of Natural Wonders, and a hands-on Discovery Room.

Parks, Gardens, and Zoos

A walk through the **Crystal Bridge Tropical Conservatory,** a glass botanical tube at the 17-acre **Myriad Botanical Gardens** (⊠ 301 W. Reno Ave., ☎ 405/297–3995; ☎ $4), takes visitors through habitats ranging from desert to rain forest, complete with a 35-ft waterfall.

One of the Southwest's oldest, the **Oklahoma City Zoological Park** (⊠ 2101 N.E. 50th St., ☎ 405/424–3344; ☎ $6) has natural habitats for primates, wildcats, and other species. In the 4.2-acre **Cat Forest/Lion Overlook,** lions, snow leopards, and other wild cats roam. Swing by **Great EscApe,** a lush tropical rain forest that's home to gorillas, chimpanzees, and orangutans.

Thoroughbred and quarter-horse pari-mutuel races are held at **Remington Park** (⊠ I–4 and Martin Luther King Blvd., ☎ 405/424–9000 or 800/456–9000; ☎ $3.50 including parking) in fall, spring, and summer. It's closed Tuesday; call ahead for race dates and reservations.

Cruise 68 mi south of Norman for one of Oklahoma's scenic wonders, **Turner Falls Park** (✉ east of Exit 51 on I–35, ☎ 580/369–2917; ☞ $6 in summer, $2.50 in winter). Surrounded by the ancient cliffs of the Arbuckle Mountains is the state's largest waterfall at 77 ft. Trails and caves are enjoyable, but on a hot summer day, people are drawn to the deliciously cool waters below the waterfall.

Dining and Lodging

Two-centuries-old brick warehouses in downtown Oklahoma City have turned Bricktown into a favorite dining district for locals. Western Avenue north of 50th Street is known as Restaurant Row.

Ames

$$ ⊞ **Island Guest Ranch.** At this 2,800-acre working ranch 90 mi north
★ of Oklahoma City, guests help herd cattle, ride horses, fish, hike, and attend staged powwows and team roping and penning in the ranch's own rodeo arena. Rooms, each with private bath, are in two rustic bunkhouses; hearty meals are served in the main log lodge. Rates include all meals and activities; reservations should be made at least several weeks in advance. ✉ *Ames 73718,* ☎ *580/753–4574 or 800/928–4574,* ℻ *580/753–4574. 10 rooms. MC, V. Closed Oct.–Mar. FAP.*

Guthrie

$ ✕ **Granny Had One.** Though this is both an antiques store and tearoom, the menu is the main draw: It includes everything from peanut-butter-and-jelly sandwiches to smoked salmon to steak, with great homemade soups and breads. ✉ *113 W. Harrison St.,* ☎ *405/282–4482. AE, D, DC, MC, V.*

$ ✕ **Stables Café.** Huge platters of steak, ribs, sandwiches, and burgers are doled out at this typically rustic barbecue joint in the heart of downtown. ✉ *223 N. Division St.,* ☎ *405/282–0893. D, MC, V.*

$$ ⊞ **Harrison House Inn.** Each room in the inn's four historical buildings is named after a famous historical figure. The Teddy Roosevelt Room is a guest favorite, and all rooms are in high Victorian style. ✉ *124 W. Harrison St., 73044,* ☎ *405/282–1000,* ℻ *405/282–1000. 34 rooms. AE, D, DC, MC, V. BP.*

Norman

$ ✕ **The Greek House.** The area north of the University of Oklahoma has long been home to a culturally diverse mix of shops and restaurants. One of the oldest eateries is this family-owned operation, where authentic Greek "fast food" is much in demand. People travel great distances for the aromatic, mouthwatering gyros. ✉ *768 Jenkins,* ☎ *405/364–6400. No credit cards. Closed Sun.*

$$–$$$ ⊞ **Montford Inn Bed & Breakfast.** Native American collectibles and foot-
★ ball memorabilia (the University of Oklahoma is nearby) blend seamlessly with antiques in this supremely comfortable inn. Rooms have fireplaces, whirlpool tubs, and writing desks. Two cottages and a detached house have kitchenettes. ✉ *322 W. Tonhawa St., 73069,* ☎ *405/321–2200 or 800/321–8969,* ℻ *405/321–8347. 15 rooms, 2 cottages, 1 house. AE, D, MC, V. BP.* ✎

Oklahoma City

$$$$ ✕ **Coach House.** The dark-wood-paneled walls of this small, cozy restaurant are covered with images of the hunt, a theme reflected in the contemporary menu, which features pheasant and quail. Another specialty is scallops with roasted corn cakes. ✉ *6437 Avondale Dr.,* ☎ *405/842–1000. AE, MC, V.*

$$ ✕ **Abuelo Mexican Embassy.** While you'll find many Mexican restaurants in Oklahoma City, Abuelo's is an original. Based on central Mexico cuisine, Abuelo's offers 10 varieties of enchiladas that can be ordered in any combination. One house specialty is the Enchiladas de Cozumel, avocado enchiladas with a seafood and mushroom white sauce. ⊠ *17 E. Sheridan,* ☎ *405/235–1422. AE, D, MC, V.*

$–$$ ✕ **Cattlemen's Steakhouse.** Beef is the star attraction at this classic steak
★ house in the heart of Stockyards City. Cowboys clad in spurs look right at home among the western murals, cattle-branding irons, and other western paraphernalia. ⊠ *1309 S. Agnew Ave.,* ☎ *405/236–0416. AE, D, DC, MC, V.*

$ ✕ **Bricktown Brewery.** Even the shrimp are steamed in beer in this airy
★ brewpub, where historical photographs are displayed against exposed brick. Land Run Lager and Copperhead Ale complement the chicken potpie, fish-and-chips, and hot links (spicy smoked sausages). ⊠ *1 Oklahoma Ave.,* ☎ *405/232–2739. AE, D, DC, MC, V.*

$$–$$$ ▥ **Waterford Marriott.** This elegant hotel in northwest Oklahoma City has a popular restaurant with summer jazz concerts. ⊠ *6300 Waterford Blvd., 73118,* ☎ *405/848–4782 or 800/992–2009,* ℻ *405/848–7810. 197 rooms. 2 restaurants, pool, health club. AE, D, DC, MC, V.*☜

$$–$$$ ▥ **Westin Oklahoma City.** This 15-story glass-and-stone building in the heart of downtown has extensive business facilities and access to the Myriad Convention Center by underground tunnel. ⊠ *1 N. Broadway, 73102,* ☎ *405/235–2780 or 800/285–2780,* ℻ *405/272–0369. 395 rooms. Restaurant, pool, exercise room. AE, D, DC, MC, V.*☜

$–$$ ▥ **Clarion Hotel and Conference Center.** The Clarion is conveniently close to museums and the Capitol. Unlike most other hotels in the area, the Clarion has several concierge floors. ⊠ *4345 N. Lincoln Blvd., 73105,* ☎ *405/528–2741 or 800/741–2741,* ℻ *405/525–8185. 307 rooms. 2 restaurants, pool, tennis. AE, D, DC, MC, V.*

Motels

▥ **Holiday Inn Airport** (⊠ 2101 S. Meridian St., 73108, ☎ 405/685–4000 or 800/622–7666, ℻ 405/685–0574), 245 rooms; restaurant, pool, exercise room; $$. ▥ **Motel 6 Oklahoma City Airport** (⊠ 820 S. Meridian St., 73108, ☎ 405/946–6662, ℻ 405/946–4058), 128 rooms; pool; $.

Shopping

Malls are abundant and do include locally owned shops amid the familiar chains. Popular malls include **Crossroads** (⊠ I–40 and I–35 junction) and **Quail Springs** (⊠ Memorial Rd. and May Ave.). The downtown areas of Guthrie, Oklahoma City, and Norman are all thriving and provide a variety of merchandise. A fun place to shop is the eclectic Campus Corner area north of the University of Oklahoma in Norman. The **Route 66** gallery and gift shop (⊠ 50 Penn Pl., 5000 N. Pennsylvania Ave., ☎ 405/848–6166) sells jewelry and work by regional artists, including picture frames made of recycled vintage auto parts, from side mirrors to radiators.

NORTHEASTERN OKLAHOMA

More than half of Oklahoma's state parks can be found in northeastern Oklahoma, where the western boundaries of the Ozark and Ouachita mountains can be found. Some of the most beautiful, unspoiled scenery in the region can be discovered here. Lakes, rivers, and creeks help keep everything a vibrant green. The eastern half of Oklahoma was once Indian Territory, the place where Native Americans of the southeastern United States were relocated after the tragic journey known as the Trail of Tears. One of the largest tribes in the United States, the Cherokee, have their tribal headquarters here.

Visitor Information

Tahlequah: Chamber of Commerce (✉ 123 E. Delaware St., 74464, ☎ 918/456–3742 or 800/456–3742). **Tulsa:** Visitor Information Center and Chamber of Commerce (✉ 616 S. Boston St., 74119, ☎ 918/585–1201).

Arriving and Departing

By Bus

Greyhound (✉ 317 S. Detroit St., ☎ 800/231–2222) serves Tulsa.

By Car

In Tulsa I–44 and I–244 form a downtown loop. The Keystone, Cherokee, and Broken Arrow expressways also lead downtown. From Tulsa U.S. 75 leads north to the Bartlesville area. Interstate 44 is the main route northeast from Tulsa and connects with many smaller, more scenic highways. Interstate 44 is also a toll road ($3) linking Tulsa and Oklahoma City.

By Plane

Tulsa International Airport (☎ 918/838–5000), 10 mi northeast of downtown Tulsa, is served by major domestic airlines. Average cab fare to the downtown area is about $17.

Exploring Northeastern Oklahoma

Tulsa, Oklahoma's second-largest city, was created by the oil barons of days gone by. The skyline speaks to that origin—sleek, modern skyscrapers erupting from the prairie and stretching to the heavens. The oil barons also left a legacy of culture, art, and widespread Art Deco architecture second only to those of New York and Miami. Stop by the chamber of commerce (☞ Visitor Information, *above*) for a walking-tour map that includes more than a dozen downtown buildings. The **Greenwood Historical District** (✉ Greenwood and Archer, ☎ 918/585–2084) is nearby. Once known as the "Black Wall Street," Greenwood continues to be a thriving area for business and culture. For a bit of nature, head west to Riverside Drive. Join others in walking, jogging, and biking along the winding paths that follow the Arkansas River.

About 3 mi from the downtown area is the **Gilcrease Museum** (✉ 1400 Gilcrease Museum Rd., ☎ 918/596–2700; ✉ $5 suggested donation). Its collection, dedicated to western art and Americana, includes paintings by such artists as Frederic Remington and Charles Russell, as well as Native American art and artifacts. A few miles southeast of downtown, the wide-ranging collection of Italian Renaissance paintings and Native American art of the **Philbrook Museum of Art** (✉ 2727 S. Rockford Rd., ☎ 918/749–7941; ✉ $5) occupies former oil baron Waite Phillips's historic Italian villa. Not only is the title song of the famous Rodgers and Hammerstein musical Oklahoma's state song, but *Oklahoma!* is also a summertime tradition at **Discoveryland** (✉ 5 mi west of 41st and Rte. 97, ☎ 918/245–6552; ✉ $15; closed Sun.), where nightly performances can be seen in an outdoor amphitheater. An optional barbecue is held before each performance.

Located north of Tulsa on Route 123, about 12 mi southwest of
★ Bartlesville, is **Woolaroc** (☎ 918/336–0307; ✉ $5), whose name is de-

Northeastern Oklahoma

rived from the words *wood, lake,* and *rock.* Once the ranch of oilman Frank Phillips, Woolaroc is now a drive-through wildlife preserve that's home to bison and 40 other species (visitors must remain in their vehicles). The preserve surrounds a museum packed with memorabilia of art and artifacts of the Southwest.

Southeast of Woolaroc by way of Nowata lies the Dog Iron Ranch and **Will Rogers Birthplace** (⊠ 2 mi east of Oologah, ☎ 918/275–4201; ⊠ free). The great humorist's childhood home, built in 1875, is a two-story clapboard structure containing period furnishings; you'll also find longhorn cattle and barnyard animals on the grounds of the working ranch. On Route 88 in Claremore is the sandstone **Will Rogers Memorial Museum** (⊠ 1720 N. Will Rogers Blvd., ☎ 918/341–0719 or 800/324–9455; ⊠ free), where Oklahoma's favorite son and members of his family are buried; it also has memorabilia, theaters that show Rogers's movies and newsreels, and a hands-on children's museum.

Take I–44 and U.S. 59 to **Grove** and the **Grand Lake O' the Cherokees.** Numerous recreational options here include a dinner cruise or sightseeing tour aboard the *Cherokee Queen* riverboat (⊠ 11350 U.S. Hwy. 59N at Sailboat Bridge, ☎ 918/786–4272; ⊠ 2-hr sightseeing tour $8.50, 3-hr dinner cruise $19.50).

About 50 mi south of Grove on Route 10 is **Tahlequah,** capital of the Cherokee Nation. The **Cherokee Heritage Center** (⊠ Willis Rd., ☎ 918/456–6007; ⊠ $6; closed Sun.), 3 mi south of Tahlequah off U.S. 62, chronicles the history of the Cherokee Nation, from the time of the Trail of Tears to the present. Within the Heritage Center are the **Cherokee National Museum,** where an exhibit focuses on the oral tradition of the elders; the **Ancient Village at Tsa-La-Gi,** where costumed tribal members demonstrate basket weaving, pottery, stickball games, and other Cherokee traditions; and **Adams Corner Rural Village,** a re-created pioneer village from the 1800s. Tsa-La-Gi and Adams Corner are only open from Monday to Saturday during summer. The nearby **Illinois River** (☎ 918/456–3251 or 800/456–4860) is a popular site for casual rowing. Canoes and kayaks can be rented along Route 10.

South from Tulsa on the Muskogee Turnpike is the quintessential Oklahoma town of **Muskogee.** Known for its azaleas, Muskogee is also home to Bacone College, which started as an Indian Art School. To learn about Oklahoma's Native American Heritage, visit the **Five Civilized Tribes Museum** (⊠ Honor Heights Dr., ☎ 918/683–1701; ⚏ $2).

Dining and Lodging

$–$$ ✕ **The Bistro at Brookside.** Think light contemporary American fare in a charming French bistro. It's no wonder this restaurant in Tulsa's trendy shopping and dining area is a favorite. ⊠ 3523 Peoria, Tulsa, ☎ 918/749–7737. AE, D, DC, MC, V.

$$$ ✕⊞ **Adam's Mark Hotel.** Next door to the Performing Arts Center, the Adam's Mark has the most highly regarded staff in Tulsa. At Bravo Ristorante, the hotel's dining room, traditional Italian cuisine is served by a waitstaff who deliver arias with your meal. ⊠ 100 E. 2nd St., Tulsa 74103, ☎ 918/582–9000 or 800/444–2326, FAX 918/560–2232. 462 rooms. Restaurant, pool, exercise room. AE, D, DC, MC, V. ⬧

$$$ ✕⊞ **Doubletree Inn Downtown.** Visitors are welcomed with chocolate chip cookies in this modern high-rise, connected by skywalk to the Tulsa Convention Center. The Grille draws a crowd with its innovative southwestern cuisine. ⊠ 616 W. 7th St., Tulsa 74127, ☎ 918/587–8000, FAX 918/587–1642. 432 rooms. 2 restaurants, pool, exercise room. AE, D, DC, MC, V. ⬧

$$–$$$ ⊞ **Western Hills Guest Ranch.** Sitting on a scenic peninsula on Fort Gibson Lake, this ranch provides a taste of the cowboy life with horseback riding and chuck-wagon cookouts. For more gentrified sensibilities, there's also golf and tennis. ⊠ 12 mi east of SH 51, Wagoner 74467, ☎ 918/772–2545 or 800/654–8240, FAX 918/587–1642. 101 rooms, 54 cottages. Restaurants. AE, MC, V.

Motels

⊞ **Best Western Trade Winds Central Motor Hotel** (⊠ 3141 E. Skelly Dr., Tulsa 74105, ☎ 918/749–5561, FAX 918/749–6312), 167 rooms; pool, exercise room.

⊞ **Motel 6** (⊠ 1011 S. Garnett Rd., Tulsa 74128, ☎ 918/234–6200, FAX 918/234–9421), 121 rooms; pool; $–$$$.

Campgrounds

⚹ **Greenleaf State Park** (⊠ SH 10-A, north of Gore, ☎ 918/487–5196) is one of the loveliest state parks, with a sparkling blue 900-acre lake. The cabins and shelters at ⚹ **Osage Hills State Park** (⊠ HC73, Box 84, Pawhuska 74056, ☎ 918/336–4141) were built in the 1930s by the Civilian Conservation Corps on rolling hills covered with blackjack oak. It's 11 mi west of Bartlesville on U.S 60.

The Arts

Tulsa's downtown **Performing Arts Center** (⊠ 110 E. 2nd St., ☎ 918/596–7122) hosts the **Tulsa Philharmonic** (☎ 918/747–7473) between September and May and the **Tulsa Opera** (☎ 918/582–4035) from October through May. The nationally acclaimed **Tulsa Ballet Theatre** (⊠ 4512 S. Peoria Ave., ☎ 918/749–6006) performs from September through April.

Outdoor Activities and Sports

Fishing

The sports section of the city's daily newspaper, *Tulsa World,* has up-to-date fishing information, or check with the **Department of Wildlife and Conservation** (☎ 405/521–3851). Fishing licenses can be purchased in most tackle shops.

Hiking

Every park in the area has hiking trails. For general information call the **Tourism and Recreation Department** (☞ Statewide Visitor Information, *above*).

Shopping

The **Brookside** and **Cherry Street** districts are home to charming boutiques, antiques shops, and a variety of dining establishments. **Utica Square,** at Utica Avenue and 21st Street, is an outdoor mall with upscale chain stores, including Saks Fifth Avenue, and such specialty shops as Petty's Fine Foods, and Miss Jackson's, one of Oklahoma's best-known designer fashion stores.

SOUTHWESTERN OKLAHOMA

The frontier doesn't seem far away in this rugged, sparsely populated region; oceans of grass are broken by blue-granite mountains, and almost every small town has a saddle shop. During the 19th century this was the domain of the buffalo and the Kiowa and Comanche tribes; travelers may still spot Native American tepees and brush arbors in rural areas during the summer.

Visitor Information

Lawton/Fort Sill: Chamber of Commerce and Industry (⊠ 607 Southwest C [Box 1376], Lawton 73502, ☎ 580/355–3541 or 800/872–4540).

Arriving and Departing

By Bus

Jefferson Lines (⊠ 15 N.E. 20th St., ☎ 580/353–1010).

By Car

As with the rest of the state, you'll need a car to tour this region. Most of the area lies between I–44 and I–40 southwest of Oklahoma City; U.S. and state highways connect with these interstates.

By Plane

The **Will Rogers World Airport** (☞ Central Oklahoma, *above*) gives the best access to the region.

Exploring Southwestern Oklahoma

At the foot of the Wichita Mountains, **Lawton** makes a good base for exploring the region. It's the largest of the Wichita Mountain communities and the business center for southwestern Oklahoma. The **Museum of the Great Plains** (⊠ 601 Ferris Ave., ☎ 580/581–3460; ☜ $3) has a reproduction trading post and an outdoor fort recalling the pre–Louisiana Purchase days.

A short drive north of Lawton on I–44 brings you to the **Fort Sill Military Reservation** (⊠ Key Gate off Sheridan Rd., ☎ 580/442–8111 or 580/442–5123; ☜ free), which was built in 1869. The guardhouse where

Geronimo, Fort Sill's most famous prisoner, was held is one of several buildings open to the public. Chief's Knoll, located east of the base, features Apache and Comanche cemeteries.

★ Just north of Lawton I–44 crosses Route 49, which runs along the northern border of Fort Sill and westward to the **Wichita Mountains Wildlife Refuge** (☎ 580/429–3222 in Indiahoma, one of the most beautiful areas in the state. Here the wildlife is thick and the scenery—boulder-topped mountains overlooking clear, still lakes—often breathtaking. The refuge is home to bison, longhorn cattle, and other wildlife. It's also the best place in the state for rock climbing. Hiking trails are abundant and camping is allowed, but backcountry camping and biking are by permit only.

From the western end of the Wichita Mountains Wildlife Refuge, Route 54 and U.S. 62 lead southwest to Altus. From here travel north on U.S. 283/Route 44 to **Quartz Mountain State Park** (☎ 580/563–2238). The scenery is worth the trip—bare rock outcroppings reflected in pristine Lake Altus-Lugert and abundant wildflowers in spring. You can also enjoy the lake's sandy beaches, visit the park's nature center, or take advantage of guided tours and special programs.

In **Anadarko,** north of Lawton on Route 281 and 8, learn how the Southern Plains Indian tribes once lived and enjoy the art and culture of today's Native Americans. **Indian City USA** (⊠ 2 mi southeast on Rte. 8, ☎ 405/247–5661 or 800/433–5661; ☞ $7.50) is an outdoor museum showing how different Plains tribes once lived. View fine art and authentic crafts at the **Southern Plains Indian Museum and Craft Center** (⊠ U.S. 62E, 715 E. Central Blvd., ☎ 405/247–6221; ☞ $3; closed Mon. during winter). Afterward, go next door for a look at our country's most famous Native Americans at the **National Hall of Fame for Famous American Indians** (⊠ 115 U.S. 62E, ☎ 405/247–5555; ☞ free).

★ Drive north on U.S. 183 to reach Clinton, where you can relive travel on the Mother Road at the **Oklahoma Route 66 Museum** (⊠ 2229 W. Gary Blvd., off I–40, Clinton, ☎ 580/323–7866, ☞ $3; closed Mon.). Exhibits are organized by decade, beginning with the road's construction in the 1920s, continuing through the Dust Bowl in the '30s, the military highway days of the '40s, and the vacation-oriented '50s (complete with a re-created diner and drive-in movie theater).

Dining and Lodging

When possible, pack lunches for park picnics; at night you'll probably have to content yourself with chain restaurants. Unless you plan to camp, your hotel will probably be little more than a convenient base for exploring.

Altus

$$–$$$$ 🏨 **Quartz Mountain Resort Park Lodge.** Overlooking the 4,500-acre state park, this lodge reopened in the summer of 2000 after reconstruction. Once the sacred grounds of the Kiowa and Comanche, Quartz Mountain is now a popular location for artists and for retreats. ⊠ 17 mi north of Altus on SH44A, 73655, ☎ 580/563–2424. 145 rooms, 16 cottages. Restaurant, golf. AE, MC, V.

Lawton

$ ★ ✕ **Woody's BBQ.** Seated under a ceiling fan in one of two rustic dining rooms, you'll be treated to pork ribs or beef brisket with side dishes such as okra, fried mushrooms, and "wood chips" (fried potatoes with melted cheese and bacon). ⊠ 1107 W. Lee Blvd., ☎ 580/ 355–4950. AE, D, MC, V.

$ 🏨 **Howard Johnson Hotel and Convention Center.** The public areas of this low-rise stucco hotel just off I–44 are a hodgepodge of decorative themes, from Victorian-style frosted glass to a rustic chandelier of antlers. ⊠ *1125 E. Gore Blvd., 73501,* ☎ *580/353–0200,* FAX *580/353–6801. 145 rooms. Restaurant, pool, tennis. AE, D, DC, MC, V.* ✎

Meers

$ ✕ **Meers Store.** All that's left of a boomtown that grew up during a brief gold rush in 1901 are this eatery and a seismographic station by the cash register. The restaurant's claim to fame is the Meersburger— a 7-inch burger made of 100% longhorn beef, voted "Best Burger" in Oklahoma by the *Tulsa World.* ⊠ *Rte. 115, 4 mi east of the Wichita Mountains Wildlife Refuge,* ☎ *580/429–8051. No credit cards.*

Motels

🏨 **Best Western Tradewinds** (⊠ 2128 Gary Blvd., Clinton 73601, ☎ 580/323–2610 or 800/528–1234, FAX 580/353–6162), 76 rooms; restaurant, pool, fitness center; $.

Campgrounds

⚠ **Doris Campgrounds** is a fully developed camping area surrounded by the wild beauty of the Wichita Mountains Wildlife Refuge (☞ Exploring Southwestern Oklahoma, *above*). Nearby lakes offer fishing for largemouth bass, sunfish, crappie, and channel catfish.

Outdoor Activities and Sports

Fishing

The best bets are Lake Altus-Lugert or any of the lakes at the Wichita Mountains Wildlife Refuge (☞ Exploring Southwestern Oklahoma, *above*). The sports section in the *Daily Oklahoman* has fishing reports for the lakes in the area, or contact the **Department of Wildlife and Conservation** (☎ 405/521–3851).

Hiking

The best hiking is found at the larger state parks including **Quartz Mountain Resort Park, Red Rock Canyon** (☞ National and State Parks, *above*) and **Foss State Park** (⊠ 14 mi west of Clinton on Rte. 73, ☎ 580/592–4433).

SOUTHEASTERN OKLAHOMA

The green and hilly southeastern corner of the state seems a world apart from the rest of Oklahoma. Here are pine and hardwood forests, populated by plentiful game and traversed by fast-running mountain streams. Outdoor enthusiasts favor this part of the state, where food, lodging, and entertainment tend toward the rustic. Much of southeastern Oklahoma belonged to the Choctaw Indians during Indian Territory days. The Choctaw Tribe is still a powerful presence with a tribal headquarters in Durant. The original Choctaw Capitol and council grounds in Tushka Homma (Tuskahoma) continue to be the site of cultural festivities. The word "Oklahoma" actually comes from the Choctaw language and means "red people."

Visitor Information

Kiamichi Country: Regional Tourism Association (⊠ Box 638, Rte. 2N, Wilburton 74578, ☎ 918/465–2367 or 800/722–8180).

Arriving and Departing

By Bus

Greyhound provides bus service to Wilburton (☎ 800/231–2222).

By Car

Much of southeastern Oklahoma is accessible only by two-lane roads. From I–40 near Sallisaw U.S. 259 leads south. From I–35 take U.S. 70 east.

By Plane

The **Will Rogers World Airport** (☎ 405/680–3200) in southwest Oklahoma City provides the best access to the northern Ouachita National Forest area. Extreme southeastern Oklahoma is closer to Dallas and the **Dallas–Fort Worth International Airport** (☎ 972/574–6701).

Getting Around Southeastern Oklahoma

This sprawling, mountainous region requires a car. Highways are generally well marked, but navigating along winding mountain roads can require patience and a little extra time. Be especially careful along county and rural roads—some are not paved and can be treacherous after rain.

Exploring Southeastern Oklahoma

Robbers Cave State Park (⊠ Rte. 2, 5 mi north of Wilburton, Box 9, 74578, ☎ 918/465–2562) enjoys a colorful history. Outlaws once found Indian Territory a good place to hide from federal marshals, as the Native Americans in the area didn't much care for the federal lawmen either. One place in particular was deep in the San Bois Mountains, where caves nearly hidden by the forests existed. Outlaws like the James and Dalton gangs occasionally used Robbers Cave to hide themselves or the profits from their heists. Today, people can explore the caves independently or take a tour with a park ranger.

A place with even more history is **Spiro Mounds Archaeological Park** (⊠ south of I–40 near Arkansas border, 6 mi east of town of Spiro, ☎ 918/962–2062; 🖾 free; closed Mon. and Tues.). Spiro Mounds is believed to be one of the most significant prehistoric Indian sites east of the Rocky Mountains. Twelve mounds and a center with artifacts explain how these ancient people may have once lived. If you're interested in seeing the countryside in comfort and style, you'll want to take Route 70 to Hugo and ride the vintage train at **Hugo Historic Railroad** (⊠ 309 "B" St., ☎ 580/326–6630 or 888/773–3768; 🖾 ticket prices vary depending on route, but most excursions start at about $17 [reservations required]). It's open Saturday from April to November. While you're waiting, take a look at the train museum or stop by the restored Harvey House Restaurant.

Spectacular views can be seen from the **Talimena Scenic Byway,** marked SH–1 and running east–west through the heart of the Ouachita National Forest. The highway extends west into the Sans Bois Mountain area and intersects with U.S. 259, which continues into the Kiamichi Mountains.

The scenic byway intersects with U.S. 259, which takes travelers south about 40 mi to **Beavers Bend Resort Park** (⊠ Hwy. 259A, 7 mi north of Broken Bow, Box 10, Broken Bow, ☎ 580/494–6300). Built on the Mountain Fork River at the edge of the Ouachita National Forest, the park is so secluded that wild turkeys have been spotted strolling on the resort's golf fairways. The history and culture of the forest from prehistoric times to the present are interpreted at the park's **Forest Heritage Center** (☎ 580/494–6497; 🖾 free).

Dining and Lodging

Lodging is rustic in southeast Oklahoma, and room service is virtually nonexistent. Many restaurants close by 9 PM.

Hochatown

$ ✕ **Stevens Gap Restaurant.** Enjoy catfish fillets served with hush puppies, or southern-fried chicken. You can also get breakfast (biscuits, gravy, and the works) all day long. It's about 2½ mi north from Hochatown State Park's main entrance via U.S. 259. ⊠ *U.S. 259 and Stevens Gap Rd.,* ☎ *580/494–6350. No credit cards.*

$$ ★ ⌂ **Lakeview Lodge.** Every room at this state-operated lodge has a balcony view of Broken Bow Lake. Breakfast is served in the lodge's Great Room, where a fire roars in a native stone fireplace when weather warrants. ⊠ *U.S. 259, Box 10, Broken Bow 74728,* ☎ *580/494–6177. 40 rooms. Golf. AE, D, DC, MC, V. CP.* ❧

Krebs

$ ★ ✕ **Pete's Place.** Pete Prichard started selling sandwiches and illicit beer out of his house in 1925; now his grandchildren operate a sprawling restaurant with a (legal) microbrewery and 25 private dining rooms clustered around three main dining areas. Krebs is about 30 mi west of Wilburton via U.S. 270. ⊠ *120 S.W. 8th St.,* ☎ *918/423–2042. No lunch Mon.–Sat. AE, D, DC, MC, V.*

Octavia

$$$–$$$$ ⌂ **Eagle Creek Guest Cottages.** Twelve secluded log cottages are spread out over 40 acres on the backside of a mountain; some are on the banks of Big Eagle Creek or on a private lake. The luxury log cabins have kitchens, stone fireplaces, whirlpools, and big back porches. Smithville is 6 mi south of Octavia via U.S. 270. ⊠ *U.S. 259, HC 15, Box 250, Smithville 74957,* ☎ *580/244–7597. 12 cottages. AE, MC, V.* ❧

Wilburton

$$ ⌂ **Belle Starr View Lodge.** Overlooking a valley in Robbers Cave State Park, the lodge has comfortable rooms with color TVs but no phones. Breakfast (not included in the rates) requires a bit of a hike to the park restaurant. ⊠ *Rte. 2, Box 9, Wilburton 74578,* ☎ *918/465–2562,* FAX *918/465–5763. 20 rooms. AE, D, DC, MC, V.*

Outdoor Activities and Sports

Ten areas in **Ouachita National Forest** (☞ National and State Parks, *above*) feature recreational opportunities. Most provide camping and hiking, and some offer fishing and hunting.

Boating and Fishing

Mountain Fork River is stocked with rainbow trout; there are brown trout in the Lower Mountain Fork. The required trout-fishing stamp is obtainable at park offices and bait shops. The Mountain Fork River is also popular with canoeists. **Beavers Bend River Floats** (⊠ Beavers' Bend Resort Park, ☎ 580/494–6070) rents canoes March–October. **WW Trading Post and Canoes** (⊠ Mountain Fork Park Rd., 6 mi from Broken Bow, ☎ 580/584–6856) rents fly-fishing equipment and supplies, along with canoes March–October.

Hiking

The **Ouachita Trail,** a 192-mi frontier trail through the Ouachita mountains, was pieced together from bison paths, military roads, and centuries-old footpaths. Forty miles of trails through the Ouachita National Forest can be hiked in Oklahoma. Backcountry camping is allowed all along the trail; numerous campgrounds have also been established. For more information, contact the Choctaw Ranger District (⊠ HC 64, Box 3467, Heavener 74937, ☎ 918/653–2991).

OREGON

By Donald S. Olson

Updated by Jeffrey Boswell

Capital	Salem
Population	3,316,000
Motto	She Flies with Her Own Wings
State Bird	Western meadowlark
State Flower	Oregon grape
Postal Abbreviation	OR

Statewide Visitor Information

Oregon Tourism Commission (✉ 775 Summer St. NE, Salem 97310, ☎ 800/547–7842).

Scenic Drives

The **Columbia Gorge Scenic Highway** (Route 30) twists and turns its way above I–84 through the heavily wooded, waterfall-laced Columbia Gorge east of Portland. **U.S. 101** hugs the largely unspoiled Oregon coastline. **Highway 138** from Roseburg to Crater Lake is a national scenic byway through rugged canyons and past waterfalls, mountain lakes, and camping areas.

National and State Parks

National Parks
Crater Lake National Park (✉ Box 7, Crater Lake 97604, ☎ 541/594–2211; 🎫 $10 per vehicle) has guided boat trips of the pristine lake, and many nature trails (☞ Ashland/The Rogue Valley *in* Elsewhere in Oregon, *below*). In the high-desert country of eastern Oregon, **John Day Fossil Beds National Monument** (✉ HCR 82, Box 126, Kimberly 97848–9701, ☎ 541/987–2333; 🎫 free) contains the richest concentration of prehistoric plant and animal fossils in the world. **Newberry National Volcanic Monument,** administered by the Deschutes National Forest (✉ 1645 Hwy. 20E, Bend 97701, ☎ 541/388–2715; 🎫 $3 per vehicle), provides recreation for campers, cross-country skiers, snowmobilers, fishers, and hikers. **Oregon Caves National Monument** (✉ 19000 Caves Hwy., Cave Junction 97523, ☎ 541/592–2100; 🎫 $7.50) conducts guided tours of the Marble Halls of Oregon. **Oregon Dunes National Recreation Area** (✉ 855 Highway Ave., Reedsport 97467, ☎ 541/271–3611; 🎫 $3 per vehicle) covers 40 mi of undulating camel-color sand and freshwater lakes (☞ Exploring the Oregon Coast, *below*).

State Parks
Oregon's 225 state parks run the gamut from sage-scented desert to mountains to sea. The **Oregon State Parks and Recreation Department** (✉ 1115 Commercial St. NE, Salem 97310, ☎ 800/551–6949) has information on the parks, campsite availability, and facilities. Many parks require day-use permits, which are $3 per vehicle. Call for details.

PORTLAND

Portland, one of America's most important gateways to the Pacific Rim, has a reputation as a well-planned, relaxing city. Straddling the banks of the wide Willamette River, this is one of the largest inland ports on the West Coast. It also has flower-filled parks, efficient mass transit, excellent hotels and restaurants, and restored historic buildings. The Rose Festival, held in June, is a monthlong series of parades and events drawing more than 2 million people each year from around the world.

Visitor Information

Portland/Oregon Visitors Association (✉ 2 World Trade Center, 26 S.W. Salmon St., 97204, ☎ 503/222–2223 or 800/962–3700). Portland Guides in green jackets walk the sidewalks downtown; they can assist with directions and answer questions about the city.

Arriving and Departing

By Bus
Greyhound (✉ 550 N.W. 6th Ave., ☎ 800/231–2222).

By Car
Interstate 84 (Banfield Freeway) and Highway 26 (the Sunset) run east–west; I–5, I–205, and I–405 run north–south. I–405 runs west of the downtown district. I–205 bypasses downtown on the city's east side.

By Plane
Portland International Airport (✉ 7000 N.E. Airport Way, ☎ 503/460–4234), in northeast Portland about 10 mi from the city center, is served by major domestic carriers. Transportation to and from the airport is available through **Portland Taxi** (☎ 503/256–5400) and **Broadway Cab** (☎ 503/227–1234), as well as hotel shuttle services. A taxi ride downtown costs about $25. **Evergreen Gray Line** (☎ 503/285–9845) buses leave from the airport every 30 minutes and serve most major downtown hotels. The fare is $12 one-way or $22 round-trip.

By Train
Amtrak serves Union Station (✉ 800 N.W. 6th Ave., ☎ 503/273–4865 or 800/872–7245) with daily service to Seattle, California, and Chicago.

Getting Around Portland

The metropolitan area is laid out in a grid system, with numbered avenues running north–south and named streets running east–west. Locations with northwest or southwest addresses are on the west side of the Willamette River, northeast and southeast on the east side. Burnside Street separates north from south addresses. The **MAX light rail line** links eastern and western Portland suburbs to the downtown core, the Lloyd Center District, the Convention Center, and the Rose Quarter, which includes Memorial Coliseum and the Rose Garden sports arena. The Westside MAX line includes a stop at the Oregon Zoo in Washington Park. At 260 ft below the surface, the transit station is the deepest in the nation. A 5½-mi extension to Portland International Airport will open in fall 2001. The **Tri-Met bus system** covers the metro area extensively. Call 503/238–7433 for schedules and routes for both buses and MAX.

Exploring Portland

Downtown
Four **Vintage Trolleys** run from Lloyd Center to Pioneer Courthouse Square on the MAX light rail line. They operate daily from May to December and weekends only in March and April. There is no service in January and February. ✉ *Board at Lloyd Center or Pioneer Courthouse Square.* ◙ *Free.*

Pioneer Courthouse Square (✉ S.W. Broadway and S.W. Morrison St.), the downtown area's main gathering place and people-watching venue, sits across from the classically sedate **Pioneer Courthouse,** the oldest public building in the Northwest, built in 1869.

★ The 1930s-era **Portland Art Museum** is one of several interesting buildings that line the South Park Blocks, a tree-lined boulevard of parks with

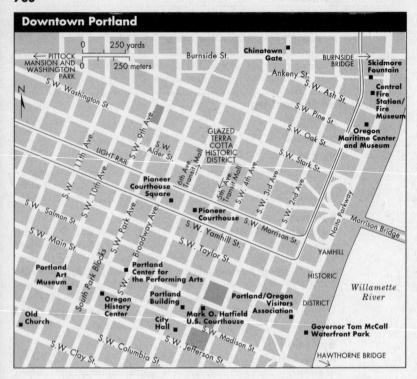

Downtown Portland

states and fountains. Portland State University is at its southern end. The museum contains 35 centuries of Asian, European, and Native American art and is a regional venue for large traveling exhibitions. ✉ *1219 S.W. Park Ave.,* ☎ *503/226–2811.* 🎫 *$7.50. Closed Mon.*

Across from the art museum, towering murals of Lewis and Clark and the Oregon Trail frame the entrance to the **Oregon History Center,** where the state's history from prehistoric times to the present is documented in dramatic galleries and hands-on exhibits. ✉ *1200 S.W. Park Ave.,* ☎ *503/222–1741.* 🎫 *$6. Closed Mon.*

The **Old Church,** built in 1882, is a prime example of Carpenter Gothicarchitecture, complete with rough-cut lumber, tall spires, and the original stained-glass windows. Free concerts are held on Wednesday at noon. ✉ *1422 S.W. 11th Ave.,* ☎ *503/222–2031.* 🎫 *Free. Closed Sun.*

Architect Michael Graves's **Portland Building** (✉ 1120 S.W. 5th Ave.) was one of the country's first postmodern designs. **Portlandia,** the second-largest hammered-copper sculpture in the world (after the Statue of Liberty), kneels on the second-story balcony. Across Madison Street from the Portland Building is the classically styled and restored **city hall,** built in 1895, with high ceilings, marble hallways, a glass-roofed atrium, and pillars inside. The **Mark O. Hatfield U.S. Courthouse** (✉ 1000 S.W. 3rd Ave.), completed in 1997, has rooftop terraces with sweeping vistas of the city and the Willamette River.

Across Naito Parkway along the Willamette River you'll find **Governor Tom McCall Waterfront Park,** a grassy 2-mi expanse (a former expressway) used as a venue for festivals and concerts as well as picnicking, jogging, and biking. From the park you can see some of the many distinctive bridges that have earned Portland the name Bridgetown.

Many fine examples of 19th-century cast-iron architecture are preserved in the **Yamhill and Skidmore National Historic districts,** which begin on Naito Parkway across from the waterfront park. The former commercial waterfront of Portland is now a district of galleries, fountains, and shops that is particularly lively on weekends.

The main mast of the battleship *Oregon,* which served in three wars, stands at the foot of Oak Street. The exterior of the **Oregon Maritime Center and Museum** incorporates fine street-level examples of cast-iron architecture. Inside are models of ships that once plied the Columbia River. The admission fee allows you to board the last operating stern-wheeler tug in the United States, docked across the street. ⊠ *113 S.W. Naito Pkwy.,* ☏ *503/224–7724.* ⊡ *$4. Closed Mon. and Tues.*

The **Portland Saturday Market** (☏ 503/222–6072), underneath the west end of the Burnside Bridge and open weekends from March through Christmas, has live entertainment and 300 merchants selling ethnic foods, arts, and crafts. Graceful **Skidmore Fountain,** built in 1888, is the splashing centerpiece of Ankeny Square, the Saturday Market's western boundary.

The official entrance to Portland's **Chinatown** is the ornate **Chinatown Gate** (⊠ N.W. 4th Ave. and W. Burnside St.). The area covers several blocks and has many Chinese restaurants, shops, and grocery stores. The adjacent **Old Town** area has several good restaurants and a few gay bars.

The **Children's Museum,** just south of downtown, has hands-on, interactive exhibits. In early 2001 the museum will move into the former OMSI building across from the Oregon Zoo in Washington Park. ⊠ *3037 S.W. 2nd Ave.,* ☏ *503/823–2227.* ⊡ *$4. Closed Mon.*

Pittock Mansion (⊠ *3229 N.W. Pittock Dr.,* ☏ *503/823–3624;* ⊡ $4.50), 1,000 ft above the city about 2 mi west of downtown, yields superb views of the skyline, rivers, and Cascade Mountains. The 1914 mansion was built for Henry Pittock, former editor of *The Oregonian.* Set in its own scenic park, the opulent manor is filled with art and antiques of the 1880s.

★ ☺ The **Oregon Museum of Science and Industry** is housed in a restored steam plant on the Willamette's east bank. It has touring exhibits, permanent displays, a planetarium, a submarine, laser shows, and an Omnimax theater. ⊠ *1945 S.E. Water Ave.,* ☏ *503/797–4000.* ⊡ *$6.50–$14. Closed Mon.*

Other Neighborhoods

In an attempt to ward off suburban sprawl, fast-growing Portland—the metro area has a population of about 2 million—has put a new emphasis on "urban density" and revitalization of its inner-city neighborhoods. As a result, several areas have been transformed. Many of the storefronts and warehouses in the formerly industrial **Pearl District,** bordered by Burnside and Marshall streets and Northwest 8th and Northwest 15th avenues, have been converted during the past 10 years into lofts, art galleries, furniture and design stores, and restaurants. A few blocks west of the Pearl District, grand old Portland houses, some dating back 100 years, line the streets of **Nob Hill,** one of the city's oldest neighborhoods. At the heart of Nob Hill are the fashion-conscious blocks of **Northwest 23rd Avenue between Burnside and Vaughn streets**—now a citywide destination for dining and café hopping. Several of the avenue's old homes have been turned into upscale boutiques, with everything from women's clothing to antique linens. **Northwest 21st Avenue between Everett and Vaughn streets** is also home to many trendy restaurants and watering holes. Finding parking in this neighborhood has become such a challenge that the city has decided to put in a European-style streetcar line. Now under construction and expected to go into service in mid-2001, the Central City Streetcar line will run from Legacy Good Samaritan Hospital in Nob Hill, through the Pearl District, rendezvous with MAX light rail near Pioneer Courthouse Square downtown, and then continue up 10th Avenue to Portland State University. Across the Willamette River, **Southeast Hawthorne Boulevard between 30th and 39th avenues** has become the east side's most popular stomping ground. More down-to-earth than Northwest 23rd and still countercultural around the edges, Southeast Hawthorne is lined with bookstores, coffeehouses, taverns, restaurants, antiques stores, and unusual boutiques.

Parks, Gardens, and Zoos

Washington Park (✉ 611 S.W. Kingston Ave., ☎ 503/823–7529), covering 322 acres in the West Hills, is the site of the renowned **International Rose Test Garden** (☎ 503/823–3636; ⊡ free),and directly above it, the serene **Japanese Gardens** (☎ 503/223–1321; ⊡ $6) is considered one of the most authentic outside Japan.

★ ☾ The **Oregon Zoo** (✉ 4001 S.W. Canyon Rd., ☎ 503/226–7627, ⊡ $6.50) has Asian elephants, an African section, and animals indigenous to the Pacific Northwest. The Washington Park MAX station is adjacent to the zoo entrance.

The **Grotto,** officially known as the Sanctuary of Our Sorrowful Mother, is owned by the Catholic Church. There are more than 100 statues and shrines displayed in 62 acre of woods. The park provides a fantastic view of the Columbia River and the Cascades. ✉ *Sandy Blvd. at N.E. 85th Ave.,* ☎ *503/254–7371.* ⊡ *Grotto free, upper garden level $2.*

Dining

Bounteous local produce from land and sea receives star billing at many Portland dining establishments, and recent Pacific Rim immigrants have added depth and spice to the restaurant scene.

$$$$ ✕ **Genoa.** Widely regarded as the finest restaurant in Portland, Genoa
★ serves a seven-course, prix-fixe menu on Friday and Saturday evenings. Weekdays they serve four courses. The menu changes every two weeks. The cuisine is authentic Italian, and the decor and harkens to Tuscany. Seating is limited to a few dozen diners, so service is excellent. ✉ 2822 *S.E. Belmont,* ☎ *503/238–1464. Reservations essential. AE, D, DC, MC, V. Closed Sun. No lunch.*

$$–$$$$ ✕ **Higgins.** Higgins focuses on Pacific Northwest ingredients but in-
★ corporates traditional French cooking styles and other international influences into the menu. Fresh seafood dishes are excellent. Higgins is dedicated to organic herbs and produce. ✉ *1239 S.W. Broadway,* ☎ *503/222–9070. AE, MC, V. No lunch weekends.*

$$–$$$$ ✕ **Paley's Place.** This charming bistro features Pacific Northwest–style French cuisine. Weather permitting, seating is available on the front porch and back patio. Among the entrées are dishes featuring duck, New York steak, chicken, and halibut. Paley's has a fine selection of Willamette Valley and French wines. ✉ *1204 N.W. 21st Ave.,* ☎ *503/ 243–2403. AE, MC, V. No lunch.*

$–$$$$ ✕ **Jake's Famous Crawfish.** White-coated waiters at this revered restaurant serve up fresh seafood, selected from a lengthy sheet of daily specials, in a warren of old-fashioned wood-paneled dining rooms. Alder-smoked salmon and crab-crawfish-salmon cakes are consistent standouts. ✉ *401 S.W. 12th Ave.,* ☎ *503/226–1419. Reservations essential. AE, D, DC, MC, V. No lunch weekends.*

$$–$$$ ✕ **Heathman Restaurant.** Master chef Philippe Boulot assembles Pacific Northwest ingredients with a French flair. Duck, lamb, salmon, specialty seafood dishes, and local free-range game—venison, veal, rabbit—appear on the hotel restaurant's seasonally changing menu. ✉ *1001 S.W. Broadway,* ☎ *503/790–7752. Reservations essential. AE, D, DC, MC, V.*

$$–$$$ ✕ **Southpark.** The specialty here is wood-fired Mediterranean seafood. The decor has touches of deco and the atmosphere is comfortable. There's a wide selection of fresh Pacific Northwest oysters and fine regional wines available by the glass. Southpark is near the Arlene Schnitzer Concert Hall, the Portland Art Museum, and many downtown hotels. ✉ *901 S.W. Salmon St.,* ☎ *503/326–1300. AE, MC, V. No lunch.*

$$–$$$ ✕ **Wildwood.** Executive chef Cory Schreiber won the prestigious James Beard Foundation Award in 1998, the first Portland area restaurateur to do so. Blond wooden chairs and a stainless steel open kitchen accent this restaurant serving fresh Pacific Northwest cuisine. Wildwood also has a Sunday brunch and a family-style Sunday supper menu. ✉ *1221 N.W. 21st Ave.,* ☎ *503/248–9663. AE, MC, V.*

$–$$ ★ ✕ **Typhoon!** This trendy restaurant serves excellent Thai food at reasonable prices in a cozy but lively atmosphere. Spicy chicken or shrimp with crispy basil, curry and noodle dishes, and vegetarian spring rolls are standouts. It's packed for lunch. ✉ *400 S.W. Broadway,* ☎ *503/224–8285. AE, D, DC, MC, V. No lunch weekends.*

Brewpubs

Portland has one of the largest microbrewery scenes in North America. Its dozens of small breweries and affiliated pubs offer both satisfying dining and good value. The **Bridgeport Brew Pub** (✉ 1313 N.W. Marshall St., ☎ 503/241–7179) serves thick hand-thrown pizzas; wash them down with creamy pints of Bridgeport real ale. **McMenamins Edgefield** (✉ 2126 S.W. Halsey St., Troutdale, ☎ 503/669–8610) is the showpiece of the vast microbrewing empire of the McMenamin brothers; the 12-acre estate has its own pub, restaurant, movie theater, 105-room inn, winery, and brewery. Portland Brewing's **Brewhouse Taproom and Grille** (✉ 2730 N.W. 31st Ave., ☎ 503/228–5269), part of a 27,000-square-ft brewery complex, has a large restaurant. The McMenamin brothers' newest venture, **Ringlers** restaurant (✉ 1332 W. Burnside St., ☎ 503/225–0543), occupies the first floor of a historic Portland building that houses the Crystal Ballroom (☞ Nightlife, *below*).

Lodging

You'll find many national and regional chains near the airport. The city center and waterfront support both elegant new and historic hotels. Bed-and-breakfasts cluster in the West Hills and across the river in the Lloyd Center/Convention Center area. **Northwest Bed & Breakfast** (☎ 503/243–7616) is a good source for information and reservations in Portland and the entire coastal region.

$$$–$$$$ ★ **The Benson.** Portland's grandest hotel, built in 1912, has maintained its turn-of-the-20th-century splendor, with Russian-walnut–paneled walls in the guest rooms and a piano in the lobby. ✉ *309 S.W. Broadway, 97205,* ☎ *503/228–2000 or 800/426–0670,* FAX *503/226–4603. 287 rooms. 2 restaurants, exercise room. AE, D, DC, MC, V.*

$$$–$$$$ **The Governor.** This distinctive hotel has a clubby lobby with mahogany walls and a mural of Northwest Indians fishing in Celilo Falls. Guest rooms, painted in soothing earth tones, have large windows and whirlpool tubs; some also have fireplaces and balconies. Jake's Grill, famous for its steaks and Sunday brunch, is located off the lobby. ✉ *611 S.W. 10th Ave., 97205,* ☎ *503/224–3400 or 800/554–3456,* FAX *503/241–2122. 100 rooms. Restaurant. AE, D, DC, MC, V.*

$$$–$$$$ ⊡ **The Heathman.** Superior service, an award-winning restaurant, an
★ elegant tea court, and a library of signed first editions by authors who
have been guests here have earned the Heathman a reputation for qual-
ity. ⊠ *1001 S.W. Broadway, 97205,* ☎ *503/241–4100 or 800/551–
0011,* FAX *503/790–7110. 150 rooms. Restaurant, exercise room. AE,
D, DC, MC, V.* ☙

$$$–$$$$ ⊡ **Hilton Portland.** Portland's first large, full-service business and con-
vention hotel recently underwent a $25 million renovation. The Hilton
is in walking distance of the Performing Arts Center, Pioneer Courthouse
Square, the Portland Art Museum, and MAX light rail. ⊠ *921 S.W. 6th
Ave., 97204,* ☎ *503/226–1611 or 800/445–8667,* FAX *503/220–2565.
455 rooms. 2 restaurants, pool, health club. AE, D, DC, MC, V.* ☙

$$$–$$$$ ⊡ **Hotel Vintage Plaza.** As the hotel's name might suggest, the names
of the rooms take their theme from Oregon's wine country, and there's
also a complimentary wine hour each evening. Top-floor rooms have
skylights and wall-to-wall conservatory-style windows. ⊠ *422 S.W.
Broadway, 97205,* ☎ *503/228–1212 or 800/243–0555,* FAX *503/228–
3598. 107 rooms. 2 restaurants, exercise room. AE, D, DC, MC, V.* ☙

$$$–$$$$ ⊡ **Marriott City Center.** The lobby of this new 20-story property, in the
heart of Portland's downtown arts and dining area, is accented with a
grand staircase, maple paneling, marble floors, and a large chandelier.
The Chinook Grill bistro-style restaurant features Pacific Northwest cui-
sine. MAX light rail is two blocks away. ⊠ *520 S.W. Broadway, 97205,*
☎ *503/226–6300 or 800/228–9290,* FAX *503/227–7515. 249 rooms.
Restaurant, bar, exercise room. AE, D, DC, MC, V. www.marriott.com.*

$$$–$$$$ ⊡ **Westin Portland.** This dependable chain is in the heart of downtown,
convenient to the city's arts and entertainment venues, MAX light rail,
and many restaurants. ⊠ *750 S.W. Alder St., 97205,* ☎ *503/294–9000,*
FAX *503/241–9565. 205 rooms. Restaurant, health club. AE, D, DC,
MC, V. www.westin.com.*

$$–$$$$ ⊡ **Doubletree Hotel Portland–Lloyd Center.** At Portland's second-largest
hotel, service runs like a well-oiled machine. Many of the large rooms
with balconies have views of the mountains or the city center. Lloyd
Center shopping and MAX light rail are across the street. ⊠ *1000 N.E.
Multnomah St., 97232,* ☎ *503/281–6111,* FAX *503/284–8553. 476
rooms. 3 restaurants, pool, exercise room. AE, D, DC, MC, V.* ☙

$$–$$$ ⊡ **MacMaster House.** This 17-room Colonial Revival mansion, built
in 1886, is comfortable and funky. Fashionable Northwest 23rd Avenue is less than 10 minutes away by foot. ⊠ *1041 S.W. Vista Ave.,
97205,* ☎ *503/223–7362 or 800/774–9523. 7 rooms, 2 with bath. AE,
D, DC, MC, V. BP.* ☙

$$–$$$ ⊡ **Portland's White House.** Hardwood floors with Oriental rugs, chan-
★ deliers, antiques, and fountains create a warm and romantic mood at
this elegant bed-and-breakfast inn in a Greek Revival mansion. All rooms
have private baths. A full gourmet breakfast is included in the room
rate. Smoking and pets are not permitted. ⊠ *1914 N.E. 22nd Ave.,
97212,* ☎ *503/287–7131 or 800/272–7131,* FAX *503/249–1641. 9
rooms. Dining room. AE, D, MC, V.* ☙

$$ ⊡ **Mallory Hotel.** The rooms are on the small side, but this Portland
stalwart, five blocks from the city center, is clean and friendly. Pets are
allowed for $10 extra. ⊠ *729 S.W. 15th Ave., 97205,* ☎ *503/223–6311
or 800/228–8657,* FAX *503/223–0522. 136 rooms. Restaurant. AE, D,
DC, MC, V.* ☙

Nightlife and the Arts

The *Oregonian,* Portland's daily newspaper, and *Willamette Week*
(available free in the metro area) list arts and entertainment events. *Just
Out* (available free in the metro area) is the city's gay newspaper.

Nightlife

The **Crystal Ballroom** (⊠ S.W. 14th and Burnside St., ☎ 503/225–0047), dating from 1914 and completely restored, hosts dancing to live bands on its huge "elastic" floor, built on ball bearings. The top jazz spots in Portland are **Brasserie Montmartre** (⊠ 626 S.W. Park Ave., ☎ 503/224–5552) and **Jazz De Opus** (⊠ 33 N.W. 2nd Ave., ☎ 503/222–6077).

Atwater's (⊠ 111 S.W. 5th Ave., ☎ 503/275–3600) is the place to go to enjoy a panoramic city view and live music with your cocktail. The Pearl District's **Bima** (⊠ 1338 N.W. Hoyt St., ☎ 503/241–3465) has a large lounge with a good bar menu.

For comedy try **Harvey's Comedy Club** (⊠ 436 N.W. 6th Ave., ☎ 503/241–0338), which presents headliners with a national reputation.

Embers (⊠ 110 N.W. Broadway, ☎ 503/222–3082), a full-throttle gay disco, is also popular with straights. Several gay bars line Southwest Stark Street downtown, including **Scandals** (⊠ 1038 S.W. Stark St., ☎ 503/227–5887), a neighborhood bar, and **Boxxes/Panorama/Fish Grotto** (⊠ 1035 S.W. Stark St., ☎ 503/221–7262), a video bar, disco, and restaurant.

Performing Arts

The **Portland Center for the Performing Arts** (⊠ 1111 S.W. Broadway, ☎ 503/796–9293), which includes the Arlene Schnitzer Concert Hall and (across the street) the Performing Arts Building, presents rock and symphony orchestra concerts, theater, dance, lectures, and touring Broadway musicals. Portland Center Stage performs from November to April at the Performing Art Building's **Newmark Theater** (⊠ 1111 S.W. Broadway, ☎ 503/248–4335). The **Oregon Symphony** (☎ 503/228–1353) performs more than 40 concerts each season at the Arlene Schnitzer Concert Hall. The **Portland Opera** (☎ 503/241–1802) and the **Oregon Ballet Theater** (☎ 503/222–5538) perform at the **Civic Auditorium** (⊠ 222 S.W. Clay St., ☎ 503/796–9293).

Major rock concerts are scheduled at the 20,000-seat **Rose Garden Arena** (⊠ 1 Center Ct., east end of Broadway Bridge, ☎ 503/231–8000).

Spectator Sports

Basketball: The NBA **Portland Trail Blazers** (⊠ Rose Garden Arena, 1 Center Ct., east end of Broadway Bridge, ☎ 503/231–8000).

Shopping

For local products try the **Made In Oregon** shops, with locations at Portland International Airport, Lloyd Center, the Galleria, Old Town, Washington Square, and Clackamas Town Center. Merchandise ranges from books to smoked salmon, hazelnuts, honey, dried fruits, local wines, and Pendleton woolen products.

Pioneer Place (⊠ 700 S.W. 5th Ave., ☎ 503/228–5800) is the jewel in the city's shopping crown. More than 80 specialty shops are anchored by a gleaming **Saks Fifth Avenue** (⊠ 850 S.W. 5th Ave., ☎ 503/226–3200) store. The original **Meier & Frank** (⊠ 621 S.W. 5th Ave., ☎ 503/223–0512) department store, a Portland landmark since 1857, sits across the street from Pioneer Place. **Nordstrom** (⊠ 701 S.W. Broadway, ☎ 503/224–6666), across from Pioneer Courthouse Square, has quality apparel and accessories and a large shoe department. High-tech **Niketown** (⊠ 930 S.W. 6th Ave., ☎ 503/221–6453), the original branch of a now-national chain, is part sports shrine, part sales outlet.

With more than a million new and used volumes, **Powell's City of Books** (⊠ 1005 W. Burnside St., ☎ 503/228–4651) is one of the largest bookstores in the world. The **Portland Pendleton Shop** (✉ 900 S.W. 5th Ave., ☎ 503/242–0037) carries men's and women's wear, including the Oregon mill's famous Pendleton shirts and blankets.

Across the Willamette River on Portland's east side, **Lloyd Center** (✉ N.E. Multnomah St. at N.E. 9th Ave., ☎ 503/282–2511), which is on the MAX light rail line, contains more than 170 shops, including Nordstrom, Sears, and Meier & Frank, a large food court, a multiscreen cinema, and an ice-skating pavilion.

The **Hawthorne District,** along Southeast Hawthorne Boulevard from Southeast 17th Avenue to Southeast 43rd Avenue, has attracted bohemian and artsy types with its coffeehouses, music clubs, funky shops, and galleries. **Sellwood,** in the city's southeast corner between Southeast Tacoma Street and Southeast 13th Avenue, is a modest neighborhood known for its antiques stores and restaurants.

THE OREGON COAST

Oregon has 400 mi of white-sand beaches, not a grain of which is privately owned. U.S. 101 parallels the coast from Astoria south to California, past monoliths of sea-tortured rock, brooding headlands, hidden beaches, historic lighthouses, tiny ports, and, of course, the tumultuous Pacific.

Visitor Information

Astoria–Warrenton area: Chamber of Commerce (✉ 143 S. Hwy. 101, 97103, ☎ 503/861–1031 or 800/875–6807). **Cannon Beach:** Chamber of Commerce (✉ 2nd and Spruce Sts., 97110, ☎ 503/436–2623). **Coos Bay/North Bend area:** Chamber of Commerce (✉ 50 Central Ave., Coos Bay 97420, ☎ 541/269–0215 or 800/824–8486). **Florence area:** Chamber of Commerce (✉ 270 Hwy. 101, 97439, ☎ 541/997–3128). **Lincoln City:** Visitors Center (✉ 801 S.W. Hwy. 101, Suite 1, 97367, ☎ 541/994–8378 or 800/452–2151).

Arriving and Departing

By Bus
Greyhound (☎ 800/231–2222) serves coastal communities such as Coos Bay, Florence, Newport, and Lincoln City.

By Car
The best way to see the coast is by car, but all travel is by two-lane highways. U.S. 26 connects Portland to U.S. 101 at Seaside. The direct route to Lincoln City is I–5 south to Highway 99W, west to McMinnville, where it connects with Highway 18.

Exploring the Oregon Coast

Astoria, founded in 1811 at the site where the mighty Columbia River meets the Pacific Ocean, is believed to be the first official settlement established by the United States on the West Coast. Here Lewis and Clark wept with joy when they first saw the Pacific. The Victorian houses once owned by fur, timber, and fishing magnates still dot the flanks of Coxcomb Hill; some are now inviting B&Bs. Patterned after Trajan's Column in Rome, the 125-ft **Astor Column** atop Coxcomb Hill rewards a climb up 164 spiral stairs with breathtaking views over Astoria, the Columbia, the Coast Range, and the ocean.

The **Columbia River Maritime Museum** (✉ 1792 Marine Dr., ☎ 503/325–2323; ✆ $5) has exhibits ranging from the fully operational

Western Oregon

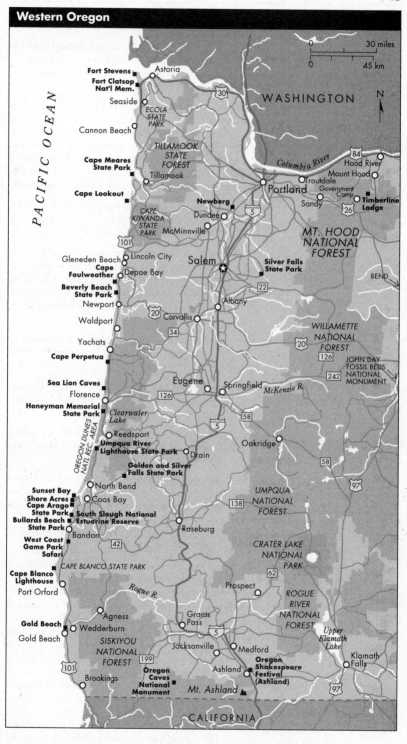

Fort Stevens ■
Fort Clatsop
Nat'l Mem. ■
Astoria ○
Seaside ○
ECOLA STATE PARK
WASHINGTON
N

Cannon Beach ○
TILLAMOOK STATE FOREST
84
Hood River ○

PACIFIC OCEAN

Cape Meares State Park ■
Tillamook ○
Columbia River
Mount Hood ○

Cape Lookout ■
Portland ○
Troutdale ○
Government Camp
Sandy ○
26
Timberline Lodge ■

CAPE KIWANDA STATE PARK
Newberg ○
Dundee ○
McMinnville ○
5

MT. HOOD NATIONAL FOREST

Gleneden Beach ○
Lincoln City ○
Cape Foulweather ●
Depoe Bay ○
Salem ☆
Silver Falls State Park ○
BEND

Beverly Beach State Park ■
Newport ○
20
22

Waldport ○
Corvallis ○
Albany ○
34

Yachats ○
WILLAMETTE NATIONAL FOREST
20

Cape Perpetua ■
126
JOHN DAY FOSSIL BEDS NATIONAL MONUMENT
242

Sea Lion Caves ■
Florence ○
Eugene ○
Springfield ○
McKenzie R.
126

Honeyman Memorial State Park ■
Clearwater Lake
5
58

OREGON DUNES NATL. REC. AREA
Reedsport ○
Oakridge ○
58

Umpqua River Lighthouse State Park ■
Drain ○
97

Golden and Silver Falls State Park
138
UMPQUA NATIONAL FOREST

North Bend ○
Sunset Bay Shore Acres State Park
Cape Arago State Park
Coos Bay ○
South Slough National Estuarine Reserve
Bullards Beach State Park ■
Bandon ○
Roseburg ○
CRATER LAKE NATIONAL PARK

West Coast Game Park Safari
42
62
ROGUE RIVER NATIONAL FOREST

CAPE BLANCO STATE PARK
Cape Blanco Lighthouse
Port Orford ○
Rogue R.
Prospect ○
Upper Klamath Lake

Gold Beach ■
Agness ○
Grants Pass ○
Wedderburn ○
Gold Beach ○
5
Klamath Falls ○

SISKIYOU NATIONAL FOREST
199
Jacksonville ○
Medford ○

101
Brookings ○
Oregon Caves National Monument
Ashland ○
Oregon Shakespeare Festival (Ashland)
97

Mt. Ashland ▲

CALIFORNIA

30 miles
45 km

lightship *Columbia* to poignant personal belongings from some of the 2,000 ships that have been wrecked at the mouth of the river since 1811.

★ Five and a half miles southeast of Astoria is the **Fort Clatsop National Memorial** (⊠ Fort Clatsop Loop Rd., ☎ 503/861–2471, 🖅 $4 per vehicle), a replica of the log stockade depicted in Clark's journal, commemorating the achievement of Lewis and Clark.

Thirty miles south of Astoria and close enough to Portland to make it
★ a popular weekend getaway, **Cannon Beach** draws visitors to its long and sandy beach, restaurants, and weathered-cedar shopping district, especially in June, when the Cannon Beach Sandcastle Contest takes place (☞ Festivals and Seasonal Events *in* the United States Region by Region chapter). **Haystack Rock**, a 235-ft offshore sea stack with tide pools at its base, is one of the most photographed sites on the coast.

At the north end of Cannon Beach, **Ecola State Park** (☎ 503/436–2844; 🖅 $3 per vehicle) is a playground of sea-sculpted rock, sandy beach, tide pools, green headlands, and panoramic views.

South of Tillamook Bay, on the lush coastal plain that is Oregon's dairy country, **Tillamook** is famous for its cheese and ice cream. Both can be tasted at the **Tillamook County Creamery** (⊠ 4175 Hwy. 101 N, ☎ 503/842–4481). The **Three Capes Scenic Loop,** west of Tillamook, encompasses magnificent coastal scenery, a lighthouse, offshore wildlife refuges, sand dunes, camping areas, and hiking trails.

Bustling **Lincoln City,** 43 mi south of Tillamook on U.S. 101, is known for its excellent seafood restaurants, lodgings, and proximity to some of the Oregon coast's most scenic landscapes.

Chinook Winds Casino and Convention Center (⊠ 1777 N.W. 44th St., ☎ 800/863–3314), on the beach in Lincoln City, has slot machines, gaming tables, a buffet, and oceanfront dining.

Twenty-five miles south of Lincoln City, **Newport,** with its fishing fleet, art galleries, and seafoodmarkets along a charming old bay front, is a fine place for an afternoon stroll.

★ ℭ Across Yaquina Bay, the **Oregon Coast Aquarium** has more than 4 acres of outdoor pools, cliffs, and caves for frolicking sea otters, plus sea lions. It was the temporary home of Keiko, the orca featured in the *Free Willy* movies. Indoor galleries are devoted to Oregon's coastal habitats and native marine life. ⊠ 2820 S.E. Ferry Slip Rd., ☎ 541/867–3474. 🖅 *$8.75. Closed Christmas.* ℘

South of Newport, the coast takes on a very different character—slower paced, less touristy, far less crowded, but just as rich in scenery
★ and outdoor sporting activities. **Cape Perpetua** (⊠ 9 mi south of Yachats, off U.S. 101, ☎ 541/547–3289; 🖅 $3), the highest lookout point on the Oregon coast, towers 800 ft above the rocky shoreline
ℭ and has hiking trails and an informative visitor center. The **Sea Lion Caves** (⊠ 91560 U.S. 101, 12 mi south of Cape Perpetua, ☎ 541/547–3111; 🖅 $6.50) is a huge vaulted chamber where kids can get a close view of hundreds of sea lions, the largest of which weigh a ton or more.
★ ℭ The peaceful village of Florence is the northern gateway to the **Oregon Dunes National Recreation Area** (☞ National and State Parks, *above*), a remarkable 40-mi swath of tawny sand. The dunes, some more than 500 ft high, are popular with campers, hikers, mountain bikers, dune-buggy enthusiasts, and even dogsledders. Children particularly enjoy the sandy slopes surrounding cool Cleawox Lake. **Umpqua River Lighthouse State Park** (⊠ 460 Lighthouse Rd., 1 mi west of U.S. 101, ☎ 541/271–4118) adjoins an operating lighthouse and encompasses a small fresh-

water lake and campground. Also in the park are a whale-watching station, 500-ft-high sand dunes, and the **Douglas County Coastal Visitors Center** (☎ 541/271–4631; ☞ free), which has local history exhibits.

Coos Bay is the Oregon coast's largest metropolitan area. At the end of a gravel road in **Golden and Silver Falls State Park** (⊠ 24 mi northeast of Coos Bay off U.S. 101, ☎ 541/888–4902; ☞ free), Glenn Creek pours over a high rock ledge deep in the old-growth forest. West of Coos Bay, the Cape Arago Highway presents spectacular scenery at three state parks (☎ 541/888–4902): **Sunset Bay** (☞ free) has a white-sand beach, picnicking, and campgrounds. **Shore Acres** (☞ $3 per vehicle), once the estate of a timber baron, has a 7½-acre formal garden and a glass-enclosed storm-watch viewpoint. **Cape Arago** (☞ free), overlooking the **Oregon Islands National Wildlife Refuge**, is a prime site for viewing sea lions and seabirds. Four miles south of the small fishing village of Charleston, the rich tidal estuaries of **South Slough National Estuarine Reserve** (⊠ Seven Devils Rd., ☎ 541/888–5558; ☞ free) support life ranging from algae to bald eagles and black bears.

★ **Bullards Beach State Park** (☎ 541/332–3501; ☞ free), 2 mi north of Bandon, spreads over miles of shoreline and sand dunes. It has a campground as well as the restored Coquille River Lighthouse. **West Coast Game Park Safari** (⊠ U.S. 101, 7 mi south of Bandon, ☎ 541/347–3106; ☞ $7.95), closed weekdays in January and February, keeps animals of more than 75 exotic species, some of which children can pet. **Cape Blanco Lighthouse,** west of the community of Sixes, was built in 1870 and is still operating. It is the most westerly lighthouse in the contiguous 48 states. Adjacent **Cape Blanco State Park** (☎ 541/332–6774; ☞ free) has sweeping views of rocks and beaches plus a campground.

Many knowledgeable coastal travelers consider the 63-mi stretch of U.S. 101 between Port Orford and Gold Beach to be Oregon's most beautiful. The highway soars up green headlands, some hundreds of feet high, past awesome scenery: caves, towering arches, natural and man-made bridges. Take time to admire the views by making use of the many turnouts along the way.

Gold Beach, about 30 mi north of the California border, is notable mainly as the place where the wild Rogue River meets the ocean. Daily jet-boat excursions roar up the scenic, rapids-filled Rogue from Wedderburn, Gold Beach's sister city across the bay, from late spring to late fall. Gold Beach also marks the entrance to Oregon's banana belt, where milder temperatures encourage a blossoming trade in lilies and daffodils. You'll even see a few palm trees here.

Dining and Lodging

Astoria

$–$$ ✕ **Cannery Café.** Housed in a 100-year-old renovated cannery on a pier, this bright, contemporary restaurant has windows that look onto the Columbia River. Fresh salads, large sandwiches, clam chowder, and crab cakes are lunch staples. ⊠ *1 6th St.,* ☎ *503/325–8642. MC, V. Closed Mon.*

$–$$ ⊞ **Franklin Street Station Bed & Breakfast.** The ticking of a grandfather clock and the mellow marine light shining through leaded-glass windows set a relaxed tone at this B&B, built in 1900. Breakfasts are huge, hot, and satisfying. ⊠ *1140 Franklin St., 97103,* ☎ *503/325–4314 or 800/448–1098. 6 rooms. MC, V. BP.*

Brookings

$$–$$$ ⊞ **Chetco River Inn.** Acres of private forest surround this modern fish-
★ ing lodge 17½ mi up the Chetco River from Brookings. Fishing guides

are available on request, as are eclectic dinners cooked by the B&B's owner, Sandra Burgger; she's also a font of information on the many hiking trails in the area. Quilts and fishing gear decorate the comfortable bedrooms. ⊠ *21202 High Prairie Rd., 97415,* ☎ *541/670–1645 or 800/327–2688. 4 rooms. MC, V. BP.* ✥

Cannon Beach

$$–$$$ ✕ **The Bistro.** Cannon Beach's most romantic restaurant is candlelit and intimate. The three-course prix-fixe menu features imaginatively prepared fresh seafood. ⊠ *263 N. Hemlock St.,* ☎ *503/436–2661. Reservations essential. MC, V. Closed most of Jan. and Tues.–Wed. in winter.*

$–$$ ✕ **Dooger's.** This comfortable family-style eatery's fresh, well-prepared seafood, exquisite clam chowder, and low prices keep 'em coming back for more. ⊠ *1371 S. Hemlock St.,* ☎ *503/436–2225. AE, D, MC, V.*

$$$–$$$$ ✕🏠 **Stephanie Inn.** Sophisticated country-style furnishings, fireplaces,
★ large bathrooms with Jacuzzi bathtubs, and balconies featuring outstanding views of Haystack Rock make this oceanfront hotel a treat. The inn also serves four-course prix-fixe dinners of Pacific Northwest cuisine; reservations are essential. Room rates include generous country breakfasts and evening wine and hors d'oeuvres. ⊠ *2740 S. Pacific, 97110,* ☎ *503/436–2221 or 800/633–3466,* ﬀ *503/436–9711. 50 rooms. Restaurant. AE, D, DC, MC, V. BP.* ✥

Coos Bay

$–$$ ✕ **Blue Heron Bistro.** You'll get subtle preparations of local seafood, chicken, and homemade pasta with an international flair at this busy bistro. There are no flat spots on the far-ranging menu; the innovative soups and desserts are also excellent. ⊠ *100 Commercial St.,* ☎ *541/ 267–3933. AE, D, MC, V. Closed Sun. in winter.*

$–$$ ✕ **Portside Restaurant.** At this unpretentious spot with picture windows overlooking the busy Charleston boat basin, you'll be treated to seafood straight off the local fishing boats. Try the steamed Dungeness crab with drawn butter, a local specialty, or the all-you-can-eat seafood buffet on Friday night. ⊠ *8001 Kingfisher Rd. (follow Cape Arago Hwy. from Coos Bay),* ☎ *541/888–5544. AE, DC, MC, V.*

$$ 🏠 **Coos Bay Manor.** Built in 1912 on a quiet residential street in Coos Bay, this 15-room Colonial Revival manor is listed on the National Register of Historic Places. An unusual open balcony on the second floor leads to the five large, comfortable guest rooms. Breakfast is served in the wainscoted dining room or, weather permitting, outside on the second-floor porch. ⊠ *955 S. 5th St., 97420,* ☎ *541/269–1224 or 800/ 269–1224. 5 rooms, 3 with bath. D, MC, V. FP.*

Depoe Bay

$$–$$$ ✕ **Sea Hag.** This friendly restaurant has been specializing in fresh
★ seafood for more than 30 years. Friday night features a seafood buffet, while Saturday the focus is on prime rib with Yorkshire pudding. ⊠ *53 Hwy. 101,* ☎ *541/765–2734. AE, D, DC, MC, V.*

Florence

$–$$ ✕ **Bridgewater Seafood Restaurant.** The salty ambience of Florence's photogenic Old Town permeates this spacious, creaky-floored fish house. Steaks, salads, and, of course, plenty of fresh seafood are the mainstays. ⊠ *1297 Bay St.,* ☎ *541/997–9405. MC, V.*

Gleneden Beach

$$$$ ✕🏠 **Westin Salishan Lodge and Golf Resort.** Nestled into a 350-acre hillside forest preserve, Salishan embodies northwestern elegance—from the soothing silvered-cedar tone of its guest rooms (all with fireplaces) to its collection of original art. The dining room is famous for its seasonal Northwest cuisine and wine list. Guests have use of an 18-hole

championship golf course, tennis courts, and hiking trails. ⊠ *7760 N. Hwy. 101, 97388,* ☎ *541/764–3605,* 𝔽𝔸𝕏 *541/764–3681. 205 rooms. 2 restaurants, indoor pool, exercise room AE, D, DC, MC, V.* ♨

Gold Beach

$$$ ✕🏨 **Tu Tu Tun Lodge.** Private decks at this lavishly appointed fishing
★ resort overlook the clear blue Rogue River. All units have an upscale rustic charm. Four-course prix-fixe gourmet dinners are served at one sitting each night. ⊠ *96550 North Bank Rogue, 97444,* ☎ *541/247–6664 or 800/864–6357,* 𝔽𝔸𝕏 *541/247–0672. 18 rooms, 1 3-bedroom house. Restaurant, pool. D, MC, V. Dining room closed Nov.–Apr.*

$ 🏨 **Ireland's Rustic Lodges.** Original one- and two-bedroom cabins filled with rough-and-tumble charm plus newer motel rooms and three houses are set amid landscaped grounds. Most units have a fireplace and a deck overlooking the sea. ⊠ *29330 Ellensburg Ave. (U.S. 101), 97444,* ☎ *541/247–7718,* 𝔽𝔸𝕏 *541/247–0225. 7 cabins; 30 motel rooms; 2-, 3-, and 4-bedroom houses. MC, V.*

Lincoln City

$–$$ ✕ **Bay House.** This bungalow serves meals to linger over while you enjoy
★ views across sunset-gilded Siletz Bay. The seasonal Northwest cuisine includes shellfish linguine, fresh halibut Parmesan, and roast duckling with dried cherries and Pinot Noir sauce. The wine list is extensive, the service impeccable. ⊠ *5911 S.W. Hwy. 101,* ☎ *541/996–3222. AE, D, MC, V. Closed Mon.–Tues., Nov.–Apr. No lunch.*

$–$$ ✕ **Kyllo's.** Perched on stilts beside the world's shortest river (the D) and bestowing views of Pacific surf and sand, Kyllos is a spacious, light-filled aerie. It's also one of the best places in Lincoln City to enjoy simple but satisfying seafood, meat, and pasta dishes. ⊠ *1110 N.W. 1st Ct.,* ☎ *541/994–3179. AE, D, MC, V.*

$$ 🏨 **Shilo Inn Oceanfront Resort.** This motel is popular because of its location: it's on the beach, next to Chinook Winds Casino, and within walking distance of shopping. A newer building has suites with kitchenettes, fireplaces, and balconies. ⊠ *1501 N.W. 40th Pl., 97367,* ☎ *541/994–3655 or 800/222–2244,* 𝔽𝔸𝕏 *503/994–2199. 248 rooms. Restaurant, pool, exercise room. AE, D, DC, MC, V.* ♨

Newport

$$–$$$ ✕ **Whale's Tale.** Fresh local seafood, thick clam chowder, burgers, and hearty sandwiches are all on the lunch and dinner menu of this casual, family-oriented Bay Front eatery; the breakfasts are considered the best in Newport. ⊠ *452 S.W. Bay Blvd.,* ☎ *541/265–8660. AE, D, DC, MC, V. Closed Wed. Nov.–Apr.*

$–$$ ✕ **Canyon Way Restaurant and Bookstore.** The best dining (and bookstore) in Newport is just up the hill from the center of the Bay Front. Cod, Dungeness crab cakes, bouillabaisse, and Umpqua Bay oysters are among the specialties served inside or on the outdoor patio. There's also a deli counter for takeout. ⊠ *S.W. Canyon Way,* ☎ *541/265–8319. AE, D, MC, V. No dinner Mon.*

$–$$$ ✕🏨 **Sylvia Beach Hotel.** Each of the phoneless, TV-less, antiques-filled
★ guest rooms at this restored 1912 B&B is named for a famous writer and decorated accordingly. (A pendulum swings over the bed in the Poe Room.) Upstairs is a well-stocked library with a fireplace, a slumbering cat, and too-comfortable chairs. Tables of Content, the hotel's restaurant, serves a filling, multicourse prix-fixe dinner; reservations are essential. ⊠ *267 N.W. Cliff St., 97365,* ☎ *541/265–5428. 20 rooms. Restaurant. AE, MC, V. No lunch. BP.*

Waldport

$–$$$ ✕ **La Serre.** Perhaps the best restaurant on the Oregon coast, La Serre
★ serves fresh seafood dishes, including razor clams lightly breaded and

flash-fried in lemon-garlic butter, fishermen's stew, and a famous Seafood Extravaganza with grilled salmon, blackened cod, and Dungeness crab cakes. ⊠ *2nd and Beach Sts.,* ☎ *541/547–3420. AE, MC, V. Closed Tues. and Jan. No lunch.*

Yachats

$$$ ⊞ **Ziggurat.** It's hard to miss this terraced, pyramid-shape B&B; it's located just south of Yachats, one of the most charming small communities on the coast. Two large suites opening onto a grassy cliff are on the first floor; a third guest room, with two balconies and outstanding views, is on the fourth level. ⊠ *95320 Hwy. 101, 97498,* ☎ *541/547–3925. 3 rooms. No credit cards. BP.*

Campgrounds

Seventeen state parks along the coast have campgrounds, most with trailer hookups and tent sites. Many are near the shore, and some have group facilities and hiker/biker or horse camps. The Oregon State Parks and Recreation Department (☞ National and State Parks, *above*) has details. △ **Honeyman State Park** (⊠ 84505 Hwy. 101, Florence 97439, ☎ 541/997–3641; ⌷ $3 per vehicle day use) adjoins the Oregon Dunes National Recreation Area. Reserve well ahead.

Outdoor Activities and Sports

Biking

The **Oregon Coast Bike Route** parallels U.S. 101 and the coast from Astoria south to Brookings.

Fishing

Salmon, delectable Dungeness crab, and dozens of species of bottom fish are the quarry here, accessible from jetties, docks, and riverbanks from Astoria to Brookings. Charter boats and guides are plentiful; contact local chambers of commerce (☞ Visitor Information, *above*) for information on fishing permits, seasons, rates, and schedules.

Golf

The Oregon coast has about 20 public and private courses, including **Salishan Golf Links** (⊠ 7760 N. Hwy. 101, Gleneden Beach, ☎ 541/764–3632), the coast's most challenging course, with 18 holes. Newport has the 9-hole **Agate Beach Golf Course** (⊠ 4100 N. Coast Hwy., ☎ 541/265–7331). In Florence the 18-hole **Ocean Dunes Golf Links** (⊠ 3345 Munsel Lake Rd., ☎ 541/997–3232) draws amateurs and professionals. Gold Beach's **Cedar Bend Golf Course** (⊠ 34391 Squaw Valley Rd., ☎ 541/247–6911) has 9 holes.

Beaches

Virtually the entire 400-mi coastline of Oregon consists of clean white-sand beaches, accessible to all. Thanks to its sea-sculpted stone, **Face Rock Wayside,** in Bandon, is thought by many to have the most beautiful walking beach in the state. The placid, semicircular lagoon at **Sunset Bay State Park,** on Cape Arago, is Oregon's safest swimming beach. Fossils, clams, mussels, and other eons-old marine creatures embedded in soft sandstone cliffs make **Beverly Beach State Park,** 5 mi north of Newport, a favorite with young beachcombers.

Shopping

Hemlock Street, the main drag of Cannon Beach, is the best place on the coast to browse for unusual clothing, souvenirs, picnic supplies, books, and gifts. Newport's **Bay Boulevard** is a good place to find local artwork, gifts, and fresh seafood. There are bargains galore at the **Lin-**

coln City Factory Stores (⊠ 1500 E. Devils Lake Rd.,☎ 541/996–5000). Particularly good deals on vintage items can be found in the antiques malls in Astoria, Seaside, and Lincoln City.

ELSEWHERE IN OREGON

Mt. Hood and Bend

Arriving and Departing

Mt. Hood lies about an hour east of Portland on U.S. 26; the only way to get there is by car. Continue east on U.S. 26, then south on U.S. 97 for the resort town of Bend, two hours beyond Mt. Hood. **Redmond Municipal Airport** (☎ 541/548–6059), about 14 mi north of Bend, is served by **Horizon Airlines** (☎ 800/547–9308) and **United Express** (☎ 800/241–6522).

What to See and Do

★ ☾ Mt. Hood, 11,235 ft high and surrounded by the 1.1-million-acre **Mt. Hood National Forest** (⊠ 16400 Champion Way, Sand 97055, ☎ 503/668–1700), is an all-season playground that attracts more than 7 million visitors annually for skiing, snowboarding, camping, hiking, and fishing.

The skiing is excellent near **Bend,** which occupies a tawny high-desert plateau in the very center of Oregon, framed on the west by three 10,000-ft Cascade peaks. With its plentiful dining and lodging options, Bend makes a fine base camp for skiing at nearby **Mt. Bachelor,** whitewater rafting on the **Deschutes River,** world-class rock climbing at **Smith Rocks State Park,** and other outdoor activities. Don't miss the ar-
☾ chaeological and wildlife displays at the **High Desert Museum** (⊠ 59800 S. Hwy. 97, 3½ mi south of Bend, ☎ 541/382–4754; ☲ $6.25). **Newberry National Volcanic Monument** (☞ National and State Parks, *above*), 25 mi southeast of Bend, contains more than 50,000 acres of lakes, lava flows, and spectacular geological features.

$$–$$$ ✕⊞ **Timberline Lodge.** Everything at this National Historic Landmark
★ (off U.S. 26 a few miles east of Government Camp) has a handcrafted, rustic feel, from the wrought-iron chairs with rawhide seats to the massive hand-hewn beams. The expert cuisine at the Cascade Dining Room incorporates the freshest Oregon ingredients. ⊠ *Timberline Rd., Timberline 97028,* ☎ *503/231–5400 or 800/547–1406,* ℻ *503/727–3710. 60 rooms. Restaurant, pool, outdoor hot tub, skiing. AE, D, MC, V.* ✆

Columbia River Gorge

Arriving and Departing

Several popular attractions are in the Columbia River Gorge, a short drive east of Portland on I–84. Multnomah Falls is 20 mi east of Troutdale; Bonneville Dam is another 10 mi east; Hood River is 30 mi farther.

What To See and Do

Multnomah Falls, a 620-ft-high double-decker torrent, is the fifth-highest waterfall in the nation. The scenic highway leads down to a parking lot; from there, a paved path winds to a bridge over the lower falls. A much steeper trail climbs to a viewing point overlooking the upper falls.

Bonneville Dam (1937) is Oregon's most impressive man-made attraction. Its generators have a capacity of nearly a million kilowatts, enough to supply power to more than 200,000 single-family homes. There is a modern visitor center on Bradford Island, complete with underwater windows for viewing migrating salmon as they struggle up fish ladders. ⊠ *From I–84 take Exit 40, head northeast, and follow signs 1 mi to visitor center,* ☎ *541/374–8820.* ⌒ *Free.*

Hood River, a town 60 mi east of Portland on I–84 in the spectacular Columbia Gorge, is the self-proclaimed sailboarding capital of the world. **Columbia Gorge Sailpark** (⊠ Port Marina, ☎ 541/386–2000), on the river downtown, has a boat basin, a swimming beach, jogging trails, and picnic tables.

Dining

$–$$ ✗ Multnomah Falls Lodge. The lodge, built in 1925 and listed on the National Register of Historic Places, has vaulted ceilings and classic stone fireplaces. Freshwater trout, salmon, and a platter of prawns, halibut, and scallops are the specialties. The restaurant is famous for its wild-huckleberry daiquiris and desserts. ⊠ *Historic Columbia River Hwy. (or Exit 31 off I–84),* ☎ *503/695–2376. AE, D, MC, V.*

Willamette Valley/Wine Country

Arriving and Departing

I–5, the state's main north–south freeway, runs straight down the center of the Willamette Valley from Portland. **Eugene Airport** (⊠ 28855 Lockheed Dr., ☎ 541/687–5430) is served by Horizon, United, and United Express.

What to See and Do

Oregon's **wine country** occupies the wet, temperate trough between the Coast Range to the west and the Cascades to the east. More than 60 wineries dot the hills west of Portland and Salem, and dozens more are scattered from Newport to as far south as Ashland, on the California border. Although tiny in comparison with California's, Oregon's wine industry is booming. Cool-climate varietals such as pinot noir, chardonnay, and Johannesberg Riesling have gained the esteem of international connoisseurs.

The best way to tour is by car. *Discover Oregon Wineries,* an indispensable map and guide to the wine country, is available free at wine shops and wineries or by calling the **Oregon Wine Winegrowers Association** (☎ 800/242–2363).

Salem, the state capital, makes a good base for exploring; in addition to its hotels, B&Bs, and restaurants, there are some fine gardens and museums.

A gilded 23-ft-high bronze statue of the Oregon Pioneer atop the 106-ft capitol dome is the centerpiece of the **Capitol** (⊠ 900 Court St., ☎ 503/986–1388), where Oregon's legislators convene every two years. Across from the Capitol are the tradition-steeped brick buildings of **Willamette University,** the oldest college in the West, founded in 1842. Just south of downtown Salem, **Bush's Pasture Park** (⊠ 600 Mission St. SE) includes **Bush House** (☎ 503/363–4714; ⌒ $3), a Victorian mansion with 10 fireplaces and original furnishings, and **Bush Barn,** an art center with two exhibition rooms and a sales gallery. **Deepwood Estate** (⊠ 1116 Mission St. SE, ☎ 503/363–1825; ⌒ $4), on the National Register of Historic Places, encompasses 5½ acres of lawns, formal English gardens, and a fanciful 1894 Queen Anne mansion with splendid interior woodwork and original stained glass. **Mission Mill Village** (⊠ 1313 Mill St. SE, ☎ 503/585–7012; ⌒ $5) offers tours of its historic circa 1889 woolen mill and collection of pioneer homes. **Silver Falls State Park** (⊠ Hwy. 214, 26 mi east of Salem, ☎ 503/873–8681, ⌒ $3 per vehicle) covers 8,700 acres and includes 10 waterfalls accessible to hikers.

Liberal-minded **Eugene** is Oregon'ssecond-largest city and the home of the **University of Oregon,** which lies southeast of the city center. Eugene's two best museums are affiliated with the university. The collection of Asian art at the **University of Oregon Museum of Art** (✉ 1430 Johnson La., ☎ 541/346–3027), next to the library, includes examples of Chinese imperial tomb figures, textiles, and furniture. Relics of a more localized nature are on display at the **University of Oregon Museum of Natural History** (✉ 1680 E. 15th Ave., ☎ 541/346–3024).

☺ **Wistec,** Eugene's imaginative, hands-on Willamette Science and Technology Center, assembles rotating exhibits designed for curious young minds. The adjacent **planetarium,** one of the largest in the Pacific Northwest, presents star shows and entertainment events. ✉ *2300 Leo Harris Pkwy.,* ☎ *541/682–3020 for museum, 541/687–7827 for planetarium.* ✇ *$4. Closed Sat.–Tues.*

South of Eugene, the sleepy farming community of **Roseburg,** on the Umpqua River, is famous among anglers. West of town are a dozen of the region's wineries. The **Douglas County Museum** (✉ Douglas County Fairgrounds, I–5, Exit 123, ☎ 541/440–4507; ✇ free) has an exceptional fossil collection.

Dining and Lodging
Northwest Bed & Breakfast (☎ 503/243–7616 or 503/370–9033) can help you with reservations for the Willamette Valley's extensive B&B network.

$$$–$$$$ ✕▦ **Valley River Inn.** Many of the rooms at this four-star hotel set on
★ the picturesque banks of the Willamette River have outdoor patios or balconies with river or pool views. Its restaurant, Sweetwaters, features Pacific Northwest cuisine. ✉ *1000 Valley River Way, Eugene, 97401,* ☎ *503/629–9465 or 800/543–8266. 257 rooms. Restaurant, pool, exercise room. AE, D, DC, MC, V.* ✉

$–$$$ ✕▦ **Excelsior Inn.** This small, stylish hotel across from the University
★ of Oregon campus is quietly sophisticated, with cherry-wood doors and moldings, marble-and-tile baths, and in-room VCRs and modem lines. A full breakfast is served in the appealing Excelsior Café, which also has a seasonal menu for lunch and dinner. ✉ *754 E. 13th St., Eugene 97401,* ☎ *541/342–6963 or 800/321–6963,* ℻ *541/342–1417. 14 rooms. Restaurant. AE, D, DC, MC. BP.*

Ashland/The Rogue Valley

Arriving and Departing
Ashland is midway between Portland and San Francisco on I–5, about 15 mi north of the California border. **Rogue Valley International Airport** (✉ 3650 Biddle Rd., ☎ 541/772–8068), in nearby Medford, is served by Horizon Airlines and United Express.

What to See and Do
★ Ashland is home to the Tony Award–winning **Oregon Shakespeare Festival** (✉ 15 S. Pioneer St., 97520, ☎ 541/482–4331), which annually attracts more than 100,000 visitors to this relaxing Rogue Valley town. The local arts scene, a warm climate, and opulent B&Bs and sumptuous restaurants make this a pleasant place for a holiday. A few miles south of Ashland you'll find excellent downhill and Nordic skiing atop 7,523-ft **Mt. Ashland.** West of Ashland, the famous Rogue River boils and churns through the rugged, remote Kalmiopsis Wilderness in **Siskiyou National Forest** (☎ 541/471–6500). The local wineries are also worth a visit.

Jacksonville, west of Ashland, preserves the look and feel of an Old West pioneer settlement; the entire town is a National Historic Landmark. Each summer from mid-June to Labor Day Jacksonville hosts the **Britt Festivals** (☏ 541/773–6077 or 800/882–7488), a concert series featuring some of the world's best jazz and classical musicians performing in an outdoor amphitheater.

★ The main attraction at **Crater Lake National Park** (☞ National and State Parks, *above*) was created 6,800 years ago, when Mt. Mazama decapitated itself in a huge explosion. Rain and snowmelt eventually filled the caldera, creating a sapphire-blue lake so clear that sunlight penetrates to a depth of 400 ft. Visitors can drive or hike the park's 25-mi **Rim Drive**, explore nature trails, and (in summer) take guided boat trips around the lake itself. The park is about 80 mi northeast of Jacksonville along Highway 62.

★ ☉ **Wildlife Safari** lets you come face to face with free-roaming animals from the comfort of your car at this 600-acre, drive-through wildlife park. There's also a petting zoo, a miniature train, and elephant rides. The admission price includes two drive-throughs in the same day. ⊠ *Box 1600, Winston 97496,* ☏ *800/355–4848.* ☞ *$11.95. AE, D, MC, V.*

Lodging

$$–$$$ ☷ **Crater Lake Lodge.** The historic 1915 lodge on the rim of the caldera features lodgepole pine columns, gleaming wood floors, and stone fireplaces that grace the common areas. There are no televisions or electronic diversions of any kind. ⊠ *1211 Ave. C, White City 97503,* ☏ *541/830–8700,* FAX *541/830–8514. 71 rooms. Restaurant. MC, V. Closed mid-Oct.–mid-May.* ✎

$$–$$$ ☷ **Mt. Ashland Inn.** Built from hand-hewn cedar logs close to the summit ski area on Mt. Ashland, this modern, 5,500-square-ft lodge provides magnificent views of Mt. Shasta and the Siskiyou range. Antiques and hand-stitched quilts lend character to the guest rooms; a sauna and outdoor hot tub overlooking the mountains add to the alpine splendor. ⊠ *550 Mt. Ashland Rd., 97520,* ☏ *541/482–8707 or 800/830–8707,* FAX *541/482–8707. 5 rooms. D, MC, V. BP.* ✎

PENNSYLVANIA

Updated by
Robert
DiGiacomo
and Clark
Henderson

Capital	Harrisburg
Population	12,020,000
Motto	Virtue, Liberty, and Independence
State Bird	Ruffed grouse
State Flower	Mountain laurel
Postal Abbreviation	PA

Statewide Visitor Information

Pennsylvania Department of Commerce, Office of Travel and Tourism
(⊠ 453 Forum Bldg., Harrisburg 17120, ☎ 717/787–5453 or 800/847–
4872). **Welcome centers** are on major highways.

Scenic Drives

In Bucks County, **River Road** (Route 32) wends 40 mi along the
Delaware River, past 18th- and 19th-century stone farmhouses, tucked-
away villages, and fall foliage along wooded hills. In the Poconos, **Route
209,** from Stroudsburg to Milford, passes untouched forests and natural waterfalls. The Lancaster County countryside, with its Amish
farms and roadside stands, can best be seen along the side roads between **Routes 23** and **340.**

National and State Parks

National Parks

Pennsylvania has 17 national parks, historic sites, and monuments over-
seen by the **National Park Service** (⊠ 200 Chestnut St., Philadelphia
19106, ☎ 215/597–7013), a few of which have camping. The **Delaware
Water Gap National Recreation Area** (⊠ Bushkill 18324, ☎ 570/588–
2451), a 40-mi-long preserve in the northeast corner of the state, has
camping, fishing, river rafting, and tubing. The 500,000-acre **Allegheny
National Forest** (⊠ Box 847, Warren 16365, ☎ 814/723–5150), in the
northwestern part of the state, has hiking and cross-country skiing trails,
three rivers suitable for canoeing, and outstanding stream fishing.

State Parks

Pennsylvania's 116 state parks have more than 7,000 campsites. The
Bureau of State Parks (⊠ Rachel Carson State Bldg., Box 8551, Harrisburg 17105, ☎ 717/772–0239 or 888/727–2757) provides information and campsite reservations. In the Poconos the wooded
15,480-acre **Hickory Run State Park** (⊠ R.D. 1, Box 81, White Haven
18661, ☎ 570/443–0400) offers fishing, camping, and Boulder Field,
an area of rock formations dating to the Ice Age. The 19,140-acre
Ohiopyle State Park (⊠ Box 105, Ohiopyle 15470, ☎ 724/329–8591)
has camping, cross-country skiing, and a 27-mi hiking and biking trail
along the Youghiogheny River. **Presque Isle State Park** (⊠ Rte. 832,
Erie 16505, ☎ 814/833–7424), a 3,200-acre peninsula that extends 7
mi into Lake Erie, is popular for fishing, swimming, and boating.

PHILADELPHIA

Almost a century after English Quaker William Penn founded Philadelphia in 1682, the city became the birthplace of the nation and the home
of its first government. Today, Philadelphia is synonymous with Independence Hall, the Liberty Bell, cheese steaks and hoagies, ethnic
neighborhoods, theaters—and city streets teeming with life. Penn's

"City of Brotherly Love" is the fifth-largest city in the country, yet it maintains the feel of a friendly small town.

Visitor Information

The **Philadelphia Visitors Center** (⊠ 16th St. and John F. Kennedy Blvd., 19102, ☎ 215/636–1666 or 800/321–9563) is a good first stop for brochures, maps, and discount coupons for tourist sites.

Arriving and Departing

By Bus
Greyhound (⊠ 10th and Filbert Sts., ☎ 800/231–2222).

By Car
The main north–south highway through Philadelphia is I–95; to reach Center City, as the downtown area is called, take the Vine Street exit off I–95S or the Broad Street exit off I–95N. From the west the Schuylkill Expressway (I–76) has several exits to Center City. From the east the New Jersey Turnpike and I–295 provide access to either U.S. 30/I–676, which enters the city via the Benjamin Franklin Bridge, or New Jersey Route 42 and the Walt Whitman Bridge.

By Plane
Philadelphia International Airport (⊠ 8800 Essington Ave., ☎ 215/937–6937), 8 mi southwest of downtown, has scheduled flights on most major domestic and foreign carriers. A **SEPTA** (☞ Getting Around Philadelphia, *below*) rail line connects the airport with Center City stations; the trip takes 20 minutes and costs $5. Airport shuttle services, such as **U.S.A. Limousine** (☎ 215/782–8818) and **SuperShuttle** (☎ 800/258–3826), charge about $10 per person. Taxis cost $20, plus tip.

By Train
Amtrak serves 30th Street Station (⊠ 30th and Market Sts., ☎ 800/872–7245). **New Jersey Transit** (⊠ 10th and Filbert Sts., ☎ 215/569–3752) trains connect with SEPTA (☞ Getting Around Philadelphia, *below*) trains at Trenton.

Getting Around Philadelphia

The traditional heart of the city is the intersection of Broad and Market streets, where city hall now stands. Market Street divides the city north and south. North–south streets are numbered, starting at the Delaware River with Front (1st) Street and increasing to the west. Most historical and cultural attractions are easy walks from the midtown area, which is safe during the day. After dark ask hotel personnel about the safety of places you're interested in visiting, but in general, taking a cab is safer than walking.

By Car
The city's narrow streets were designed for Colonial traffic of the four-legged kind, and driving can be difficult. On-street parking is often forbidden during rush hours (parking facilities include those at 41 North 6th Street; 16th and Arch streets; and 10th and Locust streets). During rush hours avoid the major arteries leading into and out of the city, particularly I–95, U.S. 1, and the Schuylkill Expressway.

By Public Transportation
SEPTA operates an extensive network of buses, trolleys, subways, and commuter trains; the fare is $1.60, transfers 40¢, and exact change is required. Tokens can be purchased from machines at stations for the discounted price of $1.15 each. Certain lines run 24 hours a day. SEPTA's **Day Pass**, good for a day's unlimited riding, can be purchased

at the visitor center (☞ Visitor Information, *above*) for $5. Bus Route 76 connects the zoo in western Fairmount Park with Penn's Landing at the Delaware River. The purple **Phlash** buses do the downtown loop.

By Taxi

Cabs are plentiful during the day—especially along Broad Street and near hotels and train stations. At night and outside Center City, taxis can be scarce, and you may have to call for service. Fares start at $1.80 and increase by 30¢ for every subsequent mile. The main companies are **Quaker City Cab** (☎ 215/728–8000), **Bell Taxi** (☎ 215/425–7000), and **Yellow Cab** (☎ 215/922–8400).

Orientation Tours

Gray Line Tours (☎ 215/569–3666) leads a tour of historic and cultural areas April through October. To combine a meal with a cruise on the Delaware River, climb aboard the *Spirit of Philadelphia* (☞ *below*).

Boat Tours

The *Spirit of Philadelphia* (☎ 215/923–1419) and the *Liberty Belle* (☎ 215/629–1131) runs cruises along the Delaware River. Both dock at Penn's Landing at the foot of Lombard Street.

Carriage Tours

Philadelphia Carriage Co. (☎ 215/922–6840), **'76 Carriage Co.** (☎ 215/923–8516), and **Society Hill Carriage Co.** (☎ 215/627–6128) run tours of the historic area in antique horse-drawn carriages.

Walking Tours

Each night (April–November) starting at dusk **Lights of Liberty** (☎ 877/462–1776; ☒ $18) gives visitors head phones, turns on surround-sound narration, and leads tours through Independence National Historic Park, where five 3-D acts about the events leading to the American Revolution are digitally projected onto the buildings where the events took place more than 200 years ago. **Historic Philadelphia, Inc.** (☎ 800/764–4786; ☒ $20) runs the early evening Tippler's Tour, which includes stops and Colonial-style cheer at several historic houses and City Tavern. **Centipede Tours** (☎ 215/735–3123; ☒ $5) organizes candlelight strolls through Old Philadelphia. **CityPass** (☒ $27.50) allows visitors to attend six of the area's most popular attractions—Philadelphia Museum of Art, the Franklin Institute Science Museum, the Philadelphia Zoo, the Academy of Natural Sciences, Independence Seaport Museum, and the New Jersey State Aquarium and Camden Children's Garden—for half the amount of the sights' combined admission. The CityPass can be purchased at any of the six facilities.

Exploring Philadelphia

The *Calendar of Events* at the visitor center (☞ Visitor Information, *above*) lists Philadelphia's myriad free events and attractions.

Historic District

Even if you're not a history buff, it's hard not to get excited by the "most ★ historic square mile in America"— **Independence National Historical Park** (☎ 215/597–8974, ☒ free).

The **visitor center** (☒ 3rd and Chestnut Sts., ☎ 215/597–8974) has park rangers staffing the information desk. Across the street stands the 1797 **First Bank of the United States** (☒ 120 S. 3rd St.), the oldest bank building in the country. Note the outstanding mahogany wood carving on the pediment. In **Carpenter's Court** (☒ Chestnut St. between 3rd and 4th Sts.) you'll find **Carpenter's Hall**, where the first Continental Congress convened in 1774, and the **New Hall Military Museum**.

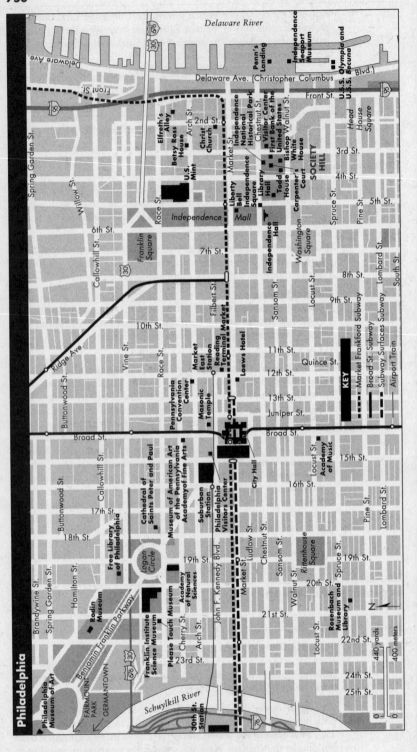

Philadelphia

★ You can almost hear "When in the course of human events . . ." when you stand behind **Independence Hall** (⊠ Chestnut St. between 5th and 6th Sts.) on the spot where the Declaration of Independence was first read to the public, and it's easy to imagine the impact those words and this setting had on the colonists on July 8, 1776. Still an impressive building, the hall opened in 1732 as the state house for the colony of Pennsylvania. It was the site of many historic events: the Second Continental Congress, convened on May 10, 1775; the adoption of the Declaration of Independence a year later; the signing of the Articles of Confederation in 1778; and the formal signing of the Constitution by its framers on September 17, 1787. In front of the hall, next to the **statue of George Washington,** note the plaques marking the spots where Abraham Lincoln and John F. Kennedy stood and delivered speeches. Tours of Independence Hall are given year-round; though a timed-ticket system has just about eliminated the long lines here, expect crowds from early May to Labor Day.

Philadelphia's best-known symbol is the **Liberty Bell** (⊠ Market St. between 5th and 6th Sts.), currently housed in a glass-enclosed pavilion. During the day park rangers relate the facts and the legends about the 2,080-pound bell. After hours you can press a button on the outside walls to hear a recorded account of the bell's history. In its current home you can still touch the bell and read its biblical inscription: PROCLAIM LIBERTY THROUGHOUT ALL THE LAND UNTO ALL THE INHABITANTS THEREOF.

Christ Church (⊠ 2nd St. north of Market St., ☎ 215/922–1695; ⊠ free) is where noted colonists, including 15 signers of the Declaration of Independence, worshiped.

Elfreth's Alley (⊠ off Front and 2nd Sts. between Arch and Race Sts.) is the oldest continuously occupied residential street in America, dating from 1702; **two houses** (⊠ 124–126 Elfreth's Alley, ☎ 215/574–0560; ⊠ $2) have been restored, one as the home of a Colonial-era Windsor chair maker, the other of a seamstress.

The **Betsy Ross House** (⊠ 239 Arch St., ☎ 215/627–5343; ⊠ donation) is a splendid example of a Colonial Philadelphia home, although the story that she lived here and sewed the first American flag in this house hangs by only a few threads of historical evidence.

The **U.S. Mint** (⊠ 5th and Arch Sts., ☎ 215/408–0114; ⊠ free; closed weekends Sept.–Apr.), built in 1969, is the largest mint in the world and stands two blocks from the first U.S. mint, which opened in 1792. Tours and exhibits on coin making are available.

The Waterfront and Society Hill

★ **Society Hill** was—and still is—Philadelphia's showplace. It is easily the city's most charming and photogenic neighborhood. A treasure trove of Federal brick row houses and quaint streets stretch from the Delaware River to 6th Street. (The *Society* in the neighborhood's moniker refers not to the wealthy Anglicans who first settled here but to the Free Society of Traders, a group of business investors who moved here on William Penn's advice.)

At Society Hill's eastern edge, the spot where William Penn stepped ashore in 1682 is today a 37-acre park known as **Penn's Landing** (⊠ Delaware Riverfront from Lombard to Market St., ☎ 215/922–2386), with festivals and concerts from spring to fall.

★ ☺ The **Independence Seaport Museum** (⊠ 211 S. Columbus Blvd., ☎ 215/925–5439, ⊠ $5 museum only, $7.50 museum with admission to the Olympia and Becuna) has nautical artifacts, ship displays, and kid-pleasing interactive exhibits. Docked together are the handsomely restored **USS *Olympia,*** Commodore George Dewey's flagship in the Spanish-

American War, and the **USS Becuna** (⊠ Penn's Landing at Spruce St., ☎ 215/922–1898; ⊡ $5 for both ships), a World War II submarine whose guides are sub veterans.

The *Gazela of Philadelphia,* built in 1883, is the last of a Portuguese fleet of cod-fishing ships, also known as "The White Fleet," and the oldest wooden square-rigger still sailing. ⊠ *Penn's Landing at Market St.,* ☎ *215/218–0110.* ⊡ *Free. Closed Oct.–May.*

You can take a 10-minute ride on the **Riverlink Ferry** ⊠ (Penn's Landing at Walnut St., ☎ 215/922–2386; ⊡ $5) across the Delaware River to Camden (☞ New Jersey). There's no service January–March.

The **Bishop White House** (⊠ 309 Walnut St.; ⊡ $2 tour includes Todd House), built in 1786 as the home of the rector of Christ Church, has been restored to its Colonial elegance. The simply furnished **Todd House** (⊠ 4th and Walnut Sts., ☎ 215/597–8974; ⊡ $2 tour includes Bishop White House) has been restored to its 1790s appearance, when its best-known resident, Dolley Payne Todd (later Mrs. James Madison), lived here.

Head House Square (⊠ 2nd and Pine Sts., ☎ 215/790–0782) was once an open-air Colonial marketplace. Today it is the site of crafts fairs, festivals, and other activities on weekends Memorial Day through the end of September.

City Hall and Environs

★ At the geographic center of Penn's original city stands **city hall**—the largest city hall in the country (it has 642 rooms) and the tallest masonry-bearing building in the world. For a tour of the interior and a 360-degree view of the city from the William Penn statue, go to Room 121 via the northeast corner of the courtyard and ride the elevator to the top of the 548-ft tower. ⊠ *Broad and Market Sts.,* ☎ *215/686–1776; 215/686–2840 for tour information.* ⊡ *Free. Closed weekends.*

Philadelphia is the mother city of American Freemasonry, and the **Masonic Temple** is home to the Grand Lodge of Free and Accepted Masons of Pennsylvania. ⊠ *1 N. Broad St.,* ☎ *215/988–1917.* ⊡ *Free. Closed Sun.*

The **Academy of Music** (⊠ Broad and Locust Sts., ☎ 215/893–1900; 215/893–1999 for tickets), modeled on Milan's La Scala opera house, is home to the Philadelphia Orchestra and the Opera Company of Philadelphia. The orchestra will move to its new home at the Regional Performing Arts Center in fall 2001.

The **Pennsylvania Convention Center** (⊠ 12th and Arch Sts., ☎ 215/418–4700; 215/418–4989 for events) includes the restored **Reading Train Shed.** Free tours of the facility can be arranged. Below Reading Train Shed is the not-to-be-missed **Reading Terminal Market** (☞ Dining, *below*), food heaven for locals and visitors alike.

★ The city's most elegant park, **Rittenhouse Square** (⊠ Walnut St. between 18th and 19th Sts.) resembles a Parisian park and frequently hosts arts festivals. The **Rosenbach Museum and Library** (⊠ 2010 Delancey Pl., ☎ 215/732–1600; ⊡ $5) offers a 90-minute tour of its sumptuous collection of paintings, rare books (including the original manuscript of James Joyce's *Ulysses*), and objets d'art.

Museum District

The **Benjamin Franklin Parkway** angles across the grid of city streets from city hall to Fairmount Park. Lined with distinguished museums, hotels, and apartment buildings, this 250-ft-wide boulevard inspired by the Champs-Elysées was built in the 1920s. The **Free Library of**

Philadelphia (✉ north side of Benjamin Franklin Pkwy. at 19th St., ☎ 215/686–5322) has more than 1 million volumes. The **Academy of Natural Sciences** (✉ south side of Benjamin Franklin Pkwy. at 19th St., ☎ 215/299–1020; ✆ $8.50), America's first museum of natural history, features "Dinosaur Hall," a permanent exhibit with six fossil skeletons, an interactive paleontology lab, and a "rain forest" with live, tropical butterflies. The **Please Touch Museum** (✉ 210 N. 21st St., ☎ 215/963–0667; ✆ $6.95), designed for children ages seven and younger, encourages hands-on participation. The **Rodin Museum** (✉ 22nd St., ☎ 215/763–8100; ✆ free) has the largest collection outside France of Auguste Rodin's works, including masterworks like *The Kiss, The Thinker,* and *The Burghers of Calais.* The **Franklin Institute Science Museum** (✉ 20th St. and Benjamin Franklin Pkwy., ☎ 215/448–1200; ✆ $9.75) is as clever as its namesake and offers a wealth of hands-on and high-tech exhibits. The museum has a planetarium and an Omniverse theater.

★ The crown jewel of the parkway is the **Philadelphia Museum of Art.** Modeled on a larger-scale version of ancient Greek temples, the 200 galleries house more than 300,000 works. The collections include paintings by Renoir, Picasso, Matisse, and Duchamp; Early American furniture; Amish and Shaker crafts; and reconstructions, including a 12th-century French cloister and a 16th-century Indian temple. ✉ *26th St. and Benjamin Franklin Pkwy.,* ☎ *215/763–8100.* ✆ *$8, free Sun. 10–1. Closed Mon.*

Along both banks of the Schuylkill River is **Fairmount Park** (✉ accesses from Kelly Dr., West River Dr., and Belmont Ave., ☎ 215/685–0000), one of the largest city parks in the world, with woodlands, meadows, and rolling hills. Within its 4,500 acres you'll find tennis courts, ball fields, playgrounds, trails, the **Ellen Phillips Samuel Memorial Sculpture Garden,** and some fine Early American country houses (**Laurel Hill, Strawberry Mansion,** and others). **Boathouse Row,** 11 architecturally varied 19th-century buildings on the banks of the Schuylkill that are home to 13 rowing clubs, is best viewed from the West River Drive. Built in 1998, **Lloyd Hall** (☎ 215/685–3936), behind the art museum at the eastern end of Boathouse Row, has rental equipment, a café, and public rest rooms. In the northwest section of the park is the **Wissahickon,** a 5½-mi-long forested gorge carved out by Wissahickon Creek. At **Valley Green Inn** (✉ Wissahickon Creek and Springfield Ave., ☎ 215/247–1730), a restaurant halfway up the valley, you can dine on the porch and watch the ducks swimming in the creek.

★ The **Pennsylvania Academy of the Fine Arts** (✉ Broad and Cherry Sts., ☎ 215/972–7600, ✆ $5, free Sun. 3–5), in one of the finest extant buildings by Philadelphia architect Frank Furness, is the oldest art institution in the United States (founded 1804). Its collection ranges from Winslow Homer and Benjamin West to Red Grooms.

The Italian Renaissance–style **Cathedral of Sts. Peter and Paul** (✉ 18th and Race Sts., ☎ 215/561–1313), built between 1846 and 1864, is the basilica of the Roman Catholic archdiocese of Philadelphia.

Germantown

In 1683 Francis Pastorius led 13 Mennonite families out of Germany to seek religious freedom in the New World; they settled 6 mi northwest of Philadelphia in what is now **Germantown,** and many became Quakers. **Cliveden** (✉ 6401 Germantown Ave., ☎ 215/848–1777; ✆ $6; closed Dec.–Mar.), an elaborate country house built in 1763, was occupied by the British during the Revolution. On October 4, 1777, George Washington's attempt to dislodge them resulted in the Yankees' defeat in the

Battle of Germantown. During the yellow fever epidemic of 1793–94, Washington lived in the **Deshler-Morris House** (⊠ 5442 Germantown Ave., ☏ 215/596–1748; ⬙ $1; closed Dec.–Mar.) to avoid the unhealthy air of sea-level Philadelphia. Contact the **Germantown Historical Society** (⊠ 5501 Germantown Ave., ☏ 215/844–0514) for information.

Other Attractions

The **University of Pennsylvania Museum** (⊠ 33rd and Spruce Sts., ☏ 215/898–4000; ⬙ $5) is one of the finest archaeology-anthropology museums in the world. The newest permanent exhibit, "Canaan and Ancient Israel," is dedicated to the archaeology of ancient Israel and neighboring lands. The **Mutter Museum** (⊠ 19 S. 22nd St., ☏ 215/563–3737; ⬙ $8), a medical museum with a plethora of anatomical and pathological specimens, is best visited on an empty stomach.

★ One of the world's great collections of Impressionist and post-Impressionist art—175 Renoirs, 66 Cézannes, 65 Matisses, plus masterpieces by van Gogh, Degas, Picasso, and others—is at the **Barnes Foundation,** 8 mi west of Center City. Reservations are required, as the number of visitors per day is limited. ⊠ *300 Latches La., Merion,* ☏ *610/667–0290. ⬙ $5, by reservation only. Closed Mon.–Thurs. Jan.–June and Sept.–Dec.; Sat.–Tues. July and Aug.*

★ ⓒ **Sesame Place,** a 45-minute drive north of the city, is an amusement park for children ages 3–13, based on the television show. ⊠ *100 Sesame Rd., Langhorne,* ☏ *215/757–1100. ⬙ $29.95. Closed Sept.–Apr.*

Parks, Gardens, and Zoos

Fairmount Park (☞ Exploring Philadelphia, *above*) is the city's largest, encompassing varied terrains as well as many cultural sites. The University of Pennsylvania's **Morris Arboretum** (⊠ Hillcrest Ave. between Germantown and Stenton Aves., Chestnut Hill, ☏ 215/247–5777; ⬙ $6) is 92 acres of romantically landscaped seclusion. America's first ⓒ zoo, the **Philadelphia Zoological Gardens** (⊠ 34th St. and Girard Ave., ☏ 215/243–1100; ⬙ $10.50) is home to 1,700 animals on 42 acres; opened in spring 1999, the Primate Reserve is a state-of-the-art habitat designed to break down barriers between "us" and "them."

Dining

$$$$ ★ ✕ **The Fountain.** Nestled in the lavish yet dignified lobby of the Four Seasons (☞ Lodging, *below*), with windows overlooking Logan Circle's Swann Fountain, this oasis serves American entrées, such as Dover sole–wrapped sea scallops with preserved lemon and chicken *jus,* or sautéed, aged sirloin with potato and beef osso buco hash in a mustard sauce. A four- or six-course tasting menu is available, and the Sunday brunch has become a Philadelphia tradition. ⊠ *1 Logan Sq.,* ☏ *215/963–1500. Reservations essential. Jacket and tie. AE, D, DC, MC, V.*

$$$$ ★ ✕ **Le Bec-Fin.** The Fine Beak (or more loosely, "the Fine Palate") is arguably the best restaurant in Philadelphia. Louis XV furniture, apricot silk walls, and crystal chandeliers create a luxurious mise-en-scène. Owner-chef Georges Perrier oversees every detail of the excellent European service and the haute French six-course prix-fixe menu ($118). The $36 three-course lunch is a relative bargain. ⊠ *1523 Walnut St.,* ☏ *215/567–1000. Reservations essential. Jacket and tie. AE, D, DC, MC, V. Closed Sun.*

$$$–$$$$ ★ ✕ **Striped Bass Restaurant and Bar.** The visually stunning room with 28-ft ceilings is the setting for such specialties as sautéed red trout with

creamy basil polenta, and melted tomatoes drizzled with balsamic vinegar. Oysters from the raw bar are a true luxury. ⊠ *1500 Walnut St.,* ☎ *215/732–4444. Reservations essential. AE, MC, V.*

$$$–$$$$ ✕ **Susanna Foo.** The handsome renovated dining room sets the tone
★ for chef-owner Susanna Foo's nationally acclaimed cuisine, which combines French technique and Western ingredients with pure, essentially Chinese dishes. Favorites include Hundred-Corner Crab Cakes and rack of lamb with curry oil. The pastry chef prepares an array of fine French and Asian desserts. ⊠ *1512 Walnut St.,* ☎ *215/545–2666. Reservations essential. Jacket and tie. AE, DC, MC, V.*

$$–$$$ ✕ **Buddakan.** In a sleek yet theatrical setting, Philadelphia restaurateur Stephen Starr presents a pan-Asian menu as stylish as the bustling main dining room, with its white draped walls, cherrywood floors, and giant, gold Buddha statue. Dishes include the Thai lobster crepe, wasabi-crusted filet mignon, and Japanese black cod with miso glaze. ⊠ *325 Chestnut St.,* ☎ *215/574–9440. AE, DC, MC, V.*

$$ ✕ **Fork.** This intimate American bistro—with an open kitchen, 7-ft-high padded banquettes, and custom light fixtures with hand-painted shades—manages to be both comfortable and sophisticated. Choices might include Greek-marinated lamb chops; port-roasted pear with Stilton, endive, and watercress; or crispy striped bass in Thai red curry sauce. ⊠ *306 Market St.,* ☎ *215/625–9425. AE, DC, MC, V.*

$$ ✕ **Friday, Saturday, Sunday.** Locals have been filling the cheek-by-jowl tables at this neighborhood spot since its opening 20 years ago. Fabrics are draped from the ceiling; mirrors and pin lights line the walls. Popular entrées include duck, salmon, and striped bass. ⊠ *261 S. 21st St.,* ☎ *215/546–4232. AE, D, DC, MC, V.*

$–$$ ✕ **Beau Monde.** This refreshing, handsome restaurant, a block off trendy South Street, serves the most authentic crepes this side of Brittany. You can choose such fillings as roasted chicken, leeks, goat cheese, and olives, or make up your own combination. ⊠ *6th and Bainbridge Sts.,* ☎ *215/592–0656. AE, DC, MC, V.*

$–$$ ✕ **Dmitri's.** The largest of chef Dmitri Chimes's popular trio of Mediterranean-inspired seafood restaurants, this casual, chic restaurant serves a mix of Greek favorites and new interpretations of classic Spanish tapas. Grilled octopus and garlicky shrimp are standouts. ⊠ *225 S. 12th St.,* ☎ *215/627–9059. AE, D, MC, V.*

$ ✕ **Jim's Steaks.** A Philadelphia phenomenon, a cheese steak is shaved slices of beef, fried onions, and melted cheese loaded onto an untoasted roll, all dripping with oil and juices. Add some greasy fries topped with more melted cheese and a Tastykake for dessert, and you have a unique Philadelphia dining experience. ⊠ *400 South St.,* ☎ *215/928–1911. No credit cards.*

$ ✕ **Reading Terminal Market.** A Philadelphia treasure, this potpourri
★ of 80 stalls, shops, and lunch counters offers a smorgasbord of cuisines, including Chinese, Greek, Mexican, Japanese, soul food, Middle Eastern, and Pennsylvania Dutch. Arrive early to beat the daily lunch rush. ⊠ *12th and Arch Sts.,* ☎ *215/922–2317. Closed Sun. No dinner.*

Lodging

As Philadelphia becomes a more popular destination for major events—including the Republican National Convention—hotel rooms become less available. The dozen or so new hotels that have recently opened should offset the increased demand. Most bed-and-breakfasts operate under the auspices of booking agencies, such as **Bed and Breakfast, Center City** (⊠ 1804 Pine St., 19103, ☎ 215/735–1137 or 800/354–8401) and **Bed and Breakfast Connections** (⊠ Box 21, Devon 19333, ☎ 610/687–3565 or 800/448–3619).

$$$$ ★ 🏨 **Four Seasons.** Built in 1983, this eight-story hotel is the city's classiest and most expensive. Rooms are furnished in a classic style with contemporary touches, and the best have views overlooking the fountains in Logan Circle. Six of the floors are no-smoking. ⊠ *1 Logan Sq., 19103,* ☎ *215/963–1500,* FAX *215/963–9506. 365 rooms. 2 restaurants, pool, exercise room. AE, D, DC, MC, V.* 🐾

$$$$ ★ 🏨 **The Rittenhouse.** This small luxury hotel, which contains condominium residences on other floors of the building, takes full advantage of its Rittenhouse Square location: Many of the rooms and both restaurants overlook the city's classiest park. ⊠ *210 W. Rittenhouse Sq., 19103,* ☎ *215/546–9000 or 800/635–1042,* FAX *215/732–3364. 98 rooms. 2 restaurants, pool, health club. AE, D, DC, MC, V.* 🐾

$$$–$$$$ 🏨 **Philadelphia Marriott.** This 23-story full-service convention hotel—the biggest in Pennsylvania—takes up an entire city block. The spacious guest rooms have large windows and traditional cherry furniture. ⊠ *1201 Market St., 19107,* ☎ *215/625–2900,* FAX *215/625–6000. 1,200 rooms. 4 restaurants, pool, health club. AE, D, DC, MC, V.* 🐾

$$$–$$$$ 🏨 **The Warwick Hotel & Towers.** The spacious guest rooms in this centrally located, freshly renovated landmark hotel come in three distinct categories—standard, deluxe, and the large Towers rooms. The Circles off the Square restaurant serves a fine mix of traditional dishes and contemporary creations, while Capriccio, a European-style café, offers desserts and espresso until late at night. ⊠ *1701 Locust St., 19103,* ☎ *215/735–6000 or 800/523–4210,* FAX *215/790–7766. 544 rooms. 2 restaurants. AE, DC, MC, V.*

$$–$$$$ 🏨 **Latham.** At this small, elegant hotel with a European accent and an emphasis on personal service, guest rooms have marble-top bureaus and French writing desks; most have minibars. ⊠ *135 S. 17th St., 19103,* ☎ *215/563–7474,* FAX *215/568–0110. 139 rooms. Restaurant, exercise room. AE, D, DC, MC, V.*

$$–$$$$ 🏨 **Sheraton Rittenhouse Square Hotel.** This 193-room hotel promises eco-friendly features such as fresh, filtered air; organic cotton linens; and a bamboo garden designed to oxygenate air in the lobby. ⊠ *227 S. 18th St., 19103,* ☎ *215/546–9400 or 800/854–8002. 193 rooms. 4 restaurants. AE, D, DC, MC, V.* 🐾

$$$ 🏨 **Adam's Mark.** Guest rooms are small here, with a contemporary motif; request one on an upper floor facing south toward Fairmount Park and the downtown skyline. The hotel's big attractions are its nightclub, sports bar, and fine restaurant—the Marker. ⊠ *City Ave. and Monument Rd., 19131,* ☎ *215/581–5000,* FAX *215/581–5089. 515 rooms. 2 restaurants, 2 pools, health club. AE, D, DC, MC, V.* 🐾

$$–$$$ ★ 🏨 **Penn's View Inn.** In a refurbished 19th-century commercial building, this cosmopolitan little hotel is on the fringe of the city's oldest warehouse district. Deluxe rooms, in somber tapestry, have windows overlooking the Delaware River. Accommodations are comfortable and rather European, if not strictly stylish, though street noise can be a concern. The hotel's Ristorante Panorama has a great wine bar. ⊠ *14 N. Front St., 19106,* ☎ *215/922–7600 or 800/331–7634,* FAX *215/922–7642. 28 rooms. Restaurant. AE, DC, MC, V. CP.*

$$ ★ 🏨 **Thomas Bond House.** Spend the night in the heart of the Old City, the way Philadelphians did more than two centuries ago. Built in 1769, this four-story house has rooms with marble fireplaces and four-poster Thomasville beds—and whirlpool baths. ⊠ *129 S. 2nd St., 19106,* ☎ *215/923–8523 or 800/845–2663,* FAX *215/923–8504. 12 rooms. AE, D, DC, MC, V. CP weekdays; BP weekends.*

$ 🏨 **Bank Street Hostel.** On the cusp of Old City and Society Hill, this clean, well-run establishment offers a dormitory arrangement that is a downtown Philly lodging bargain. ⊠ *32 S. Bank St., 19106,* ☎ *215/922–0222 or 800/392–4678,* FAX *215/922–4082. 70 beds. No credit cards.*

Nightlife and the Arts

Philadelphia magazine (at newsstands), *Calendar of Events* (free at the visitor center), the *Philadelphia Weekly* and the *City Paper* (weeklies available free from news boxes in Center City), and the *Inquirer* and the *Daily News* (the city's daily papers) list arts and entertainment events. Tickets, often at a discount, for more than 75 performing and cultural organizations can be obtained at **UpStages** (⊠ 1412 Chestnut St., ☎ 215/569–9700).

Nightlife

South Street from Front to 7th Street still attracts nighttime crowds, but the big noise is the **Delaware Waterfront** entertainment boom, with more than a dozen clubs opening in the past few years. In the northwestern part of the city, **Main Street** in **Manayunk** has joined **Germantown Avenue** in **Chestnut Hill** as an area in which to dine, shop, and stroll. On Wednesday night downtown shops and some museums stay open late; outside, street bands entertain smiling crowds. On the **First Friday** of every month 25 art galleries in Old City stay open late. Call **Electric Factory Concerts** (☎ 215/568–3222) to learn what's happening around town.

BARS, LOUNGES, AND CABARETS

A former diner, the **Continental Restaurant & Martini Bar** (⊠ 138 Market St., ☎ 215/923–6069) draws a hip crowd for cocktails and dinner. **Copa Too** (⊠ 263 S. 15th St., ☎ 215/735–0848), considered by some to have the best margaritas in town, is an informal gathering spot for burgers and beer. **Shampoo** (⊠ 417 N. 8th St., ☎ 215/922–7500) is one of Philly's hottest clubs. **Woody's** (⊠ 202 S. 13th St., ☎ 215/545–1893) is the city's most popular gay bar. Head for **Zanzibar Blue** (⊠ downstairs at the Bellevue, Broad and Walnut Sts., ☎ 215/732–5200) for top local and national names in jazz.

MISCELLANEOUS

By day **Painted Bride Art Center** (⊠ 230 Vine St., ☎ 215/925–9914) is an art gallery, by night a stage featuring performance art, readings, dance, and theater. Since 1975 the **Cherry Tree Music Co-op** (⊠ 3916 Locust Walk, ☎ 215/386–1640) has staged Sunday-night folk concerts. It's closed June–August.

The Arts

CONCERTS

The **Philadelphia Orchestra** performs at the Academy of Music (⊠ Broad and Locust Sts., ☎ 215/893–1900) in winter and at the **Mann Music Center** (⊠ W. Fairmount Park, ☎ 215/878–7707) in summer. The **Philly Pops,** conducted by Peter Nero, performs at the Academy of Music.

DANCE

The **Pennsylvania Ballet** (☎ 215/551–7000) dances at the Academy of Music from October to June. The **Philadelphia Dance Company** (☎ 215/387–8200) performs modern and jazz dance and ballet at the University of Pennsylvania's Annenberg Theater in spring and fall.

OPERA

The **Opera Company of Philadelphia** (☎ 215/928–2100) performs at the Academy of Music from October to May.

THEATER

Performances by touring companies and pre-Broadway productions can be seen at the **Merriam Theater** (⊠ 250 S. Broad St., ☎ 215/732–5446), the **Forrest Theater** (⊠ 1114 Walnut St., ☎ 215/923–1515), and the **Walnut Street Theater** (⊠ 9th and Walnut Sts., ☎ 215/574–3550). The **Arden Theatre Company** (⊠ 40 N. 2nd St., ☎ 215/922–8900) and the **Wilma Theater** (⊠ Broad and Spruce Sts., ☎ 215/546–7824) have gained a reputation for innovative work with American and European drama and musicals. **Freedom Theater** (⊠ 1346 N. Broad St., ☎ 215/765–2793) is the oldest and most active black theater in Philadelphia.

Outdoor Activities and Sports

Golf
Of the six 18-hole courses in Philadelphia open to the public, **Cobbs Creek and Karakung** (⊠ 7200 Lansdowne Ave., ☎ 215/877–8707) are the most challenging.

Jogging and Running
Philly runners' favorite is the **river loop**—an 8.2-mi circuit starting at the Art Museum and heading up Kelly Drive along the Schuylkill River, then across Falls Bridge and down West River Drive.

Spectator Sports
Baseball: Philadelphia Phillies (⊠ Veterans Stadium, Broad St. and Pattison Ave., ☎ 215/463–1000). **Basketball: Philadelphia 76ers** (⊠ First Union Center, Broad St. and Pattison Ave., ☎ 215/336–3600). **Football: Philadelphia Eagles** (⊠ Veterans Stadium, ☎ 215/463–5500). **Hockey: Philadelphia Flyers** (⊠ First Union Center, ☎ 215/336–3600). **Horse Racing: Philadelphia Park** (⊠ Street Rd., Bensalem, ☎ 215/639–9000) has Thoroughbred racing year-round. For offtrack betting, try the **Turf Club Center City** (⊠ 1635 Market St., ☎ 215/246–1556).

Shopping

There is no sales tax on clothing, medicine, or food bought in stores. Otherwise, Pennsylvania has a 6% sales tax, 7% in Philadelphia.

Shopping Districts
Walnut Street between Broad Street and Rittenhouse Square (a.k.a. Rittenhouse Row) and the intersecting streets just north and south are filled with upscale boutiques and galleries. At 16th and Chestnut streets, the **Shops at Liberty Place** offer more than 70 stores and restaurants under a 90-ft glass-roof atrium. **Jewelers' Row**, centered on Sansom Street between 7th and 8th streets, is one of the world's oldest and largest markets of precious stones. Pine Street from 9th to 12th Street is **Antiques Row**. Along **South Street** are more than 300 stores selling everything from New Age books to avant-garde art. For local color visit the outdoor stalls and indoor stores of the **Italian Market,** on 9th Street between Christian Street and Washington Avenue.

Department Stores
Philadelphia's premier department store, John Wanamaker, was bought by the May Company in 1995, but Philadelphians still rendezvous at the eagle statue in the grand court of what is now **Lord & Taylor** (⊠ 13th and Market Sts., ☎ 215/241–9000). **Strawbridge's** (⊠ 8th and Market Sts., ☎ 215/829–0346) is the anchor store for the **Gallery at Market East** (☎ 215/925–7162), a four-level indoor mall.

Specialty Stores
AIA Bookstore (⊠ 117 S. 17th St., ☎ 215/569–3188) specializes in books on architecture, interior design, and furnishings and carries posters and unusual gifts. **Anthropologie** (⊠ 1801 Walnut St., ☎ 215/568–2114), from the same company as the funky Urban Outfitters chain, features upscale, casual women's wear and items for children and the home in this Beaux Arts mansion. **Architectural Antiques Exchange** (⊠ 715 N. 2nd St., ☎ 215/922–3669) handles everything from embellishments of Victorian saloons and apothecary shops to stained and beveled glass. **Boyd's** (⊠ 1818 Chestnut St., ☎ 215/564–9000), the largest single-store men's

clothier in the country, also has a small women's department. **J. E. Caldwell** (⊠ 1339 Chestnut St., ☎ 215/864–7800), since 1839 a local landmark for jewelry, is adorned with antique handblown crystal chandeliers by Baccarat. The family-owned **Fante's Cookware** (⊠ 1006 S. 9th St., ☎ 215/922–5557), in the heart of the Italian Market, is a good source for fine cookware, cookbooks, French copper, cutlery, coffee, and tea.

Side Trip to the Brandywine Valley

Arriving and Departing

Take U.S. 1S from Philadelphia about 25 mi to the valley.

What to See and Do

The Brandywine River valley has inspired generations of Wyeths and du Ponts—the Wyeths to capture its peaceful harmony on canvas, the du Ponts to recontour the landscape with grand gardens, mansions, and mills. The **Brandywine River Museum** (⊠ U.S. 1 and Rte. 100, Chadds Ford, ☎ 610/388–7601; ⊒ $5), in a preserved 19th-century gristmill, ★ celebrates the Brandywine school of artists. **Longwood Gardens** (⊠ U.S. 1, Kennett Sq., ☎ 610/388–6741, ⊒ $12), Pierre-Samuel du Pont's 350 acres of ultimate estate gardens, has an international reputation. The **Brandywine Battlefield State Park** (⊠ U.S. 1, Chadds Ford, ☎ 610/459–3342; ⊒ $3.50 for buildings, park free) is near the site of the British defeat of Washington and his troops on September 11, 1777. The region is dotted with antiques shops and cozy inns. The **Brandywine Valley Tourist Information Center** (⊠ 300 Greenwood Rd., Kennett Sq. 19348, ☎ 610/388–2900 or 800/228–9933) has information.

Side Trip to Bucks County

Arriving and Departing

From Philadelphia follow I–95 north to the Yardley exit, and then go north on Route 32 toward New Hope. The trip takes one hour.

What to See and Do

Bucks County is known for antiques, covered bridges, and country inns. **New Hope** is a hodgepodge of art galleries, old stone houses, and shops along crooked little streets. William Penn's reconstructed Georgian-style mansion, **Pennsbury Manor** (⊠ 400 Pennsbury Memorial Rd., Tyburn Rd. E off U.S. 13, between Morrisville and Bristol, ☎ 215/946–0400; ⊒ $5) presents living history demonstrations of 17th-century life. **Washington Crossing Historic Park** (⊠ Rtes. 532 and 32, ☎ 215/493–4076; ⊒ $4 historic houses, park free) is where George Washington and his troops crossed the river on Christmas night 1776. Contact the **Bucks County Conference and Visitors Bureau** (⊠ 152 Swamp Rd., Doylestown 18901, ☎ 215/345–4552 or 800/836–2825) or the **New Hope Information Center** (⊠ 1 W. Mechanic St., at Main St., 18938, ☎ 215/862–5880 or 215/862–5030) for more information.

Side Trip to Valley Forge

Arriving and Departing

By car take the Schuylkill Expressway (I–76) west from Philadelphia to Exit 25; then take Route 363 to North Gulph Road and follow the signs to Valley Forge National Historical Park, 18 mi from the city. By bus take SEPTA Route 125 from 16th Street and John F. Kennedy Boulevard.

What to See and Do

The monuments, huts, and headquarters on the 3,500 acres of rolling hills of the **Valley Forge National Historical Park** (⊠ Rte. 23 and N. Gulph Rd., Valley Forge, ☎ 610/783–1077; ⊒ $2 Washington's Headquarters, Apr.–Nov.) preserve the moment in American history when

George Washington's Continental Army endured the bitter winter of 1777–78. The former home of John James Audubon, **Mill Grove** (✉ Audubon and Pauling Rds., Audubon, ☎ 610/666–5593; ☞ donations accepted) is now a museum displaying the naturalist's work. The
★ **Wharton Esherick Museum** (✉ Horseshoe Trail, Paoli, ☎ 610/644–5822; ☞ $6; closed Jan. and Feb.) has more than 200 examples of this eccentric artist's paintings, furniture, and sculpture. With more than 450 stores, including 9 department stores, the **Court and the Plaza** (✉ Rte. 202 and N. Gulph Rd., King of Prussia, ☎ 610/265–5727) is the nation's second-largest shopping complex. For more information contact the **Valley Forge Convention and Visitors Bureau** (✉ 600 W. Germantown Pike, Suite 130, Plymouth Meeting 19462, ☎ 610/834–1550 or 800/441–3549).

PENNSYLVANIA DUTCH COUNTRY

First of all, the Pennsylvania Dutch aren't Dutch; the name comes from *Deutsch* (German). In the 18th century this rolling farmland 65 mi west of Philadelphia became home to the Amish, the Mennonites, and other German and Swiss immigrants escaping religious persecution. Today their descendants continue to turn their backs on the modern world—and in doing so attract the world's attention. In summer, buses jam Route 30, the main thoroughfare. But there is still charm on the back roads, where you will discover Amish farms, hand-painted signs advertising quilts, fields worked with mules, and horse-drawn buggies.

Visitor Information

Pennsylvania Dutch Convention and Visitors Bureau (✉ 501 Greenfield Rd., Lancaster 17601, ☎ 717/299–8901 or 800/723–8824). **Mennonite Information Center** (✉ 2209 Millstream Rd., Lancaster 17602, ☎ 717/299–0954).

Getting There

By Bus
Greyhound (☎ 800/231–2222) has three runs daily from Philadelphia to Lancaster.

By Car
From Philadelphia (65 mi away) take the Schuylkill Expressway (I–76) west to the Pennsylvania Turnpike, exiting at Exit 20, 21, or 22.

By Train
Amtrak (☎ 800/872–7245) has service from Philadelphia to Lancaster.

Exploring Pennsylvania Dutch Country

Lancaster, a charming Colonial city, is the heart of Pennsylvania Dutch Country. The **Historic Lancaster Walking Tour** (☎ 717/392–1776), a two-hour stroll through the city, is conducted by guides who impart lively anecdotes about local architecture and history. **Central Market** (✉ Penn Sq., ☎ 717/291–4723), one of the oldest covered markets in the country and now housed in an 1889 Romanesque structure, is where the locals shop for fresh produce, meats, and baked goods. The old city hall, reborn as the **Heritage Center of Lancaster County** (✉ King and Queen Sts., ☎ 717/299–6440; ☞ free), shows the work of Lancaster County artisans and craftspeople from the past.

Several furnished farmhouses offer simulated up-close looks at how the Amish live, including the **Amish Farm and House** (✉ 2395 Lincoln Hwy. E, ☎ 717/394–6185; ☞ $6.50). Abe, of **Abe's Buggy Rides** (✉

Rte. 340, Bird-in-Hand, ☎ 717/392–1794; ⌨ $10), chats about the Amish during a 2-mi spin down country roads in an Amish family carriage. **Wheatland** (⊠ 1120 Marietta Ave. [Rte. 23], 1½ mi west of Lancaster, ☎ 717/392–8721; ⌨ $5.50; closed Dec.–Feb.), a restored 1828 Federal mansion, was the home of the only president from Pennsylvania, James Buchanan.

Strasburg has a half dozen museums and sights devoted to trains. The **Strasburg Railroad** (⊠ Rte. 741E, ☎ 717/687–7522; ⌨ $8.50) is a scenic 9-mi round-trip excursion on a wooden coach pulled by a steam locomotive. The **Railroad Museum of Pennsylvania** (⊠ Rte. 741, ☎ 717/687–8628; ⌨ $6) displays colossal engines, railcars, and memorabilia documenting railroading in the state.

In **Ephrata** the 18th-century Protestants of the **Ephrata Cloister** (⊠ Rtes. 272 and 322, ☎ 717/733–6600; ⌨ $6) led an ascetic life, following William Penn's "holy experiment." Guides now give tours of the restored medieval-style German buildings.

Lititz was founded by Moravians who settled in Pennsylvania to do missionary work among Native Americans. It's a lovely town with a tree-shaded main street of 18th-century cottages and shops. At the **General Sutter Inn** (⊠ 14 E. Main St., ☎ 717/626–2115) pick up the Historical Foundation's brochure that details a walking tour of the town.

Dining and Lodging

Like the German cuisine from which it derives, Pennsylvania Dutch cooking is hearty. To sample such regional fare as ham, buttered noodles, chowchow, and shoofly pie, eat at one of the bustling family-style restaurants where diners share tables and the food is passed around.

Bird-in-Hand

$ ✕ **Bird-in-Hand Family Restaurant.** This family-owned spot specializes in hearty Pennsylvania Dutch home cooking, served buffet-style for $9.95 or à la carte. ⊠ *Rte. 340 just west of N. Ronks Rd.,* ☎ *717/768–8266. MC, V. Closed Sun.*

Ephrata

$–$$$ ✕ **The Restaurant at Doneckers.** Classic and country-French cuisine is
★ served downstairs amid Colonial antiques and upstairs in a country garden. A lower-priced bistro menu is also available. ⊠ *333 N. State St.,* ☎ *717/738–9501. AE, D, DC, MC, V. Closed Wed. and Sun.*

Lancaster

$$–$$$ ✕ **Carr's.** The cuisine is American, and steaks, seafood, and veal are served in a cozy dining room with upholstered armchairs and 19th-century paintings, drawings, and photographs. Homemade soups and breads highlight the diverse menu. ⊠ *Market and Grant Sts.,* ☎ *717/ 299–7090. AE, D, DC, MC, V.*

$$–$$$ ☷ **Best Western Eden Resort Inn.** Spacious contemporary rooms and attractive grounds contribute to the pleasant atmosphere. The suites have kitchens and fireplaces. ⊠ *222 Eden Rd. (U.S. 30 and Rte. 272), 17601,* ☎ *717/569–6444,* 𝖥𝖠𝖷 *717/569–4208. 315 rooms. 2 restaurants, 2 pools, tennis, exercise room. AE, D, DC, MC, V.* ✑

Lititz

$$ ☷ **General Sutter Inn.** Built in 1764, the oldest continuously run inn
★ in the state is a Victoriana lover's delight. Furnishings range from Pennsylvania folk art to Louis XIV sofas and marble-top tables. At the crossroads of town, the inn is within easy walking distance of the historic district. ⊠ *14 E. Main St., 17543,* ☎ *717/626–2115,* 𝖥𝖠𝖷 *717/626– 0992. 17 rooms, Restaurant. AE, D, MC, V.* ✑

Mount Joy

$–$$ ✕ **Groff's Farm.** Hearty Mennonite farm fare, including chicken, relishes, and cracker pudding, is served family-style in a restored 1756 farmhouse. ⊠ *650 Pinkerton Rd.,* ☎ *717/653–2048. Reservations essential. AE, D, DC, MC, V.*

Strasburg

$–$$$ ✕▣ **Historic Strasburg Inn.** This Colonial-style inn is set on 58 peace-
★   ful acres overlooking farmland. Rooms have crown moldings, rocking chairs, and dried floral arrangements. The dinner menu is filled with French-influenced Continental specialties. ⊠ *1 Historic Dr., 17579,* ☎ *717/687–7691 or 800/872–0201,* ℻ *717/687–6098. 101 rooms. 2 restaurants, pool, exercise room. AE, D, DC, MC, V. BP.* ✏

Campgrounds

The Convention and Visitors Bureau (☞ Visitor Information, *above*) has a list of area campgrounds. Two of the best are ⌂ **Mill Bridge Campresort** (⊠ ½ mi south of U.S. 30 on S. Ronks Rd.; Box 7, Paradise 17562, ☎ 717/687–8181) and ⌂ **Spring Gulch Resort Campground** (⊠ Rte. 897; 475 Lynch Rd., New Holland 17557, ☎ 717/354–3100). Campers at both facilities can visit **Mill Bridge Village,** a restored 18th-century village adjacent to Mill Bridge Campresort.

Nightlife and the Arts

The **American Music Theatre** (⊠ 2425 Lincoln Hwy. E, ☎ 717/397–7700 in Lancaster or 800/648–4102) is a 1,600-seat facility presenting shows that celebrate American music. Plays and concerts, as well as performances by the Lancaster Symphony Orchestra and the Lancaster Opera, are presented at the **Fulton Opera House** (⊠ 12 N. Prince St., ☎ 717/394–7133), a restored 19th-century Victorian theater.

Outdoor Activities and Sports

Hot-Air Ballooning

Great Adventure Balloon Club (☎ 717/397–3623) offers a bird's-eye view of Pennsylvania Dutch Country.

Shopping

Antiques

Antiques malls are on Route 272 between Adamstown and Denver, 2 mi east of Pennsylvania Turnpike Exit 21; **Barr's Auctions** (☎ 717/336–2861), **Renninger's Antique and Collector's Market** (☎ 717/336–2177), and **Stoudt's Black Angus** (☎ 717/484–4385) all feature indoor and outdoor sales.

Crafts

Places to see fine local crafts include the **Weathervane Shop** at the Landis Valley Museum (⊠ 2451 Kissel Hill Rd., Lancaster, ☎ 717/569–9312), the **Tin Bin** (⊠ 20 Valley Rd. off Rte. 501, Neffsville, ☎ 717/569–6210), and the 30-shop **Kitchen Kettle Village** (⊠ Rte. 340, Intercourse, ☎ 717/768–8261 or 800/732–3538). International crafts, ideal for Christmas gifts and stocking stuffers, can be found at the **Ten Thousand Villages** (⊠ 240 N. Reading Rd., Ephrata, ☎ 717/721–8400), owned and operated by the Mennonite Central Committee.

Farmers Markets

In addition to Lancaster's **Central Market** (☞ Exploring Pennsylvania Dutch Country, *above*), the **Green Dragon Farmers Market and Auction** (⊠ 955 N. State St., just off Rte. 272, Ephrata, ☎ 717/738–

1117) is an old, traditional agricultural market with a country-carnival atmosphere, open Friday year-round.

Side Trip to Gettysburg

Arriving and Departing

From Lancaster take U.S. 30 east to Gettysburg (about 1½ hours).

What to See and Do

The battle of Gettysburg, fought in July 1863, was, along with Ulysses S. Grant's successful Vicksburg campaign, the turning point of the Civil ★ War. At the **Gettysburg National Military Park** (⊠ Visitor Center, 97 Taneytown Rd., ☎ 717/334–1124) you can follow the course of the fighting on a 750-square-ft electronic map or obtain brochures that will guide you along roads through the battleground. The **Gettysburg Convention and Visitors Travel Bureau** (⊠ 35 Carlisle St., 17325, ☎ 717/334–6274) provides information on the region.

Side Trip to Hershey

Arriving and Departing

Take I–76 to Exit 20 and follow the signs—it's about 45 minutes from Lancaster.

What to See and Do

The streets have names like Cocoa Avenue, and the streetlights look like Hershey's Kisses at **Hersheypark** (⊠ U.S. 422, ☎ 717/534–3900; ☎ $32.95), a family-oriented amusement park. At **Chocolate World** (⊠ Park Blvd., ☎ 717/534–4900; ☎ free) you can take a 12-minute ride through the process of chocolate making. Contact the **Hershey Information Center** (⊠ Hershey 17033, ☎ 800/437–7439).

Side Trip to Reading

Arriving and Departing

From Exit 22 off the Pennsylvania Turnpike take I–276 north and U.S. 422 west into downtown Reading, about an hour from Lancaster.

What to See and Do

Reading, a 19th-century industrial city, today promotes itself as the "outlet capital of the world." **Skyline Drive** is a meandering road with miles of unspoiled vistas and an expansive view of the city. The **Daniel Boone Homestead** (⊠ Daniel Boone Rd., off U.S. 422, Birdsboro, ☎ 610/582–4900; ☎ $4) is a renovation of the frontiersman's home. For information contact **Reading and Berks County Visitors Bureau** (⊠ 352 Penn St., Reading 19602, ☎ 610/375–4085 or 800/443–6610).

PITTSBURGH

Pittsburgh lies where the Allegheny and Monongahela rivers meet to form the Ohio River, in the hills of southwestern Pennsylvania. First an 18th-century French fortress and trading post, Fort Duquesne, then the British Fort Pitt, the city emerged as an industrial powerhouse in the 1800s, mostly due to iron and steel production. Today, the days of steel manufacturing are mostly gone, and with them the industrial pollution that earned the city the nickname "Smoky City." Pittsburgh has been recast into a pleasing blend of turn-of-the-20th-century architectural masterpieces and modern skyscrapers and consistently ranks among the nation's most livable cities.

Visitor Information

Greater Pittsburgh Convention and Visitors Bureau (✉ 4 Gateway Center, 15222, ☎ 800/366–0093). Information can be accessed via the Convention and Visitors Bureau's phone number 24 hours a day. The same phone number connects to all **Visitor Information Centers,** conveniently located throughout the city: **Downtown** (✉ Liberty Ave., adjacent to Gateway Center), **Oakland** (✉ Forbes Ave., next to the Cathedral of Learning), **Mount Washington** (✉ 315 Grandview Ave.), and **Airport** (✉ lower level near baggage claim).

Arriving and Departing

By Bus

Greyhound (✉ 11th St. and Liberty Ave., ☎ 800/231–2222).

By Car

From the north or south take I–79 to I–279, which leads into downtown. From the east take the Pennsylvania Turnpike (I–76), then I–376 to the Grant Street exit. From the west take I–76 to I–79 south, and then follow I–279 to downtown.

By Plane

Greater Pittsburgh International Airport (✉ 1000 Airport Blvd., ☎ 412/472–3525), served by most major airlines, is 14 mi west of downtown; a cab ride there is about $30. **Airlines Transportation Co.** (☎ 412/471–8900) provides motor-coach or van service to the major downtown hotels for $12 one-way and $20 round-trip. **Port Authority Transit** (☎ 412/442–2000) operates daily bus service (No. 28X) from around 5:30 AM to midnight between the airport and downtown and Oakland ($1.95).

By Train

Amtrak (✉ 1100 Liberty St., ☎ 800/872–7245) has daily service to Pittsburgh from Chicago and Philadelphia.

Getting Around Pittsburgh

Port Authority Transit (☎ 412/442–2000) operates daily bus and trolley service. Within the central business district, the subway, called the T, is always free, and buses are free during the day. Two **cable cars**—the *Duquesne Incline,* from West Carson Street on the Ohio River to the restaurant area of Grandview Avenue, and the *Monongahela Incline,* from Station Square on the Monongahela to Grandview Avenue—carry passengers from river level to the top of Mt. Washington, which has a magnificent view of the city.

Exploring Pittsburgh

Downtown, an area framed by the three rivers and called the Golden Triangle, contains **Point State Park** (☞ Parks and Gardens, *below*) and major hotels, restaurants, and theaters. Philip Johnson's postmodern **PPG Place** (✉ Stanwix St. and 4th Ave., ☎ 412/434–3131), whose spires and towers were modeled after London's Houses of Parliament, exemplifies the Pittsburgh renaissance. Several beautifully restored or maintained commercial and public buildings date from Pittsburgh's early boom days. Inside the Flemish-Gothic **Two Mellon Bank Center** (✉ 5th Ave. and Grant St., ☎ 412/234–5000), formerly the Union Trust Building, is an exquisite stained-glass dome above the central lobby. Daniel Burnham's Union Station is now an apartment building, the **Pennsylvanian** (✉ Grant St. and Liberty Ave., ☎ 412/391–6730). The **Allegheny County Courthouse and Jail** (✉ 5th Ave. and Grant St., ☎ 412/350–5313), designed by the influential architect Henry Hobson Richardson and completed in 1888,

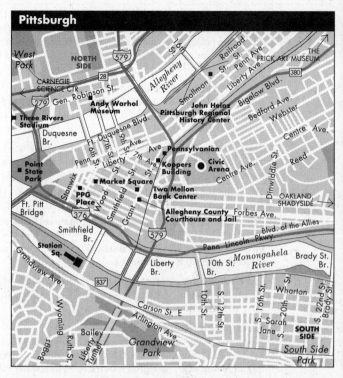

Pittsburgh

is one of the country's outstanding Romanesque buildings. The **Koppers Building** (⊠ 7th Ave. and Grant St., ☎ 412/227–2919), one of Pittsburgh's first skyscrapers, has a beautiful Art Deco lobby dating to 1929. **Station Square** (☎ 412/261–2811), on the Monongahela across the historic Smithfield Bridge, is a restored turn-of-the-20th-century rail station with boutiques and restaurants (☞ Dining, *below*).

★ East of downtown, **Oakland** is home to many of the city's cultural, educational, and medical institutions. The **Carnegie** (⊠ 4400 Forbes Ave., ☎ 412/622–3131; 412/622–3289 for group tours, ⊡ $6; closed Mon.) is an opulent cultural center, with the **Museum of Art**, the **Museum of Natural History**, the **Music Hall**, and the **Carnegie Library** all under one Beaux Arts roof. Don't miss the 19th-century French and American paintings, the Hall of Architecture, the dinosaur collection, and the extravagant Music Hall lobby.

★ Towering over Oakland is the University of Pittsburgh's Gothic skyscraper, the **Cathedral of Learning** (⊠ 4200 5th Ave., ☎ 412/624–6000; ⊡ free, tours $2), with 26 **Nationality Classrooms**, meticulously and lavishly executed to represent Pittsburgh's ethnic communities.

The **Frick Art and Historical Center** (⊠ 7227 Reynolds St., ☎ 412/371–0606; ⊡ museums are free; tour of Clayton $8; closed Mon.) includes **Clayton**, the turn-of-the-20th-century home of Henry Clay Frick, which preserves the original furnishings and art; a car and carriage museum; the **Frick Art Museum**, which possesses a small but choice collection of Old Master works; a Victorian greenhouse; and a café serving an excellent lunch in the center's garden.

The **John Heinz Pittsburgh Regional History Center** (⊠ 1212 Smallman St., ☎ 412/454–6000; ⊡ $6) focuses on western Pennsylvania history; a long-term exhibit explores glassmaking in the region.

One of America's oldest amusement parks and a National Historic Landmark, **Kennywood** (⊠ 4800 Kennywood Blvd., ☎ 412/461–0500; ☎ admission prices vary; closed early Sept.–late Apr.) features water rides and several roller coasters—including three of wooden construction dating from the 1920s.

Many of Pittsburgh's cultural attractions are across the Allegheny River on the historic **North Side**, also the site of the Pirates' new baseball stadium, PNC Park, and the Steelers' new football stadium, both to open in 2001.

The **Carnegie Science Center** (⊠ 1 Allegheny Ave., ☎ 412/237–3300; ☎ $6.50) has a planetarium, an aquarium, hands-on science exhibits, and a four-story Omnimax theater.

The **Andy Warhol Museum** (⊠ 117 Sandusky St., ☎ 412/237–8300; ☎ $7; closed Mon. and Tues.) devotes seven floors to the work of the native Pittsburgher and pop art icon. The **Mattress Factory** (⊠ 505 Jacksonia St., ☎ 412/231–3169; ☎ $6; closed Mon.), in the North Side's historic Mexican War Streets district, has permanent and visiting exhibits devoted to installation art.

The **National Aviary** (⊠ Allegheny Commons W, ☎ 412/323–7234; ☎ $5) has more than 200 species of birds, including parrots, bald eagles, and a condor.

Outside Pittsburgh

Northeast of Pittsburgh, the **Laurel Highlands** region has Revolutionary War–era forts and battlefields, restored inns and taverns, and lush mountain scenery. The region is noted for white-water rafting, hiking, and skiing. Contact **Laurel Highlands Visitors Bureau** (⊠ Ligonier Town Hall, 120 E. Main St., Ligonier, ☎ 724/238–5661 or 800/925–7669) for a visitor's guide. ★ **Fallingwater** is Frank Lloyd Wright's residential masterwork—a stone, concrete, and glass house dramatically cantilevered over a waterfall. ⊠ *Rte. 381, Mill Run,* ☎ *724/329–8501.* ☎ *$10 weekdays, $15 weekends; detailed tour $40 weekdays, $50 weekends. Reservations essential. Closed Mon. Apr.–mid-Nov. and weekdays mid-Nov.–Mar.*

Parks and Gardens

In the 36-acre **Point State Park** (☎ 412/471–0235) are the **Ft. Pitt Block-house** (☎ 412/471–1764) and **Ft. Pitt Museum** (☎ 412/281–9284). **Schenley Park** has a lake, trails, golf, tennis courts, ice skating, and cross-country skiing. The beautiful iron-and-glass **Phipps Conservatory** (⊠ 1 Schenley Park, ☎ 412/622–6914; ☎ $5), dating from 1893, contains 13 gardens, with everything from tropical and desert plants to a fine Bonsai collection.

Dining

$$$ ✕ **Casbah.** An eclectic menu creatively influenced by the cuisines of southern France, Italy, Greece, Turkey, and Tunisia includes dishes ranging from grilled quail with red-grape relish and saffron basmati rice to salmon steamed in grape leaves with a lemon–pine nut vinaigrette. Casbahs's extensive wine list, with more than 40 labels available by the glass, nicely complements any meal. ⊠ *229 S. Highland Ave.,* ☎ *412/661–5656. AE, D, DC, MC, V.*

$$ ✕ **Monterey Bay Fish Grotto.** On top of Mt. Washington, this restaurant offers an impressive selection of fresh fish and an unrivaled view of the downtown skyline. It's one of the city's best new additions. ⊠ *1411 Grandview Ave.,* ☎ *412/481–4414. AE, D, DC, MC, V.*

$$ ✕ **Grand Concourse/Gandy Dancer Saloon.** Set in a dazzlingly restored Beaux Arts railroad terminal, the restaurant features seafood, homemade pastas, and gracious service. In the Saloon the emphasis is on raw-bar platters and lighter dishes. ⊠ *1 Station Sq., Carson and Smithfield Sts.,* ☎ *412/261–1717. AE, D, DC, MC, V.*

$ ✕ **Primanti Brothers.** What started out in 1933 as a working-class bar is now a Pittsburgh favorite with eight locations. The cheese steak comes with fries, coleslaw, and tomato—all *in* the sandwich. ⊠ *46 18th St.,* ☎ *412/263–2142;* ⊠ *11 Cherry Way,* ☎ *412/566–8051;* ⊠ *Market Sq.,* ☎ *412/261–1599. No credit cards.*

$ ✕ **Spice Island Tea House.** This Oakland restaurant serves Southeast Asian cuisine, ranging from the classic pad thai to delicious curries and exotic salads. Its single, dimly lit dining room is tasteful and usually crowded with people from the nearby universities. ⊠ *253 Atwood St.,* ☎ *412/687–8821. AE, D, DC, MC, V.*

Lodging

$$$ ▦ **Doubletree Hotel Pittsburgh.** The dramatically designed lobby leads to a 26-story tower housing rooms with contemporary decor. ⊠ *1000 Penn Ave., 15222,* ☎ *412/281–3700,* FAX *412/227–4500. 616 rooms. Restaurant, pool, exercise room. AE, D, DC, MC, V.* 🐾

$$$ ▦ **Ramada Plaza Suites and Conference Center.** In the Golden Triangle, across from the Civic Arena and adjacent to the Steel Plaza subway station, the Ramada is a convenient hotel with conventionally furnished rooms. ⊠ *1 Bigelow Sq., 15219,* ☎ *412/281–5800 or 800/ 225–5858,* FAX *412/281–8467. 311 suites. Restaurant, pool, health club. AE, D, DC, MC, V. CP.* 🐾

$$$ ▦ **Westin William Penn.** Pittsburgh's grand hotel has a sumptuous lobby
★ with a coffered ceiling and crystal chandeliers where people relax over drinks. The guest rooms are filled with light, and many are large enough for a couch and a wing chair. ⊠ *530 William Penn Pl., Mellon Sq., 15230,* ☎ *412/281–7100,* FAX *412/553–5252. 595 rooms. 2 restaurants, exercise room. AE, D, DC, MC, V.* 🐾

$$ ▦ **Clubhouse Inn Pittsburgh.** At this garden-style hotel 9 mi from the
★ airport, guest rooms overlook a courtyard. ⊠ *5311 Campbells Run Rd., 15205,* ☎ *412/788–8400,* FAX *412/788–2577. 152 rooms. Pool, exercise room. AE, D, DC, MC, V. BP.* 🐾

$$ ▦ **Holiday Inn Select–University Center.** This modern nine-story hotel in the heart of Oakland is within easy walking distance of the universities and the Carnegie Institute. ⊠ *100 Lytton Ave., 15213,* ☎ *412/ 682–6200 or 800/864–8287,* FAX *412/681–4749. 251 rooms. Restaurant, pool, exercise room. AE, D, DC, MC, V.* 🐾

$$ ▦ **The Priory.** This European-style hotel is furnished with antiques and
★ reproductions. It's located on the North Side but provides complimentary shuttle service to the downtown area. ⊠ *614 Pressley St., 15212,* ☎ *412/231–3338,* FAX *412/231–4838. 24 rooms. AE, D, DC, MC, V. CP.*

Nightlife and the Arts

Nightlife

The **Strip District** (⊠ between Liberty Ave. and Smallman St., and 16th and 22nd Sts.) has become Pittsburgh's nightlife center, with many bars and nightclubs. For live music try **Rosebud** (⊠ 1650 Smallman St., ☎ 412/261–2221); next door is **Metropol** (⊠ 1600 Smallman St., ☎ 412/ 261–4512), where DJs spin dance music. **Valhalla** (⊠ 1150 Smallman St., ☎ 412/434–1440) is the most recent microbrewery bar–restaurant to open in Pittsburgh and often features live music. Another active nightlife district is along **East Carson Street,** across the Monongahela on the revitalized **South Side. Dee's Cafe** (⊠ 1314 E. Carson St., ☎

412/431–1314) has several pool tables and attracts a twentysomething crowd while **Paparazzi** (⊠ 2100 E. Carson St., ☎ 412/488–0800), regularly features live jazz. Pittsburgh's best-known place for live jazz, though, is the North Side's **James Street Tavern** (⊠ 422 Foreland St., ☎ 412/323–2222), which serves Cajun cuisine. **Pegasus** (⊠ 818 Liberty Ave., ☎ 412/281–2131), located downtown, is Pittsburgh's most popular gay dance club.

The Arts

The world-class **Pittsburgh Symphony Orchestra,** conducted by Mariss Jansons, appears at the Heinz Hall for the Performing Arts (⊠ 600 Penn Ave., ☎ 412/392–4800). The **Pittsburgh Opera** (☎ 412/281–0912) and the **Pittsburgh Ballet** (☎ 412/281–0360) are at the **Benedum Center for the Performing Arts** (⊠ 719 Liberty Ave., ☎ 412/456–6666), which also hosts many Broadway shows. The **Pittsburgh Public Theater** (⊠ O'Reilly Theater, 621 Penn Ave., ☎ 412/316–1600), now in a new downtown facility designed by Michael Graves, consistently offers interesting, quality productions.

Outdoor Activities and Sports

Golf

The **North Park Golf Course** (⊠ Kummer Rd., North Park, ☎ 724/935–1967) is one of the more than 50 courses within a 30-minute drive of downtown, all of which are open to the public.

Jogging

Point State Park (☎ 412/471–0235) has an upper and a lower path, each forming a circuit of about 1 mi in length, with views of the skyline and the city's three rivers.

Spectator Sports

Baseball: Pittsburgh Pirates (⊠ Three Rivers Stadium, 600 Stadium Circle, ☎ 412/321–2827). **Football: Pittsburgh Steelers** (⊠ Three Rivers Stadium, 300 Stadium Circle, ☎ 412/323–1200). **Hockey: Pittsburgh Penguins** (⊠ Mellon Arena, 300 Auditorium Pl., ☎ 412/642–7367).

Shopping

Pittsburgh's best downtown department stores, **Saks Fifth Avenue** (⊠ 513 Smithfield St., ☎ 412/263–4800) and **Kaufmann's** (⊠ 400 5th Ave., at Smithfield St., ☎ 412/232–2000), have recently been joined by **Lazarus** (⊠ 301 5th Ave., at Wood St., ☎ 412/291–2200). Nearby are the shopping complexes **Fifth Avenue Place** (⊠ Penn and 5th Aves.), **One Oxford Centre** (⊠ Grant St. and 4th Ave.), and **PPG Place** (⊠ Stanwix St. and 4th Ave). In the Strip District (☞ Nightlife and the Arts, *above*) are streets lined with market stalls and sellers of imported food and dry goods. East of Oakland in **Shadyside,** which is one of Pittsburgh's most desirable neighborhoods, is **Walnut Street** which has upscale clothing boutiques, housewares stores, restaurants, and cafés. The artsier **Ellsworth Avenue,** along Shadyside's northern edge, has galleries and vintage-clothing stores. Explore the unique clothing stores, antiques shops, used-book stores, and art galleries along East Carson Street on the **South Side. Station Square** (☞ Exploring Pittsburgh, *above*) has numerous shops and restaurants.

ELSEWHERE IN PENNSYLVANIA

The Poconos

Getting There

I–80 leads to the Delaware Water Gap, I–84 to Milford. From the south U.S. 611 skirts the Delaware River and takes you into Stroudsburg, which is 98 mi from Philadelphia, 135 mi from Harrisburg, and 318 mi from Pittsburgh.

What to See and Do

The Poconos, in the northeastern corner of the state, encompass 2,400 square mi of wilderness bordering the Delaware River, with lakes, streams, waterfalls, resorts, and country inns. A back-roads drive will turn up quaint villages such as **Jim Thorpe** (⊠ Rte. 209), a late-Victorian mountain-resort town that has first-rate antiques shops and galleries. Winter brings downhill and cross-country skiing, skating, and snowmobiling; summer offers golfing, boating, horseback riding, and hiking. The **Pocono Mountains Vacation Bureau** (⊠ 1004 Main St., Stroudsburg 18360, ☎ 570/421–5791 or 800/762–6667) provides information.

Lodging

$$–$$$ ⊞ **French Manor.** Forget the heart-shape bathtubs and other honeymoon hokeyness this area is known for—the French Manor is *the* most romantic spot in the Poconos. The chateau-style mansion, secluded on the top of a mountain, offers panoramic views, luxurious amenities, and excellent French cuisine. ⊠ *Huckleberry Rd., South Sterling 18460,* ☎ *570/676–3244 or 800/523–8200,* 𝖥𝖠𝖷 *570/676–9786. 9 rooms. Restaurant. AE, D, DC, MC, V.*

$$ ⊞ **Sterling Inn.** Built in 1857 on an historic Native American site, the clapboard main house and cluster of cottages, including 10 suites with fireplaces and Jacuzzis, have a bright country ambience. ⊠ *Rte. 191, South Sterling 18460,* ☎ *570/676–3311 or 800/523–8200,* 𝖥𝖠𝖷 *570/676–9786. 65 rooms. Restaurant, pool. AE, D, DC, MC, V.*

RHODE ISLAND

Updated by
K. D. Weaver

Capital	Providence
Population	987,000
Motto	Hope
State Bird	Rhode Island red hen
State Flower	Violet
Postal Abbreviation	RI

Statewide Visitor Information

Rhode Island Tourism Division (✉ 1 W. Exchange St., Providence 02903, ☎ 401/222–2601; 800/556–2484 for literature).

Scenic Drives

From Wickford to Point Judith, travel **Route 1A** and **Ocean Road** to see 19th-century mansions, a lighthouse, and various historic sights. Two bridges on **Route 138** link Newport to Narragansett; this drive affords unbeatable views of Narragansett Bay. **Route 77** runs through the idyllic towns of Tiverton and Little Compton. And nothing compares with the grand mansions along **Newport's Bellevue and Ocean Avenues.**

State Parks

Rhode Island's 37 state parks and recreational grounds encompass beaches, tidal marshes, swamp lands, woodlands, and bay shores. **Burlingame State Park, Charlestown Breachway, Fishermen's Memorial State Park, George Washington Camping Area,** and the **Ninigret Conservation Area** allow camping. For state parks information contact **Rhode Island Division of Parks and Recreation** (☎ 401/884–2010) or the Rhode Island Tourism Division (☞ Statewide Visitor Information, *above*).

THE SOUTH COAST

Visitor Information

South County (common name for Washington County): Tourism Council (✉ 4808 Tower Hill Rd., Wakefield 02879, ☎ 401/789–4422 or 800/548–4662).

Arriving and Departing

By Bus
RIPTA (Rhode Island Public Transportation Authority; ☎ 401/847–0209; 800/244–0444 in RI) provides service from Providence and Warwick to Kingston, Wakefield, Narragansett, and Galilee.

By Car
I–95 passes 10 mi north of Westerly before heading inland toward Providence. Routes 1 and 1A follow the coastline along Narragansett Bay and are the primary routes through the South County (Washington County) resort towns.

By Train
Amtrak (☎ 800/872–7245) stops at Westerly and Kingston.

Exploring the South Coast

Beautiful beaches line the southern coast of Rhode Island. **Misquamicut State Beach** in Westerly, **Charlestown Beach** in Charlestown, and **Scarborough State Beach** in Narragansett are three of the best.

Watch Hill is a Victorian-era resort village with miles of beautiful beaches and a lighthouse. **Napatree Point** is one of the best long beach walks in Rhode Island. A walk to the end of Bay Street and a left onto Fort Road will lead you to the beach. The **Flying Horse Carousel** (⊠ Bay St.; ☞ 50¢), which operates from mid-June to Labor Day, is the oldest merry-go-round in America, built in 1861.

The 15 villages of **South Kingstown** draw visitors to various historic sights, crafts shops, and galleries; the town also boasts Matunuck Beach. At the **Washington County Jail,** built in 1792, you can tour jail cells, Colonial-period rooms, and a Colonial garden. ⊠ *1348 Kingstown Rd.,* ☎ *401/783–1328.* ☞ *Free. Closed Mon., Wed., Fri., Sun., and Nov.–Apr.*

Built in 1751, the **Gilbert Stuart Birthplace** was the home of America's foremost portraitist of George Washington. It lies on a pretty country road and is adjacent to the first snuff mill in America. ⊠ *815 Gilbert Stuart Rd.,* ☎ *401/294–3001.* ☞ *$3. Closed Tues.–Wed. and Nov.–May.*

Theatre-by-the-Sea (⊠ Cards Pond Rd., ☎ 401/782–8587) presents summer-stock musicals and plays in a playhouse listed on the National Register of Historic Places.

Narragansett, which includes the maritime village of Galilee and the Point Judith Lighthouse, is a top summer destination for its beaches, bay vistas, and restaurants. The **Towers** (⊠ Ocean Rd., Narragansett Pier) are all that remains of the casino that was once the centerpiece of the beachside village known as Narragansett Pier.

☙ **South County Museum** houses 20,000 artifacts dating from 1800. ⊠ *Anne Hoxie La., off Rte. 1A,* ☎ *401/783–5400.* ☞ *$3.50. Closed Mon.–Tues. and Nov.–Apr.*

The fishing port of **Galilee** is a departure point for ferries to Block Island and charter fishing trips. The **Frances Fleet** (⊠ 2 State St., ☎ 401/783–4988 or 800/662–2824) conducts whale-watching excursions ($30) between June and September. On Ocean Road are public beaches and, at land's end, the **Point Judith Lighthouse** (☎ 401/789–0444).

Dining and Lodging

If you're interested in local fare, try the stuffies—large native clams called quahogs (pronounced *ko*-hog) that are stuffed and baked. "Shore dinners" consist of clam chowder, steamers, clam cakes, sausage, corn-on-the-cob, lobster, watermelon, and Indian pudding (a steamed pudding made with cornmeal and molasses). And just so you're not surprised, Rhode Island clam chowder is made with a clear broth. Along the south shore and in North Kingstown are many small motels and B&Bs.

Narragansett

$$–$$$ ✕ **Coast Guard House.** This restaurant, which dates from 1888 and was a lifesaving station for 50 years, displays interesting photos of Narragansett Pier and the Casino. The menu is American—seafood, pasta, veal, steak, and lamb. ⊠ *40 Ocean Rd.,* ☎ *401/789–0700. AE, D, DC, MC, V.*

$$ ★ ✕ **Spain Restaurant.** The cuisine and service in this spacious eatery near the Point Judith Lighthouse are the work of well-trained professionals. Generously portioned main courses include lobster and steak

dishes, as well as a variety of paellas. Even basic fare, like chicken with rice, is unforgettable. ⊠ *1144 Ocean Rd.,* ☎ *401/783–9770. AE, D, DC, MC, V.*

$$$ 🏨 **Stone Lea.** In the Millionaire's Mile section of private homes, this B&B is replete with rotundas, bay windows, and carved-wood paneling. Rising from the foyer's parquet floor is an impressive staircase designed to mimic the curves of a grand piano. ⊠ *40 Newton Ave., 02882,* ☎ *401/783–8237,* FAX *401/783–9546. 7 rooms. AE, MC, V. BP.*

$–$$ 🏨 **The Richards.** Imposing and magnificent, this English manor–style mansion has a broodingly Gothic mystique. Some rooms have 19th-century English antiques, floral-upholstered furniture, and fireplaces. Two of the rooms share a bath. ⊠ *144 Gibson Ave., 02882,* ☎ *401/ 789–7746. 5 rooms. No credit cards. BP.*

Shopping

The **Fantastic Umbrella Factory** (⊠ 4920 Old Post Rd., off Rte. 1, ☎ 401/364–6616) comprises four rustic shops and a barn built around a wild garden where peacocks, pheasants, and chickens parade. For sale in the backyard bazaar are kites, crafts, tapestries, incense, and blown-glass jewelry.

The Colonial village of **Wickford,** 10 mi north of Narragansett Pier along Route 1A, has a little harbor, dozens of 18th- and 19th-century homes, and numerous antiques and curiosity shops. This bayside spot is a shoppers paradise.

NEWPORT

Newport is one of the great sailing cities of the world and the host to world-class jazz, blues, folk, and classical music festivals. More than 200 Colonial homes and shops still stand from the city's first period of prosperity, the 18th-century golden age. In the 19th century, during what became known as the gilded age, Newport was a summer playground for America's wealthiest families.

Visitor Information

Newport County: Gateway Information Center (⊠ 23 America's Cup Ave., Newport 02840, ☎ 401/849–8048 or 800/326–6030) provides long-term parking and a wide array of visitors' resources.

Arriving and Departing

By Bus
Bonanza (☎ 401/751–8800 or 800/556–3815) runs from Boston. **RIPTA** (☎ 401/847–0209; 800/244–0444 in RI) serves Newport from Providence and elsewhere in Rhode Island.

By Car
From Providence take I–95 east into Massachusetts and head south on Route 24. From South County take Route 1 north to Route 138 east. From Boston take I–93 south to Route 24 south.

By Ferry
Jamestown and Newport Ferry Company (☎ 401/423–9900) runs frequently from Jamestown.

By Plane
Newport State Airport (⊠ 500 Airport Rd., ☎ 401/846–9400) is 3 mi northeast of Newport. Charter companies fly from here to T. F. Green State Airport in Warwick. By reservation, **Cozy Cab** (☎ 401/846–

Newport

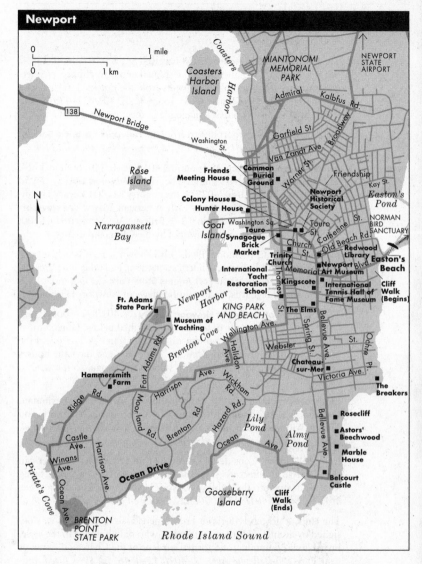

2500) runs a shuttle service ($15) between the airport and Newport's visitor's bureau.

Some travelers choose to fly into **T. F. Green State Airport** (⊠ Rte. 1, Warwick, ☎ 401/737–4000), 10 mi south of Providence, and drive a rental car to Newport. Take I–95 south to Route 4, then Route 138 to Newport; it's a 25-minute drive.

Exploring Newport

★ The French admiral de Ternay used the 1748 **Hunter House** as his Revolutionary War headquarters. The elliptical arch in the central hall is a typical Newport detail. ⊠ 54 *Washington St.,* ☎ *401/847–7516.* ☞ *$8. Closed Nov.–Apr. and weekdays Oct.*

The **Brick Market** (⊠ Thames St.) served as Newport's trading center for more than a century. The building now houses the **Museum of Newport History** (☎ 401/841–8770; ☞ $5). **Colony House** faces the Brick

Market on Washington Square. Built in 1739, it was the government's headquarters—from its balcony the Declaration of Independence was read to Newporters.

The **Friends Meeting House** (✉ 29 Farewell St., ☎ 401/846–0813; 🎫 $5) was built in 1699 and is the oldest Quaker meetinghouse in America; tours are by appointment. Austere from the outside but elaborate within, the **Touro Synagogue** (✉ 85 Touro St., ☎ 401/847–4794), dedicated in 1763, is the oldest synagogue in the country.

Walking tours of Newport depart from the **Newport Historical Society.** ✉ *82 Touro St.,* ☎ *401/846–0813.* 🎫 *Free. Closed Sun. and Mon.*

Trinity Church (✉ Queen Anne Sq., ☎ 401/846–0660), built in 1724, has a three-tier wineglass pulpit. The 1748 **Redwood Library** (✉ 50 Bellevue Ave., ☎ 401/847–0292), the country's oldest library in continuous use, houses paintings by early American artists. The **Newport Art Museum and Art Association** (✉ 76 Bellevue Ave., ☎ 401/848–8200; 🎫 $4) exhibits contemporary works by New England artists.

Easton's Beach (✉ Memorial Blvd.), also known as First Beach, is popular for its expansive beach, children's aquarium, and other amusements. A small, sheltered beach at **Fort Adams State Park** (✉ Ocean Dr.) has a picnic area, lifeguards, and beautiful views of Newport Harbor.

The **Preservation Society of Newport County** (☎ 401/847–1000) maintains 12 mansions, some of which are described below. Guided tours are given of each; you can purchase a combination ticket at any of the properties for a substantial discount. The hours and days the houses are open during the off-season are subject to change, so it's wise to call ahead.

Kingscote was built in 1839 for a plantation owner from Savannah, Georgia. It's decorated with antique furniture, glass, Asian art, and Tiffany windows. ✉ *Bowery St. off Bellevue Ave.,* ☎ *401/847–1000.* 🎫 *$8. Closed Nov.–Mar. and weekdays Apr. and Oct.*

Isaac Bell House. Considered one of the finest examples of American shingle-style architecture, this Bellevue Avenue home currently being restored is open to the public as a work in progress. ✉ *Bellevue Ave. at Perry St.,* ☎ *401/847–1000.* 🎫 *$9. Closed Nov.–Apr.*

The **Elms,** a graceful 48-room French neoclassical mansion, was designed by architect Horace Trumbauer, who paid homage to the style, broad lawn, fountains, and formal gardens of the Château d'Asnières near Paris. ✉ *Bellevue Ave.,* ☎ *401/842–0546.* 🎫 *$9. Closed mid-Nov.–Thanksgiving Day and weekdays Jan.–Mar.*

Chateau-sur-Mer, the first of Bellevue Avenue's stone mansions, was built in the Victorian Gothic style in 1852. Some rooms were created by leading 19th-century designers. ✉ *Bellevue Ave.,* ☎ *401/847–1000.* 🎫 *$8. Closed weekdays Oct.–mid-Nov. and weekdays Jan.–Mar.*

★ The **Breakers,** a four-story Italian Renaissance palace built in 1893 for railroad heir Cornelius Vanderbilt II, contains such marvels as a gold-ceiling music room and a blue-marble fireplace. To build the Breakers today would cost about $400 million. ✉ *Ochre Point Ave.,* ☎ *401/847–6544.* 🎫 *$10. Closed Dec. (most yrs), Jan.–Mar., weekends in Apr., weekdays in Nov.*

Rosecliff, Newport's most romantic mansion (complete with heart-shape staircase), was modeled after the Grand Trianon palace at Versailles. ✉ *Bellevue Ave.,* ☎ *401/847–5793.* 🎫 *$8. Closed Nov.–Mar.*

The **Marble House,** perhaps the most opulent Newport mansion, was the gift of William Vanderbilt to his wife in 1892. ⊠ *Bellevue Ave.,* ☎ *401/847–1000.* ☞ *$9. Closed Nov. and (most yrs) Dec. and weekdays Jan.–Mar.*

At **Astors' Beechwood,** which was built for the wealthy Astor family, actors in period costume play the parts of family members, servants, and household guests. ⊠ *580 Bellevue Ave.,* ☎ *401/846–3772.* ☞ *$9. Closed Jan. and weekdays Feb.–Apr.*

Belcourt Castle is so filled with European and Asian treasures that locals have dubbed it the Metropolitan Museum of Newport. ⊠ *Bellevue Ave.,* ☎ *401/846–0669 or 401/849–1566.* ☞ *$8. Closed Jan.*

★ **Hammersmith Farm** was the childhood summer home of Jacqueline Bouvier Kennedy Onassis, and a summer White House during the Kennedy Administration. The home is no longer open to the pubic. ⊠ *Ocean Dr. near Fort Adams.*

The **International Tennis Hall of Fame Museum** (⊠ 194 Bellevue Ave., ☎ 401/849–3990; ☞ $8) is in the magnificent Newport Casino. The **Museum of Yachting** (⊠ Fort Adams Park, Ocean Dr., ☎ 401/847–1018; ☞ $3; closed Nov.–Apr.) has four galleries of sailing exhibits.

Shipwrights overhaul historic oceangoing vessels, and the public is welcome to watch, at the **International Yacht Restoration School** (⊠ 449 Thames St., ☎ 401/848–5577).

☾ **Old Colony & Newport Railway** (⊠ 19 America's Cup Ave., ☎ 401/624–6951; ☞ $6), a vintage diesel train, follows an 8-mi route along Narragansett Bay from Newport to the Green Animals Topiary Gardens in Portsmouth.

☾ Just north of Second Beach, the **Norman Bird Sanctuary** (⊠ 583 3rd Rd., Middletown, ☎ 401/846–2577; ☞ $4) is a 450-acre nature preserve with hiking trails, guided tours, and a small natural history museum.

Dining and Lodging

Entering Newport from the direction of Providence, you will find a number of motels whose room rates are considerably lower than those downtown.

$$–$$$$ ✕ **Asterix & Obelix.** Fine dining here is as fun and colorful as the mad-
★ cap French cartoon strip after which this eatery was named. Occasional Asian twists enliven the French and Mediterranean fare. "Crispy duck" is roasted with honey and ginger and served with stir fry; sole meunière is topped with a spinach anglaise. ⊠ *599 Thames St.,* ☎ *401/841–8833. AE, D, DC, MC, V.*

$$–$$$$ ✕ **Black Pearl.** Tourists and yachters flock to this dignified converted dock shanty, where award-winning clam chowder is sold by the quart. Dining is in the casual tavern or the formal Commodore's Room (jacket required), where the French and American entrées include swordfish with Dutch pepper butter. ⊠ *Bannister's Wharf,* ☎ *401/846–5264. Reservations essential in the Commodore's Room. AE, MC, V.*

$$–$$$$ ✕ **Scales & Shells.** This busy restaurant serves as many as 15 types of superbly fresh wood-grilled fish. The dining is more formal upstairs at Upscales. ⊠ *527 Thames St.,* ☎ *401/848–9378. Reservations not accepted downstairs. No credit cards.*

$–$$$ ✕ **Puerini's.** The aroma of garlic and basil greets you as soon as you enter this laid-back neighborhood restaurant. The intriguing menu includes green noodles with chicken in marsala wine sauce and tortellini with seafood. ⊠ *24 Memorial Blvd.,* ☎ *401/847–5506. Reservations not accepted. MC, V. Closed Mon. in winter. No lunch.*

$–$$ ✕ **Flo's Clam Shack.** Fried seafood, steamed clams, cold beer, and the best raw bar in town keep the lines long here in summer. The upstairs bar serves baked, chilled lobster, and outside seating is available. It's located across the street from First Beach. ⊠ *4 Wave Ave.,* ☎ *401/847–8141. Reservations not accepted. MC, V.*

$$$–$$$$ ✕🏨 **Vanderbilt Hall.** The city's most sophisticated inn and restaurant is located downtown in a building formerly owned by the Vanderbilt family. All the rooms are individually decorated with antiques. A fire crackles in the somber dining room ($$$$), where a veteran and meticulous waitstaff tends to your needs. The inn has a whirlpool, sauna, and steam room. ⊠ *41 Mary St., 02840,* ☎ *401/846–6200,* FAX *401/846–0701. 50 rooms. Dining room, pool. AE, DC, MC, V.* 🍴

$$$–$$$$ 🏨 **Castle Hill Inn and Resort.** Much of the furniture at this inn is original to the structure, a summer home built in 1874 on a cliff at the mouth of the Narragansett Bay. The inn, 3 mi from the center of Newport, is famous for its Sunday brunches. Three of the rooms share a bath. ⊠ *Ocean Dr., 02840,* ☎ *401/849–3800. 38 rooms. Restaurant. AE, D, MC, V. Restaurant closed Nov.–Mar. BP.* 🍴

$$$–$$$$ 🏨 **Francis Malbone House.** This 1760 structure was tastefully doubled
★ in size in the mid-1990s; the nine newer rooms have whirlpool tubs and fireplaces. The rooms in the main house are all in corners (with two windows) and look out over the courtyard, which has a fountain, or across the street to the harbor. Six of these rooms have fireplaces. ⊠ *392 Thames St., 02840,* ☎ *401/846–0392 or 800/846–0392. 18 rooms. AE, MC, V. BP.* 🍴

$$$–$$$$ 🏨 **Hotel Viking.** Listed on the National Register of Historical Places, this elegant redbrick hotel has a prestigious address that makes it easy to walk to the waterfront, the historic district, and many nearby shops. The wood paneling and original chandeliers, among other details, evoke the hotel's sophisticated history. ⊠ *One Bellevue Ave., 02840,* ☎ *401/847–3300 or 800/556–7126,* FAX *401/848–4864. 227 rooms. Restaurant, pool. AE, D, DC, MC, V.* 🍴

$$$ 🏨 **Ivy Lodge.** This grand (though small by Newport's standards) Vic-
★ torian B&B with large and lovely rooms has gables and a turret. The defining feature is a Gothic-style 33-ft-high oak entryway with a three-story turned baluster staircase and a dangling wrought-iron chandelier. ⊠ *12 Clay St., 02840,* ☎ *401/849–6865. 8 rooms. AE, MC, V. BP.*

$–$$ 🏨 **Harbor Base Pineapple Inn.** All the rooms at this basic motel, a five-minute drive from downtown, contain two double beds; some also have kitchenettes. ⊠ *372 Coddington Hwy., 02840,* ☎ *401/847–2600. 48 rooms. AE, D, DC, MC, V.*

Nightlife

Thames Street is the nexus of Newport's lively nightlife. **Newport Blues Café** (⊠ 286 Thames St., ☎ 401/841–5510) hosts great blues performers. **One Pelham East** (⊠ 270 Thames St., ☎ 401/847–9460) draws a young crowd for progressive rock, reggae, and R&B.

Outdoor Activities and Sports

Adventure Sports (⊠ The Inn at Long Wharf, America's Cup Ave., ☎ 401/849–4820) rents waverunners, sailboats, kayaks, and canoes. **Old Port Marine Services** (⊠ Sayer's Wharf, ☎ 401/847–9109) operates harbor tours and crewed yacht charters. **Sail Newport** (⊠ Fort Adams State Park, ☎ 401/846–1983) rents sailboats by the hour.

Ten Speed Spokes (✉ 18 Elm St., ☎ 401/847–5609) rents bikes.

Tennis Indoor Club (✉ Memorial Blvd., one block east of Bellevue, ☎ 401/846–4777) rents indoor courts for $25 per hour.

Shopping

Many of Newport's arts and antiques shops are on Thames Street; others are on Spring Street, Franklin Street, and at Bowen's and Bannister's wharves. The **Brick Market** area—between Thames Street and America's Cup Avenue—has more than 40 shops that carry crafts, clothing, antiques, and toys. Stores at **Bannister's Wharf** stock clothing and gifts with a nautical theme. **Arnold Art Store and Gallery** (✉ 210 Thames St., ☎ 401/847–2273) has a large collection of marine-inspired paintings and prints. The delicate and dramatic blown-glass gifts at **Thames Glass** (✉ 688 Thames St., ☎ 401/846–0576) are designed by Matthew Buechner and created in the adjacent studio.

Side Trip to Block Island

Visitor Information
Block Island Chamber of Commerce (✉ Drawer D, Water St., 02807, ☎ 401/466–2982) offers information on available lodgings.

Arriving and Departing
BY FERRY

Interstate Navigation Co. (✉ Galilee State Pier, Narragansett, ☎ 401/783–4613; ✉ $8.40 from Galilee) has ferry service from Galilee to Block Island. **Nelesco Navigation Co.** (✉ 2 Ferry St., New London, CT, ☎ 860/442–7891; ✉ $15) operates car and passenger ferry service from New London to Block Island daily from June to September. **Viking Ferry Lines** (✉ West Lake Dr., Montauk, NY, ☎ 516/668–5709; ✉ $16) operates passenger and bicycle service from Montauk, Long Island, from mid-May to mid-October. None of these ferries take passenger reservations.

BY PLANE

Block Island State Airport (☎ 401/466–5511) is served by **New England Airlines** (☎ 401/596–2460 or 800/243–2460) from Westerly.

What to See and Do
Approaching 10-square-mi Block Island by sea from New London or Point Judith, you'll see the **Old Harbor** area. Here in the island's only village are most of the inns, shops, and restaurants. Three docks, two hotels, and four restaurants huddled in the southeast corner of the Great Salt Pond make up the **New Harbor** commercial area, where two ferries dock. Hiking paths at **Rodman's Hollow,** a fine example of a glacial outwash basin, lead to pristine beaches. The **Southeast Lighthouse** (✉ Mohegan Trail, ☎ 401/466–5009) is a National Historic Landmark that was built in 1875.

PROVIDENCE

New England's third-largest city (behind Boston and Worcester) is a prime example of how U.S. cities can be redesigned and culturally revived. In the past decade, Providence rivers have been rerouted and unsightly railroad tracks have been placed underground. In downtown Providence, a convention center, an outdoor ice rink, a riverfront park, and an upscale shopping mall now draw tourists and visitors from outlying towns. In addition, many travelers now prefer revamped T. F. Green Airport over Boston's Logan Airport.

Central Providence

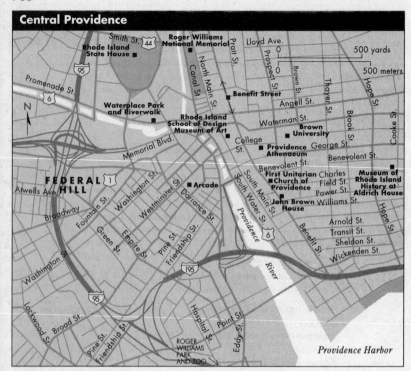

Providence Harbor

Visitor Information

Greater Providence Convention and Visitors Bureau (⊠ 1 W. Exchange St., 02903, ☎ 401/274–1636).

Arriving and Departing

By Bus

Greyhound (☎ 800/231–2222). **Bonanza** (☎ 800/556–3815). **RIPTA** (☎ 401/781–9400; 800/224–0444 in RI) provides local transportation in Providence and service to other parts of the state.

By Car

I–95 cuts diagonally across the state and is the fastest route to Providence from Boston, coastal Connecticut, and New York City. I–195 links Providence with New Bedford and Cape Cod. U.S. 1 follows the coast east from Connecticut before turning north to Providence.

By Plane

T. F. Green State Airport (⊠ 2000 Post Rd. [also Rte. 1]), Warwick, ☎ 401/737–4000), 10 mi south of Providence, is served by major U.S. airlines and regional carriers. **Airport Van Shuttle** (☎ 888/736–1900) provides service to downtown Providence and elsewhere.

By Train

Amtrak (☎ 800/872–7245) trains stop at **Providence Station** (⊠ 100 Gaspee St., ☎ 401/727–7379). **MBTA** Commuter Rail (☎ 617/722–3200) runs between Boston and Providence weekday mornings and evenings.

Exploring Providence

The **Providence Athenaeum** (⊠ 251 Benefit St., ☎ 401/421–6970; ☜ free), established in 1753 and one of the oldest lending libraries in the world, displays Rhode Island art and artifacts, as well as an original set of the folio *Birds of America* prints by John J. Audubon.

The small but comprehensive **Rhode Island School of Design Museum of Art** contains textiles, Japanese prints, Paul Revere silver, 18th-century porcelain, French Impressionist paintings, and a mummy dating from circa 300 BC. ✉ *224 Benefit St.,* ☎ *401/454–6500.* 🎫 *$5. Closed Mon.*

Also on **Benefit Street**—known as the Mile of History—is a row of Colonial and Revolutionary War houses crammed shoulder to shoulder on a steep hill overlooking downtown Providence. The **Providence Preservation Society** (✉ 21 Meeting St., at Benefit St., ☎ 401/831–7440) has maps and pamphlets with self-guided tours.

The **Arcade** (✉ 65 Weybosset St., ☎ 401/598–1199), America's first shopping mall, was built in 1828. A National Historic Landmark, this graceful Greek Revival building, which is closed on Sunday, has three tiers of shops and restaurants.

The **First Unitarian Church of Providence** (✉ 1 Benevolent St., ☎ 401/421–7970; 🎫 free), built in 1816, houses the largest bell ever cast in Paul Revere's foundry—a 2,500 pounder.

The awe-inspiring **Rhode Island State House** was built in 1900. Its dome, one of the world's largest, was modeled after St. Peter's Basilica in Rome. On display is the original parchment charter granted by King Charles to the colony of Rhode Island in 1663. Booklets for self-guided tours are available in Room 220. ✉ *82 Smith St.,* ☎ *401/222–2357. Closed weekends.*

Roger Williams contributed so significantly to the concepts leading to the Declaration of Independence and the Constitution that the National Park Service dedicated the 4½-acre **Roger Williams National Memorial** (✉ 282 N. Main St., ☎ 401/521–7266; 🎫 free) to his memory. Displays offer a quick course in the life and times of Rhode Island's extraordinary founder.

Waterplace Park and Riverwalk (✉ Boat House Clock Tower, 2 American Express Way, ☎ 401/751–1177) was completed in 1997. The 4-acre tract with Venetian-style footbridges, cobblestone walkways, and an amphitheater encircling a tidal pond on the Providence River is a critical component of the ongoing revitalization of the downtown.

★ The 1786 **John Brown House,** one of America's first mansions, is named for a China trader famous for his Revolutionary-era role in the burning of the British customs ship *Gaspee.* The three-story Georgian mansion has elaborate woodwork and furniture, silver, linens, Chinese porcelain, and an antique doll collection. ✉ *52 Power St.,* ☎ *401/331–8575.* 🎫 *$6. Closed weekdays Jan. and Feb.*

☺ **Roger Williams Park and Zoo** (✉ Elmwood Ave., ☎ 401/785–3510; 🎫 $6) is a beautiful 430-acre Victorian park. The zoo is home to more than 900 animals and 150 different species. In the park you can have a picnic, feed the ducks in the lakes, ride a pony, or rent a paddleboat.

Dining and Lodging

$$–$$$$ ✕ **L'Epicureo.** Formerly a Federal Hill butcher shop, this refined Italian bistro has won high marks for its wood-grilled steaks, veal chops, and pasta dishes, such as fettuccine tossed with arugula, garlic, and lemon. ✉ *238 Atwells Ave.,* ☎ *401/454–8430. AE, D, DC, MC, V. Closed Sun. and Mon. No lunch.*

$$–$$$$ ✕ **The Gatehouse.** Views of the Seekonk River and fine modern art by
★ local artists complement the New Orleans–influenced New England

cuisine served here. Dishes might include slow-roasted duck with sautéed vegetables, served with spiced pumpkin gravy. There's a Sunday brunch. ⊠ *4 Richmond Sq.,* ☎ *401/521–9229. Reservations essential weekends. AE, DC, MC, V. No lunch Sat.*

$$–$$$$ ✕ **Pot au Feu.** For a quarter century Pot au Feu has worked to perfect
★ basics such as pâté du foie gras, beef bourguignon, and potatoes au gratin. The dining experience is more casual at the downstairs Bistro than at the upstairs Salon. ⊠ *44 Custom House St.,* ☎ *401/273–8953. AE, DC, MC, V. Salon closed Sun. and Mon.*

$$–$$$ ✕ **Al Forno.** Roasted clams and spicy sausage served in a tomato broth
★ and charcoal-seared tournedos of beef with mashed potatoes are among the entrées at this regionally renowned contemporary eatery. Made-to-order desserts include crepes with apricot puree and crème anglaise. ⊠ *577 S. Main St.,* ☎ *401/273–9760. Reservations not accepted. AE, DC, MC, V. Closed Sun. and Mon. No lunch.*

$ ✕ **Angelo's Civita Farnese.** On Federal Hill in the heart of Little Italy, lively (even boisterous) Angelo's is a family-run place with Old World charm. Locals come here for good-size portions of fresh and simply prepared pasta. ⊠ *141 Atwells Ave.,* ☎ *401/621–8171. Reservations not accepted. No credit cards.*

$$$–$$$$ ▦ **Westin Hotel.** The 25-story Westin towers over Providence's compact downtown, but its redbrick facade and neo-turrets allow it to blend a little better into historic Providence than other contemporary peers. The newest hotel in the city, the Westin is chock-full of luxuries, and its Agora was named one of America's best new restaurants by *Esquire* magazine. ⊠ *1 W. Exchange St., 02903,* ☎ *401/598–8000 or 800/937–8461,* ℻ *401/598–8200. 386 rooms, 22 suites. Restaurant, pool, health club. AE, D, DC, MC, V.* ◈

$$$ ▦ **Providence Biltmore.** The Biltmore, completed in 1922, has a sleek
★ Art Deco exterior, an external glass elevator with delightful views of Providence, a grand ballroom, and an interesting history. The attentiveness of its staff, the downtown location, and modern amenities make this hotel one of the city's best. ⊠ *Kennedy Plaza, Dorrance and Washington Sts., 02903,* ☎ *401/421–0700 or 800/294–7209,* ℻ *401/421–0210. 238 rooms. Restaurant, exercise room. AE, DC, MC, V.* ◈

$$–$$$ ▦ **Days Hotel on the Harbor.** Half the rooms at this plain but comfortable hotel have harbor views; the other half overlook I–95. ⊠ *220 India St., 02903,* ☎ *401/272–5577,* ℻ *401/272–5577. 136 rooms. Restaurant, exercise room. AE, D, DC, MC, V.* ◈

$$–$$$ ▦ **Marriott Hotel.** Tones of peach and green grace the good-size rooms at this hotel, which has all the modern conveniences. The Blue Fin Grille restaurant specializes in local seafood prepared with a French flair. ⊠ *Charles and Orms Sts., near Exit 23 off I–95, 02904,* ☎ *401/272–2400 or 800/937–7768,* ℻ *401/273–2686. 351 rooms. Restaurant, pools, health club. AE, D, DC, MC, V.* ◈

$–$$ ▦ **C. C. Ledbetter's.** The unmarked somber green exterior of innkeeper C. C. Ledbetter's mansard-roof 1770 home gives few hints of the vibrancy within—lively art, photographs, quilts, and a shrewd blend of contemporary furnishings and antiques fill the place. Two rooms share a bath. ⊠ *326 Benefit St., 02903,* ☎ ℻ *401/351–4699. 4 rooms. D, MC, V. CP.*

Nightlife and the Arts

The **Custom House Tavern** (⊠ 36 Weybosset St., ☎ 401/751–3630) is a friendly downtown gathering place. The **Hot Club** (⊠ 575 S. Water St., ☎ 401/861–9007) is a waterside bar where scenes from *Something About Mary* were filmed. **Lupo's Heartbreak Hotel** (⊠ 239 Westminster St., ☎ 401/272–5876), a nightclub, books local and international musical talents. The **Providence Performing Arts Center** (⊠ 220 Weybosset St., ☎ 401/421–2787) hosts touring Broadway shows, concerts, and other events. **Snookers** (⊠ 145 Clifford St., ☎ 401/351–7665) is a stylish billiard hall in the Jewelry District. **Trinity Square Repertory Company** (⊠ 201 Washington St., ☎ 401/351–4242), one of New England's best theater companies, presents plays in the renovated Majestic movie house.

Outdoor Activities and Sports

Biking
For trail information call **Rhode Island Tourism Division** (☎ 800/556–2484). The **East Bay Bicycle Path** is a 14½-mi paved trail linking Providence's India Point Park to Bristol.

Tennis
Roger Williams Park (⊠ Off Elmwood Ave., ☎ 401/785–9450) has eight public courts.

Shopping

The upscale **Providence Place Mall** (⊠ 1 Providence Pl., Francis and Hayes Sts., ☎ 401/270–1000) is anchored by Filene's, Lord & Taylor, and Nordstrom; 150 other shops and restaurants complete the mix. Antiques stores and art galleries line **Wickenden Street. Tilden-Thurber** (⊠ 292 Westminster St., ☎ 401/272–3200) carries high-end Colonial- and Victorian-era furniture, antiques, and estate jewelry.

SOUTH CAROLINA

Updated by
Mary Sue
Lawrence

Capital	Columbia
Population	3,684,000
Mottoes	While I Breathe, I Hope; Prepared in Mind and Resources
State Bird	Carolina wren
State Flower	Yellow jessamine
Postal Abbreviation	SC

Statewide Visitor Information

South Carolina Department of Parks, Recreation and Tourism (⊠ 1205 Pendleton St., Box 71, Columbia 29202, ☎ 803/734–0235 or 800/872–3505). **Welcome centers:** U.S. 17 near Little River; I–95 near Dillon, Santee, and Lake Marion, and Hardeeville; I–77 near Fort Mill; I–85 near Blacksburg and Fair Play; I–26 near Landrum; I–20 at North Augusta, Georgia; and U.S. 301 near Allendale.

Scenic Drives

The **Cherokee Foothills Scenic Highway** (Route 11) passes small towns, peach orchards, and historical sites as it traverses 130 mi of Blue Ridge foothills in the northwest corner of the state. The **Ashley River Road** (Route 61), which runs parallel to the river for about 11 mi north of Charleston, leads to famous plantations and gardens. The **Savannah River Scenic Highway** (follow signs from Route 28 near North Augusta to Route 24 near Westminster) traces the Savannah River for 100 mi along the Georgia border, winding past three lakes.

National and State Parks

National Parks

At **Cowpens National Battlefield** (⊠ Rte. 11, Box 308, Chesnee 29323, ☎ 864/461–2828; ⊠ free) the American patriots defeated the British in 1781; exhibits in the visitor center explain the battle. **Kings Mountain National Military Park** (⊠ I–85 near Blacksburg, Box 40, Kings Mountain, NC 28086, ☎ 864/936–7921; ⊠ free), where patriot forces whipped the redcoats in 1780, has exhibits depicting the famous battle and a self-guided trail. For white-water enthusiasts, the **Chattooga National Wild and Scenic River** (⊠ U.S. Forest Service, 4931 Broad River Rd., Columbia 29210-4021, ☎ 803/561–4000; ⊠ free) forms the border between South Carolina and Georgia for 40 mi. **Congaree Swamp National Monument** (⊠ Old Bluff Rd., Hopkins 29061, ☎ 803/776–4396; ⊠ free) contains the oldest and largest trees east of the Mississippi River.

State Parks

Several of South Carolina's 48 state parks operate like resort communities, with everything from deluxe accommodations to golf. **Hickory Knob State Resort Park** (⊠ Rte. 1, Box 199-B, McCormick 29835, ☎ 864/391–2450 or 800/491–1764), on Strom Thurmond Lake in the western part of South Carolina, has opportunities for fishing, golfing, and skeet shooting. **Devil's Fork State Park** (⊠ 161 Holcombe Circle, Salem 29676, ☎ 864/944–2639), in Sumter National Forest in the northwest corner of the state, has luxurious accommodations overlooking beautiful Lake Jocassee. **Calhoun Falls State Park** (⊠ Rte. 81, Calhoun Falls 29628, ☎ 864/447–9367), on the western edge of the state, has a full-service marina, a campground, nature trails, and a picnic area.

The state's **coastal parks**—known for broad beaches, camping facilities, and nature preserves—draw the most visitors and are often booked months in advance. **Huntington Beach State Park** (✉ Murrells Inlet 29576, ☎ 843/237–4440) has a splendid beach, surf fishing, and a salt-marsh boardwalk, as well as Atalaya, a Moorish-style mansion. **Myrtle Beach State Park** (✉ U.S. 17, Myrtle Beach 29577, ☎ 843/238–5325) has cabins and year-round nature programs. **Hunting Island State Park** (✉ St. Helena Island 29920, ☎ 843/838–2011), a secluded beach domain, has beachfront cottages, nature trails, and varied fishing. **Edisto Beach State Park** (✉ Rte. 174, Edisto Island 29438, ☎ 843/869–2156) has cabins by the marsh and campsites by the ocean. For more information contact the **South Carolina Division of State Parks** (✉ 1205 Pendleton St., Columbia 29201, ☎ 803/734–0159).

CHARLESTON

The port city of Charleston has withstood three centuries of epidemics, earthquakes, fires, and hurricanes to become one of the South's best-preserved and most beloved cities. Residents have lovingly restored old downtown homes and commercial buildings, as well as more than 180 historic churches—so many that Charlestonians call their home the "Holy City." Each spring the city—festooned with dogwood and azaleas—celebrates its heritage with symphony galas, plantation oyster roasts, candlelight tours of historic homes and churches, and the renowned Spoleto Festival USA, a celebration of the arts staged in streets and performance halls throughout the city.

Visitor Information

Charleston Area Convention and Visitors Bureau (✉ Box 975, 375 Meeting St., 29402, ☎ 843/853–8000 or 800/868–8118).

Arriving and Departing

By Boat

Boaters arriving at Charleston Harbor via the Intracoastal Waterway may dock at **City Marina** (✉ Lockwood Blvd., ☎ 843/723–5098), **Ashley Marina** (✉ Lockwood Blvd., ☎ 843/722–1996), and at the Isle of Palms's **Wild Dunes Yacht Harbor** (✉ Palm Blvd., ☎ 843/886–5100).

By Bus

Greyhound (✉ 3610 Dorchester Rd., North Charleston, ☎ 800/231–2222).

By Car

I–26 crosses the state from northwest to southeast and ends at Charleston. U.S. 17, a north–south coastal route, passes through the city.

By Plane

Charleston International Airport (✉ 5500 International Blvd., ☎ 843/767–1100), 12 mi west of downtown Charleston along I–26, is served by Continental, Comair, Delta, Midway Express, United Express, Northwest, TWA, and US Airways. **Low Country Limousine Service** (☎ 843/767–7111 or 800/222–4771) charges $15 per person (or $10 per person for two or more) to downtown; make reservations in advance. Some hotels also provide shuttle service.

By Train

Amtrak (✉ 4565 Gaynor Ave., North Charleston, ☎ 843/744–8264 or 800/872–7245).

Getting Around Charleston

You can park your car and walk in the city's historic district, but you'll need a car to see attractions in outlying areas. **Charleston Transit** (☎ 843/747–0922) provides bus service within the city and to James Island, Isle of Palms, Sullivan's Island, Mount Pleasant, and North Charleston. It also operates the trolley-style Downtown Area Shuttle buses, called DASH. Fare for either is 75¢, exact change, or $2 for a one-day DASH pass, which can be bought on the bus. **Taxi companies** include **Yellow Cab** (☎ 843/577–6565), **Safety Cab** (☎ 843/722–4066), and **Low Country Limousine** (☞ Arriving and Departing *above*).

Guided tours are a popular option for seeing Charleston. Guides are generally knowledgeable and often provide snippets of history and humor. **Old South Carriage Co.** (☎ 843/577–0042), the city's oldest horse-drawn-carriage tour company, conducts one-hour tours of the historic district. **Charleston Tea Party Walking Tour** (☎ 843/577–5896 or 843/722–1779) offers city walking tours. **Gullah Tours** (☎ 843/763–7551), a bus-tour company, focuses on African-American influences on Charleston architecture, history, and culture.

Exploring Charleston

You can get a quick orientation to the city by viewing *Forever Charleston,* a 24-minute multimedia presentation shown by the Charleston Area Convention and Visitors Bureau (☞ Visitor Information, *above*).

★ ☾ The **Charleston Museum,** founded in 1773, has 500,000 items in its collection, including Charleston silver, fashions, toys, and snuffboxes, as well as exhibits on natural history, archaeology, and ornithology. Also part of the museum are two historic homes. The **Joseph Manigault House** (✉ 350 Meeting St.) was designed in 1803 and is noted for its carved-wood mantels and elaborate plasterwork. Furnishings are British, French, and American antiques, including rare Wedgwood pieces. The **Heyward-Washington House** (✉ 87 Church St.) was the residence of President George Washington during his 1791 visit and the setting for DuBose Heyward's novel *Porgy.* The mansion is notable for fine period furnishings by local craftspeople and includes a restored 18th-century kitchen. ✉ *360 Meeting St.,* ☎ *843/722–2996.* ✄ *Museum $8; combination ticket for museum and houses $18, for any 2 of the 3 sites $12.*

The stately 1819 **Aiken-Rhett House** mansion, with original wallpaper, paint colors, and some furnishings, was the headquarters of Confederate general P. G. T. Beauregard during his 1864 Civil War defense of Charleston. The house, kitchen, slave quarters, and work yard are much as they were when the original occupants lived here, making this one of the most complete examples of African-American urban life of the period. ✉ *48 Elizabeth St.,* ☎ *843/723–1159.* ✄ *$7; combination ticket with Nathaniel Russell House (☞ below) $12; with Nathaniel Russell House and the Old Powder Magazine (☞ below) $14.*

The heart of Charleston is the **Old City Market,** between Meeting and East Bay streets, with restaurants, shops, and produce stands. Here you can buy vegetables, fruits, benne-seed (sesame) wafers, sweet-grass baskets, jewelry, seashells, and other craft items.

The **Old Powder Magazine,** on one of Charleston's few remaining cobblestone thoroughfares, was built in 1713 and used during the Revolutionary War. It is now a museum with a fascinating audiovisual tour, costumes, armor, and other artifacts from 18th-century Charleston. ✉ *79 Cumberland St.,* ☎ *843/805–6730.* ✄ *$7; combination ticket with*

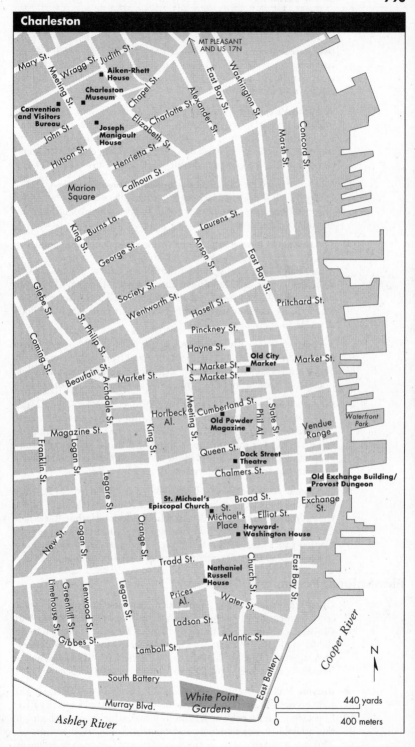

Charleston

Mary St.

Meeting St.

Wragg St.

Judith St.

Aiken-Rhett House

Charleston Museum

Chapel St.

Charlotte St.

Elizabeth St.

Alexander St.

East Bay St.

Washington St.

MT PLEASANT AND US 17N

Convention and Visitors Bureau

John St.

Joseph Manigault House

Hutson St.

Henrietta St.

Calhoun St.

Marsh St.

Concord St.

Marion Square

King St.

Burns La.

George St.

Laurens St.

Anson St.

East Bay St.

Pritchard St.

Glebe St.

Coming St.

St. Philip St.

Society St.

Wentworth St.

Hasell St.

Pinckney St.

Hayne St.

Market St.

Beautain St.

Archdale St.

Market St.

N. Market St.

S. Market St.

Old City Market

Market St.

Franklin St.

Magazine St.

Logan St.

King St.

Horlbeck Al.

Meeting St.

Cumberland St.

Old Powder Magazine

State St.

Phil Al.

Vendue Range

Waterfront Park

Queen St.

Dock Street Theatre

Chalmers St.

Old Exchange Building/ Provost Dungeon

Legare St.

Orange St.

St. Michael's Episcopal Church

St. Michael's Place

Broad St.

Elliot St.

Exchange St.

New St.

Logan St.

Heyward-Washington House

Tradd St.

Nathaniel Russell House

Prices Al.

Water St.

Church St.

East Bay St.

Greenhill St.

Lenwood St.

Legare St.

Ladson St.

Atlantic St.

Limehouse St.

Gibbes St.

Lamboll St.

South Battery

White Point Gardens

East Battery

Cooper River

Murray Blvd.

Ashley River

N

0   440 yards

0   400 meters

Aiken-Rhett House (☞ above) $12; with Aiken-Rhett House and Nathaniel Russell House (☞ below) $14.

Dock Street Theatre (✉ 135 Church St., ☎ 843/720–3968; 🎫 free) combines the reconstructed early Georgian playhouse that originally stood on the site with the 1809 Planter's Hotel to form one theater; call for tour information.

St. Michael's Episcopal Church (✉ 14 St. Michael's Alley, ☎ 843/723–0603; 🎫 free), modeled on London's St. Martin's-in-the-Fields, stands at the corner of Meeting and Broad streets. Completed in 1761, this beautiful structure is Charleston's oldest surviving church. Its steeple clock and bells were imported from England in 1764.

🕲 The British used the **Old Exchange Building/Provost Dungeon** (✉ 122 E. Bay St., ☎ 843/727–2165; 🎫 $6), originally a customs house, for prisoners during the Revolutionary War. Today a tableau of lifelike mannequins recalls this era.

★ The **Nathaniel Russell House,** one of the nation's finest examples of Federal architecture, was built in 1808. The interior is notable for its ornate detailing, its lavish period furnishings, and a "flying" circular staircase that spirals three stories with no apparent support. ✉ *51 Meeting St.,* ☎ *843/724–8481.* 🎫 *$8; combination ticket with Aiken–Rhett House (☞ above) $12; with Aiken-Rhett House and Old Powder Magazine (☞ above) $14.*

Across the Cooper River bridges, via U.S. 17N, is the town of **Mount Pleasant,** named for a plantation in England from which some of the area's settlers hailed. In its Old Village neighborhood are antebellum homes and a sleepy, old-time town center with shops and cafés.

🕲 **Patriot's Point** (✉ foot of Cooper River bridges, ☎ 843/884–2727; 🎫 $11) is the world's largest naval and maritime museum and home to the Medal of Honor Society. Berthed here are the aircraft carrier *Yorktown,* the nuclear ship *Savannah,* the World War II submarine *Clamagore,* the cutter *Ingham,* and the destroyer *Laffey.* Tours, included in the admission price, are offered on all vessels.

★ **Fort Sumter National Monument** (☎ 843/722–1691; 🎫 ferry $11), which can be reached from either Charleston's Municipal Marina or Patriot's Point, is on a man-made island in Charleston Harbor. It was here that the first shot of the Civil War was fired, on April 12, 1861, by Confederate forces. National Park Service rangers conduct free tours of the restored structure, which includes a historical museum.

Plantations, Parks, and Gardens

Charleston is famous for public parks, magnificent plantations, and secret gardens that lie behind the walls of private homes. **White Point Gardens,** on the point of the narrow Battery Peninsula bounded by the Ashley and Cooper rivers, is a popular gathering spot. **Waterfront Park,** along Concord Street on the Cooper River, has a fishing pier, unique interactive fountains, a picnic area, and landscaped gardens.

★ **Drayton Hall** (✉ 3390 Ashley River Rd., ☎ 843/766–0188, 🎫 $8), built between 1738 and 1742, is the only plantation on the Ashley River that survived the Civil War. It is unfurnished, which serves to highlight the original plaster moldings and opulent hand-carved woodwork. This is considered one of the finest examples of Georgian Palladian architecture.

★ **Magnolia Plantation and Gardens** (✉ Ashley River Rd. [Rte. 61], 2 mi beyond Drayton Hall, ☎ 843/571–1266 or 800/367–3517, 🎫

$11, house tour $6 extra, tram tour $5 extra, swamp tour $5 extra) was begun in 1865. Its gardens hold one of the largest collections of azaleas and camellias in North America. Nature lovers can canoe through the 125-acre Waterfowl Refuge, see the 60-acre Audubon Swamp Garden along boardwalks and bridges, explore 500 acres of wildlife trails, and visit the petting zoo.

Middleton Place (⊠ Ashley River Rd. [Rte. 61], 4 mi north of Magnolia Plantation, ☎ 843/556–6020 or 800/782–3608; ☜ $15, house tour $8 extra) has the nation's oldest landscaped gardens, dating from 1741. Much of the mansion was destroyed during the Civil War, but a restored wing houses impressive silver, furniture, paintings, and historical documents. Children will enjoy the lively stableyards.

An avenue of oaks leads to **Boone Hall Plantation** (⊠ 1253 Long Point Rd., Mt. Pleasant, ☎ 843/884–4371; ☜ $12.50), which is said to have been the inspiration for Tara in the film *Gone With the Wind*. You can explore the gardens, the first floor of the mansion, and the original slave quarters. Lunch is served in the old cotton-gin building.

Charles Towne Landing State Park (⊠ Rte. 171, ☎ 843/852–4200; ☜ $5), across the Ashley River Bridge, is built on the site of a 1670 settlement. It includes a reconstructed village and fortifications, a replica of a 17th-century sailing vessel, gardens with bike trails and walking paths, and an animal park.

Cypress Gardens (⊠ 24 mi north of Charleston via U.S. 52, ☎ 843/553–0515; ☜ $7) was created from a swamp that was once the freshwater reserve of a vast rice plantation. You can explore the inky waters by boat or walk along paths lined with moss-draped cypress trees and flowering bushes.

Dining

Best known for Low Country specialties like she-crab soup, sautéed shrimp, grits, and pecan pie, Charleston is also famous for contemporary cookery blending down-home cooking with haute cuisine.

$$$$ ✕ **Woodlands Inn.** Residents regularly make the 30-mi drive from
★ Charleston for superb meals at this luxury inn's restaurant. Delicate sauces and subtle touches are key in entrées such as Angus beef with celery-root home fries and Barolo-wine reduction. There are multicourse tasting menus with wine. ⊠ *125 Parsons Rd., Summerville, ☎ 843/875–2600 or 800/774–9999. AE, D, DC, MC, V.*

$$$–$$$$ ✕ **McCrady's.** With a new menu and a sleek new bar area and dining room, this revamped restaurant, in a 1778 tavern, has locals raving over its potato gnocchi, grouper with creamy leek sauce and truffle oil, herb-marinated rack of lamb with mint drizzle, and molten chocolate cake. ⊠ *2 Unity Alley, ☎ 843/577–0025. AE, MC, V.*

$$–$$$$ ✕ **Peninsula Grill.** Surrounded by olive-green wall coverings, black iron
★ chandeliers, and 18th-century-style portraits, diners at this sophisticated restaurant in the Planters Inn feast on such delights as lobster martini, wild mushroom grits with oysters, and New Zealand benne-seed-encrusted rack of lamb. For dessert, try the lemon tart with lemon sorbet. ⊠ *112 N. Market St., ☎ 843/723–0700. AE, D, DC, MC, V.*

$$–$$$$ ✕ **Slightly North of Broad.** This whimsical eatery has several seats that overlook the action-packed kitchen. Low Country cuisine is given trendy treatment here: Try the shiitake mushroom filled with foie gras mousse or the grilled, barbecued tuna. ⊠ *192 E. Bay St., ☎ 843/723–3424. Reservations not accepted. AE, D, DC, MC, V.*

$–$$$$ ✕ **Carolina's.** Always bustling, Carolina's has black-and-white bistro decor that includes terra-cotta tiles and 1920s French posters. Fans return for the pasta with crawfish and *tasso* (spiced ham) in a spicy cream sauce, crab wontons, and pecan brittle basket with fruit and ice cream. ✉ *10 Exchange St.,* ☎ *843/724–3800. AE, MC, V. No lunch.*

$$–$$$ ✕ **Magnolias.** Housed in an 1823 warehouse and decorated in a mag-
★ nolia theme, this self-designated "uptown/down South" restaurant is prized for its Low Country fare, including shrimp and sausage over creamy grits, down-South egg roll with collard greens and tasso, and fried chicken gumbo. ✉ *185 E. Bay St.,* ☎ *843/577–7771. AE, MC, V.*

$$–$$$ ✕ **Sermet's Corner.** Chef Sermet Aslan is also an artist whose colorful and bold work decorates the walls of this lively eatery. The Mediter-ranean-influenced menu offers great starters, panini sandwiches, seafood, flavorful pastas, and a lovely lavender-scented pork tender-loin. ✉ *276 King St.,* ☎ *843/853–7775. AE, MC, V.*

$–$$ ✕ **Gaulart and Maliclet French Café.** Chic and upbeat, this café serves
★ ethnic and bistro French food. The menu of soups, salads, and sand-wiches is enlivened by such evening specials as seafood Normandy and chicken sesame. "G & M" is open throughout the day. ✉ *98 Broad St.,* ☎ *843/577–9797. AE, DC, MC, V.*

$–$$ ✕ **The Wreck.** Full of wacky character, this dockside spot serves up tra-ditional dishes like boiled peanuts, fried shrimp, shrimp pilaf, deviled crab, and oyster platters in a shabby, candlelit, screened-in porch and small dining area. ✉ *106 Haddrell St., Mount Pleasant,* ☎ *843/884–0052. Reservations not accepted. No credit cards. No lunch.*

$ ✕ **Alice's Fine Foods.** The food Southerners crave is here in its origi-
★ nal, beloved form: Baked or fried chicken, ribs, fried fish, or other en-trées come with a choice of three vegetables, including green beans, collard greens, okra and tomatoes, lima beans, yams, and squash. ✉ *468–470 King St.,* ☎ *843/853–9366. MC, V.*

Lodging

Hotels and inns on the peninsula are generally more expensive than those in outlying areas of the city. Rates tend to increase during festi-vals, when reservations are essential, and on weekends. From Decem-ber 1 to March 1 some rates drop by as much as 50%. Nearby world-class accommodations include the Kiawah Island, Wild Dunes, and Seabrook Island resorts. Bed-and-breakfast reservation services in-clude **Historic Charleston B&B** (✉ 60 Broad St., 29401, ☎ 843/722–6606 or 800/743–3583), **Southern Hospitality B&B Reservations** (✉ 110 Amelia Dr., Lexington 29464, ☎ 843/356–6238 or 800/374–7422), and **RSVP Reservation Service** (✉ 9489 Whitefield Ave., Box 49, Savannah, GA 31406, ☎ 800/729–7787).

$$$$ 🏨 **Charleston Place.** This graceful, luxurious hotel, an Orient-Express
★ property, has rooms with period reproductions, French bed linens, and fax machines. It's near upscale shops in the historic district. The Charleston Grill, with its mahogany-paneled walls, provides an elegant dining experience. ✉ *130 Market St., 29401,* ☎ *843/722–4900 or 800/611–5545,* FAX *843/724–7215. 440 rooms. 2 restaurants, pool, exer-cise room. AE, D, DC, MC, V.* 🕸

$$$$ 🏨 **John Rutledge House Inn.** The 1763 main house, built by a signa-
★ tory of the U.S. Constitution, has ornate ironwork on its facade. Two carriage houses (each with four rooms) complete this luxury B&B. Rooms have plaster molding, wood floors, antiques, and four-poster beds. ✉ *116 Broad St., 29401,* ☎ *843/723–7999 or 800/476–9741,* FAX *843/720–2615. 19 rooms. AE, D, DC, MC, V. CP.* 🕸

$$$–$$$$ 🏨 **Governor's House Inn.** The inn, which dates to the mid-18th cen-tury, has opulent parlors, hardwood floors, 12-ft ceilings, nine fireplaces, and 19th-century antiques. Some of the palatial guest rooms have private piazzas; the third-floor "Roofscape" rooms are cozy, with outstanding city views. ⊠ *117 Broad St., 29401,* ☎ *843/720–2070 or 800/ 720–9812. 9 rooms. No credit cards. CP.* ✆

$$$–$$$$ 🏨 **Hayne House Bed and Breakfast.** Trees shade the brick courtyard of the Hayne House, built in 1755, in the now-prestigious South of Broad neighborhood. Rooms are filled with family heirlooms and watercolors by local artists. Four rooms are in the kitchen house, with its narrow stairway, Colonial brickwork, and chimney. ⊠ *30 King St., 29401,* ☎ *843/577–2633,* 𝔽𝔸𝕏 *843/577–5906. 6 rooms. MC, V. BP.* ✆

$$$–$$$$ 🏨 **Kiawah Island Resort.** Choose from inn rooms and one- to five-bedroom villas and private homes in two luxurious resort villages on 10,000 mostly undeveloped acres. Most rooms have an ocean or wooded view. There are 10 mi of fine broad beaches and an array of recreational opportunities. ⊠ *21 mi south of Charleston via U.S. 17; 12 Kiawah Beach Dr., Kiawah Island 29455,* ☎ *843/768–2121 or 800/ 654–2924,* 𝔽𝔸𝕏 *843/768–6099. 150 rooms, 430 villas and homes. 8 restaurants, golf, tennis. AE, D, DC, MC, V.* ✆

$$$ 🏨 **Doubletree Guest Suites Hotel Historic Charleston.** This deluxe hotel at the Old City Market has a restored entrance portico from an 1874 bank, a refurbished 1866 firehouse, and three lush gardens. The spacious suites, decorated with 18th-century reproductions and canopy beds, include full kitchens or wet bars. ⊠ *181 Church St., 29401,* ☎ *843/577–2644 or 800/527–1133,* 𝔽𝔸𝕏 *843/577–2697. 182 rooms. Exercise room. AE, D, DC, MC, V. BP.*

$$$ 🏨 **Francis Marion Hotel.** The largest hotel in the Carolinas when it was
★ built in 1924, this recently restored property retains big-band and tea-dance glamour with its windowed ballrooms, wrought-iron railings, columns, high ceilings, and scenic views of Marion Square and the harbor. A few rooms have original pedestal sinks and deep tubs. ⊠ *387 King St., 29403,* ☎ *843/722–0600,* 𝔽𝔸𝕏 *843/723–4633. 226 rooms. Restaurant, exercise room. AE, D, DC, MC, V.*

$$–$$$ 🏨 **1837 Bed and Breakfast and Tea Room.** Though not as fancy as some of the other B&Bs in town, this inn is long on hospitality; you'll get a sense of what it's really like to live in one of Charleston's beloved homes. Rooms are filled with antiques, including romantic canopy beds. A breakfast of homemade breads and sausage pie or ham frittata is included, as is afternoon tea. ⊠ *126 Wentworth St., 29401,* ☎ *803/723– 7166. 8 rooms. AE, MC, V. BP.*

$$–$$$ 🏨 **Meeting Street Inn.** Originally built as a tavern in 1874, this inn in the historic district overlooks a lovely courtyard with fountains and gardens. Spacious rooms have hardwood floors, high ceilings, and reproductions including four-poster beds. Afternoon refreshments are complimentary. ⊠ *173 Meeting St., 29401,* ☎ *843/723–1882 or 800/842– 8022,* 𝔽𝔸𝕏 *843/577–0851. 56 rooms. AE, D, DC, MC, V. CP.*

Motel

🏨 **Red Roof Inn** (⊠ 301 Johnnie Dodds Blvd., 29464, ☎ 843/884–1411 or 800/843–7663, 𝔽𝔸𝕏 843/971–0726), 126 rooms; pool; *$–$$.*

Nightlife and the Arts

Nightlife

Charlie's Little Bar, above Saracen's Restaurant (⊠ 141 E. Bay St., ☎ 843/723–6242), is a cozy, popular cocktail spot. **Lowcountry Legends Music Hall** (⊠ 30 Cumberland St., ☎ 843/722–1829 or 800/348– 7270) is Charleston's Preservation Hall, serving up music, legends, and folktales unique to the region. Favored by an elegant, older crowd, the **Mills House Hotel** (⊠ 115 Meeting St., ☎ 843/577–2400) has a hopping bar and live big band–swing music on Tuesdays. The **Music Farm**

(✉ 32 Ann St., ☎ 843/853–3276) features live national and local alternative bands. **Mitchell's** (✉ 102 N. Market St., ☎ 843/722–7032) has live music. **Southend Brewery** (✉ 161 E. Bay St., ☎ 843/853–4677) has a lively bar with beer brewed on the premises. You can dine and dance on the yacht *Spirit of Carolina* (☎ 843/722–2628; board at Patriot's Point). Try **Trio Lounge** (✉ 139 Calhoun St., ☎ 843/965–5333) for big-band or dance music Wednesday through Saturday. **Vickery's Bar & Grill** (✉ 15 Beaufain St., ☎ 843/577–5300) is a festive nightspot with a spacious outdoor patio. **Windjammer** (✉ 1000 Ocean Blvd., ☎ 843/886–8596), on the Isle of Palms, is an oceanfront spot with live rock music.

The Arts

Spoleto Festival USA (☞ Festivals and Seasonal Events *in* the United States Region by Region chapter), a world-class annual celebration, showcases opera, dance, theater, symphonic and chamber music, jazz, and the visual arts in late spring. **Piccolo Spoleto Festival** (☎ 843/724–7305) is the spirited companion festival of Spoleto Festival USA, with the best in local and regional talent from every artistic discipline. Most performances are free. The **Charleston Symphony Orchestra** (☎ 843/723–7528) presents a variety of series at Gaillard Municipal Auditorium (✉ 77 Calhoun St., ☎ 843/577–4500), and chamber and pops series elsewhere.

Outdoor Activities and Sports

Golf

For a listing of area golf packages, contact the Charleston Area Convention and Visitors Bureau (☞ Visitor Information, *above*). Nonguests may play on a space-availability basis at **private island resorts** such as **Kiawah Island** (☎ 843/768–2121), Seabrook Island (☎ 843/768–2529), and **Wild Dunes** (☎ 843/886–2180) on the Isle of Palms. The prestigious Pete Dye–designed **Ocean Course at Kiawah Island** (☎ 843/768–7272) was the site of the 1991 Ryder Cup.

Top public courses in the area include **Charleston Municipal** (✉ 2110 Maybank Hwy., ☎ 843/795–6517), **Charleston National Country Club** (✉ 1360 National Dr., Mount Pleasant, ☎ 843/884–7799), the **Dunes West Golf Club** (✉ 3535 Wando Plantation Way, Mount Pleasant, ☎ 843/856–9000), **Links at Stono Ferry** (✉ 5365 Forest Oaks Dr., Hollywood, ☎ 843/763–1817), **Oak Point Golf Course** (✉ 4255 Bohicket Rd., Johns Island, ☎ 843/768–7431), **Patriot's Point Links** (✉ 1 Patriots Point Rd., Mount Pleasant, ☎ 843/881–0042), and **Shadowmoss Golf Club** (✉ 20 Dunvegan Dr., Charleston, ☎ 843/556–8251).

Beaches

South Carolina's climate allows swimming from April through October. There are **public beaches** at Beachwalker Park on Kiawah Island; Folly Beach County Park and Folly Beach on Folly Island; the Isle of Palms; and Sullivan's Island. Resorts with private beaches include Fairfield Ocean Ridge on Edisto Island; Kiawah Island Resort (☞ Lodging, *above*); Seabrook Island; and Wild Dunes Resort on the Isle of Palms. For more information contact the Charleston Area Convention and Visitors Bureau (☞ Visitor Information, *above*).

Shopping

The three-block **Old City Market** (☞ Exploring Charleston, *above*) yields colorful produce and varied gifts, including the sweet-grass baskets unique to this area. The craft, originally introduced by West Africans brought here as slaves, is now practiced by only a handful of their descendants. The baskets are priced from $15 to more than $200. The **Shops at Charleston Place** (⊠ 130 Market St., ☎ 843/722–4900), in the historic district, includes Gucci, Brookstone, and Crabtree & Evelyn. **King Street** is lined with both small boutiques and popular national stores including Banana Republic, Gap, Ann Taylor, and Abercrombie & Finch. There is a small but pleasant **Saks Fifth Avenue** (⊠ 211 King St., ☎ 843/853–9888). The **Rainbow Market** (⊠ 40 N. Market St., ☎ 843/577–0380) is in two interconnected 150-year-old buildings. **Olde Colony Bakery** (⊠ 280 King St., ☎ 843/722–2147) sells Charleston's famed benne-seed wafers.

Elegant antiques shops line the lower part of King Street. **Geo. C. Birlant & Co.** (⊠ 191 King St., ☎ 843/722–3842) has 18th- and 19th-century English selections and the famous Charleston Battery bench. **Livingston and Sons Antiques** (⊠ 163 King St., ☎ 843/723–9697; 2137 Savannah Hwy., ☎ 843/556–6162) sells period furniture, clocks, and other items. At **Historic Charleston Reproductions** (⊠ 105 Broad St., ☎ 843/723–8292), you can find superb replicas of Charleston furniture and accessories approved by the Historic Charleston Foundation. Royalties from sales contribute to restoration projects.

Among the town's chic art galleries is the **Marty Whaley Adams Gallery** (⊠ 2 Queen St., ☎ 843/853–8512), which carries original watercolors and monotypes plus prints and posters by this Charleston artist. **Charleston Crafts** (⊠ 87 Hasell St., ☎ 843/723–2938) has a fine selection of pottery, weavings, sculptures, and jewelry fashioned by local artists. **Charleston Gardens** (⊠ 61 Queen St., ☎ 843/723–0252) has lovely garden ornamentations and home accessories, including Charleston-style iron gates and contemporary lighting. The **Elizabeth O'Neill Verner Studio & Museum** (⊠ 79 Church St., ☎ 843/722–4246), in a 17th-century house, is open to the public. Prints of Elizabeth O'Neill Verner's pastels and etchings are on sale at the adjacent **Tradd Street Press** (⊠ 38 Tradd St., ☎ 843/722–4246). **Reflections South** (⊠ 125 Meeting St., ☎ 843/577–9351) sells original paintings and limited-edition lithographs of Charleston scenes.

THE COAST

The South Carolina coast is a land of extremes, from glitzy to gracious. The Grand Strand, from the state's northeastern border to historic Georgetown, is one of the East Coast's family-vacation megacenters and the state's top tourist area. Here you'll find 60 mi of white-sand beaches, championship golf courses, campgrounds, seafood restaurants, malls and factory outlets, and, at last count, nearly a dozen live-entertainment theaters with everything from country-and-western music to magic acts. The Low Country is the area between Georgetown and the state's southeastern boundary, including Beaufort, as well as the barrier islands of Hilton Head, Edisto, and Fripp. Beaufort is a charming antebellum town with a compact historic district of lavish 18th- and 19th-century homes. Hilton Head's exclusive resorts and genteel good life make it one of the coast's most popular vacation getaways.

Visitor Information

Beaufort: Chamber of Commerce (⊠ 1006 Bay St., Box 910, 29901-0910, ☎ 843/524–3163). **Georgetown:** Chamber of Commerce and Information Center (⊠ 102 Broad St., Box 1776, 29442, ☎ 843/546–8436 or 800/777–7705). **Hilton Head Island:** Chamber of Commerce (⊠ Box 5647, 29938, ☎ 843/785–3673). **Myrtle Beach:** Area Chamber of Commerce and Information Center (✉ 1200 N. Oak St., Box 2115, 29578-2115, ☎ 843/626–7444; 800/356–3016 ext. 136 for brochures). **Pawleys Island:** Pawleys Island Chamber of Commerce (✉ U.S. 17, Box 569, 29585, ☎ 843/237–1921).

Arriving and Departing

By Boat

The South Carolina coast is accessible by boat via the Intracoastal Waterway. At **Myrtle Beach** you may dock at **Hague Marina** (✉ 1 Hague Dr., ☎ 843/293–2141), **HarbourGate** (✉ 1 Harper Place, ☎ 843/249–8888), and **Marlin Quay** (✉ 1398 S. Waccamaw Dr., ☎ 843/651–4444). **Hilton Head** has several marinas, including **Shelter Cove Marina** (✉ 1 Shelter Cove La., ☎ 843/842–7002), **Harbour Town Yacht Basin** (✉ 149 Lighthouse Rd., ☎ 843/671–2704), and **Schilling Boathouse** (✉ 405 Squire Pope Rd., ☎ 843/681–2628).

By Bus

Greyhound (☎ 800/231–2222) serves Myrtle Beach and Beaufort.

By Car

Major interstates connect with U.S. 17, the principal north–south coastal route. Hilton Head Island has a 6-mi-long toll bridge, the Cross Island Parkway, that leads to the south end of the island, where most of the resorts and attractions are located (toll $1).

By Plane

The **Myrtle Beach International Airport** (1100 Jetport Blvd., ☎ 843/448–1589) is served by Air Canada, Air Tran, ASA/Delta/Comair, Continental, Midway/Corporate, Spirit, US Airways, and Vanguard. **Hilton Head Island Airport** (✉ 120 Beach City Rd., ☎ 843/689–5400) is served by US Air Express and Continental. **Savannah International Airport** (☞ Savannah *in* Georgia) is about an hour's drive from Hilton Head.

By Train

Amtrak (☎ 800/872–7245) does not make stops in this area, although several of its stops are within driving distance: Florence is about 70 mi northwest of the Grand Strand; Yemassee, about 22 mi northwest of Beaufort; and Savannah, about 40 mi southwest of Hilton Head.

Exploring the Coast

With its high-rise beachfront hotels, nightlife, and amusement parks, **Myrtle Beach** is the hub of the Grand Strand. Downtown Myrtle Beach has a festive look, with its T-shirt shops, ice cream parlors, and amusement venues, including the **Myrtle Beach Pavilion and Amusement Park** (✉ 9th Ave. N and Ocean Blvd., ☎ 843/448–6456; ⌨ fees for individual attractions; $23.60 one-day pass for unlimited access to most rides), **Ripleys Believe It or Not Museum** (✉ 901 N. Ocean Blvd., ☎ 843/448–2331; ⌨ $8.95), and the **Myrtle Beach National Wax Museum** (✉ 1000 N. Ocean Blvd., ☎ 843/448–9921; ⌨ $5). **Ripley's Aquarium** (✉ 9th Ave. N and U.S. 17N Bypass, ☎ 843/916–0888 or 800/734–8888; ⌨ $13.95) has touch tanks, an underwater tunnel exhibit longer than a football field, and exotic marine creatures from poisonous lionfish to moray eels and an octopus.

Myrtle Beach is the minigolf capital of the world, with courses that mimic Jurassic Park and Never-Never Land, and **Hawaiian Rumble** (✉ 3210 U.S. 17S, ☎ 843/272–7812; ⌨ $8 all day [9 AM–5 PM], $6 per round after 5 PM) is the crown jewel. The best part of the course is the volcano that erupts fire and rumbles at timed intervals. Another fun course, featuring a fire-breathing dragon, is **Dragon's Lair** (✉ Hwy. 17

at Broadway at the Beach, ☎ 843/444–3215; 🖃 $8.50 all day [10 AM–6 PM], $6.50 per round after 6 PM).

🐾 South of Myrtle Beach, **Wild Water** (✉ 910 U.S. 17S, Surfside, ☎ 843/238–9453; 🖃 $17, $12 after 3 PM) provides splashy family fun for all ages.

Murrells Inlet, south of Myrtle Beach via U.S. 17, is a picturesque fishing village where you'll find fishing charters and some of the most popular seafood restaurants on the Strand.

★ **Brookgreen Gardens** (☎ 843/237–4218 or 800/849–1931, 🖃 $8.50 for 3-day pass), a few miles south of Murrells Inlet off U.S. 17, is set on four former Colonial rice plantations. Begun in 1931, the gardens contain more than 2,000 plant species as well as more than 500 sculptures, including works by Frederic Remington. Several miles down U.S. 17 from Brookgreen Gardens, **Pawleys Island** has weathered old summer cottages nestled in groves of oleander and oak. The famed Pawleys Island hammocks have been made by hand here since 1880.

Georgetown, on the shores of Winyah Bay at the end of the Grand Strand, was founded in 1729 and soon became the center of America's Colonial rice empire. Today you can enjoy its quaint waterfront and historic homes and churches. The **Rice Museum** (✉ Front and Screven Sts., ☎ 843/546–7423; 🖃 $2) traces the history of rice cultivation through maps, tools, and dioramas. It is housed in a graceful structure topped by an 1842 clock and tower.

Beaufort, about 18 mi east of U.S. 17 on U.S. 21 (about 70 mi southeast of Charleston), is a handsome waterfront town. Established in 1710, it achieved prosperity at the end of the 18th century, when Sea Island cotton became a major cash crop. A few lavish houses built by landowners and merchants have been converted into B&Bs or museums; others are open for tours part of the year. The **Arsenal/Beaufort Museum,** housed in an arsenal built in 1795 and remodeled in the Gothic style in 1852, has exhibits on prehistoric relics, Native American pottery, the Revolutionary and Civil wars, and decorative arts. ✉ 713 Craven St., ☎ 843/525–7077. 🖃 $2. Closed Wed. and Sun.

St. Helena Island, 9 mi southeast of Beaufort via U.S. 21, is the site of the **Penn Center Historic District** and **York W. Bailey Museum.** Penn Center (✉ Martin Luther King, Jr. Dr., ☎ 843/838–8563), established in the middle of the Civil War as the South's first school for freed slaves, is now an educational and cultural resource center. The **York W. Bailey Museum** (✉ Land's End Rd., ☎ 843/838–2432; 🖃 donation suggested) has photos and artifacts reflecting the heritage and lifestyles of sea island blacks. These islands are where Gullah, a musical language that combines English and African, developed.

Hilton Head Island, a 42-square-mi semitropical barrier island settled by cotton planters in the 1700s, has developed as a resort destination. Oak and pine woods, lagoons, and a temperate climate provide an incomparable environment for tennis, water sports, and golf. Choice stretches of the island are occupied by resorts, many of which have shops, restaurants, marinas, and several recreational facilities.

Hilton Head is blessed with vast nature preserves, including the **Sea Pines Forest Preserve** (✉ at southwest tip of island, via U.S. 278, ☎ 843/842–1449; 🖃 $3 per car for nonguests), a 605-acre wilderness tract within the Sea Pines Plantation resort. The preserve's most interesting site is the 3,400-year-old Native American shell ring. On 4,000 acres of salt marsh and small islands, **Pinckney Island National Wildlife**

Refuge (⊠ Coastal Discovery Museum, 100 William Hilton Pkwy., ☎ 843/689–6767; 🎫 free) is laced with walking and bike trails.

Dining and Lodging

Freshwater and ocean fish and shellfish reign supreme throughout the region, from family-style restaurants—where they're served with hush puppies and coleslaw—to elegant resorts and upscale restaurants featuring haute cuisine. You can have your choice of hotels, cottages, villas, or high-rise condominiums. Attractive package plans are available between Labor Day and spring break.

Beaufort

$–$$ ✕ **11th Street Dockside Restaurant.** Succulent fried oysters, shrimp and fish, plus other local specialties such as a steamed seafood pot, are available at this classic wharfside spot with a screened porch and water views from nearly every table. ⊠ *11th St. W,* ☎ *843/524–7433. AE, D, DC, MC, V. No lunch.*

$$$ ✕🏨 **Beaufort Inn.** Guest rooms in this 1897 Victorian have pine floors, tasteful floral and plaid fabrics, and comfortable chairs. The inn's superb restaurant serves guests sumptuous complimentary breakfasts and afternoon tea (reservations required); it's open to the public for unique Low Country fare like Parmesan grits and she-crab soup. ⊠ *809 Port Republic St., 29902,* ☎ *843/521–9000,* 𝖥𝖠𝖷 *843/521–9500. 11 rooms. Restaurant. AE, MC, V. BP.* 🐾

$$$–$$$$ 🏨 **Rhett House Inn.** This stately 1820 Greek Revival mansion in the
★ center of town is filled with antiques and reproductions, original artwork, and Oriental rugs. A recently remodeled house across the street expands the inn by six more rooms, each with gas fireplace, whirlpool tub, and private entrance and porch. ⊠ *1009 Craven St., 29902,* ☎ *843/524–9030,* 𝖥𝖠𝖷 *843/524–1310. 16 rooms. AE, MC, V. CP.* 🐾

$$$ 🏨 **Cuthbert House Inn.** This pillared 1790 home overlooks the bay and has original Federal fireplaces. The owners have filled it with 18th- and 19th-century heirlooms; rooms are elegant but cozy, with Oriental rugs on pine floors and handmade quilts on the beds. ⊠ *1203 Bay St., 29902,* ☎ *843/521–1315 or 800/327–9275,* 𝖥𝖠𝖷 *843/521–1314. 8 rooms. AE, D, MC, V. BP.* 🐾

$ 🏨 **Howard Johnson.** This hotel sits on the edge of the marsh a few miles from the historic district. Rooms are spacious and have desks; many have views of the river and marsh. ⊠ *3651 Trask Pkwy. (U.S. 21), 29902,* ☎ *843/524–6020 or 800/528–1234,* 𝖥𝖠𝖷 *843/524–2027. 43 rooms. Pool. AE, D, DC, MC, V. CP.*

Georgetown

$ ✕ **Kudzu Bakery.** Here you'll find the greatest deep-dish pecan pie anywhere and other delectables; you can grab them to go or eat them at the small counter. Other than pies and pastries, there are a few sandwiches on homemade breads, cheeses, and local specialty items. ⊠ *714 Front St.,* ☎ *843/546–1847. MC, V. Closed Wed., Sun. No dinner.*

$$ 🏨 **1790 House.** Built in the center of town after the Revolution, at the peak of Georgetown's rice culture, this restored white Georgian house with a wraparound porch contains Colonial antique and reproduction furnishings. ⊠ *630 Highmarket St., 29440,* ☎ *843/546–4821 or 800/890–7432. 6 rooms. AE, D, MC, V. BP.*

Hilton Head Island

$$–$$$$ ✕ **Old Fort Pub.** Tucked away on a quiet site overlooking the marshlands and beside the Civil War ruins of Fort Mitchell, this restaurant specializes in oyster stew, corn-crusted pork chops, and mesquite-smoked filet mignon with mushroom cabernet sauce. The ambience is publike casual but the service is not. There's a Sunday brunch. ⊠ *65 Skull Creek Dr.,* ☎ *843/681–2386. AE, D, DC, MC, V.*

$$–$$$$ × **Starfire Contemporary Bistro.** Ultrafresh ingredients are served in a
★ pleasingly unique way at this small, hip eatery. Try the wild mushroom soup with roasted rosemary, and salmon with spiced seed crust atop a crunchy cucumber salad. Next door, the more casual Starfire Winebar and Grill offers many wines by the glass, great burgers, and pizza. ⊠ *37 New Orleans Rd.,* ☎ *843/785–3434. AE, DC, MC, V. No lunch.*

$–$$ × **Brick Oven Cafe.** Velvet drapes, massive chandeliers, leather booths,
★ and 1940s lounge-style entertainment plus good, reasonably priced food served late have made this the trendy place to eat. Located just outside the gates of Sea Pines, Brick Oven has pizzas, hamburgers, salads, and pastas as well as a nice selection of wines. ⊠ *Park Plaza,* ☎ *843/ 686–2233. Reservations essential. AE, D, DC, MC, V. No lunch.*

$$$$ ⊞ **Main Street Inn.** Outside it resembles an Italianate villa; inside, rooms have velvet and silk brocade linens, feather duvets, and porcelain and brass sinks. Included in the rate are a European breakfast of cheeses, quiche, and pastries; afternoon tea; and cookies at turndown. ⊠ *2200 Main St., 29926,* ☎ *843/681–3001 or 800/471–3001,* FAX *843/ 681–5541. 34 rooms. Pool. AE, MC, V. CP* ✍

$$$–$$$$ ⊞ **Disney's Hilton Head Island Resort.** The island's newest resort op-
★ tion has Adirondack lodge–country themes carried out in fun detail. More than 100 villas (from studios to three bedrooms, four baths with sleeping accommodations for up to 12) have fully furnished kitchen, dining, living, sleeping, and porch areas; all have marsh or marina views. About a mile away, the resort's 13,000-square-ft beach house has a fireplace in the living room, a heated pool, and an arcade. ⊠ *22 Harbourside La., 29928,* ☎ *843/341–4100 or 800/453–4911,* FAX *843/341– 4130. 102 units. Restaurant, pool. AE, MC, V.*

$$$–$$$$ ⊞ **Hilton Resort.** The Hilton, on the Palmetto Dunes Resort, has spacious oceanfront rooms with kitchenettes and a colorful Caribbean motif. ⊠ *23 Ocean La., 29928,* ☎ *843/842–8000 or 800/845–8001,* FAX *843/842–4988. 323 rooms. Restaurant, pool. AE, D, DC, MC, V.* ✍

$$$–$$$$ ⊞ **Westin Resort, Hilton Head Island.** One of the island's most luxu-
★ rious properties, this sprawling hotel has a lushly landscaped oceanfront setting. Guest rooms have down pillows, warm colors, and comfortable wicker and contemporary furniture. For dinner, try the resort's Barony Grill Restaurant. ⊠ *2 Grass Lawn Ave., 29928,* ☎ *843/ 681–4000 or 800/228–3000,* FAX *843/681–1087. 450 rooms. 3 restaurants, pool, health club. AE, D, DC, MC, V.* ✍

MOTEL
⊞ **Red Roof Inn** (⊠ 5 Regency Pkwy., 29928, ☎ 843/686–6808 or 800/ 843–7663, FAX 843/842–3352), 112 rooms; pool; *$–$$.*

Myrtle Beach

$$–$$$$ × **Collectors Cafe.** A restaurant, art gallery, and coffeehouse rolled into
★ one, this unpretentiously arty spot has bright funky paintings and tile work covering its walls and tabletops. You can shop for a painting while enjoying the scallop cake, veal-stuffed ravioli, or tuna with black bean sauce and mango salsa. ⊠ *7726 N. Kings Hwy.,* ☎ *843/449–9370. AE, D, DC, MC, V. Closed Sun. No lunch.*

$$–$$$ × **Villa Katrina's Underground Cantina.** Head downstairs into a fun, tavernlike space for Mexican fare of the elegant variety, including flaming coffees and desserts. Lunch is festive, too. ⊠ *821 Main St.,* ☎ *843/946–6216. AE, D, MC, V. Closed Sun.*

$$ × **Sea Captain's House.** This picturesque restaurant with nautical decor and a fireplace has sweeping ocean views. Home-baked breads and desserts accompany Low Country fare. ⊠ *3002 N. Ocean Blvd.,* ☎ *843/448–8082. AE, D, MC, V.*

$-$$ ✕ **Croissants Bakery & Cafe.** The lunch crowd loves this spot, which has an on-site bakery. Try the chicken or broccoli salad, the Monte Cristo sandwich, and the peanut butter cheesecake. ✉ *504 A 27th. Ave. N,* ☎ *843/448–2253. D, MC, V. Closed Sun. No dinner.*

$$$–$$$$ 🏨 **Kingston Plantation—Embassy Suites.** Set amid 145 acres of oceanside woodlands, this resort—the nicest in town—includes a 20-story hotel, restaurants, and one- to four-bedroom condos. Guest rooms in the oceanfront inn have VCRs, Nintendo Game Boys, and kitchenettes. ✉ *9800 Lake Dr., 29572,* ☎ *843/449–0006 or 800/876–0010,* 🖷 *843/ 497–1110. 255 suites, 510 condos. 2 restaurants, pools, tennis, health club. AE, D, DC, MC, V.* ✍

$$$ 🏨 **Breakers Resort Hotel.** The Breakers is one of the better values along the Grand Strand. There are 24 types of rooms—the suites with kitchenettes are ideal for families. All the major attractions are within walking distance. ✉ *2006 N. Ocean Blvd., Box 485, 29578-0485,* ☎ *843/444–4444 or 800/845–0688,* 🖷 *843/626–5001. 390 rooms. Restaurant, pools, exercise room. AE, D, DC, MC, V.*

MOTELS

🏨 **Red Roof Inn** (✉ 2801 S. Kings Hwy., 29577, ☎ 843/626–4444 or 800/843–7663, 🖷 843/626–0753), 166 rooms; pool; $$.

🏨 **Days Inn at Waccamaw** (✉ 3650 U.S. 501, 29577, ☎ 843/236–1950 or 800/325–2525, 🖷 843/236–9415), 160 rooms; restaurant, pool; $–$$.

Pawleys Island

$-$$ ✕ **Island Country Store.** This little restaurant has terrific crab cakes plus hickory-smoked barbecue, roast chicken, and pizza (and they deliver). Summer nights, the tiki torches blaze outside and live music rocks the place. ✉ *The Island Shops, U.S. 17,* ☎ *843/237–8465. AE, MC, V.*

$$$ ✕🏨 **Pelican Inn.** This unusual inn, with the beach out back and creek out front, gives you a look at how families have idled away the summer at Pawleys for years. Rooms are no-fuss beachy (some share baths) with hardwood floors and throw rugs. There's no air-conditioning, but with the breezes and ceiling fans you'll barely miss it. Rates include two big family-style meals: full breakfast and a midday "dinner." ✉ *500 Myrtle Ave., Box 154, 29585,* ☎ *843/237–2295 or 843/288–8255. 6 rooms. Restaurant. No credit cards. Closed Nov.–Mar. MAP.*

$$–$$$$ 🏨 **Litchfield Beach and Golf Resort.** A diverse range of rentals, from condos to villas, are within the resort's expansive grounds, which also include three private golf clubs. The beach is a short walk away. The resort also includes the beachfront, 140-room Litchfield Inn, with standard motel-style rooms. ✉ *U.S. 17, 2 mi north of Pawleys Island, Drawer 320, 29585,* ☎ *843/237–3000 or 800/845–1897,* 🖷 *843/237–4282. 236 rooms; 254 condominiums, cottages, and villas. Restaurant, pools, golf, tennis, health club. AE, D, DC, MC, V.* ✍

Nightlife and the Arts

Nightlife

Country-and-western shows are popular along the Grand Strand, which is fast emerging as the eastern focus of country-music culture. Music lovers have several venues to choose from, including the 2,250-seat **Alabama Theater** (✉ at Barefoot Landing, 4750 U.S. 17, North Myrtle Beach, ☎ 843/272–1111 or 800/342–2262); **Carolina Opry** (✉ 82nd Ave. N, Myrtle Beach, ☎ 843/238–8888 or 800/843–6779); **Dolly Parton's Dixie Stampede** (✉ 8901-B U.S. 17 Business, next door to Carolina Opry, Myrtle Beach, ☎ 843/497–9700 or 800/433–4401); and **Legends in Concert** (✉ 301 U.S. 17 Business, Surfside Beach, ☎ 843/238–7827 or 800/843–6779). The **House of Blues** (✉ 4640 U.S.

17S, N. Myrtle Beach, ☎ 843/272–3000), adjacent to Barefoot Landing, presents blues, rock, jazz, and country on stages in its restaurant and in its concert hall; there's a gospel brunch on Sundays.

Shagging (the state dance) is popular at **Duck's** (⊠ 229 Main St., North Myrtle Beach, ☎ 843/249–3858). You can also try the shag at **Studebaker's** (⊠ U.S. 17 at 21st Ave. N, Myrtle Beach, ☎ 843/626–3855 or 843/448–9747). At **Broadway at the Beach** (⊠ U.S. 17 Bypass between 21st and 24th Sts., North Myrtle Beach, ☎ 843/444–3200) you'll find an assortment of bars and nightclubs, including Hard Rock Cafe, Planet Hollywood, and the NASCAR Cafe. Locals looking for great blues music along with a great wine list hit **Gypsy's** (⊠ 501 8th Ave. N, Myrtle Beach, ☎ 843/916–2244).

Hilton Head's hotels and resorts stage a variety of musical entertainment. **Monkey Business** (⊠ Park Plaza, ☎ 843/686–3545) is a dance nightclub in Hilton Head. Try the **Blue Nite** (⊠ 4 Target Rd., ☎ 843/842–6683) for live music or **Hilton Head Brewing Co.** (⊠ Hilton Head Plaza, ☎ 843/785–2739) for late-night discoing every Wednesday. In Beaufort, **Bananas** (⊠ 910 Bay St., ☎ 843/522–0910) and **Plum's** (⊠ 904½ Bay St., ☎ 843/525–1946) have live bands on the weekends.

The Arts

Festivals in Myrtle Beach include the Canadian/American Days Festival in March, the Sun Fun Festival (☞ Festivals and Seasonal Events *in* the United States Region-by-Region Chapter) in early June, and the Atalaya Arts Festival in fall. At Art in the Park, held in Myrtle Beach's Chapin Park three times each summer, you can buy handmade crafts and original artwork by local artists.

Hilton Head's **Self Family Arts Center** (⊠ Shelter Cove La., ☎ 843/842–2787) has an art gallery, a theater, and a theater program for kids. During the warmer months there are free **outdoor concerts** at Harbour Town and Shelter Cove in Hilton Head.

Outdoor Activities and Sports

Biking

Pedaling is popular along the beaches and pathways of **Hilton Head Island.** Rentals are available at most hotels and resorts and at such shops as **Harbour Town Bicycles** (⊠ Heritage Plaza, ☎ 843/785–3546) and **South Beach Cycles** (⊠ Sea Pines Plantation, ☎ 843/671–2453).

Fishing

Fishing is usually good from early spring through December. Licenses, required for fresh- and saltwater fishing from a private boat, can be purchased at local tackle shops. The **Grand Strand** has several piers and jetties, and fishing and sightseeing excursions depart from Murrells Inlet, North Myrtle Beach, Little River, and the Intracoastal Waterway at Route 544. Fishing tournaments are popular. On **Hilton Head** you can fish, pick oysters, dig for clams, or cast for shrimp.

Golf

The **Grand Strand** has 100 golf courses, most of them public and many of championship quality. **Myrtle Beach Golf Holiday** (☎ 843/448–5942 or 800/845–4653) offers package plans throughout the year; most area hotels have golf packages, too. **Tee Times Central** (☎ 800/344–5590) books for several area courses in Myrtle Beach. Some of **Hilton Head**'s 29 courses are among the world's best; several are open to the public, including **Palmetto Dunes** (⊠ 7 Trent Jones La., ☎ 843/785–1138), **Sea Pines** (☎ 843/842–8484), and **Port Royal** (⊠ 10A Grass-lawn Ave., ☎ 843/689–5600). Sea Pines' Harbour Town Golf Links hosts the annual **MCI Classic** in April (☎ 843/671–2448).

Horseback Riding

On Hilton Head trails wind through woods; horses can be rented at Sea Pines' **Lawton Stables** (☎ 843/671–2586).

Tennis

There are more than 200 courts throughout the **Grand Strand,** including free municipal courts in Myrtle Beach, North Myrtle Beach, and Surfside Beach. **Hilton Head** has more than 300 courts; four resorts on the island—Sea Pines, Shipyard Plantation, Palmetto Dunes, and Port Royal—are rated among the top 50 tennis destinations in the United States.

Water Sports

In Myrtle Beach surfboards, Hobie Cats, Jet Skis, Windsurfers, and sailboats are for rent at **Downwind Sails** (✉ Ocean Blvd. at 29th Ave. S, ☎ 843/448–7245). On Hilton Head you can take windsurfing or kayaking lessons and rent equipment from **Outside Hilton Head** at either **Sea Pines Resort's South Beach Marina** (☎ 843/671–2643) or **Shelter Cove Plaza** (☎ 843/686–6996).

Beaches

Almost all **Grand Strand** beaches are open to the public. The widest expanses are in North Myrtle Beach. The ocean side of **Hilton Head Island** is a 12-mi stretch of gently sloping white sand. Although resort beaches on Hilton Head are reserved for guests and residents, there are about 35 public-beach entrances, from Folly Field to South Forest Beach near Sea Pines.

Shopping

The **Grand Strand** is a great place to find bargains. **Waccamaw Pottery and Factory Shoppes** (✉ U.S. 501 at the Waterway, Myrtle Beach, ☎ 843/236–6152) is a large outlet center including Gap, Nike, and Off Saks 5th Ave stores. In North Myrtle Beach shoppers head for the **Myrtle Beach Factory Stores** (✉ Hwy. 501 and Waccamaw Pines Dr., ☎ 843/903–1614) for Brooks Brothers, Donna Karan, and Eddie Bauer stores. The **Hammock Shops at Pawleys Island** (✉ U.S. 17, ☎ 843/237–8448) sell the famous handmade hammocks; there are about a dozen boutiques and restaurants, too. Hilton Head specialty shops include **Red Piano Art Gallery** (✉ 220 Cordillo Pkwy., ☎ 843/785–2318) and, for shell and sand-dollar jewelry, the **Bird's Nest** (✉ Coligny Plaza, off Coligny Circle, ☎ 843/785–3737). **Hilton Head Factory Stores I and II** (✉ U.S. 278 at the island gateway, ☎ 843/837–4339) have more than 80 outlets, including London Fog, J. Crew, and the Gap. On St. Helena Island near Beaufort, the **Red Piano Too Art Gallery** (✉ 853 Sea Island Pkwy., ☎ 843/838–2241) is filled with quirky folk and southern art, beads, and pottery.

ELSEWHERE IN SOUTH CAROLINA

Columbia

Visitor Information

Columbia Metropolitan Convention and Visitors Bureau (✉ 1012 Gervais St., Box 15, 29202, ☎ 803/254–0479 or 800/264–4884).

Arriving and Departing

I–20 leads northeast from Georgia to Columbia. I–77 runs south to Columbia, where it terminates. I–26 runs north–south through town.

By Plane

The **Columbia Metropolitan Airport** (✉ 120 Beach City Rd., ☎ 803/822–5000) is served by Delta, US Airways, Continental, and Comair.

What to See and Do

Columbia, founded in 1786 as the capital city, was a center of political, commercial, cultural, and social activity. However, in early 1865, General Sherman invaded South Carolina and incinerated two-thirds of Columbia; only a few homes and public buildings were spared. Today the city is a sprawling blend of modern office blocks, suburban neighborhoods, and the occasional antebellum home. The **State House** (✉ Main and Gervais Sts., ☎ 803/734–2430; ☜ free), built in 1855 from local granite, contains marble and mahogany accents and a replica of Houdon's statue of George Washington. You can still see where Sherman shelled the State House, each hit marked with a bronze star.

The **South Carolina State Museum** (✉ 301 Gervais St., ☎ 803/737–4595; ☜ $4), set in a refurbished textile mill, interprets state history through exhibits on archaeology, fine arts, and scientific and technological accomplishments.

★ ♻ Two miles from the capitol area is **Riverbanks Zoological Park and Botanical Garden** (✉ I–26 at Greystone Blvd., ☎ 803/779–8717; ☜ $6.25), with more than 2,000 animals and birds, some endangered, in natural habitats. Walk along pathways and through landscaped gardens to see sea lions, polar bears, Siberian tigers, and black rhinos. A 70-acre botanical garden on the west bank of the Saluda River includes a forested section with trails past historic ruins and spectacular views.

Dining and Lodging

$$–$$$ ✕ **Motor Supply Co. Bistro.** Dine on cuisine from around the world at this restaurant in the heart of town. Fresh seafood and homemade desserts are among the many offerings. On Sunday there's a brunch, but no lunch. ✉ 920 Gervais St., ☎ 803/256–6687. AE, DC, MC, V.

$–$$$ ✕ **Mangia! Mangia!** Hammered copper and mosaic tiles transform this
★ turn-of-the-20th-century building; a lively outdoor patio has heaters for chilly nights. Try the mussels steamed in wine-garlic sauce, followed by wild mushroom pizza baked in the wood-burning oven or lamb shank roasted in red wine with herbs. ✉ 100 State St., West Columbia, ☎ 803/791–3443. AE, MC, V.

$ ✕ **Maurice Gourmet Barbecue–Piggie Park.** One of the South's best-
★ known barbecue chefs, Maurice Bessinger has a fervent national following for his mustard sauce–based, pit-cooked ham barbecue. He also serves barbecued chicken, ribs, and baked beans. ✉ 1600 Charleston Hwy., ☎ 803/796–0220. D, MC, V.

$$–$$$ 🏨 **Adam's Mark.** Public areas of this downtown hotel have leather armchairs, suspended lights, and brass accents. Guest rooms have period reproduction armoires and desks. Finlay's Restaurant, in a spectacular atrium, serves American fare. ✉ 1200 Hampton St., 29201, ☎ 803/771–7000 or 800/444–2326, ℻ 803/254–2911. 300 rooms. Restaurant, pool, health club. AE, D, DC, MC, V.

$$–$$$ 🏨 **Richland Street B&B.** Relax on the front porch or in the spacious
★ common area of this inn in the heart of Columbia's historic district. Each antiques-furnished room has its own personality. There are afternoon refreshments. ✉ 1425 Richland St., 29201, ☎ 803/779–7001 or 800/779–7011, ℻ 803/765–0370. 8 rooms. AE, MC, V. BP. ✍

$$ 🏨 **Claussen's Inn.** This small hotel, in a converted bakery warehouse in the attractive Five Points neighborhood, is near nightlife and specialty shops. It has an airy lobby with a Mexican tile floor; the rooms, some two stories, are arranged around it. ✉ 2003 Greene St., 29205,

☎ *803/765–0440 or 800/622–3382,* FAX *803/799–7924. 29 rooms. AE, MC, V.*

$ 🏨 **La Quinta Motor Inn.** At this three-story inn on a quiet street near the zoo, the rooms are spacious and well lit, with large working areas. ⊠ *1335 Garner La., 29210,* ☎ *803/798–9590 or 800/531–5900,* FAX *803/731–5574. 122 rooms. Pool. AE, D, DC, MC, V.*

SOUTH DAKOTA

Updated by
Tom Griffith

Capital	Pierre
Population	738,000
Motto	Great Faces, Great Places
State Bird	Chinese ring-necked pheasant
State Flower	Pasqueflower
Postal Abbreviation	SD

Statewide Visitor Information

The **South Dakota Department of Tourism** (⊠ 711 E. Wells Ave., Pierre 57501, ☎ 800/732–5682) dispenses state highway maps and the annual *South Dakota Vacation Guide* free of charge. Call the **Department of Transportation** (☎ 605/773–3571 or 605/773–3536) for maps of road construction in summer and reports on road conditions in winter.

Scenic Drives

The beautiful **Needles Highway** (Route 87) passes some spectacular, needle-sharp granite spires. **Iron Mountain Road** (U.S. 16A) has views of Mt. Rushmore over pigtail bridges and through tunnels. Both highways run through Custer State Park (☞ National and State Parks, *below*). U.S. 14A follows scenic **Spearfish Canyon.**

National and State Parks

National Parks

For **Badlands National Park** and **Black Hills National Forest,** *see* The Black Hills, Deadwood, and the Badlands, *below.* **Jewel Cave National Monument,** 53 mi southwest of Rapid City on U.S. 16 (⊠ R.R. 1, Box 60AA, Custer 57730, ☎ 605/673–2288), gets its name from the calcite crystals lining the walls of one of the world's longest caves. Scenic, historic, and spelunking tours are offered June–August. **Wind Cave National Park,** 50 mi south of Rapid City on U.S. 385 (⊠ R.R. 1, Box 190, Hot Springs 57747, ☎ 605/745–4600), is 28,000 acres of prairie and forest above one of the world's longest caves with perhaps the world's best collection of box work—a honeycomb-like calcite formation. Five different guided tours are offered daily June–August.

State Parks

South Dakota's state-park system encompasses 13 parks. The crown jewel is **Custer State Park** (⊠ HC 83, Box 70, Custer 57730, ☎ 605/ 255–4515; 800/710–2267 for campground reservations), which has 73,000 spectacular acres of grasslands and pine-covered hills that are home to bison, deer, bighorn sheep, prairie dogs, and pronghorn.

THE BLACK HILLS, DEADWOOD, AND THE BADLANDS

Unlike the agricultural eastern half of the state, western South Dakota is a land of mountain meadows, pine forests, and desolate, rocky landscapes. It's also where most tourists go, to visit such places as Deadwood, the 19th-century mining town turned gambling mecca; the mountain carving in progress know as Crazy Horse; and Mt. Rushmore, whose giant stone carvings of four U.S. presidents have retained their stern grandeur for 60 years.

Affordable Adventures (⊠ Box 546, Rapid City 57709, ☎ 605/342–7691, FAX 605/341–6301) specializes in individual and group tours to many of western South Dakota's most scenic and historic locations, including Rapid City, Mt. Rushmore, Custer State Park, Crazy Horse Memorial, Badlands National Park, Wounded Knee, and Pine Ridge.

Visitor Information

Black Hills, Badlands and Lakes Association (⊠ 1861 Discovery Circle, Rapid City 57701, ☎ 605/355–3600, FAX 605/355–3601). **Deadwood Area Chamber of Commerce & Visitor Bureau** (⊠ 735 Main St., 57732, ☎ 605/578–1876 or 800/999–1876, FAX 605/578–2429). **Rapid City Chamber of Commerce and Convention & Visitors Bureau** (⊠ Civic Center, Box 747, 444 N. Mt. Rushmore Rd., 57709, ☎ 605/343–1744 or 800/487–3223, FAX 605/348–9217). **USDA Forest Service Buffalo Gap National Grasslands Visitor Center** (⊠ Box 425, Wall 57790, ☎ 605/279–2125,) has 24 exhibits informing travelers on local history, flora and fauna, and activities in the national grasslands.

Arriving and Departing

By Bus

Gray Line of the Black Hills (⊠ Box 1106, Rapid City 57709, ☎ 605/342–4461) offers bus tours of the region, including trips to Mt. Rushmore and Black Hills National Forest. **Jack Rabbit Lines** (⊠ 301 N. Dakota, Sioux Falls 57103, ☎ 800/444–6287) serves Wall, Rapid City, Mitchell, and Pierre, the capital.

By Car

Unless you're traveling with a package tour, a car is essential here. Make rental reservations early; Rapid City has many business travelers, and rental agencies are often booked. I–90 bisects the state slightly south of its center; it leads to Wall and Rapid City. From Rapid City, U.S. 14 leads to towns and attractions in the northern part of the Black Hills, while U.S. 16 winds through its southern half. Route 44 is an alternate route between the Black Hills and the Badlands. The Black Hills have seven tunnels with limited clearance; they are marked on state maps and in the state's tourism booklet.

By Plane

Rapid City Regional Airport (⊠ 4550 Terminal Rd., Suite 102, Rapid City 57703-8706, ☎ 605/393–9924), 10 mi southeast of downtown via Route 44, is served by Northwest Airlines, Skywest (a Delta connection), and United Express.

Exploring the Black Hills, Deadwood, and the Badlands

The Black Hills

As with the rest of the state, many of this region's attractions are open only in the summer; be sure to call ahead before you visit. To the locals **Rapid City** is West River, meaning west of the Missouri. South Dakota's second-largest city, a cross between western town and progressive community, is a good base from which to explore the Black Hills. Cowboy boots are common here, and business leaders often travel by pickup truck or four-wheel-drive vehicle. Yet the city supports a convention center, museum, and a modern, acoustically advanced performance hall as well as numerous book, gift, and specialty shops downtown and a modern shopping mall on the outskirts.

The **Journey** (⊠ 222 New York St., near the Rushmore Plaza Civic Center, ☎ 605/394–6923; ☞ $7) combines the collections of the **Sioux Indian Museum**, the **Minnilusa Pioneer Museum**, the **Museum of Ge-**

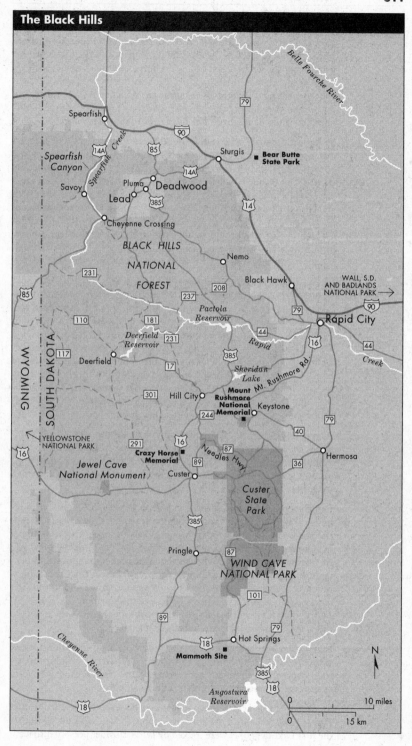

The Black Hills

ology, the State Archaeological Research Center, and a private collection of Native American artifacts into a sweeping pageant of the history and evolution of the Black Hills. The **South Dakota Air & Space Museum** is in Box Elder, just outside Rapid City and the Ellsworth Air Force Base (☒ 2890 Davis Dr., ¾ mi north of I–90, Exit 66, ☏ 605/385–5188; ☞ free). It has a model of a Stealth bomber that's 60% actual size; General Dwight D. Eisenhower's Mitchell B-25 bomber; and more than two dozen other planes, as well as a once-operational missile silo. Tours of the base and silo are available in summer.

In Rapid City itself, **Storybook Island** (☒ near intersection of Jackson Blvd. and Sheridan Lake Rd., ☏ 605/342–6357; ☞ free) lets children romp through scenes from fairy tales and nursery rhymes. **Reptile Gardens** (☒ 6 mi south on U.S. 16, ☏ 605/342–5873; ☞ $9.50) features the world's largest reptile collection, 50,000 flowers, and a variety of staged animal shows. It is open from April through October. **Bear Country U.S.A.** (☒ 8 mi south of Rapid City on U.S. 16, ☏ 605/343–2290; ☞ $8.50) is a drive-through wildlife park featuring black bears, wolves, and most other North American wildlife, as well as a walk-through wildlife center with bear cubs, wolf pups, and other offspring.

The vast **Black Hills National Forest** (☒ R.R. 2, Box 200, Custer 57730, ☏ 605/673–2251; ☞ free) covers 1.3 million acres on the state's western edge. Its most famous attraction is Keystone's **Mt. Rushmore National Memorial** (☒ 21 mi southwest of Rapid City on U.S. 16, ☏ 605/574–2523, ☞ free), the granite cliff where the faces of Presidents Washington, Jefferson, Lincoln, and Theodore Roosevelt are carved. Sculptor Gutzon Borglum labored at this monumental task for more than 14 years; his son, Lincoln, provided the finishing touches following the sculptor's death in 1941. The memorial is spectacular in the morning light and at night, when a special lighting ceremony (June–mid-September) dramatically illuminates the carving.

Also in Keystone, the **Rushmore-Borglum Story** museum (☒ 342 Winter St., ☏ 605/666–4448; ☞ $7) contains newsreel footage of the original blasting of the rock face, as well as exhibits, artwork, paintings, and drawings of Mount Rushmore sculptor Gutzon Borglum. It is open from May through September.

Nineteen miles southwest of Keystone on U.S. 16/385, another monumental likeness is emerging; when finished, the **Crazy Horse Memorial** (☏ 605/673–4681, ☞ $8 per person or $19 per car) will depict the Lakota warrior who defeated General Custer at Little Bighorn. The site includes an impressive new orientation and communications center, the **Indian Museum of North America, Native American Educational & Cultural Center**, the sculptor's studio home and workshop, indoor and outdoor sculpture galleries, and the Laughing Water Restaurant. Expect frequent blasting at this work-in-progress, which will be the world's largest sculpture when completed.

Flintstones, Bedrock City (☒ intersection of U.S. 16 and 385, Custer, ☏ 605/673–4079; ☞ $6) is a full-scale tribute to those enduring cartoon characters, complete with a curio shop, a train ride, a drive-in restaurant serving brontoburgers, and a campground.

Southeast of Custer is **Wind Cave National Park** (☞ National and State Parks, *above*). Lakota tradition holds that it was at Wind Cave that the first Lakota people were tricked by *Iktomi* (spider person) into leaving their ancestral home.

The fossilized remains of ancient mammoths at the **Mammoth Site** (☒ 1 block north of the U.S. 18 Bypass, Hot Springs, ☏ 605/745–6017,

✉ $5) should prove fascinating to children and adults alike. Discovered in 1974, the site is believed to contain up to 100 mammoths (52 have been unearthed so far) and 35 other species in the sinkhole where the mammoths came to drink some 26,000 years ago. A visitor center is built over the area; excavation is in progress.

Sturgis, 29 mi northwest of Rapid City via I–90, is a sleepy town of about 5,600 whose population swells to more than a quarter-million during the first full week of August. The **Sturgis Motorcycle Rally** (☎ 605/347–9190) has drawn enthusiasts from around the world since 1938 (☞ Festivals and Seasonal Events in the United States Region by Region chapter).

In Spearfish, about 45 mi northwest of Rapid City via I–90, the **Black Hills Passion Play** (☎ 605/642–2646; ✉ $12–$18) has since 1939 been recounting the last seven days in the life of Jesus; performances are Tuesday, Thursday, and Sunday at 8 PM from June through August.

The films *Dances with Wolves* (winner of the 1990 Academy Award for best picture) and *Thunderheart* have generated new interest—and new businesses—in the Black Hills. The **Ft. Hays Dances with Wolves Movie Set** (⊠ Moon Meadows Rd. and Hwy. 16, Rapid City, ☎ 605/394–9653; ✉ free) displays photos and shows a video taken during the making of the film. A chuck-wagon dinner show ($12) is offered Memorial Day through Labor Day.

Deadwood

A decade after the legalization of gaming in South Dakota, the town of **Deadwood** stands as a testament to an unlikely benefactor. In 1989, South Dakota voters approved limited-stakes gaming for Deadwood—the nation's third largest gambling venue, behind Nevada and Atlantic City—on the condition that a portion of revenues be devoted to historic preservation. Since then, $150 million has gone into restoring and preserving this once infamous gold-mining boomtown, earning Deadwood a designation as a National Historic Landmark. Streets have been repaved with bricks, and guests are greeted by old-time trolleys, period lighting, and original Victorian architecture. Small gaming halls, good restaurants, and hotels occupy virtually every storefront on Main Street, where half the fun is ducking in and out of the doorways of these charming spots. Today's visitor walks in the same footsteps as legendary lawman Wild Bill Hickok, cigar-smoking Poker Alice Tubbs, and the fabled Calamity Jane, who swore she could out-drink, out-spit, and out-swear any man—and usually did.

Mt. Moriah Cemetery (⊠ Top of Lincoln St., ☎ 605/578–2600; ✉ $1), above Deadwood, is the final resting place of Hickok, Calamity Jane, and other notable Deadwood residents. Currently in the midst of a major restoration project, this classic "Boot Hill" has the best panoramic view of the town and the gold-filled gulch. The **Adams Museum** (⊠ 54 Sherman St., ☎ 605/578–1714; ✉ donations accepted) has three floors of displays, including the first locomotive used in the Black Hills, photos of the town's early days, and the largest gold nugget ever discovered in the Black Hills.

The **Adams House Museum** (⊠ 22 Van Buren St., ☎ 605/578–3751; ✉ $4) recounts the tragedies and triumphs of two of the community's founding families. Restored and preserved, the house was opened to the public in July 2000, revealing an incredible time capsule.

Lead (pronounced *leed*), 50 mi north of Rapid City via I–90 and Alternate Route 14A, is a mining community born in the Black Hills goldrush frenzy of the late 19th century. **Homestake Visitor Center** (⊠ 160 W. Main St., ☎ 605/584–3110; ✉ free, tour $5.25) offers surface tours of the oldest operating underground gold mine in the western hemisphere, including an area for viewing the mine's massive open cut. Free ore samples are available. The town has a number of historic houses, many once home to immigrant miners. **Black Hills Mining Museum** (⊠ 323 W. Main, ☎ 605/584–1605; ☞ $4.25) shows the history of mining through life-size models, videos, gold-panning, and guided tours through a simulated mine.

The Badlands

Badlands National Park (⊠ Box 6, Interior 57750, ☎ 605/433–5361; ☞ $10 per car), 80 mi east of Rapid City off I–90, can seem like another planet. Millions of years of erosion have left these 244,000 acres with desolate gorges and ridges in rust, pink, and gold. The **Ben Reifel Visitor Center**, 2 mi north of Interior via Route 377 or from I–90 off Exit 131 or 110, has maps and information.

South of the park, on the Pine Ridge Indian Reservation, is the **Wounded Knee Massacre Monument,** a small obelisk that commemorates the site where more than 300 Sioux, mostly women and children, were killed when soldiers opened fire after a brief skirmish in 1890.

If you're traveling on I–90, you'll see the signs every few miles for **Wall Drug** (⊠ 510 Main St., ☎ 605/279–2175), the pharmacy turned tourist mecca that enticed depression-era travelers with offers of free ice water. The store has nearly every tourist trinket imaginable plus a restaurant seating more than 500, a bookstore with an excellent selection of western literature, a chapel, a selection of knives and boots, and western art. **Wall** itself, a quiet community on the edge of the Badlands, has several motels and restaurants.

Dining and Lodging

In the summer, reservations are helpful and often required to ensure lodging; calling two or three days ahead is usually adequate.

Deadwood

$$ ✕ **Jakes.** This elegant restaurant takes up the fourth floor of the Midnight Star Casino, owned by actor Kevin Costner. (The rest of the building contains a bar-and-grill and a gaming hall.) Costumes worn by Costner in his numerous feature films are displayed throughout the facility. ⊠ 677 Main St., ☎ 605/578–1555. AE, D, DC, MC, V.

$ ✕ **Deadwood Social Club.** On the second floor of historic Saloon No.
★ 10, this warm restaurant wraps you in wood and old-time photos of Deadwood's past. The menu stretches from wild mushroom cavatappi and seafood nest with basil cream to chicken piccata and melt-in-your-mouth rib eyes. ⊠ 657 Main St., ☎ 605/578–3346. AE, MC, V.

$$ ▥ **Bullock Hotel.** In this 1895 hotel, guest rooms are furnished with Vic-
★ torian reproductions and have large windows. The first floor, which contains the gaming hall, has high ceilings and brass-and-crystal chandeliers. ⊠ 633 Main St., 57732, ☎ 605/578–1745 or 888/428–5562, FAX 605/578–1382. 36 rooms. Restaurant, exercise room. AE, D, MC, V. ✎

$$ ▥ **The Days Inn at Deadwood Gulch Resort.** The Black Hills' most complete resort includes a 100-room hotel, casinos, a creek-side restaurant, lounges, a convention center, and immediate access to the vast Black Hills trail system. An amusement park, arcade and campground are located across the road. ⊠ Hwy. 85S (Box 643), 57732, ☎ 605/578–1294 or 800/695–1876, FAX 605/578–2505. 98 rooms. Restaurant, pool. AE, D, MC, V. ✎

Interior

$ ✕▥ **Cedar Pass Lodge.** The wood-frame cabins in this Badlands lodge
★ have knotty pine interiors and a vintage 1950s look. The restaurant specializes in Native American tacos (fried bread covered with tradi-

tional taco fixings), and serves meat-and-potatoes fare. ✉ *1 Cedar St. (Box 5), Interior 57750,* ☎ *605/433–5460,* FAX *605/433–5560. 24 cabins. Restaurant. AE, D, MC, V. Closed Nov.–mid-Mar.*

Rapid City

$$ ✕ **Fireside Inn Restaurant & Lounge.** One of its two dining rooms has tables around a slate fireplace. Guests also may dine on an outdoor deck, weather permitting. The large menu features 54 entrées and includes prime rib, seafood, and Italian dishes. ✉ *6½ mi west of Rapid City on Rte. 44,* ☎ *605/342–3900. AE, D, DC, MC, V.*

$$ ✕ **Landmark Restaurant and Lounge.** This hotel restaurant is popular for its lunch buffet, and for dinner specialties that include prime rib, beef Wellington, Cajun dishes, and wild game. ✉ *Alex Johnson Hotel, 523 6th St., Rapid City,* ☎ *605/342–1210. AE, D, DC, MC, V.*

$$ ✕ **Minerva's.** A well-appointed pub and pool room complement this spacious new restaurant, conveniently located next to hotels and the city's largest shopping mall. Specialties include linguine Minerva, rotisserie chicken, and the scrumptious Hunter's Ribeye. It's in the Best Western Ramkota Hotel & Conference Center. ✉ *2111 N. LaCrosse St.,* ☎ *605/394–9505. AE, D, DC, MC, V.*

$ ✕ **Botticelli Ristorante Italiano.** With a wide selection of delectable veal and chicken dishes as well as creamy pastas, Botticelli's offers a welcome respite from traditional midwestern meat and potatoes. ✉ *523 Main St., Rapid City,* ☎ *605/346–0089. MC, V.*

$ ✕ **Flying T Chuckwagon.** Ranch-style meals of barbecued beef, grilled chicken, potatoes, and baked beans are served on tin plates in this converted barn. At 6:30 PM, dinner is followed by a western show featuring music and cowboy comedy. ✉ *6 mi south of Rapid City on U.S. 16,* ☎ *605/342–1905. Reservations essential. D, MC, V. Closed mid-Sept.–mid-May. No lunch.*

$$$ ⌂ **Audrie's Bed & Breakfast.** Victorian antiques and an air of romance greet you at this out-of-the-way B&B, 7 mi west of Rapid City on U.S. 44. Suites, cottages, and creek-side cabins come with old-world furnishings, fireplaces, private baths, hot tubs, and big-screen TVs. Children are not allowed. ✉ *23029 Thunderhead Falls Rd., Rapid City 57702,* ☎ *605/ 342–7788. 5 suites, 6 cottages and cabins sleeping 2. No credit cards.*

$$ ⌂ **Alex Johnson Hotel.** The hotel was officially dedicated to the Lakota
★ Indians, so Native American patterns and artwork predominate this landmark building. Rooms have replicas of their original furniture (the hotel opened in 1928). The lobby has a torch chandelier made of Lakota war lances. ✉ *523 6th St., Rapid City 57701,* ☎ *605/342–1210 or 800/888–2539. 143 rooms. Restaurant. AE, D, DC, MC, V.* 🐾

$$ ⌂ **Holiday Inn Rushmore Plaza.** This eight-story hotel has a central lobby with an atrium, glass elevators, and a 60-ft waterfall. ✉ *505 N. 5th St., Rapid City 57701,* ☎ *605/348–4000,* FAX *605/348–9777. 251 rooms. Restaurant, exercise room. AE, D, DC, MC, V.* 🐾

Sturgis

$ ✕ **World Famous Roadkill Cafe.** Started by two bike-rally enthusiasts, the café promises to bring food "from your grill to ours!" including the "Chicken That Didn't Quite Cross the Road" and the daily special, "Guess That Mess!" These clever monikers hide the fact that the café offers fairly standard stuff—breakfast, tuna melts, buffalo and beef burgers. ✉ *1333 Main St., Sturgis,* ☎ *605/347–4502. Reservations not accepted. MC, V. Closed Sept.–May.*

Wall

$ ✕ **Cactus Family Restaurant and Lounge.** This all-day restaurant in downtown Wall specializes in delicious hotcakes and pies. A giant roast-beef buffet is offered in summer. ⊠ *519 Main St., Wall,* ☎ *605/279–2561. D, MC, V.*

$ ✕ **Elkton House Restaurant.** This comfortable restaurant with wood
★   paneling and a sunroom has fast service and a terrific hot roast-beef
sandwich, served on white bread with gravy and mashed potatoes. ⊠
South Blvd., Wall, ☎ *605/279–2152. D, MC, V.*

Motel

🔟 **Super 8 Motel** (⊠ 1–90, Exit 100, Box 426, Wall 57790, ☎ 605/
279–2688), 29 rooms; *$$.*

Campgrounds

For information on state campgrounds contact the **Department of
Game, Fish, and Parks** (⊠ 523 E. Capitol Ave., Pierre 57501, ☎ 605/
773–3485; 800/710–2267 for camping reservations).

Around Deadwood: ⚠ **Custer Crossing Campground and Store** (⊠ HCR
73, Box 1527, Deadwood 57732, ☎ 605/584–1009), 15 mi south of
town. ⚠ **Deadwood KOA** (⊠ Box 451, Deadwood 57732, ☎ 605/
578–3830), 1 mi west of town; ⚠ **Whistler Gulch Campground** (⊠ 235
Cliff St., Deadwood 57732, ☎ 605/578–2092 or 800/704–7139) on
the southern edge of town; and ⚠ **Wild Bill's Campground** (⊠ HCR
73, Box 1101, Deadwood 57732, ☎ 605/578–2800), on U.S. 385.

Around the Badlands: ⚠ **Circle 10 Campground** (⊠ Rte. 1, Box 51½,
Philip 57567, ☎ 605/433–5451).

Outdoor Activities and Sports

Biking

The **George S. Mickelson Trail** is South Dakota's longest, skinniest state
park and one of the newest outdoor attractions in the Black Hills. Span-
ning 110 mi, from sagebrush-flat to ponderosa-pine forest, the trail is
ideal for hiking, biking, horseback riding, and skiing. For more infor-
mation contact the South Dakota Department of Tourism (☞ Statewide
Visitor Information, *above*) or the Department of Game, Fish, and Parks
(☞ Campgrounds, *above*).

Fishing

Some of the best fishing in the state lies east of the Badlands in the large
reservoirs of the Missouri River, but mountain streams throughout the
Black Hills offer good trout fishing. Custer State Park and Pactola and
Sheridan lakes have excellent trout fishing. For more information contact
the **fishing division** of the state Department of Tourism (☎ 800/445–3474).

Hiking

The 111-mi **Centennial Trail** runs through the Black Hills National For-
est, from the Plains Indians' sacred site at Bear Butte in the north to
Wind Cave National Park, passing from grasslands into the hills in the
high country. For more information contact the state Department of
Tourism (☞ Statewide Visitor Information, *above*).

Snowmobiling

With 335 mi of marked and groomed trails, the Black Hills are a pre-
mier spot in the country for snowmobiling. A map of the trail network
is available from the state Department of Tourism (☞ Statewide Vis-
itor Information, *above*). For **trail conditions,** updated three times
weekly, call 800/445–3474.

Ski Areas

The Black Hills' winter-sports magazine, *Romancing the Snow,* has in-
formation on cross-country and downhill skiing; it's available from the

Black Hills, Badlands and Lakes Association (☞ Visitor Information, *above*). For **ski reports** call 800/445–3474.

Cross-Country Skiing

The Black Hills offer skiing on 600 mi of abandoned logging roads, railroad beds, and fire trails, as well as several trail networks, including the **Big Hill** (16 mi of trails on the rim of Spearfish Canyon). Contact **Ski Cross Country** (⊠ 701 3rd St., Spearfish 57783, ☎ 605/642–3851), a ski-equipment sales and rental shop, for information.

Downhill Skiing

Deer Mountain Ski Area (⊠ Box 622, Deadwood 57732, ☎ 605/584–3230) has 39 trails, an 850-ft vertical drop, one double lift, one triple chair, two Poma lifts (akin to T-bars), snowmaking equipment, and 10 mi of cross-country trails. The base lodge offers rentals and lessons and a full-service restaurant and lounge.

Terry Peak Ski Area (⊠ Box 774, Lead 57754, ☎ 605/584–2165; 800/456–0524 for ski conditions) offers a 1,100-ft vertical drop, five chairlifts, and state-of-the-art snowmaking. Each of the two lodges has a restaurant, lounge, and gift shop, and one rents equipment.

Shopping

Rapid City stores carry western souvenirs, crafts, and clothing. Nearly every gift shop carries the locally famous "Black Hills Gold," a combination of metals that produce distinctive green and red tints; you can watch jewelry being made at **Landstrom's Original Black Hills Gold Creations** (⊠ 405 Canal St., Rapid City, ☎ 800/770–5000). **Prairie Edge Trading Co. & Galleries** (⊠ 606 Main St., Rapid City, ☎ 605/342–3086) displays fine arts and crafts of the Plains Indians, as well as works by various other Great Plains artists, in a restored 1886 three-story building. A turn-of-the-20th-century-style trading company in the same building has books, regional crafts, and a world-class collection of Italian glass beads. **Prince & Pauper Bookshop** (⊠ 612 St. Joseph St., Rapid City, ☎ 605/342–7964 or 800/354–0988) has a large selection of books by regional and Native American authors, as well as rare and out-of-print local-history books. **Alex Johnson's Mercantile** (⊠ 608 St. Joseph St., Rapid City, ☎ 605/343–2383) sells books, wood carvings, jewelry, and unique gifts.

Rushmore Mall (⊠ Just off I–90 north of Rapid City, ☎ 605/348–3378) contains department stores, specialty shops, and western stores. Among the latter is RCC-Western Stores (☎ 605/341–6633), which has one of the area's largest selections of boots and can outfit you from head to toe in the latest western fashions.

For Native American art, jewelry, baskets, and other goods, visit the gift shop of the **Indian Museum of North America,** at the Crazy Horse Memorial (☞ The Black Hills *in* Exploring the Black Hills, Deadwood, and the Badlands, *above*).

ELSEWHERE IN SOUTH DAKOTA

Sioux Falls

Visitor Information

Sioux Falls Convention and Visitors Bureau (⊠ Box 1425, Sioux Falls 57101-1425, ☎ 605/336–1620 or 800/333–2072, ℻ 605/336–6499).

Arriving and Departing

Sioux Falls is in the southeastern corner of the state, at the intersection of I–90 and I–29. **Sioux Falls Regional Airport** (⊠ 2801 Jaycee

La., Sioux Falls 57104, ☎ 605/336–0762) is served by Northwest, TWA, and United.

What to See and Do

Sioux Falls, South Dakota's largest city, is an ideal starting point for most attractions in the eastern part of the state. Restaurants, hotels, and shops are numerous in this commercial hub. Besides live animals, the **Great Plains Zoo and Delbridge Museum of Natural History** (⊠ 805 S. Kiwanis Ave., ☎ 605/367–7059; ☞ $6) has one of the world's largest collections of mounted animals. The **Old Courthouse Museum** (⊠ 200 W. 6th St., ☎ 605/367–4210; ☞ free) is a massive Romanesque structure made of a native red stone called Sioux quartzite; it has exhibits on the history of this area, including Native American artifacts. Built in 1889, the **Pettigrew Home and Museum** (⊠ 131 N. Duluth Ave., ☎ 605/367–7097; ☞ free) was later the home of South Dakota's first full-term U.S. senator, Richard F. Pettigrew. The Queen Anne–style home contains period furnishings and Native American and natural-history exhibits.

Dining

$$ ✕ **Minerva's.** Wooden floors, a salad bar, and a strong wine list complement a menu that focuses on pasta, fresh seafood, and aged steak. ⊠ 301 S. Phillips, ☎ 605/334–0386. AE, D, DC, MC, V. Closed Sun.

$ ✕ **Champps Sports Cafe.** A lively atmosphere and great pub fare—pastas, sandwiches, hamburgers, fries, onion rings—make this a fun, reliable spot. ⊠ 2101 W. 41st St., in Western Mall, ☎ 605/331–4386. AE, D, DC, MC, V.

Mitchell

Visitor Information

Mitchell Department of Tourism (⊠ Box 776, 57301, ☎ 605/996–7311 or 800/257–2676, ℻ 605/996–8273).

Arriving and Departing

Mitchell is 70 mi west of Sioux Falls on I–90.

What to See and Do

The city of Mitchell trumpets the "world's only" **Corn Palace** (⊠ 604 N. Main St., ☎ 605/996–7311 or 800/257–2676; ☞ free). This fanciful structure, built in 1892, is topped by gaily painted Moorish domes and covered with multicolored corn, grain, and grass murals. Inside is an exhibition hall built to showcase the state's agricultural production. The exterior designs are changed annually. Across the street from the Corn Palace is the **Enchanted World Doll Museum** (⊠ 615 N. Main St., ☎ 605/996–9896; ☞ $3.50), with 4,800 antique and modern dolls displayed in 435 scenes.

Dining

$ ✕ **Chef Louie's Steakhouse.** Steaks, barbecued ribs, and seafood are served in a casual setting. Pheasant is served in summer and fall. ⊠ 601 E. Havens, ☎ 605/996–7565. AE, D, DC, MC, V. Closed Sun.

DeSmet

Visitor Information

Glacial Lakes and Prairies Association (⊠ Box 244, Watertown 57201, ☎ 605/886–7305 or 800/244–8860, ℻ 605/886–7935).

Arriving and Departing

From Sioux Falls follow I–29 north for 49 mi, then U.S. 14 west for about 37 mi.

What to See and Do

Fans of the *Little House* children's books may want to visit the town where author Laura Ingalls Wilder lived for 15 years. The Ingalls family moved to DeSmet in 1879, when Laura was 12, and lived first in a surveyor's house, next in a shanty, then in a farmhouse, and finally in town, in a home that Pa Ingalls built in 1887. The surveyor's house and town home are open to the public and contain period furnishings and memorabilia. The last weekend in June and first two weekends in July, the community hosts the annual **Laura Ingalls Wilder Pageant** (✉ Laura Ingalls Wilder Memorial Society, Box 406, DeSmet 57231, ☎ 605/854–3383), where food, period costumes, and crafts demonstrations are topped off by dramatizations of the *Little House* books themselves.

Dining and Lodging

$ ✕ **The Oxbow.** There's a little of everything—burgers, steaks, fish— on the menu at this homey restaurant, run by the Myers family. ✉ *Hwy. 14,* ☎ *605/854–9988. No credit cards.*

$ ▥ **Cottage Inn Motel.** Across the street from the Oxbow, and also run by the Myers family, this motel has clean, spacious rooms. ✉ *Hwy. 14, 57231,* ☎ *605/854–3396 or 800/848–0215. 37 rooms. AE, D, DC, MC, V.*

Pierre

Visitor Information

Pierre Convention and Visitors Bureau (✉ Box 548, Pierre 57501-0548, ☎ 605/224–7361 or 800/962–2034, ℻ 605/224–6485).

Arriving and Departing

Pierre (pronounced *peer*) is on U.S. 83, about 225 mi west of Sioux Falls.

What to See and Do

The **state capitol** (✉ 500 E. Capitol Ave., ☎ 605/773–3765; ▭ free), a magnificent Greek Revival building completed in 1910, has a rich interior decorated with mosaic floors, stained-glass skylights, allegorical murals, and an impressive columned staircase. The state historical society has a museum and archives at the **Cultural Heritage Center** (✉ 900 Governors Dr., ☎ 605/773–3458; ▭ $3); exhibits focus on the history of South Dakota. The first of three phases for a permanent exhibit (South Dakota Experience) was completed in 1992. It offers a taste of the state from 1743, the year European trappers first arrived, through the beginning of the 20th century. The second phase, completed in 1994, focuses on the culture of the Sioux Indians. The third phase, scheduled for completion in 2002, will cover the 20th century.

Dining

$ ✕▥ **Best Western Ramkota Inn.** The largest hotel in Pierre is also one of the capital's social hubs. Hearty breakfasts and buffets are hallmarks. ✉ *920 W. Sioux St., 57501,* ☎ *605/224–6877,* ℻ *605/224–1042. 151 rooms. Restaurant, pool, exercise room. AE, D, DC, MC, V.* ▨

TENNESSEE

Updated by
Katherine Price

Capital	Nashville
Population	5,368,000
Motto	Agriculture and Commerce
State Bird	Mockingbird
State Flower	Iris
Postal Abbreviation	TN

Statewide Visitor Information

Tennessee Department of Tourist Development (✉ 320 6th Ave. N, Nashville 37243, ☎ 615/741–2159 or 800/462–8366).

Scenic Drives

U.S. 421 from Bristol to Trade passes through the Cherokee National Forest and crosses the Appalachian Trail. **Route 73** south from Townsend leads through a high valley ringed by the Great Smoky Mountains to the pioneer village of Cades Cove in Great Smoky Mountains National Park. **Route 25** from Gallatin to Springfield travels through an area of Thoroughbred farms and antebellum houses. Between Monteagle and Chattanooga **I–24** winds through the Cumberland Mountains.

National and State Parks

National Parks
Great Smoky Mountains National Park (✉ Gatlinburg 37738, ☎ 423/436–1200) encompasses tall peaks and lush valleys, with camping and fishing sites and more than 900 mi of horse and hiking trails.

State Parks
The State Parks Division of the **Tennessee Department of Environment and Conservation** (✉ 401 Church St., L&C Tower, 7th floor, Nashville 37243, ☎ 615/532–0001 or 800/421–6683) provides information on Tennessee's 50-plus state parks. The 16,000-acre **Fall Creek Falls State Resort Park** (✉ Rte. 3, Pikeville 37367, ☎ 423/881–5241 or 423/881–3297) has the highest waterfall east of the Rockies. Thick stands of cypress trees make **Reelfoot Lake State Resort Park** (✉ Rte. 1, Box 296, Tiptonville 38079, ☎ 901/253–7756), in northwestern Tennessee, a favorite wintering ground for the American bald eagle. **Roan Mountain State Resort Park** (✉ 527 Hwy. 143, Roan Mountain 37687, ☎ 423/772–3303), in northeastern Tennessee, has a 600-acre natural rhododendron garden that blooms in late June.

MEMPHIS

On the bluffs overlooking the Mississippi River, Memphis is Tennessee's largest city and the commercial and cultural center of the western part of the state. It is a blend of southern tradition and modern efficiency, where aging cotton warehouses stand near sleek new office buildings and old-fashioned paddle wheelers steam upriver past the city's unusual landmark, the gleaming stainless-steel Pyramid Arena. Memphis is perhaps best known for its music and for the two extraordinary men who introduced that music to the world: W. C. Handy, the Father of the Blues, and Elvis Presley, the King of Rock and Roll.

Visitor Information

Convention & Visitors Bureau (✉ 47 Union Ave., 38103, ☎ 901/543–5300 or 800/873–6282). **Memphis Visitors Center** (✉ 119 N. Riverside Dr., ☎ 901/543–5333).

Arriving and Departing

By Boat

Memphis is one stop on the paddle-wheeler cruises of the **Delta Queen Steamboat Company** (✉ Robin Street Wharf, New Orleans, LA 70130, ☎ 800/543–1949). The *Delta Queen,* the *Mississippi Queen,* and the *American Queen* travel between St. Louis and New Orleans.

By Bus

Greyhound (✉ 203 Union Ave., ☎ 800/231–2222).

By Car

You can access Memphis via the north–south I–55 or the east–west I–40. I–240 loops around the city.

By Plane

Memphis International Airport (✉ 2491 Winchester Rd., ☎ 901/922–8000), 9 mi southeast of downtown, is served by most major airlines and is a hub for Northwest Airlines. Driving time to downtown is about 15 minutes on I–240. Cab fare (**Yellow Cab,** ☎ 901/577–7700) runs about $20 plus tip.

By Train

Amtrak (✉ 545 S. Main St., ☎ 800/872–7245) provides limited service.

Getting Around Memphis

Memphis's streets are well marked, and there's plenty of parking, so the city is best explored by car. The **Memphis Area Transit Authority** (☎ 901/274–6282) operates buses ($1.10) throughout downtown and the suburbs (additional fare for zones outside the city limits); a trolley (50¢) runs a 5-mi route linking the north and south ends of downtown via a riverfront loop.

Exploring Memphis

Downtown

Memphis begins at the Mississippi River, which is celebrated in a 52-acre river park (☎ 901/576–6595 or 800/507–6507; ⊞ $8) on **Mud Island.** A footbridge and monorail at 125 Front Street get you to the island, where a five-block **River Walk** replicates the Mississippi's every twist, turn, and sandbar from Cairo, Illinois, to New Orleans, Louisiana. Also in the park are the **Mississippi River Museum,** the famed World War II B-17 bomber *Memphis Belle,* an amphitheater, shops, and a pool.

The 32-story, 22,000-seat stainless-steel **Pyramid Arena** (✉ 1 Auction Ave., ☎ 901/521–9675; ⊞ tours $4), opposite the south end of Mud Island, hosts concerts, athletic games, and conventions. **Magevney House** (✉ 198 Adams Ave., ☎ 901/526–4464; ⊞ free; closed Mon.), built in the 1830s by a pioneer schoolteacher, is Memphis's oldest dwelling. It's a 20-minute walk from the Pyramid Arena.

The beautifully restored **Peabody Hotel** (☞ Lodging, *below*) stands on Union Avenue between 2nd and 3rd streets. **Beale Street,** where W. C. Handy played the blues in the early decades of the 20th century, is once again thriving with clubs and restaurants. The **W. C. Handy Memphis**

Home and Museum (⊠ 352 Beale St., ☎ 901/522–1556; 🖭 $2) recalls the influential blues musician through a variety of memorabilia.

The **Hunt-Phelan Home** (⊠ 533 Beale St., ☎ 901/344–3166 or 800/350–9009; 🖭 $10), with costumed docents, transports visitors to the mid-1800s. Ulysses S. Grant and Jefferson Davis were among the home's historic visitors (at different times, of course).

Exhibits in the **Memphis Music Hall of Fame Museum** (⊠ 97 S. 2nd St., ☎ 901/525–4007; 🖭 $7.50)—rare photographs, film footage, audiotapes, and memorabilia—trace the development of blues, country, and rock and roll, as well as the city's role in it all.

Sun Studio (⊠ 706 Union Ave., ☎ 901/521–0664; 🖭 $8.50), the birthplace of rock and roll, is where Elvis Presley, Jerry Lee Lewis, B. B. King, and Roy Orbison launched their careers. Tours are given daily; the studio is seven blocks east of downtown.

South of downtown, the motel where Dr. Martin Luther King Jr. was assassinated in 1968 has been transformed into the **National Civil Rights Museum,** an outstanding facility that documents the movement through exhibits and clever audiovisual displays. ⊠ *450 Mulberry St.,* ☎ *901/521–9699.* 🖭 *$6, free Mon. 3–5. Closed Tues.*

Other Attractions

★ **Graceland,** the estate once owned by Elvis Presley, is 12 mi south of downtown. A guided tour of the mansion, automobile museum, and burial site reveals the spoils of stardom. Graceland might be the only Colonial suburban home on record to have a jungle room, a pink Cadillac, and more than 700,000 guests annually. Reservations are recommended. ⊠ *3717 Elvis Presley Blvd.,* ☎ *901/332–3322 or 800/238–2000.* 🖭 *Mansion only $10, all attractions $19.50. Closed Tues. Nov.–Mar.*

The **Memphis Brooks Museum of Art,** east of downtown in Overton Park, houses a collection of fine and decorative arts from antiquity to the present, including Renaissance and Baroque works, English portraiture, Hellenistic and classical Roman art, as well as contemporary local artists. ⊠ *1934 Poplar Ave.,* ☎ *901/722–3500.* 🖭 *$5. Closed Mon.*

☺ At the **Children's Museum of Memphis** (⊠ 2525 Central Ave., ☎ 901/458–2678; 🖭 $5) youngsters can touch, climb, and explore their way through a child-size city. The **Memphis Pink Palace Museum and Planetarium** (⊠ 3050 Central Ave., ☎ 901/320–6320; 🖭 museum $6, planetarium $3.50) has a mix of natural history and cultural history exhibits, planetarium laser shows, and an IMAX theater. **Chucalissa Archaeological Museum** (⊠ 1987 Indian Village Dr., ☎ 901/785–3160; 🖭 $2) is a reconstruction of a Native American village that existed from AD 1000 to AD 1500. Skilled Choctaw craftspeople fashion jewelry, weapons, and pottery outside the **C. H. Nash Museum,** which houses historic originals of the same articles.

Parks, Gardens, and Zoos

Overton Park, a few miles east of downtown on Poplar Avenue, offers picnic areas, sports fields, hiking and biking trails, a nine-hole golf course, an art museum (☞ Other Attractions, *above*). Also in the park is the popular 70-acre **Memphis Zoo** (⊠ 2000 Galloway Ave., ☎ 901/725–3400; 🖭 $8), which includes 9-acre Cat Country and Primate Canyon. In East Memphis the 96-acre **Memphis Botanic Garden** (⊠ 750 Cherry Rd., ☎ 901/685–1566; 🖭 $2) has scores of species, from camellias to cacti.

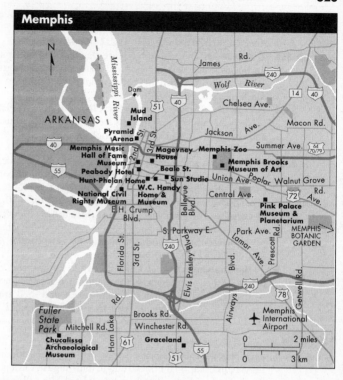

Memphis

Dining

Although Memphis has a satisfying variety of restaurants, the local passion is barbecue; the city has 70-odd barbecue places. The popular meat-and-threes (diners serving meat with three vegetable side dishes), such as the Cupboard (☞ *below*), specialize in turnip greens, fried chicken, corn bread, and other southern specialties.

$$$$ ✕ **Chez Philippe.** Chef José Gutierrez serves sophisticated dishes in an
★ ornate setting. Nightly creations may include beef tenderloin, roasted wild boar, or Chilean snapper with Portobello mushrooms on a horseradish reduction. ⊠ *Peabody Hotel, 149 Union Ave.,* ☎ *901/529–4188. Jacket required. AE, DC, MC, V. Closed Sun. No lunch.*

$$$$ ✕ **Erling Jensen.** Jensen first earned a loyal following as the chef at La Tourelle (☞ *below*) but opened his eponymous restaurant in 1996. The Dane's cuisine is global; most noteworthy is his rack of lamb. ⊠ *1044 S. Yates Rd.,* ☎ *901/763–3700. Reservations essential. AE, DC, MC, V. No lunch.*

$$$$ ✕ **Raji.** World-renowned chef and published author Raji Jallepalli blends Indian seasonings with nouvelle styles. She serves a prix-fixe four-course meal at 7 PM and occasional special-theme dinners. ⊠ *712 W. Brookhaven Circle,* ☎ *901/685–8723. Reservations essential. AE, MC, V. Closed Sun.–Mon. No lunch.*

$$–$$$$ ✕ **Landry's Seafood House.** A converted riverfront warehouse, this place packs 'em in for such seafood dishes as fried shrimp and stuffed flounder. ⊠ *263 Wagner Pl.,* ☎ *901/526–1966. AE, D, DC, MC, V.*

$$–$$$$ ✕ **La Tourelle.** This turn-of-the-20th-century bungalow in Overton Square has the romantic ambience of a French country inn. Five-course prix-fixe meals with an emphasis on French cuisine supplement the à la carte menu. Men will feel most comfortable in a jacket and tie. ⊠ *2146 Monroe Ave.,* ☎ *901/726–5771. MC, V.*

$$–$$$ ✕ **Cafe Max.** The atmosphere is lively at this bistro in East Memphis, where selections include pasta, seafood, and grilled meats. ⊠ *6161 Poplar Ave.,* ☎ *901/767–3633. AE, MC, V. No lunch.*

$$–$$$ ✕ **Paulette's.** This Overton Square classic serves delicious crepes (try
★ the hot chocolate dessert crepe) and salads and excellent grilled chicken, salmon, and swordfish in the atmosphere of a European inn. ⊠ *2110 Madison Ave.,* ☎ *901/726–5128. AE, D, DC, MC, V.*

$–$$ ✕ **Cafe Olé.** This popular midtown hangout offers a healthy version of Mexican cuisine (no animal fats are used), including spinach enchiladas and chile rellenos (cheese-stuffed fried green chilies). ⊠ *959 S. Cooper St.,* ☎ *901/274–1504. AE, D, DC, MC, V.*

$–$$ ✕ **Charlie Vergos' Rendezvous.** Tourists and locals alike flock to this downtown basement restaurant to savor Vergos's "dry" barbecued pork ribs and other barbecue specialties. ⊠ *52 S. 2nd St.,* ☎ *901/523–2746. AE, D, DC, MC, V. Closed Sun. and Mon. No lunch Tues.–Thurs.*

$–$$ ✕ **Corky's.** There's always a line at this no-frills East Memphis bar-
★ becue restaurant. Once you taste the ribs (or sandwiches, or beef or pork platters), you'll understand why. ⊠ *5259 Poplar Ave.,* ☎ *901/ 685–9744. AE, D, DC, MC, V.*

$ ✕ **The Cupboard.** Owner Charles Cavallo knows fresh produce, and his cooks turn out masterful "meat-and-three" plates. Lucky is the soul who visits when both macaroni and cheese and fried green tomatoes are offered. ⊠ *1495 Union Ave.,* ☎ *901/276–8015. AE, D, MC, V.*

Lodging

Memphis hotels are especially busy during the monthlong Memphis-in-May International Festival and in mid-August, during Elvis Tribute Week; book well ahead at these times. For bed-and-breakfasts contact the **Bed & Breakfast Reservation Service** (⊠ Box 111141, Memphis 38111–1141, ☎ 901/327–6129 or 800/336–2087, ℻ 901/458–1003).

$$$–$$$$ 🏨 **Adam's Mark Memphis.** Set in the flourishing eastern suburbs near
★ I–240, this 27-story glass tower has views of the sprawling metropolis and its outskirts. ⊠ *939 Ridge Lake Blvd., 38120,* ☎ *901/684–6664 or 800/444–2326,* ℻ *901/762–7411. 408 rooms. Restaurant, pool, health club. AE, D, DC, MC, V.* 🕭

$$$–$$$$ 🏨 **Peabody Hotel.** Even if you're not staying here, it's worth a stop to
★ see this 12-story downtown landmark, built in 1925. The lobby has the original stained-glass skylights and the travertine-marble fountain that is home to the hotel's resident ducks. The rooms are decorated in a variety of period styles. ⊠ *149 Union Ave., 38103,* ☎ *901/529–4000 or 800/732–2639,* ℻ *901/529–3600. 468 rooms. 4 restaurants, pool, health club. AE, D, DC, MC, V.* 🕭

$$–$$$ 🏨 **French Quarter Suites.** This pleasant Overton Square hotel is reminiscent of a New Orleans–style inn. All suites have oversize whirlpool tubs, and some have balconies. ⊠ *2144 Madison Ave., 38104,* ☎ *901/ 728–4000 or 800/843–0353,* ℻ *901/278–1262. 105 suites. Restaurant, pool, health club. AE, D, DC, MC, V.*

$$ 🏨 **Holiday Inn East.** Close to I–240 and the bustling Poplar/Ridgeway office complex, this sleek 10-story hotel is popular with business travelers. ⊠ *5795 Poplar Ave., 38119,* ☎ *800/465–4329,* ℻ *901/682–7881. 243 rooms. Restaurant, pool, health club. AE, D, DC, MC, V.* 🕭

$$ 🏨 **Radisson Hotel.** Across the street from the Peabody is this downtown hotel with its own lobby fountain and waterfall. Glass-walled elevators whisk guests to rooms around a 10-story atrium. ⊠ *185 Union Ave., 38103,* ☎ *901/528–1800,* ℻ *901/526–3226. 280 rooms. Restaurant, pool. AE, D, DC, MC, V.* 🕭

$–$$ 🏨 **Guest House, Inn & Suites.** This three-story hotel in East Memphis has many of the comforts of home, such as kitchenettes. The decor includes teal carpeting and Aztec-pattern draperies. ⊠ *4300 American Way, 38118,* ☎ *901/214–8378,* FAX *901/366–7835. 120 suites. Pool. AE, D, DC, MC, V. CP.*

$–$$ 🏨 **La Quinta Inn–Medical Center.** This two-story inn is convenient to midtown and has spacious, well-maintained rooms. ⊠ *42 S. Camilla St., 38104,* ☎ *901/526–1050,* FAX *901/525–3219. 130 rooms. Pool. AE, D, DC, MC, V. CP.* ✎

$–$$ 🏨 **Quality Inn.** All units have private patios or balconies; many have refrigerators and microwave ovens, and four have kitchens. ⊠ *1541 Sycamore View, 38134,* ☎ *901/388–1300. 96 rooms. Pool, coin laundry. AE, D, DC, MC, V. CP.* ✎

$ 🏨 **Executive Inn.** This four-story motor lodge near Graceland has spacious, well-appointed rooms with tasteful touches of country decor. ⊠ *3222 Airways Blvd., 38116,* ☎ *901/332–3800 or 800/221–2222,* FAX *901/345–8118. 118 rooms. Pool, exercise room. DC, MC, V. CP.*

Nightlife and the Arts

Call the Memphis **events hot line** (☎ 901/753–5847) for information about performances in the city.

Nightlife

To hear the blues as they were meant to be played, head for the clubs on Beale Street. Among the most popular clubs is **B. B. King's Blues Club** (⊠ 143 Beale St., ☎ 901/524–5464), where B. B. himself occasionally performs. **Blues Hall/Rum Boogie Cafe** (⊠ 182 Beale St., ☎ 901/528–0150) is a good spot for the blues.

The Arts

The **Orpheum Theatre** (⊠ 203 S. Main St., ☎ 901/525–3000, 901/678–2706, or 901/737–7322) hosts touring Broadway shows, as well as performances by Opera Memphis and Ballet Memphis. The **Memphis Symphony Orchestra** (☎ 901/324–3627) performs at various locations from September through May.

Spectator Sports

Baseball: The **Memphis Redbirds,** the St. Louis Cardinals AAA farm team, play at AutoZone Park (⊠ 8 S. Third St., ☎ 901/721–6050), the new stadium downtown, which opened in April 2000. **Golf:** Southwind Tournament Players Club (⊠ 3325 Club Rd., at Southwind, ☎ 901/748–0534) hosts the **St. Jude FedEx Classic Golf Tournament** each summer, drawing the PGA tour's top pros. **Tennis:** The **Kroger St. Jude International Indoor Tennis Tournament** (☎ 901/765–4400) is played in February at the Racquet Club (⊠ 5111 Sanderlin Ave., East Memphis).

Shopping

The **Mid America Mall,** on Main Street between Beale and Poplar, is one of the nation's longest pedestrian malls—better known for its trolley rides and people-watching than for shopping. Two antique districts bracket Mid America Mall, **South Main,** on Main Street between Beale and Calhoun, and the **Pinch District,** just north of downtown between Front and 3rd streets, also known for its bars and restaurants. For more local color, midtown's **Cooper Young District,** at the intersection of Cooper Street and Young Avenue, offers a handful of funky shops, vintage clothing stores, and cafés. Also in midtown, **Overton Square** (⊠ 24 S. Cooper St., ☎ 901/278–6300)—a three-block shopping, restaurant, and entertainment complex in vintage buildings and newer structures—has upscale boutiques and specialty shops. **Oak Court Mall** (⊠ 4465 Poplar Ave., ☎ 901/682–8928), in the busy Poplar/Perkins area of East Memphis, has 70 specialty stores and two department stores. At **Wolfchase Galleria** (⊠ 2760 N. Germantown Pkwy., at U.S. 64, about 18 mi east of downtown Memphis, ☎ 901/381–2769), the four anchor stores are Goldsmith's, Dillard's, Sears, and JCPenney. A large carousel attracts scores of children, and a multiplex cinema shows a wide range of movies. **Belz Factory Outlet Mall** (⊠ 3536 Canada Rd., Exit 20 off I–40, 20 mi east of downtown Memphis, Lakeland, ☎ 901/386–3180) includes 50 stores, from Bugle Boy to Van Heusen.

NASHVILLE

Hailed as Music City, U.S.A. (country music, that is), and the birthplace of the Nashville Sound, Tennessee's capital city is also a leading center of higher education, appropriately known as the Athens of the South. The city has spawned such dissimilar institutions as the Grand Ole Opry and Vanderbilt University and has prospered from them both, becoming one of the mid-South's most vibrant communities.

Visitor Information

Nashville Convention & Visitors Bureau (⊠ 161 4th Ave. N, 37219, ☎ 615/259–4700). **Visitor information center** (⊠ 501 Broadway, 37219, ☎ 615/259–4747).

Arriving and Departing

By Bus
Greyhound (⊠ 200 8th Ave. S, ☎ 800/231–2222).

By Car
I–65 leads into Nashville from the north and south; I–24, from the northwest and southeast; I–40, from the east and west. I–440 loops around the city.

By Plane
Nashville International Airport (⊠ 1 Terminal Dr., ☎ 615/275–1600), about 8 mi east of downtown, is served by most major airlines. To reach downtown by car, take I–40 west. Cab fare runs about $20 plus tip. **Downtown Airport Express** (☎ 615/275–1180) has service to downtown hotels for $9.

Getting Around Nashville

The central city is bisected by the Cumberland River; numbered avenues are west of and parallel to it, and numbered streets east of and parallel to it.

By Bus
Metropolitan Transit Authority (MTA) buses (☎ 615/862–5950) serve the county; fare is $1.35 in exact change.

By Trolley
Nashville Trolley Company (☎ 615/862–5969) trolleys cover downtown and Music Row in summer months; the fare is 90¢.

Exploring Nashville

Downtown
Downtown attractions can be covered easily on foot. Overlooking the river is **Fort Nashborough** (⊠ 170 1st Ave. N; ▭ free), a replica of the crude log fort built in 1779 by Nashville's first settlers. In the **District,**

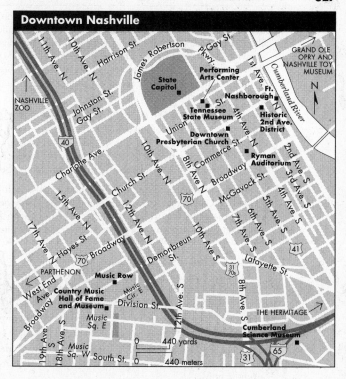

Downtown Nashville

the historic 2nd Avenue area south of Church Street, 19th-century buildings have been handsomely restored to house restaurants, clubs, boutiques, offices, and residences.

The **Downtown Presbyterian Church** (✉ 5th Ave. and Church St., ☎ 615/254–7584; 🎟 free), an Egyptian Revival tabernacle (circa 1851), was designed by noted Philadelphia architect William Strickland. **Ryman Auditorium and Museum** (✉ 116 5th Ave. N, ☎ 615/254–1445; 615/889–6611 for tickets to events; 🎟 tours $8), the home of the Grand Ole Opry from 1943 to 1974, is a shrine for die-hard fans. The renovated Ryman once again hosts performances.

The James K. Polk Office Building is home to the **Tennessee State Museum,** where more than 6,000 artifacts trace the history of life in Tennessee. ✉ 505 Deaderick St., ☎ 615/741–2692. 🎟 Free. Closed Mon.

In a park along Charlotte Avenue is the Greek Revival **state capitol** (☎ 615/741–2692; 🎟 free), designed by William Strickland, who is interred here, as are the 11th U.S. president, James Polk, and his wife.

Other Attractions

Music Row (✉ Demonbreun St. exit off I–40) is the heart of Nashville's recording industry and the center of numerous country music attractions. A ticket to the **Country Music Hall of Fame and Museum** (✉ 4 Music Sq. E, ☎ 615/255–5333; 🎟 $10.75) includes admission to the legendary **RCA Studio B**, a few blocks away, where Elvis, Dolly Parton, and other greats once recorded. In late spring of 2001, the country shrine will move across from Nashville Arena downtown.

★ Since 1974, the **Grand Ole Opry** (✉ 2804 Opryland Dr., ☎ 615/889–3060, 🎟 $19.50 for shows) has been staged at the complex that housed the Opryland U.S.A. theme park, which closed in 1997. Each weekend top stars perform at the Opry, which is the nation's oldest continuous radio show, first airing in 1925. The Opry is broadcast from the world's largest broadcast studio (it seats 4,424); advance ticket purchase is advised. The musical lineup for the Friday- and Saturday-night shows is announced on Wednesday evenings. The Opry survives and thrives, even as the former theme park's grounds have been converted into Opry Mills, a 200-store shopping, dining, and entertainment complex that opened in 2000.

The **Hermitage** (⊠ 4580 Rachel's La., Hermitage, ☎ 615/889–2941; ✑ $9.50), 12 mi east of downtown (Exit 221 off I–40), was built by Andrew Jackson, the seventh U.S. president, for his wife, Rachel. Their life and times are reflected with great care in the mansion, visitor center, and grounds. Both Jackson and his wife are entombed here.

Two miles west of downtown in Centennial Park—built for the 1897 Tennessee Centennial Exposition—stands the **Parthenon,** an exact copy of the Athenian original and now used as an art gallery. *Athena Parthenos* is a 42-ft copy of a statue in the original Parthenon. ⊠ *West End and 25th Aves.,* ☎ *615/862–8431.* ✑ *$2.50. Closed Mon.*

☺ At the **Cumberland Science Museum** (⊠ 800 Ridley Blvd., ☎ 615/862–5160; ✑ $6), children are invited to touch, smell, climb, and explore.

☺ The toy collection at the **Nashville Toy Museum** (⊠ 2613 McGavock Pike, ☎ 615/883–8870; ✑ $3.50) spans more than 150 years.

Parks, Gardens, and Zoos

The 50-acre **Nashville Zoo** (⊠ 1710 Ridge Rd. Circle, Joelton, Exit 31 off I–24W, ☎ 615/833–1534; ✑ $6) includes an African savanna and a reptile house.

The 14,200-acre **J. Percy Priest Lake** (⊠ 11 mi east of downtown off I–40, ☎ 615/889–1975) is surrounded by parks where you can swim, fish, camp, hike, bike, picnic, paddle, or ride. Thirty acres of gardens at the

★ **Cheekwood–Tennessee Botanical Gardens and Museum of Art** (⊠ 1200 Forrest Park Dr., ☎ 615/353–2140; ✑ $6) showcase annuals, perennials, and wildflowers. The museum reopened in 1999 after extensive renovations restored the neo-Georgian mansion close to its original state. **Riverfront Park** (⊠ 1st Ave. and Broadway) is home to the Tennessee Fox Trot Carousel, with horses and figures by artist Red Grooms, a Nashville native whose sculpture and painting have been exhibited worldwide.

Dining

Nashville dining is not all corn bread, turnip greens, and grits. Here you will find some of Tennessee's most sophisticated restaurants alongside the classic "meat-and-threes" (diners serving meat with three vegetable side dishes).

$$$–$$$$ ✕ **Mario's.** Country music stars, visiting celebrities, and local society
★ come here to see and be seen—and to savor the memorable osso buco and saltimbocca from chef Ricardo Bacilieri. ⊠ *2005 Broadway,* ☎ *615/327–3232. Reservations essential. Jacket and tie. AE, D, DC, MC, V. Closed Sun. No lunch.*

$$$–$$$$ ✕ **Wild Boar.** This restaurant serves excellent contemporary French cuisine, such as game, trout, duck, and beef; it also has an outstanding wine cellar. ⊠ *2014 Broadway,* ☎ *615/329–1313. AE, D, DC, MC, V. No lunch weekends.*

$$–$$$$ ✕ **Mère Bulles.** This intimate District restaurant has river-view dining, a Continental menu, and an extensive wine list. There's live entertainment nightly, often jazz or folk music. ⊠ *152 2nd Ave. N,* ☎ *615/256–1946. AE, D, MC, V.*

$$–$$$ ✕ **F. Scott's.** This elegant café and wine bar has one of the largest wine se-
★ lections in town. Try the roasted half duck with root vegetable ragout and
cranberries. ✉ *2210 Crestmoor,* ☎ *615/269–5861. AE, D, DC, MC, V.*

$$–$$$ ✕ **The Merchants.** An outdoor patio is an extra feature at this opulent
three-level restaurant. Specialties include fresh seafood, grilled meats,
and key lime pie. ✉ *401 Broadway,* ☎ *615/254–1892. AE, D, DC,
MC, V. No lunch weekends.*

$$–$$$ ✕ **Sunset Grill.** Don't be surprised to see your favorite country stars at
this hip, postmodern hangout. The hickory-smoked Tennessee trout is
terrific. In summer, the outdoor courtyard is the place to be seen. ✉ *2001A
Belcourt Ave.,* ☎ *615/386–3663. AE, D, DC, MC, V. No lunch Sat.*

$ ✕ **Elliston Place Soda Shop.** Come to this old-fashioned soda shop for
great burgers, frothy ice-cream sodas, and a 1950s atmosphere. The
chocolate shake is Nashville's best. ✉ *2111 Elliston Pl.,* ☎ *615/327–
1090. MC, V. Closed Sun.*

$ ✕ **Hermitage House Smorgasbord.** No need to be shy about helping
yourself to the bountiful spread of salads, meats, vegetables, and
desserts here. Don't miss the apple fritters. ✉ *3131 Lebanon Rd., Hermitage,* ☎ *615/883–9525. MC, V.*

$ ✕ **Loveless Cafe.** Down-home southern cooking is the draw: fried
chicken, country ham and red-eye gravy, featherlight homemade biscuits and preserves. ✉ *8400 Rte. 100,* ☎ *615/646–9700. AE, MC, V.*

$ ✕ **Old Spaghetti Factory.** This 2nd Avenue District spot offers a wide
range of pasta dishes in a lively atmosphere that's great for families.
✉ *160 2nd Ave. N,* ☎ *615/254–9010. D, MC, V.*

$ ✕ **Sylvan Park Restaurant.** The original location is a beacon for "meat-
and-three" fans; purists say the three spin-off eateries aren't quite as
good. ✉ *4502 Murphy Rd.,* ☎ *615/292–9275. No credit cards.*

Lodging

Nashville hotels are especially busy during the second week of June,
when the International Country Music Fan Fair takes over the city. Many
tour companies offer packages, but plan ahead; this is country music's
premier event and it sells out months in advance.

For information on B&Bs in the area, contact **Bed & Breakfast About
Tennessee** (✉ Box 110227, Nashville 37222, ☎ 615/331–5244) or **Ten-
nessee Bed & Breakfast Innkeepers' Association** (✉ Box 120428,
Nashville 37212, ☎ 800/820–8144).

$$$$ ▥ **Loews Vanderbilt Plaza.** This beautiful hotel near Vanderbilt University has a well-deserved reputation for attentive service. ✉ *2100 West
End Ave., 37203,* ☎ *615/320–1700 or 800/235–6397,* FAX *615/320–
5019. 351 rooms. 2 restaurants. AE, D, MC, V.* ❧

$$$$ ▥ **Opryland Hotel.** This massive plantation-style hotel adjacent to
★ Opryland has a 2-acre glass-walled conservatory filled with 10,000 tropical plants and a skylighted indoor area with water cascades and a half-
acre lake. The 18-hole golf course was designed by Larry Nelson. ✉
2800 Opryland Dr., 37214, ☎ *615/889–1000,* FAX *615/871–7741.
2,883 rooms. 7 restaurants, pools, exercise room. AE, D, MC, V.* ❧

$$$ ▥ **Renaissance Nashville Hotel.** This ultracontemporary high-rise ad-
joins the Nashville Convention Center. The spacious rooms have pe-
riod reproduction furnishings. ✉ *611 Commerce St., 37203,* ☎ *615/
255–8400 or 800/468–3571,* FAX *615/255–8163. 673 rooms. 2 restau-
rants, pool, health club. AE, D, DC, MC, V.* ❧

$$ ▥ **Courtyard by Marriott–Airport.** This handsome low-rise motor inn
★ offers some amenities found in higher-price hotels: spacious rooms, king-
size beds, and oversize desks. ✉ *2508 Elm Hill Pike, 37214,* ☎ *615/*

883–9500 or 800/321–2211, FAX *615/883–0172. 145 rooms. Restaurant, pool, exercise room. AE, D, DC, MC, V.* ⊛

$$ ⊞ **Hampton Inn Vanderbilt.** The rooms at this contemporary inn near Vanderbilt University are colorful and spacious. There's a hospitality suite for social or business use. ⊠ *1919 West End Ave., 37203,* ☎ *615/ 329–1144 or 800/426–7866,* FAX *615/320–7112. 171 rooms. Pool. AE, D, DC, MC, V. CP.* ⊛

$ ⊞ **Comfort Inn Hermitage.** Near the Hermitage is this inn offering comfortable accommodations, some with water beds or whirlpool baths. ⊠ *5768 Old Hickory Blvd., 37076,* ☎ *615/889–5060,* FAX *615/871– 4137. 106 rooms. Pool. AE, D, DC, MC, V. CP.* ⊛

$ ⊞ **La Quinta Inn–Metro Center.** Guest rooms are spacious and well lighted, with a large working area and an oversize bed. ⊠ *2001 Metrocenter Blvd., 37228,* ☎ *615/259–2130 or 800/531–5900,* FAX *615/ 242–2650. 121 rooms. Pool. AE, D, DC, MC, V. CP.* ⊛

$ ⊞ **Wilson Inn.** Three miles from the Grand Ole Opry, this five-story hotel is clean and convenient. Many rooms have kitchens. ⊠ *600 Ermac Dr. (Elm Hill Pike exit from Briley Pkwy.), 37214,* ☎ *615/889– 4466 or 800/333–9457,* FAX *615/889–0484. 110 rooms. Pool. AE, D, DC, MC, V. CP.* ⊛

Nightlife and the Arts

Nightlife

The **Grand Ole Opry** (☞ Exploring, *above*) has packed in the crowds on Friday and Saturday nights since 1925. At the famous **Bluebird Cafe** (⊠ 4104 Hillsboro Rd., Green Hills, ☎ 615/383–1461), country singers try out their latest material. The **Stock Yard Bull Pen Lounge** (⊠ 901 2nd Ave. N, ☎ 615/255–6464) is a restaurant-lounge with nightly live country entertainment and dancing. There's a variety of live music downtown at **Mère Bulles** (☞ Dining, *above*). **Exit/In** (⊠ 2208 Elliston Pl., ☎ 615/ 321–4400) showcases blues and rock. In the **District** (☞ Exploring, *above*), check out the **Wild Horse Saloon** (⊠ 120 2nd Ave. N, ☎ 615/251–1000) and local versions of **Planet Hollywood** (⊠ 322 Broadway, ☎ 615/313– 7827) and the **Hard Rock Cafe** (⊠ 100 Broadway, ☎ 615/742–9900).

The Arts

The **Tennessee Performing Arts Center** (⊠ 505 Deaderick St., ☎ 615/ 782–4000) is the venue for performances by the **Nashville Ballet** (☎ 615/244–7233), **Nashville Opera** (☎ 615/292–5710), **Nashville Symphony Orchestra** (☎ 615/255–5600), and **Tennessee Repertory Theatre** (☎ 615/244–4878). The center's Andrew Jackson Hall also hosts touring Broadway shows. Call **Ticketmaster** (☎ 615/737–4849) for tickets and information about arts events. In the second week of June, the **International Country Music Fan Fair** brings country music stars and their fans face to face at the Tennessee State Fairgrounds.

Spectator Sports

Football: Nashville's new **Adelphia Coliseum** (⊠ 1 Titans Way, ☎ 615/ 565–4000 or 888/313–8326) is home to the NFL's **Tennessee Titans,** formerly Houston Oilers. The 67,000-seat, natural grass stadium, which opened in 1999, sits on the banks of the Cumberland River. **Hockey: Nashville Arena** (⊠ 501 Broadway, ☎ 615/770–2000) hosts the NHL's **Nashville Predators,** an expansion team that first played here in 1998. **Baseball:** The **Nashville Sounds,** an AAA farm team of the Pittsburgh Pirates, play at Herschel Greer Stadium (⊠ 534 Chestnut St., ☎ 615/242–4371) just south of downtown, off I–65.

Shopping

New **Opry Mills** (✉ 2802 Opryland Dr.), offers more than a million square feet of stores, restaurants, and entertainment spots. In addition to mall perennials such as Bass, Barnes & Noble, and multiple movie screens, this supercomplex also houses a bluegrass showcase, a simulated race-car speedway, and an IMAX theater, among others. The huge **Bellevue Center** mall, in southwest Nashville (✉ Bellevue exit from I–40, ☎ 615/646–8690), has more than 120 stores. Twenty-five miles east of Nashville, the **Prime Outlets of Lebanon** (✉ Hwy. 231, Lebanon, ☎ 615/444–0433), are a favorite of locals looking for deals on Brooks Brothers, Ralph Lauren, Nike, and more. The shops along **8th Avenue South** make a good browsing ground for antiques lovers. For the latest look in country-and-western wear, two-step over to the **District** (☞ Exploring Nashville, *above*).

EAST TENNESSEE

From the Great Smoky Mountains to the rippling waters of the Holston, French Broad, Nolichucky, and Tennessee rivers, East Tennessee offers a cornucopia of scenic grandeur and recreational opportunities. Mountain folkways may persist in certain smaller communities, but cities such as Knoxville and Chattanooga are modern and quite diverse.

Visitor Information

Chattanooga: Area Convention and Visitors Bureau (✉ 1001 Market St., 37402, ☎ 423/756–8687 or 800/322–3344). **Knoxville:** Area Convention and Visitors Bureau (✉ 601 W. Summit Hill, Suite 200B, 37902, ☎ 423/523–7263 or 800/727–8045).

Arriving and Departing

By Bus
Greyhound (☎ 800/231–2222) has stops in Chattanooga and in Knoxville.

By Car
I–75 runs north–south from Kentucky through Knoxville, then to Chattanooga. I–81 heads southwest from the Virginia border at Bristol, ending at I–40 northeast of Knoxville. I–40 enters from North Carolina and continues west to Knoxville, Nashville, and Memphis.

By Plane
Knoxville Airport (✉ 2055 Alcoa Hwy., ☎ 865/970–2773), served by Airtran, American Eagle, Continental Express, Delta, Northwest, TWA, United, and US Airways, is about 12 mi from town. The **Chattanooga Airport** (✉ 1001 Airport Rd., ☎ 423/855–2200), served by ASA, ComAir, Delta, Northwest Airlink, United Express, and US Airways, is about 8 mi from town.

Exploring East Tennessee

Founded in 1786, **Knoxville** became the first state capital when Tennessee was admitted to the Union in 1796. This scenic city at the foothills of the Great Smoky Mountains continues to grow with **Volunteer Landing,** a development along the Tennessee River with shops, restaurants, and residential space. Knoxville is home to the main campus of the **University of Tennessee,** as well as the headquarters of the **Tennessee Valley Authority** (TVA), with its vast complex of hydroelectric dams and recreational lakes. The TVA was a massive work project initiated by Franklin Delano Roosevelt in 1933 as part of the New Deal.

Among the historic sites in Knoxville is the 1792 **Governor William Blount Mansion,** where the governor and his associates planned the admission of Tennessee as the 16th state in the Union. ⊠ *200 W. Hill Ave.,* ☎ *423/525–2375.* ☞ *$4. Closed Mon.*

The **Armstrong-Lockett House,** an 1834 farm mansion, is a showcase of American and English furniture and English silver. ⊠ *2728 Kingston Pike,* ☎ *423/637–3163.* ☞ *$4.50. Closed Mon. and Jan.–Feb.*

Housed in the 1874 U.S. Customs House, the **East Tennessee Historical Center** displays books and artifacts relating to the history of the state. ⊠ *800 Market St.,* ☎ *423/544–5744.* ☞ *Free. Closed Mon.*

The **Knoxville Museum of Art** has four exhibition galleries with contemporary prints, drawings, and paintings. Shows feature a wide range of local, national, and international artists and have included Indian art, landscapes, photography, and late 1980s art. ⊠ *1050 World's Fair Park Dr.,* ☎ *423/525–6101.* ☞ *Free except during special exhibits. Closed Mon.*

The **Knoxville Zoological Gardens** (⊠ Rutledge Pike S, Exit 392 off I–40, ☎ 423/637–5331; ☞ $3.50) is famous for its reptile complex and for its breeding of large cats and African elephants.

Youngsters like the hands-on displays and audiovisual exhibits at the **East Tennessee Discovery Center and Akima Planetarium** (⊠ 516 N. Beaman St., ☎ 423/594–1480; ☞ $3).

Gatlinburg, the busy, tourist-oriented northern gateway to **Great Smoky Mountains National Park** (☞ National and State Parks, *above*), is southeast of Knoxville via U.S. 441/321. Set in the narrow valley of the Little Pigeon River (actually a turbulent mountain stream), Gatlinburg has an abundance of family attractions, including the **Gatlinburg Sky Lift** (☎ 423/436–4307; ☞ $7) to the top of Crockett Mountain.

Pigeon Forge, about 6 mi north of Gatlinburg on U.S. 441, has factory outlet malls and family attractions. One Pigeon Forge highlight is **Dollywood,** Dolly Parton's popular theme park, with rides, live music, and a re-created mountain village. Dolly performs annually, usually when the season opens. Other concerts between May and October are apt to include such stars as the Oak Ridge Boys or Lorrie Morgan. ⊠ *700 Dollywood La.,* ☎ *423/428–9488 or 800/365–5996.* ☞ *$33.15. Closed Jan.–mid-Apr.*

The **Gatlinburg/Pigeon Forge area** is home to many amusement parks and offbeat museums, such as Gatlinburg's **Guinness World Records Museum** (☎ 423/436–9100; ☞ $7.95). **Newfound Gap,** south from Gatlinburg on scenic U.S. 441, provides a haunting view of the Tennessee–North Carolina border. From here a 7-mi spur road leads to **Clingmans Dome**—at 6,643 ft, the highest point in Tennessee.

Chattanooga, a city of Civil War battlefields, museums of all kinds (art, antiques, history, even knives and tow trucks), and a famous choo-choo, is southwest of Knoxville off I–75. Begin your meandering here with a stop at the **Chattanooga Visitors Center** (⊠ 2 Broad St., ☎ 423/266–7111). Dominating Chattanooga's skyline is 2,215-ft **Lookout Mountain,** 6 mi away, with panoramic views and the world's steepest **Incline Railway** (⊠ 827 E. Brow Rd., ☎ 423/821–4224; ☞ $8). From Lookout Mountain Scenic Highway, tours depart every 15 minutes to the 145-ft **Ruby Falls** (⊠ 1550 Scenic Hwy., ☎ 423/821–2544; ☞ $9), 1,120 ft underground and reached by elevator.

★ The **Tennessee Aquarium** (⊠ 1 Broad St., ☎ 423/265–0695, ☞ aquarium $10.95, IMAX theater $6.95) is the world's largest freshwater aquarium, with 350 species of fish, mammals, birds, reptiles, and amphibians; an IMAX theater is nearby. Surrounding the aquarium is **Ross's Landing Park and Plaza,** commemorating Chattanooga's Civil War history as well as its role as a major railroad town.

A restored classic revival mansion is home to the **Hunter Museum of American Art** (⊠ 10 Bluff View, ☎ 423/267–0968; ☑ $5), whose collection spans American art from the Colonial period to the present day. The paintings, sculpture, furniture, and other art represent diverse artists such as Winslow Homer, Mary Cassatt, Thomas Hart Benton, George Segal, Duane Hanson, and Robert Rauschenberg.

Ⓒ The **Creative Discovery Children's Museum** (⊠ 321 Chestnut St., ☎ 423/756–2738; ☑ $7.75) has exhibits in four areas: invention, art, music, and science.

Oak Ridge, about 100 mi northeast of Chattanooga (take U.S. 27 to I–40E or I–75 to I–40W), is where atomic energy was secretly developed during World War II. The **American Museum of Science and Energy** (⊠ 300 S. Tulane Ave., ☎ 423/576–3200; ☑ free) focuses on the uses of nuclear, solar, and geothermal energy.

Dining and Lodging

Expect hearty food in the mountains: barbecued ribs, thick pork chops, and country ham with red-eye gravy.

For reservations in hotels, motels, chalets, and condominiums in Gatlinburg, contact **Smoky Mountain Accommodations Reservation Service** (⊠ 103 Silverbell La., Gatlinburg 37738, ☎ 423/436–9700 or 800/231–2230).

Chattanooga

$$-$$$ ✕ **The Loft.** Locals and visitors alike flock to this cozy, candlelit restaurant for the clublike ambience, extensive wine list, and hearty specialties. The varied entrées include king crab legs, seafood fettuccine, and steak—all served with soup, salad, home-baked bread, fresh vegetables, and a baked potato or wild rice pilaf. ⊠ 328 Cherokee Blvd., ☎ 423/266–3601. AE, D, DC, MC, V.

$-$$$ ✕ **212 Market.** Creative American cuisine is served at this hip spot di-
★ rectly across from the Tennessee Aquarium. The fish entrées are especially good, the homemade breads scrumptious, and the wine list impressive. ⊠ 212 Market St., ☎ 423/265–1212. AE, D, DC, MC, V.

$-$$ ✕ **Big River Grille Brewing & Works.** This restored trolley-warehouse has high ceilings, exposed-brick walls, and hardwood floors. You can watch the inner workings of the microbrewery through a soaring glass wall by the bar. The sandwiches and salads are large; wash them down with the sampler of six brews. ⊠ 222 Broad St., ☎ 423/267–2739. AE, D, DC, MC, V.

$-$$ ✕ **Town & Country.** Even though this classic "meat-and-three" across the bridge from the Tennessee Aquarium seats more than 425, expect to wait a bit for the mouthwatering southern cuisine, from vegetable plates to steaks. ⊠ 110 N. Market St., ☎ 423/267–8544. AE, D, DC, MC, V.

$$-$$$$ 🏠 **Bluff View Inn.** Chattanooga's best B&B, this 1928 Colonial Revival mansion hugs a bluff high above the Tennessee River and is part of the Bluff View Art District, which comprises five houses, three restaurants, and a sculpture garden. Tastefully decorated bedrooms in the main inn and two other houses have whirlpool baths and fireplaces. ⊠ 412 E. 2nd St., 37403, ☎ 423/265–5033 or 800/725–8338, ℻ 423/757–0120. 16 rooms. 3 restaurants. AE, DC, MC, V. BP. ✎

$$ 🏨 **Chattanooga Choo-Choo Holiday Inn.** The hotel adjoins the 1905 Southern Railway Terminal, now a 30-acre complex with restaurants, shops, gardens, tennis courts, and an operating trolley. Rooms are comfortably furnished, and you can also stay in one of the 48 parlor cars. ⊠ *1400 Market St., 37402,* ☎ *423/266–5000 or 800/872–2529,* FAX *423/265–4635. 351 rooms. 4 restaurants, pools. AE, D, DC, MC, V.* 🐕

$$ 🏨 **Chattanooga Marriott.** One of the city's largest hotels, it's convenient to town attractions. Rooms compare to any Marriott, offering corporate comfort a couple of notches above Holiday Inn. ⊠ *2 Carter Plaza, 37402,* ☎ *423/756–0002 or 800/841–1674,* FAX *423/266–2254. 343 rooms. Restaurant, pools, health club. AE, D, DC, MC, V.* 🐕

$$ 🏨 **Radisson Read House.** The Georgian-style Read House, on the Na-
★ tional Register of Historic Places, dates from the 1920s and has been impeccably restored to its original grandeur. Guest rooms in the main hotel continue the Georgian motif; rooms in the annex are more contemporary. ⊠ *827 Broad St., 37402,* ☎ *423/266–4121 or 800/333–3333,* FAX *423/267–6447. 238 rooms. 2 restaurants, pool. AE, D, DC, MC, V.* 🐕

Gatlinburg

$-$$$ ✕ **Burning Bush Restaurant.** Reproduction furnishings evoke a Colonial atmosphere, but the menu leans toward Continental. Specialties include broiled Tennessee quail. ⊠ *1151 Parkway,* ☎ *423/436–4669. AE, D, DC, MC, V.*

$-$$ ✕ **Smoky Mountain Trout House.** Trout is prepared eight ways; otherwise, choose prime rib, country ham, or fried chicken. This restaurant is a truly rustic mountain cottage. ⊠ *410 N. Parkway,* ☎ *423/436–5416. AE, DC, MC, V. Closed Dec.–Mar.*

$$-$$$$ 🏨 **Buckhorn Inn.** This country inn about 6 mi outside town has wel-
★ comed guests to its rustic rooms and cottages since 1938. The mountain views are spectacular. Breakfast and dinner are available for an extra charge. ⊠ *2140 Tudor Mountain Rd., 37738,* ☎ *423/436–4668. 6 rooms, 4 1-bedroom cottages, two 2-bedroom guest houses. Restaurant. D, MC, V.* 🐕

$$ 🏨 **Holiday Inn SunSpree Resort.** Near the Convention Center and the
★ Ober Gatlinburg aerial tramway, this hotel offers the Holidome Indoor Recreation Center, with a general store, whirlpool, sauna, and game area. ⊠ *520 Airport Rd., 37738,* ☎ *423/436–9201 or 800/435–9201,* FAX *423/436–7974. 402 rooms. 2 restaurants, pools, exercise room. AE, D, DC, MC, V.* 🐕

$-$$ 🏨 **Best Western Twin Islands Motel.** Even though it's in busy downtown Gatlinburg, this motel has a peaceful air, thanks to the Little Pigeon River, which flows past each room. ⊠ *539 Parkway, 37738,* ☎ *423/436–5121,* FAX *423/436–6208. 97 rooms, 10 suites. Restaurant, pool. AE, D, DC, MC, V.* 🐕

Knoxville

$$-$$$ ✕ **Regas Restaurant.** This cozy Knoxville classic, with fireplaces and
★ original art, has been around for 70 years. The specialty, prime rib, is sliced to order and served with horseradish sauce. ⊠ *318 Gay St.,* ☎ *423/637–9805. AE, D, DC, MC, V. Closed Sun. No lunch Sat.*

$-$$ ✕ **Copper Cellar/Cumberland Grill.** A favorite of the college crowd and young professionals, the original downstairs Copper Cellar has an intimate atmosphere. Upstairs, the Cumberland Grill serves salads and sandwiches. Both serve outstanding desserts. ⊠ *1807 Cumberland Ave.,* ☎ *423/673–3411. AE, DC, MC, V.*

$$-$$$ 🏨 **Hyatt Regency Knoxville.** This handsome, contemporary adaptation
★ of an Aztec pyramid sits atop a hill overlooking the city and nearby mountains. The nine-story atrium lobby blends modern furnishings with artwork in Central American motifs. ⊠ *500 Hill Ave. SE, 37915,* ☎

423/637–1234 or 800/233–1234, FAX *423/522–5911. 385 rooms. Restaurant, pool, exercise room. AE, D, DC, MC, V.*

$ 🏨 **Best Western Luxbury Hotel.** Between downtown Knoxville and Oak Ridge, this affordable hotel has oversize rooms with spacious work areas. ⊠ *420 Peters Rd. N, 37922,* ☎ *423/539–0058 or 800/252–7748,* FAX *423/539–4887. 97 rooms. Pool. AE, D, DC, MC, V. CP.*

Nightlife and the Arts

Chattanooga

The **Tivoli Theater** (⊠ 399 McCaulley Ave., ☎ 423/757–5050) and **Tivoli Theater** (⊠ 709 Broad St., ☎ 423/757–5050) present concerts and operas. The **Chattanooga Theatre Center** (⊠ 400 River St., ☎ 423/267–8534) stages productions year-round. For rock or blues head to **Sandbar** (⊠ 1011 Riverside Dr., ☎ 423/622–4432).

Gatlinburg

Sweet Fanny Adams Theatre and Music Hall (⊠ 461 Parkway, ☎ 423/436–4038) stages original musical comedies and Gay '90s revues, and hotel lounges offer DJs and live entertainment. At Ober Gatlinburg, the **Heidelberg Restaurant** (⊠ 148 Parkway, ☎ 423/430–3094) has dancing and a show starring international entertainers, mostly German, from 5:30 to 11.

Knoxville

The **Bijou Theater** (⊠ 803 S. Gay St., ☎ 423/522–0832) offers seasonal ballet, concerts, and plays. **Clarence Brown/Carousel Theatre,** on the University of Tennessee campus (☎ 423/974–5161), is a theater-in-the-round with student and professional actors. **Old City,** on the north side of downtown, has lively restaurants, clubs, and shops. Try **Lucille's** (⊠ 106 N. Central St., ☎ 423/546–3742), in Old City, for jazz. For dancing, there's the **Underground** (⊠ 214 W. Jackson Ave., ☎ 423/525–3675), in Old City. **Patrick Sullivan's** (⊠ 100 N. Central St., ☎ 423/694–9696) has saloon-style food and live rock and roll on weekends.

Outdoor Activities and Sports

Fishing

East Tennessee's lakes offer seasonal angling for striped bass, walleye, white bass, and muskie. **Gatlinburg**'s streams and rivers are stocked with trout from April to November. There are boat-launch ramps at **Norris Dam State Resort Park** (☎ 423/426–7461), north of Knoxville, and **Booker T. Washington State Park** (☎ 423/894–4955), near Chattanooga.

Golf

East Tennessee courses open to the public include 18-hole, par-72 **Brainerd Golf Course** (☎ 423/855–2692), in Chattanooga; 18-hole, par-70 **Whittle Springs Municipal Golf Course** (☎ 423/525–1022), in Knoxville; and 18-hole, par-72 **Bent Creek Mountain Inn and Country Club** (☎ 423/436–2875), in Gatlinburg.

Hiking

A scenic portion of the **Appalachian Trail** runs along high ridges in the Great Smoky Mountains National Park (⊠ Gatlinburg, ☎ 423/436–1200). The trail can be reached at Newfound Gap, off U.S. 441.

Horseback Riding

McCarter's Riding Stables (⊠ U.S. 441 south of Gatlinburg, ☎ 423/436–5354) is open mid-March–October.

Rafting and Canoeing

East Tennessee has five white-water rivers: Ocoee, Hiwassee, French Broad, Tellico, and Nolichucky. The rafting season runs from April to early November; for canoe rentals and guided raft trips contact **Out-door Adventures** (⊠ Ocoee, ☎ 800/627–7636), **Wildwater, Ltd.** (⊠ Ducktown, ☎ 800/451–9972), and **Rafting in the Smokies** (⊠ Gatlinburg, ☎ 423/436–5008).

Shopping

At the **Great Smoky Arts and Crafts Community** (⊠ Glades and Buckhorn Rds. off U.S. 321, 3 mi east of Gatlinburg, ☎ 423/671–3600, ext. 3504), a collection of 80 shops and crafts studios along 8 mi of country road, you can watch crafters at work and buy their wood carvings, dulcimers, quilts, and other Appalachian folk crafts. Pigeon Forge is famous for its **factory outlet malls** on U.S. 441. **Warehouse Row** (⊠ 12th and Market Sts., ☎ 423/267–1111) in Chattanooga contains factory outlets for such top brands as Ellen Tracy, Ralph Lauren, Tommy Hilfiger, and Perry Ellis. Chattanooga's **Bluff View Art District,** around East 2nd Street and Bluff View, on the cliffs overlooking the Tennessee River, is a pleasant destination for art lovers. It offers a handful of restaurants, galleries, and bakeries along narrow, cobblestone streets next to the Hunter Museum of American Art.

TEXAS

Updated by
Kim Harwell,
Elizabeth
McGuire,
and Kay
Winzenried

Capital	Austin
Population	20,044,141
Motto	Friendship
State Bird	Mockingbird
State Flower	Bluebonnet
Postal Abbreviation	TX

Statewide Visitor Information

Texas Department of Tourism (⊠ Box 12728, Austin 78711, ☎ 800/888–8839).

Scenic Drives

In far southwest Texas, **Route 170** from Lajitas through Presidio and into the Chinati Mountains is one of the most spectacular drives in the state, plunging over mountains and through canyons along the Rio Grande (thus its name: El Camino del Rio, or River Road). **U.S. 83** from Leakey to Uvalde is a roller coaster of a ride through the lush western edges of Hill Country, in central Texas. In the northern panhandle, **I-27** from Lubbock to Amarillo carries you through the buffalo grass and sheer cliffs of the Llano Estacado (Staked Plain, so named because its lack of trees forced pioneers to tie their horses to stakes). From Center, a small town near the Louisiana border, south into the Sabine National Forest, **Route 87** takes you over several dramatic lakes and through one of the huge pine forests for which east Texas is famous.

National and State Parks

National Parks

★ **Big Bend National Park** (⊠ Box 129, U.S. 385 from Marathon; Superintendent, Big Bend National Park, 79834, ☎ 915/477–2251), the state's premier natural attraction, is an 801,163-acre landscape laid bare by millions of years of erosion, with spectacular canyons, a junglelike floodplain, the sprawling Chihuahuan Desert, and the cool woodlands of the Chisos Mountains. Though the park has hundreds of campsites, the only hotel is the **Chisos Mountain Lodge** (☎ 915/477–2291), which is often booked months in advance.

Canoeing and camping are top draws to **Davy Crockett National Forest** (⊠ Ratcliff Lake, 1240 E. Loop 304, Crockett 75835, ☎ 409/544–2046), a 161,842-acre park in the "piney woods" of east Texas, about 20 mi east of the historic town of Crockett on Route 7.

Aransas National Wildlife Refuge (⊠ Box 100, Rte. 2040, Austwell 77950, ☎ 512/286–3559), on a peninsula jutting 12 mi into the Gulf of Mexico near Rockport, is the principal wintering ground of the endangered whooping crane; the best time to spot them and some 300 other species of birds is between November and March.

State Parks

You can call a **central reservations number** (☎ 512/389–8900) to book any campsite in the Texas state park system.

In East Texas, **Caddo Lake State Park** (⊠ Rte. 43, Karnack 75661, ☎ 903/679–3351), 8,017 acres on the southern shore of the lake, has campgrounds and cabins, as well as facilities for fishing, swimming, and boating.

Named after the local term for "high plains," **Caprock Canyons State Park** (⊠ Rte. 1065, Quitaque 79255, ☎ 806/455–1492), in the panhandle, is marked by canyons, striking geologic formations, and an abundance of wildlife, including African aoudad, mule deer, buffalo, antelope, and golden eagles.

Enchanted Rock State Natural Area (⊠ 16710 Ranch Rd. 965, Fredericksburg 78624, ☎ 915/247–3903), 18 mi north of Fredericksburg in the Hill Country, is so named because of the noises emitted by the underground heating and cooling of its massive, 425-ft-high dome of solid pink granite. The rock is the reputed site of ancient human sacrifices and is the second-largest batholith (underground rock formation uncovered by erosion) in the United States.

Fishing is king at **Inks Lake State Park** (⊠ 3630 Park Rd. 4 W., Burnet 78611, ☎ 512/793–2223), northwest of Austin at the edge of the Hill Country.

★ On the high plains 12 mi east of the panhandle town of Canyon is **Palo Duro Canyon State Park** (⊠ Rte. 217, Park Rd. 5, Canyon 79015, ☎ 806/488–2227), site of the last great battle with the Comanche. Among its rock spires and precipitous cliffs is an outdoor amphitheater where the historical drama *Texas* is presented each year.

HOUSTON AND GALVESTON

Unbridled energy has always been **Houston**'s trademark. The forceful, wildcatter temperament that transformed what was once a swamp near the junction of the Buffalo and White Oak bayous into the nation's fourth-largest city also made the city a world energy center and pushed exploration into outer space—indeed, the first words spoken from the moon broadcast its name throughout the universe: "Houston, Tranquility Base here. The Eagle has landed." This same wild spirit explains much about the unrestricted growth that resulted in the city's patchwork layout: It's not unusual to find a luxury apartment complex next to a muffler repair shop. Magnificent glass-and-metal towers dominate the downtown corridor, but for the most part Houston's cityscape is characterized by random upcroppings of impressive architecture interspersed with groomed greenbelts and lively neighborhoods.

Houston is nevertheless an international business hub and the energy capital of the United States, evidenced by the Texas-size conventions that periodically fill its major hotels to bursting points. Medical institutions spawned from the discoveries of the famous heart transplant team of Cooley and DeBakey and research conducted at M.D. Anderson Cancer Center have earned Houston the title of "healing center." Top-notch museums, galleries, and performance halls affirm the city's commitment to creativity and expression, and its many ethnic restaurants add to the cosmopolitan flavor.

One of Texas's most popular year-round coastal destinations, **Galveston** is an island in the Gulf of Mexico 50 mi southeast of Houston, connected to the mainland by a causeway and bridge. The restored Victorian Strand district, resort hotels, and beachfront businesses give a commercial feel to the north end of the island, while miles of private and rental residences on the southern end offer solitude and open beach access.

Once one of the world's great port cities, Galveston was nearly devastated by a hurricane in 1900. In the 1950s, preservationists launched Galveston's renaissance by restoring stately homes and building up commercial districts with modern facilities. The result: a resort city with a southern flair—a petite and blended version of New Orleans and Charleston.

Visitor Information

Greater Houston: Convention & Visitors Bureau (⊠ 901 Bagby St., 77002, ☎ 713/437–5200 or 800/446–8786).

Galveston Island: Convention & Visitors Bureau (⊠ 2428 Seawall Blvd., 77550, ☎ 409/763–4311 or 888/425–4753), Historical Society Strand Visitors Center (⊠ 2016 Strand, ☎ 409/766–1572).

Arriving and Departing

By Bus

Greyhound (⊠ 2121 Main St., Houston, ☎ 800/231–2222). **Kerrville Bus Company** (⊠ 714 25th St., Galveston, ☎ 409/765–7731).

By Car

Houston is ringed by I–610 and Beltway 8. A tighter loop, comprising several expressways, circles the downtown and provides remarkable views of the city, especially at dawn and dusk. Radiating out from these rings like spokes of a wheel are I–10, heading east to Louisiana and west to San Antonio; U.S. 59, northeast to Longview or southwest to Victoria; and I–45, southeast to Galveston (about an hour away) or north to Dallas. High Occupancy Vehicle (HOV) lanes, tollways, and crosstown connectors have reduced traffic congestion, but all these highways can be extremely crowded during rush hours.

By Plane

Houston's two major airports are served by about 22 airlines between them. (Be sure to check which airport you will be using, as many airlines serve both.) **Southwest Airlines** (☎ 281/922–1221 or 800/435–9792) has particularly extensive, frequent, and inexpensive service among nine Texas cities and other U.S. destinations. Headquartered here, **Continental Airlines** (☎ 800/523–3273) offers flexible and competitive domestic and international routes. The airport more convenient to downtown is **W. P. Hobby Airport** (⊠ 7800 Airport Blvd., 77061, ☎ 713/640–3000), 9 mi to the southeast. During rush hour, the trip into the city takes about 45 minutes; taxi fare is about $20. **George Bush Intercontinental Airport** (⊠ 2800 North Terminal Rd., 77032, ☎ 281/230–3100), 15 mi north of downtown, is the city's international airport. The trip downtown during peak hours takes up to an hour; cab fare is about $32; confirm the fee with your driver before setting out. **Airport Express** (☎ 713/523–8888) van service connects several Houston hotels to both Hobby ($12) and the George Bush ($17). **Metro** city express bus service (☎ 713/635–4000) to the George Bush costs $1.50.

Galveston Limousine Service (☎ 409/744–5466 in Galveston; 800/640–4826 elsewhere in TX) has regularly scheduled service to island locations from both Houston airports for $21–$26.

By Train

In Houston, **Amtrak** (☎ 713/224–1577 or 800/872–7245) trains arrive from Florida and California at the old **Southern Pacific Station** (⊠ 902 Washington Ave.).

Getting Around Houston and Galveston

Both Houston and Galveston demand cars, as attractions are spread out. Public transportation, though available, is not easy to figure out and may require multiple transfers. Houston's city bus system, **Metro**

(☎ 713/635–4000), is most useful for straight-line routes. A free-**Downtown Trolley** (☎ 713/635–4000) provides shuttle service between the George R. Brown Convention Center and the theater district. Colorful trolleys run throughout the day and late at night stopping at hotels, restaurants, and entertainment centers. Galveston has island bus service, but of far more interest is the **Galveston Island Trolley** (✉ 2100 Seawall Blvd. or 2016 Strand, ☎ 409/797–3900; ☎ 60¢), or **Treasure Island Tour Train** (✉ 2106 Seawall Blvd., ☎ 409/765–9564; ☎ $5.50), which departs regularly for a 1½-hour narrated excursion from outside the Convention Center called "Beach Central" at 21st Street and Seawall Boulevard.

Exploring Houston and Galveston

Houston

Houston can be divided neatly into three major areas. One is its very modern downtown (including the theater district), which spurred one architecture critic to declare the city "America's future." Another is the area a couple of miles south of downtown, where some of the Southwest's leading museums are found along with Rice University and the internationally renowned Texas Medical Center. Finally, there is the thriving shopping and business center west of downtown, known as both the Galleria and Uptown.

DOWNTOWN

You may want to start by taking in the entire urban panorama from the observation deck (weekdays only) of I. M. Pei's 75-story **Chase Tower** (✉ 600 Travis St.), built in 1981. **Texas Avenue,** visible from the tower, is 100 ft wide, precisely the width needed to accommodate 14 Texas longhorns tip to tip in the days when cattle were driven to market along this route. **Tranquility Park** (✉ between Walker and Rusk Sts. east of Smith St.), a cool, human-scale oasis of fountains and diagonal walkways among the skyscrapers, was built to commemorate the first landing on the moon by the *Apollo 11* mission.

The major buildings of the theater district are a few steps from Tranquility Park. The **Jesse H. Jones Hall for the Performing Arts** (✉ 615 Louisiana St., ☎ 713/227–1910 or 800/828–2787), home to the Houston Symphony Orchestra and the Society for the Performing Arts, is a huge hall that appears almost encased by a second, colonnaded building; its teak auditorium is more attractive than the exterior. The **Alley Theatre** (✉ 615 Texas Ave., ☎ 713/228–8421 or 800/259–2553), a fortresslike but innovative low-lying structure, is the venue of the city's resident professional theater company. At the **Gus S. Wortham Theater Center** (✉ 500 Texas Ave., ☎ 713/237–1439 or 800/828–2787), the Houston Grand Opera and the Houston Ballet perform in two side-by-side theaters. A newer addition to the cultural neighborhood is **Bayou Place** (✉ 520 Texas Ave., ☎ 713/693–1600), with live performances from jazz to comedy at the **Aerial Theater. City Hall** (✉ 901 Bagby St.), which houses a comprehensive visitor center on the ground floor, is just northwest of Tranquility Park, in a 1939 modernist structure of Texas limestone designed by Joseph Finger, Houston's premier architect of the time.

Architectural additions to the skyline have spread out from the **Smith-Louisiana corridor,** a daunting canyon formed by towers of glass and steel, running south from Tranquility Park on the west side of downtown. A walk down these streets may be the truest measure of the city's modernism, intensified by the **outdoor sculptures** of Joan Miró, Claes Oldenburg, Louise Nevelson, and Jean Dubuffet. (Dubuffet's *Monument au Fantôme*, on Louisiana Street between Lamar and Dallas streets, is

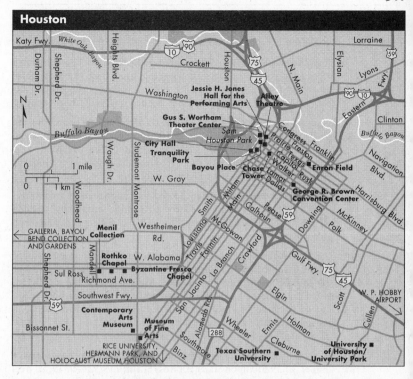

a particular delight to children.) The downtown area is experiencing a vigorous revival with residential and entertainment space being reclaimed in famous old commercial buildings such as the stately Rice Hotel (1913) and the Albert Thomas Convention Center (1963). A new retractable-roof baseball stadium, **Enron Field,** opened with the first game of the 2000 season. It incorporates the 1911 **Union Station** (designed by Warren and Wetmore of New York's Grand Central Station fame), which is being renovated to house retail stores, restaurants, the front offices for the ball club, and a theater. More than 70 of the major business and government buildings downtown are connected by a 6¾-mi labyrinth of **underground tunnels and skywalks,** used by those in the know as a welcome escape from the heat and humidity for which Houston is justly infamous. Walking tours of Houston's remarkable downtown art and architecture, as well as its fascinating tunnel system, are available through **Greater Houston Preservation Alliance** (☎ 713/216–5000), **Discover Houston Tours** (☎ 713/222–9255), and the **Houston Chapter of the American Institute of Architects** (☎ 713/520–0155).

THE MUSEUM DISTRICT

Most museums are clustered within an area bordering the verdant campus of **Rice University,** one of Texas's finest educational institutions, and **Hermann Park,** the city's playground. Walking from one institution to the other is possible, but the expanse can be taxing; it's best to segment your visit.

The **Museum of Fine Arts** is remarkable for the completeness of its enormous collection; it is housed in a complicated series of wings and galleries, many designed by Ludwig Mies van der Rohe. The Audrey Jones Beck Building, the work of famed Spanish architect Rafael Maneo, opened in 2000, doubling the museum's size. Renaissance and 18th-century art, and Impressionist and Post-Impressionist works are particularly well represented. ✉ *1001 Bissonnet St., north of Rice University, between Montrose Blvd. and Main St.,* ☎ *713/639–7300.* ⊠ *$5, free Thurs. Closed Mon.*

The **Lillie and Hugh Roy Cullen Sculpture Garden** (✉ 1001 Bissonnet St., at Montrose Ave.; ⊠ free), across the street from the Museum of Fine Arts, displays 19th- and 20th-century sculptures by Rodin, Matisse, Giacometti, and Stella in a setting designed by Isamu Noguchi.

Housed in a stark, cylindrical edifice, the **Holocaust Museum Houston** (✉ 5401 Caroline St., ☎ 713/942–8000; ⊠ free) is an education center as well as a memorial. The main exhibit, "Bearing Witness: A Community Remembers," can be viewed individually or by tour. The 30-minute film *Voices* is a moving oral history by local survivors.

The **Contemporary Arts Museum,** housed in an aluminum-sheathed trapezoid, is the home of avant-garde art in Houston, with many traveling exhibitions. ✉ *5216 Montrose Blvd.,* ☎ *713/284–8250.* ⊠ *Free. Closed Mon.*

★ The **Menil Collection** is the one of the city's premier cultural treasures. Italian architect Renzo Piano designed the spacious building, with its airy galleries. John and Dominique de Menil collected the eclectic art, which ranges from tribal African sculptures to Andy Warhol's paintings of Campbell's soup cans. A separate gallery across the street houses the paintings of American artist Cy Twombly. ✉ *1515 Sul Ross St.,* ☎ *713/525–9400.* ⊠ *Free. Closed Mon. and Tues.*

Adjacent to the lawns surrounding the Menil complex, the moody **Rothko Chapel** (✉ 3900 Yupon St., at Sul Ross St., ☎ 713/524–9839; ⊠ free) is an octagonal sanctuary designed by Philip Johnson. Fourteen Mark Rothko paintings panel the chapel's walls. Outside the ecumenical chapel is Barnett Newman's sculpture *Broken Obelisk,* which symbolizes the life and assassination of Martin Luther King Jr.

Frescoes from a 13th-century votive chapel have been preserved in the **Byzantine Fresco Chapel Museum,** just a block from the Rothko (✉ 4011 Yupon St., ☎ 713/521–3990; ⊠ free). The dome and apse were rescued from thieves and restored under a unique arrangement with the Greek Orthodox Church and the Republic of Cyprus. Suspended in a black reliquary box are frosted-glass panels replicating the tiny chapel structure.

Across town in the River Oaks neighborhood, the **Bayou Bend Collection and Gardens** (✉ 1 Westcott St., ☎ 713/639–7750; ⊠ home $10, gardens $3 or $7 for guided tour) lets you step back in time to witness the elegant lifestyle of the first half of this century. Noted Houston philanthropist and collector Ima Hogg donated the 28-room mansion, complete with period pieces dating back to the 1600s, to the Fine Arts Museum. The home is surrounded by gardens and natural woods. Guided and self-guided tours must be scheduled in advance.

THE GALLERIA, OR UPTOWN, AREA

The **Galleria** (aka Uptown) is one of the country's most upscale commercial zones. On the west side of Houston, near the intersection of Westheimer Road and I–610, it started out as a single mall. Shopping complexes, office towers, hotels, and other businesses have sprung up around that mall, making the area one of the most important business districts in the city. Many of Houston's best restaurants are here; and the River Oaks neighborhood, with its multimillion-dollar mansions and garden parkways, is nearby.

OTHER NEIGHBORHOODS

Kids and adults can learn about space exploration at **Space Center Houston** (⊠ 1601 NASA Rd. 1 off I–45, ☎ 281/244–2100; ☞ $12.95), 25 mi south of the city. Life on the deck of a space shuttle is simulated in the **Space Center Plaza.** In the **Kids Space Place,** children can ride on the lunar rover and try out tasks in the *Apollo* command module. The adjacent **Johnson Space Center** tour includes a visit to Mission Control and laboratories that simulate weightlessness and other space-related concepts. Allow several hours for your visit.

Perennial favorites, **Six Flags AstroWorld** and **WaterWorld** are enormous amusement and water parks adjacent to each other within the city perimeter (⊠ 9001 Kirby Dr. at I–610, ☎ 713/799–1234; ☞ $31.95 AstroWorld, $16.95 WaterWorld).

OFF THE
BEATEN PATH

Detour off I–45 between Houston and Galveston or take the back roads from NASA to the **Kemah Boardwalk,** a cluster of restaurants, amusement rides, game arcades, and inns on the bustling ship channel—an upmarket Coney Island. It's a family-oriented destination featuring seafood eateries with outdoor decks where you can catch a gulf breeze and watch personal and commercial marine craft motor by.
⊠ Bradford and 2nd St., Kemah, ☎ 877/285–3624.

Galveston

History and the waterfront are the main draws to Galveston, once the largest city in Texas. Its wealthy classes built the Victorian homes that give the island its elegant, turn-of-the-20th-century appearance. These homes as well as some beautifully restored iron-front commercial buildings are concentrated on the northern, or bay, side of the island—especially along a street known as the Strand—and on Broadway, a boulevard that runs east–west through Galveston's midsection. Also hugging the north rim of the island, from 9th to 51st Street, is the harbor, port to small fishing boats and shrimp trawlers and to the *Elissa,* the tall ship that is Galveston's pride and joy. The southern, or ocean, side of the island is lined with beaches (☞ Beaches, *below*), hotels, parks, and restaurants. The laid-back, easy-chair atmosphere explodes twice yearly for one of the county's largest Mardi Gras celebrations (12 days in late February, early March) and the Christmas favorite, Dickens on the Stand (first weekend of December), with seasonal food and song.

THE STRAND AND BROADWAY

The **Strand,** especially the five blocks from 20th to 25th Street, Register of Historic Places). When Galveston was still a powerful port city—before the Houston Ship Channel was dug, diverting most boat traffic inland—this stretch, formerly the site of stores, offices, and warehouses, was known as the Wall Street of the South.

As you stroll up the Strand, you'll pass dozens of shops, outlet stores, and restaurants. The **Center for Transportation and Commerce** (⊠ 2500 Strand, ☎ 409/765–5700), which also houses the **Railroad Museum,** is an Art Deco building that was once the Santa Fe Railroad terminal. The **Tremont House,** a block from the Center for Transportation and Commerce, is an 1879 dry-goods warehouse converted into a hotel; full of Victorian elegance, it's considered the top hotel on the island. Two blocks south of the Strand, on Postoffice Street, is the revitalized arts area **Gallery Row,** home to art galleries, antiques stores, and the **Grand 1894 Opera House** (☞ Nightlife and the Arts, *below*).

Broadway, a major thoroughfare just five minutes by car (or 20 minutes by foot) south of the Tremont House, is home to the "Broadway Beauties," three of the finest examples of historic restoration in Texas.

The Victorian **Bishop's Palace** (✉ 1402 Broadway, ☎ 409/762–2475; ☞ $6), a limestone-and-granite castle built in 1886 for Colonel Walter Gresham, has 11 rare stone and wood mantels—a testament to the colonel's fondness for fireplaces—and a wooden staircase that took 61 craftsmen seven years to carve.

Ashton Villa (✉ 2328 Broadway, ☎ 409/762–3933; ☞ $5), a formal Italianate villa, was built in 1859 of brick—appropriately so, as owner James Moreau Brown started out as a humble mason. A freethinking man, Brown had to install curtains to shield modest guests from the naked Cupids painted on one wall. The **Moody Mansion** (✉ 2618 Broadway, ☎ 409/762–7668; ☞ $6), home to generations of one of Texas's most powerful families, was completed in 1895. Designed by English architect Wiliam Tyndall, the brick Richardsonian Romanesque manse withstood the great storm of 1900. Its interiors of exotic woods and gilded trim are filled with the family heirlooms and personal effects.

THE ELISSA

In 1961 a marine archaeologist and naval historian named Peter Throckmorton spotted a rotting iron hulk in the shipyards outside Athens, Greece, and realized the 150-ft wreck was what remained of a beautiful square-rigger constructed in 1877. After almost 20 years, the Scottish-built **Elissa**—the oldest ship on the Lloyd's Register—has been restored by the Galveston Historical Foundation and hundreds of volunteers. The ship, which in the last century carried cargoes to Galveston Harbor, may be toured above and below decks and is the centerpiece of the **Texas Seaport Museum** (✉ Pier 21, ☎ 409/763–1877; ☞ $6).

From the seawall you will see dozens of offshore oil rigs. Climb aboard the **Ocean Star** (✉ Pier 19, ☎ 409/766–7827; ☞ $5) for a first-hand view of how the rigs operate and what life is like out on the huge platforms.

★ ⊙ **Moody Gardens** (✉ 1 Hope Blvd., ☎ 409/741–8484 or 800/582–4673, ☞ $7–$10 per venue, discount combination tickets available) is a multifaceted complex that teaches, entertains, and fascinates. Attractions include the stunning 13-story **Aquarium Pyramid**, showcasing marine life from four oceans in tanks and touch pools; **Rainforest Pyramid**, a 40,000-square-ft tropical habitat for exotic flora and fauna; **Discovery Pyramid**, a joint venture with NASA featuring more than 40 interactive exhibits; and two **IMAX theaters**, one of which has a space adventure ride. Also, don't miss the **botanical garden** or **Hope Therapy Program**, an internationally recognized hippotherapy (rehabilitation through horseback riding) treatment center.

⊙ Another family favorite is the free, 15-minute ride on the **Port Bolivar Ferry** (✉ north of Stewart Beach on Ferry Rd.; parking available adjacent to ferry landing), which crosses Galveston Bay.

Parks, Gardens, and Zoos

Houston

Hermann Park, with its 545 acres of trees, lawns, duck-filled reflecting pools, picnic areas, and 18-hole golf course, is only a short drive south of downtown on Main Street. Sitting on the northern perimeter of the Texas Medical Center, the park is also home to the **Houston Zoological Gardens** (✉ 1513 N. MacGregor St., ☎ 713/523–5888; ☞ $2.50), which includes a primate rain forest, petting zoo, and aquarium. The excellent **Museum of Natural Science** (✉ 1 Hermann Circle Dr., ☎ 713/639–4600; ☞ $4 entry fee, plus additional charges for each venue; combination discount tickets available), also on park grounds, includes the **Baker Planetarium, Cockrell Butterfly Center,** and **Wortham IMAX Theatre,** with a six-story-high projection screen.

Memorial Park, several miles west of downtown between the 610 Loop and South Shepherd Drive, has 1,500 acres of mostly virgin woodland—prime territory for walking, jogging, and biking. An **Arboretum and Nature Center** creates a sanctuary for native species.

The small downtown **Sam Houston Park,** bounded by Bagby, McKinney, and Dallas streets, is a green space where several of the city's 19th-century buildings have been moved. Tickets for daily guided tours are available at the Heritage Society (☎ 713/655–1912; ☒ $4), on the Bagby side.

Galveston

Stewart Beach Park (☒ 6th St. and Seawall Blvd., ☎ 409/765–5023; ☒ $5 parking; closed mid-Oct.–mid-Mar.), a bit of Coney Island on the Gulf, has a bathhouse, amusement park, bumper boats, miniature golf course, and water coaster.

⚠ **Galveston Island State Park,** toward the western, unpopulated end of the island (☒ 3 Mile Rd., ☎ 409/737–1222; ☒ $3), is a 2,000-acre natural habitat ideal for birding, walking, and camping.

Dining

Houston

$$$$ **✗ Tony's.** Houston's culinary icon, Tony Vallone introduced European
★ cuisine to the city when he opened his restaurant. An exceptional wine list complements artfully prepared dishes such as Sweetwater Hen Nancy (roasted hen served atop a wild-mushroom risotto with a morel-and-sherry sauce) and pan-seared halibut Strauss, blanketed with lump crabmeat, caviar, and smoked salmon. ☒ *1801 Post Oak Blvd.,* ☎ *713/ 622–6778. AE, D, DC, MC, V. Reservations essential.*

$$$–$$$$ **✗ Cafe Annie.** Chef Robert Del Grande, one of the founders of south-
★ western cuisine, serves up the best of his innovative, fiery cookery at this acclaimed restaurant. Start any meal with the layered gulf crabmeat tostada. The three-course, city lunch menu, offering a range of Del Grande's signature dishes, is well priced. ☒ *1728 Post Oak Blvd.,* ☎ *713/840–1111. Reservations essential. AE, DC, MC, V.*

$$–$$$ **✗ Grotto.** This trendy and highly acclaimed bistro has a more casual menu than its siblings, Tony's (☞ *above*) and Anthony's, which are also owned by Tony Vallone. Rich Italian heritage goes into every item on the menu. The risotto *frutti di mare* is a medley of fresh shellfish. ☒ *3920 Westheimer Blvd.,* ☎ *713/622–3663. AE, D, DC, MC, V.*

$$–$$$ **✗ Ouisie's Table.** Here American cuisine is prepared with eclectic, southern accents. Request a table on Lucy's Porch for a view of the herb plantings snipped daily by the kitchen staff. Enjoy such favorites as Ouisie's chicken fried steak salad with Roquefort dressing or a grilled lime redfish *chalupa* (a fried corn tortilla). There's a fabulous Saturday brunch and an afternoon "little bites" menu. ☒ *3939 San Felipe Rd.,* ☎ *713/528–2264. AE, D, DC, MC, V. Closed Sun. and Mon.*

$–$$$ **✗ Mo Mong.** You'll have to look hard to find this Vietnamese gem hidden behind the Hollywood Video store. With soaring two-story matte steel partitions and Asian minimalist accents, the restaurant's stunning decor highlights the creativity of the fusion cuisine. The *Ca Kho To* (seasoned catfish baked in a clay pot) and the Vietnamese fajitas convert typically southern ingredients into Asian specialties. ☒ *1201B Westheimer Rd.,* ☎ *713/524–5664. AE, D, DC, MC, V.*

$–$$ ✕ **Solero.** After-work professionals and arts patrons pack this chic downtown restaurant for Spanish and South American tapas—assorted hot and cold small plates. Mix-and-match menu items by tapa (single portion) or ración (full serving). Exceptional paella and bouillabaise showcase fresh gulf coast seafood. Solero is an excellent choice for vegetarians. ✉ *910 Prairie Ave.,* ☎ *713/227–2665. AE, D, MC, V.*

$ ✕ **Cafe Express.** Each of the sporty, gourmet cafés in this chain developed by Robert Del Grande (of Cafe Annie) serves flavorful pasta, salads, and burgers. The Post Oak branch is in the heart of the busy Galleria area. ✉ *1800 Post Oak Blvd.,* ☎ *713/963–9222 (call for additional locations). AE, D, DC, MC, V.*

$ ✕ **Goode Company.** Down-home Texas barbecue is prepared ranch-style—smoked, and served with tasty red sauce. Patrons line up on the sidewalk to eat at picnic tables on the covered patio. A standard order is the chopped-beef brisket sandwich on jalapeño-cheese bread. ✉ *5109 Kirby Dr.,* ☎ *713/522–2530. AE, D, DC, MC, V.*

$ ✕ **Irma's.** Irma and her family dish out home-style Mexican specialties to a wait-in-line breakfast and lunch crowd. There's no menu: Your server will tell you what is available. Opt for the chicken and spinach enchiladas with green chili sauce—hand-patted tortillas chock full of freshly sautéed spinach and chunks of chicken. ✉ *22 N. Chenevert St.,* ☎ *713/222–0767. AE, DC, MC, V. Closed weekends.*

Galveston

$$–$$$ ✕ **Luigi's Restorante Italiano.** Northern Italian cuisine is served trattoria-style in this converted 1895 bank building. The muted sienna walls, fruitwood-paneled bar, and mural-size replicas of classical Italian artists create a warm setting. One taste of the *pollo Parmigiano* (chicken Parmesan) or *vitello piccata* (veal piccata) and you will think you walked in off a piazza in Florence instead of the Strand on Galveston Bay. ✉ *2318 The Strand,* ☎ *409/763–6500. AE, D, DC, MC, V.*

$–$$$ ✕ **Fisherman's Wharf.** New restaurants have joined this harborside institution on the renovated piers that front the Strand, but locals keep coming here for the fresh seafood, reasonable prices, and good times. Dine indoors or out, keeping an eye on traffic in the ship channel. Start off with a cold combo—boiled shrimp and grilled rare tuna. The fresh fish, shrimp, and oysters from the grill or fryer are hard to beat. ✉ *3901 Ave. O,* ☎ *409/765–5708. AE, D, DC, MC, V.*

$–$$$ ✕ **Gaido's and Casey's.** Dine on linen at the venerable Gaido's or kick back casually at the adjacent Casey's. These family-owned restaurants have the same lineage, dating back to 1911, when Grandfather Gaido opened an eatery atop Murdoch's bathhouse. Adamant that the seafood be fresh, the kitchen here peels, shucks, and fillets by hand, just as in the early days. Gulf views are blocks wide at this landmark. ✉ *37th to 39th St. and Seawall Blvd.,* ☎ *409/762–9625. AE, DC, MC, V.*

$ ✕ **The Phoenix.** Every community needs a gathering place for breakfast and this is it. The Phoenix brews a flavorful cup of java and espresso. Selections range from New Orleans beignets to country-style bacon and eggs. The pastry case, packed with baked goods, is impossible to resist. Dining hours extend through lunch, with freshly prepared soups and sandwiches. ✉ *221 Tremont St.,* ☎ *409/763–4611. AE, D, DC, MC, V.*

$ ✕ **The Spot.** Brightly painted beach cottages connected by walkways and decks make up this retail-restaurant compound. Po'boy sandwiches, burgers, spuds, and ice cream are dispensed with casual friendliness. Watch out, the scent of freshly baked breads, pastries, and cookies from Maddie's Place Bakery will demand a stop. Dine in the cool air-conditioning or take your tray out on the deck. ✉ *3204 Seawall Blvd.,* ☎ *409/621–5237. AE, D, DC, MC, V.*

Lodging

Houston

$$$$ 🏨 **Four Seasons Hotel.** This elegant, city-center hotel is in the hub of it all. Convenient to the Convention Center, downtown businesses, and the new ballpark, the Four Seasons offers deluxe amenities and top-notch service, making it a discriminating traveler's first choice. ⊠ *1300 Lamar St., 77010,* ☎ *713/650–1300 or 800/332–3442,* 𝐅𝐀𝐗 *713/650–8169. 399 rooms. 2 restaurants, pool, health club. AE, D, DC, MC, V.* ✎

$$$$ 🏨 **Houstonian Hotel, Club and Spa.** Spread over 18 acres in a heavily wooded area near Memorial Park, just west of downtown and near the Galleria, the Houstonian has luxurious rooms and sports and fitness facilities galore—golf, tennis, a climbing wall, and indoor racket games. ⊠ *111 N. Post Oak La., 77024,* ☎ *713/680–2626 or 800/231–2759,* 𝐅𝐀𝐗 *713/680–2992. 286 rooms. 3 restaurants, pools, health club. AE, D, DC, MC, V.* ✎

$$$$ 🏨 **Lancaster.** In the heart of the theater district, this small luxury hotel has the feel of a European manor house. Chippendale furniture, plaid upholstered chairs, oil landscapes and portraits, and brass cachepots create an intimate setting that contrasts with its steel-and-glass surroundings. ⊠ *701 Texas Ave., 77002,* ☎ *713/228–9500,* 𝐅𝐀𝐗 *713/223–4528. 93 rooms. Restaurant, exercise room. AE, D, DC, MC, V.* ✎

$$$–$$$$ 🏨 **J. W. Marriott.** Across from the Galleria, Houston's premiere shopping mall, and surrounded by speciality stores, this hotel is a shopper's haven. Business travelers enjoy easy access to Fortune 500 companies headquartered in the I–610/Uptown corridor. Guests can play basketball and racquetball. ⊠ *5150 Westheimer Rd., 77056,* ☎ *713/961–1500 or 800/228–9290,* 𝐅𝐀𝐗 *713/961–5045. 513 rooms. Restaurant, pool, health club. AE, D, DC, MC, V.* ✎

$$$ 🏨 **Warwick Park Plaza.** The best location for museum hopping or having medical center appointments, the restored Warwick is noted for its spectacular views of Hermann Park and the downtown skyline. The richly paneled Hunt Room restaurant with its Old World antique furnishings is the perfect setting for special-occasion dining. ⊠ *5701 Main St., 77005,* ☎ *713/526–1991 or 800/670–7275,* 𝐅𝐀𝐗 *713/526–0359. 308 rooms. 3 restaurants, pool, exercise room. AE, D, DC, MC, V.* ✎

Galveston

$$$–$$$$ 🏨 **Moody Gardens Hotel.** This is one of the latest additions to the popular Moody Gardens complex, which includes a series of natural habitats housed in huge pyramids, parks, theaters, and water attractions. This contemporary high-rise hotel, with its brightly colored tropical decor, boasts the best views of the gulf, bay, gardens, and pyramids. A good choice for families, it is just steps away from all attractions and exhibits. The Texas-size outdoor pool surrounded by lush gardens and waterfalls is a playground for all ages. ⊠ *1 Hope Blvd., 77554,* ☎ *409/744–1745 or 800/582–4673, ext. 215,* 𝐅𝐀𝐗 *409/744–1631. 303 rooms. 2 restaurants, pools, exercise room, beauty salon, spa. AE, D, DC, MC, V.* ✎

$$$–$$$$ 🏨 **Tremont House.** Just steps off the Strand, this hotel recalls the grandeur of Victorian days. Once a busy dry-goods warehouse, Tremont House has rooms with soaring ceilings and 11-ft windows, as well as period furnishings. The four-story atrium lobby, with ironwork balconies and full-size palm trees, showcases an 1872 hand-carved, rosewood bar. ⊠ *2300 Ship's Mechanic Row, 77550,* ☎ *409/763–0300 or 800/996–3426,* 𝐅𝐀𝐗 *409/763–1539. 127 rooms. Restaurant, pool, golf and tennis privileges. AE, DC, MC, V.* ✎

$$$ 🏨 **Hotel Galvez.** This seaside grande dame was once called "Queen of the Gulf." The six-story Spanish colonial hotel, built in 1911, has been restored to its original splendor. The lobby, music hall, parlors, loggia, and veranda evoke memories of a bygone era. A pool, swim-up bar, and outdoor grill have been added to the tropical garden facing the sea. ⊠ *2024 Seawall Blvd., 77550,* ☎ *409/765–7721 or 800/996– 3426,* ℻ *409/765–5780. 231 rooms. Restaurant, pool, golf privileges. AE, DC, MC, V.* 🍽

$$$ 🛏 **Stacia Leigh.** Step aboard a 120-ft vintage schooner for a harbor-side stay at a unique floating bed-and-breakfast berthed alongside the historic *Elissa.* Commissioned in the early 1900s by the founder of Renault automobile works, the yacht changed many hands and was once owned by Facist Italian dictator Benito Mussolini. Completely restored from the hull out, the 11 staterooms and elegant salon use wicker furniture and multicolor quilts to create a coastal Americana feel. Guests enjoy ample cabins with en-suite baths and showers, some with Jacuzzi tubs. ⊠ *Pier 22, Harborside Dr., 77550,* ☎ *409/750–8858. 11 rooms. AE, D, DC, MC, V.*

$$–$$$ 🛏 **The Victorian.** This condominium at the beach has ocean views from many of its balconies. One- and two-bedroom units have fully equipped kitchens. ⊠ *6300 Seawall Blvd., 77551,* ☎ *409/740–3555 or 800/231–6363,* ℻ *409/744–3801. 254 suites. Restaurant, pool, tennis, exercise room. AE, D, DC, MC, V.*

Nightlife and the Arts

Nightlife

There are other hot spots around the city, but Downtown has become the magnet for after-hours activity with hip clubs and chic restaurants springing up among renovated storefronts and warehouses. **Bayou Place** (⊠ 500 Texas Ave.), Houston's largest entertainment complex, is a hub of evening activity, with restaurants, clubs, and the **Angelika Film Center** (⊠ 510 Texas Ave., ☎ 713/255–1470), a sophisticated NYC spin-off with independent and foreign films and before- or after-theater gourmet dining. For jazz, head to **Sambuca** (⊠ 909 Texas Ave., ☎ 713/ 224–5299); for blues, **Silky's** (⊠ 4219 Washington Ave., ☎ 713/880– 2990) is hard to beat. The **Swank Lounge,** upstairs at Solero's (⊠ 910 Prairie Ave., ☎ 713/227–2665), and the **Mercury Room** (⊠ 1008 Prairie Ave., ☎ 713/225–6372) are popular late-night hangouts with live music.

The Arts

HOUSTON

Houston is one of the few cities in the United States with four resident performance companies, which stage shows at **Jones Hall, Alley Theatre,** and **Wortham Theater Center** (☞ Downtown *in* Exploring Houston and Galveston, *above*). Ticket information on the city's **symphony orchestra, opera, ballet,** and **theater** may be obtained by calling a **central ticketing facility** (☎ 713/227–2787 or 800/828–2787).

The largest professional African-American theater company, the **Ensemble Theater** (⊠ 3535 Main St., ☎ 713/520–0055) appears in gripping performances on its own stage in the theater district.

Complete listings of events are carried in the *Houston Chronicle (Friday Weekend Preview), Houston Press,* and *Where* magazine.

GALVESTON

The **Grand 1894 Opera House** (⊠ 2020 Postoffice St., ☎ 409/765– 1894 or 800/821–1894), where performances of various kinds are held year-round, is worth visiting for the architecture alone. Sarah Bernhardt and Anna Pavlova both performed on this storied stage. The **Strand Street Theater** (⊠ 2317 Ship's Mechanic Row, ☎ 409/763–4591) is another venue for variety theater.

Spectator Sports

Baseball: Houston Astros (⊠ Enron Field, 1920 Preston Ave., ☎ 713/799–9500). **Basketball: Houston Rockets** (⊠ Compaq Center, 10 Greenway Plaza, ☎ 713/627–3865). **Houston Comets (WNBA)** (⊠ Compaq Center, 10 Greenway Plaza, ☎ 713/627–9622). **Hockey: Houston Aeros** (⊠ Compaq Center, 10 Greenway Plaza, ☎ 713/627–2376).

Motor sports: TEXACO/Havoline Grand Prix roars through the streets of Downtown the last weekend of September as part of CART's (Championship Auto Racing Team) street circuit racing (☎ 713/739–7223).

Beaches

Galveston's ocean beaches are all open to the public. The eastern end of the island, especially around Stewart Beach Park, has amenities of all kinds, including rentals of surfboards, windsurfers, sailboats, chairs, and umbrellas. To the west are quieter, less crowded beaches. The seawall along the waterfront attracts runners, cyclists, and rollerbladers.

Shopping

Houston

The city's premier shopping area is the **Galleria,** or Uptown. Here, the **Galleria mall** (⊠ Post Oak Blvd. and Westheimer Rd.) is famous for high-quality stores like Neiman Marcus, Saks Fifth Avenue, and Tiffany & Co. The **Pavilion on Post Oak,** a mall north of the Galleria mall, and **Westheimer Road,** on the east side of the I–610 Freeway, expand this shopping area with specialty retailers, superstores, and galleries. The headquarters for boots and other western gear is **Stelzig's Western Wear** (⊠ 3123 Post Oak Blvd., ☎ 713/629–7779). Gift packs of sauces, cooking equipment, and stylish western wear are found at **Goode Company BBQ Hall of Flame** (⊠ 5015 Kirby Dr., ☎ 713/643–5263). The **Village** (⊠ University Blvd. and Kirby Dr.), next to Rice University, was Houston's first mall; it still has many small shops as well as some national names. For antiques, vintage clothing, and folk art, try the stores in the **Heights,** a re-gentrified neighborhood north of I–10 (19th Street between Heights Boulevard and Yale Street). You will find everything from treasures to junk at **Trader's Village Flea Market and RV Park** (⊠ 7979 Eldridge Rd.), a 60-acre sprawl of merchants and peddlers open on Saturday and Sunday only. Admission is $2.

Galleries are scattered throughout the Museum District. Two notables are **Gremillion & Co.** (⊠ 2501 Sunset Blvd., ☎ 713/522–2701), for contemporary art, and **Nolan-Rankin** (⊠ 4621 Montrose Blvd., ☎ 713/528–0664), for the European masters.

Galveston

The historic stretches along the Strand and Gallery Row (Postoffice Street) are the best places to shop in Galveston. The **Old Strand Emporium** (⊠ 2112 Strand, ☎ 409/763–9445) is a charming deli and gourmet grocery that is reminiscent of an old-fashioned ice cream parlor and sandwich shop, with candy bins, packaged nuts, and more. The shops at the Tremont House, **Gatherings and Sean Miles** (⊠ 2300 Strand, ☎ 409/763–1770 or 409/763–7177), offer a finely edited selection of upscale women's apparel, accessories, and gifts. More than 50 antiques dealers are represented at **Eiband's Gallery** (⊠ 2001 Postoffice, ☎ 409/763–5495), an upscale showroom filled with furniture, books, art, and jewelry.

SAN ANTONIO AND THE HILL COUNTRY

The Alamo—symbol either of Texan heroism or Anglo arrogance—is by no means the only reason to visit **San Antonio.** A mélange of easily mingling ethnic groups, it is in many ways Texas's most beautiful and atmospheric city. Northwest of San Antonio is the **Hill Country,** an anomaly in generally flat Texas, rich with pretty landscapes, early American history, and echoes of the linen-to-silk story of Lyndon Baines Johnson, the nation's 36th president.

Visitor Information

Bandera: Convention & Visitors Bureau (✉ 1606 Hwy. 16S, Box 171, 78003, ☎ 830/796–3045 or 800/364–3833). **Fredericksburg:** Convention & Visitors Bureau (✉ 106 N. Adams St., 78624, ☎ 830/997–6523). **Kerrville:** Convention & Visitors Bureau (✉ 2108 Sidney Baker St., 78028, ☎ 830/792–3535 or 800/221–7958). **San Antonio:** Alamo Visitor Center (✉ 1331 N. Pine, 78202, ☎ 210/225–8587); Convention & Visitors Bureau (✉ 203 S. St. Mary's St., 78205, ☎ 210/207–6700 or 800/447–3372; ✉ 317 Alamo Plaza, near the Alamo).

Arriving and Departing

By Bus
Buses run out of San Antonio's **Greyhound station** (✉ 500 N. St. Mary's St., ☎ 210/270–5824 or 800/231–2222) to all major cities and most local towns.

By Car
The area is served by good highways, including I–35 from Dallas and Austin and I–10 from Houston. I–410 rings the city, and several highways take you downtown.

By Plane
More than a dozen airlines serve **San Antonio International Airport** (✉ 9800 Airport Blvd., 78216, ☎ 210/207–3411), about a 15-minute drive north of downtown. **Shuttle services** (☎ 210/281–9900 or 210/824–3000) transport groups or individuals citywide. **Southwest Airlines** (☎ 210/617–1221 or 800/435–9792) provides regional service.

By Train
Amtrak (☎ 210/223–3226 or 800/872–7245) serves San Antonio's station (✉ 350 Hoefgren St.) with thrice-weekly trains north to Fort Worth, Dallas, east Texas, and Chicago and east to New Orleans and beyond; on Monday, Thursday, and Saturday there is service west to Los Angeles.

Exploring San Antonio and the Hill Country

Much of San Antonio can be explored on foot, although some of its attractions will require transportation. For the Hill Country, a car is a must; you can visit several towns in a day, catching some of the landscapes in between as you drive.

San Antonio
At the heart of San Antonio, the **Alamo** (✉ Alamo Plaza, ☎ 210/225–1391; ☞ free) stands as a repository of Texas history, a monument to the 189 volunteers who died there in 1836 during a 13-day siege by the Mexican dictator and general Santa Anna. Today the historic chapel and barracks contain the guns and other paraphernalia used by

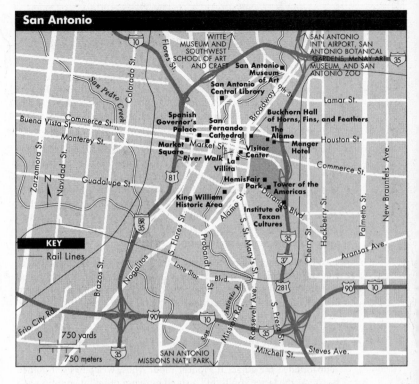

San Antonio

William Travis, Davy Crockett, James Bowie, and other Texas heroes. Outside in the peaceful courtyard, a history wall elucidates the history of the Alamo and of the Mission San Antonio de Valero, as this mission—San Antonio's first—was originally called. In the Rivercenter mall, the **Alamo IMAX Theatre** (⊠ 849 E. Commerce St., ☎ 210/225–4629 or 800/354–4629; 🎟 $7.25) shows a 45-minute film, *Alamo . . . The Price of Freedom,* on a giant screen five times a day.

On Alamo Plaza is the 1859 **Menger Hotel,** San Antonio's most historic lodging. As legend has it, William Menger built the hotel to accommodate the many carousers who frequented his brewery, which stood on the same site. Step inside the hotel to see its moody, mahogany bar, a precise replica of the pub in London's House of Lords. Here Teddy Roosevelt supposedly recruited his Rough Riders, cowboys fresh from the Chisholm Trail who drank to excess and fought, and cattlemen closed deals with a handshake over three fingers of rye.

The **Texas Star Trail,** which begins and ends at the Alamo, is a 2½-mi walking tour designated by blue disks in the sidewalks. Information on the trail, which takes you past 80 historic sites and landmarks, is available at the Alamo Visitor Center at Alamo Plaza.

★ **River Walk,** or Paseo del Rio, is the city's leading tourist attraction. Built a full story below street level, it comprises about 3 mi of scenic stone pathways lining both banks of the San Antonio River as it flows through downtown. In some places the walk is peaceful and quiet; in others it is a mad conglomeration of restaurants, bars, hotels, and strolling mariachi bands, all of which can also be seen from river taxis and charter boats (Yanaguana Riverboat Rides, ☎ 210/244–5700 or 800/417–4139). Near La Mansion del Rio hotel (☞ Dining and Lodging, *below*), at the Navarro Street Bridge, is the huge retail-and-entertainment complex known as **South Bank.** Each January parts of the river are drained to clear the bottom of debris, and locals revel in the River Walk Mud Festival and Mud Parade. During the annual Fiesta River Parade (April) and Holiday River Parade (November), colorfully festooned floats create a spectacle.

HemisFair Park, at one time the site of a World's Fair and currently home to the 750-ft **Tower of the Americas** (⊠ 600 HemisFair Way, ☎ 210/207–8615; 🎫 observation deck $3), is southeast of River Walk. The observation deck and rotating restaurant atop the tower afford bird's-eye views of the city.

☾ The University of Texas's **Institute of Texan Cultures** (⊠ 801 S. Bowie St., ☎ 210/458–2300; 🎫 $4; closed Mon.), just beyond the Tower of the Americas, is an interactive museum focusing on the 30 ethnic groups who made Texas what it is today. Here you can walk through a re-created sharecropper's house; observe and listen to an animated, recorded conversation that might have taken place between a Spanish governor and a Comanche chief in the 1790s; or learn how and when your ancestors settled in Texas.

Leading German merchants settled the **King William Historic Area** in the late 19th century. The elegant Victorian mansions, set in a quiet, leafy neighborhood, are a pleasure to behold; Madison, Guenther, and King William streets are particularly pretty for a stroll or drive. Stop in for a guided tour of the 1876 Victorian **Steves Homestead** (⊠ 509 King William St., ☎ 210/225–5924; 🎫 $3) and pick up a walking guide brochure for the entire neighborhood. The 1860 **Guenther House** (⊠ 205 E. Guenther St., ☎ 210/227–1061; 🎫 free), home of the family that founded the adjacent Pioneer Flour Mills, welcomes self-guided tours. At the latter you'll find a small museum of mill memorabilia, a gift shop, and a cheerful restaurant serving fine German pastries and full breakfasts and lunches.

Except for the Alamo, all of San Antonio's historic missions constitute **San Antonio Missions National Park** (🎫 free). Established along the San Antonio River in the 18th century, the missions stand as reminders of Spain's most successful attempt to extend its New World dominion northward from Mexico. All of the missions are active parish churches, and all are beautiful, in their way. Start your tour at the stunning **Misión San José** (⊠ 6701 San José Dr., ☎ 210/922–0543), the "Queen of Missions," where a National Park Service visitor center illuminates the history of the missions. San José's outer wall, Native American dwellings, granary, water mill, and workshops have been restored. Here you can pick up a map of the **Mission Trail** that connects San José with the other missions. **Misión Concepción** (⊠ 807 Mission Rd., ☎ 210/534–1540) is known for its frescoes; **San Juan** (⊠ 9102 Graf, ☎ 210/532–3914), with its Romanesque arches, has a serene chapel; and **Espada** (⊠ 10040 Espada Rd., ☎ 210/627–2021), the southernmost mission, includes an Arab-inspired aqueduct that was part of the missions' famous *acequia* water management system.

Now in the Buckhorn Saloon, the **Buckhorn Hall of Horns, Fins, and Feathers** (⊠ 318 E. Houston St., ☎ 210/247–4000; 🎫 $9.95) is said to contain the world's largest collection of animal horns. The **San Fernando Cathedral** (⊠ 115 Main Plaza, ☎ 210/227–1297; 🎫 free), in town, just west of the river, is where Santa Anna raised his flag—an ominous message of no mercy—to intimidate the Alamo defenders. The seat of a bishopric, it was visited by Pope John Paul II in 1987. The beautiful 18th-century **Spanish Governor's Palace** (⊠ 105 Plaza de Armas, ☎ 210/224–0601; 🎫 $1), seat of Spanish power in Texas, is an ideal picnic site.

San Antonio has a thriving arts scene. The **San Antonio Museum of Art** (✉ 200 W. Jones Ave., ☎ 210/978–8100; ✆ $5; closed Mon.) houses choice collections of pre-Columbian, Native American, and Spanish colonial art, as well as the Nelson A. Rockefeller Center for Latin American Art, the nation's largest such facility, with more than 2,500 folk art objects donated from the Rockefeller collection. The **Southwest School of Art and Craft** (✉ 300 Augusta St., ☎ 210/224–1848; ✆ free) is filled with a contemporary art gallery and local crafts made by artists-in-residence, but the school may be most remarkable for its building, once an Ursuline school for girls—a fine example of San Antonio's adaptive use of historic structures.

You can't miss the 240,000-square-ft **San Antonio Central Library** (✉ 600 Soledad St., ☎ 210/207–2500): Its burnt-orange color, locally known as enchilada-red, and its modern design by the Mexican architect Ricardo Legoretta have been a source of contention among traditionalists. Inside, the library's collection of books, videos, CDs, and laser discs is cataloged on computer with a bilingual (English/Spanish) interface.

☾ At the **Witte Museum** (✉ 3801 Broadway, Brackenridge Park, ☎ 210/357–1900; ✆ $5.95), a four-level "science tree house" is filled with interactive exhibits that let kids lift themselves with pulleys and ropes, play music with laser beams, and launch tennis balls 30 ft in the air.

The **San Antonio Zoo** (✉ 3903 N. St. Mary's St., ☎ 210/734–7183; ✆ $7) has the nation's third-largest animal collection, most in outdoor habitats.

On the outskirts of the city, the **McNay Art Museum** (✉ 6000 N. New Braunfels Ave., ☎ 210/824–5368; ✆ donations requested), in a private mansion with handsome tile floors and a Moorish-style courtyard, has an impressive collection of post-Impressionist and modern paintings and sculpture, along with a theater arts library. Not far from the McNay Art Museum are the **San Antonio Botanical Gardens** (✉ 555 Funston Pl., ☎ 210/207–3250; ✆ $4), 33 acres containing formal gardens, wildflower-spangled meadows, native Texas vegetation, and a "touch and smell" garden specially designed for blind people.

The Hill Country

A drive through the Hill Country from San Antonio makes a pleasant excursion. Starting toward the northwest, it's less than an hour's trip on I–10 to the Kerrville area. However, you may want to take the far prettier Route 16, a hilly road that leads to **Bandera** (population: 877), one of the nation's oldest Polish communities (dating from 1855) and site of an 1854 Mormon colony.

Boerne (population: 5,200), on I–10, was founded by Germans and named after a German writer. One of its fine early buildings is the **Kuhlmann-King House** (✉ 402 E. Blanco St., ☎ 830/249–2030 or 830/249–8000; ✆ donations accepted), which can be toured by appointment with the local historical society. About 4 mi from Boerne, **Cascade Caverns** (✉ Exit 543 off I–10, San Antonio, ☎ 830/755–8080; ✆ $8.50) has a 90-ft underground waterfall and visitor facilities, including RV campsites and a pool.

Kerrville, a town made for taking it easy, is said to have the best climate in the nation. This has led to a proliferation of hotels, children's summer camps, guest ranches, and religious centers, along with an annual 18-day folk music festival that draws national talents to its stage. **Kerrville State Park** (☎ 830/257–5392; ✆ $3), 500 acres along the cypress-edged Guadalupe River, is a good place to spot the area's abundant white-tail deer.

Fredericksburg, the Hill Country's prettiest town and the heart of its predominantly German-American population, is just 24 mi north of Kerrville, on Route 16. Its main street (bilingually signposted as HAUPT-STRASSE) is a sort of German version of a classic western movie scene except that it's lined with chic stores, antiques shops, and small German eateries. One of Fredericksburg's famous sons was Chester W. Nimitz, commander in chief of the U.S. Pacific fleet in World War II. The restored Nimitz Steamboat Hotel now forms part of the **Admiral Nimitz National Museum of the Pacific War** (⊠ 340 E. Main St., ☎ 830/997–4379; ☞ $5), which displays restored hotel rooms, exhibits on the war in the Pacific, and the Garden of Peace, donated by the Japanese government.

Eighteen miles north of Fredericksburg, eons of uplift and erosion have exposed a sleeping giant at **Enchanted Rock State Natural Area** (⊠ 16710 Ranch Rd. 965, ☎ 915/247–3903; ☞ $5), where an enormous pink granite rock swells 425 ft above ground and covers 640 acres. The views atop the behemoth make the short but steep hike worthwhile.

Luckenbach is only a speck (population: 25) on the map. A little east of Fredericksburg on Route 1376, Luckenbach was founded in 1850 and remains largely unchanged, with one unpainted general store and tavern, a rural dance hall, and a blacksmith's shop. Although the rustic little complex is open daily except Wednesday, you may want to stop by on Sunday afternoon, when informal groups of fiddlers, guitarists, and banjo pickers gather under the live oaks.

The **Lyndon Baines Johnson National Historical Park** is separated into two districts: one in Johnson City and the other near Stonewall, 14 mi away. At the center of **Johnson City** (U.S. 281, 60 mi north of San Antonio; U.S. 290, 50 mi west of Austin)—the poor, dusty town where our 36th President was born and raised—is the **visitor center** (⊠ 100 Lady Bird La., ☎ 830/868–7128), with books, films and exhibits on the area. Nearby are LBJ's small, white-frame **boyhood home,** where rangers give free guided tours daily, and the **Johnson Settlement** (☞ free), a ranch complex once owned by LBJ's family. On certain weekends, costumed interpreters demonstrate the skills and trades of frontier Texas; call for a schedule. A worthwhile **bus tour** (☞ $3) departs daily from the **LBJ Ranch District** (⊠ east of Stonewall on U.S. 290, ☎ 830/644–2420), with stops at Johnson's birthplace, the one-room school he attended, and his grave; along the way you'll also pass the **White House,** where Lady Bird Johnson still lives.

Blanco (just south of Johnson City on U.S. 281), the onetime county seat, is ornamented by a fine bit of classic Texas: the Second Empire–style **Old Blanco County Courthouse.**

The drive back to San Antonio on U.S. 281 is pleasant, but if you have time, go by way of **San Marcos** on Route 32. This road, which skips along parts of a ridge called the **Devil's Backbone,** leads through classic Hill Country landscapes. If time permits, make a short detour to ☾ **Natural Bridge Caverns** (⊠ follow signs from Rte. 1863 between San Antonio and New Braunfels, ☎ 210/651–6101; ☞ $9), a mile-long series of multicolored subterranean rooms and corridors. "Thunder ☾ lizard" tracks dating from 100 million years ago can be found at **Dinosaur Flats** (⊠ Rte. 306, 2 mi southwest of Sattler), a feature of a trail along the south edge of Canyon Lake.

Dining and Lodging

The Bandera and Kerrville visitor centers (☞ Visitor Information, *above*) have information on guest ranches. The Hill Country is chock-full of bed-and-breakfasts, particularly in popular towns like Fredericksburg. Ask for listings at local convention and visitor centers or try the reservation services **Be My Guest** (⊠ 110 N. Milan St., Fredericksburg 78624, ☎ 830/997–7227 or 800/364–8555) and **Gastehaus Schmidt** (⊠ 231 W. Main St., Fredericksburg 78624, ☎ 830/997–5612).

San Antonio

$$$$ ✕ **Biga.** Chef-owner Bruce Auden's inventive southwestern-American
★ restaurant relocated to the Riverwalk in spring 2000 and added patio seating, private dining, a full bar, and valet parking. ⊠ *203 S. St. Mary's St.,* ☎ *210/225–0722. AE, DC, MC, V.*

$$$$ ✕ **Polo's.** Inside the elegant Fairmount hotel (☞ *below*) is the equally classic Polo's, which serves artfully blended contemporary southwestern and Asian cuisine—black pasta stuffed with lobster and crab, for example. Polo's has been featured on the cover of *Texas Monthly* magazine. ⊠ *401 S. Alamo St.,* ☎ *210/224–8800. AE, DC, MC, V. Closed Sun.*

$$$ ✕ **Boudro's.** Among the better River Walk options, this cavelike southwestern original serves seafood, steak, and extras such as guacamole prepared tableside. The wine list is commendable. ⊠ *421 E. Commerce St.,* ☎ *210/224–8484. AE, D, DC, MC, V.*

$$–$$$ ✕ **Liberty Bar.** Built in 1890 and leaning conspicuously at its foundation (attributed to a 1921 flood), the former Liberty Schooner Saloon serves old-time favorites like pot roast and excellent pies. The rustic bar is a comfortable place to sip a beer. ⊠ *328 E. Josephine St.,* ☎ *210/227–1187. AE, D, DC, MC, V.*

$$ ✕ **Zuni Grill.** With a bright industrial-warehouse brick interior and out-
★ door seating with an idyllic river view, this predominantly southwestern restaurant along the River Walk is known for its fajitas and its Zuni Burger (served with white cheddar). Try a cactus margarita, made with cactus juice and aged tequila. ⊠ *511 River Walk St.,* ☎ *210/227–0864. AE, D, DC, MC, V.*

$–$$ ✕ **County Line Barbecue.** Texas is famous for its barbecued ribs, smoked brisket, and related fare. In San Antonio there's only one contender, with two locations. ⊠ *On the Riverwalk: 111 W. Crockett, Suite 104,* ☎ *210/229–1941; 10101 I–10W,* ☎ *210/641–1998. AE, D, DC, MC, V.*

$$$$ ☷ **Fairmount.** This historic luxury hotel made the *Guinness Book of Records* when its 3.2-million-pound brick bulk was moved six blocks in 1985 to its present location. Canopy beds, overstuffed chairs, and marble baths create a super-refined atmosphere. ⊠ *401 S. Alamo St., 78205,* ☎ *210/224–8800 or 800/996–3426,* FAX *210/224–2767. 37 rooms. Restaurant. AE, D, DC, MC, V.*

$$$$ ☷ **Hyatt Regency Hill Country Resort.** On the western edge of the city, near Sea World, this sophisticated Texas country resort occupies 200 acres on former ranch land. On the grounds is a 4-acre water park with a man-made river where you can go tubing. ⊠ *9800 Hyatt Dr., 78251,* ☎ *210/647–1234,* FAX *210/681–9681. 500 rooms. 2 restaurants, pools, tennis, golf, health club. AE, D, DC, MC, V.* ✍

$$$$ ☷ **La Mansion del Rio.** A Spanish motif marks this large hotel on a quiet portion of River Walk. Inside and out it's replete with Mediterranean tiles, archways, and soft wood tones. Rooms are very modern. ⊠ *112 College St., 78205,* ☎ *210/225–2581 or 800/292–7300,* FAX *210/226–0389. 337 rooms. 2 restaurants, pool. AE, D, DC, MC, V.* ✍

$$$–$$$$ ☷ **Havana Riverwalk Inn.** San Antonio's most bohemian boutique hotel
★ occupies a Mediterranean Revival structure built in 1914. Every room is an experience: You'll find carved teak and wicker chairs from India,

beds fashioned from the grillwork of old buildings, and vintage chairs from French hotels and bistros. Don't miss Club Cohiba, the martini bar in the basement, and Siboney restaurant. ⊠ *1015 Navarro St., 78205,* ☎ *210/222–2008 or 888/224–2008,* FAX *210/222–2717. 27 rooms. Restaurant. AE, D, DC, MC, V.*

$$$ 🏨 **The Gunter.** Since 1909 this downtown hotel has been a favorite of cattlemen and business travelers. The marble lobby has a beautiful coffered ceiling supported by massive columns. Rooms have antique reproduction furniture and modern conveniences such as large desks with data ports. ⊠ *205 E. Houston St., 78205,* ☎ *210/227–3241 or 888/ 999–2089,* FAX *210/227–4705. 322 rooms. Restaurant, pool, exercise room. AE, D, DC, MC, V.*

$$$ 🏨 **Menger Hotel.** Since its 1859 opening, the Menger has lodged,
★ among others, Robert E. Lee, Ulysses S. Grant, Teddy Roosevelt, Oscar Wilde, Sarah Bernhardt, and Roy Rogers and Dale Evans. Guests appreciate the charming three-story Victorian lobby, sunny dining room, flowered courtyard, and four-poster beds (in the oldest part of the hotel only). ⊠ *204 Alamo Plaza, 78205,* ☎ *210/223–4361 or 800/345–9285,* FAX *210/228–0022. 317 rooms. Restaurant, pool, health club. AE, D, DC, MC, V.* 🐾

$ 🏨 **Bullis House.** The rooms in this historic mansion are spacious and well restored—and a good deal in a town where lodging is surprisingly expensive. Next door in a separate building is a modern youth hostel. Internet access is available. ⊠ *621 Pierce St., 78208,* ☎ *210/223–9426. 10 rooms; hostel has 42 beds. Pool. AE, D, MC, V. CP.*

The Hill Country

$ ✕ **Friedhelm's.** This Bavarian restaurant is known as the best in town, no small feat in an area full of such eateries. Try the Bavarian schnitzel, a breaded cutlet topped with Emmentaler cheese and jalapeño sauce. ⊠ *905 W. Main St., Fredericksburg,* ☎ *830/997–6300. AE, D, MC, V. Closed Mon.*

$$ 🏨 **Holiday Inn Y.O. Ranch.** This sprawling ranch-theme hotel is named after a well-known 50,000-acre dude ranch to which regular excursions are arranged. The large rooms—sporting cattle horns and the like— carry out the western theme. ⊠ *2033 Sidney Baker St., Kerrville 78028,* ☎ *830/257–4440 or 877/967–3767,* FAX *830/896–8189. 200 rooms. Restaurant, pool, tennis. AE, D, DC, MC, V.*

Nightlife and the Arts

Nightlife

Around the 3000 block of San Antonio's **North St. Mary's Street,** you'll find a colorful assortment of bars and restaurants in converted commercial buildings, many with live entertainment. River Walk favorites include **Durty Nellie's Pub** (⊠ Hilton Palacio del Rio, 200 S. Alamo St., ☎ 210/222–1400), where sing-alongs are popular. World-class Jim Cullum's Jazz Band plays superb Dixieland at the **Landing** (⊠ Hyatt Regency Hotel, 123 Losoya St., ☎ 210/223–7266). Don't miss the **Menger Hotel bar** (☞ Dining and Lodging, *above*).

The Arts

At San Antonio's **Mexican Cultural Institute** (⊠ 102 N. Main St., ☎ 210/227–0123; 🎟 free; closed weekends), Mexican culture is depicted in film, dance, art, and other media. A 1929 movie-vaudeville theater has been restored to its baroque splendor as the **Majestic Performing Arts Center** (⊠ 224 E. Houston St., ☎ 210/226–5700), a venue for touring Broadway shows and home to the San Antonio Symphony Orchestra. **Kerrville** annually hosts one of the country's largest folk music festivals, usually beginning the Thursday before Memorial Day and running for 24 hours a day for 18 days; contact the **Convention & Visitors Bureau** (☎ 830/792–3535 or 800/221–7958).

Outdoor Activities and Sports

Water Sports

Rafting, tubing, and canoeing are popular on the **Guadalupe River** between Canyon Lake, north of San Antonio, and New Braunfels. For rentals and guided trips try **Jerry's Rentals** (⊠ 4970 River Rd., north of New Braunfels, ☎ 830/625–2036); **Rockin' R River Rides** (⊠ 1405 Gruene Rd., ☎ 830/629–9999), on the river in New Braunfels; or **Gruene River Co.** (⊠ 1404 Gruene Rd., ☎ 830/625–2800), on the river in New Braunfels. With its surrounding steep evergreen hills, **Canyon Lake** is one of the most scenic lakes in Texas and has two yacht clubs, two marinas, a waterskiing club, and excellent fishing (an 86-pound flathead catfish is just one local record). Within 20 minutes of downtown San Antonio are two Texas-size amusement parks: **Six Flags Fiesta Texas** (⊠ 17000 I–10W, at La Cantera Pkwy., ☎ 800/473–4378) and **Sea World of Texas** (⊠ 10500 Sea World Dr., ☎ 210/523–3611).

Spectator Sports

Baseball: San Antonio Missions (⊠ 5757 U.S. 90W and Callahan, ☎ 210/675–7275). **Basketball: San Antonio Spurs** (⊠ Alamodome, 100 Montana St., ☎ 210/554–7787 or 800/884–3663). **Horse Racing: Retama Park** (⊠ I–35, Exit 174A, San Antonio, ☎ 210/651–7000); April–October, Friday–Sunday, but some Wednesdays and Thursday in the fall; simulcasts daily, year-round.

Shopping

San Antonio

With its rich ethnic heritage, this city is a wonderful place to buy Mexican imports, most of them inexpensive and many of high quality. **El Mercado** is the Mexican market building that is part of **Market Square** (⊠ 514 W. Commerce St., ☎ 210/207–8600). The building contains about 35 shops, including stores selling blankets, Mexican dresses, men's guayabera shirts, and strings of brightly painted papier-mâché vegetables. The lively **Farmer's Market** is another area of Market Square worth visiting. **La Villita** (⊠ 418 Villita St., ☎ 210/207–8610), a block of restored buildings on the southern edge of downtown, includes crafts shops and small restaurants, some in adobe buildings dating from the 1820s. It's noteworthy for its Latin American importers and demonstrations by its resident glassblower. **Rivercenter** (⊠ 849 E. Commerce St., ☎ 210/225–0000) is a fairly standard, if very ritzy, shopping mall right on the river. **Paris Hatters** (⊠ 119 Broadway, ☎ 210/223–3453) is an atmospheric place to buy western hats.

The Hill Country

Fredericksburg's main street is lined with upscale antiques shops, fragrant German bakeries, imaginative boutiques, and western saloons.

AUSTIN

Created as the capital of the then-new Republic of Texas in 1839, **Austin** is a liberal enclave in a generally conservative state and a heavily treed, hilly town in a land commonly known for its monotonous flatness. For many years a quiet university town, Austin has grown rapidly within the past two decades, developing into another Silicon Valley, home to many semiconductor and computer companies. The growth of high-tech industry, combined with the state government and the university, has made for a vital and culturally diverse community; indeed, Austin now has one of the country's fastest-growing job markets.

With numerous clubs and music venues, Austin draws many top musicians. Billing itself as the "live music capital of the world," the city has been on the national music map since 1984 when *Austin City Limits,* a showcase for bands that taped at the University of Texas campus, began airing nationwide. Austin then cemented its music reputation by putting on the annual music industry conference called South by Southwest, which also draws equal numbers of film and interactive notables from around the world every March.

Visitor Information

Austin Convention and Visitors Bureau (⊠ 201 E. 2nd St., 78701, ☎ 512/478–0098 or 800/926–2282). **Chamber of Commerce** (⊠ 111 Congress Ave., 78701, ☎ 512/478–9383).

Arriving and Departing

Between Dallas–Fort Worth and San Antonio on I–35, Austin is accessible from Houston via U.S. 290. Handling all local flights is the **Austin Bergstrom International Airport** (⊠ 3600 Presidential Blvd., 78719, ☎ 512/530–2242). **Amtrak** (⊠ 250 N. Lamar Blvd., ☎ 512/476–5684 or 800/872–7245) serves the city with three trains weekly west to Los Angeles and the same number north to Chicago. **Greyhound** has a station in Austin (⊠ 916 E. Koenig La., ☎ 512/454–9699 or 800/739–5020).

Exploring Austin

Austin's downtown is dominated by its impressive **capitol** (⊠ 1100 Congress Ave., ☎ 512/463–0063), constructed in 1888 of Texas pink granite. Free, historical tours run from 8:30 to 4:30. Visitors who wish to see the nearby **governor's mansion** ⊠ (1010 Colorado, ☎ 512/463–5518) should arrive early for the free, first-come, first-served tours. The Capitol Complex Visitors Center (⊠ 112 E. 11th St., 78701, ☎ 512/305–8400) offers temporary exhibits, videos, and a gift shop.

The **University of Texas** campus flanks the capitol's north end. The campus is home to the **Lyndon Baines Johnson Presidential Library and Museum** (⊠ 2313 Red River St., ☎ 512/916–5136; ⬚ free). Also of interest on the UT campus is the **Jack S. Blanton Museum of Art,** formerly the Huntington Art Gallery (⊠ 23rd and San Jacinto Sts. and 21st and Guadalupe Sts., ☎ 512/471–7324; ⬚ free), which is the permanent home of one of the largest and most important private collections of old master paintings and drawings; it comprises 700 works by Poussin, Veronese, Rubens, Tiepolo, Boucher, Corregio, and other Italian, French, and German artists of the 14th to the 18th century. Austin's **Lyric Opera** (☎ 512/472–5927), the **Austin Symphony** (☎ 512/476–6064), and **Ballet Austin** (☎ 512/476–9051) all perform at the Performing Arts Center and Bass Concert Hall. **Guadalupe Street,** also known as "the Drag," borders the west side of the UT campus and is lined with trendy boutiques and restaurants.

With the stately capitol seated at its north end, **Congress Avenue**—specifically, the bridge at its southern downtown end—is also home to a colony of hundreds of thousands of Mexican bats. Attracted to the small space between the arches of the bridge and the road above, the nocturnal critters swarm into town every evening at dusk from May until October, creating a creepy but memorable cocktail-hour spectacle for hundreds of onlookers. The grassy areas on the bridge's northeastern or southeastern ends are good vantage points.

Parks, Gardens, and Zoos

Many people and companies have moved to Austin for a quality of life enhanced by pristine waterways and extensive greenbelts for hiking, biking, and running. **Zilker Park** (✉ 2100 Barton Springs Rd., ☎ 512/499–6700), the city's largest public park, connects to **Town Lake's hike and bike trail. Barton Springs** (☎ 512/476–9044; ⊡ $2.50; closed Thurs. afternoons), a huge natural-spring pool, is Zilker Park's main attraction. Built in the early 1900s when the city dammed Barton Creek, the pool is more than ¼ mi long and a constant 68°F. It is considered one of the nation's premier swimming holes, and Austinites cherish it as the jewel of their city. Little ones enjoy the pool and free rides on the **miniature Amtrak train** that circles the park's perimeter April–October.

The **Zilker Botanical Gardens** (✉ 2220 Barton Springs Rd., ☎ 512/477–8672; ⊡ free), across from Zilker Park, has more than 26 acres of horticultural delights, including butterfly trails and Xeriscape gardens with native plants that thrive in an arid southwestern climate. The **Austin Nature and Science Center** (✉ 301 Nature Center Dr., ☎ 512/327–8180; ⊡ donations requested), adjacent to the botanical gardens, has 80 acres of trails, interactive exhibits teaching about the environment, and animal exhibits.

The **Lady Bird Johnson Wildflower Center** (✉ 4801 LaCrosse Ave., ☎ 512/292–4100; ⊡ $4; closed Mon.) includes a 43-acre complex sponsored by Lady Bird Johnson and has educational programs and extensive plantings of wildflowers that bloom all year-round.

Just off the western thoroughfare of Austin sits 227-acre **Wild Basin Wilderness Preserve** (✉ 805 N. Capital of Texas Hwy., ☎ 512/327–7622; ⊡ donations requested), where even in the midst of a growing city unobstructed views of the verdant hill country are readily available. Call for guided tour information.

Dining

$$$$ ✕ **Hudson's on the Bend.** A bit outside town, overlooking a bend in beautiful Lake Austin (a portion of the Colorado River northwest of Austin), Hudson's serves such exotic dishes as Jamaican jerked Australian kangaroo with chipotle cream sauce. ✉ 3509 Ranch Rd. 620, ☎ 512/266–1369. Reservations essential. AE, DC, MC, V. No lunch.

$$–$$$ ✕ **Castle Hill Café.** Here you'll find great tortilla soup, imaginative salads, and eclectic entrées such as grilled Indian lamb loin with Makhani cream and cauliflower-ginger relish. The menu changes weekly. ✉ 1101 W. 5th St., ☎ 512/476–7218. AE, D, MC, V. Closed Sun.

$$ ✕ **Bitter End.** A sleek, slightly industrial interior sets the scene for the see-and-be-seen crowd at this sleek brewpub. Duck liver pâté, wood-fired pizzas, and an ever-updated Italian-tinged menu are all enhanced by outstanding home-brewed ales. ✉ 311 Colorado St., ☎ 512/478–2337. AE, D, DC, MC, V.

$ ✕ **Güeros.** The ceiling is high, the floorboards worn, and the windows long and tall in this former feed store, now a favorite Mexican restaurant with a spacious, rustic bar and adored salsas. ✉ 1412 S. Congress Ave., ☎ 512/447–7688. AE, D, DC, MC, V.

$ ✕ **Threadgill's.** Southern-style food and a friendly atmosphere make Threadgill's a local legend, having drawn the likes of Janis Joplin to sample its massive chicken-fried steak. Homemade cobbler and live music add to the appeal. ✉ 6416 N. Lamar Blvd., ☎ 512/451–5440; 301 W. Riverside Dr., ☎ 512/472–9304. MC, V.

Lodging

$$$$ 🏨 **Four Seasons.** Built along the banks of Town Lake in downtown Austin, this luxury hotel has beautiful views of sunsets over the water and the loveliest lakeside Sunday brunch in town. It is also a prime location in summer for watching the bat exodus from under the Congress Avenue Bridge (☞ Exploring Austin, *above*). Rooms are spacious and have a classical decor. ⊠ *98 San Jacinto Blvd., 78701,* ☎ *512/478–4500 or 800/332–3442,* FAX *512/478–3117. 291 rooms. Restaurant, pool. AE, DC, MC, V.* 🍽

$$$ 🏨 **Driskill Hotel.** Fronting Congress Avenue, Austin's main downtown street, this historic Renaissance Revival edifice built in 1886. Step inside to see its elegant lobby highlighted by vaulted ceilings. After a complete renovation, the hotel combines Victorian and contemporary design. ⊠ *604 Brazos St., 78701,* ☎ *512/474–5911 or 800/252–9367,* FAX *512/474–2214. 185 rooms. Restaurant. AE, D, DC, MC, V.*

$$–$$$ 🏨 **Doubletree Guest Suites.** Conveniently located between downtown and the university, this all-suite hotel is only a block away from the capitol, which is visible from many of the rooms. ⊠ *303 W. 15th St., 78701,* ☎ *512/478–7000,* FAX *512/478–5103. 189 suites. Restaurant, pool, exercise room. AE, D, DC, MC, V.* 🍽

Nightlife

Numerous traveling and homegrown bands play nightly in the city's many music venues, most of which are clustered around downtown's **6th Street,** between Red River Street and Congress Avenue. To find out who's playing where, pick up a free *Austin Chronicle* or Thursday's *Austin American Statesman.* Some of the town's most distinctive clubs are removed from the 6th Street scene: If live country music and dancing are your thing, two-step down to the venerable **Broken Spoke** (⊠ 3201 S. Lamar Blvd., ☎ 512/442–6189). Rustic, quirky, and no bigger than your parents' basement, the smoky, no-frills **Continental Club** (⊠ 1315 S. Congress Ave., ☎ 512/441–2444) plays country-tinged rock. **Antone's** (⊠ 213 E. 5th St., ☎ 512/474–5315) is another local musical institution, booking legendary blues and funk acts. A restored downtown movie palace, the **Paramount** (⊠ 713 Congress Ave., ☎ 512/472–5470) is home to both musical shows and touring theater companies. Local theater thrives at the **Zachary Scott Theatre** (⊠ 1510 Toomey Rd., ☎ 512/476–0594), named for an Austin native son who was successful in 1930s Hollywood.

DALLAS AND FORT WORTH

These twin cities, separated by 30 mi of suburbs, are an odd couple. **Dallas** is glitzy and ritzy, a swelling, modernistic business metropolis where style takes precedence over substance and image is everything. **Fort Worth,** sneered at as "Cowtown" by its neighbors, lives in the shadow of its wild history as a rip-roaring cowboy town, a place of gunfights and cattle drives—even though its cultural establishment is superior to Dallas's. In Fort Worth, that fellow in the faded jeans and cowboy hat could well be the president of the bank. In Dallas, people tend to be a bit more formal.

Visitor Information

Dallas: Convention & Visitors Bureau (⊠ 1201 Elm St., Suite 2000, 75270, ☎ 214/746–6677 or 800/232–5527; 214/746–6679 for recorded schedule of events); information booths are **downtown in the Old Red Courthouse** (⊠ Main and Houston Sts.), in **NorthPark Center** (⊠ Northwest Hwy. at Central Expressway), and at the **West End MarketPlace** (⊠ 603 Munger Ave., Suite 124). **Fort Worth:** Convention & Visitors Bureau (⊠ 415 Throckmorton St., 76102, ☎ 817/336–8791 or 800/433–5747); information centers are **downtown** (⊠ 4th St. at Throckmorton St.), in the **Cultural District** (⊠ Will Rogers Center, Lancaster Ave. at University Dr.), and at the **Stockyards** (⊠ 130 E. Exchange Ave.). **Dallas–Fort Worth International Airport** (⊠ 3200 E. Airfield Dr., 75261, ☎ 972/574–3694) also has information booths.

Arriving and Departing

By Bus

Greyhound (☎ 214/655–7082 or 800/231–2222) has stations in **Dallas** (⊠ 205 S. Lamar St.) and **Fort Worth** (⊠ 901 Commerce St.).

By Car

The **Metroplex,** as the Greater Dallas–Fort Worth area is known, is well served by interstates. The main approaches include I–35 from Oklahoma to the north and Waco to the south (this interstate splits near Denton, with I–35E heading to Dallas and I–35W branching off to Fort Worth); I–30 from Arkansas; I–20 from Louisiana and New Mexico; and I–45 from Houston. The twin cities are linked by I–20, which is the southern route, and I–30, generally the more useful road for visitors because many tourist destinations are in the northern part of town. There are three tollways in the Dallas area, the Dallas North Tollway, running from I–35E north of downtown into Collin County to the north; George Bush Turnpike (State Highway 190), an east–west route in the area's northern suburbs; and Mountain Creek Bridge, in southwestern Dallas County. Three major expressways, I–30, I–35, and I–635, have High Occupancy Vehicle (HOV) lanes for vehicles with two or more occupants. Though the highway number designations are easy to find on a map, many of these thoroughfares are also known and referred to locally by name, which can make getting directions somewhat confusing. For example, Route 183, which leads to the south entrance of DFW Airport, is often referred to as Airport Freeway, and U.S. 75 is known to locals as Central Expressway. Dallas is circled by the I–635 ring road, known as LBJ Freeway; Fort Worth is looped by I–820.

By Plane

Dallas–Fort Worth International Airport (⊠ 3200 E. Airfield Dr., 75261, ☎ 972/574–3694), midway between Dallas and Fort Worth, is the main airport for both cities and is currently the second-largest airport in the United States and the third largest in the world. Taxi service to either downtown Dallas or downtown Fort Worth generally runs $25–$30. Cheaper van service is provided by the 24-hour **Supershuttle** (☎ 817/329–2000). Fort Worth's public transportation system, the **T** (☎ 817/215–8600), runs a $10 shuttle between the airport and downtown Fort Worth. Ritzier service is provided by **Aadvantage Limousine** (☎ 972/618–7313).

Love Field (⊠ 8008 Cedar Springs Rd., at Mockingbird La., Dallas 75235, ☎ 214/670–6073), a $10–$15 taxi ride from downtown Dallas, is the hub of **Southwest Airlines** (☎ 972/263–1717 or 800/435–9792).

By Train

Amtrak (☎ 214/653–1101 or 800/872–7245) service connects Dallas–Fort Worth to San Antonio, St. Louis, and Chicago. Dallas service originates at **Union Station** (⊠ 400 Houston St., ☎ 214/653–1101). In Fort Worth, service originates from the old **Santa Fe Depot** (⊠ 1501 Jones St., ☎ 817/332–2931), across from the convention center.

Getting Around Dallas and Fort Worth

A car is the best way to see Dallas and Forth Worth, though both cities have bus systems. Public transportation in Dallas is run by **Dallas Area Rapid Transit** (DART; ☎ 214/979–1111) and consists of buses that service Dallas and 12 suburban cities along with a light-rail system with a limited route.

Exploring Dallas and Fort Worth

Dallas

Many thousands visit Dallas, in spite of—or in some cases because of—the city's unhappy legacy as the assassination site of President John F. Kennedy, which occurred downtown. Also downtown is one of the most remarkable flowerings of skyscraping architecture anywhere—that same skyline familiar to the world from the television show *Dallas*—and a multitude of restaurants and shops in the **West End,** a former warehouse district. Near the West End are several major cultural institutions, and only a little farther away is **Deep Ellum,** the lively center of the city's alternative arts and music scene. A short car trip from downtown are several historic areas that give a sense of the old Dallas. To the north, where the city's establishment has long been entrenched, there's shopping galore.

DOWNTOWN

On November 22, 1963, shots rang out on Dealey Plaza, at the west end of downtown, as the presidential motorcade rounded the corner from Houston Street onto the Elm Street approach to the Triple Underpass. Eventually the Warren Commission would conclude—to the continuing disbelief of many Americans—that President Kennedy was gunned down by Lee Harvey Oswald, acting alone and firing from the

★ sixth floor of the **Texas School Book Depository** (⊠ 411 Elm St., ☎
⚑ 214/747–6660, ⚐ $6). Today, the **Sixth Floor** exhibit reveals the details of the assassination, along with an account of the conspiracy theories that continue to emerge.

The grassy knoll from which many believe a second gunman fired is just to the right of the Book Depository, on the Elm Street side. **Dealey Plaza,** where visitors inevitably congregate to look up at the so-called sniper's perch, is directly across the street. The stark **cenotaph,** designed like an empty house by architect Philip Johnson as a personal tribute to his friend Kennedy, is a short walk from Dealey Plaza, at Main and Market streets.

Those with more of an *X-Files* view of life can check out the **Conspiracy Museum** (⊠ 110 S. Market, ☎ 214/741–3040; ⚐ $7), where the history of presidential assassinations and cover-ups from 1835 to the present is meticulously examined.

The **West End Historic District** is an area of brick warehouses built between 1900 and 1930 and brought back to life in 1976. Now filled with restaurants and shops, it is one of the city's biggest draws both day and night. Within the historic district is the **West End MarketPlace** (⊠ 603 Munger Ave., ☎ 214/748–4801), once a candy-and-cracker factory and now a lively, five-story shopping-and-eating center built around an atrium.

The **Old Red Courthouse** (⊠ Main St. at Houston St.) faces Philip Johnson's cenotaph. This 1892 Romanesque building of red sandstone is one of the city's oldest surviving structures and a familiar landmark. The **John Neely Bryan Cabin,** a restored log cabin similar to one

Downtown Dallas

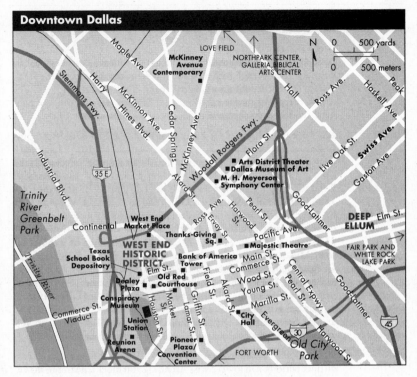

erected in 1841 by city founder Bryan, is adjacent to the courthouse on the Dallas County Historical Plaza.

Almost all the major skyscrapers that make up the famous Dallas skyline were completed in the 1980s, many by renowned architect I. M. Pei. The **Dallas City Hall** (⊠ 1500 Marilla St.), a striking Pei creation, is notable for the stunning bronze Henry Moore sculpture on the broad plaza outside. Next to City Hall in **Pioneer Plaza** stands Robert Summer's interpretation of life on the old Shawnee Trail: 70 longhorn steer and three cowboys. It is said to be the largest bronze sculpture in the world.

The **Bank of America Tower** (⊠ 901 Main St.), formerly the Nations-Bank Tower, is visible for miles, thanks to its 72 stepped stories outlined in green lights. Lending a peculiar, science-fiction twist to the skyline is **Reunion Tower** (⊠ 300 Reunion Blvd., ☎ 214/651–1234), with an observation deck (⊡ $2) and a revolving rooftop restaurant and bar. **Thanks-Giving Square** (⊠ Pacific Ave. and Ervay St., ☎ 214/969–1977), a small triangular plaza designed by Philip Johnson, contains quiet gardens and a chapel with stained glass by Gabriel Loire.

Housed in a series of low, white limestone galleries built off a central barrel vault, the **Dallas Museum of Art** is in the Arts District, on the north edge of downtown. Standout exhibits are Claes Oldenburg's *Stake Hitch*, a huge stake and rope sculpture, and Frederic Church's chilling painting *The Icebergs*. ⊠ 1717 N. Harwood St., ☎ 214/922–1200. ⊡ *Free. Closed Mon.*

The I. M. Pei–designed **Morton H. Meyerson Symphony Center** (⊠ 2301 Flora St., ☎ 214/670–3600) is a place of sweeping, dramatic curves, ever-changing vanishing points, and surprising views. Inside is the **Herman W. Lay Family Organ**, a hand-built and -installed Fisk organ with 4,535 pipes. **De Musica,** a solid iron sculpture by the great Basque sculptor Eduardo Chillida, rests in front of the Symphony Center.

OTHER ATTRACTIONS

Deep Ellum, a 20-minute walk east from downtown, was born as the city's first black neighborhood. Today it is the throbbing center of Dallas's avant-garde, with art galleries, bars, clubs, and restaurants. The area centers on Commerce, Main, and Elm streets; its name is a phonetic rendering of *deep elm* pronounced with a southern drawl.

★ **Fair Park** (⊠ 1300 Robert B. Cullum Blvd., ☎ 214/670–8400), just southeast of Deep Ellum, is a 277-acre National Historic Landmark comprising the largest collection of 1930s Art Deco architecture in the United States. Most of the grounds date from the 1936 Texas Centennial Exhibition, although the park has hosted the State Fair of Texas since 1886. In the **Hall of State** (⊠ 3939 Grand Ave., ☎ 214/421–4500; ☑ free) murals tell the story of Texas in heroic terms. Fair Park also contains six major exhibit spaces: the **African American Museum** (⊠ 3536 Grand Ave., ☎ 214/565–9026; ☑ free); the **Age of Steam Railroad Museum** (⊠ 1105 N. Washington Ave., ☎ 214/428–0101; ☑ $4); the **Dallas Aquarium** (⊠ 1st Ave. at Martin Luther King Blvd., ☎ 214/670–8443; ☑ $3); the **Dallas Horticulture Center** (⊠ 3601 Martin Luther King Blvd., ☎ 214/428–7476; ☑ free); the **Dallas Museum of Natural History** (⊠ 3535 Grand Ave., ☎ 214/421–3466; ☑ $5); and the **Science Place** (⊠ 1318 2nd Ave., ☎ 214/428–5555; ☑ $6), which also houses one of Dallas's **IMAX theaters** (☑ $6).

In east Dallas, **Swiss Avenue** has the city's best representations of two distinct periods. On lower Swiss Avenue (2900 block), nearer to downtown, the **Wilson Block Historic District** is an unaltered block of turn-of-the-20thcentury frame houses restored as offices for nonprofit groups. Set-back Prairie-style and other mansions are common in the **Swiss Avenue Historic District** (particularly the 5000–5500 blocks).

McKinney Avenue, just north of downtown in the city's burgeoning Uptown neighborhood, is lined with bustling bars and trendy restaurants. Authentic, restored **trolleys** (☎ 214/855–0006; ☑ $1.50 round-trip) run up McKinney from outside the Dallas Museum of Art. The **McKinney Avenue Contemporary** (⊠ 3120 McKinney Ave., ☎ 214/953–1622; ☑ free), locally known as "the MAC," consists of a theater, gallery space, and video installation space.

In the **Biblical Arts Center** (⊠ 7500 Park La., ☎ 214/691–4661; ☑ $6), a bit north of McKinney Avenue, sound and light bring a 124-ft by 20-ft biblical mural to life. Here you'll also find a replica of Christ's tomb at Calvary.

Anyone interested in the entertainment industry will be starstruck by the **Studios at Las Colinas** (⊠ 6301 N. O'Connor Rd., Irving, ☎ 972/869–3456; ☑ $12.95), about 25 minutes northwest of downtown. Tours include a visit to the soundstage facilities used in the filming of such movies as *JFK, Silkwood,* and *Robocop.*

Just minutes north of Dallas lies one of the city's most enduring landmarks, **Southfork Ranch** (⊠ 3700 Hogge Dr., Parker, ☎ 972/442–7800; ☑ $6.95). Built in 1970, the ranch became one of the city's best-known symbols when the TV show *Dallas* premiered in 1978. Visitors can still tour the mansion, have lunch at Miss Ellie's Deli, and try to remember who shot J. R.

Fort Worth

Downtown Fort Worth is where you'll find the city's financial core, most of its historic buildings, and Sundance Square, the restored turn-of-the-20th-century neighborhood that is one of the city's main attractions. The Stockyards and adjacent western-theme stores, restaurants, and hotels are a few miles north of downtown, clustered around Main Street and Exchange Avenue. The cultural district, west of downtown on Lancaster Avenue, is home to four well-known museums, a coliseum complex, and several parks.

DOWNTOWN

In Fort Worth's underrated downtown, modern glass-and-steel towers stand face-to-face with human-scale century-old Victorian buildings. The billionaire Bass brothers of Fort Worth are to be thanked for what may be the most eye-pleasing juxtaposition of scale: Rather than tear down several blocks of brick buildings to accommodate the twin towers of their giant City Center development, they created **Sundance Square** (bounded by Houston, Commerce, 2nd, and 3rd streets) by restoring the area as a center of tall-windowed restaurants, shops, nightclubs, and offices.

Sundance Square's name recalls the Sundance Kid (Harry Longbaugh), who with Butch Cassidy (Robert Leroy Parker) hid out around 1898 in the nearby neighborhood, south and east of the present square, known as Hell's Half-Acre. This was a violent quarter of dank saloons, drunken cowboys, and dirty brothels. The **Sid Richardson Collection of Western Art** (✉ 309 Main St., ☎ 817/332–6554; 🎫 free) conjures up parts of this dark world in the idealized oils of Frederic Remington and Charles Russell.

☻ In Sundance Square, the **Fire Station No. 1** (✉ 215 Commerce St., ☎ 817/732–1631; 🎫 free) houses an exhibit on 150 years of city history. The 1907 building—site of the city's first fire station and first city hall—fronts on the street where cattle headed for the Chisholm Trail used to pass.

The wedge-shape **Flatiron Building** (✉ 1000 Houston St.), also downtown, is topped by gargoyles and panthers. Built in 1907 as medical offices, it was patterned on similar Renaissance Revival structures in New York and Philadelphia. Near the Flatiron Building, the former **Texas Hotel,** now the Radisson Plaza (✉ 815 N. Main St., ☎ 817/870–2100), is where President Kennedy spent his last night.

The **Tarrant County Courthouse** (✉ 100 W. Weatherford St.), on the northern edge of downtown, is an 1895 Beaux Arts building of native red granite. A sad reminder of American history, the building that now houses the Ellis Pecan Company was once the **Ku Klux Klan Building** (✉ 1012 N. Main St.).

THE STOCKYARDS

☻ The **Stockyards National Historic District** recalls the prosperity brought to the city in 1902 when two major Chicago meatpackers, Armour and Swift, set up plants here to ship meat across the country in refrigerator cars. In the **Livestock Exchange Building** (✉ 131 E. Exchange Ave.), where cattle agents kept their offices, you'll find the **Stockyards Collection Museum** (☎ 817/625–5082; 🎫 free). Across the street from the Livestock Exchange Building, **Stockyards Station** (✉ 130 E. Exchange Ave., ☎ 817/625–9715) is a fast-growing marketplace of shops and restaurants, all housed in former sheep and hog pens. **Cowtown Coliseum** (✉ 121 E. Exchange Ave., ☎ 817/625–1025 or 888/269–8696) was constructed in 1908 to house what became the Southwestern Exposition and Fat Stock Show; today it is the site of Friday- and Saturday-night rodeos. The **Tarantula Train** (✉ 140 E. Exchange Ave., ☎ 817/251–0066; 🎫 $22 round-trip), a restored historic 1896 steam locomotive, links the Stockyards with nearby **Grapevine** (☎ 817/481–

0454 or 800/457–6338), where you can find tasting rooms for five of Texas's numerous wineries. Information on the Stockyards area is available at the **Stockyards Visitors Center** (⊠ 130 E. Exchange Ave., ☎ 817/624–4741).

THE CULTURAL DISTRICT

★ Architect Louis Kahn's last and finest building was the **Kimbell Art Museum,** six long concrete vaults with skylights running the length of each. Here are top-notch collections of both early 20th-century European art and old masters, including Munch's *Girls on a Jetty* and Goya's *The Matador Pedro Romero,* depicting the great bullfighter who killed 5,600 of the animals. ⊠ *3333 Camp Bowie Blvd.,* ☎ *817/332–8451.* 🈯 *Free. Closed Mon.*

The **Amon Carter Museum,** along with the city's two other major museums, is a short walk from the Kimbell. Designed by Philip Johnson, the Amon Carter has a collection of American art centered on Remingtons and Russells. The museum has been temporarily closed for an expansion that will more than triple its exhibition space and is expected to reopen in the fall of 2001. In the interim, a temporary space downtown (⊠ 500 Commerce St., ☎ 817/738–1933) will display approximately 25 works of art at a time from the Amon Carter's collection. ⊠ *3501 Camp Bowie Blvd.,* ☎ *817/738–1933.* 🈯 *Free. Closed Mon.*

Texas's oldest art museum, the **Modern Art Museum of Fort Worth** focuses on such painters as Picasso, Rauschenberg, and Warhol. ⊠ *1309 Montgomery St.,* ☎ *817/738–9215.* 🈯 *Free. Closed Mon.*

Biology, geology, computer science, and astronomy are the order of the day at the **Fort Worth Museum of Science and History** (⊠ 1501 Montgomery St., ☎ 817/255–9300; 🈯 $6), which also incorporates the **Noble Planetarium** (🈯 $3) and the **Omni Theater** (🈯 $6).

The **Will Rogers Memorial Center** (⊠ 3300 W. Lancaster Ave., ☎ 817/871–8150), near Fort Worth's museums, is a partially restored coliseum-and-stock-pen complex named after the humorist and Fort Worth booster, who described the city as "where the West begins" (and Dallas as "where the East peters out"). The center includes an equestrian arena that's used for horse and livestock shows.

Parks, Gardens, and Zoos

Dallas

Fair Park (☞ Exploring Dallas and Fort Worth, *above*), with its many museums and formal gardens, is one of the city's most visited parks; every fall it hosts Texas's largest State Fair (☞ Festivals and Seasonal Events *in* the United States Region by Region chapter). At **White Rock Lake Park** (⊠ 8300 Garland Rd., ☎ 214/670–8283), a 9⅓-mi jogging and bicycling path circles the sailboat-dotted lake. White Rock Lake Park is also home to the **Dallas Arboretum and Botanical Garden** (⊠ 8617 Garland Rd., ☎ 214/327–8263; 🈯 $6), 66 acres of gardens and lawns. **Old City Park,** just south of downtown (⊠ 1717 Gano St., ☎ 214/421–5141; 🈯 $6), is an outdoor museum consisting of 38 historic buildings, including log cabins, antebellum mansions, and a Victorian bandstand. At the **Dallas Zoo** (⊠ 621 E. Clarendon Dr., ☎ 214/670–5656; 🈯 $6), a monorail brings you past the most noted exhibit: lowland gorillas in a natural habitat.

Fort Worth

★ **Water Gardens Park** (⊠ 15th and Commerce Sts.), a free, outdoor public sculpture garden, holds a dramatic blend of modern sculpture and cascading fountains designed by Philip Johnson and John Burgee. In one area, visitors can stand 38 ft below street level and view 1,000 gallons of water tumbling down a 710-ft wall. Just south of the cultural district, the **Fort Worth Botanic Garden** (⊠ 3220 Botanic Garden Dr., at University Dr., ☎ 817/871–7686; ☞ $1, Japanese garden $2.50) ★ ☾ has a 10,000-square-ft conservatory. In Forest Park is the **Fort Worth Zoo** (⊠ 1989 Colonial Pkwy., ☎ 817/871–7050, ☞ $7), with more than 5,000 exotic and native animals, including Komodo dragons, koala bears, and a rare white tiger.

Dining

Dallas

$$$–$$$$ ✕ **Abacus.** High-profile, high-dollar eateries like Abacus are one reason why Texas can't shake that "everything's bigger" image. The interior—warm cherry woods, metal and glass sculpture, soft lighting—cost a reported $6 million. The food melds southwestern influences with Asian accents to create offerings like lobster "shooters" flavored with red chile and sake. ⊠ 4511 McKinney Ave., ☎ 214/559–3111. Reservations essential. AE, D, DC, MC, V. Closed Sun. No lunch.

$$$–$$$$ ✕ **AquaKnox.** Since the restaurant opened to critical acclaim in late 1997, folks have lined up to sample rock shrimp pot stickers and oak-roasted lobster. A short time ago, the bar area was transformed into Fishbowl, a more-casual lounge attuned to small-plate noshing and drinking. ⊠ 3214 Knox St., ☎ 214/219–2782. Reservations essential. AE, D, DC, MC, V. No lunch.

$$–$$$$ ✕ **Del Frisco's.** Even in Dallas, cattle is king, and you can't get a better piece of beef than in this legendary steak house. ⊠ 5251 Spring Valley Rd., ☎ 972/490–9000. AE, D, DC, MC, V. Closed Sun. No lunch.

$$–$$$$ ✕ **Star Canyon.** This is still one of the hottest tickets in town (read: ★ reserve well in advance for a weekend dinner). Prepare to be dazzled by southwestern-inspired inventions such as tamale tart with roast-garlic custard or red-chile- and Shiner Bock–braised osso buco. The dining room has a branded ceiling, and a barbed-wire motif is etched into the bar area's glass panels. ⊠ 3102 Oak Lawn Ave., ☎ 214/520–7827. Reservations essential. AE, D, MC, V. No lunch Sat.–Sun.

$$$ ✕ **Green Room.** In Deep Ellum, an area of town known more for its hipster music vibe, the restaurant has a menu that fuses together disparate elements nicely—think coconut risotto or soft-shell crab–laden paella—and a special chef's tasting menu (four courses for $36 or $58 with wine) is one of the best bargains in town. ⊠ 2715 Elm St., ☎ 214/748–7666. AE, D, DC, MC, V. No lunch.

$–$$$ ✕ **Liberty.** This tiny, trendy pan-Asian eatery features standards (Vietnamese spring rolls) cuddled up to more ethnic offerings (Japanese udon noodle bowls). The "Big Soups"—particularly the heavenly chicken-coconut—are pricey, but worth it. ⊠ 5631 Alta Ave., ☎ 214/887–8795. Reservations recommended. AE, D, DC, MC, V. Closed Mon.

$–$$$ ✕ **Matt's Rancho Martinez.** Tex-Mex is served up for the masses in this Dallas institution. Specialties include chicken-fried steak, chile rellenos, and the signature "Bob Armstrong" dip. ⊠ 6332 La Vista Dr., ☎ 214/823–5517. AE, D, DC, MC, V. Closed Sun.

Fort Worth

$$–$$$$ ✕ **Angeluna.** A see-and-be-seen crowd and a sometimes-raucous atmosphere make this Sundance Square hot spot an exciting place to dine. You'll find eclectic winners such as black-and-blue tuna with spoonbread and key lime tart. ⊠ 215 E. 4th St., ☎ 817/334–0080. AE, DC, MC, V.

$$–$$$$ ✕ **Bistro Louise.** People drive 30 mi from Dallas to dine on tea-smoked duck, macadamia-crusted shrimp, and the like. Wood-beam ceilings and

flowered tablecloths add to the charming French setting. ⊠ *2900 S. Hulen St.,* ☎ *817/922–9244. AE, D, DC, MC, V. Closed Sun.*

$$$ ✕ **Saint-Emilion.** Though it doesn't look like much from the outside,
★ this is one of Tarrant County's best restaurants, with a legendary crispy-roast duck and excellent daily specials. The wine list is so extensive that it has its own table of contents. ⊠ *3617 W. 7th St.,* ☎ *817/ 737–2781. Reservations essential. AE, D, DC, MC, V. Closed Mon. No lunch.*

$–$$$ ✕ **Reata.** This is about as Texan as restaurants get in the Metroplex, with leather-trimmed menus, cowhide-covered chairs, and beef straight from the owner's ranch. Other selling points include a great view, good food, and friendly service. ⊠ *500 Throckmorton St., Bank One Tower, 35th floor,* ☎ *817/336–1009. AE, MC, V.*

$ ✕ **Angelo's Barbecue.** Angelo's is famous for its succulent smoked ribs, so tender that the meat falls off the bone. Arrive early, as they've been known to run out of ribs well before closing. ⊠ *2533 White Settlement Rd.,* ☎ *817/332–0357. Reservations not accepted. No credit cards. Closed Sun.*

$ ✕ **Joe T. Garcia's.** This is the ultimate Tex-Mex joint, where cowboy-
★ boot-clad customers drink Mexican beer and the bartenders mix potent margaritas. There's usually a wait for tables, which on Saturday nights can stretch to an hour. It's worth it. ⊠ *2201 N. Commerce St.,* ☎ *817/626–4356. Reservations not accepted. No credit cards.*

Dining and Lodging

$$$$ ✕🖬 **Hotel St. Germain.** Built as a private residence in 1906, this tiny
★ boutique hotel with white-glove service is one of the most romantic in the city. The beautiful rooms are filled with antiques and collectibles. The dining room (closed Sunday and Monday, no lunch) is known for its $75-per-person prix-fixe menu, which might include French Riviera bouillon, classic *terrine de foie gras,* or rack of lamb. ⊠ *2516 Maple Ave., 75201,* ☎ *214/871–2516,* 🅵🅰🆇 *214/871–0740. 7 suites. Restaurant. AE, D, DC, MC, V. CP.*

$$$$ ✕🖬 **Mansion on Turtle Creek.** The Mansion is the only five-star, five-
★ diamond hotel in the Southwest. Rooms here are appointed with antiques and original artwork. The service is legendary, as is the food in the dining room (reservations essential, jacket required). Chef Dean Fearing helped pioneer southwestern cuisine, and he continues to wow his customers with amazing renditions of tortilla soup, warm lobster tacos, and even halibut with cashews in basil sauce. Count on finding Dallas–Fort Worth's most beautiful, celebrated, and powerful crowd inside this opulent room. There's valet parking. ⊠ *2821 Turtle Creek Blvd., 75219,* ☎ *214/559–2100,* 🅵🅰🆇 *214/528–4187. 141 rooms. 2 restaurants, pool, health club. AE, D, DC, MC, V.* ✎

Lodging

Dallas

$$$$ 🖬 **Four Seasons Resort and Club.** Looking like a Frank Lloyd Wright–
★ designed country club, this hotel is quite possibly the city's best. Rooms have balconies that overlook the Tournament Players Course golf course, site of the Professional Golfers' Association's GTE Byron Nelson Classic. The resort has an indoor track. ⊠ *4150 N. MacArthur Blvd., Irving, 75038,* ☎ *972/717–0700 or 800/332–3442,* 🅵🅰🆇 *972/717– 2550. 357 rooms. 3 restaurants, pools, golf, tennis, health club. AE, D, DC, MC, V.* ✎

$$$–$$$$ 🏨 **Adolphus.** Beer baron Adolphus Busch created this Beaux Arts building, Dallas's finest old hotel, in 1912, sparing nothing in the way of rich ornamentation. The romantic, Old World decor of the rooms is complemented by modern amenities. The celebrated French Room restaurant (closed Sunday and Monday, no lunch) serves classics such as roasted duck breast in port sauce. ⊠ *1321 Commerce St., 75202,* ☎ *214/742–8200 or 800/221–9083,* FAX *214/651–3561. 445 rooms. 3 restaurants, exercise room. AE, D, DC, MC, V.*

$$$–$$$$ 🏨 **Wyndham Anatole.** Political bigwigs such as George Bush and Colin Powell have made this huge glass-and-chrome complex their home away from home. The rooms are standard, but the Anatole has seven bars, a nightclub, and a piano bar to keep you entertained. There's a beauty salon, sauna, and indoor and outdoor pools as well. ⊠ *2201 Stemmons Fwy., 75207,* ☎ *214/748–1200 or 800/996–3426,* FAX *214/761–7242. 1,620 rooms. 6 restaurants, pools, tennis, health club. AE, D, DC, MC, V.* 🐾

$$–$$$$ 🏨 **Hotel Inter-Continental.** This North Dallas deluxe hotel, formerly the Grand Kempinski, is one of the best bargains in town. You can't beat the location or the posh surroundings. The luxury hotel rooms are what you would expect of an Inter-Continental. ⊠ *15201 Dallas Pkwy., 75248,* ☎ *972/386–6000 or 800/327–0200,* FAX *972/991–6937. 529 rooms. 3 restaurants, pools, tennis, health club. AE, CB, D, DC, MC, V.* 🐾

$$–$$$ 🏨 **Stoneleigh.** Just north of downtown, this elegant, old brick hotel has long been favored by celebrities. It's in the tony Turtle Creek neighborhood, just blocks away from the McKinney Avenue shopping and restaurant district. Rooms are comfortable and gracious but not fancy. The sushi bar here is a plus. ⊠ *2927 Maple Ave., 75201,* ☎ *214/ 871–7111 or 800/255–9299,* FAX *214/871–9379. 158 rooms. 2 restaurants, exercise room. AE, D, DC, MC, V.* 🐾

Fort Worth

$$$–$$$$ 🏨 **The Worthington.** This 12-story ultramodern, white-concrete struc-
★ ture stretches along two city blocks, forming a dramatic glassed-in bridge (where lunch, brunch, and tea are served) over Houston Street. This is Fort Worth's only four-star, four-diamond hotel. ⊠ *200 Main St., 76102,* ☎ *817/870–1000 or 800/433–5677,* FAX *817/338–9176. 504 rooms. 3 restaurants, pool, health club. AE, D, DC, MC, V.* 🐾

$$–$$$ 🏨 **Miss Molly's.** Once a prim little inn, then a raucous bordello, this place above the Star Café, just outside the Stockyards, has been reincarnated as an attractive B&B. Each room is different, but all are furnished with Old West antiques. Only one has a private bath. ⊠ *109½ W. Exchange Ave., 76106,* ☎ *817/626–1522 or 800/996–6559,* FAX *817/ 625–2723. 8 rooms. AE, D, DC, MC, V. CP.*

$$–$$$ 🏨 **Stockyards Hotel.** A storybook place that's seen more than its share of cowboys, rustlers, gangsters, and oil barons, this hotel has been used in many a movie. There are four styles of rooms to choose from: Victorian, Native American, Mountain Man, and Old West. In the Booger Red Saloon, the bar stools are saddles. Complimentary breakfast is provided weekdays only. ⊠ *109 E. Exchange Ave., 76106,* ☎ *817/625– 6427 or 800/423–8471,* FAX *817/624–2571. 52 rooms. Restaurant. AE, D, DC, MC, V. CP.*

$–$$ 🏨 **Green Oaks Park Hotel.** From the outside, the Green Oaks Park is certainly unimpressive, but the interior is clean, the staff is efficient, and it's one of the few places in the Metroplex where you can get a decent room for under $100. ⊠ *6901 West Fwy., 76116,* ☎ *817/738– 7311 or 800/433–2174,* FAX *817/377–1308. 282 rooms. Restaurant, pools, golf, tennis, exercise room. AE, D, DC, MC, V.*

Nightlife and the Arts

Nightlife

DALLAS

Bars and Nightclubs. Much of Dallas bar life swirls around lower and upper **Greenville Avenue,** north of downtown. **Mick's** (⊠ 2825 Greenville Ave., ☎ 214/827–0039) is a sophisticated place to swill martinis, while the **Dubliner** (⊠ 2818 Greenville Ave., ☎ 214/818–0911) offers a rowdy Irish pub atmosphere in which to hoist a few pints or throw a game of darts. For country music and two-stepping, try **Country 2000** (⊠ 10580 N. Stemmons Fwy., ☎ 214/654–9595).

Poor David's Pub (⊠ 1924 Greenville Ave., ☎ 214/821–9891) is one of Dallas's better-known music venues.

Connected to Dallas's premier art-house movie theater, the **Lounge at the Inwood** (⊠ 5458 W. Lovers La., ☎ 214/350–7834) is a sleek, art deco–inspired watering hole.

Dance Clubs. At **Red Jacket** (⊠ 3606 Greenville Ave., ☎ 214/823–8333) you can dance to everything from lounge to swing to 1980s retro. The scene is young and avant-garde in Deep Ellum, where **Curtain Club** (⊠ 2800 Main St., ☎ 214/742–6207) is one of several trendsetting music spots. The **Club Clearview** complex (⊠ 2806 Elm St., ☎ 214/939–0077) offers scenesters four distinct connected clubs , and **Trees** (⊠ 2707 Elm St., ☎ 214/748–5009) serves up loud local and touring bands in a warehouselike setting. At the eastern end of Deep Ellum, **Gypsy Tea Room** (⊠ 2548 Elm St., ☎ 214/744–9779), which is actually two rooms— a 600-person capacity ballroom and a connecting more-intimate performance spot—spotlights local and touring cutting-edge country and rock acts. In Oak Lawn, **Village Station** (⊠ 3911 Cedar Springs Rd., ☎ 214/526–7171) caters to a predominately gay and lesbian crowd; there's '70s disco music on Sunday nights.

FORT WORTH

The area around the Stockyards is crammed with distinctly western-style saloons. The best may be the more-than-a-century-old **White Elephant Saloon** (⊠ 106 E. Exchange Ave., ☎ 817/624–1887), a legendary Wild West bar with live country music seven nights a week. The most famous honky-tonk is **Billy Bob's Texas** (⊠ 2520 Rodeo Plaza, ☎ 817/624–7117 or 817/589–1711), built in an old cattle-pen building, with big-name country music performers. Downtown, **Caravan of Dreams** (⊠ 312 Houston St., ☎ 817/877–3000) is a world-class music venue specializing in jazz and blues greats, including top performers like Lyle Lovett. Don't miss the rooftop cactus garden. Fort Worth's beautiful people flock to downtown's **8.0** (⊠ 111 E. 3rd, ☎ 817/336–0880), one of the trendiest bars in a decidedly untrendy city.

The Arts

DALLAS

The top performing-arts attraction in Dallas is whatever's on at the **Morton H. Meyerson Symphony Center** (☞ Exploring Dallas and Fort Worth, *above*), home to the **Dallas Symphony Orchestra** (☎ 214/692–0203). The **Dallas Theater Center** performs at the **Kalita Humphreys Theatre** (⊠ 3636 Turtle Creek Blvd., ☎ 214/522–8499), the only theater ever designed by Frank Lloyd Wright, and the **Arts District Theater** (⊠ 2401 Flora, ☎ 214/522–8499). The **Majestic Theatre** (⊠ 1925 Elm St., ☎ 214/880–0137), a beautifully restored 1920s vaudeville house and movie palace, hosts various performance groups. In Fair Park, the outdoor **Starplex** amphitheater (⊠ 1818 1st Ave., ☎ 214/421–1111) hosts most of the big-name bands that come to town; smaller acts and those performing during winter months play **Bronco Bowl** (⊠ 2600 Fort

Worth Ave., ☎ 214/943–1777), a 3,000-seat arena paired with a 38-lane bowling alley. The **Music Hall at Fair Park** is the site of performances by the **Dallas Opera** (☎ 214/443–1043) and the **Dallas Summer Musicals** (☎ 214/421–5678).

FORT WORTH

Casa Mañana Theater (✉ 3101 W. Lancaster Ave., ☎ 817/332–9319), a theater-in-the-round under one of Buckminster Fuller's first geodesic domes, hosts the city's summer series of musicals. Other local theaters include the **Jubilee Theatre** (✉ 506 Main St., ☎ 817/338–4411), **Circle Theatre** (✉ 230 W. 4th St., ☎ 817/877–3040), and **Stage West** (✉ 3055 S. University Dr., ☎ 817/784–9378).

Sundance Square's majestic **Nancy Lee and Perry R. Bass Performance Hall** (✉ 555 Commerce St., ☎ 817/212–4300) is the home of the **Fort Worth-Dallas Ballet** (☎ 817/763–0207), the **Fort Worth Opera** (☎ 817/731–0833), and the **Fort Worth Symphony Orchestra** (☎ 817/665–6000).

Spectator Sports

Auto racing: Texas Motor Speedway (✉ I–35W and Hwy. 114, Fort Worth, ☎ 817/215–8500). **Texas Motorplex** (✉ 7500 W. Hwy. 287, Ennis, ☎ 972/878–2641). **Baseball: Texas Rangers** (✉ The Ballpark at Arlington, 1000 Ballpark Way, Arlington, ☎ 817/273–5100). **Basketball: Dallas Mavericks** (✉ Reunion Arena, 777 Sports St., Dallas, ☎ 972/988–3865). **Football: Dallas Cowboys** (✉ Texas Stadium, 2401 E. Airport Fwy., Irving, ☎ 972/579–5000). **Hockey: Dallas Stars** (✉ Reunion Arena, 777 Sports St., Dallas, ☎ 214/467–8277). **Fort Worth Brahmas** (✉ Fort Worth Convention Center, 1111 Houston St., Fort Worth, ☎ 817/335–7825 or 817/884–2222). **Fort Worth Fire** (✉ Tarrant County Convention Center, 100 W. Weatherford, Fort Worth, ☎ 817/336–1992). **Horse racing: Lone Star Park** (✉ 1000 Lone Star Pkwy., Grand Prairie, ☎ 972/263–7223). **Soccer: Dallas Sidekicks** (✉ Reunion Arena, 777 Sports St., Dallas, ☎ 972/988–3865). **Dallas Burn** (✉ Cotton Bowl, Fair Park, Dallas, ☎ 214/979–0303).

Shopping

Dallas

Ever since 1873, when Dallas ensured its future by successfully finagling to become the site of the intersection of two intercontinental rail lines, the city has been the southwestern hub of American commerce. The **Galleria** (✉ LBJ Fwy. at the Dallas North Tollway, ☎ 972/702–7100), with more than 200 retailers and anchor stores Macy's, Nordstrom, and Saks Fifth Avenue, is one of Dallas's best-known malls. Also well known for its collection of high-end retailers, **Highland Park Village** (✉ Mockingbird La. at Preston Rd., ☎ 214/559–2740) is touted as one of the first planned shopping centers in America. **NorthPark Center** (✉ Central Expressway at Northwest Hwy., ☎ 214/363–7441), developed as the nation's first indoor mall by art collector Ray Nasher, has rotating exhibits of world-class art on its walls. In downtown Dallas, the original **Neiman Marcus** (✉ 1618 Main St., ☎ 214/741–6911) is a huge draw.

If you're in the mood for the fresh fruit and vegetables that have made the Rio Grande Valley famous, stop by the **Dallas Farmer's Market** (✉ 1010 S. Pearl St., ☎ 214/939–2808), on the southeastern edge of downtown. There are some fine clothing stores on trendy **McKinney Avenue,** and the elegant **Crescent** (✉ 500 Crescent Ct., off McKinney Ave.), a complex of offices, retail stores, and a hotel, has *very* ritzy shops, including Stanley Korshak.

Shop-a-holics shouldn't miss **Grapevine Mills Mall** (✉ 3000 Grapevine Mills Pkwy., Grapevine, ☎ 972/724–4900), with more than 1.5 million square ft of discount shopping; it is 25 mi northwest of Dallas.

Fort Worth

Both Fort Worth's attitude and its economy have always pointed west, and that's reflected in the shopping here. Most visitors head right to the **Stockyards,** where there are several good western-wear outlets. Check out **Fincher's** (✉ 115 E. Exchange Ave., ☎ 817/624–7302), a western store since 1902 in a building that began life as a bank; you can still walk into the old vaults. A great place for boots is **M. L. Leddy's Boot and Saddlery** (✉ 2455 N. Main St., ☎ 817/624–3149).

Downtown's **Sundance Square** is a perennial draw, with several small stores. **Fort Worth Outlet Square** (✉ 150 Throckmorton St., ☎ 817/390–3720 or 800/414–2817), a large, modern indoor mall with its own privately operated subway, is attached to Sundance Square and is a better choice for shopping. **Barber's Book Store** (✉ 215 W. 8th St., ☎ 817/335–5469), specializing in Texana and rare and fine books, is the oldest bookstore in Texas.

ELSEWHERE IN TEXAS

East Texas

Arriving and Departing

Between Dallas and Shreveport, Louisiana, lies east Texas, whose main east–west artery is I–20. Marshall, the heart of the region, is about a three-hour drive from Dallas or a half hour from the Louisiana line. **Amtrak** trains serve Marshall three times a week. The station in Marshall is on Washington Street, but there is no Amtrak staff there.

What to See and Do

Heading into east Texas from the Dallas–Fort Worth area, you'll pass two great boundaries: a natural line, marking the start of a piney, hilly region totally unlike the Great Plains; and a man-made one, the beginning of what was the slaveholding part of the United States. In every way, east Texas—a region once dependent on cotton—feels more southern than western. After Texas seceded from the union in 1861, **Marshall** became the seat of civil authority west of the Mississippi and the wartime capital of Missouri; five Confederate generals are buried in its cemetery. Marshall is full of historic homes, some of which—like the **Starr Family Home** (✉ 407 W. Travis St., ☎ 903/935–3044; ✏ $3)—can be toured; others are small hostelries. One of Marshall's charms is beautiful **Stagecoach Road** (take Poplar Street, which heads east from U.S. 59, and follow markers); in places you can see the results of the stages cutting some 2 ft into the ground on this undisturbed section of the old main road to Shreveport. Off U.S. 59 signs lead to **Marshall Pottery** (✉ 4901 Elysian Field Rd., ☎ 903/938–9201; ✏ free), a huge working pottery factory.

Jefferson, a 20-minute drive north of Marshall, is one of Texas's most historic towns, a charming place on Big Cypress Bayou that once served hundreds of steamboats coming up from New Orleans. When his offer to run track through the town was rebuffed, railroad baron Jay Gould is said to have angrily scrawled in the hotel register of the Excelsior House the prophetic words "The End of Jefferson." Today the superb **Excelsior House** (✉ 211 W. Austin St., ☎ 903/665–2513), built in the 1850s, is a tribute to the restorer's art (reservations are required months in advance). **Gould's private railroad car** is across the street from the Excelsior House.

Caddo Lake, overhung with Spanish moss and edged with bald cypresses, is a major fishing destination straddling the Texas-Louisiana border. At various times it has been home to the beleaguered Caddo Indians, to bootleggers hiding out in its dense shore growth, to the great singer of spirituals Leadbelly (reared at Swanson's Landing), to thriving steamboat traffic from New Orleans, and to all manner of legend. **Caddo Lake State Park** (☞ National and State Parks, *above*) is on the south shore.

Lodging

$$ 🏠 **Caddo Cottage.** This is the ideal place for a family looking for a quiet time along one of the most beautiful parts of Caddo Lake. The two-story lake house sleeps four. ⊠ *Rte. 2, Box 66, Uncertain 75661,* ☎ *903/789–3988. 1 cottage. No credit cards.* 🐾

$$ 🏠 **Pride House.** Ornate woodwork and original stained glass distinguish this old Victorian mansion, one of Jefferson's finest B&Bs. ⊠ *409 E. Broadway, Jefferson 75657,* ☎ *903/665–2675. 10 rooms. AE, D, MC, V. BP.*

El Paso

Visitor Information

El Paso Convention & Visitors Bureau (⊠ 1 Civic Center Plaza, 79901, ☎ 915/534–0696 or 800/351–6024).

Arriving and Departing

At Texas's far southwestern corner, El Paso is an 11-hour drive from San Antonio; about 12 hours from Dallas–Fort Worth; 6 from Santa Fe, New Mexico; and 5 from Phoenix, Arizona. The major local carrier at **El Paso International Airport** (6701 Convair Dr., ☎ 915/772–4271) is Southwest Airlines (☎ 800/435–9792). **Amtrak** (⊠ Union Station, 700 San Francisco St., ☎ 800/872–7245) provides train service to and from the city.

What to See and Do

Dramatically situated a few miles between the southern end of the Rockies and the northern terminus of Mexico's Sierra Madre range, **El Paso** (population 591,610), established by the Spanish in 1598, was a major stopping point on the way west during the California gold rush. Outside the city, in El Paso's lower valley, are several important historic ★ sites, including the famed **Mission Trail.** The trail includes **Mission Socorro** (⊠ 328 S. Nevarez, ☎ 915/859–7718), known for its fine vigas (the carved ceiling beams that mark local architecture); **Presidio Chapel San Elceario** (⊠ 1556 San Elizario Rd., ☎ 915/851–2333), a fort built to protect the missions; and **Mission Ysleta** (⊠ 119 S. Old Pueblo Dr., ☎ 915/859–9848), the oldest Spanish mission in the Southwest. Adjacent to Mission Ysleta is the **Tigua Indian Reservation** (☎ 915/859–7913), home of the oldest ethnic group in Texas, where Tigua pottery, jewelry, art, and replicas of ancient Native American homes are for sale.

The history of the U.S. Border Patrol from the Old West to the present is portrayed at the **Border Patrol Museum** (⊠ 4315 Transmountain Rd., ☎ 915/759–6060; 🎫 free), with displays of aircraft and vehicles used by the patrol, surveillance equipment, and confiscated items.

Across the Rio Grande from El Paso is the Mexican city of **Juarez,** where the shopping is often sensational; you can take the **El Paso–Juarez International Trolley** (⊠ Santa Fe and San Francisco Sts., ☎ 915/544–0061; 🎫 $11 round-trip). Panoramic views of El Paso can be seen from **Scenic Drive,** which you'll find by driving north on Mesa Street and then right on Rim Road. **Transmountain Road,** off I–10 west of downtown, takes you through Smuggler's Gap, a dramatic cut across the Franklin Mountains.

Lodging

$$$ 🏨 **Camino Real Hotel.** This elegant, brick downtown hotel is listed on the National Register of Historic Places. The jewel of the lobby is the dark-wood circular Dome Bar, which sits under a superb 1912 Tiffany skylight. Guest rooms are functional and large. ⊠ *101 S. El Paso St., 79901,* ☎ *915/534–3000 or 800/722–6466,* ℻ *915/534–3024. 359 rooms. 2 restaurants, pool, exercise room. AE, D, DC, MC, V.* 🐾

South Padre Island

Visitor Information

South Padre Island Convention & Visitors Bureau (⊠ 600 Padre Island Blvd., Box 3500, 78597, ☎ 956/761–6433 or 800/767–2373).

Arriving and Departing

South Padre Island, with Texas's most beautiful beaches, is in the southeastern corner of the state, near the Mexican border town of Matamoros. The island is reached by a bridge across the Intracoastal Waterway from Port Isabel, which, in turn, is accessible from Routes 48 and 100.

What to See and Do

At the southern tip of one of the largest barrier islands in the world—113-mi-long Padre Island—the resort town and white-sand beaches of **South Padre Island** (population: 2,050) attract college students at spring break but delight nature seekers, beach- and sun-lovers, and fishermen the rest of the year. North of South Padre Island, the 80½-mi
★ **Padre Island National Seashore** (⊠ 9405 South Padre Island Dr., Corpus Christi 78418, ☎ 361/949–8173) is essentially unchanged from the days when scavenging Karankawa Indians roamed among its sand dunes, sea oats, and morning glories.

UTAH

By Stacey
Clark

Updated by
Kurt Repanshek

Capital	Salt Lake City
Population	2,059,000
Motto	Industry
State Bird	California gull
State Flower	Sego lily
Postal Abbreviation	UT

Statewide Visitor Information

Utah Travel Council (⊠ Council Hall, Capitol Hill, Salt Lake City 84114, ☎ 801/538–1030 or 800/200–1160). Ten **regional visitor information centers** (call the Utah Travel Council for locations) supply brochures and travel advice, and **welcome centers** are near all major entrances to the state. The **Salt Lake Organizing Committee for the Olympic Winter Games of 2002** (⊠ 299 S. Main St., Salt Lake City 84111, ☎ 801/212–2002) provides information on venues for the games, which will be hosted by Salt Lake City.

Scenic Drives

From Logan **U.S. 89** runs north through a limestone canyon with steep, striated walls, cresting above Bear Lake on the Utah–Idaho border. In northeastern Utah **U.S. 191** jogs north out of Vernal and past geologic formations that are up to a billion years old before meeting **Route 44,** which yields an elongated view of Flaming Gorge National Recreation Area. **Route 12,** in southwestern Utah, turns east from U.S. 89, skirting through Bryce Canyon National Park and Grand Staircase-Escalante National Monument, and then north over aspen-covered Boulder Mountain to Capitol Reef National Park. Utah has 27 officially designated scenic byways; visitor and welcome centers provide information on these.

National and State Parks

National Parks

Utah's five national parks are **Bryce Canyon,** filled with unusual geologic formations; **Capitol Reef,** distinguished by colorfully striped rock walls and ancient petroglyphs; **Zion,** with towering cliffs (for all three, ☞ Exploring Southwestern Utah, *below*); **Canyonlands,** with drives through three geologically distinct districts; and **Arches,** known for its sandstone formations (for both, ☞ Exploring Southeastern Utah, *below*).

Utah's seven national monuments include the excavations at **Dinosaur National Monument** (☞ Elsewhere in Utah, *below*); the limestone caverns of **Timpanogos Cave** (⊠ RR 3, Box 200, American Fork 84003, ☎ 801/756–5238 visitor center; 801/756–5239 headquarters); and the giant, stream-formed spans of **Natural Bridges National Monument** (☞ Exploring Southeastern Utah, *below*). You can fish or boat at **Glen Canyon National Recreation Area** (☞ Exploring Southeastern Utah, *below*) and **Flaming Gorge National Recreation Area** (☞ Elsewhere in Utah, *below*). **Grand Staircase–Escalante National Monument** (⊠ 180 W., 300 North, Kanab 84741, ☎ 435/644–4300) achieved monument status in 1996. Though amenities and services remain few, it has stunning river canyons and geologic formations.

State Parks

The **Division of State Parks** (⊠ 1594 W. North Temple St., Salt Lake City 84114, ☎ 801/538–7220) publishes a directory of Utah's 45 state parks. **Goblin Valley State Park** (⊠ Box 637, Green River 84525, ☎ 435/564–3633), off I–70 on Route 24 in eastern Utah, has acres of wind-eroded sandstone "goblins" around a desert campground. **This Is the Place Heritage Park** (⊠ 2601 Sunnyside Ave., Salt Lake City 84108, ☎ 801/584–8391), on the eastern bench of the Salt Lake Valley, details the trek of Mormon pioneers and re-creates an 1850s township, complete with cooking, crafts making, and blacksmithing demonstrations.

SALT LAKE CITY

A growing, dynamic metropolis, Salt Lake City is a high-tech hub of the Rocky Mountains, a center for biomedical research, and the gateway to the red-rock wonders of southern Utah. The city has evolved into a world-class destination for winter sports; it's no surprise that the 2002 Olympic Winter Games will be held here. Salt Lake City's roots date to July 24, 1847, when Mormon leader Brigham Young looked out over the Salt Lake Valley and announced to the ragged party behind him, "This is the right place." So began the religious settlement that nurtured the Church of Jesus Christ of Latter-Day Saints, as the Mormon Church is officially known.

Visitor Information

Convention and Visitors Bureau (⊠ Salt Palace Convention Center, 90 S. West Temple St., 84101, ☎ 801/521–2822).

Arriving and Departing

By Bus
Greyhound (⊠ 160 W. South Temple St., ☎ 800/231–2222).

By Car
I–15 runs north–south through Salt Lake, I–80 east–west. I–215 circles the valley.

By Plane
Salt Lake International Airport (⊠ 776 North Terminal Dr., ☎ 801/575–2400) is 7 mi west of downtown. Major hotels provide shuttles, and **Utah Transit Authority** (☎ 801/287–4636) buses link the airport to regular city routes for $1. Taxi fare to downtown averages $13–$15 including tip.

By Train
Amtrak (☎ 800/872–7245) serves the city's **Rio Grande Depot** (⊠ 320 S. Rio Grande St., ☎ 801/531–0188).

Getting Around Salt Lake City

Salt Lake City streets are laid out geometrically and numbered in increments of 100 in each direction, with Temple Square as their root. Parking is inexpensive. **Utah Transit Authority** (☎ 801/287–4636) buses and trolleys serve the valley. The fare is $1, with a free-fare zone in downtown shopping areas. A light-rail train system runs north and south through Salt Lake City.

Exploring Salt Lake City

City attractions fan out from Temple Square. To the north is the Capitol Hill District, to the south are shopping and arts locations, to the west is the Great Salt Lake, and to the east lie the ski resorts of the Wasatch Mountains.

Historic **Temple Square** (⊠ North Visitors' Center, 50 W. North Temple St., ☎ 801/240–2534) is the 10-acre center of sites important to

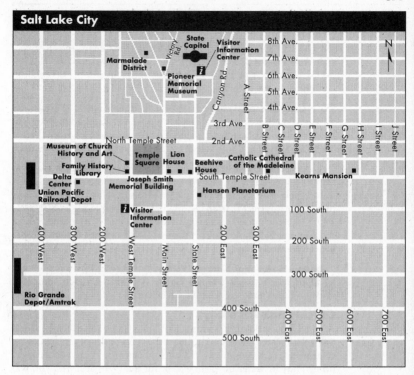

Salt Lake City

Mormonism. Two visitor centers house exhibits and art with religious themes. The **Mormon Tabernacle Choir** rehearses at 8 PM on Thursdays and performs at 9:30 AM Sundays in the squat, domed Salt Lake Tabernacle. The six-spired granite **Salt Lake Temple** is open only to church members, but the public may enter (free of charge) the other buildings and monuments on the beautifully landscaped grounds.

East of Temple Square and across Main Street, the **Joseph Smith Memorial Building** (☎ 801/240–1266 or 800/537–9703; ☒ free) details the history of the LDS Church and contains a computerized genealogical research center where visitors can trace their family heritage. Visitors also can watch an hour-long film on early Mormon history and the emigration of Mormons to the Salt Lake Valley in the mid-19th century. The center, set in what was once the elegant Hotel Utah, also has two restaurants.

On West Temple Street directly west of Temple Square is the **Museum of Church History and Art** (☎ 801/240–3310; ☒ free), displaying Mormon artifacts, paintings, fabric art, and sculptures. Also on West Temple Street, the **Family History Library** (☎ 801/240–2331) provides free public access to the Mormons' huge collection of genealogical records.

On the corner of South Temple and State streets, one block east of Temple Square, is the 1854 **Beehive House** (☎ 801/240–2671; ☒ free), the home of Brigham Young while he served as territorial governor; free tours are conducted daily. The **Lion House** (☎ 801/363–5466) received the overflow of Young's large family. It is now a social center and restaurant.

Another impressive turn-of-the-20th-century structure, half a block south of the Beehive House, houses the **Hansen Planetarium** (☒ 15 S. State St., ☎ 801/538–2098; ☒ free, shows $3.50–$7.50), where a moon rock display is among the exhibits. A domed theater hosts star shows and laser shows set to music.

On a hill at the north end of State Street sits the Renaissance Revival–style **state capitol** (✉ 300 N. State St., ☎ 801/538–1563 or 801/538–3000), completed in 1915. Free hourly tours take in the depression-era murals in the rotunda, which depict events from Utah's past.

The **Pioneer Memorial Museum** (✉ 300 N. Main St., ☎ 801/538–1050; ✉ free; donations accepted), directly west of the state capitol grounds, holds thousands of artifacts, including tools and carriages from the late 1800s and a doll and toy collection. The museum is closed on Sunday.

The **Marmalade District**—the streets bisecting the western slope of Capitol Hill—contains many pioneer houses. Other well-preserved historic houses are on South Temple Street east of Temple Square. Among them is the **Kearns Mansion** (✉ 603 E. South Temple St., ☎ 801/538–1005), the governor's residence, accessible only by free guided tours. Also on South Temple Street is the early 20th-century **Catholic Cathedral of the Madeleine** (✉ 331 E. South Temple St., ☎ 801/328–8941).

The **Utah Museum of Natural History** (✉ 1390 E. Presidents Circle, ☎ 801/581–6927; ✉ $4) has Native American artifacts, dinosaur skeletons, and hands-on science adventures.

Outside Salt Lake City

About 17 mi west of downtown Salt Lake City via I–80 is the **Great Salt Lake.** Water flows into it, but there is no outlet other than evaporation. This traps minerals and salts, causing the lake to be the most saline body of water on earth except for the Dead Sea. Yes, you will float. There are two beaches here, each with showers. The south and west shores and neighboring wetlands are prime nesting grounds for many species of migratory, shore, and wading birds. Perhaps the best way to experience the lake is to travel to **Antelope Island State Park** (☎ 801/773–2941), which is accessed from I–15 north of Salt Lake City via a 7½-mi causeway ($7 per vehicle). Beaches take you down to the water while inland trails provide breathtaking views of the lake and glimpses of the island's bison and antelope herds.

Rising to more than 11,000 ft east of the Salt Lake Valley, the **Wasatch Mountains** provide an impressive backdrop and recreational escape for city dwellers. Southeast of Salt Lake City are two scenic canyons, Big Cottonwood on Route 190 and Little Cottonwood on Route 210. Resorts here offer hiking, biking, arts festivals and concerts in summer, and skiing in winter (☞ Ski Areas, *below*).

Over the ridge line but merely 29 mi east of Salt Lake City via I–80 is **Park City,** Utah's premier ski destination. Park City's three ski areas and the Utah Winter Sports Park will host many events during the 2002 Olympic Winter Games. Park City's historic Main Street has a museum, galleries, shops, and restaurants. The town also offers fine bed-and-breakfasts, three golf courses, and an outlet mall nearby.

Parks, Gardens, and Zoos

Red Butte Gardens and Arboretum (☎ 801/581–4747; ✉ $5), east of Salt Lake City's University of Utah campus and Research Park, has 150 acres of trees, a children's garden, shrubs, herbs, wildflowers, and stream-fed pools tucked into a private canyon in the Wasatch foothills. A concert series is held each summer.

⏾ In the city's eastern foothills, **Hogle Zoo** (✉ 2600 E. Sunnyside Ave., ☎ 801/582–1631; ☜ $6) has more than 1,300 animals. Bring walking shoes and a hat—exhibits are spread out, and shade is at a premium.

Dining

Although liquor laws have some peculiarities, mixed drinks, wine, and beer are available at most restaurants. When in doubt, call ahead.

$$$–$$$$ ✕ **Glitretind.** It's pricey, but dishes such as almond-crusted salmon with
★ honey coucous and a roasted red pepper and olive vinaigrette make it worthwhile. ✉ *Stein Eriksen Lodge, Deer Valley,* ☎ *435/649–3700. AE, DC, MC, V.*

$$–$$$$ ✕ **Baci Trattoria.** Northern Italian food is served in an elegant setting of marble and stained glass. ✉ *134 W. Pierpont Ave.,* ☎ *801/328–1500. AE, D, DC, MC, V. Closed Sun.*

$$–$$$$ ✕ **Log Haven Restaurant.** Tucked away in Millcreek Canyon, this
★ restaurant set in an historic log mansion offers scenery, atmosphere, and an eclectic menu with entrées such as stone-grilled chicken served on jalapeño-cheddar crushed potatoes and grilled sirloin of lamb accompanied by Mediterranean eggplant puree in a roasted Portobello mushroom. ✉ *4 mi up Millcreek Canyon, Box 9154, Salt Lake City,* ☎ *801/272–8255. AE, D, MC, V.*

$$–$$$$ ✕ **Market Street Grill.** The stylish black-and-white decor is catchy, but creative preparations of seafood, steaks, and chicken steal the show. ✉ *48 Market St.,* ☎ *801/322–4668. AE, D, DC, MC, V.*

$$–$$$ ✕ **Creekside Restaurant.** The seasonal colors of the Wasatch Mountains and views of ski runs add to the allure of this Mediterranean-style restaurant. Wood-oven-baked pizzas have gourmet toppings; pasta, chicken, and steak round out the menu. ✉ *Solitude Resort, 12000 Big Cottonwood Canyon,* ☎ *801/536–5787. AE, D, MC, V.*

$–$$ ✕ **Lamb's Restaurant.** Lamb's claims to be Utah's oldest restaurant; it opened in 1919 and still has a turn-of-the-20th-century feel. On the menu are beef, and chicken, plus sandwiches. ✉ *169 S. Main St.,* ☎ *801/364–7166. AE, D, DC, MC, V. Closed Sun.*

$–$$ ✕ **Santa Fe Restaurant.** Inside a streamside lodge in scenic Emigration
★ Canyon, 15 minutes east of downtown, Santa Fe Restaurant earns acclaim for its creative regional dishes such as chicken roulade stuffed with vegetables, and rainbow trout, both served with unusual sauces. ✉ *2100 Emigration Canyon Rd.,* ☎ *801/582–5888. D, DC, MC, V.*

Lodging

Contact the **Utah Travel Council** (✉ Council Hall, Capitol Hill, Salt Lake City 84111, ☎ 801/538–1030 or 800/200–1160) for further suggestions. Prices vary widely with the seasons. The ski resorts listed below are no more than 30 mi away from Salt Lake City.

$$$–$$$$ ▦ **Cliff Lodge at Snowbird Resort.** The large guest rooms in this an-
★ gular gray building have wide glass walls providing spectacular views winter and summer. The lobby, draped with a private collection of Persian rugs, is sumptuous. On the grounds is a full-service day spa. ✉ *Snowbird Resort 84092,* ☎ *801/933–2222 or 800/453–3000, ℻ 801/947–8227. 511 rooms. 3 restaurants, 2 bars, 2 pools, hot tub, spa, exercise room. AE, D, DC, MC, V.* ☜

$–$$$$ ▦ **Shadow Ridge Resort.** This lodging is positioned so that guests can virtually ski straight into Park City Mountain Resort's lift lines from most of its rooms, which range from a single hotel room to a two-bedroom condominium suite with full kitchen. ✉ *50 Shadow Ridge St., Box 1820, Park City 84060,* ☎ *435/655–3315 or 800/451–3031, ℻*

435/649–5951. *150 rooms. Restaurant, pool, hot tub, sauna, exercise room. AE, D, DC, MC, V.*

$$–$$$ 🏨 **Little America Hotel & Towers.** Salt Lake's largest hotel has 17 floors of elegant rooms with textured fabrics, plush seating, and variable lighting. The lobby and mezzanine have enormous brick fireplaces. ⊠ *500 S. Main St., 84101,* ☎ *801/363–6781 or 800/453–9450,* ℻ *801/596–5911. 850 rooms. 2 restaurants, pool, exercise room. AE, D, DC, MC, V.* ❧

$$–$$$ 🏨 **Saltair Bed & Breakfast.** The history of this 1903 Victorian home
   ★   landed it on the state and national registers of historic places. Fine oak woodwork and period antiques lend elegance to the setting. Sitting in the formal parlor with a book before a roaring fire is the perfect way to end a day. ⊠ *164 S. 900 East, 84102,* ☎ *801/533–8184 or 800/733–8184,* ℻ *801/595–0332. 17 rooms. AE, D, DC, MC, V. BP.* ❧

$–$$$ 🏨 **Anton Boxrud Bed & Breakfast.** This antiques-filled Victorian manor near the governor's mansion is a pleasant 15-minute walk from the city center. The complimentary evening snacks and beverages served near the parlor's bay window are as delicious as the bountiful breakfasts, which could feature French toast stuffed with fresh fruit. ⊠ *57 S. 600 East, 84102,* ☎ *801/363–8035 or 800/524–5511,* ℻ *801/596–1316. 7 rooms. AE, D, DC, MC, V. BP.* ❧

Motels

🏨 **Holiday Inn Express** (⊠ 2080 W. North Temple St., 84116, ☎ 801/355–0088 or 800/465–4329, ℻ 801/355–0099), 92 rooms; restaurant, pool; *$$.*

🏨 **Travelodge** (⊠ 524 S. West Temple, 84101, ☎ 801/531–7100 or 800/578–7878, ℻ 801/359–3814), 60 rooms; pool; *$.*

Nightlife and the Arts

A calendar of events is available at the **Salt Lake Convention and Visitors Bureau** (☞ Visitor Information, *above*). The free *City Weekly* newspaper is widely available throughout the city. Both the *Salt Lake Tribune* and the *Deseret News* carry daily arts-and-entertainment listings.

Nightlife

Many nightspots are private clubs due to Utah's unusual liquor laws, meaning that membership is required (temporary memberships cost about $5). Weekends are wild at the **Dead Goat Saloon** (⊠ 165 S. West Temple St., ☎ 801/328–4628), a subterranean hangout with live music and a busy dance floor. A good place to spot Utah Jazz basketball players is **Port O' Call** (⊠ 78 W. 400 South, ☎ 801/521–0589), a sports bar with 14 satellite dishes and 35 TVs. The art deco–style **Zephyr Club** (⊠ 301 S. West Temple St., ☎ 801/355–2582) has nationally touring acts that provide live blues, rock, reggae, and dancing. The **Bay** (⊠ 404 S. West Temple St., ☎ 801/363–2623) is a smoke- and alcohol-free club with three dance floors. The **Hard Rock Cafe** (⊠ 505 S. 600 East, ☎ 801/532–7625) features burgers and rock-and-roll memorabilia.

The Arts

Salt Lake's best performing arts bets are **Ballet West** (⊠ 50 W. 200 South, ☎ 801/355–2787), **Pioneer Theater Company** (⊠ 300 S. 1340 East, ☎ 801/581–6961), **Salt Lake Acting Company** (⊠ 168 W. 500 North, ☎ 801/363–7522), **Utah Opera Company** (⊠ 50 W. 200 South, ☎ 801/355–2787), and **Utah Symphony** (⊠ Abravanel Hall, 123 W. South Temple St., ☎ 801/533–6683). Concerts are presented at the **Delta Center** (⊠ 301 W. South Temple St., ☎ 801/325–7328), and the **"E" Center** (⊠ 3200 S. Decker Lake Dr., ☎ 801/988–8888).

Spectator Sports

Baseball: Pacific Coast League Salt Lake Buzz (⊠ 77 W. 1300 South, ☎ 801/485–3800). **Basketball: NBA Utah Jazz** and **WNBA Utah Starzz** (⊠ Delta Center, 300 W. South Temple St., ☎ 801/355–3865). **Hockey: International Hockey League Utah Grizzlies** (⊠ 3200 S. Decker La., West Valley City, ☎ 801/988–8000).

Ski Areas

Cross-Country

Solitude (⊠ Rte. 190, ☎ 801/536–5774 or 800/748–4754) and **White Pine Touring** (⊠ Park City, ☎ 435/649–8701) offer cross-country ski-ing tours, rentals, lessons, and advice. **Sundance Nordic Center** (⊠ RR 3, Box A-1, Sundance, ☎ 801/225–4107) features 15 km of skiing and offers night skiing lit by lanterns.

Downhill

Alta (⊠ Rte. 210, ☎ 801/359–1078), 40 runs and bowls, 13 lifts, 2,020-ft vertical drop. **Brighton** (⊠ Rte. 190, ☎ 801/532–4731 or 800/873–5512), 64 runs, 7 lifts, 1,745-ft drop. The **Canyons** (⊠ The Canyons Dr., off Rte. 224, Park City, ☎ 435/649–5400 or 800/754–1636), 125 runs, 12 lifts, gondola, 3,190-ft drop. **Deer Valley** (⊠ Rte. 224, Park City, ☎ 435/649–1000 or 800/424–3337), 87 runs, 19 lifts, 3,000-ft drop. **Park City Mountain Resort** (⊠ Rte. 224 off I–80, Park City, ☎ 435/649–8111 or 800/222–7275), 100 runs, 14 lifts, 3,100-ft drop. **Solitude** (⊠ Rte. 190, ☎ 801/534–1400 or 800/748–4754), 63 runs and bowls, 7 lifts, 2,047-ft drop, 12 mi of groomed cross-country track. **Snowbird** (⊠ Rte. 210, ☎ 801/742–2222 or 800/453–3000), 66 runs and bowls, 9 lifts and a high-speed tram, 3,240-ft drop.

Shopping

Directly south of Temple Square, **Crossroads Plaza** (⊠ 50 S. Main St., ☎ 801/531–1799) has four floors of stores, theaters, and restaurants. East across Main Street, **ZCMI Center** (⊠ 36 S. State St., ☎ 801/321–8745) has 80 stores and restaurants. A few blocks south and east, **Trol-ley Square** (⊠ 600 S. 700 East, ☎ 801/521–9877) once housed elec-tric trolleys; today it has the city's most varied shopping under one roof, as well as restaurants and movie theaters. Clustered around a flour mill built in 1877 are the shops of **Gardner Village** (⊠ 1100 W. 7800 South St., ☎ 801/566–8903). East of I–15 in the south end of the city, the **Factory Stores of America Mall** (⊠ 12101 S. Factory Outlet Dr., ☎ 801/571–2933) has three dozen discount outlets with everything from cookware and coats to Doc Martens.

SOUTHWESTERN UTAH

Southwestern Utah is a panoply of natural wonders. Heading the list are Zion, Capitol Reef, and Bryce Canyon national parks, where clear air and high elevations create spectacular 100-mi vistas. The picturesque towns of St. George, Cedar City, Springdale, and Torrey are full of historic sites. The weather here is mild year-round, though summers can be hot.

Visitor Information

St. George Area Convention and Visitor Bureau (⊠ 1835 Convention Center Dr., St. George 84790, ☎ 435/628–7003 or 800/869–6635). **Capi-tol Reef Country** (⊠ Rte. 24, Box 7, Teasdale 84773, ☎ 800/858–7951).

Arriving and Departing

By Bus
Greyhound (☎ 800/231–2222) stops in St. George and Cedar City.

By Car
I–15 and U.S. 89 pass north–south through the region.

By Plane
St. George and Cedar City airports are served by **SkyWest** (☎ 800/453–9417).

Exploring Southwestern Utah

At **Bryce Canyon National Park** millions of years of geologic mayhem have created gigantic bowls filled with strange pinnacles and quilted drapes of stone. An 18-mi scenic drive skirts the western rim, providing views of the amphitheaters. ✉ *Box 170001, Hwy. 63, Bryce Canyon 84717,* ☎ *435/834–5322.* ✆ *$10 per vehicle. Some roads closed Nov.–Mar.*

Once called "Land of the Sleeping Rainbow" because of its colorfully striped cliffs, **Capitol Reef National Park** is dominated by a 100-mi-long stone uplift called the Waterpocket Fold. At the base of this soaring "reef" are still-flourishing riverside orchards planted by early settlers. Hikes lead to petroglyphs and hidden formations. The park also has an impressive backcountry scenic route ($4 per vehicle). ✉ *Hwy. 24, HCR 70, Box 15, Torrey 84775,* ☎ *435/425–3791.*

The Virgin River carved the towering cliffs of Zion Canyon and still flows along its floor. Spring-fed hanging gardens sprout lush greens along the walls. The roads, tram tours, and horseback and hiking trails of **Zion National Park** (✉ *Springdale 84767,* ☎ *435/772–3256;* ✆ *$20 per vehicle*) provide access to the beauties of this vividly hued canyon and its tributaries. The park can be very crowded in summer and early fall. As a result of the crowds, those without a reservation at Zion Lodge must ride a shuttle into the park from Springdale.

Southwest of Zion National Park, in St. George, you can tour the historic district and **Brigham Young's winter home** (✉ 67 W. 200 N. St., ☎ 435/673–2517; ✆ free). In Santa Clara the **house of missionary Jacob Hamblin** (✉ 3386 Santa Clara Dr., ☎ 435/673–2161; ✆ free) has a vineyard. Both sites are operated by the Mormon Church.

Dining and Lodging

Travel Utah Reservations (☎ 800/259–3343) provides area-wide lodging recommendations.

Bryce Canyon
$–$$ ✕🗓 **Bryce Canyon Lodge.** A huge limestone fireplace and a log and wrought-iron chandelier dominate the lobby of this National Historic Landmark building inside the park. Guests have their choice of motel-style rooms with porches, or cozy lodgepole-pine cabins, some with fireplaces. Reserve far in advance, or call the day before your arrival—cancellations occasionally make last-minute reservations possible. ✉ *#1 Bryce Canyon Lodge, Bryce Canyon 84717,* ☎ *303/297–2757 advance reservations; 435/834–5361 same-day availability;* ℻ *435/586–3157. 74 rooms, 40 cabins. Restaurant. AE, D, DC, MC, V. Closed Nov.–Apr.* ✍

$–$$ ✕🗓 **Best Western Ruby's Inn.** Just north of the park entrance, this is Grand Central Station for visitors to Bryce. A nightly rodeo takes place nearby during the summer. Rooms vary in age, with sprawling wings added as the park gained popularity. ✉ *Rte. 63, Box 1, 84764,*

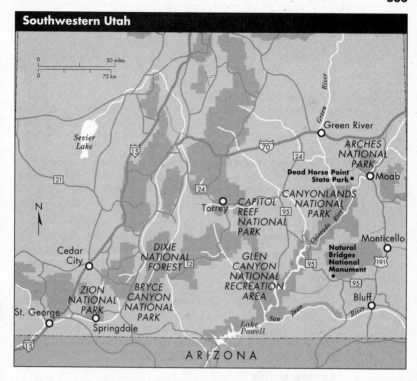

Southwestern Utah

☏ *435/834–5341 or 800/468–8660,* ⅢⅩ *435/834–5265. 369 rooms.*
Restaurant, pool. AE, D, DC, MC, V. ☜

Cedar City

\$–\$\$\$\$ ✕ **Milt's Stage Stop.** Locals swear by the 12-ounce rib-eye steak, prime
★ rib, and seafood at this restaurant in scenic Cedar Canyon. In winter,
deer feed in front of the restaurant as a fireplace blazes inside. The mountain views are splendid year-round. ✉ *5 mi east of town on Rte. 14,*
☏ *435/586–9344. AE, D, DC, MC, V.*

St. George

\$–\$\$\$ ✕ **Basila's Cafe.** Gyros, lamb kebabs, salads, and other Mediterranean
specialties fill the menu here. The surrounding red rock makes outdoor
dining particularly captivating at sunset. ✉ *2 W. St. George Blvd.,* ☏
435/673–7671. AE, D, MC, V. Closed Sun. and Mon.

\$ ✕ **Pancho and Lefty's.** The Mexican cuisine ranges from authentic
tamales wrapped in corn husks to avocado-laced taco salads, all further enlivened by spirited decor and tart margaritas. ✉ *1050 S. Bluff
St.,* ☏ *435/628–4772. AE, MC, V.*

\$ ⌂ **Ramada Inn.** On St. George's major thoroughfare and close to
restaurants, shopping, and the historic district, this is one of the city's
most convenient and best-appointed properties. ✉ *1440 E. St. George
Blvd., 84790,* ☏ *435/628–2828 or 800/713–9435,* ⅢⅩ *435/628–0505.
136 rooms. Pool, hot tub, business services, meeting rooms. AE, D,
DC, MC, V.* ☜

Springdale

\$\$–\$\$\$ ✕ **Bit and Spur Restaurant and Saloon.** This low-slung eatery serves
★ healthful Southwestern-style Mexican food. Works by local artists fill
the pine-paneled interior, and the patio is redolent of scents from the
herb garden. ✉ *1212 Zion Park Blvd.,* ☏ *435/772–3498. MC, V.*

$–$$ ✕ **Flannigan's.** Named for one of Springdale's original settlement families, this intimate restaurant has wide windows with views of Zion Canyon, and a collection of Everett Ruess woodcut prints inside. Pastas, chicken, fish, and steaks, some prepared with a southwestern flare, compose the menu. ⊠ *428 Zion Park Blvd.,* ☎ *435/772–3244 or 800-765–7787. AE, D, MC, V.*

$$–$$$ 🏨 **Cliffrose Lodge and Gardens.** Acres of lawn, trees, and gardens surround this hotel on the banks of the Virgin River, ¼ mi from Zion. Rooms are warm with desert hues. ⊠ *281 Zion Park Blvd., 84767,* ☎ *435/772–3234 or 800/243–8824,* 𝖥𝖠𝖷 *435/772–3900. 36 rooms. Pool. AE, D, MC, V.* ✎

$$–$$$ 🏨 **Snow Family Guest Ranch.** Just minutes from Zion National Park in
★   the town of Virgin, this western-style B&B has inviting common areas—both indoors and out. ⊠ *633 E. Hwy. 9, Box 790190, Virgin 84779,* ☎ *435/635–2500 or 800/308–7669. 9 rooms. Pool. AE, D, MC, V. BP.* ✎

Torrey

$–$$ ✕ **Café Diablo.** Come here for innovative Southwest cuisine such as hearty *chipotle*-baked ribs, local trout crusted with pumpkin seeds, pork tenderloin with mango salsa, and vegetarian dishes. ⊠ *599 W. Main St.,* ☎ *435/425–3070. MC, V. Closed Nov.–Apr.*

$$–$$$ 🏨 **SkyRidge Bed & Breakfast.** This three-story inn has comfortable guest
★   rooms, two with private outdoor hot tubs. There are 75 windows in the building, and all have exceptional views of the desert and mountains surrounding Capitol Reef National Park. Evening hors d'oeuvres are served by the fireplace. ⊠ *950 E. Hwy. 24, Box 750220, 84775,* ☎ 𝖥𝖠𝖷 *435/425–3222. 6 rooms. MC, V. BP.* ✎

Campgrounds

You can choose from among more than 100 campgrounds in this region, both public and private; for more information contact the **Utah Travel Council** (☞ Statewide Visitor Information, *above*).

Outdoor Activities and Sports

Biking

A spin along Route 9 through Zion, Route 18 through Snow Canyon, along the lift-served trails at the Brian Head Resort, or the Bryce Canyon Scenic Loop yields classic southwestern scenery. Route 24 through Capitol Reef accesses historic sites and off-road riding. **Utah Travel Council** (☎ 800/200–1160) provides a free directory of biking routes.

Golf

St. George attracts golfers year-round to more than a dozen courses, including **Dixie Red Hills** (⊠ 645 W. 1250 North, ☎ 435/634–5852), with nine holes; **Entrada at Snow Canyon** (⊠ 2511 W. Entrada Trail, ☎ 435/674–7500), with 18 holes; and **South Gate** (⊠ 1975 Tonaquint Dr., ☎ 435/628–0000), with 18 holes. The **St. George Area Convention and Visitor Bureau** (☎ 435/628–7003 or 800/869–6635) has more golfing information.

Hiking and Backpacking

Bryce Canyon, Capitol Reef, and Zion national parks have many trails of varying difficulty. Zion's paved **Gateway to the Narrows Trail** follows the Virgin River. Bryce's moderately difficult **Navajo Loop Trail** yields views of towering Thor's Hammer. Capitol Reef's **Hickman Bridge Trail** is a short nature trail through a sheltered canyon to the base of a natural bridge.

SOUTHEASTERN UTAH

For years the canyon country of southeastern Utah has captured the imagination of filmmakers, serving as the site of such western and adventure films as *Stagecoach, Indiana Jones and the Last Crusade,* and *Thelma and Louise.* Rugged Arches and Canyonlands national parks invite exploration via scenic drives, four-wheeling, hiking, rock climbing, river running, and cycling.

Visitor Information

Grand County Travel Council and Visitor Center (⊠ Main and Center Sts., Box 550, Moab 84532, ☎ 435/259–8825 or 800/635–6622). **San Juan County Travel Council and Visitor Center** (⊠ 117 S. Main St., Box 490, Monticello 84535, ☎ 435/587–3235 or 800/574–4386).

Arriving and Departing

By Car

I–70 runs east–west through the region; U.S. 191 slices north–south.

By Plane

Sunrise Airlines (☎ 800/842–8211) flies weekdays from Salt Lake City to **Canyonlands Field,** in Moab.

Exploring Southeastern Utah

The town of **Green River,** at the junction of I–70 and U.S. 6/191, is named for the river running through it and is the major "put-in" for raft trips on the Green River to its confluence with the Colorado.

A sweeping view of the Canyonlands' multicolor upside-down geography is found at **Dead Horse Point State Park** (⊠ Box 609, Moab 84532, ☎ 435/259–2614; ⌨ $6 per vehicle), named for a band of wild horses once stranded on this isolated peninsula.

Arches National Park (⊠ U.S. 191, Box 907, Moab 84532, ☎ 435/259–8161; ⌨ $10 per vehicle), just northwest of Moab, contains sandstone formations carved by wind and water. Trails and two scenic roads lead past towering pillars and arches.

Moab, below I–70 on U.S. 191, has become a major destination for mountain bikers, with bike shops, T-shirt stores, restaurants, and motels on virtually every corner. Just south of Moab, Utah's oldest and largest commercial winery, **Arches Vineyard** (⊠ 420 W. Kane Creek Blvd., ☎ 435/259–5397; ⌨ free), gives tours and has a tasting room.

The landscape of **Canyonlands National Park** (⊠ 2282 South West Resource Blvd., Moab 84532, ☎ 435/259–7164; ⌨ $10 per vehicle), southwest of Moab, is divided into three geologically distinct districts; the Island in the Sky and Needles districts offer visitor centers. Scenic loops, trails, and four-wheel-drive roads lead to views of massive canyons or uplifts crowded with stone spires and other bizarre features.

The city of **Monticello** is 53 mi south of Moab on U.S. 191, but at a 7,000-ft elevation compared to Moab's 4,000, it has much cooler temperatures. South and west of Monticello, just north of Route 95, a 9-mi scenic drive takes in views of three river-carved bridges at **Natural Bridges National Monument** (⊠ Box 1, Lake Powell 84533, ☎ 435/692–1234; ⌨ $6 per vehicle).

Southwest of Monticello—take U.S. 191 south and U.S. 95 west or U.S. 95 and Route 276 west—at **Lake Powell,** part of the **Glen Canyon National Recreation Area** (☎ 520/608–6404; ⌨ $10 per watercraft, $5 per vehicle), is a stark meeting of water and stone, with nearly 2,000 mi of meandering shoreline resulting from the construction of Glen Canyon Dam on the Colorado River. Side canyons and coves hold Indian ruins, rock art, and natural wonders such as the **Rainbow Bridge National Monument.** Spring and fall are the best times to visit—summer temperatures are often over 100°F.

The town of **Bluff,** 48 mi south of Monticello on U.S. 191, rests on the bank of the San Juan River at the border of the vast Navajo Nation. Houses built in the 1880s of sandstone and red adobe are clustered at the town's center.

East of Bluff, **Hovenweep National Monument** (☎ 970/749–0510; ✉ $6 per vehicle) has several tower structures built by Anasazi Indians about 800 years ago.

Dining and Lodging

An enjoyably diverse cuisine can be found in southeastern Utah, ranging from gourmet pizzas to creative entrées more typical of large metropolitan areas.

Bluff

$ ★ ✕ **Cow Canyon Trading Post.** Southwestern, Greek, Italian—you never know what might appear on the menu at this small restaurant adjacent to a funky trading post. Choices could range from chicken-and-vegetable shish kebabs on a bed of wild rice or a phyllo pie stuffed with spinach and ham to cold carrot soup with spring greens. ⊠ *Hwy. 163 Mission Rd.,* ☎ *435/672–2208. MC, V.*

$ ▥ **Recapture Lodge.** This locally owned property is unassuming, clean, and comfortable. Evening slide shows feature local geology, art, and history. ⊠ *U.S. 191, Box 309, 84512,* ☎ *435/672–2281,* ᴀ̶x̶ *435/ 672–2284. 28 rooms. Pool. AE, D, MC, V.*

Green River

$ ✕ **Ray's Tavern.** Half-pound hamburgers topped with slabs of tomato and onion and served on a heap of hearty fries share the menu with steaks, chops, and seafood at this watering hole revered by river runners, tourists, and locals looking for lunch and a game of pool. ⊠ *25 S. Broadway,* ☎ *435/564–3511. AE, D, MC, V.*

Moab

$$–$$$$ ★ ✕ **Center Café.** The "globally inspired" menu at this side-street café might feature grilled prawns with basil-crab flan and spicy gazpacho sauce, lamb with chanterelle mushrooms, and sautéed free-range chicken breast, among other culinary delights. ⊠ *92 E. Center St.,* ☎ *435/259–4295. D, MC, V.*

$–$$ ✕ **Rio Colorado.** The Rio has standard decor, but its varied menu includes southwestern-Mexican entrées, steak, chicken, and salads. Sunday brunch gets a big turnout. ⊠ *2 S. 100 West,* ☎ *435/259–6666. AE, D, MC, V.*

$–$$ ✕ **Slickrock Cafe.** Sandwiches and burgers share the lunch and dinner menus with steaks, seafood, pastas, and salads. In the morning, though, start the day with a bowl of "Slickrock" granola. ⊠ *5 N. Main St.,* ☎ *435/259–8004. AE, MC, V. Closed early Nov.–Feb.*

$–$$$$ ▥ **Pack Creek Ranch.** This bed-and-breakfast on a forested mountain loop has rustic log cabins and activities ranging from horseback riding to swimming and biking. Breakfasts are included in the rates, although guests can cook for themselves in each cabin's full kitchen. ⊠ *La Sal Mt. Loop Rd. (Box 1270), Moab 84532,* ☎ *435/259–5505,* ᴀ̶x̶ *435/259–8879. 9 cabins, one 4-bedroom ranch house that sleeps 12. Pool. AE, D, MC, V.* ✺

$$-$$$ 🎴 **Sunflower Hill Bed and Breakfast.** Moab's best bed-and-breakfast con-
★ sists of two separate buildings, the Garden Cottage and the Farmhouse,
connected by perennial gardens. For breakfast, a hot entrée is served with
yogurt and homemade bread or huge fruit muffins. ⊠ *185 N. 300 East,
84532,* ☎ *435/259–2974. 11 rooms. AE, D, MC, V. BP.* 🐢

Monticello

$$–$$ 🎴 **Grist Mill Inn.** Housed in a three-story flour mill built in 1933, the
★ Grist Mill is full of antiques and unique accessories like treadle sewing
machines and vintage telephones. Lodgings are in suite-size rooms
and a next-door cottage. ⊠ *64 S. 300 East, 84535,* ☎ *435/587–2597
or 800/645–3762. 11 rooms. AE, D, DC, MC, V. BP.* 🐢

Campgrounds

Campground directories are provided by the **Grand County Travel
Council** and the **San Juan County Travel Council** (☞ Visitor Information, *above*).

Outdoor Activities and Sports

Biking

Southeastern Utah has hundreds of charted mountain-biking trails, including the **Moab Slickrock Trail,** 4 mi east of Moab, a 10-mi roller-
coaster route marked only by dashes of paint on raw rock. Bikes are
ideal for exploring the landscape and roads of **Hovenweep National
Monument** (☞ Exploring Southeastern Utah, *above*). The **Abajo Mountain Loop,** west of Monticello, winds through cool pine and aspen forests.
For area-wide rentals and advice, try **Moab Cyclery and Kaibab Outfitters** (⊠ 391 S. Main St., Moab, ☎ 435/259–7423 or 800/451–
1133, FAX 435/259–6135).

Hiking and Backpacking

Call the travel councils of Grand County or San Juan (☞ Visitor Information, *above*) for advice on trails. Remember to bring water along
on any hike in this region.

Rafting

Outfitters operate float trips and white-water treks on the Colorado
River through black-granite-walled Westwater Canyon and the rapids
of Cataract Canyon and also on the Green River through Desolation
and Gray canyons, both of which shelter Anasazi Indian ruins. Float
trips on the San Juan River wind through petroglyph-etched cliffs. Call
the Utah Travel Council at 800/200–1160 for a free rafting directory.

ELSEWHERE IN UTAH

Northeastern Utah

Dinosaurs have left their remains in these mountains. Many, many years
later, Butch Cassidy and other outlaws stashed caches of "loot" as they
fled through the canyons. Sheep- and cattle-ranching and oil and gas
development are the predominant industries today. Some working
ranches arrange horseback riding adventures and even full-fledged
cattle drives. Call the Utah Travel Council at 800/200–1160 for a free
small inns directory.

Visitor Information

Dinosaurland Travel Board (⊠ 25 E. Main St., ☎ 435/789–6932 or
800/477–5558).

Arriving and Departing

U.S. 40 runs east–west through the region. U.S. 191 runs north–south.

What to See and Do

The excavations at **Dinosaur National Monument** (✉ Quarry Visitor Center, Box 128, Jensen 84035, ☎ 435/789–2115; 💳 $10 per vehicle) showcase the largest collection of Jurassic-period fossils ever unearthed. Some 2,000 dinosaur bones—discoveries began in 1909—lie exposed in a sandstone face inside the visitor center, 20 mi east of Vernal.

Flaming Gorge National Recreation Area (✉ Box 279, Manila 84046, ☎ 435/784–3445; 💳 $5 per vehicle) is north of Dinosaur National Monument via U.S. 191. Behind 500-ft-high Flaming Gorge Dam, Flaming Gorge Lake stretches north for 91 mi between twisting redrock canyon walls. The lake is good for boating, camping, and trophy trout fishing. South of the dam, the Green River is known for excellent fishing and calm-water rafting.

Dining and Lodging

$–$$$$ ✕ **The Curry Manor.** The diverse menu in this two-story historic home
★   includes entrées such as linguine Roxanne—jumbo shrimp, bay scallops and snow crab sautéed and served over linguine—as well as prime rib of pork served with an apricot glaze. ✉ *189 S. Vernal Ave., Vernal,* ☎ *435/789–2289. AE, D, MC, V.*

$$$–$$$$ 🏨 **Falcon's Ledge Lodge.** Falconry and fly-fishing are part of the ex-
★   perience at this lodge in a pristine canyon, which suggests multiday packages but also offers overnight stays with a full breakfast. Vaulted ceilings, sweeping views, and jetted tubs in most guest rooms make it a luxurious getaway. Gourmet dinner specialties include fresh trout, "olive lover's" steak, and bread baked fresh daily. ✉ *Stillwater Canyon, Box 67, Altamont 84001,* ☎ *435/454–3737,* 📠 *435/454–3392. 9 rooms. AE, MC, V.* 🐾

$–$$ 🏨 **Best Western Antlers Motel.** Locals favor this clean, comfortable motel with a pool, hot tub, exercise room, and playground. Rooms are equipped for computer modems. ✉ *423 W. Main St., Vernal 84078,* ☎ *435/789–1202. 44 rooms. Restaurant, pool. AE, D, DC, MC, V.* 🐾

$–$$ 🏨 **Flaming Gorge Lodge.** With a good restaurant, raft rentals, and guided fishing service, this is the best lodging choice near Flaming Gorge. ✉ *155 Greendale, U.S. 191, Dutch John 84023,* ☎ *435/889–3773,* 📠 *435/889–3788. 21 motel rooms, 24 condos. Restaurant. AE, D, MC, V.* 🐾

VERMONT

Updated by
Bill and Kay
Scheller

Capital	Montpelier
Population	589,000
Motto	Freedom and Unity
State Bird	Hermit thrush
State Flower	Red clover
Postal Abbreviation	VT

Statewide Visitor Information

Vermont Travel Division (⊠ 134 State St., Montpelier 05602, ☎ 802/828–3237 or 800/837–6668). **Vermont Chamber of Commerce** (⊠ Box 37, Montpelier 05602, ☎ 802/223–3443).

Scenic Drives

Route 100 passes through the eastern edge of Green Mountain National Forest, the Mad River valley, and the town of Stowe, then continues on to Canada.

National and State Parks

National Park

The 355,000-acre **Green Mountain National Forest** (⊠ 231 N. Main St., Rutland 05701, ☎ 802/747–6700) runs through the center of the state, from Bristol south to the Massachusetts border. **Marsh-Billings-Rockefeller National Historical Park** (⊠ Rte. 12, Woodstock, 05091, ☎ 802/457–3368) is a 500-acre park dedicated to the land-management legacy of Vermont conservationist George Perkins Marsh.

State Parks

The 50 parks maintained by the **Department of Forests, Parks, and Recreation** (⊠ Waterbury 05671, ☎ 802/241–3655) offer nature and hiking trails, campsites, swimming, boating facilities, and fishing. Especially popular are the **Champlain Islands** sites: Burton Island, Kill Kare, North Hero, Grand Isle, Knight Point, and Sand Bar.

SOUTHERN VERMONT

Many of the southern Vermont towns with village greens and white-spired churches were founded in the early 18th century as frontier outposts and later became trading centers. In the western region, the Green Mountain Boys fought off both the British and land-hungry New Yorkers. The influx of new residents in the past 20 years means the quaintness often comes with a patina of sophistication or funk; shoppers can find not only antiques but New Age crystals, Vermont-made salsa, and the highest-tech ski gear.

Visitor Information

Bennington: Chamber of Commerce (⊠ Veterans Memorial Dr., 05201, ☎ 802/447–3311). **Brattleboro:** Chamber of Commerce (⊠ 180 Main St., 05301, ☎ 802/254–4565). **Manchester and the mountains:** Chamber of Commerce (⊠ 5046 Main St., 05255, ☎ 802/362–2100). **Rutland:** Chamber of Commerce, Convention and Visitors Division (⊠ 256 N. Main St., 05701, ☎ 802/773–2747 or 800/756–8880). **Woodstock:** Chamber of Commerce (⊠ 18 Central St., Box 486, 05091, ☎ 802/457–3555 or 888/496–6378).

Arriving and Departing

By Bus
Vermont Transit (a subsidiary of Greyhound; ☏ 802/864–6811 or 800/451–3292; 800/642–3133 in VT). **Bonanza** (☏ 800/556–3815).

By Car
I–91 runs north–south along the eastern edge of Vermont. U.S. 7 goes north–south through western Vermont, and Route 9 runs east–west across the state through Bennington and Brattleboro.

By Train
Amtrak (☏ 800/872–7245) stops at Brattleboro, Bellows Falls, Rutland, and White River Junction.

Exploring Southern Vermont

It was at **Bennington** that Ethan Allen formed the Green Mountain Boys, who helped capture Fort Ticonderoga in 1775. The **Bennington Battle Monument** (✉ 15 Monument Ave., ☏ 802/447–0550; 🎫 $1.50), a 306-ft stone obelisk, commemorates General John Stark's defeat of the British in their attempt to capture Bennington's stockpile of supplies. It is closed from late October to mid-April. The artifacts at the **Bennington Museum** (✉ W. Main St./Rte. 9, ☏ 802/447–1571; 🎫 $6) include the largest public collection of the work of Grandma Moses, who lived and painted in the area; the only surviving automobile of Bennington's Martin Company; and one of the oldest Stars and Stripes in existence.

The tree-shaded marble sidewalks and stately houses of **Manchester** reflect the luxurious summer-resort lifestyle of a century ago, while upscale factory-outlet stores appeal to the ski crowd. **Hildene** (✉ Rte. 7A, 2 mi south of intersection with Rtes. 11 and 30, ☏ 802/362–1788; 🎫 $8) was the summer home of Abraham Lincoln's son Robert. Noteworthy features in the 24-room mansion include its Georgian Revival symmetry, formal gardens, grand curved staircase, and 1,000-pipe organ. The house is closed from November to mid-May.

The **American Museum of Fly Fishing** (✉ Rte. 7A, ☏ 802/362–3300; 🎫 $3) displays the tackle of such noted anglers as Jimmy Carter, Winslow Homer, and Bing Crosby.

The steep 5-mi drive to the top of **Mt. Equinox** brings you to the summit via the **Saddle**, where the views are outstanding. *✉ Rte. 7A, ☏ 802/362–1114. 🎫 $6 car and driver, $2 each additional adult. Closed Nov.–Apr.*

In **Rutland** there are strips of shopping centers and a seemingly endless row of traffic lights. The **Chaffee Center for the Visual Arts** (✉ 16 S. Main St., ☏ 802/775–0356) houses the work of more than 200 Vermont artists (closed Tuesday). At the **Vermont Marble Exhibit**, northwest of Rutland, visitors can watch the transformation of rough stone into slabs, blocks, and gift items. *✉ 62 S. Main St., off Rte. 3, Proctor, ☏ 802/459–2300 or 800/427–1396. 🎫 $5. Closed Sun. and Nov.–late May.*

Woodstock is the quintessential New England town, on the eastern side of Vermont on U.S. 4. Exquisitely preserved Federal houses surround the tree-lined village green. The **Vermont Institute of Natural Science's Raptor Center** has nature trails and 23 living species of birds of prey. *✉ Church Hill Rd., ☏ 802/457–2779. 🎫 $6. Closed Sun. Nov.–Apr.*

A half mile north of the center of Woodstock, the reconstructed farmhouse, school, and general store at the **Billings Farm and Museum** demonstrate the daily activities of early Vermonters. *✉ Rte. 12, ☏ 802/457–2355. 🎫 $7. Closed Jan.–May and weekdays Nov. and Dec.*

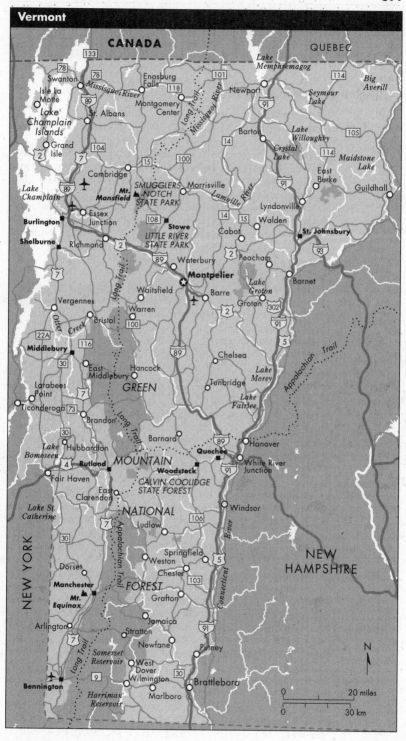

Vermont

CANADA

QUEBEC

133

78

Swanton

78

Isle la Motte

Missisquoi River

Enosburg Falls

118

101

Lake Memphremagog

Newport

114

Big Averill

Montgomery Center

Seymour Lake

105

89

St. Albans

Lake Champlain Islands

104

Barton

Lake Willoughby

114

Maidstone Lake

2

Grand Isle

7

15

14

91

Crystal Lake

East Burke

Guildhall

100

Cambridge

Mt. Mansfield

SMUGGLERS NOTCH STATE PARK

Morrisville

Lamoille River

Lyndonville

89

Lake Champlain

108

Stowe

14

15

Walden

St. Johnsbury

Burlington

Essex Junction

LITTLE RIVER STATE PARK

Cabot

93

Shelburne

Richmond

2

Waterbury

89

Montpelier

2

Peacham

Barnet

7

Waitsfield

Barre

Lake Groton

Vergennes

Warren

2

Groton

302

91

Otter Creek

Bristol

100

5

22A

116

89

Appalachian Trail

Middlebury

30

East Middlebury

Hancock

Chelsea

GREEN

Lake Morey

Larabees Point

7

Tunbridge

Lake Fairlee

Ticonderoga

73

Brandon

Barnard

89

Hanover

Long Trail

30

Hubbardton

Quechee

White River Junction

Lake Bomoseen

4

Rutland

MOUNTAIN

Woodstock

91

Fair Haven

East Clarendon

CALVIN COOLIDGE STATE FOREST

NATIONAL

Windsor

Lake St. Catherine

30

7

Ludlow

106

NEW YORK

Springfield

5

NEW HAMPSHIRE

Dorset

Weston

Chester

103

Manchester

FOREST

Grafton

Connecticut River

Mt. Equinox

Appalachian Trail

91

Arlington

7

Jamaica

Stratton

Newfane

Somerset Reservoir

West Dover

Putney

Bennington

9

Wilmington

30

Brattleboro

Harriman Reservoir

Marlboro

N

0   20 miles

0   30 km

The mile-long **Quechee Gorge** is visible from U.S. 4, but you can also scramble down one of several descents. The town of **Quechee** is perched astride the Ottauquechee River. Here you can watch potters and glassblowers and purchase their creations at **Simon Pearce** (⊠ Main St., ☎ 802/295–2711 or 800/774–5277; ⊡ free).

Dining and Lodging

Bennington

$–$$$ ✕ **Blue Benn Diner.** Breakfast is available all day in this authentic diner, which serves some twists to standard fare, such as turkey hash and burritos with scrambled eggs, sausage, and chili. The menu includes all kinds of pancakes as well as many vegetarian selections. You may have to wait for a seat on weekends. ⊠ *Rte. 7 N,* ☎ *802/442–5140. No credit cards. No dinner Sat.–Tues.*

$$$ 🏠 **South Shire Inn.** Canopy beds in plushly carpeted rooms, ornate plaster molding on the ceilings, and the mahogany fireplace in the library add up to turn-of-the-20th-century grandeur in a quiet residential neighborhood. Most rooms have fireplaces; some have whirlpool baths. ⊠ *124 Elm St., 05201,* ☎ *802/447–3839,* 🖷 *802/442–3547. 9 rooms. AE, MC, V. BP.* 🐾

$$ 🏠 **Molly Stark Inn.** This gem of a B&B makes you feel as if you were
★   staying with old friends. Blue-plaid wallpaper, hardwood floors, antique furnishings, and a woodstove in the brick alcove of the sitting room give a country charm to this 1860 Queen Anne Victorian. ⊠ *1067 E. Main St. (Rte. 9), 05201,* ☎ *802/442–9631 or 800/356–3076,* 🖷 *802/442–5224. 7 rooms. AE, D, MC, V. BP.* 🐾

Manchester

$$$$ ✕ **Chantecleer.** Intimate dining rooms have been created in a dairy barn that has a large fieldstone fireplace. The menu reflects the chef's Swiss background: The appetizers include *Bundnerfleisch* (air dried Swiss beef) and frogs' legs in garlic butter; among the entrées are rack of lamb, whole Dover sole filleted tableside, and veal chops. The restaurant is 5 mi north of Manchester. ⊠ *Rte. 7A, East Dorset,* ☎ *802/362–1616. Reservations essential. AE, DC, MC, V. Closed Mon. and Tues. in winter, Tues. in summer. No lunch.*

$$–$$$ ✕ **Bistro Henry's.** Just outside town, this spacious restaurant attracts a devoted clientele for its authentic French bistro fare, extensive wine list, and attention to detail. Popular items are merlot-braised lamb shank with balsamic glazed onions and an eggplant, mushroom, and fontina terrine Provençale. ⊠ *Rte. 11/30, Manchester,* ☎ *802/362–4982. AE, DC, MC, V. Closed Mon. No lunch.*

$$$–$$$$ 🏠 **The Equinox.** This grand white-columned resort was a landmark on Vermont's tourism scene even before Abraham Lincoln's family began summering here. Rooms have pine furnishings, and the front porch is perfect for watching the passing parade. There's a medically supervised spa program and a falconry school. ⊠ *Rte. 7A, Manchester Village 05254,* ☎ *802/362–4700 or 800/362–4747,* 🖷 *802/362–1595. 155 rooms, 10 3-bedroom town houses. 2 restaurants, 2 pools, golf, tennis. AE, D, DC, MC, V.* 🐾

$$–$$$$ 🏠 **1811 House.** Staying here is like staying at an elegant English coun-
★   try house. Six rooms have fireplaces; the Robinson room has a marble-enclosed tub. The pub-style bar serves 58 single-malt scotches. ⊠ *Rte. 7A, Box 39, 05254,* ☎ *802/362–1811 or 800/432–1811,* 🖷 *802/ 362–2443. 14 rooms. No smoking. AE, D, MC, V. BP.* 🐾

$$–$$$ 🏠 **Barnstead Inn.** This 1830s barn was transformed in 1968 into a handful of rooms that combine exposed beams and barn-board walls with modern plumbing and cheerful wallpaper. ⊠ *Rte. 30, 05255,* ☎ *800/ 331–1619,* 🖷 *802/362–0688. 14 rooms. Pool. AE, MC, V.* 🐾

Rutland

$-$$
★
  ✕ **Back Home Cafe.** Wood booths, black-and-white linoleum tile, and exposed brick lend atmosphere at this second-story café, where dinner might be chicken breast stuffed with roasted red peppers and goat cheese. There is often weekend entertainment. ⊠ *21 Center St.,* ☎ *802/775–9313. AE, MC, V.*

$$-$$$
  🏨 **Inn at Rutland.** In this Victorian mansion an ornate oak staircase leads to rooms with such turn-of-the-20th-century touches as botanical prints, elaborate ceiling moldings, and frosted glass. Guests can relax in the inn's hot tub. ⊠ *70 N. Main St., 05701,* ☎ *802/773–0575 or 800/808–0575,* FAX *802/775–3506. 12 rooms. AE, D, DC, MC, V. BP fall and winter; CP spring and summer.* ✍

$-$$$
  🏨 **Comfort Inn.** Rooms at this chain hotel are a cut above the standard, with upholstered wing chairs and blond-wood furnishings. ⊠ *19 Allen St., 05701,* ☎ *802/775–2200 or 800/432–6788,* FAX *802/775–2694. 104 rooms. Restaurant, pool, hot tub, sauna. AE, D, DC, MC, V. CP.* ✍

Woodstock

$$$-$$$$
★
  ✕ **Prince and the Pauper.** Nouvelle French dishes with a Vermont accent are served in a romantically candlelit Colonial setting. Standouts include seared paillard of tuna with Cajun spices and veal scallop *forestière* (with wild mushrooms). ⊠ *24 Elm St.,* ☎ *802/457–1818. AE, D, MC, V. No lunch.*

$-$$$
  ✕ **Bentleys.** Antique silk-fringed lamp shades and long lace curtains lend a tongue-in-cheek Victorian air to burgers, chili, soups, and entrées such as roasted Maple Leaf Farm duckling with sweet mango sauce. ⊠ *3 Elm St.,* ☎ *802/457–3232. AE, DC, MC, V.*

$$$-$$$$
  ✕🏨 **Kedron Valley Inn.** One of the state's oldest hotels—built in the 1840s—has rooms decorated with family quilts and antiques. The motel units in back have exposed log walls. The pond has a beach that is a great place to spend a summer afternoon. The dining room prepares dishes using classic French technique and Vermont ingredients. Try the salmon fillet stuffed with seafood mousse and wrapped in puff pastry or the pasta with basil pesto. ⊠ *Rte. 106, 05071,* ☎ *802/457–1473 or 800/836–1193,* FAX *802/457–4469. 26 rooms. Restaurant. AE, D, MC, V. Closed Apr. and 10 days before Thanksgiving. MAP.* ✍

$$$-$$$$
  ✕🏨 **Woodstock Inn and Resort.** Patchwork quilts and landscape paintings enliven the standard modern ash furnishings at this inn owned by the Rockefeller family. The dining room (jacket and tie required) serves nouvelle New England fare. Among the many activities are croquet, and cross-country and downhill skiing. ⊠ *U.S. 4, 05091,* ☎ *802/457–1100 or 800/448–7900,* FAX *802/457–6699. 144 rooms. 2 restaurants, pool, golf, 12 tennis courts, health club. AE, MC, V.* ✍

$$
★
  🏨 **Winslow House.** An unpretentious place with great cross-country skiing and golf nearby, this farmhouse (1872) has a small common area but two spacious upstairs quarters with separate sitting rooms. ⊠ *38 Rte. 4, 05091,* ☎ *802/457–1820,* FAX *802/457–1820. 4 rooms. D, DC, MC, V. BP.* ✍

Motels

🏨 **Aspen Motel** (⊠ Box 548, Manchester Center 05255, ☎ 802/362–2450, FAX 802/362–1348), 24 rooms; pool; *$-$$.*

🏨 **Harwood Hill Motel** (⊠ Rte. 7A, Bennington 05201, ☎ 802/442–6278, FAX 802/442–6278), 16 rooms, 3 cottages; *$.*

🏨 **Pond Ridge Motel** (⊠ U.S. 4, Woodstock 05091, ☎ 802/457–1667, FAX 802/457–1667), 21 rooms; *$.*

Campgrounds

The state park system runs over 40 campgrounds with more than 2,000 campsites. Contact the **Department of Forests, Parks, and Recreation** (⊠ 103 S. Main St., Waterbury 05671, ☎ 802/241–3655) for a copy of the Vermont Campground Guide. The official state map also lists private campgrounds.

At ⚠ **Green Mountain National Forest** (⊠ 231 N. Main St., Rutland, 05701, ☎ 802/747–6700), one camping area can be reserved in advance; the remaining areas are first-come, first-served.

Nightlife and the Arts

Most nightlife is concentrated at and around the ski resorts or in the larger towns and cities. The **Marlboro Music Festival** (⊠ Marlboro Music Center, ☎ 802/254–2394; 215/569–4690 Sept.–June) presents chamber music in weekend concerts during July and August. **New England Bach Festival** (⊠ Brattleboro Music Center, ☎ 802/257–4523), held in October, is a popular classical music festival.

Outdoor Activities and Sports

Biking

Bike Vermont (⊠ Box 207, Woodstock 05091, ☎ 802/457–3553 or 800/257–2226) focuses on inn-to-inn tours along the Connecticut River valley and in other scenic corners of Vermont.

Vermont Bicycle Touring (⊠ Box 711, Bristol 05443, ☎ 802/453–4811 or 800/245–3868) conducts guided tours throughout Vermont.

Canoeing

The **Connecticut River** and the **Battenkill** offer easygoing canoe outings. Rentals are available from **Battenkill Canoe** (⊠ Rte. 7A, Arlington, ☎ 802/362–2800 or 800/421–5268). **Wilderness Trails** (⊠ Quechee Inn, Clubhouse Rd., Quechee, ☎ 802/295–7620) offers canoe rentals, put-in and take-out service, and maps for touring the White, Ottauquechee, and Connecticut rivers.

Fishing

The **Battenkill River** is famous for trout. **Orvis** (⊠ Rte. 7A, Manchester, ☎ 802/362–3900 or 800/235–9763) runs a fly-fishing school. The necessary fishing license is available through tackle shops, or call the **Department of Fish and Wildlife** (☎ 802/241–3700).

Hiking and Backpacking

The southern half of the **Long Trail** is part of the **Appalachian Trail** and runs from just east of Rutland to Vermont's southern boundary. The **Green Mountain Club** (⊠ Rte. 100, Waterbury Center 05677, ☎ 802/244–7037) maintains the trail, staffs its huts in summer, and maps hiking elsewhere in Vermont.

Ski Areas

For up-to-date snow conditions in the state, call 802/828–3239. All listed downhill ski areas have snowmaking equipment.

Cross-Country

Mt. Snow/Haystack (⊠ 400 Mountain Rd., Mt. Snow 05356, ☎ 802/464–3333), 62 mi of trails. **Stratton** (⊠ Stratton Mountain 05155, ☎ 802/297–2200 or 800/843–6867), 20 mi of trails.

Downhill

Bromley (⊠ Box 1130, Manchester Center 05255, ☎ 802/824–5522), 41 runs, 9 lifts, 1,334-ft vertical drop. **Killington/Pico** (⊠ 400 Killington Rd., Killington 05751, ☎ 802/422–3333 or 800/621–6867), 212 runs, 3 gondolas, 34 lifts, 3,150-ft drop. **Mt. Snow/Haystack** (⊠ 400 Mountain Rd., Mt. Snow 05356, ☎ 802/464–3333), 135 trails, 26 lifts, 1,700-ft drop. **Stratton** (⊠ Stratton Mountain 05155, ☎ 802/297–2200 or 800/843–6867), 90 trails, gondola, 12 lifts, 2,000-ft drop.

Shopping

Antiques and traditional and contemporary crafts are everywhere. Particularly good is **U.S. 7** north of Manchester to Danby. The **Vermont Country Store** (⊠ Rte. 100, Weston, ☎ 802/824–3184) carries such forgotten items as Monkey Brand black tooth powder, Flexible Flyer sleds, and pickles in a barrel. **East Meets West** (⊠ Rte. 7, Pittsford, north of Rutland, ☎ 802/443–2242 or 800/443–2242) stocks international arts and crafts. The **Bennington Potters Yard** (⊠ 324 County St., ☎ 802/447–7531 or 800/205–8033) carries firsts and seconds. **Manchester** has many designer and factory outlets.

NORTHERN VERMONT

Northwestern Vermont is more mountainous than the southern part of the state and has the closest thing Vermont has to a seacoast, Lake Champlain; the nation's smallest state capital, Montpelier; and Burlington, Vermont's largest and most cosmopolitan city. The region's recorded history dates from 1609, when Samuel de Champlain explored the lake now named for him. Northeastern Vermont, known as the Northeast Kingdom, is the least populated part of the state. A great pleasure here is driving through pastoral scenery and discovering charming small towns such as Peacham, Greensboro Bend, and Craftsbury Common.

Visitor Information

Central Vermont: Chamber of Commerce (⊠ Box 336, Barre 05641, ☎ 802/229–5711). **Lake Champlain:** Chamber of Commerce (⊠ 60 Main St., Suite 100, Burlington 05401, ☎ 802/863–3489 or 877/686–5253). **Northeast Kingdom Chamber of Commerce** (⊠ 30 Western Ave., St. Johnsbury 05819, ☎ 802/748–3678 or 800/639–6379). **Smugglers' Notch:** Chamber of Commerce (⊠ Box 364, Jeffersonville 05464, ☎ 802/644–2239). **Stowe:** Area Association (⊠ Main St., Box 1320, Stowe 05672, ☎ 802/253–7321 or 800/247–8693).

Arriving and Departing

By Bus
Vermont Transit (☎ 802/864–6811 or 800/451–3292; 800/642–3133 in Vermont).

By Car
I–89 runs from White River Junction to Vermont's northwestern corner at the Canadian border. To get to the eastern part of the state, drive up I–91.

By Plane
Burlington Airport (☎ 802/863–1889 or 802/828–2093, in South Burlington, is 4½ mi east of town off Route 2 and is served by major airlines. Private planes are accommodated at several state airports; call the Department of Transportation, Aeronautics Division (☎ 802/863–1889 or 802/828–2709) for information.

By Train
Amtrak (☎ 800/872–7245) stops at Montpelier, Waterbury, Essex Junction, and St. Albans.

Exploring Northern Vermont

Middlebury is Robert Frost country; Vermont's late poet laureate spent 23 summers at a farm near here. The **Robert Frost Wayside Trail,** east of Middlebury on Route 125, winds through quiet woodland and has Frost quotations posted along the way.

The University of Vermont's **Morgan Horse Farm** offers tours of its stables and paddocks. ⊠ *Follow signs off Rte. 23, 2½ mi from Middlebury,* ☎ *802/388–2011.* ☒ *$4. Closed Nov.–Apr.*

Shelburne, a town on the banks of Lake Champlain, is known for two ★ attractions. The 37 buildings of the **Shelburne Museum** (⊠ U.S. 7, 5 mi south of Burlington, ☎ 802/985–3346,, ☒ $17.50 for 2 consecutive days, $7 for 1 day in winter) contain one of the largest Americana collections in the nation. Exhibits include 18th- and 19th-century houses and furniture, fine and folk art, farm tools, carriages and sleighs, and an old side-wheel steamship. At the 1,400-acre **Shelburne Farms** (⊠ east of U.S. 7, 6 mi south of Burlington, ☎ 802/985–8686; ☒ day pass $5, tour additional $5) visitors can see a working dairy farm, attend nature lectures, visit farm animals at the Children's Farmyard, and stroll along a stretch of Lake Champlain's waterfront. Tours are given from mid-May until mid-October; grounds are open year-round, weather permitting. The landscaping, designed by Frederick Law Olmsted, creator of New York's Central Park, gently channels the eye to expansive vistas.

Burlington is home to the University of Vermont and three smaller colleges. **Church Street Marketplace**—with its down-to-earth shops, chic boutiques, and appealing menagerie of sidewalk cafés, food and crafts vendors, and street performers—is an animated downtown focal point. There are narrated tours during the day—and **evening dinner-and-dance cruises**—on the *Spirit of Ethan Allen,* a 500-passenger, triple-deck cruise vessel. ⊠ *Burlington Boat House, College St. at Battery St.,* ☎ *802/862–8300.* ☒ *$8. Closed mid-Oct.–May.*

Smugglers' Notch is the scenic pass beneath the brow of Mt. Mansfield said to have been a route of 18th-century outlaws. There are roadside picnic tables and a spectacular waterfall. Take Route 15 to Jeffersonville; then go south on narrow, twisting Route 108.

Stowe Mountain Resort (⊠ Entrance on Mountain Rd., 8 mi from Rte. 100 at Stowe Village, ☎ 802/253–3000) is a venerable ski center. From June to late October you can take the 4½-mi toll road (☒ $12 per car) from the resort to the top of Vermont's highest peak, **Mt. Mansfield.** At the road's end is a short and beautiful walk. Another way to ascend Mt. Mansfield is in the **gondola** (☒ $10) that shuttles from the base of the ski area up 4,393 ft to the section known as the Chin, where there are scenic views and a restaurant. The toll road is closed mid-October–mid-May. The gondola is closed mid-October–mid-June (open to skiers only early December–late April).

Nine miles south of Stowe village is the mecca, the nirvana, the veritable Valhalla for ice cream lovers: **Ben & Jerry's Ice Cream Factory** (⊠ Rte. 100, 1 mi north of I–89, ☎ 802/244–8687; ☒ $2).

Montpelier, which has fewer than 9,000 residents, is the nation's least-populated state capital. The impressive **Vermont State House** has a gleaming gold dome and columns 6 ft in diameter fashioned from granite from neighboring Barre. ⊠ *State St.,* ☎ *802/828–2228.* ☒ *Free. Closed Sun. and mid-Oct.–June.*

The **Vermont Museum** has intriguing informative exhibits; its docents can answer New England trivia questions such as "Why does the area have covered bridges?" ⊠ *109 State St.,* ☎ *802/828–2291.* ⊠ *$3. Closed Mon.*

The chief city of the Northeast Kingdom is **St. Johnsbury.** The **Fairbanks Museum and Planetarium** (⊠ Main and Prospect Sts., ☎ 802/748–2372; ⊠ $5) engrosses visitors with its eclectic ethnographic, natural history, and Vermontiana collections and a 50-seat planetarium (closed weekdays September–June; additional fee). The **St. Johnsbury Athenaeum** is an architectural gem, with dark paneling, polished Victorian woodwork, and a gallery displaying 19th-century artworks, most notably Albert Bierstadt's *Domes of Yosemite.* ⊠ *30 Main St.,* ☎ *802/748–8291.* ⊠ *Free. Closed Tues. and Sun.*

Dining and Lodging

Burlington

$$–$$$ ✕ **Trattoria Delia.** Didn't manage to rent that villa in Umbria this year? The next best thing is this superb Italian country eatery just around the corner from City Hall Park. Local game and produce are the stars, as in roast rabbit marinated in herbs, wine, and olive oil. The chef's passion for the truly homemade extends to wild boar sausage, salami, and fresh mozzarella. Wood-grilled items are a specialty. ⊠ *152 St. Paul St.,* ☎ *802/864–5253. AE, D, DC, MC, V. No lunch.*

$$–$$$$ ✕🏠 **Inn at Shelburne Farms.** Built at the turn of the 20th century, this
★ Tudor-style inn overlooks Lake Champlain, the distant Adirondacks, and the sea of pastures on this 1,400-acre working farm. Each guest room is different, from the wallpaper to the period antiques. The seasonal contemporary menu makes clever use of local ingredients. Try the rack of lamb with sun-dried tomato crust. Guests can play tennis and fish or boat on the property. ⊠ *Harbor Rd., Shelburne 05482,* ☎ *802/985–8498,* FAX *802/985–8123. 24 rooms. Restaurant. AE, D, DC, MC, V. Closed mid-Oct.–mid-May.* ⊠

$$ ✕ **Isabel's.** Inspired American cuisine artfully presented is the hallmark
★ here. The menu changes weekly and has included Thai seafood pasta and vegetable Wellington. Weekend brunch is popular. ⊠ *112 Lake St.,* ☎ *802/865–2522. AE, D, DC, MC, V. No dinner Sun. and Mon. Nov.–Apr.*

$$–$$$ 🏠 **Willard Street Inn.** Perched high in the historic hill section is this grand house, which incorporates elements of Queen Anne and Colonial–Georgian Revival styles and has an exterior marble staircase and English gardens. Guest rooms are individually; some have lake views and canopy beds. ⊠ *349 S. Willard St., 05401,* ☎ *802/651–8710 or 800/577–8712,* FAX *802/651–8714. 15 rooms. Afternoon tea. AE, D, DC, MC, V. BP.* ⊠

Middlebury

$$ ✕ **Woody's.** In addition to cool jazz, diner-deco light fixtures, and ab-
★ stract paintings, Woody's has a view of Otter Creek just below. The menu has nightly specials that might include Vermont lamb or a vegetarian grill. ⊠ *5 Bakery La.,* ☎ *802/388–4182. AE, MC, V. Closed Tues. and Nov. and Dec.*

$$–$$$ ✕🏠 **Swift House Inn.** The main building at Swift House, the Georgian home of a 19th-century governor, contains white-panel wainscoting, elaborately carved mahogany and marble fireplaces, and cherry paneling in the dining room. The rooms—each with Oriental rugs and nine with fireplaces—have canopy beds, curtains with swags, and claw-foot tubs. Rooms in the gatehouse suffer from street noise but are charming; a carriage house holds six luxury rooms. The inn has a sauna and steam room, as well as a pub and restaurant. A standout menu item

is herb-crusted rack of lamb with rosemary and Madeira sauce. ⊠ *25 Stewart La., 05753,* ☎ *802/388–9925,* 𝔽𝔸𝕏 *802/388–9927. 21 rooms. Restaurant. AE, D, DC, MC, V. CP.* ⊗

Montpelier

$$–$$$ ✕ **Chef's Table.** The staff at the Chef's Table and its sister restaurant, **Main Street Bar and Grill,** are New England Culinary Institute students. Upstairs at the Chef's Table, the menu changes daily but always offers well-prepared, inventive dishes, such as swordfish with spinach and cherry tomatoes. Downstairs at the Grill, the atmosphere is more casual but the food no less delicious. ⊠ *118 Main St.,* ☎ *802/229–9202; 802/223–3188 for the Grill. AE, D, MC, V. Chef's Table closed Sun. No lunch Sat.*

$ ✕ **Horn of the Moon.** The bowls of honey and the bulletin board plastered with political notices hint at Vermont's prominent progressive contingent. This vegetarian restaurant's cuisine includes a little Mexican, a little Thai, a lot of flavor, and not too much tofu. ⊠ *8 Langdon St.,* ☎ *802/223–2895. No credit cards. Closed Mon.*

$$ ⌂ **Inn at Montpelier.** This spacious early 1800s house has antique four-posters, tapestry-upholstered wing chairs, and classical guitar on the stereo. The sitting room has a Federal feel to it, and the wide wraparound Colonial Revival porch is perfect for reading or watching the townsfolk stroll by. ⊠ *147 Main St., 05602,* ☎ *802/223–2727,* 𝔽𝔸𝕏 *802/223–0722. 19 rooms. AE, D, DC, MC, V. CP.* ⊗

St. Johnsbury

$$$–$$$$ ✕⌂ **Rabbit Hill Inn.** Some rooms have canopy beds, whirlpool baths, mountain views, and fireplaces. Eclectic, regional cuisine is served in the low-ceiling dining room, which is open to the public. Meat and fish are smoked on the premises, and the herbs and vegetables often come from gardens out back. Guests can indulge in canoeing, cross-country skiing, or sipping cocktails in the pub. ⊠ *Rte. 18, Lower Waterford 05848,* ☎ *802/748–5168 or 800/762–8669,* 𝔽𝔸𝕏 *802/748–8342. 21 rooms. Restaurant. Afternoon tea. AE, MC, V. Closed 1st 3 wks in Apr., 1st 2 wks in Nov. MAP.* ⊗

$$$ ✕⌂ **Wildflower Inn.** Guest rooms in the restored Federal-style main
★ house, as well as in the carriage houses, are decorated simply with reproductions and contemporary furnishings; nearly all have incredible views of the property's 500 acres. Meals feature hearty country-style food, with freshly made breads and vegetables from the garden. The many activities available include fishing, ice-skating, cross-country skiing, and sleigh riding. There's a hot tub and sauna as well as a recreation room, and afternoon snacks are served. ⊠ *North of St. Johnsbury on Darling Hill Rd., Lyndonville 05851,* ☎ *802/626–8310 or 800/627–8310,* 𝔽𝔸𝕏 *802/626–3039. 21 rooms. Restaurant, pool, tennis. MC, V. Closed Apr. and Nov. BP.* ⊗

Stowe

$$–$$$ ✕ **Villa Tragara.** Romance reigns in the intimate dining nooks carved
★ out of this farmhouse. Among the menu highlights are woodland mushrooms sautéed with garlic, shallots, brandy, and cream served over grilled Italian bread, and risotto with baby shrimp, mussels, scallops, clams, and squid. The chef has also introduced Italian tapas—smaller portions of many of the Villa's most popular offerings, moderately priced to allow patrons to pick and share dishes. There's live entertainment on Friday. ⊠ *Rte. 100, 6 mi south of Stowe,* ☎ *802/244–5288. AE, MC, V. Closed Tues. No lunch.*

$$$$ ✕⌂ **Topnotch at Stowe Resort and Spa.** The lobby of this resort, one of the state's poshest, has floor-to-ceiling windows, a freestanding circular stone fireplace, and cathedral ceilings. Rooms have thick carpeting and accents such as painted barn-board walls or Italian prints. Aerobics, horseback riding, cross-country skiing, and sleigh rides are among the many available activities. ⊠ *Mountain Rd., Stowe 05672,* ☎ *802/253–8585 or 800/451–8686,* FAX *802/253–9263. 90 rooms; 20 1-, 2-, and 3-bedroom town houses. Restaurant, pool, golf, tennis, health club. AE, D, DC, MC, V. BP.* ✍

$$–$$$ 🏨 **Inn at the Brass Lantern.** Home-baked cookies in the afternoon, a basket of logs by your fireplace, and stenciled hearts along the wainscoting reflect the care taken in turning this 18th-century farmhouse into a place of welcome. All rooms in this B&B have country antiques and locally made quilts; most are oversize and some have fireplaces and whirlpool tubs. ⊠ *Rte. 100, 1 mi north of Stowe, 05672,* ☎ *802/253–2229 or 800/729–2980,* FAX *802/253–7425. 9 rooms. AE, MC, V. BP.* ✍

Motels

🏨 **Econo Lodge** (⊠ 101 Northfield St., Montpelier 05602, ☎ 802/223–5258, FAX 802/223–0716), 54 rooms; restaurant; CP; $$.

🏨 **Greystone Motel** (⊠ U.S. 7, Middlebury 05753, ☎ 802/388–4935), 10 rooms; $–$$.

Nightlife and the Arts

Nightlife

Burlington's nightlife caters to its college-age population, with pubs and a few dance spots. Touring and local musicians come to **Higher Ground** (⊠ 1 Main St., Winooski, ☎ 802/654–8888). **Comedy Zone** (⊠ Radisson Hotel, 60 Battery St., Burlington, ☎ 802/658–6500) provides the laughs in town on weekends. The **Metronome** (⊠ 188 Main St., Burlington, ☎ 802/865–4563) entertains with an eclectic mix of live music almost every night. **Nectar's** (⊠ 188 Main St., Burlington, ☎ 802/658–4771) is always jumping to the sounds of local bands and never charges a cover. The **Vermont Pub and Brewery** (⊠ College and St. Paul Sts., Burlington, ☎ 802/865–0500) makes its own beers and seltzers.

The Arts

Burlington and environs host the summer-long **Vermont Mozart Festival** (☎ 802/862–7352 or 800/639–9097) and the **Flynn Theater for the Performing Arts** (☎ 802/652–4500), which schedules the Vermont Symphony Orchestra, theater, dance, big-name musicians, and lectures. Stowe has a summer **performing arts festival** (☎ 802/253–7792).

Outdoor Activities and Sports

Biking

In addition to the numerous back roads in the Champlain Valley, Stowe has a recreational path, and Burlington has a 9-mi path along its waterfront. Several operators offer guided tours through the state, among them **Vermont Bicycle Touring** (⊠ Box 711, Bristol 05443, ☎ 802/453–4811 or 800/245–3868) and **P.O.M.G. Bike Tours of Vermont** (⊠ Box 1080, Richmond 05477, ☎ 802/434–2270 or 888/635–2453).

Boating

Lake Champlain has marinas with rentals and charters in or near Vergennes and Burlington. The **North Beaches** border the northern edge of Burlington and are popular for swimming and sailboarding. **Burlington Community Boathouse** (⊠ Foot of College St., Burlington Harbor, ☎ 802/865–3377) has sailboard and boat rentals. **True North Kayak Tours** (⊠ 53 Nash Pl., Burlington, ☎ 802/860–1910) gives guided tours of Lake Champlain.

Fishing

Lake Champlain contains salmon, lake trout, bass, pike, and more. Marina services are offered by **Malletts Bay Marina** (⊠ 228 Lakeshore Dr., Colchester, ☎ 802/862–4072) and **Point Bay Marina** (⊠ 1401 Thompson's Point Rd., Charlotte, ☎ 802/425–2431).

Golf

Public courses include **Ralph Myhre's** 18 holes, run by Middlebury College (⊠ Rte. 30, Middlebury, ☎ 802/443–5125), and the new Jack Nicklaus–designed **Vermont National Country Club** (⊠ 1227 Dorset St., South Burlington, ☎ 802/864–7770).

Hiking and Backpacking

Aside from the **Long Trail** (The Green Mountain Club; ⊠ Rte. 100, R.R. 1, Box 650, Waterbury Center 05677, ☎ 802/244–7037), day hikes in northern Vermont include the **Little River** area in Mt. Mansfield State Forest, near Stowe, and **Stowe Pinnacle.**

Ski Areas

For statewide snow conditions call 802/828–3239. All downhill areas listed except Mad River Glen have snowmaking.

Cross-Country

Alpine resorts that have cross-country trails include **Burke Mountain,** 57 mi; **Jay Peak,** 20 mi; **Smugglers' Notch,** 23 mi; **Stowe,** 22 mi of groomed trails, 24 mi of backcountry trails; and **Sugarbush,** 15 mi.

Downhill

Burke Mountain (⊠ Box 247, East Burke 05832, ☎ 802/626–3305 or 800/541–5480 for lodging), 41 trails, 4 lifts, 2,000-ft vertical drop. **Jay Peak** (⊠ Rte. 242, Jay 05859, ☎ 802/988–2611 or 800/451–4449), 66 trails, 8 lifts, 2,153-ft vertical drop. **Mad River Glen** (⊠ Rte. 17, Waitsfield 05673, ☎ 802/496–3551), 44 runs, 4 lifts, 2,037-ft drop. **Smugglers' Notch** (⊠ Smugglers' Notch 05464, ☎ 802/644–8851 or 800/451–8752), 67 runs, 9 lifts, 2,610-ft drop. **Stowe** (⊠ 5781 Mountain Rd., Stowe 05672, ☎ 802/253–3000; 800/253–4754 for lodging), 47 trails, 11 lifts, 2,360-ft drop. **Sugarbush** (⊠ R.R. 1, Box 350, Warren 05674, ☎ 802/583–2381; 800/537–8427 for lodging), 135 trails, 26 lifts, 2,400- and 2,600-ft drops.

Shopping

Burlington's **Church Street Marketplace** is a pedestrian thoroughfare lined with boutiques. The **Vermont State Craft Center** (⊠ Church St., ☎ 802/863–6458) is a display of the work of more than 200 Vermont artisans. The center also has a shop on Mill Street, Middlebury (☎ 802/388–3177).

VIRGINIA

By Francis X.
Rocca

Updated by
John A. Kelly
and CiCi
Williamson

Capital	Richmond
Population	6,677,200
Motto	Thus Always to Tyrants
State Bird	Cardinal
State Flower	Dogwood
Postal Abbreviation	VA

Statewide Visitor Information

Virginia Division of Tourism (⊠ 901 E. Byrd St., Richmond 23219, ☎ 804/786–2051 or 800/932–5827) will mail travel brochures and travel information to you. Call **Visit Virginia** (☎ 800/847–4882) for visitor information and a free state map. **Welcome centers** are in Bracey (on I–85), Bristol (I–81), Clearbrook (I–81), Covington (I–64), Fredericksburg (I–95), Lambsburg (I–77), Manassas (I–66), New Church (U.S. 13), Rocky Gap (I–77), and Skippers (I–95).

Scenic Drives

Skyline Drive, the **Blue Ridge Parkway,** and **Goshen Pass** wind through spectacular mountain scenery (☞ Charlottesville and the Shenandoah Valley, *below*). A 25-mi drive north along **Route 20** from Charlottesville to Orange takes you through gently rolling countryside, past stately horse farms and vineyards. For a stirring panorama of the famous buildings and monuments of Washington, D.C., drive north from Alexandria on the **George Washington Memorial Parkway.** Between Virginia Beach and the Eastern Shore stretches the 17½-mi **Chesapeake Bay Bridge-Tunnel,** an engineering wonder that has you surrounded by sea without leaving your car; a fishing and observation pier and a restaurant are along the way.

National and State Parks

National Parks

Shenandoah National Park (⊠ 3655 U.S. 211E, Luray 22835, ☎ 540/999–3500)—196,500 acres with a vertical change in elevation of 3,500 ft—offers hiking, horseback riding, and fishing. The 1.8-million-acre **George Washington and Jefferson National Forests** (⊠ 5162 Valleypointe Pkwy., Roanoke 24019, ☎ 540/265–5100 or 888/265–0019) offer camping, boating, hiking, fishing, swimming, and horseback riding. **Mt. Rogers National Recreation Area** (⊠ 3714 Hwy. 16, Marion 24354, ☎ 540/783–5196) is a 116,000-acre expanse, including the state's highest point—5,729 ft above sea level.

State Parks

The **Department of Conservation and Recreation** (⊠ 203 Governor St., Richmond 23219, ☎ 804/786–1712) has information on Virginia's 28 state parks, which range in size from 500 to 4,500 acres. Two of the most popular are **Douthat State Park** (⊠ Rte. 629, Box 212, Millboro 24460, ☎ 540/862–8100) and **First Landing/Seashore State Park** (⊠ 2500 Shore Dr., Virginia Beach 23451, ☎ 757/481–2131).

CHARLOTTESVILLE AND THE SHENANDOAH VALLEY

Residents of Charlottesville, in the Piedmont region of rolling hills, call it "Mr. Jefferson's Country." They speak of the Sage of Monticello as if he were still writing, building, and governing. Immersed as it may be in the past, Charlottesville is anything but backward. Home to a top-ranked state university and a fashionable retreat for tycoons, movie stars, and a smattering of celebrity writers, it is one of America's most sophisticated small cities.

In and along the Shenandoah Valley are small towns that were once frontier outposts; well-traveled driving routes with turnouts overlooking breathtaking scenery; many opportunities for outdoor recreation, on water and solid ground; and accommodations and restaurants to suit all tastes.

Visitor Information

Bath County: Chamber of Commerce (✉ U.S. 220, Box 718, Hot Springs 24445, ☎ 540/839–5409). **Charlottesville:** Charlottesville-Albemarle Convention and Visitors Bureau (✉ Rte. 20S, Box 178, 22902, ☎ 804/977–1783 or 877/386–1102). **Lexington:** Visitor Center (✉ 106 E. Washington St., 24450, ☎ 540/463–3777 or 877/453–9822). **Roanoke Valley:** Convention and Visitors Bureau (✉ 114 Market St., Roanoke 24011, ☎ 540/342–6025 or 800/635–5535). **Shenandoah Valley:** Travel Association (✉ Box 1040, New Market 22844, ☎ 540/740–3132). **Winchester:** Chamber of Commerce (✉ 1360 S. Pleasant Valley Rd., 22601, ☎ 540/662–4135 or 800/662–1360).

Arriving and Departing

By Bus
Greyhound (☎ 800/231–2222) serves **Charlottesville** (✉ 310 W. Main St.), **Lexington** (✉ 211 W. 21st St., Buena Vista), **Roanoke** (✉ 26 Salem Ave.), and **Staunton** (✉ 1143 Richmond Rd.).

By Car
Charlottesville is where U.S. 29 (north–south) meets I–64. I–81 and U.S. 11 run north–south the length of the Shenandoah Valley and continue south into Tennessee. I–66 meets I–81 and U.S. 11 at the northern end of the valley; I–64 connects I–81 and U.S. 11 with Charlottesville. Route 39 runs through Bath County and connects with I–81/I–64, just north of Lexington.

By Plane
Charlottesville-Albemarle Airport (☎ 804/973–8341) is 8 mi north of town at the intersection of Rtes. 606 and 649, off U.S. 29. **Roanoke Regional Airport** (☎ 540/362–1999) is 6 mi north of town, off I–581.

By Train
Amtrak (☎ 800/872–7245) has service to Charlottesville's **Union Station** (✉ 810 W. Main St.), to Clifton Forge (✉ 400 Ridgeway St.)—for the Homestead resort in **Bath County**—and to **Staunton** (✉ 1 Middlebrook Ave.).

Exploring Charlottesville and the Shenandoah Valley

Charlottesville
★ Jefferson built his beloved **Monticello** (✉ Rte. 53, ☎ 804/984–9800, ✉ $11) on a "little mountain" over a period of 40 years, from 1769 to 1809. In details and overall conception Monticello was a revolutionary

structure, a neoclassical repudiation of the Colonial style with all its political connotations. Throughout the house are Jefferson's inventions, including a seven-day clock and a "polygraph," a clever two-pen contraption that allowed him to copy letters as he wrote them.

The cozy rooms of **Ash Lawn–Highland** (⊠ Rte. 795, southwest of Rte. 53, ☎ 804/293–9539; ☞ $7.50), James Monroe's modest farmhouse retreat, evoke the fifth president—our first to spring from the middle class. Outside, sheep and peacocks roam the grounds of this 550-acre working plantation.

In downtown Charlottesville, a six-block-long pedestrian shopping mall along Main Street bustles with boutiques, art galleries, bookshops, restaurants, movie theaters, and even a skating rink. At the eastern end is the **Virginia Discovery Museum** (⊠ 524 E. Main St., ☎ 804/977–1025; ☞ $4; closed Mon.) where children can step inside a giant kaleidoscope and observe bees in action in a working hive. At the west end of town is the **University of Virginia** (☎ 804/924–1019; ☞ free), founded and designed by Thomas Jefferson. The centerpiece of his revered "academical village" is the Rotunda, a half-scale replica of Rome's Pantheon, which is flanked by pavilions and a terraced expanse known as the Lawn.

The Shenandoah Valley

At the top of the valley, and almost at the northernmost tip of the state, is **Winchester.** Long known as Virginia's Apple Capital, the town hosts parades, concerts, and a beauty pageant during the **Shenandoah Apple Blossom Festival** every May (☎ 540/662–3863). Because of its strategic location, Winchester has drawn more than its share of military action over the years. A young Colonel George Washington spent more than a year here during the French and Indian Wars; the log cabin in which he worked is now **George Washington's Office Museum** (⊠ 32 W. Cork St., ☎ 540/662–4412; ☞ $3.50; closed Nov.–Mar.). **Stonewall Jackson's headquarters** (⊠ 415 N. Braddock St., ☎ 540/667–3242; ☞ $3.50; closed Mon.–Thurs. Nov.–Mar.) is furnished as it was when the Confederate general used it during the Valley Campaign of 1861–62, down to his prayer book and camp table.

Belle Grove (⊠ U.S. 11, ☎ 540/869–2028; ☞ $7; closed weekdays Nov.; Dec.–Mar.), just south of Middletown, is a grand 1794 limestone mansion designed with advice from Thomas Jefferson. It served as headquarters for victorious Union forces during the Battle of Cedar Creek (1864) and is today a working farm. Group tours can still be arranged when it closes in winter.

Shenandoah National Park (⊠ 3655 U.S. 211E, Luray 22835, ☎ 540/999–3500; ☞ park and Skyline Drive: $10 for cars; $5 for motorcycles, bicycles, and pedestrians), encompassing some 60 peaks, runs more than 80 mi along the Blue Ridge, south from Front Royal to Waynesboro. Heavily forested, the park is home to deer, bear, bobcat, and other wild animals and sanctuary to a colorful array of bird species. Hiking, camping, fishing, and horseback riding are all available. For information on seasonal activities pick up the free *Shenandoah Overlook* when you enter the park.

★ **Skyline Drive** winds 105 mi over the mountains of the park, affording panoramas of the valley to the west and the rolling country of the Piedmont to the east. On holidays and weekends in spring and fall, expect congestion, as crowds slow down traffic to far below speed limit. Many lodges, campsites, eating places, and sometimes stretches of the drive itself are closed from November through April.

Luray Caverns (⊠ U.S. 211, Luray, ☎ 540/743–6551; 🎟 $14), the largest caves in the eastern United States, are just west of Skyline Drive. Water seepage over millions of years has created towering rock and mineral formations, a section of which has been transformed into the world's only "stalacpipe organ." Tours begin every 20 minutes.

At **New Market,** the site of a costly Confederate victory late in the Civil War, the **New Market Battlefield Historical Park** (⊠ 8895 Collins Dr.; I–81, Exit 264, ☎ 540/740–3102; 🎟 $5) has exhibits on the battle and maps for self-guided walking tours.

★ The **Museum of American Frontier Culture** (⊠ 1250 Richmond Rd., ☎ 540/332–7850, 🎟 $8), just outside Staunton (pronounced *Stan*-ton), re-creates early agrarian life in the Shenandoah Valley through four authentic farmsteads: Scots-Irish, German, English, and American.

The 470-mi **Blue Ridge Parkway,** a continuation of Skyline Drive, runs south through the **George Washington National Forest** (☞ National and State Parks, *above*) to Great Smoky Mountains National Park in North Carolina. Less pristine than the drive, the parkway offers better, higher views—and free admission. At the **Peaks of Otter Recreation Area,** just off the Blue Ridge Parkway northeast of Roanoke (at milepost 86), there's a 360-degree panorama and a crystalline mountain lake, to boot.

In Lexington, **Washington and Lee University,** founded in 1749, is named for the first U.S. president (an early benefactor) and the Confederate commander Robert E. Lee, who served as college president after the Civil War. Among the campus's white-columned neoclassical buildings is the tiny, picturesque **Lee Memorial Chapel and Museum** (☎ 540/463–8768; 🎟 free), where a recumbent statue of the general marks his tomb. The lower level preserves Lee's office as he left it on September 28, 1870.

Adjacent to Washington and Lee University are the imposing neo-Gothic buildings of the **Virginia Military Institute.** An all-male institution since its founding in 1839, it became coeducational in 1997. On display at the **Institute Museum** (☎ 540/464–7232; 🎟 free) are some 15,000 military artifacts, including antique firearms and Civil War-era cadet equipment and uniforms. Near the Virginia Military Institute, the **Stonewall Jackson House** (⊠ 8 E. Washington St., ☎ 540/463–2552; 🎟 $5) offers a glimpse of the Confederate general's private life.

About 20 mi from Lexington is **Bath County,** where thermal springs with supposed medicinal powers have made it a popular resort area for more than 200 years. Between Lexington and Bath County runs **Goshen Pass,** a stunning 3-mi stretch of Route 39 that follows the Maury River as it winds its way through the Alleghenies.

★ **Natural Bridge** (⊠ I–81, Exit 175 or 180, ☎ 540/291–2121 or 800/533–1410, 🎟 $8), south of Lexington, is a 215-ft-high, 90-ft-long arch that was created as the creek below gradually carved out the limestone. Called the Bridge of God by the Monocan Indians who discovered it, the formation today really *is* a bridge, supporting U.S. 11.

Roanoke is a lively railroad hub and the largest city off of the Blue Ridge Parkway. A restored downtown warehouse called **Center in the Square** (⊠ Market Sq., ☎ 540/342–5700) houses a theater, a local historical museum, an art gallery, and the **Science Museum of Western Virginia** (☎ 540/342–5710; 🎟 $6), with interactive exhibits including computer games that entertain and inform youngsters on topics such as energy resources, oceanography, geology, and meteorology. A planetarium gives shows. The **Virginia Museum of Transportation** (✉ 303 Norfolk Ave., ☎ 540/342–5670; 🎟 $5; closed Mon. Jan. and Feb.) houses the largest collection of diesel and steam locomotives in the country.

A restored 19th-century tobacco farm southeast of Roanoke, **Booker T. Washington National Monument** (✉ Rte. 122, ☎ 540/721–2094; 🎟 free) is the birthplace of the great black educator and a living museum of life under slavery.

About two hours east of Roanoke and less than two hours south of Charlottesville is **Appomattox Courthouse National Historical Park** (✉ Rte. 24, Appomattox, ☎ 804/352–8987; 🎟 $2), a village of 27 buildings restored to their appearance on April 9, 1865, when Lee surrendered to Grant in the parlor of the McLean House here.

Dining and Lodging

Bed-and-breakfast reservations in the region can be made through **Blue Ridge Bed & Breakfast** (✉ Rte. 2, Box 3895, Berryville 22611, ☎ 540/955–1246 or 800/296–1246, 𝖥𝖠𝖷 540/955–4240) and **Guesthouses** (✉ Box 5737, Charlottesville 22905, ☎ 804/979–7264).

Bath County

$$$$ ✕⌑ **The Homestead.** Famous since 1766 for its mineral waters, this
★ resort ranks as one of the country's most luxurious. Elegant rooms in the older section have Chippendale-reproduction furnishings, while the newer section has duplexes with fireplaces. The 15,000-acre property has 100 mi of riding trails, nine ski slopes, and 4 mi of streams stocked with rainbow trout. The resort has a full-service spa, and an orchestra performs nightly in the formal dining room, which serves up Continental and traditional Virginia cuisine. ✉ *U.S. 220, Hot Springs 24445,* ☎ *540/839–1766 or 800/838–1766,* 𝖥𝖠𝖷 *540/839–7670. 517 rooms. 10 restaurants, 2 pools, golf, tennis, exercise room. AE, D, DC, MC, V. MAP.* 🐾

$$$ ✕⌑ **Inn at Gristmill Square.** The rooms of this state historical landmark are scattered throughout a 19th-century miller's house, blacksmith's shop, hardware store, and gristmill and feature a rustic Colonial decor. The Waterwheel Restaurant, also in the gristmill, has entrées that include breast of chicken stuffed with wild rice, sausage, apple, and pecans. ✉ *Rte. 645, Box 359, Warm Springs 24484,* ☎ *540/839–2231,* 𝖥𝖠𝖷 *540/839–5770. 16 rooms, 1 apartment. Restaurant, pool, tennis. D, MC, V. CP.* 🐾

Blue Ridge Parkway

$$$–$$$$ ⌑ **Wintergreen.** From December through March guests at this 11,000-acre mountain resort are sometimes able to ski and golf on the same day; and there are plenty of additional sports options all year long. There's also tennis, hiking, horseback riding, boating, and bicycling, as well as a spa. Accommodations range from studio mountain condos to seven-bedroom houses. ✉ *Rte. 664, Wintergreen 22958,* ☎ *804/ 325–2200 or 800/325–2200,* 𝖥𝖠𝖷 *804/325–8003. 300 units. 6 restaurants, 2 pools, exercise room. AE, D, MC, V.* 🐾

$$–$$$ ⌑ **Doe Run Lodge.** This resort's spot on the crest of the Blue Ridge at Groundhog Mountain guarantees grand vistas of the Piedmont and proximity to golfing, skiing, and hunting. Guests can enjoy tennis, volleyball, basketball, hiking, and fishing, as well as the pool and sauna. Each chalet or villa has a fireplace and floor-to-ceiling windows. Some rooms have whirlpools or hot tubs. ✉ *Milepost 189, Blue Ridge Pkwy., Rte. 2, Box 338, Hillsville 24348,* ☎ *540/398–2212 or 800/ 325–6189,* 𝖥𝖠𝖷 *540/398–2833. 39 chalets, 2 villas. Restaurant, pool, tennis. AE, MC, V. EP.* 🐾

Charlottesville

$$$–$$$$
★ ✕ **Métropolitain.** The kitchen is center stage here, situated right in the middle of the sleek, airy dining room. The cuisine is eclectic French-American; popular dishes include salmon "filet mignon" with horseradish crust, sweet onions, chard, and cabernet glaze. Also a good bet is the six-course tasting menu for $42. ✉ *214 W. Water St.,* ☎ *804/977–1043. AE, MC, V. No lunch.*

$$–$$$ ✕ **Duner's.** Locals flock to this eatery 5 mi west of Charlottesville, because its fanciful menu, which changes daily, never disappoints. Fresh, seasonal fare, including seafood and pasta dishes, predominates. Try the grilled shrimp with flying fish roe and sesame seaweed salad or the rack of lamb with pecan barbecue sauce. Sunday brunch is a big draw. ✉ *Rte. 250W, Ivy,* ☎ *804/293–8352. Reservations not accepted. MC, V. No lunch.*

$–$$$ ✕ **C&O Restaurant.** A dingy-looking storefront hung with an old, illuminated Pepsi sign conceals one of the most venerated restaurants in town. The formal dining room upstairs (seatings at 6:30 and 9) and the bistro below share a menu that is French influenced, with Pacific Rim and American Southwest touches. Try the flank steak panfried with tamari and fresh ginger cream. ✉ *515 E. Water St.,* ☎ *804/971–7044. AE, MC, V. No lunch weekends.*

$$$$
★ ✕🖾 **Keswick Hall at Monticello.** This sprawling Tuscan villa built in 1912 is set on 600 lush acres. All of the guest rooms and common areas are furnished with English and American antiques. Some rooms offer whirlpool baths and balconies. The facilities of the private Keswick Club are open to overnight guests. There's an 18-hole golf course, tennis, croquet, fishing, and bicycling. The formal dining room features classic European cuisine with a modern twist; a five-course meal, prix-fixe at $58, features entrées such as striped Virginia bass with smoked trout tortellini and a chive beurre blanc. ✉ *701 Club Dr., 5 mi east of Charlottesville, Keswick 22947,* ☎ *804/979–3440 or 800/274–5391,* 𝔽𝔸𝕏 *804/ 977–4171. 48 rooms. 2 restaurants, 2 pools, health club. AE, DC, MC, V. BP available.* 🕾

$$$–$$$$ ✕🖾 **Boar's Head Inn.** Built around a restored gristmill that dates from 1834, this resort is set on two small lakes and has the feel of an English country inn. The rooms boast king-size four-poster beds and Italian Anichini linens; many have balconies. Some of the suites offer fireplaces. In addition to tennis and golf, there's racquetball, squash, and fishing. Regional offerings in the Old Mill Room include pan-seared moulard duck with apple potato pancakes. ✉ *U.S. 250W (Box 5307), 22905,* ☎ *804/296–2181 or 800/476–1988,* 𝔽𝔸𝕏 *804/972–6024. 175 rooms. 3 restaurants, 4 pools, health club. AE, D, DC, MC, V.* 🕾

$$–$$$
★ ✕🖾 **Silver Thatch Inn.** This 1780 white-clapboard farmhouse has been transformed into an intimate inn, with four-poster beds and period antiques accenting the rooms, some of which have fireplaces. In the restaurant, provisioned by organic farms, the fish is always fresh and the rabbits and chickens are often locally raised. The chef's grilled beef tenderloin is renowned, and the wine cellar wins national awards. ✉ *3001 Hollymead Dr., 22911,* ☎ *804/978–4686 or 800/261–0720,* 𝔽𝔸𝕏 *804/973–6156. 7 rooms. Restaurant (reservations essential), pool. AE, DC, MC, V. BP.* 🕾

Lexington

$–$$$ ✕🖾 **Maple Hall.** This former 1850 plantation house is set on 56 acres, where guests can hike and fish. Rooms have period antiques and modern amenities. A notable entrées on the seasonal menu includes chicken Chesapeake (a chicken breast stuffed with spinach and crabmeat). ✉ *Rte. 11 (6 mi north of Lexington), 24450,* ☎ *540/463–6693 or 877/*

463–2044, FAX *540/463–7262. 21 rooms. Restaurant, pool, tennis. D, MC, V. BP.*

Roanoke

$$–$$$ ✕🏨 **Hotel Roanoke and Conference Center.** This elegant Tudor Revival building, listed on the National Register of Historic Places, has a richly paneled lobby and Florentine marble floors. The rooms are furnished with reproduction antiques. The Regency Dining Room features regional southern cuisine; kept on the menu by demand are the peanut soup, spoon bread, and steak Diane. ✉ *110 Shenandoah Ave., 24016,* ☎ *540/985–5900 or 800/222–8733,* FAX *540/853–8264. 332 rooms. 2 restaurants, pool, exercise room. AE, D, DC, MC, V.* ♻

Staunton

$$–$$$ ✕🏨 **Belle Grae Inn.** Canopy beds, antiques, and rocking chairs in this restored Victorian house give the guest rooms a turn-of-the-20th-century mood. The food is gourmet American. Entrées in the formal dining room include hazelnut-crusted halibut with ginger and pear chutney. The adjacent bistro is more casual and less expensive; entrées range from chicken Parmesan to London broil. ✉ *515 W. Frederick St., 24401,* ☎ *540/886–5151 or 888/541–5151,* FAX *540/886–6641. 17 rooms. 2 restaurants. AE, MC, V. BP.* ♻

$$ 🏨 **Sampson Eagon Inn.** In the historic Gospel Hill section of town, this circa-1840 Greek Revival home has been restored to its period charm. The spacious guest rooms feature antique canopy beds, cozy sitting areas, and modern amenities. Don't miss the Grand Marnier soufflé pancakes for breakfast. ✉ *238 E. Beverley St., 24401,* ☎ *540/886–8200 or 800/ 597–9722,* FAX *540/886–8200. 5 rooms. AE, MC, V. BP.* ♻

Winchester

$$–$$$ ✕ **Violino Ristorante Italiano.** Owners Franco and Marcello Stocco (he's the chef; she manages the dining room) serve up their native northern Italian cuisine at this eatery in the city's Old Town. Notable entrées include angel hair pasta sautéed with broccoli and shrimp in a white wine sauce. ✉ *181 N. Loudoun St.,* ☎ *540/667–8006. AE, D, DC, MC, V. Closed Sun.*

$$$–$$$$ ✕🏨 **L'Auberge Provençale.** The owners from Avignon bring the warm
★   elegance of the south of France to this 1750s country inn. Rooms are eclectically decorated with French art and fabrics and Victorian wicker and antiques, and some have fireplaces. The gourmet breakfast includes fresh homemade croissants and apple crepes with maple syrup. The nationally acclaimed restaurant features authentic Provençale cuisine ($67 prix-fixe). Memorable entrées include fois gras with mango and ginger. ✉ *Rte. 340 (Box 190), White Post, VA (10 mi east of Winchester), 22663,* ☎ *540/837–1375 or 800/638–1702,* FAX *540/837–2004. 14 rooms. Restaurant, pool. AE, D, MC, V. Closed Jan. Restaurant closed Mon. and Tues. No lunch. Reservations essential on weekends. BP.* ♻

Motels

🏨 **Best Western Inn at Valley View Mall** (✉ 5050 Valley View Blvd., Roanoke 24012, ☎ 800/362–2410, FAX 540/362–2400), 85 rooms; pool; $.

🏨 **Roseloe Motel** (✉ Rte. 1, Box 590, Hot Springs 24445, ☎ 540/839–5373), 14 rooms; $.

Campgrounds

In Shenandoah National Park (☞ National and State Parks, *above*) the ⛺ **Big Meadows Campground** (☎ 540/999–3500 or 800/365–2267) requires reservations for stays between May and November. Other campsites in the park are available on a first-come, first-served basis; for information contact the park.

Nightlife and the Arts

Nightlife

In Charlottesville the large and comfortable **Miller's** (✉ 109 W. Main St., Downtown Mall, ☎ 804/971–8511) hosts blues and jazz musicians. Many national acts appear at **Trax** (✉ 122 11th St. SW, ☎ 804/295–8729) Charlottesville's main alternative music club. At the **Homestead** in Hot Springs (☞ Dining and Lodging, *above*) there's nightly dancing to live music.

The Arts

CHARLOTTESVILLE

For details on performances at the University of Virginia, check the free *C'ville Weekly* or *Cavalier Daily*. **McGuffey Art Center** (✉ 201 2nd St. NW, ☎ 804/295–7973) contains the Second Street Gallery and the studios of painters, metal workers, and sculptors, all of which are open to the public.

SHENANDOAH VALLEY

Garth Newel Music Center (✉ Hot Springs, ☎ 540/839–5018) hosts chamber music concerts throughout the year. **Mill Mountain Theatre** (☎ 540/342–5740) offers year-round professional theater, plus a festival of new works. **Roanoke Ballet Theatre** (☎ 540/345–6099) performs in spring and fall. The **Theater at Lime Kiln** (✉ Lexington, ☎ 540/463–3074) is an outdoor rock-wall pit (the ruins of a lime kiln) where musicals and concerts of every genre—folk, bluegrass, classical, and more—take place throughout the summer.

Outdoor Activities and Sports

Canoeing

Downriver Canoe (✉ Rte. 613, ☎ 540/635–5526) and **Front Royal Canoe** (✉ U.S. 340, ☎ 540/635–5440) are both near Front Royal. **James River Runners Inc.** (✉ 10082 Hatton Ferry Rd., Scottsville, ☎ 804/286–2338) is about 25 mi south of Charlottesville. **Shenandoah River Outfitters** (✉ Rte. 684, ☎ 540/743–4159) is near Luray.

Fishing

To take advantage of the abundance of trout in some 50 streams of **Shenandoah National Park,** get a five-day Virginia fishing license at concession stands along Skyline Drive.

Golf

Caverns Country Club Resort (✉ U.S. 211, Luray, ☎ 540/743–6551). The **Homestead** (✉ U.S. 220, Hot Springs, ☎ 540/839–1766 or 800/838–1766). **Meadowcreek Golf Course** (✉ 1400 Pen Park Rd., Charlottesville, ☎ 804/977–0615). **Wintergreen** (✉ Rte. 664, Wintergreen, ☎ 804/325–2200 or 800/325–2200).

Hiking

The stretch of the **Appalachian Trail** running through Shenandoah National Park takes hikers along the skyline of the Blue Ridge to stunning views of the Piedmont and the Shenandoah Valley in the distance; white-tailed deer often step quietly into view. The main pathway's proximity to Skyline Drive and frequent parking lots make hike lengths flexible. For deep-wilderness hikes, 500 mi of marked side trails lead into the backcountry.

Tennis

Caverns Country Club Resort, the **Homestead,** and **Wintergreen Resort** (☞ Golf, *above*) offer tennis.

Spectator Sports

Equestrian events: The **Virginia Horse Center** (✉ Rte. 39, Lexington, ☎ 540/463–2194) stages show jumping, hunter trials, and multibreed shows year–round. **Football, soccer, basketball, softball, golf, tennis, lacrosse, and field hockey:** The **University of Virginia** (☎ 804/924–8821) is nationally ranked in several varsity sports. The *Cavalier Daily* has listings.

Ski Areas

The **Homestead** (☞ Golf, *above*) has cross-country, downhill, and night skiing. **Massanutten Resort** (✉ Rte. 644 off U.S. 33, McGaheysville, ☎ 540/289–9441) has 15 slopes, a snow-tubing park, and equipment rental. **Wintergreen** (☞ Golf, *above*) maintains 17 slopes and trails.

Shopping

Lewis Glaser Quill Pens (✉ 1700 Sourwood Pl., Charlottesville, ☎ 804/973–7783 or 800/446–6732) sells handcrafted feather pens and pewter inkwells of the kind it has made for the U.S. Supreme Court and the British royal family. The Downtown Mall in Charlottesville has a concentration of used and antiquarian bookstores with rare and hard-to-find tomes; try **Blue Whale Books** (✉ 115 W. Main St., ☎ 804/296–4646), and **Daedalus Bookshop** (✉ 123 4th St. NE, ☎ 804/293–7595).

NORTHERN VIRGINIA

The affluent and cosmopolitan residents of this region have closer ties to neighboring Washington, D.C., than to the rest of the state, yet they take pride in being Virginians and in protecting the historic treasures they hold in trust for the rest of the nation. Here are some of America's most precious acreage, including Arlington National Cemetery, Mount Vernon, and the Civil War battlefield of Manassas (Bull Run). In the rural Hunt Country, around Leesburg and Middleburg, the gracious Old South lives on in fox hunting and steeplechases.

Visitor Information

Fairfax County: Convention and Visitors Bureau (✉ 8300 Boone Blvd., Suite 450, Vienna 22182, ☎ 703/790–3329 or 800/732–4732); Visitors Center (✉ 8180 Silverbrook Rd., off I–95S at Exit 163, Lorton, ☎ 800/732–4732). **Loudoun County:** Tourism Council (✉ 108D South St. SE, Leesburg 20175, ☎ 703/771–2170 or 800/752–6118). **Alexandria:** Convention and Visitors Association (✉ 221 King St., 22314, ☎ 703/838–4200 or 800/388–9119). **Fredericksburg:** Visitor Center (✉ 706 Caroline St., 22401, ☎ 540/373–1776 or 800/678–4748).

Arriving and Departing

By Bus

Greyhound (☎ 800/231–2222) serves **Fairfax** (✉ 4103 Rust St.), **Arlington** (✉ 3860 S. Four Mile Run Dr.), **Fredericksburg** (✉ 1400 Jefferson Davis Hwy.), and **Springfield** (✉ 6583 Backlick Rd.).

By Car

I–95 runs north–south along the eastern side of the region. I–66 runs east–west. Fredericksburg is 50 mi south of Washington, D.C., on I–95.

By Plane

Two major airports serve both northern Virginia and the Washington, D.C., area. The busy **Ronald Reagan Washington National Airport** (☎ 703/417–8000), in Arlington, has scheduled daily flights by all major

U.S. carriers. **Dulles International Airport** (☎ 703/572–2700), 26 mi west of Washington, is a modern facility served by major U.S. airlines and many international carriers.

Baltimore–Washington International Airport (☎ 410/859–7100), 10 mi south of Baltimore, also serves the metropolitan Washington area and has its own train station for Amtrak and Maryland trains.

By Train

Amtrak (☎ 800/872–7245) stops in **Alexandria** (✉ 110 Callahan Dr.) and **Fredericksburg** (✉ Caroline St. and Lafayette Blvd.); some travelers find it easiest to arrive in the capital's Union Station. The **Virginia Rail Express** (VRE; ☎ 800/743–3873) provides more frequent workday commuter service between **Alexandria, Fredericksburg, Manassas,** and **Washington,** with additional stops near hotels in Crystal City, L'Enfant Plaza, and elsewhere. Tickets prices are about a third those of Amtrak.

Exploring Northern Virginia

★ George Washington's **Mount Vernon** (✉ southern end of George Washington Pkwy., ☎ 703/780–2000, ✑ $9) is the nation's best-known country house. Washington inherited the land in 1761 and farmed what was then an 8,000-acre plantation before taking command of the Continental Army. Throughout the house are small symbols of Washington's eminence, including his presidential chair.

Woodlawn (✉ Rte. 1, via Rte. 235, ☎ 703/780–4000; ✑ $6 for either or $10 for both Woodlawn and the Pope-Leighey House), designed by the amateur architect of the Capitol, William Thornton, and completed in 1805, was built for Washington's step-granddaughter, Nelly Custis, who married his favorite nephew, Lawrence Lewis. The small **Pope-Leighey House,** by Frank Lloyd Wright, is of interest only to his real devotees. Built in 1940, it was moved here from Falls Church in 1964.

South of Mount Vernon is the lesser-known **Gunston Hall** (✉ 10709 Gunston Rd., Mason Neck, ☎ 703/550–9220 or 800/811–6966; ✑ $5), the 1755 Georgian plantation home of George Mason, one of the framers of the Constitution and author of the Virginia Declaration of Rights, the basis of our Bill of Rights.

North of Mount Vernon is **Alexandria,** a couple of miles from and much older than Washington, D.C. On the Potomac, it enjoys a colorful past, linked to the most significant events and personages of the Colonial, Revolutionary, and Civil War periods. **Old Town** is a picturesque neighborhood of mostly redbrick 18th- and 19th-century town houses with a few cobblestone streets. Its major sights can be seen on foot within 20 blocks or so, and the area has scores of import and specialty shops, galleries, and restaurants, including some with exotic cuisine. Parking is usually scarce, but the **Convention and Visitors Association** (☞ Visitor Information, *above*) provides a free 24-hour pass that allows out-of-town visitors free parking at two-hour meters.

Alexandria's visitor center—the best place to start a tour—is in the town's oldest structure, **Ramsay House** (✉ 221 King St., ☎ 703/838–4200), believed to have been built around 1724 in Dumfries (25 mi south) and moved here in 1749. The 1753 **Carlyle House** (✉ 121 N. Fairfax St., ☎ 703/549–2997; ✑ $4), built by Scottish merchant John Carlyle, is still the grandest house in town. The **Old Presbyterian Meeting House** (✉ 321 S. Fairfax St., ☎ 703/549–6670; ✑ free) was both a church and a gathering place for Scottish patriots during the Revolution. John Carlyle and other Alexandria notables are buried here.

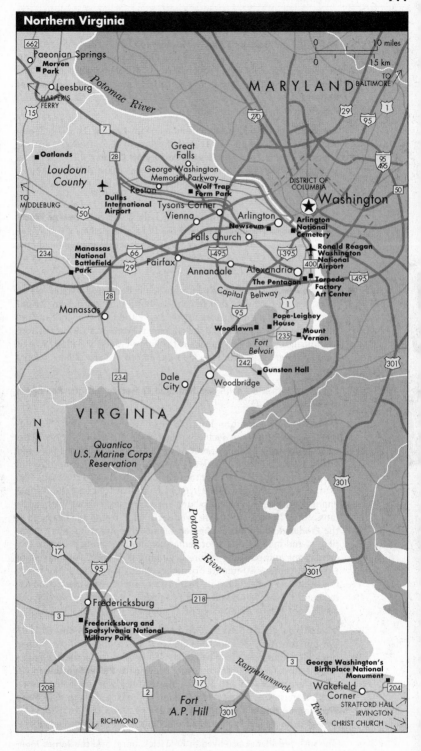

Northern Virginia

662
Paeonian Springs
Morven Park
Leesburg
HARPER'S FERRY
15
Potomac River
7
Oatlands
28
Loudoun County
TO MIDDLEBURG
50
Great Falls
George Washington Memorial Parkway
Reston
Dulles International Airport
Wolf Trap Farm Park
Tysons Corner
Vienna
Falls Church
234
Manassas National Battlefield Park
66
29
Fairfax
28
Manassas
234
Dale City
Woodbridge
242
N
VIRGINIA
Quantico U.S. Marine Corps Reservation
Potomac River
1
17
95
Fredericksburg
3
Fredericksburg and Spotsylvania National Military Park
208
218
2
17
Fort A.P. Hill
301
RICHMOND

MARYLAND
TO BALTIMORE
29
1
270
95
95 495
DISTRICT OF COLUMBIA
50
Washington
Arlington
Newseum
Arlington National Cemetery
I-395
Ronald Reagan Washington National Airport
400
I-495
Alexandria
The Pentagon
Torpedo Factory Art Center
Capital Beltway
1
95
Pope-Leighey House
Woodlawn
235
Mount Vernon
Fort Belvoir
Gunston Hall
301
301
Rappahannock River
3
George Washington's Birthplace National Monument
Wakefield Corner
204
STRATFORD HALL
IRVINGTON
CHRIST CHURCH

0   10 miles
0   15 km

George Washington frequented the buildings housing the **Stabler-Leadbeater Apothecary Museum** (✉ 105 S. Fairfax St., ☎ 703/836–3713; 🖾 $2.50) and **Gadsby's Tavern Museum** (✉ 134 N. Royal St., ☎ 703/838–4242; 🖾 $4). He also frequented **Christ Church** (✉ 118 N. Washington St., ☎ 703/549–1450; 🖾 free). Another member (or "pewholder") of Christ Church was Robert E. Lee; the **boyhood home of Robert E. Lee** (✉ 607 Oronoco St., ☎ 703/548–8454; 🖾 $4) is about three blocks from Christ Church.

Alexandria's cultural heritage is honored at the **Lyceum** (✉ 201 S. Washington St., ☎ 703/838–4994), with displays of decorative arts and exhibits on local history. The **Torpedo Factory Art Center** (✉ 105 N. Union St., ☎ 703/838–4565) is a former munitions plant that now houses the workshops and galleries of about 160 professional artists. Both sites have free admission.

Farther away but visible from a distance is the 333-ft-high **George Washington Masonic National Memorial** (✉ 101 Callahan Dr., ☎ 703/683–2007; 🖾 free). Here you'll see relics of the first president and exhibits on the Masonic Order. At the top, there's a spectacular view of Alexandria and Washington, D.C., 6 mi away.

★ The **Newseum,** the world's only museum dedicated exclusively to news, features exhibits that trace the evolution of journalism. Multimedia galleries allow visitors to try their hand at TV anchoring and radio broadcasts. Adjacent to the museum is **Freedom Park,** which honors journalists who have died in the line of duty. ✉ *1101 Wilson Blvd., Arlington,* ☎ *703/284–3544 or 888/639–7386.* 🖾 *Free. Closed Mon. and Tues.* ✍

For information on **Arlington National Cemetery** and the **Pentagon,** *see* Washington, D.C.

Fredericksburg, about an hour south of Washington, D.C., has numerous sites of interest including the town's 40-block National Historic District, which contains more than 350 original 18th- and 19th-century buildings. Fredericksburg rivals Alexandria and Mount Vernon for associations with the Washington family. From ages 6 to 20 the future first president lived at Ferry Farm across the Rappahannock River from Fredericksburg. For information about Washington family sites as well as the other venues in and around the town, go to the **Fredericksburg Visitor Center.** Beyond the usual booklets, pamphlets, and maps, this visitor center has money-saving passes to city attractions and parking. Before beginning your tour, you may want to see the center's 10-minute orientation slide show. (The center building itself was constructed in 1824 as a residence and confectionery; during the Civil War it was used as a prison.) ✉ *706 Caroline St.,* ☎ *540/373–1776 or 800/678–4748.*

Washington's sister Betty and her husband lived at **Kenmore** (✉ 1201 Washington Ave., ☎ 540/373–3381; 🖾 $6), a house whose simple, brick facade and slate roof belie a lavish interior. The home of Charles Washington, George's brother, later became the **Rising Sun Tavern** (✉ 1306 Caroline St., ☎ 540/371–1494; 🖾 $4), a watering hole for such revolutionaries as Patrick Henry and Thomas Jefferson. The **Mary Washington House** (✉ 1200 Charles St., ☎ 540/373–1569; 🖾 $4) is a modest house George bought for his mother during her last years.

The fifth president once lived in Fredericksburg, and the **James Monroe Museum and Memorial Library** (✉ 908 Charles St., ☎ 540/654–1043; 🖾 $4) is in the tiny one-story building where he practiced law from 1787 to 1789.

At the **Hugh Mercer Apothecary Shop** (⊠ 1020 Caroline St., ☎ 540/ 373–3362; ⌑ $4), the guide's explicit descriptions of amputations, cataract operations, and tooth extractions can make latter-day visitors wince.

★ **Fredericksburg Area Museum and Cultural Center.** The museum's six permanent exhibits tell the story of the area from prehistoric times through the Revolutionary and Civil wars to the present. Displays include dinosaur footprints from a nearby quarry, Native American artifacts, and Confederate memorabilia. The museum is in an 1816 building once used as a market and town hall. ⊠ *907 Princess Anne St.,* ☎ *540/371–3037.* ⌑ *$4.*

★ **Fredericksburg/Spotsylvania National Military Park.** The park includes four battlefields and three historic buildings, all accessible for a single admission price. In season, park rangers lead walking tours. The centers offer tape-recorded tour cassettes and maps that show how to reach hiking trails at the Wilderness, Chancellorsville, and Spotsylvania Court House battlefields (all within 15 mi of Fredericksburg). ⊠ *Fredericksburg Battlefield Visitor Center, Lafayette Blvd. and Sunken Rd.,* ☎ *540/373–6122; Chancellorsville Battlefield Visitor Center, Rte. 3 W (Plank Road),* ☎ *540/786–2880.* ⌑ *$3 (includes all 4 battlefields, Chatham Manor, and other historic buildings; valid for 1 wk; children 16 and under free).*

Twenty-six miles west of Washington is the monumentally important **Manassas National Battlefield Park,** or Bull Run (⊠ 12521 Lee Hwy., north of I–66, Exit 47, ☎ 703/361–1339, ⌑ $2), where the Confederacy won two major victories and Stonewall Jackson earned his nickname.

About an hour west of Washington is horse country. In **Loudoun County**'s fashionable towns of **Leesburg** and **Middleburg,** well-heeled residents (many of them Yankee transplants) keep up the local traditions of fox hunts and steeplechases. The Tourism Council in Leesburg (☞ Visitor Information, *above*) can suggest scenic drives.

The 1,200-acre mansion at **Morven Park** (⊠ Old Waterford Rd., take Morven Park Road, 1 mi north of Leesburg), ☎ 703/771–6034; ⌑ $6), a White House look-alike and last home of Governor Westmoreland Davis, contains two museums: one of horse-drawn carriages, the other of hounds and hunting.

Dining and Lodging

Alexandria's restaurants are varied and, on weekend nights, crowded. Arlington has several Latin American restaurants throughout the county. Little Saigon, on and around Wilson Boulevard, has several affordable Vietnamese restaurants.

Bed-and-breakfasts tend to be more expensive here because many serve as romantic weekend hideaways for regular customers from Washington. The state of Virginia provides information about bed-and-breakfasts, including lists and brochures (☎ 800/262–1293), and operates a reservation service (☎ 800/934–9184).

Alexandria

$$$–$$$$ ✕ **La Bergerie.** This Old Town restaurant serves food of the Basque
★ region of France. Offerings include duck confit and Parillade of Seafood (assorted seafood in light garlic tomato sauce), Galette Basque (almond tart with Sabayon sauce), and raspberry soufflé. ⊠ *218 Lee St.,* ☎ *703/ 683–1007,* 𝔽𝔸𝕏 *703/519–6114. AE, DC, MC, V. Closed Sun.*

$$-$$$ ✕ **Warehouse Bar and Grill.** Framed caricatures of the rich and famous decorate the walls in this restaurant on the main street of Alexandria's historic district. Across the street from Ramsay House—Alexandria's visitor center—they serve a variety of seafood, beef, and Virginia specialties. ✉ *214 King St.,* ☎ *703/683–6868. AE, D, DC, MC, V.*

$-$$ ✕ **Aegean Taverna.** Parking is free and easy at this restaurant near the
★ center of the Clarendon district, one block from Wilson Boulevard. They serve excellent, authentic Greek food, including favorites like pastit-sio, moussaka, and spinach pie. There's dining outside in good weather. Greek musicians perform Friday and Saturday nights. ✉ *2950 Claren-don Blvd.,* ☎ *703/841–9494. AE, D, DC, MC, V.*

$$$$ ✕🏨 **Morrison House.** Though established in 1985, this small hotel was
★ built in a traditional Federal style. Inside, the tasteful ruse continues with reproductions of antiques and fireplaces of the period. Amenities, though, are fully modern. The Elysium restaurant serves a mix of American, traditional French, and southwestern meals. ✉ *116 S. Alfred St., 22314,* ☎ *703/838–8000 or 800/367–0800,* 🖷 *703/684–6283. 45 rooms. 2 restaurants. AE, DC, MC, V.* 🐾

$$$ 🏨 **Holiday Inn Select Old Town.** Marble bathtubs, modem-ready phones, and extraordinary service—an exercise bike will be brought to your room on request—make this an exceptional member of the chain. Bicycles are available for guests, and free shuttle service to the airport and the Metro is provided. ✉ *480 King St., 22314,* ☎ *703/549–6080 or 800/368–5047,* 🖷 *703/684–6508. 227 rooms. Restaurant, pool, exercise room. AE, D, DC, MC, V.* 🐾

Arlington

$-$$ ✕ **Queen Bee.** Arlington's Little Saigon area has several good Vietnamese
★ restaurants; this is one of the best. Moist and delicately flavored spring rolls and the Saigon pancake—accented with a mix of crab, pork, and shrimp—are two reasons that diners are willing to wait for a table. ✉ *3181 Wilson Blvd.,* ☎ *703/527–3444,* 🖷 *703/525–2750. AE, MC, V.*

$$$$ 🏨 **Ritz-Carlton Pentagon City.** This 18-story Ritz-Carlton at the Pen-
★ tagon City Metro stop is more convenient to downtown Washington than many D.C. hotels. Public spaces are full of 18th- and 19th-century art and antiques. Many rooms have views of the monuments across the river. The lobby is connected with the Pentagon City Fashion Centre mall. ✉ *1250 S. Hayes St., 22202,* ☎ *703/415–5000 or 800/241–3333,* 🖷 *703/415–5060. 366 rooms. Restaurant, bar, pool, health club. AE, DC, MC, V.* 🐾

$ 🏨 **Travelodge Cherry Blossom.** This economical, three-story lodging is less than 2 mi from the Pentagon and two Metro stations. Local calls, HBO, and microwave ovens on request are included. Rooms with kitchenettes are available. The Rincome, a Thai restaurant, is on the premises, but there are many nearby restaurants. ✉ *3030 Columbia Pike, Arlington, VA 22204,* ☎ *703/521–5570,* 🖷 *703/271–0081. 76 rooms. Restaurant, exercise room. AE, D, DC, MC, V. CP.* 🐾

Fredericksburg

$$-$$$ ✕ **La Petite Auberge.** Housed in a prerevolutionary brick general store, this restaurant actually has three dining rooms in varied decor and a small bar. They specialize in house-cut beef, French onion soup, and seafood with a Continental accent. The proprietors speak French and Spanish. A prix-fixe ($14) three-course dinner is served from 5:30 to 7 Monday–Thursday. ✉ *311 William St.,* ☎ *540/371–2727. AE, D, MC, V. Closed Sun.*

$$-$$$ 🏨 **Richard Johnston Inn.** This elegant B&B was constructed in the late 1700s and served as the home of Richard Johnston, mayor of Fredericksburg (1809–10). Guest rooms—each with a private bath—are decorated with period antiques and reproductions. The inn is just across

from the visitor center and two blocks from the train station. ✉ *711 Caroline St., 22401,* ☎ *540/899–7606. 8 rooms. AE, MC, V.* ✍

$ 🏨 **Fredericksburg Colonial Inn.** This 1920s motel with cream-color brick and green awnings conceals a lobby staircase reminiscent of the one in *Gone with the Wind*'s Tara. Indeed, rooms are furnished with authentic antiques and appointments from the Civil War period. No-smoking. ✉ *1707 Princess Anne St., 22401,* ☎ *540/371–5666,* ℻ *540/371–5884. 30 rooms. CP. AE, MC, V.* ✍

$ 🏨 **Hampton Inn.** This may be a typical chain motel, but it's neat and clean, and the extensive Continental breakfast is complimentary. Because it's on a main artery in a busy retail area, ask for a room facing the interior courtyard. Several restaurants are a short walk away. ✉ *2310 William St. (Exit 130-A off I–95) 22401,* ☎ *540/371–0330,* ℻ *540/371–1753. 166 rooms. Pool. AE, D, DC, MC, V.* ✍

Great Falls

$$$–$$$$ ✕ **L'Auberge Chez François.** White stucco, dark exposed beams, and
★ a garden just outside create a country-inn ambience 20 minutes from Tysons Corner. The Alsatian cuisine includes salmon soufflé with salmon-and-scallop mousse and lobster sauce. ✉ *332 Springvale Rd., Rte. 674,* ☎ *703/759–3800. Jacket and tie. AE, D, DC, MC, V. Closed Mon. No lunch.*

Middleburg

$$$ ✕🏨 **Red Fox Inn.** This handsome fieldstone tavern in Middleburg's center has been in operation since 1728. Its cozy rooms are furnished in an 18th-century manner, with antique four-poster beds and period wallpaper; some have fireplaces. The restaurant ($$–$$$) serves Continental cuisine, from crab and artichoke casserole to filet mignon. ✉ *2 E. Washington St., 22117,* ☎ *540/687–6301 or 800/223–1728,* ℻ *540/687–6187. 24 rooms. Restaurant. AE, MC, V.* ✍

Nightlife and the Arts

Nightlife

The **Birchmere** (✉ 3701 Mount Vernon Ave., Alexandria, ☎ 703/549–7500) hosts nationally known bluegrass, acoustic, and folk music acts. **Two Nineteen** (✉ 219 King St., Alexandria, ☎ 703/549–1141) has jazz nightly Tuesday through Saturday.

The Arts

George Mason University (☎ 703/993–2787) has several concert halls and stages that offer a full range of entertainment, from ballet and drama performances to opera and pop music concerts and sporting events. **Wolf Trap Farm Park** (✉ 1551 Trap Rd., Vienna, ☎ 703/255–1860) presents top musical and dance performers in a grand outdoor pavilion during the warmer months and in the **Barns**, 18th-century farm buildings the rest of the year (✉ 1635 Trap Rd., ☎ 703/938–2404). The facility also hosts many children's activities, including mime, puppet, and animal shows.

Outdoor Activities and Sports

Biking

The 19-mi **Mount Vernon Bicycle Trail** runs along the Potomac, from Rosslyn to Mount Vernon and through Alexandria. The Arlington Parks and Recreation Bureau (☎ 703/228–4747) will mail a free map of the county **Bikeway System.**

Golf

Burke Lake Park (✉ Fairfax Station, ☎ 703/323–1641) and **Penderbrook** (✉ 3700 Golf Trail La., Fairfax, ☎ 703/385–3700) have public courses.

Water Sports

Belle Haven Marina (⊠ George Washington Pkwy., south of Old Town Alexandria, ☎ 703/768–0018) rents canoes, board sailers, and three different types of sailboats and provides lessons on the Potomac River.

Shopping

Potomac Mills Mall (⊠ 2700 Potomac Mills Circle, I–95, Dale City) is the state's most visited attraction; Swedish furniture giant IKEA is one of 220 outlets. **Tysons Corner Center** (⊠ 1961 Chain Bridge Rd., junction of Rtes. 7 and 123 and I–495) houses 240 retailers, including Bloomingdale's and Nordstrom. **Galleria at Tysons II** (⊠ 2001 International Dr.) has 125 retailers, including Saks Fifth Avenue and Neiman Marcus. The old towns of Alexandria and Fredericksburg are dense with **antiques** shops, many quite expensive, that are particularly strong on the Federal and Victorian periods. The town visitor centers (☞ Visitor Information, *above*) have maps and lists of the stores.

RICHMOND AND TIDEWATER

Tidewater Virginia is the eastern region affected by the tides of the Atlantic and the Chesapeake Bay. But "Tidewater" also has broader connotations, summoning images of the genteel Old South. Although Richmond is about 70 mi up the James River from the Chesapeake Bay, it is the heart of Tidewater gentility. Richmond lies at the fall line—the point on the James River beyond which further ship traffic upriver is not possible. Bridging the flat, swampy Tidewater and hilly Piedmont regions, it also bridges Virginia's past and present, with remnants of the Confederacy preserved in the midst of the urgent commercial bustle of a modern state capital. An hour southeast are two former capitals: Colonial Williamsburg, a restored 18th-century town, and Jamestown, Virginia's original capital, long deserted and all the more stirring for it. With Yorktown, where the Colonies won their independence, these prerevolutionary towns form the Historic Triangle. On the nearby Northern Neck—which cradles the birthplaces of George Washington and Robert E. Lee—visitors can combine historic sightseeing with fishing, water sports, and excursions to interesting residential islands in the Chesapeake Bay.

Visitor Information

Metro Richmond: Visitors centers (⊠ 1710 Robin Hood Rd., Exit 78 off I–95/I–64, 23220, ☎ 804/358–5511, 804/782–2777, or 800/365–7272, Bell Tower at Capitol Sq., 9th and Franklin Sts., 23219, ☎ 804/648–3146); for mailed information, write to 6th St. Marketplace (⊠ 550 E. Marshall St., 23219, ☎ 804/358–5511, 804/782–2777, or 800/370–9004, FAX 804/780–2577. **Northern Neck:** Visitor Information Service (⊠ Box 312, Reedville 22539, ☎ 800/453–6167). **Petersburg:** Visitors Center (⊠ 425 Cockade Alley, 23803, ☎ 804/733–2400 or 800/368–3595). **Williamsburg:** Convention and Visitors Bureau (⊠ 201 Penniman Rd., Box 3583, 23185, ☎ 757/253–0192 or 800/368–6511, FAX 757/229–2047). **Colonial Williamsburg** (⊠ Box 1776, 23187-1776, ☎ 757/220–7645 or 800/447–8679). **Yorktown:** Jamestown–Yorktown Foundation (⊠ Dept. BC, Box 1607, Williamsburg 23187, ☎ 757/253–4838 or 888/593–4682).

Arriving and Departing

By Bus

Greyhound (☎ 800/231–2222) serves Richmond (⊠ 2910 N. Boulevard), Petersburg (⊠ 108 E. Washington St.), and Williamsburg (⊠ 468 N. Boundary St.). There is no bus service to the Northern Neck.

By Car

Richmond is at the intersection of I–95 and I–64; U.S. 1 runs north–south by the city. Petersburg is 20 mi south of Richmond on I–95. Route 3 runs the length of the Northern Neck. Williamsburg is 51 mi east of Richmond via I–64; the Colonial Parkway joins it with Jamestown and Yorktown.

By Plane

Richmond International Airport (☎ 804/226–3000) is served by several major airlines. **Newport News–Williamsburg International Airport** (☎ 757/877–0924), in Newport News, and **Norfolk International Airport** (☎ 757/857–3351) also serve the region.

By Train

Amtrak (☎ 800/872–7245) serves **Richmond** (✉ 7519 Staples Mill Rd.), Petersburg (✉ 3516 South St.), and **Williamsburg** (✉ 468 N. Boundary St.).

Exploring Richmond and Tidewater

Richmond

Most of Richmond's historic attractions lie north of the James River, which bisects the city in a sweeping curve. West of downtown is the **Fan District,** so named because the streets fan out from downtown Richmond. The neighborhood has been restored and architecturally diverse turn-of-the-20th-century town houses abound. Its grandest street is Monument Avenue, a wide and leafy boulevard of stately homes lined with equally imposing statues of Civil War notables and other heroes.

The heart of old Richmond is the **Court End District,** which contains seven National Historic Landmarks, three museums, and 11 more buildings on the National Register of Historic Places—all within eight blocks. At either of the following museums you will receive a self-guided walking tour with the purchase of a discount block ticket ($15), good for all admission fees in this district. The 1790 **John Marshall House** (✉ 9th and Marshall Sts., ☎ 804/648–7998; 🎫 $3), one of the Court End museums, was the home of the early U.S. chief justice. The **Museum and White House of the Confederacy** (✉ 1201 E. Clay St., ☎ 804/649–1861, 🎫 $8) was the official residence of Confederate president Jefferson Davis. Adjacent to this 1818 house is the museum, which claims to have the world's largest collection of Confederate memorabilia.

★ The **Virginia State Capitol** (✉ Capitol Sq., ☎ 804/698–1788; 🎫 free), designed by Thomas Jefferson in 1785, contains a life-size statue of George Washington by Houdon, the only existing work for which he posed.

In the Church Hill Historic District, east of downtown, is **St. John's Episcopal Church** (✉ 2401 E. Broad St., ☎ 804/648–5015; 🎫 free). It was here on March 23, 1775, that Patrick Henry demanded of the Second Virginia Convention: "Give me liberty or give me death!"

The visitor center for **Richmond National Battlefield Park** (✉ 3215 E. Broad St., ☎ 804/226–1981; 🎫 free) provides a movie and a slide show about the three campaigns fought here, as well as maps for a self-guided tour.

ⓒ West of downtown you'll find the newly renovated **Science Museum of Virginia,** which was originally the Broad Street train station. People of all ages have fun engaging in hundreds of hands-on exhibits on everything from life sciences and biological timing to aerospace and undersea exploration. The Ethyl IMAX®DOME and Planetarium features giant screen films and planetarium shows. ✉ *2500 W. Broad St.,*

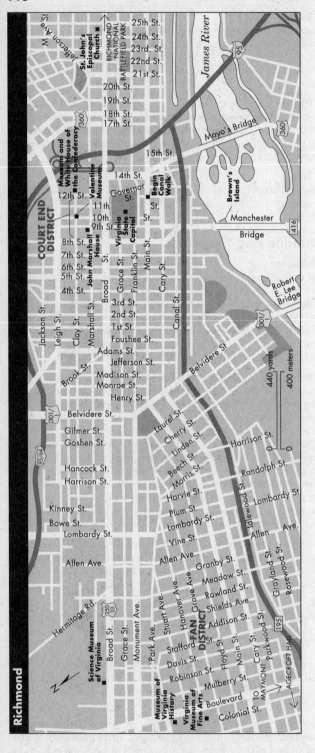

Richmond

James River

25th St.
24th St.
23rd. St.
22nd St.
21st St.
20th St.
19th St.
18th St.
17th St.
15th St.
14th St.

Jefferson Ave. St.

St. John's
Episcopal
Church

RICHMOND
NATIONAL
BATTLEFIELD PARK

360

Mayo's Bridge

360

Museum and White House of the Confederacy

Valentine Museum

Governor St.

Begin Canal Walk

Brown's Island

Manchester

12th St.
11th
10th
9th St.
8th St.
7th St.
6th St.
5th St.
4th St.
3rd St.
2nd St.
1st St.

COURT END DISTRICT

John Marshall House

Virginia State Capitol

Broad St.

Grace St.

Franklin St.

Main St.

Cary St.

Canal St.

Bridge

416

Robert
E. Lee
Bridge

301

Jackson St.
Leigh St.
Clay St.
Marshall St.
Brook St.

Foushee St.
Adams St.
Jefferson St.
Madison St.
Monroe St.
Henry St.

Belvidere St.
Gilmer St.
Goshen St.

Hancock St.
Harrison St.

Kinney St.
Bowe St.
Lombardy St.

Allen Ave.

301

95/64

Belvidere St.

Laurel St.
Cherry St.
Linden St.
Beech St.
Morris St.

Harvie St.

Plum St.

Lombardy St.

Vine St.

Allen Ave.

440 yards
400 meters

Harrison St.

Randolph St.

Idlewood St.

Lombardy St

Allen Ave.

Granby St.
Meadow St.
Rowland St.
Shields Ave.
Addison St.

Grayland St.
Rosewood St.

Hermitage Rd.

150
33

Science Museum of Virginia

Broad St.
Grace St.
Monument Ave.

Park Ave.
Stuart Ave.
Hanover Ave.
Grove Ave.

Stafford Ave.
Davis Ave.

Robinson St.

Museum of Virginia History

Virginia Museum of Fine Arts

FAN DISTRICT

Floyd St.
Main St.

Mulberry St.

Boulevard

Colonial St.

Cary St.

195

TO MAYMONT
Parkwood St.

AGECROFT HALL

☎ *804/367–6552 or 800/659–1727.* ☜ *Exhibits $5; exhibits and film $9–$10.*

★ Aptly situated in the heart of the artsy Fan District is the **Virginia Museum of Fine Arts,** whose diverse collections include art nouveau, Art Deco, Indian, Roman, Asian, contemporary, impressionist, British sporting art, and five Fabergé eggs. ⊠ *2800 Grove Ave. at the Boulevard,* ☎ *804/367–0844.* ☜ *$4 suggested donation. Closed Mon.*

Just southwest of the Fan District stands **Agecroft Hall** (⊠ 4305 Sulgrave Rd., ☎ 804/353–4241, ☜ $5), a 15th-century English house rescued from destruction and reassembled here in 1926. Formal gardens surround the manor, which is extensively furnished with Tudor and early Stuart art and furniture.

☾ North of Richmond, the 100-plus rides at **Paramount's Kings Dominion** include simulated white-water rafting and 10 roller coasters. ⊠ *I–95 Doswell Exit 98,* ☎ *804/876–5000.* ☜ *$32, plus $5 for parking. Closed Nov.–Mar.*

Petersburg

Twenty miles south of Richmond on I–95 lies **Petersburg,** the so-called last ditch of the Confederacy: Its siege in 1865 led to the fall of Richmond and the surrender at Appomattox. At **Petersburg National Battlefield** (⊠ Washington St., off Rte. 36, ☎ 804/732–3531; ☜ $4 for cars, $2 for bicycles and pedestrians) you can tread the ground where 70,000 soldiers died. The 1,500-acre park, laced with miles of earth-

★ works, includes two forts. The **Pamplin Historical Park** (⊠ 6125 Boydton Plank Rd., off U.S. 1, Petersburg, ☎ 804/861–2408, ☜ $10), where Union troops successfully penetrated General Robert E. Lee's defense line, includes an interpretive center and the **Museum of the Civil War Soldier,** as well as a 2-mi-long battle trail, reconstructed soldier huts, and an 1812 plantation home.

In Old Town Petersburg the Civil War is examined from a local perspective at the **Siege Museum** (⊠ 15 W. Bank St., ☎ 804/733–2404; ☜ $3). Outstanding relics of antebellum Petersburg include the eccentric **Trapezium House** (⊠ 244 N. Market St., ☎ 804/733–2404; ☜ $3), built with no right angles. The prerevolutionary **Blanford Church** (⊠ 319 S. Crater Rd., ☎ 804/733–2396; ☜ $3) is today a Confederate shrine. Behind the church through an archway is the memorial area where 30,000 southern dead are buried. The church's 15 stained-glass Tiffany windows are memorials donated by Confederate states.

Northern Neck

Route 3 east of Fredericksburg takes you into the **Northern Neck,** a narrow peninsula bounded by the Potomac and Rappahannock rivers. At the top of the Neck is Westmoreland County, which produced both the Father of Our Country and one of the greatest tragic heroes of the Civil War, Robert E. Lee. **George Washington's Birthplace National Monument** (⊠ Rte. 3, ☎ 804/224–1732; ☜ $2), in Oak Grove, preserves the memory of the first president with a working farm and a reproduction of the original early 18th-century plantation house (the original burned down on Christmas Day 1779). Washington's family members are buried on the property.

Stratford Hall (⊠ Rte. 214, off Rte. 3, Stratford, ☎ 804/493–8038; ☜ $7) is the birthplace of Robert E. Lee. It is a massive Georgian built in the 1730s by Lee's grandfather, Colonel Thomas Lee. Farmers still cultivate 1,600 of the original acres, and their yield, a variety of cereals, is for sale. Lunch is served in a log cabin from April through October.

At the far end of the Northern Neck is a jewel of Tidewater architecture: Irvington's **Christ Church** (✉ junction of Rtes. 646 and 709, ☎ 804/438–6855; ☞ free), a redbrick sanctuary of cruciform design, built in 1735.

Water Sports

The Northern Neck gives sailors, water-skiers, and windsurfers access to two rivers and the Chesapeake Bay. For information contact the **Northern Neck Tourism Council** (☎ 804/453–6303 or 800/393–6180).

The James River Plantations

Southeast of Richmond on Route 5, along the north bank of the James River, lie four historical plantations. **Shirley** (✉ 501 Shirley Plantation Rd., ☎ 804/232–1613; ☞ $7.50), the oldest plantation in Virginia, has belonged to the same family, the Carters, for 10 generations. The plantation was founded in 1613, six years after the English landed at Jamestown. The 1723 Georgian manor is filled with family silver, ancestral portraits, and rare books.

The **Berkeley** plantation (✉ Rte. 5, ☎ 804/829–6018; ☞ $8.50) is the birthplace of Benjamin Harrison, a signer of the Declaration of Independence, and William Henry Harrison, the short-termed ninth president. The 1726 Georgian brick house has been restored and furnished with period antiques, and the boxwood gardens are well tended. In addition to a restaurant, there are outdoor tables for picnickers.

At 300 ft, **Sherwood Forest** (✉ Rte. 5, ☎ 804/829–5377; ☞ $8.50 house, $3 grounds) may be the longest frame house in the country. The circa 1730 house was the retirement home of John Tyler, the 10th U.S. president, and remains in his family. The house, furnished with heirloom antiques, and the five outbuildings are open daily.

The Historic Triangle

★ ☾ **Colonial Williamsburg** (✉ I–64, Exits 238 and 242, ☎ 757/220–7645 or 800/447–8679, ☞ $30 for an all-day pass, which allows admission to multiple sights) is a marvel: a tidy, sanitized, but otherwise convincing re-creation of the city that was the capital of Virginia from 1699 until 1780. The restoration project, financed by John D. Rockefeller Jr., began in 1926; the work of archaeologists and historians of the Colonial Williamsburg Foundation continues to this day. An extensive packet of information is available (☞ Visitor Information, *above*).

On Colonial Williamsburg's 173 acres, 88 original 18th- and early 19th-century structures, such as the **Courthouse,** have been painstakingly restored; another 50, including the **Capitol** and the **Governor's Palace,** were reconstructed on their original sites.

All year hundreds of costumed interpreters, wearing bonnets or three-cornered hats, rove and ride through the cobblestone streets. Dozens of craftspeople (also "in character"), such as the shoemaker and gunsmith, demonstrate and explain their trades inside their workshops; their wares are for sale nearby. The restored area must be toured on foot, as all vehicles are banned between 8 AM and 6 PM. Free shuttle buses (available to ticket holders only) run continually to and from the visitor center and around the edge of the restored area. Vehicles for visitors with disabilities are permitted by prior arrangement.

Anchoring the western end of the restored area and part of the campus of the College of William and Mary is the 1695 **Sir Christopher Wren Building** (✉ College of William and Mary, ☎ 757/221–4000; ☞ free), the oldest college building in the country. Designed by the celebrated London architect that bears its name, this redbrick edifice has survived two wars and three fires and still houses classrooms and faculty offices.

Add another dimension to the Colonial experience by visiting the **De-Witt Wallace Decorative Arts Gallery** (⌧ Francis St., ☎ 757/220–7724; ⌸ $11 or free with day pass), which houses a vast and varied collection of English and American decorative arts from 1600 to 1830. Prized among this 8,000-piece collection is the full-length portrait of George Washington by Charles Willson Peale. Enter through the Public Hospital.

☝ East of Williamsburg is **Busch Gardens Williamsburg.** Rides include an especially fast and steep roller coaster as well as other traditional rides. Nine re-creations of European and French Canadian hamlets present the cuisine and entertainment of different countries. ⌧ *U.S. 60,* ☎ *757/253–3350.* ⌸ *$37. Closed Dec.–Mar.*

Jamestown Island (⌧ Colonial Pkwy., ☎ 757/229–1733; ⌸ $5), site of the first permanent English settlement in North America (1607) and the capital of Virginia until 1699, is now uninhabited. Foundation walls show the layout of the settlement, and push-button audio stations narrate the local history. A 5-mi nature drive ringing the island is posted with historical markers.

☝ Adjacent to Jamestown Island is **Jamestown Settlement** (⌧ Rte. 31 off Colonial Pkwy., ☎ 757/229–1607; ⌸ $9.75; $13.50 combination ticket with the Yorktown Victory Center), a living-history museum with a reconstructed fort staffed by docents dressed as colonists and an "Indian village" inhabited by buckskin-clad interpreters. At the pier are full-scale replicas of the *Godspeed,* the *Discovery,* and the *Susan Constant,* the ships that carried the settlers to the New World.

In 1781, American and French forces surrounded British troops and forced an end to the American War of Independence at **Yorktown Battlefield** (⌧ Colonial Pkwy., ☎ 757/898–3400; ⌸ $4). Today the museum here displays George Washington's original field tent; dioramas, illuminated maps, and a short movie tell the story. You can rent the taped audio tour and explore the battlefield by car or join a ranger-led walking tour.

☝ The **Yorktown Victory Center** (⌧ Rte. 238 off Colonial Pkwy., ☎ 757/253–4838 or 888/593–4682; ⌸ $7.25; $13.50 combination ticket with Jamestown Settlement), next door to the Yorktown Battlefield, consists of a Continental Army encampment, with tents, a covered wagon, and interpreters—costumed as soldiers or female auxiliaries—who speak to visitors in the regional dialects of the time. Also on site are a small working tobacco farm and a museum focusing on the experience of ordinary people during the Revolutionary War.

Unlike Jamestown, **Yorktown** remains a living community, albeit a tiny one. Its **Main Street** is lined with preserved 18th-century buildings on a bluff overlooking the York River. The elegant **Nelson House** (☎ 757/898–3400 for Nelson and Moore houses; ⌸ $4 for Nelson and Moore houses) was the residence of a Virginia governor and signer of the Declaration of Independence. Along the Battlefield Tour Road is **Moore House,** where the terms of surrender were negotiated. Nelson and Moore houses are both open for tours daily in summer and weekends in spring and fall.

Dining and Lodging

The established upmarket dining rooms of Richmond compare favorably with those in cities renowned for their restaurants. The luxurious trappings and innovative menus here are pricy but not nearly so much as in larger cities. Additionally, favorite local haunts offer delicious meals at moderate prices—especially in the Fan District just west of the downtown area and in Shockoe, an in-vogue renovated warehouse area east of the Capitol and near the James River. Richmond's hotel rates are slightly below those of big eastern cities and accommodations vary from pre–Civil War historic properties to ultramodern glass towers. In Williamsburg, dining rooms within walking distance of the restored area are often crowded, and reservations are advised—mandatory some months in advance for the historic taverns. The Colonial capital of Virginia has a greater range of lodging options for the money, but there will be fewer choices at the height of the summer tourist season.

Richmond

\$\$–\$\$\$\$ ✕ **The Frog and the Redneck.** The daily-changing menu is an adven-
★ turous cross of modern French and American cuisine. Local products are incorporated into the innovative offerings, which include seafood, exotic meats and poultry, and vegetables. ⊠ *1423 E. Cary St.,* ☎ *804/ 648–3764. Reservations essential. AE, MC, V. Closed Sun. No lunch.*

\$\$–\$\$\$ ✕ **Amici Ristorante.** Homemade pasta, breads, and desserts, and seafood and game specialties appear regularly on a menu with a range of authentic northern Italian dishes. Flowered tapestries and oil paintings of Italy create a cozy mood, and alfresco dining is available at this Carytown eatery. ⊠ *3343 W. Cary St.,* ☎ *804/353–4700. AE, MC, V. Closed Mon. No lunch Sun. and Tues.*

\$–\$\$ ✕ **Siné Irish Pub and Restaurant.** A recent addition to Richmond's Shockoe Slip, this Irish pub and restaurant serves lunch and dinner daily. There is an old-fashioned bar surrounded by booths and pub tables to enjoy traditional Irish dishes and a variety of other choices. ⊠ *1327 E. Cary St.,* ☎ *804/649–7767. AE, DC, MC, V.*

\$\$–\$\$\$ ✕☶ **Mr. Patrick Henry's.** Two houses circa 1858 were restored and joined
★ to create this restaurant and inn, where the three suites each have a fireplace. Antiques and fireplaces in the dining room contribute to the Colonial ambience. Menu favorites include crab cakes and crisp roast duck with bing cherry sauce. Breakfast is included for inn guests. ⊠ *2300 E. Broad St., 23223,* ☎ *804/644–1322 or 800/932–2654. 3 suites. Restaurant. AE, D, DC, MC, V. Closed Sun. No lunch Sat.*

\$\$\$–\$\$\$\$ ☶ **Jefferson Hotel.** This 1895 National Historic Landmark retains an
★ opulence matched by no other hotel in Richmond. The guest rooms have poster beds and reproduction 19th-century furnishings. In 1999, a new indoor heated pool was added and Lemaire, the hotel's beautiful dining room, was expanded with a glassed area. ⊠ *Franklin and Adams Sts., 23220,* ☎ *804/788–8000 or 800/424–8014,* FAX *804/225– 0334. 275 rooms. 2 restaurants, health club. AE, D, DC, MC, V.* ♻

\$\$\$ ☶ **Tides Inn.** At this 500-acre waterfront resort on a tributary in the Northern Neck, all the rooms have water views. Guests can take a dinner or luncheon cruise on one of the inn's two yachts and have access to a nearby fitness center. ⊠ *480 King Carter Dr., Irvington 22480,* ☎ *804/438–5000 or 800/843–3746,* FAX *804/438–5222. 194 rooms. 5 restaurants, 2 pools, golf, tennis. MAP. AE, D, DC, MC, V.* ♻

\$\$–\$\$\$ ☶ **Commonwealth Park Suites Hotel.** The original hostelry on this site
★ burned down during the Civil War battle for Richmond and was rebuilt around 1896 as a 10-story hotel. The refurbished building with its spacious suites-only lodgings, just across the street from the capitol and its magnolia-filled park, has the atmosphere of a small European-style hotel. Still, its reproduction 18th-century mahogany furniture, museum prints, and brass chandeliers confirm that you are in a southern state. ⊠ *901 Bank St., 23219,* ☎ *804/343–7300,* FAX *804/343–1025. 51 suites. Restaurant. AE, D, DC, MC, V.*

\$\$ ☶ **Linden Row Inn.** This handsome inn, on the National Register of
★ Historic Places, is composed of a row of restored 1840s Greek Revival

town houses. Guest rooms have high ceilings, tall windows, and 19th-century furnishings throughout. There is complimentary transportation anywhere within 3 mi. ⊠ *100 E. Franklin St., 23219,* ☎ *804/783–7000 or 800/348–7424,* ﬀﬄ *804/648–7504. 71 rooms. Restaurant. AE, D, DC, MC, V.*

Williamsburg

$$–$$$ ╳ **Le Yaca.** This country-French dining room is done in soft pastels with hardwood floors, candlelight, and a central open fireplace. Four prix-fixe menus include such specialties as leg of lamb with rosemary garlic sauce. ⊠ *1915 Pocahontas Trail,* ☎ *757/220–3616. AE, DC, MC, V. Closed Sun. and early Jan. No lunch Mon.*

$$–$$$ ╳ **The Trellis.** Hardwood floors, ceramic tiles, and green plants evoke
★ Napa Valley, setting the mood for world-class American cuisine. Save room for Death by Chocolate: seven layers of chocolate topped with cream sauce. ⊠ *Merchants Sq.,* ☎ *757/229–8610. AE, MC, V.*

$$$$ ╳▥ **Williamsburg Inn.** This is the grandest local hotel, built in 1937
★ and decorated in English Regency style. At the hotel's esteemed Regency Room restaurant, crystal chandeliers, Asian silk-screen prints, and full silver service set the tone. Chateaubriand is carved tableside; other specialties are lobster bisque and rich ice-cream desserts. Reservations for the restaurant are essential; jacket and tie are required for dinner and Sunday brunch. Hotel guests are entertained with croquet, hiking, golf, tennis, and lawn bowling. There are also children's programs and a pool. ⊠ *136 E. Francis St., Box 1776, 23187,* ☎ *757/229–1000 or 800/447–8679,* ﬀﬄ *757/565–8797. 135 rooms. Restaurant, pool, exercise room. AE, D, DC, MC, V.*

$$$ ▥ **Liberty Rose B&B Inn.** At this 1920s hilltop estate 1 mi from the historic area, rooms are individually appointed with European antiques and rich silk and damask; each has windows on three sides. ⊠ *1022 Jamestown Rd., 23185,* ☎ *757/253–1260 or 800/545–1825. 4 rooms. AE, MC, V. BP.* ⊗

$$ ▥ **Williamsburg Sampler.** Walking into this B&B is like stepping back in time. Antiques from the 18th and 19th centuries adorn the Colonial-style house, which exudes an unmistakable warmth. With nice-size rooms, this spot provides a wonderful overlook of Colonial Williamsburg. ⊠ *922 Jamestown Rd., 23185,* ☎ *757/253–0398 or 800/722–1169. 6 rooms. AE, D, DC, MC, V. BP.*

Yorktown

$–$$$ ╳ **Nick's Seafood Pavilion.** Atlantic seafood with a distinctly Mediterranean flavor is served in ample portions at this delightfully gaudy riverside restaurant. House specialties include lobster *dien bien* (a casserole of lobster meat mixed with a savory, buttery herbal brown rice) and seafood shish kebab. ⊠ *Water St.,* ☎ *757/887–5269. Reservations not accepted. AE, DC, MC, V.*

Motels

▥ **Williamsburg Woodlands** (⊠ 102 Visitor Center Dr., Williamsburg 23185, ☎ 757/229–1000 or 800/447–8679, ﬀﬄ 757/565–8942), 315 rooms; restaurant, 2 pools, golf, tennis; $$.

▥ **Duke of York Motel** (⊠ 508 Water St., Yorktown 23690, ☎ 757/898–3232, ﬀﬄ 757/898–5922), 57 rooms; restaurant, pool; $.

Nightlife and the Arts

Nightlife

Bogart's (⊠ 203 N. Lombardy St., Richmond, ☎ 804/353–9280) has late-night entertainment, but never on Sunday. **Chowning's Tavern** (⊠ Duke of Gloucester St., Williamsburg, ☎ 757/229–1000 or 800/447–

8679) has lively "gambols," or Colonial games, with music and other entertainment, daily from 9 PM to 1 AM; a family version is offered from 7 PM to 9 PM.

The Arts

Barksdale Theatre (⊠ 1601 Willow Lawn Dr., Richmond, ☎ 804/282–2620), founded in 1953, is the area's oldest theater company. Comedies, dramas, and musicals are presented year-round. The **Richmond Ballet** (⊠ 614 N. Lombardy St., ☎ 804/359–0906) is the city's classical ballet company. The **Richmond Symphony** (⊠ 300 W. Franklin St., ☎ 804/788–1212) often features internationally known soloists. **TheatreVirginia** (⊠ 2800 Grove Ave., Richmond, ☎ 804/353–6100), an Equity theater maintained by the Virginia Museum of Fine Arts, presents six shows September–May. The **Company of Colonial Players** (⊠ Box 1776, Williamsburg 23187-1776, ☎ 757/229–1000) presents rollicking 18th-century plays.

Outdoor Activities and Sports

Open to the public in Richmond—for free or at a nominal charge—are more than 150 tennis courts, 11 swimming pools, a golf driving range, and about 7 mi of fitness trails. The **Department of Parks, Recreation, and Community Facilities** (☎ 804/780–5944) has listings.

Biking

In Colonial Williamsburg ticket holders can rent bicycles at the **Williamsburg Lodge** (☎ 757/229–1000 or 800/447–8679) on South England Street. Also try **Bikesmith** (⊠ 515 York St., ☎ 757/229–9858).

Golf

Colonial Williamsburg (☎ 757/220–7696 or 800/447–8679) operates three courses. **Crossings Golf Club** (⊠ junction of I–95 and I–295, Glen Allen, ☎ 804/266–2254), north of Richmond, has an 18-hole course open to the public. **Kingsmill Resort** (☎ 757/253–3906), east of Williamsburg near Busch Gardens, has one 9-hole and three 18-hole courses. The **Tides Inn** (⊠ Irvington, ☎ 804/438–5501; ☞ Dining and Lodging, *above*) has 9- and 18-hole courses.

Water Sports

From March through November **Richmond Raft** (☎ 804/222–7238 or 800/540–7238) offers guided white-water rafting on the James River (Class III and IV rapids) and float trips. Costs are Sunday–Friday $54 per person, Saturday $58 per person. Price includes a light meal on the river. Minimum age requirement for a trip is 12 years. **Adventure Challenge** (☎ 804/276–7600) offers trips, lessons, and tours in white-water kayaking, coastal kayaking, river tubing, and white-water rafting.

Tennis

Colonial Williamsburg (☎ 757/220–7794 or 800/447–8679) has 10 tennis courts, and **Kingsmill** (☎ 757/253–3945) has 15 courts open to the public. Additional public courts in Williamsburg are at **Kiwanis Park**, on Long Hill Road, and **Quarterpath Park**, on Pocahontas Street.

Shopping

Fresh produce is for sale (no bargains here) at Richmond's **Farmers' Market** (⊠ 17th and Main Sts.); myriad art galleries, boutiques, and antiques shops are nearby and in **Shockoe Slip**, on East Cary Street between 12th and 15th streets. The **Williamsburg Pottery Factory** (⊠ U.S. 60 W, Lightfoot, ☎ 757/564–3326) is an enormous outlet store that sells clothing, furniture, tools, china, pottery, food, and wine. All along the same stretch of U.S. 60 are dozens of other outlet malls.

ELSEWHERE IN VIRGINIA

Hampton Roads, Virginia Beach, and the Eastern Shore

Visitor Information

Virginia Beach Visitor Information Center (⊠ 2100 Parks Ave., 23451, ☎ 757/437–4888 or 800/446–8038). **Chincoteague Chamber of Commerce** (⊠ Box 258, 23336, ☎ 757/336–6161). **Eastern Shore of Virginia Chamber of Commerce** (⊠ Box 460, Melfa 23410, ☎ 757/787–2460). **Norfolk Convention and Visitors Bureau** (⊠ 232 E. Main St., 23510, ☎ 757/664–6620 or 800/368–3097).

Arriving and Departing

Norfolk International and **Newport News–Williamsburg International airports** (☞ Richmond and Tidewater, *above*) are served by most major airlines. I–64 connects Richmond with Hampton Roads. U.S. 58 and Route 44 connect I–64 with Virginia Beach. U.S. 13 runs between Virginia Beach and the Eastern Shore via the Chesapeake Bay Bridge-Tunnel. **Greyhound** (☎ 800/231–2222) serves **Hampton** (⊠ 2 W. Pembrook Ave., ☎ 757/722–9861), **Norfolk** (⊠ 701 Monticello Ave., ☎ 757/625–7500), **Virginia Beach** (⊠ 1017 Laskin Rd., ☎ 757/422–2998), and various locations along U.S. 13 on the Eastern Shore.

What to See and Do

The cities of Newport News and Hampton on the north and Norfolk on the south flank the enormous port of **Hampton Roads,** where the James empties into the Chesapeake Bay. In Newport News the **Mariner's Museum** (⊠ I–64, Exit 258A, ☎ 757/595–0368 or 800/581–7245, ☎ $5) displays tiny hand-carved models of ancient vessels and full-size specimens of more recent ones, including a gondola and a Chinese sampan. The history of flight and space exploration can be viewed in Hampton at the futuristic **Virginia Air and Space Center** (⊠ 600 Settlers Landing Rd., ☎ 757/727–0800; ☎ $6); exhibits include a 3-billion-year-old lunar rock and an *Apollo* capsule.

At Hampton's **Fort Monroe** (⊠ U.S. 258, ☎ 757/727–3391; ☎ free), the **Casemate Museum** (⊠ Casemate 20 Bernard Rd., ☎ 757/727–3391; ☎ free) tells the Civil War history of this moat-enclosed Union stronghold, which was the object of the battle between the *Monitor* and the *Merrimac* and later where President Jefferson Davis was imprisoned after the Confederacy's defeat.

Norfolk is best known for the **U.S. Naval Base** (⊠ Hampton Blvd., ☎ 757/444–7955 or 757/444–1577; ☎ $5), the world's largest naval installation and home to about 115 ships of the Atlantic and Mediterranean fleets, including the nuclear-powered USS *Theodore Roosevelt*—the world's second-largest warship. Norfolk shows off its naval heritage at **Nauticus** (⊠ Waterside Dr., ☎ 757/664–1000; ☎ $7.50) with more than 150 exhibits on commercial, military, and exotic natural ocean subjects. The sights are gentler at the **Norfolk Botanical Gardens** (⊠ I–64, airport Exit 279, ☎ 757/441–5831; ☎ $5), with 155 acres of azaleas, camellias, and roses—plus an unusual fragrance garden for the blind. The collections at the **Chrysler Museum of Art** (⊠ 245 W. Olney Rd., ☎ 757/664–6200, ☎ $5), one of America's major art museums, range from Gainsborough to Roy Lichtenstein. The **General Douglas MacArthur Memorial** (⊠ Bank St. and City Hall Ave., ☎ 757/441–2965; ☎ donation suggested), in the restored former city hall, is the burial place of the controversial war hero.

The heart of **Virginia Beach,** 6 mi of crowded public beach and a raucous 40-block boardwalk, has been a popular summer gathering place for many years. One advantage of the commercialism is easy access to sailing, surfing, and scuba renting. Be mindful, however, that the beach gets extremely crowded mid-summer. Almost 2 mi inland, at the southern end of Virginia Beach, is one of the state's most visited museums, the **Virginia Marine Science Museum** (✉ 717 General Booth Blvd., ☏ 757/425–3474; 🎟 $7.95), where visitors can bird-watch in a salt marsh and use computers to predict the weather. On the Eastern Shore U.S. 13 takes you past historic 17th- to 19th-century towns such as **Eastville,** with its 1730 courthouse. **Onancock** has a working general store established in 1842 and a wharf where you just might be able to witness a sunset over the bay.

★ **Assateague Island** is a 37-mi-long wildlife refuge and recreational area that extends north into Maryland (☞ Maryland). Despite invasive tourism and overdevelopment, **Chincoteague Island** has had at least one tradition survive from a simpler time: Every July wild ponies from Assateague are driven across the channel and placed at auction here; those unsold swim back home.

On nearby Wallops Island is NASA's **Wallops Flight Facility** (✉ Rte. 175, ☏ 757/824–2298; 🎟 free), where a museum tells the story of the space program on the site of early rocket launchings.

Dining and Lodging

$–$$$$ **✕ La Galleria.** Large urns imported from Italy, Corinthian columns,
★ and a softly playing pianist create a warm ambience in this restaurant, known for its excellent pastas. Other good choices include a salmon sautéed in herbs, garlic, and white wine. ✉ *120 College Pl., Norfolk,* ☏ *757/623–3939. AE, MC, V.*

$$–$$$ **✕ Coastal Grill.** Chef-owner Jerry Bryan prepares American classics with
★ an innovative twist. Spinach salad is paired with sautéed chicken livers and balsamic vinaigrette, and the fresh seafood dishes are sublime. ✉ *1427 Great Neck Rd., Virginia Beach,* ☏ *757/496–3348. Reservations not accepted. AE, D, MC, V. No lunch.*

$$–$$$ **✕ The Wild Monkey Gourmet Diner.** The eclectic menu, which in-
★ cludes zesty pork and ginger dumplings, jumbalaya, and Angus beef meat loaf, is set off by a fantastic wine list. This small restaurant in the heart of Norfolk's Ghent neighborhood might be a bit off the beaten path, but it's worth it. ✉ *1603 Colleye Ave.,* ☏ *757/627–6462. AE, D, DC, MC, V.*

$$–$$$$ **The Cavalier.** The historic Cavalier (1927) has a marvelous view of the
★ ocean, exceptional service, and a well-manicured 18-hole golf course and is one of the state's premier hotels. ✉ *42nd and Atlantic Aves.,* ☏ *757/425–8555 or 888/SINCE–27. 394. Restaurant, golf, health club. AE, D, DC, MC, V.* 🐾

$$$ **🏨 Norfolk Waterside Marriott.** This modern hotel next door to the convention center is connected by a walkway to Waterside's shops and restaurants. ✉ *235 E. Main St., 23510,* ☏ *757/627–4200 or 800/228–9290,* 🖷 *757/628–6466. 404 rooms. 2 restaurants, pool, health club. AE, D, DC, MC, V.* 🐾

$$–$$$ **🏨 Ramada Plaza Resort Oceanfront.** With its 17-story tower, the Ramada is the city's tallest hotel. Rooms that do not face the ocean still have a partial view of it or overlook the swimming pool. All are equipped with a microwave, refrigerator, coffeemaker, iron, and ironing board. ✉ *57th St. and Oceanfront, Virginia Beach 23451,* ☏ *757/428–7025 or 800/365–3032,* 🖷 *757/428–2921. 245 rooms. 2 restaurants, pool, exercise room. AE, D, DC, MC, V.* 🐾

WASHINGTON

By Tom Gauntt

Updated by
John Doerper

Capital	Olympia
Population	5,756,360
Motto	By-and-by
State Bird	American goldfinch
State Flower	Rhododendron
Postal Abbreviation	WA

Statewide Visitor Information

Washington Tourism Development Division (✉ Box 42500, Olympia 98504-2500, ☎ 360/586–2088 or 800/544–1800).

Scenic Drives

About 80 mi north of Seattle, starting from just south of Bellingham on I–5, Highway 11 winds 25 mi along **Chuckanut Bay.** On one side of Highway 11 rise the steep, heavily wooded cliffs of Chuckanut Mountain and on the other are sweeping views of Puget Sound and the San Juan Islands. The area has several fine restaurants. Near the Oregon border, Highway 14 winds east from Vancouver into the **Columbia River National Scenic Area.** The road clings to the steep slopes of the gorge and traverses several tunnels and picturesque towns such as Carson, known for its hot springs, white salmon, and incredible windsurfing.

National and State Parks

National Parks
Mt. Rainier National Park (✉ Tahoma Woods, Star Rte., Ashford 98304, ☎ 360/569–2211), about 85 mi southeast of Seattle, comprises 14,411-ft Mt. Rainier—the fifth-highest mountain in the lower 48 states—and nearly 400 square mi of surrounding wilderness. The Jackson Memorial Visitor Center at Paradise has exhibits, films, and a 360-degree view of the summit and surrounding peaks. Call for off-season hours. For a vision of the apocalypse, head for the **Mount St. Helens National Volcanic Monument** (✉ 42218 N.E. Yale Bridge Rd., Amboy 98601). The visitor center (☎ 360/247–3900) is on Highway 504, 5 mi east of the Castle Rock exit off I–5, and the monument is 45 mi east of Castle Rock. Although the crater still steams and small earthquakes are common, excellent views are available within 5 mi of the mountain. **Olympic National Park** (✉ 600 E. Park Ave., Port Angeles 98362, ☎ 360/452–4501) is one of the most outstanding places of natural beauty in the United States, with such diverse areas as its jagged wilderness coastline; a lush, temperate rain forest; 60-odd active glaciers; and Hurricane Ridge, with its alpine contours. **North Cascades National Park** (✉ 2105 State Rte. 20, Sedro-Woolley 98284, ☎ 360/856–5700), a beautiful and remote park about 120 mi northeast of Seattle, holds some of the state's most rugged mountains, craggy peaks, and jewel-like lakes. Heavy snows in the Cascades close State Route 20 through the park most winters from October through April.

State Park
Leadbetter Point State Park (✉ Robert Gray Dr., 2 mi south of Ilwaco, Box 488, 98624, ☎ 360/642–3078), at the northernmost end of the Long Beach Peninsula, is a wildlife refuge that's good for bird-watching. The dunes at the very tip are closed from April to August to protect the nesting snowy plover. Black brant, sandpipers, turnstones,

yellowlegs, sanderlings, knots, and plovers are among the 100 species known to inhabit the point.

SEATTLE

Seattle is growing by leaps and bounds. Constant traffic on all the main highways and thoroughfares is the first and most obvious indication that city planning has not been sufficient to meet the needs of this expanding Pacific Rim metropolis. Certain high-profile businesses in the region (e.g., Boeing, Microsoft, Starbucks) have brought a great deal of wealth to the city, resulting in a burst of construction and renovation. In the works is a regional transit authority that will construct light-rail lines from the city to the suburbs. Though it is plain to see that the area's growing pains show no sign of ending anytime soon, there are already countless wonderful restaurants, full-service hotels, and entertainment venues springing up everywhere. Add that to the natural beauty of the city and its environs and you'll probably be too enthralled to notice the gray skies.

Visitor Information

Seattle/King County: Stop by Convention and Visitors Bureau (⊠ 520 Pike St., Suite 1300, 98101, ☎ 206/461–5800) or the **visitor center** on the third floor of Westlake Center (⊠ 5th Ave. and Pine St.). Or write to the **Visitor Information Center** (⊠ 520 Pike St., Suite 1300, 98101).

Arriving and Departing

By Bus
Greyhound (⊠ 8th Ave. and Stewart St., ☎ 800/231–2222).

By Car
I–5 enters Seattle from the north and south, I–90 from the east (traffic and pass information: ☎ 800/695–7623).

By Plane
Seattle-Tacoma International Airport (Sea-Tac; ⊠ 17801 Pacific Hwy. S, 98168-0727, ☎ 206/433–4444) is 20 mi south of downtown and is served by major American and some foreign airlines. A cab ride between the airport and downtown takes about 30 to 45 minutes and costs about $25. **Gray Line Airport Express** (☎ 206/626–6088) buses run to and from major downtown hotels; fare is $8.50 one-way, $14 round-trip.

By Train
Amtrak (⊠ 303 S. Jackson St., ☎ 800/872–7245).

Getting Around Seattle

A car is the handiest way to cover metropolitan Seattle, but bus service is convenient and efficient, too. Despite occasional steep hills, downtown is good for walking.

By Car
Hills, tunnels, reversible express lanes, and rush hours can make driving a chore. Main thoroughfares into downtown are Aurora Avenue (Highway 99 is called the Alaskan Way Viaduct along the waterfront) and I–5.

By Public Transportation
Metropolitan Transit (☎ 206/553–3000) provides free rides in the downtown-waterfront area until 7 PM; fares to other destinations range from $1 to about $1.60, depending on the zone and time of day. The elevated **monorail** (☎ 206/441–6038) runs the 2 mi from the Seattle Center to Westlake Center every 15 minutes; the fare ranges from free to $1.

By Taxi

Either pick up a cab at any hotel taxi stand or call the cab company directly. Fare is $1.80 at the flag drop and then $1.80 per mile. Major companies are **Farwest** (☎ 206/622–1717 or 425/454–5055) and **Yellow Cab** (☎ 206/622–6500 or 425/455–4999).

Orientation Tour

Boat Tour

Argosy Cruises (✉ Pier 55, ☎ 206/623–1445; 🎫 $15–$28) operates one-hour tours of Elliott Bay, the Port of Seattle, Lake Union, Hiram M. Chittenden Locks, and Lake Washington.

Bus Tour

Gray Line Tour (✉ Washington State Convention and Trade Center, 800 Convention Pl., ☎ 206/626–5208; 🎫 $29–$60) provides guided bus tours of the city and environs ranging from a daily 2½-hour spin to the 6-hour Grand City Tour, which runs in spring, summer, and fall.

Train Tour

Spirit of Washington Dinner Train (✉ 625 S. 4th St., Renton, ☎ 425/227–7245; 🎫 $50–$70) involves seven vintage railcars that transport diners on a four-hour round-trip excursion from Renton to Woodinville, along the eastern shore of Lake Washington, passing through Mercer Island, Bellevue, Kirkland, and the Sammamish River valley. During the 45-minute stop in Woodinville, guests are invited to tour the Columbia Winery and visit the tasting room.

Exploring Seattle

Downtown

Downtown Seattle is bounded by Safeco Field to the south, the Seattle Center to the north, I–5 to the east, and the waterfront to the west. You can reach most points of interest by foot, bus, or monorail. But remember that Seattle is a city of hills, so wear your walking shoes.

★ The five-story **Seattle Art Museum** (✉ 100 University St., ☎ 206/654–3100, 🎫 $7), by postmodern theorist Robert Venturi, is a work of art in itself, with a limestone exterior and vertical fluting accented by terra-cotta, cut granite, and marble. Inside are extensive collections of Asian, Native American, African, Oceanic, and pre-Columbian art, a café, and a gift shop.

Pike Place Market (✉ 1st Ave. at Pike St., ☎ 206/682–7453) got its start in 1907, when the city issued permits allowing farmers to sell produce from their wagons parked at Pike Place. Sold here are fresh seafood (which can be packed in dry ice for your flight home), produce, cheese, Northwest wines, bulk spices, teas, coffees, and arts and crafts.

At the base of the Pike Street Hillclimb at Pier 59 is the **Seattle Aquarium** (☎ 206/386–4320; 🎫 $8.50), showcasing Northwest marine life. Sea otters and seals swim and dive in their pools, and the State of the Sound exhibit shows aquatic life and the ecology of Puget Sound.

★ An 1889 fire destroyed many of the wood-frame buildings in the area now known as **Pioneer Square,** but the residents rebuilt them with brick and mortar. This area was in a state of decline from the depression until the 1970s, when buildings were restored and stores and cafés moved in. Some older saloons remain, giving the area a historical flavor. College kids party hearty here at night; during the day you can browse through the art galleries and eclectic shops. **Gallery Walk** (☎ 206/587–0260) is a free open house hosted the first Thursday of every month by Seattle's art galleries, most of them in Pioneer Square.

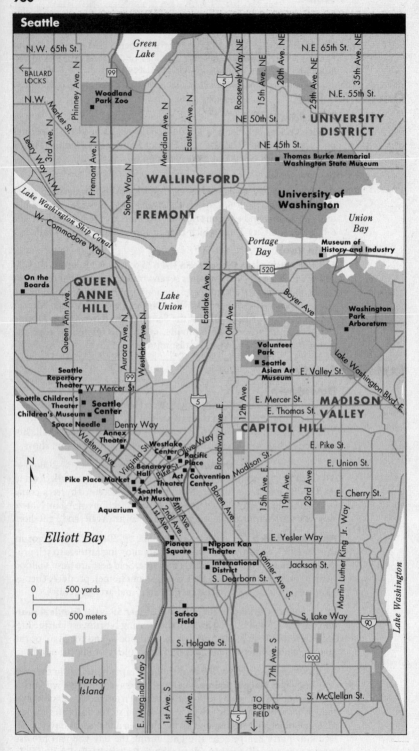

Southeast of Pioneer Square is the **International District** (known locally as the ID), where a third of the residents are ethnic Chinese, a third Filipino, and a third from elsewhere in Asia. The ID began as a haven for Chinese workers after they'd finished building the transcontinental railroad. Today the district is full of Chinese, Japanese, and Korean restaurants, as well as herbalists, massage parlors, and acupuncturists. The area is bordered by Yesler Way to the north, 4th Avenue to the west, Dearborn on the south, and I–5 on the east. The **Nippon Kan Theater** (✉ 628 S. Washington St., ☎ 206/224–0181) was historically the focal point for Japanese-American activities. It includes the Kabuki theater, now a national historic site, which hosts many Asian-oriented productions.

North of Downtown

From Westlake Center (☞ Shopping, *below*), a shopping complex completed in 1989, you can catch the monorail to **Seattle Center,** a 74-acre complex built for the 1962 Seattle World's Fair. It includes an amusement park, theaters, a renovated coliseum, exhibition halls, museums, and shops. Look for the **Pacific Science Center** (☎ 206/443–2001; ✇ $7.50) with its planetarium and six-story Boeing IMAX Theater. Also within Seattle Center is the **Tropical Butterfly House and Insect Village** and the **Children's Museum** (☎ 206/441–1768; ✇ $5.50), with hands-on exhibits replicating home life around the globe, as well as intergenerational programs, special exhibits, and workshops. The museum is on the first level of the Center House. Also within the Seattle Center is the **Space Needle** (☎ 206/443–2111; ✇ $9), a Seattle landmark that is visible from almost anywhere in the downtown area and looks like something from *The Jetsons*. Take the glass elevator to the observation deck for a sweeping view of the city.

On the northwest corner of the **University of Washington** campus is the **Burke Museum of Natural History and Culture** (✉ 17th Ave. NE and N.E. 45th St., ☎ 206/543–5590; ✇ $5.50), Washington's natural history and anthropological museum. South of the university's Husky Stadium, across the Montlake Cut, is the **Museum of History and Industry** (✉ 2700 24th Ave. E, ☎ 206/324–1125; ✇ $3).

Parks, Gardens, and Zoos

Near the university at the **Washington Park Arboretum** (✉ 2300 Arboretum Dr. E, ☎ 206/543–8800), Rhododendron Glen and Azalea Way are in bloom from March through June. The Hiram M. Chittenden Locks, better known as the **Ballard Locks** (✉ 3015 N.W. 54th St., west of the Ballard Bridge, ☎ 206/783–7059), control the 8-mi-long Lake Washington Ship Canal, which connects freshwater Lake Washington to Puget Sound. Animals at the 92-acre **Woodland Park Zoo** (✉ N. 50th St. and Fremont Ave., ☎ 206/684–4800; ✇ $9) roam freely within "bioclimatic" zones that re-create their native habitats. From downtown or the Seattle Center head north on Highway 99 (Aurora Avenue North), across the Aurora Bridge to the 45th Street exit.

Dining

$$$$ ✕ **Campagne.** Overlooking Pike Place Market and Elliott Bay, Campagne is intimate and urbane with its white walls, picture windows, and colorful modern prints. The flavors of Provence pervade the menu in dishes such as striped bass fillet grilled with fennel and served with lemon-thyme sabayon. Downstairs is a more casual café. ✉ *Inn at the Market, 86 Pine St.,* ☎ *206/728–2800. Reservations essential. Jacket required. AE, MC, V.*

$$$$ ✕ **Rover's.** Dishes of particular note at this intimate Madison Valley
★   restaurant are the diver's sea scallops with foie gras, served over chestnut puree, and the duck breast with wild mushrooms and huckleberry
sauce, all available as part of the five- and eight-course prix-fixe menus.
⊠ 2808 E. Madison, ☎ 206/325–7442. Reservations essential. AE,
DC, MC, V. Closed Sun. and Mon. No lunch.

$–$$$ ✕ **Anthony's Bell Street Diner and Pier 66.** In addition to having one
of the best views of Elliott Bay, this waterfront diner has become
known for its Manila clam chili, mahimahi tacos, and wild blackberry
cobbler. It's also convenient to the market and the waterfront. ⊠ 2201
Alaskan Way, ☎ 206/448–6688. AE, D, DC, MC, V.

$–$$ ✕ **Cactus.** In a charming neighborhood shopping district on the shores
of Lake Washington, Cactus is a casual outpost of southwestern and
Mexican cuisines. Of particular note are the extensive tapas menu and
specialty drinks such as the spicy Saguaro martini. Try the Navajo fry
bread and the grilled ancho-cinnamon chicken served with plantain cakes
and sautéed greens. ⊠ 4220 E. Madison, ☎ 206/324–4140. D, DC,
MC, V. No lunch Sun.

$–$$ ✕ **Wild Ginger.** The specialty is Pacific Rim cookery, including tasty
★   southern Chinese, Vietnamese, Thai, and Korean dishes served in a warm,
clubby dining room. Daily specials are based on seasonally available
products. ⊠ 1400 Western Ave., ☎ 206/623–4450. AE, D, DC, MC,
V. No lunch Sun.

Lodging

Seattle has an abundance of lodgings, from deluxe downtown hotels
to less expensive digs in the University District. For information on bed-
and-breakfasts, contact the **Pacific Bed & Breakfast Agency** (⊠ Box
46894, Seattle 98146, ☎ 206/439–7677, FAX 206/431–0932).

$$$$ 🛏 **Alexis.** At this intimate hotel in a restored 1901 building near the wa-
★   terfront, guest rooms are done in subdued colors. Some suites have whirlpool baths; others have wood-burning fireplaces. Pets are welcome. ⊠
1007 1st Ave., 98104, ☎ 206/624–4844 or 800/426–7033, FAX 206/621–
9009. 109 rooms. Restaurant, exercise room. AE, D, DC, MC, V. 🕾

$$$$ 🛏 **Four Seasons Olympic Hotel.** Restored to its 1920s grandeur, the
★   Olympic is Seattle's most elegant hotel. Public rooms are furnished with
marble, thick rugs, wood paneling, and potted plants. The less luxurious guest rooms are homey, with comfortable reading chairs and flo-
ral-print fabrics. ⊠ 411 University St., 98101, ☎ 206/621–1700 or
800/332–3442, FAX 206/682–9633. 450 rooms. 3 restaurants, pool, health
club. AE, D, DC, MC, V. 🕾

$$$$ 🛏 **Hotel Monaco.** Goldfish in your room (upon request) are just one of
the eclectic touches you'll find at this luxury hotel in the heart of Seattle's financial district. Spacious guest rooms with bold colors and patterns
all come with CD players and fax machines. Join the other hotel guests
around the fireplace in the lobby for complimentary evening wine. ⊠ 1101
4th Ave., 98101, ☎ 206/621–1770 or 800/945–2240, FAX 206/621–7779.
189 rooms. Restaurant, exercise room. AE, D, DC, MC, V. 🕾

$$$–$$$$ 🛏 **Edgewater.** The only hotel on Elliott Bay has comfortably rustic rooms
with unfinished wood furnishings and plaid fabric in red, green, and blue.
⊠ Pier 67, 2411 Alaskan Way, 98121, ☎ 206/728–7000 or 800/624–
0670, FAX 206/441–4119. 236 rooms. Restaurant. AE, D, DC, MC, V. 🕾

$$$–$$$$ 🛏 **Inn at the Market.** Adjacent to the Pike Place Market, this hotel com-
★   bines the best aspects of a small, deluxe hotel with the informality of the
Pacific Northwest. Rooms are spacious, with contemporary furnishings
and ceramic sculptures and views of either the city, Elliott Bay, and Pike
Place Market, or the hotel courtyard. ⊠ 86 Pine St., 98101, ☎ 206/443–
3600, FAX 206/448–0631. 65 rooms. AE, D, DC, MC, V. 🕾

$$$ 🏨 **Edmond Meany Tower Hotel.** At this art deco–style hotel a few blocks from the University of Washington campus, nearly all the rooms have views of the Cascades or the Olympic mountains, the University of Washington, or Lake Union. ✉ *4507 Brooklyn Ave. NE, 98105,* ☎ *206/634–2000,* FAX *206/547–6029. 155 rooms. 2 restaurants. AE, DC, MC, V.* 🍴

$ 🏨 **Seattle YMCA.** This member of the American Youth Hostels Association has single and double rooms that are clean and plainly furnished with bed, phone, desk, and lamp. Ten dollars extra gets you a room with a private bath; for another $3 or $4 you'll have a view of Elliott Bay. ✉ *909 4th Ave., 98104,* ☎ *206/382–5000. 120 beds, 3 rooms with baths. Pool, health club. D, MC, V.*

Motels

🏨 **Seattle Airport Hilton** (✉ International Blvd. at S. 176th St., Seattle 17620, ☎ 206/244–4800, FAX 206/248–4495). 178 rooms; restaurant, pool, exercise room; $$$.

🏨 **University Plaza Hotel** (✉ 400 N.E. 45th St., 98105, ☎ 206/634–0100, FAX 206/633–2743), 135 rooms; restaurant, pool, exercise room; $$–$$$.

Nightlife and the Arts

Nightlife

For a relatively small city, Seattle has a strong and diverse music scene. The most famous development to come out of the city so far has been grunge rock, a movement of the early 1990s.

BARS AND NIGHTCLUBS

Comet Tavern (✉ 922 E. Pike St., ☎ 206/323–9853) is Seattle's oldest post-Prohibition tavern turned hippie hangout turned upscale singles watering hole. **Entros** (✉ 823 Yale Ave. N, ☎ 206/624–0057) bills itself as an "intelligent amusement park," where patrons play socially interactive games such as "interface, the high-tech trust walk." **Meridian** (✉ 1900 N. Northlake Way, ☎ 206/547–3242) has a lounge with giant windows overlooking Gas Works Park and Lake Union. **Palace Kitchen** (✉ 2030 5th Ave., ☎ 206/448–2001) is a happening bar with great food. A Seattle favorite, **Ray's Boathouse** (✉ 6049 Seaview Ave. NW, ☎ 206/789–3770) is on the shore of Shilshole Bay, a perfect spot for watching the sun set behind the Olympic Mountains.

BREWPUBS

The **Elysian Brewing Company** (✉ 1221 E. Pike St., ☎ 206/860–1920) serves lunch and dinner in a remodeled furniture warehouse on Capitol Hill. Near Safeco Field and the waterfront is the bigger, more mainstream **Pyramid Alehouse** (✉ 1201 1st Ave., ☎ 206/682–3377), serving lunch and dinner, with daily tours. The **Trolleyman Pub** (✉ 3400 Phinney Ave. N., ☎ 206/548–8000), in the eclectic Fremont neighborhood, is the smaller of the two Red Hook breweries; the other is in Woodinville. The emphasis is on beer rather than food, but some sandwiches are available.

BLUES/R&B CLUBS

The **Ballard Firehouse** (✉ 5429 Russell St. NW, ☎ 206/784–3516) is a mostly blues mecca in Ballard. The **Central Tavern** (✉ 207 1st Ave. S, ☎ 206/622–0209), an often crowded club in Pioneer Square, presents local and national blues and reggae acts.

COMEDY CLUB

Comedy Underground (✉ 222 Main St., ☎ 206/628–0303), a Pioneer Square club that's literally underground, beneath Swannie's, presents stand-up comedy and open-mike nights.

Fenix (✉ 315 2nd Ave. S, ☎ 206/467–1111) pulsates with recorded dance music. **Fenix Underground** (✉ 323 2nd Ave. S, ☎ 206/467–1111) is one of several popular clubs in Pioneer Square. On Capitol Hill **Neighbors** (✉ 1509 Broadway E, ☎ 206/324–5358) attracts a good mix of gay men and everyone else.

JAZZ CLUB
Downtown, **Dimitriou's Jazz Alley** (✉ 2037 6th Ave., ☎ 206/441–9729) books nationally known performers every night except Monday, when local talent is showcased. Dinner is served before the first show.

ROCK CLUBS
Alibi Room (✉ 85 Pike St., ☎ 206/623–3180), in the Pike Place Market, is a restaurant and bar with live music, disco dancing, and independent film screenings in conjunction with the Seattle Film Festival. **Crocodile Cafe** (✉ 2200 2nd Ave., ☎ 206/448–2114) rocks with live local groups from Tuesday through Saturday. At the **OK Hotel** (✉ 212 Alaskan Way S, ☎ 206/621–7903), closed Monday, you'll find grunge, acoustic, and jazz, plus occasional poetry readings.

The Arts

Thursday's editions of the *Seattle Times* and the Friday calendar insert of the *Post-Intelligencer* list the coming week's events. Seattle's free weekly papers, the *Seattle Weekly* (Wednesdays) and the *Stranger* (Thursdays), cover the arts.

To charge tickets, call **Ticketmaster** (☎ 206/628–0888). **Ticket/Ticket,** with two locations (✉ 401 Broadway E; 1st Ave. and Pike St., ☎ 206/324–2744), sells half-price same-day tickets for cash only.

DANCE
The **Pacific Northwest Ballet** (✉ Opera House, Seattle Center, ☎ 206/441–2424) is a resident company and school that presents 60–70 performances annually. **On the Boards** (✉ 100 W. Roy, ☎ 206/217–9886) is the foremost center in the region for contemporary dance, theater, music, and multimedia presentation.

MUSIC
The **Seattle Symphony** (✉ Benaroya Hall, Second Ave. and University St., ☎ 206/215–4747), which presents some 160 concerts a year in and around town, opened a brand-new symphony hall for the 1998–99 season. **Northwest Chamber Orchestra** (☎ 206/343–0445), the Northwest's only professional chamber orchestra, presents a full spectrum of music, from Baroque to modern, at various venues.

OPERA
The **Seattle Opera** (✉ Opera House, Seattle Center, ☎ 206/389–7600), considered one of the top companies in America, presents five productions during its August–May season.

THEATER
The **Seattle Repertory Theater** (✉ Bagley Wright Theater, Seattle Center, 155 Mercer St., ☎ 206/443–2222) presents high-quality programming in nine productions during its October–May season. The **Seattle Children's Theater** (✉ 2nd Ave. N and Thomas St., at the Seattle Center, ☎ 206/441–3322) has a strong reputation. **Annex Theatre** (✉ 1916 4th Ave., ☎ 206/728–0933) is Seattle fringe theater at its best, with six main productions throughout the year. **Theater Schmeater** (✉ 1500 Summit Ave., ☎ 206/324–5801) also offers exceptional drama as well as its long-running, late-night spoofs of the *Twilight Zone*. **A Contemporary Theatre** (ACT; ✉ 7th Ave. and Union St., ☎ 206/292–7676) develops works by new playwrights.

Spectator Sports

Baseball: **Seattle Mariners** (✉ 83 S. King St., Suite 300, ☎ 206/346–4000). Basketball: **Seattle SuperSonics** (✉ Key Arena, 1st Ave. N, ☎ 206/281–5850). Football: **Seattle Seahawks** (✉ 421 First Ave. S, ☎ 206/682–2800).

Shopping

Shopping Centers

City Centre (✉ 1420 5th Ave., ☎ 206/467–9670), a gleaming marble tower, houses upscale shops such as Ann Taylor and Barneys of New York. **Pacific Place** (✉ 600 Pine St., ☎ 206/405–2655) is Seattle's newest upscale shopping center, with 50 shops, including Tiffany's and J. Crew. **Westlake Center** (✉ 1601 5th Ave., ☎ 206/467–1600) is a three-story steel-and-glass building with 80 shops and covered walkways that connect it to branches of Seattle's major department stores, Nordstrom and the Bon.

Food Market

Vendors at the partially open-air **Pike Place Market** (☞ Exploring Seattle, *above*) sell fresh meat, seafood, produce, flowers, and crafts.

Specialty Stores

CLOTHING

Mario's (✉ 1513 6th Ave., ☎ 206/223–1461) has trendy and designer fashions for men. **Boutique Europa** (✉ 1420 5th Ave., ☎ 206/587–6292) carries sophisticated European clothing. On the edge of the Pike Place Market, **Local Brilliance** (✉ 1535 1st Ave., ☎ 206/343–5864) showcases fashions by local designers. **Nubia's** (✉ 1507 6th Ave., ☎ 206/622–0297) sells unconstructed knits for women's business and casual wear as well as belts, beads, and other accessories.

OUTDOOR WEAR AND EQUIPMENT

★ With its 65-ft climbing wall, the 8,000-square-ft flagship branch of **REI** (✉ 222 Yale Ave. N, ☎ 206/223–1944) has become Seattle's second-most-visited landmark (after the Space Needle). **Eddie Bauer** (✉ 5th Ave. and Union St., ☎ 206/622–2766) specializes in classic sports and outdoor apparel.

TOYS

Children will love **Magic Mouse Toys** (✉ 603 1st Ave., ☎ 206/682–8097), with its two floors of toys, from small windups to giant plush animals.

Side Trip to Whidbey Island

On a nice day there's no better short excursion from Seattle than a ferry trip across Puget Sound to Whidbey Island. It's a great way to watch seagulls, sailboats, and massive container vessels in the sound—not to mention the scenery, including the Kitsap Peninsula and Olympic Mountains, Mt. Rainier, the Cascade Range, and the Seattle skyline.

Arriving and Departing

BY CAR

Whidbey Island can be reached by ferry via I–5 from Mukilteo (follow direction signs), or you can drive from Seattle north on I–5, then head west on Highway 20 and cross the dramatic Deception Pass via the bridge at the north end of the island.

BY FERRY

The **Washington State Ferry System** (☎ 206/464–6400 or 800/843–3779) provides car and passenger service from Mukilteo, on Highway 525, 30 mi north of Seattle, to Clinton, on Whidbey Island.

From Seattle-Tacoma International Airport, **Harbor Airlines** (☎ 800/359–3220) flies to Oak Harbor. **Kenmore Air** (☎ 425/486–1257 or 800/543–9595), on Lake Union, provides sea plane charter service.

What to See and Do

Whidbey Island is mostly rural, with undulating hills, gentle beaches, and little coves. **Langley,** a quaint town with inviting inns and a handful of good restaurants, shops, and galleries, sits atop a 50-ft bluff overlooking the southeastern shore. A little over halfway up 50-mi-long Whidbey Island is **Coupeville,** site of many restored Victorian houses and one of the largest National Historic Districts in the state. The town was founded in 1852 by Captain Thomas Coupe, whose house, built the next year, is one of the state's oldest.

Ebey's Landing National Historic Reserve (☎ 360/678–4636), headquartered in Coupeville, is a 17,000-acre area including Keystone, Coupeville, and Penn Cove. Established by Congress in 1978, the reserve is the first and largest of its kind, dotted with 91 nationally registered historic structures along with farmland, parks, and trails. At **Deception Pass State Park** (☎ 360/675–2417), at the north end of Whidbey Island, you can take in the spectacular view while strolling among the madrona trees, with their peeling reddish-brown bark.

Dining

$$$$ ✕ **The Captain Whidbey Inn Dining Room.** The small, rustic dining room at the Captain Whidbey Inn has great views of the shore and the tranquil waters of Penn Cove. For more than 20 years, the inn has served delectable, locally raised Penn Cove mussels, as well as local oysters, and seasonal Whidbey Island produce. ⊠ *3072 Captain Whidbey Inn Rd., Coupeville,* ☎ *360/678–4110. Reservations essential. AE, D, MC, V. No lunch.*

$$$$ ✕ **Country Kitchen.** Tables for two line the walls of this intimate restaurant. The prix-fixe, five-course menu might include locally gathered mussels in a black bean sauce, breast of duck in a loganberry sauce, or Columbia River salmon. ⊠ *Inn at Langley, 400 1st St., Langley,* ☎ *360/221–3033. Reservations essential. MC, V.*

$$ ✕ **Garibyan Brothers Café Langley.** Mediterranean fare is served at this casual café. ⊠ *113 1st St., Langley,* ☎ *360/221–3090. AE, MC, V. Closed Tues. in winter.*

Side Trip to Tacoma

Seattleite skepticism notwithstanding, Tacoma has a strong cultural scene, restored residential neighborhoods and historic theaters, fine bay views, and a world-class zoo.

Visitor Information

Tacoma–Pierce County Visitors and Convention Bureau (⊠ 906 Broadway, Tacoma 98402, ☎ 253/627–2836).

Arriving and Departing

Tacoma is about 35 mi south of Seattle via I–5. Sea-Tac Airport is about a 30-minute drive away. The city is served by major bus, train, and air carriers.

What to See and Do

Union Station (⊠ 1717 Pacific Ave., ☎ 253/593–6313) is an heirloom from the golden age of railroads, when Tacoma was the western terminus for the transcontinental Northern Pacific Railroad. Built by Reed and Stem, the architects of New York City's Grand Central Station, the massive copper-domed Beaux Arts depot was opened in 1911. It now houses federal district courts, but the rotunda is open to the public. Across the street is the **University of Washington, Tacoma campus,** housed in beautifully restored 19th-century warehouses. The **Washington State Historical Society Museum** (✉ 1911 Pacific Ave., ☎ 253/272–3500; ☞ $7) near Union Station houses exhibits on the natural, Native American, pioneer, maritime, and industrial history of the state. It's closed Mondays.

Downtown on Broadway is **Antique Row,** with antiques shops, two restored theaters, and funky boutiques. The **Tacoma Art Museum** (✉ 1123 Pacific Ave., ☎ 253/272–4258; ☞ $5) contains a rich collection of American and French paintings, as well as Chinese jades and imperial robes. **Wright Park** (✉ 6th and Division Sts., I and G Sts.) is a 30-acre park just north of downtown. Within the park is the W. W. Seymour Botanical Conservatory (✉ 316 S. G St., ☎ 253/591–5330; ☞ free), a Victorian-style greenhouse with an extensive collection of exotic flora.

Northeast of Tacoma, the 700-acre **Point Defiance Park** is one of the largest urban parks in the country. The **Point Defiance Zoo and Aquarium,** founded in 1888, is now one of the top zoos in America. ✉ *5400 N. Pearl St.,* ☎ *253/591–5337.* ☞ *$7.*

Dining

$ ✕ **Swiss.** You'll find good pub fare and Northwest microbrews at this restaurant in a distinctive 1913 building that was once Tacoma's Swiss Hall. ✉ *1904 S. Jefferson Ave.,* ☎ *253/572–2821. No credit cards.*

Side Trip to Olympia

Arriving and Departing

Olympia is on I–5, about 60 mi southwest of Seattle and 25 mi southwest of Tacoma.

What to See and Do

Olympia, Washington's state capital, is fairly quiet except when the legislature is in session. You can tour the **Legislative Building** (✉ Capitol Way between 10th and 14th Aves.), a handsome Romanesque structure with a 287-ft dome that closely resembles the Capitol in that *other* Washington.

Dining

$$–$$$ ✕ **Louisa.** Ten minutes south of downtown Olympia is Louisa, an elegant setting for sophisticated Northwest cuisine. Housemade butternut squash ravioli, served with sage pesto and goat cheese, is the perfect treat on a rainy day on the Sound. ✉ *211 Cleveland Ave., Tumwater,* ☎ *360/352–3732. MC, V. Closed Sun. and Mon. No lunch Sat.*

THE OLYMPIC PENINSULA

The rugged Olympic Peninsula forms the northwest corner of the continental United States. Much of it is wilderness, with the Olympic National Park and National Forest at its heart. The peninsula has tremendous variety: the wild Pacific shore, the sheltered waters along the Hood Canal and the Strait of Juan de Fuca, the rivers of the Olympic's rain forests, and the towering Olympic Mountains.

Visitor Information

North Olympic Peninsula Visitor & Convention Bureau (✉ Box 670, Port Angeles 98362, ☎ 360/452–8552 or 800/942–4042). **Port Angeles:** Visitor center (✉ 121 E. Railroad Ave., 98362, ☎ 360/452–2363).

Arriving and Departing

By Bus
Olympic Van Tours and Bus Lines (☎ 360/452–3858) serves the Olympic Peninsula.

By Car
U.S. 101 loops around the Olympic Peninsula, which can be reached from Olympia via Routes 8 and 101 and from Tacoma, 50 mi away, via Highway 16.

By Ferry
The **Washington State Ferry System** (☎ 206/464–6400 or 800/843–3779) provides car and passenger service from downtown Seattle to Bremerton. The **Black Ball Ferry Line** (☎ 360/457–4491) operates between Port Angeles, on the Olympic Peninsula, and Victoria, British Columbia.

By Plane
Horizon Air (☎ 800/547–9308) flies into Port Angeles from the Seattle-Tacoma airport. Private charter airlines fly into Port Angeles, Forks, and Hoquiam.

Exploring the Olympic Peninsula

From Olympia go west along Highway 101 and Routes 8 and 12 to **Gray's Harbor** and the twin seaports of **Hoquiam** and **Aberdeen.** From Hoquiam you can drive north on **Route 109,** which sticks to the coast and passes through resorts and ample beach areas such as Copalis Beach, Pacific Beach, and Moclips. Route 109 eventually leads to the Quinault Indian Reservation and the tribal center of **Taholah,** whose main draw is pristine, expansive scenery.

Route 109 dead-ends at Taholah, and you must backtrack to return to U.S. 101. About 20 mi north of Aberdeen on U.S. 101, 1½ mi north of the Hoh River Bridge, is Hoh River Rainforest Road, which goes

★ east to the **Hoh Rain Forest** (☎ 360/452–4501), part of the Olympic National Park. This complex ecosystem of conifers, hardwoods, grasses, mosses, and other flora shelters such wildlife as elks, otters, beavers, salmon, and flying squirrels. The average annual rainfall here is 145 inches. The Hoh Visitor Center (often unstaffed September–May) at the campground and the ranger station at road's end (18 mi east of U.S. 101) have interpretive displays and information on nature trails.

On U.S. 101 north of Hoh River Rainforest Road is the small logging town of **Forks,** a former lumber town that is changing into a hot spot for rain-forest visitors and back-country hikers. From Forks, La Push Road leads west about 15 mi to **La Push,** a coastal village and the tribal center of the Quileute Indians. Several points along this road have short trails with access to the ocean, fabulous views of nearby islands, and dramatic rock formations.

Returning to U.S. 101, which swings to the east as you go north from Forks, you go through the **Sol Duc River valley,** famous for its salmon fishing. The **Soleduck Fish Hatchery** (☎ 360/327–3246) has interpretive displays on fish breeding. A few miles past the tiny town of Sappho are the deep azure waters of **Lake Crescent.** The area has abundant campsites, resorts, trails, canoeing, and fishing. The original lodge buildings (☞ Dining and Lodging, *below*)—constructed in 1915 and now well worn but comfortable—are still in use.

Twelve miles south of Lake Crescent on Soleduck Road (which meets U.S. 101 1 mi west of the western tip of Lake Crescent) is an entrance to Olympic National Park and to **Sol Duc Hot Springs** (☎ 360/327–

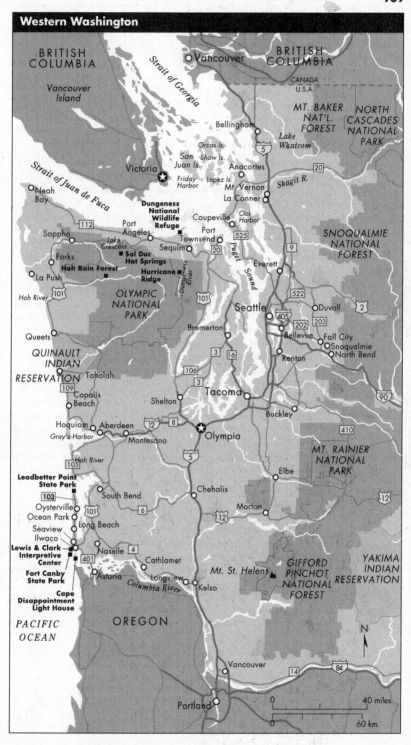

Western Washington

BRITISH COLUMBIA

Vancouver Island

Strait of Georgia

BRITISH COLUMBIA

CANADA
U.S.A.

MT. BAKER NAT'L. FOREST

NORTH CASCADES NATIONAL PARK

Bellingham

Lake Whatcom

5

Strait of Juan de Fuca

Victoria

San Juan Is.
Orcas Is.
Shaw Is.
Anacortes

Friday Harbor
Lopez Is.

Mt. Vernon

20

Skagit R.

La Conner

Neah Bay

Dungeness National Wildlife Refuge

Coupeville

Oak Harbor

SNOQUALMIE NATIONAL FOREST

112

Sappho

Port Angeles

Port Townsend

525

9

Lake Crescent

Sequim

20

Everett

Forks

Sol Duc Hot Springs

Hoh Rain Forest

Hurricane Ridge

Dungeness River

522

La Push

Puget Sound

Seattle

Duvall

2

Hoh River

101

OLYMPIC NATIONAL PARK

101

405

202

203

Bellevue

Fall City

Queets

Bremerton

Renton

Snoqualmie

North Bend

QUINAULT INDIAN RESERVATION

Taholah

3

16

90

109

Copalis Beach

106

3

Tacoma

Shelton

Buckley

Hoquiam

Aberdeen

Gray's Harbor

12

8

410

Montesano

Olympia

MT. RAINIER NATIONAL PARK

Hoh River

105

5

Elbe

12

Leadbetter Point State Park

Chehalis

103

South Bend

Morton

Oysterville

6

12

Ocean Park

101

Seaview

Ilwaco

Lewis & Clark Interpretive Center

Long Beach

Naselle

4

Cathlamet

GIFFORD PINCHOT NATIONAL FOREST

YAKIMA INDIAN RESERVATION

401

Mt. St. Helens ▲

Fort Canby State Park

Astoria

Longview

Columbia River

Kelso

Cape Disappointment Light House

PACIFIC OCEAN

OREGON

N

Vancouver

14

84

Portland

0   40 miles

0   60 km

3583), closed from October to April, where you can dip into three hot sulfur pools ranging from 98°F to 104°F.

On the northern tip of the Olympic Peninsula, on U.S. 101E, is **Port Angeles,** a once bustling commercial fishing port and mill town that's reinventing itself into the main jump-off point for visitors to the Olympic National Park (☞ National Parks, *above*), at 3002 Mt. Angeles Road. A bus will take you or you can drive up the road to **Hurricane Ridge,** 17 mi south of Port Angeles, which rises nearly a mile above sea level as it enters the park and yields spectacular views of the Olympics, the Strait of Juan de Fuca, and Vancouver Island.

Seventeen miles east of Port Angeles on U.S. 101 is the charming town of **Sequim** (pronounced *squim*). Animal life present and past can be found at the **Museum and Arts Center** (⊠ 175 W. Cedar St., ☎ 360/683–8110; ☜ free) in the Sequim-Dungeness Valley, where you can view the remains of an Ice Age mastodon and exhibits on the early Klallam Indians and the town's pioneer history. In the fertile plain at the mouth of the Dungeness River, 4 mi northwest of Sequim, the **Dungeness National Wildlife Refuge** (☎ 360/457–8451) is home to thousands of migratory waterfowl, as well as clams, oysters, and seals.

About 10 mi east of Sequim, Route 20 turns northward 12 mi to **Port Townsend.** Its waterfront is lined with carefully restored brick buildings from the 1870s that house shops and restaurants. High on the bluff are large gingerbread-trim Victorian homes, many of which have been turned into B&Bs. Driving south on U.S. 101 through the oyster and mill town of **Shelton** will bring you back to Olympia.

Dining and Lodging

Hoquiam

$–$$$ ⛆ **Sandpiper Beach Resort.** Within the four-story Sandpiper complex
★   are 31 suites, most with a sitting room, dining area, fireplace, small kitchen, and porch. With no in-room phones, no pool, no TVs, and no restaurant, this is the place to get away from it all. ⊠ *4159 Rte. 109, 1½ mi south of Pacific Beach, Box A, 98571,* ☎ *360/276–4580 or 800/567–4737,* FAX *360/276–4464. 31 suites. MC, V.* ☙

Port Angeles

$$$ ✕ **C'est Si Bon.** This locally famous spot run by a French couple is probably the most elegant restaurant on the informal Olympic Peninsula. Fine art on the walls competes with views of the flower-laden terrace and the Olympic Mountains beyond. The cuisine, of course, is French. ⊠ *23 Cedar Park Dr. (4 mi east of town),* ☎ *360/452–8888. Reservations essential. AE, D, MC, V. Closed Mon. No lunch.*

$–$$$ ⛆ **Lake Crescent Lodge.** This old but comfortable accommodation with a big main lodge and small cabins overlooks Lake Crescent. Units in the lodge are minimal—some are dimly lighted, with bathrooms down the hall—but the setting makes up for sparse amenities. ⊠ *416 Lake Crescent Rd., Port Angeles 98363,* ☎ *360/928–3211. 52 rooms, 47 with bath. Restaurant. AE, DC, MC, V. Closed late Oct.–Apr.* ☙

$$ ⛆ **Sol Duc Hot Springs Resort.** This casual resort dates from the turn of the 20th century. Some of the minimally outfitted cabins are rustic; others are more modern. Guests have access to three hot springs, and there are plenty of hiking trails nearby. ⊠ *12 mi south of U.S. 101 on Soleduck Rd., Box 2169, 98362,* ☎ *360/327–3398,* FAX *360/327–3593. 32 units, camping and RV facilities. Restaurant, pool. AE, D, MC, V. Closed Nov.–Mar.* ☙

Port Townsend

$–$$ ✕ **Fountain Café.** This small café off the main tourist drag is one of
★ the best restaurants in town. Count on seafood and pasta specialties
with imaginative twists, such as oysters in anchovy-wine sauce. ✉ *920
Washington St.,* ☎ *360/385–1364. MC, V. Closed Tues. No lunch.*

$–$$ ✕ **Salal Café.** Featuring home-style cooking and daily specials, this co-
operatively run restaurant stands out for its ample breakfasts—try one
of many variations on the potato-egg scramble—and regionally inspired
seafood dishes such as mussels in miso broth and oyster-mushroom
risotto. ✉ *634 Water St.,* ☎ *360/385–6532. Reservations not accepted. MC, V. No dinner Tues. and Wed.*

$$–$$$ 🏨 **James House.** Commanding a spot on the bluff overlooking down-
town and the waterfront, this antiques-filled Victorian B&B is a great
place to see how the well-heeled lived in the late 1800s. ✉ *1238 Washington St., 98368,* ☎ *360/385–1238 or 800/385–1238. 12 rooms.
AE, MC, V. BP.* 🐾

$–$$$ 🏨 **Palace Hotel.** This friendly hotel in the historic section of downtown
is pleasingly decorated to reflect its 1889 construction date and its one-
time history as a bordello. Rooms have no phones, but they do have
cable TV. ✉ *1004 Water St., 98368,* ☎ *360/385–0773 or 800/962-
0741,* FAX *360/385–0780. 15 units. AE, D, MC, V.*

Quinault

$$–$$$ 🏨 **Lake Quinault Lodge.** This deluxe lodge, built in 1926 of cedar shin-
gles, is set on a perfect glacial lake in the midst of the Olympic Na-
tional Forest. The lobby has antique reproductions and a fireplace. ✉
345 S. Shore Rd., Box 7, 98575, ☎ *360/288–2571,* FAX *360/288-
2901. 92 rooms. Restaurant, pool. AE, MC, V.* 🐾

Campgrounds

Some of the best campgrounds in Olympic National Park are ⚑ **Hoh
River** (☎ 360/374–6925), ⚑ **Mora** (☎ 360/374–5460), and ⚑ **Fairholm**
(☎ 360/928–3380). Elsewhere on the peninsula are ⚑ **Bogachiel State
Park** (☎ 360/374–6356), near Forks, closed after dusk in winter; ⚑
Fort Flagler State Park (☎ 360/385–1259), near Port Townsend, closed
for overnight camping November–February; ⚑ **Ocean City State Park**
(✉ 148 Rte. 115, Hoquiam 98550, ☎ 360/289–3553); and ⚑ **Pacific
Beach State Park** (☎ 360/276–4297). There is also camping at ⚑ **Sol
Duc Hot Springs Resort** (☞ Port Angeles, *above*).

Outdoor Activities and Sports

Biking

Biking is popular in the flatter parts of Port Townsend and within
Olympic National Park. There are bike-rental shops in Port Townsend
and other resort areas on the peninsula.

Fishing

Trout and salmon were once abundant in rivers throughout the penin-
sula, but that hasn't slowed down the traffic of anglers who cast their
lines with hope. Contact the area tourist office (☞ Visitor Informa-
tion, *above*) for details.

Hiking

Ocean and mountain areas contain hiking trails for all levels. Contact
the **Olympic National Forest** (☎ 360/288–2525) or **Olympic National
Park Visitor Center** (✉ 3002 Mt. Angeles Rd., Port Angeles 98362, ☎
360/452–0330).

Skiing

Hurricane Ridge (☞ Exploring the Olympic Peninsula, *above*) has 25
mi of cross-country ski trails.

Beaches

A long, sandy beach stretches from Ocean Shores north to Taholah, but north of there and along Juan de Fuca Strait, there are mostly small pocket beaches (many of them rocky and surf-swept). Keep in mind that the beaches on tribal or private lands are not generally accessible. Also, remember that the North Pacific is not for swimming—unless you wear a wet suit and are a very strong and experienced swimmer. For walking and exploring, the main beaches are Copalis and Pacific, north of Hoquiam; a series of scenic, unnamed beaches north of Kalaloch; and Rialto Beach, near La Push.

Shopping

Confirmed shoppers head for the waterfront boutiques and stores of **Port Townsend,** all of which showcase Northwest arts and crafts.

LONG BEACH PENINSULA

Where the turbulent waters of the Pacific and the Columbia River clash, ever-shifting sandbanks present a threat to boats and ships of all sizes. Upriver from Astoria, the low, densely vegetated islands are home to only a few fishermen, but a hundred years ago, during the heyday of salmon fishing, the northern bank of the river was lined with canneries and boat docks. Only a 3½-hour drive southwest of Seattle and 2 hours northwest of Portland, the small beach towns of the Long Beach Peninsula have been among the regions's favorite weekend getaways for more than a century. But there is still a lot of open space, and there's no development directly on the beach, which is divided from the communities by a wide strip of sand dunes. The peninsula separates the Pacific Ocean and Willapa Bay and is known for excellent bird-watching, beachcombing, hiking, and fine dining.

Visitor Information

Visitors Bureau (⊠ intersection of Hwys. 101 and 103, Seaview 98631, ☎ 360/642–2400 or 800/451–2542).

Arriving and Departing

By Car

Long Beach is accessible from the east via Highway 4, which connects with I–5 near Longview, and from the north and south via U.S. 101.

Exploring Long Beach Peninsula

U.S. 101 crosses the broad Columbia River between Astoria, Oregon, and Megler, Washington, on a long bridge, which starts out as a high, graceful span and soon drops down to a low-level elevated roadway that barely skims the surface of the river. Signs will tell you that the bridge runs to "Megler, WA," but don't look for that former cannery town. It vanished decades ago. A few miles downriver, on Highway 103, is **Ilwaco,** a small fishing community of about 1,000. The **Ilwaco Heritage Museum** (⊠ 115 S.E. Lake St., ☎ 360/642–3446; ⊠ $3) uses dioramas to present the history of southwestern Washington.

A couple of miles south of Ilwaco is the **Cape Disappointment Lighthouse,** first used in 1856 and one of the oldest lighthouses on the West Coast. The cape was named by John Meares, an English trader in 1788 in honor of his unsuccessful attempt to find the mouth of the Columbia River (and a rich, new source of furs).

Fort Canby State Park (⊠ 3 mi west of Ilwaco, off U.S. 101, ☎ 360/ 642–3078) was an active military installation until 1957, when it was turned over to the Washington State Parks and Recreation Commission. Now it is best known for great views of the Columbia River Bar during winter storms. The **Lewis & Clark Interpretive Center** (⊠ Robert Gray Dr., ☎ 360/642–3029, ☒ free) documents the 8,000-mi round-trip journey of the famous pair, from Wood River, Illinois, to the mouth of the Columbia.

The town of **Long Beach** has beach activities and an old-fashioned amusement park with go-carts and bumper cars. About halfway up the peninsula is **Ocean Park,** the area's commercial center. A few miles north of Ocean Park is **Oysterville,** established as an oystering town in 1854. When the native shellfish were fished to extinction, a Japanese oyster was introduced. The town never made a comeback as a commercial center, but the village's old homes, schoolhouse, and church have been beautifully preserved. Maps inside the vestibule of the restored **Oysterville Church** direct you through town, which is now on the National Register of Historic Places. At the northern tip of the peninsula is **Leadbetter Point State Park** (☞ National and State Parks, *above*).

Dining and Lodging

Ilwaco

$$–$$$ 🏠 **The Inn at Ilwaco.** This B&B is set in a renovated New England–style church. The cozy guest accommodations—most of them upstairs in the old Sunday-school rooms—have eyelet or printed chintz curtains and coverlets. ⊠ *120 Williams Ave. NE, 98624,* ☎ *360/642–8686 or 888/244–2523. 9 rooms. MC, V.*

Nahcotta

$$ 🏠 **Moby Dick Hotel and Oyster Farm.** This small, historic 1930s inn sits on spacious grounds above the Willapa Bay shoreline at the "quiet and peaceful" end of the peninsula. The Moby Dick has eight guest rooms, wildflower and organic gardens, and a separate bayside sauna pavilion. A restaurant serves dinners by advance reservation only. ⊠ *25814 Sandridge Rd.; O Box 82, 98627,* ☎ *206/665–4543,* FAX *206/ 665–6887. 8 rooms. Restaurant. No credit cards.*☜

Seaview

$$–$$$$ ✕ **Shoalwater Restaurant.** The acclaimed dining room at the Shelburne Inn features dishes with seafood brought straight from the fishing boats to the restaurant's back door, as well as mushrooms and salad greens gathered from the peninsula's woods and gardens. ⊠ *Pacific Hwy. and N. 45th St.,* ☎ *360/642–4142. AE, D, MC, V.*

$–$$ ✕ **42nd Street Cafe.** Chef Cheri Walker spent more than a decade hon-
★   ing her skills at the Shoalwater Restaurant (☞ *above*) before opening her own place, which is now by far the best restaurant on the peninsula. Her fare is inspired, original, and reasonably priced. In 1999, Walker was nominated for a James Beard Award. ⊠ *Hwy. 103 and 42nd St.,* ☎ *360/642–2323. MC, V.*

$ ✕ **My Mom's Pie Kitchen.** Fresh blackberry, banana-cream, chocolate-almond, and sour-cream-raisin are among the pie varieties you'll find in this cozy restaurant inside a Victorian house. Also on the menu are clam chowder and quiche. Call ahead, as hours are erratic. ⊠ *4316 S. Pacific Hwy.,* ☎ *360/642–2342. MC, V. No dinner.*

$$–$$$ 🏠 **Shelburne Inn.** This bright and cheerful antiques-filled inn built in 1896, complete with a pub, is on the National Register of Historic Places. It is also right on the highway; the quietest rooms are on the west side. ⊠ *4415 Pacific Way, Box 250, Seaview 98644,* ☎ *360/642–2442 or 800/ 466–1896,* FAX *360/642–8904. 18 rooms. Restaurant. AE, MC, V.*☜

$–$$ 🏨 **Sou'wester.** Choose from rooms and apartments in a historic lodge, in cabins, or in classic mobile-home units on the surrounding property just behind the beach. The lodge was built in 1892 as the summer retreat of a wealthy businessman and politician from Portland. ⌂ *Beach Access Rd., 38th Place, Box 102, 98644,* ☎ *360/642–2542. 9 rooms, 6 with bath; 4 cabins; 10 trailers. D, MC, V.*

Campgrounds
You can camp at 🏕 **Fort Canby State Park** (☞ Exploring Long Beach Peninsula, *above*).

Outdoor Activities and Sports

Biking
Good areas for bicycling on the peninsula include Fort Canby and North Head roads, and Sandridge Road to Ocean Park and Oysterville. While Highway 103, which runs up the west side of the peninsula, is too busy to be safe for bicyclists, it is paralleled by quiet residential roads, which are perfect for bicycling. U.S. 101 from Naselle to Seaview makes for a scenic ride but can be dangerous on weekends, because the road is narrow in places and locals are known to drive fast and cut corners. Rentals are available in virtually every town.

Fishing
Salmon, rock cod, lingcod, flounder, perch, sea bass, and sturgeon are plentiful. A guide is available from the **Pacific Salmon Charters** (⌂ Box 519, 98624, ☎ 800/831–2695). The clamming season varies depending on the supply; for details call the **Department of Fisheries and Wildlife** (☎ 360/902–2200) or the **Shellfish Lab: Nahcotta Field Station** (☎ 360/665–4166). There are tackle shops all over Long Beach Peninsula, and most sell fishing licenses.

Golf
Peninsula Golf Course (☎ 360/642–2828) has nine holes at the north end of Long Beach. **Surfside Golf Course** (☎ 360/665–4148), 2 mi north of Ocean Park, has nine holes.

Hiking
There are hiking trails at **Fort Canby State Park** (☞ Exploring Long Beach Peninsula, *above*) and **Leadbetter Point State Park** (☞ National and State Parks, *above*).

Shopping

The **Bookvendor** (⌂ 101 Pacific Ave., Long Beach, ☎ 360/642–2702) stocks children's books, classics, and travel books and features an excellent selection of local history titles. **North Head Gallery** (⌂ 600 S. Pacific Ave., Long Beach, ☎ 360/642–8884) has the largest selection of Elton Bennett originals, plus Bennett reproductions and works from other Northwest artists.

ELSEWHERE IN WASHINGTON

The San Juan Islands

The wooded knobs, rocky cliffs, and pebble beaches of the San Juan Islands provide a sunny reprieve to rain-weary mainlanders. While many rocky islets barely rise above high tide, the lofty peaks of the larger islands rise to a height of more than 2,000 ft. Hike the back-country trails, paddle among the tidal rocks in a seaworthy kayak, go on a whale-watching cruise, or just sit quietly on a grassy outcropping and watch the eagles circle overhead.

Visitor Information

The **San Juan Islands Visitor Information Service** (⊠ Box 65, Lopez Island 98261, ☎ 360/468–3663).

Arriving and Departing

BY CAR

By car from Seattle, drive north on I–5 to La Conner; go west on Route 534 to Route 20 and follow signs to Anacortes; then pick up the ferry for the San Juan Islands.

BY FERRY

The **Washington State Ferry System** (☎ 206/464–6400 or 800/843–3779) provides car and passenger service from Anacortes, about 90 mi north of Seattle, to the San Juan Islands. The **San Juan Islands Shuttle Express** (⊠ Alaska Ferry Terminal, 355 Harris Ave., No. 105, Bellingham 98225, ☎ 888/373–8522 or 360/671–1137) provides daily passenger service from Bellingham to Orcas Island and San Juan Island's Friday Harbor along with a lecture on the wildlife and natural history of the area. You can also take a three-hour whale-watching trip out of Friday Harbor.

The **San Juan Island Commuter** (⊠ Alaska Ferry Terminal, 355 Harris Ave, Bellingham 98225, ☎ 360/734–8180 or 888/734–8180) provides daily passenger service during the summer season from Bellingham to Orcas Island and San Juan Island's Friday Harbor and makes special drop-off and pick-up trips, on request, to *all* of the San Juan Islands, as far north as remote Sucia. A special bow ramp allows the boat to unload passengers, gear, and kayaks directly on a lonely beach.

BY PLANE

From Seattle-Tacoma International Airport, **Harbor Airlines** (☎ 800/359–3220) flies to San Juan Island. **Kenmore Air** (☎ 425/486–1257 or 800/543–9595) flies sea planes from Lake Union in Seattle to the San Juan Islands. **West Isle Air** (☎ 360/293–4691 or 800/874–4434) flies to San Juan Island from Anacortes, Bellingham, and Seattle.

What to See and Do

The major islands are **Lopez Island,** with old orchards, weathered barns, and sheep and cow pastures; **Shaw Island,** where Franciscan nuns in traditional habits run the ferry dock; **Orcas,** a large, mountainous horseshoe-shape island with marvelous hilltop views and several good restaurants; and **San Juan Island,** with the colorful, active waterfront town of Friday Harbor. Lopez, Orcas, and San Juan all have excellent bed-and-breakfast accommodations.

Dining

$$$–$$$$ ✕ **Christina's.** Some of the best salmon entrées in Washington compete for diners' attention with romantic water views at this Orcas Island favorite. ⊠ *N. Beach Rd. and Horseshoe Hwy., Eastsound,* ☎ *360/376-4904. AE, D, DC, MC, V. Closed Tues. and Wed. Oct.–Apr.*

★

$$–$$$ ✕ **Springtree Café.** Chef James Boyle plans a daily menu around fresh seafood and organic Waldron Island produce. Try the Caesar salad made with tofu instead of eggs, followed by king salmon in pesto sauce or ginger shrimp with mango and rum. ⊠ *310 Spring St., Friday Harbor,* ☎ *360/378-4848. AE, MC, V. Closed Tues.–Thurs.*

Lodging

$$$–$$$$ 🏨 **Mariella Inn and Cottages.** An 8-acre cove just outside Friday Harbor is the site of this antiques-filled 100-year-old country house. Rooms look out on either the water or the exquisite gardens. ⊠ *630 Turn Point Rd., Friday Harbor 98250,* ☎ *360/378-6868 or 800/700-7668,* 𝖥𝖠𝖷 *360/378-6822. 11 rooms, 12 cottages. AE, MC, V.* ✺

$$–$$$ ☒ **Edenwild.** This large, gray Victorian-style farmhouse is surrounded by gardens and framed by Fisherman's Bay. The boldly painted rooms are airy; some have fireplaces. ☒ *Eades La. at Lopez Village Rd., Lopez Island 98261,* ☎ *360/468–3238,* FAX *360/468–4080. 8 rooms. D, MC. BP.* ☜

The North Cascades

Visitor Information
Leavenworth Chamber of Commerce (☒ 894 Hwy. 2, 98826, ☎ 509/ 548–5807).

Arriving and Departing
Three highways pierce the Cascade Range in northern Washington, and one—the North Cascades Highway (Highway 20) through the North Cascades National Park—is closed in winter. Highway 2 from Everett crosses Stevens Pass before Leavenworth and continues east to Spokane. There is no passenger train or air service to the North Cascades, but the area is served by Greyhound buses, which stop at Leavenworth.

What to See and Do
Cross-country skiers flock to the eastern slopes of the North Cascades for high dry-powder snow from early November until May. The small Bavarian-theme town of Leavenworth is especially popular; trails on the local golf course are groomed for skiers. Mission Ridge downhill ski area is nearby.

In summer rafters can run the rapids of the Wenatchee River, or there's hiking above the tree line in the nearby **Wenatchee National Forest** to Enchantment Lakes; an advance permit is required from the Leavenworth Ranger Station (☎ 509/548–6977).

Dining
$$–$$$ ✗ **Restaurant Osterreich.** The sophisticated menu with Austrian influences includes appetizers like marinated duck breast in a dumpling coating, and entrées of elk stew. The atmosphere is infinitely more casual than the food. ☒ *Tyrolean Ritz Hotel, 633A Front St., Leavenworth,* ☎ *509/548–4031. MC, V. Closed Mon.*

Lodging
$$–$$$ ☒ **Pension Anna.** This family-run Austrian-style pension in the heart of the village has a homey mood, with antique pine furniture, fresh flowers, and comforters on the beds. A hearty European-style breakfast (cold cuts, cheeses, and soft-boiled eggs) is included. ☒ *926 Commercial, 98826,* ☎ *509/548–6273 or 800/509–2662,* FAX *509/548–4656. 15 rooms. AE, D, MC, V. BP.* ☜

Yakima Valley

Visitor Information
Yakima Valley Visitor and Convention Bureau (☒ 10 N. 8th St., Yakima 98901–2515, ☎ 509/575–3010).

Arriving and Departing
The Yakima valley encompasses the lower course of the Yakima River, from Union Gap to its junction with the Columbia River at Richland/Kennewick. It is traversed by I–82, which branches off I–90 at Ellensburg and runs south from Kennewick to the Columbia River (it merges into I–84 in Oregon). The drive from Seattle to Yakima via I–90 and I–82 is about 150 mi and takes about 1½ hours (Snoqualmie Pass slows things down). Yakima has a small airport with limited service from Seattle, Spokane, and Portland on Horizon Air. There is no

passenger train service, but the area is served by Greyhound buses, which stop in Yakima, Toppenish, Sunnyside, Wapato, and Prosser.

What to See and Do

Aside from the views of 12,688-ft Mt. Adams to the south and 14,411-ft Mt. Rainier to the west, the main attractions are the dozens of small wineries in this fertile area. Some of the best known are **Hogue Cellars, Château Ste. Michelle,** and **Covey Run Winery.** The **Yakima Valley Wine Growers Association** (☎ 509/786–1304) publishes maps of the region and a brochure that lists local wineries with tasting-room tours.

Dining

$ ✕ **Grant's Brewery Pub.** North America's oldest brewpub is a Yakima institution. Burgers, salads, and sandwiches complement the suds daily, and there's live jazz on weekends. ⊠ *32 N. Front St., Yakima,* ☎ *509/575–2922. AE, MC, V.*

Lodging

$$–$$$ 🏨 **Birchfield Manor.** The only true luxury accommodation in the val-
★ ley sits on a perfectly flat plateau, surrounded by fields and grazing cattle. The Old Manor House contains an award-winning restaurant and four upstairs rooms. A recently constructed cottage house has a country ambience and modern conveniences such as TVs, whirlpool tubs, steam-sauna showers, and gas fireplaces. ⊠ *2018 Birchfield Rd., Moxee City 98901,* ☎ *509/452–2334,* FAX *509/452–2334. 11 rooms. AE, DC, MC, V.* 🍽

Spokane

Spokane (pronounced spo-*can*) takes its name from a local Indian tribe, the "Children of the Sun." Indeed, Spokane is aptly named, for the city has more than its share of sunny days and is particularly beautiful when the rays of the rising or setting sun bathe the city's tall office and church towers in golden hues. The "Capital of the Inland Empire," a city of about 400,000, radiates outward from the falls of the Spokane River in a series of low river terraces. It is a city of parks and beautiful mansions, educational institutions, and centers for the visual and performing arts.

Visitor Information

Spokane Area Convention & Visitors Bureau. (⊠ 801 W. Riverside, Suite 301, 99201, ☎ 509/624–1341).

Arriving and Departing

Spokane International Airport (⊠ 9000 W. Airport Dr., ☎ 509/455–6455) is served by Horizon, Northwest, Alaska, Delta, and United airlines. Amtrak and Greyhound both serve Spokane. By car Spokane can be reached by I–90 (east–west), by U.S. 195 from the south, by U.S. 395 from the south and the north, and by U.S. 2 from the west and the east.

What to See and Do

In town the main attraction is **Riverfront Park** (⊠ 507 N. Howard St., ☎ 509/625–4386), 100 acres covering several islands in the Spokane River, including a spectacular falls. Developed from old downtown railroad yards to be the site of the Expo '74 world's fair, Riverfront Park retains one of the ultramodernist buildings from that exposition. The U.S. Pavilion houses an IMAX theater, a skating rink (winters only), and exhibition space. At the southern edge of the park, the 1909 carousel hand-carved by master builder Charles Looff is a local landmark. In sharp architectural contrast to Riverfront Park's Expo '74 building is the tall stone clock tower of the (demolished) 1902 **Great Northern Railroad Station,** close to the center of the park near Washington Street.

Two miles south on Grand Boulevard at 18th Avenue, **Manito Park** has a formal English garden, a conservatory, rose and perennial gardens, a Japanese garden complete with ponds stocked with koi, and a duck pond. It's a pleasant place to stroll in summer; in winter bring ice skates for a turn or two on the frozen duck pond.

Dining

$$–$$$ ✕ **Luna.** Luna's seasonal cuisine has strong southwestern and Californian influences. The focus on fruits and vegetables is natural, as the building was once a produce market. ⊠ *5620 S. Perry St.,* ☎ *509/448–2383. AE, D, MC, V.*

$$–$$$ ✕ **Patsy Clark's.** One of Spokane's finest mansions—complete with Italian marble, wood carvings and clocks, and a Tiffany stained-glass
★ window—is a suitably elegant place to dine on Continental cuisine. Entrées might include veal medallions stuffed with wild mushrooms, prosciutto, and spinach, doused with blackberry-port demi-glace. ⊠ *2208 W. 2nd Ave.,* ☎ *509/838–8300. AE, D, DC, MC, V.*

$–$$$ ✕ **Clinkerdagger's.** In a building that housed a flour mill in Spokane's early days, Clinks, as it's known locally, has a fine view of the Spokane River and Riverfront Park to the south. There might be four or five specials when fresh seafood is available. ⊠ *621 W. Mallon Ave.,* ☎ *509/328–5965. AE, D, DC, MC, V.*

Lodging

$$–$$$ 🏨 **Cavanaugh's Inn at the Park.** This hotel's greatest asset is its location, adjacent to Riverfront Park and two blocks from the downtown shopping district. All five floors in the main building open onto the spacious atrium lobby; more guest rooms are in two newer wings. ⊠ *303 W. North River Dr., 99201,* ☎ *509/326–8000 or 800/843–4667,* FAX *509/325–7329. 402 rooms. 2 restaurants. AE, D, DC, MC, V.* 🐾

The Arts

The **Spokane Symphony,** under the direction of Brazilian-born conductor Fabio Mechetti, plays a season of classical and pops concerts from September to April in the Opera House (⊠ 601 W. Riverside Dr., ☎ 509/624–1200). **Interplayers Ensemble** (⊠ 174 S. Howard St., ☎ 509/455–7529) is a professional theater company with productions from October through June. Call 509/747–2787 for more listings.

Outdoor Activities and Sports

Just 30 mi east of Spokane on I–90 is Idaho's **Lake Coeur d'Alene** (☞ Idaho), which has fishing, camping, hiking, water sports, and resort accommodations. A walking path named the Centennial Trail flanks the Spokane River continuously from west of downtown Spokane to east of Coeur d'Alene.

GOLF

The most challenging Spokane golf course is the 18-hole **Creek at Qualchan** (⊠ 301 E. Meadow La., ☎ 509/448–9317).

SKIING

Skiers flock to **Mt. Spokane** (⊠ Hwy. 206, 31 mi north of Spokane, ☎ 509/238–6281, 509/238–6845 for cross-country ski area), which holds the modest **49 Degrees North** (⊠ Hwy. 395, 58 mi north of Spokane near Chewelah, ☎ 509/935–6649) downhill resort and 11 mi of groomed cross-country ski trails. A state Sno-Park pass, available at the resort and numerous outlets throughout the state, is required at the cross-country ski areas.

SPECTATOR SPORTS

Baseball: Spokane Indians (⊠ Seafirst Stadium, Broadway and Havana St., ☎ 509/535–2922) play in the Class A Northwest League.

Hockey: Spokane Chiefs (⊠ Spokane Arena, 701 Mallon Ave.; at N. Howard St., ☎ 509/328–0450) play in the Western Hockey League.

The Palouse

Visitor Information

Walla Walla: Chamber of Commerce (⊠ 29 E. Sumach St., 99362, ☎ 509/525–0850). **Pullman:** Chamber of Commerce (⊠ 415 N. Grande Ave., 99163, ☎ 509/334–3565).

Arriving and Departing

From Spokane drive south on Highway 195 to Pullman or at Colfax take Highways 26, 127, and then 12 to Walla Walla. Pullman has a small airport that it shares with Moscow, Idaho, 8 mi to the east, with limited service from Lewiston, Idaho. There is no passenger-train service, but the area is served by Greyhound buses, which stop in Pullman and Walla Walla.

What to See and Do

The Palouse is rich in Northwest history. The Lewis and Clark expedition passed through in 1805, and in 1836 missionary Marcus Whitman built a medical mission 7 mi west of present-day Walla Walla. A band of Cayuse Indians massacred Whitman and more than a dozen other settlers in 1847; a **visitor center** (⊠ off U.S. 12, 7 mi west of Walla Walla, ☎ 509/529–2761) now marks the site. Nearby **Fort Walla Walla Park** (⊠ 755 Myra Rd., ☎ 509/525–7703) has 14 historic buildings and a pioneer museum.

The U.S. Calvary lost an important battle to Nez Percé Indians on the site of the **Steptoe Battlefield,** north of Pullman on Highway 195 near Rosalia. On Highway 12 between Colfax and Walla Walla, **Dayton** is worth a stop just to see the impressive 88 Victorian buildings listed on the National Register of Historic Places. A brochure with two self-guided walking tours of Dayton is available from the **Dayton Chamber of Commerce** (⊠ 166 E. Main St., ☎ 509/382–4825).

History buffs can take a walking or bicycle tour of Walla Walla, one of the earliest settlements in the Inland Northwest. Maps are available from the Chamber of Commerce (☞ Visitor Information, *above*). **Pioneer Park** (⊠ E. Alder St.), which has a fine aviary, was landscaped by the sons of Frederick Law Olmsted, who designed New York City's Central Park.

In winter, skiers head southeast of Walla Walla to the Blue Mountains, to **Ski Bluewood** (⊠ Touchet River Rd., 21 mi south of Dayton, ☎ 509/382–4725), for downhill and snowboarding.

Just north of the confluence with the Snake River, the **Palouse River** gushes over a basalt cliff higher than Niagara Falls and drops 198 ft into a steep-walled basin. Surefooted hikers venture to the overlook above the falls, which are at their fastest during spring runoff in March.

Dining and Lodging

$$–$$$ ✕ **Paisano's.** This Italian mainstay has the largest wine inventory in Walla Walla, with local vineyards well represented. Breads and desserts are baked fresh daily. ⊠ 26 E. Main St., Suite 1, Walla Walla, ☎ 509/527–3511. MC, V. Closed Sun.

$$ ☷ **Green Gables Inn.** A 1909 Craftsman-style mansion houses this lovely Walla Walla B&B, whose rooms are equipped with terry robes, bath amenities, and cable TV. A full breakfast is served by candlelight on antique china. ⊠ 922 Bonsella, Walla Walla, 99362, ☎ 509/525–5501 or 888/525–5501. 5 rooms. AE, D, MC, V. BP.

WASHINGTON, D.C.

By John F. Kelly

Updated by
Lisa Greaves

Population   598,000
Motto   Justice to All
Official Bird   Wood thrush
Official Flower   American Beauty rose

Washington, the District of Columbia, was founded in 1791 as the world's first planned national capital. It's a city of architectural splendors and unforgettable memorials, where the striking image of the Washington Monument is never far from sight and the stirring memories of a young democratic republic are never far from mind. Of course, the capital's attractions are more than monumental and governmental. Washington's museums, arts scene, parks, and gardens make it an American showcase, its arms open to the world.

Visitor Information

Washington, D.C., Convention and Visitors Association information center (⊠ 1212 New York Ave. NW, 6th floor, 20005, ☎ 202/789–7000, FAX 202/789–7037). **Dial-A-Park** (☎ 202/619–7275), a recording of events at National Park Service attractions. The **White House Visitor Center** (⊠ 1450 Pennsylvania Ave. NW, 20230, ☎ 202/208–1631).

Arriving and Departing

By Bus
Greyhound (⊠ 1005 1st St. NE, ☎ 800/231–2222) and **Peter Pan Trailways** (⊠ 1000 1st St. NE, ☎ 800/343–9999).

By Car
I–95 approaches Washington from the north and south, skirting east of the city as part of the Capital Beltway. I–495 is the western loop of the Beltway. I–395 connects D.C. with the Beltway to the south. Connecticut Avenue is the best approach from the north, dropping down from the Beltway in Maryland.

By Plane
Ronald Reagan Washington National Airport (☎ 703/417–8000), in Arlington, Virginia, 4 mi south of downtown Washington, has scheduled flights by most major domestic carriers. The renovated and expanded airport is a convenient 20-minute Metro (short for Metrorail) ride from the city center ($1.10 or $1.40, depending on the time of day). Cab fare to downtown averages $13, including tip. Many transcontinental and international flights arrive at **Dulles International Airport** (☎ 703/572–2700), a modern facility 26 mi west of Washington in Virginia. **Baltimore–Washington International Airport** (BWI; ☎ 410/859–7100) is in Maryland, about 25 mi northeast of D.C.

Bus service is provided to Reagan National and Dulles airports by the **Washington Flyer** (☎ 703/685–1400) and to National, Dulles, and BWI by the **SuperShuttle** (☎ 800/258–3826).

By Train
Amtrak trains pull into Union Station (⊠ 50 Massachusetts Ave. NE, ☎ 800/872–7245).

Getting Around Washington, D.C.

Washington's best-known sights are a short walk—or a short Metro ride—from one another.

By Car

A car can be a drawback in D.C. Traffic is horrendous, especially at rush hours (6:30 AM–9:30 AM and 3:30 PM–7 PM). One-way and diagonal streets can make the city seem like a maze, and parking is an adventure. There's free, three-hour parking around the Mall on Jefferson Drive and Madison Drive, but good luck grabbing a spot! You can also park for free—in some spots all day—in areas south of the Lincoln Memorial, on Ohio and West Basin drives in West Potomac Park. Private lots are expensive (up to $4 an hour and $13 a day).

By Public Transportation

The **Washington Metropolitan Area Transit Authority** (☎ 202/637–7000; 202/638–3780 TTY) provides Metrorail and Metrobus service in D.C. and the Maryland and Virginia suburbs. The base rail fare is $1.10. The final fare depends on the time of day and the distance you travel. All bus rides within D.C. are $1.10; a $5 **Metro Tourist Pass** entitles you to one day of unlimited subway travel weekdays from 9:30 AM to midnight or all day any weekend or holiday (except July 4).

By Taxi

Taxis in D.C. operate on a zone system, with a one-zone fare of $4. There are charges for extra passengers as well as rush-hour surcharges, so ask the driver for the total fare before you depart. Two major companies are **Capitol Cab** (☎ 202/546–2400) and **Diamond Cab** (☎ 202/387–6200). Maryland and Virginia taxis are metered and cannot take you between points within D.C.

Orientation Tours

Gray Line Tours (☎ 301/386–8300) offers a four-hour motor-coach tour of Washington, Embassy Row, and Arlington National Cemetery; four-hour tours of Mount Vernon and Alexandria; and a combination of both. Buses from **Old Town Trolley Tours** (☎ 301/985–3021) and **Tourmobile** (☎ 202/554–7950 or 202/554–5100) ply routes around the city's major attractions, allowing you to get on and off as often as you like.

Walking Tour

Not a specific walking route but groups of sites within historic neighborhoods, the **Black History National Recreation Trail** (brochure available from National Park Service: ✉ 1100 Ohio Dr. SW, 20242, ☎ 202/619–7222) illustrates aspects of African-American history in Washington, from slavery days to the New Deal.

Exploring Washington, D.C.

The major museums and galleries of the Smithsonian Institution surround the Mall. The U.S. Capitol is at the east end, the city's major monuments are to the west, and the White House is just a stone's throw away from the Mall and the monuments. Start your visit here to see Washington the capital; then venture farther afield for Washington the city. Since virtually every major sight in Washington is appropriate to visit with children, child-friendly attractions are not specifically noted.

The Mall

The first museum built by the Smithsonian was architect James Renwick's Norman-style **Castle.** Today it's home to the **Smithsonian Information Center.** An orientation film inside provides an overview of the various Smithsonian offerings, and television monitors announce the day's special events. All museums and monuments on the Mall are free. ✉ *1000 Jefferson Dr. SW,* ☎ *202/357–2700 for all Smithsonian museums.*

Washington, D.C.

WASHINGTON NAT'L. CATHEDRAL

California St.

NATIONAL ZOOLOGICAL PARK

ADAMS-MORGAN

T St.

16th St.

15th St.

14th St.

Massachusetts Ave.

S St.

S St.

Florida Ave.

Decatur Pl.

New Hampshire Ave.

R St.

DUMBARTON OAKS

R St.

Sheridan Circle

Phillips Collection

Corcoran St.

Q St.

Massachusetts Ave.

Q St.

R St.

Church St.

Q St.

Church St.

DUPONT CIRCLE

Dupont Circle

P St.

O St.

Scott Circle

Rhode Island Ave.

GEORGE-TOWN

P St.

28th St.

29th St.

27th St.

Rock Creek

O St.

N St.

N St.

National Geographic Society's Explorer Hall

Thomas Circle

C&O CANAL

M St.

29

M St.

New Hampshire Ave.

M St.

M St.

L St.

L St.

FARRAGUT NORTH

Hay-Adams Hotel

St. John's Episcopal Church

McPHERSON SQUARE

25th St.

26th St.

29

Washington Circle

L St.

K St.

National Museum Women in th

FOGGY BOTTOM

I St.

FARRAGUT WEST

Decatur House

H St.

5th St.

New York

66

24th St.

23rd St.

22nd St.

Pennsylvania Ave.

Lafayette Square

14th St.

Renwick Gallery

Blair House

Virginia Ave.

G St.

Old Executive Office Building

Octagon House

The White House

Treasury Building

Willo Co De Blc Nati Aqua

F St.

Corcoran Gallery of Art

Hotel Washington

50

E St.

Memorial Continental Hall (DAR Museum)

The Ellipse

FED TRIA

D St.

C St.

17th St.

Constitution Ave.

Vietnam Veterans Memorial

National Museum of American History

Vietnam Women's Memorial

Washington Monument

ARLINGTON NATIONAL CEMETARY

Lincoln Memorial

Reflecting Pool

SMI

Korean War Veterans Memorial

U.S. Holocaust Memorial Museum

Memorial Bridge

Independence Ave

Kutz Bridge

FDR Memorial

West

Ohio Dr.

Potomac River

W. Basin Dr.

Tidal Basin

Outlet Bridge

Potomac Park

Columbia Island

N

Jefferson Memorial

1

395

NW ◄► NE

SHAW/HOWARD U.

T St.
S St.
R St.
Q St.
O St.
N St.
M St.
L St.

Vermont Ave.
Rhode Island Ave.
Florida Ave.
New Jersey Ave.
3rd St.
1st St.
Lincoln Rd.

NATIONAL ARBORETUM

R St.
Q St.
O St.
M St.

New York Ave.

North Capitol St.

9th St.
8th St.
7th St.
6th St.
5th St.
4th St.
10th St.
11th St.
12th St.

sachusetts Ave.

Mt. Vernon Square
MT. VERNON

H St.
National Portrait Gallery, Museum of American Art
G St.

GALLERY PLACE

Pension Building (Nat'l Building Museum)

JUDICIARY SQUARE

UNION STATION

Massachusetts Ave.

New Jersey Ave.

Columbus Memorial Fountain

TRO
TER
l
Ford's Theatre
F St.
CHINA-TOWN
E St.
J. Edgar Hoover FBI Building
D St.
Navy Memorial
ARCHIVES / NAVY MEMORIAL

Pennsylvania Ave.

Louisiana Ave.

2nd St.

Supreme Court

Dr.
Smithsonian Castle/ Information Center
National Archives
National Museum of Natural History
National Gallery of Art
U.S. Capitol

NE

E. Capitol St.

THE MALL
Jefferson Dr.
National Air and Space Museum
Maryland Ave.
National Botanic Garden
Library of Congress (Jefferson Bldg)

SE

Arthur M. Sackler Gallery
Freer Gallery of Art
Arts and Industries Bldg.
National Museum of African Art
Hirshhorn Museum
Independence Ave.
U.S. Botanic Garden
Folger Shakespeare Library

u of
ving
rinting
D St.
C St.
L'ENFANT PLAZA
Canal St.
D St.
CAPITOL SOUTH
E St.

FEDERAL CENTER S.W.

Dep't of Trans.

New Jersey Ave.

s Case
rial Br.
PENTAGON
Washington Navy Yard
Southwest Fwy.
395
G St.
Virginia Ave.
395
FRED. DOUGLASS NAT'L HIST. SITE

0   500 yards
0   500 meters

SW ◄► SE

A clutch of Smithsonian museums surrounds the Castle. The **Freer Gallery of Art** (✉ 12th St. and Jefferson Dr. SW) is a repository of Asian works that's also known for James McNeill Whistler's stunning painting *Peacock Room*. The **Arthur M. Sackler Gallery** (✉ 1050 Independence Ave. SW) houses a collection including works from China, the Indian subcontinent, Persia, Thailand, and Indonesia. It's connected to the Freer Gallery by an underground tunnel. The **National Museum of African Art** (✉ 950 Independence Ave. SW) is dedicated to the collection, exhibition, and study of the traditional arts of sub-Saharan Africa. The **Arts and Industries Building** (✉ 900 Jefferson Dr. SW), just east of the Castle, features various changing exhibitions.

Walking counterclockwise around the Mall from the Castle, you'll come first to the cylindrical **Hirshhorn Museum and Sculpture Garden** (✉ 7th St. and Independence Ave. SW), which exhibits modern art both indoors and in its outdoor sculpture garden.

★ The **National Air and Space Museum** is the most visited museum in the world. Twenty-three galleries tell the story of aviation, from our earliest attempts at flight to travels beyond this solar system. Sensational IMAX films are shown on the five-story screen of the museum's Langley Theater (admission charged), while images of celestial bodies are projected on a domed ceiling in the Albert Einstein Planetarium. ✉ *Jefferson Dr. at 6th St. SW.*

★ The two **National Gallery of Art** buildings stand on the north side of the Mall. In its hundred-odd galleries, architect John Russell Pope's elegant, domed **West Building** presents masterworks of Western art from the 13th to the 20th century. I. M. Pei's angular **East Building**, with its stunning interior spaces, generally shows modern works. ✉ *Madison Dr. and 4th St. NW,* ☎ *202/737–4215.*

The **National Museum of Natural History** is filled with bones, fossils, stuffed animals, and other natural delights, including the popular Dinosaur Hall, the Hope Diamond, and a sea-life display featuring a living coral reef. ✉ *Madison Dr. between 9th and 12th Sts. NW.*

Exhibits on the three floors of the **National Museum of American History** trace the social, political, and technological history of the United States. You'll find a 280-ton steam locomotive, a collection of first ladies' inaugural gowns, and a perennially popular pendulum. ✉ *Madison Ave. between 12th and 14th Sts. NW.*

Alongside the city's many museums celebrating the best of humanity's accomplishments is one that illustrates what humans at their worst are
★ capable of. The **United States Holocaust Memorial Museum** tells the story of the 11 million Jews, Gypsies, homosexuals, political prisoners, and others killed by the Nazis between 1933 and 1945. Arrive early (by 9 AM to be safe) to get free, same-day, timed-entry tickets. Advance tickets are available through **Protix** (☎ 703/218–6500 or 800/400–9373) for a service charge ($1.75 per ticket plus a $1 charge per phone order). ✉ *100 Raoul Wallenberg Pl. SW (15th St. and Independence Ave. SW),* ☎ *202/488–0400.*

The Monuments

Washington is a city of monuments. Those dedicated to the most famous Americans are west of the Mall on filled-in former marshy flats on the Potomac. Entrance to all monuments is free.

The tallest, of course, is the recently restored **Washington Monument,** toward the Mall's west end. Construction of the 555-ft obelisk was started in 1848, interrupted by the Civil War—the reason for the color change about a third of the way up—and completed in 1884. Pick up free timed-tickets at the kiosk on 15th Street for the elevator ride to the monument's top, where the view is unequaled. ⌧ *Constitution Ave. at 15th St. NW,* ☎ *202/426–6840.*

The **Franklin Delano Roosevelt Memorial,** which was unveiled in May 1997, is a 7½-acre memorial to the 32nd president. It has waterfalls, reflection pools, and four outdoor gallery rooms—each symbolizing one of his four terms as president—and 10 bronze sculptures. ⌧ *West side of Tidal Basin,* ☎ *202/619–7222.*

The exquisitely classical **Jefferson Memorial,** honoring America's third president, rests on the south bank of the **Tidal Basin.** One of the best views of the White House is from the top steps of the memorial, John Russell Pope's reinterpretation of the Pantheon in Rome. ☎ *202/426–6821.*

★ Cherry trees, beautiful in their early April blossoms, ring the approach to the **Lincoln Memorial,** at the west end of the Mall. Henry Bacon's monument is considered by many to be the most moving spot in the city, its mood set by Daniel Chester French's somber statue of the seated president gazing over the **Reflecting Pool.** Visit this memorial at night for best effect. ☎ *202/426–6895.*

Adjacent to the Lincoln Memorial on the west end of the Mall is the **Korean War Veterans Memorial,** with its 19 statues of multiethnic patrolmen in Korea reflected in a black granite wall of etched faces bearing the inscription "Freedom Is Not Free." ☎ *202/426–6895.*

★ In Constitution Gardens, the **Vietnam Veterans Memorial**—a black granite V designed by Maya Lin, with sculpture by Frederick Hart—is another landmark that encourages introspection. The names of more than 58,000 Americans who died in Vietnam are etched on the face of the wall in the order of their deaths. The **Vietnam Women's Memorial** was dedicated on Veterans Day 1993 and sits southeast of the Vietnam Veterans Memorial. ⌧ *23rd St. and Constitution Ave. NW,* ☎ *202/634–1568.*

The President's Neighborhood

★ The **White House,** one of the world's most famous residences, has pride of place on Pennsylvania Avenue. The building was designed by Irishman James Hoban, who drew upon the Georgian design of Leinster Hall, near Dublin, and other Irish country houses. For a glimpse of some of the public rooms—including the East Room and the State Dining Room—get a ticket (up to four per person) at the White House Visitor Center (☞ Visitor Information, *above*) from March through September, or line up at the southeast gate the rest of the year; arrive by 8 AM to be safe. ⌧ *1600 Pennsylvania Ave. NW,* ☎ *202/619–7222; 202/456–7041 for recorded information.* ⌧ *Free. Closed Sun. and Mon.*

Lafayette Square (also known as Lafayette Park) is an intimate oasis in the midst of downtown Washington. It served as a campsite for soldiers of both the 1812 and Civil wars—in full view of presidents Madison and Lincoln across the way in the White House. At the top of the square, golden-domed **St. John's Episcopal Church** (⌧ 16th and H Sts. NW, ☎ 202/347–8766) is known as the Church of the Presidents. The opulent **Hay-Adams Hotel** (☞ Lodging, *below*), across 16th Street from St. John's, is a favorite with Washington insiders and visiting notables.

The first floor of the Federal-style redbrick **Decatur House** (⌧ 748 Jackson Pl. NW, ☎ 202/842–0920; ⌧ $4) is decorated as it was when occupied by naval hero Stephen Decatur in 1819. The green canopy at 1651 Pennsylvania Avenue marks the entrance to **Blair House,** the residence used by visiting heads of state. Flags from their respective countries fly from the outside lampposts when these dignitaries are in town to see the president. The busy, monumental, French Empire–style **Old**

Executive Office Building (⊠ 17th St. and Pennsylvania Ave. NW) houses many executive branch employees. Former vice president Dan Quayle had his office in here.

While most of the Smithsonian museums are on the Mall, the **Renwick Gallery,** devoted to American decorative arts, is downtown. ⊠ *Pennsylvania Ave. and 17th St. NW.* ⊠ *Free.*

Washington's largest nonfederal art museum is the **Corcoran Gallery of Art.** Its collection ranges from works by early-American artists to late-19th- and early 20th-century paintings from Europe. A highlight is the entire 18th-century Grand Salon from the Hôtel d'Orsay in Paris. ⊠ *17th St. and New York Ave. NW,* ☎ *202/639–1700.* ⊠ *Donation requested. Closed Tues.*

Despite its name, the **Octagon,** built in 1801, has six sides. The Treaty of Ghent, ending the War of 1812, was signed in an upstairs study. The building now houses the museum of the American Architectural Foundation, with exhibits relating to architecture, decorative arts, and Washington history. ⊠ *1799 New York Ave. NW,* ☎ *202/638–3105.* ⊠ *$3. Closed Mon.*

Memorial Continental Hall is the headquarters of the Daughters of the American Revolution. The 50,000-item collection of the **DAR Museum** includes fine examples of Colonial and Federal silver, china, porcelain, stoneware, earthenware, and glass. ⊠ *1776 D St. NW,* ☎ *202/879–3241.* ⊠ *Free. Closed Sat.*

Another building with an excellent aerial view of the downtown area around the White House is the venerable **Hotel Washington.** The view from the rooftop Sky Terrace, which is open May–October, is one of the best in the city. ⊠ *515 15th St. NW,* ☎ *202/638–5900.*

The huge Greek Revival **Treasury Building** is in fact home to the Department of the Treasury. Tours lead past the Andrew Johnson suite, which he used as the executive office while Mrs. Lincoln moved out of the White House, and the two-story marble cash room. Tours are given Saturdays at 10, 10:20, and 10:40. ⊠ *15th St. and Pennsylvania Ave. NW,* ☎ *202/622–0896.* ⊠ *Free.*

The magazine comes to life at the **National Geographic Society's Explorers Hall.** Interactive exhibits encourage you to learn about the world. The centerpiece is a hand-painted globe, 11 ft in diameter, that floats and spins on a cushion of air, showing off different features of the planet. ⊠ *17th and M Sts. NW,* ☎ *202/857–7588.* ⊠ *Free.*

Capitol Hill
Pierre L'Enfant, the French designer of Washington, called Capitol Hill (then known as Jenkins Hill) "a pedestal waiting for a monument."
★ That monument is the **U.S. Capitol,** the gleaming white-dome building in which elected officials toil. George Washington laid the cornerstone on September 18, 1793, and in November 1800 Congress moved down from Philadelphia. The Capitol has grown over the years and today contains some of the city's most inspiring art, from Constantino Brumidi's *Apotheosis of Washington,* the fresco at the center of the dome, to the splendid Statuary Hall. There are also live attractions: senators and representatives speechifying in their respective chambers. If you want to test your architectural eyes, spend a minute or two looking at the dome from afar: Does it fit or is it a bit too large? ⊠ *East end of the Mall,* ☎ *202/224–3121 or 202/225–6827.*

East of the Capitol are the three buildings that make up the **Library of Congress,** which contains 115 million items, of which only a quarter are books. The remainder includes manuscripts, prints, films, photographs, sheet music, and the largest collection of maps in the world. The **Jefferson Building** (⊠ 1st St. and Independence Ave. SE, ☎ 202/707–8000), with its grand, octagonal Main Reading Room and mahogany readers' tables, is the centerpiece of the system. The **Adams Building**, on 2nd Street behind the Jefferson, was added in 1939. The **James Madison Building** opened in 1980; it's just south of the Jefferson Building, between Independence Avenue and C Street.

The **Folger Shakespeare Library** is home to a world-class collection of Shakespeareana. Inside are a reproduction of an inn-yard theater and a gallery—designed in the manner of an Elizabethan great hall—that hosts exhibits from the library's collection of works by and about the Bard. ⊠ 201 E. Capitol St. SE, ☎ 202/544–4600. ☞ Free. Closed Sun.

After being shunted around several locations, including a spell in a tavern, the **Supreme Court** got its own building in 1935. The impressive, colonnaded white-marble temple was designed by Cass Gilbert. ⊠ 1st and E. Capitol Sts. NE, ☎ 202/479–3000. ☞ Free. Closed weekends.

Union Station is now a shopping center as well as a train terminal and subway station. The Beaux Arts building's wonderful main waiting room is a perfect setting for the inaugural ball that's held here every four years. ⊠ 50 Massachusetts Ave. NE.

Old Downtown and Federal Triangle

Before the glass office blocks around 16th and K streets NW became the business center of town, Washington's mercantile hub was farther east. The open-air markets are gone, but some of the 19th-century character of Washington's east end remains. In the 1930s the humongous **Federal Triangle** complex was built to accommodate the expanding federal bureaucracy.

The massive redbrick **Pension Building** went up in the 1880s to house workers who processed the pension claims of veterans and their survivors. It's currently home to the **National Building Museum** (⊠ F St. between 4th and 5th Sts. NW, ☎ 202/272–2448; ☞ free), devoted to architecture and related arts.

Judiciary Square is Washington's legal core, with local and district court buildings arrayed around it. At the center is the **National Law Enforcement Officers Memorial**, a 3-ft-high wall bearing the names of more than 15,000 American police officers killed in the line of duty since 1794. Washington's compact **Chinatown** is bordered roughly by G, H, 6th, and 8th streets NW.

Two Smithsonian museums share the Greek Revival **Old Patent Office Building.** The **National Portrait Gallery**, on the south side, contains paintings and photographs of presidents and other notable Americans. The north side's **National Museum of American Art** has a collection with items from Colonial times to the present. Both these museums are closed for renovation and are scheduled to reopen in 2003. ⊠ 8th and G Sts. NW.

Ford's Theatre (⊠ 511 10th St. NW, ☎ 202/426–6924; ☞ free), where Abraham Lincoln was assassinated by John Wilkes Booth on April 14, 1865, now houses a museum (in the basement) that displays items connected with Lincoln's life and untimely death.

The Beaux Arts **Willard Hotel** (⊠ 14th St. and Pennsylvania Ave. NW) is one of the most luxurious in Washington. As the story goes, its lobby is the origin of the term "lobbyist": President U. S. Grant would occasionally escape from the White House to have a brandy and cigar in the Willard's lobby, where interested parties would descend on him, trying to bend his ear.

The **Commerce Department Building** forms the base of Federal Triangle. Inside Commerce is the **National Aquarium,** the country's oldest public aquarium, featuring tropical and freshwater fish, moray eels, frogs, turtles, piranhas, even sharks. ⊠ *14th St. and Pennsylvania Ave. NW,* ☎ *202/482–2825.* ⊠ *$2.*

The tour of the hulking **J. Edgar Hoover Federal Bureau of Investigation Building** outlines the work of the FBI and ends with a live-ammo firearms demonstration. From the end of March through June the wait to get inside may be as long as three hours. ⊠ *10th St. and Pennsylvania Ave. NW (tour entrance at 9th and E Sts. NW),* ☎ *202/324–3447.* ⊠ *Free. No tours weekends.*

The Declaration of Independence, the Constitution, and the Bill of Rights are on display in the rotunda of the **National Archives.** ⊠ *Constitution Ave. between 7th and 9th Sts. NW,* ☎ *202/501–5000.* ⊠ *Free.*

The statue of a lone sailor staring out over the largest map in the world marks the site of the **Navy Memorial** (⊠ *7th St. and Pennsylvania Ave. NW*). In summer the memorial's concert stage (☎ *202/737–2300*) is the site of military-band performances.

The **National Museum of Women in the Arts** displays the works of prominent female artists from the Renaissance to the present, including Georgia O'Keeffe, Mary Cassatt, Elisabeth Vigée-Lebrun, and Judy Chicago. ⊠ *1250 New York Ave. NW,* ☎ *202/783–5000.* ⊠ *Donations accepted.*

Georgetown

At one time a tobacco port, this poshest of Washington neighborhoods is home to some of its wealthiest and best-known citizens. It's also the nucleus of the district's nightlife scene, with dozens of hot spots dotting Wisconsin Avenue and M Street, Georgetown's crossroads.

Downhill from the main bustle of G-town, the **Chesapeake & Ohio Canal** allows for a scenic getaway from the streets. Dug in the 19th century as an alternative to the rough and rocky Potomac, it was used to transport lumber, coal, iron, and flour into northwest Maryland. Runners now tread its scenic towpath, and in summer mule-drawn barges ply its placid waters; tickets are available at the Foundry Mall (⊠ *1057 Thomas Jefferson St. NW,* ☎ *202/653–5190*).

The **Shops at Georgetown Park** (⊠ *3222 M St. NW,* ☎ *202/298–5577*), home to such high-ticket stores as F. A. O. Schwarz and Polo–Ralph Lauren, is a multilevel shopping extravaganza that answers the question "If the Victorians had invented shopping malls, what would they look like?"

Georgetown University, the oldest Jesuit school in the country, has its campus at the western edge of the neighborhood. When seen from the Potomac or from Washington's high ground, the Gothic spires of the university's older buildings give it an almost medieval look.

Dumbarton Oaks, an estate comprising two museums—one of Byzantine works, the other of pre-Columbian art—is surrounded by 10 acres of stunning formal gardens designed by landscape architect Beatrix Farrand. *Art collections:* ⊠ *1703 32nd St. NW,* ☎ *202/339–6401.* ⊠ *$1 donation Apr.–Oct. Closed Mon. Gardens:* ⊠ *31st and R Sts. NW.* ⊠ *$4 Apr.–Oct.*

Other Attractions

The **Bureau of Engraving and Printing** is the birthplace of all paper currency in the United States. Although there are no free samples, the 40-minute guided tour—which takes you past presses that turn out $696 million worth of currency a day—is one of the city's most popular. ⊠ *14th and C Sts. SW,* ☎ *202/874–3019.* ☜ *Free. Closed weekends.*

★ The **Frederick Douglass National Historic Site** is at Cedar Hill, the Washington home of the noted abolitionist. The house displays mementos from Douglass's life and has a wonderful view of the Federal City, across the Anacostia River. ⊠ *1411 W St. SE,* ☎ *202/426–5961.* ☜ *$3.*

The **Phillips Collection** was the first permanent museum of modern art in the country. Holdings include works by Braque, Cézanne, Klee, Matisse, Renoir, and John Henry Twachtman. ⊠ *1600 21st St. NW,* ☎ *202/387–2151.* ☜ *$6.50, $5 Thurs. evening. Closed Mon.*

It took 83 years to complete the Gothic Revival **Washington National Cathedral,** the sixth-largest cathedral in the world. Besides flying buttresses, a nave, transepts, and rib vaults that were built stone by stone, it is adorned with fanciful gargoyles created by skilled stone carvers. ⊠ *Wisconsin and Massachusetts Aves. NW,* ☎ *202/537–6200.*

The **Washington Navy Yard** is the navy's oldest shore establishment. A former shipyard and ordnance facility, the yard today is home to the **Navy Museum** and the **Marine Corps Museum,** which outline the history of those two services from their inception to the present. ⊠ *9th and M Sts. SE,* ☎ *202/433–4882 for Navy Museum; 202/433–3840 for Marine Corps Museum.* ☜ *Free.*

Arlington, Virginia

Though the attractions here are across the Potomac, it's well worth making them a part of your visit to the nation's capital. (For more suburban Virginia sights, including Mount Vernon and Old Town Alexandria, *see* Virginia.)

At **Arlington National Cemetery,** you can trace America's history through the aftermath of its battles. Dominating the cemetery is the Greek Revival **Arlington House,** onetime home of Robert E. Lee, which offers a breathtaking view across the Potomac to the Lincoln Memorial and the Mall. On a hillside below are the **Kennedy graves.** John Fitzgerald Kennedy is buried under an eternal flame. Jacqueline Bouvier Kennedy Onassis lies next to him. Robert Francis Kennedy is buried nearby, his grave marked by a simple white cross. The **Tomb of the Unknowns** is also in the cemetery. ⊠ *West end of Memorial Bridge,* ☎ *703/607–8052.*

Just north of Arlington Cemetery is the **United States Marine Corps War Memorial,** honoring marines who have given their lives since the corps was formed in 1775. The memorial statue, sculpted by Felix W. de Weldon, is based on Joe Rosenthal's Pulitzer Prize–winning photograph of six soldiers raising a flag atop Iwo Jima's Mt. Suribachi on February 19, 1945.

The **Pentagon,** headquarters of the Department of Defense, is an exercise in immensity: 23,000 military and civilian employees work here; it's as wide as three Washington Monuments laid end to end; and inside it contains 685 drinking fountains, 7,748 windows, and 17½ mi of corridors. There is a 75-minute tour on weekdays every hour from 9 AM to 3 PM, limited to 30 people. The ticket window opens at 8:45 and tours fill up quickly; a photo ID is required. ⊠ *Off I–395,* ☎ *703/ 695–1776.* ☜ *Free.*

Parks, Gardens, and Zoos

The 444-acre **National Arboretum** blooms with all manner of plants; clematis, peonies, rhododendrons, and azaleas are among its showier inhabitants. The National Bonsai Collection, National Herb Garden, and an odd and striking hilltop construction of old marble columns from the U.S. Capitol are also well worth seeing. ⊠ *3501 New York Ave. NE,* ☎ *202/245–2726.* ⊡ *Free.*

The 160-acre **National Zoological Park,** part of the Smithsonian Institution, is one of the foremost zoos in the world. Innovative compounds show animals in naturalistic settings, and the ambitious Amazonia recreates the ecosystem of a South American rain forest. ⊠ *3001 Connecticut Ave. NW,* ☎ *202/673–4800.* ⊡ *Free.*

Rock Creek Park is a cool tongue of green jutting down into the center of Washington. Its 1,800 acres include picnic sites and biking, hiking, and equestrian trails that wend through groves of dogwood, beech, oak, and cedar. ⊠ *Park starts roughly at P St. on edge of Georgetown and runs along both sides of creek all the way to Montgomery County, MD.* ☎ *202/426–6829.*

The **United States Botanic Garden,** just below the Capitol, is a peaceful plant-filled conservatory that includes a cactus house, a fern house, and a subtropical house filled with orchids. Note that the garden is closed until spring 2001 while it undergoes renovations. ⊠ *1st St. and Maryland Ave. SW,* ☎ *202/225–8333.* ⊡ *Free.*

Dining

As the nation's capital, Washington hosts an international array of visitors and new residents. This infusion of cultures means that D.C. restaurants are getting better and better. (And sometimes, cheaper and cheaper: more of the top dining rooms now offer reasonably priced fare and fixed-price specials.) Good ethnic meals can be found in Adams-Morgan (lots of Ethiopian), Georgetown (Afghani to Indonesian), and Chinatown.

$$$$ ✕ **Citronelle.** The essence of California chic, Citronelle's glass-front
  ★ kitchen lets you see all the action as chefs scurry to and fro. Loin of venison is served with an endive tart and garnished with dried apples. ⊠ *3000 M St. NW, Georgetown,* ☎ *202/625–2150. AE, DC, MC, V.*

$$$–$$$$ ✕ **i Ricchi.** At this airy Tuscan restaurant, the spring-summer menu in-
  ★ cludes such offerings as rolled pork and rabbit roasted in wine and fresh herbs, while the fall-winter list brings grilled lamb chops and sautéed beef fillet. ⊠ *1220 19th St. NW, Downtown,* ☎ *202/835–0459. AE, DC, MC, V. Closed Sun. No lunch Sat.*

$$$–$$$$ ✕ **Sam and Harry's.** The surroundings at this quintessential steak house are understated and genteel, with five private dining rooms available. The main attractions are porterhouse steak and filet mignon. ⊠ *1200 19th St. NW, Downtown,* ☎ *202/296–4333. AE, D, DC, MC, V. Closed Sun. No lunch Sat.*

$$–$$$$ ✕ **Occidental Grill.** Part of the stately Willard Hotel complex (☞ Lodging, *below*), this popular restaurant offers innovative dishes, attentive service, and lots of photos of politicians and other power brokers past and present. The menu changes frequently, but you can count on grilled poultry, fish, and steak, as well as salads and sandwiches. ⊠ *1475 Pennsylvania Ave. NW, Downtown,* ☎ *202/783–1475. AE, MC, V.*

$$–$$$ ✕ **Bombay Club.** One block from the White House, the Bombay tries
  ★ to re-create a private club like those established for 19th-century British colonials in India. The menu includes unusual seafood specialties and a large number of vegetarian dishes, but the real standouts are the breads and the seafood appetizers. ⊠ *815 Connecticut Ave. NW, Downtown,* ☎ *202/659–3727. AE, DC, MC, V. No lunch Sat.*

$$–$$$ ✕ **Georgia Brown's.** An elegant "new South" eatery and a favorite hangout of local politicians, Georgia Brown's serves shrimp Carolina-style (with the head on and steaming grits on the side) and beef tenderloin medallions with a bourbon-pecan sauce. Fried green tomatoes are given the gourmet treatment. ⊠ *950 15th St. NW, Downtown,* ☎ *202/ 393–4499. AE, DC, MC, V. No lunch Sat.*

$$–$$$ ✕ **La Colline.** The menu here, at one of the city's best French restau-
★ rants, emphasizes seafood, with offerings that range from simple grilled preparations to fricassees and food served au gratin with imaginative sauces. Other items include duck with orange sauce and veal with chanterelle mushrooms. ⊠ *400 N. Capitol St. NW, Capitol Hill,* ☎ *202/737–0400. AE, DC, MC, V. Closed Sun. No lunch Sat.*

$–$$$ ✕ **City Lights of China.** This restaurant always makes critics' lists. The
★ traditional Chinese fare is excellent. Less common specialties, such as lamb in a tangy peppery sauce and shark's fin soup, are deftly cooked as well. Jumbo shrimp with spicy salt are baked in their shells, then stir-fried with ginger and spices. ⊠ *1731 Connecticut Ave. NW, Dupont Circle,* ☎ *202/265–6688. AE, D, DC, MC, V.*

$$ ✕ **Jaleo.** A lively Spanish bistro, Jaleo features a long list of hot and
★ cold tapas, although such entrées as grilled fish and paella—which comes in four different versions—are just as tasty. ⊠ *480 7th St. NW, Downtown,* ☎ *202/628–7949. AE, D, DC, MC, V.*

$–$$ ✕ **Aditi.** Aditi's two-story dining room seems too elegant for a moderately priced Indian restaurant. Tandoori and curry dishes are expertly prepared and not aggressively spiced; if you want your food spicy, request it. Rice *biryani* (cooked with meats and vegetables) entrées are good for lighter appetites. ⊠ *3299 M St. NW, Georgetown,* ☎ *202/ 625–6825. AE, D, MC, V.*

$–$$ ✕ **Café Nema.** The menu here combines Somali, North African, and Middle Eastern cuisines. Entrées are simple but flavorful, such as grilled chicken, lamb, and beef kabobs. There's also a good selection of pastas, salads, and sandwiches. At $4, the generous falafel sandwich is one of the best bargains in the city. ⊠ *1334 U St. NW,* ☎ *202/667– 3215. AE, D, DC, MC, V.*

$–$$ ✕ **Meskerem.** Meskerem is distinctive for a balcony where you can eat
★ Ethiopian style: seated on leather floor cushions with large woven baskets for tables. Stews served with *injera* (spongy flat bread) are made with teff, a grain grown only in Ethiopia and Idaho that imparts a distinctive sourness. ⊠ *2434 18th St. NW, Adams Morgan,* ☎ *202/462– 4100. AE, DC, MC, V.*

$–$$ ✕ **Georgetown Café.** With its unpretentious decor, cheap prices, and eclectic, lowbrow menu, this café is a bit of a neighborhood oddball. Students and other locals are known to frequent it for its pasta, pizzas, and gyros as well as its roast beef and baked chicken. ⊠ *1623 Wisconsin Ave. NW, Georgetown,* ☎ *202/333–0215. D, MC, V.*

$–$$ ✕ **Peyote Café/Roxanne Restaurant/On the Rooftop.** Mexican influences on traditional southern food define the menus at these two connected restaurants, where you can order from both menus. Grilled rib-eye steak, grilled salmon, and Sweat Hot Fire Shrimp are specialties. ⊠ *2319 18th St. NW, Adams Morgan,* ☎ *202/462–8330. AE, DC, MC, V. No lunch Mon.–Sat.*

$–$$ ✕ **Teaism.** A novel counterpoint to all the area's coffee bars, Teaism offers not only an impressive selection of more than 50 teas but also delicious Japanese, Indian, and Thai foods. ⊠ *2009 R St. NW, Dupont Circle,* ☎ *202/667–3827. AE, MC, V.*

$ ✕ **Burma.** Batter-fried eggplant and squash are deliciously paired with complex, peppery sauces at this exquisite jewel in Chinatown. Such entrées as mango pork, tamarind fish, and Kokang chicken are equally satisfying. ⊠ *740 6th St. NW, Downtown,* ☎ *202/638–1280. AE, D, DC, MC, V. No lunch weekends.*

$ ✕ **Sholl's Colonial Cafeteria.** Suited federal workers line up with tourists to grab a bite at this Washington institution, where favorites include chopped steak, liver and onions, and baked chicken and fish. Sholl's is famous for its apple, blueberry, and other fruit pies. ⊠ *1990 K St. NW, Downtown,* ☎ *202/296–3065. No credit cards.*

Lodging

Many Washington hotels, particularly those downtown, offer special **reduced rates** and package deals on weekends, and some are available midweek; be sure to ask about them at the hotel of your choice. **Capitol Reservations** (☎ 202/452–1270 or 800/847–4832 from 9 to 6 weekdays) books rooms at more than 70 better hotels in good locations at rates 20%–40% off; it also offers group packages with tours and meals. **Washington D.C. Accommodations** (☎ 202/289–2220 or 800/554–2220 from 8:30 to 5:30 weekdays) will book rooms at any hotel in town, with discounts of 20%–40% available at about 90 locations.

To find reasonably priced accommodations in small guest houses and private homes, contact **Bed & Breakfast Accommodations Ltd. of Washington, D.C.** (⊠ Box 12011, 20005, ☎ 202/328–3510, FAX 202/332–3885) or **Bed & Breakfast League, Ltd./Sweet Dreams & Toast** (⊠ Box 9490, 20016-9490, ☎ 202/363–7767, FAX 202/363–8396).

$$$$ ⊞ **Four Seasons Hotel.** This contemporary hotel, conveniently situated
★   between Georgetown and Foggy Bottom, is a gathering place for Washington's elite. The quieter rooms face the courtyard; others have a view of the C&O Canal. ⊠ *2800 Pennsylvania Ave. NW, 20007,* ☎ *202/342–0444,* FAX *202/944–2076. 262 rooms. 2 restaurants, pool, health club. AE, D, DC, MC, V.* ✿

$$$$ ⊞ **Hay-Adams Hotel.** This grand White House neighbor is a common
★   choice for state policy-making meetings. Its elegance extends to guest rooms, where you might feel like you're in a mansion in disguise. ⊠ *1 Lafayette Sq., 20006,* ☎ *202/638–6600 or 800/424–5054,* FAX *202/638–2716. 143 rooms. Restaurant. AE, D, DC, MC, V.*

$$$$ ⊞ **Hilton Washington and Towers.** This busy high-rise attracts travel-
★   ers who like to be where the action is. The light-filled but compact guest rooms are furnished in standard modern hotel style and have marble bathrooms. ⊠ *1919 Connecticut Ave. NW, 20009,* ☎ *202/483–3000,* FAX *202/232–0438. 1,122 rooms. 3 restaurants, pool, tennis, health club. AE, D, DC, MC, V.* ✿

$$$$ ⊞ **Hyatt Regency on Capitol Hill.** Close to Union Station and the Mall, the elegant 11-story Hyatt Regency features a spectacular garden atrium. Suites on the south side have a view of the Capitol dome just a few blocks away, as does the rooftop Capitol View Club restaurant. ⊠ *400 New Jersey Ave. NW, 20001,* ☎ *202/737–1234,* FAX *202/737–5773. 865 rooms. 2 restaurants, pool, health club. AE, DC, MC, V.* ✿

$$$–$$$$ ⊞ **St. Regis.** Formerly the Carlton, the hotel looks like an Italian man-
★   sion, with gilded ornamental ceilings and Louis XVI furnishings. In a bustling business sector near the White House, it offers cordial, dignified service, including day and night butler service. ⊠ *923 16th St. NW, 20006,* ☎ *202/638–2626 or 800/325–3535,* FAX *202/638–4231. 193 rooms. Restaurant, exercise room. AE, D, DC, MC, V.*

$$$–$$$$ ⊞ **Westin Fairfax.** Formerly a Sheraton property, this hotel near Dupont
★   Circle is exclusive and intimate. Rooms have views of Embassy Row or Georgetown. ⊠ *2100 Massachusetts Ave. NW, 20008,* ☎ *202/293–2100 or 800/325–3589,* FAX *202/835–0641. 209 rooms. Restaurant, exercise room. AE, DC, MC, V.* ✿

$$$–$$$$ ⊞ **Willard Inter-Continental.** The Willard is an opulent Beaux Arts feast
★   for the eye, as the main lobby with its great columns, huge chande-

liers, and elaborately carved ceilings attests. The hotel's formal restaurant has won nationwide acclaim. ⊠ *1401 Pennsylvania Ave. NW, 20004,* ☎ *202/628–9100,* FAX *202/637–7326. 340 rooms. 2 restaurants, health club. AE, D, DC, MC, V.*

$$$ ★ **Washington Courtyard by Marriott.** One of the city's best values for budget travelers, Marriott's Washington Courtyard hotel is a good alternative for international tourists and businesspeople who can't find rooms at the Washington Hilton (☞ *above*). Guest rooms on the west and south have good views. ⊠ *1900 Connecticut Ave. NW, 20009,* ☎ *202/332–9300 or 800/842–4211,* FAX *202/328–7039. 147 rooms. Restaurant, pool, health club. AE, D, DC, MC, V.*

$$–$$$ **Holiday Inn on the Hill.** For clean, comfortable, low-price rooms with high-price views, this is the place. They offer the same magnificent vistas of the Capitol as those at the pricier Hyatt (☞ *above*). Children under age 18 stay free. ⊠ *415 New Jersey Ave. NW, 20001,* ☎ *202/638–1616 or 800/638–1116,* FAX *202/638–0707. 342 rooms. Restaurant, pool. AE, D, DC, MC, V. CP.*

$$–$$$ **Latham Hotel.** A small hotel in the city's liveliest neighborhood, this redbrick neo-Colonial is popular with Europeans and devotees of Georgetown. Rooms are sleek and contemporary. Some are underground; others have views of the C&O Canal or busy M Street. The restaurant here, Citronelle (☞ Dining, *above*), is considered one of Washington's best. ⊠ *3000 M St. NW, 20007,* ☎ *202/726–5000,* FAX *202/ 337–4250. 143 rooms. Restaurant, pool. AE, D, DC, MC, V. CP.*

$–$$$ ★ **Jurys Normandy Inn.** A small European-style hotel on a quiet street in the exclusive embassy area of Connecticut Avenue, the Normandy is near restaurants and some of the most expensive residential real estate in Washington. Rooms are standard and comfortable; all have refrigerators. ⊠ *2118 Wyoming Ave. NW, 20008,* ☎ *202/483–1350 or 800/424–3729,* FAX *202/387–8241. 75 rooms. AE, D, DC, MC, V. CP.*

$$ **Capitol Hill Suites.** On a quiet residential street beside the Library of Congress, this all-suite hotel's rooms—which are actually renovated apartments—are large and cozy and have kitchenettes. ⊠ *200 C St. SE, 20003,* ☎ *202/543–6000 or 800/424–9165,* FAX *202/547–2608. 152 suites. Exercise room. AE, DC, MC, V.*

$$ **Phoenix Park Hotel.** Just steps from Union Station and four blocks from the Capitol, this Irish-style hotel has wood-panel-and-brass decor and is the home of the Dubliner bar (☞ Nightlife and the Arts, *below*). Guest rooms are bright, traditionally furnished, and quiet. ⊠ *520 N. Capitol St. NW, 20001,* ☎ *202/638–6900 or 800/824–5419,* FAX *202/ 393–3236. 156 rooms. Restaurant, health club. AE, D, DC, MC, V.*

$–$$ **Tabard Inn.** Three Victorian town houses near Dupont Circle were linked in the 1920s to form this inn. Furnishings are broken-in Victorian and American Empire antiques; a Victorian-inspired carpet cushions the labyrinthine hallways. ⊠ *1739 N St. NW, 20036,* ☎ *202/785–1277,* FAX *202/785–6173. 40 rooms, 25 with bath. Restaurant. AE, DC, MC, V. CP.*

Nightlife and the Arts

Area arts and entertainment events are listed in the "Weekend" section of Friday's *Washington Post*, in the free *City Paper*, in *Washingtonian* magazine (on newsstands), and in *Where: Washington* (free in hotels).

Nightlife

Georgetown, Adams-Morgan, Dupont Circle, and **Capitol Hill** are the main nightlife centers in DC.

BARS

The **Brickskeller** (⊠ 1523 22nd St. NW, ☎ 202/293–1885) sells more than 700 brands of beer—from Central American lagers to U.S.-microbrewed ales. The **Dubliner** (✉ Phoenix Park Hotel, 520 N. Capitol St. NW, ☎ 202/737–3773) features snug paneled rooms, thick and tasty Guinness, and nightly live Irish entertainment.

CABARET

The **Capitol Steps** (☎ 202/298–8222 or 703/683–8330) performs political song and satire regularly in Georgetown; performance locations vary, so call for details.

JAZZ

Blues Alley (✉ Rear 1073 Wisconsin Ave. NW, ☎ 202/337–4141) books some of the biggest names in jazz.

ROCK

The **Black Cat** (✉ 1831 14th St. NW, ☎ 202/667–7960) features live rock. The **9:30 Club** (✉ 815 V St. NW, ☎ 202/393–0930) books an eclectic mix of local, national, and international artists, mostly playing so-called alternative rock.

The Arts

All manner of cultural events, from ballet to classical music, are offered at the **John F. Kennedy Center for the Performing Arts** (✉ New Hampshire Ave. and Rock Creek Pkwy. NW, ☎ 202/467–4600 or 800/444–1324). **TicketPlace** (✉ Old Post Office Pavilion, 1100 Pennsylvania Ave. NW, ☎ 202/842–5387) sells half-price day-of-performance tickets; it's closed Sunday and Monday. **Ticketmaster** (☎ 202/432–7328 or 800/551–7328) takes phone charges for events around the city.

DANCE

Dance Place (✉ 3225 8th St. NE, ☎ 202/269–1600) hosts a wide array of modern and ethnic dance. The **Washington Ballet** (☎ 202/362–3606) performs at the Kennedy Center and the Warner Theatre (13th and E Sts. NW).

MUSIC

The **Armed Forces Concert Series** (☎ 202/767–5658 air force; 703/696–3718 army; 202/433–4011 marines; 202/433–2525 navy) offers free military-band performances June–August, nightly except Wednesday and Saturday, on the West Terrace of the Capitol and at the Sylvan Theater on the Washington Monument grounds.

The **National Symphony Orchestra** (☎ 202/416–8100, 703/255–1900, 202/416–8100, or 703/255–1900) performs at the Kennedy Center from September through June and during the summer at Wolf Trap Farm Park. For more on Wolf Trap Farm Park, *see* Virginia.

OPERA

The **Washington Opera** (☎ 202/295–2420 or 800/876–7372) presents eight operas each season in the Kennedy Center's Opera House and in the Kennedy Center's Eisenhower Theater.

THEATER

Arena Stage (✉ 6th St. and Maine Ave. SW, ☎ 202/488–3300) has three theaters and is the city's most respected resident company. The historic **Ford's Theatre** (✉ 511 10th St. NW, ☎ 202/347–4833) is host mainly to musicals. The **National Theatre** (✉ 1321 Pennsylvania Ave. NW, ☎ 202/628–6161) presents tryouts and national touring companies of Broadway shows. The **Shakespeare Theatre** (✉ 450 7th St. NW, ☎ 202/547–1122) presents classics by the Bard. Many scrappy smaller companies—including the Source, the Studio, and the Woolly Mammoth—are clustered near 14th and P streets NW.

Spectator Sports

Basketball: Wizards and **Mystics** (⊠ MCI Center, 7th and F Sts. NW, ☎ 202/432–7328; 800/551–7328 for tickets; 202/628–3200 for schedule). **Football:** The **Redskins** are now based in nearby Landover, Maryland (⊠ Jack Kent Cooke Stadium, ☎ 301/276–6050), with about 20,000 more seats than their old home at RFK Stadium, but all tickets are held by season-ticket holders. If you're willing to pay dearly, you can get tickets from brokers who advertise in the *Washington Post*. **Hockey: Capitals** (⊠ MCI Center, ☎ 202/432–7328; 800/551–7328 for tickets; 202/628–3200 for schedule).

Shopping

Shopping Districts

Georgetown (centered on Wisconsin Ave. and M St. NW) is probably Washington's densest shopping area, with specialty shops selling everything from antiques to designer fashions. In **Adams-Morgan** (around 18th St. and Columbia Rd. NW) you'll find used-book stores, vintage clothing shops, and a bohemian atmosphere.

The **Shops at National Place** (⊠ 13th and F Sts. NW, ☎ 202/662–1250) is a glittering three-story collection of stores, including B. Dalton, Footlocker, Filene's Basement, and Casual Corner. **Union Station** (⊠ 50 Massachusetts Ave. NE, ☎ 202/371–9441) has clothing boutiques and special-interest shops. **Mazza Gallerie** (⊠ 5300 Wisconsin Ave. NW, ☎ 202/966–6114) is an upscale mall that straddles the Maryland border and is anchored by the ritzy Neiman Marcus and a Filene's Basement.

Department Stores

Hecht's (⊠ 12th and G Sts. NW, ☎ 202/628–6661) is downtown Washington's sole remaining department store, as its former neighbors—Garfinckel's, Woodward & Lothrop, Lansburgh's—have all pulled up stakes in the last decade. It's near the Metro Center subway stop.

Specialty Stores

Every museum in Washington has a gift shop, and in each the range of items reflects the museum's collection and extends far beyond the mere souvenir. The largest is probably in the **National Museum of American History** (☞ Exploring Washington, D.C., *above*). The **Indian Craft Shop,** in the Department of the Interior (⊠ 1849 C St. NW, ☎ 202/208–4056), sells a variety of handicrafts from more than 35 Native American tribes.

WEST VIRGINIA

Updated by
Kay Michael

Capital	Charleston
Population	1,816,000
Motto	Mountaineers Are Always Free
State Bird	Cardinal
State Flower	Rhododendron maximum
Postal Abbreviation	WV

Statewide Visitor Information

West Virginia Division of Tourism (✉ 2101 Washington St. E, Charleston 25305, ☎ 304/558–2200 or 800/225–5982, FAX 304/558–0108).

Scenic Drives

In the eastern mountains a **National Scenic Byway** (W.Va. 39/55 and connecting W.Va. 150) roams between Richwood and U.S. 219/W.Va. 55 north of Edray, in the Monongahela National Forest. The **Midland Trail** follows historic U.S. 60, running east–west for 120 mi between White Sulphur Springs and Charleston, tracing the 200-year-old path through the Appalachians first used by Native Americans. The **Coal Heritage Trail** begins at Chimney Corner and continues through Beckley, Sophia, Mullens, and into Bluefield.

National and State Parks

National Parks

Harpers Ferry National Historical Park (✉ Box 65, Harpers Ferry 25425, ☎ 304/535–6298; 🎟 $2 per day, 7-day pass $5) is situated at the picturesque confluence of the Potomac and Shenandoah rivers. The **New River Gorge National River** (✉ Box 246, Glen Jean 25846, ☎ 304/465–0508), a 53-mi section of the New River, contains a wide variety of some of America's best white-water recreation. The **Monongahela National Forest** (✉ 200 Sycamore St., Elkins 26241, ☎ 304/636–1800) and **George Washington National Forest** (✉ Lee Ranger District, Rte. 4, Box 515, Edinburg, VA 22824, ☎ 540/984–4101) encompass 900,000 and 100,000 acres, respectively, near the Virginia border.

State Parks

Eight of West Virginia's 46 state parks, forests, and wildlife management facilities have fine lodges with restaurants and resort amenities, such as downhill skiing or championship golf courses. Most have cottages, cabins, and campsites with full hookups. **Cacapon Resort State Park** (✉ Rte. 1, Box 230, Berkeley Springs 25411, ☎ 304/258–1022 or 800/225–5982) is noted for its Robert Trent Jones golf course; amenities include 30 cottages and a 49-room lodge with restaurant. At **Canaan Valley Resort State Park** (✉ HC 70, Box 330, Davis 26260, ☎ 304/866–4121 or 800/225–5982), the 250-room lodge, 23 deluxe cabins, restaurant, and lounge are bustling year-round; the park has an alpine-skiing area, ice-skating, an 18-hole golf course, and outdoor and indoor pools and fitness center. **Pipestem Resort State Park** (✉ Box 150, Pipestem 25979, ☎ 304/466–1800 or 800/225–5982), southeast of Beckley, has two lodges (143 rooms) with restaurants, 25 deluxe cottages, and 82 campsites as well as golf, tennis, horseback riding, indoor and outdoor pools, an aerial tramway, cross-country skiing, and tobogganing.

EASTERN WEST VIRGINIA

West Virginia's easternmost counties are replete with captivating, yet largely unsung, Colonial and Civil War history. The towns of Harpers Ferry, Berkeley Springs, Charles Town, Martinsburg, and Shepherdstown predate the Revolutionary War, bear the scars of the Civil War and have remained largely untouched, architecturally, in the last 50 years. To the west the scene changes to one of rugged splendor in a swath of mountain land blessed with Canadian weather patterns—and the ski industry to prove it. In spring the focus shifts to white-water rafting on some of the nation's most exciting rivers.

Visitor Information

Potomac Highlands: Jefferson County Visitors and Convention Bureau (⊠ Box A, Harpers Ferry 25425, ☎ 304/535–2627 or 800/848–8687, FAX 304/535–2131); **Martinsburg/Berkeley County Convention and Visitors Bureau** (⊠ 208 S. Queen St., Martinsburg 25401, ☎ 304/264–8801 or 800/498–2386); **Southern West Virginia:** Convention and Visitors Bureau (⊠ Box 1799, Beckley 25802, ☎ 304/252–2244, FAX 304/252–2252); **Travel Berkeley Springs** (⊠ 304 Fairfax St., Berkeley Springs 25411, ☎ 304/258–9147 or 800/447–8797).

Arriving and Departing

By Bus
Greyhound (☎ 800/231–2222) serves major towns.

By Car
Three interstates traverse the region: I–64, between White Sulphur Springs and Beckley; I–77, Princeton to Charleston; and I–81, in the eastern panhandle. U.S. 340 enters Harpers Ferry from the east. From the west U.S. 50, I–79, and I–64 provide the best access.

By Plane
The region is served by Beckley's **Raleigh County Memorial Airport** (☎ 304/255–0476), Chantilly's **Dulles International Airport** (☎ 703/572–2700), Hagerstown's **Washington County Regional Airport** (☎ 301/791–3333), Lewisburg's **Greenbrier Valley Airport** (☎ 304/645–3961), and **Winchester Regional Airport** (☎ 540/662–5786).

By Train
Amtrak (☎ 800/872–7245) has stations in Harpers Ferry, Martinsburg, and White Sulphur Springs.

Exploring Eastern West Virginia

Old and new mingle here in surprising harmony. In one day in the eastern panhandle you can explore pre-Revolutionary buildings, shop for the latest fashions, and relax in a Roman bath. To the west and south, the mountain roads are scenic but sometimes narrow and limited to 40 mph. Do your driving by day to enjoy the many scenic overlooks and small towns reminiscent of the 1950s.

★ At the panhandle's southeastern tip is **Harpers Ferry National Historical Park** (☞ National and State Parks, *above*) where the Shenandoah and Potomac rivers join. Hand-carved stone steps lead to the overlook where Thomas Jefferson proclaimed the view "worth a trip across the Atlantic." The township of Harpers Ferry grew around a U.S. armory built between 1798 and 1802, and many of its original buildings have been preserved. Lining the cobblestone streets are shops and museums, where park employees in period costume demonstrate Early American skills and interpret the evolution of American firearms. Each second Saturday in October the park service stages Election Day 1860 (☞ Festivals and Seasonal Events *in* the United States Region-by-Region chapter). Near the park, the **John Brown Wax Museum** (☎ 304/535–2792; ✆ $2.50) depicts the abolitionist's raid on the town.

Charles Town, named for George Washington's brother, an early resident, is irrevocably linked with Harpers Ferry, for it is where John Brown (1800–59) was hanged for treason. The Jefferson County Courthouse here houses a museum that includes among its artifacts the wagon that delivered Brown to his fate on the courthouse square.

In **Martinsburg** two **pre–Civil War roundhouses** (circular buildings for housing and repairing locomotives) at the foot of Martin Street attract railroad buffs, though they're in poor condition. Downtown, there are pre–Civil War structures in the Federal and Greek Revival styles on John, Race, and North Spring streets.

Shepherdstown, on the Potomac River northwest of Harpers Ferry, is one of the region's oldest towns, established in 1730 as Mechlenberg. Today its quaint wooden storefronts and tree-lined brick streets are the framework for a collection of specialty shops, small inns, and restaurants that lure city folk from the Washington-Baltimore area.

Berkeley Springs was officially chartered in 1776 as the Town of Bath by George Washington and speculating friends, who envisioned the site of these ancient healing springs as a spa. The buoyant warm waters still flow freely, attracting a thriving community of massage therapists, homeopathic specialists, and artists. A variety of small inns, antiques shops, spa retreats, and services make this a year-round haven for relaxation. **Berkeley Springs State Park** (⊠ 121 S. Washington St., Berkeley Springs 25411, ☎ 304/258–2711 or 800/225–5982) offers heated Roman baths and massages.

☾ **Potomac Eagle Scenic Rail Excursions** (⊠ 1 mi north of Romney on W.Va. 28, ☎ 800/223–2453; ✆ $22–$49, depending on type of railcar and time of year) takes passengers in vintage railcars into the wilderness of the South Branch of the Potomac River, where bald-eagle sightings are common.

★ A southwesterly route leads through the Potomac Highlands—rich in outdoor recreation—to the **National Radio Astronomy Observatory** (⊠ Rte. 28/92, ☎ 304/456–2011, ✆ free), in Green Bank, where huge radio telescopes listen for life in outer space. Bus tours and a slide presentation are available, though tours must be arranged in advance from November through May.

Cass Scenic Railroad State Park encompasses an authentic turn-of-the-20th-century lumber town and offers visitors a tow up to the second-highest peak in West Virginia in open railcars once used to haul logs off the mountain. Trains are drawn by geared Shay steam locomotives, built at the turn of the 20th century to negotiate steep terrain. ⊠ *Rte. 66, Cass,* ☎ *304/456–4300 or 800/225–5982.* ✆ *$12 weekdays, $14 weekends. Closed Nov.–mid-May.*

☾ The **Youth Museum of Southern West Virginia** (⊠ New River Park, Box 1815, Beckley 25802, ☎ 304/252–3730; ✆ $2) has a permanent village of reconstructed or relocated log structures that depict agricultural
☾ life in the area before the advent of mining. The **Beckley Exhibition Coal Mine** (⊠ New River Park, Drawer A.J., Beckley 25802, ☎ 304/256–1747; ✆ $8) has 1,500 ft of restored passages accessible by guided tours and is open April through October.

The **Lewisburg National Historic District** (⊠ U.S. 219, ☎ 304/645–1000 or 800/833–2068) encompasses 236 acres and more than 60 18th-century buildings, many of native limestone or brick. At night, gas lamps flicker on quaint storefronts and signs—no overhead power lines spoil the image of a bygone era.

The mammoth **State Fair of West Virginia** (⊠ 3 mi south of I–64 on Rte. 219, Lewisburg, ☎ 304/645–1090; ☞ $6.25) fills two weeks in August with livestock shows, harness racing, crafts, and entertainment. Master artists offer more than 300 classes in traditional music, dance, crafts, and folklore at the **Augusta Heritage Workshops** (⊠ 100 Campus Dr., Elkins 26241, ☎ 304/637–1209), held at Davis & Elkins College. The engineering marvel of the **New River Gorge Bridge,** the world's longest steel arch span, is celebrated annually near Fayetteville on the third Saturday in October; more than 200 food and crafts vendors sell their wares while crowds watch parachutists leap hundreds of feet into the New River Gorge.

Dining and Lodging

Real West Virginia cooking is hearty, simple, and usually made from local ingredients—buckwheat cakes for breakfast, beef stew for lunch, brook trout or game for dinner—but more urbane fare is available. Local bed-and-breakfasts (☎ 800/225–5982 for B&B listings and booklet) afford the best access to the state's greatest treasure: its hospitable people.

Berkeley Springs

$$ ✕ **Country Inn.** This restaurant's atmosphere suits its name—lots of natural wood and old prints. The best entrées are crab cakes and lamb. ⊠ 207 S. Washington St., ☎ 304/258–2210 or 800/822–6630. AE, D, DC, MC, V.

$$–$$$ ✕⊡ **Coolfont Resort & Spectrum Spa.** Accommodations are in chalets,
★ rustic cabins, or lodge rooms, and the spa offers programs to learn about nutrition, exercise, and stress reduction. In the restaurant, the soup-salad-bread bar is exceptional, as is the daily buffet. ⊠ 1777 Cold Run Valley Rd., 25411, ☎ 304/258–4500 or 800/888–8768, FAX 304/258–6314. 82 units. Restaurant, pool, tennis, health club. AE, D, DC, MC, V. MAP.☜

$ ⊡ **Cacapon Resort State Park.** Locally crafted heavy oak pieces fur-
★ nish the guest rooms and woodsy dining room in the main lodge, which overlooks the golf course and Cacapon Ridge. Rustic cabins are tucked into the surrounding woods. ⊠ Off 522, Rte. 1 (Box 230), 25411, ☎ 304/258–1022, FAX 304/258–5323. 49 rooms, 30 cabins. Restaurant, tennis. AE, MC, V.☜

Davis

$–$$ ✕ **Blackwater Falls State Park.** The park's stone-pillar dining room, furnished in handmade red oak, perches on the rim of the Blackwater Canyon. Favorites are the breakfast bar, charbroiled chicken breast, and prime rib. ⊠ Rte. 32 to Blackwater Falls State Park Rd., ☎ 304/259–5216, FAX 304/259–5881. AE, MC, V.☜

$–$$$ ⊡ **Canaan Valley Resort State Park.** The rooms here are motel style but spacious, and the resort's wooded setting is superb. Golf, downhill skiing, snowboarding, and ice-skating are popular activities. ⊠ HC 70, Box 320, 26260, ☎ 304/866–4121 or 800/622–4121, FAX 304/866–2172. 250 rooms, 23 cabins. Restaurant, pools. D, DC, MC, V.☜

Durbin

$$$–$$$$ ⊡ **Cheat Mountain Club.** Originally an exclusive men's-sports hideaway,
★ this 100-year-old hand-hewn-spruce log cabin is surrounded by the 901,000-acre Monongahela National Forest and close to skiing, hiking,

mountain biking, and hunting. The pine-paneled guest rooms on the lodge's second floor are immaculately kept, and room rates include meals. The restaurant's three daily menus feature hearty homemade fare; prime rib and lemon-pepper pasta with lemon zest, olive oil, and garlic are typical dinner entrées. ⊠ *Rte. 250 (Box 28), Durbin 26264,* ☎ *304/456–4627,* FAX *304/456–3192. 9 rooms, 5-bed dormitory. MC, V. FAP.*

Lewisburg

$$
★ ✕🅃 **The General Lewis.** Dating from 1834, this inn is one of 60 historic structures in the Lewisburg National Historic District. After touring the town, you can relax in a rocking chair on the veranda; browse through the collection of antique tools, guns, household utensils, and musical instruments in Memory Hall; or feast on such local specialties as country ham and fried chicken. ⊠ *301 E. Washington St., 24901,* ☎ *304/645–2600,* FAX *304/645–2601. 26 rooms. Restaurant. AE, D, MC, V.* 🐾

Shepherdstown

$$–$$$$ ✕🅃 **Bavarian Inn and Lodge.** In various alpine chalets overlooking the Potomac River and the gardens, the Bavarian has luxurious rooms with canopy beds, fireplaces, and whirlpool tubs. The dining areas are decorated with antiques and fine china. The German and American cuisine includes wild pheasant, venison, and boar. ⊠ *Rte. 1 (Box 30), 25443,* ☎ *304/876–2551,* FAX *304/876–9355. 73 units. Restaurant, pool, tennis. AE, D, DC, MC, V.*

Snowshoe/Slatyfork

$$$ ✕ **Red Fox Restaurant.** A cozy tavern room, plush seating, and green-
★ house windows set this restaurant apart, as do its extensive menu and exceptional service. The chefs use local meats, fish, herbs, and cheeses in such specialties as wild game pâtés and roast quail cooked with apples, country ham, sausages, and applejack brandy. ⊠ *No. 1 Whistlepunk, Snowshoe,* ☎ *304/572–1111,* FAX *304/572–2222. AE, D, MC, V.*

$$$–$$$$ 🅃 **Snowshoe/Silver Creek Mountain Resort.** This gargantuan resort can
★ accommodate up to 9,000 guests. Lodging varies from motel-style rooms to luxury condos. Snowshoe has an assortment of natural-wood structures in the forest fringing the ski slopes; Silver Creek has rooms in a high-rise. ⊠ *Off U.S. 219; 10 Snowshoe Dr., 26209,* ☎ *304/572–1000. 1,250 houses and condos, 302 rooms. 9 restaurants, pools, tennis, exercise room. AE, MC, V.* 🐾

White Sulphur Springs

$$$$ 🅃 **The Greenbrier.** Rated a five-diamond resort by AAA—indicating world-
★ class accommodation—this 6,500-acre spa is decorated in grand turn-of-the-20th-century style. Massive white columns rise six stories against a white facade, and nine lobbies provide vast, chandeliered common areas. Every guest room is different, but all are decorated in Dorothy Draper pastel prints. The gourmet cuisine offers such dishes as farm-raised striped bass and rack of lamb. Horseback riding and golf are among the many leisure options. ⊠ *300 W. Main St., White Sulphur Springs 24986,* ☎ *304/536–1110 or 800/624–6070,* FAX *304/536–7854. 640 units. 4 dining rooms, pool, tennis, health club. AE, DC, MC, V.* 🐾

Motel

🅃 **Holiday Inn** (⊠ 301 Foxcroft Ave., Martinsburg 25401, ☎ 304/267–5500 or 800/862–6282), 120 rooms; restaurant, pools, health club; *$$$.*

Campgrounds

State-park camping facilities and more than 100 commercial campgrounds are listed in the booklet available from the West Virginia Division of Tourism (☞ Statewide Visitor Information, *above*).

Nightlife and the Arts

At Grandview State Park's **Theatre West Virginia** (☎ 304/256–6800 or 800/666–9142), you'll find the state's premier outdoor theatrical productions: *Honey in the Rock,* a Civil War story; *Hatfields and Mc-Coys,* depicting the famous feud; and a different musical each season.

Outdoor Activities and Sports

Biking

Rentals, instruction, and tours are available from **Blackwater Bikes** (✉ Davis, ☎ 304/259–5286), the **Elk River Touring Center** (✉ Slatyfork, ☎ 304/572–3771), and **Snowshoe Mountain Biking Centers** (✉ Snowshoe, ☎ 304/572–1000).

Canoeing

The **Greenbrier River** is one of the best paddling rivers in the country. Area outfitters can put you on this and other waterways; for a list of operators contact the West Virginia Division of Tourism (☞ Statewide Visitor Information, *above*).

Fishing

Trout are abundant in faster streams, while bass, crappie, and walleye lurk in big rivers and lakes. Licenses, which are required, are available at sporting and convenience stores. Most rafting companies organize fishing trips. **Elk Mountain Outfitters** (✉ Corner Rte. 66 and Rte. 219; Box 8, Slatyfork 26291, ☎ 304/572–3000) runs fly-fishing schools and trout expeditions.

Golf

Cacapon and **Canaan Valley Resort state parks** (☞ National and State Parks, *above*) have 18 holes each; the **Greenbrier,** in White Sulphur Springs (☞ Dining and Lodging, *above*), 54 holes; **Locust Hill** (☎ 304/728–7300), in Charles Town, 18 holes; **Pipestem Resort State Park** (☞ National and State Parks, *above*), 27 holes; **Stonebridge** (☎ 304/263–4653), in Martinsburg, 18 holes; the **Woods** (☎ 304/754–7977 or 800/248–2222), in Hedgesville, 27 holes.

Hiking

State and national parks have extensive trail systems. The **Appalachian Trail** (✉ Harpers Ferry 25425, ☎ 304/535–6331) and the **Big Blue Trail** (✉ Potomac Appalachian Trail Club, 118 Park St. SE, Vienna, VA 22180, ☎ 703/242–0693) run through this region.

Horseback Riding

You can horseback-ride on trails in most state parks. Stables at **Glade Springs Resort & Conference Center** (✉ 3000 Lake Dr., Daniels 25832, ☎ 800/634–5233) offer a range of activities, from short rides to overnight expeditions and wagon rides. The horse farm **Swift Level** (✉ Rte. 2, Box 269, Lewisburg 24901, ☎ 304/645–1155 or 888/645–1155) offers multiday long-distance treks for experienced equestrians.

Rafting

The **New, Gauley,** and **Shenandoah** are West Virginia's most heavily traveled rivers, followed by the **Tygart** and **Cheat.** First-timers can tackle all but the Gauley. For information on more than 30 commercial outfitters that run white-water excursions, contact the West Virginia Division of Tourism (☞ Statewide Visitor Information, *above*).

Ski Areas

Cross-Country

Elk River Touring Center (☞ Biking *in* Outdoor Activities and Sports, *above*) and the **White Grass Ski Touring Center** (⊠ Rte. 1, Box 299, Davis 26260, ☎ 304/866–4114) offer rentals, instruction, and tours.

Downhill

Call 800/225–5982 for snow conditions at these ski areas: **Canaan Valley Resort State Park** (⊠ Davis), 34 slopes and trails, 3 chairlifts, vertical drop 850 ft, 1¼-mi run; **Snowshoe/Silver Creek** (⊠ Snowshoe), 56 trails, 11 chairlifts, vertical drop 1,500 ft, 1½-mi run; **Timberline** (⊠ Davis), 35 trails, 3 chairlifts, vertical drop 1,000 ft, 2-mi run, terrain park (for snowboarding, tubing, and sledding), 200-ft half-pipe for snowboarders; and **Winterplace** (⊠ Flat Top), 27 trails, 7 chairlifts, vertical drop 603 ft, 1¼-mi run.

Shopping

West Virginia's many **fairs and festivals** are perfect places to shop for mountain handicrafts; check with the state Division of Tourism for a calendar of events. The works of 1,500 artists and craftspeople whose works have passed muster with a state jury are sold at **Tamarack** (⊠ 1 Tamarack Park, Beckley, ☎ 304/256–6843), a sprawling center just off I–77/64. **Berkeley Springs** is home to two large antiques consortiums and several independent dealers in glass, collectibles, and political memorabilia. **Harpers Ferry's Bolivar District** houses wall-to-wall antiques and specialty shops. **Martinsburg** offers antiques stores and several outlet malls, including the **Blue Ridge Outlet Center** (⊠ 315 W. Stephen St., ☎ 304/263–7467 or 800/445–3993), which houses 40 select manufacturers and designers of quality goods.

WESTERN WEST VIRGINIA

The Charleston-Huntington area is a center of commerce and culture, quite different from the mountain wilderness to the east and the farmland to the north. Skilled craftspeople, such as those who supplied the Kennedy White House with glassware, make their homes in this area in the central Ohio River valley. Its northern panhandle suffers from steel-industry troubles, but its fine old mansions and Victorian architecture are reminders of better times. Wheeling's Oglebay Resort and Conference Center is a cultural jewel and one of the finest municipal parks in the nation.

Visitor Information

Charleston: Convention and Visitors Bureau (⊠ 200 Civic Center Dr., 25301, ☎ 304/344–5075 or 800/733–5469, FAX 304/344–1241). **Huntington:** Cabell-Huntington Convention and Visitors Bureau (⊠ Box 347, 25708, ☎ 304/525–7333 or 800/635–6329). **Wheeling:** Convention and Visitors Bureau (⊠ 1401 Main St., Heritage Sq., 26003, ☎ 304/233–7709 or 800/828–3097, FAX 304/233–1320). **Northern West Virginia:** Convention and Visitors Bureau (⊠ 709 Beechurst Ave., Morgantown 26505, ☎ 304/292–5081 or 800/458–7373, FAX 304/291–1354).

Arriving and Departing

By Car

Major routes covering the region are I–64W; I–77 north–south; I–79 north–south; U.S. 50 between Clarksburg and Parkersburg; and I–70 crossing the northern panhandle at Wheeling.

By Plane

The region is served by Charleston's **Yeager Airport** (☎ 304/344–8033 or 800/241–6522), Huntington's **Tri-State Airport** (☎ 304/453–6165), Parkersburg's **Wood County Airport** (☎ 304/464–5113), Clarksburg/Fairmont's **Benedum Airport** (☎ 304/842–3400), and the **Morgantown Municipal Airport/Hart Field** (☎ 304/291–7461).

By Train

Amtrak (☎ 800/872–7245) provides service from White Sulphur Springs through Charleston to Huntington.

Exploring Western West Virginia

This area is heavily influenced by the early history and commerce of the Ohio River. Charleston, Huntington, and Parkersburg set an urban tone with museums, shopping malls, and cultural and entertainment centers, but the activity is balanced by lazy days on the river. Moving north through valley farmland, you can watch glassblowers and other craftspeople at work. The boom of the 1890s is reflected throughout the area in grand mansions and nicely preserved Victorian architecture.

Charleston, first settled in 1794, has been the state capital since 1885 and is the hub of the Great Kanawha Valley. The Italian Renaissance **capitol,** designed by Cass Gilbert (1859–1934) in 1932, is considered one of America's most beautiful state capitols. From the massive gilt dome, which rises 300 ft above the street, hangs a 2-ton chandelier of hand-cut crystal. ⊠ *1900 Kanawha Blvd. E,* ☎ *304/558–3456.* ☞ *Free. Closed Sun.*

Within the capitol complex is the **Cultural Center** (⊠ Greenbrier and Washington Sts., ☎ 304/558–0162, 800/723–4687 for information, 304/342–5757 for tickets; ☞ free), with its marble **Great Hall** and the **State Museum,** which traces West Virginia history. **Mountain Stage** (☎ 800/723–4687 for information, 304/342–5757 for tickets; ☞ prices vary), a live contemporary-music radio show, is taped here before an audience from 6 to 8 most Sunday evenings; each show has a different emphasis, from world beat to jazz, blues, folk, and rock.

Overlooking the capitol is **Sunrise Museum,** comprising two historic mansions that house art galleries, a hands-on science center, and a planetarium. Outside are 16 acres of wooded grounds with gardens and trails. ⊠ *746 Myrtle Rd.,* ☎ *304/344–8035.* ☞ *$3.50. Closed Mon. and Tues.*

Downtown are a large civic center and the pleasant **Charleston Town Center** shopping area (☞ Shopping, *below*). Eight styles of 19th-century architecture are represented in the **East End Historic District,** bordered by Bradford, Quarrier, and Michigan streets and Kanawha Boulevard.

Charleston takes pride in downtown **Haddad Riverfront Park,** which bustles the week before Labor Day during the annual Sternwheeler Regatta.

It takes an hour by I–64 to reach metropolitan **Huntington,** the state's second-largest city, a river and rail town whose meticulously laid out streets are lined with stately turn-of-the-20th-century houses. In the **9th Street West Historic District** the streets are brick, and the houses Victorian frame bordered with wrought-iron fences. The **Huntington Museum of Art,** the state's largest museum, covers 52 acres and houses the Junior Art Museum, a celestial observatory, and an amphitheater. ⊠ *2033 McCoy Rd.,* ☎ *304/529–2701.* ☞ *Donations accepted. Closed Mon.*

Near Huntington, at Milton, is the **Blenko Glass Visitor Center and Factory Outlet,** one of several handblown-glass factories between Huntington and Parkersburg. ⊠ *Exit 28 off I–64 to U.S. 60,* ☎ *304/743–9081. Factory closed 1st 2 wks in July, last 2 wks in Dec.*

Charleston, West Virginia

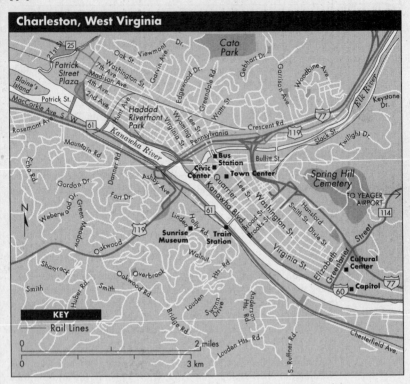

Parkersburg, another thriving Ohio River town, has many restored turn-of-the-20th-century houses, but its main attraction is **Blennerhassett Island Historical State Park.** In 1800 Harman Blennerhassett's magnificent island estate was the talk of the Northwest Territory, but he was later arrested with Aaron Burr for treason. Besides the Palladian-style mansion, you can visit a crafts village and tour the island by horse-drawn wagon. For $6, you ride to the island itself aboard a stern-wheeler. ⊠ *Blennerhassett Museum of Regional History, 2nd and Juliana Sts.,* ☎ *304/420–4800 or 800/225–5982. Island closed Nov.–Apr.*

In the heart of the state is the Mountain Lakes region, dotted with prime fishing areas and a number of Civil War landmarks, such as **Carnifex Ferry Battlefield State Park.** The battle here dashed the South's hopes of controlling the Kanawha Valley. Within the park, the **Patterson House,** which marked the line between Union and Confederate forces, has been restored as a museum. ⊠ *Rte. 2, Summersville at Carnifex Ferry Battlefield,* ☎ *304/872–0825.* ▨ *Free. Museum closed Labor Day–Memorial Day.*

North of Clarksburg is **Morgantown,** an industrial and educational center known internationally for its glass. It is the home of **West Virginia University,** where the world's first fully automated transportation system has carried students between campuses since the 1970s. There's all the bustle of a college town here, plus the 1,700-acre **Cheat Lake,** a perfect place to wind down for a bit.

In the northern panhandle, **Wheeling** was once the gateway to the West. Parks, museums, riverboat rides, and a wealth of restored Victorian houses—for instance, the **Eckhart House Tours** (☎ 304/232–5439; ▨ $10 for 4-house tour)—are reminders of the old days. **Oglebay Resort and Conference Center** (☎ 304/243–4000 or 800/624–6988) is a 1,500-acre municipal park–resort with a hotel (☞ Dining and Lodging, *below*), a 65-acre petting zoo, a planetarium, a museum, indoor and outdoor swimming pools, naturalist programs for all ages, and two championship golf courses; prices for activities vary. From early November through mid-January both the park and downtown Wheeling explode into gigantic thematic displays for the immense **Winter Festival of Lights**—touted as the largest festival of its kind in the nation.

Dining and Lodging

Charleston

$$–$$$$ ✕🏨 **Embassy Suites.** In the heart of downtown, this comfortable all-suite hotel is two blocks from the Civic Center and across from the Town Center Mall. Rooms have standard but well-kept furnishings. The Athletic Club Sports Bar & Grill serves hearty soups, salads, sandwiches, and pasta dishes for lunch and dinner. ✉ *300 Court St., 25301,* ☎ *304/347–8700 or 800/362–2779,* ℻ *304/347–8737. 253 suites. Restaurant, pool, exercise room. AE, D, DC, MC, V. BP.* ✨

$$–$$$ ✕🏨 **Charleston Marriott Town Center.** Within walking distance of the Civic Center and the Charleston Town Center Mall, this hotel offers upscale dining in the Tarragon Room and less formal meals at Allie's American Grill. ✉ *200 Lee St. E, 25301,* ☎ *304/345–6500 or 800/228–9290,* ℻ *304/347–8737. 357 rooms. Pool, health club. AE, D, DC, MC, V.* ✨

Morgantown

$$$ ✕🏨 **Lakeview Scanticon Resort and Conference Center.** This country
★ club turned resort sits on a dramatic cliff overlooking Cheat Lake. A warren of halls and stairways leads to comfortable motel-style rooms. Two golf courses and a $2 million fitness center serve the convention trade. Prime rib and poached salmon are the main attractions in the Reflections on the Lake restaurant. The Grill Restaurant serves light, healthy fare. ✉ *One Lakeview Dr., 26508,* ☎ *304/594–1111 or 800/624–8300,* ℻ *304/594–9472. 187 rooms. 2 restaurants, pools, tennis, exercise room. AE, D, DC, MC, V.* ✨

Wheeling

$$ ✕🏨 **Stratford Springs.** This historic inn, composed of two turn-of-the-
★ 20th-century houses, stands on 30 wooded, secluded acres. The rooms are Colonial style, with cherry furniture. Among the restaurants, which cater mainly to nonguests, the formal Stratford Room (jacket and tie) serves such dishes as stuffed strip steak and baby coho salmon. ✉ *355 Oglebay Dr., 26003,* ☎ *304/233–5100 or 800/521–8435,* ℻ *304/232–6447. 3 rooms. Restaurant, pool, exercise room. AE, MC, V.*

$$–$$$ 🏨 **Oglebay Resort and Conference Center.** Connected to the rustic lodge, which has a huge stone-floor lobby and a stone fireplace, are motel-style rooms and once-detached chalets. The nearby cabins sleeping 12 to 20 are rustic outside and ultramodern inside. ✉ *Rte. 88N, 26003,* ☎ *304/243–4000 or 800/624–6988,* ℻ *304/243–4070. 220 rooms, 50 cabins. Restaurant, pools, tennis. AE, D, DC, MC, V.* ✨

Motel

🏨 **Elk River Town Center Inn** (✉ 2 Kanawha Blvd. E., Charleston 25301, ☎ 304/343–4521 or 800/765–6566), 259 rooms; restaurant, pool, exercise room; *$$.*

Campgrounds

The West Virginia Division of Tourism (☞ Statewide Visitor Information, *above*) has listings of commercial campgrounds as well as facilities in more than a dozen state parks.

Nightlife and the Arts

Wheeling's **Capitol Music Hall** (⊠ 1015 Main St., ☎ 800/624–5456), home of WWVA radio's *Jamboree USA,* has live performances by country-music greats and two big-name jamborees in July and August.

Outdoor Activities and Sports

Canoeing

The area's many lakes are ideal for canoeing; contact the **Army Corps of Engineers** (☎ 304/529–5211).

Fishing

Native trout are abundant in the faster streams and rivers, while bass, crappie, and walleye lurk in the lakes. Licenses are available at sporting and convenience stores. Rafting companies organize fishing trips. **Sutton Lake** (⊠ Sutton, ☎ 304/765–2705) and **Stonewall Jackson Lake** (⊠ Weston, ☎ 304/269–0523) are prime areas.

Golf

Coonskin Golf Course (⊠ 2000 Coonskin Dr., Charleston, ☎ 304/341–8013), 18 holes; **Lakeview Scanticon Resort's Lakeview and Mountainview courses** (⊠ One Lakeview Dr., Morgantown, ☎ 304/594–1111 or 800/624–8300), 36 holes; **Oglebay Park's Crispin and Speidel courses** (⊠ Oglebay, Rte. 88N, Wheeling, ☎ 304/243–4000 or 800/624–6988), 36 holes; **Twin Falls Resort State Park Golf Course** (⊠ Rte. 97, Mullens, ☎ 304/294–4000 or 800/225–5982), 18 holes; **Worthington Golf Club** (⊠ 3414 Roseland Ave., Parkersburg, ☎ 304/428–4297), 18 holes.

Hiking and Backpacking

The **Allegheny Trail** (⊠ 633 West Virginia Ave., Morgantown 26505, ☎ 304/296–5158) and the **Kanawha Trace** (⊠ 733 7th Ave., Huntington 25701, ☎ 304/523–3408) pass through state and national forests and wilderness areas with rocky overlooks and thickets of rhododendron and mountain laurel.

Rafting

The white waters of the **Cheat** and **Tygart** rivers flow through this region. Call 800/225–5982 for brochures on guided trips and a list of more than 50 licensed outfitters.

Shopping

Antiques and local crafts, particularly handblown glass, are abundant here; vendors vary from roadside shops to outdoor fairs to sprawling glass-factory outlets (☞ Exploring Western West Virginia, *above*). The largest showcase of West Virginia wares is the **Mountain State Art & Craft Fair** (☎ 800/225–5982; ⊡ $5), held in Ripley the week of July 4. In downtown Charleston, next to the Charleston Marriott Town Center, the **Charleston Town Center** (⊠ Quarrier and Lee Sts., ☎ 304/345–9525) has 135 shops.

WISCONSIN

By Don
Davenport

Updated by
Jim Umhoefer

Capital	Madison
Population	5,169,700
Motto	Forward
State Bird	Robin
State Flower	Wood violet
Postal Abbreviation	WI

Statewide Visitor Information

Wisconsin Department of Tourism (✉ Box 7976, Madison 53707–
7976, ☎ 608/266–2161 or 800/432–8747).

Information centers: I–90N at Rest Area 22, near Beloit; I–94E at Rest
Area 25, near Hudson; I–94N at Rest Area 26, near Kenosha; I–90E
at Rest Area 31, near La Crosse; Route 12N at Rest Area 24, near Genoa
City; Prairie du Chien, at the Route 18 bridge; 201 W. Washington Ave.,
Madison; Highways 2 and 53 in Superior; Highways 151 and 61 near
Dickeyville; Highways 51 and 2 in Hurley; 1680 Bridge St. in Marinette;
and at 52 W. Adams St., in Chicago, Illinois.

Scenic Drives

As part of the **Great River Road,** scenic Route 35 follows the Mississippi River between Prairie du Chien and Prescott. Route 107, between
Merrill and Tomahawk, travels along the 400-mi-long **Wisconsin River
valley.** In northeastern Wisconsin Routes 57 and 42 circle the **Door
County Peninsula,** providing 250 mi of spectacular Lake Michigan
scenery.

National and State Parks

National Park
Apostle Islands National Lakeshore (☞ Elsewhere in Wisconsin, *below*).

State Parks
Wisconsin's state park system includes 48 parks and recreation areas,
nine forests, and numerous trails. Camping is allowed in 36 state parks
and seven state forests. The **Wisconsin Department of Natural Resources** (✉ Bureau of Parks and Recreation, Box 7921, Madison
53707, ☎ 608/266–2181) provides information.

Devil's Lake State Park (✉ S5975 Park Rd., Baraboo 53913, ☎ 608/
356–8301) is one of the state's most popular, with hiking trails, campsites, and 500-ft-high bluffs overlooking Devil's Lake. **Pattison State
Park** (✉ 6294 S. State Rd. 35, Superior 54880, ☎ 715/399–3111) is
distinguished by its 165-ft Big Manitou Falls, Wisconsin's highest waterfall and the fourth highest east of the Rocky Mountains. **Peninsula
State Park** (✉ Hwy. 42, Fish Creek 54212, ☎ 920/868–3258) covers
nearly 4,000 acres on the shores of Green Bay. With golf, hiking, bicycling, and lakeshore camping facilities, it is one of the state's most
heavily used parks. **Wyalusing State Park** (✉ 13081 State Park La.,
Bagley 53801, ☎ 608/996–2261) stands at the confluence of the Wisconsin and Mississippi rivers, providing sweeping views of the river
valleys.

MILWAUKEE

A small-town atmosphere prevails in Milwaukee, as it's not so much a city as a large collection of neighborhoods situated on the shores of Lake Michigan. The city, Wisconsin's largest, is an international seaport and the state's primary commercial and manufacturing center. Modern steel-and-glass high-rises occupy much of the downtown area but share the skyline with restored and well-kept 19th-century buildings from Milwaukee's early heritage. First settled by Potawatomi and later by French fur traders in the late 18th century, the city boomed in the 1840s with the arrival of German brewers, whose influence is still present. Milwaukee is known as a city of festivals, the biggest being Summerfest and the Great Circus Parade (☞ Festivals and Seasonal Events *in* the United States Region by Region chapter).

Visitor Information

Greater Milwaukee: Convention and Visitors Bureau (⊠ 510 W. Kilbourn Ave., 53203, ☎ 414/273–7222 or 800/554–1448).

Arriving and Departing

By Bus
Greyhound (⊠ 606 N. 7th St., ☎ 800/231–2222).

By Car
From the north, I–43 provides controlled access into downtown Milwaukee. I–94 leads to downtown from Chicago and other points south and west of the city. If you are traveling to sites in the wider metropolitan area, from I–94 you can connect to I–894, which bypasses central Milwaukee.

By Plane
General Mitchell International Airport (⊠ 5300 S. Howell Ave., ☎ 414/747–5300), 6 mi south of downtown via I–94, is served by several domestic and international carriers. **Milwaukee County Transit System** (☎ 414/344–6711) operates buses to and from the airport; fare is $1.35, and exact change is required. Taxis between the airport and downtown take about 20 minutes; fare runs from $20 to $22.

By Train
Amtrak (⊠ 433 W. St. Paul Ave., ☎ 800/872–7245).

Getting Around Milwaukee

Lake Michigan is the city's eastern boundary; Wisconsin Avenue is the main east–west thoroughfare. The Milwaukee River divides the downtown area east and west. The East–West Expressway (I–94/I–794) is the dividing line between north and south. Streets are numbered in ascending order from the Milwaukee River west well into the suburbs. Many downtown attractions are near the Milwaukee River and can be reached on foot. **Milwaukee County Transit System** (☞ Arriving and Departing by Plane, *above*) provides bus service. Taxis can be ordered by phone; try **Yellow Cab** (☎ 414/271–1800) or **City Veteran** (☎ 414/291–8900).

Exploring Milwaukee

Downtown
Milwaukee's central business district is 1 mi long, a few blocks wide, and is divided by the Milwaukee River. On the east side the **Iron Block Building** (⊠ N. Water St. and E. Wisconsin Ave.) is one of the few remaining ironclad buildings in the United States. It was designed by George

H. Johnson and built between 1860 and 1861. The metal facade was brought in by ship from an eastern foundry and installed during the Civil War. In the 1860s Milwaukee exported more wheat than any other port in the world; the mass exportation gave impetus to the building of the **Grain Exchange Room** in the Mackie Building (⊠ 225 E. Michigan St.). The 10,000-square-ft trading room has three-story-high columns and painted ceiling panels depicting Wisconsin wildflowers. The building was designed by Edward Townsend Mix and built between 1879 and 1880. The **City of Milwaukee Public Library** (⊠ 814 W. Wisconsin Ave.), located on Wisconsin Ave. near the business district, is an impressive example of the Classical Revival style; it was built between 1893 and 1897 by the architectural firm Ferry & Clas.

★ The **Milwaukee Art Museum** (⊠ 750 N. Lincoln Memorial Dr., ☎ 414/224–3200, ⌨ $5), in the lakefront War Memorial Center, houses notable collections of paintings, drawings, sculpture, photography, and decorative arts. Its permanent collection is strong in European and American art of the 19th and 20th centuries. The museum is closed on Monday.

En route from the lakefront to the river, stop a moment at **Cathedral Square** (⊠ E. Kilbourn Ave. and Jefferson St.). This quiet park was built on the site of Milwaukee's first courthouse. Across the street from Cathedral Square, **St. John's Cathedral,** dedicated in 1853, was the first Roman Catholic cathedral built in Wisconsin.

The **Milwaukee County Historical Center** (⊠ 910 N. Old World 3rd St., ☎ 414/273–8288; ⌨ free), a museum in a former bank building, displays early firefighting equipment, military artifacts, toys, and women's fashions. It also has a research library with naturalization records and genealogical resources.

The banks of the Milwaukee River, especially along the striking downtown riverwalk, are busy in summer when downtown workers lunch in the nearby parks and public areas such as **Père Marquette Park** (⊠ Old World 3rd St. and W. Kilbourn Ave.), on the river.

There are also **river cruises** of Milwaukee's harbor and lakefront during warm weather; call the Convention and Visitors Bureau (☞ Visitor Information, *above*) for details on cruise companies.

As you cross the river to the west side, notice that the east-side streets are not directly opposite the west-side streets and that the bridges across the river are built at an angle. This layout dates from the 1840s, when the area east of the river was called Juneautown and the region to the west was known as Kilbourntown. The rival communities had a fierce argument over which would pay for the bridges that connected them; the antagonism was so intense that citizens venturing into rival territory carried white flags. The Great Bridge War, as it was called, was finally settled by the state legislature in 1845, but the streets on either side of the river were never aligned.

★ ☺ Considered among the best natural history museums in the country, the **Milwaukee Public Museum** (⊠ 800 W. Wells St., ☎ 414/278–2700, ⌨ $6.50, $10.50 for museum and IMAX) is known for its collection of more than 6 million specimens and artifacts. Its award-winning walk-through exhibits include the "Streets of Old Milwaukee," depicting the city in the 1890s; a two-story rain forest; and the "Third Planet" (complete with full-size dinosaurs), where visitors walk into the interior of Earth to learn about its history. Within the museum, the **Humphrey IMAX Dome Theater** (⌨ $6.50) is run in cooperation with Discovery World.

Discovery World, as the **James Lovell Museum of Science, Economics, and Technology** (⊠ 817 N. James Lovell St., ☎ 414/765–9966; ⌨ $5.50)

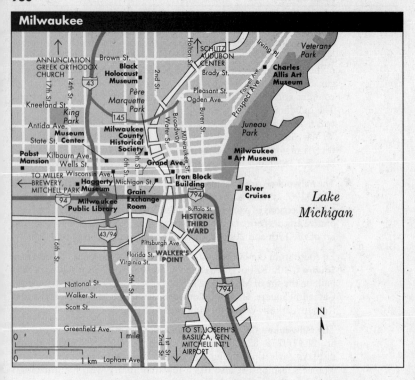

in the Milwaukee Public Museum is called, has more than 140 interactive exhibits on magnets, motors, electricity, health, and computers. It also puts on the "Great Electric Show" and the "Light Wave–Laser Beam Show" on weekends and some weekdays.

America's Black Holocaust Museum (☒ 2233 N. 4th St., ☎ 414/264–2500; ☒ $5), near Old World 3rd Street, educates visitors about race, racism, and the era of slavery and lynchings in America. It's closed Wednesdays.

St. Joan of Arc Chapel (☎ 414/288–6873; ☒ free), a small, stone 15th-century chapel, was moved from its original site near Lyon, France, in 1964 and reconstructed on the central mall of the Marquette University campus. One of the stones was reputedly kissed by Joan before she was sent to her death and is discernibly colder than the others.

The **Patrick and Beatrice Haggerty Museum of Art** (☒ 13th and Clybourn Sts., ☎ 414/288–1669; ☒ free) houses Marquette University's collection of more than 6,000 works of art, including Renaissance, Baroque, and modern paintings, sculpture, prints, photography, and decorative arts. It also has changing exhibitions.

★ The **Pabst Mansion** (☒ 2000 W. Wisconsin Ave., ☎ 414/931–0808, ☒ $7), completed in 1892 for the beer baron Captain Frederick Pabst, is one of Milwaukee's treasured landmarks. The 37-room Flemish Renaissance–style mansion, designed by the architectural firm Ferry & Clas, has a tan pressed-brick exterior with carved-stone and terra-cotta ornamentation. Inside are woodwork, ironwork, marble, tile, and stained glass. It's closed on Monday.

★ Milwaukee's **Mitchell Park Conservatory** (☒ 524 S. Layton Blvd., ☎ 414/649–9800, ☒ $4) consists of three 85-ft-high glass domes housing tropical, arid, and seasonal plants and flowers; its lilies and poinsettias are spectacular at Easter and Christmas.

Other Attractions

The **Allen-Bradley Co. Clock** (⊠ 1201 S. 2nd St.) is a Milwaukee landmark and, according to the *Guinness Book of Records,* "the largest four-faced clock in the world." Great Lakes ships often use the clock as a navigational reference point.

The **American Geographical Society Collection** (⊠ 2311 E. Hartford Ave., ☎ 414/229–6282; ☐ free), in the Golda Meir Library on the University of Wisconsin–Milwaukee campus, has an exceptional assemblage of maps, old globes, atlases, and charts, plus about 200,000 books and journals. It's closed on weekends.

The **University of Wisconsin** (☎ 414/229–5070) has three worthwhile art venues: the **Institute of Visual Arts** (⊠ 3253 N. Downer Ave.), **Gallery Three** (⊠ 2400 E. Kenwood Blvd.), and **Gallery Two** (⊠ 3203 N. Downer Ave.). All three venues show avant-garde exhibits by regional, national, and international artists, and all three are closed Monday and Tuesday. Admission is free.

The **Charles Allis Art Museum** (⊠ 1801 N. Prospect Ave., ☎ 414/278–8295; ☐ $3), closed Monday and Tuesday, occupies an elegant Tudorstyle house built in 1911 for the first president of the Allis-Chalmers Manufacturing Company. The home has stained-glass windows by Louis Comfort Tiffany and a stunning worldwide collection of paintings and objets d'art, including works by major 19th- and 20th-century French and American painters.

The **Lowell Damon House** (⊠ Wauwatosa Ave. and Rogers St., Wauwatosa, ☎ 414/771–1265; ☐ free), completed in 1847, is a classic example of Colonial-style architecture. It is open Wednesday and Sunday, or by appointment.

The **Annunciation Greek Orthodox Church** (⊠ 9400 W. Congress St., ☎ 414/461–9400; ☐ $2) was Frank Lloyd Wright's last major work; the famed Wisconsin architect called it his "little jewel." Since it opened in 1961, the blue-domed Byzantine-style church has drawn visitors from all over the world. It can only be seen on Tuesday and Friday by prearranged group tour.

Built by immigrant parishioners and local craftsmen at the turn of the 20th century, **St. Josephat's Basilica** (⊠ 601 W. Lincoln Ave., ☎ 414/645–5623; ☐ $3) has a copper dome modeled after the one atop St. Peter's in Rome. Inside is a remarkable collection of relics. Tours are Sunday mornings or by appointment.

The **Pettit National Ice Center** (⊠ 500 S. 84th St., ☎ 414/266–0100; ☐ $5) has an Olympic-size skating rink, two hockey rinks, and plenty of space for jogging. Visitors can spend time on the ice or watch local Olympic speed skaters practice.

Betty Brinn Children's Museum (⊠ 929 E. Wisconsin Ave., ☎ 414/291–0888; ☐ $4), closed Monday, is a hands-on museum for children ages 10 and under.

Outside Milwaukee

★ **Old World Wisconsin** (⊠ S103 W37890 Rte. 67, ☎ 262/594–6300, ☐ $11), the State Historical Society's living history museum near Eagle, celebrates the state's ethnic heritage in architecture, with more than 65 historic buildings on 576 acres in the Southern Kettle Moraine State Forest. The restored farm and village buildings gathered from across the state depict 19th- and 20th-century rural Wisconsin. All were originally built and inhabited by European immigrants; they are grouped in German, Norwegian, Danish, and Finnish farmsteads. Costumed interpreters representing each ethnic group relate the story of immigration to Wisconsin and perform chores, such as making soap, that were intrinsic to rural life two centuries ago. The museum is open from May through October and during the Christmas holidays. From January through March, the forest is open for **cross-country skiing** (⊠ $4).

Kohler is a planned, landscaped village surrounding the factories of the plumbing-fixtures manufacturer Kohler Company. The **Kohler Design Center** (⊠ 101 Upper Rd., ☎ 920/457–3699; ⊠ free) houses the company's ceramic art collection, archives, and artifacts from an earlier factory and village, and an elaborate showroom of model bathrooms. There are daily guided tours of **Waelderhaus** (⊠ W. Riverside Dr., ☎ 920/452–4079; ⊠ free), a reproduction of founder John M. Kohler's ancestral home in Austria. The **Woodlake Kohler Complex,** in nearby Sheboygan, comprises more than 25 shops, galleries, and restaurants. The **American Club** (⊠ Highland Dr., ☎ 920/457–8000 or 800/344–2838), built in 1918 as a company-owned hotel for workers, is now a posh resort hotel on the National Register of Historic Places. The compound has two 18-hole golf courses, an indoor sports complex, a 500-acre wilderness preserve, and several restaurants.

Parks, Gardens, and Zoos

★ The 660-acre **Whitnall Park** (⊠ 5879 S. 92nd St., in suburban Hales Corners), one of the largest municipal parks in the nation, has an 18-hole golf course, recreational facilities, picnic areas, and nature and cross-country skiing trails. Within the park are the internationally famous **Alfred L. Boerner Botanical Gardens** (☎ 414/425–1130; ⊠ free), with trees, shrubs, and flowers in formal and informal gardens. The park's **Wehr Nature Center** (☎ 414/425–8550; ⊠ free) has wildlife exhibits, woodlands and wetlands, a lake, nature trails, and wild gardens.

Forests, ponds, marshland, and nature trails attract nature lovers to the **Schlitz Audubon Center** (⊠ 1111 E. Brown Deer Rd., ☎ 414/352–2880; ⊠ $4), a 225-acre wildlife area with an environmental research and education center. It's closed on Monday.

★ ☾ The **Milwaukee County Zoo** (⊠ 10001 W. Bluemound Rd., ☎ 414/771–3040, ⊠ $8) has more than 3,000 wild animals and birds, including endangered species. Educational programs, a petting zoo, narrated tram tours, miniature-train rides, and cross-country skiing trails also draw visitors.

Dining

Milwaukee is known for its wide variety of good ethnic restaurants, especially those that serve German cuisine. Despite its small-town atmosphere, many of the city's restaurants could hold their own with those in New York and Chicago.

$$$–$$$$ ✕ **English Room.** In the Pfister Hotel (☞ Lodging, *below*), Milwaukee's premier hotel restaurant has a formal atmosphere and plenty of
★ original 19th-century paintings. Recommended dishes are rack of lamb, seared crab cakes, and lobster-and-shrimp bisque. ⊠ 424 E. Wisconsin Ave., ☎ 414/273–8222. AE, D, DC, MC, V. No lunch.

$$$–$$$$ ✕ **Sanford.** Nationally acclaimed chef Sanford D'Amato serves contemporary American cuisine in this elegant restaurant, which occupies
★ a remodeled grocery store on Milwaukee's east side. ⊠ 1547 N. Jackson St., ☎ 414/276–9608. AE, D, DC, MC, V. Closed Sun. No lunch.

$–$$$$ ✕ **Boder's on the River.** With tieback curtains, fireplaces, and antiques, this family-owned and -operated restaurant in the suburbs has a cheerful country look. Roast duckling and baked whitefish are a few of the Wisconsin specialties. Come for Sunday brunch or the Friday-night seafood buffet. ⊠ *11919 N. River Rd. 43W, Mequon,* ☎ *262/242–0335. AE, D, DC, MC, V. Closed Mon.*

$$$ ✕ **Harold's.** Velvet-back booths, low lighting, etched glass, and rich greenery set a romantic, if slightly generic, mood at this restaurant in the Four Points Sheraton Hotel. Oysters Rockefeller and rack of lamb Provençal are typical of the traditional fare. ⊠ *4747 S. Howell Ave.,* ☎ *414/481–8000. AE, D, DC, MC, V. Closed Sun. No lunch Sat.*

$$–$$$ ✕ **Boulevard Inn.** This elegant restaurant overlooking Lake Michigan serves Continental cuisine. Enjoy Caesar salad or honey duck while listening to contemporary piano music. A sit-down brunch is served on Sundays. Reservations are recommended. ⊠ *925 E. Wells St.,* ☎ *414/765–1166,* ℻ *414/765–1161. AE, D, DC, MC, V.*

$$–$$$ ✕ **Grenadier's.** Imaginative dishes such as tenderloin of veal with
★ raspberry sauce combine French classics with Asian or Indian flavors and are served in the dining room and handsome, darkly furnished piano bar. ⊠ *747 N. Broadway St.,* ☎ *414/276–0747,* ℻ *414/276–1424. Jacket required. AE, D, DC, MC, V. Closed Sun. No lunch Sat.*

$$–$$$ ✕ **Jake's.** There are two locations for this longtime Milwaukee favorite, which earned its reputation with perfectly prepared steaks and heaps of french-fried onion rings. Not to be missed are the fresh fish selections, escargots, roast duckling, and Bailey's chocolate-chip cheesecake. ⊠ *6030 W. North Ave., Wauwatosa,* ☎ *414/771–0550; 21445 W. Capitol Dr., Brookfield,* ☎ *262/781–7995. AE, DC, MC, V. No lunch.*

$–$$$ ✕ **Bartolotta.** On a quaint street in the village of Wauwatosa, this place is known for its rustic Italian cuisine, especially fresh fish. ⊠ *7616 W. State St.,* ☎ *414/771–7910. AE, D, DC, MC, V. No lunch weekends.*

$–$$$ ✕ **Giovanni's.** This bright Sicilian eatery serves large portions of rich Italian food. Veal steak Giovanni is excellent, and pasta is a sure bet. ⊠ *1683 N. Van Buren St.,* ☎ *414/291–5600. AE, D, DC, MC, V. No lunch weekends.*

$–$$$ ✕ **Steven Wade's Cafe.** Creative dishes distinguish Steven Wade's: Try
★ marinated duck breasts pan-roasted with cranberry-pecan Chambord sauce, or seared steer tenderloin with coffee-cognac demi-glace and garlic-mashed potatoes. The café, once a residence, has a casual, intimate atmosphere with a small bar. ⊠ *17001 W. Greenfield Ave., New Berlin,* ☎ *262/784–0774. AE, D, DC, MC, V. Closed Sun. No lunch Sat. and Mon.*

$$ ✕ **Elsa's on the Park.** Across from Cathedral Square Park, this chic but casual restaurant has frequently changing art exhibits and serves big, juicy hamburgers and pork-chop sandwiches. ⊠ *833 N. Jefferson St.,* ☎ *414/765–0615. AE, MC, V. No lunch weekends.*

$$ ✕ **Karl Ratzsch's Old World Restaurant.** In the authentic German
★ atmosphere of this family-owned restaurant, dirndl-skirted waitresses serve schnitzel, roast duckling, and sauerbraten. The main dining room is decked out with murals, chandeliers made from antlers, and antique beer steins. Piano music on Friday and Saturday nights adds to the fun. ⊠ *320 E. Mason St.,* ☎ *414/276–2720. AE, D, DC, MC, V. Closed Sun. No lunch.*

$–$$ ✕ **Chip and Py's.** In the northern suburbs, this stylish restaurant has light gray dual-level dining rooms, a huge fireplace, and contemporary art. There's an eclectic menu and live jazz on weekends and Wednesday evenings. ⊠ *1340 W. Town Square Rd., Mequon,* ☎ *262/241–9589. AE, D, DC, MC, V. Closed Mon. No lunch Sun.*

$-$$ ✕ **Coquette Cafe.** This French café is in a large, renovated warehouse in Milwaukee's trendy Third Ward district. Here, fine food is served in a casual atmosphere. ⊠ *316 N. Milwaukee St.,* ☎ *414/291–2655. AE, D, DC, MC, V. Closed Sun.*

$-$$ ✕ **Three Brothers.** Set in an 1887 tavern, one of Milwaukee's revered ethnic restaurants serves chicken *paprikash* (a stewed chicken dish with paprika), roast goose and duck, boneless leg of lamb stuffed with spinach and cheese, Serbian salad, and homemade desserts at old-style kitchen tables. It's about 10 minutes from downtown, on the near south side. ⊠ *2414 S. St. Clair St.,* ☎ *414/481–7530. No credit cards. Closed Mon. No lunch.*

$ ✕ **De Marinis.** These popular Italian-American restaurants have excellent pizza and pasta. The pesto-and-artichoke-packed Garden Pizza is one of the best. ⊠ *N88 W15229 Main St., Menomonee Falls,* ☎ *262/253–1568;* ⊠ *1211 E. Conway St.,* ☎ *414/481–2348. D, MC, V.*

$ ✕ **Watts Tea Shop.** This genteel spot for breakfast, lunch, or tea with scones is above George Watts & Sons, Milwaukee's premier store for china, crystal, and silver. Indulge in fresh-squeezed juice and a custard-filled sunshine cake. ⊠ *761 N. Jefferson St.,* ☎ *414/290–5720. AE, D, MC, V. Closed Sun. No dinner.*

Lodging

In summer make reservations in advance, especially for weekends.

$$$-$$$$ 🏨 **Pfister Hotel.** Milwaukee's grandest old hotel dates from 1893. Rooms
★   in the tower, which was added in 1975, are bright and contemporary with a Victorian accent in keeping with the original style. A collection of 19th-century art hangs in the elegant Victorian lobby. ⊠ *424 E. Wisconsin Ave., 53202,* ☎ *414/273–8222 or 800/558–8222,* FAX *414/390–3839. 307 rooms. 3 restaurants, pool. AE, D, DC, MC, V.* ✉

$$-$$$$ 🏨 **Hyatt Regency.** This centrally located high-rise hotel has an 18-story open atrium, a revolving rooftop restaurant, and an enclosed walkway to the Grand Avenue Shopping Center. ⊠ *333 W. Kilbourn Ave., 53203,* ☎ *414/276–1234 or 800/233–1234,* FAX *414/276–6338. 484 rooms. 2 restaurants, exercise room. AE, D, DC, MC, V.* ✉

$$$ 🏨 **Wyndham Milwaukee Center.** In the center of the city's growing the-
★   ater district by the river, the Wyndham has an opulent lobby tiled with Italian marble. Guest rooms are contemporary, with mahogany furnishings. The hotel, near the Grand Avenue Shopping Center, has an excellent pasta bar. ⊠ *139 E. Kilbourn Ave., 53202,* ☎ *414/276–8686 or 800/996–3426,* FAX *414/276–8007. 221 rooms. Restaurant, health club. AE, D, DC, MC, V.* ✉

$$-$$$ 🏨 **Embassy Suites–Milwaukee West.** The sweeping atrium lobby, with
★   fountains, potted plants, and glass elevators, is the focal point of this hotel in the western suburbs. The hotel, which has two-bedroom suites, is within walking distance of a large shopping center. ⊠ *1200 S. Moorland Rd., Brookfield 53005,* ☎ *262/782–2900 or 800/444–6404,* FAX *262/796–9159. 203 suites. Restaurant, pool, exercise room. AE, D, DC, MC, V. CP.* ✉

$$-$$$ 🏨 **Four Points Sheraton Hotel Milwaukee Airport.** The Four Points, across from the airport, is the largest hotel in the state, with a cinema and nightclub as well as extensive sports and recreation facilities. The marble-walled lobby is illuminated with chandeliers. ⊠ *4747 S. Howell Ave., 53207,* ☎ *414/481–8000 or 800/558–3862,* FAX *414/615–8065. 510 rooms. 2 restaurants, pool, exercise room. AE, D, DC, MC, V.* ✉

$$ 🏨 **Hilton Milwaukee City Center.** Adjacent to Milwaukee's convention center, and minutes from the Grand Avenue Shopping Center, this elegant hotel has recently undergone a major renovation. ⊠ *509 W. Wis-*

consin Ave., 53203, ☎ *414/271–7250 or 800/445–8667,* ℻ *414/271–1039. 498 rooms. Restaurant, exercise room. AE, D, DC, MC, V.* 🐾

Motels

🏨 **Best Western Midway Hotel–Airport** (✉ 5105 S. Howell Ave., 53207, ☎ 414/769–2100 or 800/528–1234, ℻ 414/769–0064), 139 rooms; restaurant, pool; CP; *$$.*

🏨 **Radisson Hotel Milwaukee Airport** (✉ 6331 S. 13th St., 53221, ☎ 414/764–1500 or 800/303–8002, ℻ 414/764–6531), 159 rooms; restaurant, pool, exercise room; *$$.*

🏨 **Holiday Inn Express** (✉ 11111 W. North Ave., Wauwatosa 53226, ☎ 414/778–0333 or 800/465–4329, ℻ 414/778–0331); 122 rooms; CP; *$–$$.*

Nightlife and the Arts

Milwaukee Magazine (on newsstands) lists arts and entertainment events. Also check the daily entertainment sections of the *Milwaukee Journal Sentinel.*

Nightlife

You'll find clubs, bars, and a slew of friendly saloons. The **Safe House** (✉ 779 N. Front St., ☎ 414/271–2007), with a James Bond spy-hide-out decor, is a favorite hangout for young people and out-of-towners who want to eat, drink, dance, or watch a magician. **Major Goolsby's** (✉ 340 W. Kilbourn Ave., ☎ 414/271–3414) is regarded as one of the country's top-10 sports bars. It's also known for its great brats and burgers. Jazz fans go to the **Estate** (✉ 2423 N. Murray Ave., ☎ 414/964–9923).

The Arts

Milwaukee's theater district is in a two-block downtown area bounded by the Milwaukee River, East Wells Street, North Water Street, and East State Street. Most tickets are sold at box offices.

The **Riverside Theater** (✉ 116 W. Wisconsin Ave., ☎ 414/224–3000) hosts touring theater companies, Broadway shows, and other entertainment. The **Pabst Theater** (✉ 144 E. Wells St., ☎ 414/286–3663) presents live entertainment. The Milwaukee Center (✉ 108 E. Wells St., ☎ 414/224–9490) is home to the **Milwaukee Repertory Theater.** The **Marcus Center for the Performing Arts** (✉ 929 N. Water St., ☎ 414/273–7206) comprises the **Milwaukee Symphony Orchestra, Milwaukee Ballet Company, Florentine Opera Company,** and **First Stage Milwaukee.**

Spectator Sports

Baseball: Milwaukee Brewers (✉ Miller Park, 201 S. 46th St., ☎ 414/933–9000). **Basketball: Milwaukee Bucks** (✉ Bradley Center, 1001 N. 4th St., ☎ 414/227–0500). **Football: Green Bay Packers** (✉ Lambeau Field, 1265 Lombardi Ave., Green Bay, ☎ 920/496–5700). Green Bay is about a two-hour drive from Milwaukee. **Hockey: Milwaukee Admirals** (✉ Bradley Center, 1001 N. 4th St., ☎ 414/227–0550).

Beaches

Lake Michigan is the place to swim, but be prepared: Mid-summer water temperatures linger in the 50s and 60s. Among the most popular of the narrow sandy beaches are **Bradford Beach** (✉ 2400 N. Lincoln Memorial Dr.), **Doctors Beach** (✉ 1870 E. Fox La., Fox Point), **Grant Beach** (✉ 100 Hawthorne Ave., South Milwaukee), and **McKinley Beach** (✉ 1750 N. Lincoln Memorial Dr.). The **Milwaukee County Parks Swimming Pools and Beaches Office** (☎ 414/645–4806) has information about beaches.

Shopping

Using the downtown skywalk system, it's possible to browse in hundreds of stores over several blocks without once setting foot outside. Downtown Milwaukee's major shopping area is on Wisconsin Avenue west of the Milwaukee River. The major downtown retail center, the **Grand Avenue Mall** (⊠ 275 W. Wisconsin Ave.), spans four city blocks and has 130 specialty shops and kiosks and 17 eateries. **Historic Third Ward,** a turn-of-the-20th-century wholesale and manufacturing district listed on the National Register of Historic Places, borders the harbor, the river, and downtown. Two Milwaukee landmarks, **Usinger's Sausage** and **Mader's Restaurant,** are on Old World 3rd Street, along with several interesting stores and markets. **Jefferson Street,** stretching four blocks from Wisconsin to Kilbourn, is lined with upscale stores and shops. **George Watts and Son, Inc.** (⊠ 761 N. Jefferson St., ☎ 414/291–5120) has more than a thousand patterns of china, silver, and crystal.

In the metropolitan area, near the Milwaukee County Zoo, **Mayfair Mall** (⊠ 2500 N. Mayfair Rd., Wauwatosa) has more than 160 shops that surround a multistory atrium complete with swaying bamboo. Some 145 stores at **Northridge Shopping Center** (⊠ 7700 W. Brown Deer Rd.) include a Younkers department store, Boston Store, Sears, and JCPenney. Wisconsin's largest shopping center, **Southridge Mall** (⊠ 5300 S. 76th St., Greendale) has more than 145 specialty stores and five major department stores. **Brookfield Square** (⊠ 95 N. Moorland Rd., Brookfield) is a sprawling suburban complex with about 100 stores. **Bayshore** (⊠ 5900 N. Port Washington Rd., Glendale) has about 70 stores, including Sears and the Boston Store.

About 40 minutes south of downtown Milwaukee, on I–94E, you'll find two large discount shopping malls. The **Factory Outlet Centre,** just off Highway 50, has more than 100 stores with brand-name merchandise. Two miles south of the Factory Outlet Centre, off Highway 165, is **Lakeside Market Place,** with more than 75 designer outlet stores.

Side Trip to Cedarburg

Visitor Information
Cedarburg Chamber of Commerce and Visitors Center (⊠ W63 N645 Washington Ave., Box 104, Cedarburg 53012, ☎ 262/377–9620 or 800/237–2874).

Arriving and Departing
Take I–94 west to I–43 north; then get off at the Cedarburg Exit (County C). Drive west to Washington Avenue, Cedarburg's main street.

What to See and Do
The entire downtown district of Cedarburg, most of it built of Niagara limestone by 19th-century pioneers, is on the National Register of Historic Places. Victorian "Painted Ladies" with beautifully landscaped yards abound. Throughout a nine-block area you'll find antiques shops, crafts shops, candy stores, and restaurants. Weekend flea markets take place in May, July, September, and October. Within the Wittenberg Woolen Mill, first built in 1864, **Cedar Creek Settlement** (⊠ N70 W6340 Bridge Rd., ☎ 800/827–8020) is a collection of specialty and antiques shops. Also within the mill is a **winery** (⊠ $2). Wisconsin's last remaining **covered bridge** (⊠ on Covered Bridge Road) crosses Cedar Creek 3 mi north of town. The 120-ft white-pine bridge was built in 1876 and retired in 1962. The small park beside the bridge invites picnicking.

ELSEWHERE IN WISCONSIN

Madison and Southern Wisconsin

Visitor Information

Greater Madison Convention and Visitors Bureau (✉ 615 E. Washington Ave., 53703, ☎ 608/255–2537 or 800/373–6376, ℻ 608/258–4950).

Arriving and Departing

Take I–94 west from Milwaukee to Madison or I–90 west from Chicago.

What to See and Do

Madison, named after President James Madison, is the state capital and home to the University of Wisconsin. The center of the city lies on an eight-block-wide isthmus between Lakes Mendota and Monona. The Roman Renaissance–style **Wisconsin State Capitol** (☎ 608/266–0382; 🎫 free), built between 1906 and 1917, dominates the downtown skyline; there are tours daily. A **farmers' market** is held on Capitol Square every Saturday from May through October. The **State Historical Society Museum** (✉ 30 N. Carroll St., Capitol Sq., ☎ 608/264–6555; 🎫 free for Wisconsin residents, $2 for nonresidents) has permanent and changing exhibits on Wisconsin history, from prehistoric Native American cultures to contemporary social issues. The museum is closed Mondays.

Capitol Square is connected to the university's campus by State Street, a mile-long tree-lined shopping district of imports shops, ethnic restaurants, and artisans' galleries. The **Madison Art Center,** in the lobby of the **Civic Center** (✉ 211 State St., ☎ 608/257–0158; 🎫 free), has a large permanent collection and frequent temporary exhibitions. It's closed on Mondays.

The **University of Wisconsin,** which opened in 1849 with 20 students, now has an enrollment of about 40,000. The university's **Elvehjem Museum of Art** (✉ 800 University Ave., ☎ 608/263–2246; 🎫 free) is one of the state's best, with a permanent collection of paintings, traveling exhibits, sculpture, and decorative arts dating from 2300 BC to the present. Away from downtown, the **University Arboretum** (✉ 1207 Seminole Hwy., ☎ 608/263–7888; 🎫 free) has more than 1,200 acres of natural plant and animal communities, such as prairie and forest landscapes, and horticultural collections of upper Midwest specimens.

On the shore of Lake Monona, **Monona Terrace Community and Convention Center** (✉ 1 John Nolen Dr., ☎ 608/261–4000; 🎫 free, $3 for tours), Madison's newest downtown showpiece, includes a rooftop garden, café, gift shop, and a memorial to singer Otis Redding, who died in a plane crash not far from the center. Designed by Frank Lloyd Wright in 1937 but not completed until 1997, the 250,000-square-ft structure is open to the public for guided tours daily.

The **Henry Vilas Zoo** (✉ 702 S. Randall Ave., ☎ 608/266–4732; 🎫 free) has exhibits of nearly 200 animal species, plus a petting zoo. On Madison's east side, **Olbrich Botanical Gardens** (✉ 3330 Atwood Ave., ☎ 608/246–4550; 🎫 gardens free, conservatory $1) has 14 acres of outdoor rose, herb, and rock gardens and a glass-pyramid conservatory with tropical plants and flowers.

Blue Mounds is at the eastern edge of Wisconsin's lead-mining region. At **Blue Mound State Park** (✉ 2 mi northwest of Blue Mounds, ☎ 608/437–5711), towers on one of the hill's summits provide glorious vistas. **Cave of the Mounds** (✉ Cave of the Mounds Rd., ☎ 608/437–3038; 🎫 $10) is small but filled with diverse and colorful mineral formations. It's closed weekdays from mid-November to mid-March.

Nestled in a picturesque valley near Blue Mounds is **Little Norway** (✉ 3576 Hwy. JG N, Blue Mounds, ☎ 608/437–8211; ☜ $8), a restored 1856 Norwegian homestead with its original log buildings and an outstanding collection of Norwegian antiques and pioneer arts and crafts. It's open from May through October.

Founded in 1845 by Swiss settlers from the canton of Glarus, the village of **New Glarus** retains its Swiss character in language, food, architecture, and festivities. The **Swiss Historical Village** (✉ 612 7th Ave., ☎ 608/527–2317; ☜ $6) contains original buildings and reconstructions from early New Glarus, as well as displays that trace Swiss immigration to America. It's closed November through April.

Frank Lloyd Wright chose the farming community of **Spring Green,** on the Wisconsin River, for his home Taliesin and for his architectural school. Wright's influence is evident in a number of buildings in the village; notice the use of geometric shapes, low flat-roofed profiles, cantilevered projections, and steeplelike spires. There are summertime walking tours of the Wright-designed buildings at **Taliesin** (✉ 3 mi south of Spring Green on Hwy. 23, ☎ 608/588–7900), including his home and office for nearly 50 years, the 1903 Hillside Home School, galleries, a drafting studio, and a theater. Tours range from $10 to $60; the more expensive ones include admission to buildings along the way. In November and April, tours are by shuttle bus ($10).

The extraordinary multilevel stone **House on the Rock** (✉ 5754 Hwy. 23, ☎ 608/935–3639; ☜ $19.50), closed from January through mid-March, stands atop a 60-ft chimney of rock overlooking the Wyoming Valley. Begun by artist Alex Jordan in the early 1940s and opened to the public in 1961, the complex now contains re-creations of historic village streets complete with shops, as well as extensive collections of dolls, cannons, and musical machines. Here you'll also find the world's largest carousel.

The renowned **American Players Theater** (✉ 5950 Golf Course Rd., Spring Green, ☎ 608/588–7401; ☜ $21–$40) presents Shakespeare and other classics in a beautiful, wooded outdoor amphitheater near the Wisconsin River every evening but Monday from mid-June through mid-October.

On the western edge of the state, **Prairie du Chien** dates from 1673, when explorers Marquette and Joliet reached the confluence of the Wisconsin and Mississippi rivers 6 mi to the south. It became a flourishing fur market in the late 17th century. Now a bustling river community, it's a summertime destination of the steamers *Delta Queen* and *Mississippi Queen*. The family of the fur trader Hercules Dousman (Wisconsin's first millionaire) built the **Villa Louis Mansion** (✉ 521 Villa Louis Rd., ☎ 608/326–2721; ☜ $8) in 1870. Open to the public from May through October, it contains one of the finest collections of Victorian decorative arts in the country. The **Fur Trade Museum** on the villa grounds has exhibits on the fur trade of the upper Mississippi. Near the fur warehouse is **Wyalusing State Park** (☞ National and State Parks, *above*).

Dining

$–$$ ✕ **Pasta Per Tutti.** Fresh pasta and seafood and homemade breads and
★ desserts make this contemporary Italian restaurant near the theater district a local favorite. ✉ *2009 Atwood Ave.,* ☎ *608/242–1800.* MC, V. *No lunch.*

$–$$ ✕ **White Horse Inn.** Behind the civic center, this local favorite serves a
★ dynamite chicken Mafalda, a mélange of grilled chicken, sausage, leeks, and pasta in cream sauce. Sunday brunch draws a crowd. ✉ *202*

N. Henry St., behind the Civic Center, ☎ 608/255–9933. *AE, DC, MC, V. No lunch.*

Lodging

Reservations in Madison should be made well in advance.

$$–$$$ ⊞ **Madison Concourse Hotel and Governor's Club.** The marble lobby welcomes visitors into this conveniently located hotel near Manona Terrace and the State Street shops. ⊠ *1 W. Dayton St., 53703,* ☎ *608/ 257–6000 or 800/356–8293,* 𝔽𝔸𝕏 *608/257–5280. 360 rooms. 2 restaurants, pool, exercise room. AE, D, DC, MC, V.* ♨

$$–$$$ ⊞ **Sheraton Madison.** Across from the Dane County Expo Center and minutes from the State Capitol and campus, is this Sheraton with modern, comfortable rooms. ⊠ *706 John Nolen Dr., 53713,* ☎ *608/ 251–2300 or 800/325–3535,* 𝔽𝔸𝕏 *608/251–1189. 279 rooms. 2 restaurants, pool, exercise room. AE, D, DC, MC, V.* ♨

Wisconsin Dells and Baraboo

Visitor Information

Baraboo Chamber of Commerce (⊠ 600 Chestnut St., 53913, ☎ 608/ 356–8333 or 800/227–2266).

Wisconsin Dells Visitor and Convention Bureau (⊠ 701 Superior St., Wisconsin Dells 53965, ☎ 608/254–8088 or 800/223–3557).

Arriving and Departing

Take I–90 west from Milwaukee to Madison, then I–90/94 northwest to the Dells. Baraboo is off U.S. 12 to the south of I–90/94.

What to See and Do

One of the state's foremost natural attractions is the **Wisconsin Dells,** nearly 15 mi of soaring, eroded rock formations created over thousands of years as the Wisconsin River cut into soft sandstone. The two small communities encompassed by the Dells—Wisconsin Dells and Lake Delton, with a combined population of fewer than 4,000—draw nearly 3 million visitors annually to frolic in the water parks, play miniature golf, and enjoy the rides, shows, and other planned attractions that today nearly overshadow the area's scenic wonders.

During the summer and fall tourist seasons you can view the river and its spectacular rock formations on cruise boats or aboard World War II amphibious vehicles. Several water parks have slides, wave pools, and inner-tube and raft rides. The notorious Confederate spy Belle Boyd, who died here while on a speaking tour in 1910, is buried in **Spring Grove Cemetery.**

Scenic **Mirror Lake State Park** (⊠ just south of the Dells off U.S. 12, ☎ 608/254–2333) has campgrounds, hiking trails, and 20 mi of cross-country ski trails. **Rocky Arbor State Park** (⊠ 1 mi north off U.S. 12, ☎ 608/254–8001 in summer; 608/254–2333 off-season) is another good choice for downtime, with camping, hiking, and great scenery.

South of Wisconsin Dells is **Baraboo,** former site of an early 19th-century fur-trading post run by a Frenchman named Baribault. It is best known as the place where the five Ringling brothers began their circus careers in 1882, and as the winter headquarters of their Ringling Brothers Circus from 1884 to 1918. The **Circus World Museum** (⊠ 426 Water St., ☎ 608/356–8341; ▨ $14), a State Historical Society site, preserves the history of the more than 100 circuses that began in Wisconsin. Along with an outstanding collection of antique circus wagons, the museum presents **big-top performances** from mid-May through Labor Day, featuring circus stars of today.

Dining and Lodging

$–$$$$ ✕ **Dell-Bar Steak House.** More than 55 years-old, this restaurant built in the Frank Lloyd Wright style serves seafood and meat dishes such as Killer Shrimp, panfried walleye, osso buco, lamb chops, and prime rib. Expect a crackling fire in winter, and piano music year-round. ⊠ *800 Wisconsin Dells Pkwy., Lake Delton,* ☎ *608/253–1861. AE, D, DC, MC, V.*

$$$–$$$$ 🏨 **Black Wolf Lodge.** This Northwoods–theme hotel and recreation facility has huge indoor and outdoor water activity centers including water slides and seven indoor and outdoor pools. Of the seven different styles of rooms, some have lofts, whirlpools, fireplaces, big-screen televisions, and/or patios. ⊠ *I–90/94 and Hwy. 12, Wisconsin Dells 53965,* ☎ *800/559–9653,* 𝔽𝔸𝕏 *608/253–2224. 309 rooms. Restaurant, pools, exercise room. AE, D, DC, MC, V.* ✏

Door County

Arriving and Departing

Take I–43 north from Milwaukee to Green Bay, then Route 57 north.

What to See and Do

Jutting out from the Wisconsin mainland like the thumb on a mitten, 70-mi-long **Door County Peninsula** is bordered by the waters of Lake Michigan and Green Bay. It was named for the Porte des Morts (Door of Death), a treacherous strait separating the peninsula from nearby islands. Scores of ships have come to grief in Door County waters, but today large Great Lakes freighters often slip through the Door to seek shelter in the lee of the islands during Lake Michigan's autumn storms. Soil conditions and climate make the peninsula ideal for cherry and apple production, and its orchards produce more than 20 million pounds of fruit each year. The peninsula is carpeted in blossoms when the trees bloom in late May.

A visit to the peninsula can include stops at a half dozen quaint lakeshore towns, each filled with charming restaurants, shops, and inns. First-time visitors often make a circle tour via Routes 57 and 42. The Lake Michigan side of the peninsula is somewhat less settled and the landscape rougher. The peninsula's rugged beauty attracts large numbers of artists, whose works are shown in studios, galleries, and shops in all the villages.

Sturgeon Bay, the peninsula's chief community and a busy shipbuilding port, sits on a partially man-made ship canal connecting the waters of Lake Michigan and Green Bay. Here the **Door County Maritime Museum** (⊠ 120 N. Madison Ave., at the foot of the bridge leading into town, ☎ 920/743–5958; 🎟 $5) has displays on local shipbuilding and commercial fishing.

Beside Route 57, along the peninsula's Lake Michigan side, you can see the rocky shoreline and sea caves at **Cave Point County Park,** near Valmy. Just north of **Jacksonport** you'll cross the 45th parallel, halfway between the equator and the north pole.

Northport, at the tip of the Door County Peninsula, is the port of departure for the daily car ferries to **Washington Island,** 6 mi offshore; passenger ferries leave from nearby Gills Rock. The island's 600 inhabitants celebrate their heritage with an annual **Scandinavian festival,** in August. Narrated tram tours aboard the Washington Island *Cherry Train* (☎ 920/847–2039; 🎟 $6.50) or the *Viking Tour Train* (☎ 920/ 854–2972; 🎟 $6.50, $14 for tour-and-ferry package) leave from the ferry dock between late May and mid-October. The island has nearly 100 mi of roads that are great for cycling. You may take your own bicycle on the ferry or rent one on the island. To get away from it all, take the ferry from Washington Island to remote **Rock Island State Park,** a wilderness area permitting only hiking and backpack camping.

Back on the mainland, villages on the **Green Bay** side of the peninsula evoke New England in atmosphere and charm and provide exceptional views of Green Bay, where sunsets can be breathtaking. **Fish Creek** is home to the **Peninsula Players Theater** (☎ 920/868–3287; ☙ $21–$27); America's oldest professional resident summer theater allows visitors from June through October. Here, too, is beautiful **Peninsula State Park,** where hiking and bicycling trails abound.

Complete your visit to Door County by sampling the region's famed **fish boil,** which originated more than 100 years ago. It's a simple but delicious meal that has reached legendary status in the region. A huge caldron of water is brought to a boil over a wood fire. A basket of red potatoes is cooked in the caldron, followed by a basket of fresh local whitefish steaks. At the moment the fish is cooked to perfection, kerosene is dumped on the fire, and the flames shoot high in the air, causing the caldron to boil over, expelling most of the fish oils and fat. The steaming whitefish is then served with melted butter, potatoes, coleslaw, and another favorite, Door County cherry pie. The **Door County Chamber of Commerce** (✉ Box 406, Sturgeon Bay 54235, ☎ 920/743–4456 or 800/527–3529) provides information on county attractions.

Dining and Lodging

$–$$ ✕ **Al Johnsons Swedish Restaurant and Butik.** Goats graze on the grass roof of this locally famous restaurant, a breakfast hot spot. Specialties include Swedish limpa bread, fruit soups, and wafer-thin pancakes topped with fresh fruit and whipped cream. ✉ *702 N. Bay Shore Dr., Sister Bay,* ☎ *920/854–2626. AE, D, MC, V.*

$–$$ ✕ **Kortes English Inn.** Continental cuisine is served in a formal yet cozy setting. The inn, which is surrounded by trees, has stained glass, polished wood, and fireplaces. There is also an extensive wine list and specialty coffees. ✉ *3713 Hwy. 42, Fish Creek,* ☎ *920/868–3076. DC, MC, V. Closed Nov.–Apr.*

$ ✕ **The Cookery.** Door County products—mostly cherries—are used in many of the dishes on this restaurant's breakfast, lunch, and dinner menus. Don't miss the cherry muffins and cherry-chocolate-chip coffee cake. The pantry offers goodies to go. ✉ *Main St. and Hwy. 42, Fish Creek,* ☎ *920/868–3634. Closed Mar.; first 3 weeks of Dec.; weekdays Nov. and Jan.–Feb.; first 2 weeks of Apr.*

$ ✕ **Sister Bay Café.** This quaint café on Sister Bay's main street serves Scandinavian-American specials such as Norwegian farmer's stew, heart-shape waffles topped with strawberries and whipped cream, and *risegrot,* a hot, creamy rice pudding–like dish that's a breakfast favorite. ✉ *611 Bay Shore Dr., Sister Bay,* ☎ *920/854–2429. DC, MC, V. Closed Jan.–Mar., and some weekends off-season.*

$$–$$$$ ✕▥ **White Gull Inn.** Since 1896 the White Gull has provided intimate
★ lodging and excellent food. Cottages and rooms are rustic and old-fashioned, with hardwood floors, canopy beds, braided rugs, and porches. Lamb, beef, and seafood dishes with unusual sauces are served in the candlelit, antiques-filled restaurant. ✉ *4225 Main St., Fish Creek 54212,* ☎ *920/868–3517,* ℻ *920/868–2367. 13 rooms, 4 cottages. Restaurant. AE, D, DC, MC, V.* ☙

$$–$$$ ✕▥ **Inn at Cedar Crossing.** At this inn in Sturgeon Bay's historic dis-
★ trict you can sample some of the area's best cuisine before retiring upstairs in a room with a four-poster bed, fireplace, whirlpool, and sitting area. ✉ *336 Louisiana St., Sturgeon Bay 54235,* ☎ *920/743–4200,* ℻ *920/743–4422. 9 rooms. D, MC, V. CP.* ☙

$$$–$$$$ 🏨 **Landmark Resort and Conference Center.** The largest resort in Door County, the Landmark is in a wooded area overlooking a golf course and rolling farmland. Many of its traditionally styled suites have spectacular views. ⊠ *7643 Hillside Rd., Egg Harbor 54209,* ☎ *920/868–3205 or 800/273–7877,* 𝖥𝖠𝖷 *920/868–2569. 293 suites. Restaurant, 4 pools, tennis, exercise room. AE, D, DC, MC, V.* 🐾

$$–$$$$ 🏨 **Baileys Harbor Yacht Club Resort.** A 1,000-acre wildlife sanctuary
★ and nature preserve near the waterfront provide the backdrop for the rooms, suites, villas, and cottages of this resort. Some suites have gas fireplaces and large whirlpool baths. ⊠ *8151 Ridges Rd., Baileys Harbor 54202,* ☎ *920/839–2336 or 800/927–2492,* 𝖥𝖠𝖷 *920/839–2093. 83 rooms. Pool, tennis. D, MC, V.* 🐾

$$–$$$$ 🏨 **High Point Inn.** This modern facility overlooks the town of Ephraim. Clean and comfortable one-, two-, and three-bedroom condominium suites are available. ⊠ *10386 Water St., Ephraim 54211,* ☎ *920/854–9773 or 800/595–6894,* 𝖥𝖠𝖷 *920/854–9738. 42 rooms. 2 pools, exercise room. D, MC, V.* 🐾

$$–$$$ 🏨 **White Lace Inn.** Guest rooms at this inn have plenty of white lace, as well as antiques, fireplaces, and whirlpools. Gardens surround the four houses, which are connected by a gazebo. There's also a cozy lobby with Victorian furniture and original hardwood floors, walls, and ceilings. ⊠ *16 N. 5th Ave., Sturgeon Bay 54235,* ☎ *920/743–1105. 18 rooms. AE, D, MC, V. BP.* 🐾

Bayfield and the Apostle Islands

Visitor Information

Bayfield Chamber of Commerce (⊠ Box 138, 54814, ☎ 715/779–3335 or 800/447–4094, 𝖥𝖠𝖷 715/779–5080).

Madeline Island Chamber of Commerce (⊠ Box 274, La Pointe 54850, ☎ 715/747–2801 or 888/475–3386, 𝖥𝖠𝖷 715/747–2800).

Arriving and Departing

Take I–94 west from Milwaukee to Portage, U.S. 51 north to Hurley, U.S. 2 west to Ashland, and then Hwy. 13 north to Bayfield.

What to See and Do

Known as the gateway to the Apostle Islands National Lakeshore, the commercial fishing village of **Bayfield,** population 700, also has some worthwhile attractions of its own. The **Maritime Museum** (⊠ Wilson and 1st St., ☎ 800/323–7619; ⛴ $5) depicts the story of the Bayfield area, highlighting its fishing and logging heritage. It's open from Memorial Day through mid-October.

From fall through spring, **Lake Superior Big Top Chautauqua** (⊠ 3 mi south of Bayfield off Hwy. 13, ☎ 715/373–5552 or 888/244–8368; ⛴ $10–$35) hosts concerts, plays, lectures, and original historical musicals under canvas in the spirit of old-time summer tent shows.

★ Accessible from Bayfield, the **Apostle Islands National Lakeshore** comprises 21 of Lake Superior's 22 Apostle Islands and a segment of mainland near Bayfield. Named by French missionaries who mistakenly thought the islands numbered 12, the Apostles encompass 42,000 acres spread over 600 square mi of Lake Superior. Primitive camping and hiking are allowed on most of the islands. Sailing is a favorite pastime here, as is charter-boat fishing for lake trout or whitefish. At **Lakeshore headquarters** (⊠ Washington Ave. and 4th St., Box 4, Bayfield 54814, ☎ 715/779–3397) you'll find publications, exhibits, and a movie about the Apostle Islands. In summer, the **Little Sand Bay Visitor Center** (⊠ 13 mi north of Bayfield on Hwy. 13) has exhibits and daily guided tours of a former commercial fishing operation. **Stockton**

Island, the largest island in the national lakeshore, has a visitor center with natural and cultural history exhibits and a park naturalist on duty. There are guided tours of the **Raspberry Island Lighthouse** buildings and gardens as well as historic **Manitou Island Fish Camp,** on Manitou Island (closed Labor Day to Memorial Day).

From April to December the car- and passenger-carrying **Madeline Island Ferry** (⊠ Washington Ave., Bayfield, ☎ 715/747–2051) connects Bayfield to **Madeline Island.** Here the village of **La Pointe** was established in the early 17th century as a French trading post. The **Madeline Island Historical Museum** (⊠ Ferry Dock, La Pointe, ☎ 715/747–2415; ☙ $5), on the site of a former fur-trading post, houses exhibits on island history. It's open June through September. Narrated island tours are given by **Madeline Island Bus Tours** (⊠ Ferry Dock, La Pointe, ☎ 715/747–2051; ☙ $8.50) from mid-June through Labor Day. **Big Bay State Park** (☎ 715/747–6425) has camping, a long sandy beach, picnic areas, and hiking and nature trails; sea kayaking and biking are especially popular.

Dining and Lodging

$–$$ ✗ **Maggie's Restaurant.** "Real food, real drinks, real fun, and fake flamingos" is the slogan at this eatery, where flamingos and flamingo memorabilia are ubiquitous. Great burgers share the menu with more sophisticated fare. ⊠ *257 Manypenny Ave., Bayfield,* ☎ *715/779–5641. MC, V.*

$–$$$ 🏠 **Winfield Inn.** Flower gardens and a large deck overlooking the bay and Madeline Island set this inn apart. The six apartments have kitchens. ⊠ *225 E. Lynde Ave., Bayfield 54814,* ☎ *715/779–3252,* 🖷 *715/779–5180. 37 rooms. AE, D, MC, V.* ⊗

WYOMING

By Geoffrey
O'Gara

Updated by
Candy
Moulton

Capital	Cheyenne
Population	481,000
Motto	Equal Rights
State Bird	Meadowlark
State Flower	Indian paintbrush
Postal Abbreviation	WY

Statewide Visitor Information

Wyoming Division of Tourism (⊠ I–25 at College Dr., Cheyenne 82002, ☎ 307/777–7777; 800/225–5996 for recorded ski reports). **Information centers** in Cheyenne, Evanston, Jackson, and Sheridan are open year-round. Those in Pine Bluffs, Chugwater, and near Laramie close in winter.

Scenic Drives

North of Cody and east of Yellowstone is the 60-mi **Beartooth Highway,** U.S. 212. Switchbacking across Beartooth Pass at 10,947 ft, it's the state's highest highway and open only in summer. Add a few miles to your drive and take the **Chief Joseph Scenic Highway** (Route 296, south from Beartooth Highway toward Cody) to see the gorge carved by the Clarks Fork of the Yellowstone River. There is more scenery than service on these roads, so gas up in Cody or at the northeastern end of the route, in Red Lodge or in Cooke City, Montana.

National and State Parks

National Parks
Yellowstone National Park (☞ Exploring Yellowstone, Grand Teton, Jackson, and Cody, *below*) is widely considered the crown jewel of the national park system. **Grand Teton National Park** (☞ Exploring Yellowstone, Grand Teton, Jackson, and Cody, *below*) encompasses the jagged Teton Range, the Snake River, and, in between, a string of pristine lakes. **Devils Tower National Monument** (☞ Elsewhere in Wyoming, *below*) is a site sacred to Native Americans.

State Parks
Wyoming's state parks are listed on the Division of Tourism's state road map. Historic sites include **South Pass City** (⊠ 125 South Pass Main, ☎ 307/332–3684), a history-rich gold camp near the Oregon Trail, and **Fort Bridger State Historic Site** (⊠ Fort Bridger, ☎ 307/782–3842), the pioneer trading post started by Jim Bridger and later used by the military. **Hot Springs State Park** (☎ 307/864–2176), in Thermopolis on U.S. 20, has the world's largest hot spring.

YELLOWSTONE, GRAND TETON, JACKSON, AND CODY

When John Colter's descriptions of **Yellowstone** were reported in St. Louis newspapers in 1810, most readers dismissed them as tall tales. Colter had left the Lewis and Clark expedition to trap and explore in a region virtually unknown to whites, and his reports of giant elk roaming among fuming mud pots, waterfalls, and geysers in a wilderness of evergreens and towering peaks were just too far-fetched to be taken seriously. Sixty years and several expeditions later, however, the nation was convinced, and in 1872 Yellowstone became the country's first national park.

The **Snake River** runs through Jackson Hole Valley, making its way south and west along the foot of the Grand Tetons and through **Grand Teton National Park,** which is nestled between the Tetons and the Gros Ventre Mountains. The town of **Jackson** was first a rendezvous for fur trappers, then the gateway to the nearby parks and dude ranches, and later the center of a booming ski industry.

Visitor Information

Jackson Hole: Chamber of Commerce (⌂ Box E, 83001, ☎ 307/733–3316); Visitors Council (⌂ Box 982, Dept. 8, 83001, ☎ 800/782–0011). **Cody:** Chamber of Commerce (⌂ 836 Sheridan Ave., 82414, ☎ 307/587–2297).

Arriving and Departing

By Bus

Jackson Hole Express (☎ 307/733–1719 or 800/652–9510) operates the only direct bus service to Jackson, a shuttle service from Salt Lake City, Utah, with pickups at the Salt Lake City International Airport, Amtrak station, and Greyhound bus station. Buses run daily during the winter ski season, four times each week in the summer, and fewer days in spring and fall; the cost is $45 each-way. During ski season **START** buses (☎ 307/733–4521) operate between town and the Jackson Hole Ski Resort; the fare is $2 one-way. The **Targhee Express** (☎ 307/733–3101 or 800/827–4433) crosses Teton Pass on its way to the Grand Targhee Ski Resort. **AmFac Parks and Resorts** (☎ 307/344–7901) has bus tours of Yellowstone in summer and snow-coach tours in winter.

By Car

To reach Yellowstone through the Teton Valley and Jackson Hole, turn north off I–80 at Rock Springs and take U.S. 191 the 177 mi to Jackson; Yellowstone is 60 mi farther north on U.S. 191/89. You can also approach Yellowstone from the east through Cody, 52 mi from Yellowstone on U.S. 14/16/20; or through central Wyoming via U.S. 287 and U.S. 26 through Dubois; for north and west entrances *see* Montana. Grand Teton National Park is 10 mi north of Jackson on U.S. 191/89.

By Plane

American, Delta/Sky West, United, and United Express have daily service from Denver and Salt Lake City into **Jackson Hole Airport** (☎ 307/733–7682), 9 mi north of town and about 40 mi south of Yellowstone National Park. Major car-rental agencies serve the airport. **Yellowstone Regional Airport** (☎ 307/587–5096), at Cody on the park's east side, is served by commuter airlines out of Denver. For information on additional services, *see* Montana.

Exploring Yellowstone, Grand Teton, Jackson, and Cody

Yellowstone

Yellowstone National Park (⌂ Box 168, Mammoth 82190-0168, ☎ 307/344–7381) preserves and provides access to natural treasures such as **Yellowstone Lake,** with its 110-mi shoreline and lake cruises, wildlife, waterfowl, and trout fishing; **Grand Canyon of the Yellowstone,** a 24 mi-long, 1,200-ft deep expanse of red and ocher surrounded by emerald-green forest; the multicolored, steaming **Mammoth Hot Springs;** and 900 mi of horse trails, 1,000 mi of hiking trails, and 370 mi of public roads. Visitor centers throughout the park are the departure points for guided hikes and are the sites of evening talks and campfire programs (check the park newsletter *Discover Yellowstone* for details). Park

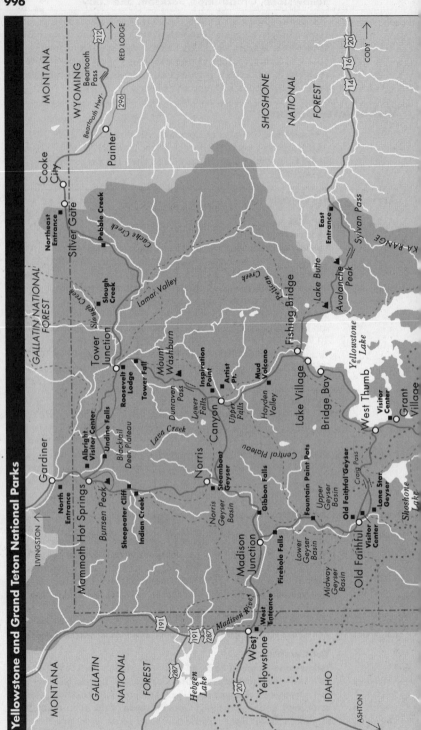

Yellowstone and Grand Teton National Parks

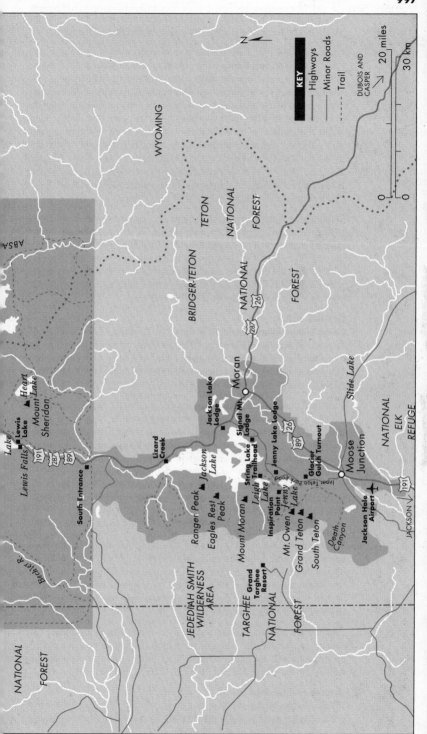

KEY
— Highways
— Minor Roads
⋯ Trail

20 miles
30 km

WYOMING

TETON

NATIONAL

FOREST

BRIDGER-TETON

NATIONAL

FOREST

DUBOIS AND CASPER

26

287

ABSA

Heart Lake

Mount Sheridan

Lewis Lake

Lewis Falls

Lake

191
287
89

South Entrance

Bechler R.

NATIONAL

FOREST

JEDEDIAH SMITH

WILDERNESS

AREA

TARGHEE

NATIONAL

FOREST

Grand Targhee Resort

Ranger Peak

Eagles Rest Peak

Mount Moran

Inspiration Point

Mt. Owen

Grand Teton

South Teton

Lizard Creek

Jackson Lake

String Lake

Leigh Lake

Jenny Lake

Jackson Lake Lodge

Signal Mt. Lodge

Jenny Lake Lodge

Glacier Gulch Turnout

Death Canyon

Inner Teton Park Road

Moran

26

89

Slide Lake

NATIONAL

ELK

REFUGE

Moose Junction

Jackson Hole Airport

191

JACKSON

service literature and warnings about interaction with the wildlife—grizzly bears and bison, especially—should be taken seriously.

Roads from all five Yellowstone entrances eventually join the figure-8 that is **Grand Loop Road,** which makes many areas accessible by vehicle. If you enter from the south, start in the Old Faithful area. The best-known geyser is, of course, **Old Faithful,** the crowd pleaser that erupts every 80 minutes or so. Earthquakes have affected the geyser schedule, but it still spouts to about 140 ft, approximately the same height that it always has. Wooden walkways wind by other geysers, mud pots, and colorful springs and along nearby Firehole River. Stay on the walkways—geysers can be dangerous. Elk and bison frequent this area. Near the west park entrance is **Norris Geyser Basin.** Among its hundreds of springs and geysers is the unpredictable Steamboat Geyser, which shoots water more than 300 ft into the air.

A short hike from **Canyon,** at the intersection of the loops, are Inspiration, Grandview, and Lookout points, where the vistas confirm Colter's accounts. The **North Rim Trail** leads to views of the 308-ft Upper Falls and 109-ft Lower Falls. In the northeast corner of the park is beautiful **Lamar Valley,** which attracts bison in the summer. Winter activities include snow-coach touring, snowmobiling, and cross-country skiing, particularly in the Old Faithful area.

Grand Teton

Grand Teton National Park (⊠ Moose 83012, ☎ 307/739–3300 or 307/739–3399) was established in 1929 and expanded to its present size when the Rockefeller family donated land it owned in Jackson Hole. The park is south of Yellowstone and linked to it by the John D. Rockefeller Memorial Parkway (U.S. 89).

Technical climbers rope up and drag themselves to the 13,770-ft summit of the **Grand,** but day hikers find many rewards, too—from a journey up Cascade Canyon to a lakeshore ramble. Jenny, Leigh, and Jackson lakes, strung along the base of the Tetons, attract fishing enthusiasts and canoeists; windsurfers and sailors favor Jackson Lake. The **Snake River** is great for rafting, with smooth and fast-moving water and occasional moose or bison sightings on the shore. Willow Flats and Oxbow Bend are excellent places to see waterfowl, and Signal Mountain Road affords a top-of-the-park view of the Tetons.

Jackson

The raised wooden sidewalks and old-fashioned storefronts of **Jackson** may make it look like a western-movie set, but it's the real thing. The town remains compact and folksy, a place where genuine cowboys rub shoulders with the store-bought variety and where the antler-arched town square, whoop-it-up nightlife, and surrounding wilderness are pretty much intact.

Jackson is walk-around size and easy to relax in after white-water rafting, hiking, or skiing. Whether your idea of relaxation is enjoying an epicurean meal, lolling in a hot tub, or two-stepping at the **Cowboy Bar** (⊠ 25 N. Cache Dr., ☎ 307/733–2207), Jackson fills the bill.

☺ **Granite Hot Springs,** south of Jackson off U.S. 191 and 10 mi into Bridger–Teton National Forest along a gravel road, has a creekside campground, a hot-springs pool, hiking trails, and scenery, plus dogsledding
☺ in the winter. The **National Elk Refuge** (⊠ Elk Refuge Visitor's Center, 2820 Rungius Rd., Jackson 83001, ☎ 307/733–3534), 3 mi north of Jackson, operates horse-drawn sleigh trips through the herd of more than 7,000 elk in their winter preserve. Trips run from December 15 through March; the cost is $8 per person.

Cody

Most people use Cody as a way station en route to or from Yellowstone's east entrance, but the town's museum is a must-see for anyone interested in the history of the American West. The **Buffalo Bill Historical Center** (✉ 720 Sheridan Ave., ☎ 307/587–4771) has a **Plains Indian Museum**, the **Cody Firearms Museum**, the **Buffalo Bill Museum**, and the **Whitney Gallery of Western Art**. Annual events such as Cowboy Songs and Range Ballads in April, the Plains Indian Powwow in June, a Frontier Festival in July, and an Old West art show in September add to the cultural experience. For more information about these events, call the **Chamber of Commerce** (☎ 307/587–2297).

Dining and Lodging

You can make reservations for a stay in Jackson or Jackson Hole Ski Resort through **Central Reservations** (☎ 800/443–6931). **Jackson Hole Bed & Breakfast Association** (✉ Box 6396, Jackson 83002, ☎ 800/542–2632) can make reservations at any of the 14 bed-and-breakfasts in the area. For information about the many guest ranches between Cody and Yellowstone, contact the **East Yellowstone Valley Lodges** (✉ 1231 Yellowstone Hwy., Cody 82414, ☎ 307/587–9595).

Cody

$–$$ ✕ **Proud Cut Saloon.** Looking straight out of the Old West, with game mounts and vintage photos, this popular downtown eatery serves what it bills as "kick-ass cowboy cuisine": steak, prime rib, fish, and chicken. ✉ *1227 Sheridan Ave.,* ☎ *307/527–6905. D, MC, V.*

$–$$ ✕🏨 **Irma Hotel.** An ornate cherry-wood bar is one of the highlights of this lodging. Some rooms have a turn-of-the-century western style. ✉ *1192 Sheridan Ave., 82414,* ☎ FAX *307/587–4221. 40 rooms. Restaurant, bar. AE, D, DC, MC, V.* ⊗

$$ 🏨 **Pahaska Teepee Resort.** Buffalo Bill's original getaway in the high country is 2 mi east of Yellowstone's East Entrance. Guided fishing, horseback, and snowmobile treks as well as cross-country skiing are available on the grounds. Cabins have two, four, or six rooms. ✉ *183 Yellowstone Hwy., 82414,* ☎ *307/527–7701 or 800/628–7791,* FAX *307/527–4019. 52 cabins. Restaurant. D, MC, V.*

Grand Teton

Grand Teton Lodge Company operates three of the park's lodges—Jackson Lake, Jenny Lake, and Colter Bay Village (☞ *below*). ✉ *Box 240, Moran 83013,* ☎ *307/543–3100 or 800/628–9988,* FAX *307/543–3143. AE, D, DC, MC, V.* ⊗

$$$$ ✕🏨 **Jenny Lake Lodge.** Set amid pines and a wildflower meadow, this
★ lodge has cabins and rooms that are rustic yet luxurious. Handmade quilts and electric blankets cover the sturdy pine beds. In the restaurant you can sample Rocky Mountain cuisine such as roast prime rib of buffalo or breast of pheasant. ✉ *Jenny Lake Rd. 37 cabins. Restaurant, bar. AE, D, DC, MC, V. Closed mid-Oct.–early June.*

$$–$$$ ✕🏨 **Jackson Lake Lodge.** This brown stone edifice has huge windows overlooking Willow Flats. Guest rooms in the adjacent buildings are larger and more attractive than those in the main lodge. The Mural Room's menu sometimes features local game such as venison or antelope. The lodge has the park's only swimming pool. ✉ *Off U.S. 89 north of Jackson Lake Junction. 385 rooms. 2 restaurants, bar, pool. AE, D, DC, MC, V. Closed late Oct.–mid-May.*

$$ ✕🏨 **Signal Mountain Lodge.** On the shore of Jackson Lake, the lodge's
★ main building is made of volcanic stone and pine shingle; inside is a cozy lounge with a fireplace, a piano, and Adirondack furniture. Guest rooms are in a separate cluster of cabinlike units, some with kitchenettes.

Aspens restaurant serves such dishes as shrimp linguine and medallions of elk. ⊠ *Inner Teton Park Rd., Moran 83013,* ☎ *307/543–2831,* ℻ *307/543–2569. 79 rooms. Restaurant, bar. AE, DC, MC, V. Closed mid-Oct.–early May.* ⌘

$–$$ ✕🏨 **Colter Bay Village.** There are log cabins and less expensive tent cabins (canvas-covered wood frames) at this resort near the shore of Jackson Lake. The restaurant serves lasagna, trout, and barbecued spareribs. ⊠ *Off U.S. 89. 166 cabins, 66 tent cabins, 112 RV spaces. 2 restaurants. AE, D, DC, MC, V. Closed early Oct.–late May.*

Jackson

$$ ✕ **Nani's Genuine Pasta House.** The ever-changing menu at this cozy
★   Italian restaurant may include braised veal shanks with saffron risotto and other regional dishes. ⊠ *240 N. Glenwood St.,* ☎ *307/733–3888. MC, V.*

$$ ✕ **Sweetwater Restaurant.** Mediterranean meals are served in a log-
★   cabin atmosphere. Start with smoked buffalo carpaccio or eggplant rouille; then go on to lamb dishes, chicken, roast pork, or fresh fish. ⊠ *King and Pearl Sts.,* ☎ *307/733–3553. AE, D, DC, MC, V.*

$ ✕ **The Bunnery.** This pine-paneled whole-grain bakery and restaurant serves irresistible breakfasts, from omelets with Swiss cheese and sautéed spinach to home-baked pastries. Sandwiches, burgers, and Mexican dishes are served for lunch and dinner. ⊠ *130 N. Cache St.,* ☎ *307/733–5474. Reservations not accepted. MC, V.*

$$–$$$$ ✕🏨 **Spring Creek Ranch.** You can spend all day gazing at the Tetons
★   from this luxury resort atop Gros Ventre Butte, near Jackson. Other activities include tennis, horseback riding, cross-country skiing, and sleigh rides. There are 36 hotel rooms, plus a mix of studios, suites, and condos with lofts and kitchenettes, and executive homes. Native American art decorates the fine Granary restaurant, where reservations are essential. ⊠ *1800 Spirit Dance Rd., 83001,* ☎ *307/733–8833 or 800/443–6139,* ℻ *307/733–1524. 117 units. Restaurant, pool, 2 tennis courts. AE, D, DC, MC, V.* ⌘

$$–$$$$ 🏨 **Painted Porch Bed & Breakfast.** This 1901 farmhouse 8 mi north of Jackson has antiques-filled rooms, some with Japanese soaking tubs. ⊠ *Teton Village Rd., Box 6955, 83001,* ☎ *307/733–1981. 4 rooms. MC, V. BP.* ⌘

$$$ 🏨 **Cowboy Village Resort.** Each of the pine-log cabins in this quiet complex has bunk beds and a kitchenette, making it a good choice for families and groups who don't mind close quarters. ⊠ *120 S. Flat Creek Dr., 83001,* ☎ *307/733–3121 or 800/962–4988,* ℻ *307/739–1955. 82 cabins. AE, D, MC, V.* ⌘

MOTELS

🏨 **Days Inn** (⊠ 350 S. Hwy. 89, Jackson 83001, ☎ 307/733–0033 or 800/329–7466, ℻ 307/733–0044), 91 rooms; CP; *$$–$$$.*

🏨 **Antler Inn** (⊠ 43 W. Pearl St., Jackson 83001, ☎ 307/733–2535 or 800/483–8667, ℻ 307/733–4158), 110 rooms; exercise room; *$–$$.*

🏨 **Virginian Motel** (⊠ 750 W. Broadway, Jackson 83001, ☎ 307/ 733–2792 or 800/262–4999, ℻ 307/733–4063), 170 rooms; restaurant, bar, pool, outdoor hot tub; *$–$$.*

🏨 **Motel 6** (⊠ 600 S. Hwy. 89, Jackson 83001, ☎ 307/733–1620, ℻ 307/734–9175), 155 rooms; pool; *$.*

Teton Village

$–$$$ ✕ **Mangy Moose.** Folks pour in off the ski slopes for food and talk at
★   this two-level restaurant plus bar with an outdoor deck. This place is full of antiques and oddities, including a caribou and sleigh suspended

from the ceiling. There's a high noise level but decent food at fair prices. ⊠ *South end of Teton Village,* ☎ *307/733–4913. AE, MC, V.*

$$$–$$$$ ✕▥ **Alpenhof.** This European-style hotel is close to Jackson Hole's ski
★ lifts. The restaurant, which serves veal, wild game, and seafood, is small, quiet, and comfortable. The upstairs Alpenhof Bistro has a more limited menu of wild game, pork, and beef at reasonable prices. ⊠ *Teton Village Rd., Box 288, Teton Village, 83025,* ☎ *307/733–3242,* 𝐅𝐀𝐗 *307/ 739–1516. 43 rooms. 2 restaurants, pool. AE, D, DC, MC, V.*

Yellowstone

The lodgings and restaurants within Yellowstone are operated by **AmFac Parks and Resorts.** There are gas stations, snack bars, and other services throughout the park. ⊠ *Yellowstone National Park, 82190,* ☎ *307/344–7901,* 𝐅𝐀𝐗 *307/344–2456. AE, D, DC, MC, V.*

$$–$$$ ✕▥ **Lake Yellowstone Hotel.** The park's oldest (late 1800s) and most
★ elegant resort, at the north end of the lake, has a pale-yellow neoclassical facade. The lobby's tall windows overlook the water, and some rooms have brass beds and vintage fixtures. Cabins are much more rustic. The restaurant (☎ 307/242–3701) serves Thai curried shrimp, fettuccine with smoked salmon and snow peas, and other eclectic fare; reservations are essential. ⊠ *Lake Village Rd., Lake Village. 194 rooms, 110 cabins. Restaurant. Closed mid-Oct.–mid-May.*

$$–$$$ ✕▥ **Old Faithful Snow Lodge.** Built in 1998, this establishment brings
★ back the grand tradition of classic western park lodges with large beams, western furnishings, unique lighting, a fireplace in the spacious lobby, and another centered between the bar and restaurant. In the long sitting room there are Molesworth-style writing desks and overstuffed chairs in which to relax. The small second-floor mezzanine has wicker chairs and a view of the lobby. Enjoy hiking, cross-country skiing, and snowmobiling. ⊠ *Off Old Faithful Bypass Rd., next to visitor center, Old Faithful. 100 rooms. Restaurant, bar. Closed mid-Oct.–mid-Dec., mid-Mar.–mid-May.*

$–$$$ ✕▥ **Old Faithful Inn.** You can loll in front of the lobby's immense stone
★ fireplace and look up six stories at wood balconies that seem to disappear into the night sky. Guest rooms are a mixed bag: In some you might find brass beds and Victorian cherry-wood furnishings; others have inexpensive motel-style furniture. The dining room (☎ 307/344–7901, ext. 4999), a huge hall centered on a fireplace of volcanic stone, serves shrimp scampi and other delights; dinner reservations are essential. ⊠ *First left turn off Old Faithful Bypass Rd., Old Faithful. 325 rooms, 248 with bath. Restaurant. Closed mid-Oct.–mid-May.*

$–$$ ✕▥ **Mammoth Hot Springs Hotel.** The smallish cabins here are arranged around "auto courts"; four have hot tubs. The dining room (☎ 307/ 344–7901) serves regional American fare, including prime rib and chicken with Brie and raspberry sauce. The cafeteria-style Terrace Grill, across from the lodge, has large windows that take in the scenic outdoors. Horseback riding can be arranged. ⊠ *North entrance to park, Mammoth. 128 cabins, 98 hotel rooms. 2 restaurants. Closed mid-Oct.– mid-Dec., early Mar.–late May.*

$ ✕▥ **Roosevelt Lodge.** Near the Lamar Valley in the park's northeast
★ corner, this simple, homey log lodge is more ranch house than resort. The dining room serves barbecued ribs, Roosevelt beans, and other western fare. Accommodations are in nearby cabins. ⊠ *Tower–Roosevelt Junction on Grand Loop Rd., Tower-Roosevelt. 62 cabins, 17 with bath. Restaurant. Closed early Sept.–early June.*

Campgrounds

In Grand Teton the **Grand Teton National Park** (⊠ Drawer 170, Moose 83012, ☎ 307/739–3300) has five campgrounds, none with RV hookups, but all with fire grates and rest rooms. There are also back-country campsites; a $15 nonrefundable fee is charged for advanced reservations at these sites. The privately run **Colter Bay Trailer Village** (✉ Grand Teton Lodge Co., Box 240, Moran 83013, ☎ 307/543–3100) has 112 full RV hookups.

Among the 11 **Yellowstone National Park** (☎ 307/344–7381) camp-site areas and one RV park, **Bridge Bay** (420 sites and a marina) is the largest, and **Slough Creek** (32 tent-trailer sites) is the smallest. There are also 300 backcountry campsites, for which you need a permit from park rangers.

Outdoor Activities and Sports

The **Jackson Hole Chamber of Commerce** (☞ Visitor Information, *above*) has lists of outfitters and news about winter and summer ac-tivities. For sports in the parks—including skiing, horseback riding, hik-ing, and climbing—contact the visitor centers.

Boating
You can rent boats on Jackson Lake through **Colter Bay Marina** (☎ 307/543–3100) or **Signal Mountain Marina** (☎ 307/543–2831).

Climbing
Two options for climbers are **Jackson Hole Mountain Guides** (☎ 307/ 733–4979) and **Exum Mountain Guides** (☎ 307/733–2297).

Fishing
Blue-ribbon trout streams thread through northwestern Wyoming, and Jackson Lake has set records for Mackinaw trout. The license for fishing in Yellowstone costs $10 for seven days or $20 for the season; in Grand Teton a license is $6 per day. You can buy licenses at entrance gates or park offices in both parks. For fishing elsewhere, buy licenses at sporting goods or general merchandise stores, or contact **Wyoming Game and Fish** (✉ 5400 Bishop Blvd., Cheyenne 82002, ☎ 307/777–4600). Fly shops in Jackson include **Jack Dennis Sporting Goods** (✉ 50 E. Broadway, ☎ 307/733–3270) and **High Country Flies** (✉ 165 N. Center St., ☎ 307/733–7210).

Golf
Jackson Hole Golf and Tennis Club (✉ off U.S. 89, 8 mi north of Jack-son, ☎ 307/733–3111) and **Teton Pines Golf Club** (✉ 3450 N. Club-house Dr., ☎ 307/733–1733) have 18 holes.

Rafting and Canoeing
Peaceful, scenic floats on the Upper Snake include the beautiful Oxbow, which you can navigate by canoe or kayak. Guided rafting trips are avail-able from **Barker-Ewing Scenic Float Trips** (✉ Moose, ☎ 307/733–1800 or 800/365–1800), **Snake River Kayak & Canoe School** (✉ Jackson, ☎ 307/733–3127 or 800/529–2501), and **Triangle X** (✉ Moose, ☎ 307/ 733–5500). For guided white-water trips in Snake River Canyon, try **Dave Hansen Whitewater** (✉ Jackson, ☎ 307/733–6295), **Barker-Ewing Float Trips** (✉ Jackson, ☎ 800/448–4202), **Mad River Boat Trips** (✉ Jackson, ☎ 307/733–6203 or 800/458–7238), or **Lewis & Clark Expeditions** (✉ Jackson, ☎ 307/733–4022 or 800/824–5375). Rent canoes and kayaks in Jackson from **Leisure Sports** (✉ 1075 S. U.S. 89, ☎ 307/733–3040) and **Teton Aquatics** (✉ 155 W. Gill St., ☎ 307/733–3127).

Ski Areas

Cross-Country
Cross-country skiing and snowshoeing are permitted in parts of both Yellowstone and Grand Teton national parks and surrounding forests.

Cowboy Village Resort at Togwotee (⊠ Box 91, Moran 83013, ☎ 307/543–2847), at Togwotee Pass within Bridger–Teton and Shoshone national forests (U.S. 26/287), operates 13½ mi of trails. **Spring Creek Ranch** (⊠ 1800 Spirit Dance Rd., Box 3154, 83001, ☎ 307/733–8833 or 800/443–6139) has 8 mi of trails. **Jackson Hole Nordic Center** (⊠ Box 290, Teton Village 83025, ☎ 307/733–2292) has 12 mi of trails.

Downhill
Grand Targhee (⊠ Box SKI, Alta 83422, ☎ 307/353–2300 or 800/827–4433), 64 runs, 3 lifts, 1 rope tow, 2,400-ft vertical drop. **Jackson Hole Nordic Center** (⊠ Box 290, Teton Village 83025, ☎ 307/733–2292 or 800/443–6931), 76 runs, 9 lifts including 3 high-speed quads, 4,139-ft drop (the longest of any U.S. ski area), increased snowmaking, ice skating rink, children's center with day care and playground, snowboard demo center. **Snow King** (⊠ Box SKI, Jackson 83001, ☎ 307/733–5200 or 800/522–5464), 400 acres of slopes, 3 lifts, 1,571-ft drop.

Shopping

Shopping in Jackson is centered on the town square. Western wear and outdoor clothing, some of it locally made, dominate in such stores as **Cattle Kate** (⊠ 120 E. Broadway Ave., ☎ 307/733–4803), **Jackson Hole Clothiers** (⊠ 45 E. Deloney St., ☎ 307/733–7211), and **Hide Out Leather** (⊠ 40 Center St., ☎ 307/733–2422). Specialists in the latest outdoor equipment include **Teton Mountaineering** (⊠ 170 N. Cache St., ☎ 307/733–3595) and **Skinny Skis** (⊠ 65 W. Deloney St., ☎ 307/733–6094). **Trailside Gallery** (⊠ 105 N. Center St., ☎ 307/733–3186) features western jewelry and art. For photographic art try **Tom Mangelsen Images of Nature Gallery** (⊠ 170 N. Cache St., ☎ 307/733–9752).

ELSEWHERE IN WYOMING

Cheyenne

Visitor Information
Cheyenne: Chamber of Commerce (⊠ Box 1147, 82003, ☎ 307/638–3388, FAX 307/778–1450).

Arriving and Departing
Both I–80 and I–25 pass through Cheyenne. Commuter airlines fly between Denver and **Cheyenne Municipal Airport** (☎ 307/634–7071). **Greyhound** (☎ 800/231–2222) provides bus service.

What to See and Do
The **Frontier Days** rodeo (☎ 307/778–7222 or 800/227–6336), held the last week of July, is a reminder that the state's capital city was once nicknamed Hell on Wheels. Outside the gold-domed **state capitol** is a statue of Esther Hobart Morris, who helped gain equal rights for Wyoming women; she got the vote in 1869, 51 years before the rest of the nation. Morris was the first woman to hold U.S. public office and was appointed a justice of the peace in 1870.

The **Cheyenne Frontier Days Old West Museum** (⊠ Frontier Park, 4610 N. Carey Ave., ☎ 307/778–7290 or 800/778–7290; ☞ $4) has 125 carriages among its vast collection of westernabilia. During Frontier Days, top western wildlife and landscape artists from around the country exhibit their work here. Guided tours are tailored for children.

Dining and Lodging
$–$$$ ×🏠 **Best Western Hitching Post Inn.** State legislators frequent this hotel near the capitol. The Hitch, as locals call it, books country-western performers in its lounge. ⊠ 1700 W. Lincolnway, 82001, ☎ 307/

638–3301, FAX 307/638–3301. *166 rooms. 5 restaurants, bar, 2 pools, health club. AE, D, DC, MC, V.* ✎

$$ ✕🏨 **Little America Hotel and Resort.** This resort at the intersection of I–80 and I–25 has a nine-hole golf course. The large pastel rooms have double vanities and comfy beds with plenty of pillows. ✉ *2800 W. Lincolnway, 82001,* ☎ *307/775–8400 or 800/445–6945,* FAX *307/775–8425. 188 rooms. Restaurant, 9-hole golf course. AE, D, DC, MC, V.*

$ 🏨 **Rainsford Inn.** The inn is on historic Cattleman's Row, in the heart of downtown Cheyenne; its masculine "Cattle Baron Corner" room overlooks 17th Street, where Cheyenne's cattle barons lived in the late 1800s. All rooms have whirlpool tubs, and one has a gas fireplace. ✉ *219 E. 18th St., 82001,* ☎ *307/638–2337,* FAX *307/634–4506. 7 rooms, 2 with shared bath. AE, D, DC, MC, V. BP.*

Devils Tower Area

Arriving and Departing
Devils Tower is 6 mi off U.S. 15 on Route 24.

What to See and Do
Native American legend has it that the corrugated **Devils Tower** was formed when a tree stump turned into granite and grew taller to protect some stranded children from a clawing bear. Geologists say that the rock tower, rising 1,280 ft above the Belle Fourche River, is the core of a defunct volcano. It was a tourist magnet long before a spaceship landed on top of it in the movie *Close Encounters of the Third Kind,* and the tower is still a sacred site for Native Americans. For information contact **Devils Tower National Monument** (✉ Devils Tower, Box 10, 82714, ☎ 307/467–5383).

Dining and Lodging
$ ✕ **Country Cottage.** This one-stop shop sells gifts, flowers, and simple daytime meals such as submarine sandwiches. ✉ *423 Cleveland St., Sundance,* ☎ *307/283–2450. MC, V. No dinner.*

$ ✕ **Log Cabin Café.** Locals crowd this small log-cabin restaurant full of country crafts for burgers, steaks, and seafood. ✉ *E. Hwy. 14,* ☎ *307/ 283–3393. MC, V.*

$$ 🏨 **Best Western Inn at Sundance.** Rooms here are spacious with dark-green carpet and plum-color drapes. Guests enjoy the indoor pool and hot tub. ✉ *2719 E. Cleveland St., Box 927, Sundance 82729,* ☎ *307/ 283–2800 or 800/238–0965,* FAX *307/283–2727. 44 rooms. Indoor pool, hot tub. AE, D, DC, MC, V. CP.* ✎

$ 🏨 **Bear Lodge Motel.** This downtown motel has a cozy lobby with a stone fireplace and wildlife mounts on the walls. There's also an indoor hot tub. ✉ *218 Cleveland St., Sundance 82729,* ☎ *307/283–1611,* FAX *307/283–2537. 33 rooms. AE, D, DC, MC, V.* ✎

Saratoga

Visitor Information
Saratoga Platte Valley Chamber of Commerce (✉ Box 1095, 82331, ☎ 307/326–8855).

Arriving and Departing
Saratoga is in south-central Wyoming, 20 mi south of I–80. It's also accessible via Wyoming 130 (the Snowy Range Road) in summer only, or via Wyoming 230 year-round.

What to See and Do
Recreational opportunities abound in the **Medicine Bow National Forest;** and the North Platte and Encampment rivers are known for excellent white-water floating, kayaking, rafting, and fishing. The **Grand**

Encampment Museum (✉ Box 43, Encampment 82325, ☎ 307/327–5308), 18 mi south of Saratoga, has a complete historic town and a modern interpretive center. For information on hunting and dude-ranch opportunities, contact the Saratoga Platte Valley Chamber of Commerce (☞ Visitor Information, *above*).

Dining and Lodging

$$–$$$$ ✕🏨 **Saratoga Inn.** Pole-frame furniture gives a western flair to southern Wyoming's most elegant inn. The North Platte River runs through the inn's property, so fishing is literally right out the back door. The inn brews all its own beers, which guests can sample during the daily social hour. ✉ *E. Pic-Pike Rd., Box 869, 82331, ☎ 307/326–5261. 50 rooms. Restaurant, bar, pool, mineral baths, 9-hole golf course, 2 tennis courts, horseback riding, fishing, skiing. AE, DC, MC, V.*

$–$$ ✕🏨 **Hotel Wolf.** This Victorian downtown hotel on the National Register of Historic Places has suites and rooms on the second and third floors (there are no elevators). The restaurant ($–$$$), with antique oak tables, crystal chandeliers, and lacy drapes, serves the best prime rib and steak in town, and the Wolf Burger is hard to beat. ✉ *101 E. Bridge St., 82331, ☎ 307/326–5525. 7 rooms. Restaurant. AE, DC, MC, V.*

Casper

Visitor Information
Casper Chamber of Commerce (✉ 500 N. Center St., 82601, ☎ 307/234–5311 or 800/852–1889).

Arriving and Departing
Commuter airlines, including **United Express** (☎ 800/241–6522) from Denver and **Delta/Skywest** (☎ 307/234–0607) from Salt Lake City, fly to **Natrona County International Airport. Powder River Transportation** (☎ 307/682–0960) buses connect with national carriers. Casper is in central Wyoming, 140 mi south of Sheridan and 178 mi north of Cheyenne via I-25.

What to See and Do
Oil and gas exploration have contributed to Casper's growth as the state's largest city. Five major emigrant trails passed near or through Casper between 1843 and 1870, including the Oregon, California, and Mormon trails, which crossed the North Platte River near Casper. You can learn about these emigrant trails and central Wyoming's military history at **Fort Caspar Historic Site** (✉ 4001 Fort Caspar Rd., ☎ 307/235–8462; 🎫 free). The **Casper Planetarium** (✉ 904 N. Poplar St., ☎ 307/577–0310; 🎫 $2) has multimedia programs on astronomy and space subjects. **Werner Wildlife Museum** (✉ 405 E. 15th St., ☎ 307/235–2108; 🎫 free; closed Sun., and Sat. in winter) has displays of birds and animals indigenous to Wyoming.

Dining and Lodging

$–$$ ✕ **Sandfords Grub & Pub.** Street signs, stoplights, and other memorabilia make this a lively setting. Pasta, pizza, burgers, chicken, and steaks are all good accompaniments to the pub selections. Children are welcome. ✉ *241 S. Center St., ☎ 307/234–4555. AE, D, DC, MC, V.*

$ ✕🏨 **Parkway Plaza.** Guest rooms are large and quiet. Furnishings are contemporary in the rooms but western in the public areas. Poor Boys Steakhouse ($–$$$) is one of Casper's best, with western-style blue-and-white checked tablecloths and hearty portions of steak, seafood, and chicken. ✉ *123 W. "E" St., 82601, ☎ 307/235–1777, FAX 307/235–8068. 272 rooms. Restaurant, pool. AE, D, MC, V.* 🐾

$–$$ 🏨 **Radisson.** The large rooms are contemporary and comfortable. There's an indoor pool and a hot tub. ✉ *I–25 and N. Poplar St., 82601,*

☎ 307/266–6000, FAX 307/473–1010. 228 rooms. Restaurant, pool. AE, D, DC, MC, V. ✉

Sheridan

Visitor Information
Sheridan Chamber of Commerce (✉ Box 707, 82801, ☎ 307/672–2485 or 800/453–3650, FAX 307/672–7321).

Arriving and Departing
Commuter airlines fly from Denver to **Sheridan County Airport** (☎ 307/674–4222). **Powder River Transportation** (☎ 307/674–6188) buses connect with national carriers. Sheridan is 130 mi south of Billings, Montana, via I–90 and 140 mi north of Casper via I–25.

What to See and Do
This is authentic cowboy country, with a touch of dudish sophistication. The **Trail End State Historic Site** (✉ 400 Clarendon Ave., ☎ 307/674–4589) includes authentic furnishings in a Flemish Revival home completed for cattleman John B. Kendrick in 1913. Mosey into **King's Saddlery and Ropes** (✉ 184 N. Main St., ☎ 307/672–2702 or 800/443–8919) to view hundreds of lariats, as well as hand-tooled leather saddles. Or see western collectibles, saddles, and tack in the store's museum.

Dining and Lodging

$–$$$$ ✕ **Ciao Bistro.** Nine tables are squeezed into this European-style café's cramped quarters, but the menu is full of tempting choices such as lamb shanks, Chilean sea bass, and horseradish-crusted halibut. ✉ 120 N. Main St., ☎ 307/672–2838. MC, V.

$$ ✕⛻ **Sheridan Holiday Inn.** This five-floor lodging with a four-story atrium is five minutes from downtown. Facilities include a pool, sauna, hot tub, putting green, exercise room, racquetball court, and beauty salon. ✉ 1809 Sugarland Dr., 82801, ☎ 307/672–8931, FAX 307/672–6388. 212 rooms. Restaurant, pool, exercise room. AE, D, DC, MC, V. ✉

$$$ ⛻ **Eaton's Guest Ranch.** Credited with creating the dude ranch, Eaton's is still going strong after nearly a century as a working cattle ranch that takes guests. The price includes all meals and activities such as horseback riding, fishing, cookouts, and pack trips. The ranch is west of Sheridan on the edge of the Bighorn National Forest. Make summer reservations by March. ✉ 270 Eaton Ranch Rd., Wolf 82844, ☎ 307/655–9285 or 307/655–9552, FAX 307/655–9269. 51 cabins. Pool. D, MC, V. Closed Oct.–May. FAP.

INDEX

Icons and Symbols

★ Our special recommendations

✕ Restaurant

🏠 Lodging establishment

✕🏠 Lodging establishment whose restaurant warrants a special trip

🕳 Good for kids (rubber duck)

☞ Sends you to another section of the guide for more information

✉ Address

☎ Telephone number

🕐 Opening and closing times

🎫 Admission prices

🔗 Sends you to www.fodors.com/urls for up-to-date links to the property's Web site

Numbers in white and black circles ③ ❸ that appear on the maps, in the margins, and within the tours correspond to one another.

A

Abbe Museum, 421
Aberdeen, WA, 938
Abiel Smith School, 451
Abilene, KS, 368–369
Abraham Lincoln Birthplace National Historic Site, 381
Academy of Music, 760
Academy of Natural Sciences, 761
Acadia National Park, 412, 421
Acadian Cultural Center, 407
Acadian Village, 407
Ace of Clubs House, 116
Acoma Pueblo, 606
Adams Building, 957
Adams Corner Rural Village, 730
Adams House Museum, 813
Adams Museum, 813
Adirondack Museum, 664
Adirondack Park, 663
Adler Planetarium, 326
Admiral Nimitz National Museum of the Pacific War, 854
Admiralty Island, AK, 59
Adventure Island, 247
Aegon Center, 378
Aerial Lift Bridge, 502
Aerial Theater, 840
Aerospace Education Center, 106

African-American culture and history
Atlanta, 264
Baltimore, 434
Birmingham, 46, 47
Boston, 451
Dallas, 864
Detroit, 480, 482
Indianapolis, 345, 346
Kansas, 368, 372
Kansas City, MO, 523–524
Little Rock, 106
Memphis, 822
Milwaukee, 980
Missouri, 527
Nebraska, 546
New York City, 629
Ohio, 721
South Carolina, 801
Virginia, 905
Washington, DC, 959
African American Museum, 864
African Meeting House, 451
Agate Fossil Beds National Monument, 549
Age of Steam Railroad Museum, 864
Agecroft Hall, 919
Aiken-Rhett House, 792
Air Force Academy, 175
Air Mobility Command Museum, 211
Airforce Armament Museum, 260
Airliewood Mansion, 512
Airports, xxii
Akaka Falls State Park, 292
Akron, OH, 721–722
Alabama, 45–55
arts in, 48–49
beaches, 50
central Alabama, 45–49
children, attractions for, 46–47
festivals and seasonal events, 48–49, 50, 55
hotels/restaurants, 47–48, 52–53, 55
Mobile and the Gulf Coast, 49–54
outdoor activities and sports, 53–54
parks, state, 45
scenic drives, 45
shopping, 49
transportation, 45–46, 49, 54, 55
visitor information, 45, 49, 54, 55
Alabama Jazz Hall of Fame, 46
Alabama Music Hall of Fame and Museum, 55
Alabama Shakespeare Festival, 48–49

Alabama Sports Hall of Fame Museum, 46
Alabaster Caverns State Park, 723
Aladdin resort, 558
Alamo, 850–851
Alamo IMAX Theatre, 851
Alamo Lake State Park, 75
Alamosa National Wildlife Refuge, 188
Alaska, 56–74
Arctic region, 73–74
arts/nightlife, 66
camping, 60, 66, 70
cruising, 56
hotels/restaurants, 59–60, 64–66, 69–71
interior region, 68–72
outdoor activities and sports, 60–61, 66–67, 71
parks, national and state, 56–57
shopping, 61, 67–68, 71–72
South Central region, 61–68
Southeast region, 57–61
Southwest region, 72–73
transportation, 57–58, 62, 68, 72, 73
visitor information, 56, 62, 68, 72, 73
wilderness camps and lodges, 70
Alaska Chilkat Bald Eagle Preserve, 61
Alaska State Museum, 58
Alaskaland Park, 69
Albany, NY, 656
Albright-Knox Art Gallery, 670
Albuquerque, NM, 604–608
arts/nightlife, 608
camping, 607–608
children, attractions for, 605–606
hotels/restaurants, 606–607
outdoor activities and sports, 608
shopping, 608
transportation, 604
visitor information, 604
Albuquerque Aquarium, 605
Albuquerque Biological Park, 605
Albuquerque Children's Museum, 605–606
Albuquerque Museum of Art and History, 605
Alcott, Louisa May, 461
Aldrich Museum of Contemporary Art, 192
Aleutian Islands, AK, 72–73
Alexander & Baldwin Sugar Museum, 297
Alexander Ramsey House, 496
Alexandre Mouton House, 407

NOTES

NOTES

NOTES

NOTES